DATE DUE

Statistical Abstract of the United States: 2002 122nd Edition

The National Data Book

Issued December 2002

U.S. Department of Commerce
Donald L. Evans,
Secretary

Economics and Statistics
Administration
Kathleen B. Cooper,
Under Secretary for Economic Affairs

U.S. CENSUS BUREAU
Charles Louis Kincannon,
Director

OUACHITA TECHNICAL COLLEGE

BUSINESS PRESS

SUGGESTED CITATION

U.S. Census Bureau,
*Statistical Abstract of the
United States: 2002*
(122nd Edition)
Washington, DC, 2001

Library of Congress
Card No. 4-18089

ECONOMICS
AND STATISTICS
ADMINISTRATION

U.S. CENSUS BUREAU

Charles Louis Kincannon,
Director

Vacant,
Deputy Director and
Chief Operating Officer

Nancy A. Potok,
Principal Associate Director
and Chief Financial Officer

Ted A. Johnson, Associate Director
for Finance and Administration

Walter C. Odom, Chief, Administrative
and Customer Services Division

Acknowledgments

Lars B. Johanson was responsible for the technical supervision and coordination of this volume under the general direction of **Glenn W. King,** Chief, Statistical Compendia Branch. Assisting in the research and analytical phases of assigned sections and in the developmental aspects of new tables were **Rosemary E. Clark, David J. Fleck, Stacey M. Lowe,** and **Jean F. Maloney. Catherine Lavender** provided primary editorial assistance. Other editorial assistance was rendered by **Susan Antroinen, Deena Grover, Kristen Iversen, Patricia S. Lancaster, Connie Nadzadi, Barbara Shugart,** and **Daphanie Smallwood.**

Maps were designed and produced by **Connie Beard** and **Scott Wilcox** of the Cartographic Operations Branch within the Geography Division.

Greg Carroll, Penny Heiston, Gloria Davis, Shirley Clark, Jan Sweeney, Patricia Edwards, and **Arlene C. Butler** of the Administrative and Customer Services Division, **Walter C. Odom,** Chief, provided publications and printing management, graphics design and composition, and editorial review for print and electronic media. General direction and production management were provided by **Gary J. Lauffer,** Chief, Publications Services Branch.

The cooperation of many contributors to this volume is gratefully acknowledged. The source note below each table credits the various government and private agencies that have collaborated in furnishing information for the *Statistical Abstract*. In a few instances, contributors have requested that their data be designated as subject to copyright restrictions, as indicated in the source notes to the tables affected. Permission to use copyright material should be obtained directly from the copyright owner.

For sale by Hoover's Business Press for $38.00
5800 Airport Blvd., Austin, Texas 78752
Phone: 800-486-8666 (orders only) or 512-374-4500

Features

Visit us on the Web at
http://www.census.gov/statab/www/

Introduction to Hoover's Edition of
the *Statistical Abstract of the United States 2002*

The *Statistical Abstract of the United States* is the single most useful reference book available to anyone interested in knowing about the vital statistics of our country. It is compiled by the Bureau of the Census and has been published annually for 122 years by the Government Printing Office.

This hardcover edition of the *Statistical Abstract of the United States 2002* was prepared by Hoover's Business Press to provide an affordable, accessible edition of this great reference book. Except for this introduction and the addition of some information on our company's other reference products in the back of this book, Hoover's edition is the same as the version published by the GPO. For the convenience of libraries, we have also added an ISBN designation.

We would like to thank Glenn W. King and Lars B. Johanson at the Bureau of the Census and Spurgeon Johnson at the Government Printing Office for their cooperation and assistance with this project. These dedicated public servants were instrumental in inspiring us and helping us complete this book.

—The Editors
January 2003

This Hoover's edition was published in 2003 by Hoover's Business Press, Austin, Texas. No copyright of this work is claimed by Hoover's, Inc. Manufactured in the United States of America.

10 9 8 7 6 5 4 3 2 1

Publisher Cataloging-in-Publication Data

Statistical Abstract of the United States. U.S. Department of Commerce, Bureau of the Census

Various pagings chiefly tables. Includes bibliographic references and index.
1. U.S. — Statistics. 2. Statistics — U.S.
HA202 S797
L/C Dewey 317.73 S79

ISBN 1-57311-085-X • Clothbound $38.00 list price

The Hoover's edition of the *Statistical Abstract of the United States* is available through all major U.S. book distributors and directly from Hoover's. The following companies are authorized distributors:

DIRECT SALES: US and World
Hoover's, Inc.
5800 Airport Blvd.
Austin, Texas 78752
Phone: 512-374-4500
Fax: 512-374-4538
e-mail: orders@hoovers.com

Europe
William Snyder Publishing Associates
5 Five Mile Drive
Oxford OX2 8HT
England
Phone and Fax: +44-186-551-3186
e-mail: snyderpub@aol.com

Preface

The *Statistical Abstract of the United States,* published since 1878, is the standard summary of statistics on the social, political, and economic organization of the United States. It is designed to serve as a convenient volume for statistical reference and as a guide to other statistical publications and sources. The latter function is served by the introductory text to each section, the source note appearing below each table, and Appendix I, which comprises the Guide to Sources of Statistics, the Guide to State Statistical Abstracts, and the Guide to Foreign Statistical Abstracts.

This volume includes a selection of data from many statistical publications, both government and private. Publications cited as sources usually contain additional statistical detail and more comprehensive discussions of definitions and concepts than can be presented here. Data not available in publications issued by the contributing agency but obtained from unpublished records are identified in the source notes as unpublished data. More information on the subjects covered in the tables so noted may generally be obtained from the source.

Except as indicated, figures are for the United States as presently constituted. Although emphasis in the *Statistical Abstract* is primarily given to national data, many tables present data for regions and individual states and a smaller number for metropolitan areas and cities. Appendix II, Metropolitan Area Concepts and Components, presents explanatory text, a complete current listing and population data for metropolitan statistical areas (MSAs), the primary metropolitan statistical areas (PMSAs), and the consolidated metropolitan statistical areas (CMSAs) defined as of June 30, 1999. Table 30, in Section 1, presents population numbers for MSAs with population of 250,000 or more. Statistics for the Commonwealth of Puerto Rico and for outlying areas of the United States are included in many state tables and are supplemented by information in Section 29.

Additional information for states, cities, counties, metropolitan areas, and other small units, as well as more historical data are available in various supplements to the *Abstract* (see inside back cover).

Statistics in this edition are generally for the most recent year or period available by summer 2002. Each year over 1,400 tables and charts are reviewed and evaluated; new tables and charts of current interest are added, continuing series are updated, and less timely data are condensed or eliminated. Text notes and appendices are revised as appropriate.

USA Statistics in Brief, a pocket-size pamphlet highlighting many statistical series in the *Abstract* is available and will be provided along with this edition. Additional copies can be obtained free from U.S. Census Bureau, Customer Service, Call Center, Washington, DC 20233 (telephone 301-763-INFO(4636). We attempt to update the pamphlet several times during the year. The latest data can be found on our Web site: <http://www.census.gov/statab/www/brief.html>.

Changes in this edition—This year we have added a new section which includes Census 2000 Sample Data. The 30 new tables in this section include data covering the educational attainment, disability status, ancestry of and language spoken at home by the resident population, as well as household income, poverty and selected housing characteristics. The layout of Appendix III has been revised. In this edition, Appendix III has been organized by the source agency and title of the survey rather than by section and table number in which the survey data appeared, as was the format in earlier editions.

In addition to the above, we have introduced 49 new tables throughout our core sections. These cover a variety of topics including unmarried households, state children's health insurance programs, limitation of activity level caused by chronic

v

conditions, characteristics of home-schooled students, computer use by children, firearm use offenders, home-based work and flexible schedules by workers, computer use in the workplace, employee benefits in private industry as well as computer and internet use. For a complete list of new tables see Appendix VI, p. 942.

Statistical Abstract on other media— The *Abstract* is available on the Internet and on CD-ROM, an enhanced version (except for a few copyrighted tables deleted by the request of source organizations). Our Internet site, <http://www.census.gov/statab/www>, contains this 2002 edition and earlier editions of the book, as well as— Statistics in Brief.

The CD-ROM version of the *Abstract* is also available. Information for the CD-ROM is located in the inside back cover.

Statistics for counties and cities— Extensive data for counties can be found in the *County and City Data Book: 2000*. It features 191 data items covering everything from age and agriculture to water use and wholesale trade for all states and counties with U.S. totals for comparison. Also included are 103 data items for cities with population of 25,000 or more. The primary sources are Census 2000 and the 1997 Economic Census. Two tables present 11 data items from Census 2000 for all places and MCDs with a population of 2,500 or more.

This publication, as well as selected rankings will be available on our Internet site at <http://www.census.gov/statab/www/ccdb.html>. Some data items that appear in the book from private sources are not available on the Internet or CD-ROM versions because we did not receive copyright permission to release the data items in these formats. For a database with over 5,000 county items, check out USA Counties at <http://www.census.gov/statab/www/county.html>.

Statistics for states and metropolitan areas—Extensive data for the states and metropolitan areas of the United States can be found in the *State and Metropolitan Area Data Book: 1997-98*.

This publication minus some data items, as well as selected rankings of the states and metropolitan areas, is available on our Internet site at <http://www.census.gov/statab/www/smadb.html>. The CD-ROM version is also available. See the inside back cover for more information.

Limitations of the data—The contents of this volume were taken from many sources. All data from either censuses and surveys or from administrative records are subject to error arising from a number of factors: Sampling variability (for statistics based on samples), reporting errors in the data for individual units, incomplete coverage, nonresponse, imputations, and processing error. (See also Appendix III, pp. 903.) The Census Bureau cannot accept the responsibility for the accuracy or limitations of the data presented here, other than those for which it collects. The responsibility for selection of the material and for proper presentation, however, rests with the Census Bureau.

For additional information on data presented—Please consult the source publications available in local libraries or write to the agency indicated in the source notes. Write to the Census Bureau only if it is cited as the source.

Suggestions and comments—Users of the Statistical Abstract and its supplements (see inside back cover) are urged to make their data needs known for consideration in planning future editions. Suggestions and comments for improving coverage and presentation of data should be sent to the Director, U.S. Census Bureau, Washington, DC 20233.

Contents

[Numbers following subjects are page numbers]

U.S. Census Bureau, Statistical Abstract of the United States: 2002

Example of Table Structure

No. 301. Immigration and Naturalization Service Enforcement Activities: 1990 to 2000

[**For fiscal years ending in year shown.** See text, Section 8, State and Local Government Finances and Employment]

Item	Unit	1990	1994	1995	1996	1997	1998	1999	2000
Deportable aliens located.	1,000	1,169.9	1,094.7	1,394.6	1,650.0	1,536.5	1,679.4	1,714.0	1,814.7
Border Patrol	1,000	1,103.4	1,031.7	1,324.2	1,549.9	1,413.0	1,555.8	1,579.0	1,676.4
Southwestern border	1,000	(NA)	979.1	1,271.4	1,507.0	1,368.7	1,516.7	1,537.0	1,643.7
Mexican	1,000	1,054.8	999.9	1,293.5	1,523.1	1,387.7	1,522.9	1,534.5	1,636.9
Canadian	1,000	5.7	3.4	3.5	2.7	2.9	2.3	2.7	2.2
Other	1,000	42.8	28.4	27.2	24.0	22.4	30.5	41.8	37.3
Number of seizures by									
Border Patrol	Number . . .	17,275	9,134	9,327	11,129	11,792	14,401	16,803	17,269
Value of seizures by Border Patrol.	Mil. dol. . . .	843.6	1,622.0	2,011.8	1,256.0	1,094.6	1,405.0	2,004.0	1,945.0
Narcotics	Mil. dol. . . .	797.8	1,555.7	1,965.3	1,208.8	1,046.3	1,340.0	1,919.0	1,848.0
Aliens expelled:									
Formal removals [1]	1,000	30.0	45.7	45.2	69.7	114.4	173.0	180.3	184.8
Voluntary departures [2]	1,000	1,022.5	1,029.1	1,313.8	1,573.4	1,440.7	1,570.1	1,574.5	1,675.3

NA Not available.   [1] Include deportations, exclusions, and removals.   [2] Includes aliens under docket control required to depart and voluntary departures not under docket control.

Source: U.S. Immigration and Naturalization Service, Statistical Yearbook, annual; and unpublished data.

Headnotes immediately below table titles provide information important for correct interpretation or evaluation of the table as a whole or for a major segment of it.

Footnotes below the bottom rule of tables give information relating to specific items or figures within the table.

Unit indicators show the *specified quantities* in which data items are presented. They are used for two primary reasons. Sometimes data are not available in absolute form and are estimates (as in the case of many surveys). In other cases we round the numbers in order to save space to show more data, as in the case above.

EXAMPLES OF UNIT INDICATOR INTERPRETATION FROM TABLE

Year	Item	Unit Indicator	Number shown	Multiplier
1990	Deportable aliens located	Thousands	1,169.9	1,000
1990	Value of seizures by Border Patrol . .	$ Millions	843.6	1,000,000

To Determine the Figure It Is Necessary to Multiply the Number Shown by the Unit Indicator:
Deportable aliens located - 1,169.9 x 1,000 = 1,169,900 (over 1 million)
Value of seizures by Border Patrol - 843.6 x $1,000,000 - $843,600,000 (over $843 million).

When a table presents data with more than one unit indicator, they are found in the headnotes and column headings (Tables 2 and 4), spanner (Table 40), stub (Table 27), or unit column (shown above). When the data in a table are shown in the same unit indicator, it is shown in boldface as the first part of the headnote (Table 2). If no unit indicator is shown, data presented are in absolute form (Table 1).

Vertical rules are used to separate independent sections of a table, (Table 1), or in tables where the stub is continued into one or more additional columns (Table 2).

Averages—An average is a single number or value that is often used to represent the "typical value" of a group of numbers. It is regarded as a measure of "location" or "central tendency" of a group of numbers.

The *arithmetic mean* is the type of average used most frequently. It is derived by summing the individual item values of a particular group and dividing the total by the number of items. The arithmetic mean is often referred to as simply the "mean" or "average."

The *median* of a group of numbers is the middle number or value when each item in the group is arranged according to size (lowest to highest or visa versa); it generally has the same number of items above it as well as below it. If there is an even number if items in the group, the median is taken to be the average of the two middle numbers.

Per capita (or per person) quantities. A per capita figure represents an average computed for every person in a specified group (or population). It is derived by taking the total for an item (such as income, taxes, or retail sales) and dividing it by the number of persons in the specified population.

U.S. Census Bureau, Statistical Abstract of the United States: 2002

Index numbers—An index number is the measure of difference or change, usually expressed as a percent, relating one quantity (the variable) of a specified kind to another quantity of the same kind. Index numbers are widely used to express changes in prices over periods of time but may also be used to express differences between related subjects for a single point in time.

To compute a price index, a base year or period is selected. The base year price (of the commodity or service) is then designated as the base or reference price to which the prices for other years or periods are related. Many price indexes use the year 1982 as the base year; in tables this is shown as "1982=100." A method of expressing the price relationship is: The price of a set of one or more items for a related year (e.g. 1990) **divided by** the price of the same set of items for the base year (e.g. 1982). The result multiplied by 100 provides the index number. When 100 is subtracted from the index number, the result equals the percent change in price from the base year.

Average annual percent change—Unless otherwise stated in the *Abstract* (as in Section 1, Population), average annual percent change is computed by use of a *compound interest formula.* This formula assumes that the rate of change is constant throughout a specified compounding period (1 year for average annual rates of change). The formula is similar to that used to compute the balance of a savings account which receives compound interest. According to this formula, at the end of a compounding period the amount of accrued change (e.g. school enrollment or bank interest) is added to the amount which existed at the beginning the period. As a result, over time (e.g., with each year or quarter), the same rate of change is applied to a larger and larger figure.

The *exponential formula,* which is based on continuous compounding, is often used to measure population change. It is preferred by population experts because they view population and population-related subjects as changing without interruption, ever ongoing. Both exponential and compound interest formulas assume a constant rate of change. The former, however, applies the amount of change continuously to the base rather than at the end of each compounding period. When the average annual rates are small (e.g., less than 5 percent) both formulas give virtually the same results. For an explanation of these two formulas as

they relate to population, see U.S. Census Bureau, *The Methods and Materials of Demography,* Vol. 2, 3d printing (rev.), 1975, pp. 372-381.

Current and constant dollars—Statistics in some tables in a number of sections are expressed in both current and constant dollars (see, for example, Table 643 in Section 13, Income, Expenditures, and Wealth). Current dollar figures reflect actual prices or costs prevailing during the specified year(s). Constant dollar figures are estimates representing an effort to remove the effects of price changes from statistical series reported in dollar terms. In general, constant dollar series are derived by dividing current dollar estimates by the appropriate price index for the appropriate period (for example, the Consumer Price Index). The result is a series as it would presumably exist if prices were the same throughout, as in the base year—in other words as if the dollar had constant purchasing power. Any changes in this constant dollar series would reflect only changes in real volume of output, income, expenditures, or other measure.

Explanation of Symbols

The following symbols, used in the tables throughout this book, are explained in condensed form in footnotes to the tables where they appear:

- Represents zero or rounds to less than half the unit of measurement shown.

B Base figure too small to meet statistical standards for reliability of a derived figure.

D Figure withheld to avoid disclosure pertaining to a specific organization or individual.

NA Data not enumerated, tabulated, or otherwise available separately.

NS Percent change irrelevant or insignificant.

S Figure does not meet publication standards for reasons other than that covered by symbol B, above.

X Figure not applicable because column heading and stub line make entry impossible, absurd, or meaningless.

Z Entry would amount to less than half the unit of measurement shown.

In many tables, details will not add to the totals shown because of rounding.

Telephone and Internet Contacts

To help *Abstract* users find more data and information about statistical publications, we are issuing this list of contacts for federal agencies with major statistical programs. The intent is to give a single, first-contact point-of-entry for users of statistics. These agencies will provide general information on their statistical programs and publications, as well as specific information on how to order their publications. We are also including the Internet (World Wide Web) addresses for many of these agencies. These URLs were current in August 2002.

Executive Office of the President
Office of Management and Budget
Administrator
Office of Information and Regulatory
 Affairs
Office of Management and Budget
725 17th Street, N.W.
Washington, DC 20503
Information: 202-395-3080
Internet address:
 http://www.whitehouse.gov/omb

Department of Agriculture
Economic Research Service
Information Center
U.S. Department of Agriculture
1800 M St. N.W., Rm. North 3050
Washington, DC 20036-5831
Information and Publications:
 202-694-5050
Internet address:
 http://www.ers.usda.gov/

National Agricultural Statistics Service
National Agricultural Statistics Service
U.S. Department of Agriculture
1400 Independence Ave., S.W., Rm. 5829
Washington, DC 20250
Information hotline: 1-800-727-9540
Internet address:
 http://www.usda.gov/nass/

Department of Commerce
U.S. Census Bureau
Customer Services Branch
U.S. Census Bureau
U.S. Department of Commerce
Washington, DC 20233
Information and Publications:
 301-763-4636
Internet address:
 http://www.census.gov/

Bureau of Economic Analysis
Bureau of Economic Analysis
U.S. Department of Commerce
Washington, DC 20230
Information and Publications:
 202-606-9900
Internet address: http://www.bea.gov/

Department of Commerce —Con.
International Trade Administration
Trade Statistics Division
Office of Trade and Economic Analysis
International Trade Administration
Room 2814 B
U.S. Department of Commerce
Washington, DC 20230
Information and Publications:
 202-482-2185
Internet address:
 http://www.ita.doc.gov/tradestats/

*National Oceanic and Atmospheric
 Administration*
National Oceanic and Atmospheric
 Administration Central Library
U.S. Department of Commerce
1315 East-West Highway
2nd Floor
Silver Spring MD 20910
Library: 301-713-2600
Internet address:
 http://www.lib.noaa.gov/

Department of Defense
Department of Defense
Office of the Assistant Secretary of
 Defense (Public Affairs)
Room 2E765
Attention: Press Operations
1400 Defense Pentagon
Washington, DC 20301-1400
Information: 703-697-5131/5132
Internet address:
 http://www.defenselink.mil

Department of Education
National Library of Education
U.S. Department of Education
400 Maryland Avenue, S.W.
Washington, DC 20202-5621
Education Information and Statistics:
 1-800-424-1616
Education Publications: 1-877-433-7827
Internet address: http://www.ed.gov/

Department of Energy
Energy Information Administration
National Energy Information Center
U.S. Department of Energy
1000 Independence Ave., S.W.
1E238-EI-30
Washington, DC 20585
Information and Publications:
202-586-8800
Internet address:
http://www.eia.doe.gov/

Department of Health and Human Services
Health Resources and Services Administration
HRSA Office of Communications
5600 Fishers Lane, Room 14-15
Rockville, MD 20857
Information Center: 301-443-3376
Internet address: http://www.hrsa.gov/

Substance Abuse Mental Health Services Administration
U.S. Department of Health and Human Services
5600 Fishers Lane, Room 12-105
Rockville, MD 20857
Information: 301-443-4795
Publications: 1-800-729-6686
Internet address:
http://www.samhsa.gov/

Centers for Disease Control and Prevention
Office of Public Affairs
1600 Clifton Road, N.E.
Atlanta, GA 30333
Public Inquiries: 1-800-311-3435
Internet address: http://www.cdc.gov/

Centers for Medicare and Medicaid Services (CMS)
Office of Public Affairs
U.S. Department of Health and Human Services
Room 303D, Humphrey Building
200 Independence Ave., S.W.
Washington, DC 20201
Media Relations: 202-690-6145
Internet address: http://www.cms.gov/

National Center for Health Statistics
U.S. Department of Health and Human Services - Centers for Disease Control and Prevention
National Center for Health Statistics
Data Dissemination Branch
6525 Belcrest Rd., Rm. 1064
Hyattsville, MD 20782
Information: 301-458-4636
Internet address:
http://www.cdc.gov/nchswww

U.S. Department of Housing and Urban Development
Office of the Assistant Secretary for Community Planning and Development
451 7th St., S.W.
Washington, DC 20410-0555
Information and Publications:
1-800-998-9999
Internet address: http://www.hud.gov/

Department of the Interior
Geological Survey
Earth Science Information Center
Geological Survey
U.S. Department of the Interior
507 National Center
Reston, VA 20192
Information and Publications:
1-888-275-8747
Internet address for minerals:
http://minerals.usgs.gov/
Internet address for other materials:
http://ask.usgs.gov/

Department of Justice
Bureau of Justice Statistics
Statistics Division
810 7th St., N.W., 2nd Floor
Washington, DC 20531
Information and Publications:
202-307-0765
Internet address:
http://www.ojp.usdoj.gov/bjs/

National Criminal Justice Reference Service
Box 6000
Rockville, MD 20849-6000
Information and Publications:
301-519-5500
Publications: 1-800-732-3277
Internet address: http://www.ncjrs.org/

Federal Bureau of Investigation
U.S. Department of Justice
J. Edgar Hoover FBI Building
935 Pennsylvania Ave., N.W.
Washington, DC 20535-0001
202-324-3000
National Press Office: 202-324-3691
Research and Communications Unit:
202-324-5611
Internet address: http://www.fbi.gov/

Immigration and Naturalization Service
Statistics Division
Immigration and Naturalization Service
U.S. Department of Justice
425 I St., N.W., Rm. 4034
Washington, DC 20536
Information and Publications:
202-305-1613
Internet address:
http://www.ins.gov/graphics/ index.htm

Department of Labor
Bureau of Labor Statistics
Office of Publications and Special Studies
Services
Division of Information
Bureau of Labor Statistics
2 Mass. Ave., N.E., Room 2850
Washington, DC 20212
Information and Publications:
202-691-5200
Internet address: http://www.bls.gov/

Employment and Training Administration
Office of Public Affairs
Employment and Training Administration
U.S. Department of Labor
200 Constitution Ave., N.W., Room
C4517
Washington, DC 20210
Information and Publications:
202-693-3900
Internet address: http://www.doleta.gov/

Department of Transportation
Federal Aviation Administration
U.S. Department of Transportation
800 Independence Ave., S.W.
Washington, DC 20591
Information and Publications:
202-267-3484
Internet address: http://www.faa.gov/
Bureau of Transportation Statistics
400 7th St., S.W., Room 3103
Washington, DC 20590
Products: 202-366-3282
Statistical Information:800-853-1351
Internet address: http://www.bts.gov/

Federal Highway Administration
Office of Public Affairs
Federal Highway Administration
U.S. Department of Transportation
400 7th St., S.W.
Washington, DC 20590
Information: 202-366-0660
Internet address:
http://www.fhwa.dot.gov/

*National Highway Traffic Safety
Administration*
Office of Public & Consumer Affairs
National Highway Traffic Safety
Administration
U.S. Department of Transportation
400 7th St., S.W.
Washington, DC 20590
Information: 202-366-4000
Publications: 202-366-8892
Internet address:
http://www.nhtsa.dot.gov/

Department of the Treasury
Internal Revenue Service
Statistics of Income Division
Internal Revenue Service
P.O. Box 2608
Washington, DC 20013-2608
Information and Publications:
202-874-0410
Internet address:
http://www.irs.gov/tax_stats

Department of Veterans Affairs
Office of Public Affairs
Department of Veterans Affairs
810 Vermont Ave., N.W.
Washington, DC 20420
Information: 202-273-5400
Internet address: http://www.va.gov/

Independent Agencies
Administrative Office of the U.S. Courts
Statistics Division
1 Columbus Circle, N.E.
Washington, DC 20544
Information: 202-502-1455
Internet address:
http://www.uscourts.gov/
Environmental Protection Agency
US EPA Headquarters Library,
Room EPA 3340
Environmental Protection Agency West
1200 Pennsylvania Avenue, N.W.
Mail Code 3404T
Washington, DC 20460-0001
Information: 202-566-0556
Internet address: http://www.epa.gov/

Federal Reserve Board
Division of Research and Statistics
Federal Reserve Board
Washington, DC 20551
Information: 202-452-3301
Publications: 202-452-3245
Internet address:
http://www.federalreserve.gov/

National Science Foundation
Office of Legislation and Public Affairs
National Science Foundation
4201 Wilson Boulevard
Arlington, Virginia 22230
Information: 703-292-8070
Publications: 703-292-8129
Internet address: http://www.nsf.gov/

Telephone & Internet Contacts   xiii

Independent Agencies —Con.

Securities and Exchange Commission

Office of Public Affairs
Securities and Exchange Commission
450 5th St., N.W., Room 2500
Mail Stop 0211
Washington, DC 20549
Information: 202-942-0020
Publications: 202-942-4040
Internet address: http://www.sec.gov/

Independent Agencies —Con.

Social Security Administration

6400 Security Blvd
Baltimore, MD 21235
Information and Publications:
 1-800-772-1213
Internet Address: http://www.ssa.gov/

U.S. Census Bureau, Statistical Abstract of the United States: 2002

Population

This section presents statistics on the growth, distribution, and characteristics of the U.S. population. The principal source of these data is the U.S. Census Bureau, which conducts a decennial census of population, a monthly population survey, a program of population estimates and projections, and a number of other periodic surveys relating to population characteristics. For a list of relevant publications, see the Guide to Sources of Statistics in Appendix I.

Decennial censuses—The U.S. Constitution provides for a census of the population every 10 years, primarily to establish a basis for apportionment of members of the House of Representatives among the states. For over a century after the first census in 1790, the census organization was a temporary one, created only for each decennial census. In 1902, the Census Bureau was established as a permanent federal agency, responsible for enumerating the population and also for compiling statistics on other population and housing characteristics.

Historically, the enumeration of the population has been a complete count. That is, an attempt is made to account for every person, for each person's residence, and for other characteristics (sex, age, family relationships, etc.). Since the 1940 census, in addition to the complete count information, some data have been obtained from representative samples of the population. In the 1990 and 2000 censuses, variable sampling rates were employed. For most of the country, 1 in every 6 households (about 17 percent) received the long form or sample questionnaire; in governmental units estimated to have fewer than 2,500 inhabitants, every other household (50 percent) received the sample questionnaire to enhance the reliability of sample data for small areas. Exact agreement is not to be expected between sample data and the 100-percent count. Sample data may be used with confidence where large numbers are involved and assumed to indicate trends and relationships where small numbers are involved.

Census Bureau data presented here have not been adjusted for underenumeration. Results from the evaluation program for the 1990 census indicate that the overall national undercount was between 1 and 2 percent. The estimate from the Post Enumeration Survey (PES) was 1.6 percent, and the estimate from Demographic Analysis (DA) was 1.8 percent. Both the PES and DA estimates show disproportionately high undercounts for some demographic groups. For example, the PES estimates of percent net undercount for Blacks (4.4 percent), Hispanics (5.0 percent), and American Indians (4.5 percent) were higher than the estimated undercount of non-Hispanic Whites (0.7 percent). Historical DA estimates demonstrate that the overall undercount rate in the census has declined significantly over the past 50 years (from an estimated 5.4 percent in 1940 to 1.8 percent in 1990), yet the undercount of Blacks has remained disproportionately high.

Current Population Survey (CPS)—This is a monthly nationwide survey of a scientifically selected sample representing the noninstitutional civilian population. The sample is located in 754 areas with coverage in every state and the District of Columbia and is subject to sampling error. At the present time, about 60,000 occupied households are eligible for interview every month; of these about 7.5 percent are, for various reasons, unavailable for interview.

While the primary purpose of the CPS is to obtain monthly statistics on the labor force, it also serves as a vehicle for inquiries on other subjects. Using CPS data, the Bureau issues a series of publications under the general title of *Current Popula-tion Reports*, which cover population char-acteristics (P20), consumer income (P60), special studies (P23), and other topics.

Estimates of population characteristics based on the CPS will not agree with the counts from the census because the CPS and the census use different procedures for collecting and processing the data for racial groups, the Hispanic population, and other topics. Caution should also be used when comparing estimates for vari-ous years because of the periodic intro-duction of changes into the CPS. Begin-ning in January 1994, a number of changes were introduced into the CPS that effect all data comparisons with prior years. These changes include the results of a major redesign of the survey ques-tionnaire and collection methodology and the introduction of 1990 census popula-tion controls, adjusted for the estimated undercount. This change in population controls had relatively little impact on derived measures such as means, medi-ans, and percent distribution, but did have a significant impact on levels.

Population estimates and projec-tions—National population estimates start with decennial census data as benchmarks and add annual population component of change data. Component of change data come from various agencies, as follows: National Center for Health Sta-tistics (births and deaths), Immigration and Naturalization Service (legal immi-grants), Office of Refugee Resettlement (refugees), U.S. Census Bureau's Interna-tional Programs Center (net movement between Puerto Rico and the U.S. main-land), Armed Forces, Department of Defense, and Office of Personnel Manage-ment (movement of military and civilian citizens abroad). Emigration and net undocumented immigration are projected based on research using census data. Esti-mates for states, counties, and smaller areas are based on the same component of change data and sources as the national estimates. School statistics from state departments of education and paro-chial school systems, federal income tax returns from the Internal Revenue Service, group quarters from the Federal-State Cooperative program and the Veterans

Administration, and medicare data from the Centers for Medicare and Medicaid Services are also included.

Data for the population by age for April 1, 1990 (shown in Table 12) are modified counts. The review of detailed 1990 infor-mation indicated that respondents tended to provide their age as of the date of completion of the questionnaire, not their age as of April 1, 1990. In addition, there may have been a tendency for respon-dents to round-up their age if they were close to having a birthday. A detailed explanation of the age modification pro-cedure appears in 1990 Census of Popula-tion and Housing Data Paper Listing (CPH-L-74).

Population estimates and projections are published in the P25 Series of *Current Population Reports* and on the Census Bureau Internet site <http://www.census.gov>. These estimates and projec-tions are generally consistent with official decennial census figures and do not reflect the amount of estimated census underenumeration. However, these esti-mates and projections by race have been modified and are not comparable to the census race categories (see section below under "Race"). For details on methodol-ogy, see the sources cited below the indi-vidual tables.

Immigration—The principal source of immigration data is the *Statistical Year-book of the Immigration and Naturaliza-tion Service*, published annually by the Immigration and Naturalization Service (INS), a unit of the Department of Justice. Immigration statistics are prepared from entry visas and change of immigration status forms. Immigrants are aliens admit-ted for legal permanent residence in the United States. The procedures for admis-sion depend on whether the alien is resid-ing inside or outside the United States at the time of application for permanent residence. Eligible aliens residing outside the United States are issued immigrant visas by the U.S. Department of State. Eli-gible aliens residing in the United States are allowed to change their status from temporary to permanent residence at INS district offices. The category, immigrant, includes persons who may have entered the United States as nonimmigrants or

2   Population

refugees, but who subsequently changed their status to that of a permanent resident. Nonresident aliens admitted to the United States for a temporary period are nonimmigrants (Table 1243). Refugees are considered nonimmigrants when initially admitted into the United States but are not included in nonimmigrant admission data. A refugee is an alien outside the United States who is unable or unwilling to return to his or her county of nationality because of persecution or a well-founded fear of persecution.

U.S. immigration law gives preferential immigration status to persons with a close family relationship with a U.S. citizen or legal permanent resident, persons with needed job skills, or persons who qualify as refugees. Immigration to the United States can be divided into two general categories: (1) those subject to the annual worldwide limitation and (2) those exempt from it. The Immigration Act of 1990 established major revisions in the numerical limits and preference system regulating legal immigration. The numerical limits are imposed on visas issued and not on admissions. The maximum number of visas allowed to be issued under the preference categories in 2000 was 436,900 – 294,601 for family-sponsored immigrants and 142,299 for employment-based immigrants. There are nine categories among which the family-sponsored and employment-based immigrant visas are distributed, beginning in fiscal year 1992. The family-sponsored preferences are based on the alien's relationship with a U.S. citizen or legal permanent resident (see Table 6). The employment-based preferences are (1) priority workers (persons of extraordinary ability, outstanding professors and researchers, and certain multinational executives and managers); (2) professionals with advanced degrees or aliens with exceptional ability; (3) skilled workers, professionals without advanced degrees, and needed unskilled workers; (4) special immigrants; and (5) employment creation immigrants (investors). Within the overall limitations the per-country limit for independent countries is set to 7 percent of the total family-sponsored and employment-based limits, while dependent areas are limited to 2 percent of the total. The 2000 limit allowed no more than 30,583 preference

visas for any independent country and 8,738 for any dependency. Those exempt from the worldwide limitation include immediate relatives of U.S. citizens, refugees and asylees adjusting to permanent residence, and other various classes of special immigrants (see Table 6).

The Refugee Act of 1980, effective April 1, 1980, provides for a uniform admission procedure for refugees of all countries, based on the United Nations' definition of refugees. Authorized admission ceilings are set annually by the President in consultation with Congress. After 1 year of residence in the United States, refugees are eligible for immigrant status. The Immigration Reform and Control Act of 1986 (IRCA) allows two groups of illegal aliens to become temporary and then permanent residents of the United States: aliens who have been in the United States unlawfully since January 1, 1982 (legalization applicants), and aliens who were employed in seasonal agricultural work for a minimum period of time (Special Agricultural Worker (SAW) applicants). The application period for temporary residency for legalization applicants began on May 5, 1987, and ended on May 4, 1988, while the application period for SAW applicants began on June 1, 1987, and ended on November 30, 1988. Legalization applicants became eligible for permanent residence beginning in fiscal year 1989. Beginning 1989 immigrant data include temporary residents who were granted permanent residence under the legalization program of IRCA.

Metropolitan Areas (MAs)—The general concept of a metropolitan area is one of a core area containing a large population nucleus, together with adjacent communities that have a high degree of social and economic integration with that core. Metropolitan statistical areas (MSAs), consolidated metropolitan statistical areas (CMSAs), and primary metropolitan statistical areas (PMSAs) are defined by the Office of Management and Budget (OMB) as a standard for federal agencies in the preparation and publication of statistics relating to metropolitan areas. The entire territory of the United States is classified as metropolitan (inside MSAs or CMSAs—PMSAs are components of CMSAs) or nonmetropolitan (outside MSAs or CMSAs).

U.S. Census Bureau, Statistical Abstract of the United States: 2002

MSAs, CMSAs, and PMSAs are defined in terms of entire counties except in New England, where the definitions are in terms of county subdivisions (primarily cities and towns). The OMB also defines New England County Metropolitan Areas (NECMAs), which are county-based alternatives to the MSAs and CMSAs in the six New England states. Over time, new MAs are created and the components of others change. The analysis of historical trends, therefore, must be made cautiously. For descriptive details and a listing of titles and components of MAs, see Appendix II.

Urban and rural—For Census 2000, the Census Bureau classified as urban all territory, population, and housing units located within urbanized areas (UAs) and urban clusters (UCs). A UA consists of densely settled territory that contains 50,000 or more people, while a UC consists of densely settled territory with at least 2,500 people but fewer than 50,000 people. (UCs are a new type of geographic entity for Census 2000.) Prior to Census 2000—from the 1950 census through the 1990 census—the urban population consisted of all people living in UAs and most places outside of UAs with a census population of 2,500 or more.

UAs and UCs encompass territory that generally consists of:

- A cluster of one or more block goups or census blocks each of which has a population density of at least 1,000 people per square mile at the time,
- Surrounding block groups and census blocks each of which has a population density of at least 500 people per square mile at the time, and
- Less densely settled blocks that form enclaves or indentations, or are used to connect discontiguous areas with qualifying densities.

They also may include an airport located adjacent to qualifying densely settled area if it has an annual enplanement (aircraft boarding) of at least 10,000 people.

"Rural" for Census 2000 consists of all territory, population, and housing units located outside of UA's and UCs. Prior to Census 2000, rural consisted of all territory, population, and housing outside of UAs and outside of other places designated as "urban." For Census 2000, many more geographic entities, including metropolitan areas, counties, county subdivisions, and places, contain both urban and rural territory, population, and housing units.

Residence—In determining residence, the Census Bureau counts each person as an inhabitant of a usual place of residence (i.e., the place where one usually lives and sleeps). While this place is not necessarily a person's legal residence or voting residence, the use of these different bases of classification would produce the same results in the vast majority of cases.

Race—For the 1990 census, the Census Bureau collected and published racial statistics as outlined in Statistical Policy Directive No. 15 issued by the U.S. Office of Management and Budget. This directive provided standards on ethnic and racial categories for statistical reporting to be used by all federal agencies. According to the directive, the basic racial categories were American Indian or Alaska Native, Asian or Pacific Islander, Black, and White. (The directive identified Hispanic origin as an ethnicity.) The question on race for Census 2000 was different from the one for the 1990 census in several ways. Most significantly, respondents were given the option of selecting one or more race categories to indicate their racial identities. Because of these changes, the Census 2000 data on race are not directly comparable with data from the 1990 census or earlier censuses. Caution must be used when interpreting changes in the racial composition of the U.S. population over time. Census 2000 adheres to the federal standards for collecting and presenting data on race and Hispanic origin as established by the Office of Management and Budget (OMB) in October 1997. Starting with Census 2000, the OMB requires federal agencies to use a minimum of five race categories: White, Black or African American, American Indian or Alaska Native, Asian, and Native Hawaiian or Other Pacific Islander. For respondents unable to identify with any of these five race categories, OMB approved and included a sixth category—"Some other

U.S. Census Bureau, Statistical Abstract of the United States: 2002

race"—on the Census 2000 questionnaire. The Census 2000 question on race included 15 separate response categories and three areas where respondents could write in a more specific race group. The response categories and write-in answers can be combined to create the five minimum OMB race categories plus "Some other race." People who responded to the question on race by indicating only one race are referred to as the race *alone* population, or the group that reported only one race category. Six categories make up this population: White *alone*; Black or African American *alone*; American Indian and Alaska Native *alone*; Asian *alone*; Native Hawaiian and Other Pacific Island *alone*; and Some other race *alone*. Individuals who chose more than one of the six race categories are referred to as the *Two or more races* population, or as the group that reported *more than one race.*

The concept of race the Census Bureau uses reflects self-identification by respondents; that is the individual's perception of his/her racial identity. The concept is not intended to reflect any biological or anthropological definition. Furthermore, the Census Bureau recognizes that the categories of the race item include both racial and national origin or sociocultural groups.

Data for the population by race for April 1, 1990 (shown in Table 10) are modified counts and are not comparable to the 1990 census race categories. These numbers were computed using 1990 census data by race which had been modified to be consistent with the guidelines in Federal Statistical Policy Directive No. 15 issued by the Office of Management and Budget. A detailed explanation of the race modification procedure appears in 1990 Census of Population and Housing Data Paper Listing (CPH-L-74).

In the CPS and other household sample surveys in which data are obtained through personal interview, respondents are asked to classify their race as: (1) White; (2) Black; (3) American Indian, Aleut, or Eskimo; or (4) Asian or Pacific Islander. The procedures for classifying persons of mixed races who could not provide a single response to the race question are generally similar to those used in the census.

Hispanic population—The question on Hispanic origin for Census 2000 was similar to the 1990 census question, except for its placement on the questionnaire. For Census 2000, the question on Hispanic origin was asked directly before the question on race. For the 1990 census, the order was reversed—the question on race preceded questions on age and marital status, which were followed by the question on Hispanic origin. In the 1990 census, the Census Bureau collected data on the Hispanic origin population in the United States by using a self-identification question. Persons of Spanish/Hispanic origin are those who classified themselves in one of the specific Hispanic origin categories listed on the questionnaire—Mexican, Puerto Rican, Cuban, as well as those who indicated that they were of Other Spanish/Hispanic origin. Persons of Other Spanish/Hispanic origin are those whose origins are from Spain, the Spanish-speaking countries of Central or South America, or the Dominican Republic. In 1980, 1990, and 2000, the Hispanic-origin question contained prelisted categories for the largest Hispanic-origin groups—Mexican, Puerto Rican, Cuban, and Other Spanish/Hispanic. The 1990 Hispanic-origin question differed from the 1980 question in that it contained a write-in line for the Other Spanish/Hispanic category. This was coded only for sample data. Another difference between the 1980 and 1990 Hispanic-origin question is that in 1980 the wording of the Hispanic-origin question read: "Is this person of Spanish/Hispanic origin or descent?" while in 1990 the word "descent" was dropped from the question. Persons of Hispanic origin may be of any race.

In the CPS information on Hispanic persons is gathered by using a self-identification question. Persons classify themselves in one of the Hispanic categories in response to the question: "What is the origin or descent of each person in this household?" Hispanic persons in the CPS are persons who report themselves as

U.S. Census Bureau, Statistical Abstract of the United States: 2002

Mexican-American, Chicano, Mexican, Puerto Rican, Cuban, Central or South American (Spanish countries), or other Hispanic origin.

Nativity—The native population consists of all persons born in the United States, Puerto Rico, or an outlying area of the United States. It also includes persons born in a foreign country who had at least one parent who was a U.S. citizen. All other persons are classified as "foreign born."

Mobility status—The U.S. population is classified according to mobility status on the basis of a comparison between the place of residence of each individual at the time of the survey or census and the place of residence at a specified earlier date. Nonmovers are all persons who were living in the same house or apartment at the end of the period as at the beginning of the period. Movers are all persons who were living in a different house or apartment at the end of the period than at the beginning of the period. Movers are further classified as to whether they were living in the same or different county, state, or region or were movers from abroad. Movers from abroad include all persons, either U.S. citizens or noncitizens, whose place of residence was outside the United States at the beginning of the period; that is, in Puerto Rico, an outlying area under the jurisdiction of the United States, or a foreign country.

Living arrangements—Living arrangements refer to residency in households or in group quarters. A "household" comprises all persons who occupy a "housing unit," that is, a house, an apartment or other group of rooms, or a single room that constitutes "separate living quarters." A household includes the related family members and all the unrelated persons, if any, such as lodgers, foster children, wards, or employees who share the housing unit. A person living alone or a group of unrelated persons sharing the same housing unit is also counted as a household. See text, Section 20, Construction and Housing, for definition of housing unit.

All persons not living in housing units are classified as living in group quarters. These individuals may be institutionalized, e.g., under care or custody in juvenile facilities, jails, correctional centers, hospitals, or nursing homes; or they may be residents in noninstitutional group quarters such as college dormitories, group homes, or military barracks.

Householder—The householder is the first adult household member listed on the questionnaire. The instructions call for listing first the person (or one of the persons) in whose name the home is owned or rented. If a home is owned or rented jointly by a married couple, either the husband or the wife may be listed first. Prior to 1980, the husband was always considered the household head (householder) in married-couple households.

Family—The term family refers to a group of two or more persons related by birth, marriage, or adoption and residing together in a household. A family includes among its members the householder.

Subfamily—A subfamily consists of a married couple and their children, if any, or one parent with one or more never-married children under 18 years old living in a household. Subfamilies are divided into "related" and "unrelated" subfamilies. A related subfamily is related to, but does not include, the householder. Members of a related subfamily are also members of the family with whom they live. The number of related subfamilies, therefore, is not included in the count of families. An unrelated subfamily may include persons such as guests, lodgers, or resident employees and their spouses and/or children; none of whom is related to the householder.

Married couple—A married couple is defined as a husband and wife living together in the same household, with or without children and other relatives.

Statistical reliability—For a discussion of statistical collection and estimation, sampling procedures, and measures of statistical reliability applicable to Census Bureau data, see Appendix III.

U.S. Census Bureau, Statistical Abstract of the United States: 2002

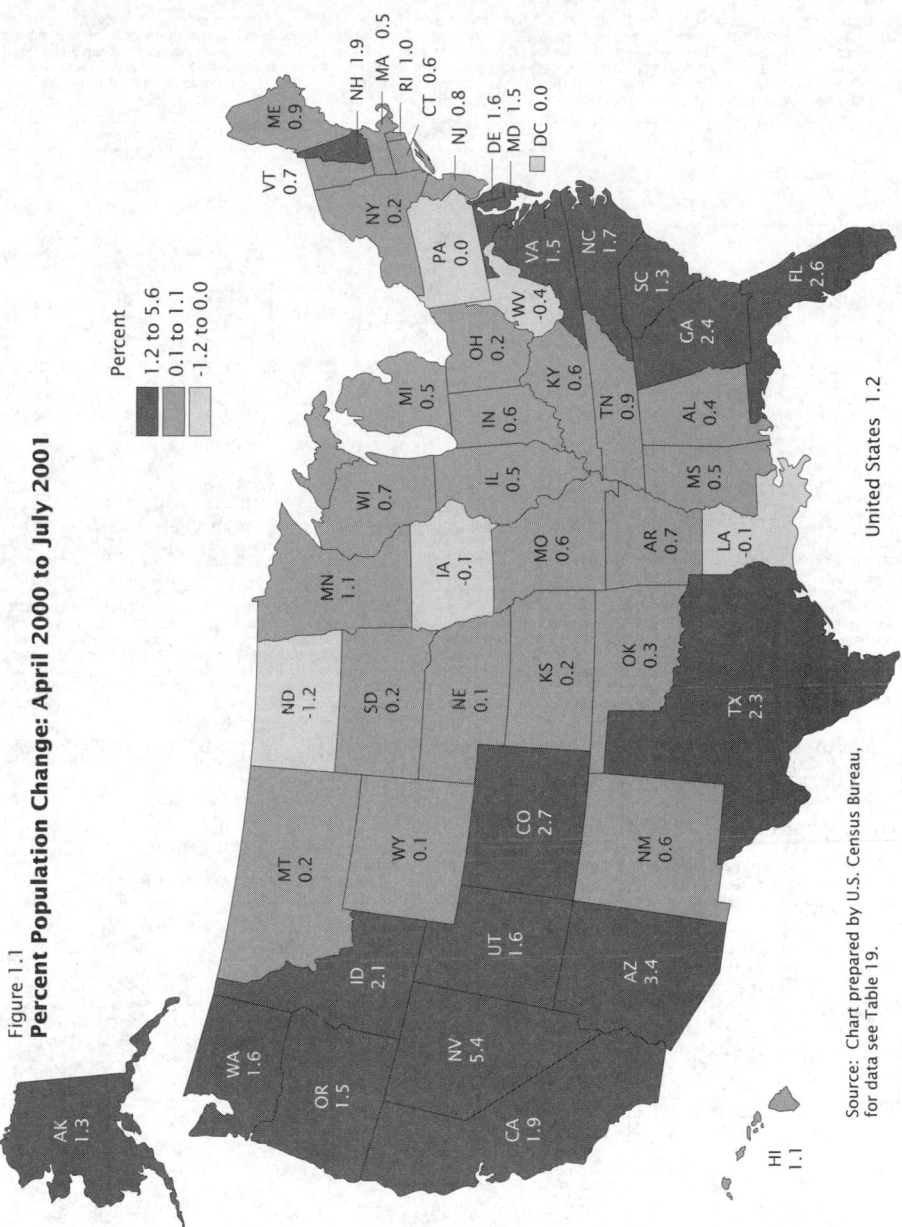

Figure 1.1
Percent Population Change: April 2000 to July 2001

Percent
1.2 to 5.6
0.1 to 1.1
-1.2 to 0.0

United States 1.2

AK 1.3
WA 1.6
OR 1.5
CA 1.9
NV 5.4
ID 2.1
UT 1.6
AZ 3.4
MT 0.2
WY 0.1
CO 2.7
NM 0.6
ND -1.2
SD 0.2
NE 0.1
KS 0.2
OK 0.3
TX 2.3
MN 1.1
IA -0.1
MO 0.6
AR 0.7
LA -0.1
WI 0.7
IL 0.5
MS 0.5
MI 0.5
IN 0.6
KY 0.6
TN 0.9
AL 0.4
OH 0.2
WV -0.4
VA 1.5
NC 1.7
SC 1.3
GA 2.4
FL 2.6
PA 0.0
NY 0.2
VT 0.7
ME 0.9
NH 1.9
MA 0.5
RI 1.0
CT 0.6
NJ 0.8
DE 1.6
MD 1.5
DC 0.0
HI 1.1

Source: Chart prepared by U.S. Census Bureau,
for data see Table 19.

Population 7

No. 1. Population and Area: 1790 to 2000

[Area figures represent area on indicated date including in some cases considerable areas not then organized or settled, and not covered by the census. Total area figures for 1790 to 1970 have been recalculated on the basis of the remeasurement of states and counties for the 1980 census, but not on the basis of the 1990 census. The land and water area figures for past censuses have not been adjusted and are not strictly comparable with the total area data for comparable dates because the land areas were derived from different base data, and these values are known to have changed with the construction of reservoirs, draining of lakes, etc. Density figures are based on land area measurements as reported in earlier censuses]

Census date	Resident population		Increase over preceding census		Area (square miles)		
	Number	Per square mile of land area	Number	Percent	Total	Land	Water [1]
1790 (Aug. 2)	3,929,214	4.5	(X)	(X)	891,364	864,746	24,065
1800 (Aug. 4)	5,308,483	6.1	1,379,269	35.1	891,364	864,746	24,065
1810 (Aug. 6)	7,239,881	4.3	1,931,398	36.4	1,722,685	1,681,828	34,175
1820 (Aug. 7)	9,638,453	5.5	2,398,572	33.1	1,792,552	1,749,462	38,544
1830 (June 1)	12,866,020	7.4	3,227,567	33.5	1,792,552	1,749,462	38,544
1840 (June 1)	17,069,453	9.8	4,203,433	32.7	1,792,552	1,749,462	38,544
1850 (June 1)	23,191,876	7.9	6,122,423	35.9	2,991,655	2,940,042	52,705
1860 (June 1)	31,443,321	10.6	8,251,445	35.6	3,021,295	2,969,640	52,747
1870 (June 1)	[2]39,818,449	[2]11.2	8,375,128	26.6	3,612,299	3,540,705	52,747
1880 (June 1)	50,189,209	14.2	10,370,760	26.0	3,612,299	3,540,705	52,747
1890 (June 1)	62,979,766	17.8	12,790,557	25.5	3,612,299	3,540,705	52,747
1900 (June 1)	76,212,168	21.5	13,232,402	21.0	3,618,770	3,547,314	52,553
1910 (Apr. 15)	92,228,496	26.0	16,016,328	21.0	3,618,770	3,547,045	52,822
1920 (Jan. 1)	106,021,537	29.9	13,793,041	15.0	3,618,770	3,546,931	52,936
1930 (Apr. 1)	123,202,624	34.7	17,181,087	16.2	3,618,770	3,551,608	45,259
1940 (Apr. 1)	132,164,569	37.2	8,961,945	7.3	3,618,770	3,551,608	45,259
1950 (Apr. 1)	151,325,798	42.6	19,161,229	14.5	3,618,770	3,552,206	63,005
1960 (Apr. 1)	179,323,175	50.6	27,997,377	18.5	3,618,770	3,540,911	74,212
1970 (Apr. 1)	[3]203,302,031	[3]57.5	23,978,856	13.4	3,618,770	[3]3,536,855	[3]78,444
1980 (Apr. 1)	[4]226,542,199	64.0	23,240,168	11.4	3,618,770	3,539,289	79,481
1990 (Apr. 1)	[5]248,718,302	70.3	22,176,103	9.8	[6]3,717,796	[6]3,536,278	[6]181,518
2000 (Apr. 1)	[7]281,422,426	79.6	32,704,124	13.1	3,794,083	3,537,438	256,645

X Not applicable.   [1] Data for 1790 to 1980 cover inland water only. Data for 1990 comprises Great Lakes, inland, and coastal water. Data for 2000 comprises Great Lakes, inland, territorial and coastal water.   [2] Revised to include adjustments for underenumeration in southern states; unrevised number is 38,558,371 (13.0 per square mile).   [3] Figures corrected after 1970 final reports were issued.   [4] Total population count has been revised since the 1980 census publications. Numbers by age, race, Hispanic origin, and sex have not been corrected.   [5] The April 1, 1990, census count includes count question resolution corrections processed through December 1997, and does not include adjustments for census coverage errors.   [6] Data reflect corrections made after publication of the results.   [7] The revised April 1, 2000 census count includes count question resolution corrections processed through May 2002, and does not include adjustments for census coverage errors.

Source: U.S. Census Bureau, *1990 Census of Population and Housing, Population and Housing Unit Counts* (CPH-2); 1990 Census of Population and Housing Listing (1990 CPH-L-157); American Factfinder, GCT-PH1-R, Population, Housing Units, Area, and Density (geographies ranked by total population): 2000; and unpublished data.

No. 2. Population: 1960 to 2001

[In thousands, except percent (180,671 represents 180,671,000). Estimates as of July 1. Total population includes Armed Forces abroad; civilian population excludes Armed Forces. For basis of estimates, see text of this section]

Year	Total		Resident population	Civilian population	Year	Total		Resident population	Civilian population
	Population	Percent change [1]				Population	Percent change [1]		
1960	180,671	1.60	179,979	178,140	1981	229,966	0.98	229,466	227,818
1961	183,691	1.67	182,992	181,143	1982	232,188	0.97	231,664	229,995
1962	186,538	1.55	185,771	183,677	1983	234,307	0.91	233,792	232,097
1963	189,242	1.45	188,483	186,493	1984	236,348	0.87	235,825	234,110
1964	191,889	1.40	191,141	189,141	1985	238,466	0.90	237,924	236,219
1965	194,303	1.26	193,526	191,605	1986	240,651	0.92	240,133	238,412
1966	196,560	1.16	195,576	193,420	1987	242,804	0.89	242,289	240,550
1967	198,712	1.09	197,457	195,264	1988	245,021	0.91	244,499	242,817
1968	200,706	1.00	199,399	197,113	1989	247,342	0.95	246,819	245,131
1969	202,677	0.98	201,385	199,145	1990	250,132	1.13	249,623	247,983
1970	205,052	1.17	203,984	201,895	1991	253,493	1.34	252,981	251,370
1971	207,661	1.27	206,827	204,866	1992	256,894	1.34	256,514	254,929
1972	209,896	1.08	209,284	207,511	1993	260,255	1.31	259,919	258,446
1973	211,909	0.96	211,357	209,600	1994	263,436	1.22	263,126	261,714
1974	213,854	0.92	213,342	211,636	1995	266,557	1.18	266,278	264,927
1975	215,973	0.99	215,465	213,789	1996	269,667	1.17	269,394	268,108
1976	218,035	0.95	217,563	215,894	1997	272,912	1.20	272,647	271,394
1977	220,239	1.01	219,760	218,106	1998	276,115	1.17	275,854	274,633
1978	222,585	1.06	222,095	220,467	1999	279,295	1.15	279,040	277,841
1979	225,055	1.11	224,567	222,969	2000	282,339	1.09	282,125	280,939
1980	227,726	1.19	227,225	225,621	2001	285,024	0.95	284,797	283,624

[1] Percent change from immediate preceding year.

Source: U.S. Census Bureau, *Current Population Reports*, P25-802 and P25-1095; "Table CO-EST2001-12-00 - Time Series of Intercensal State Population Estimates: April 1, 1990 to April 1, 2000"; published 11 April 2002; <http://eire.census.gov/popest/data/counties/tables/CO-EST2001-12/CO-EST2001-12-00.php>; "Table NA-MON - Monthly National Population Estimates", published 1 July 2002; <http://eire.census.gov/popest/data/national/tables/NA-EST2001-04.php>; and unpublished data.

No. 3. Resident Population Projections: 2002 to 2100

[In thousands (280,306 represents 280,306,000). As of July 1. The projections are based on assumptions about future childbearing, mortality, and migration. The level of childbearing among women for the middle series is assumed to remain close to present levels, with differences by race and Hispanic origin diminishing over time. Mortality is assumed to decline gradually with less variation by race and Hispanic origin than at present. International migration is assumed to vary over time and decrease generally relative to the size of the population. Assumptions for the lowest and highest series are summarized in "Methodology and Assumptions for the Population Projections of the United States: 1999 to 2100, Working Paper #38"]

Year	Middle series [1]	Lowest series [2]	Highest series [3]	Zero international migration series [4]
2002	280,306	278,801	282,087	276,709
2003	282,798	280,624	285,422	278,112
2004	285,266	282,352	288,841	279,493
2005	287,716	284,000	292,339	280,859
2006	290,153	285,581	295,911	282,219
2007	292,583	287,106	299,557	283,579
2008	295,009	288,583	303,274	284,945
2009	297,436	290,018	307,060	286,322
2010	299,862	291,413	310,910	287,710
2011	302,300	292,778	314,846	289,108
2012	304,764	294,120	318,893	290,514
2013	307,250	295,436	323,044	291,924
2014	309,753	296,723	327,293	293,334
2015	312,268	297,977	331,636	294,741
2016	314,793	299,197	336,069	296,144
2017	317,325	300,379	340,589	297,539
2018	319,860	301,521	345,192	298,921
2019	322,395	302,617	349,877	300,288
2020	324,927	303,664	354,642	301,636
2025	337,815	308,229	380,397	307,923
2030	351,070	311,656	409,604	313,219
2035	364,319	313,819	441,618	317,534
2040	377,350	314,673	475,949	321,167
2045	390,398	314,484	512,904	324,449
2050	403,687	313,546	552,757	327,641
2075	480,504	303,970	809,243	349,032
2100	570,954	282,706	1,182,390	377,444

[1] Total fertility rate in 2050 = 2,219; life expectancy in 2050 = 83.9 years; and annual net immigration in 2050 = 984,000. These are middle level assumptions. For explanation of total fertility rate; see headnote, Table 71.   [2] Total fertility rate in 2050 = 1,800; life expectancy in 2050 = 82.2 years; and annual net immigration in 2050 = 169,000. These are lowest level assumptions.   [3] Total fertility rate in 2050 = 2,647; life expectancy in 2050 = 86.1 years; and annual net immigration in 2050 = 2,812,000. These are highest level assumptions.   [4] Middle level assumptions for fertility and mortality; zero level assumption for international migration.

Source: U.S. Census Bureau, "Annual Projections of the Total Resident Population as of July 1: Middle, Lowest, Highest, and Zero International Migration Series, 2000 to 2100"; published: 14 February 2000; <http://www.census.gov/population/projections/nation/summary/np-t1.txt>.

No. 4. Components of Population Change—Projections, 2005 to 2050

[286,549 represents 286,549,000. Resident population. Based on middle series of assumptions. See footnote 1, Table 3]

Year	Popula-tion as of Jan. 1 (1,000)	Calendar year					Rate per 1,000 midyear population			
		Net increase		Births (1,000)	Deaths (1,000)	Net migra-tion [2] (1,000)	Net growth rate	Birth rate	Death rate	Net migration rate [2]
		Total (1,000)	Per-cent [1]							
2005	286,549	2,443	0.9	4,045	2,480	878	8.5	14.1	8.6	3.1
2010	298,710	2,425	0.8	4,283	2,578	720	8.1	14.3	8.6	2.4
2015	311,069	2,521	0.8	4,476	2,695	740	8.1	14.3	8.6	2.4
2020	323,724	2,530	0.8	4,613	2,840	757	7.8	14.2	8.7	2.3
2025	336,566	2,621	0.8	4,736	3,033	918	7.8	14.0	9.0	2.7
2030	349,789	2,688	0.8	4,878	3,257	1,067	7.7	13.9	9.3	3.0
2040	376,123	2,601	0.7	5,286	3,702	1,018	6.9	14.0	9.8	2.7
2050	402,420	2,699	0.7	5,661	3,952	990	6.7	14.0	9.8	2.5

[1] Percent of population at beginning of period.   [2] Covers net international migration and movement of Armed Forces, federally affiliated civilian citizens, and their dependents.

Source: U.S. Census Bureau, "Population Projections of the Total Resident Population by Quarter: Middle Series, April 1, 1999, to January 1, 2101"; published 13 January 2000; <http://www.census.gov/population/projections/nation/summary/np-t2.txt>; and "Components of Change for the Total Resident Population: Middle Series, 1999 to 2100"; published 13 January 2000; <http://www.census.gov/population/projections/nation/summary/np-t6-a.txt> and <http://www.census.gov/population/projections/nation/summary/np-t6-b.txt>.

Population   9

No. 5. Immigration: 1901 to 2000

[In thousands, except rate (8,795 represents 8,795,000). **For fiscal years ending in year shown**; see text, Section 8, State and Local Government Finances and Employment. For definition of immigrants, see text of this section. Data represent immigrants admitted. Rates based on Census Bureau estimates as of July 1 for resident population through 1929 and for total population thereafter (excluding Alaska and Hawaii prior to 1959)]

Period	Number	Rate [1]	Year	Number	Rate [1]
1901 to 1910	8,795	10.4	1990	1,536	6.1
1911 to 1920	5,736	5.7	1991	1,827	7.2
1921 to 1930	4,107	3.5	1992	974	3.8
1931 to 1940	528	0.4	1993	904	3.5
1941 to 1950	1,035	0.7	1994	804	3.1
1951 to 1960	2,515	1.5	1995	720	2.7
1961 to 1970	3,322	1.7	1996	916	3.4
1971 to 1980	4,493	2.1	1997	798	3.0
1981 to 1990	7,338	3.1	1998	654	2.4
1991 to 2000	9,095	3.4	1999	647	2.4
			2000	850	3.1

[1] Annual rate per 1,000 U.S. population. Rate computed by dividing sum of annual immigration totals by sum of annual U.S. population totals for same number of years.

Source: U.S. Immigration and Naturalization Service, *Statistical Yearbook*, annual.

No. 6. Immigrants Admitted by Class of Admission: 1990 to 2000

[**For fiscal year ending September 30**. For definition of immigrants, see text of this section]

Class of admission	1990	1995	1997	1998	1999	2000
Immigrants, total	**1,536,483**	**720,461**	**798,378**	**654,451**	**646,568**	**849,807**
New arrivals	435,729	380,291	380,719	357,037	401,775	407,402
Adjustments	1,100,754	340,170	417,659	297,414	244,793	442,405
Preference immigrants, total	272,742	323,458	303,938	268,997	273,700	342,304
Family-sponsored immigrants, total	214,550	238,122	213,331	191,480	216,883	235,280
Unmarried sons/daughters of U.S. citizens and their children	15,861	15,182	22,536	17,717	22,392	27,707
Spouses, unmarried sons/daughters of alien residents, and their children . . . . . ;	107,686	144,535	113,681	88,488	108,007	124,595
Married sons/daughters of U.S. citizens [1]	26,751	20,876	21,943	22,257	24,040	22,833
Brothers or sisters of U.S. citizens [1]	64,252	57,529	55,171	63,018	62,444	60,145
Employment-based immigrants, total	58,192	85,336	90,607	77,517	56,817	107,024
Priority workers [1]	(X)	17,339	21,810	21,408	14,898	27,706
Professionals with advanced degrees [1]	(X)	10,475	17,059	14,384	8,581	20,304
Skilled workers, professionals, unskilled workers [1]	(X)	50,245	42,596	34,317	27,966	49,736
Special immigrants [1]	4,463	6,737	7,781	6,584	5,086	9,052
Employment creation [1]	(X)	540	1,361	824	286	226
Professional or highly skilled immigrants [1][2]	26,546	(X)	(X)	(X)	(X)	(X)
Needed skilled or unskilled workers [1][2]	27,183	(X)	(X)	(X)	(X)	(X)
Immediate relatives	231,680	220,360	321,008	283,368	258,584	347,870
Spouses of U.S. citizens	125,426	123,238	170,263	151,172	127,988	197,525
Children of U.S. citizens	46,065	48,740	76,631	70,472	69,113	82,726
Orphans	7,088	9,384	12,596	14,867	16,037	18,120
Parents of U.S. citizens	60,189	48,382	74,114	61,724	61,483	67,619
Refugees and asylees	97,364	114,664	112,158	52,193	42,852	65,941
Refugee adjustments	92,427	106,827	102,052	44,645	39,495	59,083
Asylee adjustments	4,937	7,837	10,106	7,548	3,357	6,858
Immigration Reform and Control Act of 1986 legalization adjustments	880,372	4,267	2,548	955	8	421
Other immigrants	54,325	57,712	58,726	48,938	71,424	93,271
Diversity Programs [3]	29,161	47,245	49,374	45,499	47,571	50,945
Amerasians (P.L. 100-202) [4]	13,059	939	738	346	239	943
Children born abroad to alien residents	2,410	1,894	1,432	902	978	1,009
Legalization dependents [5]	(X)	277	64	21	-	55
Nicaraguan Adjustment and Central American Relief Act, Sec. 202 entrants (P.L. 105-100)	(X)	(X)	(X)	1	11,267	23,641
Other	9,695	7,357	7,118	2,169	11,369	16,678

- Represents zero.   X Not applicable.   [1] Includes spouses and children.   [2] Category was eliminated in 1992 by the Immigration Act of 1990.   [3] Includes categories of immigrants admitted under three laws intended to diversify immigration: P.L. 99-603, P.L. 100-658, and P.L. 101-649.   [4] Under Public Law 100-202, Amerasians are aliens born in Vietnam between January 1, 1962, and January 1, 1976, who were fathered by U.S. citizens.   [5] Spouses and children of persons granted permanent resident status under provisions of the Immigration Reform and Control Act of 1986.

Source: U.S. Immigration and Naturalization Service, *Statistical Yearbook*, annual.

No. 7. Immigrants by Country of Birth: 1981 to 2000

[In thousands (7,338.1 represents 7,338,100). For fiscal years ending Sept. 30. For definition of immigrants, see text of this section]

Country of birth	1981-90, total	1991-98, total	1999	2000	Country of birth	1981-90, total	1991-98, total	1999	2000
All countries	7,338.1	7,599.0	646.6	849.8	Thailand	64.4	42.3	2.4	3.8
Europe [1]	705.6	1,086.2	92.7	132.5	Turkey	20.9	21.5	2.2	2.6
Bosnia and					Vietnam	401.4	374.0	20.4	26.7
Herzegovina.	(X)	[2]21.9	5.4	11.8	**Africa**[1]	192.3	301.6	36.7	44.7
France	23.1	21.8	2.2	3.5	Egypt	31.4	37.8	4.4	4.5
Germany	70.1	54.9	5.2	7.6	Ethiopia	27.2	41.0	4.3	4.1
Greece	29.1	11.9	0.7	1.0	Ghana	14.9	27.6	3.7	4.3
Ireland	32.8	56.8	0.8	1.3	Nigeria	35.3	52.7	6.8	7.9
Italy	32.9	18.5	1.5	2.5	South Africa.	15.7	18.2	1.6	2.8
Poland	97.4	150.7	8.8	10.1	**Oceania** [1]	(NA)	39.2	3.7	5.1
Portugal	40.0	20.3	1.1	1.4	Australia	13.9	14.8	1.1	2.1
Romania	38.9	45.0	5.7	6.9	**North America** [1]	3,125.0	3,301.2	271.4	344.8
Russia	(X)	[2]98.6	12.3	17.1	Canada.	119.2	112.5	8.9	16.2
Soviet Union [3]	84.0	95.5	5.1	3.3	Mexico	1,653.3	1,929.9	147.6	173.9
Ukraine	(X)	[2]115.4	10.1	15.8	Caribbean [1]	892.7	836.2	71.7	88.2
United Kingdom	142.1	114.8	7.7	13.4	Cuba.	159.2	145.9	14.1	20.8
Yugoslavia [3]	19.2	21.2	1.9	2.8	Dominican				
Asia[1]	2,817.4	2,427.4	199.4	265.4	Republic.	251.8	305.5	17.9	17.5
Afghanistan	26.6	15.5	0.9	1.0	Haiti	140.2	142.9	16.5	22.4
Bangladesh	15.2	52.7	6.0	7.2	Jamaica.	213.8	142.8	14.7	16.0
Cambodia	116.6	15.0	1.4	2.1	Trinidad and				
China	[4]388.8	346.7	32.2	45.7	Tobago	39.5	52.3	4.3	6.7
Hong Kong	63.0	63.7	4.9	5.4	Central America [1]	458.7	422.2	43.2	66.4
India	261.9	311.0	30.2	42.0	El Salvador	214.6	180.2	14.6	22.6
Indonesia	14.3	12.3	1.2	1.8	Guatemala	87.9	85.8	7.3	10.0
Iran	154.8	96.9	7.2	8.5	Honduras	49.5	56.0	4.8	5.9
Iraq	19.6	32.2	3.4	5.1	Nicaragua	44.1	60.3	13.4	24.0
Israel	36.3	27.3	1.9	2.8	Panama.	29.0	20.5	1.6	1.8
Japan	43.2	50.2	4.2	7.1	**South America** [1]	455.9	442.2	41.6	56.1
Jordan	32.6	32.5	3.3	3.9	Argentina	25.7	20.6	1.4	2.3
Korea	338.8	142.7	12.8	15.8	Brazil	23.7	41.4	3.9	7.0
Laos	145.6	41.4	0.9	1.4	Chile.	23.4	14.1	1.1	1.7
Lebanon	41.6	36.8	3.0	3.7	Colombia.	124.4	106.5	10.0	14.5
Pakistan	61.3	96.5	13.5	14.5	Ecuador	56.0	59.8	8.9	7.7
Philippines.	495.3	432.1	31.0	42.5	Guyana	95.4	61.8	3.3	5.7
Syria.	20.6	21.7	2.1	2.4	Peru	64.4	87.7	8.4	9.6
Taiwan	(4)	90.6	6.7	9.0	Venezuela	17.9	22.7	2.5	4.7

NA Not available.   X Not applicable.   [1] Includes countries not shown separately.   [2] Covers years 1992-1998.   [3] Prior to 1992, data include independent republics; beginning in 1992, data are for unknown republic only.   [4] Data for Taiwan included with China.

Source: U.S. Immigration and Naturalization Service, *Statistical Yearbook,* annual; and releases.

No. 8. Immigrants Admitted as Permanent Residents Under Refugee Acts by Country of Birth: 1981 to 2000

[For fiscal years ending September 30]

Country of birth	1981-90, total	1991-98, total	1999	2000	Country of birth	1981-90, total	1991-98, total	1999	2000
Total [1]	1,013,620	912,473	42,852	65,941	Afghanistan	22,946	9,558	54	113
Europe [1].	155,512	371,658	21,801	33,106	Cambodia	114,064	6,313	39	36
Albania	289	3,145	44	66	China [5]	7,928	6,690	431	487
Azerbaijan	(X)	[2]11,245	372	455	Iran.	46,773	22,327	1,030	956
Belarus	(X)	[2]22,588	766	1,227	Iraq.	7,540	17,239	1,835	3,483
Bosnia and					Laos	142,964	36,174	383	708
Herzegovina . . .	(X)	[2]20,666	5,298	11,627	Syria	2,145	1,816	160	149
Bulgaria.	1,197	1,621	20	38	Thailand	30,259	21,569	380	810
Czechoslovakia [3].	8,204	1,235	12	8	Vietnam.	324,453	196,778	4,503	5,576
Georgia	(X)	[2]2,359	100	134	**Africa** [1]	22,149	46,100	2,184	3,365
Hungary	4,942	1,269	7	9	Ethiopia [6].	18,542	17,412	183	270
Kazakhstan	(X)	[2]3,587	210	472	Liberia	109	3,442	124	273
Latvia	48	2,497	126	134	Somalia.	70	13,741	1,279	1,817
Moldova	(X)	[2]10,615	373	729	Sudan.	739	4,828	153	210
Poland	33,889	7,407	36	57	**Oceania**	22	265	2	24
Romania	29,798	15,577	63	68	**North America** [1] . .	121,840	161,014	9,086	15,233
Russia.	(X)	53,577	2,842	3,985	Cuba.	113,367	121,662	8,588	14,362
Soviet Union [4] . .	72,306	83,696	4,394	2,443	Haiti	(NA)	8,920	122	322
Ukraine	(X)	[2]97,041	4,956	7,742	El Salvador	1,383	3,950	47	76
Uzbekistan	(X)	[2]17,815	759	965	Nicaragua	5,590	22,234	103	149
Yugoslavia [4] . . .	324	4,493	625	1,156	**South America** [1] . .	1,986	4,627	417	813
Asia [1].	712,092	328,705	9,300	13,342	Peru	251	2,112	117	278

NA Not available.   X Not applicable.   [1] Includes other countries and unknown, not shown separately.   [2] Covers years 1992-1998.   [3] Prior to 1993, data include independent republics; beginning in 1993, data are for unknown republic only.   [4] Prior to 1992, data include independent republics; beginning in 1992, data are for unknown republic only.   [5] Includes Taiwan.   [6] Prior to 1993, data include Eritrea.

Source: U.S. Immigration and Naturalization Service, *Statistical Yearbook,* annual; and releases.

No. 9. Immigrants Admitted by State and Leading Country of Birth: 2000

[For year ending September 30. For definition of immigrants, see text of this section]

State and other area	Total [1]	Mexico	China	Philip-pines	India	Vietnam	Nicara-gua	El Salvador	Haiti
Total	849,807	173,919	45,652	42,474	42,046	26,747	24,029	22,578	22,364
Alabama.	1,904	259	172	66	230	78	16	6	5
Alaska	1,374	136	47	327	12	21	4	27	1
Arizona.	11,980	6,301	304	335	374	464	62	81	10
Arkansas	1,596	606	93	75	124	77	12	89	4
California	217,753	85,551	13,232	16,773	9,313	10,251	5,176	9,987	81
Colorado.	8,216	2,915	503	151	286	351	31	101	6
Connecticut.	11,346	278	544	441	594	208	114	51	497
Delaware	1,570	182	117	49	153	33	5	10	80
District of Columbia	2,542	39	122	75	53	65	79	544	35
Florida	98,391	4,597	1,119	1,922	1,438	994	14,400	651	11,044
Georgia	14,778	2,099	659	310	1,323	752	106	166	127
Hawaii	6,056	62	551	3,053	23	196	-	1	1
Idaho	1,922	1,083	100	41	18	35	8	6	4
Illinois	36,180	8,600	1,475	2,738	3,239	433	112	135	98
Indiana	4,128	759	333	185	328	99	34	35	7
Iowa	3,052	699	90	64	145	298	13	27	3
Kansas.	4,582	1,794	226	129	190	350	52	57	5
Kentucky	2,989	164	176	88	149	144	9	3	8
Louisiana	3,016	194	229	97	211	335	154	40	13
Maine.	1,133	29	81	40	32	49	1	4	1
Maryland	17,705	487	1,102	748	1,228	379	475	1,480	194
Massachusetts.	23,483	193	2,023	267	1,227	902	79	290	1,943
Michigan.	16,773	935	832	783	1,490	320	36	33	21
Minnesota.	8,671	591	505	208	441	536	48	43	9
Mississippi	1,083	127	109	163	122	48	16	5	12
Missouri	6,053	636	394	227	359	331	18	43	15
Montana	493	44	25	39	11	2	4	1	2
Nebraska	2,230	834	86	64	70	281	9	47	1
Nevada	7,827	3,120	283	859	141	173	278	322	11
New Hampshire	2,001	40	116	123	101	43	4	6	26
New Jersey.	40,013	700	1,862	1,845	4,364	428	431	712	2,101
New Mexico	3,973	2,717	139	82	77	138	9	14	2
New York	106,061	1,883	8,930	1,927	3,581	665	741	2,548	5,507
North Carolina	9,251	1,390	514	386	785	352	137	152	24
North Dakota.	420	15	9	10	21	12	-	1	5
Ohio	9,263	345	712	281	804	280	44	19	5
Oklahoma.	4,586	1,565	210	174	288	365	12	24	3
Oregon.	8,543	2,699	597	286	345	511	24	46	5
Pennsylvania.	18,148	1,081	1,494	464	1,714	879	93	42	269
Rhode Island.	2,526	49	85	55	44	25	11	30	68
South Carolina	2,267	191	167	165	201	72	15	9	7
South Dakota	465	26	26	27	7	16	3	1	2
Tennessee	4,882	504	326	364	352	148	20	31	6
Texas.	63,840	31,211	2,293	2,025	3,528	2,275	644	2,677	21
Utah	3,710	1,036	146	79	57	152	30	52	3
Vermont	810	11	54	17	32	56	1	1	1
Virginia.	20,087	777	868	1,046	1,465	827	329	1,794	29
Washington.	18,486	3,256	1,058	1,216	578	1,216	39	89	8
West Virginia	573	24	47	35	35	10	-	4	3
Wisconsin	5,057	952	290	148	308	57	68	22	6
Wyoming	248	60	20	18	3	3	1	2	-
Guam	1,556	-	54	1,267	11	11	1	-	-
Northern Mariana Islands	122	-	12	83	-	-	-	-	-
Puerto Rico.	2,649	71	85	6	6	1	21	17	1
Virgin Islands.	1,328	1	4	5	13	-	-	-	24
Armed Services posts . . .	116	1	2	23	2	-	-	-	-

- Represents zero. [1] Includes other countries, not shown separately.

Source: U.S. Immigration and Naturalization Service, *Statistical Yearbook,* annual.

U.S. Census Bureau, Statistical Abstract of the United States: 2002

No. 10. Resident Population—Selected Characteristics, 1950 to 1990, and Projections, 2005 to 2050

[In thousands (75,187 represents 75,187,000)]

Date	Sex		Race				
	Male	Female	White	Black	American Indian, Eskimo, Aleut	Asian, Pacific Islander	Hispanic origin [1]
NUMBER							
1950 (Apr. 1)......	75,187	76,139	135,150	15,045	(NA)	(NA)	(NA)
1960 (Apr. 1) [2]...	88,331	90,992	158,832	18,872	(NA)	(NA)	(NA)
1970 (Apr. 1) [3][4]...	98,926	104,309	178,098	22,581	(NA)	(NA)	(NA)
1980 (Apr. 1) [3][5]...	110,053	116,493	194,713	26,683	1,420	3,729	14,609
1990 (Apr. 1) [3][5]...	121,284	127,507	208,741	30,517	2,067	7,467	22,379
2005 (July 1) [6]....	140,698	147,018	234,221	37,619	2,625	13,251	38,189
2010 (July 1) [6]....	146,679	153,183	241,770	39,982	2,821	15,289	43,688
2015 (July 1) [6]....	152,744	159,524	249,468	42,385	3,016	17,399	49,255
2020 (July 1) [6]....	158,856	166,071	257,394	44,736	3,207	19,589	55,156
2025 (July 1) [6]....	165,009	172,806	265,306	47,089	3,399	22,020	61,433
2050 (July 1) [6]....	197,047	206,640	302,453	59,239	4,405	37,589	98,229
PERCENT DISTRIBUTION							
1980 (Apr. 1) [3][4]...	48.6	51.4	85.9	11.8	0.6	1.6	6.4
1990 (Apr. 1) [3][5]...	48.7	51.3	83.9	12.3	0.8	3.0	9.0
2025 (July 1) [6].....	48.8	51.2	78.5	13.9	1.0	6.5	18.2
2050 (July 1) [6].....	48.8	51.2	74.9	14.7	1.1	9.3	24.3

NA Not available. [1] Persons of Hispanic origin may be of any race. [2] The revised 1970 resident population count is 203,302,031; which incorporates changes due to errors found after tabulations were completed. The race and sex data shown here reflect the official 1970 census count. [3] The race data shown have been modified; see text of this section for explanation. [4] See footnote 4, Table 1. [5] The April 1, 1990, estimates base (248,790,925) includes count resolution corrections processed through August 1997. It generally does not include adjustments for census coverage errors. However, it includes adjustments estimated for the 1995 Test Census in various localities in California, New Jersey, and Louisiana; and the 1998 census dress rehearsals in localities in California and Wisconsin. These adjustments amounted to a total of 81,052 persons. [6] Middle series projection; for assumptions, see Table 3.

Source: U.S. Census Bureau, *U.S. Census of Population, 1950,* Vol. II, Part 1; *1960,* Vol. I, Part 1; *1970,* Vol. I, Part B; and *Current Population Reports,* P25-1095; "National Estimates, Annual Population Estimates by Sex, Race and Hispanic Origin, Selected Years from 1990 to 2000"; published 26 May 2000; <http://www.census.gov/population/www/estimates/nation3.html>; and "National Population Projections-Summary Tables"; published 13 January 2000; <http://www.census.gov/population/www/projections/natsum-T3.html>.

No 11. Resident Population by Sex and Age Group: 1990 to 2001

[248,710 represents 248,710,000. As of April 1 except 2001 as of July 1. 1990 data are uncorrected counts. Minus sign (-) indicates decrease]

Characteristic	Number (1,000)			Percent distribution			Percent change	
	1990	2000	2001	1990	2000	2001	1990-2000	2000-2001
Total population	248,710	281,422	284,797	100.0	100.0	100.0	13.2	1.2
Male	121,239	138,054	139,813	48.7	49.1	49.1	13.9	1.3
Female.............	127,470	143,368	144,984	51.3	50.9	50.9	12.5	1.1
Under 5 years........	18,354	19,176	19,369	7.4	6.8	6.8	4.5	1.0
5 to 9 years.........	18,099	20,550	20,184	7.3	7.3	7.1	13.5	-1.8
10 to 14 years.......	17,114	20,528	20,881	6.9	7.3	7.3	19.9	1.7
15 to 19 years.......	17,754	20,220	20,267	7.1	7.2	7.1	13.9	0.2
20 to 24 years.......	19,020	18,964	19,681	7.6	6.7	6.9	-0.3	3.8
25 to 34 years.......	43,176	39,892	39,607	17.4	14.2	13.9	-7.6	-0.7
35 to 44 years.......	37,579	45,149	45,019	15.1	16.0	15.8	20.1	-0.3
45 to 54 years.......	25,223	37,678	39,188	10.1	13.4	13.8	49.4	4.0
55 to 59 years.......	10,532	13,469	14,190	4.2	4.8	5.0	27.9	5.4
60 to 64 years.......	10,616	10,805	11,118	4.3	3.8	3.9	1.8	2.9
65 to 74 years.......	18,107	18,391	18,313	7.3	6.5	6.4	1.6	-0.4
75 to 84 years.......	10,055	12,361	12,574	4.0	4.4	4.4	22.9	1.7
85 years and over	3,080	4,240	4,404	1.2	1.5	1.5	37.6	3.9
18 years and over	185,105	209,128	212,245	74.4	74.3	74.5	13.0	1.5
Male.............	88,655	100,994	102,650	35.6	35.9	36.0	13.9	1.6
Female	96,450	108,134	109,595	38.8	38.4	38.5	12.1	1.4
65 years and over	31,242	34,992	35,291	12.6	12.4	12.4	12.0	0.9
Male.............	12,565	14,410	14,583	5.1	5.1	5.1	14.7	1.2
Female	18,677	20,582	20,708	7.5	7.3	7.3	10.2	0.6

Source: U.S. Census Bureau, "Table DP-1 Profile of General Demographic Characteristics for the United States"; published 15 May 2001; <http://www.census.gov/Press-Release/www/2001/cb01cn67.html>; and unpublished data.

Population 13

[In thousands, except as indicated (226,546 represents 226,546,000). 1980, 1990, and 2000 data are enumerated population as of April 1; data for other years are estimated population as of July 1. Excludes Armed Forces overseas. For definition of median, see Guide to Tabular Presentation]

Year and sex	Total, all years	Under 5 years	5-9 years	10-14 years	15-19 years	20-24 years	25-29 years	30-34 years	35-39 years	40-44 years	45-49 years	50-54 years	55-59 years	60-64 years	65-74 years	75-84 years	85 years and over	5-13 years	14-17 years	18-24 years	Median age (yr.)
1980, total[1]	226,546	16,348	16,700	18,242	21,168	21,319	19,521	17,561	13,965	11,669	11,090	11,710	11,615	10,088	15,581	7,729	2,240	31,159	16,247	30,022	30.0
Male	110,053	8,362	8,539	9,316	10,755	10,663	9,705	8,677	6,862	5,708	5,388	5,621	5,482	4,670	6,757	2,867	682	15,923	8,298	15,054	28.8
Female	116,493	7,986	8,161	8,926	10,413	10,655	9,816	8,884	7,104	5,961	5,702	6,089	6,133	5,418	8,824	4,862	1,559	15,237	7,950	14,969	31.3
1985, total	237,924	17,842	16,665	17,027	18,727	21,265	21,671	20,025	17,604	14,087	11,606	10,854	11,229	10,906	16,858	8,890	2,667	29,893	14,888	28,902	31.4
1990, total[2]	248,791	18,765	18,042	17,067	17,893	19,143	21,336	21,838	19,851	17,593	13,747	11,315	10,489	10,627	18,048	10,014	3,022	31,839	13,345	26,961	32.8
Male	121,284	9,603	9,236	8,742	9,178	9,749	10,708	10,866	9,837	8,679	6,741	5,494	5,009	4,947	7,908	3,745	842	16,301	6,860	13,744	31.6
Female	127,507	9,162	8,806	8,325	8,714	9,394	10,629	10,973	10,014	8,914	7,006	5,821	5,480	5,679	10,140	6,268	2,180	15,538	6,485	13,217	34.0
1991, total	252,981	19,208	18,281	17,756	17,270	19,234	20,923	22,301	20,577	18,752	14,129	11,691	10,443	10,603	18,294	10,329	3,189	32,609	13,491	26,442	33.1
1992, total	256,514	19,528	18,431	18,246	17,246	19,188	20,503	22,494	21,184	19,185	15,413	12,135	10,521	10,477	18,486	10,555	3,315	33,199	13,775	26,137	33.4
1993, total	259,919	19,729	18,646	18,721	17,474	18,990	20,069	22,584	21,727	19,684	16,013	12,851	10,736	10,292	18,693	10,764	3,446	33,761	14,096	25,703	33.6
1994, total	263,126	19,777	19,025	19,001	17,876	18,656	19,740	22,590	22,135	19,684	16,791	13,362	11,009	10,150	18,790	10,980	3,561	34,217	14,637	25,482	33.9
1995, total	266,278	19,627	19,438	19,207	18,374	18,300	19,680	22,492	22,786	20,219	17,624	13,856	11,182	10,138	18,866	11,222	3,681	34,825	15,013	25,275	34.2
1996, total	269,394	19,408	19,861	19,435	18,920	17,877	19,864	21,945	22,904	20,766	18,611	14,189	11,481	10,109	18,824	11,524	3,795	35,375	15,443	25,479	34.4
1997, total	272,647	19,233	20,254	19,601	19,398	17,910	19,899	21,446	22,926	21,325	18,687	15,491	11,905	10,194	18,684	11,812	3,905	35,915	15,769	25,479	34.7
1998, total	275,854	19,145	20,510	19,825	19,840	18,167	19,804	20,953	22,926	21,822	19,114	16,118	12,589	10,422	18,570	12,016	4,033	36,454	15,829	26,059	34.9
1999, total	279,040	19,136	20,606	20,213	20,085	18,591	19,575	20,603	22,883	22,194	19,654	16,924	13,085	10,693	18,419	12,225	4,154	36,804	16,007	26,685	35.2
2000, total	281,422	19,176	20,550	20,528	20,220	18,964	19,381	20,510	22,707	22,442	20,092	17,586	13,469	10,805	18,391	12,361	4,240	37,025	16,093	27,143	35.3
Male	138,054	9,811	10,523	10,520	10,391	9,688	9,799	10,322	11,319	11,129	9,890	8,608	6,509	5,137	8,303	4,879	1,227	18,964	8,285	13,874	34.0
Female	143,368	9,365	10,026	10,008	9,829	9,276	9,583	10,189	11,388	11,313	10,203	8,978	6,961	5,669	10,088	7,482	3,013	18,061	7,808	13,270	36.5
2001, total	284,797	19,369	20,184	20,881	20,267	19,681	18,926	20,681	22,243	22,776	20,769	18,419	14,190	11,118	18,313	12,574	4,404	37,002	16,181	27,831	35.6
Male	139,813	9,905	10,337	10,696	10,423	10,062	9,593	10,421	11,105	11,298	10,225	9,011	6,865	5,289	8,297	4,987	1,299	18,952	8,306	14,260	34.0
Female	144,984	9,464	9,847	10,185	9,844	9,619	9,333	10,261	11,138	11,477	10,544	9,408	7,325	5,830	10,016	7,587	3,105	18,050	7,875	13,571	36.0
Percent:																					
1980[1]	100.0	7.2	7.4	8.1	9.3	9.4	8.6	7.8	6.2	5.2	4.9	5.2	5.1	4.5	6.9	3.4	1.0	13.8	7.2	13.3	(X)
1990[2]	100.0	7.5	7.3	6.9	7.2	7.7	8.6	8.8	8.0	7.1	5.5	4.5	4.2	4.3	7.3	4.0	1.2	12.8	5.4	10.8	(X)
2000	100.0	6.8	7.3	7.3	7.2	6.7	6.9	7.3	8.1	8.0	7.1	6.2	4.8	3.8	6.5	4.4	1.5	13.2	5.7	9.6	(X)
2001	100.0	6.8	7.1	7.3	7.1	6.9	6.6	7.3	7.8	8.0	7.3	6.4	5.0	3.9	6.4	4.4	1.5	13.0	5.7	9.8	(X)
Male	100.0	7.1	7.4	7.3	7.5	7.2	6.9	7.5	7.9	8.1	7.3	6.4	4.9	3.8	5.9	3.6	0.9	13.6	5.9	10.2	(X)
Female	100.0	6.5	6.8	7.0	6.8	6.6	6.4	7.1	7.7	7.9	7.3	6.5	5.1	4.0	6.9	5.2	2.1	12.4	5.4	9.4	(X)

X Not applicable. [1] Total population count has been revised since the 1980 census publications. Numbers by age, race, Hispanic origin, and sex have not been corrected. [2] The data shown have been modified from the official 1990 census counts. See text of this section for explanation. The April 1, 1990, estimates base (248,790,925) includes count resolution corrections processed through August 1997. It generally does not include adjustments for census coverage errors. However, it includes adjustments estimated for the 1995 Test Census in various localities in California, New Jersey, and Louisiana; and the 1998 census dress rehearsals in localities in California and Wisconsin. These adjustments amounted to a total of 81,052 persons.

Source: U.S. Census Bureau, Current Population Reports, P25-1095; and "Resident Population Estimates of the United States by Age and Sex: April 1, 1990, to July 1, 1999", with short-term projections to April 1, 2000"; published 24 May 2000; <http://www.census.gov/population/estimates/nation/intfile2-1.txt>; and unpublished data.

No. 13. Resident Population Projections by Sex and Age: 2005 to 2050

[In thousands, except as indicated (287,716 represents 287,716,000). As of July. Data shown are for middle series; for assumptions, see Table 3]

Age	2005 Total	2005 Male	2005 Female	2010 Total	2010 Male	2010 Female	2015	2020	2025	2030	2035	2040	2045	2050	Pct 2005	Pct 2010	Pct 2015	Pct 2020	Pct 2025	Pct 2050
Total	287,716	140,698	147,018	299,862	146,679	153,183	312,268	324,927	337,815	351,070	364,319	377,350	390,398	403,687	100.0	100.0	100.0	100.0	100.0	100.0
Under 5 years	19,212	9,815	9,397	20,099	10,272	9,827	21,179	21,951	22,551	23,183	24,016	25,014	26,013	26,914	6.7	6.7	6.8	6.8	6.7	6.7
5 to 9 years	19,122	9,774	9,348	19,438	9,936	9,502	20,321	21,403	22,197	22,845	23,509	24,358	25,364	26,366	6.6	6.5	6.5	6.6	6.6	6.5
10 to 14 years	20,634	10,564	10,069	19,908	10,183	9,724	20,229	21,146	22,289	23,166	23,870	24,571	25,459	26,503	7.2	6.6	6.5	6.5	6.6	6.6
15 to 19 years	20,990	10,788	10,202	21,668	11,132	10,536	20,892	21,224	22,203	23,449	24,380	25,100	25,813	26,715	7.3	7.2	6.7	6.5	6.3	6.6
20 to 24 years	20,159	10,269	9,889	21,151	10,776	10,375	21,748	21,020	21,411	22,728	23,748	24,660	25,360	26,054	7.0	7.1	7.0	6.5	6.3	6.5
25 to 29 years	18,351	9,144	9,207	19,849	9,901	9,948	20,765	21,384	21,020	21,257	22,333	23,552	24,430	25,104	6.4	6.3	6.6	6.6	6.1	6.2
30 to 34 years	18,582	9,146	9,436	19,002	9,385	9,617	20,484	21,410	21,615	21,257	22,174	23,254	23,928	25,354	6.5	6.3	6.6	6.6	6.5	6.3
35 to 39 years	20,082	9,927	10,155	19,039	9,380	9,659	19,442	20,938	22,111	22,728	22,281	22,845	24,475	25,152	7.0	6.3	6.2	6.4	6.5	6.2
40 to 44 years	22,634	11,222	11,412	20,404	10,069	10,334	19,346	19,773	21,926	21,615	23,222	22,783	23,349	24,436	7.9	6.8	6.2	5.9	5.8	6.1
45 to 49 years	22,230	10,965	11,264	22,227	10,967	11,260	20,057	19,473	19,473	21,031	22,112	22,953	22,522	23,072	7.7	7.4	6.4	6.1	5.8	5.7
50 to 54 years	19,661	9,578	10,082	21,934	10,739	11,195	21,929	19,717	18,818	19,318	20,884	21,966	22,798	22,373	6.8	7.3	7.0	6.6	5.7	5.5
55 to 59 years	16,842	8,101	8,741	19,177	9,248	9,929	21,400	21,412	19,366	18,452	18,989	20,543	21,622	22,445	5.9	6.4	6.9	6.6	5.8	5.7
60 to 64 years	12,848	6,086	6,762	16,252	7,725	8,528	18,519	20,696	20,759	18,853	18,027	18,575	20,123	21,199	4.5	5.4	5.9	6.4	6.1	5.6
65 to 69 years	10,086	4,661	5,425	12,159	5,640	6,520	15,410	17,598	19,717	19,844	18,104	17,349	17,962	19,477	3.5	4.1	4.9	5.4	5.8	5.3
70 to 74 years	8,375	3,757	4,618	8,995	4,066	4,929	10,897	13,864	15,886	17,878	18,068	16,555	15,912	16,537	2.9	3.0	3.5	4.3	4.7	4.1
75 to 79 years	7,429	3,172	4,257	7,175	3,110	4,065	7,772	9,484	12,159	14,029	15,895	16,170	14,908	14,407	2.6	2.4	2.5	2.9	3.6	3.6
80 to 84 years	5,514	2,157	3,356	5,600	2,247	3,353	5,484	6,024	7,439	9,638	11,220	12,820	13,140	12,225	1.9	1.9	1.8	1.9	2.2	3.0
85 to 89 years	3,028	1,046	1,982	3,476	1,242	2,234	3,612	3,611	4,045	5,077	6,678	7,884	9,123	9,463	1.1	1.2	1.2	1.1	1.2	2.3
90 to 94 years	1,402	404	998	1,625	497	1,128	1,930	2,074	2,135	2,457	3,155	4,243	5,115	6,030	0.5	0.5	0.6	0.6	0.6	1.5
95 to 99 years	442	104	338	556	139	417	678	844	948	1,015	1,213	1,606	2,226	2,764	0.2	0.2	0.2	0.3	0.3	0.7
100 years and over	96	18	77	129	26	103	177	235	313	381	441	551	757	1,095	(Z)	(Z)	0.1	0.1	0.1	0.3
5 to 13 years	35,475	18,144	17,331	35,321	18,056	17,265	36,497	38,361	40,054	41,377	42,592	44,004	45,740	47,582	12.3	11.8	11.7	11.8	11.9	11.8
14 to 17 years	16,931	8,709	8,222	16,681	8,583	8,098	16,437	16,839	17,741	18,653	19,325	19,881	20,477	21,252	5.9	5.6	5.3	5.2	5.3	5.3
18 to 24 years	28,498	14,543	13,956	30,163	15,388	14,774	30,254	29,593	30,305	31,910	33,590	34,803	35,779	36,804	9.9	10.1	9.7	9.1	9.0	9.1
16 years and over	224,447	108,336	116,111	236,301	114,175	122,126	246,455	256,230	266,342	277,222	288,108	298,453	308,456	318,601	78.0	78.8	78.9	78.9	78.8	78.9
18 years and over	216,098	104,030	112,068	227,761	109,768	117,993	238,155	247,776	257,469	267,857	278,386	288,450	298,168	307,938	75.1	76.0	76.3	76.3	76.2	76.3
16 to 49 years	163,661	82,026	81,635	163,247	81,794	81,453	162,961	165,609	171,482	178,100	184,120	189,717	195,335	202,390	56.9	54.4	52.2	51.1	50.8	50.1
16 to 64 years	188,077	93,017	95,059	196,586	97,208	99,377	200,496	202,498	203,701	206,903	213,334	221,276	229,314	236,602	65.4	65.6	64.2	62.3	60.3	58.6
55 years and over	66,060	29,505	36,555	75,145	33,939	41,206	85,878	95,841	102,766	107,624	111,790	116,295	120,888	125,643	23.0	25.1	27.5	29.5	30.4	31.1
65 years and over	36,370	15,318	21,052	39,715	16,966	22,749	45,959	55,733	62,641	70,319	74,774	77,177	79,142	81,999	12.6	13.2	14.7	16.5	18.5	20.3
85 years and over	4,968	1,572	3,396	5,786	1,904	3,882	6,396	6,763	7,441	8,931	11,486	14,284	17,220	19,352	1.7	1.9	2.0	2.1	2.2	4.8
Median age (years)	36.7	35.4	37.9	37.4	36.0	38.8	37.6	38.1	38.5	38.9	39.1	39.0	38.8	38.8	(X)	(X)	(X)	(X)	(X)	(X)

X Not applicable. Z Less than 0.05 percent.

Source: U.S. Census Bureau, "National Population Projections-Summary Tables"; published 13 January 2000; <http://www.census.gov/population/www/projections/natsum-T3.html>.

U.S. Census Bureau, Statistical Abstract of the United States: 2002

No. 14. Resident Population by Race, Hispanic Origin, and Single Years of Age: 2001

[In thousands (284,797 represents 284,797,000). As of July]

Age	Race Total	White	Black	American Indian, Alaska Native	Asian	Native Hawaiian and Other Pacific Islander	Two or more races	Hispanic origin [1]	Non-Hispanic White
Total	284,797	230,290	36,247	2,726	10,983	476	4,076	36,972	196,219
Under 5 yrs. old . .	19,369	14,784	2,932	236	728	41	649	3,817	11,329
Under 1 yr. old . .	4,034	3,076	606	49	150	9	144	817	2,337
1 yr. old	3,867	2,954	578	47	146	8	134	769	2,258
2 yrs. old	3,814	2,911	578	47	141	8	129	753	2,230
3 yrs. old	3,836	2,924	586	47	146	8	125	746	2,249
4 yrs. old	3,819	2,918	584	46	145	8	118	732	2,254
5-9 yrs. old	20,184	15,412	3,215	249	722	43	543	3,691	12,055
5 yrs. old	3,922	3,002	602	47	147	8	116	743	2,326
6 yrs. old	3,955	3,022	620	48	144	9	112	739	2,350
7 yrs. old	4,026	3,070	646	50	143	9	108	738	2,399
8 yrs. old	4,098	3,122	666	52	144	9	105	738	2,451
9 yrs. old	4,186	3,196	681	53	144	9	103	733	2,528
10-14 yrs. old . . .	20,881	16,049	3,320	269	734	43	467	3,365	12,984
10 yrs. old	4,261	3,258	689	55	149	9	101	723	2,600
11 yrs. old	4,287	3,281	696	55	148	9	98	705	2,639
12 yrs. old	4,184	3,213	669	54	146	9	93	669	2,604
13 yrs. old	4,086	3,153	638	53	146	8	88	641	2,568
14 yrs. old	4,064	3,145	627	52	146	8	86	627	2,573
15-19 yrs. old	20,267	15,753	3,049	256	772	43	394	3,167	12,850
15 yrs. old	4,053	3,145	621	52	144	8	83	615	2,584
16 yrs. old	4,048	3,147	611	52	149	8	81	614	2,585
17 yrs. old	4,017	3,123	605	51	151	9	78	617	2,557
18 yrs. old	4,058	3,154	606	51	161	9	77	647	2,560
19 yrs. old	4,092	3,184	607	50	167	9	75	675	2,564
20-24 yrs. old	19,681	15,364	2,862	228	859	47	322	3,523	12,117
20 yrs. old	4,129	3,210	616	49	171	10	73	696	2,570
21 yrs. old	4,097	3,191	604	48	175	10	69	710	2,537
22 yrs. old	3,920	3,060	573	45	169	9	64	702	2,412
23 yrs. old	3,818	2,991	547	44	167	9	60	705	2,340
24 yrs. old	3,720	2,913	522	42	177	9	57	710	2,257
25-29 yrs. old	18,926	14,809	2,593	205	1,019	43	258	3,553	11,509
25 yrs. old	3,700	2,899	513	42	183	9	54	719	2,233
26 yrs. old	3,743	2,927	515	41	199	9	52	721	2,258
27 yrs. old	3,715	2,904	504	40	207	9	51	705	2,248
28 yrs. old	3,769	2,941	519	40	211	8	50	700	2,290
29 yrs. old	3,999	3,138	541	42	219	8	51	709	2,479
30-34 yrs. old	20,681	16,433	2,726	204	1,037	40	241	3,309	13,361
30 yrs. old	4,194	3,311	558	42	222	9	52	694	2,668
31 yrs. old	4,320	3,426	572	42	220	9	51	704	2,773
32 yrs. old	4,109	3,267	535	40	211	8	48	657	2,658
33 yrs. old	4,028	3,209	530	40	196	8	45	639	2,616
34 yrs. old	4,028	3,219	531	40	187	7	44	616	2,647
35-39 yrs. old	22,243	17,894	2,890	216	972	39	233	2,979	15,131
35 yrs. old	4,178	3,334	558	41	192	8	45	617	2,762
36 yrs. old	4,451	3,562	591	44	199	8	47	626	2,981
37 yrs. old	4,534	3,645	588	44	202	8	47	601	3,087
38 yrs. old	4,514	3,647	578	43	191	8	47	579	3,109
39 yrs. old	4,565	3,707	574	43	188	7	46	555	3,192
40-44 yrs. old	22,776	18,574	2,833	208	900	35	225	2,473	16,283
40 yrs. old	4,584	3,732	575	43	181	7	46	537	3,234
41 yrs. old	4,701	3,816	598	43	189	8	47	533	3,321
42 yrs. old	4,518	3,685	561	41	179	7	45	485	3,236
43 yrs. old	4,532	3,707	558	41	176	6	44	472	3,270
44 yrs. old	4,437	3,634	540	40	174	6	43	446	3,221
45-49 yrs. old	20,769	17,129	2,431	178	810	28	193	1,921	15,352
45 yrs. old	4,338	3,557	525	38	170	6	42	426	3,162
46 yrs. old	4,321	3,545	518	37	174	6	41	414	3,162
47 yrs. old	4,156	3,430	485	36	160	6	39	384	3,075
48 yrs. old	4,022	3,331	458	34	157	5	37	357	3,001
49 yrs. old	3,932	3,266	445	32	149	5	35	340	2,951
50-54 yrs. old	18,419	15,412	1,983	145	698	23	159	1,477	14,042
50 yrs. old	3,762	3,116	430	31	147	5	33	323	2,817
51 yrs. old	3,790	3,132	435	31	154	5	33	322	2,834
52 yrs. old	3,641	3,035	401	29	140	4	32	293	2,763
53 yrs. old	3,696	3,122	377	28	134	4	31	279	2,862
54 yrs. old	3,529	3,007	340	26	123	4	29	259	2,766
55-59 yrs. old	14,190	12,075	1,401	102	481	16	115	1,053	11,092
55 yrs. old	3,096	2,625	309	23	100	4	26	241	2,401
56 yrs. old	2,822	2,381	290	21	103	3	24	224	2,172
57 yrs. old	2,829	2,411	279	20	93	3	23	209	2,216
58 yrs. old	2,786	2,384	268	19	90	3	22	195	2,202
59 yrs. old	2,655	2,273	255	18	86	3	20	184	2,101

See footnotes at end of table.

U.S. Census Bureau, Statistical Abstract of the United States: 2002

No. 14. Resident Population by Race, Hispanic Origin, and Single Years of Age: 2001—Con.

[In thousands (284,797 represents 284,797,000). As of July]

Age	Race							Hispanic origin [1]	Non-Hispanic White
	Total	White	Black	American Indian, Alaska Native	Asian	Native Hawaiian and Other Pacific Islander	Two or more races		
60-64 yrs. old	11,118	9,471	1,104	75	374	12	83	794	8,728
60 yrs. old	2,388	2,031	237	17	82	3	18	171	1,871
61 yrs. old	2,311	1,959	235	16	80	3	18	170	1,800
62 yrs. old	2,214	1,889	218	15	74	2	16	157	1,742
63 yrs. old	2,158	1,842	213	14	71	2	16	152	1,700
64 yrs. old	2,050	1,750	202	13	68	2	15	143	1,615
65-69 yrs. old	9,533	8,193	916	55	296	9	63	631	7,600
65 yrs. old	2,010	1,719	197	13	65	2	14	140	1,588
66 yrs. old	1,980	1,693	196	12	64	2	13	135	1,566
67 yrs. old	1,870	1,606	180	11	58	2	13	124	1,489
68 yrs. old	1,837	1,580	177	10	56	2	12	118	1,469
69 yrs. old	1,837	1,596	166	10	53	1	11	114	1,489
70-74 yrs. old	8,781	7,711	735	40	236	7	50	505	7,234
70 yrs. old	1,820	1,592	155	9	51	2	11	111	1,487
71 yrs. old	1,815	1,586	156	9	52	1	11	110	1,482
72 yrs. old	1,744	1,530	148	8	47	1	10	101	1,435
73 yrs. old	1,730	1,525	141	8	45	1	10	95	1,435
74 yrs. old	1,674	1,479	136	7	42	1	9	88	1,395
75-79 yrs. old	7,425	6,613	570	28	172	4	38	353	6,279
75 yrs. old	1,609	1,424	130	7	39	1	8	82	1,346
76 yrs. old	1,579	1,402	124	6	38	1	8	77	1,329
77 yrs. old	1,501	1,339	113	6	34	1	8	71	1,272
78 yrs. old	1,392	1,242	105	5	32	1	7	64	1,181
79 yrs. old	1,345	1,206	98	5	28	1	7	58	1,151
80-84 yrs. old	5,149	4,640	365	17	101	3	24	201	4,449
80 yrs. old	1,270	1,145	89	4	25	1	6	52	1,096
81 yrs. old	1,110	993	83	4	24	1	5	47	949
82 yrs. old	1,040	935	76	3	20	1	5	39	897
83 yrs. old	914	828	62	3	17	-	4	34	796
84 yrs. old	815	738	56	2	15	-	4	29	711
85-89 yrs. old	2,888	2,614	202	9	49	1	13	104	2,516
90-94 yrs. old	1,176	1,061	87	4	18	1	5	42	1,021
95-99 yrs. old	292	260	26	1	4	-	1	11	249
100 yrs. old and over	48	39	7	-	1	-	1	3	37
Median age (yr.) . .	35.6	36.9	30.3	28.1	33.0	27.3	19.8	26.2	39.0

- Represents or rounds to zero.   [1] Persons of Hispanic origin may be of any race.

Source: U.S. Census Bureau, unpublished data.

U.S. Census Bureau, Statistical Abstract of the United States: 2002

No. 15. Resident Population by Race, Hispanic Origin, and Age: 2000 and 2001

[In thousands (281,422 represents 281,422,000), except as indicated. 2000 as of April and 2001 as of July. For definition of median, see Guide to Tabular Presentation]

Age group	Total 2000	Total 2001	White 2000	White 2001	Black 2000	Black 2001	American Indian, Alaska Native 2000	American Indian, Alaska Native 2001	Asian 2000	Asian 2001	Native Hawaiian, Other Pacific Islander 2000	Native Hawaiian, Other Pacific Islander 2001	Two or more races 2000	Two or more races 2001	Hispanic origin[1] 2000	Hispanic origin[1] 2001	Non-Hispanic White 2000	Non-Hispanic White 2001
Total	281,422	284,797	228,104	230,290	35,704	36,247	2,664	2,726	10,589	10,983	463	476	3,898	4,076	35,306	36,972	195,575	196,219
Under 5 years	19,176	19,369	14,656	14,784	2,925	2,932	233	236	708	728	41	41	613	649	3,718	3,817	11,287	11,329
5 to 9 years	20,550	20,184	15,687	15,412	3,320	3,215	258	249	716	722	44	43	524	543	3,624	3,691	12,392	12,055
10 to 14 years	20,528	20,881	15,842	16,049	3,221	3,320	264	269	715	734	42	43	443	467	3,163	3,365	12,961	12,984
15 to 19 years	20,220	20,267	15,746	15,753	3,024	3,049	251	256	776	772	44	43	380	394	3,172	3,167	12,837	12,850
20 to 24 years	18,964	19,681	14,827	15,364	2,729	2,862	218	228	848	859	46	47	297	322	3,409	3,523	11,682	12,117
25 to 29 years	19,381	18,926	15,217	14,809	2,645	2,593	204	205	1,019	1,019	42	43	254	258	3,385	3,553	12,077	11,509
30 to 34 years	20,510	20,681	16,348	16,433	2,710	2,726	202	204	980	1,037	39	40	231	241	3,125	3,309	13,451	13,361
35 to 39 years	22,707	22,243	18,371	17,894	2,910	2,890	217	216	937	972	38	39	233	233	2,825	2,979	15,752	15,131
40 to 44 years	22,442	22,776	18,346	18,574	2,772	2,833	202	208	870	900	33	35	219	225	2,304	2,473	16,213	16,283
45 to 49 years	20,092	20,769	16,615	17,129	2,330	2,431	169	178	770	810	27	28	183	193	1,775	1,921	14,972	15,352
50 to 54 years	17,586	18,419	14,793	15,412	1,846	1,983	135	145	641	698	21	23	149	159	1,361	1,477	13,530	14,042
55 to 59 years	13,469	14,190	11,479	12,075	1,332	1,401	95	102	443	481	15	16	106	115	960	1,053	10,581	11,092
60 to 64 years	10,805	11,118	9,214	9,471	1,082	1,104	70	75	350	374	11	12	78	83	750	794	8,511	8,728
65 to 69 years	9,534	9,533	8,238	8,193	895	916	52	55	279	296	8	9	61	63	599	631	7,675	7,600
70 to 74 years	8,857	8,781	7,799	7,711	742	735	38	40	224	236	6	7	49	50	477	505	7,348	7,234
75 to 79 years	7,416	7,425	6,634	6,613	557	570	27	28	159	172	4	4	36	38	327	353	6,325	6,279
80 to 84 years	4,945	5,149	4,446	4,640	350	365	15	17	90	101	2	3	22	24	180	201	4,296	4,449
85 to 89 years	2,790	2,888	2,525	2,614	200	202	8	9	43	49	1	1	12	13	98	104	2,432	2,516
90 to 94 years	1,113	1,176	1,007	1,061	82	87	3	3	15	18	1	1	5	5	39	42	970	1,021
95 to 99 years	287	292	254	260	27	26	-	1	4	4	-	1	1	1	11	11	243	249
100 years and over	50	48	41	39	7	7	-	1	1	1	-	-	1	1	3	3	39	37
5 to 13 years	37,025	37,002	28,381	28,316	5,923	5,907	471	466	1,288	1,311	78	78	885	924	6,186	6,428	22,753	22,466
14 to 17 years	16,093	16,181	12,522	12,560	2,426	2,463	205	207	590	590	33	33	315	328	2,438	2,473	10,290	10,300
18 to 24 years	27,143	27,831	21,199	21,702	3,944	4,074	315	330	1,178	1,187	64	64	444	474	4,744	4,844	16,829	17,241
16 years and over	217,149	220,309	178,789	180,901	25,633	26,161	1,857	1,920	8,305	8,654	328	340	2,237	2,334	24,204	25,485	156,351	157,267
18 years and over	209,128	212,245	172,545	174,631	24,430	24,945	1,755	1,817	8,003	8,354	311	323	2,084	2,175	22,964	24,253	151,244	152,125
16 to 64 years	182,157	185,019	147,825	149,769	22,773	23,252	1,713	1,765	7,490	7,778	305	316	2,051	2,139	22,470	23,635	127,022	127,881
55 years and over	59,266	60,600	51,656	52,678	5,274	5,414	310	332	1,608	1,732	48	52	371	392	3,444	3,697	48,421	49,205
65 years and over	34,992	35,291	30,964	31,132	2,860	2,909	144	155	815	876	23	24	186	195	1,734	1,850	29,329	29,386
85 years and over	4,240	4,404	3,827	3,974	316	322	13	14	63	72	2	2	18	20	151	160	3,685	3,823
Median age (yrs)	35.3	35.6	36.6	36.9	30.0	30.3	27.7	28.1	32.5	33.0	26.8	27.3	19.8	19.8	25.8	26.2	38.6	39.0

- Represents or rounds to zero.   [1] Persons of Hispanic origin may be of any race.

Source: U.S. Census Bureau, unpublished data.

U.S. Census Bureau, Statistical Abstract of the United States: 2002

No. 16. Resident Population by Race and Hispanic Origin Status—Projections: 2005 to 2050

[In thousands, except as indicated (287,716 represents 287,716,000). As of July. These data are consistent with the 1980 and 1990 decennial enumerations and have been modified from the official census counts; see text of this section for explanation. Based on middle series of assumptions. See footnote 1, Table 3]

Year	Total	White	Black	American Indian, Eskimo, Aleut	Asian, Pacific Islander	Hispanic origin [1]	Not of Hispanic origin			
							White	Black	American Indian, Eskimo, Aleut	Asian, Pacific Islander
2005	287,716	234,221	37,619	2,625	13,251	38,189	199,414	35,446	2,171	12,497
2010	299,862	241,770	39,982	2,821	15,289	43,688	201,956	37,483	2,300	14,436
2015	312,268	249,468	42,385	3,016	17,399	49,255	204,590	39,551	2,428	16,444
2020	324,927	257,394	44,736	3,207	19,589	55,156	207,145	41,549	2,550	18,527
2025	337,815	265,306	47,089	3,399	22,020	61,433	209,340	43,528	2,668	20,846
2030	351,070	273,079	49,535	3,599	24,858	68,168	210,984	45,567	2,787	23,564
2040	377,350	287,787	54,462	4,006	31,095	82,692	212,475	49,618	3,023	29,543
2050	403,687	302,453	59,239	4,405	37,589	98,229	212,991	53,466	3,241	35,760
Percent distribution:										
2005	100.0	81.4	13.1	0.9	4.6	13.3	69.3	12.3	0.8	4.3
2010	100.0	80.6	13.3	0.9	5.1	14.6	67.3	12.5	0.8	4.8
2015	100.0	79.9	13.6	1.0	5.6	15.8	65.5	12.7	0.8	5.3
2020	100.0	79.2	13.8	1.0	6.0	17.0	63.8	12.8	0.8	5.7
2025	100.0	78.5	13.9	1.0	6.5	18.2	62.0	12.9	0.8	6.2
2030	100.0	77.8	14.1	1.0	7.1	19.4	60.1	13.0	0.8	6.7
2040	100.0	76.3	14.4	1.1	8.2	21.9	56.3	13.1	0.8	7.8
2050	100.0	74.9	14.7	1.1	9.3	24.3	52.8	13.2	0.8	8.9
Percent change:										
2010-2020	8.5	6.5	12.7	14.9	31.3	29.0	2.6	11.6	11.8	31.6
2020-2030	8.4	6.5	11.9	13.7	28.1	26.3	2.6	10.8	10.9	28.3
2030-2040	8.2	6.3	11.1	12.7	26.6	24.7	2.3	10.1	9.9	26.8
2040-2050	8.0	6.1	10.7	12.2	26.9	23.6	1.9	9.7	9.3	27.2

[1] Persons of Hispanic origin may be of any race.

Source: U.S. Census Bureau, "(NP-T4) Projections of the Total Resident Population by 5-Year Age Groups, Race, and Hispanic Origin With Special Age Categories: Middle Series, 1999 to 2100"; published 13 January 2000; <http://www.census.gov/population/www/projections/natsum-T3.html>.

U.S. Census Bureau, Statistical Abstract of the United States: 2002

No. 17. Resident Population by Race, Hispanic Origin Status, and Age—Projections: 2005 and 2010

[In thousands (287,716 represents 287,716,000), except as indicated. As of July. For definition of median, see Guide to Tabular Presentation. Projections are based on middle series of assumptions; see footnote 1, Table 3]

Age group	Total 2005	Total 2010	White 2005	White 2010	Black 2005	Black 2010	Am. Ind., Eskimo, Aleut 2005	Am. Ind., Eskimo, Aleut 2010	Asian, Pac. Isl. 2005	Asian, Pac. Isl. 2010	Hispanic origin 2005	Hispanic origin 2010	NH White 2005	NH White 2010	NH Black 2005	NH Black 2010	NH Am.Ind. 2005	NH Am.Ind. 2010	NH Asian 2005	NH Asian 2010
Total	287,716	299,862	234,221	241,770	37,619	39,982	2,625	2,821	13,251	15,289	38,189	43,688	199,414	201,956	35,446	37,483	2,171	2,300	12,497	14,436
Under 5 years	19,212	20,099	15,041	15,609	2,907	3,103	222	240	1,042	1,147	4,027	4,476	11,353	11,514	2,686	2,854	176	188	970	1,067
5 to 9 years	19,122	19,438	15,074	15,127	2,829	2,953	212	232	1,006	1,126	3,681	4,129	11,707	11,352	2,625	2,724	171	182	937	1,050
10 to 14 years	20,634	19,908	15,965	15,506	3,246	2,977	238	237	1,073	1,187	3,622	3,914	12,781	11,940	3,039	2,757	196	190	996	1,108
15 to 19 years	20,990	21,668	16,405	16,804	3,370	3,444	259	242	957	1,178	3,307	4,011	13,409	13,149	3,176	3,215	212	197	887	1,096
20 to 24 years	20,159	21,151	14,490	16,524	3,000	3,303	236	255	958	1,068	3,224	3,599	13,022	13,253	2,827	3,099	192	206	894	995
25 to 29 years	18,351	19,849	14,642	15,586	2,711	2,915	207	240	944	1,109	3,011	3,336	11,737	12,546	2,551	2,735	166	192	885	1,040
30 to 34 years	18,582	19,002	16,049	14,891	2,661	2,775	195	208	1,084	1,127	2,888	3,212	13,464	11,958	2,504	2,601	157	166	1,026	1,065
35 to 39 years	20,082	19,039	16,737	14,894	2,744	2,744	183	193	1,107	1,207	2,851	3,011	15,936	12,151	2,573	2,575	147	155	1,047	1,147
40 to 44 years	22,634	20,404	18,447	16,247	2,931	2,775	184	182	1,072	1,199	2,767	2,926	16,288	13,596	2,762	2,598	152	145	1,016	1,139
45 to 49 years	22,230	22,404	18,354	18,095	2,741	2,855	168	175	967	1,102	2,278	2,738	14,816	15,609	2,600	2,687	141	144	921	1,048
50 to 54 years	19,661	21,934	16,429	18,119	2,270	2,676	140	159	822	980	1,778	2,270	13,103	16,060	2,161	2,535	120	133	785	936
55 to 59 years	16,842	19,177	14,334	16,041	1,749	2,194	109	130	650	813	1,352	1,759	10,120	14,444	1,669	2,085	95	111	623	778
60 to 64 years	12,848	16,252	11,022	13,824	1,274	1,676	80	101	472	652	989	1,330	6,721	12,613	1,216	1,595	70	88	453	626
65 to 69 years	10,086	12,159	8,621	10,393	1,042	1,230	59	71	365	465	770	963	6,130	9,516	995	1,170	52	63	351	447
70 to 74 years	8,375	8,995	7,270	7,724	780	872	45	52	279	346	599	716	4,685	7,070	746	830	40	46	268	333
75 to 79 years	7,429	7,175	6,563	6,237	621	648	36	39	209	251	470	544	2,601	4,617	596	616	32	35	202	242
80 to 84 years	5,514	5,600	4,972	4,976	383	428	26	28	134	168	308	387	1,184	2,925	368	409	23	25	129	162
85 to 89 years	3,028	3,476	2,746	3,131	202	230	14	18	66	96	155	220	361	1,361	195	221	13	17	64	92
90 to 94 years	1,402	1,625	1,257	1,453	105	118	9	10	31	44	78	98	72	449	101	114	8	10	30	43
95 to 99 years	442	556	386	485	42	49	4	5	10	16	27	38	—	96	40	48	4	5	10	16
100 years and over	96	129	78	105	13	17	2	3	3	4	7	11	—	—	13	16	2	2	3	4
5 to 13 years	35,475	35,321	27,827	27,494	5,391	5,334	400	421	1,858	2,072	6,590	7,280	21,813	20,845	5,020	4,929	325	334	1,726	1,933
14 to 17 years	16,931	16,681	13,160	12,940	2,747	2,593	212	194	812	955	2,708	3,137	10,707	10,087	2,588	2,413	174	157	753	887
18 to 24 years	28,498	30,163	22,532	23,527	4,309	4,750	333	351	1,324	1,534	4,536	5,235	18,398	18,762	4,060	4,453	271	284	1,234	1,429
16 years and over	224,447	236,301	184,689	192,336	27,936	30,313	1,898	2,065	9,925	11,587	26,176	30,390	160,849	164,666	26,435	28,556	1,582	1,702	9,405	10,988
18 years and over	216,098	227,761	178,193	185,727	26,575	28,952	1,791	1,967	9,539	11,115	24,863	28,794	155,540	159,509	25,152	27,287	1,495	1,622	9,047	10,549
16 to 64 years	188,077	196,586	152,796	157,833	24,749	26,720	1,703	1,837	8,828	10,196	23,763	27,412	131,179	132,896	23,379	25,133	1,407	1,498	8,349	9,647
55 years and over	66,060	75,145	57,249	64,369	6,210	7,462	383	459	2,218	2,855	4,754	6,067	52,892	58,827	5,940	7,104	341	402	2,132	2,745
65 years and over	36,370	39,715	31,893	34,504	3,187	3,592	194	228	1,097	1,391	2,413	2,978	29,670	31,770	3,055	3,423	175	203	1,057	1,341
85 years and over	4,968	5,786	4,467	5,174	362	414	29	37	110	161	266	368	4,218	4,830	350	398	27	34	107	156
Median age (yrs)	36.7	37.4	37.9	38.8	31.5	32.3	28.4	29.3	33.1	33.7	27.0	27.6	40.1	41.1	31.7	32.5	29.2	29.9	33.4	34.1

Source: U.S. Census Bureau, "Projections of the Total Resident Population by 5-Year Age Groups, Race, and Hispanic Origin With Special Age Categories: Middle Series, 1999 to 2100"; published 13 January 2000; <http://www.census.gov/population/www/projections/natsum-T3.html>.

Figure 1.2
Center of Population: 1970 to 2000

[Prior to 1960, excludes Alaska and Hawaii. The median center is located at the intersection of two median lines, a north-south line constructed so that half of the nation's population lives east and half lives west of it, and an east-west line selected so that half of the nation's population lives north and half lives south of it. The mean center of population is that point at which an imaginary, flat, weightless, and rigid map of the United States would balance if weights of identical value were placed on it so that each weight represented the location of one person on the date of the census]

Year	Median center		Mean center		
	Latitude-N	Longitude	Latitude-N	Longitude-W	Approximate location
1790 (August 2)	(NA)	(NA)	39 16 30	76 11 12	In Kent County, MD, 23 miles E of Baltimore MD
1850 (June 1)..	(NA)	(NA)	38 59 00	81 19 00	In Wirt County, WV, 23 miles SE of Parkersburg, WV[1]
1900 (June 1)..	40 03 32	84 49 01	39 09 36	85 48 54	In Bartholomew County, IN, 6 miles SE of Columbus, IN
1950 (April 1)..	40 00 12	84 56 51	38 50 21	88 09 33	In Richland County, IL, 8 miles NNW of Olney, IL
1960 (April 1)..	39 56 25	85 16 60	38 35 58	89 12 35	In Clinton County, IL, 6.5 miles NW of Centralia, IL
1970 (April 1) .	39 47 43	85 31 43	38 27 47	89 42 22	In St. Clair County, IL, 5.3 miles ESE of Mascoutah, IL
1980 (April 1)..	39 18 60	86 08 15	38 08 13	90 34 26	In Jefferson County, MO, .25 mile W of DeSoto, MO
1990 (April 1)..	38 57 55	86 31 53	37 52 20	91 12 55	In Crawford County, MO, 10 miles SE of Steelville, MO
2000 (April 1)..	38 45 23	86 55 51	37 41 49	91 48 34	In Phelps County, MO, 3 miles E of Edgar Springs, MO

NA Not available.   [1]West Virginia was set off from Virginia, Dec. 31, 1862, and admitted as a state, June 19, 1863.

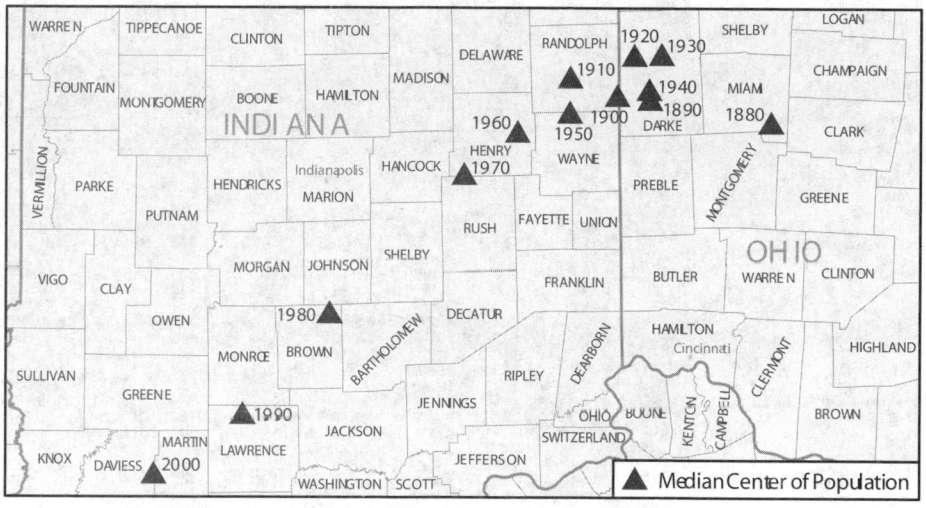

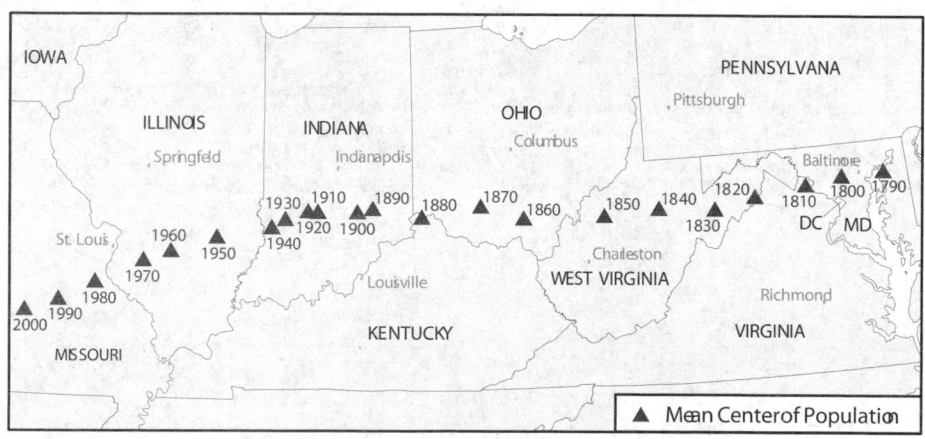

U.S. Census Bureau, Statistical Abstract of the United States: 2002

No. 18. Resident Population—States: 1980 to 2001

[In thousands (226,546 represents 226,546,000). 1980, 1990, and 2000 data as of April 1, data for other years as of July 1. Insofar as possible, population shown for all years is that of present area of state]

State	1980 [1]	1990 [2]	1995	1996	1997	1998	1999	2000	2001
United States	226,546	248,791	266,278	269,394	272,647	275,854	279,040	281,422	284,797
Alabama.	3,894	4,040	4,297	4,331	4,368	4,405	4,430	4,447	4,464
Alaska	402	550	604	609	613	620	625	627	635
Arizona.	2,718	3,665	4,432	4,587	4,737	4,883	5,024	5,131	5,307
Arkansas	2,286	2,351	2,535	2,572	2,601	2,626	2,652	2,673	2,692
California	23,668	29,811	31,697	32,019	32,486	32,988	33,499	33,872	34,501
Colorado.	2,890	3,294	3,827	3,920	4,018	4,117	4,226	4,301	4,418
Connecticut.	3,108	3,287	3,324	3,337	3,349	3,365	3,386	3,406	3,425
Delaware	594	666	730	741	751	763	775	784	796
District of Columbia	638	607	581	572	568	565	570	572	572
Florida	9,746	12,938	14,538	14,853	15,186	15,487	15,759	15,982	16,397
Georgia	5,463	6,478	7,328	7,501	7,685	7,864	8,046	8,186	8,384
Hawaii	965	1,108	1,197	1,204	1,212	1,215	1,210	1,212	1,224
Idaho	944	1,007	1,177	1,203	1,229	1,252	1,276	1,294	1,321
Illinois	11,427	11,431	12,008	12,102	12,186	12,272	12,359	12,419	12,482
Indiana.	5,490	5,544	5,851	5,906	5,955	5,999	6,045	6,080	6,115
Iowa	2,914	2,777	2,867	2,880	2,891	2,903	2,918	2,926	2,923
Kansas.	2,364	2,478	2,601	2,615	2,635	2,661	2,678	2,688	2,695
Kentucky	3,661	3,687	3,887	3,920	3,953	3,985	4,018	4,042	4,066
Louisiana	4,206	4,222	4,379	4,399	4,421	4,440	4,461	4,469	4,465
Maine.	1,125	1,228	1,243	1,249	1,255	1,259	1,267	1,275	1,287
Maryland	4,217	4,781	5,070	5,112	5,157	5,204	5,255	5,296	5,375
Massachusetts.	5,737	6,016	6,141	6,180	6,226	6,272	6,317	6,349	6,379
Michigan.	9,262	9,295	9,676	9,759	9,809	9,848	9,897	9,938	9,991
Minnesota.	4,076	4,376	4,660	4,713	4,763	4,813	4,873	4,919	4,972
Mississippi	2,521	2,575	2,723	2,748	2,777	2,805	2,828	2,845	2,858
Missouri	4,917	5,117	5,378	5,432	5,481	5,522	5,562	5,595	5,630
Montana.	787	799	877	886	890	892	898	902	904
Nebraska	1,570	1,578	1,657	1,674	1,686	1,696	1,705	1,711	1,713
Nevada	800	1,202	1,582	1,666	1,764	1,853	1,935	1,998	2,106
New Hampshire	921	1,109	1,158	1,175	1,189	1,206	1,222	1,236	1,259
New Jersey.	7,365	7,748	8,083	8,150	8,219	8,287	8,360	8,414	8,484
New Mexico	1,303	1,515	1,720	1,752	1,775	1,793	1,808	1,819	1,829
New York	17,558	17,991	18,524	18,588	18,657	18,756	18,883	18,976	19,011
North Carolina	5,882	6,632	7,345	7,501	7,657	7,809	7,949	8,049	8,186
North Dakota.	653	639	648	650	650	648	644	642	634
Ohio	10,798	10,847	11,203	11,243	11,277	11,312	11,335	11,353	11,374
Oklahoma.	3,025	3,146	3,308	3,340	3,373	3,405	3,437	3,451	3,460
Oregon.	2,633	2,842	3,184	3,247	3,304	3,352	3,394	3,421	3,473
Pennsylvania.	11,864	11,883	12,198	12,220	12,228	12,246	12,264	12,281	12,287
Rhode Island.	947	1,003	1,017	1,021	1,025	1,031	1,040	1,048	1,059
South Carolina.	3,122	3,486	3,749	3,796	3,860	3,919	3,975	4,012	4,063
South Dakota	691	696	738	742	744	746	750	755	757
Tennessee	4,591	4,877	5,327	5,417	5,499	5,570	5,639	5,689	5,740
Texas.	14,229	16,986	18,959	19,340	19,740	20,158	20,558	20,852	21,325
Utah	1,461	1,723	2,014	2,068	2,120	2,166	2,203	2,233	2,270
Vermont	511	563	589	594	597	600	605	609	613
Virginia.	5,347	6,189	6,671	6,751	6,829	6,901	7,000	7,079	7,188
Washington.	4,132	4,867	5,481	5,570	5,675	5,770	5,843	5,894	5,988
West Virginia.	1,950	1,793	1,824	1,823	1,819	1,816	1,812	1,808	1,802
Wisconsin.	4,706	4,892	5,185	5,230	5,266	5,298	5,333	5,364	5,402
Wyoming.	470	454	485	485	488	489	491	492	494

[1] See footnote 4, Table 1. [2] The April 1, 1990, census counts include corrections processed through August 1997, results of special censuses and test censuses, and do not include adjustments for census coverage errors.

Source: U.S. Census Bureau, *1990 Census of Population and Housing, Population and Housing Unit Counts* (CPH-2); "Table CO-EST2001-12-00 - Time Series of Intercensal State Population Estimates: April 1, 1990, to April 1, 2000"; published 11 April 2002; <http://eire.census.gov/popest/data/counties/tables/CO-EST2001-12/CO-EST2001-12-00.php>; and "Table ST-2001EST-01 - Time Series of State Population Estimates: April 1, 2000 to July 1, 2001"; published 27 December 2001; <http://eire.census.gov/popest/data/ states/tables/ST-EST2001-01.php>.

OUACHITA TECHNICAL COLLEGE

U.S. Census Bureau, Statistical Abstract of the United States: 2002

No. 19. State Population—Rank, Percent Change, and Population Density: 1980 to 2001

[As of April 1, except 2001 as of July 1. Insofar as possible, population shown for all years is that of present area of state. For area figures of states, see Table 335. Minus sign (-) indicates decrease]

State	Rank				Percent change			Population per sq. mile of land area [1]		
	1980	1990	2000	2001	1980-1990	1990-2000	2000-2001	1980	1990	2001
United States.	(X)	(X)	(X)	(X)	9.8	13.1	1.2	64.0	70.3	80.5
Alabama	22	22	23	23	3.8	10.1	0.4	76.7	79.6	88.0
Alaska	50	49	48	47	36.9	14.0	1.3	0.7	1.0	1.1
Arizona	29	24	20	20	34.8	40.0	3.4	23.9	32.3	46.7
Arkansas	33	33	33	33	2.8	13.7	0.7	43.9	45.1	51.7
California	1	1	1	1	26.0	13.6	1.9	151.8	191.1	221.2
Colorado	28	26	24	24	14.0	30.6	2.7	27.9	31.8	42.6
Connecticut	25	27	29	29	5.8	3.6	0.6	641.4	678.5	707.0
Delaware	47	46	45	45	12.1	17.6	1.6	304.2	341.0	407.5
District of Columbia . . .	(X)	(X)	(X)	(X)	-4.9	-5.7	(-Z)	10,396.3	9,884.4	9,313.1
Florida	7	4	4	4	32.7	23.5	2.6	180.7	239.9	304.1
Georgia	13	11	10	10	18.6	26.4	2.4	94.3	111.9	144.8
Hawaii	39	41	42	42	14.9	9.3	1.1	150.2	172.6	190.6
Idaho	41	42	39	39	6.7	28.5	2.1	11.4	12.2	16.0
Illinois	5	6	5	5	(Z)	8.6	0.5	205.6	205.6	224.6
Indiana	12	14	14	14	1.0	9.7	0.6	153.1	154.6	170.5
Iowa	27	30	30	30	-4.7	5.4	-0.1	52.2	49.7	52.3
Kansas	32	32	32	32	4.8	8.5	0.2	28.9	30.3	32.9
Kentucky	23	23	25	25	0.7	9.6	0.6	92.1	92.8	102.3
Louisiana	19	21	22	22	0.4	5.9	-0.1	96.6	96.9	102.5
Maine	38	38	40	40	9.2	3.8	0.9	36.4	39.8	41.7
Maryland	18	19	19	19	13.4	10.8	1.5	431.5	489.1	550.0
Massachusetts	11	13	13	13	4.9	5.5	0.5	731.8	767.4	813.7
Michigan	8	8	8	8	0.4	6.9	0.5	163.1	163.6	175.9
Minnesota	21	20	21	21	7.4	12.4	1.1	51.2	55.0	62.5
Mississippi	31	31	31	31	2.2	10.5	0.5	53.7	54.9	60.9
Missouri	15	15	17	17	4.1	9.3	0.6	71.4	74.3	81.7
Montana	44	44	44	44	1.6	12.9	0.2	5.4	5.5	6.2
Nebraska	35	36	38	38	0.5	8.4	0.1	20.4	20.5	22.3
Nevada	43	39	35	35	50.1	66.3	5.4	7.3	10.9	19.2
New Hampshire	42	40	41	41	20.5	11.4	1.9	102.7	123.7	140.4
New Jersey	9	9	9	9	5.2	8.6	0.8	992.9	1,044.5	1,143.9
New Mexico	37	37	36	36	16.3	20.1	0.6	10.7	12.5	15.1
New York	2	2	3	3	2.5	5.5	0.2	371.9	381.0	402.7
North Carolina	10	10	11	11	12.8	21.4	1.7	120.7	136.2	168.1
North Dakota	46	47	47	48	-2.1	0.5	-1.2	9.5	9.3	9.2
Ohio	6	7	7	7	0.5	4.7	0.2	263.7	264.9	277.8
Oklahoma	26	28	27	28	4.0	9.7	0.3	44.1	45.8	50.4
Oregon	30	29	28	27	7.9	20.4	1.5	27.4	29.6	36.2
Pennsylvania	4	5	6	6	0.2	3.4	(Z)	264.7	265.1	274.2
Rhode Island	40	43	43	43	5.9	4.5	1.0	906.4	960.3	1,013.4
South Carolina	24	25	26	26	11.7	15.1	1.3	103.7	115.8	134.9
South Dakota	45	45	46	46	0.8	8.5	0.2	9.1	9.2	10.0
Tennessee	17	17	16	16	6.2	16.7	0.9	111.4	118.3	139.3
Texas	3	3	2	2	19.4	22.8	2.3	54.4	64.9	81.5
Utah	36	35	34	34	17.9	29.6	1.6	17.8	21.0	27.6
Vermont	48	48	49	49	10.0	8.2	0.7	55.3	60.8	66.3
Virginia	14	12	12	12	15.8	14.4	1.5	135.0	156.3	181.5
Washington	20	18	15	15	17.8	21.1	1.6	62.1	73.1	90.0
West Virginia	34	34	37	37	-8.0	0.8	-0.4	81.0	74.5	74.8
Wisconsin	16	16	18	18	4.0	9.6	0.7	86.6	90.1	99.5
Wyoming	49	50	50	50	-3.4	8.9	0.1	4.8	4.7	5.1

X Not applicable.   Z Less than 0.05 percent.   [1] Persons per square mile were calculated on the basis of land area data from the 2000 census.

Source: U.S. Census Bureau, *1990 Census of Population and Housing, Population and Housing Unit Counts* (CPH-2); "ST-99-3 State Population Estimates: Annual Time Series, July 1, 1990, to July 1, 1999"; published 29 December 1999; <http://www.census.gov/population/estimates/state/st-99-3.txt>; *Population Change and Distribution: 1990 to 2000, Census 2000 Brief*, (C2KBR/01-2), April 2001; and "Table ST-2001EST-01 - Time Series of State Population Estimates: April 1, 2000, to July 1, 2001"; published 27 December 2001; <http://eire.census.gov/popest/data/states/tables/ST-EST2001-01.php>.

No. 20. Resident Population—Components of Change for States: 2000-2001

[Covers period April 1, 2000, to July 1, 2001. Minus sign (-) indicates net decrease]

State	Numeric population change	Births	Deaths	Net international migration	Net internal migration	Federal civilian movement	Residual [1]
United States	3,374,981	5,042,426	2,999,064	1,339,827	-	-8,208	-
Alabama.	17,256	80,131	56,534	3,793	-9,400	-81	-653
Alaska	7,960	12,624	3,628	1,709	-2,702	-124	81
Arizona.	176,699	104,781	50,703	28,918	92,892	-143	954
Arkansas	18,690	47,970	34,843	3,618	2,065	-30	-90
California	629,482	660,126	285,733	343,693	-88,514	-1,179	1,089
Colorado.	116,453	79,847	34,144	19,660	50,139	-202	1,153
Connecticut.	19,509	53,343	37,832	14,824	-9,628	-49	-1,149
Delaware	12,565	13,862	8,592	2,077	5,463	-26	-219
District of Columbia	-237	10,181	7,589	4,034	-6,791	-31	-41
Florida	414,137	256,107	204,172	122,430	236,764	-462	3,470
Georgia	197,462	168,353	79,804	28,376	78,036	-487	2,988
Hawaii	12,861	23,452	10,357	6,493	-6,224	-292	-211
Idaho	27,053	24,583	11,976	3,707	10,424	-27	342
Illinois	63,008	231,194	134,303	75,160	-110,286	-156	1,399
Indiana.	34,260	107,126	69,179	9,344	-12,522	-5	-504
Iowa	-3,145	46,648	35,033	4,606	-18,790	-2	-574
Kansas.	6,223	48,712	31,045	7,927	-19,306	-114	49
Kentucky	23,787	68,762	49,431	3,803	1,378	-193	-532
Louisiana	-3,546	87,433	51,633	3,797	-42,929	-129	-85
Maine.	11,747	16,505	15,512	888	10,133	-25	-242
Maryland	78,670	94,603	54,845	26,903	12,639	-237	-393
Massachusetts.	30,207	101,062	70,785	25,710	-24,431	-29	-1,320
Michigan.	52,373	169,278	109,292	24,215	-30,422	-14	-1,392
Minnesota.	52,815	82,541	47,363	11,876	5,653	-13	121
Mississippi	13,371	56,970	35,931	1,870	-9,428	-112	2
Missouri	34,496	94,677	68,762	8,151	887	-99	-358
Montana.	2,238	13,320	10,165	470	-1,377	-22	12
Nebraska	1,972	30,192	18,878	3,975	-13,022	-52	-243
Nevada	107,817	37,234	18,588	16,939	70,483	-54	1,803
New Hampshire	23,395	17,683	12,137	1,694	16,232	-5	-72
New Jersey.	70,081	138,856	89,267	60,361	-39,215	-62	-592
New Mexico	10,100	33,732	16,862	5,935	-12,481	-73	-151
New York	34,921	323,772	197,846	159,126	-249,636	-145	-350
North Carolina	136,955	150,843	89,957	21,191	55,683	-670	-135
North Dakota.	-7,752	9,452	7,379	567	-10,389	-39	36
Ohio	20,401	195,720	136,432	12,563	-49,578	-41	-1,831
Oklahoma.	9,443	60,327	43,267	6,439	-13,616	-175	-265
Oregon.	51,468	55,999	36,994	13,797	19,126	-13	-447
Pennsylvania.	6,096	180,121	163,050	22,545	-30,640	-27	-2,853
Rhode Island.	10,601	15,375	12,571	3,655	4,512	-19	-351
South Carolina	50,999	71,330	46,194	5,563	21,224	-254	-670
South Dakota	1,756	12,866	8,822	643	-2,883	-21	-27
Tennessee	50,738	99,246	68,953	7,654	13,179	-86	-302
Texas.	473,198	447,418	185,621	134,547	75,014	-785	2,625
Utah	36,620	57,516	15,429	9,367	-14,916	-34	116
Vermont	4,263	7,872	6,428	836	2,145	-1	-161
Virginia.	109,219	124,540	70,495	28,340	26,418	-980	1,396
Washington.	93,852	99,727	55,046	27,301	22,420	-361	-189
West Virginia.	-6,428	25,477	26,372	620	-5,853	-1	-299
Wisconsin	38,231	85,327	58,334	7,627	4,510	-5	-894
Wyoming	641	7,610	4,956	490	-2,440	-22	-41

- Represents zero.   [1] State estimates are constrained to sum to an independently derived estimate of the national population. The residual is the difference between a state's population before and after imposing this constraint. The residual is not a demographic component of population change; rather, it is a statistical artifact of the procedures employed to produce the estimates.

Source: U.S. Census Bureau, "Table ST-2001EST-02 - Estimated State Demographic Components of Change: April 1, 2000, to July 1, 2001"; published 27 December 2001; <http://eire.census.gov/popest/data/states/tables/ST-EST2001-02.php>; and unpublished data.

No. 21. Resident Population by Age and State: 2000

[In thousands, except percent (281,422 represents 281,422,000). As of April. Includes Armed Forces stationed in area]

State	Total	Under 5 years	5 to 17 years	18 to 24 years	25 to 34 years	35 to 44 years	45 to 54 years	55 to 64 years	65 to 74 years	75 to 84 years	85 years and over	Percent 65 years and over
U.S.	281,422	19,176	53,118	27,143	39,892	45,149	37,678	24,275	18,391	12,361	4,240	12.4
AL	4,447	296	827	440	603	686	600	416	317	196	67	13.0
AK	627	48	143	57	89	114	95	45	23	11	3	5.7
AZ	5,131	382	985	514	743	769	628	442	364	235	69	13.0
AR	2,673	182	499	262	353	398	350	257	198	129	46	14.0
CA	33,872	2,487	6,763	3,366	5,229	5,485	4,332	2,614	1,888	1,282	426	10.6
CO	4,301	298	803	430	664	737	614	339	226	142	48	9.7
CT	3,406	223	618	272	452	581	481	309	232	174	64	13.8
DE	784	52	143	75	109	128	104	72	56	35	11	13.0
DC	572	33	82	73	102	88	75	50	36	25	9	12.2
FL	15,982	946	2,701	1,331	2,084	2,485	2,069	1,559	1,452	1,024	331	17.6
GA	8,186	595	1,574	838	1,299	1,354	1,080	661	436	262	88	9.6
HI	1,212	78	218	115	171	191	171	107	85	58	18	13.3
ID	1,294	98	271	139	169	193	170	108	76	52	18	11.3
IL	12,419	877	2,369	1,211	1,812	1,984	1,627	1,041	772	536	192	12.1
IN	6,080	423	1,151	615	831	961	817	530	395	266	92	12.4
IA	2,926	188	545	298	363	445	393	257	212	159	65	14.9
KS	2,688	189	524	276	349	420	354	220	176	129	52	13.3
KY	4,042	266	729	402	568	643	557	373	274	173	58	12.5
LA	4,469	317	902	474	601	692	586	379	283	175	59	11.6
ME	1,275	71	231	104	158	213	193	123	96	64	23	14.4
MD	5,296	353	1,003	451	749	916	755	470	321	211	67	11.3
MA	6,349	397	1,103	579	927	1,063	873	546	428	316	117	13.5
MI	9,938	672	1,924	932	1,362	1,598	1,368	863	643	434	142	12.3
MN	4,919	330	957	470	673	824	666	405	296	213	86	12.1
MS	2,845	204	571	311	382	425	362	246	186	115	43	12.1
MO	5,595	370	1,058	536	739	888	742	507	393	264	99	13.5
MT	902	55	175	86	103	142	135	85	63	43	15	13.4
NE	1,711	117	333	174	223	264	226	142	116	83	34	13.6
NV	1,998	146	366	180	307	322	269	190	132	70	17	11.0
NH	1,236	76	234	103	160	221	184	110	78	51	18	12.0
NJ	8,414	564	1,524	677	1,189	1,435	1,159	754	575	402	136	13.2
NM	1,819	131	378	178	234	282	246	159	118	71	23	11.7
NY	18,976	1,239	3,451	1,765	2,757	3,074	2,553	1,688	1,276	861	311	12.9
NC	8,049	540	1,425	807	1,213	1,287	1,085	724	534	330	105	12.0
ND	642	39	121	73	77	98	85	53	46	34	15	14.7
OH	11,353	755	2,133	1,057	1,520	1,805	1,566	1,009	790	541	177	13.3
OK	3,451	236	656	357	452	524	454	316	242	156	57	13.2
OR	3,421	223	624	328	471	527	507	304	219	161	57	12.8
PA	12,281	728	2,194	1,094	1,560	1,948	1,705	1,132	969	712	238	15.6
RI	1,048	64	184	107	140	170	142	89	74	58	21	14.5
SC	4,012	265	745	408	561	625	550	373	270	165	50	12.1
SD	755	51	152	78	91	115	98	62	53	39	16	14.3
TN	5,689	375	1,024	549	816	903	787	533	383	239	81	12.4
TX	20,852	1,625	4,262	2,199	3,162	3,322	2,611	1,598	1,143	692	238	9.9
UT	2,233	209	509	317	327	300	238	143	102	67	22	8.5
VT	609	34	114	57	75	102	94	57	41	27	10	12.7
VA	7,079	462	1,276	679	1,037	1,201	999	632	432	273	87	11.2
WA	5,894	394	1,120	559	841	975	846	497	337	241	84	11.2
WV	1,808	102	301	172	229	272	270	185	148	97	32	15.3
WI	5,364	342	1,026	521	706	876	732	458	355	252	96	13.1
WY	494	31	98	50	60	79	74	45	31	20	7	11.7

Source: U.S. Census Bureau, "Demographic Profiles: Census 2000"; <http://www.census.gov/Press-Release/www/2001/demoprofile.html>.

Population   25

[281,422 represents 281,422,000. As of April]

State	Number (1,000)							
		One race						
	Total population	White	Black or African American	American Indian, Alaska Native	Asian	Native Hawaiian and Other Pacific Islander	Some other race	Two or more races
U.S.	281,422	211,461	34,658	2,476	10,243	399	15,359	6,826
AL.	4,447	3,163	1,156	22	31	1	29	44
AK.	627	435	22	98	25	3	10	34
AZ.	5,131	3,874	159	256	92	7	597	147
AR.	2,673	2,139	419	18	20	2	40	36
CA.	33,872	20,170	2,264	333	3,698	117	5,682	1,608
CO	4,301	3,560	165	44	95	5	310	122
CT.	3,406	2,780	310	10	82	1	147	75
DE.	784	585	151	3	16	(Z)	16	13
DC	572	176	343	2	15	(Z)	22	13
FL.	15,982	12,465	2,336	54	266	9	477	376
GA	8,186	5,327	2,350	22	173	4	196	114
HI	1,212	294	22	4	504	114	15	259
ID	1,294	1,177	5	18	12	1	55	26
IL	12,419	9,125	1,877	31	424	5	723	235
IN	6,080	5,320	510	16	59	2	98	76
IA	2,926	2,749	62	9	37	1	37	32
KS.	2,688	2,314	154	25	47	1	91	56
KY.	4,042	3,641	296	9	30	1	23	42
LA.	4,469	2,856	1,452	25	55	1	31	48
ME	1,275	1,236	7	7	9	(Z)	3	13
MD	5,296	3,391	1,477	15	211	2	96	104
MA	6,349	5,367	343	15	238	2	237	146
MI	9,938	7,966	1,413	58	177	3	130	192
MN	4,919	4,400	172	55	142	2	66	83
MS	2,845	1,746	1,034	12	19	1	14	20
MO	5,595	4,748	629	25	62	3	46	82
MT	902	817	3	56	5	(Z)	5	16
NE.	1,711	1,533	69	15	22	1	48	24
NV.	1,998	1,502	135	26	90	8	159	76
NH	1,236	1,187	9	3	16	(Z)	7	13
NJ.	8,414	6,105	1,142	19	480	3	451	214
NM	1,819	1,214	34	173	19	2	310	66
NY.	18,976	12,894	3,014	82	1,045	9	1,342	590
NC	8,049	5,805	1,738	100	114	4	187	103
ND	642	593	4	31	4	(Z)	3	7
OH	11,353	9,645	1,301	24	133	3	89	158
OK	3,451	2,628	261	273	47	2	83	156
OR	3,421	2,962	56	45	101	8	145	105
PA.	12,281	10,484	1,225	18	220	3	188	142
RI	1,048	891	47	5	24	1	53	28
SC.	4,012	2,696	1,185	14	36	2	40	40
SD.	755	669	5	62	4	(Z)	4	10
TN.	5,689	4,563	933	15	57	2	56	63
TX.	20,852	14,800	2,405	118	562	14	2,438	515
UT.	2,233	1,993	18	30	37	15	93	47
VT	609	589	3	2	5	(Z)	1	7
VA.	7,079	5,120	1,390	21	261	4	139	143
WA	5,894	4,822	190	93	322	24	229	214
WV	1,808	1,719	57	4	9	(Z)	3	16
WI	5,364	4,770	304	47	89	2	85	67
WY	494	455	4	11	3	(Z)	12	9

See footnotes at end of table.

26 Population

No. 22. Resident Population by Race and State: 2000—Con.

[See headnote on pg. 26]

State	Percent distribution						
	One race					Some other race	Two or more races
	White	Black or African American	American Indian, Alaska Native	Asian	Native Hawaiian and Other Pacific Islander		
U.S.	**75.1**	**12.3**	**0.9**	**3.6**	**0.1**	**5.5**	**2.4**
AL.	71.1	26.0	0.5	0.7	(Z)	0.7	1.0
AK.	69.3	3.5	15.6	4.0	0.5	1.6	5.4
AZ.	75.5	3.1	5.0	1.8	0.1	11.6	2.9
AR.	80.0	15.7	0.7	0.8	0.1	1.5	1.3
CA.	59.5	6.7	1.0	10.9	0.3	16.8	4.7
CO	82.8	3.8	1.0	2.2	0.1	7.2	2.8
CT.	81.6	9.1	0.3	2.4	(Z)	4.3	2.2
DE.	74.6	19.2	0.3	2.1	(Z)	2.0	1.7
DC	30.8	60.0	0.3	2.7	0.1	3.8	2.4
FL.	78.0	14.6	0.3	1.7	0.1	3.0	2.4
GA	65.1	28.7	0.3	2.1	0.1	2.4	1.4
HI	24.3	1.8	0.3	41.6	9.4	1.3	21.4
ID	91.0	0.4	1.4	0.9	0.1	4.2	2.0
IL	73.5	15.1	0.2	3.4	(Z)	5.8	1.9
IN	87.5	8.4	0.3	1.0	(Z)	1.6	1.2
IA	93.9	2.1	0.3	1.3	(Z)	1.3	1.1
KS.	86.1	5.7	0.9	1.7	(Z)	3.4	2.1
KY.	90.1	7.3	0.2	0.7	(Z)	0.6	1.1
LA.	63.9	32.5	0.6	1.2	(Z)	0.7	1.1
ME	96.9	0.5	0.6	0.7	(Z)	0.2	1.0
MD	64.0	27.9	0.3	4.0	(Z)	1.8	2.0
MA	84.5	5.4	0.2	3.8	(Z)	3.7	2.3
MI	80.2	14.2	0.6	1.8	(Z)	1.3	1.9
MN	89.4	3.5	1.1	2.9	(Z)	1.3	1.7
MS	61.4	36.3	0.4	0.7	(Z)	0.5	0.7
MO	84.9	11.2	0.4	1.1	0.1	0.8	1.5
MT	90.6	0.3	6.2	0.5	0.1	0.6	1.7
NE.	89.6	4.0	0.9	1.3	(Z)	2.8	1.4
NV.	75.2	6.8	1.3	4.5	0.4	8.0	3.8
NH	96.0	0.7	0.2	1.3	(Z)	0.6	1.1
NJ.	72.6	13.6	0.2	5.7	(Z)	5.4	2.5
NM	66.8	1.9	9.5	1.1	0.1	17.0	3.6
NY.	67.9	15.9	0.4	5.5	(Z)	7.1	3.1
NC	72.1	21.6	1.2	1.4	(Z)	2.3	1.3
ND	92.4	0.6	4.9	0.6	(Z)	0.4	1.2
OH	85.0	11.5	0.2	1.2	(Z)	0.8	1.4
OK	76.2	7.6	7.9	1.4	0.1	2.4	4.5
OR	86.6	1.6	1.3	3.0	0.2	4.2	3.1
PA.	85.4	10.0	0.1	1.8	(Z)	1.5	1.2
RI	85.0	4.5	0.5	2.3	0.1	5.0	2.7
SC.	67.2	29.5	0.3	0.9	(Z)	1.0	1.0
SD.	88.7	0.6	8.3	0.6	(Z)	0.5	1.3
TN.	80.2	16.4	0.3	1.0	(Z)	1.0	1.1
TX.	71.0	11.5	0.6	2.7	0.1	11.7	2.5
UT.	89.2	0.8	1.3	1.7	0.7	4.2	2.1
VT.	96.8	0.5	0.4	0.9	(Z)	0.2	1.2
VA.	72.3	19.6	0.3	3.7	0.1	2.0	2.0
WA	81.8	3.2	1.6	5.5	0.4	3.9	3.6
WV	95.0	3.2	0.2	0.5	(Z)	0.2	0.9
WI	88.9	5.7	0.9	1.7	(Z)	1.6	1.2
WY	92.1	0.8	2.3	0.6	0.1	2.5	1.8

Z Less than 500 or 0.05 percent.

Source: U.S. Census Bureau, "Demographic Profiles: Census 2000"; <http://www.census.gov/Press-Release/www/2001/demoprofile.html>.

Population   27

No. 23. Resident Population by Hispanic or Latino Origin and State: 2000

[In thousands, except percent (281,422 represents 281,422,000). As of April. Persons of Hispanic or Latino origin may be of any race]

State		Hispanic or Latino						Not Hispanic or Latino	
	Total population	Total		Mexican	Puerto Rican	Cuban	Other Hispanic or Latino	Total	White alone
		Number	Percent of total population						
U.S.	281,422	35,306	12.5	20,641	3,406	1,242	10,017	246,116	194,553
AL.	4,447	76	1.7	45	6	2	23	4,371	3,126
AK.	627	26	4.1	13	3	1	9	601	424
AZ.	5,131	1,296	25.3	1,066	18	5	207	3,835	3,274
AR.	2,673	87	3.2	61	2	1	22	2,587	2,100
CA.	33,872	10,967	32.4	8,456	141	72	2,298	22,905	15,817
CO	4,301	736	17.1	451	13	4	268	3,566	3,203
CT.	3,406	320	9.4	23	194	7	95	3,085	2,639
DE.	784	37	4.8	13	14	1	9	746	568
DC	572	45	7.9	5	2	1	36	527	159
FL.	15,982	2,683	16.8	364	482	833	1,004	13,300	10,459
GA	8,186	435	5.3	275	36	13	112	7,751	5,129
HI	1,212	88	7.2	20	30	1	37	1,124	277
ID	1,294	102	7.9	79	2	(Z)	20	1,192	1,139
IL	12,419	1,530	12.3	1,144	158	18	210	10,889	8,424
IN	6,080	215	3.5	153	20	3	39	5,866	5,219
IA	2,926	82	2.8	61	3	1	18	2,844	2,710
KS.	2,688	188	7.0	148	5	2	33	2,500	2,234
KY.	4,042	60	1.5	31	6	4	19	3,982	3,608
LA.	4,469	108	2.4	32	8	8	59	4,361	2,794
ME	1,275	9	0.7	3	2	(Z)	4	1,266	1,230
MD	5,296	228	4.3	40	26	7	156	5,069	3,287
MA	6,349	429	6.8	22	199	9	198	5,920	5,198
MI	9,938	324	3.3	221	27	7	69	9,615	7,807
MN	4,919	143	2.9	96	7	3	39	4,776	4,337
MS	2,845	40	1.4	22	3	2	14	2,805	1,728
MO	5,595	119	2.1	78	7	3	31	5,477	4,686
MT	902	18	2.0	12	1	(Z)	5	884	808
NE.	1,711	94	5.5	71	2	1	21	1,617	1,494
NV.	1,998	394	19.7	286	10	11	86	1,604	1,303
NH	1,236	20	1.7	5	6	1	9	1,215	1,175
NJ.	8,414	1,117	13.3	103	367	77	570	7,297	5,557
NM	1,819	765	42.1	330	4	3	428	1,054	813
NY.	18,976	2,868	15.1	261	1,050	63	1,494	16,109	11,761
NC	8,049	379	4.7	247	31	7	94	7,670	5,647
ND	642	8	1.2	4	1	(Z)	3	634	589
OH	11,353	217	1.9	91	66	5	55	11,136	9,538
OK	3,451	179	5.2	133	8	2	37	3,271	2,556
OR	3,421	275	8.0	215	5	3	52	3,146	2,858
PA	12,281	394	3.2	55	229	10	100	11,887	10,322
RI	1,048	91	8.7	6	25	1	58	957	858
SC.	4,012	95	2.4	53	12	3	27	3,917	2,652
SD.	755	11	1.4	6	1	(Z)	4	744	665
TN.	5,689	124	2.2	77	10	4	32	5,565	4,506
TX.	20,852	6,670	32.0	5,072	70	26	1,502	14,182	10,933
UT.	2,233	202	9.0	136	4	1	60	2,032	1,904
VT.	609	6	0.9	1	1	(Z)	3	603	585
VA.	7,079	330	4.7	74	41	8	206	6,749	4,966
WA	5,894	442	7.5	330	16	5	91	5,453	4,652
WV	1,808	12	0.7	4	2	(Z)	6	1,796	1,710
WI	5,364	193	3.6	127	30	2	33	5,171	4,682
WY	494	32	6.4	20	1	(Z)	11	462	439

Z Less than 500.

Source: U.S. Census Bureau, Census 2000 Redistricting Data (P.L. 94-171) Summary File for states, Tables PL1 and PL2.

No. 24. Resident Population, by Region, Race, and Hispanic Origin: 2000

[As of April (281,422 represents 281,422,000). For composition of regions, see map, inside front cover]

Race and Hispanic origin	Population (1,000)					Percent distribution				
	United States	North-east	Mid-west	South	West	United States	North-east	Mid-west	South	West
Total population	281,422	53,594	64,393	100,237	63,198	100.0	19.0	22.9	35.6	22.5
One race.	274,596	52,366	63,370	98,390	60,470	100.0	19.1	23.1	35.8	22.0
White	211,461	41,534	53,834	72,819	43,274	100.0	19.6	25.5	34.4	20.5
Black or African American . . .	34,658	6,100	6,500	18,982	3,077	100.0	17.6	18.8	54.8	8.9
American Indian and Alaska Native	2,476	163	399	726	1,188	100.0	6.6	16.1	29.3	48.0
Asian	10,243	2,119	1,198	1,922	5,004	100.0	20.7	11.7	18.8	48.8
Asian Indian	1,679	554	293	441	391	100.0	33.0	17.5	26.3	23.3
Chinese	2,433	692	212	343	1,186	100.0	28.4	8.7	14.1	48.8
Filipino.	1,850	202	151	245	1,253	100.0	10.9	8.2	13.2	67.7
Japanese	797	76	63	77	580	100.0	9.6	7.9	9.7	72.8
Korean.	1,077	246	132	224	474	100.0	22.9	12.3	20.8	44.0
Vietnamese.	1,123	115	107	336	564	100.0	10.3	9.5	29.9	50.3
Other Asian [1]	1,285	233	239	257	556	100.0	18.2	18.6	20.0	43.2
Native Hawaiian and Other Pacific Islander	399	21	22	51	304	100.0	5.2	5.6	12.8	76.3
Native Hawaiian.	141	4	6	12	118	100.0	3.2	4.1	8.9	83.8
Guamanian or Chamorro . .	58	5	5	15	34	100.0	7.9	7.9	25.1	59.1
Samoan	91	4	5	9	73	100.0	4.2	5.6	9.7	80.5
Other Pacific Islander [2] . . .	109	8	7	15	79	100.0	7.3	6.4	14.0	72.2
Some other race	15,359	2,430	1,417	3,889	7,623	100.0	15.8	9.2	25.3	49.6
Two or more races	6,826	1,228	1,022	1,847	2,728	100.0	18.0	15.0	27.1	40.0
Hispanic or Latino (of any race).	35,306	5,254	3,125	11,587	15,341	100.0	14.9	8.8	32.8	43.5
Mexican.	20,641	479	2,200	6,548	11,413	100.0	2.3	10.7	31.7	55.3
Puerto Rican	3,406	2,075	325	759	247	100.0	60.9	9.6	22.3	7.2
Cuban	1,242	169	45	921	106	100.0	13.6	3.6	74.2	8.5
Other Hispanic or Latino. . . .	10,017	2,531	554	3,358	3,574	100.0	25.3	5.5	33.5	35.7
Not Hispanic or Latino	246,116	48,340	61,268	88,650	47,857	100.0	19.6	24.9	36.0	19.4
White alone	194,553	39,327	52,386	65,928	36,912	100.0	20.2	26.9	33.9	19.0

[1] Other Asian alone, or two or more Asian categories. [2] Other Pacific Islander alone or two or more Native Hawaiian and Other Pacific Islander categories.

Source: U.S. Census Bureau, "Demographic Profiles: Census 2000"; <http://www.census.gov/Press-Release/www/2001/demoprofile.html>.

No. 25. Mobility Status of the Population by Selected Characteristics: 1980 to 2000

[As of March (221,641 represents 221,641,000). For persons 1 year old and over. Excludes members of the Armed Forces except those living off post or with their families on post. Based on Current Population Survey; see text of this section and Appendix III]

Mobility period and characteristic		Percent distribution						
			Movers (different house in United States)					
					Different county			
	Total (1,000)	Non-movers	Total	Same county	Total	Same state	Different state	Movers from abroad
1980-81.	221,641	83	17	10	6	3	3	1
1985-86.	232,998	82	18	11	7	4	3	1
1990-91.	244,884	83	16	10	6	3	3	1
1995-96.	260,406	84	16	10	6	3	3	1
1999-2000, total	270,219	84	15	9	6	3	3	1
1 to 4 years old.	15,740	77	22	14	8	4	4	1
5 to 9 years old.	20,379	82	17	11	6	3	3	1
10 to 14 years old	20,328	86	13	8	6	3	3	1
15 to 19 years old	20,102	83	16	9	7	3	3	1
20 to 24 years old	18,441	65	34	20	13	7	6	2
25 to 29 years old	18,268	68	31	18	13	7	6	1
30 to 44 years old	64,323	83	16	10	7	3	3	1
45 to 64 years old	60,017	92	8	4	4	2	2	(Z)
65 to 74 years old	17,796	95	4	2	2	1	1	(Z)
75 to 84 years old	11,685	96	4	2	2	1	1	(Z)
85 years old and over	3,140	95	5	2	2	1	1	(Z)
Persons 16 years and over	209,845	84	15	9	6	3	3	1
Civilian labor force.	140,454	83	17	10	7	4	3	1
Employed.	134,338	83	17	10	7	4	3	1
Unemployed	6,116	75	24	14	10	5	5	1
Armed Forces.	777	59	35	11	23	4	20	6
Not in labor force	68,613	89	11	6	5	2	3	1
Tenure:								
Owner-occupied units	189,408	91	9	5	4	2	2	(Z)
Renter-occupied units	80,811	68	31	19	12	6	6	2

Z Less than 0.5 percent.

Source: U.S. Census Bureau, Current Population Reports, P20-538.

OUACHITA TECHNICAL COLLEGE

U.S. Census Bureau, Statistical Abstract of the United States: 2002

No. 26. Mobility Status of Households by Household Income: 1999-2000

[As of March (104,711 represents 104,711,000). See headnote, Table 25]

Household income in 1999		Percent distribution						
			Movers (different house in United States)					
	Total (1,000)	Non-movers	Total	Same county	Different county			Movers from abroad
					Total	Same state	Different state	
Householders, 15 years and over...	**104,711**	**85**	**15**	**9**	**6**	**3**	**3**	**(Z)**
Less than $5,000	3,010	74	24	13	11	5	6	2
$5,000 to $9,999	6,646	81	19	12	7	4	3	1
$10,000 to $14,999	7,660	84	16	10	6	3	3	(Z)
$15,000 to $24,999	14,720	82	18	11	7	3	3	(Z)
$25,000 to $34,999	13,273	82	17	11	6	3	3	(Z)
$35,000 to $49,999	16,539	85	15	9	6	3	3	(Z)
$50,000 to $74,999	19,274	87	13	7	6	3	3	(Z)
$75,000 and over	23,589	89	10	5	5	3	2	(Z)

Z Less than 0.5 percent.

Source: U.S. Census Bureau, *Current Population Reports*, P20-538.

No. 27. Population in Coastal Counties: 1970 to 2001

[**Enumerated population as of April 1, except as indicated (3,536 represents 3,536,000).** Areas as defined by U.S. National Oceanic and Atmospheric Agency, 1992. Covers 673 counties and equivalent areas with at least 15 percent of their land area either in a coastal watershed (drainage area) or in a coastal cataloging unit (a coastal area between watersheds)]

Year	Total	Counties in coastal regions					Balance of United States
		Total	Atlantic	Gulf of Mexico	Great Lakes	Pacific	
Land area, 1990 (1,000 sq. mi.)	3,536	888	148	114	115	510	2,649
POPULATION							
1970 (mil.)......................	203.3	110.0	51.1	10.0	26.0	22.8	93.3
1980 (mil.)......................	226.5	119.8	53.7	13.1	26.0	27.0	106.7
1990 (mil.)......................	248.7	133.4	59.0	15.2	25.9	33.2	115.3
2000 (mil.)......................	281.4	148.3	65.2	18.0	27.3	37.8	133.1
2001 (July 1) (mil.)	284.8	150.0	65.9	18.3	27.4	38.4	134.8
1970 (percent)...................	100	54	25	5	13	11	46
1980 (percent)...................	100	53	24	6	11	12	47
1990 (percent)...................	100	54	24	6	10	13	46
2000 (percent)...................	100	53	23	6	10	13	47
2001 (July 1) (percent)	100	53	23	6	10	13	47

Source: U.S. Census Bureau, *U.S. Census of Population: 1970; 1980 Census of Population*, Vol. 1, Chapter A (PC80-1-A-1), *U.S. Summary; 1990 Census of Population and Housing* (CPH1); and unpublished data.

No. 28. Number and Population of Metropolitan Areas by Population Size of Area in 2000: 2000

[As of April (226.0 represents 226,000,000). Data exclude Puerto Rico. CMSA=consolidated metropolitan statistical area. MSA=metropolitan statistical area. PMSA=primary metropolitan statistical area. Areas are as defined by U.S. Office of Management and Budget, June 30, 1999. For area definitions, see Appendix II]

Population size of metropolitan area in 2000	CMSAs and MSAs			MSAs and PMSAs		
		Population			Population	
	Number	Total (mil.)	Percent in each class	Number	Total (mil.)	Percent in each class
Total, all metropolitan areas ...	**276**	**226.0**	**100**	**331**	**226.0**	**100**
1,000,000 or more	49	161.5	71	61	146.7	65
2,500,000 or more	19	117.4	52	18	79.8	35
1,000,000 to 2,499,999	30	44.1	20	43	66.9	30
250,000 to 999,999	95	45.1	20	121	56.7	25
500,000 to 999,999	32	22.1	10	42	28.3	13
250,000 to 499,999	63	22.9	10	79	28.4	13
100,000 to 249,999	112	17.7	8	129	20.8	9
Less than 100,000	20	1.7	1	20	1.7	1

Source: U.S. Census Bureau, unpublished data.

No. 29. Metropolitan and Nonmetropolitan Area Population by State: 1980 to 2000

[As of April (177,505 represents 177,505,000). Metropolitan refers to 258 metropolitan statistical areas and 18 consolidated metropolitan statistical areas as defined by U.S. Office of Management and Budget, June 30, 1999; nonmetropolitan is the area outside metropolitan areas; see Appendix II. Minus sign (-) indicates decrease]

State	Metropolitan population						Nonmetropolitan population					
	Total (1,000)			Percent change, 1990-2000	Percent of state		Total (1,000)			Percent change, 1990-2000	Percent of state	
	1980	1990	2000	2000	1990	2000	1980	1990	2000	2000	1990	2000
U.S.	177,505	198,407	225,982	13.9	79.8	80.3	49,037	50,311	55,440	10.2	20.2	19.7
AL	2,636	2,797	3,109	11.2	69.2	69.9	1,258	1,244	1,338	7.6	30.8	30.1
AK	174	226	260	15.0	41.1	41.5	227	324	367	13.3	58.9	58.5
AZ	2,339	3,202	4,527	41.4	87.4	88.2	378	463	604	30.4	12.6	11.8
AR	1,026	1,109	1,321	19.1	47.2	49.4	1,260	1,242	1,352	8.9	52.8	50.6
CA	22,907	28,797	32,750	13.7	96.8	96.7	760	961	1,121	16.6	3.2	3.3
CO	2,408	2,779	3,608	29.8	84.4	83.9	482	515	694	34.7	15.6	16.1
CT	2,982	3,148	3,257	3.5	95.8	95.6	126	140	149	6.5	4.2	4.4
DE	496	553	627	13.4	83.0	80.0	98	113	157	38.3	17.0	20.0
DC	638	607	572	-5.7	100.0	100.0	(X)	(X)	(X)	(X)	(X)	(X)
FL.	9,039	12,024	14,837	23.4	92.9	92.8	708	915	1,145	25.2	7.1	7.2
GA	3,507	4,351	5,667	30.2	67.2	69.2	1,956	2,127	2,520	18.5	32.8	30.8
HI.	763	836	876	4.8	75.5	72.3	202	272	335	23.3	24.5	27.7
ID.	322	362	508	40.4	35.9	39.3	622	645	786	21.9	64.1	60.7
IL	9,461	9,574	10,542	10.1	83.8	84.9	1,967	1,857	1,878	1.1	16.2	15.1
IN	3,885	3,962	4,390	10.8	71.5	72.2	1,605	1,582	1,691	6.9	28.5	27.8
IA	1,198	1,200	1,326	10.5	43.2	45.3	1,716	1,577	1,600	1.5	56.8	54.7
KS	1,184	1,333	1,521	14.1	53.8	56.6	1,180	1,145	1,167	2.0	46.2	43.4
KY	1,735	1,780	1,973	10.9	48.3	48.8	1,925	1,907	2,069	8.5	51.7	51.2
LA	3,125	3,160	3,370	6.7	74.9	75.4	1,082	1,061	1,099	3.6	25.1	24.6
ME	405	443	467	5.4	36.1	36.6	721	785	808	2.9	63.9	63.4
MD	3,920	4,438	4,911	10.7	92.8	92.7	297	343	385	12.5	7.2	7.3
MA	5,530	5,788	6,101	5.4	96.2	96.1	207	229	248	8.4	3.8	3.9
MI.	7,719	7,698	8,169	6.1	82.8	82.2	1,543	1,598	1,769	10.7	17.2	17.8
MN	2,674	3,011	3,463	15.0	68.8	70.4	1,402	1,364	1,456	6.7	31.2	29.6
MS	806	874	1,024	17.1	34.0	36.0	1,715	1,701	1,821	7.1	66.0	64.0
MO	3,314	3,491	3,795	8.7	68.2	67.8	1,603	1,626	1,800	10.7	31.8	32.2
MT	265	270	306	13.2	33.8	33.9	522	529	597	12.7	66.2	66.1
NE	728	787	900	14.3	49.9	52.6	842	791	811	2.6	50.1	47.4
NV	666	1,014	1,748	72.4	84.4	87.5	135	188	251	33.4	15.6	12.5
NH	535	659	740	12.3	59.4	59.9	386	450	496	10.1	40.6	40.1
NJ.	7,365	7,730	8,414	8.9	100.0	100.0	(X)	(X)	(X)	(X)	(X)	(X)
NM	675	842	1,035	23.0	55.6	56.9	628	673	784	16.4	44.4	43.1
NY	16,144	16,516	17,473	5.8	91.8	92.1	1,414	1,475	1,503	1.9	8.2	7.9
NC	3,749	4,380	5,437	24.2	66.0	67.5	2,131	2,253	2,612	15.9	34.0	32.5
ND	234	257	284	10.3	40.3	44.2	418	381	358	-6.1	59.7	55.8
OH	8,791	8,826	9,214	4.4	81.4	81.2	2,007	2,021	2,139	5.9	18.6	18.8
OK	1,724	1,870	2,098	12.2	59.4	60.8	1,301	1,276	1,352	6.0	40.6	39.2
OR	1,867	2,056	2,502	21.7	72.3	73.1	766	787	919	16.8	27.7	26.9
PA	10,067	10,084	10,392	3.0	84.9	84.6	1,798	1,799	1,890	5.1	15.1	15.4
RI.	886	938	986	5.1	93.5	94.1	61	65	62	-5.2	6.5	5.9
SC	2,114	2,422	2,807	15.9	69.5	70.0	1,006	1,064	1,205	13.2	30.5	30.0
SD	194	221	261	18.3	31.7	34.6	497	475	494	3.9	68.3	65.4
TN	3,058	3,311	3,862	16.7	67.9	67.9	1,533	1,567	1,827	16.6	32.1	32.1
TX	11,539	14,166	17,692	24.9	83.4	84.8	2,686	2,821	3,160	12.0	16.6	15.2
UT	1,132	1,341	1,708	27.4	77.8	76.5	329	382	525	37.4	22.2	23.5
VT	133	152	169	11.8	26.9	27.8	378	411	439	6.9	73.1	72.2
VA	3,966	4,775	5,528	15.8	77.2	78.1	1,381	1,414	1,550	9.6	22.8	21.9
WA	3,366	4,036	4,899	21.4	82.9	83.1	766	830	995	19.8	17.1	16.9
WV	796	748	766	2.3	41.7	42.3	1,155	1,045	1,043	-0.2	58.3	57.7
WI.	3,176	3,331	3,640	9.3	68.1	67.9	1,530	1,561	1,723	10.4	31.9	32.1
WY	141	134	148	10.2	29.6	30.0	329	319	346	8.3	70.4	70.0

X Not applicable.

Source: U.S. Census Bureau, *1990 Census of Population and Housing, Population and Housing Unit Counts* (CPH-2-1); and unpublished data.

Population 31

No. 30. Large Metropolitan Areas—Population: 1980 to 2000

[In thousands, except percent (825 represents 825,000). As of April 1. Covers 18 consolidated metropolitan statistical areas (CMSAs), their 73 component primary metropolitan statistical areas (PMSAs), and the remaining 126 MSAs with 250,000 and over population in 2000 as defined by the U.S. Office of Management and Budget as of June 30, 1999. For definitions and components of metropolitan areas and population of NECMAs (New England County Metropolitan Areas), see Appendix II. Minus sign (-) indicates decrease]

Metropolitan area	Number (1,000)			Rank		Percent change		Popula-tion per square mile, 2000
	1980	1990 [1]	2000	1990	2000	1980-1990	1990-2000	
Albany-Schenectady-Troy, NY MSA.	825	862	876	49	56	4.5	1.6	272
Albuquerque, NM MSA.	485	589	713	66	61	21.4	21.0	120
Allentown-Bethlehem-Easton, PA MSA.	551	595	638	64	65	8.0	7.2	579
Anchorage, AK MSA	174	226	260	141	138	29.8	15.0	153
Appleton-Oshkosh-Neenah, WI MSA	291	315	358	113	115	8.2	13.7	256
Atlanta, GA MSA	2,233	2,960	4,112	13	11	32.5	38.9	672
Augusta-Aiken, GA-SC MSA	363	415	477	85	86	14.2	15.0	195
Austin-San Marcos, TX MSA	585	846	1,250	52	37	44.6	47.7	296
Bakersfield, CA MSA	403	545	662	70	64	35.2	21.4	81
Baton Rouge, LA MSA	494	528	603	71	69	6.9	14.1	380
Beaumont-Port Arthur, TX MSA	373	361	385	101	106	-3.2	6.6	179
Biloxi-Gulfport-Pascagoula, MS MSA	300	312	364	115	113	4.1	16.5	204
Binghamton, NY MSA	263	264	252	127	140	0.4	-4.6	206
Birmingham, AL MSA	815	840	921	53	54	3.0	9.7	289
Boise City, ID MSA	257	296	432	117	96	15.2	46.1	263
Boston-Worcester-Lawrence, MA-NH-ME-CT CMSA .	5,122	5,455	5,819	7	7	6.5	6.7	1,034
Boston, MA-NH PMSA	3,149	3,228	3,407	(X)	(X)	2.5	5.5	1,685
Brockton, MA PMSA	225	236	255	(X)	(X)	5.1	8.1	859
Fitchburg-Leominster, MA PMSA.	125	138	142	(X)	(X)	10.5	3.0	511
Lawrence, MA-NH PMSA.	298	353	396	(X)	(X)	18.4	12.2	906
Lowell, MA-NH PMSA.	249	281	302	(X)	(X)	12.5	7.5	1,208
Manchester, NH PMSA	146	174	198	(X)	(X)	18.9	14.2	628
Nashua, NH PMSA	134	168	191	(X)	(X)	25.4	13.5	590
New Bedford, MA PMSA	167	176	175	(X)	(X)	5.4	-0.3	818
Portsmouth-Rochester, NH-ME PMSA	189	223	241	(X)	(X)	18.0	7.8	384
Worcester, MA-CT PMSA.	439	478	511	(X)	(X)	8.9	6.9	594
Brownsville-Harlingen-San Benito, TX MSA.	210	260	335	131	120	24.0	28.9	370
Buffalo-Niagara Falls, NY MSA.	1,243	1,189	1,170	33	42	-4.3	-1.6	747
Canton-Massillon, OH MSA	404	394	407	93	100	-2.6	3.3	419
Charleston-North Charleston, SC MSA	430	507	549	73	76	17.8	8.3	212
Charleston, WV MSA	270	250	252	136	141	-7.1	0.5	201
Charlotte-Gastonia-Rock Hill, NC-SC MSA	971	1,162	1,499	34	33	19.6	29.1	444
Chattanooga, TN-GA MSA.	418	424	465	83	89	1.6	9.6	255
Chicago-Gary-Kenosha, IL-IN-WI CMSA	8,115	8,240	9,158	3	3	1.5	11.1	1,322
Chicago, IL PMSA	7,246	7,411	8,273	(X)	(X)	2.3	11.6	1,634
Gary, IN PMSA	643	605	631	(X)	(X)	-5.9	4.4	690
Kankakee, IL PMSA	103	96	104	(X)	(X)	-6.5	7.9	153
Kenosha, WI PMSA	123	128	150	(X)	(X)	4.1	16.7	548
Cincinnati-Hamilton, OH-KY-IN CMSA	1,726	1,818	1,979	22	23	5.3	8.9	520
Cincinnati, OH-KY-IN PMSA.	1,468	1,526	1,646	(X)	(X)	4.0	7.9	493
Hamilton-Middletown, OH PMSA	259	291	333	(X)	(X)	12.6	14.2	712
Cleveland-Akron, OH CMSA	2,938	2,860	2,946	14	16	-2.7	3.0	816
Akron, OH PMSA	660	658	695	(X)	(X)	-0.4	5.7	768
Cleveland-Lorain-Elyria, OH PMSA	2,278	2,202	2,251	(X)	(X)	-3.3	2.2	832
Colorado Springs, CO MSA.	309	397	517	91	80	28.3	30.2	243
Columbia, SC MSA	410	454	537	79	79	10.7	18.3	369
Columbus, GA-AL MSA	255	261	275	130	136	2.4	5.3	175
Columbus, OH MSA.	1,214	1,345	1,540	29	32	10.8	14.5	490
Corpus Christi, TX MSA	326	350	381	104	108	7.3	8.8	249
Dallas-Fort Worth, TX CMSA	3,046	4,037	5,222	9	9	32.5	29.3	574
Dallas, TX PMSA	2,055	2,676	3,519	(X)	(X)	30.2	31.5	569
Fort Worth-Arlington, TX PMSA.	991	1,361	1,703	(X)	(X)	37.4	25.1	584
Davenport-Moline-Rock Island, IA-IL MSA	385	351	359	103	114	-8.8	2.3	210
Dayton-Springfield, OH MSA	942	951	951	43	52	1.0	-0.1	565
Daytona Beach, FL MSA.	270	399	493	88	82	48.1	23.5	311
Denver-Boulder-Greeley, CO CMSA	1,742	1,980	2,582	21	19	13.7	30.4	304
Boulder-Longmont, CO PMSA	190	225	291	(X)	(X)	18.8	29.3	392
Denver, CO PMSA	1,429	1,623	2,109	(X)	(X)	13.6	30.0	561
Greeley, CO PMSA.	123	132	181	(X)	(X)	6.8	37.3	45
Des Moines, IA MSA	368	393	456	94	90	6.9	16.1	264
Detroit-Ann Arbor-Flint, MI CMSA	5,293	5,187	5,456	8	8	-2.0	5.2	831
Ann Arbor, MI PMSA.	455	490	579	(X)	(X)	7.7	18.1	285
Detroit, MI PMSA	4,388	4,267	4,442	(X)	(X)	-2.8	4.1	1,140
Flint, MI PMSA.	450	430	436	(X)	(X)	-4.4	1.3	682
El Paso, TX MSA.	480	592	680	65	63	23.3	14.9	671
Erie, PA MSA	280	276	281	125	135	-1.5	1.9	350
Eugene-Springfield, OR MSA.	275	283	323	123	123	2.8	14.2	71
Evansville-Henderson, IN-KY MSA	276	279	296	124	131	1.0	6.2	202
Fayetteville, NC MSA	247	275	303	126	129	11.1	10.3	464
Fayetteville-Springdale-Rogers, AR MSA	179	211	311	148	128	18.1	47.5	173
Fort Collins-Loveland, CO MSA	149	186	251	158	142	24.8	35.1	97
Fort Myers-Cape Coral, FL MSA.	205	335	441	110	94	63.3	31.6	549
Fort Pierce-Port St. Lucie, FL MSA	151	251	319	135	125	66.1	27.2	283
Fort Wayne, IN MSA.	445	456	502	78	81	2.6	10.1	205
Fresno, CA MSA	578	756	923	56	53	30.8	22.1	114
Grand Rapids-Muskegon-Holland, MI MSA.	841	938	1,089	45	47	11.5	16.1	395
Greensboro—Winston-Salem—High Point, NC MSA .	951	1,050	1,252	39	36	10.5	19.2	323
Greenville-Spartanburg-Anderson, SC MSA	744	830	962	55	51	11.6	15.9	300

See footnotes at end of table.

U.S. Census Bureau, Statistical Abstract of the United States: 2002

[In thousands, except percent (825 represents 825,000). As of April 1. Covers 18 consolidated metropolitan statistical areas (CMSAs), their 73 component primary metropolitan statistical areas (PMSAs), and the remaining 126 MSAs with 250,000 and over population in 2000 as defined by the U.S. Office of Management and Budget as of June 30, 1999. For definitions and components of metropolitan areas and population of NECMAs (New England County Metropolitan Areas), see Appendix II. Minus sign (-) indicates decrease]

Metropolitan area	Number (1,000)			Rank		Percent change		Population per square mile, 2000
	1980	1990 [1]	2000	1990	2000	1980-1990	1990-2000	
Harrisburg-Lebanon-Carlisle, PA MSA	556	588	629	67	66	5.7	7.0	316
Hartford, CT MSA	1,081	1,158	1,183	35	41	7.1	2.2	705
Hickory-Morganton-Lenoir, NC MSA	270	292	342	120	118	8.1	16.9	209
Honolulu, HI MSA	763	836	876	54	55	9.7	4.8	1,461
Houston-Galveston-Brazoria, TX CMSA	3,118	3,731	4,670	10	10	19.6	25.2	606
Brazoria, TX PMSA.	170	192	242	(X)	(X)	13.0	26.1	174
Galveston-Texas City, TX PMSA	196	217	250	(X)	(X)	11.1	15.1	628
Houston, TX PMSA.	2,753	3,322	4,178	(X)	(X)	20.7	25.8	706
Huntington-Ashland, WV-KY-OH MSA	336	313	316	114	126	-7.1	1.0	146
Huntsville, AL MSA	243	293	342	118	117	20.6	16.8	249
Indianapolis, IN MSA	1,306	1,380	1,607	28	28	5.7	16.4	456
Jackson, MS MSA	362	395	441	92	95	9.2	11.5	187
Jacksonville, FL MSA	722	907	1,100	46	45	25.5	21.4	418
Johnson City-Kingsport-Bristol, TN-VA MSA	434	436	480	80	84	0.6	10.1	168
Kalamazoo-Battle Creek, MI MSA.	421	429	453	82	91	2.1	5.4	241
Kansas City, MO-KS MSA	1,449	1,583	1,776	25	25	9.2	12.2	329
Killeen-Temple, TX MSA	215	255	313	133	127	19.0	22.6	148
Knoxville, TN MSA.	546	586	687	69	62	7.2	17.3	281
Lafayette, LA MSA	331	345	386	105	105	4.3	11.8	149
Lakeland-Winter Haven, FL MSA	322	405	484	87	83	26.0	19.4	258
Lancaster, PA MSA	362	423	471	84	88	16.7	11.3	496
Lansing-East Lansing, MI MSA.	420	433	448	81	92	3.1	3.5	262
Las Vegas, NV-AZ MSA	528	853	1,563	51	31	61.5	83.3	40
Lexington, KY MSA	371	406	479	86	85	9.4	18.0	250
Lincoln, NE MSA	193	214	250	147	144	10.8	17.2	298
Little Rock-North Little Rock, AR MSA	474	513	584	72	73	8.1	13.8	201
Los Angeles-Riverside-Orange County, CA CMSA . . .	11,498	14,532	16,374	2	2	26.4	12.7	482
Los Angeles-Long Beach, CA PMSA	7,477	8,863	9,519	(X)	(X)	18.5	7.4	2,344
Orange County, CA PMSA	1,933	2,411	2,846	(X)	(X)	24.7	18.1	3,606
Riverside-San Bernardino, CA PMSA	1,558	2,589	3,255	(X)	(X)	66.1	25.7	119
Ventura, CA PMSA	529	669	753	(X)	(X)	26.4	12.6	408
Louisville, KY-IN MSA	954	949	1,026	44	49	-0.5	8.1	495
Macon, GA MSA	273	291	323	121	124	6.6	10.8	211
Madison, WI MSA	324	367	427	99	97	13.5	16.2	355
McAllen-Edinburg-Mission, TX MSA	283	384	569	95	74	35.4	48.5	363
Melbourne-Titusville-Palm Bay, FL MSA.	273	399	476	90	87	46.2	19.4	468
Memphis, TN-AR-MS MSA	939	1,007	1,136	40	43	7.3	12.7	378
Miami-Fort Lauderdale, FL CMSA	2,644	3,193	3,876	11	12	20.8	21.4	1,230
Fort Lauderdale, FL PMSA.	1,018	1,256	1,623	(X)	(X)	23.3	29.3	1,347
Miami, FL PMSA.	1,626	1,937	2,253	(X)	(X)	19.2	16.3	1,158
Milwaukee-Racine, WI CMSA.	1,570	1,607	1,690	24	20	2.4	5.1	942
Milwaukee-Waukesha, WI PMSA.	1,397	1,432	1,501	(X)	(X)	2.5	4.8	1,028
Racine, WI PMSA.	173	175	189	(X)	(X)	1.1	7.9	567
Minneapolis-St. Paul, MN-WI MSA	2,198	2,539	2,969	15	15	15.5	16.9	490
Mobile, AL MSA.	444	477	540	77	78	7.5	13.3	191
Modesto, CA MSA	266	371	447	97	93	39.3	20.6	299
Montgomery, AL MSA	273	293	333	119	121	7.3	13.9	166
Naples, FL MSA	86	152	251	177	143	76.9	65.3	124
Nashville, TN MSA.	851	985	1,231	41	38	15.8	25.0	302
New London-Norwich, CT-RI MSA	273	291	294	122	132	6.5	1.0	443
New Orleans, LA MSA	1,304	1,285	1,338	31	34	-1.5	4.1	394
New York-Northern New Jersey-Long Island, NY-NJ-CT-PA CMSA.	18,906	19,550	21,200	1	1	3.4	8.4	2,029
Bergen-Passaic, NJ PMSA.	1,293	1,279	1,373	(X)	(X)	-1.1	7.4	3,274
Bridgeport, CT PMSA	439	444	459	(X)	(X)	1.2	3.6	1,755
Danbury, CT PMSA	175	194	218	(X)	(X)	10.3	12.6	563
Dutchess County, NY PMSA.	245	259	280	(X)	(X)	5.9	8.0	350
Jersey City, NJ PMSA.	557	553	609	(X)	(X)	-0.7	10.1	13,044
Middlesex-Somerset-Hunterdon, NJ PMSA	886	1,020	1,170	(X)	(X)	15.1	14.7	1,120
Monmouth-Ocean, NJ PMSA	849	986	1,126	(X)	(X)	16.1	14.2	1,016
Nassau-Suffolk, NY PMSA	2,606	2,609	2,754	(X)	(X)	0.1	5.5	2,297
New Haven-Meriden, CT PMSA	500	530	542	(X)	(X)	5.9	2.3	1,261
New York, NY PMSA.	8,275	8,547	9,314	(X)	(X)	3.3	9.0	8,159
Newark, NJ PMSA	1,964	1,916	2,033	(X)	(X)	-2.4	6.1	1,289
Newburgh, NY-PA PMSA	278	336	388	(X)	(X)	20.8	15.5	284
Stamford-Norwalk, CT PMSA	326	330	354	(X)	(X)	1.3	7.2	1,683
Trenton, NJ PMSA	308	326	351	(X)	(X)	5.8	7.7	1,553
Waterbury, CT PMSA	205	222	229	(X)	(X)	8.1	3.3	981
Norfolk-Virginia Beach-Newport News, VA-NC MSA . .	1,201	1,445	1,570	27	30	20.3	8.6	668
Ocala, FL MSA	122	195	259	149	139	59.1	32.9	164
Oklahoma City, OK MSA.	861	959	1,083	42	48	11.4	13.0	255
Omaha, NE-IA MSA	605	640	717	60	60	5.6	12.1	290
Orlando, FL MSA.	805	1,225	1,645	32	27	52.2	34.3	471
Pensacola, FL MSA	290	344	412	106	99	18.9	19.7	245
Peoria-Pekin, IL MSA	366	339	347	108	116	-7.3	2.4	193
Philadelphia-Wilmington-Atlantic City, PA-NJ-DE-MD CMSA	5,649	5,893	6,188	6	6	4.3	5.0	1,043
Atlantic-Cape May, NJ PMSA	276	319	355	(X)	(X)	15.6	11.1	435
Philadelphia, PA-NJ PMSA.	4,781	4,922	5,101	(X)	(X)	2.9	3.6	1,323

See footnotes at end of table.

Population   33

No. 30. Large Metropolitan Areas—Population: 1980 to 2000—Con.

[In thousands, except percent (825 represents 825,000). As of April 1. Covers 18 consolidated metropolitan statistical areas (CMSAs), their 73 component primary metropolitan statistical areas (PMSAs), and the remaining 126 MSAs with 250,000 and over population in 2000 as defined by the U.S. Office of Management and Budget as of June 30, 1999. For definitions and components of metropolitan areas and population of NECMAs (New England County Metropolitan Areas), see Appendix II. Minus sign (-) indicates decrease]

Metropolitan area	Number (1,000)			Rank		Percent change		Popula-tion per square mile, 2000
	1980	1990 [1]	2000	1990	2000	1980-1990	1990-2000	
Vineland-Millville-Bridgeton, NJ PMSA	133	138	146	(X)	(X)	3.9	6.1	299
Wilmington-Newark, DE-MD PMSA	459	513	586	(X)	(X)	11.9	14.2	757
Phoenix-Mesa, AZ MSA	1,600	2,238	3,252	19	14	39.9	45.3	223
Pittsburgh, PA MSA	2,571	2,395	2,359	18	21	-6.9	-1.5	510
Portland-Salem, OR-WA CMSA	1,584	1,793	2,265	23	22	13.3	26.3	326
Portland-Vancouver, OR-WA PMSA	1,334	1,515	1,918	(X)	(X)	13.6	26.6	382
Salem, OR PMSA	250	278	347	(X)	(X)	11.3	24.9	180
Providence-Fall River-Warwick, RI-MA MSA	1,077	1,134	1,189	36	39	5.4	4.8	1,042
Provo-Orem, UT MSA	218	264	369	129	111	20.9	39.8	184
Raleigh-Durham-Chapel Hill, NC MSA	665	859	1,188	50	40	29.1	38.4	341
Reading, PA MSA	313	337	374	109	109	7.7	11.0	435
Reno, NV MSA	194	255	339	134	119	31.5	33.3	54
Richmond-Petersburg, VA MSA	761	866	997	47	50	13.7	15.1	338
Rochester, NY MSA	1,031	1,062	1,098	38	46	3.1	3.4	321
Rockford, IL MSA	326	330	371	111	110	1.2	12.6	239
Sacramento-Yolo, CA CMSA	1,100	1,481	1,797	26	24	34.7	21.3	353
Sacramento, CA PMSA	986	1,340	1,628	(X)	(X)	35.8	21.5	399
Yolo, CA PMSA	113	141	169	(X)	(X)	24.6	19.4	167
Saginaw-Bay City-Midland, MI MSA	422	399	403	89	101	-5.3	0.9	227
St. Louis, MO-IL MSA	2,414	2,492	2,604	17	18	3.2	4.5	407
Salinas, CA MSA	290	356	402	102	102	22.5	13.0	121
Salt Lake City-Ogden, UT MSA	910	1,072	1,334	37	35	17.8	24.4	825
San Antonio, TX MSA	1,089	1,325	1,592	30	29	21.7	20.2	479
San Diego, CA MSA	1,862	2,498	2,814	16	17	34.2	12.6	670
San Francisco-Oakland-San Jose, CA CMSA	5,368	6,250	7,039	5	5	16.4	12.6	955
Oakland, CA PMSA	1,762	2,080	2,393	(X)	(X)	18.1	15.0	1,642
San Francisco, CA PMSA	1,489	1,604	1,731	(X)	(X)	7.7	8.0	1,705
San Jose, CA PMSA	1,295	1,498	1,683	(X)	(X)	15.6	12.4	1,304
Santa Cruz-Watsonville, CA PMSA	188	230	256	(X)	(X)	22.1	11.3	574
Santa Rosa, CA PMSA	300	388	459	(X)	(X)	29.5	18.1	291
Vallejo-Fairfield-Napa, CA PMSA	334	450	519	(X)	(X)	34.6	15.2	328
Santa Barbara-Santa Maria-Lompoc, CA MSA	299	370	399	98	103	23.7	8.0	146
Sarasota-Bradenton, FL MSA	351	489	590	74	72	39.6	20.5	450
Savannah, GA MSA	231	258	293	132	133	11.8	13.6	216
Scranton—Wilkes-Barre—Hazleton, PA MSA	659	639	625	61	67	-3.2	-2.2	280
Seattle-Tacoma-Bremerton, WA CMSA	2,409	2,970	3,555	12	13	23.3	19.7	492
Bremerton, WA PMSA	147	190	232	(X)	(X)	28.9	22.3	586
Olympia, WA PMSA	124	161	207	(X)	(X)	29.8	28.6	285
Seattle-Bellevue-Everett, WA PMSA	1,652	2,033	2,415	(X)	(X)	23.1	18.8	546
Tacoma, WA PMSA	486	586	701	(X)	(X)	20.7	19.6	417
Shreveport-Bossier City, LA MSA	377	376	392	96	104	-0.1	4.2	169
South Bend, IN MSA	242	247	266	137	137	2.2	7.5	581
Spokane, WA MSA	342	361	418	100	98	5.7	15.7	237
Springfield, MO MSA	228	264	326	128	122	15.9	23.2	178
Springfield, MA MSA	570	588	592	68	71	3.2	0.7	805
Stockton-Lodi, CA MSA	347	481	564	76	75	38.4	17.3	403
Syracuse, NY MSA	723	742	732	57	59	2.7	-1.4	238
Tallahassee, FL MSA	190	234	285	140	134	22.7	21.8	241
Tampa-St. Petersburg-Clearwater, FL MSA	1,614	2,068	2,396	20	20	28.2	15.9	938
Toledo, OH MSA	617	614	618	62	68	-0.4	0.7	453
Tucson, AZ MSA	531	667	844	59	57	25.5	26.5	92
Tulsa, OK MSA	657	709	803	58	58	7.9	13.3	160
Utica-Rome, NY MSA	320	317	300	112	130	-1.1	-5.3	114
Visalia-Tulare-Porterville, CA MSA	246	312	368	116	112	26.9	18.0	76
Washington-Baltimore, DC-MD-VA-WV CMSA	5,791	6,726	7,608	4	4	16.2	13.1	795
Baltimore, MD PMSA	2,199	2,382	2,553	(X)	(X)	8.3	7.2	979
Hagerstown, MD PMSA	113	121	132	(X)	(X)	7.3	8.7	288
Washington, DC-MD-VA-WV PMSA	3,478	4,223	4,923	(X)	(X)	21.4	16.6	756
West Palm Beach-Boca Raton, FL MSA	577	864	1,131	48	44	49.7	31.0	573
Wichita, KS MSA	442	485	545	75	77	9.7	12.4	184
York, PA MSA	313	340	382	107	107	8.5	12.4	422
Youngstown-Warren, OH MSA	645	601	595	63	70	-6.8	-1.0	380

X Not applicable. [1] Reflects revisions to an area's 1990 census population count that may occur as the result of (1) post-1990 census corrections of political boundaries or geographic misallocations or documented underenumerations or overenumerations and (2) geographic boundary updates made after the 1990 census, resulting from annexations, de-annexations, new incorporations, and governmental mergers. Includes revisions processed through January 1, 1998.

Source: U.S. Census Bureau, *1990 Census of Population and Housing, Supplementary Reports, Metropolitan Areas as Defined by the Office of Management and Budget, June 30, 1993* (CPH-S-1-1); "(MA-99-1) Metropolitan Area Population Estimates for July 1, 1999, and Population Change for April 1, 1990, to July 1, 1999 (includes April 1, 1990 Population Estimates Base)"; published: 20 October 2000; <http://www.census.gov/population/estimates/metro-city/ma99-01.txt>; "Ranking Tables for Metropolitan Areas: 1990 and 2000 (PHC-T-3)"; published: 2 April 2001; <http://www.census.gov/population/www/cen2000/phc-t3.html>. and American FactFinder, GCT-PH1. Population, Housing Units, Area, and Density: 2000, Census 2000 Summary File 1 (SF1) 100-Percent Data, United States and Puerto Rico Metropolitan Area

No. 31. Incorporated Places by Population Size: 1970 to 2000

[131.9 represents 131,900,000]

Population size	Number of incorporated places				Population (mil.)				Percent of total			
	1970	1980	1990	2000	1970	1980	1990	2000	1970	1980	1990	2000
Total	18,666	19,097	19,262	19,452	131.9	140.3	152.9	173.5	100.0	100.0	100.0	100.0
1,000,000 or more. . . .	6	6	8	9	18.8	17.5	20.0	22.9	14.2	12.5	13.0	13.2
500,000 to 999,999 . . .	20	16	15	20	13.0	10.9	10.1	12.9	9.8	7.8	6.6	7.4
250,000 to 499,999 . . .	30	33	41	37	10.5	11.8	14.2	13.3	7.9	8.4	9.3	7.7
100,000 to 249,999 . . .	97	114	131	172	13.9	16.6	19.1	25.5	10.5	11.8	12.5	14.7
50,000 to 99,999.	232	250	309	363	16.2	17.6	21.2	24.9	12.2	12.3	13.9	14.3
25,000 to 49,999.	455	526	567	644	15.7	18.4	20.0	22.6	11.9	13.1	13.0	13.0
10,000 to 24,999.	1,127	1,260	1,290	1,435	17.6	19.8	20.3	22.6	13.3	14.1	13.3	13.0
Under 10,000	16,699	16,892	16,901	16,772	26.4	28.0	28.2	28.7	20.0	20.0	18.4	16.6

Source: U.S. Census Bureau, *Census of Population: 1970* and *1980*, Vol. I; *1990 Census of Population and Housing, Population and Housing Unit Counts* (CPH-2-1); and *County and City Data Book 2000*.

No. 32. Households—Cities with 350,000 or More Population: 2000

[As of April (183.2 represents 183,200). For definitions of household and family, see text, this section]

City	Households (1,000)							Average household size
	Family households					Nonfamily households		
	Total [1]			Married couple			House-holder living alone	
	Total	Total	With own children under 18 years	Total	With own children under 18 years	Total		
Albuquerque, NM	183.2	112.6	55.4	79.9	35.5	70.6	55.8	2.40
Atlanta, GA	168.1	83.2	37.7	41.2	15.5	85.0	64.7	2.30
Austin, TX.	265.6	141.6	71.3	101.1	49.1	124.1	87.0	2.40
Baltimore, MD	258.0	147.2	65.8	68.8	25.7	110.8	90.1	2.42
Boston, MA	239.5	115.1	54.3	65.7	28.2	124.4	88.9	2.31
Charlotte, NC	215.4	132.4	66.0	94.0	44.3	83.1	63.6	2.45
Chicago, IL	1,061.9	632.6	306.5	373.0	179.4	429.4	345.8	2.67
Cleveland, OH	190.6	112.0	57.1	54.2	23.2	78.6	67.2	2.44
Colorado Springs, CO	141.5	93.0	48.1	72.8	34.9	48.5	38.2	2.50
Columbus, OH	301.5	165.4	84.5	108.7	49.8	136.2	102.9	2.30
Dallas, TX	451.8	266.8	136.9	175.3	87.8	185.0	148.9	2.58
Denver, CO	239.2	119.3	55.6	83.0	35.9	119.9	94.0	2.27
Detroit, MI	336.4	218.5	114.0	89.7	42.1	117.9	99.9	2.77
El Paso, TX	182.1	141.1	77.2	99.4	54.1	41.0	35.0	3.07
Fort Worth, TX	105.1	127.5	67.7	94.4	40.2	67.5	55.8	2.67
Fresno, CA	140.1	97.9	56.6	64.6	35.5	42.2	32.6	2.99
Honolulu, HI [2]	140.3	87.4	33.2	63.8	24.6	53.0	41.7	2.57
Houston, TX	717.9	457.5	237.7	310.1	159.3	260.4	212.7	2.67
Indianapolis, IN [3]	324.3	195.5	96.8	132.0	58.4	128.9	103.8	2.39
Jacksonville, FL	284.5	190.5	96.4	132.8	61.8	94.0	74.5	2.53
Kansas City, MO	184.0	107.4	51.7	70.0	29.8	76.6	62.7	2.35
Las Vegas, NV	176.8	117.5	56.4	85.4	38.1	59.3	44.3	2.66
Long Beach, CA	163.1	99.7	57.1	64.0	35.2	63.4	48.2	2.77
Los Angeles, CA	1,275.4	798.7	427.3	535.0	288.8	476.7	363.5	2.83
Memphis, TN.	250.7	158.5	78.6	85.5	37.1	92.3	76.6	2.52
Mesa, AZ	146.6	99.9	48.9	77.3	35.2	46.8	35.5	2.68
Miami, FL	134.2	83.3	35.3	49.1	19.7	50.9	40.8	2.61
Milwaukee, WI	232.2	135.2	70.9	74.8	33.3	97.0	77.8	2.50
Minneapolis, MN . . . . . [3]	162.4	73.9	36.7	47.0	20.8	88.4	65.5	2.25
Nashville-Davidson, TN [3].	237.4	138.1	63.3	94.8	39.2	99.3	79.2	2.30
New Orleans, LA	188.3	113.0	55.1	58.0	25.0	75.3	62.4	2.48
New York, NY	3,021.6	1,853.2	897.9	1,124.3	532.4	1,168.4	962.6	2.59
Oakland, CA	150.8	86.3	43.2	51.3	24.8	64.4	49.0	2.60
Oklahoma City, OK	204.4	129.4	63.0	93.6	41.3	75.1	62.8	2.41
Omaha, NE.	156.7	94.9	47.1	68.6	31.3	61.8	50.1	2.42
Philadelphia, PA.	590.1	352.3	162.9	189.3	79.9	237.7	199.5	2.48
Phoenix, AZ	465.8	307.2	166.4	218.5	113.2	158.6	118.4	2.79
Portland, OR	223.7	118.4	54.7	85.3	36.2	105.3	77.3	2.30
Sacramento, CA.	154.6	91.1	46.7	59.3	28.1	63.4	49.5	2.57
San Antonio, TX.	405.5	280.8	145.6	194.9	97.7	124.6	101.6	2.77
San Diego, CA.	450.7	271.4	136.1	201.2	98.1	179.3	126.2	2.61
San Francisco, CA	329.7	145.2	54.7	104.3	40.3	184.5	127.4	2.30
San Jose, CA	276.6	203.7	105.9	155.0	82.7	72.9	50.9	3.20
Seattle, WA.	258.5	113.4	46.3	84.6	32.3	145.1	105.5	2.08
Tucson, AZ	192.9	112.5	56.0	76.5	34.5	80.4	62.3	2.42
Tulsa, OK	165.7	99.1	47.3	71.4	30.4	66.6	56.2	2.31
Virginia Beach, VA	154.5	111.0	59.9	86.0	44.2	43.5	31.4	2.70
Washington, DC.	248.3	114.2	49.1	56.6	20.7	134.2	108.7	2.16

[1] Includes family householders with no spouse present, not shown separately. [2] The population shown in this table is for the census designated place (CDP). [3] Represents the portion of a consolidated city that is not within one or more separately incorporated places.

Source: U.S. Census Bureau, *2000 Census of Population and Housing, Profiles of General Demographic Characteristics*.

Population 35

No. 33. Incorporated Places With 100,000 or More Inhabitants in 2000—Population, 1970 to 2000, and Land Area, 2000

[Population: As of April 1 (90 represents 90,000). Data for 1990 and 2000 refer to boundaries in effect on January 1, 2000; data for 1970 and 1980 refer to boundaries in effect for those censuses. Minus sign (-) indicates decrease]

Incorporated place	1970, total population (1,000)	1980, total population (1,000)	1990, total population (1,000)	Population, 2000 Total (1,000)	Rank	Percent change, 1990-2000	Per square mile	Land area, 2000 (square miles)
Abilene, TX	90	98	107	116	193	8.4	1,103	105.1
Akron, OH	275	237	223	217	81	-2.7	3,497	62.1
Albuquerque, NM	245	332	387	449	35	15.9	2,483	180.6
Alexandria, VA	111	103	111	128	166	15.4	8,452	15.2
Allentown, PA	110	104	105	107	215	1.1	6,011	17.7
Amarillo, TX	127	149	158	174	118	10.0	1,932	89.9
Anaheim, CA	166	219	267	328	55	23.0	6,702	48.9
Anchorage, AK	48	174	226	260	65	15.0	153	1,697.2
Ann Arbor, MI	100	108	110	114	195	3.5	4,221	27.0
Arlington, TX	90	160	262	333	53	27.1	3,475	95.8
Arvada, CO	50	85	90	102	231	13.8	3,128	32.7
Athens-Clarke County, GA [1]	(NA)	(NA)	87	100	239	15.9	852	117.8
Atlanta, GA	495	425	394	416	39	5.8	3,161	131.7
Augusta-Richmond County, GA [1]	(NA)	(NA)	186	195	97	4.8	646	302.1
Aurora, CO	75	159	222	276	61	24.6	1,940	142.5
Aurora, IL	74	81	100	143	147	42.6	3,712	38.5
Austin, TX	254	346	494	657	16	32.8	2,610	251.5
Bakersfield, CA	70	106	184	247	69	34.3	2,184	113.1
Baltimore, MD	905	787	736	651	17	-11.5	8,058	80.8
Baton Rouge, LA	166	220	222	228	74	2.5	2,965	76.8
Beaumont, TX	118	118	114	114	196	-0.5	1,339	85.0
Bellevue, WA	61	74	99	110	206	11.1	3,564	30.7
Berkeley, CA	114	103	103	103	227	-0.1	9,823	10.5
Birmingham, AL	301	284	266	243	71	-8.7	1,620	149.9
Boise City, ID	75	102	135	186	105	37.5	2,913	63.8
Boston, MA	641	563	574	589	20	2.6	12,166	48.4
Bridgeport, CT	157	143	142	140	152	-1.4	8,721	16.0
Brownsville, TX	53	85	115	140	151	21.3	1,738	80.4
Buffalo, NY	463	358	328	293	58	-10.8	7,206	40.6
Burbank, CA	89	87	94	100	238	7.1	5,782	17.3
Cambridge, MA	96	95	96	101	233	5.7	15,766	6.4
Cape Coral, FL	(²)	32	75	102	230	36.1	972	105.2
Carrollton, TX	14	41	83	110	205	32.7	3,005	36.5
Cedar Rapids, IA	111	110	109	121	181	10.9	1,913	63.1
Chandler, AZ	14	30	91	177	114	94.7	3,051	57.9
Charlotte, NC	241	315	427	541	26	26.7	2,232	242.3
Chattanooga, TN	120	170	153	156	129	1.8	1,151	135.2
Chesapeake, VA	90	114	152	199	90	31.1	585	340.7
Chicago, IL	3,369	3,005	2,784	2,896	3	4.0	12,750	227.1
Chula Vista, CA	68	84	135	174	120	28.3	3,551	48.9
Cincinnati, OH	454	385	365	331	54	-9.1	4,249	78.0
Clarksville, TN	32	55	77	103	224	35.2	1,091	94.9
Clearwater, FL	52	85	97	109	208	11.9	4,302	25.3
Cleveland, OH	751	574	505	478	33	-5.4	6,167	77.6
Colorado Springs, CO	136	215	283	361	48	27.5	1,943	185.7
Columbia, SC	114	101	114	116	191	1.6	929	125.2
Columbus, GA [1]	155	169	179	186	106	4.0	860	216.1
Columbus, OH	540	565	636	711	15	11.8	3,384	210.3
Concord, CA	85	104	111	122	177	9.5	4,041	30.1
Coral Springs, FL	1	37	79	118	186	48.5	4,917	23.9
Corona, CA	28	38	76	125	170	64.0	3,556	35.1
Corpus Christi, TX	205	232	258	277	60	7.4	1,794	154.6
Costa Mesa, CA	73	83	97	109	209	12.3	6,956	15.6
Dallas, TX	844	905	1,007	1,189	8	18.1	3,470	342.5
Daly City, CA	67	79	92	104	223	12.4	13,704	7.6
Dayton, OH	243	194	182	166	123	-8.9	2,979	55.8
Denver, CO	515	493	468	555	24	18.6	3,617	153.4
Des Moines, IA	201	191	193	199	92	2.8	2,621	75.8
Detroit, MI	1,514	1,203	1,028	951	10	-7.5	6,855	138.8
Downey, CA	89	83	91	107	212	17.3	8,642	12.4
Durham, NC	95	101	148	187	103	26.0	1,976	94.6
El Monte, CA	70	79	106	116	192	9.2	12,139	9.6
El Paso, TX	322	425	516	564	22	9.3	2,263	249.1
Elizabeth, NJ	113	106	110	121	182	9.5	9,865	12.2
Erie, PA	129	119	109	104	222	-4.6	4,723	22.0
Escondido, CA	37	64	109	134	160	22.5	3,681	36.3
Eugene, OR	79	106	114	138	156	21.1	3,403	40.5
Evansville, IN	139	130	126	122	178	-3.6	2,987	40.7
Fayetteville, NC	54	60	113	121	180	7.4	2,059	58.8
Flint, MI	193	160	141	125	171	-11.6	3,715	33.6
Fontana, CA	21	37	88	129	163	46.7	3,570	36.1
Fort Collins, CO	43	65	89	119	185	33.5	2,549	46.5
Fort Lauderdale, FL	140	153	149	152	130	2.4	4,803	31.7
Fort Wayne, IN	178	172	203	206	84	1.3	2,606	79.0
Fort Worth, TX	393	385	448	535	27	19.3	1,828	292.5
Fremont, CA	101	132	173	203	85	17.3	2,652	76.7
Fresno, CA	166	217	355	428	37	20.3	4,098	104.4
Fullerton, CA	86	102	113	126	169	11.1	5,676	22.2
Garden Grove, CA	121	123	144	165	124	15.0	9,165	18.0
Garland, TX	81	139	181	216	82	19.3	3,778	57.1
Gary, IN	175	152	117	103	226	-11.9	2,046	50.2
Gilbert, AZ	2	6	30	110	204	265.6	2,554	43.0

See footnotes at end of table.

U.S. Census Bureau, Statistical Abstract of the United States: 2002

No. 33. Incorporated Places With 100,000 or More Inhabitants in 2000—Population, 1970 to 2000, and Land Area, 2000—Con.

[Population: As of April 1 (90 represents 90,000). Data for 1990 and 2000 refer to boundaries in effect on January 1, 2000; data for 1970 and 1980 refer to boundaries in effect for those censuses. Minus sign (-) indicates decrease]

Incorporated place	1970, total population (1,000)	1980, total population (1,000)	1990, total population (1,000)	Population, 2000				Land area, 2000 (square miles)
				Total (1,000)	Rank	Percent change, 1990-2000	Per square mile	
Glendale, AZ	36	97	151	219	80	45.0	3,930	55.7
Glendale, CA	133	139	180	195	98	8.3	6,362	30.6
Grand Prairie, TX	51	71	99	127	168	28.1	1,785	71.4
Grand Rapids, MI	198	182	190	198	93	4.3	4,431	44.6
Green Bay, WI	88	88	97	102	229	5.8	2,332	43.9
Greensboro, NC	144	156	192	224	77	16.9	2,138	104.7
Hampton, VA	121	123	134	146	143	9.5	2,828	51.8
Hartford, CT.	158	136	137	122	179	-11.4	7,025	17.3
Hayward, CA	93	94	115	140	150	22.1	3,159	44.3
Henderson, NV.	16	24	65	175	116	169.4	2,201	79.7
Hialeah, FL	102	145	188	226	75	20.5	11,767	19.2
Hollywood, FL	107	121	123	139	153	13.5	5,097	27.3
Honolulu, HI [3]	325	365	377	372	46	-1.4	4,337	85.7
Houston, TX	1,234	1,595	1,698	1,954	4	15.1	3,372	579.4
Huntington Beach, CA	116	171	183	190	101	3.7	7,184	26.4
Huntsville, AL.	139	143	160	158	127	-1.3	909	174.0
Independence, MO	112	112	112	113	198	0.8	1,446	78.3
Indianapolis, IN [1]	737	701	732	782	12	6.9	2,163	361.5
Inglewood, CA	90	94	110	113	200	1.9	12,323	9.1
Irvine, CA	([2])	62	111	143	146	28.4	3,098	46.2
Irving, TX	97	110	155	192	100	23.5	2,850	67.2
Jacksonville, FL	504	541	635	736	14	15.8	971	757.7
Jackson, MS	154	203	197	184	109	-6.3	1,756	104.9
Jersey City, NJ	260	224	228	240	72	5.1	16,094	14.9
Joliet, IL	79	78	79	106	217	35.2	2,791	38.1
Kansas City, KS	168	161	151	147	142	-3.0	1,182	124.3
Kansas City, MO.	507	448	435	442	36	1.5	1,408	313.5
Knoxville, TN	175	175	173	174	117	0.4	1,877	92.7
Lafayette, LA	69	81	103	110	203	7.5	2,317	47.6
Lakewood, CO	93	114	126	144	144	14.2	3,465	41.6
Lancaster, CA	([2])	48	98	119	184	20.6	1,263	94.0
Lansing, MI	131	130	127	119	183	-6.1	3,399	35.0
Laredo, TX	69	91	125	177	115	41.2	2,251	70.5
Las Vegas, NV	126	165	260	478	32	84.1	4,223	113.3
Lexington-Fayette, KY	108	204	225	261	64	15.6	916	284.5
Lincoln, NE	150	172	193	226	76	17.0	3,022	74.6
Little Rock, AR	132	159	177	183	110	3.4	1,576	116.2
Livonia, MI.	110	105	101	101	237	-0.3	2,815	35.7
Long Beach, CA	359	361	430	462	34	7.4	9,150	50.4
Los Angeles, CA.	2,812	2,969	3,485	3,695	2	6.0	7,877	469.1
Louisville, KY.	362	299	270	256	66	-5.0	4,125	62.1
Lowell, MA	94	92	103	105	218	1.7	7,636	13.8
Lubbock, TX	149	174	187	200	89	6.9	1,738	114.8
Madison, WI	172	171	191	208	83	9.0	3,030	68.7
Manchester, NH	88	91	99	107	214	7.9	3,241	33.0
McAllen, TX	38	66	86	106	216	24.3	2,315	46.0
Memphis, TN	624	646	619	650	18	5.0	2,327	279.3
Mesa, AZ	63	152	290	396	42	36.6	3,171	125.0
Mesquite, TX	55	67	102	125	172	22.4	2,868	43.4
Miami, FL	335	347	360	362	47	0.7	10,161	35.7
Milwaukee, WI	717	636	628	597	19	-5.0	6,214	96.1
Minneapolis, MN.	434	371	368	383	45	3.9	6,970	54.9
Mobile, AL.	190	200	198	199	91	0.3	1,687	117.9
Modesto, CA	62	107	166	189	102	13.5	5,277	35.8
Montgomery, AL	133	178	191	202	87	5.6	1,297	155.4
Moreno Valley, CA	([2])	([2])	119	142	148	19.9	2,779	51.2
Naperville, IL	23	43	87	128	165	47.6	3,628	35.4
Nashville-Davidson, TN [1]	426	456	488	546	25	11.7	1,153	473.3
New Haven, CT	138	126	130	124	175	-5.0	6,558	18.9
New Orleans, LA	593	558	497	485	31	-2.5	2,684	180.6
New York, NY	7,896	7,072	7,323	8,008	1	9.4	26,402	303.3
Newark, NJ	382	329	275	274	63	-0.6	11,495	23.8
Newport News, VA	138	145	171	180	113	5.1	2,638	68.3
Norfolk, VA	308	267	261	234	73	-10.3	4,363	53.7
North Las Vegas, NV.	46	43	48	115	194	140.8	1,471	78.5
Norwalk, CA	94	85	94	103	225	9.7	10,667	9.7
Oakland, CA	362	339	400	399	41	-0.1	7,127	56.1
Oceanside, CA.	40	77	129	161	125	25.2	3,967	40.6
Oklahoma City, OK	368	404	445	506	29	13.8	834	607.0
Omaha, NE	347	314	358	390	44	9.0	3,371	115.7
Ontario, CA	64	89	133	158	128	18.6	3,174	49.8
Orange, CA.	77	91	111	129	164	16.4	5,506	23.4
Orlando, FL	99	128	163	186	104	13.8	1,989	93.5
Overland Park, KS	78	82	112	149	139	33.3	2,627	56.7
Oxnard, CA	71	108	142	170	122	19.6	6,730	25.3
Palmdale, CA.	9	12	77	117	190	50.9	1,112	105.0
Pasadena, CA	113	118	132	142	149	7.5	3,208	44.2
Pasadena, TX	90	113	119	134	159	12.2	5,799	23.1
Paterson, NJ	145	138	158	149	138	-5.6	17,675	8.4
Pembroke Pines, FL	15	36	65	137	157	110.0	4,158	33.1
Peoria, AZ	5	12	51	108	210	111.8	784	138.2
Peoria, IL	127	124	114	113	199	-0.8	2,543	44.4

See footnotes at end of table.

U.S. Census Bureau, Statistical Abstract of the United States: 2002

[Population: As of April 1 (90 represents 90,000). Data for 1990 and 2000 refer to boundaries in effect on January 1, 2000; data for 1970 and 1980 refer to boundaries in effect for those censuses. Minus sign (-) indicates decrease]

Incorporated place	1970, total population (1,000)	1980, total population (1,000)	1990, total population (1,000)	Population, 2000 Total (1,000)	Population, 2000 Rank	Population, 2000 Percent change, 1990-2000	Population, 2000 Per square mile	Land area, 2000 (square miles)
Philadelphia, PA	1,949	1,688	1,586	1,518	5	-4.3	11,233	135.1
Phoenix, AZ	584	790	989	1,321	6	33.6	2,782	474.9
Pittsburgh, PA	520	424	370	335	52	-9.6	6,019	55.6
Plano, TX	18	72	129	222	78	72.8	3,102	71.6
Pomona, CA	87	93	132	149	137	13.0	6,544	22.8
Portland, OR	380	368	486	529	28	8.9	3,939	134.3
Portsmouth, VA	111	105	104	101	236	-3.2	3,033	33.2
Providence, RI	179	157	160	174	119	8.3	9,401	18.5
Provo, UT	53	74	87	105	219	20.7	2,653	39.6
Pueblo, CO	98	102	99	102	232	3.1	2,266	45.1
Raleigh, NC	123	150	220	276	62	25.3	2,409	114.6
Rancho Cucamonga, CA	(2)	55	101	128	167	26.0	3,411	37.4
Reno, NV	73	101	135	180	112	33.9	2,611	69.1
Richmond, VA	249	219	203	198	94	-2.4	3,293	60.1
Riverside, CA	140	171	227	255	67	12.6	3,267	78.1
Rochester, NY	295	242	231	220	79	-4.8	6,133	35.8
Rockford, IL	147	140	144	150	136	4.3	2,680	56.0
Sacramento, CA	257	276	395	407	40	3.0	4,189	97.2
Salem, OR	69	89	109	137	158	25.8	2,994	45.7
Salinas, CA	59	80	109	151	134	38.8	7,948	19.0
Salt Lake City, UT	176	163	160	182	111	13.6	1,666	109.1
San Antonio, TX	654	786	997	1,145	9	14.8	2,809	407.6
San Bernardino, CA	107	119	171	185	108	8.3	3,152	58.8
San Buenaventura (Ventura), CA	58	74	94	101	235	7.8	4,791	21.1
San Diego, CA	697	876	1,111	1,223	7	10.1	3,772	324.3
San Francisco, CA	716	679	724	777	13	7.3	16,634	46.7
San Jose, CA	460	629	783	895	11	14.2	5,118	174.9
Santa Ana, CA	156	204	294	338	51	14.8	12,452	27.1
Santa Clara, CA	86	88	93	102	228	9.7	5,566	18.4
Santa Clarita, CA	(2)	(2)	124	151	133	22.2	3,159	47.8
Santa Rosa, CA	50	83	120	148	140	22.5	3,678	40.1
Savannah, GA	118	142	138	132	162	-4.4	1,760	74.7
Scottsdale, AZ	68	89	130	203	86	55.8	1,100	184.2
Seattle, WA	531	494	516	563	23	9.1	6,717	83.9
Shreveport, LA	182	206	198	200	88	0.9	1,941	103.1
Simi Valley, CA	60	78	100	111	202	11.0	2,842	39.2
Sioux Falls, SD	72	81	101	124	174	22.2	2,201	56.3
South Bend, IN	126	110	106	108	211	1.6	2,786	38.7
Spokane, WA	171	171	178	196	96	9.8	3,387	57.8
Springfield, IL	92	100	107	111	201	3.9	2,064	54.0
Springfield, MA	164	152	157	152	131	-3.1	4,738	32.1
Springfield, MO	120	133	141	152	132	7.4	2,072	73.2
Stamford, CT	109	102	108	117	187	8.3	3,102	37.7
Sterling Heights, MI	61	109	118	124	173	5.7	3,397	36.6
Stockton, CA	110	150	211	244	70	15.3	4,456	54.7
St. Louis, MO	622	453	397	348	49	-12.2	5,623	61.9
St. Paul, MN	310	270	272	287	59	5.5	5,442	52.8
St. Petersburg, FL	216	239	240	248	68	3.3	4,163	59.6
Sunnyvale, CA	96	107	117	132	161	12.3	6,006	21.9
Syracuse, NY	197	170	164	147	141	-10.1	5,871	25.1
Tacoma, WA	154	159	177	194	99	9.1	3,865	50.1
Tallahassee, FL	73	82	125	151	135	20.1	1,574	95.7
Tampa, FL	278	272	281	303	57	8.1	2,708	112.1
Tempe, AZ	64	107	142	159	126	11.7	3,959	40.1
Thousand Oaks, CA	36	77	104	117	188	12.5	2,133	54.9
Toledo, OH	383	355	333	314	56	-5.8	3,890	80.6
Topeka, KS	125	119	121	122	176	1.3	2,185	56.0
Torrance, CA	135	130	133	138	155	3.5	6,716	20.5
Tucson, AZ	263	331	417	487	30	16.7	2,500	194.7
Tulsa, OK	330	361	367	393	43	7.0	2,152	182.6
Vallejo, CA	72	80	111	117	189	5.3	3,868	30.2
Vancouver, WA	42	43	105	144	145	37.3	3,355	42.8
Virginia Beach, VA	172	262	393	425	38	8.2	1,713	248.3
Waco, TX	95	101	104	114	197	9.4	1,351	84.2
Warren, MI	179	161	145	138	154	-4.7	4,032	34.3
Washington, DC	757	638	607	572	21	-5.7	9,316	61.4
Waterbury, CT	108	103	108	107	213	-0.9	3,755	28.6
West Covina, CA	68	80	96	105	220	9.6	6,525	16.1
West Valley City, UT	(2)	(2)	87	109	207	25.2	3,076	35.4
Westminster, CO	20	50	74	101	234	36.1	3,204	31.5
Wichita Falls, TX	96	94	97	104	221	7.7	1,474	70.7
Wichita, KS	277	280	309	344	50	11.5	2,536	135.8
Winston-Salem, NC	134	132	167	186	107	11.1	1,707	108.9
Worcester, MA	177	162	170	173	121	1.8	4,597	37.6
Yonkers, NY	204	195	188	196	95	4.2	10,847	18.1

NA Not available. [1] Represents the portion of a consolidated city that is not within one or more separately incorporated places. [2] Not incorporated. [3] The population shown in this table is for the census designated place (CDP).

Source: U.S. Census Bureau, *1990 Census of Population and Housing, Population and Housing Unit Counts*, (CPH-2); "Population Estimates for Cities with Populations of 10,000 and Greater (Sorted Within State by 1999 Population Size): July 1, 1999 (includes April 1, 1990 Population Estimates Base)"; published 20 October 2000; <http://www.census.gov/population/estimates/metro-city/SC10K-T3.txt>; *2000 Census of Population and Housing, Profiles of General Demographic Characteristics*; and American FactFinder, GCT-PH1-R. Population, Housing Units, Area, and Density (geographies ranked by total population): 2000, Census 2000 Summary File 1 (SF 1) 100-Percent Data, Geographic Area: United States—Places and (in selected states) County Subdivisions with 50,000 or More Population: and for Puerto Rico.

38 Population

No. 34. Cities With 250,000 or More Inhabitants in 2000—Selected Racial Groups: 2000

[In thousands (448.6 represents 448,600). **As of April.** Data refer to boundaries in effect on January 1, 2000]

City	Total population	White	Black or African American	American Indian, Alaska Native	Asian	Native Hawaiian and Other Pacific Islander	Some other race	Two or more races
Albuquerque, NM	448.6	321.2	13.9	17.4	10.1	0.5	66.3	19.3
Anaheim, CA	328.0	179.6	8.7	3.0	39.3	1.4	79.4	16.5
Anchorage, AK	260.3	188.0	15.2	18.9	14.4	2.4	5.7	15.6
Arlington, TX	333.0	225.4	45.7	1.8	20.0	0.5	29.8	9.8
Atlanta, GA	416.5	138.4	255.7	0.8	8.0	0.2	8.3	5.2
Aurora, CO	276.4	190.3	37.1	2.2	12.1	0.5	22.5	11.7
Austin, TX.	656.6	429.1	66.0	3.9	31.0	0.5	106.5	19.7
Baltimore, MD	651.2	206.0	419.0	2.1	10.0	0.2	4.4	9.6
Boston, MA.	589.1	320.9	149.2	2.4	44.3	0.4	46.1	25.9
Buffalo, NY	292.6	159.3	109.0	2.3	4.1	0.1	10.8	7.2
Charlotte, NC	540.8	315.1	177.0	1.9	18.4	0.3	19.2	9.0
Chicago, IL	2,896.0	1,215.3	1,065.0	10.3	126.0	1.8	393.2	84.4
Cincinnati, OH.	331.3	175.5	142.2	0.7	5.1	0.1	2.1	5.6
Cleveland, OH.	478.4	198.5	243.9	1.5	6.4	0.2	17.2	10.7
Colorado Springs, CO.	360.9	291.1	23.7	3.2	10.2	0.8	18.1	13.9
Columbus, OH.	711.5	483.3	174.1	2.1	24.5	0.4	8.3	18.8
Corpus Christi, TX	277.5	198.7	13.0	1.8	3.6	0.2	51.6	8.7
Dallas, TX.	1,188.6	604.2	308.0	6.5	32.1	0.6	204.9	32.4
Denver, CO.	554.6	362.2	61.6	7.3	15.6	0.6	86.5	20.8
Detroit, MI.	951.3	116.6	775.8	3.1	9.3	0.3	24.2	22.0
El Paso, TX.	563.7	413.1	17.6	4.6	6.3	0.6	102.3	19.2
Fort Worth, TX.	534.7	319.2	108.3	3.1	14.1	0.3	75.1	14.5
Fresno, CA	427.7	214.6	35.8	6.8	48.0	0.6	99.9	22.1
Honolulu, HI [1]	371.7	73.1	6.0	0.7	207.6	25.5	3.3	55.5
Houston, TX . . . [2]	1,953.6	962.6	494.5	8.6	103.7	1.2	321.6	61.5
Indianapolis, IN [2]	781.9	540.2	199.4	2.0	11.2	0.3	15.9	12.9
Jacksonville, FL.	735.6	474.3	213.5	2.5	20.4	0.4	9.8	14.6
Kansas City, MO	441.5	267.9	137.9	2.1	8.2	0.5	14.2	10.8
Las Vegas, NV	478.4	334.2	49.6	3.6	22.9	2.1	46.6	19.4
Lexington-Fayette, KY.	260.5	211.1	35.1	0.5	6.4	0.1	3.2	4.1
Long Beach, CA	461.5	208.4	68.6	3.9	55.6	5.6	95.1	24.3
Los Angeles, CA	3,694.8	1,734.0	415.2	29.4	369.3	5.9	949.7	191.3
Louisville, KY.	256.2	161.3	84.6	0.6	3.7	0.1	1.7	4.3
Memphis, TN.	650.1	223.7	399.2	1.2	9.5	0.2	9.4	6.8
Mesa, AZ	396.4	323.7	10.0	6.6	5.9	0.9	38.3	11.1
Miami, FL	362.5	241.5	80.9	0.8	2.4	0.1	19.6	17.2
Milwaukee, WI	597.0	298.4	222.9	5.2	17.6	0.3	36.4	16.2
Minneapolis, MN . . . . [2] . .	382.6	249.2	68.8	8.4	23.5	0.3	15.8	16.7
Nashville-Davidson, TN [2] . . .	545.5	359.6	146.2	1.6	13.0	0.4	13.7	11.0
New Orleans, LA	484.7	136.0	325.9	1.0	11.0	0.1	4.5	6.2
New York, NY	8,008.3	3,576.4	2,129.8	41.3	787.0	5.4	1,074.4	394.0
Newark, NJ	273.5	72.5	146.3	1.0	3.3	0.1	38.4	11.9
Oakland, CA	399.5	125.0	142.5	2.7	60.9	2.0	46.6	19.9
Oklahoma City, OK.	506.1	346.2	77.8	17.7	17.6	0.4	26.7	19.7
Omaha, NE.	390.0	305.7	51.9	2.6	6.8	0.2	15.3	7.5
Philadelphia, PA.	1,517.6	683.3	655.8	4.1	67.7	0.7	72.4	33.6
Phoenix, AZ	1,321.0	938.9	67.4	26.7	26.4	1.8	216.6	43.3
Pittsburgh, PA	334.6	226.3	90.8	0.6	9.2	0.1	2.2	5.4
Portland, OR	529.1	412.2	35.1	5.6	33.5	2.0	18.8	22.0
Raleigh, NC	276.1	174.8	76.8	1.0	9.3	0.1	8.9	5.2
Riverside, CA	255.2	151.4	18.9	2.8	14.5	1.0	53.6	13.0
Sacramento, CA.	407.0	196.5	63.0	5.3	67.6	3.9	44.6	26.1
San Antonio, TX.	1,144.6	774.7	78.1	9.6	17.9	1.1	221.4	41.9
San Diego, CA.	1,223.4	736.2	96.2	7.5	167.0	5.9	151.5	59.1
San Francisco, CA	776.7	385.7	60.5	3.5	239.6	3.8	50.4	33.3
San Jose, CA	894.9	425.0	31.3	6.9	240.4	3.6	142.7	45.1
Santa Ana, CA.	338.0	144.4	5.7	4.0	29.8	1.2	137.4	15.5
Seattle, WA.	563.4	394.9	47.5	5.7	73.9	2.8	13.4	25.1
St. Louis, MO	348.2	152.7	178.3	1.0	6.9	0.1	2.8	6.5
St. Paul, MN	287.2	192.4	33.6	3.3	35.5	0.2	11.0	11.1
Tampa, FL	303.4	194.9	79.1	1.2	6.5	0.3	12.6	8.8
Toledo, OH	313.6	220.3	73.9	1.0	3.2	0.1	7.2	8.1
Tucson, AZ	486.7	341.4	21.1	11.0	12.0	0.8	82.0	18.4
Tulsa, OK	393.0	275.5	60.8	18.6	7.2	0.2	13.6	17.3
Virginia Beach, VA	425.3	303.7	80.6	1.6	20.9	0.4	6.4	11.7
Washington, DC.	572.1	176.1	343.3	1.7	15.2	0.3	22.0	13.4
Wichita, KS	344.3	258.9	39.3	4.0	13.6	0.2	17.6	10.7

[1] The population shown in this table is for the census designated place (CDP). [2] Represents the portion of a consolidated city that is not within one or more separately incorporated places.

Source: U.S. Census Bureau, *2000 Census of Population and Housing, Profiles of General Demographic Characteristics.*

Population 39

No. 35. Cities With 250,000 or More Inhabitants in 2000—Hispanic and Non-Hispanic Groups: 2000

[In thousands, except percent (448.6 represents 448,600). As of April. Data refer to boundaries in effect on January 1, 2000]

City	Total population	Hispanic or Latino — Total Number	Hispanic or Latino — Percent of total population	Mexican	Puerto Rican	Cuban	Other Hispanic or Latino	Not Hispanic or Latino — Total	Not Hispanic or Latino — White alone
Albuquerque, NM	448.6	179.1	39.9	68.5	1.7	1.7	107.1	269.5	223.9
Anaheim, CA	328.0	153.4	46.8	126.0	1.3	0.9	25.2	174.6	117.6
Anchorage, AK	260.3	14.8	5.7	7.2	1.7	0.3	5.6	245.5	182.0
Arlington, TX	333.0	60.8	18.3	46.8	2.1	0.3	11.6	272.2	198.6
Atlanta, GA	416.5	18.7	4.5	12.7	1.1	0.9	4.0	397.8	130.2
Aurora, CO	276.4	54.8	19.8	38.3	1.6	0.3	14.6	221.6	163.6
Austin, TX	656.6	200.6	30.5	153.9	2.5	1.4	42.8	456.0	347.6
Baltimore, MD	651.2	11.1	1.7	3.0	2.2	0.5	5.3	640.1	201.6
Boston, MA	589.1	85.1	14.4	4.1	27.4	2.2	51.3	504.1	291.6
Buffalo, NY	292.6	22.1	7.5	1.0	17.3	0.4	3.4	270.6	151.5
Charlotte, NC	540.8	39.8	7.4	22.2	2.4	1.1	14.1	501.0	297.8
Chicago, IL	2,896.0	753.6	26.0	530.5	113.1	8.1	102.0	2,142.4	907.2
Cincinnati, OH	331.3	4.2	1.3	1.5	0.6	0.2	1.8	327.1	173.8
Cleveland, OH	478.4	34.7	7.3	3.0	25.4	0.5	5.9	443.7	185.6
Colorado Springs, CO	360.9	43.3	12.0	23.0	2.7	0.3	17.3	317.6	271.7
Columbus, OH	711.5	17.5	2.5	8.7	2.8	0.6	5.4	694.0	475.9
Corpus Christi, TX	277.5	150.7	54.3	98.1	0.7	0.3	51.5	126.7	106.9
Dallas, TX	1,188.6	422.6	35.6	350.5	2.4	2.3	67.4	766.0	410.8
Denver, CO	554.6	175.7	31.7	120.7	1.6	0.7	52.7	378.9	288.0
Detroit, MI	951.3	47.2	5.0	33.1	6.6	0.9	6.5	904.1	99.9
El Paso, TX	563.7	431.9	76.6	359.7	3.7	0.5	68.0	131.8	103.4
Fort Worth, TX	534.7	159.4	29.8	132.9	1.9	0.6	24.0	375.3	245.0
Fresno, CA	427.7	170.5	39.9	144.8	1.1	0.3	24.4	257.1	159.5
Honolulu, HI [1]	371.7	16.2	4.4	4.0	4.6	0.2	7.4	355.4	69.5
Houston, TX	1,953.6	730.9	37.4	527.4	6.9	5.0	191.5	1,222.8	601.9
Indianapolis, IN [2]	781.9	30.6	3.9	21.1	1.9	0.5	7.2	751.2	527.7
Jacksonville, FL	735.6	30.6	4.2	6.1	11.1	3.2	10.2	705.0	457.5
Kansas City, MO	441.5	30.6	6.9	24.0	0.7	0.8	5.0	410.9	254.5
Las Vegas, NV	478.4	113.0	23.6	83.5	2.9	3.4	23.2	365.5	277.7
Lexington-Fayette, KY	260.5	8.6	3.3	6.0	0.5	0.2	1.8	252.0	206.2
Long Beach, CA	461.5	165.1	35.8	127.1	2.3	1.1	34.6	296.4	152.9
Los Angeles, CA	3,694.8	1,719.1	46.5	1,091.7	13.4	12.4	601.5	1,975.7	1,099.2
Louisville, KY	256.2	4.8	1.9	1.6	0.4	1.5	1.3	251.5	158.7
Memphis, TN	650.1	19.3	3.0	14.1	0.7	0.5	4.0	630.8	216.2
Mesa, AZ	396.4	78.3	19.7	63.5	1.5	0.4	12.9	318.1	290.2
Miami, FL	362.5	238.4	65.8	3.7	10.3	123.8	100.7	124.1	42.9
Milwaukee, WI	597.0	71.6	12.0	43.3	19.6	0.6	8.1	525.3	271.0
Minneapolis, MN	382.6	29.2	7.6	19.8	1.2	0.5	7.6	353.4	239.1
Nashville-Davidson, TN [2]	545.5	25.8	4.7	16.1	1.9	0.8	7.0	519.8	349.1
New Orleans, LA	484.7	14.8	3.1	2.6	1.0	1.6	9.6	469.8	128.9
New York, NY	8,008.3	2,160.6	27.0	186.9	789.2	41.1	1,143.4	5,847.7	2,801.3
Newark, NJ	273.5	80.6	29.5	2.3	39.7	3.0	35.7	192.9	39.0
Oakland, CA	399.5	87.5	21.9	65.1	2.3	0.6	19.5	312.0	94.0
Oklahoma City, OK	506.1	51.4	10.1	41.0	1.2	0.4	8.8	454.8	327.2
Omaha, NE	390.0	29.4	7.5	23.3	0.6	0.3	5.2	360.6	293.9
Philadelphia, PA	1,517.6	128.9	8.5	6.2	91.5	2.7	28.5	1,388.6	644.4
Phoenix, AZ	1,321.0	450.0	34.1	375.1	5.1	2.0	67.8	871.1	736.8
Pittsburgh, PA	334.6	4.4	1.3	1.2	0.8	0.3	2.1	330.1	224.0
Portland, OR	529.1	36.1	6.8	25.1	1.0	1.3	8.6	493.1	399.4
Raleigh, NC	276.1	19.3	7.0	12.2	1.3	0.4	5.4	256.8	166.4
Riverside, CA	255.2	97.3	38.1	79.0	1.6	0.6	16.1	157.9	116.3
Sacramento, CA	407.0	88.0	21.6	70.8	2.1	0.5	14.7	319.0	165.0
San Antonio, TX	1,144.6	671.4	58.7	473.4	7.8	1.5	188.7	473.3	364.4
San Diego, CA	1,223.4	310.8	25.4	259.2	5.9	1.9	43.7	912.6	603.9
San Francisco, CA	776.7	109.5	14.1	48.9	3.8	1.6	55.2	667.2	338.9
San Jose, CA	894.9	270.0	30.2	221.1	4.1	1.0	43.8	625.0	322.5
Santa Ana, CA	338.0	257.1	76.1	222.7	0.7	0.6	33.1	80.9	42.0
Seattle, WA	563.4	29.7	5.3	17.9	1.5	0.8	9.6	533.7	382.5
St. Louis, MO	348.2	7.0	2.0	4.1	0.5	0.4	2.0	341.2	149.3
St. Paul, MN	287.2	22.7	7.9	16.6	1.0	0.4	4.8	264.4	183.9
Tampa, Fl	303.4	58.5	19.3	6.3	17.5	14.7	20.0	244.9	154.9
Toledo, OH	313.6	17.1	5.5	13.3	0.7	0.2	2.9	296.5	212.7
Tucson, AZ	486.7	173.9	35.7	145.2	2.1	0.6	25.9	312.8	263.7
Tulsa, OK	393.0	28.1	7.2	21.1	1.1	0.3	5.5	364.9	263.8
Virginia Beach, VA	425.3	17.8	4.2	4.9	6.3	0.6	6.0	407.5	295.4
Washington, DC	572.1	45.0	7.9	5.1	2.3	1.1	36.4	527.1	159.2
Wichita, KS	344.3	33.1	9.6	27.0	0.8	0.3	5.1	311.2	246.9

[1] The population shown in this table is for the census designated place (CDP).   [2] Represents the portion of a consolidated city that is not within one or more separately incorporated places.

Source: U.S. Census Bureau, 2000 Census of Population and Housing, Profiles of General Demographic Characteristics.

No. 36. Demographic and Economic Profiles of Selected Racial and Hispanic Origin Populations

[**211,461 represents 211,461,000**. Hispanic persons may be of any race. Population data based on 2000 Census of Population. Other items except business ownership based on Current Population Survey, see text, this section]

Characteristic	White	Black	Asian	Native Hawaiian and Other Pacific Islander	American Indian, Alaskan Native	Hispanic
POPULATION, 2000						
Total persons (1,000)	211,461	34,658	10,243	399	2,476	35,306
Percent of total population	75.1	12.3	3.6	0.1	0.9	12.5
Under 5 years old	12,860	2,805	670	33	213	3,718
5-14 years old	28,268	6,327	1,365	72	485	6,787
15-44 years old	89,850	16,253	5,254	206	1,194	18,221
45-64 years old	50,078	6,451	2,153	66	445	4,847
65 years old and over	30,406	2,823	801	21	138	1,734
Five states with largest number of specified group [1]	CA (20.2) TX (14.8) NY (12.9) FL (12.5) PA (10.5)	NY (3.0) TX (2.4) GA (2.4) FL (2.3) CA (2.3)	CA (3.7) NY (1.0) TX (.6) HI (.5) NJ (.5)	CA (.117) HI (.114) WA (.024) UT (.015) TX (.014)	CA (.333) OK (.273) AZ (.256) NM (.173) TX (.118)	CA (11.0) TX (6.7) NY (2.9) FL (2.7) IL (1.5)
Five states with largest percent of specified group	ME (97%) VT (97%) NH (96%) WV (95%) IA (94%)	DC (60%) MS (36%) LA (33%) SC (30%) GA (29%)	HI (42%) CA (11%) NJ (6%) NY (6%) WA (6%)	HI (9.4%) UT (0.7%) AK (0.5%) WA (0.4%) NV (0.4%)	AK (16%) NM (10%) SD (8%) OK (8%) MT (6%)	NM (42%) CA (32%) TX (32%) AZ (25%) NV (20%)
EDUCATIONAL ATTAINMENT, 2000						
Persons 25 years old and over (1,000)	147,067	20,036	[2]6,667	[2]	(NA)	17,150
Percent high school graduate or more	84.9	78.5	[2]85.7	[2]	(NA)	57.0
Percent bachelor's degree or more	26.1	16.5	[2]43.9	[2]	(NA)	10.6
Percent with advanced degree	8.8	5.1	[2]15.3	[2]	(NA)	3.3
VOTING PARTICIPATION, 2000						
Percent reporting they registered	65.6	63.6	[2]30.7	[2]	(NA)	34.9
Percent reporting they voted	56.4	53.5	[2]25.4	[2]	(NA)	27.5
FAMILY INCOME IN 2000						
Total families (1,000)	60,222	8,814	(NA)	(NA)	(NA)	7,728
Percent distribution—						
Less than $10,000	4.0	11.7	(NA)	(NA)	(NA)	8.4
$10,000 to $14,999	4.0	8.3	(NA)	(NA)	(NA)	7.9
$15,000 to $24,999	10.7	16.8	(NA)	(NA)	(NA)	18.3
$25,000 to $34,999	11.8	14.1	(NA)	(NA)	(NA)	15.4
$35,000 to $49,999	15.9	16.8	(NA)	(NA)	(NA)	18.1
$50,000 to $74,999	22.2	16.7	(NA)	(NA)	(NA)	17.9
$75,000 or more	31.4	15.6	(NA)	(NA)	(NA)	14.1
Median income (dol.)	53,256	34,192	(NA)	(NA)	(NA)	35,054
POVERTY, 2000						
Families below poverty level (percent)	6.9	19.1	[2]8.8	[2]	(NA)	18.5
Persons below poverty level (percent)	9.4	22.1	[2]10.8	[2]	(NA)	21.2
BUSINESSES OWNED BY SPECIFIED GROUP, 1997						
All firms:						
Number (1,000)	(NA)	823	[2]913	[2]	197	1,200
Sales and receipts (mil. dol.)	(NA)	71,215	[2]306,933	[2]	34,344	186,275
Firms with paid employees:						
Number (1,000)	(NA)	93	[2]290	[2]	33	212
Sales and receipts (mil. dol.)	(NA)	56,378	[2]278,294	[2]	29,226	158,675
Employees (1,000)	(NA)	718	[2]2,203	[2]	299	1,389
Payroll, annual (mil. dol.)	(NA)	14,322	[2]46,180	[2]	6,624	29,830

NA Not available. [1] Number in parentheses in millions. [2] Native Hawaiian and Other Pacific Islander included in data for Asian population.

Source: U.S. Census Bureau, 2000 Census of Population, Summary File 1, <http://www.census.gov/Press-Release/www/2001/sumfile1.html>; *Current Population Reports*, P20-536, P20-542, P60-213, and P60-214; and "1997 Economic Census, Minority- and Women-Owned Businesses, United States"; published 24 May 2001; <http://www.census.gov/epcd/mwb97/us/us.html>.

Population   41

No. 37. Social and Economic Characteristics of the White and Black Populations: 1990 to 2000

[As of March, except labor force status, annual average (134,687 represents 134,687,000). Excludes members of Armed Forces except those living off post or with their families on post. Data for 1990 are based on 1980 census population controls; 1995 and 2000 data based on 1990 census population controls. Based on Current Population Survey; see text, this section, and Appendix III]

Characteristic	Number (1,000)						Percent distribution			
	White			Black			White		Black	
	1990	1995	2000	1990	1995	2000	1990	2000	1990	2000
EDUCATIONAL ATTAINMENT										
Persons 25 years old and over	134,687	141,113	147,067	16,751	18,457	20,036	100.0	100.0	100.0	100.0
Elementary:										
0 to 8 years	14,131	11,101	10,035	2,701	1,800	1,417	10.5	6.8	16.1	7.1
High school:										
1 to 3 years	14,080	[1]12,882	[1]12,153	2,969	[1]3,041	[1]2,899	10.5	[1]8.3	17.7	[1]14.5
4 years	52,449	[2]47,986	[2]49,105	6,239	[2]6,686	[2]7,050	38.9	[2]33.4	37.2	[2]35.2
College:										
1 to 3 years	24,350	[3]35,321	[3]37,353	2,952	[3]4,486	[3]5,366	18.1	[3]25.4	17.6	[3]26.8
4 years or more	29,677	[4]33,824	[4]38,421	1,890	[4]2,444	[4]3,303	22.0	[4]26.1	11.3	[4]16.5
LABOR FORCE STATUS [5]										
Civilians 16 years old and over	160,625	166,914	174,428	21,477	23,246	25,218	100.0	100.0	100.0	100.0
Civilian labor force	107,447	111,950	117,574	13,740	14,817	16,603	66.9	67.4	64.0	65.8
Employed	102,261	106,490	113,475	12,175	13,279	15,334	63.7	65.1	56.7	60.8
Unemployed	5,186	5,459	4,099	1,565	1,538	1,269	3.2	2.3	7.3	5.0
Unemployment rate [6]	4.8	4.9	3.5	11.4	10.4	7.6	(X)	(X)	(X)	(X)
Not in labor force	53,178	54,965	56,854	7,737	8,429	8,615	33.1	32.6	36.0	34.2
FAMILY TYPE										
Total families	56,590	58,437	60,251	7,470	8,093	8,664	100.0	100.0	100.0	100.0
With own children [7]	26,718	27,951	28,107	4,378	4,682	4,782	47.2	46.6	58.6	55.2
Married couple	46,981	47,899	48,790	3,750	3,842	4,144	83.0	81.0	50.2	47.1
With own children [7]	21,579	22,005	21,809	1,972	1,926	2,093	38.1	36.2	26.4	24.2
Female householder, no spouse present	7,306	8,031	8,380	3,275	3,716	3,814	12.9	13.9	43.8	45.1
With own children [7]	4,199	4,841	4,869	2,232	2,489	2,409	7.4	8.1	29.9	27.8
Male householder, no spouse present	2,303	2,507	3,081	446	536	706	4.1	5.1	6.0	7.8
With own children [7]	939	1,105	1,429	173	267	280	1.7	2.4	2.3	3.2
FAMILY INCOME IN PREVIOUS YEAR IN CONSTANT (1999) DOLLARS										
Total families [8]	56,590	58,444	60,256	7,470	8,093	8,664	100.0	100.0	100.0	100.0
Less than $5,000	(NA)	(NA)	1,083	(NA)	(NA)	543	1.8	1.8	7.2	6.3
$5,000 to $9,999	(NA)	(NA)	1,554	(NA)	(NA)	721	3.0	2.6	11.7	8.3
$10,000 to $14,999	(NA)	(NA)	2,514	(NA)	(NA)	793	4.6	4.2	9.7	9.1
$15,000 to $24,999	(NA)	(NA)	6,970	(NA)	(NA)	1,384	11.8	11.6	18.0	16.0
$25,000 to $34,999	(NA)	(NA)	7,090	(NA)	(NA)	1,176	12.6	11.8	13.3	13.6
$35,000 to $49,999	(NA)	(NA)	10,046	(NA)	(NA)	1,326	18.3	16.7	15.4	15.3
$50,000 or more	(NA)	(NA)	30,998	(NA)	(NA)	2,723	47.9	51.4	24.6	31.4
Median income (dol.) [9]	48,334	45,960	51,224	27,152	27,764	31,778	(X)	(X)	(X)	(X)
POVERTY										
Families below poverty level [10]	4,409	5,312	4,377	2,077	2,212	1,898	7.8	7.3	27.8	21.9
Persons below poverty level [10]	20,785	25,379	21,922	9,302	10,196	8,360	10.0	9.8	30.7	23.6
HOUSING TENURE										
Total occupied units	80,163	83,737	87,671	10,486	11,655	12,849	100.0	100.0	100.0	100.0
Owner-occupied	54,094	57,449	62,077	4,445	4,888	6,055	67.5	70.8	42.4	47.1
Renter-occupied	24,685	24,793	24,253	5,862	6,547	6,563	30.8	27.7	55.9	51.1
No cash rent	1,384	1,494	1,340	178	220	231	1.7	1.5	1.7	1.8

NA Not available.   X Not applicable.   [1] Represents those who completed 9th to 12th grade, but have no high school diploma.   [2] High school graduate.   [3] Some college or associate degree.   [4] Bachelor's or advanced degree.   [5] Source: U.S. Bureau of Labor Statistics, *Employment and Earnings*, January issues. See footnote 2, Table 560.   [6] Total unemployment as percent of civilian labor force.   [7] Children under 18 years old.   [8] Includes families in group quarters.   [9] For definition of median, see Guide to Tabular Presentation.   [10] For explanation of poverty level, see text, Section 13, Income, Expenditures, and Wealth.

Source: Except as noted, U.S. Census Bureau, Black Population in the U.S.: March 2000, PPL-142; *Current Population Reports*, P60-209, P60-210, and earlier reports; and unpublished data.

No. 38. Social and Economic Characteristics of the Asian and Pacific Islander Population: 1990 and 2000

[As of March (6,679 represents 6,679,000). Excludes members of Armed Forces except those living off post or with their families on post. Data for 1990 are based on 1980 census population controls; 2000 data are based on 1990 census population controls. Based on Current Population Survey; see text, this section, and Appendix III]

Characteristic	Number (1,000)		Percent distribution	
	1990	2000	1990	2000
Total persons	6,679	10,925	100.0	100.0
LABOR FORCE STATUS [1]				
Civilians 16 years old and over.	4,849	8,225	100.0	100.0
Civilian labor force.	3,216	5,458	66.3	66.4
Employed	3,079	5,246	63.5	63.8
Unemployed	136	212	2.8	2.6
Unemployment rate [2]	4.2	3.9	(X)	(X)
Not in labor force.	1634	2,767	33.7	33.6
FAMILY TYPE				
Total families	1,531	2,506	100.0	100.0
Married couple	1,257	1,996	82.1	79.6
Female householder, no spouse present	188	331	12.3	13.2
Male householder, no spouse present	86	179	5.6	7.1
HOUSING TENURE				
Total occupied units	1,988	3,337	100.0	100.0
Owner-occupied	976	1,766	49.1	52.9
Renter-occupied	982	1,526	49.4	45.7
No cash rent.	30	46	1.5	1.4

X Not applicable.   [1] Data beginning 1994 not directly comparable with earlier years. See text, Section 12, Labor Force.
[2] Total unemployment as percent of civilian labor force.
Source: U.S. Census Bureau, *Current Population Reports*, P20-459, and "The Asian and Pacific Islander Population in the United States: March 2000 (Update)" (PPL-146).

No. 39. Persons 65 Years Old and Over—Characteristics by Sex: 1980 to 2000

[As of March, except as noted (24.2 represents 24,200,000). Covers civilian noninstitutional population. Excludes members of Armed Forces except those living off post or with their families on post. Data for 1980 and 1990 are based on 1980 census population controls; 1995 and 2000 data based on 1990 census population controls. Based on Current Population Survey; see text, this section, and Appendix III]

Characteristic	Total				Male				Female			
	1980	1990	1995	2000	1980	1990	1995	2000	1980	1990	1995	2000
Total (million)	24.2	29.6	31.7	32.6	9.9	12.3	13.2	13.9	14.2	17.2	18.5	18.7
PERCENT DISTRIBUTION												
Marital status:												
Never married	5.5	4.6	4.2	3.9	4.9	4.2	4.2	4.2	5.9	4.9	4.2	3.6
Married	55.4	56.1	56.9	57.2	78.0	76.5	77.0	75.2	39.5	41.4	42.5	43.8
Spouse present.	53.6	54.1	54.7	54.6	76.1	74.2	74.5	72.6	37.9	39.7	40.6	41.3
Spouse absent	1.8	2.0	2.2	2.6	1.9	2.3	2.5	2.6	1.7	1.7	1.9	2.5
Widowed.	35.7	34.2	33.2	32.1	13.5	14.2	13.5	14.4	51.2	48.6	47.3	45.3
Divorced	3.5	5.0	5.7	6.7	3.6	5.0	5.2	6.1	3.4	5.1	6.0	7.2
Family status:												
In families [1]	67.6	66.7	66.6	67.4	83.0	81.9	80.6	79.7	56.8	55.8	56.7	58.2
Nonfamily householders.	31.2	31.9	32.4	31.1	15.7	16.6	18.4	18.2	42.0	42.8	42.4	40.7
Secondary individuals	1.2	1.4	1.0	1.5	1.3	1.5	1.0	2.1	1.1	1.4	0.9	1.1
Living arrangements:												
Living in household	99.8	99.7	99.9	100.0	99.9	99.9	100.0	100.0	99.7	99.5	99.9	100.0
Living alone	30.3	31.0	31.5	30.1	14.9	15.7	17.3	17.0	41.0	42.0	41.7	39.6
Spouse present.	53.6	54.1	54.7	54.6	76.1	74.3	74.5	72.6	37.9	39.7	40.6	41.3
Living with someone else	15.9	14.6	13.7	15.3	8.9	9.9	8.1	10.4	20.8	17.8	17.6	19.1
Not in household [2]	0.2	0.3	0.1	0.1	0.1	0.1	-	0.1	0.3	0.5	0.1	0.1
Years of school completed:												
8 years or less	43.1	28.5	[3]21.0	[4]16.7	45.3	30.0	[3]22.0	[4]17.8	41.6	27.5	[3]20.3	[4]15.9
1 to 3 years of high school	16.2	16.1	[3]15.2	[3]13.8	15.5	15.7	[3]14.5	[3]12.7	16.7	16.4	[3]15.6	[3]14.7
4 years of high school	24.0	32.9	[4]33.8	[4]35.9	21.4	29.0	[4]29.2	[4]30.4	25.8	35.6	[4]37.1	[4]39.9
1 to 3 years of college	8.2	10.9	[5]17.1	[5]18.0	7.5	10.8	[5]17.1	[5]17.8	8.6	11.0	[5]17.0	[5]18.2
4 years or more of college	8.6	11.6	[6]13.0	[6]15.6	10.3	14.5	[6]17.2	[6]21.4	7.4	9.5	[6]9.9	[6]11.4
Labor force participation: [7]												
Employed	12.2	11.5	11.7	12.4	18.4	15.9	16.1	16.9	7.8	8.4	8.5	9.1
Unemployed	0.4	0.4	0.5	0.4	0.6	0.5	0.7	0.6	0.3	0.3	0.3	0.3
Not in labor force	87.5	88.1	87.9	87.2	81.0	83.6	83.2	82.5	91.9	91.3	91.2	90.6
Percent below poverty level [8]	15.2	11.4	11.7	9.7	11.1	7.8	7.2	6.9	17.9	13.9	14.9	11.8

- Represents zero.   [1] Excludes those living in unrelated subfamilies.   [2] In group quarters other than institutions.
[3] Represents those who completed 9th to 12th grade, but have no high school diploma.   [4] High school graduate.   [5] Some college or associate degree.   [6] Bachelor's or advanced degree.   [7] Annual averages of monthly figures. Source: U.S. Bureau of Labor Statistics, *Employment and Earnings*, January issues. See footnote 2, Table 560.   [8] Poverty status based on income in preceding year.
Source: Except as noted, U.S. Census Bureau, *Current Population Reports*, P20-537, and earlier reports; P60-210; and unpublished data.

No. 40. Social and Economic Characteristics of the Hispanic Population: 2000

[As of March, except labor force status, annual average (32,804 represents 32,804,000). Excludes members of the Armed Forces except those living off post or with their families on post. Based on Current Population Survey; see text of this section and Appendix III]

Characteristic	Number (1,000)						Percent distribution					
	His- panic, total	Mexi- can	Puerto Rican	Cuban	Cen- tral and South Ameri- can	Other His- panic	His- panic, total	Mexi- can	Puerto Rican	Cuban	Cen- tral and South Ameri- can	Other His- panic
Total persons	32,804	21,701	2,959	1,300	4,743	2,101	100.0	100.0	100.0	100.0	100.0	100.0
Under 5 years old	3,665	2,701	278	67	404	215	11.2	12.4	9.4	5.1	8.5	10.2
5 to 14 years old	6,346	4,453	571	129	788	405	19.3	20.5	19.3	9.9	16.6	19.3
15 to 44 years old	16,277	10,842	1,414	526	2,534	960	49.6	50.0	47.8	40.5	53.4	45.7
45 to 64 years present	4,764	2,769	518	305	794	377	14.5	12.8	17.5	23.4	16.7	18.0
65 years old and over	1,752	936	178	273	222	143	5.3	4.3	6.0	21.0	4.7	6.8
EDUCATIONAL ATTAINMENT												
Persons 25 years old and over	17,150	10,625	1,612	965	2,768	1,180	100.0	100.0	100.0	100.0	100.0	100.0
High school graduate or higher	9,783	5,416	1,037	705	1,781	845	57.0	51.0	64.3	73.0	64.3	71.6
Bachelor's degree or higher	1,821	738	209	222	481	171	10.6	6.9	13.0	23.0	17.4	14.5
LABOR FORCE STATUS [1]												
Civilians 16 years old and over	22,393	14,386	2,025	1,104	3,456	1,422	100.0	100.0	100.0	100.0	100.0	100.0
Civilian labor force	15,368	9,955	1,278	680	2,486	969	68.6	69.2	63.1	61.6	71.9	68.1
Employed	14,492	9,364	1,196	650	2,365	917	64.7	65.1	59.1	58.9	68.4	64.5
Unemployed	876	591	82	30	120	53	3.9	4.1	4.0	2.7	3.5	3.7
Unemployment rate [2]	5.7	5.9	6.4	4.4	4.8	5.5	(X)	(X)	(X)	(X)	(X)	(X)
Male	4.9	5.1	5.7	4.1	4.1	4.8	(X)	(X)	(X)	(X)	(X)	(X)
Female	6.7	7.2	7.1	4.7	5.8	6.3	(X)	(X)	(X)	(X)	(X)	(X)
Not in labor force	7,025	4,430	747	424	970	454	31.4	30.8	36.9	38.4	28.1	31.9
FAMILY TYPE												
Total families	7,561	4,794	770	385	1,109	504	100.0	100.0	100.0	100.0	100.0	100.0
Married couple	5,133	3,352	437	296	721	326	67.9	69.9	56.8	77.1	65.0	64.7
Female householder, no spouse present	1,769	1,013	275	70	272	138	23.4	21.1	35.8	18.3	24.6	27.4
Male householder, no spouse present	658	428	57	18	115	40	8.7	8.9	7.4	4.6	10.4	7.9
FAMILY INCOME IN 1999												
Total families [3]	7,561	4,794	770	385	1,109	504	100.0	100.0	100.0	100.0	100.0	100.0
Less than $5,000	323	187	53	14	47	21	4.3	3.9	6.9	3.6	4.3	4.2
$5,000 to $9,999	434	270	66	18	49	31	5.7	5.6	8.6	4.6	4.5	6.2
$10,000 to $14,999	674	425	72	43	86	48	8.9	8.9	9.4	11.2	7.7	9.5
$15,000 to $24,999	1,489	1,002	144	52	206	85	19.7	20.9	18.7	13.4	18.6	16.8
$25,000 to $34,999	1,202	775	102	60	199	67	15.9	16.2	13.2	15.6	17.9	13.3
$35,000 to $49,999	1,263	806	134	46	189	89	16.7	16.8	17.4	12.0	17.0	17.6
$50,000 or more	2,177	1,330	200	152	333	163	28.8	27.7	25.9	39.6	30.0	32.4
Median income (dol.) [4]	31,663	31,123	30,129	38,312	33,105	34,935	(X)	(X)	(X)	(X)	(X)	(X)
Families below poverty level [5]	1,525	1,018	177	58	181	91	20.2	21.2	23.0	15.0	16.3	18.1
Persons below poverty level [5]	7,439	5,214	760	224	789	452	22.8	24.1	25.8	17.3	16.7	21.6
HOUSING TENURE												
Total occupied units	9,319	5,733	1,004	523	1,372	687	100.0	100.0	100.0	100.0	100.0	100.0
Owner-occupied	4,243	2,739	352	307	515	330	45.5	47.8	35.0	58.7	37.6	48.0
Renter-occupied [6]	5,075	2,993	652	216	857	357	54.5	52.2	65.0	41.3	62.4	52.0

X Not applicable.   [1] Source: U.S. Bureau of Labor Statistics, *Employment and Earnings*, January 2001.   [2] Total unemployment as percent of civilian labor force.   [3] Includes families in group quarters.   [4] For definition of median, see Guide to Tabular Presentation.   [5] For explanation of poverty level, see text, Section 13, Income, Expenditures, and Wealth.   [6] Includes no cash rent.

Source: Except as noted, U.S. Census Bureau, *Current Population Reports*, P20-535.

No. 41. Native and Foreign-Born Population by Place of Birth: 1950 to 2000

[In thousands, except percent (150,216 represents 150,216,000). Data are based on a sample from the census; for details, see text, this section. See source for sampling variability]

Year	Total popula-tion	Native population						Foreign born	
		Total	Born in state of resi-dence	Born in other states	State of birth not reported	Born in outlying areas [1]	Born abroad or at sea of Ameri-can parents	Number	Percent of total population
1950	150,216	139,869	102,788	35,284	1,370	330	96	10,347	6.9
1960	178,467	168,806	118,802	44,264	4,526	817	397	9,661	5.4
1970	203,194	193,454	131,296	51,659	8,882	873	744	9,740	4.8
1980	226,546	212,466	144,871	65,452	(NA)	1,088	1,055	14,080	6.2
1990	248,710	228,943	153,685	72,011	(NA)	1,382	1,864	19,767	7.9
2000	281,422	250,314	168,729	78,057	(NA)	1,607	1,921	31,108	11.1

NA Not available.   [1] 1950, includes Alaska and Hawaii. Includes Puerto Rico.

Source: U.S. Census Bureau, *1970 Census of Population*, Vol. II, PC(2)-2A; and *1990 Census of Population Listing* (1990CPH-L-121) and *2000 Census of Population and Housing, Profiles of General Demographic Characteristics.*

No. 42. Foreign-Stock Population by Nativity and Parentage: 1960 to 2000

[34.1 represents 34,100,000. Information on the birthplace of parents may be used to classify the native population by parentage: native of native parentage (both parents native), native of foreign parentage (both parents foreign born), and native of mixed parentage (one parent native and one parent foreign born). The term foreign stock includes the foreign-born population and the native population of foreign or mixed parentage. For 1960 and 1970, resident population. For 2000, civilian noninstitutional population plus Armed Forces living off post or with their families on post]

Nativity and parentage	Number (mil.)			Percent of total population		
	1960	1970	2000	1960	1970	2000
Foreign stock, total	34.1	33.6	55.9	19.0	16.5	20.4
Native population of foreign or mixed parentage. .	24.3	24.0	27.5	13.6	11.8	10.0
Foreign parentage	14.1	(NA)	14.8	7.9	(NA)	5.4
Mixed parentage	10.2	(NA)	12.7	5.7	(NA)	4.6
Foreign born	9.7	9.6	28.4	5.4	4.7	10.4

NA Not available.

Source: U.S. Census Bureau, *Current Population Reports*, P23-206.

No. 43. Foreign-Born Population by Country of Origin and Citizenship Status: 2000

[In thousands, except percent (28,379 represents 28,379,000). See headnote, Table 44]

Country of origin	Foreign-born, total		Naturalized citizen		Not U.S. citizen	
	Number	Percent	Number	Percent	Number	Percent
All countries	**28,379**	**100.0**	**10,622**	**100.0**	**17,758**	**100.0**
Mexico	7,841	27.6	1,592	15.0	6,249	35.2
Cuba	952	3.4	552	5.2	400	2.3
Dominican Republic	692	2.4	234	2.2	458	2.6
El Salvador	765	2.7	151	1.4	614	3.5
Great Britain	613	2.2	273	2.6	341	1.9
China and Hong Kong	1,067	3.8	507	4.8	560	3.2
India	1,007	3.5	362	3.4	644	3.6
Korea	701	2.5	341	3.2	361	2.0
Philippines	1,222	4.3	774	7.3	448	2.5
Vietnam	863	3.0	411	3.9	453	2.5
Elsewhere	12,655	44.6	5,424	51.1	7,230	40.7

Source: U.S. Census Bureau, *Current Population Reports*, P20-534.

U.S. Census Bureau, Statistical Abstract of the United States: 2002

No. 44. Native and Foreign-Born Populations by Selected Characteristics: 2000

[In thousands (245,708 represents 245,708,000). As of March. The foreign-born population includes some undocumented immigrants, refugees, and temporary residents such as students and temporary workers as well as legally-admitted immigrants. Based on Current Population Survey; see text, this section, and Appendix III]

Characteristic	Native population	Foreign-born population				
		Total	Year of entry			
			Before 1970	1970 to 1979	1980 to 1989	1990 to 2000
Total............................	245,708	28,379	4,547	4,605	8,022	11,206
Under 5 years old.....................	19,319	289	(X)	(X)	(X)	289
5 to 17 years old	50,169	2,548	(X)	(X)	545	2,003
18 to 24 years old....................	23,384	3,148	(X)	148	891	2,110
25 to 29 years old....................	15,366	2,902	(X)	332	778	1,792
30 to 34 years old....................	16,284	3,233	85	407	1,224	1,517
35 to 44 years old....................	38,571	6,235	626	1,273	2,497	1,838
45 to 64 years old....................	53,108	6,910	1,910	2,065	1,640	1,295
65 years old and over	29,507	3,115	1,926	381	446	362
Male.............................	119,733	14,200	2,079	2,243	4,186	5,692
Female...........................	125,975	14,179	2,468	2,362	3,836	5,514
White............................	205,545	19,261	3,874	3,052	4,838	7,498
Black............................	33,288	2,221	217	396	752	856
American Indian/Eskimo/Aleut..........	2,656	191	26	36	55	75
Asian or Pacific Islander	4,218	6,706	430	1,121	2,377	2,778
Hispanic origin [1].....................	19,962	12,841	1,448	2,057	3,809	5,527
EDUCATIONAL ATTAINMENT						
Persons 25 years old and over	152,836	22,394	4,547	4,457	6,586	6,804
Not high school graduate	20,456	7,397	1,368	1,445	2,337	2,247
High school grad/some college	93,312	9,219	2,087	1,813	2,733	2,586
Bachelor's degree....................	26,225	3,615	562	778	979	1,297
Graduate or professional degree	12,843	2,162	530	421	538	674
INCOME IN 1999						
Persons 16 years old and over	187,401	26,372	4,547	4,605	7,777	9,443
Without income	14,116	4,021	207	381	1,109	2,324
With income	173,285	22,351	4,340	4,224	6,668	7,119
$1 to $9,999 or loss..................	45,926	6,465	1,284	969	1,815	2,397
$10,000 to $19,999	36,876	6,097	1,020	938	1,877	2,263
$20,000 to $34,999	40,134	4,679	869	999	1,537	1,273
$35,000 to $49,999	22,749	2,150	394	548	693	514
$50,000 or more	27,600	2,960	773	770	746	672
POVERTY STATUS [2]						
In poverty	27,507	4,751	379	528	1,222	2,623
Not in poverty	217,638	23,597	4,168	4,077	6,797	8,555
HOMEOWNERSHIP						
In owner-occupied unit.................	177,393	14,224	3,568	3,053	4,128	3,475
In renter-occupied unit.................	68,315	14,155	978	1,552	3,893	7,731

X Not applicable.   [1] Persons of Hispanic origin may be of any race.   [2] Persons for whom poverty status is determined.

Source: U.S. Census Bureau, *Current Population Reports*, P20-534.

No. 45. Living Arrangements of Persons 15 Years Old and Over by Selected Characteristics: 2000

[In thousands (213,773 represents 213,773,000). As of March. Based on Current Population Survey which includes members of Armed Forces living off post or with families on post, but excludes other Armed Forces; see text, this section, and Appendix III]

Living arrangement	Total	15 to 19 years old	20 to 24 years old	25 to 34 years old	35 to 44 years old	45 to 54 years old	55 to 64 years old	65 to 74 years old	75 years old and over
Total [1]	**213,773**	**20,102**	**18,441**	**37,786**	**44,805**	**36,631**	**23,387**	**17,796**	**14,825**
Alone	26,724	127	1,016	3,848	4,109	4,304	3,538	4,091	5,692
With spouse..........	112,920	344	3,350	20,246	29,316	25,451	16,388	11,326	6,500
With other persons	74,129	19,631	14,075	13,692	11,380	6,876	3,461	2,379	2,633
White	177,581	15,843	14,671	30,320	36,915	30,790	20,163	15,528	13,352
Alone	22,307	91	770	2,959	3,291	3,500	2,942	3,542	5,212
With spouse..........	99,191	315	2,994	17,479	25,318	22,246	14,583	10,248	6,009
With other persons	56,083	15,437	10,907	9,882	8,306	5,044	2,638	1,738	2,131
Black	25,855	3,057	2,762	5,163	5,699	4,103	2,316	1,624	1,130
Alone	3,605	25	176	628	680	691	526	461	418
With spouse..........	8,392	14	215	1,620	2,518	1,885	1,136	671	333
With other persons	13,858	3,018	2,371	2,915	2,501	1,527	654	492	379
Hispanic origin [2]	22,793	2,889	2,755	5,660	4,974	3,019	1,745	1,132	621
Alone	1,296	12	73	246	215	207	184	211	147
With spouse..........	11,189	103	774	3,269	3,212	1,909	1,042	609	270
With other persons	10,308	2,774	1,908	2,145	1,547	903	519	312	204

[1] Includes other races and persons not of Hispanic origin, not shown separately.   [2] Persons of Hispanic origin may be of any race.

Source: U.S. Census Bureau, *Current Population Reports*, P20-537; and unpublished data.

No. 46. Marital Status of the Population by Sex, Race, and Hispanic Origin: 1980 to 2000

[In millions, except percent (159.5 represents 159,500,000). As of March. Persons 18 years old and over. Excludes members of Armed Forces except those living off post or with their families on post. Based on Current Population Survey, see text, this section, and Appendix III]

Marital status, race, and Hispanic origin	Total				Male				Female			
	1980	1990	1995	2000	1980	1990	1995	2000	1980	1990	1995	2000
Total [1]...............	**159.5**	**181.8**	**191.6**	**201.8**	**75.7**	**86.9**	**92.0**	**96.9**	**83.8**	**95.0**	**99.6**	**104.9**
Never married	32.3	40.4	43.9	48.2	18.0	22.4	24.6	26.1	14.3	17.9	19.3	22.1
Married................	104.6	112.6	116.7	120.1	51.8	55.8	57.7	59.6	52.8	56.7	58.9	60.4
Widowed...............	12.7	13.8	13.4	13.7	2.0	2.3	2.3	2.6	10.8	11.5	11.1	11.1
Divorced	9.9	15.1	17.6	19.8	3.9	6.3	7.4	8.5	6.0	8.8	10.3	11.3
Percent of total	100.0	100.0	100.0	100.0	100.0	100.0	100.0	100.0	100.0	100.0	100.0	100.0
Never married	20.3	22.2	22.9	23.9	23.8	25.8	26.8	27.0	17.1	18.9	19.4	21.1
Married................	65.5	61.9	60.9	59.5	68.4	64.3	62.7	61.5	63.0	59.7	59.2	57.6
Widowed...............	8.0	7.6	7.0	6.8	2.6	2.7	2.5	2.7	12.8	12.1	11.1	10.5
Divorced	6.2	8.3	9.2	9.8	5.2	7.2	8.0	8.8	7.1	9.3	10.3	10.8
White, total	**139.5**	**155.5**	**161.3**	**168.1**	**66.7**	**74.8**	**78.1**	**81.6**	**72.8**	**80.6**	**83.2**	**86.6**
Never married	26.4	31.6	33.2	36.0	15.0	18.0	19.2	20.3	11.4	13.6	14.0	15.7
Married................	93.8	99.5	102.0	104.1	46.7	49.5	50.6	51.8	47.1	49.9	51.3	52.2
Widowed...............	10.9	11.7	11.3	11.5	1.6	1.9	1.9	2.2	9.3	9.8	9.4	9.3
Divorced	8.3	12.6	14.8	16.5	3.4	5.4	6.3	7.2	5.0	7.3	8.4	9.3
Percent of total	100.0	100.0	100.0	100.0	100.0	100.0	100.0	100.0	100.0	100.0	100.0	100.0
Never married	18.9	20.3	20.6	21.4	22.5	24.1	24.6	24.9	15.7	16.9	16.9	18.1
Married................	67.2	64.0	63.2	62.0	70.0	66.2	64.9	63.5	64.7	61.9	61.7	60.2
Widowed...............	7.8	7.5	7.0	6.8	2.5	2.6	2.5	2.7	12.8	12.2	11.3	10.7
Divorced	6.0	8.1	9.1	9.8	5.0	7.2	8.1	8.8	6.8	9.0	10.1	10.7
Black, total	**16.6**	**20.3**	**22.1**	**24.0**	**7.4**	**9.1**	**9.9**	**10.7**	**9.2**	**11.2**	**12.2**	**13.3**
Never married	5.1	7.1	8.5	9.5	2.5	3.5	4.1	4.3	2.5	3.6	4.4	5.1
Married................	8.5	9.3	9.6	10.1	4.1	4.5	4.6	5.0	4.5	4.8	4.9	5.1
Widowed...............	1.6	1.7	1.7	1.7	0.3	0.3	0.3	0.3	1.3	1.4	1.4	1.4
Divorced	1.4	2.1	2.4	2.8	0.5	0.8	0.8	1.1	0.9	1.3	1.5	1.7
Percent of total	100.0	100.0	100.0	100.0	100.0	100.0	100.0	100.0	100.0	100.0	100.0	100.0
Never married	30.5	35.1	38.4	39.6	34.3	38.4	41.7	40.2	27.4	32.5	35.8	38.3
Married................	51.4	45.8	43.2	42.1	54.6	49.2	46.7	46.7	48.7	43.0	40.4	38.3
Widowed...............	9.8	8.5	7.6	7.1	4.2	3.7	3.1	2.8	14.3	12.4	11.3	10.5
Divorced	8.4	10.6	10.7	11.7	7.0	8.8	8.5	10.3	9.5	12.0	12.5	12.8
Hispanic, [2] **total**	**7.9**	**13.6**	**17.6**	**21.1**	**3.8**	**6.7**	**8.8**	**10.4**	**4.1**	**6.8**	**8.8**	**10.7**
Never married	1.9	3.7	5.0	5.9	1.0	2.2	3.0	3.4	0.9	1.5	2.1	2.5
Married................	5.2	8.4	10.4	12.7	2.5	4.1	5.1	6.2	2.6	4.3	5.3	6.5
Widowed...............	0.4	0.5	0.7	0.9	0.1	0.1	0.2	0.2	0.3	0.4	0.6	0.7
Divorced	0.5	1.0	1.4	1.6	0.2	0.4	0.6	0.7	0.3	0.6	0.8	1.0
Percent of total	100.0	100.0	100.0	100.0	100.0	100.0	100.0	100.0	100.0	100.0	100.0	100.0
Never married	24.1	27.2	28.6	28.0	27.3	32.1	33.8	32.7	21.1	22.5	23.5	23.4
Married................	65.6	61.7	59.3	60.2	67.1	60.9	57.9	59.6	64.3	62.4	60.7	60.7
Widowed...............	4.4	4.0	4.2	4.2	1.6	1.5	1.8	1.9	7.1	6.5	6.6	6.5
Divorced	5.8	7.0	7.9	7.6	4.0	5.5	6.6	6.7	7.6	8.5	9.2	9.3

[1] Includes persons of other races, not shown separately.   [2] Hispanic persons may be of any race.

Source: U.S. Census Bureau, *Current Population Reports*, P20-537, and earlier reports; and unpublished data.

No. 47. Married Couples of Same or Mixed Races and Origins: 1980 to 2000

[In thousands (49,714 represents 49,714,000). As of March. Persons 15 years old and over. Persons of Hispanic origin may be of any race. Except as noted, based on Current Population Survey; see headnote, Table 51]

Race and origin of spouses	1980	1990	1995	1999	2000
Married couples, total.	**49,714**	**53,256**	**54,937**	**55,849**	**56,497**
RACE					
White/White.	44,910	47,202	48,030	48,455	48,917
Black/Black.	3,354	3,687	3,703	3,868	3,989
Black/White.	167	211	328	364	363
Black husband/White wife.	122	150	206	240	268
White husband/Black wife.	45	61	122	124	95
White/other race [1]	450	720	988	1,086	1,051
Black/other race [1].	34	33	76	31	50
All other couples [1]	799	1,401	1,811	2,045	2,127
HISPANIC ORIGIN					
Hispanic/Hispanic.	1,906	3,085	3,857	4,480	4,739
Hispanic/other origin (not Hispanic)	891	1,193	1,434	1,647	1,743
All other couples (not of Hispanic origin).	46,917	48,979	49,646	49,722	50,015

[1] Excluding White and Black.

Source: U.S. Census Bureau, *Current Population Reports*, P20-537, and earlier reports; and unpublished data.

Population   47

No. 48. Marital Status of the Population by Sex and Age: 2000

[As of March (96,900 represents 96,900,000). Persons 18 years old and over. Excludes members of Armed Forces except those living off post or with their families on post. Based on Current Population Survey; see text, this section, and Appendix III]

Sex and age	Number of persons (1,000)					Percent distribution				
	Total	Never married	Married	Wid-owed	Divorced	Total	Never married	Married	Wid-owed	Divorced
Male	**96,900**	**26,124**	**59,631**	**2,601**	**8,544**	**100.0**	**27.0**	**61.5**	**2.7**	**8.8**
18 to 19 years old	4,082	4,011	70	-	1	100.0	98.3	1.7	-	-
20 to 24 years old	9,208	7,710	1,397	-	101	100.0	83.7	15.2	-	1.1
25 to 29 years old	8,943	4,625	3,967	9	342	100.0	51.7	44.4	0.1	3.8
30 to 34 years old	9,621	2,899	5,996	15	712	100.0	30.0	62.3	0.2	7.4
35 to 39 years old	11,032	2,241	7,440	42	1,308	100.0	20.3	67.4	0.4	11.9
40 to 44 years old	11,103	1,740	7,842	54	1,467	100.0	15.7	70.6	0.5	13.2
45 to 54 years old	17,889	1,697	13,660	157	2,377	100.0	9.5	76.4	0.9	13.3
55 to 64 years old	11,137	612	8,809	329	1,387	100.0	5.5	79.1	3.0	12.5
65 to 74 years old	8,051	348	6,411	667	625	100.0	4.3	79.6	8.3	7.8
75 years old and over . . .	5,838	242	4,044	1,327	225	100.0	4.1	69.3	22.7	3.9
Female	**104,863**	**22,089**	**60,436**	**11,054**	**11,284**	**100.0**	**21.1**	**57.6**	**10.5**	**10.8**
18 to 19 years old	4,009	3,727	270	2	10	100.0	93.0	6.7	-	0.2
20 to 24 years old	9,232	6,720	2,333	11	168	100.0	72.8	25.3	0.1	1.8
25 to 29 years old	9,326	3,627	5,106	18	575	100.0	38.9	54.8	0.1	6.2
30 to 34 years old	9,897	2,172	6,758	63	904	100.0	21.9	68.3	0.6	9.1
35 to 39 years old	11,288	1,610	8,061	131	1,486	100.0	14.3	71.4	1.2	13.2
40 to 44 years old	11,382	1,341	8,163	172	1,706	100.0	11.8	71.7	1.5	15.0
45 to 54 years old	18,742	1,606	13,191	725	3,220	100.0	8.6	70.4	3.9	17.2
55 to 64 years old	12,251	606	8,333	1,441	1,871	100.0	4.9	68.0	11.8	15.3
65 to 74 years old	9,748	363	5,424	3,055	906	100.0	3.7	55.6	31.3	9.3
75 years old and over . . .	8,988	317	2,799	5,435	438	100.0	3.5	31.1	60.5	4.9

- Represents or rounds to zero.

Source: U.S. Census Bureau, *Current Population Reports*, P20-537 and earlier reports.

No. 49. Unmarried-Partner Households by Sex of Partners: 2000

[As of April]

Item	Number
Total households	**105,480,101**
Unmarried-partner households.	5,475,768
Male householder and male partner	301,026
Male householder and female partner	2,615,119
Female householder and female partner	293,365
Female householder and male partner.	2,266,258
All other households	100,004,333

Source: U.S. Census Bureau, American FactFinder, PCT14. Unmarried-Partner Households by Sex of Partners; Census 2000 Summary File 1 (SF 1) 100-Percent Data.

No. 50. Households, 1980 to 2000, and Persons in Households, 2000, by Type of Household

[As of March (80,776 represents 80,776,000). Based on Current Population Survey; see headnote, Table 51]

Type of household	Households					Persons in households, 2000		Persons per house-hold, 2000
	Number (1,000)			Percent distribution				
	1980	1990	2000	1990	2000	Number (1,000)	Percent distribu-tion	
Total households	**80,776**	**93,347**	**104,705**	**100**	**100**	**273,901**	**100**	**2.62**
Family households	59,550	66,090	72,025	71	69	233,115	85	3.24
Married couple family.	49,112	52,317	55,311	56	53	180,224	66	3.26
Male householder, no spouse present. . .	1,733	2,884	4,028	3	4	12,734	5	3.16
Female householder, no spouse present .	8,705	10,890	12,687	12	12	40,156	15	3.17
Nonfamily households	21,226	27,257	32,680	29	31	40,787	15	1.25
Living alone	18,296	22,999	26,724	25	26	26,724	10	1.00
Male householder	8,807	11,606	14,641	12	14	19,674	7	1.34
Living alone	6,966	9,049	11,181	10	11	11,181	4	1.00
Female householder	12,419	15,651	18,039	17	17	21,112	8	1.17
Living alone	11,330	13,950	15,543	15	15	15,543	6	1.00

Source: U.S. Census Bureau, *Current Population Reports*, P20-537, and earlier reports; and unpublished data.

No. 51. Households, Families, Subfamilies, and Married Couples: 1980 to 2000

[In thousands, except as indicated (80,776 represents 80,776,000). As of March. Based on Current Population Survey; includes members of Armed Forces living off post or with their families on post, but excludes all other members of Armed Forces; see text, this section, and Appendix III. For definition of terms, see text, this section. Minus sign (-) indicates decrease]

Type of unit	1980	1985	1990	1995	1997	1998	1999	2000	Percent change 1980-90	Percent change 1990-2000
Households	**80,776**	**86,789**	**93,347**	**98,990**	**101,018**	**102,528**	**103,874**	**104,705**	16	12
Average size	2.76	2.69	2.63	2.65	2.64	2.62	2.61	2.62	(X)	(X)
Family households	59,550	62,706	66,090	69,305	70,241	70,880	71,535	72,025	11	9
Married couple	49,112	50,350	52,317	53,858	53,604	54,317	54,770	55,311	7	6
Male householder [1]	1,733	2,228	2,884	3,226	3,847	3,911	3,976	4,028	66	40
Female householder [1]	8,705	10,129	10,890	12,220	12,790	12,652	12,789	12,687	25	17
Nonfamily households	21,226	24,082	27,257	29,686	30,777	31,648	32,339	32,680	28	20
Male householder	8,807	10,114	11,606	13,190	13,707	14,133	14,368	14,641	32	26
Female householder	12,419	13,968	15,651	16,496	17,070	17,516	17,971	18,039	26	15
One person	18,296	20,602	22,999	24,732	25,402	26,327	26,606	26,724	26	16
Families	**59,550**	**62,706**	**66,090**	**69,305**	**70,241**	**70,880**	**71,535**	**72,025**	11	9
Average size	3.29	3.23	3.17	3.19	3.19	3.18	3.18	3.17	(X)	(X)
With own children [2]	31,022	31,112	32,289	34,296	34,665	34,760	34,613	34,605	4	7
Without own children [2]	28,528	31,594	33,801	35,009	35,575	36,120	36,922	37,420	18	11
Married couple	49,112	50,350	52,317	53,858	53,604	54,317	54,770	55,311	7	6
With own children [2]	24,961	24,210	24,537	25,241	25,083	25,269	25,066	25,248	-2	3
Without own children [2]	24,151	26,140	27,780	28,617	28,521	29,048	29,703	30,062	15	8
Male householder [1]	1,733	2,228	2,884	3,226	3,847	3,911	3,976	4,028	66	40
With own children [2]	616	896	1,153	1,440	1,709	1,798	1,706	1,786	87	55
Without own children [2]	1,117	1,332	1,731	1,786	2,138	2,113	2,270	2,242	55	30
Female householder [1]	8,705	10,129	10,890	12,220	12,790	12,652	12,789	12,687	25	17
With own children [2]	5,445	6,006	6,599	7,615	7,874	7,693	7,841	7,571	21	15
Without own children [2]	3,261	4,123	4,290	4,606	4,916	4,960	4,948	5,116	32	19
Unrelated subfamilies	360	526	534	674	615	575	522	571	48	7
Married couple	20	46	68	64	50	41	50	37	(B)	(B)
Male reference persons [1] . . .	36	85	45	59	77	72	64	57	(B)	(B)
Female reference persons [1] . . .	304	395	421	550	487	463	408	477	39	13
Related subfamilies	1,150	2,228	2,403	2,878	2,907	2,870	2,901	2,984	109	24
Married couple	582	719	871	1,015	1,012	947	1,029	1,149	50	32
Father-child [1]	54	116	153	195	244	250	281	201	(B)	31
Mother-child [1]	512	1,392	1,378	1,668	1,651	1,673	1,591	1,634	169	19
Married couples	**49,714**	**51,114**	**53,256**	**54,937**	**54,666**	**55,305**	**55,849**	**56,497**	7	6
With own household	49,112	50,350	52,317	53,858	53,604	54,317	54,770	55,311	7	6
Without own household	602	764	939	1,079	1,062	988	1,079	1,186	56	26
Percent without	1.2	1.5	1.8	2.0	1.9	1.8	1.9	2.1	(X)	(X)

B Not shown; base less than 75,000.   X Not applicable.   [1] No spouse present.   [2] Under 18 years old.

Source: U.S. Census Bureau, *Current Population Reports*, P20-537, and earlier reports.

No. 52. Households by Age of Householder and Size of Household: 1980 to 2000

[In millions (80.8 represents 80,800,000). As of March. Based on Current Population Survey; see headnote, Table 51]

Age of householder and size of household	1980	1985	1990	1995	1999	2000 Total [1]	2000 White	2000 Black	2000 His-panic [2]
Total	**80.8**	**86.8**	**93.3**	**99.0**	**103.9**	**104.7**	**87.7**	**12.8**	**9.3**
Age of householder:									
15 to 24 years old	6.6	5.4	5.1	5.4	5.9	5.9	4.5	1.0	0.9
25 to 29 years old	9.3	9.6	9.4	8.4	8.5	8.5	6.7	1.3	1.1
30 to 34 years old	9.3	10.4	11.0	11.1	10.3	10.1	8.1	1.4	1.3
35 to 44 years old	14.0	17.5	20.6	22.9	24.0	24.0	19.8	3.1	2.5
45 to 54 years old	12.7	12.6	14.5	17.6	20.2	20.9	17.5	2.6	1.5
55 to 64 years old	12.5	13.1	12.5	12.2	13.6	13.6	11.6	1.5	0.9
65 to 74 years old	10.1	10.9	11.7	11.8	11.4	11.3	9.9	1.1	0.6
75 years old and over	6.4	7.3	8.4	9.6	10.2	10.4	9.5	0.8	0.4
One person	18.3	20.6	23.0	24.7	26.6	26.7	22.3	3.6	1.3
Male	7.0	7.9	9.0	10.1	11.0	11.2	9.2	1.6	0.7
Female	11.3	12.7	14.0	14.6	15.6	15.5	13.1	2.0	0.6
Two persons	25.3	27.4	30.1	31.8	34.3	34.7	30.1	3.4	1.9
Three persons	14.1	15.5	16.1	16.8	17.4	17.2	13.8	2.5	1.8
Four persons	12.7	13.6	14.5	15.3	15.0	15.3	12.8	1.7	1.9
Five persons	6.1	6.1	6.2	6.6	7.0	7.0	5.7	0.9	1.3
Six persons	2.5	2.3	2.1	2.3	2.4	2.4	1.8	0.4	0.6
Seven persons or more	1.8	1.3	1.3	1.4	1.3	1.4	1.1	0.2	0.5

[1] Includes other races, not shown separately.   [2] Hispanic persons may be of any race.

Source: U.S. Census Bureau, *Current Population Reports*, P20-537, and earlier reports; and unpublished data.

Population   49

No. 53. Households—States: 2000

[As of April (105,480 represents 105,480,000). For definitions of household and family, see text, this section]

State	Households (1,000)									Average household size
	Family households							Nonfamily households		
	Total [1]		Married couple		Female family householder [2]					
	Total	Total	With own children under 18 years	Total	With own children under 18 years	Total	With own children under 18 years	Total	Householder living alone	
U.S.	105,480	71,787	34,588	54,493	24,836	12,900	7,562	33,693	27,230	2.59
AL	1,737	1,216	561	907	391	246	141	521	454	2.49
AK	222	152	88	116	63	24	17	69	52	2.74
AZ	1,901	1,287	608	986	429	211	130	614	472	2.64
AR	1,043	732	335	566	237	127	77	310	267	2.49
CA	11,503	7,920	4,117	5,877	2,990	1,449	835	3,583	2,708	2.87
CO	1,658	1,084	544	859	405	159	102	574	436	2.53
CT	1,302	881	419	676	307	157	91	421	344	2.53
DE	299	205	95	153	66	39	23	94	75	2.54
DC	248	114	49	57	21	47	25	134	109	2.16
FL	6,338	4,211	1,780	3,192	1,215	759	438	2,127	1,687	2.46
GA	3,006	2,112	1,051	1,549	733	435	258	895	711	2.65
HI	403	287	129	216	97	50	24	116	88	2.92
ID	470	336	170	277	132	41	27	134	105	2.69
IL	4,592	3,106	1,515	2,354	1,114	564	316	1,486	1,230	2.63
IN	2,336	1,603	768	1,251	556	259	160	734	605	2.53
IA	1,149	770	361	633	275	98	64	380	313	2.46
KS	1,038	702	345	568	261	97	63	336	280	2.51
KY	1,591	1,104	516	858	375	188	111	486	414	2.47
LA	1,656	1,156	572	809	374	275	162	500	419	2.62
ME	518	341	157	272	113	49	32	178	140	2.39
MD	1,981	1,359	662	995	461	280	159	622	495	2.61
MA	2,444	1,577	749	1,198	548	290	164	867	684	2.51
MI	3,786	2,576	1,237	1,948	873	474	284	1,210	994	2.56
MN	1,895	1,255	626	1,018	478	169	111	640	509	2.52
MS	1,046	747	363	521	234	181	106	299	258	2.63
MO	2,195	1,477	700	1,141	497	254	157	718	600	2.48
MT	359	237	112	192	82	32	21	121	98	2.45
NE	666	443	218	361	166	60	40	223	184	2.49
NV	751	498	239	373	166	83	51	253	187	2.62
NH	475	324	158	262	120	43	27	151	116	2.53
NJ	3,065	2,155	1,026	1,638	776	387	197	910	751	2.68
NM	678	467	235	342	158	90	56	211	172	2.63
NY	7,057	4,639	2,231	3,290	1,527	1,038	573	2,417	1,983	2.61
NC	3,132	2,159	996	1,645	708	390	227	973	795	2.49
ND	257	166	80	137	62	20	14	91	75	2.41
OH	4,446	2,993	1,410	2,286	996	537	323	1,453	1,216	2.49
OK	1,342	922	435	718	312	153	94	421	359	2.49
OR	1,334	878	411	693	296	131	83	456	348	2.51
PA	4,777	3,208	1,431	2,468	1,043	555	298	1,569	1,321	2.48
RI	408	265	125	197	86	53	32	143	117	2.47
SC	1,534	1,073	495	783	334	227	131	461	383	2.53
SD	290	194	95	157	71	26	18	96	80	2.50
TN	2,233	1,548	707	1,174	499	288	166	685	576	2.48
TX	7,393	5,248	2,723	3,990	2,002	938	564	2,146	1,752	2.74
UT	701	535	300	443	246	66	40	166	125	3.13
VT	241	158	76	126	56	22	15	83	63	2.44
VA	2,699	1,848	882	1,426	646	320	187	851	677	2.54
WA	2,271	1,499	742	1,182	542	225	147	772	594	2.53
WV	736	504	213	397	157	79	42	232	200	2.40
WI	2,085	1,387	665	1,109	494	200	129	698	558	2.50
WY	194	130	63	106	47	17	12	63	51	2.48

[1] Includes male family householders with no spouse present, not shown separately.   [2] No spouse present.

Source: U.S. Census Bureau, *2000 Census of Population and Housing, Profiles of General Demographic Characteristics.*

No. 54. Family Groups with Children Under 18 Years Old by Race and Hispanic Origin: 1980 to 2000

[In thousands. As of March (32,150 represents 32,150,000). Family groups comprise family households, related subfamilies, and unrelated subfamilies. Excludes members of Armed Forces except those living off post or with their families on post. Based on Current Population Survey; see text, this section, and Appendix III]

Race and Hispanic origin of householder or reference person	1980	1990	1995	2000 Total	2000 Family house-holds	2000 Subfamilies Total	2000 Subfamilies Related	2000 Subfamilies Unrelated
All races, total [1]	**32,150**	**34,670**	**37,168**	**37,496**	**34,605**	**2,890**	**2,346**	**544**
Two-parent family groups	25,231	24,921	25,640	25,771	25,248	523	512	11
One-parent family groups	6,920	9,749	11,528	11,725	9,357	2,368	1,834	534
Maintained by mother	6,230	8,398	9,834	9,681	7,571	2,110	1,633	477
Maintained by father	690	1,351	1,694	2,044	1,786	258	201	57
White, total.	**27,294**	**28,294**	**29,846**	**30,079**	**28,107**	**1,973**	**1,558**	**415**
Two-parent family groups	22,628	21,905	22,320	22,241	21,809	433	422	11
One-parent family groups	4,664	6,389	7,525	7,838	6,298	1,540	1,136	404
Maintained by mother	4,122	5,310	6,239	6,216	4,869	1,347	995	352
Maintained by father	542	1,079	1,286	1,622	1,429	193	140	53
Black, total.	**4,074**	**5,087**	**5,491**	**5,530**	**4,782**	**748**	**642**	**106**
Two-parent family groups	1,961	2,006	1,962	2,135	2,093	41	41	-
One-parent family groups	2,114	3,081	3,529	3,396	2,689	706	600	106
Maintained by mother	1,984	2,860	3,197	3,060	2,409	651	550	101
Maintained by father	129	221	332	335	280	55	50	5
Hispanic, total [2]	**2,194**	**3,429**	**4,527**	**5,503**	**4,814**	**688**	**596**	**92**
Two-parent family groups	1,626	2,289	2,879	3,625	3,423	203	194	9
One-parent family groups	568	1,140	1,647	1,877	1,391	486	402	84
Maintained by mother	526	1,003	1,404	1,565	1,145	420	347	73
Maintained by father	42	138	243	313	246	66	55	11

- Represents or rounds to zero.   [1] Includes other races, not shown separately.   [2] Hispanic persons may be of any race.

Source: U.S. Census Bureau, *Current Population Reports*, P20-537, and earlier reports; and unpublished data.

No. 55. Families by Number of Own Children Under 18 Years Old: 1980 to 2000

[As of March (59,550 represents 59,550,000) and based on Current Population Survey; see headnote, Table 56]

Race, Hispanic origin, and year	Number of families (1,000) Total	Number of families (1,000) No chil-dren	Number of families (1,000) One child	Number of families (1,000) Two chil-dren	Number of families (1,000) Three or more chil-dren	Percent distribution Total	Percent distribution No chil-dren	Percent distribution One child	Percent distribution Two chil-dren	Percent distribution Three or more children
ALL FAMILIES [1]										
1980	59,550	28,528	12,443	11,470	7,109	100	48	21	19	12
1990	66,090	33,801	13,530	12,263	6,496	100	51	20	19	10
1995	69,305	35,009	14,088	13,213	6,995	100	51	20	19	10
2000	72,025	37,420	14,311	13,215	7,080	100	52	20	18	10
Married couple	55,311	30,062	9,402	10,274	5,572	100	54	17	19	10
Male householder [2]	4,028	2,242	1,131	483	171	100	56	28	12	4
Female householder [2]	12,687	5,116	3,777	2,458	1,336	100	40	30	19	11
WHITE FAMILIES										
1980	52,243	25,769	10,727	9,977	5,769	100	49	21	19	11
1990	56,590	29,872	11,186	10,342	5,191	100	53	20	18	9
1995	58,437	30,486	11,491	10,983	5,478	100	52	20	19	9
2000	60,251	32,144	11,496	10,918	5,693	100	53	19	18	9
Married couple	48,790	26,981	8,023	8,970	4,816	100	55	16	18	10
Male householder [2]	3,081	1,652	885	400	144	100	54	29	13	5
Female householder [2]	8,380	3,511	2,588	1,548	732	100	42	31	18	9
BLACK FAMILIES										
1980	6,184	2,364	1,449	1,235	1,136	100	38	23	20	18
1990	7,470	3,093	1,894	1,433	1,049	100	41	25	19	14
1995	8,093	3,411	1,971	1,593	1,117	100	42	24	20	14
2000	8,664	3,882	2,101	1,624	1,058	100	45	24	19	12
Married couple	4,144	2,050	838	754	501	100	49	20	18	12
Male householder [2]	706	427	196	62	21	100	60	28	9	3
Female householder [2]	3,814	1,405	1,066	807	536	100	37	28	21	14
HISPANIC FAMILIES [3]										
1980	3,029	946	680	698	706	100	31	22	23	23
1990	4,840	1,790	1,095	1,036	919	100	37	23	21	19
1995	6,200	2,216	1,408	1,406	1,171	100	36	23	23	19
2000	7,561	2,747	1,791	1,693	1,330	100	36	24	22	18
Married couple	5,133	1,710	1,139	1,276	1,008	100	33	22	25	20
Male householder [2]	658	412	141	68	38	100	63	21	10	6
Female householder [2]	1,769	625	511	350	284	100	35	29	20	16

[1] Includes other races, not shown separately.   [2] No spouse present.   [3] Hispanic persons may be of any race.

Source: U.S. Census Bureau, *Current Population Reports*, P20-537, and earlier reports; and unpublished data.

No. 56. Families by Size and Presence of Children: 1980 to 2000

[In thousands, except as indicated (59,550 represents 59,550,000). As of March. Excludes members of Armed Forces except those living off post or with their families on post. Based on Current Population Survey; see text, this section, and Appendix III. For definition of families, see text, this section]

Characteristic	Number					Percent distribution				
	1980	1985	1990	1995	2000	1980	1985	1990	1995	2000
Total.	59,550	62,706	66,090	69,305	72,025	100	100	100	100	100
Size of family:										
Two persons	23,461	25,349	27,606	29,176	31,455	39	40	42	42	44
Three persons	13,603	14,804	15,353	15,903	16,073	23	24	23	23	22
Four persons	12,372	13,259	14,026	14,624	14,496	21	21	21	21	20
Five persons	5,930	5,894	5,938	6,283	6,526	10	9	9	9	9
Six persons	2,461	2,175	1,997	2,106	2,226	4	4	3	3	3
Seven or more persons . .	1,723	1,225	1,170	1,213	1,249	3	2	2	2	2
Average per family	3.29	3.23	3.17	3.19	3.17	(X)	(X)	(X)	(X)	(X)
Own children under age 18:										
None	28,528	31,594	33,801	35,009	37,420	48	50	51	51	52
One	12,443	13,108	13,530	14,088	14,311	21	21	20	20	20
Two	11,470	11,645	12,263	13,213	13,215	19	19	19	19	18
Three	4,674	4,486	4,650	5,044	5,063	8	7	7	7	7
Four or more	2,435	1,873	1,846	1,951	2,017	4	3	3	3	3
Own children under age 6:										
None	46,063	48,505	50,905	53,695	57,039	77	77	77	77	79
One	9,441	9,677	10,304	10,733	10,454	16	15	16	15	15
Two or more	4,047	4,525	4,882	4,876	4,533	7	7	7	7	6

X Not applicable.

Source: U.S. Census Bureau, *Current Population Reports*, P20-537, and earlier reports; and unpublished data.

No. 57. Families by Type, Race, and Hispanic Origin: 2000

[In thousands, except as indicated (72,025 represents 72,025,000). As of March. Excludes members of Armed Forces except those living off post or with their families on post. Based on Current Population Survey; see text of this section and Appendix III. For definition of families, see text of this section]

Characteristic	Married couple families				Female family householder [3]				Male family house-holder, [3] all races
	All families	All races [1]	White	Black	His-panic [2]	All races [1]	White	Black	His-panic [2]	
All families	72,025	55,311	48,790	4,144	5,133	12,687	8,380	3,814	1,769	4,028
Age of householder:										
Under 25 years old.	3,353	1,450	1,298	93	315	1,342	770	502	213	560
25 to 34 years old	13,007	9,390	8,128	783	1,436	2,732	1,586	1,039	433	886
35 to 44 years old	18,706	14,104	12,271	1,194	1,534	3,499	2,455	918	512	1,102
45 to 54 years old	15,803	12,792	11,174	984	911	2,299	1,555	658	307	713
55 to 64 years old	9,569	8,138	7,269	554	509	1,080	701	323	158	351
65 to 74 years old	7,025	5,929	5,380	360	291	894	632	229	102	203
75 years old and over.	4,562	3,508	3,270	175	136	841	681	146	44	213
Without own children under 18. .	37,420	30,062	26,981	2,050	1,710	5,116	3,511	1,405	625	2,242
With own children under 18. . . .	34,605	25,248	21,809	2,093	3,423	7,571	4,869	2,409	1,145	1,786
One own child under 18	14,311	9,402	8,023	838	1,139	3,777	2,588	1,066	511	1,131
Two own children under 18 . .	13,215	10,274	8,970	754	1,276	2,458	1,548	807	350	483
Three or more own children under 18.	7,080	5,572	4,816	501	1,008	1,336	732	536	284	171
Average per family with own children under 18.	1.87	1.94	1.93	1.99	2.14	1.75	1.66	1.91	1.95	1.50
Marital status of householder:										
Married, spouse present	55,311	55,311	48,790	4,144	5,133	(X)	(X)	(X)	(X)	(X)
Married, spouse absent.	2,434	(X)	(X)	(X)	(X)	1,878	1,210	567	404	555
Separated	1,757	(X)	(X)	(X)	(X)	1,426	908	463	301	331
Other	677	(X)	(X)	(X)	(X)	452	302	104	103	224
Widowed	2,797	(X)	(X)	(X)	(X)	2,371	1,764	522	252	426
Divorced.	5,820	(X)	(X)	(X)	(X)	4,431	3,431	874	475	1,389
Never married	5,665	(X)	(X)	(X)	(X)	4,007	1,974	1,851	639	1,658

X Not applicable.   [1] Includes other races not shown separately.   [2] Persons of Hispanic origin may be of any race.   [3] No spouse present.

Source: U.S. Census Bureau, *Current Population Reports*, P20-537.

No. 58. Family Households With Own Children Under Age 18 by Type of Family, 1980 to 2000, and by Age of Householder, 2000

[As of March (31,022 represents 31,022,000). Excludes members of Armed Forces except those living off post or with their families on post. Based on Current Population Survey; see text, this section, and Appendix III]

Family type	1980	1990	2000 Total	15 to 24 years old	25 to 34 years old	35 to 44 years old	45 to 54 years old	55 to 64 years old	65 years old and over
NUMBER (1,000)									
Family households with children...	**31,022**	**32,289**	**34,605**	**2,000**	**9,886**	**15,104**	**6,617**	**865**	**133**
Married couple	24,961	24,537	25,248	834	6,830	11,405	5,401	671	107
Male householder [1]	616	1,153	1,786	123	530	737	305	74	15
Female householder [1]	5,445	6,599	7,571	1,042	2,525	2,962	911	119	11
HOUSEHOLDS WITH CHILDREN, AS A PERCENT OF ALL FAMILY HOUSEHOLDS BY TYPE									
Family households with children, total	**52**	**49**	**48**	**60**	**76**	**81**	**42**	**9**	**1**
Married couple	51	47	46	58	73	81	42	8	1
Male householder [1]	36	40	44	22	60	67	43	21	4
Female householder [1]	63	61	60	78	92	85	40	11	1

[1] No spouse present.

Source: U.S. Census Bureau, *Current Population Reports*, P20-537 and earlier reports.

No. 59. Nonfamily Households by Sex and Age of Householder: 2000

[In thousands (14,641 represents 14,641,000). As of March. See headnote, Table 56]

Item	Male householder Total	15 to 24 yr. old	25 to 44 yr. old	45 to 64 yr. old	65 yr. old and over	Female householder Total	15 to 24 yr. old	25 to 44 yr. old	45 to 64 yr. old	65 yr. old and over
Total	**14,641**	**1,286**	**6,709**	**4,116**	**2,530**	**18,039**	**1,221**	**4,161**	**5,031**	**7,626**
One person (living alone) . .	11,181	556	4,848	3,422	2,355	15,543	588	3,108	4,420	7,427
Nonrelatives present	3,460	731	1,860	693	175	2,496	634	1,052	612	199
Never married.	7,274	1,246	4,465	1,188	374	5,671	1,169	2,910	1,119	472
Married [1]	1,180	25	527	460	166	980	19	293	390	278
Widowed	1,684	-	36	269	1,380	7,018	5	73	1,047	5,894
Divorced	4,503	15	1,680	2,198	610	4,371	28	885	2,476	982

- Represents or rounds to zero.   [1] No spouse present.

Source: U.S. Census Bureau, *Current Population Reports*, P20-537.

No. 60. Persons Living Alone by Sex and Age: 1980 to 2000

[As of March (18,296 represents 18,296,000). Based on Current Population Survey; see headnote, Table 56]

Sex and age	Number of persons (1,000) 1980	1985	1990	1995	2000	Percent distribution 1980	1985	1990	1995	2000
Both sexes	**18,296**	**20,602**	**22,999**	**24,732**	**26,724**	**100**	**100**	**100**	**100**	**100**
15 to 24 years old	1,726	1,324	1,210	1,196	1,144	9	6	5	5	4
25 to 34 years old	[1]4,729	3,905	3,972	3,653	3,848	[1]26	19	17	15	14
35 to 44 years old	([1])	2,322	3,138	3,663	4,109	([1])	11	14	15	15
45 to 64 years old	4,514	4,939	5,502	6,377	7,842	25	24	24	26	29
65 to 74 years old	3,851	4,130	4,350	4,374	4,091	21	20	19	18	15
75 years old and over	3,477	3,982	4,825	5,470	5,692	19	19	21	22	21
Male.	**6,966**	**7,922**	**9,049**	**10,140**	**11,181**	**38**	**39**	**39**	**41**	**42**
15 to 24 years old	947	750	674	623	556	5	4	3	3	2
25 to 34 years old	[1]2,920	2,307	2,395	2,213	2,279	[1]16	11	10	9	9
35 to 44 years old	([1])	1,406	1,836	2,263	2,569	([1])	7	8	9	10
45 to 64 years old	1,613	1,845	2,203	2,787	3,422	9	9	10	11	13
65 to 74 years old	775	868	1,042	1,134	1,108	4	4	5	5	4
75 years old and over	711	746	901	1,120	1,247	4	4	4	5	5
Female.	**11,330**	**12,680**	**13,950**	**14,592**	**15,543**	**62**	**62**	**61**	**59**	**58**
15 to 24 years old	779	573	536	572	588	4	3	2	2	2
25 to 34 years old	[1]1,809	1,598	1,578	1,440	1,568	[1]10	8	7	6	6
35 to 44 years old	([1])	916	1,303	1,399	1,540	([1])	4	6	6	6
45 to 64 years old	2,901	3,095	3,300	3,589	4,420	16	15	14	15	17
65 to 74 years old	3,076	3,262	3,309	3,240	2,983	17	16	14	13	11
75 years old and over	2,766	3,236	3,924	4,351	4,444	15	16	17	18	17

[1] Data for persons 35 to 44 years old included with persons 25 to 34 years old.

Source: U.S. Census Bureau, *Current Population Reports*, P20-537, and earlier reports; and unpublished data.

U.S. Census Bureau, Statistical Abstract of the United States: 2002

No. 61. Population in Group Quarters by Sex, Age, and Group Quarters Type: 2000

[In thousands (7,779 represents 7,779,000). As of April. For definitions of group quarters, see text, this section]

Group quarters type	Total population	Male Total	Male Under 18 years	Male 18 to 64 years	Male 65 years and over	Female Total	Female Under 18 years	Female 18 to 64 years	Female 65 years and over
Total	**7,779**	**4,502**	**215**	**3,740**	**548**	**3,276**	**108**	**1,722**	**1,446**
Institutionalized population	4,059	2,534	122	1,968	444	1,525	36	292	1,197
Correctional institutions.........	1,976	1,806	19	1,773	14	170	2	166	2
Nursing homes	1,721	488	-	88	401	1,232	-	75	1,157
Hospitals/wards and hospices for chronically ill	40	20	1	10	9	20	1	6	14
Mental (psychiatric) hospitals or wards................	79	50	7	37	6	29	4	18	7
Juvenile institutions	128	101	88	13	-	27	24	2	-
Other institutions	115	68	8	47	14	47	5	25	18
Noninstitutionalized population	3,720	1,968	93	1,772	104	1,751	72	1,431	249
College dormitories [1]	2,064	958	5	952	-	1,107	5	1,101	-
Military quarters	355	307	1	306	-	48	1	47	-
Other noninstitutional group quarters	1,300	703	86	513	104	597	66	283	249

- Represents or rounds to zero.   [1] Includes college quarters off campus.

Source: U.S. Census Bureau, American FactFinder, PCT17. Group Quarters Population by Sex by Age by Group Quarters Type, Census 2000 Summary File 1 (SF 1) 100-Percent Data.

No. 62. Population in Group Quarters—States: 2000

[As of April. For definitions of group quarters, see text, this section]

State	Group quarters population [1]	Correctional institutions	Nursing homes	College dormitories [2]	State	Group quarters population [1]	Correctional institutions	Nursing homes	College dormitories [2]
U.S., total ..	**7,778,633**	**1,976,019**	**1,720,500**	**2,064,128**	MS.	95,414	25,778	18,382	29,238
					MO	162,058	35,206	48,708	44,587
					MT.....	24,762	4,124	6,470	7,035
AL	114,720	33,542	26,697	31,086	NE......	50,818	6,060	16,195	18,376
AK......	19,349	3,331	803	1,748	NV.....	33,675	15,940	4,895	2,498
AZ......	109,850	45,783	13,607	17,340	NH......	35,539	3,468	9,316	17,574
AR......	73,908	20,565	21,379	18,280	NJ	194,821	47,941	51,493	45,222
CA......	819,754	248,516	120,724	126,715	NM.....	36,307	10,940	6,810	7,921
CO......	102,955	30,136	18,495	23,631	NY......	580,461	108,088	123,852	174,111
CT......	107,939	20,023	32,223	38,051	NC.....	253,881	46,614	50,892	76,018
DE.....	24,583	5,965	4,852	9,394	ND.....	23,631	1,518	7,254	10,137
DC......	35,562	2,838	3,759	19,322	OH......	299,121	68,873	93,157	91,713
FL	388,945	139,148	88,828	54,085	OK......	112,375	33,919	28,021	26,643
GA.....	233,822	81,773	34,812	47,910	OR......	77,491	19,523	14,677	18,831
HI	35,782	3,233	2,949	4,716	PA	433,301	76,553	114,113	147,542
ID	31,496	7,401	5,735	8,006	RI	38,816	3,576	9,222	20,551
IL......	321,781	67,820	91,887	90,463	SC.....	135,037	34,909	20,867	39,360
IN	178,154	34,676	48,745	69,147	SD.....	28,418	4,479	7,791	8,998
IA	104,169	11,771	33,428	41,171	TN	147,946	38,481	36,994	45,030
KS.....	81,950	16,703	25,248	24,492	TX	561,109	244,363	105,052	92,246
KY.....	114,804	28,388	29,266	31,883	UT......	40,480	9,921	6,853	9,837
LA	135,965	49,854	31,521	26,959	VT.....	20,760	1,219	4,037	12,863
ME.....	34,912	2,864	9,339	13,793	VA	231,398	64,036	38,865	65,557
MD.....	134,056	35,698	26,716	35,371	WA	136,382	28,871	23,275	30,858
MA.....	221,216	23,513	55,837	103,583	WV	43,147	10,505	11,601	14,300
MI	249,889	65,330	50,113	69,854	WI	155,958	31,068	41,370	51,397
MN.	135,883	16,999	40,506	44,835	WY	14,083	4,176	2,869	3,850

[1] Includes other group quarters types not shown separately.   [2] Includes college quarters off campus.

Source: U.S. Census Bureau, *2000 Census of Population and Housing, Profiles of General Demographic Characteristics*; and Census 2000 Summary File 1.

No. 63. Religious Bodies—Selected Data

[**Membership data: 2,500 represents 2,500,000.** Includes the self-reported membership of religious bodies with 65,000 or more as reported to the *Yearbook of American and Canadian Churches*. Groups may be excluded if they do not supply information. The data are not standardized so comparisons between groups are difficult. The definition of "church member" is determined by the religious body]

Religious body	Year reported	Churches reported	Membership (1,000)	Pastors serving parishes [1]
African Methodist Episcopal Church.	2000	6,200	2,500	(NA)
African Methodist Episcopal Zion Church	2000	3,218	1,297	3,231
American Baptist Association, The.	1998	1,760	275	1,740
American Baptist Churches in the U.S.A.	2000	5,756	1,437	4,714
Antiochian Orthodox Christian Archdiocese of North America, The.	2000	227	70	300
Armenian Apostolic Church of America.	2000	36	360	36
Assemblies of God.	2000	12,084	2,578	18,304
Baptist Bible Fellowship International	2000	4,500	1,200	(NA)
Baptist General Conference	2001	(NA)	143	(NA)
Baptist Missionary Association of America.	1999	1,334	235	1,525
Christian and Missionary Alliance, The	2000	1,959	365	1,731
Christian Brethren (a.k.a. Plymouth Brethren)	2000	1,125	95	(NA)
Christian Church (Disciples of Christ).	2000	3,781	820	3,305
Christian Churches and Churches of Christ.	1988	5,579	1,072	5,525
Christian Congregation, Inc., The	2000	1,439	119	1,437
Christian Methodist Episcopal Church	1999	3,069	784	2,058
Christian Reformed Church in North America.	1999	739	197	675
Church Of God In Christ, The.	1991	15,300	5,500	28,988
Church of God of Prophecy.	2000	1,865	73	(NA)
Church of God (Anderson, Indiana).	1998	2,353	234	3,034
Church of God (Cleveland, Tennessee)	2000	6,426	896	4,578
Church of Jesus Christ of Latter-day Saints, The	2000	11,562	5,209	34,686
Church of the Brethren	2000	1,071	136	843
Church of the Nazarene	2000	5,070	637	4,504
Churches of Christ	1999	15,000	1,500	14,500
Community of Christ.	1999	1,236	137	(NA)
Conservative Baptist Association of America	1998	1,200	200	(NA)
Coptic Orthodox Church	2000	100	300	140
Cumberland Presbyterian Church	2000	779	87	540
Episcopal Church.	2000	7,359	2,311	7,741
Evangelical Covenant Church, The	2000	800	101	679
Evangelical Free Church of America, The	1995	1,224	243	1,936
Evangelical Lutheran Church in America.	2000	10,816	5,126	9,406
Full Gospel Fellowship of Churches and Ministers International	2000	896	325	2,070
General Association of Regular Baptist Churches.	1999	1,398	92	(NA)
General Conference of Mennonite Brethren Churches.	1996	368	82	590
Greek Orthodox Archdiocese of America	2000	508	1,500	893
International Church of the Foursquare Gospel	2000	1,793	278	5,644
International Council of Community Churches	2000	217	200	249
International Pentecostal Holiness Church	2000	1,868	198	1,625
Jehovah's Witnesses	2000	11,636	998	(NA)
Jewish [2].	2001	(NA)	6,150	(NA)
Lutheran Church— Missouri Synod (LCMS), The.	2000	6,150	2,554	5,196
Mennonite Church.	2000	1,063	120	(NA)
National Association of Congregational Christian Churches	2000	430	66	530
National Association of Free Will Baptists	2000	2,472	199	2,472
National Baptist Convention of America, Inc.	2000	(NA)	3,500	(NA)
National Baptist Convention USA, Inc.	(NA)	[3]	[3]	(NA)
National Missionary Baptist Convention of America.	1992	(NA)	2,500	(NA)
Old Order Amish Church	1993	898	81	3,592
Orthodox Church in America, The.	2000	721	1,000	760
Pentecostal Assemblies of the World, Inc.	1998	1,750	1,500	4,500
Pentecostal Church of God	2000	1,212	102	(NA)
Presbyterian Church in America	2000	1,458	306	(NA)
Presbyterian Church (U.S.A.)	2000	11,178	3,485	8,891
Progressive National Baptist Convention, Inc.	1995	2,000	2,500	(NA)
Reformed Church in America	2000	898	289	773
Religious Society of Friends (Conservative).	1994	1,200	104	(NA)
Roman Catholic Church, The	2000	19,544	63,683	(NA)
Salvation Army, The	1999	1,410	473	3,072
Serbian Orthodox Church in the U.S.A. and Canada.	1986	68	67	60
Seventh-Day Adventist Church	2000	4,486	881	2,484
Southern Baptist Convention	2000	41,588	15,960	77,810
Unitarian Universalist Association of Congregations	2000	1,051	220	(NA)
United Church of Christ	2000	5,923	1,377	4,202
United Methodist Church, The	2000	35,469	8,341	24,991
Wesleyan Church, The	2000	1,602	123	1,974
Wisconsin Evangelical Lutheran Synod	2000	1,241	722	1,245

NA Not available.   [1] Does not include retired clergy or clergy not working with congregations.   [2] Source: American Jewish Committee, New York, NY, *American Jewish Year Book* (copyright). See Table 65.   [3] Church reports 8,000 to 10,000 churches and 4 to 6 million inclusive members.

Source: Except as noted, National Council of the Churches of Christ in the USA, New York, NY, *2002 Yearbook of American and Canadian Churches,* annual (copyright). (For more information, visit www.ncccusa.org).

Population   55

No. 64. Religious Preference, Church Membership, and Attendance: 1980 to 2000

[In percent. Covers civilian noninstitutional population, 18 years old and over. Data represent averages of the combined results of several surveys during year or period indicated. Data are subject to sampling variability, see source]

Year	Religious preference							Church/ synagogue members	Persons attending church/ syna- gogue [1]
	Protes- tant	Catholic	Jewish	Ortho- dox	Mormon	Other specific	None		
1980	61	28	2	(NA)	(NA)	2	7	69	40
1985	57	28	2	(NA)	(NA)	4	9	71	42
1990	56	25	2	(NA)	(NA)	6	11	65	40
1995	56	27	2	1	1	5	[2]8	69	43
1996	58	25	3	1	1	3	[2]9	65	38
1997	58	26	2	1	1	4	[2]8	67	40
1998	59	27	2	2	1	4	[2]8	70	40
1999	55	28	2	1	2	2	[2]10	70	43
2000	56	27	2	1	1	5	[2]8	68	44

NA Not available.   [1] Persons who attended a church or synagogue in the last 7 days.   [2] Includes those respondents who did not designate.

Source: The Gallup Organization, Princeton, NJ, "Gallup Poll Releases-Easter Season Finds a Religious Nation"; published 13 April 2001; <http://www.gallup.com/poll/releases/pr010413.asp>.

No. 65. Christian Church Adherents, 2000, and Jewish Population, 2001—States

[Christian church adherents were defined as "all members, including full members, their children and the estimated number of other regular participants who are not considered as communicant, confirmed or full members." The Jewish population includes Jews who define themselves as Jewish by religion as well as those who define themselves as Jewish in cultural terms. Data on Jewish population are based primarily on a compilation of individual estimates made by local Jewish federations. Additionally, most large communities have completed Jewish demographic surveys from which the Jewish population can be determined]

State	Christian adherents, 2000		Jewish population, 2001		State	Christian adherents, 2000		Jewish population, 2001	
	Number (1,000)	Percent of population [1]	Number (1,000)	Percent of population [1]		Number (1,000)	Percent of population [1]	Number (1,000)	Percent of population [1]
U.S.	133,377	47.4	6,150	2.2	MO	2,813	50.3	62	1.1
AL	2,418	54.4	9	0.2	MT......	401	44.4	1	0.1
AK......	210	33.6	3	0.5	NE......	995	58.2	7	0.4
AZ......	1,946	37.9	82	1.6	NV......	604	30.2	77	3.8
AR......	1,516	56.7	2	0.1	NH......	571	46.2	10	0.8
CA......	14,328	42.3	999	2.9	NJ......	4,262	50.7	485	5.7
CO......	1,604	37.3	73	1.7	NM......	1,041	57.2	11	0.6
CT......	1,828	53.7	111	3.2	NY......	9,569	50.4	1,657	8.7
DE......	299	38.2	14	1.7	NC......	3,598	44.7	26	0.3
DC......	331	57.8	25	4.5	ND......	468	72.9	(Z)	0.1
FL......	5,904	36.9	620	3.9	OH......	4,912	43.3	149	1.3
GA......	3,528	43.1	93	1.1	OK......	2,079	60.3	5	0.1
HI	431	35.6	7	0.6	OR......	1,029	30.1	32	0.9
ID	624	48.3	1	0.1	PA......	6,751	55.0	282	2.3
IL.......	6,457	52.0	270	2.2	RI	646	61.7	16	1.5
IN	2,578	42.4	18	0.3	SC......	1,874	46.7	11	0.3
IA	1,698	58.0	6	0.2	SD......	510	67.6	(Z)	0.1
KS......	1,307	48.6	14	0.5	TN......	2,867	50.4	18	0.3
KY......	2,141	53.0	11	0.3	TX......	11,316	54.3	131	0.6
LA......	2,599	58.2	16	0.4	UT......	1,659	74.3	4	0.2
ME......	450	35.3	9	0.7	VT......	230	37.8	6	0.9
MD......	2,012	38.0	213	4.0	VA......	2,807	39.7	66	0.9
MA......	3,725	58.7	275	4.3	WA	1,872	31.8	43	0.7
MI	3,970	39.9	110	1.1	WV	646	35.7	2	0.1
MN......	2,974	60.5	42	0.9	WI	3,198	59.6	28	0.5
MS......	1,549	54.5	1	0.1	WY	229	46.4	(Z)	0.1

Z Fewer than 500.   [1] Based on U.S. Census Bureau data for resident population enumerated as of April 1, 2000, and estimated as of July 1, 2001.

Source: Christian church adherents—Dale E. Jones, Sherri Doty, Clifford Grammich, James E. Horsch, Richard Houseal, John P. Marcum, Kenneth M. Sanchagrin, and Richard H. Taylor, *Religious Congregations and Membership in the United States: 2000*, 2002, Glenmary Research Center, Nashville, TN, <www/glenmary.org/grc> (copyright); Jewish population—American Jewish Committee, New York, NY, *American Jewish Year Book, 2002* (copyright).

U.S. Census Bureau, Statistical Abstract of the United States: 2002

Section 2
Vital Statistics

This section presents vital statistics data on births, deaths, abortions, fetal deaths, fertility, life expectancy, marriages, and divorces. Vital statistics are compiled for the country as a whole by the National Center for Health Statistics (NCHS) and published in its annual report, *Vital Statistics of the United States,* in certain reports of the *Vital and Health Statistics* series, and in the *National Vital Statistics Reports* (formerly *Monthly Vital Statistics Report*). Reports in this field are also issued by the various state bureaus of vital statistics. Data on fertility, on age of persons at first marriage, and on marital status and marital history are compiled by the U.S. Census Bureau from its Current Population Survey (CPS; see text, Section 1) and published in *Current Population Reports,* P20 Series. Data on abortions are published by the Alan Guttmacher Institute, New York, NY, in selected issues of *Family Planning Perspectives.*

Registration of vital events—The registration of births, deaths, fetal deaths, and other vital events in the United States is primarily a state and local function. The civil laws of every state provide for a continuous and permanent birth- and death-registration system. Many states also provide for marriage- and divorce-registration systems. Vital events occurring to U.S. residents outside the United States are not included in the data.

Births and deaths—The live-birth, death, and fetal-death statistics prepared by NCHS are based on vital records filed in the registration offices of all states, of New York City, and of the District of Columbia. The annual collection of death statistics on a national basis began in 1900 with a national death-registration area of 10 states and the District of Columbia; a similar annual collection of birth statistics for a national birth-registration area began in 1915, also with 10 reporting states and the District of Columbia. Since 1933, the birth- and death-registration areas have comprised the entire United States, including Alaska (beginning 1959) and Hawaii (beginning 1960). National statistics on fetal deaths were first compiled for 1918 and annually since 1922.

Prior to 1951, birth statistics came from a complete count of records received in the Public Health Service (now received in NCHS). From 1951 through 1971, they were based on a 50-percent sample of all registered births (except for a complete count in 1955 and a 20- to 50-percent sample in 1967). Beginning in 1972, they have been based on a complete count for states participating in the Vital Statistics Cooperative Program (VSCP) (for details, see the technical appendix in *Vital Statistics of the United States*) and on a 50-percent sample of all other areas. Beginning 1986, all reporting areas participated in the VSCP. Mortality data have been based on a complete count of records for each area (except for a 50-percent sample in 1972). Beginning in 1970, births to and deaths of nonresident aliens of the United States and U.S. citizens outside the United States have been excluded from the data. Fetal deaths and deaths among Armed Forces abroad are excluded. Data based on samples are subject to sampling error; for details, see annual issues of *Vital Statistics of the United States.*

Mortality statistics by cause of death are compiled in accordance with World Health Organization regulations according to the *International Classification of Diseases* (ICD). The ICD is revised approximately every 10 years. The tenth revision of the ICD was employed beginning in 1999. Deaths for prior years were classified according to the revision of the ICD in use at the time. Each revision of the ICD introduces a number of discontinuities in mortality statistics; for a discussion of those between the ninth and tenth revisions of the ICD, see *National Vital Statistics Reports,* Vol. 49, Nos. 2 and 8. Preliminary mortality data are based on a percentage of death records weighted up to the total

U.S. Census Bureau, Statistical Abstract of the United States: 2002

number of deaths reported for the given year; for a discussion of preliminary data, see *National Vital Statistics Reports,* Vol. 49, No. 3. Information on tests of statistical significance, differences between death rates, and standard errors can also be found in the reports mentioned above.

Some of the tables present age-adjusted death rates in addition to crude death rates. Age-adjusted death rates shown in this section were prepared using the direct method, in which age-specific death rates for a population of interest are applied to a standard population distributed by age. Age adjustment eliminates the differences in observed rates between points in time or among compared population groups that result from age differences in population composition.

Fertility and life expectancy—The total fertility rate, defined as the number of births that 1,000 women would have in their lifetime if, at each year of age, they experienced the birth rates occurring in the specified year, is compiled and published by NCHS. Other data relating to social and medical factors which affect fertility rates, such as contraceptive use and birth expectations, are collected and made available by both NCHS and the Census Bureau. NCHS figures are based on information in birth and fetal death certificates and on the periodic National Surveys of Family Growth; Census Bureau data are based on decennial censuses and the CPS.

Data on life expectancy, the average remaining lifetime in years for persons who attain a given age, are computed and published by NCHS. For details, see *National Vital Statistics Reports, Vol. 50, No. 6.*

Marriage and divorce—The compilation of nationwide statistics on marriages and divorces in the United States began in 1887-88 when the National Office of Vital Statistics prepared estimates for the years 1867-86. Although periodic updates took place after 1888, marriage and divorce statistics were not collected and published annually until 1944 by that office. In 1957 and 1958, respectively, the same office established marriage- and divorce-registration areas. Beginning in 1957, the marriage-registration area comprised 30 states, plus Alaska, Hawaii, Puerto Rico, and the Virgin Islands; it currently includes 42 states and the District of Columbia. The divorce-registration area, starting in 1958 with 14 states, Alaska, Hawaii, and the Virgin Islands, it currently includes a total of 31 states and the Virgin Islands. Procedures for estimating the number of marriages and divorces in the registration states are discussed in *Vital Statistics of the United States,* Vol. III—Marriage and Divorce. Total counts of events for registration and nonregistration states are gathered by collecting already summarized data on marriages and divorces reported by state offices of vital statistics and by county offices of registration.

Vital statistics rates—Except as noted, vital statistics rates computed by NCHS are based on decennial census population figures as of April 1 for 1940, 1950, 1960, 1970, 1980, and 1990; and on mid-year population figures for other years, as estimated by the Census Bureau (see text, Section 1).

Race—Data by race for births, deaths, marriages, and divorces from NCHS are based on information contained in the certificates of registration. The Census Bureau's Current Population Survey obtains information on race by asking respondents to classify their race as (1) White, (2) Black, (3) American Indian, Eskimo, or Aleut, or (4) Asian or Pacific Islander.

Beginning with the 1989 data year, NCHS is tabulating its birth data primarily by race of the mother. In 1988 and prior years, births were tabulated by race of the child, which was determined from the race of the parents as entered on the birth certificate.

Trend data by race shown in this section are by race of mother beginning with the 1980 data. Hispanic origin of the mother is reported and tabulated independently of race. Thus persons of Hispanic origin maybe of any race. In 1994, 91 percent of women of Hispanic origin were reported as White.

No. 66. Live Births, Deaths, Marriages, and Divorces: 1950 to 2001

[3,632 represents 3,632,000. Prior to 1960, excludes Alaska and Hawaii. Beginning 1970, excludes births to, and deaths of nonresidents of the United States. See Appendix III]

Year	Number (1,000)					Rate per 1,000 population				
		Deaths		Mar-riages [3]	Di-vorces [4]		Deaths		Mar-riages [3]	Di-vorces [4]
	Births [1]	Total	Infant [2]			Births [1]	Total	Infant [2]		
1950	3,632	1,452	104	1,667	385	24.1	9.6	29.2	11.1	2.6
1955	4,097	1,529	107	1,531	377	25.0	9.3	26.4	9.3	2.3
1957	4,300	1,633	112	1,518	381	25.3	9.6	26.3	8.9	2.2
1960	4,258	1,712	111	1,523	393	23.7	9.5	26.0	8.5	2.2
1965	3,760	1,828	93	1,800	479	19.4	9.4	24.7	9.3	2.5
1970	3,731	1,921	75	2,159	708	18.4	9.5	20.0	10.6	3.5
1971	3,556	1,928	68	2,190	773	17.2	9.3	19.1	10.6	3.7
1972	3,258	1,964	60	2,282	845	15.6	9.4	18.5	10.9	4.0
1973	3,137	1,973	56	2,284	915	14.8	9.3	17.7	10.8	4.3
1974	3,160	1,934	53	2,230	977	14.8	9.1	16.7	10.5	4.6
1975	3,144	1,893	51	2,153	1,036	14.6	8.8	16.1	10.0	4.8
1976	3,168	1,909	48	2,155	1,083	14.6	8.8	15.2	9.9	5.0
1977	3,327	1,900	47	2,178	1,091	15.1	8.6	14.1	9.9	5.0
1978	3,333	1,928	46	2,282	1,130	15.0	8.7	13.8	10.3	5.1
1979	3,494	1,914	46	2,331	1,181	15.6	8.5	13.1	10.4	5.3
1980	3,612	1,990	46	2,390	1,189	15.9	8.8	12.6	10.6	5.2
1981	3,629	1,978	43	2,422	1,213	15.8	8.6	11.9	10.6	5.3
1982	3,681	1,975	42	2,456	1,170	15.9	8.5	11.5	10.6	5.1
1983	3,639	2,019	41	2,446	1,158	15.6	8.6	11.2	10.5	5.0
1984	3,669	2,039	40	2,477	1,169	15.6	8.6	10.8	10.5	5.0
1985	3,761	2,086	40	2,413	1,190	15.8	8.8	10.6	10.1	5.0
1986	3,757	2,105	39	2,407	1,178	15.6	8.8	10.4	10.0	4.9
1987	3,809	2,123	38	2,403	1,166	15.7	8.8	10.1	9.9	4.8
1988	3,910	2,168	39	2,396	1,167	16.0	8.9	10.0	9.8	4.8
1989	4,041	2,150	40	2,403	1,157	16.4	8.7	9.8	9.7	4.7
1990	4,158	2,148	38	2,443	1,182	16.7	8.6	9.2	9.8	4.7
1991	4,111	2,170	37	2,371	1,187	16.3	8.6	8.9	9.4	4.7
1992	4,065	2,176	35	2,362	1,215	15.9	8.5	8.5	9.3	4.8
1993	4,000	2,269	33	2,334	1,187	15.5	8.8	8.4	9.0	4.6
1994	3,953	2,279	31	2,362	1,191	15.2	8.8	8.0	9.1	4.6
1995	3,900	2,312	30	2,336	1,169	14.8	8.8	7.6	8.9	4.4
1996	3,891	2,315	28	2,344	1,150	14.7	8.7	7.3	8.8	4.3
1997	3,881	2,314	28	2,384	1,163	14.5	8.6	7.2	8.9	4.3
1998[5]	3,942	2,337	28	2,256	1,135	14.6	8.6	7.2	8.3	4.3
1999[5]	3,959	2,391	28	2,358	(NA)	14.5	8.8	7.1	8.6	4.1
2000[5]	4,059	2,403	28	2,329	(NA)	14.7	8.7	6.9	8.5	4.2
2001[5]	4,028	2,419	28	2,327	(NA)	14.5	8.7	6.9	8.4	4.0

NA Not available.   [1] Prior to 1960, data adjusted for underregistration.   [2] Infants under 1 year, excluding fetal deaths; rates per 1,000 registered live births.   [3] Includes estimates for some states through 1965 and also for 1976 and 1977 and marriage licenses for some states for all years except 1973 and 1975. Beginning 1978, includes nonlicensed marriages in California. [4] Includes reported annulments and some estimated state figures for all years.   [5] Divorce rates excludes data for California, Colorado, Indiana, and Louisiana; population for this rate also excludes these states.

Source: U.S. National Center for Health Statistics, *Vital Statistics of the United States*, annual; and *National Vital Statistics Reports (NVSR)* (formerly *Monthly Vital Statistics Report*); and unpublished data.

No. 67. Live Births by Race and Type of Hispanic Origin—Selected Characteristics: 1990 and 2000

[4,158 represents 4,158,000. Represents registered births. Excludes births to nonresidents of the United States. Data are based on Hispanic origin of mother and race of mother. Hispanic origin data are available from only 48 states and the District of Columbia in 1990]

Race and Hispanic origin	Number of births (1,000)		Births to teen-age mothers, percent of total		Births to unmarried mothers, per-cent of total		Prenatal care beginning first trimester		Late or no prenatal care		Percent of births with low birth weight [1]	
	1990	2000	1990	2000	1990	2000	1990	2000	1990	2000	1990	2000
Total	4,158	4,059	12.8	11.8	26.6	33.2	74.2	83.2	6.0	3.9	7.0	7.6
White	3,290	3,194	10.9	10.6	16.9	27.1	77.7	85.0	4.9	3.3	5.7	6.5
Black	684	623	23.1	19.7	66.7	68.5	60.7	74.3	10.9	6.7	13.3	13.0
American Indian, Eskimo, Aleut .	39	42	19.5	19.7	53.6	58.4	57.9	69.3	12.9	8.6	6.1	6.8
Asian and Pacific Islander [2] . . .	142	201	5.7	4.5	(NA)	14.8	(NA)	84.0	(NA)	3.3	(NA)	7.3
Filipino.	26	32	6.1	5.3	15.9	20.3	77.1	84.9	4.5	3.0	7.3	8.5
Chinese	23	34	1.2	0.9	5.0	7.6	81.3	87.6	3.4	2.2	4.7	5.1
Japanese	9	9	2.9	1.9	9.6	9.5	87.0	91.0	2.9	1.8	6.2	7.1
Hawaiian	6	7	18.4	17.4	45.0	50.0	65.8	79.9	8.7	4.2	7.2	6.8
Hispanic origin [3]	595	816	16.8	16.2	36.7	42.7	60.2	74.4	12.0	6.3	6.1	6.4
Mexican	386	582	17.7	17.0	33.3	40.7	57.8	72.9	13.2	6.9	5.5	6.0
Puerto Rico.	59	58	21.7	20.0	55.9	59.6	63.5	78.5	10.6	4.5	9.0	9.3
Cuban	11	13	7.7	7.5	18.2	27.3	84.8	91.7	2.8	1.4	5.7	6.5
Central and South American .	83	113	9.0	9.9	41.2	44.7	61.5	77.6	10.9	5.4	5.8	6.3
Other and unknown Hispanic .	56	49	(NA)	14.8	(NA)	46.2	(NA)	75.8	(NA)	5.9	(NA)	7.8

NA Not available.   [1] Births less than 2,500 grams (5 lb.-8 oz.).   [2] Includes other races not shown separately.   [3] Hispanic persons may be of any race. Includes other types, not shown separately.

Source: U.S. National Center for Health Statistics; *Vital Statistics of the United States*, annual; *National Vital Statistics Report (NVSR)* (formerly *Monthly Vital Statistics Report*); and unpublished data.

Vital Statistics   59

No. 68. Births and Birth Rates by Race, Sex, and Age: 1980 to 2000

[Births in thousands. (3,612 represents 3,612,000). Births by race of mother. Excludes births to nonresidents of the United States. For population bases used to derive these data, see text this section, and Appendix III]

Item	1980	1985	1990	1993	1994	1995	1996	1997	1998	1999	2000
Live births [1]	3,612	3,761	4,158	4,000	3,953	3,900	3,891	3,881	3,942	3,959	4,059
White	2,936	3,038	3,290	3,150	3,121	3,099	3,093	3,073	3,119	3,134	3,194
Black	568	582	684	659	636	603	595	600	610	607	623
American Indian	29	34	39	39	38	37	38	39	40	41	42
Asian or Pacific Islander	74	105	142	153	158	160	166	170	173	182	201
Male	1,853	1,928	2,129	2,049	2,023	1,996	1,990	1,986	2,016	2,028	2,077
Female	1,760	1,833	2,029	1,951	1,930	1,903	1,901	1,895	1,925	1,934	1,982
Males per 100 females	105	105	105	105	105	105	105	105	105	106	105
Age of mother:											
Under 20 years old	562	478	533	514	518	512	503	493	494	485	478
20 to 24 years old	1,226	1,141	1,094	1,038	1,001	966	945	942	965	982	1,018
25 to 29 years old	1,108	1,201	1,277	1,129	1,089	1,064	1,071	1,069	1,083	1,078	1,088
30 to 34 years old	550	696	886	901	906	905	898	887	889	892	929
35 to 39 years old	141	214	318	357	372	384	400	410	425	434	452
40 to 44 years old	(NA)	(NA)	(NA)	(NA)	(NA)	(NA)	72	76	81	83	90
45 to 49 years old	(NA)	(NA)	(NA)	(NA)	(NA)	(NA)	3	3	4	4	4
Birth rate per 1,000 population	**15.9**	**15.8**	**16.7**	**15.5**	**15.2**	**14.8**	**14.7**	**14.5**	**14.6**	**14.5**	**14.7**
White	15.1	15.0	15.8	14.7	14.4	14.2	14.1	13.9	14.0	14.9	14.1
Black	21.3	20.4	22.4	20.5	19.5	18.2	17.8	17.7	17.7	18.4	17.6
American Indian	20.7	19.8	18.9	17.8	17.1	16.6	16.6	16.6	17.1	17.8	17.1
Asian or Pacific Islander	19.9	18.7	19.0	17.7	17.5	17.3	17.0	16.9	16.4	17.7	17.8
Plural birth ratio [2]	19.3	21.0	23.3	25.2	25.7	26.1	27.4	28.6	30.0	30.7	31.1
White	18.5	20.4	22.9	24.9	25.5	26.0	27.5	28.7	30.2	30.9	31.2
Black	24.1	25.3	27.0	28.7	29.4	28.8	29.8	30.9	32.0	32.9	34.0
Fertility rate per 1,000 women [3]	**68.4**	**66.2**	**70.9**	**67.6**	**66.7**	**65.6**	**65.3**	**65.0**	**65.6**	**65.9**	**67.5**
White [3]	65.6	64.1	68.3	65.4	64.9	64.4	64.3	63.9	64.6	65.1	66.5
Black [3]	84.9	78.8	86.8	80.5	76.9	72.3	70.7	70.7	71.0	70.1	71.7
American Indian [3]	82.7	78.6	76.2	73.4	70.9	69.1	68.7	69.1	70.7	70.7	71.4
Asian or Pacific Islander [3]	73.2	68.4	69.6	66.7	66.8	66.4	65.9	66.3	64.0	66.6	70.7
Age of mother:											
10 to 14 years old	1.1	1.2	1.4	1.4	1.4	1.3	1.2	1.1	1.0	1.9	0.9
15 to 19 years old	53.0	51.0	59.9	59.6	58.9	56.8	54.4	52.3	51.1	50.6	48.5
20 to 24 years old	115.1	108.3	116.5	112.6	111.1	109.8	110.4	110.4	111.2	112.0	112.3
25 to 29 years old	112.9	111.0	120.2	115.5	113.9	111.2	113.1	113.8	115.9	118.8	121.4
30 to 34 years old	61.9	69.1	80.8	80.8	81.5	82.5	83.9	85.3	87.4	90.6	94.1
35 to 39 years old	19.8	24.0	31.7	32.9	33.7	34.3	35.3	36.1	37.4	39.3	40.4
40 to 44 years old	3.9	4.0	5.5	6.1	6.4	6.6	6.8	7.1	7.3	8.4	7.9
45 to 49 years old	0.2	0.2	0.2	0.3	0.3	0.3	0.3	0.4	0.4	1.4	0.5

NA Not available. [1] Includes other races not shown separately. [2] Number of multiple births per 1,000 live births. [3] Per 1,000 women, 15 to 44 years old in specified group. The rate for age of mother 45 to 49 years old computed by relating births to mothers 45 years old and over to women 45 to 49 years old.
Source: U.S. National Center for Health Statistics, *Vital Statistics of the United States,* annual; *National Vital Statistics Report (NVSR)* (formerly *Monthly Vital Statistics Report*); and unpublished data. See also <http://www.cdc.gov/nchs.htm>.

No. 69. Teenagers—Births and Birth Rates by Race and Sex: 1990 to 2000

[Birth rates per 1,000 women in specified group, see text, this section]

Item	1990	1992	1993	1994	1995	1996	1997	1998	1999	2000
NUMBER OF BIRTHS										
All races, total [1]	**521,826**	**505,415**	**501,093**	**505,488**	**499,873**	**494,272**	**489,211**	**484,975**	**476,050**	**468,990**
15-17 years	183,327	187,549	190,535	195,169	192,508	186,762	183,324	173,252	163,588	157,209
18-19 years	338,499	317,866	310,558	310,319	307,365	307,509	305,886	311,724	312,462	311,781
White	354,482	342,739	341,817	348,081	349,635	346,509	342,029	340,894	337,888	333,013
15-17 years	114,934	118,786	121,309	126,388	127,165	124,031	121,864	116,699	111,624	106,786
18-19 years	239,548	223,953	220,508	221,693	222,470	222,477	220,164	224,195	226,264	226,227
Black	151,613	146,800	143,153	140,968	133,694	131,059	130,401	126,865	121,166	118,954
15-17 years	62,881	63,002	63,156	62,563	59,112	56,218	54,883	50,062	45,919	44,618
18-19 years	88,732	83,798	79,997	78,405	74,582	74,841	75,518	76,803	75,247	74,336
BIRTH RATE										
All races, total [1]	**59.9**	**60.7**	**59.6**	**58.9**	**56.8**	**54.4**	**52.3**	**51.1**	**49.6**	**48.5**
15-17 years	37.5	37.8	37.8	37.6	36.0	33.8	32.1	30.4	28.7	27.4
18-19 years	88.6	94.5	92.1	91.5	89.1	86.0	83.6	82.0	80.3	79.2
White	50.8	51.8	51.1	51.1	50.1	48.1	46.3	45.4	44.6	43.6
15-17 years	29.5	30.1	30.3	30.7	30.0	28.4	27.1	25.9	24.8	23.6
18-19 years	78.0	83.8	82.1	82.1	81.2	78.4	75.9	74.6	73.5	72.7
Black	112.8	112.4	108.6	104.5	96.1	91.4	88.2	85.4	81.0	79.4
15-17 years	82.3	81.3	79.8	76.3	69.7	64.7	60.8	56.8	52.0	50.4
18-19 years	152.9	157.9	151.9	148.3	137.1	132.5	130.1	126.9	122.8	121.3

[1] Includes races other than White and Black.
Source: U.S. National Center for Health Statistics, *Monthly Vital Statistics Report*, Vol. 50, No. 5, Supplement. See also <http://www.cdc.gov/nchs.htm>.

No. 70. Live Births by State: 2000

[Number of births, except rate. Registered births. Excludes births to nonresidents of the United States. By race of mother. See Appendix III]

State	All races [1]	White Total	White Non-Hispanic	Black Total	Black Non-Hispanic	Hispanic [2]	Birth rate [3]	Fertility rate [4]
United States..	**4,058,814**	**3,194,005**	**2,362,968**	**622,598**	**604,346**	**815,868**	**14.7**	**67.5**
Alabama.........	63,299	42,061	40,154	20,512	20,498	1,901	14.4	65.0
Alaska..........	9,974	6,364	5,770	462	383	597	16.0	74.6
Arizona.........	85,273	74,760	39,873	2,787	2,602	34,695	17.5	84.4
Arkansas	37,783	29,071	26,657	7,969	7,950	2,343	14.7	69.1
California	531,959	429,638	171,552	35,046	33,835	258,105	15.8	70.7
Colorado.........	65,438	59,684	41,822	3,031	2,902	18,237	15.8	73.1
Connecticut.......	43,026	35,819	28,785	5,273	4,946	6,472	13.0	61.2
Delaware	11,051	8,009	6,999	2,634	2,606	1,022	14.5	63.5
Dist. of Columbia ...	7,666	2,323	1,463	5,157	5,108	876	14.8	63.0
Florida	204,125	150,608	106,200	47,367	46,233	45,856	13.3	66.9
Georgia	132,644	84,646	70,521	44,161	43,418	13,363	16.7	71.4
Hawaii	17,551	4,022	3,285	472	440	2,302	14.9	72.3
Idaho...........	20,366	19,705	17,021	75	74	2,599	16.0	74.8
Illinois	185,036	142,390	103,267	34,317	34,079	39,313	15.2	69.5
Indiana..........	87,699	76,845	71,214	9,521	9,447	5,456	14.7	66.8
Iowa............	38,266	35,887	33,608	1,234	1,203	2,135	13.3	64.0
Kansas..........	39,666	35,297	30,181	2,870	2,820	4,761	14.9	69.2
Kentucky	56,029	50,216	49,133	5,127	5,107	1,089	14.1	63.6
Louisiana	67,898	38,125	36,592	28,351	28,298	1,532	15.5	69.1
Maine...........	13,603	13,185	13,019	112	104	141	10.8	49.4
Maryland	74,316	45,554	41,013	24,910	24,676	4,812	14.2	61.9
Massachusetts.....	81,614	68,553	60,419	8,086	6,436	9,279	13.2	59.2
Michigan.........	136,171	107,362	92,551	24,314	23,868	6,949	13.7	62.0
Minnesota........	67,604	58,431	52,098	4,450	4,378	3,952	14.0	63.8
Mississippi	44,075	23,540	22,879	19,893	19,889	623	15.8	70.3
Missouri	76,463	63,168	60,502	11,474	11,437	2,661	13.9	64.0
Montana.........	10,957	9,470	8,835	45	34	330	12.3	61.3
Nebraska	24,646	22,261	19,200	1,377	1,355	2,596	14.8	68.9
Nevada	30,829	26,033	15,724	2,369	2,283	10,195	16.4	79.8
New Hampshire	14,609	14,070	13,135	182	141	373	12.0	52.2
New Jersey.......	115,632	84,844	64,098	21,131	19,078	22,457	14.1	65.8
New Mexico	27,223	22,890	9,055	498	477	13,941	15.6	72.7
New York	258,737	183,668	125,365	54,822	47,869	53,847	14.2	65.0
North Carolina.....	120,311	86,428	73,966	29,369	29,229	12,557	15.5	71.6
North Dakota......	7,676	6,709	6,395	82	79	132	12.2	58.7
Ohio	155,472	128,527	124,378	23,726	23,495	4,150	13.8	63.0
Oklahoma........	49,782	38,787	34,120	4,787	4,702	4,357	14.7	69.9
Oregon..........	45,804	41,710	34,291	1,020	996	7,401	13.7	65.8
Pennsylvania......	146,281	121,256	113,556	20,684	20,227	7,549	12.2	58.2
Rhode Island......	12,505	10,795	7,825	1,121	1,005	2,103	12.6	58.1
South Carolina.....	56,114	35,341	33,175	19,734	19,709	2,261	14.3	63.3
South Dakota	10,345	8,424	8,224	106	104	223	14.0	66.7
Tennessee	79,611	61,224	58,028	16,909	16,876	3,220	14.4	65.2
Texas...........	363,414	309,552	142,142	41,308	40,657	166,931	17.8	80.0
Utah	47,353	44,896	38,809	328	318	5,938	21.9	94.5
Vermont	6,500	6,367	6,173	32	31	33	10.9	48.8
Virginia..........	98,938	71,187	63,528	22,529	22,369	7,725	14.2	61.2
Washington.......	81,036	68,676	55,774	3,497	3,307	11,367	13.9	63.2
West Virginia......	20,865	19,967	19,867	778	770	50	11.6	55.9
Wisconsin........	69,326	59,790	55,418	6,502	6,442	4,493	13.1	60.4
Wyoming	6,253	5,870	5,309	57	56	568	13.0	62.7

[1] Includes other races not shown separately.   [2] Persons of Hispanic origin may be of any race. Births by Hispanic origin of mother.   [3] Per 1,000 estimated population.   [4] Per 1,000 women aged 15-44 years estimated.

Source: U.S. National Center for Health Statistics, *Vital Statistics of the United States*, annual; and *National Vital Statistics Reports (NVSR)* (formerly *Monthly Vital Statistics Report*, Vol. 50, No. 5). See also <http://www.cdc.gov/nchs/nvss.htm>.

No. 71. Total Fertility Rate of Natural Increase: 1970 to 2000

[Based on race of child and registered births only, thru 1979. Beginning 1980, based on race of mother. Beginning 1970, excludes births to nonresidents of United States. The *total fertility rate* is the number of births that 1,000 women would have in their lifetime if, at each year of age, they experienced the birth rates occurring in the specified year. A total fertility rate of 2,110 represents "replacement level" fertility for the total population under current mortality conditions (assuming no net immigration). The *intrinsic rate of natural increase* is the rate that would eventually prevail if a population were to experience, at each year of age, the birth rates and death rates occurring in the specified year and if those rates remained unchanged over a long period of time. Minus sign (-) indicates decrease. See also Appendix III]

Annual average and year	Total fertility rate			Annual average and year	Total fertility rate		
	Total	White	Black and other[1]		Total	White	Black and other[1]
1970	2,480	2,385	3,067	1986	1,838	1,776	2,136
1971	2,267	2,161	2,920	1987	1,872	1,805	2,198
1972	2,010	1,907	2,628	1988	1,934	1,857	2,298
1973	1,879	1,783	2,443	1989	2,014	1,931	2,433
1974	1,835	1,749	2,339	1990	2,081	2,003	2,480
1975	1,774	1,686	2,276	1991	2,073	1,996	2,480
1976	1,738	1,652	2,223	1992	2,065	1,994	2,442
1977	1,790	1,703	2,279	1993	2,046	1,982	2,385
1978	1,760	1,668	2,265	1994	2,036	1,985	2,300
1979	1,808	1,716	2,310	1995	2,019	1,989	2,175
1980	1,840	1,773	2,177	1996	2,040	2,006	2,144
1981	1,812	1,748	2,118	1997	2,040	2,009	2,154
1982	1,828	1,767	2,107	1998	2,058	2,041	2,171
1983	1,799	1,741	2,066	1999	2,075	2,065	2,147
1984	1,807	1,749	2,071	2000	2,130	2,114	2,193
1985	1,844	1,787	2,109				

[1] Data for 1984 and earlier includes races other than Black.

Source: U.S. National Center for Health Statistics, *Vital Statistics of the United States,* annual; and unpublished data. See also <http://www.cdc.gov/nchs/>.

No. 72. Projected Fertility Rates by Race, Origin, and Age Group: 2000 and 2010

[For definition of total fertility rate, see headnote, Table 71. Birth rates represent live births per 1,000 women in age group indicated. Projections are based on middle fertility assumptions. For explanations of methodology, see text, Section 1, Population]

Age group	All races[1]		White		Black		American Indian, Eskimo, Aleut		Asian and Pacific Islanders		Hispanic[2]	
	2000	2010	2000	2010	2000	2010	2000	2010	2000	2010	2000	2010
Total fertility rate . .	2,130	2,123	2,114	2,098	2,193	2,140	2,101	2,451	2,073	2,252	3,108	2,818
Birth rates:												
10 to 14 years old. . . .	0.9	1.3	0.6	0.9	2.4	3.5	1.3	2.0	0.3	0.7	1.9	2.3
15 to 19 years old. . . .	48.5	43.6	43.6	54.3	79.4	95.6	67.8	93.6	21.6	29.6	94.4	95.7
20 to 24 years old. . . .	112.3	107.9	107.9	112.6	144.2	137.1	135.6	159.6	72.0	83.7	184.6	175.2
25 to 29 years old. . . .	121.4	124.3	124.3	118.5	105.3	95.5	106.9	118.6	125.8	134.5	170.8	146.7
30 to 34 years old. . . .	94.1	97.4	97.4	90.0	67.5	63.4	68.3	77.3	120.8	128.2	109.0	91.6
35 to 39 years old. . . .	40.4	40.7	40.7	36.6	32.2	28.9	32.5	33.7	60.4	59.0	48.7	41.9
40 to 44 years old. . . .	7.9	7.8	7.8	7.1	7.2	6.0	7.3	7.4	12.7	13.8	11.6	9.9
45 to 49 years old. . . .	0.5	0.4	0.4	0.3	0.4	0.3	0.4	0.3	0.9	0.9	0.6	0.6

[1] Includes other races not shown separately.   [2] Persons of Hispanic origin may be of any race.

Source: U.S. Census Bureau, Population Division Working Paper No. 38.

No. 73. Birth Rates by Live-Birth Order and Race: 1980 to 2000

[**Births per 1,000 women 15 to 44 years old in specified racial group.** Live-birth order refers to number of children born alive. Figures for births of order not stated are distributed. See also headnote, Table 68]

Live-birth order	All races[1]					White					Black				
	1980	1990	1995	1999	2000	1980	1990	1995	1999	2000	1980	1990	1995	1999	2000
Total	68.4	70.9	65.6	65.9	67.5	65.6	68.3	64.4	65.1	66.5	84.9	86.8	72.3	70.1	71.7
First birth	29.5	29.0	27.3	26.6	27.1	28.8	28.4	26.9	26.4	26.8	33.7	32.4	28.7	26.5	26.9
Second birth	21.8	22.8	21.1	21.5	21.9	21.3	22.4	21.1	21.6	21.9	24.7	25.6	20.7	20.9	21.3
Third birth	10.3	11.7	10.5	10.9	11.3	9.6	11.1	10.3	10.8	11.2	14.0	15.6	12.0	12.4	12.8
Fourth birth	3.9	4.5	4.0	4.2	4.3	3.4	4.0	3.8	4.0	4.1	6.5	7.4	5.7	5.7	5.9
Fifth birth	1.5	1.7	1.5	1.5	1.6	1.3	1.4	1.3	1.4	1.4	2.9	3.2	2.6	2.5	2.6
Sixth and seventh	1.0	1.0	0.9	0.9	0.9	0.8	0.8	0.7	0.8	0.8	2.1	2.0	1.8	1.7	1.7
Eighth and over	0.4	0.3	0.3	0.3	0.3	0.3	0.2	0.2	0.2	0.3	0.9	0.5	0.6	0.6	0.6

[1] Includes other races not shown separately.

Source: U.S. National Center for Health Statistics, *Vital Statistics of the United States,* annual; and *National Vital Statistics Reports (NVSR)* (formerly *Monthly Vital Statistics Report).*

No. 74. Births to Teens, Unmarried Mothers, and Prenatal Care: 1990 to 2000

[In percent. Represents registered births. See headnote, Table 67]

Characteristics	1990	1995	1996	1997	1998	1999	2000
Percent of births to teenage mothers.	**12.8**	**13.1**	**12.9**	**12.7**	**12.5**	**12.3**	**11.8**
White	10.9	11.5	11.3	11.2	11.1	10.9	10.6
Black	23.1	23.1	22.8	22.2	21.5	20.7	19.7
American Indian, Eskimo, Aleut.	19.5	21.4	20.9	20.8	20.9	20.2	19.7
Asian and Pacific Islander [1]	5.7	5.6	5.3	5.2	5.4	5.1	4.5
Filipino	6.1	6.2	6.1	5.9	6.2	5.9	5.3
Chinese.	1.2	0.9	0.9	0.9	0.9	0.9	0.9
Japanese.	2.9	2.5	2.5	2.2	2.4	2.1	1.9
Hawaiian	18.4	19.1	18.4	18.6	18.8	18.2	17.4
Other	(NA)	6.3	5.8	5.7	5.8	5.5	4.8
Hispanic origin [2].	16.8	17.9	17.4	17.0	16.9	16.7	16.2
Mexican	17.7	18.8	18.1	17.7	17.5	17.4	17.0
Puerto Rican	21.7	23.5	23.1	22.3	21.9	21.1	20.0
Cuban.	7.7	7.7	7.6	7.4	6.9	7.7	7.5
Central and South American	9.0	10.6	10.5	10.5	10.3	10.0	9.9
Other and unknown Hispanic.	(NA)	20.1	19.8	19.8	20.2	19.5	18.8
Percent births to unmarried mothers .	**26.6**	**32.2**	**32.4**	**32.4**	**32.8**	**33.0**	**33.2**
White	16.9	25.3	25.7	25.8	26.3	26.8	27.1
Black	66.7	69.9	69.8	69.2	69.1	68.9	68.5
American Indian, Eskimo, Aleut.	53.6	57.2	58.0	58.7	59.3	58.9	58.4
Asian and Pacific Islander [1]	(NA)	16.3	16.7	15.6	15.6	15.4	14.8
Filipino	15.9	19.5	19.4	19.5	19.7	21.1	20.3
Chinese.	5.0	7.9	9.2	6.5	6.4	6.9	7.6
Japanese.	9.6	10.8	11.4	10.1	9.7	9.9	9.5
Hawaiian	45.0	49.0	49.9	49.1	51.1	50.4	50.0
Hispanic origin [2].	36.7	40.8	40.7	40.9	41.6	42.2	42.7
Mexican	33.3	38.1	37.9	38.9	39.6	40.1	40.7
Puerto Rican	55.9	60.0	60.7	59.4	59.5	59.6	59.6
Cuban.	18.2	23.8	24.7	24.4	24.8	26.4	27.3
Central and South American	41.2	44.1	44.7	41.8	42.0	43.7	44.7
Percent of mothers beginning prenatal care 1st trimester	**74.2**	**81.3**	**81.9**	**82.5**	**82.8**	**83.2**	**83.2**
White	77.7	83.6	84.0	84.7	84.8	85.1	85.0
Black	60.7	70.4	71.4	72.3	73.3	74.1	74.3
American Indian, Eskimo, Aleut.	57.9	66.7	67.7	68.1	68.8	69.5	69.3
Asian and Pacific Islander [1]	(NA)	79.9	81.2	82.1	83.1	83.7	84.0
Filipino	77.1	80.9	82.5	83.3	84.2	84.2	84.9
Chinese.	81.3	85.7	86.8	87.4	88.5	88.5	87.6
Japanese.	87.0	89.7	89.3	89.3	90.2	90.7	91.0
Hawaiian	65.8	75.9	78.5	78.0	78.8	79.6	79.9
Hispanic origin [2].	60.2	70.8	72.2	73.7	74.3	74.4	74.4
Mexican	57.8	69.1	70.7	72.1	72.8	73.1	72.9
Puerto Rican	63.5	74.0	75.0	76.5	76.9	77.7	78.5
Cuban.	84.8	89.2	89.2	90.4	91.8	91.4	91.7
Central and South American	61.5	73.2	75.0	76.9	78.0	77.6	77.6
Percent of mothers beginning prenatal care 3d trimester or no care .	**6.0**	**4.2**	**4.0**	**3.9**	**3.9**	**3.8**	**3.9**
White	4.9	3.5	3.3	3.2	3.3	3.2	3.3
Black	10.9	7.6	7.3	7.3	7.0	6.6	6.7
American Indian, Eskimo, Aleut.	12.9	9.5	8.6	8.6	8.5	8.2	8.6
Asian and Pacific Islander [1]	(NA)	4.3	3.9	3.8	3.6	3.5	3.3
Filipino	4.5	4.1	3.3	3.3	3.1	2.8	3.0
Chinese.	3.4	3.0	2.5	2.4	2.2	2.0	2.2
Japanese.	2.9	2.3	2.2	2.7	2.1	2.1	1.8
Hawaiian	8.7	5.1	5.0	5.4	4.7	4.0	4.2
Hispanic origin [2].	12.0	7.4	6.7	6.2	6.3	6.3	6.3
Mexican	13.2	8.1	7.2	6.7	6.8	6.7	6.9
Puerto Rican	10.6	5.5	5.7	5.4	5.1	5.0	4.5
Cuban.	2.8	2.1	1.6	1.5	1.2	1.4	1.4
Central and South American	10.9	6.1	5.5	5.0	4.9	5.2	5.4
Percent of births with low birth weight [3]	**7.0**	**7.3**	**7.4**	**7.5**	**7.6**	**7.6**	**7.6**
White	5.7	6.2	6.3	6.5	6.5	6.6	6.5
Black	13.3	13.1	13.0	13.0	13.0	13.1	13.0
American Indian, Eskimo, Aleut.	6.1	6.6	6.5	6.8	6.8	7.1	6.8
Asian and Pacific Islander [1]	(NA)	6.9	7.1	7.2	7.4	7.4	7.3
Filipino	7.3	7.8	7.9	8.3	8.2	8.3	8.5
Chinese.	4.7	5.3	5.0	5.1	5.3	5.2	5.1
Japanese.	6.2	7.3	7.3	6.8	7.5	7.9	7.1
Hawaiian	7.2	6.8	6.8	7.2	7.2	7.7	6.8
Hispanic origin [2].	6.1	6.3	7.4	6.4	6.4	6.4	6.4
Mexican	5.5	5.8	5.9	6.0	6.0	5.9	6.0
Puerto Rican	9.0	9.4	9.2	9.4	9.7	9.3	9.3
Cuban.	5.7	6.5	6.5	6.8	6.5	6.8	6.5
Central and South American	5.8	6.2	6.0	6.3	6.5	6.4	6.3

NA Not available.   [1] Includes other races not shown separately.   [2] Hispanic persons may be of any race. Includes other types, not shown separately.   [3] Births less than 2,500 grams (5 lb.-8 oz.).

Source: U.S. National Center for Health Statistics, *Vital Statistics of the United States*, annual; and *National Vital Statistics Reports (NVSR)* (formerly *Monthly Vital Statistics Report*).

No. 75. Births to Unmarried Women by Race of Child and Age of Mother: 1990 to 2000

[Excludes births to nonresidents of United States. Marital status is inferred from a comparison of the child's and parents' surnames on the birth certificate for those States that do not report on marital status. No estimates included for misstatements on birth records or failures to register births. See also Appendix III]

Race of child and age of mother	1990	1995	1998	1999	2000	Race of child and age of mother	1990	1995	1998	1999	2000
NUMBER (1,000)						30 to 34 years	10.1	10.6	9.6	9.5	9.7
Total live births [1]	**1,165**	**1,254**	**1,294**	**1,308**	**1,347**	35 to 39 years	(NA)	5.8	4.7	5.9	6.0
White	647	785	821	840	866	40 years and over.	(NA)	(NA)	1.1	1.1	(NA)
Black	473	421	421	417	427	**AS PERCENT OF ALL**					
Under 15 years	11	11	9	9	8	**BIRTHS IN RACIAL**					
15 to 19 years	350	376	381	374	369	**GROUPS**					
20 to 24 years	404	432	460	476	504						
25 to 29 years	230	229	243	247	255	**Total** [1]	**26.6**	**32.2**	**32.8**	**33.0**	**33.2**
30 to 34 years	118	133	125	125	130	White	16.9	25.3	26.3	26.8	27.1
35 to 39 years	(NA)	60	61	63	65	Black	66.7	69.9	69.1	68.9	68.5
40 years and over.	(NA)	13	14	14	16	**BIRTH RATE** [2]					
PERCENT						**Total** [1] [3]	**43.8**	**45.1**	**44.3**	**44.4**	**45.2**
DISTRIBUTION						White [3]	31.8	37.5	37.5	38.1	38.9
Total [1]	**100.0**	**100.0**	**100.0**	**100.0**	**100.0**	Black [3]	93.9	75.9	73.3	71.5	72.5
White	55.6	62.6	63.5	64.1	64.3	15 to 19 years	42.5	44.4	41.5	40.4	39.6
Black	40.6	33.6	32.6	31.9	31.7	20 to 24 years	65.1	70.3	72.3	72.9	74.5
Under 15 years	0.9	0.9	0.7	0.7	0.6	25 to 29 years	56.0	56.1	58.4	60.2	62.2
15 to 19 years	30.0	30.0	29.4	28.6	27.4	30 to 34 years	37.6	39.6	39.1	39.3	40.7
20 to 24 years	34.7	34.5	35.6	36.4	37.4	35 to 39 years	(NA)	(NA)	19.0	19.3	20.0
25 to 29 years	19.7	18.2	18.8	18.9	18.9	40 to 44 years	(NA)	(NA)	4.6	4.6	5.0

NA Not available. [1] Includes other races not shown separately. [2] Rate per 1,000 unmarried women (never-married, widowed, and divorced) estimated as of July 1. [3] Covers women aged 15 to 44 years.

Source: U.S. National Center for Health Statistics, *Vital Statistics of the United States*, annual; and *National Vital Statistics Reports (NVSR)* (formerly *Monthly Vital Statistics Report*).

No. 76. Live Births by Plurality of Birth and Ratios and Race of Mother: 1995 to 2000

Plurality and race of mother	1995	1996	1997	1998	1999	2000
NUMBER						
Live births, total [1]	3,899,589	3,891,494	3,880,894	3,941,553	3,959,417	4,058,814
White	3,098,885	3,093,057	3,072,640	3,118,727	3,132,501	3,194,005
Black	603,139	594,781	599,913	609,902	605,970	622,598
Live births in single deliveries [1]	3,797,880	3,784,805	3,770,020	3,823,258	3,837,789	3,932,573
White	3,018,184	3,007,997	2,984,532	3,024,693	3,035,757	3,094,219
Black	585,787	577,057	581,394	590,372	586,027	601,451
Live births in twin deliveries [1]	96,736	100,750	104,137	110,670	114,307	118,916
White	76,196	79,677	82,090	87,163	90,191	93,235
Black	17,000	17,285	17,989	19,001	19,374	20,626
Live births in higher-order multiple deliveries [1] . . .	4,973	5,939	6,737	7,625	7,321	7,325
White	4,505	5,383	6,018	6,871	6,553	6,551
Black	352	439	530	529	569	521
RATIO PER 1,000 LIVE BIRTHS						
All multiple births [1]	26.1	27.4	28.6	30.0	30.7	31.1
White	26.0	27.5	28.7	30.2	30.9	31.2
Black	28.8	29.8	30.9	32.0	32.9	34.0
Twin births [1]	24.8	25.9	26.8	28.1	28.9	29.3
White	24.6	25.8	26.7	27.9	28.8	29.2
Black	28.2	29.1	30.0	31.2	32.0	33.1
RATIO PER 100,000 LIVE BIRTHS						
Higher-order multiple births [1]	127.5	152.6	173.6	193.5	184.9	180.5
White	145.4	174.0	195.9	220.3	209.2	205.1
Black	58.4	73.8	88.3	86.7	93.9	83.7

[1] Includes races other than White and Black.

Source: U.S. National Center for Health Statistics, Advance report of Final Natality Statistics, and *National Vital Statistics Reports (NVSR)* (formerly *Monthly Vital Statistics Report*).

No. 77. Low Birth Weight and Births to Teenage Mothers and to Unmarried Women—States: 1990 to 2000

[Represents registered births. Excludes births to nonresidents of the United States. Based on 100 percent of births in all states and the District of Columbia. See Appendix III]

State	Percent of births with low birth weight [1]			Births to teenage mothers percent of total [2]			Births to unmarried women percent of total		
	1990	1995	2000	1990	1995	2000	1990	1995	2000
U.S.	7.0	7.3	7.6	12.8	13.1	11.8	26.6	32.2	33.2
AL.	8.4	9.0	9.7	18.2	18.5	15.7	30.1	34.5	34.3
AK.	4.8	5.3	5.6	9.7	11.2	11.8	26.2	29.9	33.0
AZ.	6.4	6.8	7.0	14.2	15.1	14.3	32.7	38.2	39.3
AR.	8.2	8.2	8.6	19.7	19.6	17.3	29.4	32.9	35.7
CA.	5.8	6.1	6.2	11.6	12.4	10.6	31.6	32.1	32.7
CO	8.0	8.4	8.4	11.3	12.1	11.7	21.2	24.9	25.0
CT.	6.6	7.1	7.4	8.2	8.6	7.8	26.6	30.6	29.3
DE.	7.6	8.4	8.6	11.9	13.2	12.3	29.0	34.9	37.9
DC	15.1	13.4	11.9	17.8	16.3	14.2	64.9	65.8	60.3
FL.	7.4	7.7	8.0	13.9	13.7	12.6	31.7	35.8	38.2
GA	8.7	8.8	8.6	16.7	16.3	13.9	32.8	35.2	37.0
HI	7.1	7.0	7.5	10.5	10.1	10.3	24.8	29.2	32.2
ID	5.7	5.9	6.7	12.3	14.0	11.6	16.7	19.9	21.6
IL	7.6	7.9	7.9	13.1	12.9	11.4	31.7	33.8	34.5
IN	6.6	7.5	7.4	14.5	14.7	12.5	26.2	31.9	34.7
IA	5.4	6.0	6.1	10.2	11.0	10.0	21.0	25.2	28.0
KS.	6.2	6.4	6.9	12.3	13.1	12.0	21.5	25.9	29.0
KY.	7.1	7.6	8.2	17.5	17.2	14.1	23.6	28.5	31.0
LA.	9.2	9.7	10.3	17.6	19.1	17.0	36.8	42.4	45.6
ME	5.1	6.1	6.0	10.8	10.3	9.4	22.6	27.8	31.0
MD	7.8	8.5	8.6	10.5	10.3	9.9	29.6	33.3	34.6
MA	5.9	6.3	7.1	8.0	7.5	6.6	24.7	25.6	26.5
MI	7.6	7.7	7.9	13.5	12.5	10.5	26.2	34.3	33.3
MN	5.1	5.9	6.1	8.0	8.4	8.3	20.9	23.9	25.8
MS	9.6	9.8	10.7	21.3	22.2	18.8	40.5	45.3	46.0
MO	7.1	7.6	7.6	14.4	14 4	13.1	28.6	32.1	34.6
MT	6.2	5.8	6.2	11.5	12.6	11.6	23.7	26.5	30.8
NE.	5.3	6.3	6.8	9.8	10.0	10.2	20.7	24.3	27.2
NV.	7.2	7.4	7.2	12.6	13.7	12.7	25.4	42.0	36.4
NH	4.9	5.5	6.3	7.2	7.6	6.8	16.9	22.2	24.7
NJ.	7.0	7.6	7.7	8.4	8.2	7.1	24.3	27.6	28.9
NM	7.4	7.5	8.0	16.3	18.4	17.4	35.4	42.6	45.6
NY.	7.6	7.6	7.7	9.1	9.3	8.2	33.0	37.9	36.6
NC	8.0	8.7	8.8	16.2	15.2	13.0	29.4	31.4	33.3
ND	5.5	5.3	6.4	8.6	9.6	9.2	18.4	23.5	28.3
OH	7.1	7.6	7.9	13.8	13.7	12.1	28.9	33.0	34.6
OK	6.6	7.0	7.5	16.2	17.1	15.9	25.2	30.5	34.3
OR	5.0	5.5	5.6	12.0	13.0	11.3	25.7	28.9	30.1
PA	7.1	7.4	7.7	10.9	10.8	9.9	28.6	32.4	32.7
RI	6.2	6.8	7.2	10.5	10.1	10.2	26.3	31.1	35.5
SC.	8.7	9.3	9.7	17.1	17.3	15.3	32.7	37.4	39.8
SD.	5.1	5.6	6.2	10.8	11.4	11.6	22.9	28.0	33.5
TN.	8.2	8.7	9.2	17.6	16.9	14.7	30.2	33.1	34.5
TX.	6.9	7.1	7.4	15.6	16.6	15.3	17.5	30.0	30.5
UT.	5.7	6.3	6.6	10.3	10.8	8.9	13.5	15.7	17.3
VT.	5.3	5.4	6.1	8.5	8.2	8.0	20.1	24.9	28.1
VA.	7.2	7.7	7.9	11.7	11.4	9.9	26.0	29.3	29.9
WA	5.3	5.5	5.6	10.8	11.5	10.2	23.7	26.7	28.2
WV	7.1	7.9	8.3	17.8	17.2	15.9	25.4	30.5	31.7
WI	5.9	6.0	6.5	10.2	10.5	10.2	24.2	27.4	29.3
WY	7.4	7.4	8.3	13.6	15.2	13.5	19.8	26.4	28.8
Puerto Rico.	(NA)	(NA)	10.8	(NA)	(NA)	(NA)	(NA)	(NA)	49.7
Virgin Islands.	(NA)	(NA)	9.1	(NA)	(NA)	(NA)	(NA)	(NA)	66.7
Guam	(NA)	(NA)	7.6	(NA)	(NA)	(NA)	(NA)	(NA)	54.8
American Samoa	(NA)	(NA)	2.7	(NA)	(NA)	(NA)	(NA)	(NA)	35.5
Northern Marianas	(NA)	(NA)	8.9	(NA)	(NA)	(NA)	(NA)	(NA)	(NA)

NA Not available.   [1] Less than 2,500 grams (5 pounds-8 ounces).   [2] Defined as mothers who are 20 years of age or younger.

Source: U.S. National Center for Health Statistics, *Vital Statistics of the United States*, annual; and *National Vital Statistics Reports (NVSR)* (formerly *Monthly Vital Statistics Report*). See also <http://www.cdc.gov/nchs/>.

No. 78. Live Births by Place of Delivery, Median and Low Birth Weight, and Prenatal Care: 1990 to 2000

[Represents registered births. Excludes births to nonresidents of the United States. For total number of births, see Table 68. See Appendix III]

Item	1990	1994	1995	1996	1997	1998	1999	2000
Births attended (1,000):								
In hospital [1]	4,110	3,912	3,861	3,854	3,881	3,904	3,923	4,021
By physician, not in hospital	14	7	6	6	5	6	5	5
By midwife and other, not in hospital [2]	21	21	21	20	20	21	21	21
Median birth weight [3]	7 lb.-7 oz.	(NA)	(NA)	7 lb.-7 oz.	7 lb.-7 oz.	7 lb.-7 oz.	(NA)	7 lb.-7 oz.
Percent of births with low birth weight	7.0	7.3	7.3	7.4	7.5	7.6	7.6	7.6
White	5.7	6.1	6.2	6.3	6.5	6.5	6.6	6.5
Black	13.3	13.2	13.1	13.0	13.0	13.0	13.1	13.0
Percent of births by period in which prenatal care began:								
1st trimester	74.2	80.2	81.3	81.9	82.5	82.8	83.2	83.2
3d trimester or no prenatal care	6.0	4.4	4.2	4.0	3.9	3.9	3.8	3.9

NA Not available. [1] Includes all births in hospitals or institutions and in clinics. [2] Includes births with attendant not specified. [3] Median birth weight based on race of mother; prior to 1990, based on race of child.

Source: U.S. National Center for Health Statistics, *Vital Statistics of the United States*, annual; and *National Vital Statistics Reports* (NVSR) (formerly *Monthly Vital Statistics Report*), and unpublished data. See also <http://www.cdc.gov/nchs/births.htm>.

No. 79. Method of Delivery by Race: 1990 to 2000

[In thousands (4,111 represents 4,111,000), except rate. 1990 excludes data for Oklahoma, which did not report method of delivery on the birth certificate]

Item	1990	1995	2000	Item	1990	1995	2000
Births by method of delivery	4,111	3,900	4,059	Repeat	53	46	56
Vaginal	3,111	3,064	3,108	Not stated	16	4	4
After previous cesarean	84	112	90	Hispanic births by method of			
Cesarean deliveries	914	807	924	delivery (1,000)	595	680	816
Primary	575	510	578	Vaginal	458	540	633
Repeat	339	297	346	After previous cesarean	10	17	17
Not stated	85	29	27	Cesarean deliveries	123	137	180
				Primary	76	83	105
White births by method of delivery	3,252	3,099	3,194	Repeat	47	54	75
Vaginal	2,454	2,435	2,449	Not stated	14	3	3
After previous cesarean	67	91	70	Cesarean delivery rate [1]	22.7	20.8	22.9
Cesarean deliveries	733	640	723	White	23.0	20.8	22.8
Primary	459	401	449	Black	22.1	21.8	24.3
Repeat	274	239	274	Primary [2]	16.0	14.7	16.1
Not stated	66	24	22	White	16.1	14.6	15.9
				Black	15.7	15.7	17.3
Black births by method of delivery	679	603	623	Rate of vaginal birth			
Vaginal	517	469	468	after previous cesarean [3]	19.9	27.5	20.6
After previous cesarean	13	16	14	White	19.7	27.6	20.4
Cesarean deliveries	146	130	150	Black	20.3	26.1	20.5
Primary	93	84	95				

[1] Cesarean rates are the number of cesarean deliveries per 100 total deliveries for specified category. [2] Number of primary cesareans per 100 live births to women who have not had a previous cesarean. [3] Number of vaginal births after previous cesarean delivery per 100 live births to women with a previous cesarean delivery.

Source: U.S. National Center for Health Statistics, *Vital Statistics of the United States*, annual.

No. 80. Women Who Have Had a Child in the Last Year by Age and Labor Force Status: 1980 to 2000

[3,247 represents 3,247,000. See headnote, Table 81]

Year	Total, 18 to 44 years old			18 to 29 years old			30 to 44 years old		
		In the labor force			In the labor force			In the labor force	
	Number (1,000)	Number (1,000)	Percent	Number (1,000)	Number (1,000)	Percent	Number (1,000)	Number (1,000)	Percent
1980	3,247	1,233	38	2,476	947	38	770	287	37
1981	3,381	1,411	42	2,499	1,004	40	881	407	46
1982	3,433	1,508	44	2,445	1,040	43	988	469	48
1983	3,625	1,563	43	2,682	1,138	42	942	425	45
1984	3,311	1,547	47	2,375	1,058	45	936	489	52
1985	3,497	1,691	48	2,512	1,204	48	984	488	50
1986	3,625	1,805	50	2,452	1,185	48	1,174	620	53
1987	3,701	1,881	51	2,521	1,258	50	1,180	623	53
1988	3,667	1,866	51	2,384	1,177	49	1,283	688	54
1990 [1]	3,913	2,068	53	2,568	1,275	50	1,346	793	59
1992 [1]	3,688	1,985	54	2,346	1,182	50	1,342	802	60
1994 [1]	3,890	2,066	53	2,389	1,209	51	1,501	857	57
1995 [1]	3,696	2,034	55	2,252	1,150	51	1,444	884	61
1998 [1]	3,671	2,155	59	(NA)	(NA)	(NA)	(NA)	(NA)	(NA)
2000 [1]	3,934	2,170	55	2,432	1,304	54	1,502	866	58

NA Not available. [1] Lower age limit is 15 years old.

Source: U.S. Bureau of the Census, *Current Population Reports*, P20-543; and unpublished data.

66   Vital Statistics

No. 81. Women Who Have Had a Child in the Last Year by Age: 1980 to 2000

[3,247 represents 3,247,000. Excludes births to nonresidents of the United States. Data are by place of residence. Metropolitan statistical areas (MSAs), consolidated metropolitan statistical areas (CMSAs), and New England county metropolitan areas (NECMAs) are defined by the U.S. Office of Management and Budget as of June 30, 1990. See Appendix II for definitions and components]

Age of mother	Women who had a child in last year (1,000)			Total births per 1,000 women			First births per 1,000 women		
	1980	1990	2000	1980	1990	2000	1980	1990	2000
Total	**3,247**	**3,913**	**3,934**	**71.1**	**67.0**	**64.6**	**28.5**	**26.4**	**26.7**
15 to 29 years old [1] ...	2,476	2,568	2,432	103.7	90.8	85.9	48.6	43.2	43.1
15 to 19 years old ..	(NA)	338	586	(NA)	39.8	59.7	(NA)	30.1	38.7
20 to 24 years old ..	1396	1038	850	96.6	113.4	91.8	(NA)	51.8	47.1
25 to 29 years old ..	1,081	1,192	996	114.8	112.1	107.9	(NA)	46.2	43.7
30 to 44 years old	770	1,346	1,502	35.4	44.7	46.1	6.3	10.6	12.5
30 to 34 years old ..	519	892	871	60.0	80.4	87.9	(NA)	21.9	27.5
35 to 39 years old ..	192	377	506	26.9	37.3	45.1	(NA)	6.5	9.6
40 to 44 years old ..	59	77	125	9.9	8.6	10.9	(NA)	1.2	2.3

NA Not available. [1] For 1980-88, 18 to 29 years old.

Source: U.S. Census Bureau, *Current Population Reports*, P20-375, P20-454, P20-470, and P20-499.

No. 82. Characteristics of Women Who Have Had a Child in the Last Year: 1995 and 2000

[As of June. Covers civilian noninstitutional population. Since the number of women who had a birth during the 12-month period was tabulated and not the actual numbers of births, some small underestimation of fertility for this period may exist due to the omission of: (1) Multiple births, (2) Two or more live births spaced within the 12-month period (the woman is counted only once), (3) Women who had births in the period and who did not survive to the survey date, (4) Women who were in institutions and therefore not in the survey universe. These losses may be somewhat offset by the inclusion in the CPS of births to immigrants who did not have their children born in the United States and births to nonresident women. These births would not have been recorded in the vital registration system. Based on Current Population Survey (CPS); see text, Section 1, and Appendix III]

Characteristic	1995			2000		
	Women who have had a child in the last year			Women who have had a child in the last year		
	Number of women (1,000)	Total births per 1,000 women	First births per 1,000 women	Number of women (1,000)	Total births per 1,000 women	First births per 1,000 women
Total [1]	**60,225**	**61.4**	**23.2**	**60,873**	**64.6**	**26.7**
White.....................	48,603	59.2	22.6	48,506	65.4	27.2
Black	8,617	70.6	26.4	8,939	63.2	21.9
Hispanic [2]	6,632	79.6	25.0	8,002	95.1	38.6
Currently married	31,616	85.5	30.3	30,497	88.8	35.5
Married, spouse present	29,202	87.2	31.4	28,215	90.8	37.0
Married, spouse absent [3]	2,414	64.5	17.4	2,282	64.5	16.6
Widowed or divorced	5,762	28.4	4.1	5,281	31.0	6.8
Never married	22,846	36.3	18.0	25,095	42.3	20.2
Educational attainment:						
Less than high school	12,629	57.3	19.6	13,006	70.7	29.5
High school, 4 years	18,404	67.4	25.5	17,205	70.0	29.5
College: 1 or more years	29,192	59.3	23.2	30,662	59.0	24.0
No degree	12,724	56.1	21.2	12,603	51.6	19.2
Associate degree...........	4,663	56.9	19.2	4,955	60.6	23.6
Bachelor's degree	8,884	65.3	27.0	9,926	61.7	27.7
Graduate or professional degree .	2,921	59.2	26.8	3,178	77.7	32.0
Labor force status:						
Employed	39,989	46.5	20.9	41,369	47.7	20.7
Unemployed	3,287	53.5	22.8	2,493	79.4	31.1
Not in labor force	16,949	98.1	28.5	17,011	103.7	40.6
Occupation of employed women:						
Managerial-professional	11,059	46.2	22.3	12,481	52.2	22.9
Technical, sales, admin. support ...	16,997	48.6	21.5	16,561	44.0	20.3
Service workers	7,612	44.0	16.6	8,102	51.0	20.1
Farming, forestry, and fishing	501	41.0	27.9	473	69.6	71.8
Precision prod, craft, repair.......	813	56.6	37.5	880	42.3	15.1
Operators, fabricators, laborers	3,007	39.5	17.8	2,872	38.1	17.2
Family income:						
Under $10,000	6,957	91.0	32.8	4,249	86.8	32.5
$10,000 to $19,999............	8,159	64.3	25.8	6,203	74.8	25.3
$20,000 to $24,999............	4,542	60.6	20.3	3,439	76.2	37.3
$25,000 to $29,999............	4,364	57.0	18.9	3,761	78.9	34.0
$30,000 to $34,999............	4,076	60.6	24.3	3,572	62.4	27.3
$35,000 to $49,999............	9,949	59.1	20.8	8,864	64.9	25.3
$50,000 to $74,999............	9,720	52.5	23.3	10,646	61.2	26.8
$75,000 and over	7,088	53.1	19.2	12,506	60.1	24.3

[1] Includes women of other races and women with family income not reported, not shown separately. [2] Persons of Hispanic origin may be of any race. [3] Includes separated women.

Source: U.S. Census Bureau, *Current Population Reports*, P20-375, P20-499, and unpublished data..

U.S. Census Bureau, Statistical Abstract of the United States: 2002

No. 83. Number of Pregnancies, Live Births, and Induced Abortions by Age and Race of Woman: 1980 to 1996

[Due to rounding, figures may not add to totals]

Age and race of woman	1980	1985	1990	1991	1992	1993	1994	1995	1996
ALL PREGNANCIES									
Total [1]	5,912	6,144	6,778	6,674	6,596	6,494	6,373	6,245	6,240
Under 15 years	29	30	29	29	30	30	30	28	26
15 to 19 years	1,146	981	1,013	975	939	928	923	904	893
20 to 24 years	1,956	1,891	1,847	1,843	1,813	1,762	1,682	1,602	1,570
25 to 29 years	1,626	1,764	1,908	1,827	1,771	1,701	1,637	1,598	1,617
30 to 34 years	844	1,045	1,319	1,313	1,326	1,332	1,333	1,322	1,312
35 to 39 years	258	373	562	581	603	622	642	659	683
40 years and over	54	60	100	106	113	119	127	132	140
Race:									
White	4,585	4,733	5,117	5,006	4,924	4,834	4,755	4,692	(NA)
All other	1,328	1,411	1,660	1,668	1,671	1,660	1,618	1,553	(NA)
LIVE BIRTHS									
Total	3,612	3,761	4,158	4,111	4,065	4,000	3,953	3,900	3,891
Race:									
White	2,936	3,038	3,290	3,241	3,202	3,150	3,121	3,099	3,093
All other	676	723	868	870	863	850	832	801	798
INDUCED ABORTIONS									
Total	1,554	1,589	1,609	1,557	1,529	1,500	1,431	1,364	1,366
Under 15 years	15	17	13	12	13	12	12	11	10
15 to 19 years	445	399	351	314	295	289	276	264	264
20 to 24 years	549	548	532	533	526	514	478	442	434
25 to 29 years	304	336	360	348	341	332	316	308	318
30 to 34 years	153	181	216	213	213	211	205	196	195
35 to 39 years	67	87	108	107	110	111	111	110	112
40 years and over	21	21	29	29	31	31	32	32	33
Race:									
White	1,094	1,076	1,039	982	944	911	861	820	(NA)
All other	460	513	570	574	585	589	570	544	(NA)

NA Not available. [1] Includes fetal losses not shown.

Source: U.S. National Center for Health Statistics, *Vital and Health Statistics, Trends in Pregnancies and Pregnancy Rates by Outcome: 1976-96,* Series 21, No. 56.

No. 84. Contraceptive Use by Women, 15 to 44 Years of Age: 1995

[60,201 represents 60,201,000. Based on samples of the female population of the United States; see source for details. See Appendix III]

Contraceptive status and method	All women [1]	Age 15-24 years	Age 25-34 years	Age 35-44 years	Non-Hispanic White	Non-Hispanic Black	His-panic	Never married	Currently married	Formerly married
All women (1,000)	60,201	18,002	20,758	21,440	42,522	8,210	6,702	22,679	29,673	7,849
PERCENT DISTRIBUTION										
Sterile [2]	29.7	2.6	25.0	57.0	30.2	31.5	28.4	6.9	43.2	45.1
Surgically sterile	27.9	1.8	23.6	54.0	28.5	29.7	26.3	5.7	41.1	42.5
Nonsurgically sterile [3]	1.7	0.7	1.3	2.8	1.6	1.8	2.0	1.1	2.0	2.2
Pregnant, postpartum	4.6	5.9	6.9	1.3	4.3	4.5	6.3	3.1	6.4	1.9
Seeking pregnancy	4.0	2.1	6.2	3.5	3.7	4.6	4.0	1.5	6.4	2.1
Other nonusers	22.3	44.4	13.3	12.6	21.1	23.1	26.3	46.8	4.7	18.4
Never had intercourse	10.9	30.8	3.4	1.4	10.4	8.9	12.1	28.9	-	-
No intercourse in last month [4]	6.2	7.0	5.3	6.5	5.7	7.2	8.6	11.5	0.5	12.7
Had intercourse in last month [4]	5.2	6.6	4.7	4.7	5.0	7.0	5.6	6.4	4.2	5.7
Nonsurgical contraceptors	39.7	45.0	49.1	26.1	41.2	36.1	35.1	41.8	39.7	32.4
Pill	17.3	23.1	23.7	6.3	18.8	14.8	13.6	20.4	15.6	14.6
IUD	0.5	0.1	0.6	0.8	0.5	0.5	0.9	0.3	0.7	0.4
Diaphragm	1.2	0.2	1.2	2.0	1.5	0.5	0.4	0.5	1.8	0.9
Condom	13.1	13.9	15.0	10.7	13.0	12.5	12.1	13.9	13.3	10.1
Periodic abstinence	1.5	0.5	1.8	2.0	1.6	0.7	1.3	0.6	2.3	0.7
Natural family planning	0.2	-	0.3	0.3	0.3	-	0.1	-	0.4	-
Withdrawal	2.0	1.6	2.3	1.9	2.1	0.9	2.0	1.5	2.3	1.8
Other methods [5]	3.9	5.6	4.2	2.1	3.4	6.2	4.7	4.6	3.3	3.9

- Represents or rounds to zero. [1] Includes other races, not shown separately. [2] Total sterile includes male sterile for unknown reasons. [3] Persons sterile from illness, accident, or congenital conditions. [4] Data refer to no intercourse in the 3 months prior to interview. [5] Includes implants, injectables, morning-after-pill, suppository, Today™ sponge, and less frequently used methods.

Source: U.S. National Center for Health Statistics, special tabulations from the 1995 National Survey of Family Growth.

No. 85. Live Births—Mothers Who Smoked During Pregnancy: 1999

[Excludes California, Indiana, New York State (but includes New York City), and South Dakota, which did not require reporting of tobacco use during pregnancy]

Smoking measure and race of mother	Total	Age of mother 15-19 years	20-24 years	25-29 years	30-34 years	35-39 years	40-54 years
All races [1]	**3,430,385**	**418,240**	**858,770**	**937,236**	**768,339**	**367,719**	**72,082**
White	2,702,289	289,581	644,752	758,986	641,781	304,505	58,810
Black	570,478	115,514	182,883	130,504	84,909	43,654	9,161
PERCENT DISTRIBUTION							
All races smoker	100.0	100.0	100.0	100.0	100.0	100.0	100.0
10 cigarettes or less	70.1	78.7	72.2	66.9	65.1	62.8	60.7
11-20 cigarettes	26.5	19.4	24.8	29.3	30.5	31.8	33.2
21 cigarettes or more	3.5	1.8	3.0	3.9	4.5	5.4	5.9
White smoker	100.0	100.0	100.0	100.0	100.0	100.0	100.0
10 cigarettes or less	67.7	77.1	70.0	64.4	62.3	59.2	56.9
11-20 cigarettes	28.6	21.0	26.8	31.5	32.8	34.6	36.1
21 cigarettes or more	3.7	2.0	3.2	4.1	4.9	6.1	6.9
Black smoker	100.0	100.0	100.0	100.0	100.0	100.0	100.0
10 cigarettes or less	84.1	90.1	86.6	82.1	80.4	79.3	75.2
11-20 cigarettes	14.2	9.0	11.9	16.1	17.3	18.6	21.8
21 cigarettes or more	1.6	0.9	1.3	1.7	2.2	1.8	2.0

[1] Includes races other than White and Black.

Source: U.S. National Center for Health Statistics, National Vital Statistics Reports (NVSR) (formerly *Monthly Vital Statistical Report*).

No. 86. Percent Low Birthweight by Smoking Status, Age, and Race of Mother: 1999

[Low birthweight is defined as weight of less than 2,500 grams (5 lb. 8 oz.). Excludes California, Indiana, New York State (but includes New York City), and South Dakota, which did not require reporting of tobacco use during pregnancy]

Smoking status and race of mother	All ages	Under 15 years	Age of mother 15-19 years Total	15-17 years	18-19 years	20-24 years	25-29 years	30-34 years	35-39 years
All races [1]	**7.8**	**13.4**	**9.9**	**10.8**	**9.5**	**7.8**	**6.9**	**7.1**	**8.6**
Smoker	12.1	15.7	11.6	12.4	11.3	10.6	11.5	13.2	16.7
Nonsmoker	7.2	13.2	9.6	10.5	9.0	7.3	6.3	6.6	7.7
White	6.7	11.5	8.4	9.2	8.1	6.6	6.0	6.3	7.5
Smoker	10.8	15.1	10.9	11.6	10.6	9.8	10.2	11.4	14.4
Nonsmoker	6.1	11.1	7.7	8.5	7.2	5.8	5.4	5.8	6.7
Black	13.2	15.5	13.8	14.3	13.5	12.3	12.3	13.6	16.1
Smoker	21.0	19.4	17.3	18.0	17.0	16.7	21.5	25.0	29.2
Nonsmoker	12.4	15.4	13.5	14.1	13.1	11.8	11.3	12.3	14.0

[1] Includes races other than White and Black.

Source: U.S. National Center for Health Statistics, *National Vital Statistics Reports (NVSR)* (formerly *Monthly Vital Statistical Report*).

No. 87. Live Births to Mothers With Selected Complications of Labor and/or Delivery and Rates by Age of Mother: 1999

[Rates are number of live births with specified complication per 1,000 live births in specified group]

Complication	Number of Complication reported	All ages	Under 20 years	Age of mother 20-24 years	25-29 years	30-34 years	35-39 years	40-54 years
All races [1]								
Febrile	59,904	15.3	18.5	15.6	15.9	14.5	12.3	11.1
Meconium, moderate/heavy	213,698	54.7	59.7	55.2	53.5	52.5	55.1	55.5
Premature rupture of membrane	100,130	25.6	26.7	24.3	25.1	25.8	27.3	30.9
Abruption placenta	21,999	5.6	5.4	5.2	5.3	5.8	7.0	8.6
Placenta previa	12,492	3.2	1.1	1.7	2.8	4.3	6.5	8.9
Other excessive bleeding	21,930	5.6	5.2	5.2	5.5	5.8	6.4	8.2
Seizures during labor	1,331	0.3	0.7	0.4	0.3	0.2	0.3	0.3
Precipitous labor	77,848	19.9	14.3	18.9	19.8	22.1	23.6	23.3
Prolonged labor	30,683	7.9	8.4	8.0	7.8	7.8	7.3	7.9
Dysfunctional labor	105,795	27.1	26.5	25.5	27.4	27.7	28.2	31.2
Breech/Malpresentation	152,084	38.9	29.2	31.5	39.1	44.7	50.4	58.1
Cephalopelvic disproportion	71,604	18.3	17.4	16.7	19.2	19.2	18.6	20.6
Cord Prolapse	7,773	2.0	1.6	1.8	1.9	2.1	2.5	2.8
Anesthetic complication [2]	2,299	0.6	0.4	0.5	0.7	0.7	0.8	0.9
Fetal distress [2]	140,756	39.6	43.7	38.5	38.0	38.6	41.7	49.7

[1] Includes races other than White and Black.   [2] Texas does not report this complication.

Source: U.S. National Center for Health Statistics, *Vital Statistics of the United States,* annual; and unpublished data.

Vital Statistics   69

No. 88. Abortions—Number, Rate, and Ratio by Race: 1975 to 1997

	All races				White				Black and other			
		Abortions				Abortions				Abortions		
Year	Women 15-44 years old (1,000)	Number (1,000)	Rate per 1,000 women	Ratio per 1,000 live births [1]	Women 15-44 years old (1,000)	Number (1,000)	Rate per 1,000 women	Ratio per 1,000 live births [1]	Women 15-44 years old (1,000)	Number (1,000)	Rate per 1,000 women	Ratio per 1,000 live births [1]
1975 ..	47,606	1,034	21.7	331	40,857	701	17.2	276	6,749	333	49.3	565
1979 ..	52,016	1,498	28.8	420	44,266	1,062	24.0	373	7,750	435	56.2	625
1980 ..	53,048	1,554	29.3	428	44,942	1,094	24.3	376	8,106	460	56.5	642
1981 ..	53,901	1,577	29.3	430	45,494	1,108	24.3	377	8,407	470	55.9	645
1982 [2] .	54,679	1,574	28.8	428	46,049	1,095	23.8	373	8,630	479	55.5	646
1983 [2] .	55,340	1,575	28.5	436	46,506	1,084	23.3	376	8,834	491	55.5	670
1984 ..	56,061	1,577	28.1	423	47,023	1,087	23.1	366	9,038	491	54.3	646
1985 [2] .	56,754	1,589	28.0	422	47,512	1,076	22.6	360	9,242	513	55.5	659
1986 [2] .	57,483	1,574	27.4	416	48,010	1,045	21.8	350	9,473	529	55.9	661
1987 ..	57,964	1,559	27.1	405	48,288	1,017	21.1	338	9,676	542	56.0	648
1988 [2] .	58,192	1,591	27.3	401	48,325	1,026	21.2	333	9,867	565	57.3	638
1989 [2] .	58,365	1,567	26.8	380	48,104	1,006	20.9	309	10,261	561	54.7	650
1990 [2] .	58,700	1,609	27.4	389	48,224	1,039	21.5	318	10,476	570	54.4	655
1991 ..	59,080	1,557	26.3	379	48,406	982	20.3	303	10,674	574	53.8	661
1992 [2] .	59,020	1,529	25.9	380	48,161	943	19.6	298	10859	585	53.9	681
1993 [2] .	59,143	1,500	25.4	378	48,137	911	18.9	291	11,007	589	53.5	700
1994 [2] .	59,284	1,431	24.1	364	48,121	861	17.9	277	11,163	570	51.1	699
1995 ..	59,442	1,364	22.9	351	48,140	820	17.0	265	11,302	544	48.1	686
1996 ..	59,606	1,366	22.9	351	48,120	800	16.6	259	11,486	566	49.2	701
1997 ..	59,688	1,328	22.2	340	48,081	773	16.1	250	11,607	555	47.8	680

[1] Live births are those which occurred from July 1 of year shown through June 30 of the following year (to match time of conception with abortions). Births are classified by race of child 1972-1988, and by race of mother after 1988.   [2] Total numbers of abortions in 1983 and 1986 have been estimated by interpolation; 1989, 1990, 1993, and 1994 have been estimated using trends in CDC data.

No. 89. Abortions by Selected Characteristics: 1990 to 1997

[Number of abortions from surveys conducted by source; characteristics from the U.S. Centers for Disease Control's (CDC) annual abortion surveillance summaries, with adjustments for changes in states reporting data to the CDC each year. Total number of abortions in 1990 have been estimated using trends in CDC data]

Characteristic	Number (1,000)			Percent distribution			Abortion ratio [1]		
	1990	1995	1997	1990	1995	1997	1990	1995	1997
Total abortions	1,609	1,364	1,328	100	100	100	280	260	254
Age of woman:									
Less than 15 years old	13	11	10	1	1	1	515	480	496
15 to 19 years old	351	264	254	22	19	19	403	348	345
20 to 24 years old	532	442	420	33	32	32	328	317	306
25 to 29 years old	360	308	313	22	23	24	224	225	225
30 to 34 years old	216	196	189	13	14	14	196	179	175
35 to 39 years old	108	110	109	7	8	8	249	220	207
40 years old and over.	29	32	34	2	2	3	354	310	290
Race of woman:									
White.	1,039	820	773	65	60	58	241	210	200
Black and other	570	544	555	35	40	42	396	409	405
Marital status of woman: [2]									
Married	341	269	253	21	20	19	104	93	87
Unmarried	1,268	1,095	1,074	79	80	81	516	466	459
Number of prior live births:									
None	780	614	562	49	45	42	316	277	262
One	396	359	367	25	26	28	230	223	224
Two	280	248	251	17	18	19	292	285	282
Three	102	95	97	6	7	7	279	284	282
Four or more	50	48	50	3	4	4	223	228	236
Number of prior induced abortions:									
None	891	721	680	55	53	51	(NA)	(NA)	(NA)
One	443	383	376	28	28	28	(NA)	(NA)	(NA)
Two or more	275	260	271	17	19	20	(NA)	(NA)	(NA)
Weeks of gestation: [3]									
Less than 9 weeks	825	728	732	51	53	55	(NA)	(NA)	(NA)
9 to 10 weeks	416	317	292	26	23	22	(NA)	(NA)	(NA)
11 to 12 weeks	195	153	146	12	11	11	(NA)	(NA)	(NA)
13 weeks or more	173	166	157	11	12	12	(NA)	(NA)	(NA)

NA Not available.   [1] Number of abortions per 1,000 abortions and live births. Live births are those which occurred from July 1 of year shown through June 30 of the following year (to match time of conception with abortions).   [2] Separated women included with unmarried.   [3] Data not exactly comparable with prior years because of a change in the method of calculation.

Source of Tables 88 and 89: S.K. Henshaw and J. Van Vort, eds., Abortion Factbook, 1992 Edition: Readings, Trends, and State and Local Data to 1988, The Alan Guttmacher Institute, New York, NY, 1992 (copyright); S.K. Henshaw and J. Van Vort, Abortion Services in the United States, 1991 and 1992, Family Planning Perspectives, 26:100, 1994; S.K. Henshaw, Abortion Incidence and Services in the United States, 1995-1996, Family Planning Perspectives, 30:263, 1998; and unpublished data.

No. 90. Abortions—Number and Rate by State: 1992 and 1996

[Number of abortions from surveys of hospitals, clinics, and physicians identified as providers of abortion services conducted by The Alan Guttmacher Institute. Abortion rates are computed per 1,000 women 15 to 44 years of age on July 1 of specified year]

State	Number (1,000) 1992	Number (1,000) 1996	Rate [1] 1992	Rate [1] 1996	State	Number (1,000) 1992	Number (1,000) 1996	Rate [1] 1992	Rate [1] 1996
U.S.	1,529	1,366	25.9	22.9	MO	14	11	11.6	9.1
AL	17	15	18.2	15.6	MT	3	3	18.2	15.6
AK	2	2	16.5	14.6	NE	6	4	15.7	12.3
AZ	21	19	24.1	19.8	NV	13	15	44.2	44.6
AR	7	6	13.5	11.4	NH	4	3	14.6	12.7
CA	304	238	42.1	33.0	NJ	55	63	31.0	35.8
CO	20	18	23.6	20.9	NM	6	5	17.7	14.4
CT	20	16	26.2	22.5	NY	195	168	46.2	41.1
DE	6	4	35.2	24.1	NC	36	34	22.4	20.2
DC	21	21	138.4	154.5	ND	1	1	10.7	9.4
FL	85	94	30.0	32.0	OH	50	43	19.5	17.0
GA	40	37	24.0	21.1	OK	9	8	12.5	11.8
HI	12	7	46.0	27.3	OR	16	15	23.9	21.6
ID	2	2	7.2	6.1	PA	50	40	18.6	15.2
IL	68	69	25.4	26.1	RI	7	5	30.0	24.4
IN	16	15	12.0	11.2	SC	12	10	14.2	11.6
IA	7	6	11.4	9.4	SD	1	1	6.8	6.5
KS	13	11	22.4	18.9	TN	19	18	16.2	14.8
KY	10	8	11.4	9.6	TX	97	91	23.1	20.7
LA	14	15	13.4	14.7	UT	4	4	9.3	7.8
ME	4	3	14.7	9.7	VT	3	2	21.2	17.1
MD	31	31	26.4	26.3	VA	35	30	22.7	18.9
MA	41	41	28.4	29.3	WA	33	26	27.7	20.9
MI	56	49	25.2	22.3	WV	3	3	7.7	6.6
MN	16	15	15.6	13.9	WI	15	14	13.6	12.3
MS	8	4	12.4	7.2	WY	-	-	4.3	2.7

- Represents or rounds to zero.   [1] Rate per 1,000 women, 15 to 44 years old.

Source: S.K. Henshaw and J. Van Vort, *Abortion Services in the United States, 1991 and 1992, Family Planning Perspectives,* 26:100, 1994; and S.K. Henshaw, Abortion Incidence and Services in the United States, 1995-1996, *Family Planning Perspectives,* 30:263, 1998.

No. 91. Expectation of Life at Birth, 1970 to 2000, and Projections, 2005 and 2010

[**In years.** Excludes deaths of nonresidents of the United States]

Year	Total			White			Black and other			Black		
	Total	Male	Female	Total	Male	Female	Total	Male	Female	Total	Male	Female
1970	70.8	67.1	74.7	71.7	68.0	75.6	65.3	61.3	69.4	64.1	60.0	68.3
1975	72.6	68.8	76.6	73.4	69.5	77.3	68.0	63.7	72.4	66.8	62.4	71.3
1980	73.7	70.0	77.4	74.4	70.7	78.1	69.5	65.3	73.6	68.1	63.8	72.5
1982	74.5	70.8	78.1	75.1	71.5	78.7	70.9	66.8	74.9	69.4	65.1	73.6
1983	74.6	71.0	78.1	75.2	71.6	78.7	70.9	67.0	74.7	69.4	65.2	73.5
1984	74.7	71.1	78.2	75.3	71.8	78.7	71.1	67.2	74.9	69.5	65.3	73.6
1985	74.7	71.1	78.2	75.3	71.8	78.7	71.0	67.0	74.8	69.3	65.0	73.4
1986	74.7	71.2	78.2	75.4	71.9	78.8	70.9	66.8	74.9	69.1	64.8	73.4
1987	74.9	71.4	78.3	75.6	72.1	78.9	71.0	66.9	75.0	69.1	64.7	73.4
1988	74.9	71.4	78.3	75.6	72.2	78.9	70.8	66.7	74.8	68.9	64.4	73.2
1989	75.1	71.7	78.5	75.9	72.5	79.2	70.9	66.7	74.9	68.8	64.3	73.3
1990	75.4	71.8	78.8	76.1	72.7	79.4	71.2	67.0	75.2	69.1	64.5	73.6
1991	75.5	72.0	78.9	76.3	72.9	79.6	71.5	67.3	75.5	69.3	64.6	73.8
1992	75.8	72.3	79.1	76.5	73.2	79.8	71.8	67.7	75.7	69.6	65.0	73.9
1993	75.5	72.2	78.8	76.3	73.1	79.5	71.5	67.3	75.5	69.2	64.6	73.7
1994	75.7	72.3	79.0	76.4	73.2	79.6	71.7	67.5	75.8	69.6	64.9	74.1
1995	75.8	72.5	78.9	76.5	73.4	79.6	71.9	67.9	75.7	69.6	65.2	73.9
1996	76.1	73.0	79.0	76.8	73.8	79.6	72.6	68.9	76.1	70.3	66.1	74.2
1997	76.5	73.6	79.4	77.1	74.3	79.9	(NA)	(NA)	(NA)	71.1	67.2	74.7
1998 [1]	76.7	73.8	79.5	77.3	74.5	80.0	(NA)	(NA)	(NA)	71.3	67.6	74.8
1999 [2]	76.7	73.9	79.4	77.3	74.6	79.9	(NA)	(NA)	(NA)	71.4	67.8	74.7
2000 [2]	76.9	74.1	79.5	77.4	74.8	80.0	(NA)	(NA)	(NA)	71.7	68.2	74.9
Projections:												
2005	77.8	74.9	80.7	78.3	75.4	81.1	(NA)	(NA)	(NA)	73.5	69.9	76.8
2010	78.5	75.6	81.4	79.0	76.1	81.8	(NA)	(NA)	(NA)	74.5	70.9	77.8

NA Not available.   [1] The 1998 life table values are based upon an 85 percent sample of deaths.   [2] Based on middle mortality assumptions; for details, see source. Source: U.S. Census Bureau, Population Division Working Paper No. 38.

Source: Except as noted, U.S. National Center for Health Statistics, *Vital Statistics of the United States,* annual, and *National Vital Statistics Reports (NVSR)* (formerly *Monthly Vital Statistics Reports*).

No. 92. Selected Life Table Values: 1979 to 2000

Age and sex	Total[1] 1979-1981	Total 1985	Total 1990	Total 1995	Total 1997	Total 1998	Total 1999	Total 2000	White 1979-1981	White 1985	White 1990	White 1995	White 1997	White 1998	White 1999	White 2000	Black 1979-1981	Black 1985	Black 1990	Black 1995	Black 1997	Black 1998	Black 1999	Black 2000
AVERAGE EXPECTATION OF LIFE IN YEARS																								
At birth: Male	70.1	71.1	71.8	72.5	73.6	73.8	73.9	74.1	70.8	71.8	72.7	73.4	74.3	74.5	74.6	74.8	64.1	65.0	64.5	65.4	67.3	67.6	67.8	68.2
Female	77.6	78.2	78.8	78.9	79.2	79.5	79.4	79.5	78.2	78.7	79.4	79.6	79.8	80.0	79.9	80.0	72.9	73.4	73.6	74.0	74.7	74.8	74.7	74.9
Age 20: Male	51.9	52.6	53.3	53.8	54.7	55.0	55.0	55.2	52.5	53.2	54.0	54.5	55.3	55.5	55.6	55.7	46.4	47.1	46.7	47.3	49.1	49.5	49.6	49.9
Female	59.0	59.3	59.8	59.9	60.1	60.0	60.2	60.3	59.4	59.8	60.3	60.3	60.5	60.8	60.7	60.7	54.9	55.2	55.3	55.5	56.1	56.2	56.2	56.3
Age 40: Male	33.6	34.2	35.1	35.6	36.2	36.4	36.5	36.7	34.0	34.7	35.6	36.1	36.6	36.8	36.9	37.1	29.5	29.8	30.1	30.6	31.7	31.9	31.9	32.3
Female	39.8	40.0	40.6	40.7	40.8	41.1	41.0	41.0	40.2	40.4	41.0	41.0	41.1	41.4	41.3	41.3	36.3	36.4	36.8	37.0	37.4	37.5	37.4	37.5
Age 50: Male	25.0	25.6	26.4	27.0	27.4	27.6	27.7	27.9	25.3	25.8	26.7	27.3	27.7	27.9	28.0	28.2	22.0	22.1	22.5	23.1	23.8	23.9	24.0	24.2
Female	30.7	30.8	31.3	31.4	31.6	31.8	31.7	31.8	31.0	31.1	31.6	31.7	31.8	32.0	32.0	32.0	27.8	27.8	28.2	28.5	28.8	28.8	28.7	28.9
Age 65: Male	14.2	14.3	15.1	15.6	15.8	16.0	16.1	16.3	14.3	14.5	15.2	15.7	15.9	16.1	16.1	16.3	13.3	13.0	13.2	13.7	14.2	14.3	14.3	14.5
Female	18.4	18.5	18.9	18.9	19.0	19.2	19.1	19.2	18.6	18.7	19.1	19.0	19.1	19.3	19.2	19.2	17.1	16.9	17.2	17.2	17.4	17.4	17.3	17.4
EXPECTED DEATHS PER 1,000 ALIVE AT SPECIFIED AGE[2]																								
At birth: Male	13.9	12.0	10.3	(NA)	(NA)	(NA)	7.7	(NA)	12.3	10.6	8.6	(NA)	(NA)	(NA)	6.4	(NA)	23.0	19.9	19.7	(NA)	(NA)	(NA)	15.9	(NA)
Female	11.2	9.4	8.2	(NA)	(NA)	(NA)	6.4	(NA)	9.7	8.0	6.6	(NA)	(NA)	(NA)	5.2	(NA)	19.3	16.5	16.3	(NA)	(NA)	(NA)	13.2	(NA)
Age 20: Male	1.8	1.5	1.6	(NA)	(NA)	(NA)	1.3	(NA)	1.8	1.4	1.4	(NA)	(NA)	(NA)	1.2	(NA)	2.2	1.9	2.7	(NA)	(NA)	(NA)	2.7	(NA)
Female	0.6	0.5	0.5	(NA)	(NA)	(NA)	0.5	(NA)	0.6	0.5	0.5	(NA)	(NA)	(NA)	0.4	(NA)	0.7	0.6	0.7	(NA)	(NA)	(NA)	0.6	(NA)
Age 40: Male	3.0	2.8	3.1	(NA)	(NA)	(NA)	2.6	(NA)	2.6	2.5	2.7	(NA)	(NA)	(NA)	2.3	(NA)	6.9	6.5	7.1	(NA)	(NA)	(NA)	4.8	(NA)
Female	1.6	1.4	1.4	(NA)	(NA)	(NA)	1.4	(NA)	1.4	1.3	1.2	(NA)	(NA)	(NA)	1.2	(NA)	3.2	2.9	3.1	(NA)	(NA)	(NA)	2.9	(NA)
Age 50: Male	7.8	6.8	6.2	(NA)	(NA)	(NA)	5.6	(NA)	7.1	6.2	5.6	(NA)	(NA)	(NA)	5.1	(NA)	14.9	13.3	12.8	(NA)	(NA)	(NA)	11.3	(NA)
Female	4.2	3.8	3.5	(NA)	(NA)	(NA)	3.2	(NA)	3.8	3.5	3.2	(NA)	(NA)	(NA)	2.9	(NA)	7.7	6.8	6.6	(NA)	(NA)	(NA)	6.0	(NA)
Age 65: Male	28.2	26.1	23.9	(NA)	(NA)	(NA)	20.5	(NA)	27.4	25.2	23.0	(NA)	(NA)	(NA)	19.8	(NA)	38.5	28.5	36.8	(NA)	(NA)	(NA)	30.5	(NA)
Female	14.3	14.1	13.5	(NA)	(NA)	(NA)	12.8	(NA)	13.6	13.5	12.8	(NA)	(NA)	(NA)	12.3	(NA)	21.6	21.4	21.4	(NA)	(NA)	(NA)	18.3	(NA)
NUMBER SURVIVING TO SPECIFIED AGE PER 1,000 BORN ALIVE																								
Age 20: Male	973	977	979	(NA)	(NA)	(NA)	984	(NA)	975	979	981	(NA)	(NA)	(NA)	986	(NA)	961	966	963	(NA)	(NA)	(NA)	971	(NA)
Female	982	985	986	(NA)	(NA)	(NA)	989	(NA)	984	986	988	(NA)	(NA)	(NA)	990	(NA)	972	976	976	(NA)	(NA)	(NA)	980	(NA)
Age 40: Male	933	941	938	(NA)	(NA)	(NA)	952	(NA)	940	946	946	(NA)	(NA)	(NA)	958	(NA)	885	897	880	(NA)	(NA)	(NA)	917	(NA)
Female	965	970	971	(NA)	(NA)	(NA)	974	(NA)	969	973	975	(NA)	(NA)	(NA)	977	(NA)	941	948	944	(NA)	(NA)	(NA)	954	(NA)
Age 50: Male	890	902	899	(NA)	(NA)	(NA)	917	(NA)	901	912	912	(NA)	(NA)	(NA)	926	(NA)	801	820	801	(NA)	(NA)	(NA)	850	(NA)
Female	941	948	950	(NA)	(NA)	(NA)	954	(NA)	947	953	957	(NA)	(NA)	(NA)	960	(NA)	896	908	904	(NA)	(NA)	(NA)	915	(NA)
Age 65: Male	706	727	741	(NA)	(NA)	(NA)	777	(NA)	724	744	760	(NA)	(NA)	(NA)	793	(NA)	551	571	571	(NA)	(NA)	(NA)	633	(NA)
Female	835	844	851	(NA)	(NA)	(NA)	863	(NA)	848	855	864	(NA)	(NA)	(NA)	874	(NA)	733	746	751	(NA)	(NA)	(NA)	777	(NA)

NA Not available. [1] Includes other races not shown separately. [2] See footnote 1, Table 93.

Source: U.S. National Center for Health Statistics, *U.S. Life Tables and Actuarial Tables, 1959-61, 1969-71, and 1979-81; Vital Statistics of the United States,* annual; and unpublished data.

No. 93. Expectation of Life and Expected Deaths by Race, Sex, and Age: 1999

Age (years)	Expectation of life in years					Expected deaths per 1,000 alive at specified age [1]				
	Total	White		Black		Total	White		Black	
		Male	Female	Male	Female		Male	Female	Male	Female
At birth	76.7	74.6	79.9	67.8	74.7	7.06	6.35	5.16	15.92	13.16
1	76.3	74.1	79.3	67.9	74.7	0.53	0.49	0.44	1.11	0.83
2	75.3	73.1	78.4	67.0	73.8	0.36	0.37	0.28	0.65	0.53
3	74.3	72.2	77.4	66.0	72.8	0.27	0.29	0.22	0.42	0.38
4	73.4	71.2	76.4	65.0	71.9	0.22	0.20	0.17	0.44	0.31
5	72.4	70.2	75.4	64.1	70.9	0.20	0.20	0.16	0.38	0.29
6	71.4	69.2	74.4	63.1	69.9	0.19	0.19	0.15	0.36	0.25
7	70.4	68.2	73.4	62.1	68.9	0.18	0.18	0.14	0.34	0.23
8	69.4	67.2	72.5	61.1	67.9	0.16	0.16	0.13	0.30	0.21
9	68.4	66.2	71.5	60.2	67.0	0.14	0.14	0.12	0.26	0.19
10	67.4	65.3	70.5	59.2	66.0	0.13	0.12	0.11	0.22	0.18
11	66.4	64.3	69.5	58.2	65.0	0.13	0.12	0.11	0.21	0.18
12	65.5	63.3	68.5	57.2	64.0	0.17	0.18	0.14	0.28	0.20
13	64.5	62.3	67.5	56.2	63.0	0.26	0.30	0.19	0.45	0.24
14	63.5	61.3	66.5	55.2	62.0	0.38	0.46	0.25	0.68	0.29
15	62.5	60.3	65.5	54.3	61.0	0.51	0.64	0.33	0.94	0.35
16	61.5	59.4	64.5	53.3	60.1	0.63	0.80	0.40	1.18	0.41
17	60.6	58.4	63.6	52.4	59.1	0.73	0.93	0.44	1.41	0.47
18	59.6	57.5	62.6	51.5	58.1	0.79	1.02	0.46	1.63	0.52
19	58.7	56.5	61.6	50.5	57.1	0.84	1.08	0.45	1.84	0.58
20	57.7	55.6	60.7	49.6	56.2	0.88	1.20	0.44	2.08	0.64
21	56.8	54.7	59.7	48.7	55.2	0.92	1.20	0.43	2.33	0.70
22	55.8	53.7	58.7	47.9	54.2	0.96	1.25	0.42	2.50	0.76
23	54.9	52.8	57.7	47.0	53.3	0.97	1.26	0.43	2.56	0.81
24	53.9	51.8	56.8	46.1	52.3	0.96	1.25	0.44	2.53	0.85
25	53.0	50.9	55.8	45.2	51.4	0.95	1.23	0.45	2.46	0.90
26	52.0	50.0	54.8	44.3	50.4	0.95	1.22	0.47	2.42	0.95
27	51.1	49.0	53.8	43.4	49.5	0.96	1.22	0.49	2.41	1.00
28	50.1	48.1	52.9	42.5	48.5	0.98	1.24	0.51	2.45	1.06
29	49.2	47.2	51.9	41.6	47.6	1.02	1.27	0.54	2.55	1.12
30	48.2	46.2	50.9	40.7	46.6	1.06	1.32	0.57	2.66	1.19
31	47.3	45.3	49.9	39.8	45.7	1.11	1.36	0.60	2.77	1.27
32	46.3	44.3	49.0	38.9	44.7	1.17	1.43	0.65	2.89	1.39
33	45.4	43.4	48.0	38.1	43.8	1.24	1.50	0.71	3.02	1.54
34	44.4	42.5	47.0	37.2	42.9	1.33	1.59	0.78	3.16	1.71
35	43.5	41.5	46.1	36.3	41.9	1.42	1.68	0.85	3.31	1.89
36	42.6	40.6	45.1	35.4	41.0	1.51	1.78	0.92	3.48	2.06
37	41.6	39.7	44.2	34.5	40.1	1.61	1.89	1.00	3.71	2.25
38	40.7	38.7	43.2	33.7	39.2	1.73	2.02	1.07	4.01	2.46
39	39.8	37.8	42.2	32.8	38.3	1.87	2.17	1.16	4.38	2.68
40	38.8	36.9	41.3	31.9	37.4	2.01	2.33	1.25	4.78	2.92
41	37.9	36.0	40.3	31.1	36.5	2.17	2.50	1.35	5.19	3.16
42	37.0	35.1	39.4	30.2	35.6	2.34	2.70	1.45	5.67	3.41
43	36.1	34.2	38.5	29.4	34.7	2.53	2.92	1.57	6.24	3.66
44	35.2	33.3	37.5	28.6	33.9	2.74	3.17	1.70	6.89	3.93
45	34.3	32.4	36.6	27.8	33.0	2.99	3.45	1.85	7.65	4.22
46	33.4	31.5	35.6	27.0	32.1	3.25	3.76	2.02	8.47	4.54
47	32.5	30.6	34.7	26.2	31.3	3.53	4.09	2.21	9.27	4.88
48	31.6	29.7	33.8	25.5	30.4	3.81	4.40	2.42	9.98	5.23
49	30.7	28.9	32.9	24.7	29.6	4.09	4.72	2.65	10.63	5.60
50	29.8	28.0	32.0	24.0	28.7	4.39	5.09	2.90	11.31	6.02
51	29.0	27.1	31.0	23.2	27.9	4.73	5.45	3.18	12.11	6.49
52	28.1	26.3	30.1	22.5	27.1	5.12	5.89	3.48	13.00	7.02
53	27.2	25.4	29.2	21.8	26.3	5.57	6.43	3.82	14.01	7.60
54	26.4	24.6	28.4	21.1	25.5	6.10	7.06	4.21	15.12	8.23
55	25.5	23.8	27.5	20.4	24.7	6.73	7.80	4.67	16.33	8.94
56	24.7	22.9	26.6	19.8	23.9	7.42	8.64	5.19	17.62	9.71
57	23.9	22.1	25.7	19.1	23.1	8.16	9.53	5.75	18.98	10.50
58	23.1	21.3	24.9	18.5	22.4	8.92	10.43	6.34	20.39	11.30
59	22.3	20.6	24.0	17.8	21.6	9.71	11.37	6.95	21.83	12.10
60	21.5	19.8	23.2	17.2	20.9	10.58	12.41	7.65	23.36	12.96
61	20.7	19.0	22.4	16.6	20.1	11.57	13.60	8.45	24.96	13.89
62	20.0	18.3	21.6	16.0	19.4	12.65	14.94	9.32	26.53	14.90
63	19.2	17.6	20.8	15.5	18.7	13.83	16.43	10.25	27.98	15.99
64	18.5	16.8	20.0	14.9	18.0	15.09	18.06	11.24	29.33	17.16
65	17.7	16.1	19.2	14.3	17.3	16.41	19.77	12.30	30.54	18.33
70	14.3	12.9	15.5	11.6	14.0	25.28	31.12	19.30	42.74	28.25
75	11.2	10.0	12.1	9.2	11.1	38.24	46.82	30.47	62.24	42.53
80	8.5	7.5	9.1	7.3	8.6	59.50	72.70	50.12	85.72	61.59

[1] Based on the proportion of the cohort who are alive at the beginning of an indicated age interval who will die before reaching the end of that interval. For example, out of every 1,000 people alive and exactly 50 years old at the beginning of the period, between 4 and 5 (4.44) will die before reaching their 51st birthdays.

Source: U.S. National Center for Health Statistics, *Vital Statistics of the United States*, annual; and *National Vital Statistics Report*, Vol. 50, No. 15, and unpublished data.

Vital Statistics 73

No. 94. Deaths and Death Rates by Sex and Race: 1970 to 2000

[1,921 represents 1,921,000. **Rates are per 1,000 population for specified groups.** Excludes deaths of nonresidents of the United States and fetal deaths. For explanation of age-adjustment, see text, this section. The standard population for this table is the total population of the United States enumerated in 1940. See Appendix III]

Sex and race	1970	1975	1980	1985	1986	1987	1988	1989	1990	1991	1992	1993	1994	1995	1996	1997	1998	1999	2000
Deaths [1] (1,000)	1,921	1,893	1,990	2,086	2,105	2,123	2,168	2,150	2,148	2,170	2,176	2,269	2,279	2,312	2,315	2,314	2,337	2,391	2,405
Male [1] (1,000)	1,078	1,051	1,075	1,098	1,104	1,108	1,126	1,114	1,113	1,122	1,122	1,162	1,163	1,173	1,164	1,154	1,157	1,175	1,178
Female [1] (1,000)	843	842	915	989	1,001	1,015	1,042	1,036	1,035	1,048	1,053	1,107	1,116	1,139	1,151	1,160	1,180	1,216	1,227
White (1,000)	1,682	1,660	1,739	1,819	1,831	1,843	1,877	1,854	1,853	1,869	1,874	1,951	1,960	1,987	1,993	1,996	2,016	2,061	2,074
Male (1,000)	942	918	934	950	953	953	965	951	951	956	957	988	989	997	992	987	990	1,005	1,008
Female (1,000)	740	743	805	869	879	890	911	903	902	912	917	963	971	990	1,001	1,010	1,026	1,056	1,066
Black (1,000)	226	218	233	244	250	255	264	268	266	270	269	282	282	286	282	277	278	285	285
Male (1,000)	128	124	130	134	137	140	144	146	145	147	147	154	153	154	149	144	143	146	144
Female (1,000)	98	94	103	111	113	115	120	121	120	122	123	129	129	132	133	132	135	139	140
Death rates [1]	9.5	8.8	8.8	8.8	8.8	8.8	8.9	8.7	8.6	8.6	8.5	8.8	8.8	8.8	8.7	8.6	8.6	8.8	8.7
Male [1]	10.9	10.0	9.8	9.5	9.4	9.4	9.5	9.3	9.2	9.1	9.0	9.2	9.2	9.1	9.0	8.8	8.8	8.8	8.7
Female [1]	8.1	7.6	7.9	8.1	8.1	8.2	8.3	8.2	8.1	8.1	8.1	8.4	8.4	8.5	8.5	8.5	8.5	8.7	8.7
White	9.5	8.9	8.9	9.0	9.0	9.0	9.1	8.9	8.9	8.9	8.8	9.1	9.1	9.3	9.1	9.0	9.0	9.2	9.2
Male	10.9	10.0	9.8	9.6	9.6	9.5	9.6	9.4	9.3	9.3	9.2	9.4	9.3	9.3	9.2	9.1	9.0	9.1	9.1
Female	8.1	7.8	8.1	8.4	8.4	8.5	8.7	8.5	8.5	8.5	8.4	8.8	8.8	8.9	9.0	9.0	9.0	9.2	9.3
Black	10.0	8.8	8.8	8.5	8.6	8.7	8.9	8.9	8.8	8.6	8.5	8.8	8.6	8.6	8.4	8.1	8.1	8.2	8.1
Male	11.9	10.6	10.3	9.9	10.0	10.1	10.3	10.3	10.1	10.0	9.8	10.1	9.9	9.8	9.4	8.9	8.8	8.8	8.6
Female	8.3	7.3	7.3	7.3	7.4	7.5	7.6	7.6	7.5	7.4	7.4	7.6	7.5	7.6	7.5	7.4	7.5	7.6	7.6
Age-adjusted death rates [1]	12.2	10.9	10.4	9.9	9.8	9.7	9.8	9.5	9.4	9.3	9.1	9.3	9.2	9.2	9.0	8.9	8.8	8.8	8.7
Male [1]	15.4	14.2	13.5	12.8	12.6	12.5	12.5	12.2	12.0	11.8	11.6	11.8	11.6	11.5	11.2	10.9	10.6	10.6	10.4
Female [1]	9.7	8.6	8.2	7.8	7.8	7.7	7.8	7.6	7.5	7.4	7.3	7.5	7.5	7.5	7.4	7.4	7.3	7.4	7.4
White	11.9	10.7	10.1	9.6	9.5	9.4	9.5	9.2	9.1	9.0	8.8	9.0	8.9	8.9	8.8	8.6	8.5	8.6	8.5
Male	15.1	13.9	13.2	12.5	12.3	12.1	12.2	11.8	11.7	11.5	11.3	11.4	11.2	11.1	10.9	10.6	10.4	10.4	10.2
Female	9.4	8.3	8.0	7.6	7.6	7.5	7.6	7.4	7.3	7.2	7.1	7.3	7.2	7.3	7.2	7.2	7.2	7.3	7.2
Black	15.2	13.3	13.1	12.6	12.7	12.6	12.8	12.8	12.5	12.4	12.2	12.5	12.2	12.2	11.9	11.5	11.4	11.5	11.2
Male	18.7	17.0	17.0	16.3	16.5	16.5	16.8	16.7	16.4	16.2	15.9	16.3	15.9	15.8	15.1	14.5	14.1	14.1	13.7
Female	12.3	10.4	10.3	9.9	9.9	9.9	10.1	9.8	9.8	9.7	9.5	9.8	9.7	9.7	9.6	9.4	9.4	9.6	9.4

[1] Includes other races, not shown separately.

Source: U.S. National Center for Health Statistics, *Vital Statistics of the United States*, annual; and *National Vital Statistics Reports (NVSR)* (formerly *Monthly Vital Statistics Report*).

No. 95. Death Rates by Age: 1940 to 2000

[Rates per 100,000 population]

Sex, year, and race	All ages [1]	Under 1 year	1-4 years	5-14 years	15-24 years	25-34 years	35-44 years	45-54 years	55-64 years	65-74 years	75-84 years	85 years and older
MALE												
1940	1,197.4	6,189.8	311.5	117.8	228.9	338.4	588.1	1,248.8	2,612.0	5,462.3	12,126.4	24,639.0
1950	1,106.1	3,728.0	151.7	70.9	167.9	216.5	428.8	1,067.1	2,395.3	4,931.4	10,426.0	21,636.0
1960	1,104.5	3,059.3	119.5	55.7	152.1	187.9	372.8	992.2	2,309.5	4,914.4	10,178.4	21,186.3
1970	1,090.3	2,410.0	93.2	50.5	188.5	215.3	402.6	958.5	2,282.7	4,873.8	10,010.2	17,821.5
1980	976.9	1,428.5	72.6	36.7	172.3	196.1	299.2	767.3	1,815.1	4,105.2	8,816.7	18,801.1
1990	918.4	1,082.8	52.4	28.5	147.4	204.3	310.4	610.3	1,553.4	3,491.5	7,888.6	18,056.6
2000 [2]	873.8	794.8	36.3	21.6	116.2	148.4	254.0	545.8	1,250.5	3,020.0	6,863.3	16,673.5
White:												
1980	983.3	1,230.3	66.1	35.0	167.0	171.3	257.4	698.9	1,728.5	4,035.7	8,829.8	19,097.3
1985	963.6	1,056.5	52.8	30.1	134.2	158.8	243.1	611.7	1,625.8	3,770.7	8,486.1	18,980.1
1990	930.9	896.1	45.9	26.4	131.3	176.1	268.2	548.7	1,467.2	3,397.7	7,844.9	18,268.3
1995	932.1	717.5	38.8	24.5	122.3	177.7	287.7	534.6	1,330.8	3,199.0	7,320.6	18,152.9
1996	918.1	683.3	37.1	23.2	113.9	154.8	259.6	515.5	1,305.2	3,158.3	7,205.5	17,870.5
1997	906.3	678.1	35.1	22.1	109.0	140.3	235.3	495.8	1,252.4	3,122.7	7,086.0	17,767.1
1998	904.4	673.8	32.5	21.2	107.6	133.9	232.7	489.6	1,215.5	3,082.3	6,988.5	17,048.3
1999	911.2	658.1	33.9	20.3	104.9	134.5	231.5	494.2	1,200.2	3,043.2	6,965.1	17,202.1
2000 [2]	907.0	662.9	32.1	20.5	106.8	133.1	232.1	497.5	1,178.8	2,958.7	6,838.8	16,991.0
Black:												
1980	1,034.1	2,586.7	110.5	47.4	209.1	407.3	689.8	1,479.9	2,873.0	5,131.1	9,231.6	16,098.8
1985	989.3	2,219.9	90.1	42.3	173.6	351.9	630.2	1,292.9	2,779.8	5,172.4	9,262.3	15,774.2
1990	1,008.0	2,112.4	85.8	41.2	252.2	430.8	699.6	1,261.0	2,618.4	4,946.1	9,129.5	16,954.9
1995	980.7	1,590.8	77.5	40.2	249.2	416.5	721.2	1,273.0	2,437.5	4,610.5	8,778.8	16,728.7
1996	939.9	1,748.2	71.4	38.1	233.0	361.0	629.2	1,190.6	2,395.1	4,431.5	8,614.9	16,006.3
1997	893.9	1,671.6	67.2	34.8	215.8	308.6	523.7	1,114.1	2,320.0	4,298.3	8,296.8	16,083.5
1998	877.7	1,717.8	69.2	35.6	194.6	282.0	483.1	1,082.6	2,269.3	4,186.0	8,311.4	15,540.9
1999	880.0	1,694.0	66.0	34.6	185.6	268.4	473.6	1,081.9	2,244.0	4,182.8	8,352.6	16,047.8
2000 [2]	861.3	1,586.5	62.3	29.3	177.6	267.2	449.9	1,039.2	2,137.0	4,027.8	8,115.6	15,352.6
Hispanic:[3]												
1980	(NA)	(NA)	(NA)	(NA)	(NA)	(NA)	(NA)	(NA)	(NA)	(NA)	(NA)	(NA)
1985	(NA)	(NA)	(NA)	(NA)	(NA)	(NA)	(NA)	(NA)	(NA)	(NA)	(NA)	(NA)
1990	(NA)	(NA)	(NA)	(NA)	(NA)	(NA)	(NA)	(NA)	(NA)	(NA)	(NA)	(NA)
1995	(NA)	(NA)	(NA)	(NA)	(NA)	(NA)	(NA)	(NA)	(NA)	(NA)	(NA)	(NA)
1996	(NA)	(NA)	(NA)	(NA)	(NA)	(NA)	(NA)	(NA)	(NA)	(NA)	(NA)	(NA)
1997	360.5	654.3	34.1	18.7	129.1	154.5	235.7	456.1	957.8	2,251.7	4,750.3	10,487.1
1998	366.4	678.5	33.1	20.2	128.8	148.4	226.6	449.3	906.3	2,284.9	4,564.6	9,946.7
1999	367.9	655.3	34.3	19.4	124.9	151.6	226.0	456.3	962.6	2,219.4	4,525.1	9,842.3
2000 [2]	366.3	663.4	32.3	19.4	130.7	154.1	221.5	442.0	940.5	2,118.3	4,437.6	9,295.6
FEMALE												
1940	954.6	4,774.3	267.0	89.1	181.1	274.3	452.2	860.7	1,800.4	4,222.2	10,368.6	22,759.1
1950	823.5	2,854.6	126.7	48.9	89.1	142.7	290.3	641.5	1,404.8	3,333.2	8,399.6	19,194.7
1960	809.2	2,321.3	98.4	37.3	61.3	106.6	229.4	526.7	1,196.4	2,871.8	7,633.1	19,008.4
1970	807.8	1,863.7	75.4	31.8	68.1	101.6	231.1	517.2	1,098.9	2,579.7	6,677.6	15,518.0
1980	785.3	1,141.7	54.7	24.2	57.5	75.9	159.3	412.9	934.3	2,144.7	5,440.1	14,746.9
1990	812.0	855.7	41.0	19.3	49.0	74.2	137.9	342.7	878.8	1,991.2	4,883.1	14,274.3
2000 [2]	873.3	657.2	28.8	15.3	43.5	66.0	142.1	314.0	775.5	1,948.6	4,922.7	14,827.1
White:												
1980	806.1	962.5	49.3	22.9	55.5	65.4	138.2	372.7	876.2	2,066.6	5,401.7	14,979.6
1985	840.1	799.3	40.0	19.5	48.1	59.4	121.9	341.7	869.1	2,027.1	5,111.6	14,745.4
1990	846.9	690.0	36.1	17.9	45.9	61.5	117.4	309.3	822.7	1,923.5	4,839.1	14,400.6
1995	891.3	571.6	31.2	16.6	44.3	64.3	125.8	294.4	788.4	1,924.5	4,831.1	14,639.1
1996	896.2	558.0	28.5	16.4	42.7	62.7	121.6	290.5	779.5	1,919.8	4,826.5	14,642.9
1997	897.8	546.0	28.0	15.6	43.8	60.0	120.9	285.0	766.3	1,900.5	4,786.3	14,681.4
1998	903.7	563.6	27.5	15.0	41.2	58.5	122.0	278.3	740.6	1,912.9	4,792.7	14,620.4
1999	924.1	532.6	27.4	14.9	42.2	58.4	123.3	281.8	739.1	1,916.2	4,869.7	15,053.8
2000 [2]	928.8	544.4	25.1	14.2	41.0	57.4	124.8	282.0	735.2	1,901.7	4,893.6	15,028.7
Black:												
1980	733.3	2,123.7	84.4	30.5	70.5	150.0	323.9	768.2	1,561.0	3,057.4	6,212.1	12,367.2
1985	734.2	1,821.4	71.1	28.6	59.6	137.6	276.5	667.6	1,532.5	2,967.8	6,078.0	12,703.0
1990	747.9	1,735.5	67.6	27.5	68.7	159.5	298.6	639.4	1,452.6	2,865.7	5,688.3	13,309.5
1995	759.0	1,342.0	62.9	26.5	70.3	166.6	327.7	619.0	1,350.3	2,823.7	5,840.3	13,472.2
1996	753.5	1,444.0	63.7	25.9	66.8	153.8	316.4	610.1	1,311.7	2,787.0	5,775.9	13,398.5
1997	742.8	1,383.9	51.0	27.2	62.0	134.6	287.1	590.4	1,307.3	2,739.7	5,669.3	13,701.7
1998	746.4	1,390.1	53.9	23.1	58.0	130.0	284.9	582.0	1,272.2	2,724.6	5,813.8	13,580.5
1999	761.3	1,403.3	51.5	22.6	60.1	122.0	282.6	581.0	1,255.7	2,732.1	6,002.7	14,262.9
2000 [2]	756.0	1,338.6	50.1	21.2	59.4	124.2	268.7	588.6	1,196.7	2,629.8	5,871.6	14,266.8
Hispanic:[3]												
1980	(NA)	(NA)	(NA)	(NA)	(NA)	(NA)	(NA)	(NA)	(NA)	(NA)	(NA)	(NA)
1985	(NA)	(NA)	(NA)	(NA)	(NA)	(NA)	(NA)	(NA)	(NA)	(NA)	(NA)	(NA)
1990	(NA)	(NA)	(NA)	(NA)	(NA)	(NA)	(NA)	(NA)	(NA)	(NA)	(NA)	(NA)
1995	(NA)	(NA)	(NA)	(NA)	(NA)	(NA)	(NA)	(NA)	(NA)	(NA)	(NA)	(NA)
1996	(NA)	(NA)	(NA)	(NA)	(NA)	(NA)	(NA)	(NA)	(NA)	(NA)	(NA)	(NA)
1997	288.0	572.3	28.4	15.6	38.3	54.6	101.1	228.3	580.3	1,381.9	3,220.5	8,708.6
1998	283.6	568.7	27.6	14.1	34.0	51.0	96.7	225.8	543.6	1,384.3	3,140.1	8,336.3
1999	293.7	565.9	29.8	14.4	36.4	51.8	99.9	226.7	536.0	1,366.8	3,245.6	8,838.0
2000 [2]	290.4	571.4	28.5	14.3	34.6	50.7	102.5	222.4	522.3	1,326.5	3,166.4	8,327.0

NA Not available   [1] Figures for age not stated are included in "All ages" but not distributed among age groups. [2] Preliminary data.   [3] The death rates for Hispanic origin and specified races other than White and Black should be interpreted with caution because of inconsistencies between reporting Hispanic origin and race on death certificates and censuses and surveys.

Source: U.S. National Center for Health Statistics, *Vital Statistics of the United States*, annual.

No. 96. Age-Adjusted Death Rates by Race and Sex: 1940 to 2000

[Age adjusted rates per 100,000 population. Populations enumerated as of April 1 for census years and estimated as of July 1 for all other years. Beginning 1970, excludes deaths of nonresidents of the United States. Data for specified races other than White and Black should be interpreted with caution because of inconsistencies reporting race on death certificates and on censuses and surveys.]

Year	All races [1]			White			Black			American Indian [2]			Asian or Pacific Islander [3]		
	Total	Male	Female	Total	Male	Female	Total	Male	Female	Total	Male	Female	Total	Male	Female
1940	1,785.0	1,976.0	1,599.4	1,735.3	1,925.2	1,550.4	(NA)	(NA)	(NA)	(NA)	(NA)	(NA)	(NA)	(NA)	(NA)
1950	1,446.0	1,674.2	1,236.0	1,410.8	1,642.5	1,198.0	(NA)	(NA)	(NA)	(NA)	(NA)	(NA)	(NA)	(NA)	(NA)
1960	1,339.2	1,609.0	1,105.3	1,311.3	1,586.0	1,074.4	1,577.5	1,811.1	1,369.7	(NA)	(NA)	(NA)	(NA)	(NA)	(NA)
1970	1,222.6	1,542.1	971.4	1,193.3	1,513.7	944.0	1,518.1	1,873.9	1,228.7	(NA)	(NA)	(NA)	(NA)	(NA)	(NA)
1980	1,039.1	1,348.1	817.9	1,012.7	1,317.6	796.1	1,314.8	1,697.8	1,033.3	867.0	1,111.5	662.4	589.9	786.5	425.9
1981	1,007.1	1,308.2	792.7	984.0	1,282.2	773.6	1,258.4	1,626.6	986.6	784.6	1,030.2	588.0	544.7	710.3	405.3
1982	985.0	1,279.9	776.6	963.6	1,255.9	758.7	1,221.3	1,580.4	960.1	757.0	940.1	604.4	550.4	738.2	410.3
1983	990.0	1,284.5	783.3	967.3	1,259.4	763.9	1,240.5	1,600.7	980.7	757.3	945.0	605.5	565.1	718.8	428.8
1984	982.5	1,271.4	779.8	959.7	1,245.9	760.7	1,236.7	1,600.8	976.9	761.7	946.0	567.9	574.4	724.7	443.1
1985	988.1	1,278.1	784.5	963.6	1,249.8	764.3	1,261.2	1,634.5	994.4	731.7	926.1	577.2	586.5	755.4	456.7
1986	978.6	1,261.7	778.7	952.8	1,230.5	758.1	1,266.7	1,650.1	994.4	720.8	926.7	549.3	576.4	730.5	445.4
1987	970.0	1,246.1	774.2	943.4	1,213.4	753.3	1,263.1	1,650.3	989.7	719.8	899.3	583.7	577.3	732.4	448.1
1988	975.7	1,250.7	781.0	947.6	1,215.9	759.1	1,284.3	1,677.6	1,006.8	718.6	917.4	563.6	584.2	732.0	451.0
1989	950.5	1,215.0	761.8	920.2	1,176.6	738.8	1,275.5	1,670.1	998.1	761.6	999.8	586.3	581.3	729.6	458.4
1990	938.7	1,202.8	750.9	909.8	1,165.9	728.8	1,250.3	1,644.5	975.1	716.3	916.2	561.8	582.0	716.4	469.3
1991	925.5	1,182.6	741.6	897.0	1,146.4	719.8	1,237.0	1,622.0	968.0	710.5	889.0	567.7	558.3	697.9	444.4
1992	910.9	1,161.2	731.2	882.9	1,125.6	709.5	1,216.9	1,591.4	954.4	709.7	899.2	560.3	558.5	698.3	445.3
1993	931.5	1,181.8	751.0	902.0	1,143.0	728.9	1,247.2	1,629.3	977.7	740.8	925.9	596.6	603.4	769.0	475.2
1994	920.2	1,160.9	745.0	891.6	1,123.4	723.5	1,224.6	1,589.8	965.0	708.6	882.5	567.7	607.6	775.7	480.6
1995	918.5	1,150.3	748.2	890.0	1,112.7	726.6	1,224.5	1,582.3	970.1	716.5	864.2	592.8	616.0	788.1	488.4
1996	902.4	1,117.5	742.8	877.6	1,086.1	723.3	1,188.7	1,513.9	956.3	702.6	838.5	590.5	539.7	678.0	433.2
1997	887.3	1,090.5	736.3	864.9	1,062.5	718.3	1,151.5	1,446.7	940.7	711.6	880.3	574.0	533.9	671.1	429.7
1998	875.8	1,064.6	732.7	854.7	1,038.5	715.1	1,135.7	1,410.6	938.2	705.2	856.7	582.2	516.8	642.3	420.4
1999	881.9	1,061.8	743.6	860.7	1,035.8	725.7	1,147.1	1,412.5	955.0	716.1	842.0	608.5	517.5	640.6	424.0
2000 [4]	872.4	1,042.7	739.8	853.2	1,019.3	723.4	1,124.8	1,371.3	943.9	697.7	828.2	588.7	502.0	620.1	412.3

NA Not available.   [1] For 1940-91 includes deaths among races not shown separately; see Other races and, race not stated, in the Technical Notes for information for 1992 to present.   [2] Includes Aleuts and Eskimos.   [3] Incudes Chinese, Filipino, Hawaiian, Japanese, and Other Asian or Pacific Islander.   [4] Preliminary data.

Source: U.S. National Center for Health Statistics, Vital Statistics of the United States, annual.

76   Vital Statistics

No. 97. Deaths and Death Rates by State: 1990 to 2000

[2,148 represents 2,148,000.] By state of residence. Excludes deaths of nonresidents of the United States, except as noted. Caution should be used in comparing death rates by state; rates are affected by the population composition of the area. See also Appendix III]

State	Number of deaths (1,000)							Rate per 1,000 population [1]						
	1990	1995	1996	1997	1998	1999	2000 [2]	1990	1995	1996	1997	1998	1999	2000 [2]
United States..	2,148	2,312	2,315	2,314	2,337	2,391	2,405	8.6	8.8	8.7	8.6	8.6	8.8	8.7
Alabama.........	39	42	43	43	44	45	45	9.7	10.0	10.0	10.0	10.1	10.3	10.3
Alaska..........	2	3	3	3	3	3	3	4.0	4.2	4.3	4.2	4.2	4.4	4.7
Arizona.........	29	35	37	37	38	40	41	7.9	8.4	8.3	8.1	8.2	8.4	8.3
Arkansas	25	27	27	28	28	28	28	10.5	10.8	10.6	11.0	10.8	10.9	11.0
California	214	224	223	225	227	229	230	7.2	7.1	7.0	7.0	6.9	6.9	6.8
Colorado.........	22	25	26	26	27	27	27	6.6	6.7	6.7	6.6	6.7	6.7	6.6
Connecticut.......	28	29	30	29	30	29	30	8.4	9.0	9.0	9.0	9.1	9.0	9.2
Delaware	6	6	7	7	7	7	7	8.7	8.8	9.0	8.9	8.8	8.8	9.0
Dist. of Columbia ...	7	7	7	6	6	6	6	12.0	12.4	12.2	11.6	11.6	11.7	11.5
Florida..........	134	153	153	155	158	163	164	10.4	10.8	10.7	10.5	10.1	10.8	10.7
Georgia	52	58	59	59	60	62	64	8.0	8.1	8.0	7.9	7.9	8.0	8.1
Hawaii	7	8	8	8	8	8	8	6.1	6.4	6.7	6.7	6.8	7.0	7.0
Idaho...........	7	9	9	9	9	10	10	7.4	7.3	7.3	7.4	7.5	7.7	7.5
Illinois	103	108	106	103	104	108	107	9.0	9.2	9.0	8.7	8.7	8.9	8.8
Indiana..........	50	53	53	53	53	55	56	8.9	9.2	9.1	9.1	9.1	9.3	9.3
Iowa	27	28	28	28	28	28	28	9.7	9.9	9.8	9.7	9.9	9.9	9.8
Kansas..........	22	24	24	24	24	24	25	9.0	9.3	9.3	9.2	9.2	9.2	9.3
Kentucky	35	37	37	38	38	39	40	9.5	9.6	9.6	9.7	9.6	9.9	9.9
Louisiana	38	40	40	40	40	41	41	8.9	9.1	9.1	9.2	9.2	9.4	9.4
Maine...........	11	12	11	12	12	12	12	9.0	9.5	9.4	9.7	9.8	9.8	9.8
Maryland	38	42	42	42	42	43	44	8.0	8.3	8.3	8.2	8.2	8.3	8.4
Massachusetts.....	53	55	55	55	55	56	56	8.8	9.1	9.1	8.9	9.0	9.0	9.1
Michigan.........	79	84	84	83	85	87	87	8.5	8.8	8.7	8.5	8.7	8.8	8.8
Minnesota........	35	38	37	37	37	39	38	7.9	8.1	8.0	7.9	7.9	8.1	7.8
Mississippi	25	27	27	28	28	28	29	9.8	10.0	9.8	10.1	10.1	10.2	10.3
Missouri.........	50	54	54	54	55	56	55	9.8	10.2	10.1	10.1	10.1	10.2	10.0
Montana.........	7	8	8	8	8	8	8	8.6	8.8	8.8	8.8	9.1	9.2	9.1
Nebraska	15	15	15	15	15	16	15	9.4	9.3	9.4	9.2	9.1	9.4	9.0
Nevada	9	13	13	13	14	15	15	7.8	8.2	8.2	8.0	8.3	8.3	8.1
New Hampshire....	8	9	9	9	9	10	10	7.7	8.0	8.1	8.1	8.0	7.9	8.0
New Jersey.......	70	74	73	72	72	74	76	9.1	9.3	9.2	9.0	8.8	9.1	9.2
New Mexico.......	11	13	12	13	13	14	13	7.0	7.4	7.3	7.3	7.4	7.9	7.7
New York	169	168	164	159	157	160	158	9.4	9.3	9.0	8.7	8.6	8.8	8.7
North Carolina.....	57	65	66	66	68	70	72	8.6	9.0	9.1	8.9	9.0	9.1	9.3
North Dakota......	6	6	6	6	6	6	6	8.9	9.3	9.3	9.2	9.3	9.6	9.3
Ohio	99	106	105	105	106	109	(NA)	9.1	9.5	9.4	9.4	9.4	9.6	(NA)
Oklahoma........	30	33	33	34	34	35	35	9.7	10.0	10.0	10.2	10.1	10.3	10.4
Oregon..........	25	28	29	29	29	29	30	8.8	9.0	9.0	8.9	9.0	8.9	8.8
Pennsylvania......	122	128	129	128	127	130	131	10.3	10.6	10.7	10.6	10.6	10.9	10.9
Rhode Island......	10	10	10	10	10	10	10	9.5	9.8	9.6	9.9	9.8	9.8	10.1
South Carolina.....	30	34	34	34	35	36	37	8.5	9.1	9.2	9.0	9.1	9.3	9.4
South Dakota	6	7	7	7	7	7	7	9.1	9.5	9.3	9.3	9.3	9.5	9.5
Tennessee	46	51	51	53	53	54	55	9.5	9.8	9.7	9.8	9.8	9.8	10.0
Texas...........	125	138	140	143	143	147	149	7.4	7.4	7.3	7.3	7.2	7.3	7.3
Utah	9	11	11	12	12	12	12	5.3	5.6	5.6	5.6	5.6	5.7	5.7
Vermont	5	5	5	5	5	5	5	8.2	8.5	8.3	8.6	8.4	8.4	8.6
Virginia..........	48	53	54	54	54	55	56	7.8	8.0	8.0	8.0	8.0	8.0	8.1
Washington.......	37	41	42	41	43	44	44	7.6	7.5	7.6	7.4	7.5	7.6	7.6
West Virginia......	19	20	20	21	21	21	21	10.8	11.1	11.2	11.5	11.5	11.6	11.7
Wisconsin........	43	45	45	45	46	47	47	8.7	8.8	8.7	8.7	8.8	8.9	8.8
Wyoming	3	4	4	4	4	4	4	7.1	7.7	7.5	7.8	8.0	8.4	8.1
Puerto Rico.......	26	30	30	29	29	28	28	7.3	8.1	7.9	7.6	7.7	7.4	7.2
Virgin Islands......	-	1	1	1	1	1	1	4.6	5.8	5.1	5.4	5.2	5.5	5.3
Guam	1	1	1	1	1	1	1	3.9	4.1	4.1	4.2	4.2	4.6	4.2
American Samoa ...	(NA)	(NA)	(NA)	-	-	-	(NA)	(NA)	(NA)	(NA)	4.3	3.9	3.9	(NA)
Northern Marianas ..	(NA)	(NA)	(NA)	(NA)	-	-	(NA)	(NA)	(NA)	(NA)	(NA)	2.4	2.3	(NA)

- Represents zero.   NA Not available.   [1] Rates based on enumerated resident population as of April 1 for 1990 and 2000; estimated resident population as of July 1 for all other years.   [2] Preliminary data.

Source: U.S. National Center for Health Statistics, *Vital Statistics of the United States*, annual; *National Vital Statistics Reports (NVSR)* (formerly *Monthly Vital Statistics Report*).

U.S. Census Bureau, Statistical Abstract of the United States: 2002

No. 98. Infant, Maternal, and Neonatal Mortality Rates by Race: 1980 to 1999

[Deaths per 1,000 live births, except as noted. Excludes deaths of nonresidents of the United States. Beginning 1989, race for live births tabulated according to race of mother, for maternal mortality rates and mortality rates. See also Appendix III]

Item	1980	1990	1994	1995	1996	1997	1998	1999 [1]
Infant deaths [2]................	12.6	9.2	8.0	7.6	7.3	7.2	7.2	7.1
White...............	10.9	7.6	6.6	6.3	6.1	6.0	6.0	5.8
Black and other........	20.2	15.5	13.5	12.6	12.2	11.8	11.9	11.9
Black......	22.2	18.0	15.8	15.1	14.7	14.2	14.3	14.6
Maternal deaths [3]	9.2	8.2	8.3	7.1	7.6	8.4	7.1	9.9
White...............	6.7	5.4	6.2	4.2	5.1	5.8	5.1	6.8
Black and other........	19.8	19.1	16.2	18.5	16.9	18.3	14.9	21.4
Black......	21.5	22.4	18.5	22.1	20.3	20.8	17.1	25.4
Neonatal deaths [4]	8.5	5.8	5.1	4.9	4.8	4.8	4.8	4.7
White...............	7.4	4.8	4.2	4.1	4.0	4.0	4.0	3.9
Black and other........	13.2	9.9	8.6	8.1	7.9	7.7	7.9	7.9
Black......	14.6	11.6	10.2	9.8	9.6	9.4	9.5	9.8

[1] Beginning 1999, deaths are classified according to the Tenth Revision of the International Classification of Diseases; earlier years classified according to the revision in use at the time, see text, this section.   [2] Represents deaths of infants under 1 year old, exclusive of fetal deaths.   [3] Per 100,000 live births from deliveries and complications of pregnancy, childbirth, and the puerperium.   [4] Represents deaths of infants under 28 days old, exclusive of fetal deaths.

No. 99. Infant Mortality Rates by Race—States: 1980 to 1999

[Deaths per 1,000 live births, by place of residence. Represents deaths of infants under 1 year old, exclusive of fetal deaths. Excludes deaths of nonresidents of the United States. See Appendix III]

State	Total [1]				White				Black			
	1980	1990	1995	1999	1980	1990	1995	1999	1980	1990	1995	1999
U.S	12.6	9.2	7.6	7.1	10.9	7.6	6.3	5.8	22.2	18.0	15.1	14.6
Alabama	15.1	10.8	9.8	9.8	11.6	8.1	7.1	6.9	21.6	16.0	15.2	16.0
Alaska	12.3	10.5	7.7	5.7	9.4	7.6	6.1	4.7	19.5	(B)	(B)	(B)
Arizona.............	12.4	8.8	7.5	6.8	11.8	7.8	7.2	6.2	18.4	20.6	17.0	19.1
Arkansas...........	12.7	9.2	8.8	8.0	10.3	8.4	7.2	7.0	20.0	13.9	14.3	12.0
California.............	11.1	7.9	6.3	5.4	10.6	7.0	5.8	5.0	18.0	16.8	14.4	12.9
Colorado............	10.1	8.8	6.5	6.7	9.8	7.8	6.0	6.3	19.1	19.4	16.8	16.2
Connecticut	11.2	7.9	7.2	6.1	10.2	6.3	6.5	5.7	19.1	17.6	12.6	10.6
Delaware............	13.9	10.1	7.5	7.4	9.8	9.7	6.0	3.9	27.9	20.1	13.1	18.0
District of Columbia	25.0	20.7	16.2	15.0	17.8	0.0	(B)	(B)	26.7	24.6	19.6	19.0
Florida	14.6	9.6	7.5	7.4	11.8	6.7	6.0	5.6	22.8	16.8	13.0	13.6
Georgia.............	14.5	12.4	9.4	8.2	10.8	7.4	6.5	5.4	21.0	18.3	15.1	13.8
Hawaii	10.3	6.7	5.8	7.0	11.6	6.1	(B)	(B)	(B)	(B)	(B)	(B)
Idaho	10.7	8.7	6.1	6.7	10.7	8.6	5.8	6.6	(NA)	(B)	(B)	(B)
Illinois.............	14.8	10.7	9.4	8.5	11.7	7.9	7.2	6.3	26.3	22.4	18.7	18.4
Indiana	11.9	9.6	8.4	8.0	10.5	7.9	7.3	7.0	23.4	17.4	17.5	17.0
Iowa	11.8	8.1	8.2	5.7	11.5	7.9	7.8	5.3	27.2	21.9	21.2	20.6
Kansas	10.4	8.4	7.0	7.3	9.5	8.0	6.2	6.8	20.6	17.7	17.6	14.4
Kentucky.............	12.9	8.5	7.6	7.6	12.0	8.2	7.4	7.1	22.0	14.3	10.7	12.7
Louisiana.............	14.3	11.1	9.8	9.2	10.5	8.1	6.2	5.9	20.6	16.7	15.3	14.2
Maine	9.2	6.2	6.5	4.8	9.4	6.7	6.3	4.7	(B)	(B)	(B)	(B)
Maryland	14.0	9.5	8.9	8.4	11.6	6.8	6.0	5.1	20.4	17.1	15.3	14.6
Massachusetts	10.5	7.0	5.2	5.2	10.1	6.1	4.7	4.8	16.8	11.9	9.0	9.8
Michigan	12.8	10.7	8.3	8.1	10.6	7.4	6.2	6.0	24.2	21.6	17.3	17.9
Minnesota	10.0	7.3	6.7	6.2	9.6	6.7	6.0	5.4	20.0	23.7	17.6	15.4
Mississippi.............	17.0	12.1	10.5	10.1	11.1	7.4	7.0	6.8	23.7	16.2	14.7	14.2
Missouri	12.4	9.4	7.4	7.8	11.1	7.9	6.4	5.8	20.7	18.2	13.8	18.9
Montana	12.4	9.0	7.0	6.7	11.8	6.0	7.0	5.9	(NA)	(B)	(B)	(B)
Nebraska	11.5	8.3	7.4	6.8	10.7	6.9	7.3	5.9	25.2	18.9	(B)	18.9
Nevada	10.7	8.4	5.7	6.6	10.0	8.2	5.5	6.1	20.6	14.2	(B)	13.2
New Hampshire	9.9	7.1	5.5	5.8	9.9	6.0	5.5	5.7	22.5	(B)	(B)	(B)
New Jersey	12.5	9.0	6.6	6.7	10.3	6.4	5.3	5.2	21.9	18.4	13.3	14.1
New Mexico	11.5	9.0	6.2	6.9	11.3	7.6	6.1	6.5	23.1	(B)	(B)	(B)
New York	12.5	9.6	7.7	6.4	10.8	7.4	6.2	5.5	20.0	18.1	13.9	10.6
North Carolina	14.5	10.6	9.2	9.1	12.1	8.0	6.7	6.9	20.0	16.5	15.9	15.5
North Dakota	12.1	8.0	7.2	6.8	11.7	7.2	6.7	5.8	27.5	(B)	(B)	(B)
Ohio	12.8	9.8	8.7	8.2	11.2	7.8	7.3	6.6	23.0	19.5	17.5	17.6
Oklahoma	12.7	9.2	8.3	8.5	12.1	9.1	8.0	8.0	21.8	14.3	15.1	15.6
Oregon	12.2	8.3	6.1	5.8	12.2	7.0	5.9	5.7	15.9	(B)	(B)	(B)
Pennsylvania	13.2	9.6	7.8	7.3	11.9	7.4	6.2	5.8	23.1	20.5	17.6	16.8
Rhode Island	11.0	8.1	7.2	5.7	10.9	7.0	7.0	5.0	(B)	(B)	(B)	(B)
South Carolina	15.6	11.7	9.6	10.2	10.8	8.1	6.7	6.7	22.9	17.3	14.6	16.9
South Dakota	10.9	10.1	9.5	8.9	9.0	8.0	7.9	7.7	(NA)	(B)	(B)	(B)
Tennessee.............	13.5	10.3	9.3	7.7	11.9	7.3	6.8	5.7	19.3	17.9	17.9	15.2
Texas	12.2	8.1	6.5	6.2	11.2	6.7	5.9	5.5	18.8	14.7	11.7	12.5
Utah	10.4	7.5	5.4	4.8	10.5	6.0	5.3	4.8	27.3	(B)	(B)	(B)
Vermont	10.7	6.4	6.0	5.8	10.7	5.9	6.2	5.9	(B)	(B)	(B)	(B)
Virginia	13.6	10.2	7.8	7.3	11.9	7.4	5.7	5.6	19.8	19.5	15.3	13.0
Washington	11.8	7.8	5.9	5.0	11.5	7.3	5.6	4.7	16.4	20.6	16.2	15.0
West Virginia	11.8	9.9	7.9	7.4	11.4	8.1	7.6	7.3	21.5	(B)	(B)	(B)
Wisconsin	10.3	8.2	7.3	6.7	9.7	7.7	6.3	5.8	18.5	19.0	18.6	16.0
Wyoming	9.8	8.6	7.7	6.9	9.3	7.5	6.8	6.8	25.9	(B)	(B)	(B)

B Base figure too small to meet statistical standards for reliability.   NA Not available.   [1] Includes other races, not shown separately.

Source: U.S. National Center for Health Statistics, *Vital Statistics of the United States,* annual; and unpublished data.

No. 100. Deaths by Major Causes: 1960 to 2000

[Age-adjusted death rates per 100,000 population.]

Year	Heart disease	Cancer	Cerebro-vascular diseases	Chronic lower respiratory diseases	Acci-dents	Diabetes mellitus	Influenza and pneumonia	Inten-tional self-harm (suicide)	Chronic liver disease and cirrhosis	Assault (homi-cide)
1960	559.0	193.9	177.9	12.5	63.1	22.5	53.7	12.5	13.3	5.2
1961	545.3	193.4	173.1	12.6	60.6	22.1	43.4	12.2	13.3	5.2
1962	556.9	193.3	174.0	14.2	62.9	22.6	47.1	12.8	13.8	5.4
1963	563.4	194.7	173.9	16.5	64.0	23.1	55.6	13.0	14.0	5.4
1964	543.3	193.6	167.0	16.3	64.1	22.5	45.4	12.7	14.2	5.7
1965	542.5	195.6	166.4	18.3	65.8	22.9	46.8	13.0	14.9	6.1
1966	541.2	196.5	165.8	19.2	67.6	23.6	47.9	12.7	15.9	6.5
1967	524.7	197.3	159.3	19.2	66.2	23.4	42.2	12.5	16.3	7.5
1968	531.0	198.8	162.5	20.7	65.5	25.3	52.8	12.4	16.9	8.1
1969	516.8	198.5	155.4	20.9	64.9	25.1	47.9	12.7	17.1	8.3
1970	492.7	198.6	147.7	21.3	62.2	24.3	41.7	13.1	17.8	9.0
1971	492.9	199.3	147.6	21.8	60.3	23.9	38.4	13.1	17.8	9.8
1972	490.2	200.3	147.3	22.8	60.2	23.7	41.3	13.3	18.0	10.0
1973	482.0	200.0	145.2	23.6	59.3	23.0	41.2	13.1	18.1	10.2
1974	458.8	201.5	136.8	23.2	52.7	22.1	35.5	13.2	17.9	10.5
1975	431.2	200.1	123.5	23.7	50.8	20.3	34.9	13.6	16.7	10.2
1976	426.9	202.5	117.4	24.9	48.7	19.5	38.8	13.2	16.4	9.2
1977	413.7	203.5	110.4	24.7	48.8	18.2	31.0	13.7	15.8	9.2
1978	409.9	204.9	103.7	26.3	48.9	18.3	34.5	12.9	15.2	9.2
1979	401.6	204.0	97.1	25.5	46.5	17.5	26.1	12.6	14.8	9.9
1980	412.1	207.9	96.4	28.3	46.4	18.1	31.4	12.2	15.1	10.5
1981	397.0	206.4	89.5	29.0	43.4	17.6	30.0	12.3	14.2	10.1
1982	389.0	208.3	84.2	29.1	40.1	17.2	26.5	12.5	13.2	9.4
1983	388.9	209.1	81.2	31.6	39.1	17.6	29.8	12.4	12.8	8.4
1984	378.8	210.8	78.7	32.4	38.8	17.2	30.6	12.6	12.7	8.1
1985	375.0	211.3	76.6	34.5	38.5	17.4	34.5	12.5	12.3	8.0
1986	365.1	211.5	73.1	34.8	38.6	17.2	34.8	13.0	11.8	8.6
1987	355.9	211.7	71.6	35.0	38.2	17.4	33.8	12.8	11.7	8.3
1988	352.5	212.5	70.6	36.5	38.9	18.0	37.3	12.5	11.6	8.5
1989	332.0	214.2	66.9	36.6	37.7	20.5	35.9	12.3	11.6	8.8
1990	321.8	216.0	65.5	37.2	36.3	20.7	36.8	12.5	11.1	9.5
1991	313.8	215.8	63.2	38.0	34.9	20.7	34.9	12.3	10.7	10.1
1992	306.1	214.3	62.0	37.9	33.4	20.8	33.1	12.1	10.5	9.6
1993	309.9	214.6	63.1	40.9	34.5	22.0	35.2	12.2	10.3	9.8
1994	299.7	213.1	63.1	40.6	34.6	22.7	33.9	12.1	10.2	9.4
1995	296.3	211.7	63.9	40.5	34.9	23.4	33.8	12.0	10.0	8.6
1996	288.3	208.7	63.2	41.0	34.9	24.0	33.2	11.7	9.8	7.8
1997	280.4	205.7	61.8	41.5	34.8	24.0	33.6	11.4	9.6	7.3
1998	272.4	202.4	59.6	42.0	35.0	24.2	34.6	11.3	9.5	6.7
1999	267.8	202.7	61.8	45.8	35.9	25.2	23.6	10.7	9.7	6.2
2000[1]	257.5	200.5	60.2	44.9	33.9	24.9	24.3	10.3	9.5	5.8

[1] Preliminary data.

Source: U.S. National Center for Health Statistics, Vital Statistics of the United States, annual.

U.S. Census Bureau, Statistical Abstract of the United States: 2002

No. 101. Deaths, Death Rates by Selected Causes: 1999 and 2000

[**Rates per 100,000 population.** Figures for 2000 are weighted data rounded to the nearest individual, so categories may not add to total or subtotal. Excludes deaths of nonresidents of the United States, except as noted. Deaths classified according to tenth revision of *International Classification of Diseases;* see also Appendix III]

Cause of death	1999			2000, prel.		
	Number	Rate	Age-adjusted rate	Number	Rate	Age-adjusted rate
All causes...............	2,391,399	877.0	881.9	2,404,624	873.6	872.4
Major cardiovascular diseases.........	950,314	348.5	350.9	934,110	339.3	338.8
Diseases of heart................	725,192	265.9	267.8	709,894	257.9	257.5
Acute rheumatic fever and chronic rheumatic heart disease...........	3,676	1.3	1.4	3,585	1.3	1.3
Hypertensive heart disease.........	22,702	8.3	8.4	23,330	8.5	8.5
Hypertensive heart and renal disease...	3,327	1.2	1.2	2,707	1.0	1.0
Ischemic heart disease............	529,659	194.2	195.6	513,758	186.6	186.4
Other heart diseases.............	165,828	60.8	61.2	166,515	60.5	60.4
Essential (primary) hypertension and hypertensive renal disease.........	16,968	6.2	6.3	17,964	6.5	6.5
Cerebrovascular diseases...........	167,366	61.4	61.8	166,028	60.3	60.2
Atherosclerosis................	14,979	5.5	5.5	14,413	5.2	5.2
Malignant neoplasms.............	549,838	201.6	202.7	551,833	200.5	200.5
Malignant neoplasms of lip, oral cavity, and pharynx.................	7,486	2.7	2.8	7,436	2.7	2.7
Malignant neoplasms of colon, rectum and anus.................	57,155	21.0	21.1	57,344	20.8	20.8
Malignant neoplasms of kidney and renal pelvis...................	11,116	4.1	4.1	11,751	4.3	4.3
Malignant neoplasms of lymphoid, hematopoietic and related tissue.....	56,318	20.7	20.7	56,262	20.4	20.4
Leukemia..................	21,014	7.7	7.7	21,298	7.7	7.7
Accidents (unintentional injuries)........	97,860	35.9	35.9	93,592	34.0	33.9
Motor vehicle accidents...........	42,401	15.5	15.5	41,804	15.2	15.2
Accidental discharge of firearms.....	824	0.3	0.3	808	0.3	0.3
Accidental drowning and submersion...	3,529	1.3	1.3	3,343	1.2	1.2
Accidental exposure to smoke, fire and flames.................	3,348	1.2	1.2	3,265	1.2	1.2
Accidental poisoning and exposure to noxious substances..............	12,186	4.5	4.5	9,893	3.6	3.6
Other acute lower respiratory infections...	540	0.2	0.2	453	0.2	0.1
Chronic lower respiratory diseases......	124,181	45.5	45.8	123,550	44.9	44.9
Bronchitis, chronic and unspecified....	1,172	0.4	0.4	1,188	0.4	0.4
Emphysema..................	17,787	6.5	6.5	16,936	6.2	6.1
Asthma....................	4,657	1.7	1.7	4,426	1.6	1.6
Other chronic lower respiratory diseases.	100,565	36.9	37.0	100,999	36.7	36.7
Influenza and pneumonia...........	63,730	23.4	23.6	67,024	24.3	24.3
Influenza....................	1,665	0.6	0.6	2,175	0.8	0.8
Pneumonia..................	62,065	22.8	22.9	64,849	23.6	23.5
Tuberculosis.................	930	0.3	0.3	751	0.3	0.3
Septicemia..................	30,680	11.3	11.3	31,613	11.5	11.5
Human immunodeficiency virus (HIV) disease..................	14,802	5.4	5.4	14,370	5.2	5.2
Anemias....................	4,503	1.7	1.6	4,450	1.6	1.6
Diabetes mellitus...............	68,399	25.1	25.2	68,662	24.9	24.9
Nutritional deficiencies............	4,289	1.6	1.6	4,342	1.6	1.6
Meningitis...................	850	0.3	0.3	770	0.3	0.3
Parkinsons disease..............	14,593	5.4	5.4	15,690	5.7	5.7
Alzheimers disease..............	44,536	16.3	16.5	49,044	17.8	17.8
Chronic liver disease and cirrhosis......	26,259	9.6	9.7	26,219	9.5	9.5
Alcoholic liver disease...........	11,958	4.4	4.4	11,755	4.3	4.3
Other chronic liver disease and cirrhosis.	14,301	5.2	5.3	14,464	5.3	5.3
Nephritis, nephrotic syndrome and nephrosis.................	35,525	13.0	13.1	37,672	13.7	13.7
Renal failure.................	34,719	12.7	12.8	36,904	13.4	13.4
Other disorders of kidney..........	35	(Z)	(Z)	47	(Z)	(Z)
Infections of kidney..............	846	0.3	0.3	781	0.3	0.3
Pregnancy, childbirth and the puerperium..	406	0.1	0.2	370	0.1	0.1
Congenital malformations, deformations and chromosomal abnormalities.......	10,393	3.8	3.8	10,472	3.8	3.8
All other diseases (Residual)..........	171,683	63.0	63.4	177,980	64.7	64.6
Intentional self-harm (suicide)..........	29,199	10.7	10.7	28,332	10.3	10.3
Assault (homicide)................	16,889	6.2	6.2	16,137	5.9	5.8
Legal intervention................	398	0.1	0.2	345	0.1	0.1
Events of undetermined intent.........	3,917	1.4	1.4	3,422	1.2	1.2
Operations of war and their sequelae.....	23	(Z)	(Z)	17	(B)	(B)
Complications of medical and surgical care.	2,823	1.0	1.0	2,886	1.0	1.0
Injury by firearms [1].............	28,874	10.6	10.6	28,117	10.2	10.2
Drug-induced deaths [1]...........	19,102	7.0	7.0	15,852	5.8	5.8
Alcohol-induced deaths [1]...........	19,171	7.0	7.1	18,539	6.7	6.7
Injury at work..................	5,651	2.6	2.6	5,291	2.4	2.4

B Base figure too small to meet statistical standards for reliability; see text, this section.   Z Less thank 0.05.   [1] Included in selected categories.

Source: U.S. National Center for Health Statistics, *Vital Statistics of the United States,* annual; National Vital Statistics Reports (NVSR) (formerly *Monthly Statistics Report);* and unpublished data.

No. 102. Deaths by Selected Causes: 1999 to 2000

[Deaths in thousands (2,391 represents 2,391,000). Deaths are classified according to the Tenth Revision of the International Classification of Diseases. See Appendix III]

1999

Cause of Death	All ages	Under 1 year	1-4 years	5-14 years	15-24 years	25-34 years	35-44 years	45-54 years	55-64 years	65-74 years	75-84 years	85 years over
All causes	2,391	28	5	8	31	41	89	153	239	453	699	646
Tuberculosis	1	-	-	-	-	-	-	-	-	-	-	-
Viral hepatitis	5	-	-	-	-	-	1	2	1	1	1	1
Human immunodeficiency virus (HIV) disease	15	-	-	-	-	3	6	4	1	1	-	-
Malignant neoplasms	550	-	-	1	2	4	17	47	89	152	163	75
Malignant neoplasms of colon, rectum and anus	57	-	-	-	-	-	1	4	8	14	18	11
Malignant neoplasms of trachea, bronchus and lung	152	-	-	-	-	-	3	11	29	52	44	12
Malignant neoplasm of breast	42	-	-	-	-	1	3	6	7	9	10	6
Leukemia	21	-	-	1	1	-	1	1	3	5	7	3
Diabetes mellitus	68	-	-	-	-	1	2	5	9	17	22	13
Nutritional deficiencies	4	-	-	-	-	-	-	-	-	-	1	2
Alzheimers disease	45	-	-	-	-	-	-	-	-	3	16	25
Major cardiovascular diseases	950	1	-	1	1	4	17	43	78	163	303	341
Diseases of heart	725	1	-	1	1	3	14	35	64	129	226	252
Hypertensive heart disease	23	-	-	-	-	-	1	2	3	4	6	8
Ischemic heart diseases	530	-	-	-	1	1	8	25	48	99	169	179
Acute myocardial infarction	199	-	-	-	-	-	3	11	21	41	65	57
Influenza and pneumonia	64	-	-	-	-	-	1	2	3	7	19	31
Chronic lower respiratory diseases	124	-	-	-	-	-	1	3	11	33	49	27
Chronic liver disease and cirrhosis	26	-	-	-	-	-	3	6	6	6	4	1
Accidents (unintentional injuries)	98	845	2	3	14	12	15	12	7	8	12	12
Transport accidents	46	189	1	2	11	7	8	6	4	4	3	1
Motor vehicle accidents	42	184	1	2	10	7	7	5	3	3	3	1
Intentional self-harm (suicide)	29	(X)	(X)	-	4	5	6	5	3	3	2	1
Assault (homicide)	17	331	1	1	5	4	3	2	1	1	-	-
Complications of medical and surgical care	3	54	-	-	-	-	-	-	1	1	1	-

2000

Cause of Death	All ages	Under 1 year	1-4 years	5-14 years	15-24 years	25-34 years	35-44 years	45-54 years	55-64 years	65-74 years	75-84 years	85 years over
All causes	2,403	28	5	7	31	40	90	160	241	441	700	658
Tuberculosis	1	-	-	-	-	-	-	-	-	-	-	-
Viral hepatitis	5	-	-	-	-	-	1	2	1	1	1	1
Human immunodeficiency virus (HIV) disease	14	-	-	-	-	2	6	4	1	-	-	-
Malignant neoplasms	553	-	-	1	2	4	17	48	89	150	165	77
Malignant neoplasms of colon, rectum and anus	57	-	-	-	-	-	1	4	8	14	18	11
Malignant neoplasms of trachea, bronchus and lung	156	-	-	-	-	-	3	12	30	52	46	13
Malignant neoplasm of breast	42	-	-	-	-	1	3	6	8	9	10	6
Leukemia	21	-	-	1	1	1	1	1	2	5	7	4
Diabetes mellitus	69	-	-	-	-	1	2	5	9	17	22	14
Nutritional deficiencies	4	-	-	-	-	-	-	-	-	-	1	2
Alzheimers disease	50	-	-	-	-	-	-	-	-	3	17	28
Major cardiovascular diseases	937	1	-	1	1	4	17	44	77	156	296	340
Diseases of heart	711	1	-	1	1	3	13	35	63	122	220	251
Hypertensive heart disease	24	-	-	-	-	-	1	2	3	4	6	8
Ischemic heart diseases	515	-	-	-	1	1	8	25	48	93	164	177
Acute myocardial infarction	193	-	-	-	-	-	3	11	21	38	62	57
Influenza and pneumonia	65	-	-	-	-	1	1	2	3	7	20	32
Chronic lower respiratory diseases	122	-	-	-	-	-	1	3	11	31	48	27
Chronic liver disease and cirrhosis	27	-	-	-	-	-	3	7	6	5	4	1
Accidents (unintentional injuries)	98	1	2	3	14	12	15	12	8	8	12	12
Transport accidents	47	2	2	3	11	7	8	6	4	3	3	1
Motor vehicle accidents	43	2	2	2	11	7	7	5	4	3	3	1
Intentional self-harm (suicide)	29	(X)	(X)	-	4	5	7	5	3	3	2	1
Assault (homicide)	17	(X)	1	1	5	4	3	2	1	1	-	-
Complications of medical and surgical care	3	(X)	-	-	-	-	-	-	1	1	-	-

- Represents zero.   X Not applicable.

Source: U.S. National Center for Health Statistics, *Vital Statistics of the United States*, annual; *National Vital Statistics Reports (NVSR)* (formerly *Monthly Vital Statistics Report*).

U.S. Census Bureau, Statistical Abstract of the United States: 2002

No. 103. Deaths and Death Rates by Leading Causes of Death and Age: 2000

[Data are based on the tenth revision of the ICD. Rates per 100,000 population in specified group. Numbers are based on weighted data rounded to the nearest individual, so categories may not add to totals]

Age	Number	Rate
ALL AGES [1]		
All causes	2,404,624	873.6
Diseases of heart	709,894	257.9
Malignant neoplasms	551,833	200.5
Cerebrovascular diseases	166,028	60.3
Chronic lower respiratory diseases	123,550	44.9
Accidents (unintentional injuries)	93,592	34.0
Motor vehicle accidents	41,804	15.2
All other accidents	51,788	18.8
Diabetes mellitus	68,662	24.9
Influenza and pneumonia	67,024	24.3
Alzheimers disease	49,044	17.8
Nephritis, nephrotic syndrome and nephrosis	37,672	13.7
Septicemia	31,613	11.5
Other causes (residual)	505,712	183.7
1-4 YEARS		
All causes	4,942	32.6
Accidents (unintentional injuries)	1,780	11.7
Motor vehicle accidents	630	4.2
All other accidents	1,150	7.6
Congenital malformations	471	3.1
Malignant neoplasms	393	2.6
Assault (homicide)	318	2.1
Diseases of heart	169	1.1
Influenza and pneumonia	96	0.6
Septicemia	91	0.6
Certain conditions originating in the perinatal period	84	0.6
In situ neoplasms	56	0.4
Cerebrovascular diseases	45	0.3
All other causes (residual)	1,439	9.5
5-14 YEARS		
All causes	7,340	18.5
Accidents (unintentional injuries)	2,878	7.3
Motor vehicle accidents	1,716	4.3
All other accidents	1,163	2.9
Malignant neoplasms	1,017	2.6
Congenital malformations	387	1.0
Assault (homicide)	364	0.9
Intentional self-harm (suicide)	297	0.7
Diseases of heart	236	0.6
Chronic lower respiratory diseases	130	0.3
In situ neoplasms	106	0.3
Influenza and pneumonia	83	0.2
Cerebrovascular diseases	78	0.2
All other causes (Residual)	1,764	4.4
15-24 YEARS		
All causes	30,959	80.7
Accidents (unintentional injuries)	13,616	35.5
Motor vehicle accidents	10,357	27.0
All other accidents	3,259	8.5
Assault (homicide)	4,796	12.5
Intentional self-harm (suicide)	3,877	10.1
Malignant neoplasms	1,668	4.3
Diseases of heart	931	2.4
Congenital malformations	425	1.1
Cerebrovascular diseases	193	0.5
Influenza and pneumonia	188	0.5
Chronic lower respiratory diseases	180	0.5
Human immunodeficiency virus (HIV) disease	178	0.5
All other causes	4,907	12.8
25-44 YEARS		
All causes	128,779	156.4
Accidents	24,817	30.1
Motor vehicle accidents	13,261	16.1
All other accidents	11,556	14.0
Malignant neoplasms	20,200	24.5
Diseases of heart	15,267	18.5
Intentional self-harm (suicide)	10,884	13.2
Human immunodeficiency virus (HIV) disease	8,302	10.1
Assault (homicide)	7,156	8.7
Chronic liver disease and cirrhosis	3,644	4.4
Cerebrovascular diseases	3,122	3.8
Diabetes mellitus	2,416	2.9
Influenza and pneumonia	1,437	1.7
All other causes	31,534	38.3
45-64 YEARS		
All causes	399,008	652.8
Malignant neoplasms	136,363	223.1
Diseases of heart	97,334	159.2
Accidents (unintentional injuries)	18,252	29.9
Motor vehicle accidents	8,483	13.9
All other accidents	9,769	16.0
Cerebrovascular diseases	15,735	25.7
Chronic lower respiratory diseases	14,086	23.0
Diabetes mellitus	13,958	22.8
Chronic liver disease and cirrhosis	12,206	20.0
Intentional self-harm (suicide)	8,052	13.2
Human immunodeficiency virus (HIV) disease	5,336	8.7
Nephritis, nephrotic syndrome and nephrosis	4,821	7.9
All other causes	72,865	119.2
65 YEARS AND OLDER		
All causes	1,805,187	5,190.8
Diseases of heart	595,440	1,712.2
Malignant neoplasms	392,082	1,127.4
Cerebrovascular diseases	146,725	421.9
Chronic lower respiratory diseases	107,888	310.2
Influenza and pneumonia	60,261	173.3
Diabetes mellitus	52,102	149.8
Alzheimers disease	48,492	139.4
Nephritis, nephrotic syndrome and nephrosis	31,588	90.8
Accidents (unintentional injuries)	31,332	90.1
Motor vehicle accidents	7,165	20.6
All other accidents	24,167	69.5
Septicemia	25,143	72.3
All other causes	314,134	903.3

[1] Includes deaths under 1 year of age.

Source: U.S. National Center for Health Statistics. Vital Statistics of the United States, annual; National Vital Statistics Reports (NVSR); and unpublished data.

No. 104. Death Rates for Major Causes of Death—States: 1999

[Deaths per 100,000 resident population enumerated as of April 1. By place of residence. Excludes nonresidents of the United States. Causes of death classified according to tenth revisions of International Classification of Diseases]

State	Total	Heart disease	Cancer	Cerebro-vascular dis-eases	Acci-dents	Motor vehicle acci-dents	Chronic lower respira-tory dis-eases	Diabe-tes Mellitus	HIV [1]	Inten-tional self-harm (sui-cide)	Assault (homi-cide)
United States .	877.0	265.9	201.6	61.4	35.9	15.5	45.5	25.1	5.4	10.7	6.2
AL	1,025.3	307.1	217.5	72.0	52.9	26.6	49.9	30.7	4.1	12.7	10.0
AK	437.1	90.9	102.2	27.6	47.5	14.0	23.6	10.8	(B)	15.5	8.2
AZ	838.2	226.0	188.5	54.4	46.3	19.8	53.4	22.2	3.2	16.0	9.8
AR	1,094.5	325.9	240.5	88.4	50.4	25.4	53.2	27.1	2.6	13.2	7.0
CA	692.0	217.0	160.1	54.2	27.8	11.0	39.7	19.3	4.8	9.3	6.2
CO	668.5	158.3	144.5	45.2	37.4	15.3	46.7	15.8	2.6	14.2	4.9
CT	897.2	278.1	214.9	58.9	31.5	9.4	43.7	21.1	6.2	8.3	3.7
DE	884.6	266.9	230.5	48.4	35.4	13.0	43.4	23.8	8.6	11.4	3.2
DC	1,170.7	318.3	258.2	57.2	31.0	6.9	32.0	42.6	51.3	5.8	35.8
FL	1,080.1	340.4	254.6	69.9	39.4	19.0	60.4	28.8	11.0	13.4	6.4
GA	796.4	225.9	169.8	56.7	39.5	19.5	39.2	18.6	10.1	11.2	8.1
HI	697.6	203.3	161.6	64.3	24.7	7.6	24.5	17.8	2.4	11.5	3.2
ID	765.3	202.3	172.7	61.6	47.7	22.2	45.4	21.3	(B)	14.5	2.5
IL	894.1	275.3	206.3	63.6	34.0	12.7	42.5	24.8	4.5	8.4	8.4
IN	930.6	280.4	217.0	68.3	38.9	16.6	51.4	26.8	1.9	10.6	6.5
IA	990.1	303.2	221.2	80.7	39.1	18.4	57.3	23.8	0.7	10.6	1.8
KS	922.1	262.8	201.0	69.4	42.4	21.5	52.2	24.5	1.6	11.3	5.2
KY	992.7	305.4	225.3	68.4	43.7	20.6	58.8	28.6	1.9	11.9	5.3
LA	943.2	274.6	215.3	61.4	44.4	22.3	36.8	38.6	8.5	11.8	11.1
ME	978.5	272.8	242.2	70.1	36.6	15.9	59.9	27.8	(B)	14.0	2.0
MD	833.2	233.6	196.1	55.9	25.1	11.8	37.6	27.5	11.4	8.4	10.3
MA	904.3	257.0	224.3	57.5	21.1	7.1	46.3	21.9	4.2	7.0	2.2
MI	884.4	280.8	200.2	61.2	32.3	14.3	43.8	26.2	2.4	9.9	7.7
MN	807.0	199.6	186.2	62.8	37.1	13.5	41.8	26.2	1.5	9.2	2.9
MS	1,018.0	337.2	221.9	67.0	59.3	34.5	45.8	21.4	5.6	11.0	11.3
MO	1,022.8	328.7	222.8	72.2	45.1	19.4	56.1	28.4	2.7	12.8	7.0
MT	920.7	232.1	210.0	67.4	52.2	23.8	64.1	27.6	(B)	18.4	3.7
NE	935.1	269.9	204.7	70.6	40.1	17.7	56.7	22.3	1.2	10.6	3.7
NV	833.6	233.9	196.5	48.7	39.2	18.4	56.9	15.8	5.8	22.3	9.2
NH	794.0	229.0	200.5	55.7	27.4	10.7	49.3	24.5	(B)	11.4	1.7
NJ	908.5	288.5	223.2	50.6	27.3	8.9	38.4	29.9	11.2	6.9	3.7
NM	786.0	198.4	164.2	47.0	55.7	23.9	48.7	29.7	1.7	18.3	9.6
NY	878.9	324.2	206.7	44.6	26.4	9.7	38.9	20.9	13.1	6.6	5.3
NC	909.7	250.8	206.7	73.5	43.0	20.9	46.9	26.8	6.1	11.6	8.5
ND	963.1	289.3	215.6	81.0	42.1	21.1	43.1	32.0	(B)	11.5	(B)
OH	964.0	294.9	224.2	64.3	32.2	12.7	52.0	32.6	2.2	9.8	4.0
OK	1,033.3	335.4	217.7	73.9	47.9	20.4	52.1	29.4	3.1	14.7	6.9
OR	887.2	219.0	208.2	84.4	36.2	13.1	53.2	25.9	2.3	14.4	3.2
PA	1,086.2	347.7	252.7	71.7	38.5	13.2	51.2	31.2	4.2	10.7	5.3
RI	979.8	303.6	248.6	63.9	24.5	9.0	50.0	23.8	3.5	9.7	3.6
SC	927.8	256.9	208.2	76.5	48.9	25.6	45.1	28.8	7.9	10.8	8.1
SD	948.4	276.1	222.6	74.6	47.9	23.7	45.7	26.7	(B)	14.0	3.1
TN	980.5	296.9	217.8	74.8	48.8	24.1	50.1	26.2	4.7	13.2	7.7
TX	732.7	216.6	163.4	52.0	36.1	18.3	37.5	24.6	5.3	10.0	6.6
UT	566.1	130.8	112.4	40.8	30.5	17.1	26.2	22.2	1.4	13.2	2.4
VT	840.9	226.0	211.4	57.9	35.2	14.0	50.5	30.1	(B)	10.6	(B)
VA	804.9	223.0	194.5	59.8	32.2	13.1	39.3	21.6	3.9	11.5	6.1
WA	762.0	200.0	185.1	64.6	33.3	12.7	47.1	22.7	1.9	14.2	3.3
WV	1,164.9	377.5	263.5	73.2	44.2	21.4	68.4	40.6	1.2	12.7	5.5
WI	888.9	263.3	204.8	73.7	37.2	14.8	43.2	24.2	1.2	11.3	3.8
WY	842.8	210.4	187.4	55.3	53.8	30.0	70.5	28.1	(B)	20.4	(B)
PR	744.7	165.7	118.1	46.6	33.7	12.4	33.3	61.5	17.6	7.4	17.1
VI	550.9	151.3	97.8	31.8	34.3	(B)	(B)	33.4	(B)	(B)	22.6
GU	456.0	129.6	67.1	43.4	25.7	17.8	19.7	16.5	(B)	23.7	(B)
AS	385.7	70.6	56.4	(B)	(B)	(B)	(B)	34.5	(B)	(B)	(B)
MP	234.0	43.3	31.8	(B)	31.8	(B)	(B)	(B)	(B)	(B)	(B)

B Figure does not meet standards of reliability or precision.   [1] Human immunodeficiency virus.

Source: U.S. National Center for Health Statistics, *National Vital Statistics Report (NVSR)*.

Vital Statistics   83

No. 105. Death Rates From Heart Disease by Sex and Age: 1990 to 1999

[**Rates per 100,000 population.** For explanation of age-adjustment, see text, this section]

Characteristic	Male						Female					
	1990	1995	1996	1997	1998	1999 [1]	1990	1995	1996	1997	1998	1999 [1]
All ages, age adjusted . . .	412.4	372.7	360.7	349.6	336.6	328.1	257.0	239.7	234.1	228.1	223.1	220.9
All ages, crude	297.6	282.7	277.4	272.2	268.0	263.8	281.8	278.8	275.5	271.1	268.3	268.0
Under 1 year .	21.9	17.5	17.4	18.0	16.2	13.8	18.3	16.7	15.7	14.7	16.1	13.6
1-14 years . . .	1.9	1.7	1.4	1.5	1.5	1.3	1.9	1.5	1.4	1.2	1.3	1.1
5-14 years . . .	0.9	0.8	0.9	0.9	1.0	0.8	0.8	0.7	0.8	0.7	0.7	0.6
15-24 years . .	3.1	3.6	3.3	3.6	3.5	3.4	1.8	2.2	2.0	2.4	2.1	2.2
25-34 years . .	10.3	11.4	11.0	10.8	10.8	10.6	5.0	5.6	5.6	5.8	5.8	5.6
35-44 years . .	48.1	47.2	44.2	43.7	44.0	43.3	15.1	17.1	16.8	16.5	17.3	17.6
45-54 years . .	183.0	168.6	161.8	157.7	152.2	145.7	61.0	56.0	56.9	54.3	52.8	51.9
55-64 years . .	537.3	465.4	453.8	434.6	411.1	391.6	215.7	193.9	189.3	182.1	173.9	167.5
65-74 years . .	1,250.0	1,102.3	1,065.0	1,031.1	997.3	961.6	616.8	557.8	543.8	529.4	522.6	503.2
75-84 years . .	2,968.2	2,615.0	2,529.4	2,443.6	2,377.2	2,308.9	1,893.8	1,715.2	1,674.7	1,616.6	1,579.5	1,562.5
86 years and over	7,418.4	7,039.6	6,834.0	6,658.5	6,330.6	6,313.3	6,478.1	6,267.8	6,108.0	6,013.7	5,876.6	5,913.8

[1] Starting with 1999 data, cause of death is coded according to ICD-10. Discontinuity between 1998 and 1999 due to ICD-10 coding and classification changes is measured by the comparability ratio. For explanation, see text, this section.

Source: U.S. National Center for Health Statistics , *Vital Statistics of the United States,* annual; *National Vital Statistics Reports (NVSR)* (formerly *Monthly Statistics Report);* and unpublished data.

No. 106. Death Rates From Cerebrovascular Diseases by Race, Sex, and Age: 1950 to 1999

[**Rates per 100,000 population.** For explanation of age-adjustment, see text, this section]

Characteristic	1950 [1]	1960 [1]	1970	1980	1985	1990	1995	1996	1997	1998	1999 [2]
All ages, age adjusted .	180.7	177.9	147.7	96.4	76.6	65.5	63.9	63.2	61.8	59.6	61.8
Under 1 year	5.1	4.1	5.0	4.4	3.7	3.8	5.8	6.2	7.0	7.8	2.7
1-4 years	0.9	0.8	1.0	0.5	0.3	0.3	0.4	0.3	0.4	0.4	0.3
1-14 years	0.5	0.7	0.7	0.3	0.2	0.2	0.2	0.2	0.2	0.2	0.2
15-24 years	1.6	1.8	1.6	1.0	0.8	0.6	0.5	0.5	0.5	0.5	0.5
25-34 years	4.2	4.7	4.5	2.6	2.2	2.2	1.8	1.8	1.7	1.7	1.5
35-44 years	18.7	14.7	15.6	8.5	7.2	6.5	6.5	6.3	6.3	6.0	5.7
45-54 years	70.4	49.2	41.6	25.2	21.3	18.7	17.6	17.9	16.9	16.5	15.5
55-64 years	194.2	147.3	115.8	65.2	54.8	48.0	46.1	45.3	44.4	42.6	41.2
65-74 years	554.7	469.2	384.1	219.5	172.8	144.4	137.2	135.5	134.8	130.0	132.2
75-84 years	1,499.6	1,491.3	1,254.2	788.6	601.5	499.3	481.4	477.0	462.0	455.4	472.8
86 years and over	2,990.1	3,680.5	3,014.3	2,288.9	1,865.1	1,633.9	1,636.5	1,612.7	1,584.6	1,500.0	1,606.3
Male all ages, age adjusted	186.4	186.1	157.4	102.4	80.2	68.7	66.3	65.3	63.9	60.1	62.4
Under 1 year	6.4	5.0	5.8	5.0	4.6	4.4	6.3	6.5	7.6	9.0	3.4
1-4 years	1.1	0.9	1.2	0.4	0.4	0.3	0.4	0.3	0.5	0.3	0.3
1-14 years	0.5	0.7	0.8	0.3	0.2	0.2	0.2	0.2	0.2	0.2	0.2
15-24 years	1.8	1.9	1.8	1.1	0.7	0.7	0.5	0.5	0.6	0.6	0.5
25-34 years	4.2	4.5	4.4	2.6	2.2	2.1	1.9	1.7	1.7	1.7	1.6
35-44 years	17.5	14.6	15.7	8.7	7.4	6.8	7.1	6.7	6.5	6.2	5.9
45-54 years	67.9	52.2	44.4	27.3	23.2	20.5	19.8	20.0	19.2	18.5	17.1
55-64 years	205.2	163.8	138.7	74.7	63.5	54.4	53.4	52.5	51.4	49.5	47.6
65-74 years	589.6	530.7	449.5	259.2	201.4	166.8	155.9	154.7	153.1	145.7	149.1
75-84 years	1,543.6	1,555.9	1,361.6	868.3	661.2	552.7	517.1	508.7	488.7	474.7	494.4
86 years and over	3,048.6	3,643.1	2,895.2	2,199.2	1,730.1	1,533.2	1,537.7	1,512.7	1,500.7	1,347.2	1,455.0
Female all ages, age adjusted	175.8	170.7	140.0	91.9	73.5	62.7	61.5	60.9	59.7	58.3	60.5
Under 1 year	3.7	3.2	4.0	3.8	2.7	3.1	5.2	5.9	6.3	6.6	2.1
1-4 years	0.7	0.7	0.7	0.5	0.3	0.3	0.3	0.3	0.3	0.4	0.3
1-14 years	0.4	0.6	0.6	0.3	0.3	0.2	0.2	0.2	0.2	0.2	0.2
15-24 years	1.5	1.6	1.4	0.8	0.8	0.6	0.4	0.4	0.5	0.4	0.5
25-34 years	4.3	4.9	4.7	2.6	2.1	2.2	1.7	1.8	1.7	1.8	1.5
35-44 years	19.9	14.8	15.6	8.4	6.9	6.1	6.0	5.9	6.2	5.7	5.6
45-54 years	72.9	46.3	39.0	23.3	19.4	17.0	15.5	15.9	14.8	14.6	14.0
55-64 years	183.1	131.8	95.3	56.9	47.2	42.2	39.4	38.8	37.9	36.3	35.5
65-74 years	522.1	415.7	333.3	189.0	150.7	126.9	122.2	120.1	120.1	117.2	118.5
75-84 years	1,462.2	1,441.1	1,183.1	741.6	566.3	467.4	458.7	456.5	444.4	442.6	458.3
86 years and over	2,949.4	3,704.4	3,081.0	2,328.2	1,918.9	1,672.7	1,675.0	1,652.4	1,618.4	1,563.3	1,670.2
White male age adjusted . .	182.1	181.6	153.7	99.0	77.4	65.7	63.2	62.7	61.5	57.6	60.1
Black male age adjusted. . .	228.8	238.5	206.4	142.1	112.7	102.5	96.7	93.2	88.5	86.3	87.4
White female age adjusted .	169.7	165.0	135.5	89.2	70.9	60.5	59.5	59.1	57.9	56.6	58.8
Black female age adjusted .	238.4	232.5	189.3	119.8	99.4	84.0	81.0	79.0	76.1	75.3	78.1

[1] Includes deaths of persons who were not residents of the 50 states and the District of Columbia.   [2] Starting with 1999 data, cause of death is coded according to ICD-10. Discontinuity between 1998 and 1999 due to ICD-10 coding and classification changes is measured by the comparability ratio. For explanation, see text, this section.

Source: U.S. National Center for Health Statistics. *Vital Statistics of the United States,* annual; *National Vital Statistics Reports* (NVSR); and unpublished data.

No. 107. Death Rates From Malignant Neoplasms by Race, Sex, and Age: 1950 to 1999

[Rates per 100,000 population. For explanation of age-adjustment, see text, this section]

Characteristic	1950 [1]	1960 [1]	1970	1980	1985	1990	1995	1996	1997	1998	1999 [2]
Total, age adjusted . . .	193.9	193.9	198.6	207.9	211.3	216.0	211.7	208.7	205.7	202.4	202.7
Under 1 year	8.7	7.2	4.7	3.2	3.1	2.3	1.8	2.3	2.4	2.1	1.8
1-4 years	11.7	10.9	7.5	4.5	3.8	3.5	3.1	2.7	2.9	2.4	2.8
5-14 years	6.7	6.8	6.0	4.3	3.5	3.1	2.7	2.7	2.7	2.6	2.6
15-24 years	8.6	8.3	8.3	6.3	5.4	4.9	4.6	4.5	4.5	4.6	4.6
25-34 years	20.0	19.5	16.5	13.7	13.2	12.6	11.9	12.0	11.6	11.3	10.5
35-44 years	62.7	59.7	59.5	48.6	45.9	43.3	40.3	39.3	38.9	38.2	37.3
45-54 years	175.1	177.0	182.5	180.0	170.1	158.9	142.2	137.9	135.1	132.3	130.4
55-64 years	390.7	396.8	423.0	436.1	454.6	449.6	416.0	406.5	395.7	383.8	380.8
65-74 years	698.8	713.9	754.2	817.9	845.5	872.3	868.2	861.6	847.3	841.3	836.2
75-84 years	1,153.3	1,127.4	1,169.2	1,232.3	1,271.8	1,348.5	1,364.8	1,351.5	1,335.2	1,326.3	1,339.8
85 years and over	1,451.0	1,450.0	1,320.7	1,594.6	1,615.4	1,752.9	1,823.8	1,798.3	1,805.0	1,749.4	1,796.2
Male all ages, age adjusted.	208.1	225.1	247.6	271.2	274.4	280.4	268.8	263.2	258.0	252.4	251.6
Female all ages, age adjusted.	182.3	168.7	163.2	166.7	171.2	175.7	175.4	173.4	171.6	169.2	169.9
White male all ages, age adjusted.	210.0	224.7	244.8	265.1	267.1	272.2	261.8	256.8	251.9	246.9	246.4
Black male all ages, age adjusted.	178.9	227.6	291.9	353.4	373.9	397.9	372.8	365.3	354.7	343.1	340.5
White female all ages, age adjusted.	182.0	167.7	162.5	165.2	169.9	174.0	173.7	172.1	170.0	167.7	168.6
Black female all ages, age adjusted.	174.1	174.3	173.4	189.5	195.5	205.9	206.0	202.3	204.4	200.0	200.0
DEATH RATES FOR MALIGNANT NEOPLASM OF BREASTS FOR FEMALES											
All ages, age adjusted	31.9	31.7	32.1	31.9	33.0	33.3	30.8	29.8	28.6	27.9	27.0
All ages, crude	24.7	26.1	28.4	30.6	32.8	34.0	32.6	31.8	30.7	30.2	29.5
Under 25 years.	(B)	(B)	(B)	(B)	-	(B)	(B)	-	(B)	(B)	(B)
25-34 years	3.8	3.8	3.9	3.3	3.0	2.9	2.7	2.7	2.6	2.6	2.3
35-44 years	20.8	20.2	20.4	17.9	17.5	17.8	15.0	14.2	14.0	13.4	12.1
45-54 years	46.9	51.4	52.6	48.1	47.1	45.4	41.4	38.8	37.8	35.0	33.5
55-64 years	69.9	70.8	77.6	80.5	84.2	78.6	69.8	67.4	64.4	62.2	59.9
65-74 years	95.0	90.0	93.8	101.1	107.8	111.7	103.3	99.1	94.1	93.3	89.9
75-84 years	139.8	129.9	127.4	126.4	136.2	146.3	142.0	139.8	132.2	131.4	131.3
85 years and over	195.5	191.9	157.1	169.3	178.5	196.8	203.7	204.9	198.5	194.7	202.6
DEATH RATES FOR MALIGNANT NEOPLASM OF TRACHEA, BRONCHUS, AND LUNG											
All ages, age adjusted	15.0	24.1	37.1	49.9	54.6	59.3	58.9	58.4	58.1	57.6	56.0
All ages, crude	12.2	20.3	32.1	45.8	51.5	56.8	57.5	57.3	57.3	57.2	55.8
Under 25 years.	0.1	-	0.1	-	-	-	-	-	-	-	-
25-34 years	0.8	1.0	0.9	0.6	0.6	0.7	0.7	0.7	0.6	0.6	0.5
35-44 years	4.5	6.8	11.0	9.2	7.8	6.8	6.0	6.2	6.2	6.1	6.1
45-54 years	20.4	29.6	43.4	54.1	50.9	46.8	38.0	36.8	34.6	33.3	31.9
55-64 years	48.7	75.3	109.1	138.2	153.8	160.6	142.9	138.7	134.3	131.4	125.5
65-74 years	59.7	108.1	164.5	233.3	261.2	288.4	297.1	296.1	295.7	296.7	284.6
75-84 years	55.8	91.5	163.2	240.5	282.0	333.3	361.4	364.4	368.5	367.7	364.4
85 years and over	42.3	65.6	101.7	176.0	195.2	242.5	284.0	280.9	297.6	289.9	295.6

- Represents zero or rounds to less than half the unit of measurement shown.   B Base figure too small to meet statistical standards for reliability.   [1] Includes deaths of persons who were not residents of the 50 states and the District of Columbia. [2] Starting with 1999 data, cause of death is coded according to ICD-10. Discontinuity between 1998 and 1999 due to ICD-10 coding and classification changes is measured by the comparability ratio. For explanation, see text, this section.

Source: U.S. National Center for Health Statistics, Vital Statistics of the United States, annual; National Vital Statistics Reports (NVSR); and unpublished data.

No. 108. Death Rates From Suicide by Sex and Race: 1950 to 1999

[Rates per 100,000 population. For explanation of age-adjustment, see text, this section]

Characteristic	1950 [1] [2]	1960 [1]	1970	1980	1985	1990	1995	1996	1997	1998	1999 [3]
All ages, age adjusted	13.2	12.5	13.1	12.2	12.5	12.5	12.0	11.7	11.4	11.3	10.7
All ages, crude.	11.4	10.6	11.6	11.9	12.4	12.4	11.9	11.6	11.4	11.3	10.7
Under 1 year	(X)	(X)	(X)	(X)	(X)	(X)	(X)	(X)	(X)	(X)	(X)
1-4 years	(X)	(X)	(X)	(X)	(X)	(X)	(X)	(X)	(X)	(X)	(X)
5-14 years	0.2	0.3	0.3	0.4	0.8	0.8	0.9	0.8	0.8	0.8	0.6
15-24 years	4.5	5.2	8.8	12.3	12.8	13.2	13.3	12.0	11.4	11.1	10.3
25-44 years	11.6	12.2	15.4	15.6	15.0	15.2	15.3	15.0	14.8	14.6	14.0
25-34 years	9.1	10.0	14.1	16.0	15.3	15.2	15.4	14.5	14.3	13.8	13.5
35-44 years	14.3	14.2	16.9	15.4	14.6	15.3	15.2	15.5	15.3	15.4	14.4
45-64 years	23.5	22.0	20.6	15.9	16.3	15.3	14.1	14.4	14.2	14.1	13.5
45-54 years	20.9	20.7	20.0	15.9	15.7	14.8	14.6	14.9	14.7	14.8	14.2
55-64 years	26.8	23.7	21.4	15.9	16.8	16.0	13.3	13.7	13.5	13.1	12.4
65 years and over	30.0	24.5	20.8	17.6	20.4	20.5	18.1	17.3	16.8	16.9	15.9
65-74 years	29.6	23.0	20.8	16.9	18.7	17.9	15.8	15.0	14.4	14.1	13.6
75-84 years	31.1	27.9	21.2	19.1	23.9	24.9	20.7	20.0	19.3	19.7	18.3
86 years and over	28.8	26.0	19.0	19.2	19.4	22.2	21.6	20.2	20.8	21.0	19.2
White male all ages, age adjusted.	22.3	21.1	20.8	20.9	22.4	22.8	21.9	21.3	20.6	20.6	19.4
Black male all ages, age adjusted.	7.5	8.4	10.0	11.4	11.8	12.8	12.5	11.9	11.4	10.6	10.4
White female all ages, age adjusted.	6.0	5.9	7.9	6.1	5.7	5.2	4.7	4.7	4.8	4.7	4.4
Black female all ages, age adjusted.	1.8	2.0	2.9	2.4	2.3	2.4	2.1	2.0	2.0	1.8	1.6

X Not applicable. [1] Includes deaths of persons who were not residents of the 50 States and the District of Columbia. [2] In 1950 rate is for the age group 75 years and over. [3] Starting with 1999 data, cause of death is coded according to ICD-10.
Source: U.S. National Center for Health Statistics, *Vital Statistics of the United States,* annual; *National Vital Statistics Reports* (NVSR) (formerly *Monthly Statistics Report);* and unpublished data.

No. 109. Death Rates From Human Immunodeficiency Virus (HIV) Disease by Race, Sex, and Age: 1990 to 1999

[Rates per 100,000 population. For explanation of age-adjustment, see text, this section]

Characteristic	1990	1992	1993	1994	1995	1996	1997	1998	1999 [1]
All ages, age adjusted.	10.2	13.2	14.5	16.2	16.3	11.7	6.1	4.9	5.4
Under 1 year.	2.7	2.5	2.2	2.5	1.5	1.1	(B)	(B)	(B)
1-4 years	0.8	1.0	1.3	1.3	1.3	0.9	0.4	0.2	0.2
5-14 years	0.2	0.3	0.4	0.5	0.5	0.5	0.3	0.1	0.2
15-24 years	1.5	1.6	1.7	1.8	1.7	1.1	0.8	0.5	0.5
25-34 years.	19.7	24.6	27.0	29.3	29.1	19.9	10.1	7.5	7.2
35-44 years.	27.4	35.6	39.1	44.1	44.4	31.4	16.1	12.9	13.9
45-54 years.	15.2	20.3	22.6	25.6	26.3	19.3	10.4	9.0	10.9
55-64 years.	6.2	8.5	8.8	10.4	11.0	8.4	4.9	4.3	4.9
65-74 years.	2.0	2.8	2.9	3.1	3.6	2.7	1.8	1.6	2.2
75-84 years.	0.7	0.8	0.8	0.9	0.7	0.8	0.6	0.5	0.6
85 years and over	(B)	(B)	(B)	(B)	(B)	(B)	(B)	(B)	(B)
Male ages, age adjusted . .	18.5	23.5	25.4	27.8	27.7	19.2	9.7	7.7	8.4
Under 1 year.	2.4	2.3	2.1	2.1	1.7	1.1	(B)	(B)	(B)
1-4 years	0.8	1.1	1.3	1.2	1.2	0.9	0.3	(B)	(B)
5-14 years	0.3	0.4	0.4	0.5	0.5	0.5	0.3	0.1	0.2
15-24 years	2.2	2.3	2.3	2.3	2.1	1.3	0.8	0.5	0.5
25-34 years.	34.5	42.2	46.0	48.5	47.1	31.4	15.1	10.7	10.2
35-44 years.	50.2	63.5	68.5	76.2	75.9	51.8	25.5	20.1	21.1
45-54 years.	29.1	38.1	41.7	46.3	46.9	33.6	17.4	15.2	17.9
55-64 years.	12.0	15.9	16.5	19.1	19.9	14.9	8.5	7.3	8.5
65-74 years.	3.7	5.3	5.4	5.8	6.4	5.1	3.4	2.9	3.9
75-84 years.	1.1	1.6	1.4	1.4	1.3	1.5	1.0	0.9	1.0
85 years and over	(B)	(B)	(B)	(B)	(B)	(B)	(B)	(B)	(B)
Female age adjusted	2.2	3.2	3.9	4.9	5.3	4.3	2.7	2.3	2.6
Under 1 year.	3.0	2.7	2.4	2.9	1.2	(B)	(B)	(B)	(B)
1-4 years	0.8	1.0	1.3	1.3	1.5	1.0	0.4	(B)	(B)
5-14 years	0.2	0.2	0.4	0.5	0.5	0.4	0.2	0.2	0.2
15-24 years.	0.7	0.9	1.1	1.3	1.4	1.0	0.7	0.6	0.6
25-34 years.	4.9	6.9	8.0	10.1	11.1	8.5	5.1	4.4	4.3
35-45 years.	5.2	8.2	10.2	12.5	13.4	11.3	6.8	5.8	6.8
45-54 years.	1.9	3.4	4.4	5.8	6.7	5.7	3.8	3.1	4.2
55-64 years.	1.1	1.9	1.9	2.6	2.9	2.5	1.6	1.6	1.6
65-74 years.	0.8	0.9	1.0	1.0	1.4	0.8	0.5	0.6	0.8
75-84 years.	0.4	0.4	0.4	0.6	0.3	0.3	0.4	0.3	0.3
85 years and over	(B)	(B)	(B)	(B)	(B)	(B)	(B)	(B)	(B)
Race, age-adjusted									
White male	15.7	19.0	20.0	21.2	20.7	13.2	6.0	4.6	5.0
Black male	46.3	65.5	74.5	87.2	90.4	71.5	41.7	34.0	37.1
White female.	1.1	1.6	1.9	2.0	2.6	1.9	1.0	0.8	1.0
Black female	10.1	14.8	17.8	22.6	24.7	21.1	13.9	12.2	13.4

B Base figure too small to meet statistical standards for reliability of a derived figure. [1] Starting with 1999 data, cause of death is coded according to ICD-10. Discontinuity between 1998 and 1999 due to ICD-10 coding and classification changes is measured by the comparability ratio. For explanation, see text, this section.
Source: U.S. National Center for Health Statistics. Vital Statistics of the United States, annual; National Vital Statistics Reports (NVSR); and unpublished data.

No. 110. Deaths—Life Years Lost and Mortality Costs by Age, Sex, and Cause: 1998 and 1999

[*Life years lost:* Number of years person would have lived in absence of death. *Mortality cost:* value of lifetime earnings lost by persons who die prematurely, discounted at 6 percent]

Characteristic	Number of deaths (1,000)	Life years lost [1] Total (1,000)	Life years lost [1] Per death	Mortality cost [2] Total (mil. dol.)	Mortality cost [2] Per death (dol.)
Total, 1998	**2,337**	**37,959**	**16.2**	**391,290**	**167,444**
Under 5 yrs. old	34	2,564	76.3	28,013	833,170
5 to 14 yrs. old	8	537	68.9	7,924	1,017,102
15 to 24 yrs. old	31	1,792	58.5	37,917	1,238,041
25 to 44 yrs. old	131	5,650	43.0	133,550	1,016,498
45 to 64 yrs. old	326	9,884	30.3	145,852	446,900
65 yrs old and over	1,807	17,532	9.7	38,034	21,047
Heart disease	725	9,151	12.6	112,162	154,748
Cancer	542	8,944	16.5	81,201	149,950
Cerebrovascular diseases	158	1,868	11.8	11,373	71,778
Accidents and adverse effects	98	3,248	33.2	61,550	629,827
Other	814	14,748	18.1	125,005	153,501
Male	**1,157**	**19,969**	**17.3**	**284,930**	**246,279**
Under 5 yrs. old	19	1,379	73.7	17,416	931,033
5 to 14 yrs. old	5	312	66.6	5,272	1,125,097
15 to 24 yrs. old	23	1,296	57.1	30,077	1,324,005
25 to 44 yrs. old	86	3,585	41.5	98,959	1,145,973
45 to 64 yrs. old	232	5,695	24.6	106,308	458,499
65 yrs. old and over	793	7,702	9.7	26,897	33,934
Heart disease	354	4,818	13.6	79,487	224,628
Cancer	282	4,325	15.3	51,467	182,470
Cerebrovascular diseases	61	750	12.3	7,355	120,296
Accidents and adverse effects	63	2,193	34.8	48,812	775,530
Other	397	7,883	19.9	97,809	246,408
Female	**1,180**	**17,989**	**15.2**	**106,360**	**90,143**
Under 5 yrs. old	15	1,185	79.4	10,597	710,441
5 to 14 yrs. old	3	225	72.6	2,652	854,119
15 to 24 yrs. old	8	496	62.7	7,840	991,157
25 to 44 yrs. old	45	2,065	45.9	34,590	768,195
45 to 64 yrs. old	95	4,188	44.3	39,544	418,442
65 yrs. old and over	1,014	9,830	9.7	11,137	10,979
Heart disease	371	4,333	11.7	32,675	88,086
Cancer	259	4,619	17.8	29,734	114,599
Cerebrovascular diseases	97	1,118	11.5	4,017	41,290
Accidents and adverse effects	35	1,054	30.3	12,738	366,192
Other	417	6,864	16.4	27,196	65,152
Total, 1999	**2,391**	**38,383**	**16.1**	**410,022**	**171,483**
Under 5 yrs. old	33	2,530	76.2	28,788	867,464
5 to 14 yrs. old	8	525	69.1	8,011	1,054,831
15 to 24 yrs. old	31	1,795	58.6	39,585	1,291,249
25 to 44 yrs. old	130	5,595	42.9	137,676	1,056,427
45 to 64 yrs. old	337	10,209	30.3	157,184	466,226
65 yrs old and over	1,852	17,728	9.6	38,779	20,937
Heart disease	725	9,037	12.5	70,855	97,711
Cancer	550	9,007	16.4	84,739	154,119
Cerebrovascular diseases	167	1,902	11.4	11,349	67,810
Accidents and adverse effects	98	3,262	33.4	64,910	664,012
Other	851	15,176	17.8	178,170	209,377
Male	**1,175**	**20,148**	**17.1**	**299,386**	**254,757**
Under 5 yrs. old	19	1,375	73.8	18,149	974,632
5 to 14 yrs. old	4	300	66.8	5,288	1,177,258
15 to 24 yrs. old	22	1,280	57.1	31,185	1,391,335
25 to 44 yrs. old	85	3,545	41.5	102,445	1,199,680
45 to 64 yrs. old	238	5,881	24.7	114,472	480,202
65 yrs. old and over	806	7,767	9.6	27,846	34,554
Heart disease	352	4,751	13.5	55,514	157,899
Cancer	286	4,367	15.3	54,112	189,318
Cerebrovascular diseases	64	759	11.8	7,345	113,908
Accidents and adverse effects	63	2,219	35.0	51,829	816,959
Other	410	8,051	19.6	130,586	318,617
Female	**1,216**	**18,236**	**15.0**	**110,636**	**90,994**
Under 5 yrs. old	15	1,155	79.3	10,639	730,453
5 to 14 yrs. old	3	225	72.5	2,723	877,603
15 to 24 yrs. old	8	516	62.6	8,399	1,019,066
25 to 44 yrs. old	45	2,051	45.6	35,230	784,149
45 to 64 yrs. old	99	4,329	43.8	42,712	432,491
65 yrs. old and over	1,046	9,961	9.5	10,933	10,449
Heart disease	374	4,286	11.5	15,340	41,065
Cancer	264	4,639	17.6	30,627	116,011
Cerebrovascular diseases	103	1,143	11.1	4,004	38,916
Accidents and adverse effects	34	1,043	30.4	13,081	381,230
Other	441	7,125	16.2	47,584	107,876

Vital Statistics   87

U.S. Census Bureau, Statistical Abstract of the United States: 2002

No. 111. Marriages and Divorces—Number and Rate by State: 1990 to 2001

[2443.0 represents 2,443,000. By place of occurrence]

State	Marriages [1] Number (1,000)			Marriages [1] Rate per 1,000 population [2]			Divorces [3] Number (1,000)			Divorces [3] Rate per 1,000 population [2]		
	1990	1995	2001	1990	1995	2001	1990	1995	2001	1990	1995	2001
U.S. [4]	2,443.0	2,336.0	2,327.0	9.8	8.9	8.4	1,182.0	1,169.0	(NA)	4.7	4.4	4.0
Alabama	43.3	42.0	42.2	10.6	9.9	9.6	25.3	26.0	23.4	6.1	6.1	5.3
Alaska.	5.7	5.5	5.1	10.2	9.0	8.2	2.9	3.0	2.6	5.5	5.0	4.1
Arizona	37.0	38.9	40.0	10.0	9.2	8.0	25.1	27.6	21.1	6.9	6.6	4.2
Arkansas	35.7	36.6	38.4	15.3	14.7	14.8	16.8	16.0	17.1	6.9	6.5	6.6
California [5]	236.7	199.6	224.2	7.9	6.3	6.6	128.0	(NA)	(NA)	4.3	(NA)	(NA)
Colorado	31.5	34.3	36.5	9.8	9.2	8.7	18.4	(NA)	(NA)	5.5	(NA)	(NA)
Connecticut	27.8	22.6	18.6	7.9	6.7	5.6	10.3	10.6	9.7	3.2	2.9	2.9
Delaware	5.6	5.4	5.2	8.4	7.5	6.7	3.0	3.7	3.1	4.4	5.1	4.0
Dist. of Columbia. .	4.7	3.5	3.5	8.2	6.4	6.8	2.7	1.9	1.2	4.5	3.4	2.3
Florida.	142.3	144.3	151.3	10.9	10.2	9.7	81.7	79.5	84.6	6.3	5.6	5.4
Georgia	64.4	61.5	51.3	10.3	8.5	6.3	35.7	37.2	30.6	5.5	5.2	3.8
Hawaii.	18.1	18.8	24.0	16.4	15.8	20.4	5.2	5.5	4.5	4.6	4.6	3.8
Idaho	15.0	15.5	14.7	13.9	13.3	11.4	6.6	6.8	7.2	6.5	5.8	5.6
Illinois	97.1	83.2	89.8	8.8	7.0	7.3	44.3	38.8	39.7	3.8	3.3	3.2
Indiana	54.3	50.4	34.1	9.6	8.7	5.7	(NA)	(NA)	(NA)	(NA)	(NA)	(NA)
Iowa	24.8	22.0	20.9	9.0	7.8	7.2	11.1	10.5	9.3	3.9	3.7	3.2
Kansas	23.4	22.1	20.3	9.2	8.6	7.6	12.6	10.7	8.7	5.0	4.2	3.2
Kentucky	51.3	47.6	36.6	13.5	12.3	9.1	21.8	22.9	22.0	5.8	5.9	5.5
Louisiana.	41.2	40.8	37.5	9.6	9.4	8.6	(NA)	(NA)	(NA)	(NA)	(NA)	(NA)
Maine	11.8	10.8	11.4	9.7	8.7	9.0	5.3	5.5	4.9	4.3	4.4	3.9
Maryland	46.1	42.8	37.5	9.7	8.5	7.1	16.1	15.0	15.9	3.4	3.0	3.0
Massachusetts . . .	47.8	43.6	40.0	7.9	7.2	6.4	16.8	13.5	14.8	2.8	2.2	2.4
Michigan	76.1	71.0	66.5	8.2	7.4	6.7	40.2	39.9	38.9	4.3	4.2	3.9
Minnesota	33.7	32.8	33.0	7.7	7.1	6.8	15.4	15.8	16.0	3.5	3.4	3.3
Mississippi	24.3	21.5	18.7	9.4	8.0	6.7	14.4	13.1	15.1	5.5	4.8	5.4
Missouri.	49.3	44.9	42.2	9.6	8.4	7.6	26.4	26.8	23.8	5.1	5.0	4.3
Montana	7.0	6.6	6.4	8.6	7.6	7.2	4.1	4.2	2.3	5.1	4.8	2.6
Nebraska.	12.5	12.1	13.6	8.0	7.4	8.1	6.5	6.3	6.2	4.0	3.8	3.7
Nevada	123.4	134.8	146.1	99.0	88.1	75.0	13.3	12.4	13.2	11.4	8.1	6.8
New Hampshire . .	10.6	9.6	10.6	9.5	8.4	8.6	5.3	4.9	6.1	4.7	4.2	5.0
New Jersey	58.0	52.4	54.1	7.6	6.7	6.6	23.6	24.3	28.5	3.0	3.1	3.5
New Mexico	13.2	15.1	13.9	8.8	9.0	7.9	7.7	11.3	9.0	4.9	6.7	5.1
New York	169.3	147.4	145.5	8.6	8.1	7.9	57.9	56.0	54.1	3.2	3.1	3.0
North Carolina . . .	52.1	61.6	61.1	7.8	8.6	7.8	34.0	37.0	34.9	5.1	5.1	4.5
North Dakota	4.8	4.6	4.1	7.5	7.2	6.6	2.3	2.2	1.7	3.6	3.4	2.7
Ohio	95.8	90.1	82.3	9.0	8.1	7.3	51.0	48.7	45.6	4.7	4.4	4.0
Oklahoma	33.2	28.5	16.6	10.6	8.7	4.9	24.9	21.8	11.5	7.7	6.7	3.4
Oregon	25.2	25.7	26.0	8.9	8.2	7.7	15.9	15.0	16.5	5.5	4.8	4.9
Pennsylvania	86.8	75.8	71.4	7.1	6.3	6.0	40.1	39.4	38.0	3.3	3.3	3.2
Rhode Island	8.1	7.4	8.6	8.1	7.5	8.6	3.8	3.7	3.3	3.7	3.7	3.3
South Carolina . . .	55.8	44.6	36.8	15.9	12.1	9.3	16.1	14.8	13.8	4.5	4.0	3.5
South Dakota	7.7	7.4	6.7	11.1	10.0	9.1	2.6	2.9	2.5	3.7	4.0	3.4
Tennessee	66.6	82.3	77.7	13.9	15.7	13.9	32.3	33.1	28.8	6.5	6.3	5.2
Texas	182.8	188.5	194.9	10.5	10.1	9.4	94.0	99.9	85.4	5.5	5.3	4.1
Utah	19.0	21.6	23.2	11.2	11.1	10.6	8.8	8.9	9.7	5.1	4.6	4.4
Vermont	6.1	6.1	6.0	10.9	10.3	9.9	2.6	2.8	2.4	4.5	4.8	4.0
Virginia	71.3	67.9	63.4	11.4	10.3	9.0	27.3	28.9	30.2	4.4	4.4	4.3
Washington	48.6	42.0	42.2	9.5	7.7	7.2	28.8	29.7	26.3	5.9	5.5	4.5
West Virginia	13.2	11.2	14.2	7.2	6.1	7.9	9.7	9.4	9.3	5.3	5.1	5.2
Wisconsin	41.2	36.3	34.9	7.9	7.1	6.5	17.8	17.5	17.3	3.6	3.4	3.2
Wyoming.	4.8	5.2	5.0	10.7	10.7	10.3	3.1	3.2	2.9	6.6	6.7	6.1

NA Not available.   [1] Data are counts of marriages performed, except as noted.   [2] Based on total population residing in area; population enumerated as of April 1 for 1990; estimated as of July 1 for all other years.   [3] Includes annulments.   [4] U.S. totals for the number of divorces is an estimate which includes states not reporting (CA, CO, IN, and LA).   [5] Marriage data include nonlicensed marriages registered.

Source: U.S. National Center for Health Statistics, *Vital Statistics of the United States,* annual; *National Vital Statistics Reports (NVSR)* (formerly *Monthly Vital Statistical Report).*

Section 3
Health and Nutrition

This section presents statistics on health expenditures and insurance coverage, including medicare and medicaid, medical personnel, hospitals, nursing homes and other care facilities, injuries, diseases, disability status, nutritional intake of the population, and food consumption. Summary statistics showing recent trends on health care and discussions of selected health issues are published annually by the U.S. National Center for Health Statistics (NCHS) in *Health, United States*. Data on national health expenditures, medical costs, and insurance coverage are compiled by the U.S. Centers for Medicare & Medicaid Services (CMS) (formerly Health Care Financing Administration), and appear in the quarterly *Health Care Financing Review* and in the annual *Medicare and Medicaid Statistical Supplement* to the *Health Care Financing Review*. Statistics on health insurance are also collected by NCHS and are published in Series 10 of *Vital and Health Statistics*. U.S. Census Bureau also publishes data on utilization of insurance coverage. Statistics on hospitals are published annually by the Health Forum, L.L.C., an American Hospital Association Company, in *Hospital Statistics*. Primary sources for data on nutrition are the quarterly *National Food Review* and the annual *Food Consumption, Prices, and Expenditures*, both issued by the U.S. Department of Agriculture. NCHS also conducts periodic surveys of nutrient levels in the population, including estimates of food and nutrient intake, overweight and obesity, hypercholesterolemia, hypertension, and clinical signs of malnutrition.

National health expenditures—CMS compiles estimates of national health expenditures (NHE) to measure spending for health care in the United States. The NHE accounts are structured to show spending by type of expenditure (i.e., hospital care, physician and clinical care, dental care, and other professional care; home health care; retail sales of prescription drugs; other medical nondurables;

vision products and other medical durables; nursing home care and other personal health expenditures; plus non-personal health expenditures for such items as public health, research, construction of medical facilities, administration, and the net cost of private health insurance) and by source of funding (e.g., private health insurance, out-of-pocket payments, and a range of public programs including medicare, medicaid, and those operated by the Department of Veterans Affairs (VA)).

Data used to estimate health expenditures come from existing sources which are tabulated for other purposes. The type of expenditure estimates rely upon statistics produced by such groups as the American Hospital Association, the Census Bureau, and the Department of Health and Human Services (HHS). Source of funding estimates are constructed using administrative and statistical records from the medicare and medicaid programs, the Department of Defense and VA medical programs, the Social Security Administration, Census Bureau's *Governmental Finances,* state and local governments, other HHS agencies, and other nongovernment sources. More information and detailed descriptions of sources and methods are available on the HCFA home page at <http://cms.hhs.gov/statistics/nhe/default.asp >.

Medicare and medicaid—Since July 1966, the federal medicare program has provided two coordinated plans for nearly all people age 65 and over: (1) A hospital insurance plan which covers hospital and related services and (2) a voluntary supplementary medical insurance plan, financed partially by monthly premiums paid by participants, which partly covers physicians' and related medical services. Such insurance also applies, since July 1973, to disabled beneficiaries of any age after 24 months of entitlement to cash

U.S. Census Bureau, Statistical Abstract of the United States: 2002

benefits under the social security or railroad retirement programs and to persons with end stage renal disease.

Medicaid is a health insurance program for certain low-income people. These include: certain low-income families with children; aged, blind, or disabled people on Supplemental Security Income; certain low-income pregnant women and children; and people who have very high medical bills. Medicaid is funded and administered through a state-federal partnership. Although there are broad federal requirements for medicaid, states have a wide degree of flexibility to design their program. States have authority to establish eligibility standards, determine what benefits and services to cover, and set payment rates. All states, however, must cover these basic services: inpatient and outpatient hospital services, laboratory and X-ray services, skilled nursing and home health services, doctor's services, family planning, and periodic health checkups, diagnosis and treatment for children.

Health resources—Hospital statistics based on data from the American Hospital Association's yearly survey are published annually in *Hospital Statistics* and cover all hospitals accepted for registration by the Association. To be accepted for registration, a hospital must meet certain requirements relating to number of beds, construction, equipment, medical and nursing staff, patient care, clinical records, surgical and obstetrical facilities, diagnostic and treatment facilities, laboratory services, etc. Data obtained from NCHS cover all U.S. hospitals which meet certain criteria for inclusion. The criteria are published in *Vital and Health Statistics* reports, Series 13. NCHS defines a hospital as a nonfederal short-term general or special facility with six or more inpatient beds with an average stay of less than 60 days.

Statistics on the demographic characteristics of persons employed in the health occupations are compiled by the U.S. Bureau of Labor Statistics and reported in *Employment and Earnings* (monthly) (see Table 588, Section 12, Labor Force, Employment, and Earnings). Data based

on surveys of health personnel and utilization of health facilities providing long-term care, ambulatory care, and hospital care are presented in NCHS Series 13 *Data on Health Resources Utilization and Advance Data from Vital and Health Statistics*. Statistics on patient visits to health care providers, as reported in health interviews, appear in NCHS Series 10, *National Health Interview Survey Data*.

The CMS's *Health Care Financing Review* and its annual *Medicare and Medicaid Statistical Supplement* present data for hospitals and nursing homes as well as extended care facilities and home health agencies. These data are based on records of the medicare program and differ from those of other sources because they are limited to facilities meeting federal eligibility standards for participation in medicare.

Disability and illness—General health statistics, including morbidity, disability, injuries, preventive care, and findings from physiological testing are collected by NCHS in its National Health Interview Survey and its National Health and Nutrition Examination Surveys and appear in *Vital and Health Statistics*, Series 10 and 11, respectively. The Department of Labor compiles statistics on occupational injuries (see Section 12, Labor Force, Employment, and Wealth). Annual incidence data on notifiable diseases are compiled by the Public Health Service (PHS) at its Centers for Disease Control and Prevention in Atlanta, Georgia, and are published as a supplement to its *Morbidity and Mortality Weekly Report*. The list of diseases is revised annually and includes those which, by mutual agreement of the states and PHS, are communicable diseases of national importance.

Nutrition—Statistics on annual per capita consumption of food and its nutrient value are estimated by the U.S. Department of Agriculture and published quarterly in *National Food Review*. Historical data can be found in *Food Consumption, Prices, and Expenditures*, and online at <http://www.ers.gov/data/consumption>. Statistics on food insufficiency and food and nutrient intake are collected by NCHS to estimate the diet of the nation's population. NCHS also collects physical examination data to assess the population's nutritional status, including growth, overweight/obesity, nutritional deficiencies, and prevalence of nutrition-related conditions, such as hypertension, hypercholesterolemia, and diabetes.

Statistical reliability—For discussion of statistical collection, estimation, and sampling procedures and measures of reliability applicable to data from NCHS and CMS, see Appendix III.

No. 112. National Health Expenditures—Summary, 1960 to 2000, and Projections, 2001 to 2011

[In billions of dollars (27 represents $27,000,000,000). Includes Puerto Rico and outlying areas]

Year	Private expenditures				Public expenditures			Health services and supplies				
	Total expenditures [1]	Total [2]	Out-of-pocket	Insurance	Total	Federal	State and local	Total [3]	Hospital care	Physician and clinical services	Prescription drugs	Nursing home care
1960	27	20	13	6	7	3	4	25	9	5	3	1
1961	29	21	13	7	7	3	4	27	10	6	3	1
1962	31	23	14	7	8	4	4	29	11	6	3	1
1963	34	25	15	8	9	4	5	31	12	7	3	1
1964	38	28	17	9	9	4	5	34	13	8	3	1
1965	41	31	18	10	10	5	6	37	14	8	4	2
1966	45	32	19	10	14	7	6	41	16	9	4	2
1967	51	32	19	11	19	12	7	47	18	10	4	2
1968	58	36	21	12	22	14	8	53	21	11	5	3
1969	65	40	23	13	24	16	9	59	24	12	5	4
1970	73	45	25	16	28	18	10	67	28	14	6	4
1971	81	50	26	18	31	20	11	75	31	16	6	5
1972	91	56	29	21	35	23	12	84	34	17	6	6
1973	101	61	32	23	39	25	14	93	39	19	7	6
1974	114	67	35	26	46	30	16	106	45	22	7	7
1975	130	75	37	30	55	36	19	121	52	25	8	9
1976	149	87	41	37	62	43	20	139	60	28	9	10
1977	169	99	45	45	70	47	23	160	68	33	9	12
1978	189	110	48	52	80	54	26	179	76	35	10	13
1979	214	124	53	60	90	61	29	203	87	41	11	15
1980	246	141	58	68	105	71	34	234	102	47	12	18
1981	285	164	66	81	121	83	39	271	119	55	13	20
1982	321	187	72	94	134	92	42	305	135	61	15	23
1983	354	206	79	104	148	102	46	336	146	68	17	26
1984	390	229	86	118	161	113	48	372	156	77	20	28
1985	427	252	96	130	175	122	52	409	167	90	22	31
1986	457	267	103	135	190	132	59	439	178	100	24	34
1987	498	289	109	148	209	143	66	478	192	112	27	36
1988	558	332	119	175	226	154	72	535	209	127	31	41
1989	623	371	126	205	252	172	79	599	229	142	35	46
1990	696	414	137	234	283	193	90	670	254	158	40	53
1991	762	441	142	254	321	222	99	735	280	175	45	58
1992	827	469	146	274	359	251	107	797	302	190	48	62
1993	888	498	147	298	390	274	116	856	320	201	51	66
1994	937	510	144	312	427	299	129	905	332	211	55	68
1995	990	534	147	330	456	322	134	958	344	221	61	75
1996	1,040	558	152	345	482	344	138	1,006	356	229	67	80
1997	1,091	589	162	359	502	359	144	1,054	368	241	76	85
1998	1,150	629	175	383	521	368	153	1,112	379	257	87	89
1999	1,216	667	184	409	549	385	164	1,175	392	270	104	89
2000	1,300	712	195	444	587	412	176	1,256	412	286	122	92
2001, proj . .	1,424	776	210	487	648	453	195	1,377	446	311	142	99
2002, proj . .	1,546	849	227	537	697	484	213	1,497	476	336	161	104
2003, proj . .	1,653	913	243	580	741	511	230	1,601	502	361	182	107
2004, proj . .	1,773	980	259	624	794	546	248	1,718	532	388	204	113
2005, proj . .	1,902	1,050	276	672	853	585	268	1,843	565	415	228	120
2006, proj . .	2,037	1,121	294	720	916	626	290	1,973	599	443	253	126
2007, proj . .	2,175	1,192	311	767	983	670	313	2,107	632	469	280	134
2008, proj . .	2,320	1,263	330	813	1,057	719	338	2,248	666	498	309	141
2009, proj . .	2,476	1,340	351	862	1,136	771	365	2,399	701	528	341	149
2010, proj . .	2,639	1,417	372	912	1,222	828	394	2,557	737	559	376	157
2011, proj . .	2,816	1,500	396	966	1,316	891	425	2,728	775	593	414	166

[1] Includes medical research and medical facilities construction, not shown separately. [2] Includes other private expenditures, not shown separately. [3] Includes other objects of expenditure, not shown separately.

Source: U. S. Centers for Medicare and Medicaid Services, "Health Accounts"; <http://cms.hhs.gov/statistics/nhe/default.asp>.

No. 113. National Health Expenditures by Type: 1990 to 2000

[In billions of dollars (696.0 represents $696,000,000,000), except percent. Includes Puerto Rico and outlying areas]

Type of expenditure	1990	1994	1995	1996	1997	1998	1999	2000
Total	696.0	937.2	990.3	1,040.0	1,091.2	1,149.8	1,215.6	1,299.5
Annual percent change [1]	11.8	5.5	5.7	5.0	4.9	5.4	5.7	6.9
Percent of gross domestic product	12.0	13.3	13.4	13.3	13.1	13.1	13.1	13.2
Private expenditures	413.5	510.3	534.1	558.2	588.8	628.8	666.5	712.3
Health services and supplies	401.9	496.8	521.6	545.0	573.9	613.3	651.1	695.6
Out-of-pocket payments	137.3	143.9	146.5	152.1	162.3	174.5	184.4	194.5
Insurance premiums [2]	233.5	312.1	330.1	344.8	359.4	383.2	409.4	443.9
Other	31.1	40.7	44.9	48.2	52.1	55.6	57.3	57.2
Medical research	1.0	1.4	1.4	1.6	1.6	2.0	2.2	2.3
Medical facilities construction	10.7	12.1	11.1	11.6	13.3	13.6	13.3	14.3
Public expenditures	282.5	427.0	456.2	481.8	502.4	520.9	549.0	587.2
Percent federal of public	68.2	69.9	70.6	71.4	71.4	70.6	70.1	70.1
Health services and supplies	267.7	408.0	436.1	460.8	480.1	498.2	524.0	559.9
Medicare [3]	110.2	165.8	182.7	197.5	208.2	209.5	212.6	224.4
Public assistance medical payments [4]	78.7	139.2	149.5	157.6	164.8	176.6	191.8	208.5
Temporary disability insurance [5]	0.1	0.1	0.1	0.1	0.1	0.1	0.1	0.1
Workers' compensation (medical) [5]	17.5	22.2	21.9	21.9	20.5	20.8	22.5	23.3
Defense Dept. hospital, medical	10.4	11.8	12.1	12.0	12.1	12.2	12.5	13.0
Maternal, child health programs	1.8	2.2	2.2	2.3	2.3	2.4	2.5	2.6
Public health activities	20.2	30.0	31.4	33.0	35.5	37.9	40.9	44.2
Veterans' hospital, medical care	11.3	15.1	15.4	16.3	16.3	16.9	17.7	18.9
Medical vocational rehabilitation	0.5	0.7	0.7	0.7	0.7	0.8	0.7	0.8
State and local hospitals [6]	13.1	15.3	14.1	13.6	13.4	14.2	14.8	15.6
Other [7]	3.8	5.6	6.0	6.0	6.1	6.9	7.8	8.7
Medical research	11.7	14.8	15.7	16.2	17.1	18.6	20.9	23.0
Medical facilities construction	3.1	4.2	4.4	4.8	5.2	4.1	4.2	4.3

[1] Change from immediate prior year. For explanation of average annual percent change, see Guide to Tabular Presentation. [2] Covers insurance benefits and amount retained by insurance companies for expenses, additions to reserves, and profits (net cost of insurance). [3] Represents expenditures for benefits and administrative cost from federal hospital and medical insurance trust funds under old-age, survivors, disability, and health insurance programs; see text, of this section. [4] Payments made directly to suppliers of medical care (primarily medicaid). [5] Includes medical benefits paid under public law by private insurance carriers, state governments, and self-insurers. [6] Expenditures not offset by other revenues. [7] Covers expenditures for Substance Abuse and Mental Health Services Administration, Indian Health Service; school health and other programs.

Source: U.S. Centers for Medicare and Medicaid Services, "Health Accounts"; <http://cms.hhs.gov/statistics/nhe/default.asp>.

No. 114. National Health Expenditures by Object, 1990 to 2000, and Projections, 2001

[In billions of dollars (696.0 represents $696,000,000,000). Includes Puerto Rico and outlying areas]

Object of expenditure	1990	1994	1995	1996	1997	1998	1999	2000	2001, proj.
Total	696.0	937.2	990.3	1,040.0	1,091.2	1,149.8	1,215.6	1,299.5	1,423.8
Spent by—									
Consumers	370.8	456.1	476.7	496.8	521.8	557.7	593.8	638.4	697.1
Out-of-pocket	137.3	143.9	146.5	152.1	162.3	174.5	184.4	194.5	210.4
Private insurance	233.5	312.1	330.1	344.8	359.4	383.2	409.4	443.9	486.7
Government	282.5	427.0	456.2	481.8	502.4	520.9	549.0	587.2	648.1
Other [1]	42.8	54.2	57.4	61.4	67.0	71.1	72.7	73.8	78.6
Spent for—									
Health services and supplies	669.6	904.8	957.7	1,005.7	1,053.9	1,111.5	1,175.0	1,255.5	1,377.3
Personal health care expenses	609.4	816.5	865.7	911.9	959.2	1,009.9	1,062.6	1,130.4	1,235.2
Hospital care	253.9	332.4	343.6	355.9	367.5	379.2	392.2	412.1	446.3
Physician and clinical services	157.5	210.5	220.5	229.4	241.0	256.8	270.2	286.4	310.6
Dental services	31.5	41.4	44.5	46.8	50.2	53.2	56.4	60.0	64.4
Other professional services [2]	18.2	25.7	28.5	30.9	33.4	35.5	36.7	39.0	42.7
Home health care	12.6	26.1	30.5	33.6	34.5	33.6	32.3	32.4	35.9
Prescription drugs	40.3	54.6	60.8	67.2	75.7	87.2	103.9	121.8	141.8
Other nondurable medical products	22.5	24.3	25.6	27.1	27.9	28.6	30.4	31.2	32.8
Durable medical equipment [3]	10.6	13.3	14.2	15.3	16.2	16.5	17.6	18.5	19.9
Nursing home care	52.7	68.3	74.6	79.9	85.1	89.1	89.3	92.2	99.2
Other personal health care	9.6	19.9	22.9	25.8	27.8	30.2	33.7	36.7	41.5
Government administration and net cost of private health insurance [4]	40.0	58.3	60.6	60.9	59.2	63.7	71.5	80.9	92.7
Government public health activities	20.2	30.0	31.4	33.0	35.5	37.9	40.9	44.2	49.5
Medical research [5]	12.7	16.3	17.1	17.8	18.7	20.6	23.1	25.3	26.6
Medical facilities construction	13.7	16.2	15.5	16.4	18.5	17.7	17.5	18.6	19.8

[1] Includes nonpatient revenues, privately funded construction, and industrial inplant. [2] Includes services of registered and practical nurses in private duty, podiatrists, optometrists, physical therapists, clinical psychologists, chiropractors, naturopaths, and Christian Science practitioners. [3] Includes expenditures for eyeglasses, hearing aids, orthopedic appliances, artificial limbs, crutches, wheelchairs, etc. [4] Includes administrative expenses of federally financed health programs. [5] Research and development expenditures of drug companies and other manufacturers and providers of medical equipment and supplies are excluded from research expenditures, but are included in the expenditure class in which the product falls.

Source: U.S. Centers for Medicare and Medicaid Services, "Health Accounts"; <http://cms.hhs.gov/statistics/nhe/default.asp>.

No. 115. Health Services and Supplies—Per Capita Consumer Expenditures by Object: 1990 to 2000

[In dollars, except percent. Based on Social Security Administration estimates of total U.S. population as of July 1, including Armed Forces and federal employees abroad and civilian population of outlying areas. Excludes research and construction]

Object of expenditure	1990	1994	1995	1996	1997	1998	1999	2000
Total, national	**2,635**	**3,411**	**3,576**	**3,723**	**3,865**	**4,038**	**4,231**	**4,481**
Annual percent change [1]	10.6	4.6	4.8	4.1	3.8	4.5	4.8	5.9
Hospital care	999	1,253	1,283	1,317	1,348	1,378	1,412	1,471
Physician and clinical services	620	794	824	849	884	933	973	1,022
Dental services.	124	156	166	173	184	193	203	214
Other professional services [2]	71	97	107	114	122	129	132	139
Home health care	49	98	114	124	127	122	116	116
Prescription drugs.	159	206	227	249	278	317	374	435
Other nondurable medical products	88	91	95	100	102	104	109	112
Durable medical equipment [2]	42	50	53	57	59	60	63	66
Nursing home care	207	258	278	296	312	324	321	329
Other personal health care	38	75	86	96	102	110	121	131
Government administration and net cost of private health insurance	157	220	226	225	217	231	258	289
Government public health activities	80	113	117	122	130	138	147	158
Total, private consumer [3]	**1,459**	**1,720**	**1,780**	**1,839**	**1,913**	**2,026**	**2,138**	**2,278**
Hospital care	426	459	457	458	465	489	504	524
Physician and clinical services	386	490	498	510	532	556	574	606
Dental services.	120	149	158	165	175	184	194	204
Other professional services [2]	47	62	69	75	83	88	90	95
Home health care	20	32	37	43	49	53	51	50
Prescription drugs.	132	165	181	197	220	250	294	340
Other nondurable medical products	86	88	91	96	98	100	105	107
Durable medical equipment [2]	33	37	38	41	42	43	45	47
Nursing home care	90	86	96	100	106	117	117	115
Net cost of private health insurance	117	152	153	153	144	147	164	190

[1] Change from immediate prior year. [2] See footnotes for corresponding objects in Table 114. [3] Represents out-of-pocket payments and private health insurance.

No. 116. Government Expenditures for Health Services and Supplies: 2000

[In millions of dollars (559,940 represents $559,940,000,000). Includes Puerto Rico and outlying areas. Excludes medical research and construction]

Type of service	Total [1]	Federal	State and local	Medicare [2] (OASDHI)	Public assist- ance [3]	Other health services		
						Veterans	Defense Dept. [4]	Workers' compensa- tion [5]
Total [1]	**559,940**	**391,194**	**168,746**	**224,366**	**208,468**	**18,924**	**12,953**	**23,272**
Hospital care	243,209	192,887	50,322	125,734	72,117	14,287	9,032	8,248
Physician and clinical services	95,161	79,168	15,993	59,550	20,137	1,071	2,170	7,449
Prescription drugs	26,500	15,157	11,343	2,296	22,882	30	541	618
Nursing home care	55,931	37,768	18,163	9,518	44,551	1,862	-	-
Gov't administration	26,694	15,868	10,825	7,333	14,526	79	146	4,303
Public health activities. . .	44,238	4,892	39,346	-	-	-	-	-

- Represents zero. [1] Includes other items not shown separately. [2] Covers hospital and medical insurance payments and administrative costs under old-age, survivors, disability, and health insurance program. [3] Covers medicaid and other medical public assistance. Excludes funds paid into medicare trust fund by states to cover premiums for public assistance recipients and medically indigent persons. [4] Includes care for retirees and military dependents. [5] Medical benefits.

No. 117. Personal Health Care—Third Party Payments and Private Consumer Expenditures, 1990 to 2000, and Projections, 2001

[In billions of dollars (609.4 represents $609,400,000,000), except percent. See headnote, Table 118]

Item	1990	1994	1995	1996	1997	1998	1999	2000	2001, proj
Personal health care expenditures.	609.4	816.5	865.7	911.9	959.2	1,009.9	1,062.6	1,130.4	1,235.2
Third party payments, total	**472.1**	**672.5**	**719.2**	**759.8**	**796.9**	**835.4**	**878.2**	**935.9**	**1,024.7**
Percent of personal health care	77.5	82.4	83.1	83.3	83.1	82.7	82.6	82.8	83.0
Private insurance payments	203.6	271.8	289.1	303.3	320.2	342.7	363.9	390.7	423.9
Government expenditures.	237.9	360.6	385.8	409.0	425.3	438.0	458.0	489.0	541.1
Other [1]	30.6	40.1	44.3	47.5	51.4	54.7	56.3	56.1	59.7
Private consumer expenditures [2]	**340.9**	**415.8**	**435.7**	**455.4**	**482.5**	**517.2**	**548.3**	**585.3**	**634.4**
Percent met by private insurance	59.7	65.4	66.4	66.6	66.4	66.3	66.4	66.8	66.8
Hospital care	108.4	121.8	122.4	123.7	126.9	134.5	140.0	146.9	156.5
Percent met by private insurance	89.6	90.9	91.4	91.4	91.2	91.2	91.0	91.1	91.3
Physician and clinical services.	98.1	129.8	133.4	137.9	145.0	153.1	159.4	169.9	183.6
Percent met by private insurance	69.0	78.4	80.3	80.5	80.2	80.0	80.2	80.4	80.4
Prescription drugs	33.6	43.8	48.5	53.3	60.0	68.7	81.7	95.3	111.2
Percent met by private insurance	29.2	40.0	46.5	50.3	53.6	55.8	57.6	59.1	59.2

[1] Includes nonpatient revenues and industrial inplant health services. [2] Includes expenditures not shown separately. Represents out-of-pocket payments and private health insurance benefits. Excludes net cost of insurance.

Source of Tables 115-117: U. S. Centers for Medicare and Medicaid Services, "Health Accounts"; <http://cms.hhs.gov/statistics/nhe/default.asp>.

No. 118. Personal Health Care Expenditures by Object and Source of Payment: 2000

[In millions of dollars (1,130,414 represents $1,130,414,000,000), except as indicated. Includes Puerto Rico and outlying areas. Covers all expenditures for health services and supplies, except net cost of insurance and administration, government public health activities, and expenditures of philanthropic agencies for fund raising activities]

Object of expenditure	Total	Private payments					Govern-ment	Third party pay-ments [2]
		Total	Consumer					
			Total	Out of pocket pay-ments	Private health insur-ance	Other [1]		
Total	1,130,414	641,406	585,278	194,543	390,735	56,128	489,008	935,871
Hospital care.................	412,103	168,894	146,896	13,014	133,882	21,998	243,209	399,089
Physician and clinical services	286,439	191,278	169,932	33,245	136,687	21,346	95,161	253,194
Dental services	59,958	57,193	57,041	26,903	30,138	152	2,765	33,055
Other professional services [3]	38,979	29,611	26,688	11,666	15,022	2,923	9,368	27,313
Home health care..............	32,426	15,510	13,994	6,355	7,638	1,516	16,916	26,071
Prescription drugs	121,808	95,308	95,308	39,010	56,298	-	26,500	82,797
Other nondurable medical products ...	31,189	29,842	29,842	29,842	-	-	1,347	1,347
Durable medical equipment	18,537	13,268	13,268	9,631	3,637	-	5,269	8,906
Nursing home care..............	92,247	36,316	32,309	24,877	7,432	4,007	55,931	67,371
Other personal health care.........	36,729	4,186	-	-	-	4,186	32,543	36,729

- Represents zero.   [1] Includes nonpatient revenues and industrial plant.   [2] Covers private health insurance, other private payments, and government.   [3] See footnotes for corresponding items on Table 114.

Source: U.S. Centers for Medicare and Medicaid Services, "Health Accounts"; <http://cms.hhs.gov/statistics/nhe/default.asp>.

No. 119. Hospital Care and Physician and Clinical Service Expenditures by Source of Payment: 1990 to 2000

[In billions of dollars (253.9 represents $253,900,000,000)]

Source of payment	Hospital care					Physician and clinical services				
	1990	1995	1998	1999	2000	1990	1995	1998	1999	2000
Total	253.9	343.6	379.2	392.2	412.1	157.5	220.5	256.8	270.2	286.4
Out-of-pocket payments	11.2	10.5	11.9	12.6	13.0	30.4	26.3	30.7	31.5	33.2
Third-party payments	242.7	333.0	367.3	379.6	399.1	127.1	194.3	226.1	238.7	253.2
Private health insurance	97.1	111.9	122.6	127.4	133.9	67.7	107.2	122.4	127.8	136.7
Other private funds	10.3	14.7	19.5	20.6	22.0	11.3	17.6	22.1	22.4	21.3
Government	135.2	206.5	225.1	231.5	243.2	48.2	69.5	81.6	88.5	95.2
Federal................	102.7	166.2	179.9	183.9	192.9	38.7	56.2	67.6	73.4	79.2
State and local...........	32.4	40.3	45.2	47.7	50.3	9.4	13.3	14.0	15.0	16.0
Medicare [1]	67.8	107.0	119.9	120.4	125.7	30.2	41.7	51.3	55.3	59.6
Medicaid [2]	27.6	54.5	61.0	66.0	69.7	7.0	14.8	16.7	17.6	19.0

[1] Medicare expenditures come from federal funds.   [2] Medicaid expenditures come from federal and state and local funds.

Source: U.S. Centers for Medicare and Medicaid Services, "Health Accounts"; <http://cms.hhs.gov/statistics/nhe/default.asp>.

No. 120. Retail Prescription Drug Sales: 1995 to 2001

[2,125 represents 2,125,000,000]

Sales outlet	Number of prescriptions (millions)					Retail sales (bil. dol.)				
	1995	1998	1999	2000	2001	1995	1998	1999	2000	2001
Total	2,125	2,481	2,707	2,865	3,009	68.6	103.0	121.7	138.3	155.8
Traditional chain	914	1,129	1,246	1,344	1,415	27.4	43.1	51.6	58.5	64.6
Independent.................	666	651	680	689	700	20.0	24.8	28.1	29.9	32.3
Mass merchant...............	238	272	289	293	314	7.2	10.4	12.0	12.8	14.4
Supermarkets................	221	306	357	394	418	7.0	11.4	13.4	16.6	18.9
Mail order	86	123	134	146	161	7.0	13.4	16.6	20.6	25.7

Source: National Association of Chain Drug Stores, Alexandria, VA, The Chain Pharmacy Industry Profile, 2002 (copyright).

No. 121. Personal Health Care Expenditures by State, 1990 to 1998, and by Selected Object, 1998

[In millions of dollars (612,245 represents $612,245,000,000). This series of state health expenditures (SHE) uses the same definitions and, to the extent possible, the same data sources as does the national health expenditures series. For health services, this structure clusters spending according to the establishment providing those services. For retail purchases of medical products, it groups spending according to product classification. Thus, SHE is establishment-based, grouping services together according to place of service or of product sale rather than according to type of service. Establishment-based expenditures are those in which spending is located in the state of the provider rather than in the beneficiary's state of residence. Because people are able to cross state borders to receive health care services, health care spending by provider location is not necessarily an accurate reflection of spending on behalf of persons residing in that state]

State	1990	1995	1996	1997	1998 Total [1]	1998 Hospital care	1998 Physician and other professional services	1998 Prescription drugs	1998 Nursing home care
U.S.	612,245	876,212	920,970	965,701	1,016,383	380,050	296,102	90,648	87,826
AL.	9,163	13,654	14,537	15,519	16,056	6,618	4,609	1,552	1,064
AK.	1,347	1,921	2,042	2,133	2,299	986	568	133	42
AZ.	8,562	12,352	13,146	13,834	14,782	4,977	5,135	1,397	839
AR.	4,925	7,149	7,539	8,033	8,463	3,324	2,225	903	776
CA.	74,369	99,215	102,378	105,790	110,057	34,948	44,239	7,537	5,626
CO	7,740	11,395	12,004	12,776	13,669	4,850	4,314	970	904
CT.	10,013	13,662	13,952	14,600	15,221	4,686	4,292	1,354	2,264
DE.	1,728	2,619	2,698	2,915	3,106	1,166	792	300	290
DC	3,564	4,184	4,223	4,205	4,258	2,585	781	180	245
FL.	35,789	51,328	54,404	56,754	59,724	19,742	18,985	6,204	4,880
GA	15,303	23,096	24,489	25,940	27,219	10,396	8,510	2,460	1,545
HI	2,745	4,168	4,427	4,452	4,658	1,775	1,594	311	204
ID	1,697	2,758	2,994	3,194	3,397	1,236	935	334	264
IL	27,618	39,000	40,738	42,267	44,305	17,996	11,975	3,964	3,924
IN	12,692	18,388	18,727	20,207	21,259	8,515	5,613	2,058	2,337
IA	6,067	8,513	9,073	9,496	10,198	4,084	2,457	945	1,186
KS.	5,540	7,989	8,417	8,890	9,394	3,580	2,538	854	920
KY.	7,820	11,790	12,651	13,592	14,414	5,731	3,785	1,564	1,283
LA.	9,975	14,673	15,272	15,946	16,500	7,139	4,249	1,507	1,248
ME	2,695	3,908	4,242	4,554	4,925	1,846	1,219	456	476
MD	11,755	16,838	17,824	18,596	19,646	7,313	5,978	1,678	1,695
MA	19,027	25,997	27,033	28,471	30,039	11,305	8,322	2,172	3,568
MI	22,133	31,089	32,888	34,435	35,647	14,641	9,186	3,885	2,459
MN	11,462	16,826	17,776	18,858	20,313	6,540	7,183	1,491	1,964
MS	4,729	7,447	7,997	8,431	8,882	3,848	2,212	962	687
MO	12,690	18,024	18,900	19,783	20,911	8,828	5,310	1,814	2,002
MT	1,628	2,445	2,496	2,680	2,838	1,224	695	234	222
NE.	3,531	5,091	5,500	5,721	6,095	2,597	1,367	626	697
NV.	2,806	4,471	4,795	5,170	5,606	1,865	1,918	478	164
NH	2,558	3,779	4,033	4,333	4,658	1,559	1,405	391	425
NJ.	20,169	29,504	30,865	31,580	32,695	11,191	9,506	3,545	3,233
NM	2,917	4,430	4,839	5,075	5,344	2,317	1,415	402	257
NY.	53,926	75,183	78,503	81,100	85,785	32,036	20,103	7,122	10,586
NC	13,748	21,966	23,773	25,584	27,327	10,987	7,106	2,566	2,347
ND	1,639	2,373	2,461	2,542	2,680	1,282	612	192	287
OH	26,896	37,246	39,470	40,552	42,581	16,763	11,024	3,898	4,978
OK	6,357	9,454	10,095	10,419	10,988	4,218	2,978	1,056	954
OR	6,247	9,182	9,637	10,259	10,840	3,545	3,285	918	838
PA.	32,635	45,050	46,398	48,853	51,322	20,213	13,434	5,035	5,883
RI.	2,728	3,783	3,900	4,149	4,515	1,702	1,095	400	468
SC.	6,806	10,616	11,199	12,363	13,204	5,597	3,254	1,315	907
SD.	1,513	2,301	2,479	2,635	2,842	1,257	747	201	286
TN.	12,213	18,820	20,026	21,154	22,021	8,276	6,719	2,129	2,001
TX.	37,682	56,504	60,410	64,245	67,750	25,322	20,071	6,023	4,346
UT.	3,233	4,807	5,229	5,622	5,944	2,290	1,648	564	300
VT.	1,172	1,762	1,821	1,933	2,066	712	563	183	177
VA.	13,252	18,712	19,899	21,103	22,261	8,689	6,265	2,130	1,546
WA	11,276	16,810	17,461	18,214	19,292	6,362	5,908	1,603	1,492
WV	3,930	6,024	6,314	6,692	7,037	2,955	1,793	776	515
WI.	11,441	16,739	17,738	18,738	19,945	7,252	5,844	1,745	2,110
WY	793	1,179	1,260	1,313	1,407	582	343	133	113

[1] Includes other expenditures not shown separately.

Source: U.S. Centers for Medicare and Medicaid Services, "Health Accounts"; <http://cms.hhs.gov/statistics/nhe/default.asp>.

No. 122. Consumer Price Indexes of Medical Care Prices: 1980 to 2001

[1982-1984=100. Indexes are annual averages of monthly data based on components of consumer price index for all urban consumers; for explanation, see text, Section 14, Prices]

Year	Medical care, total	Medical care services					Medical care commodities		Annual percent change [3]		
			Professional services			Hospital and related services		Prescrip-tion drugs and medical supplies	Medical care, total	Medical care services	Medical care com-modities
		Total [1]	Total [1]	Physi-cians	Dental		Total [2]				
1980....	74.9	74.8	77.9	76.5	78.9	69.2	75.4	72.5	11.0	11.3	9.3
1985....	113.5	113.2	113.5	113.3	114.2	116.1	115.2	120.1	6.3	6.1	7.2
1990....	162.8	162.7	156.1	160.8	155.8	178.0	163.4	181.7	9.0	9.3	8.4
1994....	211.0	213.4	192.5	199.8	197.1	245.6	200.7	230.6	4.8	5.2	2.9
1995....	220.5	224.2	201.0	208.8	206.8	257.8	204.5	235.0	4.5	5.1	1.9
1996....	228.2	232.4	208.3	216.4	216.5	269.5	210.4	242.9	3.5	3.7	2.9
1997....	234.6	239.1	215.4	222.9	226.6	278.4	215.3	249.3	2.8	2.9	2.3
1998....	242.1	246.8	222.2	229.5	236.2	287.5	221.8	258.6	3.2	3.2	3.0
1999....	250.6	255.1	229.2	236.0	247.2	299.5	230.7	273.4	3.5	3.4	4.0
2000....	260.8	266.0	237.7	244.7	258.5	317.3	238.1	285.4	4.1	4.3	3.2
2001....	272.8	278.8	246.5	253.6	269.0	338.3	247.6	300.9	4.6	4.8	4.0

[1] Includes other services not shown separately.   [2] Includes other commodities not shown separately.   [3] Percent change from the immediate prior year.

Source: U.S. Bureau of Labor Statistics, *CPI Detailed Report*, January 2002.

No. 123. Average Annual Expenditures per Consumer Unit for Health Care: 1985 to 2000

[In dollars, except percent. See text, Section 13, Income, Expenditures, and Wealth, and headnote, Table 650. For composition of regions, see map, inside front cover]

Item	Health care, total					Percent distribution		
	Amount	Percent of total expendi-tures	Health insur-ance	Medical services	Drugs and medical supplies [1]	Health insur-ance	Medical services	Drugs and medical supplies [1]
1985	1,108	4.7	375	496	238	33.8	44.8	21.5
1990	1,480	5.2	581	562	337	39.3	38.0	22.8
1995	1,732	5.4	860	512	360	49.7	29.6	20.8
1997	1,841	5.3	881	531	428	47.9	28.8	23.2
1998	1,903	5.4	913	542	448	48.0	28.5	23.5
1999	1,959	5.3	923	558	479	47.1	28.5	24.5
2000	2,066	5.4	983	568	515	47.6	27.5	24.9
Age of reference person:								
Under 25 years old	504	2.2	211	178	115	41.9	35.3	22.8
25 to 34 years old..........	1,256	3.2	640	367	250	51.0	29.2	19.9
35 to 44 years old..........	1,774	3.9	850	555	369	47.9	31.3	20.8
45 to 54 years old..........	2,200	4.8	976	699	525	44.4	31.8	23.9
55 to 64 years old..........	2,508	6.4	1,132	721	655	45.1	28.7	26.1
65 to 74 years old..........	3,163	10.3	1,608	686	870	50.8	21.7	27.5
75 years old and over	3,338	15.2	1,631	658	1,049	48.9	19.7	31.4
Race of reference person:								
White and other	2,198	5.6	1,030	620	548	46.9	28.2	24.9
Black	1,107	3.9	639	191	276	57.7	17.3	24.9
Origin of reference person:								
Hispanic	1,243	3.8	600	364	280	48.3	29.3	22.5
Non-Hispanic	2,144	5.6	1,019	587	538	47.5	27.4	25.1
Region of residence:								
Northeast	1,862	4.8	908	504	450	48.8	27.1	24.2
Midwest	2,172	5.5	1,047	575	550	48.2	26.5	25.3
South	2,147	6.2	1,063	533	552	49.5	24.8	25.7
West..................	2,001	4.8	853	669	479	42.6	33.4	23.9
Size of consumer unit:								
One person	1,488	6.5	657	418	413	44.2	28.1	27.8
Two or more persons........	2,307	5.2	1,119	631	557	48.5	27.4	24.1
Two persons	2,596	6.7	1,241	663	692	47.8	25.5	26.7
Three persons	2,080	4.6	1,031	575	474	49.6	27.6	22.8
Four persons	2,143	4.1	1,062	651	429	49.6	30.4	20.0
Five persons or more	2,018	4.1	970	588	460	48.1	29.1	22.8
Income before taxes:								
Complete income reporters [2]...	2,120	5.3	985	583	552	46.5	27.5	26.0
Quintiles of income:								
Lowest 20 percent	1,470	8.2	690	339	441	46.9	23.1	30.0
Second 20 percent......	1,988	7.5	945	424	619	47.5	21.3	31.1
Third 20 percent	1,964	5.7	943	524	497	48.0	26.7	25.3
Fourth 20 percent.......	2,312	4.9	1,090	659	563	47.1	28.5	24.4
Highest 20 percent......	2,864	3.8	1,254	968	642	43.8	33.8	22.4
Incomplete reporters of income .	1,919	6.0	977	524	419	50.9	27.3	21.8

[1] Includes prescription and nonprescription drugs.   [2] A complete reporter is a consumer unit providing values for at least one of the major sources of income.

Source: Bureau of Labor Statistics, *Consumer Expenditure Survey,* annual.

No. 124. Medicare Enrollees: 1980 to 2000

[In millions (28.5 represents 28,500,000). As of July 1. Includes Puerto Rico and outlying areas and enrollees in foreign countries and unknown place of residence]

Item	1980	1985	1990	1995	1997	1998	1999	2000
Total...................	28.5	31.1	34.2	37.5	38.4	38.8	39.1	39.6
Aged......................	25.5	28.2	30.9	33.1	33.6	33.8	33.9	34.2
Disabled...................	3.0	2.9	3.3	4.4	4.8	5.0	5.2	5.4
Hospital insurance............	28.1	30.6	33.7	37.1	38.1	38.4	38.7	39.2
Aged..................	25.1	27.7	30.5	32.7	33.2	33.4	33.5	33.8
Disabled................	3.0	2.9	3.3	4.4	4.8	5.0	5.2	5.4
Supplementary medical insurance....	27.4	30.0	32.6	35.7	36.5	36.8	37.0	37.4
Aged..................	24.7	27.3	29.7	31.7	32.2	32.3	32.4	32.6
Disabled................	2.7	2.7	2.9	3.9	4.3	4.5	4.6	4.8

Source: U.S. Centers for Medicare and Medicaid Services, Office of the Actuary, "Medicare Enrollment Trends 1966-1999"; published 16 November 2000; <http://www.hcfa.gov/stats/enrltrnd.htm> and unpublished data.

No. 125. Medicare Disbursements by Type of Beneficiary: 1980 to 2000

[In millions of dollars (35,025 represents $35,025,000,000). For years ending Sept. 30. Distribution of benefits by type is estimated and subject to change]

Type of beneficiary	1980	1990	1995	1996	1997	1998	1999	2000
Total disbursements	35,025	109,709	180,096	194,263	210,342	213,412	211,959	219,275
Hospital insurance disbursements [1]	24,288	66,687	114,883	125,317	137,789	137,140	131,441	130,284
Benefits......................	23,776	65,721	113,394	123,908	136,007	134,321	129,107	125,992
Aged......................	20,951	58,503	100,107	109,379	120,239	118,467	113,321	110,142
Disabled..................	2,825	7,218	13,288	14,529	15,768	15,854	15,786	15,850
Disabled..................	2,654	6,467	12,320	13,474	14,659	14,791	14,731	14,768
ESRD [2]	171	751	968	1,055	1,109	1,063	1,056	1,082
Peer review activity	14	191	189	180	168	188	177	236
Administrative expenses [3].........	497	774	1,300	1,229	1,614	1,653	1,978	2,350
Supplementary medical insurance disbursements [1]..............	10,737	43,022	65,213	68,946	72,553	76,272	80,518	88,991
Benefits......................	10,144	41,498	63,490	67,165	71,117	75,782	79,151	88,876
Aged......................	8,497	36,837	54,830	57,807	60,989	65,118	67,996	76,507
Disabled..................	1,647	4,661	8,660	9,358	10,128	10,004	11,154	12,369
Disabled..................	1,256	3,758	7,363	7,943	8,604	9,156	9,668	10,750
ESRD [2]	391	903	1,297	1,415	1,524	1,508	1,486	1,619
Peer review activity	-	-	2	11	16	33	36	43
Administrative expenses.........	593	1,524	1,722	1,771	1,420	1,435	1,510	1,779

- Represents zero.   [1] Beginning 1998 home health agency transfers are excluded from total supplementary medical insurance disbursements and included in total hospital insurance disbursements.   [2] Represents persons entitled because of End Stage Renal Disease only. Benefits for those who have ESRD but would be entitled due to their aged or disabled status are included in aged and disabled benefits.   [3] Includes costs of experiments and demonstration projects. Includes costs of the health care fraud and abuse control program.

Source: U.S. Centers for Medicare and Medicaid Services, unpublished data.

No. 126. Medicare Benefits by Type of Provider: 1980 to 2000

[In millions of dollars (23,776 represents $23,776,000,000). For years ending Sept. 30. Distribution of benefits by type is estimated and subject to change]

Type of provider	1980	1990	1995	1996	1997	1998	1999	2000
Hospital insurance benefits, total...	23,776	65,721	113,394	123,908	136,007	134,321	129,107	125,992
Inpatient hospital...............	22,860	57,012	81,095	84,513	88,541	86,942	85,696	86,566
Skilled nursing facility.............	392	2,761	8,683	10,416	12,388	13,377	11,488	10,593
Home health agency	524	3,295	15,715	17,157	17,938	14,115	8,994	4,552
Hospice......................	(NA)	318	1,854	1,969	2,082	2,080	2,494	2,818
Managed care	(NA)	2,335	6,047	9,853	15,059	17,807	20,435	21,463
Supplementary medical insurance benefits, total................	10,144	41,498	63,490	67,165	71,117	75,782	79,151	88,876
Physician fee schedule............	(NA)	(NA)	31,110	31,569	31,958	32,338	33,379	35,947
Durable medical equipment..........	(NA)	(NA)	3,576	3,785	4,112	4,104	4,278	4,573
Carrier lab [1].................	(NA)	(NA)	2,819	2,654	2,414	2,166	2,085	2,201
Other carrier [2]	(NA)	(NA)	4,513	4,883	5,452	5,854	6,400	7,164
Hospital [3]....................	(NA)	(NA)	8,448	8,683	9,251	8,977	8,473	8,439
Home health.................	(NA)	(NA)	223	236	246	189	405	4,570
Intermediary lab [4]	(NA)	(NA)	1,437	1,338	1,419	1,478	1,517	1,622
Other intermediary [5]	(NA)	(NA)	5,110	5,664	6,372	6,543	5,642	6,013
Managed care	(NA)	(NA)	6,253	8,353	9,893	14,132	16,970	18,348

NA Not available.   [1] Lab services paid under the lab fee schedule performed in a physician's office lab or an independent lab.   [2] Includes free-standing ambulatory surgical centers facility costs, ambulance, and supplies.   [3] Includes the hospital facility costs for Medicare Part B services which are predominantly in the outpatient department. The physician reimbursement associated with these services is included on the "Physician Fee Schedule" line.   [4] Lab fee services paid under the lab fee schedule performed in a hospital outpatient department.   [5] Includes ESRD free-standing dialysis facility payments and payments to rural health clinics, outpatient rehabilitation facilities, psychiatric hospitals, and federally qualified health centers.

Source: U.S. Centers for Medicare and Medicaid Services, unpublished data.

Health and Nutrition   97

No. 127. Medicare Trust Funds: 1980 to 2001

[In billions of dollars (23.9 represents $23,900,000,000)]

Type of trust fund	1980	1990	1995	1996	1997	1998	1999	2000	2001
HOSPITAL INSURANCE (HI)									
Net contribution income [1]	23.9	72.2	103.3	115.9	119.5	130.7	140.3	154.5	160.9
Interest received [2]	1.1	8.5	10.8	10.2	9.6	9.3	10.1	11.7	14.0
Benefit payments [3]	25.1	66.2	116.4	128.6	137.8	134.0	128.8	128.5	141.2
Assets, end of year	13.7	98.9	130.3	124.9	115.6	120.4	141.4	177.5	208.7
SUPPLEMENTARY MEDICAL INSURANCE (SMI)									
Net premium income	3.0	11.3	19.7	18.8	19.3	[4]20.9	[4]19.0	20.6	22.8
Transfers from general revenue	7.5	33.0	39.0	65.0	60.2	[4]64.1	[4]59.1	65.9	72.8
Interest received [2]	0.4	1.6	1.6	1.8	2.5	2.7	2.8	3.5	3.1
Benefit payments [3]	10.6	42.5	65.0	68.6	72.8	76.1	80.7	88.9	99.7
Assets, end of year	4.5	15.5	13.1	28.3	36.1	46.2	44.8	44.0	41.3

[1] Includes income from taxation of benefits beginning in 1995. Includes premiums from aged ineligibles enrolled in HI.
[2] Includes recoveries of amounts reimbursed from the trust fund. [3] Beginning 1998 monies transferred to the SMI trust fund for home health agency costs, as provided for by P.L. 105-33, are included in HI benefit payments but excluded from SMI benefit payments. [4] Premiums withheld from check and associated general revenue contributions that were to occur on Jan. 3, 1999, actually occurred on December 31, 1998. These amounts are therefore excluded from 1999 data.

Source: U.S. Centers for Medicare and Medicaid Services, *Annual Report of the Board of Trustees of the Federal Hospital Insurance Trust Fund* and *Annual Report of the Board of Trustees of the Federal Supplementary Medical Insurance Trust Fund.*

No. 128. Medicare—Summary by State and Other Areas: 1995 and 2000

[For fiscal year ending in year shown (37,535 represents 37,535,000)]

State and area	Enrollment [1] (1,000)		Payments [2] (mil. dol.)		State and area	Enrollment [1] (1,000)		Payments [2] (mil. dol.)	
	1995	2000	1995	2000		1995	2000	1995	2000
All areas	37,535	39,140	176,884	214,868	MO	833	854	3,821	4,274
U.S.	36,758	38,286	175,976	213,555	MT	130	135	489	575
					NE	249	252	840	1,225
AL	642	677	3,042	3,885	NV	194	229	894	1,069
AK	34	40	133	189	NH	156	167	597	629
AZ	602	658	2,717	2,938	NJ	1,168	1,195	5,603	6,767
AR	423	436	1,638	2,083	NM	211	229	710	854
CA	3,633	3,837	20,406	23,621	NY	2,630	2,694	13,904	18,653
CO	421	458	1,835	2,338	NC	1,027	1,111	4,276	5,942
CT	502	512	2,584	3,291	ND	103	103	412	501
DE	101	110	445	430	OH	1,666	1,692	7,262	9,310
DC	78	76	1,164	784	OK	488	504	2,178	2,137
FL	2,628	2,771	14,828	19,221	OR	469	484	1,685	1,853
GA	833	898	4,090	4,111	PA	2,071	2,088	10,796	13,257
HI	149	162	580	622	RI	168	170	772	1,075
ID	150	161	463	639	SC	509	555	1,926	2,947
IL	1,617	1,629	7,276	7,309	SD	117	119	563	564
IN	823	845	3,491	4,720	TN	771	815	4,083	4,907
IA	474	476	1,527	1,453	TX	2,080	2,223	11,504	14,538
KS	383	389	1,545	1,915	UT	187	201	708	918
KY	586	615	2,401	3,153	VT	83	88	284	315
LA	581	597	3,448	4,383	VA	818	876	2,979	4,038
ME	201	213	707	793	WA	688	725	2,603	2,843
MD	602	635	2,868	3,998	WV	330	336	1,208	1,656
MA	933	954	5,496	5,466	WI	762	777	2,673	3,498
MI	1,347	1,389	6,237	6,269	WY	60	64	180	247
MN	631	648	2,378	3,109	PR	477	525	875	1,224
MS	397	414	1,723	2,248	Other areas	300	330	33	89

[1] Hospital and/or medical insurance enrollment for 1995 as of July and for 2000 as of September. [2] Distribution of benefit payments by state is based on a methodology which considered actual payments to health maintenance organizations and estimated payments for other providers of medicare services.

Source: U.S. Centers for Medicare and Medicaid Services, "Medicare Beneficiaries Enrolled as of July 1 of each year. Years 1995-1998"; published 29 July 1999; <http://www.hcfa.gov/stats/histenr1.htm> and "Medicare Estimated Benefit Payments By State for Fiscal Year 2000"; <http://www.hcfa.gov/stats/BENEPAY/bnpay00i.htm>.

No. 129. Medicaid—Selected Characteristics of Persons Covered: 2000

[In thousands, except percent (28,360 represents 28,360,000). Represents number of persons as of March of following year who were enrolled at any time in year shown. Excludes unrelated individuals under age 15. Person did not have to receive medical care paid for by medicaid in order to be counted. See headnote, Table 514]

Poverty status	Total [1]	White	Black	Hispanic [2]	Under 18 years old	18-44 years old	45-64 years old	65 years old and over
Persons covered, total......	**28,360**	**19,290**	**7,164**	**6,226**	**14,486**	**7,098**	**3,484**	**3,293**
Below poverty level..........	12,349	7,536	4,020	2,871	6,750	3,207	1,495	897
Above poverty level	16,011	11,754	3,144	3,355	7,736	3,891	1,989	2,395
Percent of population covered..	10.3	8.5	20.0	18.5	20.1	6.5	5.6	10.0
Below poverty level..........	39.8	35.5	51.1	40.1	58.4	28.0	31.9	26.7
Above poverty level	6.5	5.7	11.3	12.6	12.8	4.0	3.5	8.1

[1] Includes other races not shown separately.   [2] Persons of Hispanic origin may be of any race.

Source: U.S. Census Bureau, "Table 24. Health Insurance Coverage Status and Type of Coverage by Selected Characteristics for All People in Poverty Universe: 2000"; published 10 December 2001; <http://ferret.bls.census.gov/macro/032001/pov/new24001.htm>.

No. 130. Medicaid—Selected Utilization Measures: 1980 to 1998

[In thousands (2,255 represents 2,255,000). For year ending September 30. Includes Virgin Islands. See text, this section]

Measure	1980	1985	1990	1994	1995	1996	1997	1998
General hospitals:								
Recipients discharged	2,255	2,390	3,261	3,890	3,743	3,300	3,135	2,793
Total days of care	24,089	29,562	27,471	28,941	25,711	23,072	21,532	19,091
Nursing facilities: [1]								
Total recipients	1,395	1,375	1,461	1,639	1,667	1,594	1,497	1,555
Total days of care	273,497	277,996	360,044	400,785	400,123	409,663	388,985	384,549
Intermediate care facilities: [2]								
Total recipients	121	147	146	159	151	140	146	124
Total days of care	250,124	47,324	49,730	54,105	56,878	56,625	62,423	50,636

[1] Includes skilled nursing facilities and intermediate care facilities for all other than the mentally retarded.   [2] Mentally retarded.

Source: U.S. Centers for Medicare and Medicaid Services, Office of Information Systems, *Statistical Report on Medical Care: Eligibles, Recipients, Payments, and Services.*

No. 131. Medicaid—Recipients and Payments: 1990 to 1998

[For year ending September 30 (25,255 represents 25,255,000). Includes Puerto Rico and outlying areas. Medical vendor payments are those made directly to suppliers of medical care]

Basis of eligibility and type of service	Recipients (1,000)					Payments (mil. dol.)				
	1990	1995	1996	1997	1998	1990	1995	1996	1997	1998
Total [1]............	**25,255**	**36,282**	**36,118**	**34,872**	**40,649**	**64,859**	**120,141**	**121,685**	**124,430**	**142,318**
Age 65 and over	3,202	4,119	4,285	3,955	3,964	21,508	36,527	36,947	37,721	40,602
Blindness...............	83	92	95	(NA)	(NA)	434	848	869	(NA)	(NA)
Disabled [2]..............	3,635	5,767	6,126	6,129	6,638	23,969	48,570	51,196	54,130	60,375
AFDC [3] program	17,230	24,767	23,866	22,594	26,872	17,690	31,487	29,819	29,851	37,639
Other and unknown	1,105	1,537	1,746	2,195	3,176	1,257	2,708	2,853	2,727	3,702
Inpatient services in—										
General hospital........	4,593	5,561	5,362	4,746	4,273	16,674	26,331	25,176	23,143	21,499
Mental hospital.........	92	84	93	87	135	1,714	2,511	2,040	2,009	2,801
Intermediate care facilities, mentally retarded	147	151	140	136	126	7,354	10,383	9,555	9,798	9,482
Nursing facility services [4]....	1,461	1,667	1,594	1,603	1,646	17,693	29,052	29,630	30,504	31,892
Physicians	17,078	23,789	22,861	21,170	18,555	4,018	7,360	7,238	7,041	6,070
Dental	4,552	6,383	6,208	5,935	4,965	593	1,019	1,028	1,036	901
Other practitioner........	3,873	5,528	5,343	5,142	4,342	372	986	1,094	979	587
Outpatient hospital	12,370	16,712	15,905	13,632	12,158	3,324	6,627	6,504	6,169	5,759
Clinic.................	2,804	5,322	5,070	4,713	5,285	1,688	4,280	4,222	4,252	3,921
Laboratory [5]	8,959	13,064	12,607	11,074	9,381	721	1,180	1,208	1,033	939
Home health [6]..........	719	1,639	1,727	1,861	1,225	3,404	9,406	10,868	12,237	2,702
Prescribed drugs	17,294	23,723	22,585	20,954	19,338	4,420	9,791	10,697	11,972	13,522
Family planning	1,752	2,501	2,366	2,091	2,011	265	514	474	418	449
Prepaid health care	(NA)	(NA)	(NA)	(NA)	20,203	(NA)	(NA)	(NA)	(NA)	19,296

NA Not available.   [1] Recipient data do not add due to small number of recipients that are reported in more than one category. Includes recipients of, and payments for, other care not shown separately.   [2] Permanently and totally. Beginning 1997, includes blind.   [3] Aid to families with dependent children includes children, adults, and foster care.   [4] Nursing facility services includes skilled nursing facility services and intermediate care facility services for all other than the mentally retarded.   [5] Includes radiological services.   [6] Data for 1998 not comparable with earlier years.

Source: U.S. Centers for Medicare and Medicaid Services, Office of Information Systems, *Statistical Report on Medical Care: Eligibles, Recipients, Payments, and Services.*

No. 132. Medicaid—Summary by State and Other Area: 1995 and 1999

[For year ending September 30 (36,282 represents 36,282,000). Data for 1999 includes managed care recipients and capitation payments]

State and area	Recipients [1] (1,000) 1995	Recipients [1] (1,000) 1999	Payments [2] (mil. dol.) 1995	Payments [2] (mil. dol.) 1999	State and area	Recipients [1] (1,000) 1995	Recipients [1] (1,000) 1999	Payments [2] (mil. dol.) 1995	Payments [2] (mil. dol.) 1999
All areas .	36,282	(NA)	120,141	(NA)	MO	695	877	2,039	2,798
U.S.	35,210	40,844	119,885	152,629	MT	99	96	326	365
					NE	168	223	608	876
AL	539	650	1,455	1,695	NV	105	153	350	459
AK	68	99	252	398	NH	97	105	473	527
AZ	494	644	218	1,878	NJ	790	841	3,813	4,386
AR	353	483	1,376	1,365	NM	287	370	714	1,123
CA	5,017	6,217	10,521	15,440	NY	3,035	3,327	22,086	25,357
CO	294	352	1,063	1,641	NC	1,084	1,182	3,175	4,266
CT	380	410	2,125	2,671	ND	61	62	297	346
DE	79	113	324	462	OH	1,533	1,390	5,585	6,329
DC	138	145	532	759	OK	394	525	1,055	1,434
FL	1,735	2,116	4,802	6,440	OR	452	534	1,327	1,596
GA	1,147	1,237	3,076	3,232	PA	1,230	1,773	4,633	6,133
HI	52	(NA)	258	(NA)	RI	135	155	673	881
ID	115	94	360	520	SC	496	725	1,438	2,459
IL	1,552	1,696	5,600	6,339	SD	74	92	305	369
IN	559	668	1,878	2,750	TN	1,466	1,533	2,772	3,285
IA	304	313	1,036	1,364	TX	2,562	2,676	6,565	8,126
KS	256	260	831	1,096	UT	160	198	464	797
KY	641	677	1,945	2,598	VT	100	139	320	421
LA	785	775	2,708	2,534	VA	681	691	1,833	2,207
ME	153	201	760	1,206	WA	639	895	1,461	2,575
MD	414	628	2,019	3,044	WV	389	377	1,169	1,344
MA	728	1,043	3,972	4,953	WI	460	563	1,894	2,246
MI	1,168	1,335	3,409	4,707	WY	51	52	171	199
MN	473	587	2,550	3,038	PR	1,055	(NA)	244	(NA)
MS	520	545	1,266	1,600	VI	17	(NA)	12	(NA)

NA Not available.   [1] Persons who had payments made on their behalf at any time during the fiscal year.   [2] Payments are for fiscal year and reflect federal and state contribution payments. Data exclude disproportionate hospital share payments. Disproportionate share hospitals receive higher medicaid reimbursement than other hospitals because they treat a disproportionate share of medicaid patients.

Source: U.S. Centers for Medicare and Medicaid Services, Office of Information Systems, 1995 data, *Statistical Report on Medical Care: Eligibles, Recipients, Payments, and Services*; 1999 data, Medicaid Statistical Information System, unpublished data.

No. 133. Medicaid Managed Care Enrollment by State and Other Area: 1995 to 2000

[For year ending June 30 (33,373 represents 33,373,000)]

State and area	Total medicaid (1,000)	Managed care enrollment Number (1,000)	Managed care enrollment Percent of total	State and area	Total medicaid (1,000)	Managed care enrollment Number (1,000)	Managed care enrollment Percent of total	State and area	Total medicaid (1,000)	Managed care enrollment Number (1,000)	Managed care enrollment Percent of total
1995	33,373	9,800	29.4	IL.	1,392	138	9.9	NC.	876	599	68.3
1999	31,940	17,757	55.6	IN	563	376	66.8	ND.	43	24	55.1
				IA	202	182	90.3	OH.	1,121	239	21.4
2000, total . .	33,690	18,786	55.8	KS	192	108	56.3	OK.	404	279	69.1
				KY.	575	464	80.7	OR.	376	312	83.1
U.S.	32,720	17,958	54.9	LA.	772	49	6.3	PA	1,343	975	72.6
AL	543	325	59.9	ME.	162	57	35.4	RI	151	104	68.7
AK	81	-	-	MD.	479	386	80.5	SC.	538	32	6.0
AZ	479	442	92.4	MA.	911	583	64.0	SD.	73	68	92.7
AR	389	222	57.1	MI	1,064	1,064	100.0	TN	1,323	1,323	100.0
CA	5,037	2,525	50.1	MN.	466	291	62.5	TX	1,789	606	33.9
CO	282	254	90.2	MS.	559	218	39.1	UT.	133	119	89.5
CT	321	230	71.7	MO	754	304	40.4	VT.	119	56	46.7
DE.	95	76	79.4	MT.	69	42	61.1	VA.	479	281	58.6
DC.	119	79	66.2	NE.	183	140	76.7	WA	800	800	100.0
FL	1,701	1,017	59.8	NV	96	38	39.5	WV	262	91	34.6
GA.	842	806	95.7	NH.	79	4	5.6	WI	479	210	43.9
HI	164	122	73.9	NJ	628	372	59.2	WY	37	-	-
ID	108	32	29.9	NM.	312	199	63.8	PR	951	828	87.1
				NY	2,751	691	25.1	VI	19	-	-

- Represents zero.

Source: U.S. Centers for Medicare and Medicaid Services, *"Medicaid Statistics and Data"*; <http://www.hcfa.gov/medicaid/mcaidsad.htm\>; (accessed 25 April 2002).

No. 134. State Children's Health Insurance Program-Enrollment by State: 1999 to 2001

[In thousands (1,959 represents 1,959,000). For year ending September 30. Represents the number of children ever enrolled during the year. This program provides health benefits coverage to children living in families whose incomes exceed the eligibility limits for medicaid. Although it is generally targeted to families with incomes at or below 200 percent of the federal poverty level, each state may set its own income eligibility limits, within certain guidelines. States have three options: they may expand their medicaid programs, develop a separate child health program that functions independently of medicaid, or do a combination of both]

State	1999	2000	2001	State	1999	2000	2001	State	1999	2000	2001
U.S.	1,959	3,334	4,601	KS	14	26	34	ND	(Z)	3	3
				KY	19	56	67	OH	84	111	158
AL	39	38	68	LA	22	50	70	OK	40	58	39
AK	8	13	22	ME	14	23	27	OR	27	37	41
AZ	27	61	87	MD	18	93	110	PA	82	120	141
AR	1	2	3	MA	68	113	105	RI	7	12	17
CA	222	478	693	MI	27	37	76	SC	46	60	66
CO	24	35	46	MN	(Z)	(Z)	(Z)	SD	3	6	9
CT	10	19	19	MS	13	20	52	TN	10	15	9
DE	2	4	6	MO	50	74	107	TX	51	131	501
DC	3	2	3	MT	1	8	14	UT	13	25	35
FL	155	227	299	NE	10	11	14	VT	2	4	3
GA	48	121	183	NV	8	16	28	VA	17	38	73
HI	-	2	7	NH	5	4	6	WA	-	3	8
ID	8	12	13	NJ	76	89	100	WV	8	22	33
IL	43	63	84	NM	5	6	10	WI	13	47	57
IN	31	44	57	NY	521	769	873	WY	-	3	5
IA	10	20	23	NC	57	104	99				

- Represents zero.   Z Less than 500.

Source: U.S. Centers for Medicare & Medicaid Services, *The State Children's Health Insurance Program, Annual Enrollment Report.*

No. 135. Health Maintenance Organizations (HMOs): 1980 to 2001

[As of January 1, except 1980 as of June 30 (9.1 represents 9,100,000). An HMO is a prepaid health plan delivering comprehensive care to members through designated providers, having a fixed periodic payment for health care services, and requiring members to be in a plan for a specified period of time (usually 1 year). A group HMO delivers health services through a physician group that is controlled by the HMO unit or contracts with one or more independent group practices to provide health services. An individual practice association (IPA) HMO contracts directly with physicians in independent practice, and/or contracts with one or more associations of physicians in independent practice, and/or contracts with one or more multispecialty group practices. Data are based on a census of HMOs]

Model type	Number of plans						Enrollment [1] (mil.)					
	1980	1990	1995	1999	2000	2001	1980	1990	1995	1999	2000	2001
Total	235	572	550	643	568	541	9.1	33.0	46.2	81.3	80.9	79.5
I.P.A.	97	360	323	309	278	257	1.7	13.7	17.4	32.8	33.4	33.1
Group	138	212	107	126	102	104	7.4	19.3	12.9	15.2	15.2	15.6
Mixed	(NA)	(NA)	120	208	188	180	(NA)	(NA)	15.9	32.6	32.3	30.8

NA Not available.   [1] 1980-95 excludes enrollees participating in open-ended plans; beginning 1999 includes open-ended enrollment.

No. 136. Persons Enrolled in Health Maintenance Organizations (HMOs) by State: 2000 and 2001

[79,534 represents 79,534,000. Data are based on a census of health maintenance organizations. Pure and open-ended enrollment as of January 1]

State	Number 2001 (1,000)	Percent of population		State	Number 2001 (1,000)	Percent of population		State	Number 2001 (1,000)	Percent of population	
		2000	2001			2000	2001			2000	2001
U.S. [1] .	79,534	29.7	27.9	KS	432	17.9	16.1	ND	8	2.5	1.3
				KY	1,228	31.5	30.4	OH	2,652	25.1	23.4
AL	288	7.2	6.5	LA	696	17.0	15.6	OK	480	14.7	13.9
AK	-	-	-	ME	356	22.3	27.9	OR	1,214	41.1	35.5
AZ	1,661	30.9	32.4	MD	2,032	43.9	38.4	PA	4,100	33.9	33.4
AR	281	10.4	10.5	MA	2,814	53.0	44.3	RI	367	38.1	35.0
CA	18,074	53.5	53.4	MI	2,653	27.1	26.7	SC	383	9.9	9.5
CO	1,566	39.5	36.4	MN	1,385	29.9	28.2	SD	73	6.7	9.7
CT	1,353	44.6	39.7	MS	25	1.1	0.9	TN	1,880	33.0	33.0
DE	178	22.0	22.8	MO	1,733	35.2	31.0	TX	3,656	18.5	17.5
DC	177	35.2	31.0	MT	70	7.0	7.7	UT	793	35.3	35.5
FL	4,757	31.4	29.8	NE	170	11.2	9.9	VT	26	4.6	4.2
GA	1,304	17.4	15.9	NV	408	23.5	20.4	VA	1,144	18.5	16.2
HI	386	30.0	31.8	NH	485	33.7	39.3	WA	901	15.2	15.3
ID	55	7.9	4.3	NJ	2,664	30.9	31.7	WV	197	10.3	10.9
IL	2,387	21.0	19.2	NM	507	37.7	27.9	WI	1,588	30.2	29.6
IN	712	12.4	11.7	NY	6,637	35.8	35.0	WY	9	1.4	1.7
IA	191	7.4	6.5	NC	1,311	17.8	16.3				

- Represents zero.   [1] Includes Guam and Puerto Rico not shown separately.

Source of Tables 135 and 136: InterStudy Publications, St. Paul, MN, *The InterStudy Competitive Edge*, annual (copyright).

U.S. Census Bureau, Statistical Abstract of the United States: 2002

No. 137. Health Insurance Coverage Status by Selected Characteristics: 1990 to 2000

[Persons as of following year for coverage in the year shown (248.9 represents 248,900,000). Government health insurance includes medicare, medicaid, and military plans. Based on Current Population Survey; see text, Section 1, Population, and Appendix III]

Characteristic	Number (mil.)							Percent			
	Total persons	Covered by private or government health insurance					Not covered by health insurance	Covered by private or government health insurance			Not covered by health insurance
		Total [1]	Private		Government			Total [1]	Private	Medicaid [3]	
			Total	Group health [2]	Medicare	Medicaid [3]					
1990	248.9	214.2	182.1	150.2	32.3	24.3	34.7	86.1	73.2	9.7	13.9
1995 [4]	264.3	223.7	185.9	161.5	34.7	31.9	40.6	84.6	70.3	12.1	15.4
1999 [4]	274.1	231.5	194.6	172.0	36.1	27.9	42.6	84.5	71.0	10.2	15.5
1999 [4][5]	274.1	234.8	197.5	174.1	36.1	28.2	39.3	85.7	72.1	10.3	14.3
2000, total [4][5][6]	276.5	237.9	200.2	177.3	37.0	28.6	38.7	86.0	72.4	10.4	14.0
Age:											
Under 18 years	72.6	64.1	51.2	48.1	0.5	14.7	8.4	88.4	70.6	20.3	11.6
Under 6 years . . .	23.7	21.0	15.9	15.3	0.2	5.7	2.6	88.9	67.1	24.2	11.1
6 to 11 years . . .	24.8	22.0	17.5	16.6	0.1	5.1	2.8	88.5	70.5	20.6	11.5
12 to 17 years . . .	24.1	21.1	17.8	16.2	0.2	3.9	2.9	87.8	74.0	16.2	12.2
18 to 24 years	27.0	19.6	17.5	14.4	0.2	2.3	7.4	72.7	64.8	8.7	27.3
25 to 34 years	37.4	29.5	27.0	25.5	0.4	2.4	7.9	78.8	72.1	6.3	21.2
35 to 44 years	44.8	37.8	35.2	33.3	0.8	2.4	6.9	84.5	78.6	5.4	15.5
45 to 54 years	38.0	33.5	31.1	29.0	1.3	1.9	4.6	88.0	81.6	4.9	12.0
55 to 64 years	23.8	20.5	18.0	15.9	2.1	1.6	3.2	86.3	75.8	6.8	13.7
65 years and over . .	33.0	32.7	20.3	11.2	31.7	3.3	0.2	99.3	61.5	10.0	0.7
Sex: Male	135.2	115.1	98.4	88.3	16.2	12.7	20.1	85.1	72.8	9.4	14.9
Female	141.3	122.8	101.8	89.0	20.8	15.9	18.5	86.9	72.1	11.3	13.1
Race: White	226.4	197.2	169.8	149.3	32.0	19.4	29.2	87.1	75.0	8.6	12.9
Black	35.9	29.3	21.2	19.6	3.8	7.3	6.6	81.5	58.9	20.3	18.5
Asian and Pacific Islander	11.3	9.3	7.9	7.1	0.9	1.3	2.0	82.0	69.9	11.3	18.0
Hispanic origin [7]	33.9	23.0	16.3	15.1	2.2	6.3	10.8	68.0	47.9	18.6	32.0
Household income:											
Less than $25,000 . .	61.1	47.2	25.2	16.9	17.6	16.9	13.9	77.3	41.2	27.7	22.7
$25,000-$49,999 . . .	75.4	62.6	52.9	45.9	11.1	7.4	12.8	83.0	70.2	9.8	17.0
$50,000-$74,999 . . .	59.3	52.8	49.4	45.9	4.2	2.5	6.5	89.0	83.3	4.3	11.0
$75,000 or more . . .	80.8	75.3	72.8	68.6	4.2	1.7	5.5	93.1	90.1	2.2	6.9
Persons below poverty .	31.1	21.9	8.6	5.8	4.6	12.3	9.2	70.4	27.8	39.8	29.6

[1] Includes other government insurance, not shown separately. Persons with coverage counted only once in total, even though they may have been covered by more that one type of policy. [2] Related to employment of self or other family members. [3] Beginning 1997 persons with no coverage other than access to Indian Health Service are no longer considered covered by health insurance; instead they are considered to be uninsured. The effect of this change on the overall estimates of health insurance coverage is negligible; however, the decrease in the number of people covered by medicaid may be partially due to this change. [4] Data based on 1990 census adjusted population controls. [5] Estimates reflect results of follow-up verification questions. [6] Includes other races not shown separately. [7] Persons of Hispanic origin may be of any race.

No. 138. Persons With and Without Health Insurance Coverage by State: 2000

[237,857 represents 237,857,000. Based on the Current Population Survey and subject to sampling error; see text, Section 1, Population, and Appendix III]

State	Total persons covered (1,000)	Total persons not covered		Children not covered		State	Total persons covered (1,000)	Total persons not covered		Children not covered	
		Number (1,000)	Percent of total	Number (1,000)	Percent of total			Number (1,000)	Percent of total	Number (1,000)	Percent of total
U.S.	237,857	38,683	14.0	8,405	11.6	MO	4,930	586	10.6	124	8.5
						MT	714	162	18.5	39	18.7
AL	3,851	600	13.5	98	8.5	NE	1,494	164	9.9	40	8.8
AK	522	125	19.3	38	17.7	NV	1,680	311	15.6	90	14.9
AZ	4,124	793	16.1	173	12.8	NH	1,155	85	6.8	23	7.0
AR	2,261	364	13.9	82	11.6	NJ	7,257	1,049	12.6	203	9.3
CA	28,454	6,281	18.1	1,507	15.4	NM	1,366	427	23.8	105	20.2
CO	3,665	563	13.3	154	13.7	NY	15,608	2,802	15.2	486	10.5
CT	3,056	263	7.9	22	2.6	NC	6,541	980	13.0	187	10.1
DE	705	82	10.4	15	7.2	ND	538	69	11.3	18	11.9
DC	434	73	14.4	10	9.9	OH	10,284	1,255	10.9	309	9.5
FL	12,537	2,620	17.3	570	16.5	OK	2,651	636	19.3	134	16.8
GA	6,638	1,135	14.6	154	8.1	OR	2,935	465	13.7	111	12.9
HI	1,039	117	10.1	23	8.3	PA	11,063	905	7.6	145	4.9
ID	1,061	196	15.6	51	14.7	RI	881	55	5.9	5	2.5
IL	10,627	1,659	13.5	371	10.8	SC	3,321	448	11.9	68	8.6
IN	5,117	701	12.1	201	13.9	SD	615	82	11.8	20	11.6
IA	2,615	248	8.7	46	6.2	TN	5,003	577	10.3	63	4.7
KS	2,306	301	11.5	75	11.3	TX	16,167	4,425	21.5	1,273	21.5
KY	3,462	513	12.9	73	7.7	UT	1,913	296	13.4	75	10.1
LA	3,423	810	19.1	162	15.7						
ME	1,121	145	11.5	22	7.8	VT	564	67	10.7	15	8.5
MD	4,618	501	9.8	92	7.4	VA	6,091	886	12.7	206	11.7
MA	5,661	595	9.5	124	7.8	WA	5,075	780	13.3	126	8.1
MI	8,964	982	9.9	179	6.7	WV	1,524	254	14.3	37	9.8
MN	4,354	430	9.0	117	9.3	WI	5,032	386	7.1	56	3.7
MS	2,425	364	13.1	71	9.2	WY	418	70	14.4	16	12.5

Source of Tables 137 and 138: U.S. Census Bureau; *Current Population Reports*, P60-215; and unpublished data.

No. 139. Percent of Workers Participating in Health Care Benefit Programs and Percent of Participants Required to Contribute: 1999

[Based on National Compensation Survey, a sample survey of 3,168 private industry establishments of all sizes, representing over 107 million workers; see Appendix III. See also Table 620]

Characteristic	Percent of workers participating—			Single coverage medical care			Family coverage medical care		
	Medical care	Dental care	Vision care	Employee contributions not required (percent)	Employee contributions required (percent)	Average monthly contribution[1] (dol.)	Employee contributions not required (percent)	Employee contributions required (percent)	Average monthly contribution[1] (dol.)
Total	**53**	**32**	**18**	**33**	**67**	**48.30**	**19**	**81**	**169.84**
Worker characteristics:									
Professional, technical, and related employees	68	49	30	31	69	45.34	16	84	163.31
Clerical and sales employees	51	30	14	29	71	47.70	15	85	174.18
Blue-collar and service employees	48	27	15	37	63	50.67	24	76	171.12
Full time[2]	64	39	22	52	48	48.65	46	54	129.08
Part time[2]	14	10	6	30	70	48.27	14	86	173.77
Union[3]	73	52	39	34	66	47.81	19	81	168.68
Nonunion[3]	51	30	15	22	78	57.49	15	85	192.65
Region:[4]									
Northeast	54	35	21	27	73	54.18	20	80	178.99
South	51	27	13	30	70	51.85	12	88	187.46
Midwest	54	32	17	32	68	42.33	23	77	144.99
West	54	39	25	44	56	42.50	26	74	156.11

[1] The average is presented for all covered workers and excludes workers without the plan provision. Averages are for plans stating a flat monthly cost. [2] Employees are classified as working either a full-time or part-time schedule based on the definition used by each establishment. [3] Union workers are those whose wages are determined through collective bargaining. [4] See map, inside front cover.

Source: U.S. Bureau of Labor Statistics, *News*, USDL 01-473, December 19, 2001.

No. 140. Medical Care Benefits of Workers by Amount and Type of Employee Contribution: 1999

[In percent except as indicated (38,060 represents 38,060,000). See headnote, Table 139]

Type and amount of contribution	Individual coverage				Type and amount of contribution	Family coverage			
	All employees	Professional, technical, and related	Clerical and sales	Blue-collar and service		All employees	Professional, technical, and related	Clerical and sales	Blue-collar and service
Number with contributory coverage (1,000)	38,060	10,495	11,333	16,233	Number with contributory coverage (1,000)	45,994	12,882	13,489	19,623
Total with contributory coverage	100	100	100	100	Total with contributory coverage	100	100	100	100
Flat monthly amount	66	66	67	65	Flat monthly amount	69	68	69	69
Less than $5.00	1	(Z)	1	1	Less than $40.00	4	3	4	5
$5.00-$9.99	2	1	1	2	$40.00-$49.99	3	2	3	3
$10.00-$14.99	4	4	5	4	$50.00-$59.99	2	2	2	2
$15.00-$19.99	4	4	3	6	$60.00-$69.99	2	2	3	2
$20.00-$29.99	10	13	10	9	$70.00-$79.99	3	6	2	2
$30.00-$39.99	10	10	11	10	$80.00-$89.99	3	4	2	3
$40.00-$49.99	10	12	11	8	$90.00-$99.99	3	3	4	3
$50.00-$59.99	7	6	9	7	$100.00-$124.99	8	7	8	9
$60.00-$69.99	6	7	7	5	$125.00-$149.99	8	10	8	7
$70.00-$79.99	4	2	3	4	$150.00-$174.99	6	6	5	6
$80.00-$89.99	2	1	3	1	$175.00-$199.99	5	6	5	4
$90.00-$99.99	2	1	2	2	$200.00-$224.99	4	4	4	3
$100.00-$124.99	2	2	1	2	$225.00-$249.99	4	3	4	4
$125.00 or more	3	2	2	4	$250.00-$299.99	5	4	5	6
Dollar amount unspecified	(Z)	-	(Z)	(Z)	$300 or more	10	8	10	11
Composite rate[1]	3	2	2	4	Composite rate[1]	3	4	2	3
Varies[2]	10	9	12	9	Varies[2]	10	9	13	9
Other	(Z)	(Z)	(Z)	(Z)	Other	(Z)	(Z)	(Z)	(Z)
Flexible benefits[3]	8	11	5	7	Flexible benefits[3]	7	10	5	6
Percent of earnings	1	(Z)	1	1	Percent of earnings	1	(Z)	1	1
Exists, but unknown	13	11	13	14	Exists, but unknown	10	9	10	11

- Represents zero. Z Less than 0.5 percent. [1] A composite rate is a set contribution covering more than one benefit area; for example, health care and life insurance. Cost data for individual plans cannot be determined. [2] Based on worker attributes. For example, employee contributions may vary based on earnings, length of service, or age. [3] Amount varies by options selected under a "cafeteria plan" or employer-sponsored reimbursement account.

Source: U.S. Bureau of Labor Statistics, *News*, USDL 01-473, December 19, 2001.

U.S. Census Bureau, Statistical Abstract of the United States: 2002

No. 141. Health Care Firms—Establishments, Receipts, Payroll, and Employees by Kind of Business (NAICS Basis): 1997

Kind of business	NAICS code [1]	All firms		Employer firms			
		Establish-ments (number)	Receipts (mil. dol.)	Establish-ments (number)	Receipts (mil. dol.)	Annual payroll (mil. dol.)	Paid employ-ees [2] (1,000)
TAXABLE FIRMS							
Ambulatory health care services	621	1,047,100	334,762	440,200	310,012	137,979	3,744.3
Offices of physicians	6211	348,283	182,542	195,449	171,629	84,977	1,571.1
Offices of dentists	6212	144,292	50,027	114,178	48,482	18,227	641.7
Offices of other health practitioners [3]	6213	304,658	35,399	88,886	28,282	10,457	406.6
Offices of chiropractors	62131	49,094	7,431	30,487	6,570	1,886	91.7
Offices of optometrists	62132	28,077	6,906	17,875	6,362	1,773	79.5
Offices of PT/OT/speech therapy & audiology [4]	62134	47,665	9,718	14,277	8,684	4,377	141.5
Outpatient care centers	6214	15,863	17,817	11,828	17,306	5,502	173.8
Medical & diagnostic laboratories	6215	22,174	16,960	9,076	16,317	5,402	151.3
Home health care services	6216	78,641	22,756	16,315	21,474	10,941	681.5
Other ambulatory health care services	6219	133,189	9,259	4,468	6,521	2,475	118.2
Hospitals [3]	622	(NA)	(NA)	1,345	40,146	13,886	511.6
General medical & surgical hospitals	6221	(NA)	(NA)	792	34,213	11,570	421.3
Nursing & residential care facilities [3]	623	67,331	56,847	32,833	55,844	24,626	1,484.8
Nursing care facilities	6231	(NA)	(NA)	12,517	44,485	20,193	1,160.5
Community care facilities for the elderly	6233	(NA)	(NA)	11,637	7,088	2,533	196.1
TAX-EXEMPT FIRMS							
Ambulatory health care services [3]	621	(NA)	(NA)	15,181	45,428	17,884	669.3
Outpatient care centers	6214	(NA)	(NA)	9,940	31,561	11,158	346.5
Home health care services	6216	(NA)	(NA)	3,375	10,104	5,426	267.5
Hospitals	622	(NA)	(NA)	5,340	339,032	141,910	4,421.5
General medical & surgical hospitals	6221	(NA)	(NA)	4,695	319,920	131,054	4,105.3
Psychiatric & substance abuse hospitals	6222	(NA)	(NA)	412	10,689	6,983	201.0
Other specialty hospitals	6223	(NA)	(NA)	233	8,423	3,874	115.1
Nursing & residential care facilities [3]	623	(NA)	(NA)	24,526	37,235	17,527	985.9
Nursing care facilities	6231	(NA)	(NA)	3,088	15,249	7,396	396.6
Residential mental retardation/health facilities	6232	(NA)	(NA)	12,940	7,973	4,126	246.1
Community care facilities for the elderly	6233	(NA)	(NA)	3,951	9,304	3,742	226.0

NA Not available. [1] North American Industry Classification System, see text, Section 15, Business Enterprise. [2] For pay period including March 12. [3] Includes other kinds of business not shown separately. [4] Offices of physical, occupational and speech therapists, and audiologists.

Source: U.S. Census Bureau, *1997 Economic Census, Health Care and Social Assistance*, Series EC97562A-US, issued October 1999 and *Nonemployer Statistics*.

No. 142. Annual Receipts/Revenue for Health Care Industries: 1998 to 2000

[In millions of dollars (399,518 represents $399,518,000,000). Based on the North American Industry Classification System (NAICS), see text, Section 15, Business Enterprise. All firms in NAICS 6211, 6212, 6213, and 6215 are defined as taxable. Estimates for the nonemployer portion are derived from administrative records data provided by other federal agencies. These data are available only at the total revenue level. Estimates for tax-exempt firms are derived only from a sample of employer firms]

Kind of business	NAICS code	Total, all firms [1]			Employer firms, 2000		
		1998	1999	2000	Total	Taxable firms	Tax-exempt firms
Ambulatory health care services	621	399,518	416,580	443,040	414,722	364,834	49,888
Offices of physicians	6211	192,639	201,386	215,221	202,913	202,913	(X)
Offices of dentists	6212	53,156	56,389	60,774	58,812	58,812	(X)
Offices of other health practitioners [2]	6213	37,778	39,224	41,580	32,512	32,512	(X)
Offices of chiropractors	62131	7,907	8,324	8,661	7,576	7,576	(X)
Offices of optometrists	62132	7,454	7,932	8,612	7,941	7,941	(X)
Offices of PT/OT/speech therapy & audiology [3]	62134	10,173	9,788	9,807	8,531	8,531	(X)
Outpatient care centers	6214	52,447	55,943	58,929	58,271	23,611	34,660
Medical & diagnostic laboratories	6215	19,236	20,385	23,196	22,215	22,215	(X)
Home health care services	6216	31,942	30,649	29,977	28,431	18,581	9,851
Other ambulatory health care services	6219	12,321	12,605	13,363	11,568	6,191	5,377
Hospitals	622	397,373	413,035	430,329	430,329	44,847	385,482
General medical & surgical hospitals	6221	(NA)	(NA)	(NA)	402,578	37,256	365,322
Psychiatric & substance abuse hospitals	6222	(NA)	(NA)	(NA)	14,944	4,406	10,537
Other specialty hospitals	6223	(NA)	(NA)	(NA)	12,807	3,185	9,622
Nursing and residential care facilities	623	100,138	102,336	108,607	107,174	63,186	43,988
Nursing care facilities	6231	(NA)	(NA)	(NA)	65,774	48,182	17,592
Residential mental retardation/health facilities [3]	6232	(NA)	(NA)	(NA)	14,353	4,203	10,151
Residential mental retardation facilities	62321	(NA)	(NA)	(NA)	9,301	2,834	6,467
Community care facilities for the elderly	6233	(NA)	(NA)	(NA)	21,257	10,107	11,150

NA Not available.   X Not applicable.   [1] Includes taxable nonemployer firms, not shown separately.   [2] Includes other kinds of business not shown separately.   [3] Offices of physical, occupational and speech therapists, and audiologists.
Source: U.S. Census Bureau, *Service Annual Survey, 2000*.

No. 143. Receipts for Selected Health Service Industries by Source of Revenue: 1999 and 2000

[In millions of dollars (190,049 represents $190,049,000,000). Based on the North American Industry Classification System (NAICS), see text, Section 15, Business Enterprise. Based on a sample of employer firms only and does not include nonemployer revenue]

Source of revenue	Offices of physicians (NAICS 6211)		Offices of dentists (NAICS 6212)		Hospitals (NAICS 622)		Nursing and residential care facilities (NAICS 623)	
	1999	2000	1999	2000	1999	2000	1999	2000
Total	**190,049**	**202,913**	**54,592**	**58,812**	**413,035**	**430,329**	**101,049**	**107,174**
Medicare	44,934	48,370	(S)	(S)	134,311	138,843	11,670	12,699
Medicaid	12,856	13,896	1,209	1,416	50,050	52,305	41,645	43,834
Other government [1]	1,842	2,025	(S)	(S)	21,648	22,687	5,988	7,157
Worker's compensation	6,880	7,419	(S)	(S)	4,614	4,720	(S)	(S)
Private insurance	90,466	97,193	28,395	30,232	143,402	155,206	6,193	6,231
Patient (out-of-pocket)	21,258	22,865	23,638	25,747	22,383	22,928	[2]25,290	[2]27,019
Other patient care sources, n.e.c [3]	6,928	7,299	472	(S)	13,237	10,622	3,095	3,300
Nonpatient care revenue	4,886	3,846	(S)	(S)	23,389	23,019	7,140	6,910

S Figure does not meet publication standards. [1] Veterans, National Institute of Health, Indian Affairs, etc. [2] Represents payment from patients and their families plus patients' assigned social security benefits. [3] N.e.c. represents not elsewhere classified.

Source: U.S. Census Bureau, *Service Annual Survey: 2000.*

No. 144. Employment in the Health Service Industries: 1980 to 2001

[In thousands (5,278 represents 5,278,000). See headnote Table 603]

Industry	1987 SIC code [1]	1980	1990	1995	1999	2000	2001
Health services [2]	80	**5,278**	**7,814**	**9,230**	**9,977**	**10,095**	**10,344**
Offices and clinics of MDs	801	802	1,338	1,609	1,875	1,924	1,979
Offices and clinics of dentists	802	(NA)	513	592	667	686	703
Offices and clinics of other practitioners	804	96	277	397	441	439	451
Nursing and personal care facilities	805	997	1,415	1,691	1,786	1,796	1,823
Skilled nursing care facilities	8051	(NA)	989	1,253	1,364	1,366	1,386
Intermediate care facilities	8052	(NA)	200	211	203	206	210
Other, n.e.c [3]	8050	(NA)	227	227	219	224	227
Hospitals	806	2,750	3,549	3,772	3,974	3,990	4,095
General medical and surgical hospitals	8062	(NA)	3,268	3,474	3,674	3,689	3,776
Psychiatric hospitals	8063	(NA)	104	91	75	74	76
Specialty hospitals, exc. psychiatric	8069	(NA)	176	208	224	228	242
Medical and dental laboratories	807	(NA)	166	190	203	209	216
Home health care services	808	(NA)	291	629	636	643	650

NA Not available. [1] Based on the 1987 Standard Industrial Classification code; see text, Section 15, Business Enterprise. [2] Includes other industries not shown separately. [3] N.e.c. means not elsewhere classified.

Source: U.S. Bureau of Labor Statistics, *Employment and Earnings,* monthly, March and June issues.

No. 145. Registered Nurses by Employment Status: 1996 and 2000

[As of March (2,559 represents 2,559,000). Based on a sample and subject to sampling variability; see source for details]

Age, race, and Hispanic-origin status	Total (1,000)	Employed in nursing		Not employed in nursing (1,000)
		Number (1,000)	Percent distribution	
1996	2,559	2,116	100.0	443
2000	**2,697**	**2,202**	**100.0**	**495**
Less than 25 years	66	65	2.9	2
25 to 29 years	177	166	7.5	11
30 to 34 years	248	225	10.2	24
35 to 39 years	360	316	14.4	44
40 to 44 years	464	409	18.6	55
45 to 49 years	465	406	18.5	58
50 to 54 years	342	288	13.1	55
55 to 59 years	238	180	8.2	58
60 to 64 years	156	87	4.0	69
65 years and over	154	41	1.9	113
Unknown age	25	19	0.8	6
White non-Hispanic	2,334	1,891	85.9	443
Black non-Hispanic	133	113	5.1	20
Asian non-Hispanic	93	83	3.8	11
Native Hawaiian/Pacific Islander	6	6	0.3	1
American Indian/Alaska Native	13	11	0.5	2
Hispanic [1]	55	48	2.2	7
Two or more races non-Hispanic	33	27	1.2	6
Unknown race/ethnic	29	23	1.1	6

[1] Persons of Hispanic origin may be of any race.

Source: U.S. Dept. of Health and Human Services, Health Resources and Services Administration, *The Registered Nurse Population, March 2000,* September 2001.

No. 146. Physicians by Selected Activity: 1980 to 2000

[In thousands (467.7 represents 467,700). As of Dec. 31, except 1990 as of Jan. 1, and as noted. Includes Puerto Rico and outlying areas]

Activity	1980	1990	1995	1997	1998	1999	2000
Doctors of medicine, total	**467.7**	**615.4**	**720.3**	**756.7**	**777.9**	**797.6**	**813.8**
Professionally active	435.5	560.0	646.0	684.6	707.0	720.9	737.5
Place of medical education:							
U.S. medical graduates	343.6	437.2	492.2	519.7	533.4	542.2	554.2
Foreign medical graduates [1]	91.8	122.8	153.8	164.9	173.7	178.7	183.4
Sex: Male	386.7	463.9	505.9	527.0	538.9	544.1	551.7
Female	48.7	96.1	140.1	157.7	168.1	176.7	185.8
Active nonfederal	417.7	539.5	624.9	665.2	688.0	702.8	718.1
Patient care	361.9	487.8	564.1	603.7	606.4	610.7	631.4
Office-based practice	271.3	359.9	427.3	458.2	468.8	473.2	490.4
General and family practice	47.8	57.6	59.9	62.0	64.6	66.2	67.5
Cardiovascular diseases	6.7	10.7	13.7	15.0	15.1	15.6	16.3
Dermatology	4.4	6.0	7.0	7.4	7.6	7.8	8.0
Gastroenterology	2.7	5.2	7.3	7.9	7.9	8.2	8.5
Internal medicine	40.5	57.8	72.6	81.4	83.3	84.6	88.7
Pediatrics	17.4	26.5	33.9	36.8	38.4	40.5	42.2
Pulmonary diseases	2.0	3.7	5.0	5.0	4.9	5.7	6.1
General surgery	22.4	24.5	24.1	27.9	27.5	26.8	24.5
Obstetrics and gynecology	19.5	25.5	29.1	30.1	31.2	31.1	31.7
Ophthalmology	10.6	13.1	14.6	15.1	15.6	15.2	15.6
Orthopedic surgery	10.7	14.2	17.1	18.5	18.5	17.0	17.4
Otolaryngology	5.3	6.4	7.1	7.4	7.5	7.3	7.6
Plastic surgery	2.4	3.8	4.6	5.3	5.3	5.1	5.3
Urological surgery	6.2	7.4	8.0	8.4	8.4	8.2	8.5
Anesthesiology	11.3	17.8	23.8	25.6	26.2	26.6	27.6
Diagnostic radiology	4.2	9.8	12.8	14.1	14.2	14.3	14.6
Emergency medicine	(NA)	8.4	11.7	12.5	13.3	13.9	14.5
Neurology	3.2	5.6	7.6	8.2	8.5	8.1	8.6
Pathology, anatomical/clinical	6.0	7.3	9.0	10.2	10.0	10.1	10.3
Psychiatry	15.9	20.0	23.3	24.5	25.0	24.4	25.0
Other specialty	31.9	28.8	35.0	35.0	35.9	36.4	42.0
Hospital-based practice	90.6	127.9	136.8	145.3	137.6	137.2	141.0
Residents and interns [2]	59.6	89.9	93.7	95.8	92.3	92.5	95.1
Full-time hospital staff	31.0	38.0	43.1	49.5	45.3	44.8	45.9
Other professional activity [3]	35.2	39.0	40.3	41.5	41.6	41.2	41.6
Not classified	20.6	12.7	20.6	20.0	40.0	50.9	45.1
Federal	17.8	20.5	21.1	19.4	19.0	18.1	19.4
Patient care	14.6	16.1	18.1	16.9	15.3	14.7	16.0
Other professional activity [3]	3.2	4.4	3.0	2.4	3.7	3.4	3.4
Inactive/unknown address	32.1	55.4	74.3	72.1	70.8	76.8	76.3
Doctors of osteopathy [4]	**18.8**	**30.9**	**35.7**	**38.9**	**40.8**	**43.5**	**44.9**

NA Not available. [1] Foreign medical graduates received their medical education in schools outside the United States and Canada. [2] Includes clinical fellows. [3] Includes medical teaching, administration, research, and other. [4] As of July. Total DOs. Data from American Osteopathic Association, Chicago, IL.
Source: Except as noted, American Medical Association, Chicago, IL, *Physician Characteristics and Distribution in the U.S.*, annual (copyright).

No. 147. Active Nonfederal Physicians, 2000, and Nurses, 1999 by State

[As of December. Excludes doctors of osteopathy, federally-employed persons, and physicians with addresses unknown. Includes all physicians not classified according to activity status]

State	Physicians Total	Physicians Rate [1]	Nurses Total	Nurses Rate [1]	State	Physicians Total	Physicians Rate [1]	Nurses Total	Nurses Rate [1]
United States	**708,463**	**251**	**2,201,810**	**789**	Missouri	12,849	229	53,730	966
Alabama	8,929	201	34,070	769	Montana	1,814	201	7,330	817
Alaska	1,124	179	4,910	786	Nebraska	3,815	223	16,400	962
Arizona	10,060	195	32,220	641	Nevada	3,480	172	10,380	537
Arkansas	5,027	188	18,750	707	New Hampshire	2,945	238	11,320	926
California	84,361	248	184,330	550	New Jersey	25,121	298	67,280	805
Colorado	10,096	234	31,700	750	New Mexico	3,830	210	11,930	660
Connecticut	11,974	351	32,070	947	New York	72,181	380	160,010	847
Delaware	1,847	235	7,340	947	North Carolina	18,634	231	69,060	869
District of Columbia	3,857	675	9,580	1,680	North Dakota	1,412	220	7,040	1,093
Florida	37,635	234	125,440	796	Ohio	27,125	239	100,140	883
Georgia	16,950	206	55,880	695	Oklahoma	5,653	164	21,910	637
Hawaii	3,215	265	8,520	704	Oregon	7,796	227	27,120	799
Idaho	2,004	154	8,230	645	Pennsylvania	35,631	290	124,000	1,011
Illinois	32,669	263	101,660	823	Rhode Island	3,448	328	11,540	1,109
Indiana	12,076	198	46,240	765	South Carolina	8,581	213	29,230	735
Iowa	5,105	174	31,020	1,063	South Dakota	1,440	191	8,510	1,134
Kansas	5,565	207	23,780	888	Tennessee	13,798	242	49,630	880
Kentucky	8,482	210	33,660	838	Texas	42,027	201	126,440	615
Louisiana	11,173	250	37,380	838	Utah	4,453	199	13,230	600
Maine	3,077	241	13,070	1,032	Vermont	1,996	327	5,830	964
Maryland	19,798	373	45,320	002	Virginia	17,415	245	50,360	719
Massachusetts	26,500	417	75,800	1,200	Washington	14,158	240	43,480	744
Michigan	22,747	229	79,350	802	West Virginia	3,929	217	15,520	857
Minnesota	12,668	257	47,100	966	Wisconsin	12,461	232	47,900	898
Mississippi	4,685	164	21,340	754	Wyoming	847	171	3,850	783

[1] Per 100,000 resident population. Based on U.S. Census Bureau estimates as of July 1.
Source: Physicians: American Medical Association, Chicago, IL, *Physician Characteristics and Distribution in the U.S.*, annual (copyright); Nurses: U.S. Dept. of Health and Human Services, Health Resources and Services Administration, unpublished data.

No. 148. Health Professions—Practitioners and Schools: 1990 to 2000

[(**540 represents 540,000**). Data on the number of schools and total enrollment are reported as of the beginning of the academic year; all other school data are reported as of the end of the academic year. Data are based on reporting by health professions schools]

Year	Medi-cine	Oste-opathy	Registered nursing Total	Bacca-laureate	Associ-ate degree	Diploma	Licensed practi-cal nursing	Den-tistry [1]	Optom-etry	Phar-macy
ACTIVE PERSONNEL (1,000)										
1990	540	28	1,790	[2]682	[3]1,107	([3])	(NA)	148	26	162
1995	637	36	2,116	[2]881	[3]1,235	([3])	(NA)	159	29	182
1998	707	41	2,180	(NA)	(NA)	(NA)	(NA)	163	(NA)	(NA)
1999	711	43	2,202	(NA)	(NA)	(NA)	(NA)	165	(NA)	(NA)
NUMBER OF SCHOOLS [4]										
1990	126	15	1,470	489	829	152	1,154	58	17	74
1995	125	16	1,516	521	876	119	(NA)	54	17	75
1998	125	19	(NA)	(NA)	(NA)	(NA)	(NA)	55	17	81
1999	125	19	(NA)	(NA)	(NA)	(NA)	(NA)	55	17	81
2000	125	19	(NA)	(NA)	(NA)	(NA)	(NA)	55	17	82
TOTAL ENROLLMENT										
1990	65,016	6,615	201,458	74,865	106,175	20,418	46,720	16,412	4,723	23,013
1995	67,072	8,146	268,350	112,659	135,895	19,796	59,428	16,353	5,201	27,667
1998	66,900	9,434	(NA)	(NA)	(NA)	(NA)	(NA)	16,926	(NA)	28,345
1999	66,517	9,882	(NA)	(NA)	(NA)	(NA)	(NA)	(NA)	5,313	28,646
2000	66,444	(NA)	(NA)	(NA)	(NA)	(NA)	(NA)	(NA)	(NA)	(NA)
GRADUATES										
1990	15,398	1,529	66,088	18,571	42,318	5,199	35,417	4,233	1,115	6,956
1995	15,888	1,843	97,052	31,254	58,749	7,049	44,234	3,908	1,219	7,837
1998	16,314	2,096	(NA)	(NA)	(NA)	(NA)	(NA)	4,041	1,237	7,400
1999	15,996	2,169	(NA)	(NA)	(NA)	(NA)	(NA)	4,095	(NA)	7,141
2000	15,704	2,304	(NA)	(NA)	(NA)	(NA)	(NA)	(NA)	(NA)	7,260

NA Not available.   [1] Personnel data exclude dentists in military service, U.S. Public Health Service, and U.S. Dept. of Veterans Affairs.   [2] Includes nurses with advanced degrees.   [3] Diploma nurses included with associate degree nurses.   [4] Some nursing schools offer more than one type of program. Numbers shown for nursing are number of nursing programs.

Source: U.S. Dept. of Health and Human Services, Bureau of Health Professions, unpublished data; American Medical Association, Chicago, IL, *Physician Characteristics and Distribution in the U.S.*, annual; and American Association of Colleges of Osteopathic Medicine, Rockville, MD, Annual Statistical Report.

No. 149. Percent Distribution of Number of Visits to Health Care Professionals by Selected Characteristics: 1999 and 2000

[Covers ambulatory visits to doctor's offices and emergency departments, and home health care visits during a 12-month period. Based on the redesigned National Health Interview Survey, a sample survey of the civilian noninstitutionalized population]

Characteristic	None 1999	None 2000	1-3 visits 1999	1-3 visits 2000	4-9 visits 1999	4-9 visits 2000	10 or more visits 1999	10 or more visits 2000
All persons [1]	17.5	16.6	45.8	45.4	23.3	24.7	13.4	13.3
Age:								
Under 6 years	5.9	6.3	45.9	44.3	36.8	38.3	11.3	11.2
6-17 years	15.5	15.1	58.5	58.2	19.4	20.7	6.7	6.0
18-44 years	24.2	23.2	45.8	45.3	17.8	19.2	12.3	12.2
45-64 years	16.9	15.0	42.4	43.4	25.0	25.7	15.7	15.8
65-74 years	8.6	9.0	36.9	34.5	33.2	34.4	21.3	22.1
75 years and over	7.2	5.8	31.1	29.3	35.1	39.3	26.6	25.6
Sex: [1]								
Male	23.1	21.5	45.5	46.0	20.6	22.4	10.8	10.1
Female	12.0	11.9	46.1	44.8	25.9	27.0	15.9	16.4
Race: [1][2]								
White only	16.9	16.0	45.7	45.1	23.8	25.3	13.6	13.7
Black or African American only	18.4	17.3	46.1	46.7	22.1	23.4	13.5	12.6
American Indian or Alaska Native only	20.7	21.2	35.6	42.9	25.6	20.0	18.1	15.8
Asian only	23.1	20.2	47.3	49.2	19.4	20.9	10.2	9.7
Two or more races	15.2	12.1	40.8	41.6	22.2	28.3	21.8	17.9
Race and Hispanic origin: [1]								
White, non-Hispanic	15.5	14.5	45.9	45.4	24.5	26.0	14.1	14.1
Black, non-Hispanic	18.3	17.2	46.1	46.9	22.1	23.4	13.5	12.6
Hispanic	26.2	26.5	44.3	41.8	19.2	20.0	10.3	11.7

[1] Estimates are age adjusted to the year 2000 standard using six age groups: Under 18 years, 18-44 years, 45-54 years, 55-64 years, 65-74 years, and 75 years and over.   [2] Estimates by race and Hispanic origin are tabulated using the 1997 Standards for Federal data on race and ethnicity. Estimates for specific race groups are shown when they meet requirements for statistical reliability and confidentiality. The categories "White only," "Black or African American only," "American Indian and Alaska Native (AI/AN) only," and "Asian only" include persons who reported only one racial group; and the category "two or more races" includes persons who reported more than one of the five racial groups in the 1997 Standards or one of the five racial groups and "Some other race."

Source: U.S. National Center for Health Statistics, *Health, United States, 2002.*

No. 150. Medical Practice Characteristics by Selected Specialty: 1985 to 1999

[Dollar figures in thousands (112.2 represents $112,200). Based on a sample telephone survey of nonfederal office and hospital based patient care physicians, excluding residents. For details, see source. For definition of mean, see Guide to Tabular Presentation]

Specialty	1985	1990	1995	1996	1997	1998	1999
MEAN PATIENT VISITS PER WEEK							
All physicians [1]	117.1	120.9	107.6	109.4	110.6	105.0	106.7
General/Family practice	138.1	146.0	133.7	133.1	130.1	125.0	122.9
Internal medicine	105.2	112.0	99.7	104.7	106.4	102.8	103.0
Surgery	108.2	107.6	97.1	95.1	99.3	93.5	95.8
Pediatrics	130.8	134.0	125.9	121.1	125.5	110.9	120.5
Obstetrics/Gynecology	112.0	120.0	94.0	104.2	103.8	99.3	101.8
MEAN HOURS IN PATIENT CARE PER WEEK							
All physicians [1]	51.3	53.3	51.3	53.4	53.2	51.7	51.6
General/Family practice	53.6	55.0	52.9	53.5	53.1	51.3	50.6
Internal medicine	52.4	55.7	53.9	57.2	56.0	54.3	54.2
Surgery	51.2	53.1	53.2	54.2	55.0	51.7	53.3
Pediatrics	50.6	52.4	50.4	51.0	51.6	48.6	49.5
Obstetrics/Gynecology	56.9	60.4	54.6	60.5	59.9	59.9	59.0
MEAN NET INCOME							
All physicians [1]	112.2	164.3	195.5	199.0	199.6	194.4	(NA)
General/Family practice	77.9	102.7	131.2	139.1	140.9	142.5	(NA)
Internal medicine	102.0	152.5	185.7	185.7	193.9	182.1	(NA)
Surgery	155.0	236.4	269.4	275.2	261.4	268.2	(NA)
Pediatrics	76.2	106.5	140.5	140.6	143.5	139.6	(NA)
Obstetrics/Gynecology	124.3	207.3	244.3	231.0	228.7	214.4	(NA)
MEAN LIABILITY PREMIUM							
All physicians [1]	10.5	14.5	15.0	14.1	14.2	16.8	(NA)
General/Family practice	6.8	7.8	9.0	8.4	12.0	10.9	(NA)
Internal medicine	5.8	9.2	9.4	8.9	9.4	16.5	(NA)
Surgery	16.6	22.8	23.3	21.7	19.7	22.8	(NA)
Pediatrics	4.7	7.8	7.9	8.3	12.3	9.0	(NA)
Obstetrics/Gynecology	23.5	34.3	38.6	35.2	33.0	35.8	(NA)

NA Not available. [1] Includes other specialties not shown separately.
Source: American Medical Association, Chicago IL, *Physician Socioeconomic Statistics, 1999-2000* (copyright) and *Physician Socioeconomic Statistics, 2000-2002* (copyright).

No. 151. Ambulatory Care Visits to Physicians' Offices and Hospital Outpatient and Emergency Departments: 2000

[1,014.8 represents 1,014,800,000. Based on the annual National Ambulatory Medical Care Survey and National Hospital Ambulatory Medical Care Survey and subject to sampling error; see source for details. For composition of regions, see map inside front cover]

Characteristic	Number of visits (mil.)				Visits per 100 persons			
	Total	Physician offices	Outpatient dept.	Emergency dept.	Total	Physician offices	Outpatient dept.	Emergency dept.
Total	**1,014.8**	**823.5**	**83.3**	**108.0**	**370**	**300**	**30**	**39**
Age:								
Under 15 years old	184.1	142.5	18.2	23.4	305	236	30	39
15 to 24 years old	93.8	67.2	9.0	17.7	244	174	23	46
25 to 44 years old	250.0	196.8	20.8	32.4	305	240	25	39
45 to 64 years old	255.9	216.8	20.8	18.3	422	358	34	30
65 to 74 years old	116.5	102.4	7.5	6.5	656	577	42	37
75 years old and over	114.5	97.8	7.0	9.7	766	654	47	65
Sex:								
Male	419.9	335.3	33.7	50.9	314	251	25	38
Female	595.0	488.2	49.6	57.1	424	348	35	41
Race:								
White	856.9	710.8	63.0	83.1	381	316	28	37
Black/African-American	115.1	76.0	17.2	21.9	324	214	48	62
Asian/Native Hawaiian/Other Pacific Islander	37.7	32.9	2.6	2.2	335	292	23	20
American Indian/Alaska Native	2.9	2.0	[1]0.3	0.6	118	79	[1]13	25
More than one race reported	2.2	1.9	([1])	([1])	(NA)	(NA)	(NA)	(NA)
Region:								
Northeast	225.8	183.0	23.1	19.6	432	351	44	38
Midwest	257.5	206.7	23.7	27.1	381	306	35	40
South	318.9	251.3	25.2	42.4	329	259	26	44
West	212.7	182.5	11.3	18.9	371	318	20	33
Primary source of payment:								
Private insurance	542.6	467.0	32.1	43.5	(X)	(X)	(X)	(X)
Medicare	192.8	162.5	14.1	16.2	(X)	(X)	(X)	(X)
Medicaid	107.2	70.8	18.4	18.0	(X)	(X)	(X)	(X)
Worker's compensation	18.6	14.5	[1]1.1	3.0	(X)	(X)	(X)	(X)
Self pay	71.1	44.7	7.6	18.8	(X)	(X)	(X)	(X)
No charge	7.2	6.0	[1]0.8	[1]0.4	(X)	(X)	(X)	(X)
Other	38.5	30.0	5.7	2.8	(X)	(X)	(X)	(X)
Unknown	36.9	28.0	3.5	5.4	(X)	(X)	(X)	(X)

NA Not available. X Not applicable. [1] Figures do not meet standard of reliability or precision.
Source: U.S. National Center for Health Statistics, *Advance Data*, Nos. 326, 327, and 328; April 22, 2002; June 4, 2002; and June 5, 2002.

108   Health and Nutrition

No. 152. Visits to Office-Based Physicians and Hospital Outpatient Departments by Diagnosis: 1995 and 2000

[307.0 represents 307,000,000. See headnote, Table 151]

Leading diagnoses [1]	Number (mil.) 1995	2000	Rate per 1,000 persons [2] 1995	2000	Leading diagnoses [1]	Number (mil.) 1995	2000	Rate per 1,000 persons [2] 1995	2000
MALE					**FEMALE**				
All ages	307.0	369.0	2,406	2,760	**All ages**	457.3	537.8	3,404	3,829
Under 15 years old [3]	75.2	85.3	2,471	2,765	Under 15 years old [3]	71.4	75.4	2,457	2,556
Routine infant or child health check	10.4	17.9	341	580	Routine infant or child health check	10.2	17.5	351	593
Acute respiratory infections [4]	7.7	8.5	252	276	Acute respiratory infections [4]	9.1	8.1	313	276
Otitis media [5]	9.8	7.1	322	231	Otitis media [5]	8.5	6.6	293	222
Attention deficit disorder	1.3	3.4	41	110	Acute pharyngitis	2.8	2.3	95	78
Asthma	1.8	3.1	59	101	Chronic sinusitis	1.5	2.2	52	74
15 to 44 years old [3]	90.8	98.9	1,540	1,660	15 to 44 years old [3]	173.9	194.8	2,888	3,199
General medical examination	4.5	3.9	76	66	Normal pregnancy	22.2	24.5	369	402
Acute respiratory infections [4]	3.7	3.6	63	60	General medical examination	7.4	6.6	123	108
Essential hypertension	1.8	2.7	31	46	Complications of pregnancy, childbirth, and the puerperium	2.0	6.2	43	102
Psychoses, excluding major depressive disorder	1.2	2.5	20	43	Gynecological examination	2.6	6.1	44	100
Diabetes mellitus	1.0	2.0	17	34	Acute respiratory infections [4]	6.4	6.0	107	98
45 to 64 years old [3]	69.8	96.5	2,795	3,294	45 to 64 years old [3]	104.6	141.0	3,911	4,511
Essential hypertension	4.3	6.8	172	233	Essential hypertension	5.2	8.3	193	264
Diabetes mellitus	2.7	5.8	109	199	Malignant neoplasms	3.2	5.7	120	184
Malignant neoplasms	2.2	2.7	88	93	Diabetes mellitus	3.5	5.6	131	181
General medical examination	1.3	2.3	53	79	Follow-up examination	1.2	3.4	45	109
Ischemic heart disease	2.3	2.2	93	77	Gynecological examination	1.0	3.1	36	100
65 years old and over [3]	71.2	88.2	5,405	6,340	65 years old and over [3]	107.5	126.6	5,861	6,736
Malignant neoplasms	4.8	7.1	365	507	Essential hypertension	7.7	11.8	421	628
Essential hypertension	3.8	6.6	286	478	Diabetes mellitus	3.8	6.0	206	318
Ischemic heart disease	3.3	4.9	252	349	Malignant neoplasms	4.3	5.9	234	312
Diabetes mellitus	2.7	4.8	209	344	Cataract	4.6	4.0	254	212
Heart disease, excluding ischemic	3.1	4.1	237	296	Heart disease, excluding ischemic	4.2	3.6	227	194

[1] Based on the International Classification of Diseases, 9th Revision, Clinical Modification, (ICD-9-CM).   [2] Based on U.S. Census Bureau estimated civilian population as of July 1.   [3] Includes other first-listed diagnoses, not shown separately.   [4] Excluding pharyngitis.   [5] Includes Eustachian tube disorders.

Source: U.S. National Center for Health Statistics, *Advance Data*, Nos. 327 and 328, June 4, 2002 and June 5, 2002.

No. 153. Visits to Hospital Emergency Departments by Diagnosis: 2000

[50,887 represents 50,887,000. See headnote, Table 151]

Leading diagnoses [1]	Number (1,000)	Rate per 1,000 persons [2]	Leading diagnoses [1]	Number (1,000)	Rate per 1,000 persons [2]
MALE			**FEMALE**		
All ages	50,887	381	**All ages**	57,130	407
Under 15 years old [3]	13,255	429	Under 15 years old [3]	10,135	344
Acute upper respiratory infections [4]	1,272	41	Acute respiratory infections [4]	1,050	36
Otitis media [5]	1,080	35	Otitis media [5]	909	31
Open wound of head	964	31	Contusions with intact skin surfaces	618	21
Contusions with intact skin surfaces	700	23	Open wound of head	378	13
Pyrexia of unknown origin	471	15	Pyrexia of unknown origin	377	13
15 to 44 years old [3]	22,545	378	15 to 44 years old [3]	27,511	452
Contusions with intact skin surfaces	1,200	20	Contusions with intact skin surfaces	1,329	22
Open wound, excluding head, hand, and fingers	1,043	18	Abdominal pain	1,238	20
Strains and sprains of neck and back	1,006	17	Complications of pregnancy, childbirth, and the puerperium	1,138	19
Open wound of hand and fingers	853	14	Sprains and strains of neck and back	991	16
Open wound of head	694	12	Acute respiratory infections [4]	821	13
45 to 64 years old [3]	8,684	296	45 to 64 years old [3]	9,655	309
Chest pain	583	20	Chest pain	666	21
Contusions with intact skin surfaces	346	12	Abdominal pain	374	12
Abdominal pain	249	8	Contusions with intact skin surfaces	293	9
Ischemic heart disease	246	8	Sprains and strains of neck and back	288	9
Open wound of hand and fingers	242	8	Chronic and unspecified bronchitis	278	9
65 years old and over [3]	6,403	460	65 years old and over [3]	9,829	523
Heart disease, excluding ischemic	471	34	Heart disease, excluding ischemic	539	29
Chest pain	370	27	Chest pain	530	28
Ischemic heart disease	255	18	Contusions with intact skin surfaces	395	21
Abdominal pain	197	14	Abdominal pain	391	21
Pneumonia	187	13	Cerebrovascular disease	328	17

[1] Based on the International Classification of Diseases, 9th Revision, Clinical Modification, (ICD-9-CM).   [2] Based on U.S. Census Bureau estimated civilian population as of July 1.   [3] Includes other first-listed diagnoses, not shown separately.   [4] Excluding pharyngitis.   [5] Includes Eustachian tube disorders.

Source: U.S. National Center for Health Statistics, *Advance Data*, No. 326, April 22, 2002.

No. 154. Hospitals—Summary Characteristics: 1980 to 2000

[For beds, 1,365 represents 1,365,000. Covers hospitals accepted for registration by the American Hospital Association; see text, this section. Short-term hospitals have an average patient stay of less than 30 days; long-term, an average stay of longer duration. Special hospitals include obstetrics and gynecology; eye, ear, nose, and throat; rehabilitation; orthopedic; and chronic and other special hospitals except psychiatric, tuberculosis, alcoholism, and chemical dependency hospitals]

Item	1980	1985	1990	1995	1996	1997	1998	1999	2000
Number:									
All hospitals	6,965	6,872	6,649	6,291	6,201	6,097	6,021	5,890	5,810
With 100 beds or more	3,755	3,805	3,620	3,376	3,347	3,267	3,216	3,140	3,102
Nonfederal [1]	6,606	6,529	6,312	5,992	5,911	5,812	5,746	5,626	5,565
Community hospitals [2]	5,830	5,732	5,384	5,194	5,134	5,057	5,015	4,956	4,915
Nongovernmental nonprofit	3,322	3,349	3,191	3,092	3,045	3,000	3,026	3,012	3,003
For profit	730	805	749	752	759	797	771	747	749
State and local government	1,778	1,578	1,444	1,350	1,330	1,260	1,218	1,197	1,163
Long-term general and special	157	128	131	112	112	125	125	129	131
Psychiatric	534	610	757	657	636	601	579	516	496
Tuberculosis	11	7	4	3	3	4	3	4	4
Federal	359	343	337	299	290	285	275	264	245
Beds (1,000):									
All hospitals [3]	1,365	1,318	1,213	1,081	1,062	1,035	1,013	994	984
Rate per 1,000 population [4]	6.0	5.5	4.9	4.1	3.9	3.8	3.7	3.6	3.5
Beds per hospital	196	190	182	172	171	170	168	169	169
Nonfederal [1]	1,248	1,197	1,113	1,004	989	973	956	939	931
Community hospitals [2]	988	1,001	927	873	862	853	840	830	824
Rate per 1,000 population [4]	4.3	4.2	3.7	3.3	3.2	3.1	3.0	3.0	2.9
Nongovernmental nonprofit	692	707	657	610	598	591	588	587	583
For profit	87	104	102	106	109	115	113	107	110
State and local government	209	189	169	157	155	148	139	136	131
Long-term general and special	39	31	25	19	19	17	18	20	18
Psychiatric	215	169	158	110	106	100	95	87	87
Tuberculosis	2	1	(Z)	(Z)	(Z)	(Z)	(Z)	(Z)	(Z)
Federal	117	112	98	78	73	62	57	55	53
Average daily census (1,000):									
All hospitals	1,060	910	844	710	685	673	662	657	650
Community hospitals [2]	747	649	619	548	531	528	525	526	526
Nongovernmental nonprofit	542	476	455	393	379	376	377	381	382
For profit	57	54	54	55	56	60	60	58	61
State and local government	149	119	111	100	96	92	87	86	83
Expenses (bil. dol.): [5]									
All hospitals	91.9	153.3	234.9	320.3	330.5	342.3	355.5	372.9	395.4
Nonfederal [1]	84.0	141.0	219.6	300.0	308.3	319.6	332.9	349.2	371.5
Community hospitals [2]	76.9	130.5	203.7	285.6	293.8	305.8	318.8	335.2	356.6
Nongovernmental nonprofit	55.8	96.1	150.7	209.6	216.0	225.3	238.0	251.5	267.1
For profit	5.8	11.5	18.8	26.7	28.4	31.2	31.7	31.2	35.0
State and local government	15.2	22.9	34.2	49.3	49.4	49.3	49.1	52.5	54.5
Long-term general and special	1.2	1.9	2.7	2.2	2.3	2.5	2.6	2.8	2.8
Psychiatric	5.8	8.3	12.9	11.7	12.0	11.0	11.2	11.0	11.9
Tuberculosis	0.1	0.1	0.1	0.4	(Z)	0.1	(Z)	(Z)	(Z)
Federal	7.9	12.3	15.2	20.2	22.3	22.7	22.6	23.7	23.9
Personnel (1,000): [6]									
All hospitals	3,492	3,625	4,063	4,273	4,276	4,333	4,407	4,369	4,454
Nonfederal [1]	3,213	3,326	3,760	3,971	3,981	4,036	4,071	4,074	4,157
Community hospitals [2]	2,873	2,997	3,420	3,714	3,725	3,790	3,831	3,838	3,911
Nongovernmental nonprofit	2,086	2,216	2,533	2,702	2,711	2,765	2,834	2,862	2,919
For profit	189	221	273	343	359	385	383	362	378
State and local government	598	561	614	670	654	640	614	614	614
Long-term general and special	56	58	55	38	40	37	37	42	41
Psychiatric	275	263	280	215	212	204	198	191	200
Tuberculosis	3	2	1	1	1	1	1	1	1
Federal	279	299	303	301	295	296	336	295	297
Outpatient visits (mil.)	263.0	282.1	368.2	483.2	505.5	520.6	545.5	573.5	592.7
Emergency	82.0	80.1	92.8	99.9	97.6	97.4	99.0	103.8	106.9

Z Less than 500 beds or $50 million. [1] Includes hospital units of institutions. [2] Short term (average length of stay less than 30 days) general and special (e.g., obstetrics and gynecology; eye, ear, nose and throat; rehabilitation etc. except psychiatric, tuberculosis, alcoholism and chemical dependency). Excludes hospital units of institutions. [3] Beginning 1990, number of beds at end of reporting period; prior years, average number in 12 month period. [4] Based on Census Bureau estimated resident population as of July 1. Estimates reflect revisions based on the 2000 Census of Population. [5] Excludes new construction. [6] Includes full-time equivalents of part-time personnel.

Source: Health Forum, An American Hospital Association Company, Chicago, IL, *Hospital Statistics 2002 Edition*, and prior years (copyright).

U.S. Census Bureau, Statistical Abstract of the United States: 2002

No. 155. Average Cost to Community Hospitals Per Patient: 1980 to 2000

[In dollars, except percent. Covers nonfederal short-term general or special hospitals (excluding psychiatric or tuberculosis hospitals and hospital units of institutions). Total cost per patient based on total hospital expenses (payroll, employee benefits, professional fees, supplies, etc.). Data have been adjusted for outpatient visits]

Type of expense and hospital	1980	1985	1990	1994	1995	1996	1997	1998	1999	2000
Average cost per day, total......	245	460	687	931	968	1,006	1,033	1,067	1,103	1,149
Annual percent change [1].......	12.9	11.9	7.8	5.7	4.0	4.0	2.6	3.3	3.3	4.2
Nongovernmental nonprofit........	246	463	692	950	994	1,042	1,074	1,111	1,140	1,182
For profit....................	257	501	752	924	947	946	962	968	999	1,057
State and local government.......	239	433	635	859	878	903	914	949	1,007	1,064
Average cost per stay, total	1,851	3,245	4,947	6,230	6,216	6,225	6,262	6,386	6,512	6,649
Nongovernmental nonprofit	1,902	3,307	5,001	6,257	6,279	6,344	6,393	6,526	6,608	6,717
For profit...................	1,676	3,033	4,727	5,529	5,425	5,207	5,219	5,262	5,350	5,642
State and local government.......	1,750	3,106	4,838	6,513	6,445	6,419	6,475	6,612	6,923	7,106

[1] Change from immediate prior year.

Source: Health Forum, An American Hospital Association Company, Chicago, IL, *Hospital Statistics 2002 Edition* (copyright).

No. 156. Community Hospitals—States: 1990 to 2000

[For beds, 928.1 represents 928,100. For definition of community hospitals see footnote 2, Table 154]

State	Number of hospitals			Beds (1,000)			Patients admitted (1,000)		Average daily census [1] (1,000)		Outpatient visits (mil.)	
	1990	1995	2000	1990	1995	2000	1995	2000	1995	2000	1995	2000
United States ...	5,384	5,194	4,915	928.1	872.7	823.6	30,945	33,089	547.6	525.7	414.3	521.4
Alabama.........	120	115	108	18.6	18.3	16.4	642	680	10.7	9.8	6.4	8.0
Alaska..........	16	17	18	1.2	1.3	1.4	40	47	0.7	0.8	0.8	1.3
Arizona.........	61	61	61	9.9	9.9	10.9	427	539	5.6	6.8	4.0	5.3
Arkansas	86	85	83	10.9	10.1	9.8	342	368	6.0	5.7	3.6	4.4
California	445	424	389	80.5	75.0	72.7	3,029	3,315	45.0	47.8	39.5	44.9
Colorado.........	69	69	69	10.4	9.3	9.4	340	397	5.4	5.4	5.5	6.7
Connecticut.......	35	34	35	9.6	7.5	7.7	338	349	5.5	5.8	5.7	6.7
Delaware	8	8	5	2.0	1.9	1.8	81	83	1.5	1.4	1.4	1.5
District of Columbia .	11	12	11	4.5	3.8	3.3	154	129	2.7	2.5	1.2	1.3
Florida..........	224	212	202	50.7	49.7	51.2	1,772	2,119	29.4	31.0	16.9	21.8
Georgia	163	160	151	25.7	26.1	23.9	859	863	15.8	15.0	9.6	11.2
Hawaii	18	21	21	2.9	3.0	3.1	97	100	2.4	2.3	2.1	2.5
Idaho...........	43	41	42	3.2	3.4	3.5	104	123	1.8	1.8	1.7	2.2
Illinois	210	207	196	45.8	42.0	37.3	1,452	1,531	25.0	22.4	20.6	25.1
Indiana..........	113	115	109	21.8	19.4	19.2	699	700	11.3	10.8	11.8	14.1
Iowa	124	116	115	14.3	12.6	11.8	361	360	7.1	6.8	6.2	9.2
Kansas..........	138	132	129	11.8	10.8	10.8	291	310	5.8	5.7	4.0	5.3
Kentucky	107	104	105	15.9	15.1	14.8	534	582	9.0	9.1	6.1	8.7
Louisiana	140	130	123	19.1	19.1	17.5	622	654	10.6	9.8	8.0	10.0
Maine...........	39	39	37	4.5	4.0	3.7	142	147	2.6	2.4	2.5	3.2
Maryland	52	50	49	13.6	12.6	11.2	574	587	8.8	8.2	4.9	6.0
Massachusetts.....	101	96	80	21.7	18.9	16.6	751	740	13.0	11.7	13.5	16.7
Michigan.........	176	167	146	33.9	29.6	26.1	1,120	1,106	19.3	16.9	19.2	24.9
Minnesota........	152	142	135	19.4	17.4	16.7	496	571	11.3	11.2	5.7	7.3
Mississippi	103	97	95	12.9	12.6	13.6	388	425	7.6	8.0	3.2	3.7
Missouri	135	126	119	24.3	21.9	20.1	714	773	12.6	11.7	0.0	14.8
Montana,........	55	56	52	4.6	4.2	4.3	96	99	2.7	2.9	1.3	2.6
Nebraska	90	91	85	8.5	7.9	8.2	183	209	4.5	4.8	2.5	3.4
Nevada	21	20	22	3.4	3.6	3.8	149	199	2.2	2.7	1.4	2.2
New Hampshire....	27	29	28	3.5	3.4	2.9	110	111	2.1	1.7	1.8	2.8
New Jersey.......	95	92	80	28.9	29.9	25.3	1,068	1,074	21.4	17.3	12.8	16.3
New Mexico	37	36	35	4.2	3.7	3.5	156	174	2.1	2.0	2.5	3.1
New York	235	230	215	74.7	73.9	66.4	2,398	2,416	59.1	52.1	38.9	46.4
North Carolina.....	120	119	113	22.0	22.7	23.1	833	971	15.5	16.0	8.8	12.4
North Dakota......	50	43	42	4.4	4.2	3.9	89	89	2.7	2.3	1.3	1.7
Ohio	190	180	163	43.1	37.8	33.8	1,375	1,404	22.2	20.6	22.0	26.9
Oklahoma........	111	110	108	12.4	11.5	11.1	368	429	6.1	6.2	3.8	4.7
Oregon..........	70	64	59	8.1	7.2	6.6	296	330	3.8	3.9	5.8	7.3
Pennsylvania......	238	225	207	52.6	48.5	42.3	1,810	1,796	33.8	28.8	26.9	31.8
Rhode Island......	12	11	11	3.2	2.7	2.4	119	119	1.8	1.7	1.7	2.1
South Carolina.....	69	66	63	11.3	11.3	11.5	410	495	7.2	8.0	4.7	7.8
South Dakota	53	50	48	4.2	4.6	4.3	94	99	3.0	2.8	1.0	1.7
Tennessee	134	126	121	23.6	20.9	20.6	740	737	12.5	11.5	7.4	10.3
Texas...........	428	416	403	59.2	57.2	55.9	2,029	2,367	31.1	33.1	22.7	29.4
Utah	42	42	42	4.4	4.2	4.3	171	194	2.2	2.4	3.2	4.5
Vermont	15	14	14	1.7	1.8	1.7	55	52	1.3	1.1	1.0	1.2
Virginia	97	96	88	20.0	18.6	16.9	699	727	11.5	11.4	7.2	9.5
Washington.......	91	88	84	12.0	10.8	11.1	467	505	6.0	6.6	8.4	9.6
West Virginia......	59	59	57	8.4	8.1	8.0	271	288	4.9	4.8	4.0	5.2
Wisconsin........	129	127	118	18.6	17.0	15.3	550	558	10.2	9.1	8.2	10.9
Wyoming	27	25	24	2.2	2.0	1.9	43	48	1.1	1.1	0.7	0.9

[1] Inpatients receiving treatment each day; excludes newborn.

Source: Health Forum, An American Hospital Association Company, Chicago, IL, *Hospital Statistics 2002 Edition*, and prior years (copyright).

U.S. Census Bureau, Statistical Abstract of the United States: 2002

No. 157. Hospital Use Rates by Type of Hospital: 1980 to 2000

Type of hospital	1980	1985	1990	1995	1997	1998	1999	2000
Community hospitals: [1]								
Admissions per 1,000 population [2]	159	141	125	116	116	115	116	117
Admissions per bed.	37	33	34	35	37	38	39	40
Average length of stay [3] (days)	7.6	7.1	7.2	6.5	6.1	6.0	5.9	5.8
Outpatient visits per admission	5.6	6.5	9.7	13.4	14.3	14.9	15.3	15.8
Outpatient visits per 1,000 population [2]	890	919	1,207	1,556	1,651	1,719	1,775	1,848
Surgical operations (million [4])	18.8	20.1	21.9	23.2	24.2	25.3	26.3	26.1
Number per admission	0.5	0.6	0.7	0.7	0.8	0.8	0.8	0.8
Nonfederal psychiatric:								
Admissions per 1,000 population [2]	2.5	2.5	2.9	2.7	2.7	2.7	2.4	2.4
Days in hospital per 1,000 population [2]	295	224	190	122	107	101	94	93

[1] For definition of community hospitals, see footnote 2, Table 154.   [2] Based on U.S. Census Bureau estimated resident population as of July 1. Estimates reflect revisions based on the 2000 Census of Population.   [3] Number of inpatient days divided by number of admissions.   [4] 18.8 represents 18,800,000.

Source: Health Forum, An American Hospital Association Company, Chicago, IL, *Hospital Statistics 2002 Edition*, and prior years (copyright).

No. 158. Hospital Utilization Rates: 1980 to 2000

[37,832 represents 37,832,000. Represents estimates of inpatients discharged from noninstitutional, short-stay hospitals, exclusive of federal hospitals. Excludes newborn infants. Based on sample data collected from the National Hospital Discharge Survey, a sample survey of hospital records of patients discharged in year shown; subject to sampling variability. Comparisons beginning 1990 with data for 1980 should be made with caution as estimates of change may reflect improvements in the survey design rather than true changes in hospital use]

Item and sex	1980	1990	1994	1995	1996	1997	1998	1999	2000
Patients discharged (1,000).	37,832	30,788	30,843	30,722	30,545	30,914	31,827	32,132	31,706
Patients discharged per 1,000 persons, total [1]	168	122	117	116	114	114	117	117	114
Male	139	100	96	94	92	93	93	95	92
Female	194	143	138	136	135	135	139	138	135
Days of care per 1,000 persons, total [1] . .	1,217	784	674	620	597	582	589	581	560
Male	1,068	694	599	551	533	508	517	510	491
Female	1,356	869	745	686	657	653	658	649	627
Average stay (days).	7.3	6.4	5.7	5.4	5.2	5.1	5.1	5.0	4.9
Male	7.7	6.9	6.2	5.8	5.8	5.5	5.5	5.4	5.3
Female	7.0	6.1	5.4	5.0	4.9	4.8	4.7	4.7	4.6

[1] Based on U.S. Census Bureau estimated civilian population as of July 1. Estimates for 1980 do not reflect revisions based on the 1990 Census of Population. Beginning with 1997 data, rates are based on the U.S. Census Bureau estimates of the civilian population that have been adjusted for net underenumeration in the 1990 census. Since population estimates for the 2000 census were not available when this table was prepared, the 2000 population estimates were based on the 1990 census.

Source: U.S. National Center for Health Statistics, *Vital and Health Statistics*, Series 13; and unpublished data.

No. 159. Hospital Discharges and Days of Care: 1995 and 2000

[30,722 represents 30,722,000. See headnote, Table 158. For composition of regions, see map, inside front cover]

Age, race, and region	Discharges				Days of care per 1,000 persons [1]		Average stay (days)	
	Number (1,000)		Per 1,000 persons [1]					
	1995	2000	1995	2000	1995	2000	1995	2000
Total	30,722	31,706	116	114	620	560	5.4	4.9
Age:								
Under 1 year old	790	782	198	196	1,083	1,113	5.5	5.7
1 to 4 years old	744	703	46	45	153	145	3.3	3.2
5 to 14 years old	872	898	22	22	99	98	4.5	4.5
15 to 24 years old	2,943	2,819	80	72	271	241	3.4	3.3
25 to 34 years old	4,201	3,717	102	98	354	328	3.5	3.4
35 to 44 years old	3,449	3,433	81	76	381	327	4.7	4.3
45 to 64 years old	6,168	6,958	119	114	657	565	5.5	5.0
65 to 74 years old	4,832	4,678	260	260	1,685	1,469	6.5	5.7
75 years old and over. . .	6,724	7,718	459	468	3,248	2,891	7.1	6.2
Race:								
White.	19,951	19,165	91	84	491	414	5.4	4.9
Black.	3,887	3,572	113	98	658	520	5.8	5.3
Asian/Pacific Islander . . .	486	381	51	33	278	187	5.4	5.6
American Indian/Eskimo/ Aleut	107	142	46	56	240	279	5.2	5.0
Region:								
Northeast	7,051	7,103	136	136	858	770	6.3	5.7
Midwest	6,004	7,207	113	113	586	510	5.2	4.5
South	11,373	12,016	122	122	643	595	5.0	4.9
West	5,303	5,380	91	85	410	383	4.5	4.5

[1] Based on Census Bureau estimated civilian population that, beginning in 1997, has been adjusted for the net underenumeration in the 1990 Census of Population. Since population estimates for the 2000 census were not available when this table was prepared, the 2000 population estimates were based on the 1990 census.

Source: U.S. National Center for Health Statistics, *Vital and Health Statistics*, Series 13; and unpublished data.

No. 160. Hospital Discharges and Days of Care by Sex: 2000

[**12,514 represents 12,514,000.** Represents estimates of inpatients discharged from noninstitutional, short-stay hospitals, exclusive of federal hospitals. Diagnostic categories are based on the International Classification of Diseases, Ninth Revision, Clinical Modification. See headnote, Table 158]

Age and first-listed diagnosis	Discharges		Days of care per 1,000 per- sons [1]	Aver- age stay (days)	Age and first-listed diagnosis	Discharges		Days of care per 1,000 per- sons [1]	Aver- age stay (days)
	Num- ber (1,000)	Per 1,000 per- sons [1]				Num- ber (1,000)	Per 1,000 per- sons [1]		
MALE					FEMALE				
All ages [2]	12,514	99.9	540	5.4	All ages [2]	19,192	129.8	592	4.6
Under 18 years [3]	1,515	40.8	195	4.8	Under 18 years [3]	1,397	39.4	161	4.1
Pneumonia	199	5.4	17	3.2	Pneumonia	168	4.7	17	3.6
Injuries and poisoning	185	5.0	21	4.3	Injuries and poisoning	111	3.1	[5]12	[5]3.8
Asthma	129	3.5	7	2.1	Asthma	85	2.4	6	2.3
18 to 44 years [3]	2,498	45.5	220	4.8	18 to 44 years [3]	6,941	125.7	404	3.2
Injuries and poisoning	408	7.4	34	4.5	Delivery	3,588	65.0	161	2.5
Serious mental illness [4] . . .	[5]296	[5]5.4	[5]44	[5]8.2	Serious mental illness [4] . . .	[5]300	[5]5.4	[5]41	[5]7.6
Alcohol and drug [6]	224	4.1	19	4.7	Injuries and poisoning	237	4.3	18	4.2
Diseases of heart	148	2.7	10	3.5					
45 to 64 years [3]	3,424	115.8	586	5.1	45 to 64 years [3]	3,534	112.6	546	4.8
Diseases of heart	802	27.1	104	3.8	Diseases of heart	470	15.0	61	4.1
Injuries and poisoning	266	9.0	51	5.7	Injuries and poisoning	248	7.9	42	5.3
Malignant neoplasms	188	6.3	43	6.8	Malignant neoplasms	195	6.2	36	5.7
Serious mental illness [4] . . .	[5]120	[5]4.1	[5]36	[5]8.8	Serious mental illness [4] . . .	146	4.7	44	9.4
Cerebrovascular diseases . .	116	3.9	20	5.2					
Diabetes	114	3.8	23	6.0	65 to 74 years [3]	2,479	215.9	1,430	5.7
					Diseases of heart	525	53.3	262	4.9
65 to 74 years [3]	2,199	269.7	1,517	5.6	Injuries and poisoning	185	18.8	113	6.0
Diseases of heart	586	71.9	338	4.7	Malignant neoplasms	142	14.4	103	7.2
Injuries and poisoning	149	18.3	108	5.9	Cerebrovascular diseases . .	124	12.6	61	4.8
Malignant neoplasms	146	17.9	123	6.9	Pneumonia	117	11.9	75	6.3
75 years old and older [3] .	2,878	461.5	2,852	6.2	75 years old and older [3] .	4,840	472.3	2,915	6.2
Diseases of heart	697	111.8	593	5.3	Diseases of heart	1,045	102.0	539	5.3
Pneumonia	229	36.7	230	6.3	Injuries and poisoning	472	46.0	284	6.2
Injuries and poisoning	207	33.2	255	7.7	Pneumonia	322	31.4	216	6.9
Cerebrovascular diseases . .	186	29.9	169	5.7	Cerebrovascular diseases . .	292	28.4	161	5.7
Malignant neoplasms	135	21.6	163	7.6	Malignant neoplasms	186	18.1	129	7.1

[1] Based on Census Bureau estimated civilian population as of July 1. Population figures are adjusted for net underenumeration using the 1990 National Population Adjustment Matrix from the U.S. Census Bureau. [2] Average length of stay and rates per 1,000 population are age-adjusted to the year 2000 standard using six age groups; Under 18 years, 18-44 years, 45-54 years, 55-64 years, 65-74 years, and 75 years and over. [3] Includes other first-listed diagnoses not shown separately. [4] Excludes discharges from other types of facilities such as the Dept. of Veterans Affairs or long-term hospitals. [5] Estimates are considered unreliable. [6] Includes abuse, dependence, and withdrawal. Excludes discharges from other types of facilities such as the Dept. of Veterans Affairs or day treatment programs.

Source: U.S. National Center for Health Statistics, *Health, United States, 2002*.

No. 161. Organ Transplants and Grafts: 1990 to 2001

[**As of end of year.** Based on reports of procurement programs and transplant centers in the United States, except as noted]

Procedure	Number of procedures						Number of centers		Number of people waiting, 2001	1-year patient survival rates, 2000 (percent)
	1990	1995	1998	1999	2000	2001	1990	2001		
Transplant: [1]										
Heart	2,095	2,342	2,308	2,159	2,172	2,202	148	140	4,148	85.5
Heart-lung	52	69	43	49	47	27	79	81	212	66.2
Lung	203	869	862	884	955	1,054	70	75	3,821	76.5
Liver	2,631	3,818	4,358	4,594	4,816	5,177	85	120	17,546	85.9
Kidney	9,358	10,957	12,245	12,455	13,258	14,152	232	242	52,216	(NA)
Kidney-pancreas . .	459	915	968	933	910	884	(NA)	(NA)	2,540	95.2
Pancreas	60	103	230	350	420	468	84	138	1,317	95.9
Intestine	1	21	27	37	29	112	(NA)	38	192	74.7
Multi-organ [2]	71	124	182	133	166	(NA)	(NA)	(NA)	(NA)	(NA)
Cornea grafts [2] . . .	40,631	44,652	(NA)	45,765	46,949	46,532	[3]107	[3]93	(NA)	(NA)
Bone grafts	350,000	450,000	500,000	650,000	800,000	875,000	30	(NA)	(X)	(NA)
Skin grafts [4]	5,500	5,500	5,000	9,000	10,000	20,000	25	(NA)	(X)	(NA)

NA Not available. X Not applicable. [1] Kidney-pancreas and heart-lung transplants are each counted as one organ. All other multi-organ transplants, excluding kidney-pancreas and heart-lung, are included in the multi-organ row. The data and analyses reported in the 2001 Annual Report of the U.S. Organ Procurement and Transplantation Network and the Scientific Registry of Transplant Recipients have been supplied by UNOS under contract with HHS. The authors alone are responsible for the reporting and interpretation of these data. [2] 1990, number of procedures and eye banks include Canada. [3] Eye banks. [4] Procedure data are shown in terms of square feet.

Source: Transplants, *2001 Annual Report of the U.S. Organ Procurement and Transplantation Network and the Scientific Registry for Transplant Recipients: Transplant Data: 1991-2000.* U.S. Department of Health and Human Services, Health Resources and Services Administration, Office of Special Programs, Division of Transplantation, Rockville, MD; United Network for Organ Sharing, Richmond, VA; University Renal Research and Education Association, Ann Arbor, MI; American Association of Tissue Banks, McLean, VA; and Eye Bank Association of America, Washington, DC; and unpublished data.

U.S. Census Bureau, Statistical Abstract of the United States: 2002

No. 162. Procedures for Inpatients Discharged From Short-Stay Hospitals: 1990 to 2000

[23,051 represents 23,051,000. Excludes newborn infants and discharges from federal hospitals. See headnote, Table 158]

Sex and type of procedure	Number of procedures (1,000)				Rate per 1,000 population [1]			
	1990	1995	1999	2000	1990	1995	1999	2000
Surgical procedures, total [2]	23,051	22,530	23,833	23,244	92.4	86.2	86.5	83.6
Cardiac catheterization	995	1,068	1,271	1,221	4.0	4.1	4.6	4.4
Removal of coronary artery obstruction [3]	285	434	1,069	1,025	1.2	1.7	3.9	3.7
Reduction of fracture [4]	609	577	628	628	2.4	2.2	2.3	2.3
Coronary artery bypass graft	392	573	571	519	1.6	2.2	2.1	1.9
Male, total [2]	8,538	8,388	8,949	8,689	70.6	65.9	66.5	63.9
Cardiac catheterization	620	660	758	732	5.1	5.2	5.6	5.4
Removal of coronary artery obstruction [3]	200	285	708	655	1.7	2.2	5.3	4.8
Coronary artery bypass graft	286	423	389	371	2.4	3.3	2.9	2.7
Female, total [2].	14,513	14,142	14,884	14,556	113.0	105.3	105.6	102.4
Repair of current obstetric laceration	795	964	1,116	1,136	6.2	7.2	7.9	8.0
Cesarean section.	945	785	841	855	7.4	5.8	6.0	6.0
Hysterectomy	591	583	616	633	4.6	4.3	4.4	4.5
Diagnostic and other nonsurgical procedures [5]	17,455	17,278	17,482	16,737	70.0	66.1	63.5	60.2
Angiocardiography and arteriography [6].	1,735	1,834	2,034	2,005	7.0	7.0	7.4	7.2
Respiratory therapy	1,164	1,127	1,117	991	4.7	4.3	4.1	3.6
Diagnostic ultrasound	1,608	1,181	1,022	886	6.4	4.5	3.7	3.2
CAT scan [7]	1,506	967	871	754	6.0	3.7	3.2	2.7
Male, total [5]	7,378	7,261	7,421	6,965	61.0	57.1	55.1	51.2
Angiocardiography and arteriography [6].	1,051	1,076	1,145	1,157	8.7	8.5	8.5	8.5
Respiratory therapy	586	572	560	507	4.9	4.5	4.2	3.7
CAT scan [7]	736	473	408	345	6.1	3.7	3.0	2.5
Female, total [5].	10,077	10,016	10,061	9,772	78.5	74.6	71.4	68.8
Manual assisted delivery	750	866	802	898	5.9	6.5	5.7	6.3
Fetal EKG and fetal monitoring.	1,377	935	756	750	10.8	7.0	5.4	5.5
Diagnostic ultrasound	941	682	571	501	7.3	5.1	4.1	3.5

[1] Based on Census Bureau estimated civilian population as of July 1. Beginning 1999 population figures are adjusted for net underenumeration in the 1990 census using the 1990 National Population Adjustment Matrix from the Census Bureau. Since population estimates for the 2000 census were not available when this table was prepared the 2000 population estimates were based on the 1990 census.   [2] Includes other types of surgical procedures not shown separately.   [3] Beginning 1999 includes separately coded "insertion of stent."   [4] Excluding skull, nose, and jaw.   [5] Includes other nonsurgical procedures not shown separately.   [6] Using contrast material.   [7] Computerized axial tomography.

Source: U.S. National Center for Health Statistics, *Vital and Health Statistics,* Series 13; and unpublished data.

No. 163. Hospital Utilization Measures for HIV Patients: 1985 to 2000

[HIV represents human immunodeficiency virus. See headnote, Table 158]

Measure of utilization	Unit	1985	1990	1995	1998	1999	2000
Number of patients discharged [1]	1,000. . . .	23	146	249	189	180	173
Rate of patient discharges [2]	Rate	1.0	5.8	9.4	6.9	6.5	6.2
Number of days of care.	1,000. . . .	387	2,188	2,326	1,503	1,310	1,257
Rate of days of care [2]. [3]	Rate	16.3	86.9	87.6	55.0	47.5	45.2
Average length of stay [3]	Days	17.1	14.9	9.3	8.0	7.3	7.3

[1] Comparisons beginning 1990 with data for earlier years should be made with caution as estimates of change may reflect improvements in the 1988 sample design rather than true changes in hospital use.   [2] Per 10,000 population. Based on Census Bureau estimated civilian population as of July 1. Population estimates for the 1980's do not reflect revised estimates based on the 1990 Census of Population. Beginning 1998, rates are based on civilian population estimates that have been adjusted for net underenumeration in the 1990 census. Since population estimates for the 2000 census were not available when this table was prepared, the 2000 population estimates were based on the 1990 census.   [3] For similar data on all patients, see Table 158.

Source: National Center for Health Statistics, *Vital and Health Statistics,* Series 13; and unpublished data.

No. 164. Skilled Nursing Facilities: 1980 to 1999

[448 represents 448,000. Covers facilities and beds certified for participation under medicare as of midyear. Includes facilities which have transfer agreements with one or more participating hospitals, and are engaged primarily in providing skilled nursing care and related services for the rehabilitation of injured, disabled, or sick persons]

Item	Unit	1980	1990	1995	1996	1997	1998	1999
Skilled nursing facilities	Number .	5,155	9,008	13,281	14,177	14,860	15,037	14,913
Beds	1,000. . .	448	512	657	672	685	723	837
Per 1,000 medicare enrollees [1] .	Rate . . .	16.0	15.2	17.7	17.8	18.0	18.8	21.6

[1] Based on total number of beneficiaries enrolled in the medicare hospital insurance program as of July 1 of year stated.

Source: U.S. Health Care Financing Administration, *Medicare Participating Providers and Suppliers of Health Services, 1980;* and unpublished data.

No. 165. Home Health and Hospice Care Agencies by Selected Characteristics: 2000

[In percent, except as indicated (11.4 represents 11,400). Based on the National Home and Hospice Care Survey. Home health care is provided to individuals and families in their place of residence. Hospice care is available in both the home and inpatient settings. See source for details. For composition of regions, see map, inside front cover]

Agency characteristic	Agencies, total	Current patients [1]			Discharges [2]		
		Total	Home health care	Hospice care	Total	Home health care	Hospice care
Total (1,000).................	11.4	1,460.8	1,355.3	105.5	7,800.1	7,179.0	621.1
PERCENT DISTRIBUTION							
Ownership:							
Proprietary......................	44.7	33.2	34.1	22.3	24.2	25.0	15.8
Voluntary nonprofit	42.5	57.8	56.6	73.2	66.9	65.8	80.0
Government and other............	12.8	9.0	9.3	4.4	8.9	9.3	4.2
Region:							
Northeast......................	15.9	31.2	31.9	22.0	39.3	41.0	20.1
Midwest.......................	26.1	20.6	20.7	19.5	18.4	17.8	25.7
South.........................	42.7	37.3	37.3	37.7	29.8	29.5	33.7
West..........................	15.3	10.9	10.1	20.8	12.5	11.7	20.6

[1] Patients on the rolls of the agency as of midnight the day prior to the survey. [2] Patients removed from the rolls of the agency during the 12 months prior to the day of the survey. A patient could be included more than once if the individual had more than one episode of care during the year.

Source: U.S. National Center for Health Statistics, unpublished data.

No. 166. Home Health and Hospice Care Patients by Selected Characteristics: 2000

[In percent, except as indicated (1,460.8 represents 1,460,800). See headnote, Table 165]

Item	Current patients [1]			Discharges [2]		
	Total	Home health care	Hospice care	Total	Home health care	Hospice care
Total (1,000)...............	1,460.8	1,355.3	105.5	7,800.1	7,179.0	621.1
PERCENT DISTRIBUTION						
Age: [3]						
Under 45 years old	13.2	13.9	4.5	13.7	14.5	3.9
45-54 years old	6.5	6.7	5.1	6.2	6.3	5.0
55-64 years old	8.9	8.9	8.9	10.2	10.0	11.5
65 years old and over	71.3	70.5	81.4	70.0	69.1	79.6
65-69 years old.............	7.1	7.1	7.3	9.4	9.4	10.1
70-74 years old.............	10.2	10.2	9.9	11.1	10.8	14.5
75-79 years old.............	17.1	16.8	20.9	15.5	15.8	12.5
80-84 years old.............	14.6	14.5	16.1	16.2	16.2	15.9
85 years old and over	22.3	21.9	27.2	17.8	17.0	26.5
Sex:						
Male......................	35.8	35.2	42.6	37.3	36.2	49.8
Female	64.2	64.8	57.4	62.7	63.8	50.2
Race:						
White	76.3	76.0	82.8	79.5	79.1	84.1
Black and other [4]	14.6	14.8	12.3	12.2	12.4	10.3
Black....................	12.4	12.6	10.6	9.8	10.0	8.1
Unknown..................	9.0	9.4	5.0	8.3	8.5	5.5
Marital status: [3]						
Married	32.7	31.9	42.7	40.9	40.3	47.2
Widowed..................	34.9	34.8	36.7	29.9	29.6	33.2
Divorced or separated	5.5	5.5	6.3	5.3	5.2	5.7
Never married	17.4	18.0	9.2	14.7	15.3	7.7
Unknown..................	9.5	9.9	5.0	9.3	9.5	6.2
Primary admission diagnosis:						
Neoplasms	8.6	5.1	52.6	9.7	5.5	58.4
Endocrine, nutritional and metabolic and immunity disorders	8.8	9.5	0.3	5.8	6.2	0.3
Diseases of the nervous system and sense organs	2.3	2.4	0.4	0.7	0.7	0.2
Diseases of the circulatory system . .	23.0	23.6	15.6	21.4	22.3	11.7
Diseases of the respiratory system. .	6.8	6.8	6.5	9.2	9.4	6.9
Diseases of the musculoskeletal system and connective tissue	9.1	9.8	0.1	11.2	12.1	1.0
Injuries and poisoning	9.6	10.2	0.9	11.3	12.3	0.5

[1] Patients on the rolls of the agency as of midnight the day prior to the survey. [2] Patients removed from the rolls of the agency during the 12 months prior to the day of the survey. A patient could be included more than once if the individual had more than one episode of care during the year. [3] For current patients, current age or marital status; for discharged patients, age or marital status at time of discharge. [4] Patients with multiple races are coded in the "other" category.

Source: U.S. National Center for Health Statistics, Health, United States, 2002.

No. 167. Elderly Home Health Patients: 2000

[1,041 represents 1,041,000. Covers the civilian population 65 years old and over who are home health care patients. Age of patient is based on age at the time of interview. Home health care is provided to individuals and families in their place of residence. Based on the 2000 National Home and Hospice Care Survey]

Item	Current patients [1] Number (1,000)	Current patients [1] Percent	Discharges [2] Number (1,000)	Discharges [2] Percent	Item	Current patients [1] Number (1,000)	Current patients [1] Percent	Discharges [2] Number (1,000)	Discharges [2] Percent
Total 65 yrs. old & over.	1,041	100.0	5,456	100.0	Own income	61	5.9	85	1.6
Received help with—					Medicare	705	67.8	4,867	89.2
Bathing or showering	544	52.3	2,172	39.8	Medicaid	141	13.5	150	2.8
Dressing	480	46.1	1,900	34.8					
Eating	166	15.9	537	9.9	Services rendered: [5]				
Transferring in/out of					Nursing services	782	75.1	4,672	85.6
a bed or chair	373	35.9	1,737	31.8	Social services	138	13.3	977	17.9
Using the toilet room	289	27.8	1,092	20.0	Counseling	37	3.6	255	4.7
Doing light housework . .	379	36.4	1,031	18.9	Medications	106	10.2	599	11.0
Managing money.	17	1.6	[3]30	[3]0.5	Physical therapy	285	27.4	2,216	40.6
Shopping for groceries									
or clothes	127	12.2	261	4.8	Homemaker-household				
Using the telephone.	31	3.0	113	2.1	services	289	27.8	691	12.7
Preparing meals	227	21.8	549	10.1	Nutrition services.	53	5.1	204	3.7
Taking medications	216	20.7	1,017	18.6	Physician services.	48	4.6	307	5.6
Primary source of					Occupational therapy	83	8.0	543	10.0
payment [4]:					Speech therapy/				
Private insurance	44	4.2	251	4.6	audiology	19	1.8	102	1.9

[1] Patients on the rolls of the agency as of midnight the day prior to the survey.   [2] Patients removed from the rolls of the agency during the 12 months prior to the day of the survey. A patient could be included more than once if the individual had more than one episode of care during the year.   [3] Figure does not meet standard of reliability or precision.   [4] For current patients, the expected source; for discharges the actual source for the entire episode.   [5] For current patients, services currently being provided; for discharges services provided during the 30 days prior to discharge.

Source: U.S. National Center for Health Statistics, unpublished data.

No. 168. Nursing Homes—Selected Characteristics: 1985 to 1999

[Beds: 1,624 represents 1,624,000. Covers licensed and/or certified nursing homes in the conterminous United States that had three or more beds. Based on the 1999 National Nursing Home Survey, a two-stage survey sample of nursing homes and their residents. Subject to sampling variability. For composition of regions, see map, inside front cover]

Characteristic	Beds Nursing homes	Beds Number (1,000)	Beds Per nursing home	Current residents Number (1,000)	Current residents Occupancy rate [1]	Full-time equivalent employment — Administrative, medical, and therapeutic Number (1,000)	Full-time equivalent employment — Administrative, medical, and therapeutic Rate per 100 beds	Full-time equivalent employment — Nursing Number (1,000)	Full-time equivalent employment — Nursing Rate per 100 beds
1985	19,100	1,624	85	1,491	91.8	89.4	5.5	704	43.4
1995	16,700	1,771	106	1,549	87.4	90.5	5.1	916	51.7
1997	17,000	1,821	107	1,609	88.4	100.0	5.5	950	52.2
1999, total	18,000	1,965	109	1,627	82.8	96.6	4.9	961	48.9
Ownership:									
Proprietary.	12,000	1,291	108	1,048	81.2	60.2	4.6	597	46.2
Voluntary nonprofit	4,800	523	109	446	85.3	29.1	5.6	280	53.5
Government and other. . . .	1,200	151	126	133	88.1	7.4	4.7	84	55.6
Certification:									
Medicare and medicaid									
certified	14,700	1,698	116	1,414	83.3	83.2	4.9	842	49.6
Medicare only.	[2]600	49	82	37	75.5	2.8	5.7	26	53.1
Medicaid only.	2,100	177	89	143	80.8	9.0	5.1	75	42.4
Not certified	[2]500	40	80	33	82.5	1.6	4.0	18	45.0
Bed size:									
Less than 50 beds	2,000	72	36	59	81.9	7.1	9.9	43	59.7
50-99 beds	7,000	503	72	414	82.3	28.8	5.7	252	50.1
100-199 beds.	7,500	998	133	826	82.8	45.0	4.5	476	47.7
200 beds or more	1,400	392	280	328	83.7	15.7	4.0	190	48.5
Region:									
Northeast	3,200	443	138	382	86.2	21.7	4.9	244	55.1
Midwest	6,000	619	103	498	80.4	28.3	4.6	272	43.9
South	6,000	652	109	531	81.6	30.5	4.7	311	47.7
West	2,800	251	90	215	85.7	16.1	6.4	133	53.0
Affiliation: [3]									
Chain	10,800	1,179	109	977	82.9	58.7	5.0	556	47.2
Independent.	7,200	781	108	646	82.7	37.7	4.8	404	51.7

[1] Number of residents divided by number of available beds multiplied by 100.   [2] Figure does not meet standards of reliability or precision.   [3] Excludes a small number of homes, beds, and residents with unknown affiliation.

Source: U.S. National Center for Health Statistics, Vital and Health Statistics, Series 13, No. 152.

No. 169. Nursing Home Residents 65 Years Old and Over by Selected Characteristics: 1999

[1,470 represents 1,470,000. Covers licensed and/or certified nursing homes in the conterminous United States that had three or more beds. Based on the National Nursing Home Survey, a two-stage sample survey of nursing homes and their residents. Subject to sampling variability]

Characteristic [1]	Number (1,000)	Percent distri-bution	Item	Percent of elderly resi-dents	Functional status	Percent of elderly residents receiving assis-tance
Total [2]	1,470	100.0	Type of aids used:		ADLs: [6]	
			Wheelchair	62.6	Bathing, showering. . .	94.7
Male.	378	25.7	Walker	26.1	Dressing.	87.5
Female	1,092	74.3			Eating	47.1
					Transferring in or	
65 to 74 years	195	13.3	Vision impaired	28.5	out of beds or chair .	30.2
75 to 84 years	518	35.2	Hearing impaired.	22.8	Using toilet room	57.6
85 years and over.	757	51.5				
Living quarters before						
admission:			Primary source		IADLs: [7]	
Private residence	447	30.4	of payment: [3]		Care of personal	
Retirement home.	23	1.6	Private sources [4]	26.3	possessions	74.3
Board and care,			Medicare	32.8	Managing money	70.7
assisted living, and/or			Medicaid	37.5	Securing personal	
residential facility	81	5.5	Other [5]	3.4	items	72.9
Nursing home	164	11.1			Using telephone	62.2
Hospital.	679	46.2				
Other health facility	76	5.2				

[1] At time of survey.   [2] Includes other and/or unknown, not shown separately.   [3] At admission.   [4] Includes private insurance, own income, family support, social security benefits, and retirement funds.   [5] Includes supplemental security income, other government assistance or welfare, religious organizations, foundations, agencies, Veterans Administration contract, pensions, or other compensation, payment source not yet determined, and other and unknown sources.   [6] Activities of daily living.   [7] Instrumental activities of daily living.

Source: U.S. National Center for Health Statistics, *Vital and Health Statistics*, Series 13, No. 152.

No. 170. Mental Health Facilities—Summary by Type of Facility: 1998

[Beds: 261.9 represents 261,900. Facilities, beds and inpatients as of year-end; Excludes private psychiatric office practice and psychiatric service modes of all types in hospitals or outpatient clinics of federal agencies other than U.S. Dept. of Veterans Affairs. Excludes data from Puerto Rico, Virgin Islands, Guam, and other territories]

Type of facility	Number of facilities	Inpatient beds		Inpatients		Inpatient care episodes [2]
		Total (1,000)	Rate [1]	Total (1,000)	Rate [1]	
Total	3,729	261.9	97.3	215.9	80.3	2,099
Mental hospitals:						
State and county	229	63.5	23.6	57.0	21.2	186
Private [3]	809	67.1	24.9	51.9	19.3	527
General hospitals [4]	1,593	54.3	20.2	37.0	13.8	1,137
Veterans Administration [5]	123	13.3	4.9	10.9	4.0	128
Other [6]	975	63.7	23.7	59.1	22.0	121

[1] Rate per 100,000 population. Based on Census Bureau estimated civilian population as of July 1.   [2] "Inpatient care episodes" is defined as the number of residents in inpatient facilities at the beginning of the year plus the total additions to inpatient facilities during the year.   [3] Includes residential treatment centers for emotionally disturbed children.   [4] Nonfederal hospitals with separate psychiatric services.   [5] Includes U.S. Department of Veterans Affairs (VA) neuropsychiatric hospitals, VA general hospitals with separate psychiatric settings and VA freestanding psychiatric outpatient clinics.   [6] Includes free-standing psychiatric outpatient facilities that provide only psychiatric outpatient services and other multiservice mental health facilities with two or more settings, which are not elsewhere classified, as well as freestanding partial care facilities which only provide psychiatric partial care services. Number of facilities data also include freestanding psychiatric partial care facilities.

Source: U.S. Substance Abuse and Mental Health Services Administration, Center for Mental Health Services, unpublished data.

No. 171. Injury and Poisoning Episodes and Conditions by Age and Sex: 1999

[31,268 represents 31,268,000. Covers all medically attended injuries and poisonings occurring during the 3-month period prior to the survey interview. There may be more than one condition per episode. Based on the redesigned National Health Interview Survey, a sample survey of the civilian noninstitutionalized population; see Appendix III]

External cause and nature of injury	Total	Both sexes — Total, age-adjusted[1]	Under 12 years old	12 to 21 years old	22 to 44 years old	45 to 64 years old	65 years old and over	Male, total	Female, total
EPISODES									
Number (1,000)	31,268	(X)	4,890	6,462	10,738	5,602	3,576	17,370	13,897
Annual rate per 1,000 population, total[2]	115.1	115.0	101.1	165.9	115.1	95.6	110.1	131.1	99.8
Fall	33.8	34.0	36.2	37.4	22.4	31.5	62.6	29.7	37.7
Struck by or against a person or an object	19.8	19.6	22.0	47.8	16.6	11.6	6.6	27.0	12.8
Transportation[3]	17.8	17.7	11.3	28.3	22.3	12.1	12.3	20.5	15.3
Overexertion	14.1	14.1	[4]2.2	14.9	19.4	17.2	9.9	16.2	12.1
Cutting, piercing instruments	8.2	8.2	6.9	10.6	10.1	6.6	4.8	11.6	4.9
Poisoning	4.6	4.6	9.7	[4]3.0	4.6	[4]1.8	[4]4.4	3.8	5.5
CONDITIONS[5]									
Annual rate per 1,000 population, total[2]	137.2	137.4	102.3	199.1	139.4	118.0	143.4	155.7	119.6
Sprains/strains	33.8	33.8	9.6	53.6	42.3	33.2	22.7	36.3	31.4
Open wounds	24.5	24.3	38.7	32.0	23.0	15.7	14.4	33.2	16.1
Fractures	20.8	21.0	17.3	34.9	14.1	17.8	33.7	22.4	19.3
Contusions	13.9	14.1	8.1	19.9	11.1	12.0	27.0	13.4	14.5

X Not applicable.   [1] Data were age-adjusted by the direct method to the 2000 projected population.   [2] Includes other items not shown separately.   [3] Includes the categories "Motor vehicle traffic"; "Pedal cycle, other"; "Pedestrian, other"; and "Transport, other."   [4] Figure does not meet standard of reliability or precision.   [5] Poisoning episodes are assumed to have a single condition resulting from the episode.

Source: U.S. National Center for Health Statistics, *Vital and Health Statistics*, Series 10, No. 202, and unpublished data.

No. 172. Injuries Associated With Consumer Products: 1999

[For products associated with more than 40,000 injuries in 1999. Estimates calculated from a representative sample of hospitals with emergency treatment departments in the United States. Data are estimates of the number of emergency room treated cases nationwide associated with various products. Product involvement does not necessarily mean the product caused the accident. Products were selected from the U.S. Consumer Product Safety Commission's National Electronic Injury Surveillance System]

Product	Number	Product	Number
Home workshop equipment:		Ceilings and walls	259,301
Saws (hand or power)	96,658	Household cabinets, racks, and shelves	240,629
Hammers	40,015	Nails, screws, tacks, or bolts	162,597
Household packaging and containers:		Windows	129,276
Household containers and packaging	196,111	Porches, balconies, open-side floors	139,105
Bottles and jars	75,581	Fences or fence posts	117,175
Housewares:		Home entertainment equipment:	
Knives	446,225	Televisions	40,634
Tableware and flatware	112,665	Personal use items:	
Home furnishing:[1]		Footwear	94,170
Beds	455,027	Jewelry	65,127
Tables	304,758	Yard and garden equipment:	
Chairs	292,406	Lawn mowers	70,640
Bathtubs and showers	195,324	Sports and recreation equipment:	
Ladders	163,138	Bicycles	595,679
Sofas, couches, davenports, etc.	120,653	Trampolines	98,889
Carpets, rugs	117,156	Swings or swing sets	79,893
Toilets	56,424	Playground climbing equipment	78,576
Home structures, construction:[2]		Swimming pools	81,809
Stairs or steps	1,029,418	All-terrain vehicles	84,800
Floors or flooring materials	1,024,522	Skateboards	59,964
Other doors (excl. garage)	331,344	Slides or sliding boards	51,423

[1] Includes accessories.   [2] Includes materials.

No. 173. Costs of Unintentional Injuries: 2000

[512.4 represents $512,400,000,000. Covers costs of deaths or disabling injuries together with vehicle accidents and fires]

Cost	Amount (bil. dol.) — Total[1]	Motor vehicle	Work	Home	Other	Percent distribution — Total[1]	Motor vehicle	Work	Home	Other
Total	512.4	201.5	131.2	111.9	82.6	100.0	100.0	100.0	100.0	100.0
Wage and productivity losses[2]	259.8	71.5	67.6	70.9	53.6	50.7	35.5	51.5	63.4	64.9
Medical expense	93.5	24.6	24.2	26.4	19.6	18.2	12.2	18.4	23.6	23.7
Administrative expenses[3]	72.6	48.0	22.3	4.9	4.5	14.2	23.8	17.0	4.4	5.4
Motor vehicle damage	55.5	55.5	2.2	(NA)	(NA)	10.8	27.5	1.7	(NA)	(NA)
Employer cost[4]	20.9	1.9	11.5	4.4	3.5	4.1	0.9	8.8	3.9	4.2
Fire loss	10.1	(NA)	3.4	5.3	1.4	2.0	(NA)	2.6	4.7	1.7

NA Not available.   [1] Excludes duplication between work and motor vehicle ($14.8 billion in 2000).   [2] Actual loss of wages and household production, and the present value of future earnings lost.   [3] Home and other costs may include costs of administering medical treatment claims for some motor-vehicle injuries filed through health insurance plans.   [4] Estimate of the uninsured costs incurred by employers, representing the money value of time lost by noninjured workers.

Source of Tables 172 and 173: National Safety Council, Itasca, IL, *Injury Facts, 2001 Edition* (copyright).

No. 174. Specified Reportable Diseases—Cases Reported: 1980 to 2000

[190.9 represents 190,900. Figures should be interpreted with caution. Although reporting of some of these diseases is incomplete, the figures are of value in indicating trends of disease incidence. Includes cases imported from outside the United States]

Disease	1980	1985	1990	1995	1996	1997	1998	1999	2000
AIDS [1]	(2)	8,249	41,595	71,547	66,885	58,492	46,521	45,104	40,758
Botulism [3]	89	122	92	97	119	132	116	154	138
Brucellosis (undulant fever)	183	153	85	98	112	98	79	82	87
Chickenpox [4] (1,000)	190.9	178.2	173.1	120.6	83.5	98.7	82.5	46.0	27.4
Cholera	9	4	6	23	4	6	17	6	5
Cryptosporidiosis	(2)	(2)	(2)	(NA)	(NA)	2,566	3,793	2,361	3,128
Diphtheria	3	3	4	-	2	4	1	1	1
Escherichia coli 0157:H7	(2)	(2)	(2)	2,139	2,741	2,555	3,161	4,513	4,528
Haemophilus influenza	(2)	(2)	(2)	1,180	1,170	1,162	1,194	1,309	1,398
Hansen disease (Leprosy)	223	361	198	144	112	122	108	108	91
Hepatitis: B (serum) (1,000)	19.0	26.6	21.1	10.8	10.6	10.4	10.3	7.7	8.0
A (infectious) (1,000)	29.1	23.2	31.4	31.6	31.0	30.0	23.2	17.0	13.4
C/Non-A, non-B (1,000) [5]	(2)	4.2	2.6	4.6	3.7	3.8	3.5	3.1	3.2
Legionellosis	(2)	830	1,370	1,241	1,198	1,163	1,355	1,108	1,127
Lyme disease	(2)	(2)	(2)	11,700	16,455	12,801	16,801	16,273	17,730
Malaria	2,062	1,049	1,292	1,419	1,800	2,001	1,611	1,666	1,560
Measles (1,000)	13.5	2.8	27.8	0.3	0.5	0.1	0.1	0.1	0.1
Meningococcal infections	2,840	2,479	2,451	3,243	3,437	3,308	2,725	2,501	2,256
Mumps (1,000)	8.6	3.0	5.3	0.9	0.8	0.7	0.7	0.4	0.3
Pertussis [6] (1,000)	1.7	3.6	4.6	5.1	7.8	6.6	7.4	7.3	7.9
Plague	18	17	2	9	5	4	9	9	6
Poliomyelitis, acute [7]	9	7	6	7	5	5	1	-	-
Psittacosis	124	119	113	64	42	33	47	16	17
Rabies, animal	6,421	5,565	4,826	7,811	6,982	8,105	7,259	6,730	6,934
Rabies, human	-	1	1	5	3	2	1	-	4
Rocky Mountain spotted fever	1,163	714	651	590	831	409	365	579	495
Rubella [8]	3,904	630	1,125	128	238	181	364	267	176
Salmonellosis [9] (1,000)	33.7	65.3	48.6	46.0	45.5	41.9	43.7	40.6	39.6
Shigellosis [10] (1,000)	19.0	17.1	27.1	32.1	26.0	23.1	23.6	17.5	22.9
Tetanus	95	83	64	41	36	50	41	40	35
Toxic-shock syndrome	(2)	384	322	191	145	157	138	113	135
Trichinosis	131	61	129	29	11	13	19	12	16
Tuberculosis [11] (1,000)	27.7	22.2	25.7	22.9	21.3	19.9	18.4	17.5	16.4
Typhoid fever	510	402	552	369	396	365	375	346	377
Sexually transmitted diseases:									
Gonorrhea (1,000)	1,004	911	690	393	326	325	356	360	359
Syphilis (1,000)	69	68	134	69	53	47	38	30	32
Chlamydia (1,000)	(2)	(2)	(2)	478	499	527	604	657	702
Chancroid (1,000)	0.8	2.1	4.2	0.6	0.4	0.2	0.2	0.1	0.1

- Represents zero. NA Not available. [1] Acquired immunodeficiency syndrome was not a notifiable disease until 1984. Figures are shown for years in which cases were reported to the CDC. Beginning 1995, based on revised classification system and expanded surveillance case definition. [2] Disease was not notifiable. [3] Includes foodborne, infant, wound, and unspecified cases. [4] Chickenpox was taken off the nationally notifiable list in 1991 but many states continue to report. [5] Includes some persons positive for antibody to hepatitis C virus who do not have hepatitis. [6] Whooping cough. [7] Revised. Data subject to annual revisions. [8] German measles. Excludes rubella, congenital syndrome. [9] Excludes typhoid fever. [10] Bacillary dysentery. [11] Newly reported active cases.

Source: U.S. Centers for Disease Control and Prevention, Atlanta, GA, *Summary of Notifiable Diseases, United States, 2000, Morbidity and Mortality Weekly Report,* Vol. 49, No. 53, June 14, 2002.

No. 175. Children Immunized Against Specified Diseases: 1995 to 2000

[In percent. Covers civilian noninstitutionalized population ages 19 months to 35 months. Based on estimates from the National Immunization Survey. The health care providers of the children are contacted to verify and/or complete vaccination information. Results are based on race/ethnic status of the child]

Vaccination	1995, total	1999, total	2000					
			Total	White non-Hispanic	Hispanic	Black non-Hispanic	American Indian/ Alaskan Native [1]	Asian/ Pacific Islander [1]
Diphtheria-tetanus-pertussis (DTP)/ diphtheria-tetanus:								
3+ doses	95	96	94	95	93	92	91	95
4+ doses	79	83	82	84	79	76	75	85
Polio: 3+ doses	88	90	90	91	88	87	90	93
Hib [2]: 3+ doses	92	94	93	95	91	93	90	92
Measles, mumps, rubella vaccine	90	92	91	92	90	88	87	90
Hepatitis B: 3+ doses	68	88	90	91	88	89	91	91
Varicella [3]	(NA)	58	68	66	70	67	62	77
4+ DTP/3+ polio/1+ MCV [4]	76	80	78	80	75	72	70	79
4+ DTP/3+ polio/1+ MCV/3+ hiB [4]	74	78	76	79	73	71	69	75

NA Not available. [1] Non-Hispanic. [2] Haemophilus B. [3] Data collection for varicella (chicken pox) began in July 1996. [4] MCV=Measles containing vaccine.

Source: U.S. Centers for Disease Control and Prevention, Atlanta, GA, *Morbidity and Mortality Weekly Report,* Vol. 49, No. 26, July 7, 2000; and "Immunization Coverage in the U.S."; <http://www.cdc.gov/nip/coverage/default.htm>.

U.S. Census Bureau, Statistical Abstract of the United States: 2002

No. 176. AIDS Cases Reported by Patient Characteristic: 1981 to 2001

[**Provisional.** For cases reported in the year shown. Includes Puerto Rico, Virgin Islands, Guam, and U.S. Pacific Islands. Acquired immunodeficiency syndrome (AIDS) is a specific group of diseases or conditions which are indicative of severe immunosuppression related to infection with the human immunodeficiency virus (HIV). Data are subject to retrospective changes and may differ from those data in Table 174]

Characteristic	1981-2001, total	2001	Characteristic	1981-2001, total	2001
Total [1]	816,149	43,158	Transmission category:		
			Males, 13 years and over	666,026	31,901
Age:			Men who have sex with men. . . .	368,971	13,265
Under 5 years old	6,975	(NA)	Injecting drug use	145,750	5,261
5 to 12 years old	2,099	(NA)	Men who have sex with men and		
13 to 19 years old	4,428	(NA)	injecting drug use	51,293	1,502
20 to 29 years old	133,725	(NA)	Hemophilia/coagulation disorder .	5,000	97
30 to 39 years old	362,021	(NA)	Heterosexual contact [2]	22,914	2,213
40 to 49 years old	216,387	(NA)	Heterosexual contact with		
50 to 59 years old	66,060	(NA)	injecting drug user	9,821	549
60 years old and over	24,453	(NA)	Transfusion [3]	5,057	105
Sex:			Undetermined [4]	57,220	8,909
Male	670,687	31,994	Females, 13 years and over . .	141,048	11,082
Female	145,461	11,164	Injecting drug use	55,576	2,212
Race/ethnic group:			Hemophilia/coagulation disorder .	292	9
Non-Hispanic White	343,889	13,237	Heterosexual contact [2]	35,660	3,205
Non-Hispanic Black	313,180	21,031	Heterosexual contact with		
Hispanic	149,752	8,209	injecting drug user	21,736	937
Asian/Pacific Islander	6,157	430	Transfusion [3]	3,914	113
American Indian/Alaska Native.	2,537	194	Undetermined [4]	23,870	4,606

NA Not available. [1] Includes persons with characteristics unknown. [2] Includes persons who have had heterosexual contact with a bisexual male, a person with hemophilia, a transfusion recipient with human immunodeficiency virus (HIV) infection, or an HIV-infected person, risk not specified. [3] Receipt of blood transfusion, blood components, or tissue. [4] Includes persons for whom risk information is incomplete (because of death, refusal to be interviewed, or loss to followup), persons still under investigation, men reported only to have had heterosexual contact with prostitutes, and interviewed persons for whom no specific risk is identified.

Source: U.S. Centers for Disease Control and Prevention, Atlanta, GA, *HIV/AIDS Surveillance Report*, Volume 13, No. 2.

No. 177. Estimated Persons Living With Acquired Immunodeficiency Syndrome (AIDS) by Selected Characteristics: 1995 to 2000

[These numbers do not represent actual cases of persons living with AIDS. Rather, these numbers are point estimates of persons living with AIDS derived by subtracting the estimated cumulative number of deaths in persons with AIDS from the estimated cumulative number of persons with AIDS diagnosed. Estimated AIDS incidence and estimated deaths are adjusted for reporting delays, but not for incomplete reporting]

Characteristic	1995	1996	1997	1998	1999	2000
Total	214,674	237,687	265,494	289,568	312,673	337,731
RACE/ETHNICITY						
White, not Hispanic	90,878	97,677	106,365	113,606	120,541	127,838
Black, not Hispanic	80,868	91,772	104,768	116,339	127,393	139,522
Hispanic	40,369	45,332	51,111	56,054	60,801	65,991
Asian/Pacific Islander	1,617	1,856	2,086	2,306	2,563	2,841
American Indian/Alaska Native	724	805	894	969	1,054	1,180
MALE ADULT/ADOLESCENT EXPOSURE CATEGORY						
Male total	173,115	189,856	210,666	228,566	245,915	264,149
Men who have sex with men	100,135	109,321	120,969	131,093	140,977	151,325
Injecting drug use	43,795	47,984	52,885	56,784	60,493	64,522
Men who have sex with men and inject drugs . . .	15,882	16,741	18,053	19,061	19,879	20,528
Hemophilia/coagulation disorder	1,725	1,733	1,786	1,816	1,845	([1])
Heterosexual contact	9,739	12,145	14,908	17,592	20,348	23,333
Receipt of blood transfusion, blood components, or tissue	937	1,002	1,094	1,202	1,308	([1])
Risk not reported or identified	902	930	972	1,018	1,065	[1]4,441
FEMALE ADULT/ADOLESCENT EXPOSURE CATEGORY						
Female total	38,136	44,327	51,221	57,290	62,990	69,775
Injecting drug use	18,308	20,277	22,582	24,321	25,777	27,475
Hemophilia/coagulation disorder	132	158	193	221	235	([1])
Heterosexual contact	18,464	22,537	26,952	31,115	35,206	40,051
Receipt of blood transfusion, blood components, or tissue	862	952	1,044	1,145	1,247	([1])
Risk not reported or identified	371	403	450	488	525	[1]2,249
Pediatric [2] exposure category	3,423	3,504	3,606	3,711	3,768	3,806

[1] Statistical estimates for AIDS prevalence in 2000 among persons exposed to HIV through hemophilia/coagulation disorder or receipt of blood transfusion, blood components, or tissue are not presented, but are included in the exposure category "other." The relatively small number of AIDS cases in these categories in recent years does not provide information that results in reliable annual estimates of prevalence. [2] Less than 13 years old.

Source: U.S. Centers for Disease Control and Prevention, Atlanta, GA, *unpublished data*.

No. 178. AIDS, Syphilis, and Tuberculosis Cases Reported by State: 2000

State	AIDS	Syphilis	Tuber-culosis	State	AIDS	Syphilis	Tuber-culosis	State	AIDS	Syphilis	Tuber-culosis
U.S.	[1]40,758	31,575	16,377	KS	128	67	77	ND	3	1	5
				KY	212	253	147	OH	599	282	340
AL	483	752	310	LA	679	973	331	OK	352	327	154
AK	22	6	108	ME	40	7	24	OR	210	49	119
AZ	460	847	261	MD	1,465	1,172	282	PA	1,692	685	383
AR	194	367	199	MA	1,197	447	285	RI	102	38	49
CA	4,737	3,354	3,297	MI	767	984	287	SC	810	853	286
CO	313	63	97	MN	185	77	178	SD	8	1	16
CT	620	151	105	MS	431	685	173	TN	863	1,708	383
DE	221	45	28	MO	459	299	211	TX	2,667	3,297	1,506
DC	875	516	85	MT	16	-	21	UT	151	59	49
FL	4,976	2,768	1,171	NE	79	7	24	VT	38	-	4
GA	1,237	1,635	703	NV	286	52	96	VA	891	537	292
HI	115	22	136	NH	31	19	22	WA	515	171	258
ID	22	11	16	NJ	1,929	801	565	WV	63	13	33
IL	1,761	1,646	743	NM	144	98	46	WI	218	184	92
IN	389	747	145	NY	6,204	2,945	1,744	WY	11	5	4
IA	94	55	40	NC	696	1,494	447				

- Represents zero.   [1] Includes 98 cases among persons with unknown state of residence.

Source: U.S. Centers for Disease Control and Prevention, Atlanta, GA, *Summary of Notifiable Diseases, United States, 2000, Morbidity and Mortality Weekly Report,* Vol. 49, No. 53, June 14, 2002.

No. 179. Persons With Limitation of Activity Caused by Chronic Conditions: 1997 and 1999

[**In percent**. Limitation of activity is assessed by asking respondents a series of questions about limitations in their ability to perform activities usual for their age group because of a physical, mental, or emotional problem. Respondents are asked about limitations in activities of daily living, or instrumental activities of daily living, play, school, work, difficulty walking or remembering, and any other activity limitations. For reported limitations, the causal health conditions are determined and respondents are considered limited if one or more of these conditions is chronic. Based on the National Health Interview Survey, a sample survey of the civilian noninstitutionalized population; see Appendix III]

Characteristic	1997	1999	Characteristic	1997	1999
Total [1][2]	13.3	12.2	Male [2]	13.1	12.1
Under 18 years	6.6	6.0	Female [2]	13.4	12.2
18 to 44 years	7.0	6.3			
45 to 54 years	14.2	13.1	White, non-Hispanic [2]	13.2	12.3
55 to 64 years	22.2	21.1	Black, non-Hispanic [2]	17.0	15.3
65 to 74 years	30.0	27.5	Hispanic [2][3]	12.8	10.4
75 years and over	50.2	45.6	Mexican [2][3]	12.5	9.6

[1] Includes all other races not shown separately.   [2] Estimates for all persons are age adjusted to the year 2000 standard using six age groups: Under 18 years, 18-44 years, 45-54 years, 55-64 years. 65-74 years, and 75 years and over.   [3] Persons of Hispanic origin may be of any race.

No. 180. Persons 65 Years Old and Over With Limitation of Activity Caused by Chronic Conditions: 1997 to 1999

[**In percent**. Covers noninstitutionalized persons 65 years old and over. To determine activities of daily living (ADL) limitations respondents were asked "Because of a physical, mental, or emotional problem, does (this person) need the help of other persons with personal care needs, such as eating, bathing, dressing, or getting around inside this home?" Instrumental activities of daily living (IADL) were determined by asking respondents "Because of a physical, mental, or emotional problem, does (this person) need the help of other persons in handling routine needs, such as everyday household chores, doing necessary business, shopping, or getting around for other purposes?" See also headnote, Table 179]

Characteristic	Percent with ADL limitation			Percent with IADL limitation		
	1997	1998	1999	1997	1998	1999
Total [1][2]	6.7	6.3	6.3	13.7	13.5	12.4
65 to 74 years	3.4	3.3	3.1	6.9	7.1	6.2
75 years and over	10.4	9.6	9.9	21.2	20.5	19.1
Male [2]	5.2	5.1	4.9	9.1	9.2	8.4
Female [2]	7.7	7.1	7.2	16.9	16.4	15.1
White, non-Hispanic [2]	6.1	5.6	5.7	13.0	12.4	11.5
Black, non-Hispanic [2]	11.7	11.1	11.9	21.2	21.8	20.8
Hispanic [2][3]	10.8	9.9	8.6	16.3	19.3	14.1
Mexican [2][3]	11.4	12.3	8.9	18.8	24.7	15.6

[1] Includes other races not shown separately.   [2] Estimates are age adjusted to the year 2000 standard using two age groups: 65-74 years and 75 years and over.   [3] Persons of Hispanic origin may be of any race.

Source of Tables 179 and 180: U.S. National Center for Health Statistics, *Health, United States, 2001.*

U.S. Census Bureau, Statistical Abstract of the United States: 2002

No. 181. Substance Abuse Treatment Facilities and Clients: 1995 to 2000

[As of October 1. Based on the Uniform Facility Data Set (UFDS) survey, a census of all known facilities that provide substance abuse treatment in the United States and associated jurisdictions. Selected missing data for responding facilities were imputed]

Primary focus	Number	Primary focus	Number	Type of care and type of problem	Number
FACILITIES		CLIENTS		Total clients	[1]1,000,896
1995	10,746	1995	1,009,127	Outpatient rehab	877,298
1996	10,641	1996	940,141	Outpatient detoxification .	14,249
1997	10,860	1997	929,086	24-hour rehab.	94,710
1998	13,455	1998	1,038,378	24-hour detoxification. . . .	14,639
1999	15,239				
2000, total	**13,428**	**2000, total**	**1,000,896**	Drug only.	287,008
Substance abuse		Substance abuse		Alcohol only	222,193
treatment services	8,147	treatment services	668,835	Both alcohol & drug. . . .	475,096
Mental health services. . .	1,260	Mental health services . .	54,936		
General health care	381	General health care. . . .	32,273	Total with a drug	
Both substance abuse		Both substance abuse		problem [2]	762,104
and mental health.	3,303	and mental health	226,326	Total with an	
Other	337	Other	18,526	alcohol problem [3]	697,289

[1] Includes clients at facilities that did not provide data on type of substance abuse problem treated.   [2] The sum of clients with a drug problem and clients with both diagnoses.   [3] The sum of clients with an alcohol problem and clients with both diagnoses.

Source: U.S. Substance Abuse and Mental Health Services Administration, *Uniform Facility Data Set (UFDS): Annual surveys for 1995, 1996, 1997, 1998, and 1999* and National Survey of Substance Abuse Treatment Services (N-SSATS) 2000.

No. 182. Drug Use by Type of Drug and Age Group: 1999 and 2000

[In percent. Current users are those who used drugs at least once within month prior to this study. Based on a representative sample of the U.S. population age 12 and older, including persons living in households and in some group quarters such as dormitories and homeless shelters. Estimates are based on computer-assisted interviews of about 72,000 respondents. Subject to sampling variability; see source]

Age and type of drug	Ever used		Current user		Age and type of drug	Ever used		Current user	
	1999	2000	1999	2000		1999	2000	1999	2000
12 YEARS OLD AND OVER					18 TO 25 YEARS OLD				
Any illicit drug	39.7	38.9	6.3	6.3	Any illicit drug	52.6	51.2	16.4	15.9
Marijuana and hashish . . .	34.6	34.2	4.7	4.8	Marijuana and hashish . . .	46.8	45.7	14.2	13.6
Cocaine.	11.5	11.2	0.7	0.5	Cocaine.	11.9	10.9	1.7	1.4
Crack.	2.7	2.4	0.2	0.1	Hallucinogens.	19.3	19.3	1.9	1.8
Heroin	1.4	1.2	0.1	0.1	Inhalants	14.1	12.8	0.6	0.6
Hallucinogens	11.3	11.7	0.4	0.4	Any psychotherapeutic [1]. .	20.9	19.6	3.7	3.6
LSD.	8.7	8.8	0.2	0.2	Alcohol	83.9	84.0	57.2	56.8
PCP	2.6	2.6	-	-	"Binge" alcohol use [2] . . .	(NA)	(NA)	37.9	37.8
Inhalants	7.8	7.5	0.3	0.3	Cigarettes	68.9	67.3	39.7	38.3
Any psychotherapeutic [1] .	15.4	14.5	1.8	1.7	Smokeless tobacco	25.8	23.6	5.7	5.0
Pain relievers [1]	9.0	8.6	1.2	1.2	Cigars.	43.9	42.3	11.5	10.4
Tranquilizers [1]	6.3	5.8	0.5	0.4	26 TO 34 YEARS OLD				
Stimulants [1]	7.2	6.6	0.4	0.4					
Methamphetamine [1] .	4.3	4.0	0.2	0.2	Any illicit drug	53.2	50.9	6.8	7.8
Sedatives [1]	3.5	3.2	0.1	0.1	Marijuana and hashish . . .	47.7	46.0	5.4	5.9
Alcohol	81.3	81.0	46.4	46.6	Cocaine.	17.8	15.1	1.2	0.8
"Binge" alcohol use [2] . . .	(NA)	(NA)	20.2	20.6	Hallucinogens	16.4	15.8	0.1	0.4
Cigarettes	68.2	66.5	25.8	24.9	Inhalants	11.4	11.0	0.2	0.2
Smokeless tobacco	19.1	18.5	3.4	3.4	Any psychotherapeutic [1] .	18.6	16.9	1.5	2.1
Cigars.	35.6	34.2	5.5	4.8	26 YEARS OLD AND OVER				
Pipes	17.7	16.4	1.1	1.0					
					Alcohol	86.1	85.8	48.7	49.0
12 to 17 YEARS OLD					"Binge" alcohol use [2] . . .	(NA)	(NA)	18.6	19.1
					Cigarettes	72.3	70.7	24.9	24.2
Any illicit drug	27.6	26.9	9.8	9.7	Smokeless tobacco	19.2	19.1	3.2	3.3
Marijuana and hashish . . .	18.7	18.3	7.2	7.2	Cigars.	36.3	35.2	4.5	3.9
Cocaine.	2.4	2.4	0.5	0.6	35 YEARS OLD AND OVER				
Hallucinogens	5.7	5.8	1.1	1.2					
Inhalants	9.1	8.9	1.1	1.0	Any illicit drug	35.7	35.5	3.4	3.3
Any psychotherapeutic [1] .	10.9	10.9	2.9	3.0	Marijuana and hashish . . .	31.5	31.6	2.2	2.3
Alcohol	42.9	41.7	16.5	16.4	Cocaine.	11.4	11.8	0.4	0.3
"Binge" alcohol use [2] . . .	(NA)	(NA)	10.1	10.4	Hallucinogens	9.4	10.1	0.1	-
Cigarettes	37.1	34.6	14.9	13.4	Inhalants	5.3	5.3	0.1	0.1
Smokeless tobacco	9.8	8.6	2.3	2.1	Any psychotherapeutic [1] .	14.2	13.5	1.3	1.0
Cigars.	19.6	17.1	5.4	4.5					

- Represents or rounds to zero.   NA Not available.   [1] Nonmedical use of any prescription-type pain reliever, tranquilizer, stimulant, or sedative; does not include over-the-counter drugs.   [2] Binge use is defined as drinking five or more drinks on the same occasion on at least one day in the past 30 days.

Source: U.S. Substance Abuse and Mental Health Services Administration, *Summary of Findings from the 2000 National Household Survey on Drug Abuse*, <http://www.samhsa.gov/oas/nhsda.htm>.

No. 183. Estimated Use of Selected Drugs by State: 1999

[15,193 represents 15,193,000. Current users are those persons 12 years old and over who used drugs at least once within month prior to this study. Based on national sample of respondents (see also headnote, Table 182). The state estimates were produced by combining the prevalence rate based on the state sample data and the prevalence rate based on a national regression model applied to local-area county and census block group/tract-level estimates from the state. The parameters of the regression model are estimated from the entire national sample. For comparison purposes, the data shown here display estimates for all 50 States and the District of Columbia utilizing the modeled estimates for all 51 areas]

State	Estimated current users (1,000)					Current users as percent of population				
	Any illicit drug [1]	Mari- juana	Any illicit drug other than mari- juana [1]	Ciga- rettes	Binge alcohol [2]	Any illicit drug [1]	Mari- juana	Any illicit drug other than mari- juana [1]	Ciga- rettes	Binge alcohol [2]
U.S.	15,193	11,476	6,645	57,296	44,486	6.9	5.2	3.0	25.9	20.1
AL.	184	129	95	1,013	621	5.1	3.6	2.6	28.0	17.2
AK.	52	35	18	127	105	10.7	7.2	3.7	26.4	21.8
AZ.	267	203	130	919	725	7.1	5.4	3.4	24.4	19.2
AR.	106	80	55	614	399	5.0	3.7	2.6	28.8	18.7
CA.	2,110	1,598	887	5,247	4,692	8.3	6.3	3.5	20.6	18.4
CO	310	273	113	821	738	9.3	8.1	3.4	24.6	22.1
CT.	208	139	96	625	558	7.7	5.2	3.6	23.2	20.7
DE.	53	43	21	180	142	8.5	6.9	3.4	28.9	22.8
DC	32	31	14	106	74	7.6	7.4	3.4	24.9	17.5
FL.	843	696	360	3,146	2,181	6.8	5.6	2.9	25.2	17.5
GA	363	267	172	1,649	1,132	5.8	4.3	2.7	26.4	18.1
HI	69	59	22	217	201	7.1	6.0	2.2	22.4	20.8
ID	68	48	29	259	197	6.4	4.5	2.8	24.5	18.7
IL	670	514	283	2,647	2,122	6.9	5.3	2.9	27.2	21.8
IN	369	259	144	1,425	988	7.5	5.3	2.9	29.0	20.1
IA	131	83	57	648	582	5.5	3.5	2.4	27.2	24.4
KS.	127	88	59	532	471	5.9	4.1	2.7	24.9	22.1
KY.	198	128	103	1,080	612	6.0	3.9	3.1	33.1	18.7
LA.	202	132	101	976	768	5.7	3.7	2.8	27.5	21.7
ME	74	65	35	269	209	7.1	6.2	3.4	25.8	20.0
MD	226	215	103	939	649	5.3	5.1	2.4	22.1	15.3
MA	514	399	199	1,289	1,244	10.1	7.8	3.9	25.3	24.4
MI	628	454	260	2,299	1,709	8.0	5.7	3.3	29.1	21.7
MN	263	233	106	1,137	946	6.7	5.9	2.7	29.0	24.2
MS	131	85	56	648	413	5.8	3.8	2.5	28.8	18.3
MO	297	229	117	1,374	1,026	6.6	5.1	2.6	30.6	22.8
MT	59	48	22	193	170	7.7	6.2	2.9	25.3	22.3
NE.	76	58	36	336	344	5.6	4.2	2.6	24.7	25.3
NV.	143	86	59	430	331	9.6	5.8	4.0	28.9	22.2
NH	69	62	26	256	208	7.0	6.3	2.6	25.7	20.9
NJ.	511	338	208	1,582	1,328	7.7	5.1	3.1	23.7	19.9
NM	130	106	57	394	315	8.9	7.2	3.9	27.0	21.6
NY.	1,030	738	463	3,768	3,062	7.0	5.0	3.1	25.5	20.7
NC	392	315	169	1,876	1,038	6.3	5.0	2.7	30.0	16.6
ND	29	23	13	151	153	5.4	4.3	2.4	28.3	28.7
OH	606	436	256	2,832	2,074	6.5	4.7	2.8	30.6	22.4
OK	140	98	83	821	500	5.1	3.6	3.0	30.2	18.4
OR	214	187	97	716	525	7.7	6.7	3.5	25.7	18.9
PA.	707	493	299	2,682	2,160	7.0	4.9	3.0	26.6	21.4
RI	71	63	26	223	175	8.7	7.7	3.1	27.2	21.4
SC.	166	126	78	802	539	5.4	4.1	2.5	25.9	17.4
SD.	37	27	15	153	155	6.0	4.4	2.4	25.0	25.3
TN.	254	186	117	1,319	788	5.5	4.0	2.5	28.7	17.1
TX.	850	594	447	3,868	3,373	5.4	3.8	2.8	24.5	21.3
UT.	104	82	59	322	258	6.2	4.9	3.5	19.2	15.4
VT.	35	29	15	119	107	6.8	5.7	3.0	23.6	21.2
VA.	264	231	131	1,297	1,021	4.7	4.1	2.4	23.2	18.3
WA	398	328	158	1,202	839	8.4	7.0	3.4	25.5	17.8
WV	80	60	45	479	271	5.1	3.8	2.9	30.9	17.4
WI	306	255	119	1,177	1,141	7.0	5.9	2.7	27.1	26.3
WY	30	24	13	103	101	7.3	5.8	3.2	24.7	24.2

[1] Any illicit drug indicates use at least once of marijuana/hashish, cocaine (including crack), inhalants, hallucinogens (including PCP and LSD), heroin, or any prescription-type psychotherapeutic used nonmedically. Any illicit drug other than marijuana indicates use at least once of any of these listed drugs, regardless of marijuana/hashish use; marijuana/hashish users who also have used any of the other listed drugs are included. [2] Binge use is defined as drinking five or more drinks on the same occasion on at least 1 day in the past 30 days. By "occasion" is means at the same time or within a couple hours of each other.

Source: U.S. Substance Abuse and Mental Health Services Administration, *National Household Survey on Drug Abuse*. 1999.

U.S. Census Bureau, Statistical Abstract of the United States: 2002

No. 184. Current Cigarette Smoking: 1985 to 2000

[In percent. Prior to 1995, a current smoker is a person who has smoked at least 100 cigarettes and who now smokes. Beginning 1995, definition includes persons who smoke only "some days." Excludes unknown smoking status. Based on the National Health Interview Survey; for details, see Appendix III]

Sex, age, and race	1985	1990	1995	2000	Sex, age, and race	1985	1990	1995	2000
Total smokers, age-adjusted [1]	29.9	25.3	24.6	23.1	Black, total	39.9	32.5	28.5	26.1
					18 to 24 years	27.2	21.3	[2]14.6	20.8
					25 to 34 years	45.6	33.8	25.1	23.3
Male	32.2	28.0	26.5	25.2	35 to 44 years	45.0	42.0	36.3	30.8
Female	27.9	22.9	22.7	21.1	45 to 64 years	46.1	36.7	33.9	32.2
White male...........	31.3	27.6	26.2	25.5	65 years and over.....	27.7	21.5	28.5	14.2
Black male...........	40.2	32.8	29.4	25.7	Female, total	27.9	22.8	22.6	21.0
White female	27.9	23.5	23.4	22.0	18 to 24 years	30.4	22.5	21.8	25.1
Black female..........	30.9	20.8	23.5	20.7	25 to 34 years.........	32.0	28.2	26.4	22.5
					35 to 44 years.........	31.5	24.8	27.1	26.2
Total smokers.......	30.1	25.5	24.7	23.3	45 to 64 years.........	29.9	24.8	24.0	21.6
					65 years and over	13.5	11.5	11.5	9.3
Male, total	32.6	28.4	27.0	25.7	White, total	27.7	23.4	23.1	21.6
18 to 24 years.........	28.0	26.6	27.8	28.5	18 to 24 years	31.8	25.4	24.9	28.7
25 to 34 years.........	38.2	31.6	29.5	29.0	25 to 34 years	32.0	28.5	27.3	25.1
35 to 44 years.........	37.6	34.5	31.5	30.2	35 to 44 years	31.0	25.0	27.0	26.6
45 to 64 years.........	33.4	29.3	27.1	26.4	45 to 64 years	29.7	25.4	24.3	21.4
65 years and over	19.6	14.6	14.9	10.2	65 years and over.....	13.3	11.5	11.7	9.1
White, total	31.7	28.0	26.6	25.8	Black, total	31.0	21.2	23.5	20.8
18 to 24 years	28.4	27.4	28.4	30.9	18 to 24 years	23.7	10.0	[2]8.8	14.2
25 to 34 years	37.3	31.6	29.9	29.9	25 to 34 years	36.2	29.1	26.7	15.5
35 to 44 years	36.6	33.5	31.2	30.6	35 to 44 years	40.2	25.5	31.9	30.2
45 to 64 years	32.1	28.7	26.3	25.8	45 to 64 years	33.4	22.6	27.5	25.6
65 years and over.....	18.9	13.7	14.1	9.8	65 years and over.....	14.5	11.1	13.3	10.2

[1] Estimates are age adjusted to the year 2000 standard using five age groups: 18-24 years, 25-34 years, 35-44 years, 45-64 years, 65 years and over.   [2] Data have a relative standard error of 20-30 percent.

Source: U.S. National Center for Health Statistics, *Health, United States*, annual.

No. 185. Current Cigarette Smoking by Sex and State: 2000

[In percent. Current cigarette smoking is defined as persons who reported having smoked 100 or more cigarettes during their lifetime and who currently smoke every day or some days. Based on the Behavioral Risk Factor Surveillance System, a telephone survey of health behaviors of the civilian, noninstitutionalized U.S. population, 18 years old and over; for details, see source]

State	Total	Male	Female	State	Total	Male	Female	State	Total	Male	Female
U.S. [1] ..	23.3	24.4	21.2	KS	21.1	24.2	18.2	ND	23.3	25.9	20.7
				KY	30.5	33.4	27.9	OH	26.3	26.7	26.0
AL	25.3	29.0	22.0	LA	24.1	26.7	21.8	OK	23.3	23.7	23.0
AK......	25.0	26.8	23.1	ME	23.8	24.6	23.1	OR	20.8	22.3	19.3
AZ	18.6	18.4	18.8	MD	20.6	22.0	19.2	PA	24.3	25.4	23.3
AR......	25.2	26.2	24.2	MA	20.0	20.2	19.8	RI	23.5	23.8	23.2
CA......	17.2	20.1	14.4	MI	24.2	26.0	22.5	SC	24.7	28.5	21.3
CO......	20.1	19.5	20.6	MN	19.8	20.7	18.9	SD	22.0	22.6	21.4
CT......	20.0	20.5	19.5	MS	23.5	25.3	21.9	TN	25.7	27.7	23.8
DE......	23.0	25.8	20.3	MO	27.2	30.1	24.6	TX	22.0	25.3	18.8
DC......	20.9	22.1	19.9	MT	18.9	18.0	19.7	UT	12.9	14.5	11.4
FL	23.2	24.5	22.1	NE	21.4	22.1	20.7	VT	21.5	21.8	21.2
GA......	23.6	26.5	21.0	NV	29.1	28.7	29.5	VA	21.5	24.4	18.8
HI	19.7	22.9	16.5	NH	25.4	26.9	23.9	WA	20.7	21.7	19.7
ID	22.4	22.9	21.9	NJ	21.0	23.5	18.6	WV	26.1	27.8	24.7
IL	22.3	24.9	20.0	NM	23.6	26.2	21.2	WI	24.1	24.4	23.9
IN	27.0	28.5	25.5	NY	21.6	22.5	20.9	WY	23.8	23.2	24.3
IA	23.3	25.9	20.9	NC......	26.1	28.4	24.1				

[1] Represents median value among the states and DC. For definition of median, see Guide to Tabular Presentation.

Source: U.S. Centers for Disease Control and Prevention, Atlanta, GA, *Morbidity and Mortality Weekly Report*, Vol. 50, No. 49, December 14, 2001.

No. 186. Use of Mammography for Women 40 Years Old and Over by Patient Characteristics: 1990 to 2000

[Percent of women having a mammogram within the past 2 years. Covers civilian noninstitutional population. Based on National Health Interview Survey; see Appendix III]

Characteristic	1990	1994	2000	Characteristic	1990	1994	2000
Total [1]	51.4	60.9	70.3	Years of school completed:			
40 to 49 years old	55.1	61.3	64.2	Less than 12 years.........	36.4	48.2	57.7
50 years old and over.	49.7	60.6	73.6	12 years	52.7	61.0	69.6
50 to 64 years old	56.0	66.5	78.6	13 years or more	62.8	69.7	76.1
65 years old and over	43.4	55.0	68.0				
White, non-Hispanic...........	52.7	61.3	72.1	Poverty status: [3]			
Black, non-Hispanic	46.0	64.4	67.9	Below poverty	28.7	44.4	55.2
Hispanic origin [2]	45.2	51.9	61.4	At or above poverty	54.8	64.8	72.2

[1] Includes all other races not shown separately and unknown education level and poverty status.   [2] Persons of Hispanic origin may be of any race.   [3] For explanation of poverty level, see text, Section 13, Income, Expenditures, and Wealth.

Source: U.S. National Center for Health Statistics, *Health United States,* annual.

No. 187. Cancer—Estimated New Cases, 2002, and Survival Rates, 1980-82 to 1992-98

[1,285 represents 1,285,000. The 5-year relative survival rate, which is derived by adjusting the observed survival rate for expected mortality, represents the likelihood that a person will not die from causes directly related to their cancer within 5 years. Survival data shown are based on those patients diagnosed while residents of an area listed below during the time periods shown. Data are based on information collected as part of the National Cancer Institute's Surveillance, Epidemiology and End Results (SEER) program, a collection of population-based registries in Connecticut, New Mexico, Utah, Iowa, Hawaii, Atlanta, Detroit, Seattle-Puget Sound, and San Francisco-Oakland]

Site	Estimated new cases,[1] 2002 (1,000)			5-year relative survival rates (percent)							
				White				Black			
	Total	Male	Female	1980-82	1986-88	1989-91	1992-98	1980-82	1986-88	1989-91	1992-98
All sites[2]	1,285	638	647	52.1	56.7	60.3	63.8	39.7	42.6	46.2	52.6
Lung[3]	169	90	79	13.5	13.5	14.3	15.0	12.1	11.9	10.7	12.3
Breast[3]	205	2	204	77.1	83.9	86.1	87.6	65.7	69.2	71.1	72.5
Colon and rectum	148	73	76	54.9	60.8	62.3	62.6	46.5	52.5	54.0	52.8
Colon	107	50	57	55.7	61.6	63.1	62.7	49.3	52.9	53.9	52.8
Rectum	41	23	18	53.1	59.1	60.5	62.4	37.9	51.1	54.3	52.7
Prostate	189	189	(X)	74.5	82.7	91.8	97.8	64.7	69.3	80.6	92.6
Bladder	57	42	15	78.9	80.7	82.1	82.3	58.3	62.3	61.9	64.5
Corpus uteri	39	(X)	39	82.8	84.4	85.6	86.0	55.1	57.1	57.5	60.5
Non-Hodgkin's lymphoma[4]	54	28	26	51.9	52.9	51.9	56.1	50.2	50.2	43.7	46.1
Oral cavity and pharynx	29	19	10	55.6	55.2	55.4	58.8	31.0	34.7	32.6	34.9
Leukemia[4]	31	18	13	39.5	44.2	45.8	47.3	32.9	38.0	34.1	38.4
Melanoma of skin	54	30	24	83.2	87.9	88.7	89.3	60.9	69.0	79.1	65.5
Pancreas	30	15	16	2.8	3.1	4.1	4.3	4.5	6.2	3.8	3.9
Kidney	32	19	13	51.1	57.5	60.7	62.4	55.8	53.3	58.0	60.0
Stomach	22	13	8	16.5	19.1	18.4	20.9	19.4	19.3	24.8	20.0
Ovary	23	(X)	23	38.7	41.9	49.6	52.5	39.1	38.6	41.6	52.5
Cervix uteri[5]	13	(X)	13	68.2	71.7	72.3	72.1	61.3	55.5	62.6	59.9

X Not applicable. [1] Estimates provided by American Cancer Society are based on rates from the National Cancer Institute's SEER program. [2] Includes other sites not shown separately. [3] Survival rates for female only. [4] All types combined. [5] Invasive cancer only.

Source: U.S. National Institutes of Health, National Cancer Institute, *Cancer Statistics Review*, annual.

No. 188. Cancer—Estimated New Cases and Deaths by State: 2002

[In thousands (1,284.9 represents 1,284,900). Excludes basal and squamous cellskin cancers and in situ carcinomas except urinary bladder]

State	New cases[1]			Deaths		
	Total[2]	Lung	Female breast	Total[2]	Lung	Female breast
U.S.	1,284.9	169.4	203.5	555.5	154.9	40.0
AL	22.6	3.2	3.1	9.8	2.9	0.6
AK	1.6	0.2	0.3	0.7	0.2	0.1
AZ	22.1	2.9	3.5	9.6	2.7	0.7
AR	14.2	2.2	2.0	6.2	2.0	0.4
CA	119.9	14.3	19.9	51.8	13.1	3.9
CO	14.5	1.0	2.4	6.3	1.5	0.5
CT	16.1	2.0	2.6	7.0	1.8	0.5
DE	4.1	0.6	0.6	1.8	0.5	0.1
DC	2.7	0.3	0.6	1.2	0.3	0.1
FL	92.2	13.0	13.1	39.9	11.9	2.6
GA	31.6	4.4	5.2	13.7	4.0	1.0
HI	4.7	0.6	0.7	2.0	0.5	0.1
ID	5.2	0.6	0.9	2.3	0.6	0.2
IL	57.4	7.4	9.7	24.8	6.7	1.9
IN	30.0	4.3	4.6	13.0	4.0	0.9
IA	14.8	1.9	2.4	6.4	1.7	0.5
KS	12.3	1.7	1.8	5.3	1.5	0.4
KY	21.1	3.4	3.1	9.1	3.1	0.6
LA	21.9	2.9	3.5	9.5	2.7	0.7
ME	7.0	1.0	1.0	3.0	0.9	0.2
MD	23.5	3.2	4.1	10.2	2.9	0.8
MA	31.7	4.0	4.7	13.7	3.6	0.9
MI	45.8	6.1	7.3	19.8	5.5	1.4
MN	20.8	2.5	3.2	9.0	2.3	0.6
MS	14.4	2.1	2.2	6.2	1.9	0.4
MO	28.6	4.2	4.0	12.3	3.8	0.8
MT	4.4	0.6	0.6	1.9	0.5	0.1
NE	7.7	1.0	1.2	3.3	0.9	0.2
NV	9.5	1.4	1.3	4.1	1.3	0.3
NH	5.8	0.8	0.8	2.5	0.7	0.2
NJ	41.1	4.9	6.9	17.8	4.5	1.4
NM	7.1	0.8	1.2	3.0	0.7	0.2
NY	83.7	10.0	14.7	36.2	9.1	2.9
NC	38.2	5.5	5.9	16.5	5.0	1.2
ND	3.1	0.3	0.5	1.3	0.3	0.1
OH	58.7	7.9	9.5	25.4	7.3	1.9
OK	16.9	2.5	2.7	7.3	2.3	0.5
OR	16.8	2.2	2.6	7.3	2.0	0.5
PA	68.9	8.7	11.0	29.8	8.0	2.2
RI	5.6	0.8	0.8	2.4	0.7	0.2
SC	19.5	2.6	3.1	8.4	2.4	0.6
SD	3.7	0.4	0.5	1.6	0.4	0.1
TN	29.1	4.4	4.4	12.6	4.0	0.9
TX	79.7	10.8	13.1	34.5	9.9	2.6
UT	5.9	0.5	1.1	2.5	0.4	0.2
VT	2.9	0.4	0.4	1.3	0.4	0.1
VA	31.3	4.2	5.0	13.5	3.8	1.0
WA	25.6	3.4	3.7	11.1	3.1	0.7
WV	11.0	1.7	1.5	4.7	1.5	0.3
WI	25.3	3.0	3.9	11.0	2.8	0.8
WY	2.3	0.3	0.3	1.0	0.2	0.1

[1] Estimates are offered as a rough guide and should be interpreted with caution. They are calculated according to the distribution of estimated 2002 cancer deaths by state. [2] Includes other types of cancer, not shown separately.

Source: American Cancer Society, Inc., Atlanta, Georgia, *Cancer Facts and Figures—2002* (copyright).

No. 189. Cumulative Percent Distribution of Population by Height and Sex: 1988-94

[Height was measured without shoes. Based on sample and subject to sampling variability; see source]

Height	Males						Females					
	20-29 years	30-39 years	40-49 years	50-59 years	60-69 years	70-79 years	20-29 years	30-39 years	40-49 years	50-59 years	60-69 years	70-79 years
Percent under—												
4'8"	-	-	-	-	-	-	0.6	0.1	-	-	0.2	1.7
4'9"	-	-	-	-	-	-	0.7	0.2	0.3	0.1	0.7	3.3
4'10"	-	-	-	-	0.1	-	1.2	0.7	0.7	1.9	1.7	4.9
4'11"	-	-	-	-	0.1	0.1	3.1	2.6	1.7	3.1	4.4	9.8
5'	0.1	-	0.2	-	0.4	0.1	6.0	5.5	5.3	6.6	9.9	15.4
5'1"	0.1	-	0.4	0.1	0.5	0.6	11.5	10.4	9.9	11.9	19.0	28.9
5'2"	0.5	0.8	0.7	0.2	0.7	1.9	21.8	18.5	18.8	24.4	34.3	45.6
5'3"	1.3	1.4	0.9	1.0	2.2	2.7	34.3	30.7	31.9	38.6	48.3	61.2
5'4"	3.4	2.2	1.7	2.5	5.8	7.8	48.9	42.9	49.2	52.6	65.5	74.5
5'5"	6.9	5.1	5.6	6.0	9.4	16.5	62.7	59.1	64.3	69.9	76.5	85.9
5'6"	11.7	10.1	12.1	11.7	15.8	27.3	74.0	71.8	77.0	81.6	87.8	93.9
5'7"	20.8	18.9	19.6	20.5	27.4	39.5	84.7	84.1	87.0	89.3	92.5	97.3
5'8"	32.0	28.3	28.0	32.6	38.6	53.4	92.4	91.6	94.5	95.6	96.7	99.2
5'9"	46.3	44.3	42.1	43.9	55.1	68.7	96.2	95.6	97.3	99.0	99.3	99.9
5'10"	58.7	58.0	58.1	60.6	68.8	79.5	98.6	98.1	98.9	99.6	99.8	100.0
5'11"	70.1	70.4	71.1	75.2	81.4	89.2	99.5	99.5	99.4	100.0	100.0	100.0
6'	81.2	79.7	81.5	85.4	90.0	94.1	100.0	100.0	100.0	100.0	100.0	100.0
6'1"	87.4	86.2	89.0	92.4	95.2	97.2	100.0	100.0	100.0	100.0	100.0	100.0
6'2"	94.7	92.4	94.4	96.4	98.2	99.3	100.0	100.0	100.0	100.0	100.0	100.0
6'3"	97.9	98.1	97.2	98.2	99.5	99.9	100.0	100.0	100.0	100.0	100.0	100.0

- Represents or rounds to zero.

Source: U.S. National Center for Health Statistics, unpublished data.

No. 190. Percent of U.S. Adults Who Were Overweight and Percent Who Were Obese: 1999

[Percent who are overweight includes those who are obese and represent those who have a body mass index (BMI) equal to or above 25. Percent who are obese represent those who have a BMI equal to or above 30. BMI is a measure that adjusts body weight for height. It is calculated as weight in kilograms divided by height in meters squared. These estimates are based on definitions provided in the *Dietary Guidelines for Americans*, published by the U.S. Dept. of Agriculture and the U.S. Dept. of Health and Human Services. Based on the National Health Interview Survey; for details, see Appendix III]

Characteristic	Both sexes		Males		Females	
	Overweight	Obese	Overweight	Obese	Overweight	Obese
All ages (age-adjusted) [1]	56.5	21.1	65.0	21.6	48.3	20.6
All ages (unadjusted) [1]	56.4	21.1	65.0	21.7	48.3	20.6
18-24 years old.	37.6	13.4	41.7	13.5	33.5	13.2
25-44 years old.	56.2	21.2	67.7	22.2	44.7	20.2
45-64 years old.	65.5	26.1	73.0	26.7	58.1	25.5
65 years old and over	55.7	18.3	61.9	17.5	51.0	18.8
Hispanic	63.8	24.1	68.8	23.0	58.6	24.9
White, Non-Hispanic	55.0	20.1	65.1	21.4	45.0	18.7
Black, Non-Hispanic.	65.7	28.8	65.2	23.1	65.8	33.2
Asian/Other Pacific Islander, Non-Hispanic	29.5	6.1	36.6	8.2	23.9	4.5
Educational attainment:						
Fewer than 9 grades	63.1	24.9	65.5	22.2	60.7	27.4
Grades 9 - 11	59.3	24.7	63.8	26.3	55.0	23.5
General equivalency degree	63.3	27.2	68.8	27.3	56.4	27.3
High school graduate	58.3	23.4	66.7	24.0	50.6	22.8
Some college - no degree	57.5	22.5	65.4	23.4	50.3	21.7
Associate of Arts - Technical	57.0	20.6	65.0	18.8	49.2	22.0
Associate of Arts - Academic	56.2	19.3	70.4	20.7	45.3	18.4
Bachelor of Arts or Science	51.4	15.7	63.4	16.7	38.9	14.8
Graduate degree	47.5	14.0	56.5	13.3	36.7	14.4

[1] Age-specific rates are unadjusted; all other estimates were adjusted to the 2000 projected population.

Source: U.S. National Center for Health Statistics, unpublished data.

126   Health and Nutrition

No. 191. Percentage of Adults Engaging in Leisure-Time Physical Activity: 2000

[In percent. Covers persons 18 years old and over. Based on responses to questions about physical activity in prior month from the Behavioral Risk Factor Surveillance System. Estimates are age-adjusted to the year 2000 standard population. Based on a survey sample of approximately 180,000 persons in 50 states and the District of Columbia in 2000]

Characteristic	Persons who meet recommended activity [1]	Persons with insufficient activity [2]	Persons who are physically inactive [3]
Total...........	26.2	46.2	27.6
Male..............	27.1	47.5	25.3
Female............	25.5	44.8	29.7
White, non-Hispanic ...	27.5	48.3	24.2
Black, non-Hispanic....	21.9	43.3	34.8
Hispanic............	21.1	37.9	41.0
Other	27.3	42.9	29.8
Males:			
18 to 29 years old ...	26.9	54.6	18.5
30 to 44 years old ...	23.7	52.2	24.2
45 to 64 years old ...	26.0	45.5	28.5
65 to 74 years old ...	33.7	38.7	27.6
75 years old and over.	35.9	29.2	34.9
Females:			
18 to 29 years old ...	25.4	49.3	25.3
30 to 44 years old ...	24.7	47.1	28.2
45 to 64 years old ...	25.7	44.9	29.4
65 to 74 years old ...	24.6	40.9	34.4
75 years old and over.	28.4	27.8	43.8
School years completed:			
Less than 12 years ..	14.5	36.2	49.3
12 years	21.9	44.7	33.4
Some college (13-15 years)	28.3	48.2	23.5
College (16 or more years)	34.2	50.0	15.8
Household income:			
Less than $10,000...	18.9	36.7	44.5
$10,000 to $19,999 ..	18.9	40.2	40.9
$20,000 to $34,999 ..	23.3	44.3	32.4
$35,000 to $49,999 ..	27.8	47.8	24.5
$50,000 and over ...	33.5	50.3	16.3

[1] Recommended activity is physical activity at least 5 times/week x 30 minutes/time or vigorous physical activity for 20 minutes at a time at least 3 times/week. [2] Persons whose reported physical activity does not meet recommended level. [3] Persons with no reported physical activity.

Source: U.S. National Center for Chronic Disease Prevention and Health Promotion, "Nutrition and Physical Activity"; <http://www.cdc.gov/nccdphp/dnpa>; (accessed: 21 June 2002) and unpublished data.

No. 192. Households and Persons Having Problems With Access to Food: 1995 to 2000

[100,445 represents 100,445,000. Food secure means that a household had access at all times to enough food for an active healthy life, with no need for recourse to emergency food sources or other extraordinary coping behaviors to meet their basic food needs. A food insecure household did not have this same access to enough food to fully meet basic needs at all times. Food insecure households with hunger were those with one or more household members who were hungry at least sometime during the period due to inadequate resources for food. The omission of homeless persons may be a cause of underreporting. The Federal food security measure was developed through a collaborative process between private non-government experts, academic researchers, and a Federal interagency working group, with leadership from the U.S. Dept. of Agriculture and the U.S. Dept. of Health and Human Services. The severity of food insecurity and hunger in households is measured through a series of questions about experiences and behaviors known to characterize households that are having difficulty meeting basic food needs. These experiences and behaviors generally occur in an ordered sequence as the severity of food insecurity increases. As resources become more constrained, adults in typical households first worry about having enough food, then they stretch household resources and juggle other necessities, then decrease the quality and variety of household members' diets, then decrease the frequency and quantity of adults' food intake, and finally decrease the frequency and quantity of children's food intake. All questions refer to the previous 12 months and include a qualifying phrase reminding respondents to report only those occurrences that resulted from inadequate financial resources. Restrictions to food intake due to dieting or busy schedules are excluded. Data are from the Food Security Supplement to the Current Population Survey (CPS); for details about the CPS, see text, Section 1, Population, and Appendix III]

Household food security level	Number (1,000)				Percent distribution			
	1995	1998 [1]	1998 [2]	2000	1995	1998 [1]	1998 [2]	2000
Households, total........	100,445	103,480	103,309	106,043	100.0	100.0	100.0	100.0
Food secure	90,097	92,972	91,121	94,942	89.7	89.8	88.2	89.5
Food insecure	10,348	10,509	12,188	11,101	10.3	10.2	11.8	10.5
Without hunger...........	6,402	6,820	8,353	7,786	6.4	6.6	8.1	7.3
With hunger............	3,946	3,689	3,835	3,315	3.9	3.6	3.7	3.1
With hunger among children [3]..	(NA)	(NA)	331	255	(NA)	(NA)	0.9	0.7
Adult members	191,063	197,423	197,084	201,922	100.0	100.0	100.0	100.0
Food secure	172,862	178,631	174,964	181,586	90.5	90.5	88.8	89.9
Food insecure	18,200	18,792	22,120	20,336	9.5	9.5	11.2	10.1
Without hunger...........	11,611	12,657	15,632	14,763	6.1	6.4	7.9	7.3
With hunger............	6,589	6,135	6,488	5,573	3.4	3.1	3.3	2.8
Child members	70,279	71,463	71,282	71,763	100.0	100.0	100.0	100.0
Food secure	58,048	59,090	57,255	58,868	82.6	82.7	80.3	82.0
Food insecure	12,231	12,373	14,027	12,895	17.4	17.3	19.7	18.0
Without hunger...........	8,131	9,114	10,658	9,945	11.6	12.8	15.0	13.9
With hunger [4]	4,100	3,259	3,369	2,950	5.8	4.6	4.7	4.1
With hunger among children [3]..	(NA)	(NA)	716	562	(NA)	(NA)	1.0	0.8

NA Not available. [1] Adjusted data. These data are comparable to those of earlier years. [2] Data as collected. These data are comparable to those for 2000. [3] One or more children in these households was hungry because of the household's food insecurity. Percent distribution of households with hunger among children excludes households with no child from the denominator. [4] Most of these children did not, themselves, face hunger, but adults or older children in the household did.

Source: U.S. Dept. of Agriculture, Economic Research Service, Household Food Security in the United States, 1999, Food Assistance and Nutrition Research Report #8; Fall 2000 and Household Food Security in the United States, 2000, Food Assistance and Nutrition Research Report No. 21; February 2002.

Health and Nutrition 127

No. 193. Nutrition—Nutrients in Foods Available for Civilian Consumption Per Capita Per Day: 1970 to 1999

[Computed by the Center for Nutrition Policy and Promotion (CNPP). Based on Economic Research Service (ERS) estimates of per capita quantities of food available for consumption from "Food Consumption, Prices, and, Expenditures," on imputed consumption data for foods no longer reported by ERS, and on CNPP estimates of quantities of produce from home gardens. Food supply estimates do not reflect loss of food or nutrients from further marketing or home processing. Enrichment and fortification levels of iron, zinc, thiamin, riboflavin, niacin, vitamin A, vitamin B_6, vitamin B_{12}, and ascorbic acid are included]

Nutrient	Unit	1970-79	1980-89	1990-99	1995	1999
Food energy	Calories	3,200	3,400	3,700	3,700	3,800
Carbohydrate	Grams	387	411	478	481	500
Dietary fiber	Grams	19	20	23	23	24
Protein	Grams	95	98	108	108	111
Total fat [1]	Grams	149	156	159	158	164
Saturated	Grams	51	52	51	51	52
Monounsaturated	Grams	60	63	67	67	70
Polyunsaturated	Grams	28	31	33	33	34
Cholesterol	Milligrams	440	420	410	410	430
Vitamin A	Micrograms RE [2]	1,540	1,560	1,710	1,720	1,780
Carotenes	Micrograms RE [2]	550	590	730	730	800
Vitamin E	Milligrams α-TE [3]	13.9	15.5	17.3	17.1	17.8
Vitamin C	Milligrams	110	117	127	127	132
Thiamin	Milligrams	2.2	2.5	2.9	2.9	3.0
Riboflavin	Milligrams	2.5	2.7	2.9	2.9	2.9
Niacin	Milligrams	24.0	28.0	32.0	32.0	33.0
Vitamin B_6	Milligrams	2.0	2.2	2.4	2.5	2.5
Folate	Micrograms	310	343	432	384	641
Vitamin B_{12}	Micrograms	8.9	8.1	8.0	8.1	8.1
Calcium	Milligrams	910	910	970	970	990
Phosphorus	Milligrams	1,470	1,520	1,660	1,650	1,690
Magnesium	Milligrams	330	340	380	380	390
Iron	Milligrams	16.1	19.4	23.1	23.1	23.6
Zinc	Milligrams	12.9	13.9	15.2	15.3	15.5
Copper	Milligrams	1.6	1.8	1.9	1.9	2.0
Potassium	Milligrams	3,490	3,530	3,790	3,760	3,890
Selenium	Milligrams	130	139	162	158	178
Sodium [4]	Milligrams	1,360	1,350	1,370	1,370	1,360

[1] Includes other types of fat not shown separately. [2] Retinol equivalents. [3] Alpha-Tocopherol equivalents. [4] Does not include amount from processed foods; underestimates actual availability.

Source: U.S. Dept. of Agriculture, Center for Nutrition Policy and Promotion, *Nutrient Content of the U.S. Food Supply, 1909-99*, 2001. Data also published by Economic Research Service in *Food Consumption, Prices, and Expenditures*, annual.

No. 194. Sources of Calcium, Iron, and Cholesterol in the U.S. Food Supply: 1970 and 1999

[In percent. See headnote, Table 193]

Commodity group	Calcium 1970	Calcium 1999	Commodity group	Iron 1970	Iron 1999	Commodity group	Cholesterol 1970	Cholesterol 1999
Total	100	100	Total	100	100	Total	100	100
Whole milk	35	11	Grains and breakfast cereals	35	53	Meat, poultry, fish [1]	39	43
Low-fat and skim milk	11	21	Meat, poultry, fish [1]	32	23	Eggs	40	35
Cheese	11	25	Eggs	4	2	Whole milk	8	3
Other dairy	19	15	Vegetables	14	10	Low-fat and skim milk	1	2
Vegetables	6	7	Fruits	3	3	Cheese	3	7
Other foods	18	21	Dairy products	2	2	Other dairy	3	4
			Other foods	10	7	Other foods	6	6

[1] Includes meat alternatives.

Source: U.S. Dept. of Agriculture, Center for Nutrition Policy and Promotion, *Nutrient Content of the U.S. Food Supply, 1909-99*, 2001.

No. 195. Per Capita Consumption of Major Food Commodities: 1980 to 2000

[In pounds, retail weight, except as indicated. Consumption represents the residual after exports, nonfood use and ending stocks are subtracted from the sum of beginning stocks, domestic production, and imports. Based on Census Bureau estimated population]

Commodity	Unit	1980	1985	1990	1995	1998	1999	2000
Red meat, total (boneless, trimmed weight) [1] [2]	Pounds . . .	126.4	124.9	112.3	113.6	113.3	115.1	113.5
Beef.	Pounds . . .	72.1	74.6	63.9	63.6	63.6	64.4	64.4
Veal	Pounds . . .	1.3	1.5	0.9	0.8	0.7	0.6	0.5
Lamb and mutton	Pounds . . .	1.0	1.1	1.0	0.9	0.9	0.8	0.8
Pork . . . . [2]	Pounds . . .	52.1	47.7	46.4	48.4	48.2	49.4	47.7
Poultry (boneless, trimmed weight) [2]	Pounds . . .	40.8	45.5	56.3	62.1	63.7	66.8	66.5
Chicken	Pounds . . .	32.7	36.4	42.4	48.2	49.8	52.9	52.9
Turkey	Pounds . . .	8.1	9.1	13.8	13.9	13.9	13.8	13.6
Fish and shellfish (boneless, trimmed weight) . .	Pounds . . .	12.4	15.0	15.0	14.8	14.5	14.9	15.2
Eggs	Number. . .	271	255	234	232	239	249	250
Shell.	Number. . .	236	217	186	172	173	177	177
Processed . . . . [3] . . .	Number. . .	35	39	48	59	66	72	73
Dairy products, total [3]	Pounds . . .	543.2	593.7	568.3	576.6	572.8	584.9	593.0
Fluid milk products [4]	Gallons . .	27.9	27.1	26.2	24.6	23.8	23.7	23.2
Beverage milks	Gallons . .	27.6	26.7	25.7	24.0	23.2	23.1	22.6
Plain whole milk.	Gallons . .	16.5	13.9	10.2	8.4	7.8	7.9	7.8
Plain reduced-fat milk (2%)	Gallons . .	6.3	7.9	9.1	8.1	7.4	7.3	7.1
Plain light and skim milks.	Gallons . .	3.1	3.2	4.9	6.2	6.5	6.3	6.1
Flavored whole milk	Gallons . .	0.6	0.4	0.3	0.3	0.3	0.4	0.4
Flavored milks other than whole	Gallons . .	0.6	0.7	0.8	0.8	1.0	1.0	1.0
Buttermilk	Gallons . .	0.5	0.5	0.4	0.3	0.3	0.3	0.3
Yogurt (excl. frozen).	1/2 pints . .	4.6	7.3	7.4	9.3	9.2	9.0	9.9
Fluid cream products [5]	1/2 pints . .	10.5	13.5	14.3	15.7	17.0	17.9	18.6
Cream [6]	1/2 pints . .	6.3	8.2	8.7	9.4	10.6	11.4	11.8
Sour cream and dips	1/2 pints . .	3.4	4.3	4.7	5.4	5.6	5.7	6.2
Condensed and evaporated milks	Pounds . . .	7.0	7.5	7.9	6.8	6.1	6.5	5.8
Whole milk.	Pounds . . .	3.8	3.6	3.2	2.3	2.0	2.1	1.8
Skim milk	Pounds . . .	3.3	3.8	4.8	4.5	4.1	4.4	3.8
Cheese [7]	Pounds . . .	17.5	22.5	24.6	26.9	27.8	29.0	29.8
American [8]	Pounds . . .	9.6	12.2	11.1	11.7	11.9	12.6	12.7
Cheddar	Pounds . . .	6.9	9.8	9.0	9.1	9.6	10.1	(NA)
Italian [8]	Pounds . . .	4.4	6.5	9.0	10.4	11.3	11.8	(NA)
Mozzarella	Pounds . . .	3.0	4.6	6.9	8.1	8.8	9.2	(NA)
Other [8]	Pounds . . .	3.4	3.9	4.5	5.0	4.8	5.0	(NA)
Swiss.	Pounds . . .	1.3	1.3	1.4	1.1	1.1	1.1	(NA)
Cream and Neufchatel	Pounds . . .	1.0	1.2	1.7	2.1	2.3	2.4	(NA)
Cottage cheese, total.	Pounds . . .	4.5	4.1	3.4	2.7	2.7	2.6	2.6
Lowfat.	Pounds . . .	0.8	1.0	1.2	1.2	1.3	1.3	1.3
Frozen dairy products	Pounds . . .	26.4	27.9	28.4	29.1	29.0	28.6	27.8
Ice cream.	Pounds . . .	17.5	18.1	15.8	15.5	16.4	16.7	16.5
Lowfat ice cream	Pounds . . .	7.1	6.9	7.7	7.4	8.1	7.5	7.3
Sherbet	Pounds . . .	1.2	1.3	1.2	1.3	1.3	1.3	1.2
Frozen yogurt	Pounds . . .	(NA)	(NA)	2.8	3.4	2.1	1.9	1.8
Fats and oils:								
Total, fat content only	Pounds . . .	56.9	64.1	63.0	65.4	64.3	67.0	74.5
Butter (product weight)	Pounds . . .	4.5	4.9	4.4	4.5	4.4	4.7	4.6
Margarine (product weight)	Pounds . . .	11.3	10.8	10.9	9.1	8.2	7.9	8.2
Lard (direct use)	Pounds . . .	2.3	1.6	1.6	1.6	2.0	2.0	1.9
Edible beef tallow (direct use)	Pounds . . .	1.1	2.0	0.6	2.7	3.1	3.6	4.0
Shortening	Pounds . . .	18.2	22.9	22.2	22.2	20.5	21.1	23.1
Salad and cooking oils	Pounds . . .	21.2	23.5	25.2	26.5	27.3	28.8	33.7
Other edible fats and oils	Pounds . . .	1.5	1.6	1.2	1.6	1.3	1.5	1.5
Flour and cereal products [9]	Pounds . . .	144.7	156.5	181.0	190.3	196.1	196.9	199.9
Wheat flour	Pounds . . .	116.9	124.6	136.0	140.1	144.9	144.0	146.3
Rice, milled	Pounds . . .	9.4	9.1	15.8	18.7	18.3	19.5	19.7
Corn products	Pounds . . .	12.9	17.2	21.4	24.9	27.2	27.8	28.4
Oat products	Pounds . . .	3.9	4.0	6.5	5.4	4.4	4.4	4.3
Caloric sweeteners, total [10]	Pounds . . .	123.0	128.8	136.8	148.0	152.6	155.0	152.4
Sugar, refined cane and beet	Pounds . . .	83.6	62.7	64.4	64.7	65.0	66.4	65.6
Corn sweeteners [11]	Pounds . . .	38.2	64.8	71.1	82.0	86.3	87.2	85.3
High-fructose corn syrup	Pounds . . .	19.0	45.2	49.6	57.6	62.9	64.8	63.8
Other:								
Cocoa beans	Pounds . . .	3.4	4.6	5.4	4.5	5.4	5.6	5.9
Coffee (green beans).	Pounds . . .	10.3	10.5	10.3	7.9	9.3	9.8	10.3
Peanuts (shelled)	Pounds . . .	4.8	6.3	6.0	5.6	5.8	6.0	5.7
Tree nuts (shelled)	Pounds . . .	1.8	2.5	2.4	1.9	2.2	2.5	2.5

NA Not available.   [1] Excludes edible offals.   [2] Excludes shipments to Puerto Rico and the other U.S. possessions.
[3] Milk-equivalent, milkfat basis. Includes butter.   [4] Fluid milk figures are aggregates of commercial sales and milk produced and consumed on farms.   [5] Includes eggnog, not shown separately.   [6] Heavy cream, light cream, and half and half.   [7] Excludes full-skim American, cottage, pot, and baker's cheese.   [8] Includes other cheeses not shown separately.   [9] Includes rye flour and barley products not shown separately. Excludes quantities used in alcoholic beverages.   [10] Dry weight. Includes edible syrups (maple, molasses, etc.) and honey not shown separately.   [11] Includes glucose and dextrose not shown separately.

Source: U.S. Department of Agriculture, Economic Research Service, *Food Consumption, Prices, and Expenditures, 1970-2000; Agricultural Outlook,* monthly; and online at <http://www.ers.usda.gov/data/consumption>.

Health and Nutrition   129

No. 196. Per Capita Utilization of Commercially Produced Fruits and Vegetables: 1980 to 2000

[In pounds, farm weight. Domestic food use of fresh fruits and vegetables reflects the fresh-market share of commodity production plus imports and minus exports]

Commodity	1980	1985	1990	1995	1996	1997	1998	1999	2000
Fruits and vegetables, total [1]	608.0	629.3	659.6	690.5	698.1	708.0	699.2	705.4	707.7
Fruits, total	270.5	270.0	272.2	282.0	279.0	289.6	284.1	289.8	279.4
Fresh fruits	104.8	110.6	116.3	122.6	126.1	129.5	128.9	129.5	126.8
Noncitrus	78.7	89.1	94.9	98.8	101.5	103.0	102.3	109.2	103.3
Apples	19.2	17.3	19.6	18.7	18.6	18.1	19.0	18.5	17.4
Bananas	20.8	23.5	24.4	27.1	27.6	27.2	28.0	30.7	28.4
Cantaloupes	5.8	8.5	9.2	9.0	10.3	10.5	10.7	11.5	10.6
Grapes	4.0	6.8	7.9	7.4	6.8	7.9	7.1	8.0	7.3
Peaches and nectarines	7.1	5.5	5.5	5.3	4.4	5.5	4.8	5.4	5.4
Pears	2.6	2.8	3.2	3.4	3.0	3.4	3.3	3.3	3.2
Pineapples	1.5	1.5	2.0	1.9	1.9	2.3	2.8	3.0	3.2
Plums and prunes	1.5	1.4	1.5	0.9	1.4	1.5	1.2	1.3	1.2
Strawberries	2.0	3.0	3.2	4.1	4.3	4.1	3.9	4.4	4.7
Watermelons	10.7	13.5	13.3	15.2	16.6	15.5	14.3	15.4	13.7
Other [2]	3.5	5.3	5.1	5.8	6.6	7.0	7.3	7.7	8.2
Fresh citrus	26.1	21.5	21.4	23.8	24.6	26.5	26.6	20.3	23.4
Oranges	14.3	11.6	12.4	11.8	12.6	13.9	14.6	8.4	11.7
Grapefruit	7.3	5.5	4.4	6.0	5.8	6.2	5.9	5.8	5.1
Other [3]	4.5	4.4	4.6	6.0	6.2	6.4	6.1	6.2	6.5
Processed fruits	165.7	159.5	155.9	159.4	152.9	160.2	155.2	160.3	152.7
Frozen fruits [4]	3.1	3.3	3.8	4.2	3.9	3.6	4.1	3.7	3.7
Dried fruits [5]	11.2	12.8	12.1	12.7	11.1	10.6	12.1	10.2	10.5
Canned fruits [6]	24.6	20.9	21.0	17.3	18.4	20.1	17.0	19.2	17.4
Fruit juices [7]	126.1	122.2	118.8	125.0	119.2	125.2	121.6	126.8	120.6
Vegetables, total	337.5	359.2	387.3	408.5	419.1	418.4	415.1	415.6	428.3
Fresh vegetables	150.4	157.4	170.9	180.9	186.0	190.2	186.4	191.9	201.7
Asparagus (all uses)	0.3	0.5	0.6	0.6	0.6	0.7	0.7	0.9	1.0
Broccoli	1.4	2.6	3.4	4.3	4.5	5.0	5.1	6.5	5.5
Cabbage	8.1	8.8	8.8	8.2	8.4	9.2	8.5	7.6	9.2
Carrots	6.2	6.5	8.3	11.2	12.4	14.1	12.7	11.3	11.1
Cauliflower	1.1	1.8	2.2	1.6	1.7	1.8	1.5	1.9	2.0
Celery (all uses)	7.4	6.9	7.2	6.9	7.0	6.6	6.5	6.6	6.2
Corn	6.5	6.4	6.7	7.8	8.3	8.3	9.3	9.1	9.0
Cucumbers	3.9	4.4	4.7	5.6	5.9	6.4	6.5	6.8	6.6
Head lettuce	25.6	23.7	27.8	22.2	21.6	23.9	21.6	23.9	24.3
Mushrooms	1.2	1.8	2.0	2.1	2.1	2.3	2.5	2.5	2.6
Onions	11.4	13.6	15.1	17.8	18.4	18.8	18.3	18.4	18.4
Snap beans	1.3	1.3	1.1	1.6	1.5	1.4	1.7	1.9	2.0
Bell peppers (all uses)	2.9	3.8	4.5	6.2	7.1	6.4	6.4	6.7	7.9
Potatoes	51.1	46.3	46.8	49.3	50.0	48.5	47.0	48.0	47.2
Sweetpotatoes (all uses)	4.4	5.4	4.6	4.4	4.5	4.5	4.1	4.0	4.3
Tomatoes	12.8	14.9	15.5	16.9	17.4	16.8	17.6	17.8	17.3
Other fresh vegetables [8]	4.8	8.7	11.6	14.2	14.6	15.6	16.5	18.0	27.1
Processed vegetables	187.1	201.8	216.5	227.5	233.0	228.2	228.8	223.7	226.6
Selected vegetables for freezing	51.5	64.5	66.8	78.9	83.4	81.6	80.5	81.0	79.7
Selected vegetables for canning	102.8	99.2	111.5	109.4	107.8	106.0	107.1	103.3	104.7
Vegetables for dehydrating [9]	10.5	12.8	14.6	14.6	17.5	16.8	17.7	14.7	17.7
Potatoes for chips	16.5	17.6	16.4	16.4	16.4	15.9	14.8	15.9	16.0
Pulses [10]	5.8	7.6	7.1	8.3	7.9	7.9	8.7	8.8	8.6

[1] Excludes wine grapes. [2] Apricots, avocados, cherries, cranberries, kiwifruit, mangoes, papayas, and honeydew melons.
[3] Lemons, limes, tangerines, and tangelos. [4] Apples, apricots, blackberries, blueberries, boysenberries, cherries, loganberries, peaches, plums, prunes, raspberries, and strawberries. [5] Apples, apricots, dates, figs, peaches, pears, prunes, and raisins.
[6] Apples, apricots, cherries, olives, peaches, pears, pineapples, plums, and prunes. [7] Apple, cranberry, grape, grapefruit, lemon, lime, orange, pineapple, and prunes. [8] Artichokes, brussels sprouts, eggplant, escarole, endive, garlic, romaine, leaf lettuce, radishes, spinach, and squash. Beginning 2000, includes collard greens, kale, mustard greens, okra, pumpkin, and turnip greens. [9] Onions and potatoes. [10] Dry peas, lentils, and dry edible beans.

No. 197. Per Capita Consumption of Selected Beverages by Type: 1980 to 2000

[In gallons. See headnote, Table 195]

Commodity	1980	1985	1990	1995	1996	1997	1998	1999	2000
Nonalcoholic	(NA)	(NA)	128.3	128.6	130.3	131.5	136.2	141.8	(NA)
Milk (plain and flavored)	27.6	26.7	25.7	24.0	24.0	23.6	23.2	23.1	22.6
Whole	17.0	14.3	10.5	8.6	8.5	8.3	8.2	8.2	8.1
Reduced-fat, light, and skim	10.5	12.3	15.2	15.4	15.4	15.3	15.1	14.9	14.5
Tea	7.3	7.1	6.9	7.9	7.6	7.3	8.3	8.2	7.8
Coffee	26.7	27.4	26.9	20.3	22.1	23.3	23.9	25.1	26.3
Bottled water	2.4	4.5	8.0	11.5	12.3	12.9	15.7	17.7	(NA)
Carbonated soft drinks	35.1	35.7	46.2	47.5	46.7	46.8	47.9	49.7	49.3
Diet	5.1	7.1	10.7	10.9	10.6	10.6	11.0	11.5	11.6
Regular	29.9	28.7	35.6	36.5	36.0	36.2	36.8	38.2	37.7
Fruit juices	7.4	7.8	7.9	8.7	8.7	8.7	8.5	9.3	8.4
Fruit drinks, cocktails, and ades	(NA)	(NA)	6.3	7.7	7.9	8.2	7.7	7.7	(NA)
Canned iced tea	(NA)	(NA)	0.1	0.7	0.7	0.8	0.7	0.7	(NA)
Vegetable juices	(NA)	(NA)	0.3	0.3	0.3	0.3	0.3	0.3	(NA)
Alcoholic	28.3	28.0	27.5	24.7	24.8	24.7	24.8	25.0	24.0
Beer	24.3	23.8	23.9	21.8	21.7	21.6	21.7	21.8	21.7
Wine [1]	2.1	2.4	2.0	1.7	1.9	1.9	1.9	2.0	2.0
Distilled spirits	2.0	1.8	1.5	1.2	1.2	1.2	1.2	1.2	1.3

NA Not available. [1] Beginning 1985, includes wine coolers.
Source of Tables 196 and 197: U.S. Dept. of Agriculture, Economic Research Service, *Food Consumption, Prices, and Expenditures,* annual; *Agricultural Outlook,* monthly; and online at <http://www.ers.usda.gov/data/consumption>.

Section 4
Education

This section presents data primarily concerning formal education as a whole, at various levels, and for public and private schools. Data shown relate to the school-age population and school enrollment, educational attainment, education personnel, and financial aspects of education. In addition, data are shown for charter schools, computer usage in schools, distance education, and adult education. The chief sources are the decennial census of population and the Current Population Survey (CPS), both conducted by the U.S. Census Bureau (see text, Section 1, Population); annual, biennial, and other periodic surveys conducted by the National Center for Education Statistics (NCES), a part of the U.S. Department of Education; and surveys conducted by the National Education Association.

The censuses of population have included data on school enrollment since 1840 and on educational attainment since 1940. The CPS has reported on school enrollment annually since 1945 and on educational attainment periodically since 1947.

The NCES is continuing the pattern of statistical studies and surveys conducted by the U.S. Office of Education since 1870. The annual *Digest of Education Statistics* provides summary data on pupils, staff, finances, including government expenditures, and organization at the elementary, secondary, and higher education levels. It is also a primary source for detailed information on federal funds for education, projections of enrollment, graduates, and teachers. *The Condition of Education,* issued annually, presents a summary of information on education of particular interest to policymakers. NCES also conducts special studies periodically.

The census of governments, conducted by the Census Bureau every 5 years (for the years ending in "2" and "7"), provides data on school district finances and state and local government expenditures for education. Reports published by the

Bureau of Labor Statistics contain data relating civilian labor force experience to educational attainment (see also Tables 564, 590, and 598 in Section 12, Labor Force, Employment, and Earnings).

Types and sources of data—The statistics in this section are of two general types. One type, exemplified by data from the Census Bureau, is based on direct interviews with individuals to obtain information about their own and their family members' education. Data of this type relate to school enrollment and level of education attained, classified by age, sex, and other characteristics of the population. The school enrollment statistics reflect attendance or enrollment in any regular school within a given period; educational attainment statistics reflect the highest grade completed by an individual, or beginning 1992, the highest diploma or degree received.

Starting in October 1994, the CPS used 1990 census population controls plus adjustment for undercount. Also the survey changed from paper to computer assisted technology. For years 1981 through 1993, 1980 census population controls were used; 1971 through 1980, 1970 census population controls had been used. These changes had little impact on summary measures (e.g., medians) and proportional measures (e.g., enrollment rates); however, use of the controls may have significant impact on absolute numbers.

The second type, generally exemplified by data from the NCES and the National Education Association, is based on reports from administrators of educational institutions and of state and local agencies having jurisdiction over education. Data of this type relate to enrollment, attendance, staff, and finances for the nation, individual states, and local areas.

Unlike the NCES, the Census Bureau does not regularly include specialized vocational, trade, business, or correspondence

U.S. Census Bureau, Statistical Abstract of the United States: 2002

schools in its surveys. The NCES includes nursery schools and kindergartens that are part of regular grade schools in their enrollment figures. The Census Bureau includes all nursery schools and kindergartens. At the higher education level, the statistics of both agencies are concerned with institutions granting degrees or offering work acceptable for degree-credit, such as junior colleges.

School attendance—All states require that children attend school. While state laws vary as to the ages and circumstances of compulsory attendance, generally they require that formal schooling begin by age 6 and continue to age 16.

Schools—The NCES defines a school as "a division of the school system consisting of students composing one or more grade groups or other identifiable groups, organized as one unit with one or more teachers to give instruction of a defined type, and housed in a school plant of one or more buildings. More than one school may be housed in one school plant, as is the case when the elementary and secondary programs are housed in the same school plant."

Regular schools are those which advance a person toward a diploma or degree. They include public and private nursery schools, kindergartens, graded schools, colleges, universities, and professional schools.

Public schools are schools controlled and supported by local, state, or federal governmental agencies; private schools are those controlled and supported mainly by religious organizations or by private persons or organizations.

The Census Bureau defines *elementary* schools as including grades 1 through 8; *high* schools as including grades 9 through 12; and *colleges* as including junior or community colleges, regular 4-year colleges, and universities and graduate or professional schools. Statistics reported by the NCES and the National Education Association by type of organization, such as elementary level and secondary level, may not be strictly comparable with those from the Census Bureau because the grades included at the two levels vary, depending on the level assigned to the middle or junior high school by the local school systems.

School year—Except as otherwise indicated in the tables, data refer to the school year which, for elementary and secondary schools, generally begins in September of the preceding year and ends in June of the year stated. For the most part, statistics concerning school finances are for a 12-month period, usually July 1 to June 30. Enrollment data generally refer to a specific point in time, such as fall, as indicated in the tables.

Statistical reliability—For a discussion of statistical collection, estimation, and sampling procedures and measures of statistical reliability applicable to the Census Bureau and the NCES data, see Appendix III.

No. 198. School Enrollment: 1965 to 2011

[In thousands (54,394 represents 54,394,000). As of fall]

Year	All levels			K through grade 8		Grades 9 through 12		College [1]	
	Total	Public	Private	Public	Private	Public	Private	Public	Private
1965	54,394	46,143	8,251	30,563	4,900	11,610	1,400	3,970	1,951
1970	59,838	52,322	7,516	32,558	4,052	13,336	1,311	6,428	2,153
1975	61,004	53,654	7,350	30,515	3,700	14,304	1,300	8,835	2,350
1980	58,305	50,335	7,971	27,647	3,992	13,231	1,339	9,457	2,640
1981	57,916	49,691	8,225	27,280	4,100	12,764	1,400	9,647	2,725
1982	57,591	49,262	8,330	27,161	4,200	12,405	1,400	9,696	2,730
1983	57,432	48,935	8,497	26,981	4,315	12,271	1,400	9,683	2,782
1984	57,150	48,686	8,465	26,905	4,300	12,304	1,400	9,477	2,765
1985	57,226	48,901	8,325	27,034	4,195	12,388	1,362	9,479	2,768
1986	57,709	49,467	8,242	27,420	4,116	12,333	1,336	9,714	2,790
1987	58,254	49,982	8,272	27,933	4,232	12,076	1,247	9,973	2,793
1988	58,485	50,349	8,136	28,501	4,036	11,687	1,206	10,161	2,894
1989	59,436	51,120	8,316	29,152	4,162	11,390	1,193	10,578	2,961
1990	60,267	52,061	8,206	29,878	4,095	11,338	1,137	10,845	2,974
1991	61,605	53,356	8,248	30,506	4,074	11,541	1,125	11,310	3,049
1992	62,686	54,208	8,478	31,088	4,212	11,735	1,163	11,385	3,103
1993	63,241	54,654	8,587	31,504	4,280	11,961	1,191	11,189	3,116
1994	63,986	55,245	8,741	31,898	4,360	12,213	1,236	11,134	3,145
1995	64,764	55,933	8,831	32,341	4,465	12,500	1,197	11,092	3,169
1996	65,743	56,732	9,011	32,764	4,551	12,847	1,213	11,120	3,247
1997	66,470	57,323	9,147	33,073	4,623	13,054	1,218	11,196	3,306
1998	66,983	57,677	9,306	33,346	4,702	13,193	1,235	11,138	3,369
1999	67,667	58,166	9,501	33,488	4,765	13,369	1,254	11,309	3,482
2000, proj.	68,146	58,758	9,388	33,709	4,678	13,514	1,266	11,535	3,444
2001, proj.	68,457	58,988	9,469	33,587	4,668	13,626	1,276	11,775	3,525
2002, proj.	68,837	59,305	9,532	33,574	4,660	13,784	1,292	11,947	3,580
2003, proj.	69,198	59,593	9,605	33,475	4,644	13,957	1,310	12,161	3,651
2004, proj.	69,523	59,854	9,668	33,276	4,620	14,218	1,334	12,360	3,714
2005, proj.	69,787	60,063	9,723	33,091	4,603	14,445	1,351	12,527	3,769
2006, proj.	69,998	60,222	9,777	32,947	4,592	14,569	1,358	12,706	3,827
2007, proj.	70,127	60,302	9,824	32,868	4,588	14,562	1,355	12,872	3,881
2008, proj.	70,224	60,349	9,876	32,860	4,592	14,426	1,341	13,063	3,943
2009, proj.	70,358	60,424	9,933	32,913	4,604	14,265	1,327	13,246	4,002
2010, proj.	70,526	60,532	9,993	33,034	4,625	14,096	1,313	13,402	4,055
2011, proj..	70,810	60,743	10,067	33,179	4,649	13,991	1,303	13,573	4,115

[1] Data beginning 1996 based on new classification system. See footnote 1, Table 257.

Source: U.S. National Center for Education Statistics, *Digest of Education Statistics*, annual, and *Projections of Education Statistics*, annual.

No. 199. School Expenditures by Type of Control and Level of Instruction in Constant (2000-2001) Dollars: 1960 to 2001

[In billions of dollars (142.2 represents $142,200,000,000). For school years ending in year shown. Total expenditures for public elementary and secondary schools include current expenditures, interest on school debt and capital outlay. Data deflated by the Consumer Price Index, wage earners, and clerical workers through 1975; thereafter, all urban consumers, on a school year basis (supplied by the National Center for Education Statistics). See also Appendix III]

Year	Elementary and secondary schools				Colleges and universities [2]		
	Total	Total	Public	Private [1]	Total	Public	Private
1960	142.2	99.6	93.0	6.6	42.6	23.3	19.3
1970	317.3	200.2	188.6	11.6	117.2	75.2	41.9
1975	367.4	232.7	219.2	13.5	134.6	91.2	43.4
1980	373.6	232.7	216.4	16.2	140.9	93.4	47.4
1985	410.0	247.3	226.8	20.5	162.7	105.5	57.2
1986	433.6	260.3	239.1	21.2	173.3	112.7	60.5
1987	459.6	275.8	253.3	22.5	183.8	117.4	66.5
1988	473.7	284.2	261.0	23.1	189.5	120.7	68.8
1989	501.2	302.5	278.8	23.7	198.7	125.8	72.8
1990	526.1	318.5	293.4	25.1	207.6	132.9	74.7
1991	539.5	325.5	300.0	25.5	214.1	136.5	77.5
1992	548.5	331.0	305.4	25.6	217.6	137.7	79.9
1993	560.3	337.0	310.7	26.3	223.3	141.5	81.8
1994	571.5	344.3	317.7	26.6	227.2	143.2	84.0
1995	586.6	352.0	324.8	27.2	234.6	148.5	86.1
1996	600.2	360.7	332.8	27.9	239.5	150.4	89.1
1997	619.6	373.7	345.0	28.6	246.0	153.8	92.1
1998 [3]	646.2	391.2	361.9	29.3	254.9	158.8	96.1
1999 [4]	674.1	408.7	378.7	30.0	265.4	163.9	101.5
2000 [1]	691.9	418.2	387.8	30.3	273.8	168.8	105.0
2001 [1]	699.7	422.7	392.2	30.5	277.0	171.0	106.0

[1] Estimated.   [2] Data beginning 1996 based on new classification system. See footnote 1, Table 257.   [3] Data for college and universities are estimated.   [4] Preliminary data for public elementary and secondary schools and estimates for colleges and universities.

Source: U.S. National Center for Education Statistics, *Digest Education Statistics*, annual.

Education 133

No. 200. School Enrollment, Faculty, Graduates, and Finances With Projections: 1999 to 2005

[As of fall, except as indicated (52,875 represents 52,875,000)]

Item	Unit	1999	2000, proj.	2001, proj.	2002, proj.	2003, proj.	2004, proj.	2005, proj.
ELEMENTARY AND SECONDARY SCHOOLS								
School enrollment, total	1,000. . .	52,875	53,168	53,157	53,310	53,386	53,449	53,491
Kindergarten through grade 8	1,000. . .	38,253	38,387	38,255	38,234	38,119	37,896	37,694
Grades 9 through 12	1,000. . .	14,623	14,780	14,902	15,076	15,267	15,552	15,796
Public	1,000. . .	46,857	47,223	47,213	47,358	47,432	47,494	47,536
Kindergarten through grade 8 . . .	1,000. . .	33,488	33,709	33,587	33,574	33,475	33,276	33,091
Grades 9 through 12	1,000. . .	13,369	13,514	13,626	13,784	13,957	14,218	14,445
Private	1,000. . .	6,018	5,944	5,944	5,952	5,954	5,955	5,954
Kindergarten through grade 8 . . .	1,000. . .	4,765	4,678	4,668	4,660	4,644	4,620	4,603
Grades 9 through 12	1,000. . .	1,254	1,266	1,276	1,292	1,310	1,334	1,351
Enrollment rate:								
5 and 6 year olds	Percent .	96.0	95.6	(NA)	(NA)	(NA)	(NA)	(NA)
7 to 13 year olds	Percent .	98.7	98.2	(NA)	(NA)	(NA)	(NA)	(NA)
14 to 17 year olds	Percent .	95.8	95.7	(NA)	(NA)	(NA)	(NA)	(NA)
Classroom teachers, total [1]	1,000. . .	3,308	3,381	3,551	3,541	3,564	3,590	3,576
Public	1,000. . .	2,911	2,953	3,119	3,111	3,132	3,155	3,142
Private	1,000. . .	397	428	432	430	432	435	434
High school graduates, total [2]	1,000. . .	2,820	2,820	2,849	2,916	2,921	2,929	2,986
Public	1,000. . .	2,546	2,541	2,568	2,632	2,636	2,641	2,691
Public schools: [2]								
Average daily attendance (ADA) . . .	1,000. . .	43,433	43,613	43,763	73,898	43,966	44,024	44,063
Current dollars:								
Teachers' average salary [3]	Dol. . . .	41,724	42,898	43,166	44,165	45,436	46,629	(NA)
Current school expenditure [3] . . .	Bil. dol. .	314.3	334.5	353.5	367.8	387.2	406.4	(NA)
Per pupil in ADA [3]	Dol. . . .	7,237	7,670	8,077	8,378	8,807	9,232	(NA)
Constant (1999-2000) dollars:								
Teachers' average salary [3]	Dol. . . .	41,724	41,626	41,062	41,342	41,815	42,109	(NA)
Current school expenditure [3] . . .	Bil. dol. .	314.3	324.6	336.3	344.2	356.3	367.0	(NA)
Per pupil in ADA [3]	Dol. . . .	7,237	7,443	7,684	7,842	8,105	8,337	(NA)
HIGHER EDUCATION								
Enrollment, total	1,000. . .	14,791	14,979	15,300	15,527	15,812	16,074	16,296
Male	1,000. . .	6,491	6,538	6,644	6,708	6,786	6,862	6,922
Full time	1,000. . .	4,026	4,005	4,091	4,133	4,196	4,255	4,301
Part time	1,000. . .	2,465	2,533	2,554	2,575	2,590	2,607	2,620
Female	1,000. . .	8,301	8,441	8,656	8,819	9,026	9,212	9,374
Full time	1,000. . .	4,761	4,792	4,945	5,038	5,171	5,290	5,394
Part time	1,000. . .	3,540	3,648	3,711	3,782	3,855	3,922	3,980
Public	1,000. . .	11,309	11,535	11,775	11,947	12,161	12,360	12,527
Four-year institutions	1,000. . .	5,970	6,055	6,202	6,300	6,427	6,538	6,634
Two-year institutions	1,000. . .	5,339	5,479	5,573	5,647	5,735	5,822	5,893
Private	1,000. . .	3,482	3,444	3,525	3,580	3,651	3,714	3,769
Four-year institutions	1,000. . .	3,229	3,191	3,265	3,316	3,382	3,440	3,491
Two-year institutions	1,000. . .	253	254	260	263	269	274	278
Undergraduate	1,000. . .	12,681	12,894	13,182	13,378	13,628	13,855	14,048
Graduate	1,000. . .	1,807	1,787	1,816	1,844	1,875	1,905	1,929
First-time professional	1,000. . .	303	298	301	305	309	314	318
Full-time equivalent	1,000. . .	10,944	11,018	11,286	11,454	11,683	11,891	12,068
Public	1,000. . .	8,020	8,146	8,343	8,466	8,633	8,786	8,916
Private	1,000. . .	2,924	2,872	2,944	2,990	3,049	3,105	3,153
Faculty, total	1,000. . .	1,028	(NA)	(NA)	(NA)	(NA)	(NA)	(NA)
Public	1,000. . .	713	(NA)	(NA)	(NA)	(NA)	(NA)	(NA)
Private	1,000. . .	315	(NA)	(NA)	(NA)	(NA)	(NA)	(NA)
Degrees conferred, total [2]	1,000. . .	2,385	2,328	2,355	2,378	2,403	2,440	2,472
Associate's	1,000. . .	565	562	569	574	582	587	594
Bachelor's	1,000. . .	1,238	1,209	1,227	1,241	1,251	1,275	1,294
Master's	1,000. . .	457	428	432	436	442	448	453
Doctorate's	1,000. . .	45	47	47	47	47	48	48
First-professional	1,000. . .	80	82	80	80	80	81	84

NA Not available.   [1] Full-time equivalents.   [2] For school year ending June the following year.   [3] Financial projections after 2004-2005 are not shown due to the uncertain behavior of inflation over the long term.

Source: U.S. National Center for Education Statistics, *Digest of Education Statistics,* annual, and *Projections of Educational Statistics,* annual.

No. 201. Federal Funds for Education and Related Programs: 1999 to 2001

[In millions of dollars (82,863.6 represents $82,863,600,000), except percent. For fiscal years ending in September. Figures represent on-budget funds]

Level, agency, and program	1999	2000	2001 [1]
Total, all programs	**82,863.6**	**85,502.6**	**92,774.5**
Percent of Federal budget outlays	4.7	4.7	4.7
Elementary/secondary education programs	**39,937.9**	**43,809.0**	**48,707.0**
Department of Education [2]	17,026.7	20,039.6	22,931.4
Grants for the disadvantaged	7,554.2	8,529.1	8,470.2
School improvement programs	1,328.0	2,550.0	3,287.6
Indian education	56.8	65.3	84.5
Special education	4,444.1	4,949.0	5,814.8
Vocational and adult education	1,364.0	1,463.0	1,723.0
Education reform—Goals 2000	887.1	1,243.5	1,962.7
Department of Agriculture [2]	9,367.9	10,051.3	10,041.5
Child nutrition programs	[3]8,877.9	[3]9,554.0	[3]9,541.5
Agricultural Marketing Service—commodities [4]	400.0	400.0	400.0
Special milk program [2]	([3])	([3])	([3])
Department of Defense [2]	1,379.0	1,485.6	1,489.1
Overseas dependents schools	882.3	210.4	218.4
Section VI schools [5]	329.1	370.4	374.8
Department of Health and Human Services	5,429.9	6,011.0	6,979.6
Head Start	4,658.0	5,267.0	6,200.0
Department of the Interior [2]	709.9	729.0	770.6
Social security student benefits	593.3	725.4	812.6
Mineral Leasing Act and other funds	37.7	78.1	13.9
Indian Education	554.6	645.3	797.8
Department of Justice	204.8	224.8	244.4
Inmate programs	201.8	223.8	243.4
Department of Labor	5,402.0	4,683.2	5,628.0
Job Corps	1,253.0	1,256.0	1,412.0
Department of Veterans Affairs	417.9	445.1	427.2
Vocational rehab for disabled veterans	411.6	438.6	419.2
Other agencies and programs	116.5	143.1	153.1
Higher education programs [2]	**17,651.2**	**15,010.4**	**15,310.1**
Department of Education [2]	13,715.6	10,727.3	10,026.8
Student financial assistance	9,124.7	9,060.3	10,006.5
Federal Family Education Loans	2,805.5	2,707.5	-1,788.1
Department of Agriculture	29.7	30.7	32.7
Department of Commerce	3.6	3.8	3.6
Department of Defense	983.2	1,147.8	1,198.1
Tuition assistance for military personnel	280.5	263.3	284.5
Service academies [6]	115.1	212.7	237.0
Senior ROTC	321.8	363.5	361.2
Professional development education	265.7	308.3	315.3
Department of Health and Human Services [2]	880.2	954.2	1,204.3
Health professions training programs	301.7	340.4	587.9
National Health Service Corps scholarships [7]	28.5	16.0	31.0
National Institutes of Health training grants [7]	509.2	550.2	539.0
Department of the Interior—Shared revenues, Mineral Leasing Act and other receipts—estimated education share	132.2	187.2	234.5
Indian programs	47.8	98.7	144.0
Department of State	84.4	88.4	90.8
Department of Transportation	290.0	319.0	321.0
Department of Veterans Affairs [2]	60.3	60.3	76.9
Post-Vietnam veterans	1,134.9	1,132.3	1,678.8
All-volunteer-force educational assistance	3.7	4.0	4.3
Other agencies and programs [2]	988.7	984.1	1,494.8
National Endowment for the Humanities	421.5	447.9	533.3
National Science Foundation	28.5	28.4	28.5
United States Information Agency	369.0	389.0 ([8])	478.0 ([8])
Other education programs [2]	**5,318.0**	**5,485.1**	**5,976.4**
Department of Education [2] Administration	3,123.3	3,223.4	3,430.4
Rehabilitative services and handicapped research	439.9	458.1	555.8
Department of Agriculture	2,675.2	2,755.5	2,858.7
Department of Health and Human Services	428.3	444.5	453.8
Department of Justice	181.0	214.0	246.0
Department of State	33.8	34.7	24.4
Department of the Treasury [2]	56.9	69.3	73.3
Other agencies and programs [2]	65.0	83.0	92.0
Agency for International Development	1,429.7	1,416.2	1,656.5
Library of Congress	313.0	299.0	396.0
National Endowment for the Arts	350.0	299.0	305.0
National Endowment for the Humanities	6.3	4.0	5.3
National Science Foundation	63.2	70.8	71.0
Research programs at universities and related institutions [2]	**19,956.5**	**21,198.0**	**22,781.1**
Department of Education [2]	492.4	581.4	501.5
Department of Agriculture	1,750.1	1,799.6	1,788.9
Department of Defense	3,354.5	3,373.9	3,535.2
Department of Energy	9,044.4	10,422.6	11,037.4
Department of Health and Human Services	2,087.7	2,089.7	2,091.7
National Aeronautics and Space Administration	2,360.7	2,396.3	3,017.5
National Science Foundation			

[1] Estimated. [2] Includes other programs and agencies, not shown separately. [3] The Special Milk Program is included in the Child Nutrition Program. [4] Purchased under Section 32 of the Act of August 1935 for use in child nutrition programs. [5] Program provides for the education of dependents of federal employees residing on federal property where free public education is unavailable in the nearby community. [6] Instructional costs only including academics, audiovisual, academic computer center, faculty training, military training, physical education, and libraries. [7] Includes alcohol, drug abuse, and mental health training programs. [8] Program transferred to the Department of State in fiscal year 1998.

Source: U.S. National Center for Education Statistics, *Digest of Education Statistics*, 2001.

No. 202. School Enrollment by Age: 1970 to 2000

[As of October (60,357 represents 60,357,000). Covers civilian noninstitutional population enrolled in nursery school and above. Based on Current Population Survey, see text, Section 1, Population]

Age	1970	1980	1985	1990	1995	1996	1997	1998	1999	2000
ENROLLMENT (1,000)										
Total 3 to 34 years old .	60,357	57,348	58,013	60,588	66,939	67,317	69,041	69,277	69,601	69,560
3 and 4 years old	1,461	2,280	2,801	3,292	4,042	3,959	4,194	4,164	4,273	4,097
5 and 6 years old	7,000	5,853	6,697	7,207	7,901	7,893	7,964	7,902	7,774	7,648
7 to 13 years old.	28,943	23,751	22,849	25,016	27,003	26,936	27,616	27,846	28,209	28,296
14 and 15 years old.	7,869	7,282	7,362	6,555	7,651	7,598	7,744	7,653	7,741	7,885
16 and 17 years old.	6,927	7,129	6,654	6,098	6,997	7,220	7,538	7,456	7,611	7,341
18 and 19 years old.	3,322	3,788	3,716	4,044	4,274	4,539	4,618	4,914	4,840	4,926
20 and 21 years old.	1,949	2,515	2,708	2,852	3,025	3,017	3,231	3,197	3,256	3,314
22 to 24 years old	1,410	1,931	2,068	2,231	2,545	2,605	2,754	2,607	2,664	2,731
25 to 29 years old	1,011	1,714	1,942	2,013	2,216	2,265	2,223	2,216	2,018	2,030
30 to 34 years old	466	1,105	1,218	1,281	1,284	1,286	1,159	1,322	1,215	1,292
35 years old and over. . .	(NA)	1,290	1,766	2,439	2,830	2,979	2,989	2,831	2,794	2,653
ENROLLMENT RATE										
Total 3 to 34 years old .	56.4	49.7	48.3	50.2	53.7	54.1	55.6	55.8	56.0	55.8
3 and 4 years old	20.5	36.7	38.9	44.4	48.7	48.3	52.6	52.1	54.2	52.1
5 and 6 years old	89.5	95.7	96.1	96.5	96.0	94.0	96.6	95.6	96.0	95.6
7 to 13 years old.	99.2	99.3	99.2	99.6	98.9	97.7	99.1	98.9	98.7	98.2
14 and 15 years old.	98.1	98.2	98.1	99.0	98.9	98.0	98.9	98.4	98.2	98.7
16 and 17 years old.	90.0	89.0	91.7	92.5	93.6	92.8	94.3	93.9	93.6	92.8
18 and 19 years old.	47.7	46.4	51.6	57.3	59.4	61.5	61.5	62.2	60.6	61.2
20 and 21 years old.	31.9	31.0	35.3	39.7	44.9	44.4	45.9	44.8	45.3	44.1
22 to 24 years old	14.9	16.3	16.9	21.0	23.2	24.8	26.4	24.9	24.5	24.6
25 to 29 years old	7.5	9.3	9.2	9.7	11.6	11.9	11.8	11.9	11.1	11.4
30 to 34 years old	4.2	6.4	6.1	5.8	6.0	6.1	5.7	6.6	6.2	6.7
35 years old and over. . .	(NA)	1.4	1.6	2.1	2.2	2.3	2.3	2.1	1.8	1.9

NA Not available.

Source: U.S. Census Bureau, *Current Population Reports*, PPL-148; and earlier PPL and P-20 reports.

No. 203. School Enrollment by Race, Hispanic Origin, and Age: 1980 to 2000

[(47,673 represents 47,673,000). See headnote, Table 202.]

Age	White			Black			Hispanic origin [1]		
	1980	1990	2000	1980	1990	2000	1980	1990	2000
ENROLLMENT (1,000)									
Total 3 to 34 years old	47,673	48,899	54,257	8,251	8,854	11,115	4,263	6,073	9,928
3 and 4 years old	1,844	2,700	3,091	371	452	725	172	249	518
5 and 6 years old	4,781	5,750	5,959	904	1,129	1,219	491	835	1,390
7 to 13 years old	19,585	20,076	22,061	3,598	3,832	4,675	2,009	2,794	4,373
14 and 15 years old	6,038	5,265	6,176	1,088	1,023	1,260	568	739	1,093
16 and 17 years old	5,937	4,858	5,845	1,047	962	1,106	454	592	959
18 and 19 years old	3,199	3,271	3,924	494	596	716	226	329	617
20 and 21 years old	2,206	2,402	2,688	242	305	416	111	213	311
22 to 24 years old.	1,669	1,781	2,101	196	274	393	93	121	309
25 to 29 years old.	1,473	1,706	1,473	187	162	353	84	130	198
30 to 34 years old.	942	1,090	939	124	119	252	54	72	160
35 years old and over	1,104	2,096	2,087	186	238	387	(NA)	145	235
ENROLLMENT RATE									
Total 3 to 34 years old	48.9	49.5	55.1	53.9	51.9	59.0	49.8	47.4	51.3
3 and 4 years old	36.3	44.9	50.2	38.2	41.6	59.9	28.5	29.8	35.9
5 and 6 years old	95.8	96.5	95.3	95.4	96.3	96.3	94.5	94.8	94.3
7 to 13 years old	99.2	99.6	98.2	99.4	99.8	98.0	99.2	99.4	97.5
14 and 15 years old	98.3	99.1	98.4	97.9	99.2	99.6	94.3	99.0	96.2
16 and 17 years old	88.6	92.5	92.8	90.6	91.7	91.4	81.8	85.4	87.0
18 and 19 years old	46.3	57.1	61.3	45.7	55.2	57.2	37.8	44.1	49.5
20 and 21 years old	31.9	41.0	44.9	23.4	28.4	36.6	19.5	27.2	26.1
22 to 24 years old.	16.4	20.2	23.7	13.6	20.0	24.2	11.7	9.9	18.2
25 to 29 years old.	9.2	9.9	10.4	8.8	6.1	14.3	6.9	6.3	7.4
30 to 34 years old.	6.3	5.9	6.0	6.8	4.4	9.6	5.1	3.6	5.6
35 years old and over	1.3	2.1	1.8	1.8	2.1	2.6	(NA)	2.1	2.0

NA Not available.   [1] Persons of Hispanic origin may be of any race.

Source: U.S. Census Bureau, *Current Population Reports*, PPL-148; and earlier PPL and P-20 reports.

No. 204. Enrollment in Public and Private Schools: 1960 to 2000

[In millions (39.0 represents 39,000,000), except percent. As of October. For civilian noninstitutional population. For 1960, 5 to 34 years old; for 1970 to 1985, 3 to 34 years old; beginning 1986, for 3 years old and over]

Year	Public						Private					
	Total	Nur-sery	Kinder-garten	Ele-mentary	High School	College	Total	Nur-sery	Kinder-garten	Ele-mentary	High School	College
1960	39.0	(NA)	(1)	27.5	9.2	2.3	7.2	(NA)	(1)	4.9	1.0	1.3
1970	52.2	0.3	2.6	30.0	13.5	5.7	8.1	0.8	0.5	3.9	1.2	1.7
1975	52.8	0.6	2.9	27.2	14.5	7.7	8.2	1.2	0.5	3.3	1.2	2.0
1980	(NA)	0.6	2.7	24.4	(NA)	(NA)	(NA)	1.4	0.5	3.1	(NA)	(NA)
1982	49.2	0.7	2.7	24.4	13.0	8.4	8.2	1.4	0.6	3.0	1.1	2.6
1983	48.7	0.8	2.7	24.2	12.8	8.2	9.0	1.5	0.7	3.0	1.2	2.6
1984	49.0	0.8	3.0	24.1	12.7	8.5	8.3	1.6	0.5	2.7	1.1	2.4
1985 [2]	49.0	0.9	3.2	23.8	12.8	8.4	9.0	1.6	0.6	3.1	1.2	2.5
1986 [2]	51.2	0.8	3.4	24.2	13.0	9.8	9.4	1.7	0.6	3.0	1.2	2.9
1987 [2]	51.7	0.8	3.4	24.8	12.7	10.0	8.9	1.7	0.6	2.8	1.1	2.8
1988 [2]	52.2	0.9	3.4	25.5	12.2	10.3	8.9	1.8	0.5	2.8	1.0	2.8
1989 [2]	52.5	0.9	3.3	25.9	12.1	10.3	8.9	1.9	0.6	2.7	0.8	2.9
1990 [2]	53.8	1.2	3.3	26.6	11.9	10.7	9.2	2.2	0.6	2.7	0.9	2.9
1991 [2]	54.5	1.1	3.5	26.6	12.2	11.1	9.4	1.8	0.6	3.0	1.0	3.0
1992 [2]	55.0	1.1	3.5	27.1	12.3	11.1	9.4	1.8	0.6	3.1	1.0	3.0
1993 [2]	56.0	1.2	3.5	27.7	12.6	10.9	9.4	1.8	0.7	2.9	1.0	3.0
1994 [2]	58.6	1.9	3.3	28.1	13.5	11.7	10.7	2.3	0.6	3.4	1.1	3.3
1995 [2]	58.7	2.0	3.2	28.4	13.7	11.4	11.1	2.4	0.7	3.4	1.2	3.3
1996 [2]	59.5	1.9	3.4	28.1	14.1	12.0	10.8	2.3	0.7	3.4	1.2	3.2
1997 [2]	61.6	2.3	3.3	29.3	14.6	12.1	10.5	2.2	0.7	3.1	1.2	3.3
1998 [2]	60.8	2.3	3.1	29.1	14.3	12.0	11.3	2.3	0.7	3.4	1.2	3.6
1999 [2]	60.8	2.3	3.2	29.2	14.4	11.7	11.4	2.3	0.7	3.6	1.3	3.5
2000 [2]	61.2	2.2	3.2	29.4	14.4	12.0	11.0	2.2	0.7	3.5	1.3	3.3
Percent White:												
1960.	85.7	(NA)	(1)	84.3	88.2	92.2	95.7	(NA)	(1)	95.3	96.7	96.3
1970.	84.5	59.5	84.4	83.1	85.6	90.7	93.4	91.1	88.2	94.1	96.1	92.8
1980.	(NA)	68.2	80.7	80.9	(NA)	(NA)	(NA)	89.0	87.0	90.7	(NA)	(NA)
1990.	79.8	71.7	78.3	78.9	79.2	84.1	87.4	89.6	83.2	88.2	89.4	85.0
1995.	78.0	71.3	76.9	77.5	76.9	81.9	85.0	88.7	84.1	86.1	86.0	81.1
1999.	77.2	69.2	76.5	77.1	77.7	78.8	84.3	87.4	81.2	85.2	87.0	80.9
2000.	77.0	69.4	77.3	76.7	78.0	78.0	83.5	84.9	82.8	85.9	84.6	79.8

NA Not available. [1] Included in elementary school. [2] See Table 268 for college enrollment 35 years old and over. Also data beginning 1986 based on a revised edit and tabulation package.

Source: U.S. Census Bureau, Current Population Reports, PPL-148; and earlier PPL and P-20 reports.

No. 205. School Enrollment by Sex and Level: 1960 to 2000

[In millions (46.3 represents 46,300,000). As of Oct. For the civilian noninstitutional population. For 1960, persons 5 to 34 years old; 1970-1979, 3 to 34 years old; beginning 1980, 3 years old and over. Elementary includes kindergarten and grades 1-8; high school, grades 9-12; and college, 2-year and 4-year colleges, universities, and graduate and professional schools. Data for college represent degree-credit enrollment]

Year	All levels [1]			Elementary			High school			College		
	Total	Male	Female	Total	Male	Female	Total	Male	Female	Total	Male	Female
1960	46.3	24.2	22.0	32.4	16.7	15.7	10.2	5.2	5.1	3.6	2.3	1.2
1970	60.4	31.4	28.9	37.1	19.0	18.1	14.7	7.4	7.3	7.4	4.4	3.0
1975	61.0	31.6	29.4	33.8	17.3	16.5	15.7	8.0	7.7	9.7	5.3	4.4
1980	58.6	29.6	29.1	30.6	15.8	14.9	14.6	7.3	7.3	11.4	5.4	6.0
1981	59.9	30.3	29.6	31.0	15.9	15.0	14.7	7.5	7.3	12.1	5.8	6.3
1982	59.4	30.0	29.4	30.7	15.8	14.9	14.2	7.2	7.0	12.3	5.9	6.4
1983	59.3	30.1	29.2	30.6	15.7	14.8	14.1	7.1	7.0	12.4	6.0	6.3
1984	58.9	29.9	29.0	30.3	15.6	14.7	13.9	7.1	6.8	12.3	6.0	6.3
1985	59.8	30.0	29.7	30.7	15.7	15.0	14.1	7.2	6.9	12.5	5.9	6.6
1986 [2]	60.5	30.6	30.0	31.1	16.1	15.0	14.2	7.2	7.0	12.7	6.0	6.7
1987	60.6	30.7	29.9	31.6	16.3	15.3	13.8	7.0	6.8	12.7	6.0	6.7
1988	61.1	30.7	30.5	32.2	16.6	15.6	13.2	6.7	6.4	13.1	5.9	7.2
1989	61.5	30.8	30.7	32.5	16.7	15.8	12.9	6.6	6.3	13.2	6.0	7.2
1990	63.0	31.5	31.5	33.2	17.1	16.0	12.8	6.5	6.4	13.6	6.2	7.4
1991	63.9	32.1	31.8	33.8	17.3	16.4	13.1	6.8	6.4	14.1	6.4	7.6
1992	64.6	32.2	32.3	34.3	17.7	16.6	13.3	6.8	6.5	14.0	6.2	7.8
1993	65.4	32.9	32.5	34.8	17.9	16.9	13.6	7.0	6.6	13.9	6.3	7.6
1994	69.3	34.6	34.6	35.4	18.2	17.2	14.6	7.4	7.2	15.0	6.8	8.2
1995	69.8	35.0	34.8	35.7	18.3	17.4	15.0	7.7	7.3	14.7	6.7	8.0
1996	70.3	35.1	35.2	35.5	18.3	17.3	15.3	7.9	7.4	15.2	6.8	8.4
1997	72.0	35.9	36.2	36.3	18.7	17.6	15.8	8.0	7.7	15.4	6.8	8.6
1998	72.1	36.0	36.1	36.4	18.7	17.7	15.6	7.9	7.6	15.5	6.9	8.6
1999	72.4	36.3	36.1	36.7	18.8	17.9	15.9	8.2	7.7	15.2	7.0	8.2
2000	72.2	35.8	36.4	36.7	18.9	17.9	15.8	8.1	7.7	15.3	6.7	8.6

[1] Beginning 1970, includes nursery schools, not shown separately. [2] Revised. Data beginning 1986, based on a revised edit and tabulation package.

Source: U.S. Census Bureau, Current Population Reports, PPL-148; and earlier PPL and P-20 reports.

Education   137

No. 206. School Enrollment by Control and Level: 1980 to 1999

[In thousands (58,305 represents 58,305,000). As of fall. Data are for regular day schools and exclude independent nursery schools and kindergartens, residential schools for exceptional children, subcollegiate departments of colleges, Federal schools for Indians, and federally operated schools on Federal installations. College data include degree-credit and nondegree-credit enrollment. For projections, see Table 198]

Control of school and level	1980	1990	1992	1993	1994	1995	1996	1997	1998	1999
Total............	58,305	60,267	62,686	63,241	63,986	64,764	65,743	66,470	66,983	67,667
Public.............	50,335	52,061	54,208	54,654	55,245	55,933	56,731	57,323	57,677	58,166
Private	7,971	8,206	8,478	8,587	8,741	8,831	9,011	9,147	9,306	9,501
Kindergarten through 8 ..	31,639	33,973	35,300	35,784	36,258	36,806	37,315	37,696	38,048	38,253
Public.............	27,647	29,878	31,088	31,504	31,898	32,341	32,764	33,073	33,346	33,488
Private	3,992	4,095	4,212	4,280	4,360	4,465	4,551	4,623	4,702	4,765
Grades 9 through 12....	14,570	12,475	12,898	13,152	13,449	13,697	14,060	14,272	14,428	14,623
Public.............	13,231	11,338	11,735	11,961	12,213	12,500	12,847	13,054	13,193	13,369
Private	1,339	1,137	1,163	1,191	1,236	1,197	1,213	1,218	1,235	1,254
College [1]	12,097	13,819	14,487	14,305	14,279	14,262	14,368	14,502	14,507	14,791
Public.............	9,457	10,845	11,385	11,189	11,134	11,092	11,120	11,196	11,138	11,309
Private	2,640	2,974	3,103	3,116	3,145	3,169	3,247	3,306	3,369	3,482

[1] Data beginning 1996 reflects new classification system. See footnote 1, Table 257.

Source: U.S. National Center for Education Statistics, *Digest of Education Statistics,* annual.

No. 207. Students Who Are Foreign Born or Who Have Foreign-Born Parents: 2000

[In thousands (48,668 represents 48,668,000), except percent. As of October. Covers civilian noninstitutional population enrolled in elementary school and above. Based on Current Population Survey, see text, Section 1, Population and Appendix III]

Characteristic	All students	Students with at least one foreign-born parent					
		Total		Foreign-born student		Native student	
		Number	Percent	Number	Percent	Number	Percent
ELEMENTARY AND HIGH SCHOOL							
Total [1].....................	48,668	9,544	19.6	2,606	5.4	6,938	14.3
White............................	37,955	6,883	18.1	1,787	4.7	5,096	13.4
White, non-Hispanic................	30,824	2,161	7.0	418	1.4	1,743	5.7
Black............................	7,983	887	11.1	246	3.1	641	8.0
Asian and Pacific Islander	2,018	1,664	82.5	544	27.0	1,120	55.5
Hispanic [2].......................	7,477	4,931	66.0	1,440	19.3	3,491	46.7
COLLEGE, 1 TO 4 YEARS							
Total [1].....................	12,401	2,518	20.3	1,257	10.1	1,261	10.2
White............................	9,688	1,508	15.6	605	6.2	903	9.3
White, non-Hispanic................	8,523	755	8.9	291	3.4	464	5.4
Black............................	1,841	295	16.0	179	9.7	116	6.3
Asian and Pacific Islander	787	702	89.2	466	59.2	236	30.0
Hispanic [2].......................	1,228	788	64.1	326	26.5	462	37.6
GRADUATE SCHOOL							
Total [1].....................	2,913	748	25.7	509	17.5	239	8.2
White............................	2,311	458	19.8	242	10.5	216	9.3
White, non-Hispanic................	2,113	344	16.3	185	8.7	159	7.5
Black............................	323	38	11.9	31	9.6	7	2.2
Asian and Pacific Islander	262	252	96.3	236	90.0	16	6.1
Hispanic [2].......................	198	114	57.7	58	29.1	56	28.3

[1] Includes other races, not shown separately.   [2] Persons of Hispanic origin may be of any race.

Source: U.S. Census Bureau, *Current Population Reports,* PPL-148; and earlier PPL and P-20 reports.

No. 208. Educational Attainment by Race and Hispanic Origin: 1960 to 2000

[In percent. For persons 25 years old and over. 1960, 1970, and 1980 as of April 1 and based on sample data from the censuses of population. **Other years as of March** and based on the Current Population Survey; see text, Section 1, Population, and Appendix III. See Table 209 for data by sex]

Year	Total [1]	White	Black	Asian and Pacific Islander	Hispanic [2] Total [3]	Mexican	Puerto Rican	Cuban
HIGH SCHOOL GRADUATE OR MORE [4]								
1960	41.1	43.2	20.1	(NA)	(NA)	(NA)	(NA)	(NA)
1970	52.3	54.5	31.4	(NA)	32.1	24.2	23.4	43.9
1980	66.5	68.8	51.2	(NA)	44.0	37.6	40.1	55.3
1985	73.9	75.5	59.8	(NA)	47.9	41.9	46.3	51.1
1990	77.6	79.1	66.2	80.4	50.8	44.1	55.5	63.5
1995	81.7	83.0	73.8	(NA)	53.4	46.5	61.3	64.7
1996	81.7	82.8	74.3	83.2	53.1	46.9	60.4	63.8
1997	82.1	83.0	74.9	84.9	54.7	48.6	61.1	65.2
1998	82.8	83.7	76.0	(NA)	55.5	48.3	63.8	67.8
1999	83.4	84.3	77.0	84.7	56.1	49.7	63.9	70.3
2000	84.1	84.9	78.5	85.7	57.0	51.0	64.3	73.0
COLLEGE GRADUATE OR MORE [4]								
1960	7.7	8.1	3.1	(NA)	(NA)	(NA)	(NA)	(NA)
1970	10.7	11.3	4.4	(NA)	4.5	2.5	2.2	11.1
1980	16.2	17.1	8.4	(NA)	7.6	4.9	5.6	16.2
1985	19.4	20.0	11.1	(NA)	8.5	5.5	7.0	13.7
1990	21.3	22.0	11.3	39.9	9.2	5.4	9.7	20.2
1995	23.0	24.0	13.2	(NA)	9.3	6.5	10.7	19.4
1996	23.6	24.3	13.6	41.7	9.3	6.5	11.0	18.8
1997	23.9	24.6	13.3	42.2	10.3	7.5	10.7	19.7
1998	24.4	25.0	14.7	(NA)	11.0	7.5	11.9	22.2
1999	25.2	25.9	15.4	42.4	10.9	7.1	11.1	24.8
2000	25.6	26.1	16.5	43.9	10.6	6.9	13.0	23.0

NA Not available. [1] Includes other races, not shown separately. [2] Persons of Hispanic origin may be of any race. [3] Includes persons of other Hispanic origin, not shown separately. [4] Through 1990, completed 4 years of high school or more and 4 years of college or more.

Source: U.S. Census Bureau, *U.S. Census of Population, U.S. Summary,* PC80-1-C1 and *Current Population Report,* P20-536, earlier reports, and unpublished data. Internet site <http://www.census.gov/population/www/socdemo/educ-attn.html>.

No. 209. Educational Attainment by Race, Hispanic Origin, and Sex: 1960 to 2000

[In percent. See Table 208 for headnote and totals for both sexes]

Year	All races [1] Male	Female	White Male	Female	Black Male	Female	Asian and Pacific Islander Male	Female	Hispanic [2] Male	Female
HIGH SCHOOL GRADUATE OR MORE [3]										
1960	39.5	42.5	41.6	44.7	18.2	21.8	(NA)	(NA)	(NA)	(NA)
1970	51.9	52.8	54.0	55.0	30.1	32.5	(NA)	(NA)	37.9	34.2
1980	67.3	65.8	69.6	68.1	50.8	51.5	(NA)	(NA)	67.3	65.8
1985	74.4	73.5	76.0	75.1	58.4	60.8	(NA)	(NA)	48.5	47.4
1990	77.7	77.5	79.1	79.0	65.8	66.5	84.0	77.2	50.3	51.3
1995	81.7	81.6	83.0	83.0	73.4	74.1	(NA)	(NA)	52.9	53.8
1996	81.9	81.6	82.7	82.8	74.3	74.2	86.0	80.7	53.0	53.3
1997	82.0	82.2	82.9	83.2	73.5	76.0	(NA)	(NA)	54.9	54.6
1998	82.8	82.9	83.6	83.8	75.2	76.7	(NA)	(NA)	55.7	55.3
1999	83.4	83.4	84.2	84.3	76.7	77.2	86.9	82.8	56.0	56.3
2000	84.2	84.0	84.8	85.0	78.7	78.3	88.2	83.4	56.6	57.5
COLLEGE GRADUATE OR MORE [3]										
1960	9.7	5.8	10.3	6.0	2.8	3.3	(NA)	(NA)	(NA)	(NA)
1970	13.5	8.1	14.4	8.4	4.2	4.6	(NA)	(NA)	7.8	4.3
1980	20.1	12.8	21.3	13.3	8.4	8.3	(NA)	(NA)	9.4	6.0
1985	23.1	16.0	24.0	16.3	11.2	11.0	(NA)	(NA)	9.7	7.3
1990	24.4	18.4	25.3	19.0	11.9	10.8	44.9	35.4	9.8	8.7
1995	26.0	20.2	27.2	21.0	13.6	12.9	(NA)	(NA)	10.1	8.4
1996	26.0	21.4	26.9	21.8	12.4	14.6	46.4	37.3	10.3	8.3
1997	26.2	21.7	27.0	22.3	12.5	13.9	(NA)	(NA)	10.6	10.1
1998	26.5	22.4	27.3	22.8	13.9	15.4	(NA)	(NA)	11.1	10.9
1999	27.5	23.1	28.5	23.5	14.2	16.4	46.2	39.0	10.7	11.0
2000	27.8	23.6	28.5	23.9	16.3	16.7	47.6	40.7	10.7	10.6

NA Not available. [1] Includes other races, not shown separately. [2] Persons of Hispanic origin may be of any race. [3] Through 1990, completed 4 years of high school or more and 4 years of college or more.

Source: U.S. Census Bureau, *U.S. Census of Population, 1960, 1970, and 1980, Vol. 1;* and *Current Population Reports* P20-536; earlier reports, and unpublished data. Internet site <http://www.census.gov/population/www/socdemo/educ-attn.html>.

Education   139

No. 210. Educational Attainment by Selected Characteristic: 2000

[For persons 25 years old and over (175,230 represents 175,230,000). As of March. Based on the Current Population Survey; see text, Section 1, Population, and Appendix III. For composition of regions, see map inside front cover]

Characteristic	Population (1,000)	Percent of population—highest level					
		Not a high school graduate	High school graduate	Some college, but no degree	Associ-ate's degree [1]	Bachelor's degree	Advanced degree
Total persons	**175,230**	**15.8**	**33.1**	**17.6**	**7.8**	**17.0**	**8.6**
Age:							
25 to 34 years old	37,786	11.8	30.6	19.5	8.8	22.7	6.6
35 to 44 years old	44,805	11.4	33.7	18.4	9.5	18.4	8.6
45 to 54 years old	36,630	11.1	31.0	18.7	9.0	18.7	11.5
55 to 64 years old	23,387	18.3	35.7	16.3	6.2	13.1	10.4
65 to 74 years old	17,796	26.4	37.4	14.2	4.5	10.4	7.1
75 years old or over	14,825	35.4	34.1	13.2	3.9	8.7	4.7
Sex:							
Male	83,611	15.8	31.9	17.4	7.1	17.8	10.0
Female	91,620	16.0	34.3	17.7	8.4	16.3	7.3
Race:							
White	147,067	15.1	33.4	17.4	8.0	17.3	8.8
Black	20,036	21.5	35.2	20.0	6.8	11.4	5.1
Other	8,127	16.6	23.8	14.0	7.3	25.2	13.2
Hispanic origin:							
Hispanic	17,150	43.0	27.9	13.5	5.0	7.3	3.3
Non-Hispanic	158,080	13.0	33.7	18.0	8.1	18.1	9.1
Region:							
Northeast	34,145	15.0	35.3	13.5	7.7	18.0	10.5
Midwest	40,079	13.1	35.5	18.2	8.3	16.8	8.0
South	62,292	18.3	34.0	17.1	7.0	15.7	7.8
West	38,713	15.7	27.4	21.1	8.6	18.6	8.6
Marital status:							
Never married	26,045	14.9	29.9	17.8	7.5	21.5	8.4
Married spouse present	109,296	13.4	33.0	17.4	8.2	18.3	9.8
Married spouse absent [2]	2,560	28.0	32.8	14.6	5.5	11.6	7.3
Separated	4,141	24.6	38.0	17.8	6.3	10.1	3.2
Widowed	13,641	35.8	36.1	13.1	4.9	6.8	3.2
Divorced	19,549	13.8	35.4	21.6	8.8	13.3	7.0
Civilian labor force status:							
Employed	114,600	9.7	31.8	18.8	9.0	20.4	10.4
Unemployed	3,908	23.5	36.0	18.7	7.0	10.2	4.7
Not in the labor force	56,095	28.3	35.9	14.8	5.4	10.7	5.0

[1] Includes vocational degrees.   [2] Excludes those separated.

Source: U.S. Census Bureau, *Current Population Reports*, P20-536; and unpublished data.

No. 211. Mean Earnings by Highest Degree Earned: 1999

[In dollars. For persons 18 years old and over with earnings. Persons as of March the following year. Based on Current Population Survey; see text, Section 1, Population, and Appendix III. For definition of mean, see Guide to Tabular Presentation]

Characteristic	Total persons	Level of highest degree							
		Not a high school graduate	High school graduate only	Some college, no degree	Asso-ciate's	Bache-lor's	Master's	Profes-sional	Doctorate
All persons [1]	**32,356**	**16,121**	**24,572**	**26,958**	**32,152**	**45,678**	**55,641**	**100,987**	**86,833**
Age:									
25 to 34 years old	29,901	16,916	24,040	26,914	28,088	39,768	46,768	58,043	60,852
35 to 44 years old	36,900	18,984	27,444	34,219	35,370	50,153	56,816	100,240	94,936
45 to 54 years old	41,465	19,707	28,883	36,935	37,508	54,922	62,158	116,327	87,659
55 to 64 years old	38,577	22,212	27,558	34,240	35,703	50,141	57,580	132,326	97,214
65 years old and over	24,263	12,121	18,704	19,052	17,609	30,624	35,639	104,055	78,333
Sex:									
Male	40,257	18,855	30,414	33,614	40,047	57,706	68,367	120,352	97,357
Female	23,551	12,145	18,092	20,241	25,079	32,546	42,378	59,792	61,136
White	33,326	16,623	25,270	27,674	32,686	46,894	55,622	103,450	87,746
Male	41,598	19,320	31,279	34,825	41,010	59,606	68,831	123,086	97,076
Female	23,756	12,405	18,381	20,188	24,928	32,507	41,845	57,314	64,080
Black	24,979	13,569	20,991	24,101	28,772	37,422	48,777	75,509	(B)
Male	28,821	16,391	25,849	27,538	31,885	42,530	54,642	(B)	(B)
Female	21,694	10,734	16,506	21,355	26,787	33,184	44,761	(B)	(B)
Hispanic [2]	22,096	16,106	20,704	23,115	29,329	36,212	50,576	64,029	(B)
Male	24,970	18,020	23,736	27,288	36,740	42,733	60,013	(B)	(B)
Female	19,107	12,004	16,663	18,792	22,695	29,249	41,118	(B)	(B)

B Base figure too small to meet statistical standards for reliability of a derived figure.   [1] Includes other races, not shown separately.   [2] Persons of Hispanic origin may be of any race.

Source: U.S. Census Bureau, *Current Population Reports*, P20-536.

No. 212. Educational Attainment by State: 1990 and 2000

[In percent. As of March 2000 and April 1990. For persons 25 years old and over, except as indicated. Based on the 1990 Census of Population and the Current Population Survey; see text, Section 1, Population, and Appendix III]

State	1990 Not a high school graduate	1990 High school graduate or more	1990 Bachelors degree or more Total	1990 Bachelors degree or more Bachelor's degree	1990 Bachelors degree or more Advanced degree	1990 Drop-outs [1]	2000 High school graduate or more	2000 College graduate or more
United States.........	24.8	75.2	20.3	13.1	7.2	11.2	84.1	25.6
Alabama..............	33.1	66.9	15.7	10.1	5.5	12.6	77.5	20.4
Alaska	13.4	86.6	23.0	15.0	8.0	10.9	90.4	28.1
Arizona..............	21.3	78.7	20.3	13.3	7.0	14.4	85.1	24.6
Arkansas	33.7	66.3	13.3	8.9	4.5	11.4	81.7	18.4
California	23.8	76.2	23.4	15.3	8.1	14.2	81.2	27.5
Colorado.............	15.6	84.4	27.0	18.0	9.0	9.8	89.7	34.6
Connecticut...........	20.8	79.2	27.2	16.2	11.0	9.0	88.2	31.6
Delaware	22.5	77.5	21.4	13.7	7.7	10.4	86.1	24.0
District of Columbia	26.9	73.1	33.3	16.1	17.2	13.9	83.2	38.3
Florida	25.6	74.4	18.3	12.0	6.3	14.3	84.0	22.8
Georgia	29.1	70.9	19.3	12.9	6.4	14.1	82.6	23.1
Hawaii	19.9	80.1	22.9	15.8	7.1	7.5	87.4	26.3
Idaho...............	20.3	79.7	17.7	12.4	5.3	10.4	86.2	20.0
Illinois	23.8	76.2	21.0	13.6	7.5	10.6	85.5	27.1
Indiana..............	24.4	75.6	15.6	9.2	6.4	11.4	84.6	17.1
Iowa	19.9	80.1	16.9	11.7	5.2	6.6	89.7	25.5
Kansas..............	18.7	81.3	21.1	14.1	7.0	8.7	88.1	27.3
Kentucky	35.4	64.6	13.6	8.1	5.5	13.3	78.7	20.5
Louisiana	31.7	68.3	16.1	10.5	5.6	12.5	80.8	22.5
Maine...............	21.2	78.8	18.8	12.7	6.1	8.3	89.3	24.1
Maryland	21.6	78.4	26.5	15.6	10.9	10.9	85.7	32.3
Massachusetts.........	20.0	80.0	27.2	16.6	10.6	8.5	85.1	32.7
Michigan.............	23.2	76.8	17.4	10.9	6.4	10.0	86.2	23.0
Minnesota............	17.6	82.4	21.8	15.6	6.3	6.4	90.8	31.2
Mississippi	35.7	64.3	14.7	9.7	5.1	11.8	80.3	18.7
Missouri	26.1	73.9	17.8	11.7	6.1	11.4	86.6	26.2
Montana.............	19.0	81.0	19.8	14.1	5.7	8.1	89.6	23.8
Nebraska............	18.2	81.8	18.9	13.1	5.9	7.0	90.4	24.6
Nevada	21.2	78.8	15.3	10.1	5.2	15.2	82.8	19.3
New Hampshire.........	17.8	82.2	24.4	16.4	7.9	9.4	88.1	30.1
New Jersey............	23.3	76.7	24.9	16.0	8.8	9.6	87.3	30.1
New Mexico	24.9	75.1	20.4	12.1	8.3	11.7	82.2	23.6
New York	25.2	74.8	23.1	13.2	9.9	9.9	82.5	28.7
North Carolina	30.0	70.0	17.4	12.0	5.4	12.5	79.2	23.2
North Dakota	23.3	76.7	18.1	13.5	4.5	4.6	85.5	22.6
Ohio	24.3	75.7	17.0	11.1	5.9	8.9	87.0	24.6
Oklahoma.............	25.4	74.6	17.8	11.8	6.0	10.4	86.1	22.5
Oregon..............	18.5	81.5	20.6	13.6	7.0	11.8	88.1	27.2
Pennsylvania...........	25.3	74.7	17.9	11.3	6.6	9.1	85.7	24.3
Rhode Island...........	28.0	72.0	21.3	13.5	7.8	11.1	81.3	26.4
South Carolina.........	31.7	68.3	16.6	11.2	5.4	11.7	83.0	19.0
South Dakota	22.9	77.1	17.2	12.3	4.9	7.7	91.8	25.7
Tennessee	32.9	67.1	16.0	10.5	5.4	13.4	79.9	22.0
Texas	27.9	72.1	20.3	13.9	6.5	12.9	79.2	23.9
Utah	14.9	85.1	22.3	15.4	6.8	8.7	90.7	26.4
Vermont	19.2	80.8	24.3	15.4	8.9	8.0	90.0	28.8
Virginia..............	24.8	75.2	24.5	15.4	9.1	10.0	86.6	31.9
Washington...........	16.2	83.8	22.9	15.9	7.0	10.6	91.8	28.6
West Virginia..........	34.0	66.0	12.3	7.5	4.8	10.9	77.1	15.3
Wisconsin............	21.4	78.6	17.7	12.1	5.6	7.1	86.7	23.8
Wyoming	17.0	83.0	18.8	13.1	5.7	6.9	90.0	20.6

[1] For persons 16 to 19 years old. A dropout is a person who is not in regular school and who has not completed the 12th grade or received a general equivalency degree.

Source: U.S. Census Bureau, *1990 Census of Population*, CPH-L-96, and *Current Population Reports*, P20-536.

Education 141

No. 213. Nonfatal Crimes Against Students: 1998 and 1999

[For students aged 12 through 18 (2,715.6 represents 2,715,600). For crimes occurring at school or going to or from school. Based on the National Crime Victimization Survey; see Appendix III]

Student characteristic	1998				1999			
			Violent				Violent	
	Total	Theft	Total	Serious [1]	Total	Theft	Total	Serious [1]
Total (1,000)............	**2,715.6**	**1,562.3**	**1,153.2**	**252.7**	**2,489.7**	**1,605.5**	**884.1**	**185.6**
RATE PER 1,000 STUDENTS								
Total [2]................	101	58	43	9	92	59	33	7
Sex:								
Male..................	111	59	52	10	98	62	37	8
Female................	91	58	33	8	85	57	28	6
Age:								
12 to 14 years old.........	125	65	60	14	120	74	46	11
15 to 18 years old.........	83	53	30	6	70	48	23	4
Race/ethnicity:								
White, non-Hispanic	105	60	45	9	98	64	34	6
Black, non-Hispanic........	111	64	48	12	106	63	43	14
Hispanic	82	48	34	11	62	40	21	6
Other, non-Hispanic........	89	57	32	[3]4	77	52	26	[3]5
Urbanicity: [4]								
Urban.................	117	68	49	13	93	63	29	9
Suburban	97	56	40	7	94	58	36	8
Rural	93	50	43	11	86	58	28	[3]2
Household income:								
Less than $7,500	110	56	53	[3]17	86	38	48	[3]15
$7,500 to $14,999.........	97	38	59	[3]12	70	42	29	[3]4
$15,000 to $24,999........	126	64	62	10	90	58	32	[3]9
$25,000 to $34,999........	102	50	52	15	77	51	26	[3]2
$35,000 to $49,999........	86	57	29	[3]6	108	66	42	[3]6
$50,000 to $74,999........	110	68	42	10	100	61	39	12
$75,000 and over.........	112	75	37	[3]6	108	85	23	[3]6

[1] Includes rape, sexual assault, robbery and aggravated assault. [2] Includes those whose race/ethnicity or incomes are unknown. [3] Estimate based on fewer than 10 cases. [4] Urban: The largest city (or groupings of cities) of an MSA; suburban: those portions of metro areas outside central cities: rural: places outside MSAs.

Source: U.S. National Center for Education Statistics and U.S. Bureau of Justice Statistics, *Indicators of School Crime and Safety 2001*, October 2001, NCES 2002-113; and earlier issues.

No. 214. Public Schools Reporting Criminal Incidents to the Police: 1996-97

[In percent. For crimes that took place in school buildings, on school buses or grounds, and places holding school-sponsored events. Based on the National Center for Education Statistics' Fast Response Survey System; see source for details]

School characteristic	Any incidents					Serious violent incidents [2]				
	Total	City [1]	Urban fringe [1]	Town [1]	Rural [1]	Total	City [1]	Urban fringe [1]	Town [1]	Rural [1]
Total	**56.7**	**59.3**	**58.4**	**63.2**	**46.9**	**10.1**	**16.8**	**11.2**	**5.4**	**7.8**
Instructional level:										
Elementary school	45.1	46.9	47.0	52.6	34.2	4.2	6.1	3.3	2.0	5.1
Middle school	74.1	86.7	78.8	70.0	62.0	18.7	35.8	21.7	7.0	15.0
High school	76.9	88.8	84.0	84.2	64.1	20.6	48.0	33.0	12.7	9.4
School enrollment:										
Less than 300..............	37.8	(B)	(B)	44.9	38.0	3.9	(B)	(B)	8.8	2.5
300 to 999	59.6	54.2	59.2	67.3	56.8	9.3	12.5	9.0	3.2	13.9
1,000 or more	89.1	93.1	86.7	86.5	(B)	32.9	44.2	29.8	15.9	(B)
Minority enrollment:										
Less than 5 percent	46.7	(B)	47.2	53.9	40.8	5.8	(B)	5.9	3.3	7.3
5 to 19 percent	57.7	52.0	62.9	64.0	45.0	10.9	14.5	11.3	10.6	6.8
20 to 49 percent	58.1	54.7	58.5	66.7	53.3	11.1	19.1	10.1	5.0	8.0
50 percent or more	68.3	64.8	62.3	81.5	74.9	14.7	17.6	17.8	4.4	11.6
Free/reduced price lunch eligibility:										
Less than 20 percent	54.4	50.6	57.3	64.2	41.2	8.6	12.2	9.9	7.1	5.6
20 to 34 percent	53.2	56.0	65.5	57.2	39.5	11.7	18.4	13.3	7.1	11.6
35 to 49 percent	59.4	76.1	53.3	63.1	52.5	11.6	34.2	8.6	3.0	8.6
50 to 74 percent	58.8	60.8	54.7	66.6	52.0	8.9	22.9	10.3	2.0	2.3
75 percent or more	59.2	58.5	(B)	(B)	(B)	10.2	8.4	(B)	(B)	(B)

B Base figure too small to meet statistical standards for reliability of a derived figure. [1] City: central city of an MSA; urban fringe: a place within an MSA but not its central city; town: a place outside an MSA, with a population greater than or equal to 2,500 and defined as urban by the U.S. Census Bureau; rural: a place with a population under 2,500 and defined as urban by the U.S. Census Bureau. [2] Includes murder, rape or other sexual battery, suicide, physical attack or fight with a weapon, or robbery.

Source: U.S. National Center for Education Statistics and U.S. Bureau of Justice Statistics, *Indicators of School Crime and Safety 1999*, September 1999, NCES 1999-057.

No. 215. Children Whose Parents Are Involved in School Activities: 1999

[In percent, except as indicated (23,355 represents 23,355,000). Based on the National Household Education Survey; see source for details]

Parental involvement	Students in grades K to 5					Students in grades 6 to 8				
	Two-parent families	One-parent families				Two-parent families	One-parent families			
	Total		Total	Mother	Father	Total		Total	Mother	Father
Total students, 1999 (1,000) .	23,355	15,841	7,514	6,634	880	11,252	7,747	3,506	3,010	496
Any adult attending a meeting	84.9	88.6	77.1	77.3	75.7	81.1	85.3	72.0	71.2	77.0
Only mother attended	39.4	25.7	68.2	77.3	(X)	38.7	28.5	61.2	71.2	(X)
Only father attended	5.7	4.1	8.9	(X)	75.7	6.9	5.1	10.9	(X)	77.0
Both attended	39.8	58.7	(X)	(X)	(X)	35.6	51.7	(X)	(X)	(X)
Any adult attending a conference . .	87.7	89.4	84.1	85.1	76.7	71.1	72.3	68.5	68.1	70.8
Only mother attended	52.0	41.0	75.1	85.1	(X)	41.0	33.1	58.8	68.1	(X)
Only father attended	6.4	5.1	9.0	(X)	76.7	7.1	5.8	10.0	(X)	70.8
Both attended	29.4	43.3	(X)	(X)	(X)	23.0	33.4	(X)	(X)	(X)
Any adult attending a class event . .	70.8	74.0	64.1	63.1	71.2	67.8	72.6	57.3	55.9	66.1
Only mother attended	31.5	20.0	55.7	63.1	(X)	24.6	14.1	48.0	55.9	(X)
Only father attended	5.1	3.6	8.3	(X)	71.2	5.3	3.5	9.3	(X)	66.1
Both attended	34.2	50.4	(X)	(X)	(X)	37.9	55.0	(X)	(X)	(X)
Any adult acted as a volunteer . . .	48.9	55.5	34.8	36.3	23.1	31.7	36.1	21.9	22.1	20.6
Only mother attended	37.0	39.3	32.1	36.3	(X)	21.8	23.0	19.0	22.1	(X)
Only father attended	3.2	3.4	2.7	(X)	23.1	3.1	3.1	2.9	(X)	20.6
Both attended	8.6	12.7	(X)	(X)	(X)	6.8	9.9	(X)	(X)	(X)
Number of activities at least one parent participated in:										
None	3.5	2.2	6.5	6.2	8.3	7.3	4.4	13.7	14.1	11.2
One	7.4	5.7	11.0	11.1	10.3	11.7	11.0	13.4	13.9	10.8
Two	19.7	17.6	24.3	24.2	25.0	25.8	24.8	27.9	28.0	27.3
Three	32.0	31.7	32.5	31.7	39.0	32.2	33.5	29.2	28.5	33.5
Four	37.4	42.9	25.7	26.8	17.4	23.0	26.2	15.7	15.5	17.2
Number of activities both parents participated in:										
None	24.0	24.0	(X)	(X)	(X)	27.0	27.0	(X)	(X)	(X)
One	21.7	21.7	(X)	(X)	(X)	24.8	24.8	(X)	(X)	(X)
Two	26.0	26.0	(X)	(X)	(X)	24.2	24.2	(X)	(X)	(X)
Three	21.5	21.5	(X)	(X)	(X)	19.5	19.5	(X)	(X)	(X)
Four	6.7	6.7	(X)	(X)	(X)	4.5	4.5	(X)	(X)	(X)

X Not applicable.

Source: U.S. National Center for Education Statistics, *National Household Education Survey*, 1999.

No. 216. Children's Involvement in Home Literacy Activities: 1993 and 1999

[In percent, except number of children (8,579 represents 8,579,000). For children 3 to 5 years old not yet enrolled in kindergarten who participated in activities with a family member. Based on the National Education Household Survey; see source. See also Table 219]

Characteristic	Children (1,000)		Read to [1]		Told a story [1]		Taught letters, words, or numbers [1]		Visited a library [2]	
	1993	1999	1993	1999	1993	1999	1993	1999	1993	1999
Total	8,579	8,549	78	81	43	50	58	64	38	36
Age:										
3 years old	3,889	3,827	79	81	46	52	57	65	34	33
4 years old	3,713	3,722	78	81	41	49	58	63	41	39
5 years old	976	1,001	76	79	36	44	58	64	38	41
Race/ethnicity:										
White, non-Hispanic	5,902	5,296	85	89	44	53	58	65	42	39
Black, non-Hispanic	1,271	1,258	66	71	39	45	63	68	29	35
Hispanic	1,026	1,421	58	61	38	40	54	55	26	25
Other	381	574	73	81	50	53	59	69	43	43
Mother's home language: [3]										
English	7,805	7,599	81	84	44	52	58	66	39	39
Not English	603	683	42	48	36	31	52	45	26	19
Mother's highest education: [3]										
Less than high school	1,036	952	60	61	37	36	56	60	22	18
High school	3,268	2,556	76	76	41	48	56	63	31	30
Vocational ed or some college . .	2,624	2,586	83	85	45	52	60	67	44	40
College degree	912	1,455	90	91	48	55	56	65	55	50
Graduate/professional training or degree	569	734	90	93	50	54	60	62	59	48
Family type:										
Two parents	6,226	5,997	81	85	44	52	57	64	41	40
None or one parent	2,353	2,553	71	72	41	44	59	65	30	29
Poverty status:										
Above threshold	6,323	6,575	82	85	44	52	57	66	41	40
Below threshold	2,256	1,975	68	69	39	42	59	58	28	24

[1] Three or more times in the past week. [2] At least once in the past month. [3] Excludes children with no mother in the household and no female guardian.

Source: U.S. National Center for Education Statistics, *Statistical Brief*, NCES 2000-026, November 1999.

Education 143

No. 217. Children Who Speak a Language Other Than English At Home: 1979 to 1999

[In percent, except total (3.8 represents 3,800,000). For children 5 to 17 years old. For children reported to speak English less than "very well." Based on the Current Population Survey; see text Section 1, Population, and Appendix III]

Characteristic	1979	1989	1992	1995 [1]	1999 [1]
Children who speak another language at home (mil) .	3.8	5.3	6.4	6.7	8.8
Percent of children 5 to 17 years old	8.5	12.6	14.2	14.1	16.7
Race and Hispanic origin:					
White, non-Hispanic	3.2	3.5	3.7	3.6	3.9
Black, non-Hispanic	1.3	2.4	4.2	3.0	4.5
Hispanic [2]	75.1	71.2	76.6	73.9	70.9
Other, non-Hispanic [3]	44.1	53.4	58.3	45.5	51.0
Region: [4]					
Northeast	10.5	13.5	16.2	15.1	17.7
Midwest	3.7	4.9	5.6	5.9	7.5
South	6.8	10.7	11.1	11.7	14.3
West	17.0	24.2	27.2	26.4	28.8
Children who speak another language at home and have difficulty speaking English (mil)	1.3	1.9	2.2	2.4	2.6
Percent of children 5 to 17 years old	2.8	4.4	4.9	5.1	5.0
Race and Hispanic origin:					
White, non-Hispanic	0.5	0.8	0.6	0.7	1.0
Black, non-Hispanic	0.3	0.5	1.3	0.9	1.0
Hispanic [2]	28.7	27.4	29.9	31.0	23.4
Other, non-Hispanic [3]	19.8	20.4	21.0	14.1	11.7
Region: [4]					
Northeast	2.9	4.8	5.3	5.0	4.4
Midwest	1.1	1.3	1.6	2.3	2.0
South	2.2	3.8	3.5	3.4	3.6
West	6.5	8.8	10.4	11.4	10.5

[1] Reflects revised interviewing techniques and/or change in population controls to the 1990 Census-based estimates. [2] Persons of Hispanic origin may be of any race. [3] Includes mostly Asian/Pacific Islanders, but also American Indian/Alaska Native children. [4] For composition of regions, see map, inside front cover.

Source: Federal Interagency Forum on Child and Family Statistics, *America's Children: Key National Indicators of Well-Being,* 2001.

No. 218. Preprimary School Enrollment—Summary: 1970 to 2000

[As of October. (10,949 represents 10,949,000). Civilian noninstitutional population. Includes public and nonpublic nursery school and kindergarten programs. Excludes 5 year olds enrolled in elementary school. Based on Current Population Survey; see text, Section 1, Population, and Appendix III]

Item	1970	1975	1980	1985	1990	1995	1998	1999	2000
NUMBER OF CHILDREN (1,000)									
Population, 3 to 5 years old	10,949	10,183	9,284	10,733	11,207	12,518	12,078	11,920	11,858
Total enrolled [1]	4,104	4,954	4,878	5,865	6,659	7,739	7,788	7,844	7,592
Nursery	1,094	1,745	1,981	2,477	3,378	4,331	4,512	4,506	4,326
Public	332	570	628	846	1,202	1,950	2,212	2,209	2,146
Private	762	1,174	1,353	1,631	2,177	2,381	2,300	2,298	2,180
Kindergarten	3,010	3,211	2,897	3,388	3,281	3,408	3,276	3,338	3,266
Public	2,498	2,682	2,438	2,847	2,767	2,799	2,674	2,777	2,701
Private	511	528	459	541	513	608	602	560	565
White	3,443	4,105	3,994	4,757	5,389	6,144	5,985	6,093	5,861
Black	586	731	725	919	964	1,236	1,346	1,264	1,265
Hispanic [2]	(NA)	(NA)	370	496	642	1,040	1,170	1,189	1,155
3 years old	454	683	857	1,035	1,205	1,489	1,498	1,505	1,540
4 years old	1,007	1,418	1,423	1,765	2,086	2,553	2,666	2,768	2,556
5 years old	2,643	2,852	2,598	3,065	3,367	3,697	3,624	3,571	3,496
ENROLLMENT RATE									
Total enrolled [1]	37.5	48.6	52.5	54.6	59.4	61.8	64.5	65.8	64.0
White	37.8	48.6	52.7	54.7	59.7	63.0	63.6	65.3	63.2
Black	34.9	48.1	51.8	55.8	57.8	58.9	68.6	67.9	68.5
Hispanic [2]	(NA)	(NA)	43.3	43.3	49.0	51.1	54.0	53.2	52.6
3 years old	12.0	21.5	27.3	28.8	32.6	35.9	37.6	39.0	39.2
4 years old	27.8	40.5	46.3	49.1	56.0	61.6	66.6	68.8	64.9
5 years old	69.3	81.3	84.7	86.5	88.8	87.5	88.7	88.5	87.6

NA Not available. [1] Includes races not shown separately. [2] Persons of Hispanic origin may be of any race. The method of identifying Hispanic children was changed in 1980 from allocation based on status of mother to status reported for each child. The number of Hispanic children using the new method is larger.

Source: U.S. Census Bureau, *Current Population Reports,* PPL-148; and earlier PPL and P-20 reports.

No. 219. Children's School Readiness Skills: 1993 and 1999

[In percent. For children 3 to 5 years old not yet enrolled in kindergarden. Based on the National Education Household Survey, see source for details. See also Table 216]

Characteristic	Recognizes all letters		Counts to 20 or higher		Writes name		Reads or pretends to read storybooks		Has 3-4 skills	
	1993	1999	1993	1999	1993	1999	1993	1999	1993	1999
Total	21	24	52	57	50	51	72	74	35	39
Age:										
3 years old	11	15	37	41	22	24	66	70	15	20
4 years old	28	28	62	67	70	70	75	76	49	50
5 years old	36	44	78	81	84	87	81	77	65	69
Sex:										
Male	19	21	49	54	47	47	68	70	32	35
Female	23	27	56	60	53	56	76	77	39	43
Race/ethnicity:										
White, non-Hispanic	23	25	56	60	52	54	76	79	39	42
Black, non-Hispanic	18	25	53	60	45	49	63	66	31	35
Hispanic.	10	14	32	41	42	43	59	57	22	25
Other.	22	30	49	59	52	57	70	79	36	48
Mother's home language:										
English	22	25	55	60	51	53	73	76	37	41
Not English.	9	8	24	25	38	34	52	45	17	14
Mother's highest education:										
Less than high school.	8	7	30	36	40	32	55	53	19	15
High school	17	17	48	48	48	49	70	69	30	31
Vocational education or some college.	23	25	59	60	51	52	79	79	39	42
College degree	31	35	68	73	58	61	84	84	52	54
Graduate/professional training or degree	39	40	68	73	59	64	83	83	55	57
Mother's employment status:										
Employed.	23	24	57	59	52	53	75	75	39	40
Unemployed	17	15	41	53	46	39	67	64	29	32
Not in the labor force	18	24	49	54	47	50	68	73	32	38
Family type:										
Two parents	22	26	54	58	51	53	74	75	37	41
None or one parent	18	19	49	54	47	48	65	69	31	33
Poverty status:										
Above threshold	24	28	57	62	53	56	74	77	40	45
Below threshold.	12	10	41	39	41	37	64	63	23	19

Source: U.S. National Center for Education Statistics, *Home Literacy Activities and Signs of Children's Emerging Literacy, 1993* and *1999,* NCES 2000-026, November 1999.

No. 220. Public Charter Schools—Selected Characteristics: 1999-2000

[A public charter school is a public school that, in accordance with an enabling state statue, has been granted a charter exempting it from selected state and local rules and regulations. All schools open as public charter schools during 1998-99 and still open in the 1999-2000 school year were surveyed. Based in the School and Staffing Survey; see source for details]

Characteristic	Schools	Principals	Teachers	Students
Total.	1,010	988	17,477	266,721
Region: [1]				
Northeast	108	106	2,113	24,608
Midwest	231	226	3,437	52,081
South.	253	248	4,785	67,432
West	418	407	7,142	122,600
School level:				
Elementary	586	574	10,604	158,801
Secondary	235	219	3,546	58,218
Combined.	190	195	3,327	49,702
Enrollment:				
Fewer than 100	293	280	2,162	17,359
100 to 199	289	296	3,451	41,937
200 to 349	196	191	3,714	50,545
350 to 499	85	80	2,110	34,693
500 or more	147	141	6,040	122,187
School origin:				
Newly created	744	710	11,127	166,060
Pre-existing public school.	166	170	4,919	83,811
Pre-existing private school.	100	108	1,430	16,849

[1] For composition of regions, see map inside front cover.

Source: U.S. National Center for Education Statistics, NCES 2002-313, May 2002.

U.S. Census Bureau, Statistical Abstract of the United States: 2002

No. 221. Public Elementary and Secondary Schools—Summary: 1980 to 2001

[For school year ending in year shown, except as indicated (48,041 represents 48,041,000). Data are estimates]

Item	Unit	1980	1985	1990	1995	1999	2000	2001
School districts, total	Number.	16,044	15,812	15,552	14,947	14,903	14,999	15,000
ENROLLMENT								
Population 5-17 years old [1]	1,000. . .	48,041	44,787	44,949	48,854	52,283	52,811	53,118
Percent of resident population	Percent .	21.4	19.0	18.2	18.6	19.0	18.9	18.9
Fall enrollment [2]	1,000. . .	41,778	39,354	40,527	43,898	46,308	46,625	46,972
Percent of population 5-17 years old	Percent .	87.0	87.9	90.2	89.9	90.9	90.8	88.4
Elementary [3]	1,000. . .	24,397	23,830	26,253	28,148	29,198	29,337	29,499
Secondary [4]	1,000. . .	17,381	15,524	14,274	15,750	17,110	17,288	17,473
Average daily attendance (ADA)	1,000. . .	38,411	36,530	37,573	40,792	43,032	43,493	44,025
High school graduates	1,000. . .	2,762	2,424	2,327	2,282	2,478	2,528	2,553
INSTRUCTIONAL STAFF								
Total [5]	1,000. . .	2,521	2,473	2,685	2,924	3,176	3,258	3,317
Classroom teachers.	1,000. . .	2,211	2,175	2,362	2,565	2,799	2,871	2,919
Average salaries:								
Instructional staff.	Dollar . .	16,715	24,666	32,638	38,339	42,306	43,679	45,334
Classroom teachers.	Dollar . .	15,970	23,600	31,367	36,675	40,534	41,754	43,335
REVENUES								
Revenue receipts	Mil. dol. .	97,635	141,013	208,656	273,255	345,095	364,056	384,426
Federal	Mil. dol. .	9,020	9,533	13,184	18,764	24,363	26,024	27,955
State	Mil. dol. .	47,929	69,107	100,787	129,958	169,851	182,760	193,028
Local	Mil. dol. .	40,686	62,373	94,685	124,533	150,881	155,272	163,443
Percent of total:								
Federal	Percent .	9.2	6.8	6.3	6.9	7.0	6.9	7.3
State	Percent .	49.1	49.0	48.3	47.6	49.7	50.7	50.2
Local	Percent .	41.7	44.2	45.4	45.6	43.3	42.4	42.4
EXPENDITURES								
Total	Mil. dol. .	96,105	139,382	209,698	276,584	351,559	371,613	392,091
Current expenditures (day schools)	Mil. dol. .	85,661	127,230	186,583	242,995	302,278	318,184	336,351
Other current expenditures [6]	Mil. dol. .	1,859	2,109	3,341	5,564	6,388	6,857	7,238
Capital outlay	Mil. dol. .	6,504	7,529	16,012	21,646	34,373	36,904	38,494
Interest on school debt	Mil. dol. .	2,081	2,514	3,762	6,379	8,520	9,669	10,008
Percent of total:								
Current expenditures (day schools)	Percent .	89.1	91.3	89.0	87.9	85.7	85.6	85.8
Other current expenditures [6]	Percent .	1.9	1.5	1.6	2.0	1.9	1.9	1.8
Capital outlay	Percent .	6.8	5.4	7.6	7.8	9.9	9.9	9.8
Interest on school debt	Percent .	2.2	1.8	1.8	2.3	2.4	2.5	2.5
In current dollars:								
Revenue receipts per pupil enrolled	Dollar . .	2,337	3,583	5,149	6,225	7,452	7,808	8,184
Current expenditures per pupil enrolled	Dollar . .	2,050	3,233	4,604	5,535	6,528	6,824	7,161
In constant (2001) dollars: [7]								
Revenue receipts per pupil enrolled	Dollar . .	5,279	5,937	7,107	7,255	7,941	8,085	8,184
Current expenditures per pupil enrolled	Dollar . .	4,632	5,357	6,355	6,452	6,956	7,066	7,161

[1] Estimated resident population as of July 1 of the previous year, except 1980, 1990, and 2000 population enumerated as of April 1. Estimates reflect revisions based on the 2000 Census of Population. [2] Fall enrollment of the previous year. [3] Kindergarten through grade 6. [4] Grades 7 through 12. [5] Full-time equivalent. [6] Current expenses for summer schools, adult education, post-high school vocational education, personnel retraining, etc., when operated by local school districts and not part of regular public elementary and secondary day-school program. [7] Compiled by U.S. Census Bureau. Deflated by the Consumer Price Index, all urban consumers (for school year) supplied by U.S. National Center for Education Statistics.

Source: Except as noted, National Education Association, Washington, DC, Estimates of School Statistics Database (copyright).

U.S. Census Bureau, Statistical Abstract of the United States: 2002

No. 222. Public Elementary and Secondary Schools by Type and Size of School: 1999-2000

[Enrollment in thousands (46,689 represents 46,689,000). Data reported by schools, rather than school districts]

Enrollment size of school	Number of schools					Enrollment [1]				
	Total	Elemen-tary [2]	Second-ary [3]	Com-bined [4]	Other [5]	Total	Elemen-tary [2]	Second-ary [3]	Com-bined [4]	Other [5]
Total	92,012	64,131	22,365	4,042	1,474	46,689	30,460	15,112	1,052	66
PERCENT										
Total	100.0	100.0	100.0	100.0	100.0	100.0	100.0	100.0	100.0	100.0
Under 100 students	10.4	6.3	15.8	42.7	66.1	0.9	0.6	1.0	6.3	21.0
100 to 199 students	9.6	8.7	10.7	16.8	13.9	2.7	2.8	2.2	8.6	15.3
200 to 299 students	11.3	12.4	8.3	9.4	8.8	5.4	6.6	2.9	8.2	17.2
300 to 399 students	13.3	15.5	7.7	7.2	5.8	8.9	11.4	3.8	9.0	16.1
400 to 499 students	13.2	15.9	6.6	5.4	2.4	11.4	15.0	4.2	8.5	8.7
500 to 599 students	11.2	13.3	6.4	4.7	0.9	11.8	15.3	5.0	9.1	4.1
600 to 699 students	8.4	9.7	5.6	4.1	0.8	10.5	13.2	5.2	9.3	4.0
700 to 799 students	6.1	6.6	5.2	2.1	-	8.7	10.4	5.5	5.7	-
800 to 999 students	7.0	6.8	8.4	3.5	0.8	12.0	12.7	10.7	11.1	5.3
1,000 to 1,499 students . . .	6.0	4.0	12.7	2.7	0.2	13.8	9.9	22.1	11.3	2.1
1,500 to 1,999 students . . .	2.1	0.5	7.0	0.7	0.2	6.8	1.8	17.1	4.4	3.0
2,000 to 2,999 students . . .	1.2	0.1	4.7	0.4	0.2	5.5	0.4	15.7	3.7	3.4
3,000 or more students . . .	0.2	(Z)	0.9	0.3	-	1.7	0.1	4.7	4.9	-
Average enrollment	(X)	(X)	(X)	(X)	(X)	521	477	706	282	123

- Represents zero.   X Not applicable.   Z Less than 0.05 percent.   [1] Data for those schools reporting enrollment. [2] Includes schools beginning with grade 6 or below and with no grade higher than 8.   [3] Includes schools with no grade lower than 7.   [4] Includes schools with both elementary and secondary grades.   [5] Includes special education, alternative, and other schools not classified by grade span.

Source: U.S. National Center for Education Statistics, *Digest of Education Statistics,* annual.

No. 223. Students Who Are Homeschooled by Selected Characteristics: 1999

[As of spring. (50,188 represents 50,188,000). For students 5 to 17 with a grade equivalent of K-12. Homeschoolers are students whose parents reported them to be schooled at home instead of a public or private school. Excludes students who were enrolled in school for more than 25 hours a week or were homeschooled due to a temporary illness. Based on the Parent Survey of the National Household Education Surveys Program; see source for details]

Characteristic	Number of students (1,000)			Percent distribution		
	Total	Home-schooled	Percent home-schooled	All stu-dents	Home-schooled	Non-home-schooled
Total	50,188	850	1.7	100.0	100.0	100.0
Grade equivalent: [1]						
K-5	24,428	428	1.8	48.7	50.4	48.7
Kindergarten	3,790	92	2.4	7.6	10.8	7.5
Grades 1 to 3	12,692	199	1.6	25.3	23.5	25.3
Grades 4 to 5	7,946	136	1.7	15.8	16.0	15.8
Grades 6 to 8	11,788	186	1.6	23.5	21.9	23.5
Grades 9 to 12	13,954	235	1.7	27.8	27.7	27.8
Sex:						
Male	25,515	417	1.6	50.8	49.0	50.9
Female	24,673	434	1.8	49.2	51.0	49.1
Race/ethnicity:						
White, non-Hispanic	32,474	640	2.0	64.7	75.3	64.5
Black, non-Hispanic	8,047	84	1.0	16.0	9.9	16.1
Hispanic	7,043	77	1.1	14.0	9.1	14.1
Other	2,623	49	1.9	5.2	5.8	5.2
Number of children in the household:						
One child	8,226	120	1.5	16.4	14.1	16.4
Two children	19,883	207	1.0	39.6	24.4	39.9
Three or more children	22,078	523	2.4	44.0	61.6	43.7
Number of parents in the household:						
Two parents	33,007	683	2.1	65.8	80.4	65.5
One parent	15,454	142	0.9	30.8	16.7	31.0
Nonparental guardians	1,727	25	1.4	3.4	2.9	3.5
Parents' participation in the labor force:						
Two parents-one in labor force	9,628	444	4.6	19.2	52.2	18.6
Two parents-both in labor force	22,880	237	1.0	45.6	27.9	45.9
One parent in labor force	13,907	98	0.7	27.7	11.6	28.0
No parent in labor force	3,773	71	1.9	7.5	8.3	7.5
Household income:						
$25,000 or less	16,776	262	1.6	33.4	30.9	33.5
25,001 to 50,000	15,220	278	1.8	30.3	32.7	30.3
50,001 to 75,000	8,576	162	1.9	17.1	19.1	17.1
75,001 or more	9,615	148	1.5	19.2	17.4	19.2
Parents' highest educational attainment:						
High school diploma or less	18,334	160	0.9	36.5	18.9	36.8
Voc/tech degree or some college	15,177	287	1.9	30.2	33.7	30.2
Bachelor's degree	8,269	213	2.6	16.5	25.1	16.3
Graduate/professional school	8,407	190	2.3	16.8	22.3	16.7

[1] Excludes those ungraded.

Source: U.S. National Center for Education Statistics, *Homeschooling in the United States: 1999,* NCES 2001-033, July 2001.

Education   147

No. 224. Public Elementary and Secondary School Enrollment by State: 1980 to 2000

[In thousands (27,647 represents 27,647,000), except rate. As of fall. Includes unclassified students]

State	Enrollment								Enrollment rate [2]			
	K through grade 8 [1]				Grades 9 through 12							
	1980	1990	1999	2000, prel.	1980	1990	1999	2000, prel.	1980	1990	1999	2000, prel.
United States ...	27,647	29,878	33,488	33,709	13,231	11,338	13,369	13,514	86.2	91.2	91.4	88.9
Alabama.	528	527	539	539	231	195	202	201	87.6	93.2	95.5	89.5
Alaska	60	85	96	94	26	29	39	39	94.0	97.4	91.4	93.2
Arizona.	357	479	624	641	157	161	229	237	88.9	93.3	89.9	89.1
Arkansas	310	314	318	318	138	123	133	132	90.3	95.8	93.5	90.2
California	2,730	3,615	4,337	4,409	1,347	1,336	1,702	1,733	87.1	92.6	94.0	90.8
Colorado.	374	420	507	517	172	154	202	208	92.2	94.6	91.1	90.2
Connecticut.	364	347	404	406	168	122	150	156	83.3	90.2	90.8	90.9
Delaware	62	73	80	81	37	27	33	34	79.5	87.2	85.3	80.2
District of Columbia .	71	61	60	54	29	19	17	15	91.8	100.6	113.5	83.6
Florida	1,042	1,370	1,725	1,760	468	492	656	675	84.4	92.6	91.0	90.2
Georgia	742	849	1,044	1,060	327	303	379	385	86.8	93.7	96.3	91.8
Hawaii	110	123	133	132	55	49	53	52	83.4	87.4	88.9	84.7
Idaho	144	160	169	170	59	61	76	75	95.4	96.9	95.2	90.3
Illinois	1,335	1,310	1,462	1,474	649	512	565	575	82.6	86.9	88.0	86.5
Indiana.	708	676	699	703	347	279	289	286	88.0	90.4	88.6	85.9
Iowa	351	345	336	334	183	139	161	161	88.4	92.1	92.6	90.8
Kansas.	283	320	326	323	133	117	146	147	88.7	92.5	91.8	89.8
Kentucky	464	459	459	472	206	177	189	194	83.7	90.5	91.8	91.3
Louisiana	544	586	548	547	234	199	209	197	80.2	88.1	86.4	82.3
Maine.	153	155	149	146	70	60	60	61	91.6	96.5	93.7	89.8
Maryland	493	527	607	609	258	188	239	244	83.9	89.1	87.9	85.1
Massachusetts.	676	604	706	703	346	230	265	273	88.6	88.8	90.3	88.4
Michigan.	1,227	1,145	1,245	1,256	570	440	481	488	86.9	90.3	90.5	90.6
Minnesota.	482	546	580	578	272	211	274	277	87.2	91.3	89.9	89.2
Mississippi	330	372	365	364	147	131	135	134	79.6	91.3	91.0	87.2
Missouri	567	588	649	645	277	228	265	268	83.8	86.5	88.2	86.3
Montana.	106	111	107	105	50	42	50	50	92.9	94.1	92.3	88.4
Nebraska	189	198	197	195	91	76	91	91	86.6	88.7	87.6	85.9
Nevada	101	150	240	251	49	51	86	90	93.4	98.6	93.4	93.1
New Hampshire	112	126	147	147	55	46	60	61	85.3	89.1	89.7	89.1
New Jersey.	820	784	954	953	426	306	335	355	81.5	85.9	88.3	85.8
New Mexico	186	208	229	225	85	94	96	95	89.5	94.4	89.1	84.7
New York	1,838	1,828	2,034	2,029	1,033	770	854	853	80.8	86.6	89.5	83.5
North Carolina	786	783	935	945	343	304	341	348	90.1	94.8	90.7	90.8
North Dakota.	77	85	75	72	40	33	38	37	85.9	92.6	93.3	89.9
Ohio	1,312	1,258	1,296	1,294	645	514	540	541	84.8	88.0	87.3	86.0
Oklahoma.	399	425	447	445	179	154	180	178	92.9	95.1	96.5	95.0
Oregon.	319	340	378	379	145	132	167	167	88.5	90.6	89.7	87.6
Pennsylvania.	1,231	1,172	1,262	1,258	678	496	555	556	80.4	83.5	84.9	82.7
Rhode Island.	98	102	114	114	51	37	43	44	80.1	87.5	87.3	85.5
South Carolina.	426	452	484	493	193	170	183	184	88.1	93.9	94.9	90.9
South Dakota	86	95	90	88	42	34	41	41	87.4	89.9	88.4	84.8
Tennessee	602	598	664	668	252	226	252	241	87.8	93.5	94.1	88.8
Texas.	2,049	2,511	2,896	2,943	851	872	1,096	1,117	92.4	98.4	97.8	95.2
Utah	250	325	329	333	93	122	151	148	98.2	97.8	96.6	94.6
Vermont	66	71	72	70	29	25	32	32	87.9	94.3	97.4	89.9
Virginia.	703	728	817	816	307	270	317	329	90.7	94.2	93.4	89.7
Washington.	515	613	695	694	242	227	309	310	91.7	94.1	91.5	89.7
West Virginia.	270	224	203	201	113	98	88	85	92.6	95.7	96.4	95.3
Wisconsin.	528	566	596	595	303	232	281	285	82.1	86.1	86.4	85.7
Wyoming	70	71	62	60	28	27	30	30	97.3	97.7	95.5	91.8

[1] Data include a small number of prekindergarten students.   [2] Percent of persons 5-17 years old. Based on enumerated resident population as of April 1, 1980, 1990, and 2000, and estimated resident population as of July 1 for other years. Data not adjusted for revisions based on the 1990 Census of Population.

Source: U.S. National Center for Education Statistics, *Digest of Education Statistics*, annual.

No. 225. Public Elementary and Secondary School Enrollment by Grade: 1980 to 2000

[In thousands (40,877 represents 40,877,000). As of fall of year. Kindergarten includes nursery schools]

Grade	1980	1985	1990	1992	1993	1994	1995	1996	1997	1998	1999	2000, proj.
Pupils enrolled ...	40,877	39,422	41,217	42,823	43,465	44,111	44,840	45,611	46,127	46,539	46,857	47,223
Kindergarten and												
grades 1 to 8.......	27,647	27,034	29,878	31,088	31,504	31,898	32,341	32,764	33,073	33,346	33,488	33,709
Kindergarten	2,689	3,192	3,610	3,817	3,922	4,047	4,173	4,202	4,198	4,172	4,148	4,178
First.............	2,894	3,239	3,499	3,542	3,529	3,593	3,671	3,770	3,755	3,727	3,684	3,635
Second...........	2,800	2,941	3,327	3,431	3,429	3,440	3,507	3,600	3,689	3,681	3,656	3,633
Third.............	2,893	2,895	3,297	3,361	3,437	3,439	3,445	3,524	3,597	3,696	3,691	3,673
Fourth............	3,107	2,771	3,248	3,342	3,361	3,426	3,431	3,454	3,507	3,592	3,686	3,708
Fifth.............	3,130	2,776	3,197	3,325	3,350	3,372	3,438	3,453	3,458	3,520	3,604	3,703
Sixth.............	3,038	2,789	3,110	3,303	3,356	3,381	3,395	3,494	3,492	3,497	3,564	3,658
Seventh	3,085	2,938	3,067	3,299	3,355	3,404	3,422	3,464	3,520	3,530	3,541	3,624
Eighth............	3,086	2,982	2,979	3,129	3,249	3,302	3,356	3,403	3,415	3,480	3,497	3,532
Unclassified [1]......	924	511	543	539	515	494	502	401	442	451	417	366
Grades 9 to 12	13,231	12,388	11,338	11,735	11,961	12,213	12,500	12,847	13,054	13,193	13,369	13,514
Ninth	3,377	3,439	3,169	3,352	3,487	3,604	3,704	3,801	3,819	3,856	3,935	3,958
Tenth	3,368	3,230	2,896	3,027	3,050	3,131	3,237	3,323	3,376	3,382	3,415	3,487
Eleventh	3,195	2,866	2,612	2,656	2,751	2,748	2,826	2,930	2,972	3,021	3,034	3,080
Twelfth	2,925	2,550	2,381	2,431	2,424	2,488	2,487	2,586	2,673	2,722	2,782	2,799
Unclassified [1]......	366	303	282	269	248	242	245	206	214	212	203	189

[1] Includes ungraded and special education.

Source: U.S. National Center for Education Statistics, *Digest of Education Statistics*, annual.

No. 226. School Enrollment Below Postseconday—Summary by Sex, Race, and Hispanic Origin: 2000

[In thousands (56,900 represents 56,900,000), except percent and rate. As of October. Covers civilian noninstitutional population enrolled in nursery school through high school. Based on Current Population Survey, see text, Section 1, Population, and Appendix III]

Characteristic		Sex		Race and Hispanic origin				
				White				
	Total [1]	Male	Female	Total	Non-Hispanic	Black	Asian and Pacific Islander	Hispanic [2]
All students	56,900	29,156	27,745	44,345	36,024	9,339	2,393	8,737
Nursery	4,401	2,212	2,189	3,392	2,854	726	222	574
Full day	2,102	1,071	1,032	1,462	1,170	499	102	306
Part day	2,299	1,141	1,158	1,930	1,684	228	120	268
Kindergarten............	3,832	1,983	1,849	2,998	2,346	629	152	687
Elementary	32,898	16,884	16,014	25,562	20,574	5,481	1,350	5,224
High school.............	15,770	8,077	7,693	12,392	10,250	2,502	668	2,253
Students in public schools ...	49,198	25,157	24,041	37,789	29,963	8,562	2,094	8,214
Nursery	2,217	1,123	1,094	1,539	1,149	531	91	419
Full day	1,124	584	540	724	513	331	31	222
Part day	1,093	539	554	814	636	201	60	197
Kindergarten	3,173	1,633	1,540	2,453	1,846	547	124	639
Elementary	29,378	15,014	14,364	22,538	17,747	5,133	1,257	5,012
High school............	14,431	7,387	7,044	11,259	9,222	2,350	622	2,144
Population 15 to 17 years old: Percent below modal grade [3].	30	34	26	30	29	35	22	34
Students, 10th to 12th grade: Annual dropout rate	5	5	4	4	4	6	3	7
Population 18 to 24 years old ..	26,658	13,338	13,319	21,257	17,327	4,013	1,143	4,134
Dropouts	3,315	1,837	1,478	2,598	1,316	615	52	1,335
High school graduates	21,822	10,622	11,200	17,512	15,187	3,090	1,038	2,462
Enrolled in college	9,452	4,343	5,109	7,566	6,709	1,216	639	899

[1] Includes other races, not shown separately.   [2] Persons of Hispanic origin may be of any race.   [3] The modal grade is the grade most common for a given age.

Source: U.S. Census Bureau, *Current Population Reports*, PPL-148.

U.S. Census Bureau, Statistical Abstract of the United States: 2002

No. 227. Employed Students by Selected Characteristic: 1998-99

[In percent. For students 15 to 17 years old at the beginning of the 1998-99 school year who held a job with an employer during the school year or following summer. Excludes freelance work, such as babysitting or mowing lawns. Based on the National Longitudinal Survey of Youth 1997; see source for details]

Characteristic	Students with an employer job	Students who worked during the school year [1]			
		Total	School year and summer	School year only	Summer only [2]
Total, age 15 [3]	**59.4**	**44.1**	**38.5**	**5.6**	**15.3**
Male	61.7	47.1	41.5	5.6	14.6
Female	57.0	41.0	35.3	5.6	16.1
White, non-Hispanic	67.4	50.9	45.2	5.7	16.5
Black, non-Hispanic	45.0	28.2	22.3	6.0	16.8
Hispanic origin	45.4	35.8	29.3	6.5	9.7
Enrolled in grade 9	46.5	33.8	25.8	8.0	12.6
Enrolled in grade 10	64.7	47.8	43.0	4.8	17.0
Total, age 16 [3]	**77.4**	**67.0**	**58.2**	**8.8**	**10.4**
Male	78.5	67.0	59.8	7.3	11.5
Female	76.2	67.0	56.4	10.6	9.3
White, non-Hispanic	82.5	73.1	64.8	8.3	9.4
Black, non-Hispanic	66.1	52.7	44.0	8.8	13.3
Hispanic origin	67.6	57.9	45.7	12.2	9.7
Enrolled in grade 10	72.5	58.7	50.0	8.7	13.8
Enrolled in grade 11	80.3	71.0	63.4	7.6	9.2
Total, age 17 [3]	**86.6**	**77.7**	**67.4**	**10.3**	**8.9**
Male	88.4	78.3	67.8	10.5	10.2
Female	84.7	77.1	67.1	10.0	7.6
White, non-Hispanic	90.1	82.6	74.0	8.6	7.5
Black, non-Hispanic	79.3	66.1	52.3	13.9	13.2
Hispanic origin	77.4	69.2	57.2	12.0	8.2
Enrolled in grade 11	81.3	71.9	63.0	8.9	9.4
Enrolled in grade 12	89.2	78.7	69.8	8.9	10.5

[1] September 1998 through May 1999, excluding last week of December and first week of January.   [2] June, July, and August 1999.   [3] Includes other races, not shown separately.

Source: U.S. Bureau of Labor Statistics, *Employment Experience of Youths: Results from a Longitudinal Survey,* USDL 01-479, December 20, 2001.

No. 228. Elementary and Secondary Schools—Teachers, Enrollment, and Pupil-Teacher Ratio: 1960 to 2000

[In thousands (1,600 represents 1,600,000), except ratios. As of fall. Data are for full-time equivalent teachers]

Item	Teachers			Enrollment			Pupil-teacher ratio		
	Total	Public	Private	Total	Public	Private	Total	Public	Private
1960	1,600	1,408	192	42,181	36,281	5,900	26.4	25.8	30.7
1965	1,933	1,710	223	48,473	42,173	6,300	25.1	24.7	28.3
1970	2,292	2,059	233	51,257	45,894	5,363	22.4	22.3	23.0
1975	2,453	2,198	255	49,819	44,819	5,000	20.3	20.4	19.6
1976	2,457	2,189	268	49,478	44,311	5,167	20.1	20.2	19.3
1977	2,488	2,209	279	48,717	43,577	5,140	19.6	19.7	18.4
1978	2,479	2,207	272	47,635	42,550	5,085	19.2	19.3	18.7
1979	2,461	2,185	276	46,651	41,651	5,000	19.0	19.1	18.1
1980	2,485	2,184	301	46,208	40,877	5,331	18.6	18.7	17.7
1981	2,440	2,127	313	45,544	40,044	5,500	18.7	18.8	17.6
1982	2,458	2,133	325	45,165	39,566	5,600	18.4	18.6	17.2
1983	2,476	2,139	337	44,967	39,252	5,715	18.2	18.4	17.0
1984	2,508	2,168	340	44,908	39,208	5,700	17.9	18.1	16.8
1985	2,549	2,206	343	44,979	39,422	5,557	17.6	17.9	16.2
1986	2,592	2,244	348	45,205	39,753	5,452	17.4	17.7	15.7
1987	2,631	2,279	352	45,487	40,008	5,479	17.3	17.6	15.6
1988	2,668	2,323	345	45,430	40,189	5,242	17.0	17.3	15.2
1989	2,734	2,357	377	45,741	40,543	5,198	16.7	17.2	13.8
1990	2,753	2,398	355	46,451	41,217	5,234	16.9	17.2	14.7
1991	2,787	2,432	355	47,322	42,047	5,275	17.0	17.3	14.9
1992	2,822	2,459	363	48,145	42,823	5,322	17.1	17.4	14.7
1993	2,870	2,504	366	48,813	43,465	5,348	17.0	17.4	14.6
1994	2,926	2,552	374	49,609	44,111	5,498	17.0	17.3	14.7
1995	2,978	2,598	380	50,502	44,840	5,662	17.0	17.3	14.9
1996	3,054	2,667	387	51,375	45,611	5,764	16.8	17.1	14.9
1997	3,134	2,746	388	51,968	46,127	5,841	16.6	16.8	15.1
1998	3,221	2,830	391	52,476	46,539	5,937	16.3	16.4	15.2
1999	3,304	2,907	397	52,875	46,857	6,018	16.0	16.1	15.2
2000, est.	3,381	2,953	428	53,104	47,160	5,944	15.7	16.0	13.9

Source: U.S. National Center for Education Statistics, *Digest of Education Statistics,* annual.

U.S. Census Bureau, Statistical Abstract of the United States: 2002

No. 229. Public Elementary and Secondary School Teachers—Selected Characteristics: 1999-2000

[For school year (509 represents 509,000). Based on School and Staffing Survey and subject to sampling error; for details, see source Web site at <http://nces.ed.gov/surveys/sass/>. Excludes prekindergarten teachers. See Table 243 for similar data on private school teachers]

Characteristic	Unit	Age				Sex		Race/ethnicity		
		Under 30 years old	30 to 39 years old	40 to 49 years old	Over 50 years old	Male	Female	White [1]	Black [1]	Hispanic
Total teachers [2]	1,000 . .	509	661	953	879	754	2,248	2,532	228	169
Highest degree held:										
Bachelor's	Percent .	78.3	57.2	47.2	39.5	49.9	53.3	51.6	51.5	65.8
Master's	Percent .	20.6	39.1	48.2	53.5	44.0	42.8	44.2	42.0	29.3
Education specialist.	Percent .	0.6	2.8	3.2	4.7	3.2	3.1	3.0	4.0	3.0
Doctorate	Percent .	(Z)	0.4	0.7	1.5	1.4	0.5	0.6	1.6	1.2
Full-time teaching experience:										
Less than 3 years	Percent .	64.0	17.3	8.3	2.9	18.4	18.1	17.1	20.8	28.4
3 to 9 years	Percent .	36.0	45.7	16.9	6.8	22.7	23.8	23.2	22.0	29.3
10 to 20 years	Percent .	(X)	37.0	41.4	24.5	23.4	30.2	29.1	24.5	24.6
20 years or more	Percent .	(X)	(X)	33.4	65.7	35.6	27.9	30.6	32.7	17.7
Full-time teachers.	1,000 . .	475	600	863	805	700	2,042	2303	214	157
Earned income	Dol. . . .	33,583	38,468	44,375	50,278	46,891	41,596	43,032	43,150	41,241
Salary	Dol. . . .	30,386	35,502	41,407	47,138	41,104	39,475	40,022	39,377	38,488

X Not applicable.   Z Less than 0.05 percent.   [1] Non-Hispanic.   [2] Includes teachers with no degrees and associates degrees, not shown separately.

Source: U.S. National Center for Education Statistics, unpublished data.

No. 230. Public Elementary and Secondary Schools—Number and Average Salary of Classroom Teachers, 1980 to 2001, and by State, 2001

[Estimates for school year ending in June of year shown (2,211 represents 2,211,000). Schools classified by type of organization rather than by grade-group; elementary includes kindergarten]

Year and state	Teachers [1] (1,000)			Avg. salary ($1,000)			Year and state	Teachers [1] (1,000)			Avg. salary ($1,000)		
	Total	Elementary	Secondary	All teachers	Elementary	Secondary		Total	Elementary	Secondary	All teachers	Elementary	Secondary
1980	2,211	1,206	1,005	16.0	15.6	16.5	ME	15.7	10.8	4.9	36.4	36.2	36.9
1985	2,175	1,212	963	23.6	23.2	24.2	MD	52.5	31.4	21.0	46.0	45.1	46.8
1990	2,362	1,390	972	31.4	30.8	32.0	MA	54.3	26.3	27.9	47.8	47.8	47.8
1992	2,429	1,466	963	34.1	33.5	34.8	MI	97.6	50.7	46.9	50.7	50.7	50.7
1993	2,466	1,496	970	35.0	34.4	35.9	MN	55.6	28.5	27.0	42.2	42.7	41.6
1994	2,512	1,517	995	35.7	35.2	36.6	MS	31.0	17.2	13.8	32.0	31.5	32.6
1995	2,565	1,517	1,048	36.7	36.1	37.5	MO	64.8	33.9	30.9	36.7	35.9	37.6
1996	2,605	1,543	1,062	37.6	37.1	38.4	MT	10.4	7.1	3.3	33.2	32.5	33.8
1997	2,671	1,586	1,086	38.5	38.0	39.2	NE	20.7	13.7	7.1	34.2	34.2	34.2
1998	2,729	1,626	1,103	39.4	39.0	39.9	NV	18.2	11.0	7.2	40.4	40.4	40.4
1999	2,799	1,671	1,128	40.5	40.3	41.0	NH	14.4	10.0	4.4	38.3	38.3	38.3
2000	2,871	1,718	1,153	41.8	41.4	42.3	NJ	95.7	60.3	35.5	53.3	53.3	53.3
2001, U.S. .	2,919	1,746	1,173	43.3	43.1	43.7	NM	20.3	14.3	6.1	33.8	33.5	34.4
AL.	48.6	28.1	20.5	38.0	38.0	38.0	NY	205.7	103.1	102.6	52.0	49.8	52.8
AK.	7.9	5.1	2.8	48.1	48.1	48.1	NC	82.2	51.8	30.3	41.2	41.2	41.2
AZ.	45.8	35.3	10.5	36.3	36.3	36.3	ND	8.1	5.2	2.9	30.9	31.1	30.5
AR.	30.6	15.0	15.6	34.6	35.2	37.2	OH	115.5	77.4	38.1	42.8	42.4	43.4
CA.	292.8	215.4	77.3	52.5	52.1	54.8	OK	41.3	21.6	19.7	34.5	34.3	34.7
CO	42.0	21.0	21.0	39.2	39.2	39.2	OR	28.9	19.8	9.1	41.7	41.7	42.0
CT.	41.1	29.4	11.7	52.7	52.1	54.0	PA.	117.0	61.4	55.6	49.5	49.4	49.7
DE.	7.5	3.8	3.7	47.0	46.9	47.2	RI	12.5	7.4	5.1	48.5	48.5	48.5
DC	4.4	3.1	1.3	48.7	47.1	50.8	SC.	44.0	30.8	13.2	37.9	37.9	37.9
FL.	134.5	68.4	66.1	38.2	38.2	38.2	SD.	9.2	6.4	2.8	30.3	30.2	30.4
GA	91.1	53.0	38.2	42.2	41.6	43.0	TN.	56.6	41.0	15.6	37.4	37.1	38.3
HI	11.0	5.9	5.1	40.1	40.1	40.1	TX.	274.8	140.1	134.8	38.4	38.0	38.8
ID	13.8	7.1	6.8	36.4	36.4	36.3	UT.	22.0	11.9	10.1	36.4	36.4	37.0
IL	130.0	92.0	38.0	47.8	45.9	52.5	VT.	8.7	4.4	4.3	38.3	38.1	38.5
IN	59.2	31.8	27.4	43.3	43.4	43.3	VA.	89.9	54.2	35.6	40.2	40.2	40.2
IA	34.4	16.3	18.2	36.5	35.5	37.3	WA	50.9	28.6	22.3	42.1	42.2	42.0
KS.	32.7	16.4	16.3	35.9	35.9	35.9	WV	20.8	14.3	6.5	35.9	35.7	36.4
KY.	37.9	26.8	11.1	36.6	36.3	37.3	WI	58.5	40.3	18.2	42.1	41.9	42.7
LA.	49.3	34.6	14.7	33.6	33.6	33.6	WY	6.7	3.3	3.5	34.7	34.7	34.6

[1] Full-time equivalent.

Source: National Education Association, Washington, DC, Estimates of School Statistics Database (copyright).

Education   151

No. 231. Average Salary and Wages Paid in Public School Systems: 1980 to 2001

[**In dollars.** For school year ending in year shown. Data reported by a stratified sample of school systems enrolling 300 or more pupils. Data represent unweighted means of average salaries paid school personnel reported by each school system]

Position	1980	1985	1990	1995	1997	1998	1999	2000	2001
ANNUAL SALARY									
Central office administrators:									
Superintendent (contract salary) . . .	39,344	56,954	75,425	90,198	98,106	101,519	106,122	112,158	118,496
Deputy/assoc. superintendent	37,440	52,877	69,623	81,266	88,564	90,226	92,936	97,251	104,048
Assistant superintendent	33,452	48,003	62,698	75,236	80,176	82,339	86,005	88,913	94,137
Administrators for—									
Finance and business	27,147	40,344	52,354	61,323	65,797	67,724	71,387	73,499	77,768
Instructional services	29,790	43,452	56,359	66,767	70,788	73,058	75,680	79,023	82,725
Public relations/information	24,021	35,287	44,926	53,263	55,928	57,224	59,214	60,655	65,505
Staff personnel services	29,623	44,182	56,344	65,819	70,088	71,073	73,850	76,608	80,969
Subject area supervisors	23,974	34,422	45,929	54,534	58,776	60,359	61,083	63,103	64,659
School building administrators:									
Principals:									
Elementary.	25,165	36,452	48,431	58,589	62,903	64,653	67,348	69,407	72,587
Junior high/middle	27,625	39,650	52,163	62,311	66,859	68,740	71,499	73,877	77,382
Senior high.	29,207	42,094	55,722	66,596	72,410	74,380	76,768	79,839	83,367
Assistant principals:									
Elementary.	20,708	30,496	40,916	48,491	52,284	53,206	54,306	56,419	59,080
Junior high/middle	23,507	33,793	44,570	52,942	56,451	57,768	59,238	60,842	63,709
Senior high.	24,816	35,491	46,486	55,556	59,739	60,999	62,691	64,811	67,593
Classroom teachers.	15,913	23,587	31,278	37,264	39,580	40,133	41,351	42,213	43,658
Auxiliary professional personnel:									
Counselors	18,847	27,593	35,979	42,486	45,365	46,162	47,287	48,195	50,003
Librarians	16,764	24,981	33,469	40,418	43,315	44,310	45,680	46,732	49,007
School nurses	13,788	19,944	26,090	31,066	33,720	34,619	35,520	35,540	37,188
Secretarial/clerical personnel:									
Central office:									
Secretaries.	10,331	15,343	20,238	23,935	25,709	26,316	27,540	28,405	29,514
Accounting/payroll clerks.	10,479	15,421	20,088	24,042	25,881	26,249	27,630	28,498	29,898
Typists/data entry clerks	8,359	12,481	16,125	18,674	20,726	21,633	22,474	22,853	24,232
School building level:									
Secretaries.	8,348	12,504	16,184	19,170	20,709	21,215	21,831	22,630	23,630
Library clerks	6,778	9,911	12,152	14,381	15,349	15,742	16,033	16,509	17,052
HOURLY WAGE RATE									
Other support personnel:									
Teacher aides:									
Instructional	4.06	5.89	7.43	8.77	9.25	9.46	9.80	10.00	10.41
Noninstructional	3.89	5.60	7.08	8.29	8.88	8.82	9.31	9.77	10.15
Custodians	4.88	6.90	8.54	10.05	10.65	10.79	11.22	11.35	11.85
Cafeteria workers	3.78	5.42	6.77	7.89	8.30	8.56	8.82	9.02	9.41
Bus drivers	5.21	7.27	9.21	10.69	11.50	11.55	12.04	12.48	12.99

Source: Educational Research Service, Arlington, VA, *National Survey of Salaries and Wages in Public Schools,* annual, Vols. 2 and 3. (All rights reserved. Copyright.)

No. 232. Public School Employment: 1982 and 1998

[**In thousands (3,082 represents 3,082,000).** Covers full-time employment. Excludes Hawaii. 1982 also excludes District of Columbia and New Jersey. 1982 based on sample survey of school districts with 250 or more students. 1998 based on sample survey of school districts with 100 or more employees; see source for sampling variability]

Occupation	1982					1998				
	Total	Male	Female	White [1]	Black [1]	Total	Male	Female	White [1]	Black [1]
All occupations	3,082	1,063	2,019	2,498	432	3,890	1,040	2,850	3,028	515
Officials, administrators	41	31	10	36	3	50	27	23	42	5
Principals and assistant										
principals.	90	72	19	76	11	105	53	52	81	16
Classroom teachers [2]	1,680	534	1,146	1,435	186	2,157	544	1,613	1,805	208
Elementary schools	798	129	669	667	98	1,079	151	928	895	103
Secondary schools	706	363	343	619	67	795	331	464	677	73
Other professional staff	235	91	144	193	35	277	61	216	228	32
Teachers aides [3].	215	14	200	146	45	389	43	346	257	78
Clerical, secretarial staff.	210	4	206	177	19	266	11	255	203	29
Service workers [4]	611	316	295	434	132	646	301	345	411	147

[1] Excludes individuals of Hispanic origin.   [2] Includes other classroom teachers, not shown separately.   [3] Includes technicians.   [4] Includes craftworkers and laborers.

Source: U.S. Equal Employment Opportunity Commission, *Elementary-Secondary Staff Information (EEO-5),* biennial.

No. 233. Public Elementary and Secondary School Price Indexes: 1975 to 1998

[1983=100. For years ending June 30. Reflects prices paid by public elementary secondary schools. For explanation of average annual percent change, see Guide to Tabular Presentation]

Year	Personnel compensation					Contracted services, supplies and equipment						
	Index, total	Total	Professional salaries	Nonprofessional salaries	Fringe benefits	Total	Services	Supplies and materials	Equipment replacement	Library materials and textbooks	Utilities	Fixed costs
1975 ..	52.7	53.4	56.0	55.6	40.9	50.4	55.7	58.0	53.7	53.8	34.5	45.2
1980 ..	76.6	75.9	76.7	77.8	71.0	79.2	77.4	85.9	79.6	82.1	71.1	77.9
1984 ..	105.1	106.0	105.7	104.5	108.3	101.7	105.6	99.6	103.4	107.8	94.3	105.4
1985 ..	112.1	113.7	113.4	111.3	117.1	106.0	112.4	103.2	107.2	111.0	96.1	110.8
1986 ..	118.5	121.1	121.4	117.6	123.3	108.3	117.4	103.0	109.3	120.8	93.7	116.2
1987 ..	123.3	127.4	128.4	121.9	128.8	107.5	123.7	101.5	112.9	126.5	75.3	122.7
1988 ..	129.8	134.5	135.5	127.5	137.0	111.7	126.1	105.9	113.4	140.0	78.1	128.4
1989 ..	136.3	141.6	142.2	133.3	147.0	116.1	131.8	112.0	116.0	149.4	75.1	134.6
1990 ..	144.5	150.0	150.1	139.4	159.3	123.5	137.7	119.2	121.2	171.7	82.1	140.3
1991 ..	152.3	158.3	158.1	146.5	169.8	129.6	142.5	122.7	125.7	189.5	92.6	144.9
1992 ..	158.5	165.5	165.9	152.4	175.8	131.9	148.0	122.5	128.5	199.8	90.8	148.9
1993 ..	162.2	169.6	169.3	155.1	184.5	133.9	151.5	121.9	131.8	205.6	90.4	153.8
1994 ..	167.1	175.2	175.1	159.3	190.2	136.5	154.0	122.7	135.4	218.6	90.6	158.8
1995 ..	170.9	179.2	178.9	163.7	194.9	139.3	157.2	124.4	138.7	230.4	89.7	163.9
1996 ..	177.5	185.6	185.7	169.2	200.3	146.6	161.8	138.1	143.2	243.0	91.0	169.1
1997 ..	182.0	190.2	190.2	174.5	204.2	150.8	165.2	137.2	145.2	263.7	100.1	172.9
1998 ..	189.5	199.2	199.1	184.5	213.4	152.3	172.1	135.2	145.6	295.8	87.5	178.3

Source: Research Associates of Washington, Arlington, VA, *Inflation Measures for Schools, Colleges, and Libraries*, periodic (copyright).

No. 234. Finances of Public Elementary and Secondary School Systems by Enrollment-Size Group: 1999-2000

[In millions of dollars (373,961 represents $373,961,000,000), except as indicated. Data are estimates, subject to sampling variability. For details, see source. See also Appendix III]

Item	All school systems	School systems with enrollment of—						
		50,000 or more	25,000 to 49,999	15,000 to 24,999	7,500 to 14,999	5,000 to 7,499	3,000 to 4,999	Under 3,000
Fall enrollment (1,000)	46,857	9,447	5,441	4,640	6,793	4,362	5,511	10,664
General revenue	373,961	75,640	41,430	34,085	53,289	35,346	44,531	89,641
From federal sources	26,672	6,683	3,027	2,204	3,453	1,968	2,594	6,744
Through state	24,147	6,189	2,801	2,048	3,056	1,800	2,353	5,900
Compensatory programs	3,271	456	613	437	547	307	310	602
Handicapped programs	10,192	2,162	1,254	892	1,414	807	1,099	2,564
Child nutrition programs	6,440	1,758	837	619	844	511	648	1,223
Direct	2,525	494	225	156	397	168	241	844
From state sources [1]	186,191	36,330	21,707	18,610	26,886	16,524	20,938	45,196
General formula assistance	127,261	22,385	14,314	13,090	18,696	11,584	14,818	32,373
Handicapped programs	10,192	2,162	1,254	892	1,414	807	1,099	2,564
From local sources	161,098	32,626	16,695	13,271	22,950	16,854	20,999	37,701
Taxes	106,495	16,750	11,156	8,889	16,061	12,308	14,753	26,578
Contributions from parent government	27,412	11,518	2,417	1,772	3,188	2,005	3,052	3,460
From other local governments	3,833	579	398	341	314	257	521	1,423
Current charges	9,663	1,459	1,027	919	1,429	929	1,186	2,713
School lunch	5,429	763	577	548	866	583	741	1,353
Other	13,695	2,320	1,697	1,350	1,958	1,356	1,487	3,527
General expenditure	380,416	76,990	41,619	34,677	54,169	36,197	45,034	91,731
Current spending	325,661	65,577	35,442	29,492	46,445	30,806	38,672	79,227
By function:								
Instruction	198,352	40,295	21,418	18,126	28,565	18,998	23,814	47,136
Support services	109,339	21,248	11,960	9,694	15,364	10,278	12,881	27,914
Other current spending	17,969	4,033	2,064	1,671	2,516	1,530	1,976	4,178
By object:								
Total salaries and wages	210,849	42,730	23,506	19,555	30,493	20,152	25,127	49,285
Total employee benefits	53,826	10,833	5,830	4,974	8,050	5,253	6,464	12,421
Other	60,987	12,014	6,106	4,962	7,903	5,400	7,080	17,521
Capital outlay	44,654	9,530	5,077	4,316	6,264	4,285	5,024	10,159
Interest on debt	8,727	1,809	988	797	1,225	891	1,155	1,863
Payments to other governments	1,373	74	112	72	234	215	183	482
Debt outstanding	178,366	35,010	18,962	15,931	25,714	18,833	24,186	39,730
Long-term	173,145	34,451	18,531	15,680	25,036	18,307	23,504	37,635
Short-term	5,222	559	431	251	678	526	682	2,095
Long-term debt issued	24,965	3,011	2,763	2,103	3,556	2,789	3,638	7,105
Long-term debt retired	12,714	1,557	1,189	1,064	1,770	1,212	1,926	3,996

[1] Includes other sources, not shown separately.

Source: U.S. Census Bureau, Internet site <http://www.census.gov/govs/www/school.html>

Education 153

No. 235. Public Elementary and Secondary Estimated Finances, 1980 to 2001, and by State, 2001

[In millions of dollars (101,724 represents $101,724,000,000), except as noted. For school years ending in June of year shown]

Year and state	Receipts						Expenditures				
	Total	Revenue receipts				Non-revenue re-ceipts[1]	Total[2]	Per capita[3] (dol.)	Current expenditures	Average per pupil in ADA[4]	
		Total	Source						Ele-mentary and second-ary day schools	Amount (dol.)	Rank
			Federal	State	Local						
1980	101,724	97,635	9,020	47,929	40,686	4,089	96,105	427	85,661	2,230	(X)
1985	146,976	141,013	9,533	69,107	62,373	5,963	139,382	591	127,230	3,483	(X)
1990	218,126	208,656	13,184	100,787	94,685	9,469	209,698	850	186,583	4,966	(X)
1994	275,121	259,587	18,434	119,443	121,710	15,534	262,485	1,010	230,773	5,749	(X)
1995	288,501	273,255	18,764	129,958	124,533	15,246	276,584	1,051	242,995	5,957	(X)
1996	306,189	286,600	19,319	137,488	129,793	19,588	292,378	1,098	254,483	6,137	(X)
1997	325,007	303,400	19,965	148,184	135,251	21,607	310,719	1,153	269,824	6,401	(X)
1998	349,787	324,429	21,668	159,596	143,164	25,359	330,952	1,214	285,213	6,666	(X)
1999	371,621	345,095	24,363	169,851	150,881	26,526	351,559	1,274	302,278	7,024	(X)
2000	386,398	364,056	26,024	182,760	155,272	22,342	371,613	1,332	318,184	7,316	(X)
2001, total	408,282	384,426	27,955	193,028	163,443	23,866	392,091	1,393	336,351	7,640	(X)
Alabama	5,375	4,389	452	2,785	1,152	986	4,697	1,056	3,863	5,512	47
Alaska	1,381	1,232	155	783	295	149	1,357	2,165	1,255	11,066	3
Arizona	5,418	4,894	305	2,586	2,002	524	5,529	1,078	4,450	5,218	48
Arkansas	3,019	2,745	225	1,708	812	273	2,945	1,102	2,499	5,966	45
California	49,937	47,937	4,584	29,275	14,078	2,000	46,539	1,374	39,581	6,837	33
Colorado	5,750	5,341	274	2,198	2,868	409	5,759	1,339	4,666	6,945	31
Connecticut	6,494	6,484	324	2,691	3,469	10	6,494	1,907	5,776	10,258	5
Delaware	1,263	1,151	94	770	287	112	1,219	1,555	1,075	10,177	6
Dist. Columbia	840	840	101	-	739	-	1,022	1,786	851	13,525	1
Florida	19,165	17,931	1,597	8,686	7,647	1,234	18,722	1,171	14,778	6,368	41
Georgia	12,501	12,263	783	5,833	5,646	238	12,328	1,506	10,643	7,903	21
Hawaii	1,758	1,682	141	1,511	30	75	1,410	1,164	1,214	7,066	27
Idaho	1,681	1,605	116	963	526	77	1,557	1,203	1,393	6,029	43
Illinois	19,718	17,950	1,443	5,537	10,969	1,767	20,126	1,621	16,992	9,118	10
Indiana	9,214	8,939	468	4,663	3,809	275	9,089	1,495	7,481	8,200	18
Iowa	3,938	3,741	183	1,969	1,588	197	3,603	1,231	3,150	6,790	34
Kansas	3,811	3,522	221	2,201	1,100	289	3,430	1,276	3,076	7,355	25
Kentucky	4,948	4,939	380	3,108	1,451	9	4,823	1,193	4,316	7,516	24
Louisiana	5,371	4,973	580	2,414	1,979	398	5,180	1,159	4,396	6,461	40
Maine	1,819	1,714	125	821	769	105	1,819	1,427	1,637	8,531	14
Maryland	7,381	7,153	341	2,640	4,172	228	7,479	1,412	6,370	7,934	20
Massachusetts	9,873	9,871	529	4,468	4,874	1	9,594	1,511	9,018	9,827	7
Michigan	14,080	13,433	610	9,949	2,873	648	14,781	1,487	12,801	8,107	19
Minnesota	8,492	7,603	366	4,506	2,731	889	8,452	1,718	6,804	8,564	13
Mississippi	3,193	2,970	420	1,639	911	223	2,960	1,041	2,618	5,624	46
Missouri	7,480	6,979	498	2,589	3,893	501	6,899	1,233	5,539	6,524	38
Montana	1,123	1,093	121	490	482	30	1,113	1,233	990	7,058	28
Nebraska	1,923	1,907	105	776	1,026	16	2,044	1,194	1,822	6,905	32
Nevada	2,742	2,266	111	683	1,472	476	2,630	1,316	1,908	5,982	44
New Hampshire	1,816	1,684	72	742	870	132	1,560	1,262	1,466	7,528	23
New Jersey	13,692	13,598	403	5,067	8,128	94	14,044	1,669	13,285	10,892	4
New Mexico	2,368	2,249	298	1,667	284	119	2,224	1,222	2,011	6,976	30
New York	32,680	31,650	2,152	14,519	14,979	1,030	33,839	1,783	29,809	11,089	2
North Carolina	9,602	8,972	687	6,330	1,955	630	9,363	1,163	8,006	6,720	36
North Dakota	811	771	90	296	385	40	551	859	498	4,459	50
Ohio	17,750	15,950	950	6,900	8,100	1,800	14,700	1,295	12,600	7,639	22
Oklahoma	4,286	4,039	412	2,386	1,241	247	4,077	1,181	3,941	6,787	35
Oregon	5,014	4,634	318	2,657	1,659	380	4,608	1,347	4,126	8,593	12
Pennsylvania	16,908	16,906	881	6,828	9,198	2	15,021	1,223	14,269	8,525	15
Rhode Island	1,339	1,339	55	500	783	-	1,467	1,399	1,403	9,744	8
South Carolina	5,446	4,916	387	2,484	2,046	530	5,071	1,264	4,197	6,644	37
South Dakota	967	890	87	359	444	78	887	1,176	731	6,102	42
Tennessee	5,958	5,323	503	2,494	2,325	635	5,533	973	5,091	6,029	43
Texas	34,810	31,170	2,835	13,638	14,697	3,640	33,415	1,602	26,793	6,979	29
Utah	2,728	2,727	205	1,590	932	1	2,570	1,151	2,127	4,755	49
Vermont	1,038	1,013	61	732	221	24	1,018	1,672	888	9,355	9
Virginia	10,409	9,783	555	4,281	4,947	627	8,334	1,177	7,309	6,465	39
Washington	8,415	7,892	625	5,072	2,195	523	8,466	1,436	6,752	7,200	26
West Virginia	2,463	2,380	271	1,430	679	83	2,437	1,347	2,235	8,440	16
Wisconsin	9,257	8,175	389	4,412	3,374	1,083	8,543	1,593	7,167	8,695	11
Wyoming	839	819	69	400	351	20	765	1,549	685	8,223	17

- Represents or rounds to zero.   X Not applicable.   [1] Amount received by local education agencies from the sales of bonds and real property and equipment, loans, and proceeds from insurance adjustments.   [2] Includes interest on school debt and other current expenditures not shown separately.   [3] Based on U.S. Census Bureau estimated resident population, as of July 1, the previous year, except 1980 and 1990 population enumerated as of April 1.   [4] Average daily attendance.

Source: National Education Association, Washington, DC, Estimates of School Statistics Database (copyright).

No. 236. Public Schools With Internet Access: 1995 to 2000

[**In percent. As of fall.** Excludes special education, vocational education, and alternative schools. Based on sample and subject to sampling error; see source for details]

School characteristic	Percent of schools with Internet access				Percent of instructional classrooms with Internet access				Students per instructional computer with Internet access, 2000	Schools with Internet available to students outside of regular school hours, 2000
	1995	1998	1999	2000	1995	1998	1999	2000		
Total [1]	50	89	95	98	8	51	64	77	7	54
Instructional level:										
Elementary	46	88	94	97	8	51	62	76	8	46
Secondary	65	94	98	100	8	52	67	79	5	80
Size of enrollment:										
Less than 300	39	87	96	96	9	54	71	83	4	49
300 to 999	52	89	94	98	8	53	64	78	7	53
1,000 or more	69	95	96	99	4	45	58	70	7	79
Percent minority enrollment:										
Less than 6 percent	52	91	95	98	9	57	74	85	6	46
6 to 20 percent	58	93	97	100	10	59	78	83	6	59
21 to 49 percent.	55	91	96	98	9	52	64	79	7	54
50 percent or more.	39	82	92	96	3	37	43	64	8	61
Percent of students eligible for free or reduced-price lunch:										
Less than 35 percent	60	92	95	99	9	57	73	82	6	58
35 to 49 percent.	48	93	98	99	6	60	69	81	6	47
50 to 74 percent.	41	88	96	97	6	41	61	77	7	52
75 percent or more.	31	79	89	94	3	38	38	60	9	56

[1] Includes combined schools.

Source: U.S. National Center for Education Statistics, *Internet Access in U.S. Public Schools and Classrooms: 1994-2000*, NCES 2001-071, May 2001.

No. 237. Advanced Telecommunications in Private Schools: 1995 and 1999

[**For fall 1995 and school year 1998-99.** Based on the Fast Response Survey System; for details, see source]

Characteristic	Number of students per computer		Internet access (percent)						Percent of schools without access that plan to have access in the future, 1999	Percent of teachers using computers for teaching, 1999 [1]
			Schools with access		Instructional rooms with access		Students enrolled in schools with access			
	1995	1999	1995	1999	1995	1999	1995	1999		
All private schools .	9	6	25	67	5	25	41	81	46	45
Affiliation:										
Catholic.	10	7	35	83	4	27	43	86	74	48
Other religious	9	7	16	54	2	18	30	72	41	41
Nonsectarian	6	4	32	66	13	41	59	84	38	49
Instructional level:										
Elementary	9	7	23	64	3	21	32	77	46	45
Secondary.	7	5	57	90	6	32	70	97	31	47
Combined	8	5	19	64	8	28	41	80	46	44
Size of enrollment:										
Less than 150	7	5	13	48	2	16	16	60	38	41
150 to 299.	9	7	27	77	3	17	28	77	60	43
300 or more.	9	6	50	85	8	34	56	87	77	47
Minority enrollment:										
Less than 6 percent . .	9	7	24	59	3	28	38	83	13	41
6 to 20 percent.	7	6	29	75	9	27	51	86	71	46
21 to 49 percent.	8	6	29	76	3	32	44	85	59	45
50 percent or more . . .	11	8	18	52	2	10	24	59	59	47

[1] Percent of teachers using computers or advanced telecommunications (e.g. networked computers and interactive television) for teaching.

Source: U.S. National Center for Education Statistics, *Advanced Telecommunications in U.S. Private Schools, Fall 1995* and *1998-99*, NCES 97-394 and 2001-037.

Education 155

No. 238. Computers for Student Instruction in Elementary and Secondary Schools: 2000-2001 and 2001-2002

[53,006 represents 53,006,000. Market Data Retrieval collects student use computer information in elementary and secondary schools nationwide through a comprehensive annual technology survey that utilizes both mail, telephone, and Internet data methods]

Level	Total schools	Total enroll-ment (1,000)	Number of com-puters [1] (1,000)	Stu-dents per com-puter	Schools with a local area network (LAN) (percent)	Schools, by location of computer [2] (percent)			Schools with high speed Internet access (percent) [2][3]
						Class-rooms	Com-puter lab	Library/media center	
U.S. total, 2000-01 . . .	111,134	53,066	12,169	4.4	84.8	82.3	75.2	77.7	67.4
U.S. total, 2001-02 . . .	111,444	53,408	13,629	3.9	84.7	84.5	78.0	77.2	70.2
Public schools, total	89,958	48,162	12,663	3.8	89.9	90.1	79.8	83.0	76.1
Elementary	52,691	23,836	5,738	4.2	88.8	89.1	74.4	83.3	71.2
Middle/junior high.	13,842	9,034	2,429	3.7	92.4	91.6	91.5	91.9	83.7
Senior High.	16,324	12,916	3,816	3.4	92.3	92.3	88.2	83.1	84.7
K-12/other	7,101	2,375	681	3.5	87.2	89.9	78.2	62.1	75.4
Catholic schools, total	8,112	2,647	455	5.8	79.7	61.6	79.9	61.7	52.8
Elementary	6,732	1,954	314	6.2	77.0	59.0	77.6	56.3	48.6
Secondary	1,209	631	129	4.9	94.6	75.1	92.4	88.4	73.7
K-12/other	171	62	12	5.1	83.3	65.2	78.8	77.3	58.9
Other private schools, total .	13,374	2,600	510	5.1	52.2	59.5	58.6	42.6	40.1
Elementary	6,608	1,089	187	5.8	51.9	63.7	53.7	37.7	38.7
Secondary	1,052	234	65	3.6	69.0	64.0	79.2	64.5	63.1
K-12/other	5,714	1,277	258	5.0	49.5	51.8	62.0	45.7	36.9

[1] Includes estimates for schools not reporting number of computers. [2] Statistics based on responses of those indicating location of Internet access computers. [3] High speed includes Internet connection types: T1, T3, cable modem, digital satellite.

Source: Market Data Retrieval, Shelton, CT, unpublished data (copyright).

No. 239. Public School Teachers Using Computers or the Internet for Classroom Instruction During Class Time: 1999

[In percent. Based on the Fast Survey Response System conducted in the spring of 1999 and subject to sampling error; see source]

Characteristic	Teachers using computers or Internet for class-room in-struction [1]	Teacher assigns to a moderate or large extent							
		Com-puter applica-tions [2]	Practice drills	Research using the Internet	Solve problems and analyze data	Research using CD-ROM	Produce multi-media reports/projects	Graphi-cal presen-tation of materials	Demon-stration/simu-lations
Teachers with access to computers or the Internet at schools. . .	53	41	31	30	27	27	24	19	17
School instructional level:									
Elementary school . . .	56	41	39	25	31	27	22	17	15
Secondary school	44	42	12	41	20	27	27	23	21
Percent of students in school eligible for free or reduced-price school lunch:									
Less than 11 percent. .	61	55	26	39	25	32	29	26	22
11 to 30 percent	52	45	29	35	29	27	23	18	16
31 to 49 percent	53	39	33	29	26	30	23	16	17
50 to 70 percent	47	33	33	25	27	24	25	19	13
71 percent or more . . .	50	31	35	18	27	19	22	19	16
Hours of professional development:									
0 hours	30	21	19	20	14	16	16	10	8
1-8 hours	46	36	26	28	24	24	20	16	13
9-32 hours.	61	47	35	32	30	31	26	21	19
More than 32 hours. . .	71	55	43	42	41	34	37	31	29

[1] Includes corresponding with others (e.g. authors, experts) via e-mail or Internet, not shown separately. [2] For example, word processing or spreadsheets.

Source: U.S. National Center for Education Statistics, Fast Response Survey System, *Teacher Use of Computers and the Internet in Public Schools,* NCES 2000-090, April 2000.

156 Education

No. 240. Children's Access to Home Computer and Use of the Internet at Home: 2000

[As of August. (60,635 represents 60,635,000). For children 3 to 17 years old. Based on the Current Population Survey and subject to sampling error; see source for details]

Characteristic	Children (1,000)	Home computer access Number (1,000)	Home computer access Percent	Use of the Internet at home Number (1,000)	Use of the Internet at home Percent
Total..............................	60,635	39,430	65.0	18,437	30.4
Age:					
3 to 5 years........................	11,915	6,905	58.0	864	7.3
6 to 11 years	24,837	15,924	64.1	6,135	24.7
12 to 17 years	23,884	16,600	69.5	11,439	47.9
Sex:					
Male..............................	31,055	20,273	65.3	9,392	30.2
Female............................	29,580	19,156	64.8	9,045	30.6
Race and Hispanic origin:					
White	47,433	33,062	69.7	15,940	33.6
White non-Hispanic	38,438	29,731	77.3	14,773	38.4
Black	9,779	4,161	42.5	1,441	14.7
Asian and Pacific Islander	2,581	1,855	71.9	909	35.2
Hispanic [1]	9,568	3,546	37.1	1,229	12.8
Householder's educational attainment:					
Less than high school diploma	10,159	3,060	30.1	1,126	11.1
High school diploma/GED............	18,915	10,559	55.8	4,600	24.3
Some college.......................	16,994	12,712	74.8	5,926	34.9
Bachelor's degree or more	14,567	13,098	89.9	6,786	46.6
Household type:					
Family households	60,012	39,119	65.2	18,284	30.5
Married-couple household............	42,936	31,593	73.6	15,050	35.1
Male householder	3,092	1,508	48.8	740	23.9
Female householder	13,984	6,017	43.0	2,493	17.8
Nonfamily household................	620	310	50.0	154	24.8
Family income:					
Total children in families	59,288	38,729	65.3	18,139	30.6
Under $15,000	7,480	2,041	27.3	578	7.7
15,000 to 19,999	2,896	1,044	36.0	373	12.9
20,000 to 24,999	3,596	1,507	41.9	547	15.2
25,000 to 34,999	6,967	3,755	53.9	1,463	21.0
35,000 to 49,999	8,463	6,044	71.4	2,694	31.8
50,000 to 74,999	10,374	8,574	82.6	4,142	39.9
75,000 and over....................	12,115	11,294	93.2	6,263	51.7
Not reported	7,395	4,470	60.4	2,079	28.1

[1] Persons of Hispanic origin may be of any race.

Source: U.S. Bureau of the Census, *Current Population Reports*, Series P23-107.

No. 241. Children and Youth With Disabilities Served by Selected Programs: 1991 to 2000

[For school year ending in year shown (4,361.8 represents 4,361,800). Excludes outlying areas. Through 1994, includes children with disabilities served under Chapter 1 of of ESEA (Elementary and Secondary Education Act), SOP (State Operated Programs); beginning 1995, Individuals with Disabilities ACT (IDEA), Parts B and C]

Item	1991	1994	1995	1996	1997	1998	1999	2000
NUMBER (1,000)								
Total	4,361.8	4,779.4	4,907.5	5,079.0	5,230.8	5,397.0	5,539.9	5,683.7
Specific learning disabilities..........	2,144.0	2,427.7	2,510.2	2,601.9	2,674.4	2,754.5	2,815.7	2,872.0
Speech impairments	987.8	1,018.0	1,020.3	1,026.9	1,048.7	1,063.6	1,074.2	1,090.0
Mental retardation	551.5	553.8	570.5	585.6	593.6	603.3	610.7	614.4
Emotional disturbance	390.8	415.0	428.0	439.2	446.3	454.4	462.8	470.1
Multiple disabilities...............	97.6	109.7	89.6	94.5	99.4	107.3	107.8	113.0
Hearing impairments	59.2	64.7	65.2	68.0	68.8	69.7	70.9	71.7
Orthopedically impairments	49.3	56.9	60.5	63.2	66.3	67.4	69.4	71.4
Other health impairments	56.3	83.1	107.1	134.2	161.4	191.1	221.8	254.1
Visually impaired.................	23.7	24.8	24.7	25.5	25.8	26.0	26.1	26.6
Autism............................	(NA)	19.1	22.7	29.1	34.4	42.5	54.1	65.4
Deaf-blind	1.5	1.4	1.3	1.4	1.2	1.4	1.6	1.8
Traumatic brain injury.............	(NA)	5.4	7.3	9.6	10.5	11.9	13.0	13.9
Developmental delay [1]	(NA)	(NA)	(NA)	(NA)	(NA)	3.8	11.9	19.3

NA Not available.   [1] For children 3 to 9 years old.

Source: U.S. Department of Education, Office of Special Education Programs, Data Analysis System (DANS).

Education   157

No. 242. Private Schools: 1999-2000

[**5,163 represents 5,163,000.** Based on the Private School Survey, conducted every 2 years; see source for details. For composition of regions, see map, inside front cover]

Characteristic	Schools				Students (1,000)				Teachers [1] (1,000)			
	Num-ber	Ele-mentary	Sec-ondary	Com-bined	Num-ber	Ele-mentary	Sec-ondary	Com-bined	Num-ber	Ele-mentary	Sec-ondary	Com-bined
Total	27,223	16,530	2,538	8,155	5,163	2,831	807	1,525	395	188	63	145
School type:												
Catholic.	8,102	6,707	1,114	282	2,511	1,815	608	89	150	101	41	8
Parochial	4,607	4,352	193	63	1,307	1,209	80	18	72	66	6	1
Diocesan	2,598	2,053	481	64	835	543	274	19	49	30	18	1
Private.	897	302	440	155	368	63	254	52	28	5	18	5
Other religious . . .	13,232	6,843	718	5,672	1,844	750	112	981	153	58	11	84
Conservative Christian	4,989	1,789	225	2,975	773	230	29	514	60	17	2	41
Affiliated.	3,531	2,200	287	1,044	554	275	52	226	47	23	5	19
Unaffiliated. . . .	4,712	2,853	206	1,653	517	245	31	240	45	18	3	23
Nonsectarian	5,889	2,981	707	2,201	808	267	87	455	93	29	11	53
Regular	2,494	1,396	262	837	547	163	56	328	58	16	7	35
Special emphasis	2,131	1,387	257	487	175	92	22	61	20	11	2	7
Special education	1,264	198	188	878	86	11	9	66	15	2	1	11
Program emphasis:												
Regular elem/sec .	22,263	14,278	1,963	6,021	4,752	2,674	751	1,327	346	170	57	119
Montessori.	1,190	1,045	(B)	139	77	63	(B)	13	8	7	(B)	1
Special program emphasis.	606	280	111	216	111	36	21	54	11	4	2	5
Special education .	1,409	232	202	975	95	13	10	72	16	2	2	12
Vocational/tech . .	(B)	(B)	(B)	(B)	(B)	(B)	(B)	(B)	(B)	(B)	(B)	(B)
Alternative	1,617	579	254	784	120	39	23	58	13	4	2	6
Early childhood. . .	133	116	-	(B)	6	5	-	(B)	1	(B)	-	(B)
Size:												
Less than 150	15,303	8,961	1,103	5,240	912	557	63	293	98	53	8	37
150 to 299.	6,571	4,811	429	1,332	1,424	1,042	94	288	102	67	9	27
300 to 499.	3,219	2,019	419	782	1,229	768	164	297	84	45	13	26
500 to 749.	1,352	629	285	440	805	366	173	267	54	18	12	24
750 or more.	778	110	305	362	792	99	314	380	57	5	20	32
Region:												
Northeast	6,452	4,049	776	1,628	1,295	750	264	281	104	49	22	32
Midwest	6,991	5,001	622	1,367	1,345	892	244	210	91	55	17	19
South	8,240	4,131	594	3,515	1,576	652	159	764	131	49	13	70
West.	5,540	3,349	546	1,645	947	537	140	269	69	35	10	24

- Represents zero.   B Does not meet standard of reliability or precision.   [1] Full-time equivalents.

Source: U.S. National Center for Education Statistics, Office of Educational Research and Improvement, *Private School Universe Survey*, NCES 2001-330, August 2001.

No. 243. Private Elementary and Secondary School Teachers— Selected Characteristics: 1999-2000

[**For school year (87 represents 87,000).** Based on School and Staffing Survey and subject to sampling error; for details, see source web site at <http://nces.ed.gov/surveys/sass/>. See Table 229 for similar data on public school teachers]

Characteristic	Unit	Age				Sex		Race/ethnicity		
		Under 30 years old	30 to 39 years old	40 to 49 years old	Over 50 years old	Male	Fe-male	White [1]	Black [1]	His-panic
Total teachers [2] . . .	1,000 . . .	87	101	131	131	107	342	402	17	21
Highest degree held:										
Bachelor's	Percent .	75.9	59.6	56.3	46.7	48.8	60.9	58.3	59.1	55.4
Master's.	Percent .	14.0	28.4	33.4	42.1	39.0	28.6	31.8	18.7	26.7
Education specialist .	Percent .	0.2	1.2	2.0	3.1	2.6	1.6	1.7	2.1	2.8
Doctorate	Percent .	0.3	1.6	1.3	3.4	4.9	0.8	1.8	0.7	1.5
Full-time teaching experience:										
Less than 3 years . .	Percent .	72.5	31.4	21.4	9.2	30.9	29.6	29.1	37.6	36.6
3 to 9 years	Percent .	27.2	39.4	26.5	11.2	22.6	25.8	25.0	24.8	26.1
10 to 20 years.	Percent .	0.3	29.2	36.7	34.0	22.7	28.6	27.4	22.5	28.7
20 years or more . . .	Percent .	(Z)	(Z)	15.4	45.7	23.8	15.9	18.5	15.1	8.7
Full-time teachers . .	1,000 . . .	76	81	104	105	86	280	327	14	17
Earned income	Dol.	25,289	29,841	29,638	33,278	36,524	27,771	29,942	27,593	29,508
Salary	Dol.	22,299	26,828	27,229	31,063	31,438	25,922	27,340	24,374	27,162

Z Less than 0.05 percent.   [1] Non-Hispanic.   [2] Includes teachers with no degrees and associates degrees, not shown separately.

Source: U.S. National Center for Education Statistics, unpublished data.

No. 244. Scholastic Assessment Test (SAT) Scores and Characteristics of College-Bound Seniors: 1967 to 2001

[**For school year ending in year shown.** Data are for the SAT I: Reasoning Tests. SAT I: Reasoning Test replaced the SAT in March 1994. Scores between the two tests have been equated to the same 200-800 scale and are thus comparable. Scores for 1995 and prior years have been recentered and revised]

Type of test and characteristic	Unit	1967	1970	1975	1980	1985	1990	1995	1999	2000	2001
AVERAGE TEST SCORES [1]											
Verbal, total [2]	Point . . .	543	537	512	502	509	500	504	505	505	506
Male	Point . . .	540	536	515	506	514	505	505	509	507	509
Female	Point . . .	545	538	509	498	503	496	502	502	504	502
Math, total [2]	Point . . .	516	512	498	492	500	501	506	511	514	514
Male	Point . . .	535	531	518	515	522	521	525	531	533	533
Female	Point . . .	495	493	479	473	480	483	490	495	498	498
PARTICIPANTS											
Total [3]	1,000 . . .	(NA)	(NA)	996	922	977	1,026	1,068	1,220	1,260	1,276
Male	Percent .	(NA)	(NA)	49.9	48.2	48.3	47.8	46.4	46.1	46.2	46.4
White	Percent .	(NA)	(NA)	86.0	82.1	81.0	73.0	69.2	66.9	66.4	66.0
Black	Percent .	(NA)	(NA)	7.9	9.1	7.5	10.0	10.7	11.1	11.2	11.3
Obtaining scores [1] of—											
600 or above:											
Verbal	Percent .	(NA)	(NA)	(NA)	(NA)	(NA)	20.3	21.9	21.2	21.1	21.3
Math	Percent .	(NA)	(NA)	(NA)	(NA)	(NA)	20.4	23.4	23.7	24.2	24.5
Below 400:											
Verbal	Percent .	(NA)	(NA)	(NA)	(NA)	(NA)	17.3	16.4	16.1	15.9	15.8
Math	Percent .	(NA)	(NA)	(NA)	(NA)	(NA)	15.8	16.0	15.7	14.7	14.7
Selected intended area of study:											
Business and commerce	Percent .	(NA)	(NA)	11.5	18.6	21.0	20.9	13.3	13.8	13.6	13.7
Engineering	Percent .	(NA)	(NA)	6.7	11.1	11.7	10.2	8.8	8.5	8.5	8.6
Social science	Percent .	(NA)	(NA)	7.7	7.8	7.5	12.6	11.6	10.5	10.6	10.2
Education	Percent .	(NA)	(NA)	9.1	6.1	4.7	7.5	8.1	8.9	8.8	8.7

NA Not available. [1] Minimum score 200; maximum score, 800. [2] 1967 and 1970 are estimates based on total number of persons taking SAT. [3] 996 represents 996,000.

Source: College Entrance Examination Board, New York, NY, *National College-Bound Senior,* annual (copyright).

No. 245. ACT Program Scores and Characteristics of College-Bound Students: 1970 to 2001

[**For academic year ending in year shown.** Except as indicated, test scores and characteristics of college-bound students. Through 1980, data based on 10 percent sample; thereafter, based on all ACT tested graduating seniors]

Type of test and characteristic	Unit	1970	1975	1980	1985	1990 [1]	1995 [1]	1998 [1]	1999 [1]	2000 [1]	2001 [1]
TEST SCORES [2]											
Composite	Point . . .	19.9	18.6	18.5	18.6	20.6	20.8	21.0	21.0	21.0	21.0
Male	Point . . .	20.3	19.5	19.3	19.4	21.0	21.0	21.2	21.1	21.2	21.1
Female	Point . . .	19.4	17.8	17.9	17.9	20.3	20.7	20.9	20.9	20.9	20.9
English	Point . . .	18.5	17.7	17.9	18.1	20.5	20.2	20.4	20.5	20.5	20.5
Male	Point . . .	17.6	17.1	17.3	17.6	20.1	19.8	19.9	20.0	20.0	20.0
Female	Point . . .	19.4	18.3	18.3	18.6	20.9	20.6	20.8	20.9	20.9	20.8
Math	Point . . .	20.0	17.6	17.4	17.2	19.9	20.2	20.8	20.7	20.7	20.7
Male	Point . . .	21.1	19.3	18.9	18.6	20.7	20.9	21.5	21.4	21.4	21.4
Female	Point . . .	18.8	16.2	16.2	16.0	19.3	19.7	20.2	20.2	20.2	20.2
Reading [3]	Point . . .	19.7	17.4	17.2	17.4	(NA)	21.3	21.4	21.4	21.4	21.3
Male	Point . . .	20.3	18.7	18.2	18.3	(NA)	21.1	21.1	21.1	21.2	21.1
Female	Point . . .	19.0	16.4	16.4	16.6	(NA)	21.4	21.6	21.6	21.5	21.5
Science reasoning [4]	Point . . .	20.8	21.1	21.1	21.2	(NA)	21.0	21.1	21.0	21.0	21.0
Male	Point . . .	21.6	22.4	22.4	22.6	(NA)	21.6	21.8	21.5	21.6	21.6
Female	Point . . .	20.0	20.0	20.0	20.0	(NA)	20.5	20.6	20.6	20.6	20.6
PARTICIPANTS [5]											
Total [6]	1,000 . . .	788	714	822	739	817	945	995	1,019	1,065	1,070
Male	Percent .	52	46	45	46	46	44	43	43	43	43
White	Percent .	(NA)	77	83	82	79	75	76	76	76	75
Black	Percent .	4	7	8	8	9	10	11	11	11	11
Obtaining composite scores of—[7]											
27 or above	Percent .	14	14	13	14	12	13	14	14	14	14
18 or below	Percent .	21	33	33	32	35	34	33	33	32	33
Planned educational major:											
Business [8]	Percent .	18	21	20	21	20	14	12	11	11	11
Engineering	Percent .	8	6	8	9	9	9	7	7	6	6
Social science [9]	Percent .	10	9	6	7	10	9	9	9	8	9
Education	Percent .	16	12	9	6	8	9	10	10	9	9

NA Not available. [1] Beginning 1990, not comparable with previous years because a new version of the ACT was introduced. Estimated average composite scores for prior years: 1989, 20.6; 1988, 1987, and 1986, 20.8. [2] Minimum score, 1; maximum score, 36. [3] Prior to 1990, social studies; data not comparable with previous years. [4] Prior to 1990, natural sciences; data not comparable with previous years. [5] Beginning 1985, data are for seniors who graduated in year shown and had taken the ACT in their junior or senior years. Data by race are for those responding to the race question. [6] 788 represents 788,000. [7] Prior to 1990, 26 or above and 15 or below. [8] Includes political and persuasive (e.g. sales) fields through 1975; 1980 and 1985 business and commerce; thereafter, business and management and business and office. [9] Includes religion through 1975.

Source: ACT, Inc., Iowa City, IA, *High School Profile Report,* annual.

No. 246. Proficiency Test Scores for Selected Subjects by Characteristic: 1977 to 2001

[Based on The National Assessment of Educational Progress Tests which are administered to a representative sample of students in public and private schools. Test scores can range from 0 to 500, except as indicated. For details, see source]

Test and year	Total	Male	Fe-male	White[1]	Black[1]	His-panic origin	Less than high school	High school	More than high school Total	Some college	College gradu-ate
READING											
9 year olds:											
1979-80	215	210	220	221	189	190	194	213	226	(NA)	(NA)
1987-88	212	208	216	218	189	194	193	211	220	(NA)	(NA)
1998-99	212	209	215	221	186	193	199	206	220	(NA)	(NA)
13 year olds:											
1979-80	259	254	263	264	233	237	239	254	271	(NA)	(NA)
1987-88	258	252	263	261	243	240	247	253	265	(NA)	(NA)
1998-99	259	254	265	267	238	244	238	251	270	(NA)	(NA)
17 year olds:											
1979-80	286	282	289	293	243	261	262	278	299	(NA)	(NA)
1987-88	290	286	294	295	274	271	267	282	300	(NA)	(NA)
1998-99	288	282	295	295	264	271	265	274	298	(NA)	(NA)
WRITING[2]											
4th graders:											
1983-84	204	201	208	211	182	189	179	192	217	208	218
1987-88	206	199	213	215	173	190	194	199	212	211	212
1995-96	207	200	214	216	182	191	190	203	(NA)	205	214
8th graders:											
1983-84	267	258	276	272	247	247	258	261	276	271	278
1987-88	264	254	274	269	246	250	254	258	271	275	271
1995-96	264	251	276	271	242	246	245	258	(NA)	270	274
11th graders:											
1983-84	290	281	299	297	270	259	274	284	299	298	300
1987-88	291	282	299	296	275	274	276	285	298	296	299
1995-96	283	275	292	289	267	269	260	275	(NA)	287	291
MATHEMATICS											
9 year olds:											
1977-78	219	217	220	224	192	203	200	219	231	230	231
1985-86	222	222	222	227	202	205	201	218	231	229	231
1998-99	232	233	231	239	211	213	214	224	(NA)	237	240
13 year olds:											
1977-78	264	264	265	272	230	238	245	263	280	273	284
1985-86	269	270	268	274	249	254	252	263	278	274	280
1998-99	276	277	275	283	251	259	256	264	(NA)	279	286
17 year olds:											
1977-78	300	304	297	306	268	276	280	294	313	305	317
1985-86	302	305	299	308	279	283	279	293	310	305	314
1998-99	308	310	307	315	283	293	289	299	(NA)	308	317
SCIENCE											
9 year olds:											
1976-77	220	222	218	230	175	192	199	223	233	237	232
1985-86	224	227	221	232	196	199	204	220	235	236	235
1998-99	229	231	228	240	199	206	213	218	(NA)	234	237
13 year olds:											
1976-77	247	251	244	256	208	213	224	245	264	260	266
1985-86	251	256	247	259	222	226	229	245	262	258	264
1998-99	256	259	253	266	227	227	229	243	(NA)	261	268
17 year olds:											
1976-77	290	297	282	298	240	262	265	284	304	296	309
1985-86	289	295	282	298	253	259	258	277	300	295	304
1998-99	295	300	291	306	254	276	264	281	(NA)	297	307
HISTORY, 2001											
4th graders	209	209	209	220	188	186	177	197	(NA)	214	216
8th graders	262	264	261	271	243	243	241	251	(NA)	264	270
12th graders	287	288	286	292	269	274	263	276	(NA)	287	296
GEOGRAPHY, 2001											
4th graders	209	212	207	222	181	184	186	197	(NA)	216	216
8th graders	262	264	260	273	234	240	238	250	(NA)	265	272
12th graders	285	287	282	291	260	270	263	274	(NA)	286	294
CIVICS, 1997-98[3]											
4th graders	150	149	151	159	132	126	124	153	(NA)	150	153
8th graders	150	148	152	159	133	127	123	144	(NA)	143	160
12th graders	150	148	152	158	131	130	124	140	(NA)	145	160

NA Not available.   [1] Non-Hispanic.   [2] Writing scores revised from previous years; previous writing scores were recorded on a 0 to 400 rather than 0 to 500 scale.   [3] Civics uses a scale of 0 to 300.

Source: U.S. National Center for Education Statistics, *Digest of Education Statistics,* annual, and *NAEP 1998 Civics Report Card for the Nation* ; and *NAEP 2001 Geography* and *History Report Card for the Nation.*

No. 247. Advanced Placement Program—Summary: 2000 and 2001

[Includes exams taken by candidates abroad. In 2001, this represents 34,241 examinations taken by 23,861 students in 720 schools abroad]

| Item | Program total | | | | 2001 | | | | |
| | Schools repre- sented, 2001 | Exams taken | | Percent change, 2000-01 | Grade level of test taker | | | Sex of test taker | |
		2000	2001		10th grade	11th grade	12th grade	Male	Female
Exams taken, total [1] .	(X)	1,272,317	1,414,387	11	79,707	490,412	800,824	650,549	763,838
By subject area:									
Art History	903	9,721	11,047	14	994	2,859	6,908	3,880	7,167
Art, Drawing	1,498	4,675	5,660	21	65	1,068	4,348	2,199	3,461
Art, General	2,008	9,172	9,696	6	134	1,504	7,755	3,264	6,432
Biology	6,674	86,826	92,254	6	7,528	33,823	48,149	38,212	54,042
Calculus AB	10,007	137,276	146,771	7	1,393	20,064	121,955	77,334	69,437
Calculus BC	3,319	34,142	38,134	12	672	6,984	29,650	23,432	14,702
Chemistry.	5,099	52,786	55,406	5	2,736	27,980	23,427	30,815	24,591
Computer Science—A . .	2,188	13,646	15,827	16	1,894	6,013	7,433	13,127	2,700
Computer Science—AB .	1,360	6,876	7,595	10	722	2,786	3,846	6,764	831
Economics-Micro	1,484	17,464	18,696	7	332	2,302	15,535	10,977	7,719
Economics-Macro	1,777	23,761	28,200	19	340	3,004	24,160	15,900	12,300
English Language/ Composition	5,788	114,049	135,428	19	1,452	98,176	32,755	50,294	85,134
English Literature/ Composition	10,334	190,643	201,288	6	133	12,608	184,232	73,422	127,866
Environmental Science . .	1,198	13,698	18,880	38	605	5,847	11,833	8,225	10,655
European History.	3,572	59,708	65,776	10	31,731	10,175	22,187	31,435	34,341
French Language.	2,978	15,493	16,533	7	716	4,427	10,731	4,825	11,708
French Literature	379	1,655	1,668	1	67	385	1,151	487	1,181
German Language.	1,161	3,784	4,116	9	238	925	2,747	2,003	2,113
Government and Politics—U.S.	4,234	66,370	77,467	17	2,329	7,345	66,036	37,443	40,024
Government and Politics—Comparative . .	843	8,246	9,188	11	786	1,274	6,927	4,978	4,210
Human Geography.	305	(X)	3,272	(X)	923	771	1,202	1,685	1,587
International English Language	83	5,844	7,635	31	14	74	93	3,033	4,602
Latin—Vergil	599	3,439	3,767	10	345	1,697	1,621	1,876	1,891
Latin—Literature	409	2,343	2,419	3	88	958	1,322	1,139	1,280
Music Theory	1,427	5,304	6,135	16	464	1,821	3,689	3,163	2,972
Physics—B.	3,127	30,967	34,001	10	680	11,561	20,958	22,163	11,838
Physics—Mechanics. . . .	2,067	15,634	17,397	11	108	1,828	15,117	12,764	4,633
Physics—Electricity and Magnetism	1,262	7,465	8,362	12	59	768	7,354	6,495	1,867
Psychology.	2,242	34,035	42,978	26	857	11,919	29,157	14,647	28,331
Spanish Language	5,125	64,380	70,949	10	6,791	24,516	36,137	25,183	45,766
Spanish Literature	1,128	8,829	9,992	13	543	2,965	6,093	3,122	6,870
Statistics	2,659	34,118	41,609	22	1,425	8,123	31,123	20,842	20,767
U.S. History	8,535	180,968	206,241	9	12,543	173,862	15,193	95,421	110,820
Candidates taking exams [1] .	(X)	768,586	844,741	10	71,689	323,203	417,744	374,478	470,263

X Not applicable.   [1] Includes candidates and exams taken in other grades not shown separately.

Source: The College Board, New York, NY, Advanced Placement Program, *National Summary Report*, 2001 (copyright).

No. 248. Foreign Language Enrollment in Public High Schools: 1970 to 2000

[In thousands (13,301.9 represents 13,301,900), except percent. As of fall, for grades 9 through 12]

Language	1970	1974	1978	1982	1985	1990	1994	2000
Total enrollment.	13,301.9	13,648.9	13,941.4	12,879.3	12,466.5	11,099.6	11,847.5	13,457.8
Enrolled in all foreign languages	3,779.3	3,294.5	3,200.1	2,909.8	4,028.9	4,256.9	5,001.9	5,898.1
Percent of all students.	28.4	24.1	23.0	22.6	32.3	38.4	42.2	43.8
Enrolled in modern foreign languages [1] . .	3,514.1	3,127.3	3,048.3	2,740.2	3,852.0	4,093.0	4,813.0	5,720.7
Spanish	1,810.8	1,678.1	1,631.4	1,562.8	2,334.4	2,611.4	3,219.8	4,057.6
French.	1,230.7	977.9	856.0	858.0	1,133.7	1,089.4	1,105.9	1,075.4
German	410.5	393.0	330.6	266.9	312.2	295.4	326.0	283.3
Italian	27.3	40.2	45.5	44.1	47.3	40.4	43.8	64.1
Japanese	(NA)	(NA)	(NA)	6.2	8.6	25.1	42.3	50.9
Russian	20.2	15.1	8.8	5.7	6.4	16.5	16.4	10.6
Percent of all students [1]	26.4	22.9	21.9	21.3	30.9	36.9	40.6	42.5
Spanish	13.6	12.3	11.7	12.1	18.7	23.5	27.2	30.2
French	9.3	7.2	6.1	6.7	9.1	9.8	9.3	8.0
German	3.1	2.9	2.4	2.1	2.5	2.7	2.8	2.1
Italian.	0.2	0.3	0.3	0.3	0.4	0.4	0.4	0.5
Japanese	(NA)	(NA)	(NA)	0.1	0.1	0.2	0.4	0.4
Russian	0.2	0.1	0.1	(Z)	0.1	0.2	0.1	0.1

NA Not available.   Z Less than 0.05 percent.   [1] Includes other foreign languages, not shown separately.

Source: The American Council on the Teaching of Foreign Languages, Yonkers, NY, *Foreign Language Enrollments in Public Secondary Schools, fall 1994* and *fall 2000*.

U.S. Census Bureau, Statistical Abstract of the United States: 2002

No. 249. Public High School Graduates by State: 1980 to 2000

[In thousands (2,747.7 represents 2,747,700). For school year ending in year shown]

State	1980	1990	1995	2000, est.	State	1980	1990	1995	2000, est.
United States. . .	**2,747.7**	**2,320.3**	**2,273.5**	**2,546.1**	Missouri	62.3	49.0	48.9	52.8
					Montana	12.1	9.4	10.1	10.9
Alabama	45.2	40.5	36.3	37.8	Nebraska	22.4	17.7	18.0	20.1
Alaska	5.2	5.4	5.8	6.6	Nevada	8.5	9.5	10.0	14.6
Arizona	28.6	32.1	31.0	38.3	New Hampshire . . .	11.7	10.8	10.1	11.8
Arkansas	29.1	26.5	24.6	27.3					
California	249.2	236.3	255.2	309.9	New Jersey	94.6	69.8	67.4	74.4
					New Mexico	18.4	14.9	14.9	18.0
Colorado	36.8	33.0	32.4	38.9	New York	204.1	143.3	132.4	141.7
Connecticut	37.7	27.9	26.4	31.6	North Carolina	70.9	64.8	59.5	62.1
Delaware	7.6	5.6	5.2	6.1	North Dakota	9.9	7.7	7.8	8.6
District of Columbia .	5.0	3.6	3.0	2.7					
Florida	87.3	88.9	89.8	106.7	Ohio	144.2	114.5	109.4	111.7
					Oklahoma	39.3	35.6	33.3	37.6
Georgia	61.6	56.6	56.7	62.6	Oregon	29.9	25.5	26.7	30.2
Hawaii	11.5	10.3	9.4	10.4	Pennsylvania	146.5	110.5	104.1	114.0
Idaho	13.2	12.0	14.2	16.2	Rhode Island	10.9	7.8	7.8	8.5
Illinois	135.6	108.1	105.2	111.8					
Indiana	73.1	60.0	56.1	57.0	South Carolina	38.7	32.5	30.7	31.6
					South Dakota	10.7	7.7	8.4	9.3
Iowa	43.4	31.8	31.3	33.9	Tennessee	49.8	46.1	43.6	41.6
Kansas	30.9	25.4	26.1	29.1	Texas	171.4	172.5	170.3	212.9
Kentucky	41.2	38.0	37.6	36.8	Utah	20.0	21.2	27.7	32.5
Louisiana	46.3	36.1	36.5	38.4					
Maine	15.4	13.8	11.5	12.1	Vermont	6.7	6.1	5.9	6.7
					Virginia	66.6	60.6	58.3	65.6
Maryland	54.3	41.6	41.4	47.8	Washington	50.4	45.9	49.3	57.6
Massachusetts	73.8	55.9	47.7	53.0	West Virginia	23.4	21.9	20.1	19.4
Michigan	124.3	93.8	84.6	90.0	Wisconsin	69.3	52.0	51.7	58.5
Minnesota	64.9	49.1	49.4	57.4	Wyoming	6.1	5.8	5.9	6.5
Mississippi	27.6	25.2	23.8	24.2					

Source: U.S. National Center for Education Statistics, *Digest of Education Statistics*, annual.

No. 250. High School Dropouts by Race and Hispanic Origin: 1975 to 2000

[In percent. As of October]

Item	1975	1980	1985	1990 [1]	1993	1994	1995	1996	1997	1998	1999	2000
EVENT DROPOUTS [2]												
Total [3]	**5.8**	**6.0**	**5.2**	**4.0**	**4.2**	**5.0**	**5.4**	**4.7**	**4.3**	**4.4**	**4.7**	**4.5**
White	5.4	5.6	4.8	3.8	4.1	4.7	5.1	4.5	4.2	4.4	4.4	4.3
Male	5.0	6.4	4.9	4.1	4.1	4.6	5.4	4.8	4.9	4.4	4.1	4.7
Female	5.8	4.9	4.7	3.5	4.1	4.9	4.8	4.1	3.5	4.4	4.7	4.0
Black	8.7	8.3	7.7	5.1	5.4	6.2	6.1	6.3	4.8	5.0	6.0	5.6
Male	8.3	8.0	8.3	4.1	5.7	6.5	7.9	4.6	4.1	4.6	5.2	7.6
Female	9.0	8.5	7.2	6.0	5.0	5.7	4.4	7.8	5.7	5.5	6.8	3.8
Hispanic [4]	10.9	11.5	9.7	8.0	5.4	9.2	11.6	8.4	8.6	8.4	7.1	6.8
Male	10.1	16.9	9.3	8.7	5.7	8.4	10.9	9.2	10.4	8.6	6.9	7.1
Female	11.6	6.9	9.8	7.2	5.0	10.1	12.5	7.6	6.7	8.2	7.3	6.5
STATUS DROPOUTS [5]												
Total [3]	**15.6**	**15.6**	**13.9**	**13.6**	**12.7**	**13.3**	**13.9**	**12.8**	**13.0**	**13.9**	**13.1**	**12.4**
White	13.9	14.4	13.5	13.5	12.2	12.7	13.6	12.5	12.4	13.7	12.8	12.2
Male	13.5	15.7	14.7	14.2	13.0	13.6	14.3	12.9	13.8	15.7	13.9	13.5
Female	14.2	13.2	12.3	12.8	11.5	11.7	13.0	12.1	10.9	11.7	11.8	10.9
Black	27.3	23.5	17.6	15.1	16.4	15.5	14.4	16.0	16.7	17.1	16.0	15.3
Male	27.8	26.0	18.8	13.6	15.6	17.5	14.2	17.4	17.5	20.5	16.3	17.4
Female	26.9	21.5	16.6	16.2	17.2	13.7	14.6	14.7	16.1	14.3	15.7	13.5
Hispanic [4]	34.9	40.3	31.5	37.3	32.7	34.7	34.7	34.5	30.6	34.4	33.9	32.3
Male	32.6	42.6	35.8	39.8	34.7	36.1	34.2	36.2	33.2	39.7	36.4	36.8
Female	36.8	38.1	27.0	34.5	31.0	33.1	35.4	32.7	27.6	28.6	31.1	27.3

[1] Beginning 1990 reflects new editing procedures for cases with missing data on school enrollment. [2] Percent of students who drop out in a single year without completing high school. For grades 10 to 12. [3] Includes other races, not shown separately. [4] Persons of Hispanic origin may be of any race. [5] Percent of the population who have not completed high school and are not enrolled, regardless of when they dropped out. For persons 18 to 24 years old.

Source: U.S. Census Bureau, *Current Population Reports*, PPL-148.

No. 251. High School Dropouts by Age, Race, and Hispanic Origin: 1970 to 2000

[As of October (4,670 represents 4,670,000). For persons 14 to 24 years old. See Table 253 for definition of dropouts]

Age and race	Number of dropouts (1,000)					Percent of population				
	1970	1980	1990	1995	2000	1970	1980	1990	1995	2000
Total dropouts [1][2]....	4,670	5,212	3,854	3,963	3,775	12.2	12.0	10.1	9.9	10.9
16 to 17 years	617	709	418	406	460	8.0	8.8	6.3	5.4	5.8
18 to 21 years	2,138	2,578	1,921	1,980	2,005	16.4	15.8	13.4	14.2	12.9
22 to 24 years	1,770	1,798	1,458	1,491	1,310	18.7	15.2	13.8	13.6	11.8
White [2]	3,577	4,169	3,127	3,098	2,964	10.8	11.3	10.1	9.7	10.8
16 to 17 years	485	619	334	314	366	7.3	9.2	6.4	5.4	5.8
18 to 21 years	1,618	2,032	1,516	1,530	1,558	14.3	14.7	13.1	13.8	12.6
22 to 24 years	1,356	1,416	1,235	1,181	1,040	16.3	14.0	14.0	13.4	11.7
Black [2]	1,047	934	611	605	700	22.2	16.0	10.9	10.0	13.4
16 to 17 years	125	80	73	70	84	12.8	6.9	6.9	5.8	7.0
18 to 21 years	500	486	345	328	383	30.5	23.0	16.0	15.8	16.0
22 to 24 years	397	346	185	194	232	37.8	24.0	13.5	12.5	14.3
Hispanic [2][3]	(NA)	919	1,122	1,355	1,456	(NA)	29.5	26.8	24.7	27.8
16 to 17 years	(NA)	92	89	94	121	(NA)	16.6	12.9	10.7	11.0
18 to 21 years	(NA)	470	502	652	733	(NA)	40.3	32.9	29.9	30.0
22 to 24 years	(NA)	323	523	598	602	(NA)	40.6	42.8	37.4	35.5

NA Not available.   [1] Includes other groups not shown separately.   [2] Includes persons 14 to 15 years, not shown separately.   [3] Persons of Hispanic origin may be of any race.

Source: U.S. Census Bureau, *Current Population Reports*, PPL-148; and earlier years.

No. 252. Enrollment Status by Race, Hispanic Origin, and Sex: 1975 and 2000

[As of October (15,693 represents 15,693,000). For persons 18 to 21 years old. For the civilian noninstitutional population. Based on the Current Population Survey; see text, Section 1, Population, and Appendix III]

Characteristic	Total persons 18 to 21 years old (1,000)		Percent distribution							
			Enrolled in high school		High school graduates				Not high school graduates	
					Total		In college			
	1975	2000	1975	2000	1975	2000	1975	2000	1975	2000
Total [1]	15,693	15,553	5.7	9.4	78.0	77.6	33.5	43.5	16.3	12.9
White	13,448	12,383	4.7	8.9	80.6	78.5	34.6	44.4	14.7	12.6
Black	1,997	2,389	12.5	12.6	60.4	71.3	24.9	34.7	27.0	16.0
Hispanic [2]	899	2,439	12.0	12.5	57.2	57.2	24.4	25.3	30.8	30.0
Male [1]	7,584	7,814	7.4	11.0	76.6	74.7	35.4	38.9	15.9	14.3
White	6,545	6,313	6.2	10.6	79.7	75.7	36.9	39.8	14.1	13.7
Black	911	1,096	15.9	14.9	55.0	66.0	23.9	27.4	29.0	19.1
Hispanic [2]	416	1,269	17.3	14.4	54.6	51.8	25.2	21.9	27.9	33.7
Female [1]	8,109	7,739	4.2	7.9	79.2	80.6	31.8	48.1	16.6	11.5
White	6,903	6,070	3.2	7.1	81.4	81.3	32.4	49.3	15.3	11.4
Black	1,085	1,293	9.7	10.7	65.0	75.9	25.8	40.9	25.4	13.5
Hispanic [2]	484	1,169	7.6	10.6	59.3	63.1	23.6	28.9	33.1	26.1

[1] Includes other races not shown separately.   [2] Persons of Hispanic origin may be of any race.

Source: U.S. Census Bureau, *Current Population Reports*, PPL-148; and earlier reports.

No. 253. Employment Status of High School Graduates and School Dropouts: 1980 to 2001

[In thousands (11,622 represents 11,622,000), except percent. As of October. For civilian noninstitutional population 16 to 24 years old. Based on Current Population Survey; see text, Section 1, Population, and Appendix III]

Employment status, sex, and race	Graduates [1]				Dropouts [3]			
	1980	1990	1995 [2]	2001 [2]	1980	1990	1995 [2]	2001 [2]
Civilian population	11,622	8,370	6,627	7,395	5,254	3,800	3,876	3,774
In labor force	9,795	7,107	5,530	6,037	3,549	2,506	2,443	2,754
Percent of population	84.3	84.9	83.4	81.6	67.5	66.0	63.0	73.0
Employed	8,567	6,279	4,863	5,297	2,651	1,993	1,894	2,195
Percent of labor force	87.5	88.3	87.9	87.7	74.7	79.5	77.5	79.7
Unemployed	1,228	828	667	740	898	513	549	559
Unemployment rate, total [4]	12.5	11.7	12.1	12.3	25.3	20.5	22.5	20.3
Male	13.5	11.1	11.7	12.3	23.5	18.8	19.2	18.3
Female	11.5	12.3	12.5	12.2	28.7	23.5	28.8	23.9
White	10.8	9.0	10.5	10.3	21.6	17.0	19.1	16.4
Black	26.1	26.0	20.3	21.5	43.9	43.3	48.0	40.9
Not in labor force	1,827	1,262	1,097	1,358	1,705	1,294	1,433	1,020
Percent of population	15.7	15.1	16.6	18.4	32.5	34.1	37.0	27.0

[1] For persons not enrolled in college who have completed 4 years of high school only.   [2] See footnote 2, Table 560.   [3] For persons not in regular school and who have not completed the 12th grade nor received a general equivalency degree.   [4] Includes other races not shown separately.

Source: U.S. Bureau of Labor Statistics, Bulletin 2307; *News*, USDL 02-228, May 14, 2002; and unpublished data.

No. 254. General Educational Development (GED) Credentials Issued: 1974 to 2000

[GEDs issued in thousands (295 represents 295,000). Includes outlying areas]

Year	GEDs issued	Percent distribution by age of test taker				
		19 years old or under	20 to 24 years old	25 to 29 years old	30 to 34 years old	35 years old and over
1974	295	35	27	13	9	17
1975	342	33	26	14	9	18
1980	488	37	27	13	8	15
1985	427	33	26	15	10	16
1990	419	35	25	14	10	17
1995	513	37	25	13	10	15
1996	514	40	25	13	9	15
1997	471	41	25	12	8	14
1998	496	43	25	11	8	14
1999	517	43	25	11	8	14
2000	501	42	26	11	8	14

Source: U.S. National Center for Education Statistics, *Digest of Education Statistics*, 2001.

No. 255. College Enrollment of Recent High School Graduates: 1960 to 2000

[High school graduates in thousands (1,679 represents 1,679,000). For persons 16 to 24 who graduated from high school in the preceeding 12 months. Includes persons receiving GEDs. Based on surveys and subject to sampling error]

Year	Number of high school graduates					Percent enrolled in college [2]				
	Total [1]	Male	Female	White	Black	Total [1]	Male	Female	White	Black
1960	1,679	756	923	1,565	(NA)	45.1	54.0	37.9	45.8	(NA)
1965	2,659	1,254	1,405	2,417	(NA)	50.9	57.3	45.3	51.7	(NA)
1970	2,757	1,343	1,414	2,461	(NA)	51.8	55.2	48.5	52.0	(NA)
1975	3,186	1,513	1,673	2,825	(NA)	50.7	52.6	49.0	51.2	(NA)
1980	3,089	1,500	1,589	2,682	361	49.3	46.7	51.8	49.9	41.8
1983	2,964	1,390	1,574	2,496	392	52.7	51.9	53.4	55.0	38.5
1984	3,012	1,429	1,583	2,514	438	55.2	56.0	54.5	57.9	40.2
1985	2,666	1,286	1,380	2,241	333	57.7	58.6	56.9	59.4	42.3
1986	2,786	1,331	1,455	2,307	386	53.8	55.9	51.9	56.0	36.5
1987	2,647	1,278	1,369	2,207	337	56.8	58.4	55.3	56.6	51.9
1988	2,673	1,334	1,339	2,187	382	58.9	57.0	60.8	60.7	45.0
1989	2,454	1,208	1,245	2,051	337	59.6	57.6	61.6	60.4	52.8
1990	2,355	1,169	1,185	1,921	341	59.9	57.8	62.0	61.5	46.3
1991	2,276	1,139	1,137	1,867	320	62.4	57.6	67.1	64.6	45.6
1992	2,398	1,216	1,182	1,900	353	61.7	59.6	63.8	63.4	47.9
1993	2,338	1,118	1,219	1,910	302	62.6	59.7	65.4	62.8	55.6
1994	2,517	1,244	1,273	2,065	318	61.9	60.6	63.2	63.6	50.9
1995	2,599	1,238	1,361	2,088	356	61.9	62.6	61.4	62.6	51.4
1996	2,660	1,297	1,363	2,092	416	65.0	60.1	69.7	65.8	55.3
1997	2,769	1,354	1,415	2,228	394	67.0	63.5	70.3	67.5	59.6
1998	2,810	1,452	1,358	2,227	393	65.6	62.4	69.1	65.8	62.1
1999	2,897	1,474	1,423	2,287	453	62.9	61.4	64.4	62.8	59.2
2000	2,756	1,251	1,505	2,219	404	63.3	59.9	66.2	64.0	56.2

NA Not available.   [1] Includes other races, not shown separately.   [2] As of October.

Source: U.S. National Center for Education Statistics, *Digest of Education Statistics*, annual.

No. 256. College Enrollment by Sex and Attendance Status: 1983 to 1999

[As of fall. In thousands (12,465 represents 12,465,000)]

Sex and age	1983		1988		1993		1998 [1]		1999 [1]	
	Total	Part time	Total	Part time	Total	Part time	Total	Part time	Total	Part time
Total	12,465	5,204	13,055	5,619	14,305	6,177	14,507	5,944	14,791	6,005
Male	6,024	2,264	6,002	2,340	6,427	2,537	6,369	2,436	6,491	2,465
14 to 17 years old.	102	16	55	5	83	10	45	5	72	8
18 to 19 years old.	1,256	158	1,290	132	1,224	138	1,535	296	1,541	269
20 to 21 years old.	1,241	205	1,243	216	1,294	209	1,374	245	1,392	267
22 to 24 years old.	1,158	382	1,106	378	1,260	392	1,127	350	1,090	302
25 to 29 years old.	1,115	624	875	485	950	564	908	485	874	458
30 to 34 years old.	570	384	617	456	661	484	463	322	517	369
35 years old and over	583	494	816	668	955	739	917	733	1,005	791
Female.	6,441	2,940	7,053	3,278	7,877	3,640	8,138	3,508	8,301	3,540
14 to 17 years old.	142	16	115	17	93	6	74	21	72	6
18 to 19 years old.	1,496	179	1,536	195	1,416	172	1,847	292	1,874	297
20 to 21 years old.	1,125	204	1,278	218	1,414	279	1,437	295	1,597	360
22 to 24 years old.	884	378	932	403	1,263	493	1,250	463	1,344	470
25 to 29 years old.	947	658	932	633	1,058	689	1,083	617	995	558
30 to 34 years old.	721	553	698	499	811	575	732	506	627	438
35 years old and over	1,126	953	1,563	1,313	1,824	1,427	1,715	1,315	1,791	1,411

[1] In this table, data beginning in 1998 reflect the new classification of institutions. See footnote 1, Table 257.

Source: U.S. National Center for Education Statistics, *Digest of Education Statistics*, annual.

164   Education

No. 257. Higher Education—Summary: 1970 to 1999

[Institutions, staff, and enrollment as of fall (474 represents 474,000). Finances for fiscal year ending in the following year. Covers universities, colleges, professional schools, junior and teachers colleges, both publicly and privately controlled, regular session. Includes estimates for institutions not reporting. See also Appendix III]

Item	Unit	1970	1980	1985	1990	1995	1996	1997	1998	1999
ALL INSTITUTIONS										
Number of institutions [1]	Number.	2,556	3,231	3,340	3,559	3,706	4,009	4,064	4,048	4,084
4-year	Number.	1,665	1,957	2,029	2,141	2,244	2,267	2,309	2,335	2,363
2-year	Number.	891	1,274	1,311	1,418	1,462	1,742	1,755	1,713	1,721
Instructional staff—										
(Lecturer or above) [2]	1,000...	474	686	715	817	932	932	990	999	1,028
Percent full-time	Percent.	78	66	64	61	59	59	57	(NA)	57.5
Total enrollment [3]	1,000...	8,581	12,097	12,247	13,819	14,262	14,368	14,502	14,507	14,791
Male	1,000...	5,044	5,874	5,818	6,284	6,343	6,353	6,396	6,369	6,491
Female	1,000...	3,537	6,223	6,429	7,535	7,919	8,015	8,106	8,138	8,301
4-year institutions	1,000...	6,262	7,571	7,716	8,579	8,769	8,804	8,897	9,018	9,199
2-year institutions	1,000...	2,319	4,526	4,531	5,240	5,493	5,563	5,606	5,489	5,593
Full-time	1,000...	5,816	7,098	7,075	7,821	8,129	8,303	8,438	8,563	8,786
Part-time	1,000...	2,765	4,999	5,172	5,998	6,133	6,065	6,064	5,944	6,005
Public	1,000...	6,428	9,457	9,479	10,845	11,092	11,120	11,196	11,138	11,309
Private	1,000...	2,153	2,640	2,768	2,974	3,169	3,247	3,306	3,369	3,482
Undergraduate [4]	1,000...	7,376	10,475	10,597	11,959	12,232	12,327	12,451	12,437	12,681
Men	1,000...	4,254	5,000	4,962	5,380	5,401	5,421	5,469	5,446	5,559
Women	1,000...	3,122	5,475	5,635	6,579	6,831	6,906	6,982	6,991	7,122
First-time freshmen	1,000...	2,063	2,588	2,292	2,257	2,169	2,274	2,219	2,213	2,352
First professional	1,000...	173	278	274	273	298	298	298	302	303
Men	1,000...	159	199	180	167	174	173	170	169	165
Women	1,000...	15	78	94	107	124	126	129	134	138
Graduate [4]	1,000...	1,031	1,343	1,376	1,586	1,732	1,742	1,753	1,768	1,807
Men	1,000...	630	675	677	737	768	759	758	754	766
Women	1,000...	400	670	700	849	965	983	996	1,013	1,041
Current funds revenues [5]	Mil. dol.	23,879	65,585	100,438	149,766	197,973	(NA)	(NA)	(NA)	(NA)
Tuition and fees	Mil. dol.	5,021	13,773	23,117	37,434	55,260	(NA)	(NA)	(NA)	(NA)
Federal government	Mil. dol.	4,190	9,748	12,705	18,236	23,939	(NA)	(NA)	(NA)	(NA)
State government	Mil. dol.	6,503	20,106	29,912	39,481	45,693	(NA)	(NA)	(NA)	(NA)
Auxiliary enterprises	Mil. dol.	3,125	7,287	10,674	14,903	18,868	(NA)	(NA)	(NA)	(NA)
Current funds expenditures [5]	Mil. dol.	23,375	64,053	97,536	146,088	190,476	(NA)	(NA)	(NA)	(NA)
Educational and general [6]	Mil. dol.	17,616	50,074	76,128	114,140	151,446	(NA)	(NA)	(NA)	(NA)
Auxiliary enterprises	Mil. dol.	2,988	7,288	10,528	14,272	17,599	(NA)	(NA)	(NA)	(NA)
Endowment (market value)	Mil. dol.	13,714	23,465	50,281	72,049	128,837	(NA)	(NA)	(NA)	(NA)
2-YEAR INSTITUTIONS										
Number of institutions [1][7]	Number.	891	1,274	1,311	1,418	1,462	1,742	1,755	1,713	1,721
Public	Number.	654	945	932	972	1,047	1,088	1,092	1,069	1,068
Private	Number.	237	329	379	446	415	654	663	644	653
Instructional staff—										
(Lecturer or above) [2]	1,000...	92	192	211	(NA)	285	285	307	(NA)	314
Enrollment [3][4]	1,000...	2,319	4,526	4,531	5,240	5,493	5,563	5,606	5,489	5,593
Public	1,000...	2,195	4,329	4,270	4,996	5,278	5,314	5,361	5,246	5,339
Private	1,000...	124	198	261	244	215	249	245	243	253
Male	1,000...	1,375	2,047	2,002	2,233	2,329	2,359	2,390	2,333	2,387
Female	1,000...	945	2,479	2,529	3,007	3,164	3,204	3,216	3,156	3,205
Current funds revenue [5]	Mil. dol.	2,504	8,505	12,293	18,021	24,614	(NA)	(NA)	(NA)	(NA)
Tuition and fees	Mil. dol.	413	1,618	2,618	4,029	6,323	(NA)	(NA)	(NA)	(NA)
State government	Mil. dol.	926	3,961	5,659	8,001	9,848	(NA)	(NA)	(NA)	(NA)
Local government	Mil. dol.	701	1,623	2,027	3,044	4,324	(NA)	(NA)	(NA)	(NA)
Current funds expenditures	Mil. dol.	2,327	8,212	11,976	17,494	23,522	(NA)	(NA)	(NA)	(NA)
Education and general [6]	Mil. dol.	2,073	7,608	11,118	16,270	22,053	(NA)	(NA)	(NA)	(NA)
Instruction	Mil. dol.	1,205	3,764	5,398	7,903	10,312	(NA)	(NA)	(NA)	(NA)

NA Not available. [1] Beginning 1980, number of institutions includes count of branch campuses. Due to revised survey procedures, data beginning 1990 are not comparable with previous years. Beginning 1996 data reflect a new classification of institutions; this classification includes some additional, primarily 2-year, colleges than before and excludes a few institutions that did not award degrees. Includes institutions that were eligible to participate in Title IV Federal financial aid programs. [2] Due to revised survey methods, data beginning 1990 not comparable with previous years. [3] Beginning 1980, branch campuses counted according to actual status, e.g., 2-year branch in 2-year category; previously a 2-year branch included in university category. [4] Includes unclassified students. (Students taking courses for credit, but are not candidates for degrees.) [5] Includes items not shown separately. [6] Data for 1970 are not strictly comparable with later years. [7] Beginning 1980, includes schools accredited by the National Association of Trade and Technical Schools. 'See footnote 1 for information pertaining to data beginning 1996.

Source: U.S. National Center for Education Statistics, *Digest of Education Statistics,* annual; *Projections of Education Statistics,* annual; and unpublished data.

Education 165

No. 258. College Enrollment by Selected Characteristics: 1990 to 1999

[In thousands (13,818.6 represents 13,818,600). **As of fall**. Totals may differ from other tables because of adjustments to underreported and nonreported racial/ethnic data. Nonresident alien students are not distributed among racial/ethnic groups]

Characteristic	1990	1993	1994	1995	1996 [1]	1997 [1]	1998 [1]	1999 [1]
Total	13,818.6	14,304.8	14,278.8	14,261.8	14,367.5	14,502.3	14,507.0	14,791.2
Male	6,283.9	6,427.5	6,371.9	6,342.5	6,352.8	6,396.0	6,369.3	6,490.6
Female.	7,534.7	7,877.4	7,906.9	7,919.2	8,014.7	8,106.3	8,137.7	8,300.6
Public.	10,844.7	11,189.1	11,133.7	11,092.4	11,120.5	11,196.1	11,137.8	11,309.4
Private	2,973.9	3,115.7	3,145.1	3,169.4	3,247.0	3,306.2	3,369.2	3,481.8
2-year	5,240.1	5,565.9	5,529.7	5,492.5	5,563.3	5,605.6	5,489.3	5,592.7
4-year	8,578.6	8,738.9	8,749.1	8,769.3	8,804.2	8,896.8	9,017.7	9,198.5
Undergraduate.	11,959.2	12,324.0	12,262.6	12,232.0	12,326.9	12,450.6	12,436.9	12,681.2
Graduate	1,586.2	1,688.4	1,721.5	1,732.0	1,742.3	1,753.5	1,767.6	1,806.8
First professional . . .	273.4	292.4	294.7	297.6	298.3	298.1	302.5	303.2
White [2]	10,722.5	10,600.0	10,427.0	10,311.2	10,263.9	10,266.1	10,178.8	10,262.5
Male	4,861.0	4,755.0	4,650.7	4,594.1	4,552.2	4,548.8	4,499.4	4,539.9
Female.	5,861.5	5,845.1	5,776.3	5,717.2	5,711.7	5,717.4	5,679.4	5,722.6
Public.	8,385.4	8,226.6	8,056.3	7,945.4	7,871.9	7,857.8	7,750.6	7,794.7
Private	2,337.0	2,373.4	2,370.6	2,365.9	2,392.0	2,408.3	2,428.3	2,467.7
2-year	3,954.3	3,960.6	3,861.7	3,794.0	3,780.8	3,770.0	3,641.3	3,670.3
4-year	6,768.1	6,639.5	6,565.3	6,517.2	6,483.1	6,496.1	6,537.5	6,592.2
Undergraduate.	9,272.6	9,100.4	8,916.0	8,805.6	8,769.5	8,783.9	8,703.6	8,796.7
Graduate	1,228.4	1,273.8	1,286.8	1,282.3	1,272.6	1,261.8	1,254.3	1,246.2
First professional . . .	221.5	225.9	224.2	223.3	221.7	220.4	220.9	219.7
Black [2]	1,247.0	1,412.8	1,448.6	1,473.7	1,505.6	1,551.0	1,582.9	1,640.7
Male	484.7	543.7	549.7	555.9	564.1	579.8	584.0	603.0
Female.	762.3	869.1	898.9	917.8	941.4	971.3	999.0	1,037.7
Public.	976.4	1,114.3	1,144.6	1,160.6	1,177.4	1,205.3	1,218.8	1,252.4
Private	270.6	298.5	304.1	313.0	328.1	345.8	364.2	388.4
2-year	524.3	599.0	615.0	621.5	636.0	654.6	655.4	678.7
4-year	722.8	813.7	833.6	852.2	869.6	896.4	927.6	962.0
Undergraduate.	1,147.2	1,290.4	1,317.3	1,333.6	1,358.6	1,398.1	1,421.7	1,470.5
Graduate	83.9	102.2	110.6	118.6	125.5	131.6	138.7	147.8
First professional . . .	15.9	20.2	20.7	21.4	21.5	21.4	22.5	22.5
Hispanic	782.4	988.8	1,045.6	1,093.8	1,166.1	1,218.5	1,257.1	1,316.6
Male	353.9	441.2	464.0	480.2	506.6	525.8	538.6	562.3
Female.	428.5	547.6	581.6	613.7	659.5	692.7	718.5	754.4
Public.	671.4	851.3	898.7	937.1	990.7	1,031.6	1,057.8	1,097.8
Private	111.0	137.5	146.8	156.8	175.4	186.9	199.3	218.8
2-year	424.2	556.8	582.9	608.4	657.3	688.5	704.2	735.2
4-year	358.2	432.0	462.7	485.5	508.8	530.0	552.9	581.5
Undergraduate.	724.6	918.1	968.3	1,012.0	1,079.4	1,125.9	1,159.8	1,212.3
Graduate	47.2	57.9	63.9	68.0	72.8	78.7	82.9	89.6
First professional . . .	10.7	12.8	13.4	13.8	13.9	13.9	14.4	14.7
American Indian [2] .	102.8	121.7	127.4	131.3	137.6	142.5	144.2	145.3
Male	43.1	51.2	53.0	54.8	57.2	59.0	59.0	58.5
Female.	59.7	70.5	74.4	76.5	80.4	83.4	85.1	86.8
Public.	90.4	106.4	110.7	113.8	118.8	123.6	122.6	124.1
Private	12.4	15.3	16.6	17.5	18.8	18.8	21.5	21.2
2-year	54.9	63.2	66.2	65.6	70.2	71.0	71.5	72.1
4-year	47.9	58.5	61.2	65.7	67.3	71.5	72.6	73.2
Undergraduate.	95.5	112.7	117.4	120.7	126.5	130.8	132.2	133.3
Graduate	6.2	7.3	8.1	8.5	8.9	9.4	9.8	9.9
First professional . . .	1.1	1.7	1.8	2.1	2.2	2.3	2.2	2.1
Asian [2]	572.4	724.4	774.3	797.4	828.2	859.2	900.5	909.7
Male	294.9	363.1	385.0	393.3	405.5	417.7	433.6	435.3
Female.	277.5	361.3	389.3	404.1	422.6	441.5	466.9	474.4
Public.	461.0	586.3	622.1	638.0	657.9	680.4	713.2	714.4
Private	111.5	138.2	152.2	159.4	170.3	178.8	187.3	195.3
2-year	215.2	295.0	312.5	314.9	327.0	340.7	361.9	355.7
4-year	357.2	429.4	461.8	482.4	501.1	518.5	538.5	553.9
Undergraduate.	500.5	634.2	674.1	692.2	717.6	743.7	778.3	784.3
Graduate	53.2	65.2	72.6	75.6	79.1	82.6	87.0	89.2
First professional . . .	18.7	25.0	27.6	29.6	31.4	32.9	35.1	36.2
Nonresident alien .	391.5	457.1	455.9	454.4	466.3	465.0	443.5	516.4
Male	246.3	273.4	269.5	264.3	267.2	264.9	254.6	291.6
Female.	145.2	183.7	186.4	190.1	199.0	200.1	188.9	224.8
Public.	260.0	304.3	301.2	297.5	303.8	297.3	274.9	326.0
Private	131.4	152.7	154.7	156.9	162.5	167.7	168.7	190.4
2-year	67.1	91.2	91.4	88.1	92.0	80.7	55.0	80.7
4-year	324.3	365.9	364.5	366.2	374.3	384.3	388.5	435.7
Undergraduate.	218.7	268.2	269.4	207.0	275.3	268.2	241.3	284.2
Graduate	167.3	182.0	179.5	179.5	183.3	189.4	194.8	224.2
First professional . . .	5.4	6.9	7.0	7.3	7.6	7.5	7.4	8.0

[1] Beginning 1996 data reflect a new classification of institutions; this classification includes some additional, primarily 2-year, colleges than before and excludes a few institutions that did not award degrees.   [2] Non-Hispanic.

Source: U.S. National Center for Education Statistics, *Digest of Education Statistics*, annual.

166   Education

No. 259. Degree-Granting Institutions, Number and Enrollment by State: 1999

[**14,791 represents 14,791,000.** Number of institutions beginning in academic year. Opening fall enrollment of resident and extension students attending full time or part time. Excludes students taking courses for credit by mail, radio, or TV, and students in branches of U.S. institutions operated in foreign countries. See Appendix III]

State	Number of institutions [1]	Enrollment (1,000)										
		Total	Male	Female	Public	Private	Full time	White [2]	Minority enrollment			Nonresident alien
									Total [3]	Black [2]	Hispanic	
United States..	**4,084**	**14,791**	**6,491**	**8,301**	**11,309**	**3,482**	**8,786**	**10,262**	**4,012**	**1,641**	**1,317**	**516**
Alabama.........	77	223	97	126	197	26	149	153	65	58	2	5
Alaska	8	27	11	16	26	1	11	20	6	1	1	1
Arizona.........	69	326	146	180	276	50	164	227	90	13	53	8
Arkansas	45	115	48	67	103	12	77	91	22	18	1	3
California	410	2,017	889	1,129	1,693	325	985	959	989	153	445	69
Colorado........	71	262	119	143	219	42	142	205	48	10	26	8
Connecticut......	45	157	68	89	97	60	90	120	30	13	10	7
Delaware	10	47	19	28	37	10	28	36	10	7	1	1
District of Columbia .	16	72	31	41	5	67	49	35	29	21	3	8
Florida	149	685	296	389	541	144	359	423	237	105	107	25
Georgia	106	312	134	178	237	74	206	202	100	83	5	10
Hawaii	20	63	28	35	46	16	37	16	41	2	2	6
Idaho..........	14	65	29	36	53	12	43	59	4	(Z)	2	1
Illinois	168	733	321	412	534	200	390	495	215	97	73	23
Indiana.........	97	305	140	165	231	74	208	258	35	21	8	11
Iowa	64	187	84	102	134	53	130	166	13	5	3	8
Kansas.........	59	177	79	97	157	20	100	149	23	9	6	5
Kentucky	69	182	75	107	147	35	123	159	19	14	2	3
Louisiana	86	221	92	129	189	33	162	142	73	62	5	6
Maine..........	33	58	23	35	40	17	34	54	3	1	(Z)	1
Maryland	59	269	111	157	221	48	136	166	92	67	8	11
Massachusetts.....	123	420	183	237	182	238	272	311	77	27	21	32
Michigan........	108	559	244	315	462	97	301	439	99	64	13	21
Minnesota.......	115	283	128	155	207	75	177	247	28	10	4	8
Mississippi	45	133	55	78	121	12	98	84	47	44	1	2
Missouri........	115	317	138	179	199	118	185	262	46	31	6	9
Montana........	26	43	20	23	38	5	33	37	5	(Z)	1	1
Nebraska	36	111	50	61	88	22	70	98	10	4	3	3
Nevada	15	90	40	50	85	4	32	63	25	7	10	2
New Hampshire....	25	63	27	36	35	28	39	58	4	1	1	2
New Jersey......	58	331	144	186	264	67	189	212	104	42	36	15
New Mexico	45	112	47	65	103	9	60	56	54	3	40	2
New York	321	1,021	433	587	566	455	688	646	319	138	105	56
North Carolina	118	396	167	229	321	75	252	282	106	86	7	8
North Dakota.....	21	40	20	21	36	4	32	36	3	(Z)	(Z)	1
Ohio	175	549	242	307	412	137	352	454	78	56	9	17
Oklahoma.......	48	179	82	97	155	24	112	131	39	14	5	9
Oregon.........	55	176	80	96	148	27	101	145	24	3	7	7
Pennsylvania.....	255	605	272	333	337	268	427	497	90	53	13	19
Rhode Island.....	13	75	33	42	39	36	49	61	11	4	4	3
South Carolina....	61	184	75	108	153	30	119	129	51	46	2	4
South Dakota.....	25	42	19	23	34	8	30	37	4	(Z)	(Z)	1
Tennessee	85	253	110	143	194	59	173	198	49	41	3	5
Texas..........	193	991	445	546	862	128	559	573	384	106	225	33
Utah	23	162	81	80	121	41	100	146	11	1	5	5
Vermont	25	37	16	21	21	16	26	34	2	(Z)	1	1
Virginia.........	94	378	163	215	312	66	216	268	98	66	11	11
Washington......	71	307	136	170	263	43	188	239	57	11	13	11
West Virginia.....	35	89	39	49	77	12	63	81	6	4	1	2
Wisconsin.......	67	305	135	170	250	55	189	267	31	14	7	7
Wyoming	9	29	13	16	28	1	17	26	2	(Z)	1	1
U.S. military [4] ..	4	13	11	2	13	-	13	11	2	1	1	(Z)

- Represents zero. Z Fewer than 500. [1] Branch campuses counted as separate institutions. [2] Non-Hispanic. [3] Includes other races not shown separately. [4] Service schools.

Source: U.S. National Center for Education Statistics, *Digest of Education Statistics*, annual.

U.S. Census Bureau, Statistical Abstract of the United States: 2002

No. 260. College Enrollment by Sex, Age, Race, and Hispanic Origin: 1980 to 2000

[In thousands (11,387 represents 11,387,000). As of October for the civilian noninstitutional population, 14 years old and over. Based on the Current Population Survey; see text, Section 1, Population, and Appendix III]

Characteristic	1980	1985	1990 [1]	1993	1994	1995	1996	1997	1998	1999	2000
Total [2]	11,387	12,524	13,621	13,898	15,022	14,715	15,226	15,436	15,546	15,203	15,314
Male [3]	5,430	5,906	6,192	6,324	6,764	6,703	6,820	6,843	6,905	6,956	6,682
18 to 24 years	3,604	3,749	3,922	3,994	4,152	4,089	4,187	4,374	4,403	4,397	4,342
25 to 34 years	1,325	1,464	1,412	1,406	1,589	1,561	1,523	1,509	1,500	1,458	1,361
35 years old and over . .	405	561	772	873	958	985	1,013	899	953	1,024	918
Female [3]	5,957	6,618	7,429	7,574	8,258	8,013	8,406	8,593	8,641	8,247	8,631
18 to 24 years	3,625	3,788	4,042	4,199	4,576	4,452	4,582	4,829	4,919	4,863	5,109
25 to 34 years	1,378	1,599	1,749	1,688	1,830	1,788	1,920	1,760	1,915	1,637	1,846
35 years old and over . .	802	1,100	1,546	1,616	1,766	1,684	1,765	1,892	1,732	1,675	1,589
White [3]	9,925	10,781	11,488	11,434	12,222	12,021	12,189	12,442	12,401	12,053	11,999
18 to 24 years	6,334	6,500	6,635	6,763	7,118	7,011	7,123	7,495	7,541	7,446	7,566
25 to 34 years	2,328	2,604	2,698	2,505	2,735	2,686	2,644	2,522	2,568	2,345	2,339
35 years old and over . .	1,051	1,448	2,023	2,068	2,267	2,208	2,254	2,297	2,199	2,174	1,978
Male	4,804	5,103	5,235	5,222	5,524	5,535	5,453	5,552	5,602	5,562	5,311
Female	5,121	5,679	6,253	6,212	6,698	6,486	6,735	6,890	6,799	6,491	6,689
Black [3]	1,163	1,263	1,393	1,545	1,800	1,772	1,901	1,903	2,016	1,998	2,164
18 to 24 years	688	734	894	861	1,001	988	983	1,085	1,115	1,146	1,216
25 to 34 years	289	295	258	386	440	426	519	423	539	453	567
35 years old and over . .	156	213	207	284	323	334	354	372	340	354	361
Male	476	552	587	636	745	710	764	723	770	833	815
Female	686	712	807	909	1,054	1,062	1,136	1,180	1,247	1,164	1,349
Hispanic origin [3] [4]	443	580	748	995	1,187	1,207	1,223	1,260	1,363	1,307	1,426
18 to 24 years	315	375	435	602	662	745	706	806	820	740	899
25 to 34 years	118	189	168	249	312	250	310	254	336	334	309
35 years old and over . .	(NA)	(NA)	130	129	205	193	184	151	198	226	195
Male	222	279	364	442	529	568	529	555	550	568	619
Female	221	299	384	553	659	639	693	704	814	739	807

NA Not available. [1] Beginning 1990, based on a revised edit and tabulation package. [2] Includes other races not shown separately. [3] Includes persons 14 to 17 years old, not shown separately. [4] Persons of Hispanic origin may be of any race.

Source: U.S. Census Bureau, Current Population Reports, PPL-148; and earlier years

No. 261. Foreign (Nonimmigrant) Student Enrollment in College: 1976 to 2001

[For fall of the previous year. (179 represents 179,000)]

Region of origin	Enrollment (1,000)									Percent enrolled in—					
										Engineering		Science [1]		Business	
	1976	1980	1985	1990	1995	1998	1999	2000	2001	1980	1998	1980	1998	1980	1998
All regions . . .	179	286	342	387	453	481	491	515	548	25	16	8	8	16	21
Africa	25	36	40	25	21	23	26	30	34	20	14	9	8	19	21
Nigeria	11	16	18	4	2	2	3	4	4	19	14	9	8	22	18
Asia [2]	97	165	200	245	292	308	308	315	339	32	18	8	8	16	21
China: Taiwan . . .	11	18	23	31	36	31	31	29	29	17	15	15	6	17	24
Hong Kong	12	10	10	11	13	10	9	8	8	22	15	9	5	26	30
India	10	9	15	26	34	34	37	42	55	31	35	16	8	21	16
Indonesia	1	2	7	9	12	13	12	11	12	27	21	7	2	21	41
Iran	20	51	17	7	3	2	2	2	2	45	30	7	16	11	7
Japan	7	12	13	30	45	47	46	47	46	7	4	5	4	19	19
Malaysia	2	4	22	14	14	15	12	9	8	13	34	14	3	22	32
Saudi Arabia	3	10	8	4	4	5	5	5	5	30	31	4	4	14	13
South Korea	3	5	16	22	34	43	39	41	46	17	11	11	6	15	14
Thailand	7	7	7	7	11	15	12	11	11	17	16	6	4	26	38
Europe	14	23	33	46	65	72	74	78	81	15	9	9	9	14	22
Latin America [3]	30	42	49	48	47	51	55	62	64	20	13	8	6	14	25
Mexico	5	6	6	7	9	10	10	11	11	16	16	7	5	11	25
Venezuela	5	10	10	3	4	5	5	5	5	30	14	8	5	11	24
North America	10	16	16	19	23	23	23	24	26	8	6	6	8	13	13
Canada	10	15	15	18	23	22	23	24	25	8	6	6	8	12	13
Oceania	3	4	4	4	4	4	4	5	5	5	5	7	6	16	22

[1] Physical and life sciences. [2] Includes countries not shown separately. [3] Includes Central America, Caribbean, and South America.

Source: Institute of International Education, New York, NY, Open Doors, annual (copyright).

No. 262. College Enrollment—Summary by Sex, Race and Hispanic Origin: 2000

[In thousands (15,313 represents 15,313,000), except percent. As of October. Covers civilian noninstitutional population 15 years old and over enrolled in colleges and graduate schools. Based on Current Population Survey, see text, Section 1, Population and Appendix III]

Characteristic	Sex			Race and Hispanic origin				
				White			Asian and Pacific Islander	Hispanic [2]
	Total [1]	Male	Female	Total	Non-Hispanic	Black		
Total enrollment	**15,313**	**6,682**	**8,632**	**12,000**	**10,636**	**2,165**	**1,049**	**1,426**
15 to 17 years old.	149	61	87	116	92	19	12	25
18 to 19 years old.	3,599	1,571	2,028	2,915	2,580	455	212	349
20 to 21 years old.	3,169	1,472	1,697	2,590	2,333	375	200	268
22 to 24 years old.	2,683	1,300	1,383	2,061	1,796	387	227	283
25 to 29 years old.	1,962	844	1,118	1,432	1,274	326	188	166
30 to 34 years old.	1,244	517	728	906	770	242	81	142
35 years old and over	2,507	919	1,588	1,978	1,790	361	129	194
Type of school:								
2-year.	3,881	1,655	2,226	3,035	2,544	603	214	506
15 to 19 years old	1,232	610	622	993	820	170	64	180
20 to 24 years old	1,234	525	710	969	801	173	84	169
25 years old and over . .	1,415	519	896	1,072	923	259	65	156
4-year.	8,520	3,865	4,654	6,653	5,979	1,238	572	722
15 to 19 years old	2,478	996	1,483	2,010	1,834	293	160	183
20 to 24 years old	3,970	1,998	1,974	3,172	2,870	515	277	329
25 years old and over . .	2,071	873	1,200	1,471	1,277	427	136	208
Graduate school	2,913	1,162	1,750	2,311	2,113	324	262	198
15 to 24 years old	685	276	409	538	476	82	66	60
25 to 34 years old	1,218	498	721	944	869	143	126	75
35 years old and over . .	1,009	389	620	830	766	99	70	63
Public	12,008	5,192	6,816	9,363	8,201	1,721	831	1,219
2-year	3,591	1,511	2,079	2,826	2,365	541	198	474
4-year	6,453	2,935	3,519	5,019	4,463	939	443	598
Graduate	1,964	747	1,218	1,520	1,374	241	189	146
Percent of students:								
Employed full-time.	34.1	35.3	33.2	34.5	33.9	38.0	23.3	39.5
Employed part-time	30.3	28.8	31.5	32.1	32.1	21.5	29.1	31.1

[1] Includes other races, not shown separately. [2] Persons of Hispanic origin may be of any race.

Source: U.S. Census Bureau, *Current Population Reports*, PPL-148

No. 263. Higher Education Registrations in Foreign Languages: 1970 to 1998

[As of fall (1,111.5 represents 1,111,500)]

Item	1970	1974	1977	1980	1983	1986	1990	1995	1998
Registrations [1] (1,000)	**1,111.5**	**946.6**	**933.5**	**924.8**	**966.0**	**1,003.2**	**1,184.1**	**1,138.8**	**1,193.8**
Index (1960=100)	171.8	146.3	144.3	142.9	149.3	155.0	183.0	176.0	184.5
By selected language (1,000):									
Spanish	389.2	362.2	376.7	379.4	386.2	411.3	533.9	606.3	656.6
French	359.3	253.1	246.1	248.4	270.1	275.3	272.5	205.4	199.1
German	202.6	152.1	135.4	126.9	128.2	121.0	133.3	96.3	89.0
Italian	34.2	33.0	33.3	34.8	38.7	40.9	49.7	43.8	49.3
Japanese	6.6	9.6	10.7	11.5	16.1	23.5	45.7	44.7	43.1
Chinese	6.2	10.7	9.8	11.4	13.2	16.9	19.5	26.5	28.5
Latin	27.6	25.2	24.4	25.0	24.2	25.0	28.2	25.9	26.1
Russian	36.2	32.5	27.8	24.0	30.4	34.0	44.6	24.7	23.8
Ancient Greek	16.7	24.4	25.8	22.1	19.4	17.6	16.4	16.3	16.4
Hebrew	16.6	22.4	19.4	19.4	18.2	15.6	13.0	13.1	15.8
American Sign Language	(X)	(X)	(X)	(X)	(X)	(X)	1.6	4.3	11.4
Portuguese	5.1	5.1	5.0	4.9	4.4	5.1	6.2	6.5	6.9
Arabic	1.3	2.0	3.1	3.5	3.4	3.4	3.5	4.4	5.5

X Not applicable. [1] Includes other foreign languages, not shown separately.

Source: Association of Departments of Foreign Languages, New York, NY, *ADFL Bulletin*, Vol. 31, No. 2, and earlier issues (copyright).

No. 264. College Freshmen—Summary Characteristics: 1970 to 2001

[In percent, except as indicated (12.8 represents $12,800). As of fall for first-time full-time freshmen in 4-year colleges and universities. Based on sample survey and subject to sampling error; see source]

Characteristic	1970	1980	1985	1990	1995	1998	1999	2000	2001
Sex: Male	52.1	48.8	48.9	46.9	45.6	45.5	45.3	45.2	44.9
Female	47.9	51.2	51.1	53.1	54.4	54.5	54.7	54.8	55.1
Applied to three or more colleges	(NA)	31.5	35.4	42.9	44.4	46.2	47.7	50.5	51.3
Average grade in high school:									
A- to A+	19.6	26.6	28.7	29.4	36.1	39.8	42.7	42.9	44.1
B- to B+	62.5	58.2	57.1	57.0	54.2	52.3	50.7	50.5	49.5
C to C+	17.7	14.9	14.0	13.4	9.6	7.7	6.5	6.5	6.2
D	0.3	0.2	0.2	0.2	0.1	0.1	0.1	0.1	0.1
Political orientation:									
Liberal	35.7	21.0	22.4	24.6	22.9	23.3	23.6	24.8	26.9
Middle of the road	43.4	57.0	53.1	51.7	51.3	53.1	53.4	51.9	49.5
Conservative	17.3	19.0	21.3	20.6	21.8	19.9	19.3	18.9	19.1
Probable field of study:									
Arts and humanities	(NA)	10.5	10.1	10.5	11.2	11.8	11.3	12.1	12.6
Biological sciences	(NA)	4.5	4.5	4.9	8.3	7.0	7.2	6.6	6.9
Business	(NA)	21.2	24.6	21.1	15.4	16.4	16.4	16.7	16.6
Education	(NA)	8.4	6.9	10.3	10.1	11.1	10.6	11.0	10.1
Engineering	(NA)	11.2	11.0	9.7	8.1	8.2	9.0	8.7	9.1
Physical science	(NA)	3.2	3.2	2.8	3.1	2.4	2.3	2.6	2.6
Social science	(NA)	8.2	9.4	11.0	9.9	9.5	9.7	10.0	10.3
Professional	(NA)	15.5	13.1	13.0	16.5	14.5	13.1	11.6	12.0
Technical	(NA)	3.1	2.4	1.1	1.2	1.8	1.9	2.1	2.2
Data processing/computer programming . . .	(NA)	1.7	1.7	0.7	0.8	1.2	1.4	1.5	1.4
Other [1]	(NA)	14.0	15.1	15.8	16.0	17.3	18.0	17.9	17.5
Communications	(NA)	2.4	2.8	2.9	1.8	2.2	2.4	2.7	2.6
Computer science	(NA)	2.6	2.4	1.7	2.2	3.4	3.7	3.7	3.3
Personal objectives—very important or essential:									
Being very well off financially	36.2	62.5	69.2	72.3	72.8	72.9	72.1	73.4	73.6
Developing a meaningful philosophy of life	79.1	62.5	46.9	45.9	45.4	44.1	43.0	42.4	43.1
Keeping up to date with political affairs	57.2	45.2	(NA)	46.6	32.3	30.2	28.6	28.1	31.4
Attitudes—agree or strongly agree:									
Capital punishment should be abolished	59.4	34.8	27.6	23.1	22.0	24.1	26.7	31.2	32.2
Legalize marijuana	40.6	37.1	21.4	18.8	33.4	32.7	32.4	34.2	36.5
There is too much concern for the rights of criminals	50.7	65.0	(NA)	65.1	73.2	72.3	71.2	66.5	64.4
Abortion should be legalized	85.7	53.7	56.4	65.5	59.9	54.3	53.2	53.9	55.0
Median family income ($1,000)	12.8	24.5	37.3	46.6	54.8	58.9	61.6	64.4	67.2

NA Not available.   [1] Includes other fields, not shown separately.

Source: The Higher Education Research Institute, University of California, Los Angeles, CA, *The American Freshman: National Norms*, annual.

No. 265. Undergraduates in Postsecondary Institutions Owning Credit Cards and Balance Due: 1999-2000

[(16,539 represents 16,539,000). Based on the 1999-2000 Postsecondary Student Aid Study and subject to sampling error; for details, see source]

Characteristic	Total under-graduates (1,000)	Number of credit cards in own name (percent) [1]			Percent with balance due [2]	Balance due (dol.) [3]	
		None	One	Two or more		Average	Median
Total	16,539	29.4	42.5	28.1	44.7	3,066	1,435
Age: [4]							
18 years or younger	1,567	49.5	37.5	13.0	30.1	1,011	721
19 to 23 years	7,895	31.6	43.2	25.2	42.2	2,103	995
24 to 29 years	2,806	24.9	42.7	32.5	54.8	3,337	1,773
30 to 39 years	2,300	22.8	42.5	34.8	50.3	4,429	2,566
40 years or older	1,971	18.4	43.3	38.2	41.3	4,924	3,037
Sex:							
Male	7,231	31.6	43.9	24.5	41.6	3,166	1,421
Female	9,308	27.8	41.3	30.9	47.0	3,002	1,500
Race:							
One race: White	11,975	28.5	43.7	27.8	43.2	3,250	1,508
Black or African American	2,129	35.3	36.8	28.0	56.3	2,480	1,128
Asian	927	22.8	46.6	30.6	31.4	2,842	1,099
American Indian/Alaska Native	177	38.2	37.1	24.7	49.1	3,345	2,103
Native Hawaiian/Other Pacific Islander. .	142	27.6	41.9	30.5	42.5	2,619	1,510
Other race	905	31.7	38.4	29.9	49.9	2,648	1,513
More than one race	284	29.7	43.2	27.1	49.3	3,062	1,415
Hispanic or Latino (any race):							
Not Hispanic or Latino	14,555	29.0	42.9	28.1	43.9	3,096	1,444
Hispanic or Latino	1,984	32.7	39.0	28.3	51.6	2,854	1,513
Class level:							
Graduating senior	1,510	14.5	48.1	37.5	43.6	3,578	1,983
All other undergraduates	15,029	31.0	41.9	27.1	44.9	3,002	1,382

[1] Credit cards are billed to the student.   [2] Percent of undergraduates with credit cards who typically carry a balance.   [3] For definition of mean and median, see Guide to Tabular Presentation.   [4] As of December 31, 1999.

Source: U.S. National Center for Education Statistics, *Profile of Undergraduates in U.S. Postsecondary Education Institutions, 1999-2000*, NCES 2002-168, July 2002.

No. 266. Undergraduates Reported Disability Status by Selected Characteristic: 1999-2000

[In percent. Based on the 1999-2000 National Postsecondary Student Aid Survey; see source for details]

Characteristic	Any disability or difficulty reported [1]	None reported	Consider self with disability	Don't consider self with disability
Total.	9.3	90.7	3.6	96.4
PERCENT DISTRIBUTION				
Total.	100.0	100.0	100.0	100.0
Age: [1]				
18 years or younger	5.8	9.9	3.1	9.8
19 to 23 years old	36.3	49.3	24.5	49.1
24 to 29 years old	15.5	16.1	15.3	16.1
30 to 39 years old	19.2	13.5	23.7	13.7
40 years or older	23.3	11.1	33.4	11.5
Sex:				
Male	39.6	42.4	46.2	42.0
Female.	60.4	57.6	53.8	58.0
Race:				
White, non-Hispanic	70.8	66.7	70.8	67.1
Black, non-Hispanic	10.9	11.8	13.0	11.7
Hispanic	9.9	11.6	8.0	11.4
Asian	2.1	4.9	1.1	4.8
American Indian/Alaska Native	1.9	0.7	2.5	0.8
Native Hawaiian/Other Pacific Islander	0.8	0.8	1.4	0.7
Other race	1.4	1.5	0.8	1.6
More than one race	2.3	1.9	2.5	1.9
Parents' highest education level:				
High school or less.	40.7	36.4	45.1	36.4
Some postsecondary education	24.1	22.8	21.6	23.0
Bachelor's degree or equivalent	35.2	40.9	33.3	40.7

[1] Those who indicated they had a long lasting condition, such as blindness or deafness; or a condition substantially limiting a basic physical activity, such as walking or lifting; or a physical, emotional, or mental condition lasting six months or more which made it difficult to do any one of the following: get to school, get around campus, learn, dress, or work at a job.

Source: U.S. National Center for Education Statistics, *Profile of Undergraduates in U.S. Postsecondary Education Institutions, 1999-2000*, NCES 2002-168, July 2002.

No. 267. Undergraduates in Postsecondary Institutions Taking Distance Education Courses: 1999-2000

[16,539 represents 16,539,000. Distance education courses are courses taken for credit and exclude correspondence courses. Based on the 1999-2000 Postsecondary Student Aid Survey and subject to sampling error; see source for details]

Characteristic	Total undergraduates (1,000)	Percent taking courses	Mode of delivery of course(s) (percent)		
			Live interactive	Internet	Pre-recorded
Total.	16,539	8.4	37.0	59.0	39.1
Age: [1]					
18 years or younger	1,567	4.3	41.2	65.1	32.3
19 to 23 years old	7,895	6.9	40.2	56.9	41.8
24 to 29 years old.	2,806	10.1	35.2	56.1	42.7
30 to 39 years old.	2,300	12.5	32.6	63.0	35.7
40 years or older	1,971	10.2	36.1	60.9	34.2
Sex:					
Male.	7,231	7.3	34.5	60.8	40.1
Female	9,308	9.2	38.6	57.9	38.5
Race:					
One race:					
White	11,975	8.6	34.6	58.2	37.6
Black or African American	2,129	8.3	46.9	60.8	37.1
Asian	927	6.8	40.4	69.7	36.3
American Indian/Alaska Native.	177	10.9	52.2	44.9	41.1
Native Hawaiian/Other Pacific Islander	142	9.7	(B)	(B)	(B)
Other race	905	6.2	41.9	63.1	56.0
More than one race	284	9.3	27.7	63.6	46.9
Hispanic or Latino (any race):					
Not Hispanic or Latino	14,555	8.6	36.6	59.2	38.1
Hispanic or Latino.	1,984	6.8	41.3	56.8	50.0
Institution type:					
Public.	12,258	8.6	38.1	57.4	39.2
Private not-for-profit.	2,447	6.6	28.2	69.3	37.1
Private for-profit	809	4.5	27.9	69.8	25.4
More than one institution	1,025	12.3	40.9	57.2	44.5

B Base too small to meet statistical standards for reliability of a derived figure. [1] As of December 31, 1999.

Source: U.S. National Center for Education Statistics, *Profile of Undergraduates in U.S. Postsecondary Education Institutions, 1999-2000*, NCES 2002-168, July 2002.

Education 171

No. 268. Higher Education Price Indexes: 1970 to 1999

[1983=100. For years ending June 30. Reflects prices paid by colleges and universities]

Year	Personnel compensation					Contracted services, supplies, and equipment					
	Index, total	Total	Professional salaries	Nonprofessional salaries	Fringe benefits	Total	Services	Supplies and materials	Equipment	Library acquisitions	Utilities
1970 ..	39.5	42.1	47.7	38.8	24.7	31.9	42.8	37.6	41.9	25.7	16.3
1974 ..	49.9	52.8	57.2	50.6	38.6	41.4	52.2	46.5	49.4	41.6	24.8
1975 ..	54.3	56.3	60.3	54.6	42.9	48.5	56.8	58.0	58.3	46.7	31.8
1976 ..	57.8	60.0	63.5	59.0	47.8	51.3	59.1	60.7	61.7	52.1	34.4
1977 ..	61.5	63.5	66.4	63.1	52.8	55.7	62.6	63.8	64.8	56.8	40.5
1978 ..	65.7	67.6	69.9	68.1	58.4	60.2	66.6	66.6	69.3	63.2	45.9
1979 ..	70.5	72.4	74.1	73.4	64.5	65.1	71.2	71.7	74.7	70.0	50.3
1980 ..	77.5	78.4	79.4	80.2	72.6	75.0	77.0	84.6	81.6	77.8	64.1
1981 ..	85.8	85.8	86.3	87.7	81.8	85.9	85.2	95.6	89.6	85.9	79.7
1982 ..	93.9	93.5	93.7	94.6	91.5	94.9	94.2	100.4	96.4	93.5	92.4
1983 ..	100.0	100.0	100.0	100.0	100.0	100.0	100.0	100.0	100.0	100.0	100.0
1984 ..	104.8	105.4	104.7	105.1	108.3	103.0	104.9	99.7	102.3	105.3	102.5
1985 ..	110.8	112.0	111.4	109.2	117.7	107.1	110.8	103.0	104.8	111.3	105.3
1986 ..	116.3	118.8	118.2	112.8	127.7	109.0	115.1	102.6	107.2	121.2	103.1
1987 ..	120.9	125.4	125.0	116.3	137.4	107.4	119.7	99.0	108.9	132.9	91.0
1988 ..	126.2	131.7	130.9	120.6	147.2	109.8	123.0	101.1	120.5	140.5	87.7
1989 ..	132.8	139.6	138.8	125.3	158.8	112.8	128.8	108.3	115.1	153.5	85.3
1990 ..	140.8	148.3	147.6	130.3	171.4	118.7	134.0	114.3	119.6	167.0	90.1
1991 ..	148.2	156.5	155.6	135.4	184.3	123.3	139.8	116.4	123.3	179.8	92.4
1992 ..	153.5	162.4	160.8	140.2	194.3	126.9	145.7	115.2	126.3	193.9	93.3
1993 ..	158.0	167.6	165.0	144.2	204.3	129.4	149.5	113.2	128.6	203.4	94.7
1994 ..	163.3	173.3	170.3	148.2	213.6	133.6	154.8	114.3	130.8	213.6	98.7
1995 ..	168.1	179.1	176.1	152.5	221.4	135.3	158.0	115.7	133.5	220.2	96.8
1996 ..	173.0	184.1	181.7	157.3	224.5	139.9	163.8	130.1	137.0	230.9	93.3
1997 ..	178.4	189.0	187.2	162.1	226.7	147.2	167.3	128.6	139.3	253.4	106.1
1998 ..	184.7	195.8	193.5	168.0	236.7	151.6	172.8	126.2	141.3	266.5	111.1
1999 ..	189.1	202.0	200.7	174.1	239.2	150.8	177.0	123.2	143.3	282.1	100.5

Source: Research Associates of Washington, Arlington, VA, *Inflation Measures for Schools, Colleges, and Libraries*, periodic (copyright).

No. 269. Federal Student Financial Assistance: 1995 to 2002

[For award years July 1 of year shown to the following June 30 (35,450 represents ($35,450,000,000). Funds utilized exclude operating costs, etc., and represent funds given to students]

Award year impact data	1995	1997	1998	1999	2000	2001	2002, est.
FUNDS UTILIZED (mil. dol.)							
Total	**35,450**	**40,074**	**43,072**	**40,162**	**44,027**	**48,465**	**51,978**
Federal Pell Grants............	5,445	6,331	7,233	7,209	7,976	9,851	10,708
Federal Supplemental Educational Opportunity Grant.............	764	811	855	875	907	875	918
Federal Work-Study	764	906	913	917	939	1,215	1,215
Federal Perkins Loan	1,029	1,062	1,070	1,101	1,144	1,195	1,202
Federal Direct Student Loan (FDSL) ..	8,296	9,873	10,933	9,953	10,348	10,635	11,404
Federal Family Education Loans (FFEL)	19,152	21,091	22,068	20,107	22,712	24,694	26,531
NUMBER OF AWARDS (1,000)							
Total	**13,667**	**14,652**	**15,187**	**14,566**	**15,056**	**16,252**	**17,009**
Federal Pell Grants............	3,612	3,733	3,855	3,764	3,912	4,284	4,444
Federal Supplemental Educational Opportunity Grant.............	1,083	1,116	1,163	1,170	1,175	1,169	1,227
Federal Work-Study	702	746	744	733	713	970	970
Federal Perkins Loan	688	679	669	655	639	711	715
Federal Direct Student Loan (FDSL) ..	2,339	2,775	3,017	2,891	2,739	2,763	2,842
Federal Family Education Loans (FFEL)	5,243	5,603	5,739	5,354	5,878	6,355	6,811
AVERAGE AWARD (dol.)							
Total	**2,594**	**2,735**	**2,836**	**2,757**	**2,924**	**2,982**	**3,056**
Federal Pell Grants............	1,507	1,696	1,876	1,915	2,039	2,299	2,409
Federal Supplemental Educational Opportunity Grant.............	706	727	735	748	772	748	748
Federal Work-Study	1,087	1,215	1,228	1,252	1,318	1,252	1,252
Federal Perkins Loan	1,497	1,564	1,600	1,681	1,790	1,681	1,681
Federal Direct Student Loan (FDSL) ..	3,548	3,558	3,624	3,443	3,778	3,849	4,013
Federal Family Education Loans (FFEL)	3,653	3,764	3,845	3,756	3,864	3,886	3,895
COHORT DEFAULT RATE [1]							
Federal Perkins Loan	12.6	12.5	11.5	10.61	(NA)	(NA)	(NA)
FFEL/FDSL Combined Rates	10.4	8.8	6.9	5.6	(X)	(X)	(X)

NA Not available.   X Not applicable.   [1] As of June 30. Represents the percent of borrowers entering repayment status in year shown who defaulted in the following year.

Source: U.S. Dept. of Education, Office of Postsecondary Education, unpublished data.

No. 270. Institutions of Higher Education—Charges: 1985 to 2001

[In dollars. Estimated. For the entire academic year ending in year shown. Figures are average charges per full-time equivalent student. Room and board are based on full-time students]

Academic control and year	Tuition and required fees [1]				Board rates [2]				Dormitory charges			
	All institutions	2-yr. colleges	4-yr. colleges	Other 4-yr. schools	All institutions	2-yr. colleges	4-yr. colleges	Other 4-yr. schools	All institutions	2-yr. colleges	4-yr. colleges	Other 4-yr. schools
Public:												
1985.....	971	584	1,386	1,117	1,241	1,302	1,276	1,201	1,196	921	1,237	1,200
1990.....	1,356	756	2,035	1,608	1,635	1,581	1,728	1,561	1,513	962	1,561	1,554
1995.....	2,057	1,192	2,977	2,499	1,949	1,712	2,108	1,866	1,959	1,232	1,992	2,044
1996.....	2,179	1,239	3,151	2,660	2,020	1,681	2,192	1,937	2,057	1,297	2,104	2,133
1997.....	2,271	1,276	3,323	2,778	2,111	1,789	2,282	2,025	2,148	1,339	2,187	2,232
1998.....	2,360	1,314	3,486	2,877	2,228	1,795	2,438	2,130	2,225	1,401	2,285	2,312
1999.....	2,430	1,327	3,640	2,974	2,347	1,828	2,576	2,247	2,330	1,450	2,408	2,410
2000.....	2,506	1,338	3,768	3,091	2,364	1,834	2,628	2,239	2,440	1,549	2,516	2,521
2001, prel..	2,600	1,359	3,983	3,212	2,454	1,900	2,687	2,355	2,566	1,603	2,656	2,647
Private:												
1985.....	5,315	3,485	6,843	5,135	1,462	1,294	1,647	1,405	1,426	1,424	1,753	1,309
1990.....	8,174	5,196	10,348	7,778	1,948	1,811	2,339	1,823	1,923	1,663	2,411	1,774
1995.....	11,111	6,914	14,537	10,653	2,509	2,023	3,035	2,362	2,587	2,233	3,469	2,347
1996.....	11,864	7,094	15,605	11,297	2,606	2,098	3,218	2,429	2,738	2,371	3,680	2,473
1997.....	12,498	7,236	16,552	11,871	2,663	2,181	3,142	2,520	2,878	2,537	3,826	2,602
1998.....	12,801	7,464	17,229	12,338	2,762	2,785	3,132	2,648	2,954	2,672	3,756	2,731
1999.....	13,428	7,854	18,340	12,815	2,865	2,884	3,188	2,765	3,075	2,581	3,914	2,850
2000.....	14,081	8,235	19,307	13,361	2,882	2,922	3,157	2,790	3,224	2,808	4,070	2,976
2001, prel..	15,064	8,961	20,143	14,281	2,989	2,962	3,303	2,886	3,370	2,768	4,265	3,114

[1] For in-state students.   [2] Beginning 1990, rates reflect 20 meals per week, rather than meals served 7 days a week.

Source: U.S. National Center for Education Statistics, *Digest of Education Statistics*, annual.

No. 271. Voluntary Financial Support of Higher Education: 1990 to 2001

[For school years ending in years shown (9,800 represents $9,800,000,000); enrollment as of fall of preceding year. Voluntary support, as defined in Gift Reporting Standards, excludes income from endowment and other invested funds as well as all support received from federal, state, and local governments and their agencies and contract research]

Item	Unit	1990	1995	1996	1997	1998	1999	2000	2001
Estimated support, total	Mil. dol.	9,800	12,750	14,250	16,000	18,400	20,400	23,200	24,200
Individuals...............	Mil. dol .	4,770	6,540	7,440	8,500	10,000	10,740	12,220	12,030
Alumni...............	Mil. dol .	2,540	3,600	4,040	4,650	5,500	5,930	6,800	6,830
Business corporations	Mil. dol .	2,170	2,560	2,800	3,050	3,250	3,610	4,150	4,350
Foundations...............	Mil. dol .	1,920	2,460	2,815	3,200	3,800	4,530	5,080	6,000
Fundraising consortia and other organizations	Mil. dol .	700	940	940	1,000	1,050	1,190	1,380	1,450
Religious organizations	Mil. dol .	240	250	255	250	300	330	370	370
Current operations	Mil. dol .	5,440	7,230	7,850	8,500	9,000	9,900	11,270	12,200
Capital purposes...........	Mil. dol .	4,360	5,520	6,400	7,500	9,400	10,500	11,930	12,000
Enrollment, higher education [1]..	1,000 ..	12,835	14,078	14,044	14,022	14,098	14,264	14,311	14,623
Support per student.........	Dollars	764	906	1,015	1,141	1,305	1,430	1,621	1,655
In **2000-2001** dollars	Dollars	1,035	1,052	1,145	1,259	1,418	1,520	1,667	1,655
Expenditures, higher education .	Bil. dol .	150.56	201.53	211.35	223.30	234.80	246.30	257.80	270.00
Expenditures per student	Dollars .	11,730	14,315	15,049	15,925	16,654	17,267	18,014	18,464
In **2000-2001** dollars	Dollars .	15,895	16,635	16,987	17,572	18,095	18,355	18,527	18,464
Institutions reporting support	Number.	1,056	1,086	1,104	1,061	1,034	938	945	960
Total support reported	**Mil. dol.**	**8,214**	**10,992**	**12,251**	**13,801**	**15,771**	**17,229**	**19,419**	**20,569**
Private 4-year institutions	Mil. dol .	5,072	6,500	7,163	8,023	9,118	9,848	11,047	11,391
Public 4-year institutions......	Mil. dol .	3,056	4,382	4,943	5,654	6,556	7,252	8,254	9,026
2-year colleges............	Mil. dol .	85	110	145	124	98	129	117	152

[1] Excludes proprietary schools.

Source: Council for Aid to Education, New York, NY, *Voluntary Support of Education*, annual.

No. 272. Average Salaries for College Faculty Members: 1999 to 2001

[In thousands of dollars (55.9 represents $55,900). For academic year ending in year shown. Figures are for 9 months teaching for full-time faculty members in 4-year institutions. Fringe benefits averaged in 1999, $13,200 in public institutions and $16,600 in private institutions, in 2000, $14,200 in public institutions and $17,200 in private institutions; and in 2001, $14,300 in public institutions and $18,000 in private institutions]

Type of control and academic rank	1999	2000	2001	Type of control and academic rank	1999	2000	2001
Public: All ranks.............	55.9	57.7	58.8	Private: [1] All ranks............	63.5	66.3	69.9
Professor	71.3	74.4	76.1	Professor	83.9	88.4	93.2
Associate professor	53.4	55.3	57.1	Associate professor	56.3	59.0	62.2
Assistant professor.........	44.1	45.8	47.2	Assistant professor.........	46.8	48.8	51.7
Instructor	33.3	34.4	35.0	Instructor	36.1	37.5	39.3

[1] Excludes church-related colleges and universities.

Source: American Association of University Professors, Washington, DC, *AAUP Annual Report on the Economic Status of the Profession.*

Education 173

No. 273. Employees in Higher Education Institutions by Sex and Occupation: 1976 to 1999

[In thousands (1,863.8 represents 1,863,800). As of fall. Based on survey and subject to sampling error; see source]

| Year and status | Total | Professional staff | | | | | | | | | Nonprofessional staff, total |
| | | Total | Executive, administrative, and managerial | | Faculty[1] | | Research/instruction assistants | | Other | | |
			Male	Female	Male	Female	Male	Female	Male	Female	total
1976, total	1,863.8	1,073.1	74.6	26.6	460.6	172.7	106.5	53.6	87.5	91.0	790.7
Full time	1,339.9	709.4	72.0	25.0	326.8	107.2	18.6	9.4	76.2	74.1	630.5
Part time	523.9	363.7	2.6	1.7	133.7	65.4	87.9	44.2	11.3	16.9	160.2
1991, total	2,545.2	1,595.5	85.4	59.3	525.6	300.7	119.1	78.6	165.4	261.3	949.8
Full time	1,812.9	1,031.8	82.9	56.2	366.2	169.4	(NA)	(NA)	142.2	214.8	781.1
Part time	732.3	563.7	2.5	3.1	159.4	131.2	119.1	78.6	23.2	46.4	168.7
1999, total[2]	2,883.2	1,950.9	83.9	76.0	602.5	425.4	132.6	107.1	207.9	315.5	932.3
Full time	1,918.7	1,180.2	81.3	72.5	371.0	219.9	0.0	0.0	175.8	259.7	738.5
Part time	964.5	770.7	2.6	3.5	231.4	205.5	132.6	107.1	32.2	55.7	193.8

NA Not available.   [1] Instruction and research.   [2] Data for 1999 reflect the new classification of institutions. See footnote 1, Table 257.

Source: U.S. National Center for Education Statistics, *Fall Staff in Postsecondary Institutions, 1995* March 1998, and *Digest of Education Statistics,* 2001.

No. 274. Faculty in Institutions of Higher Education: 1970 to 1999

[In thousands (474 represents 474,000), except percent. As of fall. Based on survey and subject to sampling error; see source]

| Year | Employment status | | | Control | | Level | | Percent | | |
	Total	Full time	Part time	Public	Private	4-year	2-year	Part time	Public	2-year
1970	474	369	104	314	160	382	92	22	66	19
1975	628	440	188	443	185	467	161	30	71	26
1980	686	450	236	495	191	494	192	34	72	28
1985	715	459	256	503	212	504	211	36	70	30
1989[1]	824	524	300	577	247	584	241	36	70	29
1991	826	536	291	581	245	591	235	35	70	28
1993	915	546	370	650	265	626	289	40	71	32
1995	932	551	381	657	275	647	285	41	70	31
1997[2]	990	569	421	695	295	683	307	43	70	31
1999[2]	1,028	591	437	713	315	714	314	43	69	31

[1] Data beginning 1989 not comparable to prior years.   [2] In this table, data beginning in 1997 reflect the new classification of institutions. See footnote 1, Table 257.

Source: U.S. National Center for Education Statistics, *Fall Staff in Postsecondary Institutions, 1995* and *1997,* March 1998 and January 2000 and *Digest of Education Statistics,* 2001.

No. 275. Salary Offers to Candidates for Degrees: 1999 to 2001

[In dollars. Data are average beginning salaries based on offers made by business, industrial, government, nonprofit, and educational employers to graduating students. Data from representative colleges throughout the United States]

| Field of study | Bachelor's | | | Master's[1] | | | Doctor's | | |
	1999	2000	2001	1999	2000	2001	1999	2000	2001
Accounting.	34,644	36,710	39,720	38,152	39,839	43,196	(NA)	(NA)	(NA)
Business administration/ management[2]	33,310	36,357	37,844	50,095	50,276	50,679	(NA)	[3]65,865	[3]82,167
Marketing.	31,901	33,373	35,194	[3]54,530	[3]45,593	[3]48,833	(NA)	(NA)	(NA)
Engineering:									
Civil.	36,076	37,932	40,979	42,265	44,587	44,234	[3]58,571	[3]54,588	[3]61,606
Chemical	46,929	48,890	51,255	[3]52,068	[3]54,473	57,317	67,333	68,161	74,153
Computer	45,666	50,182	53,653	58,673	[3]57,087	60,974	[3]57,471	[3]77,700	[3]71,720
Electrical	45,180	48,613	52,092	57,162	60,828	64,188	70,848	74,423	79,383
Mechanical	43,275	45,952	48,588	51,879	53,581	56,565	64,283	[3]69,830	70,124
Nuclear[4]	[3]42,986	[3]47,070	[3]47,914	[3]54,000	[3]64,986	[3]55,496	(NA)	(NA)	(NA)
Petroleum.	50,440	50,367	54,761	[3]55,375	[3]50,369	[3]58,500	(NA)	(NA)	(NA)
Engineering technology. .	38,182	40,110	45,458	(NA)	(NA)	(NA)	(NA)	(NA)	(NA)
Chemistry	34,111	35,942	38,744	[3]38,779	[3]46,389	[3]51,467	56,885	62,901	62,067
Mathematics.	37,253	41,761	44,277	[3]41,964	[3]46,453	[3]55,482	[3]58,917	[3]60,237	[3]58,555
Physics	40,025	42,455	48,458	[3]50,552	[3]32,722	[3]61,000	[3]60,288	[3]46,500	[3]63,220
Humanities.	27,861	33,117	30,653	(NA)	(NA)	[3]32,650	(NA)	(NA)	(NA)
Social sciences[5].	28,608	30,933	31,634	(NA)	(NA)	[3]31,508	(NA)	(NA)	(NA)
Computer science	44,649	49,055	52,473	51,438	61,377	62,312	[3]58,688	[3]71,846	[3]84,033

NA Not available.   [1] Candidates with 1 year or less of full-time nonmilitary employment.   [2] For master's degree, offers are after nontechnical undergraduate degree.   [3] Fewer than 50 offers reported.   [4] Includes engineering physics.   [5] Excludes economics.

Source: National Association of Colleges and Employers, Bethlehem, PA, Salary Survey, *A Study of Beginning Offers,* annual (copyright).

No. 276. Earned Degrees Conferred by Level and Sex: 1960 to 2000

[In thousands (477 represents 477,000), except percent. Includes Alaska and Hawaii]

Year ending	All degrees Total	All degrees Percent male	Associate's Male	Associate's Female	Bachelor's Male	Bachelor's Female	Master's Male	Master's Female	First professional Male	First professional Female	Doctor's Male	Doctor's Female
1960 [1]	477	65.8	(NA)	(NA)	254	138	51	24	(NA)	(NA)	9	1
1965	660	61.5	(NA)	(NA)	282	212	81	40	27	1	15	2
1970	1,271	59.2	117	89	451	341	126	83	33	2	26	4
1975	1,666	56.0	191	169	505	418	162	131	49	7	27	7
1980	1,731	51.1	184	217	474	456	151	147	53	17	23	10
1983	1,815	49.6	204	246	479	490	145	145	51	22	22	11
1984	1,819	49.6	203	250	482	492	144	141	51	23	22	11
1985	1,828	49.3	203	252	483	497	143	143	50	25	22	11
1986	1,830	49.0	196	250	486	502	144	145	49	25	22	12
1987	1,823	48.4	191	245	481	510	141	148	47	25	22	12
1988	1,835	48.0	190	245	477	518	145	154	45	25	23	12
1989	1,873	47.3	186	250	483	535	149	161	45	26	23	13
1990	1,940	46.6	191	264	492	560	154	171	44	27	24	14
1991	2,025	45.8	199	283	504	590	156	181	44	28	25	15
1992	2,108	45.6	207	297	521	616	162	191	45	29	26	15
1993	2,167	45.5	212	303	533	632	169	200	45	30	26	16
1994	2,206	45.1	215	315	532	637	176	211	45	31	27	17
1995 [2]	2,218	44.9	218	321	526	634	179	219	45	31	27	18
1996 [2]	2,248	44.2	220	336	522	642	179	227	45	32	27	18
1997 [2]	2,288	43.6	224	347	521	652	181	238	46	33	27	19
1998 [2]	2,298	43.2	218	341	520	664	184	246	45	34	27	19
1999 [2]	2,323	42.7	218	342	519	682	186	254	44	34	25	19
2000 [2]	2,385	42.6	225	340	530	708	192	265	44	36	25	20

NA Not available.   [1] First-professional degrees are included with bachelor's degrees.   [2] Data beginning in 1996 reflect the new classification of institutions. See footnote 1, Table 257.

Source: U.S. National Center for Education Statistics, *Digest of Education Statistics*, annual.

No. 277. Degrees Earned by Level and Race/Ethnicity: 1981 to 2000

[For school year ending in year shown. Data through 1995 exclude some institutions not reporting field of study and are slight undercounts of degrees awarded]

Level of degree and race/ethnicity	Total 1981	Total 1985	Total 1990	Total 1995	Total 1999 [1]	Total 2000 [1]	Percent distribution 1981	Percent distribution 2000 [1]
Associate's degrees, total	410,174	429,815	450,263	538,545	559,954	564,933	100.0	100.0
White, non-Hispanic	339,167	355,343	369,580	419,323	408,844	408,508	82.7	72.3
Black, non-Hispanic	35,330	35,791	35,327	47,142	57,405	60,181	8.6	10.7
Hispanic	17,800	19,407	22,195	36,013	48,643	51,541	4.3	9.1
Asian or Pacific Islander	8,650	9,914	13,482	20,717	27,566	27,764	2.1	4.9
American Indian/Alaskan Native . .	2,584	2,953	3,530	5,492	6,417	6,494	0.6	1.1
Nonresident alien	6,643	6,407	6,149	9,858	11,079	10,445	1.6	1.8
Bachelor's degrees, total	934,800	968,311	1,048,631	1,158,788	1,200,303	1,237,875	100.0	100.0
White, non-Hispanic	807,319	826,106	884,376	913,377	906,305	928,013	86.4	75.0
Black, non-Hispanic	60,673	57,473	61,063	87,203	102,106	107,891	6.5	8.7
Hispanic	21,832	25,874	32,844	54,201	70,008	74,963	2.3	6.1
Asian or Pacific Islander	18,794	25,395	39,248	60,478	74,102	77,793	2.0	6.3
American Indian/Alaskan Native . .	3,593	4,246	4,392	6,606	8,418	8,711	0.4	0.7
Nonresident alien	22,589	29,217	26,708	36,923	39,364	40,504	2.4	3.3
Master's degrees, total	294,183	280,421	322,465	397,052	439,986	457,056	100.0	100.0
White, non-Hispanic	241,216	223,628	251,690	292,784	311,299	317,999	82.0	69.6
Black, non-Hispanic	17,133	13,939	15,446	24,171	32,344	35,625	5.8	7.8
Hispanic	6,461	6,864	7,950	12,907	17,708	19,093	2.2	4.2
Asian or Pacific Islander	6,282	7,782	10,577	16,842	21,803	22,899	2.1	5.0
American Indian/Alaskan Native . .	1,034	1,256	1,101	1,621	2,004	2,232	0.4	0.5
Nonresident alien	22,057	26,952	35,701	48,727	54,828	59,208	7.5	13.0
Doctor's degrees, total	32,839	32,307	38,113	44,427	44,077	44,808	100.0	100.0
White, non-Hispanic	25,908	23,934	25,880	27,826	27,492	27,520	78.9	61.4
Black, non-Hispanic	1,265	1,154	1,153	1,667	2,116	2,220	3.9	5.0
Hispanic	456	677	788	984	1,284	1,291	1.4	2.9
Asian or Pacific Islander	877	1,106	1,235	2,690	2,262	2,380	2.7	5.3
American Indian/Alaskan Native . .	130	119	99	130	192	159	0.4	0.4
Nonresident alien	4,203	5,317	8,958	11,130	10,731	11,238	12.8	25.1
First-professional degrees, total	71,340	71,057	70,744	75,800	78,439	80,057	100.0	100.0
White, non-Hispanic	64,551	63,219	60,240	59,402	58,688	59,601	90.5	74.4
Black, non-Hispanic	2,931	3,029	3,410	4,747	5,332	5,552	4.1	6.9
Hispanic	1,541	1,884	2,427	3,231	3,863	3,865	2.2	4.8
Asian or Pacific Islander	1,456	1,816	3,362	6,397	8,147	8,576	2.0	10.7
American Indian/Alaskan Native . .	192	248	257	412	612	564	0.3	0.7
Nonresident alien	669	861	1,048	1,611	1,797	1,899	0.9	2.4

[1] In this table, data beginning in 1999 reflect the new classification of institutions. See footnote 1, Table 257.

Source: U.S. National Center for Education Statistics, *Digest of Education Statistics,* annual.

Education 175

No. 278. Degrees and Awards Earned Below Bachelor's by Field: 2000

[Covers associate degrees and other awards based on postsecondary curriculums of less than 4 years in institutions of higher education]

Field of study	Less than 1-year awards		1- to less than 4-year awards		Associate degrees	
	Total	Women	Total	Women	Total	Women
Total	**119,498**	**63,682**	**140,903**	**78,483**	**564,933**	**340,212**
Agriculture and natural resources	1,526	328	1,918	563	6,667	2,314
Architecture and related programs	21	18	83	70	392	291
Area, ethnic, and cultural studies	227	165	87	74	259	203
Biological/life sciences	21	7	36	18	1,434	953
Business management and administrative services [1]	21,898	15,266	24,588	19,128	97,831	68,866
Communications and communications technologies	544	250	708	301	4463	1969
Computer and information sciences	8,984	3,221	9,177	3,425	20,450	8,750
Construction trades	2,656	160	4,701	224	2,337	117
Consumer and personal services	4,353	3,246	7,055	5,315	9,570	4,010
Education	2,014	1,458	582	539	8,226	6,524
Engineering and engineering technologies	4,798	901	6,618	878	37,147	4,902
English language and literature/letters	341	187	28	16	947	614
Foreign languages and literatures	291	206	18	13	501	266
Health professions and related sciences	31,945	25,100	41,857	36,040	84,081	72,353
Home economics and vocational home economics	6,770	4,981	4,243	3,856	8,381	7,677
Law and legal studies	794	647	1,293	1,092	7,265	6,384
Liberal/general studies and humanities	339	231	1,999	1,213	187,454	117,708
Library science	124	114	47	41	98	90
Mathematics	7	1	7	2	675	267
Mechanics and repairers	6,703	730	18,270	911	11,614	823
Multi/interdisciplinary studies	192	140	188	145	11,784	6,263
Parks, recreation, leisure, and fitness	121	67	121	62	855	344
Physical sciences	163	54	128	44	2,460	1,161
Precision production trades	4,283	724	8,691	1,327	11,814	2,614
Protective services	9,633	2,087	3,220	725	16,298	5,791
Psychology	60	54	23	19	1,455	1,129
Public administration and services	392	328	386	314	3,656	3,101
R.O.T.C. and military technologies	40	7	-	-	65	11
Social sciences and history	82	35	58	39	5,136	3,345
Theological studies, religion and philosophy	102	67	565	247	699	312
Transportation and material moving	8,560	2,171	741	66	1,021	151
Visual and performing arts	1,210	568	3,118	1,553	17,100	9,101
Undistributed and unclassified	304	163	349	223	2,798	1,808

- Represents zero.   [1] Includes marketing.

Source: U.S. National Center for Education Statistics, *Digest of Education Statistics, 2001.*

No. 279. Bachelor's Degrees Earned by Field: 1971 to 2000

Field of study	1971	1980	1990	1995	2000 [1]	Percent female	
						1971	2000 [1]
Total	**839,730**	**929,417**	**1,051,344**	**1,160,134**	**1,237,875**	**43.4**	**57.2**
Agriculture and natural resources	12,672	22,802	12,900	19,841	24,247	4.2	42.9
Architecture and environmental design	5,570	9,132	9,364	8,756	8,462	11.9	38.6
Area, ethnic and cultural studies	2,582	2,840	4,613	5,706	6,381	52.4	67.7
Biological sciences/life sciences	35,743	46,370	37,204	55,984	63,532	29.1	58.3
Business and management	114,729	184,867	248,698	234,323	257,709	9.1	49.7
Communications [2]	10,802	28,616	51,308	48,803	56,910	35.3	61.2
Computer and information sciences	2,388	11,154	27,257	24,404	36,195	13.6	28.1
Education	176,307	118,038	105,112	106,079	108,168	74.5	75.8
Engineering [2]	50,046	68,893	81,322	78,154	72,555	0.8	18.5
English language and literature/letters	64,342	32,541	47,519	51,901	50,920	65.6	67.9
Foreign languages and literatures	20,536	12,089	12,386	13,775	14,968	74.0	70.8
Health sciences	25,226	63,920	58,302	79,855	78,458	77.1	83.8
Home economics	11,167	18,411	14,491	15,345	17,779	97.3	87.9
Law and legal studies	545	683	1,592	2,032	1,925	5.0	73.0
Liberal/general studies	7,481	23,196	27,985	33,356	36,104	33.6	66.1
Library and archival sciences	1,013	398	77	50	154	92.0	50.0
Mathematics	24,937	11,872	15,176	13,723	12,070	37.9	47.1
Multi/interdisciplinary studies	6,286	11,277	16,267	26,033	27,460	22.8	66.7
Parks and recreation	1,621	5,753	4,582	12,889	19,111	34.7	52.0
Philosophy, religion, and theology	11,890	13,276	12,068	12,854	15,175	25.5	34.0
Physical sciences [2]	21,412	23,410	16,066	19,177	18,385	13.8	40.3
Protective services	2,045	15,015	15,354	24,157	24,877	9.2	43.4
Psychology	38,187	42,093	53,952	72,083	74,060	44.4	76.5
Public administration and services	5,466	16,644	13,908	18,586	20,185	68.4	81.1
R.O.T.C. and military technologies	357	38	196	27	7	0.3	(Z)
Social sciences [3]	155,324	103,662	118,083	128,154	127,101	36.8	51.2
Visual and performing arts	30,394	40,892	39,934	48,690	58,791	59.7	59.2
Unclassified [4]	662	1,535	5,628	5,397	6,186	0.9	32.1

Z Less than 0.05 percent.   [1] In this table, data for 2000 reflect the new classification of institutions. See footnote 1, Table 257.   [2] Includes technologies.   [3] Includes history.   [4] Includes precision production trades and transportation and materials moving.

Source: U.S. National Center for Education Statistics, *Digest of Education Statistics,* annual.

No. 280. Master's and Doctorate's Degrees Earned by Field: 1971 to 2000

Level and field of study	1971	1980	1990	1995	2000 [1]	Percent female	
						1971	2000 [1]
MASTER'S DEGREES							
Total	230,509	298,081	324,301	397,629	457,056	40.1	58.0
Agriculture and natural resources	2,457	3,976	3,382	4,252	4,375	5.9	46.0
Architecture and related programs	1,705	3,139	3,499	3,923	4,268	13.8	41.2
Area, ethnic and cultural studies	1,032	852	1,212	1,639	1,591	38.3	59.5
Biological sciences/life sciences	5,728	6,510	4,869	5,393	6,198	33.6	55.3
Business management and administrative services	25,977	54,484	76,676	93,809	112,258	3.9	39.8
Communications and technologies	1,856	3,082	4,362	5,609	5,605	34.6	63.3
Computer and information sciences	1,588	3,647	9,677	10,326	14,264	10.3	33.3
Education	87,666	101,819	84,881	101,242	124,240	56.2	76.4
Engineering and engineering technologies	16,443	16,243	24,772	29,670	26,522	1.1	20.9
English language and literature/letters	10,686	6,189	6,567	7,845	7,230	60.6	66.9
Foreign languages	5,217	2,854	2,760	3,136	2,780	64.2	69.6
Health sciences	5,749	15,704	20,321	31,243	42,456	55.3	77.3
Home economics	1,452	2,690	2,100	2,864	2,830	93.9	83.9
Law and legal studies	955	1,817	1,888	2,511	3,750	4.8	41.5
Liberal arts and sciences, general studies and humanities	885	2,646	1,999	2,565	3,256	44.6	64.9
Library science	7,001	5,374	4,341	5,057	4,577	81.3	79.3
Mathematics	5,695	3,382	4,146	4,181	3,412	27.1	44.9
Multi/interdisciplinary studies	821	2,306	2,834	2,457	3,064	25.0	61.7
Parks and recreation	218	647	529	1,755	2,478	29.8	50.0
Philosophy, religion, and theology	4,036	5,126	6,265	6,620	6,905	27.1	39.5
Physical sciences and science technologies	6,367	5,219	5,449	5,753	4,841	13.3	35.4
Protective services	194	1,805	1,151	1,706	2,609	10.3	41.2
Psychology	5,717	9,938	10,730	13,921	14,465	40.6	75.4
Public administration and services	7,785	17,560	17,399	23,501	25,594	50.0	73.4
R.O.T.C. and military technologies	2	46	-	124	-	-	-
Social sciences [2]	16,539	12,176	11,634	14,845	14,066	28.5	50.1
Visual and performing arts	6,675	8,708	8,481	10,277	10,918	47.4	57.2
Unclassified [3]	63	142	2,377	1,405	2,504	-	47.6
DOCTORATE'S DEGREES							
Total	32,107	32,615	38,371	44,446	44,808	14.3	44.1
Agriculture and natural resources	1,086	991	1,295	1,264	1,181	2.9	31.3
Architecture and related programs	36	79	103	141	129	8.3	34.1
Area, ethnic and cultural studies	144	151	131	186	217	16.7	51.2
Biological sciences/life sciences	3,645	3,636	3,844	4,645	4,867	16.3	44.1
Business management and administrative services	757	753	1,093	1,394	1,196	2.8	31.9
Communications and technologies	145	193	273	321	357	13.1	52.9
Computer and information sciences	128	240	627	884	777	2.3	16.9
Education	6,041	7,314	6,502	6,905	6,830	21.0	64.6
Engineering and engineering technology	3,638	2,507	4,981	6,128	5,390	0.6	15.5
English language and literature/letters	1,650	1,294	1,078	1,561	1,628	28.8	58.8
Foreign languages	988	755	724	905	915	34.6	59.0
Health sciences	466	786	1,536	2,069	2,676	16.5	61.2
Home economics	123	192	301	388	357	61.0	76.8
Law and legal studies	20	40	111	88	74	-	33.8
Liberal arts and sciences, general studies and humanities	32	192	63	90	83	31.3	50.6
Library science	39	73	42	55	68	28.2	72.1
Mathematics	1,249	763	966	1,226	1,106	7.6	25.0
Multi/interdisciplinary studies	59	209	272	238	384	6.8	47.1
Parks and recreation	2	21	35	149	134	50.0	44.0
Philosophy, religion, and theology	866	1,693	1,756	2,098	2,229	5.8	24.3
Physical sciences and science technologies	4,390	3,089	4,164	4,483	4,018	5.6	25.5
Protective services	1	18	38	26	52	-	46.2
Psychology	2,144	3,395	3,811	3,822	4,310	24.0	67.4
Public administration and services	174	342	508	556	537	24.1	57.7
Social sciences [2]	3,660	3,230	3,010	3,725	4,095	13.9	41.2
Visual and performing arts	621	655	849	1,080	1,127	22.2	52.4
Unclassified [3]	3	4	258	19	71	-	54.9

- Represents zero. [1] Data for 2000 reflect the new classification of institutions. See footnote 1, Table 257. [2] Includes history. [3] Includes precision production trades and transportation and materials moving.

Source: U.S. National Center for Education Statistics, *Digest of Education Statistics,* annual.

No. 281. First Professional Degrees Earned in Selected Professions: 1970 to 2000

[First professional degrees include degrees which require at least 6 years of college work for completion (including at least 2 years of preprofessional training). See Appendix III]

Type of degree and sex of recipient	1970	1975	1980	1985	1990	1995	1997	1998	1999	2000
Medicine (M.D.):										
Institutions conferring degrees.....	86	104	112	120	124	119	118	117	118	118
Degrees conferred, total.........	8,314	12,447	14,902	16,041	15,075	15,537	15,571	15,424	15,562	15,286
Percent to women	8.4	13.1	23.4	30.4	34.2	38.8	41.4	41.6	42.5	42.7
Dentistry (D.D.S. or D.M.D.):										
Institutions conferring degrees.....	48	52	58	59	57	53	52	53	53	54
Degrees conferred, total.........	3,718	4,773	5,258	5,339	4,100	3,897	3,784	4,032	4,144	4,250
Percent to women	0.9	3.1	13.3	20.7	30.9	36.4	36.9	38.2	35.5	40.1
Law (LL.B. or J.D.):										
Institutions conferring degrees.....	145	154	179	181	182	183	184	185	188	190
Degrees conferred, total.........	14,916	29,296	35,647	37,491	36,485	39,349	40,079	39,331	39,167	38,152
Percent to women	5.4	15.1	30.2	38.5	42.2	42.6	43.7	44.4	44.8	45.9
Theological (B.D., M.Div., M.H.L.):										
Institutions conferring degrees.....	(NA)	(NA)	(NA)	(NA)	(NA)	192	178	190	193	198
Degrees conferred, total.........	5,298	5,095	7,115	7,221	5,851	5,978	5,859	5,873	5,558	6,129
Percent to women	2.3	6.8	13.8	18.5	24.8	25.7	26.2	26.1	28.3	29.2

NA Not available.

Source: U.S. National Center for Education Statistics, *Digest of Education Statistics*, annual.

No. 282. Participation in Adult Education: 1994-95 and 1998-99

[In thousands (189,543 represents 189,543,000), except percent. For the civilian noninstitutional population 17 years old and over not enrolled full time in elementary or secondary school at the time of the survey. Adult education is considered any enrollment in any educational activity at any time in the prior 12 months, except full-time enrollment in a higher education credential program. Based on survey and subject to sampling error; see source for details]

Characteristic	Adult population (1,000)	Number taking adult ed. courses (1,000)	Percent of total	Personal/ social	Advance on the job	Train for a new job	Complete degree or diploma
					Reason for taking course (percent) [1]		
Total, 1995...............	189,543	76,261	40	44	54	11	10
Total, 1999...............	194,434	88,809	46	43	54	12	11
Age:							
17 to 24 years old............	25,276	13,029	52	34	32	20	23
25 to 34 years old............	34,880	19,431	56	38	56	16	11
35 to 44 years old............	45,258	23,047	51	41	62	13	9
45 to 54 years old............	37,153	18,972	51	44	65	6	7
55 to 64 years old............	24,309	9,003	37	49	56	7	9
65 years old and over	27,559	5,328	19	76	22	-	4
Sex:							
Male......................	92,946	40,204	43	34	59	11	13
Female	101,488	48,605	48	50	50	12	9
Race/ethnicity:							
White, Non-Hispanic	143,679	65,547	46	45	56	11	10
Black, Non-Hispanic	22,129	10,803	49	42	52	15	13
Hispanic	19,491	7,981	41	35	45	14	11
Other Non-Hispanic races.	9,135	4,478	49	35	49	14	19
Marital status:							
Never married	41,530	20,773	50	34	45	17	18
Currently married	118,568	55,966	47	46	58	10	9
Other	34,337	12,070	35	45	55	11	8
Children under 18 in household:							
Yes	83,365	43,060	52	41	55	12	12
No	111,070	45,749	41	44	53	11	10
Educational attainment:							
Up to 8th grade	11,078	1,527	14	41	39	3	21
9th to 12th grade	21,375	5,578	26	35	28	15	21
High school diploma or GED......	53,488	19,693	37	39	52	12	7
Vocational school after high school .	6,319	2,629	42	44	57	11	5
Some college...............	35,147	18,220	52	48	46	14	15
Associate's degree	11,377	6,735	59	38	60	15	14
Bachelor's or higher	55,651	34,426	62	45	63	9	8
Labor force status:							
Employed	132,227	70,849	54	37	63	12	11
Unemployed	7,963	3,433	43	39	23	32	22
Not in the labor force...........	54,244	14,527	27	72	17	7	10

- Represents or rounds to zero.   [1] Reason for taking at least one course. Includes duplication. Excludes other reasons, not shown separately.

Source: U.S. National Center for Education Statistics, *1995* and *1999 National Household Education Surveys*.

Section 5
Law Enforcement, Courts, and Prisons

This section presents data on crimes committed, victims of crimes, arrests, and data related to criminal violations and the criminal justice system. The major sources of these data are the Bureau of Justice Statistics (BJS), the Federal Bureau of Investigation (FBI), and the Administrative Office of the U.S. Courts. BJS issues several reports, including *Sourcebook of Criminal Justice Statistics, Criminal Victimization in the United States, Prisoners in State and Federal Institutions, Children in Custody, Census of State Correctional Facilities and Survey of Prison Inmates, Census of Jails and Survey of Jail Inmates, Parole in the United States, Capital Punishment*, and the annual *Expenditure and Employment Data for the Criminal Justice System*. The Federal Bureau of Investigation's major annual reports are *Crime in the United States, Law Enforcement Officers Killed and Assaulted*, annual, and *Hate Crimes*, annual. which presents data on reported crimes as gathered from state and local law enforcement agencies.

Legal jurisdiction and law enforcement—Law enforcement is, for the most part, a function of state and local officers and agencies. The U.S. Constitution reserves general police powers to the states. By act of Congress, federal offenses include only offenses against the U.S. government and against or by its employees while engaged in their official duties and offenses which involve the crossing of state lines or an interference with interstate commerce. Excluding the military, there are 52 separate criminal law jurisdictions in the United States: 1 in each of the 50 states, 1 in the District of Columbia, and the federal jurisdiction. Each of these has its own criminal law and procedure and its own law enforcement agencies. While the systems of law enforcement are quite similar among the states, there are often substantial differences in the penalties for like offenses.

Law enforcement can be divided into three parts: Investigation of crimes and arrests of persons suspected of committing them; prosecution of those charged with crime; and the punishment or treatment of persons convicted of crime.

Crime—There are two major approaches taken in determining the extent of crime. One perspective is provided by the FBI through its Uniform Crime Reporting Program (UCR). The FBI receives monthly and annual reports from law enforcement agencies throughout the country, currently representing 94 percent of the national population. Each month, city police, sheriffs, and state police file reports on the number of index offenses, hate crimes and law enforcement assaults that become known to them. Additionally, data are collected for officers killed in the line of duty.

The FBI Crime Index offenses are as follows: *Murder and nonnegligent manslaughter* is based on police investigations, as opposed to the determination of a medical examiner or judicial body, includes willful felonious homicides and excludes attempts and assaults to kill, suicides, accidental deaths, justifiable homicides, and deaths caused by negligence; *forcible rape* includes forcible rapes and attempts; *robbery* includes stealing or taking anything of value by force or violence or threat of force or violence and includes attempted robbery; *aggravated assault* includes assault with intent to kill; *burglary* includes any unlawful entry to commit a felony or a theft and includes attempted burglary and burglary followed by larceny; *larceny* includes theft of property or articles of value without use of force and violence or fraud and excludes embezzlement, "con games," forgery, etc.; *motor vehicle theft* includes all cases where vehicles are driven away and abandoned but excludes vehicles taken for temporary use and returned by the taker. Arson was added as the eighth Index offense in April 1979 following a Congressional mandate. *Arson* includes any willful or malicious burning

Law Enforcement, Courts, and Prisons   179

U.S. Census Bureau, Statistical Abstract of the United States: 2002

or attempt to burn, with or without intent to defraud, a dwelling house, public building, motor vehicle or aircraft, personal property of another, etc.

The monthly Uniform Crime Reports also contain data on crimes cleared by arrest and on characteristics of persons arrested for all criminal offenses. In summarizing and publishing crime data, the FBI depends primarily on the adherence to the established standards of reporting for statistical accuracy, presenting the data as information useful to persons concerned with the problem of crime and criminal law enforcement.

National Crime Victimization Survey (NCVS)—A second perspective on crime is provided by this survey of the Bureau of Justice Statistics. Details about the crimes come directly from the victims. No attempt is made to validate the information against police records or any other source.

The NCVS measures rape, robbery, assault, household and personal larceny, burglary, and motor vehicle theft. The NCVS includes offenses reported to the police, as well as those not reported.

Police reporting rates (percent of victimizations) varied by type of crime. In 1994, for instance, 32 percent of the rapes/sexual assaults were reported; 55 percent of the robberies; 40 percent of assaults; 33 percent of personal thefts; 51 percent of the household burglaries; and 78 percent of motor vehicle thefts.

Murder and kidnaping are not covered. Commercial burglary and robbery were dropped from the program during 1977. The so-called victimless crimes, such as drunkenness, drug abuse, and prostitution, also are excluded, as are crimes for which it is difficult to identify knowledgeable respondents or to locate data records.

Crimes of which the victim may not be aware also cannot be measured effectively. Buying stolen property may fall into this category, as may some instances of embezzlement. Attempted crimes of many types probably are under recorded

for this reason. Events in which the victim has shown a willingness to participate in illegal activity also are excluded.

In any encounter involving a personal crime, more than one criminal act can be committed against an individual. For example, a rape may be associated with a robbery or a household offense, such as a burglary, can escalate into something more serious in the event of a personal confrontation. In classifying the survey-measured crimes, each criminal incident has been counted only once—by the most serious act that took place during the incident and ranked in accordance with the seriousness classification system used by the Federal Bureau of Investigation. The order of seriousness for crimes against persons is as follows: Rape, robbery, assault, and larceny. Personal crimes take precedence over household offenses.

A *victimization,* basic measure of the occurrence of crime, is a specific criminal act as it affects a single victim. The number of victimizations is determined by the number of victims of such acts. Victimization counts serve as key elements in computing rates of victimization. For crimes against persons, the rates are based on the total number of individuals age 12 and over or on a portion of that population sharing a particular characteristic or set of traits. As general indicators of the danger of having been victimized during the reference period, the rates are not sufficiently refined to represent true measures of risk for specific individuals or households.

An *incident* is a specific criminal act involving one or more victims; therefore the number of incidents of personal crimes is lower than that of victimizations.

Courts—Statistics on criminal offenses and the outcome of prosecutions are incomplete for the country as a whole, although data are available for many states individually. The only national compilations of such statistics were made by the Census Bureau for 1932 to 1945 covering a maximum of 32 states and by the Bureau of Justice Statistics for 1986, 1988, 1990, and 1992 based on a nationally representative sample survey.

U.S. Census Bureau, Statistical Abstract of the United States: 2002

The bulk of civil and criminal litigation in the country is commenced and determined in the various state courts. Only when the U.S. Constitution and acts of Congress specifically confer jurisdiction upon the federal courts may civil or criminal litigation be heard and decided by them. Generally, the federal courts have jurisdiction over the following types of cases: Suits or proceedings by or against the United States; civil actions between private parties arising under the Constitution, laws, or treaties of the United States; civil actions between private litigants who are citizens of different states; civil cases involving admiralty, maritime, or prize jurisdiction; and all matters in bankruptcy. The Administrative Office of the United States Courts has compiled statistics on the caseload of the federal courts annually since 1940.

There are several types of courts with varying degrees of legal jurisdiction. These jurisdictions include original, appellate, general, and limited or special. A court of original jurisdiction is one having the authority initially to try a case and pass judgment on the law and the facts; a court of appellate jurisdiction is one with the legal authority to review cases and hear appeals; a court of general jurisdiction is a trial court of unlimited original jurisdiction in civil and/or criminal cases, also called a "major trial court"; a court of limited or special jurisdiction is a trial court with legal authority over only a particular class of cases, such as probate, juvenile, or traffic cases.

The 94 federal courts of original jurisdiction are known as the U.S. district courts. One or more of these courts is established in every state and one each in the District of Columbia, Puerto Rico, the Virgin Islands, the Northern Mariana Islands, and Guam. Appeals from the district courts are taken to intermediate appellate courts of which there are 13, known as U.S. courts of appeals and the United States Court of Appeals for the Federal Circuit. The Supreme Court of the United States is the final and highest appellate court in the federal system of courts.

Juvenile offenders—For statistical purposes, the FBI and most states classify as juvenile offenders persons under the age of 18 years who have committed a crime or crimes.

Delinquency cases are all cases of youths referred to a juvenile court for violation of a law or ordinance or for seriously "anti-social" conduct. Several types of facilities are available for those adjudicated delinquent, ranging from the short-term physically unrestricted environment to the long-term very restrictive atmosphere.

Prisoners—Data on prisoners in federal and state prisons and reformatories were collected annually by the Census Bureau until 1950, by the Federal Bureau of Prisons until 1971, transferred then to the Law Enforcement Assistance Administration, and, in 1979, to the Bureau of Justice Statistics. Adults convicted of criminal activity may be given a prison or jail sentence. A *prison* is a confinement facility having custodial authority over adults sentenced to confinement of more than 1 year. A *jail* is a facility, usually operated by a local law enforcement agency, holding persons detained pending adjudication and/or persons committed after adjudication to 1 year or less. Nearly every state publishes annual data either for its whole prison system or for each separate state institution.

Statistical reliability—For discussion of statistical collection, estimation and sampling procedures, and measures of statistical reliability pertaining to the National Crime Victimization Survey and Uniform Crime Reporting Program, see Appendix III.

U.S. Census Bureau, Statistical Abstract of the United States: 2002

Figure 5.1
Violent Crime Rates per 100,000 Population by State: 2000

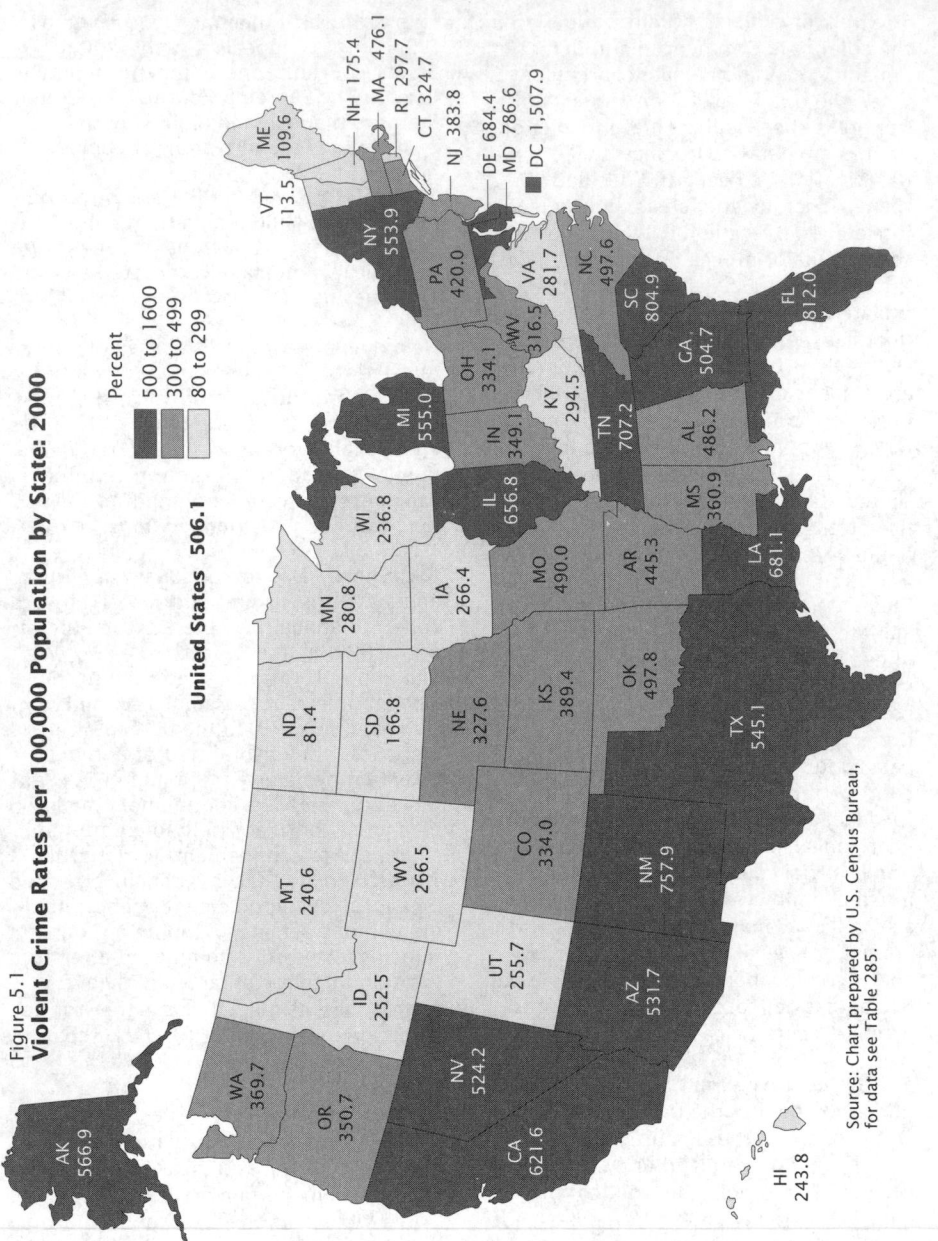

Percent

500 to 1600
300 to 499
80 to 299

United States 506.1

AK 566.9

WA 369.7

OR 350.7

CA 621.6

NV 524.2

ID 252.5

MT 240.6

WY 266.5

UT 255.7

AZ 531.7

NM 757.9

CO 334.0

ND 81.4

SD 166.8

NE 327.6

KS 389.4

OK 497.8

TX 545.1

MN 280.8

IA 266.4

MO 490.0

AR 445.3

LA 681.1

WI 236.8

IL 656.8

IN 349.1

MI 555.0

OH 334.1

KY 294.5

TN 707.2

MS 360.9

AL 486.2

GA 504.7

SC 804.9

NC 497.6

VA 281.7

WV 316.5

PA 420.0

NY 553.9

FL 812.0

HI 243.8

VT 113.5

ME 109.6

NH 175.4
MA 476.1
RI 297.7
CT 324.7
NJ 383.8
DE 684.4
MD 786.6
DC 1,507.9

Source: Chart prepared by U.S. Census Bureau,
for data see Table 285.

182   Law Enforcement, Courts, and Prisons

No. 283. Crimes and Crime Rates by Type of Offense: 1980 to 2000

[13,408 represents 13,408,000. Data refer to offenses known to the police. Rates are based on Census Bureau estimated resident population as of **July 1; 1980, 1990 and 2000, enumerated as of April 1.** See source for details. For definitions of crimes, see text, this section]

Item and year		Violent crime						Property crime			
	Total	Total	Murder [1]	Forcible rape	Robbery	Aggravated assault	Total	Burglary	Larceny/ theft	Motor vehicle theft
Number of offenses (1,000):											
1980	13,408	1,345	23.0	83.0	566	673	12,064	3,795	7,137	1,132
1985	12,430	1,328	19.0	87.7	498	723	11,103	3,073	6,926	1,103
1986	13,212	1,489	20.6	91.5	543	834	11,723	3,241	7,257	1,224
1987	13,509	1,484	20.1	91.1	518	855	12,025	3,236	7,500	1,289
1988	13,923	1,566	20.7	92.5	543	910	12,357	3,218	7,706	1,433
1989	14,251	1,646	21.5	94.5	578	952	12,605	3,168	7,872	1,565
1990	14,476	1,820	23.4	102.6	639	1,055	12,655	3,074	7,946	1,636
1991	14,873	1,912	24.7	106.6	688	1,093	12,961	3,157	8,142	1,662
1992	14,438	1,932	23.8	109.1	672	1,127	12,506	2,980	7,915	1,611
1993	14,145	1,926	24.5	106.0	660	1,136	12,219	2,835	7,821	1,563
1994	13,990	1,858	23.3	102.2	619	1,113	12,132	2,713	7,880	1,539
1995	13,863	1,799	21.6	97.5	581	1,099	12,064	2,594	7,998	1,472
1996	13,494	1,689	19.6	96.3	536	1,037	11,805	2,506	7,905	1,394
1997	13,195	1,636	18.2	96.2	499	1,023	11,558	2,461	7,744	1,354
1998	12,486	1,534	17.0	93.1	447	977	10,952	2,333	7,376	1,243
1999	11,634	1,426	15.5	89.4	409	912	10,208	2,101	6,956	1,152
2000	11,606	1,424	15.5	90.2	408	911	10,181	2,050	6,966	1,166
Rate per 100,000 population:											
1980	5,950.0	596.6	10.2	36.8	251.1	298.5	5,353.3	1,684.1	3,167.0	502.2
1985	5,224.5	558.1	8.0	36.8	209.3	304.0	4,666.4	1,291.7	2,911.2	463.5
1986	5,501.9	620.1	8.6	38.1	226.0	347.4	4,881.8	1,349.8	3,022.1	509.8
1987	5,575.5	612.5	8.3	37.6	213.7	352.9	4,963.0	1,335.7	3,095.4	531.9
1988	5,694.5	640.6	8.5	37.8	222.1	372.2	5,054.0	1,316.2	3,151.7	586.1
1989	5,774.0	666.9	8.7	38.3	234.3	385.6	5,107.1	1,283.6	3,189.6	634.0
1990	5,802.7	729.6	9.4	41.1	256.3	422.9	5,073.1	1,232.2	3,185.1	655.8
1991	5,898.4	758.2	9.8	42.3	272.7	433.4	5,140.2	1,252.1	3,229.1	659.0
1992	5,661.4	757.7	9.3	42.8	263.7	441.9	4,903.7	1,168.4	3,103.6	631.6
1993	5,487.1	747.1	9.5	41.1	256.0	440.5	4,740.0	1,099.7	3,033.9	606.3
1994	5,373.8	713.6	9.0	39.3	237.8	427.6	4,660.2	1,042.1	3,026.9	591.3
1995	5,274.9	684.5	8.2	37.1	220.9	418.3	4,590.5	987.0	3,043.2	560.3
1996	5,087.6	636.6	7.4	36.3	201.9	391.0	4,451.0	945.0	2,980.3	525.7
1997	4,927.3	611.0	6.8	35.9	186.2	382.1	4,316.3	918.8	2,891.8	505.7
1998	4,620.1	567.6	6.3	34.5	165.5	361.4	4,052.5	863.2	2,729.5	459.9
1999	4,266.5	523.0	5.7	32.8	150.1	334.3	3,743.6	770.4	2,550.7	422.5
2000	4,124.0	506.1	5.5	32.0	144.9	323.6	3,617.9	728.4	2,475.3	414.2

[1] Includes nonnegligent manslaughter.

Source: U.S. Federal Bureau of Investigation, *Crime in the United States,* annual. See also <http://www.fbi.gov/ucr/cius00/contents.pdf> (released 15 October 2001).

No. 284. Crimes and Crime Rates by Type and Area: 2000

[In thousands (11,606 represents 11,606,000), except rate. Rate per 100,000 population; see headnote, Table 283. Estimated totals based on reports from city and rural law enforcement agencies representing 96 percent of the national population. For definitions of crimes, see text, this section]

Type of crime	United States		Metropolitan areas [1]		Other cities		Rural areas	
	Total	Rate	Total	Rate	Total	Rate	Total	Rate
Total	11,606	4,124	9,954	4,428	1,020	4,485	631	1,864
Violent crime	1,424	506	1,262	561	91	401	71	210
Murder and nonnegligent manslaughter	16	6	13	6	1	4	1	4
Forcible rape	90	32	75	33	8	35	8	22
Robbery	408	145	389	173	14	60	5	16
Aggravated assault	911	324	785	349	69	302	57	168
Property crime	10,181	3,618	8,693	3,867	929	4,084	560	1,654
Burglary	2,050	728	1,697	755	173	759	180	532
Larceny-theft	6,966	2,475	5,917	2,632	711	3,125	339	1,000
Motor vehicle theft	1,166	414	1,079	480	45	199	41	122

[1] For definition, see Appendix II.

Source: U.S. Federal Bureau of Investigation, *Crime in the United States,* annual. See also <http://www.fbi.gov/ucr/cius00/contents.pdf> (released 15 October 2001).

U.S. Census Bureau, Statistical Abstract of the United States: 2002

No. 285. Crime Rates by State, 1998 to 2000, and by Type, 2000

[**Offenses known to the police per 100,000 population.** Based on Census Bureau estimated resident population **as of July 1; 2000 enumerated as of July 1.** For definitions of crimes, see text, this section]

State	1998, total	1999, total	2000 Total	Violent crime Total	Murder [1]	Forcible rape	Robbery	Aggravated assault	Property crime Total	Burglary	Larceny/ theft	Motor vehicle theft
United States	**4,619**	**4,267**	**4,124**	**506**	**5.5**	**32.0**	**145**	**324**	**3,618**	**728**	**2,475**	**414**
Alabama	4,597	4,413	4,546	486	7.4	33.3	128	317	4,060	907	2,865	288
Alaska.	4,777	4,360	4,249	567	4.3	79.3	78	405	3,683	622	2,686	375
Arizona	6,575	5,896	5,830	532	7.0	30.7	146	348	5,298	1,012	3,444	842
Arkansas	4,283	4,042	4,115	445	6.3	31.7	75	332	3,670	802	2,609	259
California	4,343	3,805	3,740	622	6.1	28.9	178	409	3,118	656	1,925	537
Colorado	4,488	4,063	3,983	334	3.1	41.2	71	219	3,649	631	2,624	394
Connecticut	3,787	3,389	3,233	325	2.9	19.9	113	189	2,908	512	2,011	385
Delaware [2]	5,363	4,838	4,478	684	3.2	54.1	178	449	3,794	666	2,726	402
District of Columbia [3] .	8,836	8,067	7,277	1,508	41.8	43.9	621	801	5,769	830	3,785	1,154
Florida.	6,886	6,205	5,695	812	5.6	44.2	199	563	4,883	1,082	3,243	558
Georgia	5,463	5,148	4,751	505	8.0	24.0	162	311	4,246	837	2,937	473
Hawaii.	5,333	4,835	5,199	244	2.9	28.6	93	120	4,955	880	3,570	505
Idaho	3,715	3,150	3,186	253	1.2	29.7	17	204	2,934	567	2,206	161
Illinois [4]	4,859	4,515	4,286	657	7.2	32.9	207	409	3,629	660	2,518	452
Indiana	4,169	3,766	3,752	349	5.8	28.9	103	211	3,403	676	2,380	347
Iowa	3,501	3,224	3,234	266	1.6	23.1	37	205	2,967	558	2,225	184
Kansas [4]	4,872	4,439	4,409	389	6.3	38.0	76	269	4,019	799	2,979	242
Kentucky [4]	3,116	2,953	2,960	295	4.8	27.0	81	182	2,665	626	1,810	230
Louisiana	6,098	5,747	5,423	681	12.5	33.5	169	467	4,742	1,036	3,230	476
Maine [4]	3,041	2,875	2,620	110	1.2	25.1	19	64	2,510	531	1,875	104
Maryland	5,366	4,920	4,816	787	8.1	29.1	256	493	4,030	744	2,746	540
Massachusetts	3,436	3,262	3,026	476	2.0	26.7	92	356	2,550	482	1,661	408
Michigan	4,683	4,325	4,110	555	6.7	50.6	138	360	3,555	702	2,292	561
Minnesota	4,047	3,598	3,488	281	3.1	45.5	76	157	3,208	531	2,404	273
Mississippi	4,384	4,270	4,004	361	9.0	35.8	95	221	3,644	946	2,452	245
Missouri.	4,826	4,578	4,528	490	6.2	24.1	136	324	4,038	745	2,851	441
Montana [4]	4,359	3,534	3,533	241	1.8	33.4	28	178	3,293	437	2,639	217
Nebraska	4,405	4,108	4,096	328	3.7	25.5	67	231	3,768	592	2,870	306
Nevada	5,281	4,653	4,269	524	6.5	43.0	227	247	3,744	877	2,208	659
New Hampshire [4] . . .	2,420	2,282	2,433	175	1.8	42.2	37	95	2,258	404	1,680	174
New Jersey	3,654	3,400	3,161	384	3.4	16.1	161	203	2,777	522	1,849	406
New Mexico	6,719	5,963	5,519	758	7.4	50.7	137	562	4,761	1,173	3,184	404
New York	3,589	3,279	3,100	554	5.0	18.6	214	317	2,546	463	1,796	286
North Carolina	5,322	5,176	4,919	498	7.0	27.1	157	307	4,422	1,216	2,892	314
North Dakota	2,681	2,394	2,288	81	0.6	26.3	9	46	2,207	326	1,727	154
Ohio	4,328	3,997	4,042	334	3.7	37.6	138	155	3,708	781	2,583	344
Oklahoma	5,004	4,684	4,559	498	5.3	41.2	76	376	4,061	918	2,785	358
Oregon	5,647	5,002	4,845	351	2.0	37.6	84	227	4,495	749	3,339	407
Pennsylvania	3,273	3,114	2,995	420	4.9	26.4	148	241	2,575	440	1,839	296
Rhode Island	3,518	3,583	3,476	298	4.3	39.3	88	166	3,179	632	2,102	445
South Carolina	5,777	5,325	5,221	805	5.8	37.7	147	615	4,417	969	3,068	379
South Dakota	2,624	2,644	2,320	167	0.9	40.4	17	108	2,153	384	1,664	106
Tennessee	5,034	4,694	4,890	707	7.2	38.4	166	495	4,183	990	2,709	484
Texas	5,112	5,032	4,956	545	5.9	37.7	145	356	4,410	906	3,057	447
Utah	5,506	4,977	4,476	256	1.9	38.6	56	160	4,220	643	3,289	289
Vermont	3,139	2,819	2,987	114	1.5	23.0	19	70	2,873	575	2,166	133
Virginia	3,660	3,374	3,028	282	5.7	22.8	89	164	2,746	430	2,065	252
Washington	5,867	5,255	5,106	370	3.3	46.4	99	221	4,736	907	3,235	594
West Virginia	2,547	2,721	2,603	317	2.5	18.3	41	254	2,286	547	1,556	183
Wisconsin [4]	3,543	3,296	3,209	237	3.2	21.7	85	127	2,972	470	2,230	273
Wyoming	3,808	3,458	3,298	267	2.4	32.4	14	218	3,032	421	2,495	116

[1] Includes nonnegligent manslaughter.   [2] Forcible rape figures furnished by the state-level uniform crime reporting (UCR) Program administered by the Delaware State Bureau of Investigation were not in accordance with the national UCR guidelines; therefore, it was necessary that the forcible rape count be estimated.   [3] Includes offenses reported by the police at the National Zoo.   [4] Complete data were not available; therefore, it was necessary for the crime counts to be estimated for Illinois, Kansas, Kentucky, and Montana, for all years shown, for Maine in 1999, and for New Hampshire and Wisconsin for 1998.

Source: U.S. Federal Bureau of Investigation, *Crime in the United States*, annual. See also <http://www.fbi.gov/ucr/cius00/contents.pdf> (released 15 October 2001).

No. 286. Crime Rates by Type—Selected Large Cities: 2000

[**Offenses known to the police per 100,000 population.** Based on U.S. Census Bureau estimated resident population enumerated as of **April 1.** For definitions of crimes, see text, this section]

City ranked by population size, 2000	Crime index, total	Violent crime Total	Murder	Forcible rape	Robbery	Aggravated assault	Property crime Total	Burglary	Larceny-theft	Motor vehicle theft
New York, NY	3,600.2	945.2	8.4	20.4	406.6	509.9	2,665.0	463.4	1,744.0	447.6
Los Angeles, CA	4,886.2	1,359.8	14.9	39.5	420.2	885.2	3,526.5	661.0	2,063.3	802.2
Chicago, IL [1]	(NA)	(NA)	21.8	(NA)	668.0	916.6	5,669.2	978.1	3,664.6	1,026.5
Houston, TX	6,741.9	1,100.1	11.8	41.6	422.6	624.1	5,641.8	1,190.3	3,434.7	1,016.8
Philadelphia, PA.......	6,457.8	1,503.2	21.0	67.3	687.0	727.9	4,954.6	796.6	3,093.9	1,064.0
San Diego, CA........	3,789.4	585.3	4.4	28.5	145.3	407.1	3,204.1	549.0	1,881.2	773.8
Phoenix, AZ	7,380.4	738.4	11.5	31.9	284.9	410.1	6,642.0	1,200.6	3,967.9	1,473.5
San Antonio, TX......	7,542.2	690.9	7.4	39.8	148.4	495.2	6,851.4	1,013.8	5,325.0	512.6
Dallas, TX..........	8,838.3	1,349.7	19.4	53.3	592.8	684.2	7,488.6	1,707.9	4,272.1	1,508.6
Detroit, MI..........	10,066.6	2,324.5	41.6	85.3	827.1	1,370.5	7,742.2	1,663.9	3,356.5	2,721.8
Las Vegas, NV	4,470.2	598.7	8.5	41.8	317.4	231.0	3,871.5	899.1	2,083.3	889.2
San Jose, CA........	2,548.5	550.6	2.1	37.7	75.6	435.2	1,997.9	298.3	1,407.4	292.2
Honolulu, HI	5,324.5	262.7	2.3	27.4	112.3	120.7	5,061.8	792.6	3,674.2	595.0
Indianapolis, IN	4,710.3	862.1	12.1	55.8	321.4	472.8	3,848.2	1,019.8	2,074.4	754.0
San Francisco, CA	5,429.4	836.7	7.6	29.5	444.9	354.7	4,592.7	733.2	3,143.4	716.2
Jacksonville, FL......	6,942.9	1,115.7	10.7	60.2	274.9	769.8	5,827.2	1,353.3	3,857.7	616.2
Columbus, OH.......	8,868.1	843.0	9.4	81.2	435.4	316.9	8,025.1	1,911.5	5,104.4	1,009.2
Baltimore, MD	10,118.3	2,457.6	40.1	56.2	1,015.6	1,345.8	7,660.7	1,641.4	4,812.5	1,206.8
El Paso, TX.........	6,151.2	779.9	3.5	33.4	129.7	613.3	5,371.3	395.3	4,542.6	433.4
Memphis, TN.........	9,170.9	1,479.2	22.6	88.3	628.7	739.6	7,691.7	2,298.6	4,055.5	1,337.6
Charlotte-Mecklenburg, NC.	7,904.0	1,201.0	12.0	49.2	423.6	716.2	6,703.0	1,533.7	4,440.5	728.8
Milwaukee, WI	7,385.9	956.7	20.4	50.8	506.1	379.4	6,429.3	1,065.9	4,011.7	1,351.7
Austin, TX..........	5,936.8	471.9	4.9	57.7	153.1	256.2	5,465.0	980.3	4,074.7	410.0
Boston, MA..........	6,088.5	1,242.8	6.6	55.2	416.0	765.0	4,845.7	687.6	2,924.3	1,233.8
Seattle, WA..........	8,040.8	769.1	6.4	32.1	293.4	437.2	7,271.7	1,092.9	4,690.3	1,488.5
Nashville, TN........	8,806.7	1,623.0	13.0	73.4	406.7	1,129.9	7,183.7	1,382.2	4,838.7	962.8
Washington, DC......	7,272.7	1,507.2	41.8	43.9	621.1	800.4	5,765.5	829.5	3,782.3	1,153.7
Denver, CO.........	4,742.2	520.2	5.8	53.4	187.3	273.7	4,222.0	898.4	2,315.4	1,008.2
Portland, OR	7,737.9	1,076.9	3.6	69.7	273.3	730.3	6,661.0	1,050.8	4,719.1	891.1
Fort Worth, TX.......	7,133.6	713.7	11.4	60.8	245.7	395.7	6,419.9	1,356.1	4,299.8	764.0
Cleveland, OH.......	6,811.0	1,262.7	14.8	128.6	644.6	474.7	5,548.3	1,554.1	2,710.9	1,283.2
Oklahoma City, OK.....	9,453.1	780.6	7.5	76.7	195.6	500.9	8,672.4	1,438.4	6,522.4	711.7
Tucson, AZ..........	9,148.4	933.2	12.3	72.9	296.7	551.3	8,215.1	1,380.9	5,619.3	1,214.9
New Orleans, LA	6,979.1	1,063.6	42.1	46.8	499.5	475.2	5,915.5	1,079.1	3,213.5	1,622.9
Kansas City, MO	10,672.8	1,626.3	25.6	70.2	513.0	1,017.6	9,046.4	1,712.6	5,699.8	1,634.0
Virginia Beach, VA	4,207.6	221.7	2.6	23.8	106.1	89.4	3,985.8	611.6	3,174.1	200.1
Long Beach, CA	3,828.0	696.8	10.6	24.7	329.1	332.4	3,131.2	684.7	1,671.4	775.0
Albuquerque, NM	8,793.2	1,144.9	7.4	53.3	344.8	739.4	7,648.3	1,587.1	5,091.8	969.4
Atlanta, GA	13,318.5	2,781.2	32.2	66.8	1,037.8	1,644.5	10,537.3	2,222.5	6,549.7	1,765.1
Sacramento, CA......	6,716.7	765.8	9.6	36.1	346.9	373.2	5,950.8	1,145.2	3,609.2	1,196.5
Fresno, CA	7,685.7	898.6	5.6	37.6	304.9	550.4	6,787.1	1,055.5	4,380.2	1,351.3
Tulsa, OK..........	6,832.0	1,122.3	8.4	61.6	187.5	864.8	5,709.7	1,369.5	3,479.7	860.5
Miami, FL..........	10,968.1	2,173.1	18.2	32.6	848.9	1,273.5	8,794.9	2,014.8	5,201.5	1,578.6
Omaha, NE.........	6,876.5	811.3	9.5	48.5	224.4	529.0	6,065.3	864.9	4,333.8	866.7
Oakland, CA........	6,273.1	1,261.1	20.0	80.1	482.9	678.1	5,012.0	877.6	2,916.8	1,217.6
Mesa, AZ	6,439.6	603.7	3.8	30.3	109.2	460.4	5,835.9	938.5	4,032.0	865.3
Minneapolis, MN	7,184.5	1,151.0	13.1	110.3	509.1	518.5	6,033.4	1,179.8	3,865.0	988.7
Colorado Springs, CO ...	4,967.2	455.0	4.2	58.5	118.3	274.0	4,512.2	851.8	3,316.8	343.6
Pittsburgh, PA	5,701.4	957.4	10.8	37.5	464.5	444.5	4,744.1	924.0	3,086.6	733.5
St. Louis, MO	14,547.6	2,279.2	35.6	32.2	925.9	1,285.5	12,268.3	2,303.3	7,714.8	2,250.2
Cincinnati, OH	6,704.8	840.1	6.6	85.7	423.8	323.9	5,864.7	1,497.2	3,755.1	612.5
Wichita, KS.........	6,293.9	604.4	9.0	51.1	172.8	371.5	5,689.5	1,091.3	4,111.1	487.1
Toledo, OH	7,661.2	758.9	3.8	52.0	328.4	374.7	6,902.3	1,627.8	4,401.8	872.7
Arlington, TX........	6,451.1	647.8	4.2	28.8	178.7	436.1	5,803.2	943.3	4,236.4	623.5
Santa Ana, CA.......	3,092.5	541.2	5.0	25.4	263.0	247.6	2,551.4	369.0	1,575.3	607.1
Buffalo, NY	6,918.9	1,249.6	13.3	60.1	531.4	644.8	5,669.3	1,433.1	3,359.3	876.8
Anaheim, CA........	3,020.9	430.8	3.4	25.6	130.5	271.3	2,590.1	478.6	1,638.3	473.2
Tampa, FL	11,094.5	2,102.8	12.5	77.4	719.4	1,293.5	8,991.7	2,035.6	5,053.9	1,902.1
Corpus Christi, TX	7,211.6	758.3	6.1	69.6	157.5	525.1	6,453.4	1,274.8	4,677.9	500.6
Newark, NJ.........	7,188.2	1,495.9	21.2	34.7	703.0	737.0	5,692.3	1,010.8	2,692.1	1,989.4
Riverside, CA	4,792.2	786.2	6.7	33.7	239.5	506.3	4,006.0	831.6	2,449.4	725.0
Raleigh, NC	7,035.3	742.1	9.4	32.2	278.5	422.0	6,293.2	1,460.7	4,311.6	520.8
St. Paul, MN	6,518.9	833.4	7.0	77.7	264.0	484.8	5,685.5	1,078.5	3,911.9	695.1
Anchorage, AK	4,943.1	585.5	3.8	74.9	132.9	373.8	4,357.6	589.0	3,380.6	388.0
Louisville, KY........	5,877.9	795.8	15.2	26.5	421.1	332.9	5,082.1	1,249.7	2,931.7	900.7
Aurora, CO	5,632.6	547.4	8.0	59.7	171.1	308.6	5,085.2	696.8	3,442.9	945.4
Birmingham, AL	8,545.0	1,213.7	32.5	93.9	402.4	684.9	7,331.4	1,679.4	4,931.6	720.3
Stockton, CA........	6,911.8	1,219.2	12.3	46.8	430.3	729.8	5,692.6	1,025.6	3,798.2	868.8
Lexington, KY	5,242.4	724.7	4.2	44.1	229.9	446.4	4,517.6	830.7	3,392.2	294.8

NA Not available.   [1] The rates for forcible rape, violent crime, and crime index are not shown because the forcible rape figures were not in accordance with national Uniform Crime Reporting guidelines.

Source: U.S. Federal Bureau of Investigation, *Crime in the United States,* annual. See also <http://www.fbi.gov/ucr/cius00/contents.pdf> (released 15 October 2001).

Law Enforcement, Courts, and Prisons   185

No. 287. Murder Victims—Circumstances and Weapons Used or Cause of Death: 1990 to 2000

[Based solely on police investigation. For definition of murder, see text, this section]

Characteristic	1990	1995	1999	2000	Characteristic	1990	1995	1999	2000
Murders, total (1,000).	20,273	20,232	13,011	12,943	Other motives.	19.4	21.6	21.0	26.2
Percent distribution	100.0	100.0	100.0	100.0	Unknown	24.8	28.9	29.6	40.3
CIRCUMSTANCES					TYPE OF WEAPON OR CAUSE OF DEATH				
Felonies, total.	20.8	17.7	17.0	21.6					
Robbery	9.2	9.3	8.1	10.5	Guns	64.3	68.2	65.2	84.9
Narcotics	6.7	5.1	4.5	5.7	Handguns.	49.8	55.8	51.2	66.9
Sex offenses	1.1	0.2	0.6	0.7	Cutting or stabbing	17.4	12.6	13.2	17.4
Other felonies	3.7	3.2	3.9	4.6	Blunt objects [1] . . . . . . [2] .	5.4	4.5	5.8	6.0
Suspected felonies	0.7	0.6	0.5	0.6	Personal weapons [2]	5.5	5.9	6.8	9.0
Argument, total	34.4	31.2	31.9	40.8	Strangulations,				
Property or money	2.5	1.7	1.6	2.1	asphyxiations	2.0	1.8	2.3	2.6
Romantic triangle	2.0	1.4	1.1	1.2	Fire.	1.4	0.8	1.0	1.3
Other arguments	29.8	28.2	29.2	37.5	All other [3]	4.0	6.1	5.8	8.2

[1] Refers to club, hammer, etc.   [2] Hands, fists, feet, etc.   [3] Includes poison, drowning, explosives, narcotics, and unknown.
Source: U.S. Federal Bureau of Investigation, *Crime in the United States*, annual. See also <http://www.fbi.gov/ucr/cius00/contents.pdf> (released 15 October 2001).

No. 288. Murder Victims by Age, Sex, and Race: 2000

Age	Total	Sex				Race			
		Male	Female	Unknown		White	Black	Other	Unknown
Total	**13,230**	10,032	3,169	29		6,417	6,303	339	171
Percent distribution	100.0	75.8	24.0	0.2		48.5	47.6	2.6	1.3
Under 18 yrs. old	1,342	902	439	1		686	604	35	17
18 yrs. old and over	11,618	8,959	2,657	2		5,615	5,607	301	95
Infant (under 1 yr. old).	226	125	100	1		127	89	3	7
1 to 4 yrs. old	286	158	128	-		151	126	7	2
5 to 8 yrs. old	89	47	42	-		53	30	5	1
9 to 12 yrs. old	63	34	29	-		38	23	2	-
13 to 16 yrs. old	378	284	94	-		179	186	9	4
17 to 19 yrs. old	1,220	1,030	190	-		546	633	31	10
20 to 24 yrs. old	2,433	2,077	356	-		946	1,427	47	13
25 to 29 yrs. old	1,881	1,557	324	-		748	1,065	52	16
30 to 34 yrs. old	1,522	1,176	345	1		704	773	37	8
35 to 39 yrs. old	1,275	900	375	-		634	593	31	17
40 to 44 yrs. old	1,160	825	335	-		642	475	33	10
45 to 49 yrs. old	765	547	218	-		430	303	26	6
50 to 54 yrs. old	507	379	128	-		311	174	17	5
55 to 59 yrs. old	345	255	90	-		213	114	13	5
60 to 64 yrs. old	217	153	64	-		147	58	8	4
65 to 69 yrs. old	157	88	69	-		101	49	5	2
70 to 74 yrs. old	162	98	64	-		118	41	3	-
75 yrs. old and over	274	128	145	1		213	52	7	2
Age unknown	270	171	73	26		116	92	3	59

- Represents zero.
Source: U.S. Federal Bureau of Investigation, *Crime in the United States*, annual. See also <http://www.fbi.gov/ucr/cius00/contents.pdf> (released 15 October 2001).

No. 289. Homicide Victims by Race and Sex: 1980 to 1999

[**Rates per 100,000 resident population in specified group.** Excludes deaths to nonresidents of United States. Deaths classified according to the tenth revision of the *International Classification of Diseases as of 1999*; see text, Section 2, Vital Statistics]

Year	Homicide victims					Homicide rate [2]				
		White		Black			White		Black	
	Total [1]	Male	Female	Male	Female	Total [1]	Male	Female	Male	Female
1980	24,278	10,381	3,177	8,385	1,898	10.7	10.9	3.2	66.6	13.5
1985	19,893	8,122	3,041	6,616	1,666	8.3	8.2	2.9	48.4	11.0
1990	24,932	9,147	3,006	9,981	2,163	10.0	9.0	2.8	69.2	13.5
1992	25,488	9,456	3,012	10,131	2,187	10.0	9.1	2.8	67.5	13.1
1993	26,009	9,054	3,232	10,640	2,297	10.1	8.6	3.0	69.7	13.6
1994	24,926	9,055	2,921	10,083	2,124	9.6	8.5	2.6	65.1	12.4
1995	22,895	8,336	3,028	8,847	1,936	8.7	7.8	2.7	56.3	11.1
1996	20,971	7,570	2,747	8,183	1,800	7.9	7.0	2.5	51.5	10.2
1997	19,846	7,343	2,570	7,601	1,652	7.4	6.7	2.3	47.1	9.3
1998	18,272	6,707	2,534	6,873	1,547	6.8	6.1	2.2	42.1	8.6
1999 [3]	16,889	6,162	2,466	6,214	1,434	6.2	5.6	2.2	37.5	7.8

[1] Includes races not shown separately. .   [2] Rate based on enumerated population figures as of April 1 for 1980 and 1990; July 1 estimates for other years.   [3] Effective with data for 1999, causes of death are classified by The Tenth Revision International Classification of Diseases (ICD-10), replacing the Ninth Revision (ICD-9) used for 1979-98 data. Breaks in the comparability of some cause of death statistics result from changes in category titles, changes in the structure and content of the classification, and changes in coding rules used to select the underlying cause of death. In ICD-9, the category Homicide also includes death as a result of legal intervention. ICD-10 has two separate categories for these two causes of death. Some caution should be used in comparing data between 1998 and 1999.
Source: U.S. National Center for Health Statistics, *Vital Statistics of the United States*, annual; and *National Vital Statistics Reports (NVSR)* (formerly *Monthly Vital Statistics Report*); and unpublished data.

No. 290. Forcible Rape—Number and Rate: 1980 to 2000

[For definition of rape, see text, this section]

Item	1980	1990	1993	1994	1995	1996	1997	1998	1999	2000
NUMBER										
Total	82,990	102,560	106,010	102,220	97,460	96,250	96,153	93,144	89,411	90,186
By force	63,599	86,541	92,360	89,297	85,249	84,053	84,931	82,823	79,697	81,111
Attempt.	19,391	16,019	13,650	12,923	12,211	12,197	11,222	10,321	9,714	9,075
RATE										
Per 100,000 population	36.8	41.1	41.1	39.3	37.1	36.3	35.9	34.5	32.8	32.0
Per 100,000 females	71.6	80.5	80.3	76.7	72.5	71.0	70.4	67.4	63.9	62.9
Per 100,000 females 12 years old and over.	86.3	96.6	96.4	92.0	87.1	85.3	84.4	80.7	76.5	69.8
AVERAGE ANNUAL PERCENT CHANGE IN RATE [1]										
Per 100,000 population	6.1	8.1	-4.0	-4.4	-5.6	-2.2	-1.0	-4.1	-5.2	-2.4
Per 100,000 females 12 years old and over.	6.0	8.2	-4.1	-4.6	-5.3	-2.1	-1.0	-4.5	-5.3	-1.8

[1] Represents annual average from prior year shown except for 1980, from 1979 and for 1990, from 1989.

Source: U.S. Federal Bureau of Investigation, *Population-at-Risk Rates and Selected Crime Indicators*, annual.

No. 291. Robbery and Property Crimes by Type and Selected Characteristic: 1990 to 2000

[For definition of crime, see text, this section]

Characteristic of offenses	Number of offenses (1,000)				Rate per 100,000 inhabitants				Average value lost (dol.)	
	1990	1995	1999	2000	1990	1995	1999	2000	1999	2000
Robbery, total [1]	639	581	409	408	256.3	220.9	150.1	144.9	1,131	1,127
Type of crime:										
Street or highway	359	315	198	188	144.2	120.0	72.6	66.7	856	858
Commercial house.	73	71	56	57	29.5	27.2	20.2	20.1	1,549	1,685
Gas station	18	13	9	12	7.1	5.1	3.2	4.1	627	679
Convenience store.	39	30	25	26	15.6	11.4	9.1	9.3	620	566
Residence	62	63	50	50	25.1	24.0	18.3	17.7	1,231	1,243
Bank.	9	9	8	9	3.8	3.5	2.9	3.1	4,552	4,379
Weapon used:										
Firearm	234	238	163	161	94.1	90.6	59.9	57.0	(NA)	(NA)
Knife or cutting instrument. . . .	76	53	35	36	30.7	20.1	12.7	12.8	(NA)	(NA)
Other dangerous weapon	61	53	41	53	24.5	20.2	14.9	18.9	(NA)	(NA)
Strongarm	268	236	171	159	107.7	90.0	62.3	56.4	(NA)	(NA)
Burglary, total	3,074	2,594	2,101	2,050	1,232.2	987.0	770.4	728.4	1,458	1,458
Forcible entry.	2,150	1,737	1,350	1,297	864.5	661.2	495.0	460.7	(NA)	(NA)
Unlawful entry.	678	657	605	615	272.8	250.1	221.8	218.7	(NA)	(NA)
Attempted forcible entry	245	201	145	138	98.7	76.4	53.2	49.0	(NA)	(NA)
Residence.	2,033	1,736	1,394	1,335	817.4	660.6	511.3	474.3	1,441	1,378
Nonresidence.	1,041	859	706	715	418.5	327.0	258.7	254.1	1,490	1,610
Occurred during the night.	1,135	905	699	699	456.4	344.4	256.2	248.3	(NA)	(NA)
Occurred during the day	1,151	1,000	798	836	462.8	380.5	292.7	297.2	(NA)	(NA)
Larceny-theft, total	7,946	7,998	6,956	6,966	3,185.1	3,043.2	2,550.7	2,475.3	678	727
Pocket picking	81	51	43	36	32.4	19.4	15.8	12.7	451	437
Purse snatching	82	51	40	37	32.8	19.5	14.8	13.2	392	387
Shoplifting.	1,291	1,205	1,003	959	519.1	458.4	367.8	340.7	165	185
From motor vehicles	1,744	1,940	1,789	1,754	701.3	738.5	656.1	623.3	693	692
Motor vehicle accessories	1,185	964	724	677	476.3	367.0	265.5	240.6	451	451
Bicycles	443	501	326	312	178.2	190.5	119.5	110.9	338	273
From buildings	1,118	1,004	947	914	449.4	382.1	347.2	324.6	1,015	1,184
From coin-operated machines. . .	63	50	46	46	25.4	18.9	17.0	16.2	376	272
Other	1,940	2,235	2,039	2,232	780.0	850.5	747.8	793.0	912	957
Motor vehicles, total [2]. . . .	1,636	1,472	1,152	1,166	655.8	560.3	422.5	414.2	6,104	6,581
Automobiles.	1,304	1,154	856	877	524.3	439.2	314.1	311.5	(NA)	(NA)
Trucks and buses	238	240	215	209	95.5	91.2	78.8	74.1	(NA)	(NA)

NA Not available. [1] Includes other crimes not shown separately. [2] Includes other types of motor vehicles not shown separately.

Source: U.S. Federal Bureau of Investigation, *Population-at-Risk Rates and Selected Crime Indicators,* annual.

U.S. Census Bureau, Statistical Abstract of the United States: 2002

No. 292. Hate Crimes—Number of Incidents, Offenses, Victims, and Known Offenders by Bias Motivation: 2000

[The FBI collected statistics on hate crimes from 11,720 law enforcement agencies representing over 238 million inhabitants in 2000. Hate crime offenses cover incidents motivated by race, religion, sexual orientation, ethnicity/national origin, and disability]

Bias motivation	Incidents reported	Offenses	Victims [1]	Known offenders [2]
Total bias motivations	8,224	9,638	10,140	7,705
Race, total	4,433	5,300	5,532	4,559
Anti-White	910	1,093	1,125	1,202
Anti-Black	2,937	3,482	3,609	2,865
Anti-American Indian/Alaskan native	59	64	66	60
Anti-Asian/Pacific Islander	282	322	347	275
Anti-multiracial group	245	339	385	157
Ethnicity/national origin, total	921	1,180	1,232	1,030
Anti-Hispanic	566	749	777	711
Anti-other ethnicity/national origin	355	431	455	319
Religion, total	1,493	1,581	1,726	598
Anti-Jewish	1,121	1,177	1,285	419
Anti-Catholic	57	62	64	33
Anti-Protestant	59	62	62	23
Anti-Islamic	29	34	37	21
Anti-other religious group	174	189	212	79
Anti-multireligious group	49	51	59	22
Anti-atheism/agnosticism/etc	4	6	7	1
Sexual orientation, total	1,332	1,524	1,596	1,474
Anti-male homosexual	905	1,033	1,070	1,098
Anti-female homosexual	192	227	244	177
Anti-homosexual	188	217	233	159
Anti-heterosexual	26	26	28	25
Anti-bisexual	21	21	21	15
Disability, total	38	38	38	36
Anti-physical	20	20	20	22
Anti-mental	18	18	18	14
Multiple bias	7	15	16	8

[1] The term "victim" may refer to a person, business, institution, or a society as a whole. [2] The term "known offender" does not imply that the identity of the suspect is known, but only that an attribute of the suspect is identified which distinguishes him/her from an unknown offender.

Source: U.S. Federal Bureau of Investigation, Hate Crime Statistics, annual; and <http://www.fbi.gov/ucr/cius00/hate.pdf> released 15 October 2001, and subsequent updates because of late data submissions.

No. 293. Hate Crimes Reported by State: 2000

[See headnote, Table 292]

State	Number of participating agencies	Population covered (1,000)	Agencies submitting incidents	Incidents reported	State	Number of participating agencies	Population covered (1,000)	Agencies submitting incidents	Incidents reported
United States	11,720	237,663	1,929	8,224	Missouri	186	3,843	26	70
Alabama	([1])	([1])	([1])	([1])	Montana	102	901	8	19
Alaska	1	261	1	4	Nebraska	202	1,361	6	17
Arizona	88	4,607	22	281	Nevada	36	1,997	8	85
Arkansas	4	77	3	3	New Hampshire	110	658	20	32
California	722	33,964	259	1,943	New Jersey	564	8,414	241	652
Colorado	234	4,299	34	102	New Mexico	44	1,084	3	15
Connecticut	97	3,316	58	152	New York	540	18,983	36	608
Delaware	52	784	9	34	North Carolina	223	4,794	15	39
Dist. of Columbia	2	572	2	6	North Dakota	80	580	5	5
Florida	491	15,955	107	240	Ohio	347	7,471	50	255
Georgia	80	1,077	4	35	Oklahoma	297	3,444	24	80
Hawaii	([1])	([1])	([1])	([1])	Oregon	171	3,411	29	142
Idaho	114	1,274	26	46	Pennsylvania	933	11,449	32	141
Illinois	46	4,463	45	183	Rhode Island	48	1,048	10	48
Indiana	167	4,416	31	106	South Carolina	352	4,009	19	36
Iowa	220	2,807	15	34	South Dakota	120	752	4	8
Kansas	24	794	24	75	Tennessee	421	5,676	73	237
Kentucky	315	3,287	38	77	Texas	941	20,609	72	287
Louisiana	173	3,828	8	12	Utah	127	2,226	29	75
Maine	181	1,270	9	28	Vermont	43	508	14	19
Maryland	146	5,294	33	218	Virginia	384	6,981	59	336
Massachusetts	341	6,278	100	470	Washington	236	5,352	57	242
Michigan	620	9,819	156	425	West Virginia	271	1,679	25	75
Minnesota	311	4,914	55	169	Wisconsin	368	5,361	22	47
Mississippi	78	1,220	1	2	Wyoming	67	493	2	9

[1] Did not report.

Source: U.S. Federal Bureau of Investigation, Hate Crime Statistics, annual; and <http://www.fbi.gov/ucr/cius00/hate00.pdf> (released: 15 October 2001) and subsequent updates because of late data submissions.

No. 294. Criminal Victimizations and Victimization Rates: 1995 to 2000

[Based on National Crime Victimization Survey; see text, this section, and Appendix III]

Type of crime	Number of victimizations (1,000)				Victimization rates [1]			
	1995	1998	1999	2000	1995	1998	1999	2000
All crimes, total	**39,926**	**31,307**	**28,780**	**25,893**	**(X)**	**(X)**	**(X)**	**(X)**
Personal crimes [2]	**10,436**	**8,412**	**7,565**	**6,597**	**46.2**	**37.9**	**33.7**	**29.1**
Crimes of violence.	10,022	8,116	7,357	6,323	44.5	36.6	32.8	27.9
Completed violence	2,960	2,564	2,278	2,044	12.9	11.6	10.1	9.0
Attempted/threatened violence	7,061	5,553	5,079	4,279	31.6	25.0	22.6	18.9
Rape/sexual assault.	363	333	383	261	1.6	1.5	1.7	1.2
Rape/attempted rape.	252	200	201	147	1.1	0.9	0.9	0.6
Rape	153	110	141	92	0.7	0.5	0.6	0.4
Attempted rape.	99	89	60	55	0.4	0.4	0.3	0.2
Sexual assault	112	133	182	114	0.5	0.6	0.8	0.5
Robbery.	1,171	886	810	732	5.3	4.0	3.6	3.2
Completed/property taken	753	610	530	520	3.5	2.7	2.4	2.3
With injury	224	170	189	160	1.0	0.8	0.8	0.7
Without injury	529	439	341	360	2.4	2.0	1.5	1.6
Attempted to take property	418	277	280	212	1.8	1.2	1.2	0.9
With injury	84	70	78	66	0.4	0.3	0.3	0.3
Without injury	335	207	202	146	1.4	0.9	0.9	0.6
Assault	8,487	6,897	6,164	5,330	37.6	31.1	27.4	23.5
Aggravated	2,050	1,674	1,503	1,293	8.8	7.5	6.7	5.7
With injury	533	547	449	346	2.4	2.5	2.0	1.5
Threatened with weapon	1,517	1,126	1,054	946	6.4	5.1	4.7	4.2
Simple	6,437	5,224	4,660	4,038	28.9	23.5	20.8	17.8
With minor injury.	1,426	1,175	998	989	6.0	5.3	4.4	4.4
Without injury	5,012	4,048	3,662	3,048	22.9	18.2	16.3	13.4
Personal theft [3]	414	296	208	274	1.7	1.3	0.9	1.2
Property crimes	**29,490**	**22,895**	**21,215**	**19,297**	**279.5**	**217.4**	**198.0**	**178.1**
Household burglary	5,004	4,054	3,652	3,444	47.4	38.5	34.1	31.8
Completed	4,232	3,380	3,064	2,909	40.0	32.1	28.6	26.9
Attempted forcible entry	773	674	587	534	7.4	6.4	5.5	4.9
Motor vehicle theft.	1,717	1,138	1,068	937	16.2	10.8	10.0	8.6
Completed	1,163	822	808	642	10.8	7.8	7.5	5.9
Attempted.	554	316	260	295	5.5	3.0	2.4	2.7
Theft.	22,769	17,703	16,495	14,916	215.9	168.1	153.9	137.7
Completed [4]	21,857	17,074	15,964	14,300	207.6	162.1	149.0	132.0
Attempted.	911	629	532	616	8.4	6.0	5.0	5.7

X Not applicable.   [1] Per 1,000 persons age 12 or older or per 1,000 households.   [2] The victimization survey cannot measure murder because of the inability to question the victim.   [3] Includes pocket picking, purse snatching, and attempted purse snatching.   [4] Includes thefts in which the amount taken was not ascertained.
Source: U.S. Bureau of Justice Statistics, *Criminal Victimization*, annual; and *Criminal Victimization 1999, Changes 1998-99 with Trends 1993-99*, Series NCJ-182734. See also <http://www.ojp.usdoj.gov/bjs/pub/pdf/cv00.pdf>.

No. 295. Victimization Rates by Type of Violent Crime and Characteristic of the Victim: 2000

[**Rate per 1,000 persons age 12 years or older**. Based on National Crime Victimization Survey; see text, this section, and Appendix III]

Characteristic	Crimes of violence							
	All crime	All crimes of violence	Rape/ sexual assault	Robbery	Assault			Personal theft
					Total	Aggra- vated	Simple	
Total	**29.1**	**27.9**	**1.2**	**3.2**	**23.5**	**5.7**	**17.8**	**1.2**
Male.	33.9	32.9	[1]0.1	4.5	28.3	8.3	19.9	1.0
Female	24.6	23.2	2.1	2.0	19.0	3.2	15.8	1.4
12 to 15 yrs. old	61.9	60.1	2.1	4.2	53.8	9.9	43.9	1.8
16 to 19 yrs. old	67.3	64.3	4.3	7.3	52.7	14.3	38.3	3.0
20 to 24 yrs. old	50.5	49.4	2.1	6.2	41.2	10.9	30.3	[1]1.1
25 to 34 yrs. old	36.3	34.8	1.3	3.9	29.5	6.8	22.7	1.5
35 to 49 yrs. old	22.7	21.8	0.8	2.7	18.4	4.7	13.7	0.9
50 to 64 yrs. old	14.2	13.7	[1]0.4	2.1	11.1	2.8	8.4	[1]0.5
65 yrs. old and over. . .	4.9	3.7	[1]0.1	[1]0.7	2.9	0.9	2.0	1.2
White	28.2	27.1	1.1	2.7	23.3	5.4	17.9	1.1
Black	35.3	35.3	1.2	7.2	26.9	7.7	19.2	1.9
Other	29.1	20.7	[1]1.1	2.8	16.7	5.2	11.5	[1]1.8
Hispanic	30.8	28.4	[1]0.5	5.0	23.0	5.6	17.4	2.4
Non-Hispanic	28.8	27.7	1.2	3.0	23.5	5.7	17.8	1.1
Household income:								
Less than $7,500. . .	62.6	60.3	5.2	7.1	48.1	14.7	33.4	[1]2.3
$7,500-$14,999	39.9	37.8	1.7	4.7	31.3	9.5	21.8	2.1
$15,000-$24,999 . . .	33.0	31.8	1.4	3.2	27.2	6.1	21.2	1.2
$25,000-$34,999 . . .	31.2	29.8	1.9	4.2	23.7	6.2	17.5	1.4
$35,000-$49,999 . . .	29.1	28.5	0.8	2.3	25.3	6.2	19.2	[1]0.6
$50,000-$74,999 . . .	24.7	23.7	1.0	3.6	19.1	3.8	15.3	1.0
$75,000 or more . . .	23.5	22.3	[1]0.2	2.0	20.2	4.4	15.7	1.2

[1] Based on 10 or fewer sample cases.
Source: U.S. Bureau of Justice Statistics, *Criminal Victimization*, annual; and *Criminal Victimization 1999, Changes 1998-99 with Trends 1993-99*, series NCJ-182734. See also <http://www.ojp.usdoj.gov/bjs/pub/pdf/cv00.pdf>.

Law Enforcement, Courts, and Prisons   189

No. 296. Victim-Offender Relationship in Crimes of Violence by Characteristics of the Criminal Incident: 2000

[In percent. Covers only crimes of violence. Based on National Crime Victimization Survey; see text, this section, and Appendix III]

Characteristics of incident	Total	Rape/ sexual assault	Robbery	Assault Total	Aggra- vated[1]	Simple
Total	100	100	100	100	100	100
Victim/offender relationship: [2]						
Relatives	11	7	4	12	8	13
Well-known	26	31	14	27	22	29
Casual acquaintance	16	24	6	17	11	19
Stranger	47	38	76	44	60	39
Time of day: [3]						
6 a.m. to 6 p.m.	51	31	41	53	48	55
6 p.m. to midnight	36	42	44	35	41	33
Midnight to 6 a.m.	10	22	13	9	10	9
Location of crime:						
At or near victim's home or lodging	29	39	26	29	29	28
Friend's/relative's/neighbor's home	8	24	2	9	9	8
Commercial places	14	4	8	15	13	16
Parking lots/garages	7	3	13	7	8	6
School	13	4	5	14	7	17
Streets other than near victim's home	19	7	36	17	24	15
Other [4]	10	19	11	10	11	9
Victim's activity:						
At work or traveling to or from work	21	4	18	22	22	22
School.	12	3	4	13	7	15
Activities at home	24	35	18	24	24	25
Shopping/errands	4	1	10	3	3	3
Leisure activities away from home	23	38	25	22	25	21
Traveling	9	8	20	8	11	7
Other	7	11	5	7	8	7
Distance from victim's home:						
Inside home or lodging.	16	39	14	15	11	16
Near victim's home	16	12	15	17	21	16
1 mile or less	18	11	25	18	22	16
5 miles or less	24	22	28	24	18	25
50 miles or less	21	11	15	23	23	23
More than 50 miles	3	3	3	3	5	3
Weapons:						
No weapons present	73	94	42	77	5	100
Weapons present	27	6	58	23	95	-
Firearm	8	3	25	6	24	-
Other type of weapon [5]	19	4	33	18	71	-

- Represents zero. [1] An aggravated assault is any assault in which an offender possesses or uses a weapon or inflicts serious injury. [2] Excludes "don't know" relationships. [3] Excludes "not known and not available" time of day. [4] Includes areas on public transportation or inside station, in apartment yard, park, field, playground, or other areas. [5] Includes knives, other sharp objects, blunt objects, and other types of weapons.
Source: U.S. Bureau of Justice Statistics, *Criminal Victimization,* annual; and *Criminal Victimization 1999, Changes 1998-99 with Trends 1993-99,* Series NCJ-182734. See also <http://www.ojp.usdoj.gov/bjs/pub/pdf/cv00.pdf>.

No. 297. Property Victimization Rates by Selected Household Characteristic: 2000

[Victimizations per 1,000 households. Based on National Crime Victimization Survey; see text, this section and Appendix III]

Characteristic	Total	Burglary	Motor vehicle theft	Theft
Total	178.1	31.8	8.6	137.7
Race:				
White	173.3	29.4	7.9	136.0
Black	212.2	47.6	13.2	151.4
Other	171.3	32.4	10.4	128.6
Ethnicity:				
Hispanic	227.0	41.7	19.7	165.6
Non-Hispanic	173.4	31.0	7.6	134.7
Household income:				
Less than $7,500	220.9	61.7	7.9	151.2
$7,500-$14,999	167.1	41.1	9.1	116.8
$15,000-$24,999.	193.1	39.3	9.9	143.8
$25,000-$34,999.	192.2	33.3	9.5	149.4
$35,000-$49,999.	192.9	32.0	9.6	151.4
$50,000-$74,999.	181.9	24.0	10.0	147.9
$75,000 or more.	197.2	27.7	7.0	162.5
Residence:				
Urban.	222.1	40.9	13.1	168.1
Suburban	163.7	27.2	8.1	128.4
Rural	152.6	29.5	4.4	110.7
Form of tenure:				
Home owned	153.4	26.2	6.7	120.6
Home rented	228.3	43.2	12.6	172.5

Source: U.S. Bureau of Justice Statistics, *Criminal Victimization,* annual; and *Criminal Victimization 2000, Changes 1999-00 with Trends 1993-00,* Series NCJ-182734. See also <http://www.ojp.usdoj.gov/bjs/pub/pdf/cv00.pdf>.

No. 298. Violence by Intimate Partners by Sex, 1993 to 1998, and by Type of Crime, 1998

[Violent acts covered include murder, rape, sexual assault, robbery, and aggravated and simple assault. Intimate partners involve current spouses, former spouses, current boy/girlfriends, and former boy/girlfriends. Based on the National Criminal Victimization Survey; see text, this section and Appendix III. Homicide data were obtained from the Federal Bureau of Investigation]

Year and type of crime	All persons		Females		Males	
	Number	Rate per 100,000 [1]	Number	Rate per 100,000 [1]	Number	Rate per 100,000 [1]
1993	1,235,660	584.2	1,072,090	982.0	163,570	159.8
1994	1,179,360	551.8	1,003,180	908.9	176,180	170.4
1995	1,069,190	495.7	953,700	855.8	115,490	110.8
1996	1,030,020	472.6	879,290	781.7	150,730	142.9
1997	956,330	433.8	848,480	747.3	107,850	100.9
1998, total	1,033,660	465.9	876,340	766.8	157,330	146.2
Murder.................	1,830	0.8	1,320	1.2	510	0.5
Rape or sexual assault	63,490	28.6	63,490	55.6	(B)	(B)
Robbery................	103,940	46.8	101,830	89.1	(B)	(B)
Aggravated Assault...........	187,970	84.7	140,050	122.5	47,910	44.5
Simple Assault...........	676,440	304.9	569,650	498.4	106,790	99.2

B Base figure too small to meet statistical standards for reliability of derived figure. In this case, 10 or fewer sample cases.
[1] Rates are the number of victimizations per 100,000 persons.

Source: U.S. Bureau of Justice Statistics, *Intimate Partner Victimization,* Series NCJ 178247, May 2000.

No. 299. Persons Arrested by Charge and Selected Characteristics: 2000

[9,117.0 represents 9,117,000. Represents arrests (not charges) reported by approximately 9,017 agencies with a total 2000 population of approximately 182 million as estimated by FBI. Age and Sex data is mandatory, while race data is optional and not always reported with arrest data; hence, two different total number of arrests.

Offense charged	Persons arrested (1,000)							
	Total	Male	Female	Total	White	Black	American Indian or Alaskan Native	Asian or Pacific Islander
Total	9,117.0	7,096.2	2,020.8	9,068.0	6,324.0	2,528.4	112.2	104.4
Serious crimes [1]:								
Murder and nonnegligent manslaughter	8.7	7.8	0.9	7.7	4.2	4.2	0.1	0.1
Forcible rape................	17.9	17.7	0.2	17.9	11.4	6.1	0.2	0.2
Robbery....................	72.3	65.0	7.3	72.1	31.9	38.9	0.4	0.9
Aggravated assault	316.6	252.9	63.7	315.7	200.6	107.5	3.5	4.1
Burglary....................	189.3	164.2	25.2	188.7	131.0	53.6	1.8	2.3
Larceny/theft................	782.1	501.1	281.0	779.2	519.7	236.8	9.9	12.8
Motor vehicle theft	98.7	83.1	15.5	98.3	54.5	40.9	1.1	1.8
Arson	10.7	9.1	1.6	10.6	8.1	2.3	0.1	0.1
All other nonserious crimes:								
Other assaults................	858.4	661.2	197.2	855.5	564.6	269.7	11.7	9.5
Forgery and counterfeiting........	71.3	43.5	27.8	70.8	48.2	21.2	0.4	1.0
Fraud	213.8	117.9	95.9	212.0	142.7	66.7	1.2	1.5
Embezzlement	12.6	6.3	6.3	12.5	8.0	4.3	0.1	0.2
Stolen property—buying, receiving, possessing	78.7	65.0	13.7	78.4	46.2	30.7	0.6	0.9
Vandalism...................	184.5	155.9	28.6	184.0	139.7	39.8	2.6	2.0
Weapons; carrying, possess ing etc. ..	105.3	96.8	8.5	105.0	64.4	38.6	0.8	1.2
Prostitution and commercialized vice..	61.4	23.2	38.1	61.3	35.6	24.2	0.5	1.0
Sex offenses (except forcible rape and prostitution)	61.2	56.7	4.5	60.9	45.3	14.1	0.7	0.8
Drug abuse violations	1,042.3	858.6	183.7	1,039.1	667.5	358.6	5.5	7.5
Gambling	7.2	6.4	0.8	7.1	2.2	4.6	-	0.3
Offenses against family and children ..	91.3	70.9	20.4	90.5	61.2	26.8	0.9	1.6
Driving under the influence	915.9	765.7	150.3	900.1	793.7	86.2	11.9	8.3
Liquor laws.................	435.7	335.6	100.1	433.6	371.2	46.1	13.1	3.3
Drunkenness.................	423.3	367.8	55.5	421.9	357.3	57.8	4.6	2.1
Disorderly conduct	421.5	325.5	96.1	419.4	273.9	136.6	6.0	2.9
Vagrancy	22.0	17.4	4.6	22.0	11.8	9.5	0.6	0.1
Suspicion	3.7	3.0	0.7	3.7	2.5	1.1	-	-
Curfew and loitering law violations ...	105.7	72.6	33.1	105.6	76.2	26.1	1.2	2.1
Runaways	93.6	38.6	55.0	93.3	71.2	16.7	1.3	4.1
All other offenses (except traffic).....	2,411.2	1,906.8	504.4	2,400.9	1,579.2	758.7	31.4	31.6

- Represents zero or rounds to zero.   [1] Includes arson.

Source: U.S. Federal Bureau of Investigation, *Crime in the United States,* annual. See also <http://www.fbi.gov/ucr/Cius00/00crime1.pdf>.

No. 300. Juvenile Arrests for Selected Offenses: 1980 to 2000

[169,439 represents 169,439,000. Juveniles are persons under 18 years of age]

Offense	1980	1990	1993	1994	1995	1996	1997	1998	1999	2000
Number of contributing agencies...............	8,178	10,765	10,277	10,693	10,037	10,026	9,472	9,589	9,502	9,904
Population covered (1,000) ...	169,439	204,543	213,705	208,035	206,762	195,805	194,925	194,612	195,324	204,965
NUMBER										
Violent crime, total	77,220	97,103	122,434	125,141	123,131	104,455	100,273	90,201	81,715	78,450
Murder	1,475	2,661	3,473	3,114	2,812	2,184	1,887	1,587	1,131	1,027
Forcible rape	3,668	4,971	5,490	4,873	4,556	4,228	4,127	3,988	3,544	3,402
Robbery	38,529	34,944	44,598	47,046	47,240	39,788	36,419	29,989	26,125	24,206
Aggravated assault	33,548	54,527	68,873	70,108	68,523	58,255	57,840	54,637	50,915	49,815
Weapon law violations......	21,203	33,123	54,414	52,278	46,506	40,145	39,358	34,122	31,307	28,514
Drug abuse, total	86,685	66,300	90,618	124,931	149,236	148,783	155,444	148,066	138,774	146,594
Sale and manufacturing ...	13,004	24,575	27,635	32,746	34,077	32,558	30,761	29,312	26,134	26,432
Heroin/cocaine	1,318	17,511	18,716	20,327	19,187	17,465	15,855	15,094	12,686	11,000
Marijuana...........	8,876	4,372	6,144	8,812	10,682	11,489	11,208	10,808	10,770	11,792
Synthetic narcotics.....	465	346	455	465	701	614	671	813	722	945
Dangerous nonnarcotic drugs.............	2,345	2,346	2,320	3,142	3,507	2,990	3,027	2,597	1,956	2,695
Possession	73,681	41,725	62,983	92,185	115,159	116,225	124,683	118,754	112,640	120,162
Heroin/cocaine	2,614	15,194	17,726	21,004	21,253	17,560	18,328	16,278	13,445	12,586
Marijuana...........	64,465	20,940	37,915	61,003	82,015	87,712	94,046	91,467	89,523	95,962
Synthetic narcotics.....	1,524	1,155	1,008	1,227	2,047	1,713	1,987	1,916	1,581	2,052
Dangerous nonnarcotic drugs.............	5,078	4,436	6,334	8,951	9,844	9,240	10,322	9,093	8,091	9,832

Source: U.S. Federal Bureau of Investigation, *Crime in the United States,* annual. See also http://www.fbi.gov/ucr/Cius_00/00crime\.pdf>.

No. 301. Immigration and Naturalization Service Enforcement Activities: 1990 to 2000

[For fiscal years ending in year shown. See text, Section 8, State and Local Government Finances and Employment]

Item	Unit	1990	1994	1995	1996	1997	1998	1999	2000
Deportable aliens located........	1,000	1,169.9	1,094.7	1,394.6	1,650.0	1,536.5	1,679.4	1,714.0	1,814.7
Border Patrol.............	1,000	1,103.4	1,031.7	1,324.2	1,549.9	1,413.0	1,555.8	1,579.0	1,676.4
Southwestern border	1,000	(NA)	979.1	1,271.4	1,507.0	1,368.7	1,516.7	1,537.0	1,643.7
Mexican..............	1,000	1,054.8	999.9	1,293.5	1,523.1	1,387.7	1,522.9	1,534.5	1,636.9
Canadian.............	1,000	5.7	3.4	3.5	2.7	2.9	2.3	2.7	2.2
Other	1,000	42.8	28.4	27.2	24.0	22.4	30.5	41.8	37.3
Number of seizures by Border Patrol..............	Number...	17,275	9,134	9,327	11,129	11,792	14,401	16,803	17,269
Value of seizures by Border Patrol.	Mil. dol....	843.6	1,622.0	2,011.8	1,256.0	1,094.6	1,405.0	2,004.0	1,945.0
Narcotics................	Mil. dol....	797.8	1,555.7	1,965.3	1,208.8	1,046.3	1,340.0	1,919.0	1,848.0
Aliens expelled: Formal removals [1]........	1,000	30.0	45.7	45.2	69.7	114.4	173.0	180.3	184.8
Voluntary departures [2]......	1,000	1,022.5	1,029.1	1,313.8	1,573.4	1,440.7	1,570.1	1,574.5	1,675.3

NA Not available. [1] Include deportations, exclusions, and removals. [2] Includes aliens under docket control required to depart and voluntary departures not under docket control.

Source: U.S. Immigration and Naturalization Service, Statistical Yearbook, annual; and unpublished data.

U.S. Census Bureau, Statistical Abstract of the United States: 2002

No. 302. Drug Use by Arrestees in Major U.S. Cities by Type of Drug and Sex: 2000

[**Percent testing positive.** Based on data from the Arrestee Drug Abuse Monitoring Program]

City	Male				Female			
	Any drug [1]	Marijuana	Cocaine	Opiates	Any drug [1]	Marijuana	Cocaine	Opiates
Albuquerque, NM	64.9	47.3	34.8	11.7	57.5	18.4	41.4	13.8
Atlanta, GA	70.4	38.2	48.5	2.8	71.7	26.3	57.6	3.4
Chicago, IL	75.9	45.7	37.1	27.0	79.5	26.4	59.2	40.0
Cleveland, OH	72.0	49.2	38.4	3.7	68.2	24.0	52.0	6.6
Dallas, TX	54.5	35.8	27.7	3.0	38.8	20.9	23.9	4.5
Denver, CO	63.7	40.9	35.4	3.4	70.8	33.8	46.9	5.8
Detroit, MI	69.5	49.8	24.4	7.8	70.6	24.2	42.4	24.2
Houston, TX	57.2	35.8	31.5	7.4	51.7	26.7	31.7	3.3
Indianapolis, IN	64.1	48.9	31.1	3.4	72.3	38.3	45.4	6.4
Las Vegas, NV	58.5	33.3	22.5	4.8	60.8	25.3	27.4	4.8
Los Angeles, CA	(NA)	(NA)	(NA)	(NA)	64.6	31.5	33.1	7.7
Miami, FL	62.8	38.5	43.5	4.0	(NA)	(NA)	(NA)	(NA)
New Orleans, LA	69.4	46.6	34.8	15.5	56.7	28.0	41.1	8.5
New York, NY	79.8	40.4	48.6	20.4	74.9	28.2	53.0	19.1
Oklahoma City, OK.	71.4	57.0	22.4	3.2	67.2	44.7	27.2	4.6
Philadelphia, PA.	71.9	49.4	30.9	11.8	59.3	22.2	40.7	11.1
Phoenix, AZ	65.5	33.7	31.9	6.6	65.9	23.1	35.0	6.4
Portland, OR	64.3	35.6	21.9	14.1	69.4	26.2	29.9	22.2
Sacramento, CA.	73.5	50.0	18.4	3.3	(NA)	(NA)	(NA)	(NA)
San Antonio, TX.	52.9	41.6	19.1	9.9	(NA)	(NA)	(NA)	(NA)
San Diego, CA.	63.7	38.6	14.8	6.0	66.4	27.2	26.1	7.5
San Jose, CA	52.9	35.9	12.1	5.9	66.7	29.4	7.8	3.9
Seattle, WA.	64.1	37.8	31.2	9.9	(NA)	(NA)	(NA)	(NA)
Tucson, AZ	69.4	45.1	40.8	8.8	70.7	28.5	49.6	17.9
Washington, DC.	(NA)	(NA)	(NA)	(NA)	(NA)	(NA)	(NA)	(NA)

NA Not available.   [1] Includes other drugs not shown separately.

Source: U.S. National Institute of Justice, *2000 Annual Report on Drug Use Among Adult and Juvenile Arrestees,* June 2001.

No. 303. Drug Arrest Rates for Drug Abuse Violations, 1990 to 2000, and by Region, 2000

[**Rate per 100,000 inhabitants.** Based on Census Bureau estimated resident population as of **July 1, except 1990, enumerated as of April 1.** For composition of regions, see map, inside front cover]

Offense	1990	1995	1999	2000					
				Total	Region				
					North-east	Midwest	South	West	
Drug arrest rate, total	**435.3**	**564.7**	**583.7**	**587.1**	**751.2**	**397.0**	**542.3**	**638.4**	
Sale and/or manufacture	139.0	140.7	126.4	122.7	201.7	97.8	97.5	108.5	
Heroin or cocaine [1]	93.7	83.7	70.1	60.8	139.1	18.4	49.5	42.4	
Marijuana.	26.4	32.7	33.8	34.2	48.0	34.3	29.0	29.7	
Synthetic or manufactured drugs	2.7	3.9	6.3	6.4	3.5	2.4	11.4	5.4	
Other dangerous nonnarcotic drugs . .	16.2	20.3	16.1	21.3	11.0	42.7	7.6	31.1	
Possession	296.3	423.9	457.3	464.4	549.6	299.2	444.8	529.9	
Heroin or cocaine [1]	144.4	157.4	142.4	138.7	196.1	50.7	123.5	170.0	
Marijuana.	104.9	192.7	237.0	244.4	322.3	192.7	276.0	182.5	
Synthetic or manufactured drugs	6.6	8.5	10.4	12.0	6.8	6.4	16.3	14.4	
Other dangerous nonnarcotic drugs . .	40.4	65.4	67.6	69.4	24.4	49.3	28.9	163.0	

[1] Includes other derivatives such as morphine, heroin, and codeine.

Source: U.S. Federal Bureau of Investigation, *Crime in the United States,* annual. See also <http://www.fbi.gov/ucr/cius_00/00crime1.pdf> (released 15 October 2001).

No. 304. Federal Drug Seizures by Type of Drug: 1990 to 2001

[**In pounds. For fiscal years ending in year shown.** Reflects the combined drug seizure effort of the Drug Enforcement Administration, the Federal Bureau of Investigation, the U.S. Customs Services, and beginning October 1993 the U.S. Border Patrol within the jurisdiction of the United States as well as maritime seizures by the U.S. Coast Guard. Based on reports to the federal-wide Drug Seizure System, which eliminates duplicate reporting of a seizure involving more than one federal agency]

Drug	1990	1994	1995	1996	1997	1998	1999	2000	2001
Total	**745,002**	**1,336,561**	**1,662,562**	**1,737,647**	**1,762,806**	**2,084,882**	**2,665,709**	**2,986,772**	**2,920,326**
Heroin.	1,515	2,830	3,407	3,014	3,592	3,214	2,538	3,694	5,530
Cocaine.	211,828	285,230	244,888	283,490	221,375	259,895	291,144	234,982	245,793
Cannabis.	531,660	1,048,502	1,414,267	1,451,142	1,537,839	1,821,773	2,372,027	2,748,096	2,669,003
Marijuana.	514,723	1,047,284	1,382,366	1,397,976	1,536,170	1,821,241	2,370,269	2,724,204	2,668,656
Hashish	16,937	1,218	31,902	53,167	1,669	532	1,758	23,892	347

Source: U.S. Drug Enforcement Administration, unpublished data from federal-wide Drug Seizure System.

Law Enforcement, Courts, and Prisons   193

No. 305. Authorized Intercepts of Communication—Summary: 1980 to 2001

[Data for jurisdictions with statutes authorizing or approving interception of wire or oral communication]

Item	1980	1985	1990	1993	1994	1995	1996	1997	1998	1999	2000	2001
Jurisdictions: [1]												
With wiretap statutes	28	32	40	41	41	41	46	45	45	45	45	46
Reporting interceptions	22	22	25	23	18	19	24	24	26	28	26	25
Intercept applications authorized .	564	784	872	976	1,154	1,058	1,149	1,186	1,329	1,350	1,190	1,491
Intercept installations	524	722	812	938	1,100	1,024	1,035	1,094	1,245	1,277	1,139	1,405
Federal	79	235	321	444	549	527	574	563	562	595	472	481
State	445	487	491	494	551	497	461	531	683	682	667	924
Intercepted communications, average [2]	1,058	1,320	1,487	1,801	2,139	2,028	1,969	2,081	1,858	1,921	1,769	1,565
Incriminating	315	275	321	364	373	459	422	418	350	390	402	333
Persons arrested [3]	1,871	2,469	2,057	2,428	2,852	2,577	2,464	3,086	3,450	4,372	3,411	3,683
Convictions [3]	259	660	420	413	772	494	502	542	911	654	736	732
Major offense specified:												
Gambling	199	206	116	96	86	95	114	98	93	60	49	82
Drugs	282	434	520	679	876	732	821	870	955	978	894	1,167
Homicide and assault	13	25	21	28	19	30	41	31	55	62	72	52
Other	70	119	215	173	173	201	173	187	228	250	175	190

[1] Jurisdictions include federal government, states, and District of Columbia.   [2] Average per authorized installation.
[3] Based on information received from intercepts installed in year shown; additional arrests/convictions will occur in subsequent years but are not shown here.

Source: Administrative Office of the U.S. Courts, *Report on Applications for Orders Authorizing or Approving the Interception of Wire, Oral or Electronic Communications* (Wiretap Report), annual. See also <http://www.uscourts.gov/wiretap01/2001wttxt.pdf>. (issued April 2002).

No. 306. Background Checks for Firearm Transfers: 1994 to 2000

[In thousands (29,953 represents 29,953,000), except rates. For "Interim period" of 1994 to November 29, 1998, covered handgun purchases from licensed firearm dealers; beginning November 29, 1998 (effective date for the Brady Handgun Violence Prevention Act, P.L. 103-159,1993) covers the transfer of both handguns and long guns from a federal firearms licensee, as well as purchases from pawnshops and retail gun shops]

Inquiries and rejections	1994-2000, period [1]	Interim period					Permanent Brady	
		1994	1995	1996	1997	1998 [2]	1999	2000
Applications and rejections:								
Applications received	29,953	2,483	2,706	2,593	2,574	3,277	8,621	7,699
Applications rejected	689	62	41	70	69	90	204	153
Rejection rate	2.3	2.5	1.5	2.7	2.7	2.9	2.4	2.0

[1] Represents from the Inception of the Brady Act on March 1, 1994 to 2000.   [2] For period January 1 to November 29, 1998. Counts are from the National Instant Criminal Background Check System and may include multiple transactions for the same application.

Source: U.S. Bureau of Justice Statistics, *Background Checks for Firearm Transfers, 1999,* Series NCJ 180882, June 2000.

No. 307. Firearm Use by Offenders: 1997

[In percent. Based on the Survey of Inmates in State and Federal Correctional Facilities]

Characteristic	Percent of prison inmates		Characteristic	Percent of prison inmates		Characteristic	Percent of prison inmates	
	State	Federal		State	Federal		State	Federal
TYPE OF FIREARM [1]			Drug	8.1	8.7	Recidivist	17.2	18.4
			Public order	19.1	27.3	Use of firearm [2]	100	100
Total	18.4	14.8						
Handgun	15.3	12.8	Gender			Fired	49.1	12.8
Rifle	1.3	1.3	Male	19.1	15.5	Killed/injured victim . .	22.8	5.0
Shotgun	2.4	2.0	Female	7.3	6.2	Other	26.3	7.8
			Age			Brandished to	73.2	46.2
CHARACTERISTIC OF INMATES WHO CARRIED FIREARMS			24 or younger	29.4	19.1	Scare someone . . .	48.6	29.3
			25-34	16.5	15.5	Defend self	41.1	24.9
			35 or older	14.8	13.6			
Offense								
Violent	30.2	35.4	Criminal history					
Property	3.1	2.9	First-time offender . . .	22.3	9.5			

[1] Percents of subtotals may not add to totals because inmates may have had more than one firearm.   [2] Percents of subtotals may not add to totals because inmates may have used a firearm in more than one way.

Source: U.S. Bureau of Justice Statistics, *Firearm Use by Offenders,* Series NCJ 189369, November 2001. See also <http://www.ojp.usdoj.gov/bjs/pub/pdf/fuo.pdf>.

194   Law Enforcement, Courts, and Prisons

No. 308. General Purpose Law Enforcement Agencies—Number and Employment: 2000

[Includes both full-time and part-time employees. State police data are based on the 49 primary law enforcement agencies; excludes agencies that perform primarily court-related duties.

Type of agency	Number of agencies [1]	Number of employees					
		Full time			Part time		
		Total	Sworn	Civilian	Total	Sworn	Civilian
Total	**15,801**	**948,544**	**660,659**	**287,885**	**86,039**	**37,872**	**48,174**
Local police............	12,674	565,881	440,888	124,993	62,197	27,351	34,853
Sheriff................	3,078	295,635	163,423	132,212	23,025	10,426	12,599
State police............	49	87,028	56,348	30,680	817	95	722

[1] The number of agencies reported here is the result of a weighted sample and not an exact enumeration.
Source: U.S. Bureau of Justice Statistics, *Law Enforcement Management and Administrative Statistics, 2000,* Series NCJ 184481, November 2001.

No. 309. U.S. Population Who Had Contact With Police by Age and Reason for Contact: 1999

[43,705 represents 43,705,000. Persons having multiple contacts or more than one reason for any single contact appear in table more than once; therefore, number of contacts may not add to total. Covers persons 16 years old and over. Based on the Police-Public Contact Survey of 94,717 persons; data subject to sampling variability]

Reason for contact	Number having contact (1,000)	Number of persons who had contact with police per 1,000 residents							
		All persons	16 to 17 years	18 to 19 years	20 to 24 years	25 to 29 years	30 to 39 years	40 to 49 years	50 years and over
Contact with police for any reason .	**43,705**	**209**	**229**	**343**	**313**	**263**	**235**	**222**	**131**
Respondent contacted police:									
Report a crime	8,373	40	24	51	56	52	50	48	23
Witness to a crime...........	1,393	7	7	9	9	9	9	8	3
Ask for assistance	5,227	25	14	19	28	33	34	29	17
Report a neighborhood problem . . .	4,001	19	5	9	15	22	27	25	14
Witness to an accident	1,674	8	5	13	10	11	10	9	5
Other reasons.............	4,031	19	10	18	18	20	21	27	15
Police contacted respondent:									
Motor vehicle stop	22,732	109	130	225	203	155	121	102	54
Involved in an accident	3,355	16	29	29	21	18	14	15	13
Witness to an accident	766	4	[1]3	7	5	4	4	4	2
Victim of crime	921	4	4	9	9	4	5	4	2
Witness to a crime...........	1,368	7	10	8	11	7	7	8	4
Suspect in a crime...........	1,314	6	22	23	16	6	5	5	2
Serve warrant..............	345	2	[1]2	[1]2	6	2	2	1	[1]-
Crime prevention............	615	3	4	[1]2	2	3	4	3	2
Other reasons.............	5,289	25	39	39	29	27	29	30	16

- Represents zero.   [1] Based on a sample of 10 or fewer cases.
Source: U.S. Bureau of Justice Statistics, *Contacts between Police and the Public Findings from the 1999 National Survey,* Series NCJ 184957, February 2001.

No. 310. Drivers Stopped by Police by Sex, Race, and Ethnicity by Age and Cause: 1999

[19,277 represents 19,277,000. Covers drivers 16 years old and over. Persons having multiple contacts or more than one reason for any based on the Police-Public Contact Survey of 94,717 persons; data subject to sampling variability]

Characteristic of driver	Drivers stopped at least once		Reason police gave for traffic stop—percent distribution					
	Number	Percent of all drivers	Speeding	Vehicle defect	Roadside check for drinking drivers	Record check	Driver suspected of something	Other traffic offense
All drivers, total	**19,277**	**10.3**	**51.2**	**11.4**	**2.3**	**9.2**	**2.3**	**22.7**
Male	11,722	12.5	49.3	12.5	2.5	8.3	3.0	23.6
Female.	7,555	8.2	54.1	9.6	1.9	10.6	1.4	21.3
White.	14,846	10.4	53.7	10.4	2.5	9.1	2.3	21.0
Black	2,232	12.3	43.4	13.4	[1]1.4	11.0	2.4	28.1
Hispanic	1,615	8.8	42.1	15.4	[1]1.3	9.7	3.0	27.9
Other.	584	8.7	45.6	15.9	[1]1.2	[1]4.0	2.3	[1]30.7
16 to 19 years old	2,032	18.2	52.3	12.1	0.7	4.4	6.1	23.6
20 to 29 years old	5,560	16.8	53.5	13.5	2.0	7.2	2.3	20.8
30 to 39 years old	4,526	11.3	51.4	11.5	2.1	10.2	1.8	22.2
40 to 49 years old	3,764	9.4	51.0	10.4	2.6	9.8	1.6	23.4
50 to 59 years old	2,094	7.7	48.8	8.8	3.8	13.4	1.8	22.6
60 years old and over . . .	1,302	3.8	43.1	7.6	3.3	13.2	[1]1.4	29.9

[1] Based on a sample of 10 or fewer cases.
Source: U.S. Bureau of Justice Statistics, *Contacts between Police and the Public Findings from the 1999 National Survey,* Series NCJ 184957, February 2001.

Law Enforcement, Courts, and Prisons   195

No. 311. Justifiable Homicide by Police and Police Officers Murdered by Felons: 1980 to 1998

[The killing of a felon is considered justified when it is done to prevent the imminent death or serious bodily injury to the officer or another person. Excludes negligent homicides, justifiable homicides by private citizens, and murders in which the victim is some-one other than an officer slain in the line of duty]

Year	Felons killed by police in justifiable homicides							Police officers killed by felons				
	Num-ber	Rate [1]	Percent of killed felons					Num-ber	Rate [2]	Percent of murdered officers		
			Male	Female	White	Black	Other race			White	Black	Other race
1980	457	2.49	97.8	2.2	51	48	1	104	26.44	86.5	13.5	-
1981	381	2.06	99.2	0.8	54	45	1	91	22.86	84.6	14.3	1.1
1982	376	2.00	98.1	1.9	52	46	2	92	22.81	83.7	15.2	1.1
1983	406	2.14	99.0	1.0	54	44	2	80	17.80	83.0	12.5	3.8
1984	332	1.73	97.9	2.1	58	41	1	72	15.41	84.7	13.9	1.4
1985	321	1.65	97.8	2.2	61	35	4	78	16.57	89.0	10.3	1.3
1986	298	1.52	98.7	1.3	58	40	2	66	13.87	89.4	10.6	-
1987	296	1.50	98.0	2.0	64	34	2	74	15.40	90.4	9.6	-
1988	339	1.70	98.2	1.8	59	39	2	78	16.06	91.0	9.0	-
1989	362	1.80	95.9	4.1	60	38	2	66	13.30	89.4	10.6	-
1990	379	1.88	96.6	3.4	62	36	2	66	12.61	80.0	18.5	1.5
1991	359	1.76	95.8	4.2	54	43	3	71	13.26	87.3	12.7	0.0
1992	414	2.01	97.8	2.2	60	38	2	64	11.76	82.3	16.1	1.6
1993	453	2.17	96.9	3.1	55	42	3	70	12.64	85.7	14.3	-
1994	459	2.18	95.9	4.1	57	40	3	79	14.07	84.2	15.0	1.3
1995	382	1.80	98.7	1.3	59	38	3	74	12.61	83.8	12.2	4.1
1996	355	1.65	97.7	2.3	61	37	2	61	10.25	80.0	14.5	5.5
1997	361	1.66	96.7	3.3	63	35	2	70	11.32	80.0	16.9	3.1
1998	367	1.67	97.5	2.5	62	35	3	61	9.51	86.9	11.5	1.6

- Represents zero.   [1] Rate per 1,000,000 persons.   [2] Rate per 100,000 sworn police officers.

Source: U.S. Bureau of Justice Statistics, *Policing and Homicide, 1976-98: Justifiable Homicide by Police, Police Officers Murdered by Felons,* Series NCJ 180987, March 2001.

No. 312. Law Enforcement Officers Killed and Assaulted: 1990 to 2000

[Covers officers killed feloniously and accidentally in line of duty; includes federal officers. For composition of regions, see map, inside front cover]

Item	1990	1993	1994	1995	1996	1997	1998	1999	2000
OFFICERS KILLED									
Total killed	133	129	141	133	112	132	142	107	135
Northeast	13	12	17	16	17	14	6	11	13
Midwest	20	27	30	19	21	25	19	17	33
South	69	57	54	63	46	55	70	56	67
West	23	22	31	32	18	31	36	22	19
Puerto Rico	8	11	9	2	10	7	9	1	3
Outlying areas, foreign countries	-	-	1	-	-	-	2	-	-
Feloniously killed	66	70	79	74	61	70	61	42	51
Firearms	57	67	78	62	57	67	58	41	47
Handgun	48	51	66	43	50	49	40	25	33
Rifle	8	13	8	14	6	12	17	11	10
Shotgun	1	3	4	5	1	6	1	5	4
Knife	3	-	-	2	1	2	1	-	1
Bomb	-	-	-	8	-	-	1	-	-
Personal weapons	2	-	-	-	1	1	-	-	-
Other	4	3	1	2	2	-	1	1	3
Accidentally killed	67	59	62	59	51	62	81	65	84
ASSAULTS									
Population (1,000) [1]	197,426	197,551	215,501	191,759	165,264	184,825	193,098	196,315	204,599
Number of—									
Agencies represented	9,343	8,814	10,246	8,503	7,803	8,120	8,153	8,174	8,940
Police officers	410,131	424,054	469,426	428,379	371,964	411,015	452,361	470,145	452,531
Total assaulted	72,091	62,933	64,967	57,762	46,608	52,149	60,673	55,026	58,398
Firearm	3,651	3,880	3,174	2,354	1,878	2,110	2,126	1,783	1,749
Knife or cutting instrument ...	1,647	1,486	1,510	1,356	871	971	1,098	990	1,015
Other dangerous weapon ...	7,423	7,155	7,197	6,414	5,069	5,800	7,415	7,392	8,132
Hands, fists, feet, etc	59,370	50,412	53,086	47,638	38,790	43,268	50,034	44,861	47,502

- Represents zero.   [1] Represents the number of persons covered by agencies shown.

Source: U.S. Federal Bureau of Investigation, *Law Enforcement Officers Killed and Assaulted,* annual.

No. 313. U.S. Supreme Court—Cases Filed and Disposition: 1980 to 2000

[Statutory term of court begins first Monday in October]

Action	1980	1990	1994	1995	1996	1997	1998	1999	2000
Total cases on docket	**5,144**	**6,316**	**8,100**	**7,565**	**7,602**	**7,692**	**8,083**	**8,445**	**8,965**
Appellate cases on docket	2,749	2,351	2,515	2,456	2,430	2,432	2,387	2,413	2,305
From prior term	527	365	377	361	375	347	326	321	351
Docketed during present term	2,222	1,986	2,138	2,095	2,055	2,085	2,061	2,092	1,954
Cases acted upon [1]	2,324	2,042	2,185	2,130	2,124	2,142	2,092	2,096	2,024
Granted review	167	114	83	92	74	75	72	78	85
Denied, dismissed, or withdrawn .	1,999	1,802	2,016	1,945	1,955	1,990	1,940	1,958	1,842
Summarily decided	90	81	52	62	66	36	44	34	63
Cases not acted upon	425	309	330	326	306	290	295	317	281
Pauper cases on docket	2,371	3,951	5,574	5,098	5,165	5,253	5,689	6,024	6,651
Cases acted upon	2,027	3,436	4,983	4,514	4,613	4,616	4,951	5,273	5,736
Granted review	17	27	10	13	13	14	9	14	14
Denied, dismissed, or withdrawn .	1,968	3,369	4,955	4,439	4,582	4,581	4,926	5,239	5,658
Summarily decided	32	28	14	55	15	14	11	16	61
Cases not acted upon	344	515	591	584	552	637	738	751	915
Original cases on docket	24	14	11	11	7	7	7	8	8
Cases disposed of during term	7	3	2	5	2	1	2	-	2
Total cases available for argument	**264**	**201**	**136**	**145**	**140**	**138**	**124**	**124**	**138**
Cases disposed of	162	131	97	93	92	97	94	87	89
Cases argued	154	125	94	90	90	96	90	83	86
Cases dismissed or remanded without argument	8	6	3	3	2	1	4	4	3
Cases remaining	102	70	39	52	48	41	30	37	49
Cases decided by signed opinion	144	121	91	87	87	93	84	79	83
Cases decided by per curiam opinion. .	8	4	3	3	3	1	4	2	4
Number of signed opinions.	123	112	82	75	80	91	75	74	77

- Represents zero.   [1] Includes cases granted review and carried over to next term, not shown separately.

Source: Office of the Clerk, Supreme Court of the United States, unpublished data.

No. 314. U.S. District Courts—Civil Cases Commenced and Pending: 1998 to 2001

[For years ending June 30]

Type of case	Cases commenced				Cases pending			
	1998	1999	2000	2001	1998	1999	2000	2001
Cases total [1]	**261,262**	**251,511**	**263,049**	**253,354**	**269,119**	**246,920**	**249,692**	**252,522**
Contract actions [1]	44,205	46,721	54,494	45,438	32,403	35,415	38,262	35,773
Recovery of overpayments [2] . . .	15,188	18,822	25,636	16,116	6,129	9,733	12,107	8,833
Real property actions	5,655	5,787	6,481	7,296	3,971	3,931	4,249	5,471
Tort actions	52,218	39,785	40,877	34,071	84,073	63,683	63,116	60,392
Personal injury	48,356	35,962	36,867	30,194	80,114	59,899	59,232	56,500
Personal injury product liability [1]	28,325	17,196	15,349	12,569	50,838	31,927	31,772	29,857
Asbestos	9,718	7,413	7,893	5,656	1,576	1,686	4,949	6,074
Other personal injury	20,031	18,766	21,518	17,625	29,276	27,972	27,460	26,643
Personal property damage	3,862	3,823	4,010	3,877	3,959	3,784	3,884	3,892
Actions under statutes [1]	159,172	159,205	161,187	166,535	148,630	158,163	144,053	150,876
Civil rights [1]	42,750	41,453	41,226	40,979	46,718	45,348	44,259	43,921
Employment	23,804	22,948	21,404	21,121	27,097	26,043	24,456	23,908
Bankruptcy suits	3,905	3,875	3,378	3,012	2,921	2,597	2,555	2,267
Commerce (ICC rates, etc.) . . .	528	650	1,007	554	510	486	444	463
Environmental matters	1,007	882	894	1,794	1,602	1,406	1,355	2,268
Prisoner petitions	55,120	56,037	57,706	59,159	44,905	42,302	43,560	46,520
Forfeiture and penalty	2,431	2,207	2,246	2,143	1,959	1,787	1,772	1,715
Labor laws.	15,039	14,325	14,229	14,880	11,807	11,265	11,267	11,569
Protected property rights [3]	7,660	8,082	8,745	8,143	7,037	7,344	7,858	7,570
Securities commodities and exchanges	2,166	2,684	2,500	3,152	2,998	3,538	3,578	4,250
Social security laws.	13,955	14,511	14,365	17,530	14,844	14,407	13,667	16,191
Tax suits	1,733	1,280	938	961	1,507	1,254	1,068	984
Freedom of information	436	350	335	350	416	386	380	377

[1] Includes other types not shown separately.   [2] Includes enforcement of judgments in student loan cases, and overpayments of veterans benefits.   [3] Includes copyright, patent, and trademark rights.

Source: Administrative Office of the U.S. Courts, *Statistical Tables for the Federal Judiciary,* annual.

U.S. Census Bureau, Statistical Abstract of the United States: 2002

No. 315. U.S. District Courts—Offenders Convicted and Sentenced to Prison and Length of Sentence: 2000

Most serious offense of conviction	Offenders convicted	Convicted offenders sentenced to prison	Mean length of sentence (mo.)
Total [1]	68,156	50,451	56.7
Violent offenses	2,557	2,360	86.5
Property offenses	12,454	7,462	24.2
Fraudulent offenses [2]	10,396	6,272	22.5
Embezzlement	917	506	14.8
Fraud [3]	8,177	5,008	23.5
Forgery	86	41	19.1
Other offenses [2]	2,058	1,190	33.2
Larceny	1,394	689	27.3
Drug offenses [2]	24,206	22,352	75.5
Possession	1,931	1,719	80.8
Trafficking and manufacturing	22,275	20,633	75.1
Public-order offenses	19,906	16,896	45.8
Regulatory offenses	1,376	647	28.4
Other offenses	18,530	16,249	46.5
Weapons	4,196	3,834	91.4
Immigration	11,125	10,073	29.5
Tax law violations [4]	655	355	18.5
Misdemeanors	8,961	1,356	10.4

[1] Total may include offenders for whom offense category could not be determined. [2] Includes offenses not shown separately. [3] Excludes tax fraud. [4] Includes tax fraud.

Source: U.S. Bureau of Justice Statistics, *Compendium of Federal Justice Statistics, 1999,* Series NCJ 186179, April 2001.

No. 316. Federal Prosecutions of Public Corruption: 1980 to 2000

[**As of Dec. 31.** Prosecution of persons who have corrupted public office in violation of Federal Criminal Statutes]

Prosecution status	1980	1985	1990	1992	1993	1994	1995	1996	1997	1998	1999	2000
Total: [1]												
Indicted	727	1,157	1,176	1,189	1,371	1,165	1,051	984	1,057	1,174	1,134	1,000
Convicted	602	997	1,084	1,081	1,362	969	878	902	853	1,014	1,065	938
Awaiting trial	213	256	300	380	403	332	323	244	327	340	329	327
Federal officials:												
Indicted	123	563	615	624	627	571	527	456	459	442	480	441
Convicted	131	470	583	532	595	488	438	459	392	414	460	422
Awaiting trial	16	90	103	139	133	124	120	64	83	85	101	92
State officials:												
Indicted	72	79	96	81	113	99	61	109	51	91	115	92
Convicted	51	66	79	92	133	97	61	83	49	58	80	91
Awaiting trial	28	20	28	24	39	17	23	40	20	37	44	37
Local officials:												
Indicted	247	248	257	232	309	248	236	219	255	277	237	211
Convicted	168	221	225	211	272	202	191	190	169	264	219	183
Awaiting trial	82	49	98	91	132	96	89	60	118	90	95	89

[1] Includes individuals who are neither public officials nor employees but who were involved with public officials or employees in violating the law, not shown separately.

Source: U.S. Department of Justice, *Federal Prosecutions of Corrupt Public Officials, 1970-1980* and *Report to Congress on the Activities and Operations of the Public Integrity Section,* annual.

No. 317. Per Capita Justice Expenditure and Employment of State and Local Governments by State: 1999

[State and local expenditure and employment data per 10,000 population]

State	Expenditure per capita (dollars)				Full-time equivalent justice employment per 10,000 population [1]			
	Total justice system	Police protection	Judicial and legal	Correc-tions	Total justice system	Police protection	Judicial and legal	Correc-tions
United States	442.1	189.8	89.9	162.4	67.4	30.2	13.3	23.9
Alabama	295.0	145.3	57.9	91.7	55.2	28.1	11.1	15.9
Alaska	724.9	283.4	195.1	246.4	70.1	26.9	20.9	22.3
Arizona	472.4	201.8	105.0	165.6	73.0	30.8	17.7	24.6
Arkansas	279.7	126.2	48.4	105.1	54.9	28.5	6.8	19.5
California	602.9	240.9	169.2	192.8	65.1	28.0	14.7	22.4
Colorado	438.3	180.9	74.3	183.1	61.2	28.4	12.5	20.4
Connecticut	455.0	193.6	107.8	153.6	68.4	30.7	12.0	25.7
Delaware	561.1	194.0	109.8	257.3	79.7	29.8	20.1	29.8
District of Columbia . . .	1,212.3	592.1	66.8	553.4	139.6	78.8	6.5	54.3
Florida	503.1	224.2	84.0	194.9	79.0	33.3	17.2	28.5
Georgia	364.8	144.6	63.1	157.2	70.7	28.2	10.9	31.5
Hawaii	429.7	182.5	136.4	110.8	70.6	28.9	22.8	18.9
Idaho	384.2	149.1	75.7	159.3	55.9	25.2	10.7	20.0
Illinois	418.2	224.4	70.6	123.3	69.7	36.4	13.2	20.1
Indiana	283.2	124.5	50.0	108.7	53.6	26.7	9.5	17.4
Iowa	314.7	135.8	82.7	96.2	48.6	23.7	10.9	14.1
Kansas	355.0	161.6	74.4	119.0	67.8	33.0	13.4	21.5
Kentucky	302.8	109.6	69.2	124.0	53.5	24.1	14.2	15.2
Louisiana	410.7	183.3	76.3	151.2	76.7	34.3	15.1	27.3
Maine	257.4	122.5	50.9	84.0	46.2	25.6	6.6	14.0
Maryland	451.1	191.2	87.8	172.1	73.3	33.2	13.1	27.0
Massachusetts	464.8	218.7	99.8	146.3	66.1	35.7	11.0	19.4
Michigan	439.3	172.3	83.2	183.7	59.6	24.9	11.5	23.2
Minnesota	363.6	166.8	85.2	111.6	48.5	21.5	11.5	15.6
Mississippi	281.7	135.7	53.6	92.5	59.7	30.0	10.2	19.4
Missouri	324.6	153.9	56.2	114.4	68.3	30.7	13.0	24.6
Montana	339.5	134.5	71.0	134.0	52.0	24.2	11.0	16.8
Nebraska	284.0	128.8	54.3	100.9	53.6	25.9	10.4	17.2
Nevada	542.7	231.7	107.8	203.2	70.4	30.7	16.2	23.5
New Hampshire	299.0	141.8	69.7	87.4	49.1	26.4	9.2	13.5
New Jersey	518.4	236.6	113.9	167.9	82.5	39.3	24.4	18.8
New Mexico	440.6	194.1	85.2	161.3	75.4	29.3	15.9	30.2
New York	630.1	292.4	113.4	224.2	92.6	44.7	15.8	32.4
North Carolina	350.9	155.4	58.1	137.5	64.4	27.6	8.2	28.5
North Dakota	243.3	102.9	66.2	74.3	46.2	22.3	11.6	12.3
Ohio	424.2	179.4	95.6	149.3	68.3	28.0	17.6	22.6
Oklahoma	301.6	119.9	51.1	130.6	63.1	31.6	11.1	20.4
Oregon	463.5	184.3	74.6	204.6	60.9	24.6	13.6	22.8
Pennsylvania	424.4	171.2	79.6	173.7	60.2	25.0	14.2	20.9
Rhode Island	408.1	179.2	94.7	134.2	58.1	29.2	11.8	17.2
South Carolina	330.9	147.0	43.9	140.0	69.4	33.3	8.8	27.3
South Dakota	268.0	115.3	49.2	103.5	49.4	22.1	9.8	17.5
Tennessee	323.3	151.0	70.2	102.1	58.9	29.6	9.6	19.8
Texas	387.6	148.5	60.0	179.2	71.1	27.8	10.5	32.8
Utah	400.4	161.4	80.7	158.4	53.3	24.2	11.7	17.5
Vermont	248.1	102.8	81.2	64.2	47.3	21.8	10.3	15.1
Virginia	388.3	156.6	67.9	163.8	66.1	25.4	9.6	31.0
Washington	418.3	162.0	83.8	172.5	55.8	23.3	12.5	20.0
West Virginia	228.0	87.3	55.7	85.0	40.0	20.2	11.3	8.5
Wisconsin	448.6	196.6	79.3	172.8	60.2	28.6	10.2	21.4
Wyoming	482.6	189.2	100.9	192.5	69.0	34.0	14.1	21.0

[1] Based on Census Bureau, Current Population Reports, Series P-25, No. 1045, as of March 1999.

Source: U.S. Bureau of Justice Statistics, *Justice Expenditure and Employment in the United States,* Series NCJ 191746, February 2002. See also <http://www.ojp.usdoj.gov/bjs/pub/pdf/jeeus99.pdf>.

No. 318. Delinquency Cases Disposed by Juvenile Courts by Reason for Referral: 1989 to 1999

[In thousands (1,220 represents 1,220,000), except rate. A delinquency offense is an act committed by a juvenile for which an adult could be prosecuted in a criminal court. Disposition of a case involves taking a definite action such as waiving the case to criminal court, dismissing the case, placing the youth on probation, placing the youth in a facility for delinquents, or such actions as fines, restitution, and community service]

Reason for referral	1989	1990	1991	1992	1993	1994	1995	1996	1997	1998	1999
All delinquency offenses .	**1,220**	**1,317**	**1,413**	**1,483**	**1,522**	**1,666**	**1,766**	**1,828**	**1,814**	**1,753**	**1,684**
Case rate [1]	48.3	51.4	54.1	55.5	55.7	60.0	62.5	64.0	62.9	60.3	57.3
Violent offenses.	78	94	106	114	118	132	137	132	111	103	88
Criminal homicide.	2	2	2	2	3	3	3	3	2	2	2
Forcible rape	5	5	6	6	7	7	7	7	6	6	4
Robbery	23	28	32	33	35	38	40	38	34	29	25
Aggravated assault	48	59	66	72	73	84	87	85	69	66	56
Property offenses.	535	564	616	620	594	609	630	639	610	550	486
Burglary	134	145	155	160	151	146	142	145	139	129	115
Larceny	327	341	382	382	372	392	424	433	412	369	323
Motor vehicle theft	67	71	71	70	62	62	54	52	50	44	39
Arson	7	7	7	8	8	10	11	9	9	8	9
Delinquency offenses	608	659	692	749	810	926	998	1,056	1,093	1,100	1,110
Simple assault	115	132	143	162	177	198	218	232	256	262	257
Vandalism	85	99	113	119	119	130	127	127	119	118	112
Drug law violations	78	71	65	73	92	131	166	184	190	192	193
Obstruction of justice.	75	80	74	78	94	111	121	139	150	150	173
Other [2]	255	278	297	317	328	356	367	375	379	377	376

[1] Number of cases disposed per 1,000 youth (ages 10 to 17) at risk.   [2] Includes such offenses as stolen property offenses, trespassing, weapons offenses, other sex offenses, liquor law violations, disorderly conduct, and miscellaneous offenses.

Source: National Center for Juvenile Justice, Pittsburgh, PA, *Juvenile Court Statistics*, annual.

No. 319. Delinquency Cases and Case Rates by Sex and Race: 1992 to 1999

[A delinquency offense is an act committed by a juvenile for which an adult could be prosecuted in a criminal court. Disposition of a case involves taking a definite action such as waiving the case to criminal court, dismissing the case, placing the youth on probation, placing the youth in a facility for delinquents, or such actions as fines, restitution, and community service. Offenses may not add to total sex and race categories due to rounding]

Sex, race, and offense	Number of cases disposed			Case rate [1]		
	1992	1998	1999	1992	1998	1999
Male, total	**1,195,100**	**1,330,700**	**1,283,500**	**87.1**	**89.2**	**85.2**
Person.	243,500	292,200	284,600	17.8	19.6	18.9
Property	692,900	606,000	541,900	50.5	40.6	35.9
Drugs.	63,600	162,000	162,100	4.6	10.9	10.8
Public order.	195,100	270,500	295,000	14.2	18.1	19.6
Female, total	**286,800**	**422,700**	**399,900**	**22.0**	**29.9**	**28.0**
Person.	65,000	111,200	104,600	5.0	7.9	7.3
Property	167,200	192,500	168,800	12.9	13.6	11.8
Drugs.	8,700	30,500	30,600	0.7	2.2	2.1
Public order.	45,900	88,500	96,000	3.5	6.3	6.7
White, total	**974,800**	**1,182,000**	**1,148,900**	**45.5**	**51.2**	**49.4**
Person.	177,200	249,900	244,100	8.3	10.8	10.5
Property	604,400	559,100	498,300	28.2	24.2	21.4
Drugs.	37,300	131,500	136,900	1.7	5.7	5.9
Public order.	155,900	241,400	269,600	7.3	10.5	11.6
Black, total	**452,900**	**508,100**	**477,400**	**112.8**	**115.2**	**106.2**
Person.	121,400	141,600	133,600	30.2	32.1	29.7
Property	221,000	205,500	183,000	55.1	46.6	40.7
Drugs.	33,400	56,000	51,200	8.3	12.7	11.4
Public order.	77,100	105,100	109,500	19.2	23.8	24.4
Other races, total	**54,200**	**63,300**	**57,200**	**41.6**	**39.9**	**35.3**
Person.	9,900	11,900	11,500	7.6	7.5	7.1
Property	34,800	33,900	29,300	26.7	21.4	18.1
Drugs.	1,700	4,900	4,500	1.3	3.1	2.8
Public order.	7,900	12,500	11,900	6.0	7.9	7.3

[1] Cases per 1,000 youth at (ages 10 to 17) risk.

Source: National Center for Juvenile Justice, Pittsburgh, PA, *Juvenile Court Statistics*, annual.

U.S. Census Bureau, Statistical Abstract of the United States: 2002

No. 320. Child Abuse and Neglect Cases Substantiated and Indicated— Victim Characteristics: 1990 to 2000

[Based on reports alleging child abuse and neglect that were referred for investigation/assessment by the respective child protective services agency in each state. The reporting period may be either calendar or fiscal year. Children are counted each time they were subjects of an investigation report. In 2000, the data are from 49 states. Victims are children whose alleged maltreatments have been substantiate, indicated, or assessed as maltreatments. A substantiated case represents a type of investigation disposition that determines that there is sufficient evidence under state law to conclude that maltreatment occurred or that the child is at risk of maltreatment. An indicated case represents a type of disposition that concludes that there was a reason to suspect maltreatment had occurred. An alternative response-victim case represents a type of disposition that identifies child as a victim within the alternative response system.]

Item	1990		1998		1999		2000	
	Number	Percent	Number	Percent	Number	Percent	Number	Percent
TYPES OF SUBSTANTIATED MALTREATMENT								
Victims, total [1]	**690,658**	**(X)**	**861,602**	**(X)**	**783,632**	**(X)**	**862,455**	**(X)**
Neglect	338,770	49.1	461,274	53.5	439,094	56.0	515,792	59.8
Physical abuse	186,801	27.0	195,891	22.7	167,703	21.4	166,232	19.3
Sexual abuse	119,506	17.3	99,278	11.5	88,801	11.3	87,480	10.1
Emotional maltreatment	45,621	6.6	51,618	6.0	59,842	7.6	66,293	7.7
Medical neglect.	(NA)	(NA)	20,338	2.4	18,809	2.4	25,450	3.0
SEX OF VICTIM								
Victims, total	**742,519**	**100.0**	**760,438**	**100.0**	**779,787**	**100.0**	**862,455**	**100.0**
Male	323,339	43.5	359,568	47.3	371,588	47.7	412,074	47.8
Female	369,919	49.8	388,187	51.0	402,051	51.6	444,793	51.6
AGE OF VICTIM								
Victims, total	**731,282**	**100.0**	**767,749**	**100.0**	**780,145**	**100.0**	**862,455**	**100.0**
1 year and younger	97,101	13.3	105,097	13.7	109,597	14.1	132,267	15.3
2 to 5 years old	172,791	23.6	187,522	24.4	186,178	23.9	204,367	23.7
6 to 9 years old	157,681	21.6	193,316	25.2	196,639	25.2	210,463	24.4
10 to 13 years old	135,130	18.5	151,126	19.7	157,879	20.2	174,854	20.3
14 to 17 years old	103,383	14.1	111,894	14.6	117,436	15.1	125,370	14.5
18 and over	4,880	0.7	4,210	0.5	4,101	0.5	995	0.1

NA Not available.   X Not applicable.   [1] A child may be a victim of more than one maltreatment. Therefore, the total for this item adds up to more than 100 percent.

No. 321. Child Abuse and Neglect Cases Reported and Investigated by State: 2000

[See headnote, Table 320]

State	Population under 18 years old	Number of reports [1]	Number of children subject of an investigation [2]	Number of child victims [3]	State	Population under 18 years old	Number of reports [1]	Number of children subject of an investigation [2]	Number of child victims [3]
U.S. [4] .	**72,293,812**	**1,732,076**	**2,915,312**	**862,455**	MO	1,427,692	47,881	74,412	7,658
					MT	230,062	10,092	21,127	3,347
AL	1,123,422	21,965	32,655	9,990	NE	450,242	6,186	9,940	3,701
AK	190,717	12,304	8,431	6,957	NV	511,799	12,797	20,437	5,775
AZ	1,366,947	32,321	51,811	7,460	NH	309,562	5,736	8,138	842
AR	680,369	16,822	23,335	7,479	NJ	2,087,558	38,330	69,305	8,727
CA	9,249,829	243,312	486,127	129,678					
CO	1,100,795	30,663	35,483	7,467	NM	508,574	12,485	20,956	6,288
CT	841,688	29,850	45,111	14,462	NY	4,690,107	140,446	230,449	74,065
DE	194,587	5,566	8,683	1,813	NC	1,964,047	61,167	123,043	36,186
DC	114,992	3,555	7,578	2,911	ND	160,849	4,054	6,985	-
FL	3,646,340	117,523	205,179	95,849	OH	2,888,339	73,798	120,712	54,084
GA	2,169,234	52,176	92,254	30,806	OK	892,360	34,791	59,955	13,861
					OR	846,526	17,728	27,616	11,381
HI	295,767	3,298	6,184	3,533	PA	2,922,221	22,694	22,694	5,002
ID	369,030	9,063	14,158	3,171	RI	247,822	7,573	11,531	3,361
IL	3,245,451	60,547	146,791	31,446	SC	1,009,641	19,084	38,844	11,246
IN	1,574,396	(NA)	(NA)	21,890					
IA	733,638	21,276	31,317	10,822	SD	202,649	7,699	10,403	3,081
KS	712,993	19,736	30,627	8,356	TN	1,398,521	51,917	51,917	16,572
KY	994,818	41,731	63,967	18,600	TX	5,886,759	119,013	193,966	45,800
LA	1,219,799	22,291	36,355	10,618	UT	718,698	15,680	25,102	8,729
ME	301,238	5,226	9,687	4,779	VT	147,523	2,948	3,609	1,347
MD	1,356,172	30,985	(NA)	(NA)	VA	1,738,262	22,511	40,799	7,416
MA	1,500,064	36,804	61,226	32,334	WA	1,513,843	24,406	38,070	7,095
MI	2,595,767	64,794	164,369	26,680	WV	402,393	16,525	27,145	8,244
MN	1,286,894	16,565	24,840	11,824	WI	1,368,756	37,455	37,455	12,001
MS	775,187	18,041	30,670	6,389	WY	128,873	2,666	3,864	1,332

- Represents zero.   NA Not available.   [1] The number of investigations includes assessments. The number of investigations is based on the total number of investigations that received a disposition in 2000.   [2] The number of Children Subject of an Investigation of Assessment is based on the total number of children for whom an alleged maltreatment was substantiated, indicated, or assessed to have occurred or the child was at risk of occurrence.   [3] Victims are defined as children subject of a substantiated, indicated, or alternative response-victim maltreatment.   [4] Includes estimates for states that did not report.

Source of Tables 320 and 321: U.S. Department of Health and Human Services, Administration on Children, Youth and Families. *Child Maltreatment 2000* (Washington, DC: U. S. Government Printing Office, 2001).

No. 322. Jail Inmates by Sex, Race, and Hispanic Origin: 1990 to 2001

[As of June 30. Excludes federal and state prisons or other correctional institutions; institutions exclusively for juveniles; state-operated jails in Alaska, Connecticut, Delaware, Hawaii, Rhode Island, and Vermont; and other facilities which retain persons for less than 48 hours. Data based on the Annual Survey of Jails, which is a sample survey and subject to sampling variability]

Characteristic	1990	1995	1996	1997	1998	1999	2000	2001
Total inmates........	405,320	507,044	518,492	567,079	592,462	605,943	621,149	631,240
Male	365,821	448,000	454,700	498,678	520,581	528,998	543,120	551,007
Female...............	37,198	51,300	55,700	59,296	63,791	67,487	70,414	72,621
White non-Hispanic........	169,600	203,300	215,700	230,300	244,900	249,900	260,500	271,700
Black non-Hispanic........	172,300	220,600	213,100	237,900	244,000	251,800	256,300	256,200
Hispanic...............	58,100	74,400	80,900	88,900	91,800	93,800	94,100	93,000
Other [1]...............	5,400	8,800	8,800	10,000	11,800	10,400	10,200	10,300

[1] Includes American Indians, Alaska Natives, Asians, and Pacific Islanders.

Source: U.S. Bureau of Justice Statistics, through 1994, *Jail Inmates,* annual; beginning 1995, *Prison and Jail Inmates at Midyear,* annual.

No. 323. State and Federal Correctional Facilities—Inmates and Staff: 1990 to 2000

[Covers all state and federal correctional institutions or places of confinement such as prisons, prison farms, boot camps, and community based halfway houses and work release centers. Excludes jails and other regional detention centers, private facilities, facilities for the military, Immigration and Naturalization Service, Bureau of Indian Affairs, U.S. Marshall Service, and correctional hospital wards not operated by correctional authorities]

Characteristic	1990	1995	2000	Characteristic	1990	1995	2000
FACILITIES				INMATES			
Total	1,287	1,500	1,668	Total	715,649	1,023,572	1,305,253
Type of facility:				Male..............	675,624	961,210	1,219,225
Confinement.......	1,037	1,196	1,280	Female	40,025	62,362	86,028
Community.......	250	304	388	Type of facility:			
Federal	80	125	84	Confinement.......	698,570	992,333	1,256,398
State............	1,207	1,375	1,584	Community........	17,079	31,239	48,855
Size of facility:				Federal	56,821	81,930	110,974
Fewer than 500.....	816	854	861	State.............	658,828	941,642	1,194,279
500-999..........	260	286	305	Custody level:			
1,000-2,499	185	306	437	Maximum/close/high..	150,205	202,174	244,797
2,500 or more......	26	54	65	Medium	292,372	415,688	509,558
Age of facility:				Minimum/low	219,907	366,227	474,353
Less than 10 years ..	314	497	444	Not classified	53,165	39,483	76,545
10-19 years old.....	163	273	398				
20-49 years old.....	373	366	380	STAFF			
50-99 years old.....	379	310	290				
100 years old or				Total	264,201	347,320	430,033
more	58	45	81	Federal............	18,451	25,379	32,700
Not reported......	-	9	75	State	245,750	321,941	397,333

- Represents zero.

Source: U.S. Bureau of Justice Statistics, *Census of State and Federal Correctional Facilities, 2000.*

No. 324. Federal and State Prisoners by Sex: 1980 to 2000

[Prisoners, **as of December 31.** Includes all persons under jurisdiction of federal and state authorities rather than those in the custody of such authorities. Represents inmates sentenced to maximum term of more than a year]

Year	Total	Rate [1]	State	Male	Female	Year	Total	Rate [1]	State	Male	Female
1980 . . .	315,974	139	295,363	303,643	12,331	1990 . . .	739,980	297	689,577	699,416	40,564
1981 . . .	353,673	154	331,504	339,375	14,298	1991 . . .	789,610	313	732,914	745,808	43,802
1982 . . .	395,516	171	371,864	379,075	16,441	1992 . . .	846,277	332	780,571	799,776	46,501
1983 . . .	419,346	179	393,015	401,870	17,476	1993 . . .	932,074	359	857,675	878,037	54,037
1984 . . .	443,398	188	415,796	424,193	19,205	1994 . . .	1,016,691	389	936,896	956,566	60,125
						1995 . . .	1,085,022	411	1,001,359	1,021,059	63,963
1985 . . .	480,568	202	447,873	459,223	21,345	1996 . . .	1,137,722	427	1,048,907	1,068,123	69,599
1986 . . .	522,084	217	485,553	497,540	24,544	1997 . . .	1,195,498	445	1,100,511	1,121,663	73,835
1987 . . .	560,812	231	521,289	533,990	26,822	1998 . . .	1,245,402	461	1,141,720	1,167,802	77,600
1988 . . .	603,732	247	560,994	573,587	30,145	1999 . . .	1,304,074	477	1,189,799	1,221,611	82,463
1989 . . .	680,907	276	633,739	643,643	37,264	2000 . . .	1,321,137	478	1,196,093	1,237,469	83,668

[1] Rate per 100,000 estimated population. Based on U.S. Census Bureau estimated resident population.

Source: U.S. Bureau of Justice Statistics, *Prisoners in State and Federal Institutions on December 31,* annual.

No. 325. State Prisons Expenditures by State: 1996

[In millions of dollars (22,033.2 represents $22,033,200,000), except as indicated. For fiscal year ending in year indicated]

State	Total expendi- tures	Operat- ing expendi- tures	Capital expendi- tures	Operating expenditures per inmate (dol.) Per year	Per day	State	Total expendi- tures	Operat- ing expendi- tures	Capital expendi- tures	Operating expenditures per inmate (dol.) Per year	Per day
U.S...	22,033.2	20,737.9	1,295.3	20,142	55.18	MO	262.8	249.4	13.4	12,832	35.16
AL	169.0	165.8	3.2	7,987	21.88	MT	42.4	41.9	0.6	20,782	56.94
AK	116.7	112.4	4.3	32,415	88.81	NE	69.9	67.9	2.0	22,271	61.02
AZ	418.1	409.2	8.9	19,091	52.30	NV	122.0	119.0	2.9	15,370	42.11
AR	133.7	124.5	9.2	13,341	36.55	NH	43.0	42.4	0.5	20,839	57.09
CA	3,031.0	2,918.8	112.2	21,385	58.59	NJ	839.3	827.1	12.2	30,773	84.31
CO	249.8	234.5	15.3	21,020	57.59	NM	125.6	123.9	1.7	29,491	80.80
CT	497.8	475.4	22.5	31,912	87.43	NY	2,220.6	1,948.8	271.8	28,426	77.88
DE	88.0	87.3	0.7	17,987	49.28	NC	756.8	733.8	23.1	25,303	69.32
DC	213.7	212.1	1.6	21,296	58.34	ND	10.7	10.6	0.2	17,154	47.00
FL	1,224.9	1,100.7	124.3	17,327	47.47	OH	1,014.9	873.6	141.3	19,613	53.74
GA	560.4	547.5	12.9	15,933	43.65	OK	198.3	193.6	4.7	10,601	29.04
HI	87.4	83.9	3.5	23,318	63.88	OR	254.3	253.4	0.9	31,837	87.22
ID	57.0	55.0	1.9	16,277	44.60	PA	978.8	902.2	76.5	28,063	76.88
IL	740.4	732.8	7.6	19,351	53.02	RI	109.6	108.7	0.9	35,739	97.92
IN	338.2	325.7	12.5	20,188	55.31	SC	315.5	277.9	37.7	13,977	38.29
IA	146.1	143.8	2.3	24,286	66.54	SD	34.2	33.6	0.6	17,787	48.73
KS	170.8	158.5	12.4	22,242	60.94	TN	350.6	349.2	1.4	22,904	62.75
KY	208.7	198.8	9.9	16,320	44.71	TX	1,713.9	1,565.2	148.7	12,215	33.47
LA	316.2	313.5	2.8	12,304	33.71	UT	113.4	111.8	1.6	32,361	88.66
ME	51.7	48.2	3.5	33,711	92.36	VT	33.5	33.4	0.1	31,094	85.19
MD	520.3	480.9	39.4	22,247	60.95	VA	476.7	452.4	24.4	16,306	44.67
MA	309.7	304.5	5.2	26,002	71.24	WA	357.9	311.1	46.7	26,662	73.05
MI	1,167.6	1,161.1	6.5	28,067	76.89	WV	46.9	43.7	3.2	17,245	47.25
MN	186.0	184.4	1.6	37,825	103.63	WI	360.4	313.4	47.1	27,771	76.08
MS	148.9	143.9	4.9	11,156	30.56	WY	29.0	27.0	2.0	19,456	53.30

Source: U.S. Bureau of Justice Statistics, State Prison Expenditures, 1996, Series NCJ 172211, August 1999.

No. 326. Prisoners Under Jurisdiction of State and Federal Correctional Authorities—Summary by State: 1980 to 2000

[For years ending December 31]

State	1980	1990	1999	2000, advance Total	Per- cent change, 1999- 2000	State	1980	1990	1999	2000, advance Total	Per- cent change, 1999- 2000
U.S. [1] ..	329,821	773,919	1,363,701	1,381,892	1.3	MO	5,726	14,943	26,155	27,323	4.5
						MT.....	739	1,425	2,951	3,105	5.2
AL	6,543	15,665	24,658	26,225	(NA)	NE.....	1,446	2,403	3,688	3,895	5.6
AK [2]	822	2,622	3,949	4,173	5.7	NV.....	1,839	5,322	9,494	10,012	5.5
AZ [3]	4,372	14,261	25,986	26,510	2.0	NH.....	326	1,342	2,257	2,257	-
AR	2,911	7,322	11,415	11,915	4.4	NJ.....	5,884	21,128	31,493	29,784	-5.4
CA	24,569	97,309	163,067	163,001	-	NM.....	1,279	3,187	5,124	5,342	4.3
CO [2]	2,629	7,671	15,670	16,833	7.4	NY.....	21,815	54,895	[6]72,899	70,198	-3.7
CT [2]	4,308	10,500	18,639	18,355	-1.5	NC.....	15,513	18,411	31,123	31,266	0.5
DE [2]	1,474	3,471	[5]6,983	6,921	-0.9	ND.....	253	483	943	1,076	14.1
DC [2]	3,145	9,947	8,652	7,456	-13.8	OH.....	13,489	31,822	46,842	45,833	-2.2
FL [3]	20,735	44,387	69,596	71,319	2.5	OK [4]	4,796	12,285	22,393	23,181	3.5
GA [3]	12,178	22,411	42,091	44,232	5.1	OR.....	3,177	6,492	9,860	10,630	7.8
HI [2]	985	2,533	4,903	5,053	3.1	PA [2]	8,171	22,290	36,525	36,847	0.9
ID	817	1,961	[6]4,842	5,526	14.1	RI [2]	813	2,392	3,003	3,286	9.4
IL [3]	11,899	27,516	44,660	45,281	1.4	SC.....	7,862	17,319	22,008	21,778	-1.0
IN	6,683	12,736	19,309	20,125	4.2	SD.....	635	1,341	2,506	2,616	4.4
IA [3]	2,481	3,967	7,232	7,955	10.0	TN.....	7,022	10,388	[6]22,502	22,166	-1.5
KS	2,494	5,775	8,567	8,344	-2.6	TX.....	29,892	50,042	[6]163,190	157,997	-3.2
KY	3,588	9,023	15,317	14,919	-2.6	UT [2]	932	2,496	[5]5,322	5,630	5.8
LA	8,889	18,599	34,066	35,047	2.9	VT [2]	480	1,049	1,536	1,697	10.5
ME......	814	1,523	1,716	1,679	-2.2	VA	8,920	17,593	29,789	30,168	1.3
MD [3] [4] ..	7,731	17,848	23,095	23,538	1.9	WA	4,399	7,995	14,590	14,915	2.2
MA [3] [4] ...	3,185	8,345	11,356	10,722	-5.6	WV.....	1,257	1,565	3,532	3,856	9.2
MI [3] [4] ...	15,124	34,267	46,617	47,718	2.4	WI.....	3,980	7,465	20,415	20,612	1.0
MN......	2,001	3,176	5,969	6,238	4.5	WY	534	1,110	1,713	1,680	-1.9
MS......	3,902	8,375	18,247	20,241	10.9						

- Represents or rounds to zero.   NA Not available.   [1] State-level data excludes federal inmates.   [2] Includes both jail and prison inmates (state has combined jail and prison system).   [3] Numbers are for custody rather than jurisdiction counts.   [4] 1980 and 1990, data are for custody counts; thereafter, jurisdiction counts are reported.   [5] Reporting criteria were expanded in 1999 to include home confinement clients in supervised custody facilities. Comparable counts for 1998 were not available.   [6] Reporting criteria changed in 1999; percent calculated based on counts adjusted for comparable reporting.

Source: U.S. Bureau of Justice Statistics, Prisoners in 2000, Series NCJ 183476; and earlier reports.

OUACHITA TECHNICAL COLLEGE

U.S. Census Bureau, Statistical Abstract of the United States: 2002

No. 327. Adults on Probation, in Jail or Prison, or on Parole: 1980 to 2000

[As of December 31, except jail counts as of June 30]

Year	Total [1]	Percent of adult population	Probation	Jail	Prison	Parole	Male	Female
1980	1,840,400	(NA)	1,118,097	[2]182,288	319,598	220,438	(NA)	(NA)
1981	2,006,600	(NA)	1,225,934	[2]195,085	360,029	225,539	(NA)	(NA)
1982	2,192,600	(NA)	1,357,264	207,853	402,914	224,604	(NA)	(NA)
1983	2,475,100	(NA)	1,582,947	221,815	423,898	246,440	(NA)	(NA)
1984	2,689,200	(NA)	1,740,948	233,018	448,264	266,992	(NA)	(NA)
1985	3,011,400	1.7	1,968,712	254,986	487,593	300,203	2,606,000	405,500
1986	3,239,400	1.8	2,114,621	272,735	526,436	325,638	2,829,100	410,300
1987	3,459,600	1.9	2,247,158	294,092	562,814	355,505	3,021,000	438,600
1988	3,714,100	2.0	2,356,483	341,893	607,766	407,977	3,223,000	491,100
1989	4,055,600	2.2	2,522,125	393,303	683,367	456,803	3,501,600	554,000
1990	4,348,000	2.3	2,670,234	403,019	743,382	531,407	3,746,300	601,700
1991	4,535,600	2.4	2,728,472	424,129	792,535	590,442	3,913,000	622,600
1992	4,762,600	2.5	2,811,611	441,781	850,566	658,601	4,050,300	712,300
1993	4,944,000	2.6	2,903,061	455,500	909,381	676,100	4,215,800	728,200
1994	5,141,300	2.7	2,981,022	479,800	990,147	690,371	4,377,400	763,900
1995	5,335,100	2.8	3,077,861	499,300	1,078,542	679,421	4,513,000	822,100
1996	5,482,700	2.8	3,164,996	510,400	1,127,528	679,733	4,629,900	852,800
1997	5,725,800	2.9	3,296,513	557,974	1,176,564	694,787	4,825,300	900,500
1998	6,175,700	3.1	3,670,441	584,372	1,224,469	696,385	(NA)	(NA)
1999	6,378,000	3.1	3,779,922	596,485	1,287,172	714,457	(NA)	(NA)
2000, advance	6,488,300	3.1	3,839,532	613,534	1,309,661	725,527	(NA)	(NA)

NA Not available. [1] Totals may not add due to individuals having multiple correctional statuses. [2] Estimated.

Source: U.S. Bureau of Justice Statistics, *Correctional Populations in the United States*, annual.

No. 328. Prisoners Under Sentence of Death by Characteristic: 1980 to 2000

[As of December 31. Excludes prisoners under sentence of death who remained within local correctional systems pending exhaustion of appellate process or who had not been committed to prison]

Characteristic	1980	1990	1991	1992	1993	1994	1995	1996	1997	1998	1999	2000
Total [1]	688	2,346	2,466	2,575	2,727	2,905	3,064	3,242	3,328	3,465	3,527	3,593
White	418	1,368	1,450	1,508	1,575	1,653	1,732	1,833	1,864	1,917	1,948	1,990
Black and other	270	978	1,016	1,067	1,152	1,252	1,332	1,409	1,464	1,548	1,579	1,603
Under 20 years	11	8	14	12	13	19	20	17	16	16	16	11
20 to 24 years	173	168	179	188	211	231	264	288	275	273	251	237
25 to 34 years	334	1,110	1,087	1,078	1,066	1,088	1,068	1,088	1,077	1,108	1,108	1,103
35 to 54 years	186	1,006	1,129	1,212	1,330	1,449	1,583	1,711	1,809	1,897	1,958	2,019
55 years and over	10	64	73	85	96	103	119	138	151	171	194	223
Years of school completed:												
7 years or less	68	178	173	181	185	186	191	196	205	208	201	214
8 years	74	186	181	180	183	198	195	201	206	218	221	233
9 to 11 years	204	775	810	836	885	930	979	1,040	1,069	1,122	1,142	1,157
12 years	162	729	783	831	887	939	995	1,037	1,084	1,128	1,157	1,184
More than 12 years	43	209	222	232	244	255	272	282	288	301	307	315
Unknown	163	279	313	315	332	382	422	486	476	488	499	490
Marital status:												
Never married	268	998	1,071	1,132	1,222	1,320	1,412	1,507	1,555	1,645	1,689	1,749
Married	229	632	663	663	671	707	718	739	740	752	731	739
Divorced [2]	217	726	746	780	823	863	924	996	1,033	1,068	1,107	1,105
Time elapsed since sentencing:												
Less than 12 months	185	231	252	265	262	280	287	306	262	293	259	208
12 to 47 months	389	753	718	720	716	755	784	816	844	816	800	786
48 to 71 months	102	438	441	444	422	379	423	447	456	482	499	507
72 months and over	38	934	1,071	1,146	1,316	1,476	1,560	1,673	1,766	1,874	1,969	2,092
Legal status at arrest:												
Not under sentence [3]	384	1,345	1,415	1,476	1,562	1,662	1,764	1,881	1,957	2,036	2,088	2,202
Parole or probation [3]	115	578	615	702	754	800	866	894	880	879	886	921
Prison or escaped	45	128	102	101	102	103	110	112	116	127	125	126
Unknown	170	305	321	296	298	325	314	355	375	423	428	344

[1] Revisions to the total number of prisoners were not carried to the characteristics except for race. [2] Includes persons married but separated, widows, widowers, and unknown. [3] Includes prisoners on mandatory conditional release, work release, leave, AWOL, or bail. Covers 28 prisoners in 1990, and 29 in 1991 and 1992, 33 in 1993 and 1995, 31 in 1994 and 1996, 30 in 1997, 26 in 1998, and 21 in 1999 and 2000.

Source: U.S. Bureau of Justice Statistics, *Capital Punishment*, annual. See also <http://www.ojp.usdoj.gov/bjs/pub/pdf/cp00.pdf> (released December 2001).

No. 329. Movement of Prisoners Under Sentence of Death: 1980 to 2000

[Prisoners reported under sentence of death by civil authorities. The term "under sentence of death" begins when the court pronounces the first sentence of death for a capital offense]

Status	1980	1990	1991	1992	1993	1994	1995	1996	1997	1998	1999	2000
Under sentence of death, Jan. 1 [1][2]	595	2,243	2,346	2,465	2,580	2,727	2,905	3,064	3,242	3,328	3,465	3,540
Received death sentence [1][2]	203	244	266	265	282	306	310	299	256	285	272	214
White	125	147	163	147	146	162	168	174	146	145	157	122
Black	77	94	101	114	130	136	138	119	106	132	104	86
Dispositions other than executions	101	108	116	124	108	112	105	99	89	93	112	76
Executions	-	23	14	31	38	31	56	45	74	68	98	85
Under sentence of death, Dec. 31 [1][2]	688	2,346	2,466	2,575	2,727	2,890	3,054	3,242	3,335	3,452	3,527	3,593
White	425	1,368	1,450	1,508	1,575	1,645	1,730	1,833	1,876	1,906	1,948	1,990
Black	268	940	1,016	1,029	1,111	1,197	1,275	1,358	1,406	1,486	1,514	1,535

- Represents zero. [1] Includes races other than White or Black. [2] Revisions to total number of prisoners under death sentence not carried to this category.

Source: U.S. Bureau of Justice Statistics, *Capital Punishment*, annual.

No. 330. Prisoners Executed Under Civil Authority by Sex and Race: 1930 to 2001

[Excludes executions by military authorities. The Army (including the Air Force) carried out 160 (148 between 1942 and 1950; 3 each in 1954, 1955, and 1957; and 1 each in 1958, 1959, and 1961). Of the total, 106 were executed for murder (including 21 involving rape), 53 for rape, and 1 for desertion. The Navy carried out no executions during the period]

Year or period	Total [1]	Male	Female	White	Black	Executed for murder Total [1]	White	Black
All years, 1930-2000	**4,542**	**4,484**	**37**	**2,173**	**2,315**	**3,692**	**1,884**	**1,770**
1930 to 1939	1,667	1,656	11	827	816	1,514	803	687
1940 to 1949 [2]	1,284	1,272	12	490	781	1,064	458	595
1950 to 1959 [2]	717	709	8	336	376	601	316	280
1960 to 1967	191	190	1	98	93	155	87	68
1968 to 1976	-	-	-	-	-	-	-	-
1977 to 2000	683	657	5	422	249	683	422	254
1985	18	-	-	11	7	18	11	7
1986	18	18	-	11	7	18	11	7
1987	25	25	-	13	12	25	13	12
1988	11	11	-	6	5	11	6	5
1989	16	16	-	8	8	16	8	8
1990	23	23	-	16	7	23	16	7
1991	14	14	-	7	7	14	7	7
1992	31	31	-	19	11	31	19	11
1993	38	38	-	23	14	38	23	14
1994	31	31	-	20	11	31	20	11
1995	56	56	-	33	22	56	33	22
1996	45	45	-	31	14	45	31	14
1997	74	74	-	45	27	74	45	27
1998	68	66	2	48	18	68	48	18
1999	98	98	-	61	33	98	61	33
2000	85	83	2	48	36	85	48	36
2001	66	63	3	48	17	66	48	17

- Represents zero. [1] Includes races other than White or Black. [2] Includes 25 armed robbery, 20 kidnapping, 11 burglary, 8 espionage (6 in 1942 and 2 in 1953), and 6 aggravated assault.

Source: Through 1978, U.S. Law Enforcement Assistance Administration; thereafter, U.S. Bureau of Justice Statistics, *Correctional Populations in the United States,* annual; and *Capital Punishment,* annual.

No. 331. Prisoners Under Sentence of Death and Executed Under Civil Authority by State: 1977 to 2001

[Alaska, District of Columbia, Hawaii, Iowa, Maine, Massachusetts, Michigan, Minnesota, New York, North Dakota, Rhode Island, Vermont, West Virginia, and Wisconsin are jurisdictions without a death penalty]

State	1977 to 2001	1998	1999	2000	2001	State	1977 to 2001	1998	1999	2000	2001	State	1977 to 2001	1998	1999	2000	2001
U.S.	**749**	**68**	**98**	**85**	**66**	IL	12	1	1	-	-	OK	48	4	6	11	18
						IN9	9	1	1	-	2	OR	2	-	-	-	-
AL	23	1	2	4	-	KY	2	-	1	-	-	PA	3	-	1	-	-
AZ	22	4	7	3	-	LA	26	-	1	1	-	SC	25	7	4	1	-
AR	24	1	4	2	1	MD	3	1	-	-	-	TN	1	-	-	1	-
CA	9	1	2	1	1	MS	4	-	-	-	-	TX	256	20	35	40	17
DE	13	-	2	1	2	MO	53	3	9	5	7	UT	6	-	1	-	-
FL	51	4	1	6	1	NE	3	-	-	-	-	VA	83	13	14	8	2
GA	27	1	-	-	4	NV	9	1	1	-	1	WA	4	1	-	-	1
ID	1	-	-	-	-	NC	21	3	4	1	5	WY	1	-	-	-	-

- Represents zero.

Source: Through 1978, U.S. Law Enforcement Assistance Administration; thereafter, U.S. Bureau of Justice Statistics, *Capital Punishment,* annual.

U.S. Census Bureau, Statistical Abstract of the United States: 2002

No. 332. Fire Losses—Total and Percent Change: 1980 to 2000

[Includes allowance for uninsured and unreported losses but excludes losses to government property and forests. Represents incurred losses]

Year	Total (mil. dol.)	Per capita [1]	Year	Total (mil. dol.)	Per capita [1]	Year	Total (mil. dol.)	Per capita [1]
1980	5,579	24.56	1987	8,504	34.96	1994	12,778	49.08
1981	5,625	24.53	1988	9,626	39.11	1995	11,887	45.23
1982	5,894	25.61	1989	9,514	38.33	1996	12,544	47.29
1983	6,320	27.20	1990	9,495	38.07	1997	12,940	48.32
1984	7,602	32.35	1991	11,302	44.82	1998	11,510	45.59
1985	7,753	32.70	1992	13,588	53.28	1999	12,428	45.58
1986	8,488	35.21	1993	11,331	43.96	2000	12,659	45.86

[1] Based on U.S. Census Bureau resident population as of July 1.

Source: Insurance Information Institute, New York, NY, *The Fact Book, Property/Casualty Insurance Facts,* annual (copyright).

No. 333. Fires—Number and Loss by Type and Property Use: 1997 to 2000

[**Number of 1,795 represents 1,795,000 and property loss of 8,525 represents $8,525,000,000.** Based on annual sample survey of fire departments. No adjustments were made for unreported fires and losses. Property loss includes direct property loss only]

Type and property use	Number (1,000)				Property loss (mil. dol.)			
	1997	1998	1999	2000	1997	1998	1999	2000
Fires, total	**1,795**	**1,755**	**1,823**	**1,708**	**8,525**	**8,629**	**10,024**	**[1]11,207**
Structure	552	517	523	506	7,087	6,717	8,490	8,501
Outside of structure [2]	57	62	64	69	99	497	123	214
Brush and rubbish	662	653	724	670	-	-	-	-
Vehicle	397	381	369	349	1,269	1,337	1,324	1,381
Other	127	142	143	114	70	78	87	111
Structure by property use:								
Public assembly	15	16	16	15	327	354	412	365
Educational	8	8	8	7	58	84	71	108
Institutional	8	9	8	7	25	23	23	20
Stores and offices	27	25	29	24	612	462	659	587
Residential	407	381	383	380	4,585	4,391	5,092	5,674
1-2 family units [3]	303	283	283	284	3,735	3,642	4,123	4,639
Apartments	93	86	88	85	718	631	842	886
Other residential [4]	11	12	12	11	132	118	127	149
Storage [5]	36	36	36	33	577	687	[6]1,375	694
Industry, utility, defense [5]	17	16	18	15	723	496	671	778
Special structures	34	26	25	25	180	220	187	275

- Represents zero.   [1] Includes $1 billion in property damage in the Cerro Grande, New Mexico Wildland Fire. Property loss by specific property type was not available.   [2] Includes outside storage, crops, timber, etc. 1998 property loss data include $390 million loss in timber from Florida wildfires.   [3] Includes mobile homes.   [4] Includes hotels and motels, college dormitories, boarding houses, etc.   [5] Data underreported as some incidents were handled by private fire brigades or fixed suppression systems which do not report.   [6] Includes estimated losses of $515 million due to two power plant fires.

Source: National Fire Protection Association, Quincy, MA, "2000 U.S. Fire Loss," *NFPA Journal,* September 2001, and prior issues (copyright 2001).

No. 334. Fires and Property Loss for Incendiary and Suspicious Fires and Civilian Fire Deaths and Injuries by Selected Property Type: 1997 to 2000

[Based on sample survey of fire departments]

Characteristic	1997	1998	1999	2000	Characteristic	1997	1998	1999	2000
NUMBER (1,000)					CIVILIAN FIRE DEATHS				
					Deaths, total [2]	**4,050**	**4,035**	**3,570**	**4,045**
Structure fires, total	**552**	**517**	**523**	**506**	Residential property	3,390	3,250	2,920	3,445
Structure fires of incendiary or suspicious origin	78	76	72	75	One- and two-family dwellings	2,700	2,775	2,375	2,920
Fires of incendiary origin	52	47	44	46	Apartments	660	445	520	500
Fires of suspicious origin	26	29	28	29	Vehicles	480	575	470	465
PROPERTY LOSS [1] (mil. dol.)					CIVILIAN FIRE INJURIES				
					Injuries, total [2]	**23,750**	**23,100**	**21,875**	**22,350**
Structure fires, total	**7,087**	**6,717**	**8,490**	**8,501**	Residential property	17,775	17,175	16,425	17,400
Structure fires of incendiary or suspicious origin	1,309	1,249	1,281	1,340	One- and two-family dwellings	12,300	11,800	11,550	12,575
					Apartments	5,000	5,000	4,500	4,400
Fires of incendiary origin	802	816	828	792	Vehicles	2,125	2,225	1,850	1,000
Fires of suspicious origin	507	433	453	548					

[1] Direct property loss only.   [2] Includes other not shown separately.

Source: National Fire Protection Association, Quincy, MA, "2000 U.S. Fire Loss," *NFPA Journal,* September 2001, and prior issues (copyright 2001).

Section 6
Geography and Environment

This section presents a variety of information on the physical environment of the United States, starting with basic area measurement data and ending with climatic data for selected weather stations around the country. The subjects covered between those points are mostly concerned with environmental trends but include related subjects such as land use, water consumption, air pollutant emissions, toxic releases, oil spills, hazardous waste sites, municipal waste and recycling, threatened and endangered wildlife, and the environmental industry.

The information in this section is selected from a wide range of federal agencies that compile the data for various administrative or regulatory purposes, such as the Environmental Protection Agency, U.S. Geological Survey, National Oceanic and Atmospheric Administration (NOAA), Natural Resources Conservation Service, and General Services Administration.

Area—For the 2000 census, area measurements were calculated by computer based on the information contained in a single, consistent geographic database, the TIGER® database, rather than relying on historical, local, and manually calculated information. New information from the 2000 census may be found in Table 335.

Geography—The U.S. Geological Survey conducts investigations, surveys, and research in the fields of geography, geology, topography, geographic information systems, mineralogy, hydrology, and geothermal energy resources as well as natural hazards. The U.S. Geological Survey provides United States cartographic data through the Earth Sciences Information Center, water resources data through the National Water Data Exchange (NAWDEX), and a variety of research and Open-File reports which are announced monthly in *New Publications of the U.S. Geological Survey*.

In a joint project with the U.S. Census Bureau, during the 1980s, the U.S. Geological Survey provided the basic information on geographic features for input into a national geographic and cartographic database prepared by the Census Bureau, called the TIGER® (Topologically Integrated Geographic Encoding and Referencing) database. Since then, using a variety of sources, the Census Bureau has updated these features and their related attributes (names, descriptions, etc.) and inserted current information on the boundaries, names, and codes of legal and statistical geographic entities; very few of these updates added aerial water features, however. Maps prepared by the Census Bureau using the TIGER database show the names and boundaries of entites and are available on a current basis.

The Census Bureau maintains a current inventory of governmental units and their legal boundaries primary through its Boundary and Annexation Survey. The information is available to the public in the several files, all available on line: TIGER/Line®, there are also several series of maps for Census 2000: P.L. County Block Maps, Census Tract Outline Maps, and Voting District/ State Legislative District Outline Maps. These maps can be obtained online via the American Fact-Finder.

An inventory of the nation's land resources by type of use/cover was conducted by the National Resource Recovery Conservation Service (formerly the Soil Conservation Service) every 5 years beginning in 1982. The most recent survey results, which were published in the 1997 National Resources Inventory, cover all nonfederal land in Puerto Rico, the Virgin Islands, and the United States except Alaska. Tables 337 and 338 provide results from the survey.

Environment—The principal federal agency responsible for pollution abatement and control activities is the Environmental Protection Agency (EPA). It is

U.S. Census Bureau, Statistical Abstract of the United States: 2002

responsible for establishing and monitoring national air quality standards, water quality activities, solid and hazardous waste disposal, and control of toxic substances. Many of these series now appear on the EPA Web site at the Center for Environmental Information and Statistics and can be accessed at <http://www.epa.gov/ceis/>.

National Ambient Air Quality Standards (NAAQS) for suspended particulate matter, sulfur dioxide, photochemical oxidants, carbon monoxide, and nitrogen dioxide were originally set by the EPA in April 1971. Every 5 years, each of the NAAQS is reviewed and revised if new health or welfare data indicates that a change is necessary. The standard for photochemical oxidants, now called ozone, was revised in February 1979. Also, a new NAAQS for lead was promulgated in October 1978 and for suspended particulate matter in 1987. Table 347 gives some of the health-related standards for the six air pollutants having NAAQS. Data gathered from state networks are periodically submitted to EPA's National Aerometric Information Retrieval System (AIRS) for summarization in annual reports on the nationwide status and trends in air quality; for details, see *National Air Quality and Emissions Trends Report*. More current information on emissions may be found on the EPA Web site at <http://www.epa.gov/ttn/chief/trends>.

The Toxics Release Inventory (TRI), published by the U.S. EPA, is a valuable source of information regarding toxic chemicals that are being used, manufactured, treated, transported, or released into the environment. Two rules, Section 313 of the Emergency Planning and Community Right-To-Know Act (EPCRA) and Section 6607 of the Pollution Prevention Act (PPA), mandate that a publicly accessible toxic chemical database be developed and maintained by U.S. EPA. This database, known as the TRI, contains information concerning waste management activities and the release of toxic chemicals by facilities that manufacture, process, or otherwise use said materials.

Data on the release of these chemicals are collected from manufacturing facilities and facilities added in 1998 that have the equivalent of 10 or more full-time employees and meet the established thresholds for manufacturing, processing, or "otherwise use" of listed chemicals. Facilities must report their releases and other waste management quantities. Federal facilities have been required to report since 1994, regardless of industry classification. In May 1997, EPA added seven new industry sectors that reported to the TRI for the first time in July 1999 for the 1998 reporting year.

Climate—NOAA, through the National Weather Service and the National Environmental Satellite, Data, and Information Service, is responsible for data on climate. NOAA maintains about 11,600 weather stations, of which over 3,000 produce autographic precipitation records, about 600 take hourly readings of a series of weather elements, and the remainder record data once a day. These data are reported monthly in the *Climatological Data* and *Storm Data,* published monthly, and annually in the *Local Climatological Data* (published by location for major cities).

The normal climatological temperatures, precipitation, and degree days listed in this publication are derived for comparative purposes and are averages for the 30-year period, 1971-2000. For stations that did not have continuous records for the entire 30 years from the same instrument site, the normals have been adjusted to provide representative values for the current location. The information in all other tables is based on data from the beginning of the record at that location through 2000, except as noted.

U.S. Census Bureau, Statistical Abstract of the United States: 2002

Figure 6.1
**Municipal Solid Waste —
Percent of Materials Recovered: 1980 to 2000**

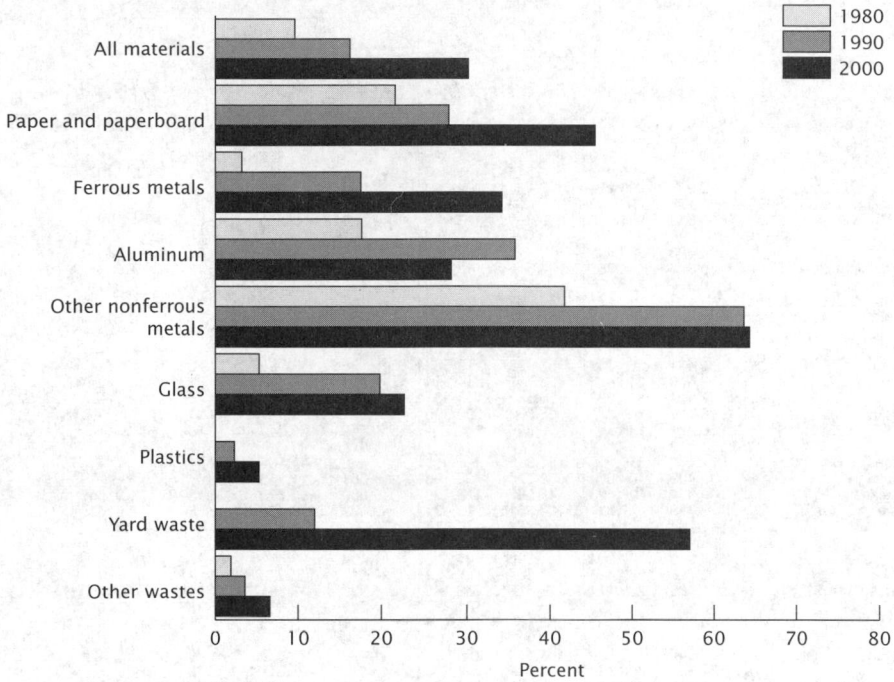

Source: Chart prepared by U.S. Census Bureau. For data, see Table 352.

Figure 6.2
Toxic Chemical Releases by Industry: 2000
(In millions of pounds)

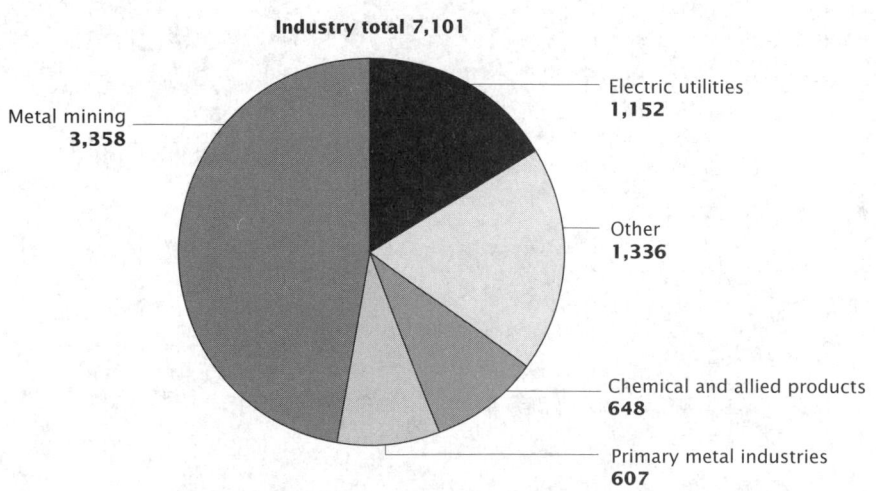

Source: Chart prepared by U.S. Census Bureau. For data, see Table 355.

Geography and Environment   209

No. 335. Land and Water Area of States and Other Entities: 2000

[One square mile=2.59 square kilometers. Area is calculated from the specific boundary recorded for each entity in the U.S. Census Bureau's geographic TIGER database]

State and other area	Total area Sq. mi.	Total area Sq. km.	Land area Sq. mi.	Land area Sq. km.	Water area Total Sq. mi.	Water area Total Sq. km.	Inland sq. mi.	Coastal sq. mi.	Great Lakes sq. mi.
Total	**3,723,033**	**9,642,657**	**3,541,447**	**9,172,346**	**181,587**	**470,310**	**79,096**	**42,241**	**60,251**
United States	**3,718,694**	**9,631,418**	**3,537,422**	**9,161,923**	**181,272**	**469,495**	**78,797**	**42,225**	**60,251**
Alabama	52,218	135,246	50,744	131,426	1,475	3,819	956	519	-
Alaska	616,240	1,596,063	571,949	1,481,347	44,292	114,716	17,243	27,049	-
Arizona	113,998	295,254	113,634	294,312	364	942	364	-	-
Arkansas	53,178	137,732	52,068	134,856	1,110	2,876	1,110	-	-
California	158,854	411,433	155,959	403,933	2,896	7,500	2,674	222	-
Colorado	104,093	269,601	103,717	268,627	376	974	376	-	-
Connecticut	5,543	14,357	4,845	12,548	699	1,809	161	538	-
Delaware	2,396	6,206	1,954	5,060	442	1,146	72	371	-
District of Columbia	68	177	61	159	7	18	7	-	-
Florida	59,909	155,165	53,927	139,670	5,983	15,495	4,672	1,311	-
Georgia	58,970	152,731	57,906	149,976	1,064	2,755	1,016	48	-
Hawaii	6,461	16,733	6,423	16,635	38	98	38	-	-
Idaho	83,570	216,446	82,747	214,314	823	2,131	823	-	-
Illinois	57,914	149,998	55,583	143,961	2,331	6,037	756	-	1,575
Indiana	36,418	94,321	35,867	92,895	551	1,427	316	-	235
Iowa	56,271	145,743	55,869	144,701	402	1,042	402	-	-
Kansas	82,276	213,096	81,815	211,900	462	1,196	462	-	-
Kentucky	40,409	104,659	39,728	102,896	681	1,763	681	-	-
Louisiana	49,650	128,595	43,562	112,825	6,089	15,770	4,154	1,935	-
Maine	33,738	87,381	30,861	79,931	2,877	7,450	2,264	613	-
Maryland	12,297	31,848	9,774	25,314	2,523	6,534	680	1,843	-
Massachusetts	9,240	23,932	7,840	20,306	1,400	3,626	423	977	-
Michigan	96,716	250,494	56,804	147,121	39,912	103,372	1,611	-	38,301
Minnesota	86,938	225,171	79,610	206,189	7,329	18,981	4,782	-	2,546
Mississippi	48,282	125,050	46,907	121,488	1,375	3,562	785	590	-
Missouri	69,704	180,533	68,886	178,414	818	2,120	818	-	-
Montana	147,042	380,838	145,552	376,979	1,490	3,859	1,490	-	-
Nebraska	77,353	200,345	76,872	199,099	481	1,247	481	-	-
Nevada	110,560	286,351	109,825	284,448	735	1,903	735	-	-
New Hampshire	9,282	24,041	8,968	23,227	314	814	314	-	-
New Jersey	8,214	21,275	7,417	19,211	797	2,065	396	401	-
New Mexico	121,589	314,915	121,355	314,309	234	606	234	-	-
New York	54,077	140,059	47,214	122,283	6,863	17,776	1,895	981	3,988
North Carolina	52,670	136,416	48,711	126,161	3,960	10,255	3,960	-	-
North Dakota	70,699	183,112	68,976	178,647	1,724	4,465	1,724	-	-
Ohio	44,825	116,096	40,948	106,056	3,877	10,040	378	-	3,499
Oklahoma	69,898	181,035	68,667	177,847	1,231	3,189	1,231	-	-
Oregon	97,126	251,557	95,996	248,631	1,130	2,927	1,050	80	-
Pennsylvania	46,055	119,283	44,816	116,074	1,239	3,208	490	-	749
Rhode Island	1,231	3,189	1,045	2,706	187	483	178	9	-
South Carolina	31,190	80,781	30,109	77,983	1,080	2,798	1,008	72	-
South Dakota	77,116	199,731	75,884	196,540	1,232	3,190	1,232	-	-
Tennessee	42,143	109,151	41,217	106,752	926	2,399	926	-	-
Texas	267,256	692,192	261,796	678,051	5,460	14,141	5,056	404	-
Utah	84,898	219,887	82,143	212,751	2,755	7,136	2,755	-	-
Vermont	9,614	24,901	9,250	23,956	365	945	365	-	-
Virginia	42,328	109,629	39,594	102,548	2,734	7,081	1,006	1,728	-
Washington	70,634	182,941	66,544	172,348	4,090	10,592	1,553	2,537	-
West Virginia	24,230	62,755	24,078	62,361	152	394	152	-	-
Wisconsin	65,498	169,639	54,310	140,663	11,188	28,976	1,830	-	9,358
Wyoming	97,813	253,336	97,100	251,489	713	1,847	713	-	-
Other areas:									
Puerto Rico	3,507	9,084	3,425	8,870	83	215	67	16	-
American Samoa	287	743	77	200	209	542	209	-	-
Guam	217	561	210	544	7	18	7	-	-
No. Mariana Islands	179	464	179	464	-	1	-	-	-
Virgin Islands of the U.S.	149	386	134	346	15	40	15	-	-

- Represents or rounds to zero.

Source: U.S. Census Bureau, *2000 Census of Population and Housing, Summary Population and Housing Characteristics,* Series PHC-1, and unpublished data on American FactFinder.

No. 336. Total and Federally Owned Land by State: 2000

[As of end of fiscal year; see text, Section 8, State and Local Government Finances and Employment. Total land area figures are not comparable with those in Table 335]

State	Total (1,000 acres)	Not owned by federal government (1,000 acres)	Owned by federal government [1] Acres (1,000)	Owned by federal government [1] Per-cent	State	Total (1,000 acres)	Not owned by federal government (1,000 acres)	Owned by federal government [1] Acres (1,000)	Owned by federal government [1] Per-cent
United States...	2,271,343	1,635,989	635,355	28.0	Missouri	44,248	39,450	4,798	10.8
Alabama	32,678	31,353	1,326	4.1	Montana	93,271	65,843	27,428	29.4
Alaska	365,482	144,630	220,852	60.4	Nebraska	49,032	48,381	651	1.3
Arizona	72,688	40,309	32,379	44.5	Nevada	70,264	11,945	58,319	83.0
Arkansas	33,599	30,190	3,410	10.1	New Hampshire	5,769	5,010	759	13.2
California	100,207	52,318	47,889	47.8	New Jersey	4,813	4,690	124	2.6
Colorado	66,486	42,377	24,108	36.3	New Mexico	77,766	51,194	26,572	34.2
Connecticut	3,135	3,121	14	0.5	New York	30,681	30,459	222	0.7
Delaware	1,266	1,250	16	1.2	North Carolina	31,403	29,414	1,989	6.3
District of Columbia	39	30	9	23.2	North Dakota	44,452	42,137	2,316	5.2
Florida	34,721	30,122	4,599	13.2	Ohio	26,222	25,781	441	1.7
Georgia	37,295	35,268	2,027	5.4	Oklahoma	44,088	42,422	1,666	3.8
Hawaii	4,106	3,467	639	15.6	Oregon	61,599	29,243	32,356	52.5
Idaho	52,933	19,827	33,106	62.5	Pennsylvania	28,804	28,088	717	2.5
Illinois	35,795	35,205	590	1.6	Rhode Island	677	674	4	0.5
Indiana	23,158	22,648	510	2.2	South Carolina	19,374	18,265	1,110	5.7
Iowa	35,860	35,631	230	0.6	South Dakota	48,882	45,762	3,120	6.4
Kansas	52,511	51,837	674	1.3	Tennessee	26,728	24,613	2,115	7.9
Kentucky	25,512	24,066	1,447	5.7	Texas	168,218	165,910	2,307	1.4
Louisiana	28,868	27,669	1,199	4.2	Utah	52,697	18,696	34,001	64.5
Maine	19,848	19,675	173	0.9	Vermont	5,937	5,562	375	6.3
Maryland	6,319	6,153	166	2.6	Virginia	25,496	23,217	2,280	8.9
Massachusetts	5,035	4,964	71	1.4	Washington	42,694	30,518	12,176	28.5
Michigan	36,492	32,417	4,076	11.2	West Virginia	15,411	14,188	1,222	7.9
Minnesota	51,206	46,989	4,217	8.2	Wisconsin	35,011	33,192	1,819	5.2
Mississippi	30,223	28,551	1,672	5.5	Wyoming	62,343	31,273	31,070	49.8

[1] Excludes trust properties.

Source: U.S. General Services Administration, *Summary Report on Real Property Owned by the United States Throughout the World*, annual. See also <http://www.gsa.gov/attachments/GSAPUBLICATIONS/extpub/OwnedReport0613.pdf>.

No. 337. Nonfederal Developed Land Use by State and Other Area: 1997

[In thousands of acres (1,944,130 represents 1,944,130,000), except percent. Excludes Alaska and District of Columbia]

State and other area	Total surface area	Developed land Total	Developed land Percent of total	Developed land Change, 1992-97	State and other area	Total surface area	Developed land Total	Developed land Percent of total	Developed land Change, 1992-97
Total	1,944,130	98,252	5.0	11,217	Montana	94,110	1,032	1.1	76
					Nebraska	49,510	1,206	2.5	55
United States	1,941,823	97,745	5.0	11,105	Nevada	70,763	381	0.6	27
Alabama	33,424	2,252	6.8	315	New Hampshire	5,941	589	10.0	63
Arizona	72,964	1,491	2.1	114	New Jersey	5,216	1,778	34.1	214
Arkansas	34,037	1,409	4.2	169	New Mexico	77,823	1,153	1.5	217
California	101,510	5,456	5.4	553	New York	31,361	3,184	10.2	318
Colorado	66,625	1,652	2.5	113	North Carolina	33,709	3,856	11.5	507
Connecticut	3,195	874	27.4	39	North Dakota	45,251	992	2.2	33
Delaware	1,534	226	14.8	23	Ohio	26,445	3,611	13.7	365
Florida	37,534	5,185	13.9	825	Oklahoma	44,738	1,926	4.4	177
Georgia	37,741	3,957	10.5	852	Oregon	62,161	1,222	2.0	104
Hawaii	4,158	180	4.4	7	Pennsylvania	28,995	3,983	13.8	545
Idaho	53,488	755	1.5	92	Rhode Island	813	201	24.7	7
Illinois	36,059	3,181	8.9	247	South Carolina	19,939	2,097	10.6	362
Indiana	23,158	2,260	9.8	195	South Dakota	49,358	960	2.0	58
Iowa	36,017	1,702	4.8	69	Tennessee	26,974	2,371	8.8	402
Kansas	52,661	1,940	3.7	97	Texas	171,052	8,567	5.1	894
Kentucky	25,863	1,738	6.8	237	Utah	54,339	662	1.3	81
Louisiana	31,377	1,624	5.2	134	Vermont	6,154	318	5.2	12
Maine	20,966	712	3.4	111	Virginia	27,087	2,626	9.7	344
Maryland	7,870	1,236	15.8	178	Washington	44,035	2,065	4.7	241
Massachusetts	5,339	1,479	27.8	212	West Virginia	15,508	874	5.7	177
Michigan	37,349	3,546	9.5	364	Wisconsin	35,920	2,418	6.8	188
Minnesota	54,010	2,186	4.1	232	Wyoming	62,603	644	1.1	34
Mississippi	30,527	1,474	4.9	206					
Missouri	44,614	2,517	5.7	224	Caribbean	2,307	507	22.0	112

Source: U.S. Department of Agriculture, National Resource and Conservation Service, and Iowa State University, Statistical Laboratory, *Summary Report, 1997 National Resources Inventory*, revised December 2000. See also <http://www.nhq.nrcs.usda.gov/NRI/1997/summaryreport/report.pdf>.

Geography and Environment 211

No. 338. Land Cover/Use by State: 1997

[In thousands of acres (1,944,130 represents 1,944,130,000), except percent. Excludes Alaska and District of Columbia]

State	Total surface area	Nonfederal rural land							
		Rural land, total	Percent of total	Crop-land	CRP land [1]	Pasture land	Range-land	Forest land	Other rural land
Total	**1,944,130**	**1,393,760**	**71.7**	**376,998**	**32,696**	**119,992**	**405,977**	**406,955**	**51,142**
United States . . .	**1,941,823**	**1,392,098**	**71.7**	**376,630**	**32,696**	**119,549**	**405,832**	**406,315**	**51,077**
Alabama.	33,424	28,950	86.6	2,954	522	3,528	74	21,261	612
Arizona.	72,964	40,858	56.0	1,212	-	73	32,323	4,216	3,035
Arkansas	34,037	28,638	84.1	7,625	230	5,351	38	15,011	384
California	101,510	47,555	46.8	9,635	173	1,049	18,269	13,936	4,494
Colorado.	66,625	40,850	61.3	8,770	1,890	1,211	24,574	3,442	964
Connecticut.	3,195	2,178	68.2	204	-	112	-	1,759	103
Delaware	1,534	988	64.4	485	1	24	-	352	128
Florida	37,534	25,498	67.9	2,752	120	4,231	3,229	12,536	2,630
Georgia	37,741	30,648	81.2	4,757	595	2,865	-	21,560	872
Hawaii	4,158	3,565	85.7	246	-	36	1,009	1,635	639
Idaho.	53,488	18,618	34.8	5,517	785	1,315	6,501	3,948	553
Illinois	36,059	31,675	87.8	24,011	726	2,502	-	3,784	652
Indiana.	23,158	20,069	86.7	13,407	378	1,830	-	3,781	674
Iowa	36,017	33,673	93.5	25,310	1,739	3,572	-	2,182	870
Kansas.	52,661	49,685	94.3	26,524	2,849	2,322	15,728	1,546	716
Kentucky	25,863	22,327	86.3	5,178	332	5,686	-	10,667	465
Louisiana	31,377	24,664	78.6	5,659	140	2,385	277	13,226	2,976
Maine.	20,966	18,794	89.6	413	30	123	-	17,691	537
Maryland	7,870	4,808	61.1	1,616	19	478	-	2,373	321
Massachusetts.	5,339	3,394	63.6	277	-	119	-	2,744	254
Michigan.	37,349	29,426	78.8	8,540	321	2,032	-	16,354	2,178
Minnesota.	54,010	45,356	84.0	21,414	1,544	3,434	-	16,248	2,716
Mississippi	30,527	26,429	86.6	5,352	799	3,679	-	16,209	389
Missouri	44,614	39,358	88.2	13,751	1,606	10,849	88	12,431	634
Montana.	94,110	64,958	69.0	15,171	2,721	3,443	36,751	5,431	1,443
Nebraska	49,510	47,187	95.3	19,469	1,245	1,801	23,089	826	757
Nevada	70,763	10,079	14.2	701	2	279	8,372	305	420
New Hampshire	5,941	4,353	73.3	134	-	94	-	3,932	193
New Jersey.	5,216	2,766	53.0	589	1	111	-	1,698	367
New Mexico	77,823	50,071	64.3	1,875	467	231	39,990	5,467	2,041
New York	31,361	26,702	85.1	5,417	54	2,722	-	17,702	808
North Carolina	33,709	24,592	73.0	5,639	131	2,039	-	15,959	824
North Dakota.	45,251	41,442	91.6	25,004	2,802	1,129	10,689	454	1,363
Ohio	26,445	22,070	83.5	11,627	324	2,006	-	7,081	1,032
Oklahoma.	44,738	40,610	90.8	9,737	1,138	7,963	14,033	7,281	459
Oregon.	62,161	28,858	46.4	3,762	483	1,961	9,286	12,643	724
Pennsylvania.	28,995	23,816	82.1	5,471	90	1,845	-	15,478	932
Rhode Island.	813	458	56.3	22	-	25	-	387	24
South Carolina.	19,939	16,018	80.3	2,574	263	1,197	-	11,188	797
South Dakota	49,358	44,411	90.0	16,738	1,686	2,108	21,876	518	1,484
Tennessee	26,974	22,597	83.8	4,644	374	4,990	-	12,042	547
Texas.	171,052	155,530	90.9	26,938	3,906	15,914	95,745	10,816	2,211
Utah	54,339	17,599	32.4	1,679	216	695	10,733	1,883	2,392
Vermont	6,154	5,183	84.2	607	-	338	-	4,150	88
Virginia.	27,087	19,886	73.4	2,918	71	2,995	-	13,316	587
Washington.	44,035	28,508	64.7	6,656	1,017	1,193	5,857	12,835	951
West Virginia.	15,508	13,252	85.5	864	-	1,527	-	10,582	279
Wisconsin.	35,920	30,374	84.6	10,613	661	2,994	-	14,448	1,658
Wyoming.	62,603	32,773	52.4	2,174	247	1,146	27,302	1,004	900
Caribbean.	2,307	1,662	72.0	368	-	443	145	640	65

- Represents or rounds to zero.   [1] Conservation Reserve Program (CRP). A federal program established under the Food Security Act of 1985 to assist private landowners to convert highly erodible cropland to vegetative cover for 10 years.

Source: U.S. Department of Agriculture, National Resource and Conservation Service, and Iowa State University, Statistical Laboratory, *Summary Report, 1997 National Resources Inventory,* revised December 2000. See also <http://www.nhq.nrcs.usda. gov/NRI/1997/summaryreport/report.pdf>.

No. 339. Extreme and Mean Elevations by State and Other Area

[One foot=.305 meter]

State and other area	Highest point Name	Elevation Feet	Elevation Meters	Lowest point Name	Elevation Feet	Elevation Meters	Approximate mean elevation Feet	Approximate mean elevation Meters
U.S.. . . .	Mt. McKinley (AK)	20,320	6,198	Death Valley (CA).	-282	-86	2,500	763
AL	Cheaha Mountain	2,405	733	Gulf of Mexico	(¹)	(¹)	500	153
AK	Mount McKinley.	20,320	6,198	Pacific Ocean.	(¹)	(¹)	1,900	580
AZ	Humphreys Peak.	12,633	3,853	Colorado River	70	21	4,100	1,251
AR	Magazine Mountain	2,753	840	Ouachita River	55	17	650	198
CA	Mount Whitney	14,494	4,419	Death Valley.	-282	-86	2,900	885
CO	Mt. Elbert	14,433	4,402	Arkansas River	3,350	1,022	6,800	2,074
CT	Mt. Frissell on South slope.	2,380	726	Long Island Sound	(¹)	(¹)	500	153
DE	Ebright Road, ² New Castle County.	448	137	Atlantic Ocean	(¹)	(¹)	60	18
DC	Tenleytown at Reno Reservoir	410	125	Potomac River	1	(Z)	150	46
FL	Sec. 30, T6N, R20W, Walton County.	345	105	Atlantic Ocean	(¹)	(¹)	100	31
GA	Brasstown Bald.	4,784	1,459	Atlantic Ocean	(¹)	(¹)	600	183
HI	Puu Wekiu	13,796	4,208	Pacific Ocean.	(¹)	(¹)	3,030	924
ID	Borah Peak	12,662	3,862	Snake River.	710	217	5,000	1,525
IL	Charles Mound	1,235	377	Mississippi River	279	85	600	183
IN	Franklin Twp., Wayne Co .	1,257	383	Ohio River	320	98	700	214
IA	Sec. 29, T100N, R41W, Osceola County ³	1,670	509	Mississippi River.	480	146	1,100	336
KS	Mount Sunflower	4,039	1,232	Verdigris River	679	207	2,000	610
KY	Black Mountain	4,139	2,162	Mississippi River	257	78	750	229
LA	Driskill Mountain	535	163	New Orleans	-8	-2	100	31
ME	Mount Katahdin	5,267	1,606	Atlantic Ocean	(¹)	(¹)	600	183
MD	Backbone Mountain	3,360	1,025	Atlantic Ocean	(¹)	(¹)	350	107
MA	Mount Greylock	3,487	1,064	Atlantic Ocean	(¹)	(¹)	500	153
MI	Mount Arvon	1,979	604	Lake Erie.	571	174	900	275
MN	Eagle Mountain, Cook Co .	2,301	702	Lake Superior.	601	183	1,200	366
MS	Woodall Mountain	806	246	Gulf of Mexico	(¹)	(¹)	300	92
MO	Taum Sauk Mountain	1,772	540	St. Francis River	230	70	800	244
MT	Granite Peak	12,799	3,904	Kootenai River	1,800	549	3,400	1,037
NE	Johnson Twp., Kimball Co .	5,424	1,654	Missouri River.	840	256	2,600	793
NV	Boundary Peak	13,140	4,007	Colorado River	479	146	5,500	1,678
NH	Mount Washington	6,288	1,918	Atlantic Ocean	(¹)	(¹)	1,000	305
NJ	High Point	1,803	550	Atlantic Ocean	(¹)	(¹)	250	76
NM.	Wheeler Peak	13,161	4,014	Red Bluff Reservoir	2,842	867	5,700	1,739
NY	Mount Marcy	5,344	1,630	Atlantic Ocean	(¹)	(¹)	1,000	305
NC	Mount Mitchell.	6,684	2,039	Atlantic Ocean	(¹)	(¹)	700	214
ND	White Butte, Slope Co . . .	3,506	1,069	Red River	750	229	1,900	580
OH	Campbell Hill	1,549	472	Ohio River.	455	139	850	259
OK	Black Mesa.	4,973	1,517	Little River.	289	88	1,300	397
OR	Mount Hood	11,239	3,428	Pacific Ocean	(¹)	(¹)	3,300	1,007
PA	Mount Davis	3,213	980	Delaware River	(¹)	(¹)	1,100	336
RI	Jerimoth Hill	812	248	Atlantic Ocean	(¹)	(¹)	200	61
SC	Sassafras Mountain	3,560	1,086	Atlantic Ocean	(¹)	(¹)	350	107
SD	Harney Peak.	7,242	2,209	Big Stone Lake	966	295	2,200	671
TN	Clingmans Dome	6,643	2,026	Mississippi River	178	54	900	275
TX	Guadalupe Peak	8,749	2,668	Gulf of Mexico	(¹)	(¹)	1,700	519
UT	Kings Peak	13,528	4,126	Beaver Dam Wash	2,000	610	6,100	1,861
VT	Mount Mansfield	4,393	1,340	Lake Champlain	95	29	1,000	305
VA	Mount Rogers	5,729	1,747	Atlantic Ocean	(¹)	(¹)	950	290
WA	Mount Rainier	14,410	4,395	Pacific Ocean.	(¹)	(¹)	1,700	519
WV	Spruce Knob.	4,861	1,483	Potomac River	240	73	1,500	458
WI	Timms Hill	1,951	595	Lake Michigan	579	177	1,050	320
WY	Gannett Peak	13,804	4,210	Belle Fourche River	3,099	945	6,700	2,044
Other areas:								
Puerto Rico	Cerro de Punta	4,390	1,339	Atlantic Ocean	(¹)	(¹)	1,800	549
American Samoa. . .	Lata Mountain.	3,160	964	Pacific Ocean	(¹)	(¹)	1,300	397
Guam	Mount Lamlam	1,332	406	Pacific Ocean.	(¹)	(¹)	330	101
Virgin Is. . . .	Crown Mountain	1,556	475	Atlantic Ocean	(¹)	(¹)	750	229

Z Less than 0.5 meter.   ¹ Sea level.   ² At DE-PA state line.   ³ "Sec." denotes section; "T," township; "R," range; "N," north; and "W," west.

Source: U.S. Geological Survey, for highest and lowest points, *Elevations and Distances in the United States, 1990*; for mean elevations, 1983 edition.

No. 340. U.S. Wetland Resources and Deepwater Habitats by Type: 1986 and 1997

[In thousands of acres (144,673.3 represents 144,677,300). Wetlands and deepwater habitats are defined separately because the term wetland does not include permanent water bodies. Deepwater habitats are permanently flooded land lying below the deepwater boundary of wetlands. Deepwater habitats include environments where surface water is permanent and often deep, so that water, rather than air, is the principal medium within which the dominant organisms live, whether or not they are attached to the substrate. As in wetlands, the dominant plants are hydrophytes; however, the substrates are In general terms, wetlands are lands where saturation with water is the dominant factor determining the nature of soil development and the types of plant and animal communities living in the soil and on its surface. The single feature that most wetlands share is soil or substrate that is at least periodically saturated with or covered by water. Wetlands are lands transitional between terrestrial and aquatic systems where the water table is usually at or near the surface or the land is covered by shallow water]

Wetland or deepwater category	1986	1997	Change, 1986 to 1997
All wetlands and deepwater habitats, total	144,673.3	144,136.8	-536.5
All deepwater habitats, total	38,537.6	38,645.1	107.5
Lacustrine [1]	14,608.9	14,725.3	116.4
Riverine [2]	6,291.1	6,255.9	-35.2
Estuarine subtidal [3]	17,637.6	17,663.9	26.3
All wetlands, total	106,135.7	105,491.7	-644
Intertidal wetlands [4]	5,336.6	5,326.2	-10.4
Marine intertidal	133.1	130.9	-2.2
Estuarine intertidal nonvegetated	580.4	580.1	-0.3
Estuarine intertidal vegetated.	4,623.1	4,615.2	-7.9
Freshwater wetlands	100,799.1	100,165.5	-633.6
Freshwater nonvegetated	5,251.0	5,914.3	663.3
Freshwater vegetated.	95,548.1	94,251.2	-1,296.9
Freshwater emergent [5]	26,383.3	25,157.1	-1,226.2
Freshwater forested [6]	51,929.6	50,728.5	-1,201.1
Freshwater shrub [7]	17,235.2	18,365.6	1,130.4

[1] The lacustrine system includes deepwater habitats with all of the following characteristics: (1) situated in a topographic depression or a dammed river channel; (2) lacking trees, shrubs, persistent emergents, emergent mosses or lichens with greater than 30 percent coverage; (3) total area exceeds 20 acres. [2] The riverine system includes deepwater habitats contained within a channel, with the exception of habitats with water containing ocean derived salts in excess of 0.5 parts per thousand. [3] The estuarine system consists of deepwater tidal habitats and adjacent tidal wetland that are usually semi-enclosed by land but have open, partly obstructed, or sporadic access to the open ocean, and in which ocean water is at least occasionally diluted by freshwater runoff from the land. Subtidal is where the substrate is continuously submerged by marine or estuarine waters. [4] Intertidal is where the substrate is exposed and flooded by tides. Intertidal includes the splash zone of coastal waters. [5] Emergent wetlands are characterized by erect, rooted, herbaceous hydrophytes, excluding mosses and lichens. This vegetation is present for most of the growing season in most years. These wetlands are usually dominated by perennial plants. [6] Forested wetlands are characterized by woody vegetation that is 20 feet tall or taller. [7] Shrub wetlands include areas dominated by woody vegetation less than 20 feet tall. The species include true shrubs, young trees, and trees or shrubs that are small or stunted because of environmental conditions.

Source: U.S. Fish and Wildlife Service, *Status and Trends of Wetlands in the Conterminous United States, 1986 to 1997*, January 2001. See also <ftp://wetlands.fws.gov/status-trends/SandT2000Reportlowres.pdf>.

No. 341. Water Areas for Selected Major Bodies of Water: 1990

[Includes only that portion of body of water under the jurisdiction of the United States, excluding Hawaii. One square mile=2.59 square kilometers]

Body of water and state	Area		Body of water and state	Area	
	Sq. mi.	Sq. km.		Sq. mi.	Sq. km.
Atlantic Coast water bodies:			San Francisco Bay (CA)	264	684
Chesapeake Bay (MD-VA)	2,747	7,115	Willapa Bay (WA)	125	325
Pamlico Sound (NC)	1,622	4,200	Hood Canal (WA).	117	303
Long Island Sound (CT-NY)	914	2,368	Interior water bodies:		
Delaware Bay (DE-NJ)	614	1,591	Lake Michigan (IL-IN-MI-WI).	22,342	57,866
Cape Cod Bay (MA)	598	1,548	Lake Superior (MI-MN-WI) [1]	20,557	53,243
Albemarle Sound (NC)	492	1,274	Lake Huron (MI) [1]	8,800	22,792
Biscayne Bay (FL)	218	565	Lake Erie (MI-NY-OH-PA) [1]	5,033	13,036
Buzzards Bay (MA).	215	558	Lake Ontario (NY) [1]	3,446	8,926
Tangier Sound (MD-VA).	172	445	Great Salt Lake (UT).	1,836	4,756
Currituck Sound (NC)	116	301	Green Bay (MI-WI)	1,396	3,617
Pocomoke Sound (MD-VA).	111	286	Lake Okeechobee (FL)	663	1,717
Chincoteague Bay (MD-VA)	105	272	Lake Sakakawea (ND).	563	1,459
			Lake Oahe (ND-SD)	538	1,394
Gulf Coast water bodies:			Lake of the Woods (MN) [1]	462	1,196
Mississippi Sound (AL-LA-MS)	813	2,105	Lake Champlain (NY-VT) [1]	414	1,072
Laguna Madre (TX)	733	1,897	Alaska water bodies:		
Lake Pontchartrain (LA).	631	1,635	Chatham Strait.	1,559	4,039
Florida Bay (FL).	616	1,596	Prince William Sound	1,382	3,579
Breton Sound (LA)	511	1,323	Clarence Strait.	1,199	3,107
Mobile Bay (AL)	310	802	Iliamna Lake	1,022	2,646
Lake Borgne (LA-MS)	271	702	Frederick Sound.	792	2,051
Matagorda Bay (TX)	253	656	Sumner Strait	791	2,048
Atchafalaya Bay (LA)	245	635	Stephens Passage	702	1,819
Galveston Bay (TX)	236	611	Kvichak Bay	640	1,659
Tampa Bay (FL).	212	549	Montague Strait	463	1,198
			Becharof Lake	447	1,158
Pacific Coast water bodies:			Icy Strait.	436	1,130
Puget Sound (WA)	808	2,092			

[1] Area measurements for Lake Champlain, Lake Erie, Lake Huron, Lake Ontario, Lake St. Clair, Lake Superior, and Lake of the Woods include only those portions under the jurisdiction of the United States.

Source: U. S. Census Bureau, unpublished data from the Census TIGER ™ database.

No. 342. Flows of Largest U.S. Rivers—Length, Discharge, and Drainage Area

River	Location of mouth	Source stream (name and location)	Length (miles) [1]	Average discharge at mouth (1,000 cubic ft. per second)	Drainage area (1,000 sq. mi.)
Missouri	Missouri.	Red Rock Creek, MT	2,540	76.2	[2]529
Mississippi	Louisiana.	Mississippi River, MN.	[3]2,340	[4]593	[2][5]1,150
Yukon	Alaska.	McNeil River, Canada	1,980	225	[2]328
St. Lawrence.	Canada	North River, MN	1,900	348	[2]396
Rio Grande.	Mexico-Texas	Rio Grande, CO	1,900	-	336
Arkansas	Arkansas	East Fork Arkansas River, CO . . .	1,460	41	161
Colorado.	Mexico	Colorado River, CO	1,450	-	246
Atchafalaya [6] . . .	Louisiana.	Tierra Blanca Creek, NM	1,420	58	95.1
Ohio	Illinois-Kentucky . . .	Allegheny River, PA	1,310	281	203
Red	Louisiana.	Tierra Blanca Creek, NM	1,290	56	93.2
Brazos	Texas	Blackwater Draw, NM.	1,280	-	45.6
Columbia	Oregon-Washington.	Columbia River, Canada.	1,240	265	[2]258
Snake	Washington	Snake River, WY.	1,040	56.9	108
Platte.	Nebraska.	Grizzly Creek, CO	990	-	84.9
Pecos	Texas	Pecos River, NM	926	-	44.3
Canadian	Oklahoma	Canadian River, CO.	906	-	46.9
Tennessee	Kentucky	Courthouse Creek, NC	886	68	40.9
Colorado (of Texas) .	Texas	Colorado River, TX	862	-	42.3
North Canadian	Oklahoma	Corrumpa Creek, NM.	800	-	17.6
Mobile	Alabama	Tickanetley Creek, GA	774	67.2	44.6
Kansas.	Kansas	Arikaree River, CO	743	-	59.5
Kuskokwim	Alaska.	South Fork Kuskokwim River, AK.	724	67	48
Yellowstone.	North Dakota	North Folk Yellowstone River, WY.	692	-	70
Tanana	Alaska.	Nabesna River, AK	659	41	44.5
Gila	Arizona	Middle Fork Gila River, NM	649	-	58.2

- Represents zero.   [1] From source to mouth.   [2] Drainage area includes both the United States and Canada.   [3] The length from the source of the Missouri River to the Mississippi River and thence to the Gulf of Mexico is about 3,710 miles.   [4] Includes about 167,000 cubic ft. per second diverted from the Mississippi into the Atchafalaya River but excludes the flow of the Red River.   [5] Excludes the drainage areas of the Red and Atchafalaya Rivers.   [6] In east-central Louisiana, the Red River flows into the Atchafalaya River, a distributary of the Mississippi River. Data on average discharge, length, and drainage area include the Red River, but exclude all water diverted into the Atchafalaya from the Mississippi River.

Source: U.S. Geological Survey, *Largest Rivers in the United States,* Open File Report 87-242, May 1990.

No. 343. U.S. Water Withdrawals and Consumptive Use Per Day by End Use: 1940 to 1995

[Includes Puerto Rico. Withdrawal signifies water physically withdrawn from a source. Includes fresh and saline water; excludes water used for hydroelectric power]

Year	Total (bil. gal.)	Per capita [1] (gal.)	Irrigation (bil. gal.)	Public supply [2] Total (bil. gal.)	Public supply [2] Per capita[3] (gal.)	Rural [4] (bil. gal.)	Industrial and misc. [5] (bil. gal.)	Steam electric utilities (bil. gal.)
WITHDRAWALS								
1940	140	1,027	71	10	75	3.1	29	23
1950	180	1,185	89	14	145	3.6	37	40
1955	240	1,454	110	17	148	3.6	39	72
1960	270	1,500	110	21	151	3.6	38	100
1965	310	1,602	120	24	155	4.0	46	130
1970	370	1,815	130	27	166	4.5	47	170
1975	420	1,972	140	29	168	4.9	45	200
1980	440	1,953	150	34	183	5.6	45	210
1985	399	1,650	137	38	189	7.8	31	187
1990	408	1,620	137	41	195	7.9	30	195
1995	402	1,500	134	40	192	8.9	29	190
CONSUMPTIVE USE								
1960	61	339	52	3.5	25	2.8	3.0	0.2
1965	77	403	66	5.2	34	3.2	3.4	0.4
1970	87	427	73	5.9	36	3.4	4.1	0.8
1975	96	451	80	6.7	38	3.4	4.2	1.9
1980	100	440	83	7.1	38	3.9	5.0	3.2
1985	92	380	74	[6]	[6]	9.2	6.1	6.2
1990	94	370	76	[6]	[6]	8.9	6.7	4.0
1995	100	374	81	[6]	[6]	9.6	4.8	3.7

[1] Based on U.S. Census Bureau resident population as of July 1.   [2] Includes commercial water withdrawals.   [3] Based on population served.   [4] Rural farm and nonfarm household and garden use, and water for farm stock and dairies.   [5] For 1940 to 1960, includes manufacturing and mineral industries, rural commercial industries, air-conditioning, resorts, hotels, motels, military and other state and Federal agencies, and miscellaneous; thereafter, includes manufacturing, mining and mineral processing, ordnance, construction, and miscellaneous.   [6] Public supply consumptive use included in end-use categories.

Source: 1940-1960, U.S. Bureau of Domestic Business Development, based principally on committee prints, *Water Resources Activities in the United States,* for the Senate Committee on National Water Resources, U.S. Senate, thereafter, U.S. Geological Survey, *Estimated Use of Water in the United States in 1995,* circular 1200, and previous quinquennial issues. Next update expected in 2003 will include data for 2000.

No. 344. Water Withdrawals and Consumptive Use—State and Other Areas: 1995

[In millions of gallons per day (401,500 represents 401,500,000,000), except as noted. Figures may not add due to rounding. Withdrawal signifies water physically withdrawn from a source. Includes fresh and saline water]

State or other area	Water withdrawn								Consumptive use,[1] fresh water
	Total	Per capita (gal. per day) fresh	Source		Selected major uses				
			Ground water	Surface water	Irrigation	Public supply	Industrial	Thermo-electric	
U.S.[2]	401,500	1,280	77,500	324,000	134,000	43,600	26,200	190,000	100,000
Alabama	7,100	1,670	445	6,650	139	875	753	5,200	532
Alaska	329	350	132	196	0.6	90	197	30	25
Arizona	6,830	1,620	2,840	3,990	5,670	846	197	62	3,830
Arkansas	8,800	3,540	5,460	3,340	5,940	419	187	1,780	4,140
California	45,900	1,130	14,700	31,300	28,900	5,740	802	9,630	25,500
Colorado	13,800	3,690	2,270	11,600	12,700	732	191	115	5,230
Connecticut	4,450	389	166	4,290	28	448	11	3,940	97
Delaware	1,500	1,050	110	1,390	48	101	64	1,270	71
District of Columbia . .	10	18	0.5	9.7	-	-	0.5	9.7	15
Florida	18,200	509	4,340	13,800	3,470	2,360	649	11,600	2,780
Georgia	5,820	799	1,190	4,630	722	1,250	676	3,070	1,170
Hawaii	1,930	853	531	1,400	652	218	20	970	542
Idaho	15,100	13,000	2,830	12,300	13,000	254	76	-	4,360
Illinois	19,900	1,680	953	19,000	180	1,950	527	17,100	857
Indiana	9,140	1,570	709	8,430	116	784	2,410	5,690	505
Iowa	3,030	1,070	528	2,510	39	418	301	2,130	290
Kansas	5,240	2,040	3,510	1,720	3,380	384	77	1,260	3,620
Kentucky	4,420	1,150	226	4,190	12	521	375	3,450	318
Louisiana	9,850	2,270	1,350	8,500	769	677	2,580	5,480	1,930
Maine	326	178	80	246	27	135	16	136	48
Maryland	7,730	289	246	7,480	57	907	331	6,360	150
Massachusetts	5,510	189	351	5,160	82	759	88	4,570	180
Michigan	12,100	1,260	862	11,200	227	1,490	1,910	8,370	667
Minnesota	3,390	736	714	2,680	157	573	438	2,090	417
Mississippi	3,200	1,140	2,590	614	1,740	377	294	375	1,570
Missouri	7,030	1,320	891	6,140	567	757	63	5,550	692
Montana	8,860	10,200	217	8,640	8,550	161	80	22	1,960
Nebraska	10,500	6,440	6,200	4,350	7,550	328	175	2,350	7,020
Nevada	2,300	1,480	896	1,400	1,640	479	95	27	1,340
New Hampshire	1,320	388	81	1,240	6.3	130	50	1,110	35
New Jersey	6,110	269	580	5,530	125	1,120	486	4,360	210
New Mexico	3,510	2,080	1,700	1,800	2,990	337	69	55	1,980
New York	16,800	567	1,010	15,800	30	3,140	321	13,100	469
North Carolina	9,290	1,070	535	8,750	239	939	385	7,420	713
North Dakota	1,120	1,750	122	1,000	117	85	17	819	181
Ohio	10,500	944	905	9,620	27	1,560	650	8,190	791
Oklahoma	2,040	543	1,220	822	864	597	285	124	716
Oregon	7,910	2,520	1,050	6,860	6,170	572	379	9.0	3,210
Pennsylvania	9,680	802	860	8,820	16	1,730	1,930	5,930	565
Rhode Island	411	138	27	383	2.3	121	7.3	275	19
South Carolina	6,200	1,690	322	5,880	53	614	703	4,810	321
South Dakota	460	631	187	273	269	97	32	5.3	249
Tennessee	10,100	1,920	435	9,640	24	831	868	8,300	233
Texas	29,600	1,300	8,780	20,800	9,450	3,420	2,920	13,500	10,500
Utah	4,460	2,200	790	3,670	3,530	506	253	48	2,200
Vermont	565	967	50	515	3.9	66	12	452	24
Virginia	8,260	826	358	7,900	30	911	622	6,620	218
Washington	8,860	1,620	1,760	7,100	6,470	1,300	652	376	3,080
West Virginia	4,620	2,530	146	4,470	-	217	1,330	3,010	352
Wisconsin	7,250	1,420	759	6,490	169	692	453	5,820	443
Wyoming	7,060	14,700	335	6,720	6,590	100	118	220	2,800
Puerto Rico	2,840	154	135	2,680	107	443	15	2,260	187
Virgin Islands	202	113	0.7	201	-	7.8	20	173	1.9

- Represents zero.   [1] Water that has been evaporated, transpired, or incorporated into products, plant or animal tissue; and therefore, is not available for immediate reuse.   [2] Includes Puerto Rico and Virgin Islands.

Source: U.S. Geological Survey, *Estimated Use of Water in the United States in 1995*, circular 1200. Next update expected in 2003 will include data for 2000.

No. 345. U.S. Water Quality Conditions by Type of Waterbody: 1998

[Section 305(b) of the Clean Water Act requires states and other jurisdictions to assess the health of their waters and the extent to which their waters support water quality standards. Section 305(b) requires that states submit reports describing water quality conditions to the Environmental Protection Agency every 2 years. Water quality standards have three elements (designated uses, criteria developed to protect each use, and an antidegradation policy. For information on survey methodology and assessment criteria, see report]

Item	Rivers and streams (miles)	Lakes, reservoirs, and ponds (acres)	Esturaries (sq. miles)	Great Lakes shoreline (miles)	Ocean shoreline (miles)
Total size.................	3,662,255	41,593,748	90,465	5,521	66,645
Amount accessed [1]............	842,426	17,390,370	28,687	4,950	3,130
Percent of total size	23	42	32	90	5
Amount accessed as—					
Good [2]	463,441	7,927,486	13,439	85	2,496
Good but threatened [3]	85,544	1,565,175	2,766	103	257
Polluted [4]	291,264	7,897,110	12,482	4,762	377
Percent of accessed as—					
Good [2]	55	46	47	2	80
Good but threatened [3]	10	9	10	2	8
Polluted [4]	35	45	44	96	12
Amount impaired by leading sources of pollution: [5]					
Agriculture.................	170,750	2,417,801	1,827	133	48
Atmospheric deposition	(NA)	616,701	2,922	1,017	(NA)
Forestry	20,020	(NA)	(NA)	(NA)	(NA)
Habitat modification...........	18,451	417,662	(NA)	(NA)	(NA)
Hydromodification	57,763	1,179,344	531	(NA)	(NA)
Industrial discharges/point sources..	13,795	502,760	1,926	140	52
Irrigated crop production	31,156	410,204	(NA)	(NA)	(NA)
Land disposal of wastes.........	19,928	381,073	1,508	(NA)	117
Municipal point sources	29,087	866,116	3,528	120	96
Natural sources	33,004	654,812	5,223	(NA)	(NA)
Nonirrigated crop production	46,484	553,064	(NA)	(NA)	(NA)
Resource extraction	25,231	(NA)	585	(NA)	(NA)
Urban runoff and storm sewers	32,310	931,567	3,482	134	236

NA Not available.   [1] Includes waterbodies accessed as not attainable for one or more uses. Most states do not assess all their waterbodies during the 2-year reporting cycle, but use a "rotating basin approach" whereby all waters are monitored over a set period of time.   [2] Based on accessment of available data, water quality supports all designated uses. Water quality meets narrative and/or numberic criteria adopted to protect and support a designated use.   [3] Although all assessed uses are currently met, data show a declining trend in water quality. Projections based on this trend indicate water quality will be impaired in the future, unless action is taken to prevent further degradation.   [4] Impaired or not attainable. The reporting state or jurisdiction has performed a "use-attainability analysis" and demonstrated that support of one or more designated beneficial uses is not attainable due to specific biological, chemical, physical, or economic/social conditions.   [5] Excludes unknown and natural sources.

Source: U.S. Environmental Protection Agency, *National Water Quality Inventory: 1998 Report to Congress*, June 2000.

No. 346. Oil Spills in U.S. Water—Number and Volume: 1997 to 2000

[Based on reported discharges into U.S. navigable waters, including territorial waters (extending 3 to 12 miles from the coastline), tributaries, the contiguous zone, onto shoreline, or into other waters that threaten the marine environment. Data found in Marine Safety Management System]

Spill characteristic	Number of spills				Spill volume (gallons)			
	1997	1998	1999	2000	1997	1998	1999	2000
Total............	8,624	8,315	8,539	8,354	942,574	885,303	1,172,449	1,431,370
Size of spill (gallons):								
1-100	8,299	7,962	8,212	8,058	39,082	38,093	39,119	39,355
101-1,000	243	259	240	219	81,895	86,606	86,530	78,779
1,001-3,000	40	54	42	37	78,117	96,743	74,582	67,529
3,001-5,000	14	15	18	12	58,016	64,609	73,798	45,512
5,001-10,000	15	15	10	16	109,288	108,148	66,274	112,415
10,001-50,000	11	8	12	6	282,176	216,335	301,510	108,400
50,001-100,000	1	-	4	4	84,000	-	245,406	266,380
100,000-1,000,000 ...	1	2	1	2	210,000	274,769	285,230	713,000
1,000,000 and over......	-	-	-	-	-	-	-	-
Waterbody:								
Atlantic ocean	87	109	148	150	40,857	6,674	29,440	135,010
Pacific ocean	505	644	758	623	32,841	192,775	150,694	36,301
Gulf of Mexico	2,341	2,190	1,756	1,838	105,462	181,372	45,786	112,069
Great Lakes..........	156	119	129	96	4,311	3,006	906	4,535
Lakes..............	29	25	31	32	210,270	63	624	349
Rivers and canals.......	1,821	1,944	1,924	1,816	182,676	280,651	504,264	663,404
Bays and sounds	811	891	1,299	1,248	46,450	24,234	136,650	49,783
Harbors.............	858	790	907	801	45,932	97,223	105,213	273,095
Other	2,016	1,603	1,587	1,750	273,775	99,305	198,872	156,824
Source:								
Tankship	124	104	92	111	22,429	56,673	8,414	608,176
Tankbarge	252	220	227	229	165,649	248,089	158,977	133,540
All other vessels........	4,971	4,848	5,361	5,220	192,801	316,473	409,084	291,927
Facilities............	838	937	1,019	1,054	204,935	166,269	367,537	311,604
Pipelines	32	45	25	25	224,122	47,863	36,140	17,021
All other nonvessels	486	571	571	566	72,208	32,584	147,704	45,136
Unknown.............	1,921	1,590	1,244	1,149	60,430	17,352	44,593	23,966

- Represents or rounds to zero.

Source: U.S. Coast Guard, <http://www.uscg.mil/hq/g-m/nmc/response/stats/Summary.htm> (accessed 05 December 2001).

Geography and Environment   217

No. 347. National Ambient Air Pollutant Concentrations: 1990 to 1999

[Data represent annual composite averages of pollutant based on daily 24-hour averages of monitoring stations, except carbon monoxide is based on the second-highest, nonoverlapping, 8-hour average; ozone, average of the second-highest daily maximum 1-hour value; and lead, quarterly average of ambient lead levels. Based on data from the Aerometric Information Retrieval System. µg/m^3=micrograms of pollutant per cubic meter of air; ppm=parts per million]

Pollutant	Unit	Monitoring stations, number	Air quality standard[1]	1990	1994	1995	1996	1997	1998	1999
Carbon monoxide .	ppm....	388	[2]9	5.8	5.1	4.6	4.3	3.9	3.8	3.7
Ozone.........	ppm....	703	[3]0.12	0.112	0.107	0.112	0.105	0.105	0.110	0.107
Ozone.........	ppm....	705	[4]0.08	0.085	0.084	0.087	0.083	0.082	0.086	0.085
Sulfur dioxide	ppm....	480	0.03	0.0081	0.0069	0.0056	0.0056	0.0054	0.0053	0.0052
Particulates (PM-10).......	µg/m^3...	954	[5]50	29.2	26.0	24.8	23.9	23.8	23.6	23.9
Nitrogen dioxide ..	ppm....	230	0.053	0.020	0.020	0.019	0.018	0.018	0.018	0.018
Lead.........	µg/m^3...	175	[6]1.5	0.1	0.05	0.05	0.04	0.04	0.04	0.04

[1] Refers to the primary National Ambient Air Quality Standard that protects the public health.   [2] Based on 8-hour standard of 9 ppm.   [3] Based on 1-hour standard of .12 ppm.   [4] Based on 8-hour standard of .08 ppm.   [5] The particulates (PM-10) standard replaced the previous standard for total suspended particulates in 1987.   [6] Based on 3-month standard of 1.5 µg/m^3.

Source: U.S. Environmental Protection Agency, *National Air Quality and Emissions Trends Report,* annual.

No. 348. National Air Pollutant Emissions: 1970 to 2000

[In thousands of tons, except as indicated. PM-10=Particulate matter of less than 10 microns. Methodologies to estimate data for 1970 to 1980 period and 1985 to present emissions differ. Beginning with 1985, the methodology for more recent years is described in the document available at <http://www.epa.gov/ttn/chief/trends/trends99/neiproc99.pdf>.

Year	PM-10	PM-10, fugitive dust[1]	Sulfur dioxide	Nitrogen dioxides	Volatile organic compounds	Carbon monoxide	Lead (tons)
1970	13,042	(NA)	31,161	20,928	30,982	129,444	220,869
1975	7,671	(NA)	28,011	22,632	26,079	116,757	159,659
1980	7,119	(NA)	25,905	24,384	26,336	117,434	74,153
1985	4,831	36,567	23,658	23,198	24,428	117,013	22,890
1990	5,068	22,813	23,679	24,170	21,053	99,119	4,975
1991	4,727	22,759	23,044	24,338	21,249	101,797	4,169
1992	4,615	22,634	22,813	24,732	20,862	99,007	3,810
1993	4,533	22,969	22,474	25,116	21,099	99,791	3,916
1994	4,753	24,003	21,875	25,474	21,683	103,713	4,047
1995	4,585	21,346	19,189	25,051	20,918	94,058	3,929
1996	4,676	18,563	19,433	25,658	19,906	104,600	4,077
1997	4,828	19,259	19,925	25,910	20,305	105,466	4,137
1998	4,452	19,261	20,045	25,572	19,258	101,246	4,057
1999	4,815	19,213	19,335	24,970	19,421	102,356	4,199
2000	5,555	19,309	18,187	24,442	20,366	109,300	4,228

NA Not available.   [1] Sources such as agricultural tilling, construction, mining and quarrying, paved roads, unpaved roads, and wind erosion.

No. 349. Air Pollutant Emissions by Pollutant and Source: 2000

[In thousands of tons, except as indicated. See headnote, Table 348]

Source	Particulates[1]	Sulfur dioxide	Nitrogen oxides	Volatile organic compounds	Carbon monoxide	Lead (tons)
Total emissions	**24,866**	**18,187**	**24,442**	**20,366**	**109,300**	**4,228**
Fuel combustion, stationary sources..........	997	14,876	9,649	1,206	4,590	501
Electric utilities	270	11,389	5,266	64	445	72
Industrial	244	2,894	3,222	185	1,221	17
Other fuel combustion	483	593	1,161	957	2,924	412
Residential	363	124	746	929	2,772	5
Industrial processes	605	1,457	858	1,399	3,836	2,349
Chemical and allied product manufacturing ...	67	268	134	407	1,112	218
Metals processing	153	411	91	79	1,735	2,078
Petroleum and related industries	30	346	146	433	369	(NA)
Other	355	432	487	480	620	53
Solvent utilization	7	1	3	4,827	2	(NA)
Storage and transport	87	5	17	1,225	74	(NA)
Waste disposal and recycling	544	35	89	582	3,609	813
Highway vehicles	273	314	8,150	5,035	48,469	20
Light-duty gas vehicles and motorcycles	59	108	2,790	2,798	26,718	14
Light-duty trucks	36	75	1,608	1,655	15,837	5
Heavy-duty gas vehicles...............	11	13	439	323	3,680	1
Diesels	168	118	3,312	260	2,234	(NA)
Off highway[2]	425	1,478	5,101	3,382	27,914	545
Miscellaneous[3]	21,027	21	676	2,710	20,806	(NA)

NA Not available.   [1] Represents both PM-10 and PM-10 fugitive dust; see Table 348.   [2] Includes emissions from farm tractors and other farm machinery, construction equipment, industrial machinery, recreational marine vessels, and small general utility engines such as lawn mowers.   [3] Includes emissions such as from forest fires and other kinds of burning, various agricultural activities, fugitive dust from paved and unpaved roads, and other construction and mining activities, and natural sources.

Source of Tables 348 and 349: U.S. Environmental Protection Agency, *National Air Quality and Emissions Trends Report, 1999,* EPA-454/R-01-004; and Internet site at <www.epa.gov/airtrends/> and <http://www.epa.gov/oar/aqtrnd00/brochure/00brochure.pdf> (released September 2001).

No. 350. Emissions of Greenhouse Gases by Type and Source: 1990 to 2000

[Emission estimates were mandated by Congress through Section 1605(a) of the Energy Policy Act of 1992 (Title XVI). Gases that contain carbon can be measured either in terms of the full molecular weight of the gas or just in terms of their carbon content. Both measures are utilized below]

Type and source	Unit	1990	1995	1996	1997	1998	1999	2000
CARBON EQUIVALENT								
Total emissions	Mil. metric tons . .	1,678.3	1,769.2	1,815.7	1,836.0	1,836.9	1,860.7	1,906.3
Carbon dioxide, total.	Mil. metric tons . .	1,355.3	1,438.2	1,487.7	1,509.0	1,510.9	1,535.7	1,583.3
Energy sources	Mil. metric tons . .	1,351.6	1,421.1	1,471.7	1,493.4	1,495.4	1,517.2	1,561.7
C02 in natural gas.	Mil. metric tons . .	3.8	4.6	4.8	4.9	4.9	4.9	5.0
Cement production	Mil. metric tons . .	9.1	10.1	10.1	10.5	10.7	10.9	11.3
Gas flaring.	Mil. metric tons . .	2.5	4.7	4.5	4.2	3.9	4.0	4.5
Other industrial.	Mil. metric tons . .	7.3	7.6	7.9	8.0	8.1	7.9	8.1
Waste combustion.	Mil. metric tons . .	4.8	6.3	6.5	7.0	6.9	7.1	7.1
Other, adjustments	Mil. metric tons . .	-23.8	-16.1	-17.9	-19.0	-19.0	-16.4	-14.3
Methane.	Mil. metric tons . .	199	195	188	186	181	180	177
Nitrous oxide	Mil. metric tons . .	94	101	101	99	99	100	99
HFCs, PFCs, and SF$_6$.	Mil. metric tons . .	30	35	39	42	46	45	47
GAS								
Carbon dioxide	Mil. metric tons . .	4,969.4	5,273.5	5,454.8	5,533.0	5,540.0	5,630.7	5,805.5
Methane, total	Mil. metric tons . .	31.67	31.08	29.94	29.64	28.88	28.66	28.2
Energy sources	Mil. metric tons . .	11.90	11.58	11.17	11.18	10.88	10.94	11.01
Waste management	Mil. metric tons . .	11.36	10.33	9.81	9.35	8.86	8.59	7.99
Agricultural sources.	Mil. metric tons . .	8.29	9.04	8.83	8.98	9.00	9.00	9.06
Industrial sources	Mil. metric tons . .	0.12	0.13	0.13	0.13	0.13	0.13	0.14
Nitrous oxide, total [1]	1,000 metric tons .	1,169	1,257	1,245	1,226	1,222	1,239	1,231
Agriculture.	1,000 metric tons .	846	861	847	866	875	870	870
Energy sources	1,000 metric tons .	210	268	264	268	270	293	285
Waste management	1,000 metric tons .	17	18	18	18	18	19	19
Industrial sources	1,000 metric tons .	96	111	116	74	58	57	56
Hydrofluorocarbons (HFCs):								
HFC-23	1,000 metric tons .	3.0	2.3	2.7	2.6	3.4	2.6	2.6
HFC-125	1,000 metric tons .	(Z)	0.5	0.7	0.9	1.1	1.3	1.6
HFC-134a	1,000 metric tons .	0.6	14.4	19.0	23.5	26.9	30.4	33.7
HFC-143a	1,000 metric tons .	(Z)	0.1	0.2	0.3	0.5	0.7	0.9
Porfluorocarbons (PFCs):								
CF$_4$	1,000 metric tons .	5	4	5	4	4	4	4
C$_2$F$_6$	1,000 metric tons .	1	1	1	1	1	1	1
C$_4$F$_{10}$	1,000 metric tons .	(Z)	(Z)	(Z)	(Z)	(Z)	(Z)	(Z)
Sulfur hexafluoride (SF$_6$)	1,000 metric tons .	2	1	1	1	1	1	1

Z Less than 50 or 500 metric tons. [1] Includes minor sources not shown separately.

Source: U.S. Energy Information Administration, *Emissions of Greenhouse Gases in the United States,* Series DOE/EIA-0573(2000), annual. See also <http://www.eia.doe.gov/pub/oiaf/1605/cdrom/pdf/ggrpt/057300.pdf> (issued November 2001).

No. 351. Municipal Solid Waste Generation, Recovery, and Disposal: 1980 to 2000

[In millions of tons (151.6 represents 151,600,000), except as indicated. Covers post-consumer residential and commercial solid wastes which comprise the major portion of typical municipal collections. Excludes mining, agricultural and industrial processing, demolition and construction wastes, sewage sludge, and junked autos and obsolete equipment wastes. Based on material-flows estimating procedure and wet weight as generated]

Item and material	1980	1990	1994	1995	1996	1997	1998	1999	2000
Waste generated	151.6	205.2	214.2	211.4	209.2	219.1	223.4	231.0	231.9
Per person per day (lb.)	3.7	4.5	4.5	4.4	4.3	4.4	4.5	4.6	4.5
Materials recovered.	14.5	33.2	50.6	54.9	57.3	59.4	61.1	64.8	69.9
Per person per day (lb.)	0.35	0.7	1.1	1.1	1.2	1.2	1.2	1.3	1.4
Combustion for energy recovery	2.7	31.9	32.5	35.5	36.1	36.7	34.4	34.0	33.7
Per person per day (lb.)	0.06	0.7	0.7	0.7	0.7	0.8	0.7	0.7	0.7
Combustion without energy recovery .	11.0	(¹)	(¹)	(¹)	(¹)	(¹)	(¹)	(¹)	(¹)
Per person per day (lb.)	0.27	(¹)	(¹)	(¹)	(¹)	(¹)	(¹)	(¹)	(¹)
Landfill, other disposal	123.4	140.1	131.1	120.9	115.8	123.1	127.1	132.1	128.3
Per person per day (lb.)	3.0	3.1	2.8	2.5	2.4	2.5	2.6	2.7	2.5
Percent distribution of generation:									
Paper and paperboard	36.4	35.4	37.7	38.6	38.1	38.5	37.7	38.2	37.4
Glass	10.0	6.4	6.2	6.1	5.9	5.5	5.7	5.6	5.5
Metals	10.2	8.1	7.6	7.5	7.7	7.7	7.5	7.7	7.8
Plastics	4.5	8.3	9.0	8.9	9.4	9.9	10.0	10.4	10.7
Rubber and leather	2.8	2.8	2.9	2.9	3.0	3.0	3.1	2.7	2.7
Textiles	1.7	2.8	3.4	3.5	3.7	3.8	3.9	3.9	4.0
Wood	4.6	6.0	5.3	4.9	5.2	5.3	5.4	5.4	5.5
Food wastes.	8.6	10.1	10.0	10.3	10.4	10.1	11.2	10.9	11.2
Yard wastes	18.1	17.1	14.7	14.0	13.3	12.8	12.4	12.0	12.0
Other wastes	3.2	3.0	3.2	3.3	3.3	3.4	3.2	3.2	3.2

[1] Combustion without energy recovery is no longer available separately.

Source: Franklin Associates, Ltd., Prairie Village, KS, *Characterization of Municipal Solid Waste in the United States: 2000.* Prepared for the U.S. Environmental Protection Agency.

No. 352. Generation and Recovery of Selected Materials in Municipal Solid Waste: 1980 to 2000

[In millions of tons (151.6 represents 151,600,000), except as indicated. Covers post-consumer residential and commercial solid wastes which comprise the major portion of typical municipal collections. Excludes mining, agricultural and industrial processing, demolition and construction wastes, sewage sludge, and junked autos and obsolete equipment wastes. Based on material-flows estimating procedure and wet weight as generated]

Item and material	1980	1990	1994	1995	1996	1997	1998	1999	2000
Waste generated, total	**151.6**	**205.2**	**214.2**	**211.4**	**209.2**	**217.0**	**223.4**	**230.9**	**231.9**
Paper and paperboard	55.2	72.7	80.8	81.7	79.7	83.3	84.2	88.3	86.7
Ferrous metals	12.6	12.6	11.8	11.6	11.8	12.3	12.4	13.3	13.5
Aluminum	1.7	2.8	3.0	3.0	3.0	3.0	3.1	3.1	3.2
Other nonferrous metals	1.2	1.1	1.3	1.3	1.3	1.3	1.4	1.4	1.4
Glass	15.1	13.1	13.4	12.8	12.3	12.0	12.6	12.9	12.8
Plastics	6.8	17.1	19.3	18.9	19.8	21.5	22.4	24.1	24.7
Yard waste	27.5	35.0	31.5	29.7	27.9	27.7	27.7	27.7	27.7
Other wastes	31.5	50.7	53.1	52.4	53.5	55.9	59.6	60.1	61.9
Materials recovered, total	**14.5**	**33.2**	**50.6**	**54.9**	**57.3**	**59.4**	**61.1**	**64.8**	**69.9**
Paper and paperboard	11.9	20.2	29.5	32.7	32.6	33.6	34.4	36.1	39.4
Ferrous metals	0.4	2.2	4.0	4.1	4.4	4.7	4.3	4.5	4.6
Aluminum	0.3	1.0	1.0	0.9	0.9	1.0	0.9	0.9	0.9
Other nonferrous metals	0.5	0.7	1.0	0.8	0.8	0.8	0.9	0.9	0.9
Glass	0.8	2.6	3.1	3.1	3.2	2.9	2.9	3.0	2.9
Plastics	-	0.4	0.9	1.0	1.1	1.1	1.2	1.3	1.3
Yard waste	-	4.2	8.0	9.0	10.4	11.5	12.6	14.2	15.8
Other wastes	0.6	1.8	3.1	3.2	3.9	3.8	3.9	3.9	4.1
Percent of generation recovered, total	**9.6**	**16.2**	**23.6**	**26.0**	**27.4**	**27.4**	**27.4**	**28.1**	**30.1**
Paper and paperboard	21.6	27.8	36.5	40.0	40.9	40.3	40.9	40.9	45.4
Ferrous metals	3.2	17.5	33.9	35.3	37.3	38.2	34.7	33.8	34.1
Aluminum	17.6	35.7	33.3	30.0	30.0	33.3	29.0	29.0	28.1
Other nonferrous metals	41.7	63.6	76.9	61.5	61.5	61.5	64.3	64.3	64.3
Glass	5.3	19.8	23.1	24.2	26.0	24.2	23.0	23.3	22.7
Plastics	-	2.3	4.7	5.3	5.6	5.1	5.4	5.4	5.3
Yard waste	-	12.0	25.4	30.3	37.3	41.5	45.5	51.3	57.0
Other wastes	1.9	3.6	5.8	6.1	7.3	6.8	6.5	6.5	6.6

- Represents zero.

Source: Franklin Associates, Ltd., Prairie Village, KS, *Characterization of Municipal Solid Waste in the United States: 2000.* Prepared for the U.S. Environmental Protection Agency.

No. 353. Curbside Recycling Programs—Number and Population Served by Region: 1995 to 2000

[For composition of regions, see map, inside front cover]

Region	Number of programs					Population served [1] (1,000)				
	1995	1996	1997	1999	2000	1995	1996	1997	1999	2000
Total	**7,375**	**8,817**	**8,969**	**9,349**	**9,247**	**121,335**	**134,630**	**136,229**	**139,826**	**133,165**
Northeast	2,210	3,427	3,406	3,414	3,459	37,256	43,052	43,200	43,162	43,482
South	1,281	1,318	1,344	1,581	1,427	31,521	32,798	36,952	37,914	37,510
Midwest	2,985	3,198	3,357	3,477	3,582	25,487	27,454	26,970	30,106	22,618
West	899	874	862	877	779	27,071	31,326	29,107	28,644	29,555

[1] Calculated using population of states reporting data.

Source: Franklin Associates, Ltd., Prairie Village, KS, *Characterization of Municipal Solid Waste in the United States: 2000.* Prepared for the U.S. Environmental Protection Agency. Also in *Biocycle Magazine.*

No. 354. Toxic Chemical Releases and Transfers by Media: 1988 to 2000

[In millions of pounds (3,211.6 represents 3,211,600,000), except as indicated. Based on reports filed as required by Section 313 of the Emergency Planning and Community Right-to-Know Act (EPCRA, or Title III of the Superfund Amendments and Reauthorization Act of 1986), Public Law 99-499. Owners and operators of facilities that are classified within Standard Classification Code groups 20 through 39, have 10 or more full-time employees, and that manufacture, process, or otherwise uses any listed toxic chemical in quantities greater than the established threshold in the course of a calendar year are covered and required to report]

Media	Core chemicals [1]					
	1988	1995	1997	1998	1999	2000
Total facilities reporting	19,824	20,173	19,608	19,400	18,913	18,680
Total releases.	**3,211.6**	**1,941.3**	**1,943.2**	**1,826.0**	**1,739.6**	**1,661.3**
On-site releases	2,790.2	1,646.9	1,496.9	1,401.5	1,311.4	1,212.3
Air emissions	2,180.5	1,205.2	993.1	928.9	862.6	800.8
Surface water	41.9	17.1	18.2	17.4	14.4	14.6
Underground injection	161.9	154.7	131.4	114.7	109.3	111.3
Releases to land	405.8	269.9	354.3	340.4	325.0	285.6
Off-site releases	421.4	294.5	446.2	424.6	428.2	449.0
Total transfers off-site for further waste management	601.1	3,043.6	2,971.5	2,795.7	2,890.2	2,839.3
Transfers to recycling	(NA)	2,206.7	2,137.4	1,995.6	2,078.9	2,009.3
Transfers to energy recovery.	(NA)	489.8	469.4	440.1	471.5	484.9
Transfers to treatment	325.9	198.3	212.7	211.7	195.7	189.0
Transfers to POTWs [2]	231.6	146.7	152.0	147.7	144.0	145.7
Other off-site transfers	43.6	2.2	0.0	0.7	0.1	10.4
Total production-related waste managed. . .	(NA)	17,684.9	17,814.7	18,080.5	18,605.9	26,960.5
Recycled on-site	(NA)	5,869.9	6,184.2	6,553.9	6,388.8	8,827.3
Recycled off-site	(NA)	2,288.1	2,150.8	2,061.6	2,135.6	2,109.0
Energy recovery on-site	(NA)	2,591.3	2,543.0	2,504.0	2,577.1	2,438.7
Energy recovery off-site	(NA)	477.7	484.0	447.8	468.9	489.8
Treated on-site	(NA)	4,181.9	4,217.9	4,347.0	4,989.2	11,141.6
Treated off-site	(NA)	394.8	371.8	387.5	348.3	350.3
Quantity released on- and off-site	(NA)	1,881.2	1,863.0	1,778.7	1,698.0	1,603.8

NA Not available. [1] Chemicals covered for all reporting years. Excludes chemicals removed from the list, those added in 1990, 1994, and 1995, and aluminum oxide, ammonia, hydrochloric acid, PBT chemicals, sulfuric acid, vanadium and vanadium compounds. [2] POTW (Publicly Owned Treatment Work) is a wastewater treatment facility that is owned by a state or municipality.

No. 355. Toxic Chemical Releases by Industry: 2000

[In millions of pounds (7,100.8 represents 7,100,800,000), except as indicated. "Original Industries" include owners and operators of facilities that are classified within Standard Classification Code groups 20 through 39, have 10 or more full-time employees, and that manufacture, process, or otherwise uses any listed toxic chemical in quantities greater than the established threshold in the course of a calendar year are covered and required to report. Beginning in 1998, additional industries (listed below as "New Industries") were required to report]

Industry	1987 SIC[1] code	Total facilities (number)	Total on and off-site releases	On-site release				Off-site releases/ transfers off-site to disposal
				Total	Air emissions	Surface water discharges	Other [2]	
Total.	**(X)**	**23,484**	**7,100.8**	**6,575.7**	**1,904.4**	**260.9**	**4,410.4**	**525.1**
ORIGINAL INDUSTRIES								
Total [3]	**(X)**	**21,352**	**2,284.4**	**1,874.4**	**1,106.6**	**255.4**	**512.5**	**410.0**
Food and kindred products	20	1,710	126.9	121.8	59.8	55.6	6.4	5.1
Tobacco products	21	27	3.1	2.9	2.4	0.6	-	0.2
Textile mill products	22	292	8.5	7.8	7.3	0.2	0.3	0.7
Apparel and other textile products . .	23	15	0.5	0.5	0.5	-	-	0.1
Lumber and wood products	24	857	34.5	33.1	32.9	0.1	0.2	1.4
Furniture and fixtures	25	324	12.3	12.2	12.2	0.0	(Z)	0.1
Paper and allied products	26	496	227.4	220.0	184.6	20.1	15.3	7.4
Printing and publishing	27	202	19.0	18.8	18.8	(Z)	(Z)	0.2
Chemical and allied products.	28	3,745	648.0	584.9	277.5	68.7	238.6	63.1
Petroleum and coal products	29	550	72.8	68.2	46.7	18.0	3.5	4.6
Rubber and misc. plastic products . .	30	1,888	105.2	89.5	88.6	(Z)	0.8	15.8
Leather and leather products.	31	75	3.7	2.0	1.9	0.1	(Z)	1.6
Stone, clay, glass products	32	757	42.8	37.2	32.3	0.2	4.8	5.6
Primary metal industries	33	1,948	606.8	381.3	94.1	68.5	218.7	225.5
Fabricated metals products	34	2,893	76.0	51.5	48.8	1.9	0.8	24.5
Industrial machinery and equipment .	35	1,109	19.2	12.7	10.1	0.1	2.4	6.6
Electronic, electric equipment	36	1,197	33.5	21.7	15.5	4.2	2.0	11.8
Transportation equipment	37	1,302	96.2	83.6	83.0	0.2	0.4	12.6
Instruments and related products . . .	38	257	9.1	8.7	7.6	1.1	(Z)	0.4
Miscellaneous.	39	302	8.2	7.2	7.2	(Z)	(Z)	1.0
NEW INDUSTRIES								
Total	**(X)**	**2,132**	**4,816.4**	**4,701.3**	**797.8**	**5.5**	**3,898.0**	**115.1**
Metal mining.	10	97	3,357.8	3,357.1	3.1	0.5	3,353.5	0.6
Coal mining	12	81	16.0	16.0	1.2	0.7	14.0	(Z)
Electric utilities	49	706	1,152.2	1,080.9	787.8	4.2	288.9	71.3
Chemical wholesalers	5169	467	1.6	1.4	1.4	(Z)	0.1	0.2
Petroleum bulk terminals	5171	566	3.9	3.4	3.4	(Z)	(Z)	0.5
RCRA/solvent recovery	4953/ 7369	215	285.0	242.4	0.9	(Z)	241.4	42.5

- Represents or rounds to zero. X Not applicable. Z Less than 50,000 pounds. [1] Standard Industrial Classification, see text, Section 12, Labor Force, Employment, and Earnings. [2] Includes underground injection for Class I and Class II to V wells and land releases. [3] Includes industries with no specific industry identified, not shown separately.

Source of Tables 354 and 355: U.S. Environmental Protection Agency, 2000 Toxics Release Inventory, annual.

Geography and Environment 221

No. 356. Toxic Releases by State: 1988 to 2000

[In millions of pounds (3,211.6 represents 3,211,600,000). Excludes delisted chemicals, chemicals added in 1990, 1994, and 1995, and aluminum oxide, ammonia, hydrochloric acid, PBT chemicals, sulfuric acid, vanadium, and vanadium compounds. See headnote, Table 354]

State and outlying area	Core chemicals					State and outlying area	Core chemicals				
	1988	1995	1998	1999	2000		1988	1995	1998	1999	2000
Total	3,211.6	1,941.3	1,826.0	1,739.6	1,661.3	MT	35.6	42.6	50.4	48.9	51.2
U.S. total. . .	3,196.1	1,931.2	1,818.5	1,733.2	1,655.2	NE	17.1	11.3	10.2	9.0	11.7
						NV	2.4	3.4	3.7	5.4	4.1
AL	110.9	100.8	66.8	63.0	56.8	NH	14.0	2.3	2.3	2.5	2.3
AK	3.7	2.2	0.3	0.2	0.2	NJ	48.3	14.7	11.8	11.8	11.6
AZ	66.3	38.3	53.5	50.2	38.8	NM	30.4	43.5	23.8	20.0	0.5
AR	41.0	26.5	40.3	40.5	47.2	NY	100.8	31.6	22.5	22.6	18.0
CA	110.1	37.7	27.8	24.7	24.6	NC	124.1	63.7	48.9	46.3	40.5
CO	15.7	3.3	3.3	3.1	2.8	ND	1.2	1.2	1.1	1.0	0.8
CT	38.5	9.3	6.1	4.5	4.5	OH	205.7	124.9	128.7	118.7	111.0
DE	8.7	5.7	5.9	5.3	5.6	OK	30.5	16.4	14.3	13.8	13.7
DC	-	0.1	(Z)	(Z)	(Z)	OR	21.6	22.3	28.1	25.7	25.2
FL	33.1	28.5	30.7	29.8	31.9	PA	136.2	97.5	89.4	82.9	89.5
GA	85.8	42.9	47.1	46.0	44.0	RI	7.8	3.2	1.6	1.2	1.1
HI	0.8	0.6	0.3	0.3	0.4	SC	66.0	49.9	51.3	56.8	51.2
ID	7.3	12.0	12.8	14.8	13.0	SD	2.4	1.9	1.4	1.1	1.2
IL	140.6	86.7	84.5	81.4	79.1	TN	126.8	99.8	85.3	88.9	81.8
IN	184.4	94.4	107.3	114.4	107.7	TX	321.6	209.4	173.5	169.1	153.4
IA	42.9	22.7	25.2	25.8	25.6	UT	123.8	69.4	99.6	82.7	103.5
KS	30.4	17.8	17.7	20.4	16.9	VT	1.7	0.6	0.2	0.2	0.2
KY	65.7	34.3	31.2	31.1	28.0	VA	112.4	40.8	40.0	39.9	35.2
LA	129.4	104.6	93.5	79.2	80.5	WA	30.6	22.7	24.4	17.3	16.9
ME	15.5	7.0	6.6	5.9	6.3	WV	39.7	19.9	16.3	11.8	10.2
MD	20.2	11.9	8.8	9.1	10.6	WI	62.3	34.8	33.9	31.9	28.9
MA	32.2	8.9	6.7	5.1	4.9	WY	2.0	1.2	1.3	1.6	1.5
MI	141.1	90.4	73.6	64.6	52.3						
MN	55.9	18.5	15.1	14.7	14.7	Guam	-	-	-	-	-
MS	59.7	46.6	40.9	40.1	41.8	Puerto Rico . . .	12.9	8.9	6.6	5.9	5.6
MO	91.1	50.6	48.7	47.8	51.6	Virgin Islands . .	2.6	1.2	0.9	0.5	0.5

- Represents zero.   Z Less than 50,000.

Source: U.S. Environmental Protection Agency, *2000 Toxics Release Inventory*. See also <http://www.epa.gov/tri/tri00/pdr/2000pdr.pdf> (released May 2002).

No. 357. Hazardous Waste Sites on the National Priority List by State: 2001

[As of December 31. Includes both proposed and final sites listed on the National Priorities List for the Superfund program as authorized by the Comprehensive Environmental Response, Compensation, and Liability Act of 1980 and the Superfund Amendments and Reauthorization Act of 1986]

State and outlying area	Total sites	Rank	Percent distribution	Federal	Non-federal	State and outlying area	Total sites	Rank	Percent distribution	Federal	Non-federal
Total	1,297	(X)	(X)	166	1,131	Montana	15	25	1.2	-	15
						Nebraska	11	39	0.9	1	10
United States . . .	1,285	(X)	100.0	165	1,120	Nevada	1	49	0.1	-	1
Alabama	15	25	1.2	3	12	New Hampshire	19	20	1.5	1	18
Alaska	7	44	0.5	6	1	New Jersey	116	1	9.0	8	108
Arizona	10	40	0.8	3	7	New Mexico	13	31	1.0	1	12
Arkansas	12	34	0.9	-	12	New York	91	4	7.1	4	87
California	99	2	7.7	24	75	North Carolina	27	15	2.1	2	25
Colorado	17	22	1.3	3	14	North Dakota	-	50	0.0	-	-
Connecticut	16	23	1.2	1	15	Ohio	33	11	2.6	5	28
Delaware	16	23	1.2	1	15	Oklahoma	12	34	0.9	1	11
District of Columbia .	1	(X)	0.1	1	-	Oregon	12	34	0.9	2	10
Florida	52	6	4.0	6	46	Pennsylvania	97	3	7.5	6	91
Georgia	15	25	1.2	2	13	Rhode Island	12	34	0.9	2	10
Hawaii	3	46	0.2	2	1	South Carolina	25	16	1.9	2	23
Idaho	10	41	0.8	2	8	South Dakota	2	47	0.2	1	1
Illinois	45	8	3.5	5	40	Tennessee	13	31	1.0	4	9
Indiana	29	14	2.3	-	29	Texas	41	9	3.2	4	37
Iowa	14	29	1.1	1	13	Utah	21	19	1.6	4	17
Kansas	12	34	0.9	2	10	Vermont	9	42	0.7	-	9
Kentucky	14	29	1.1	1	13	Virginia	30	13	2.3	11	19
Louisiana	15	25	1.2	1	14	Washington	48	7	3.7	14	34
Maine	13	31	1.0	3	10	West Virginia	9	42	0.7	2	7
Maryland	19	20	1.5	9	10	Wisconsin	40	10	3.1	-	40
Massachusetts	32	12	2.5	7	25	Wyoming	2	48	0.2	1	1
Michigan	69	5	5.4	1	68						
Minnesota	24	17	1.9	2	22	Guam	2	(X)	(X)	1	1
Mississippi	4	45	0.3	-	4	Puerto Rico	8	(X)	(X)	-	8
Missouri	23	18	1.8	3	20	Virgin Islands	2	(X)	(X)	-	2

- Represents zero.   X Not applicable.

Source: U.S. Environmental Protection Agency, *Supplementary Materials: National Priorities List, Proposed Rule,* December 2001.

222   Geography and Environment

No. 358. Environmental Industry—Revenues and Employment by Industry Segment: 1990 to 2001

[148.2 represents $148,200,000,000. Covers approximately 59,000 private and public companies engaged in environmental activities]

Industry segment	Revenue (bil. dol.)				Employment (1,000)			
	1990	1995	2000	2001	1990	1995	2000	2001
Industry total	148.2	179.2	204.9	210.7	1,174.3	1,327.0	1,414.8	1,431.5
Analytical services [1]	1.5	1.2	1.2	1.2	20.2	14.1	14.0	13.7
Wastewater treatment works [2]	18.3	23.1	28.4	29.4	95.0	101.5	117.4	120.5
Solid waste management [3]	26.1	32.5	39.0	40.0	209.5	243.4	263.5	266.8
Hazardous waste management [4]	6.3	6.2	5.1	4.9	56.9	52.5	41.8	40.1
Remediation/industrial services	11.1	11.1	11.2	11.1	107.2	98.1	110.7	105.5
Consulting & engineering	12.5	15.5	17.4	18.1	144.2	180.2	186.0	191.2
Water equipment & chemicals	13.5	16.5	19.8	20.3	97.9	110.2	130.5	132.0
Instrument manufacturing	2.0	3.0	3.6	3.8	18.8	26.2	29.4	29.8
Air pollution control equipment [5]	13.1	14.8	17.6	18.1	82.7	107.2	119.7	122.0
Waste management equipment [6]	8.7	9.9	9.9	10.1	88.8	93.8	74.6	75.1
Process & prevention technology	0.4	0.8	1.2	1.3	8.9	19.5	29.0	28.6
Water utilities [7]	19.8	25.3	30.3	31.3	104.7	118.2	131.7	134.8
Resource recovery [8]	13.1	16.9	16.0	16.4	118.4	136.0	127.2	128.3
Environmental energy sources [9]	1.8	2.4	4.2	4.8	21.1	26.1	39.3	43.1

[1] Covers environmental laboratory testing and services. [2] Mostly revenues collected by municipal entities. [3] Covers such activities as collection, transportation, transfer stations, disposal, landfill ownership and management for solid waste. [4] Transportation and disposal of hazardous, medical and nuclear waste. [5] Includes stationery and mobile sources. [6] Includes vehicles, containers, liners, processing and remediation equipment. [7] Revenues generated from the sale of water. [8] Revenues generated from the sale of recovered metals, paper, plastic, etc. [9] Includes solar, wind, geothermal and conservation devices.

Source: Environmental Business International, Inc., San Diego, CA, *Environmental Business Journal*, monthly (copyright).

No. 359. Threatened and Endangered Wildlife and Plant Species— Number: 2002

[As of April. Endangered species: One in danger of becoming extinct throughout all or a significant part of its natural range. Threatened species: One likely to become endangered in the foreseeable future]

Item	Mammals	Birds	Reptiles	Amphibians	Fishes	Snails	Clams	Crustaceans	Insects	Arachnids	Plants
Total listings	342	273	115	28	126	33	72	21	48	12	746
Endangered species, total	316	253	78	19	82	22	64	18	39	12	597
United States	65	78	14	11	71	21	62	18	35	12	596
Foreign	251	175	64	8	11	1	2	-	4	-	1
Threatened species, total	26	20	37	9	44	11	8	3	9	-	149
United States	9	14	22	8	44	11	8	3	9	-	147
Foreign	17	6	15	1	-	-	-	-	-	-	2

- Represents zero.

Source: U.S. Fish and Wildlife Service, *Endangered Species Bulletin*, bimonthly; and <http://ecos.fws.gov/tess/html/boxscore.html> (accessed 06 June 2002).

No. 360. Tornadoes, Floods, Tropical Storms, and Lightning: 1991 to 2001

Weather type	1991	1992	1993	1994	1995	1996	1997	1998	1999	2000	2001
Tornadoes, number [1]	1,132	1,297	1,173	1,082	1,235	1,170	1,148	1,424	1,343	1,071	1,104
Lives lost, total	39	39	33	69	30	25	67	130	94	40	39
Most in a single tornado	17	12	7	22	6	5	27	32	7	(NA)	(NA)
Floods and flash floods:											
Lives lost	61	62	103	91	80	131	118	136	68	38	(NA)
North Atlantic tropical storms and hurricanes [2]	8	7	8	7	19	13	7	14	12	15	15
Number of hurricanes reaching U.S. mainland	1	1	1	-	2	2	1	3	3	-	-
Direct deaths on U.S. mainland .	17	26	9	38	29	33	4	23	70	5	44
Property loss in U.S. (mil. dol.) .	1,500	26,500	57	973	3,723	3,600	100	7,299	5,862	27	5,250
Lightning:											
Deaths	73	41	43	69	85	53	42	44	46	51	(NA)
Injuries	432	292	295	577	510	309	306	570	243	364	(NA)

- Represents zero. NA Not available. [1] Source: U.S. National Weather Service, Internet site <http://www.spc.noaa.gov/climo/torn/monthlytornstats.html> (accessed 06 June 2002). A violent, rotating column of air descending from a cumulonimbus cloud in the form of a tubular- or funnel-shaped cloud, usually characterized by movements along a narrow path and wind speeds from 100 to over 300 miles per hour. Also known as a "twister" or "waterspout." [2] Source: National Hurricane Center (NHC), Coral Gables, FL, unpublished data. For data on individual hurricanes, see the NHC web site at <http://www.nhc.noaa.gov/>. Tropical storms have maximum winds of 39 to 73 miles per hour; hurricanes have maximum winds of 74 miles per hour or higher.

Source: Except as noted, U.S. National Oceanic and Atmospheric Administration (NOAA), *Storm Data*, monthly. See also NOAA web site at <http://www.nws.noaa.gov/om/hazstats.shtml>.

U.S. Census Bureau, Statistical Abstract of the United States: 2002

No. 361. Major U.S. Weather Disasters: 1980 to 2001

[5.0 represents $5,000,000,000. Covers only weather related disasters costing $1 billion or more]

Event	Description	Time period	Esti-mated cost (bil. dol.)	Deaths
Tropical Storm Allison . . .	Tropical storm produced rainfall & severe flooding in coastal portions of TX & LA & damage also in MS, FL, VA, & PA .	June 2001	5.0	43
Midwest and Ohio Valley hail and tornadoes	Storms, tornadoes, and hail in TX, OK, KS, NE, IA, MO, IL, IN, WI, MI, OH, KY, and PA.	April 2001	1.7	3
Southern drought/heat wave	Severe drought and heat over south-central and south-eastern states cause significant agricultural losses. . . .	Spring-summer 2000	Over 4.0	140
Western fire season	Severe fire season in western states due to drought and frequent winds.	Spring-summer 2000	Over 2.0	-
Hurricane Floyd	Category 2 hurricane in NC, causing severe flooding in NC and some flooding in SC, VA, MD, PA, NY, NJ, DE, RI, CT, MA, and VT	Sept. 1999	6.0	75
Drought/heat wave	Drought/heatwave over eastern U.S.	Summer 1999	1.0	256
OK-KS tornadoes	Category F4-F5 tornados hit OK, KS, TX, and TN	May 1999	1.0	55
AR-TN tornados	Two outbreaks of tornadoes in 6-day period	January 1999	1.3	31
Texas flooding	Severe flooding in southeast Texas from 2 heavy rain events with 10-20 in. totals	Oct.-Nov. 1998	1.0	31
Hurricane Georges	Category 2 hurricane in Puerto Rico, Florida Keys, and Gulf coasts of LA, MS, AL, and FL.	Sept. 1998	3-4	16
Hurricane Bonnie	Category 3 hurricane in eastern NC and VA	August 1998	1.0	2
Southern drought/heat wave	Severe drought and heat wave from TX/OK eastward to the Carolinas	Summer 1998	6.0	200
Minnesota severe storms/hail.	Very damaging severe thunderstorms with large hail over wide areas of Minnesota.	May 1998	1.5	1
Southeast severe weather	Tornadoes and flooding related to strong El Nino in the southeast	Winter/spring 1998	1.0	Over 130
Northeast ice storm	Intense ice storm hits ME, NH, VT, and NY	January 1998	1.4	16
Northern plains flooding. .	Severe flooding in Dakotas and MN due to heavy spring snowmelt	April-May 1997	2.0	11
MS and OH valleys flooding and tornadoes .	Tornadoes and severe flooding hit the states of AR, MO, MS, TN, IL, IN, KY, OH, and WV	March 1997	1.0	67
West Coast flooding	Flooding from rains & snowmelt in CA, WA, OR, ID, NV, & MT.	Dec. 1996-Jan. 1999	2-3	36
Hurricane Fran.	Category 3 hurricane in NC and VA	Sept. 1996	5.0	37
Southern Plains severe drought	Drought in agricultural areas of TX & OK	Fall 1995-summer 1996	Over 4	(NA)
Pacific Northwest severe flooding	Flooding from heavy rain & snowmelt in OR, WA, ID, and MT.	Feb. 1996	1.0	9
Blizzard of '96 followed by flooding	Heavy snowstorm followed by severe flooding in Appalachians, Mid-Atlantic, and Northeast	Jan. 1996	3.0	187
Hurricane Opal	Category 3 hurricane in FL, AL, parts of GA, TN, & Carolinas.	Oct. 1995	Over 3	27
Hurricane Marilyn.	Category 2 hurricane in Virgin Islands	Sept. 1995	2.1	13
TX/OK/LA/MS severe weather and flooding. . .	Flooding, hail, & tornadoes across TX, OK, parts of LA, MS, Dallas & New Orleans hardest hit	May 1995	5-6	32
California flooding.	Flooding from frequent winter storms across much of CA .	Jan.-Mar. 1995	3.0	27
Western fire season	Severe fire season in western states due to dry weather. .	Summer-fall 1994	1.0	(NA)
Texas flooding	Flooding from torrential rain & thunderstorms across southeast TX.	Oct. 1994	1.0	19
Tropical Storm Alberto. . .	Flooding due to 10 to 25 inch rain across GA, AL, part of FL.	July 1994	1.0	32
Southeast ice storm	Intense ice storm in pts of TX, OK, AR, LA, MS, AL, TN, GA, SC, NC, & VA	Feb. 1994	3.0	9
California wildfires	Out-of-control wildfires over southern CA	Fall 1993	1.0	4
Midwest flooding	Extreme flooding across central U.S.	Summer 1993	15-20	48
Drought/heat wave	Extreme drought/heatwave across southeastern U.S.	Summer 1993	1.0	(NA)
Storm/blizzard	"Storm of the Century" hits entire eastern seaboard.	Mar. 1993	3-6	270
Nor'easter of 1992	Slow-moving storm batters northeast U.S. coast, New England hardest hit	Dec. 1992	1-2	19
Hurricane Iniki	Category 4 hurricane hit Hawaiian island of Kauai	Sept. 1992	1.8	7
Hurricane Andrew.	Category 4 hurricane hit FL & LA	Aug. 1992	27.0	58
Oakland firestorm.	Oakland, CA firestorm due to low humidity & high winds . .	Oct. 1991	1.5	25
Hurricane Bob	Category 2 hurricane—mainly coastal NC, Long Island, & New England	Aug. 1991	1.5	18
TX/OK/LA/AR flooding. . .	Torrential rains cause flooding along Trinity, Red, and Arkansas rivers	May 1990	1.0	13
Hurricane Hugo	Category 4 hurricane hit Puerto Rico & Virgin Islands, devastated NC & SC	Sept. 1989	Over 9	86
Drought/heat wave	Drought/heatwave over central & eastern U.S.	Summer 1988	40.0	5,000-10,000
Hurricane Juan	Category 1 hurricane, flooding most severe problem, hit LA and southeast U.S.	Oct.-Nov. 1985	1.5	63
Hurricane Elena	Category 3 hurricane across FL to LA	Aug.-Sept. 1985	1.3	4
Florida freeze	Severe freeze central/northern FL, damage to citrus ind. .	Jan. 1985	1.2	-
Florida freeze	Severe freeze central/northern FL, damage to citrus ind. .	Dec. 1983	2.0	-
Hurricane Alicia	Category 3 hurricane across TX	Aug. 1983	3.0	21
Drought/heat wave	Drought/heatwave over central & eastern U.S.	June-Sept. 1980	20.0	10,000

- Represents zero.   NA Not available or not reported.

Source: U.S. National Oceanic and Atmospheric Administration, National Climatic Data Center, *"Billion Dollar U.S. Weather Disasters,1980-2001"* (release date: Jan. 1, 2002). See also <http://www.lwf.ncdc.noaa.gov/oa/reports/billionz.html>.

224   Geography and Environment

No. 362. Highest and Lowest Temperatures by State Through 2000

State	Highest temperatures			Lowest temperatures		
	Station	Temper-ature (F)	Date	Station	Temper-ature (F)	Date
U.S.	**Greenland Ranch, CA.** .	**134**	**Jul. 10, 1913**	**Prospect Creek, AK** . . .	**-80**	**Jan. 23, 1971**
AL.	Centerville	112	Sep. 5, 1925	New Market	-27	Jan. 30, 1966
AK.	Fort Yukon	100	[1]Jun. 27, 1915	Prospect Creek Camp . .	-80	Jan. 23, 1971
AZ.	Lake Havasu City	128	Jun. 29, 1994	Hawley Lake	-40	Jan. 7, 1971
AR.	Ozark	120	Aug. 10, 1936	Pond.	-29	Feb. 13, 1905
CA.	Greenland Ranch	134	Jul. 10, 1913	Boca.	-45	Jan. 20, 1937
CO	Bennett	118	Jul. 11, 1888	Maybell	-61	Feb. 1, 1985
CT.	Danbury	106	Jul. 15, 1995	Falls Village	-32	Feb. 16, 1943
DE.	Millsboro	110	Jul. 21, 1930	Millsboro	-17	Jan. 17, 1893
FL.	Monticello	109	Jun. 29, 1931	Tallahassee	-2	Feb. 13, 1899
GA	Greenville	112	Aug. 20, 1983	CCC Camp F-16	-17	[1]Jan. 27, 1940
HI	Pahala	100	Apr. 27, 1931	Mauna Kea Obs. 111.2. .	12	May 17, 1979
ID	Orofino	118	Jul. 28, 1934	Island Park Dam	-60	Jan. 18, 1943
IL	East St. Louis.	117	Jul. 14, 1954	Congerville.	-36	Jan. 5, 1999
IN	Collegeville	116	Jul. 14, 1936	New Whiteland	-36	Jan. 19, 1994
IA	Keokuk	118	Jul. 20, 1934	Elkader	-47	[2]Feb. 3, 1996
KS.	Alton (near)	121	[2]Jul. 24, 1936	Lebanon	-40	Feb. 13, 1905
KY.	Greensburg	114	Jul. 28, 1930	Shelbyville	-37	Jan. 19, 1994
LA.	Plain Dealing	114	Aug. 10, 1936	Minden	-16	Feb. 13, 1899
ME	North Bridgton	105	[2]Jul. 10, 1911	Van Buren	-48	Jan. 19, 1925
MD	Cumberland & Frederick.	109	[2]Jul. 10, 1936	Oakland	-40	Jan. 13, 1912
MA	New Bedford & Chester .	107	Aug. 2, 1975	Chester.	-35	Jan. 12, 1981
MI	Mio.	112	Jul. 13, 1936	Vanderbilt	-51	Feb. 9, 1934
MN	Moorhead	114	[2]Jul. 6, 1936	Tower	-60	Feb. 2, 1996
MS	Holly Springs	115	Jul. 29, 1930	Corinth	-19	Jan. 30, 1966
MO	Warsaw & Union	118	[2]Jul. 14, 1954	Warsaw.	-40	Feb. 13, 1905
MT	Medicine Lake	117	Jul. 5, 1937	Rogers Pass	-70	Jan. 20, 1954
NE.	Minden	118	[2]Jul. 24, 1936	Camp Clarke	-47	Feb. 12, 1899
NV.	Laughlin	125	Jun. 29, 1994	San Jacinto	-50	Jan. 8, 1937
NH	Nashua	106	Jul. 4, 1911	Mt. Washington.	-47	Jan. 29, 1934
NJ	Hunyon	110	Jul. 10, 1936	River Vale	-34	Jan. 5, 1904
NM	Waste Isolat Pilot Plt . . .	122	Jun. 27, 1994	Gavilan	-50	Feb. 1, 1951
NY.	Troy	108	Jul. 22, 1926	Old Forge	-52	[2]Feb. 18, 1979
NC	Fayetteville.	110	Aug. 21, 1983	Mt. Mitchell	-34	Jan. 21, 1985
ND	Steele.	121	Jul. 6, 1936	Parshall.	-60	Feb. 15, 1936
OH	Gallipolis (near).	113	[2]Jul. 21, 1934	Milligan	-39	Feb. 10, 1899
OK	Tipton	120	[2]Jun. 27, 1994	Watts	-27	Jan. 18, 1930
OR	Pendleton	119	Aug. 10, 1898	Seneca	-54	[2]Feb. 10, 1933
PA.	Phoenixville.	111	[2]Jul. 10, 1936	Smethport	-42	[1]Jan. 5, 1904
RI	Providence.	104	Aug. 2, 1975	Kingston	-23	Jan. 11, 1942
SC.	Camden	111	[2]Jun. 28, 1954	Caesars Head	-19	Jan. 21, 1985
SD.	Gannvalley.	120	Jul. 5, 1936	McIntosh	-58	Feb. 17, 1936
TN.	Perryville	113	[2]Aug. 9, 1930	Mountain City	-32	Dec. 30, 1917
TX.	Seymour	120	Aug. 12, 1936	Seminole	-23	[2]Feb. 8, 1933
UT.	Saint George	117	Jul. 5, 1985	Peter's Sink	-69	Feb. 1, 1985
VT.	Vernon	105	Jul. 4, 1911	Bloomfield	-50	Dec. 30, 1933
VA.	Balcony Falls	110	Jul. 15, 1954	Mtn. Lake Bio. Stn.	-30	Jan. 22, 1985
WA	Ice Harbor Dam	118	[2]Aug. 5, 1961	Mazama & Winthrop . . .	-48	Dec. 30, 1968
WV	Martinsburg	112	[2]Jul. 10, 1936	Lewisburg	-37	Dec. 30, 1917
WI	Wisconsin Dells	114	Jul. 13, 1936	Couderay	-55	Feb. 4, 1996
WY	Basin	114	Jul. 12, 1900	Riverside R.S.	-66	Feb. 9, 1933

[1] Estimated. [2] Also on earlier dates at the same or other places.

Source: U.S. National Oceanic and Atmospheric Administration, <http://www.lwf.ncdc.noaa.gov/oa/climate/severeweather/temperatures.html> (released 25 April 2002).

Geography and Environment 225

No. 363. Normal Daily Mean, Maximum, and Minimum Temperatures— Selected Cities

[**In Fahrenheit degrees.** Airport data except as noted. Based on standard 30-year period, 1971 through 2000]

State	Station	Daily mean temperature			Daily maximum temperature			Daily minimum temperature		
		Jan.	July	Annual average	Jan.	July	Annual average	Jan.	July	Annual average
AL	Mobile.........	50.1	81.5	66.8	60.7	91.2	77.4	39.5	71.8	56.2
AK	Juneau	25.7	56.8	41.5	30.6	64.3	47.6	20.7	49.2	35.3
AZ	Phoenix........	54.2	92.8	72.9	65.0	104.2	84.5	43.4	81.4	61.1
AR	Little Rock	40.1	82.4	62.1	49.5	92.8	72.7	30.8	72.0	51.5
CA	Los Angeles.....	57.1	69.3	63.3	65.6	75.3	70.6	48.6	63.3	56.1
	Sacramento	46.3	75.4	61.1	53.8	92.4	73.7	38.8	58.3	48.4
	San Diego......	57.8	70.9	64.4	65.8	75.8	70.8	49.7	65.9	58.1
	San Francisco	49.4	62.8	57.3	55.9	71.1	65.1	42.9	54.5	49.6
CO	Denver	29.2	73.4	50.1	43.2	88.0	64.2	15.2	58.7	35.8
CT	Hartford........	25.7	73.7	50.2	34.1	84.9	60.5	17.2	62.4	40.0
DE	Wilmington	31.5	76.6	54.4	39.3	86.0	63.6	23.7	67.3	45.1
DC	Washington	34.9	79.2	57.5	42.5	88.3	66.4	27.3	70.1	48.6
FL	Jacksonville	53.1	81.6	68.0	64.2	90.8	78.4	41.9	72.4	57.6
	Miami	68.1	83.7	76.7	76.5	90.9	84.2	59.6	76.5	69.1
GA	Atlanta	42.7	80.0	62.2	51.9	89.4	72.0	33.5	70.6	52.3
HI	Honolulu	73.0	80.8	77.5	80.4	87.8	84.7	65.7	73.8	70.2
ID	Boise	30.2	74.7	52.0	36.7	89.2	62.6	23.6	60.3	41.3
IL	Chicago........	22.0	73.3	49.1	29.6	83.5	58.3	14.3	63.2	39.8
	Peoria........	22.5	75.1	50.8	30.7	85.7	60.7	14.3	64.6	40.9
IN	Indianapolis	26.5	75.4	52.5	34.5	85.6	62.3	18.5	65.2	42.7
IA	Des Moines	20.4	76.1	50.0	29.1	86.0	59.8	11.7	66.1	40.2
KS	Wichita	30.2	81.0	56.4	40.1	92.9	67.4	20.3	69.1	45.2
KY	Louisville	33.0	78.4	57.0	41.0	87.0	66.0	24.9	69.8	47.9
LA	New Orleans	52.6	82.7	68.8	61.8	91.1	78.0	43.4	74.2	59.6
ME	Portland	21.7	68.7	45.8	30.9	78.8	55.2	12.5	58.6	36.3
MD	Baltimore.......	32.3	76.5	54.6	41.2	87.2	65.1	23.5	65.8	44.2
MA	Boston	29.3	73.9	51.6	36.5	82.2	59.3	22.1	65.5	43.9
MI	Detroit.........	24.5	73.5	49.8	31.1	83.4	58.4	17.8	63.6	41.0
	Sault Ste. Marie ...	13.2	63.9	40.1	21.5	75.7	49.6	4.9	52.0	30.5
MN	Duluth.........	8.4	65.5	39.1	17.9	76.3	48.7	-1.2	54.6	29.3
	Minneapolis-St. Paul.	13.1	73.2	45.4	21.9	83.3	54.7	4.3	63.0	35.9
MS	Jackson........	45.0	81.4	64.1	55.1	91.4	75.0	35.0	71.4	53.2
MO	Kansas City	26.9	78.5	54.2	36.0	88.8	64.3	17.8	68.2	44.0
	St. Louis.......	29.6	80.2	56.3	37.9	89.8	65.7	21.2	70.6	46.9
MT	Great Falls......	21.7	66.2	43.8	32.1	82.0	56.4	11.3	50.4	31.1
NE	Omaha	21.7	76.7	50.7	31.7	87.4	61.5	11.6	65.9	39.8
NV	Reno	33.6	71.3	51.3	45.5	91.2	67.4	21.8	51.4	35.2
NH	Concord	20.1	70.0	45.9	30.6	82.9	57.7	9.7	57.1	34.1
NJ	Atlantic City	32.1	75.3	53.5	41.4	85.1	63.6	22.8	65.4	43.3
NM	Albuquerque.....	35.7	78.5	56.8	47.6	92.3	70.4	23.8	64.7	43.2
NY	Albany	22.2	71.1	47.6	31.1	82.2	57.6	13.3	60.0	37.5
	Buffalo	24.5	70.8	48.0	31.1	79.6	55.9	17.8	62.1	39.9
	New York [1]......	32.1	76.5	54.6	38.0	84.2	61.7	26.2	68.8	47.5
NC	Charlotte	41.7	80.3	61.4	51.3	90.1	71.7	32.1	70.6	51.0
	Raleigh	39.7	78.8	59.6	49.8	89.1	70.6	29.6	68.5	48.6
ND	Bismarck	10.2	70.4	42.3	21.1	84.5	54.5	-0.6	56.4	30.1
OH	Cincinnati.......	29.7	76.3	54.2	38.0	86.4	64.0	21.3	66.1	44.3
	Cleveland	25.7	71.9	49.7	32.6	81.4	58.1	18.8	62.3	41.2
	Columbus	28.3	75.1	52.9	36.2	85.3	62.6	20.3	64.9	43.2
OK	Oklahoma City	36.7	82.0	60.1	47.1	93.1	71.1	26.2	70.8	49.2
OR	Portland	39.9	68.1	53.5	45.6	79.3	62.1	34.2	56.9	44.8
PA	Philadelphia	32.3	77.6	55.3	39.0	85.5	63.2	25.5	69.7	47.4
	Pittsburgh	27.5	72.6	51.0	35.1	82.7	60.4	19.9	62.4	41.5
RI	Providence.......	28.7	73.3	51.1	37.1	82.6	60.2	20.3	64.1	42.0
SC	Columbia.......	44.6	82.0	63.6	55.1	92.1	74.8	34.0	71.8	52.5
SD	Sioux Falls......	14.0	73.0	45.1	25.2	85.6	57.2	2.9	60.3	33.0
TN	Memphis	39.9	82.5	62.4	48.6	92.1	72.1	31.3	72.9	52.5
	Nashville	36.8	79.1	58.9	45.6	88.7	69.0	27.9	69.5	48.8
TX	Dallas-Fort Worth ..	44.1	85.0	65.5	54.1	95.4	75.8	34.0	74.6	55.1
	El Paso.........	45.1	83.3	64.7	57.2	94.5	77.1	32.9	72.0	52.1
	Houston	51.8	83.6	68.8	62.3	93.6	79.4	41.2	73.5	58.2
UT	Salt Lake City.....	29.2	77.0	52.0	37.0	90.6	62.9	21.3	63.4	41.2
VT	Burlington	18.0	70.6	45.2	26.7	81.4	54.5	9.3	59.8	35.8
VA	Norfolk	40.1	79.1	59.6	47.8	86.8	67.8	32.3	71.4	51.4
	Richmond	36.4	77.9	57.6	45.3	87.5	67.8	27.6	68.3	47.4
WA	Seattle-Tacoma....	40.9	65.3	52.3	45.8	75.3	59.8	35.9	55.3	44.8
	Spokane	27.3	68.6	47.3	32.8	82.5	57.4	21.7	54.6	37.2
WV	Charleston.......	33.4	73.9	54.5	42.6	84.9	65.4	24.2	62.9	43.5
WI	Milwaukee	20.7	72.0	47.5	28.0	81.1	55.9	13.4	62.9	39.2
WY	Cheyenne	25.9	67.7	45.0	37.1	81.9	57.6	14.8	53.4	32.3
PR	San Juan........	76.6	82.2	79.9	82.4	87.4	85.5	70.8	76.9	74.2

[1] City office data.

Source: U.S. National Oceanic and Atmospheric Administration, *Climatography of the United States*, No. 81.

No. 364. Highest Temperature of Record—Selected Cities

[In Fahrenheit degrees. Airport data, except as noted. For period of record through 2000]

State	Station	Length of record (yr.)	Jan.	Feb.	Mar.	Apr.	May	June	July	Aug.	Sept.	Oct.	Nov.	Dec.	Annual
AL	Mobile	59	84	82	90	94	100	102	104	105	99	93	87	81	105
AK	Juneau	56	57	57	61	72	82	86	90	83	73	61	56	54	90
AZ	Phoenix	63	88	92	100	105	113	122	121	116	118	107	93	88	122
AR	Little Rock	59	83	85	91	95	98	105	112	109	106	97	86	80	112
CA	Los Angeles	65	88	92	95	102	97	104	97	98	110	106	101	94	110
	Sacramento	50	70	76	88	95	105	115	114	110	108	101	87	72	115
	San Diego	60	88	90	93	98	96	101	95	98	111	107	97	88	111
	San Francisco	73	72	78	85	92	97	106	105	100	103	99	85	75	106
CO	Denver	61	73	76	84	90	96	104	104	101	97	89	79	75	104
CT	Hartford	46	65	73	89	96	99	100	102	101	99	91	81	76	102
DE	Wilmington	53	75	78	86	94	96	100	102	101	100	91	85	75	102
DC	Washington	59	79	82	89	95	99	101	104	105	101	94	86	79	105
FL	Jacksonville	59	85	88	91	95	100	103	105	102	100	96	88	84	105
	Miami	58	88	89	92	96	96	98	98	98	97	95	89	87	98
GA	Atlanta	52	79	80	89	93	95	101	105	102	98	95	84	79	105
HI	Honolulu	31	88	88	88	91	93	92	94	93	95	94	93	89	95
ID	Boise	61	63	71	81	92	98	109	111	110	102	94	78	65	111
IL	Chicago	42	65	72	88	91	93	104	104	101	99	91	78	71	104
	Peoria	61	70	72	86	92	93	105	103	103	100	90	81	71	105
IN	Indianapolis	61	71	76	85	89	93	102	104	102	100	90	81	74	104
IA	Des Moines	61	65	73	91	93	98	103	105	108	101	95	81	69	108
KS	Wichita	48	75	87	89	96	100	110	113	110	108	95	85	83	113
KY	Louisville	53	77	77	86	91	95	102	106	101	104	92	84	76	106
LA	New Orleans	54	83	85	89	92	96	100	101	102	101	94	87	84	102
ME	Portland	60	64	64	88	85	94	98	99	103	95	88	74	71	103
MD	Baltimore	50	75	79	89	94	98	101	104	105	100	92	83	77	105
MA	Boston	49	66	70	89	94	95	100	102	102	100	90	79	76	102
MI	Detroit	42	62	70	81	89	93	104	102	100	98	91	77	69	104
	Sault Ste. Marie	60	45	49	75	85	89	93	97	98	95	80	67	60	98
MN	Duluth	59	52	55	78	88	90	94	97	97	95	86	71	55	97
	Minneapolis-St. Paul	62	58	61	83	95	96	102	105	102	98	90	77	68	105
MS	Jackson	37	82	85	89	94	99	105	106	107	104	95	88	84	107
MO	Kansas City	28	69	77	86	93	95	105	107	109	106	92	82	70	109
	St. Louis	43	76	85	89	93	94	102	107	107	104	94	85	76	107
MT	Great Falls	63	67	70	78	89	93	101	105	106	98	91	76	69	106
NE	Omaha	64	69	78	89	97	99	105	114	110	104	96	83	72	114
NV	Reno	59	70	75	83	89	96	103	104	105	101	91	77	70	105
NH	Concord	59	68	67	89	95	97	98	102	101	98	90	80	73	102
NJ	Atlantic City	57	78	75	87	94	99	106	104	102	99	90	84	77	106
NM	Albuquerque	61	69	76	85	89	98	107	105	101	100	91	77	72	107
NY	Albany	54	65	68	89	92	94	99	100	99	100	89	82	71	100
	Buffalo	57	72	71	81	94	90	96	97	99	98	87	80	74	99
	New York [1]	132	72	75	86	96	99	101	106	104	102	94	84	75	106
NC	Charlotte	61	78	81	90	93	100	103	103	103	104	98	85	78	104
	Raleigh	56	79	84	92	95	97	104	105	105	104	98	88	80	105
ND	Bismarck	61	62	69	81	93	98	107	109	109	105	95	79	65	109
OH	Cincinnati	39	69	75	84	89	93	102	103	102	98	88	81	75	103
	Cleveland	59	73	74	83	88	92	104	103	102	101	90	82	77	104
	Columbus	61	74	75	85	89	94	102	100	101	100	90	80	76	102
OK	Oklahoma City	47	80	92	93	100	104	105	110	110	108	96	87	86	110
OR	Portland	60	63	71	80	90	100	100	107	107	105	92	73	65	107
PA	Philadelphia	59	74	74	87	94	97	100	104	101	100	96	81	73	104
	Pittsburgh	48	69	76	82	89	91	98	103	100	97	87	82	74	103
RI	Providence	47	69	72	85	98	95	97	102	104	100	86	78	77	104
SC	Columbia	53	84	84	91	94	101	107	107	107	101	101	90	83	107
SD	Sioux Falls	55	66	70	87	94	100	110	108	108	104	94	81	63	110
TN	Memphis	59	78	81	85	94	99	104	108	107	103	95	86	81	108
	Nashville	61	78	84	86	91	97	106	107	104	105	94	84	79	107
TX	Dallas-Fort Worth	47	88	95	96	95	103	113	110	108	111	102	89	88	113
	El Paso	61	80	83	89	98	104	114	112	108	104	96	87	80	114
	Houston	31	84	91	91	95	99	103	104	107	109	96	89	85	109
UT	Salt Lake City	72	62	69	78	86	95	104	107	106	100	89	75	69	107
VT	Burlington	57	66	62	84	91	93	100	100	101	94	85	75	67	101
VA	Norfolk	52	78	82	88	97	100	101	103	104	99	95	86	80	104
	Richmond	71	80	83	93	96	100	104	105	102	103	99	86	81	105
WA	Seattle-Tacoma	56	64	70	75	85	93	96	100	99	98	89	74	64	100
	Spokane	53	59	63	71	90	96	101	103	108	98	86	67	56	108
WV	Charleston	53	79	79	89	94	93	98	104	101	102	92	85	80	104
WI	Milwaukee	60	62	68	82	91	93	101	103	103	98	89	77	64	103
WY	Cheyenne	65	66	71	74	83	91	100	100	96	95	83	75	69	100
PR	San Juan	46	92	96	96	97	96	97	95	97	97	98	96	94	98

[1] City office data.

Source: U.S. National Oceanic and Atmospheric Administration, *Comparative Climatic Data*, annual.

No. 365. Lowest Temperature of Record—Selected Cities

[**In Fahrenheit degrees.** Airport data, except as noted. For period of record through 2000]

State	Station	Length of record (yr.)	Jan.	Feb.	Mar.	Apr.	May	June	July	Aug.	Sept.	Oct.	Nov.	Dec.	Annual
AL	Mobile.........	59	3	11	21	32	43	49	60	59	42	30	22	8	3
AK	Juneau.........	56	-22	-22	-15	6	25	31	36	27	23	11	-5	-21	-22
AZ	Phoenix........	63	17	22	25	32	40	50	61	60	47	34	25	22	17
AR	Little Rock.....	59	-4	-5	11	28	40	46	54	52	37	29	17	-1	-5
CA	Los Angeles.....	65	23	32	34	39	43	48	49	51	47	41	34	32	23
	Sacramento.....	50	23	23	26	31	36	41	48	49	43	36	26	18	18
	San Diego......	60	29	36	39	41	48	51	55	57	51	43	38	34	29
	San Francisco	73	24	25	30	31	36	41	43	42	38	34	25	20	20
CO	Denver........	61	-25	-30	-11	-2	22	30	43	41	17	3	-8	-25	-30
CT	Hartford.......	46	-26	-21	-6	9	28	37	44	36	30	17	1	-14	-26
DE	Wilmington......	53	-14	-6	2	18	30	41	48	43	36	24	14	-7	-14
DC	Washington	59	-5	4	11	24	34	47	54	49	39	29	16	1	-5
FL	Jacksonville	59	7	19	23	34	45	47	61	59	48	36	21	11	7
	Miami.........	58	30	32	32	46	53	60	69	68	68	51	39	30	30
GA	Atlanta........	52	-8	5	10	26	37	46	53	55	36	28	3	-	-8
HI	Honolulu.......	31	53	53	55	57	60	65	66	67	66	61	57	54	53
ID	Boise.........	61	-17	-15	6	19	22	31	35	34	23	11	-3	-25	-25
IL	Chicago........	42	-27	-19	-8	7	24	36	40	41	28	17	1	-25	-27
	Peoria.........	61	-25	-19	-10	14	25	39	47	41	26	19	-2	-23	-25
IN	Indianapolis	61	-27	-21	-7	16	28	37	44	41	28	17	-2	-23	-27
IA	Des Moines	61	-24	-26	-22	9	30	38	47	40	26	14	-4	-22	-26
KS	Wichita	48	-12	-21	-2	15	31	43	51	48	31	18	1	-16	-21
KY	Louisville	53	-22	-19	-1	22	31	42	50	46	33	23	-1	-15	-22
LA	New Orleans	54	14	16	25	32	41	50	60	60	42	35	24	11	11
ME	Portland	60	-26	-39	-21	8	23	33	40	33	23	15	3	-21	-39
MD	Baltimore.......	50	-7	-3	6	20	32	40	50	45	35	25	13	-	-7
MA	Boston	49	-12	-4	6	16	34	45	50	47	38	28	15	-7	-12
MI	Detroit.........	42	-21	-15	-4	10	25	36	41	38	29	17	9	-10	-21
	Sault Ste. Marie ...	60	-36	-35	-24	-2	18	26	36	29	25	16	-10	-31	-36
MN	Duluth........	59	-39	-39	-29	-5	17	27	35	32	22	8	-23	-34	-39
	Minneapolis-St. Paul.	62	-34	-32	-32	2	18	34	43	39	26	13	-17	-29	-34
MS	Jackson........	37	2	10	15	27	38	47	51	55	35	26	17	4	2
MO	Kansas City	28	-17	-19	-10	12	30	42	51	43	31	17	1	-23	-23
	St. Louis	43	-18	-12	-5	22	31	43	51	47	36	23	1	-16	-18
MT	Great Falls.......	63	-37	-35	-29	-6	15	31	36	30	16	-11	-25	-43	-43
NE	Omaha........	64	-23	-21	-16	5	27	38	44	43	25	13	-9	-23	-23
NV	Reno	59	-16	-16	-2	13	18	25	33	24	20	8	1	-16	-16
NH	Concord	59	-33	-37	-16	8	21	30	35	29	21	10	-5	-22	-37
NJ	Atlantic City	57	-10	-11	5	12	25	37	42	40	32	20	10	-7	-11
NM	Albuquerque......	61	-17	-5	8	19	28	40	52	50	37	21	-7	-7	-17
NY	Albany........	54	-28	-21	-21	10	26	36	40	34	24	16	5	-22	-28
	Buffalo	57	-16	-20	-7	12	26	35	43	38	32	20	9	-10	-20
	New York [1]......	132	-6	-15	3	12	32	44	52	50	39	28	5	-13	-15
NC	Charlotte	61	-5	5	4	24	32	45	53	53	39	24	11	2	-5
	Raleigh	56	-9	-	11	23	31	38	48	46	37	19	11	4	-9
ND	Bismarck.......	61	-44	-43	-31	-12	15	30	35	33	11	-10	-30	-43	-44
OH	Cincinnati.......	39	-25	-11	-11	15	27	39	47	43	31	16	1	-20	-25
	Cleveland	59	-20	-15	-5	10	25	31	41	38	32	19	3	-15	-20
	Columbus	61	-22	-13	-6	14	25	35	43	39	31	20	5	-17	-22
OK	Oklahoma City	47	-4	-3	3	20	37	47	53	51	36	16	11	-8	-8
OR	Portland	60	-2	-3	19	29	29	39	43	44	34	26	13	6	-3
PA	Philadelphia	59	-7	-4	7	19	28	44	51	44	35	25	15	1	-7
	Pittsburgh	48	-22	-12	-1	14	26	34	42	39	31	16	-1	-12	-22
RI	Providence......	47	-13	-7	1	14	29	41	48	40	33	20	6	-10	-13
SC	Columbia.......	53	-1	5	4	26	34	44	54	53	40	23	12	4	-1
SD	Sioux Falls......	55	-36	-31	-23	5	17	33	38	34	22	9	-17	-28	-36
TN	Memphis	59	-4	-11	12	29	38	48	52	48	36	25	9	-13	-13
	Nashville	61	-17	-13	2	23	34	42	51	47	36	26	-1	-10	-17
TX	Dallas-Fort Worth ..	47	4	7	15	29	41	51	59	56	43	29	20	-1	-1
	El Paso.........	61	-8	8	14	23	31	46	57	56	41	25	1	5	-8
	Houston	31	12	20	22	31	44	52	62	60	48	29	19	7	7
UT	Salt Lake City.....	72	-22	-30	2	14	25	35	40	37	27	16	-14	-21	-30
VT	Burlington	57	-30	-30	-20	2	24	33	39	35	25	15	-2	-26	-30
VA	Norfolk	52	-3	8	18	28	36	45	54	49	45	27	20	7	-3
	Richmond	71	-12	-10	11	23	31	40	51	46	35	21	10	-1	-12
WA	Seattle-Tacoma....	56	-	1	11	29	28	38	43	44	35	28	6	6	-
	Spokane	53	-22	-24	-7	17	24	33	37	35	22	10	-21	-25	-25
WV	Charleston.......	53	-16	-12	-	19	26	33	46	41	34	17	6	-12	-16
WI	Milwaukee	60	-26	-26	-10	12	21	33	40	44	28	18	-5	-20	-26
WY	Cheyenne	65	-29	-34	-21	-8	16	25	38	36	8	-1	-16	-28	-34
PR	San Juan........	46	61	62	60	64	66	69	69	70	69	67	66	63	60

- Represents zero. [1] City office data.

Source: U.S. National Oceanic and Atmospheric Administration, *Comparative Climatic Data,* annual.

No. 366. Normal Monthly and Annual Precipitation—Selected Cities

[**In inches.** Airport data, except as noted. Based on standard 30-year period, 1971 through 2000]

State	Station	Jan.	Feb.	Mar.	Apr.	May	June	July	Aug.	Sept.	Oct.	Nov.	Dec.	Annual
AL	Mobile.........	5.75	5.10	7.20	5.06	6.10	5.01	6.54	6.20	6.01	3.25	5.41	4.66	66.29
AK	Juneau.........	4.81	4.02	3.51	2.96	3.48	3.36	4.14	5.37	7.54	8.30	5.43	5.41	58.33
AZ	Phoenix.........	0.83	0.77	1.07	0.25	0.16	0.09	0.99	0.94	0.75	0.79	0.73	0.92	8.29
AR	Little Rock......	3.61	3.33	4.88	5.47	5.05	3.95	3.31	2.93	3.71	4.25	5.73	4.71	50.93
CA	Los Angeles......	2.98	3.11	2.40	0.63	0.24	0.08	0.03	0.14	0.26	0.36	1.13	1.79	13.15
	Sacramento......	3.84	3.54	2.80	1.02	0.53	0.20	0.05	0.06	0.36	0.89	2.19	2.45	17.93
	San Diego......	2.28	2.04	2.26	0.75	0.20	0.09	0.03	0.09	0.21	0.44	1.07	1.31	10.77
	San Francisco	4.45	4.01	3.26	1.17	0.38	0.11	0.03	0.07	0.20	1.04	2.49	2.89	20.11
CO	Denver.........	0.51	0.49	1.28	1.93	2.32	1.56	2.16	1.82	1.14	0.99	0.98	0.63	15.81
CT	Hartford.........	3.84	2.96	3.88	3.86	4.39	3.85	3.67	3.98	4.13	3.94	4.06	3.60	46.16
DE	Wilmington.......	3.43	2.81	3.97	3.39	4.15	3.59	4.28	3.51	4.01	3.08	3.19	3.40	42.81
DC	Washington......	3.21	2.63	3.60	2.77	3.82	3.13	3.66	3.44	3.79	3.22	3.03	3.05	39.35
FL	Jacksonville......	3.69	3.15	3.93	3.14	3.48	5.37	5.97	6.87	7.90	3.86	2.34	2.64	52.34
	Miami.........	1.88	2.07	2.56	3.36	5.52	8.54	5.79	8.63	8.38	6.19	3.43	2.18	58.53
GA	Atlanta.........	5.02	4.68	5.38	3.62	3.95	3.63	5.12	3.67	4.09	3.11	4.10	3.82	50.20
HI	Honolulu........	2.73	2.35	1.89	1.11	0.78	0.43	0.50	0.46	0.74	2.18	2.26	2.85	18.29
ID	Boise.........	1.39	1.14	1.41	1.27	1.27	0.74	0.39	0.30	0.76	0.76	1.38	1.38	12.19
IL	Chicago.........	1.75	1.63	2.65	3.68	3.38	3.63	3.51	4.62	3.27	2.71	3.01	2.43	36.27
	Peoria.........	1.50	1.67	2.83	3.56	4.17	3.84	4.02	3.16	3.12	2.76	2.99	2.40	36.03
IN	Indianapolis......	2.48	2.41	3.44	3.61	4.35	4.13	4.42	3.82	2.88	2.76	3.61	3.03	40.95
IA	Des Moines......	1.03	1.19	2.21	3.58	4.25	4.57	4.18	4.51	3.15	2.62	2.10	1.33	34.72
KS	Wichita.........	0.84	1.02	2.71	2.57	4.16	4.25	3.31	2.94	2.96	2.45	1.82	1.35	30.38
KY	Louisville........	3.28	3.25	4.41	3.91	4.88	3.76	4.30	3.41	3.05	2.79	3.80	3.69	44.54
LA	New Orleans	5.87	5.47	5.24	5.02	4.62	6.83	6.20	6.15	5.55	3.05	5.09	5.07	64.16
ME	Portland	4.09	3.14	4.14	4.26	3.82	3.28	3.32	3.05	3.37	4.40	4.72	4.24	45.83
MD	Baltimore........	3.47	3.02	3.93	3.00	3.89	3.43	3.85	3.74	3.98	3.16	3.12	3.35	41.94
MA	Boston	3.92	3.30	3.85	3.60	3.24	3.22	3.06	3.37	3.47	3.79	3.98	3.73	42.53
MI	Detroit.........	1.91	1.88	2.52	3.05	3.05	3.55	3.16	3.10	3.27	2.23	2.66	2.51	32.89
	Sault Ste. Marie ..	2.64	1.60	2.41	2.57	2.50	3.00	3.14	3.47	3.71	3.32	3.40	2.91	34.67
MN	Duluth.........	1.12	0.83	1.69	2.09	2.95	4.25	4.20	4.22	4.13	2.46	2.12	0.94	31.00
	Minneapolis-St. Paul.	1.04	0.79	1.86	2.31	3.24	4.34	4.04	4.05	2.69	2.11	1.94	1.00	29.41
MS	Jackson.........	5.67	4.50	5.74	5.98	4.86	3.82	4.69	3.66	3.23	3.42	5.04	5.34	55.95
MO	Kansas City	1.15	1.31	2.44	3.38	5.39	4.44	4.42	3.54	4.64	3.33	2.30	1.64	37.98
	St. Louis	2.14	2.28	3.60	3.69	4.11	3.76	3.90	2.98	2.96	2.76	3.71	2.86	38.75
MT	Great Falls.......	0.68	0.51	1.01	1.40	2.53	2.24	1.45	1.65	1.23	0.93	0.59	0.67	14.89
NE	Omaha.........	0.77	0.80	2.13	2.94	4.44	3.95	3.86	3.21	3.17	2.21	1.82	0.92	30.22
NV	Reno	1.06	1.06	0.86	0.35	0.62	0.47	0.24	0.27	0.45	0.42	0.80	0.88	7.48
NH	Concord	2.97	2.36	3.04	3.07	3.33	3.10	3.37	3.21	3.16	3.46	3.57	2.96	37.60
NJ	Atlantic City	3.60	2.85	4.06	3.45	3.38	2.66	3.86	4.32	3.14	2.86	3.26	3.15	40.59
NM	Albuquerque......	0.49	0.44	0.61	0.50	0.60	0.65	1.27	1.73	1.07	1.00	0.62	0.49	9.47
NY	Albany	2.71	2.27	3.17	3.25	3.67	3.74	3.50	3.68	3.31	3.23	3.31	2.76	38.60
	Buffalo .`......	3.16	2.42	2.99	3.04	3.35	3.82	3.14	3.87	3.84	3.19	3.92	3.80	40.54
	New York [1]......	4.13	3.15	4.37	4.28	4.69	3.84	4.62	4.22	4.23	3.85	4.36	3.95	49.69
NC	Charlotte	4.00	3.55	4.39	2.95	3.66	3.42	3.79	3.72	3.03	3.66	3.36	3.10	43.51
	Raleigh.........	4.02	3.47	4.03	2.80	3.79	3.42	4.29	3.78	4.26	3.18	2.97	3.04	43.05
ND	Bismarck........	0.45	0.51	0.85	1.46	2.22	2.59	2.58	2.15	1.61	1.28	0.70	0.44	16.84
OH	Cincinnati........	2.92	2.75	3.90	3.96	4.59	4.42	3.75	3.79	2.82	2.96	3.46	3.28	42.60
	Cleveland	2.48	2.29	2.94	3.37	3.50	3.89	3.52	3.69	3.77	2.73	3.38	3.14	38.71
	Columbus	2.53	2.20	2.89	3.25	3.88	4.07	4.61	3.72	2.92	2.31	3.19	2.93	38.52
OK	Oklahoma City	1.28	1.56	2.90	3.00	5.44	4.63	2.94	2.48	3.98	3.64	2.11	1.89	35.85
OR	Portland	5.07	4.18	3.71	2.64	2.38	1.59	0.72	0.93	1.65	2.88	5.61	5.71	37.07
PA	Philadelphia	3.52	2.74	3.81	3.49	3.88	3.29	4.39	3.82	3.88	2.75	3.16	3.31	42.05
	Pittsburgh	2.70	2.37	3.17	3.01	3.80	4.12	3.96	3.38	3.21	2.25	3.02	2.86	37.85
RI	Providence.......	4.37	3.45	4.43	4.16	3.66	3.38	3.17	3.90	3.70	3.69	4.40	4.14	46.45
SC	Columbia........	4.66	3.84	4.59	2.98	3.17	4.99	5.54	5.41	3.94	2.89	2.88	3.38	48.27
SD	Sioux Falls.......	0.51	0.51	1.81	2.65	3.39	3.49	2.93	3.01	2.58	1.93	1.36	0.52	24.69
TN	Memphis........	4.24	4.31	5.58	5.79	5.15	4.30	4.22	3.00	3.31	3.31	5.76	5.68	54.65
	Nashville........	3.97	3.69	4.87	3.93	5.07	4.08	3.77	3.28	3.59	2.87	4.45	4.54	48.11
TX	Dallas-Fort Worth ..	1.90	2.37	3.06	3.20	5.15	3.23	2.12	2.03	2.42	4.11	2.57	2.57	34.73
	El Paso.........	0.45	0.39	0.26	0.23	0.38	0.87	1.49	1.75	1.61	0.81	0.42	0.77	9.43
	Houston	3.68	2.98	3.36	3.60	5.15	5.35	3.18	3.83	4.33	4.50	4.19	3.69	47.84
UT	Salt Lake City.....	1.37	1.33	1.91	2.02	2.09	0.77	0.72	0.76	1.33	1.57	1.40	1.23	16.50
VT	Burlington	2.22	1.67	2.32	2.88	3.32	3.43	3.97	4.01	3.83	3.12	3.06	2.22	36.05
VA	Norfolk	3.93	3.34	4.08	3.38	3.74	3.77	5.17	4.79	4.06	3.47	2.98	3.03	45.74
	Richmond	3.55	2.98	4.09	3.18	3.95	3.54	4.67	4.18	3.98	3.60	3.06	3.12	43.91
WA	Seattle-Tacoma....	5.13	4.18	3.75	2.59	1.77	1.49	0.79	1.02	1.63	3.19	5.90	5.62	37.07
	Spokane	1.82	1.51	1.53	1.28	1.60	1.18	0.76	0.68	0.76	1.06	2.24	2.25	16.67
WV	Charleston.......	3.25	3.19	3.90	3.25	4.30	4.09	4.86	4.11	3.45	2.67	3.66	3.32	44.05
WI	Milwaukee.......	1.85	1.65	2.59	3.78	3.06	3.56	3.58	4.03	3.30	2.49	2.70	2.22	34.81
WY	Cheyenne	0.45	0.44	1.05	1.55	2.48	2.12	2.26	1.82	1.43	0.75	0.64	0.46	15.45
PR	San Juan........	3.02	2.30	2.14	3.71	5.29	3.52	4.16	5.22	5.60	5.06	6.17	4.57	50.76

[1] City office data.

Source: U.S. National Oceanic and Atmospheric Administration, *Climatography of the United States*, No. 81.

U.S. Census Bureau, *Statistical Abstract of the United States: 2002*

No. 367. Average Number of Days With Precipitation of 0.01 Inch or More— Selected Cities

[Airport data, except as noted. For period of record through 2000]

State	Station	Length of record (yr.)	Jan.	Feb.	Mar.	Apr.	May	June	July	Aug.	Sept.	Oct.	Nov.	Dec.	Annual
AL	Mobile	59	11	9	10	8	8	11	16	14	10	6	8	10	121
AK	Juneau	56	18	17	18	17	17	15	17	18	21	24	20	21	223
AZ	Phoenix	61	4	4	4	2	1	1	4	5	3	3	3	4	36
AR	Little Rock	58	10	9	10	10	10	8	8	7	7	7	8	9	104
CA	Los Angeles	65	6	6	6	3	1	1	1	(Z)	1	2	3	5	35
	Sacramento	61	10	9	9	5	3	1	(Z)	(Z)	1	3	7	9	58
	San Diego	60	7	6	7	4	2	1	(Z)	-	1	2	4	6	42
	San Francisco	73	11	10	10	6	3	1	(Z)	(Z)	1	4	7	10	63
CO	Denver	61	6	6	9	9	11	9	9	9	6	5	6	5	89
CT	Hartford	46	11	10	12	11	12	11	10	10	10	9	11	12	128
DE	Wilmington	53	11	10	11	11	11	10	9	9	8	8	9	10	117
DC	Washington	59	10	9	11	10	11	10	10	9	8	7	8	9	113
FL	Jacksonville	59	8	8	8	6	8	13	14	15	13	8	6	8	116
	Miami	58	7	6	6	6	10	15	16	18	17	14	8	7	131
GA	Atlanta	66	12	10	11	9	9	10	12	9	8	6	9	10	115
HI	Honolulu	51	9	9	9	9	7	6	7	6	7	8	9	10	97
ID	Boise	61	12	10	10	8	8	6	2	2	4	6	10	11	90
IL	Chicago	42	11	9	12	13	11	10	10	9	9	9	11	11	125
	Peoria	61	9	8	11	12	12	10	9	8	9	8	9	10	114
IN	Indianapolis	61	12	10	13	12	12	10	10	9	8	8	10	12	126
IA	Des Moines	61	7	7	10	11	11	11	9	9	9	8	7	8	108
KS	Wichita	47	5	5	8	8	11	10	8	7	8	6	5	6	86
KY	Louisville	53	11	11	13	12	12	10	10	8	8	7	10	11	124
LA	New Orleans	52	10	9	9	7	8	11	14	13	10	6	7	10	114
ME	Portland	60	11	10	11	12	13	11	10	9	9	9	11	11	129
MD	Baltimore	50	10	9	11	11	11	10	9	9	8	7	9	9	114
MA	Boston	49	12	10	12	11	12	10	9	10	9	9	11	12	127
MI	Detroit	42	13	11	13	13	11	10	10	10	10	9	12	13	135
	Sault Ste. Marie	59	19	14	13	11	11	11	10	11	13	14	17	19	165
MN	Duluth	59	12	9	11	11	12	13	12	11	12	10	11	11	134
	Minneapolis-St. Paul	62	9	7	10	10	11	12	10	10	9	8	9	9	116
MS	Jackson	37	11	9	10	9	9	9	11	9	8	6	9	10	109
MO	Kansas City	28	7	7	10	11	12	11	9	8	8	7	8	7	105
	St. Louis	43	9	8	11	11	11	9	9	8	8	8	9	9	111
MT	Great Falls	63	9	8	9	9	12	12	8	8	7	6	7	8	101
NE	Omaha	64	6	7	9	10	12	11	9	9	8	6	6	6	99
NV	Reno	58	6	6	6	4	4	3	2	2	3	3	5	6	51
NH	Concord	59	11	9	11	12	12	11	10	10	9	9	11	11	127
NJ	Atlantic City	57	11	10	11	11	10	9	9	9	8	7	9	10	113
NM	Albuquerque	61	4	4	5	3	4	4	9	10	6	5	4	4	61
NY	Albany	54	13	11	12	12	13	11	10	10	10	9	12	12	135
	Buffalo	57	20	17	16	14	13	11	10	10	11	12	16	19	169
	New York [1]	131	11	10	11	11	11	10	11	10	8	8	9	10	121
NC	Charlotte	61	10	10	11	9	9	10	11	10	7	7	8	10	111
	Raleigh	56	10	10	10	9	10	10	11	10	8	7	8	9	113
ND	Bismarck	61	8	7	8	8	10	12	9	8	7	6	7	8	96
OH	Cincinnati	53	12	11	13	13	12	11	10	9	8	8	11	12	130
	Cleveland	59	16	14	15	14	13	11	10	10	10	11	14	16	155
	Columbus	61	14	12	13	13	13	11	11	9	8	9	11	13	137
OK	Oklahoma City	61	5	6	7	8	10	9	6	6	7	7	5	6	83
OR	Portland	60	18	16	17	14	12	9	4	5	7	12	18	19	153
PA	Philadelphia	60	11	9	11	11	11	10	9	9	8	8	9	10	117
	Pittsburgh	48	16	14	15	14	13	12	11	10	10	10	13	16	152
RI	Providence	47	11	10	12	11	11	11	9	10	9	9	11	12	124
SC	Columbia	53	10	9	10	8	9	10	12	11	8	6	7	9	109
SD	Sioux Falls	55	6	7	9	10	11	11	10	9	8	6	7	6	99
TN	Memphis	50	10	9	11	10	9	9	9	7	7	6	9	10	106
	Nashville	59	11	10	12	11	11	10	10	10	8	7	9	11	119
TX	Dallas-Fort Worth	47	7	6	7	8	9	7	5	5	6	6	6	7	79
	El Paso	61	4	3	2	2	2	3	8	8	5	4	3	4	49
	Houston	31	10	8	9	7	8	9	9	9	8	8	8	9	105
UT	Salt Lake City	72	10	9	10	10	8	5	4	6	5	6	8	9	91
VT	Burlington	57	15	12	13	12	14	12	12	13	12	12	14	15	155
VA	Norfolk	52	11	10	11	10	10	9	11	10	8	7	8	9	116
	Richmond	63	10	9	11	9	11	9	11	10	8	7	8	9	114
WA	Seattle-Tacoma	56	19	16	17	14	11	9	5	6	9	13	18	19	155
	Spokane	53	14	11	11	9	10	8	5	5	6	8	13	14	113
WV	Charleston	53	15	14	15	14	13	12	13	11	9	9	12	14	151
WI	Milwaukee	60	12	10	12	12	12	11	10	9	9	9	10	11	126
WY	Cheyenne	65	6	6	9	10	12	11	11	10	8	6	6	6	101
PR	San Juan	45	17	13	12	13	16	15	19	19	18	17	19	19	197

- Represents zero. Z Less than 1/2 day. [1] City office data.

Source: U.S. National Oceanic and Atmospheric Administration, *Comparative Climatic Data*, annual.

U.S. Census Bureau, Statistical Abstract of the United States: 2002

No. 368. Snow and Ice Pellets—Selected Cities

[In inches. Airport data, except as noted. For period of record through 2000. T denotes trace]

State	Station	Length of record (yr)	Jan.	Feb.	Mar.	Apr.	May	June	July	Aug.	Sept.	Oct.	Nov.	Dec.	Annual
AL	Mobile	58	0.1	0.1	0.1	T	T	-	T	-	-	-	T	0.1	0.4
AK	Juneau	56	26.0	19.0	15.1	3.3	T	T	-	-	T	1.0	12.2	21.9	98.5
AZ	Phoenix	62	T	-	T	T	T	-	-	-	-	T	-	T	T
AR	Little Rock	56	2.4	1.5	0.5	T	T	T	-	-	-	T	0.2	0.6	5.2
CA	Los Angeles	62	T	T	T	-	-	-	-	-	-	-	-	T	T
	Sacramento	50	T	T	T	T	-	T	-	-	-	-	-	T	T
	San Diego	60	T	-	T	T	-	-	-	-	-	-	T	T	T
	San Francisco	69	T	T	T	-	-	-	-	-	-	-	-	-	T
CO	Denver	61	8.1	7.5	12.5	8.9	1.6	-	T	T	1.6	3.7	9.1	7.3	60.3
CT	Hartford	43	13.0	12.0	10.0	1.5	-	T	-	-	-	0.1	2.1	10.2	48.9
DE	Wilmington	50	6.8	6.1	3.3	0.2	T	T	T	-	-	0.1	0.9	3.3	20.7
DC	Washington	57	5.6	5.2	2.3	T	T	T	T	T	-	-	0.8	2.8	16.7
FL	Jacksonville	59	T	-	-	T	-	T	T	-	-	-	-	-	T
	Miami	58	-	-	-	-	T	-	-	-	-	-	-	-	T
GA	Atlanta	63	0.9	0.5	0.4	T	-	-	-	-	-	T	T	0.2	2
HI	Honolulu	52	-	-	-	-	-	-	-	-	-	-	-	-	-
ID	Boise	61	6.4	3.7	1.7	0.6	0.1	T	T	T	T	0.1	2.3	5.7	20.6
IL	Chicago	41	11.3	8.1	6.9	1.6	0.1	T	T	T	T	0.4	1.9	8.6	38.9
	Peoria	57	6.8	5.2	4.1	0.8	T	T	T	-	T	0.1	2.0	6.2	25.2
IN	Indianapolis	69	6.9	5.5	3.5	0.5	-	T	-	T	-	0.2	1.9	5.3	23.8
IA	Des Moines	57	8.3	7.2	6.0	1.8	-	T	T	-	T	0.3	3.1	6.7	33.4
KS	Wichita	47	4.3	4.1	2.8	0.2	T	T	T	T	T	-	1.3	3.2	15.9
KY	Louisville	53	5.4	4.5	3.2	0.1	T	T	T	T	T	0.1	1	2.3	16.6
LA	New Orleans	50	-	0.1	T	T	T	-	-	-	-	-	T	0.1	0.2
ME	Portland	60	19.5	16.7	13	2.9	0.2	-	-	-	T	0.2	3.3	14.7	70.5
MD	Baltimore	50	6.5	6.6	3.8	0.1	T	-	T	-	-	-	1.0	3.1	21.1
MA	Boston	63	12.9	11.7	8.0	0.9	-	-	-	T	-	T	1.3	7.5	42.3
MI	Detroit	42	10.7	9.2	6.9	1.7	T	-	-	-	T	0.2	2.8	10.0	41.5
	Sault Ste. Marie	57	29.2	18.2	14.6	5.8	0.5	T	T	T	0.1	2.4	15.6	31.0	117.4
MN	Duluth	57	17.9	11.5	13.6	6.7	0.7	T	T	T	0.1	1.5	13.0	15.5	80.5
	Minneapolis-St. Paul	62	10.7	8.1	10.5	2.8	0.1	T	T	T	T	0.5	7.8	9.4	49.9
MS	Jackson	37	0.5	0.2	0.2	T	-	-	-	-	-	-	T	0.1	1.0
MO	Kansas City	66	5.7	4.4	3.4	0.8	T	T	T	-	T	0.1	1.2	4.5	20.1
	St. Louis	64	5.5	4.4	3.9	0.5	-	T	T	-	-	T	1.4	3.9	19.6
MT	Great Falls	63	9.5	8.4	10.5	7.1	1.8	0.3	T	0.1	1.5	3.4	7.4	8.1	58.1
NE	Omaha	65	7.2	6.7	6.3	1.0	0.1	-	T	T	T	0.3	2.6	5.8	30.0
NV	Reno	54	5.8	5.2	4.3	1.2	0.8	-	-	-	-	0.3	2.4	4.3	24.3
NH	Concord	59	18	14.2	11.2	2.5	0.1	T	-	-	T	0.1	4.0	13.7	63.8
NJ	Atlantic City	51	5	5.3	2.5	0.3	T	T	T	-	-	T	0.4	2.2	15.7
NM	Albuquerque	61	2.5	2.1	1.8	0.6	T	T	T	T	T	0.1	1.2	2.7	11.0
NY	Albany	54	16.8	13.9	11.4	2.7	0.1	T	T	T	T	T	4.2	14.4	63.7
	Buffalo	57	24.3	17.8	12	3.2	0.2	T	T	T	T	0.3	11.6	23.1	92.5
	New York [1]	132	7.5	8.5	5.1	0.9	T	-	T	-	-	T	0.9	5.5	28.4
NC	Charlotte	61	2.1	1.6	1.2	T	T	T	-	-	-	T	0.1	0.5	5.5
	Raleigh	56	2.7	2.5	1.3	-	T	T	T	-	-	-	0.1	0.8	7.4
ND	Bismarck	61	7.8	7.1	8.5	4.1	0.9	T	T	T	0.2	1.8	7.2	7.0	44.6
OH	Cincinnati	53	7.2	5.6	4.5	0.5	-	T	T	T	-	0.3	2.0	3.8	23.9
	Cleveland	59	13.6	12	10.5	2.4	0.1	-	T	T	-	0.6	5.3	12.0	56.5
	Columbus	53	9	6.1	4.6	0.9	-	T	T	-	T	0.1	2.2	5.5	28.4
OK	Oklahoma City	61	3.2	2.4	1.5	T	T	T	T	T	T	T	0.5	1.9	9.5
OR	Portland	55	3.2	1.1	0.4	T	-	T	T	-	T	T	0.4	1.4	6.5
PA	Philadelphia	58	6.1	6.5	3.5	0.3	T	T	-	-	-	T	0.7	3.3	20.4
	Pittsburgh	48	11.8	9.1	8.6	1.7	0.1	T	T	T	T	0.4	3.5	8.1	43.3
RI	Providence	47	9.7	9.8	7.3	0.7	0.2	-	-	-	-	0.1	1.1	6.8	35.7
SC	Columbia	53	0.5	0.8	0.2	T	-	-	-	T	-	-	T	0.3	1.8
SD	Sioux Falls	55	6.9	8.1	9.3	2.9	T	T	T	-	T	0.8	6.1	7.2	41.3
TN	Memphis	49	2.2	1.4	0.8	T	T	T	-	-	-	T	0.1	0.6	5.1
	Nashville	57	3.7	3.0	1.5	-	-	-	T	-	T	-	0.4	1.4	10.0
TX	Dallas-Fort Worth	43	1.1	0.9	0.2	T	T	-	-	-	-	T	0.1	0.2	2.5
	El Paso	57	1.3	0.8	0.4	0.3	T	T	T	T	-	T	0.9	1.6	5.3
	Houston	66	0.2	0.2	T	T	T	T	-	-	-	-	T	T	0.4
UT	Salt Lake City	72	13.7	9.9	9.3	4.9	0.6	T	T	T	0.1	1.3	6.9	11.8	58.5
VT	Burlington	57	19.4	16.6	13.3	4.4	0.2	-	T	-	-	0.2	6.7	18.0	78.8
VA	Norfolk	50	2.9	3.0	1.0	-	T	T	-	T	-	-	-	0.9	7.8
	Richmond	61	5.0	3.9	2.4	0.1	T	-	-	-	-	T	0.4	2.0	13.8
WA	Seattle-Tacoma	52	4.9	1.6	1.3	0.1	T	-	T	-	T	-	1.1	2.4	11.4
	Spokane	53	15.6	7.6	3.8	0.6	0.1	T	-	-	T	0.4	6.3	14.5	48.9
WV	Charleston	49	11.1	8.7	5.4	0.9	-	T	T	T	T	0.2	2.4	5.3	34.0
WI	Milwaukee	60	14.1	9.5	8.3	1.9	0.1	T	T	T	T	0.2	3.1	10.8	48.0
WY	Cheyenne	65	6.5	6.3	11.9	9.2	3.2	0.2	T	T	1.1	3.7	7.1	6.3	55.5
PR	San Juan	45	-	-	-	-	-	-	-	-	-	-	-	-	-

- Represents zero or rounds to zero.   [1] City office data.

Source: U.S. National Oceanic and Atmospheric Administration, *Comparative Climatic Data,* annual.

U.S. Census Bureau, Statistical Abstract of the United States: 2002

No. 369. Sunshine, Average Wind Speed, Heating and Cooling Degree Days, and Average Relative Humidity—Selected Cities

[Airport data, except as noted. For period of record through 2000, except heating and cooling normals for period 1961-1990. M=morning. A=afternoon]

State	Station	Average percentage of possible sunshine [1] — Length of record (yr.)	An-nual	Average wind speed (m.p.h.) — Length of record (yr.)	An-nual	Jan.	July	Heating degree days	Cooling degree days	Average relative humidity (percent) — Length of record (yr.)	Annual M	Annual A	Jan. M	Jan. A	July M	July A
AL	Mobile	47	60	52	8.8	10.1	6.9	1,702	2,627	38	87	61	82	64	90	64
AK	Juneau	47	23	55	8.2	8.0	7.5	8,897	-	34	80	69	77	74	78	66
AZ	Phoenix	57	81	55	6.2	5.3	7.1	1,350	4,162	40	50	23	65	32	43	20
AR	Little Rock	35	60	58	7.8	8.4	6.7	3,155	2,005	36	83	58	80	63	86	57
CA	Los Angeles.	60	72	52	7.5	6.7	7.9	1,458	727	41	79	65	71	61	86	68
	Sacramento.	49	73	50	7.8	7.2	8.9	2,749	1,237	14	83	46	91	71	77	29
	San Diego.	55	72	60	7.0	6.0	7.5	1,256	984	40	77	63	72	58	82	67
	San Francisco	68	71	73	10.6	7.2	13.6	3,016	145	41	84	62	86	68	86	60
CO	Denver	61	67	47	8.6	8.6	8.3	6,020	679	35	67	40	63	49	68	34
CT	Hartford	41	52	46	8.4	9.0	7.3	6,151	677	41	77	52	72	56	79	51
DE	Wilmington	47	55	52	9.0	9.8	7.8	4,937	1,046	53	78	55	75	60	79	54
DC	Washington	48	55	52	9.4	10.0	8.3	4,047	1,549	40	75	54	70	56	76	53
FL	Jacksonville	47	61	51	7.9	8.1	7.0	1,434	2,551	64	89	56	87	58	89	59
	Miami	46	68	51	9.2	9.5	7.9	200	4,198	36	83	61	84	60	83	63
GA	Atlanta	61	59	62	9.1	10.4	7.7	2,991	1,667	40	82	56	79	60	88	59
HI	Honolulu	47	74	51	11.3	9.4	13.1	-	4,474	31	72	56	81	61	68	52
ID	Boise	56	58	61	8.7	8.0	8.4	5,861	754	61	69	43	80	70	54	22
IL	Chicago	37	52	42	10.4	11.7	8.4	6,536	752	42	80	62	78	69	82	59
	Peoria.	52	53	57	9.9	11.0	7.8	6,148	982	41	83	64	80	71	87	62
IN	Indianapolis	64	51	52	9.6	10.9	7.5	5,615	1,014	41	84	62	81	71	87	60
IA	Des Moines	46	55	51	10.7	11.4	8.9	6,497	1,036	39	80	62	77	69	83	60
KS	Wichita	39	62	47	12.2	12.0	11.3	4,791	1,628	47	80	57	79	64	79	52
KY	Louisville.	47	53	53	8.3	9.5	6.8	4,514	1,288	40	81	59	77	65	85	58
LA	New Orleans	47	60	52	8.2	9.3	6.1	1,513	2,655	52	87	65	85	68	91	67
ME	Portland	54	55	60	8.7	9.1	7.6	7,378	268	60	79	59	76	61	80	59
MD	Baltimore.	45	58	50	8.9	9.6	7.6	4,707	1,137	47	77	54	73	57	80	53
MA	Boston	60	55	43	12.4	13.8	11.0	5,641	678	36	73	58	68	58	74	57
MI	Detroit	37	49	42	10.3	12.0	8.5	6,569	626	42	81	60	80	70	82	54
	Sault Ste. Marie	54	43	59	9.2	9.6	7.8	9,316	131	59	85	66	81	74	89	62
MN	Duluth	47	49	51	11.0	11.6	9.4	9,818	180	39	81	65	77	71	85	62
	Minneapolis-St. Paul .	57	54	62	10.5	10.5	9.4	7,981	682	41	79	62	75	68	81	58
MS	Jackson	30	59	37	7.0	8.3	5.4	2,467	2,215	37	90	61	86	67	93	62
MO	Kansas City	23	59	28	10.6	11.2	9.2	5,393	1,288	28	81	63	77	66	85	62
	St. Louis	47	55	51	9.7	10.6	8.0	4,758	1,534	40	82	61	81	68	84	59
MT	Great Falls	57	51	59	12.6	14.9	10.0	7,741	388	39	68	46	67	61	68	31
NE	Omaha	49	59	64	10.5	10.9	8.8	6,300	1,072	36	81	62	79	67	85	62
NV	Reno	53	69	58	6.6	5.6	7.2	5,674	508	37	69	31	79	50	60	18
NH	Concord	54	55	58	6.7	7.3	5.7	7,554	328	35	81	53	76	59	84	51
NJ	Atlantic City	37	56	42	9.8	10.9	8.3	5,169	826	36	82	56	78	59	83	57
NM	Albuquerque	56	76	61	8.9	8.0	8.9	4,425	1,244	40	59	29	68	39	59	27
NY	Albany	57	49	62	8.9	9.8	7.5	6,894	507	35	80	58	78	64	81	55
	Buffalo	52	43	61	11.8	14.0	10.2	6,747	477	40	80	63	79	73	80	55
	New York [2]	42	64	63	9.3	10.7	7.6	4,805	1,096	66	72	56	68	60	75	55
NC	Charlotte	49	59	51	7.4	7.8	6.6	3,341	1,582	40	82	53	78	56	86	56
	Raleigh	47	59	51	7.6	8.4	6.7	3,457	1,417	36	85	54	79	55	89	58
ND	Bismarck	56	55	61	10.2	10.0	9.2	8,968	488	41	81	59	76	70	84	51
OH	Cincinnati	44	49	53	9.0	10.5	7.2	5,248	996	38	82	60	80	69	86	58
	Cleveland	54	45	59	10.5	12.2	8.6	6,201	621	40	80	62	79	70	82	57
	Columbus	46	48	51	8.3	9.8	6.5	5,708	797	41	81	59	78	68	84	56
OK	Oklahoma City	44	64	52	12.3	12.6	10.9	3,659	1,859	35	80	57	78	61	80	53
OR	Portland	47	39	52	7.9	9.9	7.6	4,522	371	60	85	59	85	75	82	45
PA	Philadelphia	55	56	60	9.5	10.3	8.2	4,954	1,101	41	76	55	73	59	79	54
	Pittsburgh	43	44	48	9.0	10.5	7.3	5,968	654	40	79	57	77	66	83	54
RI	Providence	42	55	47	10.4	11.1	9.4	5,884	606	37	75	55	71	57	77	56
SC	Columbia.	48	60	52	6.8	7.2	6.3	2,649	1,966	34	87	51	83	55	88	54
SD	Sioux Falls	50	57	52	11.0	10.9	9.8	7,809	744	37	82	63	78	71	84	58
TN	Memphis	43	59	52	8.8	10.0	7.5	3,082	2,118	61	81	58	78	64	84	59
	Nashville	54	57	59	8.0	9.1	6.5	3,729	1,616	35	83	60	79	65	88	60
TX	Dallas-Fort Worth . . .	42	64	47	10.7	11.0	9.8	2,407	2,603	37	81	58	80	62	80	52
	El Paso.	53	80	58	8.8	8.3	8.3	2,708	2,094	40	56	28	65	34	61	29
	Houston	26	59	31	7.7	8.2	6.8	1,599	2,700	31	90	63	85	67	92	61
UT	Salt Lake City	69	62	71	8.8	7.5	9.5	5,765	1,047	41	67	43	79	69	52	22
VT	Burlington	52	44	57	9.0	9.8	8.7	7,771	388	35	77	59	73	64	79	53
VA	Norfolk	47	58	52	10.5	11.5	8.9	3,495	1,422	52	78	57	75	59	82	59
	Richmond . . . [3] . . .	50	56	52	7.7	8.1	6.9	3,963	1,348	66	83	53	80	57	85	56
WA	Seattle-Tacoma [3] . . .	51	38	52	8.9	9.6	8.2	4,908	190	41	83	62	82	74	82	49
	Spokane	48	48	53	8.9	8.8	8.6	6,842	398	41	78	52	86	79	65	28
WV	Charleston.	47	40	53	5.9	7.1	4.8	4,646	1,031	53	83	56	78	63	90	60
WI	Milwaukee	55	52	60	11.5	12.6	9.7	7,324	479	40	80	65	76	70	82	63
WY	Cheyenne	60	64	43	12.9	15.3	10.4	7,326	285	41	66	45	58	51	70	38
PR	San Juan	40	76	45	8.4	8.4	9.7	-	5,558	45	79	65	82	64	79	67

- Represents zero. [1] Percent of days that are either clear or partly cloudy. [2] Airport data for sunshine. [3] Does not represent airport data.

Source: U.S. National Oceanic and Atmospheric Administration, *Comparative Climatic Data*, annual.

Section 7
Elections

This section relates primarily to presidential, congressional, and gubernatorial elections. Also presented are summary tables on congressional legislation; state legislatures; Black, Hispanic, and female officeholders; population of voting age; voter participation; and campaign finances.

Official statistics on federal elections, collected by the Clerk of the House, are published biennially in *Statistics of the Presidential and Congressional Election* and *Statistics of the Congressional Election.* Federal and state elections data appear also in *America Votes,* a biennial volume published by Congressional Quarterly, Inc., Washington, DC. Federal elections data also appear in the U.S. Congress, *Congressional Directory,* and in official state documents. Data on reported registration and voting for social and economic groups are obtained by the U.S. Census Bureau as part of the Current Population Survey (CPS) and are published in *Current Population Reports,* Series P20 (see text, Section 1).

Almost all federal, state, and local governmental units in the United States conduct elections for political offices and other purposes. The conduct of elections is regulated by state laws or, in some cities and counties, by local charter. An exception is that the U.S. Constitution prescribes the basis of representation in Congress and the manner of electing the President and grants to Congress the right to regulate the times, places, and manner of electing federal officers. Amendments to the Constitution have prescribed national criteria for voting eligibility. The 15th Amendment, adopted in 1870, gave all citizens the right to vote regardless of race, color, or previous condition of servitude. The 19th Amendment, adopted in 1919, further extended the right to vote to all citizens regardless of sex. The payment of poll taxes as a prerequisite to voting in federal elections was banned by the 24th Amendment in

1964. In 1971, as a result of the 26th Amendment, eligibility to vote in national elections was extended to all citizens, 18 years old and over.

Presidential election—The Constitution specifies how the President and Vice President are selected. Each state elects, by popular vote, a group of electors equal in number to its total of members of Congress. The 23d Amendment, adopted in 1961, grants the District of Columbia three presidential electors, a number equal to that of the least populous state. Subsequent to the election, the electors meet in their respective states to vote for President and Vice President. Usually, each elector votes for the candidate receiving the most popular votes in his or her state. A majority vote of all electors is necessary to elect the President and Vice President. If no candidate receives a majority, the House of Representatives, with each state having one vote, is empowered to elect the President and Vice President, again, with a majority of votes required.

The 22d Amendment to the Constitution, adopted in 1951, limits presidential tenure to two elective terms of 4 years each or to one elective term for any person who, upon succession to the Presidency, has held the office or acted as President for more than 2 years.

Congressional election—The Constitution provides that Representatives be apportioned among the states according to their population, that a census of population be taken every 10 years as a basis for apportionment, and that each state have at least one Representative. At the time of each apportionment, Congress decides what the total number of Representatives will be. Since 1912, the total has been 435, except during 1960 to 1962 when it increased to 437, adding one Representative each for Alaska and Hawaii. The total reverted to 435 after

Elections   233

reapportionment following the 1960 census. Members are elected for 2-year terms, all terms covering the same period. The District of Columbia, American Samoa, Guam, and the Virgin Islands each elect one nonvoting Delegate, and Puerto Rico elects a nonvoting Resident Commissioner.

The Senate is composed of 100 members, 2 from each state, who are elected to serve for a term of 6 years. One-third of the Senate is elected every 2 years. Senators were originally chosen by the state legislatures. The 17th Amendment to the Constitution, adopted in 1913, prescribed that Senators be elected by popular vote.

Voter eligibility and participation— The Census Bureau publishes estimates of the population of voting age and the percent casting votes in each state for Presidential and congressional election years. These voting-age estimates include a number of persons who meet the age requirement but are not eligible to vote, (e.g. aliens and some institutionalized persons). In addition, since 1964, voter participation and voter characteristics data have been collected during November of election years as part of the CPS. These survey data include noncitizens in the voting age population estimates but exclude members of the Armed Forces and the institutional population.

Statistical reliability—For a discussion of statistical collection and estimation, sampling procedures, and measures of statistical reliability applicable to Census Bureau data, see Appendix III.

Figure 7.1
Vote Cast for President by Major Political Party: 1972 to 2000

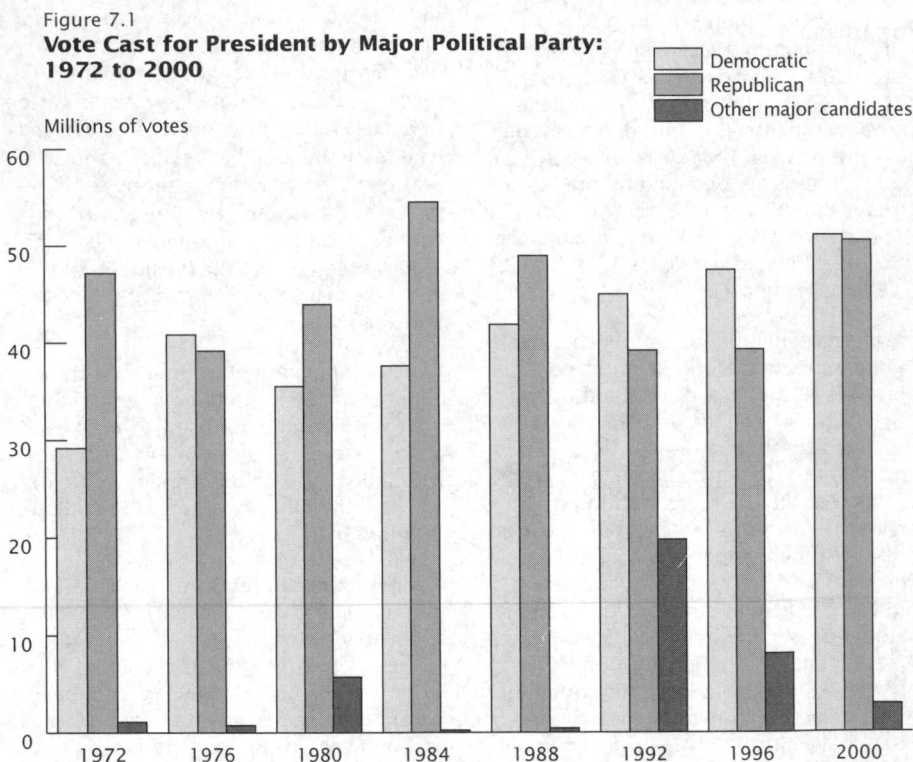

Millions of votes

Legend:
- Democratic
- Republican
- Other major candidates

[1] 1972—American, John Schmitz; 1980—Independent, John Anderson; 1992—Independent; Ross Perot, 1996 Reform, Ross Perot. 2000—Green, Ralph Nader.

Source: Chart prepared by U.S. Census Bureau. For data, see Tables 370 and 371.

No. 370. Vote Cast for President by Major Political Party: 1940 to 2000

[49,900 represents 49,900,000. Prior to 1960, excludes Alaska and Hawaii; prior to 1964, excludes DC. Vote cast for major party candidates include the votes of minor parties cast for those candidates]

	Candidates for President		Vote cast for President						
				Democratic			Republican		
Year	Democratic	Republican	Total popular vote [1] (1,000)	Popular vote		Electoral vote	Popular vote		Electoral vote
				Number (1,000)	Percent		Number (1,000)	Percent	
1940....	F. D. Roosevelt ..	Willkie	49,900	27,313	54.7	449	22,348	44.8	82
1944....	F. D. Roosevelt ..	Dewey........	47,977	25,613	53.4	432	22,018	45.9	99
1948....	Truman	Dewey.......	48,794	24,179	49.6	303	21,991	45.1	189
1952....	Stevenson	Eisenhower.....	61,551	27,315	44.4	89	33,936	55.1	442
1956....	Stevenson	Eisenhower.....	62,027	26,023	42.0	73	35,590	57.4	457
1960....	Kennedy	Nixon........	68,838	34,227	49.7	303	34,108	49.5	219
1964....	Johnson.......	Goldwater......	70,645	43,130	61.1	486	27,178	38.5	52
1968....	Humphrey	Nixon........	73,212	31,275	42.7	191	31,785	43.4	301
1972....	McGovern	Nixon........	77,719	29,170	37.5	17	47,170	60.7	520
1976....	Carter	Ford	81,556	40,831	50.1	297	39,148	48.0	240
1980....	Carter	Reagan	86,515	35,484	41.0	49	43,904	50.7	489
1984....	Mondale.......	Reagan	92,653	37,577	40.6	13	54,455	58.8	525
1988....	Dukakis	Bush........	91,595	41,809	45.6	111	48,886	53.4	426
1992....	Clinton.......	Bush........	104,425	44,909	43.0	370	39,104	37.4	168
1996....	Clinton.......	Dole	96,278	47,402	49.2	379	39,199	40.7	159
2000....	Gore	Bush........	105,397	50,992	48.4	266	50,455	47.9	271

[1] Include votes for minor party candidates, independents, unpledged electors, and scattered write-in votes.
Source: Congressional Quarterly, Inc., Washington, DC., *America at the Polls 2*, 1965, and *America Votes*, biennial, (copyright).

No. 371. Vote Cast for Leading Minority Party Candidates for President: 1940 to 2000

[See headnote, Table 370]

Year	Candidate	Party	Popular vote (1,000)	Candidate	Party	Popular vote (1,000)
1940 ..	Norman Thomas ...	Socialist	116	Roger Babson	Prohibition.........	59
1944 ..	Norman Thomas ...	Socialist	79	Claude Watson	Prohibition.........	75
1948 ..	Strom Thurmond ...	States' Rights.......	1,176	Henry Wallace.....	Progressive........	1,157
1952 ..	Vincent Hallinan....	Progressive........	140	Stuart Hamblen	Prohibition.........	73
1956 ..	T. Coleman Andrews.	States' Rights.......	111	Eric Hass	Socialist Labor......	44
1960 ..	Eric Hass	Socialist Labor......	48	Rutherford Decker ..	Prohibition.........	46
1964 ..	Eric Hass	Socialist Labor......	45	Clifton DeBerry	Socialist Workers	33
1968 ..	George Wallace....	American Independent.	9,906	Henning Blomen ...	Socialist Labor......	53
1972 ..	John Schmitz......	American..........	1,099	Benjamin Spock....	People's	79
1976 ..	Eugene McCarthy ..	Independent	757	Roger McBride.....	Libertarian.........	173
1980 ..	John Anderson	Independent	5,720	Ed Clark..........	Libertarian.........	921
1984 ..	David Bergland	Libertarian.........	228	Lyndon H. LaRouche.	Independent	79
1988 ..	Ron Paul	Libertarian.........	432	Lenora B. Fulani ...	New Alliance	217
1992 ..	H. Ross Perot	Independent	19,742	Andre Marrou......	Libertarian.........	292
1996 ..	H. Ross Perot	Reform Party	8,085	Ralph Nader	Green............	685
2000 ..	Ralph Nader	Green............	2,883	Pat Buchanan	Reform	449

Source: Congressional Quarterly, Inc. Washington, DC, *America at the Polls 1920-1996*, 1997; and *America Votes*, biennial (copyright).

No. 372. Democratic and Republican Percentages of Two-Party Presidential Vote by Selected Characteristics of Voters: 1996 and 2000

[In percent. Covers citizens of voting age living in private housing units in the contiguous United States. Percentages for Democratic presidential vote are computed by subtracting the percentage Republican vote from 100 percent; third-party or independent votes are not included as valid data. Data are from the National Election Studies and are based on a sample and subject to sampling variability; for details, see source]

Characteristic	1996		2000		Characteristic	1996		2000	
	Demo-cratic	Repub-lican	Demo-cratic	Repub-lican		Demo-cratic	Repub-lican	Demo-cratic	Repub-lican
Total [1]	**58**	**42**	**52**	**48**	Race:				
Year of birth:					White.........	51	49	46	54
1975 or later......	61	39	63	37	Black..........	99	1	92	8
1959 to 1974	58	42	46	54					
1943 to 1958	58	42	53	47	Education:				
1927 to 1942	56	44	48	52	Grade school	88	12	74	26
1911 to 1926.....	64	36	64	36	High school.......	64	36	54	46
1895 to 1910	57	43	-	100	College	49	51	50	50
Sex:									
Male	51	49	47	53	Union household.....	75	25	61	39
Female	65	35	56	44	Nonunion household ..	54	46	50	50

- Represents zero.   [1] Includes other characteristics, not shown separately.
Source: Center for Political Studies, University of Michigan, Ann Arbor, MI, National Election Studies (NES); "The NES Guide to Public Opinion and Electoral Behavior"; accessed 24 April 2002; <http://www.umich.edu/nes/nesguide/gd-index.htm#9> (copyright).

Elections 235

No. 373. Electoral Vote Cast for President by Major Political Party—States: 1960 to 2000

[D=Democratic, R=Republican. For composition of regions, see map, inside front cover]

State	1960[1]	1964	1968[2]	1972[3]	1976[4]	1980	1984	1988[5]	1992	1996	2000[6]
Democratic	303	486	191	17	297	49	13	111	370	379	266
Republican	219	52	301	520	240	489	525	426	168	159	271
Northeast:											
Democratic	121	126	102	14	86	4	-	53	106	106	102
Republican	12	-	24	108	36	118	113	60	-	-	4
Midwest:											
Democratic	71	149	31	-	58	10	10	29	100	100	68
Republican	82	-	118	145	87	135	127	108	29	29	61
South:											
Democratic	101	121	45	3	149	31	3	8	68	80	15
Republican	50	47	77	165	20	138	174	168	116	104	168
West:											
Democratic	10	90	13	-	4	4	-	21	96	93	81
Republican	75	5	82	102	97	98	111	90	23	26	38
AL	[1]D-5	R-10	([2])	R-9	D-9	R-9	R-9	R-9	R-9	R-9	R-9
AK	R-3	D-3	R-3	R-3	R-3	R-3	R-3	R-3	R-3	R-3	R-3
AZ	R-4	R-5	R-5	R-6	R-6	R-6	R-7	R-7	R-8	R-8	R-8
AR	D-8	D-6	([2])	R-6	D-6	R-6	R-6	R-6	D-6	D-6	R-6
CA	R-32	D-40	R-40	R-45	R-45	R-45	R-47	R-47	D-54	D-54	D-54
CO	R-6	D-6	R-6	R-7	R-7	R-7	R-8	R-8	D-8	R-8	R-8
CT	D-8	D-8	D-8	R-8	R-8	R-8	R-8	R-8	D-8	D-8	D-8
DE	D-3	D-3	R-3	R-3	D-3	R-3	R-3	R-3	D-3	D-3	D-3
DC	(X)	D-3	D-3	D-3	D-3	D-3	D-3	D-3	D-3	D-3	[6]D-2
FL	R-10	D-14	R-14	R-17	D-17	R-17	R-21	R-21	R-25	D-25	R-25
GA	D-12	R-12	([2])	R-12	D-12	D-12	R-12	R-12	D-13	R-13	R-13
HI	D-3	D-4	D-4	R-4	D-4	D-4	R-4	D-4	D-4	D-4	D-4
ID	R-4	D-4	R-4	R-4	R-4	R-4	R-4	R-4	R-4	R-4	R-4
IL	D-27	D-26	R-26	R-26	R-26	R-26	R-24	R-24	D-22	D-22	D-22
IN	R-13	D-13	R-13	R-13	R-13	R-13	R-12	R-12	R-12	R-12	R-12
IA	R-10	D-9	R-9	R-8	R-8	R-8	R-8	D-8	D-7	D-7	D-7
KS	R-8	D-7	R-7	R-7	R-7	R-7	R-7	R-7	R-6	R-6	R-6
KY	R-10	D-9	R-9	R-9	D-9	R-9	R-9	R-9	D-8	D-8	R-8
LA	D-10	R-10	([2])	R-10	D-10	R-10	R-10	R-10	D-9	D-9	R-9
ME	R-5	D-4	D-4	R-4	R-4	R-4	R-4	R-4	D-4	D-4	D-4
MD	D-9	D-10	D-10	R-10	D-10	D-10	R-10	R-10	D-10	D-10	D-10
MA	D-16	D-14	D-14	D-14	D-14	D-14	R-13	D-13	D-12	D-12	D-12
MI	D-20	D-21	D-21	R-21	R-21	R-21	R-20	R-20	D-18	D-18	D-18
MN	D-11	D-10	D-10	R-10	D-10	D-10	D-10	D-10	D-10	D-10	D-10
MS	([1])	R-7	([2])	R-7	D-7	R-7	R-7	R-7	R-7	R-7	R-7
MO	D-13	D-12	R-12	R-12	D-12	R-12	R-11	R-11	D-11	D-11	R-11
MT	R-4	D-4	R-4	R-4	R-4	R-4	R-4	R-4	D-3	R-3	R-3
NE	R-6	D-5	R-5	R-5	R-5	R-5	R-5	R-5	R-5	R-5	R-5
NV	D-3	D-3	R-3	R-3	R-3	R-3	R-4	R-4	D-4	D-4	R-4
NH	R-4	D-4	R-4	R-4	R-4	R-4	R-4	R-4	D-4	D-4	R-4
NJ	D-16	D-17	R-17	R-17	R-17	R-17	R-16	R-16	D-15	D-15	D-15
NM	D-4	D-4	R-4	R-4	R-4	R-4	R-5	R-5	D-5	D-5	D-5
NY	D-45	D-43	D-43	R-41	D-41	R-41	R-36	D-36	D-33	D-33	D-33
NC	D-14	D-13	[2]R-12	R-13	D-13	R-13	R-13	R-13	R-14	R-14	R-14
ND	R-4	D-4	R-4	R-3	R-3	R-3	R-3	R-3	R-3	R-3	R-3
OH	R-25	D-26	R-26	R-25	D-25	R-25	R-23	R-23	D-21	D-21	R-21
OK	[1]R-7	D-8	R-8	R-8	R-8	R-8	R-8	R-8	R-8	R-8	R-8
OR	R-6	D-6	R-6	R-6	R-6	R-6	R-7	D-7	D-7	D-7	D-7
PA	D-32	D-29	D-29	R-27	D-27	R-27	R-25	R-25	D-23	D-23	D-23
RI	D-4	D-4	D-4	R-4	D-4	D-4	R-4	D-4	D-4	D-4	D-4
SC	D-8	R-8	R-8	R-8	D-8	R-8	R-8	R-8	R-8	R-8	R-8
SD	R-4	D-4	R-4	R-4	R-4	R-4	R-3	R-3	R-3	R-3	R-3
TN	R-11	D-11	R-11	R-10	D-10	R-10	R-11	R-11	D-11	D-11	R-11
TX	D-24	D-25	D-25	R-26	D-26	R-26	R-29	R-29	R-32	R-32	R-32
UT	R-4	D-4	R-4	R-4	R-4	R-4	R-5	R-5	R-5	R-5	R-5
VT	R-3	D-3	R-3	R-3	R-3	R-3	R-3	R-3	D-3	D-3	D-3
VA	R-12	D-12	R-12	[3]R-11	R-12	R-12	R-12	R-12	R-13	R-13	R-13
WA	R-9	D-9	D-9	R-9	[4]R-8	R-9	R-10	D-10	D-11	D-11	D-11
WV	D-8	D-7	D-7	R-6	D-6	D-6	R-6	[5]D-5	D-5	D-5	R-5
WI	R-12	D-12	R-12	R-11	D-11	R-11	R-11	D-11	D-11	D-11	D-11
WY	R-3	D-3	R-3	R-3	R-3	R-3	R-3	R-3	R-3	R-3	R-3

- Represents zero.   [1] Excludes 15 electoral votes cast for Harry F. Byrd as follows: AL 6, MS 8, and OK 1.   [2] Excludes 46 electoral votes cast for American Independent George C. Wallace as follows: AL 10, AR 6, GA 12, LA 10, MS 7, and NC 1.   [3] Excludes one electoral vote cast for Libertarian John Hospers in Virginia.   [4] Excludes one electoral vote cast for Ronald Reagan in Washington.   [5] Excludes one electoral vote cast for Lloyd Bentsen for President in West Virginia.   [6] Excludes one electoral vote left blank by a Democratic elector in the District of Columbia.

Source: 1960-72, U.S. Congress, Clerk of the House, *Statistics of the Presidential and Congressional Election*, quadrennial; 1976-2000, Congressional Quarterly, Inc., Washington DC. *America Votes*, biennial (copyright).

Figure 7.2
Presidential Electoral Vote by State: 2000

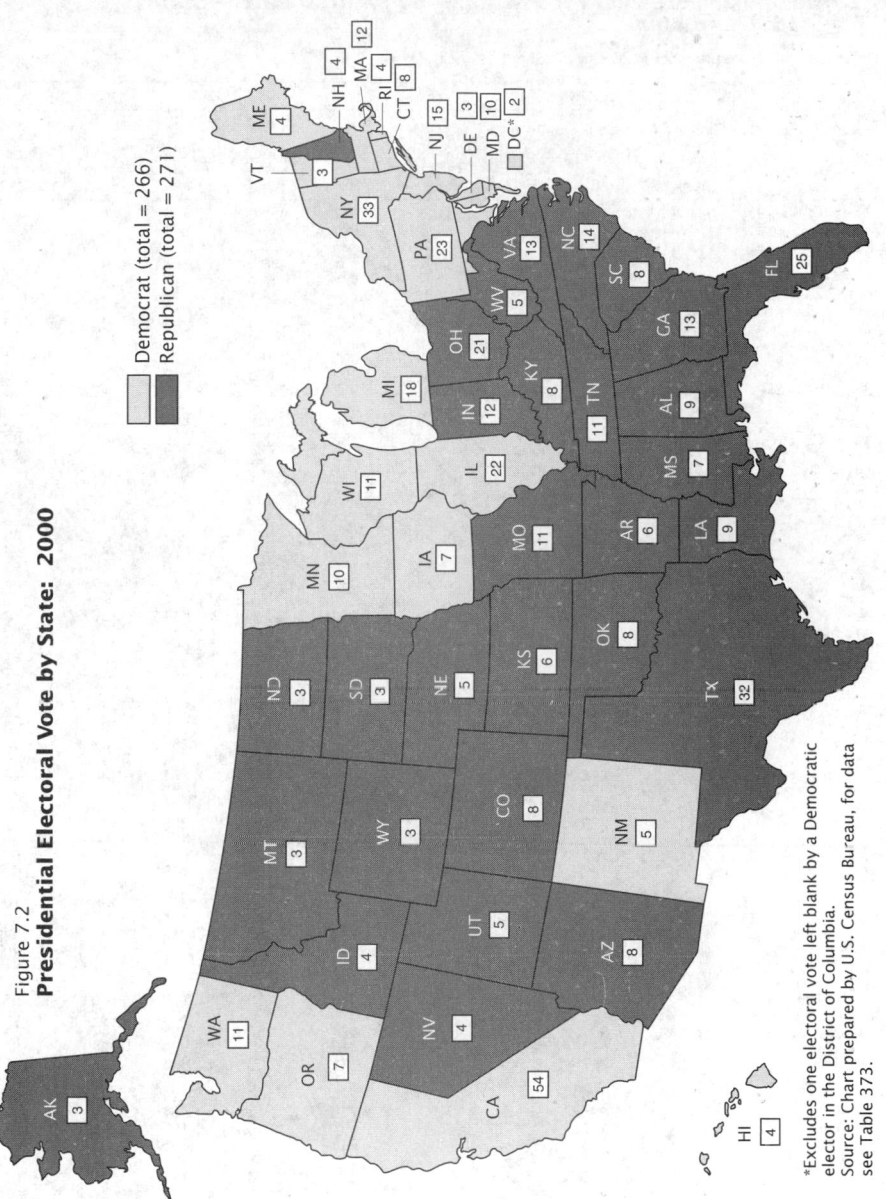

Democrat (total = 266)
Republican (total = 271)

*Excludes one electoral vote left blank by a Democratic
elector in the District of Columbia.
Source: Chart prepared by U.S. Census Bureau, for data
see Table 373.

No. 374. Popular Vote Cast for President by Political Party—States: 1996 and 2000

[In thousands (96,278 represents 96,278,000), except percent]

State	1996				2000			Percent of total vote	
	Total [1]	Demo-cratic Party	Repub-lican Party	Perot (Reform Party)	Total [1]	Demo-cratic Party	Repub-lican Party	Demo-cratic Party	Repub-lican Party
United States..	96,278	47,402	39,199	8,085	105,397	50,992	50,455	48.4	47.9
Alabama.........	1,534	662	769	92	1,666	693	941	41.6	56.5
Alaska..........	242	80	123	26	286	79	167	27.7	58.6
Arizona.........	1,404	653	622	112	1,532	685	782	44.7	51.0
Arkansas	884	475	325	70	922	423	473	45.9	51.3
California	10,019	5,120	3,828	698	10,966	5,861	4,567	53.4	41.7
Colorado.	1,511	671	692	100	1,741	738	884	42.4	50.8
Connecticut.......	1,393	736	483	140	1,460	816	561	55.9	38.4
Delaware	271	140	99	29	328	180	137	55.0	41.9
District of Columbia ..	186	158	17	4	202	172	18	85.2	9.0
Florida	5,304	2,547	2,245	484	5,963	2,912	2,913	48.8	48.8
Georgia	2,299	1,054	1,081	146	2,597	1,116	1,420	43.0	54.7
Hawaii	360	205	114	27	368	205	138	55.8	37.5
Idaho..........	492	165	257	63	502	139	337	27.6	67.2
Illinois	4,311	2,342	1,587	346	4,742	2,589	2,019	54.6	42.6
Indiana.........	2,136	887	1,007	224	2,199	902	1,246	41.0	56.6
Iowa	1,234	620	493	105	1,316	639	634	48.5	48.2
Kansas.........	1,074	388	583	93	1,072	399	622	37.2	58.0
Kentucky	1,389	637	623	120	1,544	639	872	41.4	56.5
Louisiana	1,784	928	713	123	1,766	792	928	44.9	52.6
Maine..........	606	313	186	86	652	320	287	49.1	44.0
Maryland	1,781	966	682	116	2,020	1,141	814	56.5	40.3
Massachusetts.....	2,557	1,572	718	227	2,703	1,616	879	59.8	32.5
Michigan........	3,849	1,990	1,481	337	4,233	2,170	1,953	51.3	46.1
Minnesota.......	2,193	1,120	766	258	2,439	1,168	1,110	47.9	45.5
Mississippi	894	394	440	52	994	405	573	40.7	57.6
Missouri	2,158	1,026	890	217	2,360	1,111	1,190	47.1	50.4
Montana........	407	168	180	55	411	137	240	33.4	58.4
Nebraska	677	237	363	71	697	232	434	33.3	62.2
Nevada	464	204	199	44	609	280	302	46.0	49.5
New Hampshire....	499	246	196	48	569	266	274	46.8	48.1
New Jersey.......	3,076	1,652	1,103	262	3,187	1,789	1,284	56.1	40.3
New Mexico	556	273	233	32	599	287	286	47.9	47.8
New York	6,316	3,756	1,933	503	6,822	4,108	2,403	60.2	35.2
North Carolina.....	2,516	1,108	1,226	168	2,911	1,258	1,631	43.2	56.0
North Dakota......	266	107	125	33	288	95	175	33.1	60.7
Ohio	4,534	2,148	1,860	483	4,702	2,184	2,350	46.4	50.0
Oklahoma........	1,207	488	582	131	1,234	474	744	38.4	60.3
Oregon..........	1,378	650	538	121	1,534	720	714	47.0	46.5
Pennsylvania......	4,506	2,216	1,801	431	4,913	2,486	2,281	50.6	46.4
Rhode Island......	390	233	105	44	409	250	131	61.0	31.9
South Carolina.....	1,152	506	573	64	1,383	566	786	40.9	56.8
South Dakota.....	324	139	151	31	316	119	191	37.6	60.3
Tennessee	1,894	909	864	106	2,076	982	1,062	47.3	51.1
Texas...........	5,612	2,460	2,736	379	6,408	2,434	3,800	38.0	59.3
Utah	666	222	362	66	771	203	515	26.3	66.8
Vermont	258	138	80	31	294	149	120	50.6	40.7
Virginia.........	2,417	1,091	1,138	160	2,739	1,217	1,437	44.4	52.5
Washington......	2,254	1,123	841	201	2,487	1,248	1,109	50.2	44.6
West Virginia.....	636	328	234	72	648	295	336	45.6	51.9
Wisconsin.......	2,196	1,072	845	227	2,599	1,243	1,237	47.8	47.6
Wyoming	212	78	105	26	218	60	148	27.7	67.8

[1] Includes other parties.

Source: Congressional Quarterly, Inc., Washington, DC, *America Votes*, biennial (copyright).

U.S. Census Bureau, Statistical Abstract of the United States: 2002

No. 375. Vote Cast for United States Senators, 1998 and 2000, and Incumbent Senators, 2000—States

[D=Democrat; R=Republican]

State	1998 Total (1,000)[1]	1998 Percent for leading party	2000 Total (1,000)[1]	2000 Percent for leading party	Incumbent Senators and year term expires — Name, party, and year	Incumbent Senators and year term expires — Name, party, and year
Alabama	1,293	R-63.2	(X)	(X)	Jeff Sessions (R) 2003	Richard C. Shelby (R) 2005
Alaska	222	R-74.5	(X)	(X)	Frank H. Murkowski (R) 2005	Ted Stevens (R) 2003
Arizona	1,013	R-68.7	1,397	R-79.3	John McCain (R) 2005	Jon Kyl (R) 2007
Arkansas	701	D-55.1	(X)	(X)	Blanche Lincoln (D) 2005	Tim Hutchinson (R) 2003
California	8,315	D-53.1	10,624	D-55.8	Barbara Boxer (D) 2005	Dianne Feinstein (D) 2007
Colorado	1,327	R-62.5	(X)	(X)	Ben N. Campbell (R) 2005	Wayne Allard (R) 2003
Connecticut . .	964	D-65.1	1,311	D-63.2	Christopher J. Dodd (D) 2005	Joseph I. Lieberman (D) 2007
Delaware	(X)	(X)	327	D-55.5	Joseph R. Biden Jr. (D) 2003	Thomas R. Carper (D) 2007
Florida	3,900	D-62.5	5,857	D-51.0	Bob Graham (D) 2005	Bill Nelson (D) 2007
Georgia	1,754	R-52.4	2,429	D-58.2	Max Cleland (D) 2003	Zell Miller (D) 2005
Hawaii	398	D-79.2	346	D-72.7	Daniel K. Akaka (D) 2007	Daniel K. Inouye (D) 2005
Idaho	378	R-69.5	(X)	(X)	Larry E. Craig (R) 2003	Michael D. Crapo (R) 2005
Illinois	3,395	R-50.3	(X)	(X)	Peter Fitzgerald (R) 2005	Richard J. Durbin (D) 2003
Indiana	1,589	D-63.7	2,145	R-66.6	Evan Bayh (D) 2005	Richard G. Lugar (R) 2007
Iowa	948	R-68.4	(X)	(X)	Tom Harkin (D) 2003	Charles E. Grassley (R) 2005
Kansas	727	R-65.3	(X)	(X)	Sam Brownback (R) 2005	Pat Roberts (R) 2003
Kentucky . . .	1,145	R-49.7	(X)	(X)	Jim Bunning (R) 2005	Mitch McConnell (R) 2003
Louisiana [2] . . .	969	D-64.0	(X)	(X)	John B. Breaux (D) 2005	Mary Landrieu (D) 2003
Maine	(X)	(X)	635	R-68.9	Susan Collins (R) 2003	Olympia J. Snowe (R) 2007
Maryland	1,507	D-70.5	1,947	D-63.2	Barbara A. Mikulski (D) 2005	Paul S. Sarbanes (D) 2007
Massachu- setts	(X)	(X)	2,599	D-72.7	Edward M. Kennedy (D) 2007	John F. Kerry (D) 2003
Michigan	(X)	(X)	4,168	D-49.5	Carl Levin (D) 2003	Debbie Stabenow (D) 2007
Minnesota . . .	(X)	(X)	2,420	D-48.8	Paul David Wellstone (D) 2003	Mark Dayton (D) 2007
Mississippi . . .	(X)	(X)	994	R-65.9	Thad Cochran (R) 2003	Trent Lott (R) 2007
Missouri	1,577	R-52.7	2,362	D-50.5	Christopher S. Bond (R) 2005	Jean Carnahan (D) 2003
Montana	(X)	(X)	412	R-50.6	Max Baucus (D) 2003	Conrad Burns (R) 2007
Nebraska	(X)	(X)	692	D-51.0	Chuck Hagel (R) 2003	Ben Nelson (D) 2007
Nevada	436	D-47.9	600	R-55.1	Harry Reid (D) 2005	John Ensign (R) 2007
New Hampshire . . .	315	R-67.8	(X)	(X)	Judd Gregg (R) 2005	Robert C. Smith (R) 2003
New Jersey . .	(X)	(X)	3,016	D-50.1	Robert G. Torricelli (D) 2003	Jon Corzine (D) 2007
New Mexico . .	(X)	(X)	590	D-61.7	Jeff Bingaman (D) 2007	Pete V. Domenici (R) 2003
New York	4,671	D-54.6	6,780	D-55.3	Hillary Rodham Clinton (D) 2007	Charles E. Schumer (D) 2005
North Carolina .	2,012	D-51.2	(X)	(X)	John Edwards (D) 2005	Jesse Helms (R) 2003
North Dakota . .	213	D-63.2	288	D-61.4	Byron L. Dorgan (D) 2005	Kent Conrad (D) 2007
Ohio	3,404	R-56.5	4,449	R-59.9	George V. Voinovich (R) 2005	Mike DeWine (R) 2007
Oklahoma . . .	860	R-66.4	(X)	(X)	James Inhofe (R) 2003	Don Nickles (R) 2005
Oregon	1,118	D-61.1	(X)	(X)	Gordon Smith (R) 2003	Ron Wyden (D) 2005
Pennsylvania .	2,958	R-61.3	4,736	R-52.4	Rick Santorum (R) 2007	Arlen Specter (R) 2005
Rhode Island .	(X)	(X)	392	R-56.8	Jack Reed (D) 2003	Lincoln Chafee (R) 2007
South Carolina	1,068	D-52.7	(X)	(X)	Ernest F. Hollings (D) 2005	Strom Thurmond (R) 2003
South Dakota .	262	D-62.1	(X)	(X)	Thomas A. Daschle (D) 2005	Tim Johnson (D) 2003
Tennessee . . .	(X)	(X)	1,929	R-65.1	Fred Thompson (R) 2003	Bill Frist (R) 2007
Texas	(X)	(X)	6,277	R-65.0	Kay Bailey Hutchison (R) 2007	Phil Gramm (R) 2003
Utah	495	R-64.0	770	R-65.6	Robert F. Bennett (R) 2005	Orrin G. Hatch (R) 2007
Vermont [3]	214	D-72.2	289	R-65.6	Patrick J. Leahy (D) 2005	[3]James M. Jeffords (I) 2007
Virginia	(X)	(X)	2,718	R-52.3	George F. Allen (R) 2007	John W. Warner (R) 2003
Washington . .	1,889	D-58.4	2,461	D-48.7	Patty Murray (D) 2005	Maria Cantwell (D) 2007
West Virginia .	(X)	(X)	603	D-77.8	Robert C. Byrd (D) 2007	John D. Rockefeller IV (D) 2003
Wisconsin . . .	1,761	D-50.5	2,540	D-61.5	Herb Kohl (D) 2003	Russell Feingold (D) 2005
Wyoming	(X)	(X)	214	R-73.8	Mike Enzi (R) 2003	Craig Thomas (R) 2007

X Not applicable.   [1] Includes vote cast for minor parties.   [2] Louisiana holds an open-primary election with candidates from all parties running on the same ballot. Any candidate who receives a majority is elected.   [3] Jeffords was reelected in Vermont in 2000 as a Republican, but subsequently switched to Independent status in June 2001.

Source: Congressional Quarterly, Inc., Washington, D.C. *America Votes,* biennial (copyright).

Elections   239

No. 376. Apportionment of Membership in House of Representatives by State: 1790 to 2000

[Total membership includes Representatives assigned to newly admitted states after the apportionment acts. Population figures used for apportionment purposes are those determined for states by each decennial census. No reapportionment based on 1920 population census. For method of calculating apportionment and a short history of apportionment, see House Report 91-1314, 91st Congress, 2d session, The Decennial Population Census and Congressional Apportionment]

State	1790	1800	1810	1820	1830	1840	1850	1860	1870	1880	1890	1900	1910	1930	1940	1950	1960	1970	1980	1990	2000
U.S..	106	142	186	213	242	232	237	243	293	332	357	391	435	435	435	437	435	435	435	435	435
AL	(X)	(X)	[1]1	3	5	7	7	6	8	8	9	9	10	9	9	9	8	7	7	7	7
AK	(X)	(X)	(X)	(X)	(X)	(X)	(X)	(X)	(X)	(X)	(X)	(X)	(X)	(X)	(X)	[1]1	1	1	1	1	1
AZ	(X)	(X)	(X)	(X)	(X)	(X)	(X)	(X)	(X)	(X)	(X)	(X)	[2]1	1	2	2	3	4	5	6	8
AR	(X)	(X)	(X)	(X)	[1]1	1	2	3	4	5	6	7	7	7	7	6	4	4	4	4	4
CA	(X)	(X)	(X)	(X)	(X)	[1]2	2	3	4	6	7	8	11	20	23	30	38	43	45	52	53
CO	(X)	(X)	(X)	(X)	(X)	(X)	(X)	(X)	[1]1	1	2	3	4	4	4	4	4	5	6	6	7
CT	7	7	7	6	6	4	4	4	4	4	4	5	5	6	6	6	6	6	6	6	5
DE	1	1	2	1	1	1	1	1	1	1	1	1	1	1	1	1	1	1	1	1	1
FL	(X)	(X)	(X)	(X)	(X)	[1]1	1	1	2	2	2	3	4	5	6	8	12	15	19	23	25
GA	2	4	6	7	9	8	8	7	9	10	11	11	12	10	10	10	10	10	10	11	13
HI	(X)	(X)	(X)	(X)	(X)	(X)	(X)	(X)	(X)	(X)	(X)	(X)	(X)	(X)	(X)	[1]1	2	2	2	2	2
ID	(X)	(X)	(X)	(X)	(X)	(X)	(X)	(X)	(X)	[1]1	1	1	2	2	2	2	2	2	2	2	2
IL	(X)	(X)	[1]1	1	3	7	9	14	19	20	22	25	27	27	26	25	24	24	22	20	19
IN	(X)	(X)	[1]1	3	7	10	11	11	13	13	13	13	13	12	11	11	11	11	10	10	9
IA	(X)	(X)	(X)	(X)	(X)	[1]2	2	6	9	11	11	11	11	9	8	8	7	6	6	5	5
KS	(X)	(X)	(X)	(X)	(X)	(X)	(X)	1	3	7	8	8	8	7	6	6	5	5	5	4	4
KY	2	6	10	12	13	10	10	9	10	11	11	11	11	9	9	8	7	7	7	6	6
LA	(X)	(X)	[1]1	3	3	4	4	5	6	6	6	7	8	8	8	8	8	8	8	7	7
ME	(X)	(X)	(X)	7	8	7	6	5	5	4	4	4	4	3	3	3	2	2	2	2	2
MD	8	9	9	9	8	6	6	5	6	6	6	6	6	6	6	7	8	8	8	8	8
MA	14	17	20	13	12	10	11	10	11	12	13	14	16	15	14	14	12	12	11	10	10
MI	(X)	(X)	(X)	(X)	[1]1	3	4	6	9	11	12	12	13	17	17	18	19	19	18	16	15
MN	(X)	(X)	(X)	(X)	(X)	(X)	[1]2	2	3	5	7	9	10	9	9	9	8	8	8	8	8
MS	(X)	(X)	[1]1	1	2	4	5	5	6	7	7	8	8	7	7	6	5	5	5	5	4
MO	(X)	(X)	(X)	1	2	5	7	9	13	14	15	16	16	13	13	11	10	10	9	9	9
MT	(X)	(X)	(X)	(X)	(X)	(X)	(X)	(X)	(X)	[1]1	1	1	2	2	2	2	2	2	2	1	1
NE	(X)	(X)	(X)	(X)	(X)	(X)	(X)	[1]1	1	3	6	6	6	5	4	4	3	3	3	3	3
NV	(X)	(X)	(X)	(X)	(X)	(X)	(X)	[1]1	1	1	1	1	1	1	1	1	1	1	2	2	3
NH	4	5	6	6	6	4	3	3	3	2	2	2	2	2	2	2	2	2	2	2	2
NJ	5	6	6	6	6	5	5	5	7	7	8	10	12	14	14	14	15	15	14	13	13
NM	(X)	(X)	(X)	(X)	(X)	(X)	(X)	(X)	(X)	(X)	(X)	(X)	[2]1	1	2	2	2	2	3	3	3
NY	10	17	27	34	40	34	33	31	33	34	34	37	43	45	45	43	41	39	34	31	29
NC	10	12	13	13	13	9	8	7	8	9	9	10	10	11	12	12	11	11	11	12	13
ND	(X)	(X)	(X)	(X)	(X)	(X)	(X)	(X)	(X)	[1]1	1	2	3	2	2	2	2	1	1	1	1
OH	(X)	[1]1	6	14	19	21	21	19	20	21	21	21	22	24	23	23	24	23	21	19	18
OK	(X)	(X)	(X)	(X)	(X)	(X)	(X)	(X)	(X)	(X)	(X)	[1]5	8	9	8	6	6	6	6	6	5
OR	(X)	(X)	(X)	(X)	(X)	(X)	[1]1	1	1	1	2	2	3	3	4	4	4	4	5	5	5
PA	13	18	23	26	28	24	25	24	27	28	30	32	36	34	33	30	27	25	23	21	19
RI	2	2	2	2	2	2	2	2	2	2	2	2	3	2	2	2	2	2	2	2	2
SC	6	8	9	9	9	7	6	4	5	7	7	7	7	6	6	6	6	6	6	6	6
SD	(X)	(X)	(X)	(X)	(X)	(X)	(X)	(X)	(X)	[1]2	2	2	3	2	2	2	2	2	1	1	1
TN	[1]1	3	6	9	13	11	10	8	10	10	10	10	10	9	10	9	9	8	9	9	9
TX	(X)	(X)	(X)	(X)	(X)	[1]2	2	4	6	11	13	16	18	21	21	22	23	24	27	30	32
UT	(X)	(X)	(X)	(X)	(X)	(X)	(X)	(X)	(X)	(X)	[1]1	1	2	2	2	2	2	2	3	3	3
VT	2	4	6	5	5	4	3	3	3	2	2	2	2	1	1	1	1	1	1	1	1
VA	19	22	23	22	21	15	13	11	9	10	10	10	10	9	9	10	10	10	10	11	11
WA	(X)	(X)	(X)	(X)	(X)	(X)	(X)	(X)	(X)	[1]1	2	3	5	6	6	7	7	7	8	9	9
WV	(X)	(X)	(X)	(X)	(X)	(X)	(X)	(X)	3	4	4	5	6	6	6	6	5	4	4	3	3
WI	(X)	(X)	(X)	(X)	(X)	[1]2	3	6	8	9	10	11	11	10	10	10	10	9	9	9	8
WY	(X)	(X)	(X)	(X)	(X)	(X)	(X)	(X)	(X)	[1]1	1	1	1	1	1	1	1	1	1	1	1

X Not applicable. [1] Assigned after apportionment. [2] Included in apportionment in anticipation of statehood.

Source: U.S. Census Bureau, Congressional Apportionment, Census 2000 Brief, Series C2KBR/01-7, issued July 2001; and see also <http://www.census.gov/population/www/censusdata/apportionment.html>.

No. 377. Vote Cast for United States Representatives by Major Political Party—States: 1996 to 2000

[In thousands (89,863 represents 89,863,000), except percent. R=Republican, D=Democratic, and I=Independent. In each state, totals represent the sum of votes cast in each Congressional District or votes cast for Representative at Large in states where only one member is elected. In all years there are numerous districts within the state where either the Republican or Democratic party had no candidate. In some states the Republican and Democratic vote includes votes cast for the party candidate by endorsing parties]

State	1996				1998				2000			
	Total[1]	Demo-cratic	Repub-lican	Percent for leading party	Total[1]	Demo-cratic	Repub-lican	Percent for leading party	Total[1]	Demo-cratic	Repub-lican	Percent for leading party
U.S.	89,863	43,626	43,902	R-48.9	65,897	31,482	32,255	R-48.9	97,226	46,521	46,954	R-48.3
AL	1,469	656	786	R-53.5	1,215	545	666	R-54.8	1,439	486	849	R-59.0
AK	234	85	139	R-59.4	223	77	140	R-62.6	274	45	191	R-69.6
AZ [2]	1,356	521	801	R-59.0	1,004	407	574	R-57.1	1,466	558	855	R-58.3
AR [2]	863	396	456	R-52.8	525	169	320	R-60.9	633	355	277	D-56.2
CA	9,482	4,707	4,292	D-49.6	7,990	4,040	3,510	D-50.6	10,438	5,407	4,446	D-51.8
CO	1,461	597	833	R-57.0	1,274	533	716	R-56.2	1,624	496	969	R-59.7
CT	1,294	724	547	D-55.9	954	496	442	D-51.9	1,313	699	595	D-53.2
DE	267	73	186	R-69.5	181	57	120	R-66.4	313	96	212	R-67.6
FL [2] [3]	4,692	2,037	2,640	R-56.3	1,213	581	558	D-47.9	5,011	1,976	2,852	R-56.9
GA	2,163	1,011	1,152	R-53.3	1,632	592	1,040	R-63.7	2,417	918	1,498	R-62.0
HI	353	196	136	D-55.5	397	261	119	D-65.7	340	221	111	D-65.0
ID	494	194	290	R-58.7	379	169	205	R-54.0	493	142	333	R-67.5
IL	4,128	2,267	1,813	D-54.9	3,215	1,566	1,625	R-50.5	4,393	2,454	1,907	D-55.8
IN	2,105	944	1,119	R-53.1	1,576	673	862	R-54.7	2,157	953	1,141	R-52.9
IA	1,201	533	650	R-54.1	901	338	552	R-61.3	1,276	532	717	R-56.2
KS	1,049	425	591	R-56.4	727	272	450	R-61.9	1,038	328	658	R-63.4
KY	1,238	507	731	R-59.0	1,099	456	637	R-58.0	1,435	562	825	R-57.5
LA	660	262	398	R-60.3	310	213	97	D-68.7	1,202	360	747	R-62.1
ME	600	379	211	D-63.2	415	281	125	D-67.7	638	423	203	D-66.2
MD	1,639	877	762	D-53.5	1,482	792	690	D-53.5	1,927	1,061	856	D-55.1
MA	2,409	1,585	781	D-65.8	1,742	1,306	413	D-75.0	2,347	1,968	343	D-83.8
MI	3,700	1,945	1,679	D-52.6	2,985	1,469	1,438	D-49.2	4,070	2,178	1,787	D-53.5
MN	2,141	1,180	895	D-55.1	2,040	1,090	863	D-53.5	2,364	1,234	993	D-52.2
MS	904	397	488	R-54.0	551	263	232	D-47.7	986	496	468	D-50.3
MO	2,116	1,116	833	D-52.8	1,572	788	748	D-50.1	2,326	1,136	1,136	D-48.8
MT	404	175	212	R 52.4	332	147	176	D-53.0	411	190	211	R-51.5
NE	662	204	450	R-68.0	526	105	393	R-74.7	683	178	487	R-71.2
NV	450	173	249	R-55.3	410	79	275	R-67.1	585	225	331	R-56.5
NH	491	221	247	R-50.3	318	124	190	R-59.8	556	239	303	R-54.5
NJ	2,823	1,352	1,399	R-49.6	1,815	902	858	D-49.7	2,988	1,532	1,384	D-51.3
NM	548	271	261	D-49.4	498	228	246	R-49.5	588	300	274	D-51.0
NY	5,551	3,041	2,358	D-54.8	4,267	2,278	1,858	D-53.4	5,824	3,190	2,466	D-54.8
NC	2,514	1,136	1,340	R-53.3	1,904	827	1,014	R-53.3	2,780	1,194	1,515	R-54.5
ND	263	145	114	D-55.1	213	120	88	D-56.2	286	151	127	D-52.9
OH	4,388	2,031	2,192	R-49.9	3,375	1,594	1,752	R-51.9	4,518	2,067	2,203	R-48.8
OK	1,180	430	723	R-61.3	859	314	538	R-62.7	1,088	337	702	R-64.5
OR	1,335	724	558	D-54.3	1,090	631	402	D-57.9	1,440	790	607	D-54.9
PA	4,316	2,223	2,038	D-51.5	2,896	1,381	1,472	R-50.8	4,554	2,279	2,229	D-50.0
RI	360	241	108	[3]D-66.9	293	204	77	D-69.5	384	247	89	D-64.4
SC	1,057	345	683	R-64.6	974	370	580	R-59.2	1,321	525	730	R-55.2
SD	323	120	186	R-57.7	259	64	194	R-75.1	315	78	231	R-73.4
TN	1,784	856	889	R-49.8	914	412	470	R-51.4	1,854	819	992	R-53.5
TX	5,219	2,323	2,785	R-53.4	3,462	1,531	1,787	R-51.6	5,986	2,799	2,932	R-49.0
UT	664	264	386	R-58.2	471	127	304	R-64.6	759	305	427	R-56.2
VT	255	24	83	[2]I-58.1	215	(X)	71	I-32.9	283	15	52	I-76.4
VA	2,199	1,027	1,117	R-50.8	1,149	514	542	R-47.2	2,422	1,060	1,132	R-46.7
WA	2,174	1,130	1,021	D-52.0	1,858	980	819	D-52.8	2,382	1,246	998	D-52.3
WV	522	458	64	D-87.8	351	283	29	D-80.6	580	421	109	D-72.6
WI	2,150	1,012	1,121	R-52.1	1,673	762	880	R-52.6	2,506	1,188	1,311	R-52.3
WY	210	86	116	R-55.2	174	67	101	R-57.8	212	61	142	R-66.8

X Not applicable.   [1] Includes vote cast for minor parties.   [2] Includes vote cast for nonvoting Delegate at Large in District of Columbia in 1990.   [3] State law does not require tabulation of votes for unopposed candidates.

Source: Congressional Quarterly, Inc., Washington, DC, *America Votes,* biennial (copyright).

Elections   241

No. 378. Vote Cast for United States Representatives by Major Political Party—Congressional Districts: 2000

[In some states the Democratic and Republican vote includes votes cast for the party candidate by endorsing parties]

State and district	Democratic candidate Name	Percent of total	Republican candidate Name	Percent of total	State and district	Democratic candidate Name	Percent of total	Republican candidate Name	Percent of total
AL	(X)........	(X)	(X)........	(X)	44th..	Oden......	37.9	Bono......	59.2
1st...	(¹)........	(¹)	Callahan....	91.3	45th...	Crisell.....	32.4	Rohrabacher.	62.1
2d...	Woods.....	29.2	Everett.....	68.2	46th...	Sanchez....	60.2	Tuchman...	35.0
3d...	(¹)........	(¹)	Riley......	86.9	47th...	Graham....	30.1	Cox......	65.6
4th...	Folsom....	37.4	Aderholt....	60.6	48th...	Kouvelis....	28.3	Issa......	61.4
5th...	Cramer, Jr..	88.8	(¹)........	(¹)	49th...	Davis......	49.6	Bilbray....	46.2
6th...	(¹)........	(¹)	Bachus.....	87.9	50th...	Filner.....	68.3	Divine.....	27.6
7th...	Hilliard.....	74.6	Martin.....	23.2	51st...	Barraza....	30.4	Cunningham.	64.3
AK	Greene.....	16.5	Young.....	69.6	52d...	Barkacs....	31.3	Hunter.....	64.7
AZ	(X)........	(X)	(X)........	(X)	**CO**	(X)........	(X)	(X)........	(X)
1st...	Mendoza...	42.4	Flake......	53.6	1st...	DeGette....	68.7	Thomas....	27.3
2d...	Pastor.....	68.5	Barenholtz..	26.9	2d...	Udall......	55.0	Cox......	38.6
3d...	Scharer....	31.4	Stump.....	65.7	3d...	Imrie......	29.1	McInnis....	65.8
4th...	Jankowski...	32.7	Shadegg....	64.0	4th...	(¹)........	(¹)	Schaffer....	79.5
5th...	Cunningham.	35.3	Kolbe......	60.1	5th...	(¹)........	(¹)	Hefley.....	82.7
6th...	Nelson.....	35.6	Hayworth...	61.4	6th...	Toltz......	42.1	Tancredo...	53.9
AR	(X)........	(X)	(X)........	(X)	**CT**	(X)........	(X)	(X)........	(X)
1st...	Berry......	60.1	Myshka....	39.7	1st...	Larson.....	71.9	Backlund...	28.1
2d...	Snyder.....	57.5	Thomas....	42.5	2d...	Gejdenson..	49.4	Simmons...	50.6
3d...	(¹)........	(¹)	Hutchinson..	(²)	3d...	DeLauro....	71.9	Gold......	27.5
4th...	Ross......	51.0	Dickey.....	49.0	4th...	Sanchez....	40.9	Shays.....	57.6
CA	(X)........	(X)	(X)........	(X)	5th...	Maloney....	53.6	Nielsen....	44.3
1st...	Thompson..	65.0	Chase.....	28.0	6th...	Valenti.....	32.9	Johnson....	62.6
2d...	Morgan....	28.2	Herger.....	65.7	**DE**	Miller......	30.8	Castle.....	67.6
3d...	Kent......	40.4	Ose......	56.2	**FL**	(X)........	(X)	(X)........	(X)
4th...	Norberg...	31.5	Doolittle....	63.4	1st...	(¹)........	(¹)	Scarborough.	99.5
5th...	Matsui.....	68.7	Payne.....	26.1	2d...	Boyd......	72.1	Dodd......	27.9
6th...	Woolsey...	64.3	McAuliffe...	28.3	3d...	Brown.....	57.6	Carroll.....	42.4
7th...	Miller.....	76.5	Hoffman....	21.1	4th...	Sullivan....	31.2	Crenshaw...	67.0
8th...	Pelosi.....	84.4	Sparks.....	11.7	5th...	Thurman....	64.3	Enwall.....	35.7
9th...	Lee......	85.0	Washington..	9.8	6th...	(¹)........	(¹)	Stearns....	100.0
10th..	Tauscher...	52.6	Hutchinson..	44.2	7th...	Vaughen....	36.8	Mica......	63.2
11th..	Santos.....	38.1	Pombo.....	57.8	8th...	Chapin.....	49.2	Keller.....	50.8
12th..	Lantos.....	74.5	Garza.....	20.8	9th...	(¹)........	(¹)	Bilirakis....	81.9
13th..	Stark......	70.4	Goetz.....	24.3	10th..	(¹)........	(¹)	Young.....	75.7
14th..	Eshoo.....	70.2	Quraishi....	25.8	11th..	Davis......	84.6	(¹)........	(¹)
15th..	Honda.....	54.3	Cunneen...	42.2	12th..	Stedem.....	43.0	Putnam....	57.0
16th..	Lofgren...	72.1	Thayn.....	23.3	13th..	Dunn......	36.1	Miller.....	63.8
17th..	Farr......	68.6	Engler.....	24.7	14th..	(¹)........	(¹)	Goss......	85.2
18th..	Condit.....	67.1	Wilson.....	31.3	15th..	Kurth......	39.2	Weldon....	58.8
19th..	Rosenberg..	31.7	Radanovich..	64.9	16th..	Brown.....	37.2	Foley......	60.2
20th..	Dooley.....	52.3	Rodriguez...	45.5	17th..	Meek......	100.0	(¹)........	(¹)
21st..	Martinez...	24.8	Thomas....	71.6	18th..	(¹)........	(¹)	Ros Lehtinen.	100.0
22d..	Capps.....	53.1	Stoker.....	44.3	19th..	Wexler.....	71.6	Thompson..	28.4
23d..	Case......	40.7	Gallegly....	54.1	20th..	Deutsch....	99.9	(¹)........	(¹)
24th..	Sherman...	66.0	Doyle......	29.8	21st..	(¹)........	(¹)	Diaz-Balart..	100.0
25th..	Gold......	33.2	McKeon....	62.2	22d..	Bloom.....	49.9	Shaw......	50.1
26th..	Berman....	84.1	(¹)........	(¹)	23d..	Hastings....	76.3	Lambert....	23.7
27th..	Schiff.....	52.7	Rogan.....	43.8	**GA**	(X)........	(X)	(X)........	(X)
28th..	Nelson.....	39.9	Dreier.....	56.8	1st...	Griggs.....	30.9	Kingston...	69.1
29th..	Waxman....	75.7	Scileppi....	19.2	2d...	Bishop, Jr...	53.5	Glenn.....	46.5
30th..	Becerra....	83.3	Goss......	11.8	3d...	Notti......	36.5	Collins.....	63.5
31st..	Solis......	79.4	(¹)........	(¹)	4th...	McKinney...	60.7	Warren.....	39.3
32d..	Dixon.....	83.5	Williamson..	12.1	5th...	Lewis......	77.2	Schwab....	22.8
33d..	Roybal-Allard.	84.5	Miller.....	11.5	6th...	DeHart.....	25.2	Isakson....	74.8
34th..	Napolitano..	71.3	Canales....	22.5	7th...	Kahn......	44.7	Barr......	55.3
35th..	Waters.....	86.5	McGill.....	10.8	8th...	Marshall....	41.1	Chambliss...	58.9
36th..	Harman....	48.4	Kuykendall..	46.6	9th...	Harrington..	24.8	Deal.......	75.2
37th..	Millender-McDonald...	82.3	Van......	11.3	10th..	Freeman....	36.8	Norwood....	63.2
38th..	Schipske...	47.5	Horn......	48.4	11th..	(¹)........	(¹)	Linder.....	100.0
39th..	Kanel......	31.3	Royce.....	62.9	**HI**	(X)........	(X)	(X)........	(X)
40th..	(¹)........	(¹)	Lewis......	79.9	1st...	Abercrombie.	69.0	Meyers....	28.6
41st..	Favila.....	37.4	Miller.....	58.9	2d...	Mink......	61.6	Francis.....	36.0
42d..	Baca......	59.8	Pirozzi....	35.1	**ID**	(X)........	(X)	(X)........	(X)
43d..	(¹)........	(¹)	Calvert.....	73.7	1st...	Pall......	31.4	Otter......	64.8
					2d...	Williams....	25.9	Simpson....	70.7

See footnotes at end of table.

No. 378. Vote Cast for United States Representatives by Major Political Party—Congressional Districts: 2000—Con.

[See headnote, p. 242]

State and district	Democratic candidate — Name	Percent of total	Republican candidate — Name	Percent of total
IL.....	(X).	(X)	(X)	(X)
1st...	Rush	87.8	Warding-ley	12.2
2d...	Jackson Jr.	89.8	Gordon III.	10.2
3d...	Lipinski.	75.6	Groth.	24.4
4th...	Gutierrez	88.6	(1)	(1)
5th...	Blagojevich	87.3	(1)	(1)
6th...	Christensen.	41.1	Hyde	58.9
7th...	Davis	85.9	Dallas	14.1
8th...	Pressl	39.0	Crane	61.0
9th...	Schakowsky	76.4	Driscoll	23.6
10th...	Gash	48.8	Kirk	51.2
11th...	Stevenson	43.6	Weller	56.4
12th...	Costello	100.0	(1)	(1)
13th...	Mason	33.8	Biggert.	66.2
14th...	Deljonson	26.0	Hastert.	74.0
15th...	Kelleher	46.8	Johnson.	53.2
16th...	Hendrickson	33.3	Manzullo	66.7
17th...	Evans	54.9	Baker	45.1
18th...	Harant	32.9	LaHood	67.1
19th...	Phelps	64.6	Eatherly	35.4
20th...	Cooper	36.9	Shimkus.	63.1
IN.....	(X).	(X)	(X)	(X)
1st...	Visclosky	71.6	Reynolds	27.0
2d...	Rock	38.8	Pence	50.9
3d...	Roemer	51.6	Chocola.	47.4
4th...	Foster	35.4	Souder	62.3
5th...	Goodnight.	37.5	Buyer	60.9
6th...	Griesey	26.4	Burton	70.3
7th...	Graf.	31.8	Kerns	64.8
8th...	Perry	45.3	Hostettler	52.7
9th...	Hill.	54.2	Bailey	43.8
10th...	Carson	58.5	Scott	39.7
IA.....	(X).	(X)	(X)	(X)
1st...	Simpson	36.1	Leach	61.8
2d...	Smith.	43.7	Nussle	55.4
3d...	Boswell	62.8	Marcus	33.7
4th...	Huston	36.7	Ganske	61.4
5th...	Palecek	29.2	Latham	68.8
KS.....	(X).	(X)	(X)	(X)
1st...	(1)	(1)	Moran	89.3
2d...	Wiles	29.3	Ryun	67.4
3d...	Moore	50.0	Kline	46.9
4th...	Nolla	42.0	Tiahrt.	54.4
KY.....	(X).	(X)	(X)	(X)
1st...	Roy	42.0	Whitfield.	58.0
2d...	Pedigo	31.4	Lewis.	67.7
3d...	Jordan	44.2	Northup	52.9
4th...	Lucas.	54.3	Bell.	43.5
5th...	Bailey.	26.4	Rogers.	73.6
6th...	Baesler.	34.8	Fletcher.	52.8
LA [2]....	(X).	(X)	(X)	(X)
1st...	Armato.	12.6	Vitter.	80.5
2d...	Jefferson	(3)	(1)	(1)
3d...	(1)	(1)	Tauzin	78.0
4th...	Green	25.1	McCrery.	70.5
5th...	Beall	23.9	Cooksey	69.1
6th...	Rogillio.	29.7	Baker	68.0
7th...	John	83.3	(1)	(1)
ME....	(X).	(X)	(X)	(X)
1st...	Allen	59.8	Amero.	36.5
2d...	Baldacci	73.4	Campbell	26.6
MD....	(X).	(X)	(X)	(X)
1st...	Bozman	35.5	Gilchrest	64.4
2d...	Bosley	31.3	Ehrlich.	68.6
3d...	Cardin	75.7	Harby	24.0
4th...	Wynn.	87.2	Kimble.	12.6
5th...	Hoyer.	65.1	Hutchins.	34.9
6th...	DeArmon	39.3	Bartlett.	60.6
7th...	Cummings	87.1	Kondner.	12.8
8th...	Lierman	45.5	Morella	52.0
MA....	(X).	(X)	(X)	(X)
1st...	Olver	65.3	Abair.	28.4
2d...	Neal.	77.5	(1)	(1)
3d...	McGovern.	76.5	(1)	(1)
4th...	Frank.	70.8	Travis	20.0
5th...	Meehan	74.4	(1)	(1)
6th...	Tierney.	67.6	McCarthy.	27.5
7th...	Markey.	75.6	(1)	(1)
8th...	Capuano	71.0	(1)	(1)
9th...	Moakley	71.2	Jeghelian.	18.0
10th...	Delahunt.	70.5	Bleicken.	24.4
MI.....	(X).	(X)	(X)	(X)
1st...	Stupak	58.4	Yob	40.4
2d...	Shrauger	33.2	Hoekstra	64.4
3d...	Steele	33.1	Ehlers	65.0
4th...	Hollenbeck	29.1	Camp	68.0
5th...	Barcia	74.3	Actis	23.9
6th...	Bupp	29.2	Upton	67.9
7th...	Crittendon.	35.7	Smith.	61.1
8th...	Byrum	48.7	Rogers.	48.8
9th...	Kildee	61.1	Garrett.	35.9
10th...	Bonior	64.4	Turner	33.2
11th...	Frumin	40.5	Knollenberg	55.8
12th...	Levin	64.3	Baron	32.1
13th...	Rivers	64.7	Berry	32.1
14th...	Conyers Jr.	89.1	Ashe	9.3
15th...	Kilpatrick.	88.6	Boyd-Fields	9.0
16th...	Dingell	71.0	Morse	26.5
MN....	(X).	(X)	(X)	(X)
1st...	Rieder	41.6	Gutknecht	56.4
2d...	Minge.	48.0	Kennedy	48.1
3d...	Shuff	29.8	Ramstad.	67.6
4th...	McCollum	48.0	Runbeck	30.9
5th...	Sabo	69.2	Taylor.	22.8
6th...	Luther	49.6	Kline	48.0
7th...	Peterson	68.7	Menze	29.3
8th...	Oberstar.	67.8	Lemen.	25.8
MS....	(X).	(X)	(X)	(X)
1st...	Grist	28.6	Wicker.	69.8
2d...	Thompson	65.1	Caraway.	31.2
3d...	Thrash	25.7	Pickering	73.2
4th...	Shows	58.1	Lampton	39.8
5th...	Taylor.	78.8	McDonnell	18.2
MO....	(X).	(X)	(X)	(X)
1st...	Clay.	75.2	Billingsly.	21.5
2d...	House	42.4	Akin	55.3
3d...	Gephardt	57.8	Federer	39.7
4th...	Skelton	66.9	Noland.	31.3
5th...	McCarthy	68.8	Gordon	28.6
6th...	Danner.	46.8	Graves, Jr.	50.9
7th...	Christrup.	23.9	Blunt	73.9
8th...	Camp.	28.9	Emerson	69.3
9th...	Carroll	38.3	Hulshof	59.3
MT...	Keenan	46.3	Rehberg.	51.5
NE....	(X).	(X)	(X)	(X)
1st...	Jacobsen	31.0	Bereuter.	66.2
2d...	Kiel	31.1	Terry	65.8
3d...	Reynolds	15.7	Osborne.	82.0
NV....	(X).	(X)	(X)	(X)
1st...	Berkley.	51.7	Porter	44.2
2d...	Cahill	29.8	Gibbons	64.2
NH....	(X).	(X)	(X)	(X)
1st...	Clark	45.1	Sununu	52.9
2d...	Brannen	40.7	Bass	56.2
NJ....	(X).	(X)	(X)	(X)
1st...	Andrews.	76.2	Cathcart.	21.2
2d...	Janosik	31.9	LoBiondo	66.4
3d...	Levin	41.2	Saxton.	57.3
4th...	Gusciora.	35.1	Smith.	63.2
5th...	Mercurio.	30.4	Roukema	65.4
6th...	Pallone, Jr.	67.5	Kennedy	29.8
7th...	Connelly.	45.6	Ferguson	51.6
8th...	Pascrell Jr.	67.0	Fusco	30.3
9th...	Rothman	67.9	Tedeschi	30.0
10th...	Payne	87.5	Weber	12.1
11th...	Scollo	29.6	Frelinghuysen	68.0
12th...	Holt	48.7	Zimmer	48.5
13th...	Menendez.	78.7	de Leon.	18.6

See footnotes at end of table.

U.S. Census Bureau, Statistical Abstract of the United States: 2002

[See headnote, p. 242]

State and district	Democratic candidate — Name	Percent of total	Republican candidate — Name	Percent of total	State and district	Democratic candidate — Name	Percent of total	Republican candidate — Name	Percent of total
NM	(X)	(X)	(X)	(X)	13th..	Brown	64.6	Jeric	32.0
1st...	Kelly	43.3	Wilson	50.3	14th..	Sawyer	64.8	Wood	31.0
2d...	Montoya.....	41.9	Skeen	58.1	15th..	Buckel	27.9	Pryce	67.5
3d...	Udall	67.2	Lutz	32.8	16th..	Smith......	26.8	Regula	69.2
NY	(X)	(X)	(X)........	(X)	17th..	Traficant.....	50.0	Alberty	22.7
1st...	Seltzer.....	36.1	Grucci, Jr. ...	41.2	18th..	Guthrie	33.5	Ney	64.4
2d...	Israel......	40.0	Johnson	29.1	19th..	Blanchard....	31.9	LaTourette ..	64.8
3d...	Lamagna	32.8	King.......	43.8	OK	(X)	(X)	(X)........	(X)
4th...	McCarthy	50.7	Becker	29.8	1st...	Lowe.......	29.2	Largent	69.3
5th...	Ackerman....	52.0	Elkowitz	22.9	2d...	Carson......	54.9	Ewing......	41.8
6th...	Meeks	66.7	(¹)	(¹)	3d...	(¹)	(¹)	Watkins	86.6
7th...	Crowley	51.0	Birtley	16.0	4th...	Weatherford ..	31.2	Watts, Jr. ...	64.9
8th...	Nadler	61.5	Henry	11.9	5th...	McWatters ...	27.2	Istook, Jr. ...	68.4
9th...	Weiner	52.3	Dear	22.2	6th...	Beutler.....	39.2	Lucas	59.3
10th..	Towns	66.5	Brown	3.8	OR	(X)	(X)	(X)........	(X)
11th..	Owens	64.0	Cleary	4.3	1st...	Wu	58.3	Starr	38.0
12th..	Velazquez ...	60.9	Markgraf.....	7.5	2d...	Ponsford	26.1	Walden	73.6
13th..	Johnstone ...	27.8	Fossella	47.7	3d...	Blumenauer ..	66.8	Pollock	23.6
14th..	Maloney	59.4	Rhodes	18.8	4th...	DeFazio	68.0	Lindsey	30.6
15th..	Rangel.....	70.8	Suero	3.9	5th...	Hooley.....	56.8	Boquist.....	43.1
16th..	Serrano	71.9	Justice	2.8	PA	(X)	(X)	(X)........	(X)
17th..	Engel	68.0	McManus ...	6.9	1st...	Brady	88.3	Kush	11.7
18th..	Lowey	55.6	Vonglis	23.2	2d...	Fattah	98.0	(¹)	(¹)
19th..	Graham	30.7	Kelly	50.1	3d...	Borski	68.7	Dougherty...	31.3
20th..	Feiner	32.6	Gilman	50.7	4th...	Van Horne ...	41.0	Hart	59.0
21st..	McNulty	59.0	Pillsworth ...	22.6	5th...	(¹)	(¹)	Peterson.....	85.6
22d..	McCallion....	25.6	Sweeney	54.3	6th...	Holden	66.3	Kopel	33.7
23d..	Englebrecht ..	17.0	Boehlert	49.5	7th...	Lennon	35.2	Weldon	64.8
24th..	Tallon	18.8	McHugh	58.0	8th...	Strouse	38.7	Greenwood..	59.2
25th..	Gavin	25.4	Walsh	52.1	9th...	(¹)	(¹)	Shuster	100.0
26th..	Hinchey	50.7	Moppert	31.7	10th..	Casey	47.4	Sherwood...	52.6
27th..	Pecoraro	24.8	Reynolds	51.2	11th..	Kanjorski	66.4	Urban.....	33.6
28th..	Slaughter	59.4	Johns......	26.3	12th..	Murtha	70.8	Choby	27.5
29th..	LaFalce.....	46.8	Sommer	27.9	13th..	Hoeffel.....	52.8	Greenleaf ...	45.7
30th..	Fee	25.0	Quinn......	45.6	14th..	Coyne	100.0	(¹)	(¹)
31st..	Peters	18.9	Houghton ...	60.1	15th..	O'Brien	46.7	Toomey	53.3
NC	(X)	(X)	(X)........	(X)	16th..	Yorczyk	33.1	Pitts......	66.9
1st...	Clayton	65.6	Kratzer.....	32.9	17th..	Herrmann....	28.5	Gekas	71.5
2d...	Etheridge ...	58.3	Haynes	40.9	18th..	Doyle.......	69.4	Stephens ...	30.6
3d...	McNairy	37.3	Jones......	61.4	19th..	Sanders	26.5	Platts	72.6
4th...	Price	61.6	Ward	36.6	20th..	Mascara.....	64.4	Davis	35.6
5th...	(¹)	(¹)	Burr	92.8	21st..	Flitter.......	39.2	English.....	60.8
6th...	(¹)	(¹)	Coble......	91.0	RI	(X)	(X)	(X)........	(X)
7th...	McIntyre	69.7	Adams	28.9	1st...	Kennedy	66.6	Cabral	33.2
8th...	Taylor	44.0	Hayes	55.0	2d...	Langevin	62.2	Tingle.....	14.0
9th...	McGuire.....	30.0	Myrick	68.6	SC	(X)	(X)	(X)........	(X)
10th..	Parker	29.5	Ballenger ...	68.2	1st...	Brack......	35.7	Brown	60.3
11th..	Neill	42.1	Taylor......	55.1	2d...	Frederick	40.8	Spence	57.0
12th..	Watt	64.8	Mitchell.....	33.3	3d...	Brightharp ...	29.3	Graham	67.8
ND	(¹)	(¹)	Dorso......	44.5	4th...	(¹)	0.0	DeMint.....	79.6
OH	(X)	(X)	(X)........	(X)	5th...	Spratt	58.8	Gullick.....	39.5
1st...	Cranley	44.6	Chabot.....	53.0	6th...	Clyburn.....	71.8	Ellison	26.0
2d...	Sanders	23.1	Portman	73.6	SD	Hohn.......	24.9	Thune	73.4
3d...	Hall	83.0	(¹)	(¹)	TN	(X)	(X)	(X)........	(X)
4th...	Dickman.....	29.0	Oxley	67.4	1st...	(¹)	(¹)	Jenkins	100.0
5th...	Edmon.....	25.5	Gillmor	69.8	2d...	(¹)	(¹)	Duncan, Jr. ...	89.3
6th...	Strickland....	57.7	Azinger	40.3	3d...	Callaway	34.6	Wamp	63.9
7th...	Minor......	25.1	Hobson	67.6	4th...	Dunaway	33.1	Hilleary.....	65.8
8th...	Parks......	26.2	Boehner	71.0	5th...	Clement.....	72.5	Scott	24.5
9th...	Kaptur	74.8	Bryan	21.9	6th...	Gordon	62.1	Charles	35.7
10th..	Kucinich.....	75.0	Smith	22.0	7th...	Sims	29.1	Bryant.....	69.6
11th..	Tubbs Jones..	84.8	Sykora	11.2	8th...	Tanner......	72.3	Yancy.....	27.7
12th..	O'Shaughnessy.	43.8	Tiberi	52.9	9th...	Ford, Jr.......	100.0	(¹)	(¹)

See footnotes at end of table.

[See headnote, p. 242]

Left panel

State and district	Democratic candidate — Name	Percent of total	Republican candidate — Name	Percent of total
TX	(X)	(X)	(X)	(X)
1st...	Sandlin	55.8	Willingham	43.4
2d...	Turner	91.1	([1])	([1])
3d...	Zachary	25.7	Johnson	71.6
4th...	Hall	60.3	Newton	37.9
5th...	Coggins	44.4	Sessions	54.0
6th...	([1])	([1])	Barton	88.1
7th...	Sell	24.4	Culberson	73.9
8th...	([1])	([1])	Brady	91.6
9th...	Lampson	59.2	Williams	39.7
10th..	Doggett	84.6	([1])	([1])
11th..	Edwards	54.8	Farley	44.3
12th..	Greene	36.0	Granger	62.7
13th..	Clinesmith	31.1	Thornberry	67.6
14th..	Sneary	40.3	Paul	59.7
15th..	Hinojosa	88.5	([1])	([1])
16th..	Reyes	68.3	Power	30.2
17th..	Stenholm	59.0	Clements	35.5
18th..	Jackson-Lee	76.5	Levy	22.2
19th..	([1])	([1])	Combest	91.6
20th..	Gonzalez	87.7	([1])	([1])
21st..	Green	22.2	Smith	75.9
22d..	Matranga	36.2	DeLay	60.4
23d..	Garza	38.8	Bonilla	59.3
24th..	Frost	61.8	Wright	36.7
25th..	Bentsen	60.1	Sudan	38.5
26th..	Love	25.6	Armey	72.5
27th..	Ortiz	63.4	Ahumada	33.9
28th..	Rodriguez	89.0	([1])	([1])
29th..	Green	73.3	Vu	25.6
30th..	Johnson	91.8	([1])	([1])
UT	(X)	(X)	(X)	(X)
1st...	Collinwood	27.2	Hansen	69.0
2d...	Matheson	55.9	Smith	41.3
3d...	Dunn	37.3	Cannon	58.5
VT[4]	Diamond-stone	5.3	Kerin	18.3
VA[5]	(X)	(X)	(X)	(X)

Right panel

State and district	Democratic candidate — Name	Percent of total	Republican candidate — Name	Percent of total
1st...	Davies	37.0	Davis	57.5
2d...	Wagner	48.0	Schrock	52.0
3d...	Scott	97.7	([1])	([1])
4th...	Sisisky	98.9	([1])	([1])
5th...	Boyd, Jr.	30.7	([1])	([1])
6th...	([1])	([1])	Goodlatte	99.3
7th...	Stewart	33.0	Cantor	66.9
8th...	Moran	63.3	Miller	34.1
9th...	Boucher	69.8	Osborne	30.1
10th..	([1])	([1])	Wolf	84.2
11th..	Corrigan	34.3	Davis	61.9
WA	(X)	(X)	(X)	(X)
1st...	Inslee	54.6	McDonald	42.6
2d...	Larsen	50.0	Koster	45.9
3d...	Baird	56.4	Matson	40.6
4th...	Davis	37.3	Hastings	60.9
5th...	Keefe	38.9	Nethercutt, Jr.	57.3
6th...	Dicks	64.7	Lawrence	31.1
7th...	McDermott	72.8	([1])	([1])
8th...	Behrens-Benedict	35.6	Dunn	62.2
9th...	Smith	61.7	Vance	35.0
WV	(X)	(X)	(X)	(X)
1st...	Mollohan	87.8	([1])	([1])
2d...	Humphreys	45.9	Capito	48.5
3d...	Rahall II	91.3	([1])	([1])
WI	(X)	(X)	(X)	(X)
1st...	Thomas	33.3	Ryan	66.6
2d...	Baldwin	51.4	Sharpless	(NA)
3d...	Kind	63.7	Tully	35.9
4th...	Kleczka	60.8	Riener	37.8
5th...	Barrett	77.7	Smith	22.0
6th...	Flaherty	34.9	Petri	65.0
7th...	Obey	63.3	Cronin	36.7
8th...	Reich	25.3	Green	74.6
9th...	Clawson	25.9	Sensenbrenner, Jr.	74.0
WY	Green	28.6	Cubin	66.8

X Not applicable.   [1] No candidate.   [2] According to state law, it is not required to tabulate votes for unopposed candidates. [3] Louisiana holds an open-primary election with candidates from all parties running on the same ballot. Any candidate who receives a majority is elected; if no candidate receives 50 percent, there is a run off election in November between the top two finishers. [4] Sanders, an Independent, was elected with 69.2 percent of the vote. [5] Goode, an Independent, was elected in the Virginia 5th with 67.4 percent of the vote.

Source: Congressional Quarterly Inc., *Congressional Quarterly Weekly Report* (copyright).

No. 379. Composition of Congress by Political Party: 1973 to 2002

[D=Democratic, R=Republican. Data for beginning of first session of each Congress (as of January 3), except as noted. Excludes vacancies at beginning of session]

Year	Party and President	Congress	House — Majority party	House — Minority party	House — Other	Senate — Majority party	Senate — Minority party	Senate — Other
1973 [1][2]	R (Nixon)	93d	D-239	R-192	1	D-56	R-42	2
1975 [3]	R (Ford)	94th	D-291	R-144	-	D-60	R-37	2
1977 [4]	D (Carter)	95th	D-292	R-143	-	D-61	R-38	1
1979 [4]	D (Carter)	96th	D-276	R-157	-	D-58	R-41	1
1981 [4]	R (Reagan)	97th	D-243	R-192	-	R-53	D-46	1
1983	R (Reagan)	98th	D-269	R-165	-	R-54	D-46	-
1985	R (Reagan)	99th	D-252	R-182	-	R-53	D-47	-
1987	R (Reagan)	100th	D-258	R-177	-	D-55	R-45	-
1989	R (Bush)	101st	D-259	R-174	-	D-55	R-45	-
1991 [5]	R (Bush)	102d	D-267	R-167	1	D-56	R-44	-
1993 [5]	D (Clinton)	103d	D-258	R-176	1	D-57	R-43	-
1995 [5]	D (Clinton)	104th	R-230	D-204	1	R-52	D-48	-
1997 [5]	D (Clinton)	105th	R-226	D-207	2	R-55	D-45	-
1999 [5]	D (Clinton)	106th	R-222	D-212	1	R-55	D-45	-
2001 [6]	R (Bush)	107th	R-221	D-211	2	D-50	R-50	-
2002 [6][7]	R (Bush)	107th	R-222	D-211	2	D-50	R-49	1

- Represents zero.   [1] Senate had one Independent and one Conservative-Republican.   [2] House had one Independent-Democrat.   [3] Senate had one Independent, one Conservative-Republican, and one undecided (New Hampshire).   [4] Senate had one Independent.   [5] House had one Independent-Socialist.   [6] House had one Independent-Socialist and one Independent. [7] As of beginning of second session.

Source: U.S. Congress, Joint Committee on Printing, *Congressional Directory,* annual; beginning 1977, biennial.

No. 380. Composition of Congress by Political Party Affiliation—States: 1993 to 2002

[Figures are for the beginning of the first session (as of January 3), except as noted. Dem.=Democratic; Rep.=Republican]

State	Representatives 103rd Cong.,[1] 1993 Dem.	Rep.	105th Cong.,[1][2] 1997 Dem.	Rep.	106th Cong.,[1] 1999 Dem.	Rep.	107th Cong.,[1][3] [4]2002 Dem.	Rep.	Senators 103rd Cong., 1993 Dem.	Rep.	105th Cong., 1997 Dem.	Rep.	106th Cong., 1999 Dem.	Rep.	107th Cong.,[3][5] 2002 Dem.	Rep.
U.S.	258	176	207	226	212	222	211	222	57	43	45	55	45	55	50	49
AL.	4	3	2	5	2	5	2	5	2	-	-	2	-	2	-	2
AK.	-	1	-	1	-	1	-	1	-	2	-	2	-	2	-	2
AZ.	3	3	1	5	1	5	1	5	1	1	-	2	-	2	-	2
AR.	2	2	2	2	2	2	3	1	2	-	1	1	1	1	1	1
CA.	30	22	29	23	28	24	32	20	2	-	2	-	2	-	2	-
CO.	2	4	2	4	2	4	2	4	1	1	-	2	-	2	-	2
CT.	3	3	4	2	4	2	3	3	2	-	2	-	2	-	2	-
DE.	-	1	-	1	-	1	-	1	1	1	1	1	1	1	2	-
FL.	10	13	8	15	8	15	8	15	1	1	1	1	1	1	2	-
GA	7	4	3	8	3	8	3	8	1	1	1	1	1	1	2	-
HI	2	-	2	-	2	-	2	-	2	-	2	-	2	-	2	-
ID	1	1	-	2	-	2	-	2	-	2	-	2	-	2	-	2
IL	12	8	10	10	10	10	10	10	2	-	2	-	1	1	1	1
IN	7	3	4	6	4	6	4	6	1	1	1	1	1	1	1	1
IA	1	4	1	4	1	4	1	4	1	1	1	1	1	1	1	1
KS.	2	2	-	4	1	3	1	3	-	2	-	2	-	2	-	2
KY.	4	2	1	5	1	5	1	5	1	1	1	1	-	2	-	2
LA	4	3	2	5	2	5	2	5	2	-	2	-	2	-	2	-
ME	1	1	2	-	2	-	2	-	1	1	-	2	-	2	-	2
MD	4	4	4	4	4	4	4	4	2	-	2	-	2	-	2	-
MA	8	2	10	-	10	-	10	-	2	-	2	-	2	-	2	-
MI	10	6	10	6	10	6	9	7	2	-	1	1	1	1	2	-
MN	6	2	6	2	6	2	5	3	1	1	1	1	1	1	2	-
MS	5	-	2	3	3	2	3	2	-	2	-	2	-	2	-	2
MO	6	3	5	3	5	4	4	5	-	2	-	2	-	2	1	1
MT	1	-	-	1	-	1	-	1	1	1	1	1	1	1	1	1
NE.	1	2	-	3	-	3	-	3	2	-	1	1	1	1	1	1
NV.	1	1	-	2	1	1	1	1	2	-	2	-	-	2	1	1
NH	1	1	-	2	-	2	-	2	-	2	-	2	-	2	-	2
NJ.	7	6	6	7	7	6	7	6	2	-	2	-	2	-	2	-
NM	1	2	1	2	1	2	1	2	1	1	1	1	1	1	1	1
NY.	18	13	18	13	19	12	19	12	1	1	1	1	2	-	2	-
NC	8	4	6	6	5	7	5	7	-	2	-	2	1	1	1	1
ND	1	-	1	-	1	-	1	-	2	-	2	-	2	-	2	-
OH	10	9	8	11	8	11	8	11	2	-	1	1	-	2	-	2
OK	4	2	-	6	-	6	1	5	1	1	-	2	-	2	-	2
OR	4	1	4	1	4	1	4	1	2	-	1	1	1	1	1	1
PA	11	10	11	10	11	10	10	11	1	1	-	2	-	2	-	2
RI	1	1	2	-	2	-	2	-	1	1	1	1	1	1	1	1
SC.	3	3	2	4	2	4	2	4	1	1	1	1	1	1	1	1
SD.	1	-	-	1	-	1	-	1	1	1	2	-	2	-	2	-
TN.	6	3	4	5	4	5	4	5	2	-	-	2	-	2	-	2
TX.	21	9	17	13	17	13	17	13	1	1	-	2	-	2	-	2
UT.	2	1	-	3	-	3	1	2	-	2	-	2	-	2	-	2
VT.	-	-	-	-	-	-	-	-	1	1	1	1	1	1	1	-
VA.	7	4	6	5	6	5	3	7	1	1	1	1	1	1	-	2
WA	8	1	3	6	5	4	6	3	1	1	1	1	1	1	2	-
WV	3	-	3	-	3	-	2	1	2	-	2	-	2	-	2	-
WI	4	5	5	4	5	4	5	4	2	-	2	-	2	-	2	-
WY	-	1	-	1	-	1	-	1	-	2	-	2	-	2	-	2

- Represents zero.   [1] Vermont had one Independent-Socialist Representative.   [2] Missouri had one Independent.   [3] As of beginning of second session.   [4] Virginia had one Independent Representative.   [5] Vermont had one Independent Senator.

Source: U.S. Congress, Joint Committee on Printing, *Congressional Directory*, biennial; and unpublished data.

U.S. Census Bureau, Statistical Abstract of the United States: 2002

No. 381. Members of Congress—Incumbents Reelected: 1964 to 2000

	Representatives						Senators				
	Incumbent candidates						Incumbent candidates				
			Reelected		Defeated in—			Reelected		Defeated in—	
Year	Retire-ments [1]	Total	Num-ber	Per-cent of candi-dates	Pri-mary	General election	Retire-ments [1]	Total	Num-ber	Per-cent of candi-dates	Pri-mary	General election
PRESIDENTIAL-YEAR ELECTIONS												
1964	33	397	344	86.6	8	45	2	33	28	84.8	1	4
1968	23	409	396	96.8	4	9	6	28	20	71.4	4	4
1972	40	390	365	93.6	12	13	6	27	20	74.1	2	5
1976	47	384	368	95.8	3	13	8	25	16	64.0	-	9
1980	34	398	361	90.7	6	31	5	29	16	55.2	4	9
1984	22	411	392	95.4	3	16	4	29	26	89.7	-	3
1988	23	409	402	98.3	1	6	6	27	23	85.2	-	4
1992	65	368	325	88.3	[2]19	[3]24	7	28	23	82.1	1	4
1996	50	384	361	94.0	2	21	13	21	19	90.5	1	1
2000	32	403	394	97.8	3	6	5	29	23	79.3	-	6
MIDTERM ELECTIONS												
1966	22	411	362	88.1	8	41	3	32	28	87.5	3	1
1970	29	401	379	94.5	10	12	4	31	24	77.4	1	6
1974	43	391	343	87.7	8	40	7	27	23	85.2	2	2
1978	49	382	358	93.7	5	19	10	25	15	60.0	3	7
1982	40	393	354	90.1	[2]10	29	3	30	28	93.3	-	2
1986	40	394	385	97.7	3	6	6	28	21	75.0	-	7
1990	27	406	390	96.1	1	15	3	32	31	96.9	-	1
1994	48	387	349	90.2	4	34	9	26	24	92.3	-	2
1998	23	404	395	97.8	1	6	5	29	26	89.7	-	3

- Represents zero.   [1] Does not include persons who died or resigned before the election.   [2] Number of incumbents defeated in primaries by other incumbents due to redistricting: six in 1982 and four in 1992.   [3] Five incumbents defeated in general election by other incumbents due to redistricting.

Source: Ornstein, Norman J., Thomas E. Mann, and Michael J. Malbin, *Vital Statistics on Congress, 1993-1994,* Beginning 1995, Congressional Quarterly, Inc., Washington, DC, *America Votes,* biennial (copyright).

No. 382. Members of Congress—Selected Characteristics: 1983 to 2002

[As of beginning of first session of each Congress, (January 3). Figures for Representatives exclude vacancies]

Members of congress and year	Male	Fe-male	Black [1]	API [2]	His-panic [3]	Age [4] (in years)					Seniority [5][6]				
						Under 40	40 to 49	50 to 59	60 to 69	70 and over	Less than 2 yrs.	2 to 9 yrs.	10 to 19 yrs.	20 to 29 yrs.	30 yrs. or more
REPRESENTATIVES															
98th Cong., 1983	413	21	[7]21	3	8	86	145	132	57	14	83	224	88	28	11
99th Cong., 1985	412	22	[7]21	3	10	71	154	131	59	19	49	237	104	34	10
100th Cong., 1987. . . .	412	23	[7]23	4	11	63	153	137	56	26	51	221	114	37	12
101st Cong., 1989. . . .	408	25	[7]24	5	10	41	163	133	74	22	39	207	139	35	13
102d Cong., 1991	407	28	[7]26	3	11	39	152	134	86	24	55	178	147	44	11
103d Cong., 1993 [8] . . .	388	47	[7]38	4	17	47	151	128	89	15	118	141	132	32	12
104th Cong., 1995. . . .	388	47	[9]40	4	17	53	155	135	79	13	92	188	110	36	9
106th Cong., 1999. . . .	379	56	[9]39	(NA)	19	23	116	173	87	35	41	236	104	46	7
107th Cong., 2001. . . .	381	62	[9]39	(NA)	19	14	97	167	117	35	44	155	158	63	14
SENATORS															
98th Cong., 1983	98	2	-	2	-	7	28	39	20	6	5	61	21	10	3
99th Cong., 1985	98	2	-	2	-	4	27	38	25	6	8	56	27	7	2
100th Cong., 1987. . . .	98	2	-	2	-	5	30	36	22	7	14	41	36	7	2
101st Cong., 1989. . . .	98	2	-	2	-	-	30	40	22	8	23	22	43	10	2
102d Cong., 1991	98	2	-	2	-	-	23	46	24	7	5	34	47	10	4
103d Cong., 1993 [8] . . .	93	7	1	2	-	1	16	48	22	12	15	30	39	11	5
104th Cong., 1995. . . .	92	8	1	2	-	1	14	41	27	17	12	38	30	15	5
106th Cong., 1999. . . .	91	9	-	(NA)	-	-	14	38	35	13	8	39	33	14	6
107th Cong., 2001. . . .	87	13	-	(NA)	-	-	8	39	33	18	11	34	30	14	9

- Represents zero.   NA Not available.   [1] Source: Joint Center for Political and Economic Studies, Washington, DC, *Black Elected Officials: Statistical Summary,* annual (copyright).   [2] Asians and Pacific Islanders. Source: Library of Congress, Congressional Research Service, "Asian Pacific Americans in the United States Congress," Report 94-767 GOV.   [3] Source: National Association of Latino Elected and Appointed Officials, Washington, DC, *National Roster of Hispanic Elected Officials,* annual.   [4] Some members do not provide date of birth.   [5] Represents consecutive years of service.   [6] Some members do not provide years of service.   [7] Includes District of Columbia delegate but not Virgin Islands Delegate.   [8] Includes members elected to fill vacant seats through June 14, 1993.   [9] Includes District of Columbia and Virgin Islands delegate.

Source: Except as noted, compiled by U.S. Census Bureau from data published in *Congressional Directory,* biennial.

U.S. Census Bureau, Statistical Abstract of the United States: 2002

No. 383. U.S. Congress—Measures Introduced and Enacted and Time in Session: 1985 to 2001

[Excludes simple and concurrent resolutions]

Item	99th Cong., 1985-86	100th Cong., 1987-88	101st Cong., 1989-90	102d Cong., 1991-92	103d Cong., 1993-94	104th Cong., 1995-96	105th Cong., 1997-98	106th Cong., 1999-2000	107th Cong., 2001
Measures introduced	9,885	9,588	6,664	6,775	8,544	6,808	7,732	9,158	5,603
Bills.	8,697	8,515	5,977	6,212	7,883	6,545	7,532	8,968	5,493
Joint resolutions	1,188	1,073	687	563	661	263	200	190	110
Measures enacted.	483	761	666	609	473	337	404	604	137
Public	466	713	650	589	465	333	394	580	136
Private.	17	48	16	20	8	4	10	24	1
HOUSE OF REPRESENTATIVES									
Number of days	281	298	281	280	265	290	251	272	142
Number of hours.	1,794	1,659	1,688	1,796	1,887	2,445	2,001	2,179	922
Number of hours per day . .	6.4	5.6	6.0	6.4	7.1	8.4	8.0	8.0	6.5
SENATE									
Number of days	313	307	274	287	291	343	296	303	173
Number of hours.	2,531	2,341	2,254	2,292	2,514	2,876	2,188	2,200	1,236
Number of hours per day . .	8.1	7.6	8.2	8.0	8.6	8.4	7.4	7.3	7.1

Source: U.S. Congress, *Congressional Record* and *Daily Calendar*, selected issues. <http://thomas.loc.gov/home/resume>.

No. 384. Congressional Bills Vetoed: 1961 to 2001

Period	President	Total vetoes	Regular vetoes	Pocket vetoes	Vetoes sustained	Bills passed over veto
1961-63	John F. Kennedy.	21	12	9	21	-
1963-69	Lyndon B. Johnson	30	16	14	30	-
1969-74	Richard M. Nixon	43	26	17	36	7
1974-77	Gerald R. Ford	66	48	18	54	12
1977-81	Jimmy Carter	31	13	18	29	2
1981-89	Ronald W. Reagan	78	39	39	69	9
1989-93	George Bush	44	29	15	43	1
1993-2001	William J. Clinton	38	37	1	38	2

- Represents zero.

Source: U.S. Congress, Senate Library, *Presidential Vetoes ... 1789-1968*; U.S. Congress, *Calendars of the U.S. House of Representatives and History of Legislation*, annual. <http://clerkweb.house.gov/histrecs/househis/lists/vetoes>.

No. 385. Number of Governors by Political Party Affiliation: 1970 to 2002

[Reflects figures after inaugurations for each year]

Year	Democratic	Republican	Independent/ other	Year	Democratic	Republican	Independent/ other	Year	Democratic	Republican	Independent/ other
1970	18	32	-	1991 [1] . . .	29	19	2	1997	17	32	1
1975	36	13	1	1992	28	20	2	1998	17	32	1
1980	31	19	-	1993	30	18	2	1999	17	31	2
1985	34	16	-	1994	29	19	2	2000	17	31	2
1989	28	22	-	1995	19	30	1	2001	21	27	2
1990	29	21	-	1996	18	31	1	2002	21	27	2

- Represents zero.   [1] Reflects result of runoff election in Arizona in February 1991.

Source: National Governors Association, Washington, DC, 1970-87 and 1991-2002, *Directory of Governors of the American States, Commonwealths & Territories*, annual; and 1988-90, *Directory of Governors*, annual. (copyright).

No. 386. Vote Cast for and Governor Elected by State: 1990 to 2001

[In thousands (1,216 represents 1,216,000), except percent. D=Democratic, R=Republican, I=Independent]

State	1990 Total vote [1]	1990 Percent leading party	1996 Total vote [1]	1996 Percent leading party	1998 Total vote [1]	1998 Percent leading party	2000 Total vote [1]	2000 Percent leading party	Candidate elected at most recent election
AL.........	1,216	R-52.1	(X)	(X)	1,318	D-57.7	(X)	(X)	Donald Siegelman
AK.........	195	I-38.9	(X)	(X)	220	D-51.3	(X)	(X)	Tony Knowles
AZ.........	[2]941	[2]R-52.4	(X)	(X)	1,018	R-60.9	(X)	(X)	Jane Dee Hull
AR.........	696	D-57.5	(X)	(X)	706	R-59.8	(X)	(X)	Mike Huckabee
CA.........	7,699	R-49.2	(X)	(X)	8,385	D-58.0	(X)	(X)	Gray Davis
CO.........	1,011	D-61.9	(X)	(X)	1,321	R-49.1	(X)	(X)	Bill Owens
CT.........	1,141	I-40.4	(X)	(X)	1,000	R-62.9	(X)	(X)	John G. Rowland
DE.........	(X)	(X)	271	D-69.5	(X)	(X)	324	D-59.2	Ruth Ann Minner
FL.........	3,531	D-56.5	(X)	(X)	3,964	R-55.3	(X)	(X)	Jeb Bush
GA.........	1,450	D-52.9	(X)	(X)	1,793	D-52.5	(X)	(X)	Roy Barnes
HI.........	340	D-59.8	(X)	(X)	408	D-50.1	(X)	(X)	Benjamin J. Cayetano
ID.........	321	D-68.2	(X)	(X)	381	R-67.7	(X)	(X)	Dirk Kempthorne
IL.........	3,257	R-50.7	(X)	(X)	3,359	R-51.0	(X)	(X)	George Ryan
IN.........	(X)	(X)	2,110	D-51.5	(X)	(X)	2,179	D-56.6	Frank L. O'Bannon
IA.........	976	R-60.6	(X)	(X)	956	D-52.3	(X)	(X)	Tom Vilsack
KS.[2]......	783	D-48.6	(X)	(X)	743	R-73.4	(X)	(X)	Bill Graves
KY [2]......	(X)	(X)	984	D-50.9	(X)	(X)	580	D-60.7	Paul E. Patton
LA.........	(X)	(X)	1,550	R-63.5	(X)	(X)	1,295	R-62.2	Mike Foster
ME.........	522	R-46.7	(X)	(X)	421	R-18.9	(X)	(X)	Angus King
MD.........	1,111	D-59.8	(X)	(X)	1,536	D-55.1	(X)	(X)	Parris N. Glendening
MA.........	2,343	R-50.2	(X)	(X)	1,903	R-50.8	(X)	(X)	Argeo Paul Cellucci
MI.........	2,565	R-49.8	(X)	(X)	3,027	R-62.2	(X)	(X)	John Engler
MN [2]......	1,807	R-49.6	(X)	(X)	2,091	R-34.3	(X)	(X)	Jesse Ventura
MS [2]......	(X)	(X)	819	R-55.6	(X)	(X)	764	D-49.6	Ronnie Musgrove
MO.........	(X)	(X)	2,143	D-57.2	(X)	(X)	2,347	D-49.1	Bob Holden
MT.........	(X)	(X)	405	R-79.2	(X)	(X)	410	R-51.0	Judy Martz
NE.........	587	D-49.9	(X)	(X)	545	R-53.9	(X)	(X)	Mike Johanns
NV.........	321	D-64.8	(X)	(X)	434	R-51.6	(X)	(X)	Kenny Guinn
NH [3]......	295	R-60.3	497	D-57.2	319	D-66.1	565	D-48.7	Jeanne Shaheen
NJ [3]......	2,254	D-61.2	(X)	(X)	2,418	R-46.9	2,227	D-56.4	James E. McGreevey
NM.........	411	D-54.6	(X)	(X)	499	R-54.5	(X)	(X)	Gary E. Johnson
NY.........	4,057	D-53.2	(X)	(X)	4,735	R-54.3	(X)	(X)	George E. Pataki
NC.........	(X)	(X)	2,566	D-56.0	(X)	(X)	2,942	D-52.0	Mike Easley
ND.........	(X)	(X)	264	R-66.2	(X)	(X)	289	R-55.0	John Hoeven
OH.........	3,478	R-55.7	(X)	(X)	3,354	R-50.0	(X)	(X)	Bob Taft
OK.........	911	D-57.4	(X)	(X)	874	R-57.9	(X)	(X)	Frank Keating
OR.........	1,113	D 45.7	(X)	(X)	1,113	D-64.4	(X)	(X)	John Kitzhaber
PA.........	3,053	D-67.7	(X)	(X)	3,025	R-57.4	(X)	(X)	Tom Ridge
RI.........	357	D-74.1	(X)	(X)	306	R-51.0	(X)	(X)	Lincoln C. Almond
SC.........	761	R-69.5	(X)	(X)	1,071	D-53.2	(X)	(X)	Jim Hodges
SD.........	257	R-58.9	(X)	(X)	260	R-64.0	(X)	(X)	William J. Janklow
TN.........	790	D-60.8	(X)	(X)	976	R-68.6	(X)	(X)	Don Sundquist
TX.........	3,893	D-49.5	(X)	(X)	3,738	R-68.2	(X)	(X)	George W. Bush
UT.........	(X)	(X)	672	R-75.0	(X)	(X)	762	R-55.8	Michael O. Leavitt
VT.........	211	R-51.8	255	D-70.5	218	D-55.7	293	D-50.5	Howard Dean
VA [3]......	1,789	D-50.1	(X)	(X)	1,736	R-55.8	1,887	D-52.2	Mark Warner
WA.........	(X)	(X)	2,237	D-58.0	(X)	(X)	2,470	D-58.4	Gary Locke
WV.........	(X)	(X)	629	R-51.6	(X)	(X)	648	D-50.1	Bob Wise
WI.........	1,380	R-58.2	(X)	(X)	1,756	R-59.7	(X)	(X)	Tommy G. Thompson
WY.........	160	D-65.4	(X)	(X)	175	R-55.6	(X)	(X)	Jim Geringer

X Not applicable.   [1] Includes minor party and scattered votes.   [2] Voting years 1995 and 1999.   [3] Voting years 1993, 1997, and 2001.

Source: Congressional Quarterly Inc., Washington, DC, *America Votes,* biennial; and unpublished data (copyright).

Elections   249

No. 387. Composition of State Legislatures by Political Party Affiliation: 1996 to 2001

[Data reflect election results in year shown for most states; and except as noted, results in previous year for other states. Figures reflect immediate results of elections, including holdover members in state houses which do not have all of their members running for reelection. Dem.=Democratic, Rep.=Republican. In general, Lower House refers to body consisting of state Representatives; Upper House, of state Senators]

State	Lower House								Upper House							
	1996 [1]		1998		2000 [2]		2001[3]		1996 [4]		1998 [5]		2000 [6]		2001 [7]	
	Dem.	Rep.	Dem.	Rep.	Dem.	Rep.	Dem.	Rep.	Dem.	Rep.	Dem.	Rep.	Dem.	Rep.	Dem.	Rep.
U.S.	2,886	2,539	2,903	2,580	2,818	2,600	2,809	2,604	998	931	1,041	963	995	931	990	932
AL [8]	72	33	71	34	67	36	67	38	22	12	22	13	23	12	24	11
AK [9]	16	24	15	25	13	27	13	27	7	13	6	14	6	14	6	14
AZ [10]	22	38	22	38	24	36	24	36	12	18	12	18	15	15	15	15
AR [9]	86	13	86	14	70	30	70	30	28	6	28	7	27	8	27	8
CA [9]	43	37	42	37	50	29	50	30	25	15	23	16	26	13	26	14
CO [10]	24	41	24	41	28	37	28	37	15	20	15	20	18	17	18	17
CT [9]	97	54	96	55	100	51	100	51	19	17	19	17	21	15	21	15
DE [9]	14	27	13	28	15	26	15	26	13	8	13	8	13	8	13	8
FL [9]	59	61	57	63	43	77	43	77	17	23	17	23	15	25	15	25
GA [10]	106	74	102	78	104	74	105	74	34	22	34	22	34	24	32	24
HI [9]	39	12	39	12	32	19	32	19	23	2	23	2	24	3	22	3
ID [10]	11	59	11	59	9	61	9	61	5	30	5	30	3	32	3	31
IL [11]	60	58	60	58	62	56	62	56	28	31	28	31	27	32	27	32
IN [9]	50	50	50	50	53	47	52	46	19	31	19	31	18	32	18	32
IA [9]	46	54	46	54	44	56	44	56	21	29	22	28	20	30	20	30
KS [9]	48	77	48	77	46	79	46	79	13	27	13	27	10	30	10	30
KY [9]	64	36	64	36	66	34	66	34	20	18	20	18	18	20	18	20
LA [8]	76	28	78	27	71	32	70	34	25	14	25	14	26	13	25	14
ME [10]	81	69	81	69	81	69	81	69	19	15	19	15	17	17	17	16
MD [8]	100	41	99	41	106	35	106	35	32	15	32	15	33	14	33	14
MA [10]	134	25	130	29	136	24	136	22	34	6	31	8	34	6	32	6
MI [9]	58	52	58	51	53	56	52	57	16	22	16	22	14	22	15	23
MN [9]	70	64	70	64	65	69	64	70	42	24	42	24	39	26	37	27
MS [8]	86	33	84	36	86	33	86	33	34	18	34	18	34	18	34	18
MO [9]	88	75	85	76	87	76	87	76	19	15	19	15	15	16	14	18
MT [9]	35	65	35	65	42	58	42	58	16	34	16	33	19	31	19	31
NE [12]	(12)	(12)	(12)	(12)	(12)	(12)	(12)	(12)	(12)	(12)	(12)	(12)	(12)	(12)	(12)	(12)
NV [9]	25	17	25	17	27	15	27	15	9	12	9	12	9	12	9	12
NH [10]	143	255	147	248	143	255	142	255	9	15	9	15	11	13	11	13
NJ [9]	30	50	32	48	32	48	44	36	16	24	16	24	16	24	20	20
NM [9]	42	28	42	28	42	28	42	28	25	17	25	17	24	18	24	18
NY [10]	96	54	95	52	99	51	99	51	26	35	26	35	25	36	25	36
NC [10]	59	61	59	61	62	58	62	58	30	20	30	20	35	15	35	15
ND [13]	26	72	26	71	29	69	29	69	19	30	18	29	17	32	17	32
OH [9]	39	60	39	60	40	59	39	59	12	21	12	20	12	20	11	21
OK [9]	65	36	65	36	53	48	52	48	33	15	33	15	30	18	30	18
OR [9]	29	31	29	31	27	33	28	32	10	20	10	20	14	16	14	16
PA [9]	99	104	99	104	99	104	98	104	20	30	20	30	20	28	21	29
RI [10]	84	16	84	16	85	15	87	13	41	9	42	8	44	6	43	7
SC [9]	53	70	52	71	54	69	53	71	26	20	25	21	22	24	21	25
SD [10]	23	47	22	48	20	50	20	50	13	22	13	22	11	24	11	24
TN [9]	61	38	61	38	61	38	57	41	18	15	18	15	18	15	18	15
TX [9]	82	68	82	68	77	72	78	71	14	16	14	17	15	16	15	15
UT [9]	20	55	21	54	25	50	24	51	9	20	9	20	9	20	9	20
VT [10]	89	57	89	57	62	83	62	82	17	13	17	13	16	14	16	13
VA [9]	53	46	51	48	47	52	34	64	20	20	19	21	18	22	18	22
WA [9]	45	53	41	57	49	49	50	48	23	26	23	26	25	24	25	24
WV [9]	74	25	74	26	75	25	75	25	25	9	25	9	28	6	28	6
WI [9]	47	52	46	51	43	56	43	56	17	16	17	16	18	15	18	15
WY [9]	17	43	17	43	14	46	14	46	9	21	9	21	10	20	10	20

[1] Excludes one Independent each for AK, CA, LA, and VA; two Independents each for MS and VT; four Independents for SC; members of political parties other than Democratic, Republican, or Independent (one in MA and VT, and two in NH) one undecided in GA; and one vacancy each in LA, MI, and WV; two vacancies each for CT and MA; and three vacancies for NV.   [2] Excludes one Independent each for NH and VA; two for GA; three each for ME and MS; five for VT; one vacancy each for CA, MI, NH, SC and two vacancies in AL.   [3] Excludes Lower House representatives from the following parties: MF - one Independent, one Penobscot Nation, and one Passamaquoddy Tribe; MS - three Independents; NH - one Libertarian; VT - one Independent, four Progressives; VA - two Independents.   [4] Excludes one Independent in ME, two independents in CA, one vacancy in GA, two vacancies in MS, and three vacancies in MN.   [5] Excludes one Independent for CA and one vacancy each for AL and NJ.   [6] Excludes one Independent each for ME and MN; one vacancy each in CA and OH; two vacancies for MI and PA; three vacancies for MO.   [7] Excludes two vacancies in MA, MN, and MO; one vacancy in ID, ME, OH, TX, and VT; and Upper House representatives from the following parties: MN - one Independent; and MN - one Independent.   [8] Members of both houses serve 4-year terms.   [9] Upper House members serve 4-year terms and Lower House members serve 2-year terms.   [10] Members of both houses serve 2-year terms.   [11] Illinois—4- and 2-year term depending on district.   [12] Nebraska—4-year term.   [13] North Dakota—By the 2001 session all Senators and Representatives will be serving 4-year terms.

Source: The Council of State Governments, Lexington, KY, *State Elective Officials and the Legislatures*, biennial (copyright); thereafter, National Conference of State Legislatures, Denver, CO, unpublished data.

No. 388. Political Party Control of State Legislatures by Party: 1975 to 2000

[As of beginning of year. Until 1972, there were two nonpartisan legislatures in Minnesota and Nebraska. Since then only Nebraska has had a nonpartisan legislature]

Year	Legislatures under—			Year	Legislatures under—			Year	Legislatures under—		
	Demo-cratic control	Split control or tie	Re-publican control		Demo-cratic control	Split control or tie	Re-publican control		Demo-cratic control	Split control or tie	Re-publican control
1975...	37	7	5	1987...	28	12	9	1995...	18	12	19
1977...	36	8	5	1989 [2]...	28	13	8	1996...	16	15	18
1979...	30	7	12	1990...	29	11	9	1997...	20	11	18
1981...	28	6	15	1992...	29	14	6	1999...	20	12	17
1983 [1]...	34	4	11	1993...	25	16	8	2000...	16	15	18
1985...	27	11	11	1994...	24	17	8				

[1] Two 1984 midterm recall elections resulted in a change in control of the Michigan State Senate. At the time of the 1984 election, therefore, Democrats controlled 33 legislatures.   [2] A party change during the year by a Democratic representative broke the tie in the Indiana House of Representatives, giving the Republicans control of both chambers.

Source: National Conference of State Legislatures, Denver, CO, *State Legislatures*, periodic.

No. 389. Women Holding State Public Offices by Office and State: 2001

[As of January. For data on women in U.S. Congress, see Table 382]

State	State-wide elective executive office [1]	State legisla-ture	State	State-wide elective executive office [1]	State legisla-ture	State	State-wide elective executive office [1]	State legisla-ture
United States .	**88**	**1,666**	Kentucky	-	15	North Dakota ...	2	25
Alabama	3	11	Louisiana......	2	23	Ohio	2	29
Alaska.......	1	12	Maine	-	56	Oklahoma	4	15
Arizona	4	32	Maryland	1	55	Oregon	-	30
Arkansas	2	18	Massachusetts ..	2	51	Pennsylvania ...	1	35
California	3	34	Michigan	2	33	Rhode Island ...	-	34
Colorado	1	34	Minnesota	4	58	South Carolina ..	1	18
Connecticut ...	4	56	Mississippi	1	22	South Dakota ...	3	16
Delaware	3	16	Missouri.......	2	45	Tennessee	-	21
Florida.......	1	38	Montana	2	36	Texas	2	34
Georgia	2	49	Nebraska......	3	10	Utah	1	24
Hawaii	1	19	Nevada	3	22	Vermont.......	2	50
Idaho........	1	28	New Hampshire..	1	124	Virginia	-	22
Illinois	2	46	New Jersey	-	18	Washington	2	57
Indiana	3	26	New Mexico	2	34	West Virginia ...	-	25
Iowa	2	33	New York	1	46	Wisconsin......	2	31
Kansas	2	54	North Carolina...	4	32	Wyoming	2	14

- Represents zero.   [1] Excludes women elected to the judiciary, women appointed to state cabinet-level positions, women elected to executive posts by the legislature, and elected members of university Board of Trustees or board of education.

Source: Center for the American Woman and Politics, Eagleton Institute of Politics, Rutgers University, New Brunswick, NJ, information releases, copyright.

No. 390. Public Confidence Levels in Selected Public and Private Institutions: 2001

[Based on a sample survey of 4,216 persons 21 years old and over conducted during the spring and subject to sampling variability; see source]

Institution	Level of confidence			
	A lot	Some	None	Don't know
Organized labor....................................	9.9	46.3	39.6	4.2
Media (e.g. newspapers, TV, radio)....................	5.1	48.2	45.3	1.4
Major corporations..................................	6.2	49.2	41.9	2.8
State government	9.2	58.0	31.0	1.7
Political organizations, parties	2.8	36.7	58.6	1.9
Local government	12.6	58.7	27.1	1.6
Congress	4.0	44.0	49.7	2.3

Source: Toppe, Chris, Arthur Kirsch, and Westat, Inc., Giving and Volunteering in the United States: 2001 Edition. (Copyright and published by INDEPENDENT SECTOR, Washington, 2002.)

U.S. Census Bureau, Statistical Abstract of the United States: 2002

No. 391. Black Elected Officials by Office, 1970 to 2000, and State, 2000

[As of January 2000, no Black elected officials had been identified in Hawaii, Idaho, Maine, Montana, North Dakota, South Dakota, or Wyoming

State	Total	U.S. and state legisla- tures [1]	City and county offices [2]	Law enforce- ment [3]	Educa- tion [4]	State	Total	U.S. and state legisla- tures [1]	City and county offices [2]	Law enforce- ment [3]	Educa- tion [4]
1970 (Feb.) . .	1,469	179	715	213	362	MA	31	6	20	2	3
1980 (July) . .	4,890	326	2,832	526	1,206	MI	340	22	150	55	113
1990 (Jan.) . .	7,335	436	4,485	769	1,645	MN	18	1	4	8	5
1995 (Jan.) . .	8,385	604	4,954	987	1,840	MS	897	46	604	112	135
1997 (Jan.) . .	8,617	613	5,056	996	1,952	MO	196	18	138	17	23
1998 (Jan.) . .	8,830	614	5,210	998	2,008	NE	6	1	3	-	2
1999 (Jan.) . .	8,896	618	5,354	997	1,927	NV	14	5	5	2	2
2000 (Jan.) .	**9,001**	**621**	**5,420**	**1,037**	**1,923**	NH	3	3	-	-	-
						NJ	247	16	137	1	93
AL	731	36	545	55	95	NM	4	1	-	2	1
AK	3	-	2	-	1	NY	320	32	83	80	125
AZ	14	2	1	5	6	NC	498	27	350	29	92
AR	502	15	298	67	122	OH	309	19	215	27	48
CA	238	10	69	76	83	OK	104	6	77	3	18
CO	19	4	5	9	1	OR	7	4	1	2	-
CT	71	15	45	3	8	PA	186	19	74	66	27
DE	24	4	16	1	3	RI	10	9	1	-	-
DC	204	2	[5]192	-	10	SC	540	34	334	8	164
FL	226	23	155	33	15	TN	177	17	108	26	26
GA	582	49	388	41	104	TX	475	19	313	43	100
IL	621	27	319	56	219	UT	3	-	2	1	-
IN	83	14	50	11	8	VT	1	1	-	-	-
IA	13	1	8	1	3	VA	250	16	137	15	82
KS	19	7	5	4	3	WA	24	2	12	9	1
KY	62	4	47	5	6	WV	21	4	13	4	-
LA	701	32	388	121	160	WI	31	8	13	5	5
MD	176	40	93	32	11						

- Represents zero.   [1] Includes elected state administrators.   [2] County commissioners and councilmen, mayors, vice mayors, aldermen, regional officials, and other.   [3] Judges, magistrates, constables, marshals, sheriffs, justices of the peace, and other.   [4] Members of state education agencies, college boards, school boards, and other.   [5] Includes one shadow representative.

Source: Joint Center for Political and Economic Studies, Washington, DC, *Black Elected Officials: A Statistical Summary*, annual (copyright) and <http://www.jointcenter.org/databank/graphs/99beo.pdf> (accessed 17 April 2002).

No. 392. Hispanic Public Elected Officials by Office, 1985 to 2001, and State, 2001

[As of September, For states not shown, no Hispanic public officials had been identified]

State	Total	State execu- tives and legisla- tors [1]	County and munici- pal offi- cials	Judicial and law enforce- ment	Educa- tion and school boards	State	Total	State execu- tives and legisla- tors [1]	County and munici- pal offi- cials	Judicial and law enforce- ment	Educa- tion and school boards
1985 (Sept.) .	3,147	129	1,316	517	1,185	LA	3	-	1	2	-
1988 (Sept.) .	3,360	135	1,425	574	1,226	MA	13	3	7	-	3
1989 (Sept.) .	3,783	143	1,724	575	1,341	MI	8	2	5	-	1
1990 (Sept.) .	4,004	144	1,819	583	1,458	MN	3	1	1	1	-
1991 (Sept.) .	4,202	151	1,867	596	1,588	MO	1	-	1	-	-
1992 (Sept.) .	4,994	150	1,908	628	2,308	MT	1	-	-	1	-
1993 (Sept.) .	5,170	182	2,023	633	2,332	NE	3	1	2	-	-
1994 (Sept.) .	5,459	199	2,197	651	2,412	NV	4	1	2	1	-
2000 (Sept.) .	5,205	223	1,846	454	2,682	NH	1	1	-	-	-
2001	5,205	223	1,846	454	2,682	NJ	77	6	46	-	25
CA	767	33	317	37	380	NM	618	48	316	74	180
CO	154	11	92	9	42	NY	76	14	16	8	38
CT	26	5	17	-	4	NC	1	1	-	-	-
DE	3	1	2	-	-	OH	7	-	5	2	-
DC	1	-	1	-	-	OR	7	1	5	-	1
FL	90	17	57	11	5	PA	5	1	2	1	1
GA	3	-	3	-	-	RI	3	2	1	-	-
HI	2	1	1	-	-	TX	1,828	42	768	280	738
ID	2	-	2	-	-	UT	3	1	2	-	-
IL	1,190	7	34	-	1,149	VA	1	-	-	-	1
IN	10	1	7	1	1	WA	12	3	5	-	4
IA	1	-	1	-	-	WI	12	1	6	3	2
KS	6	2	4	-	-	WY	4	1	3	-	-

- Represents zero.   [1] Includes U.S. Representatives, not shown separately.

Source: National Association of Latino Elected and Appointed Officials, Washington, DC, *National Roster of Hispanic Elected Officials*, annual.

U.S. Census Bureau, Statistical Abstract of the United States: 2002

No. 393. Voting-Age Population, Percent Reporting Registered, and Voted: 1980 to 2000

[As of November. Covers civilian noninstitutional population 18 years old and over. Includes aliens. Figures are based on Current Population Survey (see text, Section 1, Population, and Appendix III) and differ from those in Table 395 based on population estimates and official vote counts]

Characteristic	Voting-age population (mil.)							Percent reporting they registered — Presidential election years				Percent reporting they registered — Congressional election years				Percent reporting they voted — Presidential election years				Percent reporting they voted — Congressional election years			
	1980	1988	1990	1994	1996	1998	2000	1980	1992	1996	2000	1986	1990	1994	1998	1980	1992	1996	2000	1986	1990	1994	1998
Total [1]	157.1	178.1	182.1	190.3	193.7	198.2	202.6	66.9	68.2	65.9	63.9	64.3	62.2	62.0	62.1	59.2	61.3	54.2	54.7	46.0	45.0	44.6	41.9
18 to 20 years old	12.3	10.7	10.8	10.3	10.8	11.4	11.9	44.7	48.3	45.6	40.5	35.4	35.4	37.2	32.1	35.7	38.5	31.2	28.4	18.6	18.4	16.5	13.5
21 to 24 years old	15.9	14.8	14.0	14.9	13.9	14.1	14.9	52.7	55.3	51.2	49.3	46.6	43.3	45.5	35.0	43.1	45.7	33.4	35.4	24.2	22.0	22.3	19.2
25 to 34 years old	35.7	42.7	42.4	41.1	40.1	38.6	37.3	62.0	60.6	56.9	54.7	55.8	52.0	51.5	52.4	54.6	53.2	43.1	43.7	35.1	33.8	32.2	28.0
35 to 44 years old	25.6	35.2	37.9	41.9	43.3	44.4	44.5	70.6	69.2	66.5	63.8	67.9	65.5	63.3	62.4	64.4	63.6	54.9	55.0	49.3	48.4	46.0	40.7
45 to 64 years old	43.6	45.9	46.9	50.9	53.7	57.4	61.4	75.8	75.3	73.5	71.2	74.8	71.4	71.0	71.1	69.3	70.0	64.4	64.1	58.7	58.4	56.0	53.6
65 years old and over	24.1	28.8	29.9	31.1	31.9	32.3	32.8	74.6	78.0	77.0	76.1	76.9	76.5	75.6	75.4	65.1	70.1	67.0	67.6	60.9	60.3	60.7	59.5
Male	74.1	84.5	86.6	91.0	92.6	95.2	97.1	66.6	66.9	64.4	62.2	63.4	61.2	60.8	60.6	59.1	60.2	52.8	53.1	45.8	44.6	44.4	41.4
Female	83.0	93.6	95.5	99.3	101.0	103.0	105.5	67.1	69.3	67.3	65.6	65.0	63.1	63.2	63.5	59.4	62.3	55.5	56.2	46.1	45.4	44.9	42.4
White	137.7	152.9	155.6	160.3	162.8	165.8	168.7	68.4	70.1	67.7	65.6	65.3	63.8	64.2	63.9	60.9	63.6	56.0	56.4	47.0	46.7	46.9	43.3
Black	16.4	19.7	20.4	21.8	22.5	23.3	24.1	60.0	63.9	63.5	63.6	64.0	58.8	58.3	60.2	50.5	54.0	50.6	53.5	43.2	39.2	37.0	39.6
Hispanic [2]	8.2	12.9	13.8	17.5	18.4	20.3	21.6	36.3	35.0	35.7	34.9	35.9	32.3	30.0	33.7	29.9	28.9	26.7	27.5	24.2	21.0	19.1	20.0
Region: [3]																							
Northeast	35.5	37.9	38.1	38.4	38.3	38.5	38.9	64.8	67.0	64.7	63.7	62.0	61.0	60.9	60.8	58.5	61.2	54.5	55.2	44.4	45.2	45.2	41.2
Midwest	41.5	43.3	43.9	44.5	45.2	45.9	46.4	73.8	74.6	71.6	70.2	70.7	68.2	68.7	68.2	65.8	67.2	59.3	60.9	49.5	48.6	48.8	47.3
South	50.6	60.7	62.4	66.4	68.1	70.1	71.8	64.8	67.2	65.9	64.5	63.0	61.3	60.7	62.7	55.6	59.0	52.2	53.5	43.0	42.4	40.5	38.6
West	29.5	36.2	37.7	41.0	42.1	43.7	45.5	63.3	63.6	60.8	56.9	60.8	57.7	58.1	56.0	57.2	58.5	51.8	49.9	48.4	45.0	46.4	42.3
School years completed:																							
8 years or less	22.7	19.1	17.7	14.7	14.1	13.3	12.9	53.0	43.9	40.7	36.1	50.5	44.0	40.1	40.2	42.6	35.1	28.1	26.8	32.7	27.7	23.2	24.6
High school:																							
1 to 3 years [4]	22.5	21.1	21.0	20.7	21.0	21.0	20.1	54.6	50.4	47.9	45.9	52.4	47.9	44.7	43.4	45.6	41.2	33.8	33.6	33.8	30.9	27.0	25.0
4 years [5]	61.2	70.0	71.5	64.9	65.2	65.6	66.3	66.4	64.9	62.2	60.1	62.9	60.0	58.9	58.6	58.9	57.5	49.1	49.4	44.1	42.2	40.5	37.1
College:																							
1 to 3 years [6]	26.7	34.3	36.3	50.4	50.9	52.9	55.3	74.4	75.4	72.9	70.0	70.0	68.7	68.4	68.3	67.2	68.7	60.5	60.3	49.9	50.0	49.1	46.2
4 years or more [7]	24.0	33.6	35.6	39.4	42.5	45.4	48.0	84.3	84.8	80.4	77.3	77.8	77.3	76.3	75.1	79.9	81.0	73.0	72.0	62.5	62.5	63.1	57.2
Employed	95.0	113.8	115.5	122.6	125.6	130.5	133.4	68.7	69.9	67.0	64.7	64.4	62.6	62.9	62.6	61.8	63.8	55.2	55.5	45.7	45.1	45.2	41.2
Unemployed	6.9	5.8	6.7	6.5	6.4	5.2	4.9	50.3	53.7	52.5	45.1	50.6	44.6	46.4	48.5	41.2	46.2	37.2	35.1	31.2	27.9	28.3	28.4
Not in labor force [7]	55.2	58.5	59.9	61.2	61.6	62.5	64.2	65.8	66.8	65.1	63.8	65.4	63.4	61.9	62.1	57.0	58.7	54.1	54.5	48.2	46.7	45.3	44.5

[1] Includes other races not shown separately. [2] Hispanic persons may be of any race. [3] For composition of regions, see map, inside cover. [4] Beginning 1992, represents those who completed 9th to 12th grade, but have no high school diploma. [5] Beginning 1992, high school graduate. [6] Beginning 1992, some college or associate degree. [7] Beginning 1992, bachelor's or advanced degree.

Source: U.S. Census Bureau, Current Population Reports, P20-542 and earlier reports.

Elections 253

No. 394. Persons Reported Registered and Voted by State: 2000

[See headnote, Table 393]

State	Voting-age population (1,000)	Percent of voting-age population — Registered	Voted	State	Voting-age population (1,000)	Percent of voting-age population — Registered	Voted
U.S.	**202,609**	**63.9**	**54.7**	MO	4,066	74.3	65.4
AL	3,278	73.6	59.6	MT	658	70.0	62.2
AK	412	72.5	65.5	NE	1,205	71.8	58.9
AZ	3,524	53.3	46.7	NV	1,377	52.3	46.5
AR	1,893	59.4	49.4	NH	902	69.6	63.3
CA	24,749	52.8	46.4	NJ	6,109	63.2	55.2
CO	3,049	64.1	53.6	NM	1,261	59.5	51.3
CT	2,415	62.5	55.2	NY	13,725	58.6	51.0
DE	567	67.9	62.2	NC	5,629	66.1	53.2
DC	407	72.4	65.6	ND	449	91.1	69.8
FL	11,633	60.5	51.6	OH	8,301	67.0	58.1
GA	5,775	61.1	49.0	OK	2,457	68.3	58.3
HI	855	47.0	39.7	OR	2,515	68.2	60.8
ID	927	61.4	53.9	PA	8,950	65.3	55.7
IL	8,859	66.7	56.8	RI	729	69.7	60.1
IN	4,380	68.5	58.5	SC	2,929	68.0	58.9
IA	2,110	72.2	64.1	SD	530	70.9	58.7
KS	1,908	67.7	60.2	TN	4,173	62.1	52.3
KY	2,996	69.7	54.9	TX	14,533	61.4	48.2
LA	3,143	75.4	64.6	UT	1,472	64.7	56.3
ME	979	80.3	69.2	VT	458	72.0	63.3
MD	3,812	65.6	57.1	VA	5,177	64.1	57.2
MA	4,614	70.3	60.1	WA	4,314	66.1	58.6
MI	7,231	69.1	60.1	WV	1,405	63.1	52.1
MN	3,506	76.7	67.8	WI	3,884	76.5	67.8
MS	2,029	72.2	59.8	WY	350	68.6	62.5

Source: U.S. Census Bureau, *Current Population Reports*, P20-466.

No. 395. Participation in Elections for President and U.S. Representatives: 1932 to 2000

[As of November. Estimated resident population 21 years old and over, 1932-70, except as noted, and 18 years old and over thereafter; includes Armed Forces. Prior to 1960, excludes Alaska and Hawaii. District of Columbia is included in votes cast for President beginning 1964 and in votes cast for Representative from 1972 to 1994]

Year	Resident population (incl. aliens) of voting age[1] (1,000)	Votes cast — For President[2] (1,000)	Per-cent of voting-age population	For U.S. Representatives (1,000)	Per-cent of voting-age population	Year	Resident population (incl. aliens) of voting age[1] (1,000)	Votes cast — For President[2] (1,000)	Per-cent of voting-age population	For U.S. Representatives (1,000)	Per-cent of voting-age population
1932	75,768	39,758	52.5	37,657	49.7	1968	120,285	73,212	60.9	66,288	55.1
1934	77,997	(X)	(X)	32,256	41.4	1970	124,498	(X)	(X)	54,173	43.5
1936	80,174	45,654	56.9	42,886	53.5	1972	140,777	77,719	55.2	71,430	50.7
1938	82,354	(X)	(X)	36,236	44.0	1974	146,338	(X)	(X)	52,495	35.9
1940	84,728	49,900	58.9	46,951	55.4	1976	152,308	81,556	53.5	74,422	48.9
1942	86,465	(X)	(X)	28,074	32.5	1978	158,369	(X)	(X)	55,332	34.9
1944	85,654	47,977	56.0	45,103	52.7	1980	163,945	86,515	52.8	77,995	47.6
1946	92,659	(X)	(X)	34,398	37.1	1982	169,643	(X)	(X)	64,514	38.0
1948	95,573	48,794	51.1	45,933	48.1	1984	173,995	92,653	53.3	83,231	47.8
1950	98,134	(X)	(X)	40,342	41.1	1986	177,922	(X)	(X)	59,619	33.5
1952	99,929	61,551	61.6	57,571	57.6	1988	181,956	91,595	50.3	81,786	44.9
1954	102,075	(X)	(X)	42,580	41.7	1990	185,812	(X)	(X)	61,513	33.1
1956	104,515	62,027	59.3	58,426	55.9	1992	189,493	104,425	55.1	96,239	50.8
1958	106,447	(X)	(X)	45,818	43.0	1994	193,010	(X)	(X)	70,781	36.7
1960	109,672	68,838	62.8	64,133	58.5	1996	196,789	96,278	48.9	89,863	45.7
1962	112,952	(X)	(X)	51,267	45.4	1998	201,270	(X)	(X)	65,897	32.7
1964	114,090	70,645	61.9	65,895	57.8	2000	[3]205,813	105,397	51.2	97,226	47.2
1966	116,638	(X)	(X)	52,908	45.4						

X Not applicable.   [1] Population 18 and over in Georgia, 1944-70, and in Kentucky, 1956-70; 19 and over in Alaska and 20 and over in Hawaii, 1960-70. Source: U.S. Census Bureau, *Current Population Reports*, P25-1085; also see <http://www.census.gov/population/socdemo/voting/proj00/tab03.txt>.   [2] Source: 1932-58, U.S. Congress, Clerk of the House, *Statistics of the Presidential and Congressional Election*, biennial.   [3] Projection.

Source: Except as noted, Congressional Quarterly Inc., Washington, DC, *America Votes*, biennial (copyright).

No. 396. Resident Population of Voting Age and Percent Casting Votes—States: 1994 to 2000

[As of November. **Estimated population, 18 years old and over**. Includes Armed Forces stationed in each state, aliens, and institutional population]

State	Voting-age population							Percent casting votes for—				
	1994 (1,000)	1996 (1,000)	1998 (1,000)	2000 (1,000)				Presidential electors		U.S. Representatives		
				Total	Female	Black	His-panic[1]	1996	2000	1996	1998	2000
U.S.	193,010	196,789	201,270	205,813	106,865	24,635	21,305	48.9	51.2	45.8	32.8	47.3
AL	3,172	3,221	3,280	3,333	1,768	800	34	47.6	50.0	45.6	37.0	43.2
AK	413	419	425	430	203	17	16	57.7	66.4	55.8	52.5	63.8
AZ	3,059	3,245	3,421	3,625	1,853	137	700	43.3	42.3	41.8	29.3	40.4
AR	1,814	1,852	1,891	1,929	1,017	276	38	47.7	47.8	46.6	27.8	32.8
CA	22,653	23,002	23,902	24,873	12,566	1,853	6,995	43.6	44.1	41.2	33.4	42.0
CO	2,715	2,837	2,946	3,067	1,564	132	391	53.3	56.8	51.5	43.3	52.9
CT	2,476	2,475	2,489	2,499	1,307	221	182	56.3	58.4	52.3	38.3	52.6
DE	536	552	566	582	303	108	19	49.1	56.3	48.4	31.9	53.8
DC	447	428	421	411	222	230	29	43.4	49.1	(NA)	(NA)	(NA)
FL	10,721	11,078	11,398	11,774	6,155	1,600	1,784	47.9	50.6	42.4	10.6	42.6
GA	5,198	5,420	5,647	5,893	3,075	1,577	168	42.4	44.1	39.9	28.9	41.0
HI	875	886	902	909	460	27	67	40.6	40.5	39.8	44.1	37.5
ID	802	845	883	921	467	7	58	58.2	54.5	58.5	42.9	53.5
IL	8,717	8,787	8,894	8,983	4,675	1,249	837	49.1	52.8	47.0	36.2	48.9
IN	4,276	4,340	4,399	4,448	2,321	353	110	49.2	49.4	48.5	35.8	48.5
IA	2,109	2,126	2,148	2,165	1,127	45	42	58.0	60.8	56.5	41.9	58.9
KS	1,877	1,902	1,940	1,983	1,022	112	97	56.5	54.1	55.2	37.5	52.4
KY	2,864	2,918	2,959	2,993	1,568	207	25	47.6	51.6	42.4	37.1	48.0
LA	3,085	3,129	3,195	3,255	1,723	956	91	57.0	54.2	21.1	9.7	36.9
ME	930	941	955	968	503	7	7	64.4	67.3	63.8	43.4	66.0
MD	3,737	3,799	3,862	3,925	2,050	1,058	150	46.9	51.5	43.1	38.4	49.1
MA	4,616	4,652	4,701	4,749	2,500	270	255	55.0	56.9	51.8	37.1	49.4
MI	7,091	7,207	7,294	7,358	3,839	977	187	53.4	57.5	51.3	40.9	55.3
MN	3,343	3,415	3,480	3,547	1,823	106	62	64.2	68.8	62.7	58.6	66.6
MS	1,917	1,960	2,005	2,047	1,089	675	18	45.6	48.6	46.1	27.5	48.2
MO	3,932	3,984	4,046	4,105	2,155	425	68	54.2	57.5	53.1	38.9	56.7
MT	625	648	659	668	340	4	11	62.8	61.5	62.3	50.3	61.5
NE	1,186	1,208	1,222	1,234	641	49	52	56.1	56.5	54.8	43.0	55.4
NV	1,097	1,199	1,285	1,390	685	105	214	38.7	43.8	37.5	31.9	42.1
NH	846	869	889	911	468	9	14	57.4	62.5	56.5	35.7	61.1
NJ	5,979	6,042	6,144	6,245	3,272	856	750	50.9	51.0	46.7	29.5	47.9
NM	1,171	1,214	1,241	1,263	652	37	473	45.8	47.4	45.1	40.1	46.5
NY	13,633	13,606	13,721	13,805	7,294	2,309	1,833	46.4	49.4	40.8	31.1	42.2
NC	5,331	5,501	5,645	5,797	3,036	1,173	121	45.7	50.2	45.7	33.7	48.0
ND	470	476	477	477	242	4	4	56.0	60.4	55.3	44.6	59.9
OH	8,265	8,332	8,394	8,433	4,436	895	130	54.4	55.8	52.7	40.2	53.6
OK	2,384	2,427	2,477	2,531	1,316	185	91	49.7	48.8	48.6	34.7	43.0
OR	2,315	2,404	2,466	2,530	1,295	51	138	57.3	60.6	55.5	44.2	56.9
PA	9,148	9,153	9,163	9,155	4,839	820	221	49.2	53.7	47.2	31.6	49.7
RI	755	751	752	753	398	36	46	52.0	54.3	47.9	39.0	51.0
SC	2,733	2,802	2,889	2,977	1,569	816	41	41.1	46.4	37.7	33.7	44.4
SD	525	535	540	542	279	5	6	60.5	58.4	60.4	47.9	58.1
TN	3,885	4,007	4,114	4,221	2,224	635	51	47.3	49.2	44.5	22.2	43.9
TX	13,153	13,643	14,223	14,850	7,630	1,800	4,012	41.1	43.1	38.3	24.3	40.3
UT	1,285	1,350	1,411	1,465	748	16	99	49.3	52.6	49.2	33.4	51.8
VT	433	442	451	460	237	4	4	58.5	64.0	57.7	47.7	61.6
VA	4,956	5,066	5,168	5,263	2,734	1,005	197	47.7	52.1	43.4	22.2	46.0
WA	3,962	4,109	4,237	4,368	2,221	154	242	54.9	56.9	52.9	43.9	54.5
WV	1,392	1,400	1,411	1,416	746	45	9	45.5	45.8	37.3	24.9	41.0
WI	3,766	3,838	3,888	3,930	2,026	193	96	57.2	66.1	56.0	43.0	63.8
WY	340	347	354	358	180	4	19	61.0	61.0	60.5	49.2	59.3

NA Not available. [1] Persons of Hispanic origin may be of any race.

Source: Compiled by U.S. Census Bureau. Population data from U.S. Census Bureau, *Current Population Reports*, P25-1132, <http://www.census.gov/population/socdemo/voting/proj00/>; votes cast from Elections Research Center, Chevy Chase, MD, *America Votes*, annual, (copyright); and Congressional Quarterly Inc., Washington, DC (copyright).

Elections 255

No. 397. Political Party Financial Activity by Major Political Party: 1981 to 2000

[In millions of dollars ($39.3 represents $39,300,000). Covers financial activity during 2-year calendar period indicated. Some political party financial activities, such as building funds and State and local election spending, are not reported to the source. Also excludes contributions earmarked to Federal candidates through the party organizations, since some of those funds never passed through the committees' accounts]

Year and type of committee	Democratic				Republican			
	Receipts, net [1]	Dis-burse-ments, net [1]	Contribu-tions to candi-dates	Monies spent on behalf of party's nomi-nees [2]	Receipts, net [1]	Dis-burse-ments, net [1]	Contribu-tions to candi-dates	Monies spent on behalf of party's nomi-nees [2]
1981-82	39.3	40.1	1.7	3.3	215.0	214.0	5.6	14.3
1983-84	98.5	97.4	2.6	9.0	297.9	300.8	4.9	20.1
1985-86	64.8	65.9	1.7	9.0	255.2	258.9	3.4	14.3
1987-88	125.7	119.6	1.8	17.9	257.5	251.4	3.4	22.7
1989-90	85.8	90.9	1.5	8.7	206.3	213.5	2.9	10.7
1991-92	187.5	180.5	1.9	28.1	267.3	256.1	3.0	33.9
1993-94, total	151.1	149.9	2.2	21.2	254.4	243.7	3.0	20.6
1995-96, total	221.6	214.3	2.2	22.6	416.5	408.5	3.7	31.0
1997-98, total	160.0	155.3	1.2	18.6	285.0	275.9	2.6	15.7
1999-00, total [3]	**275.2**	**265.8**	**1.4**	**21.0**	**465.8**	**427.0**	**2.3**	**29.6**
National committee	124.0	122.0	-	13.5	212.8	187.4	0.4	23.7
Senatorial committee	40.5	41.5	0.3	0.1	51.5	50.7	0.4	-
Congressional committee	48.4	49.3	0.6	2.6	97.3	95.4	0.7	3.7
State and local	149.3	140.0	0.5	4.7	176.6	165.9	0.8	2.2

- Represents zero.   [1] Total receipts and disbursements do not include monies transferred among the listed committees.
[2] Monies spent in the general election.   Minus sign (-) indicates refunds for expenditures.   [3] Excludes "Other national" activity.

Source: U.S. Federal Election Commission, *FEC Reports on Financial Activity, Final Report, Party and Non-Party Political Committees*, biennial; also see <http://fecweb1.fec.gov/press/051501partyfund/tables/>.

No. 398. National Party Nonfederal Activity: 1996 to 2000

[In dollars. During the 2000 election cycle, both major parties raised record amounts of **nonfederal** or "soft money." Soft money is used to pay a portion of the overhead expenses of party organizations, as well as other shared expenses that benefit both federal and nonfederal elections. In addition, it is used for issue advocacy, as well as generic party advertising. It may also be transferred from national committees to state and local party committees as well as being used to support construction and maintenance of party headquarters]

Year and type of committee	Democratic		Republican	
	Receipts	Disbursements	Receipts	Disbursements
1996				
Total	123,877,924	121,826,562	138,199,706	149,658,099
National	101,905,186	100,483,977	113,127,010	114,401,973
Senatorial	14,176,392	14,061,273	29,395,329	29,362,653
Congressional	12,340,824	11,822,790	18,530,773	28,746,879
1998				
Total	92,811,927	92,987,711	131,615,116	127,730,744
National	56,966,353	57,411,879	74,805,286	74,325,722
Senatorial	25,880,538	25,858,673	37,866,845	37,283,103
Congressional	16,865,410	16,617,533	26,914,059	24,092,993
2000				
Total	245,202,519	244,848,838	249,861,645	252,785,565
National	136,563,419	135,332,105	166,207,843	163,521,510
Senatorial	63,717,982	63,300,415	44,652,709	44,633,117
Congressional	56,702,023	57,997,220	47,295,736	52,925,581

Source: U.S. Federal Election Commission, press release of May 31, 2001 and unpublished data.

U.S. Census Bureau, Statistical Abstract of the United States: 2002

No. 399. Political Action Committees—Number by Committee Type: 1980 to 2001

[As of December 31]

Committee type	1980	1985	1990	1995	1997	1998	1999	2000	2001
Total....................	2,551	3,992	4,172	4,016	3,844	3,798	3,835	3,706	3,907
Corporate	1,206	1,710	1,795	1,674	1,597	1,567	1,548	1,523	1,545
Labor	297	388	346	334	332	321	318	316	317
Trade/membership/health	576	695	774	815	825	821	844	812	860
Nonconnected	374	1,003	1,062	1,020	931	935	972	902	1,026
Cooperative..................	42	54	59	44	42	39	38	39	41
Corporation without stock........	56	142	136	129	117	115	115	114	118

Source: U.S. Federal Election Commission, press release of January 2002.

No. 400. Political Action Committees—Financial Activity Summary by Committee Type: 1995 to 2000

[In millions of dollars (437.4 represents $437,400,000). Covers financial activity during 2-year calendar period indicated]

Committee type	Receipts			Disbursements [1]			Contributions to candidates		
	1995-96	1997-98	1999-00	1995-96	1997-98	1999-00	1995-96	1997-98	1999-00
Total	437.4	502.6	604.9	430.0	470.8	579.4	217.9	219.9	259.8
Corporate	133.8	144.1	164.5	130.6	137.6	158.3	78.2	78.0	91.5
Labor	104.1	111.3	136.0	99.8	98.2	128.7	48.0	44.6	51.6
Trade/membership/health ..	106.0	119.6	142.9	105.4	114.4	137.2	60.2	62.3	71.8
Nonconnected	81.2	114.3	144.3	81.3	107.8	139.7	24.0	28.2	37.3
Cooperative	3.9	4.5	3.7	4.2	4.3	3.3	3.0	2.4	2.4
Corporation without stock ..	8.5	8.8	13.6	8.7	8.5	12.2	4.5	4.4	5.3

[1] Comprises contributions to candidates, independent expenditures, and other disbursements.

Source: U.S. Federal Election Commission, *FEC Reports on Financial Activity, Final Report, Party and Nonparty Political Committees*, biennial. See also <http://www.fec.gov/press/053101pacfund/tables/pachis00.htm> (accessed July 2002).

No. 401. Presidential Campaign Finances—Federal Funds for General Election: 1980 to 1996

[In millions of dollars (62.7 represents $62,700,000). Based on FEC certifications, audit reports, and Dept. of Treasury reports]

1980		1988		1992		1996	
Candidate	Amount	Candidate	Amount	Candidate	Amount	Candidate	Amount
Total	62.7	Total........	92.2	Total........	110.4	Total........	162.6
Anderson [1]	4.2	Bush.........	46.1	Bush.........	55.2	Clinton	61.8
Carter	29.4	Dukakis.......	46.1	Clinton	55.2	Dole........	61.8
Reagan	29.2	Perot	-	Perot	29.0		

- Represents zero. [1] John Anderson, as the candidate of a new party, was permitted to raise funds privately. Total receipts for the Anderson campaign, including federal funds, were $17.6 million, and total expenditures were $15.6 million.

Source: U.S. Federal Election Commission, periodic press releases.

No. 402. Presidential Campaign Finances—Primary Campaign Receipts and Disbursements: 1987 to 1996

[In millions of dollars (213.8 represents $213,800,000). Covers campaign finance activity during 2-year calendar period indicated. Covers candidates who received federal matching funds or who had significant financial activity]

Item	Total			Democratic			Republican		
	1987-88 [1]	1991-92 [2]	1995-96	1987-88	1991-92	1995-96	1987-88	1991-92	1995-96
Receipts, total [3] ...	213.8	125.2	243.9	91.9	70.0	46.2	116.0	49.7	187.0
Individual contributions.	141.1	82.4	126.4	59.4	44.7	31.3	76.8	34.4	93.1
Federal matching funds............	65.7	41.5	56.0	30.1	24.4	14.0	34.7	15.0	41.6
Disbursements....	210.7	118.7	(NA)	90.2	64.4	(NA)	114.6	48.8	(NA)

NA Not available. [1] Includes a minor party candidate who sought several party nominations and a Democratic candidate who did not receive federal matching funds, but who had significant financial activity. [2] Includes other parties, not shown separately. [3] Includes other types of receipts, not shown separately.

Source: U.S. Federal Election Commission, *FEC Reports on Financial Activity, Final Report, Presidential Prenomination Campaigns*, quadrennial.

No. 403. Congressional Campaign Finances—Receipts and Disbursements: 1995 to 2000

[Covers all campaign finance activity during 2-year calendar period indicated for primary, general, run-off, and special elections, for 1999-2000 relates to 2,083 House of Representatives candidates and 333 Senate candidates. Data have been adjusted to eliminate transfers between all committees within a campaign. For further information on legal limits of contributions, see Federal Election campaign act of 1971, as amended

Item	House of Representatives Amount (mil. dol.)			Percent distribution			Senate Amount (mil. dol.)			Percent distribution		
	1995-96	1997-98	1999-00	1995-96	1997-98	1999-00	1995-96	1997-98	1999-00	1995-96	1997-98	1999-00
Total receipts [1]	505.4	493.7	610.4	100	100	100	285.1	287.5	437.0	100	100	100
Individual contributions	272.9	253.2	315.6	55	52	52	166.9	166.5	252.1	59	58	58
Other committees	155.0	158.5	193.4	31	32	32	45.6	48.1	52.0	16	17	12
Candidate loans	42.0	46.8	61.9	8	10	10	40.3	52.2	89.0	14	18	20
Candidate contributions	7.0	5.3	6.3	1	1	1	16.4	1.3	18.7	6	(Z)	4
Democrats	233.1	233.4	286.7	46	47	47	126.5	134.1	230.4	44	47	53
Republicans	266.9	255.8	317.7	53	52	52	157.7	153.0	203.8	55	53	47
Others	5.4	4.5	6.0	1	1	1	0.9	0.4	2.8	(Z)	(Z)	1
Incumbents	279.8	293.6	361.8	56	60	59	81.8	135.5	130.6	29	47	30
Challengers [2]	119.1	92.8	127.4	24	19	21	79.2	113.9	99.6	28	40	23
Open seats [2]	101.1	102.7	121.1	14	21	20	124.1	37.7	206.7	44	13	47
Total disbursements	477.8	452.5	572.3	95	100	100	287.4	287.9	434.7	100	100	100
Democrats	221.1	211.1	266.8	44	47	47	127.4	134.6	226.3	44	47	52
Republicans	251.4	237.2	299.7	50	52	52	159.1	152.9	205.7	55	53	47
Others	5.3	4.2	5.7	1	1	1	0.9	0.4	2.7	(Z)	(Z)	1
Incumbents	258.1	257.2	327.0	51	57	57	85.4	137.3	130.2	30	48	30
Challengers [2]	119.6	94.7	125.6	24	21	22	78.9	112.5	99.3	27	39	23
Open seats [2]	100.2	100.6	119.7	20	22	21	123.1	38.1	205.1	43	13	47

Z Less than $50,000 or 0.5 percent.   [1] Includes other types of receipts, not shown separately.   [2] Elections in which an incumbent did not seek reelection.

Source: U.S. Federal Election Commission, *FEC Reports on Financial Activity, Final Report, U.S. Senate and House Campaigns*, biennial.

No. 404. Contributions to Congressional Campaigns by Political Action Committees (PAC) by Type of Committee: 1983 to 2000

[In millions of dollars. Covers amounts given to candidates in primary, general, run-off, and special elections during the 2-year calendar period indicated. For number of political action committees, see Table 399]

Type of committee	Total [1]	Democrats	Republicans	Incumbents	Challengers	Open seats [2]
HOUSE OF REPRESENTATIVES						
1983-84	75.7	46.3	29.3	57.2	11.3	7.2
1985-86	87.4	54.7	32.6	65.9	9.1	12.4
1987-88	102.2	67.4	34.7	82.2	10.0	10.0
1989-90	108.5	72.2	36.2	87.5	7.3	13.6
1991-92	127.4	85.4	41.7	94.4	12.2	20.8
1993-94	132.4	88.2	43.9	101.4	12.7	18.3
1995-96	159.8	79.4	79.7	117.2	21.4	20.1
1997-98	158.7	77.6	80.9	123.9	14.8	19.7
1999-00, total [3]	195.9	99.2	96.2	152.2	20.2	23.0
Corporate	63.1	22.2	40.7	55.3	2.4	5.3
Trade association [4]	55.7	22.5	33.0	46.3	3.5	5.7
Labor	44.0	40.3	3.6	30.5	8.1	5.3
Nonconnected [5]	27.4	11.5	15.8	15.3	5.8	6.2
SENATE						
1983-84	29.7	14.0	15.6	17.9	6.3	5.4
1985-86	45.3	20.2	25.1	23.7	10.2	11.4
1987-88	45.7	24.2	21.5	28.7	8.0	9.0
1989-90	41.2	20.2	21.0	29.5	8.2	3.5
1991-92	51.2	29.0	22.2	31.9	9.4	10.0
1993-94	47.2	24.0	23.2	26.3	5.7	15.1
1995-96	55.4	19.3	36.0	28.6	7.6	19.3
1997-98	48.1	20.7	27.3	34.3	6.6	7.2
1999-00, total [3]	61.3	23.9	37.4	42.7	7.2	11.3
Corporate	26.8	7.5	19.3	20.7	1.5	4.6
Trade association [4]	15.7	5.1	10.6	11.7	1.2	2.8
Labor	7.5	7.0	0.5	3.2	2.8	1.5
Nonconnected [5]	9.5	3.6	6.0	5.8	1.5	2.2

[1] Includes other parties, not shown separately.   [2] Elections in which an incumbent did not seek reelection.   [3] Includes other types of political action committees not shown separately.   [4] Includes membership organizations and health organizations. [5] Represents "ideological" groups as well as other issue groups not necessarily ideological in nature.

Source: U.S. Federal Election Commission, *FEC Reports on Financial Activity, Party and Nonparty Political Committees, Final Report*, biennial.

Section 8
State and Local Government Finances and Employment

This section presents data on revenues, expenditures, debt, and employment of state and local governments. Nationwide statistics relating to state and local governments, their numbers, finances, and employment are compiled primarily by the U.S. Census Bureau through a program of censuses and surveys. Every fifth year (for years ending in "2" and "7") the Census Bureau conducts a census of governments involving collection of data for all governmental units in the United States. In addition, the Census Bureau conducts annual surveys which cover all the state governments and a sample of local governments.

Annually, the Census Bureau releases information on the Internet which presents financial data for the federal government, nationwide totals for state and local governments, and state-local data by states. Also released annually is a series on state, city, county, and school finances and on state and local public employment. There is also a series of quarterly data releases covering tax revenue and finances of major public employee retirement systems.

Basic information for Census Bureau statistics on governments is obtained by mail canvass from state and local officials; however, financial data for each of the state governments and for many of the large local governments are compiled from their official records and reports by Census Bureau personnel. In over two-thirds of the states, all or part of local government financial data are obtained through central collection arrangements with state governments. Financial data on the federal government are primarily based on the *Budget* published by the Office of Management and Budget (see text, Section 9, Federal Government Finances and Employment).

Governmental units—The governmental structure of the United States includes, in addition to the federal government and

the states, thousands of local governments—counties, municipalities, townships, school districts, and numerous kinds of "special districts." In 1997, 87,453 local governments were identified by the census of governments (see Tables 413-415). As defined by the census, governmental units include all agencies or bodies having an organized existence, governmental character, and substantial autonomy. While most of these governments can impose taxes, many of the special districts—such as independent public housing authorities and numerous local irrigation, power, and other types of districts—are financed from rentals, charges for services, benefit assessments, grants from other governments, and other nontax sources. The count of governments excludes semi-autonomous agencies through which states, cities, and counties sometimes provide for certain functions—for example, "dependent" school systems, state institutions of higher education, and certain other "authorities" and special agencies which are under the administrative or fiscal control of an established governmental unit.

Finances—The financial statistics relate to government fiscal years ending June 30 or at some date within the 12 previous months. The following governments are exceptions and are included as though they were part of the June 30 group; ending September 30, the state governments of Alabama and Michigan, the District of Columbia, and Alabama school districts; and ending August 31, the state government of Texas and Texas school districts. New York State ends its fiscal year on March 31. The federal government ended the fiscal year June 30 until 1976 when its fiscal year, by an act of Congress, was revised to extend from Oct. 1 to Sept. 30. A 3-month quarter (July 1 to Sept. 30, 1976) bridged the transition.

Nationwide government finance statistics have been classified and presented in

State and Local Government Finances and Employment 259

terms of uniform concepts and categories, rather than according to the highly diverse terminology, organization, and fund structure utilized by individual governments.

Statistics on governmental finances distinguish among general government, utilities, liquor stores, and insurance trusts. *General government* comprises all activities except utilities, liquor stores, and insurance trusts. Utilities include government water supply, electric light and power, gas supply, and transit systems. Liquor stores are operated by 17 states and by local governments in 6 states. Insurance trusts relate to employee retirement, unemployment compensation, and other social insurance systems administered by the federal, state, and local governments.

Data for cities or counties relate only to municipal or county and their dependent agencies and do not include amounts for other local governments in the same geographic location. Therefore, expenditure figures for "education" do not include spending by the separate school districts which administer public schools within most municipal or county areas. Variations in the assignment of governmental responsibility for public assistance, health, hospitals, public housing, and other functions to a lesser degree also have an important effect upon reported amounts of city or county expenditure, revenue, and debt.

Employment and payrolls—These data are based mainly on mail canvassing of state and local governments. Payroll includes all salaries, wages, and individual fee payments for the month specified, and employment relates to all persons on governmental payrolls during a pay period of the month covered—including paid officials, temporary help, and (unless otherwise specified) part-time as well as full-time personnel. Beginning 1986, statistics for full-time equivalent employment have been computed with a formula using hours worked by part-time employees. A payroll based formula was used prior to 1985. Full-time equivalent employment statistics were not computed for 1985. Figures shown for individual governments cover major dependent agencies such as institutions of higher education, as well as the basic central departments and agencies of the government.

Statistical reliability—For a discussion of statistical collection and estimation, sampling procedures, and measures of statistical reliability applicable to Census Bureau data, see Appendix III.

No. 405. Number of Governmental Units by Type: 1952 to 2002

Type of government	1952 [1]	1962	1967	1972	1977	1982	1987	1992	1997	2002
Total units	**116,807**	**91,237**	**81,299**	**78,269**	**79,913**	**81,831**	**83,237**	**85,006**	**87,504**	**87,900**
U.S. Government	1	1	1	1	1	1	1	1	1	1
State government.	50	50	50	50	50	50	50	50	50	50
Local governments	116,756	91,186	81,248	78,218	79,862	81,780	83,186	84,955	87,453	87,849
County	3,052	3,043	3,049	3,044	3,042	3,041	3,042	3,043	3,043	3,034
Municipal.	16,807	18,000	18,048	18,517	18,862	19,076	19,200	19,279	19,372	19,431
Township and town . . .	17,202	17,142	17,105	16,991	16,822	16,734	16,691	16,656	16,629	16,506
School district.	67,355	34,678	21,782	15,781	15,174	14,851	14,721	14,422	13,726	13,522
Special district	12,340	18,323	21,264	23,885	25,962	28,078	29,532	31,555	34,683	35,356

[1] Adjusted to include units in Alaska and Hawaii which adopted statehood in 1959.

Source: U.S. Census Bureau, *2002 Census of Governments, Governmental Units in 2002,* series GC02-1(P). See also <http://www.census.gov/govs/cog/2002COGprelimreport.pdf>. (issued July 2002).

No. 406. Number of Local Governments by Type—States: 1997

State	All govern-mental units [1]	County	Municipal	Town-ship [1]	School district	Special district [2] Total [3]	Special district [2] Natural resources	Special district [2] Fire protection	Special district [2] Housing & community develop-ment
United States ..	87,453	3,043	19,372	16,629	13,726	34,683	6,983	5,601	3,469
Alabama	1,131	67	446	-	127	491	71	5	154
Alaska.	175	12	149	-	-	14	-	-	13
Arizona	637	15	87	-	231	304	79	152	-
Arkansas	1,516	75	491	-	311	639	232	74	126
California	4,607	57	471	-	1,069	3,010	472	369	79
Colorado	1,869	62	269	-	180	1,358	168	249	96
Connecticut	583	-	30	149	17	387	1	65	94
Delaware	336	3	57	-	19	257	236	-	3
District of Columbia	2	-	1	-	-	1	-	-	-
Florida.	1,081	66	394	-	95	526	132	56	105
Georgia	1,344	156	535	-	180	473	36	2	206
Hawaii.	19	3	1	-	-	15	14	-	-
Idaho	1,147	44	200	-	114	789	182	144	10
Illinois	6,835	102	1,288	1,433	944	3,068	935	827	113
Indiana	3,198	91	569	1,008	294	1,236	134	2	63
Iowa	1,876	99	950	-	394	433	249	68	26
Kansas	3,950	105	627	1,370	324	1,524	260	-	204
Kentucky	1,366	119	434	-	176	637	131	144	17
Louisiana.	467	60	302	-	66	39	3	-	-
Maine	832	16	22	467	98	229	16	-	30
Maryland	420	23	156	-	-	241	156	-	20
Massachusetts . . .	861	12	44	307	85	413	18	16	252
Michigan	2,775	83	534	1,242	584	332	82	2	-
Minnesota	3,501	87	854	1,794	360	406	114	-	176
Mississippi	936	82	295	-	164	395	251	-	62
Missouri.	3,416	114	944	324	537	1,497	181	273	143
Montana	1,144	54	128	-	362	600	125	159	12
Nebraska.	2,894	93	535	455	681	1,130	84	419	126
Nevada	205	16	19	-	17	153	35	16	5
New Hampshire . .	575	10	13	221	166	165	10	14	21
New Jersey	1,421	21	324	243	552	281	16	200	2
New Mexico	881	33	99	-	96	653	609	-	6
New York.	3,413	57	615	929	686	1,126	2	912	-
North Carolina	952	100	527	-	-	325	155	-	94
North Dakota	2,758	53	363	1,341	237	764	80	289	38
Ohio	3,597	88	941	1,310	666	592	97	60	73
Oklahoma	1,799	77	592	-	578	552	98	20	105
Oregon	1,493	36	240	-	258	959	195	263	22
Pennsylvania	5,070	66	1,023	1,546	516	1,919	7	-	91
Rhode Island	119	-	8	31	4	76	3	34	26
South Carolina . . .	716	46	269	-	91	310	48	97	45
South Dakota	1,810	66	309	956	177	302	107	60	34
Tennessee	940	93	343	-	14	490	112	-	100
Texas	4,700	254	1,177	-	1,087	2,182	428	103	395
Utah	683	29	230	-	40	384	77	24	17
Vermont	691	14	49	237	279	112	14	20	10
Virginia	483	95	231	-	1	156	47	-	-
Washington	1,812	39	275	-	296	1,202	163	402	45
West Virginia	704	55	232	-	55	362	15	-	39
Wisconsin	3,059	72	583	1,266	442	696	184	-	171
Wyoming	654	23	97	-	56	478	119	61	-

- Represents zero.   [1] Includes "town" governments in the six New England States and in Minnesota, New York, and Wisconsin.   [2] Single function districts.   [3] Includes other special districts not shown separately.

No. 407. County, Municipal, and Township Governments by Population Size: 1997

[Number of governments as of **January 1997**. Population enumerated as of **July 1, 1994**. Consolidated city-county governments are classified as municipal rather than county governments. Township governments include "towns" in the six New England States, Minnesota, New York, and Wisconsin]

Population-size group	County governments Number, 1997	County governments Population, 1994 Number (1,000)	County governments Population, 1994 Percent	Municipal governments Number, 1997	Municipal governments Population, 1994 Number (1,000)	Municipal governments Population, 1994 Percent	Township governments Number, 1997	Township governments Population, 1994 Number (1,000)	Township governments Population, 1994 Percent
Total	3,043	236,107	100	19,372	161,605	100	16,629	54,662	100
250,000 or more . . .	183	128,741	55	66	46,417	29	4	1,758	3
100,000 to 299,999 .	264	40,234	17	142	20,687	13	31	4,259	8
50,000 to 99,999 . . .	378	26,583	11	346	23,595	15	84	5,626	10
25,000 to 49,999 . . .	604	21,543	9	590	20,623	13	257	8,750	16
10,000 to 24,999 . . .	908	15,047	6	1,378	21,606	13	744	11,509	21
5,000 to 9,999	413	3,105	1	1,618	11,504	7	1,064	7,403	14
2,500 to 4,999	178	668	-	2,096	7,426	5	1,836	6,422	12
1,000 to 2,499	86	165	-	3,723	5,965	4	3,606	5,766	11
Less than 1,000	29	21	-	9,413	3,782	2	9,003	3,169	6

- Represents or rounds to zero.

Source of Tables 406 and 407: U.S. Census Bureau, *Census of Governments, Government Organization*, series (GC(1)-1), quinquennial.

State and Local Government Finances and Employment   261

No. 408. Government Current Receipts and Expenditures by Type: 1990 to 2001

[In billions of dollars (1,607.7 represents $1,607,700,000,000). For explanation of national income, see text, Section 13, Income, Expenditures, and Wealth]

Item	1990	1995	1996	1997	1998	1999	2000	2001
Current receipts	1,607.7	2,117.1	2,269.1	2,440.0	2,613.8	2,780.3	3,000.6	2,992.3
Personal tax and nontax receipts	609.6	778.3	869.7	968.8	1,070.4	1,159.1	1,286.4	1,292.1
Corporate profits tax accruals	140.6	211.0	223.6	237.2	238.8	247.8	259.4	199.3
Indirect business tax and nontax accruals . . .	447.3	594.6	620.0	646.2	681.3	712.9	753.6	774.8
Contributions for social insurance.	410.1	533.2	555.8	587.8	623.3	660.4	701.3	726.1
Current expenditures	1,778.0	2,293.7	2,384.5	2,462.4	2,529.3	2,630.1	2,775.8	2,951.6
Consumption expenditures	965.7	1,133.9	1,171.8	1,223.3	1,261.4	1,336.3	1,431.2	1,522.2
Transfer payments (net)	583.1	869.9	916.0	945.0	965.9	998.5	1,050.8	1,146.6
To persons	573.1	860.1	902.4	934.4	955.0	987.2	1,037.3	1,137.0
To the rest of the world (net)	10.0	9.8	13.6	10.6	11.0	11.4	13.6	9.6
Net interest paid [1]	204.3	268.0	274.4	275.3	278.8	263.1	260.1	236.0
Interest paid	297.8	357.5	366.6	371.2	372.2	360.0	363.6	341.1
To persons and business [1]	257.1	300.1	299.0	283.2	281.1	285.4	280.6	260.4
To the rest of the world	40.8	57.4	67.6	88.1	91.1	74.5	83.0	80.7
Less: Interest received by government [1] . . .	93.6	89.5	92.2	96.0	93.4	96.9	103.5	105.1
Less: Dividends received by government. . . .	0.2	0.3	0.3	0.3	0.4	0.4	0.4	0.4
Subsidies less current surplus of government enterprises.	25.3	22.2	22.6	19.1	23.5	32.5	34.1	47.3
Subsidies	26.8	33.2	33.7	33.0	35.4	44.0	44.1	55.3
Less: Current surplus of government enterprises	1.5	11.1	11.1	13.9	11.8	11.5	10.1	8.0
Less: Wage accruals less disbursements. . . .	0.1	-	-	-	-	-	-	-
Current surplus or deficit (-), national income and product accounts	-170.3	-176.7	-115.4	-22.3	84.5	150.2	224.8	40.7
Social insurance funds	46.9	23.9	19.4	31.6	58.6	96.8	118.4	93.2

- Represents zero.

Source: U.S. Bureau of Economic Analysis, *National Income and Product Accounts, 1929-97*; and *Survey of Current Business*, August 2001 and May 2002. See also <http://www.bea.doc.gov/bea/dn/nipaweb/SelectTable.asp?Selected=N> (released as 29 April 2002).

No. 409. Government Consumption Expenditures and Gross Investment by Level of Government and Type: 1990 to 2001

[In billions of dollars (1,181.4 represents $1,181,400,000,000). For explanation of national income, see text, Section 13, Income, Expenditures, and Wealth]

Level of government and type	1990	1995	1996	1997	1998	1999	2000	2001
Consumption expenditures & gross investment, total	1,181.4	1,372.0	1,421.9	1,487.9	1,538.5	1,641.0	1,751.0	1,858.0
Federal	508.4	521.5	531.6	538.2	539.2	565.0	589.2	628.1
National defense	374.9	350.6	357.0	352.6	349.1	364.3	374.9	399.9
Consumption expenditures	308.9	297.5	302.4	304.2	299.7	312.0	321.4	344.5
Durable goods	30.9	21.0	21.0	21.1	21.1	22.4	22.5	24.2
Nondurable goods.	11.0	6.3	7.7	7.5	6.9	8.1	10.4	10.5
Services	267.0	270.2	273.7	275.6	271.7	281.5	288.5	309.8
Gross investment	65.9	53.1	54.6	48.4	49.4	52.3	53.5	55.5
Structures	6.1	6.3	6.7	5.7	5.4	5.3	5.3	5.4
Equipment and software	59.8	46.9	47.9	42.7	44.0	47.4	48.2	50.0
Nondefense	133.6	170.9	174.6	185.6	190.1	200.7	214.3	228.2
Consumption expenditures	111.0	141.8	142.9	152.7	153.4	159.6	171.9	184.0
Durable goods	-0.1	0.9	1.1	1.2	-0.4	1.0	1.2	1.3
Nondurable goods.	4.6	6.5	6.1	7.9	8.1	6.3	6.4	8.7
Services	106.4	134.3	135.7	143.6	145.6	152.3	164.4	174.0
Gross investment	22.6	29.2	31.7	32.9	36.7	41.1	42.4	44.2
Structures	8.0	10.8	11.1	9.7	11.2	11.6	10.8	10.4
Equipment and software	14.6	18.4	20.5	23.2	25.5	29.4	31.6	33.8
State and local	673.0	850.5	890.4	949.7	999.3	1,076.0	1,161.8	1,229.9
Consumption expenditures	545.8	694.7	726.5	766.4	808.3	864.7	937.9	993.7
Durable goods	10.6	12.7	13.1	13.8	14.8	15.9	17.1	18.3
Nondurable goods	53.6	72.9	79.9	81.7	83.4	94.0	114.0	118.7
Services	481.5	609.0	633.6	670.9	710.1	754.7	806.8	856.7
Gross investment	127.2	155.8	163.8	183.3	191.0	211.3	223.9	236.2
Structures	98.5	117.3	122.5	139.3	142.4	158.3	167.4	177.6
Equipment and software	28.7	38.6	41.3	44.0	48.6	53.0	56.5	58.6

Source: U.S. Bureau of Economic Analysis, *National Income and Product Accounts, 1929-97*; and *Survey of Current Business*, August 2001 and May 2002. See also <http://www.bea.doc.gov/bea/dn/nipaweb/SelectTable.asp?Selected=N> (released as 29 April 2002).

No. 410. Real Government Consumption and Expenditures and Gross Investment in Chained (1996) Dollars by Level of Government and Type: 1990 to 2001

[In billions dollars (1,387.3 represents $1,387,300,000,000). For explanation of national income, see text, Section 13, Income, Expenditures, and Wealth]

Item	1990	1995	1996	1997	1998	1999	2000	2001
Total [1]	1,387.3	1,406.4	1,421.9	1,455.4	1,483.3	1,540.6	1,582.5	1,640.4
Federal	**606.8**	**536.5**	**531.6**	**529.6**	**525.4**	**537.7**	**544.4**	**570.6**
National defense	443.2	361.9	357.0	347.7	341.6	348.8	348.7	366.0
Consumption expenditures	369.7	308.7	302.4	298.5	290.6	295.3	294.1	308.9
Durable goods [2]	33.4	21.1	21.0	21.2	21.3	22.7	22.7	24.3
Nondurable goods	10.7	6.9	7.7	7.7	8.0	8.9	9.4	9.9
Services	325.0	280.7	273.7	269.6	261.4	264	262.4	275.1
Compensation of general government employees, except own-account investment [3]	172.9	139.0	133.1	128.3	124.3	120.9	120.5	121.2
Consumption of general government fixed capital [4]	61.2	63.4	63.0	62.7	62.4	62.4	62.5	62.4
Other services	91.6	78.5	77.7	78.7	74.8	80.8	79.6	91.7
Gross investment	73.2	53.2	54.6	49.1	51.0	53.7	54.8	57.3
Structures	7.7	6.5	6.7	5.5	5.1	4.8	4.6	4.6
Equipment and software	65.4	46.8	47.9	43.6	45.9	49.0	50.4	53.0
Nondefense	163.0	174.6	174.6	181.8	183.8	188.8	195.6	204.4
Consumption expenditures	140.1	145.7	142.9	148.6	146.5	147.6	153.7	161.1
Durable goods [2]	-0.7	0.8	1.1	1.3	-0.2	1.2	1.4	1.5
Nondurable goods	4.6	6.4	6.1	7.9	8.3	6.4	6.8	8.9
Commodity Credit Corporation inventory change	-2.5	-0.4	-0.4	-0.1	0.3	0.3	1.6	1.7
Other nondurables	7.1	6.8	6.5	8.0	8.1	6.0	5.2	7.2
Services	135.6	138.5	135.7	139.4	138.5	140.2	146.3	151.6
Compensation of general government employees, except own-account investment [3]	83.2	78.5	76.4	75.9	76.7	77.0	79.4	79.0
Consumption of general government fixed capital [4]	13.3	16.7	18.0	19.6	21.4	23.8	26.1	28.0
Other services	39.9	43.3	41.3	44.0	40.4	39.7	41.2	45.4
Gross investment	23.5	29.0	31.7	33.3	37.5	41.6	42.3	43.6
Structures	9.3	11.1	11.1	9.4	10.6	10.7	9.5	8.9
Equipment and software	14.2	17.9	20.5	23.9	27.0	31.2	33.3	35.4
State and local	**781.1**	**869.9**	**890.4**	**925.8**	**957.7**	**1,002.4**	**1,037.4**	**1,069.4**
Consumption expenditures	638.9	711.3	726.5	745.7	771.9	801.2	831.1	856.8
Durable goods [2]	10.9	12.7	13.1	13.9	15.0	16.1	17.2	18.3
Nondurable goods	57.8	75.6	79.9	82.3	88.4	96.2	103.0	108.7
Services	570.3	623.1	633.6	649.5	668.8	689.8	712.0	731.1
Compensation of general government employees, except own-account investment [3]	507.1	536.5	542.3	550.9	559.9	566.4	577.6	589.6
Consumption of general government fixed capital [4]	52.7	65.3	68.2	71.7	75.7	80.2	84.6	88.7
Other services	13.6	21.3	23.0	26.8	33.0	43.1	49.9	53.2
Gross investment	142.2	158.6	163.8	180.2	185.8	201.4	206.5	212.8
Structures	114.5	120.9	122.5	134.7	134.0	143.8	145.2	148.6
Equipment and software	28.4	37.8	41.3	45.4	52.3	58.4	62.7	65.9
Residual	-4.4	-0.6	-	-	-1.1	-3	-5.1	-6.8
Addenda:								
Compensation of general government employees[3]	**769.2**	**761.3**	**759.4**	**763.4**	**769.4**	**773.2**	**786.2**	**800.5**
Federal	258.4	219.0	211.0	205.7	202.6	199.4	201.4	201.6
State and local	512.4	542.4	548.4	557.7	566.8	573.8	584.9	598.9

- Represents zero. [1] Gross government investment consists of general government and government enterprise expenditures for fixed assets; inventory investment is included in government consumption expenditures. [2] Consumption expenditures for durable goods excludes expenditures classified as investment, except for goods transferred to foreign countries by the Federal Government. [3] Compensation of government employees engaged in new own-account investment and related expenditures for goods and services are classified as investment in structures and in software. The compensation of all general government employees is shown in the addenda. [4] Consumption of fixed capital, or depreciation, is included in government consumption expenditures as a partial measure of the value of the services of general government fixed assets; use of depreciation assumes a zero net return.

Source: U.S. Bureau of Economic Analysis, *National Income and Product Accounts, 1929-97*; and *Survey of Current Business*, August 2001 and May 2002. See also <http://www.bea.doc.gov/bea/dn/nipaweb/SelectTable.asp?Selected=N> (released as 29 April 2002).

State and Local Government Finances and Employment   263

No. 411. Federal Grants-in-Aid to State and Local Governments: 1980 to 2002

[91,385 represents $91,385,000,000, except as indicated. For fiscal year ending in year shown; see text, this section. Minus sign (-) indicates decrease]

Year	Current dollars							Constant (1996) dollars	
			Grants to individuals		Grants as percent of—				
	Grants, total (mil. dol.)	Annual percent change [1]	Total (mil. dol.)	Percent of total grants	State/local govt. expenditures [2]	Federal outlays	Gross domestic product	Total grants (bil. dol.)	Annual percent change [1]
1980	91,385	9.6	32,619	35.7	39.9	15.5	3.3	168.5	-1.3
1985	105,852	8.5	50,059	47.3	29.6	11.2	2.6	147.0	4.9
1990	135,325	11.0	77,264	57.1	25.2	10.8	2.4	157.9	6.6
1991	154,519	14.2	92,865	60.1	26.6	11.7	2.6	173.6	9.9
1992	178,065	15.2	112,522	63.2	28.7	12.9	2.9	195.4	12.6
1993	193,612	8.7	124,155	64.1	29.6	13.7	3.0	207.3	6.1
1994	210,596	8.8	134,153	63.7	30.9	14.4	3.0	220.7	6.5
1995	224,991	6.8	144,427	64.2	31.5	14.8	3.1	229.8	4.1
1996	227,811	1.3	146,493	64.3	30.8	14.6	3.0	227.8	-0.9
1997	234,160	2.8	148,236	63.3	30.2	14.6	2.9	229.2	0.6
1998	246,128	5.1	160,305	65.1	30.3	14.9	2.8	237.6	3.7
1999	267,081	8.5	172,384	64.5	31.2	15.7	2.9	253.4	6.6
2000	284,659	6.6	182,592	64.1	30.7	15.9	2.9	262.2	3.5
2001	317,250	11.4	203,925	64.3	32.0	17.0	3.1	285.3	8.8
2002, est	346,462	9.2	223,184	64.4	(NA)	16.9	3.3	305.8	7.2

NA Not available. [1] Average annual percent change from prior year shown. For explanation, see Guide to Tabular Presentation. For 1980, change from 1979, for 1985, from 1984, and 1990, from 1989. [2] Expenditures from own sources as defined in the national income and product accounts.

Source: U. S. Office of Management and Budget, based on *Historical Tables* and *Analytical Prospectives, Budget of the United States Government,* annual.

No. 412. Federal Aid to State and Local Governments: 1980 to 2002

[In millions of dollars (91,385 represents $91,385,000,000). For fiscal year ending in year shown; See text, this section. Includes trust funds. Minus sign (-) indicates previously disbursed funds returned to the federal government.]

Program	1980	1990	1995	1998	1999	2000	2001	2002 est.
Grant-in-aid shared revenue [1]	91,385	135,325	224,991	246,128	267,081	284,659	317,250	346,462
National defense	93	241	68	12	1	2	47	91
Energy	499	461	492	424	462	433	492	579
Natural resources and environment	5,363	3,745	4,148	3,758	4,103	4,595	4,882	5,300
Environmental Protection Agency	4,603	2,874	2,912	2,746	2,960	3,490	3,750	3,701
Agriculture	569	1,285	780	668	659	724	756	886
Commerce and housing Credit	3	-	5	9	5	3	6	11
Transportation [1]	13,022	19,174	25,787	26,144	28,904	32,222	36,673	38,686
Airports [2]	590	1,220	1,826	1,511	1,565	1,624	2,020	2,801
Highways [2]	9,208	14,171	19,475	19,791	22,590	24,711	27,098	28,040
Urban mass transit [2]	3,129	3,730	4,353	4,221	4,188	5,262	6,963	6,455
Community and regional development [1]	6,486	4,965	7,230	7,653	9,332	8,665	9,487	11,610
Appalachian regional development	335	124	182	180	136	125	86	105
Community development block grants	3,902	2,818	4,333	4,621	4,804	4,955	4,939	5,235
Education, employment, training, social services [1]	21,862	23,359	34,125	36,502	33,510	36,672	40,138	45,932
Compensatory education for the disadvantaged	3,370	4,437	6,785	7,800	7,534	8,511	8,619	9,353
School improvement programs	523	1,080	1,288	1,260	1,255	2,394	2,721	4,269
Federally affected areas impact aid	622	799	803	724	1,076	875	1,021	1,146
Vocational and adult education	854	1,287	1,449	1,425	1,338	1,448	1,651	1,756
Social services-block grants to states	2,763	2,749	2,797	2,437	1,993	1,827	1,852	1,803
Children and family services programs	1,548	2,618	4,463	5,054	5,421	5,843	6,614	7,403
Training and employment assistance	6,191	3,042	3,620	3,399	3,436	2,957	3,132	4,025
Office of libraries.	158	127	109	121	129	152	167	226
Health [1]	15,758	43,890	93,587	105,833	113,969	124,843	139,299	155,643
Alcohol, drug abuse, and mental health [3] . . .	679	1,241	2,444	2,236	2,214	1,931	2,098	2,229
Grants to states for Medicaid [3]	13,957	41,103	89,070	101,234	108,042	117,921	129,434	144,926
Income security [1]	18,495	35,189	55,122	58,870	68,885	68,653	76,064	79,954
Food stamps-administration	412	2,130	2,740	3,673	3,362	3,508	3,664	3,833
Child nutrition and special milk programs [3] . .	3,388	4,871	7,387	8,436	8,740	9,060	9,416	10,194
Veterans benefits and services [3]	90	134	253	288	317	434	405	479
Administration of justice.	529	574	1,222	3,658	4,923	5,263	6,613	4,664
General government [4]	8,616	2,309	2,172	2,309	2,011	2,144	2,388	2,616

- Represents or rounds to zero. [1] Includes items not shown separately. [2] Trust funds. [3] Includes grants for payments to individuals. [4] Includes general purpose fiscal assistance.

Source: U.S. Office of Management and Budget, *Historical Tables, Budget of the United States Government,* annual.

No. 413. Federal Aid to State and Local Governments—Selected Programs by State: 2001

[In millions of dollars (323,893 represents $323,893,000,000). For fiscal year ending September 30]

State and outlying area	Federal aid, total [1]	Department of Agriculture — Food and nutrition service					Department of Education — Office of Special Education and Rehabilitative Services				
		Total	Child nutrition programs [2]	Food stamp program [3]	Special supplemental food program (WIC)	Other	Total	Education for the disadvantaged	Special education	Rehabilitation services & disability research	Other
Total	323,893	20,035	9,380	3,739	4,098	2,817	25,474	559	5,726	2,615	16,575
United States	317,031	18,240	9,164	2,414	3,917	2,743	24,795	548	5,622	2,500	16,125
Alabama	5,085	337	179	34	69	55	416	6	91	55	264
Alaska	2,435	80	26	8	19	27	227	8	18	11	190
Arizona	5,179	346	173	36	85	51	556	9	103	51	392
Arkansas	3,134	221	110	21	42	48	255	6	57	35	157
California	37,228	2,457	1,232	288	727	210	2,897	133	629	248	1,887
Colorado	3,529	179	86	19	39	35	292	8	69	31	183
Connecticut	4,054	150	73	23	35	19	248	5	64	20	159
Delaware	896	53	26	6	9	12	81	1	15	11	53
District of Columbia . .	3,462	55	26	8	11	9	95	-	9	12	74
Florida	13,304	864	513	83	191	78	1,199	2	340	125	732
Georgia	8,093	608	368	59	112	69	689	26	158	65	441
Hawaii	1,315	92	38	8	25	20	127	15	22	10	80
Idaho	1,384	91	37	8	17	30	122	1	28	16	77
Illinois	11,957	689	367	90	142	90	951	7	227	95	622
Indiana	5,786	308	148	40	66	54	443	12	135	58	238
Iowa	2,744	181	80	21	32	48	231	8	64	32	127
Kansas	2,511	182	95	11	25	51	271	2	63	27	178
Kentucky	5,090	308	160	29	60	59	384	13	82	44	245
Louisiana	5,590	435	246	38	75	77	468	13	85	41	329
Maine	1,890	79	33	12	11	23	127	7	31	15	74
Maryland	5,657	268	134	57	47	29	380	5	110	36	229
Massachusetts	8,065	279	150	42	57	29	495	4	131	47	313
Michigan	10,270	611	237	152	123	99	902	5	195	88	615
Minnesota	5,107	310	149	56	47	59	362	17	94	43	208
Mississippi	3,958	329	169	29	57	73	341	4	55	46	236
Missouri	6,502	332	167	38	67	60	483	4	127	63	290
Montana	1,550	88	30	10	13	35	149	6	19	13	112
Nebraska	1,817	131	61	13	19	37	153	2	37	14	100
Nevada	1,414	80	42	7	22	9	108	5	34	13	56
New Hampshire.	1,158	49	18	6	9	16	84	1	23	12	48
New Jersey	8,822	356	184	71	70	31	580	1	167	44	366
New Mexico	3,255	185	107	17	33	29	342	7	99	21	215
New York	33,567	1,355	678	287	269	121	2,089	3	473	142	1,471
North Carolina.	8,769	536	292	58	99	87	606	29	152	78	347
North Dakota	1,120	64	24	7	9	23	111	12	13	11	75
Ohio	11,727	567	264	97	130	76	833	1	152	100	580
Oklahoma	4,205	297	147	37	51	61	393	10	67	47	268
Oregon	4,022	327	99	37	52	139	286	4	69	34	178
Pennsylvania	14,107	612	276	120	127	88	978	18	162	104	695
Rhode Island	1,622	58	27	6	13	12	91	20	20	9	42
South Carolina	4,382	313	165	29	63	56	326	1	85	43	197
South Dakota	1,237	81	30	10	13	29	133	4	16	11	102
Tennessee	6,899	391	193	38	89	70	484	2	121	64	298
Texas	19,001	1,572	926	165	350	130	2,016	4	419	187	1,407
Utah	2,056	147	74	23	31	20	191	63	54	23	51
Vermont	1,013	49	12	10	10	17	76	3	14	11	48
Virginia	5,295	325	132	62	76	55	510	1	143	67	299
Washington	6,167	358	152	35	89	83	493	4	115	43	332
West Virginia	2,910	148	69	12	30	38	207	18	41	26	122
Wisconsin.	5,525	269	122	38	54	55	434	2	109	51	273
Wyoming	1,163	39	15	4	7	13	77	5	13	9	50
Outlying areas.	5,163	1,774	216	1,324	181	52	675	11	104	114	446
American Samoa . .	101	19	8	5	5	1	16	1	7	1	7
Micronesia	-	-	-	-	-	-	-	-	-	-	-
Guam.	217	15	5	3	4	3	30	-	15	2	13
Marshall Islands. . .	-	-	-	-	-	-	-	-	-	-	-
Northern Marianas .	67	12	4	6	-	3	9	-	3	1	5
Palau	-	-	-	-	-	-	-	-	-	-	-
Puerto Rico.	4,509	1,697	185	1,304	167	42	596	-	69	109	418
Virgin Islands.	269	30	14	6	5	4	24	9	9	2	3
Undistributed amounts.	1,699	21	-	-	-	21	4	-	-	-	3

See footnotes at end of table.

U.S. Census Bureau, Statistical Abstract of the United States: 2002

No. 413. Federal Aid to State and Local Governments—Selected Programs by State: 2001—Con.

[In millions of dollars (2,674 represents $2,674,000,000). For fiscal year ending September 30]

State and outlying area	FEMA[4], total	Department of Housing and Urban Development							Department of Labor		
				Public housing programs						State unemployment insurance and employment service	Employment & Training Administration workforce Investment Act
		Total	Community development block grants	Low rent block	Section 8 programs	Housing certificate program	Capital programs	Other	Total[5]		
Total	2,674	33,466	4,952	3,211	489	16,720	3,474	4,620	7,475	3,122	3,444
United States	2,444	32,257	4,804	3,111	484	16,466	2,822	4,569	7,314	3,091	3,321
Alabama	51	456	62	92	2	170	79	52	122	43	50
Alaska	4	191	20	13	-	26	5	126	64	29	26
Arizona	6	423	60	14	2	141	14	192	136	41	82
Arkansas	175	214	27	21	-	117	28	21	87	29	47
California	499	3,583	650	105	37	2,106	145	540	1,141	455	609
Colorado	15	393	52	12	2	258	21	48	85	42	32
Connecticut	2	558	51	52	19	335	46	55	93	55	25
Delaware	4	97	9	8	1	48	5	26	22	11	8
District of Columbia . .	2	520	80	55	19	142	109	116	66	35	28
Florida	158	1,117	183	88	18	594	65	169	260	108	125
Georgia	34	761	129	96	13	318	127	78	153	70	65
Hawaii	9	144	25	10	-	80	17	12	56	16	35
Idaho	4	67	14	1	-	42	1	9	43	23	15
Illinois	29	1,791	226	253	31	940	167	175	311	147	127
Indiana	9	498	83	35	2	291	29	58	103	53	35
Iowa	14	226	50	2	-	141	7	27	56	29	16
Kansas	11	174	37	10	-	89	15	22	54	24	21
Kentucky	14	491	72	37	3	267	59	53	100	34	50
Louisiana	60	503	101	57	14	192	66	73	111	36	66
Maine	7	178	25	8	-	122	6	16	41	15	16
Maryland	17	633	78	80	22	312	45	96	129	66	52
Massachusetts	19	1,456	159	89	11	979	76	143	129	79	39
Michigan	70	844	177	51	3	438	41	133	249	127	88
Minnesota	46	529	78	28	-	301	48	73	94	53	29
Mississippi	31	262	43	22	1	135	30	31	75	26	40
Missouri	8	614	112	31	15	282	85	88	113	54	45
Montana	15	112	17	3	-	41	3	47	45	12	29
Nebraska	7	143	23	6	-	79	11	23	35	19	11
Nevada	3	148	17	15	-	77	13	25	48	29	15
New Hampshire	5	129	14	6	-	82	6	20	24	12	9
New Jersey	30	1,376	136	160	35	771	143	131	223	110	83
New Mexico	8	162	26	6	-	73	10	46	61	19	37
New York	202	4,215	470	815	25	1,963	480	462	559	214	303
North Carolina	240	697	93	85	21	318	66	114	173	70	59
North Dakota	67	82	18	1	-	39	4	20	25	13	10
Ohio	14	1,333	198	133	23	677	131	172	272	97	143
Oklahoma	139	395	51	22	1	156	18	146	72	27	36
Oregon	14	319	44	14	-	200	12	49	144	54	63
Pennsylvania	20	1,653	279	232	32	696	216	197	330	157	126
Rhode Island	3	225	22	15	-	143	18	27	37	16	13
South Carolina	13	315	52	26	7	165	25	39	90	39	36
South Dakota	11	99	17	2	-	43	2	35	31	10	16
Tennessee	17	538	62	86	31	225	70	64	136	46	56
Texas	238	1,616	334	89	45	800	140	207	482	164	262
Utah	10	115	30	3	-	61	4	18	53	34	13
Vermont	5	88	16	3	-	55	2	11	24	9	10
Virginia	21	574	68	59	18	311	45	74	133	52	55
Washington	21	480	66	29	16	240	31	97	196	89	76
West Virginia	20	220	60	14	1	114	8	23	74	20	46
Wisconsin	18	467	85	14	13	249	24	81	130	71	34
Wyoming	3	34	3	1	-	20	1	9	21	10	8
Outlying areas	89	729	147	100	5	253	173	51	158	31	120
American Samoa . .	-	-	-	-	-	-	-	-	2	-	1
Micronesia	-	-	-	-	-	-	-	-	-	-	-
Guam	12	21	-	2	-	12	7	1	5	-	3
Marshall Islands . . .	-	-	-	-	-	-	-	-	-	-	-
Northern Marianas .	2	-	-	-	-	-	-	-	1	-	1
Palau	-	-	-	-	-	-	-	-	-	-	-
Puerto Rico	51	653	146	79	4	228	149	47	144	27	113
Virgin Islands	25	55	2	19	1	13	18	3	8	3	3
Undistributed amounts	141	480	-	-	-	1	479	-	3	-	3

See footnotes at end of table.

U.S. Census Bureau, Statistical Abstract of the United States: 2002

No. 413. Federal Aid to State and Local Governments—Selected Programs by State: 2001—Con.

[In millions of dollars (181,412 represents $181,412,000,000). For fiscal year ending September 30]

State and outlying area	Department of Health and Human Services						Department of Transportation				Federal aid, other
		Administration for children									
	Total	Temporary assistance to needy families	Children & family services (Head start)	Foster care and adoption assistance	Health care financing administration	Other	Total	Highway trust fund	Federal transit administration	Other	
Total	181,412	17,103	5,378	5,377	133,014	20,541	37,098	26,452	7,561	3,085	16,258
United States	180,535	17,030	5,068	5,377	132,737	20,324	36,171	26,067	7,256	2,848	15,274
Alabama	2,698	134	84	24	2,142	314	764	634	38	91	241
Alaska	1,060	62	24	17	437	520	472	352	26	94	338
Arizona	2,718	239	97	65	1,948	370	591	481	46	63	404
Arkansas	1,771	66	53	34	1,445	174	320	267	15	37	89
California	21,578	3,766	607	1,278	13,887	2,040	3,720	2,051	1,421	248	1,352
Colorado	1,692	150	64	45	1,171	262	516	372	109	35	359
Connecticut	2,362	269	47	106	1,708	232	507	399	98	9	134
Delaware	451	33	11	11	333	64	136	119	11	6	52
District of Columbia . .	1,022	113	60	25	701	123	384	191	183	10	1,320
Florida	7,363	644	182	181	5,375	980	1,837	1,492	229	117	506
Georgia	4,570	368	148	77	3,261	715	1,010	790	172	49	268
Hawaii	578	104	20	25	347	82	241	157	48	36	68
Idaho	693	37	23	9	530	94	243	203	8	32	120
Illinois	6,417	602	255	350	4,407	804	1,362	883	382	97	407
Indiana	3,393	209	77	64	2,698	345	735	621	75	39	296
Iowa	1,543	132	45	61	1,125	181	377	309	25	43	115
Kansas	1,447	102	56	61	1,067	161	275	246	15	13	98
Kentucky	3,008	181	88	68	2,418	252	596	510	25	60	189
Louisiana	3,735	181	109	69	3,066	311	85	1	43	41	193
Maine	1,191	78	25	48	941	100	181	152	19	10	85
Maryland	3,372	229	124	138	1,876	1,004	632	478	127	28	226
Massachusetts	4,649	459	99	88	3,577	426	727	476	218	33	310
Michigan	6,165	800	188	232	4,251	694	1,077	851	116	110	352
Minnesota	2,922	268	73	69	2,139	373	626	409	147	70	217
Mississippi	2,434	98	127	12	1,989	207	334	289	11	34	152
Missouri	3,895	223	108	78	3,118	368	851	633	148	70	206
Montana	639	46	28	16	415	133	301	266	6	29	199
Nebraska	1,016	58	30	36	753	140	205	162	11	31	127
Nevada	587	50	18	13	371	135	264	186	20	58	175
New Hampshire	624	39	13	9	483	80	160	133	9	18	84
New Jersey	4,799	412	117	78	3,626	567	1,218	586	592	40	240
New Mexico	1,561	132	52	27	1,178	171	338	298	17	23	598
New York	21,668	2,443	365	599	16,729	1,533	2,514	1,272	1,097	145	964
North Carolina	5,230	347	126	91	4,155	511	999	861	53	85	287
North Dakota	447	28	21	13	308	77	213	177	6	31	111
Ohio	7,215	728	204	299	5,251	734	1,127	880	167	80	365
Oklahoma	2,266	152	76	48	1,579	412	371	298	25	49	272
Oregon	2,274	166	63	44	1,765	235	477	319	107	51	182
Pennsylvania	8,230	719	187	304	6,232	788	1,891	1,426	368	97	394
Rhode Island	924	95	19	19	712	78	219	171	35	13	65
South Carolina	2,711	100	65	42	2,245	259	430	375	22	34	184
South Dakota	483	21	25	7	342	88	251	226	5	20	148
Tennessee	4,388	223	90	40	3,692	344	596	493	36	67	349
Texas	10,022	563	352	164	7,718	1,225	2,445	1,846	441	158	610
Utah	993	86	32	25	689	161	339	220	63	56	208
Vermont	548	47	14	18	413	55	169	140	18	11	55
Virginia	2,528	161	142	65	1,787	373	929	755	91	83	275
Washington	3,456	402	96	50	2,465	444	783	522	212	49	380
West Virginia	1,570	112	41	24	1,231	162	480	386	14	80	191
Wisconsin	3,361	336	84	109	2,455	378	655	529	82	44	191
Wyoming	268	19	15	3	187	45	196	173	2	20	525
Outlying areas	865	73	306	-	277	209	196	82	81	32	677
American Samoa . .	17	-	3	-	6	8	6	-	-	6	41
Micronesia	-	-	-	-	-	-	-	-	-	-	-
Guam	33	3	2	-	13	15	18	14	1	4	83
Marshall Islands . . .	-	-	-	-	-	-	-	-	-	-	-
Northern Marianas .	12	-	1	-	5	7	9	3	-	6	22
Palau	-	-	-	-	-	-	-	-	-	-	-
Puerto Rico	768	67	293	-	246	162	145	55	79	10	454
Virgin Islands	34	3	8	-	7	17	18	11	1	6	77
Undistributed amounts	11	-	3	-	-	8	732	302	224	205	307

- Represents or rounds to zero.   [1] Includes programs not shown separately.   [2] Includes "special milk program."   [3] For Puerto Rico, amount shown is for nutritional assistance grant program, all other amounts are grant payments for food stamp administration.   [4] FEMA = Federal Emergency Management Agency.

Source: U.S. Census Bureau, *Federal Aid to States For Fiscal Year 2001*, series FAS/01.

U.S. Census Bureau, Statistical Abstract of the United States: 2002

No. 414. State and Local Government Receipts and Current Expenditures in the National Income and Product Accounts: 1980 to 2001

[In billions of dollars (316.6 represents $316,600,000,000). For explanation of national income, see text, Section 13, Income, Expenditures, and Wealth]

Item	1980	1990	1993	1994	1995	1996	1997	1998	1999	2000	2001
Receipts	316.6	663.4	823.2	873.8	917.9	960.4	1,011.3	1,074.4	1,144.8	1,223.6	1,293.3
Personal tax and nontax receipts	53.9	136.0	164.7	174.8	186.5	199.6	216.9	235.5	255.9	278.7	296.1
Income taxes	42.6	107.7	126.0	133.4	142.5	152.9	167.6	182.7	200.0	219.8	234.1
Nontaxes	5.0	15.6	23.4	25.0	27.1	29.2	31.1	33.7	35.9	38.1	40.6
Other	6.3	12.8	15.3	16.4	17.0	17.5	18.2	19.2	20.0	20.7	21.3
Corporate profits tax accruals	14.5	22.5	26.9	30.0	31.7	33.0	34.2	34.6	34.8	36.8	29.4
Indirect business tax and nontax accruals [1]	172.3	383.4	454.8	480.1	501.6	524.9	552.5	583.9	612.5	651.5	683.0
Sales taxes	82.9	183.2	216.0	230.9	243.6	255.6	269.3	284.2	300.6	321.5	336.8
Property taxes	68.8	161.1	191.1	197.6	203.5	211.4	220.3	230.3	239.5	248.4	258.3
Contributions for social insurance	3.6	10.0	14.1	14.5	13.6	12.5	10.8	10.1	10.1	10.0	10.6
Federal grants-in-aid	72.3	111.4	162.6	174.5	184.5	190.4	196.8	210.3	230.5	245.6	274.2
Current expenditures	307.8	660.8	821.7	865.2	902.5	939.0	980.3	1,033.7	1,101.7	1,189.8	1,275.8
Consumption expenditures	260.5	545.8	629.5	662.6	694.7	726.5	766.4	808.3	858.4	929.0	984.2
Transfer payments to persons	51.2	127.8	195.4	206.9	217.8	224.3	227.5	235.3	253.9	270.7	290.4
Net interest paid	-5.4	-6.3	5.6	4.4	0.5	0.9	-0.9	0.4	-0.1	-0.3	-0.8
Interest received by government	24.7	66.7	59.1	61.3	67.3	69.5	73.5	75.0	78.3	80.9	83.7
Less: Dividends received	0.1	0.2	0.2	0.2	0.3	0.3	0.3	0.4	0.4	0.4	0.4
Subsidies	0.4	0.4	0.4	0.3	0.3	0.3	0.4	0.4	0.4	0.4	12.5
Less: Current surplus of government enterprises	-1.2	6.7	8.9	8.8	10.5	12.8	12.8	10.3	10.5	9.7	10.2
Current surplus or deficit	8.8	2.6	1.5	8.6	15.3	21.4	31.0	40.7	42.1	32.8	17.6
Social insurance funds	1.3	2.0	4.2	4.6	4.0	2.7	1.1	0.6	0.3	-0.3	-0.2
Other	7.5	0.7	-2.7	4.0	11.4	18.7	29.9	40.0	41.7	33.1	17.7

[1] Includes other items not shown separately.

Source: U.S. Bureau of Economic Analysis, *National Income and Product Accounts* <http://www.bea.gov/dn/nipaweb/SelectTable.asp?Selected=N.> (accessed May 2002).

No. 415. State and Local Government Consumption Expenditures and Transfers in the National Income and Product Accounts: 1980 to 2001

[In billions of dollars (324.4 represents $324,400,000,000). For explanation of national income, see text, Section 13, Income, Expenditures, and Wealth]

Expenditure	1980	1985	1990	1995	1996	1997	1998	1999	2000	2001
Consumption expenditures and gross investment [1]	324.4	464.9	673.0	850.5	890.4	949.7	999.3	1,068.5	1,150.8	1,223.8
Consumption expenditures	260.5	380.5	545.8	694.7	726.5	766.4	808.3	858.4	929.0	984.2
Durable goods [2]	4.7	7.4	10.6	12.7	13.1	13.8	14.8	15.7	16.9	18.1
Nondurable goods	28.3	38.1	53.6	72.9	79.9	81.7	83.4	91.8	110.9	115.8
Services	227.5	335.0	481.5	609.0	633.6	670.9	710.1	750.8	801.2	850.3
Gross investment	64.0	84.4	127.2	155.8	163.8	183.3	191	210.1	221.8	239.6
Structures	55.1	67.6	98.5	117.3	122.5	139.3	142.4	157.3	165.0	183.1
Equipment	8.9	16.8	28.7	38.6	41.3	44.0	48.6	52.9	56.8	56.5
Transfers	51.2	77.3	127.8	217.8	224.3	227.5	235.3	253.9	270.7	(NA)
Benefits from social insurance funds	2.8	4.9	9.2	10.7	10.9	10.7	10.4	10.7	11.2	(NA)
Temporary disability insurance	0.8	1.4	2.2	2.1	2.0	2.0	2.1	2.2	2.3	(NA)
Public assistance	44.0	67.2	111.1	195.8	201.9	205	212.1	229.6	244.7	(NA)
Medical care	24.9	42.4	78.2	155.0	163.6	168.3	175.0	190.8	204.4	(NA)
Medicaid	23.9	39.7	73.1	149.6	158.2	163.1	170.0	185.1	198.3	(NA)
Family Assistance [3]	12.5	15.2	19.2	22.6	20.3	17.7	17.0	17.7	18.3	(NA)
Supplemental Security Income	2.0	2.3	3.8	3.8	3.6	3.7	3.9	4.2	4.4	(NA)
General assistance	1.4	2.2	2.9	3.5	3.3	3.3	3.5	3.5	3.5	(NA)
Energy assistance	1.3	2.1	1.6	1.5	1.3	1.4	1.3	1.4	1.7	(NA)
Other [4]	1.7	3.0	5.4	9.4	9.7	10.6	11.4	11.9	12.4	(NA)
Education	2.4	3.5	5.3	8.7	9.1	9.1	9.8	10.6	11.4	(NA)
Employment and training	1.7	0.9	0.9	1.1	0.9	1.0	1.1	1.0	1.1	(NA)
Other [5]	0.3	0.7	1.2	1.5	1.6	1.6	1.8	2	2.2	(NA)

NA Not available. [1] Gross government investment consists of general government and government enterprise expenditures for fixed assets; inventory investment is included in government consumption expenditures. [2] Consumption expenditures for durable goods excludes expenditures classified as investment, except for goods transferred to foreign countries by the Federal Government. [3] Consists of aid to families with dependent children. Beginning with 1996, assistance programs operating under the Personal Responsibility and work opportunity Act of 1996. [4] Consists of emergency assistance and medical insurance premium payments paid on behalf of indigents. [5] Consists largely of foster care, veterans benefits, Alaska dividends, and crime victim payments.

Source: U.S. Bureau of Economic Analysis, *National Income and Product Accounts* <http://www.bea.gov/dn/nipaweb/SelectTable.asp?Selected=N.> (accessed May 2002).

No. 416. State and Local Governments—Summary of Finances: 1980 to 1999

[In millions of dollars (451,537 represents $451,537,000,000), except as indicated. For fiscal year ending in year shown; see text, this section. Local government amounts are estimates subject to sampling variation; see Appendix III and source]

Item	Total (mil. dol.)				Per capita [1] (dol.)			
	1980	1990	1998	1999	1980	1990	1998	1999
Revenue [2]	451,537	1,032,115	1,720,889	1,794,557	1,993	4,150	6,368	6,581
From federal government	83,029	136,802	255,048	270,628	367	550	944	992
Public welfare	24,921	59,961	128,470	136,571	110	241	475	501
Highways	8,980	14,368	20,241	21,492	40	58	75	79
Education	14,435	23,233	38,922	42,051	64	93	144	154
Health and hospitals	2,513	5,904	13,856	14,516	11	24	51	53
Housing and community development .	3,905	9,655	18,239	18,044	17	39	67	66
Other and unallocable	28,275	23,683	35,319	37,954	125	95	131	139
From state and local sources	368,509	895,313	1,465,841	1,523,929	1,627	3,600	5,424	5,588
General, net intergovernmental.	299,293	712,700	1,110,714	1,163,836	1,321	2,865	4,110	4,268
Taxes	223,463	501,619	773,963	815,777	986	2,017	2,864	2,992
Property	68,499	155,613	230,150	240,107	302	626	852	881
Sales and gross receipts	79,927	177,885	274,883	290,993	353	715	1,017	1,067
Individual income	42,080	105,640	175,630	189,309	186	425	650	694
Corporation income	13,321	23,566	34,412	33,922	59	95	127	124
Other	19,636	38,915	58,888	61,446	87	156	218	225
Charges and miscellaneous	75,830	211,081	336,751	348,060	335	849	1,246	1,276
Utility and liquor stores	25,560	58,642	81,127	86,125	113	236	300	316
Water supply system	6,766	17,674	27,473	29,039	30	71	102	106
Electric power system	11,387	29,268	37,812	40,890	50	118	140	150
Transit system	2,397	5,216	7,546	7,708	11	21	28	28
Gas supply system	1,809	3,043	4,188	4,244	8	12	15	16
Liquor stores . . . . [3]	3,201	3,441	4,107	4,245	14	14	15	16
Insurance trust revenue [3]	43,656	123,970	274,001	273,968	193	498	1,014	1,005
Employee retirement	25,441	94,268	237,472	236,527	112	379	879	867
Unemployment compensation	13,529	18,441	23,153	22,234	60	74	86	82
Direct expenditure.	432,328	972,662	1,525,762	1,622,103	1,908	3,911	5,646	5,949
By function:								
Direct general expenditure [3]	367,340	834,786	1,314,496	1,398,533	1,622	3,356	4,864	5,129
Education [3]	133,211	288,148	450,365	483,259	588	1,159	1,666	1,772
Elementary and secondary	92,930	202,009	318,065	339,871	410	812	1,177	1,246
Higher education	33,919	73,418	112,874	122,716	150	295	418	450
Highways	33,311	61,057	87,214	93,018	147	245	323	341
Public welfare	45,552	110,518	204,640	215,190	201	444	757	789
Health	8,387	24,223	44,391	47,628	37	97	164	175
Hospitals	23,787	50,412	69,633	71,733	105	203	258	263
Police protection	13,494	30,577	50,475	53,367	60	123	187	196
Fire protection	5,718	13,186	20,269	21,262	25	53	75	78
Correction	6,448	24,635	42,479	45,598	28	100	157	167
Natural resources	5,509	12,330	17,492	18,232	24	50	65	67
Sanitation and sewerage	13,214	28,453	41,765	43,047	58	114	155	158
Housing and community development	6,062	15,479	24,697	25,234	27	62	91	93
Parks and recreation	6,520	14,326	22,365	23,417	29	58	83	86
Financial administration	6,719	16,217	25,914	27,593	30	65	96	101
Interest on general debt [4]	14,747	49,739	64,554	67,294	65	200	239	247
Utility and liquor stores [4]	36,191	77,801	102,865	108,398	160	313	381	398
Water supply system	9,228	22,101	32,069	34,089	41	89	119	125
Electric power system	15,016	30,997	35,264	38,132	66	125	130	140
Gas supply system	1,715	2,989	4,645	4,108	8	12	17	15
Transit system	7,641	18,788	27,542	28,522	34	76	102	105
Liquor stores	2,591	2,926	3,346	3,547	11	12	12	13
Insurance trust expenditure [3]	28,797	63,321	108,400	115,172	127	255	401	422
Employee retirement	14,008	38,355	80,222	85,318	56	154	297	313
Unemployment compensation	12,070	16,499	17,779	19,223	53	66	66	70
By character and object:								
Current operation	307,811	700,131	1,129,257	1,199,494	1,359	2,815	4,179	4,399
Capital outlay	62,894	123,069	181,871	198,483	278	495	673	728
Construction	51,492	89,114	135,546	147,181	227	358	502	540
Equipment, land, and existing structures	11,402	33,955	46,326	51,302	50	137	171	188
Assistance and subsidies	15,222	27,227	31,636	31,494	67	109	117	115
Interest on debt (general and utility) . .	17,604	58,914	74,597	77,459	78	237	276	284
Insurance benefits and repayments . . .	28,797	63,321	108,400	115,172	127	255	401	422
Expenditure for salaries and wages [5] . . .	163,896	341,158	495,139	522,528	723	1,372	1,832	1,916
Debt outstanding, year end	335,603	860,584	1,283,560	1,369,253	1,481	3,460	4,750	5,021
Long-term	322,456	841,278	1,266,308	1,351,408	1,423	3,382	4,686	4,956
Short-term	13,147	19,306	17,252	17,844	58	78	64	65
Long-term debt:								
Issued	42,364	108,468	204,351	229,374	187	436	756	841
Retired	17,404	64,831	144,636	153,100	77	261	535	561

[1] 1980 and 1990 based on enumerated resident population as of April 1. Other years based on estimated resident population as of July 1; see Table 2.   [2] Aggregates exclude duplicative transactions between state and local governments; see source.   [3] Includes amounts not shown separately.   [4] Interest on utility debt included in "utility expenditure." For total interest on debt, see "Interest on debt (general and utility)."   [5] Included in items shown above.

Source: U.S. Census Bureau, 1980-90, *Government Finances*, GF, No. 5, annual; thereafter, <http://www.census.gov/govs/www/estimate.html> (accessed 15 April 2002).

No. 417. State and Local Governments—Revenue and Expenditures by Function: 1999

[In millions of dollars (1,794,557 represents $1,794,557,000,000) except as indicated. For fiscal year ending in year shown; see text, this section. Local government amounts are estimates subject to sampling variation; see Appendix III and source]

Item	Amount (mil. dol.) State and local	State	Local	Per capita [1] (dol.) State and local	State	Local
Revenue [2]	1,794,557	1,152,870	952,330	6,581	4,236	3,492
Intergovernmental revenue	270,628	253,692	327,579	992	932	1,201
Total revenue from own sources	1,523,929	899,178	624,751	5,588	3,304	2,291
General revenue from own sources	1,163,836	652,384	511,452	4,268	2,397	1,876
Taxes [3]	815,777	499,943	315,833	2,992	1,837	1,158
Property	240,107	11,654	228,453	881	43	838
Individual income	189,309	172,764	16,545	694	635	61
Corporation income	33,922	30,766	3,157	124	113	12
Sales and gross receipts	290,993	239,367	51,626	1,067	879	189
General	200,627	164,378	36,249	736	604	133
Selective [3]	90,366	74,989	15,377	331	276	56
Motor fuel	30,094	29,169	925	110	107	3
Alcoholic beverages	4,191	3,900	292	15	14	1
Tobacco products	8,375	8,170	205	31	30	1
Public utilities	17,170	8,889	8,281	63	33	30
Motor vehicle and operators' licenses	16,632	15,372	1,260	61	56	5
Death and gift	7,519	7,493	26	28	28	-
Charges and miscellaneous [3]	348,060	152,441	195,619	1,276	560	717
Current charges [3]	210,885	79,308	131,577	773	291	483
Education [3]	60,406	45,471	14,935	222	167	55
School lunch sales	5,073	16	5,057	19	-	19
Higher education	50,666	44,925	5,741	186	165	21
Natural resources	2,901	1,791	1,109	11	7	4
Hospitals	51,610	17,044	34,567	189	63	127
Sewerage	23,672	28	23,645	87	-	87
Solid waste management	9,962	368	9,594	37	1	35
Parks and recreation	5,958	1,078	4,880	22	4	18
Housing and community development	4,026	434	3,593	15	2	13
Airports	10,217	745	9,472	37	3	35
Sea and inland port facilities	2,355	651	1,704	9	2	6
Highways	6,804	4,319	2,485	25	16	9
Interest earnings	65,890	32,064	33,826	242	118	124
Special assessments	3,628	78	3,549	13	-	13
Sale of property	1,558	391	1,167	6	1	4
Utility and liquor store revenue	86,125	7,956	78,169	316	29	287
Insurance trust revenue	273,968	238,838	35,130	1,005	878	129
Expenditure	1,625,939	998,365	938,641	5,963	3,668	3,442
Intergovernmental expenditure	3,836	304,933	9,970	14	1,120	37
Direct expenditure	1,622,103	693,432	928,671	5,949	2,548	3,406
General expenditure [3]	1,398,533	584,542	813,991	5,129	2,148	2,985
Education [3]	483,259	126,185	357,075	1,772	464	1,309
Elementary and secondary education	339,871	2,925	336,946	1,246	11	1,236
Higher education	122,716	102,588	20,129	450	377	74
Public welfare	215,190	182,238	32,952	789	670	121
Hospitals	71,733	29,535	42,199	263	109	155
Health	47,628	24,857	22,771	175	91	84
Highways	93,018	56,242	36,776	341	207	135
Police protection	53,367	7,810	45,557	196	29	167
Fire protection	21,262	-	21,262	78	-	78
Corrections	45,598	30,770	14,828	167	113	54
Natural resources	18,232	13,601	4,631	67	50	17
Sewerage	26,980	1,128	25,852	99	4	95
Solid waste management	16,067	1,958	14,110	59	7	52
Housing and community development	25,234	2,385	22,848	93	9	84
Governmental administration	76,699	32,558	44,141	281	120	162
Parks and recreation	23,417	3,843	19,574	86	14	72
Interest on general debt	67,294	27,785	39,508	247	102	145
Utility	104,851	8,779	96,072	385	32	352
Liquor store expenditure	3,547	2,967	579	13	11	2
Insurance trust expenditure	115,172	97,144	18,028	422	357	66
By character and object:						
Current operation	1,199,494	476,968	722,526	4,399	1,752	2,650
Capital outlay	198,483	68,509	129,974	728	252	477
Construction	147,181	53,857	93,324	540	198	342
Equip., land, and existing structures	51,302	14,652	36,650	188	54	134
Assistance and subsidies	31,494	22,229	9,266	115	82	34
Interest on debt (general and utility)	77,459	28,582	48,877	284	105	179
Insurance benefits and repayments	115,172	97,144	18,028	422	357	66
Expenditure for salaries and wages [4]	522,528	148,236	374,292	1,916	545	1,373

- Represents or rounds to zero. [1] Based on estimated resident population as of July 1. See Table 2. [2] Aggregates exclude duplicative transactions between levels of government; see source. [3] Includes amounts not shown separately. [4] Included in items shown above.

Source: U.S. Census Bureau, *Governmental Finances, 1998-99*, at Internet site <http://www.census.gov/govs/estimate/99allpub.pdf> (released September 2001).

No. 418. State and Local Governments—Capital Outlays: 1985 to 1999

[In millions of dollars (79,898 represents $79,898,000,000), except percent. For fiscal year ending in year shown; see text, this section. Local government amounts are subject to sampling variation; see Appendix III and source]

Level and function	1985	1990	1994	1995	1996	1997	1998	1999
State & local governments: Total . . .	79,898	123,102	137,501	151,440	158,911	171,414	181,871	198,483
Annual percent change [1]	13.1	4.9	0.5	1.2	10.1	4.9	6.1	9.1
Direct expenditure	656,188	972,695	1,260,642	1,347,763	1,393,714	1,456,698	1,525,762	1,622,103
Percent of direct expenditure	12.2	12.7	10.9	11.2	11.4	11.8	11.9	12.2
By function: Education [2]	13,477	25,997	29,012	35,708	40,302	44,077	49,332	54,418
Higher education	4,629	18,057	19,693	24,808	28,868	32,210	36,198	40,768
Elementary and secondary. . . .	8,358	7,441	8,959	10,461	11,006	11,279	12,590	13,114
Highways	23,900	33,867	39,503	42,561	43,453	44,962	48,067	51,906
Health and hospitals	2,709	3,848	5,157	4,883	5,166	5,065	5,692	5,699
Natural resources	1,736	2,545	2,349	2,891	3,042	3,041	3,206	3,359
Housing [3]	3,217	3,997	4,066	4,527	4,704	5,490	5,544	5,615
Air transportation	1,875	3,434	5,170	3,802	3,814	4,877	5,004	6,666
Water transportation [4]	717	924	1,483	1,101	1,246	1,376	1,252	1,487
Sewerage	5,926	8,356	7,989	8,894	9,326	9,589	9,061	9,718
Parks and recreation	2,196	3,877	3,919	4,085	4,869	5,577	6,154	6,486
Utilities	13,435	16,601	18,180	19,028	18,755	20,107	20,357	21,861
Water	4,160	6,873	6,893	7,466	7,381	8,721	8,644	10,325
Electric	5,247	3,976	4,030	3,715	3,522	3,459	3,026	3,613
Transit	3,830	310	290	340	318	399	986	389
Gas	198	5,443	6,966	7,507	7,533	7,528	7,701	7,533
Other	10,711	19,657	20,673	23,961	24,233	27,254	28,202	31,268
State governments: Total.	30,657	45,524	52,895	57,829	58,927	59,599	64,441	68,509
Annual percent change [1]	16.3	5.6	0.1	5.5	9.3	1.9	8.1	6.3
Direct expenditure	269,171	397,291	550,276	596,325	607,594	629,049	651,098	693,432
Percent of direct expenditure	11.4	11.5	9.6	9.7	9.7	9.5	9.9	9.9
By function: Education [2]	4,711	7,253	8,594	10,042	10,445	10,915	11,970	12,294
Highways	17,827	24,850	29,995	31,687	32,198	32,726	35,008	37,986
Health and hospitals	1,038	1,531	2,375	2,402	2,375	2,253	2,274	2,276
Natural resources	1,076	1,593	1,702	1,956	2,044	2,058	2,199	2,349
Housing [3]	38	119	193	187	263	225	202	202
Air transportation	280	339	389	356	356	446	339	536
Water transportation [4]	274	202	297	223	305	269	305	270
Sewerage	187	333	774	853	913	474	639	627
Parks and recreation	351	601	692	650	706	938	1,293	1,023
Utilities	1,825	2,605	2,124	2,226	2,607	2,361	2,758	3,034
Other	3,051	6,098	5,760	7,246	6,716	6,934	7,454	7,912
Local governments: Total	49,241	77,578	84,606	93,611	99,984	111,814	117,430	129,974
Annual percent change [1]	16.2	4.5	-1.3	10.6	6.8	11.8	5.0	10.7
Direct expenditure	386,753	575,404	710,366	751,438	786,120	827,648	874,664	928,671
Percent of direct expenditure	12.7	13.5	11.9	12.5	12.7	13.5	13.4	14.0
By function: Education [2]	8,766	18,744	20,418	25,667	29,858	33,162	37,362	42,124
Highways	6,073	9,017	9,508	10,874	11,255	12,235	13,059	13,920
Health and hospitals	1,671	2,316	2,782	2,481	2,790	2,811	3,418	3,423
Natural resources	660	952	647	935	998	983	1,007	1,010
Housing [3]	3,179	3,878	3,872	4,340	4,441	5,265	5,342	5,413
Air transportation	1,595	3,095	4,781	3,446	3,458	4,431	4,665	6,129
Water transportation [4]	443	722	1,185	877	941	1,107	947	1,217
Sewerage	5,738	8,023	7,215	8,040	8,413	9,116	8,422	9,091
Parks and recreation	1,845	3,276	3,228	3,435	4,163	4,639	4,861	5,463
Utilities	11,610	13,996	16,056	16,801	16,149	17,746	17,599	18,827
Other	7,660	13,559	14,913	16,715	17,518	20,320	20,748	23,356

[1] Change from prior year shown. [2] Includes other education. [3] Includes community development. [4] Includes terminals.
Source: U.S. Census Bureau, 1980-90 *Historical Statistics on Governmental Finances and Employment*; and *Government Finances*, Series GF, No. 5, annual; thereafter, <http://www.census.gov/govs/www/index.html> (accessed 22 April 2002).

No. 419. State and Local Governments—Expenditure for Public Works: 1990 to 1999

[In millions of dollars (138,851 represents $138,851,000,000) Public works include expenditures on highways, airports, water transport terminals, and sewerage, solid waste management, water supply, and mass transit systems. Represents direct expenditures excluding intergovernmental grants]

Item	Total	Highways	Airport transpor-tation	Water transport and terminals	Sewer-age	Solid waste manage-ment	Water supply	Mass transit
1990, total	161,359	68,370	9,290	2,168	22,785	12,829	24,621	21,290
State	50,206	42,056	915	572	1,097	1,304	188	4,074
Local	111,153	26,314	8,375	1,596	21,688	11,525	24,433	17,222
Capital expenditures (percent) .	41.4	54.1	58.3	45.9	45.0	11.4	26.4	24.7
1995, total	180,148	77,109	8,397	2,309	23,583	14,990	28,041	25,719
State	56,392	46,893	783	604	1,462	1,658	178	4,814
Local	123,756	30,216	7,614	1,706	22,121	13,331	27,863	20,904
Capital expenditures (percent) .	41	55	45	48	38	13	27	29
1998, total	201,833	87,214	10,459	2,785	25,647	16,118	32,069	27,542
State	62,556	51,971	810	830	1,132	1,988	172	5,653
Local	139,277	35,243	9,649	1,955	24,515	14,130	31,897	21,889
Capital expenditures (percent) .	40	55	48	45	35	11	27	28
1999, total	214,378	93,018	12,632	3,070	26,980	16,067	34,089	28,522
State	67,392	56,242	1,013	798	1,128	1,958	164	6,089
Local	146,986	36,776	11,619	2,273	25,852	14,110	33,924	22,433
Capital expenditures (percent) .	41.5	55.8	52.8	48.4	36.0	8.5	30.3	26.4

Source: U.S. Census Bureau, 1990-92, *Government Finances*, Series GF, No. 5, annual; thereafter, <http://www.census.gov/govs/www/index.html> (accessed 22 April 2002), *State and Local Government Finance Estimates by State*, annual, and unpublished data.

State and Local Government Finances and Employment 271

No. 420. State and Local Governments—Revenue by State: 1999

[In millions of dollars (1,794,557 represents $1,794,557,000,000). For fiscal year ending in year shown; see text, this section]

State					General revenue						
			Intergovernmental from Federal Government	General revenue own sources			Taxes				
	Total revenue [1]	Total			Total [1]	Property	Sales and gross receipts	Individual income	Motor vehicle	Other taxes
United States .	1,794,557	1,434,464	270,628	1,163,836	815,777	240,107	290,993	223,231	15,342	46,104
Alabama	23,621	19,322	4,651	14,671	8,770	1,192	4,386	2,278	205	710
Alaska	9,225	7,612	1,379	6,232	1,762	728	285	212	44	494
Arizona	25,714	20,958	3,952	17,005	12,238	3,584	5,471	2,644	144	395
Arkansas	13,867	11,376	2,593	8,783	6,077	1,402	2,729	1,646	107	193
California	242,469	185,731	35,955	149,776	104,977	25,425	36,268	36,192	1,663	5,430
Colorado	25,413	21,137	3,324	17,813	12,117	3,414	4,383	3,656	197	467
Connecticut	23,796	21,505	3,451	18,054	14,889	5,175	4,822	4,085	225	582
Delaware	5,526	4,872	784	4,088	2,472	349	277	1,046	30	769
District of Columbia .	6,131	5,452	1,707	3,745	2,974	680	934	1,170	18	172
Florida	88,422	72,658	10,692	61,966	40,245	13,901	20,855	1,267	910	3,311
Georgia	46,265	36,878	6,460	30,418	21,503	5,423	8,745	6,490	218	628
Hawaii	8,094	6,879	1,386	5,493	3,914	595	2,004	1,121	106	87
Idaho	6,868	5,715	1,030	4,684	3,039	816	1,021	943	108	152
Illinois	73,603	60,334	10,079	50,254	37,970	14,100	12,366	9,351	893	1,259
Indiana	30,890	27,802	4,624	23,178	15,576	5,177	4,745	5,204	142	308
Iowa	17,270	14,314	2,597	11,716	7,673	2,533	2,560	1,989	325	266
Kansas	14,141	12,343	1,969	10,374	7,292	2,115	2,824	1,950	147	257
Kentucky	22,769	18,377	4,179	14,198	9,761	1,666	3,568	3,533	212	782
Louisiana	25,698	21,639	4,856	16,784	10,533	1,620	5,965	1,822	107	1,019
Maine	8,096	6,968	1,533	5,435	4,082	1,547	1,163	1,167	82	123
Maryland	31,268	26,329	4,296	22,033	16,559	4,144	4,275	6,968	178	994
Massachusetts	41,425	35,965	5,965	30,000	22,269	7,301	4,841	9,286	234	608
Michigan	66,078	52,377	9,347	43,031	29,905	8,811	9,351	9,890	772	1,082
Minnesota	36,637	28,846	4,496	24,350	17,188	4,459	5,415	6,085	597	632
Mississippi	14,973	12,720	3,135	9,585	6,087	1,390	3,080	1,213	109	295
Missouri	29,960	24,687	5,117	19,569	14,028	3,305	5,602	4,132	264	724
Montana	5,134	4,458	1,253	3,205	2,041	891	308	573	64	206
Nebraska	10,947	8,304	1,549	6,756	4,624	1,567	1,478	1,207	94	278
Nevada	11,721	8,728	1,149	7,579	5,291	1,261	3,335	-	111	583
New Hampshire . . .	6,454	5,472	1,033	4,438	3,110	2,014	517	319	61	199
New Jersey	59,121	48,996	7,377	41,619	31,576	14,336	8,014	7,688	364	1,174
New Mexico	11,238	9,334	2,271	7,063	4,469	588	2,376	974	133	399
New York	172,301	137,114	28,448	108,665	82,154	24,759	21,274	31,872	702	3,546
North Carolina	49,073	37,545	7,687	29,858	20,266	4,351	7,041	7,507	425	942
North Dakota	4,091	3,619	1,018	2,601	1,668	497	694	276	40	162
Ohio	75,103	54,974	10,183	44,790	32,301	9,334	9,936	11,040	685	1,306
Oklahoma	17,440	14,450	2,935	11,515	7,768	1,238	3,107	2,258	580	586
Oregon	23,040	18,511	4,207	14,304	8,536	2,558	839	4,034	341	765
Pennsylvania	74,569	60,656	11,857	48,799	35,193	9,659	10,423	10,384	736	3,991
Rhode Island	7,203	5,550	1,325	4,225	3,197	1,285	925	829	53	105
South Carolina	21,640	18,400	3,870	14,530	9,067	2,476	3,279	2,556	113	643
South Dakota	4,224	3,348	871	2,476	1,653	617	786	51	49	150
Tennessee	31,368	23,364	5,914	17,450	11,748	2,684	7,127	732	297	909
Texas	117,493	90,327	17,684	72,643	49,232	18,805	25,023	-	1,137	4,267
Utah	13,292	10,443	2,091	8,353	5,469	1,192	2,332	1,641	78	226
Vermont	3,759	3,279	829	2,450	1,784	766	448	433	34	104
Virginia	39,931	32,804	4,501	28,303	19,558	5,758	5,672	6,502	400	1,226
Washington	43,831	31,563	5,302	26,260	18,118	5,763	10,697	-	393	1,264
West Virginia	10,154	8,541	2,179	6,362	4,279	812	1,802	1,183	82	400
Wisconsin	38,789	28,445	4,618	23,827	17,418	5,525	5,098	5,833	277	685
Wyoming	4,422	3,445	919	2,526	1,357	523	526	-	56	252

See footnotes at end of table.

U.S. Census Bureau, Statistical Abstract of the United States: 2002

[In millions of dollars (348,060 represents $348,060,000,000). For fiscal year ending in year shown; see text, this section]

State	General revenue								Utility and liquor stores	Insurance trust revenue
	Current charges and miscellaneous revenue									
	Current charges					Miscellaneous revenue				
	Total	Total [1]	Education	Hospitals	Sewerage	Total [1]	Interest earnings	Special assessment		
United States	348,060	210,885	60,406	51,610	23,672	137,174	65,890	3,628	86,125	273,968
Alabama	5,900	4,248	1,189	2,175	218	1,653	848	11	1,876	2,422
Alaska	4,471	718	131	57	43	3,753	1,855	4	220	1,392
Arizona	4,767	2,474	996	206	307	2,293	1,111	70	2,530	2,226
Arkansas	2,706	1,792	539	732	152	914	477	8	543	1,949
California	44,799	28,619	5,790	5,555	3,078	16,179	8,010	934	13,021	43,717
Colorado	5,696	3,640	1,357	446	413	2,056	1,052	42	1,373	2,903
Connecticut	3,165	1,553	519	297	169	1,612	706	33	470	1,821
Delaware	1,617	768	315	38	105	849	336	-	150	503
District of Columbia . . .	771	384	20	118	107	388	169	-	438	242
Florida	21,721	12,386	2,327	2,790	1,381	9,334	3,814	887	4,904	10,860
Georgia	8,915	5,693	1,245	2,211	568	3,223	1,365	19	2,676	6,710
Hawaii	1,579	1,060	215	160	139	519	333	14	182	1,032
Idaho	1,645	1,078	245	375	84	567	312	15	182	971
Illinois	12,284	6,607	2,319	705	709	5,677	3,232	90	2,593	10,677
Indiana	7,602	4,897	2,117	1,544	453	2,705	1,257	22	1,606	1,482
Iowa	4,043	2,792	1,062	1,106	225	1,251	523	15	616	2,340
Kansas	3,082	1,915	681	487	168	1,166	659	69	593	1,205
Kentucky	4,438	2,372	921	458	240	2,066	1,395	4	1,078	3,314
Louisiana	6,250	4,164	939	2,218	194	2,087	1,090	7	734	3,324
Maine	1,353	686	230	52	112	667	266	2	169	958
Maryland	5,475	3,178	1,376	75	519	2,297	952	104	641	4,297
Massachusetts	7,731	3,333	1,077	202	604	4,397	1,677	77	1,948	3,513
Michigan	13,126	8,152	3,300	1,457	1,231	4,974	2,103	85	1,898	11,802
Minnesota	7,162	3,790	1,170	000	408	3,373	1,526	266	1,304	6,486
Mississippi	3,498	2,536	598	1,459	126	962	474	4	681	1,573
Missouri	5,542	3,480	1,278	932	406	2,062	1,211	15	1,141	4,132
Montana	1,163	612	273	48	44	551	359	43	106	569
Nebraska	2,132	1,277	519	332	100	855	414	35	2,001	641
Nevada	2,288	1,542	294	429	201	746	485	35	462	2,531
New Hampshire	1,328	725	330	3	76	603	393	3	332	650
New Jersey	10,043	5,684	1,606	474	939	4,359	1,745	15	1,155	8,971
New Mexico	2,594	1,262	399	456	100	1,332	748	16	308	1,596
New York	26,511	16,118	2,263	4,648	1,253	10,394	4,610	104	7,331	27,857
North Carolina	9,592	7,028	1,763	2,955	808	2,563	1,570	12	2,744	8,784
North Dakota	933	584	246	-	25	349	168	32	77	396
Ohio	12,489	7,747	3,198	1,344	1,289	4,742	2,069	86	2,280	17,850
Oklahoma	3,747	2,671	1,000	779	190	1,076	471	5	951	2,039
Oregon	5,768	3,223	936	654	436	2,545	984	47	962	3,567
Pennsylvania	13,606	8,243	2,832	1,301	1,283	5,363	2,964	51	2,589	1,324
Rhode Island	1,028	464	221	4	57	564	307	3	105	547
South Carolina	5,463	4,096	940	2,134	194	1,367	836	21	1,823	1,417
South Dakota	823	414	160	36	41	408	223	6	146	730
Tennessee	5,702	4,421	1,067	1,848	447	1,280	683	8	5,143	2,060
Texas	23,411	13,343	4,167	3,547	1,748	10,068	4,619	61	6,297	20,869
Utah	2,884	1,831	711	366	143	1,052	488	6	1,258	1,591
Vermont	666	395	258	1	33	271	150	1	174	306
Virginia	8,746	5,453	1,794	1,266	640	3,293	1,609	21	1,384	5,743
Washington	8,142	5,555	1,511	1,179	802	2,587	1,235	74	3,776	8,493
West Virginia	2,083	1,220	398	285	117	864	428	2	186	1,427
Wisconsin	6,409	4,055	1,441	551	511	2,354	1,167	104	832	9,513
Wyoming	1,169	606	118	316	38	563	410	39	136	842

- Represents or rounds to zero.   [1] Includes items not shown separately.

Source: U.S Census Bureau; <http://www.census.gov/govs/www/estimate/9900us.html> (accessed 22 April 2002).

State and Local Government Finances and Employment 273

No. 421. State and Local Governments—Expenditures and Debt by State: 1999

[In millions of dollars (1,625,939 represents $1,625,939,000,000), except as indicated. For fiscal year ending in year shown; see text, this section]

State	Total expendi-ture [1]	Total Amount	Per capita [2] (dol.)	Direct general expendi-tures, total	Educa-tion	Public welfare	Health and hospi-tals	High-ways	Police protec-tion	Fire protec-tion	Correc-tions
United States..	**1,625,939**	**1,402,369**	**5,963**	**1,398,533**	**483,259**	**215,190**	**119,361**	**93,018**	**53,367**	**21,262**	**45,598**
Alabama	23,378	20,119	5,350	20,119	7,174	3,231	3,234	1,248	646	241	408
Alaska.	8,085	7,238	13,041	7,131	1,743	689	250	748	178	63	155
Arizona	24,062	20,302	5,036	20,302	7,402	1,885	987	1,738	1,035	386	850
Arkansas.	11,752	10,664	4,607	10,662	3,985	1,904	1,080	860	337	111	281
California.	217,970	183,165	6,576	180,875	56,688	27,133	16,764	7,383	8,131	3,398	6,531
Colorado	23,503	20,072	5,795	20,068	7,242	2,576	998	1,765	778	303	788
Connecticut	22,262	19,688	6,783	19,688	6,201	2,930	1,547	1,107	659	377	523
Delaware.	4,889	4,484	6,484	4,483	1,611	503	260	388	152	17	202
District of Columbia.	6,273	4,630	12,087	4,630	777	1,247	510	101	313	104	293
Florida.	80,663	71,631	5,338	71,631	21,321	8,848	6,600	5,055	3,583	1,436	3,116
Georgia	41,057	35,831	5,272	35,831	13,833	4,921	3,669	2,477	1,183	484	1,286
Hawaii.	7,789	6,903	6,573	6,889	1,778	956	548	403	221	90	134
Idaho	6,195	5,612	4,948	5,612	2,024	721	545	525	193	73	206
Illinois	69,283	59,729	5,713	59,727	21,190	8,657	4,176	3,814	2,787	1,049	1,531
Indiana	29,540	26,663	4,971	26,642	10,689	3,894	2,482	1,827	757	388	661
Iowa	16,138	14,722	5,625	14,687	5,692	2,078	1,619	1,607	397	139	282
Kansas	13,366	12,066	5,036	12,066	4,770	1,296	1,005	1,339	429	164	315
Kentucky	20,421	18,062	5,155	18,062	5,980	3,595	1,096	1,581	443	194	501
Louisiana.	23,810	21,118	5,446	21,118	6,870	2,982	3,078	1,548	820	271	676
Maine	6,963	6,397	5,557	6,388	2,068	1,422	393	512	156	75	107
Maryland	27,941	24,876	5,402	24,876	9,169	3,675	1,206	1,471	1,013	448	911
Massachusetts . . .	40,986	35,177	6,637	35,000	10,456	5,843	2,186	2,720	1,389	754	808
Michigan	57,058	50,616	5,784	50,558	21,213	6,452	4,235	3,043	1,713	584	1,826
Minnesota	31,874	28,160	6,674	28,160	9,755	5,501	1,725	2,223	821	241	549
Mississippi	14,299	12,940	5,164	12,940	4,420	2,041	1,929	1,142	394	147	285
Missouri.	26,585	23,881	4,862	23,881	8,559	3,809	2,102	1,923	861	462	640
Montana	4,739	4,293	5,367	4,293	1,603	511	299	481	121	40	121
Nebraska.	9,983	7,726	5,992	7,716	3,124	1,130	543	802	220	123	173
Nevada	10,848	9,302	5,997	9,296	2,939	852	675	959	463	186	406
New Hampshire . .	5,890	5,329	4,904	5,329	1,848	986	156	458	175	95	108
New Jersey	51,265	44,389	6,296	44,326	16,874	5,701	2,072	2,391	1,984	603	1,413
New Mexico	10,578	9,466	6,079	9,466	3,331	1,382	846	1,132	353	118	293
New York.	160,937	134,390	8,844	133,769	37,769	28,053	11,018	6,556	5,549	2,058	4,254
North Carolina . . .	42,198	36,769	5,515	36,769	12,953	5,691	5,298	2,512	1,251	422	1,106
North Dakota	3,783	3,487	5,967	3,487	1,194	622	52	413	66	32	48
Ohio	63,475	53,155	5,639	53,150	19,161	8,848	4,472	3,555	2,036	944	1,695
Oklahoma	15,682	13,596	4,670	13,555	5,493	1,739	1,261	1,123	414	237	445
Oregon	21,911	18,301	6,608	18,301	6,211	2,771	1,453	1,240	630	319	700
Pennsylvania	70,689	61,379	5,894	61,226	22,234	11,311	3,611	3,782	2,102	428	2,133
Rhode Island	6,137	5,305	6,192	5,281	1,774	1,042	242	298	188	141	141
South Carolina . . .	21,159	18,232	5,445	18,232	6,551	3,131	2,826	1,034	590	187	562
South Dakota	3,552	3,245	4,846	3,245	1,139	446	152	473	87	29	78
Tennessee	30,641	24,172	5,587	24,172	8,016	4,324	2,953	1,689	859	378	581
Texas	100,327	87,375	5,005	87,375	35,323	11,260	8,198	5,855	3,096	1,209	3,736
Utah	12,370	10,440	5,807	10,440	4,063	1,349	722	875	360	117	354
Vermont	3,352	3,040	5,643	3,030	1,233	550	61	316	62	23	39
Virginia	35,499	32,299	5,165	32,299	11,790	4,046	2,432	2,710	1,109	509	1,159
Washington	40,177	32,337	6,980	32,334	11,045	4,609	3,221	2,197	955	555	1,016
West Virginia	9,389	8,227	5,196	8,227	3,024	1,669	517	837	158	54	154
Wisconsin	31,673	28,216	6,033	28,043	10,892	4,128	1,609	2,387	1,055	427	927
Wyoming	3,542	3,153	7,379	3,152	1,068	251	448	397	93	26	95

See footnotes at end of table.

U.S. Census Bureau, Statistical Abstract of the United States: 2002

[See page 274]

State	General expenditure							Utility and liquor store expenditures	Employee retirement expenditures	Debt outstanding
	Environment and housing									
	Sewerage	Solid waste management	Parks and recreation	Housing [3]	Governmental administration	Interest on general debt	Other general expenditure			
United States	26,980	16,067	23,417	25,234	76,699	67,294	131,788	108,398	85,318	1,369,253
Alabama	434	204	252	322	857	640	1,227	1,919	1,149	14,250
Alaska.	72	52	74	139	483	395	2,090	294	434	7,434
Arizona	451	249	460	265	1,423	908	2,261	2,551	909	22,913
Arkansas	131	123	134	111	509	347	751	503	401	6,937
California	3,944	2,178	3,044	4,756	12,292	7,654	20,979	17,506	12,127	168,344
Colorado	348	96	608	326	1,075	1,101	2,063	1,796	1,315	22,059
Connecticut	232	316	194	433	1,275	1,291	2,603	674	1,421	22,238
Delaware.	90	52	68	89	371	302	378	154	190	4,916
District of Columbia . . .	125	42	154	60	388	254	263	1,148	432	4,939
Florida.	1,407	1,444	1,435	1,142	4,288	3,929	8,027	5,936	2,333	75,706
Georgia	717	476	502	516	1,985	1,090	2,693	3,356	1,615	26,273
Hawaii.	116	103	171	160	440	596	1,171	271	479	7,651
Idaho	107	82	79	30	379	173	474	171	223	3,144
Illinois	1,031	400	1,923	1,497	3,152	3,496	5,024	4,004	4,445	62,897
Indiana	538	187	506	363	1,311	900	2,137	1,607	1,049	18,464
Iowa	269	133	226	103	702	313	1,127	695	556	7,156
Kansas	153	97	165	97	704	437	1,096	579	583	9,737
Kentucky	273	141	210	160	865	1,375	1,646	897	1,001	22,516
Louisiana.	276	255	436	254	1,118	933	1,602	914	1,612	17,316
Maine	107	95	57	84	339	263	709	138	345	5,585
Maryland	516	411	644	595	1,465	1,121	2,231	992	1,533	23,852
Massachusetts	1,031	364	318	1,150	1,647	2,284	4,050	2,776	2,215	50,319
Michigan	1,471	396	657	298	2,448	2,230	3,992	2,171	3,272	44,095
Minnesota	499	266	635	577	1,586	1,469	2,314	1,489	1,790	26,864
Mississippi	121	98	124	106	609	450	1,076	630	624	8,577
Missouri.	386	95	365	295	1,283	934	2,167	1,287	1,124	17,605
Montana	39	47	42	60	292	226	411	101	234	3,561
Nebraska.	118	67	119	89	358	212	639	1,957	253	6,290
Nevada	124	11	353	157	782	623	767	767	387	12,300
New Hampshire	68	96	55	82	303	400	498	320	180	6,776
New Jersey	917	853	668	794	2,565	2,297	5,193	2,296	3,055	47,930
New Mexico	105	113	202	81	523	367	620	457	572	7,198
New York.	1,956	1,847	1,634	2,881	6,215	8,537	15,442	12,634	10,884	171,419
North Carolina	498	549	584	508	1,479	1,122	2,794	3,195	1,839	27,401
North Dakota	18	26	102	128	160	127	500	75	90	2,464
Ohio	1,416	411	931	982	3,291	1,910	3,499	2,712	5,328	36,510
Oklahoma	209	147	275	126	692	465	929	923	931	11,173
Oregon	469	137	339	425	1,283	616	1,707	1,359	1,449	14,346
Pennsylvania	1,381	543	608	1,183	2,941	4,062	4,908	3,617	4,137	69,465
Rhode Island	96	63	73	118	306	318	482	156	421	6,620
South Carolina	208	215	235	187	816	642	1,049	1,749	905	15,584
South Dakota	37	22	82	31	189	155	326	134	156	3,004
Tennessee	354	285	551	502	1,116	827	1,736	5,195	952	17,437
Texas	1,610	739	1,096	1,239	3,870	4,064	6,081	7,302	4,575	90,558
Utah	165	103	239	118	809	383	782	1,415	339	12,941
Vermont	49	36	21	54	194	147	243	193	76	2,786
Virginia	742	512	525	566	1,942	1,735	2,522	1,567	1,468	30,410
Washington	831	436	609	576	1,480	1,357	3,447	4,377	1,500	37,198
West Virginia	102	46	95	76	492	408	595	192	391	7,098
Wisconsin	585	379	492	331	1,398	1,283	2,152	1,093	1,885	24,643
Wyoming	41	27	48	10	208	126	313	155	135	2,350

[1] Includes items not shown separately.   [2] Based on estimated resident population as of July 1.   [3] Includes community development.

Source: U.S. Census Bureau, <http://www.census.gov/govs/www/estimate9900us.html> (accessed 22 April 2002) and <http://www.census.gov/govs/estimate/99allpub.pdf> (released September 2001).

No. 422. State and Local Governments—Summary of Finances by State: 1999

[In millions of dollars (1,794,557 represents $1,794,557,000,000), except as indicated. For fiscal year ending in year shown; see text, this section]

State	Revenue [1] All revenue	Per capita [2] (dol.)	General revenue	Per capita [2] (dol.)	From own sources	Per capita [2] (dol.)	Expenditures [1] Direct general expenditures	Per capita [2] (dol.)	Debt outstanding Total	Per capita [2] (dol.)
United States ...	1,794,557	6,581	1,434,464	5,260	1,523,929	5,588	1,398,533	5,129	1,369,253	5,021
Alabama.........	23,621	5,405	19,322	4,422	18,969	4,341	20,119	4,604	14,250	3,261
Alaska..........	9,225	14,878	7,612	12,277	7,845	12,653	7,131	11,502	7,434	11,991
Arizona.........	25,714	5,382	20,958	4,386	21,762	4,555	20,302	4,249	22,913	4,795
Arkansas	13,867	5,436	11,376	4,459	11,274	4,420	10,662	4,179	6,937	2,719
California	242,469	7,315	185,731	5,604	206,514	6,231	180,875	5,457	168,344	5,079
Colorado........	25,413	6,265	21,137	5,211	22,089	5,446	20,068	4,948	22,059	5,439
Connecticut......	23,796	7,250	21,505	6,552	20,345	6,199	19,688	5,999	22,238	6,776
Delaware	5,526	7,328	4,872	6,462	4,742	6,289	4,483	5,946	4,916	6,519
District of Columbia .	6,131	11,813	5,452	10,504	4,424	8,524	4,630	8,920	4,939	9,517
Florida	88,422	5,851	72,658	4,808	77,730	5,144	71,631	4,740	75,706	5,010
Georgia	46,265	5,940	36,878	4,735	39,805	5,111	35,831	4,601	26,273	3,373
Hawaii	8,094	6,830	6,879	5,805	6,707	5,660	6,889	5,813	7,651	6,457
Idaho...........	6,868	5,485	5,715	4,564	5,837	4,662	5,612	4,482	3,144	2,511
Illinois	73,603	6,069	60,334	4,975	63,524	5,238	59,727	4,925	62,897	5,186
Indiana.........	30,890	5,198	27,802	4,678	26,266	4,420	26,642	4,483	18,464	3,107
Iowa	17,270	6,019	14,314	4,989	14,672	5,114	14,687	5,119	7,156	2,494
Kansas.........	14,141	5,328	12,343	4,651	12,173	4,587	12,066	4,546	9,737	3,669
Kentucky	22,769	5,748	18,377	4,639	18,591	4,693	18,062	4,560	22,516	5,685
Louisiana	25,698	5,878	21,639	4,950	20,842	4,767	21,118	4,830	17,316	3,961
Maine..........	8,096	6,461	6,968	5,561	6,563	5,238	6,388	5,098	5,585	4,457
Maryland	31,268	6,046	26,329	5,091	26,972	5,215	24,876	4,810	23,852	4,612
Massachusetts.....	41,425	6,709	35,965	5,824	35,461	5,743	35,000	5,668	50,319	8,149
Michigan........	66,078	6,699	52,377	5,310	56,731	5,751	50,558	5,125	44,095	4,470
Minnesota.......	36,637	7,671	28,846	6,040	32,140	6,730	28,160	5,896	26,864	5,625
Mississippi	14,973	5,407	12,720	4,594	11,839	4,275	12,940	4,673	8,577	3,098
Missouri	29,960	5,479	24,687	4,515	24,843	4,543	23,881	4,367	17,605	3,220
Montana........	5,134	5,814	4,458	5,049	3,880	4,394	4,293	4,861	3,561	4,033
Nebraska	10,947	6,571	8,304	4,985	9,398	5,641	7,716	4,631	6,290	3,776
Nevada	11,721	6,479	8,728	4,825	10,572	5,844	9,296	5,139	12,300	6,800
New Hampshire....	6,454	5,374	5,472	4,556	5,421	4,513	5,329	4,437	6,776	5,642
New Jersey.......	59,121	7,260	48,996	6,017	51,745	6,354	44,326	5,443	47,930	5,886
New Mexico	11,238	6,459	9,334	5,364	8,967	5,153	9,466	5,440	7,198	4,137
New York	172,301	9,469	137,114	7,535	143,853	7,905	133,769	7,351	171,419	9,420
North Carolina....	49,073	6,414	37,545	4,907	41,386	5,409	36,769	4,806	27,401	3,581
North Dakota.....	4,091	6,453	3,619	5,708	3,074	4,848	3,487	5,500	2,464	3,887
Ohio	75,103	6,672	54,974	4,884	64,920	5,767	53,150	4,722	36,510	3,243
Oklahoma........	17,440	5,194	14,450	4,303	14,505	4,320	13,555	4,037	11,173	3,327
Oregon..........	23,040	6,948	18,511	5,582	18,834	5,680	18,301	5,519	14,346	4,326
Pennsylvania.....	74,569	6,217	60,656	5,057	62,712	5,229	61,226	5,105	69,465	5,792
Rhode Island.....	7,203	7,268	5,550	5,601	5,877	5,931	5,281	5,329	6,620	6,680
South Carolina....	21,640	5,569	18,400	4,735	17,770	4,573	18,232	4,692	15,584	4,010
South Dakota	4,224	5,763	3,348	4,567	3,353	4,574	3,245	4,428	3,004	4,099
Tennessee	31,368	5,720	23,364	4,260	25,454	4,641	24,172	4,408	17,437	3,180
Texas..........	117,493	5,862	90,327	4,506	99,809	4,980	87,375	4,359	90,558	4,518
Utah	13,292	6,240	10,443	4,903	11,201	5,259	10,440	4,901	12,941	6,076
Vermont	3,759	6,329	3,279	5,521	2,930	4,933	3,030	5,100	2,786	4,690
Virginia.........	39,931	5,810	32,804	4,773	35,430	5,155	32,299	4,699	30,410	4,425
Washington.......	43,831	7,615	31,563	5,483	38,529	6,694	32,334	5,617	37,198	6,463
West Virginia.....	10,154	5,619	8,541	4,727	7,975	4,413	8,227	4,553	7,098	3,928
Wisconsin.......	38,789	7,388	28,445	5,418	34,171	6,509	28,043	5,342	24,643	4,694
Wyoming	4,422	9,212	3,445	7,176	3,503	7,298	3,152	6,567	2,350	4,896

[1] Includes items not shown separately.   [2] Based on estimated resident population as of July 1.

Source: U.S Census Bureau; <http://www.census.gov/govs/www/estimate/9900us.html> (accessed 22 April 2002); and unpublished data.

No. 423. State and Local Governments—Indebtedness: 1980 to 1999

[In billions of dollars (335.6 represents $335,600,000,000), except per capita. For fiscal year ending in year shown; see text, this section. Local government amounts are estimates subject to sampling variation; see Appendix III and source]

Item	Debt outstanding						Long term		
	Total	Per capita [1] (dol.)	Long term			Shortterm	Net long term	Debt issued	Debt retired
			Local schools [2]	Utilities	All other				
1980: Total	335.6	1,481	32.3	55.2	235.0	13.1	262.9	42.4	17.4
State	122.0	540	3.8	4.6	111.5	2.1	79.8	16.4	5.7
Local	213.6	943	28.5	50.6	123.5	11.0	183.1	25.9	11.7
1990: Total	860.6	3,459	60.4	134.8	646.1	19.3	477.0	108.5	64.8
State	318.3	1,282	4.4	12.3	298.8	2.8	125.5	43.5	22.9
Local	542.3	2,180	56.0	122.4	347.4	16.5	351.5	65.0	42.0
1995: Total	1,115.3	4,244	118.2	163.9	756.0	27.0	835.3	129.3	95.1
State	427.2	1,629	11.3	17.0	345.0	6.1	205.3	52.6	37.5
Local	688.1	2,619	107.0	146.9	411.0	20.9	629.9	76.8	57.6
1996: Total	1,169.7	4,411	130.7	170.3	844.7	24.0	751.6	141.1	106.5
State	452.4	1,709	11.2	16.3	419.1	5.8	220.3	60.2	42.4
Local	717.3	2,705	119.5	154.0	425.6	18.2	531.3	80.9	64.1
1997: Total	1,224.5	4,573	139.0	179.1	889.8	16.6	797.7	151.3	109.3
State	456.7	1,710	11.7	16.0	426.8	2.1	222.6	54.4	41.1
Local	767.9	2,841	127.3	163.1	463.0	14.5	575.1	96.8	68.2
1998: Total	1,283.6	4,750	159.2	182.8	924.3	17.3	842.6	204.4	144.6
State	483.1	1,791	13.6	16.7	450.6	2.2	237.2	83.4	58.1
Local	800.4	2,962	145.5	166.1	473.8	15.1	605.4	120.9	86.5
1999: Total	1,369.3	5,021	180.7	194.9	975.7	17.8	907.3	229.4	153.1
State	510.5	1,876	15.4	16.7	475.8	2.7	249.4	83.2	55.6
Local	858.8	3,149	165.3	178.3	500.0	15.2	657.9	146.2	97.5

[1] 1980 and 1990 based on enumerated resident population as of April 1; other years based on estimated resident population as of July 1; see Table 2.   [2] Includes debt for education activities other than higher education.

Source: U.S. Census Bureau, *1980-90, State and Local Government Finance Estimates,* annual; thereafter, <http://www.census.gov/govs/www/estimate.html> (accessed 23 May 2002).

No. 424. Long-Term Municipal New Issues for State and Local Governments: 1980 to 2001

[In billions of dollars (45.6 represents $45,600,000,000)]

Item	1980	1985	1990	1995	1996	1997	1998	1999	2000	2001
Long-term municipal new issues [1]	45.6	202.4	125.9	156.2	181.5	214.3	279.7	219.2	194.3	283.5
General obligation	13.7	39.6	40.2	60.2	64.2	72.2	92.6	69.8	65.2	101.3
Revenue	31.9	162.8	85.7	96.0	117.3	142.1	187.1	149.4	129.1	182.2
Competitive	19.3	27.8	30.2	41.0	47.0	47.8	65.2	52.8	48.7	63.1
Negotiated	26.4	174.6	95.9	115.4	134.5	166.5	214.5	166.4	145.6	220.4
States with largest issuance: [2]										
California	3.6	25.3	15.7	20.2	24.9	27.7	33.9	26.5	22.9	31.7
New York	2.9	12.7	16.9	18.8	20.8	27.4	36.3	19.8	19.1	22.5
Texas	3.8	21.2	6.5	10.4	11.6	15.3	18.1	17.7	14.7	24.6
Florida	2.2	13.2	5.9	9.1	10.0	10.5	14.7	10.8	10.1	14.1
Illinois	2.3	9.2	6.3	6.6	8.8	9.6	10.1	12.4	8.9	14.1
All others	30.8	120.8	74.6	91.1	105.4	123.8	166.6	132.0	118.6	176.5
Type of issuer: [3]										
City, town, or village	8.5	36.5	22.7	27.9	30.2	34.8	44.3	33.0	29.3	45.6
College or university	0.2	2.9	1.5	2.5	4.5	3.3	4.6	4.1	3.8	5.6
County/parish	4.6	15.8	10.0	13.3	16.8	15.5	21.2	17.1	12.7	19.0
Direct issuer	-	0.4	0.2	0.4	1.4	0.8	2.1	2.0	2.6	3.1
District	3.9	15.6	15.2	22.4	27.8	33.7	43.6	34.1	27.8	47.9
Indian Tribe	(NA)	(NA)	(NA)	(NA)	(NA)	(NA)	(NA)	(NA)	(NA)	0.2
Local authority	9.2	51.1	20.7	27.9	33.5	41.5	53.9	43.2	33.1	53.1
State authority	14.1	68.1	40.6	47.2	53.0	66.0	85.2	68.1	64.2	78.9
State	5.1	12.1	15.0	14.6	14.3	18.7	24.7	17.6	20.8	30.2
General use of proceeds:										
Airports	0.4	3.0	5.2	4.7	5.2	6.4	10.2	5.5	7.4	12.3
Combined utilities	0.3	2.4	1.0	0.7	1.2	1.5	1.8	1.0	0.3	1.3
Economic development	0.2	2.5	2.1	2.5	1.8	2.9	3.5	3.6	2.9	3.9
Education	4.0	20.4	20.5	28.5	34.4	42.7	56.5	47.6	39.9	64.5
Health care	3.1	30.0	12.6	11.5	16.6	22.1	33.4	22.0	14.4	20.1
Industrial development	1.0	2.9	1.9	3.2	2.8	3.5	3.6	3.5	3.4	2.9
Multi family housing	2.5	20.2	3.1	6.1	6.6	5.4	6.4	6.1	6.2	7.3
Nursing homes/life care retirement	0.3	1.2	1.6	1.9	1.5	3.6	4.8	4.9	1.8	3.0
Other miscellaneous	11.1	37.3	36.2	44.2	55.2	57.0	71.5	58.4	52.8	81.2
Polution control	2.3	10.0	2.5	5.0	5.0	5.6	9.7	8.9	4.8	4.5
Electric & public power	4.4	23.2	5.2	4.8	5.7	6.5	15.6	4.9	5.7	11.5
Single family housing	10.6	16.4	12.5	10.0	10.5	13.6	12.9	12.6	12.0	14.0
Solid waste/resource recovery	0.4	3.8	3.0	3.3	1.6	3.6	2.4	1.2	0.5	2.1
Student loans	0.2	4.0	0.4	4.4	4.2	3.9	4.9	5.3	7.6	8.2
Transportation	1.3	11.0	7.6	11.3	9.1	16.6	20.5	16.0	15.9	18.6
Water, sewer, and gas facilities	3.1	13.4	9.3	13.2	14.5	18.2	20.9	16.4	11.3	27.1
Waterfront/seaports	0.5	1.5	0.5	0.8	1.3	1.2	0.9	1.2	1.1	1.1

- Represents or rounds to zero.   NA Not available.   [1] Excludes issues with a final maturity of less than 13 months, private placements, and not-for-profit cooperative utilities.   [2] Ranked by 1997 Long-Term Municipal New Issue Volume.   [3] Includes outlying areas.

Source: Thomson Financial Securities Data Company, Newark, NJ, Municipal New Issues Database (copyright).

No. 425. Bond Ratings for State Governments by State: 2001

[As of fourth quarter. Key to investment grade ratings are in declining order of quality. The ratings from AA to CCC may be modified by the addition of a plus or minus sign to show relative standing within the major rating categories. *S&P:* AAA, AA, A, BBB, BB, B, CCC, CC, C; *Moody's:* Aaa, Aa, A, Baa, Ba, B, Caa, Ca, C; Numerical modifiers 1, 2, and 3 are added to letter-rating. *Fitch:* AAA, AA, A, BBB, BB, B, CCC, CC, C]

State	Standard & Poor's	Moody's	Fitch	State	Standard & Poor's	Moody's	Fitch
Alabama	AA	Aa3	AA	Montana	AA-	Aa3	(1)
Alaska	(1)	Aa2	AA	Nebraska	(1)	(1)	(1)
Arizona	(1)	(1)	(1)	Nevada	AA	Aa2	AA
Arkansas	AA	Aa2	AAA	New Hampshire	AA+	Aa2	AA+
California	A+	A1	AA	New Jersey	AA	Aa2	AA+
Colorado	(1)	(1)	(1)	New Mexico	AA+	Aa1	(1)
Connecticut	AA	Aa2	AA	New York	AA	A2	AA
Delaware	AAA	Aaa	AAA	North Carolina	AAA	Aaa	AAA
Florida	AA+	Aa2	AA	North Dakota	AA-	(1)	(1)
Georgia	AAA	Aaa	AAA	Ohio	AA+	Aa1	AA+
Hawaii	AA-	Aa3	AA-	Oklahoma	AA	Aa3	AA
Idaho	(1)	(1)	(1)	Oregon	AA	Aa2	AA
Illinois	AA	Aa2	AA+	Pennsylvania	AA	Aa2	AA
Indiana	AA+	(1)	AA	Rhode Island	AA-	Aa3	AA
Iowa	AA+	(1)	(1)	South Carolina	AAA	Aaa	AAA
Kansas	AA+	(1)	(1)	South Dakota	(1)	(1)	(1)
Kentucky	AA	(1)	(1)	Tennessee	AA	Aa2	AA
Louisiana	A	A2	A	Texas	AA	Aa1	AA+
Maine	AA+	Aa2	AA+	Utah	AAA	Aaa	AAA
Maryland	AAA	Aaa	AAA	Vermont	AA+	Aa1	AA+
Massachusetts	AA-	Aa2	AA-	Virginia	AAA	Aaa	AAA
Michigan	AAA	Aaa	AA+	Washington	AA+	Aa1	AA
Minnesota	AAA	Aaa	AAA	West Virginia	AA-	Aa3	AA-
Mississippi	AA	Aa3	AA	Wisconsin	AA-	Aa3	AA
Missouri	AAA	Aaa	AAA	Wyoming	AA	(1)	(1)

[1] Not reviewed.

Sources: Standard & Poor's, New York, NY; Moody's Investors Service, New York, NY (copyright); and Fitch Ratings, New York, NY (copyright).

No. 426. Bond Ratings for City Governments by Largest Cities: 2001

[As of fourth quarter except for S&P (first quarter 2002). see headnote in table above]

Cities ranked by 2000 population	Standard & Poor's	Moody's	Fitch Ratings	Cities ranked by 2000 population	Standard & Poor's	Moody's	Fitch Ratings
New York, NY	A	A2	AA	Sacramento, CA	AA	(1)	(1)
Los Angeles, CA	AA	Aa2	AA	Oakland, CA	A+	A1	A+
Chicago, IL	A+	A1	AA-	Mesa, AZ	AA-	A1	AAA
Houston, TX	AA-	Aa3	AA	Tulsa, OK	AA	Aa2	(1)
Philadelphia, PA	BBB	Baa1	AAA	Omaha, NE	AAA	Aaa	(1)
Phoenix, AZ	AA+	Aa1	(1)	Minneapolis, MN	AAA	Aa1	(1)
San Diego, CA	AA	Aa1	AA+	Honolulu, HI	AA-	Aa3	AA
Dallas, TX	AAA	Aaa	(1)	Miami, FL	BBB+	Baa2	(1)
San Antonio, TX	AA+	Aa2	(1)	Colorado Springs, CO	AA	Aa3	(1)
Detroit, MI	A-	Baa1	AAA	St. Louis, MO	A-	A3	A-
San Jose, CA	AA+	Aa1	(1)	Wichita, KS	AA	Aa2	(1)
Indianapolis, IN	AAA	Aaa	AAA	Santa Ana, CA	(1)	(1)	(1)
San Francisco, CA	AA	Aa3	AAA	Pittsburgh, PA	A-	A3	A-
Jacksonville, FL	A	Aa2	AA	Arlington, TX	AA	Aa2	(1)
Columbus, OH	AAA	Aaa	(1)	Cincinnati, OH	AA+	Aa1	(1)
Austin, TX	AA+	Aa2	(1)	Anaheim, CA	AA	Aa2	(1)
Baltimore, MD	A+	A1	AAA	Toledo, OH	A	A3	(1)
Memphis, TN	AA	Aa2	AA	Tampa, FL	AA	Aa3	(1)
Milwaukee, WI	AA	Aa2	AA+	Buffalo, NY	BBB	Baa2	(1)
Boston, MA	AA-	Aa3	AA-	St. Paul, MN	AAA	Aa2	AA+
Washington, DC	BBB+	Baa1	AA	Corpus Christi, TX	A+	A2	AA-
El Paso, TX	AA	Aa3	AAA	Aurora, CO	AA	Aa2	AAA
Seattle, WA	AAA	Aaa	(1)	Raleigh, NC	AAA	Aaa	AAA
Denver, CO	AA+	Aa1	AA-	Newark, NJ	(1)	Baa1	(1)
Nashville-Davidson, TN	AA	Aa2	(1)	Lexington-Fayette, KY	AA+	Aa2	(1)
Charlotte, NC	AAA	Aaa	(1)	Anchorage, AK	AA-	Aa3	(1)
Fort Worth, TX	AA+	Aa1	(1)	Louisville, KY	AA-	Aa3	(1)
Portland, OR	AA+	Aaa	(1)	Riverside, CA	(1)	(1)	(1)
Oklahoma City, OK	AA	Aa2	(1)	St Petersburg, FL	(1)	(1)	(1)
Tucson, AZ	AA	Aa2	(1)	Stockton CA	(1)	(1)	(1)
New Orleans, LA	BBB+	Baa1	(1)	Birmingham, AL	AA	Aa3	AA-
Las Vegas, NV	AA-	Aa3	(1)	Jersey City, NJ	BBB	Baa3	(1)
Cleveland, OH	A+	A1	A	Norfolk, VA	AA	A1	AA
Long Beach, CA	AA-	Aa3	(1)	Baton Rouge, LA	(1)	(1)	(1)
Albuquerque, NM	AA	Aa3	AA	Rochester, NY	AA	A2	(1)
Kansas City, MO	AA	Aa3	(1)	Akron, OH	AA-	A1	AA-
Fresno, CA	AA-	A2	(1)	Mobile, AL	A+	A2	(1)
Virginia Beach, VA	AA+	Aa1	AA+	Richmond, VA	AA	A1	AA
Atlanta, GA	AA	Aa3	(1)				

[1] Not reviewed.

Sources: Standard & Poor's, New York, NY; Moody's Investors Service, New York, NY (copyright); and Fitch Ratings, New York, NY (copyright).

No. 427. State Resources, Expenditures, and Balances: 2001 and 2002

[In millions of dollars (1,044,078 represents $1,044,078,000,000). For fiscal year ending in year shown; see text; this section. General funds exclude special funds earmarked for particular purposes, such as highway trust funds and federal funds; they support most on-going broad-based state services and are available for appropriation to support any governmental activity. Minus sign (-) indicates deficit]

| State | Expenditures by fund source | | | | State general fund | | | | | |
	Total, 2001	Total [2] 2002 [1]	General fund 2002 [1]	Federal funds 2002 [1]	Resources [3][4] 2001	2002 [1]	Expenditures [4] 2001	2002 [1]	Balance [5] 2001	2002 [1]
Total.	1,044,078	1,098,610	508,726	296,922	(NA)	(NA)	(NA)	(NA)	(NA)	(NA)
United States. .	1,024,439	1,077,932	501,260	292,514	498,427	527,793	477,462	513,479	17,487	14,013
Alabama	15,390	18,835	5,322	6,347	5,268	5,347	5,248	5,362	20	25
Alaska.	(NA)	(NA)	(NA)	(NA)	2,290	(NA)	2,290	(NA)	[6]-	(NA)
Arizona	17,351	16,759	6,328	4,276	6,572	6,330	6,467	6,329	104	2
Arkansas	11,133	12,133	3,248	3,560	3,261	3,250	3,261	3,250	-	-
California	137,655	149,426	78,380	46,516	86,266	79,865	79,708	78,380	[6]6,557	1,486
Colorado	12,703	13,617	6,087	2,785	7,218	6,705	6,682	6,711	[6]537	57
Connecticut	18,953	18,583	11,899	3,304	11,914	11,686	11,413	11,899	501	-123
Delaware	5,417	5,579	2,524	835	2,569	2,844	2,467	2,524	102	[6]320
Florida.	52,390	47,540	19,232	12,672	20,465	19,736	20,465	19,267	-	469
Georgia	24,889	27,763	13,722	10,930	17,279	17,300	14,770	16,074	[6]1,128	1,226
Hawaii.	7,277	7,189	3,624	1,088	3,716	3,834	3,385	3,624	330	210
Idaho	3,984	4,536	2,002	1,485	2,024	2,002	1,844	2,002	180	-
Illinois	37,657	39,702	18,356	8,273	25,747	25,476	24,547	24,826	1,200	650
Indiana	17,767	16,856	9,579	4,650	10,570	9,594	9,742	9,579	392	16
Iowa	12,288	12,689	4,682	3,073	4,877	4,603	4,869	4,600	8	3
Kansas	8,850	9,483	4,528	2,502	4,864	4,702	4,434	4,528	430	174
Kentucky	16,849	17,817	7,415	5,277	7,124	7,429	7,124	7,251	-	24
Louisiana	15,961	17,494	6,426	5,792	6,216	6,476	6,227	6,426	[6]-	50
Maine	5,269	6,453	2,760	2,003	2,662	2,507	2,648	2,593	19	-86
Maryland	20,481	21,959	10,677	4,914	10,590	11,132	10,215	10,677	375	456
Massachusetts . . .	30,107	31,425	21,019	6,888	20,700	24,621	20,596	22,831	104	1,790
Michigan	37,952	38,281	9,307	10,325	9,831	9,290	9,831	9,290	-	-
Minnesota	20,832	21,911	13,451	4,510	14,239	14,142	13,131	12,755	[6]1,108	1,387
Mississippi	9,726	10,400	3,401	3,361	3,634	3,422	3,633	3,584	1	5
Missouri.	16,653	19,247	7,849	5,664	7,921	7,830	7,812	7,734	109	96
Montana	3,104	3,629	1,330	1,548	1,371	1,503	1,264	1,339	104	165
Nebraska	6,058	6,554	2,715	1,756	2,787	2,821	2,462	2,593	204	121
Nevada	4,780	5,084	1,807	1,289	1,918	1,946	1,875	1,847	106	138
New Hampshire . .	3,425	3,690	1,160	1,070	1,081	1,138	1,081	1,150	-	-12
New Jersey	32,267	33,736	21,785	7,797	22,338	21,730	21,057	21,207	[6]-	500
New Mexico	10,794	11,082	3,937	3,188	3,855	4,400	3,718	3,988	-	401
New York.	79,753	85,044	38,324	26,306	40,800	43,532	39,702	41,455	[6]1,098	[6]2,077
North Carolina . . .	26,958	27,036	15,002	7,066	13,720	14,713	13,720	14,530	-	1
North Dakota	2,297	2,518	865	994	864	887	826	847	38	40
Ohio	42,296	49,010	21,782	6,965	21,128	21,830	20,739	21,778	190	153
Oklahoma	11,979	13,238	5,019	4,007	5,077	5,181	4,819	5,136	259	45
Oregon	17,033	18,453	5,538	3,741	5,381	5,140	4,920	5,074	461	66
Pennsylvania	40,694	45,228	20,770	13,919	20,260	20,736	19,979	20,770	313	300
Rhode Island	4,873	5,355	2,625	1,592	2,585	2,642	2,472	2,625	113	17
South Carolina . . .	14,450	15,363	5,552	4,828	5,794	5,409	5,644	5,348	[6]150	62
South Dakota	2,353	2,509	851	995	823	864	805	853	6	-
Tennessee	17,434	18,818	7,929	7,057	7,244	7,610	7,231	7,568	-	-
Texas	52,356	54,583	30,571	15,309	(NA)	32,510	(NA)	30,572	(NA)	1,421
Utah	6,977	7,467	3,810	1,649	3,792	3,805	3,792	3,805	-	-
Vermont	2,665	2,889	881	960	899	894	897	872	-	-
Virginia	24,218	25,084	11,176	4,445	12,652	12,241	12,339	12,131	314	109
Washington	23,061	22,870	11,220	6,399	11,273	11,228	10,788	11,217	486	10
West Virginia	7,442	8,197	2,881	2,846	2,870	2,994	2,864	2,976	-	2
Wisconsin	28,092	23,244	11,534	5,481	11,324	11,259	11,030	11,074	[6]293	151
Wyoming	1,546	1,574	378	277	777	659	630	630	[6]147	10
Puerto Rico	19,639	20,678	7,466	4,408	(NA)	(NA)	(NA)	(NA)	(NA)	(NA)

- Represents zero.   NA Not available.   [1] Estimated.   [2] Includes bonds not shown separately.   [3] Includes funds budgeted, adjustments, and balances from previous year.   [4] May or may not include budget stabilization fund transfers, depending on state accounting practices.   [5] Resources less expenditures. Total excludes Puerto Rico.   [6] Ending balance includes the balance in a budget stabilization fund.

Source: Expenditures by fund from National Association of State Budget Officers, Washington, DC, *2001 State Expenditure Report*, and State General Fund from *National Governors' Association and NASBO, Fiscal Survey of the States*, semi-annual (copyright).

State and Local Government Finances and Employment   279

No. 428. State Governments—Summary of Finances: 1990 to 2000

[In millions of dollars (673,119 represents $673,119,000,000), except where indicated. For fiscal year ending in year shown; see text; this section]

Item	Total (mil. dol.)				Per capita [1] (dollars)			
	1990	1995	1999	2000	1990	1995	1999	2000
Borrowing and revenue	673,119	957,452	1,228,816	1,336,448	2,697	3,596	4,404	4,737
Borrowing	40,948	53,697	75,946	76,612	164	202	272	272
Revenue	632,172	903,756	1,152,870	1,259,835	2,533	3,394	4,132	4,466
General revenue	517,429	739,016	906,076	983,785	2,073	2,775	3,247	3,487
Taxes	300,489	399,148	499,943	539,157	1,204	1,499	1,792	1,911
Sales and gross receipts	147,069	196,851	239,367	252,147	589	739	858	894
General	99,702	132,236	164,378	174,461	399	497	589	618
Motor fuels	19,379	25,440	29,169	29,969	78	96	105	106
Alcoholic beverages	3,191	3,597	3,900	4,104	13	14	14	15
Tobacco products	5,541	7,348	8,170	8,391	22	28	29	30
Other	19,256	28,230	33,751	35,222	77	106	121	125
Licenses	18,842	26,083	30,440	32,606	75	98	109	116
Motor vehicles	9,848	12,433	14,083	15,104	39	47	50	54
Corporations in general	3,099	5,018	6,359	6,461	12	19	23	23
Other	5,895	8,632	9,998	11,041	24	32	36	39
Individual income	96,076	125,610	172,764	194,066	385	472	619	688
Corporation net income	21,751	29,075	30,766	32,522	87	109	110	115
Property	5,848	9,518	11,654	10,996	23	36	42	39
Other	10,902	12,014	14,952	16,819	44	45	54	60
Charges and miscellaneous	90,612	124,310	152,441	170,309	363	467	546	604
Intergovernmental revenue	126,329	215,558	253,692	274,318	506	810	909	972
From Federal Government	118,353	202,485	238,941	259,001	474	760	856	918
Public welfare	59,397	114,945	135,274	147,430	238	432	485	523
Education	21,271	31,944	38,738	42,114	85	120	139	149
Highways	13,931	19,419	20,874	23,376	56	73	75	83
Health and hospitals	5,475	10,344	13,205	14,235	22	39	47	50
Other	18,279	25,834	30,849	31,846	73	97	111	113
From local governments	7,976	13,073	14,751	15,317	32	49	53	54
Utility revenue	3,305	3,845	4,356	4,513	13	14	16	16
Liquor store revenue	2,907	3,073	3,599	3,895	12	12	13	14
Insurance trust revenue [2]	108,530	157,821	238,838	267,644	435	593	856	949
Employee retirement	78,898	104,451	201,500	230,166	316	392	722	816
Unemployment compensation	18,370	37,041	22,131	23,265	74	139	79	82
Expenditure and debt redemption	592,213	874,365	1,046,234	1,126,923	2,372	3,284	3,749	3,994
Expenditure	572,318	836,894	998,365	1,084,548	2,293	3,143	3,578	3,844
General expenditure	508,284	733,504	889,475	965,174	2,036	2,755	3,188	3,421
Education	184,935	249,670	318,602	346,791	741	938	1,142	1,229
Public welfare	104,971	194,854	221,167	239,021	421	732	793	847
Health	20,029	30,865	38,008	41,991	80	116	136	149
Hospitals	22,637	29,139	29,994	32,577	91	109	107	115
Highways	44,249	57,374	68,317	74,174	177	215	245	263
Police protection	5,166	6,451	8,794	9,791	21	24	32	35
Correction	17,266	26,069	32,843	35,170	69	98	118	125
Natural resources	9,909	12,534	14,482	15,977	40	47	52	57
Housing and community development	2,856	3,466	4,000	4,729	11	13	14	17
Other and unallocable	96,267	123,081	153,269	164,954	386	462	549	585
Utility expenditure	7,131	7,586	8,779	10,723	29	28	31	38
Liquor store expenditure	2,452	2,522	2,967	3,195	10	9	11	11
Insurance trust expenditure [2]	54,452	93,282	97,144	105,456	218	350	348	374
Employee retirement	29,562	47,541	67,353	75,971	118	179	241	269
Unemployment compensation	16,423	35,032	19,160	18,583	66	132	69	66
By character and object:								
Intergovernmental expenditure	175,028	240,978	304,933	327,520	701	905	1,093	1,161
Direct expenditure	397,291	595,916	693,432	757,028	1,592	2,238	2,485	2,683
Current operation	258,046	396,035	476,968	523,315	1,034	1,487	1,709	1,855
Capital outlay	45,524	57,829	68,509	76,018	182	217	246	269
Construction	34,803	46,113	53,857	59,503	139	173	193	211
Land and existing structure	3,471	39	3,953	4,643	14	-	14	16
Equipment	7,250	11,676	10,699	11,872	29	44	38	42
Assistance and subsidies	16,902	23,511	22,229	22,140	68	88	80	78
Interest on debt	22,307	25,259	28,582	30,099	90	95	102	107
Insurance benefits [3]	54,452	93,282	97,144	105,456	218	350	348	374
Debt redemption	19,895	37,471	47,869	42,374	80	141	172	150
Debt outstanding,	318,254	427,239	510,486	547,876	1,275	1,604	1,829	1,942
Long-term	315,490	421,139	507,819	541,497	1,264	1,582	1,820	1,919
Full-faith and credit	74,972	116,195	129,326	138,525	300	436	463	491
Nonguaranteed	240,518	304,944	378,493	402,972	964	1,145	1,356	1,428
Short-term	2,764	6,100	2,667	6,379	11	23	10	23
Net long-term [4]	125,524	205,348	249,432	266,870	503	771	894	946
Full-faith and credit only	63,481	100,571	119,511	120,004	254	400	428	455

- Represents or rounds to zero.   [1] Based on estimated resident population as of July 1.   [2] Includes other items not shown separately.   [3] Includes repayments.   [4] Less cash and investment assets specifically held for redemption of long-term debt.

Source: U.S. Census Bureau, 1990, *State Government Finances*, Series GF, No. 3; thereafter, <http://www.census.gov/govs/www/state00.html> (released 31 May 2002).

No. 429. State Governments—Revenue by State: 2000

[In millions of dollars (1,259,835 represents $1,259,835,000,000), except as noted. For fiscal year ending in year shown; see text, this section. Includes local shares of state imposed taxes. N.E.C. = Not elsewhere classified]

State		General revenue								
			Per capita [2]		Intergovernmental revenue		Charges and miscellaneous			Insurance trust revenue
	Total revenue [1]	Total	Total (dol.)	Rank	Total	From Federal govern- ment	Total	Current charges	Miscella- neous general revenue	
United States ..	1,259,835	983,785	3,503	(X)	274,318	259,001	170,309	86,474	83,835	267,644
Alabama	16,857	14,117	3,174	35	4,781	4,745	2,897	2,099	798	2,588
Alaska	8,584	7,330	11,691	1	1,202	1,197	4,705	327	4,378	1,229
Arizona	16,721	14,664	2,858	46	4,441	4,111	2,122	840	1,282	2,035
Arkansas	10,789	9,118	3,411	24	2,735	2,706	1,513	895	618	1,671
California	172,481	135,782	4,009	18	36,125	33,655	15,849	9,429	6,420	36,476
Colorado	17,060	12,925	3,005	40	3,301	3,280	2,549	1,341	1,208	4,135
Connecticut	17,707	15,932	4,678	6	3,395	3,387	2,367	962	1,405	1,752
Delaware	5,162	4,333	5,526	2	827	789	1,374	591	783	820
Florida	51,630	41,674	2,608	49	10,271	9,905	6,577	2,365	4,212	9,949
Georgia	29,630	23,395	2,858	45	6,459	6,411	3,424	1,633	1,791	6,235
Hawaii	6,941	5,729	4,727	3	1,128	1,124	1,266	845	421	1,212
Idaho	5,576	4,202	3,248	32	1,074	1,070	751	364	387	1,321
Illinois	48,524	38,759	3,121	39	10,214	9,275	5,756	2,242	3,514	9,766
Indiana	20,456	18,857	3,101	36	4,952	4,792	3,801	2,281	1,520	1,600
Iowa	11,340	9,892	3,381	29	2,731	2,632	1,976	1,239	737	1,340
Kansas	10,326	8,493	3,160	43	2,401	2,365	1,243	645	598	1,833
Kentucky	19,451	14,648	3,624	22	4,341	4,319	2,613	1,529	1,084	4,802
Louisiana	18,404	14,489	3,242	23	4,401	4,346	3,575	2,259	1,316	3,912
Maine	6,294	5,274	4,136	13	1,555	1,547	1,058	367	691	943
Maryland	21,366	17,956	3,391	31	4,164	4,022	3,437	1,686	1,751	3,308
Massachusetts . . .	32,011	27,418	4,319	8	5,787	5,428	5,479	1,756	3,723	4,497
Michigan	49,512	39,491	3,974	14	9,370	9,168	7,364	4,183	3,181	9,454
Minnesota	26,889	20,972	4,263	12	4,451	4,381	3,183	1,332	1,851	5,917
Mississippi	12,181	9,636	3,387	27	3,470	3,349	1,454	906	548	2,381
Missouri	20,309	16,486	2,946	41	5,256	5,205	2,658	1,351	1,307	3,824
Montana	4,204	3,496	3,876	20	1,206	1,187	879	337	542	666
Nebraska	6,136	5,657	3,306	33	1,568	1,541	1,107	533	574	479
Nevada	7,235	5,424	2,715	44	1,057	998	649	379	270	1,780
New Hampshire . .	4,993	3,876	3,136	50	1,157	994	1,023	453	570	826
New Jersey	42,341	32,237	3,831	16	7,743	7,310	6,346	3,208	3,138	9,605
New Mexico	10,570	7,888	4,336	9	2,187	2,132	1,957	759	1,198	2,683
New York	111,397	84,765	4,467	7	32,521	26,206	10,509	4,571	5,938	24,271
North Carolina . . .	34,361	27,762	3,449	25	8,591	8,055	3,856	2,385	1,471	6,599
North Dakota	3,295	2,798	4,358	11	1,002	974	623	429	194	498
Ohio	55,274	36,166	3,186	38	10,074	9,842	6,415	3,602	2,813	18,628
Oklahoma	13,116	10,783	3,125	42	3,047	2,962	1,896	1,125	771	2,046
Oregon	21,228	14,313	4,184	19	4,685	4,625	3,683	1,787	1,896	6,687
Pennsylvania	54,517	41,700	3,395	28	10,584	10,504	8,649	4,962	3,687	11,952
Rhode Island	5,530	4,047	3,862	10	1,163	1,091	849	334	515	1,472
South Carolina . . .	15,870	13,221	3,295	30	4,379	4,055	2,460	1,741	719	1,834
South Dakota	2,873	2,253	2,985	37	793	781	533	213	320	619
Tennessee	18,970	15,928	2,800	47	6,121	5,966	2,069	1,368	701	3,041
Texas	72,323	55,312	2,653	48	17,151	16,562	10,737	5,102	5,635	17,010
Utah	10,191	7,661	3,431	26	1,889	1,878	1,793	1,150	643	2,414
Vermont	3,292	2,943	4,833	5	918	877	543	295	248	320
Virginia	28,902	22,208	3,137	34	4,466	4,314	5,601	3,216	2,385	6,395
Washington	30,616	21,254	3,606	21	5,190	5,095	3,496	2,146	1,350	9,035
West Virginia	8,542	6,982	3,862	17	2,406	2,365	1,233	648	585	1,510
Wisconsin	32,119	21,183	3,949	15	4,734	4,633	3,874	2,164	1,710	10,936
Wyoming	5,740	2,357	4,770	4	855	843	537	99	438	3,339

See footnotes at end of table.

U.S. Census Bureau, Statistical Abstract of the United States: 2002

[See headnote, page 281]

State	All taxes			Property taxes	Sales and gross receipts taxes						
		Per capita[2]				General sales taxes, total	Selective sales taxes[3]				
	Total[3]	Total (dol.)	Rank		Total[3]		Total[3]	Alcoholic beverages and tobacco sales	Insurance premiums	Motor fuels sales	Public utilities
United States ...	539,157	1,920	(X)	10,996	252,147	174,461	77,686	12,495	9,750	29,969	9,231
Alabama	6,438	1,448	46	180	3,228	1,702	1,527	190	191	505	483
Alaska	1,423	2,270	45	45	138	-	138	61	29	42	3
Arizona	8,101	1,579	40	297	4,644	3,633	1,011	214	165	593	37
Arkansas	4,871	1,822	21	482	2,363	1,707	656	122	95	389	-
California	83,808	2,474	9	3,331	29,620	23,457	6,163	1,499	1,300	3,041	219
Colorado	7,075	1,645	33	-	2,709	1,849	860	95	131	544	8
Connecticut	10,171	2,986	1	-	5,054	3,420	1,634	174	184	543	198
Delaware	2,132	2,720	2	-	289	-	289	38	53	104	28
Florida	24,826	1,553	41	763	19,132	15,011	4,121	1,018	356	1,609	666
Georgia	13,511	1,651	37	48	5,746	4,630	1,116	227	257	632	-
Hawaii	3,335	2,751	3	-	2,052	1,536	516	81	70	74	120
Idaho	2,377	1,837	25	-	1,055	747	308	35	56	209	3
Illinois	22,789	1,835	23	54	10,859	6,393	4,466	595	220	1,356	1,467
Indiana	10,104	1,662	32	4	5,037	3,579	1,457	120	163	700	6
Iowa	5,185	1,772	28	-	2,479	1,723	756	109	120	346	-
Kansas	4,848	1,804	26	49	2,304	1,741	563	126	70	356	1
Kentucky	7,695	1,904	18	389	3,512	2,172	1,341	85	227	440	-
Louisiana	6,512	1,457	44	25	3,719	2,061	1,658	145	239	549	12
Maine	2,661	2,087	13	31	1,191	847	344	109	47	181	2
Maryland	10,354	1,955	19	256	4,362	2,498	1,863	234	173	652	154
Massachusetts	16,153	2,544	5	-	5,060	3,565	1,495	344	335	653	-
Michigan	22,756	2,290	7	1,703	9,785	7,666	2,118	737	192	1,075	12
Minnesota	13,339	2,712	4	9	5,775	3,724	2,052	248	172	608	-
Mississippi	4,712	1,656	31	1	3,147	2,333	814	96	115	419	1
Missouri	8,572	1,532	42	18	4,032	2,788	1,244	137	210	696	1
Montana	1,411	1,564	43	219	344	-	344	31	43	188	20
Nebraska	2,981	1,742	38	4	1,445	1,028	417	64	39	279	3
Nevada	3,717	1,861	16	93	3,154	1,942	1,212	81	129	262	10
New Hampshire	1,696	1,372	50	474	556	-	556	106	54	117	58
New Jersey	18,148	2,157	12	3	8,200	5,508	2,692	478	282	506	854
New Mexico	3,743	2,058	14	35	2,007	1,502	505	61	65	233	7
New York	41,736	2,199	11	-	13,307	8,563	4,744	851	659	522	1,606
North Carolina	15,315	1,903	17	-	5,941	3,375	2,567	235	279	1,067	387
North Dakota	1,172	1,826	24	2	655	330	325	28	22	111	28
Ohio	19,676	1,733	34	23	9,059	6,263	2,795	373	359	1,405	642
Oklahoma	5,840	1,692	35	-	2,181	1,442	739	136	161	402	15
Oregon	5,946	1,738	36	-	728	-	728	201	44	474	7
Pennsylvania	22,467	1,829	22	117	10,460	7,057	3,403	504	440	764	678
Rhode Island	2,035	1,942	15	1	1,003	621	382	69	31	131	73
South Carolina	6,381	1,591	39	13	3,241	2,458	783	159	85	370	41
South Dakota	927	1,228	49	-	732	488	244	30	40	125	2
Tennessee	7,740	1,360	47	-	5,805	4,446	1,359	159	287	788	5
Texas	27,424	1,315	48	-	22,213	14,012	8,201	1,047	739	2,689	508
Utah	3,979	1,782	27	-	1,924	1,423	501	72	83	330	-
Vermont	1,483	2,435	6	405	484	215	268	40	20	61	10
Virginia	12,141	1,715	30	34	4,352	2,472	1,880	139	251	815	102
Washington	12,567	2,132	10	1,698	9,684	7,739	1,945	440	261	775	290
West Virginia	3,343	1,849	20	4	1,800	917	883	41	101	240	183
Wisconsin	12,575	2,344	8	87	5,106	3,507	1,599	302	96	916	278
Wyoming	964	1,951	29	101	477	369	108	12	12	81	2

See footnotes at end of table.

U.S. Census Bureau, Statistical Abstract of the United States: 2002

No. 429. State Governments—Revenue by State: 2000—Con.

[See headnote, page 281]

State	License taxes					Income			Other taxes	
	Total [3]	Corpora-tion license	Hunting and fishing license	Motor vehicle and opera-tors license	Occu-pancy and business license, n.e.c.	Total	Indi-vidual income	Corpora-tion net income	Total [3]	Death and gift
United States . . .	32,606	6,461	1,110	16,450	7,195	226,588	194,066	32,522	16,819	7,998
Alabama.	542	179	14	207	129	2,315	2,071	243	174	67
Alaska	92	2	19	36	34	438	-	438	711	2
Arizona.	260	6	16	168	58	2,815	2,292	523	85	85
Arkansas	259	9	20	133	77	1,707	1,470	237	59	24
California	3,691	37	75	1,917	1,538	46,213	39,575	6,639	953	928
Colorado.	300	5	53	190	45	3,972	3,637	335	94	62
Connecticut.	365	13	3	262	75	4,400	3,974	427	352	238
Delaware	777	541	2	33	180	974	733	240	92	41
Florida	1,513	121	14	1,045	255	1,183	-	1,183	2,236	739
Georgia	467	40	24	269	64	7,077	6,365	712	173	148
Hawaii	111	3	-	77	21	1,140	1,064	75	32	23
Idaho	217	1	27	115	41	1,091	965	126	14	11
Illinois	1,571	144	28	1,087	301	9,898	7,637	2,261	406	348
Indiana.	245	5	13	160	53	4,678	3,753	925	141	140
Iowa	493	33	18	350	70	2,105	1,890	215	109	99
Kansas.	237	27	16	157	29	2,134	1,862	272	125	63
Kentucky	537	193	18	202	107	3,008	2,702	306	248	74
Louisiana	490	274	22	118	73	1,804	1,582	222	474	96
Maine.	134	3	11	78	36	1,227	1,077	150	78	59
Maryland	379	13	11	197	155	5,044	4,613	431	313	157
Massachusetts.	451	23	6	288	75	10,348	9,042	1,306	294	167
Michigan.	1,208	13	48	863	213	9,573	7,190	2,382	488	186
Minnesota.	977	4	54	673	224	6,351	5,547	803	226	83
Mississippi	279	68	11	135	53	1,234	1,007	228	50	22
Missouri	576	90	29	258	154	3,816	3,550	265	130	130
Montana.	123	1	30	59	25	616	516	100	109	19
Nebraska	190	6	12	93	59	1,314	1,174	140	28	19
Nevada	362	23	6	126	113	-	-	-	108	76
New Hampshire	143	4	6	73	49	378	66	312	146	61
New Jersey	790	151	12	384	176	8,553	7,205	1,347	602	486
New Mexico	206	2	17	152	30	1,040	881	159	455	16
New York	970	67	32	710	106	25,966	23,194	2,772	1,493	1,055
North Carolina	743	158	15	452	109	8,407	7,210	1,197	225	188
North Dakota.	87	-	4	47	36	277	199	78	151	6
Ohio	1,559	353	30	646	498	8,872	8,241	631	164	155
Oklahoma.	829	43	14	645	115	2,329	2,135	194	501	88
Oregon.	605	6	28	387	169	4,505	4,097	407	108	44
Pennsylvania.	2,273	990	52	848	309	8,467	6,771	1,697	1,148	801
Rhode Island.	91	13	2	52	23	904	829	75	36	34
South Carolina.	375	42	14	124	111	2,673	2,446	227	80	43
South Dakota	118	2	15	41	53	45	-	45	31	28
Tennessee	899	494	25	274	94	794	180	614	242	92
Texas.	3,813	2,099	63	1,043	526	-	-	-	1,398	278
Utah	138	1	23	88	22	1,825	1,651	174	91	65
Vermont	68	1	6	39	19	476	432	44	50	14
Virginia.	514	30	20	339	112	6,888	6,322	566	353	150
Washington.	608	14	29	324	183	-	-	-	577	83
West Virginia.	174	8	16	92	30	1,184	966	218	182	21
Wisconsin.	669	95	62	339	161	6,530	5,952	578	183	133
Wyoming	89	6	23	55	4	-	-	-	296	51

- Represents or rounds to zero.   [1] Duplicate intergovernmental transactions are excluded.   [2] Based on estimated resident population as of April 1, 2000.   [3] Includes categories not shown separately.

Source: U.S. Census Bureau, <http://www.census.gov/govs/www/state00.html> (released 31 May 2002).

No. 430. State Governments—Expenditures and Debt by State: 2000

[In millions of dollars (1,084,548 represents $1,084,548,000,000) except as indicated. For fiscal year ending in year shown; see text, this section]

State	Total expendi-ture [1]	General expenditure								
		Total		Inter-govern-mental	Direct expenditures					
		Amount	Per capita [2] (dol.)		Total	Educa-tion	Public welfare	Health and hospitals	High-ways	Police protection
United States..	1,084,548	965,174	3,437	327,520	637,654	138,357	198,796	59,378	61,686	8,582
Alabama	15,873	14,400	3,238	3,908	10,491	2,807	3,485	1,605	887	92
Alaska	6,611	5,972	9,525	1,027	4,945	646	803	120	630	50
Arizona	16,574	15,284	2,979	6,391	8,892	2,054	2,593	679	1,056	146
Arkansas	9,589	8,967	3,354	2,725	6,241	1,600	1,987	672	614	73
California	149,772	134,204	3,962	65,389	68,815	15,017	18,510	6,957	4,231	1,051
Colorado	13,930	12,485	2,903	3,703	8,782	2,617	2,211	420	963	77
Connecticut	16,723	14,856	4,362	3,363	11,493	1,504	3,020	1,473	751	140
Delaware	4,211	3,913	4,991	856	3,057	710	547	265	324	63
Florida	45,208	42,486	2,658	14,073	28,412	4,154	9,067	3,272	3,543	367
Georgia	24,813	23,092	2,821	7,180	15,912	4,173	5,469	1,011	1,578	193
Hawaii	6,605	5,975	4,930	158	5,818	1,854	1,019	572	226	4
Idaho	4,493	4,039	3,121	1,278	2,761	651	762	130	356	37
Illinois	41,183	36,895	2,971	12,050	24,845	4,651	8,466	2,814	1,829	336
Indiana	20,289	19,188	3,156	6,736	12,452	4,098	3,806	655	1,254	198
Iowa	11,453	10,520	3,595	3,212	7,309	1,862	2,153	768	1,017	80
Kansas	9,124	8,376	3,116	2,853	5,523	1,356	1,314	368	1,197	53
Kentucky	15,682	14,197	3,512	3,280	10,917	2,426	4,051	698	1,416	161
Louisiana	16,554	14,783	3,308	3722	11,061	2462	3,014	1,849	1056	195
Maine	5,448	4,850	3,804	912	3,938	567	1,553	322	391	45
Maryland	19,370	17,281	3,263	4,356	12,925	2,654	3,922	1,055	878	234
Massachusetts	29,478	26,821	4,225	6,241	20,581	2,722	6,247	1,935	2,609	391
Michigan	42,749	39,004	3,925	17,201	21,803	6,284	7,606	1,735	1,259	284
Minnesota	23,326	20,975	4,264	7,610	13,364	3,119	4,777	560	953	123
Mississippi	10972	10049	3532	3248	6801	1468	2295	849	776	67
Missouri	17,293	15,837	2,831	4,529	11,309	2,283	3,912	1,154	1,259	125
Montana	3,718	3,325	3,686	761	2,564	585	530	244	419	25
Nebraska	5,772	5,537	3,236	1,586	3,951	1,008	1,382	247	554	49
Nevada	6,047	5,369	2,687	2,250	3,119	711	791	194	526	58
New Hampshire	4,366	3,884	3,143	1,053	2,831	532	977	151	328	38
New Jersey	34,783	28,160	3,347	8,639	19,521	4,478	4,698	1,805	1,368	402
New Mexico	8,701	7,985	4,390	2,447	5,538	1,374	1,463	660	856	78
New York	96,925	80,617	4,248	31,273	49,344	6,225	20,698	4,519	3,147	422
North Carolina	29,615	27,242	3,384	9,301	17,941	4,203	5,158	1,732	2,256	351
North Dakota	2,856	2,569	4,001	590	1,979	512	544	73	294	12
Ohio	44,631	36,144	3,184	12,932	23,212	5,715	7,659	2,064	2,134	225
Oklahoma	10,630	9,146	2,650	3,089	6,057	2,043	864	462	977	75
Oregon	15,776	13,155	3,845	3,920	9,235	1,615	2,981	1,112	651	130
Pennsylvania	47,682	41,937	3,415	11,370	30,567	6,407	11,441	2,001	3,015	776
Rhode Island	4,648	3,987	3,805	678	3,310	569	1,135	274	220	36
South Carolina	16,237	14,195	3,538	3,806	10,389	2,404	3,441	1,330	1,116	203
South Dakota	2,403	2,228	2,951	448	1,780	321	477	107	340	18
Tennessee	16,853	15,822	2,781	4,364	11,458	2,670	4,766	999	1,184	112
Texas	60,425	54,452	2,611	16,231	38,221	8,882	11,204	3,956	4,768	338
Utah	8,592	7,956	3,563	1,978	5,979	1,819	1,452	578	765	74
Vermont	3,219	3,068	5,037	932	2,136	449	700	75	204	37
Virginia	24,314	22,609	3,194	7,132	15,476	3,943	3,540	1,871	2,142	210
Washington	25,902	21,951	3,724	6,371	15,580	4,058	5,058	1,796	1,096	153
West Virginia	7,552	6,490	3,590	1,360	5,131	1,016	1,762	237	838	52
Wisconsin	23,027	20,645	3,849	8,171	12,475	2,818	3,204	865	1,099	99
Wyoming	2,553	2,254	4,563	838	1,416	261	285	85	335	19

See footnotes at end of table.

U.S. Census Bureau, Statistical Abstract of the United States: 2002

[See headnote, page 284]

State	General expenditure—Con.									Debt outstanding	
	Direct expenditures—Con.							Insurance trust expenditures	Cash and security holdings	Total	Per capita [2] (dol.)
	Corrections	Natural resources	Parks and recreation	Governmental administration	Interest on general debt	Utility expenditures	Liquor stores expenditures				
United States..	33,048	15,011	4,052	34,510	29,198	10,723	3,195	105,456	2,518,936	547,876	1,951
Alabama	273	194	11	345	276	-	151	1,322	25,954	5,292	1,190
Alaska.	174	249	9	336	248	65	-	574	47,024	4,150	6,619
Arizona	668	168	41	441	170	26	-	1,265	35,190	3,101	604
Arkansas	266	192	75	324	121	-	-	623	17,720	2,746	1,027
California	4,118	2,117	286	5,261	2,613	114	-	15,454	336,589	57,170	1,688
Colorado	599	174	59	366	251	10	-	1,434	30,811	4,431	1,030
Connecticut	554	101	41	892	1,089	205	-	1,662	29,080	18,456	5,419
Delaware	228	65	48	288	218	51	-	247	10,747	3,261	4,159
Florida.	2,217	1,412	144	1,871	1,076	55	-	2,667	89,554	18,181	1,137
Georgia	969	496	128	566	387	-	-	1,721	49,499	7,086	866
Hawaii.	155	80	46	312	483	-	-	629	12,773	5,592	4,614
Idaho	149	135	21	204	125	-	42	412	11,782	2,279	1,761
Illinois	1,277	375	141	1,160	1,825	-	-	4,288	86,684	28,828	2,321
Indiana	537	212	61	600	373	-	-	1102	34,108	7,894	1,298
Iowa	224	236	18	410	131	-	74	859	24551	2362	807
Kansas	273	167	8	536	47	-	-	748	12,029	1,912	711
Kentucky	394	266	112	529	360	37	-	1,486	32,029	7,753	1,918
Louisiana.	397	373	168	460	411	3	-	1,768	35,791	7,770	1,739
Maine	92	135	10	210	226	-	53	545	12,346	4,060	3,184
Maryland	894	430	173	798	801	384	-	1,705	47,984	11,365	2,146
Massachusetts . . .	605	202	127	1,058	2,128	306	-	2,351	59,248	38,961	6,137
Michigan	1,483	386	125	792	920	-	465	3,281	77,922	19,445	1,957
Minnesota	293	436	99	664	349	-	-	2,351	53,967	5,602	1,139
Mississippi	242	228	50	223	182	-	133	790	21915	3222	1,132
Missouri.	514	269	38	463	543	-	-	1,456	47,592	9,820	1,755
Montana	104	153	14	187	143	-	33	360	10,184	2,557	2,835
Nebraska.	173	134	25	139	106	-	-	236	10,987	1,680	982
Nevada	218	76	18	152	120	45	-	633	18,562	2,990	1,496
New Hampshire . .	85	41	7	169	310	-	249	233	9,407	5,499	4,450
New Jersey	1,050	240	317	1,199	1,153	1,886	-	4,737	82747	28938	3,439
New Mexico	217	136	43	327	179	-	-	715	32,209	3,625	1,993
New York.	2,298	366	495	3,469	3,663	6,378	-	9,930	211,314	78,616	4,143
North Carolina . . .	906	559	152	724	585	-	-	2,373	73,229	9,336	1,160
North Dakota	29	75	9	80	77	-	-	287	6,842	1,520	2,367
Ohio	1,487	337	132	1,138	998	-	305	8,181	147,209	18,087	1,593
Oklahoma	462	183	61	388	236	278	-	1,205	24,404	5,663	1,641
Oregon	468	270	41	797	461	3	137	2,481	33,586	6,235	1,822
Pennsylvania	1,414	612	140	1,282	1,268	-	801	4,944	110,454	18,595	1,514
Rhode Island	139	41	13	256	277	59	-	602	11,458	5,681	5,422
South Carolina . . .	436	246	56	325	259	797	-	1,245	24,872	7,057	1,759
South Dakota	62	71	22	98	120	-	-	175	8,539	2,305	3,053
Tennessee	351	225	116	429	190	4	-	1,027	29,018	3,292	579
Texas	2,677	653	56	1,367	1,032	-	-	5,973	188,148	19,228	922
Utah	245	141	30	408	185	-	87	548	17,492	3,885	1,740
Vermont	66	90	7	138	124	3	29	120	4,534	2,165	3,554
Virginia	859	181	76	818	792	5	264	1,436	58,387	12,011	1,697
Washington	731	502	64	504	607	-	290	3,644	66,541	11,734	1,991
West Virginia	156	149	55	330	207	9	43	1,010	9,636	3,730	2,063
Wisconsin	746	330	54	601	687	-	-	2,381	77,051	11,454	2,135
Wyoming	73	99	11	78	64	-	38	242	9,239	1,250	2,531

- Represents or rounds to zero.   [1] Includes amounts not shown separately.   [2] Based on estimated resident population as of April 1, 2000.

Source: U.S. Census Bureau, <http://www.census.gov/govs/www/state00.html> (released 31 May 2002).

U.S. Census Bureau, Statistical Abstract of the United States: 2002

No. 431. Local Governments—Revenue by State: 1999

[In millions of dollars (952,330 represents $952,330,000,000), except as noted. For fiscal year ending in year shown; see text, this section]

State	Total revenue [1]	General revenue		Intergovernmental revenue			Taxes				
		Total	Per capita [2] (dol.)	Total	From federal government	From state governments	Total	Property	Sales and gross receipts	Income [3]	Motor licenses
United States..	952,330	839,031	3,077	327,579	31,687	295,892	315,833	228,453	51,626	19,701	1,259
Alabama	11,860	9,969	2,281	4,109	411	3,698	2,738	1,027	1,257	137	20
Alaska.	2,779	2,538	4,094	1,024	160	865	856	679	153	-	10
Arizona	16,069	13,357	2,796	5,767	559	5,208	4,695	3,316	1,176	-	-
Arkansas.	5,576	4,997	1,959	2,192	136	2,055	1,468	948	500	-	-
California.	147,304	125,175	3,777	61,086	4,805	56,281	32,590	21,582	7,949	-	-
Colorado	14,325	12,461	3,072	3,436	383	3,053	5,549	3,414	1,862	-	32
Connecticut	10,171	9,397	2,863	3,117	309	2,807	5,265	5,175	1	-	-
Delaware.	1,754	1,581	2,096	788	46	743	441	349	3	43	-
District of Columbia	6,131	5,452	10,504	1,707	1,707	-	2,974	680	934	1,170	18
Florida.	53,458	47,680	3,155	15,846	1,969	13,877	16,446	12,940	2,935	-	33
Georgia.	25,528	22,335	2,868	7,491	638	6,853	9,041	5,379	3,373	-	-
Hawaii.	1,608	1,425	1,203	282	133	149	747	595	88	-	42
Idaho	3,238	3,108	2,483	1,310	73	1,238	868	816	13	-	5
Illinois	42,289	36,628	3,020	12,695	1,531	11,164	16,759	13,890	2,371	-	113
Indiana	17,425	15,757	2,651	5,827	297	5,531	5,840	5,173	69	515	2
Iowa	8,642	8,107	2,826	3,131	220	2,911	2,805	2,533	191	40	11
Kansas	8,157	7,448	2,806	2,786	115	2,671	2,703	2,068	585	-	4
Kentucky	8,869	7,746	1,955	3,272	331	2,941	2,404	1,295	174	689	28
Louisiana.	11,701	10,826	2,476	4,056	326	3,730	4,042	1,594	2,276	-	4
Maine	3,095	2,998	2,393	980	103	877	1,542	1,504	3	-	19
Maryland	15,827	14,261	2,757	4,670	627	4,043	7,057	3,894	244	2,385	-
Massachusetts . . .	20,378	17,373	2,814	7,583	862	6,720	7,538	7,300	105	-	1
Michigan	34,623	30,856	3,128	15,846	985	14,861	8,048	7,230	55	523	1
Minnesota	18,466	16,633	3,483	7,370	507	6,863	4,706	4,450	120	-	5
Mississippi	6,948	6,423	2,320	2,711	152	2,560	1,513	1,389	52	-	-
Missouri.	14,524	12,985	2,375	4,452	428	4,025	5,464	3,288	1,684	228	13
Montana	2,071	2,001	2,266	764	119	645	696	663	4	-	13
Nebraska.	6,697	4,542	2,726	1,454	149	1,306	1,962	1,562	226	-	15
Nevada	6,505	6,072	3,357	2,522	216	2,306	1,861	1,178	410	-	-
New Hampshire . .	2,964	2,898	2,413	455	86	370	2,039	2,014	-	-	-
New Jersey	28,473	27,789	3,413	8,758	629	8,129	14,649	14,335	31	30	-
New Mexico	4,764	4,456	2,561	2,482	252	2,230	1,015	550	419	-	-
New York	105,272	92,285	5,071	32,182	2,929	29,253	43,453	24,759	8,454	8,408	126
North Carolina . . .	23,676	20,900	2,732	8,740	568	8,172	5,830	4,351	1,172	-	25
North Dakota	1,698	1,609	2,538	687	167	520	562	495	56	-	-
Ohio	35,465	33,402	2,967	12,510	1,111	11,399	14,123	9,318	1,251	3,097	99
Oklahoma	8,211	7,472	2,225	2,845	217	2,628	2,351	1,238	1,026	-	2
Oregon	11,319	10,567	3,187	4,625	737	3,888	3,195	2,558	173	-	9
Pennsylvania	37,260	33,969	2,832	13,769	1,673	12,096	13,604	9,483	369	2,436	-
Rhode Island	2,404	2,236	2,256	702	97	606	1,302	1,285	1	-	-
South Carolina . . .	10,313	9,261	2,383	3,226	290	2,936	2,906	2,468	193	-	14
South Dakota	1,785	1,616	2,204	511	77	434	782	617	106	-	16
Tennessee.	18,400	12,665	2,309	4,282	419	3,863	4,551	2,684	1,596	-	82
Texas	61,129	53,067	2,648	16,659	2,019	14,640	23,556	18,805	4,020	-	255
Utah	6,430	5,280	2,479	2,143	282	1,862	1,815	1,192	480	-	-
Vermont	1,512	1,357	2,284	804	27	777	396	380	1	-	-
Virginia	19,614	17,759	2,584	6,275	572	5,703	7,995	5,730	1,486	-	113
Washington	21,691	17,917	3,113	7,204	682	6,522	5,781	3,608	1,637	-	120
West Virginia	3,714	3,551	1,965	1,650	97	1,553	977	809	34	-	-
Wisconsin	18,163	16,890	3,217	8,055	421	7,634	5,790	5,443	208	-	1
Wyoming	2,057	1,957	4,077	738	39	699	545	423	97	-	9

See footnotes at end of table.

U.S. Census Bureau, Statistical Abstract of the United States: 2002

[See headnote, page 286]

State	Current charges & miscellaneous general revenue	Current charges				Miscellaneous general revenue			Utility revenue	Liquor store revenue	Insurance trust revenue
		Total	Education	Hospital	Sewerage	Total	Interest earnings	Special assessment			
United States.....	195,618	131,577	14,935	34,567	23,645	64,041	33,826	3,549	77,524	645	35,130
Alabama	3,121	2,262	255	1,305	218	859	408	11	1,731	-	159
Alaska.	658	404	34	57	43	254	158	4	195	-	46
Arizona	2,895	1,697	325	206	307	1,198	665	70	2,509	-	203
Arkansas	1,336	923	128	392	152	413	236	8	543	-	37
California	31,500	20,523	1,404	3,604	3,078	10,977	5,305	893	12,805	-	9,324
Colorado	3,476	2,361	259	409	413	1,115	622	42	1,373	-	492
Connecticut	1,016	550	69	-	169	466	205	33	448	-	326
Delaware.	351	230	12	-	105	121	69	-	142	-	31
District of Columbia . . .	772	384	20	118	107	388	169	-	438	-	242
Florida.	15,388	10,208	1,251	2,667	1,381	5,180	2,792	886	4,898	-	880
Georgia.	5,802	4,027	215	1,976	568	1,775	951	19	2,676	-	517
Hawaii.	396	259	-	-	139	137	76	11	182	-	-
Idaho	929	730	47	361	84	199	78	15	128	-	1
Illinois	7,174	4,477	849	462	709	2,697	1,560	90	2,593	-	3,068
Indiana	4,090	2,777	272	1,537	453	1,313	580	22	1,606	-	61
Iowa	2,171	1,612	421	627	225	559	273	15	516	-	19
Kansas	1,959	1,267	233	430	168	692	403	64	593	-	115
Kentucky	2,070	1,017	94	163	240	1,053	875	4	1,078	-	45
Louisiana.	2,728	1,912	70	1,171	194	816	557	7	728	-	147
Maine	476	342	20	49	112	134	64	2	97	-	-
Maryland	2,535	1,658	433	-	518	877	443	104	418	131	1,016
Massachusetts	2,253	1,649	173	164	604	604	265	77	1,865	-	1,139
Michigan	6,961	4,438	688	688	1,231	2,523	994	85	1,377	-	2,390
Minnesota	4,557	2,568	209	720	408	1,989	934	266	1,116	187	529
Mississippi	2,199	1,688	192	1,175	126	511	262	4	525	-	-
Missouri.	3,068	2,234	420	655	406	834	512	15	1,141	-	398
Montana	540	301	52	44	44	239	143	43	71	-	-
Nebraska.	1,125	763	161	246	100	362	190	35	2,001	-	155
Nevada	1,689	1,210	76	421	201	479	315	25	433	-	-
New Hampshire	403	294	36	-	75	109	47	3	65	-	1
New Jersey	4,381	2,664	487	202	921	1,717	588	15	670	-	14
New Mexico.	959	626	69	204	100	333	214	16	308	-	-
New York.	16,650	11,727	705	3,007	1,249	4,923	2,033	104	5,040	-	7,947
North Carolina	6,330	5,027	385	2,584	808	1,303	777	12	2,427	317	32
North Dakota	361	176	38	-	25	185	69	32	77	-	12
Ohio	6,770	4,384	871	698	1,288	2,386	1,332	86	1,828	-	235
Oklahoma	2,276	1,687	284	729	190	589	317	5	666	-	73
Oregon	2,747	1,853	344	269	436	894	455	47	751	-	1
Pennsylvania	6,596	4,093	537	24	1,282	2,503	1,726	51	1,788	-	1,502
Rhode Island	231	158	19	-	55	73	33	3	94	-	74
South Carolina	3,128	2,474	186	1,499	194	654	421	21	1,048	-	4
South Dakota	322	212	38	33	41	110	58	6	136	10	23
Tennessee	3,832	3,028	316	1,483	447	804	466	8	5,143	-	592
Texas	12,851	8,727	1,291	2,400	1,748	4,124	2,776	61	6,297	-	1,766
Utah	1,321	782	64	43	143	539	247	6	1,150	-	-
Vermont	156	98	17	-	33	58	21	1	145	-	10
Virginia	3,489	2,345	209	252	640	1,144	666	21	1,111	-	744
Washington	4,933	3,550	237	852	802	1,383	685	74	3,488	-	286
West Virginia	924	620	33	246	117	304	205	2	138	-	24
Wisconsin	3,046	2,078	346	89	511	968	485	87	831	-	441
Wyoming	673	500	41	307	38	173	99	39	95	-	5

- Represents zero.   X Not applicable. [1] Includes items not shown separately.   [2] Based on estimated resident population as of July 1.   [3] Represents individual and corporate income taxes.

Source: U.S. Census Bureau, *Governmental Finances, 1998-99*. See also <http://www.census.gov/govs/estimate/99allpub.pdf> (released September 2001).

Local Governments—Expenditures and Debt by State: 1999

[In millions of dollars, (938,641 represents $938,641,000,000), except as indicated. For fiscal year ending in year shown; see text, this section]

State	Total expen- diture [1]	General expenditure			Selected functions (direct expenditures)						
		Total amount	Per capita [2] (dol)	Direct general expen- ditures	Educa- tion	Public welfare	Health	Hospi- tals	High- ways	Police protec- tion	Fire protec- tion
United States	938,641	823,961	3,442	813,991	357,075	32,952	22,771	42,199	36,776	45,557	21,262
Alabama	12,310	10,464	2,817	10,461	4,560	36	273	1,359	515	557	241
Alaska	2,876	2,597	4,638	2,588	1,079	6	61	63	195	126	63
Arizona	16,051	13,442	3,359	13,119	5,570	476	149	270	593	895	386
Arkansas	5,456	4,939	2,139	4,939	2,547	9	37	353	296	271	111
California	141,693	120,382	4,275	119,047	43,398	10,084	4,917	5,697	3,937	7,198	3,398
Colorado	13,871	11,889	3,420	11,889	4,878	430	143	450	876	708	303
Connecticut	9,863	9,164	3,005	9,159	4,813	100	97	12	417	531	377
Delaware	1,672	1,537	2,217	1,533	931	1	12	-	94	91	17
District of Columbia . . .	6,273	4,630	12,087	4,630	777	1,247	247	263	101	313	104
Florida	51,816	45,509	3,429	45,333	17,565	349	488	3,243	1,724	3,243	1,436
Georgia	24,571	20,970	3,155	20,930	9,829	87	652	2,104	910	1,018	484
Hawaii	1,662	1,391	1,403	1,391	-	22	26	-	121	216	90
Idaho	3,182	3,053	2,542	3,048	1,454	30	49	368	212	158	73
Illinois	41,797	36,199	3,446	36,172	16,962	396	465	1,008	1,866	2,473	1,049
Indiana	17,228	15,527	2,899	15,452	6,958	438	151	1,741	624	578	388
Iowa	8,739	8,101	3,046	8,017	3,899	101	239	690	797	322	139
Kansas	7,816	7,209	2,945	7,194	3,389	49	148	437	525	382	164
Kentucky	8,894	7,986	2,245	7,984	3,767	39	264	168	290	317	194
Louisiana	11,753	10,715	2,688	10,711	4,627	52	80	1,332	581	642	271
Maine	2,949	2,861	2,353	2,860	1,520	29	14	57	174	113	75
Maryland	14,544	13,533	2,812	13,400	6,808	75	239	-	552	801	448
Massachusetts	20,132	16,533	3,260	15,932	7,988	68	82	218	650	1,012	754
Michigan	34,368	31,601	3,484	31,465	15,571	542	1,745	825	1,760	1,449	584
Minnesota	18,575	16,839	3,889	16,755	6,836	1,137	365	841	1,351	715	241
Mississippi	7,392	6,888	2,670	6,886	3,145	27	51	1,217	401	337	147
Missouri	14,520	12,995	2,655	12,976	6,495	123	207	767	809	728	462
Montana	1,939	1,869	2,196	1,865	1,033	25	39	36	95	96	40
Nebraska	6,286	4,251	3,773	4,242	2,175	24	49	258	317	175	123
Nevada	6,829	6,107	3,775	6,105	2,195	92	88	408	532	415	186
New Hampshire	2,836	2,768	2,361	2,706	1,371	129	19	-	138	141	95
New Jersey	27,251	26,603	3,347	26,294	13,042	1,204	251	265	995	1,686	603
New Mexico	4,875	4,418	2,802	4,397	2,228	43	25	214	210	283	118
New York	103,395	90,711	5,682	85,432	31,856	8,346	2,325	4,484	3,431	5,128	2,058
North Carolina	24,191	20,982	3,162	20,701	9,045	976	1,186	2,720	362	934	422
North Dakota	1,675	1,594	2,642	1,585	703	35	17	-	163	53	32
Ohio	34,560	32,069	3,070	31,881	13,949	1,724	1,765	870	1,613	1,833	944
Oklahoma	7,968	7,289	2,373	7,288	3,714	20	86	708	354	383	237
Oregon	11,622	10,340	3,505	10,338	4,633	60	464	292	583	513	319
Pennsylvania	37,260	33,670	3,107	33,656	16,509	1,728	1,632	115	1,043	1,350	428
Rhode Island	2,332	2,148	2,353	2,146	1,222	7	4	-	66	156	141
South Carolina	10,052	8,967	2,587	8,946	4,385	16	221	1,301	186	416	187
South Dakota	1,754	1,613	2,393	1,611	842	12	12	33	193	69	29
Tennessee	18,967	13,488	3,459	13,447	5,532	121	199	1,610	591	745	378
Texas	61,120	53,338	3,049	52,807	27,434	242	1,234	3,425	1,928	2,777	1,209
Utah	6,378	5,044	2,994	5,037	2,384	60	149	25	289	292	117
Vermont	1,440	1,274	2,424	1,272	822	1	5	-	110	38	23
Virginia	19,282	17,666	2,805	17,643	8,204	864	442	236	516	920	509
Washington	22,097	17,871	3,839	17,835	7,193	45	585	978	1,114	811	555
West Virginia	3,636	3,468	2,012	3,461	2,083	3	61	246	52	116	54
Wisconsin	18,960	17,654	3,611	17,616	8,329	1,218	694	165	1,450	955	427
Wyoming	1,932	1,809	4,024	1,807	826	8	18	327	75	76	26

See footnotes at end of table

U.S. Census Bureau, Statistical Abstract of the United States: 2002

[See headnote, page 288]

State	General expenditure—Con.										
	Selected functions (direct expenditures)—Con.									Insurance trust expenditure	Debt outstanding
	Corrections	Parks and recreation	Housing [4]	Sewerage	Solid waste	Governmental administration	Interest on general debt	Other	Utility expenditures		
United States	14,828	19,574	22,848	25,852	14,110	44,141	39,508	74,539	96,072	18,028	858,767
Alabama	131	237	320	434	200	521	442	636	1,777	69	9,783
Alaska.	1	64	91	72	52	169	177	368	265	13	3,524
Arizona	174	419	264	450	215	1,011	758	1,489	2,525	84	20,188
Arkansas	60	80	107	120	112	242	231	363	503	14	4,448
California	2,797	2,792	4,602	3,857	1,552	7,488	5,113	12,216	17,400	3,910	114,370
Colorado	199	558	287	348	81	722	850	1,055	1,789	193	18,000
Connecticut	-	167	378	232	162	492	262	1,118	476	224	4,733
Delaware	-	17	51	90	12	75	67	75	111	24	1,203
District of Columbia . . .	293	154	60	125	42	388	254	263	1,148	495	4,939
Florida.	1,010	1,309	1,041	1,407	1,433	2,539	2,899	5,645	5,889	418	57,881
Georgia	403	376	506	717	455	1,397	698	1,293	3,356	245	20,004
Hawaii.	-	135	64	114	103	154	109	237	271	-	2,230
Idaho	39	63	26	82	81	167	55	191	128	1	1,113
Illinois	421	1,805	1,437	1,009	368	2,034	1,784	3,094	4,004	1,594	36,315
Indiana	188	450	300	536	166	888	593	1,454	1,607	94	11,408
Iowa	75	208	99	269	129	318	228	503	626	12	4,684
Kansas	82	158	96	153	97	405	417	692	579	28	8,255
Kentucky	171	108	139	258	109	298	935	927	886	22	15,095
Louisiana	295	178	251	276	214	666	527	718	911	127	10,164
Maine	29	47	72	106	84	150	85	305	88	-	1,709
Maryland	180	473	497	457	392	723	645	1,109	517	382	12,651
Massachusetts	216	203	914	468	333	601	382	2,044	2,659	939	14,521
Michigan	361	552	263	1,471	349	1,762	1,338	2,893	1,748	1,018	27,906
Minnesota	272	533	540	499	231	890	1,044	1,261	1,310	247	21,379
Mississippi	64	73	101	121	98	388	285	430	504	-	5,353
Missouri.	154	324	229	386	90	647	435	1,122	1,287	238	8,702
Montana	27	29	26	39	47	115	79	139	70	-	1,206
Nebraska.	48	94	87	118	67	216	106	387	1,957	78	4,470
Nevada.	191	338	145	124	6	526	390	470	722	-	9,303
New Hampshire	30	49	36	66	84	144	60	344	67	1	1,350
New Jersey	413	374	606	898	746	1,425	1,121	2,665	639	9	19,998
New Mexico	86	158	69	96	111	224	197	334	457	-	4,039
New York.	2,054	1,234	2,692	1,936	1,722	2,822	5,056	10,288	7,541	5,142	94,857
North Carolina	210	416	451	496	534	785	685	1,479	2,917	14	19,173
North Dakota	11	94	117	18	26	78	58	181	75	7	1,135
Ohio	383	787	858	1,229	385	2,267	1,055	2,220	2,430	61	21,547
Oklahoma	22	217	119	209	144	314	261	500	656	24	5,610
Oregon	255	298	348	469	106	596	345	1,058	1,228	53	8,609
Pennsylvania	773	476	1,160	1,380	475	1,814	2,368	2,405	2,879	711	51,806
Rhode Island	-	35	103	59	29	81	47	195	99	85	1,155
South Carolina	125	188	159	208	211	529	425	389	1,083	3	10,502
South Dakota	20	60	22	37	22	97	40	124	125	7	900
Tennessee	234	439	493	354	267	708	621	1,158	5,191	288	14,116
Texas	1,159	1,041	1,207	1,610	643	2,520	3,193	3,187	7,302	480	75,822
Utah	136	215	101	165	92	389	205	419	1,334	-	9,160
Vermont	-	14	20	47	29	68	27	69	163	4	670
Virginia	351	462	469	680	481	1,123	875	1,511	1,313	303	18,533
Washington	354	545	445	831	388	1,001	785	2,204	4,100	126	26,119
West Virginia	29	47	62	102	43	179	205	180	147	22	3,409
Wisconsin	283	442	313	585	266	876	626	986	1,093	213	13,418
Wyoming	20	37	6	41	27	109	65	147	120	3	1,304

- Represents or rounds to zero.   [1] Duplicate intergovernmental transactions are excluded.   [2] Based on estimated resident population as of July 1.   [3] Includes items not shown separately.   [4] Includes community development.

Source: U.S. Census Bureau, *Governmental Finances, 1998-99*. See also <http://www.census.gov/govs/estimate/99allpub.pdf> (released September 2001).

OUACHITA TECHNICAL COLLEGE

No. 433. Estimated State and Local Taxes Paid by a Family of Four in Selected Cities: 2000

[Data based on average family of four (two wage earners and two school age children) owning their own home and living in a city where taxes apply. Comprises state and local sales, income, auto, and real estate taxes. For definition of median, see Guide to Tabular Presentation]

City	Total taxes paid by gross family income level (dollars)					Total taxes paid as percent of income				
	$25,000	$50,000	$75,000	$100,000	$150,000	$25,000	$50,000	$75,000	$100,000	$150,000
Albuquerque, NM . . .	1,879	3,613	6,169	8,743	14,024	7.5	7.2	8.2	8.7	9.3
Atlanta, GA	1,679	3,847	6,586	9,201	14,299	6.7	7.7	8.8	9.2	9.5
Baltimore, MD	1,792	5,352	8,461	11,264	16,781	7.2	10.7	11.3	11.3	11.2
Boston, MA	2,041	4,569	7,300	9,781	14,828	8.2	9.1	9.7	9.8	9.9
Charlotte, NC	1,967	4,125	6,781	9,575	14,813	7.9	8.2	9.0	9.6	9.9
Chicago, IL	2,110	4,016	6,386	8,403	12,378	8.4	8.0	8.5	8.4	8.3
Columbus, OH	2,189	4,312	6,996	9,694	15,316	8.8	8.6	9.3	9.7	10.2
Denver, CO	1,257	2,632	4,611	6,416	9,486	5.0	5.3	6.1	6.4	6.3
Detroit, MI.	2,330	4,587	7,264	9,728	14,703	9.3	9.2	9.7	9.7	9.8
Honolulu, HI	2,205	4,340	7,141	9,709	14,939	8.8	8.7	9.5	9.7	10.0
Houston, TX	1,707	2,584	4,040	5,202	7,306	6.8	5.2	5.4	5.2	4.9
Indianapolis, IN	2,003	3,676	5,696	7,526	11,194	8.0	7.4	7.6	7.5	7.5
Jacksonville, FL	1,262	2,282	3,726	4,852	7,049	5.0	4.6	5.0	4.9	4.7
Kansas City, MO . . .	2,326	4,344	6,852	9,377	14,729	9.3	8.7	9.1	9.4	9.8
Las Vegas, NV	1,522	2,200	3,316	4,217	5,963	6.1	4.4	4.4	4.2	4.0
Los Angeles, CA . . .	2,288	4,175	7,543	11,122	18,303	9.2	8.3	10.1	11.1	12.2
Memphis, TN.	1,831	2,516	3,810	4,914	6,960	7.3	5.0	5.1	4.9	4.6
Milwaukee, WI.	2,099	4,896	7,948	10,708	16,101	8.4	9.8	10.6	10.7	10.7
Minneapolis, MN . . .	1,511	4,216	7,273	10,110	15,911	6.0	8.4	9.7	10.1	10.6
New Orleans, LA . . .	1,434	3,136	5,605	7,658	11,675	5.7	6.3	7.5	7.7	7.8
New York City, NY . .	2,013	5,244	9,161	12,920	20,628	8.1	10.5	12.2	12.9	13.8
Oklahoma City, OK. .	2,207	3,941	6,507	8,756	13,386	8.8	7.9	8.7	8.8	8.9
Omaha, NE.	1,663	3,544	6,084	8,635	14,089	6.7	7.1	8.1	8.6	9.4
Philadelphia, PA. . . .	3,020	6,713	9,959	12,944	18,826	12.1	13.4	13.3	12.9	12.6
Phoenix, AZ	1,478	2,594	4,438	6,329	10,418	5.9	5.2	5.9	6.3	6.9
Portland, OR	1,770	3,988	6,614	9,003	13,671	7.1	8.0	8.8	9.0	9.1
Seattle, WA.	2,113	3,133	4,738	6,048	8,711	8.5	6.3	6.3	6.0	5.8
Virginia Beach, VA . .	2,048	3,988	6,391	8,661	12,953	8.2	8.0	8.5	8.7	8.6
Washington, DC. . . .	2,146	4,335	7,455	10,459	16,377	8.6	8.7	9.9	10.5	10.9
Wichita, KS.	1,356	3,192	5,687	8,104	12,798	5.4	6.4	7.6	8.1	8.5
Average [1]	2,007	4,019	6,584	8,982	13,718	8.0	8.0	8.8	9.0	9.1
Median [1]	2,003	3,954	6,507	8,986	14,024	8.0	7.9	8.7	9.0	9.3

[1] Based on selected cities and District of Columbia. For complete list of cities, see Table 434.

Source: Government of the District of Columbia, Department of Finance and Revenue, *Tax Rates and Tax Burdens in the District of Columbia: A Nationwide Comparison,* annual.

No. 434. Residential Property Tax Rates For Largest City in Each State: 2000

[Effective tax rate is amount each jurisdiction considers based upon assessment level used. Assessment level is ratio of assessed value to assumed market value. Nominal rate is announced rates it levied at taxable value of house]

City	Effective tax rate per $100		Assessment level (percent)	Nominal rate per $100	City	Effective tax rate per $100		Assessment level (percent)	Nominal rate per $100
	Rank	Rate				Rank	Rate		
Bridgeport, CT.	1	4.55	70.0	6.50	Portland, OR.	28	1.50	72.1	2.07
Providence, RI	2	3.52	100.7	3.49	Salt Lake City, UT . . .	29	1.43	99.0	1.45
Newark, NJ.	3	3.34	13.4	24.88	Boston, MA	30	1.32	100.0	1.32
Manchester, NH. . . .	4	3.05	100.0	3.05	Louisville, KY	31	1.30	100.0	1.30
Milwaukee, WI.	5	3.01	101.1	2.98	Wilmington, DE	32	1.29	56.3	2.30
Philadelphia, PA	6	2.64	32.0	8.26	Wichita, KS.	33	1.27	11.5	11.04
Houston, TX	7	2.59	100.0	2.59	Little Rock, AR	34	1.26	20.0	6.30
Des Moines, IA	8	2.45	56.3	4.36	Minneapolis, MN	35	1.25	85.9	1.45
Baltimore, MD	9	2.41	40.0	6.03	Oklahoma City, OK . .	36	1.16	11.0	10.53
Portland, ME.	10	2.40	100.0	2.40	Albuquerque, NM. . . .	37	1.15	33.3	3.46
Fargo, ND	11	2.07	4.2	49.38	Charlotte, NC	37	1.13	94.3	1.20
Burlington, VT.	12	2.06	93.7	2.20	Virginia Beach, VA . . .	39	1.12	92.0	1.22
Jacksonville, FL.	13	2.03	100.0	2.03	Seattle, WA	40	1.12	88.3	1.27
Indianapolis, IN	14	1.90	15.0	12.67	Los Angeles, CA . . .	41	1.07	100.0	1.07
Atlanta, GA.	15	1.87	40.0	4.68	Las Vegas, NV	42	1.06	35.0	3.03
Detroit, MI	16	1.81	30.4	5.94	Phoenix, AZ	43	1.00	10.0	10.00
Omaha, NE	17	1.79	95.0	1.88	Washington, DC	44	0.96	100.0	0.96
Boise City, ID	18	1.77	97.4	1.82	Chicago, IL.	45	0.93	10.0	9.31
New Orleans, LA. . . .	19	1.70	10.0	17.00	Charleston, WV.	46	0.91	60.0	1.52
Anchorage, AK	19	1.67	94.5	1.77	New York City, NY . . .	47	0.80	7.3	10.88
Jackson, MS.	21	1.64	10.0	16.39	Denver, CO	48	0.71	9.7	7.27
Columbus, OH	22	1.64	31.9	5.15	Cheyenne, WY	49	0.71	9.5	7.45
Memphis, TN	23	1.60	23.1	6.91	Birmingham, AL.	50	0.70	10.0	6.95
Sioux Falls, SD	24	1.58	100.0	1.58	Honolulu, HI	51	0.37	100.0	0.37
Billings, MT.	25	1.54	72.5	2.12					
Columbia, SC	26	1.52	4.0	37.93	Unweighted average .	(X)	1.67	56.3	6.78
Kansas City, MO . . .	27	1.50	19.0	7.88	Median	(X)	1.52	(X)	(X)

X Not applicable.

Source: Government of the District of Columbia, Department of Finance and Revenue, *Tax Rates and Tax Burdens in the District of Columbia: A Nationwide Comparison,* annual.

No. 435. Gross Revenue From Parimutuel and Amusement Taxes and Lotteries by State: 2000

[In millions of dollars (39,310 represents $39,310,000,000). For fiscal years; see text, this section]

State	Gross revenue (mil. dol.)	Amusement taxes [1]	Parimutuel taxes	Lottery revenue			
					Apportionment of funds (percent)		
				Total [2] (mil. dol.)	Prizes	Admini- stration	Proceeds available from ticket sales
United States . . .	39,310	3,638	338	35,334	20,701	2,235	12,398
Alabama.	4	-	4	(X)	(X)	(X)	(X)
Alaska	2	2	(X)	(X)	(X)	(X)	(X)
Arizona.	276	1	3	272	140	26	107
Arkansas	7	-	7	(X)	(X)	(X)	(X)
California	2,465	(X)	46	2,419	1,369	164	886
Colorado.	425	75	7	343	224	31	88
Connecticut.	1,171	319	11	840	502	80	257
Delaware	329	(X)	-	329	51	7	271
Florida	2,181	(X)	49	2,131	1,107	125	899
Georgia	2,060	(X)	(X)	2,060	1,260	122	677
Hawaii	(X)	(X)	(X)	(X)	(X)	(X)	(X)
Idaho	87	(X)	(X)	87	51	18	18
Illinois	1,881	488	24	1,369	799	62	508
Indiana.	983	448	4	531	337	32	162
Iowa	338	177	3	158	98	23	37
Kansas.	181	1	4	176	104	21	51
Kentucky	596	-	21	575	411	6	158
Louisiana	681	421	6	254	139	18	97
Maine.	148	(X)	4	143	84	16	43
Maryland	1,185	10	2	1,173	657	109	408
Massachusetts.	3,505	6	8	3,491	2,584	68	839
Michigan.	1,683	53	13	1,616	921	81	614
Minnesota.	434	62	1	370	242	71	57
Mississippi	177	177	(X)	(X)	(X)	(X)	(X)
Missouri	658	182	(X)	476	281	38	157
Montana.	70	41	-	28	16	6	7
Nebraska	76	7	1	68	36	16	16
Nevada	708	708	(X)	(X)	(X)	(X)	(X)
New Hampshire	199	2	4	193	126	6	60
New Jersey.	2,079	340	(X)	1,738	973	53	713
New Mexico	131	20	1	111	62	23	25
New York	3,352	2	36	3,314	1,768	100	1,446
North Carolina	11	11	(X)	(X)	(X)	(X)	(X)
North Dakota.	13	13	(X)	(X)	(X)	(X)	(X)
Ohio	2,172	(X)	17	2,156	1,275	95	785
Oklahoma.	12	8	4	(X)	(X)	(X)	(X)
Oregon.	1,661	-	1	1,660	842	234	584
Pennsylvania.	1,615	1	26	1,589	829	57	704
Rhode Island.	749	(X)	5	744	591	7	147
South Carolina.	38	38	(X)	(X)	(X)	(X)	(X)
South Dakota	123	-	1	122	13	8	101
Tennessee	(X)	(X)	(X)	(X)	(X)	(X)	(X)
Texas	2,691	23	12	2,657	1,509	271	878
Utah	(X)	(X)	(X)	(X)	(X)	(X)	(X)
Vermont	75	(X)	(X)	75	47	9	19
Virginia.	981	-	(X)	981	638	117	227
Washington.	455	(X)	2	453	290	62	101
West Virginia.	261	(X)	8	253	95	22	136
Wisconsin.	383	-	3	380	232	32	115
Wyoming	(X)	(X)	(X)	(X)	(X)	(X)	(X)

- Represents or rounds to zero. X Not applicable. [1] Represents nonlicense taxes. [2] Excludes commissions.

Source: U.S. Census Bureau, unpublished data.

No. 436. Lottery Sales—Type of Game: 1980 to 2001

[In millions of dollars (2,393 represents $2,393,000,000). For fiscal years]

Game	1980	1985	1990	1995	1998	1999	2000	2001
Total ticket sales	2,393	9,035	20,017	31,931	35,588	35,966	37,201	38,441
Instant [1]	527	1,296	5,204	11,511	13,882	13,933	15,459	16,420
Three digit [2].	1,554	3,376	4,572	5,737	5,643	5,237	5,341	5,245
Four digit [2]	55	693	1,302	1,941	2,232	2,655	2,711	2,776
Lotto [3]	52	3,583	8,563	10,594	9,854	9,794	9,160	8,865
Other [4]	206	88	376	2,148	3,978	4,347	4,530	5,134
State proceeds (net income) [5]	978	3,735	7,703	11,100	12,102	11,255	11,404	11,916

[1] Player scratches a latex section on ticket which reveals instantly whether ticket is a winner. [2] Players choose and bet on three or four digits, depending on game, with various payoffs for different straight order or mixed combination bets. [3] Players typically select six digits out of a large field of numbers. Varying prizes are offered for matching three through six numbers drawn by lottery. [4] Includes breakopen tickets, spiel, keno, video lottery, etc. [5] Sales minus prizes and expenses equal net government income.

Source: TLF Publications, Inc., Boyds, MD, *2002 World Lottery Almanac* annual; *LaFleur's Fiscal 2001 Lottery Report;* (copyright).

U.S. Census Bureau, Statistical Abstract of the United States: 2002

No. 437. City Governments—Revenue for Largest Cities: 1999

[In millions of dollars (56,588 represents $56,588,000,000). For fiscal years ending in year shown; see text, this section. Cities ranked by size of population estimated as of July 1, 1998. Data reflect inclusion of fiscal activity of dependent school systems where applicable]

Cities ranked by 1998 population	Total revenue	General revenue — Total	Intergovernmental — Total	Intergov — From federal govt	Intergov — From state/local govt	Intergov — From local govt	Gen. rev. from own sources — Total	Taxes — Total	Taxes — Property	Sales & gross receipts — Total	Sales — General sales	Sales — Public utilities	Current charges — Total	Current charges — Parks and recreation	Current charges — Sewerage[1]	Miscellaneous — Total	Misc — Interest earnings	Utility revenue[2]	Employee retirement revenue
New York, NY	56,588	45,994	17,477	2,171	15,219	87	28,517	21,533	7,703	4,165	3,204	309	4,987	42	914	1,996	694	2,647	7,947
Los Angeles, CA	9,598	5,064	940	350	454	136	4,124	2,129	683	947	306	542	1,436	70	463	559	322	2,740	1,793
Chicago, IL	5,657	4,382	1,140	338	802	-	3,241	1,899	677	1,031	172	440	824	-	129	518	296	293	983
Houston, TX	2,764	1,912	166	124	40	2	1,746	1,017	499	488	305	139	548	24	269	181	114	269	583
Philadelphia, PA[3]	5,562	4,216	1,762	431	1,201	130	2,454	1,822	339	162	99	41	478	17	197	154	115	603	743
San Diego, CA	1,915	1,483	413	220	193	-	1,070	509	155	99	-	80	259	38	170	302	118	212	220
Phoenix, AZ	1,873	1,636	497	110	352	35	1,139	553	148	179	179	19	429	26	137	158	97	172	65
San Antonio, TX	2,001	843	117	23	84	10	727	361	172	238	238	84	226	27	133	140	96	1,109	49
Dallas, TX	2,346	1,555	94	59	33	2	1,462	674	347	195	117	51	603	39	196	184	125	186	605
Detroit, MI[3]	4,965	3,485	2,172	298	1,853	21	1,313	817	376	195	195	51	307	16	217	189	83	217	1,262
Honolulu, HI[3]	1,089	961	146	83	62	1	816	513	403	51	-	19	212	16	182	91	51	128	-
San Jose, CA	1,530	1,095	137	24	68	44	958	522	171	224	123	83	283	17	156	153	74	14	421
San Francisco, CA[3]	5,288	4,044	1,521	263	1,251	7	2,523	1,375	541	472	240	68	871	38	150	277	185	284	960
Indianapolis, IN[3]	1,767	1,397	300	42	251	7	1,097	614	489	34	-	78	273	19	34	210	167	340	30
Jacksonville, FL[3]	2,144	1,031	139	30	108	1	892	470	264	193	105	-	200	5	104	222	188	860	253
Columbus, OH	1,011	875	130	46	79	6	744	452	30	10	-	24	217	6	138	76	42	136	493
Baltimore, MD[3]	2,696	2,136	1,164	118	988	58	972	735	477	54	58	13	122	8	71	114	58	68	61
El Paso, TX	469	354	34	19	10	4	320	177	97	75	-	14	100	4	53	43	29	54	377
Memphis, TN	2,810	1,307	873	30	464	379	435	256	206	37	-	-	125	48	57	54	27	1,125	320
Milwaukee, WI	1,122	748	383	67	315	1	365	164	154	-	-	-	108	1	44	92	36	54	199
Boston, MA	2,587	2,294	1,116	73	1,041	2	1,178	883	820	38	98	17	185	-	104	110	34	94	94
Austin, TX	1,598	628	57	47	10	-	571	298	148	133	115	83	226	17	129	48	21	774	195
Seattle, WA	1,682	1,038	139	47	66	26	899	529	153	237	237	180	264	39	201	106	30	446	198
Washington, DC	5,547	5,240	1,551	1,499	52	-	3,689	2,974	680	934	593	9	384	23	108	332	119	65	139
Nashville-Davidson, TN[3]	2,255	1,438	293	14	279	-	1,146	783	447	258	225	4	218	10	91	144	119	760	57
Charlotte, NC	321	751	172	39	133	-	578	278	207	30	-	35	201	22	94	99	54	45	25
Portland, OR[3]	780	713	111	42	66	3	602	348	222	47	-	19	164	11	111	90	50	66	1
Denver, CO[3]	1,831	1,539	166	23	143	-	1,373	593	175	358	308	-	609	39	69	170	91	129	164
Cleveland, OH	1,119	812	173	60	113	-	639	364	60	60	-	37	133	5	19	143	58	307	-
Ft Worth, TX	752	440	32	25	7	-	408	255	141	80	80	14	98	5	68	54	31	116	196
Oklahoma City, OK[3]	721	614	73	47	25	1	541	315	30	278	255	21	169	12	67	57	38	59	48
New Orleans, LA	810	714	112	23	89	-	603	361	150	189	127	-	168	11	61	74	42	54	42
Tucson, AZ	683	535	203	50	136	17	332	203	34	158	138	71	88	11	8	40	15	92	56
Kansas City, MO	928	757	82	58	23	1	676	444	73	202	89	31	148	14	45	83	54	67	103
Virginia Beach, VA	1,038	992	396	35	360	1	596	482	327	112	37	-	72	14	37	42	25	46	-

- Represents or rounds to zero.   [1] Includes solid waste management   [2] Includes water, electric, and transit.   [3] Represents, in effect, city-county consolidated government.

Source: U.S. Census Bureau, Government Finances, 1998-99. See also <http://www.census.gov/govs/estimate/99allpub.pdf> (issued September 2001).

292   State and Local Government Finances and Employment

No. 438. City Governments—Expenditures and Debt for Largest Cities: 1999

[In millions of dollars (54,100 represents $54,100,000,000). For fiscal year ending in year shown; see headnote, Table 437. Regarding intercity comparisons, see text, this section. See Appendix III]

Cities ranked by 1998 population	Total expenditure	Total direct expenditure	General expenditure — Total	Education	Housing and community development	Public welfare	Health and hospitals	Police protection	Fire protection	Correction	Highways	Parks and recreation	Sewerage	Solid waste management	Governmental administration[1]	Interest on general debt	Utility expenditure[2]	Employee retirement expenditure	Debt outstanding
New York, NY	54,100	50,555	44,140	11,353	2,391	7,551	4,229	3,018	1,079	1,306	1,152	492	1,015	765	856	3,108	4,818	5,142	53,045
Los Angeles, CA	8,125	8,071	4,913	14	191	-	35	930	331	2	193	231	265	126	303	397	2,294	918	10,429
Chicago, IL	5,469	5,400	4,500	1	175	132	138	1,004	278	-	522	48	125	169	143	500	279	689	9,620
Houston, TX	2,670	2,655	2,100	-	61	-	88	390	212	27	196	93	381	55	83	200	444	127	6,379
Philadelphia, PA[3]	5,188	5,111	4,011	19	185	338	787	427	147	247	82	81	227	88	299	124	739	439	4,783
San Diego, CA	1,810	1,803	1,435	-	105	-	4	234	98	-	49	106	294	88	56	209	288	87	2,392
Phoenix, AZ	2,025	2,017	1,667	15	76	-	-	239	121	9	99	165	137	71	119	143	311	46	3,475
San Antonio, TX	2,002	1,992	948	34	16	35	57	160	93	1	108	117	96	36	26	61	1,025	28	4,512
Dallas, TX	1,787	1,756	1,480	-	41	2	22	211	102	5	79	107	123	39	44	215	168	139	4,136
Detroit, MI	4,453	4,394	3,475	1,475	173	-	103	294	98	2	173	106	250	83	192	155	405	573	3,259
Honolulu, HI[3]	1,118	1,118	905	-	38	-	15	153	57	-	70	81	86	79	71	87	213	-	1,781
San Jose, CA	1,184	1,159	1,083	-	154	-	-	155	75	-	71	106	130	60	65	102	27	74	2,096
San Francisco, CA[3]	5,630	5,466	4,578	107	123	390	3	306	165	81	166	262	110	20	266	304	710	341	6,660
Indianapolis, IN[3]	1,975	1,964	1,607	-	122	63	792	130	47	41	72	135	95	28	169	166	328	40	2,892
Jacksonville, FL[3]	1,889	1,824	1,103	-	13	29	300	134	76	43	59	36	121	53	58	166	709	77	4,919
Columbus, OH	1,028	1,011	883	-	26	-	44	168	107	-	80	68	103	37	60	62	145	-	1,607
Baltimore, MD	2,270	2,265	1,983	780	105	2	34	216	113	9	124	45	32	54	91	74	92	195	1,363
El Paso, TX	486	484	346	-	11	-	79	70	32	-	29	25	26	14	30	28	105	35	663
Memphis, TN	2,587	2,569	1,403	709	28	-	22	147	92	-	37	160	78	35	27	33	1,058	126	960
Milwaukee, WI	998	967	762	-	86	-	-	163	73	-	58	10	109	38	50	26	103	134	535
Boston, MA	2,403	2,167	2,103	704	102	111	27	230	123	76	65	75	64	43	60	50	67	234	1,112
Austin, TX	1,650	1,650	904	-	13	-	67	91	58	-	23	54	129	27	49	87	682	64	4,013
Seattle, WA	1,797	1,682	1,165	-	60	8	64	140	78	16	140	138	125	81	96	34	546	86	2,020
Washington Dc, DC	5,405	5,236	4,798	777	60	1,247	510	313	104	293	101	154	32	42	312	254	111	432	4,663
Nashville-Davidson, TN[3]	2,423	2,423	1,470	586	-	17	135	111	69	43	36	92	32	22	84	127	857	96	3,152
Charlotte, NC	767	757	582	-	26	-	3	102	47	-	58	36	174	26	17	64	175	53	1,455
Portland, OR[3]	930	922	784	-	58	2	-	103	57	-	105	81	50	2	57	63	93	10	1,412
Denver, CO[3]	1,456	1,433	1,315	-	39	105	41	124	64	47	85	103	16	32	109	259	86	53	5,106
Cleveland, OH	1,120	1,117	778	-	64	2	31	159	70	6	43	52	31	28	74	53	342	55	1,984
Ft. Worth, TX	575	575	435	-	12	1	-	94	47	-	68	43	43	20	36	33	92	-	954
Oklahoma City, OK	609	609	532	-	29	-	6	96	80	56	40	92	41	20	36	38	69	48	854
New Orleans, LA	895	895	742	-	70	2	-	103	56	3	53	24	-	23	75	65	105	8	1,131
Tucson, AZ[3]	636	633	454	-	51	13	24	76	34	4	50	52	-	25	57	30	166	48	708
Kansas City, MO	805	781	693	-	46	-	62	112	34	-	35	65	34	15	51	58	53	16	1,030
Virginia Beach, VA	1,005	1,003	960	483	13	23	26	59	31	20	28	32	29	23	27	42	44	59	783

- Represents or rounds to zero.
[1] Excludes public buildings.
[2] Includes water, electric, and transit.
[3] Represents, in effect, city-county consolidated government.

Source: U.S. Census Bureau, Government Finances, 1998-99. See also <http://www.census.gov/govs/estimate/99allpub.pdf> (issued September 2001).

No. 439. County Governments—Revenue for Largest Counties: 1999

[In millions of dollars (15,683 represents $15,683,000,000). For fiscal year ending in year shown; see text, this section]

Counties ranked by 1998 population	Total revenue [1]	General revenue: Total [1]	Intergov: Total	Federal: Total	Federal: Housing [2]	State: Total	State: Public welfare	State: Health and hospitals	From local government	Own sources: Total	Taxes: Total [1]	Taxes: Property	Sales/gross receipts: Total	Sales: General sales	Current charges: Total	Parks and recreation	Sewerage [3]	Hospitals	Misc general revenue: Total	Misc: Interest earnings
Los Angeles, CA	15,683	13,374	9,338	290	202	8,729	4,390	1,427	319	4,037	2,054	1,863	107	47	1,081	70	52	404	901	283
Cook, IL	2,551	2,162	409	17	16	390	144	1	-	1,752	1,284	777	493	299	345	36	-	164	123	76
Harris, TX	1,875	1,875	517	73	20	393	212	120	50	1,359	783	722	25	5	327	-	2	100	249	214
Maricopa, AZ	1,736	1,736	984	67	20	896	401	16	22	752	377	355	5	5	208	3	2	155	166	108
San Diego, CA	2,566	2,195	1,549	88	63	1,353	538	256	109	646	382	319	22	16	133	3	15	-	130	43
Orange, CA	2,876	2,477	1,327	35	25	1,187	397	190	105	1,150	331	253	51	48	405	16	91	-	415	157
Metropolitan Dade, FL	4,615	4,373	866	396	189	469	103	1	-	3,507	1,224	818	339	84	1,779	22	435	643	504	305
Wayne, MI	1,334	1,334	651	44	3	537	74	264	70	684	276	271	3	-	278	4	62	314	130	51
Dallas, TX	1,098	1,098	231	2	-	206	60	60	104	867	391	351	-	-	401	-	-	-	75	54
King, WA	1,638	1,563	394	64	14	225	134	134	2	1,169	760	305	342	277	338	15	244	109	71	53
Santa Clara, CA	2,340	2,340	1,320	18	4	1,258	82	82	14	1,020	733	387	312	310	178	3	11	109	109	67
San Bernardino, CA	2,230	1,928	1,426	94	14	1,257	681	151	4	501	231	195	20	15	168	9	34	32	102	42
Broward, FL	1,396	1,357	265	91	5	146	6	6	43	1,091	566	468	76	-	344	12	133	-	182	124
Riverside, CA	1,634	1,633	1,136	84	9	975	496	72	75	498	247	207	21	17	124	2	37	28	127	57
Alameda, CA	2,042	1,755	1,081	16	2	1,000	624	207	28	674	363	215	121	114	179	-	-	44	132	59
Cuyahoga, OH	1,360	1,360	548	16	13	530	276	151	77	812	421	224	160	144	256	-	3	229	135	115
Suffolk, NY	1,871	1,770	454	7	11	427	203	39	65	1,316	1,099	412	669	667	125	8	17	-	92	44
Tarrant, TX	633	633	178	15	-	147	59	58	4	455	280	254	8	-	101	-	-	72	90	65
Bexar, TX	699	698	137	2	1	119	77	31	20	562	257	236	8	-	214	-	-	191	90	82
Nassau, NY	2,353	2,353	626	47	19	578	331	231	16	1,727	1,321	600	719	716	330	19	8	189	76	39
Allegheny, PA	1,312	1,125	610	26	18	581	177	100	16	516	281	236	44	33	188	4	7	-	47	24
Oakland, MI	794	683	427	14	5	298	99	75	-	256	174	164	2	-	47	12	7	3	35	30
Clark, NV	2,263	2,013	499	42	14	386	5	5	3	1,514	691	276	276	98	646	11	64	312	177	135
Sacramento, CA	2,318	2,012	1,090	20	15	1,029	521	132	114	922	345	185	116	93	382	11	174	228	195	108
Hennepin, MN	1,312	1,312	492	37	5	436	268	55	19	820	398	394	110	-	318	4	48	-	104	54
Palm Beach, FL	1,189	1,152	164	36	-	128	6	6	-	988	492	362	80	-	320	6	155	-	175	88
Franklin, OH	757	755	363	5	3	333	126	107	25	392	294	201	71	-	44	2	3	-	54	42
St Louis, MO	572	539	54	14	14	37	2	2	4	485	391	90	252	309	311	1	-	238	50	32
Erie, NY	1,360	1,316	339	7	-	322	213	27	11	977	570	239	313	130	291	21	181	-	96	47
Fairfax, VA	3,179	2,657	507	47	33	445	34	17	8	2,150	1,688	1,316	214	-	235	1	57	-	171	142
Hillsborough, FL	1,205	1,102	235	47	20	188	34	-	11	867	461	335	112	78	394	-	16	206	171	101
Contra Costa, CA	1,452	1,214	519	30	3	473	198	90	8	695	225	191	15	10	172	31	-	48	77	39
Milwaukee, WI	1,149	990	538	88	12	443	140	155	8	452	229	175	52	52	566	21	9	408	51	9
Westchester, NY	1,800	1,791	442	20	8	404	245	71	6	1,350	729	457	269	261	51	4	14	-	55	37
Du Page, IL	350	349	109	11	-	96	17	9	18	240	125	101	19	-	51	4	14	-	63	36

- Represents or rounds to zero.   [1] Includes revenue sources not shown separately.   [2] Includes urban development.   [3] Includes solid waste management.

Source: U.S. Census Bureau, Government Finances, 1998-99. See also <http://www.census.gov/govs/estimate/99allpub.pdf> (issued September 2001).

U.S. Census Bureau, Statistical Abstract of the United States: 2002

No. 440. County Governments—Expenditures and Debt for Largest Counties: 1999

[In millions of dollars (13,258 represents $13,258,000,000). For fiscal year ending in year shown; see text, this section. See headnote, Table 439]

Counties ranked by 1999 population	Total expenditure	Total direct expenditure	General expenditure Total[1]	Education	Housing[2]	Public welfare	Health	Hospitals	Police protection	Correction	Governmental administration	Highways	Parks and recreation	Natural resources	Sewerage and solid waste management	Interest on general debt	Utility expenditure[3]	Employee retirement expenditure	Debt outstanding
Los Angeles, CA	13,258	12,494	12,163	515	270	4,004	1,091	1,396	835	783	1,266	238	245	203	43	421	34	1,061	6,205
Cook, IL	2,249	2,234	2,105	1	13	8	48	713	76	268	460	91	103	67	-	99	-	143	1,822
Harris, TX	1,921	1,921	1,921	-	27	21	119	454	150	236	205	179	40	61	5	287	-	-	4,990
Maricopa, AZ	1,582	1,334	1,582	21	20	555	58	183	88	63	270	98	7	7	24	71	12	-	1,543
San Diego, CA	2,365	2,276	2,222	127	64	512	309	-	122	197	387	78	17	38	69	71	-	131	758
Orange, CA	2,444	2,261	2,294	169	23	498	230	-	151	186	336	73	58	17	408	192	-	150	3,531
Metropolitan Dade, FL	4,635	4,629	4,217	-	205	68	61	826	358	203	254	39	151	6	101	488	418	-	7,009
Wayne, MI	1,515	1,399	1,438	-	-	106	320	76	15	156	162	84	65	-	-	68	-	76	2,177
Dallas, TX	1,017	1,014	1,012	-	3	10	105	467	26	171	109	12	-	-	1	38	-	5	652
King, WA	1,732	1,700	1,354	1	21	6	240	52	70	70	167	97	71	48	222	167	378	-	2,377
Santa Clara, CA	2,123	1,895	2,123	197	20	484	203	352	46	197	322	36	23	24	27	39	-	97	769
San Bernardino, CA	2,160	1,937	2,058	218	4	663	135	240	139	108	180	34	14	16	92	56	5	-	1,572
Broward, FL	1,505	1,470	1,392	-	17	28	87	-	150	116	130	54	115	88	129	143	113	-	2,438
Riverside, CA	1,748	1,581	1,747	220	21	444	121	131	126	111	187	45	6	98	40	75	-	106	1,068
Alameda, CA	1,937	1,847	1,832	27	32	465	177	269	50	151	220	58	1	-	-	51	-	-	1,264
Cuyahoga, OH	1,422	1,406	1,422	232	17	288	243	387	21	84	179	33	-	-	13	105	145	-	1,553
Suffolk, NY	1,813	1,591	1,669	-	15	327	147	-	311	81	94	22	19	7	52	61	-	-	1,506
Tarrant, TX	600	599	600	-	6	8	70	234	16	73	84	14	-	-	-	60	-	1	1,411
Bexar, TX	636	590	636	217	11	48	38	299	18	58	65	20	2	8	8	64	-	-	876
Nassau, NY	2,576	2,239	2,554	27	-	484	127	294	477	155	116	63	95	3	-	147	22	45	3,079
Allegheny, PA	1,130	1,041	1,086	-	19	244	186	25	23	58	80	19	53	-	97	81	-	21	1,329
Oakland, MI	657	639	626	5	22	4	163	10	35	59	93	83	10	-	-	16	10	-	288
Clark, NV	2,198	2,185	1,946	-	7	56	30	306	222	107	162	348	159	22	63	184	252	90	4,018
Sacramento, CA	1,942	1,881	1,834	74	13	581	147	-	95	111	195	70	15	64	30	137	18	-	2,301
Hennepin, MN	1,227	1,223	1,051	-	95	216	193	313	49	82	98	38	41	-	185	23	-	-	749
Palm Beach, FL	1,127	1,090	1,090	-	6	23	33	-	128	64	156	83	47	5	50	94	76	-	1,588
Franklin, OH	757	731	756	-	18	184	227	-	18	45	103	34	24	-	99	32	1	12	562
St Louis, MO	526	389	514	-	5	15	38	-	45	26	49	58	12	19	4	23	-	-	451
Erie, NY	1,320	1,029	1,288	111	10	462	45	215	30	52	48	37	82	-	2	41	31	155	746
Fairfax, VA	2,932	2,880	2,641	1,306	4	159	109	-	115	71	75	25	27	-	27	118	136	-	2,593
Hillsborough, FL	1,116	1,105	994	-	69	41	36	-	103	65	114	76	-	29	184	109	122	91	2,110
Contra Costa, CA	1,279	1,275	1,189	47	28	237	120	247	51	73	112	41	107	18	67	53	-	79	807
Milwaukee, WI	1,056	1,056	866	-	7	226	58	126	28	96	79	24	34	-	14	26	111	-	488
Westchester, NY	1,883	1,664	1,850	78	13	417	80	420	17	69	64	37	25	1	146	69	33	-	797
Du Page, IL	362	357	361	1	9	35	27	-	18	30	62	43	25	23	18	22	1	-	448

- Represents or rounds to zero. [1] Includes expenditure categories not shown separately. [2] Includes community development. [3] Includes water, electric, and transit.

Source: U.S. Census Bureau, Government Finances, 1998-99. See also <http://www.census.gov/govs/estimate/99allpub.pdf> (issued September 2001).

State and Local Government Finances and Employment   295

No. 441. Governmental Employment and Payrolls: 1980 to 2000

[Employees in thousands (16,213 represents 16,213,000), payroll in millions of dollars (19,935 represents $19,935,000,000). For 1980 to 1995 as of October; later years as of March. 1996 data are not available. Covers both full-time and part-time employees. Local government data are estimates subject to sampling variation; see appendix III and source]

Type of government	1980	1985	1990	1993	1994	1995	1997	1998	1999	2000
EMPLOYEES (1,000)										
Total	16,213	16,690	18,369	18,823	19,420	19,521	19,540	19,854	20,306	20,876
Federal (civilian) [1]	2,898	3,021	3,105	2,999	2,952	2,895	2,807	2,765	2,799	2,899
State and local	13,315	13,669	15,263	15,824	16,468	16,626	16,733	17,089	17,506	17,976
Percent of total	82	82	83	84	85	85	86	86	86	86
State	3,753	3,984	4,503	4,673	4,694	4,719	4,733	4,758	4,818	4,877
Local	9,562	9,685	10,760	11,151	11,775	11,906	12,000	12,331	12,689	13,099
Counties	1,853	1,891	2,167	2,270	(NA)	(NA)	2,425	(NA)	(NA)	(NA)
Municipalities	2,561	2,467	2,642	2,644	(NA)	(NA)	2,755	(NA)	(NA)	(NA)
School districts	4,270	4,416	4,950	(NA)	(NA)	(NA)	455	(NA)	(NA)	(NA)
Townships	394	392	418	(NA)	(NA)	(NA)	5,675	(NA)	(NA)	(NA)
Special districts	484	519	585	(NA)	(NA)	(NA)	691	(NA)	(NA)	(NA)
OCTOBER PAYROLLS (mil. dol.)										
Total	19,935	28,945	39,228	(NA)	(NA)	(NA)	49,156	51,568	54,363	58,166
Federal (civilian) [1]	5,205	7,580	8,999	(NA)	(NA)	(NA)	9,744	10,115	10,478	11,485
State and local	14,730	21,365	30,229	34,540	36,545	37,714	39,412	41,453	43,886	46,681
Percent of total	74	74	77	(NA)	(NA)	(NA)	80	80	81	80
State	4,285	6,329	9,083	10,288	10,666	10,927	11,413	11,845	12,565	13,279
Local	10,445	15,036	21,146	24,252	25,878	26,787	27,999	29,608	31,321	33,402
Counties	1,936	2,819	4,192	4,839	(NA)	(NA)	5,750	(NA)	(NA)	(NA)
Municipalities	2,951	4,191	5,564	6,328	(NA)	(NA)	7,146	(NA)	(NA)	(NA)
School districts	4,683	6,746	9,551	(NA)	(NA)	(NA)	869	(NA)	(NA)	(NA)
Townships	330	446	642	(NA)	(NA)	(NA)	12,579	(NA)	(NA)	(NA)
Special districts	546	834	1,197	(NA)	(NA)	(NA)	1,654	(NA)	(NA)	(NA)

NA Not available.   [1] Includes employees outside the United States.

Source: U.S. Census Bureau, *Compendium of Public Employment,* and through 1990, *Public Employment,* series GE, No. 1, annual; thereafter, <http://www.census.gov/govs/www/apes.html> (accessed 05 August 2001).

No. 442. All Governments—Employment and Payroll by Function: 2000

[Employees in thousands (20,876 represents 20,876,000), payroll in millions of dollars (58,166 represents $58,166,000,000). As of March. Covers full-time and part-time employees. Local government data are estimates subject to sampling variation; see Appendix III and source]

Function	Employees (1,000)					October payrolls (mil. dol.)				
	Total	Federal (civilian) [1]	State and local			Total	Federal (civilian) [1]	State and local		
			Total	State	Local			Total	State	Local
Total	20,876	2,899	17,976	4,877	13,099	58,166	11,485	46,681	13,279	33,402
National defense [2]	695	695	(X)	(X)	(X)	2,793	2,793	(X)	(X)	(X)
Postal Service	865	865	(X)	(X)	(X)	3,047	3,047	(X)	(X)	(X)
Space research and technology	18	18	(X)	(X)	(X)	111	111	(X)	(X)	(X)
Elem and secondary educ ...	7,011	(X)	7,011	56	6,955	17,590	(X)	17,590	148	17,442
Higher education	2,613	(X)	2,613	2,089	524	5,791	(X)	5,791	4,784	1,008
Other education	125	11	114	114	-	376	52	323	323	-
Health	581	130	451	179	272	1,859	633	1,226	546	681
Hospitals	1,149	145	1,004	431	573	3,365	640	2,725	1,201	1,524
Public welfare	538	9	529	233	296	1,447	47	1,399	657	742
Social insurance administration	159	65	94	94	-	577	285	292	292	-
Police protection	1,041	106	935	103	832	3,784	559	3,225	380	2,845
Fire protection	410	(X)	410	(X)	410	1,176	(X)	1,176	(X)	1,176
Correction	729	32	697	464	233	2,219	128	2,092	1,397	695
Streets & highways	573	3	569	252	317	1,632	20	1,612	772	840
Air transportation	91	49	42	3	39	508	366	142	12	130
Water transport/terminals	18	5	13	5	8	61	16	45	16	29
Solid waste management.	119	(X)	119	2	117	314	(X)	314	8	307
Sewerage	135	(X)	135	1	133	408	(X)	408	6	402
Parks & recreation	389	25	364	39	325	694	92	602	85	517
Natural resources	395	183	211	166	45	1,389	823	566	460	105
Housing & community dev. ...	141	17	125	(X)	125	431	82	349	(X)	349
Water supply	173	(X)	173	1	172	498	(X)	498	3	495
Electric power	80	(X)	80	5	75	335	(X)	335	30	305
Gas supply	12	(X)	12	(X)	12	33	(X)	33	(X)	33
Transit	217	(X)	217	29	187	799	(X)	799	124	675
Libraries	178	4	174	1	173	303	21	282	1	281
State liquor stores	9	(X)	9	9	-	17	(X)	17	17	-
Financial administration	558	137	421	169	252	1,690	547	1,143	521	622
Other government administration	499	22	476	59	417	935	92	843	180	664
Judicial and legal	474	56	418	158	260	1,665	298	1,367	587	779
Other & unallocable	880	321	559	215	344	2,321	834	1,487	729	758

- Represents or rounds to zero.   X Not applicable.   [1] Includes employees outside the United States.   [2] Includes international relations.

Source: U.S. Census Bureau; <http://www.census.gov/pub/govs/www/apes.html> (accessed 15 October 2001).

U.S. Census Bureau, Statistical Abstract of the United States: 2002

No. 443. State and Local Government—Employer Costs Per Hour Worked: 2000

[In dollars. As of March. Based on a sample; see source for details. For additional data, see Table 618]

Occupation and industry	Total compensation	Wages and salaries	Benefits						
			Total	Paid leave	Supplemental pay	Insurance	Retirement and savings	Legally required benefits	Other [1]
Total workers	$29.05	$20.57	$8.48	$2.26	$0.25	$2.38	$1.84	$1.70	$0.05
Occupational group:									
White-collar occupations	32.17	23.36	8.81	2.33	0.14	2.51	1.96	1.82	0.05
Professional specialty and technical	38.15	28.48	9.67	2.3	0.15	2.68	2.37	2.10	0.07
Professional specialty	39.41	29.55	9.86	2.31	0.13	2.75	2.46	2.13	0.07
Teachers	42.18	32.02	10.16	2.18	0.07	2.90	2.74	2.20	0.09
Technical	24.76	17.08	7.68	2.25	0.4	1.92	1.38	1.70	0.04
Executive, admin., & managerial .	36.2	25.44	10.76	3.64	0.18	2.6	2.23	2.07	0.03
Admin. support including clerical .	18.52	12.38	6.14	1.70	0.10	2.14	1.04	1.14	0.03
Blue-collar occupations	22.78	15.05	7.72	2.18	0.36	2.28	1.31	1.57	0.03
Service occupations	22.05	14.29	7.76	2.06	0.53	2.01	1.73	1.38	0.06
Industry group:									
Services	30.61	22.37	8.25	2.04	0.16	2.44	1.84	1.73	0.05
Health services	23.74	16.03	7.70	2.4	0.6	1.91	1.08	1.68	0.04
Hospitals	24.31	16.42	7.88	2.47	0.59	1.96	1.11	1.71	0.04
Educational services	31.86	23.54	8.32	1.97	0.09	2.5	1.96	1.74	0.06
Elementary and secondary education.	31.23	23.13	8.10	1.77	0.07	2.62	1.91	1.66	0.07
Higher education	34.18	25.17	9.00	2.52	0.17	2.18	2.14	1.98	(Z)
Public administration.	26.26	17.47	8.79	2.65	0.38	2.25	1.88	1.59	0.05

Z Cost per hour worked is less than one cent.   [1] Includes severance pay and supplemental unemployment benefits.

Source: U.S. Bureau of Labor Statistics, *Compensation and Working Conditions, Fall 2000.*

No. 444. State and Local Governments—Full-Time Employment and Salary by Sex, and Race/Ethnic Group: 1980 to 1999

[As of June 30. (2,350 represents 2,350,000). Excludes school systems and educational institutions. Based on reports from state governments (47 in 1983; 42 in 1980; 49 in 1981 and 1984 through 1987; and 50 in 1989 through 1991) and a sample of county, municipal, township, and special district jurisdictions employing 15 or more nonelected, nonappointed full-time employees. Beginning 1993, only for State and Local Governments with 100 or more employees. Data for 1992, 1994, and 1996 are not available. For definition of median, see Guide to Tabular Presentation]

Year and occupation	Employment (1,000)						Median annual salary ($1,000)					
				Minority						Minority		
	Male	Female	White [1]	Total [2]	Black [1]	Hispanic [3]	Male	Female	White [1]	Total [2]	Black [1]	Hispanic [3]
1980	2,350	1,637	3,146	842	619	163	15.2	11.4	13.8	11.8	11.5	12.3
1981	2,740	1,925	3,591	1,074	780	205	17.7	13.1	16.1	13.5	13.3	14.7
1983	2,674	1,818	3,423	1,069	768	219	20.1	15.3	18.5	15.9	15.6	17.3
1984	2,700	1,880	3,458	1,121	799	233	21.4	16.2	19.6	17.4	16.5	18.4
1985	2,789	1,952	3,563	1,179	835	248	22.3	17.3	20.6	18.4	17.5	19.2
1986	2,797	1,982	3,549	1,230	865	259	23.4	18.1	21.5	19.6	18.7	20.2
1987	2,818	2,031	3,600	1,249	872	268	24.2	18.9	22.4	20.9	19.3	21.1
1989	3,030	2,227	3,863	1,394	961	308	26.1	20.6	24.1	22.1	20.7	22.7
1990	3,071	2,302	3,918	1,456	994	327	27.3	21.8	25.2	23.3	22.0	23.8
1991	3,110	2,349	3,965	1,494	1,011	340	28.4	22.7	26.4	23.8	22.7	24.5
1993	2,820	2,204	3,588	1,436	948	341	30.6	24.3	28.5	25.9	24.2	26.8
1995	2,960	2,355	3,781	1,534	993	379	33.5	27.0	31.4	26.3	26.8	28.6
1997	2,898	2,307	3,676	1,529	973	392	34.6	27.9	32.2	30.2	27.4	29.5
1999, total	2,939	2,393	3,723	1,609	1,012	417	37.0	29.9	34.8	31.1	29.6	31.2
Officials/administrators	201	106	253	54	34	13	58.7	51.0	56.4	53.9	52.4	53.7
Professionals	622	731	1,005	348	201	78	45.6	38.8	42.0	40.1	37.8	38.5
Technicians	263	191	332	122	70	34	37.0	29.9	34.4	31.6	30.3	31.8
Protective service .	843	177	729	290	185	86	37.7	31.4	37.2	35.4	32.9	39.5
Paraprofessionals .	99	275	222	152	113	29	27.3	24.3	26.0	23.8	22.9	25.7
Admin. support . .	120	770	593	297	181	86	27.2	25.1	25.3	25.5	25.2	25.1
Skilled craft	378	21	295	103	61	32	33.7	28.3	33.4	33.1	31.7	32.8
Service/maintenance	413	122	293	242	167	60	27.6	21.2	26.6	25.1	24.4	26.0

[1] Non-Hispanic.   [2] Includes other minority groups not shown separately.   [3] Persons of Hispanic origin may be of any race.

Source: U.S. Equal Employment Opportunity Commission, 1980-1991, *State and Local Government Information Report,* annual; beginning 1993, biennial.

U.S. Census Bureau, Statistical Abstract of the United States: 2002

No. 445. State and Local Government Full-Time Equivalent Employment by Selected Function and State: 2000

[In thousands (1,562.6 represents 1,562,600). For March. Local government amounts are estimates subject to sampling variation; see Appendix III and source]

State	Education Total [1] State	Local	Education Elem. & secondary State	Local	Education Higher education State	Local	Public welfare State	Local	Health State	Local	Hospitals State	Local
United States ...	1,562.6	6,277.7	45.3	5,969.3	1,415.8	308.4	229.2	272.8	172.7	236.5	409.9	519.0
Alabama	36.0	93.0	-	93.0	32.5	-	3.8	1.6	5.3	4.1	11.2	24.4
Alaska	7.8	15.3	3.0	15.3	4.4	-	1.7	0.2	0.6	0.4	0.2	0.2
Arizona	27.8	105.4	-	94.6	24.8	10.8	5.6	2.1	2.3	2.9	0.7	4.0
Arkansas	20.5	61.2	-	61.2	17.5	-	2.2	0.1	4.7	0.2	4.0	3.8
California	128.4	704.1	-	628.2	123.7	75.9	3.7	59.5	11.3	38.5	30.8	65.7
Colorado	38.5	85.4	-	83.9	37.2	1.4	1.9	5.3	1.1	2.5	3.8	9.6
Connecticut	21.5	72.4	3.6	72.4	15.1	-	4.8	1.7	2.1	1.6	10.5	-
Delaware	7.5	15.3	-	15.3	7.2	-	1.7	-	1.7	0.2	2.2	-
District of Columbia	(X)	11.4	(X)	10.5	(X)	0.8	(X)	1.0	(X)	2.0	(X)	4.2
Florida	52.8	307.6	-	284.3	50.0	23.2	13.9	5.6	19.4	5.8	6.5	30.9
Georgia	48.1	193.4	-	193.3	40.3	0.2	9.4	0.9	4.1	14.4	12.1	21.0
Hawaii	33.4	-	24.8	-	8.5	-	0.8	0.1	2.8	0.2	3.4	-
Idaho	8.9	30.8	-	29.6	8.3	1.2	1.7	0.1	1.2	0.8	1.0	4.6
Illinois	45.5	275.3	-	255.5	42.5	19.8	14.3	8.2	2.9	7.2	10.2	14.1
Indiana	47.8	130.9	-	130.9	46.7	-	5.0	1.4	1.6	3.1	5.2	23.8
Iowa	25.3	74.5	-	68.4	24.1	6.2	2.8	1.4	0.4	2.1	7.9	10.5
Kansas	18.7	78.5	-	72.2	18.1	6.3	2.7	0.5	1.0	3.5	2.8	6.4
Kentucky	29.3	98.4	-	98.4	25.2	-	6.7	0.8	2.1	4.6	5.2	4.6
Louisiana	31.9	103.9	-	103.9	28.6	-	5.5	0.5	5.4	1.3	20.6	18.0
Maine	7.4	34.2	0.1	34.2	6.1	-	2.0	0.4	1.2	0.7	0.4	0.8
Maryland	29.7	113.9	-	104.8	27.7	9.1	7.4	2.7	6.2	3.8	5.8	-
Massachusetts	26.8	142.5	-	142.5	25.7	-	7.5	2.4	7.9	5.8	8.7	0.6
Michigan	68.6	219.4	0.5	206.7	67.7	12.7	13.4	2.3	1.8	8.7	13.1	11.0
Minnesota	39.5	119.1	-	119.1	35.1	-	2.6	12.0	2.2	4.4	4.9	9.6
Mississippi	19.3	77.1	-	71.3	17.6	5.9	3.1	0.7	3.1	0.2	11.0	19.3
Missouri	29.6	126.2	-	120.5	27.5	5.6	8.2	2.4	3.5	3.9	13.6	8.7
Montana	6.9	21.6	-	21.5	6.3	0.1	1.5	0.5	0.9	0.8	0.6	0.5
Nebraska	10.5	43.6	-	40.6	10.0	3.0	2.8	1.2	0.8	0.5	4.6	4.8
Nevada	7.5	27.7	-	27.7	7.4	-	1.0	0.4	1.2	0.9	1.0	5.2
New Hampshire	7.0	29.0	-	29.0	6.7	-	1.4	2.5	0.9	0.2	0.8	-
New Jersey	44.7	192.0	12.8	182.1	28.2	9.9	6.0	10.9	2.8	3.5	15.1	2.4
New Mexico	20.8	44.3	-	41.1	19.8	3.3	1.6	0.9	2.6	0.3	6.3	0.7
New York	51.0	470.2	-	439.6	46.4	30.6	6.7	50.6	9.4	18.0	47.5	49.7
North Carolina	46.0	188.4	-	172.9	43.0	15.5	1.4	14.6	2.8	19.0	15.9	24.6
North Dakota	6.9	14.1	-	14.1	6.6	-	0.4	0.9	1.2	0.5	1.1	-
Ohio	66.6	241.8	-	235.4	64.3	6.4	2.1	24.3	3.5	16.4	12.1	12.7
Oklahoma	27.7	81.7	-	81.7	25.5	-	6.3	0.3	3.7	1.3	3.1	10.0
Oregon	14.8	71.9	-	63.9	13.8	8.0	5.7	1.0	2.4	4.2	5.1	2.5
Pennsylvania	53.9	225.8	-	219.0	50.6	6.7	12.0	21.9	1.4	5.0	13.9	-
Rhode Island	6.4	24.2	0.5	24.2	5.3	-	1.6	0.2	1.4	0.1	1.2	-
South Carolina	27.9	87.4	-	87.4	25.1	-	5.0	0.3	7.8	2.2	8.8	21.2
South Dakota	5.2	18.5	-	18.1	4.8	0.5	1.0	0.2	0.5	0.2	1.0	0.5
Tennessee	36.6	113.7	-	113.7	34.5	-	5.3	2.8	3.0	3.7	9.5	19.9
Texas	94.5	585.7	-	553.6	89.8	32.1	20.7	3.0	13.8	17.8	32.9	46.1
Utah	26.1	45.1	-	45.1	25.0	-	3.2	0.5	1.9	1.6	5.1	0.6
Vermont	5.4	17.6	-	17.6	4.9	-	1.2	-	0.6	-	0.2	-
Virginia	50.4	165.9	-	164.6	47.5	1.3	2.1	7.0	5.2	6.1	13.3	3.5
Washington	50.1	89.6	-	89.6	46.0	-	5.5	1.1	5.7	3.3	8.7	9.9
West Virginia	13.0	41.4	-	41.4	11.6	-	0.1	-	0.8	1.4	1.6	2.3
Wisconsin	28.7	130.7	-	120.6	27.6	10.1	1.4	13.7	1.9	6.1	3.9	1.6
Wyoming	3.3	16.7	-	14.9	3.1	1.8	0.8	-	0.6	0.2	1.0	4.5

See footnotes at end of table.

U.S. Census Bureau, Statistical Abstract of the United States: 2002

No. 445. State and Local Government Full-Time Equivalent Employment by Selected Function and State: 2000—Con.

[In thousands, for March. Local government amounts are estimates subject to sampling variation; see Appendix III and source]

State	Highways		Police protection		Fire protection		Corrections		Parks and recreation		Government administration	
	State	Local	State	Local	State	Local	State	Local	State	Local	State	Local
United States.....	247.0	299.2	101.3	766.0	(X)	294.5	458.7	224.8	33.2	214.7	370.7	654.8
Alabama..........	3.8	7.1	1.4	11.8	(X)	5.1	4.4	2.7	0.6	3.5	6.2	8.8
Alaska...........	2.7	0.8	0.4	1.2	(X)	0.6	1.6	0.1	0.1	0.5	2.7	2.1
Arizona..........	3.0	4.3	1.9	14.2	(X)	5.1	9.6	1.6	0.4	4.0	5.3	12.7
Arkansas.........	3.4	3.6	1.2	6.7	(X)	2.3	3.8	4.0	0.7	0.9	2.8	10.3
California........	21.0	22.4	12.8	84.0	(X)	30.0	47.3	30.6	3.1	33.0	29.7	95.9
Colorado.........	3.0	5.2	1.1	10.9	(X)	4.5	6.1	3.3	0.2	6.3	6.0	10.3
Connecticut.......	3.6	4.2	1.7	8.8	(X)	4.6	9.0	-	0.1	2.4	8.1	5.2
Delaware.........	1.6	0.6	0.9	1.5	(X)	0.2	2.4	-	0.2	0.2	2.5	1.1
District of Columbia ...	(X)	0.4	(X)	4.5	(X)	1.8	(X)	2.4	(X)	0.7	(X)	2.2
Florida...........	10.1	14.5	4.5	50.7	(X)	20.2	28.4	14.3	1.1	16.5	26.4	39.1
Georgia..........	6.0	7.8	2.2	22.1	(X)	9.5	19.3	7.3	1.6	4.1	5.6	19.8
Hawaii...........	1.0	0.8	-	3.6	(X)	1.7	2.4	-	0.2	1.7	3.4	2.5
Idaho	1.7	1.8	0.5	2.9	(X)	1.1	1.6	1.0	0.2	0.8	2.2	3.3
Illinois	8.2	12.8	4.1	40.0	(X)	16.2	15.8	9.4	0.8	17.8	11.6	32.2
Indiana	4.3	6.9	2.0	13.8	(X)	6.8	6.5	4.8	0.1	3.3	4.2	14.6
Iowa	2.9	5.6	1.0	6.3	(X)	1.7	3.4	1.1	0.1	1.9	4.8	5.8
Kansas	3.4	5.3	1.0	8.0	(X)	2.8	3.6	2.5	0.5	2.0	4.5	7.3
Kentucky.........	5.5	3.6	2.1	7.7	(X)	5.5	3.7	3.0	1.8	1.4	9.1	6.6
Louisiana.........	5.7	5.1	1.7	14.4	(X)	4.4	7.7	5.7	1.2	3.2	5.8	11.1
Maine	2.7	2.1	0.4	2.7	(X)	1.6	1.2	0.6	0.1	0.7	2.1	3.3
Maryland	4.7	5.1	2.4	14.2	(X)	5.6	11.6	2.7	0.6	6.1	9.2	8.1
Massachusetts	4.3	6.7	5.5	18.4	(X)	12.6	7.0	3.3	1.0	2.1	17.0	9.6
Michigan	3.1	10.1	3.2	22.6	(X)	8.0	18.4	5.3	0.4	5.3	6.5	24.5
Minnesota	5.2	7.3	0.9	9.7	(X)	2.3	3.7	4.2	0.6	4.7	6.0	13.4
Mississippi........	3.3	5.3	1.2	7.4	(X)	3.2	4.2	2.0	0.4	1.1	2.3	7.3
Missouri..........	6.4	6.7	2.2	14.8	(X)	6.1	11.5	2.3	0.6	4.1	7.5	10.8
Montana	2.0	1.3	0.4	1.8	(X)	0.6	1.1	0.6	0.1	0.4	1.4	2.3
Nebraska.........	2.2	2.9	0.7	3.8	(X)	1.2	2.0	1.0	0.3	1.1	1.7	4.2
Nevada..........	1.6	1.6	0.9	5.9	(X)	2.3	2.9	1.6	0.2	2.5	2.6	6.0
New Hampshire	1.9	1.9	0.4	3.8	(X)	1.5	1.2	0.5	0.2	0.4	1.7	2.4
New Jersey	7.5	10.0	3.7	29.7	(X)	7.5	9.5	6.4	1.8	4.9	20.1	18.7
New Mexico........	2.3	1.9	0.6	4.8	(X)	2.0	4.0	1.5	0.7	1.9	5.0	4.1
New York.........	13.1	25.8	5.7	80.6	(X)	24.5	35.6	25.7	2.8	10.8	37.0	39.1
North Carolina	11.9	4.2	3.4	19.7	(X)	6.4	19.1	3.8	1.1	5.4	10.0	11.6
North Dakota	0.9	1.1	0.2	1.2	(X)	0.3	0.6	0.2	0.1	0.7	1.3	1.4
Ohio	7.2	14.6	2.6	30.9	(X)	15.9	18.1	8.2	0.8	8.2	11.8	34.5
Oklahoma	3.0	6.3	1.8	9.3	(X)	4.4	6.1	1.0	1.1	2.2	5.3	6.3
Oregon	3.5	4.2	1.4	7.2	(X)	3.8	4.5	3.6	0.4	3.0	8.4	7.2
Pennsylvania	13.8	11.4	5.6	25.8	(X)	6.2	15.0	11.4	1.2	3.9	13.7	31.4
Rhode Island	0.8	0.8	0.3	3.1	(X)	2.5	1.8	-	0.1	0.5	2.7	1.5
South Carolina	4.9	2.6	3.3	10.3	(X)	3.6	9.1	2.3	0.6	2.8	3.6	8.2
South Dakota	1.0	1.6	0.3	1.4	(X)	0.4	0.9	0.5	0.1	0.5	1.2	1.7
Tennessee	4.6	6.6	1.8	16.2	(X)	6.5	6.2	4.5	1.1	4.5	5.3	11.1
Texas	15.3	19.7	3.6	55.2	(X)	19.7	47.5	21.6	1.0	13.1	16.2	42.8
Utah	1.8	1.7	0.8	4.6	(X)	1.6	3.0	1.3	0.3	2.4	3.4	4.3
Vermont	1.0	1.2	0.5	0.8	(X)	0.3	1.0	-	0.1	0.2	1.7	0.9
Virginia	10.4	4.6	2.6	16.1	(X)	7.5	15.7	6.5	0.9	6.8	8.5	14.6
Washington	6.6	6.4	2.2	11.9	(X)	6.4	8.1	4.3	0.6	5.4	5.8	16.0
West Virginia	5.1	0.9	1.1	2.7	(X)	1.0	1.3	0.3	0.6	0.8	3.7	3.8
Wisconsin	1.9	9.4	0.9	14.7	(X)	4.8	9.4	3.5	0.2	3.5	5.8	11.5
Wyoming	1.8	0.7	0.2	1.5	(X)	0.3	0.8	0.3	0.1	0.6	1.0	1.4

- Represents or rounds to zero.   X Not applicable.   [1] Totals includes other education amounts which are not shown.

Source: U.S. Census Bureau, <http://www.census.gov/pub/govs/www/apes.html>; (accessed 05 August 2001).

State and Local Government Finances and Employment   299

No. 446. State and Local Government Employment and Average Earnings by State: 1990 and 2000

[3,840 represents 3,840,000 1990, as of October; 2000 as of March]

State	Full-time equivalent employment (1,000) State		Local [1]		Full-time equivalent employment per 10,000 population [2] State		Local [1]		Average March earnings [3] (dol.) State		Local [1]	
	1990	2000	1990	2000	1990	2000	1990	2000	1990	2000	1990	2000
United States..	3,840	4,083	9,239	10,995	154	151	371	407	2,472	3,374	2,364	3,169
Alabama.........	79	80	148	182	196	183	367	417	2,196	2,841	1,749	2,431
Alaska..........	22	23	21	25	401	373	385	413	3,543	3,842	3,491	3,818
Arizona.........	50	65	136	182	137	139	370	390	2,334	3,055	2,540	2,942
Arkansas	43	49	78	96	182	192	330	380	1,922	2,842	1,545	2,175
California	325	355	1,091	1,322	109	109	367	405	3,209	4,451	3,073	4,062
Colorado........	54	66	130	164	165	166	395	414	2,765	3,779	2,292	3,076
Connecticut.......	58	66	98	111	178	201	299	338	3,018	3,909	2,854	3,856
Delaware	21	24	17	21	314	319	250	283	2,245	3,222	2,458	3,163
District of Columbia ..	(X)	(X)	57	45	(X)	(X)	939	867	(X)	(X)	3,024	3,923
Florida	160	185	497	580	123	124	384	389	2,095	3,149	2,247	2,865
Georgia	112	120	270	334	173	157	418	437	2,037	2,899	1,872	2,677
Hawaii..........	49	55	13	14	445	460	120	119	2,317	2,926	2,536	3,352
Idaho..........	19	23	37	51	186	184	372	415	2,100	3,022	1,772	2,478
Illinois	145	128	416	493	127	106	364	409	2,520	3,441	2,463	3,307
Indiana.........	89	83	196	232	161	140	354	393	2,496	2,990	2,036	2,711
Iowa	57	55	107	121	207	193	387	422	2,936	3,656	2,024	2,727
Kansas..........	50	43	104	128	200	162	421	487	2,077	3,071	1,979	2,491
Kentucky	75	74	114	149	204	188	310	379	2,141	3,051	1,823	2,339
Louisiana	85	95	155	185	200	217	368	422	2,047	2,807	1,713	2,278
Maine..........	22	21	42	51	179	165	345	413	2,352	2,983	1,978	2,609
Maryland	89	91	159	182	186	178	333	355	2,609	3,312	2,776	3,535
Massachusetts.....	93	96	196	232	155	155	325	378	2,541	3,683	2,554	3,403
Michigan........	144	142	316	351	155	145	340	357	2,858	3,934	2,646	3,518
Minnesota.......	70	73	163	206	160	155	374	436	2,936	3,892	2,552	3,255
Mississippi	47	56	105	133	183	202	407	482	1,824	2,752	1,543	2,121
Missouri	74	91	171	208	145	168	334	382	1,965	2,678	2,052	2,678
Montana.........	17	18	35	34	211	204	434	382	2,072	2,931	1,959	2,546
Nebraska	29	30	68	78	186	179	430	468	2,075	2,514	2,089	2,779
Nevada	19	22	42	61	160	128	348	352	2,502	3,444	2,574	3,817
New Hampshire....	16	19	33	46	145	158	301	386	2,352	3,079	2,215	2,830
New Jersey.......	112	133	304	316	145	164	393	389	2,859	4,075	2,698	3,967
New Mexico	40	48	57	70	262	275	379	401	2,100	2,811	1,783	2,494
New York	285	251	866	924	158	138	482	508	2,997	3,859	2,795	3,961
North Carolina.....	107	123	244	328	161	163	368	434	2,372	3,012	2,065	2,708
North Dakota......	15	16	20	23	234	247	314	353	2,057	2,826	2,138	2,778
Ohio	139	136	385	459	128	122	355	410	2,510	3,369	2,236	3,118
Oklahoma........	65	64	116	134	208	192	369	402	1,975	2,821	1,761	2,280
Oregon.........	52	53	100	124	184	163	353	379	2,302	3,269	2,322	3,332
Pennsylvania......	127	150	361	388	107	125	304	323	2,437	3,436	2,403	3,296
Rhode Island......	21	20	27	36	205	198	266	366	2,586	3,772	2,656	3,550
South Carolina.....	79	79	116	155	227	205	333	404	1,956	2,741	1,848	2,474
South Dakota	13	13	24	28	192	181	349	381	1,979	2,777	1,733	2,359
Tennessee	79	81	175	218	163	149	358	401	2,055	2,786	1,883	2,631
Texas..........	223	269	706	909	131	136	415	460	2,192	3,095	1,952	2,643
Utah	37	49	51	73	216	235	294	347	2,000	2,880	2,092	2,836
Vermont	13	14	18	23	233	231	312	384	2,302	3,153	2,090	2,534
Virginia	117	119	221	269	188	175	356	396	2,267	3,229	2,248	2,928
Washington.......	91	112	164	193	187	198	336	339	2,459	3,551	2,515	3,835
West Virginia......	34	32	59	61	188	177	326	336	1,919	2,694	1,862	2,517
Wisconsin........	67	64	183	220	136	122	375	421	2,503	3,710	2,372	3,210
Wyoming	11	11	24	29	239	233	539	595	2,045	2,589	2,110	2,660

X Not applicable.   [1] Estimates subject to sampling variation; see Appendix III and source.   [2] Based on estimated resident population as of July 1.   [3] For full-time employees.

Source: U.S. Census Bureau, 1990, *Public Employment,* Series GE, No. 1, annual; 2000, *Government Employment, March 2000.*

No. 447. City Government Employment and Payroll—Largest Cities: 1990 and 2000

[1998 for March; 1990 for October. In thousands, (456.2 represents 456,200) 1990, as of October; 2000 as of March. See footnote 3, Table 437, for those areas representing city-county consolidated governments]

Cities ranked by 1998 population	Total employment (1,000)		Full-time equivalent employment [1]				Payroll (mil. dol).		Average earnings for full-time employees (dol.)	
			Total (1,000)		Per 10,000 population [1]					
	1990	2000	1990	2000	1990	2000	1990	2000	1990	2000
New York, NY [2][3]	456.2	458.1	394.6	429.3	539	579	1,091.7	1,708.8	2,783	4,150
Los Angeles, CA	51.3	49.4	50.8	48.4	146	134	176.5	230.1	3,488	4,793
Chicago, IL	41.6	41.3	41.6	40.7	149	145	124.9	171.3	3,002	4,239
Houston, TX	19.6	25.2	19.6	24.9	120	139	40.4	75.2	2,061	3,037
Philadelphia, PA.	32.4	31.1	31.9	30.0	201	209	89.1	109.2	2,843	3,637
San Diego, CA.	10.4	12.3	9.8	11.4	88	94	28.8	46.9	3,019	4,201
Phoenix, AZ	11.9	13.0	11.4	12.7	116	106	31.7	50.3	2,876	4,024
San Antonio, TX.	13.4	16.9	12.8	15.7	134	141	28.4	48.0	2,227	3,160
Dallas, TX.	14.9	15.6	14.5	15.2	144	141	28.2	50.4	1,945	3,332
Detroit, MI.	22.1	40.7	21.2	36.1	206	372	49.8	132.1	2,390	3,693
Honolulu, HI	9.9	9.8	9.2	9.1	110	104	23.7	30.9	2,600	3,435
San Jose, CA	5.9	7.6	4.9	6.9	62	80	16.0	36.3	3,453	5,569
San Francisco, CA	25.8	27.7	25.7	27.7	356	371	93.8	141.6	3,648	5,112
Indianapolis, IN	12.8	12.4	12.5	12.0	171	161	23.1	36.7	1,910	3,115
Jacksonville, FL	10.8	10.1	9.8	9.7	154	140	23.8	35.6	2,582	3,815
Columbus, OH	7.7	9.1	7.5	8.8	118	131	17.8	30.1	2,416	3,478
Baltimore, MD [2]	29.7	30.8	29.1	29.2	395	452	73.2	95.3	2,540	3,361
El Paso, TX.	4.9	5.9	4.8	5.8	94	95	9.5	15.6	1,973	2,701
Memphis, TN [2]	21.7	28.2	21.1	26.9	341	446	47.6	80.3	2,287	3,024
Milwaukee, WI	9.0	7.9	8.6	7.7	137	133	20.6	28.5	2,431	3,706
Boston, MA [2]	20.9	23.3	20.9	22.0	363	396	49.8	80.2	2,391	3,734
Austin, TX.	10.0	10.6	9.6	10.1	203	183	20.9	31.2	2,186	3,128
Seattle, WA.	11.2	11.4	10.2	10.3	198	192	32.3	48.3	3,274	4,726
Washington, DC [2][3]	49.6	37.7	47.9	36.5	789	697	138.7	139.4	2,930	3,863
Nashville-Davidson, TN [2]	17.9	20.6	16.9	19.6	347	385	41.8	62.3	2,510	3,235
Charlotte, NC	5.0	5.2	4.8	5.1	115	100	11.5	17.1	2,399	3,408
Portland, OR	4.8	6.2	4.5	5.4	97	108	14.6	23.4	3,305	4,416
Denver, CO.	13.0	14.5	11.9	13.7	254	274	31.1	47.3	2,649	3,534
Cleveland, OH.	8.9	10.1	8.2	9.4	163	189	20.6	27.8	2,521	2,989
Fort Worth, TX.	5.5	6.1	5.2	5.7	117	117	11.1	18.9	2,171	3,394
Oklahoma City, OK	4.8	5.1	4.5	4.8	101	102	10.5	16.0	2,430	3,457
New Orleans, LA	9.8	10.5	9.6	10.1	194	216	15.5	24.4	1,623	2,446
Tucson, AZ	5.0	7.1	4.7	5.8	114	127	11.5	16.0	2,528	2,787
Kansas City, MO	6.4	6.8	6.3	6.6	145	150	14.9	21.3	2,390	3,246
Virginia Beach, VA [2]	14.4	19.7	13.1	17.4	334	402	28.4	43.4	2,232	2,679
Long Beach, CA	5.7	6.1	5.4	5.7	126	132	17.7	25.7	3,413	4,855
Albuquerque, NM	6.9	7.1	6.2	6.6	161	157	12.2	18.3	2,040	2,868
Las Vegas, NV	1.9	2.6	2.0	2.5	77	61	4.9	11.2	2,563	4,681
Sacramento, CA.	4.2	4.4	3.9	4.0	105	100	11.3	17.0	3,021	4,400
Atlanta, GA	8.3	8.0	8.1	8.6	205	213	18.4	25.6	2,286	2,974
Fresno, CA	2.9	3.2	2.7	3.1	77	79	7.9	12.7	2,944	4,073
East Baton Rouge Parish, LA.	6.0	7.1	5.0	6.0	132	152	11.0	14.7	2,255	2,653
Tulsa, OK	4.4	4.5	4.2	4.5	115	117	10.5	13.7	2,555	3,126
Omaha, NE.	2.9	3.4	2.7	2.9	79	78	7.9	10.6	3,051	3,874
Miami, FL	4.3	3.8	4.0	3.6	113	99	14.6	15.1	3,771	4,276
Oakland, CA	4.6	4.2	4.1	4.2	111	116	15.3	24.8	3,948	5,861
Mesa, AZ	2.3	3.5	2.3	3.3	81	93	6.8	13.4	2,898	4,072
Minneapolis, MN	6.4	6.3	5.7	5.8	154	164	15.2	21.3	2,815	3,866
Colorado Springs, CO	5.9	7.4	5.3	6.9	188	200	13.3	25.3	2,618	3,747
Pittsburgh, PA	5.9	4.4	5.6	4.3	152	126	12.3	15.3	2,240	3,593
St. Louis, MO	7.8	8.0	7.4	7.6	186	225	17.0	24.1	2,363	3,176
Cincinnati, OH	7.0	6.5	6.3	6.4	173	189	16.1	21.3	2,634	3,504
Wichita, KS	2.7	3.6	2.6	3.1	87	93	5.4	9.3	2,083	3,072
Toledo, OH	3.0	2.8	3.0	2.8	91	89	8.6	10.0	2,847	3,628
Arlington, TX.	1.8	3.0	1.8	2.4	68	79	4.5	7.1	2,538	3,090
Santa Ana, CA.	2.0	2.5	1.7	2.2	58	71	6.8	10.1	4,144	5,606
Buffalo, NY [2]	13.1	11.4	12.4	10.5	379	348	31.3	43.4	2,596	4,457
Anaheim, CA.	3.7	3.2	2.6	2.5	99	86	8.6	11.5	3,728	5,267
Tampa, FL	4.3	4.3	4.2	4.2	151	145	10.5	14.1	2,505	3,370
Corpus Christi, TX	3.2	3.5	3.0	3.3	116	117	5.9	8.6	2,009	2,675
Newark, NJ.	5.1	5.5	4.9	5.2	177	195	8.3	22.3	1,698	4,371
Riverside, CA	2.0	2.1	2.0	1.9	88	72	7.0	8.0	3,459	4,625
Raleigh, NC	3.0	3.2	3.0	2.9	141	113	5.0	8.9	2,297	3,114
St. Paul, MN	3.6	4.2	3.4	3.2	124	125	10.5	13.3	3,265	4,189
Louisville, KY.	4.5	4.6	4.3	4.3	159	169	9.1	11.8	2,180	2,844
Anchorage, AK	8.8	10.1	7.9	9.0	351	352	28.4	34.6	3,706	3,973
Birmingham, AL	3.9	4.2	3.8	4.1	142	163	8.4	11.5	2,243	2,799
Aurora, CO	1.9	2.5	1.9	2.5	84	98	4.8	9.0	2,586	3,682
Lexington-Fayette, KY	3.0	4.0	3.0	3.6	133	150	6.0	10.2	1,929	2,910
Stockton, CA.	2.0	2.3	1.0	1.9	47	80	5.0	7.1	3,554	4,054
St Petersburg, FL.	3.0	3.2	3.0	3.0	125	125	7.0	9.9	2,412	3,366
Jersey City, NJ	4.0	4.1	3.0	3.7	131	159	10.0	15.3	3,172	4,323
Plano, TX	(NA)	2.0	(NA)	1.8	(NA)	81	(NA)	6.4	(NA)	3,702
Rochester, NY	9.0	11.1	8.0	10.7	347	491	27.0	37.5	3,315	3,546
Akron, OH.	6.0	2.9	5.0	2.7	224	126	11.0	9.2	2,255	3,460
Norfolk, VA [2]	10.5	14.5	9.8	12.0	376	557	21.9	32.8	2,268	2,758
Lincoln, NE.	4.0	2.7	3.0	2.5	156	118	7.0	8.2	2,367	3,382

NA Not available. [1] 1990 based on enumerated resident population as of April 1, 1990. Other years based on estimated resident population as of July 1. [2] Includes city-operated elementary and secondary schools. [3] Includes city-operated university or college.

Source: U.S. Census Bureau, *1990, City Employment*, GE-90-2; and *Government Employment, March 2000*.

State and Local Government Finances and Employment   301

[As of March. See text, this section]

Counties ranked by 1998 population	Total employ-ment (1,000)	Per 10,000 popu-lation [1]	Pay-roll (mil. dol.)	Avg. earn-ings [2] (dol.)	Counties ranked by 1998 population	Total employ-ment (1,000)	Per 10,000 popu-lation [1]	Pay-roll (mil. dol.)	Avg. earn-ings [2] (dol.)
Los Angeles, CA	98.8	102	396.7	4,274	Kent, MI.	2.7	46	7.6	3,141
Cook, IL.	28.9	56	99.3	3,445	Tulsa, OK.	1.5	26	3.3	2,378
Harris, TX.	19.8	61	59.5	3,063	Delaware, PA	3.2	59	7.3	2,248
Maricopa, AZ	15.3	54	43.7	2,934	Summit, OH	3.9	71	9.8	2,560
San Diego, CA	19.5	65	66.3	3,651	Bernalillo, NM	1.6	29	4.0	2,717
Orange, CA	24.3	83	81.4	3,623	Hidalgo, TX	1.9	36	4.0	2,174
Miami-Dade, FL.....	36.0	163	130.3	3,817	Gwinnett, GA	3.8	68	11.4	3,243
Wayne, MI	6.7	32	25.8	3,914	Bristol, MA	0.8	15	2.4	3,204
Dallas, TX	12.5	58	36.4	3,055	Camden, NJ	5.5	100	18.6	3,707
King, WA	15.8	86	52.1	3,812	Jefferson, CO	2.8	50	8.8	3,464
Santa Clara, CA	14.9	87	65.3	4,655	Union, NJ.	4.5	71	11.9	3,373
San Bernardino, CA..	20.6	115	67.6	3,664	El Paso, CO	2.2	42	6.1	3,006
Broward, FL	11.0	72	37.0	3,437	Ocean, NJ	3.7	64	10.8	3,600
Riverside, CA	16.6	104	54.2	3,534	Passaic, NJ	4.1	73	14.1	4,169
Alameda, CA	12.1	79	51.1	4,619	Ramsey, MN.......	3.9	74	13.6	3,898
Cuyahoga, OH	16.1	116	49.2	3,065	New Castle, DE	1.7	32	5.4	3,690
Suffolk, NY........	12.9	82	51.9	4,686	Lake, IN.	2.4	42	4.4	2,241
Tarrant, TX........	6.9	50	19.0	2,811	Anne Arundel, MD ...	14.7	275	49.9	3,983
Bexar, TX.	9.5	67	23.6	2,619	Arapahoe, CO......	1.9	38	5.7	3,245
Nassau, NY	18.9	130	71.3	4,295	Plymouth, MA	0.6	13	2.0	3,487
Allegheny, PA	7.0	54	17.6	2,605	Brevard, FL	3.9	79	9.3	2,644
Oakland, MI	4.5	36	15.6	3,697	Morris, NJ	3.5	67	10.6	3,622
Clark, NV	16.6	131	60.3	4,169	Will, IL.	1.9	40	5.8	3,221
Sacramento, CA ...	13.3	110	50.3	4,094	Onondaga, NY	5.9	118	15.7	2,946
Hennepin, MN.	13.0	103	41.5	3,815	Lancaster, PA	2.4	50	5.5	2,675
Palm Beach, FL....	8.6	82	27.0	3,200	Polk, FL.	4.2	88	10.4	2,649
Franklin, OH	6.6	64	19.2	2,962	Jefferson, LA	10.6	214	25.8	2,692
St Louis, MO.	4.2	41	12.9	3,215	Lucas, OH	4.2	91	11.9	2,957
Erie, NY..........	10.9	105	33.4	3,578	Sedgwick, KS	2.4	53	7.1	3,015
Fairfax, VA	35.3	348	117.5	3,746	Douglas, NE.......	1.9	41	5.2	2,918
Hillsborough, FL	16.2	132	34.4	2,993	Genesee, MI	2.2	40	6.4	3,674
Contra Costa, CA ..	10.7	104	44.7	4,779	Sonoma, CA.......	6.2	125	23.5	4,581
Milwaukee, WI.	8.5	88	26.5	3,314	Johnson, KS.......	3.4	71	9.0	3,101
Westchester, NY	6.9	70	26.6	4,240	Collin, TX.	1.1	26	2.8	2,557
Du Page, IL	3.9	41	11.8	3,360	Stanislaus, CA	5.7	121	18.4	3,733
Pinellas, FL	6.2	69	18.5	3,039	Dane, WI	2.3	49	7.2	3,610
Shelby, TN	13.1	143	35.1	2,842	Volusia, FL.	3.3	63	7.3	2,776
Bergen, NJ	5.8	48	13.0	3,178	Chester, PA	2.4	54	6.3	2,859
Salt Lake, UT	5.8	53	13.4	3,252	Burlington, NJ	3.8	77	9.3	3,027
Hamilton, OH	5.9	68	15.3	2,679	Spokane, WA	1.8	44	11.1	6,181
Montgomery, MD....	37.4	342	123.1	4,619	Washington, OR	1.6	38	5.5	3,688
Orange, FL.	9.9	115	28.0	3,092	Mobile, AL	2.1	51	4.4	2,137
Pima, AZ	8.0	91	20.0	2,859	Lee, FL	3.0	75	9.3	3,230
Macomb, MI	3.0	35	8.9	3,333	Kane, IL.	1.3	32	3.5	2,755
Prince Georges, MD.	29.4	338	90.8	3,564	Santa Barbara, CA..	5.8	130	20.5	4,010
Fresno, CA........	8.6	108	26.0	3,293	Guilford, NC	13.0	295	32.3	2,862
Essex, NJ.	5.6	66	19.3	4,048	Denton, TX........	1.2	31	3.2	2,735
Fulton, GA	7.9	104	25.0	3,356	Solano, CA........	3.1	72	10.2	3,736
Ventura, CA	8.6	113	31.5	3,829	York, PA.	2.1	55	5.0	2,407
Baltimore, MD......	23.3	287	63.8	3,227	Stark, OH	2.9	74	6.6	2,372
Montgomery, PA	3.5	47	9.2	2,783	Westmoreland, PA ...	2.4	63	5.4	2,394
Middlesex, NJ	4.5	55	14.4	3,881	Knox, TN	9.4	226	19.8	2,462
Monroe, NY	7.0	83	20.4	3,430	Monterey, CA	5.5	136	17.5	3,534
Travis, TX.	3.5	49	10.6	3,057	Hillsborough, NH ...	0.7	17	1.8	2,974
El Paso, TX	4.0	56	10.4	2,685	Polk, IA.	2.1	57	6.4	3,313
San Mateo, CA	6.2	83	24.6	4,415	Berks, PA.	2.6	67	5.5	2,391
Pierce, WA........	3.4	47	13.0	4,216	Tulare, CA.	5.2	139	15.7	3,262
Jefferson, KY	3.5	51	8.9	2,610	Greenville, SC.....	2.1	56	4.9	2,506
Jefferson, AL.	4.8	72	14.7	3,122	Waukesha, WI.	1.5	40	4.5	3,242
Jackson, MO	2.1	30	5.0	2,519	Seminole, FL	2.5	67	6.7	2,926
Norfolk, MA	0.6	8	1.6	2,977	Pulaski, AR.	1.2	34	2.8	2,406
Oklahoma, OK	2.6	37	4.4	1,860	Dakota, MN	1.8	47	5.7	3,706
Kern, CA	9.2	136	30.3	3,504	Fort Bend, TX......	1.0	30	2.5	2,579
Multnomah, OR	6.0	83	15.0	3,050	Utah, UT	0.8	22	2.0	2,884
Mecklenburg, NC....	23.8	334	58.2	2,834	Clackamas, OR.....	2.2	59	7.1	3,755
Lake, IL.	3.2	48	9.6	3,277	Mercer, NJ	3.7	87	10.5	3,691
Monmouth, NJ.	5.7	85	18.3	3,673	Butler, OH	2.2	64	5.5	2,607
Dekalb, GA.	6.5	104	19.5	3,170	Orange, NY	3.2	87	9.4	3,267
Bucks, PA	2.5	40	7.3	3,181	Clark, WA.	1.4	43	4.8	3,476
Snohomish, WA.....	2.4	41	9.3	3,906	Cameron, TX	1.4	41	2.8	2,156
Wake, NC	17.8	277	44.7	2,876	Pasco, FL	2.6	77	6.1	2,457
Cobb, GA.	3.9	66	11.9	3,353	Adams, CO.	1.6	48	5.0	3,273
Montgomery, OH	4.9	82	14.4	3,065	Charleston, SC	2.5	73	5.8	2,622
Hudson, NJ	3.8	62	9.7	2,923	Nueces, TX	1.6	50	3.6	2,283
San Joaquin, CA	7.4	123	22.6	3,509	Allen, IN.	1.6	45	4.0	2,868

[1] Based on estimated resident population as of July 1, 1998.   [2] Per full-time employee.

Source: U.S. Census Bureau, *Government Employment, March 2000*.

Section 9
Federal Government Finances and Employment

This section presents statistics relating to the financial structure and the civilian employment of the federal government. The fiscal data cover taxes, other receipts, outlays, and debt. The principal sources of fiscal data are the *Budget of the United States Government* and related documents, published annually by the Office of Management and Budget (OMB), and the Department of the Treasury's *United States Government Annual Report* and its *Appendix*. Detailed data on tax returns and collections are published annually by the Internal Revenue Service. The personnel data relate to staffing and payrolls. They are published by the Office of Personnel Management and the Bureau of Labor Statistics. The primary source for data on public lands is *Public Land Statistics,* published annually by the Bureau of Land Management, Department of the Interior. Data on federally owned land and real property are collected by the General Services Administration and presented in its annual *Inventory Report on Real Property Owned by the United States Throughout the World.*

Budget concept—Under the unified budget concept, all federal monies are included in one comprehensive budget. These monies comprise both federal funds and trust funds. Federal funds are derived mainly from taxes and borrowing and are not restricted by law to any specific government purpose. Trust funds, such as the Unemployment Trust Fund, collect certain taxes and other receipts for use in carrying out specific purposes or programs in accordance with the terms of the trust agreement or statute. Fund balances include both cash balances with Treasury and investments in U.S. securities. Part of the balance is obligated, part unobligated. Prior to 1985, the budget totals, under provisions of law, excluded some federal activities—including the Federal Financing Bank, the Postal Service, the Synthetic Fuels Corporation, and the lending activities of the Rural Electrification Administration. The Balanced Budget

and Emergency Deficit Control Act of 1985 (P.L.99-177) repealed the off-budget status of these entities and placed social security (federal old-age and survivors insurance and the federal disability insurance trust funds) off-budget. Though social security is now off-budget and, by law, excluded from coverage of the congressional budget resolutions, it continues to be a federal program.

Receipts arising from the government's sovereign powers are reported as governmental receipts; all other receipts, i.e., from business-type or market-oriented activities, are offset against outlays. Outlays are reported on a checks-issued (net) basis (i.e., outlays are recorded at the time the checks to pay bills are issued).

Debt concept—For most of U.S. history, the total debt consisted of debt borrowed by the Treasury (i.e., public debt). The present debt series, includes both public debt and agency debt. The *gross federal debt* includes money borrowed by the Treasury and by various federal agencies; it is the broadest generally used measure of the federal debt. *Total public debt* is covered by a statutory debt limitation and includes only borrowing by the Treasury.

Treasury receipts and outlays—All receipts of the government, with a few exceptions, are deposited to the credit of the U.S. Treasury regardless of ultimate disposition. Under the Constitution, no money may be withdrawn from the Treasury unless appropriated by the Congress.

The day-to-day cash operations of the federal government clearing through the accounts of the U.S. Treasury are reported in the *Daily Treasury Statement*. Extensive detail on the public debt is published in the *Monthly Statement of the Public Debt of the United States*.

Budget receipts such as taxes, customs duties, and miscellaneous receipts, which are collected by government agencies, and outlays represented by checks issued and cash payments made by disbursing officers as well as government agencies are reported in the *Daily Treasury Statement of Receipts and Outlays of the United States Government* and in the Treasury's *United States Government Annual Report* and its *Appendix*. These deposits in and payments from accounts maintained by government agencies are on the same basis as the unified budget.

The quarterly *Treasury Bulletin* contains data on fiscal operations and related Treasury activities, including financial statements of government corporations and other business-type activities.

Income tax returns and tax collections—Tax data are compiled by the Internal Revenue Service of the Treasury Department. The *Annual Report of the Commissioner and Chief Counsel of the Internal Revenue Service* gives a detailed account of tax collections by kind of tax and by regions, districts, and states. The agency's annual *Statistics of Income* reports present detailed data from individual income tax returns and corporation income tax returns. The quarterly *Statistics of Income Bulletin* has, in general, replaced the supplemental *Statistics of Income* publications which presented data on such diverse subjects as tax-exempt organizations, unincorporated businesses, fiduciary income tax and estate tax returns, sales of capital assets by individuals, international income and taxes reported by corporations and individuals, and estate tax wealth.

Employment and payrolls—The Office of Personnel Management collects employment and payroll data from all departments and agencies of the federal government, except the Central Intelligence Agency, the National Security Agency, and the Defense Intelligence Agency. Employment figures represent the number of persons who occupied civilian positions at the end of the report month shown and who are paid for personal services rendered for the federal government, regardless of the nature of appointment or method of payment. Federal payrolls include all payments for personal services rendered during the report month and payments for accumulated annual leave of employees who separate from the service. Since most federal employees are paid on a biweekly basis, the calendar month earnings are partially estimated on the basis of the number of work days in each month where payroll periods overlap.

Federal employment and payroll figures are published by the Office of Personnel Management in its *Federal Civilian Workforce Statistics—Employment and Trends*. It also publishes biennial employment data for minority groups, data on occupations of white- and blue-collar workers, and data on employment by geographic area; reports on salary and wage distribution of federal employees are published annually. General schedule is primarily white-collar; wage system primarily blue-collar. Data on federal employment are also issued by the Bureau of Labor Statistics in its *Monthly Labor Review* and in Employment and Earnings and by the U.S. Census Bureau in its annual *Public Employment*.

Public lands—The data on applications, entries, selections, patents, and certifications refer to transactions which involve the disposal, under the public land laws (including the homestead laws), of federal public lands to nonfederal owners. In general, original entries and selections are applications to secure title to public lands which have been accepted as properly filed (i.e., allowed). Some types of applications, however, are not reported until issuance of the final certificate, which passes equitable title to the land to the applicant.

No. 449. Federal Budget—Receipts, Outlays, and Debt: 1960 to 2002

[In billions of dollars (92.5 represents $92,500,000,000), except percent. For fiscal years ending in year shown; see text, Section 8, State and Local Government Finances and Employment. The Balanced Budget and Emergency Deficit Control Act of 1985 put all the previously off-budget federal entities into the budget and moved social security off-budget. Minus sign (-) indicates deficit or decrease]

Year	Receipts	Outlays	Surplus or deficit(-)	Outlays as percent of GDP [1]	Gross federal debt [2]				
							Held by the public		
					Total	Federal gov't account	Total	Federal Reserve System	As percent of GDP [1]
1960	92.5	92.2	0.3	17.8	290.5	53.7	236.8	26.5	56.0
1965	116.8	118.2	-1.4	17.2	322.3	61.5	260.8	39.1	46.9
1970	192.8	195.6	-2.8	19.3	380.9	97.7	283.2	57.7	37.6
1975	279.1	332.3	-53.2	21.3	541.9	147.2	394.7	85.0	34.7
1976	298.1	371.8	-73.7	21.4	629.0	151.6	477.4	94.7	36.2
TQ [3]	81.2	96.0	-14.7	21.1	643.6	148.1	495.5	96.7	35.4
1977	355.6	409.2	-53.7	20.8	706.4	157.3	549.1	105.0	35.8
1978	399.6	458.7	-59.2	20.7	776.6	169.5	607.1	115.5	35.0
1979	463.3	504.0	-40.7	20.1	829.5	189.2	640.3	115.6	33.1
1980	517.1	590.9	-73.8	21.6	909.1	197.1	711.9	120.8	33.3
1981	599.3	678.2	-79.0	22.2	994.8	205.4	789.4	124.5	32.5
1982	617.8	745.8	-128.0	23.1	1,137.3	212.7	924.6	134.5	35.2
1983	600.6	808.4	-207.8	23.5	1,371.7	234.4	1,137.3	155.5	39.9
1984	666.5	851.9	-185.4	22.2	1,564.7	257.6	1,307.0	155.1	40.8
1985	734.1	946.4	-212.3	22.9	1,817.5	310.2	1,507.4	169.8	43.9
1986	769.2	990.5	-221.2	22.5	2,120.6	379.9	1,740.8	190.9	48.2
1987	854.4	1,004.1	-149.8	21.6	2,346.1	456.2	1,889.9	212.0	50.5
1988	909.3	1,064.5	-155.2	21.2	2,601.3	549.5	2,051.8	229.2	51.9
1989	991.2	1,143.7	-152.5	21.2	2,868.0	677.1	2,191.0	220.1	53.1
1990	1,032.0	1,253.2	-221.2	21.8	3,206.6	794.7	2,411.8	234.4	55.9
1991	1,055.0	1,324.4	-269.4	22.3	3,598.5	909.2	2,689.3	258.6	60.7
1992	1,091.3	1,381.7	-290.4	22.2	4,002.1	1,002.1	3,000.1	296.4	64.4
1993	1,154.4	1,409.5	-255.1	21.5	4,351.4	1,102.6	3,248.8	325.7	66.3
1994	1,258.6	1,461.9	-203.3	21.1	4,643.7	1,210.2	3,433.4	355.2	66.9
1995	1,351.8	1,515.8	-164.0	20.7	4,921.0	1,316.2	3,604.8	374.1	67.2
1996	1,453.1	1,560.6	-107.5	20.3	5,181.9	1,447.4	3,734.5	390.9	67.3
1997	1,579.3	1,601.2	-22.0	19.6	5,369.7	1,596.9	3,772.8	424.5	65.6
1998	1,721.8	1,652.6	69.2	19.1	5,478.7	1,757.1	3,721.6	458.2	63.2
1999	1,827.5	1,701.9	125.5	18.7	5,606.1	1,973.2	3,632.9	496.6	61.4
2000	2,025.2	1,788.8	236.4	18.4	5,629.0	2,218.9	3,410.1	511.4	57.8
2001	1,991.0	1,863.9	127.1	18.4	5,770.3	2,450.3	3,320.0	534.1	56.8
2002, est.	1,946.1	2,052.3	-106.2	19.8	6,137.1	2,659.6	3,477.5	(NA)	59.2

NA Not available. [1] Gross domestic product as of fiscal year; for calendar year GDP, see Section 13, Income, Expenditures, and Wealth. [2] See text, this section, for discussion of debt concept. [3] Prior to fiscal year 1977 the federal fiscal years began on July 1 and ended on June 30. In calendar year 1976 the July-September period was a separate accounting period (known as the transition quarter or TQ) to bridge the period required to shift to the new fiscal year.

Source: U.S. Office of Management and Budget, *Budget of the United States Government, Historical Tables*, annual. See also <http://w3.access.gpo.gov/usbudget/fy2003/pdf/hist.pdf>.

No. 450. Federal Budget Outlays—Defense, Human and Physical Resources, and Net Interest Payments: 1980 to 2002

[In billions of dollars (590.9 represents $590,900,000,000). For fiscal year ending in year shown. Minus sign (-) indicates offsets]

Outlays	1980	1990	1995	1998	1999	2000	2001	2002, est.
Federal outlays, total	590.9	1,253.2	1,515.8	1,652.6	1,701.9	1,788.8	1,863.9	2,052.3
National defense	134.0	299.3	272.1	268.5	274.9	294.5	308.5	348.0
Human resources	313.4	619.3	923.8	1,033.4	1,057.7	1,115.4	1,196.1	1,315.3
Education, training, employment and social services	31.8	37.2	51.0	50.5	50.6	53.8	57.3	71.7
Health	23.2	57.7	115.4	131.4	141.1	154.5	172.6	195.2
Medicare	32.1	98.1	159.9	192.8	190.4	197.1	217.5	226.4
Income security	86.6	148.7	223.7	237.7	242.4	253.5	269.8	310.7
Social security	118.5	248.6	335.8	379.2	390.0	409.4	433.1	459.7
Veterans benefits and services	21.2	29.1	37.9	41.8	43.2	47.1	45.8	51.5
Physical resources	66.0	126.0	59.1	74.7	81.9	84.7	99.7	112.1
Energy	10.2	3.3	4.9	1.3	0.9	-1.1	0.1	0.6
Natural resources and environment	13.9	17.1	21.9	22.3	24.0	25.0	26.3	30.2
Commerce and housing credit	9.4	67.6	-17.8	1.0	2.6	3.2	6.0	3.8
Transportation	21.3	29.5	39.4	40.3	42.5	46.9	55.2	62.1
Community and regional development	11.3	8.5	10.7	9.8	11.9	10.6	12.0	15.4
Net interest	52.5	184.4	232.2	241.2	229.8	223.0	206.2	178.4
International affairs	12.7	13.8	16.4	13.1	15.2	17.2	16.6	23.5
Agriculture	8.8	12.0	9.8	12.2	23.0	36.6	26.6	28.8
Administration of justice	4.6	10.0	16.2	22.9	26.1	28.0	30.4	34.4
General government	13.0	10.6	14.0	15.6	15.6	13.3	15.2	18.3
Undistributed offsetting receipts	-19.9	-36.6	-44.5	-47.2	-40.4	-42.6	-55.2	-55.2

Source: U.S. Office of Management and Budget, *Budget of the United States Government, Historical Tables*, annual. See also <http://w3.access.gpo.gov/usbudget/fy2003/pdf/hist.pdf>.

No. 451. Federal Budget Outlays in Constant (1996) Dollars: 1980 to 2002

[Dollar amounts in billions of dollars (1,092.5 represents $1,092,500,000,000). For fiscal year ending in year shown; see text, Section 8, State and Local Government Finances and Employment. Given the inherent imprecision in deflating outlays, the data shown in constant dollars present a reasonable perspective—not precision. The deflators and the categories that are deflated are as comparable over time as feasible. Minus sign (-) indicates offset]

Type	1980	1990	1995	1998	1999	2000	2001	2002, est.
Constant (1996) dollar outlays, total	**1,092.5**	**1,483.6**	**1,551.5**	**1,598.9**	**1,620.7**	**1,659.7**	**1,692.9**	**1,826.7**
National defense [1]	245.3	354.7	282.0	259.9	260.5	270.8	278.5	306.9
Nondefense, total:	847.3	1,128.8	1,269.5	1,338.9	1,360.3	1,388.9	1,414.4	1,520.0
Payments for individuals.	514.1	688.5	896.1	949.3	956.1	984.4	1,028.6	1,106.5
Direct payments [2]	453.8	596.1	743.9	790.7	788.3	810.5	839.1	902.9
Grants to state and local gov'ts	60.3	92.5	152.1	158.7	167.8	173.9	189.5	203.7
All other grants.	108.1	65.2	77.6	78.9	85.7	88.4	95.9	102.2
Net Interest [2]	93.8	214.3	236.8	233.2	219.4	208.6	188.5	159.6
All other [2]	173.4	209.2	106.0	122.4	136.4	145.3	149.5	198.7
Undistributed offsetting receipts [2].	-42.1	-48.4	-46.8	-44.9	-37.3	-37.9	-48.2	-47.1
Total nondefense	847.3	1,128.8	1,269.5	1,338.9	1,360.3	1,388.9	1,414.4	1,520.0
Total outlays as percent of GDP . . .	**21.6**	**21.8**	**20.7**	**19.1**	**18.7**	**18.4**	**18.4**	**19.8**
National defense [1]	4.9	5.2	3.7	3.1	3.0	3.0	3.0	3.4
Nondefense, total:	16.7	16.6	17.0	16.0	15.6	15.3	15.3	16.4
Payments for individuals.	10.2	10.2	12.0	11.3	11.0	10.9	11.1	11.9
Direct payments [2]	9.0	8.8	10.0	9.4	9.1	8.9	9.1	9.7
Grants to state and local governments	1.2	1.4	2.0	1.9	1.9	1.9	2.0	2.2
All other grants.	2.1	1.0	1.0	0.9	1.0	1.0	1.1	1.1
Net Interest [2]	1.9	3.2	3.2	2.8	2.5	2.3	2.0	1.7
All other [2]	3.2	2.9	1.4	1.5	1.6	1.6	1.6	2.2
Total nondefense	16.7	16.6	17.0	16.0	15.6	15.3	15.3	16.4
Percent of outlays, total	100.0	100.0	100.0	100.0	100.0	100.0	100.0	100.0
National defense [1]	22.7	23.9	17.9	16.2	16.2	16.5	16.6	17.0
Payments for individuals	47.1	46.7	57.9	59.4	58.9	59.1	60.6	60.2
Direct payments [2]	41.6	40.5	48.1	49.4	48.5	48.7	49.4	49.1
Grants to state and local governments . . .	5.5	6.3	9.8	9.9	10.3	10.4	11.2	11.1
All other grants	9.9	4.5	5.0	5.0	5.4	5.5	5.9	5.8
Net Interest [2]	8.9	14.7	15.3	14.6	13.5	12.5	11.1	8.7
All other [2]	14.8	13.1	6.8	7.7	8.5	8.9	8.9	11.0
Undistributed offsetting receipts [2]	-3.4	-2.9	-2.9	-2.9	-2.4	-2.4	-3.0	-2.7

[1] Includes a small amount of grants to state and local governments and direct payments for individuals.   [2] Includes some off-budget amounts; most of the off-budget amounts are direct payments for individuals (social security benefits).

Source: U.S. Office of Management and Budget, *Budget of the United States Government, Historical Tables,* annual. See also <http://w3.access.gpo.gov/usbudget/fy2003/pdf/hist.pdf>.

No. 452. Federal Outlays by Agency: 1980 to 2002

[In billions of dollars (590.9 represents $590,900,000,000). See headnote, Table 449]

Department or other unit	1980	1990	1995	1999	2000	2001	2002, est.
Outlays, total [1]	**590.9**	**1,253.2**	**1,515.8**	**1,701.9**	**1,788.8**	**1,863.9**	**2,052.3**
Legislative Branch	1.2	2.2	2.6	2.6	2.9	3.1	3.6
The Judiciary Branch	0.6	1.6	2.9	3.8	4.1	4.5	5.0
Agriculture	34.8	46.0	56.7	62.8	75.7	68.6	76.6
Commerce	3.1	3.7	3.4	5.0	7.8	5.1	5.5
Defense-Military.	130.9	289.8	259.6	261.4	281.2	294.0	330.6
Education	14.6	23.0	31.2	31.3	33.9	35.7	47.6
Energy	7.3	12.1	17.6	16.0	15.0	16.5	19.1
Health and Human Services.	68.3	175.5	303.1	359.7	382.6	426.8	459.4
Housing and Urban Development	12.7	20.2	29.0	32.7	30.8	34.0	30.9
Interior	4.5	5.8	7.5	7.8	8.0	8.2	10.3
Justice	2.6	6.5	10.8	18.3	19.6	21.3	23.1
Labor	29.5	25.2	32.1	32.5	31.4	39.4	58.6
State	2.4	4.8	6.3	6.5	6.9	7.5	11.1
Transportation	19.8	28.7	38.8	41.8	46.0	54.8	60.8
Treasury.	76.6	255.2	348.6	306.7	391.2	390.6	382.6
Veterans Affairs	21.1	29.0	37.8	43.2	47.1	45.8	51.5
Corps of Engineers.	3.2	3.3	3.7	4.2	4.3	4.8	5.0
Other Defense-Civil Programs	12.0	21.7	28.0	32.0	32.9	34.2	35.5
Environmental Protection Agency	5.6	5.1	6.4	6.8	7.2	7.5	7.8
Executive Office of the President.	0.1	0.2	0.2	0.4	0.3	0.3	0.5
Federal Emergency Management Administration . . .	1.2	2.2	3.1	4.0	3.1	4.4	5.8
General Services Administration	0.3	-0.1	0.8	(Z)	(Z)	(Z)	0.6
International Assistance Programs.	7.7	10.1	11.1	10.1	12.1	11.8	13.3
National Aeronautics and Space Administration	5.0	12.4	13.4	13.7	13.4	14.2	14.5
National Science Foundation	0.9	1.8	2.8	3.3	3.5	3.7	4.6
Office of Personnel Management	15.1	31.9	41.0	47.5	40.7	50.0	54.0
Social Security Administration (on-budget)	8.1	18.1	31.8	40.6	45.6	40.6	46.9
Social Security Administration (off-budget)	117.9	245.0	330.4	379.2	396.2	421.4	445.7
Undistributed offsetting receipts	-32.0	-98.9	-137.6	-159.0	-173.0	-199.3	-206.3

Z $50 million or less.   [1] Includes agencies and allowances not shown separately.

Source: U.S. Office of Management and Budget, *Budget of the United States Government, Historical Tables,* annual. See also <http://w3.access.gpo.gov/usbudget/fy2003/pdf/hist.pdf>.

No. 453. Federal Outlays by Detailed Function: 1980 to 2002

[In billions of dollars (590.9 represents $590,900,000,000). For fiscal years ending in year shown; see text, Section 8, State and Local Government Finances and Employment]

Superfunction and function	1980	1990	1995	1998	1999	2000	2001	2002, est.
Outlays, total	**590.9**	**1,253.2**	**1,515.8**	**1,652.6**	**1,701.9**	**1,788.8**	**1,863.9**	**2,052.3**
National defense	134.0	299.3	272.1	268.5	274.9	294.5	308.5	348.0
Department of Defense-Military	130.9	289.8	259.4	256.1	261.4	281.2	294.0	330.6
Military personnel	40.9	75.6	70.8	69.0	69.5	76.0	74.0	81.2
Operation and maintenance	44.8	88.3	91.1	93.5	96.4	105.9	114.0	133.6
Procurement	29.0	81.0	55.0	48.2	48.8	51.7	55.0	59.6
Research, development, test, and evaluation	13.1	37.5	34.6	37.4	37.4	37.6	40.6	45.1
Military construction	2.5	5.1	6.8	6.0	5.5	5.1	5.0	5.7
Family housing	1.7	3.5	3.6	3.9	3.7	3.4	3.5	3.8
Atomic energy defense activities	2.9	9.0	11.8	11.3	12.4	12.2	13.0	15.9
International affairs	12.7	13.8	16.4	13.1	15.2	17.2	16.6	23.5
International development and humanitarian assist.	3.6	5.5	7.6	5.4	5.7	6.5	7.2	7.7
International security assistance	4.8	8.7	5.3	5.1	5.5	6.4	6.6	7.5
Conduct of foreign affairs	1.4	3.1	4.2	3.3	4.2	4.7	5.1	8.7
Foreign information and exchange activities	0.5	1.1	1.4	1.2	1.2	0.8	0.8	0.9
International financial programs	2.4	-4.5	-2.0	-1.9	-1.3	-1.2	-3.1	-1.3
General science, space and technology	5.8	14.4	16.7	18.2	18.1	18.6	19.9	21.8
General science and basic research	1.4	2.8	4.1	5.4	5.7	6.2	6.6	7.8
Space flight, research, and supporting activities	4.5	11.6	12.6	12.9	12.4	12.4	13.3	14.0
Energy	10.2	3.3	4.9	1.3	0.9	-1.1	0.1	0.6
Energy supply	8.4	2.0	3.6	0.2	-0.1	-2.1	-1.1	-0.7
Energy conservation	0.6	0.4	0.7	0.6	0.6	0.7	0.8	0.8
Emergency energy preparedness	0.3	0.4	0.2	0.2	0.2	0.2	0.2	0.2
Energy information, policy, and regulation	0.9	0.6	0.5	0.2	0.2	0.2	0.3	0.3
Natural resources and environment [1]	13.9	17.1	21.9	22.3	24.0	25.0	26.3	30.2
Water resources	4.2	4.4	4.6	4.7	4.7	5.1	5.4	6.0
Conservation and land management	1.3	4.0	6.0	6.2	6.4	6.8	7.5	9.2
Recreational resources	1.4	1.4	2.0	2.1	2.6	2.6	2.3	3.0
Pollution control and abatement	5.5	5.2	6.5	6.4	6.9	7.4	7.7	8.0
Agriculture	8.8	12.0	9.8	12.2	23.0	36.6	26.6	28.8
Farm income stabilization	7.4	9.8	7.0	9.3	20.0	33.5	22.8	24.6
Agricultural research and services	1.4	2.2	2.8	2.9	3.0	3.2	3.8	4.3
Commerce and housing credit [1]	9.4	67.6	-17.8	1.0	2.6	3.2	6.0	3.8
Mortgage credit	5.9	3.8	-1.0	-2.9	0.4	-3.3	-1.1	-6.7
Postal Service	1.2	2.1	-1.8	0.3	1.1	2.1	2.4	2.8
Deposit insurance	-0.3	57.9	-17.8	-4.4	-5.3	-3.1	-1.4	0.2
Transportation [1]	21.3	29.5	39.4	40.3	42.5	46.9	55.2	62.1
Ground transportation	15.3	19.0	25.3	26.0	28.1	31.7	35.8	37.6
Air transportation	3.7	7.2	10.0	10.6	10.7	10.6	14.4	18.9
Water transportation	2.2	3.2	3.7	3.5	3.5	4.4	4.7	5.3
Community and regional development	11.3	8.5	10.7	9.8	11.9	10.6	12.0	15.4
Community development	4.9	3.5	4.7	5.1	5.1	5.5	5.3	5.9
Area and regional development	4.3	2.9	2.7	2.5	2.3	2.5	2.8	3.1
Disaster relief and Insurance	2.0	2.1	3.3	2.1	4.4	2.6	3.9	6.4
Educ./training/employment/& social services [1]	31.8	37.2	51.0	50.5	50.6	53.8	57.3	71.7
Elementary, secondary, and vocational education	6.9	9.9	14.7	16.6	17.6	20.6	22.9	27.0
Higher education	6.7	11.1	14.2	12.1	10.7	10.1	9.6	16.8
Research and general education aids	1.2	1.6	2.1	2.3	2.3	2.5	2.8	3.3
Training and employment	10.3	5.6	7.4	6.6	6.8	6.8	7.2	8.1
Other labor services	0.6	0.8	1.0	1.0	1.1	1.2	1.3	1.6
Social services	6.1	8.1	11.6	11.9	12.2	12.6	13.5	14.8
Health	23.2	57.7	115.4	131.4	141.1	154.5	172.6	195.2
Health care services	18.0	47.6	101.9	116.3	124.5	136.2	152.1	170.6
Health research and training	4.2	8.6	11.6	13.1	14.4	16.0	18.0	21.7
Consumer and occupational health and safety	1.0	1.5	1.9	2.0	2.2	2.3	2.6	2.9
Medicare	32.1	98.1	159.9	192.8	190.4	197.1	217.5	226.4
Income security [1]	86.6	148.7	223.7	237.7	242.4	253.5	269.8	310.7
Gen. retirement & disability ins. (exc. soc. sec.)	5.1	5.1	5.1	4.6	1.9	5.2	5.8	5.2
Federal employee retirement and disability	26.6	52.0	65.9	73.5	75.1	77.2	81.0	85.0
Unemployment compensation	18.1	18.9	23.6	22.1	23.6	23.0	30.2	47.4
Housing assistance	5.6	15.9	27.5	28.7	27.7	28.8	30.1	32.1
Food and nutrition assistance	14.0	24.0	37.6	33.6	33.1	32.5	34.1	38.8
Social security:								
Social security	118.5	248.6	335.8	379.2	390.0	409.4	433.1	459.7
Veterans benefits and services [1]	21.2	29.1	37.9	41.8	43.2	47.1	45.8	51.5
Income security for veterans	11.7	15.2	19.0	21.3	22.2	24.9	22.5	26.0
Veterans education, training and rehabilitation	2.3	0.3	1.1	1.1	1.3	1.3	1.2	2.0
Hospital and medical care for veterans	6.5	12.1	16.4	17.5	18.2	19.5	21.7	22.8
Veterans housing	(Z)	0.5	0.3	0.8	0.6	0.3	-0.9	-0.9
Administration of justice	4.6	10.0	16.2	22.9	26.1	28.0	30.4	34.4
General government	13.0	10.6	14.0	15.6	15.6	13.3	15.2	18.3
Net interest [1]	52.5	184.4	232.2	241.2	229.8	223.0	206.2	178.4
Interest on Treasury debt securities (gross)	74.8	264.7	332.4	363.8	353.5	362.0	359.5	338.8
Interest received by on-budget trust funds	-9.7	-46.3	-59.9	-67.2	-66.5	-69.3	-75.3	-74.3
Interest received by off-budget trust funds	-2.3	-16.0	-33.3	-46.6	-52.1	-59.8	-68.8	-76.8
Undistributed offsetting receipts	-19.9	-36.6	-44.5	-47.2	-40.4	-42.6	-55.2	-55.2

Z $50 million or less.   [1] Includes functions not shown separately.

Source: U.S. Office of Management and Budget, *Budget of the United States Government, Historical Tables*, annual. See also <http://w3.access.gpo.gov/usbudget/fy2003/pdf/hist.pdf>.

Federal Government Finances and Employment   307

No. 454. Federal Receipts by Source: 1980 to 2002

[In billions of dollars (517.1 represents $517,100,000,000). For fiscal years ending in year shown; see text, Section 8, State and Local Government Finances and Employment. Receipts reflect collections. Covers both federal funds and trust funds; see text, this section. Excludes government-sponsored but privately-owned corporations, Federal Reserve System, District of Columbia government, and money held in suspense as deposit funds]

Source	1980	1990	1995	1998	1999	2000	2001	2002, est.
Total federal receipts [1]	**517.1**	**1,032.0**	**1,351.8**	**1,721.8**	**1,827.5**	**2,025.2**	**1,991.0**	**1,946.1**
Individual income taxes	244.1	466.9	590.2	828.6	879.5	1,004.5	994.3	949.2
Corporation income taxes	64.6	93.5	157.0	188.7	184.7	207.3	151.1	201.4
Social insurance and retirement receipts . .	157.8	380.0	484.5	571.8	611.8	652.9	694.0	708.0
Excise taxes.	24.3	35.3	57.5	57.7	70.4	68.9	66.1	66.9
Social insurance and retirement receipts	**157.8**	**380.0**	**484.5**	**571.8**	**611.8**	**652.9**	**694.0**	**708.0**
Employment and general retirement	138.7	353.9	451.0	540.0	580.9	620.5	661.4	673.1
Old-age & survivors ins. (off-budget) . .	96.6	255.0	284.1	358.8	383.6	411.7	434.1	442.1
Disability insurance (off-budget)	16.6	26.6	67.0	57.0	60.9	68.9	73.5	75.1
Hospital insurance	23.2	68.6	96.0	119.9	132.3	135.5	149.7	151.7
Railroad retirement/pension fund	2.3	2.3	2.4	2.6	2.6	2.7	2.7	2.6
Unemployment insurance	15.3	21.6	28.9	27.5	26.5	27.6	27.8	30.3
Other retirement	3.7	4.5	4.6	4.3	4.5	4.8	4.7	4.6
Federal employees retirement-employee share	3.7	4.4	4.5	4.3	4.4	4.7	4.6	4.6
Excise taxes, total [1]	**24.3**	**35.3**	**57.5**	**57.7**	**70.4**	**68.9**	**66.1**	**66.9**
Federal funds	15.6	15.6	26.9	21.7	19.3	22.7	24.1	24.7
Alcohol	5.6	5.7	7.2	7.2	7.4	8.1	7.6	7.6
Tobacco	2.4	4.1	5.9	5.7	5.4	7.2	7.4	8.0
Telephone	(X)	3.0	3.8	4.9	5.2	5.7	5.8	6.0
Ozone depleting chemicals/products . .	(X)	0.4	0.6	0.1	0.1	0.1	(Z)	(Z)
Transportation fuels	(X)	(X)	8.5	0.6	0.8	0.8	1.2	1.1
Trust funds.	8.8	19.8	30.5	36.0	51.1	46.2	41.9	42.2
Highway.	6.6	13.9	22.6	26.6	39.3	35.0	31.5	31.9
Airport and airway	1.9	3.7	5.5	8.1	10.4	9.7	9.2	8.9
Black lung disability	0.3	0.7	0.6	0.6	0.6	0.5	0.5	0.6
Inland waterway	(X)	0.1	0.1	0.1	0.1	0.1	0.1	0.1
Hazardous substance superfund.	(X)	0.8	0.9	-	(Z)	(Z)	-	-
Oil spill liability.	(X)	0.1	0.2	-	-	0.2	-	-
Aquatic resources	(X)	0.2	0.3	0.3	0.4	0.3	0.4	0.4
Vaccine injury compensation	(X)	0.2	0.1	0.1	0.1	0.1	0.1	0.1

- Represents zero.   X Not applicable.   Z $50 million or less.   [1] Totals reflect interfund and intragovernmental transactions and/or other functions, not shown separately.

Source: U.S. Office of Management and Budget, *Budget of the United States Government, Historical Tables*, annual. See also <http://w3.access.gpo.gov/usbudget/fy2003/pdf/hist.pdf>.

No. 455. Federal Trust Fund Receipts, Outlays, and Balances: 1999 to 2001

[In billions of dollars (1,002 represents $1,002,000,000,000). For fiscal years ending in year shown. Receipts deposited. Outlays on a checks-issued basis less refunds collected. Balances: That which have not been spent. See text, this section, for discussion of the budget concept and trust funds]

Description	Income			Outlays			Balances [1]		
	1999	2000	2001	1999	2000	2001	1999	2000	2001
Total [2]	**1,002**	**1,063**	**1,125**	**798**	**829**	**897**	**1,876**	**2,110**	**2,340**
Airport and airway trust fund.	11	11	10	8	9	10	12	14	15
Federal employees health benefits fund . .	18	20	22	19	20	21	6	6	7
Fed./civ. employees retirement funds	76	77	79	45	46	48	492	523	554
Federal old-age, survivors and disability insurance trust funds.	517	564	597	393	412	434	855	1,007	1,170
Foreign military sales trust fund.	12	11	10	12	11	10	6	6	6
Highway trust fund	39	35	32	29	33	35	29	31	28
Health insurance trust funds:									
Medicare:									
Federal hospital insurance trust fund. . .	153	160	172	132	130	143	138	168	197
Federal supplemental medical insurance.	86	91	99	81	91	103	46	46	42
Military retirement fund	38	39	41	32	33	34	152	158	165
Railroad retirement trust funds	9	10	10	8	8	9	14	16	17
Unemployment trust funds	32	33	34	25	24	32	78	87	89
Veterans life insurance trust funds	2	2	2	2	2	2	14	14	14
Other trust funds [3]	9	11	19	13	9	18	35	35	38

[1] Balances available on a cash basis (rather than an authorization basis) at the end of the year. Balances are primarily invested in federal debt securities.   [2] Includes funds not shown separately.   [3] Effective August 9, 1989, the permanent insurance fund of the FDIC was classified under law as a federal fund.

Source: U.S. Office of Management and Budget, *Budget of the United States Government, Analytical Perspectives*, annual. See also <http://w3.access.gpo.gov/usbudget/fy2003/pdf/spec.pdf>.

No. 456. Tax Expenditures Estimates Relating to Individual and Corporate Income Taxes by Selected Function: 2001 to 2003

[In millions of dollars (2,160 represents $2,160,000,000). For years ending Sept. 30. Tax expenditures are defined as *revenue losses* attributable to provisions of the federal tax laws which allow a special exclusion, exemption, or deduction from gross income or which provide a special credit, a preferential rate of tax, or a deferral of liability]

Function and provision	2001	2002	2003	2003, rank
National defense:				
Exclusion of benefits and allowances to armed forces personnel	2,160	2,190	2,210	43
International affairs:				
Exclusion of income earned abroad by U.S. citizens	2,450	2,540	2,660	37
Exclusion of certain allowances for federal employees abroad.	760	800	840	59
Extraterritorial income exclusion	4,490	4,820	5,150	23
Inventory property sales source rules exception	1,400	1,470	1,540	48
Deferral of income from controlled foreign corporations (normal tax method)	6,600	7,000	7,450	17
General science, space, and technology:				
Expensing of research and experimentation expenditures (normal tax method) . .	2,020	1,780	2,380	39
Credit for increasing research activities	5,370	6,010	4,590	26
Agriculture:				
Capital gains treatment of certain income	990	1,040	1,100	56
Commerce and housing:				
Financial institutions and insurance:				
Exemption of credit union income	1,000	1,070	1,150	53
Exclusion of interest on life insurance savings	16,290	17,710	19,250	14
Housing:				
Exclusion of interest on owner-occupied mortgage subsidy bonds	800	830	870	58
Deductibility of mortgage interest on owner-occupied homes.	64,510	64,190	66,110	2
Deductibility of state and local property tax on owner-occupied homes	22,410	22,680	23,580	11
Deferral of income from post 1987 installment sales	1,040	1,050	1,080	57
Capital gains exclusion on home sales	19,090	19,670	20,260	12
Exception from passive loss rules for $25,000 of rental loss	4,800	4,400	4,070	30
Credit for low-income housing investments	3,220	3,330	3,460	33
Accelerated depreciation on rental housing (normal tax method)	5,190	5,440	5,710	21
Commerce:				
Capital gains (except agriculture, timber, iron ore, and coal) [1]	67,800	61,810	60,200	3
Step-up basis of capital gains at death	26,540	27,610	28,710	9
Accelerated depreciation of buildings other than rental housing [1]	4,540	4,560	4,240	28
Accelerated depreciation of machinery and equipment [1]	37,860	37,130	36,480	7
Expensing of certain small investments [1]	1,670	1,430	1,420	49
Graduated corporation income tax rate [1]	4,940	5,590	6,210	19
Transportation:				
Exclusion of reimbursed employee parking expenses	1,980	2,090	2,190	44
Education, training, employment, and social services:				
Exclusion of scholarship and fellowship income [1]	1,210	1,200	1,210	51
HOPE tax credit	4,130	4,110	3,520	32
Lifetime Learning tax credit.	2,370	2,290	2,360	40
Deduction for higher education expenses	-	430	2,290	41
Parental personal exemption for students age 19 or over	1,010	1,070	1,120	55
Deductibility of charitable contributions (education)	3,830	3,980	4,200	29
Training, employment, and social services:				
Exclusion of employee meals and lodging (other than military)	710	740	780	60
Child credit	19,840	19,760	19,680	13
Credit for child and dependent care expenses	2,670	2,610	2,670	36
Deductibility of charitable contributions, other than education and health	30,150	30,810	32,080	8
Health:				
Exclusion of employer contributions for medical insurance premiums [2]	82,800	90,910	99,260	1
Self-employed medical insurance premiums	1,520	1,730	2,420	38
Workers' compensation insurance premiums	4,730	4,870	5,080	24
Deductibility of medical expenses.	4,990	5,260	5,530	22
Exclusion of interest on hospital construction bonds	1,100	1,130	1,190	52
Deductibility of charitable contributions (health).	4,010	4,180	4,420	27
Income security:				
Exclusion of workers' compensation benefits	5,560	5,810	6,070	20
Net exclusion of pension contributions and earnings:				
Employer plans	42,070	48,070	53,080	5
401(k) plans	44,080	52,960	59,510	4
Individual Retirement Accounts	18,680	18,090	18,660	15
Low and moderate income savers credit	-	550	1,960	45
Keogh plans	6,160	6,520	6,770	18
Exclusion of other employee benefits:				
Premiums on group term life insurance	1,750	1,780	1,800	47
Special ESOP rules	1,290	1,340	1,420	50
Additional deduction for the elderly	1,970	1,890	1,950	46
Earned income tax credit	4,940	4,370	4,800	25
Social Security:				
Exclusion of social security benefits:				
Social Security benefits for retired workers	17,830	18,000	18,180	16
Social Security benefits for disabled	2,690	2,930	3,240	35
Social Security benefits for dependents and survivors	3,720	3,870	4,060	31
Veterans benefits and services:				
Exclusion of veterans death benefits and disability compensation	3,150	3,190	3,300	34
General purpose fiscal assistance:				
Exclusion of interest on public purpose state and local bonds	23,100	23,680	24,270	10
Deductibility of nonbusiness state and local taxes other than on owner-occupied .	45,520	46,160	48,150	6
Tax credit for corporations receiving income from doing business in U.S. pos. . . .	2,190	2,240	2,240	42

- Represents zero.   [1] Normal tax method.   [2] Includes premiums and medical care.

Source: U.S. Office of Management and Budget, *Budget of the United States Government, Analytical Perspectives, Fiscal Year 2003.* See also <http://www.whitehouse.gov/omb/budget/fy2003/pdf/spec.pdf> (released 04 February 2003).

No. 457. United States Government Ledger Balance Sheet—Assets and Liabilities: 1995 to 2001

[In millions of dollars (89,349 represents $89,349,000,000). For fiscal year ending in year shown]

Item	1995	1998	1999	2000	2001
Assets, total	**89,349**	**135,874**	**170,378**	**181,729**	**212,738**
Cash and monetary assets, total	84,080	85,030	103,507	98,401	104,463
U.S. Treasury operating cash:					
Federal Reserve account	8,620	4,952	6,641	8,459	9,796
Tax and loan note accounts	29,329	33,926	49,817	44,199	34,423
Special drawing rights (SDR):					
Total holdings	11,035	10,106	10,284	10,316	10,919
SDR's certificates issued to Federal Reserve banks	-10,168	-9,200	-7,200	-3,200	-2,200
Monetary assets with IMF [1]	14,682	21,155	19,982	13,690	18,407
Other cash and monetary assets:					
U.S. Treasury monetary assets	356	87	30	-	-
Cash and other assets held outside the Treasury Account	29,697	18,967	18,341	24,937	33,118
U.S. Treasury time deposits	528	4,543	5,612	5,977	13,352
Loan financing accounts:					
Guaranteed loans	-12,714	-14,362	-18,518	-22,013	-17,801
Direct loans	19,732	65,289	83,894	105,459	124,518
Miscellaneous asset accounts	-1,748	-83	1,496	-119	1,558
Total assets and excess of liabilities over assets	**3,674,266**	**3,781,596**	**3,690,740**	**3,467,448**	**3,380,867**
Excess of liabilities over assets at beginning of fiscal year	3,421,723	3,715,533	3,645,730	3,519,430	3,285,720
Add: Total deficit for fiscal year	163,916	-69,242	-124,360	-246,917	-127,021
Subtotal	3,585,639	3,646,292	3,521,370	3,283,464	3,158,698
Deduct: Other transactions not applied to surplus or deficit	*722*	*569*	*1,009*	*-3,207*	*-9,430*
Excess of liabilities over assets at close of fiscal year	3,584,917	3,645,722	3,520,361	3,285,720	3,168,129
Liabilities, total	**3,674,266**	**3,781,596**	**3,690,740**	**3,467,448**	**3,380,867**
Federal securities, total	4,920,944	5,478,704	5,606,080	5,629,009	5,770,249
Treasury debt securities, total	4,893,989	5,449,345	5,577,575	5,601,336	5,743,238
Agency securities outstanding	26,955	29,359	28,505	27,672	27,011
Deduct: Net federal securities held as investments by government accounts	*1,317,645*	*1,757,090*	*1,973,160*	*2,218,896*	*2,450,266*
Equals: Borrowing from the public, total	3,603,299	3,721,613	3,632,920	3,410,113	3,319,983
Accrued interest payable	50,611	45,448	42,603	44,211	39,483
Special drawing rights allocated by IMF [1]	7,380	6,719	6,799	6,359	6,316
Deposit fund liabilities	8,186	3,893	3,998	2,625	6,785
Miscellaneous liability accounts (checks outstanding, etc.)	4,790	3,923	4,420	4,140	8,301

- Represents zero.   [1] IMF = International Monetary Funds.

Source: U.S. Dept. of Treasury, 1995-1999, *United States Government Annual Report;* and beginning 2000, *Combined Statement of Receipts, Outlays, and Balances of the United States 2001.* See also <http://www.fms.treas.gov/annualreport/cs2001/index.html> (released 23 January 2002).

No. 458. Federal Participation in the Credit Market: 1980 to 2000

[In millions of dollars (103.2 represents $103,200,000), except percents]

Item	1980	1990	1995	1996	1997	1998	1999	2000 est.
Total, federal and federally assisted borrowing	**103.2**	**261.6**	**197.5**	**219.6**	**96.1**	**7.3**	**-27.9**	**-76.0**
Federal borrowing from the public	71.6	220.9	171.3	129.7	38.3	-51.2	-88.7	-170.9
Guaranteed borrowing	31.6	40.7	26.2	89.9	57.8	58.5	60.8	94.9
Total, federal and federally assisted lending	**55.8**	**43.5**	**27.8**	**93.9**	**70.6**	**65.3**	**74.2**	**104.8**
Direct loans	24.2	2.8	1.6	4.0	12.8	6.8	13.4	9.9
Guaranteed loans	31.6	40.7	26.2	89.9	57.8	58.5	60.8	94.9
Total net borrowing in credit market	336.9	704.1	720.4	727.1	713.5	975.3	1,091.4	(NA)
Federal borrowing participation rate (percent)	30.6	37.2	27.4	30.2	13.5	0.7	-2.6	(NA)
Total net lending in credit market	336.9	704.1	720.4	727.1	713.5	975.3	1091.4	(NA)
Federal lending participation rate (percent)	16.6	6.2	3.9	12.9	9.9	6.7	6.8	(NA)

NA Not available.

Source: U.S. Office of Management and Budget, *Budget of the United States Government, Analytical Perspectives,* annual.

No. 459. Federal Government Debt by Type and Maturity: 1990 to 2000

[In millions of dollars (3,266,073 represents $3,266,073,000,000). As of end of fiscal year]

Item	1990	1995	1998	1999	2000
Debt outstanding, total	**3,266,073**	**5,000,945**	**5,555,552**	**5,684,776**	**5,701,850**
Public debt securities	3,233,313	4,973,983	5,526,193	5,656,271	5,674,178
Agency securities	32,758	26,962	29,359	28,505	27,672
Securities held by—					
Government accounts, total	795,907	1,320,800	1,767,778	1,989,308	2,235,763
Public debt securities	795,762	1,320,784	1,763,860	1,988,674	2,235,710
Agency securities	145	16	3,917	634	51
The public, total	2,470,166	3,680,145	3,787,774	3,695,468	3,466,087
Public debt securities	2,437,551	3,653,199	3,762,333	3,667,597	3,438,469
Agency securities	32,613	26,946	25,442	27,871	27,621
Interest-bearing public debt, total	**3,210,943**	**4,950,644**	**5,518,681**	**5,647,241**	**5,622,092**
Marketable, total	2,092,759	3,260,447	3,331,030	3,232,998	2,992,752
Treasury bills	482,454	742,462	637,648	653,165	616,174
Treasury notes	1,218,081	1,980,343	2,009,115	1,828,775	1,611,326
Treasury bonds	377,224	522,643	610,444	643,695	635,263
Treasury inflation-indexed notes	(Z)	(Z)	58,823	92,365	114,988
Federal Financing Bank	15,000	15,000	15,000	15,000	15,000
Nonmarketable, total.	1,118,184	1,690,197	2,187,651	2,414,242	2,629,341
U.S. savings bonds	122,152	181,181	180,816	180,019	177,724
Foreign series: Government	36,041	40,950	35,079	30,970	25,431
Government account series, total.	779,412	1,324,270	1,777,329	2,005,166	2,242,900
Airport and airway trust fund	14,312	11,145	8,550	12,414	13,097
Bank insurance fund	8,438	20,117	27,445	28,359	29,126
Employees life insurance fund	9,561	15,839	19,377	20,755	22,372
Exchange stabilization fund	1,863	2,399	15,981	12,382	11,029
Federal disability insurance trust fund	11,254	35,150	76,947	92,622	113,667
Federal employees retirement funds	223,229	357,539	440,145	474,692	507,225
Federal hospital insurance trust fund.	96,249	129,864	118,250	153,767	168,859
Federal Housing Administration	6,678	6,277	14,518	15,152	17,267
Fed. old-age & survivors insurance trust fund . .	203,717	447,947	653,282	762,226	893,519
Fed. S&L Corp., resolution fund	929	528	2,087	2,304	2,508
Fed. supplementary medical insur. trust fund	14,286	13,513	39,502	26,528	45,075
Government life insurance fund	184	106	(Z)	(Z)	(Z)
Highway trust fund.	9,530	8,954	17,926	28,083	31,023
National service life insurance fund.	10,917	11,954	12,008	11,954	11,804
Postal Service fund	3,063	1,249	1,000	(Z)	1,086
Railroad retirement account.	8,356	12,129	19,764	22,347	22,628
Treasury deposit funds	304	130	71	71	62
Unemployment trust fund	50,186	47,098	70,598	77,357	86,399
Other	106,376	202,332	239,878	264,153	266,154
State and local government series.	161,248	113,368	164,431	168,091	153,288
Domestic series	18,886	29,995	29,995	29,995	29,996
Other	447	432	1	1	1
MATURITY DISTRIBUTION					
Amount outstanding, privately held	**1,841,903**	**2,870,781**	**2,856,637**	**2,728,011**	**2,469,152**
Maturity class:					
Within 1 year	626,297	1,002,875	940,572	915,145	858,903
1-5 years.	630,144	1,157,492	1,105,175	962,644	791,540
5-10 years.	267,573	290,111	319,331	378,163	355,382
10-20 years	82,713	87,297	157,347	149,703	167,082
20 years and over.	235,176	333,006	334,212	322,356	296,246

Z Less than $500,000.

Source: U.S. Department of the Treasury, *Treasury Bulletin*, quarterly.

No. 460. U.S. Savings Bonds: 1990 to 2001

[In billions of dollars (122.5 represents $122,500,000,000), except percent. As of end of fiscal year, see text, Section 8, State and Local Government Finances and Employment]

Item	1990	1992	1993	1994	1995	1996	1997	1998	1999	2000	2001
Amounts outstanding, total [1]	122.5	148.6	167.4	176.8	181.5	184.4	182.6	180.7	166.5	177.7	179.5
Sales	7.8	13.6	17.3	9.5	7.2	5.9	5.3	4.8	6.5	5.6	8.0
Accrued discounts	8.0	8.7	9.3	9.4	9.5	9.8	9.1	9.1	8.4	6.9	8.4
Redemptions [2]	7.5	7.4	7.8	9.4	11.8	2.5	2.1	14.3	16.6	14.5	13.8
Percent of total outstanding. . . .	6.1	5.0	4.7	5.3	6.5	1.4	1.1	7.9	10.0	8.2	7.7

[1] Interest-bearing debt only for amounts end of year. [2] Matured and unmatured bonds.

Source: U.S. Department of the Treasury, *Treasury Bulletin*, quarterly.

Federal Government Finances and Employment 311

No. 461. Federal Funds—Summary Distribution by State and Outlying Area: 2001

[In millions of dollars (1,778,884 represents $1,778,884,000,000), except as indicated. For year ending Sept. 30. Data for grants, salaries and wages and direct payments to individuals are on an expenditures basis; procurement is on obligation basis]

State and outlying area	Federal funds							
	Total	Per capita [1] (dol.)	Defense	Non-defense	Direct payments	Procurement	Grants	Salaries and wages
United States [2]	**1,778,884**	**6,268**	**255,385**	**1,523,499**	**1,005,613**	**246,219**	**338,977**	**188,075**
Alabama	31,700	7,128	5,648	26,053	18,303	5,204	5,298	2,895
Alaska	6,403	10,214	1,778	4,625	1,546	1,130	2,314	1,414
Arizona	30,376	5,921	6,641	23,735	17,009	5,260	5,190	2,917
Arkansas	16,632	6,221	1,166	15,466	11,314	692	3,448	1,178
California	188,517	5,566	31,304	157,213	101,914	28,949	39,797	17,858
Colorado	24,345	5,660	4,768	19,576	12,094	4,468	3,916	3,868
Connecticut	22,742	6,678	4,737	18,005	12,269	4,734	4,364	1,375
Delaware	4,246	5,418	423	3,822	2,779	148	892	428
District of Columbia	30,941	54,086	2,871	28,069	4,012	10,263	4,020	12,646
Florida	99,998	6,257	13,716	86,283	69,058	8,859	13,666	8,415
Georgia	47,320	5,780	10,995	36,326	25,078	7,382	7,929	6,931
Hawaii	9,722	8,025	3,728	5,995	4,217	1,467	1,514	2,525
Idaho	7,529	5,819	580	6,949	4,074	1,197	1,505	753
Illinois	65,036	5,237	4,118	60,918	42,765	4,135	11,883	6,252
Indiana	32,166	5,290	2,650	29,516	21,462	2,734	5,850	2,121
Iowa	17,401	5,946	795	16,606	12,396	897	3,079	1,029
Kansas	16,699	6,211	2,087	14,612	10,728	1,383	2,721	1,866
Kentucky	25,835	6,392	3,042	22,793	15,172	2,759	5,100	2,805
Louisiana	27,816	6,224	2,915	24,901	16,708	2,625	6,173	2,310
Maine	8,180	6,416	1,094	7,086	4,793	674	1,905	808
Maryland	48,164	9,094	8,622	39,542	20,920	10,736	7,586	8,921
Massachusetts	44,179	6,958	6,250	37,929	24,395	6,851	9,718	3,214
Michigan	51,632	5,195	3,148	48,484	34,217	3,378	10,887	3,150
Minnesota	24,935	5,069	1,870	23,065	15,721	2,049	5,260	1,904
Mississippi	20,212	7,105	2,724	17,488	12,377	1,863	4,246	1,725
Missouri	39,191	7,004	6,611	32,580	22,122	6,741	6,865	3,463
Montana	6,618	7,335	419	6,199	3,871	371	1,665	711
Nebraska	10,771	6,294	874	9,898	7,216	447	2,054	1,053
Nevada	9,624	4,816	1,188	8,436	6,121	1,041	1,442	1,019
New Hampshire	6,314	5,109	744	5,570	3,855	655	1,288	516
New Jersey	46,240	5,495	4,175	42,065	29,822	4,158	8,478	3,782
New Mexico	16,587	9,118	1,910	14,677	6,131	5,122	3,586	1,747
New York	116,366	6,132	5,166	111,200	69,180	6,168	32,897	8,122
North Carolina	44,557	5,536	6,159	38,398	26,779	3,154	9,122	5,502
North Dakota	5,948	9,262	545	5,404	3,750	280	1,284	634
Ohio	61,705	5,435	5,523	56,182	39,968	5,124	11,762	4,851
Oklahoma	22,672	6,570	3,962	18,710	13,290	2,212	4,119	3,050
Oregon	18,401	5,378	958	17,444	11,541	959	4,308	1,592
Pennsylvania	79,310	6,458	6,422	72,888	51,912	6,788	14,847	5,763
Rhode Island	6,989	6,666	807	6,182	4,241	392	1,607	747
South Carolina	24,675	6,150	3,604	21,071	14,265	3,155	4,730	2,526
South Dakota	5,807	7,693	387	5,420	3,652	301	1,254	600
Tennessee	36,758	6,461	2,228	34,530	20,985	5,811	7,027	2,935
Texas	112,530	5,397	18,128	94,403	63,102	15,649	21,675	12,104
Utah	11,377	5,095	2,381	8,996	5,284	2,084	2,244	1,765
Vermont	3,734	6,133	417	3,317	1,954	391	1,069	319
Virginia	71,257	10,067	30,020	41,237	26,069	26,935	5,908	12,345
Washington	36,903	6,261	6,328	30,576	19,684	5,480	6,794	4,945
West Virginia	12,541	6,935	402	12,139	8,038	527	2,971	1,005
Wisconsin	26,645	4,968	1,396	25,249	17,359	1,817	5,843	1,626
Wyoming	3,584	7,257	335	3,248	1,594	341	1,213	435
Outlying areas:								
American Samoa	116	1,813	6	109	41	12	58	5
Federated States of Micronesia	98	749	-	98	3	1	94	-
Guam	908	5,972	461	446	266	219	176	247
Marshall Islands	150	2,287	101	49	1	101	48	-
Northern Marianas	96	1,390	9	87	25	9	60	3
Palau	36	1,939	-	36	-	-	35	-
Puerto Rico	13,181	3,461	668	12,513	7,939	477	3,899	866
Virgin Islands	404	3,376	12	392	234	15	111	45
Undistributed	24,066	(X)	15,370	8,696	-	19,443	183	4,440

- Represents zero.   X Not applicable.   [1] Based on U.S. Census Bureau resident population as of July 1.   [2] Includes outlying areas and undistributed.

Source: U.S. Census Bureau, *Consolidated Federal Funds Report, 2001.* See also <http://www.census.gov/prod/2002pubs/01cffr.pdf> (issued April 2002).

No. 462. Per Capita Federal Balance of Payments by State: 1990 to 1999

[**In dollars, except rank. For year ending Sept. 30.** Represents federal spending within the borders of the 50 states, including defense and excluding interest payments on the federal debt. Each state runs a balance of payments surplus or deficit with the federal government. Put another way, each state indirectly subsidizes or is being subsidized by the other states]

State	Balance of payments			1999						
				Balance of pay-ments	Rank	Federal taxes	Federal spending in the state			
	1990	1995	1998				Total [1]	Defense	Non-defense	Social Security
Alabama..........	1,948	1,629	1,863	2,091	9	4,519	6,610	1,320	1,964	1,802
Alaska...........	1,025	1,063	2,155	2,777	6	4,872	7,649	2,194	3,786	657
Arizona..........	1,163	853	493	904	20	4,713	5,617	1,361	1,689	1,474
Arkansas........	1,163	1,057	1,534	1,633	13	4,238	5,871	595	1,772	1,932
California........	-481	-255	-600	-685	39	5,593	4,909	943	1,439	1,195
Colorado.........	960	-233	-444	-620	38	5,923	5,303	1,408	1,884	1,143
Connecticut.......	-1,898	-2,466	-2,432	-2,840	50	8,064	5,224	1,046	1,156	1,543
Delaware........	-1,861	-1,415	-1,050	-1,025	43	5,876	4,851	615	1,458	1,578
District of Columbia	28,482	33,259	37,804	42,514	(X)	7,451	49,965	6,295	39,471	1,242
Florida............	57	258	128	47	31	6,074	6,121	1,058	1,392	2,025
Georgia..........	-218	85	-111	-29	32	5,523	5,493	1,322	1,626	1,360
Hawaii...........	1,056	908	1,981	1,982	10	3,955	5,937	2,391	1,441	1,107
Idaho...........	1,342	552	817	829	21	4,349	5,178	1,166	1,616	1,412
Illinois..........	-1,588	-1,687	-1,535	-1,669	47	6,260	4,592	354	1,442	1,501
Indiana..........	-478	-789	-374	-399	35	5,085	4,686	493	1,318	1,663
Iowa	366	53	548	750	22	5,071	5,820	325	2,409	1,837
Kansas..........	318	46	187	373	25	5,459	5,832	898	2,083	1,646
Kentucky	1,192	1,363	2,073	1,595	14	4,516	6,111	970	1,702	1,858
Louisiana........	1,147	1,439	1,312	1,576	15	4,432	6,008	788	1,815	1,597
Maine...........	821	1,262	1,668	1,324	16	4,215	5,539	1,110	1,399	1,589
Maryland	1,306	1,731	2,148	1,770	12	6,564	8,334	1,895	3,768	1,322
Massachusetts........	89	-304	-793	-895	42	6,256	5,361	836	1,528	1,415
Michigan..........	-1,070	-1,411	-1,231	-1,042	44	5,724	4,682	265	1,197	1,742
Minnesota..........	-680	-1,454	-1,568	-1,294	45	6,069	4,775	432	1,713	1,455
Mississippi	2,364	2,409	2,351	2,684	7	3,905	6,589	1,285	1,877	1,776
Missouri.........	1,633	1,457	1,269	1,187	18	5,358	6,544	1,293	1,966	1,776
Montana.........	1,764	1,774	2,454	3,109	2	4,279	7,389	596	3,939	1,624
Nebraska........	587	-166	125	320	27	5,304	5,624	657	2,177	1,614
Nevada.........	-991	-1,420	-1,802	-1,583	46	5,938	4,355	944	1,172	1,349
New Hampshire.......	-1,644	-1,430	-1,565	-1,787	48	5,854	4,067	576	1,189	1,358
New Jersey.........	-2,404	-2,079	-2,054	-2,342	49	6,705	4,362	504	1,097	1,452
New Mexico	3,906	3,651	3,778	3,944	1	4,048	7,992	2,655	2,678	1,387
New York	-1,068	-943	-854	-890	41	5,834	4,944	305	1,370	1,473
North Carolina........	-179	-41	66	146	30	5,141	5,287	898	1,415	1,666
North Dakota........	2,167	1,870	2,568	3,043	4	4,647	7,690	1,005	3,745	1,624
Ohio...........	-186	-438	-369	-344	34	5,171	4,827	514	1,275	1,660
Oklahoma..........	1,028	1,233	1,755	1,866	11	4,332	6,198	1,255	1,864	1,685
Oregon..........	-25	-436	-441	-483	36	5,235	4,752	354	1,564	1,571
Pennsylvania........	-222	166	218	256	28	5,275	5,531	563	1,450	1,812
Rhode Island........	141	495	754	528	23	4,976	5,504	824	1,409	1,624
South Carolina........	1,592	1,119	1,159	1,265	17	4,546	5,810	1,438	1,346	1,682
South Dakota	1,682	1,053	1,838	2,327	8	4,949	7,276	638	3,720	1,678
Tennessee	700	742	1,000	961	19	5,110	6,071	686	2,029	1,722
Texas............	-100	-54	-252	-189	33	5,566	5,377	1,037	1,801	1,278
Utah.............	1,503	734	9	230	29	4,094	4,324	725	1,854	989
Vermont..........	-623	18	167	343	26	4,719	5,061	587	1,690	1,491
Virginia..........	2,454	2,970	2,969	3,069	3	5,756	8,825	3,685	2,851	1,382
Washington........	264	-31	-355	-533	37	5,872	5,339	1,377	1,490	1,325
West Virginia........	1,627	2,415	2,710	2,808	5	3,916	6,724	419	2,036	2,332
Wisconsin..........	-715	-1,149	-886	-887	40	5,409	4,521	284	1,333	1,688
Wyoming..........	836	294	243	386	24	5,951	6,338	769	3,062	1,472

X Not applicable.   [1] Includes categories of spending, not shown separately.

Source: Jay H. Walder and Herman B. Leonard, Tauber Center for State and Local Government and John F. Kennedy School of Government, Harvard University, *The Federal Budget and the States*, annual.

[In thousands (103,251 represents 103,251,000, except as indicated. Return classification as Schedule C or C-EZ (nonfarm sole proprietorships) or Schedule F (farm proprietorships) for audit examination purposes was based on the largest source of income on the return and certain other characteristics. Therefore, some returns with business activity are reflected in the nonbusiness individual income tax return statistics in the table below (and vise versa), so that the statistics for the number of returns with Schedule C is not comparable to the number of nonfarm sole proprietorship returns in Table 702]

Year and type of return	Returns filed [1]	Returns examined		By—			Average tax and penalty per return (dollars)		
		Total	Percent coverage	Revenue agents	Tax auditors	Service centers [2]	Revenue agents [3]	Tax auditors	Service centers
INDIVIDUAL RETURNS									
1990	109,868	1,145	1.04	202	517	426	309,566	1,962	2,432
1991	112,305	1,313	1.17	200	500	613	664,440	2,398	2,738
1992	113,829	1,206	1.06	210	537	459	1,365,896	2,280	2,539
1993	114,719	1,059	0.92	251	506	303	103,250	2,625	2,974
1994	113,754	1,226	1.08	364	456	406	246,785	3,113	1,963
1995	114,683	1,919	1.67	339	459	1,122	204,616	3,497	1,404
1996	116,060	1,942	1.67	252	509	1,180	818,753	3,051	1,714
1997	118,363	1,519	1.28	210	506	804	802,549	3,460	2,963
1998	120,342	1,193	0.99	168	383	625	177,830	3,372	2,760
1999	122,547	1,100	0.90	124	236	716	322,230	3,265	2,085
ALL RETURNS 2000 [4]									
Individual, total	124,887	618	0.49	92	146	367	123,337	3,337	2,602
1040A, TPI under $25,000 [5]	42,485	257	0.6	11	31	211	274,941	2,706	2,201
Non 1040, TPI under $25,000 [5]	13,763	52	0.37	6	14	30	9,365	2,627	2,074
TPI $25,000 under $50,000 [5]	29,651	64	0.21	9	30	21	23,566	1,967	1,670
TPI $50,000 under $100,000 [5]	22,337	52	0.23	10	24	16	10,024	2,644	1,692
TPI $100,000 and over [5]	8,152	69	0.84	23	14	31	138,561	5,976	8,454
Sch C—TGR under $25,000 [6]	2,541	62	2.43	5	12	44	15,124	2,908	1,264
Sch C—TGR $25,000 under $100,000 [6]	3,351	31	0.93	9	14	8	8,558	5,046	1,380
Sch C—TGR $100,000 and over [6]	1,949	29	1.48	18	6	5	89,594	9,547	6,424
Sch F—TGR under $100,000 [6]	391	1	0.35	1	1	0.56	6,718	1,638	718
Sch F—TGR $100,000 and over [6]	268	2	0.8	1	1	0.8	548,608	6,872	10,045
Corporation (except S Corporation)	2,509	28	1.12	27	(NA)	1	3,641,403	(NA)	7,076
Fiduciary	3,403	7	0.22	4	(NA)	3	53,664	(NA)	1,406
Estate	117	8	6.89	8	(NA)	0.3	5,217,777	(NA)	7,442
Gift	292	2	0.72	2	(NA)	(NA)	(NA)	(NA)	(NA)
Employment	29,000	16	0.06	14	1	0.03	158,005	3,781	418
Excise	822	10	1.25	9	1	1	82,809	3	(NA)
Windfall profit	(NA)	(NA)	-	(NA)	(NA)	(NA)	(NA)	(NA)	(NA)
Misc. taxable	-	0.4		0.04	1	0.01	218,325	(NA)	18,715
Partnerships	1,975	7	0.33	5	5	1	(NA)	(NA)	(NA)
S Corporations (nontaxable)	2,767	15	0.55	14	14	0.8	(NA)	(NA)	(NA)
Miscellaneous nontaxable [7]	(NA)	0.03	(NA)	0.03	(NA)	(NA)	(NA)	(NA)	(NA)

- Represents zero or rounds to zero.   NA Not available.   [1] Returns filed in previous calendar year.   [2] Includes taxpayer contacts by correspondence.   [3] Mostly reflects coordinated examination of large corporations and related returns.   [4] Includes activities to protect release of funds in Treasury in response to taxpayer efforts to recoup tax previously assessed and paid with penalty.   [5] Total positive income, i.e., excludes losses.   [6] TGR= Total gross receipts.   [7] Includes Domestic International Sales Corporations, Interest Charge Domestic International Sales Corporations, Real Estate Investment Mortgage Conduits, and other.

Source: U.S. Internal Revenue Service, *IRS Data Book, 2000*, Publication 55B.

No. 464. Internal Revenue Gross Collections by Source: 1990 to 2000

[1,078 represents $1,078,000,000,000. For fiscal year ending in year shown; see text, Section 8, State and Local Government Finances and Employment]

Source of revenue	Collections (bil. dol.)					Percent of total				
	1990	1995	1998	1999	2000	1990	1995	1998	1999	2000
All taxes	1,078	1,389	1,769	1,904	2,098	100.0	100.0	100.0	100.0	100.0
Individual income taxes	540	676	928	1,002	1,137	50.1	48.7	52.5	52.6	54.2
Withheld by employers	388	534	648	694	781	36.0	38.4	36.6	36.4	37.2
Employment taxes [1]	367	465	558	599	640	34.0	33.5	31.5	31.4	30.5
Old-age and disability insurance	358	455	547	587	628	33.2	32.8	30.9	30.9	29.9
Unemployment insurance	6	6	6	7	7	0.6	0.4	0.4	0.3	0.3
Corporation income taxes	110	174	213	216	236	10.2	12.5	12.0	11.4	11.2
Estate and gift taxes	12	15	25	28	30	1.1	1.1	1.4	1.5	1.4
Excise taxes	49	59	45	55	55	4.5	4.2	3.3	2.6	2.6

[1] Includes railroad retirement, not shown separately.

Source: U.S. Internal Revenue Service, *IRS Data Book*, annual. For most recent report, see <http://www.irs.gov/pub/irs-soi/01databk.pdf>.

No. 465. Federal Individual Income Tax Returns With Adjusted Gross Income (AGI)—Summary: 1998 and 1999

[Includes Puerto Rico and Virgin Islands. Includes returns of resident aliens, based on a sample of unaudited returns as filed. Data are not comparable for all years because of tax changes and other changes, as indicated. See *Statistics of Income, Individual Income Tax Returns* publications for a detailed explanation. See Appendix III]

Item	Number of returns (1,000)		Amount (mil. dol.)		Average amount (dollars)	
	1998	1999	1998	1999	1998	1999
Total returns	124,772	127,075	5,415,973	5,855,468	(X)	(X)
Adjusted gross income (AGI)	124,771	127,075	5,415,973	5,855,468	43,407	46,079
Salaries and wages	106,535	108,184	3,879,762	4,132,473	36,418	38,199
Taxable interest received	67,232	67,219	178,334	175,675	2,653	2,613
Tax-exempt interest	4,778	4,802	50,223	52,513	10,511	10,936
Dividends in AGI	30,423	32,226	118,480	132,466	3,894	4,111
Business or profession net income	13,083	13,165	226,145	233,746	17,285	17,755
Business or profession net loss	4,022	4,147	23,745	25,332	5,904	6,109
Net capital gain in AGI	20,957	22,498	455,223	552,605	21,722	24,562
Net capital loss in AGI	4,734	5,203	9,139	9,847	1,931	1,893
Sales of property other than capital assets, net gain	829	835	6,208	6,558	7,489	7,854
Sales of property other than capital assets, net loss	891	898	7,784	8,270	8,736	9,209
Pensions and annuities in AGI	20,473	21,344	280,650	304,311	13,708	14,257
Unemployment compensation in AGI	7,083	6,776	16,815	17,531	2,374	2,587
Social security benefits in AGI	8,941	9,459	68,703	75,079	7,684	7,937
Rent net income	4,339	4,356	40,610	43,460	9,359	9,977
Rent net loss	4,845	4,617	28,874	28,342	5,960	6,139
Royalty net income	1,131	1,117	5,938	6,482	5,250	5,803
Royalty net loss	53	47	198	132	3,736	2,809
Partnerships and S Corporations net income [1]	4,032	4,155	240,836	269,758	59,731	64,924
Partnerships and S Corporations net loss [1]	2,152	2,122	53,482	58,686	24,852	27,656
Estate or trust net income	485	516	10,495	10,976	21,639	21,271
Estate or trust net loss	45	40	1,031	1,092	22,911	27,300
Farm net income	673	726	8,809	9,201	13,089	12,674
Farm net loss	1,419	1,321	16,743	15,444	11,799	11,691
Statutory adjustments, total	21,998	22,660	51,531	56,699	2,343	2,502
Individual Retirement Arrangements	3,868	3,687	8,188	7,883	2,117	2,138
Student loan interest deduction	3,764	4,137	1,731	2,255	460	545
Medical savings accounts	42	50	62	82	1,476	1,640
Self-employed retirement plans	1,177	1,264	11,040	11,928	9,380	9,437
Deduction for self-employment tax	13,756	14,030	15,960	16,690	1,160	1,190
Self-employment health insurance	3,381	3,492	4,693	6,755	1,388	1,934
Exemptions, total [2]	245,593	248,657	650,347	669,241	2,648	2,691
Deductions, total	123,763	126,000	1,135,918	1,205,337	9,178	9,566
Standard deductions	85,576	85,755	459,457	463,960	5,369	5,244
Returns with additional standard deductions for age 65 or older or for blindness	11,082	11,200	14,057	14,264	1,268	1,274
Itemized deductions, total [3]	38,186	40,244	676,460	741,377	17,715	18,422
Medical and dental expenses	5,560	5,884	31,984	35,376	5,753	6,012
Taxes paid	37,576	39,564	241,783	265,365	6,435	6,707
Interest paid	32,024	33,706	271,624	291,553	8,482	8,650
Home mortgage interest paid	31,627	33,268	254,397	272,149	8,044	8,181
Charitable contributions	33,836	35,523	109,240	125,799	3,229	3,541
Taxable income	100,801	102,846	3,780,838	4,136,120	37,508	40,217
Income tax before credits	100,798	102,834	813,569	906,812	8,071	8,818
Tax credits, total [2]	34,272	36,622	30,056	35,892	877	980
Child care credit	6,128	6,182	2,661	2,675	434	433
Elderly and disabled credit	180	182	36	34	200	187
Child tax credit	24,811	26,016	15,143	19,399	610	746
Education credit	4,653	6,437	3,377	4,772	726	741
Foreign tax credit	2,995	3,267	4,677	4,941	1,562	1,512
General business credit	272	288	732	784	2,691	2,722
Income tax after credits	93,027	94,512	783,513	870,919	8,422	9,215
Income tax, total [4]	93,048	94,546	788,542	877,401	8,475	9,280
Alternative minimum tax	853	1,018	5,015	6,478	5,879	6,363
Earned income credit	19,705	19,259	31,592	31,901	1,603	1,656
Used to offset income tax before credits	5,919	5,352	2,232	1,918	377	358
Used to offset other taxes	3,165	3,137	2,358	2,379	745	758
Excess earned income credit (refundable)	16,279	16,050	27,002	27,604	1,659	1,720
Tax payments, total	117,835	119,809	893,418	981,100	7,582	8,189
Income tax withheld	109,145	111,194	636,248	695,527	5,829	6,255
Excess social security tax withheld	1,304	1,378	1,524	1,713	1,169	1,243
Estimated tax payments	13,072	13,169	177,751	196,916	13,598	14,953
Payments with requests for extension of filing time	1,541	1,510	45,640	53,984	29,617	35,751
Taxes due at time of filing	28,430	29,201	102,151	119,092	3,593	4,078
Tax overpayments, total	93,435	94,827	167,987	182,049	1,798	1,920
Overpayment refunds	90,233	91,601	144,446	155,514	1,601	1,698

X Not applicable.   [1] S Corporations are certain small corporations with up to 35 shareholders. [2] Includes items not shown separately. Beginning 1998, total exemptions amount is after limitation.   [3] Beginning 1998, total itemized deductions are after limitation.   [4] Includes minimum tax or alternative minimum tax.

Source: U.S. Internal Revenue Service, *Statistics of Income Bulletin*, and *Statistics of Income, Individual Income Tax Returns*, annual.

No. 466. Individual Income Tax Returns—Number, Income Tax, and Average Tax by Size of Adjusted Gross Income: 1998 and 1999

[In billions of dollars 5,416.0 represents $5,416,000,000,000, except as indicated]

Size of adjusted gross income	Number of returns (1,000) 1998	1999	Adjusted gross income (AGI) 1998	1999	Income tax total [1] 1998	1999	Tax as percent of AGI [2] 1998	1999	Average tax (dol.) [2] 1998	1999
Total	124,771	127,075	5,416.0	5,855.5	788.5	877.4	15.3	15.7	7,823	8,531
Less than $1,000 [3]	2,845	2,880	-52.1	-52.8	0.1	0.1	-1.8	-1.9	414	518
$1,000 to $2,999	5,753	5,922	11.5	11.9	0.1	0.1	7.2	7.0	134	132
$3,000 to $4,999	5,615	5,614	22.4	22.4	0.2	0.2	3.8	4.0	161	171
$5,000 to $6,999	5,250	5,220	31.5	31.3	0.5	0.5	5.0	5.1	290	301
$7,000 to $8,999	5,110	5,102	40.8	40.8	0.8	0.8	3.6	3.7	248	250
$9,000 to $10,999	5,313	5,069	53.0	50.5	1.5	1.4	4.8	5.0	456	464
$11,000 to $12,999	5,085	4,957	61.0	59.5	2.0	2.0	5.9	6.0	600	599
$13,000 to $14,999	5,215	4,907	73.0	68.7	2.7	2.6	6.2	6.2	678	680
$15,000 to $16,999	4,815	5,023	77.0	80.3	3.4	3.5	6.8	6.6	802	781
$17,000 to $18,999	4,638	4,609	83.4	82.9	4.1	3.9	7.3	7.2	959	923
$19,000 to $21,999	6,514	6,245	133.4	127.8	7.3	6.9	7.5	7.5	1,180	1,154
$22,000 to $24,999	5,858	5,873	137.5	137.8	9.0	8.7	8.0	7.8	1,568	1,513
$25,000 to $29,999	8,192	8,393	224.6	229.8	17.0	16.9	8.3	8.3	2,103	2,049
$30,000 to $39,999	13,135	13,288	456.2	461.8	40.3	39.7	9.1	8.9	3,093	3,007
$40,000 to $49,999	9,974	9,870	447.1	441.5	44.8	43.5	10.1	10.0	4,511	4,418
$50,000 to $74,999	15,887	16,756	969.8	1,023.7	108.9	113.2	11.3	11.1	6,868	6,770
$75,000 to $99,999	7,221	7,812	618.5	671.2	85.2	91.8	13.8	13.7	11,812	11,760
$100,000 to $199,999	6,266	7,105	822.6	934.8	143.7	162.2	17.5	17.4	22,951	22,858
$200,000 to $499,999	1,606	1,877	463.6	542.4	111.5	130.3	24.1	24.0	69,498	69,479
$500,000 to $999,999	307	348	207.6	235.7	58.5	67.0	28.2	28.4	190,498	192,428
$1,000,000 or more	172	205	533.5	653.2	146.8	182.3	27.5	27.9	853,297	889,234

[1] Consists of income after credits, and alternative minimum tax.   [2] Computed using taxable returns only.   [3] In addition to low income taxpayers, this size class (and others) includes taxpayers with "tax preferences," not reflected in adjusted gross income or taxable income which are subject to the "alternative minimum tax" (included in total income tax).
Source: U.S. Internal Revenue Service, Statistics of Income Bulletin, quarterly and Statistics of Income, Individual Income Tax Returns, annual.

No. 467. Individual Income Tax Returns—Itemized Deductions and Statutory-Adjustments by Size of Adjusted Gross Income: 1999

Item	Unit	Adjusted gross income class Total	Under $10,000	$10,000 to $19,999	$20,000 to $29,999	$30,000 to $39,999	$40,000 to $49,999	$50,000 to $99,999	$100,000 and over
Returns with itemized deductions:									
Number of returns [1]	1,000	40,244	631	2,048	3,243	4,233	4,285	17,114	8,688
Amount	Mil. dol	741,377	7,969	22,073	34,491	48,169	52,276	261,850	314,549
Medical and dental expenses:									
Returns	1,000	5,884	391	1,078	1,079	945	651	1,476	263
Amount	Mil. dol	35,376	3,473	6,664	5,100	4,603	3,374	8,803	3,358
Taxes paid:									
Returns, total	1,000	39,564	548	1,895	3,115	4,127	4,223	16,995	8,661
Amount, total	Mil. dol	265,365	1,110	3,719	7,111	11,241	13,751	83,641	144,792
State, local income taxes:									
Returns	1,000	33,609	273	1,301	2,481	3,470	3,646	14,822	7,616
Amount	Mil. dol	169,163	188	850	2,420	4,938	6,837	47,084	106,845
Real estate taxes:									
Returns	1,000	35,420	454	1,532	2,560	3,539	3,671	15,559	8,105
Amount	Mil. dol	86,651	861	2,604	4,201	5,632	6,146	32,720	34,485
Interest paid:									
Returns	1,000	33,706	389	1,299	2,420	3,484	3,621	15,046	7,448
Amount	Mil. dol	291,553	2,541	7,469	14,475	21,119	23,482	114,535	107,931
Home mortgages interest:									
Returns	1,000	33,268	378	1,284	2,398	3,459	3,605	14,940	7,204
Amount	Mil. dol	272,149	2,457	7,338	14,286	20,823	23,100	112,727	91,418
Contributions:									
Returns	1,000	35,523	392	1,511	2,546	3,539	3,702	15,555	8,280
Amount	Mil. dol	125,799	432	2,299	4,192	6,224	6,647	35,449	70,506
Returns with statutory adjustments: [2]									
Number of returns [2]	1,000	22,660	3,062	3,219	3,054	2,726	2,153	5,476	2,971
Amount of adjustments	Mil. dol	56,699	2,447	3,528	4,663	4,376	3,902	14,251	23,532
Payments to IRAs: [3]									
Returns	1,000	3,687	160	353	518	546	443	1,127	541
Amount	Mil. dol	7,883	257	621	982	995	1,021	2,480	1,528
Student loan interest deduction	1,000	4,137	217	621	880	801	571	1,046	-
Amount	Mil. dol	2,255	95	304	512	509	341	494	-
Medical savings account deduction	1,000	50	2	3	6	6	2	14	18
Amount	Mil. dol	82	3	5	5	10	3	19	37
Payments to Keogh plans	1,000	1,264	21	21	51	58	70	401	642
Amount	Mil. dol	11,928	53	52	160	219	297	2,288	8,860
Alimony paid	1,000	611	25	40	50	62	52	197	177
Amount	Mil. dol	7,248	306	237	385	338	289	1,851	3,842

- Represents zero   [1] After limitations.   [2] Includes disability income exclusion, employee business expenses, moving expenses, forfeited interest penalty, alimony paid, deduction for expense of living abroad, and other data not shown separately.   [3] Individual Retirement Account.
Source: U.S. Internal Revenue Service, Statistics of Income, Individual Income Tax Returns, annual.

No. 468. Federal Individual Income Tax Returns—Adjusted Gross Income (AGI) by Source of Income and Income Class for Taxable Returns: 1999

[In millions of dollars (5,580,849 represents $5,580,849,000,000), except as indicated. Minus sign (-) indicates net loss was greater than net income. See headnote, Table 465]

Item	Total [1]	Under $10,000	$10,000 to $19,999	$20,000 to $29,999	$30,000 to $39,999	$40,000 to $49,999	$50,000 to $99,999	$100,000 and over
Number of taxable returns (1,000)	94,546	8,052	14,770	15,175	12,802	9,742	24,480	9,526
Source of income:								
Adjusted gross income (AGI)	5,580,849	44,808	222,963	378,381	445,310	435,846	1,689,529	2,364,012
Salaries and wages	3,861,513	39,907	160,645	302,905	362,217	357,176	1,341,032	1,297,631
Percent of AGI for taxable returns . .	69.2	89.1	72.1	80.1	81.3	82.0	79.4	54.9
Interest received	163,726	3,137	12,359	12,302	11,088	9,737	37,521	77,581
Dividends in AGI	126,883	1,692	4,346	5,058	5,253	5,811	26,637	78,086
Business; profession, net profit less loss.	185,899	1,282	6,717	8,997	11,532	11,388	50,955	95,027
Sales of property, [2] net gain less loss .	534,765	4,769	4,536	5,359	6,840	7,488	46,398	459,375
Pensions and annuities in AGI	287,104	2,521	27,930	33,450	32,075	26,449	102,332	62,348
Rents and royalties, net income less loss.	26,945	114	990	670	487	216	2,302	22,166
Other sources, [3] net.	394,014	-8,614	5,440	9,639	15,818	17,582	82,353	271,797
Percent of all returns: [4]								
Number of returns	74.4	6.3	11.6	11.9	10.1	7.7	19.3	7.5
Adjusted gross income (AGI)	95.3	0.8	3.8	6.5	7.6	7.4	28.9	40.4
Salaries and wages	93.4	1.0	3.9	7.3	8.8	8.6	32.5	31.4
Interest received	93.2	1.8	7.0	7.0	6.3	5.5	21.4	44.2
Dividends in AGI	95.8	1.3	3.3	3.8	4.0	4.4	20.1	58.9
Business; profession, net profit less loss.	89.2	0.6	3.2	4.3	5.5	5.5	24.4	45.6
Sales of property, [2] net gain less loss .	98.8	0.9	0.8	1.0	1.3	1.4	8.6	84.9
Pensions and annuities in AGI	94.3	0.8	9.2	11.0	10.5	8.7	33.6	20.5
Rents and royalties, net income less loss.	105.1	0.4	3.9	2.6	1.9	0.8	9.0	86.5

[1] Includes a small number of taxable returns with no gross income not shown separately. [2] Includes sales of capital assets and other property; net gain less loss. [3] Excludes rental passive losses disallowed in the computation of adjusted gross income. [4] Without regard to taxability.

Source: U.S. Internal Revenue Service, *Statistics of Income, Individual Income Tax Returns,* annual.

No. 469. Federal Individual Income Tax Returns by State: 1999

State	Number of returns [1] (1,000)	Adjusted gross income (AGI) [2] (mil. dol.)	Income tax Total [3] (mil. dol.)	Income tax Per capita [4] (dol.)	State	Number of returns [1] (1,000)	Adjusted gross income (AGI) [2] (mil. dol.)	Income tax Total [3] (mil. dol.)	Income tax Per capita [4] (dol.)
U.S.. .	127,668	5,813,855	880,324	3,228	MO	2,530	102,312	14,094	2,577
					MT.	417	13,414	1,611	1,825
AL	1,898	70,233	9,127	2,089	NE.	804	31,864	4,256	2,555
AK	328	13,047	1,899	3,064	NV	913	43,969	7,052	3,898
AZ	2,088	91,092	12,863	2,692	NH	612	30,302	4,748	3,954
AR	1,109	37,729	4,695	1,841	NJ	3,988	231,283	39,210	4,815
CA	14,510	752,654	120,168	3,626	NM	777	26,532	3,288	1,889
CO.	2,030	100,073	15,576	3,840	NY	8,418	444,100	74,090	4,072
CT.	1,646	106,835	19,966	6,084	NC	3,578	146,643	19,563	2,557
DE.	371	17,304	2,538	3,366	ND	302	10,112	1,240	1,956
DC.	274	14,731	2,515	4,847	OH	5,527	220,984	30,171	2,680
FL	7,264	320,843	50,952	3,372	OK	1,445	51,126	6,481	1,930
GA.	3,555	156,405	22,581	2,900	OR.	1,534	65,053	8,668	2,614
HI	559	22,327	2,843	2,399	PA	5,725	246,545	36,285	3,025
ID	546	20,367	2,542	2,030	RI	482	20,682	2,895	2,921
IL	5,714	283,629	45,680	3,767	SC	1,776	66,165	8,415	2,166
IN	2,804	115,131	15,871	2,671	SD	351	12,631	1,749	2,386
IA	1,345	52,171	6,670	2,325	TN	2,537	99,017	14,042	2,561
KS	1,212	50,958	7,048	2,656	TX	8,837	380,233	59,560	2,972
KY	1,720	63,288	8,109	2,047	UT	919	37,558	4,597	2,158
LA	1,860	65,929	8,754	2,002	VT	294	11,521	1,524	2,566
ME.	595	22,367	2,816	2,247	VA	3,262	159,155	24,144	3,513
MD.	2,499	127,431	18,690	3,614	WA	2,713	143,076	24,571	4,269
MA.	3,049	172,449	29,150	4,721	WV	745	24,457	2,926	1,619
MI	4,557	207,142	30,535	3,096	WI	2,560	109,497	14,858	2,830
MN.	2,341	110,821	15,890	3,327	WY	232	9,965	1,599	3,332
MS.	1,171	37,963	4,508	1,628	Other [5] . . .	1,350	42,740	6,697	(NA)

NA Not available. [1] Includes returns constructed by Internal Revenue Service for certain self-employment tax returns. [2] Less deficit. [3] Includes additional tax for tax preferences, self-employment tax, tax from investment credit recapture and other income-related taxes. Total is before earned income credit. [4] Based on resident population as of July 1. [5] Includes returns filed from Army Post Office and Fleet Post Office addresses by members of the armed forces stationed overseas; returns by other U.S. citizens abroad; and returns filed by residents of Puerto Rico with income from sources outside of Puerto Rico or with income earned as U.S. Government employees.

Source: U.S. Internal Revenue Service, *Statistics of Income Bulletin,* quarterly.

No. 470. Federal Individual Income Tax—Tax Liability and Effective and Marginal Tax Rates for Selected Income Groups: 1990 to 1999

[Refers to income after exclusions. Effective rate represents tax liability divided by stated income. The marginal tax rate is the percentage of the first additional dollar of income which would be paid in income tax. Computations assume the low income allowance, standard deduction, zero bracket amount, or itemized deductions equal to 10 percent of adjusted gross income, whichever is greatest. Excludes self-employment tax]

Adjusted gross income	1990	1994	1995	1996	1997	1998	1999
TAX LIABILITY							
Single person, no dependents:							
$5,000	-	-306	-314	-323	-332	-341	-347
$10,000	705	563	540	518	480	455	427
$20,000	2,205	2,063	2,040	2,018	1,980	1,958	1,943
$25,000	2,988	2,813	2,790	2,768	2,730	2,708	2,693
$35,000	5,718	5,093	4,973	4,846	4,692	4,559	4,479
$50,000	9,498	8,957	8,865	8,766	8,654	8,549	8,483
$75,000	16,718	15,555	15,418	15,270	15,107	14,951	14,852
Married couple, two dependents: [1]							
$5,000	-700	-1,500	-1,800	-2,000	-2,000	-2,000	-2,000
$10,000	-953	-2,528	-3,110	-3,556	-3,556	-3,756	-3,816
$20,000	926	-359	-832	-1,324	-1,414	-1,811	-1,958
$25,000	1,703	1,275	929	479	389	-8	-155
$35,000	3,203	2,828	2,768	2,715	2,625	2,565	2,520
$50,000	5,960	5,078	5,018	4,965	4,875	4,815	4,770
$75,000	12,386	11,216	11,030	10,831	10,576	10,371	10,224
EFFECTIVE RATE							
Single person, no dependents:							
$5,000 [2]	-	-6.1	-6.3	-6.5	-6.6	-6.8	-6.9
$10,000	7.1	5.6	5.4	5.2	4.8	4.6	4.3
$20,000	11.0	10.3	10.2	10.1	9.9	9.8	9.7
$25,000	12.0	11.3	11.2	11.1	10.9	10.8	10.8
$35,000	16.3	14.6	14.2	13.8	13.4	13.0	12.8
$50,000	19.0	17.9	17.7	17.5	17.3	17.1	17.0
$75,000	22.3	20.7	20.6	20.4	20.1	19.9	19.8
Married couple, two dependents: [2]							
$5,000 [3]	-14.0	-30.0	-36.0	-40.0	-40.0	-40.0	-40.0
$10,000 [4]	-9.5	-25.3	-31.1	-35.6	-35.6	-37.6	38.2
$20,000 [4]	4.6	-1.8	-4.2	-6.6	-7.1	-9.1	-9.8
$25,000	6.8	5.1	3.7	1.9	1.6	-	-0.6
$35,000	9.2	8.1	7.9	7.8	7.5	7.3	7.2
$50,000	11.9	10.2	10.0	9.9	9.8	9.6	9.5
$75,000	16.5	15.0	14.7	14.4	14.1	13.8	13.6
MARGINAL TAX RATE							
Single person, no dependents:							
$5,000	-	7.7	-	-	-	-	-
$10,000	15	15	15	15	15	22.7	22.7
$20,000	15	15	15	15	15	15	15
$25,000	28	15	15	15	15	15	15
$35,000	28	28	28	28	28	28	28
$50,000	28	28	28	28	28	28	28
$75,000	33	31	31	31	31	31	31
Married couple, two dependents: [1]							
$5,000 [3]	-14	-30	-36	-40	-40	-40	-40
$10,000 [4]	-	-	-	-	-	-	-
$20,000 [4]	25	32.7	35.2	36.1	36.1	36.1	36.1
$25,000	15	32.7	35.2	36.1	36.1	36.1	36.1
$35,000	15	15	15	15	15	15	15
$50,000	28	15	15	15	15	15	15
$75,000	28	28	28	28	28	28	28

- Represents zero. [1] Only one spouse is assumed to work. [2] Beginning 1994, refundable earned income credit. [3] Refundable earned income credit. [4] Refundable earned income credit.

Source: U.S. Dept. of the Treasury, Office of Tax Analysis, unpublished data.

No. 471. Federal Individual Income Tax—Current Income Equivalent to 1995 Constant Income for Selected Income Groups: 1990 to 1999

[Constant 1995 dollar incomes calculated by using the NIPA Chain-Type Price Index for Person Consumption Expenditures (1996 = 100) 1990, 85.63; 1994, 95.70; 1995, 97.90; 1996, 100.0; 1997, 101.98; 1998, 102.93; and 1999, 104.57]

Adjusted gross income	1990	1994	1995	1996	1997	1998	1999
REAL INCOME EQUIVALENT							
Single person, no dependents:							
$5,000	4,280	4,790	4,900	5,000	5,100	5,150	5,230
$10,000	8,560	9,570	9,790	10,000	10,200	10,290	10,460
$20,000	17,130	19,140	19,580	20,000	20,400	20,590	20,910
$25,000	21,410	23,930	24,480	25,000	25,500	25,730	26,140
$35,000	29,970	33,500	34,270	35,000	35,690	36,030	36,600
$50,000	42,820	47,850	48,950	50,000	50,990	51,470	52,290
$75,000	64,220	71,780	73,430	75,000	76,490	77,200	78,430
Married couple, two dependents: [1]							
$5,000	4,280	4,790	4,900	5,000	5,100	5,150	5,230
$10,000	8,560	9,570	9,790	10,000	10,200	10,290	10,460
$20,000	17,130	19,140	19,580	20,000	20,400	20,590	20,910
$25,000	21,410	23,930	24,480	25,000	25,500	25,730	26,140
$35,000	29,970	33,500	34,270	35,000	35,690	36,030	36,600
$50,000	42,820	47,850	48,950	50,000	50,990	51,470	52,290
$75,000	64,220	71,780	73,430	75,000	76,490	77,200	78,430
EFFECTIVE RATE (percent)							
Single person, no dependents:							
$5,000 [2]	-	-6.4	-6.4	-6.5	-6.5	-6.6	-6.6
$10,000	5.7	5.2	5.2	5.2	5.0	4.9	4.9
$20,000	10.4	10.1	10.1	10.1	10.0	9.9	9.9
$25,000	11.3	11.1	11.1	11.1	11.0	10.9	11.0
$35,000	14.6	13.9	13.9	13.8	13.7	13.5	13.5
$50,000	18.0	17.6	17.6	17.5	17.5	17.3	17.3
$75,000	21.0	20.4	20.4	20.4	20.3	20.2	20.2
Married couple, two dependents: [1]							
$5,000 [3]	-14.0	-30.0	-36.0	-40.0	-40.0	-40.0	-40.0
$10,000 [4]	-11.1	-26.4	-31.8	-35.6	-34.9	-36.5	-36.5
$20,000 [4]	1.2	-3.3	-5.0	-6.6	-6.2	-7.8	-7.8
$25,000	5.4	3.9	3.0	1.9	2.2	1.0	1.0
$35,000	8.2	7.8	7.8	7.8	7.6	7.5	7.5
$50,000	10.2	9.9	9.9	9.9	9.9	9.8	9.8
$75,000	15.1	14.5	14.5	14.4	14.3	14.2	14.1
MARGINAL TAX RATE (percent)							
Single person, no dependents:							
$5,000	-	-	-	-	-	-	-
$10,000	15.0	15.0	15.0	15.0	15.0	15.0	15.0
$20,000	15.0	15.0	15.0	15.0	15.0	15.0	15.0
$25,000	15.0	15.0	15.0	15.0	15.0	15.0	15.0
$35,000	28.0	28.0	28.0	28.0	28.0	28.0	28.0
$50,000	28.0	28.0	28.0	28.0	28.0	28.0	28.0
$75,000	33.0	31.0	31.0	31.0	31.0	31.0	31.0
Married couple, two dependents: [1]							
$5,000 [3]	-14.0	-30.0	-36.0	-40.0	-40.0	-40.0	-40.0
$10,000 [4]	-	-	-	-	-	-	-
$20,000 [4]	25.0	32.7	35.2	36.1	36.1	36.1	36.1
$25,000	15.0	32.7	35.2	36.1	36.1	36.1	36.1
$35,000	15.0	15.0	15.0	15.0	15.0	15.0	15.0
$50,000	15.0	15.0	15.0	15.0	15.0	15.0	15.0
$75,000	28.0	28.0	28.0	28.0	28.0	28.0	28.0

- Represents zero.   [1] Only one spouse is assumed to work.   [2] Beginning 1994, refundable earned income credit.   [3] Refundable earned income credit.   [4] Refundable earned income credit.

Source: U.S. Dept. of the Treasury, Office of Tax Analysis, unpublished data.

No. 472. Paid Full-Time Federal Civilian Employment by Pay System: 1990 to 2001

[As of March 31 (2,035 represents 2,035,000). Excludes employees of Congress and federal courts, maritime seamen of Dept. of Commerce, and small number for whom rates were not reported. See text, this section, for explanation of general schedule and wage system]

Pay system	Employees (1,000)				Average pay (dol.)			
	1990	1999	2000	2001	1990	1999	2000	2001
Total, excl. postal	2,036	1,685	1,671	1,660	31,174	47,569	50,429	52,911
General Schedule	1,506	1,234	1,216	1,219	31,239	46,744	49,428	51,733
Wage System	369	214	205	199	26,565	35,767	37,082	38,416
Other	161	237	250	242	41,149	62,519	66,248	70,748
Postal pay system [1]	753	798	(NA)	(NA)	29,264	36,413	(NA)	(NA)

NA Not available.   [1] Source: Career employees—U.S. Postal Service, *Annual Report of the Postmaster General*. Average pay—U.S. Postal Service, *Comprehensive Statement of Postal Operations*, annual.

Source: Except as noted, U.S. Office of Personnel Management, *Pay Structure of the Federal Civil Service*, annual.

No. 473. Federal Civilian Employment and Annual Payroll by Branch: 1970 to 2001

[Employment in thousands (2,997 represents 2,997,000); payroll in millions of dollars (27,322 represents $27,322,000,000). For fiscal year ending in year shown; see text, Section 8, State and Local Government Finances and Employment. Includes employees in U.S. territories and foreign countries. Data represent employees in active-duty status, including intermittent employees. Annual employment figures are averages of monthly figures. Excludes Central Intelligence Agency, National Security Agency, and, as of November 1984, the Defense Intelligence Agency, and as of October 1996, the National Imagery and Mapping Agency]

Year	Employment						Payroll				
	Total	Percent of U.S. employed [1]	Executive		Legisla- tive	Judicial	Total	Executive		Legisla- tive	Judicial
			Total	Defense				Total	Defense		
1970	[2]2,997	3.81	2,961	1,263	29	7	27,322	26,894	11,264	338	89
1971	2,899	3.65	2,861	1,162	31	7	29,475	29,007	11,579	369	98
1972	2,882	3.51	2,842	1,128	32	8	31,626	31,102	12,181	411	112
1973	2,822	3.32	2,780	1,076	33	9	33,240	32,671	12,414	447	121
1974	2,825	3.26	2,781	1,041	35	9	35,661	35,035	12,789	494	132
1975	2,877	3.35	2,830	1,044	37	10	39,126	38,423	13,418	549	154
1976	2,879	3.24	2,831	1,025	38	11	42,259	41,450	14,699	631	179
1977	2,855	3.10	2,803	997	39	12	45,895	44,975	15,696	700	219
1978	2,875	2.99	2,822	987	40	13	49,921	48,899	16,995	771	251
1979	2,897	2.93	2,844	974	40	13	53,590	52,513	18,065	817	260
1980	[2]2,987	3.01	2,933	971	40	14	58,012	56,841	18,795	883	288
1981	2,909	2.90	2,855	986	40	15	63,793	62,510	21,227	922	360
1982	2,871	2.88	2,816	1,019	39	16	65,503	64,125	22,226	980	398
1983	2,878	2.85	2,823	1,033	39	16	69,878	68,420	23,406	1,013	445
1984	2,935	2.80	2,879	1,052	40	17	74,616	73,084	25,253	1,081	451
1985	3,001	2.80	2,944	1,080	39	18	80,599	78,992	28,330	1,098	509
1986	3,047	2.77	2,991	1,089	38	19	82,598	80,941	29,272	1,112	545
1987	3,075	2.73	3,018	1,084	38	19	85,543	83,797	29,786	1,153	593
1988	3,113	2.71	3,054	1,073	38	21	88,841	86,960	29,609	1,226	656
1989	3,133	2.67	3,074	1,067	38	22	92,847	90,870	30,301	1,266	711
1990	[2]3,233	2.72	3,173	1,060	38	23	99,138	97,022	31,990	1,329	787
1991	3,101	2.63	3,038	1,015	38	25	104,273	101,965	32,956	1,434	874
1992	3,106	2.62	3,040	1,004	39	27	108,054	105,402	31,486	1,569	1,083
1993	3,043	2.53	2,976	952	39	28	114,323	111,523	32,755	1,609	1,191
1994	2,993	2.43	2,928	900	37	28	116,138	113,264	32,144	1,613	1,260
1995	2,943	2.36	2,880	852	34	28	118,304	115,328	31,753	1,598	1,379
1996	2,881	2.27	2,819	811	32	29	119,321	116,385	31,569	1,519	1,417
1997	2,816	2.17	2,755	768	31	30	119,603	116,693	31,431	1,515	1,396
1998	2,783	2.12	2,721	730	31	31	121,964	118,800	30,315	1,517	1,647
1999	2,789	2.09	2,726	703	30	32	124,990	121,732	30,141	1,560	1,699
2000	[2]2,879	2.13	2,816	681	31	32	130,832	127,472	29,607	1,619	1,741
2001	2,704	2.00	2,641	672	30	33	131,964	128,502	28,594	1,682	1,780

[1] Civilian only. See Table 560. [2] Includes temporary census workers.

Source: U.S. Office of Personnel Management, *Federal Civilian Workforce Statistics—Employment and Trends*, bimonthly; and unpublished data.

No. 474. Paid Civilian Employment in the Federal Government by State: 2000

[As of December 31. (2,674 represents 2,674,000). Excludes Central Intelligence Agency, Defense Intelligence Agency, seasonal and on-call employees, and National Security Agency]

State	Total (1,000)	Percent Defense	Percent change, 1998-2000	State	Total (1,000)	Percent Defense	Percent change, 1998-2000
United States [1]	**2,674**	**23.2**	**-3.0**	Missouri	54	16.9	-5.3
Alabama	48	42.0	-7.7	Montana	11	9.8	-
Alaska	14	30.8	-	Nebraska	15	20.9	-
Arizona	43	18.4	-	Nevada	13	14.8	-
Arkansas	20	17.7	-4.8	New Hampshire	8	12.4	-
California	248	24.0	-6.4	New Jersey	62	22.4	-4.6
Colorado	51	20.4	-5.6	New Mexico	25	26.2	-3.8
Connecticut	21	11.8	-8.7	New York	134	8.3	-3.6
Delaware	5	25.4	-	North Carolina	57	29.0	-
District of Columbia	181	6.9	-	North Dakota	8	21.0	-
Florida	113	23.2	-2.6	Ohio	84	27.2	-3.4
Georgia	89	34.8	1.1	Oklahoma	43	48.8	-
Hawaii	23	70.3	-4.2	Oregon	29	10.3	-3.3
Idaho	11	12.6	-	Pennsylvania	107	23.6	-5.3
Illinois	94	13.3	-4.1	Rhode Island	10	40.4	-9.1
Indiana	37	24.1	-2.6	South Carolina	26	34.5	-3.7
Iowa	18	7.8	-10.0	South Dakota	9	11.9	-10.0
Kansas	25	21.3	-	Tennessee	50	14.0	-3.8
Kentucky	30	22.0	-3.2	Texas	162	23.1	-7.4
Louisiana	33	23.0	-5.7	Utah	30	46.1	7.1
Maine	13	41.5	-	Vermont	6	9.1	-
Maryland	130	24.2	-0.8	Virginia	145	54.8	-1.4
Massachusetts	53	12.7	-5.4	Washington	62	34.6	-1.6
Michigan	58	13.3	-1.7	West Virginia	18	9.2	-
Minnesota	34	7.0	-2.9	Wisconsin	30	9.5	-3.2
Mississippi	24	37.9	-4.0	Wyoming	6	15.2	-

- Represents zero or rounds to zero. [1] Includes employees outside the United States not shown separately.

Source: U.S. Office of Personnel Management, *Biennial Report of Employment by Geographic Area, 2000* (forthcoming).

No. 475. Federal Civilian Employment by Branch and Agency: 1990 to 2001

[For fiscal year ending in year shown; excludes Central Intelligence Agency, National Security Agency; and, as of November 1984, the Defense Intelligence Agency; and, as of October 1996, the National Imagery and Mapping Agency]

Agency	1990	1995	2000	2001	Percent change 1990-1995	Percent change 1995-2001
Total, all agencies	**3,128,267**	**2,920,277**	**2,708,101**	**2,709,956**	**-6.6**	**-7.2**
Legislative Branch, total.	37,495	33,367	31,157	30,439	-11.0	-8.8
Judicial Branch.	23,605	28,993	32,186	33,810	22.8	16.6
Executive Branch, total	3,067,167	2,857,917	2,644,758	2,645,707	-6.8	-7.4
Executive Departments.	2,065,542	1,782,834	1,592,200	1,603,426	-13.7	-10.1
State	25,288	24,859	27,983	28,122	-1.7	13.1
Treasury.	158,655	155,951	143,508	148,186	-1.7	-5.0
Defense.	1,034,152	832,352	676,268	671,591	-19.5	-19.3
Justice.	83,932	103,262	125,970	127,783	23.0	23.7
Interior	77,679	76,439	73,818	75,846	-1.6	-0.8
Agriculture	122,594	113,321	104,466	108,540	-7.6	-4.2
Commerce	69,920	36,803	47,652	40,289	-47.4	9.5
Labor.	17,727	16,204	16,040	16,376	-8.6	1.1
Health & Human Services	123,959	59,788	62,605	64,343	-51.8	7.6
Housing & Urban Development.	13,596	11,822	10,319	10,178	-13.0	-13.9
Transportation	67,364	63,552	63,598	65,542	-5.7	3.1
Energy.	17,731	19,589	15,692	16,054	10.5	-18.0
Education.	4,771	4,988	4,734	4,683	4.5	-6.1
Veterans Affairs [1]	248,174	263,904	219,547	225,893	6.3	-14.4
Independent agencies	999,894	1,073,510	1,050,900	1,040,657	7.4	-3.1
Board of Governors Federal Reserve System. .	1,525	1,704	1,644	1,680	11.7	-1.4
Commodity Futures Trading Commission.	542	544	574	551	0.4	1.3
Consumer Product Safety Commission	520	486	479	479	-6.5	-1.4
Environmental Protection Agency	17,123	17,910	18,036	18,095	4.6	1.0
Equal Employment Opportunity Commission . .	2,880	2,796	2,780	2,910	-2.9	4.1
Federal Communications Commission.	1,778	2,116	1,965	2,004	19.0	-5.3
Federal Deposit Insurance Corporation	17,641	14,765	6,958	6,402	-16.3	-56.6
Federal Emergency Management Agency	3,137	5,256	4,813	6,147	67.5	17.0
Federal Trade Commission	988	996	1,019	1,052	0.8	5.6
General Services Administration.	20,277	16,500	14,334	14,016	-18.6	-15.1
National Archives & Recds Admin.	3,120	2,833	2,702	2,878	-9.2	1.6
National Aeronautics & Space Admin	24,872	21,635	18,819	18,918	-13.0	-12.6
National Labor Relations Board	2,263	2,050	2,054	2,110	-9.4	2.9
National Science Foundation	1,318	1,292	1,247	1,287	-2.0	-0.4
Nuclear Regulatory Commission	3,353	3,212	2,858	2,871	-4.2	-10.6
Office of Personnel Management	6,636	4,354	3,780	3,349	-34.4	-23.1
Peace Corps	1,178	1,179	1,065	1,019	0.1	-13.6
Securities & Exchange Commission	2,302	2,852	2,955	3,049	23.9	6.9
Small Business Administration	5,128	5,085	4,150	4,219	-0.8	-17.0
Smithsonian Institution	5,092	5,444	5,065	4,981	6.9	-8.5
Social Security Administration	(X)	66,850	64,474	65,351	(X)	-2.2
Tennessee Valley Authority	28,392	16,545	13,145	13,430	-41.7	-18.8
U.S. Information Agency	8,555	7,480	2,436	2,372	-12.6	-68.3
U.S. Postal Service	816,886	845,393	860,726	847,621	3.5	0.3

X Not applicable.   [1] Formerly Veterans Administration.
Source: U.S. Office of Personnel Management, *Federal Civilian Workforce Statistics— Employment and Trends*, bimonthly.

No. 476. Federal Employment Trends—Individual Characteristics: 1990 to 2000

[In percent, except as indicated. Covers only federal civilian nonpostal employees]

Characteristics	1990	1993	1994	1995	1996	1997	1998	1999	2000
Average age (years) [1]	42.3	43.8	44.1	44.3	44.8	45.2	45.6	45.9	46.3
Average length of service (years) [1]	13.4	14.9	15.2	15.5	15.9	16.3	16.6	16.9	17.1
Retirement eligible:									
Civil Service Retirement System[2].	8	10	10	10	11	12	13	15	17
Federal Employees Retirement System. .	3	4	5	5	6	7	8	10	11
College-conferred [3].	35	37	38	39	39	40	40	40	41
Gender:									
Men.	57	56	56	56	56	56	56	55	55
Women	43	44	44	44	44	44	44	45	45
Race and national origin:									
Total minorities	27.4	28.2	28.5	28.9	29.1	29.4	29.7	30.0	30.4
Black.	16.7	16.7	16.7	16.8	16.7	16.7	16.7	17.0	17.1
Hispanic	5.4	5.6	5.7	5.9	6.1	6.2	6.4	6.5	6.6
Asian/Pacific Islander	3.5	3.9	4.1	4.2	4.3	4.4	4.5	4.5	4.5
American Indian/Alaska native	1.8	2.0	2.0	2.0	2.0	2.1	2.1	2.2	2.2
Disabled.	7.0	7.0	7.0	7.0	7.0	7.0	7.0	7.0	7.0
Veterans preference	30.0	27.0	27.0	26.0	26.0	25.0	25.0	25.0	24.0
Vietnam Era veterans	17.0	16.0	17.0	17.0	17.0	15.0	14.0	14.0	14.0
Retired military.	4.9	4.3	4.3	4.2	4.3	4.2	3.9	3.9	3.9
Retired officers.	0.5	0.5	0.5	0.5	0.5	0.5	0.5	0.5	0.5

[1] Represents full-time permanent employees.   [2] Represents full-time permanent employees under the Civil Service Retirement System (excluding hires since January 1984), and the Federal Employees Retirement System (since January 1984).
[3] Bachelor's degree or higher.
Source: U.S. Office of Personnel Management, Office of Workforce Information, *The Fact Book, Federal Civilian Workforce Statistics*, annual. See also <http://www.opm.gov/feddata/01factbk.pdf> (released July 2001).

No. 477. Federal Executive Branch (Nonpostal) Employment by Race and National Origin: 1990 to 2001

[As of Sept. 30. Covers total employment for only Executive Branch agencies participating in OPM's Central Personnel Data File (CPDF). For information on the CPDF, see <http://www.opm.gov/feddata/acpdf.pdf>]

Pay system	1990	1995	1999	2000	2001
All personnel	**2,150,359**	**1,960,577**	**1,766,298**	**1,755,689**	**1,764,083**
White, non-Hispanic	1,562,846	1,394,690	1,236,698	1,224,836	1,226,113
General schedule and related	1,218,188	1,101,108	979,803	961,261	968,938
Grades 1-4 ($13,870 - $24,833)	132,028	79,195	58,381	55,067	57,368
Grades 5-8 ($21,370 - $38,108)	337,453	288,755	246,759	239,128	239,253
Grades 9-12 ($32,380 - $61,040)	510,261	465,908	413,989	404,649	403,556
Grades 13-15 ($55,837 - $100,897)	238,446	267,250	260,674	262,417	268,761
Total executives/senior pay levels	9,337	13,307	13,856	14,332	14,565
Wage pay system	244,220	186,184	151,585	146,075	142,428
Other pay systems	91,101	94,091	91,454	103,168	100,182
Black	356,867	327,302	298,694	298,701	299,203
General schedule and related	272,657	258,586	241,422	241,135	243,689
Grades 1-4 ($13,870 - $24,833)	65,077	41,381	28,530	26,895	25,873
Grades 5-8 ($21,370 - $38,108)	114,993	112,962	101,742	99,937	100,079
Grades 9-12 ($32,380 - $61,040)	74,985	79,795	81,410	82,809	84,342
Grades 13-15 ($55,837 - $100,897)	17,602	24,448	29,740	31,494	33,395
Total executives/senior pay levels	479	942	1,103	1,180	1,124
Wage pay system	72,755	55,637	44,076	42,590	40,619
Other pay systems	10,976	12,137	12,093	13,796	13,771
Hispanic	115,170	115,964	114,743	115,247	118,272
General schedule and related	83,218	86,762	89,367	89,911	93,360
Grades 1-4 ($13,870 - $24,833)	15,738	11,081	8,874	8,526	8,764
Grades 5-8 ($21,370 - $38,108)	28,727	31,152	31,544	31,703	33,148
Grades 9-12 ($32,380 - $61,040)	31,615	34,056	36,474	36,813	37,820
Grades 13-15 ($55,837 - $100,897)	7,138	10,473	12,475	12,869	13,628
Total executives/senior pay levels	154	382	487	547	511
Wage pay system	26,947	22,128	17,781	16,926	16,526
Other pay systems	4,851	6,692	7,108	7,863	7,875
American Indian, Alaska Natives, Asians, and Pacific	115,476	122,621	116,163	116,905	120,495
General schedule and related	81,499	86,768	85,891	86,074	89,018
Grades 1-4 ($13,870 - $24,833)	15,286	11,854	9,603	9,340	9,556
Grades 5-8 ($21,370 - $38,108)	24,960	26,580	25,786	25,691	26,608
Grades 9-12 ($32,380 - $61,040)	31,346	33,810	33,417	33,167	33,751
Grades 13-15 ($55,837 - $100,897)	9,907	14,524	17,085	17,876	19,103
Total executives/senior pay levels [1]	148	331	462	504	555
Wage pay system	24,927	21,553	18,212	17,613	17,453
Other pay systems	8,902	13,969	11,598	12,714	13,469

Source: Office of Personnel Management, Central Personnel Data File.

No. 478. Federal General Schedule Employee Pay Increases: 1980 to 2001

[Percent change from prior year shown, except 1980, change from 1979. Represents legislated pay increases. For some years data based on range; for details, see source]

Date	Pay increase	Date	Pay increase	Date	Pay increase
1980	9.1	1988	2.0	1995	2.0
1981	4.8	1989	4.1	1996	2.0
1982	4.0	1990	3.6	1997	2.3
1984	4.0	1991	4.1	1998	2.3
1985	3.5	1992	4.2	1999	3.1
1986	-	1993	3.7	2000	3.8
1987	3.0	1994	-	2001	2.7

- Represents zero.
Source: U.S. Office of Personnel Management, *Pay Structure of the Federal Civil Service,* annual.

No. 479. Turnover Data for the Executive Branch—All Areas: 1990 to 2000

[Turnover data exclude Legislative and Judicial branches, U.S. Postal Service, Postal Rate Commission]

Year	Accessions		Separations		Total employment		
	Total	New hires	Total	Quits	Average	Change from prior year	Percent change
1990 [1]	819,554	716,066	799,237	165,099	2,348,458	114,477	5.1
1991	495,123	351,112	515,673	134,175	2,224,389	-124,069	-5.3
1992	430,021	290,883	446,126	129,167	2,238,635	14,246	0.6
1993	382,399	253,374	423,830	127,140	2,189,416	-49,219	-2.2
1994	317,509	219,026	398,134	111,096	2,114,387	-75,029	-3.4
1995	345,166	222,025	457,246	91,909	2,037,890	-76,542	-3.6
1996	266,473	199,463	356,566	80,922	1,960,892	-76,953	-3.8
1997	283,517	208,725	333,431	81,574	1,895,295	-65,597	-3.3
1998	320,830	242,637	321,292	84,124	1,855,112	-40,183	-2.1
1999	423,500	346,988	372,778	129,196	1,846,170	-8,942	-0.5
2000 [1]	1,168,783	1,092,888	1,027,653	801,684	1,946,684	100,514	5.4

[1] Includes hiring for census enumerators.
Source: U.S. Office of Personnel Management, *Federal Civilian Workforce Statistics— Employment and Trends,* bimonthly. Also in *The Fact Book, Federal Civilian Workforce Statistics,* annual.

No. 480. Accessions to and Separations From Employment in the Federal Government: 2000 and 2001

[As of September 30. Turnover data exclude Legislative and Judicial branches, U.S. Postal Service, Postal Rate Commission]

Agency	Accessions				Separations			
	Number		Rate		Number		Rate	
	2000	2001	2000	2001	2000	2001	2000	2001
Total, all agencies	1,380,937	518,104	48.8	19.5	1,233,364	508,495	43.6	19.2
Legislative Branch, total [1]	1,233	1,214	9.2	9.2	1,689	1,937	12.6	14.6
General Accounting Office	219	237	6.8	7.5	452	461	13.9	14.6
Government Printing Office	199	163	6.3	5.3	284	314	8.9	10.2
Library of Congress	322	280	7.4	6.5	509	552	11.6	12.8
Judicial Branch	-	-	(X)	(X)	-	-	(X)	(X)
Executive Branch, total	1,379,704	516,890	49.0	19.6	1,231,675	506,558	43.7	19.2
Executive Office of the President	450	706	27.3	44.5	395	760	23.9	47.9
Executive Departments	1,148,804	286,314	65.6	18.0	998,722	281,489	57.0	17.7
State	3,649	3,945	13.1	14.1	2,649	3,395	9.5	12.1
Treasury	49,878	50,679	33.1	33.2	49,254	46,343	32.6	30.3
Defense	94,329	96,062	13.8	14.3	105,734	106,933	75.5	15.9
Justice	9,985	10,866	8.0	8.6	7,397	7,601	5.9	6.0
Interior	19,008	20,834	27.0	29.0	14,110	14,799	20.0	20.6
Agriculture	27,440	32,087	27.7	31.5	27,535	28,251	27.7	27.8
Commerce [2]	892,415	12,176	434.2	29.7	742,789	25,128	361.4	61.3
Labor	1,709	2,112	10.7	13.1	1,599	1,787	10.0	11.1
Health & Human Services [3]	11,129	11,691	17.9	18.4	8,698	9,048	14.0	14.2
Housing & Urban Development	1,004	807	9.8	7.9	993	958	9.7	9.4
Transportation	3,089	5,465	4.9	8.5	4,212	4,234	6.6	6.6
Energy	1,260	1,717	8.0	10.9	1,355	1,272	8.6	8.1
Education	531	690	11.2	14.7	321	486	6.8	10.4
Veterans Affairs [4]	33,771	37,183	15.5	16.7	32,650	31,252	14.9	14.0
Independent agencies [1]	230,450	229,870	21.7	21.9	232,558	224,309	21.9	21.4
Board of Governors, Fed Reserve System	184	233	11.2	14.1	254	196	15.4	11.8
Environmental Protection Agency	1,011	1,635	5.6	9.0	1,469	1,552	8.1	8.6
Equal Employment Opportunity Comm .	86	289	2.9	10.4	161	146	5.5	5.3
Federal Deposit Insurance Corporation .	425	310	5.9	4.7	1,044	794	14.5	12.1
Fed Emergency Management Agency . . .	1,124	1,665	22.0	31.2	2,180	1,916	42.7	35.9
General Services Administration	815	961	5.8	6.9	691	1,022	4.9	7.3
National Aeronautics & Space Admin . .	1,745	1,829	9.4	9.7	1,627	1,627	8.7	8.6
National Archives & Records Admin . . .	510	649	19.2	22.9	366	365	13.8	12.9
Nuclear Regulatory Commission	239	265	8.4	9.2	251	250	8.8	8.7
Office of Personnel Management	703	617	18.7	18.5	640	654	17.0	19.6
Panama Canal Comm	332	-	14.6	0.0	8,530	1	374.8	19.2
Railroad Retirement Board	39	48	3.2	4.1	115	57	9.6	4.9
Securities and Exchange Commission . .	607	535	21.0	17.9	461	331	16.0	11.1
Small Business Administration	879	1,193	20.3	28.8	1,251	1,197	28.9	28.9
Smithsonian Institution	620	556	12.1	11.0	860	675	16.8	13.4
Tennessee Valley Authority	875	1,018	6.6	7.7	1,013	715	7.6	5.4
U.S. Information Agency	138	117	5.6	4.9	174	263	7.1	11.0
U.S. International Dev Coop Agency . . .	181	(X)	7.6	(X)	268	(X)	11.2	(X)
U.S. Postal Service	210,915	208,002	24.3	24.2	204,015	204,886	23.5	23.9

- Represents or rounds to zero.   X Not applicable.   [1] Includes other branches, or other agencies, not shown separately. [2] 2000 includes census enumerators for the decennial census.   [3] Sizable changes due to the Social Security Administration which was separated from the Department of Health and Human Services to become an independent agency effective April 1995. [4] Formerly Veterans Administration.

Source: U.S. Office of Personnel Management, *Federal Civilian Workforce Statistics— Employment and Trends*, bimonthly.

No. 481. Federal Agencies Employing 500 or More Full-Time Officers With Authority to Carry Firearms and Make Arrests—Number of Officers: 1993 to 2000

[As of June]

Selected agency	1993	1996	1998	2000
All agencies [1]	68,825	74,493	83,143	88,496
Immigration and Naturalization Service	9,466	12,403	16,552	17,654
Federal Bureau of Prisons	9,984	11,329	12,587	13,557
Federal Bureau of Investigation	10,075	10,389	11,285	11,523
U.S. Customs Service	10,120	9,749	10,539	10,522
Drug Enforcement Administration	2,813	2,946	3,305	4,161
U.S. Secret Service	2,186	3,185	3,587	4,039
Administrative Office of the U.S. Courts	3,763	2,777	2,490	3,599
U.S. Postal Inspection Service	3,587	3,576	3,490	3,412
U.S. Marshals Service	2,153	2,650	2,705	2,735
Internal Revenue Service	3,621	3,784	3,361	2,726
National Park Service	2,160	2,148	2,197	2,188
Bureau of Alcohol, Tobacco and Firearms	1,959	1,869	1,723	1,967
U.S. Capitol Police	1,080	1,031	1,055	1,199
U.S. Fish and Wildlife Service	620	869	831	888
U.S. Forest Service	732	619	601	586

[1] Includes agencies not shown separately.

Source: U.S. Bureau of Justice Statistics, *Federal Law Enforcement Officers, 1993, 1996, 1998,* and *2000* reports. See also <http://www.ojp.usdoj.gov/bjs/pub/pdf/fleo00.pdf> (issued July 2001).

Federal Government Finances and Employment   323

No. 482. Federal Land and Buildings Owned and Leased: 1990 to 2000

[For fiscal years ending in years shown; see text, Section 8, State and Local Government Finance and Employment. Covers federal real property throughout the world, except as noted. Cost of land figures represent total cost of property owned in year shown. For further details see source. For data on federal land by state, see Tables 336 and 483]

Item	Unit	1990	1995	1997	1998	1999	2000
Federally owned:							
Land, worldwide	1,000 acres . .	650,014	549,670	563,231	655,042	630,648	635,824
United States	1,000 acres . .	649,802	549,474	563,081	654,885	630,266	635,355
Buildings [1]	1,000	(NA)	(NA)	(NA)	(NA)	(NA)	435
United States	1,000	446	424	430	420	419	430
Buildings floor area (sq. ft.) [1] . . .	Mil. sq/ft.	(NA)	(NA)	(NA)	(NA)	(NA)	3,003
United States	Mil. sq/ft.	2,859	2,793	2,935	2,911	2,875	2,968
Costs	Mil. dol.	187,865	199,387	222,391	244,273	238,327	260,069
Land	Mil. dol.	(NA)	18,972	22,914	26,450	17,257	21,008
Buildings	Mil. dol.	(NA)	113,018	128,530	130,858	132,981	139,291
Structures and facilities.	Mil. dol.	(NA)	67,398	70,946	86,965	88,090	99,770
Federally leased:							
Land, worldwide	1,000 acres . .	994	1,385	1,374	1,306	1,400	1,670
United States	1,000 acres . .	938	1,351	1,340	1,272	1,342	1,611
Buildings [1]	1,000	(NA)	(NA)	(NA)	(NA)	(NA)	84
United States	1,000	47	78	77	76	77	73
Buildings floor area (sq. ft.) [1] . . .	Mil. sq/ft.	(NA)	(NA)	(NA)	(NA)	(NA)	347
United States	Mil. sq/ft.	234	275	276	276	301	313
Annual rental	Mil. dol.	2,590	3,633	3,613	3,628	3,998	3,394
United States	Mil. dol.	2,125	3,174	3,212	3,226	3,590	2,931

NA Not available.   [1] Excludes data for Dept. of Defense military functions outside of the United States.

Source: U.S. General Services Administration, *Summary Report on Real Property Owned by the United States Throughout the World*, annual; and *Summary Report of Real Property Leased by the United States Throughout the World*, annual.

No. 483. Federally Owned Property in the United States by State: 2000

[As of September 30. For data on federal land by state, see Table 336]

State	Installa-tions [1]	Buildings	Floor area (mil. sq. ft.)	Costs [2] (mil. dol.)	State	Installa-tions [1]	Buildings	Floor area (mil. sq. ft.)	Costs [2] (mil. dol.)
U.S. . .	40,439	430,373	2,968.2	254,052	MO.	994	6,288	53.0	4,575
AL	564	8,764	56.9	7,257	MT	991	5,514	12.9	2,926
AK	1,285	7,586	52.8	4,918	NE	688	3,015	18.7	1,187
AZ	809	12,108	48.4	4,644	NV	445	7,502	30.9	2,674
AR	557	5,199	24.0	2,730	NH	161	975	8.1	746
CA	2,985	62,528	416.0	30,659	NJ	608	7,582	72.7	4,038
CO	1,074	7,526	59.6	5,184	NM	710	13,066	55.9	5,962
CT	357	2,250	17.3	950	NY	1,649	11,128	107.5	7,801
DE	108	926	7.3	402	NC	790	15,730	86.4	5,576
DC	139	1,290	66.6	3,159	ND	848	4,274	21.0	2,153
FL	1,413	15,023	112.1	8,370	OH	1,131	5,878	77.0	5,914
GA	804	13,048	111.9	6,859	OK	587	7,465	39.5	3,460
HI.	552	15,502	78.3	4,566	OR	942	5,900	21.2	9,173
ID.	649	5,270	18.4	4,301	PA	1,380	6,871	71.8	5,123
IL.	1,255	7,856	87.9	6,730	RI.	172	1,336	13.4	683
IN.	617	5,039	34.2	2,191	SC	415	9,547	60.0	6,562
IA.	599	2,208	12.1	1,021	SD	623	2,699	15.6	1,779
KS	563	6,032	43.1	2,914	TN	665	8,114	70.4	11,132
KY	520	7,009	51.4	4,035	TX	2,253	28,479	206.3	16,215
LA	608	6,147	46.8	4,745	UT	570	5,957	36.4	2,378
ME	539	2,775	14.3	1,063	VT	159	329	2.1	260
MD.	636	11,523	111.8	7,813	VA	920	17,696	152.0	9,186
MA	757	3,936	35.9	2,213	WA	1,006	18,638	86.8	12,987
MI	1,244	6,069	33.6	1,904	WV	434	1,483	12.3	3,800
MN.	776	2,860	22.0	1,362	WI	743	4,493	27.0	1,314
MS.	506	5,063	34.7	5,302	WY	639	6,877	11.9	1,156

[1] An installation may consist of land, buildings, other structures and facilities, or combinations of them. Examples of installations are a national forest, national park, a hydroelectric project, a single office or warehouse building, and an unimproved site.   [2] Covers cost of land, buildings, and structures and facilities. All properties are reported at actual or estimated cost without considering depreciation, obsolescence, or economic changes in value.

Source: U.S. General Services Administration, *Summary Report of Real Property Owned by the United States Throughout the World, 2000*. See also <http://www.gsa.gov/attachments/GSAPUBLICATIONS/extpub/OwnedReport0613.pdf>.

Section 10
National Defense and Veterans Affairs

This section presents data on national defense and its human and financial costs; active and reserve military personnel; ships, equipment, and aircraft; and federally sponsored programs and benefits for veterans. The principal sources of these data are the annual *Selected Manpower Statistics* and the *Atlas/Data Abstract for the United States and Selected Areas* issued by the Office of the Secretary of Defense; *Annual Report of Secretary of Veterans Affairs, Department of Veterans Affairs,* and *The Budget of the United States Government,* Office of Management and Budget. For more data on expenditures, personnel, and ships, see Section 30.

Department of Defense (DOD)—The Department of Defense is responsible for providing the military forces of the United States. It includes the Office of the Secretary of Defense, the Joint Chiefs of Staff, the Army, the Navy, the Air Force, and the defense agencies. The President serves as Commander in Chief of the Armed Forces; from him, the authority flows to the Secretary of Defense and through the Joint Chiefs of Staff to the commanders of unified and specified commands (e.g., U.S. Strategic Command).

Reserve components—Reserve personnel of the Armed Forces consist of the Army National Guard, Army Reserve, Naval Reserve, Marine Corps Reserve, Air National Guard, Air Force Reserve, and Coast Guard Reserve. They provide trained personnel available for active duty in the Armed Forces in time of war or national emergency and at such other times as authorized by law.

The National Guard has dual federal-state responsibilities and uses jointly provided equipment, facilities, and budget support.

The President is empowered to mobilize the National Guard and to use such of the Armed Forces as he considers necessary to enforce federal authority in any state.

The ready reserve includes selected reservists who are intended to assist active forces in a war and the individual ready reserve who, in a major war, would be used to fill out active and reserve units and later would be a source of combat replacements; a portion of the ready reserve serves in an active status. The standby reserve cannot be called to active duty unless the Congress gives explicit approval. The retired reserve represents a low potential for mobilization.

Department of Veterans Affairs (VA)—The Department of Veterans Affairs administers laws authorizing benefits for eligible former and present members of the Armed Forces and for the beneficiaries of deceased members. Veterans benefits available under various acts of Congress include compensation for service-connected disability or death; pensions for nonservice-connected disability or death; vocational rehabilitation, education, and training; home loan insurance; life insurance; health care; special housing and automobiles or other conveyances for certain disabled veterans; burial and plot allowances; and educational assistance to families of deceased or totally disabled veterans, servicemen missing in action, or prisoners of war. Since these benefits are legislated by Congress, the dates they were enacted and the dates they apply to veterans may be different from the actual dates the conflicts occurred.

VA estimates of veterans cover all persons with active duty service during periods of war or armed conflict and until 1982 include those living outside the United States.

No. 484. National Defense Outlays and Veterans Benefits: 1960 to 2003

[For fiscal year ending in year shown; see text, Section 8, State and Local Government Finances and Employment. Includes outlays of Department of Defense, Department of Veterans Affairs, and other agencies for activities primarily related to national defense and veterans programs. For explanation of average annual percent change, see Guide to Tabular Presentation. Minus sign (-) indicates decline]

Year	National defense and veterans outlays				Annual percent change [1]			Defense outlays, percent of—	
	Defense outlays			Veterans outlays (bil. dol.)	Total outlays	Defense outlays	Veterans outlays	Federal outlays	Gross domestic product [2]
	Total outlays (bil. dol.)	Current dollars (bil. dol.)	Constant (1996) dollars (bil. dol.)						
1960	53.5	48.1	280.3	5.4	2.5	2.4	3.1	52.2	9.3
1965	56.3	50.6	267.7	5.7	-6.8	-7.6	0.7	42.8	7.4
1970	90.4	81.7	336.6	8.7	0.3	-1.0	13.6	41.8	8.1
1975	103.1	86.5	239.5	16.6	11.2	9.0	24.0	26.0	5.5
1980	155.1	134.0	244.7	21.1	13.9	15.2	6.3	22.7	4.9
1985	279.0	252.7	329.9	26.3	10.3	11.1	2.7	26.7	6.1
1990	328.4	299.3	354.3	29.1	-1.6	-1.4	-3.2	23.9	5.2
1991	304.6	273.3	309.3	31.3	-7.2	-8.7	7.6	20.6	4.6
1992	332.4	298.4	327.0	34.1	12.0	12.4	8.0	21.6	4.8
1993	326.8	291.1	314.1	35.7	-1.9	-2.4	4.6	20.7	4.4
1994	319.2	281.6	297.9	37.6	-2.3	-3.2	5.4	19.3	4.1
1995	310.0	272.1	281.8	37.9	-2.9	-3.4	0.8	17.9	3.7
1996	302.7	265.8	265.8	37.0	-2.3	-2.3	-2.4	17.0	3.5
1997	309.8	270.5	265.3	39.3	2.3	1.8	6.3	16.9	3.3
1998	310.2	268.5	259.9	41.8	0.1	-0.8	6.3	16.2	3.1
1999	320.2	274.9	260.5	43.2	3.2	2.4	3.4	16.1	3.0
2000	341.6	294.5	270.8	47.1	6.7	7.1	9.0	16.5	3.0
2001	354.4	308.5	278.5	45.8	3.7	4.8	-2.7	16.6	3.0
2002, est	399.5	348.0	306.9	51.5	12.7	12.8	12.4	17.0	3.4
2003, est	435.6	379.0	328.0	56.6	9.0	8.9	9.8	17.8	3.5

[1] Change from prior year shown; for 1960, change from 1955. [2] Represents fiscal year GDP; for definition, see text, Section 13, Income, Expenditures, and Wealth.

No. 485. Federal Budget Outlays for Defense Functions: 1980 to 2002

[In billions of dollars (134.0 represents $134,000,000,000), except percent. For fiscal year ending in year shown; see text, Section 8, State and Local Government Finances and Employment. Minus sign (-) indicates decline]

Defense function	1980	1990	1994	1995	1996	1997	1998	1999	2000	2001	2002, est.
Total.	134.0	299.3	281.6	272.1	265.8	270.5	268.5	274.9	294.5	308.5	348.0
Percent change [1].	15.2	-1.4	-3.2	-3.4	-2.3	1.8	-0.8	2.4	5.7	4.8	12.8
Defense Dept., military	130.9	289.8	268.6	259.4	253.2	258.3	256.1	261.4	281.2	294.0	330.6
Military personnel	40.9	75.6	73.1	70.8	66.7	69.7	69.0	69.5	76.0	74.0	81.2
Operation, maintenance.	44.8	88.3	87.9	91.1	88.8	92.5	93.5	96.4	105.9	114.0	133.6
Procurement	29.0	81.0	61.8	55.0	48.9	47.7	48.2	48.8	51.7	55.0	59.6
Research and development . .	13.1	37.5	34.8	34.6	36.5	37.0	37.4	37.4	37.6	40.6	45.1
Military construction	2.5	5.1	5.0	6.8	6.7	6.2	6.0	5.5	5.1	5.0	5.7
Family housing.	1.7	3.5	3.3	3.6	3.8	4.0	3.9	3.7	3.4	3.5	3.8
Other [2]	-1.1	-1.2	2.7	-2.4	1.8	1.2	-1.9	0.1	1.6	1.9	1.7

[1] Change from immediate prior year. [2] Revolving and management funds, trust funds, special foreign currency program, allowances, and offsetting receipts.

Source: U.S. Office of Management and Budget, *Historical Tables,* annual.

No. 486. National Defense—Budget Authority and Outlays: 1980 to 2002

[In billions of dollars (143.9 represents $143,900,000,000), except percent. For fiscal year ending in year shown, except as noted; see text, Section 8, State and Local Government Finances and Employment]

Item	1980	1990	1995	1996	1997	1998	1999	2000	2001	2002, est.
Defense (Budget authority) [1]	143.9	303.3	266.4	266.2	270.4	271.3	292.3	304.1	329.0	350.7
Department of Defense-Military	140.7	293.0	255.7	254.6	258.0	258.6	278.6	290.5	313.0	333.0
Atomic energy defense activities[1]. . . .	3.0	9.7	10.1	10.7	11.4	11.7	12.6	12.4	14.4	16.0
Defense-related activities	0.2	0.6	0.6	0.9	1.0	1.0	1.1	1.2	1.6	1.7
Defense (Outlays) [1]	134.0	299.3	272.1	265.8	270.5	268.5	274.9	294.5	308.5	348.0
Department of Defense-Military	130.9	289.8	259.4	253.2	258.3	256.1	261.4	281.2	294.0	330.6
Atomic energy defense activities [1] . . .	2.9	9.0	11.8	11.6	11.3	11.3	12.4	12.2	13.0	15.9
Defense-related activities	0.2	0.6	0.8	0.9	0.9	1.1	1.1	1.1	1.5	1.6

[1] Includes defense budget authority, balances, and outlays by other departments.

Source of Tables 484-486: U.S. Office of Management and Budget, *Historical Tables,* annual.

No. 487. Military Prime Contract Awards to All Businesses by Program: 1980 to 2001

[In billions of dollars (83.7 represents $83,700,000,000). Net values for fiscal year ending in year shown; see text, Section 8, State and Local Government Finances and Employment. Includes all new prime contracts; debit or credit changes in contracts are also included. Actions cover official awards, amendments, or other changes in prime contracts to obtain military supplies, services, or construction. Excludes term contracts and contracts which do not obligate a firm total dollar amount or fixed quantity, but includes job orders, task orders, and delivery orders against such contracts]

DOD procurement program	1980	1990	1995	1996	1997	1998	1999	2000	2001
Total	83.7	144.7	131.4	132.2	128.4	128.8	135.2	143.0	154.1
Intragovernmental [1]	10.2	10.0	12.3	13.0	11.5	9.9	11.6	14.8	13.4
For work outside the United States	5.4	7.1	5.6	6.4	6.4	5.6	7.4	7.5	7.1
Educ. and nonprofit institutions	1.5	3.5	3.3	3.3	3.6	3.5	3.9	4.3	4.5
With business firms for work in the United States [2] .	66.7	123.8	110.0	109.5	106.9	109.7	112.2	116.4	129.2
Major hard goods	41.0	79.1	56.0	55.1	52.5	56.0	57.5	59.8	67.9
Aircraft	12.5	24.0	18.8	20.3	18.4	20.8	23.3	28.8	30.5
Electronics and communication equip.	9.6	18.5	12.3	11.5	12.1	10.7	10.7	9.5	10.9
Missiles and space systems	7.9	17.1	10.6	10.2	9.5	9.9	9.5	8.2	8.2
Ships	6.0	10.3	9.1	7.1	6.8	8.6	7.8	8.3	12.0
Tanks, ammo. and weapons	5.1	9.2	5.3	5.9	5.7	6.0	6.2	5.0	6.3
Services	5.9	14.6	18.6	19.2	20.2	21.2	23.7	24.0	25.9

[1] Covers only purchases from other federal agencies and reimbursable purchases on behalf of foreign governments.
[2] Includes Department of Defense. Includes other business not shown separately. Contracts awarded for work in U.S. possessions, and other areas subject to complete sovereignty of United States; contracts in a classified location; and any intragovernmental contracts entered into overseas.

Source: U.S. Dept. of Defense, *Prime Contract Awards*, semiannual.

No. 488. Department of Defense Contract Awards, Payroll, and Civilian and Military Personnel—States: 2000

[For years ending Sept. 30. *Contracts* refer to awards made in year specified; expenditures relating to awards may extend over several years. *Civilian employees* include United States citizen and foreign national direct hire civilians subject to Office of Management and Budget (OMB) ceiling controls and civilian personnel involved in civil functions in the United States. Excludes indirect hire civilians and those direct hire civilian not subject to OMB ceiling controls. *Military personnel* include active duty personnel based ashore. Excludes personnel temporarily shore-based in a transient status, or afloat. *Payroll outlays* include the gross earnings of civilian and active duty military personnel for services rendered to the government and for cash allowances for benefits. Excludes employer's share of employee benefits, accrued military retirement benefits and most permanent change of station costs]

State	Contract awards [1] (mil. dol.)	Payroll (mil. dol.)	Personnel 1,000) Civilian	Military	State	Contract awards [1] (mil. dol.)	Payroll (mil. dol.)	Personnel 1,000) Civilian	Military
AL	3,298	2,376	20.2	11.1	MT	87	290	1.1	3.5
AK	831	902	4.8	15.7	NE	238	660	3.2	7.6
AZ	4,547	1,995	8.2	21.3	NV	276	818	2.0	7.7
AR	343	772	3.6	4.7	NH	398	262	1.0	0.7
CA	18,100	11,362	60.8	146.3	NJ	2,944	1,518	14.2	8.5
CO	2,214	2,395	11.0	29.1	NM	654	1,106	7.0	11.0
CT	2,177	541	2.6	6.5	NY	3,839	1,776	11.1	19.6
DE	95	329	1.4	3.7	NC	1,199	4,653	15.4	90.9
DC	1,899	1,218	12.6	13.0	ND	134	405	3.3	7.2
FL	6,470	6,887	26.4	60.9	OH	3,077	2,189	23.4	6.8
GA	3,665	4,934	30.4	66.0	OK	1,401	2,391	21.4	24.6
HI	1,160	2,537	17.9	40.4	OR	284	556	3.0	0.6
ID	213	399	1.4	4.2	PA	3,967	2,217	25.7	3.1
IL	1,609	2,361	12.7	32.1	RI	418	502	4.3	3.4
IN	1,611	929	9.3	1.1	SC	1,055	2,449	8.9	39.6
IA	621	272	1.5	0.4	SD	87	266	1.7	3.1
KS	891	1,136	5.5	15.5	TN	1,077	1,165	6.7	2.4
KY	910	1,856	6.1	35.8	TX	12,145	8,659	39.3	109.9
LA	1,938	1,403	8.6	15.5	UT	950	1,044	13.5	4.8
ME	772	571	5.8	2.7	VT	243	96	0.6	0.0
MD	4,977	3,726	32.0	30.4	VA	13,637	11,407	79.6	133.3
MA	4,737	826	6.9	2.3	WA	2,192	4,035	23.1	48.9
MI	1,446	867	7.7	1.0	WV	74	271	1.8	0.6
MN	1,458	440	2.5	0.7	WI	768	456	3.0	0.6
MS	1,557	1,392	9.5	16.6	WY	100	226	1.0	3.3
MO	4,508	1,604	9.4	16.2					

[1] Military awards for supplies, services, and construction. Net value of contracts of over $25,000 for work in each state and DC. Figures reflect impact of prime contracting on state distribution of defense work. Often the state in which a prime contractor is located in is not the state where the subcontracted work is done. See also headnote, Table 487. Undistributed civilians and military personnel, their payrolls, and prime contract awards for performance in classified locations are excluded.

Source: U.S. Dept. of Defense, *Atlas/Data Abstract for the United States and Selected Areas*, annual.

U.S. Census Bureau, Statistical Abstract of the United States: 2002

No. 489. U.S. Military Sales and Assistance to Foreign Governments: 1990 to 2000

[In millions of dollars, (16,614 represents $16,614,000,000). For fiscal year ending in year shown; see text, Section 8, State and Local Government Finances and Employment. Department of Defense (DOD) sales deliveries cover deliveries against sales orders authorized under Arms Export Control Act, as well as earlier and applicable legislation. For details regarding individual programs, see source]

Item	1990	1993	1994	1995	1996	1997	1998	1999	2000
Military sales agreements	16,614	29,607	12,846	8,621	9,517	8,509	8,793	11,874	11,851
Military constr. sales agrmts	636	625	58	25	125	30	430	286	287
Military sales deliveries [1]	8,065	11,634	9,632	12,036	11,532	15,545	12,999	16,989	11,604
Military sales financing . . . . [2] . . .	4,758	4,124	3,917	3,712	3,836	3,530	3,420	3,370	4,333
Military assistance programs [2] . [3] .	137	552	321	117	330	72	95	268	85
Military assist. program delivery [3] .	27	61	5	13	27	100	80	11	14
IMET program/deliveries [3]	43	43	22	26	39	43	50	50	51

[1] Includes military construction sales deliveries. [2] Also includes Military Assistance Service Funded (MASF) program data, Section 506(a) drawdown authority, and MAP Merger Funds. [3] Includes Military Assistance Service Funded (MASF) program data and Section 506(a) drawdown authority.

No. 490. U.S. Military Sales Deliveries by Major Selected Country: 1990 to 2000

[In millions of dollars (8,065 represents $8,065,000,000). For fiscal years ending in year shown. See text, Section 8, State and Local Government Finances and Employment. Represents Department of Defense military sales]

Country	1990	1993	1994	1995	1996	1997	1998	1999	2000
Total [1]	**8,065**	**11,634**	**9,632**	**12,036**	**11,532**	**15,545**	**12,999**	**16,989**	**11,604**
Australia	384	259	354	303	228	196	208	269	331
Belgium	150	12	13	8	157	107	194	250	58
China: Taiwan	455	816	845	1,347	834	2,555	1,487	2,526	923
Egypt	368	1,360	1,028	1,565	1,141	945	598	524	1,202
Germany	366	378	152	262	404	212	191	280	147
Greece	114	226	235	220	210	717	411	577	316
Israel	146	778	410	327	386	503	1,204	1,228	573
Italy	61	72	181	54	77	51	43	106	41
Japan	272	379	780	693	753	492	409	488	557
Kuwait	52	25	31	47	16	42	47	49	53
Netherlands	397	19	17	22	22	11	7	5	8
Saudi Arabia	874	82	228	88	19	71	21	12	21
Singapore	44	3,562	2,005	3,676	2,887	4,677	4150	4,808	2,144
South Korea	328	78	87	59	80	133	232	561	139
Turkey	761	755	931	368	482	1,153	538	1,278	783

[1] Includes countries not shown.

Source of Tables 489 and 490: U.S. Defense Security Assistance Agency, *Foreign Military Sales, Foreign Military Construction Sales,* and *Military Assistance Facts,* annual.

No. 491. Military and Civilian Personnel and Expenditures: 1990 to 2000

Item	1990	1995	1997	1998	1999	2000
Personnel, total [1] (1,000).	**3,693**	**3,391**	**3,081**	**2,943**	**2,863**	**2,791**
Active duty military	1,185	1,085	1,045	1,004	1,003	984
Civilian	931	768	689	654	634	634
Reserve and National Guard.	1,577	1,538	1,347	1,285	1,226	1,173
Expenditures, total [2] (mil. dol.)	**209,904**	**209,695**	**205,764**	**208,843**	**218,861**	**229,072**
Prime contract awards [3] (mil. dol.)	121,254	109,005	106,561	109,386	114,875	123,295
Grants.	(NA)	(NA)	1,907	2,079	2,175	2,330
Major area of work (mil. dol.):						
Aircraft, fixed wing	6,329	7,543	5,432	12,904	7,733	(NA)
Guided missiles	928	495	2,831	417	654	(NA)

NA Not available. [1] Includes those based ashore and excludes those temporarily shore-based, in a transient status, or afloat. [2] Includes expenditures not shown separately. [3] Represents contract awards over $25,000.

Source: U.S. Dept. of Defense, *Atlas/Data Abstract for the United States and Selected Areas,* annual.

No. 492. Department of Defense Manpower: 1950 to 2001

[In thousands (1,459 represents 1,459,000. **As of end of fiscal year;** see text, Section 8, State and Local Government Finances and Employment. Includes National Guard, Reserve, and retired regular personnel on extended or continuous active duty. Excludes Coast Guard. Other officer candidates are included under enlisted personnel]

Year	Total [1,2]	Army Total [2]	Army White	Army Black	Army Officers	Army Enlisted	Navy [3] Total [2]	Navy White	Navy Black	Navy Officers	Navy Enlisted	Marine corps Total [2]	Marine White	Marine Black	Marine Officers	Marine Enlisted	Air Force Total [2]	Air Force White	Air Force Black	Air Force Officers	Air Force Enlisted
1950	1,459	593	(NA)	(NA)	73	519	381	(NA)	(NA)	45	333	74	(NA)	(NA)	7	67	411	(NA)	(NA)	57	354
1955	2,935	1,109	(NA)	(NA)	122	986	661	(NA)	(NA)	75	583	205	(NA)	(NA)	18	187	960	(NA)	(NA)	137	823
1960	2,475	873	(NA)	(NA)	101	770	617	(NA)	(NA)	70	545	171	(NA)	(NA)	16	154	815	(NA)	(NA)	130	683
1965	2,654	969	(NA)	(NA)	112	855	670	(NA)	(NA)	78	588	190	(NA)	(NA)	17	173	825	(NA)	(NA)	132	690
1970	3,065	1,323	(NA)	(NA)	167	1,153	691	(NA)	(NA)	81	606	260	(NA)	(NA)	25	235	791	(NA)	(NA)	130	657
1971	2,713	1,124	(NA)	(NA)	149	972	622	(NA)	(NA)	75	542	212	(NA)	(NA)	22	191	755	(NA)	(NA)	126	625
1972	2,322	811	(NA)	(NA)	121	687	587	(NA)	(NA)	73	511	198	(NA)	(NA)	20	178	726	(NA)	(NA)	122	600
1973	2,252	801	(NA)	(NA)	116	682	564	(NA)	(NA)	71	490	196	(NA)	(NA)	19	177	691	(NA)	(NA)	115	572
1974	2,162	783	(NA)	(NA)	106	674	546	(NA)	(NA)	67	475	189	(NA)	(NA)	19	170	644	(NA)	(NA)	110	529
1975	2,128	784	(NA)	(NA)	103	678	535	(NA)	(NA)	66	466	196	(NA)	(NA)	19	177	613	(NA)	(NA)	105	503
1976	2,082	779	(NA)	(NA)	99	678	525	(NA)	(NA)	64	458	192	(NA)	(NA)	19	174	585	(NA)	(NA)	100	481
1977	2,075	782	(NA)	(NA)	98	680	530	(NA)	(NA)	63	462	192	(NA)	(NA)	19	173	571	(NA)	(NA)	96	470
1978	2,062	772	(NA)	(NA)	98	670	530	(NA)	(NA)	63	463	191	(NA)	(NA)	18	172	570	(NA)	(NA)	95	470
1979	2,027	759	(NA)	(NA)	97	657	523	(NA)	(NA)	62	457	185	(NA)	(NA)	18	167	559	(NA)	(NA)	96	459
1980	2,051	777	503	229	99	674	527	436	55	63	460	188	142	39	18	170	558	460	80	98	456
1981	2,083	781	502	232	102	675	540	443	58	65	470	191	145	39	18	172	570	468	83	99	467
1982	2,109	780	504	230	103	673	553	450	62	67	481	192	149	38	19	173	583	476	87	102	476
1983	2,123	780	512	220	106	669	558	462	66	68	485	194	152	37	20	174	592	483	88	105	483
1984	2,138	780	520	215	108	668	565	455	67	69	491	196	153	36	20	176	597	486	89	106	486
1985	2,151	781	523	211	110	667	571	459	70	71	495	198	152	37	20	178	602	488	90	108	489
1986	2,169	781	524	210	110	667	581	464	75	72	504	199	151	38	20	179	608	491	92	109	495
1987	2,174	781	519	212	108	668	587	467	81	72	510	200	150	38	20	179	607	489	92	107	495
1988	2,138	772	507	213	107	660	593	466	85	72	516	197	147	38	20	177	576	462	88	105	467
1989	2,130	770	497	218	107	658	593	461	91	72	516	197	146	38	20	177	571	458	87	104	463
1990	2,044	732	466	213	104	624	579	446	93	72	503	197	145	38	20	177	535	428	82	100	431
1991	1,986	711	452	204	104	603	570	439	92	71	495	194	144	36	20	174	510	409	77	97	409
1992	1,807	610	388	173	95	511	542	415	88	69	468	185	138	32	19	165	470	377	70	90	376
1993	1,705	572	365	158	88	480	510	390	84	66	439	178	134	30	18	160	444	357	65	84	356
1994	1,610	541	344	147	85	453	469	355	78	62	403	174	131	28	18	156	426	341	62	81	341
1995	1,518	509	322	137	83	422	435	326	75	59	372	175	130	28	18	157	400	318	58	78	318
1996	1,472	491	(NA)	(NA)	81	407	417	(NA)	(NA)	57	355	175	(NA)	(NA)	18	157	389	(NA)	(NA)	76	309
1997	1,439	492	(NA)	(NA)	79	408	396	(NA)	(NA)	56	335	174	(NA)	(NA)	18	156	377	(NA)	(NA)	74	299
1998	1,407	484	(NA)	(NA)	78	401	382	(NA)	(NA)	55	323	173	(NA)	(NA)	18	155	377	(NA)	(NA)	72	292
1999	1,386	479	(NA)	(NA)	77	398	373	(NA)	(NA)	54	315	173	(NA)	(NA)	18	155	361	(NA)	(NA)	70	286
2000	1,384	482	(NA)	(NA)	77	401	373	(NA)	(NA)	54	315	173	(NA)	(NA)	18	155	356	(NA)	(NA)	69	282
2001	1,385	481	(NA)	(NA)	76	400	378	(NA)	(NA)	54	320	173	(NA)	(NA)	18	155	354	(NA)	(NA)	69	280

NA Not available. [1] Beginning 1980, excludes Navy Reserve personnel on active duty for Training and Administration of Reserves (TARS). From 1969, the full-time Guard and Reserve. [2] Includes cadets and other not shown separately. [3] Prior to 1980, includes Navy Reserve personnel on active duty for TARS.

Source: U.S. Dept. of Defense, *Selected Manpower Statistics*, annual.

U.S. Census Bureau, Statistical Abstract of the United States: 2002

No. 493. United States Military and Civilian Personnel in Installations: 1999

[As of September 30]

State	Military personnel				Civilian personnel			
	Total [1]	Army	Navy/ Marine Corps	Air Force	Total [1]	Army	Navy/ Marine Corps	Air Force
United States.....	1,014,166	386,369	324,613	303,184	633,600	208,006	179,340	151,406
Alabama............	11,272	6,116	573	4,583	20,955	16,603	40	2,713
Alaska	15,684	6,196	85	9,403	4,247	2,333	7	1,622
Arizona............	21,240	5,358	4,559	11,323	8,117	3,338	414	3,337
Arkansas	4,888	369	110	4,409	3,570	2,585	6	865
California	109,697	7,697	80,572	21,428	64,086	6,899	34,986	12,376
Colorado...........	29,247	15,002	955	13,290	11,118	2,661	46	5,055
Connecticut.........	4,412	38	4,265	109	2,593	450	1,136	256
Delaware	3,898	13	13	3,872	1,370	184	-	1,102
District of Columbia	13,240	4,600	4,974	3,666	12,651	4,357	7,015	993
Florida	50,731	2,982	23,223	24,526	26,322	2,594	12,731	7,739
Georgia	62,714	49,340	4,096	9,278	30,678	11,295	4,409	11,987
Hawaii	32,354	14,692	13,179	4,483	16,318	4,293	8,864	2,026
Idaho	4,326	40	76	4,210	1,411	604	54	691
Illinois	35,674	716	29,283	5,675	12,988	6,537	1,793	2,923
Indiana............	991	416	411	164	9,266	1,436	3,164	1,160
Iowa	443	234	115	94	1,514	938	4	519
Kansas............	16,354	13,264	179	2,911	5,457	3,914	3	1,069
Kentucky	36,149	35,713	228	208	8,734	7,030	185	223
Louisiana	15,246	8,367	1,515	5,364	7,815	4,168	1,503	1,667
Maine..............	2,136	242	1,781	113	5,520	320	4,509	290
Maryland	29,859	7,548	14,085	8,226	32,101	12,037	15,633	2,313
Massachusetts.......	2,535	318	489	1,728	6,970	2,225	305	3,132
Michigan...........	1,085	488	389	208	7,664	4,614	26	1,208
Minnesota..........	862	321	320	221	2,418	1,333	26	782
Mississippi	12,069	500	3,255	8,314	9,434	3,586	2,740	2,785
Missouri	17,184	11,489	1,901	3,794	9,516	5,675	240	1,200
Montana...........	3,663	26	15	3,622	1,113	442	1	604
Nebraska	7,988	90	558	7,340	3,323	1,406	14	1,534
Nevada	7,721	91	1,003	6,627	2,068	305	334	1,199
New Hampshire.......	376	18	201	157	1,028	506	45	305
New Jersey.........	7,116	958	847	5,311	14,549	9,627	2,312	1,593
New Mexico	11,642	420	252	10,970	6,915	2,931	62	3,568
New York	20,532	17,219	2,636	677	11,365	6,886	178	2,439
North Carolina.......	86,594	38,831	38,431	9,332	16,311	5,959	7,084	1,210
North Dakota........	7,499	27	6	7,466	1,638	409	1	1,112
Ohio	7,668	578	525	6,565	23,544	1,311	82	12,335
Oklahoma..........	25,234	14,889	841	9,504	20,187	4,116	88	14,567
Oregon............	933	200	368	365	2,908	2,072	19	786
Pennsylvania........	3,261	1,252	1,604	405	25,772	7,883	8,696	1,603
Rhode Island........	3,415	97	3,160	158	4,352	264	3,743	239
South Carolina.......	38,289	11,963	17,329	8,997	9,495	2,542	3,746	1,708
South Dakota	3,171	38	8	3,125	1,264	485	1	711
Tennessee	2,679	378	1,800	501	4,939	2,468	1,029	948
Texas.............	108,835	60,945	6,909	40,981	39,993	16,050	1,788	17,716
Utah	4,844	331	148	4,365	12,419	2,079	22	8,849
Vermont	125	24	16	85	525	253	2	229
Virginia............	80,132	25,696	40,420	14,016	78,973	19,519	36,004	4,238
Washington.........	32,398	17,367	7,751	7,280	22,322	5,015	14,162	1,877
West Virginia........	614	208	299	107	1,713	1,216	76	398
Wisconsin..........	578	294	142	142	3,119	2,069	11	914
Wyoming...........	3,496	7	3	3,486	932	184	1	691

- Represents zero. [1] Includes other DOD organizations not shown separately.

Source: U.S. Dept. of Defense, *Selected Manpower Statistics*, annual.

No. 494. Military Personnel on Active Duty by Location: 1980 to 2001

[In thousands (2,051 represents 2,051,000). As of end of fiscal year; see text, Section 8, State and Local Government Finances and Employment]

Location	1980	1985	1990	1995	1996	1997	1998	1999	2000	2001
Total	2,051	2,151	2,044	1,518	1,472	1,439	1,407	1,386	1,384	1,385
Shore-based [1]	1,840	1,920	1,794	1,351	1,317	1,294	1,267	1,241	1,237	1,244
Afloat [2]	211	231	252	167	155	145	140	145	147	141
United States [3]	1,562	1,636	1,437	1,280	1,231	1,211	1,147	1,133	1,127	1,130
Foreign countries	488	516	609	238	240	227	260	253	258	255

[1] Includes Navy personnel temporarily on shore.   [2] Includes Marine Corps.   [3] Includes outlying areas.
Source: U.S. Dept. of Defense, *Selected Manpower Statistics*, annual.

No. 495. U.S. Military Personnel on Active Duty in Selected Foreign Countries: 2000

[As of end of fiscal year]

Country	2000	Country	2000	Country	2000
In foreign countries [1] .	257,817	El Salvador	27	New Zealand	6
Ashore	212,858	France	67	Norway	81
Afloat	44,959	Germany	69,203	Oman	251
Argentina	26	Greece	678	Pakistan	22
Australia	175	Greenland	125	Panama	20
Austria	18	Haiti	21	Peru	425
Bahamas, The	24	Honduras	351	Philippines	79
Bahrain	949	Hungary	375	Portugal	1,005
Belgium	1,554	Iceland	1,636	Qatar	52
Bolivia	20	India	20	Russia	101
Bosnia and Herzegovina . . .	5,708	Indonesia	51	Saudi Arabia	7,053
Brazil	38	Israel	36	Singapore	411
Canada	156	Italy	11,190	South Africa	34
Chile	26	Jamaica	11	Spain	2,007
China	74	Japan	40,159	Switzerland	19
Colombia	224	Jordan	29	Thailand	526
Croatia	138	Kenya	21	Tunisia	12
Cuba (Guantanamo)	688	Korea, Republic of	36,565	Turkey	2,006
Cyprus	41	Kuwait	4,602	Ukraine	16
Denmark	26	Macedonia, The Former		United Arab Emirates	402
Diego Garcia	625	Yugoslav, Republic of	347	United Kingdom	11,207
Ecuador	20	Mexico	29	Venezuela	28
Egypt	499	Netherlands	659	Zimbabwe	8

[1] Includes areas not shown separately.
Source: U.S. Dept. of Defense, *Selected Manpower Statistics,* annual. See also <http://web1.whs.osd.mil/mmid/m01/fy00/m01fy00.pdf>.

No. 496. Coast Guard Personnel on Active Duty: 1970 to 2001

[As of end of fiscal year; see text, Section 8, State and Local Government Finances and Employment]

Year	Total	Officers	Cadets	Enlisted	Year	Total	Officers	Cadets	Enlisted
1970	38,012	5,512	976	31,524	1994	37,472	7,401	881	29,002
1975	36,788	5,630	1,177	29,981	1995	36,731	7,295	841	28,401
1980	39,100	6,465	874	31,761	1996	35,229	7,106	802	27,129
1985	38,615	6,584	727	31,146	1997	34,890	6,939	805	26,945
1990	36,939	6,713	927	29,136	1998	35,293	6,962	777	27,363
1991	38,444	7,095	900	30,285	1999	35,534	6,942	835	27,593
1992	39,424	7,348	919	30,918	2000	35,952	6,968	856	27,964
1993	39,239	7,471	907	30,699	2001	36,137	7,033	890	28,046

Source: U.S. Dept. of Transportation, *Annual Report of the Secretary of Transportation.*

No. 497. U.S. Active Duty Military Deaths by Manner of Death: 1980 to 2000

Manner of death	1980-2000	1980	1990	1992	1993	1994	1995	1996	1997	1998	1999	2000
Deaths, total	33,686	2,391	1,526	1,332	1,245	1,109	1,055	1,008	864	815	761	774
Accident	19,888	1,577	864	712	672	548	572	518	463	420	411	400
Illness	6,098	401	275	253	215	217	167	180	177	156	126	124
Homicide	1,834	161	71	112	89	86	59	65	43	28	34	31
Self-inflicted	4,681	236	250	222	246	231	242	210	159	155	110	142
Pending/undetermined	605	15	42	32	13	8	9	14	22	53	80	60
Hostile deaths	580	1	24	1	10	19	6	21	-	3	-	17
Deaths per 100,000 of personnel strength	(X)	116.6	74.7	73.7	73.0	68.9	69.5	68.5	60.1	57.9	54.9	53.9
Nonhostile deaths per 100,000 . . .	(X)	116.5	73.5	73.7	72.4	67.7	69.1	67.1	60.1	57.7	54.9	52.7
Accidents per 100,000	(X)	76.9	42.3	39.4	39.4	34.0	37.7	35.2	32.2	29.9	29.7	27.8
Illnesses per 100,000	(X)	19.6	13.5	14.0	12.6	13.5	11.0	12.2	12.3	11.1	9.1	8.6
Homicides per 100,000	(X)	7.9	3.5	6.2	5.2	5.3	3.9	4.4	3.0	2.0	2.5	2.2
Self-inflicted per 100,000	(X)	11.5	12.2	12.3	14.4	14.3	15.9	14.3	11.1	11.0	7.9	9.9

- Represents zero.   X Not applicable.
Source: U.S. Dept. of Defense, *DOD Worldwide U.S. Active Duty Military Personnel.*

National Defense and Veterans Affairs   331

U.S. Census Bureau, Statistical Abstract of the United States: 2002

No. 498. Armed Forces Personnel—Summary of Major Conflicts

[For Revolutionary War, number of personnel serving not known, but estimates range from 184,000 to 250,000; for War of 1812, 286,730 served; for Mexican War, 78,718 served. Dates of the major conflicts may differ from those specified in various laws providing benefits for veterans]

Item	Unit	Civil War [1]	Spanish-American War	World War I	World War II	Korean conflict	Vietnam conflict
Personnel serving [2]	1,000. . . .	2,213	307	4,735	[3]16,113	[4]5,720	[5]8,744
Average duration of service	Months. . .	20	8	12	33	.19	23
Service abroad: Personnel serving	Percent . .	(NA)	[6]29	53	73	[7]56	(NA)
Average duration [8]	Months. . .	(NA)	1.5	6	16	13	(NA)
Casualties: [9] Battle deaths [2]	1,000. . . .	140	(Z)	53	292	34	[10]47
Other deaths	1,000. . . .	224	2	63	114	3	11
Wounds not mortal [2]	1,000. . . .	282	2	204	671	103	[10]153
Draftees: Classified	1,000. . . .	777	(X)	24,234	36,677	9,123	[5]75,717
Examined	1,000. . . .	522	(X)	3,764	17,955	3,685	[5]8,611
Rejected	1,000. . . .	160	(X)	803	6,420	1,189	[5]3,880
Inducted	1,000. . . .	46	(X)	2,820	10,022	1,560	[5]1,759

NA Not available.   X Not applicable.   Z Fewer than 500.   [1] Union forces only. Estimates of the number serving in Confederate forces range from 600,000 to 1.5 million.   [2] Source: U.S. Department of Defense, *Selected Manpower Statistics*, annual.   [3] Covers Dec. 1, 1941, to Dec. 31, 1946.   [4] Covers June 25, 1950, to July 27, 1953.   [5] Covers Aug. 4, 1964, to Jan. 27, 1973.   [6] Army and Marines only.   [7] Excludes Navy. Covers July 1950 through Jan. 1955. Far East area only.   [8] During hostilities only.   [9] For periods covered, see footnotes 3, 4, and 5.   [10] Covers Jan. 1, 1961, to Jan. 27, 1973. Includes known military service personnel who have died from combat related wounds.

Source: Except as noted, the President's Commission on Veterans' Pensions, Veterans' *Benefits in the United States*, Vol. I, 1956; and U.S. Dept. of Defense, unpublished data.

No. 499. Enlisted Military Personnel Accessions by Branch: 1990 to 1997

[In thousands (461.1 represents 461,100). For years ending Sept. 30]

Branch of service	1990	1995	1996	1997	Branch of service	1990	1995	1996	1997
Total	461.1	357.3	367.6	380.1	First enlistments	62.1	36.4	39.2	43.7
First enlistments	216.4	160.0	174.6	184.6	Reenlistments	58.6	41.4	40.6	41.6
Reenlistments	237.0	180.8	181.0	187.4	Marine Corps	47.7	46.7	48.7	50.0
Reserves to active duty	15.6	16.6	12.0	8.1	First enlistments	32.9	34.4	34.5	35.1
Army	181.7	135.9	146.0	162.3	Reenlistments	14.4	11.9	0.4	14.7
First enlistments	84.8	57.7	69.7	75.3	Air Force	104.4	81.3	81.6	74.5
Reenlistments	96.5	77.7	76.2	87.0	First enlistments	36.6	31.4	31.2	30.5
Navy	135.3	93.4	91.3	93.3	Reenlistments	67.5	49.7	50.3	44.0

Source: U.S. Dept. of Defense, *Selected Manpower Statistics*, annual. See also <http://web1.whs.osd.mil/mmid/m01/fy00/m01fy00.pdf>.

No. 500. Military Personnel on Active Duty by Rank or Grade: 1990 to 2001

[In thousands (2,043.7 represents 2,043,700). As of Sept. 30]

Rank/grade	1990	1995	1997	1998	1999	2000	2001
Total [1]	2,043.7	1,518.2	1,438.6	1,406.8	1,385.7	1,384.3	1,385.1
Recruit—E-1	97.6	63.4	74.1	73.6	81.2	80.0	72.5
Private—E-2	140.3	99.7	100.8	99.0	93.9	99.0	92.4
Pvt. 1st class—E-3	280.1	197.1	196.0	194.7	190.5	196.3	210.4
Corporal—E-4	427.8	317.2	264.8	262.9	262.9	251.0	240.1
Sergeant—E-5	361.5	261.4	250.6	239.9	229.5	229.5	239.7
Staff Sgt.—E-6	239.1	180.5	169.6	163.7	162.9	164.9	164.9
Sgt. 1st class—E-7	134.1	109.3	104.7	100.4	97.1	97.7	98.4
Master Sgt.—E-8	38.0	28.8	27.6	26.6	25.8	26.0	26.7
Sgt. Major—E-9	15.3	11.1	10.8	10.5	10.4	10.2	10.4
Warrant Officer—W-1	3.2	2.0	2.0	2.1	2.2	2.1	2.2
Chief Warrant—W-4	3.0	2.2	1.9	2.0	2.1	2.0	1.9
2d Lt.—O-1	31.9	25.6	24.8	23.8	24.9	26.4	28.1
1st Lt.—O-2	37.9	26.1	25.5	26.2	25.4	24.7	25.7
Captain—O-3	106.6	84.3	78.3	73.8	69.8	68.1	66.0
Major—O-4	53.2	43.9	43.1	43.3	43.5	43.2	43.1
Lt. Colonel—O-5	32.3	28.7	28.0	28.6	28.0	27.5	27.2
Colonel—O-6	14.0	11.7	11.4	11.3	11.3	11.3	11.2
Brig. General—O-7	0.5	0.4	0.4	0.4	0.4	0.4	0.4
Major General—O-8	0.4	0.3	0.3	0.3	0.3	0.3	0.3
Lt. General—O-9	0.1	0.1	0.1	0.1	0.1	0.1	0.1
General—O-10	(Z)	(Z)	(Z)	(Z)	(Z)	(Z)	(Z)

Z Fewer than 50.   [1] Includes cadets and midshipmen and warrant officers, W-2 and W-3.

Source: U.S. Dept. of Defense, *Selected Manpower Statistics*, annual.

No. 501. Military Reserve Personnel: 1990 to 2001

[As of end of fiscal year. The Ready Reserve includes the Selected Reserve which is scheduled to augment active forces during times of war or national emergency, and the Individual Ready Reserve which, during times of war or national emergency, would be used to fill out Active, Guard and Reserve units, and which would also be a source for casualty replacements; Ready Reservists serve in an active status (except for the Inactive National Guard - a very small pool within the Army National Guard). The Standby Reserve cannot be called to active duty except in situations where those members are the only available assets with specific required specialties. The Retired Reserve is categorized into three groups, based on age and length of retirement, prioritized for mobilization purposes.

Reserve status and branch of service	1990	1995	1997	1998	1999	2000	2001
Total reserves [1]	1,688,674	1,674,164	1,474,167	1,382,348	1,316,984	1,276,843	1,250,155
Ready reserve	1,658,707	1,648,388	1,450,974	1,353,428	1,288,844	1,251,452	1,225,233
Standby reserve	29,967	25,776	23,193	28,920	28,140	25,391	24,922
Retired reserve.	462,371	505,905	549,845	562,088	564,358	573,305	580,785

[1] Less retired reserves.

Source: U.S. Dept. of Defense, *Official Guard and Reserve Manpower Strengths and Statistics*, quarterly.

No. 502. Ready Reserve Personnel Profile—Race and Sex: 1990 to 2001

Item	Race					Percent distribution			
	Total	White	Black	Asian	American Indian	White	Black	Asian	American Indian
1990	1,641,475	1,289,367	271,470	14,616	7,695	78.7	16.4	0.9	0.5
1991	1,758,144	1,377,583	290,241	17,966	9,111	78.5	16.4	1.0	0.5
1992	1,857,801	1,443,155	308,807	19,944	9,180	77.8	16.5	1.1	0.5
1993	1,840,650	1,425,255	309,699	21,089	9,068	77.5	16.7	1.1	0.5
1994	1,779,436	1,366,387	297,519	22,190	8,870	76.9	16.6	1.2	0.5
1995	1,633,497	1,254,592	273,847	21,792	8,591	76.9	16.7	1.3	0.5
1996	1,522,451	1,166,628	249,114	21,240	8,226	76.7	16.3	1.4	0.6
1997	1,437,722	1,102,234	229,950	21,412	8,115	76.8	15.9	1.5	0.6
1998	1,340,557	1,022,851	209,814	21,411	7,531	76.4	15.5	1.6	0.6
1999	1,288,844	969,248	201,969	22,293	7,349	76.0	15.8	1.8	0.6
2000	1,251,452	980,037	202,574	22,610	7,589	75.3	15.9	2.1	0.7
2001	1,225,233	912,719	198,366	27,879	8,496	74.5	16.2	2.3	0.7

Source: U.S. Dept. of Defense, *Official Guard and Reserve Manpower Strengths and Statistics*, annual.

No. 503. National Guard—Summary: 1980 to 2000

[As of end of fiscal year; see text, Section 8, State and Local Government Finances and Employment. Includes Puerto Rico]

Item	Unit	1980	1985	1990	1995	1996	1997	1998	1999	2000
Army National Guard: Units . .	Number. . .	3,379	4,353	4,055	5,872	5,643	5,500	5,415	5,360	5300
Personnel [1]	1,000	368	438	444	375	373	370	362	357	353
Number of females	1,000	(NA)	(NA)	(NA)	(NA)	(NA)	(NA)	(NA)	38	38
Funds obligated [2]	Bil. dol. . . .	1.8	4.4	5.2	6.0	5.9	5.7	6.0	6.5	6.9
Value of equipment	Bil. dol. . . .	7.6	18.8	29.0	33.0	33.0	33.0	33.0	34.0	35.0
Air National Guard: Units. . . .	Number. . .	1,054	1,184	1,339	1,604	1,588	(NA)	1,541	1,541	1550
Personnel [1]	1,000	96	109	118	110	110	108	108	107	106
Number of females	1,000	(NA)	(NA)	(NA)	(NA)	(NA)	(NA)	(NA)	15	15
Funds obligated [2]	Bil. dol. . . .	1.7	2.8	3.2	4.2	4.6	4.5	4.4	4.8	5.6
Value of equipment (est.) [3] .	Bil. dol. . . .	5.2	21.4	26.4	38.3	40.1	42.0	41.0	43.0	44.0

NA Not available. [1] Officers and enlisted personnel. [2] Federal funds; includes personnel, operations, maintenance, and military construction. [3] Beginning 1985, increase due to repricing of aircraft to current year dollars to reflect true replacement value. Beginning 1994 includes value of aircraft and support equipment.

Source: National Guard Bureau, *Annual Review of the Chief, National Guard Bureau;* and unpublished data.

No. 504. Summary of U.S. Military Force Structure: 1993 to 2001

Item	1993	1994	1995	1996	1997	1998	1999	2000	2001
DEPARTMENT OF DEFENSE (DOD) STRATEGIC FORCES [1]									
Land-based ICBMs: [2]									
Minuteman II (1 warhead each) plus Minuteman III (3 warheads each)	737	625	535	530	530	500	500	500	500
Peacekeeper (10 warheads each)	50	50	50	50	50	50	50	50	50
Heavy bombers (PAI): [3]									
B-52.	84	64	74	56	56	56	56	56	56
B-1 [4]	84	84	60	60	60	70	74	80	82
B-2.	-	3	6	9	10	12	13	16	16
Submarine-launched ballistic missiles: [2]									
Poseidon (C-3) and Trident (C-4) missiles on pre-Ohio-class submarines .	96	48	-	-	-	-	-	-	-
Trident (C-4 and D-5) missiles on Ohio-class submarines.	312	336	360	384	408	432	432	432	432
DOD AIRLIFT AND SEALIFT FORCES									
Intertheater Airlift (PMAI): [5]									
C-5.	109	107	104	104	104	104	104	104	104
C-141	214	214	199	187	163	143	136	104	88
KC-10 [6]	57	54	54	54	54	54	54	54	54
C-17.	2	9	17	22	24	30	37	46	58
Intratheater Airlift (PMAI): [5]									
C-130 [7]	380	424	428	432	430	425	425	425	418
Sealift ships (Active): [8]									
Tankers.	20	18	18	12	13	10	10	10	10
Cargo	40	51	51	49	48	43	49	52	57
Sealift ships, reserve:									
RRF [9]	97	93	77	82	87	88	87	87	72
SPECIAL OPERATIONS FORCES									
Army:									
Special forces groups, (Active)	5	5	5	5	5	5	5	5	5
Special forces groups, (National Guard) .	2	2	2	2	2	2	2	2	2
Special forces groups (Reserve)	2	-	-	-	-	-	-	-	(NA)
Psychological operations groups (Active).	1	1	1	1	1	1	1	1	1
Special operations aviation regiments . . .	1	1	1	1	1	1	1	1	1
Ranger regiments	1	1	1	1	1	1	1	1	1
Civil affairs battalions (Active)	1	1	1	1	1	1	1	1	1
Civil affairs brigades (Reserve)	9	9	9	9	9	8	8	8	8
Civil affairs commands (Reserve).	3	3	3	3	3	4	4	4	4
Air Force:									
Special operations wings/groups:									
Active	3	3	3	3	3	3	3	3	3
National Guard	1	1	1	1	1	1	1	1	1
Special operations wing (Reserve)	1	1	1	1	1	1	1	1	1
Special tactics groups	1	1	1	1	1	1	1	1	1
Naval:									
Special boat squadrons	2	2	2	2	2	2	2	2	2

- Represents or rounds to zero.   NA Not available.   [1] Force levels shown are for the ends of the fiscal years in question. The actual force levels for FY 2000 and FY 2001 will depend on future decisions.   [2] Number of operational missiles. Not in maintenance or overhaul status.   [3] PAI=Primary aircraft inventory. PAI excludes backup and attrition reserve aircrafts as well as aircraft in depot maintenance. Total inventory counts will be higher than the PAI figures given here.   [4] B-1 are accountable under START I but will not be accountable under START II.   [5] PMAI = Primary mission aircraft inventory for active and reserve components. The numbers shown reflect only combat support and industrial funded PMAI aircraft and not developments/test or training aircraft.   [6] Includes 37 KC-10s allocated to an airlift code.   [7] Does not include Department of the Navy aircraft.   [8] Includes fast sea lift (FSS), afloat prepositioning, and common-user (charter) ships, plus (through FY 1998) aviation support ships. For FY 1999 on, includes LMSR and ready reserve force (RRF) ships tendered to the Military sealift command (MSC). FSS and LMSR vessels are maintained in a reserve, 4-day ready status.   [9] The RRF includes vessels assigned to 4-, 5-, 10-, or 20-day reactivation readiness groups. The ship counts shown exclude RRF vessels tendered to the MSC. Inventory figures for FY 1999, FY 2000, and FY 2001 include aviation support ships.

Source: U.S. Dept. of Defense, *Annual Report to the President and the Congress.*

U.S. Census Bureau, Statistical Abstract of the United States: 2002

No. 505. Veterans by Sex, by Period of Service, and by States: 2001

[In thousands (25,349 represents 25,349,000). As of end of fiscal year; see text, Section 8, State and Local Government Finances and Employment. Estimated starting with veteran's place of residence as of April 1, 1980, based on 1980 Census of Population data, extended to later years on the basis of estimates of veteran interstate migration, separations from the Armed Forces, and mortality; not directly comparable with earlier estimates previously published by the VA. Excludes 602,000 veterans whose only active-duty military service of less than 2 years occurred since Sept. 30, 1980, and who failed to satisfy the minimum service requirement. Also excludes a small number of National Guard personnel or reservists who incurred service-connected disabilities while on an initial tour of active duty for training only]

State	Total veterans [1]			World War I	World War II	Korean conflict	Vietnam era [1]	Persian Gulf War
	Both sexes	Male	Female					
United States ...	25,349	23,950	1,399	1	5,039	3,064	7,718	2,723
Alabama.........	462	434	28	-	84	55	137	62
Alaska.........	68	63	5	-	5	6	27	7
Arizona.........	515	483	32	-	102	59	161	50
Arkansas	283	268	15	-	55	33	86	34
California	2,318	2,180	137	-	476	283	717	214
Colorado........	411	384	27	-	62	44	138	48
Connecticut......	275	262	13	-	67	38	79	22
Delaware	78	74	4	-	15	9	24	7
District of Columbia .	47	44	3	-	10	6	14	5
Florida..........	1,784	1,676	108	-	412	210	507	183
Georgia	777	727	50	-	111	80	250	103
Hawaii	102	96	6	-	18	12	34	9
Idaho..........	125	118	7	-	22	14	39	15
Illinois	927	883	43	-	204	121	269	102
Indiana..........	562	535	27	-	106	68	173	62
Iowa	266	254	12	-	58	35	79	29
Kansas.........	245	233	12	-	50	30	76	25
Kentucky	372	354	18	-	73	45	115	41
Louisiana	388	365	23	-	75	45	114	56
Maine..........	154	145	9	-	28	17	47	18
Maryland	493	461	32	-	88	58	152	52
Massachusetts.....	533	506	27	-	128	73	153	41
Michigan........	891	846	46	-	172	106	273	105
Minnesota.......	427	408	19	-	81	53	139	39
Mississippi	252	237	15	-	50	31	71	34
Missouri	566	539	28	-	113	70	173	63
Montana........	106	100	7	-	18	12	34	14
Nebraska	157	149	9	-	31	20	47	18
Nevada	233	220	14	-	40	28	78	19
New Hampshire....	135	127	8	-	23	15	43	14
New Jersey.......	621	594	28	-	159	90	172	47
New Mexico	188	176	12	-	33	21	62	20
New York	1,294	1,231	63	-	307	176	355	131
North Carolina....	772	725	47	-	134	87	237	96
North Dakota......	56	53	3	-	11	7	18	6
Ohio	1,115	1,060	55	-	228	136	335	125
Oklahoma........	376	356	20	-	71	45	120	40
Oregon.........	367	346	22	-	68	39	119	40
Pennsylvania......	1,216	1,157	58	-	291	160	345	118
Rhode Island......	94	89	4	-	24	12	27	7
South Carolina.....	413	388	25	-	70	46	127	55
South Dakota	77	73	4	-	15	10	23	10
Tennessee	545	517	28	-	100	64	172	60
Texas..........	1,721	1,621	99	-	296	194	544	215
Utah	134	127	7	-	26	16	42	14
Vermont	59	55	3	-	11	7	18	6
Virginia.........	715	665	50	-	119	81	227	80
Washington.......	622	583	39	-	103	68	210	61
West Virginia......	202	193	9	-	42	26	61	23
Wisconsin........	487	463	24	-	95	60	152	48
Wyoming	53	50	3	-	9	6	18	6

- Represents or rounds to zero.   [1] Excludes reservists.
Source: U.S. Dept. of Veterans Affairs, Management Sciences Service (008B2), *Annual Report of the Secretary of Veterans Affairs.*

No. 506. Veterans Living by Age and by Service: 2001

[In thousands, except as indicated. (25,349 represents 25,349,000). As of July, 1. Includes Puerto Rico Estimated. Excludes 602,000 veterans whose only active duty military service of less than 2 years occurred since Sept. 30, 1980. See headnote, Table 505]

Age	Total veterans	Wartime veterans					
		Total [1]	Persian Gulf War	Vietnam era	Korean conflict	World War II	World War I
All ages.............	25,349	19,120	2,723	7,718	3,064	5,039	1
Under 35 years old	2,105	1,833	1,833	-	-	-	-
35-39 years old	1,444	432	432	-	-	-	-
40-44 years old	1,808	331	295	35	-	-	-
45-49 years old	2,028	1,487	128	1,249	-	-	-
50-54 years old	3,049	2,962	26	2,810	-	-	-
55-59 years old	3,098	2,722	6	2,667	-	-	-
60 years old and over	11,816	9,352	3	958	3,063	5,039	1
60-64 years old..........	2,263	882	2	789	69	-	-
65 years old and over	9,553	8,470	1	169	2,994	5,039	1

- Represents or rounds to zero.   [1] Veterans who served in more than one wartime period are counted only once.
Source: U.S. Dept. of Veterans Affairs, Office of Policy and Planning, *Veteran Population,* annual. See also <http://www.va.gov/vetdata/>.

National Defense and Veterans Affairs 335

No. 507. Disabled Veterans Receiving Compensation by Period of Service: 1980 to 2001

[In thousands (2,274 represents 2,274,000), except as indicated. As of end of fiscal year; see text, Section 8, State and Local Government. Represents veterans receiving compensation for service-connected disabilities. Totally disabled refers to veterans with any disability, mental or physical, deemed to be total and permanent which prevents the individual from maintaining a livelihood and are rated for disability at 100 percent]

Period of service	1980	1990	1994	1995	1996	1997	1998	1999	2000	2001
Disabled, all periods [1]	2,274	2,184	2,218	2,236	2,253	2,263	2,277	2,294	2,308	2,321
Peace time	262	444	492	514	529	539	550	561	567	569
World War I [1]	30	3	1	1	(Z)	(Z)	(Z)	(Z)	(Z)	(Z)
World War II.	1,193	876	731	692	655	616	578	541	505	470
Korea	236	209	195	191	187	182	179	175	171	166
Vietnam.	553	652	694	705	714	724	729	736	741	750
Persian Gulf.	(X)	(X)	106	134	168	202	241	282	325	366
Compensation (mil. dol.) . . .	6,104	9,284	11,056	11,644	11,072	13,004	13,791	14,542	15,489	16,529

X Not applicable.   Z Less than 500.   [1] Includes Spanish-American War and Mexican Border service, not shown separately.

Source: U.S. Dept. of Veterans Affairs, *Annual Report of the Secretary of Veterans Affairs;* and unpublished data.

No. 508. Veterans Benefits—Expenditures by Program: 1980 to 2001

[In millions of dollars (23,187 represents $23,187,000,000). For fiscal years ending in year shown; see text, Section 8, State and Local Government Finances and Employment. Beginning with fiscal year 1990, data are for outlays]

Program	1980	1990	1995	1996	1997	1998	1999	2000	2001
Total	23,187	28,998	37,775	36,915	39,277	41,776	43,166	47,087	45,037
Medical programs	6,042	11,582	16,255	16,337	16,900	17,575	18,223	19,637	21,330
Construction	300	661	641	698	597	515	521	466	421
General operating expenses	605	811	954	961	1,063	877	989	1,016	1,222
Compensation and pension	11,044	14,674	17,765	17,056	19,284	20,289	21,024	21,963	23,198
Vocational rehabilitation and education.	2,350	452	1,127	1,212	1,287	1,310	1,605	2,053	1,786
All other [1]	2,846	818	1,034	652	145	1,209	804	1,952	-2,921

[1] Includes insurance and indemnities, and miscellaneous funds and expenditures. (Excludes expenditures from personal funds of patients.)

Source: U.S. Dept. of Veterans Affairs, *Trend Data*, annual.

No. 509. Veterans Compensation and Pension Benefits—Number on Rolls by Period of Service and Status: 1980 to 2001

[As of Sept. 30. Living refers to veterans receiving compensation for disability incurred or aggravated while on active duty and war veterans receiving pension and benefits for nonservice connected disabilities. Deceased refers to deceased veterans whose dependents were receiving pensions and compensation benefits]

Period of service and veteran status	1980	1990	1995	1997	1998	1999	2000	2001
Total	4,646	3,584	3,330	3,281	3,263	3,252	3,236	3,218
Living veterans	3,195	2,746	2,669	2,667	2,668	2,673	2,672	2,669
Service connected	2,273	2,184	2,236	2,263	2,277	2,294	2,308	2,321
Nonservice connected	922	562	433	404	391	379	364	348
Deceased veterans	1,451	838	662	614	595	579	564	549
Service connected	358	320	307	305	303	304	307	307
Nonservice connected	1,093	518	355	309	291	274	257	241
Prior to World War I.	14	4	2	2	1	1	1	1
Living	(Z)	(Z)	(Z)	(Z)	(Z)	(Z)	(Z)	(Z)
World War I	692	198	89	61	51	42	34	28
Living	198	18	3	1	1	(Z)	(Z)	(Z)
World War II.	2,520	1,723	1,307	1,165	1,097	1,031	968	906
Living	1,849	1,294	961	842	785	730	676	624
Korean conflict [1]	446	390	368	351	342	333	323	313
Living	317	305	290	278	271	264	255	246
Peacetime	312	495	559	582	592	602	607	608
Living	262	444	514	539	550	561	567	569
Vietnam era [2]	662	774	868	913	932	953	969	987
Living	569	685	766	804	819	835	848	862
Persian Gulf War [3]	(X)	(X)	138	207	247	290	334	376
Living	(X)	(X)	134	203	242	283	326	368

X Not applicable.   Z Fewer than 500.   [1] Service during period June 27, 1950, to Jan. 31, 1955.   [2] Service from Aug. 5, 1964, to May 7, 1975.   [3] Service from August 2, 1990 to the present.

Source: U.S. Dept. of Veterans Affairs, *Annual Report of the Secretary of Veterans Affairs;* and unpublished data.

Social Insurance and Human Services

This section presents data related to governmental expenditures for social insurance and human services; governmental programs for old-age, survivors, disability, and health insurance (OASDHI); governmental employee retirement; private pension plans; government unemployment and temporary disability insurance; federal supplemental security income payments and aid to the needy; child and other welfare services; and federal food programs. Also included here are selected data on workers compensation and vocational rehabilitation, child support, child care, charity contributions, and philanthropic trusts and foundations.

The principal source for these data is the Social Security Administration's *Annual Statistical Supplement to the Social Security Bulletin* which presents current data on many of the programs.

Social insurance under the Social Security Act—Programs established by the Social Security Act provide protection against wage loss resulting from retirement, prolonged disability, death, or unemployment, and protection against the cost of medical care during old age and disability. The federal OASDI program provides monthly benefits to retired or disabled insured workers and their dependents and to survivors of insured workers. To be eligible, a worker must have had a specified period of employment in which OASDI taxes were paid. The age of eligibility for full retirement benefits has been 65 years old for many years. However, for persons born in 1938 or later that age will gradually increase until it reaches age 67 for those born after 1959. Reduced benefits may be obtained as early as age 62. The worker's spouse is under the same limitations. Survivor benefits are payable to dependents of deceased insured workers. Disability benefits are payable to an insured worker under full retirement age with a prolonged disability and to the disabled worker's dependents on the same basis as

dependents of retired workers. Disability benefits are provided at age 50 to the disabled widow or widower of a deceased worker who was fully insured at the time of death. Disabled children, aged 18 or older, of retired, disabled, or deceased workers are also eligible for benefits. A lump sum benefit is generally payable on the death of an insured worker to a spouse or minor children. For information on the medicare program, see Section 3, Health and Nutrition.

Retirement, survivors, disability, and hospital insurance benefits are funded by a payroll tax on annual earnings (up to a maximum of earnings set by law) of workers, employers, and the self-employed. The maximum taxable earnings are adjusted annually to reflect increasing wage levels (see Table 517). Effective January 1994, there is no dollar limit on wages and self-employment income subject to the hospital insurance tax. Tax receipts and benefit payments are administered through federal trust funds. Special benefits for uninsured persons; hospital benefits for persons aged 65 and over with specified amounts of social security coverage less than that required for cash benefit eligibility; and that part of the cost of supplementary medical insurance not financed by contributions from participants are financed from federal general revenues.

Unemployment insurance is presently administered by the U.S. Employment and Training Administration and each state's employment security agency. By agreement with the U.S. Secretary of Labor, state agencies also administer unemployment compensation for eligible ex-military personnel and federal employees. Under state unemployment insurance laws, benefits related to the individual's past earnings are paid to unemployed eligible workers. State laws vary concerning the length of time benefits are paid and their amount. In most states, benefits are payable for 26 weeks and, during periods of high unemployment, extended benefits are payable under a federal-state program to those who have exhausted their regular state benefits. Some states also supplement the basic benefit with allowances for dependents.

Unemployment insurance is funded by a federal unemployment tax levied on the taxable payrolls of most employers. Taxable payroll under the federal act and 12 state laws is the first $7,000 in wages paid each worker during a year. Forty-one states have taxable payrolls above $7,000. Employers are allowed a percentage credit of taxable payroll for contributions paid to states under state unemployment insurance laws. The remaining percent of the federal tax finances administrative costs, the federal share of extended benefits, and advances to states. About 97 percent of wage and salary workers are covered by unemployment insurance.

Retirement programs for government employees—The Civil Service Retirement System (CSRS) and the Federal Employees' Retirement System (FERS) are the two major programs providing age and service, disability, and survivor annuities for federal civilian employees. In general, employees hired after December 31, 1983, are covered under FERS and the social security program (OASDHI), and employees on staff prior to that date are members of CSRS and are covered under medicare. CSRS employees were offered the option of transferring to FERS during 1987 and 1998. There are separate retirement systems for the uniformed services (supplementing OASDHI) and for certain special groups of federal employees. State and local government employees are covered for the most part by state and local retirement systems similar to the federal CSRS. In many jurisdictions these benefits supplement OASDHI coverage.

Workers' compensation—All states provide protection against work-connected injuries and deaths, although some states exclude certain workers (e.g., domestic help). Federal laws cover federal employees, private employees in the District of Columbia, and longshoremen and harbor workers. In addition, the Social Security Administration and the Department of Labor administer "black lung" benefits programs for coal miners disabled by pneumoconiosis and for specified dependents and survivors. Specified occupational diseases are compensable to some extent. In most states, benefits are related to the worker's salary. The benefits may or may not be augmented by dependents' allowances or automatically adjusted to prevailing wage levels.

Income support—Income support programs are designed to provide benefits for persons with limited income and resources. The Supplemental Security Income (SSI) program and Temporary Assistance for Needy Families (TANF) program are the major programs providing monthly payments. In addition, a number of programs provide money payments or in-kind benefits for special needs or purposes. Several programs offer food and nutritional services. Also, various federal-state programs provide energy assistance, public housing, and subsidized housing to individuals and families with low incomes. General assistance may also be available at the state or local level.

The SSI program, administered by the Social Security Administration, provides income support to persons aged 65 or older and blind or disabled adults and children. Eligibility requirements and federal payment standards are nationally uniform. Most states supplement the basic SSI payment for all or selected categories of persons.

The Personal Responsibility and Work Opportunity Reconciliation Act of 1996 contained provisions that replaced the Aid to Families With Dependent Children (AFDC), Job Opportunities and Basic Skills (JOBS), and Emergency Assistance programs with the Temporary Assistance for Needy Families block grant program. This law contains strong work requirements, comprehensive child support enforcement, support for families moving from welfare to work, and other features. The TANF became effective as soon as each state submitted a complete plan implementing TANF, but no later than July 1, 1997. The AFDC program provided cash assistance based on need, income, resources, and family size.

U.S. Census Bureau, Statistical Abstract of the United States: 2002

Federal food stamp program—Under the food stamp program, single persons and those living in households meeting nationwide standards for income and assets may receive coupons redeemable for food at most retail food stores. The monthly amount of coupons a unit receives is determined by household size and income. Households without income receive the determined monthly cost of a nutritionally adequate diet for their household size. This amount is updated to account for food price increases. Households with income receive the difference between the amount of a nutritionally adequate diet and 30 percent of their income, after certain allowable deductions.

To qualify for the program, a household must have less than $2,000 in disposable assets ($3,000 if one member is aged 60 or older), gross income below 130 percent of the official poverty guidelines for the household size, and net income below 100 percent of the poverty guidelines. Households with a person aged 60 or older or a disabled person receiving SSI, social security, state general assistance, or veterans' disability benefits may have gross income exceeding 130 percent of the poverty guidelines. All households in which all members receive TANF or SSI are categorically eligible for food stamps without meeting these income or resource criteria. Households are certified for varying lengths of time, depending on their income sources and individual circumstances.

Health and welfare services—Programs providing health and welfare services are aided through federal grants to states for child welfare services, vocational rehabilitation, activities for the aged, maternal and child health services, maternity and infant care projects, comprehensive health services, and a variety of public health activities. For information about the medicaid program, see Section 3, Health and Nutrition.

Noncash benefits—The U.S. Census Bureau annually collects data on the characteristics of recipients of noncash (in-kind) benefits to supplement the collection of annual money income data in the Current Population Survey (see text, Section 1, Population, and Section 14, Prices). Noncash benefits are those benefits received in a form other than money which serve to enhance or improve the economic well-being of the recipient. As for money income, the data for noncash benefits are for the calendar year prior to the date of the interview. The major categories of noncash benefits covered are public transfers (e.g., food stamps, school lunch, public housing, and medicaid) and employer or union-provided benefits to employees.

Statistical reliability—For discussion of statistical collection, estimation, and sampling procedures and measures of statistical reliability applicable to HHS and Census Bureau data, see Appendix III.

U.S. Census Bureau, Statistical Abstract of the United States: 2002

No. 510. Government Transfer Payments to Individuals—Summary: 1970 to 2000

[In billions of dollars (69.3 represents $69,300,000,000)]

Year	Total	Retirement & disability insurance benefits	Medical payments	Income maintenance benefits	Unemployment insurance benefits	Veterans benefits	Federal education & training assistance payments [1]	Other [2]
1970	69.3	34.3	13.0	9.9	4.2	7.5	0.4	0.1
1975	159.3	72.0	30.7	21.5	18.2	14.0	1.0	1.9
1980	262.7	128.8	62.0	34.3	18.7	14.7	4.1	0.2
1985	394.7	197.2	114.6	44.4	15.9	16.6	5.5	0.6
1990	561.4	263.9	189.1	63.5	18.2	17.7	7.3	1.8
1991	635.7	285.7	223.5	72.5	26.9	18.1	7.3	1.8
1992	714.8	304.7	257.3	84.6	39.7	18.6	8.0	2.0
1993	760.6	320.8	284.7	90.3	34.9	19.4	9.1	1.4
1994	792.8	334.8	308.3	95.6	24.1	19.7	8.6	1.8
1995	841.0	350.0	337.5	100.4	21.9	20.5	9.0	1.6
1996	883.0	364.6	361.3	102.5	22.5	21.4	8.6	2.1
1997	914.9	379.4	379.6	100.3	20.3	22.2	11.5	1.7
1998	935.1	392.0	386.3	100.7	19.9	23.2	11.2	1.9
1999	965.2	403.0	399.6	104.4	20.7	24.1	11.4	2.1
2000	1,013.4	425.3	423.2	106.4	20.7	24.9	10.7	2.1

[1] See footnote 9, Table 511. [2] See footnote 10, Table 511.

No. 511. Government Transfer Payments to Individuals by Type: 1990 to 2000

[In millions of dollars (561,399 represents $561,399,000,000)]

Item	1990	1995	1996	1997	1998	1999	2000
Total	561,399	841,041	883,042	914,942	935,058	965,206	1,013,424
Retirement & disability insurance benefit payments	263,854	350,027	364,623	379,415	391,987	402,990	425,333
Old age, survivors, & disability insurance	244,135	327,667	341,987	356,602	369,347	379,895	401,408
Railroad retirement and disability	7,221	8,028	8,085	8,193	8,225	8,203	8,265
Worker's compensation payments (federal & state)	8,618	10,530	10,795	10,606	10,344	10,560	11,111
Other government disability insurance & retirement [1]	3,880	3,802	3,756	4,014	4,071	4,332	4,549
Medical payments	189,099	337,532	361,342	379,557	386,273	399,597	423,180
Medicare	107,929	180,283	195,581	209,198	208,755	208,126	215,882
Public assistance medical care [2]	78,176	155,017	163,629	168,288	175,475	189,464	205,281
Military medical insurance [3]	2,994	2,232	2,132	2,071	2,043	2,007	2,017
Income maintenance benefit payments	63,481	100,444	102,494	100,288	100,694	104,421	106,421
Supplemental Security Income (SSI)	16,670	27,726	28,903	29,154	30,322	31,023	31,675
Family assistance [4]	19,187	22,637	20,325	17,717	17,026	17,683	18,277
Food stamps	14,741	22,447	21,955	18,732	16,465	15,473	14,939
Other income maintenance [5]	12,883	27,634	31,311	34,685	36,881	40,242	41,530
Unemployment insurance benefit payments	18,208	21,864	22,480	20,299	19,859	20,724	20,707
State unemployment insurance compensation	17,644	20,975	21,614	19,469	19,154	20,010	19,938
Unemployment compensation for federal civilian employees	215	339	326	281	236	206	227
Unemployment compensation for railroad employees	89	62	65	72	61	65	81
Unemployment compensation for veterans	144	320	279	259	211	201	182
Other unemployment compensation [6]	116	168	196	218	197	242	279
Veterans benefit payments	17,687	20,545	21,430	22,233	23,168	24,058	24,939
Veterans pension and disability	15,550	17,565	18,286	19,061	20,049	20,904	21,885
Veterans readjustment [7]	257	1,086	1,138	1,234	1,220	1,323	1,331
Veterans life insurance benefits	1,868	1,883	1,997	1,929	1,891	1,823	1,714
Other assistance to veterans [8]	12	11	9	9	8	8	9
Federal education & training assistance payments [9]	7,300	9,007	8,568	11,481	11,189	11,366	10,729
Other payments to individuals [10]	1,770	1,622	2,105	1,669	1,888	2,050	2,115

[1] Consists largely of temporary disability payments, pension benefit guaranty payments, and black lung payments.
[2] Consists of medicaid and other medical vendor payments.   [3] Consists of payments made under the TriCare Management Program (formerly called CHAMPUS) for the medical care of dependents of active duty military personnel and of retired military personnel and their dependents at nonmilitary medical facilities.   [4] Through 1995, consists of emergency assistance and aid to families with dependent children. Beginning with 1998, consists of benefits— generally known as temporary assistance for needy families— provided under the Personal Responsibility and Work Opportunity Reconciliation Act of 1996. For 1996-97, consists of payments under all three of these programs.   [5] Consists largely of general assistance, expenditures for food under the supplemental program for women, infants, and children; refugee assistance; foster home care and adoption assistance; earned income tax credits; and energy assistance.   [6] Consists of trade readjustment allowance payments, Redwood Park benefit payments, public service employment benefit payments, and transitional benefit payments.   [7] Consists largely of veterans' readjustment benefit payments, educational assistance to spouses and children of disabled or deceased veterans, payments to paraplegics, and payments for autos and conveyances for disabled veterans.   [8] Consists largely of state and local government payments to veterans.   [9] Excludes veterans. Consists largely of federal fellowship payments (National Science Foundation fellowships and traineeships, subsistence payments to state maritime academy cadets, and other federal fellowships), interest subsidy on higher education loans, basic educational opportunity grants, and Job Corps payments.   [10] Consists largely of Bureau of Indian Affairs payments, education exchange payments, Alaska Permanent Fund dividend payments, compensation of survivors of public safety officers, compensation of victims of crime, disaster relief payments, compensation for Japanese internment, and other special payments to individuals.

Source of Tables 510 and 511: U.S. Bureau of Economic Analysis, "Regional Accounts Data, Annual State Personal Income"; <http://www.bea.doc.gov/bea/regional/spi/>; (accessed 21 May 2002).

No. 512. Government Transfer Payments to Individuals by State: 1990 to 2000

[In millions of dollars (561,399 represents $561,399,000,000)]

State	1990, total	1995, total	Total	Retirement & disability insurance benefits	Medical payments	Income maintenance benefits	Unemployment insurance benefits	Veterans benefits	Federal education & training assistance payments [1]	Other [2]
									2000	
U.S.	561,399	841,041	1,013,424	425,333	423,180	106,421	20,707	24,939	10,729	2,115
AL.	8,738	13,395	16,701	7,187	6,619	1,857	237	569	220	12
AK.	1,294	1,860	2,908	482	725	292	111	85	13	1,198
AZ.	7,864	12,653	15,802	7,560	5,771	1,426	182	554	230	80
AR.	5,459	8,063	9,841	4,429	3,636	1,049	199	422	102	4
CA.	65,912	96,576	113,693	42,244	45,834	19,407	2,509	2,115	1,471	113
CO	5,796	9,273	11,058	4,872	4,453	990	153	434	141	17
CT.	8,121	12,470	14,325	5,941	6,516	1,238	340	200	84	5
DE.	1,364	2,148	2,725	1,310	1,036	213	71	67	26	1
DC	1,676	2,318	2,676	611	1,471	429	58	61	42	4
FL.	33,029	52,572	64,371	29,533	26,597	5,058	709	1,916	524	34
GA	11,843	19,042	23,485	9,813	9,468	2,773	338	820	258	14
HI	2,139	3,480	3,893	1,655	1,341	618	108	128	40	3
ID	1,849	2,836	3,729	1,882	1,260	287	113	128	54	5
IL	25,216	36,032	41,461	18,211	16,694	4,256	1,231	601	419	48
IN	11,363	16,191	20,278	9,696	7,975	1,681	305	382	229	11
IA	6,065	8,215	9,823	5,054	3,518	699	214	214	116	7
KS.	5,264	7,298	8,810	4,300	3,331	650	178	233	109	9
KY.	8,343	12,503	15,891	6,840	6,387	1,789	293	426	150	6
LA	9,284	15,257	16,901	6,074	7,741	2,231	179	456	213	8
ME	2,814	4,203	5,155	2,141	2,137	523	86	221	44	3
MD	9,168	13,513	16,641	7,069	7,075	1,614	279	429	164	11
MA	16,490	23,068	26,888	9,889	13,144	2,221	798	582	243	11
MI	22,351	29,984	36,271	16,234	14,486	3,723	918	569	326	15
MN	9,469	13,241	15,774	7,021	6,472	1,336	399	378	153	15
MS	5,609	8,648	10,745	4,221	4,436	1,440	128	342	166	13
MO	11,277	17,029	21,186	9,241	9,079	1,808	331	502	214	11
MT	1,893	2,636	3,092	1,546	1,052	255	71	119	39	10
NE.	3,141	4,425	5,561	2,702	2,168	384	55	188	62	3
NV.	2,479	4,217	5,695	2,924	1,923	397	200	197	47	7
NH	2,013	3,461	3,931	1,915	1,580	238	27	130	30	1
NJ.	18,376	27,593	32,139	14,321	13,695	2,269	1,079	490	270	15
NM	2,786	4,586	5,906	2,406	2,202	792	86	265	91	63
NY.	54,178	82,755	95,679	30,796	49,214	11,837	1,595	1,140	1,058	39
NC	12,658	21,054	27,349	11,887	11,209	2,599	504	881	251	17
ND	1,510	1,940	2,366	1,132	932	157	33	61	29	22
OH	26,578	36,753	42,829	20,116	16,891	3,862	724	840	372	24
OK	6,615	9,937	11,954	5,418	4,496	1,141	125	607	152	15
OR	6,374	9,529	11,936	5,793	4,168	1,011	415	391	142	17
PA.	32,238	45,821	55,208	23,385	24,427	4,521	1,454	990	414	18
RI	2,776	4,027	4,793	1,880	2,136	461	151	109	50	6
SC.	6,724	10,621	13,800	6,151	5,380	1,429	211	467	150	13
SD.	1,445	2,061	2,489	1,152	949	194	16	98	40	40
TN.	10,814	17,338	22,243	8,820	10,150	2,094	387	603	175	13
TX.	29,214	49,155	60,798	23,617	26,450	6,756	1,107	2,040	766	62
UT.	2,594	3,892	4,919	2,362	1,781	408	119	130	109	10
VT.	1,163	1,743	2,179	939	877	235	45	57	25	1
VA.	10,174	15,539	19,352	9,518	6,877	1,709	197	812	227	11
WA	10,973	16,608	20,336	9,344	7,306	1,724	967	743	221	32
WV	5,125	7,426	8,627	4,318	3,012	829	120	268	77	3
WI	10,941	14,829	17,714	8,552	6,642	1,403	525	417	160	16
WY	819	1,225	1,495	823	462	110	28	52	18	2

[1] Excludes veterans. Consists largely of federal fellowship payments (National Science Foundation, fellowships and traineeships, subsistence payments to state maritime academy cadets, and other federal fellowships), interest subsidy on higher education loans, basic educational opportunity grants, and Job Corps payments.   [2] Consists largely of Bureau of Indian Affairs payments, education exchange payments, Alaska Permanent Fund dividend payments, compensation of survivors of public safety officers, compensation of victims of crime, disaster relief payments, compensation for Japanese internment, and other special payments to individuals.

Source: U.S. Bureau of Economic Analysis, "Regional Accounts Data, Annual State Personal Income"; <http://www.bea.doc.gov/bea/regional/spi/>; (accessed 21 May 2002).

Social Insurance and Human Services 341

No. 513. Number of Persons With Income by Specified Sources of Income: 2000

[In thousands (196,957 represents 196,957,000). **Persons 15 years old and over as of March 2001.** Based on Current Population Survey; see text, Sections 1, Population, and 13, Income, Expenditure, and Wealth, and Appendix III]

Source of income	Total persons with income	Under 65 years old	65 years old and over	White	Black	Hispanic origin [1]
Total	**196,957**	**164,700**	**32,257**	**165,115**	**22,648**	**19,336**
Earnings	149,816	144,256	5,559	125,050	17,467	16,077
Wages and salary	141,025	136,484	4,541	117,215	16,993	15,526
Nonfarm self-employment	12,462	11,430	1,033	10,990	798	784
Farm self-employment	2,619	2,382	237	2,363	171	112
Unemployment compensation	4,967	4,849	119	3,986	773	581
Workers compensation	2,104	1,945	159	1,751	268	258
Social security, railroad retirement	38,436	8,820	29,616	33,629	3,782	2,201
Supplemental security income (SSI)	4,685	3,479	1,206	3,193	1,180	627
Public assistance	2,253	2,187	66	1,416	696	479
TANF/Welfare (AFDC) only [2]	1,615	1,578	37	976	531	382
Other assistance only	567	537	29	409	129	90
Both	71	71	-	31	36	7
Veterans payments	2,339	1,207	1,131	1,983	300	81
Survivors benefits	2,726	962	1,764	2,468	192	112
Company or union	1,196	267	929	1,088	88	49
Disability benefits	1,537	1,316	221	1,229	264	112
Company or union	444	384	60	339	97	25
Pensions	14,375	4,357	10,018	12,937	1,184	458
Company or union	9,002	2,446	6,555	8,187	669	297
Federal government	1,260	291	969	1,073	155	46
Military retirement	865	488	377	747	83	31
State or local government	2,876	976	1,900	2,566	262	75
Interest	102,443	83,698	18,745	91,457	6,710	5,058
Dividends	39,111	32,294	6,817	35,887	1,579	1,112
Rents, royalties, estates or trusts	11,405	8,595	2,809	10,422	493	530
Education	7,578	7,527	51	6,067	1,058	570
Pell grant only	1,385	1,366	18	991	297	166
Other government only	1,083	1,070	14	899	142	107
Scholarships only	2,098	2,095	3	1,702	247	130
Child support	5,255	5,241	14	4,161	983	478
Alimony	448	406	42	407	30	16
Financial assistance	1,917	1,818	100	1,507	247	134
Other income	1,244	999	245	1,042	128	69
Combinations of income types:						
Government transfer payments	53,989	23,169	30,820	45,489	6,679	4,041
Public assistance or SSI	6,618	5,370	1,248	4,401	1,778	1,073
Property income [3]	107,294	87,749	19,545	95,713	7,078	5,392

- Represents or rounds to zero.   [1] Persons of Hispanic origin may be of any race.   [2] TANF-Temporary assistance for needy families program; AFDC=Aid to Families with Dependent Children program.   [3] Includes estates and trusts reported as survivor benefits.

Source: U.S. Census Bureau, "Table PINC-09. Source of Income in 2000—Number With Income and Mean Income of Specified Type in 2000 of People 15 Years Old and Over, by Race, Hispanic Origin and Sex"; published 10 December 2001; <http://ferret.bls.census.gov/macro/032001/perinc/new09000.htm>.

No. 514. Households Receiving Means-Tested Noncash Benefits: 1980 to 2000

[In thousands (82,368 represents 82,368,000), except percent. **Households as of March of following year.** Covers civilian noninstitutional population, including persons in the Armed Forces living off post or with their families on post. A means-tested benefit program requires that the household's income and/or assets fall below specified guidelines in order to qualify for benefits. There are general trends toward underestimation of noncash beneficiaries. Households are classified according to poverty status of family or nonfamily householder; for explanation of poverty level, see text, Section 13, Income, Expenditures, and Wealth. Data for 1980 and 1990 based on 1980 census population controls; beginning 1995, based on 1990 census population controls. Based on Current Population Survey; see text, Section 1, Population, and Appendix III]

Type of benefit received					2000			
						Below poverty level		Above poverty level
	1980	1990	1995	1999	Total	Number	Percent of total	
Total households	**82,368**	**94,312**	**99,627**	**104,705**	**106,418**	**11,881**	**100**	**94,537**
Receiving at least one noncash benefit	14,266	16,098	21,148	18,996	20,131	6,873	58	13,258
Not receiving cash public assistance	7,860	8,819	13,335	12,999	14,465	4,059	34	10,406
Receiving cash public assistance [1]	6,407	7,279	7,813	5,997	5,667	2,814	24	2,853
Total households receiving—								
Food stamps	6,769	7,163	8,388	5,738	5,563	3,501	30	2,062
School lunch	5,532	6,252	8,607	7,258	7,185	2,704	23	4,481
Public housing	2,777	4,339	4,846	4,447	4,689	2,397	20	2,292
Medicaid	8,287	10,321	14,111	13,477	14,328	5,264	44	9,064

[1] Households receiving money from aid to families with dependent children program (beginning 1999, temporary assistance for needy families program), supplemental security income program or other public assistance programs.

Source: U.S. Census Bureau, "Table NC1. Means-Tested Noncash Benefits Received by Households, by Selected Household Characteristics, Race and Hispanic Origin, and Poverty Status: 2000"; published 10 December 2001; <http://ferret.bls.census.gov/macro/032001/noncash/nc1000.htm> and *Current Population Reports*, P-60 reports.

No. 515. Government Expenditures for Income-Tested Benefits by Type of Benefit: 1980 to 2000

[In millions of dollars (105,312 represents $105,312,000,000). For years ending September 30. Programs cover:d provide cash, goods, or services to persons who make no payment and render no service in return. In case of many programs, including family cash welfare, food and housing programs, job and training programs and some educational programs, some recipients must work or study. Most of the programs base eligibility on individual, household, or family income, but some use group or area income tests; and a few offer help on the basis of presumed need. Constant dollar figures are based on the Consumer Price Index for all Urban Consumers]

Level of government and year	Total spending		Constant (2000) dollars							
	Current dollars	Constant (2000) dollars	Medical benefits	Cash aid	Food benefits	Housing benefits	Education benefits	Jobs/training	Services	Energy aid
TOTAL										
1980	105,312	224,866	69,606	61,332	28,924	21,869	11,052	18,589	9,818	3,675
1985	144,291	231,158	79,204	60,294	32,666	24,207	15,972	6,370	8,773	3,672
1990	213,055	282,815	115,250	72,019	33,326	23,926	19,102	5,631	11,267	2,294
1993	314,451	374,152	170,155	89,003	43,237	32,672	17,941	6,346	12,889	1,909
1994	352,487	408,624	187,153	100,067	43,909	34,142	18,015	6,393	16,633	2,311
1995	371,109	418,484	196,922	103,291	43,558	35,764	18,146	6,132	12,775	1,896
1996	375,310	411,725	195,199	101,426	42,876	35,656	17,967	5,138	12,090	1,373
1997	384,465	414,821	198,815	99,463	39,908	35,561	18,737	4,246	12,587	1,502
1998	394,687	414,944	203,549	96,269	36,906	34,681	19,052	5,142	17,939	1,405
1999	408,405	421,379	213,619	96,576	35,718	29,848	19,058	5,831	19,291	1,439
2000	436,985	436,985	225,858	91,703	34,347	34,906	20,385	7,347	20,724	1,715
FEDERAL										
1980	80,679	172,268	41,421	40,522	27,948	21,869	10,441	18,416	7,975	3,675
1985	106,061	169,912	44,664	39,227	31,018	24,207	15,245	6,240	5,689	3,622
1990	151,990	201,756	66,671	48,378	31,687	23,926	18,267	5,277	5,421	2,129
1993	225,768	268,632	101,200	63,479	41,374	31,089	17,030	5,677	6,958	1,825
1994	250,066	289,891	108,609	73,494	41,857	32,270	16,968	5,635	8,836	2,222
1995	262,899	296,460	114,359	76,594	41,494	33,142	17,069	5,217	6,779	1,805
1996	268,097	294,110	114,009	76,804	40,770	32,958	16,919	4,432	6,924	1,293
1997	274,153	292,947	115,176	76,773	37,799	32,937	17,641	4,056	7,130	1,434
1998	280,138	294,516	116,604	76,687	34,869	31,939	17,857	4,390	10,848	1,322
1999	291,022	300,267	123,476	76,726	33,618	29,848	17,830	4,929	12,490	1,351
2000	306,520	306,520	131,468	72,516	32,182	29,261	19,043	6,219	14,201	1,630
STATE AND LOCAL										
1980	24,633	52,598	28,185	20,810	976	-	611	173	1,843	50
1985	38,230	61,246	34,540	21,067	1,648	-	727	130	3,084	165
1990	61,065	81,059	48,579	23,641	1,639	-	835	354	5,846	84
1993	88,683	105,520	68,955	25,524	1,863	1,583	911	669	5,931	89
1994	102,421	118,733	78,544	26,573	2,052	1,872	1,047	758	7,797	91
1995	108,210	122,024	82,563	26,697	2,064	2,622	1,077	915	5,996	80
1996	107,213	117,615	81,190	24,622	2,106	2,698	1,048	706	5,166	68
1997	110,312	117,874	83,639	22,690	2,109	2,624	1,096	190	5,457	83
1998	114,549	120,428	86,945	19,582	2,037	2,742	1,195	752	7,091	88
1999	117,383	121,112	90,143	19,850	2,100	(NA)	1,228	902	6,801	88
2000	130,465	130,465	94,390	19,187	2,165	5,645	1,342	1,128	6,523	85

- Represents or rounds to zero.   NA Not available.

Source: Library of Congress, Congressional Research Service, "Cash and Noncash Benefits for Persons With Limited Income: Eligibility Rules, Recipient and Expenditure Data, FY1998-FY2000"; CRS Report RL 31228; November 19, 2001.

No. 516. Cash and Noncash Benefits for Persons With Limited Income: 1999 and 2000

[For years ending September 30, except as noted (408,405 represents $408,405,000,000). Programs covered provide cash, goods, or services to persons who make no payment and render no service in return. In case of many programs, including family cash welfare, food and housing programs, job and training programs and some educational programs, some recipients must work or study. Most of the programs base eligibility on individual, household, or family income, but some use group or area income tests; and a few offer help on the basis of presumed need]

Program	Average monthly recipients (1,000)		Expenditures (mil. dol.)					
			Total		Federal		State and local	
	1999	2000	1999	2000	1999	2000	1999	2000
Total	(X)	(X)	408,405	436,985	291,022	306,520	117,383	130,465
Medical care [1]	(X)	(X)	207,042	225,858	119,674	131,468	87,368	94,390
Medicaid [2] [3]	42,020	(NA)	190,443	207,195	107,819	117,684	82,624	89,511
Veterans [4] [5]	114	123	6,781	7,420	6,781	7,420	-	-
General assistance [5]	(NA)	(NA)	4,052	3,898	-	-	4,052	3,898
State children's health insurance program	1,980	3,300	1,182	2,474	922	1,929	260	545
Indian health services [2] [3]	1,500+	1,500+	2,240	2,391	2,240	2,391	-	-
Maternal and child health services	27,097	(NA)	1,131	1,144	699	708	432	436
Consolidated health centers [2]	9,150	9,600	925	1,018	925	1,018	-	-
Cash aid [1]	(X)	(X)	93,603	91,703	74,364	72,516	19,239	19,187
Supplemental security income [3] [8] . .	6,595	6,609	34,838	35,066	30,616	30,718	4,222	4,348
Temporary assistance for needy families (TANF) [7]	7,203	6,035	15,741	14,490	7,882	6,852	7,859	7,638
Earned income tax credit (refunded portion) [8] . .	57,300	55,320	27,344	25,800	27,344	25,800	-	-
Foster care	302	312	7,585	7,941	4,012	4,237	3,573	3,704
General assistance [8]	(NA)	(NA)	2,867	2,649	-	-	2,867	2,649
Pensions for needy veterans [9] [10]	671	635	3,084	2,953	3,084	2,953	-	-
Food benefits [1]	(X)	(X)	34,618	34,347	32,583	32,182	2,035	2,165
Food stamps [3] [11]	19,300	18,200	20,984	20,341	19,022	18,255	1,962	2,086
School lunch program [12] [13]	15,382	15,389	5,507	5,629	5,507	5,629	(NA)	(NA)
Women, infants and children [3] [14]	7,300	7,200	3,927	3,944	3,927	3,944	-	-
Child and adult care food program [15]	1,900	1,900	1,468	1,557	1,468	1,557	-	-
School breakfast [12]	6,275	6,339	1,299	1,349	1,299	1,349	-	-
Housing benefits [1]	(X)	(X)	28,929	34,906	28,929	29,261	(NA)	5,645
Low-income housing asst. (Sec. 8) [16] [17]	2,985	3,196	15,652	15,972	15,652	15,972	-	-
Low-rent public housing [18] [19] . .	1,274	1,267	5,956	6,526	5,956	6,526	(NA)	(NA)
Rural housing loans [18] [19]	54	46	3,944	3,291	3,944	3,291	-	-
Home investment partnerships [3] [19] [20]	76	86	1,600	7,275	1,600	1,636	(NA)	5,639
Education aid [1]	(X)	(X)	18,471	20,385	17,281	19,043	1,190	1,342
Pell grants [21] [22]	3,838	3,810	7,345	7,704	7,345	7,704	-	-
Head Start [21]	826	858	5,823	6,583	4,658	5,266	1,165	1,317
Stafford loans [21] [22]	5,388	5,354	2,673	3,332	2,673	3,332	-	-
Federal Work-Study Program [21] [22]	892	930	830	870	830	870	-	-
Services [1]	(X)	(X)	18,697	20,724	12,105	14,201	6,592	6,523
Social services (Title 20) [23]	(NA)	(NA)	6,149	5,623	3,171	2,854	2,978	2,769
Child care for TANF recipients and ex-recipients [24]	(NA)	(NA)	1,139	2,308	604	1,411	535	897
Child care and development block grant [25]	1,875	1,800	6,236	6,934	4,640	5,059	1,596	1,875
TANF services	(NA)	(NA)	3,095	3,687	1,612	2,705	1,483	982
Jobs and training [1]	(X)	(X)	5,651	7,348	4,777	6,219	874	1,128
TANF work activities	(X)	(X)	1,654	2,272	1,125	1,515	529	757
Training for disadvantaged adults and youth [26]	513	(NA)	1,084	1,950	1,084	1,950	-	-
Job Corps	71	70	1,307	1,357	1,307	1,357	-	-
Energy assistance [1]	(X)	(X)	1,394	1,715	1,309	1,630	85	85
Low-income energy assistance [3] [27]	4,400	4,100	1,176	1,495	1,176	1,495	(NA)	(NA)

- Represents zero. NA Not available. X Not applicable. [1] Includes other programs not shown separately. [2] Recipient data represent unduplicated annual number. [3] Expenditures include administrative expenses. [4] Medical care for veterans with a nonservice-connected disability. [5] Estimated expenditures. [6] Includes state-administered SSI supplements. [7] Excludes data for child support operations. [8] Estimated recipients. [9] Estimated recipients as of September. [10] Includes dependents and survivors. [11] Includes Puerto Rico's nutritional assistance program. [12] Free and reduced-price segments. [13] Includes estimate of commodity assistance. [14] Special supplemental food program for women, infants and children. [15] Recipient data are numbers of children receiving free or reduced price meals and snacks in child care centers and estimates of children in family day care homes with incomes below 185 percent of poverty. [16] Recipient data represent units eligible for payment at end of year. [17] Includes operating subsidies, capital grants, and HUD-administered Indian housing. [18] Recipient data represent total families or dwelling units during year. [19] Expenditure data represent amounts obligated. [20] Recipient data are housing units provided or rehabilitated. [21] Recipient data are total numbers for the school year ending in year shown. [22] Expenditure data are appropriations available for school year ending the fiscal year named. [23] Nonfederal expenditure data are rough estimates. [24] P.L. 104-193, which created TANF, established a mandatory block grant for TANF-related child care. [25] Recipient data are estimated number of children served. [26] Recipient data are total number of participants. [27] Households served during the year with heating and winter crisis aid. Federal funds include amounts transferred to other programs serving the needy.

Source: Library of Congress, Congressional Research Service, "Cash and Noncash Benefits for Persons With Limited Income: Eligibility Rules, Recipient and Expenditure Data, FY1998-FY2000"; CRS Report RL31228; November 19, 2001.

No. 517. Social Security—Covered Employment, Earnings, and Contribution Rates: 1980 to 2001

[**140.4 represents 140,400,000.** Includes Puerto Rico, Virgin Islands, American Samoa, and Guam. Represents all reported employment. Data are estimated. OASDHI=Old-age, survivors, disability, and health insurance; SMI=Supplementary medical insurance]

Item	Unit	1980	1985	1990	1995	1996	1997	1998	1999	2000	2001
Workers with insured											
status [1]	Million. .	140.4	150.9	164.0	173.2	175.3	177.7	180.0	182.4	184.8	187.3
Male	Million. .	76.6	80.7	86.5	90.2	91.1	92.1	93.0	94.0	95.0	96.1
Female	Million. .	63.8	70.1	77.5	83.0	84.2	85.7	87.1	88.4	89.7	91.1
Under 25 years old.	Million. .	25.7	22.0	21.3	18.8	18.8	19.1	19.5	20.0	20.6	21.1
25 to 34 years old	Million. .	36.5	40.1	41.6	39.4	38.9	38.2	37.5	36.9	36.4	36.2
35 to 44 years old	Million. .	23.0	29.9	36.4	40.6	41.2	41.8	42.2	42.5	42.4	42.2
45 to 54 years old	Million. .	18.6	19.2	22.8	29.5	30.8	31.9	33.1	34.4	35.8	36.9
55 to 59 years old	Million. .	9.3	9.0	8.7	9.7	10.2	10.7	11.3	11.8	12.2	13.0
60 to 64 years old	Million. .	8.2	8.8	8.8	8.5	8.5	8.8	8.9	9.2	9.4	9.7
65 to 69 years old	Million. .	7.0	7.5	8.2	8.1	8.1	8.0	7.9	7.9	7.9	8.0
70 years old and over. . .	Million. .	12.1	14.3	16.3	18.5	18.8	19.3	19.6	19.8	20.1	20.2
Workers reported with—											
Taxable earnings [2]	Million. .	113	120	134	141	143	146	149	151	154	153
Maximum earnings [2]. . . .	Million. .	10	8	8	8	9	9	9	9	10	10
Earnings in covered											
employment [2]	Bil. dol..	1,329	1,942	2,704	3,359	3,566	3,847	4,143	4,435	4,786	5,043
Reported taxable [2]	Bil. dol. .	1,178	1,725	2,359	2,920	3,074	3,285	3,522	3,745	3,991	4,198
Percent of total	Percent.	88.6	88.8	87.2	86.9	86.2	85.4	85.0	84.4	83.4	83.2
Average per worker:											
Total earnings [2]	Dollars .	11,761	16,125	20,227	23,818	24,869	26,324	27,814	29,289	31,144	32,860
Taxable earnings [2] . . .	Dollars .	10,430	14,326	17,642	20,703	21,432	22,483	23,644	24,733	25,970	27,355
Annual maximum taxable											
earnings [3]	Dollars .	25,900	39,600	51,300	61,200	62,700	65,400	68,400	72,600	76,200	80,400
Contribution rates for OASDHI: [4]											
Each employer and											
employee	Percent.	6.13	7.05	7.65	7.65	7.65	7.65	7.65	7.65	7.65	7.65
Self-employed [5].	Percent.	8.10	14.10	15.30	15.30	15.30	15.30	15.30	15.30	15.30	15.30
SMI, monthly premium [6]. . .	Dollars .	9.60	15.50	28.60	46.10	42.50	43.80	43.80	45.50	45.50	50.00

[1] Estimated number fully insured for retirement and/or survivor benefits as of end of year.   [2] Includes self-employment.
[3] Beginning 1994 upper limit on earnings subject to HI taxes was repealed.   [4] As of January 1, 2002, each employee and employer pays 7.65 percent and the self-employed pay 15.3 percent.   [5] Self-employed pays 11.8 percent in 1985. The additional amount is supplied from general revenues. Beginning 1990, self-employed pays 15.3 percent, and half of the tax is deductible for income tax purposes and for computing self-employment income subject to social security tax.   [6] 1980, as of July 1; beginning 1985, as of January 1. As of January 1, 2002, the monthly premium is $54.00.

Source: U.S. Social Security Administration, *Annual Statistical Supplement* to the *Social Security Bulletin;* and unpublished data.

No. 518. Social Security Trust Funds: 1980 to 2001

[**In billions of dollars (103.5 represents $103,500,000,000)**]

Type of trust fund	1980	1990	1995	1996	1997	1998	1999	2000	2001
Old-age and survivors insurance (OASI):									
Net contribution income [1]	103.5	272.4	310.1	328.0	357.4	380.4	407.3	433.0	453.4
Interest received [2]	1.8	16.4	32.8	35.7	39.8	44.5	49.8	57.5	64.7
Benefit payments [3]	105.1	223.0	291.6	302.9	316.3	326.8	334.4	352.7	372.3
Assets, end of year	22.8	214.2	458.5	514.0	589.1	681.6	798.8	931.0	1,071.5
Disability insurance (DI):									
Net contribution income [1]	13.3	28.7	54.7	57.7	56.5	59.5	63.9	71.8	75.7
Interest received [2]	0.5	0.9	2.2	3.0	4.0	4.8	5.7	6.9	8.2
Benefit payments [3]	15.5	24.8	40.9	44.2	45.7	48.2	51.4	55.0	59.6
Assets, end of year	3.6	11.1	37.6	52.9	66.4	80.8	97.3	118.5	141.0

[1] Includes deposits by states and deductions for refund of estimated employee-tax overpayment. Beginning in 1990, includes government contributions on deemed wage credits for military service in 1957 and later. Includes taxation of benefits beginning in 1990.   [2] In 1990, includes interest on advance tax transfers. Beginning 1990, includes interest on reimbursement for unnegotiated checks.   [3] Includes payments for vocational rehabilitation services furnished to disabled persons receiving benefits because of their disabilities. Beginning in 1990, amounts reflect deductions for unnegotiated benefit checks.

Source: U.S. Social Security Administration, *Annual Report of Board of Trustees, OASI, DI, HI, and SMI Trust Funds.* Also published in *Social Security Bulletin,* quarterly.

U.S. Census Bureau, Statistical Abstract of the United States: 2002

No. 519. Social Security (OASDI)—Benefits by Type of Beneficiary: 1980 to 2001

[35,585 represents 35,585,000. A person eligible to receive more than one type of benefit is generally classified or counted only once as a retired-worker beneficiary. OASDI=Old-age, survivors, and disability insurance. See also headnote, Table 517, and Appendix III]

Type of beneficiary	1980	1985	1990	1995	1996	1997	1998	1999	2000	2001
Number of benefits [1] (1,000)....	**35,585**	**37,058**	**39,832**	**43,387**	**43,737**	**43,971**	**44,246**	**44,596**	**45,415**	**45,878**
Retired workers [2] (1,000).........	19,562	22,432	24,838	26,673	26,898	27,275	27,511	27,775	28,499	28,837
Disabled workers [3] (1,000)........	2,859	2,657	3,011	4,185	4,386	4,508	4,698	4,879	5,042	5,274
Wives and husbands [2][4] (1,000).....	3,477	3,375	3,367	3,290	3,194	3,129	3,054	2,987	2,963	2,899
Children (1,000)................	4,607	3,319	3,187	3,734	3,803	3,772	3,769	3,795	3,803	3,839
Under age 18................	3,423	2,699	2,497	2,956	3,010	2,970	2,963	2,970	2,976	2,994
Disabled children [5].........	450	526	600	686	697	705	713	721	729	737
Students [6].................	733	94	89	92	96	97	93	104	98	109
Of retired workers...........	639	457	422	442	443	441	439	442	459	467
Of deceased workers..........	2,610	1,917	1,776	1,884	1,898	1,893	1,884	1,885	1,878	1,890
Of disabled workers..........	1,358	945	989	1,409	1,463	1,438	1,446	1,468	1,466	1,482
Widowed mothers [7] (1,000)......	562	372	304	275	242	230	221	212	203	197
Widows and widowers [2][8] (1,000)....	4,411	4,863	5,111	5,226	5,210	5,053	4,990	4,944	4,901	4,828
Parents [2] (1,000).............	15	10	6	4	4	4	3	3	3	3
Special benefits [9] (1,000).......	93	32	7	1	1	(Z)	(Z)	(Z)	(Z)	(Z)
AVERAGE MONTHLY BENEFIT, CURRENT DOLLARS										
Retired workers [2].............	341	479	603	720	745	765	780	804	844	874
Retired worker and wife [2]........	567	814	1,027	1,221	1,262	1,295	1,318	1,357	1,420	1,466
Disabled workers [3]............	371	484	587	682	704	722	733	754	786	814
Wives and husbands [2][4].........	164	236	298	354	369	379	386	398	416	430
Children of retired workers........	140	198	259	322	337	349	358	373	395	413
Children of deceased workers.......	240	331	406	469	487	500	510	526	550	571
Children of disabled workers.......	110	142	164	183	194	201	208	216	228	238
Widowed mothers [7]............	246	332	409	478	515	532	545	566	595	621
Widows and widowers, nondisabled [2].	311	433	556	680	699	731	749	775	810	841
Parents [2].................	276	378	482	591	614	636	651	674	704	729
Special benefits [9]............	105	138	167	192	197	201	204	209	217	224
AVERAGE MONTHLY BENEFIT, CONSTANT (2001) DOLLARS [10]										
Retired workers [2].............	698	774	796	829	830	838	841	844	858	874
Retired worker and wife [2]........	1,161	1,316	1,356	1,406	1,406	1,419	1,421	1,425	1,442	1,466
Disabled workers [3]............	760	782	775	785	784	791	790	792	799	814
Wives and husbands [2][4].........	336	382	394	408	411	415	417	418	423	430
Children of deceased workers.......	491	535	536	540	543	548	550	552	559	571
Widowed mothers [7]............	504	537	540	550	574	583	588	594	604	621
Widows and widowers, nondisabled [2].	637	700	734	783	778	801	807	814	823	841
Number of benefits awarded (1,000)....	**4,215**	**3,796**	**3,717**	**3,882**	**3,793**	**3,866**	**3,800**	**3,917**	**4,290**	**4,162**
Retired workers [2].............	1,620	1,690	1,665	1,609	1,581	1,719	1,631	1,690	1,961	1,779
Disabled workers [3]............	389	377	468	646	624	587	608	620	622	691
Wives and husbands [2][4].........	469	440	379	322	302	319	311	322	385	358
Children.....................	1,174	714	695	809	798	757	763	773	777	796
Widowed mothers [7]............	108	72	58	52	49	44	42	42	40	41
Widows and widowers [2][8].........	452	502	452	445	438	440	444	470	505	496
Parents [2]..................	1	(Z)	(Z)	(Z)	(Z)	(Z)	(Z)	(Z)	(Z)	(Z)
Special benefits [9]............	1	1	(Z)	(Z)	(Z)	(Z)	(Z)	(Z)	(Z)	(Z)
BENEFIT PAYMENTS DURING YEAR (bil. dol.)										
Total [11]....	**120.5**	**186.2**	**247.8**	**332.6**	**347.1**	**362.0**	**375.0**	**385.8**	**407.6**	**431.9**
Monthly benefits [12]............	120.1	186.0	247.6	332.4	346.9	361.8	374.8	385.6	407.4	431.7
Retired workers [2]...........	70.4	116.8	156.8	205.3	213.4	223.6	232.3	238.5	253.5	269.0
Disabled workers [3].........	12.8	16.5	22.1	36.6	39.6	41.1	43.5	46.5	49.8	54.2
Wives and husbands [2][4]......	7.0	11.1	14.5	17.9	18.2	18.6	18.9	18.8	19.4	19.9
Children..................	10.5	10.7	12.0	16.1	17.1	17.6	18.1	18.6	19.3	20.4
Under age 18.............	7.4	8.5	9.0	11.9	12.6	13.0	13.3	13.6	14.1	14.8
Disabled children [5].......	1.0	1.8	2.5	3.6	3.8	4.0	4.2	4.4	4.6	4.8
Students [6].............	2.1	0.4	0.5	0.6	0.6	0.6	0.7	0.7	0.7	0.7
Of retired workers.........	1.1	1.1	1.3	1.7	1.8	1.9	1.9	2.0	2.1	2.3
Of deceased workers........	7.4	7.8	8.6	10.7	11.2	11.7	11.9	12.1	12.5	13.1
Of disabled workers........	2.0	1.8	2.2	3.7	4.0	4.1	4.2	4.4	4.7	4.9
Widowed mothers [7].........	1.6	1.5	1.4	1.6	1.5	1.5	1.4	1.4	1.4	1.4
Widows and widowers [2][8]......	17.6	29.3	40.7	54.8	57.0	59.3	60.5	61.8	63.9	66.8
Parents [2]...............	0.1	0.1	(Z)	(Z)	(Z)	(Z)	(Z)	(Z)	(Z)	(Z)
Special benefits [9].........	0.1	0.1	(Z)	(Z)	(Z)	(Z)	(Z)	(Z)	(Z)	(Z)
Lump sum..................	0.4	0.2	0.2	0.2	0.2	0.2	0.2	0.2	0.2	0.2

Z Fewer than 500 or less than $50 million.   [1] Number of benefit payments in current-payment status, i.e., actually being made at a specified time with no deductions or with deductions amounting to less than a month's benefit.   [2] 62 years and over.   [3] Disabled workers under age 65.   [4] Includes wife beneficiaries with entitled children in their care and entitled divorced wives.   [5] 18 years old and over. Disability began before age 18.   [6] Full-time students aged 18-21 through 1984 and aged 18 and 19 beginning 1985.   [7] Includes surviving divorced mothers with entitled children in their care and widowed fathers with entitled children in their care.   [8] Includes widows aged 60-61, surviving divorced wives aged 60 and over, disabled widows and widowers aged 50 and over; and widowers aged 60-61.   [9] Benefits for persons aged 72 and over not insured under regular or transitional provisions of Social Security Act.   [10] Constant dollar figures are based on the consumer price index (CPI-U) for December as published by the U.S. Bureau of Labor Statistics.   [11] Represents total disbursements of benefit checks by the U.S. Dept. of the Treasury during the years specified.   [12] Distribution by type estimated.

Source: U.S. Social Security Administration, Annual Statistical Supplement to the Social Security Bulletin; and unpublished data.

No. 520. Social Security—Beneficiaries, Annual Payments, and Average Monthly Benefit, 1990 to 2001 and by State and Other Areas, 2001

[Number of beneficiaries in current-payment status **(39,832 represents 39,832,000)** and average monthly benefit as of **December**. Data based on 10-percent sample of administrative records. See also headnote, Table 519, and Appendix III]

Year, state, and other area	Number of beneficiaries (1,000)				Annual payments [2] (mil. dol.)				Average monthly benefit (dol.)		
	Total	Retired workers and dependents [1]	Survivors	Disabled workers and dependents	Total	Retired workers and dependents [1]	Survivors	Disabled workers and dependents	Retired workers [3]	Disabled workers	Widows and widowers [4]
1990.	39,832	28,369	7,197	4,266	247,796	172,042	50,951	24,803	603	587	557
1995.	43,380	30,139	7,379	5,862	332,581	224,381	67,302	40,898	720	682	680
1998.	44,247	30,819	7,091	6,338	374,772	252,659	73,940	48,173	780	734	749
1999.	44,599	31,035	7,038	6,526	385,525	258,885	75,309	51,331	804	755	775
2000.	45,417	31,761	6,981	6,675	407,431	274,645	77,848	54,938	845	787	810
2001, total [5]	45,874	32,046	6,915	6,913	431,737	290,799	81,359	59,579	875	815	841
United States.	44,756	31,354	6,696	6,707	424,880	287,061	79,653	58,167	(NA)	(NA)	(NA)
Alabama	842	522	145	175	7,428	4,467	1,550	1,411	827	784	766
Alaska	57	36	10	11	506	317	101	88	848	796	793
Arizona	813	588	106	119	7,713	5,401	1,260	1,052	888	845	870
Arkansas.	521	333	84	104	4,495	2,775	878	843	805	766	745
California.	4,247	3,078	591	578	40,358	28,010	7,179	5,169	882	828	873
Colorado.	542	382	78	82	5,004	3,365	932	707	852	808	849
Connecticut	580	438	71	72	6,015	4,438	930	647	959	841	931
Delaware.	137	98	19	20	1,357	933	239	185	914	843	905
District of Columbia. . . .	73	52	12	10	603	403	113	87	741	760	698
Florida	3,235	2,407	413	416	30,455	21,846	4,981	3,629	870	818	867
Georgia.	1,125	725	184	216	10,172	6,381	1,967	1,824	844	794	778
Hawaii	189	147	23	19	1,752	1,319	261	171	864	838	811
Idaho	200	144	28	28	1,829	1,263	329	236	854	801	851
Illinois.	1,846	1,323	287	236	18,397	12,668	3,614	2,115	915	842	903
Indiana	1,000	699	152	149	9,899	6,698	1,913	1,289	915	824	894
Iowa	541	395	81	65	5,149	3,585	1,012	552	874	788	861
Kansas	441	318	66	57	4,273	2,968	822	484	896	793	891
Kentucky.	746	444	120	175	6,578	3,729	1,379	1,470	821	805	757
Louisiana	716	431	153	132	6,248	3,533	1,637	1,077	810	816	771
Maine.	254	171	34	49	2,199	1,440	388	371	805	743	797
Maryland.	734	525	115	94	7,057	4,835	1,356	867	880	851	851
Massachusetts	1,062	757	138	168	10,161	7,007	1,711	1,444	879	806	872
Michigan	1,658	1,145	259	254	16,827	11,187	3,289	2,351	941	879	902
Minnesota	746	550	106	90	7,048	4,963	1,309	776	867	797	850
Mississippi.	523	306	92	125	4,374	2,514	896	964	792	759	714
Missouri	1,013	690	152	171	9,415	6,203	1,773	1,438	863	797	838
Montana	159	112	24	23	1,451	978	278	195	845	800	833
Nebraska	286	209	42	35	2,663	1,866	512	286	856	772	863
Nevada.	300	221	36	43	2,869	2,032	435	401	882	873	883
New Hampshire	204	147	26	32	1,970	1,377	325	268	892	816	890
New Jersey	1,356	1,001	185	170	14,221	10,201	2,411	1,609	965	879	931
New Mexico.	285	194	46	45	2,451	1,614	474	363	816	783	786
New York.	3,015	2,149	410	456	30,142	20,893	5,093	4,156	928	862	893
North Carolina	1,374	922	193	258	12,458	8,193	2,076	2,189	846	789	774
North Dakota	114	82	20	12	1,020	680	239	102	817	765	808
Ohio.	1,922	1,337	323	262	18,598	12,289	4,036	2,272	891	811	873
Oklahoma	597	409	99	89	5,429	3,545	1,123	761	835	802	812
Oregon	578	424	77	77	5,536	3,904	957	676	884	812	885
Pennsylvania	2,366	1,704	365	297	23,270	16,036	4,624	2,609	899	831	884
Rhode Island	192	138	22	31	1,821	1,283	274	264	874	797	879
South Carolina	704	457	107	140	6,355	4,041	1,122	1,192	844	803	769
South Dakota.	137	98	23	16	1,186	808	251	127	802	742	796
Tennessee.	1,011	653	164	194	9,109	5,707	1,787	1,616	842	783	785
Texas	2,673	1,835	477	361	24,367	15,948	5,397	3,021	851	807	816
Utah.	246	180	35	31	2,300	1,632	410	257	878	805	892
Vermont	105	73	14	18	973	659	165	149	862	787	843
Virginia.	1,053	718	160	175	9,707	6,365	1,831	1,511	852	816	800
Washington.	859	626	113	119	8,427	5,918	1,437	1,072	911	823	899
West Virginia	395	235	75	85	3,690	2,054	868	768	862	859	804
Wisconsin	905	669	126	111	8,818	6,274	1,585	959	896	807	884
Wyoming.	78	57	10	11	737	516	124	97	872	822	870
Puerto Rico	677	372	120	185	4,231	2,103	869	1,259	577	694	515
Guam	11	7	3	1	71	43	19	8	609	696	593
American Samoa. . . .	5	2	1	2	31	9	10	11	522	616	489
Virgin Islands	14	10	2	2	108	76	18	14	739	806	640
Northern Mariana Islands.	2	1	1	(Z)	9	5	3	1	478	449	425
Abroad	405	297	92	16	2,381	1,483	782	116	519	701	565

NA Not available.   Z Fewer than 500.   [1] Includes special benefits for persons aged 72 and over not insured under regular or transitional provisions of Social Security Act.   [2] Unnegotiated checks not deducted. 1990 and 1995 include lump-sum payments to survivors of deceased workers.   [3] Excludes persons with special benefits.   [4] Nondisabled only.   [5] Includes those with state or area unknown.

Source: U.S. Social Security Administration, *Annual Statistical Supplement to the Social Security Bulletin.*

No. 521. Public Employee Retirement Systems—Participants and Finances: 1980 to 2000

[For fiscal year of retirement system, except data for the Thrift Savings Plan are for calendar year (4,629 represents 4,629,000)]

Retirement plan	Unit	1980	1985	1990	1995	1996	1997	1998	1999	2000, proj.
TOTAL PARTICIPANTS [1]										
Federal retirement systems:										
Defined benefit:										
Civil Service Retirement System	1,000 .	4,629	4,919	4,167	3,731	3,663	3,518	3,423	3,362	(NA)
Federal Employees Retirement System [2].	1,000 .	(X)	(X)	1,180	1,512	1,615	1,679	1,757	1,879	(NA)
Military Service Retirement System [3] . . .	1,000 .	3,380	3,672	3,763	3,387	3,372	3,367	3,368	3,374	(NA)
Thrift Savings Plan [4]	1,000 .	(X)	(X)	1,625	2,195	2,254	2,303	2,300	2,400	(NA)
State and local retirement systems [5][6]	1,000 .	(NA)	15,234	16,858	14,734	15,153	15,194	16,215	16,195	16,834
ACTIVE PARTICIPANTS										
Federal retirement systems:										
Defined benefit:										
Civil Service Retirement System	1,000 .	2,700	2,800	1,826	1,525	1,343	1,189	1,099	1,042	(NA)
Federal Employees Retirement System [2].	1,000 .	(X)	(X)	1,136	1,318	1,447	1,497	1,547	1,640	(NA)
Military Service Retirement System [3] . . .	1,000 .	2,050	2,192	2,130	1,572	1,525	1,491	1,459	1,438	(NA)
Thrift Savings Plan [4]	1,000 .	(X)	(X)	1,419	1,930	1,987	2,011	1,800	1,900	(NA)
State and local retirement systems [5][6]	1,000 .	(NA)	10,364	11,345	12,524	13,051	12,817	13,059	13,472	13,917
ASSETS										
Total	Bil. dol..	258	529	1,047	1,655	1,854	2,110	2,403	2,644	2,943
Federal retirement systems	Bil. dol..	73	154	326	537	581	631	686	738	774
Defined benefit	Bil. dol..	73	154	318	502	534	570	608	643	676
Civil Service Retirement System	Bil. dol..	73	142	220	311	329	344	361	376	390
Federal Employees Retirement System [2].	Bil. dol..	(X)	(X)	18	60	70	83	97	111	126
Military Service Retirement System [3] . . .	Bil. dol..	([7])	12	80	131	135	143	150	156	160
Thrift Savings Plan [4]	Bil. dol..	(X)	(X)	8	35	47	61	77	95	98
State and local retirement systems [5]	Bil. dol..	185	374	721	1,118	1,273	1,479	1,717	1,906	2,169
CONTRIBUTIONS										
Total	Bil. dol..	83	106	103	127	129	139	137	142	143
Federal retirement systems	Bil. dol..	19	54	61	67	66	73	73	75	78
Defined benefit	Bil. dol..	19	54	59	61	60	66	65	67	69
Civil Service Retirement System	Bil. dol..	19	27	28	31	32	33	33	33	33
Federal Employees Retirement System [2].	Bil. dol..	(X)	(X)	4	6	6	7	6	8	8
Military Service Retirement System [3] . . .	Bil. dol..	([7])	27	27	24	22	26	26	26	28
Thrift Savings Plan [4]	Bil. dol..	(X)	(X)	2	6	6	7	8	8	9
State and local retirement systems [5]	Bil. dol..	64	52	42	60	63	66	64	67	65
BENEFITS										
Total	Bil. dol..	39	62	89	125	135	142	152	160	172
Federal retirement systems	Bil. dol..	27	40	53	66	70	73	76	78	81
Defined benefit	Bil. dol..	27	40	53	65	69	72	74	76	78
Civil Service Retirement System	Bil. dol..	15	23	31	37	39	41	42	43	44
Federal Employees Retirement System [2].	Bil. dol..	(X)	(X)	(Z)	1	1	1	1	1	1
Military Service Retirement System [3] . . .	Bil. dol..	12	17	22	28	29	30	31	32	33
Thrift Savings Plan [4]	Bil. dol..	(X)	(X)	(Z)	1	1	1	2	2	3
State and local retirement systems [5]	Bil. dol..	12	22	36	59	65	69	76	82	91

NA Not available.   X Not applicable.   Z Less than $500 million.   [1] Includes active, separated vested, retired employees, and survivors.   [2] The Federal Employees Retirement System was established June 6, 1986.   [3] Includes nondisability and disability retirees, surviving families, and all active personnel with the exception of active reserves.   [4] The Thrift Savings Plan (a defined contribution plan) was established April 1, 1987.   [5] Excludes state and local plans that are fully supported by employee contributions.   [6] Not adjusted for double counting of individuals participating in more than one plan.   [7] The Military Retirement System was unfunded until October 1, 1984.

Source: Employee Benefit Research Institute, Washington, DC, *EBRI Databook on Employee Benefits, Fourth Edition*, and unpublished data (copyright).

No. 522. Federal Civil Service Retirement: 1980 to 2001

[As of Sept. 30 or for year ending Sept. 30 (2,720 represents 2,720,000). Covers both Civil Service Retirement System and Federal Employees Retirement System]

Item	Unit	1980	1985	1990	1995	1997	1998	1999	2000	2001
Employees covered [1]	1,000 . .	2,720	2,750	2,945	2,668	2,681	2,658	2,668	2,764	2,655
Annuitants, total	1,000 . .	1,675	1,955	2,143	2,311	2,352	2,369	2,368	2,376	2,383
Age and service	1,000 . .	905	1,122	1,288	1,441	1,474	1,488	1,491	1,501	1,509
Disability	1,000 . .	343	332	297	263	257	253	246	242	239
Survivors	1,000 . .	427	501	558	607	621	628	631	633	635
Receipts, total [2]	Mil. dol.	24,389	40,790	52,689	65,684	70,227	72,156	74,522	75,967	77,949
Employee contributions	Mil. dol.	3,686	4,679	4,501	4,498	4,358	4,274	4,381	4,637	4,593
Federal government contributions. .	Mil. dol	15,562	22,301	27,368	33,130	35,386	36,188	36,561	37,722	38,442
Disbursements, total [3]	Mil. dol.	14,977	23,203	31,416	38,435	41,722	43,058	43,932	45,194	47,356
Age and service annuitants [4]	Mil. dol	12,639	19,414	26,495	32,070	34,697	35,806	36,492	37,546	39,397
Survivors	Mil. dol	1,912	3,158	4,366	5,864	6,518	6,763	6,978	7,210	7,533
Average monthly benefit:										
Age and service	Dollars .	902	1,189	1,369	1,643	1,749	1,796	1,830	1,885	1,967
Disability	Dollars .	723	881	1,008	1,164	1,204	1,216	1,221	1,240	1,269
Survivors	Dollars .	392	528	653	819	881	905	923	952	992
Cash and security holdings	Bil. dol.	73.7	142.3	238.0	366.2	422.2	451.3	481.3	508.1	542.6

[1] Excludes employees in leave without pay status.   [2] Includes interest on investments.   [3] Includes refunds, death claims, and administration.   [4] Includes disability annuitants.

Source: U.S. Office of Personnel Management, *Civil Service Retirement and Disability Trust Fund Annual Report*.

348   Social Insurance and Human Services

No. 523. State and Local Government Retirement Systems—Beneficiaries and Finances: 1990 to 2000

[In billions of dollars, except as indicated (4,026 represents 4,026,000). For fiscal years closed during the 12 months ending June 30]

Year and level of government	Num- ber of benefi- ciaries (1,000)	Receipts					Benefits and withdrawals			Cash and security holdings
		Total	Employee contri- butions	Government contributions		Earn- ings on invest- ments	Total	Ben- efits	With- drawals	
				State	Local					
1990: All systems.........	4,026	111.3	13.9	14.0	18.6	64.9	38.4	36.0	2.4	721
State-administered ...	3,232	89.2	11.6	14.0	11.5	52.0	29.6	27.6	2.0	575
Locally administered..	794	22.2	2.2	(Z)	7.0	12.9	8.8	8.4	0.4	145
1995: All systems.........	4,979	148.8	18.6	16.6	24.4	89.2	61.4	58.8	2.7	1,118
State-administered ...	4,025	123.3	15.7	16.2	15.4	76.0	48.0	45.8	2.2	914
Locally administered..	954	25.5	2.9	0.4	9.0	13.3	13.5	13.0	0.5	204
1999: All systems.........	5,506	264.3	23.6	17.2	23.4	200.0	85.7	81.8	3.9	1,907
State-administered ...	4,522	220.7	19.8	16.9	15.4	168.5	67.4	64.3	3.1	1,582
Locally administered..	984	43.6	3.8	0.3	8.0	31.5	18.3	17.5	0.8	325
2000: All systems.........	6,292	297.0	25.0	17.5	22.6	231.9	95.7	91.3	4.4	2,169
State-administered ...	4,786	247.4	20.7	17.2	16.7	192.8	76.0	72.2	3.8	1,798
Locally administered..	1,506	49.7	4.3	0.4	5.9	39.1	19.7	19.1	0.7	371

Z Less than $50 million.

Source: U.S. Census Bureau, Through 1995, *Finances of Employee-Retirement Systems of State and Local Governments*, Series GF, No. 2, annual; beginning 1999, "Federal, State, and Local Governments, State and Local Government Public Employee Retirement Systems"; <http://www.census.gov/govs/www/retire.html>.

No. 524. Private Pension Plans—Summary by Type of Plan: 1990 to 1998

[712.3 represents 712,300. "Pension plan" is defined by the Employee Retirement Income Security Act (ERISA) as "any plan, fund, or program which was heretofore or is hereafter established or maintained by an employer or an employee organization, or by both, to the extent that such plan (a) provides retirement income to employees, or (b) results in a deferral of income by employees for periods extending to the termination of covered employment or beyond, regardless of the method of calculating the contributions made to the plan, the method of calculating the benefits under the plan, or the method of distributing benefits from the plan." A defined benefit plan provides a definite benefit formula for calculating benefit amounts - such as a flat amount per year of service or a percentage of salary times years of service. A defined contribution plan is a pension plan in which the contributions are made to an individual account for each employee. The retirement benefit is dependent upon the account balance at retirement. The balance depends upon amounts contributed, investment experience, and, in the case of profit sharing plans, amounts which may be allocated to the account due to forfeitures by terminating employees. Employee Stock Ownership Plans (ESOP) and 401(k) plans (see Table 527) are included among defined contribution plans. Data are based on Form 5500 series reports filed with the Internal Revenue Service]

Item	Unit	Total				Defined contribution plan				Defined benefit plan			
		1990	1995	1997	1998	1990	1995	1997	1998	1990	1995	1997	1998
Number of plans [1]	1,000...	712.3	693.4	720.0	730.0	599.2	623.9	660.5	673.6	113.1	69.5	59.5	56.4
Total participants [2] [3] ..	Million...	76.9	87.5	95.0	99.5	38.1	47.7	54.6	57.9	38.8	39.7	40.4	41.6
Active participants [2] [4]	Million ..	61.8	66.2	70.7	73.3	35.5	42.7	48.0	50.3	26.3	23.5	22.7	23.0
Contributions [5]........	Bil. dol. ..	98.8	158.8	177.9	201.9	75.8	117.4	148.1	166.9	23.0	41.4	29.9	35.0
Benefits [6]	Bil. dol. ..	129.4	183.0	232.5	273.1	63.0	97.9	135.3	161.9	66.4	85.1	97.2	111.2

[1] Excludes all plans covering only one participant. [2] Includes double counting of workers in more than one plan. [3] Total participants include active participants, vested separated workers, and retirees. [4] Any workers currently in employment covered by a plan and who are earning or retaining credited service under a plan. Includes any nonvested former employees who have not yet incurred breaks in service. [5] Includes both employer and employee contributions. [6] Benefits paid directly from trust and premium payments made from plan to insurance carriers. Excludes benefits paid directly by insurance carriers.

Source: U.S. Dept. of Labor, Pension and Welfare Benefits Administration, *Private Pension Plan Bulletin*, No. 10 winter 2001, and unpublished data.

No. 525. Percent Of Workers Participating In Retirement Benefits by Worker Characteristics: 1999

[Based on National Compensation Survey, a sample survey of 3,168 private industry establishments of all sizes, representing over 107 million workers; see Appendix III. See also Table 620]

Characteristic	Total	Defined benefit	Defined contri- bution	Characteristic	Total	Defined benefit	Defined contri- bution
Total	48	21	36	Full time [1]	56	25	42
Professional, technical, and				Part time [1]	21	9	14
related employees	69	29	56				
Clerical and sales employees....	45	17	34	Union [2]	79	70	39
Blue-collar and service				Nonunion [2]	44	16	35
employees	42	21	28				

[1] Employees are classified as working either a full-time or part-time schedule based on the definition used by each establishment. [2] Union workers are those whose wages are determined through collective bargaining.

Source: U.S. Bureau of Labor Statistics, *News*, USDL 01-473, December 19, 2001.

Social Insurance and Human Services 349

No. 526. Pension Plan Coverage of Workers by Selected Characteristics: 2000

[66,814 represents 66,814,000. Covers workers as of March 2001 who had earnings in 2000. Based on Current Population Survey; see text, Section 1, Population and Appendix III]

Sex and age	Number with coverage (1,000)				Percent of total workers			
	Total [1]	White	Black	Hispanic [2]	Total [1]	White	Black	Hispanic [2]
Total	66,814	56,587	7,364	4,557	44.5	45.2	42.2	28.3
Male.	36,591	31,539	3,408	2,528	46.2	47.0	41.9	27.9
Under 65 years old	35,716	30,750	3,345	2,498	47.0	47.9	42.2	28.0
15 to 24 years old	1,929	1,640	211	188	14.9	14.9	14.9	10.0
25 to 44 years old	19,009	16,082	1,913	1,496	50.0	51.0	44.8	29.6
45 to 64 years old	14,778	13,028	1,221	814	59.2	60.3	54.6	41.4
65 years old and over	875	790	63	31	26.8	26.9	30.0	18.9
Female.	30,224	25,047	3,956	2,029	42.7	43.1	42.4	28.9
Under 65 years old	29,686	24,570	3,905	2,008	43.3	43.8	42.8	29.0
15 to 24 years old	1,699	1,364	248	169	13.8	13.5	15.0	11.1
25 to 44 years old	15,774	12,791	2,276	1,193	47.0	47.8	45.9	32.0
45 to 64 years old	12,212	10,415	1,381	646	53.9	54.2	55.1	38.6
65 years old and over	538	478	51	21	23.2	23.3	23.9	23.4

[1] Includes other races, not shown separately. [2] Hispanic persons may be of any race.

Source: U.S. Census Bureau, "Table NC8. Pension Plan Coverage of Workers by Selected Characteristics, Gender, Race and Hispanic Origin, and Poverty Status: 2000"; published 10 December 2001; <http://ferret.bls.census.gov/macro/032001/noncash/nc8000.htm>.

No. 527. 401(k) Plans—Summary: 1985 to 1998

[10,339 represents 10,339,000. A 401(k) plan is a qualified retirement plan that allows participants to have a portion of their compensation (otherwise payable in cash) contributed pretax to a retirement account on their behalf]

Item	1985	1990	1993	1994	1995	1996	1997	1998
Number of plans [1]	29,869	97,614	154,527	174,945	200,813	230,808	265,251	300,593
Active participants [2] (1,000)	10,339	19,548	23,138	26,206	28,061	30,843	33,865	37,114
Assets (bil. dol.)	144	385	616	675	864	1,062	1,264	1,541
Contributions (bil. dol.)	24	49	69	76	87	104	116	135
Benefits (bil. dol.)	16	32	44	51	62	78	93	121
Percentage of all private defined contribution plans:								
Assets	34	54	58	62	65	68	73	74
Contributions	46	65	68	72	74	78	78	81
Benefits	35	51	57	62	64	67	69	75

[1] Excludes single-participant plans. [2] May include some employees who are eligible to participate in the plan but have not elected to join. 401(k) participants may participate in one or more additional plans.

Source: Employee Benefit Research Institute, Washington, DC, *EBRI Databook on Employee Benefits, Fourth Edition* and unpublished data (copyright).

No. 528. State Unemployment Insurance by State and Other Area: 2001

[9,877 represents 9,877,000. See headnote, Table 529. For state data on insured unemployment, see Table 600]

State or other area	Beneficiaries, first payments (1,000)	Benefits paid (mil. dol.)	Avg. weekly unemployment benefits (dol.)	State or other area	Beneficiaries, first payments (1,000)	Benefits paid (mil. dol.)	Avg. weekly unemployment benefits (dol.)	State or other area	Beneficiaries, first payments (1,000)	Benefits paid (mil. dol.)	Avg. weekly unemployment benefits (dol.)
Total .	9,877	31,629	238	KY	145	413	234	OH. . . .	365	1,242	248
AL	164	285	164	LA	87	232	194	OK. . . .	62	175	228
AK	44	112	193	ME. . . .	35	101	216	OR. . . .	203	675	256
AZ	113	274	173	MD. . . .	124	393	235	PA	546	2,132	282
AR	115	277	220	MA. . . .	272	1,366	335	RI	44	174	289
CA	1,289	3,362	172	MI	526	1,632	261	SC	162	386	206
CO. . . .	94	320	291	MN. . . .	165	663	307	SD	11	24	190
CT. . . .	147	509	277	MS. . . .	82	182	163	TN	247	580	198
DE. . . .	30	95	221	MO. . . .	174	491	200	TX	485	1,546	241
DC. . . .	23	91	262	MT. . . .	26	68	194	UT	60	178	253
FL	336	965	223	NE	38	95	205	VT	25	64	233
GA	270	606	228	NV	93	292	228	VA	151	392	235
HI	40	142	297	NH. . . .	27	67	241	WA. . . .	273	1,250	311
ID	57	146	223	NJ	313	1,550	309	WV. . . .	51	132	202
IL.	446	1,902	269	NM. . . .	35	97	193	WI	327	812	242
IN	207	596	244	NY	624	2,716	269	WY. . . .	12	27	215
IA.	114	313	250	NC	383	937	248	PR	131	258	94
KS	70	240	261	ND	13	44	218	VI.	2	6	226

Source: U.S. Employment and Training Administration, *Unemployment Insurance Financial Data Handbook*.

No. 529. State Unemployment Insurance—Summary: 1980 to 2001

[3,356 represents 3,356,000. Includes unemployment compensation for state and local government employees where covered by state law]

Item	Unit	1980	1985	1990	1995	1996	1997	1998	1999	2000	2001
Insured unemployment, avg. weekly. .	1,000. . .	3,356	2,617	2,522	2,572	2,596	2,323	2,222	2,188	2,110	2,974
Percent of covered employment [1] . .	Percent .	3.9	2.9	2.4	2.3	2.3	2.0	1.9	1.8	1.7	(NA)
Percent of civilian unemployed. . . .	Percent .	43.9	31.5	35.8	34.7	35.9	34.5	35.8	37.2	45.0	(NA)
Unemployment benefits, avg. weekly .	Dollars . .	100	128	161	187	189	193	201	212	221	238
Percent of weekly wage	Percent .	36.6	35.3	36.0	35.5	34.5	33.5	32.9	31.6	32.9	(NA)
Weeks compensated	Million .	149.0	119.3	116.2	118.5	119.1	106.5	101.4	100.6	96.0	136.4
Beneficiaries, first payments	1,000. . .	9,992	8,372	8,629	8,035	7,995	7,323	7,339	6,965	7,033	9,877
Average duration of benefits [2]	Weeks . .	14.9	14.2	13.4	14.7	14.9	14.6	13.8	14.4	13.7	13.8
Claimants exhausting benefits.	1,000. . .	3,072	2,572	2,323	2,662	2,739	2,485	2,266	2,299	2,144	2,827
Percent of first payment [3]	Percent .	33.2	31.2	29.4	34.3	33.4	32.8	31.8	31.4	31.8	34.0
Contributions collected [4]	Bil. dol. .	11.4	19.3	15.2	22.0	21.6	21.2	19.8	19.2	19.9	19.7
Benefits paid	Bil. dol. .	14.2	14.7	18.1	21.3	21.8	19.8	19.6	20.6	20.5	31.6
Funds available for benefits [5]	Bil. dol. .	6.6	10.1	37.9	35.4	38.6	43.8	48.0	50.3	54.1	46.6
Average employer contribution rate [6] .	Percent .	2.37	3.13	1.95	2.44	2.28	2.13	1.92	1.76	1.75	(NA)

NA Not available. [1] Insured unemployment as percent of average covered employment in preceding year. [2] Weeks compensated divided by first payment. [3] Based on first payments for 12-month period ending June 30. [4] Contributions from employers; also employees in states which tax workers. [5] End of year. Sum of balances in state clearing accounts, benefit-payment accounts, and state accounts in Federal unemployment trust funds. [6] As percent of taxable wages.
Source: U.S. Employment and Training Administration, *Unemployment Insurance Financial Data Handbook.*

No. 530. Persons With Work Disability by Selected Characteristics: 2001

[In thousands, except percent (17,067 represents 17,067,000). As of March. Covers civilian noninstitutional population and members of Armed Forces living off post or with their families on post. Persons are classified as having a work disability if they (1) have a health problem or disability which prevents them from working or which limits the kind or amount of work they can do; (2) have a service-connected disability or ever retired or left a job for health reasons; (3) did not work in survey reference week or previous year because of long-term illness or disability; or (4) are under age 65, and are covered by medicare or receive supplemental security income. Based on Current Population Survey; see text, Section 1, Population, and Appendix III]

Age and participation status in assistance programs	Total [1]	Male	Female	White	Black	Hispanic [2]
Persons with work disability	**17,067**	**8,190**	**8,878**	**13,036**	**3,336**	**1,629**
16 to 24 years old.	1,330	627	703	951	324	135
25 to 34 years old.	2,102	1,042	1,060	1,448	556	227
35 to 44 years old	3,569	1,731	1,838	2,672	715	329
45 to 54 years old	4,841	2,407	2,434	3,723	934	433
55 to 64 years old.	5,226	2,383	2,843	4,242	807	505
Percent work disabled of total population . . .	9.6	9.4	9.8	8.9	14.7	7.8
16 to 24 years old.	3.8	3.6	4.1	3.4	6.2	2.6
25 to 34 years old.	5.7	5.7	5.6	4.9	10.9	4.1
35 to 44 years old.	8.0	7.9	8.1	7.3	12.6	6.6
45 to 54 years old.	12.7	13.0	12.5	11.7	21.9	13.5
55 to 64 years old.	22.0	21.2	22.7	20.8	33.6	26.8
Percent of work disabled—						
Receiving social security income	32.5	33.9	31.3	33.7	30.4	29.4
Receiving food stamps	16.8	13.5	19.8	13.9	27.1	20.7
Covered by medicaid.	32.8	29.8	35.5	29.7	44.0	41.2
Residing in public housing	6.9	5.5	8.2	5.1	12.8	8.7
Residing in subsidized housing	3.3	2.1	4.3	2.5	6.5	3.3

[1] Includes other races not shown separately. [2] Hispanic persons may be of any race.
Source: U.S. Census Bureau, unpublished data.

No. 531. Vocational Rehabilitation—Summary: 1980 to 1999

[For year ending September 30 (1,076 represents $1,076,000,000). Includes Puerto Rico, Guam, Virgin Islands, American Samoa, Northern Mariana Islands, and the Republic of Palau. State agencies, using matching state and federal funds, provide vocational rehabilitation services to eligible individuals with disabilities to enable them to prepare for and engage in gainful employment. Services may include counseling, guidance and work related placement services, physical and mental restoration, training and rehabilitation technology]

Item	Unit	1980	1985	1990	1994	1995	1996	1997	1998	1999
Federal and State expenditures [1]	Mil. dol .	1,076	1,452	1,910	2,517	2,714	2,844	3,046	3,081	3,138
Federal expenditures.	Mil. dol .	817	1,100	1,525	1,891	2,054	2,104	2,164	2,232	2,287
Applicants processed for program eligibility .	1,000. . .	717	594	625	675	625	578	617	624	608
Percent accepted into program	Percent .	58	60	57	72	76	76	79	75	80
Total persons rehabilitated [2]	1,000. . .	277	228	216	203	210	213	212	224	232
Rehabilitation rate [3]	Percent .	64	64	62	49	46	61	61	62	63
Severely disabled persons rehabilitated [2][4] .	1,000. . .	143	135	146	149	159	166	168	185	197
Rehabilitation rate [3].	Percent .	61	62	62	49	46	60	60	61	62
Percent of total persons rehabilitated . . .	Percent .	51	59	68	74	76	78	79	83	85
Persons served, total [5]	1,000. . .	1,095	932	938	1,194	1,250	1,226	1,267	1,211	1,202
Persons served, severely disabled [4][5]	1,000. . .	606	581	640	882	940	951	1,005	988	1,015
Percent of total persons served	Percent .	55	62	68	74	75	78	79	82	84

[1] Includes expenditures only under the basic support provisions of the Rehabilitation Act. [2] Persons successfully placed into gainful employment. [3] Persons rehabilitated as a percent of all active case closures (whether rehabilitated or not); beginning 1996, as a percent of persons who required services. [4] An individual with a severe disability is an individual whose severe physical or mental impairment seriously limits one or more functional capacities in terms of an employment outcome, and whose vocational rehabilitation can be expected to require multiple vocational rehabilitation services over an extended period of time. [5] Includes active cases accepted for rehabilitation services during year plus active cases on hand at beginning of year.
Source: U.S. Dept. of Education, Rehabilitation Services Administration, *Caseload Statistics of State Vocational Rehabilitation Agencies in Fiscal Years*, and *State Vocational Rehabilitation Agency Program Data in Fiscal Years*, both annual.

Social Insurance and Human Services   351

No. 532. Workers' Compensation Payments: 1980 to 2000

[In billions of dollars, except as indicated (79 represents 79,000,000). See headnote, Table 533]

Item	1980	1985	1990	1994	1995	1996	1997	1998	1999	2000
Workers covered [1] (mil.)	79	84	106	109	113	115	118	121	124	127
Premium amounts paid [2]	22.3	29.2	53.1	60.5	57.1	55.3	52.5	52.8	54.4	56.0
Private carriers [2]	15.7	19.5	35.1	34.0	31.6	30.5	29.5	30.1	30.8	32.6
State funds	3.0	3.5	8.0	11.2	10.5	10.2	9.5	9.8	10.6	9.8
Federal programs [3]	1.1	1.7	2.2	2.5	2.6	2.6	2.6	2.7	2.7	2.7
Self-insurers	2.4	4.5	7.9	12.8	12.5	12.0	11.0	10.2	10.4	10.9
Annual benefits paid [2]	13.6	22.2	38.2	44.6	43.4	41.8	41.1	42.2	43.1	45.9
By private carriers [2]	7.0	12.3	22.2	22.3	21.1	20.4	20.9	22.6	23.6	25.7
From state funds [4]	4.3	5.7	8.8	10.8	11.0	10.6	10.3	10.4	10.2	10.4
Employers' self-insurance [5]	2.3	4.1	7.2	11.5	11.2	10.8	9.9	9.2	9.3	9.8
Type of benefit:										
Medical/hospitalization	3.9	7.5	15.2	17.2	16.7	16.5	15.7	16.3	17.9	20.0
Compensation payments	9.7	14.7	23.1	27.5	26.7	25.3	25.4	25.9	25.2	25.9
Percent of covered payroll: [1]										
Workers' compensation costs [6][7]	1.96	1.82	2.18	2.05	1.83	1.66	1.47	1.37	1.32	1.25
Benefits [7]	1.07	1.30	1.57	1.51	1.39	1.26	1.15	1.10	1.04	1.03

[1] Data for years 1980 and 1985 not comparable with later years. [2] Premium and benefit amounts include estimated payments under insurance policy deductible provisions. Deductible benefits are allocated to private carriers and state funds. [3] Includes federal employer compensation program and that portion of federal black lung benefits program financed from employer contributions. [4] Net cash and medical benefits paid by competitive and exclusive state funds and by federal workers' compensation programs, including black lung benefit program. [5] Cash and medical benefits paid by self-insurers, plus value of medical benefits paid by employers carrying workers' compensation policies that exclude standard medical coverage. [6] Premiums written by private carriers and state funds, and benefits paid by self-insurers increased by 5-10 percent from 1980 to 1990 and by 11 percent for 1994-2000 for administrative costs. Also includes benefits paid and administrative costs of federal system for government employees. [7] Excludes programs financed from general revenue—black lung benefits and supplemental pensions in some states.

Source: 1980-1990, U.S. Social Security Administration, *Annual Statistical Supplement* to the *Social Security Bulletin.* Beginning 1994, National Academy of Social Insurance, Washington, DC, *Workers' Compensation: Benefits, Coverage, and Costs*, annual.

No. 533. Workers' Compensation Payments by State: 1990 to 2000

[In millions of dollars (38,238 represents $38,238,000,000). Calendar-year data, except fiscal-year data for federal civilian and other programs and for some states with state funds. Payments represent compensation and medical benefits and include insurance losses paid by private insurance carriers (compiled from state workers' compensation agencies and A.M. Best Co); disbursements of state funds (compiled from the A.M. Best Co. and state workers' compensation agencies); and self-insurance payments, based on information from the National Association of Insurance Commissioners and the source's estimates. Includes benefit payments under Longshore and Harbor Workers' Compensation Act for states in which such payments are made]

State	1990	1995	1998	1999	2000	State	1990	1995	1998	1999	2000
Total [1]	**38,238**	**43,373**	**42,213**	**43,137**	**45,916**	Nevada	339	365	330	373	287
						New Hampshire	169	169	164	170	168
Alabama	444	516	615	596	529	New Jersey	844	[2]972	955	987	1,067
Alaska	113	115	129	138	156	New Mexico	228	145	117	117	137
Arizona	371	386	394	427	482	New York	1,752	[2]2,780	2,686	2,782	2,828
Arkansas	229	187	161	165	188	North Carolina	480	495	766	708	788
California	6,065	[2]7,177	7,374	7,856	8,949	North Dakota	60	71	81	77	86
Colorado	595	584	710	655	769	Ohio	1,960	2,162	2,069	2,019	2,092
Connecticut	694	[2]733	711	722	667	Oklahoma	369	580	520	464	417
Delaware	75	[2]103	119	97	100						
District of Columbia	86	113	76	82	78	Oregon	573	463	431	384	413
Florida	1,976	2,518	2,208	2,080	2,273	Pennsylvania	2,019	[2]2,663	2,418	2,441	2,379
Georgia	735	699	809	814	882	Rhode Island	219	138	104	109	122
Hawaii	216	326	233	211	231	South Carolina	277	[2]353	484	512	597
Idaho	105	148	155	153	168	South Dakota	56	70	73	80	76
Illinois	1,607	1,438	1,690	1,716	1,813	Tennessee	463	396	518	513	588
Indiana	350	361	482	521	550	Texas	2,896	[2]2,006	1,494	1,673	1,949
Iowa	231	233	292	282	329	Utah	187	140	147	181	160
Kansas	266	[2]290	318	326	342	Vermont	61	65	95	104	114
Kentucky	383	498	431	461	516	Virginia	507	557	591	580	534
						Washington	883	1,129	1,309	1,418	1,499
Louisiana	575	516	429	428	455	West Virginia	389	529	629	665	741
Maine	380	286	246	249	252	Wisconsin	561	651	622	652	703
Maryland	505	522	1,045	1,152	1,195	Wyoming	49	74	74	71	46
Massachusetts	1,235	[2]775	641	634	666						
Michigan	1,205	[2]1,585	1,367	1,393	1,574	Federal programs:					
Minnesota	582	[2]733	732	745	798	Civilian employees	1,448	1,880	1,955	2,009	2,100
Mississippi	198	[2]218	235	253	269	Black lung benefits [3]	1,435	1,222	1,035	981	932
Missouri	496	733	589	591	526	Other [4]	11	(NA)	(NA)	(NA)	(NA)
Montana	150	140	171	145	150						
Nebraska	137	141	182	173	186						

NA Not available. [1] Total for 1995 includes an amount for benefits under deductible provisions not distributed by state. [2] Includes benefits under deductible provisions. [3] Includes payments by Social Security Administration and by Department of Labor. [4] Primarily payments made to dependents of reservists who died while on active duty in the Armed Forces.

Source: 1990, U.S. Social Security Administration, *Social Security Bulletin*, summer 1995, and selected prior issues. Beginning 1995, National Academy of Social Insurance, Washington, DC, *Workers' Compensation: Benefits, Coverage, and Costs*, annual.

No. 534. Supplemental Security Income—Recipients and Payments: 1980 to 2000

[As of December, except total payments, calendar year (4,142 represents 4,142,000). See also Appendix III]

Program	Unit	1980	1985	1990	1995	1996	1997	1998	1999	2000
Recipients, total [1]	1,000 . . .	**4,142**	**4,138**	**4,817**	**6,514**	**6,614**	**6,495**	**6,566**	**6,557**	**6,602**
Aged	1,000 . . .	1,808	1,504	1,454	1,446	1,413	1,363	1,332	1,308	1,289
Blind	1,000 . . .	78	82	84	84	82	81	80	79	79
Disabled	1,000 . . .	2,256	2,551	3,279	4,984	5,119	5,052	5,154	5,169	5,234
Payments, total [2]	Mil. dol .	**7,941**	**11,060**	**16,599**	**27,628**	**28,792**	**29,052**	**30,216**	**30,923**	**31,564**
Aged	Mil. dol .	2,734	3,035	3,736	4,467	4,507	4,532	4,425	4,712	4,811
Blind	Mil. dol .	190	264	334	376	372	375	366	391	394
Disabled	Mil. dol .	5,014	7,755	12,521	22,779	23,906	24,006	25,305	25,719	26,198
Average monthly payment, total [1]	Dollars . .	**168**	**226**	**299**	**358**	**363**	**351**	**359**	**368**	**378**
Aged	Dollars . .	128	164	213	251	261	268	277	289	299
Blind	Dollars . .	213	274	342	370	379	382	390	401	413
Disabled	Dollars . .	198	261	337	389	391	373	380	388	397

[1] Persons with a federal SSI payment and/or federally administered state supplementation.   [2] Includes payments not distributed by reason for eligibility.

No. 535. Supplemental Security Income (SSI)—Recipients and Payments by State and Other Area: 1995 to 2000

[Recipients as of December; payments for calendar year (6,514 represents 6,514,000). Data cover federal SSI payments and/or federally-administered state supplementation. For explanation of methodology, see Appendix III]

State and other area	Recipients (1,000)			Payments for year (mil. dol.)			State and other area	Recipients (1,000)			Payments for year (mil. dol.)		
	1995	1999	2000	1995	1999	2000		1995	1999	2000	1995	1999	2000
Total . . .	6,514	6,557	6,602	27,037	30,106	30,672	MO	114	111	112	431	463	471
U.S.	6,513	6,556	6,601	27,035	30,104	30,669	MT	14	14	14	53	56	57
AL	165	160	159	600	659	659	NE	21	21	21	76	84	85
AK	7	8	9	27	35	37	NV	21	24	25	79	101	108
AZ	73	79	81	288	340	355	NH	11	11	12	39	47	49
AR	94	88	85	326	339	333	NJ	144	146	146	594	665	672
CA	1,032	1,066	1,088	5,391	6,168	6,386	NM	45	46	47	166	187	193
CO	57	55	54	217	230	228	NY	589	609	617	2,724	3,118	3,197
CT	45	48	49	181	211	216	NC	191	192	191	639	720	732
DE	11	12	12	40	50	50	ND	9	8	8	29	30	30
DC	20	20	20	83	91	93	OH	248	243	240	1,044	1,125	1,114
FL	338	367	377	1,300	1,564	1,621	OK	74	73	72	266	297	302
GA	199	197	197	692	773	785	OR	47	51	52	183	219	228
HI	19	20	21	82	98	104	PA	265	278	284	1,159	1,339	1,367
ID	17	18	18	63	73	76	RI	24	27	28	100	124	130
IL	267	251	249	1,160	1,177	1,174	SC	111	108	107	384	423	429
IN	89	88	88	348	380	382	SD	14	13	13	47	49	48
IA	42	40	40	148	157	158	TN	180	166	164	648	666	664
KS	38	36	36	141	151	151	TX	404	408	409	1,391	1,557	1,575
KY	165	172	174	635	720	741	UT	20	20	20	80	87	87
LA	182	168	166	717	727	715	VT	13	13	13	50	51	51
ME	31	29	30	96	111	116	VA	130	132	132	471	530	535
MD	82	87	88	332	389	400	WA	92	98	101	398	469	484
MA	164	167	168	700	788	807	WV	68	71	71	276	316	318
MI	210	210	210	896	983	988	WI	112	87	85	487	363	357
MN	62	64	64	235	266	272	WY	6	6	6	21	23	23
MS	141	131	129	504	517	512	N. Mariana .	1	1	1	2	3	3

Source of Tables 534 and 535: U.S. Social Security Administration, *Annual Statistical Supplement* to the *Social Security Bulletin.*

No. 536. Temporary Assistance for Needy Families (TANF)—Families and Recipients: 1980 to 2001

[In thousands (3,712 represents 3,712,000). Average monthly families and recipients for calendar year, except 2001 for Jan.-Sept. period. Prior to TANF, the cash assistance program to families was called Aid to Families with Dependent Children (1980-1996). Under the new welfare law (Personal Responsibility and Work Opportunity Reconciliation Act of 1996), the program became TANF. See text, this section. Includes Puerto Rico, Guam, and Virgin Islands]

Year	Families	Recipients	Year	Families	Recipients	Year	Families	Recipients
1980	3,712	10,774	1988	3,749	10,915	1996	4,434	12,321
1981	3,835	11,079	1989	3,799	10,993	1997	3,740	10,376
1982	3,542	10,258	1990	4,057	11,695	1998	3,050	8,347
1983	3,686	10,761	1991	4,467	12,930	1999	2,554	6,828
1984	3,714	10,831	1992	4,829	13,773	2000	2,219	5,790
1985	3,701	10,855	1993	5,012	14,205	2001	2,110	5,420
1986	3,763	11,038	1994	5,033	14,161			
1987	3,776	11,027	1995	4,791	13,418			

Source: U.S. Administration for Children and Families, unpublished data.

U.S. Census Bureau, Statistical Abstract of the United States: 2002

No. 537. Temporary Assistance for Needy Families (TANF)—Recipients by State and Other Areas: 1995 to 2001

[In thousands (4,791 represents 4,791,000). Average monthly families and recipients for calendar year, except as noted. See headnote, Table 536]

State or other area	Families 1995	Families 2000	Families 2001 [1]	Recipients 1995	Recipients 2000	Recipients 2001 [1]	State or other area	Families 1995	Families 2000	Families 2001 [1]	Recipients 1995	Recipients 2000	Recipients 2001 [1]
Total .	4,791	2,219	2,110	13,418	5,790	5,420	MT......	11	5	5	33	13	14
U.S....	4,734	2,186	2,080	13,242	5,690	5,334	NE......	15	9	10	41	24	24
AL.....	45	19	18	114	45	43	NV......	16	6	8	41	16	20
AK.....	12	7	6	36	22	17	NH......	10	6	6	27	14	14
AZ.....	68	33	34	185	84	84	NJ......	110	50	45	310	125	112
AR.....	24	12	12	62	29	28	NM......	34	23	18	103	69	53
CA.....	916	492	471	2,675	1,283	1,219	NY......	452	250	223	1,241	695	600
CO.....	38	11	11	106	28	27	NC......	123	45	42	305	97	90
CT.....	61	27	26	169	64	59	ND......	5	3	3	14	8	9
DE.....	11	6	5	24	12	12	OH......	222	95	84	592	235	195
DC.....	26	17	16	72	46	43	OK......	44	14	14	120	35	34
FL.....	224	65	57	606	143	121	OR......	38	18	19	101	41	43
GA.....	138	52	50	378	125	119	PA......	201	88	82	582	232	213
HI.....	22	15	13	66	42	41	RI......	22	16	15	60	44	41
ID.....	9	1	1	24	2	2	SC......	48	16	17	127	37	41
IL.....	233	78	60	684	234	175	SD......	6	3	3	17	7	6
IN.....	62	37	42	177	101	118	TN......	102	57	60	271	148	156
IA.....	35	20	20	97	53	55	TX......	269	129	130	730	347	346
KS.....	28	13	13	77	32	33	UT......	16	8	7	44	22	22
KY.....	74	38	36	184	87	81	VT......	10	6	5	27	16	15
LA.....	77	27	25	251	71	64	VA......	70	31	29	179	69	64
ME.....	21	11	10	59	28	26	WA......	101	56	54	283	148	141
MD.....	80	29	28	220	72	67	WV......	38	13	15	102	33	40
MA.....	97	43	42	263	100	99	WI......	71	17	18	202	38	40
MI.....	195	72	72	578	199	197	WY......	5	1	1	14	1	1
MN.....	61	39	39	178	114	113	PR.....	54	32	26	164	88	74
MS.....	51	15	16	140	34	36	GU....	2	3	3	8	10	10
MO.....	88	47	45	249	125	121	VI.....	1	1	1	5	3	2

[1] January-September period only.

Source: U.S. Administration for Children and Families, unpublished data.

No. 538. Temporary Assistance for Needy Families (TANF)—Expenditures by State: 1999 and 2000

[In millions of dollars (22,585 represents $22,585,000,000), except as indicated. Represents federal and state funds expended in fiscal year]

State	1999, total	2000 Total [1]	2000 Percent federal funds	2000 Expenditures on assistance	State	1999, total	2000 Total [1]	2000 Percent federal funds	2000 Expenditures on assistance
U.S....	22,585	23,590	53	13,323	MO	317	321	54	189
AL.....	91	93	58	39	MT......	41	44	65	24
AK.....	88	93	46	67	NE......	116	77	63	48
AZ.....	240	265	65	118	NV......	65	56	51	23
AR.....	72	112	79	31	NH......	60	73	56	42
CA.....	6,252	6,228	53	4,761	NJ......	450	322	7	226
CO.....	160	205	42	51	NM......	130	149	73	113
CT.....	385	436	56	171	NY......	3,652	3,498	43	2,126
DE.....	59	55	56	24	NC......	394	435	59	140
DC.....	128	134	42	72	ND......	33	33	72	25
FL.....	484	765	51	265	OH......	656	987	60	394
GA.....	410	383	55	251	OK......	151	134	54	85
HI.....	168	161	52	141	OR......	286	256	64	128
ID	27	44	70	4	PA.....	1,038	891	54	496
IL.....	840	880	50	280	RI......	164	167	51	111
IN	188	342	65	113	SC......	107	124	71	29
IA	175	165	63	80	SD.....	22	21	59	21
KS.....	176	151	51	174	TN......	209	273	68	160
KY.....	208	205	65	108	TX......	591	743	66	315
LA.....	128	126	55	86	UT.....	80	91	72	45
ME.....	109	108	52	94	VT......	65	59	54	44
MD.....	328	333	47	196	VA.....	258	222	42	100
MA.....	632	587	39	255	WA.....	504	531	49	311
MI	1,034	1,198	61	384	WV	58	134	71	72
MN.....	377	382	50	193	WI	322	419	60	55
MS.....	44	62	63	37	WY	14	16	30	7

[1] Includes other items not shown separately.

Source: U.S. Administration for Children and Families, Temporary Assistance for Needy Families (TANF) Program, Annual Report to Congress.

No. 539. Child Support—Award and Recipiency Status of Custodial Parent: 1999

[In thousands except as noted (13,529 represents 13,529,000). Custodial parents 15 years and older with own children under 21 years of age present from absent parents as of spring 2000. Covers civilian noninstitutional population. Based on Current Population Survey; see text, Section 1, Population, and Appendix III. For definition of mean, see Guide to Tabular Presentation]

Award and recipiency status	All custodial parents				Custodial parents below the poverty level			
	Total				Total			
	Number	Percent distribu-tion	Mothers	Fathers	Number	Percent distribu-tion	Mothers	Fathers
Total	13,529	(X)	11,499	2,030	3,530	(X)	3,305	225
With child support agreement or award	7,945	(X)	7,150	795	1,803	(X)	1,730	73
Supposed to receive payments in 1999	6,791	100	6,133	658	1,486	100	1,421	65
Actually received payments in 1999	5,005	74	4,578	427	953	64	898	55
Received full amount	3,066	45	2,818	248	476	32	443	33
Received partial payments	1,939	29	1,760	179	477	32	455	22
Did not receive payments in 1999	1,786	26	1,555	231	533	36	523	10
Child support not awarded	5,584	(X)	4,349	1,235	1,727	(X)	1,575	152
MEAN INCOME AND CHILD SUPPORT								
Received child support payments in 1999:								
Mean total money income (dol.)	26,183	(X)	24,983	39,047	7,169	(X)	7,098	(B)
Mean child support received (dol.)	3,787	(X)	3,844	3,175	2,784	(X)	2,788	(B)
Received the full amount due:								
Mean total money income (dol.)	28,277	(X)	27,113	41,480	6,996	(X)	6,927	(B)
Mean child support received (dol.)	4,853	(X)	4,914	4,164	3,999	(X)	4,038	(B)
Received partial payments:								
Mean total money income (dol.)	22,873	(X)	21,573	35,669	7,343	(X)	7,264	(B)
Mean child support received (dol.)	2,100	(X)	2,131	1,802	1,572	(X)	1,572	(B)
Received no payments in 1999:								
Mean total money income (dol.)	23,004	(X)	19,845	44,314	6,230	(X)	6,307	(B)
Without child support agreement or award:								
Mean total money income (dol.)	21,803	(X)	16,762	39,552	5,747	(X)	5,693	6,310

B Base too small to meet statistical standards for reliability.   X Not applicable.

Source: U.S. Census Bureau, unpublished data.

No. 540. Child Support Enforcement Program—Caseload and Collections: 1990 to 2001

[For years ending Sept. 30 (12,796 represents 12,796,000). Includes Puerto Rico, Guam, and the Virgin Islands. The child support enforcement program locates absent parents, establishes paternity of children born out-of-wedlock, and establishes and enforces support orders. By law, these services are available to all families that need them. The program is operated at the state and local government level but 68 percent of administrative costs are paid by the federal government. Child support collected for families not receiving Temporary Assistance for Needy Families (TANF) goes to the family to help it remain self-sufficient. Most of the child support collected on behalf of TANF families goes to federal and state governments to offset TANF payments. Based on data reported by state agencies. Minus sign (-) indicates net outlay]

Item	Unit	1990	1995	1996	1997	1998	1999	2000	2001, prel.
Total cases	1,000	12,796	19,162	19,319	19,057	19,419	17,330	17,334	17,060
Paternities established, total	1,000	393	659	734	814	848	845	867	776
Support orders established, total	1,000	[1]1,022	1,051	1,093	1,260	1,148	1,220	1,175	1,182
FINANCES									
Collections, total	Mil. dol	6,010	10,827	12,020	13,364	14,348	15,901	17,854	18,958
TANF/FC collections [2]	Mil. dol	1,750	2,689	2,855	2,843	2,650	2,482	2,593	2,592
State share	Mil. dol	620	939	1,014	1,159	1,089	1,048	1,080	1,004
Incentive payments to states	Mil. dol	264	400	409	410	396	377	353	337
Federal share	Mil. dol	533	822	888	1,046	961	922	968	895
Non-TANF collections	Mil. dol	4,260	8,138	9,165	10,521	11,698	13,419	15,261	16,366
Administrative expenditures, total	Mil. dol	1,606	3,012	3,049	3,428	3,585	4,039	4,526	4,835
State share	Mil. dol	545	918	1,014	1,100	1,200	1,359	1,519	1,613
Federal share	Mil. dol	1,061	2,095	2,035	2,328	2,385	2,680	3,006	3,222
Program savings, total	Mil. dol	-190	-852	-738	-813	-1,139	-1,692	-2,125	-2,599
State share	Mil. dol	338	421	409	469	286	66	-87	-272
Federal share	Mil. dol	-528	-1,273	-1,147	-1,282	-1,424	-1,758	-2,038	-2,327

[1] Includes modifications to orders.   [2] Collections for current assistance cases where the children are: (1) recipients of TANF under title IV-A of the Social Security Act or (2) entitled to Foster Care (FC) maintenance under title IV-E of the Social Security Act plus collections distributed as assistance reimbursements. Includes medical support and payments to families of current assistance not shown separately.

Source: U.S. Department of Health and Human Services, Office of Child Support Enforcement, *Annual Report to Congress.*

Social Insurance and Human Services   355

No. 541. Federal Food Programs: 1990 to 2001

[20.1 represents 20,100,000. For years ending Sept. 30. Program data include Puerto Rico, Virgin Islands, Guam, American Samoa, Northern Marianas, and the former Trust Territory when a federal food program was operated in these areas. Participation data are average monthly figures except as noted. Participants are not reported for the commodity distribution programs. Cost data are direct federal benefits to recipients; they exclude Federal administrative payments and applicable state and local contributions. Federal costs for commodities and cash-in-lieu of commodities are shown separately from direct cash benefits for those programs receiving both]

Program	Unit	1990	1995	1996	1997	1998	1999	2000	2001
Food Stamp:									
Participants	Million	20.1	26.6	25.5	22.9	19.8	18.2	17.2	17.3
Federal cost	Mil. dol.	14,187	22,765	22,441	19,550	16,889	15,755	14,985	15,535
Monthly average coupon value per recipient	Dollars	58.92	71.26	73.21	71.27	71.12	72.21	72.78	74.76
Nutrition assistance program for Puerto Rico:									
Federal cost	Mil. dol.	937	1,131	1,143	1,174	1,204	1,236	1,268	1,296
National school lunch program (NSLP):									
Free lunches served	Million	1,662	2,090	2,128	2,194	2,198	2,207	2,205	2,183
Reduced-price lunches served	Million	273	309	326	347	362	392	409	424
Children participating [1]	Million	24.1	25.7	25.9	26.3	26.6	26.9	27.2	27.5
Federal cost	Mil. dol.	3,214	4,466	4,662	4,934	5,102	5,314	5,493	5,613
School breakfast (SB):									
Children participating [1]	Million	4.1	6.3	6.6	6.9	7.1	7.4	7.6	7.8
Federal cost	Mil. dol.	596	1,049	1,119	1,214	1,272	1,345	1,393	1,448
Special supplemental food program (WIC): [2]									
Participants	Million	4.5	6.9	7.2	7.4	7.4	7.3	7.2	7.3
Federal cost	Mil. dol.	1,637	2,517	2,690	2,815	2,808	2,853	2,852	3,008
Child and adult care (CC): [3]									
Participants [4]	Million	1.5	2.4	2.4	2.5	2.6	2.7	2.7	2.7
Federal cost	Mil. dol.	720	1,296	1,360	1,393	1,372	1,438	1,501	1,548
Federal cost of commodities donated to— [5]									
Child nutrition (NSLP, CC, SF [6], and SB)	Mil. dol.	646	733	734	661	774	754	704	917
Emergency feeding [7]	Mil. dol.	286	100	52	152	190	225	181	332

[1] Average monthly participation (excluding summer months of June through August). Includes children in public and private elementary and secondary schools and in residential child care institutes. [2] WIC serves pregnant and postpartum women, infants, and children up to age five. [3] Program provides year-round subsidies to feed preschool children in child care centers and family day care homes. Certain care centers serving disabled or elderly adults also receive meal subsidies. [4] Average quarterly daily attendance at participating institutions. [5] Includes the Federal cost of commodity entitlements, cash-in-lieu of commodities, and bonus foods. [6] Summer Feeding (SF) program provides free meals to children in poor areas during summer months. [7] Provides free commodities to needy persons for home consumption through food banks, hunger centers, soup kitchens, and similar nonprofit agencies. Includes the Emergency Food Assistance Program, the commodity purchases for soup kitchens/food banks program, and commodity disaster relief.

No. 542. Federal Food Stamp Program by State: 1995 to 2001

[Participation data are average monthly number (26,619 represents 26,619,000). For years ending Sept. 30. Food stamp costs are for benefits only and exclude administrative expenditures]

State	Persons (1,000)			Benefits (mil. dol.)		
	1995	2000	2001	1995	2000	2001
Total [1]	26,619	17,158	17,316	22,765	14,985	15,535
U.S.	26,579	17,120	17,280	22,714	14,928	15,480
AL	525	396	411	441	344	365
AK	45	38	38	50	46	47
AZ	480	259	291	414	240	280
AR	272	247	256	212	206	223
CA	3,175	1,832	1,668	2,473	1,639	1,582
CO	252	156	154	217	127	131
CT	226	165	157	169	138	136
DE	57	32	32	47	31	32
DC	94	81	73	93	77	70
FL	1,395	882	887	1,307	773	771
GA	816	559	574	700	489	515
HI	125	118	108	177	166	150
ID	80	58	60	59	46	47
IL	1,151	779	825	1,056	777	810
IN	470	300	347	382	268	306
IA	184	123	126	141	100	107
KS	184	117	124	144	83	92
KY	520	403	413	413	337	350
LA	711	500	518	629	448	483
ME	132	102	104	112	81	86
MD	399	219	208	365	199	191
MA	410	232	219	315	182	173
MI	971	603	641	806	457	504
MN	308	196	198	240	165	172
MS	480	276	298	383	226	254
MO	576	423	454	488	358	395
MT	71	59	62	57	51	54
NE	105	82	81	77	61	63
NV	99	61	69	91	57	65
NH	58	36	36	44	28	28
NJ	551	345	318	506	304	292
NM	239	169	163	196	140	137
NY	2,183	1,439	1,354	2,065	1,361	1,365
ND	41	32	38	32	25	27
NC	614	488	494	495	403	425
OH	1,155	610	641	1,017	520	573
OK	375	253	271	315	208	236
OR	289	234	281	254	198	238
PA	1,173	777	748	1,006	656	639
RI	93	74	71	82	59	59
SC	364	295	316	297	249	269
SD	50	43	45	40	37	39
TN	662	496	522	554	415	454
TX	2,558	1,333	1,366	2,246	1,215	1,270
UT	119	82	80	90	68	67
VT	59	41	39	46	32	31
VA	546	336	332	450	263	263
WA	476	295	309	417	241	261
WV	309	227	221	253	185	178
WI	320	193	216	220	129	152
WY	34	22	23	28	19	19

[1] Includes Guam and the Virgin Islands. Several outlying areas receive nutrition assistance grants in lieu of food stamp assistance (e.g., Puerto Rico, American Samoa and the Northern Marianas).

Source of Tables 541 and 542: U.S. Dept. of Agriculture, Food and Nutrition Service. "Food and Nutrition Service, Program Data"; <http://www.fns.usda.gov/pd/>; updated monthly.

No. 543. Selected Characteristics of Food Stamp Households and Participants: 1990 to 2000

[For years ending September 30. Data for 1990-1992 exclude Guam and the Virgin Islands. Based on a sample of households from the Food Stamp Quality Control System]

Year	Households				Participants		
	Total (1,000)	Percent of total			Total (1,000)	Percent of total	
		With children	With elderly [1]	With disabled [2]		Children	Elderly [1]
1990	7,803	60.3	18.1	8.9	20,411	49.6	7.7
1991	8,855	60.4	16.4	9.0	22,963	52.0	7.0
1992	10,049	62.2	15.4	9.5	25,743	51.9	6.6
1993	10.791	62.1	15.5	10.7	27,595	51.5	6.8
1994	11,091	61.1	15.8	12.5	28,009	51.4	7.0
1995	10,883	59.7	16.0	18.9	26,955	51.5	7.1
1996	10,552	59.5	16.2	20.2	25,926	51.0	7.3
1997	9,452	58.3	17.6	22.3	23,117	51.4	7.9
1998	8,246	58.3	18.2	24.4	19,969	52.8	8.2
1999	7,670	55.7	20.1	26.5	18,149	51.5	9.4
2000	7,335	53.9	21.0	27.5	17,091	51.3	10.0

[1] Persons 60 years old and over. [2] Beginning 1995, disabled households are defined as households with at least one member under age 65 who received SSI, or at least one member age 18 to 61 who received Social Security, veterans benefits, or other government benefits as a result of a disability. For years prior to 1995, disabled households are defined as households with SSI but no members over age 59. The substantial increase in the percentage of households with a disabled member between 1994 and 1995 is due in part to the change in the definition of disabled households. Using the previous definition, 13.3 percent of households included a disabled person in fiscal year 1995.

No. 544. Food Stamp Households and Participants—Summary: 2000

[For year ending September 30. Based on a sample of 46,963 households from the Food Stamp Quality Control System]

Household type and income source	Households		Age, sex, race, and Hispanic origin	Participants	
	Number (1,000)	Percent		Number (1,000)	Percent
Total	7,335	100.0	Total [1]	17,091	100.0
With children	3,955	53.9	Children.................	8,765	51.3
Single-parent households	2,704	36.9	Under 5 years old.........	2,846	16.7
Married-couple households	573	7.8	5 to 17 years old	5,919	34.6
Other	676	9.2	Adults	8,325	48.7
With elderly	1,542	21.0	18 to 35 years old	3,396	19.9
Living alone..................	1,226	16.7	36 to 59 years old	3,226	18.9
Not living alone...............	316	4.3	60 years old and over	1,702	10.0
Disabled	2,017	27.5			
Living alone.................	1,154	15.6	Male	6,891	40.3
Not living alone...............	863	11.8	Female	10,198	59.7
Earned income................	1,993	27.2	White, non-Hispanic	6,837	40.0
Wages and salaries.............	1,857	25.3	Black, non-Hispanic	6,123	35.8
Unearned income................	5,775	78.7	Hispanic..................	3,168	18.5
TANF [2]	1,891	25.8	Asian....................	591	3.5
Supplemental Security Income.	2,324	31.7	Native American	290	1.7
Social Security	1,870	25.5	Other....................	83	0.5
No income	617	8.4			

[1] Includes persons of unknown age not shown separately. [2] Temporary Assistance for Needy Families (TANF) program.

Source of Tables 543 and 544: U.S. Dept. of Agriculture, Food and Nutrition Service, *Characteristics of Food Stamp Households: Fiscal Year 2000*, October 2001.

No. 545. Head Start—Summary: 1980 to 2001

[For years ending September 30 (376 represents 376,000)]

Year	Enrollment (1,000)	Appropriation (mil. dol.)	Age and race	Enrollment, 2001 (percent)	Item	Number
1980 ...	376	735	Under 3 years old	7	Average cost per child (dollars):	
1985 ...	452	1,075	3 years old..........	35	1995...............	4,534
1990 ...	541	1,552	4 years old..........	54	2000...............	5,951
1992 ...	621	2,202	5 years old and over ...	4	2001.................	6,633
1993 ...	714	2,776				
1994 ...	740	3,326			Paid staff (1,000):	
1995 ...	751	3,534	White	30	1995................	147
1996 ...	752	3,569	Black	34	2000................	180
1997 ...	794	3,981	Hispanic	30	2001................	195
1998 ...	822	4,347	American Indian	4	Volunteers (1,000):	
1999 ...	826	4,658	Asian	2	1995................	1,235
2000 ...	858	5,267	Hawaiian/		2000................	1,252
2001 ...	905	6,200	Pacific Islander	1	2001................	1,345

Source: U.S. Administration for Children and Families, "Head Start Statistical Fact Sheet"; <http://www2.acf.dhhs.gov/programs/hsb/research/index.htm>.

Social Insurance and Human Services   357

No. 546. Social Assistance—Taxable Establishments, Receipts, Payroll, and Employees by Kind of Business: 1997

[18,051 represents $18,051,000,000]

Kind of business	NAICS code [1]	All firms		Employer firms			
		Establishments (number)	Receipts (mil. dol.)	Establishments (number)	Receipts (mil. dol.)	Annual payroll (mil. dol.)	Paid employees [2] (1,000)
Social assistance	624	583,203	18,051	56,691	12,599	5,766	491.1
Individual & family services	6241	43,070	3,228	9,843	2,636	1,113	68.8
Child & youth services	62411	(NA)	(NA)	1,648	539	210	11.5
Services for elderly & disabled persons . . .	62412	(NA)	(NA)	2,976	807	394	32.2
Other individual & family services	62419	(NA)	(NA)	5,219	1,290	508	25.1
Community/emergency & other relief services	6242	1,682	136	344	112	29	1.6
Community food services	62421	(NA)	(NA)	95	18	4	0.4
Community housing services	62422	(NA)	(NA)	167	74	21	1.0
Emergency & other relief services	62423	(NA)	(NA)	82	20	4	0.2
Vocational rehabilitation services	6243	5,762	1,514	2,549	1,432	676	32.0
Child day care services	6244	532,689	13,172	43,955	8,419	3,948	388.7

NA Not available.   [1] North American Industry Classification System, 1997; see text, Section 15, Business Enterprise.   [2] For pay period including March 12.

No. 547. Social Assistance—Tax-Exempt Establishments, Receipts, Payroll, and Employees by Kind of Business: 1997

[44,756 represents $44,756,000,000. Covers establishments with payroll only]

Kind of business	NAICS code [1]	Establishments (number)	Receipts (mil. dol.)	Annual payroll (mil. dol)	Paid employees [2] (1,000)
Social assistance	624	69,737	44,756	18,628	1,253.1
Individual & family services	6241	36,364	26,453	10,781	642.6
Child & youth services	62411	11,086	7,719	3,171	172.0
Services for elderly & disabled persons	62412	9,960	8,217	3,260	226.7
Other individual & family services	62419	15,318	10,516	4,350	243.9
Community/emergency & other relief services . .	6242	9,606	6,085	1,739	100.8
Community food services	62421	2,988	1,598	324	23.0
Community housing services	62422	4,737	2,954	1,079	60.2
Emergency & other relief services	62423	1,881	1,534	336	17.7
Vocational rehabilitation services	6243	5,668	6,462	3,093	269.7
Child day care services	6244	18,099	5,757	3,015	240.0

[1] North American Industry Classification System, 1997; see text, Section 15, Business Enterprise.   [2] For pay period including March 12.

Source of Tables 546 and 547: U.S. Census Bureau, *1997 Economic Census, Health Care and Social Assistance*, Series EC97S62A-US, issued October 1999 and *Nonemployer Statistics*.

No. 548. Social Assistance Services—Revenue for Employer Firms: 1998 to 2000

[In millions of dollars (60,816 represents $60,816,000,000). Based on the North American Industry Classification System (NAICS), see text, Section 15, Business Enterprise]

Kind of business	NAICS code	1998, total	1999, total	2000		
				Total	Taxable firms	Tax-exempt firms
Social assistance	624	60,816	66,191	73,754	16,417	57,337
Individual and family services	6241	30,554	33,174	37,277	3,470	33,807
Child and youth services	62411	8,294	8,937	9,993	786	9,207
Services for elderly and disabled persons . . .	62412	9,566	10,259	11,270	1,011	10,259
Other individual and family services	62419	12,694	13,979	16,014	1,674	14,340
Community, emergency and other relief services	6242	6,416	6,981	7,735	263	7,472
Community food services	62421	1,766	1,949	2,193	(S)	2,073
Community housing services	62422	3,221	3,469	3,855	123	3,732
Emergency and other relief services	62423	1,428	1,563	1,688	(S)	1,667
Vocational rehabilitation services	6243	8,719	9,373	10,558	1,991	8,567
Child day care services	6244	15,127	16,663	18,184	10,693	7,491

S Figure does not meet publication standards.

Source: U.S. Census Bureau, *Service Annual Survey, 2000.*

No. 549. Social Assistance—Nonemployer Establishments and Receipts: 1997 to 1999

[Receipts in millions of dollars (5,451 represents $5,451,000,000). Includes only firms subject to federal income tax. Nonemployers are businesses with no paid employees. Based on the North American Industry Classification System (NAICS), see text, Section 15, Business Enterprise]

Kind of business	NAICS code	Establishments			Receipts		
		1997	1998	1999	1997	1998	1999
Social assistance, total	624	526,512	560,373	605,113	5,451	6,004	6,793
Individual & family services	6241	33,227	51,399	63,775	592	753	949
Community/emergency & other relief services ..	6242	1,338	2,614	3,333	24	33	45
Vocational rehabilitation services...........	6243	3,213	5,351	6,731	82	111	134
Child day care services.................	6244	488,734	501,009	531,274	4,754	5,107	5,665

Source: U.S. Census Bureau, "Nonemployer Statistics"; published 28 March 2002; <http://www.census.gov/epcd/nonemployer/>.

No. 550. Child Care Arrangements of Preschool Children by Type of Arrangement: 1991 to 1999

[In percent, except as indicated (8,428 represents 8,428,000). Estimates are based on children 3 to 5 years old who have not entered kindergarten. Based on interviews from a sample survey of the civilian, noninstitutional population in households with telephones; see source for details]

Characteristic	Children		Type of nonparental arrangement [1]			
	Number (1,000)	Percent distribution	In relative care	In nonrelative care	In center-based program [2]	With parental care only
1991, total	8,428	100.0	16.9	14.8	52.8	31.0
1995, total	9,232	100.0	19.4	16.9	55.1	25.9
1999, total	**8,549**	**100.0**	**23.3**	**15.9**	**59.3**	**23.3**
Age:						
3 years old	3,827	44.8	25.1	16.5	45.6	30.7
4 years old	3,722	43.5	22.3	15.3	68.9	18.3
5 years old	1,001	11.7	20.3	16.2	76.1	13.5
Race-ethnicity:						
White, non-Hispanic	5,296	61.9	18.8	19.3	59.4	23.6
Black, non-Hispanic.	1,258	14.7	36.0	8.0	72.5	13.1
Hispanic	1,421	16.6	25.9	12.7	44.4	33.6
Other	574	6.7	31.0	9.9	66.0	17.5
Household income:						
Less than $10,001	1,126	13.2	28.9	12.8	56.6	26.6
$10,001 to $20,000	1,395	16.3	29.5	12.9	51.1	28.1
$20,001 to $30,000	1,327	15.5	27.7	12.2	50.8	29.6
$30,001 to $40,000	1,050	12.3	23.3	14.9	54.5	25.3
$40,001 to $50,000	792	9.3	20.9	14.2	59.7	23.1
$50,001 to $75,000	1,351	15.8	17.3	20.5	65.5	19.0
$75,001 or more	1,509	17.7	16.2	21.9	74.0	13.4

[1] Columns do not add to 100.0 because some children participated in more than one type of nonparental arrangement.
[2] Center-based programs include day care centers, head start programs, preschools, prekindergarten, and nursery schools.

Source: U.S. National Center for Education Statistics, *Digest of Education Statistics, 2000.*

No. 551. Licensed Child Care Centers and Family Child Care Providers by State: 2001

[Centers as of February; family child care providers as of August]

State	Licensed child care centers	Licensed family child care providers	State	Licensed child care centers	Licensed family child care providers	State	Licensed child care centers	Licensed family child care providers
US, total . . .	110,791	305,987	KY	2,100	7,081	OH.	3,413	14,468
AL	1,385	2,840	LA	2,110	11,666	OK.	1,945	4,184
AK	246	1,962	ME.	904	2,087	OR.	863	7,320
AZ	2,357	4,219	MD.	2,385	10,538	PA	3,693	4,869
AR	2,638	1,282	MA.	2,337	10,404	RI	415	1,056
CA.	13,829	43,909	MI	4,873	15,314	SC	1,742	1,852
CO.	2,632	4,964	MN.	1,590	15,559	SD	216	1,035
CT	1,641	3,783	MS.	1,760	888	TN	3,234	2,512
DE	302	1,766	MO	1,691	2,720	TX	10,422	15,061
DC.	369	215	MT	251	1,525	UT	320	1,886
FL	6,303	8,253	NE	798	3,304	VT	570	1,320
GA.	2,556	6,744	NV	438	616	VA	2,515	4,050
HI	500	501	NH.	830	435	WA	2,064	7,244
ID	504	1,108	NJ	3,800	5,100	WV	474	4,322
IL	3,003	10,591	NM.	992	319	WI	2,289	8,029
IN	682	3,961	NY	3,655	22,388	WY	207	646
IA	1,533	5,424	NC	3,920	5,189			
KS	1,379	7,521	ND	116	1,957			

Source: Children's Foundation, Washington, DC, *Child Care Center Licensing Study and Family Child Care Licensing Study,* annual (copyright).

Social Insurance and Human Services   359

No. 552. Charity Contributions—Average Dollar Amount: 1991 to 2000

[Estimates cover households' contribution activity (both cash and in-kind) for the year and are based on respondents' replies as to contribution and volunteer activity of household. For 2000, based on a sample survey of 4,216 persons 21 years old and over conducted during the spring of the following year and subject to sampling variability; see source]

Year and age	All contributing households — Average amount (dol.)	Percent of household income	Contributors and volunteers — Average amount (dol.)	Percent of household income	Household income	All contributing households — Average amount (dol.)	Percent of household income	Contributors and volunteers — Average amount (dol.)	Percent of household income
1991	899	2.2	1,155	2.6	**2000—**				
1995	1,017	2.2	1,279	2.6	Under $10,000	296	5.5	382	6.7
					$10,000-$19,999 . . .	465	3.3	624	4.4
2000, total .	1,623	3.2	2,295	4.0	$20,000-$29,999 . . .	916	3.9	1,299	5.5
21-24 years . .	958	2.3	1,635	3.1	$30,000-$39,999 . . .	1,036	3.1	1,408	4.2
25-34 years . .	1,002	2.3	1,411	3.1	$40,000-$49,999 . . .	1,147	2.7	1,638	3.8
35-44 years . .	1,831	2.8	2,471	3.5	$50,000-$59,999 . . .	1,566	3.0	1,989	3.8
45-54 years . .	1,818	2.9	2,632	3.8	$60,000-$74,999 . . .	1,935	3.0	2,483	3.8
55-64 years . .	1,888	3.3	2,626	4.3	$75,000-$99,999 . . .	2,119	2.6	2,530	3.1
65-74 years . .	1,798	4.5	2,307	5.5	$100,000 and over .	3,976	2.7	4,894	3.3
75 years and over	1,628	5.1	2,498	6.5					
					Itemizers [1]	2,288	3.6	2,903	4.3
White	1,693	3.2	2,359	4.0	Claimed charitable deduction . .	2,733	4.0	3,262	4.6
Black	1,488	3.3	2,300	4.3	Didn't claim charitable deduction .	868	2.4	1,207	2.9
Hispanic [2] . . .	1,276	2.5	2,285	3.6	Nonitemizers	954	2.7	1,464	3.6

[1] Persons who itemized their deductions on their 2000 federal tax returns. [2] Hispanic persons may be of any race.

No. 553. Charity Contributions—Percent of Households Contributing by Dollar Amount, 1991 to 2000, and Type of Charity, 2000

[In percent, except as noted. See headnote, Table 552]

Annual amount of household contributions	All households 1991	All households 1995	All households 2000	Givers 1991	Givers 1995	Givers 2000	Type of charity	2000 Percentage of households	2000 Average contribution [1] (dol.)
None	27.8	31.5	11.7	(X)	(X)	(X)	Arts, culture, humanities .	16.6	234
Givers	72.2	68.5	88.3	100.0	100.0	100.0	Education	29.9	508
$1 to $100. . . .	14.9	15.2	14.2	24.9	24.3	17.6	Environment.	19.0	195
$101 to $200 . .	8.1	7.2	8.6	13.5	11.6	10.6	Health.	38.0	224
$201 to $300 . .	7.3	5.7	5.7	12.2	9.2	7.1	Human services	34.7	338
$301 to $400 . .	3.3	4.7	3.8	5.6	7.5	4.7	International	6.3	254
$401 to $500 . .	3.2	5.2	4.3	5.4	8.3	5.3	Private, community		
$501 to $600 . .	2.6	3.0	3.2	4.4	4.7	4.0	foundations	7.3	238
$601 to $700 . .	2.5	2.6	3.1	4.2	4.1	3.8	Public, societal benefit . .	11.1	251
$701 to $999 . .	3.4	3.7	6.2	5.7	6.0	7.7	Recreation - adults	5.9	371
$1,000 or more. .	14.5	15.2	31.9	24.2	24.3	39.4	Religion.	60.6	1,358
Not reported . .	12.4	5.9	7.3	(X)	(X)	(X)	Youth development	33.8	254

X Not applicable. [1] Average contribution per household making a contribution to the specified type of charity.
Source of Tables 552 and 553: Toppe, Chris, Arthur Kirsch, and Westat, Inc., *Giving and Volunteering in the United States: 2001 Edition*. (Copyright and published by INDEPENDENT SECTOR, Washington, DC, 2002).

No. 554. Private Philanthropy Funds by Source and Allocation: 1990 to 2001

[In billions of dollars (101.4 represents $101,400,000,000). Estimates for sources of funds based on U.S. Internal Revenue Service reports of individual charitable deductions and household surveys of giving by Independent Sector. For corporate giving, data are corporate charitable deductions from the US Internal Revenue Service and the contributions made by corporate foundations as reported by the Foundation Center. Data about foundation donations are based upon surveys of foundations and data provided by the Foundation Center. Estimates of the allocation of funds were derived from surveys of nonprofits conducted by various sources]

Source and allocation	1990	1991	1992	1993	1994	1995	1996	1997	1998	1999	2000	2001
Total funds	101.4	105.0	110.4	116.5	119.2	124.0	138.6	157.1	174.8	199.0	210.9	212.0
Individuals	81.0	84.3	87.7	92.0	92.5	95.4	107.6	122.0	135.8	152.6	158.9	160.7
Foundations [1]	7.2	7.7	8.6	9.5	9.7	10.6	12.0	13.9	17.0	20.5	24.6	25.9
Corporations	5.5	5.3	5.9	6.5	7.0	7.3	7.5	8.6	8.5	10.2	10.3	9.1
Charitable bequests	7.6	7.8	8.2	8.5	10.0	10.7	11.5	12.6	13.6	15.6	17.1	16.3
Allocation:												
Religion.	49.8	50.0	51.0	52.9	56.4	58.1	61.9	64.7	68.2	71.2	77.4	81.0
Health.	9.9	9.7	10.2	10.8	11.5	12.6	13.9	14.0	16.9	18.0	18.8	18.4
Education	12.4	13.5	14.3	15.4	16.6	17.6	19.2	22.0	25.3	27.5	31.7	31.8
Human service	11.8	11.1	11.6	12.5	11.7	11.7	12.2	12.7	16.1	17.4	18.0	20.7
Arts, culture and humanities . .	7.9	8.8	9.3	9.6	9.7	10.0	10.9	10.6	10.5	11.1	11.5	12.1
Public/societal benefit.	4.9	4.9	5.0	5.4	6.1	7.1	7.6	8.4	10.9	11.0	11.6	11.8
Environment/wildlife	2.5	2.8	2.9	3.0	3.3	3.8	3.8	4.1	5.3	5.8	6.2	6.4
International	1.3	1.9	2.2	2.2	2.4	2.9	2.8	2.6	2.9	3.6	3.7	4.1
Gifts to foundations [1]	3.8	4.5	5.0	6.3	6.3	8.5	12.6	14.0	19.9	28.8	24.7	([2])
Unallocated [3]	-3.0	-2.0	-1.2	-1.5	-4.9	-8.2	-6.2	4.1	-1.1	4.8	7.3	25.6

[1] Data are from the Foundation Center. [2] Included in "Unallocated." [3] Money received by charities but not allocated to sources.
Source: AAFRC Trust for Philanthropy, Indianapolis, IN, researched and written by the Center on Philanthropy at Indiana University, *Giving USA*, annual (copyright).

No. 555. Foundations—Number and Finances: 1980 to 2000

[48.2 represents $48,200,000,000. Covers nongovernmental nonprofit organizations with funds and programs managed by their own trustees or directors, whose goals were to maintain or aid social, educational, religious, or other activities deemed to serve the common good. Excludes organizations that make general appeals to the public for funds, act as trade associations for industrial or other special groups, or do not currently award grants. Constant dollar figures based on Consumer Price Index, all urban consumers, supplied by US Bureau of Labor Statistics. Minus sign (-) indicates decrease]

| | | Assets | | | | Total giving [2] | | | | Gifts received | | | |
| | | Current dollars | | Constant (1975) dollars | | Current dollars | | Constant (1975) dollars | | Current dollars | | Constant (1978) dollars | |
Year	Number of foundations	Amount (bil. dol.)	Percent change[1]	Amount (bil. dol.)	Percent change[1]	Amount (bil. dol.)	Percent change[1]	Amount (bil. dol.)	Percent change[1]	Amount (bil. dol.)	Percent change[1]	Amount (bil. dol.)	Percent change[1]
1980	22,088	48.2	15.8	31.5	2.0	3.4	20.4	2.2	6.0	2.0	-10.4	1.6	-21.1
1985	25,639	102.1	37.8	51.1	33.1	6.0	19.6	3.0	15.5	4.7	40.8	2.9	35.9
1990	32,401	142.5	3.6	58.7	-1.7	8.7	9.7	3.6	4.1	5.0	-10.0	2.5	-14.6
1991	33,356	162.9	14.3	64.4	9.7	9.2	6.1	3.6	1.8	5.5	9.9	2.6	5.6
1992	35,765	176.8	8.5	67.8	5.4	10.2	10.9	3.9	7.6	6.2	13.1	2.9	9.7
1993	37,571	189.2	7.0	70.5	3.9	11.1	8.8	4.1	5.7	7.8	25.6	3.5	22.0
1994	38,807	195.8	3.5	71.1	0.9	11.3	1.6	4.1	-0.9	8.1	4.2	3.6	1.5
1995	40,140	226.7	15.8	80.1	12.6	12.3	8.6	4.3	5.6	10.3	27.0	4.4	23.5
1996	41,588	267.6	18.0	92.2	14.6	13.8	12.9	4.8	9.6	16.0	56.1	6.7	51.7
1997	44,146	329.9	23.3	110.6	19.9	16.0	15.5	5.4	12.8	15.8	-1.2	6.4	-3.4
1998	46,832	385.1	16.7	127.1	14.9	19.5	21.7	6.4	19.8	22.6	42.6	9.0	40.4
1999	50,201	448.6	16.5	144.9	14.0	23.3	19.9	7.5	17.3	32.1	42.1	12.6	39.0
2000	56,582	486.1	8.4	151.9	4.8	27.6	18.2	8.6	14.3	27.6	-13.9	10.5	-16.7

[1] Percent change from immediate preceding year. [2] Includes grants, scholarships, and employee matching gifts.

Source: The Foundation Center, New York, NY, FC Stats; <http://fdncenter.org/fcstats/index.html>; (copyright).

No. 556. Foundations—Number and Finances by Asset Size: 1999

[Figures are for latest year reported by foundations (448,612 represents $448,612,000,000). See headnote, Table 555]

| Asset size | Number | Assets (mil. dol.) | Gifts received (mil. dol.) | Expenditures (mil. dol.) | Grants (mil. dol.) | Percent distribution | | | | |
						Number	Assets	Gifts received	Expenditures	Grants
Total	50,201	448,612	32,077	28,911	23,321	100.0	100.0	100.0	100.0	100.0
Under $50,000	7,553	128	389	509	466	15.1	(Z)	1.3	1.8	2.1
$50,000-$99,999	3,413	250	106	147	127	6.8	0.1	0.3	0.5	0.5
$100,000-$249,999	6,842	1,139	252	334	287	13.6	0.3	0.8	1.2	1.2
$250,000-$499,999	6,224	2,253	357	428	368	12.4	0.5	1.1	1.5	1.6
$500,000-$999,999	6,759	4,857	528	663	549	13.5	1.1	1.6	2.3	2.4
$1,000,000-$4,999,999	12,142	27,510	2,562	2,702	2,260	24.2	6.1	8.0	9.3	9.7
$5,000,000-$9,999,999	3,019	21,137	1,896	1,899	1,562	6.0	4.7	5.9	6.6	6.7
$10,000,000-$49,999,999	3,204	67,517	4,912	5,093	4,052	6.4	15.1	15.3	17.6	17.4
$50,000,000-$99,999,999	494	34,462	2,373	2,339	1,873	1.0	7.7	7.4	8.1	8.0
$100,000,000-$249,999,999	345	51,947	3,115	3,228	2,584	0.7	11.6	9.7	11.2	11.1
$250,000,000 or more	206	237,409	15,584	11,569	9,194	0.4	52.9	48.6	40.0	39.4

Z Less than 0.05 percent.

Source: The Foundation Center, New York, NY, Foundation Yearbook, annual (copyright).

No. 557. Foundations—Grants Reported by Subject Field and Recipient Organization: 2000

[15,015 represents $15,015,000,000. Covers grants of $10,000 or more in size. Based on reports of 1,015 larger U.S. foundations. Grant sample dollar value represented half of all grant dollars awarded by private, corporate, and community foundations. For definition of foundations, see headnote, Table 555]

| Subject field | Number of grants | | Dollar value | | Recipient organization | Number of grants | | Dollar value | |
	Number	Percent distribution	Amount (mil. dol.)	Percent distribution		Number	Percent distribution	Amount (mil. dol.)	Percent distribution
Total	119,778	100.0	15,015	100.0	Community improvement organizations	6,044	5.0	606	4.0
Arts and culture	17,835	14.9	1,799	12.0	Educational institutions	31,360	26.2	5,562	37.0
Education	24,615	20.6	3,779	25.2	Colleges & universities	14,130	11.8	2,614	17.4
Environment & animals	7,368	6.2	987	6.6	Educational support				
Health	14,517	12.1	3,090	20.6	agencies	7,546	6.3	1,649	11.0
Human services	29,140	24.3	2,169	14.4	Schools	7,138	6.0	750	5.0
International affairs, development & peace	3,264	2.7	414	2.8	Environmental agencies	4,725	3.9	620	4.1
Public/societal benefit	14,859	12.4	1,692	11.3	Hospitals/medical care facilities	4,612	3.9	632	4.2
Science and technology	2,400	2.0	414	2.8	Human service agencies	22,694	18.9	1,585	10.6
Social sciences	1,837	1.5	324	2.2	Museums/historical societies	5,018	4.2	622	4.1
Religion	3,819	3.2	330	2.2	Public/general health organizations	2,890	2.4	573	3.8
Other	124	0.1	17	0.1					

Source: The Foundation Center, New York, NY, Foundation Giving Trends, annual (copyright).

U.S. Census Bureau, Statistical Abstract of the United States: 2002

No. 558. Percent of Adult Population Doing Volunteer Work: 2000

[Volunteers are persons who worked in some way to help others for no monetary pay during the previous year. Based on a sample survey of 4,216 persons 21 years old and over conducted during the spring of the following year and subject to sampling variability; see source]

Age, sex, race, and Hispanic origin	Percent of population volunteering	Average hours volunteered per month	Educational attainment and household income	Percent of population volunteering	Average hours volunteered per month	Type of activity	Percent of population involved in activity
Total.	44.0	15.1	Less than high school graduate	20.0	17.1	Arts, culture, humanities. .	2.1
						Education	7.7
21-24 years old	32.3	12.1	High school graduate	36.1	12.3	Environment	2.1
25-34 years old	40.5	15.9	Technical, trade,			Health.	7.9
35-44 years old	50.9	16.1	business school [1]	46.9	16.3	Human services	6.8
45-54 years old	47.9	14.7	4 year college degree	60.3	15.3		
55-64 years old	42.9	12.1	Some graduate school [2] . .	58.4	16.7	International, foreign	0.4
65-74 years old	41.4	14.1				Political organizations . . .	1.3
75 years old and over.	39.0	19.5	Under $10,000.	23.8	8.3	Private, community	
			$10,000-$19,999	27.2	13.1	foundations	2.2
Male	41.2	14.6	$20,000-$29,999	32.3	17.4		
Female	45.9	15.5	$30,000-$39,999	37.3	12.5	Public and societal benefit.	4.0
			$40,000-$49,999	40.4	13.7	Recreation - adults	1.5
White.	46.7	14.6	$50,000-$59,999	48.3	13.0	Religion	19.1
Black.	36.9	18.4	$60,000-$74,999	58.6	14.6	Work-related organizations.	1.0
			$75,000-$99,999	57.0	16.5	Youth development	6.6
Hispanic [3]	33.4	13.6	$100,000 or more.	55.5	18.6		

[1] Includes some college or 2-year college.   [2] Includes professional school.   [3] Hispanic persons may be of any race.

Source: Toppe, Chris, Arthur Kirsch, and Westat, Inc., *Giving and Volunteering in the United States: 2001 Edition*. (Copyright and published by INDEPENDENT SECTOR, Washington, DC, 2002).

No. 559. Community Service Participation of Students in Grades 6 Through 12: 1996 and 1999

[**12,627 represents 12,627,000**. Based on the National Household Education Survey, a sample survey of approximately 55,000 households with telephones in the civilian, noninstitutional population; for details, see source]

Characteristic	Students participating in community service (1,000)		Percent of students participating in community service		Characteristic	Students participating in community service (1,000)		Percent of students participating in community service	
	1996	1999	1996	1999		1996	1999	1996	1999
Total [1]	12,627	14,063	49	52	College graduate	2,250	2,710	58	62
Student's grade:					Graduate or professional school	2,653	3,285	64	65
Grades 6 through 8	5,462	5,610	47	48					
Grades 9 and 10	3,370	3,955	45	50	School type:				
Grades 11 and 12	3,795	4,486	56	61	Public	11,056	12,331	47	50
Sex:					Private:				
Male	5,971	6,446	45	47	Church-related	1,270	1,286	69	72
Female.	6,656	7,617	53	57	Not church-related	301	446	57	68
Race/ethnicity:					School size:				
White, non-Hispanic	9,113	9,759	53	56	Under 300 students	1,336	1,531	49	53
Black, non-Hispanic	1,761	1,993	43	47	300 to 599 students	3,892	3,887	50	50
Hispanic	1,246	1,587	38	39	600 to 999 students	3,111	3,304	48	51
Other race-ethnicity	506	724	50	53	1,000 students or more . . .	4,288	5,341	49	54
Parent's highest level of education:					School practice: Requires and arranges				
Less than high school	834	1,013	34	37	service	2,389	3,094	56	59
High school graduate or					Requires service only	74	178	19	39
equivalent	3,273	3,125	42	45	Arranges service only	9,087	9,848	52	55
Voc/tech education after					Neither requires nor				
high school or some					arranges service.	1,076	942	30	29
college	3,617	3,930	48	50					

[1] Includes students with no grade reported.

Source: U.S. National Center for Education Statistics, *Statistics in Brief*, November 1999 (NCES 2000-028).

Section 12
Labor Force, Employment, and Earnings

This section presents statistics on the labor force; its distribution by occupation and industry affiliation; and the supply of, demand for, and conditions of labor. The chief source of these data is the Current Population Survey (CPS) conducted by the U.S. Census Bureau for the Bureau of Labor Statistics (BLS). Comprehensive historical and current data are available from the BLS Internet site <http://www.bls.gov/cps/home.htm>. These data are published on a current basis by the BLS monthly publication *Employment and Earnings*. Detailed data on the labor force are also available from the Census Bureaus decennial census of population.

Types of data—Most statistics in this section are obtained by two methods: household interviews or questionnaires and reports of establishment payroll records. Each method provides data which the other cannot suitably supply. Population characteristics, for example, are readily obtainable only from the household survey, while detailed industrial classifications can be readily derived only from establishment records.

Household data are obtained from a monthly sample survey of the population. The CPS is used to gather data for the calendar week including the 12th of the month and provides current comprehensive data on the labor force (see text, Section 1, Population). The CPS provides information on the work status of the population without duplication since each person is classified as employed, unemployed, or not in the labor force. Employed persons holding more than one job are counted only once, according to the job at which they worked the most hours during the survey week.

Monthly, quarterly, and annual data from the CPS are published by the Bureau of Labor Statistics in *Employment and Earnings*. Data presented include national totals of the number of persons in the civilian labor force by sex, race, Hispanic origin, and age; the number employed; hours of work; industry and occupational groups; and the number unemployed, reasons for, and duration of unemployment. Annual data shown in this section are averages of monthly figures for each calendar year, unless otherwise specified.

The CPS also produces annual estimates of employment and unemployment for each state, 50 large metropolitan statistical areas, and selected cities. These estimates are published by BLS in its annual *Geographic Profile of Employment and Unemployment*. More detailed geographic data (e.g., for counties and cities) are provided by the decennial population censuses.

Data based on establishment records are compiled by BLS and cooperating state agencies as part of an ongoing Current Employment Statistics program. Survey data, gathered monthly from a sample of employers through electronic interviewing or mail questionnaires or electronic interviewing, are supplemented by data from other government agencies and adjusted at intervals to data from government social insurance program reports. The estimates exclude self-employed persons, private household workers, unpaid family workers, agricultural workers, and the Armed Forces. In March 2001, reporting establishments employed 6 million manufacturing workers (33 percent of the total manufacturing employment at the time), 18 million workers in private non-manufacturing industries (19 percent of the total in private nonmanufacturing), and 15 million federal, state, and local government employees (73 percent of total government).

The establishment survey counts workers each time they appear on a payroll during the reference period (as with the CPS, the week including the 12th of the month). Thus, unlike the CPS, a person with two jobs is counted twice. The establishment survey is designed to provide detailed

Labor Force, Employment, and Earnings   363

industry information for the nation, states, and metropolitan areas on non-farm wage and salary employment, average weekly hours, and average hourly and weekly earnings. Establishment survey data also are published in *Employment and Earnings*. Historical national data are available on the site <http://www.bls.gov/ces/>. Historical data for states and metropolitan areas are available on the site <http://www.bls.gov/sae/>.

In June 2000, BLS began to phase in a comprehensive sample redesign of the establishment survey, changing from a quota sample to a probability-based sample. Probability-based sample estimates for the wholesale trade industry were published at that time. In June 2001, estimates for the mining, construction, and manufacturing industries were published under the new sample design for the first time. In June 2002, estimates for the transportation and public utilities; retail trade; and finance, insurance, and real estate industries were published under the new sample design for the first time. The sample redesign will be completed in June 2003 with the publication of estimates for the services industry under the new design. More information on the sample redesign appears in "BLS Establishment Estimates Revised to Incorporate March 2001 Benchmarks" in the June 2002 issue of *Employment and Earnings*, as well as the Establishment Data portion of the Explanatory Notes and Estimates of Error section of *Employment and Earnings*.

Labor force—According to the CPS definitions, the civilian labor force comprises all civilians in the noninstitutional population 16 years and over classified as "employed" or "unemployed" according to the following criteria: Employed civilians comprise (a) all civilians, who, during the reference week, did any work for pay or profit (minimum of an hour's work) or worked 15 hours or more as unpaid workers in a family enterprise and (b) all civilians who were not working but who had jobs or businesses from which they were temporarily absent for noneconomic reasons (illness, weather conditions, vacation, labor-management dispute, etc.) whether they were paid for the time off or

were seeking other jobs. Unemployed persons comprise all civilians who had no employment during the reference week, who made specific efforts to find a job within the previous 4 weeks (such as applying directly to an employer or to a public employment service or checking with friends) and who were available for work during that week, except for temporary illness. Persons on layoff from a job and expecting recall also are classified as unemployed. All other civilian persons, 16 years old and over, are "not in the labor force."

Beginning in 1982, changes in the estimation procedures and the introduction of 1980 census data caused substantial increases in the population and estimates of persons in all labor force categories. Rates on labor force characteristics, however, were essentially unchanged. In order to avoid major breaks in series, some 30,000 labor force series were adjusted back to 1970. The effect of the 1982 revisions on various data series and an explanation of the adjustment procedure used are described in "Revisions in the Current Population Survey in January 1982," in the February 1982 issue of *Employment and Earnings*. The revisions did not, however, smooth out the breaks in series occurring between 1972 and 1979, and data users should make allowances for them in making certain data comparisons.

Beginning in January 1994, several changes were introduced into the CPS that effect all data comparisons with prior years. These changes include the results of a major redesign of the survey questionnaire and collection methodology, revisions to some of the labor force concepts and definitions, and the introduction of 1990 census population controls, adjusted for the estimated undercount. An explanation of the changes and their effects on the labor force data appears in "Revisions in the Current Population Survey Effective January 1994" in the February 1994 issue of *Employment and Earnings*.

Beginning 1996, 1990 census population controls, adjusted for the estimated undercount, were extended back to January 1990. A discussion of the changes and their effects on the labor force data appears in "Revisions In Household Survey Data Effective February 1996" in the March 1996 issue of *Employment and Earnings.*

Beginning in January 1997, the CPS reflects updated 1990 census-based population controls. The greatest impact of the new population controls was on estimates for persons of Hispanic origin. An explanation of the changes and their effects on labor force estimates appear in "Revisions in the Current Population Survey Effective January 1997" in the February 1997 issue of *Employment and Earnings.*

Beginning in January 1998, the CPS reflects the introduction of new composite estimation procedures and revised 1990 census-based population controls. An explanation of the changes and their effects on labor force estimates appear in "Revisions in the Current Population Survey Effective January 1998" in the February 1998 issue of *Employment and Earnings.*

Beginning in January 1999 and January 2000, the CPS reflects the introduction of revised 1990 census-based population controls that incorporate newly updated information on immigration. An explanation of the changes and their effects on labor force estimates appear in "Revisions in the Current Population Survey Effective January 1999" and "Revisions in the Current Population Survey Effective January 2000" in the February 1999 and February 2000 issues, respectively, of *Employment and Earnings.*

Hours and earnings—Average hourly earnings, based on establishment data, are gross earnings (i.e., earnings before payroll deductions) and include overtime premiums; they exclude irregular bonuses and value of payments in kind. Hours are those for which pay was received. Wages and salaries from the CPS consist of total monies received for work performed by an employee during the income year. It includes wages, salaries, commissions, tips, piece-rate payments, and cash bonuses earned before deductions were made for taxes, bonds, union dues, etc. Persons who worked 35 hours or more are classified as working full time.

Industry and occupational groups— Industry data derived from the CPS for 1983-91 utilize the 1980 census industrial classification developed from the 1972 SIC. CPS data from 1971 to 1982 were based on the 1970 census classification system which was developed from the 1967 SIC. Most of the industry categories were not affected by the change in classification.

Establishments responding to the establishment survey are classified according to the *Standard Industrial Classification (SIC) Manual.* Beginning in June 2003, the establishment survey will begin using the 2002 North American Industrial Classification System (NAICS) to classify establishments responding to the survey. See text, Section 15, Business Enterprise, for information about the SIC manual and NAICS.

The occupational classification system used in the 1980 census and in the CPS for 1983-91, evolved from the 1980 Standard Occupational Classification (SOC) system, first introduced in 1977. Occupational categories used in the 1980 census classification system are so radically different from the 1970 census system used in the CPS through 1982, that their implementation represented a break in historical data series. In cases where data have not yet been converted to the 1980 classifications and still reflect the 1970 classifications (e.g., Table 615), comparisons between the two systems should not be made. To help users bridge the data gap, a limited set of estimates was developed for the 1972-82 period based on the new classifications. The estimates were developed by means of applying conversion factors created by double coding a 20-percent sample of CPS occupational records for 6 months during 1981-82. For further details, contact BLS.

Beginning in January 1992, the occupational and industrial classification system used in the 1990 census were introduced into the CPS. (These systems were largely based on the 1980 Standard Occupational Classification and the 1987 Standard Industrial Classification.) There were a few breaks in comparability between the 1980 and 1990 census-based systems, particularly within the "technical, sales, and administrative support" categories.

Labor Force, Employment, and Earnings   365

The most notable changes in industry classification were the shift of several industries from "business services" to "professional services" and the splitting of some industries into smaller, more detailed categories. A number of industry titles were changed as well, with no change in content.

Productivity—BLS publishes data on productivity as measured by output per hour (labor productivity), output per combined unit of labor and capital input (multifactor productivity), and, for manufacturing industries, output per combined unit of capital, labor, energy, materials, and purchased service inputs. Labor productivity and related indexes are published for the business sector as a whole and its major subsectors: nonfarm business, manufacturing, and nonfinancial corporations, and for over 450 specific industries. Multifactor productivity and related measures are published for the private business sector and its major subsectors. Productivity indexes which take into account capital, labor, energy, materials, and service inputs are published for the 18 major industry groups which comprise the manufacturing sector, the utility services industry group, for 108 three-digit SIC manufacturing industries, and railroad transportation. The major sector data are published in the BLS quarterly news release, *Productivity and Costs* and in the annual *Multifactor Productivity Trends* release. Industry productivity measures are published annually in the news releases *Productivity and Costs, Manufacturing Industries, and Productivity and Costs, Services - Producing and Mining Industries*. Detailed information on methods, limitations, and data sources appears in the BLS *Handbook of Methods*, BLS Bulletin 2490 (1997), Chapters 10 and 11.

Unions—As defined here, unions include traditional labor unions and employee associations similar to labor unions. Data on union membership status provided by BLS are for employed wage and salary workers and relate to their principal job. Earnings by union membership status are usual weekly earnings of full-time wage and salary workers. The information is collected through the Current Population Survey. Collective bargaining settlements data are available for bargaining situations involving 1,000 or more workers in private industry and state and local government.

Work stoppages—Work stoppages include all strikes and lockouts known to BLS which last for at least 1 full day or shift and involve 1,000 or more workers. All stoppages, whether or not authorized by a union, legal or illegal, are counted. Excluded are work slowdowns and instances where employees report to work late or leave early to attend mass meetings or mass rallies.

Seasonal adjustment—Many economic statistics reflect a regularly recurring seasonal movement which can be estimated on the basis of past experience. By eliminating that part of the change which can be ascribed to usual seasonal variation (e.g., climate or school openings and closings), it is possible to observe the cyclical and other nonseasonal movements in the series. However, in evaluating deviations from the seasonal pattern—that is, changes in a seasonally adjusted series—it is important to note that seasonal adjustment is merely an approximation based on past experience. Seasonally adjusted estimates have a broader margin of possible error than the original data on which they are based, since they are subject not only to sampling and other errors, but also are affected by the uncertainties of the adjustment process itself.

Statistical reliability—For discussion of statistical collection, estimation, sampling procedures, and measures of statistical reliability applicable to Census Bureau and BLS data, see Appendix III.

No. 560. Employment Status of the Civilian Population: 1960 to 2001

[In thousands (117,245 represents 117,245,000), except as indicated. Annual averages of monthly figures. For the civilian noninstitutional population 16 years old and over. Based on Current Population Survey; see text, Section 1, Population, and Appendix III]

Year	Civilian noninsti-tutional population	Civilian labor force						Not in labor force	
		Total	Percent of population	Employed	Employ-ment/ population ratio [1]	Unemployed		Not in labor force	
						Number	Percent of labor force	Number	Percent of population
1960	117,245	69,628	59.4	65,778	56.1	3,852	5.5	47,617	40.6
1970	137,085	82,771	60.4	78,678	57.4	4,093	4.9	54,315	39.6
1980	167,745	106,940	63.8	99,303	59.2	7,637	7.1	60,806	36.2
1981	170,130	108,670	63.9	100,397	59.0	8,273	7.6	61,460	36.1
1982	172,271	110,204	64.0	99,526	57.8	10,678	9.7	62,067	36.0
1983	174,215	111,550	64.0	100,834	57.9	10,717	9.6	62,665	36.0
1984	176,383	113,544	64.4	105,005	59.5	8,539	7.5	62,839	35.6
1985	178,206	115,461	64.8	107,150	60.1	8,312	7.2	62,744	35.2
1986	180,587	117,834	65.3	109,597	60.7	8,237	7.0	62,752	34.7
1987	182,753	119,865	65.6	112,440	61.5	7,425	6.2	62,888	34.4
1988	184,613	121,669	65.9	114,968	62.3	6,701	5.5	62,944	34.1
1989 [2]	186,393	123,869	66.5	117,342	63.0	6,528	5.3	62,523	33.5
1990 [2]	189,164	125,840	66.5	118,793	62.8	7,047	5.6	63,324	33.5
1991	190,925	126,346	66.2	117,718	61.7	8,628	6.8	64,578	33.8
1992	192,805	128,105	66.4	118,492	61.5	9,613	7.5	64,700	33.6
1993	194,838	129,200	66.3	120,259	61.7	8,940	6.9	65,638	33.7
1994 [2]	196,814	131,056	66.6	123,060	62.5	7,996	6.1	65,758	33.4
1995	198,584	132,304	66.6	124,900	62.9	7,404	5.6	66,280	33.4
1996 [2]	200,591	133,943	66.8	126,708	63.2	7,236	5.4	66,647	33.2
1997 [2]	203,133	136,297	67.1	129,558	63.8	6,739	4.9	66,837	32.9
1998 [2]	205,220	137,673	67.1	131,463	64.1	6,210	4.5	67,547	32.9
1999 [2]	207,753	139,368	67.1	133,488	64.3	5,880	4.2	68,385	32.9
2000 [2]	209,699	140,863	67.2	135,208	64.5	5,655	4.0	68,836	32.8
2001	211,864	141,815	66.9	135,073	63.8	6,742	4.8	70,050	33.1

[1] Civilian employed as a percent of the civilian noninstitutional population.   [2] Data not strictly comparable with data for earlier years, See text, this section, and February 1994, March 1996, and February 1997, 1998, 1999, 2000 issues of *Employment and Earnings*.

Source: U.S. Bureau of Labor Statistics, Bulletin 2307; and *Employment and Earnings*, monthly.

No. 561. Civilian Labor Force and Participation Rates, With Projections: 1980 to 2010

[106.9 represents 106,900,000. For civilian noninstitutional population 16 years old and over. Annual averages of monthly figures. Rates are based on annual average civilian noninstitutional population of each specified group and represent proportion of each specified group in the civilian labor force. Based on Current Population Survey; see text, Section 1, Population, and Appendix III]

Race, sex, and age	Civilian labor force (millions)						Participation rate (percent)					
	1980	1990 [1]	1995	2000 [1]	2001	2010, proj.	1980	1990 [1]	1995	2000 [1]	2001	2010, proj.
Total [2]	106.9	125.8	132.3	140.9	141.8	157.7	63.8	66.5	66.6	67.2	66.9	67.5
White	93.6	107.4	112.0	117.6	118.1	128.0	64.1	66.9	67.1	67.4	67.2	67.6
Male	54.5	59.6	61.1	63.9	64.1	68.2	78.2	77.1	75.7	75.4	75.1	73.8
Female	39.1	47.8	50.8	53.7	54.0	59.9	51.2	57.4	59.0	59.8	59.7	61.6
Black	10.9	13.7	14.8	16.6	16.7	20.0	61.0	64.0	63.7	65.8	65.4	67.1
Male	5.6	6.8	7.2	7.8	7.9	9.0	70.3	71.0	69.0	69.0	68.5	68.2
Female	5.3	6.9	7.6	8.8	8.9	11.1	53.1	58.3	59.5	63.2	62.9	66.2
Hispanic [3]	6.1	10.7	12.3	15.4	15.8	20.9	64.0	67.4	65.8	68.6	68.1	69.0
Male	3.8	6.5	7.4	8.9	9.1	11.7	81.4	81.4	79.1	80.6	79.8	79.0
Female	2.3	4.2	4.9	6.4	6.7	9.2	47.4	53.1	52.6	56.9	56.8	59.4
Male	61.5	69.0	71.4	75.2	75.7	82.2	77.4	76.4	75.0	74.7	74.4	73.2
16 to 19 years.	5.0	4.1	4.0	4.3	4.2	4.7	60.5	55.7	54.8	53.0	50.7	52.3
20 to 24 years.	8.6	7.9	7.3	7.6	7.6	8.6	85.9	84.4	83.1	82.6	81.5	81.2
25 to 34 years.	17.0	19.9	18.7	17.1	16.8	17.9	95.2	94.1	93.0	93.4	92.7	93.1
35 to 44 years.	11.8	17.5	19.2	20.3	20.2	17.8	95.5	94.3	92.3	92.6	92.5	92.3
45 to 54 years.	9.9	11.1	13.4	16.0	16.6	18.9	91.2	90.7	88.8	88.6	88.5	87.8
55 to 64 years.	7.2	6.6	6.5	7.6	7.9	11.1	72.1	67.8	66.0	67.3	68.1	67.0
65 years and over . .	1.9	2.0	2.2	2.4	2.5	3.1	19.0	16.3	16.8	17.5	17.7	19.5
Female	45.5	56.8	60.9	65.6	66.1	75.5	51.5	57.5	58.9	60.2	60.1	62.2
16 to 19 years.	4.4	3.7	3.7	4.1	3.9	4.6	52.9	51.6	52.2	51.3	49.4	52.2
20 to 24 years.	7.3	6.8	6.3	6.8	6.9	8.1	68.9	71.3	70.3	73.3	72.9	75.7
25 to 34 years.	12.3	16.1	15.5	14.6	14.3	16.3	65.5	73.5	74.9	76.3	75.8	81.4
35 to 44 years.	8.6	14.7	16.6	17.5	17.4	16.2	65.5	76.4	77.2	77.3	77.1	80.0
45 to 54 years.	7.0	9.1	11.8	14.5	15.0	17.9	59.9	71.2	74.4	76.8	76.4	80.0
55 to 64 years.	4.7	4.9	5.4	6.4	6.7	10.1	41.3	45.2	49.2	51.8	53.0	55.2
65 years and over . .	1.2	1.5	1.6	1.8	1.8	2.3	8.1	8.6	8.8	9.4	9.7	11.1

[1] See footnote 2, Table 560.   [2] Includes other races, not shown separately.   [3] Persons of Hispanic origin may be of any race.

Source: U.S. Bureau of Labor Statistics, *Employment and Earnings*, monthly, January issues; *Monthly Labor Review*, November 2001; and unpublished data.

No. 562. Employment Status of the Civilian Population: 1970 to 2001

[In thousands (137,085 represents 137,085,000), except as indicated. Annual averages of monthly figures. For the civilian noninstitutional population 16 years old and over. Based on Current Population Survey; see text, Section 1, Population, and Appendix III]

Year, sex, race, and Hispanic origin	Civilian noninstitutional population	Civilian labor force						Not in labor force	
		Total	Percent of population	Employed	Employment/population ratio [1]	Unemployed		Number	Percent of population
						Number	Percent of labor force		
Total: [2]									
1970.........	137,085	82,771	60.4	78,678	57.4	4,093	4.9	54,315	39.6
1980.........	167,745	106,940	63.8	99,303	59.2	7,637	7.1	60,806	36.2
1985.........	178,206	115,461	64.8	107,150	60.1	8,312	7.2	62,744	35.2
1990 [3]	189,164	125,840	66.5	118,793	62.8	7,047	5.6	63,324	33.5
1995.........	198,584	132,304	66.6	124,900	62.9	7,404	5.6	66,280	33.4
1999 [3]	207,753	139,368	67.1	133,488	64.3	5,880	4.2	68,385	32.9
2000 [3]	209,699	140,863	67.2	135,208	64.5	5,655	4.0	68,836	32.8
2001.........	211,864	141,815	66.9	135,073	63.8	6,742	4.8	70,050	33.1
Male:									
1970.........	64,304	51,228	79.7	48,990	76.2	2,238	4.4	13,076	20.3
1980.........	79,398	61,453	77.4	57,186	72.0	4,267	6.9	17,945	22.6
1985.........	84,469	64,411	76.3	59,891	70.9	4,521	7.0	20,058	23.7
1990 [3]	90,377	69,011	76.4	65,104	72.0	3,906	5.7	21,367	23.6
1995.........	95,178	71,360	75.0	67,377	70.8	3,983	5.6	23,818	25.0
1999 [3]	99,722	74,512	74.7	71,446	71.6	3,066	4.1	25,210	25.3
2000 [3]	100,731	75,247	74.7	72,293	71.8	2,954	3.9	25,484	25.3
2001.........	101,858	75,743	74.4	72,080	70.8	3,663	4.8	26,114	25.6
Female:									
1970.........	72,782	31,543	43.3	29,688	40.8	1,855	5.9	41,239	56.7
1980.........	88,348	45,487	51.5	42,117	47.7	3,370	7.4	42,861	48.5
1985.........	93,736	51,050	54.5	47,259	50.4	3,791	7.4	42,686	45.5
1990 [3]	98,787	56,829	57.5	53,689	54.3	3,140	5.5	41,957	42.5
1995.........	103,406	60,944	58.9	57,523	55.6	3,421	5.6	42,462	41.1
1999 [3]	108,031	64,855	60.0	62,042	57.4	2,814	4.3	43,175	40.0
2000 [3]	108,968	65,616	60.2	62,915	57.7	2,701	4.1	43,352	39.8
2001.........	110,007	66,071	60.1	62,992	57.3	3,079	4.7	43,935	39.9
White:									
1970.........	122,174	73,556	60.2	70,217	57.5	3,339	4.5	48,618	39.8
1980.........	146,122	93,600	64.1	87,715	60.0	5,884	6.3	52,523	35.9
1985.........	153,679	99,926	65.0	93,736	61.0	6,191	6.2	53,753	35.0
1990 [3]	160,625	107,447	66.9	102,261	63.7	5,186	4.8	53,178	33.1
1995.........	166,914	111,950	67.1	106,490	63.8	5,459	4.9	54,965	32.9
1999 [3]	173,085	116,509	67.3	112,235	64.8	4,273	3.7	56,577	32.7
2000 [3]	174,428	117,574	67.4	113,475	65.1	4,099	3.5	56,854	32.6
2001.........	175,888	118,144	67.2	113,220	64.4	4,923	4.2	57,744	32.8
Black:									
1973.........	14,917	8,976	60.2	8,128	54.5	846	9.4	5,941	39.8
1980.........	17,824	10,865	61.0	9,313	52.2	1,553	14.3	6,959	39.0
1985.........	19,664	12,364	62.9	10,501	53.4	1,864	15.1	7,299	37.1
1990 [3]	21,477	13,740	64.0	12,175	56.7	1,565	11.4	7,737	36.0
1995.........	23,246	14,817	63.7	13,279	57.1	1,538	10.4	8,429	36.3
1999 [3]	24,855	16,365	65.8	15,056	60.6	1,309	8.0	8,490	34.2
2000 [3]	25,218	16,603	65.8	15,334	60.8	1,269	7.6	8,615	34.2
2001.........	25,559	16,719	65.4	15,270	59.7	1,450	8.7	8,840	34.6
Hispanic: [4]									
1980.........	9,598	6,146	64.0	5,527	57.6	620	10.1	3,451	36.0
1985.........	11,915	7,698	64.6	6,888	57.8	811	10.5	4,217	35.4
1990 [3]	15,904	10,720	67.4	9,845	61.9	876	8.2	5,184	32.6
1995.........	18,629	12,267	65.8	11,127	59.7	1,140	9.3	6,362	34.2
1999 [3]	21,650	14,665	67.7	13,720	63.4	945	6.4	6,985	32.3
2000 [3]	22,393	15,368	68.6	14,492	64.7	876	5.7	7,025	31.4
2001.........	23,122	15,751	68.1	14,714	63.6	1,037	6.6	7,371	31.9
Mexican:									
1986.........	7,377	4,941	67.0	4,387	59.5	555	11.2	2,436	33.0
1990 [3]	9,752	6,707	68.8	6,146	63.0	561	8.4	3,045	31.2
1995.........	11,609	7,765	66.9	7,016	60.4	750	9.7	3,844	33.1
1999 [3]	13,582	9,267	68.2	8,656	63.7	611	6.6	4,315	31.8
2000 [3]	14,386	9,955	69.2	9,364	65.1	591	5.9	4,430	30.8
2001.........	14,850	10,264	69.1	9,577	64.5	687	6.7	4,586	30.9
Puerto Rican:									
1986.........	1,494	804	53.8	691	46.3	113	14.0	690	46.2
1990 [3]	1,718	960	55.9	870	50.6	91	9.5	758	44.1
1995.........	1,896	1,098	57.9	974	51.4	123	11.2	798	42.1
1999 [3]	2,058	1,269	61.6	1,165	56.6	104	8.2	789	38.3
2000 [3]	2,025	1,278	63.1	1,196	59.1	82	6.4	747	36.9
2001.........	2,164	1,294	59.8	1,193	55.1	101	7.8	871	40.2
Cuban:									
1986.........	842	570	67.7	533	63.3	36	6.4	272	32.3
1990 [3]	918	603	65.7	559	60.9	44	7.2	315	34.3
1995.........	1,019	613	60.2	568	55.7	45	7.4	406	39.8
1999 [3]	1,141	714	62.6	681	59.7	33	4.6	427	37.4
2000 [3]	1,104	680	61.6	650	58.9	30	4.4	424	38.4
2001.........	1,043	608	58.3	568	54.5	40	6.5	435	41.7

[1] Civilian employed as a percent of the civilian noninstitutional population.   [2] Includes other races, not shown separately.   [3] See footnote 2, Table 560.   [4] Persons of Hispanic origin may be of any race. Includes persons of other Hispanic origin, not shown separately.

Source: U.S. Bureau of Labor Statistics, Bulletin 2307; and *Employment and Earnings*, monthly, January issues.

No. 563. Civilian Labor Force—Percent Distribution by Sex and Age: 1970 to 2001

[**82,771 represents 82,771,000.** For civilian noninstitutional population 16 years old and over annual averages of monthly figures. Based on Current Population Survey; see text, Section 1, Population, and Appendix III]

Year and sex	Civilian labor force (1,000)	16 to 19 years	20 to 24 years	25 to 34 years	35 to 44 years	45 to 54 years	55 to 64 years	65 yrs. and over
Total: 1970	82,771	8.8	12.8	20.6	19.9	20.5	13.6	3.9
1980	106,940	8.8	14.9	27.3	19.1	15.8	11.2	2.9
1990 [1]	125,840	6.2	11.7	28.6	25.5	16.1	9.2	2.7
1995	132,304	5.9	10.3	25.8	27.0	19.1	9.0	2.9
2000 [1]	140,863	5.9	10.2	22.5	26.9	21.6	9.9	3.0
2001	141,815	5.7	10.3	22.0	26.5	22.3	10.3	3.0
Male: 1970	51,228	7.8	11.2	22.1	20.4	20.3	13.9	4.2
1980	61,453	8.1	14.0	27.6	19.3	16.1	11.8	3.1
1990 [1]	69,011	5.9	11.4	28.8	25.3	16.1	9.6	2.9
1995	71,360	5.7	10.3	26.2	26.9	18.8	9.1	3.1
2000 [1]	75,247	5.7	10.0	22.7	27.0	21.2	10.1	3.2
2001	75,743	5.5	10.1	22.2	26.7	21.9	10.4	3.3
Female: 1970	31,543	10.3	15.5	18.1	18.9	20.7	13.2	3.3
1980	45,487	9.6	16.1	26.9	19.0	15.4	10.4	2.6
1990 [1]	56,829	6.5	12.0	28.3	25.8	16.1	8.7	2.6
1995	60,944	6.1	10.4	25.5	27.2	19.4	8.8	2.7
2000 [1]	65,616	6.2	10.3	22.2	26.7	22.1	9.8	2.7
2001	66,071	5.9	10.5	21.7	26.3	22.7	10.2	2.8

[1] See footnote 2, Table 560.
Source: U.S. Bureau of Labor Statistics, Bulletin Bulletin 2307, and *Employment and Earnings,* monthly, January issues.

No. 564. Civilian Labor Force and Participation Rates by Educational Attainment, Sex, Race, and Hispanic Origin: 1992 to 2001

[**102,387 represents 102,387,000 As of March.** For the civilian noninstitutional population 25 to 64 years of age. See Table 598 for unemployment data. Based on Current Population Survey; see text, Section 1, Population, and Appendix III]

Year, sex, and race	Civilian labor force Total (1,000)	Less than high school diploma	High school graduate, no degree	Less than a bachelor's degree	College graduate	Participation rate [1] Total	Less than high school diploma	High school graduates, no degree	Less than a bachelor's degree	College graduate
Total: [2]										
1992	102,387	12.2	36.2	25.2	26.4	79.0	60.3	78.3	83.5	88.4
1995	106,519	10.8	33.1	27.8	28.3	79.3	59.8	77.3	83.2	88.7
1998 [3]	111,857	10.7	32.8	27.4	29.1	80.2	63.0	78.4	83.5	88.0
1999 [3]	112,542	10.3	32.3	27.4	30.0	80.0	62.7	78.1	83.0	87.6
2000 [3]	114,052	9.8	31.8	27.9	30.4	80.3	62.7	78.4	83.2	87.8
2001	115,073	9.8	31.4	28.1	30.7	80.3	63.5	78.4	83.0	87.0
Male:										
1992	55,917	13.9	34.7	23.8	27.5	88.6	75.1	89.0	91.8	93.7
1995	57,454	12.2	32.3	25.7	29.7	87.4	72.0	86.9	90.1	93.8
1998 [3]	59,905	12.3	32.3	25.8	29.6	87.8	75.3	86.7	90.0	93.4
1999 [3]	60,030	11.7	32.0	25.8	30.5	87.5	74.4	86.6	89.4	93.0
2000 [3]	60,510	11.1	31.8	26.1	30.9	87.5	74.9	86.2	88.9	93.3
2001	61,091	11.0	31.6	26.3	31.1	87.4	75.4	85.8	89.1	92.9
Female:										
1992	46,469	10.2	37.9	26.9	25.0	70.0	45.6	69.1	76.2	82.2
1995	49,065	9.1	34.1	30.2	26.6	71.5	47.2	68.9	77.3	82.8
1998 [3]	51,953	8.8	33.3	29.3	28.6	73.0	49.8	70.9	77.8	82.3
1999 [3]	52,512	8.7	32.7	29.2	29.5	72.8	50.5	70.4	77.4	81.9
2000 [3]	53,541	8.4	31.8	30.0	29.8	73.5	50.4	71.2	78.3	82.0
2001	53,982	8.5	31.1	30.1	30.2	73.9	51.7	71.3	77.7	80.9
White:										
1992	87,656	11.3	36.1	25.5	27.1	79.8	61.5	78.7	83.8	88.7
1995	90,192	10.0	32.8	27.8	29.3	80.1	61.6	77.9	83.4	88.8
1998 [3]	93,527	10.2	32.7	27.4	29.8	80.6	63.8	78.6	83.5	88.3
1999 [3]	94,216	9.8	32.2	27.2	30.8	80.6	64.2	78.5	83.3	87.9
2000 [3]	95,073	9.5	31.8	27.7	31.0	80.8	64.2	78.7	83.1	87.9
2001	95,562	9.5	31.0	28.0	31.4	80.7	64.5	78.7	83.2	87.2
Black:										
1992	10,936	19.2	40.3	24.9	15.6	74.4	55.4	76.9	83.4	89.1
1995	11,695	14.1	38.6	29.6	17.7	74.2	51.0	74.5	82.8	90.9
1998 [3]	12,893	14.3	37.3	30.1	18.2	77.7	59.3	77.0	85.0	88.8
1999 [3]	12,945	13.0	37.2	30.4	19.5	76.5	55.1	76.5	82.9	88.6
2000 [3]	13,383	11.8	36.1	31.5	20.7	77.9	55.5	77.0	84.2	90.3
2001	13,617	12.0	37.1	31.1	19.8	78.1	58.7	76.8	83.0	90.5
Hispanic: [4]										
1992	7,702	39.1	30.2	19.3	11.4	73.8	64.6	77.5	84.2	87.1
1995	9,298	38.9	28.2	21.3	11.6	73.2	64.7	75.9	81.9	87.9
1998 [3]	10,922	37.3	29.1	20.3	13.3	75.8	67.9	78.8	82.3	86.9
1999 [3]	11,129	36.5	29.2	21.4	12.9	75.7	67.0	79.0	84.0	85.0
2000 [3]	11,800	37.1	29.4	21.0	12.5	76.9	69.9	78.5	83.5	87.0
2001	12,149	36.9	29.7	20.4	13.0	77.3	69.1	81.0	84.6	85.2

[1] See headnote, Table 561.   [2] Includes other races, not shown separately.   [3] See footnote 2, Table 560.   [4] Persons of Hispanic origin may be of any race.
Source: U.S. Bureau of Labor Statistics, unpublished data.

Labor Force, Employment, and Earnings   369

No. 565. Characteristics of the Civilian Labor Force by State: 2001

[In thousands (141,815 represents 14,815,000), except ratio and rate. Preliminary. For civilian noninstitutional population, 16 years old and over. Annual averages of monthly figures. Because of separate processing and weighting procedures, the totals for the United States may differ from results obtained by aggregating totals for states]

State	Total Number	Total Female	Employed Total	Employed Female	Employed/population ratio [1]	Unemployed Total Number	Unemployed Total Female	Rate [2] Total	Rate [2] Male	Rate [2] Female	Participation rate [3] Male	Participation rate [3] Female
United States...	141,815	66,071	135,073	62,992	63.8	6,742	3,079	4.8	4.8	4.7	74.4	60.1
Alabama........	2,148	1,020	2,033	964	59.5	114	56	5.3	5.2	5.5	70.9	55.8
Alaska.........	322	147	302	139	68.2	20	8	6.3	6.8	5.6	78.7	66.9
Arizona........	2,420	1,075	2,307	1,018	62.5	113	57	4.7	4.2	5.3	74.5	57.0
Arkansas.......	1,227	598	1,164	569	58.2	63	29	5.1	5.4	4.8	67.7	55.8
California.......	17,362	7,842	16,435	7,421	63.4	927	421	5.3	5.3	5.4	75.4	58.9
Colorado........	2,295	1,024	2,210	983	69	85	41	3.7	3.5	4.0	79.6	63.8
Connecticut.....	1,718	815	1,661	788	65.3	56	27	3.3	3.2	3.4	73.7	61.8
Delaware.......	419	202	404	195	67.9	15	7	3.5	3.7	3.3	75.8	65.3
District of Columbia.	278	140	260	131	63.1	18	9	6.5	6.5	6.5	71.1	64.3
Florida.........	7,674	3,525	7,309	3,349	60.2	365	176	4.8	4.5	5.0	70.4	56.4
Georgia	4,132	1,948	3,966	1,869	65.3	165	80	4.0	3.9	4.1	75.8	60.9
Hawaii	606	291	577	278	64.7	28	13	4.6	4.9	4.4	72.9	63.1
Idaho	682	316	648	301	66.9	34	15	5.0	5.1	4.8	77.2	63.9
Illinois.........	6,349	2,985	6,006	2,827	65	343	158	5.4	5.5	5.3	76.5	61.6
Indiana........	3,106	1,443	2,970	1,383	65.2	136	60	4.4	4.6	4.1	76.1	60.8
Iowa...........	1,588	757	1,535	732	69.8	53	25	3.3	3.4	3.3	77.6	67.1
Kansas.........	1,381	666	1,322	641	65.7	59	25	4.3	4.8	3.7	74.7	63.1
Kentucky.......	1,968	928	1,860	876	59.8	108	52	5.5	5.4	5.6	70.9	56.4
Louisiana	2,050	959	1,928	908	58.4	122	51	6.0	6.5	5.4	71.1	54.3
Maine..........	684	322	657	310	65	27	12	4.0	4.2	3.7	73.6	62.1
Maryland........	2,837	1,378	2,722	1,323	67.1	116	55	4.1	4.2	4.0	75.4	64.9
Massachusetts....	3,284	1,544	3,163	1,496	65.5	121	48	3.7	4.2	3.1	74.9	61.6
Michigan........	5,175	2,412	4,901	2,291	64.5	274	121	5.3	5.6	5.0	74.7	61.9
Minnesota.......	2,814	1,317	2,710	1,279	73.3	104	38	3.7	4.4	2.9	81.4	70.9
Mississippi......	1,296	636	1,225	600	58.3	72	36	5.5	5.3	5.7	69.2	55.5
Missouri........	2,970	1,418	2,830	1,359	67.4	140	59	4.7	5.2	4.2	76.2	65.5
Montana........	465	220	444	210	63.6	21	9	4.6	5.0	4.1	70.7	62.7
Nebraska	928	438	899	424	71.3	29	14	3.1	3.1	3.1	80.0	67.5
Nevada.........	1,023	459	969	434	66.7	55	25	5.3	5.3	5.4	77.6	63.3
New Hampshire ...	689	326	664	315	69.7	24	11	3.5	3.7	3.4	78.4	66.3
New Jersey	4,179	1,949	4,004	1,860	63.3	176	89	4.2	3.9	4.6	74.3	58.7
New Mexico......	838	398	798	380	60	40	18	4.8	5.0	4.4	70.2	56.5
New York	8,832	4,166	8,402	3,976	59.1	429	190	4.9	5.1	4.6	69.6	55.5
North Carolina....	3,995	1,898	3,773	1,794	64.4	221	105	5.5	5.6	5.5	74.1	62.6
North Dakota.....	339	163	329	159	69	10	4	2.8	3.3	2.3	75.1	67.0
Ohio...........	5,857	2,795	5,606	2,683	64.8	251	112	4.3	4.5	4.0	74.6	61.5
Oklahoma.......	1,665	760	1,602	733	62.2	64	27	3.8	4.0	3.6	73.2	56.8
Oregon.........	1,794	827	1,680	780	63.8	114	47	6.3	6.9	5.7	75.1	61.5
Pennsylvania.....	6,073	2,861	5,786	2,736	62.2	287	126	4.7	5.0	4.4	72.2	59.0
Rhode Island.....	504	245	480	234	63.4	24	11	4.7	4.9	4.5	73.0	60.8
South Carolina....	1,949	957	1,843	906	60	106	51	5.4	5.6	5.3	70.0	57.8
South Dakota.....	405	196	392	189	70.2	13	6	3.3	3.3	3.3	77.8	67.9
Tennessee.......	2,818	1,309	2,692	1,243	62.3	126	65	4.5	4.0	5.0	73.1	58.0
Texas..........	10,463	4,684	9,955	4,438	64.6	507	245	4.8	4.5	5.2	77.5	58.9
Utah...........	1,115	488	1,067	464	68.7	49	24	4.4	3.9	5.0	81.7	62.3
Vermont	335	162	323	155	67.7	12	6	3.6	3.3	3.9	75.8	65.2
Virginia........	3,675	1,765	3,548	1,702	66	127	63	3.5	3.4	3.5	74.6	62.7
Washington	2,996	1,391	2,804	1,311	62.5	192	80	6.4	7.0	5.8	73.9	60.1
West Virginia	833	380	792	365	54.9	41	15	4.9	5.7	4.0	65.5	50.5
Wisconsin	2,991	1,399	2,854	1,346	70.1	136	53	4.6	5.2	3.8	78.3	68.7
Wyoming........	271	128	261	122	69.5	11	5	3.9	3.8	4.0	78.6	66.4

[1] Civilian employment as a percent of civilian noninstitutional population. [2] Percent unemployed of the civilian labor force.
[3] Percent of civilian noninstitutional population of each specified group in the civilian labor force.

Source: U.S. Bureau of Labor Statistics, "Local Area Unemployment Statistics, Geographic Profile," Internet site <http://www.bls.gov/lau>.

U.S. Census Bureau, Statistical Abstract of the United States: 2002

No. 566. Civilian Labor Force by Selected Metropolitan Area: 2001

[**141,815 represents 141,815,000.** For the civilian noninstitutional population 16 years old and over. Annual averages of monthly figures. Data are derived from the Local Area Unemployment Statistics Program. For composition of metropolitan areas, see Appendix II]

Metropolitan areas ranked by labor force size, 2001	Civilian labor force (1,000)	Unemployment rate [1]	Metropolitan areas ranked by labor force size, 2001	Civilian labor force (1,000)	Unemployment rate [1]
U.S. total	141,815	4.8	Cincinnati, OH-KY-IN PMSA	866	3.9
Los Angeles-Long Beach, CA PMSA . . .	4,875	5.7	Indianapolis, IN MSA	865	3.4
Chicago, IL PMSA	4,241	5.4	Sacramento, CA PMSA.	830	4.0
New York, NY PMSA	4,150	5.6	Milwaukee-Waukesha, WI PMSA	813	4.7
Washington, DC-MD-VA-WV PMSA. . . .	2,740	3.1	Fort Lauderdale, FL PMSA	812	4.9
Philadelphia, PA-NJ PMSA	2,535	4.3	Charlotte-Gastonia-Rock Hill,		
Detroit, MI PMSA.	2,318	5.1	NC-SC MSA	811	5.1
Atlanta, GA MSA	2,280	3.5	Las Vegas, NV-AZ MSA	803	5.5
Houston, TX PMSA	2,201	4.3	San Antonio, TX MSA.	789	4.0
Dallas, TX PMSA.	2,007	4.8	Austin-San Marcos, TX MSA	754	3.8
Boston, MA-NH PMSA	1,826	3.2	Norfolk-Virginia Beach-Newport News,		
Minneapolis-St. Paul, MN-WI MSA	1,771	3.3	VA-NC MSA	754	3.6
Phoenix-Mesa, AZ MSA	1,620	3.9	Salt Lake City-Ogden, UT MSA	711	4.3
Riverside-San Bernardino, CA PMSA . .	1,565	5.0	Nashville, TN MSA.	670	3.3
Orange County, CA PMSA.	1,537	3.0	Middlesex-Somerset-Hunterdon,		
San Diego, CA MSA.	1,425	3.2	NJ PMSA	659	3.2
Nassau-Suffolk, NY PMSA	1,392	3.3	Bergen-Passaic, NJ PMSA	655	4.3
Seattle-Bellevue-Everett, WA PMSA . . .	1,363	5.2	Raleigh-Durham-Chapel Hill, NC MSA. .	652	3.3
St. Louis, MO-IL MSA.	1,360	4.9	Greensboro-Winston-Salem-High Point,		
Baltimore, MD PMSA	1,331	4.6	NC MSA.	644	5.0
Tampa-St. Petersburg-Clearwater,			Grand Rapids-Muskegon-Holland,		
FL MSA	1,270	3.7	MI MSA	626	5.1
Oakland, CA PMSA	1,265	4.0	New Orleans, LA MSA	612	5.2
Pittsburgh, PA MSA	1,176	4.3	Hartford, CT MSA	587	3.3
Denver, CO PMSA.	1,153	3.5	Providence-Fall River-Warwick,		
Cleveland-Lorain-Elyria, OH PMSA . . .	1,126	4.6	RI-MA MSA.	574	4.8
Miami, FL PMSA	1,080	6.9	Jacksonville, FL MSA	567	4.2
Portland-Vancouver, OR-WA PMSA. . . .	1,072	5.9	Memphis, TN-AR-MS MSA	564	4.2
Newark, NJ PMSA	1,014	4.3	Louisville, KY-IN MSA.	562	4.4
San Jose, CA PMSA	1,013	4.5	Rochester, NY MSA	555	4.5
Kansas City, MO-KS MSA.	1,009	4.4	Oklahoma City, OK MSA	555	3.9
San Francisco, CA PMSA	983	3.8	Buffalo-Niagara Falls, NY MSA.	547	5.4
Fort Worth-Arlington, TX PMSA	931	4.1	West Palm Beach-Boca Raton, FL MSA.	540	5.5
Orlando, FL MSA.	907	4.0	Monmouth-Ocean, NJ PMSA	530	3.8
Columbus, OH MSA.	876	2.8	Richmond-Petersburg, VA MSA	529	3.4

[1] Percent unemployed of the civilian labor force.

Source: U.S. Bureau of Labor Statistics, Local Area Unemployment Statistics program.

No. 567. School Enrollment and Labor Force Status: 1990 and 2001

[In thousands (**31,421 represents 31,421,000**), except percent. **As of October.** For the civilian noninstitutional population 16 to 24 years old. Based on Current Population Survey; see text, Section 1, Population, and Appendix III]

Characteristic	Population		Civilian labor force		Employed		Unemployed		
	1990	2001	1990	2001	1990	2001	1990, total	2001 Total	2001 Rate [1]
Total, 16 to 24 years [2].	**31,421**	**35,195**	**20,679**	**22,458**	**18,317**	**19,996**	**2,363**	**2,461**	**11.0**
Enrolled in school [2]	15,210	18,949	7,301	9,047	6,527	8,174	774	873	9.6
16 to 19 years	10,118	12,519	4,244	5,109	3,645	4,476	599	632	12.4
20 to 24 years	5,092	6,430	3,057	3,938	2,882	3,698	174	241	6.1
Sex:									
Male	7,704	9,331	3,635	4,202	3,215	3,738	420	464	11.0
Female	7,507	9,617	3,666	4,845	3,312	4,436	353	409	8.4
College level	8,139	9,958	4,542	5,721	4,231	5,311	311	410	7.2
Full-time.	6,810	8,289	3,376	4,219	3,117	3,900	259	319	7.6
Race:									
White	12,308	14,906	6,294	7,531	5,705	6,911	588	619	8.2
Below college	5,535	7,027	2,374	2,862	2,021	2,530	354	332	11.6
College level	6,772	7,879	3,919	4,669	3,685	4,381	234	288	6.2
Black.	2,129	2,759	718	1,009	576	817	142	193	19.1
Below college	1,207	1,480	306	349	212	247	94	102	29.3
College level	922	1,279	411	660	364	570	47	91	13.7
Not enrolled [2]	16,210	16,246	13,379	13,411	11,789	11,822	1,589	1,588	11.8
White	13,317	13,107	11,276	10,995	10,193	9,901	1,083	1,094	9.9
Black	2,441	2,497	1,752	1,898	1,298	1,482	454	416	21.9

[1] Percent unemployed of civilian labor force in each category. [2] Includes other races, not shown separately.

Source: U.S. Bureau of Labor Statistics, Bulletin 2307; *News,* USDL 02-288, May 14, 2001; and unpublished data.

U.S. Census Bureau, Statistical Abstract of the United States: 2002

No. 568. Labor Force Participation Rates by Marital Status, Sex, and Age: 1970 to 2001

[Annual averages of monthly figures. See Table 565 for definition of participation rate. Based on Current Population Survey; see text, Section 1, Population, and Appendix III]

Marital status and year	Male participation rate							Female participation rate						
	Total	16-19 years	20-24 years	25-34 years	35-44 years	45-64 years	65 and over	Total	16-19 years	20-24 years	25-34 years	35-44 years	45-64 years	65 and over
Single:														
1970 ..	65.5	54.6	73.8	87.9	86.2	75.7	25.2	56.8	44.7	73.0	81.4	78.6	73.0	19.7
1980 ..	72.6	59.9	81.3	89.2	82.2	66.9	16.8	64.4	53.6	75.2	83.3	76.9	65.6	13.9
1985 ..	73.8	56.3	81.5	89.4	84.6	65.5	15.6	66.6	52.3	76.3	82.4	80.8	67.9	9.8
1990 [1] .	74.8	55.1	81.6	89.9	84.5	67.3	15.7	66.7	51.7	74.5	80.9	80.8	66.2	12.1
1995 ..	73.7	54.4	80.3	88.7	81.4	67.0	17.9	66.8	52.2	72.9	80.2	79.5	67.3	11.6
1996 [1] .	73.3	52.8	79.8	89.1	82.1	67.4	18.2	67.1	51.5	73.3	80.9	79.4	68.5	12.2
1997 [1] .	73.1	51.9	80.1	89.0	82.1	68.5	14.8	67.9	51.0	75.1	82.3	80.1	70.8	11.5
1998 [1] .	73.3	52.9	79.7	89.1	82.5	70.2	15.2	68.5	52.4	75.3	83.0	80.9	69.9	9.7
1999 [1] .	73.4	52.5	79.7	89.5	83.5	70.6	17.3	68.7	51.1	76.1	84.2	80.8	69.6	9.9
2000 [1] .	73.5	52.7	80.5	89.4	82.8	69.7	17.1	69.0	51.3	76.3	84.1	80.9	70.0	10.8
2001 ..	72.6	50.4	79.5	88.9	83.1	69.9	15.4	68.2	49.5	75.4	83.4	81.1	69.9	12.5
Married: [2]														
1970 ..	86.1	92.3	94.7	98.0	98.1	91.2	29.9	40.5	37.8	47.9	38.8	46.8	44.0	7.3
1980 ..	80.9	91.3	96.9	97.5	97.2	84.3	20.5	49.8	49.3	61.4	58.8	61.8	46.9	7.3
1985 ..	78.7	91.0	95.6	97.4	96.8	81.7	16.8	53.8	49.6	65.7	65.8	68.1	49.4	6.6
1990 [1] .	78.6	92.1	95.6	96.9	96.7	82.6	17.5	58.4	49.5	66.1	69.6	74.0	56.5	8.5
1995 ..	77.5	89.2	94.9	96.3	95.4	82.4	18.0	61.0	51.6	64.7	72.0	75.7	62.7	9.1
1996 ..	77.6	84.4	94.5	96.4	95.4	83.2	18.3	61.2	48.6	66.0	71.7	75.8	63.7	9.0
1997 [1] .	77.7	84.6	94.9	96.1	95.7	83.6	18.3	61.6	50.1	66.1	71.9	76.0	64.6	8.9
1998 [1] .	77.6	83.8	95.0	96.4	95.8	83.7	17.5	61.2	49.8	66.1	71.6	74.5	64.9	8.9
1999 [1] .	77.5	83.2	93.7	96.5	95.9	83.4	18.3	61.2	49.8	64.5	70.9	74.6	65.3	9.6
2000 [1] .	77.3	79.6	94.0	96.7	95.8	83.1	19.0	61.3	53.4	64.2	70.5	74.8	65.4	10.1
2001 ..	77.4	79.2	93.8	95.8	95.7	83.8	19.0	61.4	46.0	64.1	70.2	74.5	66.1	10.3
Other: [3]														
1970 ..	60.7	(B)	90.4	93.7	91.1	78.5	19.3	40.3	48.6	60.3	64.6	68.8	61.9	10.0
1980 ..	67.5	(B)	92.6	94.1	91.9	73.3	13.7	43.6	50.0	68.4	76.5	77.1	60.2	8.2
1985 ..	68.7	(B)	95.1	93.7	91.8	72.8	11.4	45.1	51.9	66.2	76.9	81.6	61.0	7.5
1990 [1] .	68.9	(B)	93.1	93.0	90.7	74.9	12.0	47.2	53.9	65.4	77.0	82.1	65.0	8.4
1995 ..	66.2	(B)	92.7	90.9	88.2	72.4	12.1	47.4	55.8	67.2	77.1	80.7	67.2	8.4
1996 ..	66.4	(B)	90.6	92.0	88.8	73.1	11.5	48.1	42.6	70.7	78.5	82.1	67.7	8.0
1997 [1] .	67.4	60.8	89.9	92.1	89.6	74.7	13.2	48.6	49.7	70.4	80.2	81.9	68.6	8.1
1998 [1] .	66.9	66.2	89.1	93.0	89.1	73.7	13.1	48.8	50.4	73.7	81.0	82.8	68.6	8.4
1999 [1] .	65.9	(B)	90.2	92.3	88.7	73.4	12.3	49.1	45.3	73.6	82.4	83.4	69.1	8.4
2000 [1] .	66.6	60.4	87.7	93.2	89.8	74.0	12.7	49.4	45.8	74.0	83.2	82.9	69.7	8.7
2001 ..	66.0	58.0	85.7	92.3	89.4	73.6	14.1	49.5	46.0	75.0	81.5	82.7	69.3	9.1

B Percentage not shown where base is less than 35,000.   [1] See footnote 2, Table 560.   [2] Spouse present.   [3] Widowed, divorced, and married (spouse absent).

Source: U.S. Bureau of Labor Statistics, Bulletins 2217 and 2340; and unpublished data.

No. 569. Marital Status of Women in the Civilian Labor Force: 1970 to 2001

[Annual averages of monthly figures (31,543 represents 31,543,000). For civilian noninstitutional population 16 years old and over. Based on the Current Population Survey; see text, Section 1, Population, and Appendix III]

Year	Female civilian labor force (1,000)				Female participation rate [3]			
	Total	Single	Married [1]	Other [2]	Total	Single	Married [1]	Other [2]
1970	31,543	7,265	18,475	5,804	43.3	56.8	40.5	40.3
1975	37,475	9,125	21,484	6,866	46.3	59.8	44.3	40.1
1980	45,487	11,865	24,980	8,643	51.5	64.4	49.9	43.6
1983	48,503	12,659	26,468	9,376	52.9	65.0	51.8	44.4
1984	49,709	12,867	27,199	9,644	53.6	65.6	52.8	44.7
1985	51,050	13,163	27,894	9,993	54.5	66.6	53.8	45.1
1986	52,413	13,512	28,623	10,277	55.3	67.2	54.9	45.6
1987	53,658	13,885	29,381	10,393	56.0	67.4	55.9	45.7
1988	54,742	14,194	29,921	10,627	56.6	67.7	56.7	46.2
1989	56,030	14,377	30,548	11,104	57.4	68.0	57.8	47.0
1990 [4]	56,829	14,612	30,901	11,315	57.5	66.7	58.4	47.2
1991	57,178	14,681	31,112	11,385	57.4	66.2	58.5	46.8
1992	58,141	14,872	31,700	11,570	57.8	66.2	59.3	47.1
1993 [4]	58,795	15,031	31,980	11,784	57.9	66.2	59.4	47.2
1994 [4]	60,239	15,333	32,888	12,018	58.8	66.7	60.7	47.5
1995	60,944	15,467	33,359	12,118	58.9	66.8	61.0	47.4
1996 [4]	61,857	15,842	33,618	12,397	59.3	67.1	61.2	48.1
1997 [4]	63,036	16,492	33,802	12,742	59.8	67.9	61.6	48.6
1998 [4]	63,714	17,087	33,857	12,771	59.8	68.5	61.2	48.8
1999 [4]	64,855	17,575	34,372	12,909	60.0	68.7	61.2	49.1
2000 [4]	65,616	17,847	34,631	13,138	60.2	69.0	61.3	49.4
2001	66,071	17,987	34,671	13,413	60.1	68.2	61.4	49.5

[1] Husband present.   [2] Widowed, divorced, or separated.   [3] See footnote 3, Table 565 for definition of participation rate.   [4] See footnote 2, Table 560.

Source: U.S. Bureau of Labor Statistics, Bulletin 2307; and unpublished data.

No. 570. Employment Status of Women by Marital Status and Presence and Age of Children: 1970 to 2001

[As of March (7.0 represents 7,000,000). For the civilian noninstitutional persons 16 years and over. Based on the Current Population Survey; see text, Section 1, Population, and Appendix III]

Item	Total Single	Total Married[1]	Total Other[2]	With any children — Total Single	With any children — Total Married[1]	With any children — Total Other[2]	Children 6 to 17 only Single	Children 6 to 17 only Married[1]	Children 6 to 17 only Other[2]	Children under 6 Single	Children under 6 Married[1]	Children under 6 Other[2]
IN LABOR FORCE (mil.)												
1970	7.0	18.4	5.9	(NA)	10.2	1.9	(NA)	6.3	1.3	(NA)	3.9	0.6
1980	11.2	24.9	8.8	0.6	13.7	3.6	0.2	8.4	2.6	0.3	5.2	1.0
1985	12.9	27.7	10.3	1.1	14.9	4.0	0.4	8.5	2.9	0.7	6.4	1.1
1990	14.0	31.0	11.2	1.5	16.5	4.2	0.6	9.3	3.0	0.9	7.2	1.2
1995[3]	15.0	33.6	12.0	2.1	18.0	4.6	0.8	10.2	3.3	1.3	7.8	1.3
1998[3]	16.9	34.1	12.9	3.0	18.1	4.5	1.2	10.5	3.3	1.8	7.7	1.2
1999[3]	17.5	34.3	13.0	3.1	17.9	4.6	1.2	10.6	3.3	1.8	7.2	1.3
2000[3]	17.8	35.0	13.2	3.1	18.2	4.5	1.2	10.8	3.4	1.8	7.3	1.1
2001	17.9	35.2	13.5	3.0	18.3	4.4	1.2	11.0	3.3	1.8	7.3	1.1
PARTICIPATION RATE[4]												
1970	53.0	40.8	39.1	(NA)	39.7	60.7	(NA)	49.2	66.9	(NA)	30.3	52.2
1980	61.5	50.1	44.0	52.0	54.1	69.4	67.6	61.7	74.6	44.1	45.1	60.3
1985	65.2	54.2	45.6	51.6	60.8	71.9	64.1	67.8	77.8	46.5	53.4	59.7
1990	66.4	58.2	46.8	55.2	66.3	74.2	69.7	73.6	79.7	48.7	58.9	63.6
1995[3]	65.5	61.1	47.3	57.5	70.2	75.3	67.0	76.2	79.5	53.0	63.5	66.3
1998[3]	68.1	61.8	49.4	72.5	70.6	79.7	81.2	76.8	82.7	67.3	63.7	72.5
1999[3]	68.1	61.6	49.4	73.4	70.1	80.4	82.6	77.1	81.8	68.1	61.8	77.1
2000[3]	68.6	62.0	50.2	73.9	70.6	82.7	79.7	77.2	85.0	70.5	62.8	76.6
2001	68.4	62.1	50.3	73.8	70.8	83.7	80.6	77.7	86.5	69.7	62.5	76.2
EMPLOYMENT (mil.)												
1970	6.5	17.5	5.6	(NA)	9.6	1.8	(NA)	6.0	1.2	(NA)	3.6	0.6
1980	10.1	23.6	8.2	0.4	12.8	3.3	0.2	8.1	2.4	0.2	4.8	0.9
1985	11.6	26.1	9.4	0.9	13.9	3.5	0.3	8.1	2.6	0.5	5.9	0.9
1990	12.9	20.0	10.5	1.2	15.8	3.8	0.5	8.9	2.7	0.7	6.9	1.1
1995[3]	13.7	32.3	11.3	1.8	17.2	4.2	0.7	9.8	3.1	1.1	7.3	1.2
1998[3]	15.6	33.0	12.2	2.5	17.4	4.2	1.1	10.1	3.1	1.4	7.3	1.1
1999[3]	16.2	33.4	12.3	2.7	17.3	4.3	1.1	10.4	3.1	1.6	7.0	1.1
2000[3]	16.4	34.0	12.7	2.7	17.6	4.3	1.1	10.6	3.2	1.6	7.1	1.1
2001	16.6	34.0	12.9	2.6	17.7	4.2	1.1	10.7	3.2	1.5	7.1	1.0
UNEMPLOYMENT RATE[5]												
1970	7.1	4.8	4.8	(NA)	6.0	7.2	(NA)	4.8	5.9	(NA)	7.9	9.8
1980	10.3	5.3	6.4	23.2	5.9	9.2	15.6	4.4	7.9	29.2	8.3	12.8
1985	10.2	5.7	8.5	23.8	6.6	12.1	15.4	5.5	10.6	28.5	8.0	16.1
1990	8.2	3.5	5.7	18.4	4.2	8.5	14.5	3.8	7.7	20.8	4.8	10.2
1995[3]	8.7	3.9	5.8	16.6	4.3	8.1	11.8	3.6	7.1	19.5	5.3	10.8
1998[3]	7.5	3.2	5.0	15.1	3.8	6.7	11.8	3.2	5.3	17.5	4.5	10.6
1999[3]	7.4	2.8	5.0	11.7	2.9	6.2	8.9	2.4	4.5	13.6	3.7	10.7
2000[3]	7.3	2.7	4.3	11.0	2.9	5.1	8.7	2.6	4.8	12.6	3.5	5.9
2001	7.1	2.7	4.2	12.7	3.2	4.9	11.5	2.9	4.0	13.6	3.5	7.6

NA Not available.   [1] Husband present.   [2] Widowed, divorced, or separated.   [3] See footnote 2, Table 560.   [4] Percent of women in each specific category in the labor force.   [5] Unemployed as a percent of civilian labor force in specified group.

Source: U.S. Bureau of Labor Statistics, Bulletin 2307; and unpublished data.

No. 571. Labor Force Participation Rates for Wives, Husband Present by Age of Own Youngest Child: 1975 to 2001

[As of March. For civilian noninstitutional population, 16 years old and over. For definition of participation rate, see Table 570. Based on Current Population Survey; see text, Section 1, Population, and Appendix III]

Presence and age of child	Total 1975	Total 1985	Total 2001	White 1975	White 1985	White 2001	Black 1975	Black 1985	Black 2001
Wives, total	44.4	54.2	62.1	43.6	53.3	61.6	54.1	63.8	69.0
No children under 18	43.8	48.2	54.8	43.6	47.5	54.6	47.6	55.2	58.2
With children under 18	44.9	60.8	70.8	43.6	59.9	70.2	58.4	71.7	80.0
Under 6, total	36.7	53.4	62.5	34.7	52.1	61.7	54.9	69.6	76.0
Under 3	32.7	50.5	59.4	30.7	49.4	59.0	50.1	66.2	72.2
1 year or under	30.8	49.4	58.0	29.2	48.6	57.3	50.0	63.7	70.0
2 years	37.1	54.0	64.2	35.1	52.7	64.2	56.4	69.9	74.3
3 to 5 years	42.2	58.4	67.0	40.1	56.6	65.8	61.2	73.8	81.5
3 years	41.2	55.1	64.9	39.0	52.7	63.3	62.7	72.3	83.1
4 years	41.2	59.7	66.6	38.7	58.4	66.0	64.9	70.6	78.0
5 years	44.4	62.1	70.4	43.8	59.9	68.8	56.3	79.1	84.5
6 to 13 years	51.8	68.2	76.7	50.7	67.7	76.0	65.7	73.3	83.4
14 to 17 years	53.5	67.0	80.0	53.4	66.6	80.1	52.3	74.4	82.8

Source: U.S. Bureau of Labor Statistics, Bulletin 2340; and unpublished data.

Labor Force, Employment, and Earnings   373

No. 572. Families With Own Children—Employment Status of Parents: 1995 and 2001

[Annual average of monthly figures (33,544 represents 33,544,000). For families with own children. Based on the Current Population Survey, see text, Section 1, Population, and Appendix III]

Characteristic	Number (1,000) 1995	Number (1,000) 2001	Percent distribution 1995	Percent distribution 2001
WITH OWN CHILDREN UNDER 18				
Total families	33,544	34,365	100.0	100.0
Parent(s) employed	29,659	31,412	88.4	91.4
No parent employed	3,886	2,953	11.6	8.6
Married-couple families	24,604	24,810	100.0	100.0
Parent(s) employed	23,643	24,092	96.1	97.1
Mother employed	16,629	16,782	67.6	67.6
Both parents employed	15,491	15,676	63.0	63.2
Mother employed, not father	1,137	1,105	4.6	4.5
Father employed, not mother	7,014	7,311	28.5	29.5
Neither parent employed	962	718	3.9	2.9
Families maintained by women [1]	7,433	7,665	100.0	100.0
Mother employed	4,755	5,710	64.0	74.5
Mother not employed	2,678	1,955	36.0	25.5
Families maintained by men [1]	1,507	1,890	100.0	100.0
Father employed	1,261	1,610	83.7	85.2
Father not employed	245	280	16.3	14.8
WITH OWN CHILDREN 6 to 17				
Total families	18,270	19,608	100.0	100.0
Parent(s) employed	16,391	18,026	89.7	91.9
No parent employed	1,878	1,580	10.3	8.1
Married-couple families	13,001	13,743	100.0	100.0
Parent(s) employed	12,484	13,339	96.0	97.1
Mother employed	9,562	10,196	73.6	74.2
Both parents employed	8,846	9,488	68.0	69.0
Mother employed, not father	717	707	5.5	5.1

Characteristic	Number (1,000) 1995	Number (1,000) 2001	Percent distribution 1995	Percent distribution 2001
Father employed, not mother	2,921	3,144	22.5	22.9
Neither parent employed	517	403	4.0	2.9
Families maintained by women [1]	4,360	4,750	100.0	100.0
Mother employed	3,142	3,743	72.1	78.8
Mother not employed	1,219	1,006	27.9	21.2
Families maintained by men [1]	908	1,114	100.0	100.0
Father employed	766	944	84.3	84.7
Father not employed	143	171	15.7	15.4
WITH OWN CHILDREN UNDER 6				
Total families	15,275	14,758	100.0	100.0
Parent(s) employed	13,267	13,386	86.9	90.7
No parent employed	2,007	1,373	13.1	9.3
Married-couple families	11,604	11,067	100.0	100.0
Parent(s) employed	11,159	10,753	96.2	97.2
Mother employed	7,066	6,586	60.9	59.5
Both parents employed	6,646	6,188	57.3	55.9
Mother employed, not father	421	398	3.6	3.6
Father employed, not mother	4,092	4,167	35.3	37.7
Neither parent employed	445	314	3.8	2.8
Families maintained by women [1]	3,073	2,916	100.0	100.0
Mother employed	1,613	1,967	52.5	67.5
Mother not employed	1,460	949	47.5	32.5
Families maintained by men [1]	598	775	100.0	100.0
Father employed	496	666	82.8	85.9
Father not employed	102	110	17.1	14.2

[1] No spouse present.
Source: U.S. Bureau of Labor Statistics, News, USDL 97-195, June 16, 1997; and USDL 02-175, March 29, 2002.

No. 573. Employed Civilians and Weekly Hours: 1980 to 2001

[In thousands (99,303 represents 99,303,000), except as indicated. For civilian noninstitutional population 16 years old and over. Annual averages of monthly figures. Based on Current Population Survey; see text, Section 1, Population, and Appendix III]

Item	1980	1990 [1]	1995	1997 [1]	1998 [1]	1999 [1]	2000 [1]	2001
Total employed	99,303	118,793	124,900	129,558	131,463	133,488	135,208	135,073
Age:								
16 to 19 years old	7,710	6,581	6,419	6,661	7,051	7,172	7,276	6,889
20 to 24 years old	14,087	13,401	12,443	12,380	12,557	12,891	13,321	13,361
25 to 34 years old	27,204	33,935	32,356	31,809	31,394	30,865	30,501	29,697
35 to 44 years old	19,523	30,817	34,202	35,908	36,278	36,728	36,697	36,226
45 to 54 years old	16,234	19,525	24,378	26,744	27,587	28,635	29,717	30,592
55 to 64 years old	11,586	11,189	11,435	12,296	12,872	13,315	13,627	14,133
65 years old and over	2,960	3,346	3,666	3,761	3,725	3,882	4,070	4,174
Class of worker:								
Nonagriculture	95,938	115,570	121,460	126,159	128,085	130,207	131,903	131,930
Wage and salary worker	88,525	106,598	112,448	116,983	119,019	121,323	123,128	123,235
Self-employed	7,000	8,719	8,902	9,056	8,962	8,790	8,674	8,594
Unpaid family workers	413	253	110	120	103	95	101	101
Agriculture	3,364	3,223	3,440	3,399	3,378	3,281	3,305	3,144
Wage and salary worker	1,425	1,740	1,814	1,890	2,000	1,944	2,034	1,884
Self-employed	1,642	1,378	1,580	1,457	1,341	1,297	1,233	1,233
Unpaid family workers	297	105	45	51	38	40	38	27
Weekly hours:								
Nonagriculture:								
Wage and salary workers	38.1	39.2	39.2	39.4	39.2	39.5	39.6	39.2
Self-employed	41.2	40.8	39.4	39.7	39.6	40.1	40.0	39.4
Unpaid family workers	34.7	34.0	33.5	32.6	34.0	33.4	32.3	30.4
Agriculture:								
Wage and salary workers	41.6	41.2	41.1	41.6	40.6	41.1	41.0	40.6
Self-employed	49.3	46.8	43.5	42.7	43.3	43.3	43.0	43.3
Unpaid family workers	38.6	38.5	42.0	44.3	36.2	36.6	37.5	39.4

[1] See footnote 2, Table 560.
Source: U.S. Bureau of Labor Statistics, Employment and Earnings, monthly, January issues; and unpublished data.

No. 574. Employed Workers Actively Seeking a New Job: 2001

[As of February. In thousands (121,334 represents 121,334,000), except rate. For employed wage and salary workers 16 old and over (except as indicated) responding to the question on actively seeking work in the prior 3 months. Based on the Current Population Survey; see text, Section 1, Population, and Appendix III]

Characteristic	Total employed	Persons responding to search question		Per-cent	Characteristic	Total employed	Persons responding to search question		Per-cent
		Total	Actively seeking work				Total	Actively seeking work	
Total	121,334	118,163	4,937	4.2	Professional specialty	19,670	19,337	852	4.4
Age:					Technical and related support	4,440	4,332	258	6.0
16 to 19 years old	6,544	6,373	313	4.9	Sales	13,908	13,545	680	5.0
20 to 24 years old	12,997	12,632	902	7.1	Administrative support, including clerical	18,391	17,920	608	3.4
25 to 34 years old	28,285	27,472	1,517	5.5	Private household	592	401	44	11.0
35 to 44 years old	32,887	32,018	1,233	3.9	Protective service	2,436	2,376	79	3.3
45 to 54 years old	26,052	25,515	749	2.9	Service, except private households and protective	13,493	13,007	556	4.3
55 to 64 years old	11,743	11,426	213	1.9	Precision production, craft, and repair	12,770	12,426	395	3.2
65 years old and over	2,826	2,728	10	0.4	Machine operators, assemblers and inspectors	6,730	6,613	242	3.7
Sex: Male	62,753	61,106	2,606	4.3	Transportation and material moving occupations	5,266	5,109	191	3.7
Female	58,581	57,058	2,332	4.1	Handlers, equipment cleaners, helpers and laborers	4,846	4,675	241	5.2
Educational attainment:[1]					Farming, forestry and fishing	1,402	1,330	41	3.1
Less than high school diploma	9,515	9,172	233	2.5					
High school diploma, no college	31,280	30,297	846	2.8					
Some college or associate degree	28,984	28,320	1,175	4.1					
Bachelor's degree or more	32,014	31,370	1,469	4.7					
Occupation:									
Executive, administrative and managerial	17,390	17,091	750	4.4					

[1] Persons 25 years old and over.

Source: U.S. Bureau of Labor Statistics, Current Population Survey, February 2001, unpublished data.

No. 575. Persons at Work by Hours Worked: 2001

[129,517 represents 129,517,000. For civilian noninstitutional population 16 years old and over. Annual averages of monthly figures. Based on Current Population Survey; see text, Section 1, Population, and Appendix III]

Hours of work	Persons at work (1,000)			Percent distribution		
	Total	Agriculture industries	Non-agriculture industries	Total	Agriculture industries	Non-agriculture industries
Total	129,517	3,004	126,513	100.0	100.0	100.0
1 to 34 hours	31,175	838	30,337	24.1	27.9	24.0
1 to 4 hours	1,336	61	1,275	1.0	2.0	1.0
5 to 14 hours	4,819	197	4,622	3.7	6.6	3.7
15 to 29 hours	15,305	389	14,917	11.8	12.9	11.8
30 to 34 hours	9,715	191	9,524	7.5	6.4	7.5
35 hours and over	98,342	2,166	96,176	75.9	72.1	76.0
35 to 39 hours	8,703	169	8,534	6.7	5.6	6.7
40 hours	51,822	831	50,991	40.0	27.7	40.3
41 hours and over	37,817	1,166	36,651	29.2	38.8	29.0
41 to 48 hours	13,665	228	13,437	10.6	7.6	10.6
49 to 58 hours	14,067	360	13,706	10.9	12.0	10.8
60 hours and over	10,085	577	9,507	7.8	19.2	7.5
Average weekly hours:						
Total at work	39.2	41.6	39.2	(X)	(X)	(X)
Persons usually working full time	42.9	47.6	42.8	(X)	(X)	(X)

X Not applicable.

Source: U.S. Bureau of Labor Statistics, Employment and Earnings, monthly, January, 2001 issue.

No. 576. Persons With a Job But Not at Work: 1980 to 2001

[In thousands (5,881 represents 5,881,000), except percent. For civilian noninstitutional population 16 years old and over. Annual averages of monthly figures. Based on Current Population Survey; see text, Section 1, Population, and Appendix III]

Reason for not working	1980	1985	1990 [1]	1994 [1]	1995	1996	1997 [1]	1998 [1]	1999 [1]	2000 [1]	2001
All industries, number	5,881	5,789	6,160	5,619	5,582	5,768	5,555	5,586	5,407	5,616	5,556
Percent of employed	5.9	5.4	5.2	4.6	4.5	4.6	4.3	4.2	4.1	4.2	4.1
Reason for not working:											
Vacation	3,320	3,338	3,529	2,877	2,982	3,085	2,942	3,033	2,899	3,071	2,994
Illness	1,426	1,308	1,341	1,184	1,084	1,090	1,114	1,095	1,096	1,145	1,083
Bad weather	155	141	90	165	122	256	146	130	104	88	101
Industrial dispute	105	42	24	15	21	11	20	10	7	14	8
All other	876	960	1,177	1,378	1,373	1,325	1,334	1,318	1,300	1,298	1,370

[1] See footnote 2, Table 560.

Source: U.S. Bureau of Labor Statistics, Employment and Earnings, monthly, January issues; and unpublished data.

Labor Force, Employment, and Earnings   375

No. 577. Self-Employed Workers by Industry and Occupation: 1980 to 2001

[In thousands (8,642 represents 8,642,000). For civilian noninstitutional population 16 years old and over. Annual averages of monthly figures. Data from 1990 forward are not fully comparable with data for prior years because of the introduction of the occupational and industrial classification used in the 1990 census. Based on the Current Population Survey; see text, Section 1, Population, and Appendix III]

Item	1980	1990 [1]	1995	1997 [1]	1998 [1]	1999 [1]	2000 [1]	2001
Total self-employed............	8,642	10,097	10,482	10,513	10,303	10,087	9,907	9,826
Industry: Agriculture	1,642	1,378	1,580	1,457	1,341	1,297	1,233	1,233
Nonagriculture	7,000	8,719	8,902	9,056	8,962	8,790	8,674	8,594
Mining..........................	28	24	16	14	21	16	16	25
Construction.....................	1,173	1,457	1,460	1,492	1,519	1,545	1,581	1,519
Manufacturing....................	358	427	433	422	428	380	343	361
Transportation and public utilities	282	301	396	438	430	429	399	437
Trade	1,899	1,851	1,772	1,761	1,640	1,621	1,498	1,466
Finance, insurance, and real estate	458	630	660	629	609	661	693	644
Services	2,804	4,030	4,166	4,300	4,317	4,138	4,145	4,142
Occupation:								
Managerial and professional specialty......	(NA)	3,050	3,147	3,432	3,400	3,298	3,119	3,149
Technical, sales, and administrative support..	(NA)	2,240	2,341	2,219	2,117	2,111	2,083	1,968
Service occupations	(NA)	1,207	1,190	1,179	1,198	1,136	1,202	1,168
Precision production, craft, and repair......	(NA)	1,675	1,618	1,651	1,697	1,665	1,722	1,748
Operators, fabricators, and laborers	(NA)	567	631	629	584	607	555	579
Farming, forestry, and fishing	(NA)	1,358	1,556	1,403	1,307	1,270	1,226	1,213

NA Not available.   [1] See footnote 2, Table 560.

Source: U.S. Bureau of Labor Statistics, Bulletin 2307; *Employment and Earnings,* monthly, January issues; and unpublished data.

No. 578. Persons Doing Job-Related Work at Home: 2001

[19,759 represents 19,759,000. As of May. For persons at work 16 years and over in nonagricultural industries doing job-related work at home at least once a week as part of their primary job. Based on the Current Population Survey; see text, Section 1, Population, and Appendix III]

Characteristic	Percent distribution					Wage and salary workers paid to work at home			
	Total [1] (1,000)	Rate [2]	Wage and salary workers			Self-em-ployed [4]	Total [5] (1,000)	Percent distribution		
			Paid [3]	Unpaid				Hours vary	Usually less than 8 hours	Usually 35 hours or more
Total [6]....................	19,759	15.0	17.4	52.0		29.7	3,436	27.4	24.5	15.7
SEX										
Male.........................	10,291	14.8	16.0	50.5		32.6	1,642	30.9	23.3	14.8
Female.......................	9,468	15.2	18.9	53.7		26.5	1,794	24.2	25.7	16.5
RACE AND HISPANIC ORIGIN										
White	17,947	16.3	17.5	51.6		30.0	3,138	27.2	24.4	15.0
Black	1,152	7.6	14.9	57.9		26.0	172	29.7	22.1	28.9
Hispanic origin [7]...............	937	6.7	20.4	49.2		28.4	191	32.3	15.9	27.6
OCCUPATION										
Managerial and professional	12,628	29.8	14.2	62.8		22.4	1,798	28.0	24.1	13.9
Exec., admin., and managerial....	5,262	25.7	16.7	52.5		30.0	880	25.8	24.3	12.9
Professional	7,366	33.5	12.5	70.1		17.0	918	30.1	23.9	14.9
Technical, sales and administrative ..	4,669	12.2	24.7	40.2		33.9	1,155	27.3	22.1	16.7
Technical and related support	305	6.9	36.0	48.4		14.3	110	40.2	24.6	21.2
Sales	3,133	20.0	20.3	40.3		38.9	635	27.8	18.9	13.0
Administrative support	1,231	6.8	33.4	37.8		25.8	411	23.3	26.5	21.0
Service	972	5.3	24.1	18.4		55.1	234	25.6	19.6	33.1
Precision production, craft, and repair.	1,050	7.1	15.7	19.4		64.4	165	29.1	47.2	2.7
Operators, fabricators, and laborers ..	381	2.2	19.4	24.3		49.3	74	(B)	(B)	(B)
Farming, forestry, and fishing	59	8.7	(B)	(B)		(B)	10	(D)	(D)	(D)
INDUSTRY										
Mining	65	11.1	(B)	(B)		(B)	9	(B)	(B)	(B)
Construction	1,134	12.4	11.6	20.5		65.2	131	31.8	36.5	5.1
Manufacturing	1,806	9.3	28.7	54.9		15.7	518	27.0	21.5	12.5
Transportation and public utilities....	898	8.9	22.8	49.4		26.0	205	14.1	29.7	25.3
Wholesale trade	1,009	19.4	24.4	47.9		25.6	247	28.1	15.0	12.9
Retail trade	1,529	7.0	12.8	36.4		49.8	196	23.7	32.5	10.3
Finance, insurance, and real estate ..	1,810	20.8	18.8	48.2		33.0	340	30.7	24.0	9.5
Services	10,926	21.7	14.8	57.2		27.1	1,618	28.0	24.3	19.0
Public administration	581	9.2	29.6	69.8		-	172	33.7	27.1	12.8

B Base figure too small to meet statistical standards for reliability of a derived figure.   - Represents zero.   [1] Includes unpaid family workers and persons who did not report pay status.   [2] Persons working at home as a percent of the total employed.   [3] Persons with formal arrangements with their employers to be paid for the work done at home.   [4] Includes incorporated and unincorporated self-employed.   [5] Includes those not reporting usual number of hours worked.   [6] Includes other races, not shown separately.   [7] Persons of Hispanic origin may be of any race.

Source: U.S. Bureau of Labor Statistics, News, *Work at Home in 2001,* USDL 02-107, March 1, 2002.

U.S. Census Bureau, Statistical Abstract of the United States: 2002

No. 579. Persons on Flexible Schedules: 2001

[In thousands, (99,631 represents 99,631,000) except percent. As of May. For employed full-time wage and salary workers 16 years old and over. Excludes the self-employed. Data relate to the primary job. Based on the Current Population Survey; see text, Section 1, Population, and Appendix III]

Item	Total			Male			Female		
	Total [1]	With flexible schedules		Total [1]	With flexible schedules		Total [1]	With flexible schedules	
		Number	Percent		Number	Percent		Number	Percent
Total	**99,631**	**28,724**	**28.8**	**56,066**	**16,792**	**30.0**	**43,566**	**11,931**	**27.4**
AGE									
16 to 19 years old	1,761	339	19.2	988	167	16.9	773	171	22.2
20 to 24 years old	9,343	2,327	24.9	5,219	1,203	23.0	4,124	1,124	27.2
25 to 34 years old	24,552	7,434	30.3	14,058	4,370	31.1	10,494	3,064	29.2
35 to 44 years old	28,702	8,578	29.9	16,522	5,120	31.0	12,180	3,458	28.4
45 to 54 years old	23,946	6,990	29.2	12,902	4,032	31.2	11,044	2,958	26.8
55 to 64 years old	9,971	2,633	26.4	5,531	1,590	28.8	4,440	1,043	23.5
65 years old and over	1,357	423	31.2	847	311	36.7	510	112	22.0
RACE AND HISPANIC ORIGIN									
White	82,205	24,647	30.0	47,498	14,734	31.0	34,707	9,913	28.6
Black	12,390	2,629	21.2	5,776	1,209	20.9	6,614	1,420	21.5
Hispanic origin [2]	11,919	2,356	19.8	7,305	1,344	18.4	4,614	1,011	21.9
OCCUPATION									
Executive, administrative, and managerial	16,279	7,404	45.5	8,748	4,277	48.9	7,531	3,128	41.5
Professional specialty	16,681	5,922	35.5	8,037	3,678	45.8	8,644	2,244	26.0
Technical and related support	3,757	1,181	31.4	1,863	683	36.7	1,894	498	26.3
Sales	9,852	4,011	40.7	5,424	2,404	44.3	4,428	1,607	36.3
Administrative support, including clerical	13,997	3,426	24.5	3,206	753	23.5	10,791	2,672	24.8
Private household	377	132	35.0	5	3	(B)	371	129	34.8
Protective service	2,144	343	16.0	1,773	291	16.4	371	52	14.0
Service, exc. private household and protective	8,207	1,755	21.4	3,324	698	21.0	4,883	1,057	21.6
Precision production, craft and repair	12,061	2,209	18.3	11,000	2,026	18.4	1,061	183	17.3
Operators, fabricators, and laborers	14,621	1,999	13.7	11,324	1,689	14.9	3,297	310	9.4

B Percent not shown where base is less than 75,000.   [1] Includes persons who did not provide information on flexible schedules.   [2] Persons of Hispanic origin may be of any race.
Source: U.S. Bureau of Labor Statistics, *News*, USDL 02-225, April 18, 2002.

No. 580. Persons on Shift Schedules: 2001

[In percent, except as indicated (99,631 represents 99,631,000). As of May. For employed full-time wage and salary workers 16 years old and over. Excludes the self-employed. Data relate to the primary job. Based on the Current Population Survey; see text, Section 1, Population, and Appendix III]

Item	Total workers [1] (1,000)	Regular daytime schedules	Shift workers						
			Total	Evening shift	Night shift	Rotating shift	Split shift	Irregular shift [2]	Other shift
Total	**99,631**	**84.8**	**14.5**	**4.8**	**3.3**	**2.3**	**0.4**	**2.8**	**0.7**
AGE									
16 to 19 years old	1,761	70.2	28.8	13.5	5.4	3.4	0.3	5.3	1.0
20 to 24 years old	9,343	77.8	21.3	8.7	4.7	3.3	0.4	3.5	0.8
25 to 34 years old	24,552	84.9	14.4	4.9	3.3	2.3	0.6	2.4	0.8
35 to 44 years old	28,702	86.2	13.2	3.7	3.3	2.3	0.4	2.8	0.6
45 to 54 years old	23,946	86.3	13.1	4.1	2.9	2.3	0.3	2.6	0.8
55 to 64 years old	9,971	86.3	13.2	4.5	3.1	1.7	0.4	2.8	0.6
65 years old and over	1,357	84.9	15.0	3.9	2.1	1.7	1.3	5.5	0.5
SEX									
Male	56,066	82.9	16.4	5.2	3.6	2.8	0.5	3.3	0.9
Female	43,566	87.3	12.1	4.3	3.0	1.8	0.4	2.1	0.5
RACE AND HISPANIC ORIGIN									
White	82,205	85.8	13.6	4.4	3.0	2.2	0.4	2.8	0.7
Black	12,390	79.3	19.7	7.0	5.0	3.3	0.5	3.2	0.6
Hispanic origin [3]	11,919	84.3	14.8	5.8	3.4	2.0	0.5	2.5	0.5
OCCUPATION									
Executive, administrative, and managerial	16,279	93.9	5.6	1.6	0.7	1.0	0.2	1.8	0.3
Professional specialty	16,681	91.7	7.8	1.7	1.7	1.1	0.3	2.5	0.4
Technical and related support	3,757	83.9	15.6	3.8	4.2	2.4	0.1	3.8	1.4
Sales	9,852	84.3	15.2	4.1	1.3	3.6	0.3	5.2	0.5
Administrative support, including clerical	13,997	91.1	8.4	3.6	2.4	0.7	0.4	0.9	0.4
Private household	377	82.8	15.6	1.0	0.5	0.7	0.7	9.4	3.3
Protective service	2,144	49.8	49.0	12.4	9.7	12.3	1.1	8.1	5.4
Service, exc. private household and protective	8,207	66.9	32.0	14.5	5.9	3.9	1.3	4.7	1.5
Precision production, craft and repair	12,061	87.4	12.0	4.0	3.6	2.3	0.3	1.3	0.5
Operators, fabricators, and laborers	14,621	73.6	25.4	8.4	8.0	3.7	0.6	3.8	0.8
Farming, forestry, fishing	1,653	93.5	5.6	2.3	0.8	0.7	0.5	1.0	0.3

[1] Includes persons who did not provide information on flexible schedules.   [2] Employer arranged schedule.   [3] Persons of Hispanic origin may be of any race.
Source: U.S. Bureau of Labor Statistics, *News*, USDL 02-225, April 18, 2002.

U.S. Census Bureau, Statistical Abstract of the United States: 2002

No. 581. Multiple Jobholders: 2001

[**Annual average of monthly figures (7,319 represents 7,319,000).** For the civilian noninstitutional population 16 years old and over. Multiple jobholders are employed persons who, either 1) had jobs as wage or salary workers with two employers or more; 2) were self-employed and also held a wage and salary job; or 3) were unpaid family workers on their primary jobs but also held wage and salary job. Based on the Current Population Survey; see text, Section 1, Population, and Appendix III]

Characteristic	Total		Male		Female	
	Number (1,000)	Percent of employed	Number (1,000)	Percent of employed	Number (1,000)	Percent of employed
Total [1]	7,319	5.4	3,808	5.3	3,511	5.6
Age:						
16 to 19 years old	318	4.6	130	3.7	188	5.5
20 to 24 years old	756	5.7	345	5.0	411	6.4
25 to 54 years old	5,412	5.6	2,868	5.6	2,544	5.7
55 to 64 years old	686	4.9	372	4.9	314	4.8
65 years old and over	146	3.5	92	3.8	54	3.0
Race and Hispanic origin:						
White	6,281	5.5	3,275	5.3	3,006	5.8
Black	759	5.0	390	5.5	369	5.2
Hispanic origin [2]	504	3.4	290	3.5	214	3.2
Marital status:						
Married, spouse present	4,028	5.2	2,380	5.8	1,648	4.9
Widowed, divorced, or separated	1,297	6.0	472	5.3	824	6.6
Single, never married	1,994	5.4	956	4.8	1,038	6.6
Full- or part-time status:						
Primary job full time, secondary job part time	3,992	(X)	2,311	(X)	1,681	(X)
Both jobs part time	1,581	(X)	507	(X)	1,073	(X)
Both jobs full time	280	(X)	181	(X)	100	(X)
Hours vary on primary or secondary job	1,425	(X)	787	(X)	639	(X)

X Not applicable. [1] Includes a small number of persons who work part time on their primary job and full time on their secondary job(s), not shown separately. Includes other races, not shown separately. [2] Persons of Hispanic origin may be of any race.

Source: U.S. Bureau of Labor Statistics, *Employment and Earnings*, monthly, January 2002 issue.

No. 582. Average Number of Job Held from Ages 18 to 34: 1978 to 1998

[**In percent.** For persons 33 to 41 in 1998. A job is an uninterrupted period of work with a particular employer. Educational attainment as of 1998. Based on the National Longitudinal Survey of Youth 1979; see source for details]

Sex and educational attainment	Total [1]	Number of jobs held by age—		
		Age 18 to 24 years old	Age 25 to 29 years old	Age 30 to 34 years old
Total [2]	9.2	5.6	3.0	2.4
Less than a high school diploma	9.3	5.2	3.0	2.4
High school graduates, no college	8.7	5.2	2.8	2.4
Less than a bachelor's degree	9.6	5.8	3.2	2.5
Bachelor's degree or more	9.7	6.3	3.0	2.4
Male	9.6	5.8	3.2	2.6
Less than a high school diploma	10.7	6.1	3.5	2.8
High school graduates, no college	9.1	5.5	3.1	2.5
Less than a bachelor's degree	10.0	6.0	3.4	2.6
Bachelor's degree or more	9.3	6.0	2.9	2.4
Female	8.8	5.4	2.8	2.3
Less than a high school diploma	7.4	4.0	2.2	2.0
High school graduates, no college	8.2	4.8	2.5	2.3
Less than a bachelor's degree	9.2	5.6	3.0	2.4
Bachelor's degree or more	10.1	6.6	3.1	2.3
White, non-Hispanic	9.4	5.8	3.0	2.4
Less than a high school diploma	9.8	5.6	3.1	2.6
High school graduates, no college	8.7	5.3	2.8	2.4
Less than a bachelor's degree	9.9	6.0	3.2	2.5
Bachelor's degree or more	9.8	6.4	3.0	2.3
Black, non-Hispanic	8.5	4.7	2.9	2.5
Less than a high school diploma	8.0	3.9	2.7	2.2
High school graduates, no college	8.4	4.5	2.9	2.5
Less than a bachelor's degree	8.5	5.0	2.9	2.4
Bachelor's degree or more	9.4	6.0	3.1	2.7
Hispanic origin	8.7	5.0	2.9	2.4
Less than a high school diploma	8.8	4.9	2.8	2.2
High school graduates, no college	8.6	5.0	2.8	2.4
Less than a bachelor's degree	8.6	5.1	3.0	2.3
Bachelor's degree or more	8.9	5.3	2.7	2.6

[1] Jobs held in more than one age category were counted in each category, but only once in the total. [2] Includes other races, not shown separately.

Source: U.S. Bureau of Labor Statistics, *Number of Jobs Held, Labor Market Activity, and Earnings Growth over Two Decades: Results from a Longitudinal Survey*, USDL 00-119, April 25, 2000.

No. 583. Distribution of Workers by Tenure With Current Employer by Selected Characteristic: 2000

[120,303 represents 120,303,000. As of February. For employed wage and salary workers 16 years old and over. Based on the Current Population Survey and subject to sampling error; see source and Appendix III]

Characteristic	Number employed (1,000)	Percent distribution by tenure with current employer								Median years [1]
		12 months or less	13 to 23 months	2 years	3 to 4 years	5 to 9 years	10 to 14 years	15 to 19 years	20 years or more	
Total [2]	120,303	26.8	8.0	5.3	16.1	17.1	11.0	6.1	9.5	3.5
AGE AND SEX										
16 to 19 years old.	6,713	75.1	11.9	6.9	5.8	0.3	-	-	-	0.7
20 years old and over	113,590	24.0	7.7	5.3	16.7	18.1	11.7	6.4	10.1	4.0
20 to 24 years old	12,535	54.7	13.0	9.3	17.5	5.5	(Z)	-	-	1.1
25 to 34 years old	28,560	31.1	10.3	7.1	21.9	21.2	7.4	0.9	(Z)	2.6
35 to 44 years old	32,625	19.4	6.9	4.5	16.9	21.2	15.5	9.5	6.1	4.8
45 to 54 years old	25,650	13.7	5.4	3.3	13.0	17.7	14.9	10.0	21.8	8.2
55 to 64 years old	11,326	11.2	3.9	3.3	11.7	16.8	15.8	9.8	27.5	10.0
65 years old and over	2,893	12.9	4.9	2.7	12.6	16.9	15.4	9.2	25.5	9.5
Male.	62,306	25.6	7.7	5.3	15.8	17.3	10.9	6.5	11.0	3.8
16 to 19 years old	3,401	73.8	12.2	7.7	6.0	0.4	-	-	-	0.7
20 years old and over	58,905	22.9	7.4	5.2	16.4	18.2	11.5	6.8	11.6	4.2
20 to 24 years old	6,499	52.0	12.7	9.2	19.8	6.1	0.1	-	-	1.2
25 to 34 years old	15,222	29.4	10.0	7.3	21.8	22.1	8.4	0.9	(Z)	2.7
35 to 44 years old	17,023	17.9	6.4	4.2	15.7	20.9	16.4	11.1	7.3	5.4
45 to 54 years old	12,858	13.1	5.0	3.2	11.7	16.8	13.0	10.8	26.3	9.5
55 to 64 years old	5,841	11.2	3.9	3.2	11.4	16.9	14.5	8.2	30.6	10.2
65 years old and over.	1,461	14.4	3.4	2.5	12.2	18.5	12.7	8.1	28.0	9.1
Female	57,997	28.1	8.3	5.4	16.4	17.0	11.1	5.7	8.0	3.3
16 to 19 years old	3,312	76.5	11.7	6.0	5.6	0.1	-	-	-	0.7
20 years old and over	54,685	25.2	8.1	5.3	17.1	18.0	11.8	6.0	8.5	3.7
20 to 24 years old	6,037	57.6	13.3	9.4	15.0	4.8	-	-	-	1.0
25 to 34 years old	13,338	33.0	10.7	6.8	22.0	20.2	6.3	1.0	-	2.5
35 to 44 years old	15,601	21.0	7.4	4.9	18.2	21.5	14.4	7.8	4.8	4.3
45 to 54 years old	12,791	14.4	5.9	3.5	14.3	18.7	16.8	9.2	17.3	7.3
55 to 64 years old	5,485	11.3	3.8	3.4	11.9	16.6	17.2	11.6	24.3	9.9
65 years old and over.	1,432	11.5	6.4	2.8	12.9	15.3	18.0	10.3	22.8	9.7
RACE AND HISPANIC ORIGIN										
White	100,624	26.2	8.0	5.2	16.0	17.1	11.2	6.3	9.8	3.6
Male	52,890	24.9	7.6	5.3	15.7	17.2	11.0	6.6	11.5	3.9
Female	47,735	27.6	8.5	5.2	16.4	17.0	11.4	6.0	7.9	3.4
Black	14,199	29.3	7.0	6.1	15.6	17.6	10.0	5.3	9.2	3.3
Male	6,546	29.0	7.2	6.0	15.1	17.8	10.1	6.2	8.6	3.4
Female . . . . . ;.	7,653	29.5	6.8	6.1	16.1	17.4	9.8	4.5	9.8	3.3
Hispanic origin [3]	13,767	30.7	8.3	7.7	18.1	16.6	8.8	4.3	5.5	2.8
Male	7,971	28.7	8.0	7.6	17.7	17.6	9.6	4.8	6.0	3.0
Female	5,796	33.4	8.6	7.9	18.7	15.3	7.7	3.7	4.7	2.5

- Represents zero.   Z Less than 0.05 percent.   [1] For definition of median, see Guide to Tabular Presentation.   [2] Includes other races, not shown separately.   [3] Persons of Hispanic origin may be of any race.
Source: U. S. Bureau of Labor Statistics, News, USDL 00-245, August 29, 2000; and unpublished data.

No. 584. Part-Time Workers by Reason: 2001

[In thousands (31,175 represents 31,175,000), except hours. For persons working 1 to 34 hours per week. For civilian noninstitutional population 16 years old and over. Annual average of monthly figures. Based on the Current Population Survey and subject to sampling error; see text, Section 1, Population, and Appendix III]

Reason	All industries			Nonagriculture industries		
	Total	Usually work—		Total	Usually work—	
		Full time	Part time		Full time	Part time
Total working fewer than 35 hours	31,175	10,312	20,863	30,337	10,067	20,270
Economic reasons	3,672	1,516	2,156	3,529	1,436	2,093
Slack work or business conditions	2,355	1,256	1,099	2,266	1,203	1,063
Could find only part-time work	1,007	-	1,007	989	-	989
Seasonal work	160	111	50	130	88	42
Job started or ended during the week	149	149	-	144	144	-
Noneconomic reasons	27,503	8,797	18,707	26,808	8,632	18,177
Child-care problems.	785	87	699	772	85	686
Other family or personal obligations	5,659	772	4,887	5,515	757	4,758
Health or medical limitations	759	-	759	734	-	734
In school or training.	6,264	95	6,169	6,138	92	6,045
Retired or Social Security limit on earnings . . .	1,896	-	1,896	1,780	-	1,780
Vacation or personal day	3,520	3,520	-	3,471	3,471	-
Holiday, legal, or religious	1,162	1,162	-	1,151	1,151	-
Weather related curtailment.	294	294	-	259	259	-
Other	7,164	2,868	4,296	6,990	2,816	4,174
Average hours per week:						
Economic reasons.	23.2	24.1	22.6	23.3	24.2	22.7
Noneconomic reasons	21.5	25.3	19.7	21.6	25.3	19.8

- Represents or rounds to zero.
Source: U.S. Bureau of Labor Statistics, Employment and Earnings, monthly, January 2002 issue.

No. 585. Displaced Workers by Selected Characteristics: 2000

[In percent, except total (3,275 represents 3,275,000). As of February. For persons 20 years old and over with tenure of 3 years or more who lost or left a job between January 1997 and December 1999 because of plant closings or moves, slack work, or the abolishment of their positions. Data revised since originally published. Based on Current Population Survey and subject to sampling error; see source and Appendix III]

Characteristic	Total (1,000)	Employment status			Reason for job loss		
		Employed	Unemployed	Not in the labor force	Plant or company closed down or moved	Slack work	Position or shift abolished
Total [1]	**3,275**	**73.5**	**10.4**	**16.1**	**49.4**	**21.6**	**29.0**
20 to 24 years old	100	87.7	3.7	8.7	49.8	29.5	20.7
25 to 54 years old	2,503	79.5	10.3	10.2	48.3	22.1	29.6
55 to 64 years old	517	56.0	13.6	30.4	56.6	15.3	28.1
65 years old and over . . .	155	26.3	5.2	68.6	43.1	29.0	27.9
Males	1,765	78.9	9.6	11.5	47.1	24.0	28.9
20 to 24 years old	75	86.6	4.9	8.4	43.4	36.1	20.5
25 to 54 years old	1,331	85.1	9.1	5.8	46.2	24.0	29.8
55 to 64 years old	279	62.9	13.3	23.8	56.3	17.4	26.3
65 years old and over . . .	80	23.6	10.0	66.4	33.5	34.6	31.9
Females	1,511	67.3	11.3	21.4	52.1	18.7	29.1
20 to 24 years old	25	(2)	(2)	(2)	(2)	(2)	(2)
25 to 54 years old	1,172	73.2	11.7	15.1	50.7	19.9	29.4
55 to 64 years old	238	47.9	14.0	38.1	57.0	12.8	30.2
65 years old and over . . .	75	29.1	-	70.9	53.4	23.0	23.6
White	2,778	74.4	9.9	15.7	48.9	20.9	30.3
Black	363	72.2	12.8	15.0	53.2	26.5	20.3
Hispanic origin [3]	346	69.7	13.0	17.3	50.4	32.1	17.5

- Represents zero.   [1] Includes other races, not shown separately.   [2] Data not shown where base is less than 75,000.
[3] Persons of Hispanic origin may be of any race.

Source: U.S. Bureau of Labor Statistics, *News*, USDL 00-223, August 9, 2000.

No. 586. Labor Force Status of Persons With a Work Disability by Age: 2001

[In percent, except as indicated (21,331 represents 21,331,000). As of March. For civilians 16 to 74 who have a condition which prevents then from working or limits the amount of work they can do. Data from the Current Population Survey and subject to sampling error; see text, Section 1, Population, and Appendix III]

Labor force status	Total	Age						
		16 to 24 years old	25 to 34 years old	35 to 44 years old	45 to 54 years old	55 to 64 years old	65 to 69 years old	70 to 74 years old
Number (1,000)	**21,331**	**1,330**	**2,102**	**3,569**	**4,841**	**5,226**	**2,123**	**2,140**
In labor force	24.8	37.5	41.7	33.6	30.9	18.0	7.4	5.7
Employed	22.3	28.5	36.9	30.2	28.8	16.7	6.8	5.6
Full-time	14.4	14.4	25.2	21.5	20.2	9.9	2.0	1.7
Not in labor force	75.2	62.5	58.3	66.4	69.1	82.0	92.6	94.3
Unemployment rate	10.0	23.9	11.5	10.0	6.8	7.5	7.2	2.8

Source: U.S. Census Bureau Internet site <http://www.census.gov/hhes/www/disable/disabcps.html> (accessed 28 May 2002).

No. 587. Persons Not in the Labor Force: 2001

[In thousands (70,050 represents 70,050,000). Annual average of monthly figures. For the civilian noninstitutional population 16 years old and over. Based on the Current Population Survey; see text, Section 1, Population, and Appendix III]

Status and reason	Total	Age			Sex	
		16 to 24 years old	25 to 54 years old	55 years old and over	Male	Female
Total not in the labor force	**70,050**	**12,384**	**19,495**	**38,171**	**26,114**	**43,935**
Do not want a job now [1]	65,483	10,629	17,509	37,345	24,119	41,363
Want a job now	4,567	1,755	1,986	826	1,995	2,572
In the previous year—						
Did not search for a job	2,705	946	1,130	629	1,130	1,575
Did search for a job [2]	1,862	809	856	197	865	997
Not available for work now	591	306	248	36	227	364
Available for work now, not looking for work. . .	1,271	503	608	161	638	634
Reason for not currently looking for work:						
Discouraged over job prospects [3]	319	105	165	49	191	128
Family responsibilities	131	31	87	13	30	101
In school or training	208	174	32	2	112	96
Ill health or disability	95	16	55	24	45	50
Other [4]	518	177	268	74	260	258

[1] Includes some persons who are not asked if they want a job.   [2] Persons who had a job in the prior 12 months must have searched since the end of that job.   [3] Includes such things as believes no work available, could not find work, lacks necessary schooling or training, employer thinks too young or old, and other types of discrimination.   [4] Includes such things as child care and transportation problems.

Source: U.S. Bureau of Labor Statistics, *Employment and Earnings*, monthly, January 2002 issue.

No. 588. Employed Civilians by Occupation, Sex, Race, and Hispanic Origin: 1983 and 2001

[**100,834 represents 100,834,000.** For civilian noninstitutional population 16 years old and over. Annual average of monthly figures. Based on Current Population Survey; see text, Section 1, Population, and Appendix III. Persons of Hispanic origin may be of any race. See headnote, Table 577]

Occupation	1983				2001 [1]			
	Total employed (1,000)	Percent of total			Total employed (1,000)	Percent of total		
		Fe-male	Black	His-panic		Fe-male	Black	His-panic
Total	100,834	43.7	9.3	5.3	135,073	46.6	11.3	10.9
Managerial and professional specialty	23,592	40.9	5.6	2.6	41,894	50.0	8.3	5.1
Executive, administrative, and managerial [2]	10,772	32.4	4.7	2.8	20,338	46.0	7.9	5.6
Officials and administrators, public	417	38.5	8.3	3.8	731	51.5	14.5	7.0
Financial managers	357	38.6	3.5	3.1	752	52.1	6.6	4.2
Personnel and labor relations managers	106	43.9	4.9	2.6	224	68.2	11.4	7.3
Purchasing managers	82	23.6	5.1	1.4	152	42.6	8.9	4.3
Managers, marketing, advertising and public relations	396	21.8	2.7	1.7	766	39.3	3.7	4.3
Administrators, education and related fields	415	41.4	11.3	2.4	833	64.1	11.5	5.7
Managers, medicine and health	91	57.0	5.0	2.0	780	77.3	7.5	5.6
Managers, properties and real estate	305	42.8	5.5	5.2	583	48.8	8.2	7.7
Management-related occupations	2,966	40.3	5.8	3.5	5,139	58.6	9.7	5.7
Accountants and auditors	1,105	38.7	5.5	3.3	1,657	58.8	9.5	5.4
Professional specialty [2]	12,820	48.1	6.4	2.5	21,556	53.7	8.6	4.7
Architects	103	12.7	1.6	1.5	214	23.5	3.1	4.4
Engineers [2]	1,572	5.8	2.7	2.2	2,122	10.4	5.5	3.5
Aerospace engineers	80	6.9	1.5	2.1	89	9.4	3.0	2.3
Chemical engineers	67	6.1	3.0	1.4	78	11.4	4.4	1.1
Civil engineers	211	4.0	1.9	3.2	297	10.2	6.0	1.9
Electrical and electronic	450	6.1	3.4	3.1	739	10.0	6.9	4.5
Industrial engineers	210	11.0	3.3	2.4	261	17.3	5.4	4.1
Mechanical	259	2.8	3.2	1.1	333	6.2	4.2	3.3
Mathematical and computer scientists [2]	463	29.6	5.4	2.6	2,103	30.1	8.6	3.6
Computer systems analysts, scientists	276	27.8	6.2	2.7	1,810	27.4	8.5	3.7
Operations and systems researchers and analysts	142	31.3	4.9	2.2	237	46.9	10.5	3.5
Natural scientists [2]	357	20.5	2.6	2.1	582	34.3	4.8	2.8
Chemists, except biochemists	98	23.3	4.3	1.2	165	31.0	8.7	3.1
Geologists and geodesists	65	18.0	1.1	2.6	50	23.5	1.9	1.6
Biological and life scientists	55	40.8	2.4	1.8	126	44.0	3.0	4.5
Medical scientists	(³)	(³)	(³)	(³)	95	51.5	4.3	3.2
Health diagnosing occupations [2]	735	13.3	2.7	3.3	1,090	28.6	5.0	4.1
Physicians	519	15.8	3.2	4.5	761	29.3	5.6	4.6
Dentists	126	6.7	2.4	1.0	170	19.9	4.1	3.5
Health assessment and treating occupations	1,900	85.8	7.1	2.2	3,052	86.1	9.6	3.8
Registered nurses	1,372	95.8	6.7	1.8	2,162	93.1	9.9	3.4
Pharmacists	158	26.7	3.8	2.6	212	48.1	5.6	3.2
Dietitians	71	90.8	21.0	3.7	101	86.4	24.8	8.0
Therapists [2]	247	76.3	7.6	2.7	497	76.3	7.6	5.2
Respiratory therapists	69	69.4	6.5	3.7	87	61.1	13.3	3.9
Physical therapists	55	77.0	9.7	1.5	150	66.9	2.5	4.9
Speech therapists	51	90.5	1.5	-	111	92.1	4.3	4.2
Physicians' assistants	51	36.3	7.7	4.4	80	60.3	4.5	3.2
Teachers, college and university	606	36.3	4.4	1.8	1,003	43.3	6.1	4.1
Teachers, except college and university [2]	3,365	70.9	9.1	2.7	5,473	74.9	9.9	5.4
Prekindergarten and kindergarten	299	98.2	11.8	3.4	651	97.8	15.0	10.3
Elementary school	1,350	83.3	11.1	3.1	2,216	82.5	10.6	5.4
Secondary school	1,209	51.8	7.2	2.3	1,304	58.5	6.9	3.9
Special education	81	82.2	10.2	2.3	353	86.0	9.7	2.4
Counselors, educational and vocational	184	53.1	13.9	3.2	258	68.4	14.1	6.5
Librarians, archivists, and curators	213	84.4	7.8	1.6	231	84.5	10.0	3.5
Librarians	193	87.3	7.9	1.8	203	85.7	10.8	3.0
Social scientists and urban planners [2]	261	46.8	7.1	2.1	454	58.0	8.6	3.3
Economists	98	37.9	6.3	2.7	135	52.3	9.6	3.6
Psychologists	135	57.1	8.6	1.1	268	61.7	8.3	3.7
Social, recreation, and religious workers [2]	831	43.1	12.1	3.8	1,449	56.7	17.6	6.1
Social workers	407	64.3	18.2	6.3	782	72.2	24.5	7.5
Recreation workers	65	71.9	15.7	2.0	127	73.7	12.6	6.2
Clergy	293	5.6	4.9	1.4	360	15.1	10.7	3.9
Lawyers and judges	651	15.8	2.7	1.0	966	29.3	5.3	3.2
Lawyers	612	15.3	2.6	0.9	929	29.3	5.1	3.1
Writers, artists, entertainers, and athletes [2]	1,544	42.7	4.8	2.9	2,536	49.7	6.5	6.7
Authors	62	46.7	2.1	0.9	122	57.7	5.0	2.1
Technical writers	(³)	(³)	(³)	(³)	81	58.2	5.7	6.0
Designers	393	52.7	3.1	2.7	788	56.3	3.9	7.7
Musicians and composers	155	28.0	7.9	4.4	180	36.5	14.7	6.2
Actors and directors	60	30.8	6.6	3.4	131	42.1	7.9	8.9
Painters, sculptors, craft-artists, and artist printmakers	186	47.4	2.1	2.3	243	45.6	5.1	6.4
Photographers	113	20.7	4.0	3.4	154	38.4	5.0	4.1
Editors and reporters	204	48.4	2.9	2.1	309	51.6	5.2	4.3
Public relations specialists	157	50.1	6.2	1.9	182	60.2	9.9	5.0
Announcers	(³)	(³)	(³)	(³)	(³)	(³)	(³)	(³)
Athletes	58	17.6	9.4	1.7	114	27.4	10.3	8.3

See footnotes at end of table.

U.S. Census Bureau, Statistical Abstract of the United States: 2002

[**100,834 represents 100,834,000.** For civilian noninstitutional population 16 years old and over. Annual average of monthly figures. Based on Current Population Survey; see text, Section 1, Population, and Appendix III. Persons of Hispanic origin may be of any race. See headnote, Table 577]

Occupation	1983				2001 [1]			
	Total employed (1,000)	Percent of total			Total employed (1,000)	Percent of total		
		Female	Black	Hispanic		Female	Black	Hispanic
Technical, sales, and administrative support	**31,265**	**64.6**	**7.6**	**4.3**	**39,044**	**63.7**	**11.4**	**9.1**
Technicians and related support [2]	3,053	48.2	8.2	3.1	4,497	53.4	10.3	7.5
Health technologists and technicians [2]	1,111	84.3	12.7	3.1	1,807	81.7	14.3	8.6
Clinical laboratory technologists and technicians	255	76.2	10.5	2.9	355	78.8	16.5	7.7
Dental hygienists	66	98.6	1.6	-	116	97.8	2.5	1.6
Radiologic technicians	101	71.7	8.6	4.5	167	70.3	8.2	7.5
Licensed practical nurses	443	97.0	17.7	3.1	374	94.3	23.2	3.4
Engineering and related technologists and technicians [2]	822	18.4	6.1	3.5	1,007	21.3	8.9	7.8
Electrical and electronic technicians	260	12.5	8.2	4.6	475	19.5	9.3	7.1
Drafting occupations	273	17.5	5.5	2.3	220	20.1	4.3	9.2
Surveying and mapping technicians	(3)	(3)	(3)	(3)	68	13.6	3.4	10.6
Science technicians [2]	202	29.1	6.6	2.8	299	44.6	6.1	6.9
Biological technicians	52	37.7	2.9	2.0	124	63.4	5.8	8.8
Chemical technicians	82	26.9	9.5	3.5	70	27.1	6.2	6.6
Technicians, except health, engineering, and science [2]	917	35.3	5.0	2.7	1,384	41.6	7.0	6.1
Airplane pilots and navigators	69	2.1	-	1.6	136	3.5	0.6	1.7
Computer programmers	443	32.5	4.4	2.1	646	26.6	6.2	4.8
Legal assistants	128	74.0	4.3	3.6	400	83.5	9.5	10.5
Sales occupations	11,818	47.5	4.7	3.7	16,044	49.4	9.1	8.7
Supervisors and proprietors	2,958	28.4	3.6	3.4	4,836	41.1	6.9	6.9
Sales representatives, finance and business services [2]	1,853	37.2	2.7	2.2	2,891	44.3	7.7	5.6
Insurance sales	551	25.1	3.8	2.5	582	47.4	8.1	6.0
Real estate sales	570	48.9	1.3	1.5	811	52.2	5.2	4.9
Securities and financial services sales	212	23.6	3.1	1.1	562	29.9	6.9	4.1
Advertising and related sales	124	47.9	4.5	3.3	176	54.5	7.1	3.6
Sales representatives, commodities, except retail	1,442	15.1	2.1	2.2	1,511	23.4	3.5	5.8
Sales workers, retail and personal services	5,511	69.7	6.7	4.8	6,711	63.1	12.6	12.2
Cashiers	2,009	84.4	10.1	5.4	2,974	76.9	16.6	13.6
Sales-related occupations	54	58.7	2.8	1.3	96	67.5	10.4	3.2
Administrative support, including clerical	16,395	79.9	9.6	5.0	18,503	78.7	13.7	9.8
Supervisors	676	53.4	9.3	5.0	720	66.1	15.7	9.0
Computer equipment operators	605	63.9	12.5	6.0	324	53.0	18.4	7.8
Computer operators	597	63.7	12.1	6.0	317	53.2	17.8	7.9
Secretaries, stenographers, and typists [2]	4,861	98.2	7.3	4.5	3,086	97.7	10.2	8.5
Secretaries	3,891	99.0	5.8	4.0	2,404	98.4	9.0	8.7
Typists	906	95.6	13.8	6.4	529	95.0	17.3	8.9
Information clerks	1,174	88.9	8.5	5.5	2,029	87.8	12.1	10.4
Receptionists	602	96.8	7.5	6.6	1,047	97.0	11.7	11.6
Records processing occupations, except financial [2]	866	82.4	13.9	4.8	1,063	80.8	15.7	9.4
Order clerks	188	78.1	10.6	4.4	315	75.2	22.9	9.8
Personnel clerks, except payroll and time keeping	64	91.1	14.9	4.6	56	88.1	21.5	3.9
Library clerks	147	81.9	15.4	2.5	150	82.0	8.9	8.1
File clerks	287	83.5	16.7	6.1	328	81.5	14.4	11.4
Records clerks	157	82.8	11.6	5.6	210	85.6	10.4	8.2
Financial records processing [2]	2,457	89.4	4.6	3.7	2,205	91.8	7.9	7.4
Bookkeepers, accounting, and auditing clerks	1,970	91.0	4.3	3.3	1,621	92.9	7.5	6.4
Payroll and time keeping clerks	192	82.2	5.9	5.0	171	93.2	10.5	7.9
Billing clerks	146	88.4	6.2	3.9	210	87.9	9.3	9.7
Cost and rate clerks	96	75.6	5.9	5.3	52	71.4	7.1	18.2
Billing, posting, and calculating machine operators	(3)	(3)	(3)	(3)	151	90.6	7.2	10.6
Duplicating, mail and other office machine operators	68	62.6	16.0	6.1	59	51.3	27.2	12.6
Communications equipment operators	256	89.1	17.0	4.4	156	82.1	26.0	11.6
Telephone operators	244	90.4	17.0	4.3	140	83.3	25.5	11.5
Mail and message distributing occupations	799	31.6	18.1	4.5	936	40.7	21.7	8.3
Postal clerks, except mail carriers	248	36.7	26.2	5.2	295	49.7	35.5	6.2
Mail carrier, postal service	259	17.1	12.5	2.7	344	30.9	14.9	7.6
Mail clerks, except postal service	170	50.0	15.8	5.9	140	56.4	22.4	12.8
Messengers	122	26.2	16.7	5.2	157	31.2	10.1	9.8
Material recording, scheduling, and distributing [2] [4]	1,562	37.5	10.9	6.6	2,012	46.1	14.2	12.5
Dispatchers	157	45.7	11.4	4.3	228	52.7	12.0	9.0
Production coordinators	182	44.0	6.1	2.2	226	56.5	9.0	4.6
Traffic, shipping, and receiving clerks	421	22.6	9.1	11.1	656	30.2	15.5	17.2
Stock and inventory clerks	532	38.7	13.3	5.5	440	46.0	13.8	10.7
Expediters	112	57.5	8.4	4.3	344	68.1	15.0	12.9
Adjusters and investigators	675	69.9	11.1	5.1	1,943	74.3	17.0	10.0
Insurance adjusters, examiners, and investigators	199	65.0	11.5	3.3	476	72.1	15.0	7.3
Investigators and adjusters, except insurance	301	70.1	11.3	4.8	1,171	75.0	17.0	10.8
Eligibility clerks, social welfare	69	88.7	12.9	9.4	91	91.1	14.1	9.9
Bill and account collectors	106	66.4	8.5	6.5	205	68.7	22.9	12.1
Miscellaneous administrative support [2]	2,397	85.2	12.5	5.9	3,970	83.5	14.7	11.1
General office clerks	648	80.6	12.7	5.2	903	83.7	15.2	10.5
Bank tellers	480	91.0	7.5	4.3	444	86.9	10.6	11.7
Data entry keyers	311	93.6	18.6	5.6	692	81.9	18.8	11.3
Statistical clerks	96	75.7	7.5	3.4	111	89.7	21.3	6.1
Teachers' aides	348	93.7	17.8	12.6	779	91.6	12.8	16.0

See footnotes at end of table.

U.S. Census Bureau, Statistical Abstract of the United States: 2002

No. 588. Employed Civilians by Occupation, Sex, Race, and Hispanic Origin: 1983 and 2001—Con.

[**100,834 represents 100,834,000.** For civilian noninstitutional population 16 years old and over. Annual average of monthly figures. Based on Current Population Survey; see text, Section 1, Population, and Appendix III. Persons of Hispanic origin may be of any race. See headnote, Table 577]

Occupation	1983				2001 [1]			
	Total employed (1,000)	Percent of total			Total employed (1,000)	Percent of total		
		Female	Black	Hispanic		Female	Black	Hispanic
Service occupations	**13,857**	**60.1**	**16.6**	**6.8**	**18,359**	**60.4**	**17.9**	**16.3**
Private household [2]	980	96.1	27.8	8.5	715	96.2	12.1	32.8
Child care workers	408	96.9	7.9	3.6	239	97.0	8.1	18.8
Cleaners and servants	512	95.8	42.4	11.8	446	96.1	13.5	39.5
Protective service	1,672	12.8	13.6	4.6	2,478	20.4	19.9	9.8
Supervisors, protective service	127	4.7	7.7	3.1	212	12.3	17.3	7.8
Supervisors, police and detectives	58	4.2	9.3	1.2	111	10.3	13.6	4.5
Firefighting and fire prevention	189	1.0	6.7	4.1	264	4.1	12.3	8.1
Firefighting occupations	170	1.0	7.3	3.8	250	2.7	12.9	8.3
Police and detectives	645	9.4	13.1	4.0	1,066	17.8	17.2	9.5
Police and detectives, public service	412	5.7	9.5	4.4	574	14.1	12.6	9.7
Sheriffs, bailiffs, and other law enforcement officers	87	13.2	11.5	4.0	169	21.2	14.4	9.7
Correctional institution officers	146	17.8	24.0	2.8	323	22.5	26.8	9.2
Guards	711	20.6	17.0	5.6	936	29.9	25.6	11.2
Guards and police, except public service	602	13.0	18.9	6.2	786	24.0	27.6	12.1
Service except private household and protective	11,205	64.0	16.0	6.9	15,166	65.3	17.8	16.6
Food preparation and service occupations [2]	4,860	63.3	10.5	6.8	6,246	57.0	12.4	18.1
Bartenders	338	48.4	2.7	4.4	342	50.9	2.9	8.2
Waiters and waitresses	1,357	87.8	4.1	3.6	1,347	76.4	5.4	10.4
Cooks	1,452	50.0	15.8	6.5	2,073	42.5	17.4	24.0
Food counter, fountain, and related occupations	326	76.0	9.1	6.7	388	67.2	14.6	14.6
Kitchen workers, food preparation	138	77.0	13.7	8.1	305	71.0	11.1	12.9
Waiters' and waitresses' assistants	364	38.8	12.6	14.2	640	54.0	10.8	21.5
Health service occupations	1,739	89.2	23.5	4.8	2,680	89.1	29.4	11.5
Dental assistants	154	98.1	6.1	5.7	219	96.8	4.8	11.1
Health aides, except nursing	316	86.8	16.5	4.8	380	79.1	25.8	10.8
Nursing aides, orderlies, and attendants	1,269	88.7	27.3	4.7	2,081	90.1	32.7	11.6
Cleaning and building service occupations [2]	2,736	38.8	24.4	9.2	3,114	46.0	20.7	23.8
Maids and housemen	531	81.2	32.3	10.1	686	84.8	21.9	28.5
Janitors and cleaners	2,031	28.6	22.6	8.9	2,166	36.0	20.8	23.3
Personal service occupations [2]	1,870	79.2	11.1	6.0	3,126	80.7	15.9	11.0
Barbers	92	12.9	8.4	12.1	90	25.9	23.6	18.5
Hairdressers and cosmetologists	622	88.7	7.0	5.7	854	90.4	13.1	10.5
Attendants, amusement and recreation facilities	131	40.2	7.1	4.3	258	37.7	9.4	7.0
Public transportation attendants	63	74.3	11.3	5.9	133	80.5	12.6	9.3
Welfare service aides	77	92.5	24.2	10.5	109	84.7	30.2	8.7
Family child care providers	(NA)	(NA)	(NA)	(NA)	455	98.7	15.3	14.6
Early childhood teachers' assistants	(NA)	(NA)	(NA)	(NA)	499	94.7	20.4	10.7
Precision production, craft, and repair	**12,328**	**8.1**	**6.8**	**6.2**	**14,833**	**8.7**	**7.8**	**14.7**
Mechanics and repairers	4,158	3.0	6.8	5.3	4,807	4.9	7.8	11.4
Mechanics and repairers, except supervisors [2]	3,906	2.8	7.0	5.5	4,547	4.7	7.9	11.6
Vehicle and mobile equipment mechanics/repairers [2]	1,683	0.8	6.9	6.0	1,795	1.5	6.6	13.5
Automobile mechanics	800	0.5	7.8	6.0	817	1.5	7.5	15.2
Aircraft engine mechanics	95	2.5	4.0	7.6	123	4.1	4.0	14.4
Electrical and electronic equipment repairers [2]	674	7.4	7.3	4.5	984	11.4	11.0	9.2
Data processing equipment repairers	98	9.3	6.1	4.5	316	17.1	11.5	6.6
Telephone installers and repairers	247	9.9	7.8	3.7	290	13.8	11.8	9.9
Construction trades	4,289	1.8	6.6	6.0	6,253	2.5	7.0	17.4
Construction trades, except supervisors	3,784	1.9	7.1	6.1	5,266	2.4	7.3	19.2
Carpenters	1,160	1.4	5.0	5.0	1,486	1.7	5.2	18.3
Extractive occupations	196	2.3	3.3	6.0	132	2.0	6.2	11.9
Precision production occupations	3,685	21.5	7.3	7.4	3,641	24.6	9.0	14.4
Operators, fabricators, and laborers	**16,091**	**26.6**	**14.0**	**8.3**	**17,698**	**23.3**	**15.6**	**17.7**
Machine operators, assemblers, and inspectors [2]	7,744	42.1	14.0	9.4	6,734	36.4	14.8	19.6
Textile, apparel, and furnishings machine operators [2]	1,414	82.1	18.7	12.5	768	68.4	18.9	30.7
Textile sewing machine operators	806	94.0	15.5	14.5	368	74.2	13.5	38.3
Pressing machine operators	141	66.4	27.1	14.2	71	74.5	29.0	36.8
Fabricators, assemblers, and hand working occupations	1,715	33.7	11.3	8.7	1,833	31.6	12.5	18.3
Production inspectors, testers, samplers, and weighers	794	53.8	13.0	7.7	704	51.1	16.3	17.4
Transportation and material moving occupations	4,201	7.8	13.0	5.9	5,638	10.4	16.4	12.4
Motor vehicle operators	2,978	9.2	13.5	6.0	4,356	12.2	16.8	12.0
Trucks drivers	2,195	3.1	12.3	5.7	3,156	5.3	14.0	12.6
Transportation occupations, except motor vehicles	212	2.4	6.7	3.0	171	3.5	15.2	3.8
Material moving equipment operators	1,011	4.8	12.9	6.3	1,111	4.8	15.0	15.1
Industrial truck and tractor operators	369	5.6	19.6	8.2	542	6.3	20.8	20.8
Handlers, equipment cleaners, helpers, and laborers [2]	4,147	16.8	15.1	8.6	5,326	20.5	15.7	21.0
Freight, stock, and material handlers	1,488	15.4	15.3	7.1	2,003	24.1	18.2	15.0
Laborers, except construction	1,024	19.4	16.0	8.6	1,252	21.2	18.2	17.4
Farming, forestry, and fishing	**3,700**	**16.0**	**7.5**	**8.2**	**3,245**	**20.8**	**5.0**	**21.5**
Farm operators and managers	1,450	12.1	1.3	0.7	1,108	25.3	0.9	3.6
Other agricultural and related occupations	2,072	19.9	11.7	14.0	2,004	19.1	7.1	32.6
Farm workers	1,149	24.8	11.6	15.9	671	20.7	3.7	42.3
Forestry and logging occupations	126	1.4	12.8	2.1	90	8.3	7.4	4.5
Fishers, hunters, and trappers	53	4.5	1.8	2.5	(3)	(3)	(3)	(3)

- Represents or rounds to zero.   NA Not available.   [1] See footnote 2, Table 560.   [2] Includes other occupations, not shown separately.   [3] Level of total employment below 50,000.   [4] Includes clerks.

Source: U.S. Bureau of Labor Statistics, *Employment and Earnings*, monthly, January issues; and unpublished data.

No. 589. Employment Projections by Occupation: 2000 and 2010

[In thousands (380 represents 380,000), except percent and rank. Estimates based on the Current Employment Statistics, the Occupational Employment Statistics Program Survey, and the Current Population Survey. See source for methodological assumptions. Occupations based on the 2000 Standard Occupational Classification system]

Occupation	Employment (1,000)		Change 2000-2001		Quartile rank by 2000 median annual earnings [1]	Education and training category
	2000	2010	Number (1,000)	Percent		
FASTEST GROWING						
Computer software engineers, applications...	380	760	380	100	1	Bachelor's degree
Computer support specialists.............	506	996	490	97	2	Associate degree
Computer software engineers, systems software................................	317	601	284	90	1	Bachelor's degree
Network and computer systems administrators.........................	229	416	187	82	1	Bachelor's degree
Network systems and data communications analysts..............................	119	211	92	77	1	Bachelor's degree
Desktop publishers....................	38	63	25	67	2	Postsecondary vocational award
Database administrators...............	106	176	70	66	1	Bachelor's degree
Personal and home care aides...........	414	672	258	62	4	Short-term on-the-job training
Computer systems analysts.............	431	689	258	60	1	Bachelor's degree
Medical assistants....................	329	516	187	57	3	Moderate-term on-the-job training
Social and human service assistants......	271	418	147	54	3	Moderate-term on-the-job training
Physician assistants..................	58	89	31	53	1	Bachelor's degree
Medical records and health information technicians..........................	136	202	66	49	3	Associate degree
Computer and information systems managers.	313	463	150	48	1	Bachelor's or higher degree, plus work experience
Home health aides....................	615	907	291	47	4	Short-term on-the-job training
Physical therapist aides	36	53	17	46	3	Short-term on-the-job training
Occupational therapist aides	9	12	4	45	3	Short-term on-the-job training
Physical therapist assistants	44	64	20	45	2	Associate degree
Audiologists	13	19	6	45	1	Master's degree
Fitness trainers and aerobics instructors	158	222	64	40	3	Postsecondary vocational award
Computer and information scientists, research...........................	28	39	11	40	1	Doctoral degree
Veterinary assistants and laboratory animal caretakers...................	55	77	22	40	4	Short-term on-the-job training
Occupational therapist assistants	17	23	7	40	2	Associate degree
Veterinary technologists and technicians	49	69	19	39	3	Associate degree
Speech-language pathologists	88	122	34	39	1	Master's degree
Mental health and substance abuse social workers.............................	83	116	33	39	2	Master's degree
Dental assistants.....................	247	339	92	37	2	Moderate-term on-the-job training
Dental hygienists.....................	147	201	54	37	1	Associate degree
Special education teachers, preschool, kindergarten, and elementary school	234	320	86	37	1	Bachelor's degree
Pharmacy technicians.................	190	259	69	36	3	Moderate-term on-the-job training
LARGEST JOB GROWTH						
Combined food preparation and serving workers, including fast food	2,206	2,879	673	30	4	Short-term on-the-job training
Customer service representatives.........	1,946	2,577	631	32	3	Moderate-term on-the-job training
Registered nurses....................	2,194	2,755	561	26	1	Associate degree
Retail salespersons	4,109	4,619	510	12	4	Short-term on-the-job training
Computer support specialists...........	506	996	490	97	2	Associate degree
Cashiers, except gaming...............	3,325	3,799	474	14	4	Short-term on-the-job training
Office clerks, general	2,705	3,135	430	16	3	Short-term on-the-job training
Security guards......................	1,106	1,497	391	35	4	Short-term on-the-job training
Computer software engineers, applications...	380	760	380	100	1	Bachelor's degree
Waiters and waitresses................	1,983	2,347	364	18	4	Short-term on-the-job training
General and operations managers	2,398	2,761	363	15	1	Bachelor's or higher degree, plus work experience
Truck drivers, heavy and tractor-trailer...	1,749	2,095	346	20	2	Moderate-term on-the-job training
Nursing aides, orderlies, and attendants	1,373	1,697	323	24	3	Short-term on-the-job training
Janitors and cleaners, except maids and housekeeping cleaners	2,348	2,665	317	13	4	Short-term on-the-job training
Postsecondary teachers	1,344	1,659	315	23	1	Doctoral degree
Teacher assistants...................	1,262	1,562	301	24	4	Short-term on-the-job training
Home health aides...................	615	907	291	47	4	Short-term on-the-job training
Laborers and freight, stock, and material movers, handlers....................	2,084	2,373	289	14	3	Short-term on-the-job training
Computer software engineers, systems software................................	317	601	284	90	1	Bachelor's degree
Landscaping and groundskeeping workers ...	894	1,154	260	29	4	Short-term on-the-job training
Personal and home care aides...........	414	672	258	62	4	Short-term on-the-job training
Computer systems analysts.............	431	689	258	60	1	Bachelor's degree
Receptionists and information clerks	1,078	1,334	256	24	3	Short-term on-the-job training
Truck drivers, light or delivery services	1,117	1,331	215	19	3	Short-term on-the-job training
Packers and packagers, hand	1,091	1,300	210	19	4	Short-term on-the-job training
Elementary school teachers, except special education.........................	1,532	1,734	202	13	1	Bachelor's degree

[1] Quartile ranks based on the Occupational Employment Statistics annual earnings. Ranks: 1 = $39,700 and over; 2 = $25,760 to $39,600; 3 = $18,500 to 25,760; 4 = up to $18,490.

Source: U.S. Bureau of Labor Statistics, *Monthly Labor Review,* November 2001.

No. 590. Occupations of the Employed by Selected Characteristics: 2001

[In thousands (59,231 represents 59,231,000). Annual averages of monthly figures. For civilian noninstitutional population 25 to 64 years old. Based on Current Population Survey; see text, Section 1, Population, and Appendix III]

Sex, race, and educational attainment	Total employed	Managerial/professional	Tech./sales/administrative	Service [1]	Precision production [2]	Operators/fabricators [3]	Farming, forestry, fishing
Male, total [4]	**59,231**	**19,079**	**11,079**	**4,977**	**11,682**	**10,576**	**1,838**
Less than a high school diploma	6,397	327	448	846	1,890	2,323	562
High school graduates, no college	18,188	2,144	2,839	1,888	5,341	5,270	705
Less than a bachelor's degree	15,613	3,851	3,846	1,571	3,603	2,382	360
College graduates	19,033	12,757	3,946	672	847	600	211
White	50,327	16,665	9,437	3,718	10,380	8,458	1,667
Less than a high school diploma	5,415	281	378	627	1,664	1,963	502
High school graduates, no college	15,326	1,916	2,432	1,350	4,765	4,226	637
Less than a bachelor's degree	13,227	3,399	3,254	1,217	3,208	1,822	327
College graduates	16,359	11,071	3,373	524	743	447	201
Black	5,903	1,224	1,023	932	910	1,696	118
Less than a high school diploma	702	31	52	151	153	272	42
High school graduates, no college	2,231	160	304	417	426	874	50
Less than a bachelor's degree	1,767	319	408	282	276	455	24
College graduates	1,204	713	258	81	55	94	2
Female, total [4]	**51,416**	**19,021**	**19,315**	**7,947**	**1,138**	**3,482**	**514**
Less than a high school diploma	4,069	256	919	1,677	200	901	115
High school graduates, no college	15,823	2,470	7,355	3,511	495	1,801	191
Less than a bachelor's degree	15,685	4,809	7,621	2,172	322	624	137
College graduates	15,841	11,486	3,420	587	120	156	72
White	42,102	16,172	16,056	5,852	899	2,632	492
Less than a high school diploma	3,157	216	760	1,222	151	701	108
High school graduates, no college	13,008	2,157	6,337	2,579	389	1,364	182
Less than a bachelor's degree	12,695	4,063	6,172	1,605	266	454	136
College graduates	13,241	9,735	2,786	445	94	113	68
Black	6,752	1,920	2,423	1,631	131	635	11
Less than a high school diploma	675	28	117	378	21	126	5
High school graduates, no college	2,212	252	807	735	65	348	4
Less than a bachelor's degree	2,350	566	1,170	445	34	136	-
College graduates	1,514	1,074	329	72	12	25	2

- Represents zero.   [1] Includes private household workers.   [2] Includes craft and repair.   [3] Includes laborers.   [4] Includes other races, not shown separately.
Source: U.S. Bureau of Labor Statistics, unpublished data.

No. 591. Employment by Industry: 1980 to 2001

[In thousands (99,303 represents 99,303,000), except percent. See headnote, Table 563. Data for 1990, and also beginning 1995, not strictly comparable with other years due to changes in industrial classification. Based on Current Population Survey; see text, Section 1, and Appendix III]

Industry	1980	1990 [1]	1995	2000 [1]	2001 Total	Percent Female	Black	Hispanic [2]
Total employed	**99,303**	**118,793**	**124,900**	**135,208**	**135,073**	**46.6**	**11.3**	**10.9**
Agriculture	3,364	3,223	3,440	3,305	3,144	27.6	3.6	20.3
Mining	979	724	627	521	567	14.6	4.2	7.6
Construction	6,215	7,764	7,668	9,433	9,581	9.7	6.4	15.8
Manufacturing	21,942	21,346	20,493	19,940	18,970	31.8	10.1	12.3
Transportation, communication, and other public utilities	6,525	8,168	8,709	9,740	9,738	29.2	15.8	9.6
Wholesale and retail trade	20,191	24,622	26,071	27,832	27,672	47.0	10.0	12.4
Wholesale trade	3,920	4,669	4,986	5,421	5,102	30.1	7.5	11.1
Retail trade	16,270	19,953	21,086	22,411	22,571	50.8	10.6	12.7
Finance, insurance, real estate	5,993	8,051	7,983	8,727	8,797	58.3	10.8	7.2
Services [3]	28,752	39,267	43,953	49,695	50,478	62.1	12.6	9.3
Business and repair services [3]	3,848	7,485	7,526	9,661	9,764	37.2	11.4	11.7
Advertising	191	277	267	280	296	49.5	3.2	6.9
Services to dwellings and buildings	370	827	829	862	946	52.8	13.2	26.2
Personnel supply services	235	710	853	1,063	1,032	60.4	22.2	11.9
Computer and data processing	221	805	1,136	2,496	2,395	30.6	7.3	4.2
Detective/protective services	213	378	506	574	614	29.1	26.3	10.8
Automobile services	952	1,457	1,459	1,626	1,580	14.4	10.0	16.7
Personal services [3]	3,839	4,733	4,375	4,515	4,452	70.1	13.3	18.4
Private households	1,257	1,036	971	894	816	92.0	13.2	31.3
Hotels and lodging places	1,149	1,818	1,495	1,590	1,568	56.4	15.2	19.8
Entertainment and recreation	1,047	1,526	2,238	2,582	2,684	43.5	10.4	9.8
Professional and related services [3]	19,853	25,351	29,661	32,784	33,445	69.9	13.1	7.4
Hospitals	4,036	4,700	4,961	5,028	5,189	77.2	17.4	6.8
Health services, except hospitals	3,345	4,673	5,967	6,569	6,758	79.7	14.7	8.4
Elementary, secondary schools	5,550	5,994	6,653	7,629	7,735	75.9	11.6	8.0
Colleges and universities	2,108	2,637	2,768	2,903	3,006	53.9	10.6	6.4
Social services	1,590	2,239	2,979	3,519	3,516	82.2	20.7	10.1
Legal services	776	1,215	1,335	1,362	1,402	55.6	6.4	6.6
Public administration [4]	5,342	5,627	5,957	6,015	6,126	45.1	16.2	8.0

[1] See footnote 2, Table 560.   [2] Persons of Hispanic origin may be of any race.   [3] Includes industries not shown separately.   [4] Includes workers involved in uniquely governmental activities, e.g., judicial and legislative.
Source: U.S. Bureau of Labor Statistics, Employment and Earnings, monthly, January issues; and unpublished data.

Labor Force, Employment, and Earnings 385

No. 592. Employment Projections by Industry: 2000 to 2010

[3,887.0 represents 3,887,000. Estimates based on the Current Employment Statistics estimates. See source for methodological assumptions. Minus sign (-) indicates decline]

Industry	1987 SIC code [1]	Employment (1,000) 2000	Employment (1,000) 2010	Change (1,000), 2000-2010	Average annual rate of change, 2000-2010
LARGEST GROWTH					
Personnel supply services	736	3,887.0	5,800.0	1,913.0	4.1
Computer and data processing services	737	2,094.9	3,900.0	1,805.1	6.4
Retail trade exc. eating and drinking places	52-57,59	15,193.5	16,799.9	1,606.4	1.0
Eating and drinking places	58	8,113.7	9,600.0	1,486.3	1.7
Offices of health practitioners	801-804	3,098.8	4,344.0	1,245.2	3.4
State and local government education	(X)	9,471.8	10,548.2	1,076.4	1.1
Miscellaneous business services	732,733,738	2,300.9	3,305.0	1,004.1	3.7
Construction	15,16,17	6,697.5	7,522.3	824.8	1.2
State and local general government, n.e.c. [2]	(X)	6,592.2	7,400.0	807.8	1.2
Wholesale trade	50,51	7,023.8	7,800.0	776.2	1.1
Health services, n.e.c. [2]	807-809	1,210.2	1,900.0	689.8	4.6
Amusement and recreation services, n.e.c. [2]	791,799	1,313.6	1,850.0	536.4	3.5
Educational services	82	2,325.1	2,851.8	526.7	2.1
Residential care	836	805.9	1,318.0	512.1	5.0
Hospitals	806	3,990.3	4,500.0	509.7	1.2
Management and public relations	874	1,089.7	1,550.0	460.3	3.6
Nursing and personal care facilities	805	1,795.9	2,190.0	394.1	2.0
Legal services	81	1,009.6	1,350.0	340.4	2.9
Air transportation	45	1,281.3	1,600.0	318.7	2.2
Trucking and courier services except air	421,423	1,649.3	1,962.4	313.1	1.8
MOST RAPID GROWTH					
Computer and data processing services	737	2,094.9	3,900.0	1,805.1	6.4
Residential care	836	805.9	1,318.0	512.1	5.0
Health services, n.e.c. [2]	807-809	1,210.2	1,900.0	689.8	4.6
Cable and pay television services	484	215.8	325.0	109.2	4.2
Personnel supply services	736	3,887.0	5,800.0	1,913.0	4.1
Warehousing and storage	422	206.3	300.0	93.7	3.8
Water and sanitation	494-497	213.9	310.3	96.4	3.8
Miscellaneous business services	732,733,738	2,300.9	3,305.0	1,004.1	3.7
Miscellaneous equipment rental and leasing	735	279.4	397.5	118.1	3.6
Management and public relations	874	1,089.7	1,550.0	460.3	3.6
Child day care services	835	711.9	1,010.0	298.1	3.6
Amusement and recreation services, n.e.c. [2]	791,799	1,313.6	1,850.0	536.4	3.5
Offices of health practitioners	801-804	3,098.8	4,344.0	1,245.2	3.4
Wood buildings and mobile homes mfg.	245	90.8	127.0	36.2	3.4
Veterinary services	074	240.0	335.9	95.9	3.4
Miscellaneous transportation services	473,474,478	252.8	350.0	97.2	3.3
Landscape and horticultural services	078	808.0	1,093.0	285.0	3.1
Research and testing services	873	642.3	886.0	243.7	3.3
Accounting, auditing, and other services	872,89	720.0	963.0	243.0	3.0
Legal services	81	1,009.6	1,350.0	340.4	2.9
MOST RAPID DECLINE					
Watches, clocks, and parts mfg.	387	5.3	2.5	-2.8	-7.2
Footwear, except rubber and plastic mfg.	313,314	30.1	14.2	-15.9	-7.2
Coal mining	12	77.2	54.0	-23.2	-3.5
Metal cans and shipping containers mfg.	341	35.9	25.6	-10.3	-3.3
Luggage, handbags, and leather products, n.e.c. [2] mfg.	311,315-317,319	41.4	30.0	-11.4	-3.2
Railroad transportation	40	235.5	175.0	-60.5	-2.9
Private households	88	890.0	664.4	-225.6	-2.9
Apparel mfg.	231-238	417.9	314.9	-103.0	-2.8
Petroleum refining mfg.	291	84.6	65.0	-19.6	-2.6
Crude petroleum, natural gas, and gas liquids	131-132	129.3	100.0	-29.3	-2.5
Photographic equipment and supplies mfg	386	70.2	55.0	-15.2	-2.4
Blast furnaces and basic steel products mfg.	331	224.5	176.0	-48.5	-2.4
Federal electric utilities	(X)	27.0	21.6	-5.4	-2.2
Dairy products mfg.	202	145.5	121.1	-24.4	-1.8
Household appliances mfg.	363	116.2	96.9	-19.3	-1.8
Pipelines, except natural gas	46	13.7	11.5	-2.2	-1.7
Plastics materials and synthetics mfg.	282	154.3	130.0	-24.3	-1.7
Electrical industrial apparatus mfg	362	150.4	127.0	-23.4	-1.7
Service industries for the printing trade mfg.	279	47.2	40.0	-7.2	-1.6
Tobacco products mfg.	21	33.9	28.9	-5.0	-1.6

X Not applicable.   [1] Based on the 1987 Standard Industrial Classification; see text, this section.   [2] N.e.c. means not elsewhere classified.

Source: U.S. Bureau of Labor Statistics, *Monthly Labor Review,* November 2001.

No. 593. Unemployed Workers—Summary: 1980 to 2001

[In thousands (7,637 represents 7,637,000), except as indicated. For civilian noninstitutional population 16 years old and over. Annual averages of monthly figures. For data on unemployment insurance, see Table 529]

Age, sex, race, Hispanic origin	1980	1985	1990 [1]	1995	1998 [1]	1999 [1]	2000 [1]	2001
UNEMPLOYED								
Total [2]	7,637	8,312	7,047	7,404	6,210	5,880	5,655	6,742
16 to 19 years old	1,669	1,468	1,212	1,346	1,205	1,162	1,093	1,187
20 to 24 years old	1,835	1,738	1,299	1,244	1,081	1,042	1,025	1,203
25 to 44 years old	2,964	3,681	3,323	3,390	2,677	2,432	2,309	2,806
45 to 64 years old	1,075	1,331	1,109	1,269	1,125	1,120	1,096	1,418
65 years and over	94	93	105	153	122	124	131	129
Male	4,267	4,521	3,906	3,983	3,266	3,066	2,954	3,663
16 to 19 years old	913	806	667	744	686	633	604	660
20 to 24 years old	1,076	944	715	673	583	562	549	680
25 to 44 years old	1,619	1,950	1,803	1,776	1,308	1,195	1,143	1,453
45 to 64 years old	600	766	662	697	621	606	576	796
65 years and over	58	55	59	94	69	70	82	76
Female	3,370	3,791	3,140	3,421	2,944	2,814	2,701	3,079
16 to 19 years old	755	661	544	602	519	529	489	527
20 to 24 years old	760	794	584	571	498	480	476	523
25 to 44 years old	1,345	1,732	1,519	1,615	1,370	1,238	1,167	1,353
45 to 64 years old	473	566	447	574	503	513	521	622
65 years and over	36	39	46	60	53	54	49	53
White [3]	5,884	6,191	5,186	5,459	4,484	4,273	4,099	4,923
16 to 19 years old	1,291	1,074	903	952	876	844	805	866
20 to 24 years old	1,364	1,235	899	866	731	720	684	827
Black [3]	1,553	1,864	1,565	1,538	1,426	1,309	1,269	1,450
16 to 19 years old	343	357	268	325	281	268	239	271
20 to 24 years old	426	455	349	311	301	273	290	312
Hispanic [3] [4]	620	811	876	1,140	1,026	945	876	1,037
16 to 19 years old	145	141	161	205	214	196	181	199
20 to 24 years old	138	171	167	209	194	171	162	179
Full-time workers	6,269	6,793	5,677	5,909	4,916	4,669	4,502	5,493
Part-time workers	1,369	1,519	1,369	1,495	1,293	1,211	1,153	1,249
UNEMPLOYMENT RATE (percent) [5]								
Total [2]	7.1	7.2	5.6	5.6	4.5	4.2	4.0	4.8
16 to 19 years old	17.8	18.6	15.5	17.3	14.6	13.9	13.1	14.7
20 to 24 years old	11.5	11.1	8.8	9.1	7.9	7.5	7.1	8.3
25 to 44 years old	6.0	6.2	4.9	4.8	3.8	3.5	3.3	4.1
45 to 64 years old	3.7	4.5	3.5	3.4	2.7	2.6	2.5	3.1
65 years and over	3.1	3.2	3.0	4.0	3.2	3.1	3.1	3.0
Male	6.9	7.0	5.7	5.6	4.4	4.1	3.9	4.8
16 to 19 years old	18.3	19.5	16.3	18.4	16.2	14.7	14.0	15.9
20 to 24 years old	12.5	11.4	9.1	9.2	8.1	7.7	7.3	8.9
25 to 44 years old	5.6	5.9	4.8	4.7	3.4	3.2	3.1	3.9
45 to 64 years old	3.5	4.5	3.7	3.5	2.8	2.6	2.4	3.3
65 years and over	3.1	3.1	3.0	4.3	3.1	3.0	3.4	3.0
Female	7.4	7.4	5.5	5.6	4.6	4.3	4.1	4.7
16 to 19 years old	17.2	17.6	14.7	16.1	12.9	13.2	12.1	13.4
20 to 24 years old	10.4	10.7	8.5	9.0	7.8	7.2	7.0	7.5
25 to 44 years old	6.4	6.6	4.9	5.0	4.2	3.8	3.6	4.3
45 to 64 years old	4.0	4.6	3.2	3.3	2.6	2.5	2.5	2.9
65 years and over	3.1	3.3	3.1	3.7	3.3	3.2	2.8	2.9
White [3]	6.3	6.2	4.8	4.9	3.9	3.7	3.5	4.2
16 to 19 years old	15.5	15.7	13.5	14.5	12.6	12.0	11.4	12.7
20 to 24 years old	9.9	9.2	7.3	7.7	6.5	6.3	5.8	6.9
Black [3]	14.3	15.1	11.4	10.4	8.9	8.0	7.6	8.7
16 to 19 years old	38.5	40.2	30.9	35.7	27.6	27.9	24.7	29.0
20 to 24 years old	23.6	24.5	19.9	17.7	16.8	14.6	15.0	16.2
Hispanic [3] [4]	10.1	10.5	8.2	9.3	7.2	6.4	5.7	6.6
16 to 19 years old	22.5	24.3	19.5	24.1	21.3	18.6	16.7	17.7
20 to 24 years old	12.1	12.6	9.1	11.5	9.4	8.3	7.5	8.2
Experienced workers [6]	6.9	6.8	5.3	5.4	4.3	4.0	3.9	4.6
Women maintaining families	9.2	10.4	8.3	8.0	7.2	6.4	5.9	6.6
Married men, wife present [2]	4.2	4.3	3.4	3.3	2.4	2.2	2.0	2.7
White	3.9	4.0	3.1	3.0	2.2	2.1	2.1	2.5
Black	7.4	8.0	6.2	5.0	3.9	3.8	3.7	4.5
Percent without work for—								
Fewer than 5 weeks	43.2	42.1	46.3	36.5	42.2	43.7	45.0	42.0
5 to 10 weeks	23.4	22.2	23.5	22.0	22.1	21.8	23.0	22.3
11 to 14 weeks	9.0	8.0	8.5	9.6	9.3	9.3	8.9	9.8
15 to 26 weeks	13.8	12.3	11.7	14.6	12.3	12.8	11.8	14.1
27 weeks and over	10.7	15.4	10.0	17.3	14.1	12.3	11.4	11.8
Unemployment duration, average (weeks)	11.9	15.6	12.0	16.6	14.5	13.4	12.6	13.2

[1] See footnote 2, Table 560. [2] Includes other races, not shown separately. [3] Includes other ages, not shown separately. [4] Persons of Hispanic origin may be of any race. [5] Unemployed as percent of civilian labor force in specified group. [6] Wage and salary workers.

Source: U.S. Bureau of Labor Statistics, *Employment and Earnings*, monthly, January issues; and unpublished data.

U.S. Census Bureau, Statistical Abstract of the United States: 2002

No. 594. Computer and Internet Access and Internet Job Searching by Labor Force Status and Race: 1998 and 2000

[In percent. For December 1998 and August 2000. For the civilian noninstitutionalized population 16 and over. Based on the Current Population Survey; see text, Section 1, Population, and Appendix III]

Labor force status	Total 1998	Total 2000	White 1998	White 2000	Black 1998	Black 2000	Hispanic [1] 1998	Hispanic [1] 2000
COMPUTER AND INTERNET ACCESS								
With a computer at home	46.9	55.9	49.3	58.3	26.3	37.5	28.2	35.7
Employed:								
Working	54.6	63.2	57.2	65.7	32.7	43.7	32.4	38.6
Absent	52.6	72.5	54.6	74.8	32.2	51.0	36.9	55.3
Unemployed:								
On layoff	30.5	48.5	32.8	54.3	9.9	21.5	13.8	29.9
Jobseeker	37.5	50.1	41.7	57.6	20.0	28.0	20.2	31.5
Not in labor force:								
Retired.	22.3	31.3	23.2	32.0	10.2	22.7	17.4	23.0
Disabled.	20.3	28.1	23.5	31.3	9.4	17.2	15.4	23.1
Other.	49.1	56.5	52.8	59.6	22.9	36.0	23.9	32.1
With Internet access from home	29.4	45.7	31.4	48.0	12.7	26.7	13.9	25.4
Employed:								
Working	34.7	52.1	36.9	54.5	16.3	32.4	16.5	27.9
Absent	33.9	61.1	35.7	63.7	15.2	36.8	19.8	40.0
Unemployed:								
On layoff	16.5	39.6	18.5	45.0	2.0	12.6	4.2	15.5
Jobseeker	22.3	39.4	25.4	46.3	10.4	17.3	7.6	19.8
Not in labor force:								
Retired.	12.2	23.8	12.9	24.5	3.9	13.9	6.8	16.5
Disabled.	10.5	20.4	12.5	23.1	3.2	11.3	6.9	13.6
Other.	31.9	46.5	35.0	49.7	10.4	24.1	11.3	22.6
Internet use from any location	34.3	46.8	36.1	48.9	20.7	31.4	18.0	25.3
Employed:								
Working	42.6	56.0	44.6	58.2	27.6	39.5	21.6	29.3
Absent	39.2	64.5	41.3	66.9	22.6	45.6	27.0	40.3
Unemployed:								
On layoff	21.7	41.6	22.9	44.9	16.6	26.1	7.8	14.9
Jobseeker	30.1	45.1	33.2	51.2	18.1	26.2	14.0	28.3
Not in labor force:								
Retired.	8.5	16.7	9.3	17.6	1.7	7.8	1.8	5.2
Disabled.	8.2	14.9	9.8	17.1	2.7	8.4	3.3	6.3
Other.	34.3	45.4	37.0	48.0	17.2	29.1	17.1	21.7
INTERNET JOB SEARCH [2] RATES AMONG THOSE WITH ACCESS								
With a computer at home	10.1	14.1	9.9	13.5	12.5	18.1	8.4	13.6
Employed:								
Working	11.2	15.9	11.0	15.2	13.6	20.6	9.6	14.7
Absent	12.2	13.3	11.4	13.0	18.1	15.4	10.1	16.6
Unemployed:								
On layoff	9.5	18.3	9.6	19.4	20.1	11.8	(B)	(B)
Jobseeker	31.2	43.7	31.2	45.3	33.3	31.7	20.5	35.3
Not in labor force:								
Retired.	1.3	1.6	1.3	1.5	0.8	2.8	-	3.3
Disabled.	6.1	7.3	6.8	6.2	1.2	11.7	1.9	5.5
Other.	6.5	9.9	6.4	9.4	6.5	13.4	4.8	9.3
With Internet access from home	14.6	16.5	14.1	15.7	20.7	23.5	15.5	17.5
Employed:								
Working	15.9	18.3	15.5	17.4	21.4	25.5	16.7	18.4
Absent	16.6	15.1	16.1	14.7	(B)	17.5	(B)	22.0
Unemployed:								
On layoff	17.6	20.7	17.0	21.4	(B)	(B)	(B)	(B)
Jobseeker	49.5	54.1	47.9	54.6	64.0	52.3	(B)	48.3
Not in labor force:								
Retired.	2.3	2.1	2.4	2.0	2.0	4.6	-	4.7
Disabled.	10.4	9.7	11.2	8.0	(B)	17.5	(B)	6.6
Other.	9.0	11.7	8.6	11.0	11.0	19.0	10.7	13.3
Internet use from any location	16.1	18.9	15.4	17.7	23.0	27.9	18.0	23.9
Employed:								
Working	16.7	20.1	16.0	18.9	22.8	29.0	18.7	23.9
Absent	17.9	16.3	16.6	15.7	30.3	21.6	13.8	27.3
Unemployed:								
On layoff	22.0	24.7	21.2	24.8	(B)	(B)	(B)	(B)
Jobseeker	49.9	56.5	49.6	56.7	51.1	55.6	51.5	52.8
Not in labor force:								
Retired.	3.5	3.2	3.5	3.0	(B)	8.2	(B)	14.8
Disabled.	17.3	14.8	17.1	11.9	(B)	27.5	(B)	20.5
Other.	11.2	14.0	10.6	13.0	16.3	21.1	11.9	17.2

- Represents or rounds to zero.   B Base figure too small to meet statistical standards for reliability of a derived figure. [1] Persons of Hispanic origin may be of any race.   [2] Represents persons who responded they used the Internet regularly to search for jobs.

Source: U.S. Bureau of Labor Statistics, *Monthly Labor Review,* October 2000; and Peter Kuhn and Mikal Skuterud, "The Digital Divide in Internet Job Search, 1998-2000," unpublished data, University of California, Santa Barbara.

No. 595. Unemployed Persons by Sex and Reason: 1980 to 2001

[In thousands (4,267 represents 4,267,000). For civilian noninstitutional population 16 years old and over. Annual averages of monthly figures. Based on Current Population Survey; see text, Section 1, Population, and Appendix III]

Sex and reason	1980	1985	1990 [1]	1993	1994 [1]	1995	1996	1997 [1]	1998 [1]	1999 [1]	2000 [1]	2001
Male, total.	**4,267**	**4,521**	**3,906**	**5,055**	**4,367**	**3,983**	**3,880**	**3,577**	**3,266**	**3,066**	**2,954**	**3,663**
Job losers [2].	2,649	2,749	2,257	3,150	2,416	2,190	2,158	1,902	1,703	1,563	1,499	2,098
Job leavers.	438	409	528	507	408	407	372	414	368	389	384	419
Reentrants	776	876	806	939	1,265	1,113	1,076	1,004	931	895	855	929
New entrants.	405	487	315	459	278	273	273	257	264	219	216	217
Female, total. . . .	**3,370**	**3,791**	**3,140**	**3,885**	**3,629**	**3,421**	**3,356**	**3,162**	**2,944**	**2,814**	**2,701**	**3,079**
Job losers [2].	1,297	1,390	1,130	1,699	1,399	1,286	1,212	1,135	1,119	1,059	993	1,330
Job leavers.	453	468	513	469	383	417	402	381	366	394	391	413
Reentrants	1,152	1,380	1,124	1,259	1,521	1,412	1,435	1,334	1,201	1,111	1,102	1,100
New entrants.	468	552	373	459	326	306	307	312	257	250	215	236

[1] See footnote 2, Table 560.   [2] Beginning 1994, persons who completed temporary jobs are identified separately and are included as job losers.

Source: U.S. Bureau of Labor Statistics, *Employment and Earnings,* monthly, January issues; and Bulletin 2307; and unpublished data.

No. 596. Unemployment Rates by Industry, 1980 to 2001, and by Sex, 1980 and 2001

[In percent. For civilian noninstitutional population 16 years old and over. Annual averages of monthly figures. Rate represents unemployment as a percent of labor force in each specified group. Data for 1985-90 not strictly comparable with other years due to changes in industrial classification]

Industry	1980	1985	1990 [1]	1995	2000 [1]	2001	Male 1980	Male 2001	Female 1980	Female 2001
All unemployed [2]	**7.1**	**7.2**	**5.6**	**5.6**	**4.0**	**4.8**	**6.9**	**4.8**	**7.4**	**4.7**
Industry: [3]										
Agriculture.	11.0	13.2	9.8	11.1	7.5	9.7	9.7	9.7	15.1	9.5
Mining.	6.4	9.5	4.8	5.2	3.9	4.7	6.7	4.8	4.5	4.0
Construction	14.1	13.1	11.1	11.5	6.4	7.3	14.6	7.5	8.9	5.1
Manufacturing	8.5	7.7	5.8	4.9	3.6	5.2	7.4	4.7	10.8	6.3
Transportation and public utilities	4.9	5.1	3.9	4.5	3.1	4.1	5.1	3.9	4.4	4.5
Wholesale and retail trade	7.4	7.6	6.4	6.5	5.0	5.6	6.6	5.2	8.3	6.1
Finance, insurance, and real estate	3.4	3.5	3.0	3.3	2.3	2.8	3.2	2.7	3.5	2.8
Services	5.9	6.2	5.0	5.4	3.8	4.6	6.3	4.9	5.8	4.3
Government.	4.1	3.9	2.7	2.9	2.0	2.1	3.9	2.0	4.3	2.1

[1] See footnote 2, Table 560.   [2] Includes the self-employed, unpaid family workers, and persons with no previous work experience, not shown separately.   [3] Covers unemployed wage and salary workers.

Source: U.S. Bureau of Labor Statistics, *Employment and Earnings,* monthly, January issues.

No. 597. Unemployment by Occupation, 1990 to 2001, and by Sex, 2001

[7,047 represents 7,047,000. For civilian noninstitutional population 16 years old and over. Annual averages of monthly data. Rate represents unemployment as a percent of the labor force for each specified group. Based on Current Population Survey; see text, Section 1, Population, and Appendix III. See also headnote, Table 577]

Occupation	Number (1,000) 1990 [1]	Number (1,000) 2000 [1]	Number (1,000) 2001	Unemployment rate 1990 [1]	Unemployment rate 2000 [1]	2001 Total	2001 Male	2001 Female
Total [2]	**7,047**	**5,655**	**6,742**	**5.6**	**4.0**	**4.8**	**4.8**	**4.7**
Managerial and professional specialty	666	725	973	2.1	1.7	2.3	2.3	2.2
Executive, administrative, and managerial	350	356	491	2.3	1.8	2.4	2.3	2.5
Professional specialty	316	369	482	2.0	1.7	2.2	2.3	2.1
Technical sales, and administrative support.	1,641	1,464	1,699	4.3	3.6	4.2	3.9	4.3
Technicians and related support	116	97	133	2.9	2.2	2.9	3.4	2.4
Sales occupations.	720	684	794	4.8	4.0	4.7	3.6	5.8
Administrative support, including clerical	804	684	772	4.1	3.5	4.0	4.8	3.8
Service occupations	1,139	1,023	1,150	6.6	5.3	5.9	6.1	5.8
Private household.	47	58	53	5.6	6.9	6.9	(B)	6.6
Protective service	74	65	74	3.6	2.6	2.9	2.7	3.9
Service except private household and protective. .	1,018	900	1,023	7.1	5.6	6.3	7.3	5.8
Precision production, craft, and repair	861	554	711	5.9	3.6	4.6	4.4	6.3
Mechanics and repairers	175	129	153	3.8	2.6	3.1	3.0	4.0
Construction trades	483	312	391	8.5	4.9	5.9	5.8	9.5
Other precision production, craft, and repair. . . .	202	113	167	4.7	2.8	4.2	3.6	6.3
Operators, fabricators, and laborers.	1,714	1,228	1,481	8.7	6.3	7.7	7.3	8.9
Machine operators, assemblers, inspectors	727	455	573	8.1	5.9	7.8	7.1	9.1
Transportation and material moving occupations. .	329	253	298	6.3	4.4	5.0	4.9	6.0
Handlers, equipment cleaners, helpers, laborers. .	657	520	610	11.6	8.7	10.3	10.3	10.1
Construction laborers	177	133	155	18.1	11.6	13.1	13.0	18.0
Farming, forestry, and fishing	237	215	259	6.4	6.0	7.4	6.9	9.1

B Base less than 35,000.   [1] See footnote 2, Table 560.   [2] Includes persons with no previous work experience and those whose last job was in the Armed Forces.

Source: U.S. Bureau of Labor Statistics, *Employment and Earnings,* monthly, January issues.

Labor Force, Employment, and Earnings 389

No. 598. Unemployed and Unemployment Rates by Educational Attainment, Sex, Race, and Hispanic Origin: 1992 to 2001

[6,846 represents 6,846,000. As of March. For the civilian noninstitutional population 25 to 64 years old. See Table 564 for civilian labor force and participation rate data. Based on Current Population Survey; see text, Section 1, Population, and Appendix III]

Year, sex, and race	Unemployed (1,000)					Unemployment rate [1]				
	Total	Less than high school diploma	High school graduates, no degree	Less than a bachelor's degree	College graduate	Total	Less than high school diploma	High school graduate, no degree	Less than a bachelor's degree	College graduate
Total: [2]										
1992 . . .	6,846	1,693	2,851	1,521	782	6.7	13.5	7.7	5.9	2.9
1995 [3] . . .	5,065	1,150	1,833	1,329	753	4.8	10.0	5.2	4.5	2.5
2000 [3] . . .	3,750	883	1,364	966	537	3.3	7.9	3.8	3.0	1.5
2001 . . .	4,072	913	1,516	947	696	3.5	8.1	4.2	2.9	2.0
Male:										
1992	4,207	1,151	1,709	854	493	7.5	14.8	8.8	6.4	3.2
1995 [3]	2,925	765	1,064	656	440	5.1	10.9	5.7	4.4	2.6
2000 [3]	2,027	475	749	494	308	3.3	7.1	3.9	3.1	1.6
2001	2,281	505	885	521	371	3.7	7.5	4.6	3.2	1.9
Female:										
1992	2,639	542	1,142	666	289	5.7	11.4	6.5	5.3	2.5
1995 [3]	2,140	385	770	673	313	4.4	8.6	4.6	4.5	2.4
2000 [3]	1,723	407	615	472	229	3.2	9.1	3.6	2.9	1.4
2001	1,792	408	632	427	325	3.3	8.9	3.8	2.6	2.0
White:										
1992	5,247	1,285	2,146	1,176	641	6.0	12.9	6.8	5.3	2.7
1995 [3]	3,858	831	1,362	1,054	612	4.3	9.2	4.6	4.2	2.3
2000 [3]	2,812	676	1,006	723	407	3.0	7.5	3.3	2.7	1.4
2001	2,995	657	1,066	723	549	3.1	7.2	3.6	2.7	1.8
Black:										
1992	1,353	361	619	291	81	12.4	17.2	14.1	10.7	4.8
1995 [3]	905	225	377	218	86	7.7	13.7	8.4	6.3	4.1
2000 [3]	717	164	305	179	68	5.4	10.4	6.3	4.3	2.5
2001	890	229	390	183	88	6.5	14.0	7.7	4.3	3.3
Hispanic: [4]										
1992	757	408	224	88	36	9.8	13.6	9.6	5.9	4.2
1995 [3]	746	393	211	102	40	8.0	10.9	8.1	5.2	3.7
2000 [3]	647	363	159	78	47	5.5	8.3	4.6	3.1	3.2
2001	665	397	145	77	46	5.5	8.9	4.0	3.1	2.9

[1] Percent unemployed of the civilian labor force.   [2] Includes other races, not shown separately.   [3] See footnote 2, Table 560.   [4] Persons of Hispanic origin may be of any race.

Source: U.S. Bureau of Labor Statistics, unpublished data.

No. 599. Unemployed Persons by Reason of Unemployment: 2001

[6,742 represents 6,742,000. Annual averages of monthly data. Based on Current Population Survey; see text, Section 1, Population, and Appendix III]

Age, sex, and reason	Total unemployed (1,000)	Percent distribution by duration				
		Less than 5 weeks	5 to 14 weeks	15 weeks and over		
				Total	15 to 26 weeks	27 weeks or longer
Total 16 years old and over	6,742	42.0	32.1	25.9	14.1	11.8
16 to 19 years old	1,187	51.6	31.6	16.8	9.8	7.0
Total 20 years old and over	5,554	40.0	32.2	27.8	15.0	12.9
Males	3,003	39.0	32.3	28.7	15.5	13.2
Job losers and persons who completed temporary jobs	1,977	40.1	32.5	27.3	16.2	11.1
On temporary layoff	613	52.9	32.7	14.4	11.3	3.0
Not on temporary layoff	1,364	34.4	32.4	33.2	18.4	14.8
Permanent job losers	993	33.2	32.0	34.9	19.0	15.9
Persons who completed temporary jobs	371	37.7	33.7	28.6	16.8	11.9
Job leavers	369	43.0	33.7	23.2	12.0	11.2
Reentrants	606	34.0	30.9	35.1	15.4	19.7
New entrants	52	28.2	28.3	43.5	13.9	29.7
Females	2,551	41.0	32.1	26.9	14.4	12.5
Job losers and persons who completed temporary jobs	1,265	41.4	32.7	25.8	15.9	9.9
On temporary layoff	367	57.1	30.7	12.2	8.7	3.6
Not on temporary layoff	898	35.1	33.6	31.4	18.9	12.5
Permanent job losers	681	32.5	34.3	33.2	20.2	13.0
Persons who completed temporary jobs	217	43.1	31.3	25.6	14.7	10.9
Job leavers	362	47.7	30.9	21.4	12.3	9.1
Reentrants	835	38.0	31.6	30.4	13.2	17.2
New entrants	90	36.2	33.1	30.6	12.6	18.0

Source: U.S. Bureau of Labor Statistics, *Employment and Earnings*, monthly, January 2000 issue.

No. 600. Total Unemployed and Insured Unemployed by State: 1980 to 2001

[7,637 represents 7,637,000. For civilian noninstitutional population 16 years old and over . Annual averages of monthly figures. Total unemployment estimates based on the Current Population Survey; see text, Section 1, Population, and Appendix III. U.S. totals derived by independent population controls; therefore state data may not add to U.S. totals]

State	Total unemployed								Insured unemployed [3]			
	Number (1,000)				Percent [1]				Number (1,000)		Percent [4]	
	1980	1990 [2]	2000 [2]	2001	1980	1990 [2]	2000 [2]	2001	1999	2000	1999	2000
United States ...	7,637	7,047	5,655	6,742	7.1	5.6	4.0	4.8	[5]2,187.9	[5]2,110	[5]1.8	[5]1.7
Alabama........	147	130	99	114	8.8	6.9	4.6	5.3	28.4	29.0	1.6	1.6
Alaska.........	18	19	21	20	9.7	7.0	6.6	6.3	12.9	12.3	5.1	4.9
Arizona.........	83	99	91	113	6.7	5.5	3.9	4.7	21.2	20.5	1.0	1.0
Arkansas	76	78	55	63	7.6	7.0	4.4	5.1	24.9	23.9	2.3	2.2
California	790	874	845	927	6.8	5.8	4.9	5.3	367.0	338.5	2.7	2.4
Colorado........	88	89	63	85	5.9	5.0	2.7	3.7	15.9	15.0	0.8	0.7
Connecticut......	94	95	39	56	5.9	5.2	2.3	3.3	31.2	28.3	1.9	1.7
Delaware	22	19	16	15	7.7	5.2	4.0	3.5	5.5	5.9	1.4	1.5
District of Columbia .	24	22	16	18	7.3	6.6	5.8	6.5	6.5	5.7	1.6	1.3
Florida	251	390	269	365	5.9	6.0	3.6	4.8	73.1	70.8	1.1	1.1
Georgia	163	182	154	165	6.4	5.5	3.7	4.0	32.6	34.5	0.9	0.9
Hawaii	21	16	26	28	4.9	2.9	4.3	4.6	10.7	8.4	2.1	1.7
Idaho..........	34	29	32	34	7.9	5.9	4.9	5.0	12.5	12.1	2.4	2.3
Illinois	459	369	279	343	8.3	6.2	4.4	5.4	104.0	103.8	1.8	1.8
Indiana.........	252	149	100	136	9.6	5.3	3.2	4.4	28.6	31.8	1.0	1.1
Iowa	82	62	41	53	5.8	4.3	2.6	3.3	17.9	19.4	1.3	1.4
Kansas.........	53	57	52	59	4.5	4.5	3.7	4.3	14.7	15.6	1.2	1.2
Kentucky	133	104	82	108	8.0	5.9	4.1	5.5	24.9	25.4	1.5	1.5
Louisiana	121	117	112	122	6.7	6.3	5.5	6.0	25.9	24.0	1.4	1.3
Maine..........	39	33	24	27	7.8	5.2	3.5	4.0	9.8	8.9	1.8	1.6
Maryland	140	122	108	116	6.5	4.7	3.9	4.1	30.2	28.9	1.4	0.3
Massachusetts.....	162	195	86	121	5.6	6.0	2.6	3.7	66.2	60.1	2.2	1.9
Michigan........	534	350	185	274	12.4	7.6	3.6	5.3	79.7	81.6	1.8	1.8
Minnesota.......	125	117	90	104	5.9	4.9	3.3	3.7	29.9	31.4	1.2	1.2
Mississippi	79	90	75	72	7.5	7.6	5.7	5.5	18.4	19.7	1.7	1.8
Missouri........	167	151	101	140	7.2	5.8	3.5	4.7	40.1	41.8	1.6	1.6
Montana........	23	24	24	21	6.1	6.0	4.9	4.6	7.8	7.8	2.2	2.2
Nebraska	31	18	28	29	4.1	2.2	3.0	3.1	7.0	7.3	0.8	0.9
Nevada	27	33	40	55	6.2	4.9	4.1	5.3	18.3	19.5	2.0	2.0
New Hampshire....	22	36	19	24	4.7	5.7	2.8	3.5	3.7	3.1	0.7	0.5
New Jersey......	260	206	157	176	7.2	5.1	3.8	4.2	91.0	84.8	2.5	2.3
New Mexico	42	46	40	40	7.5	6.5	4.9	4.8	11.0	9.5	1.7	1.4
New York	597	467	408	429	7.5	5.3	4.6	4.9	157.5	146.2	2.0	1.8
North Carolina	187	144	144	221	6.6	4.2	3.6	5.5	51.3	54.3	1.4	1.5
North Dakota......	15	13	10	10	5.0	4.0	3.0	2.8	4.1	3.9	1.4	1.3
Ohio	426	310	237	251	8.4	5.7	4.1	4.3	68.1	71.6	1.3	1.3
Oklahoma.......	66	86	50	64	4.8	5.7	3.0	3.8	14.2	12.2	1.0	0.9
Oregon.........	107	83	87	114	8.3	5.6	4.9	6.3	42.4	41.2	2.8	2.7
Pennsylvania......	425	315	250	287	7.8	5.4	4.2	4.7	136.5	132.4	2.6	2.5
Rhode Island......	34	35	21	24	7.2	6.8	4.1	4.7	13.2	12.2	3.0	2.7
South Carolina.....	96	83	77	106	6.9	4.8	3.9	5.4	25.7	27.1	1.5	1.5
South Dakota	16	13	9	13	4.9	3.9	2.3	3.3	2.1	2.0	0.6	0.6
Tennessee	152	126	110	126	7.3	5.3	3.9	4.5	39.9	42.2	1.6	1.6
Texas..........	352	544	437	507	5.2	6.3	4.2	4.9	124.6	107.9	1.4	1.2
Utah	40	35	36	49	6.3	4.3	3.2	4.4	10.1	10.5	1.1	1.1
Vermont	16	15	10	12	6.4	5.0	2.9	3.6	5.3	4.8	1.9	1.7
Virginia.........	128	141	80	127	5.0	4.3	2.2	3.5	22.2	22.2	0.7	0.7
Washington.......	156	125	158	192	7.9	4.9	5.2	6.4	77.6	70.6	3.1	2.7
West Virginia......	74	64	46	41	9.4	8.4	5.5	4.9	16.1	14.1	2.4	2.1
Wisconsin.......	167	114	104	136	7.2	4.4	3.5	4.6	50.3	53.1	1.9	2.0
Wyoming	9	13	10	11	4.0	5.5	3.9	3.9	3.1	2.9	1.5	1.3

[1] Total unemployment as percent of civilian labor force.   [2] See footnote 2, Table 560.   [3] Source: U.S. Employment and Training Administration, *Unemployment Insurance, Financial Handbook,* annual updates.   [4] Insured unemployment as percent of average covered employment in the previous year.   [5] Includes 59,100 in Puerto Rico and the Virgin Islands in 1999 and 49,800 in 2000.

Source: Except as noted, U.S. Bureau of Labor Statistics, *Geographic Profile of Employment and Unemployment,* annual.

U.S. Census Bureau, Statistical Abstract of the United States: 2002

No. 601. Nonfarm Establishments—Employees, Hours, and Earnings by Industry: 1980 to 2001

[Annual averages of monthly data (90,406 represents 90,406,000). Based on data from establishment reports. Includes all full- and part-time employees who worked during, or received pay for, any part of the pay period reported. Excludes proprietors, the self-employed, farm workers, unpaid family workers, private household workers, and Armed Forces. Establishment data shown here conform to industry definitions in the 1987 Standard Industrial Classification and are adjusted to March 2000 employment benchmarks, and reflect historical corrections to previously published data. Based on the Current Employment Statistics Program; see Appendix III]

Item and year	Goods producing					Service producing						
	Total	Total	Mining	Construction	Manufacturing	Total	Transportation and public utilities	Wholesale trade	Retail trade	Finance, insurance, and real estate	Services	Government
EMPLOYEES (1,000)												
1980	90,406	25,658	1,027	4,346	20,285	64,748	5,146	5,292	15,018	5,160	17,890	16,241
1985	97,387	24,842	927	4,668	19,248	72,544	5,233	5,727	17,315	5,948	21,927	16,394
1990	109,403	24,905	709	5,120	19,076	84,497	5,777	6,173	19,601	6,709	27,934	18,304
1994	114,163	23,908	601	4,986	18,321	90,256	5,984	6,162	20,507	6,896	31,579	19,128
1995	117,191	24,265	581	5,160	18,524	92,925	6,132	6,378	21,187	6,806	33,117	19,305
1996	119,608	24,493	580	5,418	18,495	95,115	6,253	6,482	21,597	6,911	34,454	19,419
1997	122,690	24,962	596	5,691	18,675	97,727	6,408	6,648	21,966	7,109	36,040	19,557
1998	125,865	25,414	590	6,020	18,805	100,451	6,611	6,800	22,295	7,389	37,533	19,823
1999	128,916	25,507	539	6,415	18,552	103,409	6,834	6,911	22,848	7,555	39,055	20,206
2000	131,759	25,709	543	6,698	18,469	106,050	7,019	7,024	23,307	7,560	40,460	20,681
2001	132,213	25,122	563	6,861	17,698	107,092	7,070	7,014	23,488	7,624	41,024	20,873
PERCENT DISTRIBUTION												
1980	100.0	28.4	1.1	4.8	22.4	71.6	5.7	5.9	16.6	5.7	19.8	18.0
1985	100.0	25.5	1.0	4.8	19.8	74.5	5.4	5.9	17.8	6.1	22.5	16.8
1990	100.0	22.8	0.6	4.7	17.4	77.2	5.3	5.6	17.9	6.1	25.5	16.7
1994	100.0	20.9	0.5	4.4	16.0	79.1	5.2	5.4	18.0	6.0	27.7	16.8
1995	100.0	20.7	0.5	4.4	15.8	79.3	5.2	5.4	18.1	5.8	28.3	16.5
1996	100.0	20.5	0.5	4.5	15.5	79.5	5.2	5.4	18.1	5.8	28.8	16.2
1997	100.0	20.3	0.5	4.6	15.2	79.7	5.2	5.4	17.9	5.8	29.4	15.9
1998	100.0	20.2	0.5	4.8	14.9	79.8	5.3	5.4	17.7	5.9	29.8	15.7
1999	100.0	19.8	0.4	5.0	14.4	80.2	5.3	5.4	17.7	5.9	30.3	15.7
2000	100.0	19.5	0.4	5.1	14.0	80.5	5.3	5.3	17.7	5.7	30.7	15.7
2001	100.0	19.0	0.4	5.2	13.4	81.0	5.3	5.3	17.8	5.8	31.0	15.8
WEEKLY HOURS [1]												
1980	35.3	(NA)	43.3	37.0	39.7	(NA)	39.6	38.4	30.2	36.2	32.6	(NA)
1985	34.9	(NA)	43.4	37.7	40.5	(NA)	39.5	38.4	29.4	36.4	32.5	(NA)
1990	34.5	(NA)	44.1	38.2	40.8	(NA)	38.4	38.1	28.8	35.8	32.5	(NA)
1994	34.7	(NA)	44.8	38.9	42.0	(NA)	39.7	38.4	28.9	35.8	32.5	(NA)
1995	34.5	(NA)	44.7	38.9	41.6	(NA)	39.4	38.3	28.8	35.9	32.4	(NA)
1996	34.4	(NA)	45.3	39.0	41.6	(NA)	39.6	38.3	28.8	35.9	32.4	(NA)
1997	34.6	(NA)	45.4	39.0	42.0	(NA)	39.7	38.4	28.9	36.1	32.6	(NA)
1998	34.6	(NA)	43.9	38.9	41.7	(NA)	39.5	38.3	29.0	36.4	32.6	(NA)
1999	34.5	(NA)	43.2	39.1	41.7	(NA)	38.7	38.3	29.0	36.2	32.6	(NA)
2000	34.5	(NA)	43.1	39.3	41.6	(NA)	38.6	38.5	28.9	36.3	32.7	(NA)
2001	34.2	(NA)	43.4	39.2	40.7	(NA)	38.1	38.2	28.8	36.3	32.7	(NA)
HOURLY EARNINGS [1]												
1980	6.66	(NA)	9.17	9.94	7.27	(NA)	8.87	6.95	4.88	5.79	5.85	(NA)
1985	8.57	(NA)	11.98	12.32	9.54	(NA)	11.40	9.15	5.94	7.94	7.90	(NA)
1990	10.01	(NA)	13.68	13.77	10.83	(NA)	12.92	10.79	6.75	9.97	9.83	(NA)
1994	11.12	(NA)	14.88	14.73	12.07	(NA)	13.78	12.06	7.49	11.83	11.04	(NA)
1995	11.43	(NA)	15.30	15.09	12.37	(NA)	14.13	12.43	7.69	12.32	11.39	(NA)
1996	11.82	(NA)	15.62	15.47	12.77	(NA)	14.45	12.87	7.99	12.80	11.79	(NA)
1997	12.28	(NA)	16.15	16.04	13.17	(NA)	14.92	13.45	8.33	13.34	12.28	(NA)
1998	12.78	(NA)	16.91	16.61	13.49	(NA)	15.31	14.07	8.74	14.07	12.84	(NA)
1999	13.24	(NA)	17.05	17.19	13.90	(NA)	15.69	14.59	9.09	14.62	13.37	(NA)
2000	13.75	(NA)	17.24	17.88	14.38	(NA)	16.22	15.20	9.46	15.07	13.91	(NA)
2001	14.33	(NA)	17.65	18.33	14.84	(NA)	16.89	15.80	9.82	15.83	14.61	(NA)
WEEKLY EARNINGS [1]												
1980	235	(NA)	397	368	289	(NA)	351	267	147	210	191	(NA)
1985	299	(NA)	520	464	386	(NA)	450	351	175	289	257	(NA)
1990	345	(NA)	603	526	442	(NA)	496	411	194	357	319	(NA)
1994	386	(NA)	667	573	507	(NA)	547	463	216	424	359	(NA)
1995	394	(NA)	684	587	515	(NA)	557	476	221	442	369	(NA)
1996	407	(NA)	708	603	531	(NA)	572	493	230	460	382	(NA)
1997	425	(NA)	733	626	553	(NA)	592	516	241	482	400	(NA)
1998	442	(NA)	742	646	563	(NA)	605	539	253	512	419	(NA)
1999	457	(NA)	737	672	580	(NA)	607	559	264	529	436	(NA)
2000	474	(NA)	743	703	598	(NA)	626	585	273	547	455	(NA)
2001	490	(NA)	766	719	604	(NA)	644	604	283	575	478	(NA)

NA Not available.   [1] Average hours and earnings. Private production and related workers in mining, manufacturing, and construction; nonsupervisory employees in other industries.
Source: U.S. Bureau of Labor Statistics, Employment and Earnings, monthly, June issues and Internet site <http://www.bls.gov/ces/home.htm>

No. 602. Employees in Nonfarm Establishments—States: 1990 to 2001

[In thousands (109,403 represents 109,403,000). For coverage, see headnote, Table 601. National totals differ from the sum of the state figures because of differing benchmarks among states and differing industrial and geographic stratification. Based on 1987 *Standard Industrial Classification Manual*, see text, this section]

State			2001							
	1990	1995	Total [1]	Construction	Manufacturing	Transportation and public utilities	Wholesale and retail trade	Finance, insurance, and real estate	Services	Government
United States	109,403	117,191	132,213	6,861	17,698	7,070	30,502	7,624	41,024	20,873
Alabama.	1,636	1,804	1,914	105	340	96	440	92	481	352
Alaska	238	262	290	15	14	28	58	13	73	79
Arizona.	1,483	1,796	2,266	165	210	111	533	150	711	377
Arkansas	924	1,069	1,156	53	241	72	267	46	280	194
California	12,500	12,422	14,697	767	1,904	750	3,336	844	4,688	2,383
Colorado.	1,521	1,834	2,232	167	199	144	530	144	689	345
Connecticut.	1,624	1,562	1,682	65	254	78	358	143	540	244
Delaware	348	366	419	[2]24	56	17	91	52	122	57
District of Columbia	686	643	651	11	11	18	51	33	305	222
Florida	5,387	5,996	7,198	403	469	366	1,782	458	2,686	1,029
Georgia	2,992	3,402	3,954	203	550	266	966	207	1,150	605
Hawaii	528	533	554	[2]24	18	42	136	33	186	115
Idaho.	385	477	569	38	76	28	141	24	151	110
Illinois	5,288	5,593	6,005	269	908	355	1,355	404	1,860	844
Indiana.	2,522	2,787	2,938	147	642	148	696	140	750	409
Iowa	1,226	1,358	1,469	63	252	72	351	88	395	246
Kansas.	1,089	1,198	1,357	64	206	89	317	66	358	249
Kentucky	1,471	1,643	1,817	88	307	108	424	76	484	310
Louisiana	1,590	1,772	1,931	122	182	118	450	87	542	378
Maine.	535	538	609	30	81	25	151	34	187	102
Maryland	2,171	2,183	2,470	162	178	118	554	143	861	452
Massachusetts.	2,985	2,977	3,335	137	424	145	740	233	1,228	429
Michigan.	3,970	4,274	4,587	202	926	181	1,073	210	1,300	687
Minnesota.	2,127	2,379	2,674	122	423	134	633	166	789	401
Micciccippi	937	1,075	1,134	52	214	57	253	43	271	239
Missouri	2,345	2,521	2,732	144	379	175	643	171	787	428
Montana.	297	351	392	21	24	22	102	18	116	84
Nebraska	730	816	909	43	117	58	213	62	259	156
Nevada	621	786	1,054	90	46	58	221	50	453	127
New Hampshire	508	540	627	27	104	22	165	34	191	84
New Jersey	3,635	3,601	4,024	161	450	270	928	272	1,342	601
New Mexico	580	682	757	46	43	37	174	33	222	186
New York	8,212	7,892	8,633	334	843	436	1,734	741	3,067	1,473
North Carolina	3,118	3,460	3,901	229	734	183	890	190	1,048	624
North Dakota.	266	302	330	15	25	19	82	17	94	74
Ohio	4,882	5,221	5,566	237	1,027	250	1,331	313	1,602	794
Oklahoma.	1,196	1,316	1,509	64	179	85	343	75	437	296
Oregon.	1,247	1,418	1,596	79	236	79	391	95	445	269
Pennsylvania.	5,170	5,253	5,701	248	893	303	1,272	329	1,908	730
Rhode Island.	451	440	479	18	70	17	108	33	169	65
South Carolina.	1,545	1,646	1,835	111	332	96	432	84	459	320
South Dakota	289	344	379	18	46	17	94	28	102	73
Tennessee	2,193	2,499	2,712	121	479	180	639	132	755	402
Texas.	7,095	8,023	9,513	565	1,058	595	2,266	533	2,751	1,584
Utah	724	908	1,082	71	127	61	251	60	315	190
Vermont	258	270	299	15	48	12	68	13	93	50
Virginia.	2,896	3,070	3,528	214	372	188	766	193	1,155	631
Washington.	2,143	2,347	2,698	155	338	146	635	141	774	506
West Virginia	630	688	735	34	77	37	162	30	233	141
Wisconsin.	2,292	2,559	2,826	123	588	134	640	150	775	414
Wyoming	199	219	246	18	11	14	55	8	58	62

[1] Includes mining, not shown separately.   [2] Mining included with construction.

Source: U.S. Bureau of Labor Statistics, *Employment and Earnings*, monthly, May issues. Compiled from data supplied by cooperating state agencies.

Labor Force, Employment and Earnings   393

No. 603. Nonfarm Industries—Employees and Earnings: 1990 to 2001

[Annual averages of monthly figures (109,403 represents 109,403,000). Covers all full- and part-time employees who worked during, or received pay for, any part of the pay period including the 12th of the month. For mining and manufacturing, data refer to production and related workers; for construction, to employees engaged in actual construction work; and for other industries, to nonsupervisory employees and working supervisors. See also headnote, Table 601]

Industry	1987 SIC [1] code	All employees (1,000)			Production workers Total (1,000)			Production workers Average hourly earnings (dollars)		
		1990	1995	2001	1990	1995	2001	1990	1995	2001
Total	(X)	109,403	117,191	132,213	(NA)	(NA)	(NA)	(NA)	(NA)	(NA)
Private sector [2]	(X)	91,098	97,885	111,340	73,774	80,125	91,167	10.01	11.43	14.33
Mining	(B)	709	581	563	509	424	441	13.68	15.30	17.65
Metal mining	10	58	51	36	46	41	27	14.05	16.77	18.96
Coal mining	12	147	104	78	119	84	66	16.71	18.45	19.04
Oil and gas extraction	13	395	320	337	261	218	263	12.94	14.52	17.82
Nonmetallic minerals, except fuels	14	110	105	113	83	80	86	11.58	13.39	15.74
Construction	(C)	5,120	5,160	6,861	3,974	3,993	5,302	13.77	15.09	18.33
General building contractors	15	1,298	1,207	1,554	938	856	1,067	13.01	14.33	17.68
Heavy construction, except building	16	770	752	929	643	626	775	13.34	14.65	17.62
Special trade contractors	17	3,051	3,201	4,377	2,393	2,511	3,459	14.20	15.47	18.71
Manufacturing	(D)	19,076	18,524	17,698	12,947	12,826	11,922	10.83	12.37	14.84
Durable goods [3]	(X)	11,109	10,683	10,638	7,363	7,317	7,122	11.35	12.94	15.28
Lumber and wood products [3]	24	733	769	795	603	632	641	9.08	10.12	12.26
Logging	241	85	83	77	70	67	61	11.22	11.64	14.00
Sawmills and planing mills	242	198	187	177	172	161	152	9.22	10.31	12.20
Millwork, plywood, and structural members	243	262	280	327	210	224	259	9.04	10.12	12.46
Wood containers	244	45	51	58	38	44	48	6.64	7.68	9.93
Mobile homes	2451	41	62	55	33	52	44	8.67	10.26	11.91
Furniture and fixtures [3]	25	506	510	527	400	403	416	8.52	9.82	12.21
Household furniture	251	289	281	275	241	234	231	7.87	9.29	11.44
Office furniture	252	68	63	73	51	47	50	9.64	10.53	12.98
Partitions and fixtures	254	78	86	86	57	63	65	9.77	10.92	13.26
Stone, clay, and glass products [3]	32	556	540	571	432	418	446	11.12	12.41	15.03
Flat glass	321	17	16	16	13	12	13	15.15	17.94	19.02
Glass and glassware, pressed and blown	322	83	74	67	72	62	52	12.40	14.11	17.14
Products of purchased glass	323	60	62	62	46	48	48	9.75	10.92	13.38
Cement, hydraulic	324	18	18	18	14	13	13	13.90	16.34	19.13
Structural clay products	325	36	34	35	28	26	27	9.55	10.97	12.04
Pottery and related products	326	39	42	35	31	33	27	9.62	10.70	12.81
Concrete, gypsum, and plaster	327	206	205	251	157	156	200	10.76	11.93	14.97
Primary metal industries [3]	33	756	712	651	574	553	504	12.92	14.62	16.97
Blast furnaces and basic steel products	331	276	242	210	212	185	162	14.82	17.33	20.43
Iron and steel foundries	332	132	131	112	105	107	93	11.55	13.42	15.79
Primary nonferrous metals	333	46	40	33	34	31	25	14.36	15.83	19.32
Nonferrous rolling and drawing	335	172	168	167	124	127	125	12.29	13.66	15.35
Nonferrous foundries (castings)	336	84	87	86	66	71	68	10.21	11.48	13.17
Fabricated metal products [3]	34	1,419	1,437	1,479	1,045	1,080	1,100	10.83	12.13	14.26
Metal cans and shipping containers	341	50	41	36	43	35	30	14.27	15.71	17.23
Cutlery, handtools, and hardware	342	131	128	111	96	96	85	10.78	12.16	13.44
Plumbing and heating, exc. electric	343	60	57	58	43	41	40	9.75	10.75	12.79
Fabricated structural metal products	344	427	428	490	303	312	354	10.16	11.35	13.68
Screw machine products	345	96	100	99	73	79	76	10.70	11.99	14.52
Metal forgings and stampings	346	225	252	238	178	202	186	12.70	14.30	16.58
Industrial machinery and equipment [3]	35	2,095	2,067	2,014	1,260	1,295	1,226	11.77	13.24	15.91
Engines and turbines	351	89	88	80	58	56	52	14.55	15.96	18.35
Farm and garden machinery	352	106	101	93	78	74	63	10.99	12.79	15.07
Construction and related machinery	353	229	224	230	141	146	143	11.92	12.89	14.85
Metalworking machinery	354	330	340	302	236	242	207	12.27	13.99	16.99
Special industry machinery	355	159	172	156	94	99	80	11.90	13.64	16.40
General industrial machinery	356	247	252	234	158	162	146	11.32	12.95	15.01
Computer and office equipment	357	438	352	355	137	123	127	11.51	13.59	18.43
Refrigeration and service machinery	358	177	201	198	125	144	136	10.93	11.98	14.23
Electronic and other elec. equip. [3]	36	1,673	1,625	1,612	1,055	1,045	972	10.30	11.69	14.53
Electric distribution equipment	361	97	83	80	67	58	53	10.15	11.43	14.58
Electrical industrial apparatus	362	169	158	144	119	111	93	10.00	11.07	14.12
Household appliances	363	124	121	116	99	99	94	10.26	11.49	13.17
Electric lighting and wiring equip	364	189	179	171	136	129	123	10.12	11.55	14.18
Household audio and video equip	365	85	84	70	59	57	44	9.68	10.90	13.33
Communications equipment	366	264	265	254	133	131	109	11.03	12.04	14.96
Electronic components and accessories	367	582	581	647	329	349	364	10.00	11.49	15.32
Transportation equipment [3]	37	1,989	1,790	1,747	1,224	1,200	1,137	14.08	16.74	19.02
Motor vehicles and equipment	371	812	971	933	617	761	696	14.56	17.34	19.36
Aircraft and parts	372	712	451	463	345	208	221	14.79	18.02	21.03
Ship and boat building and repairing	373	188	160	156	141	124	119	10.94	12.66	14.81
Railroad equipment	374	33	38	31	25	28	21	13.41	15.07	18.08
Guided missiles, space vehicles, and parts	376	185	98	82	57	28	19	14.39	17.74	21.44
Instruments and related products	38	1,006	843	859	499	417	421	11.29	12.71	14.87
Search and navigation equipment	381	284	161	159	94	40	40	14.62	16.38	19.01
Measuring and controlling devices	382	323	288	305	180	148	150	10.68	12.56	15.00
Medical instruments and supplies	384	246	264	295	144	151	175	9.85	11.57	13.80
Ophthalmic goods	385	43	37	29	30	24	21	8.18	9.59	11.31
Photographic equipment and supplies	386	100	85	68	43	38	31	14.08	15.36	18.55

See footnotes at end of table.

U.S. Census Bureau, Statistical Abstract of the United States: 2002

[Annual averages of monthly figures (109,403 represents 109,403,000). Covers all full- and part-time employees who worked during, or received pay for, any part of the pay period including the 12th of the month. For mining and manufacturing, data refer to production and related workers; for construction, to employees engaged in actual construction work; and for other industries, to nonsupervisory employees and working supervisors. See also headnote, Table 601]

Industry	1987 SIC [1] code	All employees (1,000)			Production workers					
					Total (1,000)			Average hourly earnings (dollars)		
		1990	1995	2001	1990	1995	2001	1990	1995	2001
Watches, clocks, watchcases, and parts	387	11	8	4	8	6	3	7.70	8.90	10.77
Misc. manufacturing industries [3]	39	375	390	385	272	276	259	8.61	10.05	12.19
Jewelry, silverware, and plated ware	391	52	50	46	37	35	30	9.23	10.23	12.63
Toys and sporting goods	394	104	118	103	76	84	67	7.94	9.47	12.21
Pens, pencils, office and art supplies	395	34	31	31	24	21	21	8.89	11.08	12.24
Costume jewelry and notions	396	33	26	18	25	18	13	7.40	8.65	10.70
Nondurable goods [3]	(X)	**7,968**	**7,841**	**7,060**	**5,584**	**5,508**	**4,800**	**10.12**	**11.58**	**14.17**
Food and kindred products [3]	20	1,661	1,692	1,685	1,194	1,248	1,242	9.62	10.93	12.88
Meat products	201	422	472	512	359	402	440	7.94	8.97	10.71
Dairy products	202	155	147	145	95	95	99	10.56	12.35	14.88
Preserved fruits and vegetables	203	247	245	213	206	204	177	8.95	10.49	12.26
Grain mill products	204	128	128	119	89	91	84	11.52	13.64	15.26
Bakery products	205	213	211	197	133	142	134	10.85	11.87	14.18
Sugar and confectionery products	206	99	100	94	78	78	71	10.26	11.81	15.29
Fats and oils	207	31	31	31	22	21	21	10.10	11.63	12.52
Beverages	208	184	175	191	78	82	87	13.51	15.51	17.61
Tobacco products	21	49	42	33	36	32	24	16.23	19.41	22.29
Cigarettes	211	35	29	24	26	22	17	19.57	24.46	26.13
Textile mill products [3]	22	691	663	473	593	560	396	8.02	9.41	11.35
Broadwoven fabric mills, cotton	221	91	79	55	82	69	49	8.31	9.87	11.53
Broadwoven fabric mills, synthetics	222	77	70	48	68	59	40	8.63	10.37	12.42
Broadwoven fabric mills, wool	223	17	15	8	14	13	7	8.61	9.84	12.07
Narrow fabric mills	224	24	23	18	20	19	15	7.39	8.74	10.98
Knitting mills	225	205	194	107	179	166	88	7.37	8.64	10.74
Textile finishing, except wool	226	62	72	51	50	59	42	8.45	9.53	11.35
Carpets and rugs	227	61	63	63	50	51	55	8.25	9.37	11.13
Yarn and thread mills	228	103	94	71	92	83	63	7.68	9.17	10.74
Apparel and other textile products [3]	23	1,036	936	566	869	776	436	6.57	7.64	9.47
Men's and boys' suits and coats	231	50	36	19	42	30	14	7.34	8.10	9.46
Men's and boys' furnishings	232	274	252	116	235	214	93	6.06	7.19	8.65
Women's and misses outerwear	233	328	279	160	274	230	119	6.26	7.27	8.69
Women's and children's undergarments	234	62	48	17	51	40	12	6.18	7.24	9.14
Girls' and children's outerwear	236	56	43	11	47	36	8	5.95	6.85	8.60
Paper and allied products [3]	26	697	693	635	522	525	482	12.31	14.23	16.86
Papermills	262	180	164	135	136	127	106	15.10	17.86	21.73
Paperboard mills	263	52	51	45	40	39	35	15.26	17.93	21.66
Paperboard containers and boxes	265	209	220	213	162	172	165	10.39	12.02	14.45
Misc. converted paper products	267	241	245	230	174	178	167	10.79	12.39	14.53
Printing and publishing [3]	27	1,569	1,546	1,492	871	848	780	11.24	12.33	14.81
Newspapers	271	474	447	431	166	155	142	11.17	12.19	14.13
Periodicals	272	129	131	147	47	43	48	11.95	13.42	15.99
Books	273	121	124	124	66	66	55	10.10	11.57	15.29
Commercial printing	275	552	563	533	401	406	373	11.52	12.53	15.19
Blankbooks and bookbinding	278	72	69	54	56	54	40	8.83	9.68	11.29
Chemicals and allied products [3]	28	1,086	1,038	1,033	600	580	566	13.54	15.62	18.59
Industrial inorganic chemicals	281	138	120	96	70	54	53	14.66	17.33	19.83
Plastics materials and synthetics	282	180	158	149	116	106	100	13.97	16.10	19.27
Drugs	283	237	260	330	105	127	143	12.90	15.15	18.38
Soap, cleaners, and toilet goods	284	159	153	154	98	95	95	11.71	12.76	16.40
Paints and allied products	285	61	55	49	31	29	26	11.99	13.07	16.15
Industrial organic chemicals	286	155	146	118	86	83	66	15.97	19.11	21.91
Agricultural chemicals	287	56	53	49	34	31	29	13.73	15.73	19.69
Petroleum and coal products [3]	29	157	145	127	103	94	88	16.24	19.36	22.09
Petroleum refining	291	118	105	84	75	66	57	17.58	21.44	24.72
Asphalt paving and roofing materials	295	27	27	29	21	20	22	12.87	14.48	17.92
Rubber and misc. plastics products [3]	30	888	980	954	687	763	739	9.76	10.91	13.39
Tires and inner tubes	301	84	80	76	62	58	58	15.42	17.58	19.57
Rubber and plastics footwear	302	11	8	4	9	7	3	6.66	8.44	8.39
Leather and leather products [3]	31	133	106	64	109	83	48	6.91	8.17	10.31
Leather tanning and finishing	311	15	14	10	12	11	8	9.04	11.06	12.63
Footwear, except rubber	314	74	52	26	63	43	20	6.61	7.67	9.73
Luggage	316	11	11	8	8	8	7	6.91	8.13	9.64
Handbags and personal leather goods	317	15	12	8	12	8	5	6.08	7.43	10.32
Transp. and public utilities [3]	(E)	**5,777**	**6,132**	**7,070**	**4,781**	**5,140**	**5,933**	**12.92**	**14.13**	**16.89**
Railroad transportation	40	279	238	227	(4)	(4)	(4)	(4)	(4)	(4)
Class I railroads, plus Amtrak [5]	4011	241	212	188	(4)	(4)	(4)	16.08	17.48	18.28
Local and interurban passenger transit	41	338	419	482	308	386	442	9.23	10.55	12.42
Trucking and warehousing	42	1,395	1,587	1,854	1,215	1,382	1,623	11.68	12.73	14.69
Water transportation	44	177	175	203	(4)	(4)	(4)	(4)	(4)	(4)
Transportation by air	45	968	1,068	1,287	(4)	(4)	(4)	(4)	(4)	(4)
Pipelines, except natural gas	46	19	15	14	14	12	10	17.04	20.28	23.80
Transportation services	47	336	401	464	270	321	378	10.38	12.44	15.07

See footnotes at end of table.

U.S. Census Bureau, Statistical Abstract of the United States: 2002

[Annual averages of monthly figures (109,403 represents 109,403,000). Covers all full- and part-time employees who worked during, or received pay for, any part of the pay period including the 12th of the month. For mining and manufacturing, data refer to production and related workers; for construction, to employees engaged in actual construction work; and for other industries, to nonsupervisory employees and working supervisors. See also headnote, Table 601]

Industry	1987 SIC [1] code	All employees (1,000)			Production workers					
					Total (1,000)			Average hourly earnings (dollars)		
		1990	1995	2001	1990	1995	2001	1990	1995	2001
Communication [3]	48	1,309	1,318	1,692	978	1,017	1,313	13.51	15.56	18.50
Telephone communication	481	913	900	1,167	658	673	909	14.13	16.21	18.93
Radio and television broadcasting	483	234	236	255	193	198	204	12.71	15.31	19.10
Cable and other pay television services	484	126	156	236	105	131	182	10.50	12.10	15.50
Electric, gas, and sanitary services [3]	49	957	911	847	759	719	688	15.23	17.68	22.28
Electric services	491	454	404	354	351	316	286	15.80	18.54	22.99
Gas production and distribution	492	165	154	124	129	119	98	14.25	17.30	20.37
Combination utility services	493	193	167	151	156	128	125	17.58	21.39	26.50
Sanitary services	495	115	154	178	99	132	148	11.55	12.89	19.57
Wholesale trade	(F)	6,173	6,378	7,014	4,959	5,163	5,584	10.79	12.43	15.80
Retail trade [3]	(G)	19,601	21,187	23,488	17,358	18,639	20,612	6.75	7.69	9.82
General merchandise stores	53	2,540	2,681	2,792	2,380	2,498	2,586	6.83	7.53	9.80
Food stores	54	3,215	3,366	3,542	2,953	3,062	3,181	7.31	8.15	9.72
Automotive dealers and service stations	55	2,063	2,190	2,429	1,718	1,825	2,034	8.92	10.41	13.59
Apparel and accessory stores	56	1,183	1,125	1,218	991	919	1,003	6.25	7.47	9.71
Furniture and home furnishings stores	57	820	946	1,140	670	765	936	8.53	10.15	13.37
Eating and drinking places	58	6,509	7,354	8,216	5,905	6,631	7,392	4.97	5.59	7.15
Finance, insurance, real estate	(H)	6,709	6,806	7,624	4,860	4,961	5,590	9.97	12.32	15.83
Depository institutions	60	2,251	2,025	2,036	1,632	1,458	1,469	8.43	9.62	12.15
Nondepository institutions	61	373	463	701	270	335	466	10.40	12.53	17.31
Security and commodity brokers	62	424	525	764	(4)	(4)	(4)	(4)	(4)	(4)
Insurance carriers	63	1,462	1,529	1,596	982	1,092	1,266	11.18	14.82	18.61
Insurance, agents, brokers, service	64	663	696	759	(4)	(4)	(4)	(4)	(4)	(4)
Real estate	65	1,315	1,351	1,510	(4)	(4)	(4)	(4)	(4)	(4)
Holding and other investment offices	67	221	217	259	(4)	(4)	(4)	(4)	(4)	(4)
Services [3]	(I)	27,934	33,117	41,024	24,387	28,979	35,784	9.83	11.39	14.61
Hotels and other lodging places	70	1,631	1,668	1,915	(4)	(4)	(4)	(4)	(4)	(4)
Hotels and motels	701	1,578	1,615	1,847	1,398	1,420	1,623	6.98	7.93	9.94
Personal services [3]	72	1,104	1,163	1,276	(4)	(4)	(4)	(4)	(4)	(4)
Laundry, cleaning, garment services	721	426	432	448	379	381	390	6.82	7.53	9.47
Beauty shops	723	372	391	435	333	351	386	7.10	8.56	10.70
Business services [3]	73	5,139	6,812	9,628	4,522	6,069	8,495	9.48	10.71	14.91
Advertising	731	235	233	296	169	170	214	13.51	15.90	19.97
Personnel supply services	736	1,535	2,476	3,532	(4)	(4)	(4)	(4)	(4)	(4)
Employment agencies	7361	246	287	389	(4)	(4)	(4)	(4)	(4)	(4)
Help supply services	7363	1,288	2,189	3,143	1,245	2,127	3,016	8.09	8.80	11.69
Computer and data processing services	737	772	1,090	2,193	603	879	1,774	15.11	17.79	24.24
Prepackaged software	7372	113	181	320	(4)	(4)	(4)	(4)	(4)	(4)
Data processing and preparation	7374	197	223	298	(4)	(4)	(4)	(4)	(4)	(4)
Auto repair, services, and parking	75	914	1,020	1,302	756	842	1,074	8.77	9.92	12.33
Automotive repair shops	753	524	567	702	429	459	567	9.67	11.07	13.90
Motion pictures	78	408	488	592	344	406	501	10.95	13.59	14.71
Motion picture theaters	783	112	119	140	(4)	(4)	(4)	(4)	(4)	(4)
Amusement and recreation services	79	1,076	1,417	1,772	944	1,243	1,549	8.11	8.74	10.59
Health services [3]	80	7,814	9,230	10,344	6,948	8,178	9,174	10.41	12.45	15.49
Offices and clinics of medical doctors	801	1,338	1,609	1,979	1,105	1,315	1,630	10.58	12.54	16.08
Nursing and personal care facilities	805	1,415	1,691	1,823	1,279	1,526	1,639	7.24	8.77	11.28
Hospitals	806	3,549	3,772	4,095	3,248	3,450	3,760	11.79	14.30	17.45
Home health care services	808	291	629	650	269	582	598	8.72	10.91	12.74
Legal services	81	908	921	1,026	748	736	815	14.16	16.06	20.98
Educational services	82	1,661	1,965	2,419	(4)	(4)	(4)	(4)	(4)	(4)
Social services	83	1,734	2,336	3,051	1,494	2,024	2,632	7.11	8.33	10.32
Membership organizations	86	1,946	2,146	2,498	(4)	(4)	(4)	(4)	(4)	(4)
Engineering and management services	87	2,478	2,731	3,525	1,886	2,098	2,696	13.56	15.79	19.86
Government	(J)	18,304	19,305	20,873	(NA)	(NA)	(NA)	(NA)	(NA)	(NA)
Federal government	(X)	3,085	2,822	2,616	(NA)	(NA)	(NA)	(NA)	(NA)	(NA)
State government	(X)	4,305	4,635	4,880	(NA)	(NA)	(NA)	(NA)	(NA)	(NA)
Local government	(X)	10,914	11,849	13,377	(NA)	(NA)	(NA)	(NA)	(NA)	(NA)

NA Not available. X Not applicable. [1] 1987 Standard Industrial Classification, see text, this section. [2] Excludes government. [3] Includes industries not shown separately. [4] Included in totals; not available separately. [5] For changes in "Class I" classification, see text, Section 23, Transportation.

Source: U.S. Bureau of Labor Statistics, *Employment and Earnings*, monthly, June issues and Internet site <http://www.bls.gov/ces/home.htm>.

No. 604. Annual Indexes of Output Per Hour for Selected Three-Digit SIC Industries: 1990 to 2000

[See text, this section. Minus sign (-) indicates decrease]

Industry	1987 SIC code [1]	Indexes (1987=100)						Average annual percent change [2]
		1990	1995	1997	1998	1999	2000	
Mining:								
Bituminous coal and lignite mining	122	118.7	155.9	176.6	188.0	194.9	207.0	5.7
Crude petroleum and natural gas	131	97.0	119.4	125.2	127.5	134.5	142.5	3.9
Manufacturing:								
Meat products	201	97.1	102.3	102.5	102.3	101.8	102.9	0.6
Dairy products	202	107.3	116.4	119.3	119.3	112.7	113.5	0.6
Preserved fruits and vegetables	203	95.6	109.1	110.7	117.8	120.4	123.5	2.6
Grain mill products	204	105.4	115.4	118.2	126.2	129.3	127.5	1.9
Bakery products	205	92.7	97.3	99.1	100.9	106.4	107.6	1.5
Sugar and confectionery products	206	103.2	108.3	116.7	123.0	127.0	130.5	2.4
Beverages	208	117.0	133.5	135.5	136.4	129.7	128.6	0.9
Miscellaneous food and kindred products	209	99.2	102.9	104.0	112.4	113.9	116.3	1.6
Knitting mills	225	107.5	138.3	138.0	135.9	146.6	155.6	3.8
Yarn and thread mills	228	110.2	137.4	150.4	153.0	157.6	155.4	3.5
Men's and boys' furnishings	232	102.1	123.4	162.1	174.8	190.9	200.3	7.0
Women's and misses' outerwear	233	104.1	135.5	149.9	151.9	173.9	189.9	6.2
Miscellaneous fabricated textile products	239	99.9	109.2	119.2	117.3	128.8	132.5	2.9
Sawmills and planing mills	242	99.8	110.2	116.9	118.7	125.4	124.4	2.2
Millwork, plywood, and structural members	243	98.0	92.7	89.1	91.3	89.2	91.4	-0.7
Wood buildings and mobile homes	245	103.1	97.0	100.3	99.2	100.3	94.6	-0.9
Miscellaneous wood products	249	107.7	115.4	123.4	131.2	140.7	146.5	3.1
Household furniture	251	104.5	116.9	121.3	125.7	128.9	128.4	2.1
Office furniture	252	95.0	101.1	118.3	113.1	108.9	111.2	1.6
Partitions and fixtures	254	95.6	101.2	121.1	125.6	125.9	131.9	3.3
Paper mills	262	102.3	118.6	112.0	114.8	126.2	133.5	2.7
Paperboard containers and boxes	265	101.3	105.1	109.7	113.5	111.9	112.9	1.1
Miscellaneous converted paper products	267	101.4	113.3	119.5	123.0	126.0	128.3	2.4
Newspapers	271	90.6	79.0	79.0	83.6	86.0	88.3	-0.3
Periodicals	272	93.9	87.8	100.1	112.2	111.2	109.9	1.6
Books	273	96.6	101.6	102.6	100.9	106.1	106.1	0.9
Miscellaneous publishing	274	92.2	94.8	114.5	119.4	127.2	127.8	3.3
Commercial printing	275	102.5	107.2	108.8	109.9	115.0	118.7	1.5
Industrial inorganic chemicals	281	106.8	109.3	116.8	145.8	148.5	141.3	2.8
Plastics materials and synthetics	282	100.9	128.3	135.4	142.2	148.6	151.0	4.1
Drugs	283	103.8	108.7	112.4	104.3	105.6	106.2	0.2
Soaps, cleaners, and toilet goods	284	103.8	118.6	126.4	122.7	114.8	124.8	1.9
Industrial organic chemicals	286	101.4	98.6	111.3	105.7	120.6	127.8	2.3
Miscellaneous chemical products	289	97.3	107.8	120.3	120.8	123.3	125.6	2.6
Petroleum refining	291	109.2	132.3	149.2	155.8	170.2	180.2	5.1
Tires and inner tubes	301	103.0	131.1	149.1	144.1	142.1	145.9	3.5
Hose and belting and gaskets and packing	305	96.1	104.6	113.5	112.7	110.6	115.4	1.8
Fabricated rubber products, n.e.c. [3]	306	109.0	121.5	125.3	132.3	136.9	144.7	2.9
Miscellaneous plastics products, n.e.c. [3]	308	105.7	121.0	129.9	133.8	140.9	145.4	3.2
Concrete, gypsum, and plaster products	327	102.3	104.5	107.6	112.8	111.1	105.1	0.3
Miscellaneous nonmetallic mineral products	329	95.4	107.8	114.7	114.9	113.3	116.1	2.0
Blast furnace and basic steel products	331	109.7	142.6	155.0	151.0	155.6	160.1	3.9
Iron and steel foundries	332	106.1	112.7	120.8	121.1	128.9	132.1	2.2
Nonferrous rolling and drawing	335	92.7	99.2	111.3	115.7	121.4	118.0	2.4
Nonferrous foundries (castings)	336	104.0	117.8	127.0	131.5	129.8	129.7	2.2
Cutlery, handtools, and hardware	342	97.3	111.3	114.6	115.7	121.9	125.4	2.6
Fabricated structural metal products	344	98.8	105.8	111.9	112.7	112.8	112.8	1.3
Metal forgings and stampings	346	95.6	109.3	120.2	125.9	128.3	129.8	3.1
Metal services, n.e.c. [3]	347	104.7	127.7	124.4	127.3	126.1	135.7	2.6
Miscellaneous fabricated metal products	349	97.5	106.6	107.7	111.6	110.9	109.2	1.1
Engines and turbines	351	106.5	122.7	136.9	146.1	151.5	164.5	4.4
Farm and garden machinery	352	116.5	134.7	141.2	148.5	128.6	139.6	1.8
Construction and related machinery	353	107.0	122.1	132.5	137.6	133.6	139.8	2.7
Metalworking machinery	354	101.1	114.8	119.2	119.8	123.0	129.8	2.5
Special industry machinery	355	107.5	132.3	131.7	124.5	138.6	172.2	4.8
General industrial machinery	356	101.5	109.0	110.0	111.2	113.1	118.7	1.6
Computer and office equipment	357	138.1	469.4	960.2	1,356.6	1,862.5	2,172.0	31.7
Refrigeration and service machinery	358	103.6	112.7	115.0	121.4	124.0	122.3	1.7
Industrial machinery, n.e.c. [3]	359	107.3	138.8	129.3	127.5	135.8	141.8	2.8
Electric distribution equipment	361	106.3	143.0	142.8	147.5	148.9	155.4	3.9
Electrical industrial apparatus	362	107.7	150.8	164.2	162.3	158.3	157.0	3.8
Household appliances	363	105.8	127.3	142.9	150.2	149.5	162.4	4.4
Electric lighting and wiring equipment	364	99.9	113.7	121.8	129.2	132.4	134.8	3.0
Communications equipment	366	123.8	200.7	275.4	284.5	371.9	448.8	13.7
Electronic components and accessories	367	133.4	401.5	613.4	768.6	1,062.6	1,440.1	26.9
Miscellaneous electrical equipment & supplies	369	90.6	114.1	128.3	135.3	147.2	156.0	5.6
Motor vehicles and equipment	371	102.4	106.7	116.3	125.2	136.7	127.1	2.2
Aircraft and parts	372	98.9	107.8	114.7	140.1	138.1	132.2	2.9
Ship and boat building and repairing	373	103.7	98.1	105.5	102.5	113.1	121.6	1.6
Guided missiles, space vehicles, parts	376	116.5	116.9	133.6	138.9	156.1	113.3	-0.3

See footnotes at end of table.

U.S. Census Bureau, Statistical Abstract of the United States: 2002

[See text, this section. Minus sign (-) indicates decrease]

Industry	1987 SIC code [1]	Indexes (1987=100)						Average annual percent change [2]
		1990	1995	1997	1998	1999	2000	
Search and navigation equipment..........	381	112.7	149.5	149.5	149.1	149.6	163.7	3.8
Measuring and controlling devices..........	382	106.4	146.4	142.4	143.5	152.4	158.5	4.1
Medical instruments and supplies..........	384	116.9	131.5	147.4	158.6	160.4	167.0	3.6
Photographic equipment & supplies.........	386	107.8	129.5	121.5	128.0	160.6	169.4	4.6
Toys and sporting goods.................	394	108.1	113.6	125.7	131.6	126.6	140.4	2.7
Miscellaneous manufactures..............	399	106.5	108.1	109.4	108.5	114.9	115.9	0.8
Transportation:								
Railroad transportation.................	4011	118.5	156.2	169.8	173.3	182.5	195.8	5.1
Trucking, except local [4]................	4213	111.1	125.4	132.4	129.9	131.6	131.2	1.7
United states postal service [5]..........	431	104.0	106.5	108.3	109.8	110.9	113.6	0.9
Air transportation [4]..................	4512,13,22 (pts.)	92.9	108.6	111.6	108.4	109.1	110.7	1.8
Utilities:								
Telephone communications..............	481	113.3	148.1	160.9	170.1	186.3	201.3	5.9
Radio and television broadcasting.........	483	104.9	109.6	101.7	104.5	108.4	109.9	0.5
Cable and other pay TV services..........	484	92.6	84.5	84.7	86.1	85.0	87.6	-0.6
Electric utilities.....................	491,3 (pts.)	110.1	80.8	150.0	159.6	162.0	169.6	4.4
Gas utilities.......................	492,3 (pts.)	105.8	137.1	158.6	144.4	147.2	160.6	4.3
Trade:								
Lumber and other building materials dealers...	521	104.3	117.8	121.8	134.2	143.0	144.2	3.3
Paint, glass, and wallpaper stores.........	523	106.8	130.9	134.8	163.5	165.1	170.1	4.8
Hardware stores....................	525	115.3	115.6	119.0	137.9	147.6	145.7	2.4
Retail nurseries, lawn and garden supply stores................................	526	84.7	117.4	127.5	133.7	150.4	154.5	6.2
Department stores....................	531	96.8	116.1	129.1	135.8	146.0	160.4	5.2
Variety stores......................	533	154.6	212.4	260.1	271.2	315.0	359.8	7.9
Miscellaneous general merchandise stores....	539	118.6	167.4	170.4	185.9	199.6	224.3	6.6
Grocery stores.....................	541	96.6	93.9	91.7	92.2	95.3	96.1	-0.1
Retail bakeries.....................	546	91.2	83.0	67.6	68.1	83.1	88.4	-0.3
New and used car dealers..............	551	106.7	108.1	108.8	108.7	111.6	112.5	0.5
Auto and home supply stores............	553	103.7	109.1	108.1	113.1	115.5	119.3	1.4
Gasoline service stations..............	554	103.0	127.2	126.1	133.9	141.7	139.0	3.0
Men's and boy's wear stores............	561	115.6	121.4	136.3	145.2	154.5	165.0	3.6
Women's clothing stores...............	562	106.6	139.9	157.3	176.0	190.2	205.7	6.8
Family clothing stores.................	565	107.8	141.8	150.2	153.1	155.9	160.4	4.1
Shoe stores.......................	566	107.9	139.2	148.4	145.0	152.9	160.2	4.0
Furniture and home furnishings stores.......	571	104.6	117.4	124.2	127.3	134.5	141.1	3.0
Household appliance stores.............	572	104.6	139.6	155.2	184.2	186.4	209.3	7.2
Radio, television, computer, and music stores..	573	120.8	198.1	216.8	258.3	309.1	359.4	11.5
Eating and drinking places.............	581	104.5	102.0	101.6	102.0	104.0	107.3	0.3
Drug and proprietary stores.............	591	106.3	111.1	119.8	125.7	129.8	136.9	2.6
Liquor stores......................	592	105.9	104.7	109.9	116.5	114.5	127.7	1.9
Used merchandise stores...............	593	103.0	120.6	140.3	163.6	183.2	216.7	7.7
Miscellaneous shopping goods stores.......	594	107.4	123.2	129.4	138.7	143.7	150.6	3.4
Nonstore retailers...................	596	111.1	152.5	186.8	208.3	220.6	263.2	9.0
Fuel dealers.......................	598	84.6	111.4	109.1	105.8	115.2	117.3	3.3
Retail stores, n.e.c. [3]................	599	114.5	127.0	147.8	157.4	162.5	168.1	3.9
Finance and services:								
Commercial banks....................	602	107.7	126.4	133.0	132.6	135.9	143.2	2.9
Hotels and motels....................	701	96.2	110.5	108.2	108.2	109.9	114.1	1.7
Laundry, cleaning, and garment services.....	721	102.3	106.6	109.0	116.0	120.8	123.6	1.9
Photographic studios, portrait............	722	98.2	116.2	114.1	121.6	107.7	112.0	1.3
Beauty shops......................	723	97.5	104.8	108.5	110.5	113.4	114.5	1.6
Funeral services and crematories..........	726	91.2	100.2	101.9	104.2	100.2	93.9	0.3
Automotive repair shops................	753	107.9	121.6	117.2	124.9	126.4	128.5	1.8
Motion picture theaters................	783	118.1	105.0	103.4	106.1	108.7	112.3	-0.5

[1] 1987 Standard Industrial Classification; see text, this section. [2] Average annual percent change, 1990 to 2000, based on compound rate formula. [3] N.e.c. means not elsewhere classified. [4] Employee hours are based on employees with the assumption of constant average weekly hours. [5] Refers to output per full-time equivalent employee year on a fiscal basis.

Source: U.S. Bureau of Labor Statistics, Internet site <http://www.bls.gov/lpc/home.htm>.

No. 605. Productivity and Related Measures: 1980 to 2001

[See text, this section. Minus sign (-) indicates decrease]

Item	1980	1985	1990	1995	1997	1998	1999	2000	2001
INDEXES (1992=100)									
Output per hour, business sector............	80.4	88.7	95.2	102.6	107.8	110.7	113.4	117.3	119.6
Nonfarm business.................	82.0	89.3	95.3	102.8	107.5	110.3	112.9	116.6	118.8
Manufacturing..................	70.1	82.3	92.9	109.0	117.6	124.0	129.6	137.5	139.0
Output,[1] business sector...............	69.8	83.1	97.6	111.5	122.5	128.5	134.4	140.6	141.9
Nonfarm business.................	70.2	83.0	97.8	111.8	122.7	128.8	134.8	140.8	142.1
Manufacturing..................	75.3	86.0	97.3	113.4	124.1	130.4	135.2	141.5	135.5
Hours,[2] business sector	86.8	93.6	102.6	108.7	113.6	116.1	118.5	119.8	118.6
Nonfarm business.................	85.6	93.0	102.7	108.8	114.1	116.8	119.4	120.8	119.6
Manufacturing..................	107.5	104.6	104.8	104.0	105.5	105.2	104.3	102.9	97.5
Compensation per hour,[3] business sector	54.2	72.9	90.7	106.7	113.5	119.8	125.2	133.3	141.2
Nonfarm business.................	54.6	73.2	90.5	106.6	113.1	119.2	124.4	132.5	140.1
Manufacturing..................	55.6	75.1	90.8	107.9	111.4	117.4	122.1	130.7	140.2
Real hourly compensation,[3] business sector......	89.2	92.5	96.3	99.6	101.0	105.1	107.6	110.8	114.2
Nonfarm business.................	89.8	92.9	96.2	99.4	100.6	104.5	106.8	110.2	113.3
Manufacturing..................	91.4	95.3	96.4	100.6	99.1	103.0	104.9	108.6	113.4
Unit labor costs,[4] business sector............	67.4	82.1	95.3	104.1	105.3	108.2	110.4	113.6	118.1
Nonfarm business.................	66.5	82.0	95.0	103.7	105.2	108.0	110.2	113.6	117.9
Manufacturing..................	79.3	91.3	97.8	99.0	94.7	94.7	94.3	95.1	100.9
ANNUAL PERCENT CHANGE[5]									
Output per hour, business sector.............	-0.3	2.0	1.3	0.7	2.3	2.7	2.5	3.4	2.0
Nonfarm business.................	-0.3	1.3	1.1	0.9	2.0	2.6	2.3	3.3	1.9
Manufacturing..................	0.4	3.6	2.9	3.8	4.3	5.4	4.5	6.1	1.1
Output,[1] business sector...............	-1.1	4.2	1.5	3.1	5.2	4.9	4.6	4.6	0.9
Nonfarm business.................	-1.1	3.9	1.4	3.4	5.1	5.0	4.6	4.5	0.9
Manufacturing..................	-4.2	2.8	0.7	4.3	6.1	5.1	3.7	4.6	-4.2
Hours,[2] business sector	-0.9	2.2	0.2	2.4	2.9	2.2	2.0	1.1	-1.0
Nonfarm business.................	-0.8	2.5	0.3	2.4	3.1	2.4	2.2	1.1	-0.9
Manufacturing..................	-4.6	-0.7	-2.1	0.4	1.8	-0.2	-0.8	-1.4	-5.3
Compensation per hour,[3] business sector	10.8	4.9	5.7	2.1	3.1	5.5	4.6	6.4	6.0
Nonfarm business.................	10.8	4.7	5.5	2.1	3.0	5.4	4.4	6.5	5.8
Manufacturing..................	12.0	5.5	4.8	2.1	1.9	5.4	4.0	7.0	7.3
Real hourly compensation,[3] business sector......	-0.2	1.5	0.7	-0.3	0.9	4.0	2.4	3.0	3.1
Nonfarm business.................	-0.2	1.3	0.5	-0.3	0.8	3.9	2.2	3.1	2.9
Manufacturing..................	0.9	2.1	-0.2	-0.3	-0.3	3.9	1.9	3.6	4.4
Unit labor costs,[4] business sector............	11.1	2.9	4.3	1.4	0.8	2.8	2.0	2.9	3.9
Nonfarm business.................	11.1	3.3	4.3	1.2	0.9	2.7	2.0	3.1	3.8
Manufacturing..................	11.6	1.8	1.9	-1.7	-2.3	-	-0.5	0.9	6.1

- Represents or rounds to zero.   [1] Refers to gross sectoral product, annual weighted.   [2] Hours at work of all persons engaged in the business and nonfarm business sectors (employees, proprietors, and unpaid family workers); employees' and proprietors' hours in manufacturing.   [3] Wages and salaries of employees plus employers' contributions for social insurance and private benefit plans. Also includes an estimate of same for self-employed. Real compensation deflated by the consumer price index for all urban consumers, see text, Section 14, Prices.   [4] Hourly compensation divided by output per hour.   [5] All changes are from the immediate prior year.

Source: U.S. Bureau of Labor Statistics, News USDL 02-261, *Productivity and Costs;* and Internet site <http://www.bls.gov/lpc/home.htm>.

No. 606. Computer Use at Work by Occupation: 2001

[**In percent, except as indicated (115,065 represents 115,065,000). As of September.** For employed persons 25 years old and over. Based on the Current Population Survey and subject to sampling error; see Appendix III and source]

Occupation	Employed			Use a computer at main job		Main computer uses			
	Total (1,000)	Percent women	Median education[1]	Total (1,000)	Percent of employed	Internet, e-mail	Word processing[2]	Spreadsheets, databases	Calendar, scheduling
Total	115,065	46.3	SC	65,190	56.7	41.7	38.8	35.9	30.4
Managerial and professional . . .	39,412	50.2	CD	31,723	80.5	66.8	63.2	56.6	48.8
Technical, sales, and administrative support.	31,482	62.9	SC	22,205	70.5	49.2	45.5	43.1	34.7
Precision production, craft and repair	13,083	8.4	HS	4,152	31.7	19.0	14.8	16.6	14.6
Service	13,678	61.6	HS	3,478	25.4	13.9	14.3	11.8	12.3
Operators, fabricators and laborers................	14,504	24.3	HS	3,006	20.7	9.2	7.6	8.7	7.0
Farming, forestry and fishing.................	2,905	20.3	HS	625	21.5	14.6	13.0	13.2	9.2

[1] SC = Some college, no degree; CD = College degree; HS = High school diploma or GED. For definition of median, see Guide to Tabular Presentation.   [2] Includes desktop publishing.

Source: U.S. Department of Commerce, National Telecommunications and Information Administration, *A Nation Online: How Americans Are Expanding Their Use of the Internet,* February 2002, Internet site <http://www.ntia.doc.gov/ntiahome/dn/index.html> (accessed 17 April 2002).

No. 607. Annual Total Compensation and Wages and Salary Accruals Per Full-Time Equivalent Employee by Industry: 1990 to 2000

[In dollars. Wage and salary accruals include executives' compensation, bonuses, tips, and payments-in-kind; total compensation includes in addition to wages and salaries, employer contributions for social insurance, employer contributions to private and welfare funds, director's fees, jury and witness fees, etc. Based on the 1987 Standard Industrial Classification Code (SIC); See text, this section]

Industry	Annual total compensation				Annual wages and salary			
	1990	1995	1999	2000	1990	1995	1999	2000
Domestic industries	31,940	37,742	43,389	45,613	26,259	30,911	36,587	38,612
Private industries	30,822	36,322	42,030	44,318	25,853	30,310	36,215	38,322
Agriculture, forestry, and fishing	18,475	21,022	24,145	24,872	15,996	18,166	21,168	21,922
Mining.	45,872	56,523	64,815	68,730	38,024	46,583	55,372	58,896
Construction	33,833	37,285	42,186	43,995	27,871	30,431	36,140	37,896
Manufacturing	36,958	44,713	50,695	53,921	30,054	35,779	42,832	45,704
Transportation	36,459	40,732	45,020	46,382	28,900	32,349	37,210	38,450
Communications	46,281	59,952	73,679	75,679	38,751	48,979	62,342	64,155
Electric, gas, and sanitary services.	48,097	59,478	68,968	73,934	39,557	48,751	57,962	62,333
Wholesale trade	37,031	44,508	53,443	56,478	31,499	37,808	45,980	48,731
Retail trade	18,626	21,189	24,399	25,271	15,990	18,246	21,447	22,260
Finance, insurance, and real estate	37,501	49,272	64,114	69,559	31,982	41,661	55,391	60,348
Services	28,807	34,043	39,198	41,554	24,697	29,084	34,238	36,419
Government	37,218	44,951	50,917	52,820	28,176	33,962	38,650	40,228

Source: U.S. Bureau of Economic Analysis, *National Income and Product Accounts, Volume 1, 1929-97*, and *Survey of Current Business*, August 2001. See also <http://www.bea.gov/bea/dn/nipaweb/selecttable.asp>.

No. 608. Average Hourly and Weekly Earnings by Private Industry Group: 1980 to 2001

[In dollars. Average earnings include overtime. Data are for production and related workers in mining, manufacturing, and construction, and nonsupervisory employees in other industries. Excludes agriculture. See headnote, Table 601]

Private industry group	Current dollars					Constant (1982) dollars [1]				
	1980	1990	1995	2000	2001	1980	1990	1995	2000	2001
AVERAGE HOURLY EARNINGS										
Total	6.66	10.01	11.43	13.75	14.33	7.78	7.52	7.39	7.89	8.00
Mining	9.17	13.68	15.30	17.24	17.65	10.71	10.28	9.90	9.89	9.85
Construction	9.94	13.77	15.09	17.88	18.33	11.61	10.35	9.76	10.26	10.23
Manufacturing	7.27	10.83	12.37	14.38	14.84	8.49	8.14	8.00	8.25	8.29
Transportation, public utilities	8.87	12.92	14.13	16.22	16.89	10.36	9.71	9.14	9.31	9.43
Wholesale trade	6.95	10.79	12.43	15.20	15.80	8.12	8.11	8.04	8.72	8.82
Retail trade	4.88	6.75	7.69	9.46	9.82	5.70	5.07	4.97	5.43	5.48
Finance, insurance, real estate	5.79	9.97	12.32	15.07	15.83	6.76	7.49	7.97	8.65	8.84
Services	5.85	9.83	11.39	13.91	14.61	6.83	7.39	7.37	7.98	8.16
AVERAGE WEEKLY EARNINGS										
Total	235	345	394	474	490	275	259	255	272	274
Mining	397	603	684	743	766	464	453	442	426	428
Construction	368	526	587	703	719	430	395	380	403	401
Manufacturing	289	442	515	598	604	337	332	333	343	337
Transportation, public utilities	351	496	557	626	644	410	373	360	359	359
Wholesale trade	267	411	476	585	604	312	309	308	336	337
Retail trade	147	194	221	273	283	172	146	143	157	158
Finance, insurance, real estate	210	357	442	547	575	245	268	286	314	321
Services	191	319	369	455	478	223	240	239	261	267

[1] Earnings in current dollars divided by the Consumer Price Index (CPI-W) on a 1982 base; see text, Section 14, Prices.

Source: U.S. Bureau of Labor Statistics, *Employment and Earnings*, monthly, March and June issues; and Internet site <http://www.bls.gov/ces/home.htm>.

No. 609. Annual Percent Changes in Earnings and Compensation: 1980 to 2001

[Annual percent change from immediate prior year. Minus sign (-) indicates decrease]

Item	1980	1985	1990	1995	1997	1998	1999	2000	2001
Current dollars:									
Hourly earnings, total [1]	8.1	3.0	3.6	2.8	3.9	4.1	3.6	3.9	4.2
Hourly earnings, manufacturing [2]	8.5	3.8	3.3	2.5	3.1	2.4	3.0	3.5	3.2
Compensation per employee-hour [3]	10.7	4.6	5.5	2.1	3.0	5.4	4.4	6.5	5.8
Constant (1982) dollars:									
Hourly earnings, total [1]	-4.8	-0.4	-1.6	-0.1	1.6	2.6	1.4	0.4	1.4
Hourly earnings, manufacturing [2]	-4.5	0.3	-1.7	-0.4	0.9	1.1	0.7	-	0.5
Compensation per employee-hour [3]	-0.3	1.2	0.5	-0.3	0.8	3.9	2.2	3.1	2.9

- Represents or rounds to zero.   [1] Production or nonsupervisory workers on private nonfarm payrolls.   [2] Production and related workers.   [3] Nonfarm business sector.

Source: U.S. Bureau of Labor Statistics, News USDL 02-261, *Productivity and Costs*, May 7, 2002; and Internet site <http://www.bls.gov/lpc/>.

No. 610. Mean Hourly Earnings and Weekly Hours for Metro and Nonmetro Areas by Selected Characteristics: 2000

[Covers civilian workers in private industry establishments and state and local governments in the 50 states and DC. Excludes private households, federal government and agriculture. Based on establishment survey; see source for details]

Item	Mean hourly earnings (dol.) [1]			Mean weekly hours		
	Total	Metro areas [2]	Nonmetro areas	Total	Metro areas [2]	Nonmetro areas
Total	**15.80**	**16.08**	**13.22**	**35.8**	**35.7**	**37.0**
Private industry	15.08	15.37	11.89	35.7	35.6	37.1
State and local government	20.00	20.76	16.68	36.7	36.6	36.8
WORKER CHARACTERISTIC						
White-collar occupations	19.35	19.59	16.46	36.0	36.0	36.9
Professional specialty and technical	25.57	25.95	21.80	35.8	35.7	36.3
Professional	(NA)	(NA)	(NA)	(NA)	(NA)	(NA)
Technical	(NA)	(NA)	(NA)	(NA)	(NA)	(NA)
Executive, administrative, and managerial	28.37	28.53	25.18	40.0	40.1	39.6
Sales	13.40	13.72	9.40	33.0	32.8	35.9
Administrative support	12.55	12.66	11.14	36.4	36.3	37.6
Blue-collar occupations	13.41	13.54	12.39	38.2	38.1	38.8
Precision production, craft, and repair	17.01	17.13	15.74	39.6	39.5	40.1
Machine operators, assemblers, and inspectors	11.88	11.94	11.59	39.2	39.1	39.7
Transportation and material moving	13.31	13.24	14.14	37.3	37.4	36.2
Handlers, equipment cleaners, helpers and laborers	10.15	10.22	9.64	35.8	35.6	37.1
Service occupations	9.59	9.66	9.13	31.8	31.4	34.7
Full time	16.66	17.01	13.56	39.6	39.6	39.6
Part time	9.06	9.07	8.90	20.5	20.5	20.3
Union [3]	19.02	19.35	16.38	37.0	36.8	38.2
Nonunion	15.12	15.41	12.43	35.6	35.5	36.7
Time [4]	15.57	15.83	13.26	35.7	35.6	37.0
Incentive [4]	20.19	20.61	11.57	38.2	38.1	39.5
ESTABLISHMENT CHARACTERISTIC						
Goods producing [5]	16.37	16.83	13.27	39.5	39.4	39.9
Service producing [5]	14.55	14.82	10.77	34.4	34.3	35.1
1 to 99 workers [6]	13.71	13.76	12.46	34.7	34.7	35.3
100 to 499 workers	15.31	15.76	12.94	36.3	36.2	36.7
500 to 999 workers	17.58	17.94	15.94	36.9	36.7	37.7
1,000 to 2,499 workers	17.35	19.10	12.17	36.9	36.4	38.3
2,500 workers or more	21.44	21.45	20.97	37.3	37.3	39.7
GEOGRAPHIC REGION [7]						
New England	17.45	17.63	14.97	35.4	35.5	34.4
Middle Atlantic	18.25	18.33	15.48	34.7	34.7	35.8
East North Central	15.75	15.90	14.47	35.8	35.7	37.1
West North Central	14.99	15.36	13.20	35.3	35.1	36.4
South Atlantic	14.90	15.13	12.98	36.5	36.4	37.5
East South Central	12.64	13.96	10.07	37.0	36.5	33.0
West South Central	14.57	14.59	14.33	36.8	36.9	36.7
Mountain	14.67	14.54	15.96	35.6	35.5	36.2
Pacific	17.15	17.19	16.02	35.6	35.5	37.0

NA Not available.   [1] Earnings are straight time hourly wages or salary, including incentive pay, cost-of-living adjustments, and hazard pay. Excludes premium pay for overtime, vacations and holidays, nonproduction bonuses and tips.   [2] Metropolitan areas defined as of 1994.   [3] Workers whose wages are determined through collective bargaining.   [4] Time worker wages are based solely on an hourly rate or salary. Incentive workers wages are based at least in part on productivity payments such as piece rates or commissions.   [5] For private industry only.   [6] Private establishments employing 1 to 99 workers and state and local government establishments employing 50 to 99 workers.   [7] Composition of regions: NEW ENGLAND: Maine, New Hampshire, Vermont, Massachusetts, Rhode Island, Connecticut. MIDDLE ATLANTIC: New York, New Jersey, and Pennsylvania. EAST NORTH CENTRAL: Ohio, Indiana, Illinois, Michigan, Wisconsin. WEST NORTH CENTRAL: Minnesota, Iowa, Missouri, North Dakota, South Dakota, Nebraska, and Kansas. SOUTH ATLANTIC: Delaware, Maryland, District of Columbia, Virginia, West Virginia. North Carolina, South Carolina, Georgia, Florida. EAST SOUTH CENTRAL: Kentucky, Tennessee, Alabama, Mississippi. WEST SOUTH CENTRAL: Arkansas, Louisiana, Oklahoma, and Texas. MOUNTAIN: Montana, Idaho, Wyoming, Colorado, New Mexico, Arizona, Utah, Nevada. PACIFIC: Washington, Oregon, California, Alaska, and Hawaii.

Source: U.S. Bureau of Labor Statistics, *National Compensation Survey: Occupational Wages in the United States, 2000,* Summary 01-04, September 2001.

U.S. Census Bureau, Statistical Abstract of the United States: 2002

No. 611. Average Annual Pay by State: 1999 and 2000

[In dollars, except percent change. For workers covered by state unemployment insurance laws and for federal civilian workers covered by unemployment compensation for federal employees, approximately 99 percent of wage and salary civilian employment in 2000. Excludes most agricultural workers on small farms, all Armed Forces, elected officials in most states, railroad employees, most domestic workers, most student workers at school, employees of certain nonprofit organizations, and most self-employed individuals. Pay includes bonuses, cash value of meals and lodging, and tips and other gratuities]

State	Average annual pay 1999	Average annual pay 2000, prel.	Percent change, 1999-00	State	Average annual pay 1999	Average annual pay 2000, prel.	Percent change, 1999-00
United States.	33,340	35,296	5.9	Missouri	29,967	31,386	4.7
Alabama	28,095	29,037	3.4	Montana	23,260	24,264	4.3
Alaska	34,033	35,125	3.2	Nebraska	26,632	27,662	3.9
Arizona	30,525	32,606	6.8	Nevada.	31,213	32,276	3.4
Arkansas.	25,371	26,307	3.7	New Hampshire	32,141	34,731	8.1
California.	37,577	41,194	9.6	New Jersey	41,038	43,691	6.5
Colorado.	34,191	37,167	8.7	New Mexico.	26,267	27,498	4.7
Connecticut	42,682	45,445	6.5	New York	42,179	44,942	6.6
Delaware.	35,157	36,677	4.3	North Carolina	29,462	31,077	5.5
District of Columbia. . . .	50,885	53,018	4.2	North Dakota	23,751	24,678	3.9
Florida	28,935	30,549	5.6	Ohio.	31,395	32,510	3.6
Georgia	32,332	34,182	5.7	Oklahoma	25,813	26,980	4.5
Hawaii	29,794	30,630	2.8	Oregon	30,872	32,765	6.1
Idaho	26,044	27,709	6.4	Pennsylvania	32,696	33,999	4.0
Illinois.	36,296	38,044	4.8	Rhode Island	31,169	32,618	4.6
Indiana	30,027	31,015	3.3	South Carolina	27,132	28,173	3.8
Iowa.	26,953	27,928	3.6	South Dakota	23,767	24,803	4.4
Kansas.	28,031	29,357	4.7	Tennessee.	29,478	30,558	3.7
Kentucky.	27,783	28,829	3.8	Texas	32,898	34,948	6.2
Louisiana	27,216	27,877	2.4	Utah.	27,895	29,226	4.8
Maine	26,887	27,664	2.9	Vermont	27,597	28,920	4.8
Maryland.	34,489	36,373	5.5	Virginia	33,025	35,151	6.4
Massachusetts	40,352	44,326	9.8	Washington	35,736	37,059	3.7
Michigan	35,750	37,016	3.5	West Virginia	26,018	26,887	3.3
Minnesota	33,487	35,418	5.8	Wisconsin	29,607	30,697	3.7
Mississippi.	24,391	25,197	3.3	Wyoming.	25,647	26,837	4.6

Source: U.S. Bureau of Labor Statistics, News USDL 01-295, September 11, 2001, Average Annual Pay by State and Industry.

No. 612. Average Annual Pay by Selected Metropolitan Area: 1999 and 2000

[In dollars. Metropolitan areas ranked by average pay 2000. Includes data for metropolitan statistical areas and primary metropolitan statistical areas defined as of June 1999. In the New England areas, the New England County metropolitan area (NECMA) definitions were used. See source for details. See also headnote, Table 611]

Metropolitan area	1999	2000, prel.	Metropolitan area	1999	2000, prel.
Metropolitan areas	34,890	36,986	New London-Norwich, CT.	35,404	36,727
San Jose, CA.	61,117	76,076	Anchorage, AK.	35,706	36,619
San Francisco, CA	50,125	59,314	Sacramento, CA	34,269	36,598
New York, NY	52,467	56,377	Monmouth-Ocean, NJ	34,610	36,463
New Haven-Bridgeport-Stamford-			Flint, MI	35,808	36,418
Waterbury-Danbury, CT	47,133	50,585	Charlotte-Gastonia-Rock Hill, NC-SC .	34,374	36,193
Middlesex-Somerset-Hunterdon, NJ . .	46,200	48,977	Rochester, MN.	35,023	36,111
Newark, NJ	44,647	48,733	Dutchess County, NY	35,274	36,063
Jersey City, NJ.	43,046	47,514	Santa Cruz-Watsonville, CA	31,025	35,826
Boulder-Longmont, CO	40,002	45,565	Santa Rosa, CA	32,092	35,796
Washington, DC-MD-VA-WV	42,660	45,333	Huntsville, AL.	34,177	35,650
Boston-Worcester-Lawrence-Lowell-			Baltimore, MD	33,862	35,578
Brockton, MA-NH	40,892	45,191	Corvallis, OR	33,693	35,355
Seattle-Bellevue-Everett, WA	43,925	45,171	Saginaw-Bay City-Midland, MI.	33,947	35,335
Trenton, NJ	42,445	44,576	West Palm Beach-Boca Raton, FL. . . .	32,824	35,219
Oakland, CA	40,994	44,170	Cincinnati, OH-KY-IN	33,627	35,049
Bergen-Passaic, NJ.	41,511	43,789	Kansas City, MO-KS	33,030	34,993
Hartford, CT.	40,059	42,394	Phoenix-Mesa, AZ	32,430	34,915
Detroit, MI.	40,781	42,303	Saint Louis, MO-IL	33,354	34,913
Dallas, TX	39,259	42,133	Indianapolis, IN	33,658	34,880
Chicago, IL	39,525	41,549	Cleveland-Lorain-Elyria, OH	33,435	34,704
Denver, CO	38,115	41,413	Milwaukee-Waukesha, WI	33,372	34,612
Austin-San Marcos, TX	38,940	41,012	Fort Worth-Arlington, TX	32,941	34,587
Houston, TX	38,107	40,986	Springfield, IL.	33,988	34,529
Kokomo, IN	39,651	40,240	Richmond-Petersburg, VA	32,987	34,480
Wilmington-Newark, DE-MD	38,071	39,899	Brazoria, TX	33,264	34,361
Atlanta, GA	37,303	39,704	Bloomington-Normal, IL	32,895	34,226
Los Angeles-Long Beach, CA	37,788	39,671	Cedar Rapids, IA	32,506	34,109
Minneapolis-St. Paul, MN-WI	37,229	39,549	Columbus, OH	32,400	33,946
Orange County, CA	37,452	39,208	Lansing-East Lansing, MI	32,358	33,908
Philadelphia, PA-NJ.	37,333	39,197	Pittsburgh, PA	33,048	33,837
Nassau-Suffolk, NY.	36,948	38,941	Albany-Schenectady-Troy, NY.	31,899	33,815
Raleigh-Durham-Chapel Hill, NC	34,803	37,775	Yolo, CA	32,362	33,395
San Diego, CA	34,722	37,516	Miami, FL	32,067	33,328
Ann Arbor, MI	35,773	37,446	Birmingham, AL	32,092	33,284
Ventura, CA.	33,978	37,102	Nashville, TN	31,717	33,268
Portland-Vancouver, OR-WA	34,382	37,043	Memphis, TN-AR-MS.	32,429	33,248

Source: U.S. Bureau of Labor Statistics, News USDL 01-318, September 28, 2001, Average Annual Pay Levels in Metropolitan Areas.

No. 613. Full-Time Wage and Salary Workers—Number and Earnings: 1990 to 2001

[In current dollars of usual weekly earnings. Data represent annual averages (85,804 represents 85,804,000). See text, this section, and headnote Table 577, for a discussion of occupational data. Based on Current Population Survey; see text, Section 1, Population, and Appendix III. For definition of median, see Guide to Tabular Presentation]

Characteristic	Number of workers (1,000)				Median weekly earnings (dol.)			
	1990 [1]	1995 [1]	2000 [1]	2001	1990 [1]	1995 [1]	2000 [1]	2001
All workers [2]	85,804	89,282	99,917	99,599	412	479	576	597
Male	49,564	51,222	56,273	55,928	481	538	646	672
16 to 24 years old	6,824	6,118	6,786	6,554	282	303	376	392
25 years old and over	42,740	45,104	49,487	49,374	512	588	700	722
Female	36,239	38,060	43,644	43,671	346	406	491	511
16 to 24 years old	5,227	4,366	5,147	5,098	254	275	342	354
25 years old and over	31,012	33,695	38,497	38,573	369	428	515	542
White	72,811	74,874	82,475	82,149	424	494	591	612
Male	42,797	43,747	47,578	47,279	494	566	669	694
Female	30,014	31,127	34,897	34,871	353	415	500	521
Black	9,820	10,596	12,556	12,533	329	383	468	487
Male	4,983	5,279	5,989	5,925	361	411	503	518
Female	4,837	5,317	6,568	6,607	308	355	429	451
Hispanic origin [3]	7,812	8,719	11,738	11,790	304	329	396	414
Male	5,000	5,597	7,261	7,230	318	350	414	438
Female	2,812	3,122	4,477	4,561	278	305	364	385
Occupation, male:								
Managerial and professional	12,255	13,684	15,875	16,265	729	829	994	1,038
Exec., admin., managerial	6,389	7,172	8,142	8,349	740	833	1,014	1,060
Professional specialty	5,866	6,512	7,733	7,916	719	827	977	1,021
Technical, sales, and administrative support ...	9,677	9,894	10,828	10,733	493	556	655	667
Tech. and related support.	1,762	1,688	1,882	1,870	567	641	761	783
Sales	4,692	5,000	5,583	5,599	502	579	684	692
Admin. support, incl. clerical	3,224	3,206	3,363	3,264	436	489	563	576
Service	4,602	4,779	5,284	5,331	317	357	414	438
Private household	12	15	20	15	(B)	(B)	(B)	(B)
Protective	1,531	1,691	1,771	1,783	477	552	659	658
Other service	3,059	3,073	3,493	3,532	271	300	357	374
Precision production [4]	10,259	10,046	11,075	11,018	486	534	628	648
Mechanics and repairers	3,687	3,658	4,024	3,951	475	538	649	670
Construction trades	3,650	3,541	4,341	4,407	478	507	599	613
Other	2,922	2,847	2,709	2,660	508	574	651	684
Operators, fabricators and laborers	11,464	11,529	11,837	11,310	375	413	487	501
Machine operators, assemblers, and inspectors.	4,594	4,576	4,240	3,954	387	421	495	512
Transportation and material moving	3,752	3,870	4,221	4,149	416	482	558	587
Handlers, equipment cleaners, helpers, and laborers	3,118	3,083	3,376	3,207	306	328	394	401
Farming, forestry, and fishing	1,306	1,290	1,374	1,271	261	294	347	366
Occupation, female:								
Managerial and professional	10,575	12,609	15,580	15,956	510	605	709	732
Exec., admin., managerial	4,758	5,803	7,226	7,446	484	570	686	706
Professional specialty	5,816	6,806	8,354	8,510	534	632	725	749
Technical, sales, and administrative support ...	16,290	16,004	17,424	17,411	331	383	452	473
Tech. and related support.	1,476	1,506	1,769	1,883	417	480	541	580
Sales	3,554	3,862	4,550	4,574	290	330	407	429
Admin. support, incl. clerical	11,260	10,636	11,105	10,954	332	384	449	469
Service	4,577	4,838	5,736	5,812	230	264	316	335
Private household	305	324	348	340	171	193	261	255
Protective	217	266	341	383	405	438	500	509
Other service	4,055	4,249	5,047	5,089	230	264	314	332
Precision production [4]	900	957	1,088	1,012	316	371	445	479
Mechanics and repairers	139	150	203	201	458	550	627	594
Construction trades	50	66	88	94	393	400	475	437
Other	711	741	796	717	299	346	414	451
Operators, fabricators, and laborers	3,722	3,462	3,574	3,258	261	297	351	368
Machine operators, assemblers, and inspectors.	2,878	2,559	2,396	2,119	259	296	355	369
Transportation and material moving	227	261	366	356	314	354	407	439
Handlers, equipment cleaners, helpers, and laborers	616	642	812	783	249	284	320	342
Farming, forestry, and fishing	175	190	242	222	216	249	294	308

B Data not shown where base is less than 50,000.   [1] See footnote 2, Table 560.   [2] Includes other races, not shown separately.   [3] Persons of Hispanic origin may be of any race.   [4] Includes craft and repair.

Source: U.S. Bureau of Labor Statistics, Bulletin 2307, and *Employment and Earnings*, monthly, January issues; and unpublished data.

No. 614. Workers With Earnings by Occupation of Longest Held Job and Sex: 2000

[**Earnings as of March 2000.** Covers persons 15 years old and over, 2001 **(70,718 represents 70,718,000).** Based on Current Population Survey; see text, Section 1, Population, and Appendix III. For definition of median, see Guide to Tabular Presentation]

Major occupation of longest job held	All workers				Full-time, year-round			
	Women		Men		Women		Men	
	Number (1,000)	Median earnings	Number (1,000)	Median earnings	Number (1,000)	Median earnings	Number (1,000)	Median earnings
Total [1]	70,718	20,309	79,098	31,039	41,571	27,352	58,734	37,339
Executive, administrators, and managerial .	10,063	33,527	11,408	52,283	7,860	36,954	9,963	57,164
Professional specialty	12,152	32,428	10,289	51,280	7,353	39,319	8,129	58,363
Technical and related support	2,652	27,423	2,218	41,018	1,853	31,039	1,813	44,154
Sales	9,262	12,303	8,801	31,828	4,533	25,618	6,428	41,266
Admin. support, incl. clerical.	16,313	20,267	4,430	25,896	10,127	25,196	2,979	32,626
Precision production, craft and repair	1,374	21,237	14,480	31,266	935	26,092	11,478	35,197
Machine operators, assemblers, and inspectors	3,055	16,721	4,875	26,174	2,027	20,353	3,854	29,592
Transportation and material moving	690	14,116	5,476	27,456	320	21,826	4,117	31,148
Handlers, equipment cleaners, helpers, and laborers	1,249	11,681	5,192	15,015	635	17,387	2,659	22,153
Service workers	13,063	10,437	8,137	16,704	5,574	16,873	4,954	25,052
Private household	925	6,238	50	(B)	267	11,893	18	(B)
Service, except private household	12,138	10,725	8,087	16,755	5,306	17,085	4,936	25,056
Farming, forestry, and fishing	774	8,999	3,161	13,637	294	17,618	1,772	19,583

B Base less than 75,000. [1] Includes people whose longest job was in the Armed Forces.

Source: U.S. Census Bureau, *Current Population Reports*, P60-213; and Internet site <http›ww.census.gov/hhes/income/dinctabs.html>.

No. 615. Employment Cost Index (ECI), Compensation by Occupation and Industry: 1982 to 2001

[**As of December.** The ECI is a measure of the rate of change in employee compensation (wages, salaries, and employer costs for employee benefits). Data are not seasonally adjusted: 1982 and 1985 based on fixed employment counts from 1970 Census of Population; 1990 based on fixed employment counts from the 1980 Census of Population; Beginning 1995 based primarily on 1990 Occupational Employment Survey]

Item	Indexes (June 1989=100)						Percent change for 12 months ending Dec.—				
	1982	1985	1990	1995	2000	2001	1985	1990	1995	2000	2001
Civilian workers [1]	74.8	86.8	107.6	127.2	150.6	156.8	4.3	4.9	2.7	4.1	4.1
Workers, by occupational group:											
White-collar occupations	72.9	85.8	108.3	128.0	152.5	158.9	4.9	5.2	2.9	4.2	4.2
Blue-collar occupations	78.2	88.4	106.5	125.8	146.5	152.0	3.3	4.4	2.5	4.2	3.8
Service occupations	74.3	87.2	108.0	127.4	150.0	156.9	3.9	5.1	2.5	3.6	4.6
Workers, by industry division:											
Manufacturing	76.9	87.8	107.2	128.3	149.3	154.6	3.3	5.1	2.6	4.0	3.5
Nonmanufacturing[2]	73.9	86.4	107.8	126.8	150.7	157.2	4.7	4.9	2.8	4.1	4.3
Service industries	70.5	84.1	110.2	129.4	152.4	159.0	4.7	6.3	2.4	4.0	4.3
Public administration [3]	71.9	85.4	108.7	128.3	148.3	155.2	4.9	5.3	3.3	2.7	4.7
State and local government. . .	70.8	84.6	110.4	129.3	148.9	155.2	5.6	5.8	2.9	3.0	4.2
Workers, by occupational group:											
White-collar occupations	70.4	84.2	110.9	129.1	148.3	154.4	5.8	6.0	2.9	3.0	4.1
Blue-collar workers	73.9	86.7	108.7	128.0	147.2	153.2	5.3	4.8	2.6	3.3	4.1
Workers, by industry division:											
Service industries	70.0	84.0	111.3	129.6	148.9	154.9	5.9	6.3	2.8	3.0	4.0
Schools	69.0	83.6	111.6	129.8	149.0	154.8	6.2	6.0	2.8	3.0	3.9
Elementary and secondary	68.6	83.6	112.1	130.1	148.1	153.1	6.4	6.3	2.8	2.8	3.4
Colleges and universities	(NA)	(NA)	110.2	128.7	151.7	159.6	(NA)	5.3	2.5	3.5	5.2
Services, excluding schools [4]	73.1	85.2	110.2	129.4	148.8	156.1	4.7	6.8	3.0	3.5	4.9
Public administration [3]	71.9	85.4	108.7	128.3	148.3	155.2	4.9	5.3	3.3	2.7	4.7
Private industry workers [5]	75.8	87.3	107.0	126.7	150.9	157.2	3.9	4.6	2.6	4.4	4.2
Workers, by occupational group:											
White-collar occupations	73.7	86.4	107.4	127.6	153.6	160.1	4.9	4.9	2.8	4.6	4.2
Blue collar occupations	78.4	88.5	106.4	125.6	146.4	151.9	3.1	4.4	2.4	4.2	3.8
Service occupations	76.3	88.4	107.3	125.2	148.1	154.8	3.0	4.7	1.9	3.9	4.5
Workers, by industry division:											
Manufacturing	76.9	87.8	107.2	128.3	149.3	154.6	3.3	5.1	2.6	4.0	3.5
Nonmanufacturing[2]	75.1	87.0	106.9	125.9	151.1	157.6	4.3	4.5	2.7	4.6	4.3
Service industries[2]	(NA)	84.1	109.3	129.4	154.1	161.0	(NA)	6.2	2.2	4.4	4.5
Business services	(NA)	(NA)	107.4	126.3	158.4	166.2	(NA)	6.0	2.7	4.3	4.9
Health services	(NA)	83.7	110.8	132.2	150.6	158.4	(NA)	6.8	2.7	4.4	5.2
Hospitals	(NA)	(NA)	110.7	131.3	151.1	160.3	(NA)	7.0	2.1	4.5	6.1
Workers by bargaining status:											
Union	79.6	90.1	106.2	127.7	146.9	153.1	2.6	4.3	2.8	4.0	4.2
Nonunion	74.3	86.3	107.3	126.5	151.6	157.8	4.6	4.8	2.7	4.4	4.1

NA Not available. [1] Includes private industry and state and local government workers and excludes farm, household, and federal government workers. [2] Includes other industries not shown separately. [3] Consists of executive, legislative, judicial, administrative, and regulatory activities. [4] Includes library, social, and health services. Formerly called hospitals and other services. [5] Excludes farm and household workers.

Source: U.S. Bureau of Labor Statistics, *News, Employment Cost Index,* quarterly; and Internet site <http://www.bls.gov/ncs/ect/home.htm>.

No. 616. Federal Minimum Wage Rates: 1950 to 2000

Year	Value of the minimum wage — Current dollars	Value of the minimum wage — Constant (2000) dollars [1]	Year	Value of the minimum wage — Current dollars	Value of the minimum wage — Constant (2000) dollars [1]
1950	0.75	5.36	1976	2.30	6.96
1952	0.75	4.87	1977	2.30	6.54
1953	0.75	4.84	1978	2.65	7.00
1954	0.75	4.80	1979	2.90	6.88
1955	0.75	4.82	1980	3.10	6.48
1956	1.00	6.33	1981	3.35	6.35
1957	1.00	6.13	1982	3.35	5.98
1958	1.00	5.96	1983	3.35	5.79
1959	1.00	5.92	1984	3.35	5.55
1960	1.00	5.82	1985	3.35	5.36
1961	1.15	6.62	1986	3.35	5.26
1962	1.15	6.56	1987	3.35	5.08
1963	1.25	7.03	1988	3.35	4.88
1964	1.25	6.94	1989	3.35	4.65
1965	1.25	6.83	1990	3.80	5.01
1966	1.25	6.64	1991	4.25	5.37
1967	1.40	7.22	1992	4.25	5.22
1968	1.60	7.92	1993	4.25	5.06
1969	1.60	7.51	1994	4.25	4.94
1970	1.60	7.10	1995	4.25	4.80
1971	1.60	6.80	1996	4.75	5.21
1972	1.60	6.59	1997	5.15	5.53
1973	1.60	6.21	1998	5.15	5.44
1974	2.00	6.99	1999	5.15	5.32
1975	2.10	6.72	2000	5.15	5.15

[1] Adjusted for inflation using the CPI-U; see text, Section 14, Prices.

Source: U.S. Employment Standards Administration, Internet site: <http://www.dol.gov/esa/minwage/chart2.htm> (accessed 30 May 2002).

No. 617. Workers Paid Hourly Rates by Selected Characteristics: 2001

[Data are annual averages (72,486 represents 72,486,000). For employed wage and salary workers. Based on Current Population Survey; see text, Section 1, Population, and Appendix III]

Characteristic	Number of workers [1] (1,000) — Total paid hourly rates	At or below $5.15 — Total	At or below $5.15 — At $5.15	At or below $5.15 — Below $5.15	Percent of all workers paid hourly rates — At or below $5.15 — Total	At or below $5.15 — At $5.15	At or below $5.15 — Below $5.15	Median hourly earnings of workers paid hourly rates [2]
Total, 16 years and over [3]	72,486	2,238	636	1,602	3.1	0.9	2.2	$10.17
16 to 24 years	16,602	1,206	376	830	7.3	2.3	5.0	7.65
16 to 19 years	6,319	629	241	388	10.0	3.8	6.1	6.75
25 years and over	55,884	1,032	260	771	1.8	0.5	1.4	11.47
Male, 16 years and over	36,029	784	255	529	2.2	0.7	1.5	11.36
16 to 24 years	8,491	473	177	296	5.6	2.1	3.5	7.97
16 to 19 years	3,153	274	119	155	8.7	3.8	4.9	6.90
25 years and over	27,538	311	78	233	1.1	0.3	0.8	13.00
Women, 16 years and over	36,457	1,454	381	1,073	4.0	1.0	2.9	9.57
16 to 24 years	8,111	733	199	534	9.0	2.5	6.6	7.21
16 to 19 years	3,166	355	122	233	11.2	3.9	7.4	6.62
25 years and over	28,346	721	182	539	2.5	0.6	1.9	10.19
White	59,152	1,861	502	1,359	3.1	0.8	2.3	10.25
Black	10,014	297	114	183	3.0	1.1	1.8	9.66
Hispanic origin [4]	10,030	302	114	187	3.0	1.1	1.9	8.98
Full-time workers [5]	55,232	853	191	662	1.5	0.3	1.2	11.19
Part-time workers [5]	17,124	1,378	441	937	8.0	2.6	5.5	7.60
Private sector industries	63,520	2,100	572	1,528	3.3	0.9	2.4	10.04
Goods-producing [6]	18,496	157	64	93	0.8	0.3	0.5	11.93
Service-producing [7]	45,024	1,944	509	1,435	4.3	1.1	3.2	9.43
Public sector	8,966	138	64	74	1.5	0.7	0.8	12.33

[1] Excludes the incorporated self-employed. [2] For definition of median, see Guide to Tabular Presentation. [3] Includes races not shown separately. Also includes a small number of multiple jobholders whose full- part- time status can not be determined for their principal job. [4] Persons of Hispanic origin may be of any race. [5] Working fewer than 35 hours per week. [6] Includes agriculture, mining, construction, and manufacturing. [7] Includes transportation and public utilities; wholesale trade; finance, insurance, and real estate; private households; and other service industries.

Source: U.S. Bureau of Labor Statistics, Employment and Earnings, January 2002.

Labor Force, Employment, and Earnings 405

No. 618. Employer Costs for Employee Compensation Per Hour Worked: 2002

[In dollars. As of March, for private industry workers. Based on a sample of establishments; see source for details]

Compensation component	Total	Goods producing [1]	Service producing [2]	Manufacturing	Non-manufacturing	Union members	Non-union members	Full-time workers	Part-time workers
Total compensation . . .	**21.71**	**25.44**	**20.66**	**25.20**	**21.06**	**29.42**	**20.79**	**24.57**	**12.14**
Wages and salaries	15.80	17.47	15.33	17.19	15.55	19.33	15.38	17.61	9.76
Total benefits.	5.90	7.96	5.33	8.01	5.51	10.09	5.41	6.96	2.38
Paid leave	1.44	1.66	1.37	1.91	1.35	2.08	1.36	1.75	0.40
Vacation.	0.72	0.86	0.68	0.97	0.67	1.08	0.68	(NA)	(NA)
Holiday	0.49	0.60	0.46	0.70	0.45	0.68	0.47	(NA)	(NA)
Sick	0.17	0.12	0.18	0.14	0.17	0.23	0.16	(NA)	(NA)
Other	0.06	0.08	0.06	0.10	0.05	0.10	0.06	(NA)	(NA)
Supplemental pay	0.62	1.11	0.48	1.13	0.52	1.08	0.56	0.75	0.18
Premium pay	0.24	0.54	0.16	0.56	0.18	0.66	0.19	(NA)	(NA)
Shift pay	0.06	0.08	0.05	0.11	0.05	0.16	0.04	(NA)	(NA)
Nonproduction bonuses .	0.32	0.49	0.27	0.46	0.29	0.26	0.33	(NA)	(NA)
Insurance	1.40	2.01	1.22	2.11	1.27	2.76	1.23	1.69	0.40
Health insurance	1.29	1.84	1.13	1.92	1.17	2.57	1.13	(NA)	(NA)
Retirement and savings . . .	0.63	0.88	0.56	0.74	0.61	1.64	0.51	0.77	0.15
Defined benefit	0.23	0.42	0.17	0.30	0.21	1.16	0.12	(NA)	(NA)
Defined contributions . . .	0.40	0.46	0.39	0.44	0.40	0.48	0.39	(NA)	(NA)
Legally required	1.80	2.25	1.67	2.05	1.75	2.46	1.72	1.96	1.24
Social security.	1.32	1.49	1.27	1.48	1.29	1.65	1.28	(NA)	(NA)
Federal unemployment . .	0.03	0.03	0.03	0.03	0.03	0.03	0.03	(NA)	(NA)
State unemployment . . .	0.10	0.12	0.09	0.11	0.09	0.13	0.09	(NA)	(NA)
Workers compensation . .	0.35	0.61	0.28	0.43	0.34	0.65	0.32	(NA)	(NA)
Other benefits [3]	0.03	0.05	0.02	0.07	0.02	0.07	0.02	0.03	-

- Represents or rounds to zero. NA Not available. [1] Mining, construction, and manufacturing. [2] Transportation, communications, and public utilities, wholesale and retail trade, finance, insurance, and real estate, and services. [3] Includes severance pay and supplemental unemployment benefits.

Source: U.S. Bureau of Labor Statistics, *News, Employer Costs for Employee Compensation*, USDL, 02-346, June 19, 2002.

No. 619. Employees With Employer- or Union-Provided Pension Plans or Group Health Plans: 2000

[Total in thousands (150,006 represents 150,006,000). For wage and salary workers 15 years old and over as of **March 2001.** Based on Current Population Survey; see text, Section 1, Population, and Appendix III. Data based on 1990 population controls]

Occupation	Total (1,000)	Percent— Included in pension plan	Percent— With group health plan	Characteristic	Total (1,000)	Percent— Included in pension plan	Percent— With group health plan
Total.	**150,006**	**44.5**	**54.2**	AGE			
Executive, admin., managerial . . .	21,478	59.2	68.4	Total.	150,006	44.5	54.2
Professional specialty	22,446	62.4	68.2	15 to 24 years	25,239	14.4	23.5
				25 to 44 years old	71,545	48.6	59.3
Technical/related support	4,878	57.7	70.2	45 to 64 years	47,640	56.7	64.4
Sales workers	18,079	33.9	44.5	65 years and over	5,582	25.3	40.5
Admin. support, inc. clerical	20,801	48.4	56.4	WORK EXPERIENCE			
				Worked.	150,006	44.5	54.2
Precision prod., craft/repair	15,873	44.5	57.9	Full time	120,672	51.7	63.0
				50 weeks or more	100,365	56.2	67.6
Mach. operators, assemblers [1] . . .	7,930	45.0	62.0	27 to 49 weeks	12,086	38.0	50.5
Transportation/material moving . . .	6,189	43.4	58.3	26 weeks or fewer	8,221	16.9	25.4
Handlers, equipment cleaners [2] . .	6,459	24.9	35.4	Part time	29,335	15.0	18.0
				50 weeks or more	13,965	20.7	24.1
Service workers	21,206	24.4	32.8	27 to 49 weeks	6,197	15.7	16.7
Private households	975	2.7	6.5	26 weeks or fewer	9,173	6.1	9.4
Other	20,232	25.4	34.1	EMPLOYER SIZE			
				Under 25 persons	43,063	17.8	29.7
Farming, forestry and fishing	3,965	12.1	22.7	25 to 99 persons.	19,107	38.4	53.0
				100 to 499 persons	19,987	52.9	64.4
Armed Forces	702	67.2	38.2	500 to 999 persons	7,989	57.3	66.0
				Over 1,000 persons	59,860	61.2	67.2

[1] Includes inspectors. [2] Includes helpers and laborers.

Source: U.S. Census Bureau Internet site <http://ferret.bls.census.gov/macro/032001/noncash/toc.htm>.

No. 620. Percent of Workers With Access to Selected Employee Benefits in Private Industry: 1999

[Based on National Compensation Survey, a sample survey of 3,168 private industry establishments of all sizes, representing over 107 million workers; see Appendix III. See also Tables 139 and 140]

Characteristic	Paid vacation	Paid holidays	Employer assistance for child care	Adoption assistance	Long-term care insurance	Flexible work plans [1]	Nonwage cash payments			Section 125 cafeteria plans [4]			
							Non-production bonus [2]	Severance pay	Subsidized commuting [3]	Total	Flexible benefit plans	Reimbursement plans	Premium conversion plans
Total	79	75	6	6	6	3	42	22	4	28	7	15	6
WORKER CHARACTERISTICS													
Professional, technical, and	88	89	12	11	11	7	48	36	9	43	13	24	5
Clerical and sales employees	80	77	5	6	7	3	42	24	4	30	6	16	8
Blue-collar and service employees	75	69	4	3	3	1	39	14	3	20	10	10	4
Full time [5]	90	87	6	6	7	4	46	26	5	32	9	17	6
Part time [5]	43	36	6	2	4	1	28	8	3	14	3	8	3
Union [6]	86	82	5	7	3	2	29	28	7	24	7	12	4
Nonunion [6]	78	75	6	5	6	3	43	21	4	28	7	15	6
ESTABLISHMENT CHARACTERISTICS													
Goods producing [7]	84	84	2	7	5	3	47	25	4	26	9	12	5
Construction	63	68	1	1	1	1	50	6	2	8	1	4	3
Manufacturing	91	90	3	10	7	4	46	31	4	32	12	15	5
Service producing	77	73	7	9	6	3	40	21	5	28	7	15	7
Transportation and public utilities	92	86	1	9	12	1	53	29	11	36	14	13	8
Wholesale trade	89	91	4	5	6	8	43	24	1	30	9	16	5
Retail trade	64	50	4	2	6	1	29	13	1	18	2	11	5
Finance, insurance, and real estate	86	91	9	12	15	10	55	44	5	51	15	23	12
Services	79	77	10	5	4	2	41	19	6	28	6	17	5
1 to 99 workers	73	70	3	1	2	2	46	13	3	18	3	10	6
1 to 49 workers	70	66	3	1	2	3	46	10	1	13	3	6	5
50 to 99 workers	84	81	3	3	2	3	48	26	8	33	3	23	7
100 or more workers	86	82	10	11	10	4	37	31	6	39	13	21	6
100 to 499 workers	83	80	7	5	8	4	33	24	3	31	7	19	5
500 to 999 workers	89	87	8	12	8	2	45	33	6	39	13	19	8
1,000 to 2,499 workers	89	87	18	17	15	6	32	33	13	49	16	25	8
2,500 or more workers	88	82	14	22	19	6	48	53	12	61	33	24	4
Region: [8]													
Northeast	79	79	6	8	8	3	42	23	4	29	9	15	4
South	78	75	5	5	6	2	40	21	3	28	7	12	10
Midwest	80	76	7	5	6	4	44	21	4	28	6	15	4
West	79	72	5	4	4	3	43	23	9	26	5	18	2

[1] Arrangements permitting employees to work at home several days of the workweek. [2] A cash payment not directly related to output of the employee or group of employees, such as attendance or profit sharing bonuses. [3] Employers subsidize employees' cost of commuting to and from work via public transportation, company sponsored van pool, discounted subway fares, etc. [4] Under flexible benefit plans, employees are able to create a benefits package from among several options; reimbursement accounts are funded by employee pretax contributions to pay for health care or dependent care benefits; premium conversion plans allow medical plan participants to pay the required plan premium with pretax dollars. [5] Employees are classified as working either a full-time or part-time schedule based on the definition used by each establishment. [6] Union workers are those whose wages are determined through collective bargaining. [7] Includes mining not shown separately. [8] For composition of regions, see map, inside front cover.

Source: U.S. Bureau of Labor Statistics, Employee Benefits in Private Industry, , USDL 01-73, December 19, 2001.

Labor Force, Employment, and Earnings   407

No. 621. Workers Killed or Disabled on the Job: 1970 to 2000

[Data for 2000 are preliminary estimates (13.8 represents 13,800). Excludes homicides and suicides. Estimates based on data from the U.S. National Center for Health Statistics, State vital statistics departments, state industrial commissions and beginning 1992, Bureau of Labor Statistics, Census of Occupational Fatalities. Numbers of workers based on data from the U.S. Bureau of Labor Statistics]

Year	Deaths Total Number (1,000)	Total Rate [1]	Manufacturing Number (1,000)	Manufacturing Rate [1]	Non-manufacturing Number (1,000)	Non-manufacturing Rate [1]	Disabling injuries [2] (mil.)	Year and industry group	Deaths, 1999 Number	Rate [1]	Disabling injuries 1999 [2] (1,000)
1970 ...	13.8	18	1.7	9	12.1	21	2.2	Total	[3]5,200	3.8	3,900
1975 ...	13.0	15	1.6	9	11.4	17	2.2	Agriculture [4]	780	22.5	130
1980 ...	13.2	13	1.7	8	11.5	15	2.2	Mining and quarrying [5]	110	21.2	20
1985 ...	11.5	11	1.2	6	10.3	12	2.0	Construction	1,220	13.6	470
1990 ...	10.1	9	1.0	5	9.1	9	3.9	Manufacturing	660	3.3	630
1995 ...	5.0	4	0.6	3	4.4	4	3.6	Transportation and utilities	930	11.5	380
1996 ...	5.1	4	0.7	3	4.4	4	3.9	Trade [6]	420	1.5	750
1997 ...	5.2	4	0.7	3	4.5	4	3.8	Services [7]	630	1.3	940
1998 ...	5.1	4	0.6	3	4.5	4	3.8	Government	450	2.2	580
1999 ...	5.2	4	0.6	3	4.6	4	3.8				
2000 ...	5.2	4	0.7	3	4.5	3	3.9				

[1] Per 100,000 workers. [2] Disabling injury defined as one which results in death, some degree of physical impairment, or renders the person unable to perform regular activities for a full day beyond the day of the injury. Due to change in methodology, data beginning 1990 not comparable with prior years. [3] Includes deaths where industry is not known. [4] Includes forestry and fishing. [5] Includes oil and gas extraction. [6] Includes wholesale and retail trade. [7] Includes finance, insurance, and real estate.

Source: National Safety Council, Itasca, IL, *Accident Facts*, annual through 1998 edition; thereafter, *Injury Facts*, annual (copyright).

No. 622. Worker Deaths, Injuries, and Production Time Lost: 1995 to 2000

[45.7 represents 45,700. Data may not agree with Table 621 because data here are not revised]

Item	Deaths (1,000) 1995	1999	2000	Disabling injuries [1] (mil.) 1995	1999	2000	Production time lost (mil. days) In the current year 1995	1999	2000	In future years [2] 1995	1999	2000
All accidents	45.7	45.7	47	9.9	10.4	10.5	225	240	240	455	440	460
On the job	5.3	5.1	5.2	3.6	3.8	3.9	75	80	80	65	60	60
Off the job	40.4	40.6	41.8	6.3	6.6	6.6	150	160	160	390	380	400
Motor vehicle	22.9	21.0	22.8	1.2	1.1	1.2	(NA)	(NA)	(NA)	(NA)	(NA)	(NA)
Public nonmotor vehicle ...	7.5	9.1	8.3	2.3	3.0	2.8	(NA)	(NA)	(NA)	(NA)	(NA)	(NA)
Home	10.0	10.5	10.7	2.8	2.5	2.6	(NA)	(NA)	(NA)	(NA)	(NA)	(NA)

NA Not available. [1] See footnote 2, Table 621, for a definition of disabling injuries. [2] Based on an average of 5,850 days lost in future years per fatality and 565 days lost in future years per permanent injury.
Source: National Safety Council, Itasca, IL, *Accident Facts*, annual through 1998 edition; thereafter, *Injury Facts*, annual (copyright).

No. 623. Industries With the Highest Total Case Incidence Rates for Nonfatal Injuries and Illnesses: 1999 and 2000

[Rates per 100 full-time employees. Industries shown are those with the highest rates for 2000. For nonfarm employment data, see Table 603. Rates refer to any occupational injury or illness resulting in (1) lost workday cases, or (2) nonfatal cases without lost workdays. Incidence rates were calculated as: Number of injuries and illnesses divided by total hours worked by all employees during year multiplied by 200,000 as base for 100 full-time equivalent workers (working 40 hours per week, 50 weeks a year)]

Industry	1987 SIC [1] code	1999	2000	Industry	1987 SIC [1] code	1999	2000
Private industry	(X)	6.3	6.1	Fabricated structural metal	3441	15.2	16.7
Meat packing plants	2011	26.7	24.7	Leather tanning and finishing	311	15.7	16.5
Motor vehicles and car bodies.	3711	22.7	22.7	Public building and related furniture . .	253	14.9	15.8
Ship building and repairing	3731	20.2	22.0	Prefabricated wood buildings	2452	19.0	15.3
Gray and ductile iron foundries	3321	21.9	21.7	Automotive stampings	3465	20.1	15.3
Truck trailers	3715	16.6	21.1	Flat glass	321	12.2	15.2
Mobile homes	2451	17.3	19.7	Aluminum die-castings	3363	16.2	15.2
Truck and bus bodies	3713	18.0	19.4	Primary aluminum	3334	14.0	15.0
Transportation equipment, n.e.c. [2] ...	3799	14.1	18.9	Sausages and other prepared meats .	2013	13.5	14.7
Aluminum foundries.	3365	18.3	18.3	Air transportation, scheduled.	451	14.4	14.7
Industrial furnaces and ovens	3567	11.8	18.1	Iron and steel forgings	3462	17.8	14.6
Travel trailers and campers	3792	17.1	18.1	Bottled and canned soft drinks	2086	13.9	14.4
Structural wood members, n.e.c. [2] ...	2439	15.7	17.5	Poultry slaughtering and processing. .	2015	14.3	14.2
Metal sanitary ware.	3431	22.6	17.5	Brick and structural clay tile	3251	16.1	14.2
Plastics pipe	3084	12.9	17.2	Office furniture, except wood.	2522	12.5	14.0
Boat building and repairing	3732	14.5	17.0	Nursing and personal care facilities . .	805	13.5	13.9

X Not applicable. [1] 1987 Standard Industrial Classification; see text, this section. [2] N.e.c. means not elsewhere classified.
Source: U.S. Bureau of Labor Statistics, *Occupational Injuries and Illnesses in the United States by Industry*, annual.

No. 624. Nonfatal Occupational Injury and Illness Incidence Rates: 1999 and 2000

[Rates per 100 full-time employees. For nonfarm employment data, see Table 603. Rates refer to any occupational injury or illness resulting in (1) lost workday cases, or (2) nonfatal cases without lost workdays. Incidence rates were calculated as: Number of injuries and illnesses divided by total hours worked by all employees during year multiplied by 200,000 as base for 100 full-time equivalent workers (working 40 hours per week, 50 weeks a year)]

Industry	1987 SIC [1] code	1999	2000	Industry	1987 SIC [1] code	1999	2000
Private sector [2]	(X)	6.3	6.1	Trucking and warehousing	42	8.7	7.9
Agriculture, forestry, fishing [2]	A	7.3	7.1	Water transportation	44	8.0	7.0
Mining [3]	B	4.4	4.7	Transportation by air	45	13.3	13.9
Metal mining [3]	10	5.0	4.9	Pipelines, except natural gas	46	5.1	-
Coal mining [3]	12	7.4	7.5	Transportation services	47	3.8	3.2
Oil and gas extraction	13	3.5	4.2	Communications	48	3.1	2.6
Nonmetallic minerals, exc. fuels	14	4.3	4.3	Electric, gas, sanitary services	49	6.1	6.3
Construction	C	8.6	8.3	**Wholesale and retail trade**	F, G	6.1	5.9
General building contractors	15	8.0	7.8	Wholesale trade	F	6.3	5.8
Heavy construction, except				Retail trade	G	6.1	5.9
building	16	7.8	7.6	**Finance, insurance, real estate**	H	1.8	1.9
Special trade contractors	17	8.9	8.6	Depository institutions	60	1.5	1.4
Manufacturing	D	9.2	9.0	Nondepository institutions	61	1.0	1.1
Durable goods	(X)	10.1	9.8	Security and commodity brokers	62	0.6	.6
Lumber and wood products	24	13.0	12.1	Insurance carriers	63	1.9	1.9
Furniture and fixtures	25	11.5	11.2	Insurance agents, brokers, and			
Stone, clay, and glass products	32	10.7	10.4	service	64	0.9	1.0
Primary metal industries	33	12.9	12.6	Real estate	65	3.9	4.1
Fabricated metal products	34	12.6	11.9	Holding and other investment			
Industrial machinery and equip	35	8.5	8.2	offices	67	1.4	1.3
Electronic/other electric equip	36	5.7	5.7	**Services [4]**	I	4.9	4.9
Transportation equipment	37	13.7	13.7	Hotels and other lodging			
Instruments/related products	38	4.0	4.5	places	70	7.8	6.9
Miscellaneous manufacturing				Personal services	72	3.0	3.3
industries	39	8.4	7.2	Business services	73	3.0	3.2
Nondurable goods	(X)	7.8	7.8	Auto repair, services, and			
Food and kindred products	20	12.7	12.4	parking	75	6.1	5.0
Tobacco products	21	5.5	6.2	Miscellaneous repair services	76	5.2	4.9
Textile mill products	22	6.4	6.0	Motion pictures	78	2.9	3.4
Apparel and other textile				Amusement and recreation			
products	23	5.8	6.1	services	79	6.7	6.9
Paper and allied products	26	7.0	6.5	Health services	80	7.5	7.4
Printing and publishing	27	5.0	5.1	Legal services	81	1.0	.7
Chemicals and allied products	28	4.4	4.2	Educational services	82	2.9	3.2
Petroleum and coal products	29	4.1	3.7	Social services	83	5.6	6.1
Rubber and misc. plastics				Museums, botanical, zoological			
products	30	10.1	10.7	gardens	84	7.0	5.2
Leather and leather products	31	10.3	9.0	Membership organizations	86	3.1	3.0
Transportation/public utilities [3]	E	7.3	6.9	Engineering and management			
Railroad transportation [3]	40	3.6	3.6	services	87	1 7	1 7
Local passenger transit	41	9.1	8.0				

- Represents zero.   X Not applicable.   [1] 1987 Standard Industrial Classification; see text, this section .   [2] Excludes farms with fewer than 11 employees.   [3] Data conforming to OSHA definitions for employers in the railroad industry and for mining operators in coal, metal, and nonmetal mining. Independent mining contractors are excluded from the coal, metal, and nonmetal mining industries.   [4] Includes categories not shown separately.

Source: U.S. Bureau of Labor Statistics, *Occupational Injuries and Illnesses in the United States by Industry,* annual.

No. 625. Fatal Work Injuries by Cause: 2000

[For the 50 states and DC. Based on the 2000 Census of Fatal Occupational Injuries. Due to methodological differences, data differ from those in Table 621. For details, see source]

Cause	Number of fatalities	Percent distribu- tion	Cause	Number of fatalities	Percent distribu- tion
Total	**5,915**	**100**	Contacts with objects and equipment [1]	1,005	17
			Struck by object [1]	570	10
Transportation accidents [1]	2,571	43	Struck by falling objects	357	6
Highway accidents [1]	1,363	23	Struck by flying object	61	1
Collision between vehicles, mobile			Caught in or compressed by—		
equipment	694	12	Equipment or objects	294	5
Noncollision accidents	356	6	Collapsing materials	123	2
Nonhighway accident (farm, industrial					
premises)	399	7	Falls	734	12
Aircraft accidents	280	5	Exposure to harmful substances or		
Workers struck by a vehicle	370	6	environments	480	8
Water vehicle accidents	84	1	Contact with electric current	256	4
Railway accidents	71	1	Exposure to caustic, noxious		
			or allergenic substances	100	2
Assaults and violent acts [1]	929	16	Oxygen deficiency	93	2
Homicides [1]	677	11	Drowning, submersion	74	1
Shooting	533	9			
Stabbing	66	1	Fires and explosions	177	3
Self-inflicted injury	220	4	Other events and exposures	19	(Z)

Z Less than 0.5 percent.   [1] Includes other causes, not shown separately.

Source: U.S. Bureau of Labor Statistics, *USDL News,* Bulletin 00-261, August 14, 2001.

No. 626. Fatal Occupational Injuries by Industry and Event: 2000

[For the 50 states and DC. Based on the 2000 Census of Fatal Occupational Injuries. Due to methodological differences, data differ from those in Table 621. For details, see source]

Industry	1987 SIC [1] code	Fatal-ities [2]	Event or exposure—Percent distribution						Rate [5]
			Trans-portation incidents	Assaults/ violent acts	Contact with objects [3]	Falls	Expo-sure [4]		
Total.................	(X)	5,915	44	16	17	12	8		4
Private industry............	(X)	5,344	42	15	18	13	9		5
Agriculture, forestry, fishing........	A	720	51	7	25	9	8		21
Mining [6]...................	B	156	30	-	37	12	8		30
Coal mining...............	12	40	35	-	43	-	-		53
Oil and gas extraction........	13	83	30	-	30	12	8		27
Construction................	C	1,154	25	4	21	32	15		13
General building contractors......	15	175	14	7	18	43	12		-
Heavy construction, except building......	16	284	44	-	28	7	17		-
Special trade contractors........	17	672	20	4	19	40	15		-
Manufacturing [6]...............	D	668	31	7	38	7	10		3
Food and kindred products.......	20	68	37	-	31	9	15		4
Lumber and wood products .... [6]	24	186	31	3	57	-	5		24
Transportation and public utilities [6] ...	E	957	71	9	9	5	5		12
Local passenger transit........	41	84	42	55	-	-	-		15
Trucking and warehousing.......	42	566	80	4	9	4	2		21
Transportation by air..........	45	97	84	-	10	-	-		11
Electric, gas, sanitary services	49	84	54	-	13	-	18		8
Wholesale trade.............	F	230	54	11	17	9	6		4
Retail trade [6]...............	G	594	26	59	3	7	3		3
Food stores...............	54	145	10	86	-	-	-		4
Automotive dealer and service stations.............	55	95	41	43	-	-	-		4
Eating and drinking places.......	58	138	13	73	-	9	-		2
Finance, insurance, real estate......	H	79	41	33	6	13	8		1
Services [6].................	I	768	43	24	10	10	8		2
Business services............	73	199	45	20	8	15	10		2
Auto repair, services, and parking..................	75	132	28	30	24	-	-		8
Government..............	J	571	58	21	8	5	5		3

- No data reported or data do not meet publication standards.   X Not applicable.   [1] 1987 Standard Industrial Classification code, see text, this section.   [2] Includes 18 fatalities for which there was insufficient information to determine industry classification. Includes fatalities caused by other events and exposures, not shown separately.   [3] Includes equipment.   [4] Exposure to harmful substances or environments.   [5] Rate per 100,000 employed civilians 16 years old and over.   [6] Includes other industries, not shown separately.

Source: U.S. Bureau of Labor Statistics, *USDL News*, 01-261, August 14, 2001; and unpublished data.

No. 627. Work Stoppages: 1960 to 2001

[**896 represents 896,000.** Excludes work stoppages involving fewer than 1,000 workers and lasting less than 1 day. Information is based on reports of labor disputes appearing in daily newspapers, trade journals, and other public sources. The parties to the disputes are contacted by telephone, when necessary, to clarify details of the stoppages]

Year	Number of stop-pages [1]	Workers involved [2] (1,000)	Days idle		Year	Number of stop-pages [1]	Workers involved [2] (1,000)	Days idle	
			Number [3] (1,000)	Percent estimated working time [4]				Number [3] (1,000)	Percent estimated working time [4]
1960......	222	896	13,260	0.09	1985......	54	324	7,079	0.03
1965......	268	999	15,140	0.10	1986......	69	533	11,861	0.05
1969......	412	1,576	29,397	0.16	1987......	46	174	[5]4,481	0.02
1970......	381	2,468	52,761	0.29	1988......	40	118	[5]4,381	0.02
1971......	298	2,516	35,538	0.19	1989......	51	452	16,996	0.07
1972......	250	975	16,764	0.09	1990......	44	185	5,926	0.02
1973......	317	1,400	16,260	0.08	1991......	40	392	4,584	0.02
1974......	424	1,796	31,809	0.16	1992......	35	364	3,989	0.01
1975......	235	965	17,563	0.09	1993......	35	182	3,981	0.01
1976......	231	1,519	23,962	0.12	1994......	45	322	5,020	0.02
1977......	298	1,212	21,258	0.10	1995......	31	192	5,771	0.02
1978......	219	1,006	23,774	0.11	1996......	37	273	4,889	0.02
1979......	235	1,021	20,409	0.09	1997......	29	339	4,497	0.01
1980......	187	795	20,844	0.09	1998......	34	387	5,116	0.02
1981......	145	729	16,908	0.07	1999......	17	73	1,996	0.01
1982......	96	656	9,061	0.04	2000......	39	394	20,419	0.06
1983......	81	909	17,461	0.08	2001......	29	99	1,151	(Z)
1984......	62	376	8,499	0.04					

Z Less than 0.005 percent.   [1] Beginning in year indicated.   [2] Workers counted more than once if involved in more than one stoppage during the year.   [3] Resulting from all stoppages in effect in a year, including those that began in an earlier year.   [4] Agricultural and government employees are included in the total working time; private household and forestry and fishery employees are excluded.   [5] Revised since originally published.

Source: U.S. Bureau of Labor Statistics, *Work Stoppages Summary*, USDL 02-153, March 22, 2002.

No. 628. Labor Union Membership by Sector: 1983 to 2001

[See headnote, Table 630. **(17,717.4 represents 17,717,400)**]

Sector	1983	1985	1990	1995	1997	1998	1999	2000	2001
TOTAL (1,000)									
Wage and salary workers:									
Union members	17,717.4	16,996.1	16,739.8	16,359.6	16,109.9	16,211.4	16,476.7	16,258.2	16,288.8
Covered by unions	20,532.1	19,358.1	19,057.8	18,346.3	17,923.0	17,918.3	18,182.3	17,944.1	17,878.1
Public sector workers:									
Union members.	5,737.2	5,743.1	6,485.0	6,927.4	6,746.7	6,905.3	7,058.1	7,110.5	7,147.5
Covered by unions.	7,112.2	6,920.6	7,691.4	7,986.6	7,668.0	7,814.7	7,966.3	7,975.6	7,975.4
Private sector workers:									
Union members.	11,980.2	11,253.0	10,254.8	9,432.1	9,363.3	9,306.1	9,418.6	9,147.7	9,141.3
Covered by unions.	13,419.9	12,437.5	11,366.4	10,359.8	10,255.0	10,103.6	10,216.0	9,968.5	9,902.7
PERCENT									
Wage and salary workers:									
Union members	20.1	18.0	16.1	14.9	14.1	13.9	13.9	13.5	13.5
Covered by unions	23.3	20.5	18.3	16.7	15.6	15.4	15.3	14.9	14.8
Public sector workers:									
Union members.	36.7	35.7	36.5	37.7	37.2	37.5	37.3	37.5	37.4
Covered by unions.	45.5	43.1	43.3	43.5	42.3	42.5	42.1	42.0	41.7
Private sector workers:									
Union members.	16.5	14.3	11.9	10.3	9.7	9.5	9.4	9.0	9.0
Covered by unions.	18.5	15.9	13.2	11.3	10.6	10.3	10.2	9.8	9.7

Source: The Bureau of National Affairs, Inc., Washington, DC, *Union Membership and Earnings Data Book: Compilations from the Current Population Survey (2002 edition),* (copyright by BNA PLUS); authored by Barry Hirsch of Trinity University, San Antonio, TX and David Macpherson of Florida State University. Internet site <http://www.bna.com/bnaplus/labor/laborrpts.html>.

No. 629. Union Members by Selected Characteristics: 2001

[**Annual averages of monthly data (120,760 represents 120,760,000).** Covers employed wage and salary workers 16 years old and over. Excludes self-employed workers whose businesses are incorporated although they technically qualify as wage and salary workers. Based on Current Population Survey, see text, Section 1, Population, and Appendix III]

Characteristic	Employed wage and salary workers			Median usual weekly earnings [3] (dol.)			
		Percent					
	Total (1,000)	Union members [1]	Represented by unions [2]	Total	Union members [1]	Represented by unions [2]	Not represented by unions
Total [4]	**120,760**	**13.5**	**14.8**	**597**	**718**	**712**	**575**
16 to 24 years old	19,819	5.2	6.0	376	473	475	370
25 to 34 years old	27,710	11.5	12.8	579	654	646	563
35 to 44 years old	32,124	15.0	10.3	658	743	738	637
45 to 54 years old	26,503	18.9	20.6	693	776	774	663
55 to 64 years old	11,609	17.2	18.8	640	744	744	613
65 years and over	2,995	8.1	8.9	472	607	605	440
Men.	62,727	15.1	16.4	672	765	761	647
Women	58,033	11.7	13.1	511	643	639	494
White	**100,384**	**13.1**	**14.3**	**612**	**741**	**736**	**591**
Men.	52,970	14.8	16.0	694	784	781	669
Women	47,414	11.1	12.5	521	667	661	503
Black	**14,515**	**17.0**	**18.6**	**487**	**603**	**599**	**463**
Men.	6,660	18.9	20.4	518	649	637	498
Women	7,855	15.4	17.2	451	563	564	424
Hispanic [5].	**13,782**	**11.3**	**12.5**	**414**	**578**	**578**	**398**
Men.	7,950	11.8	12.9	438	611	612	414
Women	5,832	10.7	12.1	385	503	501	372
Full-time workers	99,599	14.9	16.3	597	718	712	575
Part-time workers	20,926	6.9	7.8	(X)	(X)	(X)	(X)
Managerial and professional specialty	36,276	12.8	14.8	859	865	860	859
Technical sales, and admin. support	35,953	8.9	10.0	521	613	606	513
Service occupations	17,156	13.3	14.4	377	556	550	352
Precision, production, craft, and repair	12,635	21.5	22.5	629	822	817	590
Operators, fabricators, and laborers.	16,888	19.9	20.9	467	620	613	425
Farming, forestry, and fishing	1,853	4.6	5.2	354	587	582	345
Private wage and salary workers.	101,605	9.0	9.7	580	684	676	566
Agricultural	1,667	1.6	2.0	371	(B)	(B)	370
Mining.	531	12.3	12.9	795	816	816	789
Construction	6,881	18.4	19.0	609	864	854	569
Manufacturing	18,149	14.6	15.5	613	645	641	607
Transportation and public utilities	7,422	23.5	24.7	705	796	792	669
Wholesale and retail trade, total.	25,045	4.7	5.1	468	540	528	464
Finance, insurance, and real estate	7,648	2.1	2.8	655	584	600	658
Services	34,261	5.9	6.8	580	599	597	579
Government	19,155	37.4	41.8	684	753	749	620

B Data not shown where base is less than 50,000.   X Not applicable.   [1] Members of a labor union or an employee association similar to a labor union.   [2] Members of a labor union or an employee association similar to a union as well as workers who report no union affiliation but whose jobs are covered by a union or an employee association contract.   [3] For full-time employed wage and salary workers.   [4] Includes races not shown separately. Also includes a small number of multiple jobholders whose full- and part- time status can not be determined for their principal job.   [5] Persons of Hispanic origin may be of any race.

Source: U.S. Bureau of Labor Statistics, *Employment and Earnings,* monthly, January 2002 issue.

No. 630. Labor Union Membership by State: 1983 and 2001

[Annual averages of monthly figures (17,717.4 represents 17,717,400). For wage and salary workers in agriculture and non-agriculture. Data represent union members by place of residence. Based on the Current Population Survey and subject to sampling error. For methodological details, see source. The 2001 figures are based on publicly released Current Population Survey files. Figures for 2001 differ slightly from annual figures compiled by the Bureau of Labor Statistics, which are based on nonpublic files that included an experimental sample during January-June 2001]

| State | Union members (1,000) | | Workers covered by unions (1,000) | | Percent of workers— | | | | | |
| | | | | | Union members | | Covered by unions | | Private sector union members | |
	1983	2001	1983	2001	1983	2001	1983	2001	1983	2001
United States..	17,717.4	16,288.8	20,532.1	17,878.1	20.1	13.5	23.3	14.8	16.5	9.0
Alabama [1]	228.2	180.7	268.2	201.7	16.9	9.9	19.8	11.0	15.3	6.5
Alaska	41.7	59.1	49.2	66.6	24.9	22.0	29.3	24.8	17.3	12.3
Arizona [1]	125.0	121.8	156.4	135.1	11.4	5.9	14.3	6.6	8.6	3.3
Arkansas [1]	82.2	64.3	103.2	79.1	11.0	6.3	13.8	7.7	10.2	4.5
California	2,118.9	2,391.7	2,505.2	2,613.6	21.9	16.4	25.9	18.0	17.7	9.7
Colorado.	177.9	177.5	209.6	204.0	13.6	9.2	16.0	10.5	11.2	6.2
Connecticut.	314.0	223.9	345.1	234.1	22.7	15.1	25.0	15.8	16.7	8.5
Delaware	49.2	45.9	54.1	50.4	20.1	12.4	22.1	13.6	15.9	8.2
District of Columbia .	52.4	40.5	69.4	50.5	19.5	16.7	25.9	20.8	15.2	11.3
Florida [1]	393.7	426.6	532.9	554.5	10.2	6.6	13.8	8.6	7.1	3.5
Georgia [1]	267.0	261.3	345.1	299.8	11.9	7.2	15.3	8.3	11.1	5.1
Hawaii	112.6	118.9	124.9	128.8	29.2	23.4	32.4	25.3	21.9	15.8
Idaho [1]	41.3	41.9	53.7	47.9	12.5	7.5	16.2	8.6	10.3	5.1
Illinois	1,063.8	999.1	1,205.1	1,059.9	24.2	18.3	27.4	19.4	21.5	13.7
Indiana	503.3	388.9	544.5	412.2	24.9	14.5	27.0	15.4	25.0	12.3
Iowa [1]	185.9	179.5	231.3	211.6	17.2	13.3	21.5	15.7	14.6	10.0
Kansas [1]	125.2	108.6	170.4	132.7	13.7	9.3	18.7	11.4	12.2	8.0
Kentucky	223.7	191.6	259.8	209.8	17.9	11.4	20.8	12.4	18.2	9.9
Louisiana [1]	204.2	137.1	267.8	178.2	13.8	7.8	18.1	10.2	11.0	4.8
Maine.	88.0	72.4	100.4	82.2	21.0	12.8	24.0	14.6	14.2	6.8
Maryland	346.5	334.6	423.1	399.3	18.5	13.7	22.6	16.4	14.4	7.8
Massachusetts.	603.2	421.0	661.4	451.7	23.7	14.8	26.0	15.9	17.6	8.7
Michigan.	1,005.4	972.7	1,084.6	1,010.9	30.4	21.8	32.8	22.7	25.3	16.3
Minnesota.	393.9	416.8	439.4	432.3	23.2	17.8	25.9	18.5	17.1	11.5
Mississippi [1]	79.4	60.3	99.7	97.8	9.9	5.5	12.5	8.8	9.0	5.2
Missouri	374.4	345.8	416.7	377.1	20.8	13.5	23.2	14.7	21.5	11.7
Montana.	49.5	48.1	55.5	54.7	18.3	13.2	20.5	15.0	14.8	7.3
Nebraska [1]	80.6	60.1	94.8	82.4	13.6	8.0	16.0	10.9	9.7	5.1
Nevada [1]	90.0	146.0	106.7	157.6	22.4	16.7	26.6	18.1	19.6	13.6
New Hampshire. . . .	48.5	56.9	60.8	63.2	11.5	9.6	14.4	10.6	7.5	4.8
New Jersey.	822.1	709.5	918.2	756.5	26.9	19.5	30.0	20.8	21.1	12.7
New Mexico	52.6	56.0	70.6	67.0	11.8	8.0	15.8	9.5	10.1	5.3
New York	2,155.6	2,024.9	2,385.9	2,099.4	32.5	26.7	36.0	27.7	24.0	16.7
North Carolina [1]	178.7	124.3	238.1	145.1	7.6	3.7	10.2	4.3	5.4	2.3
North Dakota [1]	28.4	20.5	35.1	23.4	13.2	7.2	16.3	8.2	9.5	4.4
Ohio [2]	1,011.0	899.1	1,125.0	966.5	25.1	17.7	27.9	19.0	22.5	12.4
Oklahoma [2]	131.5	115.9	168.2	128.4	11.5	8.4	14.7	9.3	9.1	5.7
Oregon.	222.9	223.2	261.9	240.8	22.3	15.5	26.2	16.7	16.4	9.1
Pennsylvania.	1,195.7	892.7	1,350.0	960.3	27.5	17.1	31.1	18.4	23.2	11.1
Rhode Island.	85.8	73.5	93.7	76.0	21.5	16.8	23.5	17.4	13.7	9.5
South Carolina [1] . . .	69.6	79.6	100.6	98.9	5.9	4.9	8.6	6.1	3.9	3.4
South Dakota [1]	26.8	19.3	34.8	24.0	11.5	5.8	14.9	7.3	8.0	3.5
Tennessee [1]	252.4	185.1	300.9	208.3	15.1	7.8	18.0	8.8	12.4	6.0
Texas [1]	583.7	502.0	712.8	598.0	9.7	5.7	11.9	6.8	8.1	3.6
Utah [1]	81.6	65.0	100.9	73.2	15.2	6.9	18.9	7.8	11.3	3.6
Vermont	25.9	29.7	31.5	34.0	12.6	10.7	15.3	12.3	6.7	5.7
Virginia [1]	268.3	172.1	346.1	215.7	11.7	5.3	15.1	6.6	10.2	3.6
Washington.	419.9	460.3	499.7	496.5	27.1	18.6	32.3	20.0	22.0	13.6
West Virginia.	142.7	106.3	160.6	115.8	25.3	14.6	28.5	15.9	26.1	12.2
Wisconsin	465.5	416.4	526.7	446.4	23.8	16.4	26.9	17.6	19.8	11.3
Wyoming [1]	27.1	19.7	31.8	24.0	13.9	9.0	16.2	11.0	10.4	6.1

[1] Right to work state.   [2] Passed right to work law in 2001.

Source: The Bureau of National Affairs, Inc., Washington, DC, *Union Membership and Earnings Data Book: Compilations from the Current Population Survey (2002 edition)*, (copyright by BNA PLUS); authored by Barry Hirsch of Trinity University, San Antonio, TX, and David Macpherson of Florida State University. Internet site <http://www.bna.com/bnaplus/labor/laborrpts.html>.

U.S. Census Bureau, Statistical Abstract of the United States: 2002

Section 13
Income, Expenditures, and Wealth

This section presents data on gross domestic product (GDP), gross national product (GNP), national and personal income, saving and investment, money income, poverty, and national and personal wealth. The data on income and expenditures measure two aspects of the U.S. economy. One aspect relates to the national income and product accounts (NIPAs), a summation reflecting the entire complex of the nation's economic income and output and the interaction of its major components; the other relates to the distribution of money income to families and individuals or consumer income.

The primary source for data on GDP, GNP, national and personal income, gross saving and investment, and fixed reproducible tangible wealth is the *Survey of Current Business,* published monthly by the Bureau of Economic Analysis (BEA). A comprehensive revision to the NIPAs was released beginning in October 1999. Discussions of the revision appeared in the August, September, October, December 1999, and the April 2000 issues of the *Survey of Current Business.* Summary historical estimates appeared in the August 2000 issue of the *Survey of Current Business.* Detailed historical data will appear in forthcoming *National Income and Product Accounts of the United States, 1929-97* report.

Sources of income distribution data are the decennial censuses of population and the Current Population Survey (CPS), both products of the U.S. Census Bureau (see text, Section 1 and new Section 31). Annual data on income of families, individuals, and households are presented in *Current Population Reports, Consumer Income,* P60 Series, in print, and many data series found on the census Web site at <http://www.census.gov/hhes/www.income.html>.

Data on individuals' saving and assets are published by the Board of Governors of the Federal Reserve System in the quarterly *Flow of Funds Accounts.* The Board also periodically conducts the *Survey of Consumer Finances,* which presents financial information on family assets and net worth. Detailed information on personal wealth is published periodically by the Internal Revenue Service (IRS) in *SOI Bulletin.*

National income and product—Gross domestic product is the total output of goods and services produced by labor and property located in the United States, valued at market prices. GDP can be viewed in terms of the expenditure categories that comprise its major components—purchases of goods and services by consumers and government, gross private domestic investment, and net exports of goods and services. The goods and services included are largely those bought for final use (excluding illegal transactions) in the market economy. A number of inclusions, however, represent imputed values, the most important of which is rental value of owner-occupied housing. GDP, in this broad context, measures the output attributable to the factors of production located in the United States. Gross state product (GSP) is the gross market value of the goods and services attributable to labor and property located in a state. It is the state counterpart of the nation's gross domestic product.

In January 1996, BEA replaced its fixed-weighted index as the featured measure of real GDP with an index based on chain-type annual weights. Changes in this measure of real output and prices are calculated as the average of changes based on weights for the current and preceding years. (Components of real output are weighted by price, and components of prices are weighted by output.) These annual changes are "chained" (multiplied) together to form a time series that allows for the effects of changes in relative prices and changes in the composition of output over time. Quarterly and monthly changes are also based on annual

Income, Expenditures, and Wealth   413

weights. The new output indexes are expressed as 1996=100, and for recent years, in 1996 dollars; the new price indexes are based to 1996=100.

Chained (1996) dollar estimates of most components of GDP are not published for periods prior to 1987, because during periods far from the base period, the levels of the components may provide misleading information about their contributions to an aggregate. Values are published in index form (1996=100) for 1929 to the present to allow users to calculate the percent changes for all components, changes which are accurate for all periods. In addition, the Bureau of Economic Analysis publishes estimates of the contribution of major components to the percent change in GDP for all periods.

Gross national product measures the output attributable to all labor and property supplied by United States residents. GNP differs from "national income" mainly in that GNP includes allowances for depreciation and for indirect business taxes (sales and property taxes); see Table 646.

In December 1991, the Bureau of Economic Analysis began featuring gross domestic product rather than gross national product as the primary measure of U.S. production. GDP is now the standard measure of growth because it is the appropriate measure for much of the short-term monitoring and analysis of the economy. In addition, the use of GDP facilitates comparisons of economic activity in the United States with that in other countries.

National income is the aggregate of labor and property earnings which arises in the current production of goods and services. It is the sum of employee compensation, proprietors' income, rental income of persons, corporate profits, and net interest. It measures the total factor costs of the goods and services produced by the economy. Income is measured before deduction of taxes.

Capital consumption adjustment for corporations and for nonfarm sole proprietorships and partnerships is the difference between capital consumption based on income tax returns and capital consumption measured using empirical evidence on prices of used equipment and structures in resale markets, which have shown that depreciation for most types of assets approximates a geometric pattern. The tax return data are valued at historical costs and reflect changes over time in service lives and depreciation patterns as permitted by tax regulations. *Inventory valuation adjustment* represents the difference between the book value of inventories used up in production and the cost of replacing them.

Personal income is the current income received by persons from all sources minus their personal contributions for social insurance. Classified as "persons" are individuals (including owners of unincorporated firms), nonprofit institutions that primarily serve individuals, private trust funds, and private noninsured welfare funds. Personal income includes transfers (payments not resulting from current production) from government and business such as social security benefits, public assistance, etc., but excludes transfers among persons. Also included are certain nonmonetary types of income—chiefly estimated net rental value to owner-occupants of their homes and the value of services furnished without payment by financial intermediaries. Capital gains (net losses) are excluded.

Disposable personal income is personal income less personal tax and nontax payments. It is the income available to persons for spending or saving. Personal tax and nontax payments are tax payments (net of refunds) by persons (except personal contributions for social insurance) that are not chargeable to business expense and certain personal payments to general government that are treated like taxes. Personal taxes include income, estate and gift, and personal property taxes and motor vehicle licenses. Nontax payments include passport fees, fines and forfeitures, and donations.

Consumer Expenditure Survey—The Consumer Expenditure Survey program was begun in late 1979. The principal objective of the survey is to collect current consumer expenditure data which provide a continuous flow of data on the

U.S. Census Bureau, Statistical Abstract of the United States: 2002

buying habits of American consumers. The data are necessary for future revisions of the Consumer Price Index.

The survey conducted by the Census Bureau for the Bureau of Labor Statistics consists of two components: (1) An interview panel survey in which the expenditures of consumer units are obtained in five interviews conducted every 3 months, and (2) a diary or recordkeeping survey completed by participating households for two consecutive 1-week periods.

Each component of the survey queries an independent sample of consumer units representative of the U.S. total population.

Over 52 weeks of the year, 5,000 consumer units are sampled for the diary survey. Each consumer unit keeps a diary for two 1-week periods yielding approximately 10,000 diaries a year. The interview sample is selected on a rotating panel basis, targeted at 5,000 consumer units per quarter. Data are collected in 88 urban and 16 rural areas of the country that are representative of the U.S. total population. The survey includes students in student housing. Data from the two surveys are combined; integration is necessary to permit analysis of total family expenditures because neither the diary nor quarterly interview survey was designed to collect a complete account of consumer spending.

Distribution of money income to families and individuals—Money income statistics are based on data collected in various field surveys of income conducted since 1936. Since 1947, the Census Bureau has collected the data on an annual basis and published them in *Current Population Reports,* P60 Series. In each of the surveys, field representatives interview samples of the population with respect to income received during the previous year. Money income as defined by the Census Bureau differs from the BEA concept of "personal income."

Data on consumer income collected in the CPS by the Census Bureau cover money income received (exclusive of certain money receipts such as capital gains)

before payments for personal income taxes, social security, union dues, medicare deductions, etc. Therefore, money income does not reflect the fact that some families receive part of their income in the form of noncash benefits (see Section 12) such as food stamps, health benefits, and subsidized housing; that some farm families receive noncash benefits in the form of rent-free housing and goods produced and consumed on the farm; or that noncash benefits are also received by some nonfarm residents which often take the form of the use of business transportation and facilities, full or partial payments by business for retirement programs, medical and educational expenses, etc. These elements should be considered when comparing income levels. For data on noncash benefits, see Section 12. None of the aggregate income concepts (GDP, national income, or personal income) is exactly comparable with money income, although personal income is the closest.

In October 1983, the Census Bureau began to collect data under the new Survey of Income and Program Participation (SIPP). The information supplied by this survey is expected to provide better measures of the status and changes in income distribution and poverty of households and persons in the United States. The data collected in SIPP will be used to study federal and state aid programs (such as food stamps, welfare, medicaid, and subsidized housing), to estimate program costs and coverage, and to assess the effects of proposed changes in program eligibility rules or benefit levels. The core questions are repeated at each interview and cover labor force activity, the types and amounts of income received, and participation status in various programs. The core also contains questions covering attendance in postsecondary schools and private health insurance coverage. Various supplements or topical modules covering areas such as educational attainment, assets and liabilities, and pension plan coverage are periodically included.

Poverty—Families and unrelated individuals are classified as being above or below the poverty level using the poverty index originated at the Social Security Administration in 1964 and revised by Federal Interagency Committees in 1969 and 1980.

The poverty index is based solely on money income and does not reflect the fact that many low-income persons receive noncash benefits such as food stamps, medicaid, and public housing. The index is based on the Department of Agriculture's 1961 Economy Food Plan and reflects the different consumption requirements of families based on their size and composition. The poverty thresholds are updated every year to reflect changes in the Consumer Price Index. The following technical changes to the thresholds were made in 1981: (1) distinctions based on sex of householder have been eliminated, (2) separate thresholds for farm families have been dropped, and (3) the matrix has been expanded to families of nine or more persons from the old cut-off of seven or more persons. These changes have been incorporated in the calculation of poverty data beginning with 1981. In the recent past, the Census Bureau has published a number of technical papers that presented experimental poverty estimates based on income definitions that counted the value of selected government noncash benefits. The Census Bureau has also published annual reports on after-tax income (see Tables 664 and 665). The annual income and poverty reports (P60 Series) have brought together the benefit and tax data that previously appeared in the separate reports. These reports have shown the distribution of income among households and the prevalence of poverty under the official definition of money income and under definitions that add or subtract income components. In addition, in July 1999, the Census Bureau released a report (P60-205) that showed the effect of using experimental poverty following the recommendations of a National Academy of Sciences panel on redefining our nation's poverty measure.

Statistical reliability—For a discussion of statistical collection and estimation, sampling procedures, and measures of statistical reliability pertaining to Census Bureau data, see Appendix III.

No. 631. Gross Domestic Product in Current and Real (1996) Dollars: 1960 to 2001

[In billions of dollars (527.4 represents $527,400,000,000). For explanation of gross domestic product and chained dollars, see text, this section]

Item	1960	1970	1980	1985	1988	1989	1990	1991	1992	1993	1994	1995	1996	1997	1998	1999	2000	2001
CURRENT DOLLARS																		
Gross domestic product	527.4	1,039.7	2,795.6	4,213.0	5,108.3	5,489.1	5,803.2	5,986.2	6,318.9	6,642.3	7,054.3	7,400.5	7,813.2	8,318.4	8,781.5	9,268.6	9,872.9	10,208.1
Personal consumption expenditures	332.3	648.9	1,762.9	2,712.6	3,356.6	3,596.7	3,831.5	3,971.2	4,209.7	4,454.7	4,716.4	4,969.0	5,237.5	5,529.3	5,856.0	6,250.2	6,728.4	7,064.5
Durable goods	43.3	85.0	214.2	363.3	450.2	467.8	467.6	443.0	470.8	513.4	560.8	589.7	616.5	642.5	693.2	760.9	819.6	858.3
Nondurable goods	152.9	272.0	696.1	928.8	1,082.9	1,165.4	1,246.1	1,278.8	1,322.9	1,375.2	1,438.0	1,497.3	1,574.1	1,641.6	1,708.5	1,831.3	1,989.6	2,055.1
Services	136.1	292.0	852.7	1,420.6	1,823.5	1,963.5	2,117.8	2,249.4	2,415.9	2,566.1	2,717.6	2,882.0	3,047.0	3,245.2	3,454.3	3,658.0	3,919.2	4,151.1
Gross private domestic investment	78.9	152.4	477.9	736.3	821.1	872.9	861.7	800.2	866.6	955.1	1,097.1	1,143.8	1,242.7	1,390.5	1,538.7	1,636.7	1,767.5	1,633.9
Fixed investment	75.7	150.4	484.2	714.5	802.7	845.2	847.2	800.4	851.6	934.0	1,034.6	1,110.7	1,212.7	1,327.7	1,465.6	1,578.2	1,718.1	1,692.4
Change in business inventories	3.2	2.0	-6.3	21.8	18.5	27.7	14.5	-0.2	15.0	21.1	62.6	33.0	30.0	62.9	73.1	58.6	49.4	-58.4
Net exports of goods and services	2.4	1.2	-14.9	-114.2	-106.3	-80.7	-71.4	-20.7	-27.9	-60.5	-87.1	-84.3	-89.0	-89.3	-151.7	-250.9	-364.0	-329.8
Exports	25.3	57.0	278.9	303.0	446.9	509.0	557.2	601.6	636.8	658.0	725.1	818.6	874.2	966.4	964.9	989.8	1,102.9	1,050.4
Imports	22.8	55.8	293.8	417.2	553.2	589.7	628.6	622.3	664.6	718.5	812.1	902.8	963.1	1,055.8	1,116.7	1,240.6	1,466.9	1,380.1
Government consumption expenditures and gross investment	113.8	237.1	569.7	878.3	1,036.9	1,100.2	1,181.4	1,235.5	1,270.5	1,293.0	1,327.9	1,372.0	1,421.9	1,487.9	1,538.5	1,632.5	1,741.0	1,839.5
Federal	65.9	116.4	245.3	413.4	462.6	482.6	508.4	527.4	534.5	527.3	521.1	521.5	531.6	538.2	539.2	564.0	590.2	615.7
National defense	55.2	90.9	169.6	312.4	355.9	363.2	374.9	384.5	378.5	364.9	355.1	350.6	357.0	352.6	349.1	364.5	375.4	399.0
State and local	47.9	120.7	324.4	464.9	574.3	617.7	673.0	708.1	736.0	765.7	806.8	850.5	890.4	949.7	999.3	1,068.5	1,150.8	1,223.8
CHAINED (1996) DOLLARS																		
Gross domestic product	2,376.7	3,578.0	4,900.9	5,717.1	6,368.4	6,591.8	6,707.9	6,676.4	6,880.0	7,062.6	7,347.7	7,543.8	7,813.2	8,159.5	8,508.9	8,856.5	9,224.0	9,333.8
Personal consumption expenditures	1,510.8	2,317.5	3,193.0	3,820.9	4,279.5	4,393.7	4,474.5	4,466.6	4,594.5	4,748.9	4,928.1	5,075.6	5,237.5	5,423.9	5,683.7	5,968.4	6,257.8	6,450.3
Durable goods	(NA)	(NA)	(NA)	(NA)	481.5	491.7	487.1	454.9	479.0	518.3	557.7	583.5	616.5	657.3	726.7	817.8	895.5	955.6
Nondurable goods	(NA)	(NA)	(NA)	(NA)	1,315.1	1,351.0	1,369.6	1,364.0	1,389.7	1,430.3	1,485.1	1,529.0	1,574.1	1,619.9	1,686.4	1,766.4	1,849.9	1,883.3
Services	(NA)	(NA)	(NA)	(NA)	2,477.2	2,546.0	2,616.2	2,651.8	2,729.7	2,802.5	2,886.2	2,963.4	3,047.0	3,147.0	3,273.4	3,393.2	3,527.7	3,633.4
Gross private domestic investment	272.8	436.2	655.3	863.4	902.8	936.5	907.3	829.5	899.8	977.9	1,107.0	1,140.6	1,242.7	1,393.3	1,558.0	1,660.1	1,772.9	1,630.8
Fixed investment	(NA)	(NA)	(NA)	(NA)	887.1	911.2	894.6	832.5	886.5	958.4	1,045.9	1,109.2	1,212.7	1,328.6	1,480.0	1,595.4	1,716.2	1,682.6
Change in business inventories	(NA)	(NA)	(NA)	(NA)	18.4	29.6	16.5	-1.0	17.1	20.0	66.8	30.4	30.0	63.8	76.7	62.1	50.6	-61.7
Net exports of goods and services	(NA)	(NA)	(NA)	(NA)	-112.1	-79.4	-56.5	-15.8	-19.8	-59.1	-86.5	-78.4	-89.0	-113.3	-221.1	-316.9	-399.1	-408.7
Exports	87.5	159.3	334.8	341.6	473.5	529.4	575.7	613.2	651.0	672.7	732.8	808.2	874.2	981.5	1,002.4	1,034.9	1,133.2	1,081.7
Imports	108.0	223.1	324.8	490.7	585.6	608.8	632.2	629.0	670.8	731.8	819.4	886.6	963.1	1,094.8	1,223.5	1,351.7	1,532.3	1,490.4
Government consumption expenditures and gross investment	661.3	931.1	1,020.9	1,190.5	1,307.5	1,343.5	1,387.3	1,403.4	1,410.0	1,398.8	1,400.1	1,406.4	1,421.9	1,455.4	1,483.3	1,531.8	1,572.6	1,628.6
Federal	(NA)	(NA)	(NA)	(NA)	586.9	594.7	606.8	604.9	595.1	572.0	551.3	536.5	531.6	529.6	525.4	536.7	545.9	560.3
National defense	(NA)	(NA)	(NA)	(NA)	446.8	443.3	443.2	438.4	417.1	394.7	375.9	361.9	357.0	347.7	341.6	348.6	349.0	365.3
State and local	(NA)	(NA)	(NA)	(NA)	721.4	749.5	781.1	798.9	815.3	827.0	848.9	869.9	890.4	925.8	957.7	994.7	1,026.3	1,067.5

NA Not available.

Source: U.S. Bureau of Economic Analysis, National Income and Product Accounts, 1929-97, and Survey of Current Business, August 2001 and May 2002. See also <http://www.bea.doc.gov/bea/dn/n/paweb/SelectTable.asp?Selected=N> (released as 29 April 2002).

Income, Expenditures, and Wealth   417

No. 632. Gross Domestic Product in Current and Real (1996) Dollars by Industry: 1990 to 2000

[In billions of dollars (5,803.2 represents $5,803,200,000,000). **Data are based on the 1987 SIC.** Data include nonfactor charges (capital consumption allowances, indirect business taxes, etc.) as well as factor charges against gross product; corporate profits and capital consumption allowances have been shifted from a company to an establishment basis]

Industry	Current dollars				Chained (1996) dollars			
	1990	1995	1999	2000	1990	1995	1999	2000
Gross domestic product [1]	5,803.2	7,400.5	9,268.6	9,872.9	6,707.9	7,543.8	8,856.5	9,224.0
Private industries	4,996.7	6,411.1	8,116.9	8,656.5	5,736.8	6,508.7	7,852.7	8,177.6
Agriculture, forestry, and fishing	108.3	109.8	127.2	135.8	118.5	123.1	153.4	166.3
Farms	79.6	73.2	74.3	79.0	84.2	85.5	106.0	120.5
Agricultural services	28.7	36.7	53.0	56.7	34.6	37.6	46.7	47.3
Mining	111.9	95.7	103.3	127.1	105.8	113.0	112.0	95.2
Metal mining	5.2	6.5	5.0	4.9	4.4	5.5	8.2	7.4
Coal mining	11.8	10.7	10.6	10.1	7.5	10.1	13.5	13.5
Oil and gas extraction	87.1	69.3	76.2	99.5	87.5	88.6	79.8	63.4
Nonmetallic minerals, except fuels	7.8	9.1	11.5	12.6	8.1	9.1	10.9	12.4
Construction	248.7	290.3	425.5	463.6	290.7	299.6	370.0	379.3
Manufacturing	1,040.6	1,289.1	1,496.8	1,566.6	1,102.3	1,284.7	1,532.1	1,594.6
Durable goods	586.6	729.8	865.7	901.7	585.1	714.9	965.1	1,034.1
Lumber and wood products	32.2	42.3	46.3	44.4	45.1	41.6	43.0	44.1
Furniture and fixtures	15.6	19.5	26.0	26.7	18.1	20.7	23.9	24.4
Stone, clay, and glass products	25.3	32.4	42.5	43.9	29.4	32.8	38.4	39.7
Primary metal industries	43.2	53.0	50.2	52.9	43.7	49.6	57.2	57.4
Fabricated metal products	69.4	87.2	107.6	108.7	76.1	90.8	98.4	99.6
Industrial machinery	118.2	132.8	157.3	167.6	93.5	124.7	214.4	236.0
Electronic & other electric equipment	105.7	146.9	165.5	181.2	68.6	128.7	255.8	327.7
Motor vehicles and equipment	47.3	98.2	118.9	120.2	68.7	103.2	114.7	116.9
Other transportation equipment	60.5	47.7	64.5	62.7	75.7	49.4	61.2	55.2
Instruments and related products	49.3	47.2	58.8	64.2	68.9	52.6	48.2	48.1
Misc. manufacturing industries	19.8	22.7	28.3	29.1	22.8	23.3	26.9	27.7
Nondurable goods	454.0	559.2	631.0	664.8	520.2	570.3	574.0	574.0
Food and kindred products	96.4	121.1	132.9	137.0	109.5	133.3	117.3	118.2
Tobacco manufactures	11.9	15.1	18.9	22.3	14.5	15.7	6.3	6.2
Textile mill products	22.0	24.8	25.5	24.7	22.8	26.0	23.6	24.1
Apparel and other textile products	25.4	27.3	24.3	23.6	27.3	28.0	22.6	22.5
Paper and allied products	45.0	58.9	58.0	59.9	52.5	52.2	57.3	50.0
Printing and publishing	73.1	80.8	102.7	105.5	102.9	89.2	88.1	86.6
Chemicals and allied products	109.9	150.8	175.1	191.1	131.1	148.0	168.7	184.2
Petroleum and coal products	31.7	29.0	30.4	36.5	22.9	26.9	34.4	25.5
Rubber and misc. plastic products	33.9	46.1	59.3	60.2	34.0	47.0	58.2	59.8
Leather and leather products	4.7	5.3	3.9	4.0	5.2	5.3	3.7	3.9
Transportation and public utilities	490.9	642.6	776.8	825.0	525.0	634.5	737.2	781.5
Transportation	177.4	233.4	302.7	313.9	180.6	225.1	268.6	281.1
Railroad transportation	19.8	23.6	23.2	22.9	18.1	22.7	22.5	23.2
Local & interurban passenger transit	9.1	12.4	17.6	18.7	12.8	13.2	16.6	18.2
Trucking and warehousing	69.4	89.0	122.0	126.0	68.1	86.6	100.3	105.7
Water transportation	10.0	11.6	13.7	14.8	10.2	11.3	11.8	11.7
Transportation by air	45.3	67.7	90.2	93.0	46.9	62.9	80.9	85.0
Pipelines, except natural gas	5.5	5.5	6.1	6.2	5.7	5.0	6.4	6.4
Transportation services	18.2	23.5	29.9	32.3	19.5	23.4	29.8	30.6
Communications	148.1	202.3	258.5	281.1	155.2	202.4	256.5	283.9
Telephone and telegraph	119.4	151.6	196.4	208.9	117.1	147.6	208.0	232.5
Radio and television broadcasting	28.7	50.7	62.1	72.2	37.5	55.2	50.3	54.1
Electric, gas, and sanitary services	165.4	206.9	215.6	230.0	190.0	207.2	212.9	217.9
Wholesale trade	376.1	500.6	633.5	674.1	395.1	483.0	688.8	708.4
Retail trade	507.8	646.8	834.9	893.9	559.5	641.4	843.7	905.7
Finance, insurance, and real estate	1,010.3	1,347.2	1,810.6	1,936.2	1,250.6	1,393.0	1,713.5	1,809.5
Depository institutions	171.3	227.4	325.6	366.5	244.0	242.4	268.1	288.2
Nondepository institutions	23.3	34.1	53.7	59.0	26.3	33.4	60.6	66.8
Security and commodity brokers	42.3	77.7	138.8	144.2	42.0	76.5	210.0	290.7
Insurance carriers	64.6	120.2	158.3	167.7	112.2	129.9	135.2	131.1
Insurance agents, brokers & services	37.7	47.2	65.4	67.3	61.4	49.9	58.9	60.1
Real estate	665.7	832.6	1,051.2	1,116.3	763.4	852.8	986.2	1,018.3
Services	1,071.5	1,462.4	1,980.9	2,164.6	1,361.9	1,510.4	1,774.8	1,865.2
Hotels and other lodging places	46.3	61.7	80.4	86.5	55.2	62.7	64.8	67.3
Personal services	38.0	46.7	57.4	60.4	46.4	48.1	52.6	53.5
Business services	203.9	302.0	502.6	571.7	241.3	313.9	452.5	490.9
Auto repair, services, and garages	50.3	65.1	88.1	93.9	61.9	65.9	80.6	83.7
Motion pictures	17.7	22.4	32.0	34.9	21.2	23.6	29.2	30.0
Amusement and recreation services	36.5	53.5	75.1	80.8	45.0	55.6	68.3	69.5
Health services	314.4	433.1	516.3	546.8	423.2	444.3	470.5	485.4
Legal services	82.7	101.1	123.0	133.5	108.8	105.1	110.4	115.6
Educational services	39.6	55.7	72.1	78.6	50.3	58.5	62.4	64.6
Social services & membership organizations	30.1	47.4	61.8	67.5	38.0	49.3	53.7	55.5
Other services	149.2	194.4	275.9	306.2	191.3	199.9	250.7	269.3
Government	806.6	989.5	1,151.7	1,216.4	1,008.2	1,017.1	1,060.7	1,085.4
Federal	300.2	342.3	369.7	387.0	384.7	354.3	346.5	353.0
State and local	506.4	647.2	782.0	829.5	624.1	662.9	714.0	732.2

[1] Includes private households and statistical discrepancy, not shown separately.

Source: U.S. Bureau of Economic Analysis, *National Income and Product Accounts, 1929-97,* (forthcoming); and *Survey of Current Business,* November 2001.

No. 633. Gross Domestic Product in Current and Real (1996) Dollars by Type of Product and Sector: 1990 to 2001

[In billions of dollars (5,803 represents $5,803,000,000,000). For explanation of chained dollars, see text, this section]

Item	1990	1993	1994	1995	1996	1997	1998	1999	2000	2001
CURRENT DOLLARS										
Gross domestic product ...	**5,803**	**6,642**	**7,054**	**7,401**	**7,813**	**8,318**	**8,782**	**9,269**	**9,873**	**10,208**
PRODUCT										
Goods..................	2,266	2,503	2,680	2,798	2,951	3,145	3,305	3,477	3,694	3,661
Durable goods............	1,002	1,108	1,197	1,273	1,351	1,469	1,569	1,654	1,770	1,681
Nondurable goods.........	1,264	1,395	1,483	1,525	1,600	1,676	1,736	1,823	1,924	1,981
Services	3,011	3,594	3,783	3,985	4,191	4,442	4,679	4,939	5,268	5,580
Structures	526	546	592	617	671	731	798	852	910	967
SECTOR										
Business	4,842	5,518	5,887	6,190	6,556	7,011	7,418	7,841	8,357	8,603
Nonfarm................	4,762	5,444	5,803	6,117	6,464	6,922	7,337	7,766	8,278	8,519
Farm...................	80	74	84	73	92	88	81	74	79	84
Households and institutions......	238	297	313	330	349	363	384	403	432	469
General government	723	827	855	880	909	945	980	1,025	1,084	1,136
Federal	260	287	287	287	292	295	299	308	324	335
State and local	464	540	567	593	617	649	681	717	760	801
CHAINED (1996) DOLLARS										
Gross domestic product ...	**6,708**	**7,063**	**7,348**	**7,544**	**7,813**	**8,160**	**8,509**	**8,857**	**9,224**	**9,334**
PRODUCT										
Goods..................	2,404	2,548	2,708	2,814	2,951	3,146	3,332	3,516	3,719	3,664
Durable goods............	1,007	1,094	1,179	1,265	1,351	1,491	1,634	1,763	1,908	1,835
Nondurable goods.........	1,400	1,457	1,531	1,549	1,600	1,655	1,701	1,759	1,822	1,834
Services	3,692	3,917	4,010	4,098	4,191	4,308	4,431	4,573	4,725	4,860
Structures	615	603	631	633	671	707	749	774	792	810
SECTOR										
Business	5,524	5,838	6,112	6,296	6,556	6,882	7,209	7,540	7,879	7,954
Nonfarm................	5,441	5,753	6,014	6,210	6,464	6,779	7,108	7,433	7,762	7,837
Farm...................	84	86	100	86	92	104	100	106	121	118
Households and institutions......	292	320	331	342	349	361	372	379	389	403
General government	895	906	906	907	909	917	929	940	959	979
Federal	331	320	310	299	292	288	286	286	290	293
State and local	565	587	596	608	617	629	643	654	669	686

Source: U.S. Bureau of Economic Analysis, *National Income and Product Accounts, 1929-97*, and *Survey of Current Business,* August 2001 and May 2002. See also <http://www.bea.doc.gov/bea/dn/nipaweb/SelectTable.asp?Selected=N> (released as 29 April 2002).

No. 634. GDP Components in Current Dollars—Annual Percent Change: 1990 to 2001

[Change from previous year; for 1990, change from 1989. For explanation of chained dollars, see text, this section. Minus sign (-) indicates decrease]

Item	1990	1993	1994	1995	1996	1997	1998	1999	2000	2001
Gross domestic product (GDP) .	**5.7**	**5.1**	**6.2**	**4.9**	**5.6**	**6.5**	**5.6**	**5.5**	**6.5**	**3.4**
Personal consumption expenditures...	6.5	5.8	5.9	5.4	5.4	5.6	5.9	6.7	7.7	5.0
Durable goods	-	9.1	9.2	5.2	4.5	4.2	7.9	9.8	7.7	4.7
Nondurable goods.............	6.9	3.9	4.6	4.1	5.1	4.3	4.1	7.2	8.6	3.3
Services	7.9	6.2	5.9	6.0	5.7	6.5	6.4	5.9	7.1	5.9
Gross private domestic investment ...	-1.3	10.2	14.9	4.2	8.7	11.9	10.7	6.4	8.0	-7.6
Fixed investment	0.2	9.7	10.8	7.4	9.2	9.5	10.4	7.7	8.9	-1.5
Nonresidential..............	2.8	9.0	9.7	10.2	9.0	11.1	10.2	6.7	10.1	-3.6
Structures...............	4.7	4.2	4.5	9.1	9.9	13.7	10.4	0.4	10.6	5.3
Producers' durable equipment .	1.9	10.8	11.6	10.6	8.7	10.3	10.1	8.8	9.9	-6.5
Residential................	-6.5	11.7	13.6	-0.1	9.7	4.8	11.0	10.7	5.3	5.0
Exports of goods and services	9.5	3.3	10.2	12.9	6.8	10.6	-0.2	2.6	11.4	-4.8
Exports of goods	7.2	2.5	10.8	14.6	5.9	11.4	-1.1	2.5	12.5	-6.3
Exports of services	15.5	5.4	8.7	8.9	9.0	8.5	2.2	2.8	8.8	-1.0
Imports of goods and services	6.6	8.1	13.0	11.2	6.7	9.6	5.8	11.1	18.2	-5.9
Imports of goods..............	4.9	8.8	14.2	12.0	6.7	9.5	5.1	12.6	18.9	-5.7
Imports of services	14.6	5.0	7.7	7.2	6.6	10.3	9.4	3.8	14.5	-6.9
Govt. consumption expenditures and gross investment	7.4	1.8	2.7	3.3	3.6	4.6	3.4	6.1	6.6	5.7
Federal..................	5.4	-1.4	-1.2	0.1	1.9	1.2	0.2	4.6	4.6	4.3
National defense	3.2	-3.6	-2.7	-1.3	1.8	-1.2	-1.0	4.4	3.0	6.3
Nondefense	12.0	4.1	2.2	3.0	2.1	6.3	2.4	4.9	7.7	0.9
State and local	9.0	4.0	5.4	5.4	4.7	6.7	5.2	6.9	7.7	6.3

Source: U.S. Bureau of Economic Analysis, *National Income and Product Accounts, 1929-97*, and *Survey of Current Business,* August 2001 and May 2002. See also <http://www.bea.doc.gov/bea/dn/nipaweb/SelectTable.asp?Selected=N> (released as 29 April 2002).

Income, Expenditures, and Wealth 419

No. 635. Gross State Product in Current and Real (1996) Dollars: 1990 to 1999

[In billions of dollars (5,706.7 represents $5,706,700,000,000). For definition of gross state product or chained dollars, see text, this section]

State	Current dollars					Chained (1996) dollars [1]				
	1990	1995	1997	1998	1999	1990	1995	1997	1998	1999
United States	5,706.7	7,309.5	8,225.0	8,752.4	9,309.0	6,630.7	7,434.0	8,093.4	8,508.0	8,934.1
Alabama.	71.6	95.5	104.2	109.0	115.1	83.2	96.6	102.6	105.7	110.1
Alaska.	24.8	24.8	26.6	25.0	26.4	27.8	26.4	26.1	25.3	25.9
Arizona.	68.9	104.6	122.3	133.5	143.7	79.0	105.4	120.8	131.3	140.1
Arkansas	38.4	53.8	59.1	61.6	64.8	44.1	54.7	58.6	60.3	62.8
California	798.9	925.9	1,045.3	1,125.6	1,229.1	927.6	941.9	1,029.2	1,096.6	1,185.6
Colorado.	74.7	109.0	129.6	141.1	153.7	87.0	111.2	127.3	136.9	147.0
Connecticut.	98.9	118.6	135.0	143.2	151.8	117.3	120.8	132.6	138.7	145.3
Delaware	20.3	27.6	31.3	33.9	34.7	25.0	28.2	30.1	31.7	31.9
District of Columbia	40.4	48.4	50.5	52.2	55.8	50.9	49.7	49.3	49.7	51.8
Florida	258.3	344.8	389.5	416.4	442.9	303.7	350.6	382.3	401.9	420.3
Georgia	141.4	203.5	235.7	255.5	275.7	164.8	206.4	231.8	246.6	260.8
Hawaii	32.3	37.2	38.5	39.6	40.9	38.1	37.9	37.7	37.9	38.3
Idaho	17.7	27.2	29.4	31.2	34.0	20.0	27.4	29.3	31.2	34.1
Illinois	275.8	359.5	400.3	424.8	445.7	317.9	364.1	394.5	413.0	429.5
Indiana.	110.8	148.4	163.0	176.1	182.2	127.0	150.0	161.1	171.6	176.0
Iowa	55.8	71.7	81.7	83.1	85.2	63.4	73.1	81.5	82.4	84.0
Kansas.	51.5	64.1	73.0	76.8	80.8	59.8	65.6	72.1	75.0	78.0
Kentucky	67.9	91.5	101.5	107.6	113.5	77.5	92.8	100.2	104.2	107.5
Louisiana	94.9	112.2	123.5	125.3	129.0	108.0	116.5	120.7	123.6	124.4
Maine.	23.5	28.0	30.4	32.1	34.1	27.8	28.3	30.0	31.1	32.3
Maryland	115.0	139.5	154.6	164.3	174.7	137.1	142.1	151.5	157.9	164.8
Massachusetts.	160.0	197.5	223.6	240.9	262.6	187.2	200.5	219.7	233.6	251.9
Michigan.	190.8	254.2	279.5	291.6	308.3	225.1	258.3	276.0	283.8	295.6
Minnesota.	100.4	131.8	152.3	162.5	173.0	116.6	133.8	150.4	158.4	167.1
Mississippi	39.2	54.6	58.7	61.4	64.3	44.9	55.4	57.8	59.6	61.9
Missouri	104.8	139.5	155.8	163.9	170.5	122.8	141.9	153.4	158.8	162.9
Montana.	13.4	17.5	18.9	19.9	20.6	15.5	17.9	18.6	19.3	20.0
Nebraska	33.5	44.1	49.3	51.7	53.7	38.6	45.2	48.9	50.7	52.2
Nevada	31.6	49.4	59.2	64.3	69.9	37.1	50.1	57.5	61.0	64.6
New Hampshire	23.9	32.4	37.5	41.2	44.2	27.3	32.6	37.1	40.7	43.5
New Jersey.	217.0	271.4	300.0	316.5	331.5	253.6	275.0	294.1	304.8	315.4
New Mexico	27.2	42.2	47.8	49.2	51.0	29.4	42.7	47.6	50.3	51.9
New York	502.2	597.6	663.4	710.9	754.6	593.4	609.1	651.1	688.1	728.9
North Carolina	141.1	194.6	221.6	236.5	258.6	162.6	197.5	218.1	227.5	240.8
North Dakota.	11.5	14.5	15.9	17.0	17.0	13.2	15.0	15.8	16.9	16.7
Ohio	230.0	295.7	326.5	346.8	362.0	265.9	299.2	322.1	337.7	348.9
Oklahoma	57.8	70.0	79.4	83.0	86.4	66.1	71.8	78.1	81.7	84.0
Oregon.	57.8	81.1	97.5	103.5	109.7	66.5	81.3	97.1	103.7	110.1
Pennsylvania	249.9	318.8	347.3	364.9	383.0	291.5	322.9	340.9	352.1	364.9
Rhode Island.	21.6	25.7	29.4	30.5	32.5	25.5	26.2	28.8	29.2	30.6
South Carolina.	66.1	86.9	95.4	101.2	106.9	76.0	87.8	94.3	98.2	102.3
South Dakota	13.0	18.3	19.8	20.9	21.6	15.1	18.7	19.7	20.6	21.3
Tennessee	95.0	136.8	151.7	161.8	170.1	110.5	138.6	149.2	156.4	161.7
Texas.	388.1	513.9	608.6	645.2	687.3	439.5	527.7	597.9	636.2	668.5
Utah	31.4	46.3	55.1	59.0	62.6	36.3	47.0	54.0	56.9	59.7
Vermont	11.8	14.0	15.5	16.2	17.2	13.4	14.1	15.3	15.9	16.6
Virginia.	148.2	189.0	212.1	228.0	242.2	174.5	192.5	207.9	218.4	225.1
Washington.	115.5	151.3	175.2	191.8	209.3	136.6	154.0	172.2	185.3	198.9
West Virginia.	28.3	36.3	38.3	39.4	40.7	31.8	36.6	37.7	38.2	39.1
Wisconsin.	100.4	133.7	148.2	158.3	166.5	115.3	135.2	146.9	155.0	161.5
Wyoming	13.4	14.9	16.2	16.5	17.4	14.3	15.6	16.0	16.5	17.2

[1] For chained (1996) dollar estimates, states will not add to U.S. total.

Source: U.S. Bureau of Economic Analysis, *Survey of Current Business,* August 2001; and Internet site at <http://www.bea.doc.gov/bea/regional/gsp/>.

No. 636. Gross State Product in Chained (1996) Dollars by Industry: 1999

[In billions of dollars (8,934.1 represents $8,934,100,000,000).** For definition of gross state product or chained dollars, see text, this section. Industries based on 1987 Standard Industrial Classification]

State	Total [1]	Farms, forestry, fisher- ies [2]	Con- struction	Manu- facturing	Trans- portation, public utilities	Whole- sale trade	Retail trade	Finance, insur- ance, real estate	Serv- ices	Govern- ment [3]
United States [4]	8,934.1	150.9	361.1	1,529.4	752.3	709.3	847.3	1,692.1	1,772.6	1,009.5
Alabama.	110.1	2.8	4.7	21.8	9.6	8.3	11.8	15.4	17.4	16.7
Alaska	25.9	0.4	1.1	1.1	4.4	0.9	1.8	2.5	3.0	4.7
Arizona.	140.1	2.4	7.2	23.9	10.1	10.6	15.2	25.0	28.1	16.0
Arkansas	62.8	3.2	2.6	14.6	6.5	4.7	7.5	6.9	9.0	7.4
California	1,185.6	26.5	41.0	192.3	86.8	91.0	112.2	251.9	257.6	121.0
Colorado.	147.0	2.7	8.0	15.8	18.4	10.6	15.0	25.4	31.7	16.9
Connecticut.	145.3	1.1	4.3	25.5	8.8	10.8	12.1	41.4	29.8	11.6
Delaware	31.9	0.4	1.3	4.7	1.7	1.5	2.4	12.2	4.8	2.9
District of Columbia	51.8	-	0.4	1.2	2.9	0.8	1.6	7.2	18.2	19.5
Florida	420.3	8.9	19.4	32.0	36.8	37.4	50.1	89.7	96.2	49.8
Georgia	260.8	4.5	11.9	43.1	30.5	27.5	25.5	39.3	47.4	30.2
Hawaii	38.3	0.6	1.4	1.0	4.1	1.7	4.4	8.9	7.9	8.3
Idaho	34.1	2.3	2.0	8.6	2.6	2.4	3.4	3.7	4.9	4.2
Illinois	429.5	4.3	17.4	75.9	39.3	39.0	36.3	85.9	89.8	40.6
Indiana.	176.0	2.3	8.0	57.3	13.0	12.3	16.7	21.9	27.0	16.8
Iowa	84.0	4.1	3.3	20.1	6.9	7.4	7.6	11.7	12.9	9.4
Kansas.	78.0	3.1	3.2	13.2	9.8	7.1	8.2	9.6	12.6	10.0
Kentucky	107.5	2.5	4.4	29.2	8.6	7.7	10.7	11.4	16.2	14.1
Louisiana	124.4	1.5	5.4	19.6	11.4	8.4	11.8	15.5	20.2	14.6
Maine.	32.3	0.7	1.3	5.2	2.3	2.2	4.1	5.9	6.1	4.4
Maryland	164.8	1.6	8.2	14.0	12.8	11.9	15.5	35.1	37.6	28.2
Massachusetts.	251.9	1.4	9.4	38.8	14.4	21.6	20.4	61.6	62.9	22.0
Michigan.	295.6	3.3	12.9	80.8	19.5	25.0	29.9	40.4	54.0	29.3
Minnesota.	167.1	3.9	7.4	32.1	12.6	15.7	16.1	30.0	32.2	16.2
Mississippi	61.9	2.2	2.6	13.5	5.9	4.2	6.9	6.7	9.9	9.5
Missouri	162.9	2.4	7.3	32.5	16.5	13.9	16.4	24.4	31.1	17.9
Montana	20.0	1.1	1.0	1.6	2.4	1.5	2.1	2.6	3.7	3.1
Nebraska	52.2	3.5	2.2	7.6	5.5	4.7	4.7	7.6	9.2	7.0
Nevada	64.6	0.5	6.2	2.8	5.4	3.6	7.2	10.9	19.4	6.6
New Hampshire	43.5	0.3	1.6	11.1	2.5	3.2	4.3	9.5	7.7	3.2
New Jersey	315.4	1.8	11.0	38.3	30.5	33.9	25.2	74.8	69.3	30.9
New Mexico	51.9	1.3	1.8	11.4	3.6	2.4	4.7	6.2	8.2	7.9
New York	728.9	3.5	19.8	75.6	54.2	49.7	52.0	248.8	155.0	70.8
North Carolina	240.8	4.9	11.1	55.4	17.5	17.5	22.8	43.6	37.8	29.7
North Dakota	16.7	1.0	0.8	1.6	1.7	1.7	1.7	2.2	2.9	2.3
Ohio	348.9	3.5	13.6	95.7	25.5	28.5	34.7	51.7	59.1	35.5
Oklahoma.	84.0	2.5	2.9	15.4	7.7	5.7	8.9	9.7	14.1	12.7
Oregon.	110.1	3.5	5.0	32.6	7.3	9.1	9.4	14.7	11.8	11.9
Pennsylvania	364.9	3.8	13.9	75.7	31.8	26.3	34.0	64.7	76.5	35.9
Rhode Island	30.6	0.2	1.5	4.1	2.1	1.9	2.9	8.0	6.3	3.6
South Carolina	102.3	1.3	5.4	23.0	9.1	7.4	11.7	13.6	15.6	14.9
South Dakota	21.3	2.1	0.8	3.3	1.7	1.7	2.3	3.5	3.4	2.5
Tennessee	161.7	1.7	6.5	35.1	13.1	14.3	19.2	22.2	31.3	18.0
Texas.	668.5	11.0	28.0	103.3	73.1	60.2	65.4	93.3	122.0	70.7
Utah	59.7	0.9	3.5	8.4	5.2	4.3	6.6	9.5	11.5	8.3
Vermont	16.6	0.5	0.7	3.3	1.3	1.1	1.7	2.8	3.4	2.0
Virginia.	225.1	2.2	9.6	27.3	21.1	15.3	20.8	39.3	48.9	40.0
Washington	198.9	5.1	8.9	25.9	16.0	16.0	20.4	34.0	46.8	25.4
West Virginia	39.1	0.3	1.6	6.4	4.5	2.5	4.0	4.2	6.5	5.8
Wisconsin	161.5	4.0	6.8	45.7	11.2	11.8	15.5	24.0	26.5	16.2
Wyoming	17.2	0.6	0.8	1.1	2.5	0.8	1.3	1.8	1.8	2.3

- Represents zero.   [1] Includes mining not shown separately.   [2] Includes agricultural services.   [3] Includes federal civilian and military and state and local government.   [4] States will not add to U.S. total as chained-dollar estimates are usually not additive.

Source: U.S. Bureau of Economic Analysis, *Survey of Current Business,* August 2001; and Internet site at <http://www.bea.doc.gov/bea/regional/gsp/>.

Income, Expenditures, and Wealth   421

No. 637. Relation of GDP, GNP, Net National Product, National Income, Personal Income, Disposable Personal Income, and Personal Saving: 1990 to 2001

[In billions of dollars (5,803.2 represents $5,803,200,000,000). For definitions, see text, this section]

Item	1990	1995	1996	1997	1998	1999	2000	2001
Gross domestic product	5,803.2	7,400.5	7,813.2	8,318.4	8,781.5	9,268.6	9,872.9	10,208.1
Plus: Receipts of factor income from the rest of the world [1]	188.3	232.3	245.6	281.3	286.1	313.8	384.2	335.2
Less: Payments of factor income to the rest of the world [2]	159.3	211.9	227.5	274.2	289.6	320.5	396.3	340.5
Equals: Gross national product	5,832.2	7,420.9	7,831.2	8,325.4	8,778.1	9,261.8	9,860.8	10,202.8
Less: Consumption of fixed capital	711.3	911.7	956.2	1,013.3	1,072.0	1,151.4	1,241.3	1,351.4
Equals: Net national product [3]	5,120.9	6,509.1	6,875.0	7,312.1	7,706.1	8,110.4	8,619.5	8,851.5
Less: Indirect business tax and nontax liability	447.3	594.6	620.0	646.2	681.3	713.1	762.7	794.0
Plus: Subsidies [4]	25.3	22.2	22.6	19.1	23.5	33.3	37.6	54.8
Equals: National income [3]	4,642.1	5,876.7	6,210.4	6,618.4	7,041.4	7,462.1	7,980.9	8,217.5
Less: Corporate profits [5]	408.6	668.8	754.0	833.8	777.4	825.2	876.4	767.1
Net interest	452.4	389.8	386.3	423.9	511.9	506.5	532.7	554.3
Contributions for social insurance.	410.1	533.2	555.8	587.8	623.3	660.7	701.5	731.2
Wage accruals less disbursements.	0.1	16.4	3.6	-2.9	-0.7	5.2	-	-
Plus: Personal interest income	772.4	792.5	810.6	864.0	964.4	950.0	1,000.6	993.6
Personal dividend income.	165.4	254.0	297.4	334.9	348.3	343.1	379.2	416.3
Government transfer payments to persons.	573.1	860.1	902.4	934.4	955.0	988.4	1,036.0	1,113.8
Business transfer payments to persons. .	21.3	25.8	26.4	27.9	28.8	31.1	33.1	35.0
Equals: Personal income.	4,903.2	6,200.9	6,547.4	6,937.0	7,426.0	7,777.3	8,319.2	8,723.5
Less: Personal tax and nontax payments . .	609.6	778.3	869.7	968.8	1,070.4	1,159.2	1,288.2	1,306.2
Equals: Disposable personal income . . .	4,293.6	5,422.6	5,677.7	5,968.2	6,355.6	6,618.0	7,031.0	7,417.3
Less: Personal outlays	3,959.3	5,120.2	5,405.6	5,715.3	6,054.1	6,457.2	6,963.3	7,298.9
Equals: Personal saving	334.3	302.4	272.1	252.9	301.5	160.9	67.7	118.4

- Represents zero. [1] Consists largely of receipts by U.S. residents of interest and dividends and reinvested earnings of foreign affiliates of U.S. corporations. [2] Consists largely of payments to foreign residents of interest and dividends and reinvested earnings of U.S. affiliates of foreign corporations. [3] Includes items not shown separately. [4] Less current surplus of government enterprises. [5] With inventory valuation and capital consumption adjustments.

Source: U.S. Bureau of Economic Analysis, *National Income and Product Accounts, 1929-97,* and *Survey of Current Business,* August 2001 and May 2002. See also <http://www.bea.doc.gov/bea/dn/nipaweb/SelectTable.asp?Selected=N> (released as 29 April 2002).

No. 638. Selected Per Capita Income and Product Measures in Current and Real (1996) Dollars: 1960 to 2001

[In dollars. Based on U.S. Census Bureau estimated population including Armed Forces abroad; based on quarterly averages. For explanation of chained dollars, see text, this section]

Year	Current dollars					Chained (1996) dollars			
	Gross domestic product	Gross national product	Personal income	Disposable personal income	Personal consumption expenditures	Gross domestic product	Gross national product	Disposable personal income	Personal consumption expenditures
1960	2,918	2,935	2,283	2,026	1,838	13,148	13,232	9,210	8,358
1965	3,705	3,733	2,868	2,567	2,286	15,583	15,702	10,965	9,764
1970	5,069	5,101	4,101	3,591	3,164	17,446	17,556	12,823	11,300
1975	7,571	7,632	6,166	5,470	4,771	18,911	19,065	14,393	12,551
1976	8,363	8,442	6,765	5,960	5,272	19,771	19,953	14,873	13,155
1977	9,221	9,315	7,432	6,519	5,803	20,481	20,685	15,256	13,583
1978	10,313	10,412	8,302	7,253	6,425	21,383	21,584	15,845	14,035
1979	11,401	11,547	9,247	8,033	7,091	21,821	22,096	16,120	14,230
1980	12,276	12,431	10,205	8,869	7,741	21,521	21,791	16,063	14,021
1981	13,614	13,765	11,301	9,773	8,453	21,830	22,066	16,265	14,069
1982	14,035	14,192	11,922	10,364	8,954	21,184	21,418	16,328	14,105
1983	15,085	15,242	12,576	11,036	9,757	21,902	22,126	16,673	14,741
1984	16,636	16,786	13,853	12,215	10,569	23,288	23,494	17,799	15,401
1985	17,664	17,771	14,738	12,941	11,373	23,970	24,112	18,229	16,020
1986	18,501	18,565	15,425	13,555	12,029	24,565	24,649	18,641	16,541
1987	19,529	19,585	16,317	14,246	12,787	25,174	25,246	18,870	16,938
1988	20,845	20,920	17,433	15,312	13,697	25,987	26,080	19,522	17,463
1989	22,188	22,271	18,593	16,235	14,539	26,646	26,742	19,833	17,760
1990	23,215	23,331	19,614	17,176	15,327	26,834	26,962	20,058	17,899
1991	23,630	23,727	20,074	17,664	15,676	26,354	26,460	19,867	17,631
1992	24,618	24,709	21,001	18,524	16,401	26,804	26,905	20,217	17,900
1993	25,544	25,637	21,574	18,979	17,131	27,160	27,257	20,233	18,262
1994	26,799	26,863	22,369	19,624	17,918	27,914	27,977	20,504	18,722
1995	27,784	27,860	23,280	20,358	18,655	28,321	28,397	20,795	19,055
1996	28,993	29,060	24,296	21,069	19,435	28,993	29,060	21,069	19,435
1997	30,497	30,523	25,433	21,881	20,272	29,915	29,947	21,464	19,886
1998	31,822	31,810	26,910	23,031	21,221	30,834	30,833	22,354	20,597
1999	33,204	33,179	27,861	20,709	22,391	31,727	31,715	22,641	21,381
2000	34,950	34,907	29,450	24,889	23,818	32,653	32,026	23,148	22,152
2001	35,704	35,686	30,511	25,943	24,709	32,646	32,645	23,687	22,561

Source: U.S. Bureau of Economic Analysis, *National Income and Product Accounts, 1929-97,* and *Survey of Current Business,* August 2001 and May 2002. See also <http://www.bea.doc.gov/bea/dn/nipaweb/SelectTable.asp?Selected=N> (released as 29 April 2002).

No. 639. Personal Consumption Expenditures in Current and Real (1996) Dollars by Type: 1990 to 2000

[In billions of dollars (3,831.5 represents $3,831,500,000,000). For definition of "chained" dollars, see text, this section]

Expenditure	Current dollars				Chained (1996) dollars			
	1990	1995	1999	2000	1990	1995	1999	2000
Total expenditures [1]	3,831.5	4,969.0	6,250.2	6,728.4	4,474.5	5,075.6	5,968.4	6,257.8
Food and tobacco [1].	677.9	802.5	965.5	1,029.5	774.4	825.1	889.7	921.6
Food purchased for off-premise consumption	401.6	459.8	536.7	569.6	452.4	473.7	511.6	531.0
Purchased meals and beverages [2] . . .	227.8	287.5	353.4	378.0	261.8	294.6	327.2	341.1
Tobacco products	41.0	46.7	65.7	72.1	52.0	48.1	43.3	42.8
Clothing, accessories, and jewelry [1]	261.7	317.3	391.0	416.2	258.2	312.9	404.9	435.3
Shoes	31.5	37.1	44.8	46.8	32.0	36.8	46.5	49.4
Clothing	172.4	210.4	255.8	272.0	165.1	207.2	265.3	285.6
Jewelry and watches	30.3	38.1	48.5	51.4	30.1	36.7	53.7	58.5
Personal care.	53.7	67.4	84.4	90.4	60.1	68.3	80.3	84.1
Housing [1]	585.6	740.8	909.0	958.8	696.2	763.7	831.6	850.1
Owner-occupied nonfarm dwellings-space rent	410.7	529.3	664.6	702.7	488.3	546.1	609.0	625.3
Tenant-occupied nonfarm dwellings-space rent.	148.7	177.0	201.3	209.3	174.6	181.6	184.3	185.1
Household operation [1]	433.6	555.0	676.5	727.4	476.8	564.2	676.6	716.0
Furniture [3]	38.4	47.5	60.0	64.1	42.2	48.1	60.3	64.7
Semidurable house furnishings [4]	22.5	29.7	36.8	39.3	21.8	29.0	38.9	42.7
Cleaning and polishing preparations . .	38.9	47.3	56.6	60.0	42.4	48.5	54.2	54.9
Household utilities	141.1	175.0	189.5	207.6	162.8	180.8	189.6	193.7
Electricity	74.2	91.0	96.4	101.2	83.2	92.5	100.6	103.9
Gas.	26.8	31.5	33.2	40.2	29.5	32.8	31.9	32.8
Water and other sanitary services . .	27.1	38.4	46.2	48.3	37.1	39.8	42.7	43.6
Fuel oil and coal	12.9	14.1	13.6	17.9	13.1	15.7	14.6	13.8
Telephone and telegraph.	60.5	87.8	122.3	131.3	62.6	88.1	127.1	141.8
Medical care [1]	619.7	888.6	1,100.5	1,173.9	807.6	907.8	1,027.8	1,064.2
Drug preparations and sundries [5]	65.4	92.1	139.2	155.5	80.3	94.1	129.4	139.9
Physicians	140.4	192.4	231.2	245.6	183.3	193.8	218.5	228.2
Dentists.	32.4	46.5	58.3	62.1	44.8	48.7	51.1	52.0
Hospitals and nursing homes [6]	265.0	370.9	446.6	472.4	340.5	381.5	419.0	429.3
Health insurance [7]	37.7	58.0	65.3	70.0	66.0	58.9	61.4	62.6
Medical care [7]	31.7	46.4	57.2	61.3	47.9	47.1	49.0	50.0
Personal business [1]	284.7	406.8	577.3	638.9	363.2	424.4	517.0	554.8
Expense of handling life insurance [8] . .	55.0	81.8	97.0	104.5	71.2	87.0	83.0	83.5
Legal services	40.9	48.0	62.4	66.1	51.9	49.7	54.7	55.1
Funeral and burial expenses	9.5	13.3	16.4	16.9	12.9	14.0	14.6	14.6
Transportation [1]	455.4	560.3	711.6	784.9	532.2	574.7	708.3	735.5
User-operated transportation [1]	419.0	517.8	658.9	727.9	493.5	532.3	657.2	682.7
New autos	89.7	82.2	98.0	105.0	104.0	83.5	99.5	106.6
Net purchases of used autos	29.3	50.0	57.6	59.1	42.0	51.2	59.7	59.6
Tires, tubes, accessories, etc. . . .	29.9	36.9	44.4	46.3	29.7	36.8	45.3	47.1
Repair, greasing, washing, parking, storage, rental, and leasing	84.9	122.2	163.6	173.4	100.8	124.5	155.1	160.1
Gasoline and oil	107.3	113.3	129.5	165.3	113.1	120.2	136.7	136.6
Purchased local transportation.	8.4	10.4	12.4	13.0	10.8	11.4	12.5	12.8
Mass transit systems	5.8	7.1	8.6	9.0	7.4	7.8	8.7	9.0
Taxicab	2.6	3.2	3.8	3.9	3.4	3.6	3.8	3.9
Purchased intercity transportation [1]. . .	28.1	32.1	40.3	44.0	28.1	31.0	38.6	39.9
Railway (commutation)	0.7	0.6	0.7	0.8	0.9	0.7	0.7	0.8
Bus	1.3	1.6	2.0	2.2	1.3	1.6	1.8	1.9
Airline	22.7	25.5	32.3	35.8	22.0	24.3	31.1	32.6
Recreation [1] [9]	284.9	401.6	527.9	574.2	292.6	398.7	559.6	614.9
Magazines, newspapers, and sheet music	21.6	26.2	32.9	36.8	27.2	27.2	31.2	34.2
Nondurable toys and sport supplies . .	32.8	47.2	60.4	64.6	33.7	47.4	67.8	76.7
Video and audio products, including musical instruments and computer goods	52.9	77.0	98.0	106.9	33.0	67.3	152.6	186.6
Computers, peripherals, and software	8.9	21.0	31.4	34.3	2.1	14.6	90.9	121.4
Education and research.	83.7	114.5	149.5	159.9	107.6	119.2	134.4	137.7
Higher education.	43.8	62.9	77.4	80.6	60.1	65.6	69.7	70.1
Religious and welfare activities	97.1	134.9	173.0	190.3	115.3	138.7	157.4	164.8
Foreign travel and other, net	-6.3	-20.7	-16.0	-15.9	-5.3	-21.4	-11.6	-7.7
Foreign travel by U.S. residents	42.7	54.1	72.3	80.7	51.7	55.3	70.9	78.0
Less: Expenditures in the United States by nonresidents	51.6	75.4	89.6	97.9	60.1	77.4	84.1	87.8

[1] Includes other expenditures not shown separately.   [2] Consists of purchases (including tips) of meals and beverages from retail, service, and amusement establishments; hotels; dining and buffet cars; schools; school fraternities; institutions; clubs; and industrial lunch rooms. Includes meals and beverages consumed both on and off-premise.   [3] Includes mattresses and bedsprings.   [4] Consists largely of textile house furnishings including piece goods allocated to house furnishing use. Also includes lamp shades, brooms, and brushes.   [5] Excludes drug preparations and related products dispensed by physicians, and other medical services.   [6] Consists of (1) current expenditures (including consumption of fixed capital) of nonprofit hospitals and nursing homes and (2) payments by patients to proprietary and government hospitals and nursing homes.   [7] Consists of (1) premiums, less benefits and dividends, for health hospitalization and accidental death and dismemberment insurance provided by commercial insurance carriers and (2) administrative expenses (including consumption of fixed capital) of Blue Cross and Blue Shield plans and of other independent prepaid and self-insured health plans.   [8] Consists of (1) operating expenses of life insurance carriers and private noninsured pension plans and (2) premiums less benefits and dividends of fraternal benefit societies. Excludes expenses allocated by commercial carriers to accident and health insurance.   [9] For additional details, see Table 1233.

Source: U.S. Bureau of Economic Analysis, *National Income and Product Accounts of the United States, 1929-97; and Survey of Current Business, May 2002.*

Income, Expenditures, and Wealth   423

No. 640. Personal Income and Its Disposition: 1990 to 2001

[In billions of dollars (4,903.2 represents $4,903,200,000,000), except as indicated. For definition of personal income and chained dollars, see text, this section]

Item	1990	1995	1996	1997	1998	1999	2000	2001
Personal income	**4,903.2**	**6,200.9**	**6,547.4**	**6,937.0**	**7,426.0**	**7,777.3**	**8,319.2**	**8,723.5**
Wage and salary disbursements	2,754.6	3,424.7	3,626.5	3,888.9	4,192.8	4,472.2	4,837.2	5,098.2
Goods-producing industries [1]	754.4	863.6	908.2	975.1	1,038.5	1,088.7	1,163.7	1,197.3
Manufacturing	561.4	647.5	673.7	718.4	756.6	782.0	830.1	842.1
Distributive industries [2]	633.6	782.1	822.4	879.6	948.9	1,021.0	1,095.6	1,145.5
Service industries [3]	849.9	1,156.3	1,254.9	1,369.9	1,512.7	1,638.2	1,809.5	1,949.4
Government	516.7	622.7	641.0	664.3	692.7	724.3	768.4	806.0
Other labor income	390.0	497.0	490.0	475.4	490.6	509.7	534.2	553.8
Proprietors' income [4]	381.0	497.7	544.7	581.2	623.8	672.0	715.0	743.5
Rental income of persons [5]	49.1	117.9	129.7	128.3	138.6	147.7	141.6	142.6
Personal dividend income	165.4	254.0	297.4	334.9	348.3	343.1	379.2	416.3
Personal interest income	772.4	792.5	810.6	864.0	964.4	950.0	1,000.6	993.6
Transfer payments to persons	594.4	885.9	928.8	962.2	983.7	1,019.6	1,069.1	1,148.8
Less: Personal contributions for social insurance	203.7	268.8	280.4	297.9	316.3	337.1	357.7	373.3
Less: Personal tax and nontax payments.	609.6	778.3	869.7	968.8	1,070.4	1,159.2	1,288.2	1,306.2
Equals: Disposable personal income . .	**4,293.6**	**5,422.6**	**5,677.7**	**5,968.2**	**6,355.6**	**6,618.0**	**7,031.0**	**7,417.3**
Less: Personal outlays	3,959.3	5,120.2	5,405.6	5,715.3	6,054.1	6,457.2	6,963.3	7,298.9
Personal consumption expenditures . .	3,831.5	4,969.0	5,237.5	5,529.3	5,856.0	6,250.2	6,728.4	7,064.5
Interest paid by persons	115.8	134.7	149.9	164.8	173.7	179.7	205.3	203.2
Personal transfer payments to the rest of the world (net).	12.0	16.5	18.2	21.2	24.3	27.2	29.6	31.2
Equals: Personal saving	**334.3**	**302.4**	**272.1**	**252.9**	**301.5**	**160.9**	**67.7**	**118.4**
Addenda:								
Disposable personal income: Total, billions of chained (**1996**) dollars	5,014.2	5,539.1	5,677.7	5,854.5	6,168.6	6,320.0	6,539.2	6,772.4
Per capita (dollars): Current dollars	17,176.0	20,358.0	21,069.0	21,881.0	23,031.0	23,708.0	24,889.0	25,943.0
Chained (**1996**) dollars	20,058.0	20,795.0	21,069.0	21,464.0	22,354.0	22,641.0	23,148.0	23,687.0
Personal saving as percentage of disposable personal income	7.8	5.6	4.8	4.2	4.7	2.4	1.0	1.6

[1] Comprises agriculture, forestry, fishing, mining, construction, and manufacturing.   [2] Comprises transportation, communication, public utilities, and trade.   [3] Comprises finance, insurance, real estate, services, and rest of world.   [4] With capital consumption and inventory valuation adjustments.   [5] With capital consumption adjustment.

Source: U.S. Bureau of Economic Analysis, *National Income and Product Accounts, 1929-97,* and *Survey of Current Business,* August 2001 and May 2002. See also <http://www.bea.doc.gov/bea/dn/nipaweb/SelectTable.asp?Selected=N> (released as 29 April 2002).

No. 641. Gross Saving and Investment: 1990 to 2001

[In billions of dollars (977.7 represents $977,700,000,000)]

Item	1990	1995	1996	1997	1998	1999	2000	2001
Gross saving	**977.7**	**1,257.5**	**1,349.3**	**1,502.3**	**1,647.2**	**1,707.4**	**1,785.7**	**1,740.8**
Gross private saving	1,016.2	1,266.0	1,290.4	1,343.7	1,375.0	1,348.0	1,323.0	1,380.5
Personal saving.	334.3	302.4	272.1	252.9	301.5	160.9	67.7	118.4
Undistributed corporate profits [1]	102.4	203.6	232.7	261.3	189.9	228.7	225.3	134.5
Undistributed profits	95.3	203.3	205.0	220.0	133.6	179.8	194.3	65.9
Inventory valuation adjustment	-12.9	-18.3	3.1	8.4	18.3	-2.9	-12.4	2.2
Capital consumption adjustment . . .	19.9	18.6	24.6	32.9	38.0	51.7	43.4	66.4
Corporate consumption of fixed capital	391.1	512.1	543.5	581.5	620.2	669.2	727.1	798.6
Noncorporate consumption of fixed capital	188.4	231.5	238.5	250.9	264.2	284.1	302.8	329.0
Wage accruals less disbursements . . .	-	16.4	3.6	-2.9	-0.7	5.2	-	-
Gross government saving	-38.6	-8.5	58.9	158.6	272.2	359.4	462.7	360.3
Federal	-104.3	-108.0	-51.5	33.4	132.0	210.9	315.0	218.6
State and local	65.7	99.4	110.4	125.1	140.2	148.5	147.8	141.8
Gross investment	**1,008.2**	**1,284.0**	**1,382.1**	**1,532.1**	**1,616.2**	**1,634.7**	**1,655.3**	**1,590.9**
Gross private domestic investment	861.7	1,143.8	1,242.7	1,390.4	1,538.7	1,636.7	1,767.5	1,633.9
Gross government investment	215.8	238.2	250.1	264.6	277.1	304.6	318.3	341.2
Net foreign investment	-69.2	-98.0	-110.7	-123.1	-199.7	-306.6	-430.5	-384.1
Statistical discrepancy	**30.6**	**26.5**	**32.8**	**29.7**	**-31.0**	**-72.7**	**-130.4**	**-149.8**
Addendum: Gross saving as a percentage of gross national product	16.8	16.9	17.2	18.0	18.8	18.4	18.1	17.1

- Represents or rounds to zero.   [1] With inventory valuation and capital consumption adjustments.

Source: U.S. Bureau of Economic Analysis, *National Income and Product Accounts, 1929-97,* and *Survey of Current Business,* August 2001 and May 2002. See also <http://www.bea.doc.gov/bea/dn/nipaweb/SelectTable.asp?Selected=N> (released as 29 April 2002).

No. 642. Personal Income in Current and Constant (1996) Dollars by State: 1980 to 2001

[In billions of dollars (2,313.9 represents $2,313,900,000,000). 2001 preliminary. Represents a measure of income received from all sources during the calendar year by residents of each state. Data exclude federal employees overseas and U.S. residents employed by private U.S. firms on temporary foreign assignment. Totals may differ from those in Tables 637, 638, and 640.

State	Current dollars					Constant (1996) dollars [1]				
	1980	1990	1995	2000	2001	1980	1990	1995	2000	2001
United States	2,313.9	4,885.5	6,192.2	8,314.0	8,621.0	4,191.1	5,705.4	6,325.1	7,732.5	7,872.4
Alabama.	30.8	64.1	83.9	104.7	109.0	55.8	74.9	85.7	97.4	99.6
Alaska	6.0	12.6	15.5	18.6	19.7	10.9	14.7	15.8	17.3	18.0
Arizona.	26.3	63.3	88.9	129.1	135.2	47.6	73.9	90.8	120.0	123.5
Arkansas	17.4	34.2	46.0	58.9	61.7	31.4	39.9	47.0	54.8	56.3
California	286.3	655.6	771.5	1,093.1	1,127.4	518.5	765.6	788.0	1,016.6	1,029.5
Colorado.	31.4	65.1	92.9	140.2	145.6	57.0	76.0	94.9	130.4	132.9
Connecticut.	38.7	87.9	104.3	138.8	143.6	70.1	102.7	106.6	129.1	131.1
Delaware	6.4	14.5	18.2	24.4	25.6	11.6	16.9	18.6	22.7	23.4
District of Columbia . . .	7.9	16.1	18.2	22.2	23.2	14.3	18.8	18.6	20.6	21.1
Florida	98.9	258.5	333.5	445.7	467.2	179.1	301.9	340.7	414.6	426.6
Georgia	46.5	115.4	159.8	228.7	238.4	84.2	134.8	163.2	212.7	217.7
Hawaii	11.1	24.9	30.2	33.8	35.0	20.2	29.1	30.8	31.4	31.9
Idaho	8.3	16.1	22.9	30.8	32.0	15.0	18.7	23.4	28.7	29.3
Illinois	126.7	237.6	304.8	396.2	408.9	229.4	277.5	311.3	368.4	373.4
Indiana.	51.9	97.9	126.5	164.0	168.3	94.0	114.3	129.2	152.5	153.7
Iowa	28.2	48.3	60.2	77.4	79.8	51.0	56.4	61.5	72.0	72.8
Kansas.	23.8	45.1	56.6	73.7	76.8	43.1	52.7	57.8	68.5	70.1
Kentucky	30.2	57.2	74.1	97.5	101.9	54.6	66.8	75.7	90.7	93.0
Louisiana	37.3	64.2	84.6	103.2	107.5	67.6	75.0	86.4	96.0	98.2
Maine.	9.5	21.5	25.0	32.4	33.9	17.2	25.1	25.6	30.1	31.0
Maryland	47.5	110.4	135.1	177.8	187.9	86.0	129.0	138.0	165.4	171.5
Massachusetts.	61.3	139.8	170.1	239.7	247.8	111.1	163.2	173.7	222.9	226.3
Michigan.	96.0	177.1	231.6	289.9	295.1	173.8	206.8	236.6	269.6	269.5
Minnesota.	42.2	87.8	113.2	157.5	163.0	76.4	102.5	115.6	146.5	148.9
Mississippi	17.9	33.9	46.2	59.5	61.9	32.4	39.6	47.2	55.4	56.5
Missouri	46.2	91.0	117.6	152.4	157.8	83.7	106.3	120.2	141.8	144.1
Montana.	7.2	12.4	10.3	20.3	21.3	13.1	14.5	16.6	18.9	19.4
Nebraska	14.6	28.6	36.3	47.3	48.9	26.4	33.4	37.1	44.0	44.7
Nevada	9.5	25.2	39.4	59.6	62.9	17.3	29.4	40.2	55.4	57.4
New Hampshire	9.2	23.0	28.6	41.1	42.7	16.6	26.9	29.3	38.2	39.0
New Jersey.	86.9	192.1	233.2	312.9	323.7	157.4	224.4	238.2	291.0	295.6
New Mexico	11.0	22.7	31.7	39.9	42.4	19.9	26.6	32.4	37.1	38.7
New York	194.9	419.7	503.2	658.7	682.2	353.0	490.2	514.0	612.6	623.0
North Carolina	48.6	115.6	157.6	217.1	224.4	88.1	135.0	161.0	202.0	205.0
North Dakota.	5.3	10.1	12.2	15.8	16.2	9.6	11.8	12.5	14.7	14.8
Ohio	109.1	204.1	255.3	317.8	325.5	197.6	238.4	260.8	295.6	297.2
Oklahoma.	29.1	51.0	63.3	81.7	85.8	52.8	59.6	64.7	76.0	78.3
Oregon.	26.9	52.2	71.2	94.9	97.2	48.8	60.9	72.7	88.2	88.8
Pennsylvania.	120.5	235.8	285.9	362.4	376.2	218.2	275.4	292.1	337.0	343.5
Rhode Island.	9.2	20.3	23.8	30.6	31.8	16.7	23.7	24.3	28.4	29.0
South Carolina.	24.4	56.2	72.1	96.6	99.9	44.2	65.6	73.6	89.8	91.2
South Dakota	5.6	11.3	14.5	19.6	19.9	10.2	13.2	14.8	18.2	18.2
Tennessee	38.3	82.3	114.3	147.9	153.6	69.3	96.1	116.7	137.6	140.3
Texas.	142.8	297.6	402.1	581.3	607.5	258.6	347.5	410.7	540.7	554.7
Utah	12.5	25.9	37.3	52.5	54.9	22.6	30.3	38.1	48.9	50.2
Vermont	4.5	10.2	12.4	16.4	17.2	8.1	11.9	12.7	15.2	15.7
Virginia.	54.6	127.6	161.4	221.1	232.1	98.9	149.0	164.9	205.6	212.0
Washington.	45.3	98.1	129.7	184.5	189.1	82.1	114.6	132.5	171.6	172.7
West Virginia.	15.9	26.1	32.6	39.3	40.9	28.9	30.5	33.3	36.5	37.4
Wisconsin.	47.9	89.0	116.0	151.0	156.2	86.7	104.0	118.4	140.4	142.6
Wyoming	5.6	8.2	10.3	13.5	14.2	10.1	9.5	10.5	12.6	13.0

[1] Constant dollar estimates are computed by the U.S. Census Bureau using the national implicit price deflator for personal consumption expenditures from the Bureau of Economic Analysis. Any regional differences in the rate of inflation are not reflected in these constant dollar estimates.

Source: U.S. Bureau of Economic Analysis, *Survey of Current Business*, May 2002, and unpublished data.

U.S. Census Bureau, Statistical Abstract of the United States: 2002

No. 643. Personal Income Per Capita in Current and Constant (1996) Dollars by State: 1980 to 2001

[In dollars, except as indicated. 2001 preliminary. See headnote, Table 642]

State	Current dollars				Constant (1996) dollars [1]				Income rank	
	1980	1990	2000	2001	1980	1990	2000	2001	1980	2001
United States . . .	10,183	19,572	29,469	30,271	18,444	22,856	27,408	27,642	(X)	(X)
Alabama.	7,892	15,826	23,521	24,426	14,295	18,482	21,876	22,305	47	42
Alaska	14,807	22,712	29,642	30,997	26,819	26,523	27,569	28,305	1	14
Arizona.	9,590	17,187	24,988	25,479	17,370	20,071	23,240	23,266	28	38
Arkansas	7,586	14,495	21,995	22,912	13,740	16,927	20,457	20,922	49	48
California	12,029	21,882	32,149	32,678	21,788	25,554	29,900	29,840	3	10
Colorado.	10,809	19,680	32,434	32,957	19,578	22,983	30,166	30,095	12	7
Connecticut.	12,439	26,712	40,702	41,930	22,530	31,195	37,855	38,289	2	1
Delaware	10,803	21,620	31,012	32,121	19,567	25,248	28,843	29,332	13	12
District of Columbia .	12,347	26,561	38,838	40,498	22,364	31,018	36,122	36,981	(X)	(X)
Florida	10,049	19,832	27,764	28,493	18,201	23,160	25,822	26,019	22	25
Georgia	8,474	17,722	27,794	28,438	15,349	20,696	25,850	25,968	37	27
Hawaii	11,512	22,375	27,851	28,554	20,851	26,130	25,903	26,074	7	23
Idaho	8,735	15,858	23,727	24,257	15,821	18,519	22,068	22,150	35	43
Illinois	11,077	20,744	31,856	32,755	20,063	24,225	29,628	29,911	10	9
Indiana.	9,449	17,616	26,933	27,532	17,115	20,572	25,049	25,141	30	31
Iowa	9,671	17,372	26,431	27,283	17,517	20,287	24,582	24,914	27	33
Kansas.	10,038	18,177	27,374	28,507	18,181	21,227	25,459	26,031	23	24
Kentucky	8,231	15,478	24,085	25,057	14,909	18,075	22,400	22,881	43	39
Louisiana	8,833	15,215	23,090	24,084	15,999	17,768	21,475	21,993	34	45
Maine.	8,408	17,473	25,380	26,385	15,229	20,405	23,605	24,094	39	35
Maryland	11,230	23,012	33,482	34,950	20,341	26,874	31,140	31,915	8	5
Massachusetts.	10,673	23,208	37,704	38,845	19,332	27,103	35,067	35,472	14	2
Michigan.	10,369	19,020	29,127	29,538	18,781	22,212	27,090	26,973	15	18
Minnesota.	10,320	20,000	31,935	32,791	18,692	23,356	29,701	29,943	16	8
Mississippi	7,076	13,156	20,900	21,643	12,817	15,364	19,438	19,763	50	50
Missouri	9,390	17,743	27,206	28,029	17,008	20,721	25,303	25,595	31	28
Montana	9,143	15,516	22,518	23,532	16,560	18,120	20,943	21,488	33	46
Nebraska	9,272	18,077	27,630	28,564	16,794	21,111	25,698	26,083	32	22
Nevada	11,780	20,639	29,506	29,860	21,337	24,103	27,442	27,267	4	17
New Hampshire	9,915	20,703	33,169	33,928	17,959	24,177	30,849	30,982	25	6
New Jersey.	11,778	24,748	37,118	38,153	21,333	28,901	34,522	34,840	5	3
New Mexico	8,402	14,944	21,931	23,162	15,218	17,452	20,397	21,151	40	47
New York	11,095	23,292	34,689	35,884	20,096	27,201	32,263	32,768	9	4
North Carolina	8,247	17,348	26,882	27,418	14,938	20,259	25,002	25,037	42	32
North Dakota.	8,095	15,872	24,708	25,538	14,662	18,536	22,980	23,320	46	37
Ohio	10,103	18,788	27,977	28,619	18,299	21,941	26,020	26,134	21	21
Oklahoma.	9,580	16,205	23,650	24,787	17,352	18,924	21,996	22,634	29	40
Oregon.	10,196	18,242	27,660	28,000	18,468	21,303	25,725	25,568	17	29
Pennsylvania.	10,151	19,810	29,504	30,617	18,386	23,134	27,440	27,958	20	15
Rhode Island.	9,742	20,167	29,113	29,984	17,645	23,551	27,077	27,380	26	16
South Carolina.	7,794	16,040	24,000	24,594	14,117	18,732	22,321	22,458	48	41
South Dakota	8,142	16,227	25,958	26,301	14,747	18,950	24,142	24,017	45	36
Tennessee	8,319	16,808	25,946	26,758	15,068	19,629	24,131	24,434	41	34
Texas.	9,957	17,446	27,752	28,486	18,035	20,374	25,811	26,012	24	26
Utah	8,464	14,983	23,436	24,202	15,331	17,497	21,797	22,100	38	44
Vermont	8,702	18,047	26,848	27,992	15,762	21,076	24,970	25,561	36	30
Virginia.	10,176	20,527	31,120	32,295	18,431	23,972	28,943	29,490	18	11
Washington.	10,913	20,017	31,230	31,582	19,766	23,376	29,046	28,839	11	13
West Virginia	8,172	14,579	21,738	22,725	14,802	17,026	20,218	20,752	44	49
Wisconsin	10,161	18,152	28,100	28,911	18,404	21,198	26,135	26,400	19	19
Wyoming	11,753	17,985	27,372	28,807	21,288	21,003	25,458	26,305	6	20

X Not applicable.

[1] Constant dollar estimates are computed by the U.S. Census Bureau using the national implicit price deflator for personal consumption expenditures from the Bureau of Economic Analysis. Any regional differences in the rate of inflation are not reflected in these constant dollar estimates.

Source: Except as noted, U.S. Bureau of Economic Analysis, *Survey of Current Business*, May 2002, and unpublished data.

No. 644. Disposable Personal Income Per Capita in Current and Constant (1996) Dollars by State: 1980 to 2001

[In dollars, except percent. 2001 preliminary. Disposable personal income is the income available to persons for spending or saving; it is calculated as personal income less personal tax and nontax payments]

State	Current dollars				Constant (1996) dollars [1]				Percent of U.S. average	
	1980	1990	2000	2001	1980	1990	2000	2001	1980	2001
United States	8,848	17,135	24,908	25,688	16,026	20,011	23,166	23,457	100.0	100.0
Alabama.	6,996	14,091	20,595	21,481	12,672	16,456	19,155	19,616	79.1	83.6
Alaska	12,738	19,931	25,856	27,131	23,072	23,276	24,048	24,775	144.0	105.6
Arizona.	8,493	15,226	21,446	21,942	15,383	17,781	19,946	20,037	96.0	85.4
Arkansas	6,741	12,975	19,280	20,151	12,210	15,152	17,932	18,401	76.2	78.4
California	10,497	19,021	26,401	26,947	19,013	22,213	24,555	24,607	118.6	104.9
Colorado.	9,347	17,232	27,131	27,683	16,930	20,124	25,233	25,279	105.6	107.8
Connecticut.	10,655	23,259	32,655	33,765	19,299	27,162	30,371	30,833	120.4	131.4
Delaware	8,984	18,598	26,200	27,237	16,272	21,719	24,368	24,872	101.5	106.0
District of Columbia	10,480	22,864	31,578	33,031	18,982	26,701	29,369	30,163	118.4	128.6
Florida	8,857	17,711	23,838	24,554	16,042	20,683	22,171	22,422	100.1	95.6
Georgia	7,442	15,523	23,648	24,296	13,479	18,128	21,994	22,186	84.1	94.6
Hawaii	10,054	19,415	24,149	24,810	18,210	22,673	22,460	22,655	113.6	96.6
Idaho	7,779	14,064	20,394	20,967	14,090	16,424	18,968	19,146	87.9	81.6
Illinois	9,519	18,032	26,860	27,711	17,241	21,058	24,981	25,305	107.6	107.9
Indiana.	8,246	15,390	23,155	23,801	14,936	17,973	21,536	21,734	93.2	92.7
Iowa	8,366	15,288	22,949	23,754	15,153	17,854	21,344	21,691	94.6	92.5
Kansas.	8,674	16,005	23,461	24,506	15,711	18,691	21,820	22,378	98.0	95.4
Kentucky	7,267	13,617	20,729	21,631	13,162	15,902	19,279	19,753	82.1	84.2
Louisiana	7,709	13,673	20,393	21,286	13,963	15,968	18,967	19,437	87.1	82.9
Maine.	7,502	15,408	21,778	22,663	13,588	17,994	20,255	20,695	84.8	88.2
Maryland	9,530	19,702	27,906	29,197	17,261	23,008	25,954	26,661	107.7	113.7
Massachusetts.	9,121	19,902	30,587	31,694	16,521	23,242	28,448	28,942	103.1	123.4
Michigan.	9,009	16,587	24,601	25,158	16,318	19,371	22,880	22,973	101.8	97.9
Minnesota.	8,867	17,318	26,816	27,622	16,060	20,224	24,940	25,223	100.2	107.5
Mississippi	6,347	11,920	18,655	19,401	11,496	13,920	17,350	17,716	71.7	75.5
Missouri	8,195	15,603	23,461	24,217	14,843	18,221	21,820	22,114	92.6	94.3
Montana	8,009	13,778	19,639	20,544	14,506	16,090	18,265	18,760	90.5	80.0
Nebraska	8,099	16,061	23,827	24,707	14,669	18,756	22,161	22,561	91.5	96.2
Nevada	10,348	18,081	25,245	25,637	18,743	21,115	23,479	23,411	117.0	99.8
New Hampshire	8,757	18,441	28,454	29,250	15,861	21,536	26,464	26,710	99.0	113.9
New Jersey.	10,137	21,487	30,645	31,693	18,361	25,093	28,502	28,941	114.6	123.4
New Mexico	7,520	13,381	19,190	20,340	13,621	15,627	17,848	18,574	85.0	79.2
New York	9,480	19,879	28,370	29,402	17,171	23,215	26,386	26,849	107.1	114.5
North Carolina	7,208	15,241	23,002	23,567	13,056	17,700	21,093	21,520	81.5	91.7
North Dakota.	7,085	14,313	21,993	22,691	12,833	16,715	20,455	20,720	80.1	88.3
Ohio	8,797	16,439	23,780	24,420	15,934	19,198	22,117	22,299	99.4	95.1
Oklahoma.	8,329	14,256	20,591	21,613	15,086	16,648	19,151	19,736	94.1	84.1
Oregon.	8,788	15,992	23,185	23,650	15,917	18,676	21,563	21,596	99.3	92.1
Pennsylvania.	8,817	17,422	25,164	26,203	15,970	20,346	23,404	23,927	99.7	102.0
Rhode Island.	8,520	17,771	24,966	25,769	15,432	20,753	23,220	23,531	96.3	100.3
South Carolina.	6,880	14,190	20,821	21,423	12,462	16,571	19,365	19,563	77.8	83.4
South Dakota	7,362	14,837	23,134	23,454	13,335	17,327	21,516	21,417	83.2	91.3
Tennessee	7,449	15,181	22,987	23,819	13,492	17,729	21,379	21,751	84.2	92.7
Texas.	8,616	15,589	24,263	25,015	15,606	18,205	22,566	22,843	97.4	97.4
Utah	7,515	13,207	20,083	20,803	13,612	15,423	18,678	18,996	84.9	81.0
Vermont	7,663	15,831	23,011	24,064	13,880	18,488	21,402	21,974	86.6	93.7
Virginia.	8,784	17,890	25,913	26,972	15,910	20,892	24,101	24,630	99.3	105.0
Washington.	9,544	17,753	26,291	26,773	17,287	20,732	24,452	24,448	107.9	104.2
West Virginia.	7,162	12,997	19,156	20,068	12,972	15,178	17,816	18,325	80.9	78.1
Wisconsin.	8,811	15,809	23,878	24,710	15,959	18,462	22,208	22,564	99.6	96.2
Wyoming	10,166	16,067	23,300	24,575	18,413	18,763	21,670	22,441	114.9	95.7

[1] Constant dollar estimates are computed by the U.S. Census Bureau using the national implicit price deflator for personal consumption expenditures from the Bureau of Economic Analysis. Any regional differences in the rate of inflation are not reflected in these constant dollar estimates.

Source: U.S. Bureau of Economic Analysis, *Survey of Current Business*, May 2002, unpublished data.

Income, Expenditures, and Wealth   427

No. 645. Personal Income by Selected Large Metropolitan Area: 1998 to 2000

[7,418,497 represents $7,418,497,000,000 as defined June 30, 1994. CMSA=Consolidated metropolitan statistical area; MSA= Metropolitan statistical area; NECMA=New England County Metropolitan areas. See Appendix II]

Metropolitan area ranked by 2000 income	Personal income				Per capita personal income			
	1998 (mil. dol.)	1999 (mil. dol.)	2000 (mil. dol.)	Annual percent change, 1999-2000	1998 (dol.)	1999 (dol.)	2000 (dol.)	Percent of national average, 2000
United States.................	7,418,497	7,769,367	8,314,032	7.01	26,893	27,843	29,469	100.0
New York-No. New Jersey-Long Island, NY-NJ-CT-PA (CMSA)	741,023	774,361	836,234	7.99	35,723	36,956	39,568	134.3
Los Angeles-Riverside-Orange County, CA (CMSA)...............	428,551	451,458	482,176	6.80	26,909	27,892	29,329	99.5
San Francisco-Oakland-San Jose, CA (CMSA).	257,252	283,762	328,725	15.85	37,277	40,660	46,586	158.1
Chicago-Gary-Kenosha, IL-IN-WI (CMSA)....	287,183	298,505	316,620	6.07	31,878	32,820	34,506	117.1
Washington-Baltimore, DC-MD-VA-WV (CMSA).................	247,605	262,832	283,865	8.00	33,416	34,955	37,168	126.1
Boston-Worcester-Lawrence-Lowell-Brockton, MA-NH (NECMA)................	199,531	212,497	235,164	10.67	33,411	35,287	38,758	131.5
Philadelphia-Wilmington-Atlantic City, PA-NJ-DE-MD (CMSA).............	187,702	194,772	206,743	6.15	30,592	31,598	33,377	113.3
Detroit-Ann Arbor-Flint, MI (CMSA)	162,694	169,368	178,609	5.46	29,973	31,114	32,694	110.9
Dallas-Fort Worth, TX (CMSA).........	150,138	160,079	174,907	9.26	30,167	31,267	33,289	113.0
Houston-Galveston-Brazoria, TX (CMSA)	136,556	142,509	155,001	8.77	30,405	30,982	33,025	112.1
Atlanta, GA (MSA)	116,796	126,048	136,832	8.56	30,121	31,435	33,013	112.0
Seattle-Tacoma-Bremerton, WA (CMSA).....	112,042	121,281	127,818	5.39	32,207	34,412	35,877	121.7
Minneapolis-St. Paul, MN-WI (MSA)......	96,082	101,215	109,236	7.92	33,308	34,518	36,666	124.4
Miami-Fort Lauderdale, FL (CMSA)	95,902	98,951	105,353	6.47	25,637	25,937	27,033	91.7
Denver-Boulder-Greeley, CO (CMSA).......	78,606	85,196	94,440	10.85	31,947	33,652	36,370	123.4
San Diego, CA (MSA)	78,156	84,493	91,850	8.71	28,558	30,289	32,515	110.3
Phoenix-Mesa, AZ (MSA)............	77,874	82,677	90,309	9.23	25,329	26,013	27,564	93.5
Cleveland-Akron, OH (CMSA).........	83,338	85,770	89,742	4.63	28,294	29,115	30,464	103.4
St. Louis, MO-IL (MSA)	75,458	77,468	81,709	5.47	29,184	29,855	31,354	106.4
Pittsburgh, PA (MSA)............	66,086	68,840	72,206	4.89	27,806	29,096	30,644	104.0
Portland-Salem, OR-WA (CMSA)........	61,119	64,272	69,210	7.68	27,732	28,687	30,453	103.3
Tampa-St. Petersburg-Clearwater, FL (MSA) ..	61,218	63,331	67,824	7.10	26,197	26,732	28,214	95.7
Cincinnati-Hamilton, OH-KY-IN (CMSA)	54,908	57,245	60,249	5.25	28,078	29,075	30,384	103.1
Kansas City, MO-KS (MSA)	50,305	53,017	56,591	6.74	28,865	30,090	31,765	107.8
Milwaukee-Racine, WI (CMSA)	49,851	51,775	54,331	4.94	29,698	30,734	32,137	109.1
Sacramento-Yolo, CA (CMSA).........	46,577	50,012	54,157	8.29	26,894	28,299	29,951	101.6
Indianapolis, IN (MSA)............	44,755	46,852	49,836	6.37	28,589	29,485	30,906	104.9
Columbus, OH (MSA)	41,976	44,389	47,299	6.56	27,896	29,114	30,619	103.9
Charlotte-Gastonia-Rock Hill, NC-SC (MSA) ..	40,359	43,205	46,600	7.86	28,212	29,360	30,901	104.9
West Palm Beach-Boca Raton, FL (MSA)	42,948	44,169	46,589	5.48	39,182	39,545	41,007	139.2
Orlando, FL (MSA)	38,426	40,731	43,921	7.83	24,508	25,330	26,523	90.0
Las Vegas, NV-AZ (MSA)...........	37,556	40,561	43,615	7.53	26,320	26,985	27,558	93.5
Hartford, CT (NECMA)............	37,637	39,103	41,761	6.80	33,179	34,261	36,295	123.2
Norfolk-Virginia Beach-Newport News, VA-NC (MSA).................	37,362	38,836	41,180	6.04	24,154	24,929	26,159	88.8
San Antonio, TX (MSA)	36,977	38,704	41,169	6.37	23,903	24,612	25,741	87.3
Austin-San Marcos, TX (MSA)........	32,797	36,972	40,483	9.50	28,382	30,526	32,039	108.7
Raleigh-Durham-Chapel Hill, NC (MSA)	33,005	35,371	38,912	10.01	29,253	30,443	32,537	110.4
Nashville, TN (MSA)	34,143	35,748	38,263	7.03	28,598	29,429	30,962	105.1
Greensboro-Winston-Salem-High Point, NC (MSA).................	32,570	33,716	35,799	6.18	26,716	27,237	28,522	96.8
Salt Lake City-Ogden, UT (MSA).........	31,226	32,672	34,868	6.72	23,953	24,738	26,075	88.5
New Orleans, LA (MSA)............	33,225	33,710	34,842	3.36	24,878	25,187	26,056	88.4
Memphis, TN-AR-MS (MSA)...........	30,687	31,775	33,329	4.89	27,625	28,222	29,275	99.3
Jacksonville, FL (MSA)	28,638	29,383	31,413	6.91	26,673	26,997	28,456	96.6
Buffalo-Niagara Falls, NY (MSA)	29,513	30,160	31,371	4.01	25,043	25,710	26,846	91.1
Richmond-Petersburg, VA (MSA).........	27,932	29,358	31,271	6.52	28,635	29,744	31,292	106.2
Rochester, NY (MSA)	29,626	30,133	31,213	3.58	27,024	27,488	28,419	96.4
Louisville, KY-IN (MSA)	28,201	29,247	31,008	6.02	27,866	28,670	30,191	102.5
Grand Rapids-Muskegon-Holland, MI (MSA) ..	27,695	28,933	30,550	5.59	26,095	26,853	27,977	94.9
Providence-Warwick-Pawtucket, RI (NECMA) .	25,106	26,176	27,693	5.80	26,519	27,393	28,709	97.4
Oklahoma City, OK (MSA)	24,684	25,793	27,606	7.03	23,226	23,969	25,436	86.3
Dayton-Springfield, OH (MSA).........	25,427	26,056	27,084	3.95	26,572	27,336	28,504	96.7
Birmingham, AL (MSA)	24,406	25,652	26,814	4.53	26,791	27,966	29,057	98.6
Honolulu, HI (MSA)	24,914	25,263	26,235	3.85	28,091	28,744	29,960	101.7
Albany-Schenectady-Troy, NY (MSA)	24,112	24,816	26,233	5.71	27,587	28,392	29,942	101.6
Greenville-Spartanburg-Anderson, SC (MSA)..	21,965	22,964	24,403	6.26	23,404	24,100	25,277	85.8
Tulsa, OK (MSA)	21,450	21,984	23,157	5.34	27,244	27,529	28,775	97.6
Omaha, NE-IA (MSA)	20,377	21,682	22,895	5.59	28,932	30,459	31,866	108.1

Source: U.S. Bureau of Economic Analysis, *Survey of Current Business*, June 2002; and Internet site <http://www.bea.doc.gov/bea/regional/reis/> (accessed 14 June 2002).

No. 646. Flow of Funds Accounts—Composition of Individuals' Savings: 1990 to 1999

[In billions of dollars (567.7 represents $567,700,000,000). Combined statement for households, farm business, and nonfarm noncorporate business. Minus sign (-) indicates decrease]

Composition of savings	1990	1992	1993	1994	1995	1996	1997	1998	1999
Increase in financial assets	567.7	448.4	439.7	502.4	485.9	497.0	441.2	586.6	556.6
Foreign deposits	1.4	1.2	-1.1	3.1	4.6	12.4	6.3	-0.3	4.3
Checkable deposits and currency	-19.4	103.7	56.4	-24.2	-53.9	-50.7	-32.8	59.2	-14.2
Time and savings deposits	48.5	-76.9	-106.5	-4.0	173.2	175.7	190.2	202.3	115.6
Money market fund shares	26.9	-40.9	-0.3	13.5	98.8	56.6	89.7	145.4	103.9
Securities	179.0	179.3	140.8	151.4	-129.4	-107.2	-277.9	-275.0	-81.4
Open market paper	6.2	-3.3	15.6	1.2	1.3	7.4	3.6	4.2	5.3
U.S. government securities	114.2	78.9	-16.3	290.2	-48.0	27.7	-161.8	-153.8	100.7
Municipal securities	27.7	-27.0	-32.1	-50.2	-43.5	-22.2	53.6	15.3	48.3
Corporate and foreign bonds	43.1	2.3	31.3	30.5	95.0	46.2	75.4	60.4	32.3
Corporate equities [1]	-39.6	-5.6	-62.8	-187.6	-228.8	-347.2	-507.1	-462.7	-401.7
Mutual fund shares	27.5	133.9	205.1	67.4	94.7	180.8	258.4	261.6	133.6
Life insurance reserves	26.5	29.1	37.1	35.5	45.8	44.5	59.3	53.3	58.6
Pension fund reserves	249.4	244.3	267.9	254.4	235.4	247.6	304.4	303.9	287.4
Investment in bank personal trusts	32.9	-7.1	0.9	17.8	4.0	-8.6	-56.3	-48.0	-31.1
Miscellaneous assets	22.4	15.7	44.5	54.9	107.3	126.7	158.2	145.8	113.6
Gross investment in tangible assets	806.3	793.8	864.4	958.8	979.9	1,061.1	1,092.5	1,206.1	1,364.1
Minus: Consumption of fixed capital	593.5	639.0	649.2	690.6	709.3	729.6	755.7	784.7	840.7
Equals: Net investment in tangible assets . . .	212.9	154.8	215.2	268.2	270.5	331.5	336.9	421.4	523.4
Net increase in liabilities	241.5	168.6	246.2	324.8	407.3	484.7	533.9	641.7	757.3
Mortgage debt on nonfarm homes	212.3	168.9	159.4	182.6	179.5	241.2	251.0	382.3	431.7
Other mortgage debt [2]	1.4	-39.4	-29.4	-29.6	-8.5	53.6	83.7	79.3	89.8
Consumer credit	11.9	6.1	58.4	124.9	138.9	88.8	52.5	67.6	94.4
Policy loans	4.1	5.7	5.6	7.8	10.5	4.5	3.2	0.1	-5.3
Security credit	-3.7	-1.6	22.6	-1.1	3.5	15.8	36.8	21.6	69.7
Other liabilities [2]	15.5	28.9	29.6	40.2	83.5	80.8	106.7	90.7	77.0
Personal saving with consumer durables [3] . . .	539.1	434.7	408.7	445.7	349.1	343.8	244.2	366.3	322.7
Personal saving, without consumer durable [3] . .	466.3	379.6	323.0	332.7	223.8	202.7	88.3	170.7	101.7
Personal saving (NIPA, excludes consumer durables) [4] . .	334.3	413.7	350.8	315.6	302.4	272.1	271.1	229.7	156.3

[1] Only directly held and those in closed-end funds. Other equities are included in mutual funds, life insurance and pension reserves, and bank personal trusts.   [2] Includes corporate farms.   [3] Flow of Funds measure.   [4] National Income and Product Accounts measure.

Source: Board of Governors of the Federal Reserve System, Flow of Funds Accounts, quarterly.

No. 647. Annual Expenditure Per Child by Husband-Wife Families by Family Income and Expenditure Type: 2001

[In dollars. Expenditures based on data from the 1990-92 Consumer Expenditure Survey updated to 2001 dollars using the Consumer Price Index. Excludes expenses for college. For more on the methodology, see report cited below]

Age of child	Expenditure type							
	Total	Housing	Food	Trans-por-tation	Clothing	Health care	Child care and educa-tion	Miscel-lan-eous [1]
INCOME: LESS THAN $39,100								
Less than 2 yrs. old	6,490	2,500	910	780	370	460	840	630
3 to 5 yrs. old	6,630	2,470	1,010	750	360	440	950	650
6 to 8 yrs. old	6,710	2,380	1,300	880	400	510	560	680
9 to 11 yrs. old	6,730	2,150	1,560	950	450	560	340	720
12 to 14 yrs. old	7,560	2,400	1,640	1,070	750	560	240	900
15 to 17 yrs. old	7,480	1,940	1,780	1,440	660	600	400	660
INCOME: $39,100-$65,800								
Less than 2 yrs. old	9,030	3,380	1,090	1,160	430	610	1,380	980
3 to 5 yrs. old	9,260	3,350	1,260	1,130	420	580	1,530	990
6 to 8 yrs. old	9,260	3,260	1,600	1,260	470	660	980	1,030
9 to 11 yrs. old	9,190	3,030	1,890	1,330	520	720	640	1,060
12 to 14 yrs. old	9,940	3,280	1,900	1,450	870	720	470	1,250
15 to 17 yrs. old	10,140	2,820	2,110	1,840	780	770	810	1,010
INCOME: MORE THAN $65,800								
Less than 2 yrs. old	13,430	5,370	1,440	1,630	570	700	2,090	1,630
3 to 5 yrs. old	13,720	5,340	1,630	1,600	560	670	2,270	1,650
6 to 8 yrs. old	13,570	5,250	1,970	1,720	610	770	1,560	1,690
9 to 11 yrs. old	13,410	5,020	2,290	1,800	670	820	1,090	1,720
12 to 14 yrs. old	14,260	5,270	2,400	1,920	1,100	830	840	1,900
15 to 17 yrs. old	14,670	4,810	2,530	2,330	1,000	870	1,470	1,660

[1] Expenses include personal care items, entertainment, and reading materials.

Source: Dept. of Agriculture, Center for Nutrition Policy and Promotion, Expenditures on Children by Families, 2000 Annual Report. See also <http://www.usda.gov/cnpp/Crc/crc2001.pdf> (accessed 17 June 2002).

Income, Expenditures, and Wealth   429

No. 648. Average Annual Expenditures of All Consumer Units by Selected Major Types of Expenditure: 1990 to 2000

[In dollars, except as indicated. Based on Consumer Expenditure Survey. Data are averages for the noninstitutional population. Expenditures reported here are out-of-pocket]

Type	1990	1994	1995	1996	1997	1998	1999	2000
Number of consumer units (1,000)	96,968	102,210	103,123	104,212	105,576	107,182	108,465	109,367
Total expenditures.	**28,381**	**31,731**	**32,264**	**33,797**	**34,819**	**35,535**	**36,995**	**38,045**
Food	4,296	4,411	4,505	4,698	4,801	4,810	5,031	5,158
Food at home	2,485	2,712	2,803	2,876	2,880	2,780	2,915	3,021
Meats, poultry, fish, and eggs . .	668	732	752	737	743	723	749	795
Dairy products	295	289	297	312	314	301	322	325
Fruits and vegetables.	408	437	457	490	476	472	500	521
Other food at home	746	825	856	889	895	858	896	927
Food away from home.	1,811	1,698	1,702	1,823	1,921	2,030	2,116	2,137
Alcoholic beverages	293	278	277	309	309	309	318	372
Housing	8,703	10,106	10,458	10,747	11,272	11,713	12,057	12,319
Shelter	4,836	5,686	5,928	6,064	6,344	6,680	7,016	7,114
Fuels, utilities, public services. . . .	1,890	2,189	2,191	2,347	2,412	2,405	2,377	2,489
Apparel and services	1,618	1,644	1,704	1,752	1,729	1,674	1,743	1,856
Transportation	5,120	6,044	6,014	6,382	6,457	6,616	7,011	7,417
Vehicle purchase	2,129	2,725	2,638	2,815	2,736	2,964	3,305	3,418
Gasoline and motor oil.	1,047	986	1,006	1,082	1,098	1,017	1,055	1,291
Other transportation	1,642	1,953	2,015	2,058	2,230	2,206	2,254	2,281
Health care.	1,480	1,755	1,732	1,770	1,841	1,903	1,959	2,066
Entertainment	1,422	1,567	1,612	1,834	1,813	1,746	1,891	1,863
Reading	153	165	162	159	164	161	159	146
Tobacco products, smoking supplies . .	274	259	269	255	264	273	300	319
Personal insurance and pensions	2,592	2,938	2,964	3,060	3,223	3,381	3,436	3,365
Life and other personal insurance	345	398	373	353	379	398	394	399
Pensions and social security	2,248	2,540	2,591	2,707	2,844	2,982	3,042	2,966

Source: U.S. Bureau of Labor Statistics, *Consumer Expenditures in 2000;* earlier reports. See also <http://www.bls.gov/cex/csxann00.pdf> (released April 2002).

No. 649. Average Annual Expenditures of All Consumer Units by Metropolitan Area: 1999-2000

[In dollars. Metropolitan areas defined June 30, 1983, CMSA=Consolidated Metropolitan Statistical Area; MSA=Metropolitan Statistical Area; PMSA=Primary Metropolitan Statistical Area. See text, Section 1, Population, and Appendix II. See headnote, Table 648]

Metropolitan area	Total expenditures [1]	Food	Housing			Transportation			Health care
			Total [1]	Shelter	Utility fuels [2]	Total [1]	Vehicle purchases	Gasoline and motor oil	
Anchorage, AK MSA	53,028	6,964	17,504	10,720	2,485	9,812	4,276	1,334	2,530
Atlanta, GA MSA	37,624	4,689	13,663	8,254	3,055	7,056	3,194	1,128	1,910
Baltimore, MD MSA	41,725	5,531	13,779	8,323	2,483	7,185	3,214	1,172	1,843
Boston-Lawrence-Salem, MA-NH CMSA	37,727	4,924	13,362	8,633	2,362	6,587	2,808	965	1,740
Chicago-Gary-Lake County, IL-IN-WI CMSA	43,437	5,452	15,322	9,396	2,796	7,418	3,374	1,120	2,033
Cincinnati-Hamilton, OH-KY-IN CMSA .	39,772	5,492	12,749	7,410	2,411	7,911	3,872	1,117	1,882
Cleveland-Akron-Lorain, OH CMSA . . .	38,834	5,274	12,567	7,156	2,584	8,277	4,253	1,073	1,770
Dallas-Fort Worth, TX CMSA	46,600	6,865	14,339	8,087	3,041	8,948	4,441	1,469	1,963
Denver-Boulder-Greeley, CO CMSA . .	46,002	5,676	15,773	10,110	2,311	8,340	3,257	1,196	2,045
Detroit-Ann Arbor, MI CMSA.	41,360	6,040	13,845	7,704	2,637	7,635	2,871	1,268	1,638
Honolulu, HI MSA.	41,972	5,771	14,084	9,717	2,113	5,775	1,553	1,071	2,211
Houston-Galveston-Brazoria, TX CMSA	46,299	6,080	13,870	7,337	2,929	9,722	4,813	1,442	2,195
Kansas City, MO-Kansas City, KS CMSA	37,647	5,302	11,513	6,606	2,645	7,889	3,824	1,341	1,931
Los Angeles-Long Beach, CA PMSA . .	44,748	5,490	16,550	10,293	2,290	7,701	2,933	1,383	1,833
Miami-Fort Lauderdale, FL CMSA	39,773	5,560	14,535	8,787	2,768	7,463	3,023	1,250	1,746
Milwaukee, WI PMSA	38,877	4,627	13,313	8,332	2,271	7,017	3,369	1,129	2,283
Minneapolis-St. Paul, MN-WI MSA . . .	49,893	5,794	15,637	9,285	2,414	8,303	3,312	1,348	2,334
New York-Northern New Jersey-Long Island, NY-NJ-CT CMSA	46,277	6,416	16,838	10,962	2,687	7,003	2,607	982	1,960
Philadelphia-Wilmington-Trenton, PA-NJ-DE-MD CMSA	39,666	5,408	14,235	8,455	2,864	6,872	2,879	931	1,779
Phoenix-Mesa, AZ MSA.	41,991	5,486	13,123	7,793	2,599	8,858	4,223	1,118	2,168
Pittsburgh-Beaver Valley, PA CMSA. . .	35,526	5,032	10,451	5,293	2,490	6,359	2,505	1,026	2,073
Portland-Vancouver, OR-WA CMSA. . .	44,331	5,655	14,654	9,095	2,344	7,800	3,304	1,248	1,984
San Diego, CA MSA	47,338	5,243	17,011	10,996	2,104	9,982	5,323	1,349	1,927
San Francisco-Oakland-San Jose, CA CMSA	55,040	7,442	19,682	12,963	2,226	9,726	4,409	1,424	2,030
Seattle-Tacoma, WA CMSA	43,602	6,543	14,644	9,489	2,225	7,401	2,766	1,300	2,514
St. Louis-East St. Louis Alton, MO-IL CMSA.	38,935	5,619	11,557	6,411	2,668	7,950	4,345	1,105	2,133
Tampa-St. Petersburg-Clearwater, FL MSA.	35,404	4,589	11,258	6,281	2,576	7,752	4,130	1,102	2,388
Washington, DC-MD-VA MSA	47,894	5,705	16,978	10,698	2,639	7,813	3,222	1,195	2,222

[1] Includes expenditures not shown separately. [2] Includes public services.

Source: U.S. Bureau of Labor Statistics, *Consumer Expenditures,* annual; and Internet <http://www.bls.gov/cex/csxann00.pdf> (released April 2002).

No. 650. Average Annual Expenditures of All Consumer Units by Race, Hispanic Origin, and Age of Householder: 2000

[**In dollars.** Based on Consumer Expenditure Survey. Data are averages for the noninstitutional population. Expenditures reported here are out-of-pocket]

Item	All con- sumer units	Black	His- panic	Age Under 25 yrs.	Age 25 to 34 yrs.	Age 35 to 44 yrs.	Age 45 to 54 yrs.	Age 55 to 64 yrs.	Age 65 yrs. and over
Expenditures, total	**38,045**	**28,152**	**32,735**	**22,543**	**38,945**	**45,149**	**46,160**	**39,340**	**26,533**
Food	5,158	4,095	5,362	3,213	5,260	6,092	6,295	5,168	3,652
Food at home	3,021	2,691	3,496	1,643	2,951	3,484	3,657	3,071	2,448
Cereals and bakery products	453	393	491	238	429	531	560	441	376
Cereals and cereal products	156	159	201	90	167	190	180	140	123
Bakery products	297	234	290	148	263	341	380	301	253
Meats, poultry, fish, and eggs	795	909	1,036	437	770	918	970	832	626
Beef	238	236	326	135	239	270	296	243	182
Pork	167	199	213	89	155	186	198	186	143
Other meats	101	106	116	55	98	120	121	99	79
Poultry	145	185	190	86	145	178	169	146	108
Fish and seafood	110	139	136	52	102	126	146	115	84
Eggs	34	43	55	21	30	37	40	43	30
Dairy products	325	245	359	175	317	383	377	321	275
Fresh milk and cream	131	102	170	73	134	157	146	126	112
Other dairy products	193	143	189	101	183	226	232	195	163
Fruits and vegetables	521	454	670	253	488	552	626	558	495
Fresh fruits	163	131	228	77	146	169	187	185	169
Fresh vegetables	159	129	228	74	148	164	201	173	146
Processed fruits	115	118	125	62	113	125	133	115	109
Processed vegetables	84	76	89	41	82	92	105	87	71
Other food at home	927	691	940	541	946	1,101	1,124	918	676
Nonalcoholic beverages	250	186	292	147	247	300	300	263	176
Food away from home	2,137	1,404	1,865	1,569	2,309	2,607	2,638	2,097	1,205
Alcoholic beverages	372	211	285	392	431	420	417	371	211
Housing	12,319	9,906	10,850	7,109	13,050	15,111	14,179	12,362	8,759
Shelter	7,114	5,678	6,437	4,574	7,905	8,930	8,297	6,587	4,597
Owned dwellings	4,602	2,607	2,949	634	4,142	6,433	5,964	4,780	3,043
Mortgage interest and charges	2,639	1,574	1,751	386	2,888	4,302	3,558	2,278	793
Property taxes	1,139	640	665	176	755	1,246	1,471	1,462	1,175
Rented dwellings	2,034	2,843	3,307	3,618	3,514	2,067	1,614	1,123	1,140
Other lodging	478	227	181	322	248	430	719	685	413
Utilities, fuels, and public services	2,489	2,571	2,170	1,248	2,341	2,810	2,057	2,756	2,198
Natural gas	307	342	242	102	273	350	344	341	310
Electricity	911	938	749	444	826	1,009	1,045	1,048	834
Fuel oil and other fuels	97	43	30	21	58	97	109	113	137
Telephone	877	986	889	589	950	1,018	1,007	909	620
Water and other public services	296	261	259	91	234	336	352	345	298
Household operations	684	468	465	226	871	896	583	542	661
Personal services	326	292	255	154	641	542	147	93	215
Other household expenses	358	176	211	72	230	354	435	449	446
Housekeeping supplies	482	303	474	104	437	570	532	585	421
Household furnishings and equipment	1,549	887	1,303	867	1,495	1,906	1,911	1,891	882
Household textiles	106	57	89	35	120	124	125	125	73
Furniture	391	283	447	270	457	499	471	361	201
Floor coverings	44	25	27	6	42	53	51	56	38
Major appliances	189	108	166	77	181	212	223	221	160
Miscellaneous household equipment	731	377	508	429	617	926	915	1,022	356
Apparel and services	1,856	1,695	2,076	1,420	2,059	2,323	2,371	1,694	925
Men and boys	440	390	483	320	511	551	577	395	196
Women and girls	725	604	691	435	704	935	977	687	400
Children under 2 years old	82	89	137	101	165	105	54	53	20
Footwear	343	352	516	363	394	401	438	300	159
Other apparel products and services	266	260	249	201	285	331	325	259	150
Transportation	7,417	5,214	6,719	5,189	8,357	8,702	8,827	7,842	4,397
Vehicle purchases (net outlay)	3,418	2,285	3,146	2,628	4,139	3,996	3,863	3,623	1,904
Cars and trucks, new	1,605	869	1,079	1,061	1,845	1,724	1,690	2,097	1,076
Cars and trucks, used	1,770	1,414	2,058	1,547	2,217	2,198	2,128	1,508	823
Gasoline and motor oil	1,291	956	1,244	947	1,341	1,577	1,592	1,349	735
Other vehicle expenses	2,281	1,705	1,945	1,397	2,482	2,677	2,868	2,375	1,374
Vehicle finance charges	328	290	274	228	436	406	391	349	115
Maintenance and repair	624	452	546	442	570	708	801	672	441
Vehicle insurance	778	634	696	449	774	884	1,002	796	557
Public transportation	427	268	385	216	395	451	505	495	385
Health care [1]	2,066	1,107	1,243	504	1,256	1,774	2,200	2,508	3,247
Entertainment [2]	1,863	1,014	1,186	1,091	1,876	2,464	2,231	1,955	1,069
Personal care products and services	564	627	564	345	576	644	682	569	426
Reading	146	72	59	57	118	151	178	179	148
Education	632	383	363	1,257	585	615	1,146	380	108
Tobacco products and smoking supplies	319	243	173	237	310	427	376	349	163
Miscellaneous	776	572	602	322	804	852	927	824	661
Cash contributions	1,192	700	645	189	648	1,003	1,537	1,301	1,828
Personal insurance and pensions	3,365	2,313	2,608	1,216	3,614	4,570	4,795	3,838	939
Life and other personal insurance	399	358	189	54	242	412	549	587	378
Pensions and Social Security	2,966	1,955	2,420	1,162	3,373	4,158	4,246	3,252	561
Personal taxes [1]	**3,117**	**1,626**	**1,581**	**931**	**2,833**	**3,874**	**4,740**	**3,999**	**1,330**

[1] For additional health care expenditures, see Table 123.   [2] For additional recreation expenditures, see Section 26, Arts, Entertainment, and Recreation section.

Source: U.S. Bureau of Labor Statistics, *Consumer Expenditures in 2000;* earlier reports. See also <http://www.bls.gov/cex/csxann00.pdf> (released April 2002).

No. 651. Average Annual Expenditures of All Consumer Units by Region and Size of Unit: 2000

[In dollars. For composition of regions, see map, inside front cover. See headnote, Table 648]

Item	Region				Size of consumer unit				
	North-east	Mid west	South	West	One person	Two per-sons	Three per-sons	Four per-sons	Five or more
Expenditures, total	38,902	39,213	34,707	41,328	23,059	38,627	45,156	52,032	49,100
Food	5,377	5,255	4,724	5,554	2,825	5,104	6,093	7,122	7,833
Food at home	3,202	2,933	2,823	3,269	1,477	2,894	3,687	4,247	5,111
Cereals and bakery products	491	444	422	480	221	421	550	647	805
Cereals and cereal products	164	152	148	167	69	138	185	229	318
Bakery products	326	292	274	313	151	282	365	419	487
Meats, poultry, fish, and eggs	883	721	779	821	352	774	1,007	1,109	1,366
Beef	248	226	230	255	100	228	317	342	399
Pork	162	160	176	164	71	171	216	218	282
Other meats	116	103	94	94	47	91	121	142	195
Poultry	174	125	142	146	68	137	176	212	252
Fish and seafood	149	78	100	124	50	112	135	154	175
Eggs	35	28	36	38	18	34	41	40	63
Dairy products	354	330	286	356	162	306	395	449	566
Fresh milk and cream	132	132	122	145	65	114	165	183	253
Other dairy products	222	197	164	211	98	193	230	266	313
Fruits and vegetables	579	482	470	592	279	522	611	695	826
Fresh fruits	181	151	141	196	93	166	182	213	258
Fresh vegetables	184	137	139	190	86	160	183	206	258
Processed fruits	131	113	103	123	60	113	139	163	176
Processed vegetables	83	81	86	84	40	83	108	114	134
Other food at home	895	957	867	1,021	462	872	1,124	1,346	1,549
Nonalcoholic beverages	240	249	238	277	125	237	310	363	395
Food away from home	2,175	2,322	1,901	2,285	1,348	2,210	2,407	2,875	2,722
Alcoholic beverages	390	388	304	449	325	429	411	329	318
Housing	13,505	11,961	10,855	13,972	8,189	12,096	14,193	16,921	15,585
Shelter	8,222	6,633	5,839	8,667	5,054	6,936	8,023	9,510	8,862
Owned dwellings	5,229	4,599	3,803	5,320	2,332	4,535	5,338	7,351	6,385
Mortgage interest and charges	2,574	2,471	2,238	3,498	1,005	2,356	3,292	4,810	4,164
Property taxes	1,780	1,224	825	987	723	1,248	1,191	1,557	1,346
Maintenance, repair, insurance, other	874	903	739	834	604	931	855	984	876
Rented dwellings	2,434	1,531	1,643	2,832	2,435	1,765	2,160	1,665	2,009
Other lodging	559	503	393	515	287	636	525	494	467
Utilities, fuels, and public services	2,570	2,513	2,596	2,226	1,628	2,545	2,839	3,156	3,348
Natural gas	413	430	190	272	208	301	336	396	446
Electricity	816	834	1,148	704	569	952	1,044	1,158	1,233
Fuel oil and other fuels	271	73	57	35	68	118	96	106	107
Telephone	856	884	891	864	607	865	1,031	1,108	1,136
Water and other public services	214	291	311	351	175	309	332	389	425
Household operations	643	670	645	796	387	501	921	1,308	846
Personal services	312	369	284	360	124	102	524	862	526
Other household expenses	331	301	361	436	264	400	398	446	320
Housekeeping supplies	530	514	440	472	224	515	553	663	755
Household furnishings and equipment	1,540	1,631	1,334	1,811	895	1,600	1,857	2,283	1,775
Household textiles	134	117	85	106	63	109	132	163	105
Furniture	388	378	338	489	226	391	521	578	407
Floor coverings	47	54	41	37	20	49	57	63	58
Major appliances	179	198	168	221	104	186	215	260	303
Small appliances, misc. housewares	91	103	72	93	49	97	99	120	105
Miscellaneous household equipment	702	782	630	865	433	769	832	1,100	798
Apparel and services	2,115	1,917	1,617	1,945	1,028	1,679	2,259	2,729	2,946
Men and boys	484	489	382	445	223	408	543	660	687
Women and girls	849	771	612	746	414	665	843	1,062	1,155
Children under 2 years old	82	88	82	75	17	39	142	165	196
Footwear	382	324	303	391	191	295	421	482	619
Other apparel products and services	318	245	238	288	183	272	310	360	289
Transportation	6,664	7,841	7,211	7,943	3,732	7,529	9,721	10,711	9,629
Vehicle purchases (net outlay)	2,719	3,759	3,566	3,430	1,456	3,397	4,805	5,282	4,435
Cars and trucks, new	1,456	1,540	1,632	1,759	797	1,767	2,493	2,072	1,458
Cars and trucks, used	1,246	2,132	1,909	1,620	628	1,606	2,275	3,093	2,937
Gasoline and motor oil	1,094	1,352	1,290	1,400	682	1,307	1,572	1,813	1,850
Other vehicle expenses	2,251	2,327	2,073	2,586	1,272	2,324	2,879	3,146	2,955
Vehicle finance charges	228	353	366	329	129	327	476	477	474
Maintenance and repair	570	610	584	749	396	646	700	823	825
Vehicle insurance	808	750	747	831	437	804	1,000	1,022	1,009
Public transportation	600	403	283	527	322	501	465	469	389
Health care [1]	1,862	2,172	2,147	2,001	1,488	2,596	2,080	2,143	2,018
Entertainment [2]	1,915	2,040	1,617	2,021	1,026	1,821	2,192	2,797	2,598
Personal care products and services	578	544	550	594	338	575	693	736	738
Reading	172	164	114	158	113	173	145	168	134
Education	823	667	477	674	407	476	841	952	986
Tobacco products and smoking supplies	326	360	334	245	203	318	399	389	436
Miscellaneous	738	798	729	859	561	855	794	990	831
Cash contributions	1,064	1,615	953	1,233	1,047	1,497	1,144	1,116	887
Personal insurance and pensions	3,071	3,490	3,077	3,679	1,778	3,480	4,191	4,930	4,160
Life and other personal insurance	423	429	407	333	155	484	480	560	499
Pensions and Social Security	2,948	3,061	2,670	3,346	1,623	2,996	3,711	4,370	3,661
Personal taxes	2,983	3,667	2,516	3,582	2,090	3,604	3,437	4,275	2,687

[1] For additional health care expenditures, see Table 123.   [2] For additional recreation expenditures, see Section 26 Arts, Entertainment, and Recreation section.

Source: U.S. Bureau of Labor Statistics, *Consumer Expenditures in 2000;* earlier reports. See also <http://www.bls.gov/cex/csxann00.pdf> (released April 2002).

No. 652. Money Income of Households—Percent Distribution by Income Level, Race, and Hispanic Origin, in Constant (2000) Dollars: 1980 to 2000

[Constant dollars based on CPI-U-RS deflator. Households as of March of following year (82,368 presents 82,368,000). Based on Current Population Survey; see text, Sections 1 and 13, and Appendix III. For definition of median, see Guide to Tabular Presentation]

Year	Number of households (1,000)	Percent distribution							Median income (dollars)
		Under $15,000	$15,000- $24,999	$25,000- $34,999	$35,000- $49,999	$50,000- $74,999	$75,000- $99,999	$100,000 and over	
ALL HOUSEHOLDS [1]									
1980	82,368	20.2	15.5	14.0	18.9	18.7	7.5	5.2	35,238
1985	88,458	19.6	15.1	13.7	17.7	18.3	8.7	6.8	36,246
1990	94,312	18.4	14.1	13.7	17.2	18.8	9.1	8.7	38,446
1995	99,627	18.3	14.9	13.1	16.4	18.3	9.4	9.6	38,262
1998	103,874	17.1	13.4	13.1	15.5	18.8	10.2	12.0	41,032
1999	104,705	16.0	13.8	12.4	15.8	18.5	10.5	13.2	42,187
2000	106,418	16.0	13.4	12.5	15.5	18.9	10.4	13.4	42,151
WHITE									
1970	57,575	19.4	14.6	16.3	21.8	18.5	5.8	3.7	35,148
1980	71,872	18.1	15.1	14.1	19.5	19.7	8.0	5.6	37,176
1985	76,576	17.6	14.7	13.8	18.2	19.2	9.2	7.4	38,226
1990	80,968	16.0	13.9	13.8	17.6	19.6	9.6	9.3	40,100
1995	84,511	16.4	14.6	13.0	16.7	19.1	9.8	10.4	40,159
1998	87,212	15.2	13.0	13.0	15.7	19.6	10.7	12.9	43,171
1999	87,671	14.2	13.6	12.2	16.0	19.1	11.1	13.8	43,932
2000	88,543	14.4	13.0	12.6	15.4	19.4	11.0	14.2	44,232
BLACK									
1980	8,847	37.6	18.9	13.7	14.4	10.7	3.4	1.3	21,418
1985	9,797	35.9	18.7	13.4	14.1	11.4	4.5	1.9	22,742
1990	10,671	35.4	15.8	13.7	14.6	12.7	4.7	3.1	23,979
1995	11,577	32.3	17.8	13.8	14.5	12.4	6.0	3.1	25,144
1998	12,579	30.5	17.0	13.6	14.5	13.4	6.1	4.9	26,751
1999	12,849	28.1	15.9	13.8	14.6	14.4	6.6	6.7	28,848
2000	13,355	26.0	16.5	12.9	16.8	15.2	6.5	6.1	30,436
HISPANIC [2]									
1980	3,906	26.2	20.1	16.2	17.0	14.0	4.2	2.2	27,161
1985	5,213	28.1	18.8	15.4	16.8	13.1	5.3	2.5	26,803
1990	6,220	26.1	18.2	15.7	16.9	14.1	5.2	3.8	28,671
1995	7,939	28.9	20.3	14.9	14.5	13.1	4.6	3.8	25,668
1998	9,060	24.7	17.1	16.3	15.7	14.6	6.0	5.0	29,894
1999	9,319	21.1	18.4	15.5	16.8	15.1	7.3	5.8	31,761
2000	9,663	18.9	18.3	14.7	17.7	17.4	7.4	5.8	33,455

[1] Includes other races not shown separately. [2] Persons of Hispanic origin may be of any race.

No. 653. Money Income of Households—Median Income by Race and Hispanic Origin, in Current and Constant (2000) Dollars: 1980 to 2000

[In dollars. See headnote, Table 652]

Year	Median income in current dollars					Median income in constant (2000) dollars				
	All households [1]	White	Black	Asian, Pacific Islander	His-panic [2]	All households [1]	White	Black	Asian, Pacific Islander	His-panic [2]
1980	17,710	18,684	10,764	(NA)	13,651	35,238	37,176	21,418	(NA)	27,162
1985	23,618	24,908	14,819	(NA)	17,465	36,246	38,226	22,742	(NA)	26,803
1986 [3]	24,897	26,175	15,080	(NA)	18,352	37,546	39,474	22,742	(NA)	27,676
1987 [3]	26,061	27,458	15,672	32,226	19,336	38,007	40,044	22,856	46,998	28,199
1988	27,225	28,781	16,407	32,267	20,359	38,309	40,499	23,087	45,404	28,648
1989	28,906	30,406	18,083	36,102	21,921	38,979	41,002	24,385	48,683	29,560
1990	29,943	31,231	18,676	38,450	22,330	38,446	40,100	23,979	49,369	28,671
1991	30,126	31,569	18,807	36,449	22,691	37,314	39,101	23,294	45,145	28,105
1992 [4]	30,636	32,209	18,755	37,801	22,597	36,965	38,863	22,630	45,611	27,266
1993	31,241	32,960	19,533	38,347	22,886	36,746	38,768	22,975	45,105	26,919
1994	32,264	34,028	21,027	40,482	23,421	37,136	39,166	24,202	46,595	26,958
1995	34,076	35,766	22,393	40,614	22,860	38,262	40,159	25,144	45,603	25,668
1996	35,492	37,161	23,482	43,276	24,906	38,798	40,623	25,669	47,307	27,226
1997	37,005	38,972	25,050	45,249	26,628	39,594	41,699	26,803	48,415	28,491
1998	38,885	40,912	25,351	46,637	28,330	41,032	43,171	26,751	49,212	29,894
1999	40,816	42,504	27,910	51,205	30,735	42,187	43,932	28,848	52,925	31,767
2000	42,151	44,232	30,436	55,525	33,455	42,151	44,232	30,436	55,525	33,455

NA Not available. [1] Includes other races not shown separately. [2] Persons of Hispanic origin may be of any race. [3] Beginning 1987, data based on revised processing procedures and not directly comparable with prior years. [4] Based on 1990 census population controls.

Source of Tables 652 and 653: U.S. Census Bureau, *Current Population Reports*, P60-213; and Internet site <http://www.census.gov/hhes/income/histinc/h05.html> (released 16 April 2002).

Income, Expenditures, and Wealth   433

No. 654. Money Income of Households—Distribution by Income Level and Selected Characteristics: 2000

[106,418 represents 106,418,000]

Characteristic	Number of households (1,000)	Under $15,000	$15,000-$24,999	$25,000-$34,999	$35,000-$49,999	$50,000-$74,999	$75,000-$99,999	$100,000 and over	Median income (dollars)
Total [1]	106,418	16,952	14,269	13,315	16,471	20,099	11,051	14,262	42,151
Age of householder:									
15 to 24 years	6,393	1,506	1,319	1,126	1,044	878	272	248	27,711
25 to 34 years	18,554	2,098	2,305	2,576	3,437	4,285	1,913	1,940	44,477
35 to 44 years	23,904	2,163	2,307	2,614	3,947	5,614	3,297	3,962	53,243
45 to 54 years	21,797	2,082	1,839	2,079	3,172	4,651	3,245	4,730	58,217
55 to 64 years	13,944	2,220	1,626	1,595	2,168	2,605	1,501	2,227	44,993
65 years and over	21,827	6,882	4,873	3,325	2,703	2,064	824	1,156	23,047
White	88,543	12,818	11,522	11,120	13,595	17,193	9,712	12,583	44,232
Black	13,355	3,472	2,199	1,728	2,244	2,030	868	815	30,436
Hispanic [2]	9,663	1,820	1,764	1,422	1,707	1,682	711	556	33,455
Region:[3]									
Northeast	20,212	3,358	2,460	2,314	2,844	3,808	2,244	3,184	45,118
Midwest	24,496	3,556	3,222	3,025	3,755	5,012	2,787	3,138	44,647
South	38,526	6,901	5,541	5,100	6,213	6,910	3,426	4,434	38,402
West	23,185	3,136	3,045	2,875	3,659	4,369	2,594	3,506	44,759
Size of household:									
One person	27,820	10,112	5,528	3,996	3,653	2,709	970	850	21,468
Two persons	35,388	3,716	4,920	5,067	5,953	7,075	3,769	4,888	44,530
Three persons	17,259	1,530	1,662	1,763	2,886	4,036	2,367	3,015	54,196
Four persons	15,430	904	1,209	1,405	2,272	3,801	2,487	3,353	61,847
Five persons	6,686	425	541	698	1,048	1,549	1,007	1,417	60,295
Six persons	2,396	154	263	239	421	579	298	442	54,841
Seven or more persons. .	1,439	108	146	147	239	350	153	296	54,663
Type of household:									
Family households	72,380	6,355	8,108	8,538	11,702	15,845	9,332	12,499	51,751
Married-couple	55,603	2,937	4,913	5,920	8,749	13,227	8,272	11,586	59,343
Male householder, wife absent	4,252	484	596	569	838	955	401	410	42,143
Female householder, husband absent	12,525	2,934	2,600	2,049	2,116	1,663	660	503	28,126
Nonfamily households. . .	34,039	10,596	6,160	4,777	4,769	4,254	1,719	1,763	25,439
Male householder. . . .	15,218	3,477	2,531	2,333	2,402	2,414	1,032	1,029	31,269
Female householder . .	18,821	7,119	3,629	2,444	2,367	1,840	687	734	20,929
Educational attainment of householder:[4]									
Total	100,026	15,446	12,950	12,189	15,427	19,221	10,780	14,014	43,556
Less than 9th grade.	6,753	2,898	1,434	868	710	534	196	112	17,557
9th to 12th grade (no diploma)	9,111	3,023	1,930	1,294	1,221	1,055	345	242	22,753
High school graduate	30,785	5,248	4,902	4,461	5,360	6,050	2,737	2,028	36,722
Some college, no degree . .	18,165	2,155	2,280	2,554	3,171	3,916	2,067	2,022	44,449
Associate degree	8,214	730	846	1,042	1,454	1,897	1,148	1,098	50,356
Bachelor's degree or more .	26,997	1,392	1,558	1,970	3,512	5,767	4,286	8,512	71,437
Bachelor's degree	17,521	1,006	1,132	1,475	2,510	3,952	2,698	4,748	65,922
Master's degree.	6,435	265	306	379	738	1,338	1,137	2,273	77,935
Professional degree	1,641	70	69	76	135	207	235	850	100,000
Doctorate degree	1,400	51	52	41	128	270	217	642	93,361
Work experience of householder:									
Total	106,418	16,952	14,269	13,315	16,471	20,099	11,051	14,262	42,151
Worked	76,040	5,605	8,106	9,240	12,911	17,278	10,014	12,886	52,147
Worked at full-time jobs.	66,002	3,566	6,625	7,936	11,420	15,648	9,139	11,667	54,398
50 weeks or more. .	56,479	1,976	5,072	6,624	9,801	13,989	8,358	10,659	57,149
27 to 49 weeks	6,234	723	917	872	1,138	1,166	643	775	42,234
26 weeks or less . . .	3,289	868	637	439	481	494	137	233	27,465
Worked at part-time jobs	10,038	2,036	1,481	1,305	1,491	1,629	876	1,219	36,898
50 weeks or more. . .	5,338	826	772	664	845	969	511	750	42,088
27 to 49 weeks	2,104	444	328	283	306	310	192	241	34,877
26 weeks or less	2,596	766	381	358	340	350	173	228	28,435
Did not work	30,379	11,347	6,162	4,075	3,559	2,822	1,037	1,376	20,821

[1] Includes other races not shown separately.　[2] Persons of Hispanic origin may be of any race.　[3] For composition of regions, see map inside front cover.　[4] Persons 25 years old and over.

Source: U.S. Census Bureau, *Current Population Reports*, P60-213; and Internet site <http://ferret.bls.census.gov/macro/032001/hhinc/new01001.htm> (released 10 December 2001).

No. 655. Money Income of Households—Median Income and Income Level by Household Type: 2000

[See headnote, Table 652]

Race and Income Interval	All house-holds	Family households				Nonfamily households		
		Total	Married couple	Male house-holder, wife absent	Female house-holder, husband absent	Total [1]	Single-person household	
							Male house-holder	Female house-holder
MEDIAN INCOME (dollars)								
All households	42,151	51,751	59,343	42,143	28,126	25,439	26,723	18,163
White	44,232	54,293	60,080	44,020	31,230	25,985	27,326	18,695
Black	30,436	36,063	50,729	37,015	21,698	20,551	21,286	14,825
Hispanic [2]	33,455	36,578	41,116	39,015	23,671	21,263	20,597	13,295
NUMBER (1,000)								
All households	106,418	72,380	55,603	4,252	12,525	34,039	15,218	18,821
Under $5,000	3,065	1,342	581	90	671	1,722	668	1,054
$5,000 to $9,999	6,475	1,915	745	177	994	4,560	1,405	3,155
$10,000 to $14,999	7,412	3,098	1,611	217	1,269	4,315	1,404	2,911
$15,000 to $19,999	7,113	3,911	2,291	244	1,374	3,202	1,280	1,921
$20,000 to $24,999	7,157	4,197	2,621	351	1,226	2,959	1,250	1,708
$25,000 to $34,999	13,315	8,537	5,919	570	2,049	4,777	2,333	2,444
$35,000 to $49,999	16,470	11,702	8,750	837	2,117	4,768	2,403	2,368
$50,000 to $74,999	20,100	15,845	13,227	956	1,664	4,253	2,415	1,840
$75,000 to $99,999	11,050	9,332	8,270	400	660	1,718	1,031	688
$100,000 and over	14,262	12,499	11,586	410	503	1,763	1,029	734

[1] Includes other nonfamily households not shown separately. [2] Persons of Hispanic origin may be of any race.

Source: U.S. Census Bureau, *Current Population Reports*, P60-213, *Money Income in the United States: 2000*. See also <http://www.census.gov/prod/2000pubs/p60-213.pdf> (released September 2001) and <http://ferret.bls.census.gov/macro/032001/hhinc/new01000.htm> (released 10 December 2001).

No. 656. Median Income of Households in Constant (2000) Dollars by State: 3-Year Averages for 1990 to 2000

[Constant dollars based on the CPI-U-RS deflator. Data based on the Current Population Survey; see text, this section and Section 1 and Appendix III. The CPS is designed to collect reliable data on income primarily at the national level and secondarily at the regional level. When the income data are tabulated by state, the estimates are considered less reliable and, therefore, particular caution should be used when trying to interpret the results]

State	1990-1992	1995-1997	1996-1998	1997-1999	1998-2000	State	1990-1992	1995-1997	1996-1998	1997-1999	1998-2000
U.S.	**37,575**	**38,885**	**39,808**	**40,938**	**41,790**						
						MO	34,232	38,557	39,663	41,463	44,250
AL	30,428	32,161	35,189	36,624	36,269	MT	30,923	31,259	31,977	32,290	32,553
AK	50,399	54,297	54,180	52,694	52,499	NE	36,047	37,092	37,575	38,544	39,019
AZ	37,005	34,756	36,251	37,512	39,653	NV	40,137	41,406	41,885	42,201	43,256
AR	29,033	28,876	28,945	29,316	30,082	NH	48,201	43,642	44,795	46,342	48,021
CA	42,184	42,152	42,698	43,626	45,072						
						NJ	48,798	50,863	51,949	51,855	51,739
CO	39,223	45,576	46,732	48,467	49,230	NM	32,075	29,599	30,966	33,014	34,034
CT	50,466	46,097	47,394	49,548	50,651	NY	39,136	38,032	38,823	39,722	40,820
DE	40,986	42,744	44,254	46,068	47,444	NC	33,525	37,724	38,361	38,253	38,409
DC	36,227	34,519	34,771	36,451	37,994	ND	32,345	33,647	33,418	33,278	33,785
FL	33,672	33,873	35,019	36,214	37,307						
						OH	37,775	38,380	38,993	40,228	41,973
GA	34,612	37,679	38,517	40,262	41,480	OK	31,118	31,027	33,042	34,386	34,026
HI	48,973	45,858	44,181	44,248	45,680	OR	37,837	39,831	39,958	41,053	41,923
ID	32,755	36,791	37,463	37,186	37,760	PA	36,970	39,019	39,820	40,194	41,394
IL	39,781	43,386	44,324	45,895	46,649	RI	38,653	39,122	40,198	41,514	43,492
IN	34,184	39,172	40,652	41,946	41,288						
						SC	34,729	35,732	36,552	36,518	36,653
IA	35,028	37,444	37,171	39,278	41,545	SD	31,250	32,420	32,881	34,520	35,983
KS	37,104	36,237	37,794	38,832	38,444	TN	29,545	33,006	34,137	35,505	35,882
KY	29,863	34,899	36,493	36,362	36,823	TX	34,774	36,552	37,147	38,525	39,294
LA	30,266	33,350	34,052	34,289	32,503	UT	38,243	42,406	44,334	46,718	46,549
ME	35,172	37,003	36,867	37,638	39,836						
						VT	38,521	36,952	38,141	40,693	40,916
MD	46,849	48,042	50,273	52,265	52,815	VA	45,294	43,166	44,858	46,332	47,689
MA	44,882	43,816	44,273	45,108	45,781	WA	41,403	42,570	45,937	48,297	46,424
MI	39,050	41,744	42,821	44,458	46,037	WV	27,184	28,315	28,396	29,337	29,214
MN	38,098	44,314	46,974	48,314	50,091	WI	39,394	44,026	43,234	44,446	45,452
MS	24,950	29,818	30,128	31,618	31,959	WY	36,752	35,000	35,598	37,203	38,291

Source: U.S. Census Bureau, *Current Population Reports,* P60-213; and <http://www.census.gov/hhes/income/histinc/h08b.html> (released 16 April 2002).

Income, Expenditures, and Wealth **435**

No. 657. Money Income of Families—Percent Distribution by Income Level, Race, and Hispanic Origin in Constant (2000) Dollars: 1980 to 2000

[Constant dollars based on CPI-U-RS deflator. Families as of March of following year (60,309 represent 60,309,000). Beginning with 1980, based on householder concept and restricted to primary families. Based on Current Population Survey; see text, this section, Section 1, Population, and Appendix III. For definition of median, see Guide to Tabular Presentation]

Year	Number of families (1,000)	Under $15,000	$15,000-$24,999	$25,000-$34,999	$35,000-$49,999	$50,000-$74,999	$75,000-$99,999	$100,000 and over	Median income (dollars)
ALL FAMILIES [1]									
1980	60,309	12.5	13.9	14.1	21.0	22.7	9.3	6.5	41,830
1985	63,558	12.9	13.6	13.6	19.0	21.7	10.7	8.5	42,564
1990	66,322	12.0	12.2	13.1	18.3	22.1	11.4	11.0	45,392
1995	69,597	12.0	12.8	12.8	17.3	21.3	11.5	12.2	45,599
1998	71,551	10.9	11.6	12.4	15.9	21.7	12.4	15.1	49,317
1999	72,031	10.2	11.5	11.6	16.3	21.1	12.9	16.4	50,594
2000	72,388	9.6	11.5	12.0	15.9	21.5	12.6	17.0	50,890
WHITE									
1980	52,710	10.4	13.2	14.1	21.6	23.9	9.9	7.0	43,583
1985	54,991	10.8	12.9	13.5	19.5	22.7	11.3	9.2	44,739
1990	56,803	9.4	11.8	13.1	18.7	23.2	12.0	11.8	47,398
1995	58,872	9.7	12.3	12.7	17.6	22.4	12.0	13.3	47,884
1998	60,077	9.0	10.8	12.3	16.1	22.6	12.9	16.3	51,729
1999	60,256	8.2	11.1	11.4	16.5	22.0	13.6	17.3	52,945
2000	60,222	8.0	10.7	11.8	15.9	22.2	13.4	18.0	53,256
BLACK									
1980	6,317	30.3	19.4	14.6	16.4	13.3	4.4	1.6	25,218
1985	6,921	30.2	18.8	14.1	15.4	13.6	5.5	2.3	25,761
1990	7,471	30.5	15.3	13.5	16.0	15.0	6.0	3.7	27,506
1995	8,055	27.2	17.2	14.1	15.9	14.1	7.5	4.0	29,160
1998	8,452	23.8	17.8	13.5	15.1	15.8	7.7	6.4	31,027
1999	8,664	23.2	15.2	14.0	15.2	16.1	8.0	8.2	32,846
2000	8,814	20.0	16.8	14.1	16.8	16.7	7.7	7.9	34,192
ASIAN AND PACIFIC ISLANDER									
1990	1,536	10.2	10.7	10.2	14.2	21.6	15.9	17.3	54,243
1995	2,125	12.8	9.3	11.1	14.5	22.8	13.0	16.4	52,050
1998	2,459	10.5	8.6	10.7	14.6	19.9	15.5	20.2	55,742
1999	2,506	10.8	9.1	8.4	14.7	18.8	13.0	25.3	58,208
2000	2,663	8.2	9.8	9.2	12.1	21.4	12.5	26.8	61,511
HISPANIC ORIGIN [2]									
1980	3,235	22.4	20.0	17.1	18.3	15.3	4.3	2.5	29,281
1985	4,206	24.5	19.0	15.8	17.6	14.4	5.7	2.9	29,200
1990	4,981	23.4	18.7	15.5	17.3	15.1	5.8	4.1	30,085
1995	6,287	24.8	21.2	15.8	15.1	13.8	5.0	4.1	27,588
1998	7,273	21.2	17.9	17.3	16.2	15.6	6.1	5.9	31,243
1999	7,561	18.4	19.1	15.6	16.9	16.0	7.8	6.1	32,727
2000	7,728	16.4	18.3	15.4	18.1	17.9	8.0	6.1	35,054

[1] Includes other races not shown separately.　　[2] Persons of Hispanic origin may be of any race.

No. 658. Money Income of Families—Median Income by Race and Hispanic Origin in Current and Constant (2000) Dollars: 1980 to 2000

[See headnote, Table 657]

Year	Median income in current dollars					Median income in constant (2000) dollars				
	All families [1]	White	Black	Asian, Pacific Islander	Hispanic [2]	All families [1]	White	Black	Asian, Pacific Islander	Hispanic [2]
1980	21,023	21,904	12,674	(NA)	14,716	41,830	43,583	25,218	(NA)	29,281
1985 [3]	27,735	29,152	16,786	(NA)	19,027	42,564	44,739	25,761	(NA)	29,200
1986	29,458	30,809	17,604	(NA)	19,995	44,425	46,462	26,548	(NA)	30,154
1987 [4]	30,970	32,385	18,406	(NA)	20,300	45,166	47,230	26,843	(NA)	29,605
1988	32,191	33,915	19,329	36,560	21,769	45,297	47,723	27,199	51,445	30,632
1989	34,213	35,975	20,209	40,351	23,446	46,135	48,511	27,251	54,412	31,616
1990	35,353	36,915	21,423	42,246	23,431	45,392	47,398	27,506	54,243	30,085
1991	35,939	37,783	21,548	40,974	23,895	44,514	46,798	26,689	50,750	29,596
1992 [5]	36,573	38,670	21,103	42,255	23,555	44,129	46,659	25,463	50,985	28,421
1993 [6]	36,959	39,300	21,542	44,456	23,654	43,472	46,226	25,338	52,290	27,822
1994 [7]	38,782	40,884	24,698	46,122	24,318	44,638	47,058	28,427	53,087	27,990
1995 [8]	40,611	42,646	25,970	46,356	24,570	45,599	47,884	29,160	52,050	27,588
1996	42,300	44,756	26,522	49,105	26,179	46,240	48,925	28,993	53,679	28,618
1997	44,568	46,754	28,602	51,850	28,142	47,687	50,026	30,603	55,478	30,111
1998	46,737	49,023	29,404	52,826	29,608	49,317	51,729	31,027	55,742	31,243
1999	48,950	51,224	31,778	56,316	31,663	50,594	52,945	32,846	58,208	32,727
2000	50,890	53,256	34,192	61,511	35,054	50,890	53,256	34,192	61,511	35,054

NA Not available.　　[1] Includes other races not shown separately.　　[2] Persons of Hispanic origin may be of any race. [3] Recording of amounts for earnings from longest job increased to $299,999.　　[4] Implementation of a new March CPS processing system.　　[5] Implementation of 1990 census population controls.　　[6] See text, Section 14, Prices, for information on data collection change.　　[7] Introduction of 1990 census sample design.　　[8] Full implementation of the 1990 census-based sample design and metropolitan definitions, 7,000 household sample reduction, and revised race edits.

Source of Tables 657 and 658: U.S. Census Bureau, *Current Population Reports*, P60-213; and Internet site <http://www.census.gov/hhes/income/histinc/f05.html> (released 16 April 2002).

No. 659. Share of Aggregate Income Received by Each Fifth and Top 5 Percent of Families: 1980 to 2000

[Families as of March of the following year (60,309 represents 60,309,000). Income in constant 2000 CPI-U-RS adjusted dollars]

Year	Number of families (1,000)	Income at selected positions (dollars)					Percent distribution of aggregate income					
		Upper limit of each fifth					Lowest 5th	Second 5th	Third 5th	Fourth 5th	Highest 5th	Top 5 percent
		Lowest	Second	Third	Fourth	Top 5 percent						
1980	60,309	20,693	34,840	49,346	69,243	109,436	5.3	11.6	17.6	24.4	41.1	14.6
1985	63,558	20,388	35,122	50,877	74,016	121,185	4.8	11.0	16.9	24.3	43.1	16.1
1986	64,491	21,113	36,344	52,963	76,263	125,773	4.7	10.9	16.9	24.1	43.4	16.5
1987 [1]	65,204	21,289	36,725	53,670	77,775	126,805	4.6	10.7	16.8	24.0	43.8	17.2
1988	65,837	21,251	36,842	54,175	78,668	129,458	4.6	10.7	16.7	24.0	44.0	17.2
1989	66,090	21,580	37,757	55,018	80,302	133,449	4.6	10.6	16.5	23.7	44.6	17.9
1990	66,322	21,630	37,292	53,978	78,951	131,425	4.6	10.8	16.6	23.8	44.3	17.4
1991	67,173	21,056	36,056	53,259	78,020	127,356	4.5	10.7	16.6	24.1	44.2	17.1
1992 [2]	68,216	20,166	35,805	53,090	77,283	127,914	4.3	10.5	16.5	24.0	44.7	17.6
1993 [3]	68,506	19,961	35,287	52,965	78,565	133,127	4.1	9.9	15.7	23.3	47.0	20.3
1994 [4]	69,313	20,649	36,026	54,097	80,568	138,170	4.2	10.0	15.7	23.3	46.9	20.1
1995 [5]	69,597	21,412	37,037	55,002	81,136	138,845	4.4	10.1	15.8	23.2	46.5	20.0
1996	70,241	21,513	37,512	55,845	82,332	139,924	4.2	10.0	15.8	23.1	46.8	20.3
1997	70,884	22,026	38,519	57,368	85,598	146,672	4.2	9.9	15.7	23.0	47.2	20.7
1998	71,551	22,792	39,773	59,113	88,313	153,215	4.2	9.9	15.7	23.0	47.3	20.7
1999	72,031	23,593	40,930	61,395	91,041	160,248	4.3	9.9	15.6	23.0	47.2	20.3
2000	72,388	24,000	41,000	61,378	91,700	160,250	4.3	9.8	15.5	22.8	47.4	20.8

[1] Implementation of a new March CPS processing system. [2] Based on 1990 census population controls. [3] See text, Section 14, for explanation of changes in data collection method. [4] Introduction of new 1990 census sample design. [5] Full implementation of the 1990 census-based sample design and metropolitan definitions, 7,000 household sample reduction, and revised race edits.

Source: U.S. Census Bureau, *Current Population Reports*, P60-213; and Internet site <http://www.census.gov/hhes/income/histinc/f02.html> (released 16 April 2002).

No. 660. Money Income of Families—Distribution by Family Characteristics and Income Level: 2000

[(72,388 represents 72,388,000). See headnote, Table 657. For composition of region, see map inside front cover.]

Characteristic	Number of families (1,000)	Income level (1,000)							Median income (dollars)
		Under $15,000	$15,000 to $24,999	$25,000 to $34,999	$35,000 to $49,999	$50,000 to $74,999	$75,000 to $99,999	$100,000 and over	
All families	**72,388**	**6,910**	**8,308**	**8,704**	**11,521**	**15,543**	**9,118**	**12,282**	**50,890**
Age of householder:									
15 to 24 years old.	3,489	911	722	564	545	484	136	128	26,536
25 to 34 years old.	12,824	1,540	1,484	1,709	2,250	3,052	1,397	1,392	45,890
35 to 44 years old.	18,581	1,384	1,599	1,879	2,906	4,506	2,820	3,487	58,084
45 to 54 years old.	16,225	850	1,056	1,271	2,153	3,776	2,815	4,304	68,082
55 to 64 years old.	9,662	824	927	1,023	1,537	2,040	1,285	2,027	55,718
65 years old and over	11,606	1,402	2,520	2,258	2,131	1,685	666	945	32,852
White.	60,222	4,787	6,456	7,119	9,604	13,371	8,073	10,810	53,256
Black.	8,814	1,757	1,478	1,247	1,482	1,474	676	700	34,192
Hispanic origin [1].	7,728	1,259	1,411	1,187	1,398	1,385	617	471	35,054
Northeast	13,422	1,212	1,247	1,492	1,967	2,907	1,847	2,748	56,128
Midwest	16,646	1,319	1,750	1,828	2,611	3,981	2,417	2,740	54,576
South.	26,602	3,004	3,399	3,473	4,456	5,438	2,915	3,916	46,009
West	15,719	1,375	1,912	1,910	2,487	3,217	1,939	2,878	51,034
Type of family:									
Married-couple families	55,611	2,968	4,928	5,947	8,753	13,231	8,246	11,537	59,184
Male householder, wife absent .	4,252	595	657	679	793	847	348	331	37,529
Female householder, husband absent.	12,525	3,347	2,723	2,078	1,975	1,465	524	413	25,794
Unrelated subfamilies	528	212	158	88	29	33	2	5	17,339
Education attainment of householder: [2]									
Total	68,899	6,000	7,587	8,140	10,977	15,059	8,982	12,155	52,166
Less than 9th grade	4,178	1,003	1,088	748	610	464	166	98	24,946
9th to 11th grade (no diploma) . . .	6,026	1,291	1,275	1,043	998	942	286	191	28,878
High school graduate (includes equivalency)	21,502	2,055	2,834	3,151	4,133	5,099	2,439	1,791	44,248
Some college, no degree.	12,593	886	1,284	1,574	2,315	3,102	1,690	1,742	51,642
Associate degree	5,869	261	497	643	1,003	1,499	1,010	955	57,814
Bachelor's degree or more.	18,732	504	609	982	1,918	3,953	3,390	7,378	84,172
Bachelor's degree.	12,016	330	446	743	1,429	2,782	2,166	4,119	77,245
Master's degree	4,518	122	109	178	360	873	894	1,983	91,126
Professional degree	1,161	27	19	43	59	129	164	720	100,000
Doctorate degree	1,036	26	34	18	69	169	166	555	100,000

[1] Persons of Hispanic origin may be of any race. [2] Persons 25 years old and over.

Source: U.S. Census Bureau, *Current Population Reports*, P60-213. See also <http://www.census.gov/prod/2001pubs/p60-213.pdf> (released September 2001) and <http://ferret.bls.census.gov/macro/032001/faminc/new01001.htm> (released 10 December 2001).

No. 661. Money Income of Families—Work Experience by Income Level: 2000

[**72,388 represents 72,388,000** See headnote, Table 657]

Characteristic	Number of families (1,000)	Under $15,000	$15,000 to $24,999	$25,000 to $34,999	$35,000 to $49,999	$50,000 to $74,999	$75,000 to $99,999	$100,000 and over	Median income (dollars)
All families	**72,388**	**6,910**	**8,308**	**8,704**	**11,521**	**15,543**	**9,118**	**12,282**	**50,890**
Number of earners:									
No earners	9,384	2,951	2,441	1,686	1,176	692	223	215	21,916
One earner	21,712	3,234	3,974	3,789	3,860	3,448	1,346	2,062	34,423
Two earners or more	41,291	726	1,893	3,229	6,486	11,403	7,550	10,005	67,600
Two earners	32,403	666	1,710	2,919	5,520	9,055	5,515	7,018	63,816
Three earners	6,601	60	172	274	810	1,870	1,417	1,998	76,566
Four earners or more	2,288	-	11	36	156	478	618	989	91,709
Work experience of householder:									
Total	72,388	6,910	8,308	8,704	11,521	15,543	9,118	12,282	50,890
Worked	54,464	3,194	4,661	5,647	8,551	13,132	8,212	11,068	59,217
Worked at full-time jobs	47,344	2,123	3,830	4,808	7,416	11,738	7,448	9,981	60,907
50 weeks or more	40,946	1,159	2,965	4,015	6,279	10,534	6,838	9,156	63,346
27 to 49 weeks	4,228	407	530	517	788	843	501	643	47,396
26 weeks or less	2,170	558	335	275	349	362	110	182	31,899
Worked at part-time jobs	7,120	1,070	831	839	1,135	1,394	764	1,087	45,707
50 weeks or more	3,848	426	438	418	620	834	449	664	50,546
27 to 49 weeks	1,411	220	142	168	225	260	184	212	44,922
26 weeks or less	1,862	425	251	253	290	300	131	211	35,060

- Represents zero.

No. 662. Median Income of Families by Type of Family in Current and Constant (2000) Dollars: 1980 to 2000

[See headnote, Table 657]

Year	Current dollars					Constant (2000) dollars				
	Married-couple families				Female householder, no husband present	Married-couple families				Female householder, no husband present
	Total	Total	Wife in paid labor force	Wife not in paid labor force	Male householder, no wife present	Total	Total	Wife in paid labor force	Wife not in paid labor force	Male householder, no wife present
1980	21,023	23,141	26,879	18,972	17,519	10,408	41,830	46,045	53,482	37,749	34,858	20,709
1985	27,735	31,100	36,431	24,556	22,622	13,660	42,564	47,728	55,910	37,685	34,717	20,964
1990	35,353	39,895	46,777	30,265	29,046	16,932	45,392	51,224	60,060	38,859	37,294	21,740
1991	35,939	40,995	48,169	30,075	28,351	16,692	44,514	50,776	59,661	37,250	35,115	20,674
1992 [1]	36,573	41,890	49,775	30,174	27,576	17,025	44,129	50,544	60,059	36,408	33,273	20,542
1993	36,959	43,005	51,204	30,218	26,467	17,443	43,472	50,584	60,227	35,543	31,131	20,517
1994 [2]	38,782	44,959	53,309	31,176	27,751	18,236	44,638	51,748	61,359	35,884	31,942	20,990
1995 [3]	40,611	47,062	55,823	32,375	30,358	19,691	45,599	52,843	62,680	36,352	34,087	22,110
1996	42,300	49,707	58,381	33,748	31,600	19,911	46,240	54,337	63,819	36,892	34,544	21,766
1997	44,568	51,591	60,669	36,027	32,960	21,023	47,687	55,201	64,914	38,548	35,266	22,494
1998	46,737	54,180	63,751	37,161	35,681	22,163	49,317	57,171	67,271	39,213	37,651	23,387
1999	48,950	56,676	66,529	38,626	37,396	23,732	50,594	58,580	68,764	39,924	38,652	24,529
2000	50,890	59,184	69,463	39,735	37,529	25,794	50,890	59,184	69,463	39,735	37,529	25,794

[1] Based on 1990 census population controls. [2] See text, this section, for information on data collection change. [3] Introduction of 1990 census sample design.

No. 663. Married-Couple Families—Number and Median Income by Work Experience of Husbands and Wives and Presence of Children: 2000

[**55,611 represents 55,611,000 as of March 2001.** Based on Current Population Survey; see text, this section, Section 1, Population, and Appendix III]

Work experience of husband or wife	Number (1,000)					Median income (dollars)				
	All married-couple families	No related children	One or more related children under 18 years old			All married-couple families	No related children	One or more related children under 18 years old		
			Total	One child	Two children or more			Total	One child	Two children or more
All married-couple families	**55,611**	**29,048**	**26,563**	**10,189**	**16,374**	**59,184**	**54,631**	**62,931**	**65,462**	**61,508**
Husband worked	44,491	19,349	25,141	9,458	15,684	66,922	69,844	64,737	67,483	62,693
Wife worked	33,454	14,692	18,761	7,481	11,280	71,432	75,544	69,016	70,972	67,524
Wife year-round, full-time worker .	20,239	9,727	10,512	4,671	5,841	76,572	80,378	73,089	75,222	71,653
Wife did not work	11,037	4,657	6,380	1,977	4,403	50,319	50,494	50,179	51,729	49,079
Husband year-round, full-time worker .	37,619	15,324	22,295	8,296	13,999	70,349	74,966	67,397	70,074	65,618
Wife worked	28,732	12,121	16,611	6,584	10,027	74,362	79,274	71,193	73,294	70,148
Wife year-round, full-time worker .	17,956	8,463	9,493	4,238	5,255	78,604	82,470	75,161	76,992	73,127
Wife did not work	8,887	3,203	5,684	1,712	3,972	53,577	55,542	52,252	53,898	51,736
Husband did not work	11,120	9,698	1,422	731	690	29,680	29,639	30,018	32,929	26,750
Wife worked	3,116	2,262	854	438	416	40,260	40,739	38,149	42,283	32,368
Wife year-round, full-time worker .	1,783	1,224	559	295	264	44,011	44,341	43,193	44,919	41,740
Wife did not work	8,003	7,436	568	293	274	26,622	26,895	22,706	24,426	19,208

Source of Tables 661-663: U.S. Census Bureau, *Current Population Reports*, P60-213; and <http://ferret.bls.census.gov/macro/032001/faminc/new04000.htm> released 10 December 2001.

No. 664. Money Income of Persons—Selected Characteristics by Income Level: 2000

[Persons as of March 2001 (104,273 represents 104,273,000). Covers persons 15 years old and over. For definition of median, see Guide to Tabular Presentation. For composition of regions, see map, inside front cover]

Characteristic	All persons (1,000)	Persons with income									Median income (dollars)
		Number (1,000)									
		Total (1,000)	Under $5,000 [1]	$5,000 to $9,999	$10,000 to $14,999	$15,000 to $24,999	$25,000 to $34,999	$35,000 to $49,999	$50,000 to $74,999	$75,000 and over	
MALE											
Total	104,273	96,983	7,716	8,278	9,352	17,556	14,573	15,346	13,347	10,815	28,269
15 to 24 years old	19,636	14,484	4,691	2,744	2,056	2,782	1,233	633	255	90	9,548
25 to 34 years old	18,451	17,822	647	854	1,466	3,868	3,536	3,688	2,451	1,312	30,633
35 to 44 years old	22,177	21,684	707	962	1,213	3,351	3,636	4,315	4,254	3,245	37,088
45 to 54 years old	18,578	18,155	618	908	974	2,235	2,671	3,615	3,683	3,451	41,072
55 to 64 years old	11,253	10,900	549	714	951	1,710	1,592	1,726	1,816	1,842	34,414
65 yr. old and over . . .	14,179	13,937	503	2,097	2,692	3,609	1,903	1,369	889	875	19,167
Northeast	19,552	18,280	1,512	1,563	1,601	2,974	2,630	2,978	2,608	2,413	30,464
Midwest	24,180	22,875	1,901	1,789	2,054	3,946	3,572	3,895	3,366	2,350	29,935
South	36,678	33,827	2,634	3,150	3,348	6,600	5,236	5,192	4,402	3,265	26,699
West	23,862	22,002	1,669	1,776	2,349	4,036	3,134	3,281	2,971	2,786	28,009
Education attainment of householder: [3]											
Total	84,637	82,499	3,025	5,535	7,296	14,774	13,339	14,713	13,092	10,725	32,092
Less than 9th grade . . .	5,853	5,499	418	1,304	1,201	1,483	630	274	124	64	14,149
9th to 12th grade [4] . . .	7,360	6,983	446	943	1,189	2,076	1,116	723	331	159	18,952
High school graduate [5] .	26,856	26,094	1,023	1,850	2,525	5,847	5,222	5,073	3,273	1,281	27,669
Some college, no degree	14,645	14,330	444	741	1,201	2,506	2,593	3,076	2,489	1,281	33,035
Associate degree	6,233	6,138	171	179	327	785	1,196	1,521	1,310	649	37,956
Bachelor's degree or more	23,691	23,455	523	518	854	2,076	2,582	4,047	5,565	7,291	53,457
Bachelor's degree . .	15,331	15,150	320	384	601	1,588	1,940	2,850	3,578	3,889	49,180
Master's degree	5,193	5,163	128	93	179	340	472	825	1,366	1,759	59,376
Professional degree .	1,707	1,695	43	23	42	86	87	184	273	957	81,606
Doctorate degree . . .	1,460	1,447	32	18	32	62	82	188	348	686	71,732
Tenure:											
Owner occupied . . .	75,119	70,314	5,493	5,036	6,019	11,067	10,315	11,783	11,121	9,480	31,665
Renter occupied . . .	27,691	25,318	2,080	3,050	3,178	6,119	4,033	3,432	2,136	1,290	21,551
Occupier paid no cash rent	1,463	1,351	143	193	154	370	224	132	90	45	18,802
FEMALE											
Total	111,735	99,974	16,767	16,879	13,481	19,411	13,629	10,443	6,495	2,869	16,188
15 to 24 years old	19,349	14,026	5,219	2,851	2,018	2,421	1,016	348	107	47	7,742
25 to 34 years old	18,989	17,140	2,403	1,767	1,987	3,908	3,204	2,274	1,101	496	20,940
35 to 44 years old	22,603	20,972	3,019	2,133	2,235	4,231	3,555	2,995	1,926	877	21,861
45 to 54 years old	19,462	18,117	2,205	1,762	1,852	3,468	3,060	2,906	2,067	798	24,193
55 to 64 years old	12,532	11,400	1,926	2,023	1,364	2,095	1,552	1,205	848	387	16,468
65 yr. old and over . . .	18,799	18,320	1,994	6,343	4,026	3,287	1,243	716	446	265	10,898
Northeast	21,618	19,740	3,401	3,238	2,594	3,604	2,679	2,061	1,512	651	16,396
Midwest	25,298	23,294	3,956	3,721	3,198	4,634	3,354	2,506	1,350	574	16,417
South	40,034	35,351	5,731	6,456	4,821	7,187	4,721	3,469	2,070	896	15,717
West	24,785	21,589	3,680	3,463	2,868	3,986	2,875	2,407	1,563	748	16,653
Education attainment of householder: [3]											
Total	92,385	85,948	11,548	14,028	11,463	16,990	12,613	10,096	6,388	2,822	18,025
Less than 9th grade . . .	6,139	5,112	932	2,222	1,016	678	141	71	36	16	8,404
9th to 12th grade [4] . . .	8,416	7,336	1,313	2,357	1,563	1,384	435	188	75	21	9,995
High school graduate [5] .	30,893	28,663	4,177	5,350	4,699	6,894	4,175	2,187	921	259	15,120
Some college, no degree	16,290	15,386	1,950	1,916	1,996	3,572	2,737	1,927	962	326	20,181
Associate degree	8,213	7,856	868	802	824	1,726	1,637	1,265	558	176	23,270
Bachelor's degree or more	22,436	21,594	2,308	1,379	1,366	2,737	3,488	4,457	3,836	2,023	33,366
Bachelor's degree . .	15,513	14,857	1,753	1,073	1,084	2,094	2,571	2,995	2,234	1,052	30,489
Master's degree	5,451	5,322	440	243	230	521	755	1,244	1,301	590	40,246
Professional degree .	879	840	68	39	30	72	95	136	159	241	45,999
Doctorate degree . . .	594	576	47	24	22	50	67	82	142	141	48,885
Tenure:											
Owner occupied . . .	79,734	72,266	12,586	11,379	9,119	13,457	9,903	8,103	5,330	2,389	16,887
Renter occupied . . .	30,482	26,459	3,887	5,190	4,163	5,731	3,618	2,262	1,145	464	14,986
Occupier paid no cash rent	1,519	1,249	295	310	199	222	108	78	20	16	10,384

[1] Includes persons with income deficit. [2] Persons 25 years and over. [3] No diploma attained. [4] Includes high school equivalency.

Source: U.S. Census Bureau, *Current Population Reports*, series P60-213. See also <http://www.census.gov/prod/2001pubs/p60-213.pdf> (released September 2001).

Income, Expenditures, and Wealth 439

No. 665. Median Income of Persons With Income in Constant (2000) Dollars by Sex, Race, and Hispanic Origin: 1980 to 2000

[Persons 15 years old and over as of March of following year (78,661 represent 78,661,000). Constant dollars based on CPI-U-RS deflator]

Item	Male					Female				
	1980	1990	1995	1999	2000	1980	1990	1995	1999	2000
NUMBER WITH INCOME (1,000)										
All races	78,661	88,220	92,066	96,023	96,983	80,826	92,245	96,007	99,613	99,974
White	69,420	76,480	79,022	81,574	82,214	70,573	78,566	80,608	82,781	82,901
Black	7,387	8,820	9,339	10,067	10,124	8,596	10,687	11,607	12,432	12,524
Asian and Pacific Islander.	(NA)	2,235	3,095	3,572	3,810	(NA)	2,333	3,025	3,568	3,687
Hispanic [1]	3,996	6,767	8,577	10,045	10,253	3,617	5,903	7,478	8,749	9,083
Non-Hispanic White.	65,564	69,987	70,754	72,027	72,400	67,084	72,939	73,506	74,496	74,294
MEDIAN INCOME IN CONSTANT (2000) DOLLARS										
All races	24,932	26,056	25,333	28,191	28,269	9,790	12,930	13,620	15,825	16,188
White	26,519	27,182	26,830	29,524	29,696	9,843	13,247	13,829	15,878	16,216
Black	15,936	16,522	17,972	21,270	21,659	9,113	10,693	12,307	15,267	16,084
Asian and Pacific Islander.	(NA)	24,901	24,884	28,663	30,445	(NA)	14,234	14,442	17,406	17,313
Hispanic [1]	19,219	17,295	16,663	18,847	19,829	8,765	9,671	10,025	11,694	12,249
Non-Hispanic White.	27,222	28,193	28,611	31,622	31,213	9,909	13,586	14,380	16,457	16,804

NA Not available.   [1] Persons of Hispanic origin may be of any race.

No. 666. Average Earnings of Year-Round Full-Time Workers by Educational Attainment: 2000

[In dollars. For persons 18 years old and over as of March 2001]

Sex and age			High school		College		
	All workers	Less than 9th grade	9th to 12th grade (no diploma)	High school graduate (includes equivalency)	Some college, no degree	Associate degree	Bachelor's degree or more
Male, total.	50,557	24,692	28,832	36,770	44,911	46,226	77,963
18 to 24 years old	24,049	17,139	18,603	23,997	22,589	27,078	40,726
25 to 34 years old	42,154	22,975	28,704	32,727	39,942	40,470	59,482
35 to 44 years old	53,478	25,705	27,464	38,150	49,902	48,389	81,528
45 to 54 years old	58,455	24,791	38,466	40,577	52,913	48,202	84,175
55 to 64 years old	61,054	30,070	33,064	46,120	46,098	61,126	93,523
65 years old and over. . . .	56,502	25,183	28,356	39,827	41,143	(B)	95,461
Female, total.	32,641	17,131	19,063	24,970	29,273	31,681	47,224
18 to 24 years old	20,183	(B)	14,370	17,653	19,744	21,337	28,109
25 to 34 years old	31,367	15,867	21,571	23,442	26,760	28,388	42,330
35 to 44 years old	35,320	15,458	18,404	25,945	32,611	33,004	53,594
45 to 54 years old	35,326	17,144	19,953	27,434	32,774	34,811	49,305
55 to 64 years old	32,703	20,843	19,670	25,706	29,658	34,525	50,137
65 years old and over. . . .	29,611	(B)	(B)	23,966	29,103	(B)	42,320

B Base too small to meet statistical standards for reliability of derived figure.

No. 667. Per Capita Money Income in Current and Constant (2000) Dollars by Race and Hispanic Origin: 1980 to 2000

[As of March of following year. In dollars. Constant dollars based on CPI-U-RS deflator]

Year	Current dollars					Constant (2000) dollars				
	All races [1]	White	Black	Asian, Pacific Islander	Hispanic [2]	All races [1]	White	Black	Asian, Pacific Islander	Hispanic [2]
1980	7,787	8,233	4,804	(NA)	4,865	15,494	16,382	9,559	(NA)	4,865
1985 [3]	11,013	11,671	6,840	(NA)	6,613	16,901	17,911	10,497	(NA)	6,613
1990	14,387	15,265	9,017	(NA)	8,424	18,472	19,600	11,578	(NA)	8,424
1991	14,617	15,510	9,170	(NA)	8,662	18,104	19,210	11,358	(NA)	8,662
1992 [4]	14,847	15,785	9,239	(NA)	8,591	17,914	19,046	11,148	(NA)	8,591
1993	15,777	16,800	9,863	15,691	8,830	18,557	19,761	11,601	18,456	8,830
1994 [5]	16,555	17,611	10,650	16,902	9,435	19,055	20,270	12,258	19,454	9,435
1995 [6]	17,227	18,304	10,982	16,567	9,300	19,343	20,552	12,331	18,602	9,300
1996	18,136	19,181	11,899	17,921	10,048	19,825	20,968	13,007	19,590	10,048
1997	19,241	20,425	12,351	18,226	10,772	20,587	21,854	13,215	19,501	10,772
1998	20,120	21,394	12,957	18,709	11,434	21,231	22,575	13,672	19,742	11,434
1999	21,181	22,375	14,397	21,134	11,621	21,893	23,127	14,881	21,844	11,621
2000	22,199	23,415	15,197	22,352	12,306	22,199	23,415	15,198	22,457	12,307

NA Not available.   [1] Includes other races not shown separately.   [2] Persons of Hispanic origin may be of any race.   [3] Beginning 1985, data based on revised Hispanic population controls.   [4] Based on 1990 population controls.   [5] Introduction to new 1990 census sample design.   [6] Full implementation of the 1990 census-based sample design.

Source of Tables 665-667: U.S. Census Bureau, Current Population Reports, P60-213, and <http://www.census.gov/hhes/income/histinc/incperdet.html> (released 05 March 2002).

No. 668. Persons Below Poverty Level and Below 125 Percent of Poverty Level Race and Hispanic Origin: 1970 to 2000

[Persons as of March of the following year (25,420 represents 25,420,000). Based on Current Population Survey; See text, this section, and Section 1, Population, and Appendix III]

Year	Number below poverty level (1,000)					Percent below poverty level					Below 125 percent of poverty level	
	All races [1]	White	Black	Asian and Pacific Islander	His-panic [2]	All races [1]	White	Black	Asian and Pacific Islander	His-panic [2]	Num-ber (1,000)	Percent of total popula-tion
1970	25,420	17,484	7,548	(NA)	(NA)	12.6	9.9	33.5	(NA)	(NA)	35,624	17.6
1975	25,877	17,770	7,545	(NA)	2,991	12.3	9.7	31.3	(NA)	26.9	37,182	17.6
1980	29,272	19,699	8,579	(NA)	3,491	13.0	10.2	32.5	(NA)	25.7	40,658	18.1
1981	31,822	21,553	9,173	(NA)	3,713	14.0	11.1	34.2	(NA)	26.5	43,748	19.3
1982	34,398	23,517	9,697	(NA)	4,301	15.0	12.0	35.6	(NA)	29.9	46,520	20.3
1983 [3]	35,303	23,984	9,882	(NA)	4,633	15.2	12.1	35.7	(NA)	28.0	47,150	20.3
1984	33,700	22,955	9,490	(NA)	4,806	14.4	11.5	33.8	(NA)	28.4	45,288	19.4
1985	33,064	22,860	8,926	(NA)	5,236	14.0	11.4	31.3	(NA)	29.0	44,166	18.7
1986 [4]	32,370	22,183	8,983	(NA)	5,117	13.6	11.0	31.1	(NA)	27.3	43,486	18.2
1987 [4]	32,221	21,195	9,520	1,021	5,422	13.4	10.4	32.4	16.1	28.0	43,032	17.9
1988	31,745	20,715	9,356	1,117	5,357	13.0	10.1	31.3	17.3	26.7	42,551	17.5
1989	31,528	20,785	9,302	939	5,430	12.8	10.0	30.7	14.1	26.2	42,653	17.3
1990	33,585	22,326	9,837	858	6,006	13.5	10.7	31.9	12.2	28.1	44,837	18.0
1991	35,708	23,747	10,242	996	6,339	14.2	11.3	32.7	13.8	28.7	47,527	18.9
1992 [5]	38,014	25,259	10,827	985	7,592	14.8	11.9	33.4	12.7	29.6	50,592	19.7
1993	39,265	26,226	10,877	1,134	8,126	15.1	12.2	33.1	15.3	30.6	51,801	20.0
1994	38,059	25,379	10,196	974	8,416	14.5	11.7	30.6	14.6	30.7	50,401	19.3
1995	36,425	24,423	9,872	1,411	8,574	13.8	11.2	29.3	14.6	30.3	48,761	18.5
1996	36,529	24,650	9,694	1,454	8,697	13.7	11.2	28.4	14.5	29.4	49,310	18.5
1997	35,574	24,396	9,116	1,468	8,308	13.3	11.0	26.5	14.0	27.1	47,853	17.8
1998	34,476	23,454	9,091	1,360	8,070	12.7	10.5	26.1	12.5	25.6	46,036	17.0
1999	32,258	21,922	8,360	1,163	7,439	11.8	9.8	23.6	10.7	22.8	44,286	16.2
2000	31,054	21,242	7,862	1,214	7,153	11.3	9.4	22.0	10.7	21.2	43,377	15.7

NA Not available.   [1] Includes other races not shown separately.   [2] Persons of Hispanic origin may be of any race.
[3] Beginning 1983, data based on revised Hispanic population controls and not directly comparable with prior years.   [4] Beginning 1987, data based on revised processing procedures and not directly comparable with prior years.   [5] Beginning 1992, based on 1990 population controls.

Source: U.S. Census Bureau, Current Population Reports, P60-214. See also <http://www.census.gov/prod/2000pubs/p60-214.pdf> (released September 2001).

No. 669. Children Below Poverty Level by Race and Hispanic Origin: 1970 to 2000

[Persons as of March of the following year (10,235 represents 10,235,000). Covers only related children in families under 18 years old. Based on Current Population Survey; see text, this section and Section 1, and Appendix III]

Year	Number below poverty level (1,000)					Percent below poverty level				
	All races [1]	White	Black	Asian and Pacific Islander	His-panic [2]	All races [1]	White	Black	Asian and Pacific Islander	His-panic [2]
1970	10,235	6,138	3,922	(NA)	(NA)	14.9	10.5	41.5	(NA)	(NA)
1975	10,882	6,748	3,884	(NA)	1,619	16.8	12.5	41.4	(NA)	33.1
1980	11,114	6,817	3,906	(NA)	1,718	17.9	13.4	42.1	(NA)	33.0
1981	12,068	7,429	4,170	(NA)	1,874	19.5	14.7	44.9	(NA)	35.4
1982 [3]	13,139	8,282	4,388	(NA)	2,117	21.3	16.5	47.3	(NA)	38.9
1983 [3]	13,427	8,534	4,273	(NA)	2,251	21.8	17.0	46.2	(NA)	37.7
1984	12,929	8,086	4,320	(NA)	2,317	21.0	16.1	46.2	(NA)	38.7
1985	12,483	7,838	4,057	(NA)	2,512	20.1	15.6	43.1	(NA)	39.6
1986	12,257	7,714	4,037	(NA)	2,413	19.8	15.3	42.7	(NA)	37.1
1987 [4]	12,275	7,398	4,234	432	2,606	19.7	14.7	44.4	22.7	38.9
1988	11,935	7,095	4,148	458	2,576	19.0	14.0	42.8	23.5	37.3
1989	12,001	7,164	4,257	368	2,496	19.0	14.1	43.2	18.9	35.5
1990	12,715	7,696	4,412	356	2,750	19.9	15.1	44.2	17.0	37.7
1991	13,658	8,316	4,637	348	2,977	21.1	16.1	45.6	17.1	39.8
1992 [5]	14,521	8,752	5,015	352	3,440	21.6	16.5	46.3	16.0	39.0
1993	14,961	9,123	5,030	358	3,666	22.0	17.0	45.9	17.6	39.9
1994	14,610	8,826	4,787	308	3,956	21.2	16.3	43.3	17.9	41.1
1995	13,999	8,474	4,644	532	3,938	20.2	15.5	41.5	18.6	39.3
1996	13,764	8,488	4,411	553	4,090	19.8	15.5	39.5	19.1	39.9
1997	13,422	8,441	4,116	608	3,865	19.2	15.4	36.8	19.9	36.4
1998	12,845	7,935	4,073	542	3,670	18.3	14.4	36.4	17.5	33.6
1999	11,510	7,123	3,644	348	3,382	16.3	12.9	32.7	11.5	29.9
2000	11,018	6,838	3,417	434	3,173	15.6	12.3	30.4	14.1	27.3

NA Not available.   [1] Includes other races not shown separately.   [2] Persons of Hispanic origin may be of any race.
[3] Beginning 1983, data based on revised Hispanic population controls and not directly comparable with prior years.   [4] Beginning 1987, data based on revised processing procedures and not directly comparable with prior years.   [5] Beginning 1992, based on 1990 population controls.

Source: U.S. Census Bureau, Current Population Reports, P60-214. See also <http://www.census.gov/prod/2000pubs/p60-214.pdf> (released September 2001).

No. 670. Weighted Average Poverty Thresholds by Size of Unit: 1980 to 2001

[**In dollars.** For information on the official poverty thresholds; see text, this section]

Size of family unit	1980[1]	1990	1995	1996	1997	1998	1999	2000	2001
One person (unrelated individual) . . .	4,190	6,652	7,763	7,995	8,183	8,316	8,501	8,794	9,044
Under 65 years	4,290	6,800	7,929	8,163	8,350	8,480	8,667	8,959	9,214
65 years and over	3,949	6,268	7,309	7,525	7,698	7,818	7,990	8,259	8,494
Two persons	5,363	8,509	9,933	10,233	10,473	10,634	10,869	11,239	11,559
Householder under 65 years	5,537	8,794	10,259	10,564	10,805	10,972	11,214	11,590	11,920
Householder 65 years and over . . .	4,983	7,905	9,219	9,491	9,712	9,862	10,075	10,419	10,715
Three persons	6,565	10,419	12,158	12,516	12,802	13,003	13,290	13,738	14,129
Four persons	8,414	13,359	15,569	16,036	16,400	16,660	17,029	17,603	18,104
Five persons	9,966	15,792	18,408	18,952	19,380	19,680	20,127	20,819	21,411
Six persons	11,269	17,839	20,804	21,389	21,886	22,228	22,727	23,528	24,197
Seven persons	12,761	20,241	23,552	24,268	24,802	25,257	25,912	26,754	27,514
Eight persons	14,199	22,582	26,237	27,091	27,593	28,166	28,967	29,701	30,546
Nine or more persons	16,896	26,848	31,280	31,971	32,566	33,339	34,417	35,060	36,058

[1] Poverty levels for nonfarm families.

Source: U.S. Census Bureau, *Current Population Reports*, P60-214. See also <http://www.census.gov/prod/2000pubs/p60-214.pdf> (released September 2001).

No. 671. Persons Below Poverty Level by Selected Characteristics: 2000

[**Persons as of March 2001 (31,054 represents 31,054,000).** Based on Current Population Survey; see text, this section and Section 1, Population, and Appendix III. For composition of regions, see map, inside front cover]

Age and region	Number below poverty level (1,000)					Percent below poverty level				
	All races [1]	White	Black	Asian and Pacific Islander	His-panic [2]	All races [1]	White	Black	Asian and Pacific Islander	His-panic [2]
Total	31,054	21,242	7,862	1,214	7,153	11.3	9.4	22.0	10.7	21.2
Male	13,417	9,241	3,267	588	3,287	9.9	8.3	19.6	10.7	19.5
Female.	17,637	12,001	4,595	626	3,866	12.5	10.5	24.1	10.8	22.9
Under 18 years old	11,553	7,283	3,487	447	3,328	16.1	12.9	30.6	14.4	28.0
18 to 24 years old	3,890	2,709	941	154	896	14.4	12.6	23.6	13.6	21.5
25 to 34 years old	3,892	2,738	882	180	1,080	10.4	9.2	17.1	8.7	19.1
35 to 44 years old	3,678	2,569	896	129	782	8.2	7.0	15.6	6.8	15.5
45 to 54 years old	2,441	1,661	582	131	395	6.4	5.2	13.6	8.8	12.3
55 to 59 years old	1,175	854	253	56	134	8.8	7.5	18.9	12.3	12.8
60 to 64 years old	1,066	828	197	31	184	10.2	9.2	18.6	9.9	22.1
65 years old and over . . .	3,359	2,601	623	86	353	10.2	8.9	22.4	10.3	18.8
65 to 74 years old	1,592	1,190	317	55	218	8.9	7.6	19.4	11.1	18.9
75 years old and over .	1,767	1,412	306	30	135	11.7	10.4	26.4	9.0	18.5
Northeast	5,363	3,598	1,466	244	1,041	10.3	8.3	22.5	12.9	22.9
Midwest	6,037	4,138	1,627	104	455	9.5	7.5	24.4	8.0	17.7
South.	12,105	7,529	4,184	195	2,422	12.5	10.1	21.7	9.7	20.6
West	7,550	5,978	584	671	3,235	11.9	11.3	18.2	11.0	21.8
Native	26,351	17,716	7,514	414	4,324	10.7	8.6	22.7	9.9	21.2
Foreign born	4,704	3,527	348	800	2,829	15.7	17.6	13.3	11.3	21.2
Naturalized citizen. . . .	1,106	737	59	305	460	9.7	10.8	5.7	8.8	13.2
Not a citizen.	3,597	2,790	289	495	2,369	19.4	21.2	18.1	13.6	24.1

[1] Includes other races not shown separately. [2] Persons of Hispanic origin may be of any race.

Source: U.S. Census Bureau, *Current Population Reports*, P60-214. See also <http://www.census.gov/prod/2000pubs/p60-214.pdf> (released September 2001) and <http://ferret.bls.census.gov/macro/032001/pov/new19007.htm> (released 10 December 2001).

442   Income, Expenditures, and Wealth

No. 672. Work Experience During 2000 by Poverty Status, Sex, and Age: 2000

[Number in thousands (100,349 represents 100,349,000). Covers only persons 16 years old and over. Based on Current Population Survey; see text, this section, and Section 1, and Appendix III]

Sex and age	Worked full-time year-round			Did not work full-time year-round			Did not work		
		Below poverty level			Below poverty level			Below poverty level	
	Number (1,000)	Number (1,000)	Percent	Number (1,000)	Number (1,000)	Percent	Number (1,000)	Number (1,000)	Percent
BOTH SEXES									
Total	100,349	2,433	2.4	49,012	5,906	12.1	62,620	12,252	19.6
16 to 17 years old	104	10	10.0	3,267	243	7.4	4,622	837	18.1
18 to 64 years old	98,242	2,395	2.4	42,166	5,527	13.1	30,601	8,221	26.9
18 to 24 years old	8,400	369	4.4	12,822	1,931	15.1	5,743	1,590	27.7
25 to 34 years old	23,884	707	3.0	8,725	1,483	17.0	4,832	1,702	35.2
35 to 54 years old	55,104	1,166	2.1	16,001	1,751	10.9	11,714	3,202	27.3
55 to 64 years old	10,855	153	1.4	4,618	362	7.8	8,312	1,727	20.8
65 years old and over	2,003	28	1.4	3,579	137	3.8	27,396	3,195	11.7
MALE									
Total	58,756	1,313	2.2	20,048	2,348	11.7	23,427	4,485	19.1
16 to 17 years old	63	6	(B)	1,671	109	6.5	2,384	449	18.8
18 to 64 years old	57,346	1,289	2.2	16,463	2,171	13.2	10,126	3,058	30.2
18 to 24 years old	4,620	175	3.8	6,232	768	12.3	2,624	625	23.8
25 to 34 years old	14,104	362	2.6	3,133	481	15.3	1,214	578	47.6
35 to 54 years old	32,256	674	2.1	5,181	741	14.3	3,318	1,227	37.0
55 to 64 years old	6,366	77	1.2	1,916	182	9.5	2,970	629	21.2
65 years old and over	1,347	18	1.4	1,915	68	3.5	10,917	977	9.0
FEMALE									
Total	41,593	1,121	2.7	28,964	3,558	12.3	39,193	7,767	19.8
16 to 17 years old	41	5	(B)	1,596	134	8.4	2,238	387	17.3
18 to 64 years old	40,896	1,107	2.7	25,703	3,355	13.1	20,476	5,163	25.2
18 to 24 years old	3,780	194	5.1	6,590	1,164	17.7	3,119	965	30.9
25 to 34 years old	9,780	345	3.5	5,591	1,002	17.9	3,618	1,125	31.1
35 to 54 years old	22,848	492	2.2	10,820	1,010	9.3	8,397	1,975	23.5
55 to 64 years old	4,489	76	1.7	2,701	179	6.6	5,342	1,098	20.6
65 years old and over	656	9	1.4	1,664	69	4.1	16,479	2,217	13.5

B Base figure too small to meet statistical standards for reliability of a derived figure.
Source: U.S. Census Bureau, <http://ferret.bls.census.gov/macro/032001/pov/new10001.htm> (released 10 December 2001).

No. 673. Persons Below Poverty Level—Number and Rate by State: 1998 to 2000 Average

[32,596 represents 32,596,000. Based on the Current Population Survey; see text, see above, and Appendix III. The CPS is designed to collect reliable data on income primarily at the national level and secondarily at the regional level. When the income data are tabulated by state, the estimates are considered less reliable and, therefore, particular caution should be used when trying to interpret the results; for additional detail, see source]

State	Number below poverty level (1,000)	Percent below poverty level	State	Number below poverty level (1,000)	Percent below poverty level
United States.	32,596	11.9	Missouri	535	9.8
			Montana	143	16.0
Alabama	640	14.7	Nebraska	180	10.7
Alaska	53	8.4	Nevada.	194	10.1
Arizona	661	13.5	New Hampshire	93	7.6
Arkansas.	407	15.8			
California.	4,745	14.0	New Jersey	663	8.1
			New Mexico.	347	19.3
Colorado.	353	8.5	New York	2,710	14.7
Connecticut	255	7.7	North Carolina	989	13.2
Delaware.	77	9.9	North Dakota	80	12.8
District of Columbia.	89	17.4			
Florida	1,798	12.0	Ohio.	1,253	11.1
			Oklahoma	459	14.1
Georgia	969	12.5	Oregon	437	12.9
Hawaii	126	10.6	Pennsylvania	1,167	9.8
Idaho	167	13.3	Rhode Island	98	10.2
Illinois	1,282	10.5			
Indiana	482	8.3	South Carolina	457	12.0
			South Dakota	66	9.4
Iowa.	225	7.9	Tennessee.	743	13.4
Kansas.	273	10.5	Texas.	3,005	14.9
Kentucky.	487	12.5	Utah.	175	8.1
Louisiana	791	18.5			
Maine.	124	9.8	Vermont	63	10.3
			Virginia	555	8.1
Maryland.	371	7.3	Washington	548	9.5
Massachusetts	626	10.2	West Virginia	279	15.8
Michigan	1,023	10.2	Wisconsin	476	9.0
Minnesota	376	7.9	Wyoming.	54	11.1
Mississippi.	429	15.5			

Source: U.S. Census Bureau, *Current Population Reports*, P60-214. See also <http://www.census.gov/prod/2000pubs/p60-214.pdf> (released September 2001).

Income, Expenditures, and Wealth   443

No. 674. Families Below Poverty Level and Below 125 Percent of Poverty by Race and Hispanic Origin: 1970 to 2000

[Families as of March of the following year (5,260 represents 5,260,000). Based on Current Population Survey, see text, this section, Section 1, and Appendix III]

Year	Number below poverty level (1,000)					Percent below poverty level					Below 125 percent of poverty level	
	All races [1]	White	Black	Asian and Pacific Islander	His-panic [2]	All races [1]	White	Black	Asian and Pacific Islander	His-panic [2]	Number (1,000)	Percent
1970	5,260	3,708	1,481	(NA)	(NA)	10.1	8.0	29.5	(NA)	(NA)	7,516	14.4
1975	5,450	3,838	1,513	(NA)	627	9.7	7.7	27.1	(NA)	25.1	7,974	14.2
1980	6,217	4,195	1,826	(NA)	751	10.3	8.0	28.9	(NA)	23.2	8,764	14.5
1981	6,851	4,670	1,972	(NA)	792	11.2	8.8	30.8	(NA)	24.0	9,568	15.7
1982	7,512	5,118	2,158	(NA)	916	12.2	9.6	33.0	(NA)	27.2	10,279	16.7
1983 [3]	7,647	5,220	2,161	(NA)	981	12.3	9.7	32.3	(NA)	25.9	10,358	16.7
1984	7,277	4,925	2,094	(NA)	991	11.6	9.1	30.9	(NA)	25.2	9,901	15.8
1985	7,223	4,983	1,983	(NA)	1,074	11.4	9.1	28.7	(NA)	25.5	9,753	15.3
1986	7,023	4,811	1,987	(NA)	1,085	10.9	8.6	28.0	(NA)	24.7	9,476	14.7
1987 [4]	7,005	4,567	2,117	199	1,168	10.7	8.1	29.4	13.5	25.5	9,338	14.3
1988	6,874	4,471	2,089	201	1,141	10.4	7.9	28.2	13.6	23.7	9,284	14.1
1989	6,784	4,409	2,077	182	1,133	10.3	7.8	27.8	11.9	23.4	9,267	14.0
1990	7,098	4,622	2,193	169	1,244	10.7	8.1	29.3	11.0	25.0	9,564	14.4
1991	7,712	5,022	2,343	210	1,372	11.5	8.8	30.4	13.0	26.5	10,244	15.3
1992 [5]	8,144	5,255	2,484	215	1,529	11.9	9.1	31.1	12.2	26.7	10,959	16.1
1993	8,393	5,452	2,499	235	1,625	12.3	9.4	31.3	13.5	27.3	11,203	16.4
1994	8,053	5,312	2,212	208	1,724	11.6	9.1	27.3	13.1	27.8	10,771	15.5
1995	7,532	4,994	2,127	264	1,695	10.8	8.5	26.4	12.4	27.0	10,223	14.7
1996	7,708	5,059	2,206	284	1,748	11.0	8.6	26.1	12.7	26.4	10,476	14.9
1997	7,324	4,990	1,985	244	1,721	10.3	8.4	23.6	10.2	24.7	10,032	14.2
1998	7,186	4,829	1,981	270	1,648	10.0	8.0	23.4	11.0	22.7	9,714	13.6
1999	6,676	4,377	1,898	258	1,525	9.3	7.3	21.9	10.3	20.2	9,320	12.9
2000	6,222	4,151	1,685	235	1,431	8.6	6.9	19.1	8.8	18.5	8,886	12.3

NA Not available. [1] Includes other races not shown separately. [2] Persons of Hispanic origin may be of any race. [3] Beginning 1983, data based on revised Hispanic population controls and not directly comparable with prior years. [4] Beginning 1987, data based on revised processing procedures and not directly comparable with prior years. [5] Beginning 1992, based on 1990 population controls.

Source: U.S. Census Bureau, *Current Population Reports*, P60-214. See also <http://www.census.gov/prod/2000pubs/p60-214.pdf> (released September 2001).

No. 675. Families Below Poverty Level by Selected Characteristics: 2000

[Families as of March 2001 (6,222 represents 6,222,000). Based on Current Population Survey; see text, this section, and Section 1, and Appendix III]

Characteristic	Number below poverty level (1,000)					Percent below poverty level				
	All races [1]	White	Black	Asian and Pacific Islander	His-panic [2]	All races [1]	White	Black	Asian and Pacific Islander	His-panic [2]
Total	6,222	4,151	1,685	235	1,431	8.6	6.9	19.1	8.8	18.5
Age of householder:										
15 to 24 years old.	847	527	290	11	196	25.5	21.6	41.3	8.4	29.1
25 to 34 years old.	1,671	1,085	500	43	478	13.0	10.7	25.0	7.6	23.1
35 to 44 years old.	1,593	1,094	407	63	395	8.6	7.2	17.0	8.2	18.2
45 to 54 years old.	820	516	211	60	169	5.1	3.8	12.0	9.5	12.3
55 to 64 years old.	639	456	145	28	88	6.6	5.5	15.5	9.2	11.6
65 years old and over	627	458	126	27	93	5.4	4.4	12.7	11.1	14.3
Education of householder: [3]										
No high school diploma	2,079	1,483	481	61	821	20.4	18.1	30.8	23.6	27.2
High school diploma, no college . . .	1,865	1,197	585	52	270	8.7	6.7	20.7	11.0	14.6
Some college, less than bachelor's degree.	982	632	264	44	94	5.3	4.1	10.9	9.4	7.1
Bachelor's degree or more	424	296	59	65	38	2.3	1.9	4.6	4.9	4.7
Work experience of householder:										
Total [4]	5,588	3,687	1,559	208	1,335	9.2	7.4	19.9	8.6	18.9
Worked during year.	3,263	2,198	877	105	804	6.3	5.1	13.7	4.9	13.8
Year-round, full-time	1,271	868	331	55	362	3.2	2.6	6.9	3.2	8.4
Not year-round, full-time	1,992	1,330	546	50	442	16.7	13.6	34.3	12.2	29.0
Did not work	2,025	1,400	682	100	531	20.2	21.4	40.4	34.0	42.7

[1] Includes other races not shown separately. [2] Hispanic persons may be of any race. [3] Householder 25 years old and over. [4] Persons 16-64 years old.

Source: U.S. Census Bureau, *Current Population Reports*, P60-214. See also <http://www.census.gov/prod/2000pubs/p60-214.pdf> (released September 2001) and <http://ferret.bls.census.gov/macro/032001/pov/new16a000.htm> (released 10 December 2001).

No. 676. Nonfinancial Assets Held by Families by Type of Asset: 1998

[**Median value in thousands of dollars**. Constant dollar figures are based on consumer price index for all urban consumers published by U.S. Bureau of Labor Statistics. Families include one-person units and, as used in this table, are comparable to the U.S. Census Bureau household concept. For definition of family, see text, Section 1, Population. Based on Survey of Consumer Finance; see Appendix III. For data on financial assets, see Table 1144. For definition of median, see Guide to Tabular Presentation]

Age of family head, and family income	Total	Vehicles	Primary residence	Other residential property	Equity in nonresidential property	Business equity	Other	Any nonfinancial asset
PERCENT OF FAMILIES OWNING ASSET								
All families, total	96.8	82.8	66.2	12.8	8.6	11.5	8.5	89.9
Age of family head:								
Under 35 years old	94.8	78.3	38.9	3.5	2.7	7.2	7.3	83.3
35 to 44 years old	97.6	85.8	67.1	12.2	7.5	14.7	8.8	92.0
45 to 54 years old	96.7	87.5	74.4	16.2	12.2	16.2	9.2	92.9
55 to 64 years old	98.2	88.7	80.3	20.4	10.4	14.3	8.5	93.8
65 to 74 years old	98.5	83.4	81.5	18.4	15.3	10.1	10.3	92.0
75 years old and over	96.4	69.8	77.0	13.6	8.1	2.7	7.0	87.2
Family income:								
Less than $10,000	83.8	51.3	34.5	(B)	(B)	3.8	2.6	62.7
$10,000 to $24,999	96.4	78.0	51.7	5.8	5.0	5.0	5.6	85.9
$25,000 to $49,999	99.2	89.6	68.2	11.4	7.6	10.3	9.4	95.6
$50,000 to $99,999	100.0	93.6	85.0	19.0	12.0	15.0	10.2	98.0
$100,000 and more	100.0	88.7	93.3	37.3	22.6	34.7	17.1	98.9
MEDIAN VALUE [1] ($1,000)								
All families, total	123.5	10.8	100.0	65.0	38.0	60.0	10.0	97.8
Age of family head:								
Under 35 years old	28.9	8.9	84.0	42.5	25.0	34.0	5.0	22.7
35 to 44 years old	128.0	11.4	101.0	45.0	20.0	62.5	8.0	103.5
45 to 54 years old	178.9	12.8	120.0	74.0	45.0	100.0	14.0	126.8
55 to 64 years old	198.2	13.5	110.0	70.0	54.0	62.5	28.0	126.9
65 to 74 years old	165.2	10.8	95.0	75.0	45.0	61.1	10.0	109.9
75 years old and over	135.0	7.0	85.0	103.0	54.0	40.0	10.0	96.1
Family income:								
Less than $10,000	11.7	4.0	51.0	(B)	(B)	37.5	5.0	16.3
$10,000 to $24,999	46.2	5.7	71.9	70.0	25.0	31.1	5.0	43.7
$25,000 to $49,999	112.0	10.2	85.0	50.0	28.0	37.5	6.0	83.5
$50,000 to $99,999	233.2	16.6	130.0	60.0	30.0	56.0	12.0	156.3
$100,000 and more	665.6	26.8	240.0	132.0	114.1	230.0	36.0	380.0

B Base too small to meet statistical standards for reliability of derived figure.   [1] Median value of financial asset for families holding such assets.

No. 677. Family Net Worth—Mean and Median Net Worth in Constant (1998) Dollars by Selected Family Characteristics: 1992 to 1998

[**Net worth in thousands of constant (1998) dollars** (212.7 represents $212,700). Constant dollar figures are based on consumer price index for all urban consumers published by U.S. Bureau of Labor Statistics. Families include one-person units and as used in this table are comparable to the Census Bureau household concept. Based on Survey of Consumer Finance; see Appendix III. For definition of median, see Guide to Tabular Presentation]

Family characteristic	1992 Percent of families	1992 Net worth Mean	1992 Net worth Median	1995 Percent of families	1995 Net worth Mean	1995 Net worth Median	1998 Percent of families	1998 Net worth Mean	1998 Net worth Median
All families	100.0	212.7	56.5	100.0	224.8	60.9	100.0	282.5	71.6
Age of family head:									
Under 35 years old	25.8	53.1	10.4	24.8	47.4	12.7	23.3	65.9	9.0
35 to 44 years old	22.8	152.7	50.9	23.0	152.8	54.9	23.3	196.2	63.4
45 to 54 years old	16.2	304.4	89.3	17.9	313.0	100.8	19.2	362.7	105.5
55 to 64 years old	13.2	384.9	130.2	12.5	404.7	122.4	12.8	530.2	127.5
65 to 74 years old	12.6	326.1	112.3	12.0	369.3	117.9	11.2	465.5	146.5
75 years old and over	9.4	244.4	99.2	9.8	273.8	98.8	10.2	310.2	125.6
Family income in constant (1998) dollars:[1]									
Less than $10,000	14.8	32.1	2.9	15.1	46.6	4.8	12.6	40.0	3.6
$10,000 to $24,999	27.0	69.8	27.1	25.4	80.3	31.0	24.8	85.6	24.8
$25,000 to $49,999	29.8	131.4	55.6	31.0	124.0	56.7	28.8	135.4	60.3
$50,000 to $99,999	20.7	245.6	129.9	21.0	258.1	126.6	25.2	275.5	152.0
$100,000 and more	7.6	1,300.8	481.9	7.4	1,411.9	511.4	8.6	1,727.8	510.8

[1] Income for year preceding the survey.

Source of Tables 676 and 677: Board of Governors of the Federal Reserve System, *Federal Reserve Bulletin*, January 2000, and unpublished data.

No. 678. Household and Nonprofit Organization Sector Balance Sheet: 1980 to 2001

[In billions of dollars (11,011 represents $11,011,000,000,000). As of December 31. For details of financial assets and liabilities, see Table 1149]

Item	1980	1990	1994	1995	1996	1997	1998	1999	2000	2001
Assets	**11,011**	**24,127**	**29,230**	**32,285**	**35,158**	**39,320**	**43,131**	**48,570**	**48,467**	**47,939**
Tangible assets [1]	4,378	9,288	10,209	10,684	11,183	11,914	12,773	13,723	15,072	16,266
Real estate	3,421	7,415	8,039	8,425	8,844	9,495	10,249	11,058	12,223	13,231
Consumer durable goods.	931	1,815	2,092	2,176	2,254	2,329	2,427	2,560	2,732	2,914
Financial assets [1]	6,633	14,839	19,021	21,601	23,975	27,405	30,358	34,847	33,395	31,673
Deposits	1,521	3,259	3,110	3,298	3,441	3,622	3,928	4,050	4,406	4,793
Checkable deposits and currency.	220	412	585	544	471	437	410	346	309	344
Time and savings deposits	1,239	2,465	2,154	2,281	2,434	2,566	2,733	2,787	3,039	3,217
Money market fund shares	62	369	352	450	501	582	747	873	1,006	1,174
Credit market instruments [1]	425	1,556	1,951	1,926	2,085	2,029	2,042	2,311	2,098	1,887
U.S. government securities.	165	555	958	898	997	863	757	953	735	511
Treasury	160	495	870	799	825	686	601	686	456	406
Savings bonds	73	126	180	185	187	187	187	186	185	190
Corporate equities	875	1,781	3,082	4,161	4,896	6,302	7,174	9,197	7,317	5,888
Mutual fund shares	46	457	997	1,159	1,495	1,941	2,401	3,113	3,094	2,970
Pension fund reserves	970	3,376	4,882	5,671	6,325	7,323	8,209	9,066	9,075	8,682
Equity in noncorporate business	2,220	3,179	3,394	3,598	3,787	4,053	4,287	4,538	4,815	4,867
Liabilities	**1,455**	**3,747**	**4,760**	**5,111**	**5,446**	**5,825**	**6,308**	**6,893**	**7,472**	**8,056**
Credit market instruments	1,404	3,625	4,575	4,914	5,224	5,557	6,011	6,513	7,078	7,693
Home mortgages	935	2,532	3,218	3,383	3,578	3,818	4,157	4,531	4,904	5,385
Consumer credit.	355	805	984	1,123	1,214	1,272	1,347	1,446	1,593	1,703
Net worth	**9,556**	**20,380**	**24,470**	**27,174**	**29,713**	**33,495**	**36,823**	**41,677**	**40,995**	**39,883**
Memo:										
Replacement cost value of structures:										
Residential	2,548	4,599	5,748	6,012	6,352	6,713	7,159	7,642	8,228	8,748
Households	2,363	4,337	5,459	5,718	6,050	6,396	6,827	7,294	7,862	8,371
Farm households	112	150	170	174	179	189	198	209	223	228
Nonprofit organizations	73	112	120	121	124	128	134	139	144	148
Nonresidential (nonprofits).	267	475	572	596	624	665	710	754	808	857
Disposable personal income	2,116	4,363	5,304	5,505	5,780	6,092	6,467	6,737	7,190	7,435
Owners' equity in household real estate .	2,010	4,076	4,063	4,247	4,432	4,736	5,036	5,417	6,102	6,642

[1] Includes types of assets and/or liabilities not shown separately.
Source: Board of Governors of the Federal Reserve System, *Balance Sheets for the U.S. Economy*, June 6, 2002. See also <http://www.federalreserve.gov/releases/Z1/Current/data.htm> (released 06 June 2002).

No. 679. Net Stock of Fixed Reproducible Tangible Wealth in Current and Real (1996) Dollars: 1980 to 2000

[In billions of dollars (10,297 represents $10,297,000,000,000). As of December 31]

Item	1980	1990	1994	1995	1996	1997	1998	1999	2000
CURRENT DOLLARS									
Net stock	**10,297**	**18,187**	**21,618**	**22,617**	**23,701**	**24,925**	**26,219**	**27,757**	**29,640**
Private.	7,213	12,760	15,204	15,909	16,723	17,653	18,650	19,767	21,165
Nonresidential equipment.	1,420	2,542	2,992	3,183	3,352	3,520	3,712	3,959	4,245
Information processing and related equipment	225	663	803	850	906	975	1,036	1,129	1,262
Industrial equipment	525	893	1,011	1,075	1,119	1,157	1,200	1,239	1,288
Transportation equipment	306	472	604	651	690	717	764	840	905
Other equipment.	319	513	575	607	637	672	712	751	791
Nonresidential structures	2,256	4,081	4,739	4,941	5,175	5,487	5,746	6,028	6,448
Nonresidential buildings, excluding farm	1,169	2,514	2,992	3,125	3,286	3,499	3,741	3,986	4,288
Utilities	695	1,005	1,148	1,190	1,229	1,265	1,283	1,311	1,368
Residential	3,537	6,087	7,414	7,723	8,131	8,581	9,124	9,711	10,398
Housing units	2,898	4,963	6,059	6,302	6,625	6,995	7,450	7,929	8,485
Government	2,151	3,612	4,322	4,533	4,725	4,943	5,142	5,430	5,743
Equipment	300	559	672	686	692	694	698	720	741
Structures.	1,952	3,053	3,651	3,847	4,033	4,249	4,444	4,710	5,002
Federal.	653	1,087	1,279	1,314	1,343	1,367	1,381	1,424	1,463
Defense	483	743	874	885	891	893	891	907	920
State and local.	1,498	2,525	3,043	3,219	3,382	3,576	3,760	4,006	4,279
Consumer durable goods	934	1,815	2,092	2,176	2,254	2,329	2,427	2,560	2,732
Motor vehicles	257	574	629	647	663	673	703	753	809
Furniture and household equipment. .	459	823	968	1,011	1,053	1,096	1,142	1,193	1,262
Other	203	417	495	519	537	560	583	614	661
CHAINED (1996) DOLLARS									
Net stock	**14,269**	**20,650**	**22,291**	**22,829**	**23,450**	**24,126**	**24,908**	**25,770**	**26,680**
Private.	9,950	14,562	15,694	16,075	16,521	17,010	17,571	18,160	18,780
Nonresidential equipment.	1,855	2,723	3,036	3,183	3,354	3,555	3,797	4,066	4,360
Nonresidential structures	3,177	4,704	4,939	5,008	5,094	5,198	5,314	5,421	5,541
Residential	4,921	7,142	7,720	7,884	8,074	8,261	8,474	8,703	8,932
Government	3,127	4,192	4,512	4,585	4,668	4,749	4,835	4,932	5,027
Federal.	969	1,291	1,326	1,326	1,334	1,329	1,327	1,329	1,328
State and local.	2,156	2,901	3,185	3,259	3,334	3,420	3,507	3,602	3,696
Consumer durable goods	1,198	1,899	2,087	2,170	2,262	2,369	2,508	2,695	2,911

Source: U.S. Bureau of Economic Analysis, *Fixed Assets and Consumer Durable Goods in the United States, 1925-97* (forthcoming); and *Survey of Current Business*, September 2001.

Section 14
Prices

This section presents indexes of producer and consumer prices, actual prices for selected commodities, and energy prices. The primary sources of these data are monthly publications of the Department of Labor, Bureau of Labor Statistics (BLS), which include *Monthly Labor Review, Consumer Price Index, Detailed Report, Producer Price Indexes,* and *U.S. Import and Export Price Indexes.* The Department of Commerce, Bureau of Economic Analysis is the source for gross domestic product measures.

Producer price index (PPI)—This index, dating from 1890, is the oldest continuous statistical series published by BLS. It is designed to measure average changes in prices received by producers of all commodities, at all stages of processing, produced in the United States.

The index has undergone several revisions (see *Monthly Labor Review,* February 1962, April 1978, and August 1988). It is now based on approximately 10,000 individual products and groups of products along with about 100,000 quotations per month. Indexes for the net output of manufacturing and mining industries have been added in recent years. Prices used in constructing the index are collected from sellers and generally apply to the first significant large-volume commercial transaction for each commodity—i.e., the manufacturer's or other producer's selling price or the selling price on an organized exchange or at a central market.

The weights used in the index represent the total net selling value of commodities produced or processed in this country. Values are f.o.b. (free on board) production point and are exclusive of excise taxes. Effective with the release of data for January 1988, many important producer price indexes were changed to a new reference base year, 1982=100, from 1967=100. The reference year of the PPI shipment weights has been taken primarily from the 1987 Census of Manufactures. For further detail regarding the PPI, see the BLS *Handbook of Methods,* Bulletin 2490 (April 1997), Chapter 16. The PPI Web page is <http://stats.bls.gov/ppihome.htm>.

Consumer price indexes (CPI)—The CPI is a measure of the average change in prices over time in a "market basket" of goods and services purchased either by urban wage earners and clerical workers or by all urban consumers. In 1919, BLS began to publish complete indexes at semiannual intervals, using a weighting structure based on data collected in the expenditure survey of wage-earner and clerical-worker families in 1917-19 (BLS Bulletin 357, 1924). The first major revision of the CPI occurred in 1940, with subsequent revisions in 1953, 1964, 1978, 1987, and 1998.

Beginning with the release of data for January 1988 in February 1988, most consumer price indexes shifted to a new reference base year. All indexes previously expressed on a base of 1967=100, or any other base through December 1981, have been rebased to 1982-84= 100. The expenditure weights are based upon data tabulated from the Consumer Expenditure Surveys for 1993, 1994, and 1995.

BLS publishes CPIs for two population groups: (1) a CPI for all urban consumers (CPI-U) which covers approximately 80 percent of the total population; and (2) a CPI for urban wage earners and clerical workers (CPI-W) which covers 32 percent of the total population. The CPI-U includes, in addition to wage earners and clerical workers, groups which historically have been excluded from CPI coverage, such as professional, managerial, and technical workers; the self-employed; short-term workers; the unemployed; and retirees and others not in the labor force.

The current CPI is based on prices of food, clothing, shelter, fuels, transportation fares, charges for doctors' and dentists' services, drugs, etc. purchased for

U.S. Census Bureau, Statistical Abstract of the United States: 2002

day-to-day living. Prices are collected in 87 areas across the country from over 50,000 housing units and 23,000 establishments. Area selection was based on the 1990 census. All taxes directly associated with the purchase and use of items are included in the index. Prices of food, fuels, and a few other items are obtained every month in all 87 locations. Prices of most other commodities and services are collected monthly in the three largest geographic areas and every other month in other areas.

In calculating the index, each item is assigned a weight to account for its relative importance in consumers' budgets. Price changes for the various items in each location are then averaged. Local data are then combined to obtain a U.S. city average. Separate indexes are also published for regions, area size-classes, cross-classifications of regions and size-classes, and for 26 local areas, usually consisting of the Metropolitan Statistical Area (MSA); see Appendix II. Area definitions are those established by the Office of Management and Budget in 1983. Definitions do not include revisions made since 1992. Area indexes do not measure differences in the level of prices among cities; they only measure the average change in prices for each area since the base period. For further detail regarding the CPI, see the BLS *Handbook of Methods*, Bulletin 2490, Chapter 17; the *Consumer Price Index*, and the CPI home page: <http://stats.bls.gov/cpihome.htm>. In January 1983, the method of measuring homeownership costs in the CPI-U was changed to a rental equivalence approach. This treatment calculates homeowner costs of shelter based on the implicit rent owners would pay to rent the homes they own. The rental equivalence approach was introduced into the CPI-W in 1985. The CPI-U was used to prepare the consumer price tables in this section.

Other price indexes—Chain-weighted price indexes, produced by the Bureau of Economic Analysis (BEA), are weighted averages of the detailed price indexes used in the deflation of the goods and services that make up the gross domestic product (GDP) and its major components. Growth rates are constructed for years and quarters using quantity weights for

the current and preceding year or quarter; these growth rates are used to move the index for the preceding period forward a year or quarter at a time. The gross domestic purchases chained price index measures the average price of goods and services purchased in the United States. It differs from the GDP chained price index, which measures of the average price of goods produced in the United States, by excluding net exports. All chain-weighted price indexes are expressed in terms of the reference year value 1996=100.

Measures of inflation—Inflation is defined as a time of generally rising prices for goods and factors of production. The Bureau of Labor Statistics samples prices of items in a representative market basket and publishes the result as the CPI. The media invariably announce the inflation rate as the percent change in the CPI from month to month. A much more meaningful indicator of inflation is the percent change from the same month of the prior year. The producer price index measures prices at the producer level only. The PPI shows the same general pattern of inflation as does the CPI but is more volatile. The PPI can be roughly viewed as a leading indicator. It often tends to foreshadow trends that later occur in the CPI.

Other measures of inflation include the gross domestic purchases chain-weighted price index, the index of industrial materials prices; the Dow Jones Commodity Spot Price Index; Futures Price Index; the Employment Cost Index, the Hourly Compensation Index, or the Unit Labor Cost Index as a measure of the change in cost of the labor factor-of production; and changes in long-term interest rates that are often used to measure changes in the cost of the capital factor of production.

International price indexes—The BLS International Price Program produces export and import price indexes for non-military goods traded between the United States and the rest of the world.

The export price index provides a measure of price change for all products sold by U.S. residents to foreign buyers. The import price index provides a measure of price change for goods purchased from

448   Prices

other countries by U.S. residents. The reference period for the indexes is 1995=100, unless otherwise indicated. The product universe for both the import and export indexes includes raw materials, agricultural products, semifinished manufactures, and finished manufactures, including both capital and consumer goods. Price data for these items are collected primarily by mail questionnaire. In nearly all cases, the data are collected directly from the exporter or importer, although in a few cases, prices are obtained from other sources.

To the extent possible, the data gathered refer to prices at the U.S. border for exports and at either the foreign border or the U.S. border for imports. For nearly all products, the prices refer to transactions completed during the first week of the month. Survey respondents are asked to indicate all discounts, allowances, and rebates applicable to the reported prices, so that the price used in the calculation of the indexes is the actual price for which the product was bought or sold.

In addition to general indexes for U.S. exports and imports, indexes are also published for detailed product categories of exports and imports. These categories are defined according to the five-digit level of detail for the Bureau of Economic Analysis End-Use Classification, the three-digit level of detail for the Standard International Trade Classification (SITC), and the four-digit level of detail for the Harmonized System. Aggregate import indexes by country or region of origin are also available.

No. 680. Purchasing Power of the Dollar: 1950 to 2001

[Indexes: PPI, 1982=$1.00; CPI, 1982-84+$1.00. Producer prices prior to 1961, and consumer prices prior to 1964, exclude Alaska and Hawaii. Producer prices based on finished goods index. Obtained by dividing the average price index for the 1982=100, PPI; 1982-84=100, CPI base periods (100.0) by the price index for a given period and expressing the result in dollars and cents. Annual figures are based on average of monthly data]

Year	Annual average as measured by—		Year	Annual average as measured by—		Year	Annual average as measured by—	
	Producer prices	Consumer prices		Producer prices	Consumer prices		Producer prices	Consumer prices
1950	3.546	4.151	1968	2.732	2.873	1986	0.969	0.913
1951	3.247	3.846	1969	2.632	2.726	1987	0.949	0.880
1952	3.268	3.765	1970	2.545	2.574	1988	0.926	0.846
1953	3.300	3.735	1971	2.469	2.466	1989	0.880	0.807
1954	3.289	3.717	1972	2.392	2.391	1990	0.839	0.766
1955	3.279	3.732	1973	2.193	2.251	1991	0.822	0.734
1956	3.195	3.678	1974	1.901	2.029	1992	0.812	0.713
1957	3.077	3.549	1975	1.718	1.859	1993	0.802	0.692
1958	3.012	3.457	1976	1.645	1.757	1994	0.797	0.675
1959	3.021	3.427	1977	1.546	1.649	1995	0.782	0.656
1960	2.994	3.373	1978	1.433	1.532	1996	0.762	0.638
1961	2.994	3.340	1979	1.289	1.380	1997	0.759	0.623
1962	2.985	3.304	1980	1.136	1.215	1998	0.766	0.614
1963	2.994	3.265	1981	1.041	1.098	1999	0.752	0.600
1964	2.985	3.220	1982	1.000	1.035	2000	0.725	0.581
1965	2.933	3.166	1983	0.984	1.003	2001	0.711	0.565
1966	2.841	3.080	1984	0.964	0.961			
1967	2.809	2.993	1985	0.955	0.928			

Source: U.S. Bureau of Labor Statistics. Monthly data in U.S. Bureau of Economic Analysis, *Survey of Current Business*.

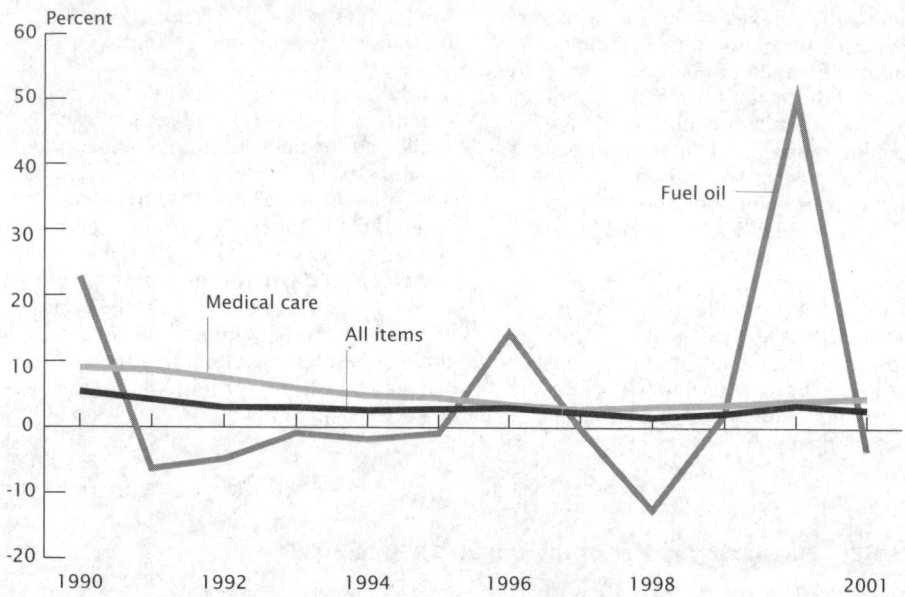

Figure 14.1
**Annual Percent Change in Consumer
Price Indexes: 1990 to 2001**

Source: Chart prepared by U.S. Census Bureau. For data, see Table 681.

Figure 14.2
**Annual Percent Change in Producer Price Indexes
by Stage of Processing: 1990 to 2001**

Source: Chart prepared by U.S. Census Bureau. For data, see Table 686.

No. 681. Consumer Price Indexes (CPI-U) by Major Groups: 1980 to 2001

[1982-84=100 except as noted. Represents annual averages of monthly figures. Reflects buying patterns of all urban consumers. Minus sign (-) indicates decrease. See text, this section]

Year	All items	Com-modities	Serv-ices	Food	Energy	All items less food and energy	Food and bever-ages	Shelter	Trans-porta-tion	Medical care	Apparel	Educa-tion and commu-nication[1]
1980	82.4	86.0	77.9	86.8	86.0	80.8	86.7	81.0	83.1	74.9	90.9	(NA)
1987	113.6	107.7	120.2	113.5	88.6	118.2	113.5	121.3	105.4	130.1	110.6	(NA)
1988	118.3	111.5	125.7	118.2	89.3	123.4	118.2	127.1	108.7	138.6	115.4	(NA)
1989	124.0	116.7	131.9	125.1	94.3	129.0	124.9	132.8	114.1	149.3	118.6	(NA)
1990	130.7	122.8	139.2	132.4	102.1	135.5	132.1	140.0	120.5	162.8	124.1	(NA)
1991	136.2	126.6	146.3	136.3	102.5	142.1	136.8	146.3	123.8	177.0	128.7	(NA)
1992	140.3	129.1	152.0	137.9	103.0	147.3	138.7	151.2	126.5	190.1	131.9	(NA)
1993	144.5	131.5	157.9	140.9	104.2	152.2	141.6	155.7	130.4	201.4	133.7	85.5
1994	148.2	133.8	163.1	144.3	104.6	156.5	144.9	160.5	134.3	211.0	133.4	88.8
1995	152.4	136.4	168.7	148.4	105.2	161.2	148.9	165.7	139.1	220.5	132.0	92.2
1996	156.9	139.9	174.1	153.3	110.1	165.6	153.7	171.0	143.0	228.2	131.7	95.3
1997	160.5	141.8	179.4	157.3	111.5	169.5	157.7	176.3	144.3	234.6	132.9	98.4
1998	163.0	141.9	184.2	160.7	102.9	173.4	161.1	182.1	141.6	242.1	133.0	100.3
1999	166.6	144.4	188.8	164.1	106.6	177.0	164.6	187.3	144.4	250.6	131.3	101.2
2000	172.2	149.2	195.3	167.8	124.6	181.3	168.4	193.4	153.3	260.8	129.6	102.5
2001	177.1	150.7	203.4	173.1	129.3	186.1	173.6	200.6	154.3	272.8	127.3	105.2
PERCENT CHANGE [2]												
1980	13.5	12.3	15.4	8.6	30.9	12.4	8.5	17.6	17.9	11.0	7.1	(NA)
1987	3.6	3.2	4.2	4.1	0.5	4.1	4.0	4.7	3.0	6.6	4.4	(NA)
1988	4.1	3.5	4.6	4.1	0.8	4.4	4.1	4.8	3.1	6.5	4.3	(NA)
1989	4.8	4.7	4.9	5.8	5.6	4.5	5.7	4.5	5.0	7.7	2.8	(NA)
1990	5.4	5.2	5.5	5.8	8.3	5.0	5.8	5.4	5.6	9.0	4.6	(NA)
1991	4.2	3.1	5.1	2.9	0.4	4.9	3.6	4.5	2.7	8.7	3.7	(NA)
1992	3.0	2.0	3.9	1.2	0.5	3.7	1.4	3.3	2.2	7.4	2.5	(NA)
1993	3.0	1.9	3.9	2.2	1.2	3.3	2.1	3.0	3.1	5.9	1.4	(NA)
1994	2.6	1.7	3.3	2.4	0.4	2.8	2.3	3.1	3.0	4.8	-0.2	3.9
1995	2.8	1.9	3.4	2.8	0.6	3.0	2.8	3.2	3.6	4.5	-1.0	3.8
1996	3.0	2.6	3.2	3.3	4.7	2.7	3.2	3.2	2.8	3.5	-0.2	3.4
1997	2.3	1.4	3.0	2.6	1.3	2.4	2.6	3.1	0.9	2.8	0.9	3.3
1998	1.6	0.1	2.7	2.2	-7.7	2.3	2.2	3.3	-1.9	3.2	0.1	1.9
1999	2.2	1.8	2.5	2.1	3.6	2.1	2.2	2.9	2.0	3.5	-1.3	0.9
2000	3.4	3.3	3.4	2.3	16.9	2.4	2.3	3.3	6.2	4.1	-1.3	1.3
2001	2.8	1.0	4.1	3.2	3.8	2.6	3.1	3.7	0.7	4.6	-1.8	2.6

NA Not available.   [1] Dec. 1997=100.   [2] Change from immediate prior year.
Source: U.S. Bureau of Labor Statistics, *Monthly Labor Review* and *Handbook of Labor Statistics*, periodic.

No. 682. Consumer Price Indexes (CPI-U)—Selected Areas: 2001

[1982-84=100, except as indicated. Represents annual averages of monthly figures. Local area CPI indexes are byproducts of the national CPI program. Each local index has a smaller sample size than the national index and is therefore, subject to substantially more sampling and other measurement error. As a result, local area indexes show greater volatility than the national index, although their long-term trends are similar. Area definitions are those established by the Office of Management and Budget in 1983. For further detail see the U.S. Bureau of Labor Statistics Handbook of Methods, Bulletin 2285, Chapter 19, the Consumer Price Index, and Report 736, the CPI: 1987 Revision. See also text, this section]

Area	All items	Food and bever-ages	Food	Housing	Apparel	Trans-porta-tion	Medical care	Fuel and other utilities
U.S. city average	**177.1**	**173.6**	**173.1**	**176.4**	**127.3**	**154.3**	**272.8**	**150.2**
Anchorage, AK MSA	155.2	156.4	156.7	139.0	131.1	153.0	282.9	159.8
Atlanta, GA MSA	176.2	180.1	185.5	178.4	127.0	139.0	276.7	174.7
Boston, MA MSA	191.5	181.6	182.5	191.3	140.0	152.1	368.2	152.0
Chicago-Gary, IL-IN CMSA	178.3	176.3	175.5	181.5	106.3	149.8	272.2	138.0
Cincinnati-Hamilton, OH-KY-IN CMSA . . .	167.9	161.7	160.1	161.0	125.8	149.9	266.2	133.4
Cleveland-Akron-Lorain, OH CMSA	172.9	176.5	178.6	172.6	123.2	154.5	240.1	157.0
Dallas-Fort Worth, TX CMSA	170.4	173.6	170.5	160.3	143.5	154.2	252.4	161.2
Denver-Boulder-Greely, CO CMSA	181.3	167.9	169.9	181.4	93.6	183.4	320.6	162.4
Detroit-Ann Arbor-Flint, MI CMSA	174.4	168.5	167.9	166.3	125.1	168.3	272.8	134.7
Honolulu, HI MSA.	178.4	169.5	169.5	179.1	101.0	174.5	(NA)	146.6
Houston-Galveston-Brazoria, TX CMSA	158.8	163.5	162.8	144.1	142.4	142.4	251.7	132.5
Kansas City, MO-KS CMSA	172.2	172.3	173.8	168.5	119.3	148.1	254.5	160.3
Los Angeles-Anaheim-Riverside, CA CMSA . . .	177.3	181.1	179.3	179.5	112.1	155.3	265.6	178.2
Miami-Fort Lauderdale, FL CMSA	173.0	180.7	181.0	164.2	150.7	159.5	253.3	130.3
Milwaukee, WI PMSA	171.7	174.1	174.9	170.2	117.5	149.6	266.6	133.7
Minneapolis-St. Paul, MN-WI MSA	176.5	185.0	181.7	163.2	137.2	162.1	265.9	143.5
New York-Northern New Jersey-Long Island, NY-NJ-CT CMSA	187.1	177.5	176.5	192.6	117.2	160.8	287.1	129.7
Philadelphia-Wilmington-Trenton, PA-NJ-DE-MD CMSA.	181.3	167.0	166.2	183.3	99.8	160.6	305.3	148.5
Pittsburgh, PA MSA	172.5	165.1	163.6	172.3	156.6	141.2	254.6	171.9
Portland, OR MSA	182.4	160.6	160.6	183.9	132.5	167.5	270.2	157.8
San Diego, CA MSA	191.2	178.4	176.6	202.4	129.7	164.9	267.9	152.4
San Francisco-Oakland-San Jose, CA CMSA . .	189.9	181.8	182.2	216.5	111.2	143.7	255.2	184.9
Seattle-Tacoma, WA CMSA	185.7	181.2	182.0	195.6	124.2	162.1	257.4	155.8
St. Louis-East St. Louis, MO-IL CMSA	167.3	169.3	167.6	161.2	120.3	151.5	268.2	150.1
Tampa-St. Petersburg-Clearwater, FL MSA [1] . .	148.8	146.9	145.9	144.0	148.8	134.3	206.1	132.3
Washington-Baltimore, DC-MD-VA-WV CMSA [2].	110.4	108.7	108.7	110.3	98.6	109.7	111.0	112.0

NA Not available.   [1] 1987=100.   [2] 1997=100; except "Apparel and upkeep" and "Transportation," 1996=100.
Source: U.S. Bureau of Labor Statistics, *Monthly Labor Review* and *CPI Detailed Report*, January issues.

Prices   451

No. 683. Consumer Price Indexes for All Urban Consumers (CPI-U) for Selected Items and Groups: 1980 to 2001

[1982-84 = 100 except as noted. Annual averages of monthly figures. See headnote, Table 681]

Item	1980	1990	1995	1996	1997	1998	1999	2000	2001
All items	**82.4**	**130.7**	**152.4**	**156.9**	**160.5**	**163.0**	**166.6**	**172.2**	**177.1**
Food and beverages	86.7	132.1	148.9	153.7	157.7	161.1	164.6	168.4	173.6
Food	86.8	132.4	148.4	153.3	157.3	160.7	164.1	167.8	173.1
Food at home	88.4	132.3	148.8	154.3	158.1	161.1	164.2	167.9	173.4
Cereals and bakery products	83.9	140.0	167.5	174.0	177.6	181.1	185.0	188.3	193.8
Cereals and cereal products	84.2	141.1	167.1	168.9	169.5	171.5	175.0	175.9	178.7
Cereal	76.3	158.6	192.5	190.0	187.5	189.9	195.2	198.0	199.7
Rice, pasta, and cornmeal	90.9	122.0	140.2	144.2	148.8	150.5	151.9	150.7	154.6
Bakery products	83.8	139.2	167.4	176.1	181.1	185.4	189.4	194.1	201.3
White bread	85.9	136.4	165.5	177.5	183.8	187.3	192.5	199.1	208.3
Cookies, cakes, and cupcakes	81.5	142.7	169.1	174.1	179.2	181.2	185.0	187.9	192.0
Meats, poultry, fish and eggs	92.0	130.0	138.8	144.8	148.5	147.3	147.9	154.5	161.3
Meats	92.7	128.5	135.5	140.2	144.4	141.6	142.3	150.7	159.3
Beef and veal	98.4	128.8	134.9	134.5	136.8	136.5	139.2	148.1	160.5
Uncooked ground beef and related products	104.6	118.1	116.1	114.3	116.4	116.1	118.4	125.2	135.5
Pork	81.9	129.8	134.8	148.2	155.9	148.5	145.9	156.5	162.4
Bacon	73.5	113.4	120.0	148.9	164.0	152.0	151.5	177.5	184.6
Chops	82.9	140.2	144.2	153.0	155.2	146.8	143.5	152.2	159.0
Ham	85.5	132.4	139.6	149.2	156.3	150.0	147.0	152.7	157.3
Poultry	93.7	132.5	143.5	152.4	156.6	157.1	157.9	159.8	164.9
Fish and seafood	87.5	146.7	171.6	173.1	177.1	181.7	185.3	190.4	191.1
Canned fish and seafood	93.7	119.5	125.5	125.9	128.4	132.6	131.5	127.4	127.3
Eggs	88.6	124.1	120.5	142.1	140.0	135.4	128.1	131.9	136.4
Dairy and related products	90.9	126.5	132.8	142.1	145.5	150.8	159.6	160.7	167.1
Fruits and vegetables	82.1	149.0	177.7	183.9	187.5	198.2	203.1	204.6	212.2
Fresh fruits and vegetables	81.8	(NA)	206.0	211.8	215.4	231.2	237.2	238.8	247.9
Fresh fruits	84.8	170.9	219.0	234.4	236.3	246.5	266.3	258.3	265.1
Apples	92.1	147.5	183.5	202.3	199.6	202.3	200.1	212.6	213.9
Bananas	91.5	138.2	153.8	159.0	159.6	160.9	159.4	162.5	166.6
Oranges, tangerines	72.6	160.6	224.5	239.3	226.1	215.3	337.0	257.0	271.7
Fresh vegetables	79.0	151.1	193.1	189.2	194.6	215.8	209.3	219.4	230.6
Potatoes	81.0	162.6	174.7	180.6	174.2	185.2	193.1	196.3	202.3
Lettuce	77.8	150.3	221.2	185.7	200.1	229.1	228.1	233.8	233.8
Tomatoes	81.9	160.8	188.3	198.2	213.6	239.2	224.1	234.7	250.0
Processed fruits and vegetables [1]	(NA)	(NA)	(NA)	(NA)	(NA)	(NA)	(NA)	105.6	109.0
Nonalcoholic beverages and beverage materials	91.4	113.5	131.7	128.6	133.4	133.0	134.3	137.8	139.2
Carbonated drinks	86.6	112.1	119.5	119.9	118.3	117.5	118.8	123.4	125.4
Coffee	111.6	117.5	163.1	149.2	168.0	163.4	154.8	154.0	146.7
Food away from home	83.4	(NA)	149.0	152.7	157.0	161.1	165.1	169.0	173.9
Alcoholic beverages	86.4	129.3	153.9	158.5	162.8	165.7	169.7	174.7	179.3
Alcoholic beverages at home	87.3	123.0	143.1	146.8	149.5	150.6	153.7	158.1	161.1
Beer ale, and other malt beverages	84.8	123.6	143.9	147.4	148.2	148.5	151.9	156.8	160.7
Distilled spirits	89.8	125.7	145.7	147.5	150.8	152.7	156.2	162.3	168.0
Wine	89.5	114.4	133.6	139.3	145.5	147.3	149.4	151.6	151.5
Alcoholic beverages away from home	82.9	144.4	176.5	182.7	189.4	195.0	201.0	207.1	215.2
Housing	81.1	128.5	148.5	152.8	156.8	160.4	163.9	169.6	176.4
Shelter	81.0	140.0	165.7	171.0	176.3	182.1	187.3	193.4	200.6
Owners' equivalent rent of primary residence [2]	(NA)	144.8	171.3	176.8	181.9	187.8	192.9	198.7	206.3
Fuels and utilities	75.4	111.6	123.7	127.5	130.8	128.5	128.8	137.9	150.2
Fuels	74.8	104.5	111.5	115.2	117.9	113.7	113.5	122.8	135.4
Fuel oil and other	86.1	99.3	88.1	99.2	99.8	90.0	91.4	129.7	129.3
Gas (piped) and electricity	71.4	109.3	119.2	122.1	125.1	121.2	120.9	128.0	142.4
Electricity	75.8	117.4	129.6	131.8	132.5	127.4	126.5	128.5	137.8
Utility natural gas service	65.7	97.3	102.9	107.2	114.6	112.4	113.0	132.0	158.3
Water and sewerage maintenance	74.0	150.2	196.5	204.5	210.0	217.3	222.0	227.5	234.6
Garbage and trash collection [3]	(NA)	171.2	241.2	246.0	250.5	256.7	263.8	269.8	275.5

See footnotes at end of table.

452 Prices

No. 683. Consumer Price Indexes for All Urban Consumers (CPI-U) for Selected Items and Groups: 1980 to 2001—Con.

[1982-84 = 100, except as noted. Annual averages of monthly figures. See headnote, Table 681]

Item	1980	1990	1995	1996	1997	1998	1999	2000	2001
Household furnishings and operations	86.3	113.3	123.0	124.7	125.4	126.6	126.7	128.2	129.1
Furniture and bedding	88.0	115.7	130.9	134.1	134.5	135.0	134.9	134.4	132.2
Bedroom furniture	83.5	118.5	136.4	139.3	141.5	141.3	141.0	138.4	136.6
Housekeeping supplies	83.2	125.2	137.1	141.1	143.1	145.7	148.1	153.4	158.4
Apparel	90.9	124.1	132.0	131.7	132.9	133.0	131.3	129.6	127.3
Men's and boy's apparel	89.4	120.4	126.2	127.7	130.1	131.8	131.1	129.7	125.7
Women's and girl's apparel	96.0	122.6	126.9	124.7	126.1	126.0	123.3	121.5	119.3
Infants' and toddlers'	85.5	125.8	127.2	129.7	129.0	126.1	129.0	130.6	129.2
Footwear	91.8	117.4	125.4	126.6	127.6	128.0	125.7	123.8	123.0
Transportation	83.1	120.5	139.1	143.0	144.3	141.6	144.4	153.3	154.3
Private transportation	84.2	118.8	136.3	140.0	141.0	137.9	140.5	149.1	150.0
New vehicles	88.5	121.4	141.0	143.7	144.3	143.4	142.9	142.8	142.1
New cars	88.4	121.0	139.0	141.4	141.7	140.7	139.6	139.6	138.9
New trucks [3]	(NA)	121.6	145.9	149.5	151.4	151.1	152.0	151.7	150.7
Used cars and trucks	62.3	117.6	156.5	157.0	151.1	150.6	152.0	155.8	158.7
Motor fuel	97.4	101.2	100.0	106.3	106.2	92.2	100.7	129.3	124.7
Motor vehicle maintenance and repair	81.5	130.1	154.0	158.4	162.7	167.1	171.9	177.3	183.5
Motor vehicle insurance	82.0	177.9	234.3	243.9	251.6	254.3	253.8	256.7	268.1
Motor vehicle fees [1]	(NA)	(NA)	(NA)	(NA)	(NA)	102.5	103.8	107.3	109.3
Public transportation	69.0	142.6	175.9	181.9	186.7	190.3	197.7	209.6	210.6
Airline fares	68.0	148.4	189.7	192.5	199.2	205.3	218.8	239.4	239.4
Medical care	74.9	162.8	220.5	228.2	234.6	242.1	250.6	260.8	272.8
Medical care commodities	75.4	163.4	204.5	210.4	215.3	221.8	230.7	238.1	247.6
Prescription drugs and medical supplies	72.5	181.7	235.0	242.9	249.3	258.6	273.4	285.4	300.9
Nonprescription drugs and medical supplies[4]	(NA)	120.6	140.5	143.1	145.4	147.7	176.7	149.5	150.6
Medical care services	74.8	162.7	224.2	232.4	239.1	246.8	255.1	266.0	278.8
Professional services	77.9	156.1	201.0	208.3	215.4	222.2	229.2	237.7	246.5
Hospital and related services	69.2	178.0	257.8	269.5	278.4	287.5	299.5	317.3	338.3
Recreation [1]	(NA)	(NA)	(NA)	(NA)	(NA)	(NA)	102.0	103.3	104.9
Video and audio	100.7	80.8	73.9	71.3	99.4	101.1	100.7	101.0	101.5
Cable television [3]	(NA)	158.4	200.7	212.6	228.7	245.2	254.6	266.8	278.4
Photography [1]	(NA)	(NA)	(NA)	(NA)	(NA)	(NA)	99.4	99.2	99.0
Sporting goods	88.5	114.9	123.5	123.4	122.6	121.9	120.3	119.0	118.5
Other recreational goods [1]	(NA)	(NA)	(NA)	(NA)	(NA)	97.1	92.3	87.8	84.6
Pets, pet products and services [1]	(NA)	(NA)	(NA)	(NA)	(NA)	101.5	103.4	106.1	109.7
Recreation services [2]	(NA)	(NA)	(NA)	(NA)	(NA)	102.4	106.9	111.7	116.1
Recreational reading materials	(NA)	(NA)	(NA)	(NA)	179.0	184.1	186.1	188.3	191.4
Tobacco and smoking products	72.0	181.5	225.7	232.8	243.7	274.8	355.8	394.9	425.2
Personal care	81.9	130.4	147.1	150.1	152.7	156.7	161.1	165.6	170.5
Personal care services	83.7	132.8	151.5	156.6	162.4	166.0	171.4	178.1	184.3
Education and communication [1]	(NA)	(NA)	(NA)	(NA)	(NA)	(NA)	101.2	102.5	105.2
Education [1]	(NA)	(NA)	(NA)	(NA)	97.3	102.1	107.0	112.5	118.5
Educational books and supplies	71.4	171.3	214.4	226.9	238.4	250.8	261.7	279.9	295.9
Tuition, other school fees and child care	71.2	175.7	253.8	267.1	280.4	294.2	308.4	324.0	341.1
College tuition and fees	70.8	175.0	264.8	279.8	294.1	306.5	318.7	331.9	348.8
Communication [1]	(NA)	(NA)	99.0	100.3	100.0	97.1	95.9	93.0	93.4
Postage [1]	76.2	125.1	160.3	160.3	160.3	160.3	165.1	165.1	171.5
Delivery services [1]	(NA)	(NA)	(NA)	(NA)	100.0	104.2	110.0	114.5	123.0
Information and information processing [1] . . .	(NA)	(NA)	98.9	100.3	100.0	96.9	95.4	92.8	92.3
Telephone services [1]	(NA)	(NA)	(NA)	(NA)	(NA)	(NA)	100.1	98.5	99.3
Telephone services, local charges [1] . . .	72.8	149.3	160.4	160.8	163.1	165.7	168.7	175.6	184.8
Telephone services, long distance charges [1]	(NA)	(NA)	(NA)	(NA)	100.0	99.9	98.6	97.8	88.8
Cellular telephone services [1]	(NA)	(NA)	(NA)	(NA)	100.0	91.7	81.1	76.0	68.1
Information and information processing other than telephone services [5]	(NA)	(NA)	61.0	53.9	47.4	34.8	28.2	25.9	21.3
Personal computers and peripheral equipment [1]	(NA)	(NA)	(NA)	(NA)	100.0	64.2	47.2	41.1	29.5
Computer software and accessories [1] . . .	(NA)	(NA)	(NA)	(NA)	100.0	90.0	88.2	85.4	79.1
Computer information processing services [1]	(NA)	(NA)	(NA)	(NA)	100.0	103.3	96.0	96.4	98.1
All commodities	86.0	122.8	136.4	139.9	141.8	141.9	144.4	149.2	150.7
All commodities less food	85.7	117.4	129.8	132.6	133.4	132.0	134.0	139.2	138.9
Energy	86.0	102.1	105.2	110.1	111.5	102.9	106.6	124.6	129.3

NA Not available. [1] December 1997=100. [2] December 1982=100. [3] December 1983=100. [4] December 1986=100. [5] December 1988=100.

Source: U.S. Bureau of Labor Statistics, *Monthly Labor Review* and *CPI Detailed Report*, January issues.

No. 684. Cost of Living Index—Selected Metropolitan Areas: Fourth Quarter 2001

[Measures relative price levels for consumer goods and services in participating areas for a mid-management standard of living. The nationwide average equals 100, and each index is read as a percent of the national average. The index does not measure inflation, but compares prices at a single point in time. Excludes taxes. Metropolitan areas as defined by the Office of Management and Budget. For definitions and components of MSAs, see source for details]

Metropolitan areas (MA)	Composite index (100%)	Grocery items (16%)	Housing (28%)	Utilities (8%)	Transportation (10%)	Health care (5%)	Misc. goods and services (33%)
Anniston, AL MSA	94.5	94.4	92.9	96.6	86.8	87.8	98.9
Birmingham, AL MSA	97.5	95.0	92.4	109.5	98.2	90.4	101.0
Decatur, AL MSA	91.4	92.4	82.2	85.2	100.4	92.0	97.4
Dothan, AL MSA	91.1	97.4	80.5	80.1	88.5	87.4	101.0
Florence, AL MSA	90.1	90.7	82.1	87.4	89.3	86.4	97.9
Huntsville, AL MSA	95.2	97.7	85.1	80.4	103.3	97.1	103.4
Mobile, AL MSA	94.3	92.7	88.7	103.6	97.2	83.9	98.2
Montgomery, AL MSA	96.3	95.9	93.3	107.1	101.7	92.1	95.4
Tuscaloosa, AL MSA	98.3	95.3	94.4	92.4	98.4	95.5	104.9
Anchorage, AK MSA	123.0	127.3	131.5	83.6	110.4	155.1	122.3
Nonmetropolitan areas:							
Fairbanks, AK	120.6	117.4	108.6	157.5	119.3	163.3	117.3
Kodiak, AK	128.9	144.6	120.5	140.3	135.6	148.5	120.5
Flagstaff, AZ-UT MSA	106.4	104.1	117.8	88.8	113.6	112.8	98.9
Las Vegas, NV-AZ MSA:							
Lake Havasu City, AZ	100.6	104.7	93.7	101.7	103.5	108.8	102.2
Phoenix-Mesa, AZ MSA:							
Phoenix, AZ.	100.4	101.8	96.9	94.8	108.4	115.6	99.4
Tucson, AZ MSA	99.3	104.8	95.3	107.0	104.6	107.3	95.3
Yuma, AZ	96.6	98.6	86.1	128.6	109.2	102.0	92.1
Fayetteville-Springdale-Rogers, AR MSA . .	90.7	87.5	89.8	89.2	92.7	87.8	93.4
Fort Smith, AR-OK MSA	88.0	87.1	76.2	91.5	89.3	86.9	97.3
Jonesboro, AR MSA	87.9	92.3	81.4	87.0	85.7	86.3	92.2
Little Rock-North Little Rock, AR MSA	87.9	90.0	81.7	92.2	87.6	85.2	91.8
Fresno, CA MSA	106.4	109.4	98.5	124.9	110.3	113.0	105.0
Los Angeles-Long Beach, CA PMSA	141.5	111.8	221.3	101.4	111.9	117.2	110.7
Riverside-San Bernardino, CA PMSA:							
Riverside City, CA.	105.5	107.2	101.8	101.3	111.2	119.8	104.9
Sacramento, CA PMSA	118.5	120.9	128.3	116.8	119.0	150.7	104.4
San Diego, CA MSA	127.6	122.2	161.3	115.4	121.4	126.8	106.6
San Francisco, CA PMSA	186.2	122.2	352.1	117.4	134.8	161.7	112.5
Visalia-Tulare-Porterville, CA MSA.	105.1	105.1	96.4	125.6	113.9	111.1	104.0
Colorado Springs, CO MSA	99.4	101.0	105.7	82.0	104.3	115.6	93.5
Denver, CO PMSA	108.3	109.9	119.9	90.4	109.4	125.4	99.2
Fort Collins-Loveland, CO MSA:							
Fort Collins, CO	106.6	111.0	115.6	97.4	105.8	113.6	98.2
Grand Junction, CO MSA	101.4	103.2	105.3	98.5	103.2	103.7	96.8
Pueblo, CO MSA	92.6	109.2	79.3	104.2	90.6	100.5	92.4
New Haven-Meriden, CT PMSA	119.8	107.5	137.8	145.8	108.2	129.3	106.2
Dover, DE MSA	101.7	103.2	100.2	124.3	92.8	93.3	100.6
Wilmington-Newark, DE-MD PMSA	108.5	109.0	111.4	123.4	102.2	115.1	103.1
Washington DC-MD-VA-WV PMSA	119.7	111.9	142.4	97.0	116.7	119.5	110.7
Daytona Beach, FL MSA	99.1	104.2	95.4	103.8	106.4	96.9	96.9
Fort Walton Beach FL, MSA.	99.6	97.3	100.6	87.5	101.6	102.5	101.8
Jacksonville, FL MSA	91.7	101.7	86.3	84.1	93.9	88.3	93.2
Orlando, FL MSA	98.8	102.4	90.9	105.3	96.2	105.9	102.0
Panama City, FL MSA.	98.3	98.8	96.5	91.9	105.5	99.6	98.6
Pensacola, FL MSA	97.3	97.7	92.2	93.8	100.5	103.0	100.4
Sarasota-Bradenton, FL MSA:							
Sarasota, FL	105.7	102.4	111.4	108.2	107.2	100.6	102.4
Tallahassee, FL MSA	108.1	108.9	108.2	110.7	104.6	103.0	108.9
Tampa-St. Petersburg-Clearwater, FL MSA							
Tampa, FL.	99.1	101.1	97.5	94.1	102.7	101.5	99.1
West Palm Beach-Boca Raton, FL MSA . . .	104.7	106.0	97.8	111.0	107.8	107.2	107.2
Albany, GA MSA	92.6	96.5	83.6	95.0	91.7	85.8	99.1
Atlanta, GA MSA:							
Atlanta, GA	101.7	101.6	107.2	90.7	103.1	104.8	98.8
Augusta-Aiken, GA-SC MSA	93.6	103.3	80.5	94.2	98.2	96.0	98.1
Boise City, ID MSA.	99.7	92.5	104.5	84.8	103.7	109.8	100.0
Pocatello, ID	97.7	98.6	94.5	94.7	101.8	100.7	99.1
Bloomington-Normal, IL MSA	104.4	100.2	99.5	113.2	103.2	103.3	109.0
Champaign-Urbana, IL MSA.	102.6	96.8	98.5	109.6	103.5	99.9	107.5
Chicago, IL PMSA:							
Joliet/Will County, IL	105.1	106.6	107.3	97.9	114.7	105.4	101.3
Decatur, IL MSA.	93.0	92.3	88.5	95.5	99.5	83.8	95.9
Peoria-Pekin, IL MSA	101.7	99.0	104.6	86.0	106.2	91.5	104.5
Rockford, IL MSA.	104.2	103.3	102.2	124.7	104.6	106.0	100.9
Springfield, IL MSA.	93.7	94.4	93.8	92.0	91.5	100.4	93.5
Elkhart-Goshen, IN MSA	95.7	95.5	90.5	97.8	97.0	95.5	99.5
Evansville-Henderson, IN-KY MSA	92.6	89.9	90.3	93.7	92.9	93.1	95.5
Lafayette, IN MSA	93.8	90.8	88.7	107.7	96.9	93.7	95.3
Muncie, IN MSA.	96.1	91.6	103.0	91.2	96.7	92.2	94.1
South Bend, IN MSA	92.9	88.6	92.2	100.7	90.3	97.2	93.7
Cedar Rapids, IA MSA	94.7	89.1	86.4	116.7	97.2	90.9	98.9
Waterloo-Cedar Falls, IA MSA	96.2	98.2	92.5	104.7	99.8	94.3	95.5
Lawrence, KS MSA	99.9	93.6	106.3	95.6	97.1	92.0	100.8
Wichita, KS MSA	100.0	97.3	93.4	109.2	102.4	104.3	103.4

See footnote at end of table.

U.S. Census Bureau, Statistical Abstract of the United States: 2002

[See headnote, page 454]

Metropolitan areas (MA)	Composite index (100%)	Grocery items (16%)	Housing (28%)	Utilities (8%)	Transportation (10%)	Health care (5%)	Misc. goods and services (33%)
Cincinnati, OH-KY-IN PMSA:							
Covington, KY	93.8	97.7	84.5	97.5	95.3	95.9	98.0
Clarksville-Hopkinsville, TN-KY MSA:	92.7	90.4	85.1	100.3	93.7	85.8	99.1
Evansville-Henderson, IN-KY MSA	93.7	95.2	96.6	83.8	90.9	83.5	95.4
Lexington, KY MSA	98.1	102.3	96.3	93.3	95.5	98.7	99.6
Louisville, KY-IN MSA	95.7	92.5	90.5	100.0	107.1	87.2	98.5
Baton Rouge, LA MSA	105.5	108.9	100.3	128.7	103.6	96.3	104.6
Lafayette, LA MSA	97.6	92.0	104.3	88.4	98.2	88.7	98.0
Lake Charles, LA MSA	96.7	90.2	97.6	109.0	100.0	93.0	95.7
Monroe, LA MSA	98.8	91.0	101.0	108.3	97.1	88.4	100.5
New Orleans, LA MSA	99.7	103.2	92.7	115.8	104.6	102.4	98.0
Shreveport-Bossier City, LA MSA	93.0	88.9	93.3	90.2	91.6	87.0	96.7
Cumberland, MD-WV MSA.	95.5	93.1	90.7	109.8	101.1	94.0	95.8
Boston, MA-NH PMSA:							
Boston PMSA (MA Part).	142.7	111.1	203.5	150.0	121.7	127.9	113.4
Grand Rapids-Muskegon-Holland, MI MSA .	110.3	109.0	125.4	85.0	109.7	95.0	106.9
Lansing-East Lansing, MI MSA.	97.6	101.5	98.2	77.7	93.4	93.0	102.1
Minneapolis-St Paul, MN-WI MSA:							
Minneapolis, MN.	112.1	98.2	121.4	113.0	112.3	126.1	108.6
St Paul, MN.	110.6	99.3	116.6	115.4	110.8	126.2	107.3
Rochester, MN MSA.	101.4	94.9	92.5	115.0	104.5	114.6	105.8
St Cloud, MN MSA.	97.7	98.5	85.1	106.3	105.8	101.5	103.0
Hattiesburg, MS MSA	94.0	90.6	90.8	111.7	85.3	86.6	97.8
Jackson, MS MSA	91.0	83.0	92.0	100.0	95.1	77.0	92.6
Columbia, MO MSA	98.2	96.1	94.7	98.3	98.0	96.3	102.5
Joplin, MO MSA.	88.0	89.4	84.5	81.4	79.7	100.6	92.5
St Joseph, MO MSA.	94.1	89.4	91.2	94.1	91.7	96.5	99.1
St Louis, MO-IL MSA	98.0	93.2	92.5	96.6	105.6	102.9	102.2
Springfield, MO MSA	91.8	96.9	86.8	78.1	94.0	98.6	95.1
Billings, MT MSA	96.8	99.8	92.7	93.2	100.0	102.6	97.7
Great Falls, MT MSA	99.2	103.5	103.0	94.8	94.6	89.5	97.8
Missoula, MT MSA	103.1	113.7	96.0	92.1	101.5	99.5	107.7
Lincoln, NE MSA	99.1	98.8	97.9	95.9	99.3	93.2	101.7
Omaha, NE-IA MSA	93.9	93.3	88.8	99.9	102.3	96.8	94.1
Las Vegas, NV-AZ MSA:							
Las Vegas, NV MSA	108.1	114.6	104.1	95.2	119.9	122.0	105.7
Reno, NV MSA	108.1	113.8	108.7	95.6	117.3	123.3	102.6
Manchester, NH PMSA	104.8	101.3	93.5	153.3	101.4	104.4	105.4
Albuquerque, NM MSA:							
Albuquerque, NM	101.9	103.1	104.0	99.7	98.3	105.6	100.7
Las Cruces, NM MSA	96.4	100.9	97.0	93.6	89.4	92.8	97.1
Santa Fe, NM MSA:	115.2	106.0	141.4	90.2	111.7	124.3	103.2
Santa Fe, NM.	115.2	106.0	141.4	90.2	111.7	124.3	103.2
Binghamton, NY MSA	96.2	95.8	86.5	125.0	98.7	91.5	97.7
Buffalo-Niagara Falls, NY MSA.	101.7	112.1	88.7	150.5	105.3	91.8	96.4
Glens Falls, NY MSA	103.9	101.4	87.6	159.0	103.7	98.5	106.5
Nassau-Suffolk, NY PMSA.	141.4	122.1	178.9	153.9	113.0	145.0	123.9
New York, NY PMSA	235.0	143.2	472.7	156.7	120.0	180.3	139.8
Asheville, NC MSA.	101.8	100.6	110.9	90.0	102.7	93.6	98.4
Charlotte-Gastonia-Rock Hill, NC-SC MSA .	96.7	100.7	91.8	89.1	101.2	96.2	99.6
Fayetteville, NC MSA	98.7	106.3	84.9	99.3	98.4	97.0	107.0
Greensboro-Winston-Salem-High Point, NC MSA							
Greensboro, NC.	99.4	93.5	105.4	88.7	107.1	97.9	97.7
Greenville, NC MSA.	97.9	95.2	103.4	111.9	88.5	96.1	94.3
Jacksonville, NC MSA.	92.2	98.1	82.4	104.8	84.3	90.2	97.2
Raleigh-Durham-Chapel Hill, NC MSA:							
Raleigh, NC.	102.5	100.8	108.0	95.7	96.1	107.2	101.4
Rocky Mount, NC MSA	98.0	101.7	93.8	102.7	99.3	90.2	99.5
Wilmington, NC MSA	101.0	104.4	106.9	98.1	87.6	96.2	99.9
Bismarck, ND MSA.	97.3	99.2	88.8	102.8	103.7	90.5	101.3
Fargo-Moorhead, ND-MN MSA	100.4	97.8	97.5	102.9	98.9	101.8	103.9
Nonmetropolitan areas:							
Minot, ND	93.5	95.6	88.6	99.3	91.2	78.4	98.2
Akron, OH PMSA.	97.6	104.0	86.9	125.0	94.6	98.8	97.7
Cincinnati, OH-KY-IN PMSA:							
Cincinnati, OH	98.1	98.5	92.0	113.3	95.8	92.1	101.0
Cleveland-Lorain-Elyria, OH PMSA	107.4	106.4	105.9	133.9	107.9	113.9	101.6
Dayton-Springfield, OH MSA	96.0	95.2	89.6	104.8	97.8	100.2	98.6
Lima, OH MSA	98.0	103.6	92.1	108.8	95.1	87.5	100.0
Mansfield, OH MSA	95.3	103.5	85.5	123.2	97.5	89.4	93.0
Toledo, OH MSA	100.3	108.9	88.8	122.3	99.4	101.9	100.7
Youngstown-Warren, OH MSA	93.1	99.6	84.1	129.6	85.2	82.9	92.7

See footnote at end of table.

U.S. Census Bureau, Statistical Abstract of the United States: 2002

No. 684. Cost of Living Index—Selected Metropolitan Areas: Fourth Quarter 2001—Con.

[See headnote, page 454]

Metropolitan areas (MA)	Composite index (100%)	Grocery items (16%)	Housing (28%)	Utilities (8%)	Transportation (10%)	Health care (5%)	Misc. goods and services (33%)
Enid, OK MSA.	94.3	93.4	83.5	103.3	93.1	93.5	102.3
Lawton, OK MSA	96.5	97.1	84.6	108.8	99.6	89.2	103.3
Oklahoma City, OK MSA	93.0	88.7	84.2	103.8	97.8	96.2	98.1
Tulsa, OK MSA	94.7	97.7	87.0	100.5	88.9	102.6	99.0
Corvallis, OR MSA	111.0	100.7	124.7	98.6	110.6	126.5	105.3
Portland-Vancover, OR-WA PMSA	104.2	105.6	96.5	92.4	115.7	119.7	107.0
Salem, OR PMSA	102.9	100.1	100.7	91.2	100.8	120.9	106.9
Lancaster, PA MSA.	99.9	91.3	98.2	114.8	104.8	94.8	101.3
Philadelphia, PA-NJ PMSA.	121.0	107.2	139.9	126.7	120.3	99.2	113.7
Pittsburgh, PA MSA	103.1	101.5	98.2	135.9	101.2	92.0	102.2
Williamsport, PA MSA	95.1	95.9	88.4	109.3	92.9	90.8	98.1
York, PA MSA:							
Hanover, PA.	99.5	90.2	99.9	123.8	98.8	83.1	100.4
York County, PA	100.3	92.5	98.6	123.7	106.1	90.0	99.5
Charleston-North Charleston, SC MSA. . . .	102.2	102.2	104.9	99.7	94.9	99.9	102.9
Columbia, SC MSA.	94.2	100.2	90.5	104.1	86.9	92.1	94.5
Myrtle Beach, SC MSA	97.8	102.8	96.0	87.4	92.7	93.6	101.6
Sumter, SC MSA	96.0	100.6	89.5	95.8	93.9	92.4	100.5
Sioux Falls, SD MSA	98.1	98.0	90.9	123.2	100.2	94.4	98.0
Chattanooga, TN-GA MSA	96.3	99.0	93.8	88.7	97.0	85.7	100.5
Clarksville-Hopkinsville, TN-KY MSA:	90.7	90.0	84.4	83.2	97.1	92.5	95.9
Jackson, TN MSA	95.5	100.9	87.0	84.1	102.2	82.8	102.8
Johnson City-Kingsport-Bristol, TN-VA MSA:							
Johnson City, TN	90.1	88.4	91.2	102.7	83.3	81.2	90.2
Kingsport, TN.	88.2	95.1	88.0	72.0	86.7	87.3	89.5
Knoxville, TN MSA	91.9	95.5	85.4	92.2	88.6	90.4	96.9
Memphis, TN-AR-MS MSA.	89.0	92.9	83.1	82.0	98.2	87.2	91.2
Nashville, TN MSA:							
Nashville-Franklin, TN	92.7	97.4	87.6	80.4	97.3	81.1	98.0
Abilene, TX MSA	92.8	86.8	85.4	104.8	97.2	91.0	97.9
Amarillo, TX MSA.	93.4	91.8	92.2	83.5	97.8	92.1	96.4
Beaumont-Port Arthur, TX MSA.	97.7	95.6	89.0	104.4	97.5	99.5	104.2
Brownsville-Harlingen-San Benito, TX MSA.	92.8	91.3	78.2	104.5	98.6	101.2	100.0
Dallas, TX PMSA	98.4	98.4	94.9	95.7	102.2	99.3	100.6
El Paso, TX MSA.	94.1	102.8	79.5	106.8	103.8	89.5	96.8
Fort Worth-Arlington, TX PMSA:							
Houston, TX PMSA:							
Houston, TX PMSA	95.3	92.8	83.9	110.4	105.7	107.9	97.7
Killeen-Temple, TX MSA	91.6	84.4	90.1	95.8	92.8	99.4	93.8
Longview-Marshall, TX MSA.	89.9	89.6	85.5	77.4	90.2	94.1	96.2
Lubbock, TX MSA	90.5	86.2	82.3	89.6	97.2	100.6	96.4
McAllen-Edinburg-Mission, TX MSA.	92.1	83.3	83.2	107.0	91.2	103.7	98.8
Odessa-Midland, TX MSA:							
Odessa, TX	91.1	87.8	81.3	98.0	93.1	98.3	97.6
San Angelo, TX MSA	91.2	89.2	81.0	74.7	95.6	95.4	102.7
San Antonio, TX MSA:	91.4	88.0	88.9	80.7	85.0	92.6	99.6
Sherman-Denison, TX MSA	95.9	96.4	86.1	107.4	99.0	103.5	99.1
Tyler, TX MSA	93.6	90.4	89.5	107.1	92.0	97.2	95.3
Victoria, TX MSA	89.7	82.2	85.2	109.7	92.6	89.4	91.4
Waco, TX MSA	93.6	90.3	83.3	97.6	97.0	93.8	101.8
Provo-Orem, UT MSA	101.3	110.7	100.2	87.1	103.9	90.4	101.9
Salt Lake City-Ogden, UT MSA.	99.0	108.9	95.4	85.7	102.6	93.4	100.3
Burlington, VT MSA	106.4	107.8	101.9	126.5	100.8	109.5	105.8
Lynchburg, VA	91.7	93.6	90.7	75.4	87.7	96.7	96.1
Norfolk-Virginia Beach-Newport News VA-NC MSA							
Hampton Roads/SE Virginia	99.7	94.4	94.7	130.3	105.2	93.5	98.5
Richmond-Petersburg, VA MSA.	103.2	99.7	110.8	106.6	103.2	90.8	99.4
Roanoke, VA MSA	90.4	93.8	90.4	74.7	86.0	92.0	93.8
Bellingham, WA MSA	107.4	108.6	112.4	90.5	104.1	116.9	106.2
Olympia, WA PMSA	103.8	107.6	99.9	89.4	104.7	129.9	104.5
Richland-Kennewick-Pasco, WA MSA	99.4	101.4	97.0	77.9	108.9	122.5	99.1
Spokane, WA MSA.	101.9	105.7	100.4	81.4	102.4	116.4	103.9
Tacoma, WA MSA	101.6	111.4	93.4	87.5	105.6	123.9	102.7
Yakima, WA MSA	102.9	107.4	104.3	78.0	94.1	126.5	104.7
Huntington-Ashland, WV-KY-OH MSA	95.9	104.2	90.5	78.7	99.8	94.3	99.6
Appleton-Oshkosh-Neenah, WI MSA	98.8	93.3	98.9	107.7	97.0	96.4	100.2
Eau Claire, WI MSA	99.6	98.6	97.3	109.0	103.4	108.5	97.2
Green Bay, WI MSA	96.6	89.7	98.7	94.3	98.0	105.4	96.8
Sheboygan, WI MSA	96.3	95.3	92.0	107.4	109.0	95.8	94.0
Wausau, WI MSA.	95.6	94.7	91.7	97.6	97.6	101.4	97.3
Cheyenne, WY MSA.	98.8	108.1	90.4	102.5	97.1	102.6	100.5

Source: ACCRA, 4232 King St., Alexandria, VA 22302-1507, *ACCRA Cost of Living Index*, Fourth Quarter 2000 (copyright).

U.S. Census Bureau, Statistical Abstract of the United States: 2002

No. 685. Annual Percent Changes From Prior Year in Consumer Prices— United States and OECD Countries: 1990 to 2000

[Covers member countries of Organization for Economic Cooperation (OECD). For consumer price indexes for OECD countries, see Section 30, Comparative International Statistics]

Country	1990	1994	1995	1996	1997	1998	1999	2000
United States	5.4	2.6	2.8	2.9	2.3	1.6	2.2	3.4
OECD	7.0	4.6	5.7	5.4	4.6	4.0	3.4	4.0
Australia	7.3	1.9	4.6	2.6	0.3	0.9	1.5	4.5
Canada	4.8	0.2	2.2	1.6	1.6	1.0	1.7	2.7
Japan	3.1	0.7	-0.1	0.1	1.7	0.7	-0.3	-0.7
New Zealand	6.1	1.7	3.8	2.3	1.2	1.3	-0.1	2.6
Austria	3.3	3.0	2.2	1.5	1.3	0.9	0.6	2.4
Belgium	3.4	2.4	1.5	2.1	1.6	1.0	1.1	2.5
Denmark	2.6	2.0	2.1	2.1	2.2	1.8	2.5	2.9
Finland	6.1	1.1	0.8	0.6	1.2	1.4	1.2	3.4
France	3.6	1.7	1.8	2.0	1.2	0.8	0.5	1.7
Greece	20.4	10.9	8.9	8.2	5.5	4.8	2.6	3.2
Ireland	3.3	2.3	2.5	1.7	1.4	2.4	1.6	5.6
Italy [1]	6.5	4.1	5.2	4.0	2.0	2.0	1.7	2.5
Luxembourg	3.3	2.2	1.9	1.3	1.4	1.0	1.0	3.2
Netherlands	2.5	2.8	1.9	2.0	2.2	2.0	2.2	2.5
Norway	4.1	5.4	2.4	1.2	2.6	2.3	2.3	3.1
Portugal [2]	13.4	5.4	4.2	3.1	2.3	2.8	2.3	2.9
Spain	6.7	4.7	4.7	3.6	2.0	1.8	2.3	3.4
Sweden	10.4	2.4	2.9	0.8	0.9	0.4	0.3	1.3
Switzerland	5.4	0.9	1.8	0.8	0.5	0.0	0.8	1.6
Turkey [2]	60.3	105.2	89.1	80.4	85.7	84.6	64.9	54.9
United Kingdom	9.5	2.5	3.4	2.4	3.1	3.4	1.6	2.9
Germany	2.7	2.8	1.7	1.4	1.9	0.9	0.6	1.9

[1] Households of wage and salary earners.   [2] Excludes rent.
Source: Organization for Economic Cooperation and Development, Paris, France, *Main Economic Indicators*, monthly (copyright).

No. 686. Producer Price Indexes by Stage of Processing: 1980 to 2001

[1982=100. Minus sign (-) indicates decline. See text, this section]

Year	Crude materials			Intermediate	Finished goods		Finished consumer foods		
	Total	Foodstuffs and feedstuffs	Fuel	Crude nonfood materials except fuel	diate materials, supplies, and components	Consumer goods	Capital equipment	Crude	Processed	Finished consumer goods excl. food
1980	95.3	104.6	69.4	91.8	90.3	88.6	85.8	93.9	92.3	87.1
1985	95.8	94.8	102.7	94.3	102.7	103.8	107.5	102.9	104.8	103.3
1986	87.7	93.2	92.2	76.0	99.1	101.4	109.7	105.6	107.4	98.5
1987	93.7	96.2	84.1	88.5	101.5	103.6	111.7	107.1	109.6	100.7
1988	96.0	106.1	82.1	85.9	107.1	106.2	114.3	109.8	112.7	103.1
1989	103.1	111.2	85.3	95.8	112.0	112.1	118.8	119.6	118.6	108.9
1990	108.9	113.1	84.8	107.3	114.5	118.2	122.9	123.0	124.4	115.3
1991	101.2	105.5	82.9	97.5	114.4	120.5	126.7	119.3	124.4	118.7
1992	100.4	105.1	84.0	94.2	114.7	121.7	129.1	107.6	124.4	120.8
1993	102.4	108.4	87.1	94.1	116.2	123.0	131.4	114.4	126.5	121.7
1994	101.8	106.5	82.4	97.0	118.5	123.3	134.1	111.3	127.9	121.6
1995	102.7	105.8	72.1	105.8	124.9	125.6	136.7	118.8	129.8	124.0
1996	113.8	121.5	92.6	105.7	125.7	129.5	138.3	129.2	133.8	127.6
1997	111.1	112.2	101.3	103.5	125.6	130.2	138.2	126.6	135.1	128.2
1998	96.8	103.9	86.7	84.5	123.0	128.9	137.6	127.2	134.8	126.4
1999	98.2	98.7	91.2	91.1	123.2	132.0	137.6	125.5	135.9	130.5
2000	120.6	100.2	136.9	118.0	129.2	138.2	138.8	123.5	138.3	138.4
2001	121.3	106.2	152.1	101.8	129.7	141.5	139.7	127.6	142.4	141.4
PERCENT CHANGE [1]										
1980	10.9	4.6	21.1	22.0	15.2	14.3	10.7	1.7	6.3	18.5
1985	-7.4	-9.5	-2.3	2.2	-0.4	0.5	2.2	-7.6	-0.1	1.1
1986	-8.5	-1.7	-10.2	-6.6	-3.5	-2.3	2.0	2.6	2.5	-4.6
1987	6.8	3.2	-8.8	-19.4	2.4	2.2	1.8	1.4	2.0	2.2
1988	2.5	10.3	-2.4	16.4	5.5	2.5	2.3	2.5	2.8	2.4
1989	7.4	4.8	3.9	-2.9	4.6	5.6	3.9	8.9	5.2	5.6
1990	5.6	1.7	-0.6	12.0	2.2	5.4	3.5	2.8	4.9	5.9
1991	-7.1	-6.7	-2.2	-9.1	-0.1	1.9	3.1	-3.0	-	2.9
1992	-0.8	-0.4	1.3	-3.4	0.3	1.0	1.9	-9.8	-	1.8
1993	2.0	3.1	3.7	-0.1	1.3	1.1	1.8	6.3	1.7	0.7
1994	-0.6	-1.8	-5.4	3.1	2.0	0.2	2.1	-2.7	1.1	-0.1
1995	0.9	-0.7	-12.5	9.1	5.4	1.9	1.9	6.7	1.5	2.0
1996	10.8	14.8	28.4	-0.1	0.6	3.1	1.2	8.8	3.1	2.9
1997	-2.4	-7.7	9.4	-2.1	-0.1	0.5	-0.1	-2.0	1.0	0.5
1998	-12.9	-7.4	-14.4	-18.4	-2.1	-1.0	-0.4	0.5	-0.2	-1.4
1999	1.4	-5.0	5.2	7.8	0.2	2.4	0.6	-1.3	0.8	3.2
2000	22.8	1.5	50.1	29.5	4.9	4.7	0.9	-1.6	1.8	6.1
2001	0.6	6.0	11.1	-13.7	0.4	2.4	0.6	3.3	3.0	2.2

- Represents or rounds to zero.   [1] Change from immediate prior year.

Source: U.S. Bureau of Labor Statistics, *Producer Price Indexes*, monthly and annual.

U.S. Census Bureau, Statistical Abstract of the United States: 2002

No. 687. Producer Price Indexes by Stage of Processing: 1990 to 2001

[1982=100, except as indicated]

Stage of processing	1990	1995	1996	1997	1998	1999	2000	2001
Finished goods	**119.2**	**127.9**	**131.3**	**131.8**	**130.7**	**133.0**	**138.0**	**140.7**
Finished consumer goods	**118.2**	**125.6**	**129.5**	**130.2**	**128.9**	**132.0**	**138.2**	**141.5**
Finished consumer foods.....................	**124.4**	**129.0**	**133.6**	**134.5**	**134.3**	**135.1**	**137.2**	**141.3**
Fresh fruits and melons....................	118.1	85.8	100.8	99.4	90.5	103.6	91.4	97.2
Fresh and dry vegetables	118.1	144.4	135.0	123.1	139.5	118.0	126.7	124.7
Eggs for fresh use (Dec. 1991=100)	(NA)	86.3	105.1	97.1	90.1	77.9	84.9	81.8
Bakery products..........................	141.0	164.3	169.8	173.9	175.8	178.0	182.3	187.8
Milled rice..............................	102.5	113.1	129.4	127.3	124.9	121.3	101.2	87.5
Pasta products (June 1985=100)...........	114.1	125.0	127.4	125.1	122.6	122.1	121.6	122.1
Beef and veal	116.0	100.9	100.2	102.8	99.4	106.3	113.7	120.4
Pork....................................	119.8	101.5	120.9	123.1	96.6	96.0	113.4	119.9
Processed young chickens.................	111.0	113.5	121.5	118.6	125.2	113.4	110.4	117.2
Processed turkeys	107.6	104.9	105.5	101.0	95.2	94.8	98.7	99.0
Finfish and shellfish	147.2	170.8	165.9	178.1	183.2	190.9	198.1	191.0
Dairy products...........................	117.2	119.7	130.4	128.1	138.2	139.2	133.7	145.3
Processed fruits and vegetables	124.7	122.4	127.6	126.4	125.7	128.1	128.6	129.4
Confectionery end products	140.0	160.7	166.9	168.3	168.7	170.4	170.6	171.3
Soft drinks	122.3	133.1	134.0	133.2	134.8	137.9	141.1	148.1
Roasted coffee	113.0	146.5	129.2	152.9	143.9	134.7	133.5	124.3
Shortening and cooking oils	123.2	142.5	138.5	137.8	143.4	140.4	132.4	132.9
Finished consumer goods excluding foods	**115.3**	**124.0**	**127.6**	**128.2**	**126.4**	**130.5**	**138.4**	**141.4**
Alcoholic beverages	117.2	128.5	132.8	135.1	135.2	136.7	140.6	145.3
Women's apparel.........................	116.1	119.6	119.9	120.5	122.3	123.9	124.6	123.4
Men's and boy's apparel	120.2	130.3	132.1	132.7	133.2	133.1	133.2	132.4
Girls', children's, and infants' apparel	115.3	121.6	122.4	122.9	121.8	118.2	117.4	116.7
Textile house furnishings	109.5	119.5	122.3	122.6	123.1	122.7	122.0	122.5
Footwear	125.6	139.2	141.6	143.7	144.7	144.5	144.9	145.8
Residential electric power (Dec. 1990=100).	(NA)	111.8	112.8	112.8	110.7	109.5	110.8	116.6
Residential gas (Dec. 1990=100)	(NA)	104.4	110.4	116.5	114.0	114.3	135.5	158.3
Gasoline................................	78.7	63.7	72.8	71.9	53.4	64.7	94.6	90.5
Fuel oil No. 2...........................	73.3	56.6	69.5	64.8	48.1	56.1	93.5	84.1
Pharmaceutical preps, ethical (Prescription)	200.8	257.0	265.4	273.5	322.9	335.0	344.4	(NA)
Pharmaceutical preps, proprietary (Overcounter)	156.8	186.5	185.1	184.8	184.5	186.0	187.7	(NA)
Soaps and synthetic detergents	117.7	122.9	125.2	126.4	126.1	126.3	128.2	130.6
Cosmetics and other toilet preparations ...	121.6	129.0	130.2	130.6	132.9	135.4	137.4	138.6
Tires, tubes, and tread	96.8	100.2	97.0	95.2	94.0	92.9	93.0	94.1
Sanitary papers and health products	135.3	144.4	149.9	147.1	145.1	144.3	146.7	147.2
Newspaper circulation	144.1	185.6	198.8	201.9	202.9	207.1	210.0	219.4
Periodical circulation.....................	150.3	176.6	180.6	188.1	193.8	196.9	198.9	200.9
Book publishing	153.4	185.0	193.9	200.1	205.9	213.0	218.2	225.4
Household furniture	125.1	141.8	144.5	146.2	148.4	150.5	152.7	154.9
Floor coverings	119.0	123.7	126.6	128.0	128.3	127.2	129.6	130.1
Household appliances.....................	110.8	112.4	112.7	110.1	108.9	108.5	107.3	105.3
Home electronic equipment	82.7	78.9	79.0	77.1	75.9	73.7	71.8	70.4
Household glassware	132.5	153.2	157.3	161.3	162.7	163.9	166.0	169.6
Household flatware	122.1	138.3	138.4	138.5	139.2	139.7	142.6	142.8
Lawn and garden equipment, except tractors	123.0	130.4	132.3	132.2	131.7	132.0	132.0	132.7
Passenger cars	118.3	134.1	135.4	133.6	131.9	131.3	132.8	132.1
Toys, games, and children's vehicles	118.1	124.3	125.3	125.2	124.4	123.1	121.9	123.4
Sporting and athletic goods	112.6	122.0	123.3	124.7	126.2	126.2	126.1	125.8
Tobacco products........................	221.4	231.3	237.4	248.9	283.6	374.0	397.2	441.9
Mobile homes	117.5	145.6	149.8	152.2	154.3	158.4	161.3	164.2
Jewelry, platinum, and karat gold	122.8	127.8	129.4	129.2	128.1	127.1	127.2	128.5
Costume jewelry and novelties	125.3	135.1	136.9	139.9	139.6	140.1	141.6	144.0
Capital Equipment	**122.9**	**136.7**	**138.3**	**138.2**	**137.6**	**137.6**	**138.8**	**139.7**
Agricultural machinery and equipment	121.7	142.9	146.8	149.0	150.4	152.1	153.7	155.7
Construction machinery and equipment	121.6	136.7	139.8	142.2	145.2	147.2	148.6	149.1
Metal cutting machine tools	129.8	148.0	152.6	156.0	159.9	160.7	161.9	158.8
Metal forming machine tools..............	128.7	145.7	149.6	153.9	157.6	159.7	161.8	164.7
Tools, dies, jigs, fixtures, and industrial molds	117.2	133.8	136.2	138.1	138.8	139.8	141.1	141.3
Pumps, compressors, and equipment	119.2	139.4	143.5	146.5	149.0	151.7	154.1	157.5
Industrial material handling equipment	115.0	125.3	127.4	129.7	131.3	132.9	134.7	136.9

See footnote at end of table.

U.S. Census Bureau, Statistical Abstract of the United States: 2002

No. 687. Producer Price Indexes by Stage of Processing: 1990 to 2001—Con.

[1982=100, except as indicated]

Stage of processing	1990	1995	1996	1997	1998	1999	2000	2001
Capital Equipment—Continued								
Electronic computers (Dec. 1990=100)	(NA)	51.8	42.4	33.2	24.7	87.2	73.0	56.6
Textile machinery	128.8	146.7	148.4	152.1	152.7	154.2	156.2	157.9
Paper industries machinery (June 1982=100)	134.8	151.0	153.8	157.4	160.3	162.6	164.7	166.9
Printing trades machinery	124.9	133.6	136.8	138.8	141.5	141.0	142.1	143.5
Transformers and power regulators	120.9	128.9	129.7	129.5	131.0	132.6	135.8	134.3
Communication/related equip. (Dec. 1985=100)	106.1	112.1	113.0	114.0	114.0	112.7	110.6	109.4
X-ray and electromedical equipment	109.8	111.8	110.9	107.4	106.7	104.3	101.5	100.1
Oil field and gas field machinery	102.4	114.1	117.8	122.8	125.8	126.5	128.2	134.6
Mining machinery and equipment	121.0	135.6	139.0	140.3	142.2	144.2	146.1	148.5
Office and store machines and equipment	109.5	111.5	112.0	112.4	112.3	112.3	112.7	112.6
Commercial furniture	133.4	148.2	151.7	154.3	155.2	156.6	158.4	160.3
Light motor trucks	130.0	159.0	160.3	158.9	155.1	157.5	157.6	155.0
Heavy motor trucks	120.3	144.1	144.5	140.4	142.1	146.5	148.0	147.9
Truck trailers	110.8	131.7	130.7	130.3	135.0	136.3	139.4	138.8
Civilian aircraft (Dec. 1985=100)	115.3	141.8	147.3	150.0	150.1	151.7	159.6	168.5
Ships (Dec. 1985=100)	110.1	132.8	138.7	143.7	145.7	145.8	146.9	148.8
Railroad equipment	118.6	134.8	137.2	134.7	134.9	135.2	135.7	135.4
Intermediate materials, supplies, and components	**114.5**	**124.9**	**125.7**	**125.6**	**123.0**	**123.2**	**129.2**	**129.7**
Intermediate foods and feeds	**113.3**	**114.8**	**128.1**	**125.4**	**116.1**	**111.1**	**111.7**	**115.9**
Flour	103.6	123.0	136.8	118.7	109.2	104.3	103.8	109.5
Refined sugar	122.7	119.3	123.7	123.6	119.8	121.0	110.6	110.0
Confectionery materials	101.2	109.1	107.9	105.4	93.8	94.0	94.2	106.3
Crude vegetable oils	115.8	130.0	118.1	116.6	131.1	90.2	73.6	70.4
Prepared animal feeds	107.4	109.1	135.3	132.9	107.9	98.3	102.9	105.1
Intermediate materials less foods and feeds	**120.9**	**135.2**	**134.0**	**134.2**	**133.5**	**123.9**	**130.1**	**130.5**
Synthetic fibers	106.7	109.4	111.3	111.1	109.8	103.8	107.2	108.6
Processed yarns and threads	112.6	112.8	114.7	114.0	112.7	108.6	107.9	105.6
Gray fabrics	117.2	121.2	121.4	121.9	121.6	114.4	113.2	114.1
Leather	177.5	191.4	177.9	182.7	178.5	176.3	182.2	200.0
Liquefied petroleum gas	77.4	65.1	84.7	84.5	60.1	73.7	127.1	122.1
Commercial electric power	115.3	131.7	131.6	131.7	130.5	129.1	131.5	139.2
Industrial electric power	119.6	130.8	131.6	130.8	130.0	128.9	131.5	141.7
Commercial natural gas (Dec. 1990=100)	(NA)	96.5	103.2	109.8	106.6	108.1	134.7	167.6
Industrial natural gas (Dec. 1990=100)	(NA)	90.9	98.9	109.3	104.2	103.3	139.0	176.2
Natural gas to electric utilities (Dec. 1990=100)	(NA)	87.7	90.4	96.9	80.5	81.6	120.7	143.7
Jet fuels	76.0	55.0	66.7	62.9	46.0	52.5	88.5	77.3
No. 2 Diesel fuel	74.1	57.0	70.0	64.5	47.3	57.0	93.3	83.6
Residual fuel	57.7	52.6	59.8	59.5	43.8	51.5	84.7	74.5
Industrial chemicals	113.2	128.4	126.7	126.4	121.6	118.9	129.1	128.4
Prepared paint	124.8	142.1	147.2	152.1	155.0	157.4	160.8	164.5
Paint materials	136.3	139.4	141.3	141.5	143.8	144.1	148.5	150.9
Medicinal and botanical chemicals	102.2	128.3	128.6	133.4	135.0	142.2	146.2	141.2
Fats and oils, inedible	88.1	126.9	133.3	132.3	116.9	88.4	70.1	77.5
Mixed fertilizers	103.3	111.1	114.7	113.6	115.3	113.7	112.4	116.5
Nitrogenates	92.3	129.4	130.5	132.3	108.2	94.6	118.2	142.9
Phosphates	96.5	109.1	116.3	110.4	112.5	112.0	96.9	95.1
Other agricultural chemicals	119.9	144.3	146.1	147.8	149.7	144.5	146.1	148.4
Plastic resins and materials	124.1	143.5	133.1	137.3	125.6	125.8	141.6	134.9
Synthetic rubber	111.9	126.3	122.2	119.3	117.2	113.9	119.1	122.9
Plastic construction products	117.2	133.8	130.9	128.2	126.2	128.0	135.8	133.1
Unsupported plastic film, sheet, and shapes	119.0	135.6	132.7	131.7	128.1	127.5	133.2	137.9
Plastic parts and components for manufacturing	112.9	115.9	117.5	117.2	117.1	117.4	117.3	116.8
Softwood lumber	123.8	178.5	189.5	206.5	182.4	196.0	178.6	170.0
Hardwood lumber	131.0	167.0	163.9	174.1	178.7	177.3	185.9	181.1
Millwork	130.4	163.8	166.6	170.9	171.1	174.7	176.4	179.1
Plywood	114.2	165.3	156.4	159.3	157.6	176.4	157.6	154.1
Woodpile	151.3	183.2	133.1	128.6	122.0	119.7	145.3	125.6
Paper	128.8	159.0	149.4	143.9	146.0	141.8	149.8	150.7
Paperboard	135.7	183.1	155.1	144.4	151.7	153.2	176.7	171.9
Paper boxes and containers	129.9	163.8	153.9	144.7	154.7	158.0	172.6	175.2
Building paper and board	112.2	144.9	137.2	129.6	132.8	141.6	138.8	128.9

See footnotes at end of table.

U.S. Census Bureau, Statistical Abstract of the United States: 2002

No. 687. Producer Price Indexes by Stage of Processing: 1990 to 2001—Con.

[1982=100, except as indicated]

Stage of processing	1990	1995	1996	1997	1998	1999	2000	2001
Intermediate materials less foods and feeds—Continued								
Commercial printing (June 1982=100)	128.0	144.5	148.3	148.7	152.1	152.2	155.2	157.6
Foundry and forge shop products	117.2	129.3	132.6	134.1	135.0	135.1	136.5	137.0
Steel mill products	112.1	120.1	115.6	116.4	113.9	105.3	108.4	101.3
Primary nonferrous metals	133.4	146.8	126.2	126.2	106.7	101.5	113.6	105.4
Aluminum mill shapes	127.9	160.4	144.8	147.5	142.1	138.1	149.0	148.5
Copper and brass mill shapes	174.6	195.2	179.0	177.3	153.4	151.2	162.3	155.4
Nonferrous wire and cable	142.6	151.5	147.5	148.1	140.9	135.6	143.7	140.6
Metal containers	114.0	117.2	110.0	108.1	108.7	106.4	106.8	106.2
Hardware	125.9	141.1	143.8	145.6	147.0	148.7	151.2	154.4
Plumbing fixtures and brass fittings	144.3	166.0	171.1	174.5	175.1	176.7	180.4	180.7
Heating equipment	131.6	147.5	151.2	152.4	153.2	154.0	155.6	157.1
Fabricated structural metal products	121.8	135.1	137.8	140.3	142.5	143.3	144.9	144.6
Fabricated ferrous wire products (June 1982=100) . .	114.6	125.7	126.8	128.0	130.1	130.6	130.0	129.8
Other miscellaneous metal products	120.7	124.9	125.7	126.2	126.2	125.5	126.0	127.0
Mechanical power transmission equipment	125.3	146.9	151.5	154.8	157.7	161.1	163.9	167.1
Air conditioning and refrigeration equipment	122.1	130.2	132.7	132.6	134.6	135.5	135.3	136.0
Metal valves, excluding fluid power (Dec. 1982=100) .	125.3	145.3	149.8	153.3	156.6	160.2	162.1	164.6
Ball and roller bearings	130.6	152.0	157.8	162.9	165.2	166.8	168.8	169.5
Wiring devices	132.2	147.2	151.2	154.0	154.2	152.5	152.9	153.7
Motors, generators, motor generator sets	132.9	143.9	145.6	144.7	145.8	145.9	146.2	146.9
Switchgear and switchboard equipment	124.4	140.3	142.6	145.6	148.3	151.0	153.0	156.8
Electronic components and accessories	118.4	113.6	108.9	104.0	100.1	98.2	97.1	93.9
Internal combustion engines	120.2	135.6	138.8	140.1	140.7	143.0	143.8	143.9
Machine shop products	124.3	131.3	133.6	135.2	136.3	136.8	138.0	140.2
Flat glass	107.5	113.2	110.0	108.4	107.2	106.4	109.7	112.0
Cement	103.7	128.1	134.0	139.4	145.7	150.6	150.1	150.2
Concrete products	113.5	129.4	133.2	136.0	140.1	143.7	147.8	151.7
Asphalt felts and coatings	97.1	100.0	100.0	99.9	99.6	99.2	104.1	107.5
Gypsum products	105.2	154.5	154.0	170.8	177.2	208.0	201.4	156.1
Glass containers	120.4	130.5	129.1	125.7	125.9	125.9	127.4	132.8
Motor vehicle parts	111.2	116.0	116.2	115.4	114.6	114.0	113.6	113.1
Aircraft engines and engine parts (Dec. 1985=100) .	113.5	132.8	134.7	135.7	136.9	138.5	141.0	145.2
Aircraft parts and auxiliary equipment, n.e.c. (June 1985=100) .	117.7	135.7	139.3	141.3	142.6	143.7	145.7	147.8
Photographic supplies	127.6	126.8	129.8	130.0	128.9	128.3	125.2	128.5
Medical/surgical/personal aid devices	127.3	141.3	143.1	143.1	143.3	144.6	146.0	148.3
Crude materials for further processing	**108.9**	**102.7**	**113.8**	**111.1**	**96.7**	**98.2**	**120.6**	**121.3**
Crude foodstuffs and feedstuffs	113.1	105.8	121.5	112.2	103.8	98.7	100.2	106.2
Wheat	87.6	118.6	136.6	108.2	87.8	79.5	80.3	85.5
Corn	100.9	109.0	158.5	110.1	91.7	78.2	76.4	78.8
Slaughter cattle	122.5	99.5	95.8	97.9	92.5	97.6	104.1	108.4
Slaughter hogs	94.1	70.2	88.6	87.0	52.2	53.8	72.7	73.4
Slaughter broilers/fryers	119.5	129.1	148.0	137.2	151.8	134.5	127.6	138.4
Slaughter turkeys	116.9	120.3	121.5	112.9	110.4	120.0	120.7	110.3
Fluid milk	100.8	93.6	107.9	97.5	112.6	106.3	92.0	112.0
Soybeans	100.8	102.2	127.9	131.0	103.4	80.1	83.4	78.6
Cane sugar, raw	119.2	119.7	118.6	116.8	117.2	113.7	101.8	111.3
Crude nonfood materials	101.5	96.8	104.5	106.4	88.3	94.3	130.4	127.3
Raw cotton	118.2	156.2	130.0	116.5	111.0	87.4	95.2	67.2
Leaf tobacco	95.8	102.5	105.1	(NA)	104.6	101.6	(NA)	105.2
Cattle hides	217.8	209.9	186.5	196.1	153.3	141.9	169.4	(NA)
Coal	97.5	95.0	94.5	96.3	93.1	90.7	87.9	96.2
Natural gas	80.4	66.6	91.2	101.7	83.7	91.2	155.5	172.7
Crude petroleum	71.0	51.1	62.2	57.5	35.7	50.3	85.2	69.6
Logs and timber	142.8	220.4	206.8	214.4	208.2	202.0	196.4	182.7
Wastepaper	138.9	371.1	141.6	163.3	146.0	183.6	282.5	148.6
Iron ore	83.3	91.8	96.7	96.3	95.5	94.9	94.8	96.2
Iron and steel scrap	166.0	202.7	191.1	188.9	164.9	139.2	142.1	119.8
Nonferrous metal ores (Dec. 1983=100)	98.3	101.6	90.2	82.2	66.9	63.1	68.0	63.4
Copper base scrap	181.3	193.5	166.3	157.7	116.3	108.2	123.7	114.8
Aluminum base scrap	172.6	209.4	173.4	195.1	162.8	161.7	177.0	156.4
Construction sand, gravel, and crushed stone	125.4	142.3	145.6	148.2	152.7	157.2	163.1	168.8

NA Not available.   N.e.c. Not elsewhere classified.

Source: U.S. Bureau of Labor Statistics, *Producer Price Indexes,* monthly and annual.

No. 688. Producer Price Indexes for the Net Output of Selected Industries: 1997 to 2001

[Indexes are based on selling prices reported by establishments of all sizes by probability sampling. Manufacturing industries selected by shipment value. N.e.c.= not elsewhere classified. See text, Section 22, Domestic Trade]

Industry	SIC code [1]	Index base [2]	1997	1998	1999	2000	2001
Iron ores.	1011	12/84	95.3	94.5	94.0	93.9	95.2
Copper ores	1021	06/88	110.4	76.8	71.3	88.7	80.9
Lead and zinc ores.	1031	12/85	138.6	107.0	111.8	118.8	89.9
Gold ores	1041	06/85	100.9	90.0	85.6	84.2	81.5
Metal mining services	1081	12/85	116.8	122.2	120.2	109.0	118.2
Metal ores, n.e.c.	1099	12/85	100.8	89.9	82.9	85.8	77.9
Bituminous coal and lignite.	1211	12/81	95.9	93.0	90.6	(NA)	(NA)
Anthracite mining	1231	12/79	159.0	160.1	158.7	157.3	161.1
Coal mining services.	1241	06/85	108.1	108.1	107.7	108.4	118.2
Crude petroleum and natural gas liquids.	1331	06/96	115.6	86.1	102.6	174.3	172.6
Drilling oil and gas wells	1381	12/85	143.7	154.6	133.1	138.2	174.0
Oil and gas exploration services	1382	12/85	105.6	114.5	92.7	80.4	72.7
Oil and gas field services, n.e.c.	1389	12/85	112.7	113.6	112.9	123.3	142.4
Dimension stone	1411	06/85	138.2	142.2	145.9	153.4	156.9
Crushed and broken limestone	1422	12/83	134.5	137.4	140.6	145.6	150.9
Crushed and broken granite, n.e.c.	1423	12/83	159.7	166.4	172.5	182.3	188.3
Crushed and broken stone, n.e.c.	1429	12/83	145.4	147.9	149.9	153.1	156.8
Construction sand and gravel	1442	06/82	155.3	163.0	169.0	175.5	181.7
Industrial sand.	1446	06/82	138.9	142.2	145.2	148.0	154.3
Kaolin and ball clay	1455	06/84	117.1	115.8	113.3	113.3	119.5
Clay and related minerals, n.e.c.	1459	06/84	131.7	133.4	133.5	135.7	140.3
Potash, soda, and borate minerals	1474	12/84	117.4	118.9	113.6	111.6	109.8
Chemicals and fertilizer mineral mining, n.e.c.	1479	12/89	92.7	93.4	95.0	90.1	85.8
Nonmetallic minerals (except fuels) services	1481	06/85	104.7	104.7	106.5	107.2	109.2
Miscellaneous nonmetallic minerals	1499	06/85	133.5	136.7	138.0	138.7	143.3
Meat packing plants	2011	12/80	113.5	101.4	104.2	113.4	120.0
Sausage and other prepared meats.	2013	12/82	118.8	113.3	113.8	121.3	125.8
Poultry slaughtering and processing	2015	12/81	124.7	127.1	119.8	118.3	121.5
Natural and processed cheese	2022	06/81	115.7	126.1	124.3	117.8	129.8
Dry, condensed, and evaporated milk products	2023	12/83	138.7	146.4	142.4	140.9	150.7
Ice cream and frozen desserts	2024	06/83	135.1	142.6	150.0	150.4	157.1
Fluid milk	2026	12/82	133.6	140.4	145.9	141.8	153.7
Canned specialties	2032	12/82	163.0	165.6	168.6	171.5	173.9
Canned fruits, vegetables, preserves, jams, and jellies	2033	06/81	137.7	136.9	138.2	139.1	142.2
Pickled fruits/veg./veg. sauces/seasonings/salad dressings	2035	06/81	161.2	162.2	163.2	163.6	162.9
Frozen fruits and vegetables	2037	06/81	139.2	138.6	141.8	141.0	140.0
Frozen specialties	2038	12/82	136.8	137.0	137.4	136.1	139.0
Flour and other grain mill products	2041	06/83	114.3	103.3	97.1	97.2	101.6
Cereal breakfast foods	2043	12/83	168.2	161.4	159.5	159.6	161.6
Wet corn milling	2046	06/85	123.6	107.1	101.3	102.6	112.6
Dog and cat food	2047	12/85	132.1	132.3	132.2	131.3	134.7
Prepared animal feeds, n.e.c.	2048	12/80	112.2	95.2	86.7	89.0	92.2
Bread and other bakery products, except cookies and crackers	2051	06/80	199.7	201.4	204.5	211.3	221.5
Cookies and crackers	2052	06/83	167.0	170.3	171.0	172.0	173.4
Candy and other confectionery products, and chewing gum	2064	06/83	146.2	146.8	149.4	150.9	152.2
Soybean oil mill products.	2075	12/79	103.2	86.7	68.0	69.1	67.6
Malt beverages	2082	06/82	128.0	128.1	131.4	136.1	140.4
Bottled and canned soft drinks	2086	06/81	140.5	142.4	145.7	152.0	156.6
Flavoring extracts and syrups, n.e.c.	2087	12/85	130.7	131.4	133.6	137.3	140.7
Fresh or frozen packaged fish	2092	12/82	145.2	151.7	160.9	171.5	161.6
Coffee	2095	06/81	161.8	153.3	145.8	144.3	136.4
Potato and corn chips, and similar snacks	2096	06/91	109.4	111.1	112.7	116.7	121.8
Macaroni, spaghetti, and noodles	2098	06/85	125.5	122.7	122.3	121.9	122.4
Food preparations, n.e.c.	2099	12/85	127.5	128.5	128.9	129.1	131.0
Cigarettes.	2111	12/82	223.3	260.4	356.7	379.2	425.8
Cigars	2121	12/82	228.5	242.7	259.6	268.8	279.1
Cotton broadwoven fabric	2211	12/80	118.5	117.4	114.1	110.6	111.7
Manmade fiber and silk broadwoven fabric	2221	06/81	115.0	114.8	108.6	108.6	109.0
Narrow fabric mills	2241	06/84	122.7	123.8	124.3	125.3	126.2
Knit outerwear	2253	12/84	118.8	118.9	116.4	117.0	116.5
Carpet and rugs	2273	06/90	105.9	106.4	105.6	107.8	108.6
Spun yarn.	2281	12/82	104.7	102.5	96.9	95.5	93.9
Men's and boys' separate trousers and slacks	2325	12/81	133.4	136.5	137.0	134.8	135.2
Women's, misses', and juniors' dresses	2335	12/80	126.0	127.0	126.3	125.8	123.4
Women's, misses', and juniors' outerwear, n.e.c.	2339	06/83	110.9	111.2	112.6	113.3	112.2
House furnishings, n.e.c.	2392	06/83	120.5	119.5	118.8	117.7	117.2
Automotive trimmings, apparel findings, and related products.	2396	12/83	120.1	124.0	122.6	123.9	124.8
Logging camps and logging contractors	2411	12/81	191.2	188.2	182.8	177.6	167.6
Sawmills and planing mills	2421	12/80	163.1	151.7	157.4	148.0	141.1
Millwork	2431	06/83	156.4	157.2	160.0	161.3	164.7
Wood kitchen cabinets	2434	06/84	150.4	153.1	155.7	159.8	162.6
Softwood plywood	2436	12/80	142.4	142.5	164.7	140.4	135.9
Mobile homes	2451	06/81	157.8	159.9	164.2	167.1	170.1
Wood household furniture, except upholstered.	2511	12/79	192.3	195.8	200.5	204.1	207.6
Upholstered wood household furniture	2512	06/82	138.1	140.1	142.0	144.4	146.2
Nonwood office furniture	2522	12/79	193.5	191.6	191.8	193.4	195.4
Public building and related furniture	2531	12/84	135.9	135.9	136.8	138.6	139.0

See footnotes at end of table.

U.S. Census Bureau, Statistical Abstract of the United States: 2002

No. 688. Producer Price Indexes for the Net Output of Selected Industries: 1997 to 2001—Con.

[See headnote, page 461]

Industry	SIC code [1]	Index base [2]	1997	1998	1999	2000	2001
Paper mills	2621	06/81	143.2	144.4	139.7	148.7	150.5
Paperboard mills	2631	12/82	158.2	165.1	167.0	192.4	187.2
Corrugated and solid fiber boxes	2653	03/80	154.9	168.8	175.5	196.8	198.0
Folding paperboard boxes	2657	12/83	142.2	143.6	142.3	145.4	146.7
Paper coated and laminated, n.e.c.	2672	06/93	110.1	109.6	109.8	111.7	113.0
Plastics, foil and coated paper bags	2673	12/83	160.9	156.5	159.0	168.6	169.2
Sanitary paper products	2676	06/83	147.8	146.0	145.1	148.3	147.9
Newspaper publishing	2711	12/79	317.7	328.5	339.3	351.2	367.7
Periodical publishing	2721	12/79	263.2	276.8	284.9	292.6	305.8
Book Publishing	2731	12/80	232.1	238.0	247.6	255.0	263.2
Miscellaneous publishing	2741	06/84	181.1	187.8	194.5	201.3	209.9
Commercial printing, lithographic	2752	06/82	149.8	153.3	153.2	156.0	158.1
Commercial printing, n.e.c.	2759	06/82	159.4	160.9	162.6	166.2	168.4
Manifold business forms	2761	12/83	165.8	167.1	170.5	185.7	192.3
Industrial inorganic chemicals, n.e.c.	2819	12/82	135.5	132.3	129.2	132.7	142.2
Plastic materials and resins	2821	12/80	153.9	139.5	142.8	164.3	160.5
Noncellulosic manmade fibers	2824	06/81	107.7	106.6	98.9	101.5	102.8
Medicinal chemicals and botanical products (in bulk)	2833	06/82	134.2	136.3	143.2	147.8	143.3
Pharmaceutical preparations	2834	06/81	259.1	289.9	298.5	306.6	314.0
In vivo and In vitro diagnostics	2835	03/80	167.4	177.8	184.5	189.9	191.9
Biological products, except diagnostics	2836	06/91	112.3	115.8	126.1	127.5	137.4
Soap and other detergents	2841	06/83	124.6	124.8	125.9	127.4	129.6
Specialty cleaning, polishing and sanitation preparations	2842	06/83	130.8	132.6	135.1	138.1	139.9
Toilet preparations	2844	03/80	168.9	171.7	174.8	177.7	179.3
Paints and Allied Products	2851	06/83	152.1	154.9	157.3	160.5	163.9
Cyclic (coal tar) crudes and intermediates, organic dyes and pigments	2865	12/82	115.2	109.3	110.1	124.3	114.3
Industrial organic chemicals, n.e.c.	2869	12/82	171.5	168.0	169.1	185.5	182.9
Agricultural chemicals, n.e.c.	2879	06/82	137.6	139.4	135.4	136.6	138.1
Adhesives and sealants	2891	12/83	148.8	151.4	151.7	153.6	158.1
Chemicals and chemical preparations, n.e.c. . . .	2899	06/85	133.2	134.3	134.8	135.8	137.9
Petroleum refining	2911	06/85	83.1	62.3	73.6	111.6	103.1
Tires and inner tubes	3011	06/81	103.4	102.2	100.4	100.4	101.6
Fabricated rubber products, n.e.c.	3069	06/83	132.1	132.4	132.2	133.1	134.6
Unsupported plastic film and sheet	3081	06/93	108.3	103.8	103.2	109.0	113.7
Plastic bottles	3085	06/93	107.1	105.5	106.1	110.4	111.3
Plastic foam products	3086	06/93	109.7	108.6	108.6	110.1	110.2
Custom compounding of purchased plastic resins	3087	06/93	106.7	107.4	104.2	111.1	113.7
Plastic products n.e.c.	3089	06/93	106.3	106.3	106.7	108.0	109.2
Products of purchased glass	3231	06/83	127.1	127.5	128.4	131.6	133.6
Concrete products	3272	12/79	151.6	156.7	161.0	166.4	172.2
Ready-mixed concrete	3273	06/81	138.0	142.3	145.6	150.2	153.4
Blast furnaces and steel mills	3312	06/82	114.2	111.4	102.0	104.1	96.9
Cold finishing of steel shapes - mfpm	3316	06/82	116.7	114.7	110.3	113.6	107.5
Steel pipe and tubes - mfpm	3317	06/82	131.8	132.7	127.1	132.1	129.5
Gray iron foundries	3321	12/80	143.0	143.3	144.5	147.1	148.1
Primary copper	3331	06/80	137.3	106.2	102.2	111.6	-
Secondary nonferrous metals	3341	06/80	94.5	85.9	84.8	88.4	85.8
Rolling, drawing and extruding of copper	3351	12/80	149.9	131.9	130.0	137.6	132.3
Aluminum sheet, plate, foil and welded tube products	3353	06/81	152.9	145.5	139.5	150.4	148.0
Nonferrous wire drawing and insulating	3357	12/82	154.5	148.1	143.7	153.2	149.3
Metal cans	3411	06/81	110.4	110.2	107.8	108.1	108.0
Hardware, n.e.c.	3429	06/85	125.0	126.0	127.4	129.7	132.0
Fabricated structural metal	3441	06/82	132.8	136.8	139.1	142.0	140.9
Metal doors, sash and trim	3442	06/83	152.5	152.9	153.6	156.1	158.2
Fabricated plate work (boiler shops)	3443	03/80	161.9	164.7	167.2	168.9	170.4
Sheet metal work	3444	12/82	138.6	139.9	140.1	141.8	141.5
Bolts, nuts, screws, rivets, and washers	3452	06/82	125.6	127.0	126.4	126.5	126.4
Automotive stampings	3465	12/82	112.8	112.1	110.4	110.6	110.1
Metal stampings, n.e.c.	3469	06/84	128.5	128.9	128.6	128.7	129.9
Metal coating and allied services	3479	12/84	119.4	119.1	118.8	119.1	122.6
Industrial valves	3491	06/91	117.3	119.7	122.4	123.9	126.3
Fabricated metal products, n.e.c.	3499	06/85	129.9	131.8	131.8	133.0	133.8
Turbines and turbine generator sets	3511	06/82	146.9	146.9	148.7	149.6	150.9
Internal combustion engines, n.e.c.	3519	12/82	135.7	136.2	138.1	139.0	140.1
Farm machinery and equipment	3523	12/82	138.8	140.4	142.2	143.9	146.3
Lawn and garden equipment	3524	12/82	126.0	124.2	124.5	124.6	125.1
Construction machinery	3531	12/80	164.4	167.8	170.8	172.7	173.5
Special tools, dies, jigs, fixtures and industrial molds	3544	06/81	144.1	144.9	145.8	147.0	146.8
Special industry machinery, n.e.c.	3559	12/81	163.3	166.0	168.2	169.4	169.8
Pumps and pumping equipment	3561	12/83	150.4	153.3	156.2	158.6	162.3
General industrial machinery, n.e.c.	3569	12/84	149.5	151.3	151.3	155.8	159.2
Electronic computers	3571	12/90	36.5	29.1	91.1	80.8	71.2
Computer storage devices	3572	12/92	51.1	45.3	95.0	85.2	77.5
Computer peripheral equipment, n.e.c.	3577	12/93	90.5	84.5	80.1	78.8	78.3
Refrigeration and heating equipment	3585	12/82	129.2	131.3	131.5	130.6	130.6
Service industry machinery, n.e.c.	3589	06/82	159.3	161.7	164.0	165.9	168.5
Machinery, except electrical, not elsewhere classified	3599	06/84	125.4	126.9	127.6	129.8	132.3
Switchgear and switchboard apparatus	3613	06/85	135.0	138.2	141.0	143.3	147.6
Electric motors and generators	3621	06/83	138.6	139.8	139.9	140.4	141.7
Relays and industrial controls	3625	06/85	137.8	140.4	142.8	144.4	148.2

See footnotes at end of table.

U.S. Census Bureau, Statistical Abstract of the United States: 2002

No. 688. Producer Price Indexes for the Net Output of Selected Industries: 1997 to 2001—Con.

[See headnote, page 461]

Industry	SIC code [1]	Index base [2]	1997	1998	1999	2000	2001
Household audio & video equipment	3651	03/80	80.5	79.7	77.8	76.1	74.6
Telephone & telegraph apparatus	3661	12/85	119.4	117.9	115.8	113.1	108.7
Radio and television broadcast and communication equipment	3663	12/91	105.7	105.5	104.1	101.5	101.7
Printed circuit boards	3672	06/91	95.0	93.9	92.2	91.7	91.8
Semiconductors and related devices	3674	06/81	76.7	70.6	97.4	91.1	87.0
Electronic components, n.e.c.	3679	06/82	114.2	114.2	113.8	114.5	109.2
Electrical equipment for internal combustion engines	3694	12/82	128.8	127.9	127.4	127.6	127.9
Electrical equipment and supplies, not elsewhere classified . .	3699	12/85	118.5	117.5	118.6	118.3	119.0
Motor vehicles and passenger car bodies	3711	06/82	138.7	136.8	137.6	138.7	137.6
Truck and bus bodies	3713	12/82	153.5	155.3	157.0	160.3	163.3
Motor vehicle parts and accessories	3714	12/82	113.1	112.6	112.0	111.6	111.4
Aircraft	3721	12/85	142.3	142.6	144.1	150.5	155.7
Aircraft engines and engine parts	3724	12/85	134.8	135.7	136.8	139.7	144.0
Aircraft parts and auxiliary equipment, n.e.c.	3728	06/85	139.0	140.9	142.2	143.3	145.8
Ship building and repairing.	3731	12/85	133.3	134.8	135.4	137.6	139.7
Railroad equipment.	3743	06/84	127.4	127.5	128.1	128.6	128.4
Search, detection, navigation, and guidance systems and aeronautical and nautical nav sys	3812	12/91	107.0	109.0	109.0	108.7	108.1
Industrial process control instruments.	3823	06/83	147.7	149.9	151.0	152.3	154.3
Electrical measuring and integrating instruments	3825	12/83	135.0	135.1	135.5	137.3	138.8
Laboratory analytical instruments	3826	12/85	117.5	118.4	116.9	119.2	121.6
Surgical and medical instruments and apparatus	3841	06/82	129.0	127.9	127.4	127.2	128.7
Surgical, orthopedic and prosthetic appliances and supplies. .	3842	06/83	158.1	160.5	163.0	166.4	170.0
Electromedical equipment	3845	06/85	104.7	103.8	101.4	98.5	96.7
Photographic equipment and supplies	3861	12/83	113.5	110.0	106.7	106.3	107.5
Sporting and athletic goods, n.e.c..	3949	12/85	127.5	129.1	128.8	127.9	127.3
Signs and advertising displays	3993	12/85	134.3	136.2	139.1	140.7	145.0
Manufacturing industries, n.e.c.	3999	12/85	124.6	125.1	126.1	127.3	128.5
Railroads, line haul operations	4011	12/84	112.1	113.4	113.0	114.5	116.9
Local trucking without storage.	4212	06/93	104.6	104.8	106.3	110.0	113.5
Trucking, except local	4213	06/92	110.7	114.1	118.0	123.5	127.1
Local trucking with storage.	4214	06/93	112.2	113.0	113.2	114.1	115.8
Courier services, except by air	4215	12/92	116.4	122.2	126.0	130.6	135.4
Farm product warehousing and storage	4221	12/92	102.9	104.1	107.1	110.6	114.1
Refrigerated warehousing and storage	4222	12/91	105.1	105.5	106.4	108.1	109.8
General warehousing and storage.	4225	06/93	105.5	107.2	111.5	113.6	116.8
United States Postal Service	4311	06/89	132.3	132.3	135.3	135.2	143.4
Deep sea foreign transportation of freight	4412	06/88	113.1	116.4	134.0	155.8	174.3
Domestic deep sea transportation of freight	4424	06/88	124.5	120.9	124.3	129.8	134.2
Freight transportation on the Great Lakes-St Lawrence Seaway	4432	12/91	106.4	107.4	107.4	107.4	108.2
Water transportation of freight, n.e.c.	4449	12/90	105.9	107.4	111.2	117.9	123.1
Marine cargo handling.	4491	12/91	103.7	105.0	106.7	109.1	111.4
Tugging and towing services	4492	12/92	113.3	115.7	119.7	124.2	125.3
Air transportation, scheduled	4512	12/80	150.9	152.6	161.2	186.5	200.6
Air courier services.	4513	12/89	115.1	113.2	117.3	128.0	133.7
Air transportation, nonscheduled	4522	06/92	104.5	106.0	109.2	114.7	119.9
Airports, flying fields, and airport services	4581	06/92	109.7	112.5	116.2	122.1	125.9
Crude petroleum pipelines	4612	06/86	96.0	96.8	95.5	101.0	110.9
Refined petroleum pipelines	4613	06/86	105.3	104.8	104.9	105.3	108.5
Travel agencies	4724	12/89	114.5	112.5	112.0	121.8	123.5
Freight transportation arrangement	4731	12/94	101.4	99.8	99.2	100.3	99.4
Telephone communications, except radiotelephone.	4813	06/95	99.6	98.5	96.0	93.9	91.3
Radio broadcasting.	4832	06/88	148.5	151.2	162.3	170.6	171.9
Cable and other pay television services	4841	06/93	108.3	112.4	116.2	120.9	125.0
Electric power and natural gas utilities	4981	12/90	112.0	110.4	109.5	114.4	123.9
Scrap and waste materials.	5093	12/86	152.7	131.7	127.9	152.8	124.2
Life insurance carriers.	6311	12/98	(X)	(X)	100.4	99.2	100.1
Property and casualty insurance	6331	06/98	(X)	(X)	100.8	102.0	104.4
Operators and lessors of nonresidential buildings.	6512	12/95	101.0	103.1	105.9	109.0	111.6
Real estate agents and managers	6531	12/95	100.8	102.5	104.4	107.8	111.4
Hotels and motels	7011	06/93	115.6	119.8	124.9	128.8	134.5
Advertising agencies.	7311	06/95	103.8	105.3	107.4	110.2	116.1
Building cleaning and maintenance services, n.e.c.	7349	12/94	104.5	105.6	108.0	111.3	116.2
Employment agencies.	7361	06/94	104.5	106.4	109.9	111.9	113.9
Help supply services.	7363	06/94	106.9	109.1	111.1	113.4	114.3
Prepackaged software.	7372	12/97	(X)	100.6	100.1	100.8	101.4
Truck rental and leasing, without drivers.	7513	06/91	104.5	104.7	104.2	108.2	108.8
Passenger car rental, without drivers	7514	12/91	130.5	132.5	129.4	134.9	133.7
Offices and clinics of doctors of medicine	8011	12/93	109.0	11.2	113.8	115.8	119.1
Skilled and intermediate care facilities	8053	12/94	114.7	119.4	124.1	131.0	139.2
General medical and surgical hospitals.	8062	12/92	113.6	114.5	116.6	119.8	123.2
Psychiatric hospitals	8063	12/92	112.0	108.2	109.2	109.1	110.5
Specialty hospitals, except psychiatric	8069	12/92	114.7	117.1	120.0	123.9	126.6
Medical laboratories	8071	06/94	106.1	106.4	105.9	108.0	112.1
Home health care services.	8082	12/96	103.3	106.1	107.1	111.1	114.0
Legal services	8111	12/96	102.5	106.2	108.7	112.5	117.9
Engineering design, analysis, and consulting services.	8711	12/96	102.3	105.0	107.9	111.1	115.5
Architectural design, analysis, and consulting services	8712	12/96	102.0	105.5	111.8	115.8	117.7
Accounting, auditing, and bookkeeping services.	8721	06/95	105.7	108.2	111.9	115.4	117.5

NA Not available.   N.e.c. Not elsewhere classified.   X Not applicable.   [1] Standard Industrial Classification code.   [2] Index base year equals 100.

Source: U.S. Bureau of Labor Statistics, *Producer Price Indexes*, monthly.

No. 689. Chain-Type Price Indexes For Personal Consumption Expenditures (PCE): 1980 to 2001

[1996=100. For explanation of "chain-type," see text, Section 13, Income]

Item	1980	1985	1990	1995	1999	2000	2001
Personal consumption expenditures .	55.2	71.0	85.6	97.9	104.7	107.5	109.5
Durable goods [1]	76.5	88.6	96.0	101.1	93.0	91.5	89.8
Motor vehicles and parts	61.0	74.2	83.8	98.4	99.1	99.6	100.1
Furniture and household equipment	106.3	116.3	113.6	104.5	85.2	81.5	77.0
Nondurable goods [1]	65.3	77.3	91.0	97.9	103.7	107.6	109.1
Food	60.8	72.9	88.2	97.3	106.1	108.6	111.9
Clothing and shoes	86.5	93.3	103.5	101.4	96.4	95.2	93.3
Gasoline, fuel oil, and other energy goods	90.6	93.3	95.2	93.7	94.6	121.9	118.2
Gasoline and oil	91.4	92.8	94.8	94.2	94.8	121.1	117.0
Fuel oil and coal	87.4	97.6	98.6	89.6	92.6	129.3	130.2
Services [1]	45.9	64.4	81.0	97.3	107.8	111.1	114.3
Housing	47.1	66.7	84.1	97.0	109.3	112.8	117.2
Household operation	56.3	81.8	87.6	98.1	100.4	102.1	106.5
Transportation	51.9	65.5	81.8	98.4	105.5	108.6	110.2
Medical care	37.2	55.9	76.0	97.9	107.1	110.2	113.4
Recreation	53.7	67.9	83.3	96.8	108.9	112.9	116.6
Addenda:							
Energy goods and services	75.5	90.3	92.5	95.6	96.3	113.3	116.9
PCE less food and energy	52.4	69.2	84.7	98.2	105.0	107.0	108.7

[1] Includes other items not shown separately.

Source: U.S. Bureau of Economic Analysis, *The National Income and Product Accounts of the United States* , 1929-97, Vol. 2; and *Survey of Current Business,* May 2002. See also <http://www.bea.gov/bea/dn/nipaweb/selecttable.asp?selected=N>.

No. 690. Chain-Type Price Indexes for Gross Domestic Product: 1980 to 2001

[1996=100. For explanation of "chain-type," see text Section 13, Income]

Item	1980	1985	1990	1995	1999	2000	2001
Gross domestic product	57.1	73.7	86.5	98.1	104.7	107.0	109.4
Personal consumption expenditures	55.2	71.0	85.6	97.9	104.7	107.5	109.5
Durable goods	76.5	88.6	96.0	101.1	93.0	91.5	89.8
Nondurable goods	65.3	77.3	91.0	97.9	103.7	107.6	109.1
Services	45.9	64.4	81.0	97.3	107.8	111.1	114.3
Gross private domestic investment	73.0	85.3	95.1	100.3	98.6	99.7	100.2
Fixed investment	71.8	84.5	94.7	100.1	98.9	100.1	100.6
Nonresidential	77.4	89.6	98.2	100.9	95.6	95.7	95.3
Structures	60.0	74.1	85.8	97.4	110.4	115.0	120.1
Producers' durable equipment. . . .	86.6	96.3	102.9	102.1	91.1	90.1	88.1
Residential	58.7	72.2	85.5	97.9	109.6	114.5	118.4
Exports of goods and services	83.3	88.7	96.8	101.3	95.7	97.3	97.1
Exports of goods	94.7	95.6	101.4	102.7	92.9	94.0	93.3
Exports of services	58.4	73.4	86.5	98.0	102.6	106.0	106.9
Imports of goods and services	90.5	85.0	99.4	101.8	91.8	95.7	92.5
Imports of goods	95.9	88.8	102.0	102.5	90.3	94.6	91.7
Imports of services	69.0	69.5	88.3	98.3	99.7	101.5	96.9
Government consumption expenditures [1]	55.8	73.8	85.2	97.6	106.6	110.7	112.9
Federal	57.5	75.7	83.8	97.2	105.1	108.1	109.9
National defense	57.9	77.2	84.6	96.9	104.6	107.6	109.2
	58.0	77.2	84.6	96.9	104.6	107.6	109.2
Nondefense	56.0	71.5	82.0	97.9	106.0	109.2	111.1
State and local	67.1	72.4	87.7	97.7	111.7	115.3	119.9

[1] And gross investment.

Source: U.S. Bureau of Economic Analysis, *The National Income and Product Accounts of the United States, 1929-97,* and *Survey of Current Business,* May 2002. See also <http://www.bea.gov/bea/dn/nipaweb/selecttable.asp?selected=N>.

No. 691. Commodity Research Bureau Futures Price Index: 1980 to 2001

[1967=100. Index computed daily. Represents unweighted geometric average of commodity futures prices (through 6 months forward) of 17 major commodity futures markets. Represents end of year index]

Item	1980	1985	1990	1993	1994	1995	1996	1997	1998	1999	2000	2001
All commodities	308.5	229.2	222.6	212.4	229.7	237.1	247.9	229.1	191.2	205.1	227.8	190.6
Softs [1]	426.0	398.2	276.0	246.9	352.3	354.4	322.2	408.7	344.8	200.9	254.4	252.8
Industrials	324.6	211.7	245.5	235.0	263.6	272.5	266.3	210.9	185.3	192.9	211.0	141.8
Grains and Oilseeds [2]	312.1	198.5	171.2	193.8	191.2	218.6	284.7	210.7	172.8	156.6	174.9	159
Energy	(NA)	96.5	246.0	151.8	173.8	180.0	224.0	180.4	135.0	221	355.8	204.9
Oilseeds [3]	314.6	245.4	223.6	239.8	259.9	277.5	307.9	(3)	(3)	(3)	(3)	(3)
Livestock and Meats	217.4	206.9	226.2	201.4	192.3	192.4	241.7	238.1	186.7	239.6	253.6	247.4
Metals (precious)	531.4	256.6	257.8	242.2	273.9	276.0	271.3	249.3	234.3	253.4	265.7	246.8

NA Not available. [1] Prior to 1997, reported as Imported. [2] Prior to 1997, reported as Grains. [3] Incorporated into Grains and Oilseeds beginning 1997.

Source: Bridge Commodity Research Bureau (CRB), Chicago, IL, *CRB Commodity Index Report,* weekly (copyright).

No. 692. Indexes of Spot Primary Market Prices: 1980 to 2001

[1967=100. Computed weekly for 1980; daily thereafter. Represents unweighted geometric average of price quotations of 23 commodities; much more sensitive to changes in market conditions than is a monthly producer price index]

Items and number of commodities	1980	1985	1990	1994	1995	1996	1997	1998	1999	2000	2001
All commodities (23)	**265.1**	**251.4**	**279.2**	**261.5**	**290.6**	**297.7**	**271.8**	**235.2**	**227.3**	**224.0**	**212.1**
Foodstuffs (10).	260.9	248.1	231.5	215.5	229.1	251.3	227.3	197.5	178.1	184.7	204.6
Raw industrials (13)	268.0	253.6	317.0	299.2	348.2	334.9	307.5	265.3	268.9	255.8	217.3
Livestock and products (5)	250.5	284.5	306.9	296.9	314.6	338.4	306.1	232.3	265.7	265.5	257.2
Metals (5)	257.9	220.2	313.9	262.1	306.7	296.7	269.8	218.5	261.6	214.3	172.5
Textiles and fibers (4)	234.7	220.8	259.4	252.6	286.0	274.6	261.5	237.5	223.8	245.7	217.4
Fats and oils (4)	229.5	273.1	193.3	209.6	228.3	245.7	257.1	236.0	174.8	163.6	175.8

Source: Bridge Commodity Research Bureau, Chicago, IL, *CRB Commodity Index Report*, weekly (copyright).

No. 693. Average Prices of Selected Fuels and Electricity: 1980 to 2001

[In dollars per unit, except electricity, in cents per kWh. Represents price to end-users, except as noted]

Type	Unit [1]	1980	1990	1994	1995	1996	1997	1998	1999	2000	2001
Crude oil, composite [2] . . .	Barrel	28.07	22.22	15.59	17.23	20.71	19.04	12.52	17.51	28.26	22.96
Motor gasoline: [3]											
Unleaded regular	Gallon.	1.25	1.16	1.11	1.15	1.23	1.23	1.06	1.17	1.51	1.46
Unleaded premium . . .	Gallon.	(NA)	1.35	1.31	1.34	1.41	1.42	1.25	1.36	1.69	1.66
No. 2 heating oil.	Gallon.	0.97	1.06	0.88	0.87	0.99	0.98	0.85	0.88	1.31	1.25
No. 2 diesel fuel.	Gallon.	0.82	0.73	0.55	0.56	0.68	0.64	0.49	0.58	0.94	0.84
Residual fuel oil	Gallon.	0.61	0.44	0.35	0.39	0.46	0.42	0.31	0.37	0.60	0.53
Natural gas, residential . .	1,000 cu/ft. .	3.68	5.80	6.41	6.06	6.34	6.94	6.82	6.69	7.76	(NA)
Electricity, residential. . . .	kWh	5.36	7.83	8.38	8.40	8.36	8.43	8.26	8.16	8.22	8.48

NA Not available. [1] See headnote. [2] Refiner acquisition cost. [3] Average, all service.

Source: U.S. Energy Information Administration, *Monthly Energy Review*.

No. 694. Weekly Food Cost by Type of Family: 1990 and 2001

[In dollars. Assumes that food for all meals and snacks is purchased at the store and prepared at home. See source for details on estimation procedures]

Family type	December 1990				December 2001			
	Thrifty-plan	Low-cost plan	Moderate-cost plan	Liberal-plan	Thrifty-plan	Low-cost plan	Moderate-cost plan	Liberal-plan
FAMILIES								
Family of two:								
20-50 years.	48.10	60.60	74.70	92.70	62.60	80.20	98.70	122.80
51 years and over	45.60	58.30	71.80	85.80	59.10	77.10	95.20	114.00
Family of four:								
Couple, 20-50 years and children—								
1-2 and 3-5 years	70.10	87.30	106.60	131.00	91.10	115.30	141.00	173.40
6-8 and 9-11 years	80.10	102.60	128.30	154.40	105.10	136.00	169.40	204.10
INDIVIDUALS [1]								
Child:								
1-2 years	12.70	15.40	18.00	21.80	16.40	20.20	23.80	28.90
3-5 years	13.70	16.80	20.70	24.90	17.80	22.20	27.50	32.90
6-8 years	16.60	22.20	27.90	32.50	22.10	29.60	36.80	42.80
9-11 years	19.80	25.30	32.50	37.60	26.10	33.50	42.90	49.70
Male:								
12-14 years.	20.60	28.60	35.70	42.00	27.10	37.90	47.00	55.30
15-19 years.	21.40	29.60	36.80	42.60	27.90	39.10	48.70	56.20
20-50 years.	22.90	29.30	36.60	44.30	29.80	38.90	48.40	58.60
51 years and over	20.90	27.90	34.30	41.10	27.10	37.00	45.50	54.60
Female:								
12-19 years.	20.80	24.80	30.10	36.30	27.10	32.70	39.60	47.90
20-50 years.	20.80	25.80	31.30	40.00	27.10	34.00	41.30	53.00
51 years and over	20.60	25.10	31.00	36.90	26.60	33.10	41.00	49.00

[1] The costs given are for individuals in four-person families. For individuals in other size families, the following adjustments are suggested: one-person, add 20 percent; two-person, add 10 percent; three-person, add 5 percent; five- or six-person, subtract 5 percent; seven- (or more) person, subtract 10 percent.

Source: U.S. Dept. of Agriculture, *Agricultural Research Service,* monthly. See also <http://www.usda.gov/fcs/cnpp.htm>.

U.S. Census Bureau, Statistical Abstract of the United States: 2002

No. 695. Food—Retail Prices of Selected Items: 1990 to 2001

[In dollars per pound, except as indicated. As of December]

Food	1990	1994	1995	1996	1997	1998	1999	2000	2001
Cereals and bakery products:									
Flour, white, all purpose	0.24	0.23	0.24	0.29	0.28	0.28	0.27	0.28	0.28
Rice, white, lg. grain, raw	0.49	0.53	0.55	0.55	0.58	0.54	0.50	(NA)	(NA)
Spaghetti and macaroni	0.85	0.87	0.88	0.85	0.88	0.88	0.88	0.88	0.91
Bread, whole wheat.	(NA)	1.12	1.15	1.30	1.30	1.32	1.36	1.36	1.46
Meats, poultry, fish and eggs:									
Ground beef, 100% beef	1.63	1.38	1.40	1.42	1.39	1.39	1.53	1.63	1.71
Ground beef, lean and extra lean.	(NA)	2.14	2.04	2.05	2.06	2.08	2.15	2.33	2.51
Sirloin steak, bone-in.	3.65	(NA)	(NA)	(NA)	(NA)	(NA)	(NA)	(NA)	(NA)
T-bone steak	5.45	5.86	5.92	5.87	6.07	6.40	6.71	6.82	7.31
Pork:									
Bacon, sliced	2.28	1.89	2.17	2.64	2.61	2.58	2.75	3.03	3.30
Chops, center cut, bone-in	3.32	3.03	3.29	3.44	3.39	3.03	3.21	3.46	3.53
Sausage	2.42	1.85	1.92	2.15	2.08	2.43	2.50	2.75	2.87
Poultry:									
Chicken, fresh, whole	0.86	0.90	0.94	1.00	1.00	1.06	1.05	1.08	1.11
Chicken breast, bone-in	2.00	1.91	1.95	2.09	1.99	2.11	2.08	2.14	2.11
Turkey, frozen, whole.	0.96	0.98	0.99	1.02	0.98	0.95	0.98	0.99	1.00
Tuna, light, chunk, canned	2.11	2.02	2.00	2.03	2.03	2.22	2.03	1.92	1.96
Eggs, Grade A, large, (dozen)	1.00	0.87	1.16	1.31	1.17	1.09	0.92	0.96	0.93
Dairy products:									
Milk, fresh, whole, fortified (1/2 gal.)	1.39	1.44	1.48	1.65	1.61	(NA)	(NA)	(NA)	(NA)
Butter, salted, grade AA, stick	1.92	1.54	1.73	2.17	2.46	3.18	2.27	2.80	3.31
Ice cream, prepack., bulk, reg. (1/2 gal.) .	2.54	2.62	2.68	2.94	3.02	3.30	3.40	3.66	3.84
Fresh fruits and vegetables:									
Apples, red delicious	0.77	0.72	0.83	0.89	0.90	0.85	0.92	0.82	0.89
Bananas	0.43	0.46	0.45	0.48	0.46	0.51	0.49	0.49	0.51
Oranges, navel.	0.56	0.55	0.64	0.59	0.58	0.61	0.64	0.62	0.71
Grapefruit	0.56	0.47	0.49	0.55	0.53	0.55	0.58	0.58	0.60
Grapes, thompson seedless	(NA)	2.13	1.86	(NA)	2.19	(NA)	2.40	2.36	(NA)
Lemons.	0.97	1.04	1.12	1.14	1.06	1.37	1.41	1.11	1.40
Pears, Anjou	0.79	(NA)	(NA)	1.06	0.85	0.98	1.03	(NA)	0.98
Potatoes, white.	0.32	0.34	0.38	0.34	0.37	0.38	0.40	0.35	0.41
Tomatoes, field grown	0.86	1.43	1.51	1.21	1.62	1.80	1.41	1.57	1.40
Cabbage	0.39	0.45	0.41	0.40	0.46	0.42	0.42	(NA)	(NA)
Carrots, short trimmed and topped.	0.44	0.48	0.53	0.54	0.50	0.54	0.52	(NA)	(NA)
Celery.	0.49	0.52	0.54	0.44	0.57	0.53	0.56	(NA)	(NA)
Cucumbers	0.56	0.69	0.53	0.60	0.58	(NA)	0.84	(NA)	(NA)
Onions, dry yellow.	(NA)	0.43	0.41	0.46	0.46	(NA)	(NA)	(NA)	(NA)
Peppers, sweet	(NA)	1.52	1.32	1.34	1.54	1.46	1.53	(NA)	(NA)

NA Not available.

Source: U.S. Bureau of Labor Statistics, *Monthly Labor Review* and *CPI Detailed Report,* January issues.

No. 696. Import Price Indexes—Selected Commodities: 1990 to 2001

[1995 = 100. Indexes are weighted by the 1990 Tariff Schedule of the United States Annotated, a scheme for describing and reporting product composition and value of U.S. imports. Import prices are based on U.S. dollar prices paid by importer. F.o.b. = Free on board; c.i.f. = Cost, insurance, and freight; n.e.s. = Not elsewhere specified]

Commodity	1990	1995 [1]	1996	1997	1998	1999	2000	2001
All commodities.	90.3	100.8	100.1	98.2	92.6	92.4	100.2	97.6
Food and live animals.	84.9	100.1	94.7	103.7	98.0	93.3	99.0	96.0
Meat.	116.3	99.1	90.4	101.9	98.3	94.5	100.8	106.2
Fish	77.9	101.6	97.5	103.6	109.4	104.3	99.3	90.0
Crustaceans; fresh, chilled, frozen, salted or dried. .	73.3	103.4	95.0	103.5	106.4	99.0	100.9	83.6
Beverages and tobacco.	86.1	99.7	103.6	107.5	109.6	110.4	100.4	101.7
Crude materials.	82.4	99.8	94.3	97.4	87.7	90.3	99.4	102.8
Mineral fuels and related products.	92.9	105.1	110.6	104.6	77.6	92.7	101.3	90.4
Crude petroleum and petroleum products	91.7	105.4	111.0	104.0	73.4	91.3	102.2	89.3
Natural gas	112.7	101.2	108.2	113.3	111.9	106.5	95.2	97.4
Chemicals and related products	88.3	100.7	98.8	96.4	93.6	90.6	99.8	100.5
Intermediate manufactured products	88.8	99.8	99.2	96.8	94.0	92.0	100.4	98.0
Machinery and transport equipment.	90.2	100.6	98.6	95.7	91.8	90.3	100.1	98.5
Computer equipment and office machines	119.2	100.4	91.7	81.2	70.4	63.1	99.9	93.6
Computer equipment	143.0	99.7	93.0	80.8	66.5	54.7	100.4	89.3
Telecommunications [2]	102.0	100.5	97.3	93.4	89.4	87.6	100.2	97.2
Electrical machinery and equipment	92.0	101.6	95.5	90.2	84.5	82.7	100.7	98.8
Road vehicles	84.3	100.0	100.4	100.8	101.1	102.3	100.1	99.8
Miscellaneous manufactured articles	92.1	100.4	100.7	100.2	98.6	97.8	99.7	99.8
Plumbing, heating & lighting fixtures.	95.3	100.4	99.5	96.2	96.0	93.0	99.2	99.2
Furniture and parts	93.7	100.7	100.8	102.9	100.2	98.7	99.6	98.5
Articles of apparel and clothing	97.6	100.1	101.5	102.6	102.7	101.8	99.6	100.6
Footwear.	97.2	100.0	101.3	101.1	100.7	100.7	99.6	100.1

[1] June 1995 and 2000 may not equal 100 because indexes were reweighted to an "average" trade value in 1995 and 2000.
[2] Includes sound recording and reproducing equipment.

Source: U.S. Bureau of Labor Statistics, *U.S. Import and Export Price Indexes,* monthly.

U.S. Census Bureau, Statistical Abstract of the United States: 2002

No. 697. Export Price Indexes—Selected Commodities: 1990 to 2001

[1990=100. Indexes are weighted by 1980 export values according to the Schedule B classification system of the U.S. Census Bureau. Prices used in these indexes were collected from a sample of U.S. manufacturers of exports and are factory transaction prices, except as noted. F.a.s. = free alongside ship. N.e.s. = not elsewhere specified. F.o.b. = free on board]

Commodities	1990	1995 [1]	1996	1997	1998	1999	2000 [1]	2001
All commodities	95.1	104.5	105.4	103.2	99.9	98.2	100.1	99.4
Food and live animals	102.4	112.1	140.4	113.3	104.6	102.6	100.6	101.1
Meat	81.4	95.7	97.4	91.3	93.7	87.6	104.8	106.1
Fish	86.8	107.1	92.8	88.5	83.8	123.0	100.6	90.8
Cereals and cereal preparations	126.5	133.2	203.3	128.9	115.4	106.0	100.0	102.6
Wheat	116.9	132.5	188.0	126.7	109.6	101.4	99.4	111.3
Maize	144.0	144.6	243.9	133.5	119.5	108.3	101.0	95.9
Fruits and vegetables	93.2	107.2	117.8	113.3	109.8	109.9	97.9	98.6
Feeding stuff for animals	99.5	104.9	130.7	135.7	101.3	92.5	100.4	101.1
Miscellaneous food products	94.0	94.8	96.6	96.9	98.3	100.1	100.0	100.1
Beverages and tobacco	84.9	98.2	98.8	99.1	98.2	99.4	100.0	98.4
Tobacco and tobacco manufactures	85.0	98.1	98.6	98.9	97.8	99.2	99.9	98.2
Crude materials	96.7	125.4	108.7	112.4	98.7	90.2	101.6	92.6
Oil seeds and oleaginous fruits	116.1	115.6	152.0	161.1	122.8	94.8	103.3	95.6
Cork and wood	76.5	117.5	109.0	107.3	94.5	94.4	99.8	92.8
Pulp and waste paper	70.9	122.2	62.3	72.1	70.1	72.3	106.9	80.6
Textile fibers	118.2	154.3	131.6	120.3	114.4	99.1	100.5	90.9
Metalliferous ores and metal scrap	105.9	132.2	113.4	116.4	97.2	89.7	99.2	91.0
Mineral fuels and related materials	67.2	68.5	73.3	74.5	69.3	68.5	97.4	103.2
Coal, coke and briquettes	109.5	106.4	109.5	108.2	106.2	104.3	99.5	106.9
Crude petroleum and petroleum products	57.5	59.6	65.4	68.7	61.4	61.9	96.8	101.8
Chemicals and related products	90.4	108.4	102.6	102.0	97.9	96.4	100.9	96.2
Organic chemicals	93.9	122.8	100.9	97.6	88.7	86.4	102.1	90.6
Chemical materials and products, n.e.s.	86.4	100.7	102.6	104.6	101.2	100.3	99.7	99.1
Intermediate manufactured products	86.8	100.6	97.7	98.1	97.7	96.7	100.2	99.5
Rubber manufactures	81.4	95.7	98.6	99.0	97.7	101.2	100.1	99.8
Paper and paperboard products	90.8	115.6	97.7	93.4	93.7	93.3	100.5	97.4
Textiles	91.2	102.8	105.5	105.0	104.9	100.8	100.2	98.5
Nonmetallic mineral manufactures	85.8	94.3	95.4	98.3	100.6	100.2	100.4	100.8
Nonferrous metals	87.1	98.2	91.9	92.0	86.7	83.7	98.5	98.0
Manufactures of metals, n.e.s.	81.2	92.3	93.6	96.3	98.6	100.2	100.9	101.5
Machinery and transport equipment [2]	97.9	102.8	103.6	103.3	101.4	100.3	100.0	100.3
Power generating machinery [3]	77.0	88.5	92.9	94.4	95.3	97.6	99.7	102.3
Rotating electric plant and parts thereof, n.e.s.	87.0	97.9	99.8	100.5	100.4	100.1	100.1	99.8
Machinery specialized for particular industries	82.7	94.0	96.5	98.0	99.0	99.8	100.2	100.3
Agricultural machinery and parts [4]	86.0	95.6	97.2	98.0	98.3	98.9	99.9	98.9
Civil engineering and contractors, plant and equip.	81.8	93.6	94.8	96.4	98.8	100.4	100.3	100.4
Metalworking machinery	82.1	92.3	94.4	96.3	100.0	100.4	99.3	101.0
General industrial machines, parts, n.e.s.	82.5	92.0	94.8	97.3	98.1	99.2	100.1	101.3
Computer equipment and office machines	193.2	147.5	137.2	123.9	112.0	104.8	99.9	95.6
Computer equipment	234.5	160.7	142.6	125.2	116.9	106.1	99.7	96.0
Telecommunications [5]	97.3	103.8	104.6	103.0	102.1	100.2	100.3	99.8
Electrical machinery and equipment	112.7	117.2	115.3	112.3	107.2	103.1	99.8	98.3
Electronic valves, diodes, transistors & integr. cir.	135.0	135.1	130.0	121.9	112.1	105.0	99.5	95.4
Road vehicles	88.7	96.1	97.2	98.0	98.1	98.6	100.0	100.2
Miscellaneous manufactured articles	90.5	98.6	99.4	100.3	99.4	99.6	99.7	100.1

NA Not available.   [1] June 1995 and 2000 may not equal 100 because indexes were reweighted to an "average" trade value in 1995 and 2000.   [2] Excludes military and commercial aircraft.   [3] Includes equipment.   [4] Excludes tractors.   [5] Includes sound recording and reproducing equipment.

Source: U.S. Bureau of Labor Statistics, *U.S. Import and Export Price Indexes,* monthly.

U.S. Census Bureau, Statistical Abstract of the United States: 2002

No. 698. Refiner/Reseller Sales Price of Gasoline by State: 1999 to 2001

[In cents per gallon. As of March. Represents all refinery and gas plant operators' sales through company-operated retail outlets. Gasoline prices exclude excise taxes]

State	Gasoline excise taxes 2000	Average, all grades			Midgrade			Premium		
		1999	2000	2001	1999	2000	2001	1999	2000	2001
United States	(NA)	63.2	111.6	102.6	68.1	117.5	109.2	76.0	125.0	117.3
Alabama	18.0	61.7	109.7	100.7	65.6	115.2	107.3	73.8	123.1	116.6
Alaska	8.0	93.8	127.6	137.1	101.6	130.2	144.6	109.7	142.7	155.8
Arizona	18.0	73.9	118.9	113.9	79.2	126.2	121.4	90.5	136.8	132.2
Arkansas	20.5	56.6	107.4	96.9	62.9	112.0	102.1	71.2	120.0	110.5
California	18.0	79.9	125.6	120.1	83.6	130.5	123.9	92.7	138.7	133.4
Colorado	22.0	66.0	109.9	107.7	72.2	120.0	115.5	82.7	125.4	123.1
Connecticut	25.0	64.2	114.8	107.0	70.3	120.6	115.0	79.3	128.1	123.8
Delaware	23.0	57.8	108.4	100.5	63.7	114.7	107.8	72.4	119.7	116.3
District of Columbia . .	20.0	(D)	(D)	(D)	(D)	(D)	(D)	(D)	(D)	(D)
Florida	13.6	61.2	110.1	98.2	66.2	116.3	104.8	73.3	122.6	112.0
Georgia	7.5	56.3	106.4	95.5	60.8	112.2	100.8	69.4	119.2	109.5
Hawaii	16.0	103.9	125.6	146.3	106.8	127.7	149.9	115.1	136.3	153.8
Idaho.	25.0	66.5	114.1	103.4	73.1	119.7	109.8	81.4	126.2	117.8
Illinois	19.0	65.8	112.6	102.4	68.6	116.6	108.8	80.9	127.6	119.3
Indiana	15.0	62.1	109.5	100.5	67.9	115.5	107.2	75.1	122.3	115.3
Iowa	20.0	59.1	107.2	99.0	63.0	109.3	101.9	67.1	116.6	108.7
Kansas	20.0	57.3	105.4	97.1	62.8	111.4	103.6	68.5	118.8	110.7
Kentucky	16.4	64.2	110.5	101.5	69.4	116.8	107.8	78.0	124.3	116.1
Louisiana	20.0	59.0	110.2	98.4	64.3	116.9	105.7	72.1	123.9	115.2
Maine	22.0	63.4	115.7	105.5	70.5	121.7	113.1	80.0	127.3	120.4
Maryland	23.5	59.7	107.9	100.5	64.7	113.3	107.1	71.1	117.4	111.2
Massachusetts	21.0	60.6	114.9	109.0	66.3	120.1	115.8	74.4	126.4	123.2
Michigan	19.0	59.9	108.7	96.6	66.6	113.4	101.6	72.7	121.7	111.4
Minnesota	20.0	68.0	113.1	108.9	70.4	117.0	110.8	78.2	125.1	119.9
Mississippi	18.4	61.7	111.2	104.7	64.9	116.2	110.7	74.5	125.5	119.9
Missouri.	17.0	57.0	108.4	99.7	62.9	116.0	106.6	72.0	124.0	115.6
Montana	27.0	58.3	115.8	101.8	(NA)	117.4	106.8	69.2	127.1	117.2
Nebraska	23.9	59.2	107.3	100.6	63.0	110.9	105.2	69.8	119.1	109.5
Nevada	24.8	79.6	131.0	126.8	86.1	140.1	138.2	94.8	145.1	141.0
New Hampshire.	19.5	62.5	114.5	107.0	68.3	119.8	114.3	77.2	126.4	121.7
New Jersey	10.5	63.4	114.7	106.7	67.8	120.0	112.7	76.1	126.5	120.0
New Mexico	18.5	64.6	111.5	102.6	70.9	120.1	110.2	78.5	126.3	117.7
New York	22.0	59.9	112.6	101.8	65.6	117.6	108.4	72.9	124.2	115.6
North Carolina.	24.3	57.9	109.0	98.1	62.0	114.6	103.7	71.7	123.6	112.1
North Dakota	21.0	66.9	112.7	109.8	72.1	118.3	114.4	70.2	120.5	115.0
Ohio	22.0	66.7	110.0	100.4	72.5	117.5	107.8	79.8	124.3	115.2
Oklahoma	17.0	57.1	107.3	92.0	60.9	113.3	96.9	67.5	119.5	104.3
Oregon	24.0	75.0	121.5	109.4	83.0	129.3	119.7	92.2	139.1	126.2
Pennsylvania	26.0	54.4	107.3	96.1	58.7	111.9	101.6	67.0	119.4	110.6
Rhode Island	29.0	57.5	109.9	102.8	63.3	114.9	110.0	71.9	121.3	116.8
South Carolina	16.0	56.5	108.6	95.4	61.5	115.4	101.7	70.4	123.6	110.7
South Dakota	22.0	64.3	114.1	109.2	66.7	114.9	115.2	77.8	125.1	118.1
Tennessee	20.0	58.0	108.0	96.2	62.3	113.7	102.0	71.2	120.2	108.6
Texas	20.0	57.4	106.3	94.4	62.5	112.8	102.1	70.6	119.7	108.7
Utah	24.5	67.8	111.7	100.0	71.2	116.5	104.2	80.4	125.5	112.9
Vermont.	20.0	63.6	116.3	106.8	67.8	121.5	112.8	75.7	128.0	118.2
Virginia	17.5	60.6	109.9	102.0	65.0	115.0	107.7	73.6	122.9	116.2
Washington	23.0	70.9	120.5	111.3	78.3	127.7	119.9	88.7	138.2	129.6
West Virginia	25.7	59.6	110.7	98.5	63.6	117.0	105.0	73.1	124.3	113.0
Wisconsin.	26.4	62.6	108.5	100.7	68.3	111.0	103.2	74.2	119.5	113.8
Wyoming	14.0	67.8	113.3	108.4	71.6	119.7	114.8	79.1	125.0	119.7

D Withheld to avoid disclosure of individual company data.   NA Not available.

Source: U.S. Energy Information Administration, *Petroleum Marketing Monthly*.

Section 15
Business Enterprise

This section relates to the place and behavior of the business firm and to business initiative in the American economy. It includes data on the number, type, and size of businesses; financial data of domestic and multinational U.S. corporations; business investments, expenditures, and profits; and sales and inventories.

The principal sources of these data are the *Survey of Current Business*, published by the Bureau of Economic Analysis (BEA), the *Federal Reserve Bulletin*, issued by the Board of Governors of the Federal Reserve System, the annual *Statistics of Income (SOI)* reports of the Internal Revenue Service (IRS), and the Census Bureau's Economic Census, *County Business Patterns,* and *Quarterly Financial Report for Manufacturing, Mining, and Trade Corporations (QFR).*

Business firms—A firm is generally defined as a business organization under a single management and may include one or more establishments. The terms firm, business, company, and enterprise are used interchangeably throughout this section. A firm doing business in more than one industry is classified by industry according to the major activity of the firm as a whole.

The IRS concept of a business firm relates primarily to the legal entity used for tax reporting purposes. A sole proprietorship is an unincorporated business owned by one person and may include large enterprises with many employees and hired managers and part-time operators. A partnership is an unincorporated business owned by two or more persons, each of whom has a financial interest in the business. A corporation is a business that is legally incorporated under state laws. While many corporations file consolidated tax returns, most corporate tax returns represent individual corporations, some

of which are affiliated through common ownership or control with other corporations filing separate returns.

Economic census—The economic census is the major source of facts about the structure and functioning of the nation's economy. It provides essential information for government, business, industry, and the general public. It furnishes an important part of the framework for such composite measures as the gross domestic product estimates, input/output measures, production and price indexes, and other statistical series that measure short-term changes in economic conditions. The Census Bureau takes the economic census every 5 years, covering years ending in "2" and "7." The economic census forms an integrated program at 5-year intervals since 1967, and before that for 1963, 1958, and 1954. Prior to that time, the individual censuses were taken separately at varying intervals.

The economic census is collected on an establishment basis. A company operating at more than one location is required to file a separate report for each store, factory, shop, or other location. Each establishment is assigned a separate industry classification based on its primary activity and not that of its parent company. Establishments responding to the establishment survey are classified into industries on the basis of their principal product or activity (determined by annual sales volume) in accordance with the *North American Industry Classification System—United States, 1997 manual* (see below).

More detailed information about the scope, coverage, classification system, data items, and publications for each of the economic censuses and related surveys is published in the *Guide to the Economic Censuses and Related Statistics*. More information on the methodology, procedures, and history of the censuses is

U.S. Census Bureau, Statistical Abstract of the United States: 2002

available in the *History of the 1997 Economic Census* found on the Census Bureau Web site at <http://www.census.gov/prod/ec97/pol00-hec.pdf>.

Data from the 1997 Economic Census were released through the Census Bureau's American FactFinder service, on CD-ROM, and in Adobe Acrobat PDF reports available on the Census Bureau Web site. For more information on these various media of release, see the following page on the Census Bureau Web site <http://www.census.gov/epcd/www/econ97.html>.

North American Industry Classification System (NAICS)—The 1997 Economic Census is the first census to present data based on the new NAICS. Previous census data were based on the Standard Industrial Classification (SIC) system. This new system of industrial classification was developed by experts on classification in government and private industry under the guidance of the Office of Information and Regulatory Affairs, Office of Management and Budget.

There are 20 NAICS sectors, which are subdivided into 96 subsectors (three-digit codes), 313 industry groups (four-digit codes), and, as implemented in the United States, 1,170 industries (five- and six-digit codes). While many of the individual NAICS industries correspond directly to industries as defined under the SIC system, most of the higher level groupings do not.

Most of the 1997 Economic Census data are issued on a NAICS basis as seen in the industry and geographic series from the census. Other related census reports remain on an SIC basis due to use of administrative records and other methodological and data processing issues. Current survey data from the Census Bureau as well as other statistical agencies are converting over time to NAICS after benchmarking to the 1997 Economic Census where appropriate or implementation of data collection on a NAICS basis.

No. 699. Number of Returns, Receipts, and Net Income by Type of Business: 1980 to 1999

[**8,932 represents 8,932,000.** Covers active enterprises only. Figures are estimates based on sample of unaudited tax returns; see Appendix III. Minus sign (-) indicates net loss]

Item	Number of returns (1,000)			Business receipts [2] (bil. dol.)			Net income (less loss) [3] (bil. dol.)		
	Nonfarm proprietor-ships [1]	Partner-ships	Corpora-tions	Nonfarm proprietor-ships [1]	Partner-ships	Corpora-tions	Nonfarm proprietor-ships [1]	Partner-ships	Corpora-tions
1980	8,932	1,380	2,711	411	286	6,172	55	8	239
1985	11,929	1,714	3,277	540	349	8,050	79	-9	240
1990	14,783	1,554	3,717	731	541	10,914	141	17	371
1991	15,181	1,515	3,803	713	539	10,963	142	21	345
1992	15,495	1,485	3,869	737	571	11,272	154	43	402
1993	15,848	1,468	3,965	757	627	11,814	156	67	498
1994	16,154	1,494	4,342	791	732	12,858	167	82	577
1995	16,424	1,581	4,474	807	854	13,969	169	107	714
1996	16,955	1,654	4,631	843	1,042	14,890	177	145	806
1997	17,176	1,759	4,710	870	1,297	15,890	187	168	915
1998	17,409	1,855	4,849	918	1,534	16,543	202	187	838
1999	17,576	1,937	4,936	969	1,829	18,009	208	228	929

[1] In 1980, represents individually owned businesses, including farms; thereafter, represents only nonfarm proprietors, i.e., business owners. [2] Excludes investment income except for partnerships and corporations in finance, insurance, and real estate before 1998. After 1997 finance and insurance, real estate, and management of companies included investment income for partnerships and corporations. Starting 1985, investment income no longer included for S corporations. [3] Net income (less loss) is defined differently by form of organization, basically as follows: (a) Proprietorships: Total taxable receipts less total business deductions, including cost of sales and operations, depletion, and certain capital expensing, excluding charitable contributions and owners' salaries; (b) Partnerships: Total taxable receipts (including investment income except capital gains) less deductions, including cost of sales and operations and certain payments to partners, excluding charitable contributions, oil and gas depletion, and certain capital expensing; (c) Corporations: Total taxable receipts (including investment income, capital gains, and income from foreign subsidiaries deemed received for tax purposes, except for S corporations beginning 1985) less business deductions, including cost of sales and operations, depletion, certain capital expensing, and officers' compensation excluding S corporation charitable contributions and investment expenses starting 1985; net income is before income tax.

Source: U.S. Internal Revenue Service, *Statistics of Income,* various publications.

No. 700. Number of Returns and Business Receipts by Size of Receipts: 1990 to 1999

[**3,717 represents 3,717,000.** Covers active enterprises only. Figures are estimates based on sample of unaudited tax returns; see Appendix III]

Size-class of receipts	Returns (1,000)					Business receipts [1] (bil. dol.)				
	1990	1995	1997	1998	1999	1990	1995	1997	1998	1999
Corporations.	3,717	4,474	4,710	4,849	4,936	10,914	13,969	15,890	16,543	18,009
Under $25,000 [2]	879	1,030	1,106	1,181	1,189	5	4	4	4	4
$25,000 to $49,999	252	288	306	287	297	9	11	11	11	11
$50,000 to $99,999	359	447	453	456	487	26	33	33	34	36
$100,000 to $499,999.	1,162	1,393	1,450	1,481	1,500	291	350	363	368	379
$500,000 to $999,999.	416	513	533	552	546	294	361	376	389	388
$1,000,000 or more	649	803	862	892	918	10,289	13,210	15,102	15,738	17,191
Partnerships	1,554	1,581	1,759	1,855	1,937	541	854	1,297	1,534	1,829
Under $25,000 [2]	963	931	987	1,038	1,036	4	4	4	4	4
$25,000 to $49,999	126	133	151	157	170	5	5	5	6	6
$50,000 to $99,999	133	142	165	157	187	10	10	12	11	14
$100,000 to $499,999.	222	245	294	320	338	51	56	68	73	79
$500,000 to $999,999.	52	59	68	77	84	36	42	48	54	59
$1,000,000 or more	57	69	94	107	122	435	738	1,160	1,385	1,667
Nonfarm proprietorships	14,783	16,424	17,176	17,409	17,576	731	807	870	918	969
Under $25,000 [2]	10,196	11,317	11,703	11,767	11,821	69	76	79	79	80
$25,000 to $49,999	1,660	1,983	2,111	2,112	2,227	58	71	75	75	79
$50,000 to $99,999	1,282	1,393	1,491	1,590	1,558	91	99	107	113	110
$100,000 to $499,999.	1,444	1,514	1,637	1,686	1,702	296	310	332	345	349
$500,000 to $999,999.	143	147	160	175	182	97	100	107	118	123
$1,000,000 or more	57	70	75	78	86	119	151	170	188	227

[1] Excludes investment income except for partnerships and corporations in finance, insurance, and real estate before 1998. After 1997 finance and insurance, real estate, and management of companies included investment income for partnerships and corporations. [2] Includes firms with no receipts.

Source: U.S. Internal Revenue Service, *Statistics of Income Bulletin;* and unpublished data.

No. 701. Number of Returns, Receipts, and Net Income by Type of Business and Industry: 1999

[17,576 represents 17,576,000. Covers active enterprises only. Figures are estimates based on sample of unaudited tax returns; see Appendix III. Based on the North American Industry Classification System. Minus sign (-) indicates net loss]

Industry	Number of returns (1,000)			Business receipts [1] (bil. dol.)			Net income (less loss) (bil. dol.)		
	Non-farm proprietor-ships	Partner-ships	Corpo-rations	Non-farm proprietor-ships	Partner-ships	Corpo-rations	Non-farm proprietor-ships	Partner-ships	Corpo-rations
Total [2]	17,576	1,937	4,936	969	1,829	18,009	208	228	929
Agriculture, forestry, fishing, and hunting [3]	307	115	142	17	14	105	1	1	1
Mining	117	28	31	4	29	110	(Z)	6	(Z)
Utilities	9	3	7	(Z)	62	479	(Z)	2	39
Construction	2,284	128	580	154	126	974	28	9	33
Special trade contractors	1,764	41	335	101	19	406	21	2	15
Manufacturing	360	37	298	27	310	4,802	4	13	247
Wholesale and retail trade [4]	2,669	142	948	228	373	4,789	17	6	92
Wholesale trade	360	33	350	43	172	2,249	5	4	44
Retail trade [5]	2,309	109	596	185	200	2,539	11	2	48
Motor vehicle and parts dealers	126	13	94	33	54	703	1	1	8
Food and beverage stores	109	13	71	32	32	391	1	(Z)	7
Gasoline stations	33	7	34	24	15	105	1	(-Z)	1
Transportation and warehousing	790	22	160	46	38	485	7	2	10
Information	237	20	108	7	116	761	2	-7	40
Broadcasting and telecommunications	36	6	30	1	79	429	(Z)	-10	22
Finance and insurance	579	219	218	86	219	3,008	14	84	361
Real estate and rental and leasing	851	858	521	43	134	185	18	50	6
Professional, scientific, and technical services [5]	2,444	123	657	107	172	576	45	41	13
Legal services	324	31	79	28	72	50	13	27	3
Accounting, tax preparation, bookkeeping, and payroll services	390	13	50	9	35	23	4	6	2
Management, scientific, and technical consulting services	590	25	166	24	19	97	13	4	4
Management of companies and enterprises	(NA)	13	43	(NA)	18	519	(NA)	7	58
Administrative and support and waste management and remediation services	1,456	33	205	37	31	284	11	2	7
Educational services	326	6	35	4	1	21	2	(Z)	1
Health care and social assistance	1,520	40	303	83	66	371	36	8	5
Arts, entertainment and recreation	1,040	34	94	19	25	71	5	(Z)	1
Accommodation and food services	315	63	252	36	82	319	2	3	10
Accommodation	61	22	34	5	47	96	(Z)	2	3
Food services and drinking places	254	41	219	31	35	223	2	1	7
Other services [5]	2,007	52	306	66	12	146	15	1	4
Auto repair and maintenance	327	16	(NA)	23	5	(NA)	3	(Z)	(NA)
Personal and laundry services	1,105	29	119	28	5	58	8	(Z)	2
Religious, grantmaking, civic, professional, and similar organizations	211	(Z)	43	2	(Z)	7	1	(Z)	(Z)
Unclassified	263	2	27	3	1	5	1	(Z)	(Z)

NA Not available.   Z Less than 500 or $500 million.   [1] Includes investment income for partnerships and corporations in finance and insurance, real estate, and management of companies industries. Excludes investment income for S corporations. [2] For corporations, includes businesses not allocable to individual industries.   [3] For corporations represents agricultural services only.   [4] For corporations includes trade business not identified as wholesale or retail.   [5] Includes other industries not shown separately.

Source: U.S. Internal Revenue Service, *Statistics of Income,* various publications.

No. 702. Nonfarm Sole Proprietorships—Selected Income and Deduction Items: 1990 to 1999

[In millions of dollars (730,606 represents $730,606,000,000) except as indicated. All figures are estimates based on sample. Tax law changes have affected the comparability of the data over time; see *Statistics of Income* reports for a description]

Item	1990	1992	1993	1994	1995	1996	1997	1998	1999
Number of returns (1,000)	14,783	15,495	15,848	16,154	16,424	16,955	17,176	17,409	17,576
Businesses with net income (1,000).	11,222	11,720	11,872	12,187	12,213	12,524	12,703	13,080	13,159
Business receipts	730,606	737,082	757,215	790,630	807,364	843,234	870,392	918,268	969,347
Income from sales and operations .	719,008	725,666	746,306	778,494	796,597	831,546	858,453	905,138	955,392
Business deductions [1]	589,250	583,147	600,765	623,833	638,127	666,461	683,872	716,157	761,428
Cost of goods sold/operations [1] . . .	291,010	274,220	289,578	301,004	306,959	316,421	319,557	341,133	370,079
Purchases	210,225	204,317	210,260	216,365	219,305	220,029	224,259	231,405	255,539
Labor costs.	22,680	18,838	20,685	23,497	24,383	26,002	24,941	27,448	28,723
Materials and supplies	30,195	28,825	32,701	34,304	34,427	40,473	37,552	42,162	41,757
Car and truck expenses	21,766	23,920	26,714	30,845	32,785	36,700	38,728	39,716	40,787
Commissions	8,816	10,457	8,707	9,029	9,592	10,792	10,986	10,722	11,228
Depreciation.	23,735	23,274	24,964	26,158	26,738	27,883	28,625	29,136	30,638
Pension and profit sharing plans . .	586	528	636	605	649	707	728	757	870
Insurance.	13,358	13,260	13,173	13,289	12,978	13,195	13,299	12,938	13,220
Interest paid.	13,312	10,406	9,431	9,170	10,057	10,567	10,884	11,159	11,224
Rent paid.	23,392	25,148	25,008	26,769	27,503	28,516	29,326	30,460	31,418
Repairs	8,941	9,706	9,847	10,385	10,172	10,715	10,897	11,350	11,697
Salaries and wages (net)	46,998	52,316	52,046	53,649	54,471	56,322	57,746	58,865	61,204
Taxes paid	10,342	12,618	13,062	13,600	13,471	13,736	13,774	13,731	14,000
Utilities	13,539	14,547	16,069	16,918	17,206	18,162	18,575	18,431	18,466
Net income (less loss) [2].	141,430	153,960	156,459	166,799	169,262	176,756	186,644	202,275	207,947
Net income [2]	161,657	173,473	176,983	187,845	191,729	200,124	210,465	226,190	233,405

[1] Includes other amounts not shown separately. [2] After adjustment for the passive loss carryover from prior years. Therefore, "business receipts" minus "total deductions" do not equal "net income."

Source: U.S. Internal Revenue Service, *Statistics of Income Bulletin.*

No. 703. Partnerships—Selected Income and Balance Sheet Items: 1990 to 1999

[In billions of dollars (1,735 represents $1,735,000,000,000), except as indicated. Covers active partnerships only. All figures are estimates based on samples. See Appendix III]

Item	1990	1992	1993	1994	1995	1996	1997	1998	1999
Number of returns (1,000)	1,554	1,485	1,468	1,494	1,581	1,654	1,759	1,855	1,937
Number with net income (1,000). . .	854	856	870	890	955	1,010	1,092	1,171	1,226
Number of partners (1,000).	17,095	15,735	15,627	14,990	15,606	15,662	16,184	15,663	15,924
Assets [1][2]	1,735	1,907	2,118	2,295	2,719	3,368	4,171	5,127	5,999
Depreciable assets (net)	681	701	698	712	767	848	980	1,153	1,314
Inventories, end of year	57	62	71	76	88	137	147	176	174
Land	215	213	207	208	221	232	257	291	326
Liabilities [1][2]	1,415	1,508	1,620	1,662	1,886	2,235	2,658	3,151	3,453
Accounts payable	67	79	80	81	91	121	159	191	244
Short-term debt [3]	88	115	131	126	124	126	127	230	232
Long-term debt [4]	498	486	489	508	544	607	706	884	989
Nonrecourse loans.	470	476	478	463	466	474	492	523	582
Partners' capital accounts [2]	320	399	499	633	832	1,133	1,513	1,976	2,546
Receipts [1]	566	597	656	762	890	1,089	1,354	1,603	1,907
Business receipts [5]	483	515	561	732	854	1,042	1,297	1,534	1,829
Interest received	21	16	16	19	31	33	41	51	62
Deductions [1]	550	554	589	680	784	943	1,186	1,416	1,679
Cost of goods sold/operations . . .	243	249	273	335	395	486	625	737	902
Salaries and wages	56	62	65	70	80	94	115	143	170
Taxes paid	9	10	11	12	13	15	18	24	27
Interest paid	30	25	27	36	43	49	60	73	74
Depreciation.	60	60	60	22	23	29	38	43	52
Net income (less loss)	17	43	67	82	107	145	168	187	228
Net income.	116	122	137	151	179	228	262	298	348

[1] Includes items not shown separately. [2] Assets, liabilities, and partners' capital accounts are understated because not all partnerships file complete balance sheets. [3] Mortgages, notes, and bonds payable in less than 1 year. [4] Mortgages, notes, and bonds payable in 1 year or more. [5] Excludes investment income except for partnerships in finance, insurance, and real estate from 1994 to 1997. After 1997 finance and insurance, real estate, and management of companies included investment income for partnerships.

Source: U.S. Internal Revenue Service, *Statistics of Income,* various issues.

U.S. Census Bureau, Statistical Abstract of the United States: 2002

No. 704. Partnerships—Selected Items by Industry: 1999

[In millions of dollars (5,998,953 represents $5,998,953,000,000), except as indicated. Covers active partnerships only. Includes partnerships not allocable by industry. Figures are estimates based on samples. Based on the North American Industry Classification System. See Appendix III]

Year	Number of partnerships (1,000) Total	With net income	With net loss	Number of partners (1,000)	Total assets [1]	Business receipts [2]	Total deductions	Net income less loss	Net income	Net loss
Total	1,937	1,226	711	15,924	5,998,953	1,829,073	1,678,733	228,438	348,468	120,030
Agriculture, forestry, fishing and hunting	115	66	49	471	65,978	13,518	17,764	1,344	4,938	3,595
Mining	28	17	11	687	85,393	28,636	26,703	6,252	10,238	3,985
Utilities	3	1	1	68	70,690	62,157	62,584	1,819	3,729	1,910
Construction	128	80	48	431	125,593	125,518	120,269	9,361	13,191	3,831
Manufacturing	37	20	18	169	255,103	309,694	308,138	13,058	21,586	8,528
Wholesale trade	33	18	15	124	56,086	172,271	170,811	4,248	6,283	2,035
Retail trade	109	56	53	310	68,811	200,423	201,783	2,193	5,627	3,434
Transportation & warehousing	22	13	10	288	63,884	38,182	39,314	2,047	4,546	2,499
Information	20	9	12	343	257,283	116,418	132,126	-6,931	20,131	27,061
Finance and insurance	219	166	53	3,797	2,811,320	219,448	135,805	83,643	93,379	9,736
Real estate & rental & leasing	858	559	299	7,604	1,662,831	134,449	91,995	49,666	83,004	33,338
Professional, scientific, and technical services	123	79	43	454	76,961	172,278	140,297	40,628	44,880	4,252
Management of companies	13	9	4	177	165,839	17,837	10,909	6,928	11,037	4,109
Admin/support and waste management/remediation services	33	21	12	81	20,767	31,147	30,613	1,513	2,387	875
Educational services	6	3	3	14	1,932	1,360	1,276	123	204	81
Health care and social assistance	40	26	14	234	45,899	65,685	61,969	8,487	11,256	2,769
Arts, entertainment and recreation	34	15	18	231	49,625	25,444	31,844	422	3,926	3,504
Accommodation and food services	63	33	30	296	105,426	81,805	82,236	2,734	6,602	3,868
Other services	52	34	18	139	8,948	12,299	11,738	884	1,417	533
Nature of business not allocable	2	1	1	6	586	505	559	19	107	88

[1] Total assets are understated because not all partnerships file complete balance sheets. [2] Finance and insurance, real estate, and management of companies includes investment income for partnerships.

Source: U.S. Internal Revenue Service, *Statistics of Income*, various issues.

No. 705. Corporate Funds—Sources and Uses: 1990 to 2001

[In billions of dollars (236 represents $236,000,000,000). Covers nonfarm nonfinancial corporate business]

Item	1990	1992	1993	1994	1995	1996	1997	1998	1999	2000	2001
Profits before tax (book)	236	257	305	381	422	459	494	460	469	502	379
-Profit tax accruals	95	91	105	128	136	150	158	154	170	186	142
-Dividends	118	134	149	158	178	201	216	241	238	267	303
+Consumption of fixed capital	371	391	408	445	472	504	540	571	618	660	707
=U.S. internal funds, book	393	424	459	540	579	612	660	636	678	708	641
+Foreign earnings retained abroad	51	45	56	39	59	60	59	63	75	99	115
+Inventory valuation adjustment (IVA)	-13	-3	-4	-12	-18	3	8	18	-3	-12	4
=Internal funds + IVA	432	465	511	567	620	676	728	717	750	795	761
Gross investment	377	440	624	609	674	718	749	780	824	857	811
Capital expenditures [1]	436	456	509	576	639	663	760	826	893	960	833
Fixed investment [2]	424	446	483	526	591	637	694	754	834	911	887
Net financial investment	-59	-15	115	34	36	56	-11	-46	-68	-103	-22
Net acquisition of financial assets [1]	124	146	333	275	426	454	272	570	665	603	264
Checkable deposits and currency	6	-4	22	11	3	28	13	28	37	38	-21
Time and savings deposits	-6	-2	16	4	3	(-Z)	20	-7	16	-3	-14
Money market fund shares	9	13	-4	3	23	8	20	26	23	40	97
Commercial paper	(-Z)	2	2	-1	1	11	5	3	4	4	6
U.S. government securities	-20	21	-1	3	10	-5	-41	-1	-2	1	7
Mortgages	-2	1	-8	4	2	-4	26	-13	-7	-5	-5
Consumer credit	3	3	7	9	-2	-7	1	-4	5	2	-15
Trade receivables	29	28	51	72	78	88	94	86	113	106	-99
Miscellaneous assets [1]	114	75	236	164	322	324	152	438	481	417	317
U.S. direct investment abroad [3]	35	41	58	79	90	77	84	129	136	122	147
Insurance receivables	13	14	7	6	8	3	2	2	1	(-Z)	11
Net increase in liabilities [1]	184	161	218	242	391	398	283	616	734	706	286
Net funds raised in markets	66	52	56	80	167	110	177	139	298	269	212
Net new equity issues	-63	27	21	-45	-58	-70	-114	-267	-143	-160	-56
Credit market instruments [1]	129	25	34	125	225	179	292	406	442	429	268
Commercial paper	10	9	10	21	18	-1	14	24	37	48	-88
Corporate bonds [3]	47	68	75	23	91	116	151	219	230	171	328
Bank loans n.e.c.	3	-19	-8	46	75	40	51	82	73	74	-58
Mortgages	14	-37	-25	(Z)	6	6	33	21	62	61	81
Trade payables	28	33	36	77	81	50	65	58	144	102	-59
Miscellaneous liabilities [1]	89	70	120	85	143	229	32	415	284	327	133
Foreign direct investment in U.S.	59	7	20	45	54	72	100	144	262	179	88

Z Less than $500 million. [1] Includes other items not shown separately. [2] Nonresidential fixed investment plus residential fixed investment. [3] Through 1992:Q4, corporate bonds include net issues by Netherlands Antillean financial subsidiaries, and U.S. direct investment abroad excludes net inflows from those bond issues.

Source: Board of Governors of the Federal Reserve System, "Federal Reserve Statistical Release, Z.1, Flow of Funds Accounts of the United States"; published: 7 March 2002; <http://www.federalreserve.gov/releases/Z1/20020307/data.htm>.

No. 706. Nonfinancial Corporate Business-Sector Balance Sheet: 1990 to 2001

[In billions of dollars (9,755 represents $9,755,000,000,000). Represents year-end outstandings. Tangible assets stated at either market value or replacement cost]

Item	1990	1994	1995	1996	1997	1998	1999	2000	2001
Assets.	9,755	10,882	11,736	12,725	13,681	14,968	16,156	17,400	17,527
Tangible assets	6,179	6,405	6,777	7,267	7,872	8,152	8,591	9,288	9,202
Real estate [1]	3,385	3,158	3,318	3,661	4,101	4,210	4,392	4,784	4,772
Equipment and software [2]	1,892	2,240	2,390	2,515	2,641	2,771	2,942	3,171	3,202
Inventories [2]	901	1,007	1,070	1,091	1,130	1,171	1,257	1,334	1,228
Financial assets [3]	3,575	4,477	4,959	5,458	5,809	6,816	7,564	8,112	8,325
Checkable deposits and currency. . . .	151	185	188	216	229	257	294	332	311
Trade receivables	967	1,107	1,185	1,273	1,367	1,453	1,566	1,672	1,573
Liabilities [3]	4,729	5,627	6,010	6,379	6,629	7,458	8,153	8,806	9,177
Credit market instruments.	2,507	2,655	2,880	3,093	3,383	3,789	4,265	4,694	4,962
Corporate bonds [4]	1,008	1,253	1,344	1,460	1,611	1,830	2,059	2,231	2,559
Bank loans n.e.c.	545	527	602	642	693	774	847	922	865
Other loans and advances	473	421	454	468	508	562	596	670	671
Trade payables	626	797	878	927	992	1,050	1,194	1,296	1,237
Net worth (market value).	5,025	5,255	5,726	6,346	7,052	7,510	8,002	8,594	8,349

[1] At market value.   [2] At replacement (current) cost.   [3] Includes items not shown separately.   [4] Through 1992, corporate bonds include net issues by Netherlands Antillean financial subsidiaries.

Source: Board of Governors of the Federal Reserve System, "Federal Reserve Statistical Release, Z.1, Flow of Funds Accounts of the United States"; published: 7 March 2002; <http://www.federalreserve.gov/releases/Z1/20020307/data.htm>.

No. 707. Corporations—Selected Financial Items: 1990 to 1999

[In billions of dollars (18,190 represents $18,190,000,000,000), except as noted. Covers active corporations only. All corporations are required to file returns except those specifically exempt. See source for changes in law affecting comparability of historical data. Based on samples; see Appendix III]

Item	1990	1992	1993	1994	1995	1996	1997	1998	1999
Number of returns (1,000)	3,717	3,869	3,965	4,342	4,474	4,631	4,710	4,849	4,936
Number with net income (1,000)	1,911	2,064	2,145	2,392	2,455	2,588	2,647	2,761	2,812
S Corporation returns [1] (1,000)	1,575	1,785	1,902	2,024	2,153	2,304	2,452	2,588	2,726
Assets [2]	18,190	20,002	21,816	23,446	26,014	28,642	33,030	37,347	41,464
Cash	771	806	812	853	962	1,097	1,299	1,336	1,597
Notes and accounts receivable	4,198	4,169	4,532	4,768	5,307	5,783	6,632	7,062	7,745
Inventories.	894	915	947	1,126	1,045	1,079	1,114	1,139	1,198
Investments in Govt. obligations	921	1,248	1,290	1,309	1,363	1,339	1,343	1,366	1,340
Mortgage and real estate	1,538	1,567	1,627	1,661	1,713	1,825	2,029	2,414	2,555
Other investments	4,137	4,971	5,701	6,265	7,429	8,657	10,756	13,201	15,799
Depreciable assets	4,318	4,755	4,969	5,284	5,571	5,923	6,208	6,541	6,936
Depletable assets	129	131	137	148	154	169	177	193	184
Land.	210	221	230	239	242	254	262	271	286
Liabilities [2]	18,190	20,002	21,816	23,446	26,014	28,642	33,030	37,347	41,464
Accounts payable	1,094	1,605	1,466	1,606	1,750	1,905	2,111	2,501	2,792
Short-term debt [3]	1,803	1,560	1,569	1,831	2,034	2,328	2,582	3,216	3,658
Long-term debt [4]	2,665	2,742	2,871	3,100	3,335	3,651	4,072	4,813	5,448
Capital stock	1,585	1,881	2,042	2,132	2,194	2,278	2,951	3,244	3,522
Paid-in or capital surplus	2,814	3,656	4,223	4,790	5,446	6,427	7,253	8,610	10,186
Retained earnings [5]	1,410	1,431	1,662	1,698	2,191	2,519	3,113	3,373	3,970
Net worth [2 6]	4,739	5,700	(NA)	7,031	8,132	9,495	11,353	13,108	15,363
Receipts [2 6]	11,410	11,742	12,270	13,360	14,539	15,526	16,610	17,324	18,892
Business receipts [6 7]	9,860	10,360	10,866	11,884	12,786	13,659	14,461	15,010	16,314
Interest [8]	977	829	808	882	1,039	1,082	1,140	1,277	1,354
Rents and royalties	133	140	130	132	145	156	176	200	223
Deductions [2 6]	11,033	11,330	11,765	12,775	13,821	14,728	15,704	16,489	17,967
Cost of sales and operations [7]	6,611	6,772	7,052	7,625	8,206	8,707	9,114	9,362	10,284
Compensation of officers	205	221	226	282	304	319	336	357	374
Rent paid on business property	185	196	201	223	232	248	265	308	347
Taxes paid.	251	274	290	322	326	341	350	355	371
Interest paid.	825	597	546	611	744	771	866	967	1,019
Depreciation	333	346	364	403	437	474	513	542	584
Advertising	126	134	140	157	163	177	188	198	216
Net income (less loss) [6 9]	371	402	498	577	714	806	915	838	929
Net income	553	570	659	740	881	987	1,118	1,091	1,229
Deficit.	182	168	161	162	166	180	202	253	300
Income subject to tax	366	378	437	494	565	640	684	663	694
Income tax before credits [10]	119	126	149	168	194	220	235	231	242
Tax credits	32	30	35	37	42	53	55	50	49
Foreign tax credit	25	22	23	25	30	40	42	37	38
Income tax after credits [11]	96	102	(NA)	136	156	171	184	182	193

NA Not available.   [1] Represents certain small corporations with up to 75 shareholders (35 for 1990-1996), mostly individuals, electing to be taxed at the shareholder level.   [2] Includes items not shown separately.   [3] Payable in less than 1 year.   [4] Payable in 1 year or more.   [5] Appropriated and unappropriated and "adjustments to shareholders' equity" which was formerly included in "retained earnings, appropriated."   [6] Receipts, deductions and net income of S corporations are limited to those from trade or business. Those from investments are excluded.   [7] Includes gross sales and cost of sales of securities, commodities, and real estate by exchanges, brokers, or dealers selling on their own accounts. Previously, net gain included in total receipts only. Excludes investment income.   [8] Includes tax-exempt interest in state and local government obligations.   [9] Excludes regulated investment companies.   [10] Consists of regular (and alternative tax) only.   [11] Includes minimum tax, alternative minimum tax, adjustments for prior year credits, and other income-related taxes.

Source: U.S. Internal Revenue Service, *Statistics of Income, Corporation Income Tax Returns*, annual.

No. 708. Corporations by Receipt-Size Class and Industry: 1998 and 1999

[Number of returns in thousands (4,849 represents 4,849,000); receipts and net income in billions of dollars (16,543 represents $16,543,000,000,000). Covers active enterprises only. Figures are estimates based on a sample of unaudited tax returns; see Appendix III. The industrial distribution is based on the North American Industry Classification System and on data collected from establishments; see text, this section]

Industry	1998, total	1999					
		Total	Under $1 mil. [1]	$1 mil.-$4.9 mil.	$5 mil.-$9.9 mil.	$10 mil.-$49.9 mil.	$50 mil. or more
Total: [2]							
Number............	4,849	4,936	4,018	681	112	99	25
Business receipts [3]	16,543	18,009	818	1,456	776	2,029	12,930
Net income (less loss)	838	929	2	35	22	86	784
Agriculture, forestry, fishing, and hunting:							
Number............	135	142	127	12	1	1	(Z)
Business receipts [3]	100	105	20	26	9	22	27
Mining:							
Number............	31	31	27	3	1	(Z)	(Z)
Business receipts [3]	117	110	5	7	4	9	86
Utilities:							
Number............	8	7	6	(Z)	(Z)	(Z)	(Z)
Business receipts [3]	451	479	1	1	1	4	473
Construction:							
Number............	552	580	437	113	17	12	1
Business receipts [3]	859	974	110	242	119	231	271
Manufacturing:							
Number............	310	298	180	76	17	19	6
Business receipts [3]	4,591	4,802	48	173	122	384	4,076
Wholesale and retail trade:							
Number............	957	948	644	215	39	40	9
Business receipts [3]	4,517	4,789	177	472	275	860	3,007
Transportation and warehousing:							
Number............	160	160	131	21	4	3	1
Business receipts [3]	470	485	24	46	28	54	332
Information:							
Number............	101	108	92	11	2	2	1
Business receipts [3]	668	761	15	25	14	43	665
Finance and insurance:							
Number............	218	218	182	22	5	6	3
Business receipts [3]	2,358	3,008	29	49	33	132	2,765
Real estate and rental and leasing:							
Number............	522	521	501	17	2	1	(Z)
Business receipts [3]	176	185	43	36	12	23	72
Professional, scientific, and technical services:							
Number............	624	657	586	57	8	5	1
Business receipts [3]	541	576	101	116	56	97	206
Management of companies & enterprises:							
Number............	31	43	37	3	1	2	(Z)
Business receipts [3]	551	519	1	7	10	32	469
Administrative and support and waste management and remediation services:							
Number............	200	205	174	25	4	2	(Z)
Business receipts [3]	264	284	36	50	25	37	136
Educational services:							
Number............	37	35	32	3	(Z)	(Z)	(Z)
Business receipts [3]	23	21	5	5	1	4	6
Health care and social services:							
Number............	307	303	254	41	5	3	(Z)
Business receipts [3]	357	371	74	82	34	49	132
Arts, entertainment, and recreation:							
Number............	93	94	85	8	1	(Z)	(Z)
Business receipts [3]	60	71	14	16	6	9	26
Accommodation and food services:							
Number............	245	252	216	32	2	1	(Z)
Business receipts [3]	296	319	56	62	17	28	156
Other services:							
Number............	300	306	282	22	1	1	(Z)
Business receipts [3]	143	146	57	42	9	12	26

Z Less than 500 returns. [1] Includes businesses without receipts. [2] Includes businesses not allocable to individual industries. [3] Includes investment income for corporations in finance and insurance, real estate, and management of companies industries. Excludes investment income for S corporations (certain small corporations with up to 75 shareholders, mostly individuals, electing to be taxed at the shareholder level).

Source: U.S. Internal Revenue Service, *Statistics of Income*, various publications; and unpublished data.

No. 709. Corporations by Asset-Size Class and Industry: 1999

[In millions of dollars (115,898 represents $115,898,000,000), except number of returns. Covers active corporations only. Excludes corporations not allocable by industry. The industrial distribution is based on the North American Industry Classification System and on data collected from companies; see text, this section. Detail may not add to total because of rounding]

Industry	Total	Under $10 mil. [1]	$10-$24.9 mil.	$25-$49.9 mil.	$50-$99.9 mil.	$100-$249.9 mil.	$250 mil. and over
Agriculture, forestry, fishing, and hunting:							
Returns	141,678	140,864	536	131	84	43	19
Total receipts	115,898	78,871	8,855	5,201	7,476	6,350	9,145
Mining:							
Returns	30,849	29,841	467	179	117	89	156
Total receipts	124,847	18,979	5,068	4,494	3,763	6,603	85,940
Utilities:							
Returns	7,044	6,654	99	51	27	41	171
Total receipts	516,184	10,066	1,303	2,715	2,112	3,513	496,476
Construction:							
Returns	580,302	575,442	3,415	828	333	159	125
Total receipts	990,662	640,958	98,168	52,609	38,976	34,743	125,207
Manufacturing:							
Returns	297,714	282,868	7,313	2,920	1,678	1,368	1,567
Total receipts	5,207,025	619,517	195,364	155,566	156,960	261,233	3,818,385
Wholesale and retail trade:							
Returns	948,371	933,835	9,431	2,513	1,175	753	664
Total receipts	4,913,444	1,733,411	457,130	240,449	201,409	259,861	2,021,184
Transportation and warehousing:							
Returns	160,195	158,642	873	277	144	140	118
Total receipts	506,308	141,271	22,824	14,993	13,767	23,639	289,813
Information:							
Returns	107,628	104,787	1,249	572	337	276	408
Total receipts	889,707	113,091	16,496	13,543	13,978	25,355	707,245
Finance and insurance:							
Returns	217,780	199,761	3,545	2,714	2,884	3,431	5,446
Total receipts	3,008,131	211,806	20,576	21,265	30,035	74,683	2,648,866
Real estate and rental and leasing:							
Returns	521,447	516,849	3,001	893	354	209	140
Total receipts	215,875	107,401	12,604	8,709	7,357	8,472	71,332
Professional, scientific, and technical services:							
Returns	657,153	654,170	1,598	584	406	234	163
Total receipts	604,083	361,051	36,862	26,259	27,852	34,213	117,846
Management of companies & enterprises:							
Returns	43,246	37,217	1,108	1,183	1,302	1,358	1,079
Total receipts	518,532	18,131	1,660	3,201	7,536	16,524	471,480
Administrative and support and waste management and remediation services:							
Returns	205,011	204,141	443	166	101	80	80
Total receipts	296,911	155,501	17,222	10,532	11,039	18,843	83,774
Educational services:							
Returns	35,196	35,065	68	28	17	11	7
Total receipts	23,084	14,973	1,615	865	1,598	1,626	2,407
Health care and social assistance:							
Returns	303,499	302,557	512	201	94	68	67
Total receipts	385,913	240,914	14,926	11,994	9,779	10,657	97,644
Arts, entertainment, and recreation:							
Returns	93,922	93,298	365	114	64	52	30
Total receipts	76,849	42,846	4,238	2,738	3,847	5,623	17,558
Accommodation and food services:							
Returns	252,113	250,924	651	203	120	96	117
Total receipts	342,084	155,121	12,356	8,252	9,032	15,779	141,544
Other services:							
Returns	305,725	305,286	267	75	49	24	23
Total receipts	151,674	118,596	5,598	3,108	4,169	3,942	16,262

[1] Includes returns with zero assets.

Source: U.S. Internal Revenue Service, *Statistics of Income, Corporation Income Tax Returns,* annual.

Kind of business	NAICS code [1]	All firms		Employer firms			
		Establish-ments (number)	Sales, receipts or ship-ments (mil. dol.)	Establish-ments (number)	Sales, receipts or ship-ments (mil. dol.)	Annual payroll (mil. dol.)	Paid employ-ees [2] (1,000)
TAXABLE							
Mining	21	117,240	178,953	25,000	173,989	20,798	509.0
Oil & gas extraction.	211	90,006	107,147	8,312	102,837	5,511	110.9
Mining (except oil & gas)	212	13,391	51,585	7,348	51,253	9,422	229.3
Support activities for mining	213	13,843	20,222	9,340	19,899	5,866	168.8
Utilities . . . [3]	22	31,406	412,228	15,513	411,713	36,595	702.7
Utilities [3]	221	31,406	412,228	15,513	411,713	36,595	702.7
Elec. power generation, transmsn. & distribution	2211	(NA)	(NA)	7,935	269,095	30,440	564.5
Natural gas distribution.	2212	(NA)	(NA)	2,747	136,995	5,110	102.9
Construction	23	2,546,680	945,682	656,448	858,581	174,185	5,664.8
Building, developing, & general contracting . .	233	611,859	421,524	199,289	386,926	42,546	1,343.0
Heavy construction	234	80,319	132,720	42,557	130,795	30,292	880.4
Special trade contractors	235	1,854,502	391,439	414,602	340,861	101,347	3,441.5
Manufacturing	31-33	666,609	3,854,381	363,753	3,842,061	572,101	16,888.0
Wholesale trade.	42	859,328	(NA)	453,470	4,059,658	214,915	5,796.6
Wholesale trade, durable goods	421	526,545	(NA)	290,629	2,179,717	133,237	3,398.3
Wholesale trade, nondurable goods	422	332,783	(NA)	162,841	1,879,940	81,678	2,398.3
Retail trade	44-45	2,949,786	2,530,304	1,118,447	2,460,886	237,196	13,991.1
Motor vehicle & parts dealers	441	240,460	660,682	122,633	645,368	50,239	1,719.0
Furniture & home furnishings stores	442	104,578	74,093	64,725	71,691	9,959	482.8
Electronics & appliance stores.	443	71,486	70,210	43,373	68,561	7,064	345.0
Bldg material & garden equip & supp dealers.	444	121,912	229,489	93,117	227,566	25,609	1,117.9
Food & beverage stores.	445	239,290	410,287	148,528	401,764	40,581	2,893.1
Health & personal care stores	446	142,491	119,056	82,941	117,701	15,191	903.7
Gasoline stations	447	137,566	199,856	126,889	198,166	11,482	922.1
Clothing & clothing accessories stores . . .	448	251,398	140,565	156,601	136,398	16,597	1,280.2
Sporting goods, hobby, book, & music stores.	451	164,753	65,572	69,149	62,011	7,113	560.8
General merchandise stores	452	56,788	331,453	36,171	330,444	30,871	2,507.5
Miscellaneous store retailers.	453	530,500	91,670	129,838	78,109	10,165	753.0
Nonstore retailers	454	888,564	137,370	44,482	123,107	12,323	506.0
Transportation & warehousing [3] [4] [5]	48-49	823,908	347,673	178,025	318,245	82,346	2,920.8
Air transportation [4]	481	19,518	20,925	3,598	20,249	2,748	89.1
Water transportation	483	9,047	24,405	1,921	24,019	2,834	72.9
Truck transportation.	484	426,345	162,104	103,798	141,225	38,471	1,293.8
Pipeline transportation	486	2,604	26,877	2,311	26,837	2,661	49.3
Transportation support activities.	488	55,616	40,930	30,675	39,758	12,592	411.6
Couriers & messengers	492	131,523	41,808	10,887	39,812	14,072	530.8
Information	51	288,500	628,981	114,475	623,214	129,482	3,066.2
Publishing industries	511	79,614	180,434	33,896	179,035	43,358	1,006.2
Motion picture & sound recording industries. .	512	71,016	57,858	22,204	55,926	9,392	276.0
Broadcasting & telecommunications	513	80,486	347,676	43,480	346,316	63,480	1,434.5
Information & data processing services	514	57,384	43,014	14,895	41,937	13,252	349.5
Finance & insurance.	52	1,074,360	2,234,737	395,203	2,197,771	264,551	5,835.2
Monetary authorities - central bank.	521	42	24,582	42	24,582	903	21.7
Credit intermediation & related activities . . .	522	330,563	817,504	166,882	808,811	98,723	2,744.9
Security, commodity contracts & like activity. .	523	242,901	291,425	54,491	274,987	71,281	706.1
Insurance carriers & related activities	524	499,365	1,084,618	172,299	1,072,784	92,230	2,327.3
Funds, trusts, & other financial vehicles (part)	525	1,489	16,608	1,489	16,608	1,413	35.3
Real estate & rental & leasing [3]	53	1,684,976	342,621	288,273	240,918	41,591	1,702.4
Real estate	531	1,557,556	252,120	221,650	153,275	27,947	1,117.2
Rental & leasing services	532	124,792	79,184	64,472	76,379	12,569	559.4
Professional, scientific, & technical services . . [3]	54	3,265,160	660,707	615,305	579,542	225,376	5,212.7
Professional, scientific, & technical services [3].	541	3,265,160	660,707	615,305	579,542	225,376	5,212.7
Legal services.	5411	383,682	136,785	173,716	127,052	49,060	1,012.1
Accounting/tax prep/bookkeep/payroll services	5412	407,005	65,942	97,512	61,117	26,104	966.5
Architectural, engineering & related services	5413	(NA)	(NA)	92,710	116,986	46,943	1,038.3
Computer systems design & related services	5415	278,512	115,696	72,278	108,968	42,151	764.7
Management, sci & tech consulting services.	5416	644,497	80,803	80,426	63,429	26,582	511.3
Scientific R&D services.	5417	24,480	23,553	7,830	23,078	9,322	177.0
Advertising & related services	5418	135,133	53,937	38,832	49,290	16,012	417.2
Other professional/scientific/technical service.	5419	979,072	42,933	25,565	15,368	5,115	212.7
Management of companies & enterprises	55	(NA)	(NA)	47,319	92,473	154,178	2,617.5
Admin/support waste mgt/remediation services .	56	1,168,621	312,912	276,393	295,936	137,337	7,347.4
Administrative & support services.	561	1,131,846	272,821	260,025	256,591	128,430	7,066.7
Waste management & remediation services.	562	36,775	40,091	16,368	39,346	8,899	280.7

See footnotes at end of table.

U.S. Census Bureau, Statistical Abstract of the United States: 2002

No. 710. Economic Census Summary (NAICS Basis): 1997—Con.

Kind of business	NAICS code [1]	All firms Establish-ments (number)	All firms Sales, receipts or ship-ments (mil. dol.)	Employer firms Establish-ments (number)	Employer firms Sales, receipts or ship-ments (mil. dol.)	Annual payroll (mil. dol.)	Paid employ-ees [2] (1,000)
Educational services . . . . [3]	61	268,937	17,731	33,783	14,933	4,903	248.7
Health care & social assistance [3]	62	1,698,979	449,806	531,069	418,602	182,256	6,231.8
Ambulatory health care services	621	1,047,100	334,762	440,200	310,012	137,979	3,744.3
Hospitals	622	1,345	40,146	1,345	40,146	13,886	511.6
Nursing & residential care facilities	623	67,331	56,847	32,833	55,844	24,626	1,484.8
Arts, entertainment, & recreation [3]	71	772,981	99,455	79,636	85,088	26,104	1,207.4
Perform arts, spectator sports, & related ind .	711	561,923	42,995	25,942	32,744	12,834	235.9
Amusement, gambling, & recreation industries	713	208,466	55,938	52,907	51,861	13,147	964.2
Accommodation & food services	72	736,073	359,434	545,068	350,399	97,007	9,451.2
Accommodation [3]	721	105,686	101,394	58,162	98,457	26,674	1,696.7
Traveler accommodation . . . . [3]	7211	78,235	97,353	47,079	94,966	25,851	1,645.7
Food services & drinking places [3]	722	630,387	258,040	486,906	251,942	70,334	7,754.6
Full-service restaurants	7221	230,732	114,592	191,245	112,450	34,435	3,641.4
Limited-service eating places	7222	246,138	109,298	214,774	107,788	27,483	3,327.0
Special food services	7223	77,690	20,706	28,062	19,408	5,766	464.9
Other services (except public administration) [3] . .	81	2,357,005	206,332	420,950	163,033	48,453	2,493.6
Repair & maintenance	811	800,207	122,886	235,466	105,154	29,875	1,276.4
TAX-EXEMPT							
Professional, scientific, & technical services . . .	54	(NA)	(NA)	5,824	15,709	6,023	148.5
Educational services	61	(NA)	(NA)	7,153	5,506	1,461	72.4
Health care & social assistance	62	(NA)	(NA)	114,784	466,452	195,949	7,329.8
Ambulatory health care services	621	(NA)	(NA)	15,181	45,428	17,884	669.3
Hospitals	622	(NA)	(NA)	5,340	339,032	141,910	4,421.5
Nursing & residential care facilities	623	(NA)	(NA)	24,526	37,235	17,527	985.9
Social assistance	624	(NA)	(NA)	69,737	44,756	18,628	1,253.1
Arts, entertainment, & recreation	71	(NA)	(NA)	19,463	19,627	6,683	380.3
Other services (except public administration) . . .	81	(NA)	(NA)	98,765	102,864	17,068	762.6

NA Not available.   [1] North American Industry Classification System, 1997.   [2] For pay period including March 12.
[3] Includes other kinds of business not shown separately.   [4] Data do not include large certificated passenger carriers that report to the Office of Airline Statistics, U.S. Department of Transportation.   [5] Railroad transportation and U.S. Postal Service are out of scope for the 1997 Economic Census.

Source: U.S. Census Bureau, *1997 Economic Census, Geographic Area Series* and *Nonemployer Statistics*.

No. 711. Nonemployer Establishments and Receipts by Industry: 1997 to 1999

[**Establishments in thousands (15,440 represents 15,440,000).** Includes only firms subject to federal income tax. Nonemployers are businesses with no paid employees. Based on the North American Industry Classification System (NAICS), see text, this section]

Industry	NAICS code	Establishments (1,000) 1997	Establishments (1,000) 1998	Establishments (1,000) 1999	Receipts (mil. dol.) 1997	Receipts (mil. dol.) 1998	Receipts (mil. dol.) 1999
All industries	(X)	15,440	15,709	16,153	586,316	643,720	667,220
Forestry, fishing & hunting, & ag support services	113-115	240	225	226	8,533	8,286	8,876
Mining	21	92	82	81	4,964	3,833	3,945
Utilities	22	16	15	14	515	504	487
Construction	23	1,890	1,908	1,986	87,101	94,390	102,909
Manufacturing	31-33	303	297	289	12,319	12,638	12,636
Wholesale trade	42	406	400	395	30,759	31,280	31,434
Retail trade	44-45	1,831	1,762	1,761	69,418	70,971	73,314
Transportation & warehousing	48-49	646	662	719	29,428	31,745	34,994
Information	51	174	195	221	5,767	6,213	7,019
Finance & insurance	52	679	708	667	36,966	38,940	40,288
Real estate & rental & leasing	53	1,397	1,565	1,648	101,704	131,728	125,513
Professional, scientific, & technical services .	54	2,650	2,415	2,388	81,165	83,081	85,443
Admin/support waste mgt/remediation services	56	892	925	990	16,975	19,237	21,777
Educational services	61	235	244	263	2,798	3,029	3,360
Health care & social assistance	62	1,168	1,185	1,254	31,203	32,328	34,097
Arts, entertainment, & recreation	71	693	713	749	14,366	15,325	16,656
Accommodation & food services	72	191	198	210	9,035	11,757	12,594
Other services (except public administration) .	81	1,936	2,209	2,293	43,299	48,438	51,876

X Not applicable.

Source: U.S. Census Bureau, "Nonemployer Statistics"; published 28 March 2002; <http://www.census.gov/epcd/nonemployer/>.

U.S. Census Bureau, Statistical Abstract of the United States: 2002

No. 712. Comparative Statistics for the United States (1987 SIC Basis): 1992 and 1997

[162.1 represents $162,100,000,000. Includes only establishments with payroll. SIC=Standard Industrial Classification]

Industry	1987 SIC code	Establishments (number)		Sales/receipts/ revenues/ shipments (bil. dol.)		Annual payroll (bil. dol.)		Paid employees (1,000)	
		1992	1997	1992	1997	1992	1997	1992	1997
Mining	B	29,497	25,251	162.1	174.5	18.6	20.9	534.7	512.0
Construction	C	572,851	639,482	539.1	834.8	117.7	171.0	4,668.3	5,567.0
Manufacturing	D	370,912	377,776	3,004.7	3,958.1	494.1	595.7	16,948.9	17,557.0
Transportation and public utilities	E	(NA)	293,575	(NA)	1,143.9	(NA)	199.7	(NA)	5,689.1
Wholesale trade.	F	495,457	521,127	3,238.5	4,235.4	173.3	234.5	5,791.3	6,509.3
Retail trade	G	1,526,215	1,561,195	1,894.9	2,545.9	222.9	290.5	18,407.5	21,165.9
Finance, insurance, and real estate	H	585,580	661,388	1,831.5	2,474.9	211.6	308.2	6,509.6	7,314.3
Services (taxable firms only).	I	1,825,435	2,077,666	1,202.6	1,843.8	452.7	688.9	19,290.4	25,278.4
Auxiliaries	(X)	47,250	48,193	(NA)	41.3	137.1	178.2	3,229.7	3,284.1

NA Not available.   X Not applicable.

Source: U.S. Census Bureau, *1997 Economic Census, Comparative Statistics, Core Business Statistics Series*, EC97X-C52, issued June 2000.

No. 713. Establishments, Employees and Payroll by Employment-Size Class: 1990 to 2000

[6,176 represents 6,176,000. Excludes most government employees, railroad employees, self-employed persons. Employees are for the week including March 12. Covers establishments with payroll. An *establishment* is a single physical location where business is conducted or where services or industrial operations are performed. For statement on methodology, see Appendix III]

Employment-size class	Unit	1990	1993	1994	1995	1996	1997	1998	1999	2000
Establishments, total	1,000 . .	6,176	6,403	6,509	6,613	6,739	6,895	6,942	7,008	7,070
Under 20 employees.	1,000 . .	5,354	5,577	5,662	5,733	5,843	5,968	5,991	6,036	6,069
20 to 99 employees	1,000 . .	684	688	704	730	741	767	786	802	826
100 to 499 employees.	1,000 . .	122	123	128	135	138	143	147	152	157
500 to 999 employees.	1,000 . .	10	9	10	10	11	11	11	12	12
1,000 or more employees . . .	1,000 . .	6	6	6	6	6	6	6	7	7
Employees, total	1,000 . .	93,476	94,789	96,733	100,335	102,199	105,299	108,118	110,706	114,065
Under 20 employees.	1,000 . .	24,373	25,233	25,373	25,785	26,115	26,883	27,131	27,289	27,569
20 to 99 employees	1,000 . .	27,414	27,443	28,138	29,202	29,697	30,631	31,464	32,193	33,147
100 to 499 employees.	1,000 . .	22,926	23,195	24,048	25,364	26,086	26,993	27,842	28,707	29,736
500 to 999 employees.	1,000 . .	6,551	6,449	6,663	7,021	7,274	7,422	7,689	7,923	8,291
1,000 or more employees . . .	1,000 . .	12,212	12,470	12,513	12,962	13,026	13,370	13,991	14,594	15,322
Annual payroll, total	Bil. dol.	2,104	2,363	2,488	2,666	2,849	3,048	3,309	3,555	3,879
Under 20 employees.	Bil. dol .	485	554	579	608	647	688	734	773	818
20 to 99 employees	Bil. dol .	547	611	650	696	747	796	866	925	1,006
100 to 499 employees.	Bil. dol .	518	582	621	675	730	786	858	931	1,031
500 to 999 employees.	Bil. dol .	174	191	202	219	240	254	277	298	336
1,000 or more employees . . .	Bil. dol .	381	424	436	467	485	524	575	628	690

Source: U.S. Census Bureau, "County Business Patterns"; published 30 May 2002; <http://www.census.gov/epcd/cbp/view/cbpview.html>.

No. 714. Establishments, Employees, and Payroll by Employment-Size Class and Industry: 1998 to 2000

[Establishments and employees in thousands (6,942 represents 6,942,000); payroll in billions of dollars. See headnote, Table 713. Based on the North American Industry Classification System (NAICS), see text, this section]

Industry	NAICS code	1998, total	1999, total	2000					
				Total	Under 20 employees	20 to 99 employees	100 to 499 employees	500 to 999 employees	1,000 or more employees
Establishments, total	(X)	6,942	7,008	7,070	6,069	826	157	12	7
Agriculture, forestry, fishing & hunting	11	27	27	26	24	1	(Z)	(Z)	(Z)
Mining	21	25	24	24	19	4	1	(Z)	(Z)
Utilities	22	16	17	17	12	4	1	(Z)	(Z)
Construction	23	692	699	710	643	59	7	(Z)	(Z)
Manufacturing	31-33	366	360	354	236	84	30	3	1
Wholesale trade	42	454	450	446	380	58	8	(Z)	(Z)
Retail trade	44-45	1,113	1,111	1,114	967	121	25	(Z)	(Z)
Transportation and warehousing	48-49	186	187	190	159	25	5	(Z)	(Z)
Information	51	121	127	134	105	22	6	1	(Z)
Finance and insurance	52	412	418	424	379	37	6	1	1
Real estate and rental and leasing	53	292	298	300	285	13	2	(Z)	(Z)
Professional, scientific, and technical services	54	687	705	723	666	48	8	1	(Z)
Management of companies and enterprises	55	44	47	47	31	11	4	1	(Z)
Admin/support waste mgt/remediation services	56	351	350	352	291	43	16	1	1
Educational services	61	65	66	68	51	13	3	(Z)	(Z)
Health care and social assistance	62	649	650	659	562	75	18	2	2
Arts, entertainment, and recreation	71	103	103	104	86	15	2	(Z)	(Z)
Accommodation and food services	72	544	540	542	388	145	9	(Z)	(Z)
Other services [1]	81	719	718	723	675	44	4	(Z)	(Z)
Auxiliaries [2]	95	14	15	15	9	4	1	(Z)	(Z)
Unclassified establishments	99	62	98	99	98	1	-	-	-
Employees, total	(X)	108,118	110,706	114,065	27,569	33,147	29,736	8,291	15,322
Agriculture, forestry, fishing & hunting	11	187	192	184	90	55	31	(D)	(D)
Mining	21	498	457	456	90	141	139	41	46
Utilities	22	682	667	655	65	169	227	96	99
Construction	23	5,798	6,202	6,573	2,556	2,245	1,273	240	259
Manufacturing	31-33	16,946	16,660	16,474	1,382	3,722	6,139	2,165	3,067
Wholesale trade	42	5,885	5,972	6,112	1,875	2,258	1,450	273	256
Retail trade	44-45	14,241	14,477	14,841	5,184	4,875	4,374	304	103
Transportation and warehousing	48-49	3,462	3,627	3,790	666	1,038	915	217	953
Information	51	3,142	3,235	3,546	475	938	1,168	426	539
Finance and insurance	52	5,770	5,965	5,963	1,682	1,427	1,282	584	988
Real estate and rental and leasing	53	1,813	1,874	1,942	1,015	499	319	(D)	(D)
Professional, scientific, and technical services	54	6,052	6,432	6,816	2,303	1,862	1,559	411	680
Management of companies and enterprises	55	2,704	2,788	2,874	172	483	918	465	835
Admin/support waste mgt/remediation services	56	7,775	8,367	9,138	1,174	1,870	3,178	954	1,962
Educational services	61	2,324	2,432	2,532	246	560	522	264	939
Health care and social assistance	62	13,758	13,865	14,109	2,906	3,010	3,409	1,168	3,615
Arts, entertainment, and recreation	71	1,584	1,640	1,741	342	632	439	113	216
Accommodation and food services	72	9,466	9,638	9,881	2,331	5,559	1,410	206	374
Other services [1]	81	5,038	5,151	5,293	2,829	1,625	660	82	97
Auxiliaries [2]	95	916	959	1,001	58	162	322	203	256
Unclassified establishments	99	78	106	144	127	16	-	-	-
Annual payroll, total	(X)	3,309	3,555	3,879	818	1,006	1,031	336	690
Agriculture, forestry, fishing & hunting	11	5	5	5	2	2	1	(D)	(D)
Mining	21	22	21	22	4	6	8	2	2
Utilities	22	38	39	41	3	10	14	7	7
Construction	23	199	219	240	79	86	54	10	11
Manufacturing	31-33	607	626	644	43	126	226	87	162
Wholesale trade	42	234	250	270	76	97	68	14	15
Retail trade	44-45	260	282	303	99	105	88	7	4
Transportation and warehousing	48-49	109	117	126	20	32	29	8	37
Information	51	147	170	209	25	45	68	28	43
Finance and insurance	52	290	313	347	76	83	82	33	73
Real estate and rental and leasing	53	50	54	59	28	16	11	(D)	(D)
Professional, scientific, and technical services	54	278	311	362	104	106	93	26	33
Management of companies and enterprises	55	176	192	211	14	33	62	33	68
Admin/support waste mgt/remediation services	56	164	183	210	35	48	66	18	43
Educational services	61	52	57	62	5	12	13	5	27
Health care and social assistance	62	395	409	431	104	83	82	35	128
Arts, entertainment, and recreation	71	36	39	43	11	12	13	3	5
Accommodation and food services	72	110	117	126	29	62	21	4	10
Other services [1]	81	96	102	110	55	34	16	2	3
Auxiliaries [2]	95	41	45	55	3	7	16	10	19
Unclassified establishments	99	1	3	4	4	-	-	-	-

- Represents zero.   D Data withheld to avoid disclosure.   X Not applicable.   Z Less than 500 establishments.   [1] Except public administration.   [2] Excludes corporate, subsidiary and regional management.

Source: U.S. Census Bureau, "County Business Patterns"; published 30 May 2002; <http://www.census.gov/epcd/cbp/view/cbpview.html>.

No. 715. Major Industries—Employer Firms, Employment, and Annual Payroll by Enterprise Size: 1999

[5,608 represents 5,608,000. A firm is an aggregation of all establishments owned by a parent company (within a geographic location and/or industry) with some annual payroll. A firm may be a single location or it can include multiple locations. Employment is measured in March and payroll is annual leading to some firms with zero employment. Numbers in parentheses represent North American Industry Classification System codes, see text, this section]

Industry and data type	Unit	All industries—employment size of enterprise								
		Total	0	1 to 4	5 to 9	10 to 19	20 to 99	100 to 499	Less than 500	More than 500
Total [1]:										
Firms	1,000	5,608	709	2,680	1,013	606	502	81	5,591	17
Employment	1,000	110,706	-	5,606	6,652	8,130	19,703	15,638	55,729	54,977
Annual payroll	Bil. dol.	3,555	34	143	167	218	565	475	1,601	1,954
Construction (23):										
Firms	1,000	691	100	337	123	71	53	6	691	1
Employment	1,000	6,202	-	707	805	953	1,977	984	5,427	775
Annual payroll	Bil. dol.	219	4	18	22	30	72	40	186	33
Manufacturing (31-33):										
Firms	1,000	312	23	96	57	49	65	16	307	5
Employment	1,000	16,660	-	219	384	675	2,668	2,896	6,841	9,819
Annual payroll	Bil. dol.	626	2	5	10	19	85	97	218	407
Wholesale trade (42):										
Firms	1,000	359	36	161	65	45	41	8	355	3
Employment	1,000	5,972	-	340	430	600	1,495	970	3,834	2,138
Annual payroll	Bil. dol.	250	2	12	15	22	56	38	144	106
Retail trade (44-45):										
Firms	1,000	730	77	341	154	87	60	9	728	2
Employment	1,000	14,477	-	754	1,013	1,140	2,235	1,241	6,382	8,094
Annual payroll	Bil. dol.	282	3	12	18	22	56	32	144	138
Transportation & warehousing (48-49):										
Firms	1,000	155	22	75	23	16	15	3	154	1
Employment	1,000	3,627	-	146	154	213	571	440	1,524	2,103
Annual payroll	Bil. dol.	117	1	3	4	5	16	13	42	75
Information (51):										
Firms	1,000	77	13	32	12	9	8	2	76	1
Employment	1,000	3,235	-	64	80	121	326	323	913	2,321
Annual payroll	Bil. dol.	170	2	3	3	4	14	16	42	129
Finance & insurance (52):										
Firms	1,000	224	24	131	32	16	15	4	222	2
Employment	1,000	5,965	-	266	207	212	617	614	1,916	4,049
Annual payroll	Bil. dol.	313	2	8	8	10	28	29	85	228
Real estate & rental & leasing (53):										
Firms	1,000	243	33	148	33	15	10	2	242	1
Employment	1,000	1,874	-	281	210	201	366	267	1,324	550
Annual payroll	Bil. dol.	54	1	7	5	5	11	8	37	17
Professional, scientific & technical services (54):										
Firms	1,000	654	95	370	96	51	35	5	652	2
Employment	1,000	6,432	-	711	622	681	1,297	879	4,190	2,243
Annual payroll	Bil. dol.	311	5	25	23	29	66	46	196	116
Admin/support waste mgt/ remediation services (56):										
Firms	1,000	299	46	140	48	29	26	8	296	3
Employment	1,000	8,367	-	288	315	384	1,035	1,354	3,377	4,990
Annual payroll	Bil. dol.	183	2	7	7	9	24	28	78	105
Health care and social assistance (62):										
Firms	1,000	524	41	232	123	64	46	13	521	3
Employment	1,000	13,865	-	521	810	854	1,844	2,482	6,510	7,355
Annual payroll	Bil. dol.	409	3	19	27	30	54	57	190	219
Arts, entertainment & recreation (71):										
Firms	1,000	96	19	39	14	10	12	2	95	1
Employment	1,000	1,640	-	77	91	141	479	345	1,133	507
Annual payroll	Bil. dol.	39	2	4	2	2	9	10	29	11
Accommodation & food services (72):										
Firms	1,000	412	53	131	78	69	71	8	410	2
Employment	1,000	9,638	-	301	526	938	2,702	1,381	5,849	3,789
Annual payroll	Bil. dol.	117	2	3	5	9	29	16	65	52
Other services (except public administration) (81):										
Firms	1,000	657	53	365	132	63	39	4	656	1
Employment	1,000	5,151	-	772	857	001	1,387	582	4,428	723
Annual payroll	Bil. dol.	102	1	13	15	16	27	13	85	17

- Represents zero. [1] Includes other industries not shown separately.

Source: U.S. Small Business Administration, Office of Advocacy, "Statistics of U.S. Businesses: Firm Size Data provided by U.S. Census Bureau"; published 21 March 2002; <http://www.sbaonline.sba.gov/ADVO/stats/data.html>.

No. 716. Employer Firms, Establishments, Employment, and Annual Payroll by Enterprise Size: 1990 to 1999

[In thousands except as noted (5,074 represents 5,074,000). Firms are an aggregation of all establishments owned by a parent company. Establishments are locations with active payroll in any quarter. Employment is measured in March and payroll is annual leading to some enterprises with zero employment. This table illustrates the changing importance of enterprise sizes over time, not job growth as enterprises can grow or decline and change enterprise size cells over time]

Item	All industries—employment size of enterprise							
	Total	0-4 [1]	5-9	10-19	20-99	100-499	Less than 500	More than 500
Firms:								
1990.	5,074	3,021	952	563	454	70	5,060	14
1992.	5,095	3,075	946	552	439	69	5,081	14
1993.	5,194	3,140	962	560	446	72	5,179	15
1994.	5,277	3,208	965	563	452	73	5,262	15
1995.	5,369	3,250	981	577	470	76	5,354	15
1996.	5,478	3,328	996	586	476	76	5,462	16
1997.	5,542	3,358	1,007	594	487	80	5,526	16
1998.	5,579	3,376	1,012	600	494	80	5,563	16
1999.	5,608	3,389	1,013	606	502	81	5,591	17
Establishments:								
1990.	6,176	3,032	971	600	590	255	5,448	728
1992.	6,319	3,082	965	606	635	284	5,572	747
1993.	6,401	3,148	981	609	632	285	5,655	746
1994.	6,509	3,218	983	609	631	284	5,725	784
1995.	6,613	3,260	998	618	639	284	5,799	814
1996.	6,738	3,338	1,013	625	636	281	5,893	846
1997.	6,895	3,364	1,023	639	683	309	6,018	877
1998.	6,942	3,383	1,026	640	675	307	6,030	911
1999.	7,008	3,398	1,027	643	671	309	6,048	960
Employment:								
1990.	93,469	5,117	6,252	7,543	17,710	13,545	50,167	43,302
1992.	92,826	5,179	6,203	7,391	17,121	13,307	49,201	43,625
1993.	94,774	5,258	6,314	7,498	17,421	13,825	50,316	44,458
1994.	96,722	5,319	6,333	7,544	17,694	14,118	51,008	45,714
1995.	100,315	5,395	6,440	7,734	18,422	14,660	52,653	47,662
1996.	102,187	5,486	6,541	7,855	18,643	14,650	53,175	49,013
1997.	105,299	5,546	6,610	7,962	19,110	15,317	54,545	50,754
1998.	108,118	5,584	6,643	8,048	19,378	15,411	55,064	53,053
1999.	110,706	5,606	6,652	8,130	19,703	15,638	55,729	54,977
Annual payroll ($bll.):								
1990.	2,104	117	114	144	352	279	1,007	1,097
1992.	2,272	125	122	153	369	298	1,067	1,205
1993.	2,363	129	127	159	385	316	1,116	1,247
1994.	2,488	135	132	166	408	336	1,176	1,312
1995.	2,666	142	137	175	437	361	1,252	1,414
1996.	2,849	151	145	185	465	384	1,330	1,518
1997.	3,048	158	151	194	495	418	1,416	1,632
1998.	3,309	168	160	207	531	446	1,513	1,797
1999.	3,555	177	167	218	565	475	1,601	1,954

[1] Employment is measured in March, thus some firms (start-ups after March, closures before March, and seasonal firms) will have zero employment and some annual payroll.

No. 717. Firm Births and Deaths by Employment Size of Enterprise: 1990 to 1999

[For employment (3,105 represents 3,105,000). Data represent activity from March of the beginning year to March of the ending year. Establishments with no employment in the first quarter of the beginning year were excluded. This table provides the number of births and deaths of initial establishments (based on plant number) as an approximation of firm births and deaths]

Item	Births (initial locations)				Deaths (initial locations)			
	Total	Less than 20	Less than 500	More than 500	Total	Less than 20	Less than 500	More than 500
Firms:								
1990-1991	541,141	515,870	540,889	252	546,518	516,964	546,149	369
1991-1992	544,596	519,014	544,278	318	521,606	492,746	521,176	430
1992-1993	564,504	539,601	564,093	411	492,651	466,550	492,266	385
1993-1994	570,587	546,437	570,337	250	503,563	476,667	503,125	438
1994-1995	594,369	568,896	594,119	250	497,246	472,441	496,874	372
1995-1996	597,792	572,442	597,503	289	512,402	485,509	512,024	378
1996-1997	590,644	564,197	590,335	309	530,003	500,014	529,481	522
1997-1998	589,982	564,804	589,706	276	540,601	511,567	540,112	489
1998-1999	579,609	554,288	579,287	322	544,487	514,293	544,040	447
Employment (1,000):								
1990-1991	3,105	1,713	2,907	198	3,208	1,723	3,044	164
1991-1992	3,201	1,703	2,864	337	3,126	1,603	2,894	232
1992-1993	3,438	1,751	3,054	384	2,906	1,516	2,698	209
1993-1994	3,106	1,760	2,890	216	3,077	1,549	2,801	276
1994-1995	3,322	1,836	3,049	273	2,823	1,517	2,634	189
1995-1996	3,256	1,845	3,056	200	3,100	1,560	2,808	291
1996-1997	3,228	1,814	3,030	198	3,275	1,621	2,961	314
1997-1998	3,205	1,812	3,002	203	3,233	1,662	2,992	242
1998-1999	3,225	1,670	2,991	235	3,180	1,645	2,969	210

Source of Tables 716 and 717: U.S. Small Business Administration, Office of Advocacy, "Statistics of U.S. Businesses: Firm Size Data provided by U.S. Census Bureau"; published 21 March 2002; <http://www.sbaonline.sba.gov/ADVO/stats/data.html>.

U.S. Census Bureau, Statistical Abstract of the United States: 2002

No. 718. U.S. Firms by Race and Hispanic Origin: 1997

[20,822 represents 20,822,000. A Hispanic firm may be of any race and, therefore may be included in more than one minority group]

Group	All firms		Firms with paid employees			
	Firms (1,000)	Sales and receipts (mil. dol.)	Firms (1,000)	Sales and receipts (mil. dol.)	Employees (1,000)	Annual payroll (mil. dol.)
All firms	20,822	18,553,243	5,295	17,907,940	103,360	2,936,493
Black	823	71,215	93	56,378	718	14,322
Hispanic	1,200	186,275	212	158,675	1,389	29,830
Cuban	125	26,492	30	23,873	176	4,163
Mexican, Mexican American, Chicano.	472	73,707	91	62,271	695	13,015
Puerto Rican	70	7,461	11	5,814	62	1,497
Spaniard	57	16,923	13	15,264	76	2,046
Hispanic Latin American.	287	40,998	43	34,798	239	5,863
Other Spanish/Hispanic/Latino. . . .	188	20,694	24	16,654	140	3,247
American Indian and Alaska Native . . .	197	34,344	33	29,226	299	6,624
Asian and Pacific Islander	913	306,933	290	278,294	2,203	46,180
Asian Indian.	167	67,503	67	61,760	491	12,586
Chinese	253	106,197	91	98,233	692	12,945
Filipino	85	11,078	15	8,966	110	2,667
Japanese	86	43,741	23	41,295	262	7,107
Korean	136	45,936	50	40,746	334	5,789
Vietnamese	98	9,323	19	6,768	79	1,166
Other Asian	71	19,016	22	16,801	202	3,136
Native Hawaiian	16	2,250	2	1,957	21	498
Other Pacific Islander	4	1,888	1	1,768	13	286
White non-Hispanic.	17,317	7,763,011	4,373	7,252,270	54,084	1,395,150
50-percent minority/50-percent nonminority	85	37,732	39	34,632	302	8,619
Other [1]	382	10,161,242	(S)	10,104,058	44,458	1,437,195

S Does not meet publication standards. [1] Includes publicly-held corporations, foreign-owned companies, and not-for-profit companies.

Source: U.S. Census Bureau, *1997 Economic Census, Company Statistics Series, Company Summary 1997,* EC97CS-1; and *Survey of Minority-Owned Business Enterprises—Asians and Pacific Islanders 1997,* EC97CS-5; and *Hispanic 1997,* EC97CS-4.

No. 719. Women-Owned Firms by Major Industry Group: 1997

[818,669,084 represents $818,669,084,000. Based on the 1987 Standard Industrial Classification code; see text, this section]

Major industry group	All firms		Firms with paid employees			
	Firms [1] (number)	Sales and receipts ($1,000)	Firms [1] (number)	Sales and receipts ($1,000)	Employees (number)	Annual payroll ($1,000)
All industries.	5,417,034	818,669,084	846,780	717,763,965	7,076,081	149,115,699
Agric. services, forestry, and fishing. . .	74,444	5,852,901	16,652	4,599,852	77,370	1,442,618
Mining	20,030	7,186,113	2,180	6,491,900	25,982	873,455
Construction [2]	157,173	67,632,059	65,707	63,738,665	518,142	15,302,000
Manufacturing	121,108	113,722,304	41,141	111,658,770	901,434	24,674,596
Transportation and public utilities	128,999	32,944,160	35,623	30,063,926	321,759	7,803,912
Wholesale trade.	125,645	188,488,639	50,459	184,574,784	468,276	14,086,123
Retail trade	919,990	152,041,311	211,583	137,296,015	1,574,747	19,520,353
Finance, insurance, and real estate . . .	479,469	56,021,358	66,375	38,920,419	276,045	7,549,811
Services	2,981,266	186,161,274	355,768	140,255,817	2,908,080	57,808,228
Industries not classified	411,596	8,618,965	3,979	163,817	4,246	54,604

[1] Firms may be classified in more than one industry group. [2] Includes SIC 6552, Subdividers and developers, formerly included in real estate.

Source: U.S. Census Bureau, *1997 Economic Census, Company Statistics Series, Survey of Women-Owned Business Enterprises, Women-Owned Businesses 1997,* Series EC97CS-2.

No. 720. Hispanic-Owned Firms by Major Industry Group: 1997

[186,274,582 represents $186,274,582,000. Based on the 1987 Standard Industrial Classification code; see text, this section]

Major industry group	All firms		Firms with paid employees			
	Firms [1] (number)	Sales and receipts ($1,000)	Firms [1] (number)	Sales and receipts ($1,000)	Employees (number)	Annual payroll ($1,000)
All industries	1,199,896	186,274,582	211,884	158,674,537	1,388,746	29,830,028
Agric. services, forestry, and fishing. . .	40,040	2,279,397	5,925	1,309,733	25,955	416,702
Mining	1,909	429,446	325	367,442	3,569	97,854
Construction [2]	152,573	21,923,384	31,478	19,146,212	168,873	4,218,419
Manufacturing	25,552	28,684,759	10,173	27,719,404	171,738	4,549,598
Transportation and public utilities	84,544	8,293,935	12,735	5,605,332	79,682	1,587,106
Wholesale trade.	31,480	40,386,625	14,125	38,746,137	94,281	2,388,988
Retail trade	155,061	32,280,310	48,713	28,599,447	324,474	3,892,182
Finance, insurance, and real estate . . .	56,629	6,644,826	9,944	4,728,312	34,783	949,006
Services	500,449	39,177,767	70,838	30,406,573	463,889	11,297,362
Industries not classified	151,931	6,174,133	7,909	2,045,945	21,502	432,812

[1] Firms may be classified in more than one industry group. [2] Includes SIC 6552, Subdividers and developers, formerly included in real estate.

Source: U.S. Census Bureau, *1997 Economic Census, Company Statistics Series, Survey of Minority-Owned Business Enterprises, Hispanic 1997,* Series EC97CS-4.

484   Business Enterprise

No. 721. Black-Owned Firms by Major Industry Group: 1997

[71,214,662 represents $71,214,662,000. Based on the 1987 Standard Industrial Classification code; see text, this section]

Major industry group	All firms		Firms with paid employees			
	Firms [1] (number)	Sales and receipts ($1,000)	Firms [1] (number)	Sales and receipts ($1,000)	Employees (number)	Annual payroll ($1,000)
All industries	**823,499**	**71,214,662**	**93,235**	**56,377,860**	**718,341**	**14,322,312**
Agricultural services, forestry, and fishing . .	12,464	417,169	1,356	259,649	5,457	77,198
Mining	231	21,551	16	12,867	186	5,319
Construction [2]	56,508	7,712,059	12,973	6,587,348	70,928	1,510,252
Manufacturing	10,447	3,682,510	1,931	3,463,861	26,624	652,787
Transportation and public utilities	71,586	6,376,645	6,184	4,252,240	47,289	909,470
Wholesale trade.	8,120	5,818,734	2,139	5,573,907	13,746	471,320
Retail trade	87,568	13,803,266	14,074	12,244,399	125,480	1,497,111
Finance, insurance, and real estate	37,934	3,088,582	4,820	2,189,556	18,379	498,318
Services	437,646	25,925,092	43,529	19,503,488	388,398	8,212,775
Industries not classified	101,128	4,369,056	6,347	2,290,545	21,853	487,761

[1] Firms may be classified in more than one industry group.   [2] Includes SIC 6552, Subdividers and developers, formerly included in Real Estate.

Source: U.S. Census Bureau, *1997 Economic Census, Company Statistics Series, Survey of Minority-Owned Business Enterprises, Black 1997*, Series EC97CS-3.

No. 722. Asian- and Pacific Islander-Owned Firms by Major Industry Group: 1997

[306,932,982 represents $306,932,982,000. Based on the 1987 Standard Industrial Classification code; see text, this section]

Major industry group	All firms		Firms with paid employees			
	Firms [1] (number)	Sales and receipts ($1,000)	Firms [1] (number)	Sales and receipts ($1,000)	Employees (number)	Annual payroll ($1,000)
All industries	**912,960**	**306,932,982**	**289,999**	**278,294,345**	**2,203,079**	**46,179,519**
Agric. services, forestry, and fishing . . .	12,988	1,140,670	1,927	791,843	11,359	226,707
Mining	660	253,329	87	229,059	1,007	33,447
Construction [2]	27,711	7,485,505	6,398	6,522,807	42,533	1,386,303
Manufacturing	23,242	28,952,417	10,553	28,271,707	238,167	5,513,875
Transportation and public utilities	37,501	5,625,483	5,916	4,427,646	52,441	1,220,240
Wholesale trade.	50,400	105,466,223	30,095	102,902,082	211,510	6,128,070
Retail trade	195,691	67,895,241	106,264	62,467,158	644,644	7,497,710
Finance, insurance, and real estate . . .	68,765	11,398,069	9,429	7,585,054	42,243	1,185,688
Services	406,010	67,762,462	107,910	57,153,191	896,731	21,719,605
Industries not classified	90,509	10,953,582	11,937	7,943,797	62,443	1,267,874

[1] Firms may be classified in more than one industry group.   [2] Includes SIC 6552, Subdividers and developers, formerly included in Real Estate.

Source: U.S. Census Bureau, *1997 Economic Census, Company Statistics Series, Survey of Minority-Owned Business Enterprises, Asians and Pacific Islanders 1997*, Series EC97CS-5.

No. 723. American Indian- and Alaska Native-Owned Firms by Major Industry Group: 1997

[34,343,907 represents $34,343,907,000. Based on the 1987 Standard Industrial Classification code; see text, this section]

Major industry group	All firms		Firms with paid employees			
	Firms [1] (number)	Sales and receipts ($1,000)	Firms [1] (number)	Sales and receipts ($1,000)	Employees (number)	Annual payroll ($1,000)
All industries	**197,300**	**34,343,907**	**33,277**	**29,226,260**	**298,661**	**6,624,235**
Agric. services, forestry, and fishing . . .	8,942	360,484	797	174,841	2,760	50,041
Mining	947	543,908	199	465,764	2,124	64,737
Construction [2]	27,435	5,384,815	6,012	4,648,924	38,419	1,021,524
Manufacturing	6,717	2,503,417	1,612	2,334,452	21,206	563,454
Transportation and public utilities	6,291	1,620,515	1,118	1,347,949	10,584	276,381
Wholesale trade.	4,365	3,155,143	1,145	3,036,534	9,801	260,713
Retail trade	14,768	4,618,484	4,645	4,245,552	31,451	441,783
Finance, insurance, and real estate . . .	4,616	1,190,741	1,004	1,025,527	4,585	133,050
Services	34,144	5,202,704	4,826	4,497,918	66,627	1,541,895
Industries not classified	89,243	9,763,696	12,086	7,448,800	111,103	2,270,656

[1] Firms may be classified in more than one industry group.   [2] Includes SIC 6552, Subdividers and developers, formerly included in Real Estate.

Source: U.S. Census Bureau, *1997 Economic Census, Company Statistics Series, Survey of Minority-Owned Business Enterprises, American Indians and Alaska Natives 1997*, Series EC97CS-6.

No. 724. Bankruptcy Petitions Filed and Pending by Type and Chapter: 1990 to 2001

[For years ending June 30. Covers only bankruptcy cases filed under the Bankruptcy Reform Act of 1978. *Bankruptcy:* legal recognition that a company or individual is insolvent and must restructure or liquidate. Petitions "filed" means the commencement of a proceeding through the presentation of a petition to the clerk of the court; "pending" is a proceeding in which the administration has not been completed]

Item	1990	1994	1995	1996	1997	1998	1999	2000	2001
Total filed	725,484	845,257	858,104	1,042,110	1,316,999	1,429,451	1,391,964	1,276,922	1,386,606
Business [1]	64,688	56,748	51,288	52,938	53,993	50,202	39,934	36,910	37,135
Nonbusiness [2]	660,796	788,509	806,816	989,172	1,263,006	1,379,249	1,352,030	1,240,012	1,349,471
Voluntary	723,886	844,087	856,991	1,040,915	1,315,782	1,428,550	1,391,130	1,276,146	1,385,840
Involuntary	1,598	1,170	1,113	1,195	1,217	901	834	776	766
Chapter 7 [3]	505,337	578,903	581,390	712,129	917,274	1,015,453	993,414	885,447	972,659
Chapter 9 [4]	7	17	12	10	9	5	3	8	10
Chapter 11 [5]	19,591	17,098	13,221	12,859	11,159	9,613	8,684	9,947	10,272
Chapter 12 [6]	1,351	976	904	1,063	1,006	845	829	732	206
Chapter 13 [7]	199,186	248,246	262,551	316,024	387,521	403,501	389,004	380,770	403,418
Section 304 [8]	12	17	26	24	29	34	30	18	41
Total pending	961,919	1,134,036	1,090,446	1,169,112	1,331,290	1,389,917	1,394,794	1,400,416	1,535,903

[1] Business bankruptcies include those filed under chapters 7, 9, 11, or 12. [2] Bankruptcies include those filed under chapters 7, 11, or 13. [3] Chapter 7, liquidation of nonexempt assets of businesses or individuals. [4] Chapter 9, adjustment of debts of a municipality. [5] Chapter 11, individual or business reorganization. [6] Chapter 12, adjustment of debts of a family farmer with regular income, effective November 26, 1986. [7] Chapter 13, adjustment of debts of an individual with regular income. [8] Chapter 11 U.S.C., Section 304, cases ancillary to foreign proceedings.

Source: Administrative Office of the U.S. Courts, *Statistical Tables for the Federal Judiciary.*

No. 725. Bankruptcy Cases Filed by State: 1995 to 2001

[In thousands (858.1 represents 858,100). For years ending June 30. Covers only bankruptcy cases filed under the Bankruptcy Reform Act of 1978. *Bankruptcy:* legal recognition that a company or individual is insolvent and must restructure or liquidate. Petitions "filed" means the commencement of a proceeding through the presentation of a petition to the clerk of the court]

State	1995	1999	2000	2001	State	1995	1999	2000	2001
Total [1]	858.1	1,392.0	1,276.9	1,386.6	Missouri	15.1	27.9	26.3	28.4
					Montana	2.1	3.7	3.3	3.7
Alabama	24.3	31.2	31.4	36.6	Nebraska	3.4	5.8	5.6	6.5
Alaska	0.9	1.5	1.4	1.5	Nevada	7.3	15.5	14.3	16.3
Arizona	14.8	23.7	21.7	22.8	New Hampshire ...	3.1	4.5	3.9	3.9
Arkansas	7.9	16.8	16.3	19.7					
California	140.4	200.2	160.6	147.9	New Jersey	25.5	44.1	38.7	40.3
					New Mexico	3.7	7.7	7.1	8.0
Colorado	13.1	17.3	15.6	17.4	New York	48.8	74.4	61.7	66.0
Connecticut	8.5	13.2	11.4	11.3	North Carolina	14.0	26.8	25.8	30.7
Delaware.	1.4	3.9	4.9	4.0	North Dakota	1.2	2.2	2.0	2.1
District of Columbia.	1.4	2.8	2.6	2.5					
Florida	43.4	79.2	74.0	80.4	Ohio	32.4	55.3	53.6	63.6
					Oklahoma	13.2	21.3	19.3	21.9
Georgia	42.1	59.3	57.9	64.9	Oregon	13.2	18.2	18.1	20.9
Hawaii	1.8	5.9	5.0	4.8	Pennsylvania	22.0	45.7	43.8	49.2
Idaho	3.7	7.3	7.3	7.9	Rhode Island	3.0	5.3	4.8	4.8
Illinois	39.2	66.6	62.3	68.2					
Indiana	22.3	38.9	37.5	43.0	South Carolina	6.9	11.6	11.7	13.0
					South Dakota.	1.3	2.3	2.1	2.4
Iowa...........	5.9	8.9	8.2	9.9	Tennessee.	35.5	48.2	47.1	55.5
Kansas	8.5	12.3	11.4	12.8	Texas	43.8	68.6	62.9	69.1
Kentucky	13.0	21.4	20.8	24.1	Utah	6.9	14.0	14.4	17.4
Louisiana	13.4	22.5	23.1	25.4					
Maine.	1.9	4.5	4.1	4.4	Vermont	0.9	1.9	1.6	1.7
					Virginia	25.5	41.2	37.1	39.2
Maryland	16.3	34.1	31.1	33.7	Washington	18.6	32.4	31.2	34.8
Massachusetts	14.3	20.9	16.7	17.0	West Virginia	3.8	8.4	8.2	9.9
Michigan	22.7	38.8	36.4	41.8	Wisconsin	11.8	18.9	18.0	20.3
Minnesota	14.1	17.4	15.4	16.9	Wyoming.	1.2	2.2	2.0	2.4
Mississippi.	10.6	18.1	17.9	20.8					

[1] Includes outlying areas not shown separately.

Source: Administrative Office of the U.S. Courts, unpublished data.

No. 726. Mergers and Acquisitions—Summary: 1990 to 2001

[**205.6 represents $205,600,000,000**. Covers transactions valued at $5 million or more. Values based on transactions for which price data revealed. *All activity* includes mergers, acquisitions, acquisitions of partial interest that involve a 40 percent stake in the target or an investment of at least $100 million, divestitures, and leveraged transactions that result in a change in ownership. *Divestiture:* sale of a business, division, or subsidiary by corporate owner to another party. *Leveraged buyout:* acquisition of a business in which buyers use mostly borrowed money to finance purchase price and incorporate debt into capital structure of business after change in ownership]

Item	Unit	1990	1994	1995	1996	1997	1998	1999	2000	2001
All activity:										
Number	Number . .	4,239	4,383	4,981	5,639	8,770	9,634	9,599	11,169	7,610
Value	Bil. dol. . .	205.6	524.9	895.8	1,059.3	1,610.3	2,480.2	3,401.6	3,440.0	1,711.1
Divestitures:										
Number.	Number . .	1,907	2,005	2,227	2,423	3,189	3,304	3,184	3,497	2,776
Value	Bil. dol. . .	90.8	236.9	365.3	319.0	616.2	554.8	677.7	891.8	654.7
Leveraged buyouts:										
Number.	Number . .	177	173	206	169	198	238	344	476	323
Value	Bil. dol. . .	17.6	10.6	23.6	17.4	24.1	27.2	58.1	86.2	58.9
Foreign acquisitions of U.S. companies:										
Number	Number . .	773	(NA)	80	73	441	483	560	741	449
Value	Bil. dol. . .	56.4	(NA)	3.5	2.9	64.8	232.5	297.0	334.5	132.4
U.S. acquisitions overseas:										
Number	Number . .	392	207	317	364	539	746	698	746	467
Value	Bil. dol. . .	20.5	21.1	62.6	59.3	87.8	127.8	158.1	136.0	114.8

NA Not available.

No. 727. Mergers and Acquisitions by Industry: 2001

[**660,654 represents $660,654,000,000**. See headnote Table 726]

Industry	U.S. Company acquiring U.S. company		Foreign company acquiring U.S. company		U.S. company acquiring foreign company	
	Number	Value (mil. dol.)	Number	Value (mil. dol.)	Number	Value (mil. dol.)
Total activity [1]	2,033	660,654	449	132,365	467	114,793
Advertising services.	15	3,223	3	47	4	41
Aerospace and aircraft.	7	1,740	2	176	3	245
Agriculture, forestry, and fishing	13	1,149	-	-	5	138
Air transportation and shipping.	9	1,765	2	326	1	28
Amusement and recreation services	26	4,102	11	513	3	201
Business services	279	24,672	83	9,329	55	6,993
Chemicals	17	9,521	7	509	9	471
Commercial banks, bank holding companies . .	111	26,300	3	7,200	6	13,864
Communications equipment	37	5,539	8	1,322	7	1,977
Computer and office equipment	27	31,160	12	702	8	1,209
Construction firms	25	4,957	5	114	3	711
Credit institutions.	18	8,288	1	9,341	2	492
Drugs	61	46,573	10	934	16	2,198
Electric, gas, water distribution.	49	44,852	12	9,739	26	16,325
Electronic and electrical equipment.	81	14,350	21	1,601	20	4,285
Food and kindred products	40	14,845	11	14,565	17	6,084
Health services	38	3,506	2	194	2	100
Holding companies, except banks	3	6,041	2	322	-	-
Hotels and casinos	22	3,610	3	286	7	593
Insurance	39	30,543	12	6,665	15	2,724
Investment & commodity firms, dealers, exchanges	99	31,883	18	8,183	23	1,683
Machinery	35	6,303	7	206	13	813
Measuring, medical, photo equip; clocks	76	16,634	27	2,119	19	1,682
Metal and metal products	36	7,165	8	2,466	8	1,628
Mining.	14	690	5	2,637	8	5,153
Motion picture production and distribution . . .	14	7,604	5	441	1	12
Oil and gas; petroleum refining	81	72,176	13	4,561	39	16,925
Paper and allied products	14	7,535	10	3,868	5	1,632
Prepackaged software	167	12,471	33	1,750	35	1,471
Printing, publishing, and allied services	26	2,302	7	2,522	4	2,850
Radio & television broadcasting stations	62	87,727	3	12,625	3	564
Real estate, mortgage bankers and brokers . .	57	17,757	6	1,671	18	2,741
Retail trade-eating and drinking places	24	1,221	3	3,948	-	-
Retail trade-food stores	9	1,135	4	766	1	279
Retail trade—general merchandise and apparel	14	1,334	-	-	-	-
Real estate, mortgage bankers and brokers . .	36	8,465	2	200	(NA)	(NA)
Soaps, cosmetics, & personal-care products .	9	6,269	1	11	-	-
Stone, clay, glass and concrete products	7	2,532	4	69	4	297
Telecommunications.	85	48,265	17	5,366	23	5,004
Textile and apparel products	26	3,739	3	57	3	301
Transportation and shipping (except air)	35	10,084	12	9,599	12	7,532
Transportation equipment	26	5,235	4	51	8	3,319
Wholesale trade—durable goods	27	3,419	17	302	12	216
Wholesale trade—nondurable goods.	21	4,700	7	2,665	7	137

- Represents zero.   NA Not available.   [1] Includes other industries not shown separately.

Source of Tables 726 and 727: Thomson Financial Securities Data, Newark, NJ, Merger & Corporate Transactions Database (copyright).

U.S. Census Bureau, Statistical Abstract of the United States: 2002

No. 728. Small Business Administration Loans to Small Businesses: 1980 to 2001

[For fiscal year ending in year shown; see text, Section 8, State and Local Government Finances and Employment. A small business must be independently owned and operated, must not be dominant in its particular industry, and must meet standards set by the Small Business Administration as to its annual receipts or number of employees]

Item	Unit	1980	1990	1995	1996	1997	1998	1999	2000	2001
Loans, all businesses	1,000. . .	31.7	18.8	60.1	52.7	49.4	47.2	48.9	48.3	48.2
Loans, minority-owned businesses. .	1,000. . .	6.0	2.4	10.4	10.1	10.6	10.9	12.1	12.1	12.0
Percent of all business loans. . . .	Percent .	19	13	19	19	22	23	25	25	25
Value of total loans [1] . . . . [2]	Mil. dol. .	3,858	4,354	9,854	10,177	10,904	10,795	12,142	12,343	12,154
Minority business loans [2]	Mil. dol. .	470	473	1,885	2,130	2,603	2,697	3,361	3,652	3,487

[1] Includes both SBA and bank portions of loans.   [2] SBA direct loans and guaranteed portion of bank loans only.

Source: U.S. Small Business Administration, Management Information Summary, unpublished data.

No. 729. Venture Capital Commitments by Source: 1980 to 2001

[In billions of dollars (2.1 represents $2,100,000,000), except as indicated. Venture capital commitment: investment in venture capital partnerships]

Source	1980	1985	1990	1995	1996	1997	1998	1999	2000	2001
Capital commitments	2.1	3.7	3.3	9.9	12.4	17.6	30.7	58.8	104.9	40.3
Corporations	0.4	0.6	0.2	0.5	2.5	4.4	3.6	8.4	3.9	1.0
Endowments & foundations.	0.3	0.4	0.5	2.0	1.5	2.9	1.9	10.1	22.1	8.8
Individuals & families	0.4	0.6	0.4	1.7	0.8	2.2	3.5	5.6	12.4	3.8
Financial & insurance.	0.3	0.5	0.3	2.0	0.4	1.1	3.2	9.1	24.4	9.9
Pension funds	0.7	1.6	1.8	3.8	7.2	6.9	18.5	25.6	42.1	16.8
PERCENT DISTRIBUTION										
Corporations	21	15	7	5	20	25	12	14	4	3
Endowments & foundations.	15	10	14	20	12	17	6	17	21	22
Individuals & families	17	17	13	17	7	12	11	10	12	9
Financial & insurance.	14	14	10	20	3	6	10	16	23	25
Pension funds	32	43	56	38	58	39	60	44	40	42

Source: Venture Economics Investor Services, Boston, MA, *Venture Capital Journal*, monthly.

No. 730. Patents and Trademarks: 1980 to 2001

[In thousands (113.0 represents 113,000). Calendar year data. Covers patents issued to citizens of the United States and residents of foreign countries. For data on foreign countries, see Table 1325]

Type	1980	1985	1990	1995	1997	1998	1999	2000	2001
Patent applications filed.	113.0	127.1	176.7	228.8	233.0	261.4	289.5	315.8	346.6
Inventions	104.3	117.0	164.6	212.4	215.3	243.0	270.2	295.9	326.5
Designs	7.8	9.6	11.3	15.4	16.5	17.1	17.8	18.3	18.3
Botanical plants	0.2	0.2	0.4	0.5	0.6	0.7	0.9	0.8	0.9
Reissues.	0.6	0.3	0.5	0.6	0.5	0.6	0.7	0.8	0.8
Patents issued.	66.2	77.3	99.2	113.8	124.1	163.1	169.1	176.0	184.0
Inventions	61.8	71.7	90.4	101.4	112.0	147.5	153.5	157.5	166.0
Individuals	13.8	12.9	17.3	17.4	17.6	22.5	22.8	22.4	21.7
Corporations:									
United States	27.7	31.2	36.1	44.0	50.2	66.1	69.4	70.9	74.3
Foreign [1]	19.1	26.4	36.0	39.1	42.9	57.9	60.3	63.3	69.0
U.S. Government.	1.2	1.1	1.0	1.0	0.9	1.0	1.0	0.9	1.0
Designs	3.9	5.1	8.0	11.7	11.4	14.8	14.7	17.4	16.9
Botanical plants	0.1	0.2	0.3	0.4	0.4	0.6	0.4	0.5	0.6
Reissues.	0.3	0.3	0.4	0.3	0.3	0.3	0.4	0.5	0.5
U.S. residents [2]	40.8	43.3	52.8	64.4	69.9	90.6	94.0	96.9	98.6
Foreign country residents [2]	25.4	33.9	46.2	49.4	54.2	72.5	75.1	79.1	85.4
Percent of total	38.4	43.9	46.7	43.4	43.7	44.4	44.4	44.9	46.4
Other published documents [3]	(Z)	(Z)	0.1	0.1	0.1	0.1	0.1	0.1	0.1
Trademarks:									
Applications filed.	46.8	65.1	127.3	188.9	234.6	246.6	328.6	296.5	232.9
Issued	24.7	71.7	60.8	92.5	145.2	136.1	191.9	115.2	133.8
Trademarks	18.9	65.8	53.6	85.6	138.2	129.9	184.9	106.4	102.3
Trademark renewals.	5.9	5.9	7.2	6.9	7.0	6.2	7.0	8.8	31.5

Z Less than 50.   [1] Includes patents to foreign governments.   [2] Includes patents for inventions, designs, botanical plants, and reissues.   [3] Includes Defensive Publications, a practice which began in November 1968 and ended in July 1986; and Statutory Invention Registrations, the current practice, which began May 1985. These documents are patent applications, which are published to provide the defensive properties of a patent, but do not have the enforceable rights of a patent.

Source: U.S. Patent and Trademark Office, "Statistical Reports Available For Viewing, Calendar Year Patent Statistics"; published 1 May 2002; <http://www.uspto.gov/web/offices/ac/ido/oeip/taf/reports.htm>.

No. 731. Patents by Industry: 1980 to 2000

[Based on the 1972 Standard Industrial Classification (SIC). Includes all patents for inventions granted to residents of the United States, its territories, and foreign citizens. Individual industries may not add to total since a patent may be recorded in more than one industry category. Data for all years have been revised to reflect the U.S. Patent Classification System as of December 2000]

Industry	SIC code	1980	1985	1990	1995	1999	2000
Total	(X)	61,819	71,661	90,364	101,419	153,485	157,495
Durable goods:							
Stone, clay, and glass products	32	1,221	1,307	1,638	1,574	2,322	2,123
Primary metals	33, 3462-3	706	780	913	901	1,031	978
Fabricated metal products [1]	34	5,012	5,560	6,771	5,931	8,390	8,550
Machinery, except electrical	35	14,325	16,841	19,144	21,272	34,524	35,416
Electronic and other electric equipment	36, 3825	10,737	13,892	19,088	25,284	40,140	44,293
Transportation equipment	37, 348	3,107	3,743	4,727	4,462	6,091	6,714
Instruments and related products [2]	38	7,443	8,938	12,297	14,396	20,500	20,648
Nondurable goods:							
Food and kindred products	20	484	546	730	601	918	927
Textile mill products	22	420	494	501	609	845	739
Chemicals and allied products	28	9,880	10,274	12,487	13,565	20,829	19,433
Oil and gas extraction, petroleum products . .	13, 29	595	802	664	643	724	750
Rubber and miscellaneous plastics products .	30	2,611	3,045	3,818	3,934	5,098	5,036
Other industries	(X)	5,279	5,440	7,586	8,249	12,073	11,887

X Not applicable.   [1] Excludes SIC groups 3462, 3463, and 348.   [2] Excludes SIC group 3825.

Source: U.S. Patent and Trademark Office, *Patenting Trends in the United States, State Country Report, 1963-2000.*

No. 732. Patents by State: 2001

[Includes only U.S. patents granted to residents of the United States and territories]

State	Total	Inventions	Designs	Botanical plants	Reissues	State	Total	Inventions	Designs	Botanical plants	Reissues
U.S. [1]	98,590	87,606	10,346	372	266	Missouri	966	841	119	3	3
Alabama	452	382	65	5	-	Montana	162	145	17	-	-
Alaska	58	50	8	-	-	Nebraska	253	215	33	4	1
Arizona	1,702	1,540	158	-	4	Nevada	371	313	56	-	2
Arkansas	222	180	36	3	3	New Hampshire . .	670	598	70	-	2
California	20,853	18,597	2,014	194	48	New Jersey	4,281	3,869	398	2	12
Colorado	2,108	1,927	177	1	3	New Mexico	391	376	15	-	-
Connecticut	2,071	1,853	213	-	5	New York	7,180	6,349	812	9	10
Delaware	423	381	38	1	3	North Carolina . . .	2,265	1,946	313	3	3
Dist. of Columbia .	73	67	5	-	1	North Dakota	107	97	9	1	-
Florida	3,147	2,649	440	44	14	Ohio	3,991	3,274	701	2	14
Georgia	1,599	1,370	223	1	5	Oklahoma	633	576	55	-	2
Hawaii	107	95	9	1	2	Oregon	1,504	1,259	231	11	3
Idaho	1,737	1,697	35	1	4	Pennsylvania . . .	3,839	3,534	271	22	12
Illinois	4,266	3,640	610	6	10	Rhode Island	334	287	46	-	1
Indiana	1,593	1,358	213	18	4	South Carolina . . .	642	565	75	2	-
Iowa	815	751	64	-	-	South Dakota . . .	85	76	9	-	-
Kansas	382	312	69	-	1	Tennessee	958	813	136	2	7
Kentucky	546	481	62	-	3	Texas	6,760	6,371	360	8	21
Louisiana	562	520	35	5	2	Utah	803	715	84	1	3
Maine	156	145	11	-	-	Vermont	507	453	53	-	1
Maryland	1,635	1,482	146	2	5	Virginia	1,275	1,115	157	1	2
Massachusetts . .	3,972	3,667	290	1	14	Washington	2,257	1,969	274	9	5
Michigan	4,235	3,853	368	3	11	West Virginia	161	148	12	-	1
Minnesota	2,926	2,635	280	1	10	Wisconsin	2,249	1,837	403	2	7
Mississippi	226	166	56	3	1	Wyoming	59	51	7	-	1

- Represents zero.   [1] Includes U.S. territories not shown separately.

Source: U.S. Patent and Trademark Office, "Statistical Reports Available For Viewing, Calendar Year Patent Statistics"; published 1 May 2002; <http://www.uspto.gov/web/offices/ac/ido/oeip/taf/reports.htm>.

No. 733. Copyright Registration by Subject Matter: 1990 to 2001

[In thousands (590.7 represents 590,700). For years ending September 30. Comprises claims to copyrights registered for both U.S. and foreign works. Semiconductor chips and renewals are not considered copyright registration claims]

Subject matter	1990	1995	2000	2001	Subject matter	1990	1995	2000	2001
Total copyright claims . . .	590.7	577.8	497.6	580.8	Works of the visual arts [3]	76.7	95.5	85.8	99.9
Monographs [1]	179.7	196.0	169.7	212.1					
Serials	111.5	88.7	69.0	62.2	Semiconductor chip				
Sound recordings	37.5	34.0	34.2	50.3	products	1.0	0.8	0.7	0.5
Musical works [2]	185.3	163.6	138.9	156.3	Renewals	51.8	30.6	16.8	19.7

[1] Includes computer software and machine readable works.   [2] Includes dramatic works, accompanying music, choreography, pantomimes, motion pictures, and filmstrips.   [3] Two-dimensional works of fine and graphic art, including prints and art reproductions; sculptural works; technical drawings and models; photographs; commercial prints and labels; works of applied arts, cartographic works, and multimedia works.

Source: The Library of Congress, Copyright Office, *Annual Report.*

No. 734. Net Stock of Fixed Private Capital by Industry: 1990 to 2000

[In billions of dollars (12,760 represents $12,760,000,000,000). Estimates as of Dec. 31. Net stock estimates are presented in terms of current cost. Based on the 1987 Standard Industrial Classification]

Industry	1990	1995	1997	1998	1999	2000
Fixed private capital	**12,760**	**15,908**	**17,653**	**18,650**	**19,767**	**21,165**
Agriculture, forestry, and fishing	481	551	594	620	643	675
Farms	447	498	532	554	571	596
Housing	161	187	202	212	224	238
Other	285	311	329	341	347	358
Agricultural services, forestry, and fishing	35	53	62	67	73	79
Mining	431	455	538	530	529	580
Metal mining	29	34	36	36	36	36
Coal mining	32	39	43	44	45	46
Oil and gas extraction	350	360	435	425	423	470
Nonmetallic minerals, except fuels	19	21	23	25	26	27
Construction	82	101	116	126	139	149
Manufacturing	1,217	1,457	1,584	1,654	1,713	1,794
Durable goods	636	747	819	860	894	937
Lumber and wood products	25	29	31	32	34	35
Furniture and fixtures	11	13	14	15	16	17
Stone, clay, and glass products	40	44	49	53	56	61
Primary metal industries	116	126	131	133	135	137
Fabricated metal products	70	81	87	90	93	97
Industrial machinery and equipment	110	126	138	146	153	162
Electronic and other electric equipment	92	120	143	153	161	171
Motor vehicles and equipment	64	85	95	100	103	106
Other transportation equipment	51	55	57	60	63	66
Instruments and related products	45	54	59	62	65	69
Miscellaneous manufacturing industries	12	14	15	15	16	17
Nondurable goods	581	711	765	794	820	858
Food and kindred products	119	146	158	165	173	183
Tobacco products	9	9	10	10	10	10
Textile mill products	34	38	39	40	41	42
Apparel and other textile products	11	13	14	14	15	15
Paper and allied products	84	98	104	107	108	110
Printing and publishing	52	59	64	66	70	77
Chemicals and allied products	157	200	219	228	236	248
Petroleum and coal products	75	93	95	96	97	98
Rubber and miscellaneous plastics products	38	52	59	64	68	73
Leather and leather products	3	3	3	3	3	3
Transportation and public utilities	1,855	2,232	2,401	2,471	2,575	2,722
Transportation	582	692	747	766	797	838
Railroad transportation	304	337	352	347	341	341
Local and interurban passenger transit	21	25	28	28	30	32
Trucking and warehousing	71	99	113	117	122	127
Water transportation	35	37	39	40	41	43
Transportation by air	85	115	131	145	169	194
Pipelines, except natural gas	38	44	47	47	49	50
Transportation services	26	34	37	41	45	50
Communications	436	549	621	653	698	755
Telephone and telegraph	377	458	507	527	560	604
Radio and television	59	91	114	125	138	151
Electric, gas, and sanitary services	837	991	1,033	1,052	1,080	1,128
Electric services	609	696	718	721	735	763
Gas services	165	205	220	231	240	253
Sanitary services	63	89	95	100	105	113
Wholesale trade	286	379	435	464	499	540
Retail trade	391	514	582	618	657	708
Finance, insurance, and real estate	7,466	9,481	10,555	11,242	11,984	12,853
Depository institutions	236	268	285	300	314	333
Nondepository institutions	114	166	210	232	260	280
Security and commodity brokers	40	63	76	86	97	110
Insurance carriers	89	139	155	167	179	194
Insurance agents, brokers, and service	8	13	16	18	20	22
Real estate	6,944	8,779	9,747	10,362	11,025	11,811
Owner-occupied housing	4,337	5,718	6,396	6,827	7,294	7,862
Tenant-occupied housing	1,640	1,880	2,048	2,153	2,263	2,372
Other	967	1,182	1,303	1,383	1,468	1,577
Holding and other investment offices	35	52	66	77	90	104
Services	552	739	848	925	1,028	1,146
Hotels and other lodging places	105	125	147	159	171	185
Personal services	27	27	28	29	31	33
Business services	99	131	155	179	222	269
Auto repair, services, and parking	62	111	122	129	136	144
Miscellaneous repair services	9	12	14	14	15	16
Motion pictures	16	28	35	39	41	44
Amusement and recreation services	34	47	54	58	65	72
Other services	200	257	292	318	347	383
Health services	98	135	153	168	182	199
Legal services	18	19	21	22	24	26
Educational services	11	14	16	18	19	21
Other [1]	73	90	102	111	122	137

[1] Consists of social services; museums, botanical and zoological gardens, membership organizations; engineering and management services; and services, not elsewhere classified.

Source: U.S. Bureau of Economic Analysis, *Survey of Current Business,* September 2001.

No. 735. Gross Private Domestic Investment in Current and Real (1996) Dollars: 1990 to 2000

[In billions of dollars (861.7 represents $861,700,000,000)]

Item	1990	1994	1995	1996	1997	1998	1999	2000
CURRENT DOLLARS								
Gross private domestic investment . . .	861.7	1,097.1	1,143.8	1,242.7	1,390.5	1,538.7	1,636.7	1,767.5
Less: Consumption of fixed capital	579.5	714.6	743.6	781.9	832.4	884.3	953.3	1,029.9
Equals: Net private domestic investment	282.2	382.5	400.1	460.8	558.1	654.4	683.4	737.6
Fixed investment	847.2	1,034.6	1,110.7	1,212.7	1,327.7	1,465.6	1,578.2	1,718.1
Less: Consumption of fixed capital . . .	579.5	714.6	743.6	781.9	832.4	884.3	953.3	1,029.9
Equals: Net fixed investment	267.7	320.0	367.1	430.8	495.2	581.3	624.9	688.2
Nonresidential	630.3	748.6	825.1	899.4	999.4	1,101.2	1,174.6	1,293.1
Residential	216.8	286.0	285.6	313.3	328.2	364.4	403.5	425.1
Change in private inventories	14.5	62.6	33.0	30.0	62.9	73.1	58.6	49.4
CHAINED (1996) DOLLARS								
Gross private domestic investment . . .	907.3	1,107.0	1,140.6	1,242.7	1,393.3	1,558.0	1,660.1	1,772.9
Less: Consumption of fixed capital	612.6	724.3	742.6	781.9	831.8	894.7	967.9	1,036.2
Equals: Net private domestic investment	294.7	382.8	398.0	460.8	561.5	663.3	692.2	736.7
Fixed investment	894.6	1,045.9	1,109.2	1,212.7	1,328.6	1,480.0	1,595.4	1,716.2
Nonresidential	641.7	744.6	817.5	899.4	1,009.3	1,135.9	1,228.6	1,350.7
Residential	253.5	302.7	291.7	313.3	319.7	345.1	368.3	371.4
Change in private inventories	16.5	66.8	30.4	30.0	63.8	76.7	62.1	50.6

Source: U.S. Bureau of Economic Analysis, *National Income and Product Accounts, Volume 1, 1929-97*, and *Survey of Current Business,* August 2001. See also <http://www.bea.gov/bea/dn/nipaweb/selecttable.asp>.

No. 736. Capital Expenditures: 1998 to 2000

[In billions of dollars (971 represents $971,000,000,000). Based on the North American Industry Classification System (NAICS), see text, this section]

Item	NAICS code	All companies			Companies with employees			Companies without employees		
		1998	1999	2000	1998	1999	2000	1998	1999	2000
STRUCTURES AND EQUIPMENT										
Total	(X)	971	1,047	1,172	896	975	1,100	74	72	71
Structures	(X)	329	320	368	300	294	341	29	26	26
New	(X)	284	296	328	260	276	308	24	20	20
Used	(X)	45	24	40	40	18	33	4	6	6
Equipment	(X)	642	727	804	596	681	759	46	46	45
New	(X)	606	690	758	570	656	726	36	33	32
Used	(X)	36	37	46	26	24	34	10	13	12
CAPITAL LEASES AND CAPITALIZED INTEREST EXPENSES										
Capital leases	(X)	17	17	20	16	17	19	1	1	(Z)
Capitalized interest	(X)	(NA)	(NA)	(NA)	10	10	11	(NA)	(NA)	(NA)
INDUSTRY										
Total expenditures	(X)	(NA)	(NA)	(NA)	896	975	1,100	(NA)	(NA)	(NA)
Forestry, fishing, and agricultural services . .	113-115	(NA)	(NA)	(NA)	1	2	1	(NA)	(NA)	(NA)
Mining	21	(NA)	(NA)	(NA)	40	31	43	(NA)	(NA)	(NA)
Utilities	22	(NA)	(NA)	(NA)	36	43	61	(NA)	(NA)	(NA)
Construction	23	(NA)	(NA)	(NA)	27	23	24	(NA)	(NA)	(NA)
Manufacturing	31-33	(NA)	(NA)	(NA)	204	196	215	(NA)	(NA)	(NA)
Durable goods	321, 327, 33	(NA)	(NA)	(NA)	118	117	134	(NA)	(NA)	(NA)
Nondurable goods	31, 322-326	(NA)	(NA)	(NA)	86	79	80	(NA)	(NA)	(NA)
Wholesale trade	42	(NA)	(NA)	(NA)	29	32	35	(NA)	(NA)	(NA)
Retail trade	44-45	(NA)	(NA)	(NA)	57	64	70	(NA)	(NA)	(NA)
Transportation and warehousing	48-49	(NA)	(NA)	(NA)	51	57	60	(NA)	(NA)	(NA)
Information	51	(NA)	(NA)	(NA)	96	123	164	(NA)	(NA)	(NA)
Finance and insurance	52	(NA)	(NA)	(NA)	118	130	134	(NA)	(NA)	(NA)
Real estate and rental and leasing	53	(NA)	(NA)	(NA)	85	101	98	(NA)	(NA)	(NA)
Professional, scientific, and technical services	54	(NA)	(NA)	(NA)	22	30	33	(NA)	(NA)	(NA)
Management of companies and enterprises	55	(NA)	(NA)	(NA)	2	6	5	(NA)	(NA)	(NA)
Admin/support waste mgt/remediation services	56	(NA)	(NA)	(NA)	13	16	17	(NA)	(NA)	(NA)
Educational services	61	(NA)	(NA)	(NA)	13	14	18	(NA)	(NA)	(NA)
Health care and social assistance	62	(NA)	(NA)	(NA)	47	51	53	(NA)	(NA)	(NA)
Arts, entertainment, and recreation	71	(NA)	(NA)	(NA)	9	13	19	(NA)	(NA)	(NA)
Accommodation and food services	72	(NA)	(NA)	(NA)	21	23	26	(NA)	(NA)	(NA)
Other services (except public administration)	81	(NA)	(NA)	(NA)	21	17	21	(NA)	(NA)	(NA)
Structure and equipment expenditures serving multiple industry categories	(X)	(NA)	(NA)	(NA)	3	2	2	(NA)	(NA)	(NA)

NA Not available.   X Not applicable.   Z Less than $500 million.
Source: U.S. Census Bureau, *Annual Capital Expenditures, 2000*, Series ACE.

No. 737. Composite Indexes of Leading, Coincident, and Lagging Economic Indicators: 1990 to 2001

Item	Unit	1990	1995	1998	1999	2000	2001
Leading index, composite	1996=100. . .	94.0	97.6	105.5	109.0	110.1	109.5
Average weekly hours, manufacturing. . .	Hours	40.8	41.6	41.8	41.7	41.6	40.7
Average weekly initial claims for unemployment insurance	1,000.	385.6	359.3	316.8	296.9	299.4	407.1
Manufacturers' new orders, consumer goods and materials (1996 dol.).	Mil. dol.	128,882	152,881	171,358	182,547	183,252	164,994
Vendor performance, slower deliveries diffusion index	Percent	47.9	52.8	51.1	53.2	53.3	48.0
Manufacturers' new orders, nondefense capital goods (1996 dol.)	Mil. dol.	36,515	40,986	52,519	55,175	63,633	53,031
Building permits, new private housing units	1,000.	1,155	1,336	1,619	1,664	1,602	1,601
Stock prices, 500 common stocks	1941-43=10 .	334.6	541.6	1,084.3	1,326.1	1,426.8	1,192.1
Money supply, M2 (1996 dol.)	Bil. dol.	3,770	3,643	4,083	4,322	4,465	4,769
Interest rate spread, 10-year Treasury bonds less federal funds	Percent	0.45	0.74	-0.09	0.67	-0.21	1.13
Index of consumer expectations	1966:1=100 .	70.2	83.2	98.3	99.3	102.7	82.3
Coincident index, composite.	1996=100. . .	88.7	97.2	108.3	111.8	115.6	115.9
Employees on nonagricultural payrolls . .	1,000.	109,404	117,188	125,845	128,901	131,757	132,228
Personal income less transfer payments (1996 dol.)	Bil. dol.	5,032	5,446	6,251	6,457	6,742	6,916
Industrial production	1992=100. . .	98.9	114.4	134.5	139.4	145.7	140.4
Manufacturing and trade sales (1996 dol.).	Mil. dol.	593,865	699,548	774,192	819,707	855,776	849,485
Lagging index, composite	1996=100. . .	101.8	98.8	102.3	104.1	107.0	105.6
Average duration of unemployment	Weeks	12.0	16.6	14.5	13.4	12.6	13.1
Inventories to sales ratio, manufacturing and trade (1996 dol.) . . .	Ratio	1.47	1.41	1.40	1.38	1.38	1.39
Change in labor cost per unit of output, manufacturing	Percent	2.8	-2.4	-0.3	-0.5	2.5	6.3
Average prime rate	Percent	10.01	8.83	8.35	7.99	9.23	6.92
Commercial and industrial loans outstanding (1996 dol.)	Mil. dol.	606,695	562,542	686,323	756,187	847,501	750,830
Consumer installment credit to personal income ratio.	Percent	16.1	16.6	17.3	17.6	17.9	18.5
Change in consumer price index for services	Percent	5.8	3.5	2.6	2.5	3.8	3.9

Source: The Conference Board, New York, NY 10022-6601, *Business Cycle Indicators*, monthly <http://www.globalindicators.org> (copyright).

No. 738. Business Cycle Expansions and Contractions—Months of Duration: 1919 to 2001

[A trough is the low point of a business cycle; a peak is the high point. Contraction, or recession, is the period from peak to subsequent trough; expansion is the period from trough to subsequent peak. Business cycle reference dates are determined by the National Bureau of Economic Research, Inc.]

Business cycle reference date				Contraction (trough from previous peak)	Expansion (trough to peak)	Length of cycle	
Trough		Peak				Trough from previous trough	Peak from previous peak
Month	Year	Month	Year				
March.	1919	January	1920	[1]7	10	[2]51	[1]17
July	1921	May	1923	18	22	28	40
July	1924	October	1926	14	27	36	41
November	1927	August	1929	13	21	40	34
March.	1933	May	1937	43	50	64	93
June.	1938	February	1945	13	80	63	93
October	1945	November	1948	8	37	88	45
October	1949	July	1953	11	45	48	56
May	1954	August	1957	10	39	55	49
April.	1958	April	1960	8	24	47	32
February	1961	December	1969	10	106	34	116
November	1970	November	1973	11	36	117	47
March	1975	January	1980	16	58	52	74
July	1980	July	1981	6	12	64	18
November	1982	July	1990	16	92	28	108
March	1991	March	2001	8	120	100	128
Average, all cycles:							
1854 to 1991 (31 cycles).				18	35	53	[3]53
1854 to 1919 (16 cycles).				22	27	48	[4]49
1919 to 1945 (six cycles).				18	35	53	53
1945 to 1991 (nine cycles).				11	50	61	61
Average, peacetime cycles:							
1854 to 1991 (26 cycles).				19	29	48	[5]48
1854 to 1919 (14 cycles).				22	24	46	[6]47
1919 to 1945 (5 cycles) .				20	26	46	45
1945 to 1991 (7 cycles) .				11	43	53	53

[1] Previous peak: August 1918. [2] Previous trough: December 1914. [3] 30 cycles. [4] 15 cycles. [5] 25 cycles. [6] 13 cycles.

Source: National Bureau of Economic Research, Inc., Cambridge, MA, "Business Cycle Expansions and Contractions"; <http://www.nber.org/cycles.html>; (accessed: 25 June 2002).

No. 739. Industrial Production Indexes by Industry: 1990 to 2001

[1992=100. Data based on 1987 Standard Industrial Classification (SIC)]

Industry	SIC code	1990	1993	1994	1995	1996	1997	1998	1999	2000	2001
Total index	(X)	98.9	103.4	109.1	114.4	119.6	127.9	134.5	139.4	145.7	140.1
Manufacturing	(D)	98.5	103.7	110.0	115.8	121.5	131.1	138.8	144.7	151.6	144.8
Durable goods	(X)	99.0	105.6	114.8	124.4	135.0	149.6	164.1	176.3	190.0	179.3
Lumber and wood products . . .	24	101.6	100.8	105.9	107.9	110.4	113.1	117.4	122.0	118.8	113.0
Furniture and fixtures	25	100.9	105.4	109.5	113.6	116.2	126.2	135.2	141.9	146.3	138.7
Stone, clay, and glass products	32	105.0	101.9	107.9	110.8	117.5	121.0	126.9	130.8	133.9	130.8
Primary metal industries	33	104.0	105.1	113.8	116.2	119.7	125.5	127.7	129.4	131.9	116.9
Iron and steel	331,2	106.4	106.0	114.4	116.6	119.1	123.9	124.0	123.9	127.3	112.6
Fabricated metal products	34	101.2	104.3	112.1	116.3	120.1	126.5	131.3	132.4	137.2	130.4
Industrial machinery and equipment [1]	35	100.1	110.4	126.0	144.7	161.1	178.3	195.2	207.9	227.1	213.3
Computer and office equipment	357	81.4	123.8	155.7	216.9	311.3	438.3	598.3	804.6	1,070.0	1,088.0
Electronic and other electric equipment	36	87.7	109.8	131.3	165.5	206.3	266.8	334.5	411.3	536.6	504.2
Transportation equipment	37	102.3	104.0	108.8	108.5	110.2	120.2	130.6	137.8	137.1	128.5
Motor vehicles and equipment	371	95.3	114.4	133.6	137.6	137.6	148.4	154.7	174.3	177.6	162.9
Autos and light trucks	371pt	99.3	113.4	130.2	129.4	130.5	139.9	143.6	163.6	164.6	154.1
Aerospace and miscellaneous	372- 6,9	109.8	93.6	84.9	80.6	83.8	93.1	107.6	103.4	99.1	96.3
Instruments and related products	38	98.4	100.8	99.8	103.2	107.8	110.4	114.0	117.7	118.6	115.3
Nondurable goods	(X)	97.9	101.5	104.8	106.5	107.4	112.0	113.4	113.7	114.8	111.4
Food and kindred products	20	97.0	102.0	103.6	105.7	105.4	107.2	110.6	112.0	113.8	112.9
Tobacco products	21	105.4	84.1	104.4	111.8	113.5	111.7	107.6	93.5	93.0	93.8
Textile mill products	22	93.2	105.2	110.6	110.1	108.6	108.2	106.2	103.9	98.9	86.7
Paper and allied products	26	96.0	103.4	107.0	107.6	106.8	112.2	113.8	114.9	113.9	108.1
Printing and publishing	27	103.1	100.5	100.5	101.1	101.1	107.3	106.3	105.3	106.9	101.6
Chemicals and allied products . .	28	97.3	100.9	103.7	106.0	108.8	115.9	118.3	119.1	122.0	121.1
Petroleum and coal products . .	29	100.3	102.9	102.7	104.5	106.9	111.0	113.1	113.4	115.0	114.3
Rubber and misc. plastics products	30	92.2	106.9	116.5	119.7	123.3	130.9	135.7	142.5	144.9	136.8
Leather and leather products . .	31	107.8	100.9	93.5	86.8	87.7	86.4	78.1	74.5	71.4	63.1
Mining	(C)	104.8	100.0	102.3	102.0	103.5	105.3	102.9	98.2	100.7	101.3
Metal mining	10	93.1	98.7	100.5	101.8	104.3	108.8	108.1	99.8	97.2	88.4
Coal mining	12	103.7	94.0	103.0	102.6	105.0	108.2	109.7	107.8	107.1	111.7
Oil and gas extraction	13	106.4	101.1	101.6	100.4	101.6	102.5	98.6	92.4	95.6	96.1
Nonmetallic minerals except fuels	14	103.3	102.3	108.6	112.9	114.9	120.1	123.4	127.5	130.4	132.6
Utilities	(X)	98.3	104.0	105.4	109.1	112.7	112.7	114.3	117.3	120.7	119.8
Electric	491,3pt	99.2	103.9	105.6	109.6	112.8	113.2	117.1	120.0	123.3	123.1
Gas	492,3pt	94.4	104.3	104.6	107.2	112.3	110.5	102.9	106.2	109.9	109.1

X Not applicable.
Source: Board of Governors of the Federal Reserve System, *Federal Reserve Bulletin*, monthly; and *Industrial Production and Capacity Utilization*, Statistical Release G.17, monthly.

No. 740. Index of Manufacturing Capacity: 1980 to 2001

[1992 output=100. Annual figures are averages of monthly data. Capacity represents estimated quantity of output relative to output in 1992 which the current stock of plant and equipment in manufacturing industries was capable of producing. Primary processing manufacturing includes textile mill products, paper and products, industrial chemicals, synthetic materials, and fertilizers, petroleum products, rubber and plastics products, lumber and products, primary metals, fabricated metals, stone, clay and glass products, semiconductors and related electronic components, and motor vehicle parts. Advanced processing manufacturing includes foods; tobacco products, apparel products, printing and publishing, chemical products and other agricultural chemicals; leather and products; furniture and fixtures, industrial machinery and equipment; electrical machinery except semiconductors and related electronic components; transportation equipment except motor vehicle parts; instruments; and miscellaneous manufactures]

Year	Index of capacity	Relation of output to capacity (percent)			Year	Index of capacity	Relation of output to capacity (percent)		
		All manu-facturing	Primary processing	Advanced process-ing			All manu-facturing	Primary processing	Advanced process-ing
1980	95	79	77	81	1991	123	78	79	78
1981	98	78	76	80	1992	126	79	82	78
1982	100	72	68	74	1993	129	80	83	79
1983	102	74	74	75	1994	133	82	87	80
1984	105	80	81	79	1995	140	83	86	80
1985	109	79	79	78	1996	149	82	84	80
1986	112	79	79	78	1997	159	83	85	81
1987	114	81	84	80	1998	171	81	83	81
1988	116	84	86	82	1999	180	81	83	79
1989	118	84	85	83	2000	188	81	84	79
1990	121	81	83	81	2001	193	75	75	75

Source: Board of Governors of the Federal Reserve System, *Industrial Production and Capacity Utilization*, G.17 (419), monthly.

U.S. Census Bureau, Statistical Abstract of the United States: 2002

No. 741. Manufacturing and Trade—Sales and Inventories: 1992 to 2001

[In billions of dollars (538 represents $538,000,000,000), except ratios. Data reflect changeover to North American Industry Classification System (NAICS)]

Item	1992	1993	1994	1995	1996	1997	1998	1999	2000	2001
Sales, average monthly [1]	**538**	**564**	**606**	**649**	**681**	**717**	**737**	**781**	**832**	**819**
Manufacturing [2]	239	249	266	284	294	313	319	330	348	329
Retail trade	154	165	179	188	200	209	220	239	255	264
Merchant wholesalers	144	151	161	176	187	195	198	212	229	226
Inventories [3]	**838**	**865**	**928**	**986**	**1,005**	**1,045**	**1,080**	**1,134**	**1,197**	**1,124**
Manufacturing [2]	376	376	396	421	426	438	446	456	476	440
Retail trade	268	286	312	330	340	351	364	393	416	396
Merchant wholesalers	194	203	220	236	239	256	269	286	305	288
Inventory-sales ratios [4]	**1.53**	**1.51**	**1.47**	**1.49**	**1.47**	**1.43**	**1.45**	**1.41**	**1.41**	**1.42**
Manufacturing [2]	1.57	1.51	1.45	1.45	1.45	1.38	1.40	1.36	1.35	1.40
Retail trade	1.68	1.69	1.67	1.72	1.68	1.65	1.62	1.59	1.59	1.55
Merchant wholesalers	1.32	1.31	1.30	1.31	1.28	1.27	1.33	1.31	1.30	1.32

[1] Averages of monthly not seasonally adjusted figures. [2] Beginning with data for March 2002, the Census Bureau announced that because of data availability, monthly estimates for shipments, order, and inventories would no longer include data on semiconductors. Historical data have been revised to exclude data on semiconductors. [3] Seasonally adjusted end-of-year data. [4] Averages of seasonally adjusted monthly ratios.

Source: U.S. Council of Economic Advisors, *Economic Indicators*, April 2002.

No. 742. Manufacturing Corporations—Number, Assets, and Profits by Asset Size: 1990 to 2001

[Corporations and assets as of end of 4th quarter; profits for entire year (2,629,458 represents $2,629,458,000,000). Through 2000 based on Standard Industrial Classification code; beginning 2001 based on North American Industry Classification System. For corporations above a certain asset value based on complete canvass. The asset value for complete canvass was raised in 1988 to $50 million and in 1995 to $250 million. Asset sizes less than these values are sampled, except as noted. For details regarding methodology, see source for first quarter, 1988. Minus sign (-) indicates loss]

Year	Unit	Asset-size class							
		Total	Under $10 mil. [1]	$10-$25 mil.	$25-$50 mil.	$50-$100 mil.	$100-$250 mil.	$250 mil.-$1 bil.	$1 bil. and over
Corporations:									
1990	Number .	(NA)	(NA)	(NA)	(NA)	834	774	597	367
1995	Number .	(NA)	(NA)	(NA)	(NA)	574	639	727	447
1996	Number .	(NA)	(NA)	(NA)	(NA)	532	620	745	484
1997	Number .	(NA)	(NA)	(NA)	(NA)	470	615	748	529
1998	Number .	(NA)	(NA)	(NA)	(NA)	416	531	753	549
1999	Number .	(NA)	(NA)	(NA)	(NA)	438	486	730	601
2000	Number .	(NA)	(NA)	(NA)	(NA)	450	499	722	635
2001	Number .	(NA)	(NA)	(NA)	(NA)	504	504	735	576
Assets:									
1990	Mil. dol. .	2,629,458	142,498	74,477	55,914	72,554	123,967	287,512	1,872,536
1995	Mil. dol. .	3,345,229	155,618	87,011	68,538	87,262	159,133	370,263	2,417,403
1996	Mil. dol. .	3,574,407	163,928	87,096	69,722	93,205	156,702	398,651	2,605,102
1997	Mil. dol. .	3,746,797	167,921	87,398	76,034	85,186	157,130	397,559	2,775,570
1998	Mil. dol. .	3,967,309	170,068	87,937	69,627	86,816	148,060	419,153	2,985,647
1999	Mil. dol. .	4,382,814	170,058	85,200	67,352	97,810	138,143	398,881	3,425,370
2000	Mil. dol. .	4,852,106	171,666	85,482	72,122	90,866	149,714	389,537	3,892,720
2001	Mil. dol. .	4,750,401	170,948	84,710	67,977	88,267	135,152	393,861	3,809,487
Net profit: [2]									
1990	Mil. dol. .	110,128	8,527	5,160	2,769	2,661	3,525	7,110	80,377
1995	Mil. dol. .	198,151	13,224	5,668	3,767	5,771	7,000	16,549	146,172
1996	Mil. dol. .	224,869	15,802	6,872	4,266	5,664	7,935	16,059	168,271
1997	Mil. dol. .	244,505	17,948	8,383	4,153	4,675	7,074	18,433	183,836
1998	Mil. dol. .	234,386	18,350	6,421	3,790	4,681	5,610	14,364	181,170
1999	Mil. dol. .	257,805	17,398	7,618	3,504	4,798	4,795	12,756	206,934
2000	Mil. dol. .	275,313	16,578	6,820	3,403	2,742	3,510	15,121	227,136
2001	Mil. dol. .	35,638	8,411	3,458	-443	519	-3,296	-5,988	32,978

NA Not available. [1] Excludes estimates for corporations with less than $250,000 in assets at time of sample selection. [2] After taxes.

Source: U.S. Census Bureau, *Quarterly Financial Report for Manufacturing, Mining and Trade Corporations.*

No. 743. Corporate Profits, Taxes, and Dividends: 1990 to 2001

[In billions of dollars (409 represents $409,000,000,000). Covers corporations organized for profit and other entities treated as corporations. Represents profits to U.S. residents, without deduction of depletion charges and exclusive of capital gains and losses; intercorporate dividends from profits of domestic corporations are eliminated; net receipts of dividends, reinvested earnings of incorporated foreign affiliates, and earnings of unincorporated foreign affiliates are added]

Item	1990	1995	1997	1998	1999	2000	2001
Corporate profits with IVA and CCA .	409	669	834	777	825	876	767
Corporate profits with IVA	389	650	801	739	773	833	701
Profits before tax	402	668	792	721	776	845	699
Profits tax liability	141	211	237	239	253	272	216
Profits after tax	261	458	555	482	523	574	483
Dividends	166	254	335	349	344	380	417
Undistributed profits	95	203	220	134	180	194	66
Inventory valuation adjustment (IVA)	-13	-18	8	18	-3	-12	2
Capital consumption adjustment (CCA)	20	19	33	38	52	43	66
Addenda:							
Corporate profits after tax with IVA/CCA [1] . .	268	458	597	539	572	605	551
Net cash flow with IVA/CCA [1]	494	716	843	810	898	952	933
Undistributed profits with IVA/CCA [1]	102	204	261	190	229	225	135
Consumption of fixed capital	391	512	582	620	669	727	799
Less: Inventory valuation adjustment (IVA) . .	-13	-18	8	18	-3	-12	2
Equals: Net cash flow	506	734	834	792	901	965	931

[1] Inventory valuation adjustment/capital consumption adjustment.

Source: U.S. Bureau of Economic Analysis, *National Income and Product Accounts, Volume 1, 1929-97,* and *Survey of Current Business,* August 2001. See also <http://www.bea.gov/bea/dn/nipaweb/selecttable.asp>.

No. 744. Corporate Profits Before Taxes by Industry: 1990 to 2000

[In millions of dollars (401,534 represents $401,534,000,000). Profits are without inventory valuation and capital consumption adjustments. Based on the 1987 Standard Industrial Classification code. See headnote, Table 743]

Industry	1990	1994	1995	1996	1997	1998	1999	2000
Corporate profits before tax . . .	401,534	573,406	668,454	726,345	792,396	721,107	776,323	845,409
Domestic industries	328,812	496,168	576,442	625,492	681,706	618,848	661,693	708,617
Agriculture, forestry, and fishing	1,638	1,385	1,842	2,950	3,059	3,019	4,651	5,669
Mining	2,502	3,348	4,517	8,124	10,972	2,115	362	4,862
Construction	10,922	13,650	17,265	21,932	25,696	32,531	38,278	43,826
Manufacturing	113,552	144,709	172,518	175,789	192,312	153,035	162,600	160,966
Transportation and public utilities	45,931	82,954	85,894	92,023	83,991	78,867	59,565	68,096
Transportation	954	10,316	11,613	16,157	18,639	21,013	15,755	14,030
Communications	20,049	36,837	33,604	35,012	25,570	22,684	5,847	12,491
Electric, gas, and sanitary services . . .	24,928	35,801	40,677	40,854	39,782	35,170	37,963	41,575
Wholesale trade	21,201	36,883	35,546	41,588	46,315	49,044	54,587	63,046
Retail trade	24,896	49,187	47,471	54,806	62,648	74,172	79,106	84,581
Finance, insurance, and real estate	88,334	117,726	160,062	171,827	195,658	174,415	207,170	220,086
Services	19,836	46,326	51,327	56,453	61,055	51,650	55,374	57,485
Rest of the world [1]	72,722	77,238	92,012	100,853	110,690	102,259	114,630	136,792

[1] Consists of receipts by all U.S. residents, including both corporations and persons, dividends from their incorporated foreign affiliates, their share of reinvested earnings of their incorporated foreign affiliates, and earnings of unincorporated foreign affiliates, net of corresponding payments.

No. 745. Corporate Profits With Inventory Valuation and Capital Consumption Adjustments—Financial and Nonfinancial Industries: 1990 to 2001

[In billions of dollars (409 represents $409,000,000,000). Based on the 1987 Standard Industrial Classification code. Minus sign (-) indicates loss. See headnote, Table 743]

Item	1990	1995	1996	1997	1998	1999	2000	2001
Corporate profits with IVA/CCA [1] . .	409	669	754	834	777	825	876	767
Domestic industries	336	577	653	723	675	711	740	618
Rest of the world	73	92	101	111	102	115	137	149
Corporate profits with IVA [1]	389	650	729	801	739	773	833	701
Domestic industries	316	558	629	690	637	659	696	551
Financial	92	154	165	186	158	191	204	180
Nonfinancial	224	404	463	505	479	468	492	371
Manufacturing	109	166	181	195	164	164	155	80
Transportation and public utilities . . .	44	86	91	85	79	59	67	52
Wholesale trade	19	29	43	49	56	54	61	40
Retail trade	21	44	53	64	74	77	82	86
Other	31	79	95	111	106	114	127	114
Rest of the world	73	92	101	111	102	115	137	149

[1] Inventory valuation adjustment and capital consumption adjustment.

Source of Tables 744 and 745: U.S. Bureau of Economic Analysis, *National Income and Product Accounts, Volume 1, 1929-97,* and *Survey of Current Business,* August 2001. See also <http://www.bea.gov/bea/dn/nipaweb/selecttable.asp>.

No. 746. Manufacturing, Mining, and Trade Corporations—Profits and Stockholders' Equity by Industry: 2001

[Averages of quarterly figures at annual rates. Manufacturing data exclude estimates for corporations with less than $250,000 in assets at time of sample selection. Based on sample; see source for discussion of methodology. Based on North American Industry Classification System; see text, this section. Minus sign indicates loss]

Industry	Ratio of profits to stockholders' equity (percent)	Profits per dollar of sales (cents)	Ratio of stockholders' equity to debt
Manufacturing	1.9	0.8	1.4
Nondurable manufacturing	14.8	5.7	1.2
Food	14.0	3.2	0.8
Beverage and tobacco products	27.5	10.1	0.8
Textile mills and textile product mills	1.2	0.3	0.9
Apparel and leather products	18.0	4.3	0.9
Paper	1.2	0.4	0.8
Printing and related support activities	8.2	1.7	0.8
Petroleum and coal products	16.5	7.4	2.8
Chemicals	17.2	8.4	1.1
Basic chemicals, resins, and synthetics	2.2	1.3	0.9
Pharmaceuticals and medicines	32.3	16.7	1.6
All other chemicals	8.8	4.1	0.9
Plastics and rubber products	1.8	1.5	0.9
Durable manufacturing	-7.1	-3.3	1.7
Wood products	4.1	1.0	1.1
Nonmetallic mineral products	-4.0	-1.5	1.0
Primary metals	-6.2	-2.3	1.0
Iron, steel, and ferroalloys	-34.3	-8.6	0.7
Nonferrous metals	5.7	2.4	1.3
Foundries	2.6	0.7	1.0
Fabricated metal products	7.8	2.6	1.1
Machinery	7.2	3.1	1.2
Computer and electronic products	-24.7	-20.4	3.4
Computer and peripheral equipment	-1.0	-0.6	2.2
Communications equipment	-69.4	-75.9	4.3
All other electronic products	-6.5	-6.2	3.3
Electrical equipment, appliances, and components	16.1	8.6	2.6
Transportation equipment	0.8	0.1	1.2
Motor vehicles and parts	-7.9	-1.9	1.0
Aerospace products and parts	11.6	4.0	1.4
Furniture and related products	8.1	2.6	1.8
Miscellaneous manufacturing	9.7	4.6	1.4
All mining	10.3	9.3	1.7
All wholesale trade	5.8	0.9	1.2
All retail trade	10.7	1.9	1.2

Source: U.S. Census Bureau, *Quarterly Financial Report for Manufacturing, Mining, and Trade Corporations.*

No. 747. Manufacturing Corporations—Selected Finances: 1980 to 2001

[In billions of dollars (1,913 represents $1,913,000,000,000). Data are not necessarily comparable from year to year due to changes in accounting procedures, industry classifications, sampling procedures, etc.; for detail, see source. Through 2000 based on Standard Industrial Classification code; beginning 2001 based on North American Industry Classification System]

Year	All manufacturing corps.					Durable goods industries					Nondurable goods industries				
		Profits [1]		Stock-hold-ers' equi-ty	Debt [2]		Profits [1]		Stock-hold-ers' equi-ty	Debt [2]		Profits [1]		Stock-hold-ers' equi-ty	Debt [2]
	Sales	Before taxes	After taxes			Sales	Before taxes	After taxes			Sales	Before taxes	After taxes		
1980	1,913	146	93	668	292	889	57	36	318	143	1,024	88	57	350	149
1985	2,331	137	88	866	454	1,143	62	39	421	167	1,189	76	49	445	267
1990	2,811	158	110	1,044	782	1,357	57	41	515	328	1,454	101	69	529	453
1991	2,761	99	66	1,064	814	1,304	14	7	507	338	1,457	85	59	557	476
1992 [3]	2,890	31	22	1,035	819	1,390	-34	-24	474	335	1,500	65	46	561	485
1993	3,015	118	83	1,040	819	1,490	39	27	483	327	1,525	79	56	557	492
1994	3,256	244	175	1,110	815	1,658	121	87	533	316	1,598	123	88	577	500
1995	3,528	275	198	1,241	862	1,808	131	94	614	333	1,721	144	104	627	529
1996	3,758	307	225	1,348	920	1,942	147	106	674	366	1,816	160	119	674	554
1997	3,922	331	244	1,464	953	2,076	167	121	744	386	1,847	164	123	721	566
1998	3,949	315	234	1,487	1,065	2,169	175	128	794	458	1,781	140	107	694	607
1999	4,149	355	258	1,637	1,199	2,314	199	140	928	551	1,835	157	117	709	648
2000	4,548	381	275	1,892	1,308	2,457	191	132	1,101	610	2,091	190	144	791	698
2001	4,308	82	36	1,827	1,296	2,332	-70	-77	1,049	640	1,976	152	112	779	656

[1] Beginning 1998, profits before and after income taxes reflect inclusion of minority stockholders' interest in net income before and after income taxes. [2] Annual data are average debt for the year (using four end-of-quarter figures). [3] Data for 1992 (most significantly 1992:I qtr.) reflect the early adoption of Financial Accounting Standards Board Statement 106 (Employer's Accounting for Post-Retirement Benefits Other Than Pensions) by a large number of companies during the fourth quarter of 1992. Data for 1993: I qtr. also reflect adoption of Statement 106. Corporations must show the cumulative effect of a change in accounting principle in the first quarter of the year in which the change is adopted.

Source: 1980, U.S. Federal Trade Commission; thereafter, U.S. Census Bureau, *Quarterly Financial Report for Manufacturing, Mining, and Trade Corporations.*

No. 748. Gross Product, Employment, and Capital Expenditures of Nonbank U.S. MNCs, U.S. Parents, and Foreign Affiliates: 1989 to 1999

[Gross product and capital expenditures in billions of dollars (1,365 represents $1,365,000,000,000); employees in thousands. See headnote, Table 749. MNC=Multinational company. MOFA=Majority-owned foreign affiliate. Minus sign (-) indicates decrease]

Item	1989	1990	1994	1995	1998	1999 [1]	Percent change at annual rates 1989-94	1989-99	1994-99
GROSS PRODUCT									
MNCs worldwide:									
Parents and all affiliates .	(NA)	(NA)	(NA)	(NA)	(NA)	(NA)	(NA)	(NA)	(NA)
Parents and MOFAs....	1,365	(NA)	1,717	1,831	2,101	2,370	4.7	5.7	6.6
Parents	1,045	(NA)	1,314	1,365	1,595	1,809	4.7	5.6	6.6
Affiliates, total.	(NA)	(NA)	(NA)	(NA)	(NA)	(NA)	(NA)	(NA)	(NA)
MOFAs	320	356	404	466	506	561	4.8	5.8	6.8
Other.	(NA)	(NA)	(NA)	(NA)	(NA)	(NA)	(NA)	(NA)	(NA)
EMPLOYEES									
MNCs worldwide:									
Parents and all affiliates .	25,388	25,264	25,670	25,921	28,004	30,287	0.2	1.8	3.4
Parents and MOFAs....	23,879	23,786	24,273	24,500	26,593	28,851	0.3	1.9	3.5
Parents	18,765	18,430	18,565	18,576	19,820	21,380	-0.2	1.3	2.9
Affiliates, total.	6,622	6,834	7,105	7,345	8,184	8,907	1.4	3.0	4.6
MOFAs	5,114	5,356	5,707	5,924	6,773	7,471	2.2	3.9	5.5
Other.	1,508	1,478	1,398	1,421	1,411	1,436	-1.5	-0.5	0.5
CAPITAL EXPENDITURES									
MNCs worldwide:									
Parents and all affiliates .	277	(NA)	328	(NA)	(NA)	502	3.5	6.1	8.9
Parents and MOFAs....	260	275	303	324	411	471	3.1	6.1	9.2
Parents	202	213	232	248	317	358	2.8	5.9	9.1
Affiliates, total.	75	(NA)	96	(NA)	(NA)	145	5.1	6.8	8.5
MOFAs	59	62	71	76	94	113	4.0	6.8	9.7
Other.	16	(NA)	25	(NA)	(NA)	31	8.8	6.7	4.6

NA Not available.   [1] Not strictly comparable with prior years; see source.
Source: U.S. Bureau of Economic Analysis, *Survey of Current Business*, March 2002.

No. 749. U.S. Multinational Companies—Selected Characteristics: 1999

[Preliminary. In billions of dollars (11,399 represents $11,399,000,000,000), except as indicated. Consists of nonbank U.S. parent companies and their nonbank foreign affiliates. U.S. parent comprises the domestic operations of a multinational and is a U.S. person that owns or controls directly or indirectly, 10 percent or more of the voting securities of an incorporated foreign business enterprise, or an equivalent interest in an unincorporated foreign business enterprise. A U.S. person can be an incorporated business enterprise. A foreign affiliate is a foreign business enterprise owned or controlled by a U.S. parent company. MOFA=Majority-owned foreign affiliate]

Industry [1]	Total assets	U.S. parents Gross prod-uct	Capital expen-ditures	Employ-ment (1,000)	All affiliates Capital expen-ditures	Employ-ment (1,000)	MOFAs Gross prod-uct	Capital expen-ditures	Employ-ment (1,000)
All industries.	11,399	1,809	357.8	21,380	144.6	8,907	561	113.4	7,471
Mining	116	18	8.7	113	24.6	156	41	21.9	134
Utilities	518	91	25.2	363	6.6	119	10	4.5	67
Manufacturing [2]	3,642	910	152.4	8,870	56.9	4,900	312	48.6	4,245
Food	144	47	6.0	614	3.2	376	19	2.9	334
Beverages and tobacco products.	133	40	5.5	249	3.5	371	27	2.5	173
Paper	149	46	6.2	420	1.8	173	9	1.6	136
Petroleum and coal products.	359	82	18.2	297	2.7	68	45	1.6	38
Chemicals [2]	529	128	21.6	955	13.9	617	58	11.2	553
Pharmaceuticals and medicines	220	52	7.4	333	3.5	205	25	3.5	198
Primary and fabricated metals	139	44	6.8	574	2.7	240	12	2.5	213
Machinery	203	51	6.0	704	2.8	392	19	1.9	341
Computers and electronic products [2] . . .	446	119	19.8	1,136	9.2	781	39	8.9	766
Computers and peripheral equipment . .	173	43	7.2	411	2.2	250	16	2.2	249
Transportation equipment.	1,192	234	46.2	2,192	11.1	943	48	9.9	839
Motor vehicles, bodies and trailers, and parts	763	130	32.7	1,122	10.9	899	46	9.8	800
Other	429	105	13.6	1,070	0.2	44	3	0.2	40
Wholesale trade.	320	69	18.0	774	6.5	658	82	5.9	620
Information [2]	1,064	241	71.6	1,899	21.2	581	19	8.5	270
Broadcasting and telecommunications [2] .	835	180	65.2	1,201	19.6	387	7	7.1	101
Telecommunications.	558	150	56.7	857	17.9	355	6	6.0	86
Finance (except depository institutions) and insurance	4,762	97	17.1	1,293	4.6	322	22	4.5	295
Finance, except depository institutions [2] .	2,019	49	7.2	464	3.9	184	9	3.8	168
Securities, commodity contracts, and other intermediation	1,841	51	5.0	401	0.9	107	9	0.8	101
Insurance carriers and related activities. .	2,743	48	10.0	829	0.7	138	13	0.6	127
Professional, scientific, and technical services	138	69	8.7	784	3.5	375	29	3.4	344
Other industries [2]	841	314	56.0	7,283	20.6	1,796	45	16.1	1,498
Retail trade	269	118	17.1	3,288	2.4	448	15	2.1	411
Transportation and warehousing	227	88	20.2	1,131	3.3	186	5	1.2	112

[1] Represents North American Industry Classification System-based industry of U.S. parent or industry of foreign affiliate.
[2] Includes other industries not shown separately.
Source: U.S. Bureau of Economic Analysis, *Survey of Current Business*, May 2002.

Business Enterprise   497

No. 750. U.S. Multinational Companies—Gross Product: 1995 and 1999

[In millions of dollars (1,831,046 represents $1,831,046,000,000). Gross product measures valued added by a firm. Consists of nonbank U.S. parent companies and their nonbank foreign affiliates. A U.S. parent comprises the domestic operations of a multinational and is a U.S. person that owns or controls 10 percent or more of the voting securities, or the equivalent, of a foreign business enterprise. A U.S. person can be an incorporated business enterprise. A majority-owned foreign affiliate is a foreign business enterprise in which a U.S. parent company owns or controls 50 percent or more of the voting securities. Based on Standard Industrial Classification code]

Industry	U.S. multinationals		U.S. parents		Majority-owned foreign affiliates	
	1995	1999	1995	1999	1995	1999
All industries.....................	1,831,046	2,369,688	1,365,470	1,808,530	465,576	561,158
Petroleum......................	205,044	215,976	110,014	108,415	95,030	107,561
Manufacturing..................	1,023,697	1,116,918	723,182	847,577	300,515	269,341
Food and kindred products...	119,282	112,192	78,223	82,971	41,059	29,221
Chemical and allied products [1]	182,827	179,486	116,949	122,980	65,878	56,506
Industrial chemicals.........	66,480	53,117	42,625	38,532	23,855	14,585
Drugs.....................	73,723	76,997	46,894	51,716	26,829	25,281
Primary and fabricated metals...	59,387	58,261	39,937	45,842	19,450	12,419
Industrial machinery and equipment [1]	139,767	122,741	88,818	88,469	50,949	34,272
Computer and office equipment....	74,748	59,811	39,934	42,672	34,814	17,139
Electronic and other electric equipment [1]...	103,693	129,559	77,286	102,363	26,407	27,196
Electronic components and accessories......	51,981	53,635	36,495	38,487	15,486	15,148
Transportation equipment............	202,108	271,571	152,834	226,610	49,274	44,961
Motor vehicles and equipment.....	144,776	164,415	103,531	122,059	41,245	42,356
Other.................. [1]	57,331	107,157	49,303	104,552	8,028	2,605
Other manufacturing [1].............	216,632	243,108	169,135	178,342	47,497	64,766
Paper and allied products.........	55,446	55,358	43,995	46,010	11,451	9,348
Wholesale trade..............	39,127	119,271	30,853	58,406	8,274	60,865
Durable goods..............	23,322	73,337	18,325	31,747	4,997	41,590
Nondurable goods.............	15,804	45,934	12,527	26,659	3,277	19,275
Finance (exc dep inst), insurance & real estate [1]...	72,489	118,468	52,813	100,263	19,676	18,205
Finance, except depository institutions.......	22,370	58,649	18,205	48,350	4,165	10,299
Insurance................	41,677	61,532	32,815	48,470	8,862	13,062
Services [1]....................	118,328	237,879	97,623	178,034	20,705	59,845
Business services [1]...........	51,915	131,258	38,667	90,279	13,248	40,979
Computer and data processing services.....	24,094	79,951	18,481	55,644	5,613	24,307
Other industries [1].............	372,360	561,174	350,984	515,835	21,376	45,339
Transportation.............	70,372	91,220	67,277	86,144	3,095	5,076
Communication.............	121,576	186,707	117,802	180,120	3,774	6,587
Electric, gas, and sanitary services..........	73,136	106,058	71,128	94,843	2,008	11,215
Retail trade...............	85,616	150,260	77,367	134,505	8,249	15,755

[1] Includes other industries not shown separately.

Source: U.S. Bureau of Economic Analysis, *Survey of Current Business,* September 1998 and March 2002.

No. 751. Nonbank U.S. Multinational Companies—U.S. Parents and Affiliates by Industry: 1999

[In billions of dollars (1,808.5 represents $1,808,500,000,000), except as noted. Data are by industry of U.S. parent, except affiliate data are by industry of affiliate. See headnote, Table 749. Based on Standard Industrial Classification code. MOFA=Majority-owned foreign affiliate]

Industry	Parents			All affiliates			MOFAs		
	Gross product	Number of employees (1,000)	Capital expenditures	Number of employees (1,000)	Capital expenditures		Gross product	Number of employees (1,000)	Capital expenditures
All industries..............	1,808.5	21,380	357.8	8,907	144.6		561.2	7,471	113.4
Petroleum..............	108.4	418	36.0	245	28.6		107.6	177	23.9
Manufacturing.............	847.6	8,807	136.2	4,857	54.4		269.3	4,227	47.1
Food and kindred products.....	83.0	824	11.2	685	6.1		29.2	451	4.9
Chemicals and allied products...	123.0	902	21.1	597	13.7		56.5	532	11.0
Primary and fabricated metals...	45.8	611	7.0	256	2.3		12.4	226	2.1
Industrial machinery and equip...	88.5	1,037	12.8	613	4.3		34.3	576	4.1
Electronic and other electric equipment.....	102.4	1,112	15.7	814	8.1		27.2	763	7.7
Transportation equipment......	226.6	2,078	45.4	826	10.5		45.0	729	9.4
Other manufacturing..........	178.3	2,243	23.0	1,066	9.2		64.8	950	7.9
Wholesale trade..............	58.4	741	11.5	614	5.1		60.9	591	5.0
Finance (except depository institutions), insurance and real estate..................	100.3	1,313	18.6	356	7.7		18.2	326	6.4
Services..............	178.0	3,115	26.2	1,146	13.7		59.8	1,031	12.9
Other industries..............	515.8	6,986	129.4	1,690	35.0		45.3	1,119	18.0

Source: U.S. Bureau of Economic Analysis, *Survey of Current Business,* May 2002.

Section 16
Science and Technology

This section presents statistics on scientific, engineering, and technological resources, with emphasis on patterns of research and development (R&D) funding and on scientific, engineering, and technical personnel; education; and employment. Also included are statistics on space program outlays and accomplishments. Principal sources of these data are the National Science Foundation (NSF) and the National Aeronautics and Space Administration (NASA).

NSF gathers data chiefly through recurring surveys. Current NSF publications containing data on funds for research and development and on scientific and engineering personnel include detailed statistical tables; issue briefs; and annual, biennial, triennial, and special reports. Titles or the areas of coverage of these reports include the following: *Science and Engineering Indicators; National Patterns of R&D Resources; Women, Minorities, and Persons with Disabilities in Science and Engineering*—science and technology data presented in chart and tabular form in a pocket-sized publication—*Federal Funds for Research and Development; Federal R&D Funding by Budget Function; Federal Support to Universities, Colleges, and Selected Nonprofit Institutions; Research and Development in Industry;* R&D expenditures and graduate enrollment and support in academic science and engineering; and characteristics of doctoral scientists and engineers and of recent graduates in the United States. Statistical surveys in these areas pose problems of concept and definition and the data should therefore be regarded as broad estimates rather than precise, quantitative statements. See sources for methodological and technical details.

The National Science Board's biennial *Science and Engineering Indicators* contains data and analysis of international and domestic science and technology, including measures of inputs and outputs.

The *Budget of the United States Government,* published by the U.S. Office of Management and Budget, contains summary financial data on federal R&D programs.

Research and development outlays— NSF defines research as "systematic study directed toward fuller scientific knowledge of the subject studied" and development as "the systematic use of scientific knowledge directed toward the production of useful materials, devices, systems, or methods, including design and development of prototypes and processes."

National coverage of R&D expenditures is developed primarily from periodic surveys in four principal economic sectors: (1) *Government,* made up primarily of federal executive agencies; (2) *industry,* consisting of manufacturing and nonmanufacturing firms and the federally funded research and development centers (FFRDCs) they administer; (3) *universities and colleges,* composed of universities, colleges, and their affiliated institutions, agricultural experiment stations, and associated schools of agriculture and of medicine, and FFRDCs administered by educational institutions; and (4) *other nonprofit institutions,* consisting of such organizations as private philanthropic foundations, nonprofit research institutes, voluntary health agencies, and FFRDCs administered by nonprofit organizations.

The R&D funds reported consist of current operating costs, including planning and administration costs, except as otherwise noted. They exclude funds for routine testing, mapping and surveying, collection of general-purpose data, dissemination of scientific information, and training of scientific personnel.

Scientists, engineers, and technicians—Scientists and engineers are defined as persons engaged in scientific and engineering work at a level requiring a knowledge of sciences equivalent at least to that acquired through completion

U.S. Census Bureau, Statistical Abstract of the United States: 2002

of a 4-year college course. Technicians are defined as persons engaged in technical work at a level requiring knowledge acquired through a technical institute, junior college, or other type of training less extensive than 4-year college training. Craftsmen and skilled workers are excluded.

Figure 16.1
Top 15 Universities - Federal Research and Development Obligations: 2000

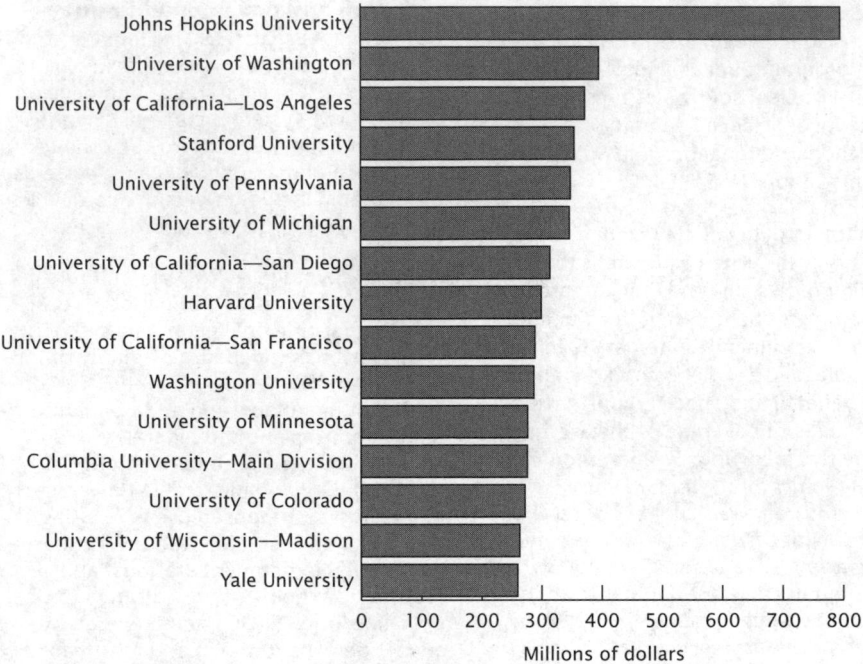

Source: Chart prepared by U.S. Census Bureau. For data, see Table 760.

U.S. Census Bureau, Statistical Abstract of the United States: 2002

No. 752. R&D Expenditures by Source and Objective: 1960 to 2000

[In millions of dollars (13,711 represents $13,711,000,000) except as indicated. For calendar years]

Year	Total	Sources of funds					Objective (percent of total)			Character of work		
		Federal govern- ment	Indus- try	Univer- sities/ col- leges	Non- profit	Non- federal govern- ment [1]	Defense related [2]	Space related [3]	Other	Basic research	Applied research	Devel- opment
1960....	13,711	8,915	4,516	67	123	90	53	3	44	1,286	3,065	9,360
1961....	14,564	9,484	4,757	75	148	101	50	6	44	1,512	3,123	9,930
1962....	15,636	10,138	5,124	84	179	112	49	7	45	1,824	3,698	10,116
1963....	17,519	11,645	5,456	96	197	125	42	14	43	2,115	3,865	11,540
1964....	19,103	12,764	5,888	114	200	138	37	19	43	2,396	4,201	12,506
1965....	20,252	13,194	6,549	136	225	150	33	21	45	2,664	4,374	13,215
1966....	22,072	14,165	7,331	165	252	160	32	20	47	2,930	4,653	14,490
1967....	23,346	14,563	8,146	200	271	168	35	14	49	3,168	4,848	15,332
1968....	24,666	14,964	9,008	221	290	185	35	14	52	3,376	5,137	16,154
1969....	25,996	15,228	10,011	233	316	208	35	11	54	3,491	5,454	17,051
1970....	26,271	14,984	10,449	259	343	237	33	10	56	3,594	5,752	16,925
1971....	26,952	15,210	10,824	290	366	262	33	10	59	3,720	5,833	17,399
1972....	28,740	16,039	11,715	312	393	282	33	8	59	3,850	6,147	18,743
1973....	30,952	16,587	13,299	343	422	302	32	7	62	4,099	6,655	20,197
1974....	33,359	17,287	14,885	393	474	320	29	7	64	4,511	7,344	21,504
1975....	35,671	18,533	15,824	432	534	348	28	8	65	4,875	8,091	22,706
1976....	39,435	20,292	17,702	480	592	369	27	8	66	5,373	8,976	25,085
1977....	43,421	22,155	19,642	569	662	394	27	7	67	6,075	9,670	27,677
1978....	48,774	24,468	22,457	679	727	443	26	6	69	6,998	10,710	31,067
1979....	55,457	27,303	26,097	785	791	482	25	6	70	7,864	12,117	35,475
1980....	63,273	30,035	30,929	920	871	519	24	5	71	8,825	13,745	40,703
1981....	72,267	33,714	35,948	1,058	967	581	24	5	70	9,844	16,393	46,030
1982....	80,848	37,233	40,692	1,207	1,095	621	26	5	68	10,863	18,286	51,698
1983....	90,075	41,576	45,264	1,357	1,220	658	28	4	67	12,110	20,394	57,571
1984....	102,344	46,571	52,187	1,514	1,351	721	29	3	67	13,503	22,517	66,323
1985....	114,778	52,748	57,962	1,743	1,491	834	30	3	66	14,885	25,403	74,489
1986....	120,337	54,711	60,991	2,019	1,647	969	32	3	65	17,287	27,251	75,799
1987....	126,299	58,548	62,576	2,262	1,849	1,065	32	3	65	18,551	27,914	79,833
1988....	133,930	60,180	67,977	2,527	2,081	1,165	30	3	66	19,813	29,545	84,572
1989....	141,914	60,489	74,966	2,852	2,333	1,274	28	4	68	21,908	32,279	87,727
1990....	152,051	61,669	83,208	3,187	2,589	1,399	25	4	70	23,069	34,974	94,008
1991....	160,914	60,822	92,300	3,457	2,852	1,483	23	4	73	27,201	38,632	95,081
1992....	165,358	60,923	96,229	3,568	3,113	1,525	22	4	74	27,628	37,938	99,793
1993....	165,714	60,515	96,640	3,708	3,387	1,556	22	4	74	28,754	37,285	99,676
1994....	169,214	60,790	99,203	3,936	3,664	1,621	20	4	76	29,578	36,613	103,023
1995....	183,611	62,961	110,870	4,108	3,924	1,750	19	5	77	29,560	40,999	113,053
1996....	197,330	63,392	123,412	4,430	4,238	1,858	18	4	78	32,812	43,169	121,348
1997....	212,379	64,783	136,231	4,846	4,593	1,926	17	4	79	36,270	47,211	128,898
1998....	226,872	66,827	147,867	5,183	5,007	1,987	16	4	81	41,294	45,702	139,875
1999....	244,143	67,711	163,397	5,562	5,390	2,083	15	3	83	44,625	51,632	147,886
2000 [4]...	264,622	69,627	181,040	5,969	5,789	2,197	14	3	83	47,903	55,041	161,679

[1] Nonfederal R&D expenditures to university and college performers. [2] R&D spending by the Department of Defense, including space activities, and a portion of the Department of Energy funds. [3] For the National Aeronautics and Space Administration only. [4] Preliminary.
Source: U.S. National Science Foundation, *National Patterns of R&D Resources*, annual.

No. 753. Federal Obligations for R&D in Current and Constant (1996) Dollars by Agency: 1980 to 2002

[In millions of dollars (29,830 represents $29,830,000,000). For fiscal years ending in year shown; see text, Section 8, State and Local Government Finances and Employment. Includes those agencies with obligations of $1 billion or more in 2000]

Agency	1980	1985	1990	1995	1998	1999	2000	2001, prel.	2002, prel.
CURRENT DOLLARS									
Obligations, total [1]...........	29,830	48,360	63,559	68,187	72,101	75,341	72,863	80,898	80,645
Dept. of Defense	13,981	29,792	37,268	33,796	35,286	35,646	33,167	36,334	34,235
Dept. of Health and Human Services .	3,780	5,451	8,406	11,455	13,902	15,915	18,426	21,355	23,816
National Aeronautics and Space Administration..................	3,234	3,327	6,533	9,015	9,568	9,526	6,882	7,221	7,259
Dept. of Energy	4,754	4,966	5,631	6,145	5,874	6,010	6,063	6,712	6,322
National Science Foundation.......	882	1,346	1,690	2,149	2,289	2,506	2,726	3,015	3,017
Dept. of Agriculture	688	943	1,108	1,380	1,441	1,614	1,747	1,980	1,806
CONSTANT (1996) DOLLARS [2]									
Obligations, total [1]...........	53,278	65,804	73,863	69,550	69,730	71,856	68,160	73,961	72,191
Dept. of Defense	24,971	40,538	43,310	34,472	34,258	33,997	31,026	33,218	30,646
Dept. of Health and Human Services .	6,752	7,417	9,769	11,684	13,445	15,179	17,237	19,524	21,319
National Aeronautics and Space Administration..................	5,776	4,527	7,592	9,195	9,289	9,085	6,438	6,602	6,498
Dept. of Energy	8,490	6,757	6,544	6,268	5,703	5,732	5,672	6,136	5,659
National Science Foundation.......	1,575	1,831	1,964	2,192	2,223	2,390	2,550	2,756	2,701
Dept. of Agriculture	1,228	1,283	1,288	1,408	1,399	1,539	1,634	1,810	1,617

[1] Includes other agencies, not shown separately. [2] Based on gross domestic product implicit price deflator.
Source: U.S. National Science Foundation, *Federal Funds for Research and Development*, annual.

No. 754. Performance Sector of R&D Expenditures 1995 to 2000

[In millions of dollars (183,611 represents $183,611,000,000). For calendar year. FFRDCs are federally funded research and development centers. For most academic institutions and the federal government before 1997 began on July 1 instead of October 1.]

Year	Total	Federal government	Industry (Total; Funded by—)				Universities and colleges (Total; Funded by—)							Other nonprofit institutions (Total; Funded by—)				
			Total	Federal government	Industry[1]	Industry FFRDCs	Total	Federal government	Non-federal government[2]	Industry	Universities & colleges	Non-profits	Universities & colleges FFRDCs[3]	Total	Federal government	Industry	Non-profits	Nonprofit FFRDCs
RESEARCH AND DEVELOPMENT TOTAL																		
1995	183,611	16,904	129,830	21,178	108,652	2,273	22,599	13,580	1,750	1,547	4,108	1,616	5,372	5,827	2,847	671	2,308	808
1996	197,330	16,585	142,371	21,356	121,015	2,297	23,686	14,067	1,858	1,667	4,430	1,665	5,410	6,209	2,906	730	2,574	772
1997	212,379	16,819	155,409	21,798	133,611	2,130	25,088	14,716	1,926	1,812	4,846	1,790	5,486	6,626	3,014	809	2,804	821
1998	226,872	17,362	167,102	22,086	145,016	2,078	26,664	15,589	1,987	1,971	5,183	1,934	5,589	7,234	3,281	880	3,073	843
1999	244,143	18,332	180,450	20,162	160,288	2,373	28,363	16,518	2,083	2,133	5,562	2,066	5,698	8,017	3,718	976	3,323	909
2000 prel.	264,621	19,143	197,260	19,635	177,645	2,575	30,154	17,475	2,197	2,310	5,969	2,203	5,801	8,750	4,079	1,085	3,586	918
BASIC RESEARCH																		
1995	29,560	2,689	5,569	190	5,379	530	15,137	9,628	1,069	945	2,509	987	2,661	2,899	1,170	390	1,338	75
1996	32,812	2,680	7,498	650	6,848	708	16,029	10,085	1,148	1,030	2,738	1,028	2,632	3,187	1,248	428	1,510	79
1997	36,270	2,746	9,795	1,029	8,766	625	17,015	10,608	1,190	1,119	2,993	1,105	2,660	3,322	1,317	449	1,557	108
1998	41,294	3,003	13,027	1,326	11,701	568	18,143	11,358	1,217	1,208	3,175	1,185	2,685	3,656	1,461	489	1,706	213
1999	44,625	3,312	14,024	1,211	12,813	649	19,439	12,154	1,281	1,312	3,421	1,271	2,759	4,092	1,705	542	1,845	351
2000 prel.	47,903	3,525	15,378	1,179	14,199	704	20,656	12,857	1,351	1,421	3,672	1,355	2,809	4,492	1,898	602	1,991	339
APPLIED RESEARCH																		
1995	40,999	4,952	26,919	3,164	23,755	535	5,653	2,774	558	494	1,311	516	1,119	1,692	934	170	589	129
1996	43,169	4,872	29,010	3,640	25,370	231	5,870	2,856	582	522	1,388	522	1,283	1,781	960	182	640	122
1997	47,211	4,997	32,430	2,648	29,782	213	6,152	2,900	604	568	1,519	561	1,364	1,926	1,011	205	711	128
1998	45,702	5,146	30,341	2,533	27,808	230	6,475	2,957	631	626	1,646	614	1,326	2,062	1,060	223	779	123
1999	51,632	5,503	35,367	3,440	31,927	274	6,814	3,075	658	673	1,756	652	1,276	2,284	1,194	247	842	114
2000 prel.	55,041	5,826	37,648	2,252	35,396	285	7,260	3,259	693	729	1,884	695	1,401	2,504	1,320	275	909	117
DEVELOPMENT																		
1995	113,053	9,262	97,342	17,824	79,518	1,208	1,809	1,177	123	108	288	113	1,592	1,236	744	111	381	603
1996	121,348	9,033	105,863	17,066	88,797	1,358	1,787	1,125	128	115	305	115	1,495	1,241	698	120	423	571
1997	128,898	9,077	113,184	18,121	95,063	1,292	1,921	1,207	132	125	333	123	1,462	1,378	687	155	536	585
1998	139,875	9,214	123,734	18,227	105,507	1,280	2,046	1,274	139	137	361	135	1,577	1,516	760	168	588	507
1999	147,886	9,517	131,060	15,512	115,548	1,450	2,110	1,290	144	148	385	143	1,663	1,641	819	187	636	445
2000 prel.	161,679	9,792	144,254	16,205	128,050	1,586	2,238	1,360	152	160	413	153	1,592	1,754	860	208	686	463

[1] For R&D funded by the federal government. FFRDCs are federally funded research and development centers. [2] Includes all nonfederal sources. [3] Includes all R&D expenditures of FFRDCs administered by academic institutions and funded by the federal government.

Source: National Science Foundation. Data derived from: *Research and Development in Industry*, annual; *Academic Research and Development Expenditures*, annual; and *Federal Funds For Research and Development* annual.

No. 755. Performance Sector of R&D Expenditures by State: 1998

[In millions of dollars (226,872 represents $226,872,000,000). Industry R&D data refer to calendar years; other R&D data refer to fiscal years but may serve as approximation to calendar year data]

State	Total R&D [1]	Federal govern- ment [2]	Industry Total	Industry Funded by— Federal govern- ment [3]	Industry Funded by— Indus- try [4]	Universities and colleges Total	Universities and colleges Funded by— Federal govern- ment	Universities and colleges Funded by— Non- federal govern- ment	Universities and colleges Funded by— Industry	Universities and colleges Funded by— U&Cs	Universities and colleges Funded by— Non- profits	Other non- profit insti- tutions funded by federal govern- ment [5]
U.S ..	226,872	17,403	169,180	24,164	145,016	26,547	15,533	1,993	1,933	5,166	1,923	3,236
AL.....	1,926	753	707	180	527	442	282	7	30	82	40	24
AK.....	(D)	44	(D)	(D)	9	76	32	4	16	24	-	4
AZ.....	2,318	138	1,727	490	1,237	406	210	12	22	147	15	8
AR.....	283	46	118	(D)	(D)	117	41	33	8	27	7	2
CA.....	43,919	1,595	35,568	3,803	31,764	3,345	2,009	146	213	702	274	519
CO	4,565	202	3,565	1,237	2,329	489	332	26	27	68	36	55
CT.....	3,559	18	3,113	179	2,935	404	262	13	26	67	35	24
DE.....	2,556	4	2,476	13	2,463	73	36	5	4	19	9	3
DC	2,606	1,718	503	90	413	233	166	2	19	26	19	150
FL.....	4,773	750	3,300	889	2,411	713	356	81	52	184	40	11
GA	2,492	236	1,444	86	1,358	802	370	70	86	246	30	10
HI	242	55	17	(D)	(D)	148	87	37	11	13	-	22
ID	1,127	25	1,028	(D)	(D)	72	25	22	8	16	1	1
IL	8,830	72	6,892	136	6,755	1,046	587	57	60	262	81	62
IN	3,089	38	2,622	(D)	(D)	425	214	26	40	126	19	3
IA	1,054	33	634	(D)	(D)	358	167	53	31	89	18	4
KS.....	1,518	25	1,279	(D)	(D)	213	80	47	12	56	17	1
KY.....	645	7	427	(D)	(D)	210	80	15	19	86	9	2
LA.....	542	84	102	14	87	352	144	78	23	87	20	4
ME	159	11	82	(D)	(D)	35	14	2	7	11	1	31
MD	8,019	4,766	1,744	655	1,089	1,330	1,014	63	42	143	69	179
MA	13,382	301	10,604	2,419	8,185	1,343	987	32	107	99	118	707
MI	13,655	111	12,648	(D)	(D)	878	472	56	59	221	69	18
MN	3,818	38	3,321	334	2,986	365	206	48	25	56	29	94
MS	366	133	73	17	57	153	80	29	10	31	2	8
MO	1,868	49	1,313	(D)	(D)	484	278	24	30	109	43	22
MT	191	33	82	(D)	(D)	72	36	14	8	13	1	3
NE.....	315	29	93	(D)	(D)	186	63	47	17	55	5	7
NV.....	571	49	434	(D)	(D)	84	45	5	5	24	4	4
NH	1,340	34	1,187	(D)	(D)	117	71	8	6	17	14	2
NJ.....	11,368	393	10,415	134	10,282	485	228	40	27	150	39	17
NM	3,032	396	1,205	(D)	(D)	229	152	13	13	46	5	15
NY.....	13,731	192	11,176	2,216	8,960	1,925	1,224	82	96	286	236	221
NC	4,560	236	3,362	12	3,350	899	516	129	121	96	36	64
ND	119	27	34	-	34	57	23	1	4	26	4	1
OH	6,970	698	5,338	605	4,732	808	444	74	88	152	49	125
OK	513	51	245	2	243	209	84	37	13	60	15	8
OR	1,910	88	1,492	26	1,467	310	203	33	10	38	25	21
PA.....	8,762	133	7,083	485	6,598	1,342	873	44	156	199	70	174
RI	1,677	222	1,320	(D)	(D)	112	78	3	2	26	3	23
SC.....	989	45	695	(D)	(D)	246	113	27	11	83	11	3
SD.....	60	28	5	-	5	25	12	8	-	3	2	2
TN.....	2,503	38	2,040	(D)	(D)	346	208	37	20	54	28	28
TX.....	10,774	597	8,408	223	8,185	1,698	910	179	140	290	179	69
UT.....	1,495	135	1,109	181	928	249	165	18	14	43	10	1
VT.....	175	4	112	32	80	58	31	3	6	12	6	1
VA.....	4,934	1,480	2,707	1,614	1,093	491	289	49	46	77	30	44
WA	8,466	184	7,476	(D)	(D)	534	384	13	42	77	19	122
WV	421	97	225	(D)	(D)	63	25	3	5	27	4	1
WI.....	2,501	38	1,919	(D)	(D)	536	300	44	20	111	61	8
WY	65	12	2	-	2	49	18	5	3	21	1	3
Unknown.	12,119	912	5,709	8,092	34,452	905	507	89	73	183	65	301

- Represents zero.   D Data withheld to avoid disclosing information about individual companies.   [1] Includes university and college Federally Funded Research and Development Centers (FFRDCs). Nonprofit FFRDCs not shown separately.   [2] For R&D funded by the federal government.   [3] Includes performance at industry Federally Funded Research and Development Centers (FFRDCs). Nonprofit FFRDCs not shown separately.   [4] Includes all nonfederal sources.   [5] Data by state are for R&D funded by the federal government.

Source: U.S. National Science Foundation. Data derived from *Research and Development in Industry*, annual; *Academic Research and Development Expenditures*, annual; and *Federal Funds For Research and Development*, annual.

Science and Technology   503

No. 756. Federal Budget Authority for R&D in Current and Constant (1996) Dollars by Selected Budget Functions: 1970 to 2002

[In millions of dollars (15,339 represents $15,339,000,000). For fiscal years ending in year shown; see text, Section 9, State and Local Government Finances and Employment. Excludes R&D plant. Represents budget authority. Functions shown are those for which $1 billion or more was authorized since 1995]

Function	1970	1980	1985	1990	1995	1999	2000	2001, prel.	2002, prel.
CURRENT DOLLARS									
Total [1]	15,339	29,739	49,887	63,781	68,791	77,637	78,664	86,756	98,029
Eight functions, percent of total	96.6	96.5	98.3	98.0	97.7	97.6	97.7	97.7	97.9
National defense	7,981	14,946	33,698	39,925	37,204	41,306	42,580	45,713	52,922
Health	1,084	3,694	5,418	8,308	11,407	15,553	17,869	20,758	23,654
Space research and technology [2]	3,606	2,738	2,725	5,765	7,916	8,245	5,363	6,126	6,556
Energy [3]	574	3,603	2,389	2,726	2,844	1,131	996	1,314	1,547
General science [3]	452	1,233	1,862	2,410	2,794	4,690	4,977	5,468	5,717
Natural resources and environment	340	999	1,059	1,386	1,988	1,842	1,999	2,096	2,159
Transportation	535	887	1,030	1,045	1,833	1,725	1,636	1,640	1,696
Agriculture	238	585	836	950	1,194	1,288	1,426	1,657	1,703
CONSTANT (1996) DOLLARS [4]									
Total [1]	53,840	53,115	67,883	73,872	70,166	74,046	73,587	79,316	87,753
National defense	28,013	26,694	45,854	46,242	37,948	39,395	39,832	41,793	47,374
Health	3,805	6,598	7,372	9,622	11,635	14,834	16,716	18,978	21,174
Space research and technology [2]	12,657	4,890	3,708	6,677	8,074	7,864	5,017	5,601	5,869
Energy [3]	2,015	6,435	3,251	3,157	2,901	1,079	932	1,201	1,385
General science [3]	1,587	2,202	2,534	2,791	2,850	4,473	4,656	4,999	5,118
Natural resources and environment	1,193	1,784	1,441	1,605	2,028	1,757	1,870	1,916	1,933
Transportation	1,878	1,584	1,402	1,210	1,870	1,645	1,530	1,499	1,518
Agriculture	835	1,045	1,138	1,100	1,218	1,228	1,334	1,515	1,524

[1] Includes other functions, not shown separately. [2] In FY 2000, the National Aeronautics and Space Administration reclassified Space Station as a physical asset and Space Station research as equipment and transferred funding for the Space Station program from R&D to R&D plant. [3] Beginning in FY 1998, a number of DOE programs were reclassified from energy (270). [4] Based on gross domestic product implicit price deflator.
Source: U.S. National Science Foundation, Federal R&D Funding by Budget Function, annual.

No. 757. National R&D Expenditures as a Percent of Gross Domestic Product by Country: 1981 to 1999

Year	Total R&D						Nondefense R&D [1]					
	United States	Japan	Unified Germany	France	United Kingdom	Italy	United States	Japan	Unified Germany	France	United Kingdom	Italy
1981	2.31	2.13	2.47	1.93	2.38	0.88	1.7	2.1	2.3	1.6	1.8	0.9
1985	2.72	2.58	2.75	2.22	2.24	1.12	1.9	2.6	2.6	1.8	1.8	1.1
1990	2.62	2.85	2.75	2.37	2.16	1.29	2.0	2.8	2.6	1.9	1.7	1.3
1994	2.40	2.63	2.26	2.34	2.07	1.05	1.9	2.6	2.2	2.0	1.8	1.0
1995	2.48	2.77	2.26	2.31	1.98	1.00	2.0	2.7	2.2	2.0	1.7	1.0
1996	2.53	2.80	2.26	2.30	1.91	1.01	2.1	2.8	2.2	2.0	1.6	1.0
1997	2.55	2.88	2.29	2.22	1.83	0.99	2.1	2.8	2.2	2.0	1.6	1.0
1998	2.58	3.01	2.31	2.18	1.83	1.02	2.2	3.0	2.2	2.0	1.6	1.0
1999	2.63	3.01	2.38	2.17	1.87	1.04	2.2	(NA)	2.3	(NA)	(NA)	(NA)

NA Not available. [1] Estimated.
Source: National Science Foundation, National Patterns of R&D Resources, annual; and Organization for Economic Cooperation and Development.

No. 758. R&D Expenditures in Science and Engineering at Universities and Colleges in Current and Constant (1996) Dollars: 1981 to 1999

[In millions of dollars (6,847 represents $6,847,000,000)]

Characteristic	1981	1990	1999	Characteristic	1981	1990	1999
CURRENT DOLLARS				CONSTANT (1996) DOLLARS			
Total	6,847	16,286	27,489	Total	11,090	18,863	26,217
Basic research	4,594	10,643	18,844	Basic research	7,441	12,327	17,972
Applied R&D	2,253	5,643	8,645	Applied R&D	3,649	6,536	8,245
Source of funds:				Source of funds:			
All governments	5,117	10,962	18,075	All governments	8,288	12,696	17,239
Institutions' own funds	1,004	3,006	5,366	Institutions' own funds	1,626	3,482	5,118
Industry	291	1,127	2,048	Industry	471	1,305	1,953
Other	435	1,191	2,000	Other	705	1,379	1,907
Fields:				Fields:			
Physical sciences	765	1,807	2,600	Physical sciences	1,239	2,093	2,480
Environmental sciences	550	1,069	1,690	Environmental sciences	891	1,238	1,612
Mathematical sciences	87	222	313	Mathematical sciences	141	257	299
Computer sciences	144	515	860	Computer sciences	233	596	820
Life sciences	3,695	8,726	15,591	Life sciences	5,985	10,107	14,870
Psychology	127	253	465	Psychology	206	293	443
Social sciences	366	703	1,262	Social sciences	593	814	1,204
Other sciences	145	336	452	Other sciences	235	389	431
Engineering	967	2,656	4,257	Engineering	1,566	3,076	4,060

[1] Based on gross domestic product implicit price deflator.
Source: U.S. National Science Foundation, Survey of Research and Development Expenditures at Universities and Colleges, annual.

504 Science and Technology

No. 759. Federal Obligations to Universities and Colleges in Current and Constant (1996) Dollars: 1970 to 2000

[In millions of dollars (3,237 represents $3,237,000,000) except percent. For fiscal years ending in year shown; see text, Section 8, State and Local Government Finances and Employment. Minus sign (-) indicates decrease]

Item	1970	1980	1990	1995	1998	1999	2000
CURRENT DOLLARS							
Federal obligations, total	**3,237**	**8,299**	**15,226**	**(NA)**	**(NA)**	**(NA)**	**(NA)**
Academic science/engineering obligations	2,188	4,791	10,471	14,461	16,094	18,058	19,879
Percent of total	67.6	57.7	68.8	(NA)	(NA)	(NA)	(NA)
Research and development	1,447	4,161	9,017	12,181	13,877	15,570	17,281
Research and development plant.	45	38	142	341	157	173	248
Other science/engineering activities	696	593	1,312	1,939	2,060	2,315	2,350
Nonscience/engineering activities	1,049	3,508	4,755	(NA)	(NA)	(NA)	(NA)
CONSTANT (1996) DOLLARS [1]							
Federal obligations, total	**11,361**	**14,822**	**17,694**	**(NA)**	**(NA)**	**(NA)**	**(NA)**
Academic science/engineering obligations	7,678	8,557	12,168	14,750	15,566	17,241	18,596
Percent of total	67.6	57.7	68.8	(NA)	(NA)	(NA)	(NA)
Research and development	5,078	7,431	10,478	12,424	13,422	14,865	16,166
Research and development plant.	157	67	165	348	151	165	232
Other science/engineering activities	2,444	1,058	1,525	1,978	1,993	2,211	2,199
Nonscience/engineering activities	3,682	6,265	5,526	(NA)	(NA)	(NA)	(NA)

NA Not available.   [1] Based on gross domestic product implicit price deflator.
Source: U.S. National Science Foundation, *Survey of Federal S&E Support to Universities, Colleges, and Nonprofit Institutions,* annual.

No. 760. Federal R&D Obligations to Selected Universities and Colleges: 1981 to 2000

[In millions of dollars (4,410.9 represents $4,410,900,000), except rank. For fiscal years ending in year shown; see text, Section 8, State and Local Government Finances and Employment. For the top 45 institutions receiving federal R&D funds in 1998. Awards to the administrative offices of university systems are excluded from totals for individual institutions because that allocation of funds is unknown, but those awards are included in "total all institutions"]

Major institution ranked by total 1999 Federal R&D obligations	Obligations				Rank			
	1981	1990	1995	2000	1981	1990	1995	2000
Total, all institutions [1]	**4,410.9**	**9,016.7**	**12,180.9**	**17,281.0**	(X)	(X)	(X)	(X)
45 institutions, percent of total	61.6	59.4	58.6	59.0	(X)	(X)	(X)	(X)
Johns Hopkins University.	363.4	469.5	569.3	795.5	1	1	1	1
University of Washington	100.0	217.2	299.7	396.1	4	4	2	2
University of California—Los Angeles.	94.9	176.7	216.4	372.4	5	5	7	3
Stanford University	106.1	248.0	266.7	355.0	3	2	4	4
University of Pennsylvania	76.1	142.5	202.3	348.5	10	13	10	5
University of Michigan.	74.0	176.4	243.6	346.7	11	6	5	6
University of California—San Diego	91.4	164.8	239.2	314.4	6	8	6	7
Harvard University	87.8	148.1	191.5	299.9	7	11	13	8
University of California—San Francisco	64.8	167.3	201.8	289.2	15	7	12	9
Washington University.	54.2	117.9	165.4	287.3	17	19	18	10
University of Minnesota	72.0	137.5	202.8	276.8	14	15	9	11
Columbia University—Main Division	83.7	153.2	185.7	276.3	9	10	14	12
University of Colorado.	46.1	116.4	165.4	272.3	22	21	17	13
University of Wisconsin—Madison	86.9	155.2	207.7	263.4	8	9	8	14
Yale University.	73.5	142.5	179.5	260.0	12	14	15	15
Massachusetts Institute of Technology	146.0	218.3	280.3	248.9	2	3	3	16
University of Pittsburgh	38.5	116.6	166.3	246.2	29	20	16	17
Cornell University.	72.7	144.7	202.2	240.1	13	12	11	18
University of North Carolina at Chapel Hill	38.4	100.2	156.3	232.7	30	24	19	19
Duke University	44.3	116.1	155.0	232.2	23	22	20	20
Pennsylvania State University.	47.1	136.4	152.5	230.1	21	16	21	21
University Southern California.	49.2	122.7	152.2	203.9	20	17	22	22
University of California—Berkeley	64.1	121.7	142.4	196.2	16	18	23	23
University of Alabama—Birmingham	30.0	74.5	120.2	182.9	44	32	26	24
Case Western Reserve University	33.7	71.3	127.4	179.4	38	34	25	25
Baylor College of Medicine.	35.1	72.3	84.1	172.3	35	33	43	26
University of Arizona.	36.3	92.8	137.1	162.7	33	26	24	27
University of California—Davis	31.8	68.9	98.9	157.2	42	37	33	28
University of Illinois—Urbana Champaign	53.6	99.7	115.7	156.1	19	25	28	29
University of Rochester	43.0	102.5	107.6	153.2	25	23	30	30
Northwestern University.	32.4	61.1	101.9	149.6	47	45	32	31
Emory University	17.4	49.6	75.8	145.6	72	57	49	32
University of Chicago	54.0	88.5	106.7	144.5	18	28	31	33
California Institute of Technology	33.0	69.2	113.7	143.1	40	36	29	34
The Scripps Research Institute	(NA)	(NA)	83.2	141.8	(NA)	(NA)	44	35
Ohio State University	42.9	80.1	96.5	140.7	26	29	34	36
Boston University	27.0	59.4	86.1	139.4	51	47	41	37
Vanderbilt University	27.4	70.6	94.4	138.4	49	35	35	38
University of Iowa.	35.3	76.8	93.9	138.2	34	30	36	39
University of Texas at Austin.	43.8	91.8	115.9	135.0	24	27	27	40
University of Florida	30.8	55.5	82.5	129.2	43	49	45	41
Indiana University.	29.3	61.4	89.0	128.3	45	44	39	42
New York University	40.6	75.7	85.5	127.0	28	31	42	43
University of Utah.	38.2	65.3	93.8	125.0	31	40	37	44
University of Virginia.	24.3	60.8	79.0	122.5	52	46	48	45

NA Not available.   X Not applicable.   [1] Includes other institutions, not shown separately.
Source: U.S. National Science Foundation, *Federal S&E Support to Universities and Colleges and Nonprofit Institutions,* annual.

Science and Technology   505

No. 761. Percentage of U.S. Scientific and Technical Articles Which Are Coauthored and Internationally Coauthored: 1989 to 1999

[Coauthorships are based on authors' corporate address. The database consists of the Institute of Scientific Information's Science and Social Science Citation Indexes (SCI, SSCI)]

Science field	Percentage coauthored				Percentage internationally coauthored			
	1989-91	1992-94	1995-97	1998-99	1989-91	1992-94	1995-97	1998-99
Science and engineering, total . . .	49.4	52.9	56.8	59.7	11.8	14.9	18.0	20.9
Physics	47.9	54.3	59.3	62.2	19.1	24.7	30.1	34.0
Chemistry	34.5	38.6	42.6	45.6	11.6	14.5	16.9	19.6
Earth & space science	53.3	58.2	63.1	67.2	20.2	24.2	28.7	33.1
Mathematics	42.8	46.8	49.6	52.3	21.0	24.3	26.8	30.2
Biology	34.5	38.6	42.5	49.0	11.6	14.5	16.9	19.4
Biomedical research	54.7	58.8	61.8	65.2	14.0	17.0	19.5	22.9
Clinical medicine	61.4	63.3	66.4	68.3	9.5	12.2	15.0	17.6
Engineering	39.3	43.3	47.0	51.2	11.5	13.8	16.5	20.2
Psychology	38.5	41.3	43.6	47.0	5.7	6.9	8.9	10.6
Social science	30.8	32.9	35.7	35.4	7.0	8.8	10.3	10.8
Health & professional fields	34.9	36.1	39.6	40.1	3.8	4.6	6.5	6.3

Source: CHI Research, Inc., Haddon Heights, NJ; and U.S. National Science Foundation, special tabulation.

No. 762. Citations on U.S. Patents to the U.S. Scientific and Technical Literature by Cited Field: 1990 to 2000

[Citations to articles with authors in different sectors are assigned fractionally to participating sectors. Citations are to articles published in a 12-year period, lagged by 3 years from the patent data. For example, 1997 citations are to articles published in 1993-95]

Science field	1990	1993	1994	1995	1996	1997	1998	1999	2000
Total [1]	19,422	38,493	40,266	46,961	66,129	102,111	143,541	143,215	142,008
Physics	3,414	4,931	5,693	5,432	5,578	6,739	7,699	8,247	9,238
Chemistry	3,451	5,961	6,190	7,070	8,373	11,594	13,007	13,009	15,009
Earth & space science	138	122	152	164	238	259	369	440	434
Mathematics	7	23	22	26	34	48	52	42	48
Biology	544	868	1,172	1,336	2,017	2,244	3,683	4,515	4,063
Biomedical research	4,999	13,812	13,709	16,389	26,537	45,273	68,074	67,264	64,276
Clinical medicine	4,682	9,986	9,789	12,576	18,339	30,549	43,823	42,988	41,454
Engineering technology	2,187	2,790	3,538	3,969	5,014	5,418	6,838	6,720	7,496

[1] Other science fields not shown separately.

Source: CHI Research, Inc., Haddon Heights, NJ; and U.S. National Science Foundation, special tabulation.

No. 763. Percentage of Citations to Foreign Articles in U.S. Scientific and Technical Public Publications: 1990 to 1999

[Citations are to 3 years' articles with 2-year lag. For example, 1997 citations are to articles published in 1993-1995]

Science field	1990	1992	1993	1994	1995	1996	1997	1998	1999
Total science & engineering . . .	29.6	30.4	31.0	31.7	32.1	32.9	33.5	34.0	35.1
Physics	34.4	34.6	35.5	36.9	38.0	39.4	40.9	41.3	43.3
Chemistry	36.4	37.3	37.6	38.6	38.1	39.3	40.7	41.8	41.9
Earth & space science	28.8	28.5	29.7	29.7	29.6	31.2	32.0	32.7	34.0
Mathematics	29.5	30.9	29.9	29.8	31.7	32.5	32.7	32.2	34.0
Biology	28.7	29.5	29.9	29.5	30.4	32.3	33.4	34.3	36.6
Biomedical research	29.8	30.4	30.9	31.5	31.6	32.0	32.3	32.4	33.1
Clinical medicine	30.0	31.4	32.0	32.8	33.4	34.2	34.5	35.4	36.6
Engineering technology	26.7	26.9	26.7	29.4	28.7	29.6	31.8	31.4	33.8
Psychology	17.8	17.5	17.7	17.7	18.2	19.2	20.2	20.6	21.3
Social science	14.7	14.4	14.7	15.1	15.6	16.9	17.2	17.2	17.1
Health & professional fields	9.5	9.3	9.8	9.9	9.9	10.1	10.7	10.7	11.9

Source: CHI Research, Inc., Haddon Heights, NJ; and U.S. National Science Foundation, special tabulation.

U.S. Census Bureau, Statistical Abstract of the United States: 2002

No. 764. Funds for Performance of Industrial R&D in Current and Constant (1996) Dollars by Source of Funds and Selected Industries: 1998 to 2000

[In millions of dollars (169,180 represents $169,180,000,000). For calendar years. Covers basic research, applied research, and development]

Source of funds and industry	NAICS [1] code	1998	1999	2000
CURRENT DOLLARS				
Total funds	(X)	**169,180**	**182,823**	**199,539**
Petroleum and coal products	324	1,395	615	(D)
Chemicals and allied products	325	18,969	20,246	20,918
Machinery	333	(D)	6,057	6,580
Navigational, measuring, electromedical, and control instruments	3345	11,232	14,337	15,116
Electrical equipment, appliances, and components	335	2,280	(D)	(D)
Motor vehicles, trailers, and parts	3361-3363	(D)	(D)	(D)
Aerospace products and parts	3364	16,359	14,425	10,319
All other [2]	(X)	(D)	(D)	(D)
Company funds	(X)	**145,016**	**160,288**	**180,421**
Petroleum and coal products	324	1,390	(D)	1,172
Chemicals	325	18,733	20,051	20,768
Machinery	333	5,831	5,658	6,539
Navigational, measuring, electromedical, and control instruments	3345	5,483	8,632	10,114
Electrical equipment, appliances, and components	335	2,139	3,820	3,390
Motor vehicles, trailers, and parts	3361-3363	13,781	17,987	18,306
Aerospace products and parts	3364	6,521	5,309	3,895
All other [2]	(X)	91,138	(D)	116,237
CONSTANT (1996) DOLLARS [3]				
Total funds	(X)	**163,934**	**174,699**	**186,415**
Petroleum and coal products	324	1,352	588	(D)
Chemicals	325	18,381	19,346	19,542
Machinery	333	(D)	5,788	6,147
Navigational, measuring, electromedical, and control instruments	3345	10,884	13,700	14,122
Electrical equipment, appliances, and components	335	2,209	(D)	(D)
Motor vehicles, trailers, and parts	3361-3363	(D)	(D)	(D)
Aerospace products and parts	3364	15,852	13,784	9,640
All other [2]	(X)	(D)	(D)	(D)
Company funds	(X)	**140,519**	**153,166**	**168,555**
Petroleum and coal products	324	1,347	(D)	1,095
Chemicals	325	18,152	19,160	19,402
Machinery	333	5,650	5,407	6,109
Navigational, measuring, electromedical, and control instruments	3345	5,313	8,248	9,449
Electrical equipment, appliances, and components	335	2,073	3,650	3,167
Motor vehicles, trailers, and parts	3361-3363	13,354	17,188	17,102
Aerospace products and parts	3364	6,319	5,073	3,639
All other [2]	(X)	88,312	(D)	108,592

D Figure withheld to avoid disclosure of information pertaining to a specific organization or individual. X Not applicable. [1] 1997 North American Industry Classification System; see text, Section 15, Business Enterprise. [2] All other manufacturing and nonmanufacturing. [3] Based on gross domestic product implicit price deflator.

Source: U.S. National Science Foundation, *Research and Development in Industry,* annual.

No. 765. R&D Funds in R&D-Performing Manufacturing Companies by Industry: 1998 to 2000

Industry	NAICS [1] code	Total R&D funds as a percent of net sales			Company R&D funds as a percent of net sales		
		1998	1999	2000	1998	1999	2000
Total [2]	(X)	**3.7**	**3.7**	**3.6**	**3.2**	**3.2**	**3.3**
Food	311	0.4	0.4	(D)	0.4	0.4	0.4
Paper, printing, and support activities	322, 326	(D)	(D)	(D)	1.0	1.4	1.6
Petroleum and coal products	324	0.8	0.4	(D)	0.8	(D)	0.3
Chemicals	325	6.3	5.2	5.9	6.2	5.1	5.9
Plastic and rubber products	326	2.0	1.9	(D)	2	1.9	1.8
Nonmetallic mineral products	327	1.3	(D)	1.8	(D)	1.5	1.8
Primary metals	331	(D)	0.4	0.5	0.5	0.4	0.5
Fabricated metal products	332	1.5	1.5	1.4	1.4	1.4	1.4
Machinery	333	(D)	3.5	3.9	3.1	3.3	3.8
Navigational, measuring, electromedical, and control instruments	3345	13.6	15.2	12.0	6.6	9.1	8.0
Electrical equipment, appliances, and components	335	2.9	(D)	(D)	2.7	2.3	2.1
Motor vehicles, trailers, and parts	3361-3363	(D)	(D)	(D)	2.2	2.9	3.2
Aerospace products and parts	3364	7.2	8.8	7.3	2.9	3.2	2.8

D Figure withheld to avoid disclosure of information pertaining to a specific organization or individual. X Not applicable. [1] 1997 North American Industry Classification System; see text, Section 15, Business. [2] Includes all manufacturing industries.

Source: U.S. National Science Foundation, *Research and Development in Industry,* annual.

Figure 16.2
Funds for Performance of Industrial R&D: 1998 to 2000

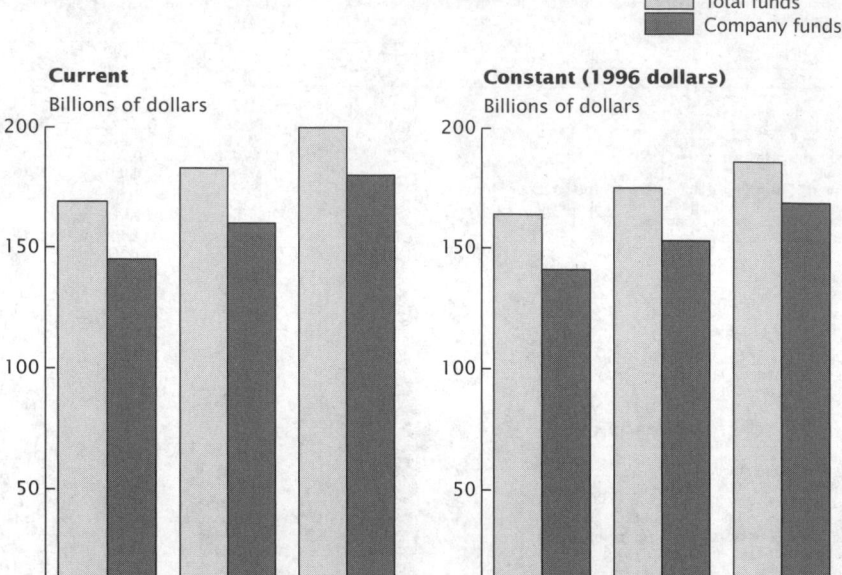

Source: Chart prepared by U.S. Census Bureau. For data, see Table 764.

Figure 16.3
Federal Funding for Research—Percent Distribution by Field of Science: 2001

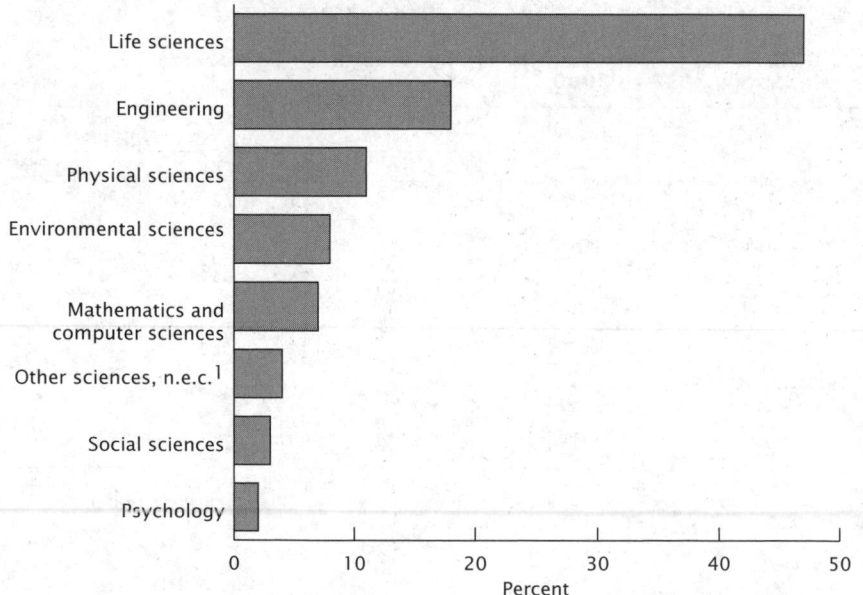

[1] n.e.c. = Not elsewhere classified.
Source: Chart prepared by U.S. Census Bureau. For data, see Table 766.

No. 766. Federal Obligations for Research in Current and Constant (1996) Dollars by Field of Science: 1980 to 2002

[In millions of dollars (11,597 represents $11,597,000,000). For fiscal years ending in year shown; see text, Section 8, State and Local Government Finances and Employment. Excludes R&D plant]

Field	1980	1985	1990	1995	1998	1999	2000	2001, prel.	2002, prel.
CURRENT DOLLARS									
Research, total	11,597	16,133	21,622	28,434	30,922	33,528	38,471	43,836	45,327
Basic	4,674	7,819	11,286	13,877	15,613	17,444	19,570	22,705	23,399
Applied	6,923	8,315	10,337	14,557	15,309	16,084	18,901	21,131	21,928
Life sciences	4,192	6,363	8,830	11,811	13,558	15,422	17,965	21,118	22,204
Psychology	199	327	449	623	591	633	1,627	1,871	2,075
Physical sciences	2,001	3,046	3,809	4,278	4,210	4,066	4,788	5,163	5,145
Environmental sciences	1,261	1,404	2,174	2,854	3,062	3,095	3,329	3,661	3,644
Mathematics and computer sciences . . .	241	575	841	1,579	1,837	1,981	2,206	2,458	2,618
Engineering	2,830	3,618	4,227	5,708	5,895	6,263	6,346	7,091	7,031
Social sciences	524	460	630	679	806	855	1,050	1,216	1,271
Other sciences, n.e.c. [1]	350	342	664	902	964	1,212	1,160	1,259	1,338
CONSTANT (1996) DOLLARS [2]									
Research, total	20,713	21,953	25,128	29,003	29,906	31,977	35,988	40,077	40,576
Basic	8,348	10,639	13,116	14,154	15,100	16,637	18,307	20,758	20,946
Applied	12,365	11,314	12,013	14,848	14,806	15,340	17,681	19,319	19,629
Life sciences	7,488	8,658	10,261	12,047	13,112	14,709	16,805	19,307	19,876
Psychology	355	445	522	635	572	604	1,522	1,711	1,857
Physical sciences	3,573	4,145	4,426	4,364	4,071	3,878	4,479	4,720	4,606
Environmental sciences	2,252	1,910	2,526	2,911	2,961	2,952	3,114	3,347	3,262
Mathematics and computer sciences . . .	430	782	977	1,611	1,776	1,889	2,064	2,247	2,344
Engineering	5,055	4,923	4,912	5,823	5,702	5,973	5,936	6,483	6,294
Social sciences	936	626	732	692	780	815	982	1,112	1,138
Other sciences, n.e.c. [1]	624	465	772	920	932	1,156	1,085	1,151	1,198

[1] N.e.c. = Not elsewhere classified.   [2] Based on gross domestic product implicit price deflator.

Source: U.S. National Science Foundation, *Federal Funds for Research and Development,* annual.

No. 767. R&D Scientists and Engineers— Employment and Cost by Industry: 1998 to 2000

[974.6 represents 974,600. Data are estimates; on average full-time-equivalent (FTE) basis]

Industry	NAICS [1] code	1998	1999	2000
EMPLOYED SCIENTISTS (1,000)				
Average FTE of scientists and engineers [2][3]	(X)	974.6	1,015.7	1,037.5
Chemicals	325	90.1	86.7	82.0
Machinery	333	104.1	74.1	51.9
Electrical equipment, appliances, and components	335	172.7	98.8	23.3
Motor vehicles, trailers, and parts.	3361-3363	63.5	69.2	75.4
Aerospace products and parts.	3364	71.7	60.9	40.2
CONSTANT (1996) DOLLARS [4] ($1,000)				
Cost per scientist or engineer [3][5]	(X)	168.2	172.0	179.7
Chemicals	325	234.1	234.6	238.3
Machinery	333	138.8	113.7	118.6
Electrical equipment, appliances, and components	335	145.8	(D)	(D)
Motor vehicles, trailers, and parts.	3361-3363	(D)	(D)	(D)
Aerospace products and parts.	3364	195.2	210.2	(D)

D Withheld to avoid disclosure.   X Not applicable.   [1] 1997 North American Industry Classification System; see text, Section 15, Business Enterprise.   [2] The mean number of FTE R&D scientists and engineers employed in January of the year shown and the following January.   [3] Includes industries not shown separately.   [4] Based on gross domestic product implicit price deflator. [5] Represents the arithmetic mean of the numbers of R&D scientists and engineers reported in each industry for January in 2 consecutive years divided into total R&D expenditures in each industry.

Source: U.S. National Science Foundation, *Research and Development in Industry,* annual.

U.S. Census Bureau, Statistical Abstract of the United States: 2002

No. 768. Civilian Employment of Scientists, Engineers, and Technicians by Occupation and Industry: 2000

[In thousands (6,412.4 represents 6,412,400). Based on sample and subject to sampling error. For details, see source]

Occupation		Wage and salary workers								Self employed [5]
	Total [1]	Mining [2]	Construction	Manufacturing	Transportation [3]	Trade	Fire [4]	Services	Government	
Scientists, engineers, and technicians, total	6,412.4	38.1	81.6	1,423.1	264.1	377.7	370.2	2,772.7	726.9	343.6
Scientists	922.8	7.4	0.5	108.1	15.2	21.7	43.8	374.0	227.0	118.0
Physical scientists	239.1	7.0	0.2	60.5	5.5	2.3	0.7	82.1	73.8	7.0
Life scientists	184.4	0.2	(6)	21.9	0.2	3.8	0.5	77.1	60.8	12.9
Mathematical scientists	89.4	0.1	(6)	6.9	2.6	1.3	23.0	37.5	17.9	(6)
Social scientists and related occupations	409.9	0.2	0.3	18.8	6.9	14.3	19.5	177.4	74.5	98.1
Computer specialists,	2,903.4	4.5	9.5	318.2	115.4	247.3	315.7	1,557.9	179.2	154.3
Engineers [7]	1,465.3	14.5	44.6	642.1	82.4	48.3	8.4	401.2	179.4	42.7
Civil engineers	232.0	0.9	19.1	3.8	2.7	0.2	1.0	120.7	70.0	12.1
Electrical/electronics	287.6	0.4	6.1	139.0	20.4	22.2	0.9	59.1	31.1	8.3
Mechanical engineers	221.4	0.6	5.4	122.3	2.5	8.2	1.0	62.5	11.8	7.1
Engineering and science technicians	1,062.6	9.2	24.6	354.7	50.2	60.3	2.1	396.2	135.5	26.1
Electrical/electronics technicians	232.7	0.8	4.0	101.7	22.1	34.0	0.5	48.3	15.0	6.3
Other engineering technicians	286.6	1.1	5.4	104.1	17.0	16.7	0.6	85.0	52.0	4.6
Drafters	213.1	0.7	15.0	65.5	4.9	5.5	0.5	103.2	6.5	10.0
Life, physical, and social science technicians	330.1	6.7	0.2	83.5	6.1	4.1	0.5	159.7	62.0	5.2
Surveyors [6]	58.3	2.5	2.5	0.1	1.0	0.1	0.4	43.4	5.8	2.5

[1] Includes agriculture, forestry, and fishing not shown separately. [2] Includes oil and gas extraction. [3] Includes communications and public utilities. [4] Finance, insurance, and real estate. [5] Includes secondary jobs. [6] Includes cartographers, photogrammetrists, and surveying and mapping technicians. [7] Includes kinds of engineers and technicians not shown separately.

Source: U.S. Bureau of Labor Statistics, *National Industry-Occupation Employment Matrix*, November 2001; and unpublished data. (Data collected biennially.)

No. 769. Graduate Science/Engineering Students in Doctorate-Granting Colleges by Characteristic and Field: 1985 to 2000

[In thousands (359.8 represents 359,800). As of fall. Includes outlying areas]

Field of science or engineering	Total			Characteristic							
				Female			Foreign		Part-time		
	1985	1990	2000	1985	1990	2000	1990	2000	1985	1990	2000
Total, all surveyed fields	359.8	404.4	435.6	124.8	152.9	196.3	102.2	121.4	118.0	127.6	119.1
Science/engineering	320.3	356.2	368.6	94.8	115.8	146.4	98.1	116.0	99.6	104.6	95.5
Engineering, total	90.8	100.7	99.1	10.4	13.7	19.6	36.7	45.6	36.2	36.4	28.2
Sciences, total	229.5	255.5	269.5	84.4	102.1	126.8	61.4	70.4	63.4	68.2	67.3
Physical sciences	29.6	32.7	29.4	6.1	7.7	8.7	12.1	11.4	3.5	3.7	3.3
Environmental	14.2	13.0	12.7	3.6	3.8	5.2	2.6	2.6	3.4	3.1	2.6
Mathematical sciences	15.7	17.8	13.9	4.6	5.4	4.9	6.3	5.7	4.4	4.5	2.8
Computer sciences	24.2	28.6	39.7	6.1	6.7	11.4	9.4	19.2	11.7	13.6	16.4
Agricultural sciences	11.0	10.7	10.9	2.8	3.1	4.6	3.1	2.3	2.1	1.9	2.2
Biological sciences	42.5	46.6	52.6	18.1	21.3	27.6	11.2	11.6	7.0	7.1	7.3
Psychology	31.4	37.0	38.2	18.8	24.4	27.4	1.7	2.1	9.9	11.1	9.7
Social sciences	61.0	69.0	72.0	24.3	29.7	37.0	14.9	15.6	21.4	23.1	23.1
Health fields, total	39.5	48.2	67.0	30.0	37.1	49.9	4.1	5.4	18.5	22.9	23.6

Source: U.S. National Science Foundation, *Survey of Graduate Science Engineering Students and Postdoctorates*, annual.

No. 770. Science and Engineering Degree Recipients in 1995 and 1996

[In thousands (708.9 represents 708,900) except for percent. Based on survey and subject to sampling error; see source for details]

Degree and field	Graduates 1995 and 1996 (1,000)	1996 [1] percent distribution				Median salary [4] ($1,000)
			Employed		Not employed or not FT students	
		In school [2]	In S&E [3]	In other		
Bachelor's recipients	**708.9**	**21**	**21**	**53**	**5**	**28.2**
All science fields	593.8	23	12	60	5	26.0
Computer and information sciences	41.0	6	57	34	3	37.7
Mathematical sciences	26.8	19	15	63	3	29.8
Life and related sciences	139.0	31	11	53	5	22.8
Physical and related sciences	36.6	38	26	33	3	27.3
Psychology	138.0	24	6	65	5	22.3
Social and related sciences	212.4	18	6	70	6	26.4
All engineering fields	115.1	13	65	18	3	37.7
Aerospace and related engineering	3.0	22	48	27	2	34.0
Chemical engineering	11.6	17	65	14	4	39.3
Civil and architectural engineering	20.7	14	63	20	3	34.4
Electrical, electronics, computer and communications engineering	32.9	10	70	16	4	40.5
Industrial engineering	5.8	8	66	24	2	37.6
Mechanical engineering	27.9	11	71	15	3	38.2
Other engineering	13.2	21	52	25	3	34.1
Master's recipients	**149.5**	**21**	**49**	**27**	**3**	**41.5**
All science fields	102.5	23	36	36	4	37.2
Computer and mathematical sciences	18.2	6	74	18	2	51.2
Mathematical sciences	7.9	27	37	32	3	39.7
Life and related sciences	15.3	32	37	27	4	32.4
Physical and related sciences	9.7	37	42	18	3	33.6
Psychology	26.4	22	29	43	5	29.7
Social and related sciences	25.1	26	15	54	5	35.0
All engineering fields	47.0	15	75	9	2	49.9
Aerospace and related engineering	1.5	31	54	15	1	48.8
Chemical engineering	2.0	33	61	4	2	47.6
Civil and architectural engineering	6.5	11	76	11	1	41.9
Electrical, electronics, computer and communications engineering	16.2	15	77	7	1	55.0
Industrial engineering	3.2	13	70	16	1	49.9
Mechanical engineering	7.2	16	72	10	2	47.7
Other engineering	10.4	10	78	9	4	49.0

[1] As of April. [2] Full-time students. [3] In science and engineering. [4] For the principal job. Excludes full-time students, the self-employed, and persons whose principal job is less than 35 hours per week.

Source: National Science Foundation, *National Survey of Recent College Graduates: 1997.*

No. 771. Doctorates Conferred by Recipients' Characteristics: 1990 and 2000

[In percent, except as indicated]

Characteristic	1990, total	2000									
		All fields [1]	Engin- eering	Physi- cal sci- ences [2]	Earth sci- ences	Math- ematics	Com- puter sci- ences	Biologi- cal sci- ences [3]	Agricul- tural	Social sci- ences [4]	Psy- chology
Total conferred (number)	**36,068**	**41,368**	**5,330**	**3,411**	**757**	**1,048**	**861**	**5,855**	**943**	**4,151**	**3,623**
Male	63.7	56.0	84.3	75.5	69.6	75.4	83.5	55.2	70.9	57.1	33.4
Female	36.3	43.8	15.7	24.5	30.4	24.6	16.5	44.8	29.1	42.9	66.6
Median age [5]	33.9	33.6	31.4	30.7	33.4	30.4	32.9	30.7	34.4	34.1	32.2
CITIZENSHIP [6]											
Total conferred (number)	**34,697**	**39,485**	**5,000**	**3,240**	**711**	**1,010**	**819**	**5,650**	**917**	**3,980**	**3,385**
U.S. citizen	71.8	75.6	51.1	64.3	71.6	56.2	55.9	75.4	54.6	73.0	95.2
Foreign citizen	28.2	24.4	48.9	35.7	28.4	43.8	44.1	24.6	45.4	27.0	4.8
RACE/ETHNICITY [7]											
Total conferred (number)	**26,604**	**29,837**	**2,556**	**2,084**	**509**	**568**	**458**	**4,260**	**501**	**2,907**	**3,221**
White [8]	86.5	79.3	73.5	80.9	84.9	81.0	73.6	77.6	82.2	79.3	80.8
Black [8]	3.8	5.9	3.2	3.0	1.4	2.5	3.9	2.9	3.6	7.2	6.0
Asian/Pacific [8]	4.9	7.8	17.5	9.7	5.7	12.3	16.8	12.9	6.2	6.2	4.6
Indian/Alaskan [8]	0.4	0.6	0.3	0.4	1.0	0.4	0.2	0.4	0.8	0.7	0.7
Hispanic	3.1	4.3	3.1	3.7	3.5	2.5	2.8	4.1	5.2	3.7	6.0
Other/unknown	1.4	2.2	2.3	2.3	3.5	1.4	2.6	2.9	2.0	2.6	1.9

[1] Includes other fields, not shown separately. [2] Astronomy, physics, and chemistry. [3] Biochemistry, botany, microbiology, physiology, zoology, and related fields. [4] Anthropology, sociology, political science, economics, international relations and related fields. [5] For definition of median, see Guide to Tabular Presentation. [6] For those with known citizenship. Includes those with temporary visas. [7] Excludes those with temporary visas. [8] Non-Hispanic.

Source: U.S. National Science Foundation, Survey of Earned Doctorates, *Selected Data on Science and Engineering Doctorate Awards,* annual.

Science and Technology   511

No. 772. Space Vehicle Systems—Net Sales and Backlog Orders: 1970 to 2000

[**In millions of dollars (1,956 represents $1,956,000,000).** Backlog orders as of Dec. 31. Based on data from major companies engaged in manufacture of aerospace products. Includes parts but excludes engines and propulsion units]

Year	Net sales			Backlog orders			Year	Net sales			Backlog orders		
	Total	Military	Non-military	Total	Military	Non-military		Total	Military	Non-military	Total	Military	Non-military
1970 .	1,956	1,025	931	1,184	786	398	1995 .	11,314	4,782	6,532	15,650	5,872	9,778
1975 .	2,119	1,096	1,023	1,304	1,019	285	1996 .	11,698	5,613	6,085	23,004	9,125	13,879
1980 .	3,483	1,461	2,022	1,814	951	863	1997 .	13,410	4,916	8,494	23,357	8,790	14,567
1985 .	6,300	4,241	2,059	6,707	4,941	1,766	1998 .	9,490	4,227	5,264	20,371	7,970	12,402
1990 .	9,691	6,556	3,135	12,462	8,130	4,332	1999 .	9,022	5,107	3,915	22,356	10,666	11,690
1994 .	10,594	5,707	4,887	12,888	6,732	6,156	2000 .	9,079	3,723	5,356	21,190	10,400	10,790

Source: U.S. Census Bureau, *Current Industrial Reports*, MA-336G, *Aerospace Industry (Orders, Sales, and Backlog)* and, beginning 1994, Internet site <http://www.census.gov/cir/www>.

No. 773. Federal Outlays in Current and Constant 1996 Dollars for General Science, Space, and Other Technology, 1970 to 2001, and Projections, 2002 to 2007

[**In billions of dollars (4.5 represents $4,500,000,000).** For fiscal years ending in year shown; see text, Section 8, State and Local Governments Finances and Employment]

Year	Current dollars			Constant (1996) dollars		
	Total	General science/basic research	Space and other technologies	Total	General science/basic research	Space and other technologies
1970	4.5	0.9	3.6	18.5	3.9	14.6
1980	5.8	1.4	4.5	11.6	2.7	8.9
1985	8.6	2.0	6.6	12.8	3.0	9.8
1990	14.4	2.8	11.6	18.4	3.6	14.8
1995	16.7	4.1	12.6	17.3	4.3	13.0
1996	16.7	4.0	12.7	16.7	4.0	12.7
1997	17.2	4.1	13.1	16.9	4.0	12.9
1998	18.2	5.4	12.9	17.5	5.1	12.4
1999	18.1	5.7	12.4	17.1	5.3	11.7
2000	18.6	6.2	12.4	17.1	5.7	11.4
2001	19.9	6.6	13.3	17.9	5.9	12.0
2002, proj.	21.8	7.8	14.0	18.9	6.7	12.3
2003, proj.	22.2	8.1	14.1	19.0	6.8	12.1
2004, proj.	22.8	8.3	14.5	19.2	6.9	12.3
2005, proj.	23.5	8.5	15.0	19.6	7.1	12.5
2006, proj.	24.0	8.7	15.4	19.6	7.1	12.6
2007, proj.	24.6	8.9	15.7	19.7	7.1	12.6

Source: U.S. Office of Management and Budget, *Budget of the United States, Historical Tables, Fiscal Year 2003*, annual.

No. 774. U.S. Commercial Space Industry Revenue by Type: 1996 to 2001

[**In billions of dollars (19.6 represents $19,600,000,000).** For calendar years]

Industry	1996	1997	1998	1999	2000	2001, est.
Revenue, total	19.6	26.7	30.5	31.9	36.9	36.5
Satellite manufacturing [1]	7.3	10.3	11.8	10.0	8.9	5.5
Launch industry	3.2	3.6	3.5	3.5	4.1	1.7
Satellite services [2]	4.8	6.3	7.4	9.8	11.8	15.9
Ground equipment manufacturing [3]	4.3	6.5	7.8	8.6	12.1	13.4

See footnotes for corresponding objects in Table 775.

No. 775. Worldwide Commercial Space Industry Revenue by Type: 1996 to 2001

[In billions of dollars (44.8 represents $44,800,000,000). For calendar years]

Industry	1996	1997	1998	1999	2000	2001, est.
Total	**44.8**	**57.5**	**63.8**	**68.0**	**82.6**	**85.1**
Satellite manufacturing [1]	12.4	15.9	18.5	15.8	17.2	14.1
Launch industry	6.9	7.9	7.0	6.6	8.5	5.0
Satellite services [2]	15.8	21.2	24.4	29.7	39.2	46.4
Ground equipment manufacturing [3]	9.7	12.5	13.9	16.0	17.7	19.6

[1] Includes revenues from the construction and sale of satellites to both commercial and government. [2] Includes revenues derived from transponder leasing and subscription/retail services such as direct-to-home television and satellite mobile and data communications. [3] Includes revenues from the manufacture of gateways and satellite control stations, satellite news-gathering trucks, very small aperture terminals, direct-to-home television equipment and mobile satellite phones.

Source of Tables 774 and 775: Satellite Industry Association/Futron Corporation, Bethesda, MD, *2000 Satellite Survey* (copyright).

No. 776. National Aeronautics and Space Administration—Budget Authority: 1999 and Projections to 2004

[In millions of dollars (13,653.0 represents $13,653,000,000)]

Item	1999	2000	2001	2002	2003	2004
Budget authority, total............	13,653.0	13,600.8	14,357.2	15,012.7	15,117.0	15,690.4
Human space flight....................	5,480.0	5,467.7	7,153.5	6,830.1	6,130.9	5,868.9
International space station	2,299.7	2,323.1	2,127.8	1,721.7	1,492.1	1,195.9
Space flight operations (space shuttle)	2,998.3	2,979.5	3,118.8	3,272.8	3,208.0	3,301.0
Payload utilization and operations	182.0	165.1	(NA)	(NA)	(NA)	(NA)
Payload and elv support..............	(X)	(X)	90.0	91.3	87.5	91.0
Investments and support..............	(X)	(X)	1,247.8	1,214.5	1,178.2	1,159.9
Science, aeronautics and technology	5,653.9	5,580.9	7,076.5	8,047.8	8,844.5	9,679.0
Space science	2,119.2	2,192.8	2,606.6	2,867.1	3,414.3	3,906.9
Earth science	1,413.8	1,443.4	1,762.2	1,625.7	1,628.4	1,620.5
Aerospace technology	1,338.9	1,124.9	2,212.8	2,507.7	2,815.8	3,124.9
Academic programs..................	138.5	138.8	132.7	227.3	143.7	143.7
Safety, mission assurance, engineering and advanced concepts	35.6	43.0	47.4	47.6	47.6	47.8
Inspector General......................	19.6	20.0	22.9	23.7	24.6	25.5

NA Not available.   X Not applicable.

Source: U.S. National Aeronautics and Space Administration, <http://ifmp.nasa.gov/codeb/budget2003/2003websites.html>.

No. 777. NASA Space Shuttle Operations Expenditures: 1996 to 2001

[In millions of dollars (2,485.4 represents $2,485,400,000). Data are funding requirements for fiscal years shown]

Operation	1996	1997	1998	1999	2000	2001
Total	2,485.4	2,464.9	2,369.4	2,998.3	2,999.9	3,165.7
Shuttle operations.....................	2,485.4	2,464.9	2,369.4	2,426.7	2,530.9	2,672.8
Orbiter and integration	521.0	492.6	502.9	608.0	746.9	724.5
Propulsion.........................	1,061.5	1,124.7	1,061.8	1,071.2	1,037.6	1,167.4
External tank.....................	327.5	352.4	341.3	363.2	359.2	318.8
Space shuttle main engine	185.0	208.3	204.6	200.0	182.7	283.4
Reusable solid rocket motor...........	395.7	412.8	380.4	339.0	347.9	377.7
Solid rocket booster	153.3	151.2	135.5	169.0	134.8	125.8
Mission and launch operations.........	902.9	847.6	804.7	747.5	746.4	780.9
Safety and performance upgrades	(X)	(X)	(X)	571.6	469.0	492.9
Orbiter improvements..................	(X)	(X)	(X)	234.8	183.7	327.2
Propulsion upgrades..................	(X)	(X)	(X)	175.7	181.6	60.2
Flight operations and launch site equipment...	(X)	(X)	(X)	147.6	92.5	90.0
Construction of facilities	(X)	(X)	(X)	13.5	11.0	15.5

X Not applicable.

Source: U.S. National Aeronautics and Space Administration, *NASA, 1996-97, Pocket Statistics,* annual; thereafter, <http://ifmp.nasa.gov/codeb/budget2003>.

No. 778 . World-Wide Successful Space Launches: 1957 to 2001

[Criterion of success is attainment of Earth orbit or Earth escape]

Country	Total, 1957-01	1957-64	1965-69	1970-74	1975-79	1980-84	1985-89	1990-94	1995-99	2000	2001
Total	4,182	289	586	555	607	605	550	466	384	82	58
Soviet Union/Russia [1]...	2,656	82	302	405	461	483	447	283	135	35	23
United States	1,237	207	279	139	126	93	61	122	161	28	21
Japan	55	-	-	5	10	12	11	9	7	-	1
ESA [2].............	137	-	-	-	1	8	21	33	54	12	8
China...............	65	-	-	2	6	6	9	15	21	5	1
France	10	-	4	3	3	-	-	-	-	-	-
India	11	-	-	-	-	3	-	3	3	-	2
Israel..............	3	-	-	-	-	-	1	1	1	-	-
Ukraine [1]	6	(NA)	(NA)	(NA)	(NA)	(NA)	(NA)	(NA)	2	2	2
Australia............	1	-	1	-	-	-	-	-	-	-	-
United Kingdom	1	-	-	1	-	-	-	-	-	-	-

- Represents zero.   NA Not available.   [1] Launches conducted by the former Soviet Union are listed separately as Russia or Ukraine.   [2] European Space Agency. Includes launches by Arianespace.

Source: Library of Congress, Congressional Research Service, Science Policy Research Division, *Space Activities of the United States, CIS, and Other Launching Countries/Organizations 1957-1999;* thereafter, Resources, Science, and Industry Division, 2001.

Science and Technology   513

Flight number	Mission date	Orbiter name	Crew size (up/down)	Days/hours duration	Flight number	Mission date	Orbiter name	Crew size (up/down)	Days/hours duration
1	04/12/81	Columbia	2	2	61	12/02/93	Endeavour	7	11
2	11/12/81	Columbia	2	2	60	02/03/94	Discovery	6	8
3	03/22/82	Columbia	2	8	62	03/04/94	Columbia	5	14
4	06/27/82	Columbia	2	7	59	04/09/94	Endeavour	6	11
5	11/11/82	Columbia	4	5	65	07/08/94	Columbia	7	15
6	04/04/83	Challenger	4	5	64	09/09/94	Discovery	6	11
7	06/18/83	Challenger	5	6	68	09/30/94	Endeavour	6	11
8	08/30/83	Challenger	5	6	66	11/03/94	Atlantis	6	11
9	11/28/83	Columbia	6	10	63	02/03/95	Discovery	6	8
10	02/03/84	Challenger	5	8	67	03/02/95	Endeavour	7	17
11	04/06/84	Challenger	5	7	71	06/27/95	Atlantis	7/8	10
12	08/30/84	Discovery	6	7	70	07/13/95	Discovery	5	9
13	10/05/84	Challenger	7	8	69	09/07/95	Endeavour	5	11
14	11/08/84	Discovery	5	8	73	10/20/95	Columbia	7	16
15	01/24/85	Discovery	5	4	74	11/08/95	Atlantis	5	8
16	04/12/85	Discovery	7	7	72	01/11/96	Endeavour	6	9
17	04/29/85	Challenger	7	7	75	02/22/96	Columbia	7	16
18	06/17/85	Discovery	7	7	76	03/22/96	Atlantis	6/5	9
19	07/29/85	Challenger	7	8	77	05/19/96	Endeavour	6	10
20	08/27/85	Discovery	5	7	78	06/20/96	Columbia	7	17
21	10/03/85	Atlantis	5	4	79	09/16/96	Atlantis	6	10
22	10/30/85	Challenger	8	7	80	11/20/96	Columbia	5	18
23	11/26/85	Atlantis	7	7	81	01/12/97	Atlantis	6	10/05
24	01/12/86	Columbia	7	6	82	02/11/97	Discovery	7	10/00
25	01/28/86	Challenger	7	-	83	04/04/97	Columbia	7	03/23
26	09/29/88	Discovery	5	4	84	05/15/97	Atlantis	7/7	09/05
27	12/02/88	Atlantis	5	4	94	07/01/97	Columbia	7	15/07
29	03/13/89	Discovery	5	5	85	08/07/97	Discovery	5	11/20
30	05/04/89	Atlantis	5	4	86	09/25/97	Atlantis	7/7	10/19
28	08/08/89	Columbia	5	5	87	11/19/97	Columbia	6	15/17
34	10/18/89	Atlantis	5	5	89	01/22/98	Endeavor	7/7	08/20
33	11/22/89	Discovery	5	5	90	04/17/98	Columbia	7	15/22
32	01/09/90	Columbia	5	11	91	06/02/98	Discovery	6/7	09/19
36	02/28/90	Atlantis	5	4	95	11/20/98	Discovery	7	08/22
31	04/24/90	Discovery	5	5	88	12/04/98	Endeavor	6	11/19
41	10/06/90	Discovery	5	4	96	05/27/99	Discovery	7	09/19
38	11/15/90	Atlantis	5	5	93	07/23/99	Columbia	5	04/24
35	12/02/90	Columbia	7	9	103	12/19/99	Atlantis	7	07/23
37	04/05/91	Atlantis	5	6	99	02/11/00	Endeavor	6	11/04
39	04/28/91	Discovery	7	8	101	05/19/00	Atlantis	7	09/21
40	06/05/91	Columbia	7	9	106	09/08/00	Atlantis	7	11/19
43	08/02/91	Atlantis	5	9	92	10/11/00	Discovery	7	12/21
48	09/12/91	Discovery	5	5	98	12/02/00	Endeavor	5	10/20
44	11/24/91	Atlantis	6	7	97	02/07/01	Atlantis	5	12/21
42	01/22/92	Discovery	7	9	102	03/08/01	Discovery	7/7	12/20
45	03/24/92	Atlantis	7	9	100	04/19/01	Endeavor	7	11/20
49	05/07/92	Endeavour	7	9	104	07/12/01	Atlantis	5	12/19
50	06/25/92	Columbia	7	14	105	10/10/01	Discovery	7/7	11/21
46	07/31/92	Atlantis	7	8					
47	09/12/92	Endeavour	7	8	FUTURE				
52	10/22/92	Columbia	6	10	MISSIONS				
53	12/02/92	Discovery	5	7	IN WORK				
54	01/13/93	Endeavour	5	6					
56	04/08/93	Discovery	5	9	108	11/30/2001	Endeavor	7/7	10
55	04/26/93	Columbia	7	10	109	1/18/2001	Columbia	7	11
57	06/21/93	Endeavour	6	10	110	2/15/2001	Atlantis	7	9
51	09/12/93	Discovery	5	10	107	4/04/2002	Columbia	7	16
58	10/18/93	Columbia	7	14	111	4/18/2002	Endeavor	4	10

- Represents zero.

Source: U.S. National Aeronautics and Space Administration, Internet site <http://www.ksc.nasa.gov/shuttle/missions/missions.html> (accessed 22 July 2002).

No. 780. Nobel Prize Laureates in Selected Sciences: 1901 to 1999

[Presented by location of award-winning research and by date of award]

Country	1901-1999				1901-1930	1931-1945	1946-1960	1961-1975	1976-1990	1991-1998	1999
	Total	Physics	Chemistry	Physiology/Medicine							
Total	459	158	132	169	93	49	74	92	98	51	4
United States	199	70	47	82	6	14	38	41	63	36	3
United Kingdom	71	21	26	24	15	11	14	20	9	2	-
Germany [1]	61	17	29	15	27	11	4	8	7	3	-
France	25	11	7	7	13	2	-	5	2	3	-
Soviet Union	10	7	1	2	2	-	4	3	1	-	-
Japan	4	3	1	-	-	-	1	2	1	-	-
Other countries	89	29	21	39	30	11	13	13	15	7	1

- Represents zero. [1] Between 1946 and 1991, data are for the former West Germany only.

Source: U.S. National Science Foundation, unpublished data.

This section presents statistics on farms and farm operators; land use; farm income, expenditures, and debt; farm output, productivity, and marketings; foreign trade in agricultural products; specific crops; and livestock, poultry, and their products.

The principal sources are the reports issued by the National Agricultural Statistics Service (NASS) and the Economic Research Service (ERS) of the U.S. Department of Agriculture. The information from the 1997 Census of Agriculture is available in printed form in the Volume 1, Geographic Area Series; in electronic format on CD-ROM; and on the Internet site <http://www.nass.usda.gov/census/>. The Department of Agriculture publishes annually *Agricultural Statistics,* a general reference book on agricultural production, supplies, consumption, facilities, costs, and returns. The ERS publishes data on farm assets, debt, and income on the Internet site <http://www.ers.usda. gov/briefing/farmincome/>. Sources of current data on agricultural exports and imports include *Foreign Agricultural Trade of the United States,* published by the ERS, and the reports of the U.S. Census Bureau, particularly *U.S. Imports of Merchandise on CD-ROM,* and *U.S. Exports of Merchandise on CD-ROM.*

The 45 field offices of the NASS collect data on crops, livestock and products, agricultural prices, farm employment, and other related subjects mainly through sample surveys. Information is obtained on some 75 crops and 50 livestock items as well as scores of items pertaining to agricultural production and marketing. State estimates and supporting information are sent to the Agricultural Statistics Board of NASS which reviews the estimates and issues reports containing state and national data. Among these reports are annual summaries such as *Crop Production, Crop Values, Agricultural Prices,* and *Livestock Production, Disposition and*

Income. For more information about concepts and methods underlying USDA's statistical series, see *Major Statistical Series of the U.S. Department of Agriculture* (Agricultural Handbook No. 671), a 12-volume set of publications.

Farms and farmland—The definitions of a farm have varied through time. Since 1850, when minimum criteria defining a farm for census purposes first were established, the farm definition has changed nine times. The current definition, first used for the 1974 census, is any place from which $1,000 or more of agricultural products were produced and sold, or normally would have been sold, during the census year.

Acreage designated as "land in farms" consists primarily of agricultural land used for crops, pasture, or grazing. It also includes woodland and wasteland not actually under cultivation or used for pasture or grazing, provided it was part of the farm operator's total operation. Land in farms includes acres set aside under annual commodity acreage programs as well as acres in the Conservation Reserve and Wetlands Reserve Programs for places meeting the farm definition. Land in farms is an operating unit concept and includes land owned and operated as well as land rented from others. All grazing land, except land used under government permits on a per-head basis, was included as "land in farms" provided it was part of a farm or ranch.

Since 1945, an evaluation of census coverage has been conducted for each census of agriculture to provide estimates of the completeness of census farm counts. According to coverage evaluation results, the past five censuses of agriculture included an average of 92 percent of U.S. farms and 98 percent of agriculture production. The 1997 coverage evaluation program was designed to measure four components of error in the census farm

U.S. Census Bureau, Statistical Abstract of the United States: 2002

counts. These components include undercount due to farms not on the mail list; overcount due to farms duplicated or enumerated more than once; undercount due to farms incorrectly classified as nonfarms; and overcount due to nonfarms incorrectly classified as farms. The first component, mail list undercount, is by far the largest component of coverage error. The percentage of farms missed in the census varies considerably by state. In general, farms not on the mail list tended to be small in acreage, production, and sales of agricultural products. For more explanation about mail list compilation and census coverage, see Appendixes A and C, *1997 Census of Agriculture,* Volume 1, reports.

Farm income—The final agricultural sector output comprises cash receipts from farm marketings of crops and livestock, federal government payments made directly to farmers for farm-related activities, rental value of farm homes, value of farm products consumed in farm homes, and other farm-related income such as machine hire and custom work. Farm marketings represent quantities of agricultural products sold by farmers multiplied by prices received per unit of production at the local market. Information on prices received for farm products is generally obtained by the NASS Agricultural Statistics Board from surveys of firms (such as grain elevators, packers, and processors) purchasing agricultural commodities directly from producers. In some cases, the price information is obtained directly from the producers.

Crops—Estimates of crop acreage and production by the NASS are based on current sample survey data obtained from individual producers and objective yield counts, reports of carlot shipments, market records, personal field observations by field statisticians, and reports from other sources. Prices received by farmers are marketing year averages. These averages are based on U.S. monthly prices weighted by monthly marketings during specific periods. U.S. monthly prices are state average prices weighted by marketings during the month. Marketing year average prices do not include allowances for outstanding loans, government purchases, deficiency payments or disaster payments.

All state prices are based on individual state marketing years, while U.S. marketing year averages are based on standard marketing years for each crop. For a listing of the crop marketing years and the participating states in the monthly program, see *Crop Values.* Value of production is computed by multiplying state prices by each state's production. The U.S. value of production is the sum of state values for all states. Value of production figures shown in Tables 813-816, 820, and 821 should not be confused with cash receipts from farm marketings which relate to sales during a calendar year, irrespective of the year of production.

Livestock—Annual inventory numbers of livestock and estimates of livestock, dairy, and poultry production prepared by the Department of Agriculture are based on information from farmers and ranchers obtained by probability survey sampling methods.

Statistical reliability—For a discussion of statistical collection and estimation, sampling procedures, and measures of statistical reliability pertaining to Department of Agriculture data, see Appendix III.

No. 781. Farms—Number and Acreage by Size of Farm: 1987 to 1997

[2,088 represents 2,088,000]

Size of farm	Number of farms (1,000)			Land in farms (mil. acres)			Cropland harvested (mil. acres)			Percent distribution, 1997		
										Num-ber of farms	All land in farms	Crop-land har-vested
	1987	1992	1997	1987	1992	1997	1987	1992	1997			
Total	2,088	1,925	1,912	964.5	945.5	931.8	282.2	295.9	309.4	100.0	100.0	100.0
Under 10 acres.	183	166	154	0.7	0.7	0.6	0.2	0.2	0.2	8.1	0.1	0.1
10 to 49 acres	412	388	411	11.1	10.3	11.0	3.9	3.5	3.6	21.5	1.2	1.2
50 to 99 acres	311	283	295	22.5	20.4	21.2	7.9	7.2	7.0	15.4	2.3	2.3
100 to 179 acres. . . .	334	301	298	45.3	40.7	40.2	17.1	15.4	14.3	15.6	4.3	4.6
180 to 259 acres. . . .	192	172	165	41.5	37.2	35.5	17.2	15.5	14.0	8.6	3.8	4.5
260 to 499 acres. . . .	286	255	238	103.0	91.7	85.4	47.3	43.6	39.3	12.4	9.2	12.7
500 to 999 acres. . . .	200	186	176	138.5	129.3	122.1	67.4	68.6	65.4	9.2	13.1	21.1
1,000 to 1,999 acres . .	102	102	101	138.8	139.0	138.8	61.1	69.3	73.8	5.3	14.9	23.9
2,000 acres and over. .	67	71	75	463.2	476.3	476.9	60.2	72.5	91.8	3.9	51.2	29.7

No. 782. Farms—Number and Acreage by Tenure of Operator: 1987 to 1997

[2,088 represents 2,088,000. *Full owners* own all the land they operate. *Part owners* own a part and rent from others the rest of the land they operate]

Item and year	Unit					Percent distribution			
		Total	Full owner	Part owner	Tenant	Total	Full owner	Part owner	Tenant
NUMBER OF FARMS									
1987	1,000. . . .	2,088	1,239	609	240	100.0	59.3	29.2	11.5
1992	1,000. . . .	1,925	1,112	597	217	100.0	57.7	31.0	11.3
1997	1,000. . . .	1,912	1,147	574	191	100.0	60.0	30.0	10.0
Under 50 acres	1,000. . . .	564	460	57	48	100.0	81.6	10.1	8.5
50 to 179 acres	1,000. . . .	593	409	131	53	100.0	69.0	22.1	8.9
180 to 499 acres	1,000. . . .	403	189	169	45	100.0	46.9	41.9	11.2
500 to 999 acres	1,000. . . .	176	50	103	23	100.0	28.4	58.5	13.0
1,000 acres or more	1,000. . . .	176	40	114	22	100.0	22.7	64.8	12.5
LAND IN FARMS									
1987	Mil. acres .	964	318	520	127	100.0	32.9	53.9	13.2
1992	Mil. acres .	946	296	527	123	100.0	31.3	55.7	13.0
1997	Mil. acres .	932	316	508	108	100.0	33.9	54.5	11.6

No. 783. Farm Operators—Tenure and Characteristics: 1992 and 1997

[In thousands, except as indicated (1,925 represents 1,925,000)]

Characteristic	All farms		Farms with sales of $10,000 and over		Characteristic	All farms		Farms with sales of $10,000 and over	
	1992	1997	1992	1997		1992	1997	1992	1997
Total operators	1,925	1,912	1,019	949	Principal occupation:				
White.	1,882	1,865	1,003	932	Farming	1,053	962	754	675
Black.	19	18	5	4	Other	872	950	265	274
American Indian, Eskimo,									
and Aleut	8	10	3	4	Place of residence: [2]				
Asian or Pacific Islander	8	9	5	5	On farm operated	1,379	1,362	736	681
Other.	8	10	3	3	Not on farm operated	409	413	215	201
Operators of Hispanic origin [1].	21	28	8	11	Years on present farm: [2]				
Female.	145	165	50	52	2 years or less	95	93	41	35
					3 to 4 years	133	127	58	46
Under 25 years old.	28	21	17	12	5 to 9 years	259	264	121	109
25 to 34 years old	179	128	112	72	10 years or more	1,113	1,114	648	616
35 to 44 years old	382	371	217	200					
45 to 54 years old	429	467	223	232	Days worked off farm: [2]				
55 to 64 years old	430	427	229	212	None	802	755	536	476
65 years old and over	478	497	220	222	Less than 100 days.	165	165	104	98
					100 to 199 days	162	168	76	76
Average age (years)	53.3	54.3	51.9	53.2	200 days or more	666	709	226	229
Full owner.	1,112	1,147	422	404					
Part owner	597	574	448	419					
Tenant	217	191	148	126					

[1] Operators of Hispanic origin may be of any race.   [2] Excludes not reported.

Source of Tables 781-783: U.S. Dept. of Agriculture, National Agricultural Statistics Service, *Census of Agriculture: 1992*, Vol. 1; and *1997*, Vol. 1.

No. 784. Farms—Number, Acreage, and Value by Type of Organization: 1992 and 1997

[1,925 represents 1,925,000]

Item	Unit	Total [1]	Individual or family	Partnership	Corporation	Total [1]	Individual or family	Partnership	Corporation
						Percent distribution			
ALL FARMS									
Number of farms:									
1992	1,000 ...	1,925	1,653	187	73	100.0	85.9	9.7	3.8
1997	1,000 ...	1,912	1,643	169	84	100.0	85.9	8.8	4.4
Land in farms:									
1992	Mil. acres.	946	604	153	123	100.0	63.9	16.2	13.0
1997	Mil. acres.	932	585	149	131	100.0	62.8	16.0	14.1
Value of land and buildings: [2]									
1992	Bil. dol. ..	687	474	109	85	100.0	69.0	15.8	12.4
1997	Bil. dol. ..	860	593	133	114	100.0	69.0	15.5	13.3
Value of farm products sold:									
1992	Bil. dol. ..	163	88	29	44	100.0	54.1	18.0	27.2
1997	Bil. dol. ..	197	103	36	57	100.0	52.6	18.4	29.1
FARMS WITH SALES OF $10,000 AND OVER									
Number of farms:									
1992	1,000 ...	1,019	820	131	61	100.0	80.5	12.8	6.0
1997	1,000 ...	949	758	114	70	100.0	79.9	12.0	7.4
Land in farms:									
1992	Mil. acres.	822	512	143	119	100.0	62.2	17.4	14.4
1997	Mil. acres.	802	485	138	126	100.0	60.5	17.2	15.7

[1] Includes other types, not shown separately.   [2] Based on a sample of farms.

No. 785. Corporate Farms—Characteristics by Type: 1997

[131.5 represents 131,500,000]

Item	Unit	All corporations	Family held corporations			Other corporations		
			Total	1-10 stockholders	11 or more stockholders	Total	1-10 stockholders	11 or more stockholders
Farms	Number...	84,002	76,103	74,308	1,795	7,899	6,870	1,029
Percent distribution	Percent...	100.0	90.6	88.5	2.1	9.4	8.2	1.2
Land in farms	Mil. acres..	131.5	119.6	109.6	10.0	11.9	8.8	3.1
Average per farm	Acres	1,565	1,571	1,474	5,571	1,507	1,284	2,994
Value of—								
Land and buildings [1]	Bil. dol. ...	113.7	99.3	91.6	7.7	14.4	9.3	5.1
Average per farm	$1,000	1,380	1,338	1,264	4,429	1,769	1,288	5,450
Farm products sold	Bil. dol. ...	56.9	45.9	40.8	5.1	11.0	7.3	3.8
Average per farm	$1,000 ...	677	603	548	2,862	1,395	1,057	3,649

[1] Based on a sample of farms.

No. 786. Farms—Number, Acreage, and Value of Sales by Size of Sales: 1997

[1,912 represents 1,912,000]

Value of products sold	Farms (1,000)	Acreage		Value of sales		Percent distribution		
		Total (mil.)	Average per farm	Total (mil. dol.)	Average per farm (dol.)	Farms	Acreage	Value of sales
Total	1,912	931.8	487	196,865	102,970	100.0	100.0	100.0
Less than $10,000	963	129.5	134	2,937	3,050	50.4	13.9	1.5
Less than $2,500	497	63.8	128	424	854	26.0	6.8	0.2
$2,500-$4,999	228	26.3	115	820	3,591	12.0	2.8	0.4
$5,000-$9,999	238	39.4	166	1,693	7,113	12.4	4.2	0.9
$10,000 or more	949	802.3	846	193,928	204,373	49.6	86.1	98.5
$10,000-$24,999	274	75.3	275	4,372	15,955	14.3	8.1	2.2
$25,000-$49,999	171	82.0	481	6,084	35,642	8.9	8.8	3.1
$50,000-$99,999	158	118.0	746	11,347	71,741	8.3	12.7	5.8
$100,000-$249,999	189	207.5	1,095	30,143	159,137	9.9	22.3	15.3
$250,000-$499,999	00	138.1	1,577	30,505	347,531	4.6	14.9	15.5
$500,000-$999,999	43	91.3	2,129	29,365	685,140	2.2	0.8	14.9
$1,000,000 or more	26	89.8	3,464	82,110	3,166,152	1.4	9.6	41.7

Source of Tables 784-786: U.S. Dept. of Agriculture, National Agricultural Statistics Service, *1997 Census of Agriculture*, Vol. 1.

No. 787. Farms—Number, Acreage, and Value by State: 1992 and 1997

[1,925 represents 1,925,000]

State	All farms								Farms with sales of $10,000 or more, 1997		
	Number of farms (1,000)		Land in farms (mil. acres)		Average size of farm (acres)		Total value [1] (mil. dol.)		Number of farms (1,000)	Land in farms (mil. acres)	Average size of farm (acres)
	1992	1997	1992	1997	1992	1997	1992	1997			
United States ...	1,925	1,912	945.5	931.8	491	487	687,432	859,839	949	802.3	846
Alabama.........	38	41	8.5	8.7	223	210	8,350	12,340	13	5.2	406
Alaska..........	1	1	0.9	0.9	1,803	1,608	249	267	(Z)	0.7	3,088
Arizona.........	7	6	35.0	26.9	5,173	4,379	10,984	10,360	3	25.5	8,681
Arkansas	44	45	14.1	14.4	322	318	12,407	16,255	20	11.4	556
California	78	74	29.0	27.7	373	374	63,689	69,768	42	25.2	605
Colorado........	27	28	34.0	32.6	1,252	1,154	14,568	19,993	15	28.9	1,943
Connecticut......	3	4	0.4	0.4	105	97	2,138	2,104	1	0.2	159
Delaware	3	2	0.6	0.6	224	236	1,351	1,499	2	0.5	319
Florida	35	35	10.8	10.5	306	300	21,801	23,048	15	8.8	596
Georgia	41	40	10.0	10.7	246	265	11,437	15,842	16	7.5	468
Hawaii	5	5	1.6	1.4	298	263	3,854	3,460	2	1.3	572
Idaho..........	22	22	13.5	11.8	609	530	9,077	11,983	12	10.3	866
Illinois	78	73	27.3	27.2	351	372	41,844	56,475	50	25.6	515
Indiana.........	63	58	15.6	15.1	249	261	21,732	30,853	33	13.5	415
Iowa...........	97	91	31.3	31.2	325	343	38,063	51,438	67	29.2	435
Kansas.........	63	62	46.7	46.1	738	748	21,725	26,517	39	42.6	1,099
Kentucky	90	82	13.7	13.3	151	162	14,775	18,943	36	9.7	268
Louisiana	26	24	7.8	7.9	306	331	7,474	9,077	10	6.3	661
Maine..........	6	6	1.3	1.2	218	209	1,396	1,456	2	0.8	337
Maryland	13	12	2.2	2.2	171	178	6,570	6,825	6	1.8	295
Massachusetts.....	5	6	0.5	0.5	100	93	2,421	2,535	3	0.3	130
Michigan........	47	46	10.1	9.9	217	215	11,517	16,490	23	8.1	359
Minnesota.......	75	73	25.7	26.0	342	354	23,319	29,927	47	23.0	486
Mississippi	32	31	10.2	10.1	318	323	7,952	10,555	10	6.9	658
Missouri	98	99	28.5	28.8	291	292	22,070	30,589	44	22.2	505
Montana........	23	24	59.6	58.6	2,613	2,414	13,578	16,970	15	52.3	3,499
Nebraska.......	53	51	44.4	45.5	839	885	22,713	29,200	40	43.6	1,092
Nevada	3	3	9.3	6.4	3,205	2,266	2,347	2,474	1	6.2	4,209
New Hampshire....	2	3	0.4	0.4	158	141	836	945	1	0.2	222
New Jersey.......	9	9	0.8	0.8	93	91	5,590	5,403	4	0.6	179
New Mexico......	14	14	46.8	45.8	3,281	3,249	9,220	8,801	5	41.6	7,593
New York	32	32	7.5	7.3	231	228	9,130	9,117	17	5.7	334
North Carolina.....	52	49	8.9	9.1	172	105	13,950	18,566	23	7.2	314
North Dakota......	31	31	39.4	39.4	1,267	1,290	13,163	15,635	23	36.4	1,590
Ohio	71	69	14.2	14.1	201	206	20,626	28,450	36	11.8	328
Oklahoma........	67	74	32.1	33.2	480	448	15,754	20,188	30	26.7	899
Oregon.........	32	34	17.6	17.4	552	513	11,824	16,316	13	15.5	1,193
Pennsylvania......	45	45	7.2	7.2	160	158	14,752	16,891	25	5.4	221
Rhode Island......	1	1	0.1	0.1	76	75	313	325	(Z)	(Z)	107
South Carolina.....	20	20	4.5	4.6	221	228	5,093	6,558	6	2.9	470
South Dakota.....	34	31	44.8	44.4	1,316	1,418	12,264	15,237	24	40.2	1,669
Tennessee	75	77	11.2	11.1	149	145	13,977	20,066	21	6.7	315
Texas...........	181	194	130.9	131.3	725	676	65,060	77,351	65	108.0	1,662
Utah	14	14	9.6	12.0	712	848	4,704	6,894	6	11.0	1,776
Vermont	5	6	1.3	1.3	235	217	1,730	1,876	3	1.0	321
Virginia.........	42	41	8.3	8.2	197	200	13,534	15,813	16	5.9	364
Washington.......	30	29	15.7	15.2	520	523	14,178	18,410	14	12.8	913
West Virginia......	17	18	3.3	3.5	192	194	2,810	3,790	4	1.5	401
Wisconsin.......	68	66	15.5	14.9	228	227	14,285	18,504	40	12.4	309
Wyoming	9	9	32.9	34.1	3,772	3,692	5,242	7,460	6	30.9	5,349

Z Less than 500 farms or 50,000 acres.   [1] Value of land and buildings. Based on reports for a sample of farms.

Source: U.S. Dept. of Agriculture, National Agricultural Statistics Service, *1997 Census of Agriculture*, Vol. 1.

U.S. Census Bureau, Statistical Abstract of the United States: 2002

No. 788. Farms—Number and Acreage: 1980 to 2001

[As of June 1 (2,440 represents 2,440,000). Based on 1974 census definition; for definition of farms and farmland, see text of this section. Data for census years (indicated by italics) have been adjusted for underenumeration and are used as reference points along with data from acreage and livestock surveys in estimating data for other years. Minus sign (-) indicates decrease]

Year	Farms		Land in farms		Year	Farms		Land in farms	
	Number (1,000)	Annual change [1] (1,000)	Total (mil. acres)	Average per farm (acres)		Number (1,000)	Annual change [1] (1,000)	Total (mil. acres)	Average per farm (acres)
1980......	2,440	3	1,039	426	1996......	2,191	-6	959	438
1985......	2,293	-41	1,012	441	1997......	2,191	-	956	436
1990......	2,146	-29	987	460	1998......	2,191	1	954	435
1992......	2,108	-9	979	464	1999......	2,192	1	947	432
1994......	2,198	-4	966	440	2000......	2,172	-20	943	434
1995......	2,196	-1	963	438	2001......	2,158	-14	941	436

- Represents or rounds to zero.   [1] Annual change from immediate preceding year.

No. 789. Farms—Number and Acreage by State: 2000 and 2001

[2,172 represents 2,172,000. See headnote, Table 788]

State	Farms (1,000)		Acreage (mil.)		Acreage per farm		State	Farms (1,000)		Acreage (mil.)		Acreage per farm	
	2000	2001	2000	2001	2000	2001		2000	2001	2000	2001	2000	2001
U.S.......	2,172	2,158	943	941	434	436	Montana.....	28	27	57	57	2,054	2,124
Alabama.....	47	47	9	9	191	189	Nebraska....	54	53	46	46	859	875
Alaska.....	1	1	1	1	1,586	1,586	Nevada......	3	3	7	7	2,267	2,267
Arizona......	8	7	27	27	3,560	3,644	New						
Arkansas.....	48	48	15	15	304	304	Hampshire...	3	3	(Z)	(Z)	135	135
California....	88	88	28	28	318	315	New Jersey...	10	10	1	1	86	86
Colorado....	30	30	32	31	1,071	1,043	New Mexico...	15	15	44	44	2,895	2,933
Connecticut...	4	4	(Z)	(Z)	92	92	New York....	38	38	8	8	203	203
Delaware.....	3	3	1	1	223	228	North Carolina..	57	56	9	9	161	163
Florida......	44	44	10	10	234	232	North Dakota..	30	30	39	39	1,300	1,300
Georgia.....	50	50	11	11	222	220	Ohio........	80	78	15	15	186	190
Hawaii.....	6	5	1	1	262	272	Oklahoma....	85	86	34	34	400	395
Idaho......	25	24	12	12	486	496	Oregon......	40	40	17	17	430	430
Illinois......	78	76	28	28	355	364	Pennsylvania..	59	59	8	8	131	131
Indiana.....	64	63	16	15	242	244	Rhode Island..	1	1	(Z)	(Z)	86	86
Iowa........	95	94	33	33	345	350	South Carolina..	24	24	5	5	200	200
Kansas.....	64	63	48	47	742	752	South Dakota..	33	33	44	44	1,354	1,354
Kentucky....	90	88	14	14	151	155	Tennessee....	90	91	12	12	130	130
Louisiana....	30	29	8	8	275	278	Texas........	226	227	130	130	575	573
Maine.....	7	7	1	1	187	188	Utah........	16	15	12	12	748	773
Maryland.....	12	12	2	2	169	169	Vermont.....	7	7	1	1	200	203
Massachusetts.	6	6	1	1	93	93	Virginia......	49	49	9	9	178	178
Michigan.....	52	52	10	10	200	200	Washington...	40	39	16	16	393	403
Minnesota....	79	79	29	29	362	361	West Virginia..	21	21	4	4	176	176
Mississippi....	43	42	11	11	258	262	Wisconsin....	77	77	16	16	210	210
Missouri.....	109	108	30	30	275	277	Wyoming....	9	9	35	35	3,761	3,761

Z Less than 500,000 acres.

Source of Tables 788 and 789: U.S. Dept. of Agriculture, National Agricultural Statistics Service, *Farm Numbers, 1975-80; Farms and Land in Farms, Final Estimates by States, 1979-1987; Farms and Land in Farms, Final Estimates, 1988-1992; Farms and Land in Farms, Final Estimates, 1993-1997;* and *Farms and Land In Farms,* February releases.

No. 790. Certified Organic Farmland Acreage and Livestock: 1992 to 1997

Item	Unit	1992	1995	1997	Crop	Certified organic acreage, 1997	
						Total (1,000)	Percent of total cropland
Certified growers.........	Number .	3,587	4,856	5,021	Total..............	1,347	0.16
					Pastureland and rangeland..	496	0.11
Certified organic acreage,					Cropland..............	850	0.23
total.................	1,000...	935	918	1,347			
Pastureland and rangeland.	1,000...	532	279	496			
Cropland..............	1,000...	403	639	850	Corn...............	43	0.1
					Wheat...............	126	0.2
Certified animals:					Oats...............	30	1.1
Beef cows............	Number .	6,796	(NA)	4,429	Barley...............	30	0.5
Milk cows.............	Number .	2,265	(NA)	12,897	Spelt...............	2	36.7
Hogs and pigs.........	Number .	1,365	(NA)	482	Buckwheat.............	8	30.1
Sheep and lambs........	Number .	1,221	(NA)	705	Soybeans.............	82	0.1
Layer hens...........	Number .	43,981	(NA)	537,826	Alfalfa...............	62	0.3
Broilers............	Number .	17,382	(NA)	38,285	Grapes.............	19	1.9
Unclassified/other.......	Number .	(NA)	(NA)	226,105	Trees for maple syrup.....	14	11.5

NA Not available.

Source: U.S. Dept. of Agriculture, Economic Research Service, "U.S. certified organic farmland acreage and livestock, 1992-97"; published 4 April 2000; <http://www.ers.usda.gov/whatsnew/issues/organic/table4.htm>; and "Certified organic and total U.S. acreage, selected crops, 1995-1997"; published 4 April 2000; <http://www.ers.usda.gov/whatsnew/issues/organic/table5.htm>.

No. 791. Gross Farm Product—Summary: 1980 to 2000

[In billions of dollars (142.9 represents $142,900,000,000). For definition of gross product, see text, Section 13, Income, Expenditures, and Wealth. Minus sign (-) indicates decrease]

Item	1980	1985	1990	1993	1994	1995	1996	1997	1998	1999	2000
CURRENT DOLLARS											
Farm output, total	142.9	152.7	185.3	187.4	203.3	197.9	222.6	226.3	214.6	208.3	214.7
Cash receipts from farm marketings	140.3	136.3	172.1	182.0	181.0	194.2	201.2	208.6	197.6	192.2	199.8
Farm housing	5.1	5.0	5.1	5.6	5.9	6.0	6.2	6.4	6.7	7.2	7.7
Farm products consumed on farms	1.2	0.9	0.7	0.6	0.6	0.5	0.5	0.5	0.5	0.5	0.6
Other farm income	2.4	4.6	4.9	5.1	5.1	6.3	6.8	7.8	9.0	9.9	8.5
Change in farm inventories	-6.1	5.8	2.4	-5.9	10.8	-9.2	7.9	2.9	0.9	-1.5	-1.8
Less: Intermediate goods and services purchased [1]	86.8	85.6	105.7	113.9	119.8	124.7	130.4	138.1	134.1	134.0	135.7
Equals: **Gross farm product**	56.1	67.1	79.6	73.6	83.6	73.2	92.2	88.3	80.6	74.3	79.0
Less: Consumption of fixed capital	18.6	21.0	22.1	23.5	23.7	24.6	25.4	26.3	27.3	29.3	28.6
Indirect business tax [2]	3.0	3.3	4.3	4.4	4.7	5.0	5.0	5.2	5.2	5.5	5.4
Plus: Subsidies to operators	1.0	6.3	7.5	11.3	6.6	6.1	6.2	6.3	10.4	18.4	19.5
Equals: **Farm national income**	35.5	49.1	60.8	56.9	61.8	49.7	68.1	63.1	58.5	58.0	64.5
CHAINED (1996) DOLLARS [3]											
Farm output, total	(NA)	(NA)	200.8	208.3	227.1	217.9	222.6	237.5	238.5	244.3	248.4
Cash receipts from farm marketings	(NA)	(NA)	186.3	202.6	202.9	214.7	201.2	218.7	219.8	226.2	232.4
Farm housing	(NA)	(NA)	6.9	6.6	6.4	6.3	6.2	6.0	6.0	6.2	6.2
Farm products consumed on farms	(NA)	(NA)	0.6	0.6	0.6	0.5	0.5	0.5	0.5	0.5	0.5
Other farm income	(NA)	(NA)	5.7	6.0	5.8	7.0	6.8	8.2	9.9	11.8	10.1
Change in farm inventories	(NA)	(NA)	2.6	-7.9	13.0	-12.3	7.9	3.2	1.6	-1.9	-2.0
Less: Intermediate goods and services purchased [1]	(NA)	(NA)	117.0	122.8	127.7	132.3	130.4	134.4	138.2	139.1	132.9
Equals: **Gross farm product**	(NA)	(NA)	84.2	85.8	100.3	85.5	92.2	103.6	100.3	106.0	120.5

NA Not available. [1] Includes rent paid to nonoperator landlords. [2] Includes nontax liability. [3] See text, Section 13, Income, Expenditures, and Wealth.

Source: U.S. Bureau of Economic Analysis, *National Income and Product Accounts, Volume 1, 1929-97,* and *Survey of Current Business,* August 2001. See also <http://www.bea.gov/bea/dn/nipaweb/selecttable.asp>.

No. 792. Value Added to Economy by Agricultural Sector: 1980 to 2000

[In billions of dollars (148.0 represents $148,000,000,000). Data are consistent with the net farm income accounts and include income and expenses related to the farm operator dwellings. The concept presented is consistent with that employed by the Organization for Economic Co-operation and Development]

Item	1980	1985	1990	1993	1994	1995	1996	1997	1998	1999	2000
Final agricultural sector output	148.0	153.5	188.8	191.6	208.2	203.5	228.4	231.0	219.5	213.8	218.6
Final crop output (sales) [1]	64.4	74.1	83.3	82.6	100.3	95.7	115.5	112.3	101.5	93.2	95.3
Final animal output (sales) [1]	70.3	68.7	90.2	92.1	89.8	87.8	92.1	96.5	94.2	95.3	99.3
Services and forestry	13.3	10.7	15.3	17.0	18.1	19.9	20.8	22.2	23.7	25.4	24.0
Machine hire and customwork	0.7	1.5	1.8	1.9	2.1	1.9	2.2	2.4	2.2	2.0	2.2
Forest products sold	1.0	1.4	1.9	2.5	2.6	2.8	2.7	2.9	3.1	2.7	2.8
Other farm income	0.6	3.2	4.5	4.6	4.3	5.8	6.2	6.9	8.7	10.2	8.7
Gross imputed rental value of farm dwellings	11.0	4.7	7.2	8.1	9.0	9.4	9.8	10.1	9.8	10.4	10.4
Less: Intermediate consumption outlays	77.0	73.5	92.9	100.7	104.9	109.7	113.2	121.0	118.6	119.6	122.4
Farm origin [2]	34.9	29.3	39.5	41.3	41.3	41.8	42.7	46.9	44.8	45.6	47.7
Feed purchased	21.0	16.9	20.4	21.4	22.6	23.8	25.2	26.3	25.0	24.5	24.5
Livestock and poultry purchased	10.7	9.2	14.6	14.7	13.3	12.5	11.3	13.8	12.6	13.8	15.8
Manufactured inputs [2]	22.4	20.2	22.0	23.1	24.4	26.1	28.6	29.2	28.2	27.1	28.7
Fertilizers and lime	9.5	7.5	8.2	8.4	9.2	10.0	10.9	10.9	10.6	9.9	10.0
Pesticides	3.5	4.3	5.4	6.7	7.2	7.7	8.5	9.0	9.0	8.6	8.5
Other intermediate expenses [2]	19.7	24.1	31.4	36.2	39.2	41.7	41.9	44.9	45.6	46.9	46.0
Repair and maintenance of capital items	7.1	6.4	8.6	9.2	9.1	9.5	10.3	10.4	10.4	10.5	10.8
Plus: Net government transactions [3]	-2.8	2.9	3.1	6.9	1.0	0.1	0.1	0.1	4.9	14.2	15.5
Direct Government payments	1.3	7.7	9.3	13.4	7.9	7.3	7.3	7.5	12.4	21.5	22.9
Property taxes	3.9	4.5	5.9	6.2	6.5	6.7	6.8	7.0	7.0	6.8	6.9
Equals: Gross value added	68.2	82.9	98.9	97.8	104.3	93.9	115.3	110.1	105.7	108.4	111.7
Less: Capital consumption	21.5	19.4	18.1	18.3	18.6	19.2	19.4	19.6	20.0	20.3	20.6
Equals: Net value added	46.7	63.5	80.8	79.5	85.7	74.8	95.9	90.5	85.8	88.1	91.1
Less: Employee compensation	8.3	8.5	12.5	13.2	13.5	14.3	15.2	16.0	16.9	17.5	17.3
Less: Net rent received by nonoperator landlords	6.1	7.7	10.2	10.9	11.8	10.9	13.0	12.9	12.7	12.8	13.2
Less: Real estate and nonreal estate interest	16.3	18.6	13.4	10.7	11.6	12.6	13.0	13.1	13.4	13.6	14.1
Equals: Net farm income	16.1	28.6	44.6	44.7	48.9	36.9	54.8	48.5	42.9	44.3	46.4

[1] Includes home consumption and value of inventory adjustment. [2] Includes other outlays not shown separately. [3] Direct Government payments minus motor vehicle registration and licensing fees and property taxes.

Source: U.S. Dept. of Agriculture, Economic Research Service, "United States and State Farm Income Data"; <http://www.ers.usda.gov/Data/farmincome/finfidmu.htm>; accessed 28 November 2001.

Agriculture 521

No. 793. Farm Income—Cash Receipts From Farm Marketings: 1995 to 2000

[In millions of dollars (188,049 represents $188,049,000,000). Represents gross receipts from commercial market sales as well as net Commodity Credit Corporation loans. The source estimates and publishes individual cash receipt values only for major commodities and major producing states. The U.S. receipts for individual commodities, computed as the sum of the reported states, may understate the value of sales for some commodities. The degree of underestimation in some of the minor commodities can be substantial]

Commodity	1995	1998	1999	2000	Commodity	1995	1998	1999	2000
Total	188,049	195,816	188,132	193,586	Vegetables [1]	14,984	15,160	15,236	15,889
					Potatoes	2,492	2,387	2,452	2,469
					Broccoli.	443	512	518	597
Livestock and					Corn, sweet	647	693	680	702
products [1]	87,217	94,121	95,547	99,473	Lettuce [1]	2,004	1,560	1,474	1,863
Cattle and calves	34,044	33,415	36,530	40,761	Head.	1,447	1,006	966	1,252
Hogs	10,255	9,444	8,622	11,772	Onions	706	803	747	775
Dairy products	19,880	24,114	23,207	20,622	Peppers, green. . . .	446	507	484	614
Broilers.	11,762	15,145	15,129	13,953	Tomatoes	1,584	1,764	1,865	1,823
Chicken eggs	3,893	4,439	4,287	4,347	Fresh	871	1,150	952	1,159
Turkeys	2,769	2,616	2,754	2,786	Processing	713	614	913	664
Horses/mules	662	1,891	1,028	1,156	Fruits/nuts [1]	11,075	11,649	12,287	12,692
Aquaculture [2]	797	814	876	876	Oranges	1,749	1,889	1,710	2,052
					Apples	1,558	1,428	1,422	1,453
Crops [1]	100,832	101,695	92,585	94,113	Grapes [3]	2,045	2,788	2,925	3,064
Rice.	1,282	1,720	1,504	1,151	Wine	965	1,492	1,556	1,909
Wheat	9,054	7,077	5,438	5,470	Strawberries.	812	1,003	1,106	1,014
Corn	18,893	17,230	14,818	15,086	Almonds	881	733	716	710
Hay	3,288	3,781	3,325	3,408					
Sorghum grain.	1,377	950	826	824	Sugarbeets	1,071	1,181	1,243	1,215
Cotton	6,853	6,073	4,698	4,555	Cane for sugar.	893	898	962	914
Tobacco	2,548	2,803	2,273	2,315	Greenhouse/nursery [1] . .	10,336	12,043	12,567	13,037
Peanuts	1,014	1,126	972	836	Floriculture.	3,329	3,965	4,097	4,568
Soybeans	13,868	15,566	12,023	12,540	Mushrooms	758	810	831	837

[1] Includes other commodities not shown separately. [2] See also Table 847. [3] Includes raisins and table grapes not shown separately.

No. 794. Cash Receipts for Selected Commodities—Leading States: 2000

[40,761 represents $40,761,000,000. See headnote, Table 793]

State	Value of receipts (mil. dol.)	Percent of total receipts	Rank	State	Value of receipts (mil. dol.)	Percent of total receipts	Rank
Cattle and calves	40,761	100.0	(X)	Vegetables	15,889	100.0	(X)
Texas	6,815	16.7	1	California.	6,802	42.8	1
Nebraska	4,948	12.1	2	Florida	1,456	9.2	2
Kansas	4,948	12.1	3	Washington	768	4.8	3
Colorado.	2,551	6.3	4	Idaho	689	4.3	4
Oklahoma	2,298	5.6	5	Arizona	682	4.3	5
Dairy products	20,622	100.0	(X)	Corn	15,086	100.0	(X)
California.	3,704	18.0	1	Iowa	2,656	17.6	1
Wisconsin	2,690	13.0	2	Illinois.	2,582	17.1	2
New York	1,544	7.5	3	Nebraska	1,725	11.4	3
Pennsylvania	1,520	7.4	4	Indiana	1,298	8.6	4
Minnesota	1,127	5.5	5	Minnesota	1,173	7.8	5

X Not applicable.

No. 795. Balance Sheet of the Farming Sector: 1980 to 2000

[In billions of dollars, except as indicated (983 represents $983,000,000,000). As of December 31]

Item	1980	1985	1990	1993	1994	1995	1996	1997	1998	1999	2000
Assets	983	773	841	910	936	967	1,005	1,053	1,085	1,141	1,188
Real estate	783	586	619	678	704	740	770	808	840	886	929
Livestock and poultry [1]	61	46	71	73	68	58	60	67	63	73	77
Machinery, motor vehicles [2]	80	83	86	86	88	89	90	90	92	92	92
Crops [3]	33	23	23	23	23	27	32	33	30	28	28
Purchased inputs	(NA)	1	3	4	5	3	4	5	5	4	5
Financial assets	27	33	38	46	48	49	49	50	55	57	57
Claims	983	773	841	910	936	967	1,005	1,053	1,085	1,141	1,188
Debt [4]	167	178	138	142	147	151	156	165	173	176	184
Real estate debt	90	100	75	76	78	79	82	85	90	94	97
Nonreal estate debt.	77	78	63	66	69	71	74	80	83	82	87
Equity	816	595	703	768	789	816	848	888	912	964	1,004
Farm debt/equity ratio (percent) . .	20.4	29.8	19.6	18.5	18.6	18.5	18.4	18.6	18.9	18.3	18.3
Farm debt/asset ratio (percent) . . .	17.0	23.0	16.4	15.6	15.7	15.6	15.5	15.7	15.9	15.5	15.5

NA Not available. [1] Excludes horses, mules, and broilers. [2] Include only farm share value for trucks and autos. [3] All non-CCC crops held on farms plus the value above loan rate for crops held under Commodity Credit Corporation. [4] Excludes debt for nonfarm purposes.

Source of Tables 793-795: U.S. Dept. of Agriculture, Economic Research Service, "United States and State Farm Income Data;" <http://www.ers.usda.gov/Data/farmincome/finfidmu.htm>; accessed 7 February 2002 and "Farm Business Balance Sheet and Financial Ratios"; published 9 October 2001; <http://www.ers.usda.gov/Data/FarmBalanceSheet/fbsdmu.htm>.

No. 796. Farm Assets, Debt, and Income by State: 1999 and 2000

[Assets and debt, as of December 31 (1,140,784 represents $1,140,784,000,000). Farm income data are after inventory adjustment and include income and expenses related to the farm operator's dwelling]

State	Assets (mil. dol.)		Debt (mil. dol.)		Debt/asset ratio (percent)		Final agricultural sector output (mil. dol.)		Net farm income (mil. dol.)	
	1999	2000	1999	2000	1999	2000	1999	2000	1999	2000
United States . . .	1,140,784	1,188,260	176,431	183,978	15.5	15.5	213,787	218,636	44,314	46,444
Alabama	15,808	16,548	2,008	2,131	12.7	12.9	4,194	3,903	1,450	1,196
Alaska	649	622	22	24	3.4	3.9	53	57	19	13
Arizona	31,288	34,323	1,450	1,487	4.6	4.3	2,570	2,604	773	617
Arkansas	21,884	22,421	4,315	4,485	19.7	20.0	5,847	5,374	1,827	1,578
California	84,783	85,978	17,173	18,578	20.3	21.6	26,948	27,162	5,262	5,349
Colorado	24,330	25,102	3,683	3,816	15.1	15.2	4,914	5,000	857	543
Connecticut	2,233	2,320	268	295	12.0	12.7	540	591	140	185
Delaware	1,708	1,738	375	391	21.9	22.5	830	837	136	136
Florida	27,054	28,699	4,760	5,009	17.6	17.5	7,203	7,236	2,807	2,713
Georgia	22,405	24,570	3,551	3,736	15.9	15.2	6,075	5,750	2,186	1,999
Hawaii	3,649	3,786	258	264	7.1	7.0	562	558	63	64
Idaho	16,225	17,014	3,001	3,097	18.5	18.2	3,754	3,752	913	832
Illinois	72,408	74,147	9,499	9,755	13.1	13.2	7,405	7,993	998	1,561
Indiana	38,231	39,623	5,728	5,907	15.0	14.9	4,859	5,301	373	822
Iowa	71,553	72,253	13,035	13,613	18.2	18.8	10,783	11,751	1,616	2,578
Kansas	35,255	36,848	7,054	7,349	20.0	19.9	8,492	8,625	1,564	956
Kentucky	23,507	25,752	3,471	3,582	14.8	13.9	3,972	4,534	885	1,663
Louisiana	11,784	11,826	1,760	1,830	14.9	15.5	2,122	2,026	530	488
Maine	1,875	1,928	370	400	19.7	20.8	565	550	101	97
Maryland	7,495	7,899	1,088	1,134	14.5	14.4	1,748	1,751	364	410
Massachusetts	3,227	3,259	375	399	11.6	12.3	447	466	54	60
Michigan	23,435	24,179	3,130	3,179	13.4	13.2	4,058	3,846	677	305
Minnesota	44,666	46,079	9,066	9,271	20.3	20.1	8,056	8,450	1,442	1,548
Mississippi	14,830	14,957	2,820	2,990	19.0	20.0	3,672	3,387	934	769
Missouri	41,435	45,077	6,155	6,260	14.9	13.9	4,845	5,453	393	972
Montana	23,295	24,549	2,755	2,786	11.8	11.4	2,100	1,967	501	292
Nebraska	41,236	43,976	9,143	9,595	22.2	21.8	9,346	9,502	1,744	1,420
Nevada	3,169	3,314	266	271	8.4	8.2	400	452	64	89
New Hampshire	958	989	104	107	10.8	10.8	182	176	25	16
New Jersey	5,760	5,980	495	483	8.6	8.1	833	946	120	222
New Mexico	11,343	11,617	1,402	1,474	12.4	12.7	2,121	2,165	629	494
New York	13,308	14,002	2,455	2,569	18.5	18.4	3,482	3,388	666	609
North Carolina	24,521	26,928	3,675	3,805	15.0	14.1	8,355	9,307	1,929	3,108
North Dakota	22,771	22,538	4,008	4,077	17.6	18.1	2,974	3,365	516	749
Ohio	36,078	37,615	4,249	4,419	11.8	11.8	5,097	5,488	790	1,177
Oklahoma	25,534	25,777	4,406	4,528	17.3	17.6	4,577	4,645	1,108	1,145
Oregon	18,326	18,692	2,579	2,619	14.1	14.0	3,601	3,620	307	343
Pennsylvania	22,667	23,492	2,759	2,935	12.2	12.5	4,480	4,774	655	949
Rhode Island	368	368	39	40	10.7	10.8	55	57	11	11
South Carolina	8,119	8,354	988	1,173	12.2	14.0	1,647	1,788	419	552
South Dakota	23,261	24,741	4,182	4,298	18.0	17.4	3,979	4,377	1,229	1,399
Tennessee	25,993	27,038	2,595	2,713	10.0	10.0	2,488	2,676	172	449
Texas	92,480	94,094	11,743	12,341	12.7	13.1	15,638	15,046	4,661	3,644
Utah	10,653	11,436	787	885	7.4	7.7	1,180	1,190	270	219
Vermont	2,582	2,708	382	392	14.8	14.5	599	595	144	163
Virginia	20,172	21,284	2,092	2,157	10.4	10.1	2,663	2,846	386	642
Washington	20,042	20,831	3,491	3,618	17.4	17.4	5,550	5,900	489	796
West Virginia	4,288	4,401	416	425	9.7	9.7	482	504	2	41
Wisconsin	32,509	36,340	5,931	6,183	18.2	17.0	6,408	5,854	940	348
Wyoming	9,615	10,225	1,076	1,100	11.2	10.8	1,039	1,052	174	114

Source: U.S. Dept. of Agriculture, Economic Research Service, "United States and State Farm Income Data;" published 31 July 2001; <http://www.ers.usda.gov/Data/farmincome/finfidmu.htm>; and "Farm Business Balance Sheet and Financial Ratios"; published 12 October 2001; <http://www.ers.usda.gov/Data/FarmBalanceSheet/fbsdmu.htm>.

Agriculture 523

No. 797. Farm Income—Farm Marketings, 1999 and 2000, and Principal Commodities, 2000 by State

[In millions of dollars (188,132 represents $188,132,000,000). Cattle include calves and greenhouse includes nursery]

State	1999			2000			State rank for total farm marketings and four principal commodities in order of marketing receipts
	Total	Crops	Live-stock and prod-ucts	Total	Crops	Live-stock and prod-ucts	
U.S. . . .	188,132	92,585	95,547	193,586	94,113	99,473	Cattle, dairy products, corn, broilers
AL	3,404	658	2,746	3,272	588	2,684	24-Broilers, cattle, chicken eggs, greenhouse
AK	50	21	29	52	20	32	49-Greenhouse, dairy products, hay, potatoes
AZ	2,224	1,233	991	2,290	1,226	1,063	29-Cattle, dairy products, cotton, hay
AR	5,213	1,816	3,397	4,887	1,639	3,248	13-Broilers, rice, cattle, soybeans
CA	24,997	18,346	6,651	25,510	19,241	6,269	1-Dairy products, grapes, greenhouse, lettuce
CO	4,321	1,305	3,016	4,561	1,229	3,332	16-Cattle, corn, hogs, dairy products
CT	483	303	180	503	337	165	44-Greenhouse, dairy products, chicken eggs, aquaculture
DE	725	159	566	741	184	557	40-Broilers, soybeans, corn, greenhouse
FL	6,856	5,495	1,361	6,951	5,573	1,378	9-Greenhouse, oranges, tomatoes, sugar cane
GA	5,230	1,901	3,329	5,050	1,945	3,105	12-Broilers, cotton, chicken eggs, peanuts
HI	532	444	88	530	444	87	41-Pineapples, greenhouse, sugar cane, macadamia nuts
ID	3,282	1,666	1,616	3,389	1,761	1,628	23-Dairy products, cattle, potatoes, wheat
IL	6,611	5,086	1,525	7,022	5,312	1,710	8-Corn, soybeans, hogs, cattle
IN	4,397	2,814	1,583	4,581	2,886	1,695	14-Corn, soybeans, hogs, dairy products
IA	9,749	5,036	4,713	10,774	5,027	5,747	3-Hogs, corn, soybeans, cattle
KS	7,477	2,464	5,012	7,905	2,417	5,488	5-Cattle, wheat, corn, sorghum grain
KY	3,554	1,301	2,254	3,605	1,271	2,335	21-Horses/mules, tobacco, cattle, broilers
LA	1,819	1,197	622	1,820	1,167	653	33-Sugar cane, cotton, cattle, rice
ME	494	208	286	504	242	262	43-Potatoes, dairy products, aquaculture, chicken eggs
MD	1,496	559	937	1,473	625	848	36-Broilers, greenhouse, dairy products, soybeans
MA	380	279	101	392	301	91	45-Greenhouse, dairy products, cranberries, apples
MI	3,467	2,139	1,328	3,475	2,140	1,335	22-Dairy products, greenhouse, soybeans, corn
MN	7,093	3,543	3,550	7,522	3,647	3,875	6-Soybeans, hogs, corn, dairy products
MS	3,156	1,012	2,145	2,922	886	2,037	27-Broilers, cotton, aquaculture, cattle
MO	4,276	1,796	2,480	4,567	1,890	2,677	15-Cattle, soybeans, hogs, corn
MT	1,719	787	932	1,806	704	1,102	34-Wheat, cattle, barley, hay
NE	8,422	2,996	5,426	8,952	3,029	5,923	4-Cattle, corn, soybeans, hogs
NV	338	126	212	386	149	237	47-Cattle, hay, dairy products, onions
NH	155	92	63	154	94	60	48-Greenhouse, dairy products, cattle, apples
NJ	729	536	193	812	619	193	39-Greenhouse, horses/mules, blueberries, dairy products
NM	1,969	529	1,441	2,086	473	1,613	31-Cattle, dairy products, hay, greenhouse
NY	3,148	1,098	2,049	3,123	1,189	1,934	25-Dairy products, greenhouse, cattle, apples
NC	6,700	2,861	3,840	7,410	3,135	4,275	7-Hogs, broilers, greenhouse, tobacco
ND	2,724	2,091	633	2,689	2,050	639	28-Wheat, cattle, soybeans, sugar beets
OH	4,472	2,695	1,777	4,405	2,654	1,751	17-Soybeans, corn, dairy products, greenhouse
OK	3,978	842	3,136	4,220	779	3,441	18-Cattle, hogs, broilers, wheat
OR	2,988	2,195	793	3,049	2,223	826	26-Greenhouse, cattle, dairy products, hay
PA	4,079	1,189	2,890	4,033	1,252	2,781	19-Dairy products, cattle, greenhouse, chicken eggs
RI	47	39	8	48	40	8	50-Greenhouse, dairy products, sweet corn, potatoes
SC	1,412	638	774	1,544	752	792	35-Broilers, greenhouse, tobacco, turkeys
SD	3,573	1,743	1,830	3,790	1,755	2,035	20-Cattle, soybeans, corn, wheat
TN	1,958	956	1,002	2,020	1,030	990	32-Cattle, broilers, greenhouse, tobacco
TX	13,071	4,588	8,484	13,344	4,181	9,162	2-Cattle, greenhouse, cotton, broilers
UT	957	244	713	1,010	240	770	37-Cattle, dairy products, hogs, hay
VT	541	69	472	508	67	441	42-Dairy products, cattle, greenhouse, maple products
VA	2,281	702	1,579	2,281	732	1,549	30-Broilers, cattle, dairy products, turkeys
WA	4,849	3,201	1,648	5,050	3,339	1,710	11-Apples, cattle, dairy products, potatoes
WV	387	53	334	391	51	339	46-Broilers, cattle, turkeys, dairy products
WI	5,498	1,362	4,136	5,221	1,416	3,804	10-Dairy products, cattle, corn, soybeans
WY	850	171	679	954	160	795	38-Cattle, sugar beets, hay, hogs

Source: U.S. Dept. of Agriculture, Economic Research Service, "Farm Income"; published 29 October 2001; <http://www.ers.usda.gov/data/farmincome/firkdmu.htm>.

No. 798. Indexes of Prices Received and Paid by Farmers: 1990 to 2001

[1990-92=100, except as noted]

Item	1990	1995	2000	2001	Item	1990	1995	2000	2001
Prices received, all products	104	102	96	103	**Prices paid, total [2]**	99	109	118	122
					Production	99	108	116	120
Crops	103	112	96	99	Feed	103	103	102	108
Food grains	100	134	86	91	Livestock & poultry	102	82	110	111
Feed grains and hay	105	112	86	91	Seed	102	110	124	132
Cotton	107	127	82	68	Fertilizer	97	121	110	122
Tobacco	97	103	107	105	Agricultural chemicals	95	116	120	121
Oil-bearing crops	105	104	85	80	Fuels	100	89	134	118
Fruits and nuts	97	97	97	106	Supplies & repairs	96	112	124	128
Commercial vegetables [1]	102	121	123	131	Autos and trucks	97	115	119	118
Potatoes & dry beans	133	107	93	100	Farm machinery	96	120	139	142
All other crops	(NA)	(NA)	108	108	Building materials	99	114	121	121
					Farm services	96	115	119	121
Livestock and products	105	92	97	108	Rent	(NA)	117	110	117
Meat animals	105	85	94	100	Interest	107	102	112	114
Dairy products	105	98	94	116	Taxes	95	109	123	124
Poultry and eggs	105	107	107	117	Wage rates	96	114	140	146
					Parity ratio (1910-14=100) [3]	51	45	38	40

NA Not available. [1] Excludes potatoes and dry beans. [2] Includes production items, interest, taxes, wage rates, and a family living component. The family living component is the Consumer Price Index for all urban consumers from the Bureau of Labor Statistics. See text, Section 14, Prices, and Table 681. [3] Ratio of prices received by farmers to prices paid.
Source: U.S. Dept. of Agriculture, National Agricultural Statistics Service, *Agricultural Prices: Annual Summary*.

No. 799. Value of Selected Commodities Produced Under Contracts: 2000

[66,394 represents $66,394,000,000. Marketing contracts refer to verbal or written agreements between a buyer and a grower that set a price and determine an outlet for a specified quantity of a commodity before harvest or before the farmer markets the commodity. Production contracts involve paying the farmer a fee for providing management, labor, facilities, and equipment, while assigning ownership of the product to the contractor. Survey based estimates (see source) exclude Alaska and Hawaii and do not represent official U.S. Dept. of Agriculture estimates of farm sector activity]

Commodity	Value of production under contract (mil. dol.)	Percent of total production [1]	Commodity	Value of production under contract (mil. dol.)	Percent of total production [1]
Total	66,394	[2]37	Sugar beets	967	88
Marketing contracts [3]	37,395	[2]21	Vegetables	2,123	25
Cattle	[4]1,680	4	Production contracts [3]	28,999	[2]16
Corn	1,944	13	Poultry and eggs [5]	12,191	74
Cotton	1,438	43	Cattle	[4]6,884	[4]18
Fruits	7,837	70	Hogs	3,918	46
Hogs	[4]1,109	[4]13	Vegetables	[4]1,057	[4]13
Soybeans	1,152	9			

[1] Represents percent of production under contract as percent of total commodity production, except as noted. [2] Percent of total value of agricultural production. [3] Includes other commodities not shown separately. [4] Data have relative standard error between 25 and 49 percent. [5] Data not available to estimate value of production for broilers.
Source: U.S. Dept. of Agriculture, Economic Research Service, Agricultural Resource Management Study, annual.

No. 800. Civilian Consumer Expenditures for Farm Foods: 1980 to 2000

[In billions of dollars, except percent (264.4 represents $264,400,000,000). Excludes imported and nonfarm foods, such as coffee and seafood, as well as food consumed by the military, or exported]

Item	1980	1985	1990	1993	1994	1995	1996	1997	1998	1999	2000
Consumer expenditures, total	264.4	345.4	449.8	489.2	512.2	529.5	546.7	566.5	585.0	625.3	661.1
Farm value, total	81.7	86.4	106.2	109.6	109.6	113.8	122.2	121.9	119.6	122.2	123.3
Marketing bill, total [1]	182.7	259.0	343.6	379.6	402.6	415.7	424.5	444.6	465.4	503.1	537.8
Percent of total consumer expenditures	69.1	75.0	76.4	77.6	78.6	78.5	77.6	78.5	79.6	80.5	81.3
At-home expenditures [2]	180.1	220.8	276.2	294.9	308.7	316.9	328.0	339.2	346.8	370.7	390.2
Farm value	65.9	66.6	80.2	76.4	75.3	76.1	81.6	79.0	77.0	78.7	79.6
Marketing bill [1]	114.2	154.2	196.0	218.5	233.4	240.8	246.4	260.2	269.8	292.0	310.6
Away-from-home expenditures	84.3	124.6	173.6	194.3	203.5	212.6	218.7	227.3	238.2	254.6	270.9
Farm value	15.8	19.8	26.0	33.2	34.3	37.7	40.6	42.9	42.6	43.5	43.7
Marketing bill [1]	68.5	104.8	147.6	161.1	169.2	174.9	178.1	184.4	195.6	211.1	227.2
Marketing bill cost components:											
Labor cost	81.5	115.6	154.0	178.0	186.1	196.6	204.6	216.9	229.9	241.5	252.9
Packaging materials	21.0	26.9	36.5	40.9	43.3	48.2	47.7	48.7	50.4	50.9	53.5
Rail and truck transport	13.0	16.5	19.8	21.2	21.8	22.3	22.9	23.6	24.4	25.2	26.4
Corporate profits before taxes	9.9	10.4	13.2	18.1	20.9	19.5	20.7	22.3	25.5	29.2	31.1
Fuels and electricity	9.0	13.1	15.2	17.2	17.9	18.6	19.6	20.2	20.7	22.0	23.1
Advertising	7.3	12.5	17.1	18.6	19.3	19.8	20.9	22.1	23.4	24.8	26.1
Depreciation	7.8	15.4	16.3	17.2	18.1	18.9	20.1	21.0	21.6	23.0	24.2
Net interest	3.4	6.1	13.5	10.1	11.0	11.6	11.4	12.5	12.9	14.4	16.9
Net rent	6.8	9.3	13.9	17.9	18.9	19.8	21.0	21.8	23.7	25.3	26.7
Repairs	3.6	4.8	6.2	7.2	7.8	7.9	8.5	8.8	9.0	9.6	10.1
Taxes	8.3	11.7	15.7	18.2	18.7	19.1	19.4	19.8	20.9	22.2	23.5
Other	11.0	16.7	22.2	15.0	18.0	18.8	13.4	7.7	6.9	3.0	23.3

[1] The difference between expenditures for domestic farm-originated food products and the farm value or payment farmers received for the equivalent farm products. [2] Food primarily purchased from retail food stores for use at home.
Source: U.S. Dept. of Agriculture, Economic Research Service, *Food Cost Review*, annual; *Food Review*, periodic; and *Agricultural Statistics*, annual.

Agriculture 525

No. 801. Indexes of Farm Production, Input Use, and Productivity: 1980 to 1999

[1996=100]

Item	1980	1985	1990	1992	1993	1994	1995	1996	1997	1998	1999
Farm output [1]	74	84	89	95	91	101	97	100	104	105	107
Livestock and products [2]	82	84	90	94	95	100	102	100	103	105	108
Meat animals	95	90	93	97	97	103	103	97	103	103	105
Dairy products	83	92	96	98	98	100	101	100	101	102	106
Poultry and eggs	53	59	76	83	87	91	95	100	102	104	109
Cereals	79	102	94	105	79	106	83	100	100	104	100
Forage	95	103	99	99	98	101	101	100	104	103	108
Industrial crops	74	83	85	94	85	106	93	100	110	104	103
Potatoes	61	79	83	89	87	96	90	100	94	95	96
Vegetables and horticulture	53	62	82	87	91	100	96	100	101	102	106
Fruits and nuts	93	88	99	104	110	116	108	109	129	113	123
Other crops	55	70	92	88	79	83	101	100	85	97	84
Farm input [3]	115	104	102	99	99	100	102	100	101	99	100
Farm labor	126	111	105	102	98	99	103	100	101	98	101
Farm real estate	114	110	105	104	102	102	101	100	99	99	98
Durable equipment	186	157	119	113	109	106	103	100	98	98	99
Energy	113	92	94	94	94	97	102	100	102	104	105
Agricultural chemicals [4]	112	90	95	98	94	101	92	100	108	105	104
Other purchased inputs [5]	98	90	96	91	97	98	101	98	99	96	98
Farm output per unit of input	64	81	88	96	91	101	95	100	103	106	107

[1] Annual production available for eventual human use. [2] Includes items not shown separately. [3] Based on physical quantities of resources used in production. [4] Includes fertilizer, lime, and pesticides. [5] Includes purchased services and miscellaneous inputs.

Source: U.S. Dept. of Agriculture, Economic Research Service, unpublished data.

No. 802. Hired Farmworkers—Selected Characteristics: 1990 to 2000

[Annual averages (886 represents 886,000). Data for 1990 are not directly comparable with data for later years. Data are calculated by source using data from the Census Bureau's Current Population Survey earnings microdata file]

Characteristic	1990	1995	1996	1997	1998	1999	2000
Number of workers (1,000)	886	849	906	889	875	840	878
PERCENT DISTRIBUTION							
Total	100.0	100.0	100.0	100.0	100.0	100.0	100.0
Age:							
Less than 25 years old	31.5	30.1	27.9	30.7	28.4	30.4	26.0
25 to 44 years old	47.6	44.2	46.0	45.6	46.7	44.0	46.9
45 to 59 years old	14.4	18.2	19.1	17.1	17.8	18.8	19.6
60 years old and over	6.5	7.5	7.0	6.6	7.1	6.8	7.5
Median age (years)	28.0	32.0	34.0	33.0	33.0	33.0	35.0
Sex:							
Male	82.9	84.5	84.2	83.3	83.8	80.7	82.1
Female	17.1	15.5	15.8	16.7	16.2	19.3	17.9
Racial/ethnic group:							
White	61.0	53.5	58.9	52.4	52.4	50.1	47.2
Hispanic	29.4	41.1	36.0	41.0	41.8	43.0	46.4
Black and other	9.6	5.3	5.1	6.6	5.8	6.4	6.4
Years of school completed:							
0 to 4 years	11.1	14.2	13.1	12.2	10.9	11.3	13.4
5 to 8 years	21.6	22.5	19.9	22.1	21.1	22.6	21.0
9 to 11 years	22.8	22.7	24.2	24.8	24.9	20.7	21.2
12 years [1]	31.4	25.9	25.4	22.3	26.5	27.1	25.7
13 years or more	13.1	14.7	17.4	18.6	16.6	18.3	18.7
Employment status:							
Part-time	21.8	18.3	22.4	18.5	18.6	20.5	19.3
Full-time [2]	78.2	81.7	77.6	81.5	81.4	79.5	80.7
Median weekly earnings (dol.): [3]							
Full-time workers [2]	316	294	304	297	304	331	319
All workers	264	271	274	268	276	289	280

[1] A person received a high school diploma, GED, or equivalent degree. [2] Full-time workers usually work 35 or more hours per week. [3] Median earnings are in 2000 dollars.

Source: U.S. Dept. of Agriculture, Economic Research Service, "The Number of Hired Farmworkers Increased in 2000 and Most Now Come From Minority Groups", *Rural America*, Vol. 16, Issue 3, Fall 2001.

No. 803. Agricultural Exports and Imports—Volume by Principal Commodities: 1990 to 2001

[In thousands of metric tons (2,707 represents 2,707,000)]

Exports	1990	1995	2000	2001	Imports	1990	1995	2000	2001
Animal products [1]	2,707	5,606	6,510	6,893	Fruits, nuts, vegetables	4,696	6,213	8,866	9,244
Wheat and products [2]	28,247	33,458	28,412	26,237	Bananas	3,094	3,664	4,031	3,841
Feed grains and products . .	61,526	67,403	55,602	55,505	Green coffee	1,174	953	1,297	1,158
Rice	2,534	3,275	3,241	2,992	Cocoa and products	716	620	999	991
Feeds and fodders	10,974	13,338	13,065	12,606	Red meat and poultry meat [5].	1,169	1,050	1,579	1,636
Protein meal.	5,079	6,404	6,462	7,402					
Oilseeds and products [3] . . .	15,820	23,596	28,017	30,064	Vegetable oils.	1,204	1,509	1,846	1,885
Vegetable oils.	1,226	2,532	2,043	2,201	Rubber, crude natural	840	1,044	1,232	1,002
Fruits, nuts, vegetables [4] . .	5,553	6,918	7,567	7,537	Sugar	1,858	1,599	1,474	1,342
Cotton and linters	1,733	2,118	1,539	1,895	Spices.	129	155	211	224
Tobacco, unmanufactured . .	223	209	180	186	Tobacco, unmanufactured. . .	173	190	216	234

[1] Includes meat and products, poultry meats, dairy products, and fats, oils and greases. Excludes live animals, hides, skins, and eggs.   [2] Includes flour and bulgur.   [3] Includes soybeans, sunflowerseeds, peanuts, cottonseed, safflowerseed, flaxseed, and nondefatted soybean flour.   [4] Excludes fruit juices.   [5] Excludes horsemeat.

Source: U.S. Dept. of Agriculture, Economic Research Service, *U.S. Agricultural Trade Update*, February 25, 2002; and *Foreign Agricultural Trade of the United States*, calendar year supplements.

No. 804. Agricultural Exports and Imports—Value: 1980 to 2001

[In billions of dollars, except percent (23.9 represents $23,900,000,000). Includes Puerto Rico. Excludes forest products and distilled liquors; includes crude rubber and similar gums (now mainly plantation products). Includes shipments under foreign aid programs]

Year	Trade balance	Exports, domestic products	Percent of all exports	Imports for consumption	Percent of all imports	Year	Trade balance	Exports, domestic products	Percent of all exports	Imports for consumption	Percent of all imports
1980. . .	23.9	41.2	18	17.4	7	1995. . .	26.1	56.3	10	30.3	4
1985. . .	9.1	29.0	13	20.0	6	1996. . .	26.9	60.4	10	33.5	4
1990. . .	16.6	39.5	11	22.9	5	1997. . .	21.1	57.2	9	36.1	4
1991. . .	16.5	39.4	10	22.9	5	1998. . .	14.9	51.8	8	36.9	4
1992. . .	18.4	43.2	10	24.8	5	1999. . .	10.7	48.4	8	37.7	4
1993. . .	17.8	42.9	10	25.1	4	2000. . .	12.3	51.2	7	39.0	3
1994. . .	19.2	46.3	10	27.0	4	2001. . .	14.4	53.7	8	39.4	3

Source: U.S. Dept. of Agriculture, Economic Research Service, *U.S. Agricultural Trade Update*, February 25, 2002; and *Foreign Agricultural Trade of the United States*, calendar year supplements. Also in *Agricultural Statistics*, annual.

No. 805. Agricultural Imports—Value by Selected Commodity, 1990 to 2001, and by Leading Countries of Origin, 2001

[In millions of dollars (22,918 represents $22,918,000,000)]

Commodity	1990	1995	1998	1999	2000	2001	Leading countries of origin, 2001
Total	22,918	30,255	36,896	37,673	38,974	39,369	Canada, Mexico, Australia
Competitive products.	17,344	21,792	27,912	29,714	31,213	32,747	Canada, Mexico, Australia
Cattle, live	978	1,413	1,144	1,001	1,152	1,461	Canada, Mexico, Norway
Beef and veal	1,872	1,447	1,842	2,136	2,399	2,712	Canada, Australia, New Zealand
Pork	938	686	682	753	997	1,047	Canada, Denmark, Poland
Dairy products	891	1,118	1,465	1,557	1,671	1,789	New Zealand, Canada, Italy
Fruits and preparations. .	2,218	2,249	2,852	3,540	3,471	3,450	Mexico, Chile, Costa Rica
Vegetables and preparations	2,317	3,189	4,374	4,583	4,740	5,252	Mexico, Canada, Spain
Wine.	917	1,153	1,876	2,187	2,207	2,250	France, Italy, Australia
Malt beverages	923	1,166	1,712	1,893	2,179	2,348	Mexico, Netherlands, Canada
Grains and feeds.	1,188	2,312	2,878	2,989	3,076	3,320	Canada, Mexico, Italy
Sugar and related products.	1,213	1,335	1,682	1,589	1,555	1,602	Canada, Mexico, Brazil
Oilseeds and products . .	952	1,746	2,067	1,818	1,847	1,626	Canada, Italy, Philippines
Noncompetitive products . .	5,574	8,464	8,984	7,959	7,761	6,623	Indonesia, Canada, Colombia
Coffee and products. . . .	1,915	3,263	3,431	2,893	2,700	1,677	Colombia, Brazil, Mexico
Rubber, crude natural. . .	707	1,629	977	704	842	613	Indonesia, Thailand, Malaysia
Cocoa and products. . . .	1,072	1,106	1,666	1,522	1,404	1,535	Canada, Cote d'Ivoire, Indonesia
Bananas and plantains . .	939	1,140	1,202	1,209	1,130	1,179	Costa Rica, Ecuador, Guatemala

Source: U.S. Dept. of Agriculture, Economic Research Service, *U.S. Agricultural Trade Update*, February 25, 2002; and *Foreign Agricultural Trade of the United States*, calendar year supplements.

No. 806. Imports' Share of Food Consumption by Commodity: 1980 to 2000

[In percent. Import share is the total quantity imported divided by the quantity available for domestic human food consumption. Calculated from supply and utilization balance sheets. A portion of the imports of some commodities is exported plus, some is diverted to such nonfood uses as feed, seed, alcohol and fuel production, and industrial uses. These can overstate the importance of imports]

Commodity	1980	1985	1990	1995	1996	1997	1998	1999	2000
Beef	8.7	8.0	9.7	8.1	7.9	9.0	9.9	10.6	11.0
Pork	3.3	7.1	5.6	3.7	3.7	3.8	3.9	4.4	5.2
Lamb	9.4	9.2	11.4	18.5	21.9	25.2	31.3	31.3	35.6
Fish and shellfish	45.3	53.8	56.3	55.3	58.5	62.1	64.7	68.1	68.3
Fresh and frozen	56.8	62.8	65.8	66.0	70.6	74.3	76.6	78.5	81.7
Canned	21.8	34.9	36.0	30.8	29.8	33.0	36.1	43.8	38.4
Dairy products	1.7	2.0	1.9	1.9	2.0	1.9	2.9	2.9	2.7
Cheese	5.8	5.6	4.8	4.7	4.5	4.1	4.5	5.3	4.8
Fruits—fresh and frozen	5.8	9.0	13.2	15.4	16.5	17.6	19.1	21.0	21.8
Citrus	2.1	3.1	3.6	7.2	6.6	7.4	8.1	13.3	11.5
Noncitrus	7.3	10.8	16.0	18.0	19.8	21.2	22.8	22.9	24.9
Apples	4.0	5.9	4.3	6.1	7.7	7.3	7.0	6.6	7.2
Avocados	1.6	1.6	7.3	11.6	12.0	14.1	18.4	31.0	26.0
Grapes	12.6	29.6	41.1	41.8	37.8	41.9	42.8	43.1	44.3
Melons	10.5	9.6	15.4	17.0	18.6	21.9	24.8	23.0	25.7
Pears	3.4	6.8	11.4	11.6	14.1	20.9	16.0	21.1	21.2
Strawberries	22.1	10.0	13.0	12.3	10.6	8.5	10.1	14.9	11.8
Fruits—processed	1.7	2.2	2.6	2.6	2.8	2.8	2.6	3.1	3.1
Fruit juices	11.6	50.3	48.6	27.2	27.2	32.5	28.7	34.7	31.6
Orange juice	8.9	55.3	50.3	16.8	15.6	20.1	18.2	23.9	20.6
Apple juice	19.3	60.2	57.9	51.5	52.5	61.1	62.0	59.0	60.2
Grape juice	2.0	11.3	33.6	21.5	46.6	60.4	29.9	53.0	38.4
Tree nuts	25.5	26.7	35.6	33.6	43.4	43.8	41.4	45.7	38.5
Pecans	1.5	2.3	21.5	43.8	53.8	34.1	46.6	51.7	36.8
Wine	20.6	23.1	13.0	15.8	18.8	23.0	20.7	19.9	21.4
Vegetables—fresh, frozen	5.9	8.0	9.6	11.2	13.6	13.3	15.5	14.7	14.0
Asparagus	10.8	16.2	29.8	53.3	48.8	49.3	54.4	57.0	59.0
Cucumbers	36.0	36.3	33.7	38.3	42.9	38.1	40.2	39.7	41.1
Onions	5.5	8.7	10.1	10.2	12.6	11.2	11.9	11.4	9.3
Peppers, bell & chili	26.5	23.7	19.7	19.1	19.8	22.5	24.8	24.4	19.6
Potatoes	1.2	3.8	6.8	6.8	11.0	10.2	14.5	14.0	14.3
Squash	(NA)	(NA)	19.8	24.3	29.4	29.3	30.0	29.3	27.1
Tomatoes	22.8	23.3	22.0	27.5	34.0	35.8	39.0	32.0	31.9
Vegetables—processed	3.1	6.7	3.6	3.5	3.3	3.9	3.9	4.8	3.9
Artichokes	19.6	24.0	20.3	32.3	39.7	42.6	50.6	41.4	40.5
Mushrooms	31.2	30.7	24.2	34.9	25.6	33.3	35.7	24.1	32.5
Olives	20.8	40.5	44.8	57.0	33.7	50.2	59.9	47.9	74.6
Vegetable oils	15.6	17.6	18.0	19.8	19.2	20.9	21.0	17.9	20.2
Olive oil [1]	96.6	98.2	103.1	109.6	106.5	105.9	104.9	104.4	104.4
Canola oil [1]	100.0	100.0	105.4	87.5	97.5	98.1	85.5	81.7	69.1
Spices	4.8	7.3	7.2	7.1	8.9	8.5	11.0	13.9	13.9
Wheat	0.3	2.1	4.1	6.9	9.3	9.4	10.4	9.3	8.7
Rice	0.3	3.4	5.1	7.2	10.3	9.0	9.4	8.3	9.6
Barley	3.3	3.5	7.7	23.7	21.4	23.4	17.5	16.1	17.0
Cane and beet sugar	45.4	34.9	29.9	19.6	29.3	28.4	22.0	18.2	16.4
Confectionery products	2.4	4.4	5.6	7.3	7.2	7.8	8.5	10.1	11.1
Malt beverages	2.6	4.2	4.5	5.8	6.5	7.2	8.3	9.0	9.9

NA Not available.   [1] When some imports are re-exported and consumption falls below import levels, import share exceeds 100 percent.

Source: U.S. Dept. of Agriculture, Economic Research Service, "The Import Share of U.S.-Consumed Food Continues to Rise," *Electronic Outlook Report*, FAU-66-01, July 2002 and online at <http://www.ers.usda.gov/data/consumption>.

No. 807. Selected Farm Products—United States and World Production and Exports: 1995 to 2001

[In metric tons, except as indicated (59 represents 59,000,000). Metric ton=1.102 short tons or 0.984 long tons]

Commodity	Unit	Amount						United States as percent of world		
		United States			World					
		1995	2000	2001	1995	2000	2001	1995	2000	2001
PRODUCTION [1]										
Wheat	Million	59	61	53	539	584	580	11.0	10.4	9.1
Corn for grain	Million	188	252	241	515	585	589	36.5	43.1	40.9
Soybeans	Million	59	75	79	125	175	185	47.4	42.9	42.7
Rice, milled	Million	5.6	5.9	6.6	371	397	395	1.5	1.5	1.7
Cotton [2]	Million bales [3]	19.7	17.0	17.2	85.9	87.5	88.8	23.0	19.4	19.4
EXPORTS [4]										
Wheat [5]	Million	33.7	27.8	26.5	99.5	103.4	107.7	33.9	26.9	24.6
Corn	Million	52.7	48.1	49.0	64.9	75.9	72.3	81.1	63.4	67.8
Soybeans	Million	23.1	27.2	27.8	31.9	55.5	58.3	72.4	49.0	47.7
Rice, milled basis	Million	3.1	2.8	2.6	21.0	22.8	24.6	14.8	12.3	10.6
Cotton [2]	Million bales [3]	9.4	6.0	6.8	28.4	27.3	26.6	33.0	24.7	25.5

[1] Production years vary by commodity. In most cases, includes harvests from July 1 of the year shown through June 30 of the following year.   [2] For production and trade years ending in year shown.   [3] Bales of 480 lb. net weight.   [4] Trade years may vary by commodity. Wheat, corn and soybean data are for trade year beginning in year shown. Rice data are for calendar year shown.   [5] Includes wheat flour on a grain equivalent.

Source: U.S. Dept. of Agriculture, Foreign Agricultural Service, *Foreign Agricultural Commodity Circular Series*, periodic.

No. 808. Agricultural Exports—Value by Principal Commodities: 1990 to 2001

[In millions of dollars, except percent (39,492 represents $39,492,000,000). See headnote, Table 804]

Commodity	Value (mil. dol.) 1990	1995	1997	1998	1999	2000	2001	Percent 1990	2000	2001
Total agricultural exports [1]	39,492	56,251	57,151	51,754	48,378	51,246	53,749	100.0	100.0	100.0
Grains and feeds [1]	14,409	18,644	15,368	14,008	13,995	13,687	13,952	36.5	26.7	26.0
Feed grains and products.......	7,150	8,341	6,219	5,210	5,747	5,372	5,498	18.1	10.5	10.2
Corn	6,026	7,304	5,180	4,382	4,924	4,469	4,497	15.3	8.7	8.4
Wheat and products	4,035	5,734	4,302	3,905	3,810	3,578	3,563	10.2	7.0	6.6
Rice	801	996	932	1,208	942	855	716	2.0	1.7	1.3
Oilseeds and products [1]	5,728	8,953	12,093	9,495	8,143	8,586	9,236	14.5	16.8	17.2
Soybeans	3,548	5,400	7,379	4,835	4,532	5,258	5,420	9.0	10.3	10.1
Soybean oilcake and meal	979	986	1,865	1,604	1,069	1,169	1,381	2.5	2.3	2.6
Vegetable oils and waxes.	832	1,852	1,802	2,272	1,599	1,259	1,255	2.1	2.5	2.3
Animals and animal products [1]	6,648	10,889	11,338	10,567	10,360	11,600	12,463	16.8	22.6	23.2
Hides and skins, incl. furskins	1,751	1,748	1,651	1,259	1,139	1,562	1,980	4.4	3.0	3.7
Cattle hides	1,369	1,465	1,337	993	924	1,227	1,528	3.5	2.4	2.8
Meats and meat products.......	2,558	4,522	4,597	4,371	4,816	5,276	5,294	6.5	10.3	9.8
Beef and veal	1,580	2,647	2,497	2,326	2,724	2,986	2,634	4.0	5.8	4.9
Fats, oils, and greases..........	424	827	541	647	507	383	334	1.1	0.7	0.6
Poultry and poultry products	906	2,345	2,779	2,530	2,121	2,232	2,638	2.3	4.4	4.9
Dairy products	353	795	932	915	958	1,018	1,130	0.9	2.0	2.1
Cotton, excluding linters	2,783	3,681	2,682	2,545	954	1,873	2,164	7.0	3.7	4.0
Tobacco, unmanufactured	1,441	1,400	1,553	1,459	1,312	1,204	1,268	3.6	2.3	2.4
Fruits and preparations	2,379	3,300	3,451	3,200	3,267	3,451	3,446	6.0	6.7	6.4
Fresh fruits	1,486	1,973	2,100	1,838	1,820	2,080	2,127	3.8	4.1	4.0
Vegetables and preparations	2,225	3,637	4,144	4,222	4,295	4,457	4,485	5.6	8.7	8.3
Nuts and preparations............	976	1,410	1,446	1,360	1,190	1,319	1,295	2.5	2.6	2.4
Other.....................	2,903	4,337	5,075	4,898	4,862	5,069	5,440	7.4	9.9	10.1

[1] Includes commodities not shown separately.

Source: U.S. Dept. of Agriculture, Economic Research Service, *U.S. Agricultural Trade Update*, February 25, 2002; and *Foreign Agricultural Trade of the United States*, calendar year supplements. Also in *Agricultural Statistics*, annual.

No. 809. Agricultural Exports—Value by Selected Countries of Destination: 1990 to 2001

[39,492 represents $39,492,000,000. See headnote, Table 804. Totals include transshipments through Canada, but transshipments are not distributed by country prior to 2000]

Country	Value (mil. dol.) 1990	1995	1997	1998	1999	2000	2001	Percent 1990	2000	2001
Total agricultural exports [1]	39,492	56,251	57,151	51,754	48,378	51,246	53,749	100.0	100.0	100.0
Asia [1]......................	17,626	28,147	25,004	20,853	20,109	22,213	22,633	44.6	43.3	42.1
Japan	8,142	11,160	10,519	9,082	8,892	9,290	8,905	20.6	18.1	16.6
Korea, South	2,650	3,754	2,855	2,224	2,448	2,546	2,598	6.7	5.0	4.8
Taiwan [2]	1,663	2,597	2,615	1,794	1,945	1,996	2,012	4.2	3.9	3.7
China [2]	818	2,633	1,601	1,335	854	1,716	1,951	2.1	3.3	3.6
Hong Kong	704	1,502	1,712	1,492	1,209	1,262	1,231	1.8	2.5	2.3
Indonesia	274	819	772	454	530	668	911	0.7	1.3	1.7
Philippines................	381	765	874	714	783	901	794	1.0	1.8	1.5
Israel	304	481	537	365	423	482	427	0.8	0.9	0.8
Saudi Arabia	482	520	618	503	447	477	430	1.2	0.9	0.8
Turkey	226	515	727	664	502	658	578	0.6	1.3	1.1
Western Europe [1] [3]	7,345	8,765	9,513	8,151	6,941	6,685	7,058	18.6	13.0	13.1
European Union [4]	7,061	8,419	8,891	7,846	6,413	6,244	6,420	17.9	12.2	11.9
Belgium-Luxembourg	380	632	668	636	542	545	624	1.0	1.1	1.2
Netherlands	1,586	2,071	1,926	1,553	1,533	1,442	1,364	4.0	2.8	2.5
Germany	1,161	1,212	1,315	1,215	923	905	925	2.9	1.8	1.7
Spain [5]	931	1,169	1,139	1,031	681	609	645	2.4	1.2	1.2
United Kingdom	813	1,041	1,302	1,245	1,079	1,035	1,063	2.1	2.0	2.0
Italy	715	700	756	686	497	551	567	1.8	1.1	1.1
Switzerland	174	211	517	205	421	352	545	0.4	0.7	1.0
Latin America [1]	5,122	8,038	10,344	11,375	10,049	10,639	11,748	13.0	20.8	21.9
Colombia.................	119	465	538	576	440	415	452	0.3	0.8	0.8
Mexico	2,561	3,538	5,174	6,154	5,624	6,410	7,411	6.5	12.5	13.8
Canada	4,217	5,791	6,767	6,993	7,058	7,640	8,117	10.7	14.9	15.1
Russia	(X)	1,032	1,204	835	728	580	917	(X)	1.1	1.7
Eastern Europe	531	289	282	271	170	170	222	1.3	0.3	0.4
Africa [1].....................	1,845	2,818	2,267	2,091	2,073	2,308	2,106	4.7	4.5	3.9
Egypt	687	1,309	964	904	966	1,050	1,022	1.7	2.0	1.9
Oceania	343	507	549	545	486	489	472	0.9	1.0	0.9

X Not applicable.   [1] Includes areas not shown separately.   [2] See footnote 2, Table 1308.   [3] Includes Canary Islands and Madeira Islands.   [4] Includes France, Denmark, Greece, Ireland, and Portugal. Beginning 1995, also includes Austria, Finland, and Sweden. For consistency, data for all years are shown on same basis.   [5] Includes Canary Islands and Spanish Africa, not elsewhere classified.

Source: U.S. Dept. of Agriculture, Economic Research Service, *Foreign Agricultural Trade of the United States*, calendar year supplements. Also in *Agricultural Statistics*, annual.

Agriculture   529

No. 810. Cropland Used for Crops and Acreages of Crops Harvested: 1980 to 2001

[In millions of acres, except as indicated (382 represents 382,000,000)]

Item	1980	1985	1990	1995	1996	1997	1998	1999	2000	2001
Cropland used for crops.....	382	372	341	332	346	349	345	344	343	337
Index (1977=100).........	101	98	90	88	92	92	91	91	91	89
Cropland harvested [1].........	342	334	310	302	314	321	315	316	312	308
Crop failure	10	7	6	8	10	7	10	8	11	10
Cultivated summer fallow	30	31	25	22	22	21	20	20	20	19
Cropland idled by all federal programs	(NA)	(NA)	62	55	34	33	30	30	31	32
Acres of crops harvested [2] ...	352	342	322	314	326	332	326	327	322	319

NA Not available.   [1] Land supporting one or more harvested crops.   [2] Area in principal crops harvested as reported by Crop Reporting Board plus acreages in fruits, vegetables for sale, tree nuts, and other minor crops.

Source: U.S. Dept. of Agriculture, Economic Research Service, *Economic Indicators of the Farm Sector: Production and Efficiency Statistics*, annual. Also in *Agricultural Statistics*, annual. Beginning 1994 *Agricultural Resources and Environmental Indicators*, periodic, and *AREI Updates: Cropland Use,* annual. See also ERS Briefing Room at <http://www.ers.usda.gov/Briefing/LandUse/Questions/Ruseqa6.htm>

No. 811. Percent of Corn, Soybean, and Cotton Acreage Planted With Genetically Modified Seed: 2000 and 2002

[In percent. Based on the June Agricultural Survey. Randomly selected farmers across the United States were asked if they planted corn, soybeans, or upland cotton seed that, through biotechnology, is resistant to herbicides, insects, or both. The states published individually below represent 81 percent of all corn planted acres, 89 percent of all soybean planted acres, and 81 percent of all upland cotton planted acres. Conventionally bred herbicide resistant varieties were excluded. Insect resistant varieties include only those containing bacillus thuringiensis (Bt). The acreage estimates are subject to sampling variability because all operations planting biotech varieties are not included in the sample]

State	Corn 2000	Corn 2002	State	Soybeans 2000	Soybeans 2002	State	Cotton 2000	Cotton 2002
US, total	25	34	US, total	54	75	US, total	61	71
IL.	17	22	AR	43	68	AR	70	90
IN	11	13	IL	44	71	CA	24	33
IA	30	41	IN	63	83	GA	82	93
KS	33	43	IA	59	75	LA	80	85
MI	12	22	KS	66	83	MS	78	88
MN	37	44	MI	50	72	NC	76	86
MO	28	34	MN	46	71	TX	46	51
NE.	34	46	MS	48	80	Other states [1]	74	86
OH.	9	9	MO	62	72			
SD.	48	66	NE	72	85			
WI	18	26	ND	22	61			
Other states [1]	17	27	OH	48	73			
			SD	68	89			
			WI	51	78			
			Other states [1]	54	70			

[1] Includes all other states in the specified commodity estimating program.

Source: U.S. Dept. of Agriculture, National Agricultural Statistics Service, *Acreage*, annual.

No. 812. Quantity of Pesticides Applied to Selected Crops: 1990 to 2000

[In million pounds of active ingredients, except as indicated (497.7 represents 497,700,000)]

Type of pesticide and commodity	1990	1994	1995	1996	1997	1998	1999	2000
Total	497.7	563.4	543.3	575.8	579.3	544.4	553.7	545.3
Herbicides	344.6	350.6	324.9	365.7	362.6	340.3	316.8	309.4
Insecticides	57.4	68.2	69.9	59.2	60.2	52.0	75.4	74.1
Fungicides	27.8	43.6	47.5	46.8	48.5	45.7	42.3	39.0
Other	67.9	101.1	101.0	104.0	108.0	106.4	119.1	122.7
Corn	240.7	233.0	201.3	227.7	227.3	212.4	186.0	176.1
Cotton	50.9	69.1	83.7	65.6	68.4	55.4	90.6	90.7
Wheat	17.8	23.8	21.5	32.9	25.5	23.9	21.4	19.9
Soybeans	74.4	69.5	68.7	78.1	83.5	78.8	77.3	79.2
Potatoes	43.8	64.2	53.1	49.5	59.4	63.6	64.6	65.1
Other vegetables.	39.8	68.2	78.0	82.8	73.3	67.8	70.5	70.7
Citrus fruit	11.0	13.6	14.0	14.5	15.0	14.1	13.3	13.1
Apples	8.3	9.1	9.0	9.7	10.6	9.3	7.9	7.6
Other deciduous fruit	10.9	12.9	14.1	14.9	16.4	19.2	22.2	22.9
POUNDS OF ACTIVE INGREDIENT PER PLANTED ACRE								
Total	2.2	2.4	2.4	2.4	2.4	2.3	2.3	2.3
Herbicides	1.5	1.6	1.4	1.5	1.5	1.4	1.3	1.3
Insecticides	0.3	0.3	0.3	0.2	0.2	0.2	0.3	0.3
Fungicides	0.1	0.2	0.2	0.2	0.2	0.2	0.2	0.2
Other	0.3	0.4	0.4	0.4	0.4	0.4	0.5	0.5

Source: U.S. Dept. of Agriculture, Economic Research Service, *Production Practices for Major Crops in U.S. Agriculture, 1990-97*, Statistical Bulletin No. 969, August 2000 and unpublished data.

No. 813. Principal Crops—Production, Supply, and Disappearance: 1990 to 2001

[67.0 represents 67,000,000. Marketing year beginning May 1 for hay, June 1 for wheat, August 1 for cotton, September 1 for soybeans and corn. Acreage, production, and yield of all crops periodically revised on basis of census data]

Item	Unit	1990	1995	1997	1998	1999	2000	2001
CORN FOR GRAIN								
Acreage harvested	Million	67.0	65.2	72.7	72.6	70.5	72.4	68.8
Yield per acre	Bushel . . .	119	114	127	134	134	137	138
Production	Mil. bu. . . .	7,934	7,400	9,207	9,759	9,431	9,915	9,507
Farm price [1]	Dol./bu. . . .	2.28	3.24	2.43	1.94	1.82	1.85	2.00
Farm value [2]	Mil. dol. . . .	18,192	24,118	22,352	18,922	17,104	18,499	19,209
Total supply [2] . . . . . [3] . . .	Mil. bu. . . .	9,282	8,974	10,099	11,085	11,232	11,639	11,416
Total disappearance [3]	Mil. bu. . . .	7,761	8,548	8,791	9,298	9,515	9,740	9,795
Exports	Mil. bu. . . .	1,725	2,228	1,504	1,984	1,937	1,935	1,925
Ending stocks	Mil. bu. . . .	1,521	426	1,308	1,787	1,718	1,899	1,621
HAY								
Acreage harvested	Million	61.0	59.8	61.1	60.1	63.2	59.9	63.5
Yield per acre	Sh. tons . .	2.40	2.58	2.50	2.53	2.53	2.54	2.47
Production . . . [3] . . .	Mil. sh. tons.	146	154	153	152	160	152	157
Farm price [4][5]	Dol./ton . . .	80.60	82.20	100.00	84.60	76.90	85.00	97.30
Farm value [2]	Mil. dol. . . .	10,462	11,042	13,250	11,607	11,014	11,417	12,612
Total supply [2] . . . . . [3] . . .	Mil. sh. tons.	173	175	170	174	185	181	178
Total disappearance [3]	Mil. sh. tons.	146	154	148	149	156	160	(NA)
Ending stocks	Mil. sh. tons.	27	21	22	25	29	21	(NA)
SOYBEANS								
Acreage harvested	Million	56.5	61.5	69.1	70.4	72.4	72.4	73.0
Yield per acre	Bushel . . .	34.1	35.3	38.9	38.9	36.6	38.1	39.6
Production	Mil. bu. . . .	1,926	2,174	2,689	2,741	2,654	2,758	2,891
Farm price [1]	Dol./bu. . . .	5.74	6.72	6.47	4.93	4.63	4.54	4.30
Farm value [2]	Mil. dol. . . .	11,042	14,617	17,373	13,494	12,205	12,467	12,440
Total supply [2] . . . . . [3] . . .	Mil. bu. . . .	2,169	2,514	2,826	2,944	3,006	3,052	3,141
Total disappearance [3]	Mil. bu. . . .	1,840	2,330	2,626	2,595	2,716	2,804	2,876
Exports	Mil. bu. . . .	557	849	873	805	975	1,000	1,020
Ending stocks	Mil. bu. . . .	329	183	200	348	290	248	265
WHEAT								
Acreage harvested	Million	69.1	61.0	62.8	59.0	53.8	53.1	48.7
Yield per acre	Bushel . . .	39.5	35.8	39.5	43.2	42.7	42.0	40.2
Production	Mil. bu. . . .	2,730	2,183	2,481	2,547	2,299	2,232	1,958
Farm price [1]	Dol./bu. . . .	2.61	4.55	3.38	2.65	2.48	2.62	2.80
Farm value [2]	Mil. dol. . . .	7,184	9,787	8,287	6,781	5,594	5,782	5,554
Total supply [2] . . . . . [3] . . .	Mil. bu. . . .	3,303	2,757	3,020	3,373	3,339	3,272	2,934
Total disappearance [3]	Mil. bu. . . .	2,435	2,381	2,298	2,427	2,390	2,396	2,201
Exports	Mil. bu. . . .	1,069	1,241	1,040	1,046	1,089	1,061	975
Ending stocks	Mil. bu. . . .	868	376	722	946	950	876	733
COTTON								
Acreage harvested	Million	11.7	16.0	13.4	10.7	13.4	13.1	13.8
Yield per acre	Pounds . . .	634	537	673	625	607	632	698
Production [6] . . . . [7]	Mil. bales [7].	15.5	17.9	18.8	13.9	17.0	17.2	20.1
Farm price [1]	Cents/lb. . .	68.2	76.5	66.2	61.7	46.8	51.6	35.1
Farm value [2] . . . . [7]	Mil. dol. . . [7].	5,076	6,575	5,976	4,120	3,810	4,260	3,384
Total supply [2] . . . . . [3] . . .	Mil. bales [7].	18.5	21.0	22.8	18.2	21.0	21.1	26.3
Total disappearance [3]	Mil. bales [7].	16.5	18.3	18.8	14.7	17.0	15.6	18.0
Exports	Mil. bales [7].	7.8	7.7	7.5	4.3	6.8	6.8	10.5
Ending stocks [8]	Mil. bales [7].	2.3	2.6	3.9	3.9	3.9	6.0	8.3

NA Not available.   [1] Except as noted, marketing year average price. U.S. prices are computed by weighting U.S. monthly prices by estimated monthly marketings and do not include an allowance for outstanding loans and government purchases and payments.   [2] Comprises production, imports, and beginning stocks.   [3] Includes feed, residual, and other domestic uses not shown separately.   [4] Prices are for hay sold baled.   [5] Season average prices received by farmers. U.S. prices are computed by weighting state prices by estimated sales.   [6] State production figures, which conform with annual ginning enumeration with allowance for cross-state ginnings, rounded to thousands and added for U.S. totals.   [7] Bales of 480 pounds, net weight.   [8] Stock estimates based on Census Bureau data which results in an unaccounted difference between supply and use estimates and changes in ending stocks.

Source: Production—U.S. Dept. of Agriculture, National Agricultural Statistics Service. In *Crop Production*, annual; and *Crop Values*, annual. Supply and disappearance—U.S. Dept. of Agriculture, Economic Research Service, *Feed Situation*, quarterly; *Fats and Oils Situation*, quarterly; *Wheat Situation*, quarterly; *Cotton and Wool Outlook Statistics*, periodic; and *Agricultural Supply and Demand Estimates*, periodic. Data are also in *Agricultural Statistics*, annual; and *Agricultural Outlook*, monthly.

Agriculture   531

No. 814. Corn—Acreage, Production, and Value by Leading States: 1999 to 2001

[70,487 represents 70,487,000. One bushel of corn=56 pounds]

State	Acreage harvested (1,000 acres)			Yield per acre (bu.)			Production (mil. bu.)			Price ($/bu.)			Farm value (mil. dol.)		
	1999	2000	2001	1999	2000	2001	1999	2000	2001	1999	2000	2001	1999	2000	2001
U.S. [1] .	70,487	72,440	68,808	134	137	138	9,431	9,915	9,507	1.82	1.85	2.00	17,104	18,499	19,209
IA.	11,800	12,000	11,400	149	144	146	1,758	1,728	1,664	1.72	1.75	2.10	3,024	3,024	3,495
IL.	10,650	11,050	10,850	140	151	152	1,491	1,669	1,649	1.91	1.90	2.05	2,848	3,187	3,381
NE	8,300	8,050	7,750	139	126	147	1,154	1,014	1,139	1.75	1.95	2.00	2,019	1,927	2,279
IN.	5,670	5,550	5,670	132	146	156	748	810	885	1.88	1.85	1.95	1,407	1,540	1,725
MN. . . .	6,600	6,650	6,200	150	145	130	990	964	806	1.60	1.75	1.85	1,584	1,649	1,491
OH	3,200	3,300	3,170	126	147	138	403	485	437	1.89	2.00	2.00	762	922	875
KS	2,980	3,170	3,050	141	130	127	420	412	387	1.81	2.05	2.05	761	824	794
SD	3,250	3,800	3,400	113	112	109	367	426	371	1.54	1.60	1.75	566	685	649
MO	2,550	2,770	2,600	97	143	133	247	396	346	1.96	1.70	2.00	485	705	692
WI	2,850	2,750	2,600	143	132	127	408	363	330	1.77	1.90	2.00	721	675	660
MI	1,950	1,950	1,900	130	124	105	254	242	200	1.78	1.90	1.90	451	459	379
TX	1,770	1,900	1,420	129	124	118	228	236	168	2.07	2.15	2.40	473	514	402
KY	1,180	1,230	1,100	105	130	142	124	160	156	2.11	2.00	1.90	261	331	297
CO	1,120	1,150	1,070	142	126	140	159	145	150	1.84	2.15	2.15	293	301	322
PA	880	1,080	990	70	127	98	62	137	97	2.41	2.00	2.30	148	287	223
TN	570	580	620	102	114	132	58	66	82	1.92	1.85	2.05	112	130	168
ND	655	930	705	117	112	115	77	104	81	1.59	1.60	1.85	122	172	150
NC	640	640	625	80	116	125	51	74	78	2.27	1.90	2.30	116	149	180
NY	590	450	540	101	98	105	60	44	57	2.24	2.20	2.30	133	104	130
MD	360	405	410	93	155	136	33	63	56	2.36	2.00	2.05	79	126	114
MS	310	365	385	117	100	130	36	37	50	2.00	1.90	2.00	73	70	100

[1] Includes other states, not shown separately.

Source: U.S. Dept. of Agriculture, National Agricultural Statistics Service, *Crop Production*, annual; and *Crop Values*, annual.

No. 815. Soybeans—Acreage, Production, and Value by Leading States: 1999 to 2001

[72,446 represents 72,446,000. One bushel of soybeans=60 pounds]

State	Acreage harvested (1,000 acres)			Yield per acre (bu.)			Production (mil. bu.)			Price ($/bu.)			Farm value (mil. dol.)		
	1999	2000	2001	1999	2000	2001	1999	2000	2001	1999	2000	2001	1999	2000	2001
U.S. [1] .	72,446	72,408	73,000	37	38	40	2,654	2,758	2,891	4.63	4.54	4.30	12,205	12,467	12,440
IA.	10,750	10,680	10,920	45	44	44	478	465	480	4.53	4.49	4.30	2,167	2,086	2,066
IL.	10,550	10,450	10,620	42	44	45	443	460	478	4.75	4.62	4.50	2,105	2,124	2,151
IN.	5,550	5,480	5,590	39	46	49	216	252	274	4.71	4.61	4.40	1,019	1,162	1,205
MN. . . .	6,900	7,150	7,200	42	41	37	290	293	266	4.42	4.38	4.15	1,281	1,284	1,106
NE	4,250	4,575	4,900	43	38	46	181	174	223	4.47	4.44	4.20	807	772	936
OH	4,500	4,440	4,580	36	42	41	162	186	188	4.72	4.63	4.40	765	863	826
MO	5,350	5,000	4,900	28	35	38	147	175	186	4.67	4.55	4.30	687	796	801
SD	4,070	4,370	4,470	36	35	31	147	153	139	4.33	4.27	4.05	634	653	561
AR	3,300	3,150	2,850	28	26	32	92	80	91	4.79	4.73	4.40	443	380	401
KS	2,800	2,500	2,730	29	20	32	81	50	87	4.53	4.50	4.15	368	225	363
ND	1,340	1,850	2,110	35	32	34	47	59	72	4.19	4.23	4.00	197	250	287
MI	1,940	2,030	2,130	40	36	30	78	73	64	4.61	4.54	4.20	358	332	268
WI	1,300	1,500	1,570	46	40	38	60	60	60	4.70	4.45	4.25	281	267	254
KY	1,160	1,160	1,220	21	39	40	24	45	49	4.83	4.71	4.40	118	213	215

[1] Includes other states, not shown separately.

Source: U.S. Dept. of Agriculture, National Agricultural Statistics Service, *Crop Production*, annual; and *Crop Values*, annual.

No. 816. Wheat—Acreage, Production, and Value by Leading States: 1999 to 2001

[53,823 represents 53,823,000. One bushel of wheat=60 pounds]

State	Acreage harvested (1,000 acres)			Yield per acre (bu.)			Production (mil. bu.)			Price ($/bu.)			Farm value (mil. dol.)		
	1999	2000	2001	1999	2000	2001	1999	2000	2001	1999	2000	2001	1999	2000	2001
U.S. [1] .	53,823	53,133	48,653	42.7	42.0	40.2	2,299	2,232	1,958	2.48	2.62	2.80	5,594	5,782	5,554
KS	9,200	9,400	8,200	47.0	37.0	40.0	432	348	328	2.25	2.65	2.75	973	922	902
ND	8,657	9,413	9,080	28.0	33.7	32.2	242	317	292	2.77	2.71	2.85	670	857	831
WA. . . .	2,290	2,420	2,380	54.2	68.1	55.7	124	165	133	2.77	2.70	3.30	345	443	443
OK	4,300	4,200	3,700	35.0	34.0	33.0	151	143	122	2.24	2.57	2.80	337	367	342
TX	3,400	2,200	3,200	36.0	30.0	34.0	122	66	109	2.28	2.52	2.85	279	166	310
MT	5,320	4,920	4,215	29.0	27.5	22.9	154	135	97	2.93	3.02	3.30	452	409	317
ID	1,350	1,300	1,200	77.4	83.4	71.0	105	108	85	2.59	2.60	3.30	260	281	279
MN	1,990	1,971	1,815	39.8	49.0	43.9	79	97	80	2.87	2.89	3.00	227	278	239

[1] Includes other states, not shown separately.

Source: U.S. Dept. of Agriculture, National Agricultural Statistics Service, *Crop Production*, annual; and *Crop Values*, annual.

532   Agriculture

No. 817. Floriculture and Nursery Crops—Receipts by Type of Product: 1990 to 2001

[In millions of dollars (8,677 represents $8,677,000,000). Represents value of grower cash receipts]

Year	Total floriculture and nursery crops [1]	Total floriculture wholesale value [2]	Commercial floriculture crops in major states [3]					Nursery crops [4]
			Cut flowers	Potted flowering plants	Foliage plants	Bedding and garden plants	Cut cultivated greens	
1990	8,677	2,652	468	550	475	829	107	6,025
1991	9,035	2,795	472	569	448	942	110	6,240
1992	9,294	3,136	458	646	427	1,118	112	6,158
1993	9,398	3,073	424	683	417	1,170	116	6,325
1994	9,853	3,247	442	662	489	1,280	119	6,607
1995	10,336	3,329	424	681	499	1,357	113	7,007
1996	10,830	3,407	413	684	509	1,428	118	7,422
1997	11,861	3,896	472	723	500	1,747	116	7,965
1998	12,043	3,948	412	737	503	1,873	118	8,096
1999	12,567	4,097	432	759	512	1,943	127	8,470
2000	13,271	4,577	430	800	560	2,095	126	8,694
2001, prel.	13,290	4,739	424	832	585	2,177	111	8,552

[1] Includes all floriculture and nursery crops except cut Christmas trees, seeds, and food crops grown under cover. [2] Includes commercial growers with less than $100,000 in floriculture crop sales in 36 major states (since 1992), not shown separately. Data for 1990 and 1991 include 29 crops in 28 states; 1992-93 includes 29 crops in 36 states; 1994 to date includes 40 crops in 36 states. [3] Based on wholesale value of sales; since 1992, includes only commercial growers with $100,000 or more in floriculture sales; 36 major states. [4] Includes nursery crops, such as annuals and perennials, bulbs, sod, nursery stock, and other products grown in nurseries and greenhouses. Excludes cut Christmas trees.

Source: U.S. Dept. of Agriculture, Economic Research Service, Floriculture and Environmental Horticulture Yearbook 2002.

No. 818. Fresh Fruits and Vegetables—Supply and Use: 1990 to 2001

[In millions of pounds, except per capita in pounds (7,327 represents 7,327,000,000)]

Year	Utilized production [1]	Imports [2]	Supply, [1] total	Consumption		Exports [2]
				Total	Per capita	
FRUITS						
Citrus:						
1990	7,327	184	7,510	5,331	21.4	2,179
1995	8,635	449	9,084	6,333	24.1	2,751
1999	6,662	756	7,418	5,648	20.7	1,769
2000	8,355	684	9,040	6,602	24.0	2,438
2001	5,392	518	5,910	4,362	15.7	1,547
Noncitrus: [3]						
1990	12,122	7,852	19,974	17,978	70.4	1,995
1995	12,983	9,388	22,371	19,521	74.3	2,850
1999	13,199	11,832	25,031	22,339	81.7	2,691
2000	13,930	11,212	25,141	21,755	78.9	3,386
VEGETABLES & MELONS						
1990	35,341	3,458	39,679	35,364	141.5	2,690
1995	39,507	4,997	45,584	40,279	151.2	3,532
1999	44,526	6,866	52,584	46,539	166.7	3,900
2000	47,237	6,629	55,081	48,910	173.1	4,188
2001	47,161	7,242	55,529	49,540	173.0	4,118
POTATOES						
1990	11,335	684	12,019	11,691	46.8	327
1995	13,020	685	13,704	13,121	49.9	584
1999	13,074	923	13,998	13,399	48.0	599
2000	12,310	806	14,015	13,338	47.2	677
2001	13,459	671	14,022	13,386	46.7	636

[1] Crop-year basis for fruits. [2] Fiscal year for fruits; calendar year for vegetables and potatoes. [3] Includes bananas.

No. 819. Nuts—Supply and Use: 1990 to 2000

[In millions of pounds (shelled) (326.2 represents 326,200,000)]

Year	Beginning stocks	Marketable production [1]	Imports	Supply, total	Con-sumption	Exports	Ending stocks
1990	326.2	961.5	198.4	1,486.1	609.6	522.6	354.0
1995	334.1	770.1	204.0	1,308.2	512.5	543.8	251.9
1998	348.7	851.8	238.8	1,439.4	602.8	612.8	223.9
1999	223.9	1,295.9	283.4	1,803.0	706.7	730.6	365.6
2000	365.6	1,111.3	280.3	1,757.1	698.3	786.9	271.9

[1] Utilized production minus inedibles and noncommercial usage.

Source of Tables 818 and 819: U.S. Dept. of Agriculture, Economic Research Service, Fruit and Tree Nuts Situation and Outlook Yearbook and Vegetables and Specialties Situation and Outlook Yearbook.

Agriculture 533

No. 820. Commercial Vegetable and Other Specified Crops—Area, Production, and Value, 1999 to 2001, and Leading Producing States, 2001

[76 **represents** 76,000. Except as noted, relates to commercial production for fresh market and processing combined. Includes market garden areas but excludes minor producing acreage in minor producing states. Excludes production for home use in farm and nonfarm gardens. Value is for season or crop year and should not be confused with calendar-year income]

Crop	Area [1] (1,000 acres)			Production [2] (1,000 short tons)			Value [3] (mil. dol.)			Leading states in order of production, 2001
	1999	2000	2001	1999	2000	2001	1999	2000	2001	
Asparagus	76	77	72	109	114	104	233	221	230	CA, WA, MI
Beans, snap	303	311	290	1,058	1,128	1,000	396	394	386	WI, OR, NY [4]
Beans, dry edible. .	1,877	1,608	1,243	1,654	1,320	977	548	414	393	ND, NE, CO
Broccoli	148	144	141	1,085	1,044	1,021	518	633	504	CA, AZ
Cabbage	80	86	87	1,268	1,508	1,484	249	336	373	NY, CA, TX [5]
Cantaloups	107	99	99	1,129	1,048	1,138	389	367	420	CA, AZ, TX
Carrots	127	123	120	2,141	2,049	2,003	565	437	578	CA, CO, MI [5]
Cauliflower	46	47	48	387	388	403	225	249	216	CA, AZ
Celery	28	26	28	936	921	941	225	341	277	CA, MI, TX
Corn, sweet	703	706	702	4,586	4,476	4,526	677	713	772	(NA)
Fresh market. . .	237	246	256	1,289	1,320	1,383	443	481	543	FL, NY, CA
Processed.	466	460	446	3,297	3,156	3,143	234	232	229	WA, MN, WI
Cucumbers.	165	158	160	1,224	1,161	1,137	367	383	381	MI, NC, FL [4]
Lettuce, head	193	185	194	3,516	3,481	3,626	936	1,208	1,273	CA, AZ, CO
Lettuce, leaf	49	50	56	554	588	587	268	349	321	CA, AZ
Lettuce, Romaine .	42	49	56	657	792	815	228	315	313	CA, AZ
Mushrooms [6]	150	151	144	424	427	419	828	829	820	(NA)
Onions.	173	166	159	3,678	3,586	3,354	633	736	703	CA, OR, WA
Peppers, green . . .	57	62	57	778	843	741	484	527	421	CA, FL, NJ
Potatoes	1,332	1,348	1,241	23,911	25,681	22,238	2,746	2,591	2,934	ID, WA, WI
Strawberries	46	48	46	916	979	833	1,133	1,086	1,085	CA, FL, OR
Sweet potatoes . . .	83	95	94	612	690	718	215	211	233	NC, LA, CA
Tomatoes	483	413	403	14,673	12,741	11,096	1,864	1,809	1,665	(NA)
Fresh market. . .	133	123	128	1,837	1,883	1,848	951	1,160	1,117	FL, CA, OH
Processed.	350	290	275	12,836	10,858	9,248	913	649	548	CA, IN, OH
Watermelons.	175	165	157	2,058	1,881	2,019	266	241	277	FL, CA, TX

NA Not available.   [1] Area of crops for harvest for fresh market, including any partially harvested or not harvested because of low prices or other factors, plus area harvested for processing.   [2] Excludes some quantities not marketed.   [3] Fresh market vegetables valued at f.o.b. shipping point. Processing vegetables are equivalent returns at packinghouse door.   [4] Processed only.   [5] Fresh market only.   [6] Area is shown in million square feet. All data are for marketing year ending June 30.

Source: U.S. Dept. of Agriculture, National Agricultural Statistics Service, *Vegetables*, annual summary. Also in *Agricultural Statistics*, annual.

No. 821. Fruits and Nuts—Utilized Production and Value, 1999 to 2001, and Leading Producing States, 2001

[5,223 **represents** 5,223,000]

Fruit or nut	Unit	Utilized production [1]			Farm value (mil. dol.)			Leading states in order of production, 2001
		1999	2000	2001	1999	2000	2001	
Apples [2]	1,000 tons . .	5,223	5,201	4,606	1,564	1,326	1,514	WA, MI, NY
Apricots	1,000 tons . .	91	88	75	35	32	26	CA, WA
Avocados	1,000 tons . .	183	240	(NA)	356	326	(NA)	CA, FL
Cherries, sweet	1,000 tons . .	213	204	219	235	274	281	WA, CA, OR
Cherries, tart	1,000 tons . .	127	141	154	56	52	51	MI, WA, NY
Cranberries	1,000 tons . .	317	274	240	109	96	110	WI, MA, NJ
Dates (CA)	1,000 tons . .	22	15	19	28	18	28	CA
Grapefruit	1,000 tons . .	2,513	2,762	2,469	334	411	270	FL, CA, TX
Grapes (13 states)	1,000 tons . .	6,235	7,687	6,520	2,927	3,072	2,794	CA, WA, NY
Lemons	1,000 tons . .	747	840	1,000	251	299	239	CA, AZ
Nectarines (CA)	1,000 tons . .	274	267	275	112	106	128	CA
Olives (CA)	1,000 tons . .	142	53	134	55	35	90	CA
Oranges	1,000 tons . .	9,824	12,997	12,390	1,688	1,666	1,636	FL, CA
Papayas	1,000 tons . .	21	28	28	16	16	14	HI
Peaches	1,000 tons . .	1,217	1,254	1,170	463	489	496	CA, GA, SC
Pears	1,000 tons . .	1,013	949	968	298	250	290	WA, CA, OR
Pineapples	1,000 tons . .	352	354	323	101	102	96	HI
Plums (CA)	1,000 tons . .	196	197	210	82	87	66	CA
Prunes (dried basis) (CA).	1,000 tons . .	165	201	133	142	155	101	CA
Tangerines	1,000 tons . .	327	458	369	117	108	99	FL, CA, AZ
Almonds (shelled basis) (CA)	Mil. lb . .	833	703	850	688	655	685	CA
Hazelnuts (in the shell)	1,000 tons . .	40	23	48	36	20	34	OR
Macadamia nuts	Mil. lb . .	57	50	54	38	30	31	HI
Pecans (in the shell) (11 states) . . .	Mil. lb . .	406	210	315	330	239	216	GA, TX, NM
Pistachios	Mil. lb . .	123	243	161	164	241	167	CA
Walnuts, English (in the shell)	1,000 tons . .	283	239	305	251	296	(NA)	CA

NA Not available.   [1] Excludes quantities not harvested or not marketed.   [2] Production in commercial orchards with 100 or more bearing age trees.

Source: U.S. Dept. of Agriculture, National Agricultural Statistics Service, *Noncitrus Fruits and Nuts*, annual; and *Citrus Fruits*, annual.

No. 822. Meat Supply and Use: 1980 to 2001

[**In millions of pounds** (carcass weight equivalent) (**53,151 represents 53,151,000,000**). Carcass weight equivalent is the weight of the animal minus entrails, head, hide, and internal organs; includes fat and bone. Covers federal and state inspected, and farm slaughter]

Year and type of meat	Production	Imports	Supply, [1] total	Consumption [2]	Exports	Ending stocks
RED MEAT AND POULTRY						
1980	53,151	2,668	57,036	54,695	1,124	1,217
1990	62,255	3,295	66,673	62,937	2,472	1,263
1995	74,068	2,838	78,636	69,911	6,956	1,768
1999	81,536	3,820	87,371	76,017	9,385	1,971
2000	82,371	4,136	88,479	76,591	9,820	2,069
2001	82,643	4,275	88,986	76,170	10,696	2,120
ALL RED MEATS						
1980	38,978	2,668	42,481	41,170	429	882
1990	38,787	3,295	42,742	40,784	1,250	707
1995	43,675	2,832	47,511	43,967	2,614	929
1999	46,284	3,813	51,091	46,483	3,694	914
2000	46,299	4,127	51,340	46,559	3,760	1,021
2001	45,804	4,257	51,082	46,082	3,840	1,160
Beef:						
1980	21,643	2,064	24,166	23,560	173	432
1990	22,743	2,356	25,434	24,031	1,006	397
1995	25,222	2,104	27,874	25,534	1,821	519
1999	26,493	2,873	29,759	26,936	2,412	411
2000	26,888	3,031	30,330	27,337	2,468	525
2001	26,212	3,161	29,898	27,022	2,271	606
Pork:						
1980	16,617	550	17,521	16,838	252	431
1990	15,354	898	16,565	16,031	238	296
1995	17,849	664	18,952	17,768	787	396
1999	19,308	827	20,720	18,954	1,277	489
2000	18,952	967	20,407	18,643	1,287	478
2001	19,160	950	20,588	18,489	1,563	536
Veal:						
1980	400	21	432	420	2	9
1990	327	(NA)	331	325	(NA)	6
1995	319	(NA)	326	319	(NA)	7
1999	235	(NA)	240	235	(NA)	5
2000	225	(NA)	230	225	(NA)	5
2001	205	(NA)	210	204	(NA)	6
Lamb and mutton:						
1980	318	33	362	351	1	9
1990	363	41	412	397	6	8
1995	285	64	359	346	6	8
1999	248	112	372	358	5	9
2000	234	130	372	354	5	13
2001	227	146	386	368	7	12
POULTRY, TOTAL						
1980	14,173	-	14,555	13,525	695	334
1990	23,468	-	23,931	22,153	1,222	556
1995	30,393	6	31,125	25,944	4,342	839
1999	35,252	7	36,281	29,534	5,691	1,058
2000	36,072	9	37,139	30,031	6,060	1,048
2001	36,839	18	37,904	30,087	6,856	961
Broilers:						
1980	11,252	-	11,364	10,682	567	115
1990	18,430	-	18,651	17,266	1,143	242
1995	24,827	1	25,286	20,832	3,894	560
1999	29,468	4	30,184	24,469	4,919	796
2000	30,209	6	31,011	24,821	5,392	798
2001	30,841	14	31,652	24,755	6,186	712
Mature chicken:						
1980	551	-	581	507	53	21
1990	523	-	530	496	25	9
1995	496	3	513	406	99	7
1999	553	2	561	162	393	8
2000	530	2	540	307	224	9
2001	515	3	527	337	182	8
Turkeys:						
1980	2,370	-	2,610	2,337	75	198
1990	4,514	-	4,750	4,390	54	306
1995	5,069	2	5,326	4,706	348	271
1999	5,231	1	5,536	4,903	379	254
2000	5,333	1	5,588	4,903	444	241
2001	5,483	1	5,725	4,996	488	241

- Represents zero.   NA Not available.   [1] Total supply equals production plus imports plus ending stocks of previous year.
[2] Includes shipments to territories.

Source: U.S. Department of Agriculture, Economic Research Service, *Food Consumption, Prices, and Expenditures, 1970-2000*; and *Agricultural Outlook*, monthly.

Agriculture   535

No. 823. Livestock Inventory and Production: 1980 to 2002

[111.2 represents 111,200,000. **Production in live weight.** Includes animals for slaughter market, younger animals shipped to other states for feeding or breeding purposes, farm slaughter and custom slaughter consumed on farms where produced, minus livestock shipped into states for feeding or breeding with an adjustment for changes in inventory]

Type of livestock	Unit	1980	1990	1995	1996	1997	1998	1999	2000	2001	2002
ALL CATTLE [1]											
Inventory: [2] Number on farms	Mil	111.2	95.8	102.8	103.5	101.7	99.7	99.1	98.2	97.3	96.7
Total value	Bil. dol. .	55.8	59.0	63.2	52.1	53.4	60.2	58.8	67.1	70.5	72.2
Value per head	Dol	502	616	615	503	525	603	594	683	725	747
Production: Quantity . . . . [1]	Bil. lb . .	40.3	39.2	42.5	40.9	40.9	41.6	42.5	42.8	42.4	(NA)
Beef, price per 100 lb . .	Dol	62.40	74.60	61.80	58.70	63.10	59.60	63.40	68.60	71.30	(NA)
Calves, price per 100 lb .	Dol	76.80	95.60	73.10	58.40	78.90	78.80	87.70	104.00	106.00	(NA)
Value of production	Bil. dol. .	25.5	29.3	24.7	22.1	24.8	24.2	26.1	28.4	29.3	(NA)
HOGS AND PIGS											
Inventory: [3] Number on farms	Mil	67.3	53.8	59.7	58.2	56.1	61.2	62.2	59.3	59.1	59.1
Total value	Bil. dol. .	3.8	4.3	3.2	4.1	5.3	5.0	2.8	4.3	4.5	4.6
Value per head	Dol	56.00	79.10	53.00	71.00	94.00	82.00	44.00	72.00	77.00	77.00
Production: Quantity	Bil. lb . .	23.4	21.3	24.4	23.1	24.0	25.7	25.8	25.7	25.9	(NA)
Price per 100 lb	Dol	38.00	53.70	40.50	51.90	52.90	34.40	30.30	42.30	44.30	(NA)
Value of production	Bil. dol. .	8.9	11.3	9.8	11.9	12.6	8.7	7.8	10.8	11.4	(NA)
SHEEP AND LAMBS											
Inventory: [2] Number on farms	Mil	12.7	11.4	9.0	8.5	8.0	7.8	7.2	7.0	7.0	6.7
Total value	Mil. dol	993	901	663	732	762	798	638	669	694	618
Value per head	Dol	78.20	79.30	74.70	86.50	96.00	102.00	88.00	95.00	100.00	92.00
Production: Quantity	Mil. lb . .	746	781	602	572	603	555	534	509	499	(NA)
Sheep, price per 100 lb .	Dol	21.30	23.20	28.00	29.90	37.90	30.60	31.10	34.30	34.60	(NA)
Lambs, price per 100 lb .	Dol	63.60	55.50	78.20	88.20	90.30	72.30	74.50	79.80	66.90	(NA)
Value of production	Mil. dol	403	374	414	441	490	354	349	361	300	(NA)

NA Not available.   [1] Includes milk cows.   [2] As of Jan. 1.   [3] As of Dec. 1 of preceding year.
Source: U.S. Dept. of Agriculture, National Agricultural Statistics Service, *Meat Animals—Production, Disposition, and Income*, annual; and annual livestock summaries. Also in *Agricultural Statistics*, annual.

No. 824. Livestock Operations by Size of Herd: 1995 to 2001

[In thousands (1,191 represents 1,191,000). An operation is any place having one or more head on hand at any time during the year]

Size of herd	1995	2000	2001	Size of herd	1995	2000	2001
CATTLE [1]				MILK COWS [2]			
Total operations	1,191	1,078	1,051	**Total operations . . . .**	140	105	98
1 to 49 head	746	671	653	1 to 49 head	79	53	48
50 to 99 head	208	186	180	50 to 99 head	39	31	29
100 to 499 head	210	192	190	100 or more head	21	21	20
500 to 999 head	18	19	19				
1,000 head or more	9	10	10	HOGS AND PIGS			
BEEF COWS [2]				**Total operations . . . .**	168	86	81
				1 to 99 head	97	48	46
Total operations	898	831	814	100 to 499 head	44	18	15
1 to 49 head	716	654	638	500 to 999 head	15	8	7
50 to 99 head	105	100	99	1,000 to 1,999 head	7	6	5
100 to 499 head	70	71	71	2,000 to 4,999 head	4	5	5
500 head or more	6	6	6	5,000 head or more	1	2	2

[1] Includes calves.   [2] Included in operations with cattle.
Source: U.S. Dept. of Agriculture, National Agricultural Statistics Service, *Cattle Final Estimates, 1994-1998*, January 1999; *Cattle*, January 2002; *Milk Cows and Production Final Estimates 1993-1997*, January 1999; *Hogs and Pigs Final Estimates 1993-1997*, December 1998; *Hogs and Pigs*, December 2001; and *Agricultural Statistics*, annual.

No. 825. Hogs and Pigs—Number, Production, and Value by State: 1999 to 2001

[59,342 represents 59,342,000. See headnote, Table 823]

State	Number on farms [1] (1,000)			Quantity produced (mil. lb.)			Value of production (mil. dol.)			Commercial slaughter [2] (mil. lb.)	
	1999	2000	2001	1999	2000	2001	1999	2000	2001	2000	2001
U.S. [3]	59,342	59,138	59,074	25,791	25,730	25,937	7,766	10,818	11,442	25,660	25,864
IA	15,400	15,100	15,100	6,495	6,479	6,408	1,891	2,675	2,752	7,294	7,246
NC	9,500	9,300	9,600	3,658	3,708	3,665	1,149	1,648	1,719	2,473	2,502
MN	5,500	5,800	5,700	2,461	2,515	2,783	735	1,083	1,235	2,086	2,208
IL	4,050	4,150	4,250	1,863	1,776	1,818	559	762	853	2,516	2,535
IN	3,260	3,350	3,150	1,535	1,388	1,476	445	547	616	1,621	1,693
NE	3,000	3,050	2,900	1,549	1,491	1,450	488	642	665	1,641	1,750
MO	3,150	2,900	3,000	1,238	1,215	1,177	379	504	513	981	(4)

[1] As of December 1.   [2] Includes slaughter in federally inspected and other slaughter plants; excludes animals slaughtered on farms.   [3] Includes other states not shown separately.   [4] Included in U.S. total. Not printed to avoid disclosing individual operation.
Source: U.S. Dept. of Agriculture, National Agricultural Statistics Service, *Meat Animals-Production, Disposition and Income*, annual; and *Livestock Slaughter*, annual.

No. 826. Cattle and Calves—Number, Production, and Value by State: 1999 to 2002

[98,198 represents 98,198,000. Includes milk cows. See headnote, Table 823]

State	Number on farms [1] (1,000)			Quantity produced (mil. lb.)			Value of production (mil. dol.)			Commercial slaughter [2] (mil. lb.)	
	2000	2001	2002	1999	2000	2001	1999	2000	2001	2000	2001
U.S. [3]	98,198	97,277	96,704	42,468	42,842	42,365	26,051	28,392	29,267	44,558	43,175
TX	13,900	13,700	13,600	7,417	7,469	7,734	4,638	5,039	5,462	7,623	7,516
NE	6,650	6,600	6,400	4,326	4,405	4,335	2,519	2,552	2,711	9,558	9,536
KS	6,600	6,700	6,600	3,973	4,097	3,937	2,442	2,418	2,460	9,858	8,717
CO	3,150	3,150	3,050	2,072	2,121	2,109	1,293	1,337	1,463	3,265	3,243
CA	5,100	5,150	5,200	1,972	1,923	1,970	862	831	924	1,309	1,348
OK	5,200	5,050	5,200	2,050	1,936	1,825	1,449	1,578	1,475	38	39
IA	3,700	3,650	3,550	1,862	1,730	1,616	1,009	1,066	1,132	846	964
SD	3,900	4,050	3,950	1,546	1,627	1,554	1,094	1,269	1,240	402	451
WI	3,400	3,350	3,300	1,068	1,214	1,204	581	698	730	2,313	2,162
MO	4,350	4,250	4,350	1,152	1,188	1,186	834	1,004	997	99	113
MN	2,550	2,550	2,550	1,083	1,157	1,107	625	714	726	911	955

[1] As of January 1.   [2] Data cover cattle only. Includes slaughter in federally inspected and other slaughter plants; excludes animals slaughtered on farms.   [3] Includes other states not shown separately.

Source: U.S. Dept. of Agriculture, National Agricultural Statistics Service, *Meat Animals-Production, Disposition and Income*, annual; and *Livestock Slaughter*, annual.

No. 827. Milk Cows—Number, Production, and Value by State: 1999 to 2001

[9,156 represents 9,156,000]

State	Number on farms [1] (1,000)			Milk produced on farms (mil. lb.)			Value of production [2] (mil. dol.)		
	1999	2000	2001	1999	2000	2001	1999	2000	2001
United States [3] . .	9,156	9,206	9,115	162,716	167,559	165,336	23,400	20,771	24,887
California	1,466	1,526	1,590	30,459	32,273	33,251	4,097	3,711	4,635
Wisconsin	1,365	1,344	1,292	23,071	23,259	22,199	3,184	2,721	3,285
New York	701	686	672	12,082	11,921	11,778	1,764	1,562	1,861
Pennsylvania	616	617	599	10,931	11,156	10,849	1,727	1,528	1,801
Minnesota	545	534	510	9,478	9,493	8,812	1,327	1,139	1,313
Idaho	318	347	366	6,453	7,223	7,757	839	766	1,047
Michigan	299	300	303	5,455	5,705	5,855	807	736	890
New Mexico	232	250	268	4,724	5,236	5,561	661	649	823
Washington	247	247	247	5,535	5,593	5,514	825	716	844

[1] Average number during year. Represents cows and heifers that have calved, kept for milk; excluding heifers not yet fresh.   [2] Valued at average returns per 100 pounds of milk in combined marketings of milk and cream. Includes value of milk fed to calves.   [3] Includes other states not shown separately.

Source: U.S. Dept. of Agriculture, National Agricultural Statistics Service, *Dairy Products*, annual; and *Milk: Production, Disposition, and Income*, annual.

No. 828. Milk Production and Manufactured Dairy Products: 1980 to 2001

[334 represents 334,000]

Item	Unit	1980	1990	1995	1996	1997	1998	1999	2000	2001
Number of farms with milk cows	1,000	334	193	140	131	124	117	111	105	98
Cows and heifers that have calved, kept for milk. .	Mil. head . .	10.8	10.0	9.5	9.4	9.3	9.2	9.2	9.2	9.1
Milk produced on farms	Bil. lb . . .	128	148	155	154	156	157	163	168	165
Production per cow	1,000 lb. . .	11.9	14.8	16.4	16.4	16.9	17.2	17.8	18.2	18.1
Whole milk sold from farms [1]	Bil. lb . . .	126	146	154	153	155	156	161	166	164
Value of milk produced	Bil. dol. . . .	16.9	20.4	20.1	23.0	21.1	24.3	23.4	20.8	24.9
Gross farm income, dairy products	Bil. dol. . . .	16.7	20.2	19.9	22.8	21.0	24.2	23.2	20.6	24.7
Cash receipts from marketing of milk and cream [1]	Bil. dol. . . .	16.6	20.1	19.9	22.8	20.9	24.1	23.2	20.6	24.7
Number of dairy manufacturing plants	Number . . .	2,257	1,723	1,495	1,422	1,384	1,323	1,192	1,163	1,164
Manufactured dairy products:										
Butter (incl. whey butter)	Mil. lb	1,145	1,302	1,264	1,174	1,151	1,168	1,277	1,256	1,237
Cheese, total [2]	Mil. lb	3,984	6,059	6,917	7,218	7,330	7,492	7,894	8,258	8,129
American (excl. full-skim American). . .	Mil. lb	2,376	2,894	3,131	3,281	3,286	3,315	3,533	3,641	3,519
Cream and Neufchatel	Mil. lb	229	431	544	575	615	621	639	687	645
All Italian varieties	Mil. lb	983	2,207	2,674	2,812	2,881	3,005	3,145	3,289	3,328
Cottage cheese: Creamed [3]	Mil. lb	825	832	711	690	706	728	720	735	742
Condensed bulk milk	Mil. lb	952	1,426	1,372	1,270	1,275	1,263	1,365	1,202	1,104
Nonfat dry milk [4]	Mil. lb	1,168	902	1,243	1,068	1,223	1,140	1,364	1,457	1,419
Dry whey [5]	Mil. lb	690	1,143	1,147	1,117	1,137	1,178	1,147	1,188	1,046
Yogurt, plain and fruit flavored.	Mil. lb	(NA)	(NA)	1,646	1,588	1,574	1,639	1,717	1,837	1,999
Ice cream, regular	Mil. gal . . .	830	824	862	879	914	935	972	980	981
Ice cream, lowfat [6]	Mil. gal . . .	293	352	357	366	386	407	381	373	407

NA Not available.   [1] Comprises sales to plants and dealers, and retail sales by farmers direct to consumers.   [2] Includes varieties not shown separately.   [3] Includes partially creamed (low fat).   [4] Includes dry skim milk for animal feed.   [5] Includes animal but excludes modified whey production.   [6] Includes freezer-made milkshake in most states.

Source: U.S. Dept. of Agriculture, National Agricultural Statistics Service, *Dairy Products*, annual; and *Milk: Production, Disposition, and Income*, annual.

Agriculture   537

No. 829. Milk Production and Commercial Use: 1980 to 2001

[In billions of pounds milkfat basis (128.4 represents 128,400,000,000)]

Year	Production	Farm use	Commercial Farm marketings	Commercial Beginning stock	Imports	Commercial supply, total	CCC net removals [1]	Commercial Ending stock	Commercial Disappearance	Milk price per 100 lb. [2] (dol.)
1980	128.4	2.3	126.1	5.3	2.1	133.5	8.8	5.6	119.0	13.05
1990	147.7	2.0	145.7	4.1	2.7	152.5	8.5	5.1	138.8	13.68
1995	155.3	1.6	153.7	4.3	2.9	160.9	2.1	4.1	154.7	12.78
1998	157.3	1.4	155.9	4.9	4.6	165.4	0.4	5.3	159.8	15.46
1999	162.7	1.3	161.4	5.3	4.8	171.4	0.3	6.1	164.9	14.38
2000	167.6	1.3	166.2	6.1	4.4	176.8	0.8	6.9	169.1	12.40
2001	165.3	1.3	164.1	6.8	5.7	176.6	0.2	7.0	169.4	14.93

[1] Removals from commercial supply by Commodity Credit Corporation. [2] Wholesale price received by farmers for all milk delivered to plants and dealers.

Source: U.S. Dept. of Agriculture, Economic Research Service, *Agricultural Outlook,* monthly.

No. 830. Broiler, Turkey, and Egg Production: 1980 to 2001

[For year ending November 30 (392 represents 392,000,000)]

Item	Unit	1980	1990	1994	1995	1996	1997	1998	1999	2000	2001
Chickens:[1]											
Number [2]	Million . .	392	353	386	388	393	410	425	436	435	441
Value per head [2]	Dollars . .	1.88	2.29	2.34	2.41	2.65	2.72	2.65	2.65	2.44	2.42
Value, total [2]	Mil. dol. .	737	808	902	935	1,039	1,113	1,144	1,155	1,061	1,069
Number sold [3]	Million . .	238	208	197	180	174	191	194	210	218	200
Price per lb. [3]	Cents . .	11.0	9.6	7.4	6.5	6.6	7.7	8.1	7.1	5.7	4.5
Value of sales [3]	Mil. dol. .	129	94	73	60	59	71	76	73	64	46
PRODUCTION											
Broilers:[4]											
Number.	Million . .	3,963	5,864	7,018	7,326	7,597	7,764	7,934	8,146	8,284	8,387
Weight	Bil. lb. . .	15.5	25.6	32.5	34.2	36.5	37.5	38.6	40.8	41.6	42.4
Price per lb	Cents . .	27.7	32.6	35.0	34.4	38.1	37.7	39.3	37.1	33.6	39.3
Production value.	Mil. dol. .	4,303	8,366	11,372	11,762	13,903	14,159	15,145	15,129	13,989	16,688
Turkeys:											
Number.	Million . .	165	282	287	292	303	301	285	270	270	272
Weight	Bil. lb. . .	3.1	6.0	6.5	6.8	7.2	7.2	7.1	6.9	6.9	7.2
Price per lb	Cents . .	41.3	39.6	40.4	41.0	43.3	39.9	38.0	40.8	40.7	39.0
Production value.	Mil. dol. .	1,272	2,393	2,643	2,769	3,124	2,884	2,679	2,810	2,823	2,790
Eggs:											
Number.	Billion . .	69.7	68.1	73.9	74.8	76.4	77.5	79.8	82.7	84.4	85.7
Price per dozen	Cents . .	56.3	70.8	61.5	62.5	75.0	70.3	66.8	62.7	61.8	62.2
Production value.	Mil. dol. .	3,268	4,021	3,790	3,893	4,776	4,540	4,439	4,323	4,345	4,445

[1] Excludes commercial broilers. [2] As of December 1. [3] Data for 1980 represent number produced and production value. [4] Young chickens of the heavy breeds and other meat-type birds, to be marketed at 2-5 lbs. live weight and from which no pullets are kept for egg production.

Source: U.S. Dept. of Agriculture, National Agricultural Statistics Service, *Poultry—Production and Value,* annual; *Turkeys,* annual; and *Layers and Egg Production,* annual.

No. 831. Broiler and Turkey Production by State: 1999 to 2001

[In millions of pounds, liveweight production (40,830 represents 40,830,000,000)]

State	Broilers 1999	Broilers 2000	Broilers 2001	Turkeys 1999	Turkeys 2000	Turkeys 2001	State	Broilers 1999	Broilers 2000	Broilers 2001	Turkeys 1999	Turkeys 2000	Turkeys 2001
U.S. [1] . .	40,830	41,625	42,435	6,886	6,943	7,155	MS.	3,676	3,700	3,827	(NA)	(NA)	(NA)
AL	4,953	5,297	5,139	(NA)	(NA)	(NA)	MO	1,124	1,080	(NA)	616	619	660
AR	5,861	5,839	5,737	491	498	473	NC	3,866	4,051	4,203	1,069	1,033	1,131
CA	(NA)	(NA)	(NA)	429	439	451	ND	(NA)	(NA)	(NA)	44	49	42
DE	1,410	1,461	1,495	(Z)	(Z)	(NA)	OH	263	224	213	172	165	181
FL	648	648	634	(NA)	(NA)	(NA)	OK	1,017	1,093	1,111	(NA)	(NA)	(NA)
GA	6,199	6,149	6,237	(NA)	(NA)	(NA)	PA	704	693	701	222	207	214
IL	(NA)	(NA)	(NA)	81	82	83	SC	924	1,004	1,049	326	335	326
IN	(NA)	(NA)	(NA)	377	383	399	SD	(NA)	(NA)	(NA)	137	141	166
IA	(NA)	(NA)	(NA)	233	214	217	TN	724	696	932	(NA)	(NA)	(NA)
KY	982	1,150	1,292	(NA)	(NA)	(NA)	TX	2,387	2,590	2,714	(NA)	(NA)	(NA)
MD	1,472	1,360	1,381	15	15	15	VA	1,317	1,298	1,330	526	553	530
MI	4	(NA)	(NA)	86	119	162	WV	358	365	368	95	89	91
MN	217	221	220	1,066	1,061	1,100	WI	159	148	138	(NA)	(NA)	(NA)

NA Not available. Z Less than 500,000 pounds. [1] Includes other states not shown separately.

Source: U.S. Dept. of Agriculture, National Agricultural Statistics Service, *Poultry—Production and Value,* annual; and *Turkeys,* annual.

This section presents data on the area, ownership, production, trade, reserves, and disposition of natural resources. Natural resources is defined here as including forestry, fisheries, and mining and mineral products.

Forestry—Presents data on the area, ownership, and timber resource of commercial timberland; forestry statistics covering the National Forests and Forest Service cooperative programs; product data for lumber, pulpwood, woodpulp, paper and paperboard, and similar data.

The principal sources of data relating to forests and forest products are *Forest Resources of the United States, 1991; Timber Demand and Technology Assessment, 2001; U.S. Timber Production, Trade, Consumption, and Price Statistics; Land Areas of the National Forest System,* issued annually by the Forest Service of the Department of Agriculture; *Agricultural Statistics* issued by the Department of Agriculture; and reports of the annual survey of manufactures, see Table 851) and the annual *Current Industrial Reports,* issued by the Census Bureau on the Internet and in print in the annual *Manufacturing Profiles.* Additional information is published in the monthly *Survey of Current Business* of the Bureau of Economic Analysis, and the annual *Wood Pulp and Fiber Statistics* and *The Statistics of Paper, Paperboard, and Wood Pulp* of the American Forest and Paper Association, Washington, DC.

The completeness and reliability of statistics on forests and forest products vary considerably. The data for forest land area and stand volumes are much more reliable for areas which have been recently surveyed than for those for which only estimates are available. In general, more data are available for lumber and other manufactured products such as particle board and softwood panels, etc., than for the primary forest products such as poles and piling and fuelwood.

Fisheries—The principal source of data relating to fisheries is *Fisheries of the United States,* issued annually by the National Marine Fisheries Service (NMFS), National Oceanic and Atmospheric Administration (NOAA). The NMFS collects and disseminates data on commercial landings of fish and shellfish. Annual reports include quantity and value of commercial landings of fish and shellfish disposition of landings and number and kinds of fishing vessels and fishing gear. Reports for the fish-processing industry include annual output for the wholesaling and fish processing establishments, annual and seasonal employment. The principal source for these data is the annual *Fisheries of the United States.*

Mining and mineral products—
Presents data relating to mineral industries and their products, general summary measures of production and employment, and more detailed data on production, prices, imports and exports, consumption, and distribution for specific industries and products. Data on mining and mineral products may also be found in Sections 19, 21, and 28 of this *Abstract;* data on mining employment may be found in Section 12.

Mining comprises the extraction of minerals occurring naturally (coal, ores, crude petroleum, natural gas) and quarrying, well operation, milling, refining and processing, and other preparation customarily done at the mine or well site or as a part of extraction activity. (Mineral preparation plants are usually operated together with mines or quarries.) Exploration for minerals is included as is the development of mineral properties.

The principal governmental sources of these data are the *Minerals Yearbook* and *Mineral Commodity Summaries,* published by the U.S. Geological Survey, Department of the Interior, and various monthly and annual publications of the Energy Information Administration, Department of

Energy. See text, Section 19, for a list of Department of Energy publications. In addition, the Census Bureau conducts a census of mineral industries every 5 years (for 1997 results, see Tables 864 and 865).

Nongovernment sources include the *Annual Statistical Report* of the American Iron and Steel Institute, Washington, DC; *Metals Week* and the monthly *Engineering and Mining Journal,* issued by the McGraw-Hill Publishing Co., New York, NY; *The Iron Age,* issued weekly by the Chilton Co., Philadelphia, PA; and the *Joint Association Survey of the U.S. Oil and Gas Industry,* conducted jointly by the American Petroleum Institute, Independent Petroleum Association of America, and Mid-Continent Oil and Gas Association.

Mineral statistics, with principal emphasis on commodity detail, have been collected by the U.S. Geological Survey and the former Bureau of Mines since 1880. Current data in U.S. Geological Survey publications include quantity and value of non-fuel minerals produced, sold or used by producers, or shipped; quantity of minerals stocked; crude materials treated and prepared minerals recovered; and consumption of mineral raw materials.

Censuses of mineral industries have been conducted by the Census Bureau at various intervals since 1840. Beginning with the 1967 census, legislation provides for a census to be conducted every 5 years for years ending in "2" and "7." The most recent results, published for 1997, are based on the North American Industry Classification System (NAICS). The censuses provide, for the various types of mineral establishments, information on operating costs, capital expenditures, labor, equipment, and energy requirements in relation to their value of shipments and other receipts. Commodity statistics on many manufactured mineral products are also collected by the Census Bureau at monthly, quarterly, or annual intervals and issued in its *Current Industrial Reports* series.

In general, figures shown in the individual commodity tables include data for outlying areas and may therefore not agree with summary tables. Except for crude petroleum and refined products, the export and import figures include foreign trade passing through the customs districts of United States and Puerto Rico but exclude shipments between U.S. territories and the customs districts.

No. 832. Gross Domestic Product of Natural Resource-Related Industries in Current and Real (1996) Dollars by Industry: 1990 to 2000

[In billions of dollars (5,803.2 represents 5,803,200,000,000). Data are based on the 1987 SIC. Data include nonfactor charges (capital consumption allowances, indirect business taxes, etc.) as well as factor charges against gross product; corporate profits and capital consumption allowances have been shifted from a company to an establishment basis]

Industry	Current dollars				Chained (1996) dollars			
	1990	1995	1999	2000	1990	1995	1999	2000
All industries, total [1]	5,803.2	7,400.5	9,268.6	9,872.9	6,707.9	7,543.8	8,856.5	9,224.0
Industries covered	297.3	306.7	334.8	367.2	321.9	329.9	365.7	355.5
Percent of all industries	5.12	4.14	3.61	3.72	4.80	4.37	4.13	3.85
Agriculture, forestry, and fishing.	108.3	109.8	127.2	135.8	118.5	123.1	153.4	166.3
Farms	79.6	73.2	74.3	79.0	84.2	85.5	106.0	120.5
Agricultural services.	28.7	36.7	53.0	56.7	34.6	37.6	46.7	47.3
Mining.	111.9	95.7	103.3	127.1	105.8	113.0	112.0	95.2
Metal mining.	5.2	6.5	5.0	4.9	4.4	5.5	8.2	7.4
Coal mining	11.8	10.7	10.6	10.1	7.5	10.1	13.5	13.5
Oil and gas extraction	87.1	69.3	76.2	99.5	87.5	88.6	79.8	63.4
Nonmetallic minerals, except fuels . . .	7.8	9.1	11.5	12.6	8.1	9.1	10.9	12.4
Timber-related manufacturing	77.2	101.3	104.2	104.4	97.6	93.8	100.3	94.1
Lumber and wood products	32.2	42.3	46.3	44.4	45.1	41.6	43.0	44.1
Paper and allied products	45.0	58.9	58.0	59.9	52.5	52.2	57.3	50.0

[1] For additional industry detail, see Table 632.
Source: U.S. Bureau of Economic Analysis, *National Income and Product Accounts, 1929-97*; and *Survey of Current Business* November 2001.

No. 833. Natural Resource-Related Industries—Employees, Annual Payroll, and Establishments by Industry: 2000

[Excludes government employees, railroad employees, self-employed persons, etc. See "General Explanation" in source for definitions and statement on reliability of data. An establishment is a single physical location where business is conducted or where services or industrial operations are performed]

Industry	NAICS code [1]	Number of employ-ees [2] (1,000)	Annual payroll (bil. dol.)	Aver-age payroll per em-ployee (dol.)	Establishment by employment size-class (1,000)				
					Total	Under 20 employ-ees	20 to 99 employ-ees	100 to 499 employ-ees	500 and over employ-ees
Natural resource-related industries, total.	(X)	1,791.3	66.58	37,166	72,932	56,913	11,929	3,758	332
Percent of all industries	(X)	1.57	1.72	109.28	1.03	0.94	1.44	2.40	1.74
Forestry, fishing, hunting and agriculture support	11	183.6	4.68	25,509	26,076	24,437	1,463	167	9
Forestry and logging.	113	83.1	2.26	27,137	13,347	12,639	681	26	1
Timber tract operations	1131	3.3	0.13	39,563	469	429	37	3	-
Forest nurseries & gathering forest products	1132	1.7	0.07	39,933	258	243	15	-	-
Logging	1133	78.1	2.06	26,331	12,620	11,967	629	23	1
Fishing, hunting & trapping	114	10.0	0.34	34,287	2,671	2,583	75	12	1
Fishing	1141	7.5	0.27	35,669	2,308	2,237	61	10	-
Hunting & trapping	1142	2.5	0.08	30,173	363	346	14	2	1
Agriculture & forestry support activities.	115	90.4	2.08	23,043	10,058	9,215	707	129	7
Crop production support activities . .	1151	57.6	1.35	23,400	5,061	4,507	453	96	5
Animal production support activities .	1152	18.2	0.38	21,086	3,450	3,300	134	16	-
Forestry support activities.	1153	14.7	0.35	24,067	1,547	1,408	120	17	2
Mining.	21	456.1	22.09	48,432	23,738	19,422	3,524	708	84
Oil & gas extraction	211	83.0	5.39	64,967	7,740	6,926	683	121	10
Oil & gas extraction.	2111	83.0	5.39	64,967	7,740	6,926	683	121	10
Mining (except oil & gas).	212	204.3	9.34	45,731	7,231	5,132	1,718	343	38
Coal mining	2121	70.7	3.54	50,125	1,253	654	416	169	14
Metal ore mining.	2122	34.8	1.72	49,353	522	402	47	53	20
Nonmetallic mineral mining & quarrying.	2123	98.8	4.08	41,313	5,456	4,076	1,255	121	4
Mining support activities	213	168.8	7.35	43,570	8,767	7,364	1,123	244	36
Mining support activities.	2131	168.8	7.35	43,570	8,767	7,364	1,123	244	36
Timber-related manufacturing	(X)	1,151.6	39.80	34,562	23,118	13,054	6,942	2,883	239
Wood product manufacturing	321	597.7	16.51	27,626	17,328	11,247	4,600	1,412	69
Sawmills & wood preservation.	3211	131.4	3.78	28,798	4,695	3,110	1,256	327	2
Veneer, plywood & engineered wood product manufacturing	3212	120.6	3.75	31,098	1,904	756	780	356	12
Other wood product manufacturing .	3219	345.8	8.95	25,882	10,729	7,381	2,564	729	55
Paper manufacturing	322	553.9	23.29	42,046	5,790	1,807	2,342	1,471	170
Pulp, paper & paperboard mills	3221	177.1	9.48	53,490	597	73	162	239	123
Converted paper product manufac-turing	3222	376.8	13.82	36,666	5,193	1,734	2,180	1,232	47

- Represents zero. X Not applicable. [1] North American Industry Classification System, 1997. [2] Covers full- and part-time employees who are on the payroll in the pay period including March 12.
Source: U.S. Census Bureau, *County Business Patterns: 2000*, Series CBP/00-1. See also <http://www.census.gov/prod/2002pubs/00cbp/cbp00-1.pdf> (issued May 2002).

Natural Resources **541**

No. 834. National Forest System—Summary: 1980 to 1998

[**For fiscal years ending in year shown;** see text, Section 8, State and Local Government Finances and Employment. Includes Alaska and Puerto Rico, except as noted]

Item	Unit	1980	1990	1993	1994	1995	1996	1997	1998
Timber cut, total value	Mil. dol. . .	737	1,192	919	787	620	548	502	450
Commercial and cost sales: [1]									
Volume.	Mil. bd. ft .	9,178	10,500	5,917	4,815	3,866	3,725	3,285	3,298
Value	Mil. dol. . .	730	1,188	915	783	616	544	498	446
Livestock grazing: [2]									
Cattle and horses [3]	1,000. . . .	1,521	1,236	1,318	1,224	1,311	1,167	1,225	1,208
Sheep and goats	1,000. . . .	1,328	958	1,111	925	1,068	859	932	909
Receipts, total.	Mil. dol. . .	703	971	504	515	387	273	285	294
Timber use	Mil. dol. . .	625	849	425	432	303	195	197	208
Grazing use	Mil. dol. . .	16	10	11	11	9	7	7	7
Special land use, etc	Mil. dol. . .	62	112	68	72	75	71	81	79

[1] Includes land exchanges.   [2] Covers number actually grazed. Excludes Puerto Rico.   [3] Excludes animals under 6 months of age.

Source: U.S. Forest Service, *Timber Demand and Technology Assessment*, RWU-4861. Also in *Agricultural Statistics*, annual.

No. 835. National Forest System Land—State and Other Area: 2000

[**In thousands of acres (232,245 represents 232,245,000). As of Sept. 30**]

State and other area	Gross area within unit bound- aries [1]	National Forest System Land [2]	State and other area	Gross area within unit bound- aries [1]	National Forest System Land [2]	State and other area	Gross area within unit bound- aries [1]	National Forest System Land [2]
Total .	**232,245**	**192,363**	IA	-	-	ND.	1,106	1,106
			KS	116	108	OH.	834	233
U.S. . . .	**232,189**	**192,335**	KY	2,210	805	OK.	772	398
			LA	1,025	604	OR.	17,501	15,662
AL	1,288	666	ME.	93	53	PA	743	513
AK	24,355	21,987	MD.	-	-	RI	-	-
AZ	11,891	11,262	MA.	-	-	SC	1,376	617
AR	3,540	2,587	MI	4,894	2,864	SD	2,369	2,013
CA	24,430	20,709	MN.	5,467	2,839	TN	1,276	700
CO	16,015	14,481	MS.	2,320	1,169	TX	1,994	755
CT	-	-	MO	3,060	1,494	UT	9,209	8,189
DE.	-	-	MT.	19,108	16,903	VT	817	386
DC.	-	-	NE	442	352	VA	3,224	1,661
FL	1,255	1,109	NV	6,275	5,835	WA	10,110	9,252
GA	1,856	866	NH.	828	728	WV	1,869	1,034
HI	-	-	NJ	-	-	WI	2,023	1,523
ID	21,653	20,463	NM.	10,455	9,417	WY	9,703	9,238
IL.	857	293	NY	16	16	PR	56	28
IN	644	199	NC.	3,167	1,247	VI	-	-

- Represents zero or rounds to zero.   [1] Comprises all publicly and privately owned land within authorized boundaries of national forests, purchase units, national grasslands, land utilization projects, research and experimental areas, and other areas. [2] Federally owned land within the "gross area within unit boundaries."

Source: U.S. Forest Service, *Land Areas of the National Forest System*, annual.

No. 836. Forest and Timberland Area, Sawtimber, and Stock: 1987 to 1996

[**As of Jan. 1. 731 acres represents 731,000,000 acres**]

Year and region	Total forest land (mil. acres)	Timberland, ownership [1] (mil. acres)				Sawtimber, net volume [3]		Growing stock, net volume [4]	
		All owner- ships	Federally owned or man- aged [2]	State and local	Private	Total (bil. bd. ft.)	Soft- wood (bil. bd. ft.)	Total (bil. cu. ft.)	Soft- wood (bil. cu. ft.)
United States, 1987.	**731**	**485**	**97**	**34**	**354**	**2,853**	**2,040**	**766**	**453**
North	165	154	11	19	124	459	126	190	48
South	203	197	16	4	177	781	388	245	106
Rocky Mountains.	142	61	39	3	20	411	394	108	100
Pacific Coast	220	72	31	8	32	1,202	1,132	223	199
United States, 1992.	**737**	**490**	**97**	**35**	**358**	**2,992**	**2,047**	**786**	**450**
North	168	158	11	19	127	540	137	207	51
South	212	199	16	4	179	842	389	251	103
Rocky Mountains.	140	63	40	3	20	415	397	110	101
Pacific Coast	217	70	30	8	32	1,196	1,124	218	195
United States, 1996.	**746**	**518**	**124**	**35**	**357**	**3,227**	**2,231**	**860**	**503**
North	170	180	32	21	127	574	146	213	49
South	214	201	16	5	180	858	393	256	105
Rocky Mountains.	143	68	44	2	21	482	457	141	126
Pacific Coast	219	69	32	7	29	1,313	1,235	250	223

[1] Timberland is forest land that is producing or is capable of crops of industrial wood and not withdrawn from timber utilization by statute or administrative regulation. Areas qualifying as timberland have the capability of producing in excess of 20 cubic feet per acre per year of industrial wood in natural stands. Currently inaccessible and inoperable areas are included.   [2] Includes Indian lands.   [3] Sawtimber is timber suitable for sawing into lumber. Live trees of commercial species containing at least one 12-foot sawlog or two noncontiguous 8-foot logs, and meeting regional specifications for freedom from defect. Softwood trees must be at least 9.0-inches diameter, and hardwood trees must be at least 11.0-inches diameter at 4 1/2 feet above ground. International 1/4-inch rule.   [4] Live trees of commercial species meeting specified standards of quality or vigor. Cull trees are excluded. Includes only trees 5.0-inches diameter or larger at 4 1/2 feet above ground.

Source: U.S. Forest Service, *Timber Demand and Technology Assessment, 1996*, RWU-4851.

No. 837. Timber-Based Manufacturing Industries—Employees, Payroll, and Shipments: 2000

[Based on the Annual Survey of Manufactures; for description, see Appendix III]

Selected industries	1987 NAICS code [1]	All employees			Value added by manufactures [2]			
			Payroll		Produc-tion workers, total (1,000)		Per produc-tion worker (dol.)	Value of ship-ments [3] (mil. dol.)
		Number (1,000)	Total (mil. dol.)	Per employee (dol.)		Total (mil. dol.)		
Manufacturing, all industries	31-33	16,681	618,217	37,060	11,959	2,002,649	167,456	4,217,852
Timber-based manufacturing, total	(X)	1,137	38,955	34,273	914	114,260	124,992	259,867
Percent of total manufacturing . . .	(X)	6.81	6.30	(X)	7.64	5.70	(X)	6.16
Wood product manufacturing	321	585	16,136	27,581	487	36,093	74,156	93,767
Sawmills & wood preservation.	3211	129	3,648	28,385	109	8,340	76,270	28,124
Sawmills	321113	117	3,333	28,506	100	7,478	74,672	23,424
Wood preservation	321114	12	316	27,169	9	861	93,673	4,700
Veneer, plywood, & engineered wood product	3212	120	3,660	30,457	100	8,474	84,984	21,269
Other wood product	3219	336	8,828	26,246	278	19,279	69,436	44,374
Millwork	32191	152	4,228	27,879	126	9,465	75,056	22,802
Wood container & pallet	32192	51	1,123	21,878	44	2,302	52,544	5,060
All other wood product	32199	133	3,478	26,069	108	7,512	69,728	16,512
Paper	322	552	22,819	41,372	427	78,166	182,896	166,099
Pulp, paper, & paperboard mills.	3221	182	9,570	52,605	143	40,735	284,574	78,515
Pulp mills.	32211	7	411	56,059	6	1,827	322,178	3,701
Paper mills.	32212	124	6,463	52,266	98	26,994	275,065	51,445
Paperboard mills	32213	51	2,695	52,927	39	11,914	302,875	23,369
Converted paper product	3222	370	13,249	35,843	284	37,432	131,690	87,584
Paperboard container.	32221	213	7,669	36,085	164	18,383	112,011	48,048
Paper bag & coated & treated paper.	32222	71	2,678	37,931	53	8,953	170,121	19,370
Stationery product	32223	47	1,499	32,003	36	3,490	96,629	8,133
Other converted paper product	32229	40	1,403	35,366	31	6,606	210,525	12,033

X Not applicable.   [1] North American Industry Classification System, 1997; see text, Section 15, Business Enterprise.
Source: U.S. Census Bureau, *Annual Survey of Manufactures, 2000*, Series M00(AS)-1. See also <http://www.census.gov/prod/2002pubs/m00-as1.pdf> (issued February 2002).

No. 838. Timber Products—Production, Foreign Trade, and Consumption by Type of Product: 1990 to 2000

[In millions of cubic feet, roundwood equivalent (15,577 represents 15,577,000,000)]

Type of product	1990	1991	1992	1993	1994	1995	1996	1997	1998	1999	2000
Industrial roundwood:											
Domestic production [1]	15,577	14,894	15,280	15,011	15,306	14,683	14,496	14,790	14,899	15,034	14,399
Softwoods.	10,968	10,402	10,563	10,090	10,268	9,795	9,700	10,180	10,097	10,390	10,186
Hardwoods	4,609	4,493	4,717	4,921	5,038	4,888	4,795	4,609	4,802	4,643	4,213
Imports	3,091	2,808	3,090	3,465	3,632	3,764	3,754	3,864	3,979	4,222	4,371
Exports	2,307	2,393	2,344	2,143	2,139	2,145	2,112	2,136	1,813	1,838	1,824
Consumption [2]	16,361	15,310	16,026	16,334	16,800	16,302	16,137	16,519	17,065	17,418	16,946
Softwoods.	11,779	11,011	11,536	11,539	11,906	11,581	11,575	12,114	12,348	12,812	12,744
Hardwoods	4,582	4,299	4,490	4,795	4,894	4,721	4,562	4,404	4,718	4,606	4,201
Lumber:											
Domestic production	7,317	6,746	6,983	6,887	7,052	6,815	6,886	7,103	7,298	7,629	7,201
Imports.	1,909	1,714	1,960	2,240	2,395	2,522	2,616	2,619	2,690	2,810	2,832
Exports.	589	619	561	532	512	460	449	452	350	404	421
Consumption	8,637	7,841	8,383	8,595	8,935	8,877	9,053	9,270	9,638	10,035	9,612
Plywood and veneer:											
Domestic production	1,423	1,267	1,294	1,293	1,320	1,303	1,281	1,213	1,201	1,208	1,172
Imports.	97	83	100	100	94	107	97	114	131	160	155
Exports.	109	95	106	100	86	89	87	103	55	45	42
Consumption	1,410	1,255	1,288	1,293	1,328	1,321	1,291	1,224	1,276	1,323	1,285
Pulp products:											
Domestic production	5,313	5,397	5,516	5,423	5,576	5,225	4,991	5,183	5,187	4,964	4,857
Imports	1,038	969	992	1,065	1,102	1,073	969	1,063	1,082	1,159	1,207
Exports	646	746	801	724	758	768	739	775	679	642	677
Consumption	5,704	5,620	5,706	5,764	5,920	5,530	5,221	5,472	5,590	5,481	5,387
Logs:											
Imports	4	2	7	15	18	13	18	20	30	47	68
Exports	674	602	524	460	429	451	422	384	316	326	331
Pulpwood chips, exports	288	332	351	326	354	377	416	422	412	422	354
Fuelwood consumption	3,019	3,028	3,044	3,084	3,134	2,937	2,739	2,542	2,523	2,542	2,561

[1] Includes log exports.   [2] Includes log imports.
Source: U.S. Forest Service, *U.S. Timber Production, Trade, Consumption, and Price Statistics, 1965-1999*, Research Paper FPL-RP-595; and unpublished data. See also <http://www.fpl.fs.fed.us/documnts/fplrp/fplrp595.pdf>.

Natural Resources   543

No. 839. Selected Timber Products—Imports and Exports: 1990 to 2000

Product	Unit	1990	1993	1994	1995	1996	1997	1998	1999	2000
IMPORTS [1]										
Lumber, total [2]	Mil. bd. ft . .	13,063	15,368	16,534	17,524	18,363	18,237	19,012	19,900	20,200
From Canada	Percent . . .	91.2	98.0	97.4	97.0	97.1	96.2	96	93	92
Logs, total	Mil. bd. ft.[3] .	23	94	110	80	115	128	185	294	427
From Canada	Percent . . .	84	95	77	70	82	83	91	95	96
Paper and board [4]	1,000 tons .	12,195	12,990	13,651	14,292	13,023	14,525	14,538	16,917	17,555
Woodpulp	1,000 tons .	4,893	5,413	5,650	5,969	5,692	6,398	5,984	6,650	7,227
Plywood	Mil. sq. ft.[5] .	1,687	1,786	1,693	1,951	1,780	2,111	2,429	2,989	2,918
EXPORTS										
Lumber, total [2]	Mil. bd. ft . .	2,549	3,280	3,115	2,958	2,898	2,933	2,189	2,549	2,700
To: Canada	Percent . . .	26	17	20	22	23	24	26	26	26
Japan	Percent . . .	14	36	34	33	33	27	16	14	12
Europe	Percent . . .	21	17	18	17	17	20	26	21	18
Logs, total	Mil. bd. ft.[3] .	4,213	2,876	2,684	2,820	2,636	2,398	1,978	2,038	2,068
To: Canada	Percent . . .	9	14	16	25	20	30	39	39	41
Japan	Percent . . .	62	65	68	61	69	56	51	49	45
China: Mainland	Percent . . .	9	5	3	1	1	1	1	-	-
Paper and board [4]	1,000 tons .	5,163	6,835	7,536	7,621	9,118	10,368	9,103	9,477	10,003
Woodpulp	1,000 tons .	5,905	6,499	6,728	8,261	7,170	6,990	6,025	5,438	6,409
Plywood	Mil. sq. ft.[5] .	1,766	1,677	1,455	1,517	1,499	1,802	970	833	758

- Represents zero.   [1] Customs value of imports; see text, Section 28.   [2] Includes railroad ties.   [3] Log scale.   [4] Includes paper and board products. Excludes hardboard.   [5] 3/8 inch basis.

Source: U.S. Forest Service, *U.S. Timber Production, Trade, Consumption, and Price Statistics, 1965-1999*, Research Paper FPL-RP-595; and unpublished data. See also <http://www.fpl.fs.fed.us/documnts/fplrp/fplrp595.pdf>.

No. 840. Lumber Consumption by Species Group and End Use: 1995 to 2000

[In million board feet (59.3 represents 59,300,000), except per capita in board feet. Per capita consumption based on estimated resident population as of July 1]

Item	1995	1997	1998	1999	2000	End-use	1995	1997	1998	1999	2000
Total	59.3	63.0	65.1	68.3	66.1	New housing	15.9	19.2	20.6	22.1	20.6
						Residential upkeep and					
Per capita	225	235	241	250	240	improvements	14.3	15.1	14.7	15.1	16.4
						New nonresidential					
Species group:						construction [1]	5.8	7.5	7.8	7.6	7.7
Softwoods . . .	47.6	50.9	52.1	54.5	54.0	Manufacturing	5.5	8.4	8.4	7.9	7.6
Hardwoods . .	11.7	12.1	13.0	13.8	12.2	Shipping	8.5	6.9	7.2	7.4	7.7
						Other [2]	10.2	6.5	6.1	7.2	6.7

[1] In addition to new construction, includes railroad ties laid as replacements in existing track and lumber used by railroads for railcar repair.   [2] Includes upkeep and improvement of nonresidential buildings and structures; made-at-home projects, such as furniture, boats, and picnic tables; made-on-the-job items such as advertising and display structures; and miscellaneous products and uses.

Source: U.S. Forest Service, *U.S. Timber Production, Trade, Consumption, and Price Statistics, 1965-1999*, Research Paper FPL-RP-595. See also <http://www.fpl.fs.fed.us/documnts/fplrp/fplrp595.pdf>.

No. 841. Selected Timber Products—Producer Price Indexes: 1990 to 2001

[1982=100. For information about producer prices, see text, Section 14, Prices]

Product	1990	1994	1995	1996	1997	1998	1999	2000	2001, prel.
Lumber and wood products.	129.7	180.0	178.1	176.1	183.8	179.1	183.6	178.2	174.3
Lumber.	124.6	188.4	173.4	179.8	194.5	179.5	188.2	178.8	171.4
Softwood lumber.	123.8	198.1	178.5	189.5	206.5	182.7	196.0	178.6	170.0
Hardwood lumber.	131.0	168.3	167.0	163.9	174.1	178.7	177.3	185.9	181.1
Millwork	130.4	162.4	163.8	166.6	170.9	171.1	174.7	176.4	179.1
General millwork	132.0	163.6	165.4	167.9	171.1	172.4	175.6	178.0	181.6
Prefabricated structural members.	122.3	169.3	163.5	167.5	177.8	170.1	178.1	175.1	173.4
Plywood.	114.2	158.6	165.3	156.4	159.3	157.3	176.4	157.6	154.1
Softwood plywood	119.6	176.8	188.1	173.7	175.5	174.9	207.0	173.3	168.0
Hardwood plywood and related products. .	102.7	122.3	122.2	124.9	127.1	126.9	128.6	130.2	129.8
Other wood products	114.7	137.7	143.7	127.5	128.4	135.2	131.1	130.5	130.5
Boxes.	119.1	141.3	145.0	147.1	149.2	150.7	152.3	155.2	154.5
Pulp, paper, and allied products	141.2	152.5	172.2	168.7	167.9	171.7	174.1	183.7	184.7
Pulp, paper, and prod., ex. bldg. paper . . .	132.9	133.1	163.4	149.7	144.7	147.0	147.9	161.4	157.6
Woodpulp	151.3	115.9	183.2	133.1	128.6	122.6	119.7	145.3	125.6
Wastepaper.	138.9	209.5	371.1	141.6	163.3	145.4	183.6	282.5	148.6
Paper.	128.8	126.0	159.0	149.4	143.9	145.4	141.8	149.8	150.7
Writing and printing papers	129.1	121.7	158.4	144.6	140.0	139.9	137.8	146.6	146.5
Newsprint	119.6	116.7	161.8	159.5	133.9	143.4	(NA)	127.5	138.4
Paperboard	135.7	140.5	183.1	155.1	144.4	151.6	153.2	176.7	171.9
Converted paper & paperboard products. .	135.2	136.7	157.0	153.4	148.4	152.2	153.5	162.7	164.5
Office supplies and accessories	121.4	116.9	134.9	132.9	131.0	131.2	129.5	133.8	136.9
Building paper & building board mill prods.	112.2	144.1	144.9	137.2	129.6	132.9	141.6	138.8	128.9

Source: U.S. Bureau of Labor Statistics, *Producer Price Indexes*, monthly.

No. 842. Selected Species—Stumpage Prices In Current and Constant (1996) Dollars: 1990 to 2000

[In dollars per 1,000 board feet. Stumpage prices are based on sales of sawtimber from National Forests]

Species	1990	1991	1992	1993	1994	1995	1996	1997	1998	1999	2000
CURRENT DOLLARS											
Softwoods:											
Douglas fir [1]	466	395	477	318	652	454	436	331	254	315	433
Southern pine [2]	127	166	198	217	266	248	241	307	288	269	142
Sugar pine [3]	285	241	492	598	625	397	318	212	177	224	183
Ponderosa pine [3][4]	218	238	292	535	291	150	274	270	205	181	155
Western hemlock [5]	203	164	165	364	335	297	248	211	161	96	46
Hardwoods:											
All eastern hardwoods [6]	146	160	167	264	352	309	259	287	241	195	341
Oak, white, red, and black [6]	188	164	211	195	317	297	237	265	270	317	258
Maple, sugar [7]	135	121	145	220	313	286	238	357	395	448	314
CONSTANT (1996) DOLLARS [8]											
Softwoods:											
Douglas fir [1]	428	362	438	292	598	417	436	304	233	289	397
Southern pine [2]	117	152	182	199	244	228	241	282	264	247	130
Sugar pine [3]	262	221	451	549	574	364	318	195	163	206	168
Ponderosa pine [3][4]	200	218	268	491	267	138	274	248	188	166	142
Western hemlock [5]	186	150	151	334	307	272	248	194	148	88	42
Hardwoods:											
All eastern hardwoods [6]	134	147	153	242	323	283	259	263	221	179	313
Oak, white, red, and black [6]	172	150	194	179	291	272	237	243	248	291	237
Maple, sugar [7]	124	111	133	202	287	262	238	328	362	411	288

[1] Western Washington and western Oregon. [2] Southern region. [3] Pacific Southwest region (formerly California region). [4] Includes Jeffrey pine. [5] Pacific Northwest region. [6] Eastern and Southern regions. [7] Eastern region. [8] Deflated by the producer price index, all commodities.

Source: U.S. Forest Service, *Timber Demand and Technology Assessment*, RWU-4851. Also in *Agricultural Statistics*, annual.

No. 843. Paper and Paperboard—Production and New Supply: 1990 to 2000

[In millions of short tons (80.45 represents 80,445,000)]

Item	1990	1993	1994	1995	1996	1997	1998	1999	2000, prel.
Production, total	80.45	86.69	90.90	91.33	92.25	96.85	96.28	98.77	96.44
Paper, total	39.36	41.75	43.36	42.87	42.48	44.70	44.76	45.98	45.64
Paperboard, total	39.32	43.11	45.72	46.64	47.96	60.33	49.70	50.97	48.99
Unbleached kraft	20.36	21.45	22.47	22.70	22.23	23.23	23.20	23.03	21.80
Semichemical	5.64	5.67	5.94	5.66	5.62	6.05	5.89	6.01	5.95
Bleached kraft	4.40	4.58	5.03	5.30	5.24	5.55	5.48	5.71	5.44
Recycled	8.92	11.41	12.28	12.98	14.87	15.51	15.14	16.22	15.80
Wet machine board E	0.15	0.15	0.15	0.15	0.10	0.10	0.10	0.10	0.10
Building paper E	0.81	0.81	0.81	0.81	0.79	0.79	0.79	0.79	0.79
Insulating board E	0.86	0.86	0.86	0.86	0.93	0.93	0.93	0.93	0.93
New supply, all grades, excluding products	87.68	93.15	97.45	98.16	98.34	101.20	102.88	107.01	105.48
Paper, total	49.49	51.25	53.08	52.77	50.69	54.15	55.13	57.30	57.30
Newsprint	13.41	12.75	12.89	12.76	11.77	12.61	12.80	13.09	13.13
Printing/writing papers	25.46	27.85	29.44	29.55	28.30	30.75	31.38	32.53	32.96
Packaging and ind. conv. papers	4.72	4.63	4.64	4.24	4.33	4.29	4.29	4.71	4.27
Tissue	5.90	6.02	6.11	6.22	6.29	6.66	6.66	6.98	6.95
Paperboard, total	36.30	39.95	42.44	43.45	43.67	45.06	45.55	47.52	46.03
Construction and other	1.90	1.95	1.94	1.95	1.99	1.99	2.20	2.19	2.14

Source: American Forest and Paper Association, Washington, DC, *Monthly Statistical Summary of Paper, Paperboard, and Woodpulp.*

Natural Resources 545

No. 844. Fishery Products—Domestic Catch, Imports, and Disposition: 1990 to 2000

[Live weight, in millions of pounds (16,349 represents 16,349,000,000). For data on commercial catch for selected countries, see Table 1339, Section 30, Comparative International Statistics]

Item	1990	1993	1994	1995	1996	1997	1998	1999	2000
Total	16,349	20,334	19,309	16,484	16,474	17,131	16,897	17,378	17,338
For human food	12,662	13,821	13,714	13,584	13,625	13,739	14,175	14,462	14,738
For industrial use	3,687	6,513	5,595	2,900	2,848	3,392	2,722	2,916	2,599
Domestic catch	9,404	10,467	10,461	9,788	9,565	9,845	9,194	9,339	9,068
For human food	7,041	8,214	7,936	7,667	7,476	7,248	7,174	6,832	6,912
For industrial use	2,363	2,253	2,525	2,121	2,090	2,597	2,020	2,507	2,157
Imports [1]	6,945	9,867	8,848	6,696	6,909	7,286	7,703	8,039	8,269
For human food	5,621	5,607	5,778	5,917	6,150	6,491	7,001	7,630	7,827
For industrial use [2] . . .	1,324	4,260	3,070	779	759	795	702	409	442
Disposition of domestic catch	9,404	10,467	10,461	9,788	9,565	9,846	9,194	9,339	9,069
Fresh and frozen	6,501	7,744	7,475	7,099	7,054	6,877	6,870	6,416	6,657
Canned	751	649	622	769	678	648	516	712	530
Cured.	126	115	95	90	93	108	129	133	119
Reduced to meal, oil, etc.	2,026	1,959	2,269	1,830	1,740	2,213	1,679	2,078	1,763

[1] Excludes imports of edible fishery products consumed in Puerto Rico; includes landings of tuna caught by foreign vessels in American Samoa.   [2] Fish meal and sea herring.

No. 845. Fisheries—Quantity and Value of Domestic Catch: 1980 to 2000

Year	Quantity (mil. lb. [1])			Value (mil. dol.)	Average price per lb. (cents)	Year	Quantity (mil. lb. [1])			Value (mil. dol.)	Average price per lb. (cents)
	Total	For human food	For industrial products [2]				Total	For human food	For industrial products [2]		
1980	6,482	3,654	2,828	2,237	34.5	1991	9,484	7,031	2,453	3,308	34.9
1981	5,977	3,547	2,430	2,388	40.0	1992	9,637	7,618	2,019	3,678	38.2
1982	6,367	3,285	3,082	2,390	37.5	1993	[3]10,467	8,214	2,253	3,471	33.2
1983	6,439	3,238	3,201	2,355	36.6	1994	10,461	7,936	2,525	3,807	36.8
1984	6,438	3,320	3,118	2,350	36.5	1995	9,788	7,667	2,121	3,770	38.5
1985	6,258	3,294	2,964	2,326	37.2	1996	9,565	7,474	2,091	3,487	36.5
1986	6,031	3,393	2,638	2,763	45.8	1997	9,842	7,244	2,598	3,448	35.0
1987	6,896	3,946	2,950	3,115	45.2	1998	9,194	7,173	2,021	3,128	34.0
1988	7,192	4,588	2,604	3,520	48.9	1999	9,339	6,832	2,507	3,467	37.1
1989	8,463	6,204	2,259	3,238	38.3	2000	9,069	6,912	2,157	3,550	39.1
1990	9,404	7,041	2,363	3,522	37.5						

[1] Live weight.   [2] Meal, oil, fish solubles, homogenized condensed fish, shell products, bait, and animal food.   [3] Represents record year.

No. 846. Domestic Fish and Shellfish Catch and Value by Major Species Caught: 1990 to 2000

Species	Quantity (1,000 lb.)				Value ($1,000)			
	1990	1995	1999	2000	1990	1995	1999	2000
Total	9,403,571	9,787,554	9,339,034	9,068,985	3,521,995	3,735,615	3,467,084	3,549,481
Fish, total [1]	8,091,068	8,520,086	7,811,868	7,689,661	1,900,097	1,915,642	1,558,292	1,594,815
Cod:								
Atlantic	95,881	29,631	21,445	25,060	61,329	28,184	23,943	26,384
Pacific.	526,396	591,399	523,987	530,505	91,384	109,680	83,227	142,330
Flounder.	254,519	423,443	331,218	412,723	112,921	150,239	89,946	109,910
Halibut	70,454	44,796	80,330	75,190	96,700	66,781	124,696	143,826
Herring, sea; Atlantic.	113,095	147,181	175,478	160,269	5,746	8,654	11,082	9,972
Herring, sea; Pacific.	108,120	117,479	91,059	74,835	32,178	49,245	14,989	12,043
Menhaden	1,962,160	1,846,959	1,989,081	1,760,498	93,896	99,131	113,082	112,403
Pollock, Alaska	3,108,031	2,852,618	2,325,889	2,000,002	268,344	259,614	162,812	160,525
Salmon.	733,146	1,020,765	814,896	628,638	612,367	486,107	359,785	270,213
Tuna	62,393	63,864	58,120	50,779	105,040	102,638	86,254	95,176
Whiting (Atlantic, silver).	44,500	33,548	30,997	26,855	11,281	14,632	14,282	11,370
Whiting (Pacific, hake).	21,232	390,302	478,154	452,718	1,229	18,002	18,593	18,809
Shellfish, total [1]	1,312,503	1,267,468	1,527,166	1,379,324	1,621,898	1,819,973	1,908,792	1,954,666
Clams	139,198	134,224	112,230	118,482	130,194	140,414	135,024	153,973
Crabs.	499,416	363,639	458,307	299,006	483,837	511,987	521,237	405,006
Lobsters: American.	61,017	66,406	87,469	83,180	154,677	214,838	322,957	301,300
Oysters	29,193	40,380	26,983	41,146	93,718	101,574	72,658	90,667
Sea	39,917	18,316	23,038	32,747	153,696	92,826	125,289	164,609
Shrimp	346,494	306,869	304,173	332,486	491,433	570,034	560,501	690,453
Squid, Pacific	36,082	155,280	199,888	259,508	2,636	22,660	34,954	27,077

[1] Includes other types of fish and shellfish, not shown separately.

Source of Tables 844-846: U.S. National Oceanic and Atmospheric Administration, National Marine Fisheries Service, *Fisheries of the United States,* annual. See also <http://www.st.nmfs.gov/st1/fus/fus00/2000-fus.pdf> (released August 2001).

No. 847. U.S. Private Aquaculture—Trout and Catfish Production and Value: 1990 to 2001

[67.8 represents 67,800,000. Periods are from Sept. 1 of the previous year to Aug. 31 of stated year. Data are for foodsize fish, those over 12 inches long]

Item	Unit	1990	1995	1996	1997	1998	1999	2000	2001
TROUT FOODSIZE									
Number sold	Millions .	67.8	60.2	56.5	59.3	57.6	61.0	58.5	54.6
Total weight.	Mil. lb . .	56.8	55.6	53.6	56.9	57.9	60.2	59.2	56.9
Total value of sales.	Mil. dol. .	64.6	60.8	57.0	60.7	60.3	64.7	63.7	64.5
Average price received	Dol./lb . .	1.14	1.09	1.06	1.07	1.04	1.07	1.08	1.13
Percent sold to processors.	Percent .	58	68	67	63	62	68	70	68
CATFISH FOODSIZE									
Number sold	Millions .	272.9	321.8	375.4	391.8	409.8	424.5	420.1	406.7
Total weight.	Mil. lb . .	392.4	481.5	526.3	569.6	601.4	635.2	633.8	647.2
Total value of sales.	Mil. dol. .	305.1	378.1	403.3	406.8	445.4	464.7	468.8	410.5
Average price received	Dol./lb . .	0.78	0.79	0.77	0.71	0.74	0.73	0.74	0.63
Fish sold to processors	Mil. lb . .	360.4	446.9	472.1	524.9	564.4	596.6	593.6	597.1
Avg. price paid by processors.	Cents/lb .	75.8	78.6	77.3	71.2	74.3	73.7	75.1	64.7
Processor sales	Mil. lb . .	183.1	227.0	237.2	261.8	281.4	292.7	297.2	296.4
Avg. price received by processors . . .	Cents/lb .	224.1	240.3	236.9	226.0	229.0	234.0	236.0	226.0
Inventory (Jan. 1)	Mil. lb . .	9.4	10.9	11.9	11.9	10.8	12.6	13.6	15.0

Source: U.S. Dept. of Agriculture, National Agricultural Statistics Service, *Trout Production* released February; *Catfish Production* released February; and *Catfish Processing* released February. Also in *Agricultural Statistics*, annual.

No. 848. Supply of Selected Fishery Items: 1990 to 2000

[In millions of pounds (734 represents 734,000,000). Totals available for U.S. consumption are supply minus exports plus imports. Round weight is the complete or full weight as caught]

Species	Unit	1990	1993	1994	1995	1996	1997	1998	1999	2000
Shrimp.	Heads-off weight. .	734	808	847	832	842	923	1,002	1,084	1,172
Tuna, canned	Canned weight. . .	856	835	850	875	859	829	912	1,020	980
Snow crab	Round weight. . .	37	66	40	42	46	110	254	216	122
Clams	Meat weight.	152	156	144	144	134	124	119	125	133
Salmon, canned	Canned weight. . .	148	114	117	147	104	82	83	123	95
American lobster	Round weight. . .	95	92	101	94	97	112	110	122	124
Spiny lobster.	Round weight. . .	89	76	76	89	81	76	100	91	97
Scallops.	Meat weight.	74	66	76	62	71	66	58	64	77
Sardines, canned.	Canned weight. . .	61	41	48	44	46	49	50	57	(NA)
Oysters	Meat weight.	56	48	50	63	58	58	61	55	71
King crab	Round weight. . . .	19	8	12	21	30	45	62	52	49
Crab meat, canned	Canned weight. . .	9	9	9	12	13	15	22	26	29

NA Not available.

Source: U.S. National Oceanic and Atmospheric Administration, National Marine Fisheries Service, *Fisheries of the United States*, annual.

No. 849. Canned, Fresh, and Frozen Fishery Products—Production and Value: 1990 to 2000

[Fresh fishery products exclude Alaska and Hawaii. Canned fishery products data are for natural pack only]

Product	Production (mil. lb.)					Value (mil. dol.)				
	1990	1995	1998	1999	2000	1990	1995	1998	1999	2000
Canned, total [1]	1,178	1,927	1,533	1,897	1,744	1,562	1,887	1,775	1,861	1,623
Tuna	581	667	681	664	671	902	939	983	946	855
Salmon.	196	244	159	234	171	366	419	274	393	288
Clam products	110	129	113	123	125	76	110	105	110	117
Sardines, Maine	13	14	12	12	(Z)	17	24	19	20	(Z)
Shrimp	1	1	2	2	2	3	7	2	10	11
Crabs . [2]	1	(Z)	(Z)	(Z)	(Z)	4	(Z)	(Z)	(Z)	(Z)
Oysters [2].	1	(Z)	(Z)	(Z)	(Z)	1	(Z)	(Z)	(Z)	(Z)
Fish fillets and steaks [3] .	441	385	422	362	369	843	841	961	807	830
Cod	65	65	67	61	56	132	152	161	108	165
Flounder	54	35	24	23	27	154	86	70	67	72
Haddock	7	3	6	5	5	24	11	22	20	21
Ocean perch, Atlantic	1	(Z)	1	1	1	1	1	2	2	2
Rockfish	33	25	16	11	11	53	38	33	23	25
Pollock, Atlantic	12	4	4	2	2	21	10	7	4	4
Pollock, Alaska.	164	135	161	144	160	174	184	190	169	179
Other	105	118	143	115	107	284	359	476	414	362

Z Less than 500,000 pounds or $500,000. [1] Includes other products, not shown separately. [2] Includes oyster specialties. [3] Fresh and frozen.

Source: U.S. National Oceanic and Atmospheric Administration, National Marine Fisheries Service, *Fisheries of the United States*, annual. See also <http://www.st.nmfs.gov/st1/fus/fus00/2000-fus.pdf> (released August 2001).

No. 850. Mining Industries—Employees, Payroll, and Shipments: 1997

[The mining sector comprises establishments that extract naturally occurring mineral solids, such as coal and ores; liquid minerals and gases, such as natural gas. The term mining is used in the broad sense to include quarrying, well operations, beneficiating (e.g., crushing, screening, washing, and flotation), and other preparation customarily performed at the mine site, or as a part of mining activity]

Selected industries	NAICS code [1]	Establishments	All employees		Payroll		Production workers, total [2]	Value added by manufactures (mil. dol.)	Value of shipments (mil. dol.)
			Number [2]		Total (mil. dol.)	Per employee (dol.)			
Mining, total	21	25,000	509,006		20,798	40,861	389,232	133,636	173,985
Oil and gas extraction	211	8,312	110,881		5,511	49,698	67,197	82,350	102,834
Oil and gas extraction.	2111	8,312	110,881		5,511	49,698	67,197	82,350	102,834
Mining (except oil & gas)	212	7,348	229,319		9,422	41,085	188,988	35,207	51,253
Coal mining	2121	1,511	87,965		3,984	45,289	75,398	15,567	23,427
Metal ore mining	2122	493	45,467		1,993	43,837	39,103	7,387	11,204
Iron ore mining	21221	32	7,920		394	49,738	6,787	992	1,938
Gold ore & silver ore mining . . .	21222	316	18,292		810	44,308	16,199	2,865	4,073
Copper, nickel, lead, and zinc mining	21223	80	15,872		640	40,291	13,447	3,050	4,549
Other metal ore mining	21229	65	3,383		149	44,110	2,670	480	644
Nonmetallic mineral mining and quarrying	2123	5,344	95,887		3,445	35,924	74,487	12,253	16,621
Stone mining & quarrying . . .	21231	2,367	44,052		1,551	35,206	35,260	5,549	7,385
Sand, gravel, clay, ceramic and refractory minerals mining and quarrying.	21232	2,674	37,052		1,261	34,044	27,646	4,080	5,541
Other nonmetallic mineral mining and quarrying	21239	303	14,783		632	42,777	11,581	2,624	3,695
Support activities for mining	213	9,340	168,806		5,866	34,751	133,047	16,079	19,899

[1] North American Industrial Classification System, 1997; see text, Section 15, Business Enterprise. [2] For pay period including March 12.

Source: U.S. Census Bureau, *1997 Economic Census, Mining,* Series EC97N21S-GS, April 2001. The next update for these data will be after the 2002 Economic Census.

No. 851. Mining Summary by State: 1997

[The mining sector comprises establishments that extract naturally occurring mineral solids, such as coal and ores; liquid minerals and gases, such as natural gas. The term mining is used in the broad sense to include quarrying, well operations, beneficiating (e.g., crushing, screening, washing, and flotation), and other preparation customarily performed at the mine site, or as a part of mining activity]

State	Establishments, total	All employees		Production workers [1]	Value added by manufactures (mil. dol.)	State	Establishments, total	All employees		Production workers [1]	Value added by manufactures (mil. dol.)
		Number [1]	Payroll (mil. dol.)					Number [1]	Payroll (mil. dol.)		
United States	25,000	509,006	20,798	389,232	133,636	Montana	294	5,328	216	3,864	1,047
						Nebraska	150	1,078	31	858	104
Alabama	291	9,066	371	7,421	1,775	Nevada.	250	14,035	626	12,451	1,959
Alaska	141	10,137	672	7,585	9,565	New Hampshire. . .	32	396	18	293	44
Arizona	206	12,889	510	10,699	2,171	New Jersey . . .	95	1,864	84	1,350	243
Arkansas.	307	3,250	98	2,602	704	New Mexico. . .	606	14,600	574	11,520	5,336
California.	910	22,110	945	16,908	7,497	New York	359	3,879	142	2,819	474
Colorado.	885	12,263	522	7,881	2,872	North Carolina . .	171	3,231	118	2,644	533
Connecticut . . .	62	626	27	467	105	North Dakota . .	227	4,098	176	3,361	1,017
Delaware [2] . . .	11	107	4	90	15	Ohio	828	11,997	454	8,961	1,746
Florida	225	6,688	249	5,424	1,009	Oklahoma	2,271	25,976	967	16,957	5,509
Georgia	205	6,354	233	4,984	1,024	Oregon	134	1,739	61	1,216	161
Hawaii	7	120	6	100	22	Pennsylvania . .	914	17,522	677	14,262	2,411
Idaho	110	3,021	118	2,418	291	Rhode Island . .	16	120	5	82	13
Illinois.	650	10,798	437	8,557	1,381	South Carolina . .	74	1,388	44	1,099	166
Indiana	347	6,007	241	5,013	795	South Dakota . .	67	1,837	67	1,635	166
Iowa.	177	1,700	55	1,428	217	Tennessee	221	4,473	137	3,614	479
Kansas	1,026	7,998	245	5,993	2,178	Texas	6,412	105,492	4,334	73,686	32,485
Kentucky.	691	22,400	832	19,413	3,297	Utah	316	8,134	335	6,593	1,875
Louisiana	1,608	52,816	2,302	38,255	21,889	Vermont	52	658	22	538	72
Maine.	21	76	1	50	4	Virginia	417	11,711	429	9,860	1,449
Maryland.	93	1,771	64	1,429	257	Washington . . .	154	2,890	114	2,170	349
Massachusetts .	72	1,063	42	704	110	West Virginia . .	766	23,927	1,042	20,450	4,161
Michigan	445	6,687	271	5,030	1,182	Wisconsin	147	2,304	92	1,598	312
Minnesota	145	7,154	348	6,071	954	Wyoming.	669	15,436	723	12,367	5,395
Mississippi. . . .	368	4,096	115	3,100	531	Offshore areas .	41	11,135	455	9,717	5,782
Missouri	306	4,561	146	3,645	503						

[1] For pay period including March 12. [2] District of Columbia is included with Delaware.

Source: U.S. Census Bureau, *1997 Economic Census, Mining,* Series EC97N21S-GS, April 2001. The next update for these data will be after the 2002 Economic Census.

548   Natural Resources

No. 852. Mining and Primary Metal Production Indexes: 1990 to 2001

[Index 1992=100]

Industry group	1990	1993	1994	1995	1996	1997	1998	1999	2000	2001
Mining	**104.8**	**100.0**	**102.3**	**102.0**	**103.5**	**105.3**	**102.9**	**98.2**	**100.7**	**101.3**
Coal	103.7	94.0	103.0	102.6	105.0	108.2	109.7	107.8	107.1	111.7
Oil and gas extraction.	106.4	101.1	101.6	100.4	101.6	102.5	98.6	92.4	95.6	96.1
Crude oil and natural gas. . . .	101.6	98.0	98.1	96.5	95.9	95.6	93.8	90.5	90.6	90.9
Oil and gas drilling	151.1	122.4	126.2	125.8	137.5	147.8	131.6	103.3	132.0	140.2
Metal mining	93.1	98.7	100.5	101.8	104.3	108.8	108.1	99.8	97.2	88.4
Iron ore	101.4	100.0	104.3	112.3	111.3	113.6	112.7	103.6	113.6	83.1
Nonferrous ores	91.9	98.5	100.0	100.4	103.4	108.1	107.5	99.4	94.5	89.3
Copper ore	89.4	102.0	104.7	104.7	108.7	109.9	105.4	90.7	81.4	76.9
Primary metals, manufacturing . .	**104.0**	**105.1**	**113.8**	**116.2**	**119.7**	**125.5**	**127.7**	**129.4**	**131.9**	**116.9**
Nonferrous metals	100.9	103.9	113.0	115.7	120.4	127.3	132.3	136.1	137.7	122.3
Copper.	81.6	116.4	111.4	121.8	103.4	109.6	133.4	124.8	100.1	102.1
Aluminum	100.4	91.7	81.8	83.7	88.5	89.4	92.1	93.7	90.8	65.5
Iron and steel	106.4	106.0	114.4	116.6	119.1	123.9	124.0	123.9	127.3	112.6

Source: Board of Governors of the Federal Reserve System, *Federal Reserve Bulletin*, monthly; and *Industrial Production and Capacity Utilization*, Statistical Release G.17, monthly.

No. 853. Mineral Industries—Employment, Hours, and Earnings: 1990 to 2001

[Based on the Current Employment Statistics Program, see Appendix III]

Industry and item	Unit	1990	2000	2001	Industry and item	Unit	1990	2000	2001
All mining:					Avg. weekly hours	Number .	43.9	41.5	41.4
All employees	1,000 . . .	709	543	563	Avg. weekly earnings . .	Dollars . .	568	718	738
Production workers	1,000 . . .	509	417	441	Metal mining:				
Avg. weekly hours . .	Number .	44.1	43.1	43.4	All employees	1,000 . . .	58	41	36
Avg. weekly earnings . .	Dollars . .	603	743	766	Production workers	1,000 . . .	46	31	27
Coal mining:					Avg. weekly hours	Number .	42.8	43.4	43.5
All employees	1,000 . . .	147	77	78	Avg. weekly earnings . .	Dollars . .	601	809	825
Production workers	1,000 . . .	119	63	66	Nonmetallic minerals,				
Avg. weekly hours	Number .	44.0	44.5	47.1	except fuels:				
Avg. weekly earnings . .	Dollars . .	735	850	897	All employees	1,000 . . .	110	114	113
Oil and gas extraction:					Production workers	1,000 . . .	83	87	86
All employees	1,000 . . .	395	311	337	Avg. weekly hours	Number .	45.3	46.2	46.8
Production workers	1,000 . . .	261	237	263	Avg. weekly earnings . .	Dollars . .	525	707	737

Source: U.S. Bureau of Labor Statistics, *Bulletin 2370* and *Employment and Earnings*, March and June issues.

No. 854. Selected Mineral Products—Average Prices: 1980 to 2001

[Excludes Alaska and Hawaii, except as noted]

Year	Nonfuels								Fuels		
	Copper, electro-lytic (cents per lb.)	Plati-num[1] (dol./ troy oz.)	Gold (dol./ fine oz.)	Silver (dol./ fine oz.)	Lead (cents per lb.)	Tin (New York) (cents per lb.)	Zinc (cents per lb.)	Sulfur, crude[2] (dol./ metric ton)	Bitumi-nous coal[3][4] (dol./ short ton)	Crude petro-leum[3] (dol./ bbl.)	Natural gas[3] (dol./ 1,000 cu. ft.)
1980	101	677	613	20.63	43	846	37	89.06	29.17	21.59	1.59
1981	84	446	460	10.52	37	733	45	111.48	31.51	31.77	1.98
1982	73	327	376	7.95	26	654	39	108.27	32.15	28.52	2.46
1983	77	424	424	11.44	22	655	41	87.24	31.11	26.19	2.59
1984	67	357	361	8.14	26	624	49	94.31	30.63	25.88	2.66
1985	67	291	318	6.14	19	596	40	106.46	30.78	24.09	2.51
1986	66	461	368	5.47	22	383	38	105.22	28.84	12.51	1.94
1987	83	553	478	7.01	36	419	42	89.78	28.19	15.40	1.67
1988	121	523	438	6.53	37	441	60	85.95	27.66	12.58	1.69
1989	131	507	383	5.50	39	520	82	86.62	27.40	15.86	1.69
1990	123	467	385	4.82	46	386	75	80.14	27.43	20.03	1.71
1991	109	371	363	4.04	34	363	53	71.45	27.49	16.54	1.64
1992	107	360	345	3.94	35	402	58	48.14	26.78	15.99	1.74
1993	92	375	361	4.30	32	350	46	31.86	26.15	14.25	2.04
1994	111	411	385	5.29	37	369	49	28.60	25.68	13.19	1.85
1995	138	425	386	5.15	42	416	56	44.46	25.56	14.62	1.55
1996	109	398	389	5.19	49	412	51	34.11	25.17	18.46	2.17
1997	107	397	332	4.89	47	381	65	36.06	24.64	17.23	2.32
1998	79	375	295	5.54	45	373	51	29.14	24.87	10.87	1.96
1999	76	379	280	5.25	44	366	54	37.81	23.88	15.56	2.19
2000	89	549	280	5.00	44	370	56	24.73	24.15	26.72	3.69
2001	77	533	272	4.39	44	315	44	(NA)	(NA)	21.84	4.12

NA Not available.   [1] Average annual dealer prices.   [2] F.o.b. works.   [3] Average value at the point of production or domestic first purchase price.   [4] Includes lignite.

Source: Nonfuels, through 1994, U.S. Bureau of Mines, thereafter, U.S. Geological Survey, *Minerals Yearbook* and *Mineral Commodities Summaries*, annual; fuels, U.S. Energy Information Administration, *Annual Energy Review*, and most recent year from the *Monthly Energy Review*.

Natural Resources   549

No. 855. Mineral Production: 1990 to 2001

[Data represent production as measured by mine shipments, mine sales or marketable production]

Mineral	Unit	1990	1995	1999	2000	2001, est.
FUEL MINERALS						
Coal, total	Mil. sh. tons	1,029.1	1,033.0	1,100.4	1,073.6	1,121.3
Bituminous	Mil. sh. tons	693.2	613.8	601.7	574.3	(NA)
Subbituminous	Mil. sh. tons	244.3	328.0	406.7	409.2	(NA)
Lignite	Mil. sh. tons	88.1	86.5	87.2	85.6	(NA)
Anthracite	Mil. sh. tons	3.5	4.7	4.8	4.6	(NA)
Natural gas (marketed production)	Tril. cu. ft	18.59	19.51	19.80	20.00	20.47
Petroleum (crude)	Mil. bbl. [1]	2,686	2,394	2,147	2,125	2,118
Uranium (recoverable content)	Mil. lb.	8.9	6.0	4.6	4.0	2.6
NONFUEL MINERALS						
Asbestos (sales)	1,000 metric tons . .	(D)	9	7	5	5
Barite, primary, sold/used by producers . .	1,000 metric tons . .	430	543	434	392	400
Boron minerals, sold or used by producers	1,000 metric tons . .	1,090	1,190	1,220	1,070	(NA)
Bromine, sold or used by producers	1,000 metric tons . .	177	218	239	228	204
Cement:						
Portland	Mil. metric tons	67	73	82	84	(NA)
Masonry	Mil. metric tons	3	4	4	4	(NA)
Clays	1,000 metric tons . .	42,900	43,100	42,200	40,800	40,600
Diatomite	1,000 metric tons . .	631	722	747	677	735
Feldspar [2]	1,000 metric tons . .	630	880	875	790	780
Fluorspar, finished shipments	1,000 metric tons . .	64	51	-	-	-
Garnet (industrial)	1,000 metric tons . .	47	46	61	60	53
Gypsum, crude	Mil. metric tons . . .	15	17	22	20	19
Helium [3]	Mil. cu. meters	85	101	114	98	100
Lime, sold or used by producers	Mil. metric tons . . .	16	19	20	20	19
Mica, scrap & flake, sold/used by producers	1,000 metric tons . .	109	108	104	101	95
Peat, sales by producers	1,000 metric tons . .	721	660	731	755	812
Perlite, processed, sold or used	1,000 metric tons . .	576	700	711	672	650
Phosphate rock (marketable)	Mil. metric tons	46	44	41	39	34
Potash (K$_2$O equivalent) sales	1,000 metric tons . .	1,710	1,480	1,200	1,300	1,200
Pumice & pumicite, producer sales	1,000 metric tons . .	443	529	643	697	687
Salt, common, sold/used by producers . .	Mil. metric tons	37	41	45	46	45
Sand & gravel, sold/used by producer . .	Mil. metric tons . . .	855	935	1,139	1,148	1,149
Construction	Mil. metric tons . . .	829	907	1,110	1,120	1,120
Industrial	Mil. metric tons . . .	26	28	29	28	29
Sodium carbonate (natural) (soda ash) . .	1,000 metric tons . .	9,100	10,100	10,200	10,200	10,300
Sodium sulfate (natural)	1,000 metric tons . .	349	327	599	491	510
Stone [4]	Mil. metric tons . . .	1,110	2,420	2,600	2,810	2,920
Crushed and broken	Mil. metric tons . . .	1,110	1,260	1,540	1,560	1,620
Dimension [5]	1,000 metric tons . .	1,120	1,160	1,250	1,250	1,300
Sulfur: Total shipments	1,000 metric tons . .	11,500	12,100	11,100	10,300	9,200
Sulfur: Frasch mines (shipments)	1,000 metric tons . .	3,680	(D)	(D)	10,500	9,100
Talc, and pyrophyllite, crude	1,000 metric tons . .	1,270	1,060	925	851	914
Vermiculite concentrate	1,000 metric tons . .	209	171	175	150	150
METALS						
Antimony ore and concentrate	Metric tons	(D)	262	449	(D)	300
Aluminum	1,000 metric tons . .	4,048	3,375	3,779	3,668	2,600
Bauxite (dried)	1,000 metric tons . .	(D)	(D)	(NA)	(NA)	(NA)
Copper (recoverable content)	1,000 metric tons . .	1,590	1,850	1,600	1,440	1,340
Gold (recoverable content)	Metric tons	294	317	341	353	350
Iron ore (gross weight) [6]	Mil. metric tons	57	61	58	63	60
Lead (recoverable content)	1,000 metric tons . .	484	394	520	468	420
Magnesium metal	1,000 metric tons . .	139	142	(D)	(D)	(D)
Manganiferous ore (gross weight) [7] . . .	1,000 metric ton . .	(D)	(D)	-	-	(NA)
Mercury [8]	Metric tons	562	(D)	(NA)	(NA)	-
Molybdenum (concentrate)	1,000 metric tons . .	62	61	43	41	38
Nickel	1,000 metric tons . .	-	2	-	-	-
Palladium metal	Kilograms	5,930	5,260	9,800	10,300	12,000
Platinum metal	Kilograms	1,810	1,590	2,920	3,110	3,600
Silicon (silicon content)	1,000 metric tons . .	418	396	423	367	301
Silver (recoverable content)	Metric tons	2,120	1,560	1,950	1,860	1,800
Titanium concentrate: Ilmenite (gross weight)	1,000 metric tons . .	(D)	(D)	(D)	(NA)	(NA)
Tungsten ore and concentrate [9]	Metric tons	(D)	(D)	-	(NA)	(NA)
Zinc (recoverable content)	1,000 metric tons . .	515	614	843	829	830

- Represents zero.   D Withheld to avoid disclosing individual company data.   NA Not available.   [1] 42 gal. bbl. [2] Beginning 1995, includes aplite.   [3] Refined.   [4] Excludes abrasive stone, bituminous limestone and sandstone, and ground soapstone, all included elsewhere in table.   Includes calcareous marl and slate.   [5] Includes Puerto Rico.   [6] Represents shipments; includes byproduct ores.   [7] 5 to 35 percent manganiferous ore.   [8] Covers mercury recovered as a by product of gold ores only.   [9] Content of ore and concentrate.

Source: Nonfuels, through 1995, U.S. Bureau of Mines, thereafter, U.S. Geological Survey, *Minerals Yearbook* and *Mineral Commodities Summaries,* annual; fuels, U.S. Energy Information Administration, *Annual Energy Review* and *Uranium Industry Annual.*

No. 856. Nonfuel Mineral Commodities—Summary: 2001

[Preliminary estimates. Average price in dollars per metric tons except as noted]

Mineral	Unit	Mineral disposition				Average price per unit (dollars)	Employment (number)
		Production	Exports	Net import reliance [1] (percent)	Consumption, apparent		
Aluminum	1,000 metric tons.	2,600	1,500	35	6,000	[2]70.00	15,700
Antimony (contained)	Metric tons	[3]300	1,500	86	49,800	[2]65.00	70
Asbestos	1,000 metric tons.	5	16	100	(NA)	206.00	20
Barite	1,000 metric tons.	400	40	87	2,960	[4]25.00	340
Bauxite and alumina	1,000 metric tons.	(NA)	(NA)	100	3,200	[4]24.00	(NA)
Beryllium (contained)	Metric tons	180	40	39	295	[2][6]338.00	(NA)
Bismuth (contained)	Metric tons	-	600	95	2,200	[2]3.80	-
Boron (B$_2$O$_3$ content)	1,000 metric tons.	650	100	([5])	482	[4][7]376.00	1,300
Bromine (contained)	1,000 metric tons.	204	20	5	214	[8][9]67.00	1,700
Cadmium (contained)	Metric tons	[3]1,400	280	3	1,440	[2][10]0.15	(NA)
Cement	1,000 metric tons.	89,600	738	21	114,000	[4]79.00	18,000
Chromium	1,000 metric tons.	[11]120	60	78	540	[4][12](NA)	-
Clays	1,000 metric tons.	40,600	5,130	([5])	35,500	(NA)	9,250
Cobalt (contained)	Metric tons	[11]2,500	3,000	78	11,200	[2]10.70	-
Copper (Mine, contained)	1,000 metric tons.	1,340	670	31	2,770	10	-
Diamond (industrial)	Million carats	418	91	83	626	[14]0.31	-
Diatomite	1,000 metric tons.	735	131	([5])	604	[4]256.00	1,000
Feldspar	1,000 metric tons.	780	5	([3])	782	[4]54.00	400
Fluorspar	1,000 metric tons.	(NA)	21	100	636	0.00	5
Garnet (industrial)	Metric tons	52,500	10,000	20	59,600	[4]50-2,000	220
Germanium (contained)	Kilograms	20,000	(NA)	(NA)	(NA)	(NA)	90
Gold (contained)	Metric tons	350	580	([5])	(NA)	[17]280.00	9,800
Gypsum (crude)	1,000 metric tons.	18,800	198	25	33,200	[4]8.46	5,900
Iodine	Metric tons	1,700	1,000	72	6,000	[8][21]14.28	30
Iron ore (usable)	Million metric tons	63	6	15	71	[4][22]25.00	6,000
Iron and steel slag (metal)	1,000 metric tons.	18,000	20	8	19,000	[4]8.60	2,700
Lead (contained)	1,000 metric tons.	420	100	20	1,650	[2]44.00	1,000
Lime	1,000 metric tons.	18,700	90	(Z)	18,800	76.00	5,500
Magnesium compounds	1,000 metric tons.	360	50	([5])	590	(NA)	450
Magnesium metal	1,000 metric tons.	(D)	20	44	120	1.25	375
Mercury	Metric tons	[11](NA)	50	(NA)	(NA)	[26]140.00	(NA)
Mica, scrap and flake	1,000 metric tons.	95	10	19	118	[4]140.00	(NA)
Molybdenum (contained)	Metric tons	38,300	32,300	([5])	22,300	[8]5.20	290
Nickel (contained)	Metric tons	-	9,040	56	128,000	[2][27]2.69	1
Nitrogen (fixed)-ammonia	1,000 metric tons.	9,500	670	29	13,500	[4][28]150.00	1,800
Peat	1,000 metric tons.	812	25	50	1,620	[4]23.00	800
Perlite	1,000 metric tons.	650	39	18	796	[4]31.55	145
Phosphate rock	1,000 metric tons.	34,200	50	2	(NA)	[4]25.00	6,000
Platinum-group metals	Kilograms	(NA)	(NA)	(NA)	(NA)	[17][29](NA)	(NA)
Potash (K$_2$O equivalent)	1,000 metric tons.	1,200	410	80	5,400	[4][30]155.00	670
Pumice and pumicite	1,000 metric tons.	687	25	35	1,050	[4]24.53	80
Salt	1,000 metric tons.	45,100	900	17	54,200	[4][31]117.00	4,100
Silicon (contained)	1,000 metric tons.	301	25	42	518	(NA)	(NA)
Silver (contained)	Metric tons	1,800	470	44	5,800	[17]5.00	1,300
Sodium carbonate (soda ash)	1,000 metric tons.	10,300	4,100	([5])	6,200	[33]105.00	2,700
Sodium sulfate	1,000 metric tons.	510	220	([5])	330	[34]114.00	225
Stone (crushed)	Million metric tons	1,620	4	1	1,631	[4]5.53	79,200
Sulfur (all forms)	1,000 metric tons.	9,200	840	12	10,400	[4][35]18.00	2,700
Talc	1,000 metric tons.	914	136	1	925	[4]118.00	620
Thallium (contained)	Kilograms	-	(NA)	100	(NA)	[8]1,295.00	(NA)
Tin (contained)	Metric tons	[11]15,500	6,800	88	56,900	[2]19.00	(NA)
Titanium dioxide	1,000 metric tons.	1,340	432	([5])	1,100	[2][36]1.00	4,600
Tungsten (contained)	Metric tons	-	5,140	59	14,000	[37]64.00	(NA)
Vermiculite	1,000 metric tons.	150	5	27	205	114.00	230
Zinc (contained)	1,000 metric tons.	830	532	60	1,500	[2]0.45	2,400
Zirconium (Z,02) content	Metric tons	(D)	41,180	(D)	(NA)	[4][39]350	(D)

- Represents or rounds to zero. D Withheld to avoid disclosure. NA Not available. [1] Calculated as a percent of apparent consumption. [2] Dollars per pound. [3] Refinery production. [4] Dollars per metric ton. [5] Net exporter. [6] Metal, vacuum-cast ingot. [7] Granulated pentahydrate borax in bulk, f.o.b. mine. [8] Dollars per kilogram. [9] Bulk, purified bromine. [10] 1- to 5-short ton lots. [11] Secondary production. [12] Turkish, chromite price. [13] Columbite price. [14] Value of imports, dollars per carat. [15] Reported consumption. [16] Zone refined. [17] Dollars per troy ounce. [18] Price of flake imports. [19] Includes employment at calcining plants. [20] 99.97% indium. [21] C.i.f. value, crude, per kilogram. [22] Price of eastern Canadian ore. [23] Delivered, No. 1 Heavy Melting composite price. [24] Year-end price. [25] 46%-48% Mn metallurgical ore, per unit contained Mn, c.i.f. U.S. ports. [26] Dollars per 76-pound flask. [27] London Metal Exchange cash price. [28] F.o.b. gulf coast. [29] Dealer price of platinum. [30] Price of K20, muriate. [31] Vacuum and open pan, bulk, pellets and packaged, f.o.b. mine and plant. [32] Ferrosilicon, 50% Si. [33] Quoted year-end price, dense, bulk, f.o.b. Green River, WY, dollars per short ton. [34] Quoted price, bulk, f.o.b. works, East, dollars per short ton. [35] Elemental sulfur, f.o.b. mine and/or plant. [36] Rutile, list, year-end. [37] Dollars per unit W03 (7.93 kilograms of contained tungsten per unit). [38] All forms. [39] Price for imported zircon, f.o.b. U.S. east coast.

Source: U.S. Geological Survey, *Mineral Commodity Summaries*, annual.

Natural Resources 551

No. 857. Value of Domestic Nonfuel Mineral Production by State: 1990 to 2001

[In millions of dollars (33,445 represents 33,445,000,000), except as indicated. For similar data on fuels, see Table 864]

State	1990	1995	1998	1998	2000	2001, prel. Total (mil. dol.)	Rank	Percent of U.S.
United States [1] . .	33,445	38,506	39,600	39,100	40,100	38,900	(X)	100.00
Alabama	559	706	1,010	1,080	1,070	938	16	2.41
Alaska.	577	538	999	1,090	1,140	1,060	13	2.73
Arizona	3,085	4,190	2,770	2,510	2,550	2,110	4	5.43
Arkansas	381	492	484	518	506	491	30	1.26
California	2,771	2,760	2,980	3,200	3,350	3,250	1	8.35
Colorado	377	570	650	555	566	676	22	1.74
Connecticut	122	93	[3]99	[3]103	[3]100	104	43	0.27
Delaware [2]	10	9	[3]12	[3]10	[3]12	13	50	0.03
Florida.	1,574	1,540	1,810	1,930	1,920	1,750	5	4.5
Georgia	1,504	1,690	1,720	1,840	1,660	1,610	7	4.13
Hawaii.	106	114	85	89	91	70	45	0.18
Idaho	375	510	453	420	398	344	35	0.88
Illinois	667	828	875	913	907	911	17	2.34
Indiana	428	589	691	717	729	718	20	1.84
Iowa	310	456	518	537	510	487	31	1.25
Kansas	349	498	551	566	624	640	23	1.64
Kentucky	359	432	498	483	497	531	26	1.37
Louisiana	368	434	347	374	404	274	37	0.7
Maine	55	68	92	101	[3]102	91	44	0.23
Maryland	368	324	352	336	357	356	33	0.92
Massachusetts	128	190	204	204	210	209	39	0.54
Michigan	1,440	1,520	1,670	1,660	1,670	1,620	6	4.17
Minnesota	1,482	1,530	1,740	1,580	1,570	1,440	8	3.7
Mississippi	111	131	149	190	157	177	41	0.45
Missouri.	1,105	1,140	1,320	1,380	1,320	1,340	9	3.45
Montana	573	574	502	491	582	514	29	1.32
Nebraska.	90	146	[3]99	163	170	163	42	0.42
Nevada	2,621	3,060	3,170	2,780	[3]2,800	2,930	2	7.53
New Hampshire	36	50	[3]68	[3]64	[3]59	60	47	0.16
New Jersey	229	243	290	300	286	348	34	0.9
New Mexico	1,103	1,130	888	671	812	615	24	1.58
New York.	773	886	972	935	970	1,050	14	2.7
North Carolina	586	735	750	761	779	744	19	1.91
North Dakota	25	31	38	38	42	39	48	0.1
Ohio	733	891	1,030	1,040	1,060	1,070	12	2.74
Oklahoma	259	357	460	475	453	530	28	1.36
Oregon	205	239	301	303	[3]439	326	36	0.84
Pennsylvania	1,031	1,080	1,230	[3]1,270	[3]1,250	1,270	11	3.27
Rhode Island	18	31	[3]25	[3]25	24	28	49	0.07
South Carolina	450	447	562	574	560	531	27	1.36
South Dakota	319	332	258	226	260	255	38	0.66
Tennessee	663	665	705	710	770	708	21	1.82
Texas	1,459	1,680	1,820	1,780	2,050	2,210	3	5.68
Utah	1,335	1,850	1,320	1,260	[3]1,420	1,310	10	3.36
Vermont	87	60	[3]74	[3]83	43	69	46	0.18
Virginia	507	515	636	667	692	751	18	1.93
Washington	483	582	609	631	691	545	25	1.4
West Virginia	133	181	170	180	[3]182	185	40	0.48
Wisconsin	215	416	323	[3]334	349	368	32	0.95
Wyoming	911	973	1,070	956	922	986	15	2.53

X Not applicable. [1] Includes undistributed not shown separately. [2] Includes District of Columbia. [3] Partial data only; excludes values withheld to avoid disclosing individual company data.

Source: U.S. Geological Survey, *Minerals Yearbook,* annual, and *Mineral Commodities Summaries,* annual. See also <http://minerals.er.usgs.gov/minerals/pubs/mcs/2002/mcs2002.pdf> (released 25 January 2002).

U.S. Census Bureau, Statistical Abstract of the United States: 2002

No. 858. Principal Fuels, Nonmetals, and Metals—World Production and the U.S. Share: 1980 to 2000

Mineral	Unit	World production				Percent U.S. of world			
		1980	1990	1995	2000	1980	1990	1995	2000
Fuels: [1]									
Coal	Mil. sh. ton	4,193	5,386	5,218	5,059	19.8	19.1	20.0	21.7
Petroleum (crude)	Bil. bbl	21.8	22.1	22.8	24.9	14.4	12.2	10.5	8.9
Natural gas (dry, marketable).	Tril. cu. ft	53.5	73.6	78.0	88.0	36.3	24.2	23.9	21.2
Natural gas plant liquids	Bil. bbl	1.3	1.7	2.0	2.3	45.7	33.7	32.1	30.9
Nonmetals:									
Asbestos	1,000 metric tons.	4,699	4,003	2,420	1,900	2	(D)	(Z)	(Z)
Barite	1,000 metric tons.	7,495	5,633	4,300	5,700	27	8	13	11
Feldspar	1,000 metric tons.	3,202	5,456	6,780	9,100	20	12	13	9
Fluorspar	1,000 metric tons.	5,006	5,131	4,050	4,480	2	1	1	-
Gypsum.	Mil. metric tons	78	100	97	110	14	15	17	23
Mica (incl. scrap).	1,000 metric tons.	228	215	253	300	46	51	43	37
Nitrogen, (fixed) - ammonia. .	Mil. metric tons .	74	97	96	104	20	13	14	13
Phosphate rock, gross wt.. . . .	Mil. metric tons .	144	162	130	139	38	29	33	29
Potash (k_2O equivalent)	Mil. metric tons .	28	28	25	27	8	6	6	5
Sulfur, elemental	Mil. metric tons .	55	58	53	57	22	20	22	19
Metals, mine basis:									
Bauxite	Mil. metric tons .	89	109	107	127	2	(D)	(D)	(NA)
Columbian concentrates									
(Nb content)	1,000 metric tons.	15	15	18	24	-	-	-	-
Copper	1,000 metric tons.	7,405	9,017	10,100	12,900	16	18	18	11
Gold	Metric tons	1,219	2,133	2,220	2,445	2	14	14	14
Iron ore	Mil. metric tons .	891	982	1,027	1,010	8	6	6	6
Lead [2]	1,000 metric tons.	3,470	3,353	2,780	2,980	17	15	14	16
Mercury	Metric tons	6,806	4,523	3,160	1,800	16	12	(D)	(D)
Molybdenum.	1,000 metric tons.	111	128	141	112	62	48	43	29
Nickel [2]	1,000 metric tons.	779	965	1,030	1,230	2	(Z)	(Z)	(Z)
Silver	1,000 metric tons.	11	16	15	18	9	13	10	12
Tantalum concentrates	Metric tons	544	400	362	513	-	-	-	-
Titanium concentrates:									
Ilmenite	1,000 metric tons.	3,726	4,072	3,970	4,000	14	(D)	(D)	(NA)
Rutile.	1,000 metric tons.	436	481	416	410	(D)	(D)	(D)	(NA)
Tungsten [2]	1,000 metric tons.	52	43	39	32	5	14	-	-
Vanadium [2]	1,000 metric tons.	37	31	35	42	12	(D)	(D)	(D)
Zinc [2]	1,000 metric tons.	5,954	7,184	7,240	8,000	6	8	9	11
Metals, smelter basis:									
Aluminum.	1,000 metric tons.	15,383	19,292	19,900	23,900	30	21	17	16
Cadmium.	1,000 metric tons.	18	20	19	19	9	8	7	6
Copper	1,000 metric tons.	7,649	9,472	10,200	12,900	14	15	16	11
Iron, pig.	Mil. metric tons .	514	532	533	571	12	9	10	9
Lead [3]	1,000 metric tons.	5,430	5,763	5,590	2,980	23	23	25	16
Magnesium [4]	1,000 metric tons.	316	354	389	284	49	39	37	(NA)
Raw Steel	Mil. metric tons .	717	771	755	833	14	12	13	13
Tin [5]	1,000 metric tons.	251	223	201	200	1	-	-	-
Zinc	1,000 metric tons.	6,049	7,550	7,550	8,000	6	5	5	11

- Represents or rounds to zero. D Withheld to avoid disclosing company data. NA Not available. Z Less than half the unit of measure. [1] Source: Energy Information Administration, *International Energy Annual*. [2] Content of ore and concentrate. [3] Refinery production. [4] Primary production; no smelter processing necessary. [5] Production from primary sources only.

Source: Nonfuels, through 1990, U.S. Bureau of Mines, thereafter, U.S. Geological Survey, *Minerals Yearbook*, annual, and *Mineral Commodities Summaries*, annual; fuels, U.S. Energy Information Administration, *International Energy Annual*.

No. 859. Federal Strategic and Critical Materials Inventory: 1990 to 2000

[**As of Dec. 31.** Covers strategic and critical materials essential to military and industrial requirements in time of national emergency]

Mineral	Unit	Quantity [1]				Value (mil. dol.) [2]			
		1990	1995	1999	2000	1990	1995	1999	2000
Bauxite [3]	1,000 lg. ton . . .	18,033	16,032	9,492	6,267	888	203	71	49
Chromium [4]	1,000 sh. ton . . .	1,074	1,192	1,068	937	917	839	628	606
Cobalt	Mil. lb.	53	44	28	23	443	1,121	295	313
Diamonds: Stones . . .	Carat 1,000	7,777	5,135	2,497	1,509	267	52	25	15
Industrial, bort	Carat 1,000	17,353	1,967	-	-	16	9	-	-
Lead 1,000 sh. ton . .	(NA)	465	277	226	(NA)	263	140	103	-
Manganese [5]	1,000 sh. ton . . .	4,017	2,817	2,144	2,146	962	464	270	255
Palladium.	1,000 troy oz . . .	(NA)	1265	1,099	842	(NA)	143	343	326
Platinum	1,000 troy oz . . .	453	453	342	217	186	154	120	84
Silver	1,000 troy oz . . .	92,151	46,667	26,203	15,942	374	158	86	61
Tantalum Group	1,000 lb	(NA)	3031	2,689	2,282	(NA)	127	126	94
Tin	1,000 metric ton .	169	130	72	60	962	908	391	323
Titanium	1,000 sh. ton . . .	37	37	35	30	402	221	124	96
Tungsten [6]	Mil. lb	82	82	79	74	253	253	174	156
Zinc	1,000 sh. ton . . .	379	301	198	151	483	281	203	152

- Represents or rounds to zero. NA Not available. [1] Consists of stockpile and nonstockpile grades and reflects uncommitted balances. [2] Market values are estimated trade values of similar materials and not necessarily amounts that would be realized at time of sale. [3] Consists of abrasive grade, metallic grade Jamaica, metallic grade Suriname, and refractory. [4] Consists of ferro-high carbon, ferro-low carbon, ferro-silicon, and metal. [5] Consists of chemical grade, dioxide battery natural, dioxide battery synthetic, electrolytic, ferro-high carbon, ferro-med. carbon, ferro-silicon, and metal. [6] Consists of carbide powder, ferro, metal powder, and ores and concentrates.

Source: U.S. Defense Logistics Agency, *Statistical Supplement, Stockpile Report to the Congress* (AP-3).

Natural Resources 553

No. 860. Net U.S. Imports of Selected Minerals and Metals as Percent of Apparent Consumption: 1980 to 2001

[In percent. Based on net imports which equal the difference between imports and exports plus or minus Government stockpile and industry stock changes]

Minerals in rank of dependency	1980	1990	1995	1996	1997	1998	1999	2000	2001
Bauxite [1]	94	98	99	100	100	100	100	100	100
Columbium	100	100	100	100	100	100	100	100	100
Manganese	98	100	100	100	100	100	100	100	100
Mica (sheet)	100	100	100	100	100	100	100	100	100
Strontium	100	100	100	100	100	100	100	100	100
Vanadium	35	(D)	84	(D)	(D)	78	80	(NA)	100
Tin	79	71	84	83	86	85	85	86	88
Barite	44	71	65	70	76	80	67	71	87
Potash	65	68	75	77	80	80	80	70	80
Tantalum	90	71	80	80	75	80	80	80	80
Chromium	91	84	80	79	75	80	80	78	78
Cobalt	93	86	79	76	76	73	73	74	78
Zinc [2]	60	41	35	33	35	35	30	60	60
Tungsten	53	81	90	89	84	77	81	68	59
Nickel	76	64	60	59	56	64	63	58	56
Silver	7	(NA)	(NA)	(NA)	([3])	14	14	52	44
Aluminum	([3])	36	23	22	23	27	30	33	35
Copper	16	15	27	14	13	14	27	37	31
Gypsum	35	46	30	29	28	28	29	22	25
Iron and steel	13	13	21	20	20	27	22	17	15
Iron ore	25	3	14	14	14	12	17	19	15
Sulfur	14	21	21	13	13	18	17	22	12
Cadmium	55	([3])	23	32	16	20	19	6	3
Mercury	27	(D)	(NA)	(NA)	(D)	(NA)	(NA)	(NA)	(NA)
Platinum group	87	88	(NA)	(NA)	(NA)	(NA)	(NA)	(NA)	(NA)
Selenium	59	46	31	38	(D)	(D)	(D)	(NA)	(NA)

D Withheld to avoid disclosure.   NA Not available.   [1] Includes alumina.   [2] Beginning 1990, effect of sharp rise in exports of concentrates. If calculated on a refined zinc-only basis, reliance would be about the same as pre-1990 level; 1990, 64 percent; 1991, 61 percent; 1992, 61 percent; 1993, 67 percent; 1994, 70 percent; 1995, 71 percent; 1996 and 1997, 70 percent; 1998, 69 percent; and 1999, 71 percent.   [3] Net exports.

Source: Through 1994, U.S. Bureau of Mines; thereafter, U.S. Geological Survey, *Mineral Commodity Summaries;* import and export data from U.S. Census Bureau.

No. 861. Federal Offshore Leasing, Exploration, Production, and Revenue: 1990 to 2001

[See source for explanation of terms and for reliability statement]

Item	Unit	1990	1995	1996	1997	1998	1999	2000	2001
Tracts offered	Number	10,459	10,995	12,230	9,870	8,205	7,453	7,992	8,790
Tracts leased	Number	825	835	1,537	1,780	1,157	333	553	942
Acres offered	Millions	56.79	59.70	70.00	26.24	44.10	40.22	42.89	49.15
Acres leased	Millions	4.30	4.34	8.15	9.62	6.34	1.77	2.92	5.00
Bonus paid for leased tracts	Bil. dol.	0.6	0.4	0.9	(NA)	1.3	0.3	0.3	1.0
New wells being drilled:									
Active	Number	120	124	835	186	173	219	224	213
Suspended	Number	266	247	1,323	244	122	110	146	97
Cumulative wells (since 1953):									
Wells completed	Number	13,167	13,475	13,583	13,546	13,702	13,676	13,718	13,921
Wells plugged and abandoned	Number	14,677	18,008	18,268	18,728	21,050	22,115	22,814	24,218
Revenue, total [1]	Bil. dol.	3.4	2.7	4.3	5.3	4.3	3.2	5.2	[4]5.8
Bonuses	Bil. dol.	0.8	0.4	0.8	1.4	1.3	0.2	0.4	[4]0.5
Oil and gas royalties [1]	Bil. dol.	2.6	2.1	3.1	3.4	2.7	2.6	4.1	[4]4.75
Rentals	Bil. dol.	0.09	0.09	0.16	0.23	0.26	0.21	0.21	[4]0.13
Sales value [2]	Bil. dol.	17.0	13.8	19.8	22.3	17.6	17.4	27.4	[4]31.4
Oil	Bil. dol.	7.0	6.3	8.0	9.0	6.2	6.5	11.5	[4]11.3
Natural gas	Bil. dol.	9.5	7.5	11.8	13.3	11.4	10.9	15.9	[4]20.1
Sales volume: [3]									
Oil	Mil. bbls.	324	409	438	479	477	513	566	[4]463
Natural gas	Bil. cu. ft	5,093	4,692	5,024	5,077	4,836	4,992	4,723	[4]3,470

NA Not available.   [1] Includes condensate royalties.   [2] Production value is value at time of production, not current value.   [3] Excludes sales volumes for gas lost, gas plant products or sulfur.   [4] Covers January through September 2001 only.

Source: U.S. Dept. of the Interior, Minerals Management Service, *Federal Offshore Statistics,* annual.

No. 862. Petroleum Industry—Summary: 1980 to 2001

[Includes all costs incurred for drilling and equipping wells to point of completion as productive wells or abandonment after drilling becomes unproductive. Based on sample of operators of different size drilling establishments]

Item	Unit	1980	1990	1995	1996	1997	1998	1999	2000	2001
Crude oil producing wells (Dec. 31).	1,000...	548	602	574	574	573	562	546	534	(NA)
Daily output per well	Bbl.....	15.9	12.2	11.4	11.3	11.3	11.1	10.8	10.9	(NA)
Completed wells drilled, total	1,000...	57.73	31.56	21.06	22.90	27.47	24.08	18.18	25.14	(NA)
Crude oil.	1,000...	30.88	12.20	7.63	8.31	10.44	7.06	4.09	4.73	(NA)
Gas	1,000...	15.25	11.04	8.35	9.30	11.33	12.11	10.51	15.21	(NA)
Dry	1,000...	11.60	8.31	5.08	5.28	5.70	4.91	3.58	5.20	(NA)
Average depth per well [1]	Feet ..	4,171	4,871	5,596	5,636	5,704	6,213	5,944	6,516	(NA)
Average cost per well [1]	$1,000..	368	384	513	496	604	769	856	(NA)	(NA)
Average cost per foot [1]	Dollars..	77.02	76.07	87.22	88.92	107.83	128.97	152.02	(NA)	(NA)
Crude oil production, total	Mil. bbl..	3,138	2,685	2,394	2,360	2,355	2,282	2,141	2,139	2,118
Value at wells	Bil. dol..	67.7	53.8	35.0	43.6	40.6	24.8	33.3	57.2	46.3
Average price per barrel	Dollars..	21.59	20.03	14.62	18.46	17.23	10.87	15.56	26.72	21.84
Lower 48 states	Mil. bbl..	2,548	2,037	1,853	1,851	1,882	1,853	1,764	1,775	1,766
Alaska	Mil. bbl..	590	647	542	508	473	429	383	354	351
Onshore	Mil. bbl..	2,760	2,290	1,838	1,789	1,753	1,664	1,508	1,494	(NA)
Offshore	Mil. bbl..	377	395	557	570	602	618	639	635	(NA)
Imports: Crude oil	Mil. bbl..	1,921	2,151	2,639	2,740	3,002	3,178	3,187	3,260	3,405
Refined petroleum products	Mil. bbl..	601	775	586	719	707	731	775	789	636
Exports: Crude oil	Mil. bbl..	104.8	39.8	34.7	40.2	39.4	40.2	43.1	18.3	7.4
Proved reserves	Bil. bbl..	29.8	26.3	22.4	22.0	22.5	21.0	21.8	22.0	(NA)
Operable refineries.	Number .	319	205	175	170	164	163	159	158	(NA)
Capacity (Jan. 1)	Mil. bbl..	6,566	5,683	5,632	5,595	5,639	5,734	5,935	6,026	(NA)
Refinery input, total.	Mil. bbl..	5,117	5,325	5,555	5,654	5,807	5,891	5,877	5,950	(NA)
Crude oil	Mil. bbl..	4,920	4,895	5,099	5,179	5,351	5,435	5,402	5,504	(NA)
Natural gas plant liquids.....	Mil. bbl..	168	172	172	164	153	146	135	135	(NA)
Other liquids	Mil. bbl..	29	259	285	307	303	310	339	310	(NA)
Refinery output, total.	Mil. bbl..	5,336	5,574	5,836	5,957	6,117	6,216	6,201	6,296	(NA)
Motor gasoline	Mil. bbl..	2,369	2,540	2,723	2,759	2,825	2,880	2,894	2,902	(NA)
Jet fuel	Mil. bbl..	365	544	518	555	566	558	573	588	(NA)
Distillate fuel oil	Mil. bbl..	971	1,066	1,153	1,212	1,237	1,248	1,241	1,307	(NA)
Residual fuel oil	Mil. bbl..	577	347	288	266	259	277	256	259	(NA)
Liquefied petroleum gases ...	Mil. bbl..	120	183	237	241	252	245	248	256	(NA)
Utilization rate	Percent .	75.4	87.1	92.0	94.1	95.2	95.6	92.6	92.6	(NA)

NA Not available.   [1] Source: American Petroleum Institute, *Joint Association Survey on Drilling Costs,* annual.
Source: Except as noted, U.S. Energy Information Administration, *Annual Energy Review, Petroleum Supply Annual; U.S. Crude Oil, Natural Gas,* and *Natural Gas Liquids Reserves*; and *Monthly Energy Review.*

No. 863. U.S. Petroleum Balance: 1980 to 2001

[In millions of barrels (6,242 represents 6,242,000,000)]

Item	1980	1990	1995	1996	1997	1998	1999	2000	2001
Petroleum products supplied for domestic use	**6,242**	**6,201**	**7,087**	**6,701**	**6,796**	**6,905**	**7,125**	**7,211**	**7,172**
Production of products	5,765	5,934	6,940	6,511	6,671	6,733	6,774	6,903	6,942
Crude input to refineries	4,934	4,894	5,718	5,195	5,351	5,434	5,403	5,514	5,522
Oil, field production...............	3,138	2,685	2,406	2,366	2,355	2,282	2,147	2,131	2,118
Alaska.......................	592	647	542	510	473	429	383	355	351
Lower 48 States	2,555	2,037	1,853	1,856	1,882	1,853	1,764	1,776	1,766
Net imports	1,821	2,112	2,604	2,708	2,963	3,137	3,144	3,301	3,398
Imports (gross excluding SPR) [1]	1,910	2,142	2,639	2,748	3,002	3,178	3,184	3,317	3,401
SPR [1] imports	16	10	-	-	-	-	3	3	4
Exports	-105	40	35	40	39	40	43	18	7
Other sources	33	98	102	122	34	15	113	82	7
Natural gas liquids (NGL), supply	577	574	708	716	721	717	757	799	801
Other liquids	253	465	514	599	599	582	614	589	619
Net imports of refined products	484	326	101	181	154	225	252	305	303
Imports	578	598	407	491	469	508	537	648	636
Exports	94	272	307	310	315	283	284	343	333
Stock withdrawal, refined products	-7	-59	46	9	-29	-53	98	2	-73
TYPE OF PRODUCT SUPPLIED									
Total products supplied for domestic use	**6,242**	**6,201**	**6,469**	**6,701**	**6,796**	**6,905**	**7,125**	**7,211**	**7,172**
Finished motor gasoline	2,407	2,641	2,843	2,888	2,926	3,012	3,077	3,101	3,143
Distillate fuel oil.	1,049	1,103	1,170	1,232	1,254	1,263	1,304	1,362	1,404
Residual fuel oil	918	449	311	311	291	324	303	333	296
Liquefied petroleum gases [2].	414	568	693	736	744	713	801	816	746
Other	1,454	1,440	1,452	1,535	1,582	1,593	1,639	1,598	1,583
ENDING STOCKS									
Ending stocks, all oils	**1,392**	**1,621**	**1,563**	**1,052**	**1,560**	**1,647**	**1,493**	**1,468**	**1,586**
Crude oil and lease condensate.	358	323	303	284	305	324	284	286	312
Strategic Petroleum Reserve (SPR) [1]	108	586	592	566	563	571	567	541	550
Other	926	712	668	202	692	752	641	641	724

- Represents zero.   [1] SPR=Strategic petroleum reserve. For more information, see Table 889.   [2] Includes ethane.
Source: U.S. Energy Information Administration, *Petroleum Supply Annual,* Volume 1. See also <http://www.eia.doe.gov/pub/oilgas/petroleum/datapublications/petroleumsupplyannual/psavolume1/current/pdf/volume1all.pdf> (released June 2002).

Natural Resources   **555**

No. 864. Crude Petroleum and Natural Gas—Production and Value by Major Producing States: 1990 to 2000

[2,685 mil. bbl. represents 2,685,000,000 bbl. or 18,594 bil. cu. ft. represents 18,594,000,000,000 cu. ft.]

State	Crude petroleum Quantity (mil. bbl.) 1990	1999	2000	Value (mil. dol.) 1990	1999	2000	Natural gas marketed production [1] Quantity (bil. cu. ft.) 1990	1999	2000	Value (mil. dol.) 1990	1999	2000
Total [2]	2,685	2,141	2,131	53,772	33,311	56,932	18,594	19,805	20,002	31,658	43,325	73,620
AL	18	11	10	387	186	289	135	547	523	373	1,263	2,087
AK	658	383	355	10,086	4,829	8,439	403	463	459	554	635	807
AR	10	7	7	222	113	193	175	170	172	360	697	898
CA	322	268	271	5,732	3,772	6,729	363	383	377	857	905	1,812
CO	31	19	18	722	333	533	243	739	753	377	1,436	2,765
FL	6	5	5	(NA)	(NA)	(NA)	6	6	6	15	(NA)	(NA)
IL	20	12	12	467	210	343	1	-	-	1	(NA)	(NA)
IN	3	2	2	73	34	59	(Z)	1	1	1	2	3
KS	59	33	34	1,359	567	970	574	553	526	893	998	1,690
KY	5	3	3	124	46	92	75	77	82	169	159	258
LA	148	110	105	3,409	1,951	3,060	5,242	5,314	5,069	9,587	11,649	18,642
MI	20	8	8	458	130	222	140	277	297	420	491	724
MS	30	19	20	630	299	520	95	111	89	167	181	293
MT	20	15	15	429	253	429	50	61	70	90	103	198
NE	5	3	3	119	46	83	1	1	1	2	2	3
NM	66	66	67	1,472	1,146	1,935	965	1,512	1,687	1,629	3,191	5,790
NY	(Z)	-	-	9	4	6	25	16	18	55	35	67
ND	39	33	33	849	549	922	52	53	52	93	123	206
OH	8	6	7	196	98	181	155	110	105	393	346	426
OK	117	71	70	2,690	1,265	2,035	2,258	1,571	1,613	3,548	3,223	5,857
PA	2	2	2	54	28	43	178	175	201	417	(NA)	(NA)
TX	674	449	443	15,060	7,769	12,681	6,343	6,118	6,205	9,939	14,106	24,384
UT	23	16	16	524	290	446	146	263	269	249	506	883
WV	2	1	1	43	23	38	178	176	264	568	(NA)	(NA)
WY	103	62	61	2,169	1,014	1,633	736	823	1,088	856	1,621	3,640
Federal offshore . .	296	534	558	6,468	8,699	28,420	(NA)	(NA)	(NA)	(NA)	(NA)	(NA)

- Represents zero.   NA Not available.   Z Less than 500,000 barrels, 500 million cubic feet, or less than $500,000.
[1] Excludes nonhydrocarbon gases.   [2] Includes other states not shown separately. State production does not include state offshore production.

Source: U.S. Energy Information Administration, *Petroleum Supply Annual* and *Petroleum Marketing Annual*; and *Natural Gas Annual*, and *Natural Gas Monthly*.

No. 865. Crude Oil, Natural Gas, and Natural Gas Liquids—Reserves by State: 1990 and 2000

[26,254 mil. bbl. represents 26,254,000,000 bbl. As of December 31. Proved reserves are estimated quantities of the mineral, which geological and engineering data demonstrate with reasonable certainty, to be recoverable in future years from known reservoirs under existing economic and operating conditions. Indicated reserves of crude oil are quantities other than proved reserves, which may become economically recoverable from existing productive reservoirs through the application of improved recovery techniques using current technology. Based on a sample of operators of oil and gas wells]

Area	1990 Crude oil Proved (mil. bbl.)	Indicated (mil. bbl.)	Natural gas (bil. cu. ft.)	Natural gas liquids (mil. bbl.)	2000 Crude oil Proved (mil. bbl.)	Indicated (mil. bbl.)	Natural gas (bil. cu. ft.)	Natural gas liquids (mil. bbl.)
United States [1]	26,254	3,483	169,346	7,586	22,045	(NA)	177,427	8,345
Lower 48 States	19,730	2,514	160,046	7,246	17,184	(NA)	168,190	8,068
Alabama	44	(Z)	[1]4,125	170	34	(NA)	4,149	150
Alaska	6,524	969	9,300	340	4,861	(NA)	9,237	277
Arkansas	60	1	1,731	9	48	(NA)	1,581	5
California	[2]4,658	[2]1,425	[2]3,185	[2]105	3,813	(NA)	2,849	101
Colorado.	305	8	4,555	169	217	(NA)	10,428	316
Florida	(NA)	(NA)	(NA)	(NA)	76	(NA)	82	11
Illinois	(NA)	(NA)	(NA)	(NA)	111	(NA)	(NA)	(NA)
Indiana	131	-	(NA)	(NA)	15	(NA)	(NA)	(NA)
Kansas.	(NA)	(NA)	(NA)	(NA)	237	(NA)	5,299	306
Kentucky	321	(Z)	9,614	313	24	(NA)	1,760	56
Louisiana	33	-	1,016	25	529	(NA)	9,239	436
Michigan.	(NA)	(NA)	(NA)	(NA)	56	(NA)	2,729	35
Mississippi	(NA)	(NA)	(NA)	(NA)	182	(NA)	618	8
Montana	(NA)	(NA)	(NA)	(NA)	235	(NA)	885	4
Nebraska	221	-	899	15	18	(NA)	(NA)	(NA)
New Mexico	(NA)	(NA)	(NA)	(NA)	719	(NA)	17,322	896
New York	687	256	17,260	990	(NA)	(NA)	322	(NA)
North Dakota.	285	-	586	60	270	(NA)	433	54
Ohio	65	-	1,214	(NA)	59	(NA)	1,185	(NA)
Oklahoma.	734	37	16,151	657	610	(NA)	13,699	734
Pennsylvania.	22	-	1,720	(NA)	15	(NA)	1,741	(NA)
Texas.	[2]7,106	618	[2]38,192	[2]2,575	5,273	426	42,082	2,819
Utah	249	44	1,510	[3]	283	(NA)	4,235	[3]
Virginia	(NA)	(NA)	138	(NA)	(NA)	(NA)	1,704	(NA)
West Virginia	31	-	2,207	86	12	(NA)	2,900	105
Wyoming	794	42	9,944	[4]812	561	(NA)	16,158	[4]947
Federal offshore.	2,805	49	31,433	619	3,770	(NA)	26,748	1,078

- Represents or rounds to zero.   NA Not available.   Z Less than 500,000 barrels.   [1] Includes miscellaneous not shown separately.   [2] Excludes federal offshore.   [3] Included with Wyoming.   [4] Includes Utah.

Source: Energy Information Administration, *U.S. Crude Oil, Natural Gas, and Natural Gas Liquids Reserves, 2000 Annual Report*, December 2001.

No. 866. World Daily Crude Oil Production by Major Producing Country: 1980 to 2000

[In thousands of barrels per day (59,600 barrels represents 59,600,000 barrels]

Country	1980	1990	1994	1995	1996	1997	1998	1999	2000
World, total [1]	59,600	60,566	60,991	62,335	63,711	65,690	66,921	65,848	68,103
Saudi Arabia	9,900	6,410	8,120	8,231	8,218	8,362	8,389	7,833	8,404
Russia	(X)	(X)	6,135	5,995	5,850	5,920	5,854	6,079	6,479
United States	**8,597**	**7,355**	**6,662**	**6,560**	**6,465**	**6,452**	**6,252**	**5,881**	**5,822**
Iran	1,662	3,088	3,618	3,643	3,686	3,664	3,634	3,557	3,696
China.	2,114	2,774	2,939	2,990	3,131	3,200	3,198	3,195	3,249
Norway.	528	1,704	2,521	2,768	3,104	3,143	3,017	3,018	3,197
Mexico	1,936	2,553	2,685	2,618	2,855	3,023	3,070	2,906	3,012
Venezuela.	2,168	2,137	2,588	2,750	2,938	3,280	3,167	2,826	2,949
Iraq	2,514	2,040	553	560	579	1,155	2,150	2,508	2,571
United Arab Emirates	1,709	2,117	2,193	2,233	2,278	2,316	2,345	2,169	2,368
United Kingdom	1,622	1,820	2,375	2,489	2,568	2,518	2,616	2,684	2,275
Nigeria	2,055	1,810	1,931	1,993	2,001	2,132	2,153	2,130	2,144
Kuwait	1,656	1,175	2,025	2,057	2,062	2,007	2,085	1,898	2,126
Canada	1,435	1,553	1,746	1,805	1,837	1,922	1,981	1,907	1,977
Indonesia	1,577	1,462	1,510	1,503	1,547	1,520	1,518	1,472	1,423
Libya	1,787	1,375	1,378	1,390	1,401	1,446	1,390	1,319	1,410
Brazil	182	631	671	695	795	841	969	1,132	1,269
Algeria	1,106	1,175	1,180	1,202	1,242	1,277	1,246	1,202	1,244
Oman	282	685	810	851	883	904	900	910	940
Argentina	491	483	650	715	756	834	847	802	761
Egypt.	595	873	896	920	922	856	834	852	748
Angola	150	475	536	646	709	714	735	745	746
Qatar	472	406	415	442	510	550	696	665	737
Australia	380	575	536	562	570	588	544	539	722
Colombia	126	440	450	585	623	652	733	816	691
Malaysia.	283	619	645	682	695	700	720	693	690
India	182	660	590	703	651	675	661	653	646
Kazakhstan	(X)	(X)	352	362	403	466	476	530	599
Syria	164	388	560	575	582	561	553	538	523
Yemen	-	193	335	345	340	362	388	409	440

- Represents or rounds to zero.   X Not applicable.   [1] Includes countries not shown separately.

Source: U.S. Energy Information Administration, *International Energy Annual, 2000.* See also <http://www.eia.doe.gov/pub/pdf/international/021900.pdf> (issued May 2002).

No. 867. Liquefied Petroleum Gases—Summary: 1980 to 2001

[In millions of 42-gallon barrels (561 barrels represents 561,000,000 barrels). Includes ethane]

Item	1980	1990	1995	1996	1997	1998	1999	2000	2001
Production	**561**	**638**	**760**	**789**	**799**	**775**	**814**	**845**	**813**
At natural gas plants	441	456	521	547	547	529	564	587	570
At refineries	121	182	234	242	252	246	250	258	243
Imports	79	68	53	61	62	71	66	79	75
Refinery input.	85	107	105	102	96	92	87	87	88
Exports	9	14	21	19	18	15	18	27	16
Stocks, Dec. 31	116	98	93	86	89	115	89	83	121

Source: U.S. Energy Information Administration, *Petroleum Supply Annual,* volume 1.

No. 868. Natural Gas Plant Liquids—Production and Value: 1980 to 2000

[Barrels of 42 gallons (576 barrels represents 576,000,000 barrels)]

Item	Unit	1980	1990	1994	1995	1996	1997	1998	1999	2000
Field production [1]	Mil. bbl . . .	576	566	630	643	670	663	642	675	699
Pentanes plus	Mil. bbl . . .	126	112	119	122	123	116	113	111	112
Liquefied petroleum gases .	Mil. bbl . . .	441	454	511	521	547	547	529	564	587
Natural gas processed	Tril. cu. ft. .	15	15	16	17	17	17	17	17	17

[1] Includes other finished petroleum products, not shown separately.

Source: U.S. Energy Information Administration, *Petroleum Supply Annual* and *Natural Gas Annual.*

Natural Resources   557

No. 869. Natural Gas—Supply, Consumption, Reserves, and Marketed Production: 1980 to 2000

[182 represents 182,000 wells]

Item	Unit	1980	1990	1994	1995	1996	1997	1998	1999	2000
Producing wells (year-end)......	1,000.....	182	269	292	299	302	311	317	302	306
Production value at wells.......	Bil. dol....	32.1	31.8	36.5	30.2	43.0	46.1	38.2	43.4	73.6
Avg. per 1,000 cu. ft	Dollars...	1.59	1.71	1.85	1.55	2.17	2.32	1.96	2.19	3.68
Proved reserves [1]	Tril. cu. ft ..	199	169	164	165	166	167	164	167	177
Marketed production [2]	**Bil. cu. ft..**	**20,180**	**18,594**	**19,710**	**19,506**	**19,812**	**19,866**	**19,961**	**19,805**	**20,002**
Minus: Extraction losses [3]	Bil. cu. ft...	777	784	889	908	958	964	938	973	1,016
Equals: Dry production	Bil. cu. ft..	19,403	17,810	18,821	18,599	18,854	18,902	19,024	18,832	18,987
Plus: Supplemental gas supplies..	Bil. cu. ft..	155	123	111	110	109	103	102	99	86
Equals: Dry production with supplemental gas	Bil. cu. ft...	19,558	17,932	18,932	18,709	18,964	19,005	19,126	18,931	19,073
Plus: Withdrawals from storage...	Bil. cu. ft..	1,972	1,986	2,579	3,025	2,981	2,894	2,432	2,808	3,550
Plus: Imports [4]	Bil. cu. ft..	985	1,532	2,624	2,841	2,937	2,994	3,152	3,586	3,782
Plus: Balancing item..........	Bil. cu. ft..	-640	-152	-416	-230	217	61	-334	-897	-827
Equals: Total supply	Bil. cu. ft...	21,875	21,299	23,719	24,345	25,099	24,954	24,376	24,427	25,577
Minus: Exports.......... [5]	Bil. cu. ft..	49	86	162	154	153	157	159	163	244
Minus: Additions to storage [5]	Bil. cu. ft..	1,949	2,499	2,865	2,610	2,979	2,870	2,961	2,636	2,721
Equals: Consumption, total	**Bil. cu. ft ..**	**19,877**	**18,715**	**20,708**	**21,581**	**21,967**	**21,959**	**21,277**	**21,620**	**22,547**
Lease and plant fuel..	Bil. cu. ft..	1,026	1,236	1,124	1,220	1,250	1,203	1,173	1,079	1,130
Pipeline fuel..........	Bil. cu. ft..	635	660	685	700	711	751	635	645	644
Residential.	Bil. cu. ft..	4,752	4,391	4,848	4,850	5,241	4,984	4,520	4,726	4,992
Commercial [6]	Bil. cu. ft..	2,611	2,623	2,895	3,031	3,158	3,215	2,999	3,045	3,218
Industrial..........	Bil. cu. ft..	7,172	7,018	8,167	8,580	8,870	8,832	8,686	9,006	9,512
Vehicle fuel	Bil. cu. ft..	(NA)	-	2	3	3	4	5	6	8
Electric utilities	Bil. cu. ft..	3,682	2,786	2,987	3,197	2,732	2,968	3,258	3,113	3,043
World production (dry)..	Tril. cu. ft ..	53.5	73.6	76.9	78.0	81.7	81.5	83.0	84.9	88.0
U.S. production (dry)........	Tril. cu. ft ..	19.4	17.8	18.8	18.6	18.9	18.9	19.0	18.8	19.0
Percent U.S. of world......	Percent ...	36.3	24.2	24.5	23.9	23.1	23.2	22.9	22.2	21.6

- Represents zero.   NA Not available.   [1] Estimated, end of year. Source: U.S. Energy Information Administration, *U.S. Crude Oil, Natural Gas,* and *Natural Gas Liquids Reserves,* annual.   [2] Marketed production includes gross withdrawals from reservoirs less quantities used for reservoir repressuring and quantities vented or flared. For 1980 and thereafter, it excludes the nonhydrocarbon gases subsequently removed.   [3] Volumetric reduction in natural gas resulting from the extraction of natural gas constituents at natural gas processing plants.   [4] Includes imports of liquefied natural gas.   [5] Includes liquefied natural gas (LNG) storage in above ground tanks.   [6] Includes deliveries to municipalities and public authorities for institutional heating and other purposes.

Source: Except as noted, U.S. Energy Information Administration, *Annual Energy Review, International Energy Annual, Natural Gas Annual,* Volume I and II, and *Monthly Energy Review.*

No. 870. World Natural Gas Production by Major Producing Country: 1980 to 2000

[In trillion cubic feet (53.35 represents 53,350,000,000,000]

Country	1980	1990	1994	1995	1996	1997	1998	1999	2000
World, total [1]	**53.35**	**73.57**	**76.93**	**77.96**	**81.65**	**81.52**	**83.03**	**84.91**	**88.03**
Russia	(X)	(X)	21.45	21.01	21.23	20.17	20.87	20.83	20.63
United States	**19.40**	**17.81**	**18.82**	**18.60**	**18.85**	**18.90**	**19.02**	**18.83**	**18.99**
Canada	2.76	3.85	5.27	5.60	5.71	5.76	5.98	6.26	6.47
United Kingdom	1.32	1.75	2.47	2.67	3.18	3.03	3.14	3.49	3.83
Algeria	0.41	1.79	1.81	2.05	2.19	2.43	2.60	2.88	2.94
Netherlands	3.40	2.69	2.95	2.98	3.37	2.99	2.84	2.67	2.57
Indonesia	0.63	1.53	2.21	2.24	2.35	2.37	2.27	2.51	2.36
Iran	0.25	0.84	1.12	1.25	1.42	1.66	1.77	2.04	2.13
Uzbekistan	(X)	(X)	1.67	1.70	1.70	1.74	1.94	1.96	1.99
Norway	0.92	0.98	1.04	1.08	1.45	1.62	1.63	1.76	1.81
Saudi Arabia	0.33	1.08	1.33	1.34	1.46	1.60	1.65	1.63	1.76
Turkmenistan	-	-	1.26	1.14	1.31	0.90	0.47	0.79	1.64
Malaysia	0.06	0.65	0.92	1.02	1.23	1.36	1.37	1.42	1.50
United Arab Emirates	0.20	0.78	0.91	1.11	1.19	1.28	1.31	1.34	1.41
Mexico	0.90	0.90	0.97	0.96	1.06	1.17	1.27	1.29	1.33
Argentina	0.28	0.63	0.79	0.88	0.94	0.97	1.04	1.22	1.32
Australia	0.31	0.72	0.93	1.03	1.06	1.06	1.10	1.10	1.12
Qatar	0.18	0.28	0.48	0.48	0.48	0.61	0.69	0.78	1.03
Venezuela	0.52	0.76	0.88	0.89	0.96	0.99	1.11	0.95	0.96
China	0.51	0.51	0.59	0.60	0.67	0.75	0.78	0.85	0.96
Pakistan	0.29	0.48	0.63	0.65	0.70	0.70	0.71	0.78	0.86
India	0.05	0.40	0.59	0.63	0.70	0.72	0.76	0.75	0.79
Germany	-	-	0.70	0.74	0.80	0.79	0.77	0.82	0.78
Thailand	-	0.21	0.34	0.37	0.43	0.54	0.57	0.63	0.66
Egypt	0.03	0.29	0.42	0.44	0.47	0.48	0.49	0.52	0.65
Ukraine	(X)	(X)	0.64	0.62	0.64	0.64	0.64	0.63	0.64
Italy	0.44	0.61	0.73	0.72	0.71	0.00	0.67	0.62	0.67
Romania	1.20	1.00	0.69	0.68	0.63	0.61	0.52	0.50	0.50
Trinidad and Tobago	0.08	0.18	0.25	0.27	0.30	0.33	0.33	0.41	0.49
Nigeria	0.04	0.13	0.16	0.18	0.19	0.21	0.21	0.25	0.44

- Represents zero.   X Not applicable.   [1] Includes countries not shown separately.

Source: U.S. Energy Information Administration, *International Energy Annual, 2000.* See also <http://www.eia.doe.gov/pub/pdf/international/021900.pdf> (issued May 2002).

No. 871. Coal and Coke—Summary: 1980 to 2000

[830 short tons represents 830,000,000 short tons. Includes coal consumed at mines. Demonstrated coal reserve base for United States on Jan. 1, 1997, was an estimated 508 billion tons. Recoverability varies between 40 and 90 percent for individual deposits; 50 percent or more of overall U.S. coal reserve base is believed to be recoverable]

Item	Unit	1980	1990	1995	1996	1997	1998	1999	2000
COAL									
Coal production, total [1] . . .	Mil. sh. tons . .	830	1,029	1,033	1,064	1,090	1,118	1,100	1,074
Value	Bil. dol.	20.45	22.39	19.45	19.68	19.77	19.75	19.42	18.02
Anthracite production	Mil. sh. tons . . .	6.1	3.5	4.7	4.8	4.7	5.3	4.8	4.6
Bituminous coal and lignite.	Mil. sh. tons . . .	824	1,026	1,028	1,059	1,085	1,112	1,096	1,069
Underground	Mil. sh. tons . . .	337	425	396	410	421	417	392	374
Surface	Mil. sh. tons . . .	487	605	637	654	669	700	709	700
Exports	Mil. sh. tons . . .	92	105.804	89	90	84	78	59	59
Imports.	Mil. sh. tons . . .	1	3	9	8	8	9	9	13
Consumption [2]	Mil. sh. tons . . .	703	896	941	1,006	1,030	1,038	1,045	1,081
Electric power utilities	Mil. sh. tons . . .	569	774	829	875	900	911	894	859
Industrial.	Mil. sh. tons . . .	126	115	106	103	102	96	94	94
Number of mines	Number.	5,598	3,243	2,104	1,903	1,828	1,726	1,591	707
Daily employment.	1,000	225	131	90	83	82	85	79	72
Production, by state:									
Alabama	Mil. sh. tons . . .	26	29	25	25	24	23	20	19
Illinois.	Mil. sh. tons . . .	63	60	48	47	41	40	40	33
Indiana	Mil. sh. tons . . .	31	36	26	30	35	37	34	28
Kentucky	Mil. sh. tons . . .	150	173	154	152	156	150	140	131
Montana	Mil. sh. tons . . .	30	38	39	38	41	43	41	38
Ohio.	Mil. sh. tons . . .	39	35	26	29	29	28	22	22
Pennsylvania	Mil. sh. tons . . .	93	71	62	68	76	81	76	75
Virginia	Mil. sh. tons . . .	41	47	34	36	36	34	32	33
West Virginia	Mil. sh. tons . . .	122	169	163	170	174	171	158	158
Wyoming.	Mil. sh. tons . . .	95	184	264	278	282	314	337	339
Other States	Mil. sh. tons . . .	140	187	192	192	195	196	200	197
World production	Mil. sh. tons . . .	4,200	5,386	5,218	5,265	5,278	5,169	5,053	5,059
Percent U.S. of world.	Percent	19.8	19.1	19.8	20.2	20.6	21.6	21.8	21.2
COKE									
Coke production [3]	Mil. sh. tons . . .	46.13	27.62	23.75	23.08	22.12	20.04	20.02	20.81
Imports.	Mil. sh. tons . . .	0.66	0.77	3.82	2.54	3.14	3.83	3.22	3.78
Exports	Mil. sh. tons . . .	2.07	0.57	1.36	1.62	1.27	1.13	0.90	1.15
Consumption	Mil. sh. tons . . .	41.28	27.82	25.85	23.97	24.02	23.11	22.42	23.24

[1] Includes bituminous coal, subbituminous coal, lignite, and anthracite.   [2] Includes some categories not shown separately.   [3] Includes beehive coke.

Source: U.S. Energy Information Administration, *Coal Industry,* annual; *Annual Energy Review, International Energy Annual,* and *Quarterly Coal Report.* See also <ftp://ftp.eia.doe.gov/pub/pdf/coal.nuclear/05842000.pdf> (issued June 2002).

No. 872. World Coal Production by Major Producing Country: 1980 to 2000

[In millions of short tons (4,188.6 represents 4,188,600,000]

Country	1980	1990	1994	1995	1996	1997	1998	1999	2000
World, total	4,188.6	5,440.9	5,082.5	5,218.0	5,265.1	5,278.3	5,169.0	5,052.9	5,059.2
China	683.6	1190.4	1403.5	1537.0	1545.3	1507.1	1429.0	1365.0	1314.4
United States	829.7	1029.1	1033.5	1033.0	1063.9	1089.9	1117.5	1100.4	1073.6
India.	125.9	233.4	279.7	297.8	314.9	326.1	322.2	328.5	345.0
Australia	116.1	225.8	248.5	266.6	272.4	292.1	316.8	322.2	337.2
South Africa	132.0	247.6	272.3	288.4	297.1	324.6	322.0	320.2	326.1
Russia	(X)	(X)	312.7	296.4	304.0	257.9	241.0	259.2	281.4
Germany [1]	532.2	513.7	291.8	274.2	265.0	251.7	233.0	226.1	225.3
Poland	253.5	237.1	220.4	220.2	193.1	221.5	196.2	187.6	178.6
Korea, North	39.7	99.2	108.0	106.9	105.7	104.7	99.5	100.5	101.4
Ukraine	(X)	(X)	104.1	94.6	83.5	84.8	85.1	91.2	90.3
Kazakhstan	(X)	(X)	115.3	91.9	84.7	80.1	76.9	64.4	82.4
Canada.	40.4	75.4	80.3	82.6	83.5	86.7	83.1	79.9	76.2
Turkey	20.2	52.6	59.9	60.7	62.1	66.1	74.3	73.9	74.2
Indonesia	0.6	11.6	34.2	45.7	55.5	60.2	66.5	71.2	73.9
Czech Republic	(X)	(X)	84.8	81.9	84.0	81.0	74.4	65.2	71.8
Greece	25.6	57.2	62.5	63.6	65.9	64.9	67.1	68.4	69.5
Colombia.	4.5	22.6	25.0	28.4	33.1	35.9	37.2	36.1	42.0
Yugoslavia	(X)	(X)	42.3	44.1	42.4	44.8	48.6	36.7	37.8
United Kingdom	143.8	104.1	53.9	52.5	55.3	53.5	44.1	39.9	35.3
Romania	38.8	42.1	44.7	45.3	46.2	37.3	28.9	25.2	32.2
Bulgaria	39.6	39.0	31.6	33.9	33.7	32.8	34.1	28.7	29.8
Spain	40.9	39.6	32.7	31.3	30.8	29.2	28.7	26.8	25.8
Thailand	1.6	13.7	18.9	20.3	23.9	25.8	22.0	20.1	19.6
Hungary	28.3	19.7	15.6	16.1	16.7	17.2	17.1	16.8	15.3
Mexico	4.0	8.6	10.1	10.3	11.1	11.5	12.4	11.3	10.9

X Not applicable.   [1] For 1980 and 1990, represents East and West Germany combined.

Source: U.S. Energy Information Administration, *International Energy Annual, 2000.* See also <http://www.eia.doe.gov/pub/pdf/international/021900.pdf> (issued May 2002).

Natural Resources   559

No. 873. Demonstrated Coal Reserves by Type of Coal and Major Producing State: 2001

[In millions of short tons. As of January 1. The demonstrated reserve base represents the sum of coal in both measured and indicated resource categories of reliability. Measured resources of coal are estimates that have a high degree of geologic assurance from sample analyses and measurements from closely spaced and geological well known sample sites. Indicated resources are estimates based partly from sample and analyses and measurements and partly from reasonable geologic projections. For more information on the classification of coal resources and related terminology, see report cited below]

State	Total reserves	Type of coal				Method of mining	
		Anthracite	Bituminous	Sub-bituminous	Lignite	Under ground	Surface
United States.....	501,059	7,465	266,629	183,160	43,805	338,525	162,534
Alabama............	4,389	-	3,306	-	1,083	1,157	3,232
Alaska.............	6,118	-	698	5,407	14	5,423	695
Colorado...........	16,552	26	8,550	3,787	4,190	11,780	4,772
Illinois	104,773	-	104,773	-	-	88,188	16,586
Indiana............	9,738	-	9,738	-	-	8,831	907
Iowa	2,189	-	2,189	-	-	1,732	457
Kentucky	31,053	-	31,053	-	-	17,797	13,257
Kentucky, Eastern....	11,326	-	11,326	-	-	1,727	9,598
Kentucky, Western ...	19,728	-	19,728	-	-	16,069	3,658
Missouri...........	5,992	-	5,992	-	-	1,479	4,513
Montana...........	119,472	-	1,385	102,329	15,758	70,958	48,514
New Mexico	12,324	2	3,658	8,664	-	6,203	6,121
North Dakota........	9,243	-	-	-	9,243	-	9,243
Ohio	23,495	-	23,495	-	-	17,679	5,816
Oklahoma..........	1,566	-	1,566	-	-	1,235	331
Pennsylvania........	28,101	7,208	20,893	-	-	23,769	4,332
Anthracite	7,208	7,208	-	-	-	3,847	3,361
Bituminous	20,893	-	20,893	-	-	19,922	971
Texas.............	12,672	-	-	-	12,672	-	12,672
Utah	5,639	-	5,638	1	-	5,371	268
Virginia............	1,960	125	1,835	-	-	1,332	628
Washington.........	1,368	-	304	1,056	8	1,332	36
West Virginia........	34,244	-	34,244	-	-	30,097	4,147
Wyoming	66,219	-	4,320	61,898	-	42,501	23,718
East of the MS River....	239,379	7,333	230,962	-	1,083	190,116	49,262
West of the MS River ...	261,680	132	35,666	183,160	42,722	148,409	113,271

- Represents or rounds to zero.

Source: U.S. Energy Information Administration, unpublished data from the Coal Reserves Database.

No. 874. Uranium Concentrate (U_3O_8) Industry—Summary: 1990 to 2001

[See also Table 898 in Section 19, Energy and Utilities]

Item	Unit	1990	1994	1995	1996	1997	1998	1999	2000	2001
Exploration and development,										
surface drilling	Mil. ft........	1.7	0.7	1.3	3.0	4.9	4.6	2.5	1.0	0.7
Expenditures	Mil. dol.......	17.1	3.7	6.0	10.1	30.4	21.7	9.0	6.7	4.8
Number of mines operated......	Number......	39	12	12	13	14	15	14	10	7
Underground	Number......	27	-	-	1	1	4	3	1	-
Openpit..................	Number......	2	-	-	-	-	-	-	-	-
In situ leaching............	Number......	7	5	5	6	7	6	6	4	3
Other sources	Number......	3	7	7	6	6	5	5	5	4
Mine production	1,000 pounds ..	5,876	2,526	3,528	4,705	4,710	4,782	4,548	3,123	2,647
Underground	1,000 pounds ..	(D)	-	-	(D)	(D)	(D)	(D)	(D)	-
Openpit.................	1,000 pounds ..	1,881	-	-	-	-	-	-	-	-
In situ leaching............	1,000 pounds ..	(D)	2,448	3,372	4,379	4,084	3,721	3,830	2,995	(D)
Other sources	1,000 pounds ..	3,995	78	156	326	626	1,062	718	128	(D)
Uranium concentrate production [1] .	1,000 pounds ..	8,886	3,352	6,043	6,321	5,643	4,705	4,611	3,958	2,639
Concentrate shipments from mills and plants	1,000 pounds ..	12,957	6,319	5,500	5,982	5,817	4,863	5,527	3,187	2,203
Employment	Person-years ..	1,335	980	1,107	1,118	1,097	1,120	848	627	423

- Represents zero.   D Data withheld to avoid disclosing figures for individual companies.   [1] U_3O_8.

Source: U.S. Department of Energy, Uranium Industry, annual. See also <http://www.eia.doe.gov/cneaf/nuclear/uia/uia.pdf> (released May 2001) and <http://www.eia.doe.gov/cneaf/nuclear/uia/contents.html> (released 27 June 2002).

Section 19
Energy and Utilities

This section presents statistics on fuel resources, energy production and consumption, electric energy, hydroelectric power, nuclear power, solar energy, wood energy, and the electric and gas utility industries. The principal sources are the U.S. Department of Energy's Energy Information Administration (EIA), the Edison Electric Institute, Washington, DC, and the American Gas Association, Arlington, VA. The Department of Energy was created in October 1977 and assumed and centralized the responsibilities of all or part of several agencies including the Federal Power Commission (FPC), the U.S. Bureau of Mines, the Federal Energy Administration, and the U.S. Energy Research and Development Administration. For additional data on transportation, see Section 23; on fuels, see Section 18; and on energy-related housing characteristics, see Section 20.

The EIA, in its *Annual Energy Review,* provides statistics and trend data on energy supply, demand, and prices. Information is included on petroleum and natural gas, coal, electricity, hydroelectric power, nuclear power, solar, wood, and geothermal energy. Among its annual reports are *Annual Energy Review, Electric Power Annual, Natural Gas Annual, Petroleum Supply Annual, State Energy Data Report, State Energy Price and Expenditure Report, Financial Statistics of Selected Electric Utilities, Performance Profiles of Major Energy Producers, Annual Energy Outlook,* and *International Energy Annual.* These various publications contain state, national, and international data on production of electricity, net summer capability of generating plants, fuels used in energy production, energy sales and consumption, and hydroelectric power. The EIA also issues the *Monthly Energy Review,* which presents current supply, disposition, and price data and monthly publications on petroleum, coal, natural

gas, and electric power. Data on residential energy consumption, expenditures, and conservation activities are available from EIA's Residential Energy Consumption Survey and are published every 4 years.

The Edison Electric Institute's monthly bulletin and annual *Statistical Year Book of the Electric Utility Industry for the Year* contain data on the distribution of electric energy by public utilities; information on the electric power supply, expansion of electric generating facilities, and the manufacture of heavy electric power equipment is presented in the annual *Year-End Summary of the Electric Power Situation in the United States.* The American Gas Association, in its monthly and quarterly bulletins and its yearbook, *Gas Facts,* presents data on gas utilities and financial and operating statistics.

Btu conversion factors—Various energy sources are converted from original units to the thermal equivalent using British thermal units (Btu). A Btu is the amount of energy required to raise the temperature of 1 pound of water 1 degree Fahrenheit (F) at or near 39.2 degrees F. Factors are calculated annually from the latest final annual data available; some are revised as a result. The following list provides conversion factors used in 2001 for production and consumption, in that order, for various fuels: Petroleum, 5.800 and 5.326 mil. Btu per barrel; total coal, 21.072 and 20.753 mil. Btu per short ton; and natural gas (dry), 1,025 Btu per cubic foot for both. The factors for the production of nuclear power and geothermal power were 10,623 and 21,017 Btu per kilowatt-hour, respectively. The fossil fuel steam-electric power plant generation factor of 10,346 Btu per kilowatt-hour was used for hydroelectric power generation and for wood and waste, wind, photovoltaic, and solar thermal energy consumed at electric utilities.

U.S. Census Bureau, Statistical Abstract of the United States: 2002

No. 875. Utilities—Establishments, Revenue, Payroll, and Employees by Kind of Business (NAICS Basis): 1997

Kind of business	NAICS code [1]	Estab- lish- ments (number)	Revenue		Annual payroll		Paid employee for pay period including March 12 (number)
			Total (mil. dol.)	Per paid employee (dol.)	Total (mil. dol.)	Per paid employee (dol.)	
Utilities	22	15,513	411,713	585,899	36,595	52,077	702,703
Electric power generation, transmission, & distribution	2211	7,935	269,095	476,676	30,440	53,921	564,525
Electric power generation	22111	1,745	73,375	493,492	8,369	56,289	148,686
Fossil fuel electric power generation . . .	221112	1,009	48,324	515,374	5,049	53,843	93,765
Nuclear electric power generation	221113	67	13,967	406,231	2,202	64,045	34,381
Other electric power generation	221119	316	8,011	608,723	725	55,069	13,160
Electric power transmission, control & distribution	22112	6,190	195,720	470,663	22,070	53,074	415,839
Electric bulk power transmission & control	221121	120	956	395,361	116	47,852	2,418
Electric power distribution	221122	6,070	194,764	471,103	21,955	53,105	413,421
Other combination utilities	2211223	30	428	630,811	52	76,771	678
Natural gas distribution	2212	2,747	136,995	1,331,629	5,110	49,666	102,878
Natural gas transmission & distribution. .	2212101	713	18,267	629,034	1,534	52,838	29,039
Natural gas distribution	2212102	1,682	87,105	1,387,135	2,955	47,059	62,795
Mixed, manu., or LP gas pro &/or dist. .	2212103	86	(D)	(NA)	(D)	(NA)	(2)
Electric & other serv. combined (natural gas distribution)	2212104	145	28,110	4,193,063	413	61,565	6,704
Gas & other serv. combined (natural gas distribution)	2212105	119	2,853	915,151	149	47,705	3,117
Water, sewage, & other systems	2213	4,831	5,623	159,284	1,045	29,614	35,300
Water supply & irrigation systems.	22131	4,052	4,454	159,447	825	29,550	27,933
Sewage treatment facilities	22132	696	596	106,399	139	24,816	5,600
Steam & air-conditioning supply	22133	83	573	324,314	81	45,838	1,767

D Withheld to avoid disclosing data of individual companies; data are included in higher level totals.　　NA Not available.
[1] North American Industry Classification System, 1997; see text, Section 15, Business Enterprise.　　[2] 1,000 to 2,499 employees.

Source: U.S. Census Bureau, *1997 Economic Census, Utilities,* Series EC97T22A-US, issued December 1999.

No. 876. Private Utilities—Employees, Annual Payroll, and Establishments by Industry: 2000

[Excludes government employees, railroad employees, self-employed persons, etc. See "General Explanation" in source for definitions and statement on reliability of data. An *establishment* is a single physical location where business is conducted or where services or industrial operations are performed]

Year and industry	NAICS code [1]	Number of employ- ees [2]	Annual payroll (mil. dol.)	Average payroll per em- ployee (dol.)	Establishment by employment size-class				
					Total	Under 20 employ- ees	20 to 99 employ- ees	100 to 499 employ- ees	500 and over employ- ees
Utilities, total	22	655,230	40,651	62,041	17,301	12,174	3,775	1,155	197
Electric power generation, transmission and distribution	2211	520,854	33,759	64,815	9,150	5,155	2,897	924	174
Electric power generation	22111	143,927	10,045	69,790	2,118	1,230	544	289	55
Hydroelectric power generation .	221111	9,736	582	59,751	463	373	68	20	2
Fossil fuel electric power gen- eration	221112	86,936	5,848	67,270	1,213	584	382	231	16
Nuclear electric power genera- tion	221113	32,876	2,653	80,690	68	14	7	17	30
Other electric power generation.	221119	14,379	962	66,895	374	259	87	21	7
Electric pwr transmsn, control & distribution	22112	376,927	23,714	62,915	7,032	3,925	2,353	635	119
Electric bulk power transmission & control	221121	5,420	344	63,436	145	98	37	9	1
Electric power distribution.	221122	371,507	23,370	62,907	6,887	3,827	2,316	626	118
Natural gas distribution.	2212	94,821	5,530	58,318	2,846	2,027	605	194	20
Water, sewage & other systems	2213	39,555	1,362	34,436	5,305	4,992	273	37	3
Water supply & irrigation systems .	22131	32,786	1,120	34,171	4,523	4,293	194	33	3
Sewage treatment facilities	22132	5,141	160	31,105	708	657	48	3	-
Steam & air-conditioning supply . .	22133	1,628	82	50,308	74	42	31	1	-

- Represents zero.　　[1] North American Industry Classification System, 1997.　　[2] Covers full- and part-time employees who are on the payroll in the pay period including March 12.

Source: U.S. Census Bureau, *County Business Patterns,* annual. See also <http://www.census.gov/epcd/cbp/view/cbpview.html> (accessed August 2002).

No. 877. Energy Supply and Disposition by Type of Fuel: 1960 to 2000

[In quadrillion British thermal units (Btu). For Btu conversion factors, see source]

	Production					Renewable energy					Consumption					
Year	Total[1]	Crude oil[2]	Natural gas	Coal	Nuclear power[3]	Total[1]	Hydro-electric power	Biofuels[4]	Solar energy	Net trade, total[5]	Total[1]	Petro-leum[6]	Natural gas[7]	Coal	Nuclear power	Renewable energy, total[1]
1960	42.80	14.94	12.66	10.82	0.01	2.93	1.61	1.32	(NA)	-2.74	45.12	19.92	12.39	9.84	0.01	2.98
1970	63.50	20.40	21.67	14.61	0.24	4.08	2.63	1.43	(NA)	-5.72	67.86	29.52	21.80	12.27	0.24	4.10
1971	62.72	20.03	22.28	13.19	0.41	4.27	2.82	1.43	(NA)	-7.41	69.31	30.56	22.47	11.60	0.41	4.31
1972	63.92	20.04	22.21	14.09	0.58	4.40	2.86	1.50	(NA)	-9.32	72.76	32.95	22.70	12.08	0.58	4.48
1973	63.59	19.49	22.19	13.99	0.91	4.43	2.86	1.53	(NA)	-12.68	75.81	34.84	22.51	12.97	0.91	4.58
1974	62.37	18.58	21.21	14.07	1.27	4.77	3.18	1.54	(NA)	-12.19	74.08	33.46	21.73	12.66	1.27	4.90
1975	61.36	17.73	19.64	14.99	1.90	4.72	3.16	1.50	(NA)	-11.75	72.04	32.73	19.95	12.66	1.90	4.79
1976	61.60	17.26	19.48	15.65	2.11	4.77	2.98	1.71	(NA)	-14.65	76.00	35.18	20.35	13.58	2.11	4.86
1977	62.05	17.45	19.57	15.76	2.70	4.25	2.33	1.84	(NA)	-18.02	78.12	37.12	19.93	13.92	2.70	4.43
1978	63.14	18.43	19.49	14.91	3.02	5.04	2.94	2.04	(NA)	-17.32	80.12	37.97	20.00	13.77	3.02	5.24
1979	65.95	18.10	20.08	17.54	2.78	5.17	2.93	2.15	(NA)	-16.75	81.04	37.12	20.67	15.04	2.78	5.38
1980	67.24	18.25	19.91	18.60	2.74	5.49	2.90	2.49	(NA)	-12.25	78.44	34.20	20.39	15.42	2.74	5.71
1981	67.01	18.15	19.70	18.38	3.01	5.47	2.76	2.59	(NA)	-9.65	76.57	31.93	19.93	15.91	3.01	5.82
1982	66.57	18.31	18.32	18.64	3.13	5.99	3.27	2.62	(NA)	-7.46	73.44	30.23	18.51	15.32	3.13	6.29
1983	64.11	18.39	16.59	17.25	3.20	6.49	3.53	2.83	(NA)	-8.31	73.32	30.05	17.36	15.89	3.20	6.86
1984	68.83	18.85	18.01	19.72	3.55	6.43	3.39	2.88	(Z)	-8.96	76.97	31.05	18.51	17.07	3.55	6.85
1985	67.72	18.99	16.98	19.33	4.15	6.03	2.97	2.86	(Z)	-7.87	76.78	30.92	17.83	17.48	4.15	6.46
1986	67.18	18.38	16.54	19.51	4.47	6.13	3.07	2.84	(Z)	-10.38	77.07	32.20	16.71	17.26	4.47	6.51
1987	67.76	17.68	17.14	20.14	4.91	5.69	2.64	2.82	(Z)	-11.91	79.63	32.87	17.74	18.01	4.91	6.17
1988	69.03	17.28	17.60	20.74	5.66	5.49	2.33	2.94	(Z)	-13.15	83.07	34.22	18.55	18.85	5.66	5.82
1989	69.47	16.12	17.85	21.35	5.68	6.32	2.86	3.06	0.06	-14.19	84.72	34.21	19.38	19.04	5.68	6.49
1990	70.84	15.57	18.36	22.46	6.16	6.15	3.05	2.66	0.06	-14.09	84.34	33.55	19.30	19.25	6.16	6.25
1991	70.53	15.70	18.23	21.59	6.58	6.17	3.02	2.70	0.07	-13.34	84.30	32.85	19.61	19.00	6.58	6.32
1992	70.07	15.22	18.38	21.63	6.61	5.92	2.62	2.85	0.07	-14.62	85.51	33.53	20.13	19.15	6.61	6.13
1993	68.38	14.49	18.58	20.25	6.52	6.17	2.89	2.80	0.07	-17.22	87.30	33.84	20.83	19.76	6.52	6.41
1994	70.85	14.10	19.35	22.11	6.84	6.09	2.68	2.94	0.07	-18.65	89.21	34.67	21.29	19.93	6.84	6.43
1995	71.30	13.89	19.10	22.03	7.18	6.69	3.21	3.07	0.07	-18.03	90.94	34.55	22.16	20.03	7.18	6.99
1996	72.60	13.72	19.36	22.68	7.17	7.16	3.59	3.13	0.08	-19.35	93.93	35.76	22.56	20.96	7.17	7.47
1997	72.55	13.66	19.39	23.21	6.68	7.15	3.72	3.00	0.07	-20.94	94.34	36.27	22.53	21.46	6.68	7.40
1998	72.91	13.24	19.46	23.94	7.16	6.75	3.35	2.98	0.07	-22.47	94.61	36.93	21.92	21.67	7.16	6.98
1999	71.98	12.45	19.13	23.19	7.74	7.02	3.31	3.22	0.07	-23.74	96.87	37.96	22.29	21.69	7.74	7.23
2000	71.90	12.38	19.74	22.66	8.01	6.56	2.84	3.28	0.07	-24.42	98.50	37.96	23.33	22.41	8.01	6.82

NA Not available. Z Less than 50 trillion. [1] Includes types of fuel not shown separately. [2] Includes lease condensate. [3] Data on the generation of electricity in the United States represent net generation, which is gross output of electricity (measured at the generator terminals) minus power plant use. Nuclear electricity generation data are gross outputs of electricity. [4] Alcohol is ethanol blended into motor gasoline. [5] Exports minus imports. [6] Petroleum products supplied, including natural gas plant liquids and crude oil burned as fuel. [7] Includes supplemental gaseous fuels.

Source: U.S. Energy Information Administration, *Annual Energy Review* and Internet site <http://tonto.eia.doe.gov/FTPROOT/multifuel/038400.pdf> (released August 2001).

U.S. Census Bureau, Statistical Abstract of the United States: 2002

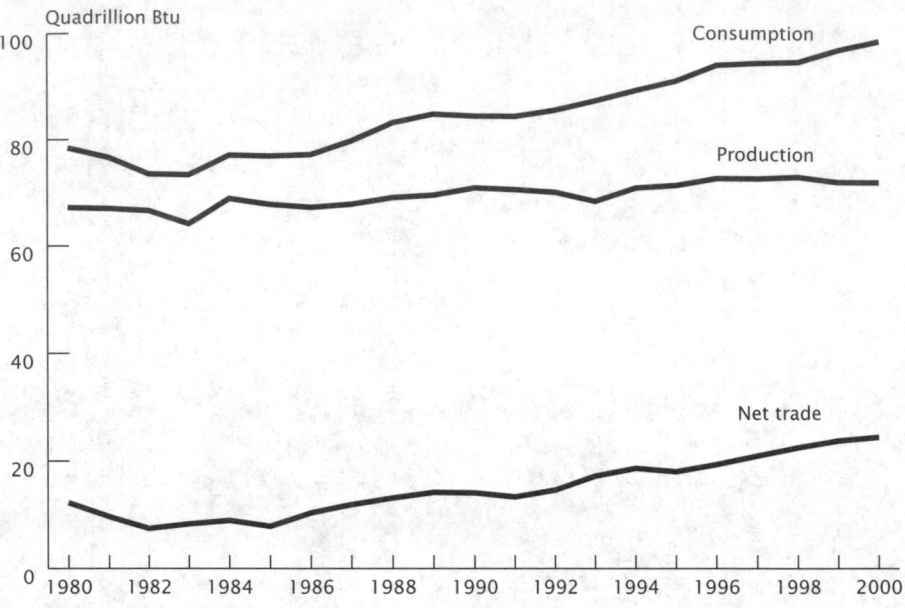

Figure 19.1
Energy Production, Trade, and Consumption: 1980 to 2000

Quadrillion Btu

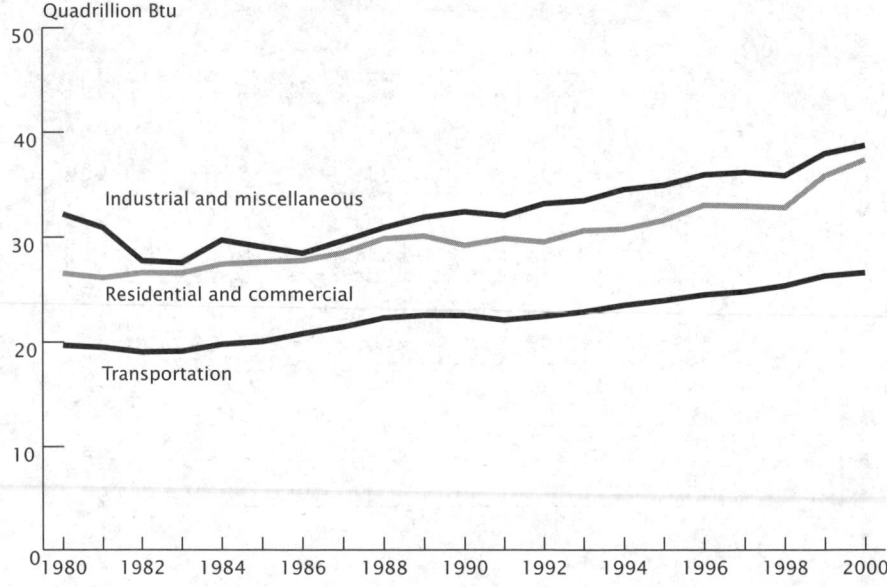

Source: Chart prepared by U.S. Census Bureau. For data, see Table 877.

Figure 19.2
Energy Consumption by End-Use Sector: 1980 to 2000

Quadrillion Btu

Source: Chart prepared by U.S. Census Bureau. For data, see Table 879.

564 Energy and Utilities

No. 878. Energy Supply and Disposition by Type of Fuel—Estimates, 1999 and 2000, and Projections, 2005 to 2020

[Quadrillion Btu (73.50 represents 73,500,000,000,000,000) per year. Btu=British thermal unit. Totals may not equal sum of components due to rounding. Projections are "reference" or midlevel forecasts. See report for methodology and assumptions used in generating projections]

Type of fuel	1999	2000	Projections			
			2005	2010	2015	2020
Production, total	**73.50**	**72.80**	**76.79**	**81.09**	**86.51**	**90.66**
Crude oil and lease condensate	12.43	12.33	11.38	10.76	11.76	11.92
Natural gas plant liquids	2.62	2.71	3.02	3.37	3.74	4.03
Natural gas, dry	19.20	19.59	21.29	24.12	27.03	29.25
Coal	23.15	22.58	24.95	26.23	26.91	28.11
Nuclear power	7.74	8.03	8.10	7.87	7.55	7.49
Renewable energy [1]	6.69	6.46	7.37	7.89	8.47	8.93
Other [2]	1.66	1.10	0.68	0.85	1.04	0.93
Imports, total	**27.37**	**29.04**	**34.39**	**38.79**	**41.46**	**44.44**
Crude oil [3]	18.96	19.69	22.63	24.36	24.04	24.45
Petroleum products [4]	4.19	4.73	5.68	7.83	10.31	12.69
Natural gas	3.66	3.85	5.01	5.64	6.04	6.20
Other imports [5]	0.56	0.76	1.07	0.95	1.07	1.09
Exports, total	**3.64**	**3.93**	**3.52**	**3.90**	**4.01**	**4.05**
Petroleum [6]	1.96	2.15	1.70	1.91	2.02	2.11
Natural gas	0.16	0.25	0.41	0.63	0.66	0.56
Coal	1.52	1.53	1.41	1.36	1.34	1.38
Consumption, total	**97.10**	**99.29**	**107.61**	**115.61**	**123.64**	**130.85**
Petroleum products [7]	38.25	38.63	41.40	45.20	48.85	51.99
Natural gas	22.57	23.43	26.16	28.85	32.14	34.63
Coal	21.56	22.34	24.03	25.41	26.16	27.35
Nuclear power	7.74	8.03	8.10	7.87	7.55	7.49
Renewable energy [1] other [8]	6.98	6.86	7.92	8.28	8.94	9.38
Net imports of petroleum	**21.19**	**22.28**	**26.61**	**30.29**	**32.33**	**35.04**
Prices (1999 dollars per unit):						
World oil price (dol per bbl) [9]	17.60	27.72	22.73	23.36	24.00	24.68
Gas wellhead price (dol. per mcf) [10]	2.27	3.60	2.66	2.85	3.07	3.26
Coal minemouth price (dol per ton)	17.01	16.45	14.99	14.11	13.44	12.79
Average electric price (cents per kWh)	6.7	6.9	6.4	6.3	6.3	6.5

[1] Includes grid-connected electricity from conventional hydroelectric; wood and wood waste; landfill gas; municipal solid waste; other biomass; wind; photovoltaic and solar thermal sources; nonelectric energy from renewable sources, such as active and passive solar systems, and wood; and both the ethanol and gasoline components of E85, but not the ethanol components of blends less than 85 percent. Excludes electricity imports using renewable sources and nonmarketed renewable energy. See Table A18 for selected nonmarketed residential and commercial renewable energy.   [2] Includes liquid hydrogen, methanol, supplemental natural gas, and some domestic inputs to refineries.   [3] Includes imports of crude oil for the Strategic Petroleum Reserve.   [4] Includes imports of finished petroleum products, imports of unfinished oils, alcohols, ethers, and blending components.   [5] Includes coal, coal coke (net), and electricity (net).   [6] Includes crude oil and petroleum products.   [7] Includes natural gas plant liquids, crude oil consumed as a fuel, and nonpetroleum based liquids for blending, such as ethanol.   [8] Includes net electricity imports, methanol, and liquid hydrogen.   [9] Average refiner acquisition cost for imported crude oil.   [10] Represents lower 48 onshore and offshore supplies.

Source: U.S. Energy Information Administration, *Annual Energy Outlook, 2002,* Series DOE/EIA-0383(2002). See also <http://www.eia.doe.gov/oiaf/aeo/pdf/0383(2002).pdf> released December 2001).

No. 879. Energy Consumption by End-Use Sector: 1970 to 2000

[There exists a discontinuity in the series between 1989 and 1990 due to the expanded coverage of nonelectric utility use of renewable energy beginning 1990. Btu=British thermal units. For Btu conversion factors, see source]

Year	Total consumption [1] (quad. Btu)	Residential and commercial (quad. Btu)	Industrial [1] (quad. Btu)	Transportation (quad. Btu)	Percent of total		
					Residential and commercial	Industrial [1]	Transportation
1970	67.86	22.13	29.63	16.10	32.6	43.7	23.7
1975	72.04	24.35	29.45	18.25	33.8	40.9	25.3
1980	78.44	26.55	32.19	19.70	33.9	41.0	25.1
1985	76.78	27.64	29.07	20.07	36.0	37.9	26.1
1990	84.34	29.22	32.42	22.54	34.6	38.4	26.7
1992	85.51	29.55	33.20	22.47	34.6	38.8	26.3
1993	87.30	30.62	33.46	22.89	35.1	38.3	26.2
1994	89.21	30.76	34.54	23.52	34.5	38.7	26.4
1995	90.94	31.61	34.95	23.97	34.8	38.4	26.4
1996	93.93	33.04	35.94	24.52	35.2	38.3	26.1
1997	94.34	32.96	36.16	24.82	34.9	38.3	26.3
1998 [2]	94.61	32.82	35.86	25.39	34.7	37.9	26.8
1999 [2]	96.87	35.83	37.96	26.31	37.0	39.2	27.2
2000	98.50	37.39	38.76	26.64	38.0	39.4	27.0

[1] Includes some fossil-fuel consumption at nonutilities.   [2] There is a discontinuity in this time series between 1998 and 1999; beginning in 1999, nonutility consumption of fossil fuels is included in electric power sector consumption and the calculation for electrical system energy losses.

Source: U.S. Energy Information Administration, *Annual Energy Review 2000,* Series DOE/EIA-0384(2000). See also <http://www.eia.doe.gov/emeu/aer/pdf/038400.pdf> (released August 2001).

No. 880. Energy Consumption—End-Use Sector and Selected Source by State: 1999

[In trillions of Btu (95,682 represents 95,682,000,000,000,000), except as indicated]

State	Total [1]	Per capita [2] (mil. Btu)	End-use sector				Source				
			Resi-dential	Com-mercial	Indus-trial	Trans-portation	Petro-leum	Natural gas (dry)	Coal	Hydro electric power	Nuclear electric power
United States..	**95,682**	**351**	**18,382**	**15,059**	**[3]35,917**	**26,325**	**37,960**	**22,295**	**20,498**	**3,449**	**7,736**
Alabama	2,005	459	341	226	977	461	551	345	855	80	328
Alaska.	695	1,122	48	63	386	198	253	420	11	9	-
Arizona	1,220	255	279	267	222	453	497	163	404	104	323
Arkansas	1,204	472	193	124	589	297	384	266	267	28	137
California	8,375	253	1,416	1,237	2,824	2,899	3,383	2,182	64	425	355
Colorado	1,156	285	261	255	273	366	426	318	355	17	-
Connecticut	839	256	245	197	162	235	440	135	-	14	135
Delaware	279	370	56	45	107	71	141	58	36	-	-
District of Columbia	170	327	34	106	4	27	34	33	-	-	-
Florida.	3,853	255	1,018	810	680	1,346	1,912	542	672	2	335
Georgia	2,798	359	553	416	957	871	1,044	341	790	28	334
Hawaii.	241	204	23	25	71	122	214	3	3	1	-
Idaho	518	414	96	87	210	126	170	72	8	140	-
Illinois	3,883	320	897	722	1,273	991	1,340	1,058	837	2	868
Indiana	2,736	460	484	301	1,306	645	899	577	1,451	4	-
Iowa	1,122	391	223	159	463	278	419	236	416	10	39
Kansas	1,050	396	201	169	392	288	437	302	329	-	97
Kentucky	1,830	462	316	219	851	444	726	220	885	27	-
Louisiana	3,615	827	325	237	2,249	805	1,452	1,558	228	8	139
Maine	529	422	98	58	260	113	250	6	3	81	-
Maryland	1,378	267	359	337	277	405	584	201	304	15	141
Massachusetts . . .	1,569	254	412	325	391	441	639	356	13	15	48
Michigan	3,240	328	744	568	1,083	845	1,098	930	823	11	155
Minnesota	1,675	351	340	218	618	500	661	346	336	59	142
Mississippi	1,209	437	203	146	451	409	483	346	138	-	90
Missouri.	1,768	323	432	334	380	623	781	270	686	18	91
Montana	412	467	62	48	196	107	174	64	174	143	-
Nebraska	602	361	130	111	166	194	246	121	196	18	107
Nevada	615	340	122	97	198	198	221	157	180	29	-
New Hampshire . .	335	279	82	56	97	101	188	21	35	25	92
New Jersey	2,589	318	540	541	645	863	1,236	641	68	[4]-1	308
New Mexico	635	365	93	106	202	234	257	225	298	3	-
New York	4,283	235	1,092	1,216	995	980	1,653	1,251	188	265	393
North Carolina . . .	2,447	320	563	440	754	691	937	229	708	40	399
North Dakota	366	577	54	43	186	82	123	59	412	28	-
Ohio	4,323	384	867	632	1,855	969	1,340	878	1,379	4	175
Oklahoma	1,378	410	259	198	518	403	500	543	334	32	-
Oregon	1,109	335	238	191	352	328	392	219	39	475	-
Pennsylvania	3,716	310	859	583	1,290	984	1,385	696	1,143	16	756
Rhode Island	261	264	66	52	77	66	99	86	(Z)	10	-
South Carolina . . .	1,493	384	288	210	618	376	467	163	403	7	540
South Dakota	239	326	53	39	62	84	115	36	46	71	-
Tennessee	2,071	378	442	328	711	590	713	286	626	74	289
Texas	11,501	574	1,323	1,147	6,482	2,549	5,565	3,982	1,535	13	391
Utah	694	326	128	120	235	211	262	169	382	13	-
Vermont	165	278	43	29	40	53	85	8	2	61	43
Virginia	2,227	324	494	463	614	656	864	275	402	-6	301
Washington	2,241	389	436	332	856	617	878	277	96	988	65
West Virginia	735	407	142	101	311	182	220	147	977	10	-
Wisconsin	1,811	345	376	285	717	432	668	379	472	23	122
Wyoming	422	879	36	42	224	120	156	102	495	12	-

- Represents zero.   Z Less than 0.05 trillion Btu.   [1] Sources of energy includes geothermal, wood and waste, and net interstate sales of electricity, including losses, not shown separately.   [2] Based on estimated resident population as of July 1.   [3] Includes 57.7 trillion Btu of net imports of coal coke not allocated.   [4] Minus sign (-) indicates when amount of energy expended exceeds amount of energy consumed.

Source: U.S. Energy Information Administration, State Energy Data Report, 1999, annual. See also <http://eia.doe.gov/pub/state. data/pdf/sedr.pdf> (released May 2001).

No. 881. Renewable Energy Consumption Estimates by Type: 1990 to 1999

[**In quadrillion Btu.** Renewable energy is obtained from sources that are essentially inexhaustible unlike fossil fuels of which there is a finite supply]

Source and sector	1990	1994	1995	1996	1997	1998	1999
Consumption, total	**6.26**	**6.39**	**6.96**	**7.45**	**7.37**	**6.99**	**7.21**
Conventional hydroelectric power [1]	3.14	2.97	3.48	3.89	3.96	3.57	3.51
Geothermal energy [2]	0.36	0.40	0.33	0.35	0.32	0.33	0.37
Biomass [3]	2.67	2.91	3.04	3.10	2.98	2.99	3.21
Solar energy [4]	0.06	0.07	0.07	0.08	0.07	0.07	0.07
Wind energy	0.03	0.04	0.03	0.04	0.03	0.03	0.05
Residential and commercial	0.68	0.66	0.72	0.72	0.56	0.50	0.53
Biomass [5]	0.62	0.58	0.64	0.64	0.48	0.42	0.46
Geothermal energy [6]	0.01	0.01	0.01	0.01	0.01	0.02	0.02
Solar [7]	0.06	0.06	0.07	0.07	0.07	0.07	0.06
Industrial [8]	2.24	2.61	2.68	2.79	2.80	2.84	3.20
Biomass [3]	1.94	2.21	2.28	2.37	2.39	2.44	2.62
Geothermal energy [6]	0.16	0.21	0.20	0.21	0.19	0.20	0.32
Conventional hydroelectric power [9]	0.10	0.14	0.15	0.17	0.18	0.15	0.20
Solar energy	0.01	0.01	0.01	0.01	0.01	0.01	0.01
Wind energy	0.03	0.04	0.03	0.04	0.03	0.03	0.05
Transportation:							
Biomass [10]	0.08	0.10	0.10	0.07	0.10	0.11	0.11
Electric utilities [11]	3.25	3.02	3.47	3.87	3.91	3.55	3.37
Biomass [3]	0.02	0.02	0.02	0.02	0.02	0.02	0.02
Geothermal energy [6]	0.19	0.17	0.10	0.11	0.12	0.11	0.04
Conventional hydroelectric power [9]	3.04	2.83	3.06	3.42	3.54	3.20	3.10
Solar and wind energy	(Z)	(Z)	(Z)	(Z)	(Z)	(Z)	(Z)

Z Less than 0.005 quadrillion Btu.   [1] Hydroelectricity generated by pumped storage is not included in renewable energy.   [2] Includes grid-connected electricity, geothermal heat pump and direct use energy.   [3] Wood, wood waste, wood liquors, peat, railroad ties, wood sludge, spent sulfite liquors, agricultural waste, straw, tires, fish oils, tall oil, sludge waste, waste alcohol, municipal solid waste, landfill gases, and other waste.   [4] Includes solar thermal and photovoltaic.   [5] Wood.   [6] Includes geothermal heat pump and direct use energy. The Industrial and Electric Utility sectors also include   [7] The solar thermal component of 0.06 quadrillion Btu for residential and commercial use is calculated by presuming an overall efficiency of 50 percent for all three categories of solar thermal collectors, a 1,500-Btu per square foot average daily insolation, and the potential thermal energy production from the 219 million square feet of thermal collectors produced between 1980 and 1999.   [8] Includes generation of electricity by cogenerators, independent power producers, and small power producers.   [9] Hydroelectricity generated by pumped storage Is not included in renewable energy.   [10] Ethanol blended into gasoline.   [11] For Btu conversion rates, see source.

Source: U.S. Energy Information Administration, *Renewable Energy Annual 2000,* Series DOE/EIA-0603(2000). See also <http://www.eia.doe.gov/cneaf/solar.renewables/page/readata/rea.pdf> (issued March 2001).

No. 882. Energy Expenditures and Average Fuel Prices by Source and Sector: 1970 to 1999

[**82,862 represents $82,862,000,000.** For definition of Btu, see text, this section. End-use sector and electric utilities exclude expenditures and prices on energy sources such as hydropower, solar, wind, and geothermal. Also excludes expenditures for reported amounts of energy consumed by the energy industry for production, transportation, and processing operations]

Source and sector	1970	1975	1980	1985	1990	1994	1995	1996	1997	1998	1999
EXPENDITURES (mil. dol.)											
Total [1][2][3]	82,862	171,828	374,360	437,321	471,940	505,771	515,358	561,803	568,242	526,224	558,742
Natural gas	10,891	20,061	51,061	72,938	64,102	77,716	74,150	85,634	91,736	81,628	83,512
Petroleum products [2]	47,942	103,372	237,628	223,597	235,328	229,976	237,110	268,447	267,621	232,367	262,912
Motor gasoline	31,596	59,446	124,408	118,048	126,558	130,068	136,647	148,344	149,668	132,730	149,260
Coal	4,594	13,047	22,648	29,723	28,372	27,186	26,861	27,369	27,523	27,195	25,920
Electricity sales	23,345	50,680	98,095	149,233	176,737	200,883	205,932	211,011	213,645	216,928	216,737
Residential sector [3]	20,151	36,988	69,524	99,009	110,057	126,963	128,423	138,030	138,954	135,044	137,348
Commercial sector [3]	10,654	22,839	46,888	70,289	78,884	89,409	91,587	95,899	100,296	98,249	98,059
Industrial sector [3]	16,678	41,068	94,268	106,835	102,330	109,196	107,599	119,712	120,042	108,282	114,318
Transportation sector [2]	35,379	70,933	163,680	161,188	180,668	180,204	187,749	208,161	208,950	184,649	209,017
Motor gasoline	30,525	57,992	121,809	115,205	123,845	128,112	134,641	146,106	147,164	130,709	147,592
Electric utilities [3]	-4,316	-16,396	-37,435	-42,558	38,325	36,138	34,820	36,677	37,808	37,573	36,550
AVERAGE FUEL PRICES (dol. per mil. Btu)											
All sectors [3]	**1.65**	**3.33**	**6.89**	**8.36**	**8.27**	**8.29**	**8.29**	**8.76**	**8.82**	**8.19**	**8.41**
Residential sector [3]	2.11	3.81	7.44	10.93	11.91	12.63	12.57	12.67	13.23	13.43	13.15
Commercial sector [3]	1.96	4.09	7.88	11.70	12.00	12.87	12.75	12.88	13.15	13.13	12.82
Industrial sector [3]	0.98	2.12	5.15	6.27	5.21	4.52	4.37	5.17	4.88	4.26	4.45
Transportation sector	2.31	4.02	8.61	8.26	8.28	7.91	8.09	8.76	8.70	7.48	8.19
Electric utilities [3]	0.32	0.96	1.75	1.85	1.46	1.30	1.23	1.28	1.30	1.24	1.21

[1] Includes electricity sales; excludes electricity generation.   [2] Includes sources or fuel types not shown separately.   [3] There are no direct fuel costs for hydroelectric, geothermal, wind, photovoltaic, or solar thermal energy.

Source: U.S. Energy Information Administration, *State Energy Price and Expenditure Report,* annual. See also <http://tonto.eia.doe.gov/FTPROOT/multifuel/037697.pdf> (released July 2001).

Energy and Utilities   567

No. 883. Energy Expenditures—End-Use Sector and Selected Source by State: 1999

[In millions of dollars (558,742 represents $558,742,000,000). End-use sector and electric utilities exclude expenditures on energy sources such as hydroelectric, photovoltaic, solar thermal, wind, and geothermal. Also excludes expenditures for reported amounts of energy consumed by the energy industry for production, transportation, and processing operations]

State	Total [1]	End-use sector				Source			
		Residential	Commercial	Industrial	Transportation	Petroleum products	Natural gas	Coal	Electricity sales
U.S.	558,742	137,348	98,059	114,318	209,017	262,912	83,512	25,920	216,737
AL.	10,076	2,463	1,465	2,527	3,621	4,221	1,200	1,284	4,367
AK.	2,040	342	354	197	1,147	1,357	235	23	515
AZ.	9,013	2,303	1,845	998	3,866	4,212	723	545	4,170
AR.	5,990	1,423	707	1,591	2,269	2,774	948	391	2,215
CA.	56,007	12,110	10,170	8,875	24,852	26,691	9,102	111	20,360
CO	7,003	1,652	1,359	835	3,156	3,510	1,123	352	2,395
CT.	7,111	2,310	1,650	770	2,380	3,414	885	(Z)	2,968
DE.	1,728	483	316	348	581	808	260	56	745
DC	1,311	266	771	18	257	287	255	(Z)	777
FL.	25,295	7,684	5,004	2,330	10,277	12,275	1,954	1,071	12,819
GA.	15,524	3,795	2,631	2,925	6,174	7,162	1,170	1,231	6,989
HI	2,144	427	408	393	917	1,243	39	5	1,107
ID	2,572	504	370	555	1,143	1,386	269	10	884
IL	23,932	6,202	4,682	5,035	8,014	9,899	4,716	1,212	9,182
IN	14,174	3,158	1,724	4,263	5,029	6,090	2,591	1,752	5,070
IA	6,631	1,586	905	1,851	2,289	3,220	1,073	381	2,255
KS.	6,033	1,372	1,009	1,536	2,116	3,071	959	315	2,091
KY.	9,110	1,764	1,086	2,624	3,636	4,877	840	991	3,268
LA.	13,436	2,278	1,498	5,147	4,513	6,569	3,140	318	4,460
ME	2,987	873	492	573	1,049	1,706	37	7	1,167
MD	9,885	2,891	2,251	1,056	3,687	4,521	1,326	417	4,158
MA	12,022	3,503	2,548	1,888	4,084	5,241	2,321	24	4,440
MI	19,786	4,999	3,831	4,115	6,842	8,483	3,814	1,126	7,354
MN	9,674	2,216	1,191	2,131	4,137	4,927	1,367	387	3,312
MS	6,091	1,351	875	1,309	2,556	3,056	834	214	2,443
MO	11,344	2,915	1,928	1,621	4,880	5,778	1,396	647	4,186
MT.	2,055	372	283	424	975	1,178	237	128	625
NE.	3,571	770	579	645	1,577	1,876	487	113	1,212
NV.	3,956	855	592	740	1,770	1,920	656	233	1,532
NH	2,631	798	523	376	934	1,369	129	54	1,147
NJ.	17,716	4,883	4,052	2,611	6,171	7,852	2,932	99	7,034
NM	3,450	668	657	495	1,631	1,951	406	396	1,169
NY.	31,999	10,696	9,209	3,496	8,598	11,766	6,910	282	13,868
NC	15,678	4,402	2,725	2,897	5,654	7,050	1,119	1,029	7,412
ND	1,713	329	227	510	647	877	148	426	497
OH	25,330	6,495	4,295	6,162	8,378	10,280	4,206	1,905	10,435
OK	7,160	1,649	1,051	1,516	2,944	3,464	1,635	311	2,499
OR	6,530	1,378	951	1,188	3,013	3,331	915	42	2,297
PA	23,152	6,916	3,763	4,342	8,131	10,203	3,990	1,562	8,590
RI	1,981	571	384	404	622	827	497	(Z)	617
SC.	8,313	2,162	1,284	1,919	2,949	3,429	718	591	4,086
SD.	1,521	363	226	247	685	876	136	48	503
TN.	11,724	2,802	2,019	2,342	4,561	5,207	1,186	732	5,208
TX.	54,085	9,658	6,973	19,974	17,481	29,927	9,070	1,860	17,976
UT.	3,669	710	568	554	1,837	2,024	545	409	1,052
VT.	1,344	415	262	161	507	726	41	5	568
VA.	13,248	3,664	2,481	1,843	5,261	8,511	1,418	575	5,435
WA	10,702	2,260	1,555	1,880	5,007	5,701	1,015	153	3,925
WV	3,754	906	558	904	1,387	1,714	533	1,194	1,373
WI.	10,551	2,557	1,572	2,501	3,920	7,615	1,792	510	3,489
WY	1,852	201	200	538	913	1,703	216	392	495

Z Less than $500,000.   [1] Includes sources not shown separately. Total expenditures are the sum of purchases for each source (including electricity sales) less electric utility purchases of fuel.

Source: U.S. Energy Information Administration, *State Energy Price and Expenditure Report, 1999*, Series DOE/EIA-0376(99). See also <http://www.eia.doe.gov/pub/state.prices/pdf/seper.pdf> (released November 2001).

U.S. Census Bureau, Statistical Abstract of the United States: 2002

No. 884. Manufacturing Energy Consumption for all Purposes by Type of Fuel and Major Industry Group: 1998

[In trillions of Btu (23,783 represents 23,783,000,000,000). Estimates represented consumption of energy for all purposes (First Use) represents unduplicated demand for energy by manufacturers. "First Use" is all energy produced offsite, all energy produced onsite, either directly from captive minesand wells or as byproducts from nonenergy materials (such as sawdust from furniture production, hydrogen from electrolysis of brine, nut shells from peanut processing). Based on the Manufacturing Energy Consumption Survey and subject to sampling variability]

Industry	NAICS [1] code	Total	Net elec- tricity [2]	Resi- dual fuel oil	Distil- late fuel oil [3]	Natural gas [4]	LPG and NGL [5]	Coal	Coke and breeze	Other [6]
All industries, total.	(X)	23,783	3,035	406	142	7,426	1,882	1,814	461	8,967
Food and kindred products	311	1,044	213	14	16	568	5	129	2	97
Beverage and tobacco products . .	312	108	24	2	2	45	1	29	-	4
Textile mills	313	256	102	12	4	103	2	20	-	14
Textile product mills	314	50	18	3	(S)	25	(Z)	3	-	(Z)
Apparel	315	48	18	2	1	23	1	1	-	4
Leather and allied products	316	8	3	(Z)	(Z)	4	(Z)	-	-	(Z)
Wood products	321	509	72	1	13	73	4	2	-	343
Paper.	322	2,733	240	151	9	586	5	277	-	1,465
Printing and Related Support . . .	323	98	51	(Z)	(Z)	44	1	(Z)	-	2
Petroleum and coal products	324	7,320	126	72	28	1,007	39	12	-	6,082
Petroleum refineries	324110	7,130	118	70	4	948	33	(Z)	-	5,957
Chemicals.	325	6,064	577	98	10	2,709	1,796	300	7	677
Petrochemicals.	325110	723	8	-	(Z)	(D)	222	(D)	-	(D)
Other basic organic chemicals. .	325199	1,740	73	3	(D)	782	639	(D)	-	201
Plastics materials and resins. . .	325211	1,067	66	2	1	259	675	17	(Z)	60
Nitrogenous fertilizers	325311	592	13	-	(Z)	572	(Z)	-	-	6
Plastics and rubber products	326	328	183	5	1	126	5	3	-	5
Nonmetallic mineral products	327	979	134	4	17	444	3	284	11	82
Primary metals.	331	2,560	545	30	9	933	3	715	437	82
Iron and Steel mills	331111	1,584	158	29	5	494	(Z)	680	388	22
Alumina and aluminum.	3313	490	246	(Z)	1	189	1	2	2	49
Primary aluminum.	331312	254	196	(Z)	(Z)	(D)	(Z)	(D)	-	41
Fabricated metal products	332	445	176	2	6	241	5	3	3	10
Machinery.	333	217	96	1	3	99	3	6	-	7
Computer and electronic products .	334	205	137	1	1	64	(Z)	(Z)	-	1
Electrical equipment, appliances, and component	335	143	55	1	1	53	2	1	(Z)	30
Transportation equipment	336	492	195	5	15	212	4	29	1	31
Furniture and related products . . .	337	88	30	(Z)	1	27	1	2	-	28
Miscellaneous	339	89	40	1	2	40	1	(Z)	-	4

- Represents or rounds to zero.   D Withheld to avoid disclosing data for individual establishments.   S Withheld because Relative Standard Error is greater than 50 percent.   X Not applicable.   Z Less than 0.5 trillion Btu.   [1] North American Industrial Classification System; see text, Section 15, Business Enterprise.   [2] Net electricity is obtained by aggregating purchases, transfers in, and generation from noncombustible renewable resources minus quantities sold and transferred out. Excludes electricity inputs from onsite cogeneration or generation from combustible fuels because that energy has already been included as generating fuel (for example, coal).   [3] Includes Nos 1, 2, and 4 fuel oils and Nos. 1, 2, and 4 diesel fuels.   [4] Includes natural gas obtained from utilities, transmission pipelines, and any other supplier such as brokers and producers.   [5] Liquid petroleum gas and natural gas liquids.   [6] Includes net steam, and other energy that respondents indicated was used to produce heat and power or as feedstock/raw material inputs.

Source: U.S. Energy Information Administration, <http://www.eia.doe.gov/emeu/mecs/mecs98/datatables/contnets.html> (accessed 22 January 2001).

No. 885. Fossil Fuel Prices in Current and Constant (1996) Dollars by Type of Fuel: 1980 to 2000

[In cents per million British thermal units (Btu), except as indicated. All fuel prices taken as close to the point of production as possible. See text, this section, for explanation of Btu conversions from mineral fuels]

Fuel	1980	1985	1990	1993	1994	1995	1996	1997	1998	1999	2000
CURRENT DOLLARS											
Composite [1]	2.04	2.51	1.84	1.67	1.53	1.47	1.82	1.81	1.40	1.64	2.57
Crude oil [2]	3.72	4.15	3.45	2.46	2.27	2.52	3.18	2.97	1.87	2.68	4.61
Natural gas [3].	1.45	2.26	1.55	1.84	1.67	1.40	1.96	2.10	1.75	1.95	3.24
Bituminous coal [4]	1.10	1.15	1.00	0.93	0.91	0.88	0.87	0.85	0.82	0.80	[5]0.80
CONSTANT (1996) DOLLARS											
Composite [1]	3.58	3.41	2.13	1.78	1.59	1.50	1.82	1.77	1.36	1.57	2.40
Crude oil [2]	6.52	5.64	3.99	2.61	2.37	2.57	3.18	2.91	1.82	2.56	4.31
Natural gas [3].	2.54	3.06	1.79	1.96	1.74	1.43	1.96	2.06	1.69	1.86	3.03
Bituminous coal [4].	1.93	1.56	1.15	0.99	0.94	0.90	0.87	0.84	0.80	0.76	[5]0.74

[1] Weighted by relative importance of individual fuels in total fuels production.   [2] Domestic first purchase prices.   [3] Wellhead prices.   [4] Includes subbituminous and lignite.   [5] Calculated using the 1999 coal price for the 2000 value.

Source: U.S. Energy Information Administration, Annual Energy Review. See also <http://www.eia.doe.gov/emeu/aer/contents.html> (released July 2001).

Energy and Utilities   569

No. 886. Energy Imports and Exports by Type of Fuel: 1980 to 2000

[In quadrillion of Btu. For definition of Btu, see text, this section]

Type of fuel	1980	1985	1990	1993	1994	1995	1996	1997	1998	1999	2000 [1]
Net imports, total [2]	**12.25**	**7.87**	**14.09**	**17.22**	**18.65**	**18.03**	**19.35**	**20.94**	**22.47**	**23.74**	**24.42**
Coal	-2.39	-2.39	-2.70	-1.76	-1.66	-2.08	-2.17	-2.01	-1.87	-1.30	-1.21
Natural gas (dry)	0.96	0.90	1.46	2.25	2.52	2.74	2.85	2.90	3.06	3.50	3.57
Petroleum [3]	13.50	8.95	15.29	16.40	17.26	16.89	18.23	19.64	20.94	21.18	21.63
Other [4]	0.18	0.41	0.03	0.32	0.53	0.47	0.45	0.40	0.34	0.36	0.43
Imports, total	15.97	12.10	18.95	21.50	22.73	22.57	24.01	25.51	26.86	27.55	28.52
Coal	0.03	0.05	0.07	0.20	0.22	0.24	0.20	0.19	0.22	0.23	0.31
Natural gas (dry)	1.01	0.95	1.55	2.40	2.68	2.90	3.00	3.06	3.22	3.66	3.81
Petroleum [3]	14.66	10.61	17.12	18.51	19.24	18.88	20.29	21.74	22.91	23.13	23.78
Other [4]	0.28	0.49	0.22	0.39	0.58	0.55	0.52	0.52	0.50	0.52	0.61
Exports, total	3.72	4.23	4.87	4.28	4.08	4.54	4.66	4.58	4.39	3.81	4.10
Coal	2.42	2.44	2.77	1.96	1.88	2.32	2.37	2.19	2.09	1.53	1.53
Natural gas (dry)	0.05	0.06	0.09	0.14	0.16	0.16	0.16	0.16	0.16	0.16	0.24
Petroleum [3]	1.16	1.66	1.82	2.12	1.99	1.99	2.06	2.10	1.97	1.95	2.15
Other [4]	0.09	0.08	0.18	0.06	0.05	0.07	0.07	0.12	0.16	0.17	0.18

[1] Preliminary. [2] Net imports equals imports minus exports. Minus sign (-) denotes an excess of exports over imports.
[3] Includes imports into the Strategic Petroleum Reserve, which began in 1977. [4] Coal coke and small amounts of electricity transmitted across U.S. borders with Canada and Mexico.

Source: U.S. Energy Information Administration, *Annual Energy Review*. See also <http://www.eia.doe.gov/pub/pdf/multi.fuel/038400.pdf> (released August 2001).

No. 887. U.S. Foreign Trade in Selected Mineral Fuels: 1980 to 2000

[Minus sign (-) indicates an excess of imports over exports]

Mineral fuel	Unit	1980	1985	1990	1995	1996	1997	1998	1999	2000 [1]
Natural gas:										
Imports	Bil. cu. ft. . . .	985	950	1,532	2,841	2,937	2,994	3,152	3,586	3,726
Exports	Bil. cu. ft. . . .	49	55	86	154	153	157	159	163	237
Net trade	Bil. cu. ft. . . .	-936	-894	-1,446	-2,687	-2,784	-2,837	-2,993	-3,423	-3,489
Crude oil:										
Imports [2]	Mil. bbl.	1,926	1,168	2,151	2,639	2,740	3,002	3,178	3,187	3,260
Exports	Mil. bbl.	105	75	40	35	40	39	40	43	18
Net trade	Mil. bbl.	-1,821	-1,093	-2,112	-2,604	-2,700	-2,963	-3,138	-3,144	-3,242
Petroleum products:										
Imports [2]	Mil. bbl.	603	681	775	586	719	707	731	773.8	788.4
Exports	Mil. bbl.	94	211	273	312	318	318	327	343.1	379.6
Net trade	Mil. bbl.	-509	-470	-502	-274	-402	-389	-404	-431	-409
Coal: [2]										
Imports	Mil. sh. tons. .	1.2	2.0	2.7	9.5	8.1	7.5	8.7	9.1	12.5
Exports	Mil. sh. tons. .	91.7	92.7	105.8	88.5	90.5	83.5	78.0	58.5	58.5
Net trade	Mil. sh. tons. .	90.5	90.7	103.1	79.1	82.4	76.1	69.3	49.4	46.0

[1] Preliminary. [2] Beginning 1980, includes strategic petroleum reserve imports.
Source: U.S. Energy Information Administration, *Annual Energy Review*. See also <http://www.eia.doe.gov/emeu/aer/contents.html> (accessed April 2002).

No. 888. Crude Oil Imports Into the U.S. by Country of Origin: 1980 to 2000

[In millions of barrels (1,921 represents 1,921,000,000). Barrels contain 42 gallons]

Country of origin	1980	1985	1990	1993	1994	1995	1996	1997	1998	1999	2000
Total imports	**1,921**	**1,168**	**2,151**	**2,477**	**2,578**	**2,639**	**2,748**	**3,002**	**3,178**	**3,187**	**3,320**
OPEC, [1] total	1,410	479	1,283	1,317	1,307	1,303	1,258	1,378	1,522	1,543	1,663
Algeria	166	31	23	9	8	10	3	2	4	9	211
Iraq	10	17	188	-	-	-	-	33	123	265	227
Kuwait [2]	10	1	29	126	112	78	86	92	109	90	96
Qatar	8	-	1	-	-	-	-	-	1	-	-
Saudi Arabia [2]	456	48	436	468	473	460	457	472	512	506	558
United Arab Emirates. . .	63	13	3	4	4	2	1	-	1	-	1
Indonesia	115	107	36	24	34	23	16	19	18	25	13
Nigeria	307	102	286	264	228	227	218	252	251	227	320
Venezuela	57	112	243	369	377	420	477	509	503	420	448
Non-OPEC, [3] total	511	689	869	1,160	1,271	1,336	1,490	1,624	1,656	1,643	1,657
Canada.	73	171	235	329	359	380	394	437	462	430	493
Ecuador [4]	6	20	14	28	33	35	35	42	36	42	46
Gabon [5]	9	19	23	55	71	84	67	84	76	61	52
Malaysia	(NA)	(NA)	(NA)	4	2	2	4	3	9	8	11
Mexico	185	261	251	315	343	375	442	496	482	458	480
'Norway.	53	11	35	50	69	94	107	105	81	96	111
Trinidad and Tobago . .	42	36	28	20	23	23	21	20	19	15	20
United Kingdom	63	101	57	114	145	124	79	62	59	104	106

- Represents zero.   NA Not available.   [1] OPEC (Organization of Petroleum Exporting Countries) includes the Persian Gulf nations shown below, except Bahrain, which is not a member of OPEC, and also includes nations shown under "Other OPEC." [2] Imports from the Neutral Zone between Kuwait and Saudi Arabia are included in Saudi Arabia.   [3] Includes petroleum imported into the United States indirectly from member of OPEC, primarily from Caribbean and West European areas, as petroleum products that were refined from crude oil produced by OPEC.   [4] Ecuador withdrew from OPEC on Dec. 31, 1992; therefore, it is included under OPEC for the period 1980 to 1992.   [5] Gabon withdrew from OPEC on Dec. 31, 1994; therefore, it is included under OPEC for the period 1980 to 1994.

Source: U.S. Energy Information Administration, *Petroleum Supply Annual*, Vol. I.

No. 889. Crude Oil and Refined Products—Summary: 1980 to 2001

[12,442 represents 12,442,000 bbl. Barrels of 42 gallons. Data are averages]

Year	Crude oil (1,000 bbl. per day)					Refined oil products (1,000 bbl. per day)			Total oil imports [2] (1,000 bbl. per day)	Crude oil stocks[3] (mil. bbl.)	
			Imports								
	Input to refiner- ies	Domestic produc- tion	Total [1]	Strate- gic reserve	Exports	Domestic demand	Imports	Exports		Total	Strategic reserve
1980	13,481	8,597	5,263	44	287	17,056	1,646	258	6,909	466	108
1985	12,002	8,971	3,201	118	204	15,726	1,866	577	5,067	814	493
1990	13,409	7,355	5,894	27	109	16,988	2,123	748	8,018	908	586
1991	13,301	7,417	5,782	-	116	16,714	1,844	885	7,627	893	569
1992	13,411	7,171	6,083	10	89	17,033	1,805	861	7,888	893	575
1993	13,613	6,847	6,787	15	98	17,237	1,833	904	8,620	922	587
1994	13,866	6,662	7,063	12	99	17,718	1,933	843	8,996	929	592
1995	13,973	6,560	7,230	-	95	17,725	1,605	855	8,835	895	592
1996	14,195	6,465	7,508	-	110	18,309	1,971	871	9,478	850	566
1997	14,662	6,452	8,225	-	108	18,620	1,936	896	10,162	868	563
1998	14,889	6,252	8,706	-	110	18,917	2,002	835	10,708	895	571
1999	14,804	5,881	8,731	8	118	19,519	2,122	822	10,852	852	567
2000	15,067	5,822	9,071	8	50	19,701	2,389	990	11,459	826	541
2001	15,130	[4]5,853	9,146	11	23	19,593	2,473	959	11,619	862	550

- Represents zero.   X Not applicable.   [1] Includes Strategic Petroleum Reserve.   [2] Crude oil (including Strategic Petroleum Reserve imports) plus refined products.   [3] End of year.   [4] Estimate.

Source: U.S. Energy Information Administration, *Monthly Energy Review,* March 2002 issue.

No. 890. Petroleum and Coal Products Corporations—Sales, Net Profit, and Profit Per Dollar of Sales: 1990 to 2001

[Represents SIC group 29. Through 2000 based on Standard Industrial Classification code; beginning 2001 based on North American Industry Classification System. Profit rates are averages of quarterly figures at annual rates. Beginning 1990, excludes estimates for corporations with less than $250,000 in assets]

Item	Unit	1990	1991	1992	1994	1995	1996	1997	1998	1999	2000	2001
Sales	Bil. dol. .	318.5	282.2	278.0	268.2	283.1	323.5	320.0	250.4	277.0	455.2	469.9
Net profit:												
Before income taxes	Bil. dol . .	23.1	12.1	2.0	17.2	16.5	32.6	36.8	9.7	20.3	55.5	47.0
After income taxes	Bil. dol . .	17.8	10.8	3.1	14.9	13.9	26.6	29.4	8.3	17.2	42.6	35.6
Depreciation[1]	Bil. dol . .	18.7	18.0	18.3	17.1	16.7	15.9	15.6	14.7	13.5	15.5	17.1
Profits per dollar of sales:												
Before income taxes	Cents . .	7.3	4.3	0.4	6.3	5.8	10.1	11.5	3.5	7.1	12.2	9.7
After income taxes	Cents . .	5.6	3.8	0.9	5.5	4.9	8.2	9.2	3.1	6.0	9.4	7.4
Profits on stockholders' equity:												
Before income taxes	Percent .	16.4	8.6	1.6	13.2	12.6	23.2	23.5	6.0	13.0	29.4	21.8
After income taxes	Percent .	12.7	7.6	2.5	11.4	10.6	18.9	18.9	5.2	11.0	22.6	16.5

[1] Includes depletion and accelerated amortization of emergency facilities.
Source: U.S. Census Bureau, *Quarterly Financial Report for Manufacturing, Mining, and Trade Corporations.*

No. 891. Major Petroleum Companies—Financial Summary: 1980 to 2001

[Data represent a composite of approximately 42 major worldwide petroleum companies aggregated on a consolidated total company basis]

Item	1980	1985	1990	1995	1996	1997	1998	1999	2000	2001
FINANCIAL DATA (bil. dol.)										
Net income	32.9	19.4	26.8	24.3	39.7	40.0	14.5	35.3	76.4	61.2
Depreciation, depletion, etc	32.5	53.0	38.7	43.1	44.4	46.0	61.0	45.0	53.3	62.2
Cash flow [1]	65.4	72.4	65.5	67.4	84.1	86.0	75.5	75.3	129.7	138.1
Dividends paid	9.3	12.0	15.9	17.6	18.9	20.1	20.9	21.7	23.0	29.6
Net internal funds available for investment or debt repayment [2]	56.1	60.4	49.6	49.8	65.2	65.9	54.6	54.1	106.7	108.6
Capital and exploratory expenditures	62.1	58.3	59.6	59.8	59.3	75.3	83.9	67.7	72.8	97.5
Long-term capitalization	211.4	272.1	300.0	304.3	336.6	372.5	382.0	456.2	516.9	535.7
Long-term debt	49.8	93.5	90.4	85.4	80.8	86.1	103.9	105.4	112.8	140.9
Preferred stock	2.0	3.3	5.2	5.7	5.8	5.1	3.9	4.8	5.4	6.5
Common stock and retained earnings [3] . .	159.6	175.3	204.4	213.2	250.0	281.3	274.2	346.0	398.7	388.3
Excess of expenditures over cash income [4]	6.0	-2.1	10.0	10.0	-5.9	9.4	29.3	13.6	-33.9	-11.1
RATIOS [5] (percent)										
Long-term debt to long-term capitalization. .	23.6	34.4	30.1	28.1	24.0	23.1	27.2	23.1	21.8	26.6
Net income to total average capital	17.0	7.0	9.1	8.1	12.4	11.3	3.8	8.9	15.7	12.3
Net income to average common equity. . . .	22.5	10.8	13.5	11.6	17.1	15.1	5.2	12.4	20.5	16.3

[1] Generally represents internally-generated funds from operations. Sum of net income and noncash charges such as depreciation, depletion, and amortization.   [2] Cash flow minus dividends paid.   [3] Includes common stock, capital surplus, and earned surplus accounts after adjustments.   [4] Capital and exploratory expenditures plus dividends paid minus cash flow.   [5] Represents approximate year-to-year comparisons because of changes in the makeup of the group due to mergers and other corporate changes.
Source: Carl H. Pforzheimer & Co., New York, NY, *Comparative Oil Company Statements,* annual.

Energy and Utilities   571

No. 892. Electric Power Industry—Sales, Prices, Net Generation, Net Summer Capability, and Consumption of Fuels: 1990 to 2000

[Net generation for calendar years; capability as of December 31]

Item	Unit	1990	1995	1997	1998	1999	2000
ELECTRIC POWER INDUSTRY							
Consumption, total.	Bil. kWh. . .	2,816.7	3,162.4	3,294.6	3,424.0	3,500.9	3,606.5
Net generation, total	Bil. kWh. . .	3,024.9	3,357.8	3,494.2	3,617.9	3,706.1	3,791.9
Electric utilities	Bil. kWh. . .	2,808.2	2,994.5	3,122.5	3,212.2	3,173.7	3,009.5
Nonutilities.	Bil. kWh. . .	216.7	363.3	371.7	405.7	532.5	782.4
Electricity imports	Bil. kWh. . .	18.4	42.9	43.0	39.5	42.9	50.4
Electricity exports	Bil. kWh. . .	16.1	3.6	9.0	13.2	14.0	14.8
Electricity losses and unaccounted for	Bil. kWh. . .	210.4	234.6	233.7	220.1	234.1	221.0
Electric utility retail sales of electricity. . .	Bil. kWh. . .	2,712.6	3,013.3	3,145.6	3,264.2	3,312.1	3,398.1
Direct use of electricity at nonutilities	Bil. kWh. . .	104.2	149.2	149.0	159.8	188.8	208.4
Electricity retail prices per kWh:							
All sectors, current dollars	Cents . . .	6.57	6.89	6.85	6.74	6.66	6.66
All sectors, real (1996) dollars	Cents . . .	7.59	7.02	6.72	6.53	6.36	6.23
Residential, current dollars.	Cents . . .	7.83	8.40	8.43	8.26	8.16	8.21
Residential, real (1996) dollars	Cents . . .	9.05	8.56	8.27	8.00	7.79	7.68
Commercial, current dollars	Cents . . .	7.34	7.69	7.59	7.41	7.26	7.20
Commercial, real (1996) dollars	Cents . . .	8.48	7.84	7.44	7.18	6.93	6.73
Industrial, current dollars	Cents . . .	4.74	4.66	4.53	4.48	4.43	4.45
Industrial, real (1996) dollars	Cents . . .	5.48	4.75	4.44	4.34	4.23	4.16
Other users, current dollars	Cents . . .	6.40	6.88	6.91	6.63	6.35	6.37
Other users, real (1996) dollars.	Cents . . .	7.40	7.01	6.78	6.42	6.06	5.96
Net generation, total [1]	Bil. kWh	3,024.9	3,357.8	3,494.2	3,617.9	3,706.1	3,791.9
Coal	Bil. kWh. . .	1,590.3	1,710.2	1,844.1	1,873.9	1,884.3	1,964.6
Petroleum	Bil. kWh. . .	124.0	75.3	93.0	126.9	123.6	108.9
Natural gas	Bil. kWh. . .	378.3	498.5	485.4	540.6	556.2	595.8
Nuclear	Bil. kWh. . .	577.0	673.4	628.6	673.7	728.3	753.9
Hydroelectric pumped storage plants . . .	Bil. kWh. . .	-3.5	-2.7	-4.0	-4.4	-6.3	-5.6
Conventional hydroelectric power plants .	Bil. kWh. . .	293.0	311.0	358.9	323.3	319.5	274.6
Geothermal	Bil. kWh. . .	15.8	14.4	14.6	14.7	16.8	14.2
Wood	Bil. kWh. . .	30.4	36.4	34.2	31.8	37.6	39.5
Waste	Bil. kWh. . .	10.8	16.9	17.6	18.1	20.2	21.2
Other waste	Bil. kWh. . .	2.3	3.4	3.0	3.2	3.3	3.4
Wind	Bil. kWh. . .	3.0	3.2	3.2	3.0	4.5	4.9
Solar	Bil. kWh. . .	0.6	0.8	0.9	0.9	0.8	0.8
Net summer capability, total [1]	Mil. kW . . .	734.9	769.5	778.5	775.9	794.9	818.5
Coal-fired plants	Mil. kW . . .	306.7	310.8	313.1	312.6	321.7	322.3
Petroleum-fired plants	Mil. kW . . .	56.7	48.0	46.3	42.2	34.8	39.3
Natural gas-fired plants	Mil. kW . . .	31.0	41.9	49.9	59.1	82.1	96.7
Dual-fired plants	Mil. kW . . .	133.5	152.4	153.6	148.0	141.4	145.5
Nuclear electric power plants	Mil. kW . . .	99.6	99.5	99.7	97.1	97.5	97.4
Hydroelectric pumped storage plants . . .	Mil. kW . . .	19.5	21.4	19.3	18.9	19.5	19.6
Conventional hydroelectric power plants .	Mil. kW . . .	74.0	78.6	79.8	79.6	79.5	79.5
Geothermal energy plants	Mil. kW . . .	2.7	3.0	2.9	2.9	2.9	2.9
Wood energy plants	Mil. kW . . .	6.2	6.8	7.1	6.8	6.7	6.8
Waste energy plants	Mil. kW . . .	2.6	3.5	3.4	3.5	4.3	4.3
Wind energy plants	Mil. kW . . .	1.9	1.7	1.6	1.7	2.3	2.3
Solar energy plants	Mil. kW . . .	0.3	0.3	0.3	0.4	0.4	0.4
Fuel consumption:							
Coal	Mil. sh. tons.	805.9	879.3	953.3	967.7	951.6	991.3
Distillate fuel and kerosene.	Mil. bbl . . .	14.8	15.6	15.2	22.0	34.8	30.8
Residual fuel	Mil. bbl . . .	209.1	121.6	145.6	210.8	160.7	143.4
Petroleum	Mil. bbl . . .	233.6	161.9	189.6	264.1	218.1	195.5
Natural gas	Bil. cu. ft. . .	4,174.1	5,500.5	5,199.8	5,924.5	5,679.9	6,325.0
ELECTRIC UTILITIES							
Net generation, total [1]	Bil. kWh . .	2,808.2	2,994.5	3,122.5	3,212.2	3,173.7	3,009.5
Coal	Bil. kWh. . .	1,559.6	1,652.9	1,787.8	1,807.5	1,767.7	1,692.3
Petroleum	Bil. kWh. . .	117.0	60.8	77.8	110.2	86.9	72.3
Natural gas	Bil. kWh. . .	264.1	307.3	283.6	309.2	296.4	289.8
Nuclear	Bil. kWh. . .	576.9	673.4	628.6	673.7	725.0	705.4
Hydroelectric pumped storage plants . . .	Bil. kWh. . .	-3.5	-2.7	-4.0	-4.4	-6.0	-5.3
Conventional hydroelectric power plants .	Bil. kWh. . .	283.4	296.4	341.3	308.8	299.9	252.9
Net summer capability, total [1]	Mil. kW . . .	690.5	706.1	711.9	686.7	639.3	602.4
Coal-fired plants	Mil. kW . . .	299.9	300.6	302.9	299.7	277.8	259.1
Petroleum-fired plants	Mil. kW . . .	55.4	46.1	43.7	39.8	31.5	26.2
Natural gas-fired plants	Mil. kW . . .	15.0	17.7	22.9	26.2	37.4	39.0
Dual-fired plants	Mil. kW . . .	127.5	143.2	144.9	127.2	103.5	99.9
Nuclear electric power plants	Mil. kW . . .	99.6	99.5	99.7	97.1	95.0	85.5
Hydroelectric pumped storage plants . . .	Mil. kW . . .	19.5	21.4	19.3	18.9	18.9	17.9
Conventional hydroelectric power plants .	Mil. kW . . .	71.4	75.3	76.2	75.5	74.1	73.7
NONUTILITY PLANTS							
Net generation, total [1]	Bil. kWh . .	216.7	363.3	371.7	405.7	532.5	782.4
Coal	Bil. kWh. . .	30.7	57.3	56.3	66.5	116.7	272.4
Petroleum	Bil. kWh. . .	7.0	14.4	15.3	16.8	36.6	36.6
Natural gas	Bil. kWh. . .	114.3	191.2	201.8	231.4	259.8	306.0
Net summer capability, total [1]	Mil. kW . . .	44.5	63.4	66.6	89.2	155.6	216.1
Coal firod plants	Mil. kW . . .	6.8	10.2	10.3	12.8	44.0	63.2
Petroleum-fired plants	Mil. kW . . .	1.2	2.0	2.7	2.4	3.4	13.0
Natural gas-fired plants	Mil. kW . . .	16.0	24.2	26.9	32.9	44.7	57.8
Dual-fired plants	Mil. kW . . .	6.0	9.2	8.8	20.8	37.9	45.5

[1] Includes types not shown separately.

Source: U.S. Energy Information Administration, *Electric Power Annual* and *Annual Energy Review*.

No. 893. Electric Utility Industry—Capability, Peak Load, and Capacity Margin: 1980 to 2000

[Excludes Alaska and Hawaii. Capability represents the maximum kilowatt output with all power sources available and with hydraulic equipment under actual water conditions, allowing for maintenance, emergency outages, and system operating requirements. Capacity margin is the difference between capability and peak load]

| Year | Capability at the time of— | | | | Noncoincident peak load | | Capacity margin | | | |
| | Summer peak load (1,000 kW) | | Winter peak load (1,000 kW) | | | | Summer | | Winter | |
	Amount	Change from prior year	Amount	Change from prior year	Summer	Winter	Amount (1,000 kW)	Percent of capability	Amount (1,000 kW)	Percent of capability
1980	558,237	13,731	572,195	17,670	427,058	384,567	131,179	23.5	187,628	32.8
1981	572,219	13,982	586,569	14,374	429,349	397,800	142,870	25.0	188,769	32.2
1982	586,142	13,923	598,066	11,497	415,618	373,985	170,524	29.1	224,081	37.5
1983	596,449	10,307	612,453	14,387	447,526	410,779	148,923	25.0	201,674	32.9
1984	604,240	7,791	622,125	9,672	451,150	436,374	153,090	25.3	185,751	29.9
1985	621,597	17,357	636,475	14,350	460,503	423,660	161,094	25.9	212,815	33.4
1986	633,291	11,694	646,721	10,246	476,320	422,857	156,971	24.8	223,864	34.6
1987	648,118	14,827	662,977	16,256	496,185	448,277	151,933	23.4	214,700	32.4
1988	661,580	13,462	676,940	13,963	529,460	466,533	132,120	20.0	210,407	31.1
1989	673,316	11,736	685,249	8,309	523,432	496,378	149,884	22.3	188,871	27.6
1990	685,091	11,775	696,757	11,508	545,537	484,014	139,554	20.4	212,743	30.5
1991	690,915	5,824	703,212	6,455	551,320	485,435	139,595	20.2	217,777	31.0
1992	695,436	4,521	707,752	4,540	548,707	492,983	146,729	21.1	214,769	30.3
1993	694,250	-1,186	711,957	4,205	575,356	521,733	118,894	17.1	190,224	26.7
1994	702,985	8,735	715,090	3,133	585,320	518,253	117,665	16.7	196,837	27.5
1995	714,222	11,237	727,679	12,589	620,249	544,684	93,973	13.2	182,995	25.1
1996	724,728	10,506	737,637	9,958	615,529	554,081	107,938	14.9	183,556	24.9
1997	725,829	1,101	736,666	-971	631,355	529,874	88,152	12.1	206,792	28.1
1998	724,193	-1,636	735,090	-1,576	660,293	567,558	63,900	8.8	167,532	22.8
1999	733,481	9,288	748,036	12,946	681,449	570,915	52,032	7.1	177,121	23.7
2000	750,771	17,290	767,505	19,469	678,413	588,426	72,358	9.6	179,079	23.3

Source: Edison Electric Institute, Washington, DC, *Statistical Yearbook of the Electric Utility Industry*, annual.

No. 894. Electric Energy Sales by Class of Service and State: 2000

[In billions of kilowatt-hours (3,309.6 represents 3,309,600,000,000)]

State	Total [1]	Resi-dential	Com-mercial	Indus-trial	State	Total [1]	Resi-dential	Com-mercial	Indus-trial
United States	3,309.6	1,183.1	1,000.9	1,017.7					
					Missouri	72.6	29.6	25.9	16.1
Alabama	83.5	28.8	19.1	35.0	Montana	12.5	3.9	3.5	4.8
Alaska	5.3	1.9	2.2	1.0	Nebraska	24.3	8.3	7.0	7.3
Arizona	61.0	24.8	21.3	12.0	Nevada	27.8	9.4	6.5	11.2
Arkansas	41.6	14.9	8.7	17.3	New Hampshire	10.0	3.6	3.6	2.6
California	221.3	78.0	82.5	53.1					
					New Jersey	62.8	24.1	27.3	10.9
Colorado	43.0	14.0	18.0	10.0	New Mexico	18.8	4.9	6.7	5.5
Connecticut	30.0	11.6	11.9	5.8	New York	124.5	41.6	47.0	23.5
Delaware	10.8	3.6	3.7	3.5	North Carolina	119.9	46.5	36.9	34.3
District of Columbia	10.6	1.6	8.3	0.3	North Dakota	9.4	3.4	2.6	3.0
Florida	195.8	99.0	72.1	18.9					
					Ohio	161.1	46.5	40.8	69.9
Georgia	119.2	44.6	37.0	36.1	Oklahoma	49.6	19.6	13.1	13.9
Hawaii	9.7	2.8	3.0	3.8	Oregon	50.3	18.2	15.3	16.4
Idaho	22.8	7.0	7.1	8.4	Pennsylvania	98.1	41.4	25.3	30.4
Illinois	125.6	40.1	39.2	36.5	Rhode Island	7.1	2.7	3.0	1.4
Indiana	97.8	28.6	20.5	48.0					
					South Carolina	77.0	25.3	17.5	33.3
Iowa	39.1	12.0	8.4	17.1	South Dakota	8.3	3.4	2.4	2.0
Kansas	35.9	12.5	12.5	10.2	Tennessee	95.7	36.6	25.8	32.3
Kentucky	78.3	23.4	13.9	37.7	Texas	318.3	116.9	84.8	101.6
Louisiana	80.7	27.7	18.2	32.0	Utah	23.2	6.5	7.9	7.9
Maine	6.4	1.3	2.8	2.3					
					Vermont	5.6	2.0	1.9	1.6
Maryland	60.6	23.9	25.8	10.1	Virginia	96.7	37.5	28.3	20.6
Massachusetts	48.9	17.5	20.9	9.8	Washington	93.2	33.0	24.0	32.1
Michigan	104.4	30.7	35.8	36.9	West Virginia	27.7	9.7	6.8	11.1
Minnesota	59.8	18.6	11.6	28.8	Wisconsin	65.1	19.9	18.3	26.2
Mississippi	45.3	17.2	11.5	15.9	Wyoming	12.4	2.1	2.7	7.3

[1] Includes "other service" not shown separately.

U.S. Energy Information Administration, *Electric Power Annual*, Volume 1. See <http://www.eia.doe.gov/cneaf/electricity/epav1/epav1.pdf> (issued August 2001).

Energy and Utilities 573

No. 895. Electric Utilities—Net Generation and Net Summer Capability by State: 1990 to 2000

[Capability as of Dec. 31. (2,808.2 represents 2,808,200,000,000) Covers utilities for public use]

State	Net generation (bil. kWh)					Net summer capability (mil. kW)			
				2000					
	1990	1995	1999	Total	Percent from coal	1990	1995	1998	1999
United States.	2,808.2	2,994.5	3,173.7	3,015.4	56.3	690.5	706.1	686.7	639.3
Alabama.	76.2	99.6	113.9	118.0	65.2	20.0	20.5	21.3	21.5
Alaska	4.5	4.8	4.6	4.9	3.7	1.5	1.7	1.7	1.7
Arizona.	62.3	69.0	83.1	88.2	46.1	14.9	15.2	15.1	15.1
Arkansas	37.1	39.5	44.1	41.5	58.0	9.6	9.6	9.6	9.3
California	114.5	121.9	87.9	85.9	-	43.7	43.3	30.7	24.3
Colorado.	31.3	32.7	36.2	40.1	87.5	6.6	6.6	6.9	7.3
Connecticut.	32.2	26.9	20.5	17.0	-	7.1	6.7	5.6	2.9
Delaware	7.1	8.3	6.2	4.1	80.2	2.0	2.2	2.3	2.3
District of Columbia	0.4	0.2	0.2	0.1	-	0.8	0.8	0.8	0.8
Florida	123.6	147.2	166.9	169.9	39.5	32.7	35.9	36.5	36.5
Georgia	97.6	102.0	110.5	116.2	68.0	20.7	22.3	23.4	23.3
Hawaii	8.0	6.2	6.5	6.5	-	1.5	1.6	1.6	1.6
Idaho	8.6	10.1	12.5	10.1	-	2.3	2.6	2.6	2.6
Illinois	127.0	145.2	149.8	113.6	26.9	32.6	33.1	30.4	17.0
Indiana.	97.7	105.2	114.2	119.7	98.2	20.6	20.7	20.3	20.4
Iowa	29.0	33.5	37.0	39.6	85.4	8.0	8.2	8.4	8.4
Kansas.	33.9	38.2	42.0	44.8	72.6	9.6	9.7	9.9	10.0
Kentucky	73.8	86.2	81.7	81.4	96.6	15.5	15.4	14.0	14.7
Louisiana	58.2	65.6	64.8	57.6	25.1	16.8	17.0	17.0	16.3
Maine.	9.1	2.7	1.2	(Z)	-	2.4	2.4	1.5	0.1
Maryland	31.5	44.7	49.3	31.8	64.0	9.8	11.0	11.0	11.0
Massachusetts.	36.5	27.0	4.4	1.7	64.2	9.9	9.3	3.4	2.2
Michigan.	89.1	92.5	87.9	89.6	74.8	22.3	22.0	21.9	22.4
Minnesota.	41.6	42.5	44.2	46.6	68.1	8.8	8.9	9.1	9.0
Mississippi	22.9	26.4	32.2	33.9	40.9	7.0	7.2	7.2	6.8
Missouri	59.0	65.4	73.5	76.3	82.1	15.2	15.7	16.3	16.8
Montana.	25.7	25.4	27.6	6.6	4.9	4.9	4.9	4.9	3.0
Nebraska	21.6	25.3	30.0	29.0	63.4	5.5	5.5	5.8	5.8
Nevada	19.3	20.0	26.5	29.3	64.5	4.9	5.6	5.6	5.4
New Hampshire	10.8	13.9	13.9	12.7	31.2	2.6	2.5	2.3	2.3
New Jersey.	36.5	27.1	38.9	25.3	21.0	13.7	13.8	13.4	12.1
New Mexico	28.5	29.4	31.7	32.9	88.5	5.0	5.1	5.3	5.3
New York	128.7	101.2	97.0	73.2	5.5	31.2	32.1	29.6	17.7
North Carolina	79.8	96.1	109.9	114.4	62.7	20.2	20.6	21.0	21.2
North Dakota.	26.8	28.8	31.3	31.1	93.0	4.5	4.5	4.7	4.7
Ohio	126.5	137.9	140.9	144.4	87.4	27.0	27.4	26.8	27.1
Oklahoma.	45.1	48.0	50.3	51.4	63.9	12.8	12.9	12.6	12.9
Oregon.	49.2	44.0	51.7	46.1	8.2	11.2	10.4	10.4	10.3
Pennsylvania.	165.7	168.9	161.6	97.1	37.8	33.4	33.7	33.8	25.3
Rhode Island.	0.6	0.7	(Z)	(Z)	-	0.3	0.4	(Z)	(Z)
South Carolina.	69.3	78.4	87.3	90.4	42.8	14.9	16.7	17.6	17.7
South Dakota	6.4	8.8	10.6	9.7	37.9	2.7	3.0	2.9	2.9
Tennessee	73.9	82.3	89.7	92.3	65.7	17.0	16.1	17.5	17.3
Texas.	234.0	261.7	292.5	297.3	46.4	62.0	64.4	65.2	65.3
Utah	32.3	32.1	36.1	35.8	95.0	4.8	4.8	5.1	5.1
Vermont	5.0	4.8	4.7	5.3	-	1.1	1.1	0.8	0.8
Virginia.	47.2	52.7	65.1	65.8	51.6	13.7	14.3	15.3	15.3
Washington.	100.5	95.7	112.1	96.2	3.4	24.2	24.3	25.2	25.2
West Virginia.	77.4	77.3	91.7	89.7	99.3	14.4	14.5	14.5	14.5
Wisconsin	45.6	51.0	54.7	55.7	73.8	10.6	11.5	11.9	12.1
Wyoming	39.4	39.7	43.0	44.6	97.2	5.8	6.0	6.0	6.0

- Represents zero. Z Represents less than 50 million kWh or 50,000 kW.

Source: U.S. Energy Information Administration, *Electric Power Annual, Electric Power Monthly*, August and December issues, and *Inventory of Power Plants in the United States*, annual. Also see <http://www.eia.doe.gov/fuelelectric.html> (accessed July 31, 2002).

No. 896. Nuclear Power Plants—Number, Capacity, and Generation: 1980 to 2001

Item	1980	1985	1990	1993	1994	1995	1996	1997	1998	1999	2000	2001
Operable generating units [1]	71	96	112	110	109	109	109	107	104	104	104	104
Net summer capability [1][2] (mil. kW)	51.8	79.4	99.6	99.1	99.1	99.5	100.8	99.7	97.1	97.4	97.4	98.1
Net generation (bil. kWh)	251.1	383.7	577.0	610.4	640.5	673.4	674.7	628.6	673.7	728.3	753.9	767.3
Percent of total electric utility generation [3]	11.0	15.5	19.1	19.1	19.7	20.1	19.6	18.0	18.6	19.7	19.8	20.3
Capacity factor [3]	56.3	58.0	66.0	70.5	73.8	77.4	76.2	71.1	78.2	85.3	88.1	89.3

[1] As of year-end.   [2] Net summer capability is the peak steady hourly output that generating equipment is expected to supply to system load, exclusive of auxiliary and other power plant, as demonstrated by test at the time of summer peak demand. [3] Weighted average of monthly capacity factors. Monthly factors are derived by dividing actual monthly generation by the maximum possible generation for the month (hours in month times net maximum dependable capacity).

Source: U.S. Energy Information Administration, *Annual Energy Review.* See also <http://www.eia.doe.gov/emeu/aer/contents.html> (released August 2001).

No. 897. Nuclear Power Plants—Number of Units, Net Generation, and Net Summer Capability by State: 1999

State	Number of units	Net generation Total (mil. kWh)	Net generation Percent of total [1]	Net summer capability Total (mil. kW)	Net summer capability Percent of total [1]	State	Number of units	Net generation Total (mil. kWh)	Net generation Percent of total [1]	Net summer capability Total (mil. kW)	Net summer capability Percent of total [1]
U.S.	104	725,036	22.8	97.07	15.2	MS	1	8,428	25.9	1.20	17.7
AL	5	30,892	27.1	4.95	23.1	MO	1	8,587	11.7	1.14	6.8
AZ	3	30,416	36.6	3.73	24.7	NE	2	10,091	33.7	1.25	21.4
AR	2	12,920	29.3	1.69	18.3	NH	1	8,676	62.4	1.16	50.7
CA	4	33,372	37.2	4.31	17.7	NJ	4	28,971	74.5	3.86	32.0
CT	2	12,675	61.6	2.01	68.9	NY	6	37,019	38.2	4.97	28.1
FL	5	31,526	18.9	3.87	10.6	NC	5	37,524	34.2	4.69	22.1
GA	4	31,478	28.6	3.95	16.9	OH	2	16,422	11.6	2.04	7.5
IL	11	81,356	54.4	10.53	62.0	PA	9	70,885	44.0	9.04	35.8
IA	1	3,640	9.8	0.52	6.2	SC	7	50,814	58.2	6.43	36.4
KS	1	9,157	21.8	1.16	11.6	TN	3	27,227	30.4	3.36	19.5
LA	2	13,112	20.3	2.01	12.3	TX	4	36,760	12.7	4.80	7.4
MD	2	13,312	26.9	1.68	15.3	VT	1	4,059	85.3	0.50	63.9
MA	1	1,931	31.3	0.67	30.0	VA	4	28,301	43.5	3.39	22.2
MI	4	14,591	16.6	3.92	17.5	WA	1	6,086	5.4	1.12	4.5
MN	3	13,316	30.2	1.63	18.1	WI	3	11,495	21.0	1.49	12.4

[1] For total capability and generation, see Table 895.

Source: U.S. Energy Information Administration, *Electric Power Annual* and *Electric Power Monthly,* December issues.

No. 898. Uranium Concentrate—Supply, Inventories, and Average Prices: 1980 to 2000

[**Years ending Dec. 31**. For additional data on uranium, see Section 18, Natural Resources, on mining]

Item	Unit	1980	1990	1994	1995	1996	1997	1998	1999	2000
Production	Mil. lb.	43.70	8.89	3.35	6.04	6.32	5.64	4.71	4.61	3.96
Exports	Mil. lb.	5.8	2.0	17.7	9.8	11.5	17.0	15.1	8.5	13.6
Imports	Mil. lb.	3.6	23.7	36.6	41.3	45.4	43.0	43.7	47.6	44.9
Utility purchases from domestic suppliers	Mil. lb.	(NA)	20.5	22.7	22.3	22.9	18.7	20.3	19.2	22.9
Loaded into U.S. nuclear reactors [1]	Mil. lb.	(NA)	(NA)	40.4	51.1	46.2	48.2	38.2	58.8	51.4
Inventories, total	Mil. lb.	(NA)	129.1	86.9	72.5	80.0	106.2	136.5	127.1	112.3
At domestic suppliers	Mil. lb.	(NA)	26.4	21.5	13.7	13.9	40.4	70.7	68.8	56.5
At electric utilities	Mil. lb.	(NA)	102.7	65.4	58.7	66.1	65.9	65.8	58.3	55.9
Average price per pound: Purchased imports	Dollars	(NA)	12.55	8.95	10.20	13.15	11.81	11.19	10.55	9.84
Domestic purchases	Dollars	(NA)	15.70	10.30	11.11	13.81	12.87	12.31	11.88	11.45

NA Not available.   [1] Does not include any fuel rods removed from reactors and later reloaded into the reactor.

Source: Except as noted, U.S. Energy Information Administration, *Annual Energy Review, Uranium Industry Annual* and unpublished data.

Energy and Utilities   575

[A nonutility power producer may be a corporation, person, agency, authority, or other legal entity or instrumentality that owns electric generating capacity and is not an electric utility. Nonutility power producers include qualifying cogenerators, qualifying small power producers, and other nonutility generators (including independent power producers) without a designated franchised service area, and which do not file forms listed in the Code of Federal Regulations, Title 18, Part 141]

Type of fuel	Unit	1990	1992	1993	1994	1995	1996	1997	1998	1999
Installed capacity ...	1,000 kW..	45,271	56,814	60,778	68,461	70,254	73,189	74,004	98,085	167,357
Coal[1]	1,000 kW..	6,937	8,503	9,772	10,372	10,877	11,370	11,027	13,712	48,501
Petroleum[2]	1,000 kW..	1,038	1,730	2,043	2,262	2,116	2,251	2,924	2,629	3,701
Natural gas	1,000 kW..	17,430	21,542	23,463	26,925	27,906	30,166	31,092	37,325	49,353
Other gas[3]	1,000 kW..	(4)	(4)	(4)	1,130	1,217	327	35	205	918
Petroleum/natural gas (combined)	1,000 kW..	6,468	8,478	8,505	9,820	10,479	10,912	10,029	23,105	40,508
Hydroelectric	1,000 kW..	1,968	2,684	2,741	3,364	3,399	3,419	3,770	4,136	5,996
Geothermal	1,000 kW..	1,086	1,254	1,318	1,335	1,295	1,346	1,303	1,449	2,698
Solar	1,000 kW..	360	360	360	354	354	354	354	385	382
Wind	1,000 kW..	1,405	1,822	1,813	1,737	1,723	1,670	1,566	1,689	2,222
Wood[5]	1,000 kW..	6,049	6,805	7,046	7,416	6,885	7,263	7,282	6,887	6,647
Waste[6]	1,000 kW..	2,323	3,006	3,131	3,150	3,430	3,463	3,394	3,488	4,316
Gross generation ...	Mil. kWh..	220,058	296,001	325,226	354,925	375,901	382,423	384,496	421,364	569,336
Coal[1]	Mil. kWh..	32,131	47,363	53,367	59,035	60,234	61,375	59,211	70,369	129,502
Petroleum[2]	Mil. kWh..	7,330	10,963	13,364	15,069	15,049	14,959	15,930	17,533	21,947
Natural gas	Mil. kWh..	116,969	158,798	174,282	179,735	196,633	198,555	207,527	238,747	295,725
Other gases[3]	Mil. kWh..	(4)	(4)	(4)	12,480	13,984	14,750	11,687	8,866	8,707
Hydroelectric	Mil. kWh..	8,153	9,446	11,511	13,227	14,774	16,555	17,902	14,633	21,748
Geothermal	Mil. kWh..	7,235	8,578	9,749	10,122	9,912	10,198	9,382	9,882	15,581
Solar	Mil. kWh..	663	746	897	824	824	903	893	887	870
Wind	Mil. kWh..	2,251	2,916	3,052	3,482	3,185	3,400	3,248	3,015	4,510
Wood[5]	Mil. kWh..	30,812	36,255	37,421	38,595	37,283	37,525	34,898	32,596	34,999
Waste[6]	Mil. kWh..	11,688	17,352	18,325	18,797	20,231	20,412	20,246	21,086	22,312
Supply and disposition:										
Gross generation	Mil. kWh..	220,058	296,001	325,226	354,925	375,901	382,423	384,496	421,364	569,336
Receipts	Mil. kWh..	60,926	83,421	85,323	94,166	89,919	103,219	88,506	90,675	89,688
Sales to utilities	Mil. kWh..	106,224	164,374	187,466	204,688	217,906	224,646	223,532	249,483	369,539
Sales to other end users	Mil. kWh..	19,824	10,786	15,569	17,626	15,548	14,284	18,147	25,777	42,983
Facility use	Mil. kWh..	154,936	204,261	207,514	226,777	232,367	246,713	231,138	236,770	250,227

[1] Includes coal, anthracite, culm and coal waste. [2] Includes petroleum, petroleum coke, diesel, kerosene, and petroleum sludge and tar. [3] Includes butane, ethane, propane, and other gases. [4] Included in "Natural gas." [5] Includes wood, wood waste, peat, wood liquors, railroad ties, pitch and wood sludge. [6] Includes municipal solid waste, agricultural waste, straw, tires, landfill gases and other waste.

Source: Energy Information Administration, *Electric Power Annual*, Vol. II; and *Inventory of Nonutility Electric Power Plants in the United States,* annual.

No. 900. Electric Utilities—Generation, Sales, Revenue, and Customers: 1980 to 2000

[Sales and revenue are to and from ultimate customers]

Class	Unit	1980	1985	1990	1995	1996	1997	1998	1999	2000
Generation[1][2]	Bil. kWh.	2,286	2,470	3,025	3,358	3,447	3,494	3,618	3,705	3,800
Sales[3]	Bil. kWh.	2,126	2,306	2,684	3,013	3,098	3,139	3,240	3,236	3,310
Residential or domestic	Bil. kWh.	734	793	916	1,043	1,082	1,079	1,128	1,141	1,183
Percent of total	Percent	34.5	34.4	34.1	35	35.0	34.4	34.8	35.3	35.7
Commercial[4]	Bil. kWh.	524	606	739	863	887	929	969	971	1,001
Industrial[5]	Bil. kWh.	794	820	932	1,013	1,030	1,028	1,040	1,040	1,018
Revenue[3]	Bil. dol.	95.5	149.2	176.5	207.7	212.5	215.1	218.4	215.5	224.2
Residential or domestic	Bil. dol.	37.6	58.6	71.7	87.6	90.5	90.9	93.2	93.1	97.1
Percent of total	Percent	39.4	39.3	40.6	42.2	42.6	42.2	42.7	43.2	43.3
Commercial[4]	Bil. dol.	27.4	44.1	54.2	66.4	67.8	70.5	71.8	70.5	73.7
Industrial[5]	Bil. dol.	27.3	41.4	44.9	47.2	47.4	46.7	46.6	45.1	46.5
Ultimate customers, Dec. 31[3]	Million..	92.7	101.6	110.1	118.3	120.0	122.2	124.0	125.2	126.0
Residential or domestic	Million	82.2	89.8	97.0	103.9	105.3	107.1	108.7	109.8	110.5
Commercial[4]	Million	9.7	10.9	12.1	13.0	13.2	13.5	13.8	14.0	14.1
Industrial[5]	Million	0.5	0.5	0.5	0.6	0.6	0.6	0.5	0.5	0.5
Avg. kWh used per customer	1,000...	23.2	22.9	24.4	(NA)	(NA)	25.7	26.1	25.8	26.3
Residential	1,000...	9.0	8.9	9.4	(NA)	(NA)	10.1	10.4	10.4	10.7
Commercial[4]	1,000...	54.5	56.1	60.9	(NA)	(NA)	68.7	70.0	69.5	71.2
Avg. annual bill per customer.	Dollar..	1,040	1,482	1,603	(NA)	(NA)	1,761	1,760	1,720.4	1,779.3
Residential	Dollar	462	658	739	(NA)	(NA)	849	857	848.2	878.6
Commercial[4]	Dollar	2,848	4,080	4,466	(NA)	(NA)	5,209	5,189	5,048.2	5,242.7
Avg. revenue per kWh sold...	Cents..	4.49	6.47	6.57	6.89	6.86	6.85	6.74	6.7	6.8
Residential	Cents.	5.12	7.39	7.83	8.40	8.36	8.43	8.26	8.2	8.2
Commercial[4]	Cents.	5.22	7.27	7.33	7.69	7.64	7.58	7.41	7.3	7.4
Industrial[5]	Cents.	3.44	5.04	4.81	4.66	4.60	4.54	4.48	4.4	4.6

NA Not available. [1] Source: U.S. Energy Information Administration, *Monthly Energy Review,* monthly. [2] Generation includes batteries, chemicals, hydrogen, pitch, sulfur, and purchased steam. [3] Includes other types not shown separately. [4] Small light and power. [5] Large light and power.
Source: Except as noted, Edison Electric Institute, Washington, DC, *Statistical Yearbook of the Electric Utility Industry,* annual.

No. 901. Major Investor-Owned Electric Utilities—Balance Sheet and Income Account of Privately Owned Companies: 1994 to 1999

[In millions of dollars (196,282 represents $196,282,000,000). As of Dec. 31. Covers approximately 180 investor-owned electric utilities that during each of the last 3 years met any one or more of the following conditions—1 mil. megawatt-hours of total sales; 100 megawatt-hours of sales for resale, 500 megawatt-hours of gross interchange out, and 500 megawatt-hours of wheeling for other]

Item	1994	1995	1996	1997	1998	1999
COMPOSITE INCOME ACCOUNTS						
Operating revenue	196,282	199,967	207,459	215,083	218,175	214,160
Electric	179,307	183,655	188,901	195,898	201,970	197,578
Gas	16,222	15,580	17,869	18,663	15,735	16,033
Other utility	753	731	689	522	470	550
Operating expenses [1]	164,207	165,321	173,920	182,796	186,498	182,258
Electric [1]	148,663	150,599	156,938	165,443	171,689	167,266
Operation	93,108	91,881	97,207	104,337	110,759	108,461
Maintenance	12,022	11,767	12,050	12,368	12,486	12,276
Depreciation	18,679	19,885	21,194	23,072	24,122	23,968
Taxes other than income taxes	13,275	13,519	13,569	13,612	12,867	12,336
Income taxes	9,626	11,480	11,195	11,862	13,037	14,843
Deferred income tax	1,832	1,474	1,617	25	-476	-2,216
Investment tax credit (net)	-585	-550	-577	-448	-651	-1,695
Gas	14,878	14,073	16,258	16,925	14,396	14,493
Other utility	667	649	725	427	413	499
Operating income	32,074	34,646	33,539	32,286	31,677	31,902
Electric	30,645	33,057	31,963	30,454	30,281	30,311
Gas	1,344	1,507	1,612	1,737	1,339	1,540
Other utility	86	82	-36	95	57	51
Total income before interest charges	33,884	36,457	35,153	34,100	32,788	33,567
Less: Net interest charges	14,162	14,421	13,990	14,086	14,057	13,691
Interest expense	13,915	14,170	13,646	13,768	13,670	13,376
Less allow. for borrowed funds used during construction	421	435	326	331	328	331
Other charges, net.	667	687	671	649	715	646
Net income before extraordinary charges	19,722	22,036	21,162	20,014	18,732	19,876
Less extraordinary items after taxes	-165	-25	-66	3,151	1,344	2,793
Equals: Net income.	19,888	22,061	21,228	16,863	17,388	17,083
Dividends declared - preferred stock	1,582	1,519	1,248	1,005	750	687
Earnings available for common stocks	18,306	20,542	19,980	15,857	16,638	16,396
Dividends declared - common stock.	15,876	16,250	16,810	17,756	17,414	18,687
Additions total earnings	2,063	4,282	2,193	-1,960	-199	-2,785
COMPOSITE BALANCE SHEET						
Total assets and other debits	**574,512**	**578,934**	**581,991**	**586,241**	**598,856**	**585,827**
Utility plant, net	397,812	397,383	396,438	385,258	362,388	344,112
Electric utility plant, net.	366,936	366,116	363,854	351,427	327,646	310,317
Electric utility plant.	535,928	553,858	569,969	579,042	575,651	567,825
Construction work in progress	17,148	13,523	11,396	11,164	11,886	12,306
Less accumulated depreciation.	186,140	201,265	217,510	238,779	259,892	269,813
Nuclear fuel, net	5,657	5,286	5,444	5,219	4,731	4,205
Other utility plant, net.	25,219	25,981	27,140	28,613	30,011	29,529
Other property and investments.	23,479	27,988	33,120	43,248	48,853	54,546
Current and accrued assets	41,263	44,140	43,515	47,639	54,901	57,324
Deferred debits	111,957	109,423	108,918	110,096	132,714	129,845
CAPITALIZATION AND LIABILITIES						
Liabilities and other credits.	**574,512**	**578,934**	**581,991**	**586,241**	**598,856**	**585,827**
Capitalization	364,725	365,775	365,783	369,079	367,052	345,786
Common stock equity (end of year)	164,483	170,497	174,325	174,467	172,239	165,341
Preferred stock	24,860	21,569	18,830	16,080	14,447	12,061
Long-term debt	175,382	173,708	172,627	178,532	180,366	168,384
Current liabilities and deferred credits.	209,787	213,159	216,208	217,162	231,803	240,041

[1] Includes items not shown separately.

Source: U.S. Energy Information Administration, *Electric Power Annual*.

No. 902. Water Power—Developed and Undeveloped Capacity by Division: 1980 to 2001

[In millions of kilowatts. (64.4 represents 64,400,000). As of Dec. 31. Excludes all capacity of reversible equipment at pumped storage projects. Also excludes capacity precluded from development due to wild and scenic river legislation. For composition of divisions, see map, inside front cover]

Division	Developed installed capacity						Estimated undeveloped capacity					
	1980	1990	1995	1999	2000	2001	1980	1990	1995	1999	2000	2001
United States	**64.4**	**73.0**	**74.2**	**73.8**	**73.8**	**73.8**	**129.9**	**73.9**	**71.0**	**64.1**	**64.1**	**64.1**
New England	1.5	1.9	1.9	2.0	2.0	2.0	4.7	4.4	4.4	3.9	3.9	3.9
Middle Atlantic	4.3	4.9	4.9	5.6	5.6	5.6	5.1	5.1	4.9	3.6	3.6	3.6
East North Central	0.9	1.1	1.2	1.2	1.2	1.2	2.0	1.7	1.7	1.5	1.5	1.5
West North Central	2.8	3.1	3.1	3.0	3.0	3.0	3.4	3.1	3.1	2.8	2.8	2.8
South Atlantic	5.9	6.7	6.7	6.8	6.8	6.8	9.6	7.0	7.2	6.8	6.8	6.8
East South Central	5.6	5.9	5.9	5.9	5.9	5.9	3.3	2.4	2.3	2.0	2.0	2.0
West South Central	2.3	2.7	2.7	2.8	2.8	2.8	4.7	4.6	4.6	4.0	4.0	4.0
Mountain	7.4	9.2	9.5	10.0	10.0	10.0	34.2	19.4	18.8	18.0	18.0	18.0
Pacific	33.7	37.5	38.3	36.5	36.5	36.5	62.9	26.2	24.0	21.5	21.5	21.5

Source: U.S. Federal Energy Regulatory Commission (formerly U.S. Federal Power Commission), *Hydroelectric Power Resources of the United States, Developed and Undeveloped*, January 1, 1988; and unpublished data from the Hydroelectric Power Resources Assessment Database Developed and Undeveloped, March 30, 2002.

Energy and Utilities   577

No. 903. Solar Collector Shipments by Type, End Use, and Market Sector: 1980 to 2000

[Shipments in thousands of square feet (19,398 represents 19,398,000). Solar collector is a device for intercepting sunlight, converting the light to heat, and carrying the heat to where it will be either used or stored. 1985 data are not available]

Year	Number of manufac- turers	Total ship- ments [1]	Collector type		End use			Market sector		
			Low tempera- ture	Medium tempera- ture, special, other [2]	Pool heating	Hot water	Space heating	Resi- dential	Com- mercial	Industrial
1980	233	19,398	12,233	7,165	12,029	4,790	1,688	16,077	2,417	488
1981	203	20,133	8,677	11,456	9,781	7,204	2,017	15,773	2,561	1,518
1982	265	18,621	7,476	11,145	7,035	7,444	2,367	13,729	3,789	560
1983	203	16,828	4,853	11,975	4,839	9,323	2,082	11,780	3,039	1,665
1984 [3]	225	17,191	4,479	11,939	4,427	8,930	2,370	13,980	2,091	289
1986 [3]	98	9,360	3,751	1,111	3,494	1,181	127	4,131	703	13
1987 [3]	59	7,269	3,157	957	3,111	964	23	3,775	305	11
1988 [3]	51	8,174	3,326	732	3,304	726	7	3,796	255	7
1989 [3]	44	11,482	4,283	1,989	4,688	1,374	205	5,804	424	42
1990	51	11,409	3,645	2,527	5,016	1,091	2	5,835	294	22
1991	48	6,574	5,585	989	5,535	989	24	6,322	225	13
1992	45	7,086	6,187	897	6,210	801	35	6,832	204	27
1993	41	6,968	6,025	931	6,040	880	15	6,694	215	31
1994	41	7,627	6,823	803	6,813	790	19	7,026	583	16
1995	36	7,666	6,813	840	6,763	755	132	6,966	604	82
1996	28	7,616	6,821	785	6,787	765	57	6,873	682	54
1997	29	8,138	7,524	606	7,528	595	10	7,360	768	7
1998	28	7,756	7,292	443	7,201	463	67	7,165	517	62
1999	29	8,583	8,152	427	8,141	373	42	7,774	785	18
2000	(NA)	8,354	7,948	(NA)	7,863	367	99	7,473	810	57

[1] Includes high temperature collectors, end uses such as process heating, and utility and other market sectors not shown separately.   [2] Includes imputation of shipment data to account for nonrespondents.   [3] Declines between 1986 and 1989 are primarily due to the expiration of the Federal energy tax credit and industry consolidation.

Source: U.S. Energy Information Administration, 1974-1993, *Solar Collector Manufacturing Activity,* annual reports; thereafter, *Renewable Energy Annual.* See also <http://www.eia.doe.gov/cneaf/solar.renewables/page/solar/table16.html> (accessed April 2002).

No. 904. Privately Owned Gas Utility Industry—Balance Sheet and Income Account: 1980 to 2000

[In millions of dollars (75,851 represents $75,851,000,000). The gas utility industry consists of pipeline and distribution companies. Excludes operations of companies distributing gas in bottles or tanks]

Item	1980	1990	1994	1995	1996	1997	1998	1999	2000
COMPOSITE BALANCE SHEET									
Assets, total	**75,851**	**121,686**	**137,911**	**141,965**	**121,328**	**134,715**	**119,715**	**155,413**	**167,176**
Total utility plant	67,071	112,863	139,372	143,636	135,179	140,268	135,092	166,134	163,641
Depreciation and amortization. . . .	*26,162*	*49,483*	*61,140*	*62,723*	*58,815*	*62,554*	*61,226*	*73,823*	*69,981*
Utility plant (net).	40,909	63,380	78,232	80,912	76,364	77,714	73,866	92,311	93,661
Investment and fund accounts	15,530	23,872	22,658	26,489	13,207	22,812	12,337	17,344	10,942
Current and accrued assets	17,243	23,268	20,728	18,564	17,393	19,084	17,348	22,443	36,007
Deferred debits [1]	2,169	9,576	14,234	13,923	11,983	12,844	13,721	20,922	24,494
Liabilities, total	**75,851**	**121,686**	**137,911**	**141,965**	**121,328**	**134,775**	**119,715**	**155,413**	**167,176**
Capitalization, total	51,382	74,958	85,728	90,581	77,440	78,887	71,718	95,244	96,929
Capital stock	29,315	43,810	50,394	54,402	43,555	42,530	37,977	859	767
Long-term debts	22,067	31,148	35,296	35,548	33,644	35,971	33,386	46,906	48,695
Current and accrued liabilities. . . .	18,119	29,550	25,438	28,272	22,098	33,507	26,953	32,683	42,686
Deferred income taxes [2]	4,149	11,360	13,787	14,393	13,326	13,636	13,239	17,120	17,309
Other liabilities and credits	2,201	5,818	12,955	8,715	8,464	8,745	7,806	10,365	10,252
COMPOSITE INCOME ACCOUNT									
Operating revenues, total . .	**85,918**	**66,027**	**63,446**	**58,390**	**63,600**	**62,617**	**57,117**	**59,142**	**72,712**
Minus: Operating expenses [3]	*81,789*	*60,137*	*56,789*	*50,760*	*56,695*	*59,375*	*50,896*	*38,752*	*53,398*
Operation and maintenance	74,508	51,627	43,879	37,966	43,742	46,070	41,026	41,415	54,910
Federal, state, and local taxes . .	4,847	4,957	6,613	6,182	6,362	7,182	5,429	5,605	6,213
Equals: Operating income	4,129	5,890	6,657	7,630	6,905	3,242	6,220	20,390	19,314
Utility operating income	4,471	6,077	6,851	7,848	7,013	3,337	6,361	16,614	15,496
Income before interest charges. . .	6,929	8,081	8,200	9,484	8,030	4,193	7,779	17,531	15,386
Net income	4,194	4,410	5,011	5,139	4,797	48	4,379	10,420	9,035
Dividends	2,564	3,191	3,928	4,037	4,138	6,258	2,263	5,595	5,448

[1] Includes capital stock discount and expense and reacquired securities.   [2] Includes reserves for deferred income taxes.
[3] Includes expenses not shown separately.

Source: American Gas Association, Arlington, VA, *Gas Facts,* annual (copyright).

No. 905. Gas Utility Industry—Summary: 1980 to 2000

[Covers natural, manufactured, mixed, and liquid petroleum gas. Based on questionnaire mailed to all privately and municipally owned gas utilities in United States, except those with annual revenues less than $25,000]

Item	Unit	1980	1985	1990	1995	1997	1998	1999	2000
End users [1]	1,000	47,223	49,971	54,261	58,728	59,790	62,421	64,071	64,115
Residential	1,000	43,489	45,929	49,802	53,955	54,993	57,465	58,939	59,061
Commercial	1,000	3,498	3,816	4,246	4,530	4,589	4,755	4,920	4,813
Industrial and other	1,000	187	179	166	181	170	164	174	161
Sales [2]	Tril. Btu [3] . .	15,413	12,616	9,842	9,221	8,880	8,630	8,889	9,052
Residential	Tril. Btu . . .	4,826	4,513	4,468	4,803	5,013	4,828	4,865	4,941
Percent of total	Percent . . .	31.3	35.8	45.4	52.0	56.3	56.3	54.7	54.6
Commercial	Tril. Btu . . .	2,453	2,338	2,192	2,281	2,234	2,157	2,087	2,116
Industrial	Tril. Btu . . .	7,957	5,635	3,010	1,919	1,511	1,528	1,868	1,904
Other	Tril. Btu . . .	177	130	171	218	123	117	69	91
Revenues [2]	Mil. dol . . .	48,303	63,293	45,153	46,436	51,531	47,930	48,423	59,667
Residential	Mil. dol . . .	17,432	26,864	25,000	28,742	33,175	31,333	31,472	37,446
Percent of total	Percent . . .	36.1	42.4	55.4	61.9	64.2	65.4	65.0	62.8
Commercial	Mil. dol . . .	8,183	12,722	10,604	11,573	12,632	11,523	11,133	13,648
Industrial	Mil. dol . . .	22,215	23,086	8,996	5,571	5,236	4,684	5,547	8,069
Other	Mil. dol . . .	473	621	553	549	488	391	272	505
Prices per mil. Btu [3]	Dollars . . .	3.13	5.02	4.59	5.05	5.80	5.55	5.45	6.59
Residential	Dollars . . .	3.61	5.95	5.60	6.00	6.62	6.49	6.47	7.58
Commercial	Dollars . . .	3.34	5.44	4.84	5.07	5.65	5.34	5.34	6.45
Industrial	Dollars . . .	2.79	4.10	2.99	2.98	3.53	3.18	3.19	4.35
Gas mains mileage	1,000	1,052	1,119	1,207	1,261	1,251	1,295	1,389	1,400
Field and gathering	1,000	84	94	90	60	43	40	40	40
Transmission.	1,000	266	271	280	264	251	256	254	251
Distribution	1,000	702	754	837	937	957	999	1,095	1,110
Construction expenditures [4] . .	Mil. dol . . .	5,350	5,671	7,899	10,760	6,830	10,978	8,320	8,697
Transmission.	Mil. dol . . .	1,583	1,562	2,886	3,380	1,319	3,656	1,785	1,604
Distribution	Mil. dol . . .	1,869	2,577	3,714	5,394	4,188	5,035	4,180	5,484
Production and storage	Mil. dol . . .	1,150	790	309	367	276	598	161	139
General	Mil. dol . . .	352	567	770	1,441	891	1,389	1,974	1,284
Underground Storage	Mil. dol . . .	396	175	219	177	156	299	220	186

[1] Annual average.　[2] Excludes sales for resale.　[3] For definition of Btu, see text, this section.　[4] Includes general.

Source: American Gas Association, Arlington, VA, *Gas Facts,* annual (copyright).

No. 906. Gas Utility Industry—Customers, Sales, and Revenues by State: 2000

[See headnote, Table 905. For definition of Btu, see text, this section]

State	Customers [1] (1,000) Total [2]	Resi-dential	Sales [3] (tril. Btu) Total [2]	Resi-dential	Revenues [3] (mil. dol.) Total [2]	Resi-dential	State	Customers [1] (1,000) Total [2]	Resi-dential	Sales [3] (tril. Btu) Total [2]	Resi-dential	Revenues [3] (mil. dol.) Total [2]	Resi-dential
U.S. . . .	64,115	59,061	9,052	4,941	59,667	37,446	MO	1,485	1,342	176	114	1,227	857
AL	877	805	113	47	766	400	MT	257	225	31	21	183	121
AK	104	91	24	16	80	57	NE	521	464	74	42	451	278
AZ	898	843	84	35	617	335	NV	552	520	47	31	287	198
AR	633	560	88	44	607	356	NH	121	101	19	9	166	79
CA	9,801	9,367	717	526	5,560	4,213	NJ	2,625	2,426	601	232	3,321	1,821
CO	1,525	1,385	195	122	1,104	753	NM	525	479	60	35	343	221
CT	508	460	96	42	803	473	NY	4,467	4,127	650	377	5,502	3,798
DE	122	112	23	10	165	79	NC	978	860	174	64	1,222	582
DC	131	120	19	10	165	89	ND	121	106	24	12	139	72
FL.	752	694	75	19	601	236	OH	3,078	2,847	416	308	2,978	2,266
GA	339	310	66	20	404	166	OK	1,000	913	109	70	764	517
HI	68	62	6	1	96	24	OR	663	586	93	45	622	349
ID	320	283	39	23	220	138	PA	2,501	2,296	362	237	2,838	1,994
IL	3,821	3,559	545	421	3,560	2,801	RI	123	112	16	9	147	90
IN	1,803	1,647	279	167	1,775	1,159	SC	528	474	95	28	641	250
IA	906	812	120	74	868	576	SD	161	142	23	13	153	93
KS	1,708	1,553	199	133	1,350	974	TN	1,065	949	169	68	1,073	495
KY	1,000	898	142	78	936	558	TX	3,987	3,672	895	200	4,415	1,515
LA	838	790	187	55	931	373	UT	1,360	1,264	181	117	979	687
ME	48	34	11	2	72	18	VT	59	30	10	3	58	25
MD	868	808	85	60	733	549	VA	942	857	129	67	1,041	628
MA	1,572	1,446	202	130	1,825	1,260	WA	1,012	913	172	84	985	554
MI.	3,327	3,084	523	379	2,593	1,922	WV	407	365	69	34	407	245
MN	1,373	1,250	276	134	1,698	939	WI.	1,604	1,457	245	135	1,653	1,010
MS	473	422	75	26	415	176	WY	159	141	25	14	129	79

[1] Averages for the year.　[2] Includes other service, not shown separately.　[3] Excludes sales for resale.

Source: American Gas Association, Arlington, VA, *Gas Facts,* annual (copyright).

U.S. Census Bureau, Statistical Abstract of the United States: 2002

No. 907. Public Drinking Water Systems by Size of Community Served and Source of Water: 2001

[As of September. Covers systems that provide water for human consumption through pipes and other constructed conveyances to a least 15 service connection or serve an average of at least 25 persons for at least 60 days a year. Based on reported data in the Safe Drinking Water Information System maintained by the Environmental Protection Agency]

Type of system	Total	Size of community served					Water source	
		500 or fewer persons	501 to 3,300 persons	3,301 to 10,000 persons	10,001 to 100,000	100,000 persons or more	Ground water	Surface water
Total systems...............	165,471	137,124	19,779	4,712	3,500	356	150,739	14,732
COMMUNITY WATER SYSTEMS [1]								
Number of systems..............	53,783	31,262	14,241	4,498	3,432	350	42,212	11,571
Percent of systems	100	58	26	8	6	1	78	22
Population served (1,000)..........	264,145	5,095	20,097	26,092	96,516	116,345	85,744	178,402
Percent of systems	100	2	8	10	37	44	32	68
NONTRANSIENT NONCOMMUNITY WATER SYSTEM [2]								
Number of systems..............	20,095	17,133	2,847	93	19	3	19,205	890
Percent of systems	100	85	14	-	-	-	96	4
Population served (1,000)..........	6,586	2,386	2,815	459	546	380	5,717	869
Percent of systems	100	36	43	7	8	6	87	13
TRANSIENT NONCOMMUNITY WATER SYSTEM [3]								
Number of systems..............	91,593	88,729	2,691	121	49	3	89,322	2,271
Percent of systems	100	97	3	-	-	-	98	2
Population served (1,000)..........	12,819	7,472	2,702	667	1,242	735	11,882	937
Percent of systems	100	58	21	5	10	6	93	7

- Represents zero.   [1] A public water system that supplies water to the same population year-round.   [2] A public water system that regularly supplies water to at least 25 of the same people at least 6 months per year, but not year-round. Some examples are schools, factories, and office buildings which have their own water systems.   [3] A public water system that provides water in a place such as a gas station or campground where people do not remain for long periods of time.

Source: U.S. Environmental Protection Agency, Internet site <http://www.epa.gov/safewater/data/getdata.html> (accessed May 2002).

No. 908. Water and Sewage Treatment Facilities: 1997

State	Water supply (NAICS 2213101)		Sewage treatment facilities (NAICS 22132)		State	Water supply (NAICS 2213101)		Sewage treatment facilities (NAICS 22132)	
	Number of establishments	Paid employees	Number of establishments	Paid employees		Number of establishments	Paid employees	Number of establishments	Paid employees
U.S. ...	3,721	26,597	696	5,600	MO	57	(4)	15	(5)
AL......	96	(1)	13	(2)	MT	35	113	6	(3)
AK......	6	(3)	(NA)	(NA)	NE......	(NA)	(NA)	(NA)	(NA)
AZ......	129	1,131	8	40	NV......	23	(5)	(NA)	(NA)
AR......	140	(4)	9	(5)	NH......	10	(2)	(NA)	(NA)
CA......	374	2,848	27	116	NJ......	49	(6)	24	(4)
CO......	71	314	14	51	NM.....	90	323	(NA)	(NA)
CT......	32	(6)	9	(5)	NY......	41	(4)	28	(2)
DE......	9	(1)	(NA)	(NA)	NC......	81	577	18	(5)
DC......	(NA)	(NA)	(NA)	(NA)	ND.....	24	(5)	(NA)	(NA)
FL......	129	1,393	88	(4)	OH......	60	686	19	(2)
GA.....	34	130	10	(5)	OK......	105	(1)	9	(2)
HI......	9	24	13	(2)	OR......	63	(2)	7	(5)
ID	35	(2)	6	20	PA......	125	2,568	59	(1)
IL......	82	(4)	27	(2)	RI	(NA)	(NA)	(NA)	(NA)
IN......	114	(6)	30	(2)	SC	48	(1)	12	(5)
IA	25	(2)	7	(5)	SD.....	29	(2)	(NA)	(NA)
KS......	38	(2)	(NA)	(NA)	TN	30	(1)	11	(2)
KY......	42	(1)	13	116	TX......	601	2,514	38	(4)
LA......	192	(4)	21	(2)	UT......	23	71	(NA)	(NA)
ME.....	22	(2)	(NA)	(NA)	VT......	7	(5)	(NA)	(NA)
MD.....	8	(5)	9	107	VA	48	(1)	12	(5)
MA.....	18	(2)	21	(1)	WA	148	(1)	8	(5)
MI	12	66	10	24	WV	40	523	20	94
MN.....	6	(5)	13	(5)	WI	(NA)	(NA)	13	47
MS.....	332	1,001	14	(5)	WY	16	(5)	(NA)	(NA)

NA Not available.   [1] 250-499 employees.   [2] 100-249.   [3] 1-19.   [4] 500-999.   [5] 20-99.   [6] 1000-2499.

Source: U.S. Census Bureau, 1997 Economic Census. See also <http://www.census.gov/epcd/www/97EC22.HTM> (accessed May 2002).

Section 20
Construction and Housing

This section presents data on the construction industry and on various indicators of its activity and costs; on housing units and their characteristics and occupants; and on the characteristics and vacancy rates for commercial buildings. This edition contains data from the 2001 American Housing Survey.

The principal source of these data is the U.S. Census Bureau, which issues a variety of current publications. Construction statistics compiled by the Census Bureau appear in its *New Residential Construction* and *New Residential Sales* press releases and Web sites <http://www.census.gov/const/www/>. Statistics on expenditures by owners of residential properties are issued quarterly and annually in *Expenditures for Residential Upkeep and Improvements. Value of New Construction Put in Place* presents data on all types of construction and includes monthly composite cost indexes. Reports of the censuses of construction industries (see below) are also issued on various topics.

Other Census Bureau publications include the *Current Housing Reports* series, which comprises the quarterly *Housing Vacancies*, the quarterly *Market Absorption of Apartments*, the biennial *American Housing Survey* (formerly *Annual Housing Survey*), and reports of the censuses of housing and of construction industries. *Construction Review*, published quarterly by the International Trade Administration, U.S. Department of Commerce, contains many of the census series and other construction statistics series from the federal government and private agencies.

Other sources include the monthly *Dodge Construction Potentials* of F. W. Dodge Division, McGraw-Hill Information Systems Company, New York, NY, which presents national and state data on construction contracts; the National Association of Home Builders with state-level data on housing starts; the NATIONAL ASSOCIATION OF REALTORS®, which presents data

on existing home sales; the Society of Industrial and Office Realtors and Oncor International on commercial office and industrial space; the Bureau of Economic Analysis, which presents data on residential capital and gross housing product; and the U.S. Energy Information Administration, which provides data on commercial buildings through its periodic sample surveys.

Censuses and surveys—Censuses of the construction industry were first conducted by the Census Bureau for 1929, 1935, and 1939; beginning in 1967, a census has been taken every 5 years (through 1997, for years ending in "2" and "7"). The latest complete reports are for 1997. The 1997 census results are part of the 1997 Economic Census. See Table 910. See also text, Section 15, Business Enterprise.

The construction sector of the economic census, covers all employer establishments primarily engaged in (1) building construction by general contractors or operative builders; (2) heavy (nonbuilding) construction by general contractors; and (3) construction by special trade contractors. The 1997 census was conducted in accordance with the 1997 *North American Industry Classification System* (NAICS); the 1992 census was conducted in accordance with the 1987 *Standard Industrial Classification* (SIC). This sector now includes construction management and land subdividers and developers, not included previously. See text, Section 15, Business Enterprise, for general information on the SIC and NAICS.

From 1850 through 1930, the Census Bureau collected some housing data as part of its censuses of population and agriculture. Beginning in 1940, separate censuses of housing have been taken at 10-year intervals. For the 1970 and 1980 censuses, data on year-round housing units were collected and issued on occupancy and structural characteristics, plumbing facilities, value, and rent; for 1990 such characteristics were presented for all housing units.

The American Housing Survey (*Current Housing Reports* Series H-150 and H-170), which began in 1973, provided an annual and ongoing series of data on selected housing and demographic characteristics until 1983. In 1984, the name of the survey was changed from the Annual Housing Survey. Currently, national data are collected every other year, and data for selected metropolitan areas are collected on a rotating basis. All samples represent a cross section of the housing stock in their respective areas. Estimates are subject to both sampling and nonsampling errors; caution should therefore be used in making comparisons between years.

Data on residential mortgages were collected continuously from 1890 to 1970, except 1930, as part of the decennial census by the Census Bureau. Since 1973, mortgage status data, limited to single family homes on less than 10 acres with no business on the property, have been presented in the American Housing Survey. Data on mortgage activity are covered in Section 25, Banking and Finance.

Housing units—In general, a housing unit is a house, an apartment, a group of rooms or a single room occupied or intended for occupancy as separate living quarters; that is, the occupants live separately from any other individual in the building, and there is direct access from the outside or through a common hall. Transient accommodations, barracks for workers, and institutional-type quarters are not counted as housing units.

Statistical reliability—For a discussion of statistical collection and estimation, sampling procedures, and measures of statistical reliability applicable to Census Bureau data, see Appendix III.

U.S. Census Bureau, Statistical Abstract of the United States: 2002

No. 909. Construction—Establishments, Employees, and Payroll by Kind of Business (NAICS Basis): 1999 and 2000

[For establishments with payroll. (6,201.6 represents 6,201,600). See Appendix III]

Industry	NAICS code [1]	Establishments 1999	Establishments 2000	Paid employees [2] (1,000) 1999	Paid employees [2] (1,000) 2000	Annual payroll (mil. dol.) 1999	Annual payroll (mil. dol.) 2000
Construction	23	698,541	709,590	6,201.6	6,572.8	219,087.1	239,910.1
Building, developing, & general contracting . .	233	216,355	216,354	1,538.1	1,604.9	55,883.8	60,798.1
Land subdivision & land development	2331	12,383	13,111	68.0	77.9	2,814.5	3,269.2
Residential building construction	2332	160,178	159,550	741.6	781.0	23,225.8	25,519.7
Single-family housing construction	23321	151,952	151,296	677.1	713.3	20,956.6	23,058.3
Multifamily housing construction	23322	8,226	8,254	64.5	67.7	2,269.2	2,461.3
Nonresidential building construction	2333	43,794	43,693	728.5	746.0	29,843.5	32,009.3
Mfg & industrial building construction. . .	23331	6,998	7,039	166.0	164.9	6,461.9	6,797.3
Commercial & institutional building construction	23332	36,796	36,654	562.5	581.2	23,381.6	25,212.0
Heavy construction	234	39,556	39,516	848.4	901.0	35,807.9	38,628.0
Highway, street, bridge, & tunnel construction	2341	11,911	11,795	284.4	304.9	13,469.4	14,316.1
Highway & street construction	23411	11,006	10,889	248.8	265.7	11,707.0	12,328.6
Bridge & tunnel construction	23412	905	906	35.6	39.3	1,762.5	1,987.5
Other heavy construction	2349	27,645	27,721	564.0	596.1	22,338.5	24,311.9
Water, sewer, & pipeline construction . .	23491	7,597	7,483	163.8	165.8	6,728.8	7,033.0
Power & communication transmission line construction.	23492	3,436	3,644	85.3	97.5	3,187.0	3,815.8
Industrial nonbuilding structure construction	23493	696	689	98.6	101.7	3,844.7	4,137.8
All other heavy construction.	23499	15,916	15,905	216.4	231.0	8,578.0	9,325.3
Special trade contractors	235	442,630	453,720	3,815.2	4,066.9	127,395.4	140,484.1
Plumbing, heating, & air-conditioning contractors.	2351	89,125	90,487	862.0	897.9	31,044.9	33,406.0
Painting & wall covering contractors	2352	39,767	40,973	212.1	221.8	5,684.3	6,121.4
Electrical contractors	2353	66,220	66,802	742.5	815.1	28,361.5	32,698.0
Masonry, drywall, insulation, & tile contractors.	2354	52,704	53,625	538.9	565.0	15,995.3	17,389.8
Masonry & stone contractors	23541	24,532	25,030	182.7	197.9	5,208.9	5,667.8
Drywall, plastering, acoustical, & insulation contractors	23542	21,515	21,774	312.7	319.3	9,454.2	10,224.4
Tile, marble, terrazzo, & mosaic contractors	23543	6,657	6,821	43.5	47.8	1,332.2	1,497.7
Carpentry & floor contractors.	2355	57,801	58,525	327.8	347.3	9,104.4	9,963.6
Carpentry contractors	23551	44,449	45,028	256.3	269.8	6,935.4	7,533.3
Floor laying & other floor contractors. . .	23552	13,352	13,497	71.5	77.5	2,169.1	2,430.3
Roofing, siding, & sheet metal contractors .	2356	30,767	30,966	257.6	260.8	7,614.4	7,928.8
Concrete contractors	2357	29,870	30,238	269.2	292.0	8,718.1	9,501.2
Water well drilling contractors	2358	3,789	3,797	20.5	21.6	636.8	688.5
Other special trade contractors	2359	72,587	78,307	584.5	644.9	20,235.7	22,786.6
Structural steel erection contractors. . . .	23591	4,945	5,382	86.6	93.6	3,199.8	3,585.8
Glass & glazing contractors	23592	5,450	5,772	42.3	45.8	1,409.8	1,570.1
Excavation contractors	23593	25,060	27,005	133.2	152.5	4,625.7	5,253.6
Wrecking & demolition contractors	23594	1,519	1,752	19.4	21.9	703.0	808.7
Building equip & other machinery installation contractors.	23595	4,374	4,820	73.4	80.9	3,472.6	3,859.6
All other special trade contractors	23599	31,239	33,576	229.6	250.1	6,824.9	7,708.7

[1] North American Industry Classification System code; see text, Section 15, Business Enterprise. [2] Employees on the payroll for the pay period including March 12.

Source: U.S. Census Bureau, "County Business Patterns"; published 30 May 2002; <http://www.census.gov/epcd/cbp/view/cbpview.html>.

U.S. Census Bureau, Statistical Abstract of the United States: 2002

No. 910. Construction—Establishments, Employees, and Payroll by Kind of Business (NAICS Basis): 1997

[For establishments with payroll (174,185 represents $174,185,000,000). Based on the 1997 Economic Census; See Appendix III]

Kind of business	NAICS code [1]	Number of establishments	Number of employees: All	Number of employees: Construction workers	Payroll (mil. dol.): All employees	Payroll (mil. dol.): Construction workers	Net value of construction work (mil. dol.)
Construction	23	**656,448**	**5,664,853**	**4,332,737**	**174,185**	**119,677**	**612,209**
Building, developing, & general contracting	233	199,289	1,342,953	885,939	42,546	23,136	198,827
Land subdivision & land development	2331	8,186	41,827	10,977	1,510	254	10,248
Residential building construction	2332	146,394	629,887	407,801	16,731	8,762	100,124
Nonresidential building construction	2333	44,710	671,239	467,161	24,305	14,119	88,455
Heavy construction	234	42,557	880,400	710,898	30,292	22,219	105,639
Highway, street, bridge, & tunnel construction	2341	12,448	325,743	265,267	11,375	8,474	46,274
Other heavy construction	2349	30,109	554,657	445,630	18,917	13,745	59,365
Special trade contractors	235	414,602	3,441,500	2,735,901	101,347	74,322	307,743
Plumbing, heating, & air-conditioning contractors	2351	84,876	788,930	599,940	25,720	18,280	78,496
Painting & wall covering contractors	2352	37,480	195,331	160,740	4,543	3,431	12,050
Electrical contractors	2353	61,414	641,985	510,921	21,680	16,261	61,121
Masonry, drywall, insulation, & tile contractors	2354	49,917	470,701	407,700	12,612	10,073	34,843
Carpentry & floor contractors	2355	56,936	290,942	228,273	7,163	5,116	24,049
Roofing, siding, & sheet metal contractors	2356	30,557	253,315	197,294	6,495	4,370	21,976
Concrete contractors	2357	30,417	262,256	222,121	6,858	5,298	23,604
Water well drilling contractors	2358	3,862	21,214	15,360	576	399	2,132
Other special trade contractors	2359	59,143	516,824	393,552	15,699	11,095	49,472

[1] North American Industry Classification System, 1997; see text, Section 15, Business Enterprise.

Source: U.S. Census Bureau, *1997 Economic Census, Construction,* Series EC97C23S-IS, issued January 2000. See Internet site: <http://www.census.gov/epcd/www/econ97.html>.

No. 911. Construction Materials—Producer Price Indexes: 1990 to 2001

[1982=100, except as noted. Data for 2001 are preliminary. For discussion of producer price indexes, see text, Section 14, Prices. This index, more formally known as the special commodity grouping index for construction materials, covers materials incorporated as integral part of a building or normally installed during construction and not readily removable. Excludes consumer durables such as kitchen ranges, refrigerators, etc. This index is not the same as the stage-of-processing index of intermediate materials and components for construction]

Commodity	1990	1994	1995	1996	1997	1998	1999	2000	2001
Construction materials	**119.6**	**133.8**	**138.8**	**139.6**	**142.1**	**141.4**	**142.8**	**144.1**	**142.8**
Interior solvent based paint	133.0	148.1	164.5	175.6	180.5	185.7	188.0	191.1	190.2
Construction products from plastics	117.2	122.9	133.8	130.9	128.2	126.2	128.0	135.8	133.1
Douglas fir, dressed	138.4	236.2	198.8	227.1	221.3	186.1	212.1	185.2	178.0
Southern pine, dressed	111.2	182.6	166.9	177.9	201.2	177.3	185.7	161.0	152.5
Millwork	130.4	162.4	163.8	166.6	170.9	171.1	174.7	176.4	179.1
Softwood plywood	119.6	176.8	188.1	173.7	175.5	174.9	207.0	173.3	168.0
Hardwood plywood and related products	102.7	122.3	122.2	124.9	127.1	126.9	128.6	130.2	129.8
Softwood plywood veneer, ex. reinforced/backed	142.3	207.8	203.5	189.3	201.7	180.1	197.4	182.2	175.7
Building paper and building board mill products	112.2	144.1	144.9	137.2	129.6	132.9	141.6	138.8	128.9
Steel pipe and tubes [1]	102.6	96.9	104.4	103.2	106.9	109.4	102.5	106.6	103.8
Builders hardware	133.0	148.0	153.2	156.5	158.4	160.8	161.9	163.8	166.4
Plumbing fixtures and brass fittings	144.3	159.6	166.0	171.1	174.5	175.1	176.7	180.4	180.7
Heating equipment	131.6	142.5	147.5	151.2	152.4	153.3	154.0	155.6	157.1
Metal doors, sash, and trim	131.4	142.0	156.5	159.3	161.0	161.3	162.2	165.1	167.1
Siding, aluminum [2]	(NA)	119.4	132.4	125.5	132.1	134.5	135.4	142.2	141.4
Outdoor lighting equipment, including parts [3]	113.0	115.4	120.8	122.9	123.2	122.8	122.3	124.7	126.0
Commercial fluorescent fixtures [4]	113.0	116.2	121.0	123.4	122.8	119.0	118.7	117.7	113.0
Architectural and ornamental metalwork [5]	118.7	123.4	128.0	131.3	133.5	135.4	136.2	139.8	141.8
Fabricated ferrous wire products [1]	114.6	122.6	125.7	126.8	128.0	130.1	130.6	130.0	129.8
Elevators, escalators, and other lifts	110.1	112.4	113.0	113.7	114.8	116.0	117.5	118.7	119.4
Stamped metal switch and receptacle box	158.0	179.1	183.5	186.3	189.0	191.5	192.8	183.0	195.4
Concrete ingredients and related products	115.3	128.7	134.7	138.8	142.5	147.6	152.1	155.6	159.1
Concrete products	113.5	124.6	129.4	133.2	136.0	140.0	143.7	147.8	151.7
Clay construction products exc. refractories	129.9	138.3	141.3	142.3	143.5	144.9	148.3	152.8	158.0
Prep. asphalt and tar roofing and siding products	95.8	92.9	97.8	97.4	96.5	95.7	95.2	100.0	103.2
Gypsum products	105.2	136.1	154.5	154.0	170.8	177.6	208.0	201.4	156.1
Insulation materials	108.4	111.9	118.8	118.9	117.7	119.7	131.7	128.6	127.5
Paving mixtures and blocks	101.2	103.2	105.8	107.6	113.2	112.5	112.9	130.4	134.6

NA Not available. [1] June 1982=100. [2] December 1982=100. [3] June 1985=100. [4] Recessed nonall. [5] December 1983=100.

Source: U.S. Bureau of Labor Statistics, *Producer Price Indexes,* monthly and annual.

No. 912. Price and Cost Indexes for Construction: 1980 to 2001

[1996=100. Excludes Alaska and Hawaii. Indexes of certain of these sources are published on bases different from those shown here]

Name of index	1980	1985	1990	1995	1997	1998	1999	2000	2001
U.S. Census Bureau Composite:									
Fixed-weighted [1]	59.3	71.8	85.5	97.7	103.2	106.0	110.3	115.3	119.6
Implicit price deflator [2]	59.0	71.1	85.0	97.8	103.3	106.1	110.4	115.4	119.6
U.S. Census Bureau houses under construction: [3]									
Fixed-weighted	58.0	69.8	84.6	98.1	102.9	105.6	110.4	115.4	120.6
Price deflator	57.0	68.3	83.4	98.1	102.9	105.6	110.4	115.5	120.5
Federal Highway Administration, composite [4]	79.7	83.6	88.9	99.8	107.5	105.2	111.9	119.3	118.7
Bureau of Reclamation composite [5]	62	75	85	98	103	105	107	111	112
Turner Construction Co.: Building construction [6]	54	74	87	97	104	109	113	118	121
Engineering News-Record: [7]									
Buildings	60.6	75.8	84.4	97.1	105.0	105.8	107.9	110.5	111.6
Construction	57.6	74.6	84.2	97.3	103.6	105.3	107.8	110.7	112.8
Handy-Whitman public utility: [8]									
Buildings	66	76	85	97	103	104	107	110	113
Electric [9]	60	74	86	98	102	104	105	109	113
Gas	60	75	86	99	102	104	107	111	114
Water [10]	64	76	85	98	102	104	107	112	116
C. A. Turner Telephone Plant [11]	79	77	87	96	102	102	101	103	106

[1] Weighted average of the various indexes used to deflate the Construction Put in Place series. In calculating the index, the weights (i.e., the composition of current dollar estimates in 1996 by category) are held constant. [2] Derived ratio of total current to constant dollar Construction Put in Place (multiplied by 100). [3] Excludes value of site. [4] Based on average contract unit bid prices for composite mile (involving specific average amounts of excavation, paving, reinforcing steel, structural steel, and structural concrete). [5] Derived from the four quarterly indexes which are weighted averages of costs of labor, materials, and equipment for the construction of dams and reclamation projects. [6] Based on firm's cost experience with respect to labor rates, materials prices, competitive conditions, efficiency of plant and management, and productivity. [7] Building construction index computed on the basis of a hypothetical unit of construction requiring 6 bbl. of portland cement, 1,088 M bd. ft. of 2" x 4" lumber, 2,500 lb. of structural steel, and 68.38 hours of skilled labor. General construction index based on same materials components combined with 200 hours of common labor. [8] Based on data covering public utility construction costs in six geographic regions. Covers skilled and common labor. [9] As derived by U.S. Census Bureau. Covers steam generation plants only. [10] As derived by U.S. Census Bureau. Reflects costs for structures and improvements at water pumping and treatment plants. [11] Computed by the Census Bureau by averaging the weighted component indexes published for six geographic regions.

Source: U.S. Census Bureau, Current Construction Reports, Series C30, Value of Construction Put in Place. Also in U.S. International Trade Administration, Construction Review, quarterly.

No. 913. Value of New Construction Put in Place: 1964 to 2001

[In millions of dollars (75,097 represents $75,097,000,000). Represents value of construction put in place during year; differs from building permit and construction contract data in timing and coverage. Includes installed cost of normal building service equipment and selected types of industrial production equipment (largely site fabricated). Excludes cost of shipbuilding, land, and most types of machinery and equipment. For methodology, see Appendix III]

Year	Current dollars					Constant (1996) dollars				
		Private					Private			
	Total	Total [1]	Residential buildings	Nonresidential buildings	Public	Total	Total [1]	Residential buildings	Nonresidential buildings	Public
1964	75,097	54,893	30,526	17,385	20,203	405,864	300,372	169,635	96,497	105,492
1970	105,890	77,982	35,863	28,171	27,908	429,041	321,940	155,113	115,372	107,101
1975	152,635	109,342	51,581	35,409	43,293	404,132	298,555	149,410	96,407	105,577
1980	273,936	210,290	100,381	72,480	63,646	464,144	364,101	175,822	129,275	100,043
1982	279,332	216,268	84,676	92,690	63,064	423,729	333,894	134,605	145,054	89,835
1983	311,887	248,437	125,833	87,069	63,450	465,073	375,193	195,028	131,289	89,880
1984	370,190	299,952	155,015	107,680	70,238	534,557	437,325	231,396	155,261	97,232
1985	403,416	325,601	160,520	127,466	77,815	567,689	463,854	234,955	178,925	103,835
1986	433,454	348,872	190,677	120,917	84,582	588,804	479,623	266,481	163,740	109,182
1987	446,643	355,994	199,652	123,247	90,648	585,103	470,575	267,063	160,363	114,528
1988	462,012	367,277	204,496	130,854	94,735	583,396	467,599	263,385	164,191	115,797
1989	477,502	379,328	204,255	139,953	98,174	579,583	463,541	252,745	169,173	116,042
1990	476,778	369,300	191,103	143,506	107,478	560,802	436,999	228,943	167,896	123,803
1991	432,592	322,483	166,251	116,570	110,109	503,711	378,245	197,526	135,389	125,467
1992	463,661	347,814	199,293	105,646	115,847	533,322	401,567	232,134	120,921	131,755
1993	491,033	375,073	225,067	107,715	115,960	544,285	415,565	249,763	118,988	128,720
1994	539,193	418,999	258,561	120,284	120,193	574,256	445,414	274,966	127,576	128,842
1995	557,818	427,885	247,351	138,015	129,933	570,188	436,738	251,953	141,218	133,450
1996	615,900	476,638	281,115	155,858	139,263	615,797	476,650	281,207	155,813	139,147
1997	653,429	502,734	289,014	173,875	150,695	632,680	487,197	280,722	167,610	145,483
1998	705,685	551,383	314,607	190,710	154,302	665,156	519,859	297,960	177,644	145,297
1999	765,876	596,331	350,562	199,935	169,545	694,123	540,220	317,236	173,429	153,904
2000	820,345	641,783	374,457	208,241	178,561	711,328	556,426	323,977	178,074	154,902
2001	842,539	650,030	388,705	201,094	192,509	704,747	542,782	322,305	166,587	161,965

[1] Includes other types of private construction, not shown separately.

Source: U.S. Census Bureau, Current Construction Reports, Series C30, Value of Construction, Put in Place, monthly. See Internet site <http://www.census.gov/ftp/pub/const/www/C30index.html>.

Construction and Housing   585

No. 914. Value of New Construction Put in Place by Type: 1990 to 2001

[In millions of dollars (476,778 represents $476,778,000,000). Represents value of construction put in place during year; differs from building permit and construction contract data in timing and coverage. Includes installed cost of normal building service equipment and selected types of industrial production equipment (largely site fabricated). Excludes cost of shipbuilding, land, and most types of machinery and equipment. For methodology, see Appendix III]

Type of construction	Current dollars					Constant (1996) dollars				
	1990	1995	1999	2000	2001	1990	1995	1999	2000	2001
Total new construction .	476,778	557,818	765,876	820,345	842,539	560,802	570,188	694,123	711,328	704,747
Private construction. . .	369,300	427,885	596,331	641,783	650,030	436,999	436,738	540,220	556,426	542,782
Residential buildings	191,103	247,351	350,562	374,457	388,705	228,943	251,953	317,236	323,977	322,305
New housing units	132,137	171,404	251,272	265,047	279,772	158,319	174,585	227,467	229,324	232,008
1 unit	112,886	153,515	223,837	236,788	249,086	135,253	156,363	202,620	204,867	206,557
2 or more units	19,250	17,889	27,434	28,259	30,686	23,066	18,222	24,848	24,457	25,451
Improvements	58,966	75,947	99,290	109,410	108,933	70,625	77,368	89,769	94,653	90,297
Nonresidential buildings . . .	143,506	138,015	193,935	208,241	201,094	167,896	141,218	173,429	178,074	166,587
Industrial	33,636	35,498	32,639	31,801	29,046	39,350	36,322	29,206	27,194	24,072
Office	35,055	25,613	47,582	55,605	52,020	41,027	26,218	42,552	47,534	43,112
Hotels, motels.	10,679	7,112	15,951	16,293	14,421	12,497	7,274	14,274	13,944	11,948
Other commercial	40,047	42,654	56,915	60,381	60,297	46,847	43,636	50,870	51,635	49,933
Religious	3,566	4,326	7,371	8,019	8,310	4,169	4,426	6,590	6,858	6,880
Educational	4,616	5,493	9,645	11,375	12,629	5,398	5,621	8,621	9,726	10,454
Hospital and institutional .	10,868	11,248	13,530	14,434	15,114	12,710	11,512	12,102	12,342	12,518
Miscellaneous [1]	5,040	6,071	10,301	10,332	9,259	5,897	6,209	9,214	8,841	7,670
Farm nonresidential.	2,801	3,014	5,059	5,988	6,134	3,276	3,084	4,519	5,115	5,076
Public utilities	28,933	36,084	44,066	50,144	51,114	33,505	36,965	42,534	46,641	46,230
Telecommunications. . . .	9,803	11,093	18,404	18,799	18,538	11,346	11,556	18,305	18,272	17,440
Other public utilities	19,130	24,991	25,662	31,345	32,576	22,159	25,409	24,229	28,370	28,789
Railroads	2,600	3,509	4,670	4,263	4,149	2,969	3,609	4,311	3,781	3,595
Electric light and power.	11,299	14,274	14,585	21,149	22,515	13,083	14,535	13,892	19,280	19,990
Gas	4,820	6,279	4,918	4,930	4,969	5,627	6,329	4,625	4,411	4,374
Petroleum pipelines . .	411	929	1,489	1,003	943	480	936	1,401	897	830
All other private [2]	2,957	3,420	2,709	2,954	2,983	3,379	3,518	2,501	2,619	2,584
Public construction.	107,478	129,933	169,545	178,561	192,509	123,803	133,450	153,904	154,902	161,965
Buildings	43,615	57,754	80,418	88,566	96,967	51,117	59,074	71,928	75,772	80,280
Housing and redevelopment	3,808	4,698	4,653	4,308	4,751	4,560	4,786	4,218	3,726	3,940
Industrial	1,434	1,508	925	1,157	1,556	1,677	1,544	827	990	1,288
Educational	16,055	25,783	42,427	49,814	55,752	18,772	26,374	37,904	42,588	46,148
Hospital	2,860	4,236	4,026	4,135	4,053	3,348	4,335	3,600	3,538	3,355
Other [3]	19,458	21,528	28,387	29,151	30,855	22,760	22,034	25,378	24,930	25,549
Highways and streets	32,105	37,616	48,851	49,262	54,026	35,879	38,952	44,559	42,764	45,415
Military facilities	2,665	3,011	2,125	2,441	2,843	3,050	3,102	1,922	2,105	2,372
Conservation and development	4,686	6,308	6,088	6,063	7,122	5,482	6,443	5,682	5,494	6,371
Sewer systems.	10,276	8,420	9,864	8,807	8,751	12,010	8,600	9,214	7,982	7,828
Water supply facilities	4,909	4,709	6,541	5,993	7,152	5,730	4,809	6,147	5,327	6,138
Miscellaneous public [4] . . .	9,223	12,116	15,658	17,429	15,648	10,535	12,468	14,453	15,459	13,561

[1] Includes amusement and recreational buildings, bus and airline terminals, animal hospitals and shelters, etc.   [2] Includes privately owned streets and bridges, parking areas, sewer and water facilities, parks and playgrounds, golf courses, airfields, etc.   [3] Includes general administrative buildings, prisons, police and fire stations, courthouses, civic centers, passenger terminals, space facilities, postal facilities, etc.   [4] Includes open amusement and recreational facilities, power generating facilities, transit systems, airfields, open parking facilities, etc.

Source: U.S. Census Bureau, *Current Construction Reports*, Series C30, *Value of Construction, Put in Place*, monthly. See Internet site <http://www.census.gov/ftp/pub/const/www/C30index.html>.

No. 915. Value of Private Nonresidential Construction Put in Place: 1993 to 2001

[In millions of dollars (110,996 represents $110,996,000,000). Represents value of construction put in place during year; differs from building permit and construction contract data in timing and coverage. Data are not directly comparable to Tables 913 and 914 due to a new classification system which bases project types on their end usage instead of building/nonbuilding and ownership types. See Appendix III]

Type of construction	1993	1994	1995	1996	1997	1998	1999	2000	2001 [1]
Total construction [2]	110,996	123,174	141,435	158,663	176,267	193,280	196,644	211,195	204,077
Lodging	4,590	4,657	7,131	10,914	12,898	14,818	15,955	16,304	14,447
Office	[2]19,999	20,443	22,996	26,530	32,813	40,394	45,052	52,407	49,621
General	17,314	18,008	20,569	23,216	29,301	37,615	41,745	49,637	47,017
Financial	2,604	2,361	2,339	3,231	3,157	2,636	3,125	2,689	2,583
Commercial [2]	31,005	36,389	41,082	45,723	49,273	51,398	54,317	58,067	58,007
Automotive [2]	2,077	2,731	4,191	5,251	5,736	5,270	5,904	5,967	5,503
Sales	473	659	883	1,250	1,743	1,542	1,573	1,629	2,008
Service/parts	1,099	1,613	2,448	2,993	3,213	2,527	3,270	3,009	2,286
Parking	421	458	860	1,008	781	1,200	1,062	1,329	1,208
Food/beverage [2]	6,201	6,133	7,169	7,478	8,566	9,118	8,277	8,786	8,696
Food	2,766	2,627	3,062	3,776	4,658	4,665	4,610	4,792	4,309
Dining/drinking	2,108	2,830	3,408	2,958	3,058	3,817	2,874	2,935	3,388
Fast food	1,243	670	699	744	850	636	793	1,058	999
Multiretail [2]	11,483	12,228	11,976	13,331	12,157	13,254	15,234	14,911	16,355
General merchandise	3,787	5,421	5,339	5,159	4,083	3,778	4,668	5,100	5,098
Shopping center	4,942	4,585	4,086	5,496	5,694	6,045	7,186	6,803	7,689
Shopping mall	1,973	1,718	2,175	2,189	1,949	2,917	2,873	2,523	2,759
Other commercial [2]	5,934	8,994	8,432	8,202	10,203	11,050	11,179	13,537	11,805
Drug store	349	326	536	750	1,007	1,409	1,645	1,682	1,216
Building supply store	850	1,194	1,372	1,201	1,323	1,742	1,588	2,592	2,914
Other stores	4,264	6,826	5,653	5,327	7,090	7,025	6,849	8,136	6,919
Warehouse [2]	5,181	6,298	9,299	11,458	12,563	12,698	13,702	14,822	15,600
General commercial	5,079	6,166	8,944	10,849	11,501	11,732	12,756	13,511	14,330
Ministorage	86	126	319	594	993	918	892	1,263	1,242
Health care	14,939	15,447	15,259	15,420	17,390	17,737	18,388	19,455	19,619
Hospital	9,754	9,891	8,807	8,348	9,968	9,469	9,490	10,182	11,504
Medical building	2,840	3,398	4,064	3,728	4,001	4,070	4,911	5,066	4,521
Special care	2,345	2,158	2,388	3,344	3,421	4,197	3,987	4,206	3,593
Educational [2]	4,814	5,009	5,699	6,985	8,802	9,829	9,756	11,684	12,863
Preschool	169	421	326	398	531	619	662	770	887
Primary/secondary	725	849	1,245	1,560	2,032	2,174	2,421	2,949	3,524
Higher education [2]	3,240	2,939	3,055	3,619	4,327	4,945	5,204	6,334	6,662
Instructional	1,806	1,937	1,712	2,028	1,991	2,469	2,258	3,058	3,287
Dormitory	521	324	483	573	789	955	1,274	1,356	1,548
Sports/recreation	220	236	192	260	475	403	515	645	707
Other educational	549	649	817	1,042	1,714	1,798	1,232	1,318	1,371
Gallery/museum	357	387	571	662	1,107	1,127	778	920	926
Religious [2]	3,894	3,871	4,348	4,537	5,782	6,604	7,372	8,030	8,318
House of worship	2804	2,808	2,951	3,211	3,844	4,549	5,056	5,656	5,974
Other religious	1,075	1,051	1,389	1,310	1,935	2,054	2,314	2,348	2,321
Auxiliary building	382	507	619	620	874	992	1,252	1,280	1,239
Public safety	215	327	185	321	569	586	465	424	273
Amusement and recreation [2]	4,601	5,108	5,886	7,016	8,537	8,589	9,551	8,768	7,662
Theme/amusement park	478	709	563	727	723	866	919	747	463
Sports	534	716	910	1,193	1,333	1,136	1,495	1,068	1,064
Fitness	509	458	637	622	801	889	1,137	1,152	1,260
Performance/meeting center	274	369	365	539	628	603	546	732	925
Social center	1,488	1,293	1,558	1,597	1,979	2,093	2,006	2,367	2,317
Movie theater/studio	331	623	848	1,271	2,199	2,441	2,376	1,461	752
Transportation [2]	1,572	1,364	1,250	1,422	1,285	1,554	1,855	2,616	2,750
Air	1,026	914	666	871	901	1,093	1,107	1,804	2,002
Land	401	233	499	396	261	376	494	644	594
Sewage and waste disposal	373	299	576	637	468	339	516	508	380
Water supply	426	567	670	468	448	543	413	714	541
Manufacturing	23,371	28,845	35,364	38,101	37,624	40,482	32,631	31,800	29,066
Food/beverage/tobacco	2,031	2,809	4,525	4,294	3,957	3,538	3,383	3,374	2,873
Textile/apparel/leather & allied	773	651	824	743	584	712	456	350	245
Wood	279	413	616	689	522	492	427	412	283
Paper	1,886	1,623	1,448	1,711	1,548	1,232	837	629	993
Print/publishing	539	739	1,197	993	930	1,104	856	718	968
Petroleum/coal	2,729	2,593	4,741	2,348	1,186	1,064	927	1,069	757
Chemical	4,937	6,270	5,531	5,445	6,034	8,264	6,181	3,222	3,711
Plastic/rubber	1,808	1,121	1,475	1,632	1,959	2,137	2,222	1,398	1,081
Nonmetallic mineral	160	222	856	1,220	1,004	1,481	1,188	1,603	1,709
Primary metal	834	2,567	2,533	2,244	2,802	2,603	1,993	1,677	621
Fabricated metal	442	744	808	1,585	2,162	2,036	1,890	1,823	1,111
Machinery	352	1,296	1,275	1,169	1,106	1,257	965	731	683
Computer/electronic/electrical	2,158	4,118	6,332	8,945	7,537	7,557	4,415	5,386	4,746
Transportation equipment	2,289	2,631	2,382	2,948	3,453	3,497	3,418	5,347	5,435
Furniture	121	260	213	308	167	296	282	349	187
Miscellaneous	2,033	788	607	1,827	2,671	3,212	3,190	3,713	3,661

[1] Preliminary. [2] Includes other types of construction, not shown separately.

Source: U.S. Census Bureau, Internet site <http://www.census.gov/pub/const/C30/newtc.html>.

U.S. Census Bureau, Statistical Abstract of the United States: 2002

No. 916. Value of State and Local Government Construction Put in Place: 1993 to 2001

[In millions of dollars (101,535 represents $101,535,000,000). See headnote, Table 915]

Type of construction	1993	1994	1995	1996	1997	1998	1999	2000	2001 [1]
Total construction [2]	101,535	105,753	114,181	123,938	136,608	139,984	155,520	164,396	177,527
Residential	3,686	3,359	4,043	4,220	4,336	4,340	4,121	3,724	4,231
Multifamily	3,441	3,233	3,976	4,144	4,238	4,242	4,103	3,703	4,166
Office	3,192	3,559	3,914	4,404	4,619	4,605	4,448	5,419	6,147
Commercial [2]	1,119	1,075	1,329	1,724	2,227	1,993	2,487	2,195	2,877
Automotive	619	750	965	1,257	1,553	1,603	1,891	1,486	2,254
Parking	430	561	794	1,020	1,425	1,549	1,683	1,378	2,237
Warehouse	252	135	231	280	295	258	338	398	344
Health care	2,676	2,856	3,156	3,442	3,501	2,884	3,120	3,413	3,389
Hospital	1,431	1,633	1,960	2,108	2,498	1,980	2,187	2,352	2,438
Medical building	751	766	801	937	657	515	487	591	569
Special care	495	458	395	396	345	389	446	470	381
Educational [2]	19,227	20,541	25,743	28,603	33,758	35,015	42,467	49,785	55,719
Primary/secondary [2]	12,781	13,348	17,545	20,009	23,853	26,064	31,498	35,896	38,869
Elementary	4,533	4,177	5,242	6,301	8,015	9,492	10,655	13,035	14,900
Middle/junior high	2,789	2,637	3,745	3,685	3,988	3,930	6,187	6,193	7,380
High	3,170	3,638	4,833	6,130	6,687	7,627	11,433	14,173	14,904
Higher education [2]	5,294	6,047	6,883	7,311	8,198	7,721	9,198	11,439	13,868
Instructional	3,311	3,977	4,277	4,746	4,459	4,307	5,439	6,725	8,272
Parking	91	133	158	169	262	331	379	544	591
Administration	107	108	128	91	189	179	279	313	192
Dormitory	346	384	324	396	388	548	829	1,147	1,500
Library	252	212	300	439	695	368	336	328	405
Student union/cafeteria	104	170	238	231	405	318	307	342	648
Sports/recreation	474	535	625	538	873	795	790	1,028	1,185
Infrastructure	537	494	788	585	654	780	726	888	876
Other educational	929	864	1,110	1,121	1,250	1,128	1,421	1,749	2,340
Library/archive	475	481	704	853	779	566	979	1,036	1,830
Public safety [2]	5,226	5,371	5,928	6,718	6,668	7,575	7,750	7,052	6,910
Correctional	4,459	4,724	4,854	5,586	5,701	6,588	6,488	5,728	5,571
Detention	3,964	4,224	4,049	4,749	4,786	5,618	5,268	4,706	4,362
Police/sheriff	495	500	804	837	916	970	1,220	1,022	1,209
Other public safety	705	634	1,025	1,126	967	988	1,262	1,324	1,339
Fire/rescue	496	457	652	831	773	795	1,076	1,197	1,143
Amusement and recreation	4,943	5,612	6,142	6,056	6,857	7,666	9,024	9,137	10,076
Sports	1,398	1,227	1,637	1,477	2,311	3,173	3,356	2,758	2,924
Performance/meeting center	1,517	1,449	1,751	2,127	1,629	1,343	1,547	2,501	3,245
Convention center	1,158	1,076	1,224	1,318	938	835	1,082	1,685	2,477
Social center	883	1,089	772	911	961	947	1,379	1,387	1,520
Neighborhood center	487	670	581	612	673	622	1,043	1,067	1,186
Park/camp	916	1,604	1,696	1,430	1,874	2,020	2,544	2,325	2,109
Transportation [2]	8,803	8,647	8,967	9,998	9,708	10,197	11,126	12,294	14,137
Air [2]	5,088	3,858	3,855	4,666	4,852	5,594	5,869	6,337	6,912
Passenger terminal	1,650	996	1,209	1,656	2,086	2,196	2,183	2,771	2,397
Runway	2,503	2,065	2,176	2,593	2,260	2,563	3,052	3,024	3,867
Land [2]	2,952	3,757	4,009	4,067	3,642	3,823	4,212	4,884	5,633
Passenger terminal	526	907	1,147	1,362	1,237	1,222	1,231	1,184	1,425
Mass transit	1,273	1,534	1,734	1,787	1,607	1,548	1,330	1,403	2,191
Railroad	327	498	462	402	401	564	1,016	1,391	1,010
Water [2]	764	1,033	1,103	1,264	1,214	780	1,044	1,073	1,592
Dock/marina	524	579	690	898	729	421	646	816	1,132
Dry dock/marine terminal	101	212	204	308	477	352	399	223	438
Power	3,159	2,763	2,879	2,503	3,101	2,495	3,911	5,831	2,561
Electrical	2,654	1,893	2,231	2,225	2,893	2,052	3,080	5,564	2,398
Distribution	920	482	733	656	1,650	1,511	1,803	2,207	809
Highway and street [2]	34,353	37,281	37,616	39,500	43,017	44,782	49,124	49,296	54,180
Pavement	26,503	29,402	29,164	30,472	32,416	33,180	36,427	36,254	39,713
Lighting	543	570	659	796	812	1,180	908	818	1,198
Retaining wall	219	325	187	176	493	711	815	1,050	606
Tunnel	393	454	346	430	539	862	924	855	1,032
Bridge	5,961	5,909	6,615	6,682	7,299	7,229	8,470	8,889	10,196
Toll/weigh	170	107	152	138	219	247	277	310	109
Maintenance building	119	158	53	159	307	362	354	281	386
Rest facility/streetscape	27	94	167	464	722	838	939	840	940
Sewage and waste disposal [2]	8,875	8,714	8,419	9,801	10,515	9,943	9,864	8,807	8,751
Sewage/dry waste	5,237	5,370	4,825	6,420	6,830	6,589	6,626	5,874	5,579
Plant	2,076	1,822	1,641	2,173	1,969	1,925	2,038	1,739	1,517
Line/pump station	2,612	3,225	2,960	4,001	4,639	4,422	4,314	3,980	3,927
Waste water	3,480	3,215	3,522	3,346	3,664	3,317	3,232	2,932	3,173
Plant	2,714	2,367	2,467	2,211	2,680	2,276	2,457	2,030	2,369
Line/drain	766	848	1,055	1,135	984	1,041	775	903	804
Water supply [2]	5,089	4,651	4,713	5,618	6,493	6,678	6,541	5,993	7,152
Plant	1,520	1,368	1,204	1,372	1,664	1,912	2,023	1,929	2,526
Well	118	170	212	260	179	247	237	238	249
Line	2,550	2,319	2,516	2,841	3,353	3,106	2,894	2,921	3,327
Pump station	193	274	286	437	349	418	540	393	426
Reservoir	317	260	208	409	514	429	385	167	261
Tank/tower	262	225	246	298	433	505	461	344	363
Conservation and development [2]	1,052	1,194	1,265	1,191	1,503	1,444	1,325	1,127	1,252
Dam/levee	149	205	329	349	631	597	517	366	284
Breakwater/jetty	320	431	358	472	360	456	375	327	563
Dredging	105	176	151	83	161	121	175	170	134

[1] Preliminary.   [2] Includes other types of construction, not shown separately.

Source: U.S. Census Bureau, Internet site <http://www.census.gov/pub/const/C30/newtc.html>.

No. 917. Construction Contracts—Value of Construction and Floor Space of Buildings by Class of Construction: 1980 to 2001

[151.8 represents $151,800,000,000. Building construction includes new structures and additions; nonbuilding construction includes major alterations to existing structures which affect only valuation, since no additional floor area is created by "alteration"]

Year	Total	Resi-dential build-ings	Nonresidential buildings										Non-build-ing con-struc-tion
			Total	Com-mer-cial [1]	Manu-fac-turing	Educa-tional [2]	Health	Public build-ings	Reli-gious	Social and recrea-tional	Mis-cella-neous		
VALUE (bil. dol.)													
1980	151.8	60.4	56.9	27.7	9.2	7.4	5.4	1.6	1.2	2.7	1.7		34.5
1985	235.6	102.1	92.1	54.6	8.1	10.0	7.8	3.1	2.0	4.0	2.5		41.4
1990	246.0	100.9	95.4	44.8	8.4	16.6	9.2	5.7	2.2	5.3	3.1		49.7
1992	252.2	110.6	87.0	32.8	8.9	17.6	10.9	5.8	2.5	5.5	3.1		54.6
1993	271.5	123.9	88.8	34.2	9.0	19.3	10.5	3.9	2.4	6.8	2.6		58.9
1994	296.7	133.6	101.5	40.8	11.2	21.0	10.5	6.1	2.5	6.5	3.0		61.6
1995	306.5	127.9	114.2	46.6	13.8	22.9	10.8	6.3	2.8	7.1	3.8		64.4
1996	332.0	146.5	120.5	51.9	13.1	23.0	11.1	6.3	2.9	8.1	4.1		65.1
1997	362.4	153.6	138.9	59.8	14.0	28.4	11.9	7.0	3.8	10.0	4.0		69.8
1998	405.6	179.8	154.4	74.0	12.1	30.1	12.9	6.6	4.3	10.8	3.6		71.3
1999	448.2	195.1	169.5	77.5	11.4	37.3	13.7	8.2	4.6	11.8	5.1		83.6
2000	474.4	208.4	174.3	81.5	8.9	41.0	12.5	7.5	4.7	13.8	4.5		91.7
2001	494.4	218.8	169.0	70.2	8.1	47.1	14.1	7.8	4.9	12.1	4.8		106.6
FLOOR SPACE (mil. sq. ft.)													
1980	3,102	1,839	1,263	738	220	103	55	18	28	49	52		(X)
1985	3,853	2,324	1,529	1,039	165	111	73	28	32	44	38		(X)
1990	3,020	1,817	1,203	694	128	152	69	47	29	51	32		(X)
1992	2,799	1,864	936	462	95	156	77	41	30	42	32		(X)
1993	3,062	2,091	971	481	110	165	75	30	30	51	29		(X)
1994	3,411	2,267	1,144	600	143	172	72	45	30	51	31		(X)
1995	3,454	2,172	1,281	700	163	186	70	40	33	56	33		(X)
1996	3,776	2,479	1,297	723	155	177	77	41	32	60	33		(X)
1997	4,126	2,586	1,540	855	191	204	89	48	42	77	35		(X)
1998	4,812	3,015	1,797	1,106	166	219	96	42	47	85	34		(X)
1999	5,103	3,256	1,847	1,118	142	262	99	50	49	88	39		(X)
2000	4,994	3,115	1,880	1,189	111	274	88	45	50	94	29		(X)
2001	4,815	3,146	1,669	986	92	296	90	44	51	82	27		(X)

X Not applicable.   [1] Includes nonindustrial warehouses.   [2] Includes science.

Source: McGraw-Hill Construction Dodge, a Division of the McGraw-Hill Companies, New York, NY (copyright).

No. 918. Construction Contracts—Value by State: 1990 to 2001

[In millions of dollars (246,022 represents $246,022,000,000). Represents value of construction in states in which work was actually done. See headnote, Table 917]

State	1990	1995	2001 Total [1]	2001 Resi-den-tial	2001 Non-resi-den-tial	State	1990	1995	2001 Total [1]	2001 Resi-den-tial	2001 Non-resi-den-tial
U.S.	246,022	306,527	494,419	218,834	168,994	MO	3,833	6,438	8,243	3,326	2,982
AL	2,939	4,308	8,402	2,557	2,728	MT	332	865	1,030	424	300
AK	1,919	1,660	1,600	580	544	NE.	1,318	1,694	2,972	1,013	1,227
AZ	4,553	8,784	14,237	8,206	3,404	NV	3,334	5,555	8,388	4,111	2,206
AR	1,438	2,903	4,640	1,762	1,058	NH	1,021	1,039	2,086	966	841
CA	37,318	29,045	54,844	24,746	18,790	NJ	6,141	6,454	11,457	3,807	5,098
CO.	3,235	6,476	12,397	7,200	3,517	NM.	1,124	2,108	2,665	1,046	912
CT	3,058	3,124	4,384	1,670	1,918	NY	14,137	13,380	22,566	6,413	11,001
DE	787	871	1,338	532	568	NC	6,614	10,599	17,624	10,050	5,065
DC	795	656	1,655	242	1,082	ND	506	791	749	280	183
FL	16,975	21,453	39,206	21,415	10,831	OH	9,885	12,430	18,201	7,603	6,213
GA	7,120	12,156	19,276	10,808	5,900	OK	2,164	2,968	6,284	1,954	2,345
HI	2,831	2,273	1,973	860	552	OR	3,101	5,451	6,493	3,341	2,046
ID	986	1,864	2,547	1,521	683	PA	10,117	9,348	15,639	4,805	5,987
IL.	10,796	11,744	19,353	7,844	7,008	RI	594	465	1,135	378	560
IN	6,350	7,896	11,875	5,786	3,848	SC	3,664	4,580	8,103	3,792	2,467
IA	2,034	2,883	4,201	1,478	1,650	SD	468	706	1,038	428	311
KS	2,193	3,264	4,125	1,860	1,420	TN	4,388	7,167	9,113	4,730	2,888
KY	3,174	4,464	6,327	2,844	1,681	TX	13,197	23,022	42,962	18,549	14,687
LA	3,191	4,354	4,678	1,544	1,785	UT	1,884	4,218	4,586	2,168	1,497
ME	897	1,076	1,668	763	614	VT	515	484	676	335	179
MD	6,056	6,299	8,829	4,072	3,243	VA	7,180	8,794	12,424	6,259	4,336
MA	5,135	7,411	10,505	3,430	5,123	WA	6,185	7,334	11,433	4,857	4,213
MI	7,646	9,947	14,371	6,282	5,149	WV	1,253	1,215	1,304	291	450
MN.	4,953	5,607	9,449	4,236	3,183	WI	4,654	5,652	8,851	4,082	3,153
MS	1,569	2,718	5,413	1,296	1,293	WY	462	532	1,016	290	274

[1] Includes nonbuilding construction, not shown separately.

Source: McGraw-Hill Construction Dodge, a Division of the McGraw-Hill Companies, New York, NY (copyright).

Construction and Housing   **589**

No. 919. New Privately-Owned Housing Units Authorized by State: 2000 and 2001

[1,592.3 represents 1,592,300. Based on about 19,000 places in United States having building permit systems]

State	Housing units (1,000) 2000	2001 Total	2001 1 unit	Valuation (mil. dol.) 2000	2001 Total	2001 1 unit	State	Housing units (1,000) 2000	2001 Total	2001 1 unit	Valuation (mil. dol.) 2000	2001 Total	2001 1 unit
U.S.	1,592.3	1,636.7	1,235.6	185,744	196,243	170,006	MO . . .	24.3	24.7	18.8	2,569	2,750	2,387
AL . . .	17.4	17.7	14.0	1,718	1,823	1,616	MT . . .	2.6	2.6	1.8	235	266	218
AK . . .	2.1	2.9	1.8	333	450	320	NE . . .	9.1	8.2	6.6	830	835	755
AZ . . .	61.5	62.5	51.8	7,158	7,783	7,163	NV . . .	32.3	36.1	27.0	3,312	3,742	3,254
AR . . .	9.2	10.4	7.5	859	1,019	896	NH . . .	6.7	6.6	5.9	937	950	905
CA . . .	145.6	146.7	107.4	23,344	23,650	20,253	NJ . . .	34.6	28.3	21.5	3,376	3,017	2,566
CO . . .	54.6	55.0	36.4	6,822	6,593	5,277	NM . . .	8.9	10.0	9.0	1,073	1,186	1,143
CT . . .	9.4	9.3	7.8	1,425	1,440	1,339	NY . . .	44.1	45.5	24.1	4,992	5,257	3,683
DE . . .	4.6	4.8	4.4	414	504	480	NC . . .	78.4	82.0	62.7	8,643	9,226	8,286
DC . . .	0.8	0.9	0.1	54	60	16	ND . . .	2.1	2.7	1.5	190	241	182
FL . . .	155.3	167.0	118.7	17,462	19,465	15,597	OH . . .	49.7	49.9	38.8	6,154	6,452	5,856
GA . . .	91.8	93.1	71.5	8,722	9,462	8,266	OK . . .	11.1	12.4	9.8	1,204	1,478	1,284
HI . . .	4.9	4.8	4.0	823	812	731	OR . . .	19.9	21.3	16.3	2,533	2,998	2,655
ID . . .	10.9	11.8	9.7	1,359	1,448	1,340	PA . . .	41.1	41.4	34.8	4,616	4,804	4,412
IL . . .	51.9	54.8	39.4	6,528	7,141	6,114	RI . . .	2.6	2.4	2.2	296	306	289
IN . . .	37.9	39.1	32.4	4,414	4,877	4,494	SC . . .	32.8	30.1	24.8	3,533	3,470	3,106
IA . . .	12.5	13.1	8.8	1,333	1,480	1,205	SD . . .	4.2	4.5	3.4	369	405	351
KS . . .	12.5	14.5	10.1	1,397	1,612	1,387	TN . . .	32.2	32.4	26.2	3,378	3,540	3,249
KY . . .	18.5	17.7	15.0	1,767	1,818	1,689	TX . . .	141.2	150.3	111.9	15,418	15,761	13,959
LA . . .	14.7	15.7	13.3	1,553	1,598	1,472	UT . . .	17.6	18.9	15.0	2,138	2,312	2,012
ME . . .	6.2	6.5	5.9	723	776	730	VT . . .	2.5	2.7	2.3	319	397	364
MD . . .	30.4	29.1	23.7	3,232	3,228	2,929	VA . . .	48.4	52.9	41.7	5,052	5,715	5,048
MA . . .	18.0	17.0	13.0	2,741	2,689	2,327	WA . . .	39.0	38.3	26.7	4,426	4,689	3,851
MI . . .	52.5	50.1	40.5	6,256	6,085	5,483	WV . . .	3.8	3.9	3.5	360	385	366
MN . . .	32.8	34.2	26.9	4,204	4,576	3,975	WI . . .	34.2	37.8	25.4	3,917	4,495	3,655
MS . . .	11.3	9.9	8.1	918	894	817	WY . . .	1.6	1.9	1.5	314	277	255

Source: U.S. Census Bureau, *Construction Reports*, Series C40, *Building Permits*, monthly; publication discontinued in 2001. See Internet site <http://www.census.gov/ftp/pub/const/www/newresconstindex.html> and *New Residential Construction*, monthly.

No. 920. New Privately-Owned Housing Units Started—Selected Characteristics: 1970 to 2001

[In thousands (1,434 represents 1,434,000). For composition of regions, see map, inside front cover]

Year	Total units	Structures with— One unit	2 to 4 units	5 or more units	Region North-east	Mid-west	South	West	Units for sale Total	Single-family	Multi-family
1970	1,434	813	85	536	218	294	612	311	(NA)	(NA)	(NA)
1975	1,160	892	64	204	149	294	442	275	576	531	45
1976	1,538	1,162	86	289	169	400	569	400	768	705	63
1977	1,987	1,451	122	414	202	465	783	538	994	904	90
1978	2,020	1,433	125	462	200	451	824	545	1,032	901	131
1979	1,745	1,194	122	429	178	349	748	470	915	742	173
1980	1,292	852	110	331	125	218	643	306	689	526	163
1981	1,084	705	91	288	117	165	562	240	584	426	158
1982	1,062	663	80	320	117	149	591	205	549	409	140
1983	1,703	1,068	113	522	168	218	935	382	923	713	210
1984	1,750	1,084	121	544	204	243	866	436	934	728	206
1985	1,742	1,072	93	576	252	240	782	468	867	713	154
1986	1,805	1,179	84	542	294	296	733	483	925	782	143
1987	1,621	1,146	65	409	269	298	634	420	862	732	130
1988	1,488	1,081	59	348	235	274	575	404	808	709	99
1989	1,376	1,003	55	318	179	266	536	396	735	648	87
1990	1,193	895	37	260	131	253	479	329	585	529	56
1991	1,014	840	36	138	113	233	414	254	531	490	41
1992	1,200	1,030	31	139	127	288	497	288	659	618	41
1993	1,288	1,126	29	133	126	298	562	302	760	716	44
1994	1,457	1,198	35	224	138	329	639	351	815	763	52
1995	1,354	1,076	34	244	118	290	615	331	763	712	51
1996	1,477	1,161	45	271	132	322	662	361	833	774	59
1997	1,474	1,134	44	296	137	304	670	363	843	784	59
1998	1,617	1,271	43	303	149	331	743	395	941	882	59
1999	1,641	1,302	32	307	156	347	746	392	981	912	69
2000	1,569	1,231	39	299	155	318	714	383	946	871	75
2001	1,603	1,273	37	293	149	330	732	391	990	919	71

NA Not available.

Source: U.S. Census Bureau, *Current Construction Reports*, Series C20, *Housing Starts*, monthly; publication discontinued in 2001. See Internet site <http://www.census.gov/const/www/newresconstindex.html> and *New Residential Construction*, monthly.

No. 921. New Privately-Owned Housing Units Started by State: 1997 to 2000

[In thousands of units (1,476 represents 1,476,000)]

State	1997	1998	1999	2000 Total units	2000 Single-family units	State	1997	1998	1999	2000 Total units	2000 Single-family units
U.S.	1,476	1,623	1,660	1,535	1,223	MO	27.9	29.7	29.6	26.0	22.2
AL	21.7	23.7	23.5	21.2	17.7	MT	2.5	2.4	2.5	2.2	1.4
AK	2.5	2.7	2.4	2.1	1.6	NE	9.8	9.8	9.7	8.4	6.2
AZ	58.2	65.2	66.5	60.0	48.2	NV	35.6	36.4	35.1	34.5	25.3
AR	13.0	12.9	13.7	12.5	9.5	NH	5.3	5.7	6.0	6.0	5.6
CA	109.1	123.0	129.9	128.2	99.9	NJ	26.8	29.7	31.9	31.2	25.4
CO	43.8	50.6	49.9	45.9	36.0	NM	10.5	9.4	9.2	8.1	7.2
CT	9.1	11.0	10.6	10.0	8.7	NY	30.5	34.0	36.3	34.9	22.7
DE	4.9	5.5	5.4	5.2	4.8	NC	74.1	81.5	85.8	74.8	59.2
DC	-	0.4	0.7	0.4	0.3	ND	3.2	3.3	3.2	2.7	1.8
FL	135.2	143.9	152.8	148.1	104.9	OH	44.6	47.0	49.8	45.3	37.7
GA	78.6	87.1	88.4	81.5	68.4	OK	13.2	16.3	16.2	15.5	12.4
HI	3.8	3.4	3.7	3.8	3.2	OR	26.6	25.6	24.5	22.2	15.8
ID	10.5	12.0	12.6	11.5	10.1	PA	38.6	40.1	41.1	37.5	32.4
IL	46.5	49.2	52.4	48.1	38.9	RI	2.6	2.7	2.9	2.7	2.5
IN	36.0	40.8	41.8	37.6	32.3	SC	31.2	33.2	35.8	33.9	27.1
IA	11.2	13.7	13.6	13.0	10.7	SD	3.4	3.8	4.1	3.5	2.8
KS	13.6	15.6	16.4	15.2	11.7	TN	37.8	37.4	37.3	33.9	29.9
KY	20.5	23.2	23.2	21.4	17.5	TX	134.0	159.8	155.2	148.4	108.3
LA	16.7	17.8	18.6	15.8	13.4	UT	19.8	21.1	20.5	19.5	16.1
ME	4.6	5.8	5.8	5.8	5.5	VT	1.8	2.2	2.4	2.4	2.1
MD	26.5	31.2	30.3	27.9	23.0	VA	46.9	50.9	53.0	50.2	42.6
MA	16.9	18.2	18.0	17.7	15.5	WA	40.7	44.0	43.7	40.9	28.4
MI	49.0	54.5	55.4	50.9	44.2	WV	5.1	5.1	5.8	5.3	4.1
MN	25.2	30.8	32.9	30.7	26.8	WI	30.7	34.3	35.4	32.0	24.7
MS	12.2	15.0	15.2	12.8	10.1	WY	1.9	2.1	2.0	1.8	1.5

- Represents or rounds to zero.

Source: National Association of Home Builders, Economics Division, Washington, DC. Data provided by the Econometric Forecasting Service.

No. 922. Characteristics of New Privately-Owned One-Family Houses Completed: 1980 to 2001

[Percent distribution, except as indicated (957 represents 957,000). Data are percent distribution of characteristics for all houses completed (includes new houses completed, houses built for sale completed, contractor-built and owner-built houses completed, and houses completed for rent). Percents exclude houses for which characteristics specified were not reported]

Characteristic	1980	1990	1995	2000	2001	Characteristic	1980	1990	1995	2000	2001
Total houses (1,000). . . .	957	966	1,066	1,242	1,256	Bedrooms.	100	100	100	100	100
						2 or less.	17	15	13	11	11
Financing [1]	100	100	100	100	100	3.	63	57	57	54	52
Mortgage	82	82	88	92	92	4 or more	20	29	30	35	37
FHA-insured	16	14	8	9	9	Bathrooms	100	100	100	100	100
VA-guaranteed	8	4	5	3	3	1 1/2 or less	27	13	11	7	6
Conventional	55	62	74	79	81	2	48	42	41	39	38
Rural Housing Service [2]	3	2	1	1	(Z)	2 1/2 or more	25	45	48	54	56
Cash or equivalent. . . .	18	18	12	8	8	Heating fuel	100	100	100	100	100
						Gas.	41	59	67	70	70
						Electricity	50	33	28	27	27
Floor area.	100	100	100	100	100	Oil.	3	5	3	3	3
Under 1,200 sq. ft	21	11	10	6	6	Other.	5	3	1	1	1
1,200 to 1,599 sq. ft. . .	29	22	22	18	18	Heating system	100	100	100	100	100
1,600 to 1,999 sq. ft. . .	22	22	23	23	21	Warm air furnace	57	65	67	71	71
2,000 to 2,399 sq. ft. . .	13	17	17	18	18	Electric heat pump	24	23	25	23	23
2,400 sq. ft. and over . .	15	29	28	35	38	Other.	19	12	9	6	5
Average (sq. ft.).	1,740	2,080	2,095	2,266	2,324	Central air-conditioning .	100	100	100	100	100
Median (sq. ft.)	1,595	1,905	1,920	2,057	2,103	With	63	76	80	85	86
						Without	37	24	20	15	14
Number of stories	100	100	100	100	100	Fireplaces.	100	100	100	100	100
1.	60	46	49	47	46	No fireplace	43	34	37	40	42
2 or more	31	49	48	52	53	1 or more	56	66	63	60	58
Split level	8	4	3	1	1	Parking facilities	100	100	100	100	100
Foundation	100	100	100	100	100	Garage	69	82	84	89	89
Full or partial basement.	36	38	39	37	35	Carport	7	2	2	1	1
Slab	45	40	42	46	48	No garage or carport . .	24	16	14	11	11
Crawl space	19	21	19	17	17						

Z Less than 1 percent.   [1] Excludes homes not yet sold.   [2] Prior to 2000, Farmers Home Administration.

Source: U.S. Census Bureau and U.S. Dept. of Housing and Urban Development, *Current Construction Reports*, Series C25, *New One-Family Houses Sold*, monthly, and *Characteristics of New Housing*, annual; publication discontinued in 2001, see Internet site <http://www.census.gov/const/www/charindex.html>.

U.S. Census Bureau, Statistical Abstract of the United States: 2002

No. 923. New Privately Owned One-Family Houses Sold by Region and Type of Financing, 1980 to 2001, and by Sales-Price Group, 2001

[In thousands (545 represents 545,000). Based on a national probability sample of monthly interviews with builders or owners of one-family houses for which building permits have been issued or, for nonpermit areas, on which construction has started. For details, see source. For composition of regions, see map inside front cover]

Year and sales-price group	Total sales	Region				Financing type			
		North-east	Midwest	South	West	Conven-tional [1]	FHA and VA	Rural Housing Service [2]	Cash
1980	545	50	81	267	145	302	196	14	32
1985	688	112	82	323	170	403	208	11	64
1990	534	71	89	225	149	337	138	10	50
1995	667	55	125	300	187	490	129	9	39
1996	757	74	137	337	209	570	140	9	38
1997	804	78	140	363	223	616	137	6	46
1998	886	81	164	398	243	693	136	9	48
1999	880	76	168	395	242	689	143	6	41
2000	877	71	155	406	244	695	138	4	40
2001	**908**	**66**	**164**	**439**	**239**	**(NA)**	**(NA)**	**(NA)**	**(NA)**
Under $100,000	75	1	11	56	6	(NA)	(NA)	(NA)	(NA)
$100,000 to $149,999	248	11	46	145	46	(NA)	(NA)	(NA)	(NA)
$150,000 to $199,999	221	12	45	107	57	(NA)	(NA)	(NA)	(NA)
$200,000 to $299,999	221	19	40	84	78	(NA)	(NA)	(NA)	(NA)
$300,000 and over	142	22	21	47	53	(NA)	(NA)	(NA)	(NA)

NA Not available. [1] Includes all other types of financing. [2] Prior to 1996, the Farmers Home Administration.

Source: U.S. Census Bureau and U.S. Dept. of Housing and Urban Development, Current Construction Reports, Series C25, Characteristics of New Housing, annual; and New One-Family Houses Sold, monthly; publications discontinued in 2001. See Internet site <http://www.census.gov/ftp/pub/const/www/newressalesindex.html> and New Residential Sales, monthly.

No. 924. Median Sales Price of New Privately Owned One-Family Houses Sold by Region: 1980 to 2001

[In dollars. For definition of median, see Guide to Tabular Presentation. For composition of regions, see map inside front cover]

Year	U.S.	North-east	Mid-west	South	West	Year	U.S.	North-east	Mid-west	South	West
1980	64,600	69,500	63,400	59,600	72,300	1995	133,900	180,000	134,000	124,500	141,400
1985	84,300	103,300	80,300	75,000	92,600	1996	140,000	186,000	138,000	126,200	153,900
1990	122,900	159,000	107,900	99,000	147,500	1997	146,000	190,000	149,900	129,600	160,000
1991	120,000	155,900	110,000	100,000	141,100	1998	152,500	200,000	157,500	135,800	163,500
1992	121,500	169,000	115,600	105,500	130,400	1999	161,000	210,500	164,000	145,900	173,700
1993	126,500	162,600	125,000	115,000	135,000	2000	169,000	227,400	169,700	148,000	196,400
1994	130,000	169,000	132,900	116,900	140,400	2001	175,200	246,400	172,600	155,400	213,600

Source: U.S. Census Bureau and U.S. Dept. of Housing and Urban Development, Current Construction Reports, Series C25, Characteristics of New Housing, annual; and New One-Family Houses Sold, monthly; publications discontinued in 2001. See Internet site <http://www.census.gov/ftp/pub/const/www/newressalesindex.html> and New Residential Sales, monthly.

No. 925. New Manufactured (Mobile) Homes Placed for Residential Use and Average Sales Price by Region: 1980 to 2001

[233.7 represents 233,700. A mobile home is a moveable dwelling, 8 feet or more wide and 40 feet or more long, designed to be towed on its own chassis, with transportation gear integral to the unit when it leaves the factory, and without need of permanent foundation. Excluded are travel trailers, motor homes, and modular housing. Data are based on a probability sample and subject to sampling variability; see source. For composition of regions, see map inside front cover]

Year	Units placed (1,000)					Average sales price (dol.)				
	Total	North-east	Mid-west	South	West	U.S.	North-east	Mid-west	South	West
1980	233.7	12.3	32.3	140.3	48.7	19,800	18,500	18,600	18,200	25,400
1985	283.4	20.2	38.6	187.6	36.9	21,800	22,700	21,500	20,400	28,700
1990	195.4	18.8	37.7	108.4	30.6	27,800	30,000	27,000	24,500	39,300
1992	212.0	15.0	42.2	124.4	30.4	28,400	30,900	28,800	25,400	39,000
1993	242.5	15.4	44.5	146.7	35.9	30,500	32,000	31,400	27,700	40,500
1994	290.9	16.3	53.3	177.7	43.6	32,800	32,900	34,000	30,200	41,900
1995	319.4	15.0	57.5	203.2	43.7	35,300	35,800	35,700	33,300	44,100
1996	337.7	16.2	58.8	218.2	44.4	37,200	37,300	38,000	35,500	45,000
1997	336.3	14.3	55.3	219.4	47.3	39,800	41,300	40,300	38,000	47,300
1998	373.7	14.7	58.3	250.3	50.4	41,600	42,200	42,400	40,100	48,400
1999	338.3	14.1	53.6	227.2	43.5	43,300	44,000	44,400	41,900	49,600
2000	280.6	14.6	49.9	177.4	38.8	46,300	47,500	47,700	44,200	54,000
2001	192.0	12.2	37.6	112.6	29.5	48,800	50,400	49,100	46,100	58,800

Source: U.S. Census Bureau, Internet site, <http://www.census.gov/ftp/pub/const/www/mhsindex.html>.

No. 926. Existing One-Family Homes Sold and Price by Region: 1970 to 2001

[1,612 represents 1,612,000. Includes existing detached single-family homes and townhomes. Based on data (adjusted and aggregated to regional and national totals) reported by participating real estate multiple listing services. For definition of median, see Guide to Tabular Presentation. For composition of regions, see map inside front cover]

Year	Houses sold (1,000)					Median sales price (dol.)				
	Total	North-east	Mid-west	South	West	Total	North-east	Mid-west	South	West
1970	1,612	251	501	568	292	23,000	25,700	20,100	22,200	24,300
1975	2,476	370	701	862	543	35,300	39,300	30,100	34,800	39,600
1980	2,973	403	806	1,092	672	62,200	60,800	51,900	58,300	89,300
1982	1,990	354	490	780	366	67,800	63,500	55,100	67,100	98,900
1983	2,697	477	692	1,004	524	70,300	72,200	56,600	69,200	94,900
1984	2,829	478	720	1,006	624	72,400	78,700	57,100	71,300	95,800
1985	3,134	561	806	1,063	704	75,500	88,900	58,900	75,200	95,400
1986	3,474	635	922	1,145	773	80,300	104,800	63,500	78,200	100,900
1987	3,436	618	892	1,163	763	85,600	133,300	66,000	80,400	113,200
1988	3,513	606	865	1,224	817	89,300	143,000	68,400	82,200	124,900
1989 [1]	3,325	490	832	1,185	818	89,500	127,700	71,800	84,400	127,100
1990	3,219	458	809	1,193	759	92,000	126,400	75,300	85,100	129,600
1991	3,186	463	812	1,173	737	97,100	129,100	79,500	88,500	135,300
1992	3,479	521	913	1,242	802	99,700	128,900	83,000	91,500	131,500
1993	3,786	550	967	1,386	882	103,100	129,100	86,000	94,300	132,500
1994	3,916	552	965	1,436	962	107,200	129,100	89,300	95,700	139,400
1995	3,888	547	945	1,433	964	110,500	126,700	94,800	97,700	141,000
1996	4,196	584	986	1,511	1,116	115,800	127,800	101,000	103,400	147,100
1997	4,382	607	1,005	1,595	1,174	121,800	131,800	107,000	109,600	155,200
1998	4,970	662	1,130	1,868	1,309	128,400	135,900	114,300	116,200	164,800
1999	5,205	656	1,148	2,015	1,386	133,300	139,000	119,600	120,300	173,900
2000	5,152	643	1,119	2,015	1,376	139,000	139,400	123,600	128,300	183,000
2001	5,296	638	1,158	2,114	1,386	147,800	146,500	130,200	137,400	194,500

[1] Beginning 1989 data not comparable to earlier years due to rebenchmarking.

Source: NATIONAL ASSOCIATION OF REALTORS®, Washington, DC, prior to 1990, *Home Sales*, monthly, and *Home Sales Yearbook: 1990*; (copyright); thereafter, *Real Estate Outlook; Market Trends & Insights*, monthly, (copyright).

No. 927. Median Sales Price of Existing One-Family Homes by Selected Metropolitan Area: 1999 to 2001

[In thousands of dollars (133.3 represents $133,300). Includes existing detached single-family homes and townhomes. Areas are metropolitan statistical areas defined by source as of 1992, except as noted]

Metropolitan area	1999	2000	2001	Metropolitan area	1999	2000	2001
United States, all areas.	**133.3**	**139.0**	**147.8**	Miami-Hialeah, FL PMSA	134.6	144.6	162.7
				Milwaukee, WI PMSA	135.3	140.7	140.4
Albuquerque, NM	130.3	130.4	133.3	Minneapolis-St. Paul, MN-WI . . .	138.7	151.4	167.4
Anaheim-Santa Ana, CA PMSA				Nashville, TN	116.4	(NA)	130.0
(Orange Co.) [1]	280.9	316.2	355.6	New Haven-Meriden, CT	145.7	151.6	168.0
Atlanta, GA	123.7	131.2	138.8	NY: Bergen-Passaic, NJ PMSA . .	221.8	261.2	288.8
Aurora-Elgin, IL [2]	151.9	163.0	178.2	NY: Middlesex-Somerset-			
Austin/San Marcos, TX	128.6	142.8	152.0	Hunterdon, NJ PMSA.	196.8	219.7	244.3
Baltimore, MD	127.4	153.0	158.2	NY: Monmouth-Ocean, NJ	164.4	179.0	208.6
Birmingham, AL	127.1	125.5	133.6	NY: Nassau-Suffolk, NY PMSA . .	190.4	214.0	248.4
Boise, ID	123.9	126.0	130.0	NY: New York-North NJ-			
Boston, MA PMSA	290.0	314.2	356.6	Long Island, NY CMSA	203.2	230.2	258.2
Bradenton, FL [2]	117.2	127.3	137.8	NY: Newark, NJ	212.0	242.4	263.1
Charleston, SC.	131.7	137.9	150.8	Philadelphia, PA-NJ PMSA.	124.8	125.2	134.8
Charlotte-Gastonia-Rock Hill,				Phoenix, AZ.	126.4	134.4	139.4
NC-SC	138.2	140.3	145.3	Portland, OR PMSA	165.0	170.1	172.3
Chicago, IL PMSA	171.2	171.8	198.5	Providence, RI PMSA	128.8	137.8	158.0
Cincinnati, OH-KY-IN PMSA	119.9	126.7	130.2	Raleigh-Durham, NC	165.0	158.4	168.2
Colorado Springs, CO	144.9	154.1	173.3	Reno, NV	150.6	157.3	165.1
Columbus, OH	125.0	129.1	135.7	Richmond-Petersburg, VA	128.5	129.8	133.3
Dallas, TX PMSA	115.7	122.5	131.1	Riverside-San Bernadino, CA			
Denver, CO PMSA	171.3	196.8	218.3	PMSA [1]	128.7	138.6	157.2
Eugene-Springfield, OR	129.5	132.8	134.6	Sacramento, CA [1]	131.5	145.2	174.2
Ft. Lauderdale-Hollywood-				Salt Lake City-Ogden, UT.	137.9	141.5	147.6
Pompano Beach, FL PMSA . . .	136.1	148.7	168.1	San Diego, CA [1]	231.6	269.4	298.6
Greensboro/Winston Salem/				San Francisco, CA Area [1]	340.8	454.6	475.9
High Point, NC	124.8	129.3	132.7	Sarasota, FL [2]	134.8	132.0	(NA)
Hartford, CT PMSA.	150.7	159.9	167.3	Seattle, WA	(NA)	230.1	245.4
Honolulu, HI.	290.0	295.0	299.9	Tacoma, WA	(NA)	151.1	159.5
Kansas City, MO-KS	120.7	127.4	135.7	Trenton, NJ	144.2	150.9	165.3
Lake County, IL	164.0	169.4	178.9	Washington, DC-MD-VA.	176.5	182.6	213.9
Las Vegas, NV	130.8	137.4	149.1	West Palm Bch-Boca Raton-			
Los Angeles-Long Beach, CA				Delray Beach, FL	131.0	138.4	149.5
PMSA [1]	199.0	215.9	241.4	Wilmington, DE-NJ-MD	120.6	127.6	136.5
Madison, WI	136.5	153.6	162.5	Worcester, MA	117.0	131.8	152.6

NA Not available.   [1] California data supplied by the California Association of REALTORS.   [2] In 1992, Bradenton and Sarasota were merged and Aurora/Elgin was incorporated into Chicago. The source still collects price data on the previous jurisdictions.

Source: NATIONAL ASSOCIATION OF REALTORS®, Washington, DC, *Real Estate Outlook: Market Trends & Insights*, monthly, (copyright).

Construction and Housing   593

No. 928. Existing Home Sales by State: 1990 to 2001

[In thousands (3,599 represents 3,599,000). Includes condos and co-ops as well as single-family homes]

State	1990	1995	2000	2001	State	1990	1995	2000	2001
United States ..	3,599	4,350	5,814	6,050	Missouri..........	77.1	100.8	118.6	122.2
Alabama	52.0	69.0	75.9	80.6	Montana	13.5	14.8	19.7	22.6
Alaska	12.3	10.2	18.9	23.1	Nebraska	23.6	25.0	31.3	32.3
Arizona	71.8	120.3	180.3	200.6	Nevada	26.9	31.0	56.7	68.8
Arkansas	33.7	45.0	54.7	56.0	New Hampshire.....	13.5	26.2	43.5	42.7
California	413.1	426.7	709.2	676.6	New Jersey	85.7	102.4	135.3	132.3
Colorado	77.7	102.5	154.1	158.7	New Mexico	24.7	27.6	30.6	37.3
Connecticut	37.4	43.3	53.2	53.4	New York	135.9	149.7	194.7	198.0
Delaware	7.9	9.5	7.7	8.2	North Carolina......	98.9	157.7	215.5	222.8
District of Columbia ..	7.2	7.0	12.7	12.7	North Dakota	8.5	8.5	10.2	10.9
Florida...........	281.1	379.6	505.4	519.1	Ohio	146.9	173.1	187.9	197.7
Georgia	91.2	101.0	144.5	164.1	Oklahoma	62.2	74.5	91.9	103.6
Hawaii	19.0	10.3	22.8	24.8	Oregon	56.6	58.7	64.0	72.0
Idaho...........	22.3	27.1	30.4	34.1	Pennsylvania	143.2	163.2	170.1	172.9
Illinois	163.3	183.4	239.0	242.3	Rhode Island	9.6	13.6	21.0	21.4
Indiana	83.6	102.6	126.8	133.7	South Carolina	54.3	70.7	97.0	108.5
Iowa	42.8	43.2	53.1	55.9	South Dakota	10.8	11.9	15.4	15.3
Kansas	36.8	50.5	64.2	68.3	Tennessee	66.2	106.6	140.2	148.4
Kentucky	47.9	61.5	71.3	78.9	Texas	311.8	367.9	518.5	539.1
Louisiana	57.1	77.3	84.2	88.4	Utah	29.4	43.5	50.9	56.9
Maine	17.0	25.5	37.9	38.7	Vermont..........	7.2	7.9	7.2	6.9
Maryland	67.0	63.5	101.0	113.5	Virginia	89.3	94.8	131.4	142.1
Massachusetts	47.9	69.4	94.1	93.8	Washington	85.9	110.9	189.9	192.8
Michigan	137.6	142.2	150.8	155.1	West Virginia	22.6	26.1	21.5	24.8
Minnesota	68.1	81.6	105.5	109.0	Wisconsin.........	62.1	78.2	94.2	101.8
Mississippi	28.2	41.3	45.1	50.4	Wyoming	8.5	11.4	13.5	16.0

Source: NATIONAL ASSOCIATION OF REALTORS®, Washington, DC, *Real Estate Outlook: Market Trends & Insights,* monthly (copyright).

No. 929. Existing Apartment Condos and Co-Ops—Units Sold and Median Sales Price by Region: 1990 to 2001

[348 represents 348,000. For definition of median, see Guide to Tabular Presentation. For composition of regions, see map inside front cover]

Year	Units sold (1,000)					Median sales price (dol.)				
	Total	North-east	Mid-west	South	West	United States	North-east	Mid-west	South	West
1990	348	45	42	151	110	85,200	110,200	70,200	66,800	105,200
1992	361	57	49	153	102	86,000	103,100	79,000	69,400	107,700
1993	400	63	53	175	108	84,400	99,200	78,900	69,300	102,700
1994	439	69	54	196	119	87,200	99,500	86,200	69,500	108,800
1995	428	70	53	188	116	87,400	94,800	90,700	70,600	105,300
1996	476	78	58	206	134	90,900	97,500	95,200	73,500	109,900
1997	524	88	64	220	152	95,500	101,100	99,100	76,300	118,300
1998	607	104	75	252	176	100,600	103,400	106,400	80,000	126,400
1999	681	118	81	292	190	108,000	112,500	114,600	84,100	132,100
2000	706	116	82	311	197	111,800	111,200	121,700	87,700	136,800
2001	746	121	88	339	198	123,200	124,200	134,900	97,100	141,900

Source: NATIONAL ASSOCIATION OF REALTORS®, Washington, DC, *Real Estate Outlook: Market Trends & Insights,* monthly (copyright).

No. 930. New Apartments Completed and Rented in 3 Months by Region: 1985 to 2001

[365.2 represents 365,200. Structures with five or more units, privately financed, nonsubsidized, unfurnished rental apartments. Based on sample and subject to sampling variability; see source for details. For composition of regions, see map, inside front cover]

Year and rent	Number (1,000)					Percent rented in 3 months				
	United States	North-east	Mid-west	South	West	United States	North-east	Mid-west	South	West
1985	365.2	8.1	54.0	166.1	137.0	65	69	72	59	68
1990 [1]	214.3	12.7	44.3	77.2	80.0	67	66	75	64	65
1995	155.0	7.1	31.7	78.5	37.7	73	74	75	72	73
2000	226.2	14.8	39.5	125.9	45.9	72	85	76	67	77
2001, prel..........	192.4	16.3	31.5	96.6	48.0	64	83	67	60	64
Less than $550	15.0	2.1	4.4	7.0	1.5	73	98	63	69	84
$550 to $749...........	45.7	0.6	11.0	28.0	6.2	64	68	71	62	64
$550 to $649	20.6	0.2	6.8	12.1	1.5	63	98	76	54	70
$650 to $749	25.1	0.4	4.2	15.9	4.7	66	50	63	68	62
$750 to $949...........	54.5	2.8	9.2	30.4	12.2	60	96	57	56	64
$750 to $849	28.1	0.1	5.0	16.5	6.6	60	43	59	60	63
$850 to $949	20.4	2.7	4.2	13.0	6.6	60	97	55	52	65
$950 or more...........	77.1	10.9	6.8	31.3	28.2	65	77	77	60	63
Median monthly asking rent ..	877	(2)	756	831	(2)	(X)	(X)	(X)	(X)	(X)

X Not applicable.   [1] Due to revised estimation procedures, data beginning 1990 not strictly comparable with prior years.
[2] Over $950.
Source: U.S. Census Bureau, *Current Housing Reports,* Series H130, *Market Absorption of Apartments,* and unpublished data. See Internet site: <http://www.census.gov/prod/www/abs/apart.html>.

U.S. Census Bureau, *Statistical Abstract of the United States: 2002*

No. 931. Total Housing Inventory for the United States: 1980 to 2001

[In thousands (87,739 represents 87,739,000), except percent. Based on the Current Population Survey and the Housing Vacancy Survey and subject to sampling error; see source for details]

Item	1980	1985	1990	1995	1996	1997	1998	1999	2000	2001
All housing units	87,739	97,333	106,283	112,655	114,139	115,621	117,282	119,044	119,628	121,480
Vacant	8,101	9,446	12,059	12,669	13,155	13,419	13,748	14,116	13,908	14,470
Year-round vacant	5,996	7,400	9,128	9,570	9,945	10,114	10,516	10,848	10,439	10,916
For rent	1,575	2,221	2,662	2,946	3,008	2,978	3,046	3,119	3,024	3,203
For sale only	734	1,006	1,064	1,022	1,082	1,133	1,205	1,184	1,148	1,301
Rented or sold	623	664	660	810	834	867	927	956	856	882
Held off market	3,064	3,510	4,742	4,793	5,022	5,136	5,338	5,589	5,411	5,530
Occasional use	814	977	1,485	1,667	1,709	1,818	1,792	1,948	1,892	1,887
Usual residence else where	568	659	1,068	801	852	885	910	965	1,037	1,064
Other	1,683	1,875	2,189	2,325	2,461	2,433	2,636	2,676	2,482	2,579
Seasonal [1]	2,106	2,046	2,931	3,099	3,209	3,305	3,232	3,268	3,469	3,554
Total occupied	79,638	87,887	94,224	99,985	100,984	102,202	103,534	104,928	105,720	107,010
Owner	52,223	56,152	60,248	64,739	66,041	67,143	68,638	70,097	71,250	72,593
Renter	27,415	31,736	33,976	35,246	34,943	35,059	34,896	34,831	34,470	34,417
PERCENT DISTRIBUTION										
All housing units	100.0	100.0	100.0	100.0	100.0	100.0	100.0	100.0	100.0	100.0
Vacant	9.2	9.7	11.3	11.2	11.5	11.6	11.7	11.9	11.6	11.9
Total occupied	90.8	90.3	88.7	88.8	88.5	88.4	88.3	88.1	88.4	88.1
Owner	59.5	57.7	56.7	57.5	57.9	58.1	58.5	58.9	59.6	59.8
Renter	31.2	32.6	32.0	31.3	30.6	30.3	29.8	29.3	28.8	28.3

[1] Beginning 1990 includes vacant seasonal mobile homes. For years shown, seasonal vacant housing units were underreported prior to 1990.

Source: U.S. Census Bureau, Internet site <http://www.census.gov/hhes/www/housing/hvs/historic/index.html>.

No. 932. Occupied Housing Inventory by Age of Householder: 1985 to 2001

[In thousands (87,887 represents 87,887,000). Based on the Current Population Survey/Housing Vacancy Survey; See source for details]

Age of householder	1985	1990	1994	1995	1996	1997	1998	1999	2000	2001
Total [1]	87,887	94,224	98,695	99,986	100,983	102,201	103,534	104,929	105,719	107,009
Less than 25 years old	5,483	5,143	5,408	5,502	5,467	5,517	5,750	6,000	6,221	6,460
25 to 29 years old	9,543	9,508	8,628	8,662	8,669	8,755	8,666	8,661	8,482	8,358
30 to 34 years old	10,288	11,213	11,284	11,206	10,936	10,622	10,494	10,440	10,219	10,301
35 to 39 years old	9,615	10,914	11,906	11,993	12,083	12,166	12,026	11,950	11,834	11,587
40 to 44 years old	7,919	9,893	10,931	11,151	11,644	11,869	12,141	12,206	12,377	12,504
45 to 49 years old	6,617	8,038	9,611	10,080	10,523	10,532	10,744	10,973	11,164	11,529
50 to 54 years old	6,157	6,532	7,637	7,882	7,081	8,650	9,040	9,412	9,834	10,288
55 to 59 years old	6,558	6,182	6,284	6,355	6,474	6,731	7,051	7,389	7,602	7,827
60 to 64 years old	6,567	6,446	5,972	5,860	5,836	5,947	6,055	6,183	6,215	6,345
65 to 69 years old	5,976	6,407	6,113	6,088	6,099	5,926	5,852	5,845	5,816	5,749
70 to 74 years old	5,003	5,397	5,681	5,693	5,602	5,574	5,583	5,621	5,567	5,496
75 years old and over	7,517	8,546	9,236	9,514	9,669	9,912	10,131	10,289	10,388	10,565

[1] 1985 total includes ages not reported. Thereafter cases allocated by age.

Source: U.S. Census Bureau, Internet site <http://www.census.gov/hhes/www/housing/hvs/historic/index.html>.

No. 933. Vacancy Rates for Housing Units—Characteristics: 1990 to 2001

[In percent. Rate is relationship between vacant housing for rent or for sale and the total rental and homeowner supply, which comprises occupied units, units rented or sold and awaiting occupancy, and vacant units available for rent or sale. Based on the Current Population/ Housing Vacancy Survey; see source for details. For composition of regions, see map, inside front cover]

Characteristic	Rental units					Homeowner units				
	1990	1995 [1]	1999	2000	2001	1990	1995 [1]	1999	2000	2001
Total units	7.2	7.6	8.1	8.0	8.4	1.7	1.5	1.7	1.6	1.8
Inside MSAs	7.1	7.6	7.8	7.7	8.0	1.7	1.5	1.5	1.4	1.6
Outside MSAs	7.6	7.9	9.6	9.5	10.4	1.8	1.6	2.1	2.1	2.3
Northeast	6.1	7.2	6.3	5.6	5.3	1.6	1.5	1.4	1.2	1.2
Midwest	6.4	7.2	8.6	8.8	9.7	1.3	1.3	1.2	1.3	1.7
South	8.8	8.3	10.3	10.5	11.1	2.1	1.7	2.0	1.9	2.1
West	6.6	7.5	6.2	5.8	6.2	1.8	1.7	1.7	1.5	1.6
Units in structure:										
1 unit	4.0	5.4	7.3	7.0	7.9	1.4	1.4	1.5	1.5	1.6
2 units or more . . .	9.0	9.0	8.7	8.7	8.9	7.1	4.8	3.6	4.7	5.0
5 units or more . . .	9.6	9.5	8.9	9.2	9.6	8.4	5.1	3.8	5.8	5.8
Units with—										
3 rooms or less . .	10.3	11.4	10.5	10.3	10.5	10.2	9.2	7.9	10.4	7.9
4 rooms	8.0	8.2	8.3	8.2	8.8	3.2	2.8	2.9	2.9	3.0
5 rooms	5.7	5.8	7.2	6.9	7.5	2.0	1.8	2.0	2.0	2.2
6 rooms or more . .	3.0	3.8	5.2	5.2	5.6	1.1	1.1	1.1	1.1	1.2

[1] Beginning 1995, based on 1990 population census controls.

Source: U.S. Census Bureau, Internet site <http://www.census.gov/hhes/www/housing/hvs/historic/index.html>.

U.S. Census Bureau, Statistical Abstract of the United States: 2002

No. 934. Housing Units and Tenure, States: 2000

[115,905 represents 115,905,000. As of April 1. Based on the 2000 Census of Population and Housing; see text, Section 1, Population, and Appendix III]

State	Housing units — Total (1,000)	Housing units — Occu- pied (1,000)	Vacant — Total	Vacant — For sea- sonal use [1]	Vacancy rate — Home- owner [2]	Vacancy rate — Renter [3]	Owner occupied units — Total (1,000)	Owner occupied units — Average house- hold size	Renter occupied units — Total (1,000)	Renter occupied units — Average house- hold size
United States.....	115,905	105,480	10,425	3,579	1.7	6.8	69,816	2.69	35,664	2.40
Alabama............	1,964	1,737	227	47	2.0	11.8	1,259	2.57	478	2.30
Alaska.............	261	222	39	21	1.9	7.8	139	2.89	83	2.49
Arizona............	2,189	1,901	288	142	2.1	9.2	1,294	2.69	608	2.53
Arkansas	1,173	1,043	130	29	2.5	9.6	724	2.54	319	2.40
California	12,215	11,503	712	237	1.4	3.7	6,546	2.93	4,957	2.79
Colorado...........	1,808	1,658	150	72	1.4	5.5	1,116	2.64	542	2.30
Connecticut.........	1,386	1,302	84	23	1.1	5.6	870	2.67	432	2.25
Delaware	343	299	44	26	1.5	8.2	216	2.61	83	2.37
District of Columbia	275	248	27	2	2.9	5.9	101	2.31	147	2.06
Florida	7,303	6,338	965	483	2.2	9.3	4,442	2.49	1,896	2.39
Georgia	3,282	3,006	275	50	1.9	8.2	2,029	2.71	977	2.51
Hawaii	461	403	57	26	1.6	8.2	228	3.07	175	2.71
Idaho..............	528	470	58	27	2.2	7.6	340	2.75	130	2.52
Illinois	4,886	4,592	294	30	1.5	6.2	3,089	2.76	1,503	2.37
Indiana............	2,532	2,336	196	34	1.8	8.8	1,669	2.64	667	2.24
Iowa	1,233	1,149	83	16	1.7	6.8	831	2.57	318	2.15
Kansas............	1,131	1,038	93	10	2.0	8.8	719	2.63	319	2.25
Kentucky	1,751	1,591	160	30	1.8	8.7	1,125	2.55	465	2.27
Louisiana	1,847	1,656	191	40	1.6	9.3	1,125	2.70	531	2.44
Maine.............	652	518	134	101	1.7	7.0	371	2.54	147	2.03
Maryland	2,145	1,981	164	39	1.6	6.1	1,342	2.73	639	2.35
Massachusetts........	2,622	2,444	178	94	0.7	3.5	1,508	2.72	936	2.17
Michigan...........	4,234	3,786	449	234	1.6	6.8	2,793	2.67	993	2.24
Minnesota..........	2,066	1,895	171	106	0.9	4.1	1,413	2.69	482	2.03
Mississippi	1,162	1,046	116	22	1.6	9.2	757	2.67	289	2.52
Missouri	2,442	2,195	247	66	2.1	9.0	1,542	2.59	652	2.20
Montana...........	413	359	54	24	2.2	7.6	248	2.55	111	2.22
Nebraska	723	666	56	12	1.8	7.6	449	2.63	217	2.20
Nevada	827	751	76	17	2.6	9.7	457	2.71	294	2.47
New Hampshire.......	547	475	72	56	1.0	3.5	331	2.70	144	2.14
New Jersey.........	3,310	3,065	246	109	1.2	4.5	2,011	2.81	1,053	2.43
New Mexico	781	678	103	32	2.2	11.6	474	2.72	204	2.41
New York	7,679	7,057	622	235	1.6	4.6	3,739	2.78	3,318	2.41
North Carolina	3,524	3,132	392	135	2.0	8.8	2,172	2.54	960	2.37
North Dakota........	290	257	33	8	2.7	8.2	171	2.60	86	2.02
Ohio	4,783	4,446	337	47	1.6	8.3	3,073	2.62	1,373	2.19
Oklahoma..........	1,514	1,342	172	32	2.5	10.6	918	2.55	424	2.36
Oregon............	1,453	1,334	119	37	2.3	7.3	857	2.59	477	2.36
Pennsylvania........	5,250	4,777	473	148	1.6	7.2	3,406	2.62	1,371	2.12
Rhode Island........	440	408	31	13	1.0	5.0	245	2.66	163	2.19
South Carolina.......	1,754	1,534	220	70	1.9	12.0	1,108	2.59	426	2.37
South Dakota	323	290	33	10	1.8	8.0	198	2.64	92	2.22
Tennessee	2,439	2,233	207	37	2.0	8.8	1,561	2.57	672	2.29
Texas.............	8,158	7,393	764	173	1.8	8.5	4,717	2.87	2,676	2.53
Utah	769	701	67	30	2.1	6.5	502	3.28	200	2.75
Vermont	294	241	54	43	1.4	4.2	170	2.58	71	2.11
Virginia............	2,904	2,699	205	55	1.5	5.2	1,838	2.62	861	2.36
Washington.........	2,451	2,271	180	60	1.8	5.9	1,467	2.65	804	2.32
West Virginia........	845	736	108	33	2.2	9.1	554	2.47	183	2.17
Wisconsin..........	2,321	2,085	237	142	1.2	5.6	1,426	2.66	658	2.15
Wyoming	224	194	30	12	2.1	9.7	136	2.58	58	2.25

[1] For seasonal, recreational or occasional use.   [2] Proportion of the homeowner housing inventory which is vacant for sale.
[3] Proportion of the rental inventory which is vacant for rent.

Source: U.S. Census Bureau, *2000 Census of Population and Housing, Profiles of General Demographic Characteristics.*

No. 935. Housing Units and Tenure for Large Cities: 2000

[115,905 represents 115,905,000. As of April 1. For cities with 200,000 or more inhabitants in 2000. Based on the 2000 Census of Population and Housing; see text, Section 1, Population, and Appendix III]

City	Housing units Total (1,000)	Housing units Occupied (1,000)	Vacant Total	Vacant For seasonal use [1]	Vacancy rate Homeowner [2]	Vacancy rate Renter [3]	Owner occupied units Total (1,000)	Owner occupied units Average household size	Renter occupied units Total (1,000)	Renter occupied units Average household size
United States.....	115,905	105,480	10,425	3,579	1.7	6.8	69,816	2.69	35,664	2.40
Albuquerque, NM......	198.5	183.2	15.2	0.8	1.9	11.8	110.6	2.55	72.6	2.16
Anaheim, CA.........	99.7	97.0	2.8	0.2	0.9	3.2	48.5	3.24	48.5	3.45
Anchorage, AK	100.4	94.8	5.5	1.1	1.4	5.3	57.0	2.81	37.9	2.46
Arlington, TX.........	130.6	124.7	5.9	0.4	1.4	6.1	68.3	2.87	56.4	2.38
Atlanta, GA..........	186.9	168.1	18.8	1.1	4.1	7.2	73.5	2.37	94.7	2.25
Aurora, CO	109.3	105.6	3.6	0.2	1.1	3.5	67.5	2.65	38.1	2.50
Austin, TX...........	276.8	265.6	11.2	1.4	1.0	3.5	119.1	2.65	146.5	2.19
Baltimore, MD........	300.5	258.0	42.5	1.4	3.6	7.6	129.9	2.57	128.1	2.27
Boston, MA..........	251.9	239.5	12.4	1.6	1.0	3.0	77.2	2.51	162.3	2.22
Buffalo, NY	145.6	122.7	22.9	0.3	4.2	11.1	53.3	2.47	69.4	2.16
Charlotte, NC	230.4	215.4	15.0	0.7	2.2	8.4	123.9	2.56	91.6	2.30
Chicago, IL..........	1,152.9	1,061.9	90.9	4.5	1.7	5.7	464.9	2.90	597.1	2.49
Cincinnati, OH........	166.0	148.1	17.9	0.6	2.2	9.9	57.7	2.43	90.4	1.97
Cleveland, OH........	215.9	190.6	25.2	0.8	2.1	10.8	92.5	2.56	98.1	2.32
Colorado Springs, CO...	148.7	141.5	7.2	0.7	1.2	6.2	86.0	2.65	55.5	2.27
Columbus, OH........	327.2	301.5	25.6	1.1	2.0	8.3	148.0	2.48	153.5	2.13
Corpus Christi, TX	107.8	98.8	9.0	1.1	2.0	9.5	58.9	2.89	39.9	2.56
Dallas, TX...........	484.1	451.8	32.3	1.5	1.4	7.0	195.3	2.78	256.5	2.44
Denver, CO..........	251.4	239.2	12.2	1.4	1.7	4.5	125.5	2.41	113.7	2.10
Detroit, MI...........	375.1	336.4	38.7	0.6	1.6	8.3	184.6	2.84	151.8	2.68
El Paso, TX..........	193.7	182.1	11.6	0.7	1.6	7.9	111.8	3.20	70.3	2.86
Fort Worth, TX........	211.0	195.1	16.0	0.6	1.9	9.1	109.1	2.84	86.0	2.44
Fresno, CA	149.0	140.1	8.9	0.4	1.9	6.4	70.9	2.94	69.2	3.05
Honolulu, HI [4]	158.7	140.3	18.3	5.2	1.7	10.2	65.9	2.75	74.5	2.40
Houston, TX	782.0	717.9	64.1	4.2	1.6	8.7	328.7	2.84	389.2	2.54
Indianapolis, IN [5]	352.4	320.1	32.3	1.2	2.0	10.9	187.6	2.53	132.5	2.18
Jacksonville, FL.......	308.8	284.5	24.3	0.9	1.8	9.0	179.7	2.64	104.8	2.34
Kansas City, MO	202.3	184.0	18.4	0.7	1.9	9.6	106.1	2.52	77.9	2.11
Las Vegas, NV	190.7	176.8	14.0	1.8	2.5	8.4	104.5	2.76	72.3	2.52
Lexington-Fayette, KY...	116.2	108.3	7.9	0.9	1.1	8.4	59.9	2.47	48.4	2.07
Long Beach, CA	171.6	163.1	8.5	0.8	2.2	4.2	66.9	2.81	96.2	2.74
Los Angeles, CA	1,337.7	1,275.4	62.3	4.9	1.8	3.5	491.9	2.99	783.5	2.73
Louisville, KY........	121.3	111.4	9.9	0.4	1.8	7.5	58.5	2.33	52.9	2.10
Memphis, TN.........	271.6	250.7	20.8	0.7	2.0	8.4	140.0	2.62	110.7	2.40
Mesa, AZ	175.7	146.6	29.1	18.1	2.4	10.7	97.3	2.74	49.3	2.54
Miami, FL	148.4	134.2	14.2	2.9	2.9	6.6	46.8	2.79	87.4	2.52
Milwaukee, WI........	249.2	232.2	17.0	0.5	1.3	6.0	105.2	2.60	127.0	2.42
Minneapolis, MN	168.0	162.4	6.3	0.8	0.7	2.8	83.4	2.43	78.9	2.05
Nashville-Davidson, TN [5].	242.5	227.4	15.0	1.1	2.0	6.5	124.0	2.43	103.4	2.13
New Orleans, LA	215.1	188.3	26.8	2.4	2.2	7.9	87.6	2.60	100.7	2.37
New York, NY	3,200.9	3,021.6	179.3	28.2	1.7	3.2	912.3	2.81	2,109.3	2.50
Newark, NJ..........	100.1	91.4	8.8	0.1	2.0	5.6	21.7	3.22	69.6	2.74
Oakland, CA	157.5	150.8	6.7	0.4	1.0	2.7	62.5	2.76	88.3	2.49
Oklahoma City, OK.....	228.1	204.4	23.7	1.1	2.2	12.3	121.5	2.51	82.9	2.27
Omaha, NE...........	165.7	156.7	9.0	0.5	1.0	7.2	93.4	2.64	63.3	2.10
Philadelphia, PA.......	662.0	590.1	71.9	1.8	1.9	7.0	349.6	2.65	240.4	2.23
Phoenix, AZ	495.8	465.8	30.0	4.5	1.4	7.9	282.7	2.89	183.2	2.63
Pittsburgh, PA	163.4	143.7	19.6	0.9	2.8	8.8	74.9	2.37	68.8	1.95
Portland, OR.........	237.3	223.7	13.6	1.0	2.3	6.2	124.8	2.47	99.0	2.08
Raleigh, NC	120.7	112.6	8.1	0.4	2.1	8.3	58.1	2.43	54.5	2.15
Riverside, CA	86.0	82.0	4.0	0.2	1.9	4.8	46.5	3.18	35.6	2.81
Sacramento, CA.......	164.0	154.6	9.4	0.6	2.0	5.4	77.5	2.65	77.1	2.50
San Antonio, TX.......	433.1	405.5	27.6	2.3	1.4	6.9	235.7	2.95	169.8	2.51
San Diego, CA........	469.7	450.7	19.0	5.1	0.8	3.2	223.3	2.71	227.4	2.52
San Francisco, CA.....	346.5	329.7	16.8	3.8	0.8	2.5	115.4	2.73	214.3	2.06
San Jose, CA	281.8	276.6	5.2	0.8	0.4	1.8	171.0	3.22	105.6	3.16
Santa Ana, CA........	74.6	73.0	1.6	0.1	0.8	1.9	36.0	4.54	37.0	4.57
Seattle, WA..........	270.5	258.5	12.0	1.8	1.2	3.5	125.2	2.32	133.3	1.84
St. Louis, MO	176.4	147.1	29.3	0.5	3.5	11.8	68.9	2.49	78.1	2.12
St. Paul, MN	115.7	112.1	3.6	0.4	0.7	2.8	61.5	2.72	50.6	2.15
Tampa, FL	135.8	124.8	11.0	0.8	2.1	7.8	68.6	2.49	56.2	2.20
Toledo, OH	139.9	128.9	10.9	0.4	1.5	8.8	77.1	2.50	51.9	2.19
Tucson, AZ	209.6	192.9	16.7	3.5	1.6	8.1	103.1	2.58	89.8	2.24
Tulsa, OK	179.4	165.7	13.7	0.9	1.6	8.7	92.2	2.41	73.5	2.18
Virginia Beach, VA	162.3	154.5	7.8	2.3	1.5	4.0	101.3	2.79	53.1	2.54
Washington, DC.......	274.8	248.3	26.5	2.2	2.9	5.9	101.2	2.31	147.1	2.06
Wichita, KS..........	152.1	139.1	13.0	0.4	2.0	12.0	85.7	2.61	53.4	2.17

[1] For seasonal, recreational or occasional use.   [2] Proportion of the homeowner housing inventory which is vacant for sale.
[3] Proportion of the rental inventory which is vacant for rent.   [4] The population shown in this table is for the census designated place (CDP).   [5] Represents the portion of a consolidated city that is not within one or more separately incorporated places.

Source: U.S. Census Bureau, 2000 Census of Population and Housing, Profiles of General Demographic Characteristics.

Construction and Housing   597

No. 936. Housing Units—Characteristics by Tenure and Region: 2001

[In thousands of units (119,117 represents 119,117,000), except as indicated. As of Oct. 1. Based on the American Housing Survey; see Appendix III. For composition of regions, see map, inside front cover]

Characteristic	Total housing units	Sea-sonal	Year-round units Occupied Total	Owner	Renter	North-east	Mid-west	South	West	Vacant
Total units	**119,117**	**3,078**	**106,261**	**72,265**	**33,996**	**20,321**	**24,758**	**38,068**	**23,115**	**9,777**
Percent distribution	100.0	2.6	89.2	60.7	28.5	17.1	20.8	32.0	19.4	8.2
Units in structure:										
Single family detached	73,427	1,900	67,129	59,239	7,890	11,121	17,307	24,576	14,125	4,399
Single family attached	8,428	167	7,305	3,722	3,583	1,920	1,165	2,583	1,637	956
2 to 4 units	9,354	105	8,200	1,291	6,909	2,544	1,860	1,953	1,843	1,049
5 to 9 units	5,682	62	4,994	503	4,490	942	1,077	1,714	1,261	626
10 to 19 units	5,367	63	4,620	502	4,118	820	884	1,757	1,159	684
20 to 49 units	3,898	65	3,253	391	2,862	936	595	805	917	580
50 or more units	4,084	89	3,543	615	2,927	1,454	654	678	757	453
Mobile home or trailer	8,876	626	7,219	6,001	1,218	584	1,217	4,002	1,416	1,031
Stories in structure: [1]										
One story	(NA)	1,334	34,145	25,665	8,480	1,234	3,934	18,667	10,310	(NA)
2 stories	(NA)	725	34,824	22,418	12,406	6,230	9,817	10,424	8,352	(NA)
3 stories	(NA)	242	22,942	15,403	7,539	8,235	8,415	3,964	2,328	(NA)
4 to 6 stories	(NA)	53	5,208	2,312	2,896	2,973	1,042	672	520	(NA)
7 or more stories	(NA)	99	1,924	466	1,458	1,065	332	338	189	(NA)
Foundation: [2]										
Full or partial basement	(NA)	424	33,092	29,556	3,536	10,996	14,045	5,134	2,919	(NA)
Crawlspace	(NA)	810	18,840	15,574	3,266	787	2,606	9,845	5,601	(NA)
Concrete slab	(NA)	591	21,947	17,434	4,513	1,173	1,704	11,955	7,115	(NA)
Other	(NA)	242	554	396	158	85	117	224	128	(NA)
Year structure built:										
Median year	1,970	1,970	1,970	1,971	1,967	1,954	1,964	1,975	1,973	1,970
1980 or later	35,747	841	31,948	23,365	8,583	3,460	6,036	14,806	7,646	2,957
1970 to 1979	23,529	675	20,917	13,868	7,048	2,660	4,468	8,529	5,261	1,936
1960 to 1969	15,894	477	14,396	9,741	4,655	2,558	3,316	5,104	3,418	1,021
1950 to 1959	13,779	366	12,501	9,068	3,433	2,665	3,209	3,855	2,771	912
1940 to 1949	8,284	246	7,278	4,775	2,504	1,694	1,694	2,317	1,574	760
1939 and earlier	21,885	472	19,221	11,448	7,773	7,284	6,035	3,457	2,445	2,190
Main heating equipment:										
Warm-air furnace	71,804	1,272	65,262	47,867	17,395	8,114	19,833	22,510	14,805	5,270
Electric heat pump	12,693	373	11,080	8,099	2,981	293	566	8,917	1,304	1,240
Steam or hot water system	14,420	94	13,441	7,801	5,640	9,661	2,190	732	858	884
Floor, wall, or pipeless furnace	6,133	174	5,343	2,365	2,978	470	515	1,409	2,949	616
Built-in electric units	5,929	269	5,063	2,385	2,678	1,266	1,156	928	1,713	597
Room heaters with flue	1,856	98	1,542	866	676	193	216	787	345	216
Room heaters without flue	1,916	75	1,558	1,019	539	34	32	1,440	52	283
Stoves	1,501	255	1,131	917	214	180	175	396	380	115
Fireplaces	274	37	209	170	39	14	18	71	107	27
Cooking stoves	213	9	193	74	118	44	7	72	69	12
None	1,017	309	401	146	255	10	6	98	287	308
Portable electric heaters	893	58	746	390	356	10	18	560	158	89
Other	467	56	292	163	128	34	24	147	87	119
Kitchen equipment:										
Lacking complete facilities	5,260	570	1,646	380	1,266	455	312	440	439	3,044
With complete facilities	113,857	2,508	104,615	71,885	32,730	19,866	24,446	37,628	22,673	6,733
Kitchen sink	118,085	2,863	105,929	72,176	33,753	20,224	24,696	37,989	23,019	9,293
Refrigerator	116,219	2,764	105,859	72,091	33,768	20,218	24,681	37,942	23,018	7,597
Cooking stove or range	115,374	2,604	105,358	71,863	33,495	20,126	24,585	37,742	22,906	7,412
Burners only, no stove or range	178	4	169	73	96	37	19	73	40	6
Microwave oven only	487	18	399	222	177	72	95	150	82	70
Dishwasher	67,251	1,023	62,352	48,852	13,501	10,321	13,074	23,645	15,312	3,876
Washing machine	90,160	1,213	85,562	68,950	16,612	15,019	20,381	32,157	18,005	3,385
Clothes dryer	87,145	1,378	81,591	66,752	14,840	13,732	20,098	30,547	17,214	4,176
Disposal in kitchen sink	52,671	718	48,604	34,329	14,276	4,661	11,412	16,523	16,009	3,348
Trash compactor	4,483	138	4,010	3,305	706	576	635	1,566	1,234	335
Air conditioning: Central	69,145	917	63,854	48,816	15,038	5,473	15,532	32,535	10,314	4,374
Percent of total units	58.0	29.8	60.1	67.6	44.2	26.9	62.7	85.5	44.6	44.7
One or more room units	29,347	675	26,563	15,519	11,042	9,930	6,749	6,724	3,159	2,110
Source of water:										
Public system or private company	102,924	1,837	92,576	60,126	32,451	17,184	20,769	33,054	21,570	8,510
Percent of total units	86.4	59.7	87.1	83.2	95.5	84.6	83.9	86.8	93.3	87.0
Well serving 1 to 5 units	15,337	972	13,245	11,767	1,478	3,032	3,901	4,833	1,479	1,121
Other	855	270	440	372	68	105	89	181	66	146
Means of sewage disposal:										
Public sewer	92,680	1,232	83,870	52,502	31,368	16,014	19,815	27,940	20,101	7,578
Percent of total units	77.8	40.0	78.9	72.7	92.3	78.8	80.0	73.4	87.0	77.5
Septic tank, cesspool, chemical toilet	25,977	1,570	22,328	19,720	2,608	4,305	4,934	10,084	3,005	2,078
Other	459	276	63	43	20	3	9	43	8	120

NA Not available. [1] Excludes mobile homes. [2] Limited to single-family units.

Source: U.S. Census Bureau, *Current Housing Reports*, Series H150/01, *American Housing Survey for the United States.*

No. 937. Housing Units—Size of Units and Lot: 2001

[In thousands (119,117 represents 119,117,000), except as indicated. As of Oct. 1. Based on the American Housing Survey; see Appendix III. For composition of regions, see map inside front cover]

Item	Total hous-ing units	Sea-sonal	Total	Owner	Renter	North-east	Mid-west	South	West	Vacant
			Year-round units							
			Occupied							
Total units	**119,117**	**3,078**	**106,261**	**72,265**	**33,996**	**20,321**	**24,758**	**38,068**	**23,115**	**9,777**
Rooms:										
1 room.	622	57	394	16	378	159	55	24	156	171
2 rooms	1,406	161	993	87	906	302	153	201	338	252
3 rooms	10,698	484	8,800	1,029	7,771	2,262	1,774	2,463	2,301	1,413
4 rooms	23,082	1,090	19,003	7,169	11,834	3,429	4,163	7,012	4,398	2,989
5 rooms	27,896	746	24,798	17,180	7,618	3,912	5,888	9,727	5,271	2,353
6 rooms	24,637	299	22,768	19,205	3,563	4,382	5,354	8,705	4,328	1,570
7 rooms	14,710	121	14,032	12,841	1,190	2,655	3,419	5,000	2,957	558
8 rooms or more	16,066	120	15,473	14,737	736	3,220	3,952	4,935	3,365	471
Complete bathrooms:										
No bathrooms	2,227	595	681	288	393	175	125	224	157	950
1 bathroom	48,464	1,484	42,113	18,408	23,705	10,289	10,723	12,883	8,217	4,867
1 and one-half bathrooms	17,756	195	16,548	13,062	3,486	4,019	5,272	4,592	2,665	1,013
2 or more bathrooms	50,670	804	46,920	40,507	6,412	5,838	8,638	20,368	12,076	2,946
Square footage of unit:										
Single detached and mobile homes [1]	82,303	2,526	74,347	65,240	9,107	11,705	18,523	28,578	15,541	5,429
Less than 500	1,198	319	725	445	280	109	113	332	170	155
500 to 749	3,047	556	2,080	1,317	764	281	479	942	378	410
750 to 999	6,875	485	5,542	4,162	1,380	646	1,487	2,332	1,077	848
1,000 to 1,499	20,267	455	18,306	15,488	2,818	2,029	4,286	7,750	4,241	1,506
1,500 to 1,999	18,574	249	17,492	15,799	1,693	2,422	4,096	6,750	4,223	833
2,000 to 2,499	12,293	128	11,699	11,043	656	2,012	3,098	4,183	2,406	466
2,500 to 2,999	6,289	74	5,955	5,685	271	1,141	1,560	2,165	1,091	259
3,000 to 3,999	5,540	76	5,231	5,036	195	1,120	1,444	1,705	962	233
4,000 or more	3,016	24	2,854	2,708	146	736	734	960	424	137
Other [2]	5,204	160	4,463	3,558	905	1,210	1,226	1,459	568	582
Median square footage	1,693	909	1,737	1,798	1,298	1,951	1,779	1,663	1,692	1,336
Lot size:										
Single detached and attached units and mobile homes	88,223	2,554	79,647	67,362	12,285	13,250	19,278	30,582	16,536	6,022
Less than one-eighth acre	12,711	562	10,942	8,282	2,660	2,167	2,580	2,994	3,201	1,207
One-eighth to one-quarter acre .	24,365	559	22,041	18,027	4,013	2,748	5,745	7,329	6,218	1,765
One-quarter to one-half acre. . . .	17,131	339	15,846	13,980	1,866	2,563	3,870	6,108	3,305	945
One-half up to one acre.	11,464	321	10,497	9,200	1,297	2,066	2,258	4,894	1,279	646
1 to 5 acres.	15,659	482	14,197	12,483	1,713	2,795	2,949	6,766	1,687	981
5 to 10 acres	2,496	45	2,352	2,157	195	340	683	1,011	318	99
10 acres or more	4,397	246	3,772	3,233	539	572	1,193	1,479	527	380
Median acreage	0.35	0.36	0.36	0.38	0.23	0.42	0.33	0.45	0.23	0.26

[1] Does not include selected vacant units.   [2] Represents units not reported or size unknown.
Source: U.S. Census Bureau, Current Housing Reports, Series H150/01, American Housing Survey for the United States.

No. 938. Occupied Housing Units—Tenure by Race of Householder: 1991 to 2001

[In thousands (93,147 represents 93,147,000), except percent. As of fall. Based on the American Housing Survey; see Appendix III]

Race of householder and tenure	1991	1993	1995	1997	1999	2001
ALL RACES [1]						
Occupied units, total	**93,147**	**94,724**	**97,693**	**99,487**	**102,803**	**106,261**
Owner occupied	59,796	61,252	63,544	65,487	68,796	72,265
Percent of occupied	64.2	64.7	65.0	65.8	66.9	68.0
Renter occupied	33,351	33,472	34,150	34,000	34,007	33,996
WHITE						
Occupied units, total	**79,140**	**80,029**	**81,611**	**82,154**	**83,624**	**85,292**
Owner occupied	53,749	54,878	56,507	57,781	60,041	62,465
Percent of occupied	67.9	68.6	69.2	70.3	71.8	73.2
Renter occupied	25,391	25,151	25,104	24,372	23,583	22,826
BLACK						
Occupied units, total	**10,832**	**11,128**	**11,773**	**12,085**	**12,936**	**13,292**
Owner occupied	4,635	4,788	5,137	5,457	6,013	6,318
Percent of occupied	42.8	43.0	43.6	45.2	46.5	47.5
Renter occupied	6,197	6,340	6,637	6,628	6,923	6,974
HISPANIC ORIGIN [2]						
Occupied units, total	**6,239**	**6,614**	**7,757**	**8,513**	**9,041**	**9,814**
Owner occupied	2,423	2,788	3,245	3,646	4,087	4,731
Percent of occupied	38.8	42.2	41.8	42.8	45.2	48.2
Renter occupied	3,816	3,826	4,512	4,867	4,955	5,083

[1] Includes other races, not shown separately.   [2] Persons of Hispanic origin may be of any race.
Source: U.S. Census Bureau, Current Housing Reports, Series H150/91, H150/93, H150/95RV, H150/97, H150/99, and H150/01, American Housing Survey for the United States.

Construction and Housing   599

No. 939. Homeownership Rates by Age of Householder and Family Status: 1985 to 2001

[**In percent**. Represents the proportion of owner households to the total number of occupied households. Based on the Current Population Survey/Housing Vacancy Survey; see source for details]

Age of householder and household type	1985	1990	1994	1995	1996	1997	1998	1999	2000	2001
United States	**63.9**	**63.9**	**64.0**	**64.7**	**65.4**	**65.7**	**66.3**	**66.8**	**67.4**	**67.8**
AGE OF HOUSEHOLDER										
Less than 25 years old.	17.2	15.7	14.9	15.9	18.0	17.7	18.2	19.9	21.7	22.5
25 to 29 years old.	37.7	35.2	34.1	34.4	34.7	35.0	36.2	36.5	38.1	38.9
30 to 34 years old.	54.0	51.8	50.6	53.1	53.0	52.6	53.6	53.8	54.6	54.8
35 to 39 years old.	65.4	63.0	61.2	62.1	62.1	62.6	63.7	64.4	65.0	65.5
40 to 44 years old.	71.4	69.8	68.2	68.6	69.0	69.7	70.0	69.9	70.6	70.8
45 to 49 years old.	74.3	73.9	73.8	73.7	74.4	74.2	73.9	74.5	74.7	75.4
50 to 54 years old.	77.5	76.8	76.8	77.0	77.2	77.7	77.8	77.8	78.5	78.2
55 to 59 years old.	79.2	78.8	78.4	78.8	79.4	79.7	79.8	80.7	80.4	81.0
60 to 64 years old.	79.9	79.8	80.1	80.3	80.7	80.5	82.1	81.3	80.3	81.8
65 to 69 years old.	79.5	80.0	80.6	81.0	82.4	81.9	81.9	82.9	83.0	82.4
70 to 74 years old.	76.8	78.4	80.1	80.9	81.4	82.0	82.2	82.8	82.6	82.5
75 years old and over	69.8	72.3	73.5	74.6	75.3	75.8	76.2	77.1	77.7	78.1
Less than 35 years old.	39.9	38.5	37.3	38.6	39.1	38.7	39.3	39.7	40.8	41.2
35 to 44 years old.	68.1	66.3	64.5	65.2	65.5	66.1	66.9	67.2	67.9	68.2
45 to 54 years old.	75.9	75.2	75.2	75.2	75.6	75.8	75.7	76.0	76.5	76.7
55 to 64 years old.	79.5	79.3	79.3	79.5	80.0	80.1	80.9	81.0	80.3	81.3
65 years and over.	74.8	76.3	77.4	78.1	78.9	79.1	79.3	80.1	80.4	80.3
TYPE OF HOUSEHOLD										
Family households:										
Married-couple families	78.2	78.1	78.8	79.6	80.2	80.8	81.5	81.8	82.4	82.9
Male householder, no spouse present.	57.8	55.2	52.8	55.3	55.5	54.0	55.7	56.1	57.5	57.9
Female householder, no spouse present.	45.8	44.0	44.2	45.1	46.1	46.1	47.0	48.2	49.1	49.9
Nonfamily households:										
One-person	45.8	49.0	49.8	50.5	51.4	51.8	52.1	52.7	53.6	54.4
Male householder.	38.8	42.4	43.1	43.8	44.9	45.2	45.7	46.3	47.4	48.2
Female householder	51.3	53.6	54.5	55.4	56.0	56.7	56.9	57.6	58.1	59.0
Other:										
Male householder.	30.1	31.7	33.6	34.2	35.5	35.9	36.7	37.2	38.0	38.6
Female householder	30.6	32.5	34.3	33.0	35.9	39.5	40.3	41.5	40.6	41.0

Source: U.S. Census Bureau, Internet site <http://www.census.gov/hhes/www/hvs.html>.

No. 940. Homeownership Rates by State: 1985 to 2001

[**In percent**. See headnote, Table 939]

State	1985	1990	1995	1999	2000	2001	State	1985	1990	1995	1999	2000	2001
United States .	**63.9**	**63.9**	**64.7**	**66.8**	**67.4**	**67.8**	Missouri	69.2	64.0	69.4	72.9	74.2	74.0
Alabama	70.4	68.4	70.1	74.8	73.2	73.2	Montana	66.5	69.1	68.7	70.6	70.2	68.3
Alaska	61.2	58.4	60.9	66.4	66.4	65.3	Nebraska	68.5	67.3	67.1	70.9	70.2	70.1
Arizona	64.7	64.5	62.9	66.3	68.0	68.1	Nevada	57.0	55.8	58.6	63.7	64.0	64.6
Arkansas	66.6	67.8	67.2	65.6	68.9	71.2	New Hampshire . . .	65.5	65.0	66.0	70.2	69.2	68.4
California	54.2	53.8	55.4	55.7	57.1	58.2	New Jersey	62.3	65.0	64.9	64.5	66.2	66.5
Colorado	63.6	59.0	64.6	68.1	68.3	68.5	New Mexico.	68.2	68.6	67.0	72.6	73.7	70.8
Connecticut	69.0	67.9	68.2	69.1	70.0	71.8	New York	50.3	53.3	52.7	52.8	53.4	53.9
Delaware.	70.3	67.7	71.7	71.6	72.0	75.4	North Carolina	68.0	69.0	70.1	71.7	71.1	71.3
Dist. of Columbia . .	37.4	36.4	39.2	40.0	41.9	42.7	North Dakota	69.9	67.2	67.3	70.1	70.7	71.0
Florida	67.2	65.1	66.6	67.6	68.4	69.2	Ohio.	67.9	68.7	67.9	70.7	71.3	71.2
Georgia	62.7	64.3	66.6	71.3	69.8	70.1	Oklahoma	70.5	70.3	69.8	71.5	72.7	71.5
Hawaii	51.0	55.5	50.2	56.6	55.2	55.5	Oregon	61.5	64.4	63.2	64.3	65.3	65.8
Idaho	71.0	69.4	72.0	70.3	70.5	71.7	Pennsylvania	71.6	73.8	71.5	75.2	74.7	74.3
Illinois	60.6	63.0	66.4	67.1	67.9	69.4	Rhode Island	61.4	58.5	57.9	60.6	61.5	60.1
Indiana	67.6	67.0	71.0	72.9	74.9	75.3	South Carolina	72.0	71.4	71.3	77.1	76.5	76.1
Iowa	69.9	70.7	71.4	73.9	75.2	76.6	South Dakota	67.6	66.2	67.5	70.7	71.2	71.5
Kansas	68.3	69.0	67.5	67.5	69.3	70.4	Tennessee.	67.6	68.3	67.0	71.9	70.9	69.7
Kentucky	68.5	65.8	71.2	73.9	73.4	73.9	Texas	60.5	59.7	61.4	62.9	63.8	63.9
Louisiana	70.2	67.8	65.3	66.8	68.1	67.1	Utah.	71.5	70.1	71.5	74.7	72.7	72.4
Maine.	73.7	74.2	76.7	77.4	76.5	75.5	Vermont	69.5	72.6	70.4	69.1	68.7	69.8
Maryland	65.6	64.9	65.8	69.6	69.9	70.7	Virginia	68.5	69.8	68.1	71.2	73.9	75.1
Massachusetts	60.5	58.6	60.2	60.3	59.9	60.6	Washington	66.8	61.8	61.6	64.8	63.6	66.4
Michigan	70.7	72.3	72.2	76.5	77.2	77.1	West Virginia	75.9	72.0	73.1	74.8	75.9	76.4
Minnesota	70.0	68.0	73.3	76.1	76.1	76.1	Wisconsin	63.8	68.3	67.5	70.9	71.8	72.3
Mississippi.	69.6	69.4	71.1	74.9	75.2	74.5	Wyoming	73.2	68.9	69.0	69.8	71.0	73.5

Source: U.S. Census Bureau, <http://www.census.gov/hhes/www/hvs.html>.

No. 941. Occupied Housing Units—Costs by Region: 2001

[As of fall. (72,265 represents 72,265,000). Specified owner-occupied units are limited to one-unit structures on less than 10 acres and no business on property. Specified renter-occupied units exclude one-unit structures on 10 acres or more. See headnote Table 942 for an explanation of housing costs. Based on the American Housing Survey; see Appendix III. For composition of regions, see map inside front cover]

Category	Number (1,000)					Percent distribution				
	Total units	North-east	Mid-west	South	West	Total units	North-east	Mid-west	South	West
OWNER OCCUPIED UNITS										
Total	72,265	12,987	18,049	26,715	14,514	100.0	100.0	100.0	100.0	100.0
Monthly housing costs:										
Less than $300	15,633	1,506	3,739	8,126	2,263	21.6	11.6	20.7	30.4	15.6
$300 to $399	6,850	1,287	1,991	2,338	1,234	9.5	9.9	11.0	8.8	8.5
$400 to $499	5,146	1,138	1,416	1,779	812	7.1	8.8	7.8	6.7	5.6
$500 to $599	4,856	1,054	1,313	1,862	627	6.7	8.1	7.3	7.0	4.3
$600 to $699	4,261	777	1,263	1,600	620	5.9	6.0	7.0	6.0	4.3
$700 to $799	4,110	698	1,235	1,510	667	5.7	5.4	6.8	5.7	4.6
$800 to $999	7,813	1,352	2,110	2,858	1,493	10.8	10.4	11.7	10.7	10.3
$1,000 to $1,249	7,214	1,424	1,798	2,385	1,608	10.0	11.0	10.0	8.9	11.1
$1,250 to $1,499	5,245	1,027	1,203	1,576	1,439	7.3	7.9	6.7	5.9	9.9
$1,500 or more	11,137	2,722	1,982	2,682	3,751	15.4	21.0	11.0	10.0	25.8
Median (dol.) [1]	686	805	645	560	938	(X)	(X)	(X)	(X)	(X)
RENTER OCCUPIED UNITS										
Total	33,996	7,334	6,709	11,353	8,600	100.0	100.0	100.0	100.0	100.0
Monthly housing costs:										
Less than $300	3,370	865	807	1,141	558	9.9	11.8	12.0	10.1	6.5
$300 to $399	2,442	416	613	971	442	7.2	5.7	9.1	8.6	5.1
$400 to $499	3,911	696	1,076	1,458	680	11.5	9.5	16.0	12.8	7.9
$500 to $599	4,686	881	1,147	1,657	1,001	13.8	12.0	17.1	14.6	11.6
$600 to $699	4,559	1,023	878	1,471	1,188	13.4	13.9	13.1	13.0	13.8
$700 to $799	3,682	815	614	1,237	1,017	10.8	11.1	9.2	10.9	11.8
$800 to $999	4,526	1,117	651	1,343	1,416	13.3	15.2	9.7	11.8	16.5
$1,000 to $1,249	2,363	559	276	641	888	7.0	7.6	4.1	5.6	10.3
$1,250 to $1,499	1,046	247	105	202	493	3.1	3.4	1.6	1.8	5.7
$1,500 or more	1,209	336	118	217	538	3.6	4.6	1.8	1.9	6.3
No cash rent	2,201	380	426	1,016	380	6.5	5.2	6.3	8.9	4.4
Median (dol.) [1]	633	661	556	596	724	(X)	(X)	(X)	(X)	(X)

X Not applicable.   [1] For explanation of median, see Guide to Tabular Presentation.

No. 942. Occupied Housing Units—Financial Summary by Selected Characteristics of the Householder: 2001

[In thousands of units (106,261 represents 106,261,000), except as indicated. As of fall. Housing costs include real estate taxes, property insurance, utilities, fuel, water, garbage collection, and mortgage. Based on the American Housing Survey; see Appendix III]

Characteristic	Total occu-pied units	Tenure		Black		Hispanic origin [1]		Elderly [2]		Households below poverty level	
		Owner	Renter	Owner	Renter	Owner	Renter	Owner	Renter	Owner	Renter
Total units [3]	106,261	72,265	33,996	6,318	6,974	4,731	5,083	17,513	4,299	6,713	7,889
Monthly housing costs:											
Less than $300	19,003	15,633	3,411	1,607	1,082	897	439	7,452	966	2,817	1,908
$300-$399	9,292	6,850	2,442	587	554	312	320	2,987	342	821	807
$400-$499	9,056	5,146	3,911	488	838	302	561	1,733	529	655	1,095
$500-$599	9,542	4,856	4,686	551	1,017	325	784	1,296	461	523	1,057
$600-$699	8,820	4,261	4,559	420	971	300	809	832	403	371	756
$700-$799	7,793	4,110	3,682	437	736	270	693	639	310	296	530
$800-$999	12,339	7,813	4,526	683	843	582	719	889	380	397	503
$1,000 or more	28,215	23,596	4,557	1,546	534	1,745	590	1,686	430	832	485
Median amount (dol.) [4]	658	686	633	587	580	786	644	339	516	356	478
Monthly housing costs as percent of income: [5]											
Less than 5 percent	5,217	4,906	311	329	84	225	27	1,043	39	29	34
5 to 9 percent	12,267	11,131	1,136	912	204	583	133	2,857	86	78	50
10 to 14 percent	15,166	12,316	2,850	995	456	626	387	2,972	182	156	83
15 to 19 percent	14,879	10,913	3,966	842	666	649	487	2,212	231	271	127
20 to 24 percent	12,616	8,544	4,072	719	822	593	596	1,562	314	309	272
25 to 29 percent	9,555	5,932	3,623	528	702	384	588	1,147	411	297	406
30 to 34 percent	6,840	4,181	2,659	414	576	362	443	846	293	275	322
35 to 39 percent	4,758	2,728	2,030	261	424	256	336	706	248	265	350
40 percent or more	19,871	10,057	9,815	1,188	2,242	957	1,741	3,512	1,868	3,540	4,307
Median amount (percent) [4]	21	18	29	20	31	22	32	19	41	62	65
Median monthly costs (dol.): [4]											
Electricity	59	65	44	68	47	65	44	58	38	59	43
Piped gas	55	61	39	68	46	44	33	61	38	60	41
Fuel oil	75	79	60	70	49	70	61	74	63	69	49

[1] Persons of Hispanic origin may be of any race.   [2] Householders 65 years old and over.   [3] Includes units with mortgage payment not reported and no cash rent not shown separately.   [4] For explanation of median, see Guide to Tabular Presentation.   [5] Money income before taxes.

Source of Tables 941 and 942: U.S. Census Bureau, *Current Housing Reports,* Series H150/01, *American Housing Survey for the United States.*

Construction and Housing 601

No. 943. Mortgage Characteristics—Owner Occupied Units: 2001

[In thousands (72,265 represents 72,265,000). As of fall. Based on the American Housing Survey; see Appendix III]

Mortgage characteristic	Total owner occu-pied units	New con-struc-tion [1]	Mobile homes	Black	His-panic [2]	Elderly [3]	Moved in past year	Below poverty level
ALL OWNERS								
Total [4]	**72,265**	**4,690**	**6,001**	**6,318**	**4,731**	**17,513**	**5,723**	**6,713**
Mortgages currently on property:								
None, owned free and clear	25,675	938	3,228	2,113	1,397	12,792	1,103	3,924
Regular and home equity mortgages	44,970	3,647	2,609	4,013	3,241	4,317	4,491	2,569
Regular mortgage only	41,717	3,559	2,450	3,785	3,093	3,490	4,384	2,367
Home equity mortgage only	4,752	233	159	343	201	498	172	196
With regular mortgage, home equity not reported	6,481	314.	78	310	278	845	234	243
No regular mortgage, home equity not reported	1,583	103	163	190	91	376	129	213
Number of regular and home equity mortgages: [4]								
1 mortgage	32,721	2,828	2,332	3,165	2,562	3,268	3,786	1,947
2 mortgages	8,470	575	126	487	434	497	446	245
3 mortgages or more	1,008	63	14	86	51	68	35	38
Type of home equity mortgage:								
Regular and home equity lump sum [4]	3,090	174	43	194	121	150	107	75
With home equity line of credit	549	30	4	43	23	45	15	25
No home equity line of credit	2,513	141	38	148	98	104	90	49
Regular no home equity lump sum [4]	38,627	3,385	2,407	3,591	2,972	3,340	4,277	2,292
With home equity line of credit	4,051	250	29	180	177	235	175	107
No home equity line of credit	31,929	2,957	2,257	3,142	2,607	2,646	3,883	1,858
Home equity lump sum no regular [4]	1,661	60	116	149	80	348	65	122
With home equity line of credit	290	5	2	7	10	87	2	31
No home equity line of credit	1,332	55	102	141	70	245	60	88
No regular or home equity lump sum [4]	28,886	1,072	3,435	2,385	1,558	13,675	1,274	4,225
With home equity line of credit	1,592	29	43	80	68	479	42	81
No home equity line of credit	25,712	940	3,230	2,115	1,400	12,820	1,103	3,931
OWNERS WITH ONE OR MORE REGULAR OR LUMP SUM HOME EQUITY MORTGAGES, 2001								
Total [4]	**43,378**	**3,618**	**2,566**	**3,934**	**3,173**	**3,838**	**4,449**	**2,488**
Type of primary mortgage:								
FHA	6,110	494	116	1,023	840	339	811	295
VA	2,177	208	70	271	174	145	279	81
Farmers Home Administration	318	36	14	48	23	30	25	43
Other types	31,796	2,694	2,211	2,225	1,919	2,766	3,086	1,646
Mortgage origination:								
Placed new mortgage(s)	42,799	3,599	2,491	3,852	3,089	3,780	4,379	2,431
Primary obtained when property acquired	30,230	3,336	2,121	2,979	2,462	2,181	4,228	1,821
Obtained later	12,569	263	369	872	626	1,599	151	610
Assumed	492	17	74	62	70	53	60	53
Wrap-around	16	2	-	2	2	2	4	-
Combination of the above	72	-	2	18	12	2	7	5
Payment plan of primary mortgage:								
Fixed payment, self amortizing	35,689	3,058	2,169	3,127	2,643	2,776	3,745	1,746
Adjustable rate mortgage	1,964	155	88	163	142	175	148	91
Adjustable term mortgage	504	21	45	41	24	106	42	59
Graduated payment mortgage	378	48	6	46	26	15	46	30
Balloon	357	23	25	18	31	29	44	17
Combination of the above	321	27	26	29	13	42	51	21
Payment plan of secondary mortgage:								
Units with two or more mortgages [4]	5,388	409	115	397	319	253	321	161
Fixed payment, self amortizing	4,501	339	112	343	276	189	274	128
Adjustable rate mortgage	187	8	-	12	4	5	7	5
Adjustable term mortgage	244	18	2	19	11	23	12	10
Graduated payment mortgage	19	-	-	-	3	-	-	-
Balloon	118	16	-	5	5	3	11	-
Other	-	-	-	-	-	-	-	-
Combination of the above	98	9	-	3	4	19	3	3
Reason primary refinanced:								
Units with a refinanced primary mortgage [5]	11,133	303	267	645	581	847	140	342
To get a lower interest rate	8,877	258	154	439	447	646	130	212
To increase payment period	319	8	15	21	11	38	5	25
To reduce payment period	1,318	19	34	78	72	73	17	32
To renew or extend a loan that has fallen due	204	4	13	10	23	17	5	13
To receive cash	1,579	11	66	137	82	164	17	57
Other reason	1,504	43	62	127	82	107	6	62
Cash received in primary mortgage refinance:								
Units receiving refinance cash	1,579	11	66	137	82	164	17	57
Median amount received (dol.)	24,513	-	14,006	24,346	21,221	26,800	-	-

- Represents or rounds to zero. [1] Constructed in the past 4 years. [2] Persons of Hispanic origin may be of any race. [3] 65 years old and over. [4] Includes don't know and not reported. [5] Persons reporting more than one reason are counted once in the total.

Source: U.S. Census Bureau, *Current Housing Reports,* Series H150/01, *American Housing Survey for the United States.*

No. 944. Occupied Housing Units—Neighborhood Indicators by Selected Characteristics of the Householder: 2001

[In thousands (106,261 represents 106,261,000). As of fall. Based on the American Housing Survey; see Appendix III]

Characteristic	Total occu-pied units	Tenure Owner	Tenure Renter	Black Owner	Black Renter	Hispanic origin[1] Owner	Hispanic origin[1] Renter	Elderly[2] Owner	Elderly[2] Renter	Households below poverty level Owner	Households below poverty level Renter
Total units[3]	**106,261**	**72,265**	**33,996**	**6,318**	**6,974**	**4,731**	**5,083**	**17,513**	**4,299**	**6,713**	**7,889**
Street noise or traffic present[3]	29,889	17,572	12,318	1,854	2,883	1,194	1,634	4,463	1,460	1,782	3,038
Condition not bothersome	18,064	10,571	7,493	1,070	1,697	666	933	3,106	1,052	1,053	1,865
Condition bothersome	11,757	6,981	4,776	782	1,167	525	698	1,353	405	727	1,164
So bothersome they want to move	4,457	2,235	2,222	306	705	215	332	321	138	242	554
Neighborhood crime present[3]	15,948	8,657	7,291	1,326	2,230	706	1,034	1,734	693	901	1,885
Condition not bothersome	6,675	3,746	2,928	510	843	283	346	859	365	359	690
Condition bothersome	9,215	4,888	4,327	811	1,373	423	685	866	328	534	1,185
So bothersome they want to move	3,934	1,538	2,397	322	863	207	451	211	115	213	744
Odors present[3]	6,462	3,771	2,691	445	757	317	479	785	232	449	762
Condition not bothersome	2,314	1,385	929	130	224	72	147	315	88	139	225
Condition bothersome	4,139	2,386	1,754	316	527	245	329	471	143	310	538
So bothersome they want to move	1,635	723	912	124	358	116	177	129	58	118	308
Other problems:											
Noise	2,652	1,554	1,098	149	267	128	178	347	87	141	286
Litter or housing deterioration	1,980	1,324	656	198	225	160	106	307	58	113	199
Poor city or county services	929	605	332	119	140	71	80	118	23	72	115
People	4,075	2,410	1,665	255	456	221	263	463	145	243	458
With public transportation[3]	58,642	34,434	24,208	3,830	5,546	2,936	4,100	8,328	3,071	2,821	5,649
Household uses it at least weekly	11,609	4,291	7,317	926	2,267	562	1,790	870	938	493	2,269
Household uses it less than weekly	9,366	5,485	3,880	660	905	456	632	1,062	462	414	856
Household does not use	36,699	24,167	12,532	2,203	2,250	1,878	1,636	6,295	1,614	1,855	2,418
No public transportation	44,409	35,683	8,726	2,343	1,267	1,682	870	8,707	1,133	3,639	2,043
Police protection:											
Satisfactory	95,179	64,906	30,273	5,446	5,992	4,096	4,451	15,862	3,960	5,787	6,855
Unsatisfactory	7,594	5,146	2,448	645	703	487	477	1,076	215	664	718
Secured communities:[4]											
Community access secured with walls or fences	7,033	3,097	3,935	196	839	332	776	905	508	285	802
Community access not secured	98,497	68,615	29,882	6,049	6,095	4,365	4,284	16,458	3,760	6,336	7,034
Secured multiunits:[4]											
Multiunit access secured	5,330	886	4,445	49	980	54	560	372	1,060	95	1,066
Multiunit access not secured	19,035	2,365	16,670	216	3,615	219	2,818	685	1,973	195	3,883
Senior citizen communities:											
Households with persons 55 years old and over	39,049	31,419	7,630	2,638	1,393	1,639	907	17,513	4,299	4,465	2,412
Community age restricted[5]	2,195	1,116	1,079	21	159	37	80	884	911	169	431
Community quality:											
Some or all activities present	40,538	26,372	14,166	2,260	3,070	1,554	1,852	6,700	2,182	2,164	3,148
Community center or clubhouse	24,039	14,580	9,459	1,134	2,017	825	1,118	4,242	1,628	1,232	2,005
Golf in the community	11,459	8,820	2,639	440	314	324	273	2,237	325	580	485
Trails in the community	18,496	13,169	5,326	942	843	759	623	2,876	628	923	969
Shuttle bus	10,313	6,330	3,983	530	726	417	537	2,014	978	593	1,064
Daycare	17,307	11,545	5,762	1,418	1,634	761	899	2,435	633	916	1,424
Private or restricted beach, park or shoreline	6,700	4,964	1,736	256	319	229	205	1,154	210	376	353
Trash, litter or junk on street:[6]											
None	94,194	65,592	28,602	5,323	5,419	4,073	4,108	16,121	3,861	5,876	6,322
Minor accumulation	6,931	3,422	3,509	557	905	342	680	653	240	407	981
Major accumulation	2,815	1,470	1,345	244	488	181	227	364	98	250	444

[1] Persons of Hispanic origin may be of any race. [2] Householders 65 years old and over. [3] Includes those not reported. [4] Public access is restricted (walls, gates, private security). Includes high rise apartments, retirement communities, resorts, etc. [5] At least one family member must be aged 55 years old or older. [6] Or on any properties within 300 feet.

Source: U.S. Census Bureau, Current Housing Reports, Series H150/01, American Housing Survey for the United States.

Construction and Housing 603

No. 945. Heating Equipment and Fuels for Occupied Units: 1993 to 2001

[As of fall. (94,724 represents 94,724,000). Based on American Housing Survey. See Appendix III]

Type of equipment or fuel	Number (1,000)					Percent distribution	
	1993	1995	1997	1999	2001	1993	2001
Occupied units, total.	94,724	97,692	99,487	102,803	106,261	100.0	100.0
Heating equipment:							
Warm air furnace.	51,248	53,165	58,603	62,018	65,262	54.1	61.4
Heat pumps	8,422	9,406	11,101	10,992	11,080	8.9	10.4
Steam or hot water	13,657	13,669	12,929	13,153	13,441	14.4	12.6
Floor, wall, or pipeless furnace. . .	4,746	4,963	5,588	5,310	5,343	5.0	5.0
Built-in electric units.	6,722	7,035	4,531	4,939	5,063	7.1	4.8
Room heaters with flue.	1,766	1,620	1,584	1,624	1,542	1.9	1.5
Room heaters without flue.	1,597	1,642	1,754	1,790	1,558	1.7	1.5
Fireplaces, stoves, portable heaters or other.	5,654	5,150	2,780	2,434	2,571	6.0	2.4
None.	911	1,044	617	544	401	1.0	0.4
House main heating fuel:							
Utility gas.	47,669	49,203	51,052	52,366	54,689	50.3	51.5
Fuel oil, kerosene, etc.	12,189	12,029	10,855	10,750	10,473	12.9	9.9
Electricity.	25,107	26,771	29,202	31,142	32,590	26.5	30.7
Bottled, tank, or LP gas	3,922	4,251	5,398	5,905	6,079	4.1	5.7
Coal or coke.	297	210	183	168	128	0.3	0.1
Wood and other fuel	4,630	4,186	2,177	1,927	1,902	4.9	1.8
None.	910	1,043	620	545	401	1.0	0.4
Cooking fuel:							
Electricity.	55,887	57,621	58,818	61,315	63,685	59.0	59.9
Gas [1]	37,996	39,218	40,083	41,051	42,161	40.1	39.7
Other fuel	479	566	113	69	66	0.5	0.1
None.	362	287	473	368	349	0.4	0.3

[1] Includes utility, bottled, tank, and LP gas.

Source: U.S. Census Bureau, *Current Housing Reports*, Series H150/93, H150/95RV, H150/97, H150/99, and H150/01, *American Housing Survey for the United States.*

No. 946. Occupied Housing Units—Housing Indicators by Selected Characteristics of the Householder: 2001

[In thousands of units (106,261 represents 106,261,000). As of fall. Based on the American Housing Survey; see Appendix III]

Characteristic	Total occu-pied units	Tenure		Black		Hispanic origin [1]		Elderly [2]		Households below poverty level	
		Owner	Renter	Owner	Renter	Owner	Renter	Owner	Renter	Owner	Renter
Total units	106,261	72,265	33,996	6,318	6,974	4,731	5,083	17,513	4,299	6,713	7,889
Amenities:											
Porch, deck, balcony or patio .	88,834	65,479	23,354	5,389	4,573	4,132	3,161	15,688	2,549	5,870	4,934
Usable fireplace	35,097	31,079	4,018	1,859	548	1,460	447	6,292	311	1,810	456
Separate dining room	50,125	40,568	9,553	3,698	2,157	2,332	1,225	9,153	913	3,171	1,852
With 2 or more living rooms or recreation rooms.	30,451	28,300	2,151	2,117	292	1,333	146	5,907	234	1,578	293
Garage or carport with home .	64,547	53,778	10,769	3,543	1,404	3,424	1,617	13,307	1,191	4,050	1,805
Cars and trucks available:											
No cars, trucks, or vans.	9,342	2,699	6,643	529	2,254	188	1,123	1,741	1,957	902	3,075
Other households without cars	11,828	8,273	3,555	478	374	697	633	1,291	198	796	666
1 car with or without trucks or vans	51,749	34,657	17,092	2,996	3,329	2,106	2,375	10,408	1,865	3,684	3,374
2 cars	25,866	20,234	5,632	1,743	896	1,324	784	3,385	250	1,057	680
3 or more cars.	7,476	6,401	1,075	572	120	416	168	690	29	275	93
With cars, no trucks or vans. .	50,031	31,832	18,199	3,276	3,666	1,789	2,368	9,899	1,880	3,167	3,434
1 truck or van with or without cars	33,775	26,617	7,158	1,942	852	1,899	1,236	4,614	357	1,919	1,061
2 or more trucks or vans	13,113	11,116	1,997	572	201	854	356	1,259	106	726	318
Selected deficiencies:											
Signs of rats in last 3 months .	1,021	482	539	47	182	87	154	82	57	78	185
Holes in floors	1,148	550	598	55	192	76	141	107	36	125	228
Open cracks or holes	5,697	2,896	2,801	372	783	319	495	472	163	434	836
Broken plaster or peeling paint (interior of unit)	2,707	1,274	1,433	199	442	127	261	203	101	199	413
No electrical wiring	72	65	7	15	-	-	-	9	-	25	5
Exposed wiring	535	300	235	22	48	21	39	86	19	47	93
Rooms without electric outlet .	1,308	706	602	76	114	56	86	167	53	115	145
Water leakage [3]	9,985	5,649	4,336	641	1,066	372	654	794	300	506	1,037

- Represents zero.   [1] Persons of Hispanic origin may be of any race.   [2] Householders 65 years old and over.   [3] During the 12 months prior to the survey.

Source: U.S. Census Bureau, *Current Housing Reports*, Series H150/01, *American Housing Survey for the United States.*

U.S. Census Bureau, Statistical Abstract of the United States: 2002

No. 947. Appliances and Office Equipment Used by Households by Region and Household Income: 2001

[In millions (107.0 represents 107,000,000). Preliminary. Represents appliances possessed and generally used by the household. Based on Residential Energy Consumption Survey; see source. For composition of regions, see inside front cover]

Type of appliance	House-holds using appli-ance	Region				Household income in 2001			
		North-east	Midwest	South	West	Under $14,999	$15,000 -$29,999	$30,000 -$49,999	$50,000 and over
Total households.	107.0	20.3	24.5	38.9	23.3	18.7	22.9	27.1	38.3
Oven [1]	101.7	19.6	23.8	36.2	22.1	18.0	22.0	26.1	35.6
Electric	63.0	9.9	14.0	26.0	13.1	10.1	12.9	16.2	23.8
Natural gas	34.3	8.6	8.7	8.7	8.2	7.1	7.8	8.6	10.9
Self cleaning oven	48.2	10.2	12.3	16.1	9.6	4.1	8.5	12.4	23.2
Range [1]	105.7	20.1	24.1	38.6	22.9	18.5	22.5	26.9	37.7
Electric	64.2	9.9	13.9	27.2	13.2	10.4	13.2	16.5	24.1
Natural gas	36.7	9.0	9.1	9.8	8.8	7.3	8.0	9.0	12.5
Refrigerator.	106.8	20.2	24.5	38.9	23.2	18.6	22.8	27.1	38.3
Frost free	96.9	18.3	21.7	36.3	20.7	15.5	19.9	25.0	36.5
Freezer	34.2	4.9	9.6	13.6	6.2	4.4	6.9	9.2	13.7
1	30.8	4.5	8.6	12.2	5.6	3.9	6.1	8.4	12.4
2 or more	3.4	0.4	1.0	1.4	0.6	0.4	0.9	0.8	1.3
Most used defrost method:									
Frost free.	12.2	1.8	2.8	5.7	1.8	1.3	2.0	3.2	5.7
Manual	22.0	3.1	6.7	7.9	4.4	3.0	4.9	6.0	8.1
Dishwasher.	56.7	9.2	12.1	22.1	13.2	3.3	9.1	14.9	29.3
Electric coffee maker	65.5	12.4	16.1	23.0	14.0	8.7	12.8	16.7	27.3
Electric toaster oven	36.1	8.5	5.5	14.7	7.4	5.1	7.7	8.9	14.3
Microwave oven.	92.1	15.2	22.3	34.7	19.9	14.0	19.4	23.8	35.0
Air conditioning	80.8	14.2	20.2	36.9	9.6	11.9	16.7	21.0	31.2
Central system	57.3	5.7	14.3	30.3	7.0	6.1	10.7	15.2	25.3
Room	23.5	8.5	5.8	6.6	2.6	5.8	6.0	5.8	5.9
Color TV.	105.8	20.0	24.4	38.4	22.9	18.1	22.7	26.9	38.0
One	29.3	5.8	6.4	9.8	7.3	8.5	8.6	6.5	5.7
Two	38.4	8.1	8.2	13.7	8.4	6.4	8.5	10.7	12.8
Three	23.3	3.8	5.9	9.2	4.3	2.5	3.8	6.1	10.9
Four.	10.2	1.6	2.7	3.9	2.0	0.6	1.4	2.6	5.7
Five or more	4.5	0.7	1.1	1.8	0.9	(S)	0.4	1.1	2.9
Large screen TV [2]	36.6	7.1	8.1	13.3	8.0	4.7	6.7	9.8	15.3
One	27.3	5.3	5.9	9.7	6.5	3.7	5.1	7.0	11.4
Two	7.9	1.4	1.8	3.3	1.4	0.9	1.5	2.2	3.2
Three or more	1.4	(S)	(S)	(S)	(S)	(S)	(S)	0.5	0.7
Cable/Satellite dish-antenna	82.2	16.3	19.1	30.2	16.6	12.1	16.2	20.9	33.0
VCR and DVD players	96.1	18.0	22.5	34.6	21.0	13.9	19.8	25.3	37.0
Stereo equipment.	80.3	15.1	18.2	28.5	18.5	10.2	15.4	20.9	33.8
Clothes washer	84.1	14.7	19.8	32.7	16.9	10.7	16.4	22.1	34.9
Clothes dryer [1]	78.8	13.3	19.2	30.3	16.0	8.4	15.0	21.3	34.1
Electric	61.1	9.2	13.4	26.6	11.9	6.9	12.2	16.8	25.1
Natural gas	16.9	4.0	5.4	3.4	4.1	1.4	2.6	4.2	8.7
Water heater [1]	107.0	20.3	24.5	38.9	23.3	18.7	22.9	27.1	38.3
Electric	40.9	4.7	6.4	22.5	7.4	8.3	9.6	10.7	12.4
Natural gas	57.9	10.8	16.9	15.4	14.9	9.3	11.6	14.1	22.9
Personal computers	60.0	10.9	14.1	20.7	14.3	3.7	8.7	16.0	31.6
Access to Internet.	50.7	9.7	11.8	16.9	12.2	2.8	6.6	13.1	28.3
Cell/mobile telephone	56.8	10.3	12.8	21.4	12.3	4.4	8.6	14.7	29.1

S Figure does not meet publication standards. [1] Includes other types, not shown separately. [2] Determined by respondent.

Source: U.S. Energy Information Administration, "2001 Housing Characteristic Tables." See Internet site <http://www.eia.doe.gov/emeu/recs/contents.html> (accessed 30 July 2001).

No. 948. Net Stock of Residential Fixed Assets: 1990 to 2000

[In billions of dollars (6,287.4 represents $6,287,400,000,000). End of year estimates]

Item	1990	1993	1994	1995	1996	1997	1998	1999	2000
Total residential fixed assets . .	6,287.4	7,161.9	7,654.5	7,973.1	8,391.5	8,850.1	9,405.1	10,006.6	10,708.1
By type of owner and legal form of organization:									
Private.	6,137.7	6,991.0	7,472.2	7,784.2	8,195.3	8,646.3	9,191.8	9,780.5	10,471.2
Corporate	68.0	73.7	76.0	78.2	81.6	86.5	91.8	97.2	101.6
Noncorporate	6,069.6	6,917.2	7,396.3	7,706.0	8,113.8	8,559.8	9,100.1	9,683.3	10,369.6
Government	149.7	170.9	182.3	188.8	196.2	203.8	213.3	226.1	237.0
Federal	52.5	57.3	60.7	62.4	64.5	66.7	69.5	73.2	76.1
State and local	97.2	113.7	121.6	126.5	131.7	137.2	143.8	152.9	160.9
By tenure group: [1]									
Owner occupied	4,486.9	5,214.1	5,628.7	5,891.6	6,228.8	6,584.7	7,025.1	7,502.8	8,084.2
Farm	150.3	161.1	169.6	174.0	178.9	188.7	198.3	209.0	222.6
Nonfarm	4,336.6	5,053.0	5,459.1	5,717.7	6,049.9	6,396.0	6,826.9	7,293.8	7,861.5
Tenant occupied	1,774.5	1,920.3	1,997.3	2,052.5	2,133.1	2,234.9	2,348.1	2,470.3	2,588.3
Farm	10.9	11.7	12.5	12.8	13.2	13.6	14.0	14.6	15.2
Nonfarm	1,763.6	1,908.6	1,984.8	2,039.7	2,119.9	2,221.4	2,334.1	2,455.8	2,573.1

[1] Excludes stocks of other nonfarm residential assets, which consists primarily of dormitories, and of fraternity and sorority houses.

Source: U.S. Bureau of Economic Analysis, *Survey of Current Business*, September 2001 issue, and <http://www.bea.doc.gov/bea/dn/faweb/> (accessed 30 May 2002).

Construction and Housing 605

No. 949. Expenditures by Residential Property Owners for Improvements and Maintenance and Repairs by Type of Property and Activity: 1990 to 2001

[In millions of dollars (115,432 represents $115,432,000,000)]

Year and type of expenditure	1-unit properties with owner occupant Total	1-unit properties with owner occupant	Other properties	Additions and alterations To structures Total	To structures Additions	To structures Alterations	To property outside of structures	Major replacements	Maintenance and repairs
1990	115,432	63,441	51,991	39,929	9,160	23,510	7,261	19,700	55,800
1991	107,692	62,608	45,084	33,662	8,609	17,486	7,567	18,526	55,505
1992	115,569	72,930	42,639	44,041	7,401	24,870	11,771	20,705	50,821
1993	121,899	77,626	44,273	53,512	16,381	27,657	9,472	22,604	45,785
1994	130,625	85,903	44,722	56,835	12,906	30,395	13,534	26,606	47,185
1995	124,971	79,003	45,968	51,011	11,197	29,288	10,526	26,928	47,032
1996	131,362	84,462	46,900	64,513	17,388	32,889	14,235	26,738	40,108
1997	133,577	90,677	42,900	65,222	14,575	37,126	13,523	27,210	41,145
1998	133,693	96,159	37,534	62,971	11,897	38,787	12,287	28,741	41,980
1999	142,900	95,778	47,122	72,056	16,164	42,058	13,833	28,493	42,352
2000, total [1]	**152,975**	**100,161**	**52,814**	**77,979**	**18,189**	**40,384**	**19,407**	**32,760**	**42,236**
Heating and air conditioning [2]	10,866	7,075	3,791	2,736	(NA)	2,736	(NA)	5,645	2,486
Plumbing	11,518	5,561	5,957	3,359	(NA)	2,186	1,172	3,035	5,123
Roofing	15,834	8,670	7,164	(NA)	(NA)	(NA)	(NA)	11,243	4,591
Painting	13,830	7,592	6,238	(NA)	(NA)	(NA)	(NA)	(NA)	13,830
2001, total [1]	**157,765**	**105,997**	**51,768**	**77,559**	**14,133**	**47,208**	**16,218**	**32,714**	**47,491**
Heating and air conditioning [2]	12,210	7,554	4,655	2,408	(NA)	2,408	(NA)	7,181	2,621
Plumbing	12,823	5,218	7,604	4,597	(NA)	3,827	769	3,465	4,761
Roofing	11,024	6,513	4,510	(NA)	(NA)	(NA)	(NA)	7,090	3,933
Painting	16,679	7,828	8,851	(NA)	(NA)	(NA)	(NA)	(NA)	16,679

NA Not available.   [1] Includes types of expenditures not separately specified.   [2] Central air-conditioning.
Source: U.S. Census Bureau, *Current Construction Reports*, Series C50, *Expenditures for Residential Improvement*, quarterly. See Internet site <http://www.census.gov/const/www/c50index.html>.

No. 950. Home Remodeling—Work Done and Amount Spent: 2001

[In thousands, except percent. (3,411 represents 3,411,000) as of fall. For work done in the prior 12 months. Based on household survey and subject to sampling error; see source]

Remodeling project	Households with work done [1] Number	Households with work done [1] Percent of households	Work done by— Household member	Work done by— Outside contractor	Amount spent Under $1,000	Amount spent $1,000 to $2,999	Amount spent Over $3,000
Conversion of garage/attic/basement into living space	3,411	1.7	2,066	853	915	767	1,054
Remodel bathroom	14,131	7.0	8,962	3,624	6,930	2,953	1,764
Remodel kitchen	9,358	4.6	5,521	2,431	3,086	1,852	2,136
Remodel bedroom	6,893	3.4	5,183	811	4,209	843	343
Remodel/convert room to home office	2,352	1.2	1,968	171	1,563	268	80
Remodel other rooms	6,910	3.4	4,822	1,029	3,396	1,023	1,002
Add bathroom	1,434	0.7	628	465	461	246	427
Add/extend garage	979	0.5	485	277	119	146	481
Add other rooms- exterior addition	1,717	0.9	695	814	100	350	905
Add deck/porch/patio	4,912	2.4	2,576	1,528	1,764	1,297	961
Roofing	10,039	5.0	2,339	5,737	1,950	2,763	3,286
Siding - vinyl/metal	3,205	1.6	967	1,482	409	884	1,036
Aluminum windows	1,532	0.8	603	614	737	290	252
Clad-wood/Wood windows	1,069	0.5	402	410	308	213	282
Vinyl windows	4,177	2.1	1,203	2,269	959	1,115	1,347
Ceramic tile floors	6,333	3.1	3,173	2,281	3,266	1,215	418
Hardwood floors	3,555	1.8	1,542	1,360	1,185	854	570
Laminate flooring	2,591	1.3	1,418	893	1,149	642	176
Vinyl flooring	4,351	2.2	2,209	1,266	2,556	496	151
Carpeting	11,157	5.5	2,503	6,837	4,537	3,384	947
Kitchen cabinets	5,287	2.6	2,196	1,702	1,634	843	1,016
Kitchen counter tops	4,697	2.3	1,663	1,905	1,855	846	549
Skylights	993	0.5	295	498	663	97	22
Exterior doors	5,695	2.8	2,771	2,046	3,268	789	184
Interior doors	3,766	1.9	2,275	808	2,155	330	156
Garage doors	3,493	1.7	748	1,869	1,499	796	64
Concrete or masonry work	3,991	2.0	1,703	1,776	1,557	883	679
Swimming pool—in ground	734	0.4	132	414	97	33	378
Wall paneling	1,601	0.8	917	301	802	175	62
Ceramic wall tile	1,966	1.0	884	618	1,103	197	84

[1] Includes no response and amount unknown.
Source: Mediamark Research Inc., *New York, NY, Top-Line Reports*, (copyright). Internet site <http://www.mediamark.com/mri/docs/TopLineReports.html>.

No. 951. Commercial Office Space—Overview for Selected Market Areas: 2001

[As of mid-October. (3,928,797 represents 3,928,797,000). For the 76 market areas with the highest vacancy rates in 2001. Data based on responses from individuals knowledgeable in the local markets]

Market area	Inventory (1,000 sq. ft.)	Vacant space (1,000 sq. ft.)	Vacancy rate (percent)	Construction (1,000 sq. ft.)	Net absorption [1] (1,000 sq. ft.)
United States, all market areas [2] ...	3,928,797	479,982	12.2	132,513	105,342
Akron..........................	5,724	781	13.6	30	305
Albuquerque.....................	11,744	1,306	11.1	81	111
Atlanta.........................	133,331	21,553	16.2	5,311	3,719
Bakersfield.....................	6,913	790	11.4	100	186
Baltimore.......................	47,329	6,367	13.5	2,762	740
Boston..........................	177,533	24,877	14.0	9,489	7,770
Bridgeport/Stratford	6,360	688	10.8	289	28
Charleston......................	4,502	599	13.3	205	120
Charlotte.......................	35,507	4,997	14.1	1,163	4,075
Chicago.........................	172,300	35,900	20.8	6,281	2,300
Cincinnati......................	26,099	3,451	13.2	909	833
Cleveland.......................	36,902	4,816	13.1	312	309
Columbus........................	37,360	4,427	11.8	508	1,414
Corpus Christi..................	2,789	466	16.7	-	77
Dallas..........................	172,630	35,545	20.6	6,351	382
Denver..........................	79,451	12,155	15.3	-	1,593
Des Moines......................	10,281	1,269	12.3	-	90
Detroit.........................	88,057	11,508	13.1	1,690	2,334
El Paso.........................	7,915	1,775	22.4	-	-
Fort Lauderdale.................	22,043	3,611	16.4	1,493	1,426
Fort Wayne......................	5,797	664	11.5	-	92
Fort Worth......................	19,681	2,432	12.4	617	908
Grand Rapids....................	11,366	1,396	12.3	176	335
Greensboro, High-Point, Winston-Salem...	15,084	2,126	14.1	1,006	156
Greenville......................	7,197	1,211	16.8	105	842
Hartford........................	22,059	3,541	16.1	191	684
Honolulu........................	11,725	1,513	12.9	-	84
Indianapolis....................	25,819	4,347	16.8	168	919
Jacksonville....................	16,281	2,914	17.9	201	46
Kansas City.....................	39,649	5,538	14.0	938	184
Knoxville.......................	7,249	912	12.6	185	283
Las Vegas.......................	19,629	2,247	11.4	1,428	1,085
Los Angeles-Central.............	27,428	5,011	18.3	-	1,153
Los Angeles-Inland Empire	7,223	887	12.3	212	281
Los Angeles-Orange County........	52,663	7,354	14.0	2,432	1,971
Los Angeles-San Fernando Valley.......	33,239	3,989	12.0	600	-
Los Angeles-San Gabriel.........	8,725	1,292	14.8	282	3
Los Angeles-South Bay...........	31,444	4,425	14.1	589	-
Louisville......................	16,212	2,406	14.8	640	123
Marin County....................	6,115	1,164	19.0	-	-
Memphis.........................	18,014	3,534	19.6	282	1,570
Milwaukee.......................	27,200	3,300	12.1	400	245
Minneapolis/St. Paul............	59,496	7,728	13.0	1,083	3,659
Mobile..........................	13,445	2,797	20.8	215	100
Nashua..........................	2,226	350	15.7	-	-
Nashville.......................	24,139	3,191	13.2	527	2,031
New Haven.......................	13,900	1,785	12.8	-	110
New Jersey Northern.............	205,165	25,666	12.5	7,167	2,941
New Orleans.....................	14,929	2,277	15.2	-	51
NYC-Long Island.................	66,516	7,404	11.1	-	198
NYC-Westchester.................	33,108	4,610	13.9	-	-
Oklahoma City...................	15,150	2,406	15.9	95	494
Omaha...........................	9,306	1,059	11.4	835	227
Orlando.........................	22,396	2,692	12.0	1,327	833
Phoenix.........................	29,281	4,228	14.4	2,488	713
Pittsburgh......................	42,760	6,214	14.5	1,442	2,062
Raleigh.........................	30,976	3,658	11.8	1,011	1,758
Richmond........................	25,459	3,124	12.3	-	1,731
Roanoke.........................	3,026	355	11.7	-	56
Rochester.......................	15,180	1,964	12.9	200	211
Salt Lake City..................	19,440	3,431	17.6	649	177
San Antonio.....................	18,249	2,364	13.0	222	133
San Diego.......................	49,448	5,407	10.9	1,093	2
San Jose........................	17,531	2,286	13.0	4,756	174
San Mateo.......................	26,380	4,192	15.9	798	1,766
Shreveport......................	3,121	343	11.0	-	-
Sioux Falls.....................	3,626	700	19.3	-	178
South Bend......................	3,039	477	15.7	-	-
Stamford/Norwalk................	25,749	3,438	13.4	216	-
St. Louis.......................	38,524	6,827	17.7	1,079	965
Tampa...........................	38,137	5,764	15.1	749	370
Toledo..........................	9,290	1,301	14.0	8	339
Tulsa...........................	15,479	1,836	11.9	-	151
West Palm Beach.................	24,052	3,607	15.0	-	-
Wilmington......................	12,387	1,739	14.0	-	611
Youngstown......................	2,700	315	11.7	20	10

- Represents zero.   [1] Net change in occupied stock.   [2] Includes other market areas, not shown separately.

Source: Society of Industrial and Office REALTORS, Washington DC, *2001 Comparative Statistics of Industrial and Office Real Estate Markets* (copyright).

Construction and Housing   607

No. 952. Commercial Buildings—Summary: 1999

[4,675 represents 4,675,000. Excludes buildings 1,000 square feet or smaller. Building type based on predominant activity in which the occupants were engaged. Based on a sample survey of building representatives conducted in 1999, therefore subject to sampling variability]

Characteristic	All build-ings (1,000)	Floor-space (mil. sq. ft.)	Mean sq. ft. per build-ing (1,000)	Characteristic	All build-ings (1,000)	Floor-space (mil. sq. ft.)	Mean sq. ft. per build-ing (1,000)
All buildings	**4,657**	**67,338**	**14.5**	1980 to 1989	846	13,931	16.5
Building floorspace (sq. ft.):				1990 to 1999	690	11,094	16.1
1,001 to 5,000	2,348	6,774	2.9	Workers (main shift):			
5,001 to 10,000	1,110	8,238	7.4	Fewer than 5	2,376	14,321	6.0
10,001 to 25,000	708	11,153	15.7	5 to 9	807	6,325	7.8
25,001 to 50,000	257	9,311	36.2	10 to 19	683	8,028	11.8
50,001 to 100,000	145	10,112	69.9	20 to 49	487	10,814	22.2
100,001 to 200,000	59	8,271	139.4	50 to 99	174	8,898	51.1
200,001 to 500,000	23	6,851	296.3	100 to 249	90	8,356	92.4
Over 500,000	7	6,628	929.0	250 or more	39	10,595	270.0
Principal activity within building:				Energy sources: [1]			
Education	327	8,651	26.4	Electricity	4,395	65,716	15.0
Food sales	174	994	5.7	Natural gas	2,669	45,507	17.0
Food service	349	1,851	5.3	Fuel oil	434	13,285	30.6
Health care	127	2,918	22.9	District heat	117	5,891	50.2
Inpatient	11	1,865	168.2	District chilled water	50	2,750	55.4
Outpatient	116	1,053	9.1	Propane	451	6,290	14.0
Lodging	153	4,521	29.5	Wood	79	570	7.2
Mercantile	667	10,398	15.6	Heating equipment: [1]			
Retail (other than mall)	534	4,766	8.9	Heat pumps	492	8,923	18.1
Enclosed mall and strip				Furnaces	1,460	14,449	9.9
center	133	5,631	42.2	Individual space heaters	894	17,349	19.4
Office	739	12,044	16.3	District heat	96	5,534	57.7
Public assembly	305	4,393	14.4	Boilers	581	19,522	33.6
Public order and safety	72	1,168	16.2	Packaged heating units	1,347	25,743	19.1
Religious worship	307	3,405	11.1	Other	185	4,073	22.1
Service	478	3,388	7.1	Cooling equipment: [1]			
Warehouse and storage	603	10,477	17.4	Residential-type central A/C . .	676	8,329	12.3
Other	102	1,222	12.0	Heat pumps	485	9,147	18.8
Vacant	253	1,908	7.6	Individual A/C	799	14,276	17.9
Year constructed:				District chilled water	50	2,750	55.4
1919 or before	419	4,034	9.6	Central chillers	130	12,909	99.7
1920 to 1945	499	6,445	12.9	Packaged A/C units	1,953	36,527	18.7
1946 to 1959	763	9,127	12.0	Swamp coolers	136	2,219	16.3
1960 to 1969	665	10,866	16.3	Other	49	1,312	26.7
1970 to 1979	774	11,840	15.3				

[1] More than one type may apply.

Source: U.S. Energy Information Administration, Internet site <http://www.eia.doe.gov/emeu/cbecs/pdf/set1.pdf> (accessed 1 May 02)

No. 953. Office Building Markets—Summary: 2001

[As of end-of-year. In thousands of square feet, except as indicated. (399,465 represents 399,465,000). For top 27 areas in market size. Excludes government owned, and occupied, owner-occupied, and medical office buildings. Minus sign (-) indicates loss. CBD means central business district]

Market area	Total market size	Total market vacancy rate (percent)	Market absorption	CBD market size	Suburban market size	CBD market construc-tion	Suburban market construc-tion	CBD rental rate [1] (dol.)
Manhattan	399,465	11.80	-26,401	399,465	(X)	9,363	(NA)	60.62
Washington, DC	294,978	11.30	-1,400	101,371	193,608	4,662	4,862	34.00
Los Angeles	287,690	11.78	14,754	39,111	248,579	-	3,436	24.65
Chicago	272,792	16.25	-4,179	136,945	135,847	6,040	2,501	31.80
Houston	170,302	11.97	1,401	39,117	131,185	3,303	1,401	27.53
Dallas/Ft. Worth	165,722	20.94	-4,658	28,319	137,403	-	1,864	23.43
Atlanta	139,465	18.10	-655	46,196	93,269	425	2,133	25.00
Boston	131,229	15.40	-12,569	52,677	78,551	2,917	2,936	46.00
Toronto	114,767	10.20	-2,665	48,439	66,327	460	1,500	33.00
Northern New Jersey . .	105,004	12.42	1,065	15,594	89,410	244	9,169	29.00
Philadelphia	85,404	11.85	2,461	38,643	46,761	350	1,758	26.00
Denver	84,178	19.14	-4,259	23,455	60,724	280	1,960	24.00
Tampa/St. Petersburg .	73,553	13.62	-459	11,536	62,017	-	144	19.80
Detroit	72,647	12.32	-156	15,829	56,817	-	1,055	26.75
Phoenix	62,999	14.57	549	16,761	46,237	-	2,245	22.50
Columbus	62,743	12.86	3,023	21,472	41,271	48	717	20.00
San Francisco	61,265	16.83	-6,563	39,933	21,332	824	1,548	42.00
Central New Jersey . . .	57,114	10.64	2,727	(X)	57,114	(NA)	3,612	(NA)
Minneapolis	53,435	12.30	507	25,195	28,240	1,465	395	28.15
San Diego	53,311	12.40	1,040	9,153	44,158	-	2,436	30.00
Sacramento	52,969	11.73	550	5,023	47,946	-	2,068	32.00
Baltimore	49,707	12.31	1,278	13,371	36,336	454	1,046	23.00
Silicon Valley	49,090	17.45	-655	8,292	40,804	1,082	3,339	51.00
Orlando	48,363	13.26	791	8,334	40,029	-	625	25.26
Calgary	46,373	9.89	819	31,777	14,596	-	267	21.50
Miami	43,598	11.09	1,136	12,686	30,912	460	1,985	31.44
St. Louis	39,224	13.72	106	10,468	28,757	-	731	22.00

- Represents zero.   NA Not available.   X Not applicable.   [1] Per square foot.
Source: ONCOR International, Houston, TX, Year-End 2001 Market Data Book (copyright).

608   Construction and Housing

Section 21
Manufactures

This section presents summary data for manufacturing as a whole and more detailed information for major industry groups and selected products. The types of measures shown at the different levels include data for establishments, employment and wages, plant and equipment expenditures, value and quantity of production and shipments, value added by manufacture, inventories, and various indicators of financial status.

The principal sources of these data are U.S. Census Bureau reports of the censuses of manufactures conducted every 5 years, the *Annual Survey of Manufactures,* and *Current Industrial Reports.* Reports on current activities of industries or current movements of individual commodities are compiled by such government agencies as the Bureau of Labor Statistics; the Economic Research Service of the Department of Agriculture; the International Trade Administration; and by private research or trade associations such as The Conference Board, Inc., the American Iron and Steel Institute, the Electronic Industries Association, and several others.

Data on financial aspects of manufacturing industries are collected by the Bureau of Economic Analysis (BEA) and the U.S. Census Bureau. Industry aggregates in the form of balance sheets, profit and loss statements, analyses of sales and expenses, lists of subsidiaries, and types and amounts of security issues are published for leading manufacturing corporations registered with the Securities and Exchange Commission. The BEA issues data on capital in manufacturing industries and capacity utilization rates in manufacturing. See also Section 15, Business Enterprise.

Several private trade associations provide industry coverage for certain sections of the economy. They include the Aluminum Association (Table 976), American Iron and Steel Institute (Tables 977-979), Consumer Electronics Association (Tables 987 and 988), and the Aerospace Industries Association (Tables 995-997). Machine tool consumption data (Table 980) is produced jointly by the Association for Manufacturing Technology and American Machine Tool Distributors Association.

Censuses and annual surveys—The first census of manufactures covered the year 1809. Between 1809 and 1963, a census was conducted at periodic intervals. Since 1967, it has been taken every 5 years (for years ending in "2" and "7"). Results from the 1997 census are presented in this section utilizing the new NAICS (North American Industry Classification System). For additional information see text, Section 15, Business Enterprise, and the Census Bureau Web site at <http://www.census.gov/epcd/www/NAICS.html>. Census data either direct reports or estimates from administrative records, are obtained for every manufacturing plant with one paid employee or more.

The *Annual Survey of Manufactures* (ASM), conducted for the first time in 1949, collects data for the years between censuses for the more general measure of manufacturing activity covered in detail by the censuses. The annual survey data are estimates derived from a scientifically selected sample of establishments. The 1999 annual survey is based on a sample of about 55,000 establishments of an approximate total of 230,000. These establishments represent all manufacturing establishments of multiunit companies and all single-establishment manufacturing companies mailed schedules in the 1997 Census of Manufactures. For the current panel of the ASM sample, all establishments of companies with 1997 shipments in manufacturing in excess of $500 million were included in the survey with certainty. For the remaining portion of the mail survey, the establishment was

U.S. Census Bureau, Statistical Abstract of the United States: 2002

defined as the sampling unit. For this portion, all establishments with 250 employees or more and establishments with a very large value of shipments also were included. Therefore, of the 58,000 establishments included in the ASM panel, approximately 33,000 are selected with certainty. These establishments account for approximately 80 percent of total value of shipments in the 1992 census. Smaller establishments in the remaining portion of the mail survey were selected by sample.

Establishments and classification—
The censuses of manufactures for 1947 through 1992 cover operating manufacturing establishments as defined in the *Standard Industrial Classification Manual* (SIC), issued by the U.S. Office of Management and Budget (see text, Section 12). The Manual is also used for classifying establishments in the annual surveys. The comparability of manufactures data over time is affected by changes in the official definitions of industries as presented in the Manual. It is important to note, therefore, that the 1987 edition of the Manual was used for the 1987 and 1992 censuses; and the 1972 edition of the Manual and the 1977 Supplement were used for the 1972 through 1982 censuses.

The Manual defines an industry as a number of establishments producing a single product or a closely related group of products. In the manual, an establishment is classified in a particular industry if its production of a product or product group exceeds in value added its production of any other product group. While some establishments produce only the products of the industry in which they are classified, few within an industry specialize to

that extent. The statistics on employment, payrolls, value added, inventories, and expenditures, therefore, reflect both the primary and secondary activities of the establishments in that industry. For this reason, care should be exercised in relating such statistics to the total shipments figures of products primary to the industry.

Most tables in this section use the new way of organizing economic statistics called the North American Industry Classification System (NAICS). For more information on this system, see *North American Industry Classification System (NAICS) - United States, 1997.*

Establishment—Establishment signifies a single physical plant site or factory. It is not necessarily identical to the business unit or company, which may consist of one or more establishments. A company operating establishments at more than one location is required to submit a separate report for each location. An establishment engaged in distinctly different lines of activity and maintaining separate payroll and inventory records is also required to submit separate reports.

Durable goods—Items with a normal life expectancy of 3 years or more. Automobiles, furniture, household appliances, and mobile homes are common examples.

Nondurable goods—Items which generally last for only a short time (3 years or less). Food, beverages, clothing, shoes, and gasoline are common examples.

Statistical reliability—For a discussion of statistical collection and estimation, sampling procedures, and measures of statistical reliability applicable to Census Bureau data, see Appendix III.

No. 954. Gross Domestic Product in Manufacturing in Current and Real (1996) Dollars by Industry: 1990 to 2000

[In billions of dollars (5,803.2 represents 5,803,200,000,000). Data are based on the 1987 Standard Industrial Classification (SIC). Data include nonfactor charges (capital consumption allowances, indirect business taxes, etc.) as well as factor charges against gross product; corporate profits and capital consumption allowances have been shifted from a company to an establishment basis]

Industry	1990	1994	1995	1996	1997	1998	1999	2000
CURRENT DOLLARS								
Gross domestic product [1]	**5,803.2**	**7,054.3**	**7,400.5**	**7,813.2**	**8,318.4**	**8,781.5**	**9,268.6**	**9,872.9**
Manufacturing.	1,040.6	1,223.2	1,289.1	1,316.0	1,379.6	1,431.5	1,496.8	1,566.6
Durable goods.	586.6	694.1	729.8	748.4	791.2	830.7	865.7	901.7
Lumber and wood products	32.2	39.8	42.3	39.9	41.2	41.9	46.3	44.4
Furniture and fixtures	15.6	18.9	19.5	20.7	22.7	24.3	26.0	26.7
Stone, clay, and glass products. . . .	25.3	30.4	32.4	33.2	37.2	38.7	42.5	43.9
Primary metal industries.	43.2	47.6	53.0	50.8	52.6	53.1	50.2	52.9
Fabricated metal products	69.4	83.2	87.2	93.1	97.6	101.7	107.6	108.7
Industrial machinery	118.2	121.0	132.8	136.3	143.2	158.6	157.3	167.6
Electronic & other electric equipment	105.7	139.3	146.9	153.2	165.9	159.2	165.5	181.2
Motor vehicles and equipment	47.3	95.2	98.2	92.2	96.5	111.5	118.9	120.2
Other transportation equipment. . . .	60.5	49.6	47.7	51.4	55.5	58.4	64.5	62.7
Instruments and related products. . .	49.3	46.8	47.2	53.7	53.6	57.5	58.8	64.2
Misc. manufacturing industries	19.8	22.3	22.7	23.8	25.2	25.9	28.3	29.1
Nondurable goods	454.0	529.1	559.2	567.6	588.4	600.8	631.0	664.8
Food and kindred products.	96.4	110.2	121.1	118.7	123.1	121.8	132.9	137.0
Tobacco manufactures.	11.9	13.2	15.1	14.8	15.4	17.3	18.9	22.3
Textile mill products.	22.0	25.6	24.8	25.3	25.7	25.8	25.5	24.7
Apparel and other textile products . .	25.4	28.5	27.3	27.0	26.5	26.0	24.3	23.6
Paper and allied products	45.0	50.1	58.9	55.9	53.8	55.7	58.0	59.9
Printing and publishing	73.1	83.5	80.8	88.2	91.1	95.6	102.7	105.5
Chemicals and allied products.	109.9	138.7	150.8	153.6	164.8	164.8	175.1	191.1
Petroleum and coal products	31.7	29.3	29.0	30.2	31.4	32.9	30.4	36.5
Rubber and misc. plastic products . .	33.9	44.9	46.1	49.7	52.1	56.8	59.3	60.2
Leather and leather products	4.7	5.0	5.3	4.2	4.3	4.1	3.9	4.0
CHAINED (1996) DOLLARS								
Gross domestic product, total [1]	**6,707.9**	**7,347.7**	**7,543.8**	**7,813.2**	**8,159.5**	**8,508.9**	**8,856.5**	**9,224.0**
Manufacturing.	1,102.3	1,206.0	1,284.7	1,316.0	1,387.3	1,444.3	1,532.1	1,594.6
Durable goods.	585.1	656.5	714.9	748.4	813.0	892.9	965.1	1,034.1
Lumber and wood products	45.1	38.9	41.6	39.9	39.5	40.1	43.0	44.1
Furniture and fixtures	18.1	20.2	20.7	20.7	22.1	22.9	23.9	24.4
Stone, clay, and glass products. . . .	29.4	32.0	32.8	33.2	36.6	36.6	38.4	39.7
Primary metal industries.	43.7	50.5	49.6	50.8	52.7	54.5	57.2	57.4
Fabricated metal products	76.1	86.4	90.8	93.1	96.2	96.5	98.4	99.6
Industrial machinery	93.5	106.8	124.7	136.3	158.4	195.8	214.4	236.0
Electronic & other electric equipment	68.6	103.3	128.7	153.2	102.2	210.8	255.8	327.7
Motor vehicles and equipment	68.7	99.1	103.2	92.2	97.1	111.6	114.7	116.9
Other transportation equipment. . . .	75.7	52.2	49.4	51.4	54.8	56.7	61.2	55.2
Instruments and related products. . .	68.9	53.8	52.6	53.7	49.8	49.0	48.2	48.1
Misc. manufacturing industries	22.8	22.6	23.3	23.8	24.8	24.9	26.9	27.7
Nondurable goods	520.2	551.2	570.3	567.6	574.7	555.5	574.0	574.0
Food and kindred products.	109.5	112.6	133.3	118.7	118.1	112.1	117.3	118.2
Tobacco manufactures.	14.5	13.8	15.7	14.8	13.9	11.9	6.3	6.2
Textile mill products.	22.8	26.9	26.0	25.3	25.0	24.1	23.6	24.1
Apparel and other textile products . .	27.3	28.4	28.0	27.0	26.5	25.2	22.6	22.5
Paper and allied products	52.5	61.3	52.2	55.9	58.3	56.2	57.3	50.0
Printing and publishing	102.9	92.6	89.2	88.2	86.4	85.6	88.1	86.6
Chemicals and allied products.	131.1	145.5	148.0	153.6	164.2	155.2	168.7	184.2
Petroleum and coal products	22.9	22.0	26.9	30.2	25.6	26.4	34.4	25.5
Rubber and misc. plastic products . .	34.0	44.9	47.0	49.7	53.2	55.6	58.2	59.8
Leather and leather products	5.2	5.1	5.3	4.2	4.2	3.8	3.7	3.9

[1] For additional industry detail, see Table 632.

Source: U.S. Bureau of Economic Analysis, *National Income and Product Accounts, 1929-97;* and *Survey of Current Business,* November 2001.

Manufactures 611

No. 955. Manufacturing—Establishments, Employees, and Annual Payroll by Industry: 1999 and 2000

[Excludes government employees, railroad employees, self-employed persons, etc. See "General Explanation" in source for definitions and statement on reliability of data. An *establishment* is a single physical location where business is conducted or where services or industrial operations are performed]

Industry	NAICS code [1]	1999			2000		
		Establishments, number	Number of employees [2] (1,000)	Annual payroll (mil. dol.)	Establishments, number	Number of employees [2] (1,000)	Annual payroll (mil. dol.)
All industries, total	(X)	7,008,444	110,706	3,554,693	7,070,048	114,065	3,879,430
Manufacturing, total	31-33	360,244	16,660	625,536	354,498	16,474	643,954
Percent of all industries	(X)	5.14	15.05	17.60	5.20	14.45	17.60
Food.	311	26,734	1,464	41,858	26,401	1,468	43,773
Beverage & tobacco product	312	2,789	172	6,992	2,869	169	7,318
Textile mills	313	4,587	362	9,694	4,449	339	9,491
Textile product mills	314	7,152	222	5,313	6,881	216	5,364
Apparel manufacturing	315	16,721	575	11,206	16,505	510	10,426
Leather & allied product	316	1,807	74	1,738	1,783	69	1,711
Wood product.	321	17,473	595	16,373	17,328	598	16,511
Paper	322	5,883	559	23,227	5,790	554	23,291
Printing & related support activities.	323	40,671	834	27,940	39,035	813	28,319
Petroleum & coal products	324	2,226	109	6,058	2,210	109	6,386
Chemical	325	13,534	886	44,738	13,426	886	45,610
Plastics & rubber products	326	16,646	1,047	33,351	16,292	1,057	34,110
Nonmetallic mineral product	327	16,541	510	18,273	16,537	524	19,123
Primary metal	331	5,900	598	24,766	6,300	602	25,545
Fabricated metal product	332	62,242	1,788	61,604	61,144	1,791	64,244
Machinery	333	30,177	1,398	55,874	29,442	1,378	58,387
Computer & electronic product.	334	17,279	1,615	83,842	17,148	1,557	90,397
Electrical equip, appliance & component	335	7,104	586	20,600	7,041	589	21,853
Transportation equipment	336	13,042	1,906	90,609	12,766	1,873	88,632
Furniture & related product	337	20,266	623	17,128	19,848	640	17,964
Miscellaneous.	339	31,470	734	24,354	31,303	732	25,500

X Not applicable. [1] North American Industry Classification System, 1997. [2] Covers full- and part-time employees who are on the payroll in the pay period including March 12.

Source: U.S. Census Bureau, *County Business Patterns*, annual. See also <http://www.census.gov/prod/2002pubs/00cbp/cbp00-1.pdf> (issued May 2002).

No. 956. Manufacturing Establishments, Employees, and Annual Payroll by State: 2000

[Excludes government employees, railroad employees, self-employed persons, etc. See "General Explanation" in source for definitions and statement on reliability of data. An *establishment* is a single physical location where business is conducted or where services or industrial operations are performed]

State	Establishments	Number of employees [1] (1,000)	Annual payroll (mil. dol.)	State	Establishments	Number of employees [1] (1,000)	Annual payroll (mil. dol.)
United States	354,498	16,474.0	643,955	Missouri	7,307	347.8	11,662
Alabama	5,261	333.8	10,600	Montana	1,200	21.0	643
Alaska	489	11.3	372	Nebraska	1,946	108.6	3,424
Arizona.	4,901	200.9	8,622	Nevada	1,693	38.1	1,379
Arkansas	3,245	235.6	6,611	New Hampshire	2,272	93.0	3,747
California.	49,137	1,753.7	80,288	New Jersey	11,038	386.1	17,270
Colorado	5,392	166.5	7,004	New Mexico.	1,563	38.1	1,145
Connecticut	5,503	232.8	11,344	New York	22,129	705.9	27,508
Delaware	687	41.8	1,772	North Carolina	10,997	731.4	23,329
District of Columbia	174	2.6	91	North Dakota	700	24.0	743
Florida	15,345	415.4	14,246	Ohio.	17,704	988.6	39,542
Georgia	8,720	518.1	17,065	Oklahoma	3,942	168.6	5,664
Hawaii	911	14.8	462	Oregon	5,616	202.7	8,271
Idaho	1,669	67.1	2,845	Pennsylvania	16,762	798.3	30,576
Illinois	17,312	852.6	34,518	Rhode Island	2,256	68.6	2,376
Indiana	9,262	639.2	25,143	South Carolina	4,431	334.7	11,449
Iowa.	3,724	244.8	8,583	South Dakota	906	46.7	1,445
Kansas	3,229	191.6	7,015	Tennessee.	7,093	475.6	15,998
Kentucky	4,209	293.7	10,576	Texas	21,409	966.4	38,737
Louisiana	3,463	161.4	6,435	Utah.	2,917	122.5	4,322
Maine	1,878	79.6	2,797	Vermont	1,208	45.2	1,749
Maryland.	3,910	158.8	6,900	Virginia	5,838	360.2	12,916
Massachusetts	9,168	397.6	19,874	Washington	7,584	315.1	13,765
Michigan	15,550	819.2	37,796	West Virginia	1,453	74.2	2,675
Minnesota	8,095	377.7	14,987	Wisconsin	9,904	572.2	21,370
Mississippi	2,843	220.0	5,984	Wyoming	553	9.7	318

[1] Covers full- and part-time employees who are on the payroll in the pay period including March 12.

Source: U.S. Census Bureau, *County Business Patterns*, annual. See also <http://www.census.gov/prod/2002pubs/00cbp/cbp00-1.pdf> (issued May 2002).

No. 957. Manufactures—Summary by Selected Industry: 2000

[16,681 represents 16,681,000. Based on the Annual Survey of Manufactures; see Appendix III]

Industry based on shipments	NAICS code [1]	All employees [2]			Production workers[2] (1,000)	Value added by manufactures [3] (mil. dol.)	Value of shipments [4] (mil. dol.)
		Number (1,000)	Payroll				
			Total (mil. dol.)	Per employee (dol.)			
Manufacturing, total	31-33	16,681	618,217	37,060	11,959	2,002,649	4,217,852
Food	311	1,508	42,671	28,303	1,150	183,482	434,261
Grain and oilseed milling	3112	57	2,389	41,637	43	17,752	44,893
Fruit and vegetable preserving and specialty food.	3114	181	5,135	28,401	154	25,898	50,347
Dairy product	3115	133	4,593	34,493	88	19,579	60,067
Meat product	3116	486	11,503	23,675	420	35,116	118,916
Bakeries and tortilla.	3118	320	8,938	27,921	198	30,953	47,779
Other food.	3119	155	4,784	30,906	114	29,871	54,155
Beverage and tobacco product	312	174	7,108	40,795	94	71,763	112,055
Beverage	3121	146	5,558	38,047	75	30,028	63,418
Tobacco	3122	28	1,550	55,060	20	41,736	48,638
Textile mills	313	337	9,200	27,303	286	21,429	51,770
Textile product mills	314	231	5,441	23,503	189	13,797	33,880
Apparel	315	526	10,374	19,723	423	28,210	60,215
Cut and sew apparel	3152	394	7,595	19,299	313	22,300	48,021
Leather and allied product	316	69	1,656	23,877	55	4,510	9,610
Wood product	321	585	16,136	27,581	487	36,093	93,767
Sawmills and wood preservation	3211	129	3,648	28,385	109	8,340	28,124
Other wood product.	3219	336	8,828	26,246	278	19,279	44,374
Paper.	322	552	22,819	41,372	427	78,166	166,099
Pulp, paper, and paperboard mills	3221	182	9,570	52,605	143	40,735	78,515
Converted paper product	3222	370	13,249	35,843	284	37,432	87,584
Printing and related support activities.	323	830	28,060	33,792	597	63,446	104,614
Printing and related support activities	3231	830	28,060	33,792	597	63,446	104,614
Petroleum and coal products	324	101	5,619	55,524	67	45,748	235,105
Petroleum and coal products.	3241	101	5,619	55,524	67	45,748	235,105
Chemical	325	890	43,711	49,131	508	235,614	451,580
Basic chemical	3251	193	10,644	55,218	109	47,671	117,734
Resin, syn rubber, and artif. & syn. fibers	3252	107	5,566	51,897	74	26,256	69,514
Pharmaceutical and medicine	3254	241	13,017	54,079	115	85,231	120,725
Soap, cleaning compound, and toilet preparation .	3256	120	4,532	37,861	75	33,271	55,783
Other chemical product	3259	118	5,103	43,347	71	20,661	39,944
Plastics and rubber products	326	1,088	34,091	31,325	862	92,333	179,295
Plastics product	3261	877	26,576	30,308	694	73,349	142,932
Rubber product	3262	211	7,516	35,541	169	18,984	36,362
Nonmetallic mineral product.	327	522	18,533	35,485	408	55,722	97,484
Cement and concrete product	3273	221	7,739	35,008	167	22,591	42,493
Primary metal	331	578	24,122	41,731	460	66,095	157,056
Iron and steel mills and ferroalloy.	3311	144	7,620	52,883	113	21,635	53,946
Alumina and aluminum production and processing	3313	82	3,295	40,263	64	11,167	31,663
Fabricated metal product	332	1,821	62,570	34,368	1,379	149,449	269,181
Architectural and structural metals	3323	418	13,604	32,549	308	32,245	63,885
Machine shops, turned product & screw, nut, bolt .	3327	430	15,309	35,621	335	31,292	47,731
Other fabricated metal product	3329	324	11,717	36,216	235	30,057	52,560
Machinery	333	1,403	56,028	39,948	920	148,798	295,754
Agriculture, construction, and mining machinery . .	3331	195	7,353	37,618	135	20,833	50,869
Industrial machinery	3332	198	8,844	44,560	114	25,123	46,474
Metalworking machinery	3335	235	10,012	42,514	170	19,071	30,638
Engine, turbine, and power transmission equipment	3336	114	5,039	44,233	76	16,807	35,840
Other general-purpose machinery	3339	350	13,888	39,681	217	33,529	68,611
Computer and electronic product.	334	1,644	80,289	48,826	848	291,125	513,038
Computer and peripheral equipment.	3341	190	10,378	54,533	74	43,380	110,028
Communications equipment	3342	291	16,591	56,991	128	66,813	119,329
Semiconductor and other electronic component . .	3344	621	26,663	42,941	398	111,625	168,455
Navigational, measuring, medical, control instr.. . .	3345	469	24,105	51,353	197	61,439	97,199
Electrical equipment, appliance, and component . . .	335	593	20,672	34,867	431	62,991	124,865
Electrical equipment	3353	196	7,079	36,039	135	19,110	36,265
Other electrical equipment and component	3359	221	7,904	35,771	159	26,210	52,135
Transportation equipment	336	1,839	86,877	47,234	1,349	240,989	638,700
Motor vehicle	3361	231	14,559	63,155	201	61,680	239,396
Motor vehicle parts	3363	803	35,280	43,932	644	85,458	204,765
Aerospace product and parts	3364	445	24,697	55,515	230	64,863	126,620
Furniture and related product	337	642	17,581	27,366	515	42,267	75,510
Miscellaneous	339	747	24,661	33,002	501	70,621	114,013
Medical equipment and supplies	3391	307	11,675	38,027	192	37,487	53,019
Other miscellaneous	3399	440	12,986	29,498	310	33,135	60,994

[1] North American Industry Classification System, 1997; see Text, Section 15, Business. [2] Includes employment and payroll at administrative offices and auxiliary units. All employees represents the average of production workers plus all other employees for the payroll period ended nearest the 12th of March. Production workers represents the average of the employment for the payroll periods ended nearest the 12th of March, May, August, and November. [3] Adjusted value added; takes into account (a) value added by merchandising operations (that is, difference between the sales value and cost of merchandise sold without further manufacture, processing, or assembly), plus (b) net change in finished goods and work-in-process inventories between beginning and end of year. [4] Includes extensive and unmeasurable duplication from shipments between establishments in the same industry classification.

Source: U.S. Census Bureau, *Annual Survey of Manufactures, Statistics for Industry Groups and Industries*, Series M00(AS)-1. See also <http://www.census.gov/prod/2002pubs/m00as-1.pdf> (issued February 2002).

Manufactures   613

[16,681 represents 16,681,000. Sum of state totals may not add to U.S. total because U.S. and state figures were independently derived]

State	All employees [1]			Production workers [1]		Value added by manufactures [2]		Value of ship-ments [3] (mil. dol.)
		Payroll					Per production worker (dol.)	
	Number (1,000)	Total (mil. dol.)	Per employee (dol.)	Total (1,000)	Wages (mil. dol.)	Total (mil. dol.)		
United States	**16,681**	**618,217**	**37,060**	**11,959**	**363,272**	**2,002,649**	**167,456**	**4,217,852**
Alabama.	337	10,479	31,131	266	7,119	29,998	112,973	70,290
Alaska	13	391	30,932	11	291	1,169	110,104	4,034
Arizona.	201	7,730	38,507	124	3,384	29,259	236,268	47,244
Arkansas	235	6,531	27,753	191	4,666	21,329	111,397	47,747
California	1,846	72,310	39,166	1,212	34,334	242,667	200,271	446,873
Colorado.	171	6,816	39,894	112	3,362	20,206	180,575	39,372
Connecticut.	238	10,675	44,848	145	5,012	27,536	189,748	46,604
Delaware	41	1,612	39,618	31	1,051	6,021	195,732	17,115
District of Columbia	3	118	40,449	2	70	98	46,904	210
Florida	426	14,145	33,193	286	7,244	41,919	146,602	80,966
Georgia	514	16,480	32,039	402	11,044	61,169	152,047	134,697
Hawaii	15	420	28,841	10	234	1,353	141,218	3,732
Idaho	65	2,806	43,200	48	1,556	14,229	297,188	22,329
Illinois	868	33,650	38,784	605	19,015	102,040	168,544	214,315
Indiana.	638	24,608	38,551	486	16,406	78,202	160,784	162,577
Iowa	248	8,518	34,301	188	5,511	31,002	165,303	66,302
Kansas.	196	6,990	35,606	144	4,400	20,869	144,965	54,549
Kentucky	293	10,500	35,825	226	7,045	32,795	145,038	90,148
Louisiana	163	6,299	38,665	121	4,204	28,258	234,191	95,345
Maine.	80	2,926	36,675	60	1,847	8,680	143,595	16,805
Maryland	167	7,049	42,133	107	3,578	18,455	172,240	36,490
Massachusetts.	389	16,845	43,285	239	7,868	48,638	203,332	85,688
Michigan.	810	36,758	45,384	616	25,361	96,411	156,632	228,923
Minnesota.	390	14,927	38,257	262	8,091	43,007	163,865	86,803
Mississippi	215	5,863	27,291	171	4,054	17,893	104,546	40,994
Missouri	362	12,575	34,693	266	7,743	41,083	154,262	90,261
Montana.	21	644	30,068	16	448	1,687	105,646	5,628
Nebraska	110	3,448	31,247	87	2,393	12,377	142,232	30,969
Nevada	40	1,370	34,297	28	785	4,529	162,953	7,953
New Hampshire	101	3,902	38,534	71	2,230	10,350	145,021	19,641
New Jersey	391	16,009	40,984	264	8,384	52,185	197,787	101,632
New Mexico	37	1,169	31,930	27	761	10,176	377,824	15,185
New York	738	27,157	36,788	511	14,960	85,467	167,289	155,355
North Carolina.	744	22,955	30,852	578	14,790	92,463	160,020	178,017
North Dakota.	24	721	30,181	17	429	2,419	138,692	5,975
Ohio	986	38,663	39,220	734	25,435	117,972	160,737	258,645
Oklahoma.	172	5,590	32,421	128	3,595	18,198	141,723	44,480
Oregon.	205	7,330	35,669	152	4,573	26,838	177,056	49,712
Pennsylvania.	795	29,154	36,679	572	17,760	92,512	161,716	187,906
Rhode Island.	74	2,469	33,341	50	1,326	6,223	123,786	11,681
South Carolina.	331	11,071	33,477	256	7,233	35,324	137,758	78,033
South Dakota	42	1,179	28,126	33	723	5,308	161,355	12,144
Tennessee	468	15,324	32,726	360	9,976	47,651	132,456	104,201
Texas.	979	36,991	37,783	673	19,897	134,088	199,181	344,998
Utah	126	4,203	33,378	86	2,390	13,174	154,006	27,598
Vermont	44	1,646	37,672	30	828	5,140	169,846	9,394
Virginia.	352	12,014	34,152	263	7,370	53,191	202,262	96,067
Washington.	322	13,316	41,323	206	7,320	37,443	181,801	89,336
West Virginia.	70	2,530	36,388	52	1,687	8,503	162,355	17,316
Wisconsin.	575	21,013	36,549	426	13,256	63,684	149,641	131,755
Wyoming	10	332	32,445	8	232	1,462	185,706	3,818

[1] Includes employment and payroll at administrative offices and auxiliary units. All employees represents the average of production workers plus all other employees for the payroll period ended nearest the 12th of March. Production workers represents the average of the employment for the payroll periods ended nearest the 12th of March, May, August, and November.   [2] Adjusted value added; takes into account (a) value added by merchandising operations (that is, difference between the sales value and cost of merchandise sold without further manufacture, processing, or assembly), plus (b) net change in finished goods and work-in-process inventories between beginning and end of year.   [3] Includes extensive and unmeasurable duplication from shipments between establishments in the same industry classification.

Source: U.S. Census Bureau, *Annual Survey of Manufactures, Geographic Area Statistics*, Series M00(AS)-3. See also <http://www.census.gov/prod/2002pubs/m00as-3.pdf> (issued March 2002).

No. 959. Manufacturers' E-Commerce Shipments by Industry: 1999 and 2000

[In millions of dollars (4,031,882 represents $4,031,882,000,000), except percent. Based on the Annual Survey of Manufactures; subject to sampling variability. E-commerce is the value of goods and services sold over computer-mediated networks (open or proprietary). Online purchases are the cost of materials purchased over computer-mediated networks]

Industry	NAICS code [1]	1999				2000			
		Ship-ments, total (mil. dol)	E-commerce			Ship-ments, total (mil.dol)	E-commerce		
			Ship-ments, total (mil.dol)	Percent of total ship-ments	Percent distri-bution		Ship-ments, total (mil.dol)	Percent of total ship-ments	Percent distri-bution
Manufacturing, total	31-33	4,031,882	729,563	18.1	100.0	4,217,852	776,942	18.4	100.0
Food products	311	426,000	45,757	10.7	6.3	434,261	54,837	12.6	7.1
Beverage and tobacco	312	106,920	35,138	32.9	4.8	112,055	42,862	38.3	5.5
Textile mills	313	54,306	6,016	11.1	0.8	51,770	5,214	10.0	0.7
Textile product mills	314	32,689	7,284	22.3	1.0	33,880	5,800	17.1	0.7
Apparel	315	62,305	16,485	26.5	2.3	60,215	12,063	20.0	1.6
Leather and allied products	316	9,653	2,336	24.2	0.3	9,610	2,122	22.1	0.3
Wood products	321	97,311	4,275	4.4	0.6	93,767	5,957	6.4	0.8
Paper	322	156,915	15,312	9.8	2.1	166,099	20,617	12.4	2.7
Printing and related support activities.	323	101,536	7,319	7.2	1.0	104,614	5,966	5.7	0.8
Petroleum and coal products . . .	324	162,620	19,881	12.2	2.7	235,105	24,770	10.5	3.2
Chemicals	325	420,320	58,827	14.0	8.1	451,580	52,974	11.7	6.8
Plastics and rubber products . . .	326	171,885	27,795	16.2	3.8	179,295	28,400	15.8	3.7
Nonmetallic mineral products. . .	327	96,153	7,282	7.6	1.0	97,484	8,174	8.4	1.1
Primary metals	331	156,647	15,470	9.9	2.1	157,056	15,403	9.8	2.0
Fabricated metal products.	332	257,072	29,509	11.5	4.0	269,181	25,798	9.6	3.3
Machinery	333	276,901	48,452	17.5	6.6	295,754	40,441	13.7	5.2
Computer and electronic products	334	467,059	65,336	14.0	9.0	513,038	77,933	15.2	10.0
Electrical equipment, appliances, and components . .	335	118,313	27,067	22.9	3.7	124,865	30,003	24.0	3.9
Transportation equipment	336	676,328	268,667	39.7	36.8	638,700	294,408	46.1	37.9
Furniture and related products. . .	337	72,659	7,623	10.5	1.0	75,510	8,400	11.1	1.1
Miscellaneous.	339	108,290	13,732	12.7	1.9	114,013	14,800	13.0	1.9

[1] North American Industry Classification System, 1997; see text, Section 15, Business Enterprise.

Source: U.S. Census Bureau, Internet site <http://www.census.gov/eos/www/papers/estatstext.pdf> and <http://www.census.gov/eos/www/papers/estatstables.pdf> (released 18 March 2002).

No. 960. Manufacturing Employer Costs for Employee Compensation Per Hour Worked: 1990 to 2002

[As of March, for private industry workers. Based on a sample of establishments; see source for details. See also Table 618, Section 12, Labor Force, Employment, and Earnings]

Compensation component	Cost (dol.)					Percent distribution				
	1990	1995	2000	2001	2002	1990	1995	2000	2001	2002
Total compensation . . .	17.33	20.47	23.41	24.30	25.20	100.0	100.0	100.0	100.0	100.0
Wages and salaries	11.86	13.72	16.01	16.66	17.19	68.4	67.0	68.4	68.6	68.2
Total benefits.	5.47	6.74	7.40	7.64	8.01	31.6	32.9	31.6	31.4	31.8
Paid leave	1.31	1.54	1.74	1.85	1.91	7.6	7.5	7.4	7.6	7.6
Vacation.	0.67	0.80	0.86	0.92	0.97	3.9	3.9	3.7	3.8	3.8
Holiday	0.48	0.57	0.65	0.68	0.70	2.8	2.8	2.8	2.8	2.8
Sick	0.12	0.12	0.13	0.15	0.14	0.7	0.6	0.6	0.6	0.6
Other	0.05	0.05	0.10	0.10	0.10	0.3	0.2	0.4	0.4	0.4
Supplemental pay	0.65	0.80	1.04	1.09	1.13	3.8	3.9	4.4	4.5	4.5
Premium pay	0.34	0.40	0.58	0.58	0.56	2.0	2.0	2.5	2.4	2.2
Nonproduction bonuses . .	0.22	0.30	0.36	0.41	0.46	1.3	1.5	1.5	1.7	1.8
Shift pay	0.09	0.09	0.10	0.11	0.11	0.5	0.4	0.4	0.5	0.4
Insurance	1.37	1.72	1.85	1.93	2.11	7.9	8.4	7.9	7.9	8.4
Health insurance	(NA)	1.58	1.69	1.75	1.92	(NA)	7.7	7.2	7.2	7.6
Retirement and savings . . .	0.56	0.75	0.75	0.75	0.74	3.2	3.7	3.2	3.1	2.9
Defined benefit	(NA)	(NA)	0.34	0.29	0.30	(NA)	(NA)	1.5	1.2	1.2
Defined contributions . . .	(NA)	(NA)	0.41	0.46	0.44	(NA)	(NA)	1.8	1.9	1.7
Legally required	1.54	1.86	1.92	1.95	2.05	8.9	9.1	8.2	8.0	8.1
Social Security	1.02	1.21	1.38	1.42	1.48	5.9	5.9	5.9	5.8	5.9
Federal unemployment . .	0.03	0.03	0.03	0.03	0.03	0.2	0.1	0.1	0.1	0.1
State unemployment . . .	0.12	0.14	0.11	0.10	0.11	0.7	0.7	0.5	0.4	0.4
Workers compensation . .	0.36	0.48	0.40	0.40	0.43	2.1	2.3	1.7	1.6	1.7
Other benefits [1]	0.04	0.09	0.09	0.07	0.07	0.2	0.4	0.4	0.3	0.3

NA Not available.   [1] Includes severance pay, and supplemental unemployment benefits.

Source: U.S. Bureau of Labor Statistics, *Employer Costs for Employee Compensation Historical Listing, annual, 1986-2001,* and Internet site at <ftp://ftp.bls.gov/pub/special.requests/ocwc/ect/ececrlse.pdf> and <ftp://ftp.bls.gov/pub/special.requests/ocwc/ect/ecechist.pdf> (issued 19 June 2002).

Manufactures 615

No. 961. Average Hourly Earnings of Production Workers in Manufacturing Industries by State: 1980 to 2001

[In dollars]

State	1980	1990	1995	2000	2001	State	1980	1990	1995	2000	2001
United States .	7.27	10.83	12.37	14.38	14.84	Missouri	7.26	10.74	12.17	14.34	14.81
Alabama	6.49	9.39	11.14	12.96	13.30	Montana	8.78	11.51	12.94	14.34	14.68
Alaska	10.22	12.46	11.00	12.46	13.27	Nebraska	7.38	9.66	11.19	12.94	13.39
Arizona	7.29	10.21	11.16	12.78	13.18	Nevada	7.72	11.05	12.62	13.85	14.11
Arkansas	5.71	8.51	10.05	11.97	12.39	New Hampshire . . .	5.87	10.83	11.94	13.39	13.77
California	7.70	11.48	12.55	14.26	14.72	New Jersey	7.31	11.76	13.56	15.47	15.88
Colorado	7.63	10.94	12.51	14.82	15.37	New Mexico	5.79	9.04	10.68	13.26	14.09
Connecticut	7.08	11.53	13.71	15.70	16.07	New York	7.18	11.11	12.50	14.24	14.76
Delaware	7.58	12.39	14.20	16.53	16.63	North Carolina	5.37	8.79	10.56	12.80	13.29
Dist. of Columbia [1] .	8.46	12.51	13.66	(NA)	(NA)	North Dakota	6.56	9.27	10.75	12.64	12.69
Florida	5.98	8.98	10.18	12.28	12.78	Ohio	8.57	12.64	14.42	16.71	17.13
Georgia	5.77	9.17	10.71	12.99	13.05	Oklahoma	7.36	10.73	11.52	13.17	12.95
Hawaii	6.83	10.99	12.82	13.59	14.19	Oregon	8.65	11.15	12.75	15.08	15.72
Idaho	7.55	10.60	11.46	14.17	15.28	Pennsylvania	7.59	11.04	12.81	14.60	14.85
Illinois	8.02	11.44	12.64	14.36	14.55	Rhode Island	5.59	9.45	10.62	12.17	12.20
Indiana	8.49	12.03	13.91	15.83	16.20	South Carolina	5.59	8.84	10.16	10.97	11.19
Iowa	8.67	11.27	12.73	14.66	14.92	South Dakota	6.50	8.48	9.36	10.70	11.45
Kansas	7.37	10.94	12.39	14.98	15.30	Tennessee	6.08	9.55	10.78	12.92	13.37
Kentucky	7.34	10.70	12.22	14.83	15.34	Texas	7.15	10.47	11.47	12.38	12.57
Louisiana	7.74	11.61	13.43	15.56	15.90	Utah	7.02	10.32	11.62	13.68	13.88
Maine	6.00	10.59	12.39	14.28	15.17	Vermont	6.14	10.52	12.21	14.23	14.32
Maryland	7.61	11.57	13.49	14.98	15.35	Virginia	6.22	10.07	11.72	13.82	14.28
Massachusetts	6.51	11.39	12.79	14.66	15.31	Washington	(NA)	12.61	14.73	16.75	17.59
Michigan	9.52	13.86	16.31	19.26	19.71	West Virginia	8.08	11.53	12.64	14.61	14.95
Minnesota	7.61	11.23	12.79	14.99	15.36	Wisconsin	8.03	11.11	12.76	14.85	15.25
Mississippi	5.44	8.37	9.76	11.64	12.14	Wyoming	7.01	10.83	11.96	16.18	16.70

NA Not available.   [1] Washington PMSA (primary metropolitan statistical area).

Source: U.S. Bureau of Labor Statistics, *Employment and Earnings,* May 2002 issue and earlier issues.

No. 962. Manufacturing Full-Time Equivalent Employees and Wages by Industry: 1990 to 2000

Industry	SIC code	Full-time equivalent (FTE) employees (1,000)				Wage and salary accruals per FTE worker (dol.)			
		1990	1995	1999	2000	1990	1995	1999	2000
Manufacturing, total	**(X)**	18,679	18,190	18,273	18,163	30,054	35,779	42,832	45,704
Durable goods	(X)	10,959	10,561	11,003	11,010	31,658	37,660	44,850	47,974
Lumber & wood products	24	725	772	843	827	21,712	25,110	29,009	30,018
Furniture & fixtures	25	493	502	539	547	21,404	25,048	29,653	30,707
Stone, clay, & glass products	32	550	530	562	572	28,342	33,283	38,616	40,685
Primary metal industries	33	749	697	692	694	33,637	40,067	44,579	45,473
Fabricated metal products	34	1,398	1,421	1,508	1,523	28,248	32,927	37,140	38,322
Industrial machinery & equipment . .	35	2,053	2,051	2,103	2,083	34,030	40,063	49,666	54,831
Electronic, other electric equipment.	36	1,664	1,607	1,647	1,699	31,055	38,922	50,370	57,325
Motor vehicles & equipment	371	816	961	1,016	1,014	38,202	46,658	53,877	55,285
Other transportation equipment . . .	372-9	1,171	809	866	828	37,348	44,611	50,084	51,896
Instruments & related products . . .	38	975	827	836	833	35,896	44,654	55,006	59,059
Miscel. manufacturing industries . . .	39	365	384	391	390	24,468	28,219	33,217	34,723
Nondurable goods.	(X)	7,720	7,629	7,270	7,153	27,777	33,176	39,776	42,211
Food & kindred products	20	1,596	1,642	1,657	1,660	25,909	30,139	34,150	36,018
Tobacco products	21	50	41	36	34	40,860	53,854	60,222	68,353
Textile mill products	22	682	654	552	527	20,217	23,985	28,451	29,440
Apparel & other textile products . . .	23	1,001	919	675	598	16,174	18,800	23,332	25,254
Paper & allied products	26	687	685	661	648	33,514	39,458	44,900	46,519
Printing & publishing	27	1,474	1,450	1,465	1,463	28,888	34,539	41,080	43,258
Chemicals & allied products	28	1,071	1,027	1,023	1,025	40,949	51,054	62,953	68,239
Petroleum & coal products	29	155	142	130	125	44,974	54,739	63,738	64,512
Rubber & misc. plastics products . .	30	872	963	995	1,002	25,500	29,867	34,462	35,590
Leather & leather products	31	132	106	76	71	18,189	22,321	27,961	29,620

X Not applicable.

Source: U.S. Bureau of Economic Analysis, *National Income and Product Accounts, 1929-97;* and *Survey of Current Business,* November 2001. See also <http://www.bea.doc.gov/bea/dn2/gpo.htm>.

616 Manufactures

No. 963. Manufacturers' Shipments, Inventories, and New Orders: 1992 to 2001

[In billions of dollars (2,904 represents $2,904,000,000,000), except ratio. Based on a sample survey; for methodology, see publication cited below. These data are now on a NAICS (North American Industry Classification System) basis and not comparable to previous data, which were based on the Standard Industrial Classification system]

Year	Shipments	Inventories (Dec. 31)[1]	Ratio of inventories to ship-ments[2]	New orders (Dec. 31)	Unfilled orders (Dec. 31)
1992	2,904	370	1.57	(NA)	454
1993	3,020	371	1.51	2,996	430
1994	3,238	391	1.48	3,247	438
1995	3,480	415	1.47	3,496	454
1996	3,597	421	1.44	3,638	495
1997	3,835	433	1.39	3,859	519
1998	3,900	439	1.38	3,885	504
1999	4,032	453	1.38	4,052	524
2000	4,218	474	1.38	4,258	565
2001	3,971	436	1.35	3,921	514

NA Not available.   [1] Inventories are stated at current cost.   [2] Ratio based on December seasonally adjusted data.

Source: U.S. Census Bureau, *Current Industrial Reports, Manufacturers' Shipments, Inventories, and Orders: 1992-2001*, Series M3-1(01). See also <http://www.census.gov/prod/2002pubs/m3-01.pdf> (released June 2002).

No. 964. Ratios of Manufacturers' Inventories to Shipments and Unfilled Orders to Shipments by Industry Group: 1993 to 2001

[Based on a sample survey; for methodology, see publication cited below. These data are now on a NAICS (North American Industry Classification System) basis and not comparable to previous data, which were based on the Standard Industrial Classification system]

Industry	1993	1994	1995	1996	1997	1998	1999	2000	2001
INVENTORIES TO SHIPMENTS RATIO									
All manufacturing industries	**1.51**	**1.48**	**1.47**	**1.44**	**1.39**	**1.38**	**1.38**	**1.38**	**1.35**
Durable goods	1.79	1.73	1.69	1.65	1.57	1.56	1.53	1.57	1.56
Wood products	1.41	1.31	1.34	1.28	1.26	1.26	1.26	1.31	1.25
Nonmetallic mineral products	1.40	1.33	1.35	1.29	1.25	1.17	1.18	1.22	1.20
Primary metals	1.71	1.70	1.61	1.66	1.61	1.59	1.69	1.67	1.68
Fabricated metals	1.78	1.75	1.72	1.69	1.61	1.56	1.56	1.55	1.50
Machinery	2.22	2.18	2.18	2.12	2.04	2.01	2.06	2.04	2.00
Computers and electronic products	1.84	1.76	1.74	1.53	1.51	1.41	1.42	1.54	1.53
Electrical equipment, appliances, and components	1.71	1.73	1.68	1.59	1.51	1.45	1.42	1.43	1.37
Transportation equipment	1.71	1.58	1.50	1.59	1.44	1.57	1.41	1.47	1.50
Furniture and related products	1.63	1.63	1.57	1.49	1.44	1.34	1.35	1.34	1.23
Miscellaneous products	1.96	1.98	2.00	2.02	1.92	1.85	1.89	1.89	1.82
Nondurable goods	1.20	1.20	1.20	1.17	1.16	1.14	1.17	1.13	1.09
Food products	0.86	0.87	0.89	0.88	0.85	0.82	0.86	0.86	0.83
Beverages and tobacco products	1.72	1.58	1.55	1.58	1.71	1.63	1.55	1.50	1.47
Textile mills	1.48	1.47	1.53	1.45	1.41	1.45	1.52	1.48	1.49
Textile product mills	1.70	1.73	1.76	1.72	1.76	1.63	1.62	1.75	1.55
Apparel	1.92	1.94	1.93	1.64	1.70	1.75	1.89	1.92	1.70
Leather and allied products	1.73	1.97	2.03	2.05	1.98	2.05	2.18	2.14	2.10
Paper products	1.27	1.20	1.20	1.20	1.21	1.15	1.16	1.11	1.16
Printing	0.92	0.96	0.97	0.89	0.88	0.80	0.81	0.79	0.74
Petroleum and coal products	0.87	0.95	0.91	0.88	0.82	0.84	0.89	0.70	0.64
Basic chemicals	1.37	1.33	1.34	1.35	1.31	1.31	1.38	1.36	1.36
Plastics and rubber products	1.26	1.28	1.27	1.27	1.22	1.19	1.20	1.21	1.15
UNFILLED ORDERS TO SHIPMENTS RATIO									
All manufacturing industries	**1.72**	**1.64**	**1.58**	**1.67**	**1.64**	**1.57**	**1.58**	**1.62**	**1.57**
Durable goods	3.24	3.01	2.90	3.03	2.93	2.74	2.74	2.88	2.87
Primary metals	1.97	2.04	1.75	1.81	1.94	1.56	1.69	1.45	1.47
Fabricated metals	1.87	1.87	1.83	1.98	2.08	1.99	2.01	2.01	1.92
Machinery	2.55	2.67	2.70	2.63	2.61	2.40	2.50	2.48	2.30
Computers and electronic products	3.73	3.38	3.25	2.98	2.81	2.93	3.56	3.59	3.64
Electrical equipment, appliances, and components	1.75	1.79	1.74	1.61	1.66	1.56	1.78	1.74	1.52
Transportation equipment	6.18	5.47	5.32	6.07	5.58	5.00	4.25	4.90	5.11
Furniture and related products	1.23	1.17	1.02	1.05	1.38	1.19	1.27	1.14	1.09
Miscellaneous products	0.27	0.30	0.31	0.39	0.44	0.46	0.49	0.63	0.43

Source: U.S. Census Bureau, *Current Industrial Reports, Manufacturers' Shipments, Inventories, and Orders: 1992-2001*, Series M3-1(00). See also <http://www.census.gov/prod/2002pubs/m3-01.pdf> (released June 2002).

No. 965. Value of Manufacturers' Shipments, Inventories, and New Orders by Industry: 1996 to 2001

[In millions of dollars (3,597,188 represents $3,597,188,000,000). Based on a sample survey; for methodology, see publication cited below. These data are now on a NAICS (North American Industry Classification System) basis and not comparable to previous data, which were based on the Standard Industrial Classification system]

Industry	1996	1997	1998	1999	2000	2001
SHIPMENTS						
All manufacturing industries	3,597,188	3,834,699	3,899,813	4,031,887	4,217,854	3,971,431
Durable goods	1,978,597	2,147,384	2,231,588	2,326,736	2,379,369	2,173,843
Wood products	81,827	88,470	91,175	97,311	93,767	88,342
Nonmetallic mineral products	81,308	86,465	92,501	96,153	97,484	90,975
Primary metals	157,638	168,118	166,109	156,648	157,057	136,334
Fabricated metals	222,995	242,812	253,720	257,071	269,181	253,528
Machinery	257,459	270,687	280,651	276,904	295,753	283,860
Computers and electronic products	399,516	439,380	443,768	467,059	513,038	418,349
Electrical equipment, appliances, and components	105,283	112,116	116,024	118,313	124,866	118,736
Transportation equipment	516,030	575,307	612,882	676,328	638,699	598,694
Furniture and related products	61,156	64,299	69,616	72,659	75,511	69,216
Miscellaneous products	95,385	99,730	105,142	108,290	114,013	115,809
Nondurable goods	1,618,591	1,687,315	1,668,225	1,705,151	1,838,485	1,797,588
Food products	404,173	421,737	428,479	426,001	434,261	453,218
Beverages and tobacco products	94,033	96,971	102,359	106,920	112,056	116,788
Textile mills	59,796	58,707	57,416	54,306	51,770	44,932
Textile product mills	28,515	31,052	31,137	32,689	33,880	34,484
Apparel	64,237	68,018	64,932	62,305	60,215	57,678
Leather and allied products	10,032	10,877	10,186	9,653	9,610	8,685
Paper products	152,860	150,296	154,984	156,915	166,099	153,378
Printing	95,072	97,485	100,297	101,536	104,614	98,760
Petroleum and coal products	174,181	177,394	137,957	162,620	235,105	220,959
Basic chemicals	385,919	415,617	416,742	420,321	451,580	434,150
Plastics and rubber products	149,773	159,161	163,736	171,885	179,295	174,556
INVENTORIES (Dec. 31)						
All manufacturing industries	420,680	433,451	438,845	452,803	474,032	436,172
Durable goods	265,170	273,330	282,698	288,362	303,655	274,829
Wood products	8,879	9,441	9,684	10,289	10,295	9,203
Nonmetallic mineral products	8,560	8,840	8,877	9,279	9,748	8,980
Primary metals	21,945	22,728	22,305	22,309	22,171	19,308
Fabricated metals	30,611	31,776	32,215	32,800	34,020	31,055
Machinery	43,869	44,490	45,728	46,050	48,745	45,764
Computers and electronic products	48,997	53,045	50,066	52,838	63,285	51,133
Electrical equipment, appliances, and components	13,342	13,530	13,503	13,510	14,367	13,140
Transportation equipment	65,927	66,414	77,014	76,781	75,384	72,212
Furniture and related products	7,426	7,527	7,599	7,983	8,242	6,987
Miscellaneous products	15,614	15,539	15,707	16,523	17,398	17,047
Nondurable goods	155,510	160,121	156,147	164,441	170,377	161,343
Food products	29,751	30,152	29,419	30,650	31,312	31,375
Beverages and tobacco products	12,731	14,188	14,294	14,167	14,356	14,581
Textile mills	6,972	6,640	6,684	6,648	6,149	5,400
Textile product mills	3,898	4,331	4,024	4,219	4,741	4,275
Apparel	8,397	9,267	9,114	9,454	9,271	7,864
Leather and allied products	1,640	1,718	1,667	1,675	1,636	1,450
Paper products	15,120	15,042	14,688	15,034	15,312	14,769
Printing	6,529	6,621	6,212	6,394	6,421	5,631
Petroleum and coal products	12,087	11,492	9,102	11,375	12,802	11,060
Basic chemicals	42,782	44,691	44,943	47,806	50,485	48,469
Plastics and rubber products	15,603	15,979	16,000	17,019	17,892	16,469
NEW ORDERS						
All manufacturing industries	3,638,149	3,859,016	3,884,868	4,051,732	4,258,435	3,920,613
Durable goods	2,019,558	2,171,701	2,216,643	2,346,581	2,419,950	2,123,025
Wood products	81,827	88,470	91,175	97,311	93,767	88,342
Paper products	81,308	86,465	92,501	96,153	97,484	90,975
Primary metals	158,066	171,407	160,743	156,968	154,176	134,090
Fabricated metals	227,447	247,839	253,847	258,116	271,200	249,161
Machinery	258,405	272,998	278,100	278,277	299,105	277,308
Computers and electronic products	398,053	442,816	449,158	496,706	528,301	392,515
Electrical equipment, appliances, and components	104,837	113,411	115,711	120,774	125,476	115,863
Transportation equipment	552,024	581,780	600,205	660,215	659,847	592,456
Furniture and related products	61,499	66,256	69,098	73,393	74,976	68,357
Miscellaneous products	96,092	100,259	106,105	108,668	115,618	113,958
Nondurable goods	1,618,591	1,687,315	1,668,225	1,705,151	1,838,485	1,797,588

Source: U.S. Census Bureau, *Current Industrial Reports, Manufacturers' Shipments, Inventories, and Orders: 1992-2001*, Series M3-1(00). See also <http://www.census.gov/prod/2002pubs/m3-01.pdf> (released June 2002).

U.S. Census Bureau, Statistical Abstract of the United States: 2002

No. 966. Value of Manufactures' Shipments, Inventories, and New Orders by Market Grouping: 1996 to 2001

[In millions of dollars (3,597,188 represents 3,597,188,000,000). Based on a sample survey; for methodology, see publication cited below. These data are now on a NAICS (North American Industry Classification System) basis and not comparable to previous data, which were based on the Standard Industrial Classification system]

Market grouping	1996	1997	1998	1999	2000	2001
SHIPMENTS						
All manufacturing industries	**3,597,188**	**3,834,699**	**3,899,813**	**4,031,887**	**4,217,854**	**3,971,431**
Consumer goods	1,309,819	1,375,603	1,364,326	1,438,519	1,516,994	1,488,780
Consumer durable goods	345,266	377,280	385,918	426,337	405,093	381,163
Consumer nondurable goods.	964,553	998,323	978,408	1,012,182	1,111,901	1,107,617
Aircraft and parts	80,582	100,126	116,812	120,242	111,023	119,079
Defense aircraft and parts	29,693	27,472	26,938	27,719	24,417	28,102
Nondefense aircraft and parts	50,889	72,654	89,874	92,523	86,606	90,977
Construction materials and supplies	355,413	385,735	418,756	434,138	446,230	420,821
Motor vehicles and parts	387,394	421,573	439,590	498,716	471,677	423,462
Computers and related products	93,926	110,055	114,482	113,162	110,028	87,277
Information technology industries.	311,028	349,846	362,564	374,384	404,616	346,013
Nondefense capital goods	630,932	702,971	747,046	768,799	811,099	730,149
Excluding aircraft.	605,295	665,074	695,717	713,042	760,797	680,111
Defense capital goods.	73,703	76,261	74,690	70,955	66,769	72,280
Durables excluding capital goods.	1,273,962	1,368,152	1,409,852	1,486,982	1,501,501	1,371,414
INVENTORIES (Dec. 31)						
All manufacturing industries	**420,680**	**433,451**	**438,845**	**452,803**	**474,032**	**436,172**
Consumer goods	115,751	118,980	116,715	123,218	127,957	122,112
Consumer durable goods	25,212	25,251	25,137	26,307	27,295	24,708
Consumer nondurable goods.	90,539	93,729	91,578	96,911	100,662	97,404
Aircraft and parts	35,905	37,509	46,921	42,599	42,501	41,314
Defense aircraft and parts.	8,641	8,380	11,376	11,052	10,867	10,506
Nondefense aircraft and parts	27,264	29,129	35,545	31,547	31,634	30,808
Construction materials and supplies	43,275	44,877	45,617	47,510	49,120	44,839
Motor vehicles and parts	20,744	20,298	20,764	22,102	22,190	19,705
Computers and related products	8,841	10,289	8,017	7,963	8,352	6,739
Information technology industries.	41,784	46,117	43,592	44,375	51,013	41,207
Nondefense capital goods	110,904	117,932	122,415	121,653	131,254	118,137
Excluding aircraft.	90,031	95,226	94,045	96,254	105,783	93,687
Defense capital goods.	17,336	14,814	17,775	19,754	18,646	18,516
Durables excluding capital goods.	136,930	140,584	142,508	146,955	153,755	138,176
NEW ORDERS						
All manufacturing industries	**3,638,149**	**3,859,016**	**3,884,868**	**4,051,732**	**4,258,435**	**3,920,613**
Consumer goods	1,305,517	1,372,919	1,364,268	1,440,903	1,518,473	1,486,072
Consumer durable goods	340,964	374,596	385,860	428,721	406,572	378,455
Consumer nondurable goods.	964,553	998,323	978,408	1,012,182	1,111,901	1,107,617
Aircraft and parts	104,614	109,077	108,004	107,336	128,715	114,334
Defense aircraft and parts.	32,520	23,280	23,854	25,717	30,932	38,015
Nondefense aircraft and parts	72,094	85,797	84,150	81,619	97,783	76,319
Construction materials and supplies	373,536	403,860	419,330	435,034	448,383	416,316
Motor vehicles and parts	385,712	422,427	440,934	499,527	469,014	421,927
Computers and related products	95,070	107,564	115,806	114,481	107,442	86,697
Information technology industries.	310,074	352,700	365,723	389,160	415,041	332,379
Nondefense capital goods	648,797	728,362	745,600	772,703	833,709	694,633
Excluding aircraft.	607,174	676,119	698,279	728,089	771,475	659,443
Defense capital goods.	88,471	64,497	64,127	67,900	78,487	80,903
Durables excluding capital goods.	1,282,290	1,378,842	1,406,916	1,505,978	1,507,754	1,347,489

Source: U.S. Census Bureau, *Current Industrial Reports, Manufacturers' Shipments, Inventories, and Orders: 1992-2001,* Series M3-1(01). See also <http://www.census.gov/prod/2002pubs/m3-01.pdf> (released June 2002).

Manufactures   619

No. 967. Finances and Profits of Manufacturing Corporations: 1990 to 2001

[In billions of dollars (2,811 represents $2,811,000,000,000). Data exclude estimates for corporations with less than $250,000 in assets at time of sample selection. See Table 746 for individual industry data]

Item	1990	1993	1994	1995	1996	1997	1998	1999	2000	2001
Net sales.	2,811	3,014	3,256	3,528	3,758	3,920	3,949	4,149	4,548	4,308
Net operating profit	173	180	242	268	277	298	298	317	348	185
Net profit:										
Before taxes	160	118	244	274	307	331	315	355	381	82
After taxes	112	83	175	198	225	245	234	258	275	36
Cash dividends.	62	67	70	81	96	108	121	104	132	102
Net income retained in business . .	49	16	105	117	129	136	114	154	143	-67

Source: U.S. Census Bureau, *Quarterly Financial Report for Manufacturing, Mining, and Trade Corporations.*

No. 968. U.S. Exports of Manufactures—Origin of World Exports of Manufacture by Major Product and Country: 1991 to 1999

[In billions of dollars (328 represents 328,000,000,000), except percent]

Item	1991	1992	1993	1994	1995	1996	1997	1998	1999
U.S. manufactures export value	328	350	365	409	464	498	566	570	587
Machinery & transport equipment.	200	215	225	252	283	308	354	359	371
Chemicals	43	45	46	52	62	63	71	69	72
Other	85	90	94	104	119	128	141	142	144
Origin of world exports of manufactures (percent):									
United States [1]	12.9	12.6	13.1	12.7	12.4	12.8	13.8	13.7	13.7
Machinery & transport equipment	15.9	15.8	16.4	15.7	14.9	15.3	16.6	16.4	16.2
Chemicals	14.4	13.4	13.9	13.5	13.3	13.1	14.2	13.6	13.7
Other	8.5	8.3	8.7	8.5	8.6	9.1	9.7	9.8	9.8
Germany [2]	14.2	13.9	12.0	11.8	12.4	11.8	11.1	11.8	11.0
Japan	11.9	11.8	12.6	11.8	11.4	10.1	9.8	8.9	9.3
Other G-7 countries [3]	21.6	21.0	20.1	19.7	20.3	20.8	20.1	20.5	19.6
East Asian NICs [4]	8.2	8.1	8.8	8.9	9.4	9.2	9.1	8.3	8.6

[1] U.S. exports are domestic exports only.   [2] Prior to 1991, data for are for former West Germany only.   [3] Other Group of Seven (G-7) Countries: Canada, France, Italy, United Kingdom.   [4] East Asian newly industrialized countries (NICs): Hong Kong, S. Korea, Singapore, Taiwan.

Source: U.S. Dept. of Commerce, International Trade Administration, Office of Trade and Economic Analysis. Based on United Nations Commodity Trade Statistics, *Statistical Yearbook of the Republic of China (Taiwan)*, and unpublished data.

No. 969. Tobacco Products—Summary: 1990 to 2001

[**Production data are for calendar years.** Excludes cigars produced in customs bonded manufacturing warehouses]

Item	Unit	1990	1994	1995	1996	1997	1998	1999	2000	2001
PRODUCTION										
Cigarettes, total	Billions .	710	726	747	758	720	680	607	580	580
Nonfilter tip	Billions .	23	15	15	14	12	12	8	7	(NA)
Filter tip	Billions .	687	710	732	744	708	669	599	573	(NA)
Cigars	Billions .	1.9	1.9	2.1	2.4	2.3	2.8	2.9	2.8	2.8
Tobacco [1]	Mil. lb. .	142	132	131	131	134	131	133	133	131
Smoking	Mil. lb. .	16	14	12	12	11	13	15	14	13
Chewing tobacco	Mil. lb. .	73	63	63	61	58	53	51	49	47
Snuff	Mil. lb. .	53	60	60	62	64	66	67	70	71
EXPORTS										
Cigarettes	Billions .	164.3	220.2	231.1	243.9	217.0	201.3	151.4	147.9	133.9
Cigars	Billions .	72	74	94	84	86	93	84	113	120
Smoking tobacco	Billions .	0.8	0.5	0.3	0.7	0.8	1.1	1.6	0.5	5.3
IMPORTS										
Cigarettes	Billions .	1.4	3.5	3.0	2.8	3.2	4.3	8.7	11.3	14.7
Cigars	Billions .	111	146	195	320	448	582	463	497	489
Smoking tobacco	Billions .	2.9	3.9	4.2	4.2	4.3	4.3	4.3	4.2	4.0
CONSUMPTION										
Consumption per person [2] .	Lb. [3] . . .	5.6	4.9	4.7	4.7	4.5	4.5	4.3	4.2	4.1
Cigarettes	1,000 . .	3	3	3	3	2	2	2	2	2
Cigars [4]	Number.	13	12	15	18	18	18	19	19	19
EXPENDITURES										
Consumer expenditures,										
total	Bil. dol. .	43.8	47.7	48.7	50.4	52.2	57.3	72.1	77.5	(NA)
Cigarettes	Bil. dol. .	41.6	44.5	45.8	47.2	48.7	53.2	68.3	72.9	(NA)
Cigars	Bil. dol. .	0.7	0.9	1.0	1.0	1.2	1.6	1.8	1.8	(NA)
Other	Bil. dol. .	1.5	2.3	2.5	2.2	2.2	2.4	2.7	2.7	(NA)

NA Not available.   [1] Smoking and chewing tobaccos and snuff output.   [2] Based on estimated population 18 years old and over, as of July 1, including Armed Forces abroad.   [3] Unstemmed processing weight equivalent.   [4] Weighing over 3 pounds per 1,000.

Source: U.S. Dept. of Agriculture, Economic Research Service, *Tobacco Situation and Outlook*, quarterly.

No. 970. Cotton, Wool, and Manmade Fibers—Consumption by End-Use: 1990 to 2000

[14,011 represents 14,011,000,000. Represents products manufactured by U.S. mills. Excludes glass fiber]

Year	Total (mil. lb.)	Cotton Total (mil. lb.)	Cotton Percent of end-use	Wool Total (mil. lb.)	Wool Percent of end-use	Manufactured fibers Total (mil. lb.)	Manufactured fibers Percent of end-use	Artificial[1] Total (mil. lb.)	Artificial[1] Percent of end-use	Synthetic[2] Total (mil. lb.)	Synthetic[2] Percent of end-use
Total:											
1990	14,011	4,699	33.5	185	1.3	9,127	65.1	599	4.3	8,528	60.9
1995	16,815	5,508	32.8	184	1.1	11,123	66.1	540	3.2	10,583	62.9
1997	17,520	5,404	30.8	208	1.2	11,908	68.0	438	2.5	11,470	65.5
1998	17,698	5,514	31.2	170	1.0	12,014	67.9	370	2.1	11,526	65.1
1999	17,735	5,328	30.0	135	0.8	12,272	69.2	330	1.9	11,902	67.1
2000	17,148	4,938	28.8	131	0.8	12,080	70.4	303	1.8	11,776	68.7
Apparel:											
1990	5,204	2,897	55.7	118	2.3	2,189	42.1	287	5.5	1,902	36.5
1995	6,877	3,640	52.9	132	1.9	3,106	45.2	306	4.4	2,800	40.7
1997	7,038	3,541	49.8	153	2.2	3,344	47.9	247	3.6	3,097	44.4
1998	6,526	3,329	51.0	113	1.7	3,083	47.3	208	3.2	2,875	44.1
1999	6,417	3,262	50.8	89	1.4	3,065	47.8	172	2.7	2,894	45.1
2000	6,057	3,007	49.6	79	1.3	2,971	49.1	150	2.5	2,822	46.6
Home textiles:											
1990	2,235	1,325	59.3	14	0.6	896	40.1	104	4.7	792	35.4
1995	2,530	1,487	58.8	12	0.5	1,030	40.7	93	3.7	937	37.0
1996	2,595	1,520	58.7	12	0.5	1,063	40.8	81	3.2	982	37.7
1997	2,767	1,626	58.8	16	0.6	1,125	40.7	79	2.8	1,046	37.8
1998	2,916	1,779	61.0	15	0.5	1,122	38.5	67	2.3	1,056	36.2
1999	2,815	1,656	58.8	15	0.5	1,145	40.7	66	2.3	1,080	38.3
Floor coverings:											
1990	3,075	18	0.6	21	0.7	3,036	98.7	-	-	3,036	98.7
1995	3,731	25	0.7	25	0.7	3,681	98.7	-	-	3,681	98.7
1997	3,956	32	0.8	26	0.6	3,897	98.6	-	-	3,897	98.6
1998	4,123	36	0.9	29	0.7	4,058	98.4	-	-	4,058	98.4
1999	4,247	39	0.9	29	0.7	4,180	98.4	-	-	4,180	98.4
2000	4,107	36	0.9	24	0.6	4,048	98.6	-	-	4,048	98.6
Industrial:[3]											
1990	2,965	313	10.6	10	0.3	2,642	89.1	179	6.0	2,463	83.1
1995	3,677	355	9.7	15	0.4	3,307	89.9	141	3.8	3,165	86.1
1997	3,871	360	9.4	16	0.4	3,495	90.2	113	2.9	3,382	87.3
1998	4,016	371	9.2	13	0.3	3,632	90.4	95	2.4	3,537	88.1
1999	4,227	372	8.8	13	0.3	3,843	90.9	93	2.2	3,750	88.7
2000	4,257	369	8.7	13	0.3	3,875	91.0	89	2.1	3,785	88.9

- Represents or rounds to zero.   [1] Rayon and acetate.   [2] Nylon, polyester, acrylic, and olefin.   [3] Includes consumer-type products.

Source: Fiber Economics Bureau, Inc., Washington, DC, Fiber Organon, monthly (copyright).

No. 971. Broadwoven and Knit Fabrics—Shipments and Foreign Trade: 2000

[3,717,511 represents 3,717,511,000. Fabric blends as shown in the report are reported based on the chief weight of the fiber; whereas, fabrics blends as shown for imports are based on the chief value of the fiber. Apparent consumption represents new domestic supply and is derived by subtracting exports for the total manufacturers' shipments plus imports]

Product description	Manufacturers' shipments (quantity)	Imports for consumption Quantity	Imports for consumption Value[1] ($1,000)	Percent imports to manufacturers' shipments	Exports of domestic merchandise Quantity	Exports of domestic merchandise Value ($1,000)	Percent exports to manufacturers' shipments
BROADWOVEN FABRICS (quantity 1,000 sq. meters)							
Cotton fabrics[2]	3,717,511	1,617,753	1,853,891	43.5	534,094	1,097,679	14.4
Manmade fiber fabrics	9,055,023	1,165,495	1,413,349	12.9	620,001	1,323,263	6.8
Silk fabrics	(D)	37,725	301,058	(D)	2,272	16,959	1,526.6
Wool fabrics	56,742	39,863	312,224	70.3	14,340	78,251	25.3
KNIT FABRICS (quantity in 1,000 kilograms)							
Total	718,548	116,478	786,913	16.2	150,766	1,135,450	21.0
Pile fabrics	69,086	20,533	182,594	29.7	42,745	285,874	61.9
Elastic fabric	31,963	12,907	130,947	40.4	16,612	235,564	52.0
Other warp knit fabrics	86,100	11,049	94,602	12.8	15,765	150,247	18.3
Other narrow knit fabrics	15,977	3,288	22,039	20.6	1,244	12,241	7.8
Other knit fabrics	515,422	68,701	356,731	13.3	74,400	451,524	14.4

D Data withheld to avoid disclosing figures for individual companies.   [1] Dollar value represents the c.i.f. (cost, insurance, and freight) at the first port of entry in the United States plus calculated import duty.   [2] Includes all cotton and chiefly cotton mixed with manmade fiber.

Source: U.S. Census Bureau, Current Industrial Reports, Series MQ313 and MA313K, annual; and <http://www.census.gov/ftp/pub/industry/1/mq22t005.pdf> (issued June 2001) and <http://www.census.gov/ftp/pub/industry/1/ma22k00.pdf> (issued July 2001).

Manufactures   621

No. 972. Footwear—Production, Foreign Trade, and Apparent Consumption: 2000

[Quantity in thousands of pairs (92,736 represents 92,736,000 pairs), value in thousands of dollars (329,484 represents $329,484,000)]

Product description	Manufacturers' shipments (quantity)	Exports of domestic merchandise		Percent exports to domestic production	Imports for consumption		Apparent consumption (quantity)	Percent imports to apparent consumption
		Quantity	Value		Quantity	Value		
Total	92,736	23,370	329,484	25.2	1,708,460	14,702,955	1,777,743	96.1
Rubber or plastic uppers and rubber or plastic soles	10,241	8,170	66,806	79.8	648,445	3,603,769	650,516	99.7
Waterproof	9,344	1,142	10,008	12.2	8,688	49,551	16,890	51.4
Not waterproof	897	7,028	56,798	783.5	639,757	3,554,218	633,626	101.0
Leather uppers	25,589	8,784	194,779	34.4	715,982	9,680,727	732,704	97.7
Athletic	1,456	5,754	103,259	395.2	548,465	6,506,943	544,167	100.8
Leather soles	7,374	1,791	59,223	24.4	51,357	1,199,862	56,907	90.2
Made with steel safety toes . .	(D)	208	10,819	(D)	10,798	215,235	(D)	(D)
Boots, ex. with steel safety toes	(D)	298	10,421	(D)	5,817	167,238	(D)	(D)
Shoes, ex. with steel safety toes	4,277	1,285	37,983	30.3	34,742	817,389	37,701	92.2
Other soles	16,759	1,239	32,297	7.4	116,160	1,973,922	131,630	88.2
Made with steel safety toes . .	2,651	-	-	(NA)	-	-	2,651	(NA)
Boots, ex. with steel safety toes	4,807	1,239	32,297	25.8	116,160	1,973,922	119,728	97.0
Shoes, ex. with steel safety toes	9,301	-	-	(NA)	-	-	9,251	(NA)
Fabric uppers	52,150	6,416	67,899	12.3	344,033	1,418,459	389,767	88.3
Rubber or plastic soles	(D)	5,325	57,513	(D)	266,249	1,019,990	(D)	(D)
Athletic	(D)	4,026	47,885	(D)	37,345	162,244	(D)	(D)
All other	(D)	1,299	9,628	(D)	228,904	857,746	(D)	(D)
With all other soles	(D)	1,091	10,386	(D)	77,784	398,469	(D)	(D)

- Represents zero.   D Data withheld to avoid disclosure.   NA Not available.

Source: U.S. Census Bureau, *Current Industrial Reports,* Series MA31A, annual. See also <ftp://ftp.census.gov/pub/industry/1/ma31a00.pdf> (released August 2001).

No. 973. Inorganic Chemicals and Fertilizers—Production: 1995 to 2000

[In thousands of short or metric tons (17,402 represents 17,402,000)]

Product description	Unit	1995	1996	1997	1998	1999	2000
INORGANIC FERTILIZERS							
Ammonia, synthetic anhydrous	1,000 sh. tons	17,402	17,923	17,891	18,475	17,337	16,806
Ammonium nitrate, original solution	1,000 sh. tons	8,489	8,498	8,604	9,079	7,630	7,498
Ammonium sulfate	1,000 sh. tons	2,647	2,662	2,711	2,787	2,875	2,868
Urea (100%)	1,000 sh. tons	8,117	8,548	8,190	8,865	8,907	7,621
Nitric acid (100%)	1,000 sh. tons	8,839	9,205	9,433	9,285	8,945	8,479
Phosphoric acid (100% P2O5)	1,000 sh. tons	13,134	13,210	13,159	13,891	13,708	13,143
Sulfuric acid, gross (100%)	1,000 sh. tons	47,519	47,770	47,929	48,513	44,756	44,032
Superphosphates and other fertilizer materials (100% P2O5)	1,000 sh. tons	10,364	10,547	10,473	10,260	9,133	8,921
INORGANIC CHEMICALS							
Chlorine gas	1,000 metric tons . .	12,395	12,460	12,922	11,650	12,114	11,912
Sodium hydroxide, total liquid	1,000 metric tons . .	11,408	11,563	11,972	11,896	11,974	10,449
Potassium hydroxide liquid	1,000 metric tons . .	(D)	500	533	450	430	489
Finished sodium bicarbonate	1,000 metric tons . .	520	502	522	493	505	487
Titanium dioxide, composite and pure	1,000 metric tons . .	1,382	1,352	1,477	1,323	1,355	1,404
Boric acid	1,000 metric tons . .	(D)	(D)	(D)	(D)	(NA)	(NA)
Hydrochloric acid	1,000 metric tons . .	3,904	4,116	4,411	4,226	4,191	4,280
Hydroflouric acid	1,000 metric tons . .	(D)	(D)	(D)	(D)	(NA)	(NA)
Aluminum oxide	1,000 metric tons . .	4,764	4,734	5,072	4,537	4,016	(D)
Aluminum sulfate (commercial)	1,000 metric tons . .	1,144	1,197	1,161	1,058	1,052	990
Sodium metal	1,000 metric tons . .	(D)	(D)	(D)	(D)	(NA)	(NA)
Sodium chlorate	1,000 metric tons . .	617	662	626	707	742	852
Sodium phosphate tribasic	1,000 metric tons . .	21	20	(D)	19	27	(NA)
Sodium phosphate tripoly	1,000 metric tons . .	(D)	(D)	(D)	205	(D)	(D)
Sodium silicats [1]	1,000 metric tons . .	1,203	1,105	1,214	1,097	992	1,034
Sodium metasilicates	1,000 metric tons . .	93	87	83	70	63	66
Sodium sulfate	1,000 metric tons . .	(D)	(D)	(D)	571	599	(NA)
Calcium carbide	1,000 metric tons . .	(D)	(D)	(D)	(D)	(NA)	(NA)
Calcium phosphorous	1,000 metric tons . .	1,567	1,507	1,486	1,798	1,808	(NA)
Carbon activated [2]	1,000 metric tons . .	156	170	173	150	151	161
Hydrogen peroxide	1,000 metric tons . .	355	343	360	324	342	(S)
Phosphorous, elemental	1,000 metric tons . .	(D)	(D)	(D)	(D)	(NA)	(NA)
Phosphorous, oxychloride and trichloride . .	1,000 metric tons . .	226	242	298	(D)	163	(D)

D Withheld to avoid disclosing data for individual companies.   NA Not available.   [1] Other than metasilicates.   [2] Granular and pulverized.

Source: U.S. Census Bureau, *Current Industrial Reports,* Series MAQ325A, and MA325B, annual. See also <ftp://ftp.census.gov/pub/industry/1/mq28a005.pdf> (issued July 2001) and <ftp://ftp.census.gov/pub/industry/1/mq28b005.pdf> (issued July 2001).

622   Manufactures

No. 974. Pharmaceutical Preparations—Value of Shipments: 1990 to 2000

[In millions of dollars (33,954 represents 33,954,000,000)]

Product description	Product code	1990	1995	1997	1998	1999	2000
Pharmaceutical preparations, except biologicals	(X)	33,954	48,864	57,419	65,712	70,171	78,908
Affecting neoplasms, endocrine systems, and metabolic disease	3254121000	2,743	4,076	5,466	7,633	7,742	8,945
Acting on the central nervous system and sense organs	3254124000	7,219	9,228	11,708	13,605	14,881	18,315
Acting on the cardiovascular system	3254127000	4,815	5,988	8,799	9,368	9,601	8,971
Acting on the respiratory system	325412A000	3,724	5,196	5,641	6,725	8,155	10,177
Acting on the digestive system	325412D000	4,840	8,593	9,482	9,502	8,741	10,077
Acting on the skin	325412G000	1,558	2,171	1,867	2,245	2,798	2,944
Vitamin, nutrient, and hematinic preps.	325412L000	2,588	4,812	5,088	5,851	6,161	6,688
Affecting parasitic and infective disease	325412P000	5,411	7,196	7,795	8,780	9,778	10,902
Pharmaceutical preps. for veterinary use	325412T000	1,057	1,605	1,572	2,003	2,314	1,888

X Not applicable.
Source: U.S. Census Bureau, 1990, *Current Industrial Reports,* Series MA28G; thereafter, MA325G(00)-1. See also <http://www.census.gov/ftp/pub/industry/1/ma28g00.pdf> (released August 2001).

No. 975. Glass Containers, Clay Construction Products, and Refractories— Quantity and Value of Shipments: 1990 to 2000

[285 represents 285,000,000]

Product description	Unit	1990	1995	1997	1998	1999	2000
Glass container shipments	Mil. of gross [1]	285	269	254	254	256	247
Brick shipments: [2]							
Quantity	Mil. of bricks	(NA)	7,244	7,838	8,081	8,553	9,100
Value	Mil. dol.	1,014	1,092	1,331	1,453	1,631	1,694
Clay floor and wall tile shipments: [3]							
Quantity	Mil. sq. ft.	(NA)	581	627	621	625	666
Value	Mil. dol.	687	728	834	837	843	857
Clay pipe and fittings shipments:							
Quantity	Mil. sq. ft	(NA)	138	162	165	177	160
Value	Mil. dol.	60	35	47	48	54	62
Refractory shipments	Mil. dol.	2,003	2,222	2,566	2,379	2,229	1,998
Clay	Mil. dol.	771	941	1,084	1,025	919	771
Nonclay	Mil. dol.	1,232	1,282	1,482	1,354	1,311	1,228

NA Not available. [1] One thousand gross = 144,000. [2] Building or common and face bricks. [3] Floor and wall tile including quarry tile.
Source: U.S. Census Bureau, 1990, *Current Industrial Reports,* Series M32G, MQ32D, and MA32C, annual; thereafter, M327G, MQ327D, and MA327C.

No. 976. Aluminum—Supply, Shipments, and Foreign Trade: 1990 to 2001

[In millions of pounds (17,334 represents 17,334,000,000)]

Item	1990	1995	1996	1997	1998	1999	2000	2001
SUPPLY								
Aluminum supply, total	17,334	20,425	20,848	21,945	22,970	24,590	23,586	20,516
Primary production	8,925	7,441	7,887	7,944	8,185	8,330	8,087	5,812
Recovery from scrap	5,276	7,028	7,291	7,819	7,589	8,146	7,606	6,900
Imports of ingot and mill products	3,133	5,956	5,671	6,183	7,196	8,113	7,893	7,804
Aluminum net shipments, total [1]	17,188	21,019	21,155	22,513	23,189	24,673	24,496	21,476
PRODUCT								
Mill products, total	13,013	15,716	15,605	16,609	17,019	17,989	17,676	15,590
Sheet, plate, and foil	9,297	11,168	10,936	11,536	11,801	12,437	12,116	11,021
Rod, bar, and wire	370	534	582	621	657	670	690	563
Electrical conductor	542	566	604	629	631	676	681	598
Extruded shapes and tube	2,546	3,102	3,139	3,473	3,559	3,817	3,792	3,058
Powder and paste	106	108	108	118	123	130	142	140
Forgings and impacts	152	238	236	232	248	259	255	210
Ingot for castings and other [2]	4,175	5,303	5,550	5,904	6,170	6,684	6,820	5,886
MARKET								
Domestic, total	14,637	18,152	18,313	19,523	20,358	21,707	21,676	19,041
Building and construction	2,663	2,679	2,921	2,921	3,070	3,237	3,204	2,895
Transportation	3,205	5,749	5,820	6,592	7,162	7,938	7,947	6,646
Consumer durables	1,122	1,369	1,443	1,529	1,599	1,675	1,692	1,445
Electrical	1,309	1,395	1,447	1,532	1,527	1,646	1,700	1,376
Machinery and equipment	992	1,257	1,254	1,381	1,386	1,458	1,496	1,284
Containers and packaging	4,772	5,088	4,796	4,895	5,012	5,106	4,992	4,851
Other	574	615	632	673	602	647	645	544
Exports	2,551	2,867	2,842	2,990	2,831	2,967	2,820	2,435
FOREIGN TRADE [3]								
Exports	3,753	3,846	3,600	3,763	3,743	3,865	4,097	3,712
Imports	3,718	6,910	6,580	7,209	8,342	9,506	9,357	8,853

[1] Data presented on this report have been adjusted to shipments and inventories plus imports by consumers. [2] Net ingot for foundry castings, export and destructive uses. [3] U.S. imports and exports of aluminum ingot, mill products and scrap.
Source: The Aluminum Association, Inc., Washington, DC, *Aluminum Statistical Review,* annual; and *Aluminum Facts at a Glance,* June 2002.

Manufactures 623

No. 977. Iron and Steel Industry—Summary: 1990 to 2001

[**95.5 represents 95,500,000 tons.** For financial data, the universe in 1992 consists of the companies that produced 68 percent of the total reported raw steel production. The financial data represent the operations of the steel segment of the companies. Minus sign (-) indicates net loss]

Item	Unit	1990	1995	1996	1997	1998	1999	2000	2001, prel.
Steel mill products, apparent supply . . .	Mil. tons [1] . .	95.5	109.6	117.5	124.6	131.6	127.9	131.9	116.9
Net shipments	Mil. tons [1] . .	85.0	97.5	100.9	105.9	102.4	106.2	109.1	99.4
Exports	Mil. tons [1] . .	4.3	7.1	5.0	6.0	5.5	5.4	6.5	6.1
Imports	Mil. tons [1] . .	17.2	24.4	29.2	31.2	41.5	31.2	29.4	30.1
Scrap consumed	Mil. tons [1] . .	50.1	62.0	62.0	64.0	64.0	62.0	65.0	(NA)
Scrap inventory	Mil. tons [1] . .	3.6	4.1	5.3	5.5	4.5	5.3	5.3	(NA)
Iron and steel products: Exports	Mil. tons [1] . .	5.3	8.2	6.2	7.4	6.9	6.7	7.7	7.2
Imports	Mil. tons [1] . .	21.9	27.3	32.1	34.4	45.4	40.2	42.6	34.4
Capacity by steelmaking process	Mil. net tons.	116.7	112.4	116.1	121.4	125.3	128.2	130.3	125.5
Revenue	Bil. dol.	30.9	35.1	34.9	36.6	38.1	36.3	38.8	(NA)
Net income	Bil. dol.	0.1	1.5	0.4	1.0	1.1	-0.5	-1.1	(NA)
Stockholders' equity.	Bil. dol.	4.3	8.6	10.2	9.8	12.5	11.8	9.9	(NA)
Total assets	Bil. dol.	28.3	35.1	35.8	38.3	42.2	43.7	43.9	(NA)
Capital expenditures [2]	Bil. dol.	2.6	2.5	2.3	2.7	3.1	2.8	2.1	(NA)
Working capital ratio [2]	Ratio	1.6	1.5	1.7	1.6	1.6	1.7	1.7	(NA)
Inventories	Bil. dol.	4.7	5.1	5.4	5.8	6.8	6.5	6.8	(NA)
Average employment	1,000	169.0	122.6	118.8	111.8	109.6	102.2	99.5	(NA)
Hours worked	Million	350.0	269.2	258.9	247.2	240.0	222.7	219.7	(NA)
Index of output, all employees [3]	1987=100 . .	109.7	142.6	147.5	155.0	151.0	155.6	160.1	(NA)

NA Not available.   [1] In millions of short tons.   [2] Current assets to current liabilities.   [3] Output per hour. Source: U.S. Bureau of Labor Statistics, Internet site <http://stats.bls.gov/iprhome.htm>.

Source: Except as noted, American Iron and Steel Institute, Washington, DC, *Annual Statistical Report* (copyright).

No. 978. Raw Steel, Pig Iron, and Ferroalloys Production: 1990 to 2001

[In millions (849.4 represents 849,400,000), except percent]

Item	1990	1995	1996	1997	1998	1999	2000	2001, prel.
Raw steel (net tons):								
World production	849.4	829.4	826.9	874.9	856.8	868.2	932.7	(NA)
U.S. production	98.9	104.9	105.3	108.6	108.8	107.4	112.2	99.3
Percent of world	11.6	12.6	12.7	12.4	12.7	12.4	12.0	(NA)
Furnace:								
Basic oxygen process . .	58.5	62.5	60.4	61.1	59.7	57.7	59.5	52.2
Electric	36.9	42.4	44.9	47.5	49.1	49.7	52.8	47.1
Open hearth	3.5	-	-	-	-	-	-	-
Grade:								
Carbon	86.6	92.7	93.6	95.9	97.1	96.5	101.5	90.8
Alloy and stainless.	12.3	12.3	11.7	12.6	11.7	10.9	10.7	8.5
Pig iron and ferroalloys production (sh. tons)	54.8	56.1	54.5	54.7	53.2	51.0	52.8	46.4

- Represents or rounds to zero.   NA Not available

Source: American Iron and Steel Institute, Washington, DC, *Annual Statistical Report* (copyright).

No. 979. Steel Products—Net Shipments by Market Classes: 1990 to 2000

[In thousands of short tons (84,981 represents 84,981,000). Comprises carbon, alloy, and stainless steel]

Market class	1990	1995	1996	1997	1998	1999	2000
Total [1]	84,981	97,494	100,878	105,858	102,420	106,201	109,050
Automotive	11,100	14,622	14,665	15,251	15,842	16,771	16,063
Steel service centers, distributors	21,111	23,751	27,124	27,800	27,751	28,089	30,108
Construction, incl. maintenance [2]	9,245	14,892	15,561	15,885	15,280	18,428	20,290
Containers, packaging, shipping	4,474	4,139	4,101	4,163	3,829	3,842	3,708
Machinery, industrial equipment, tools	2,388	2,310	2,410	2,355	2,147	1,722	1,784
Steel for converting and processing	9,441	10,440	10,245	11,263	9,975	11,309	12,708
Rail transportation	1,080	1,373	1,400	1,410	1,657	1,031	1,307
Contractors' products	2,870	([2])	([2])	([2])	([2])	([2])	([2])
Oil and gas industries	1,892	2,643	3,254	3,811	2,649	2,151	2,885
Electrical equipment	2,453	2,397	2,401	2,434	2,255	2,267	2,055
Appliances, utensils, and cutlery	1,540	1,589	1,713	1,635	1,729	1,789	1,907

[1] Includes nonclassified shipments and other classes not shown separately.   [2] Beginning 1994, contractors' products included with construction.

Source: American Iron and Steel Institute, Washington, DC, *Annual Statistical Report* (copyright).

No. 980. U.S. Machine Tool Consumption—Gross New Orders and Exports: 1999 and 2000

[Value in millions of dollars (4,459 represents $4,459,000,000)]

Item	1999				2000			
	Total	Metal cutting machines	Metal forming machines	Other manufac- turing technol- ogy	Total	Metal cutting machines	Metal forming machines	Other manufac- turing technology
New order units, total . .	**27,525**	**22,085**	**3,309**	**2,131**	**29,009**	**24,197**	**2,921**	**1,890**
Northeast [1]	5,013	4,135	532	346	5,159	4,286	546	328
South [2]	4,512	3,566	543	403	4,227	3,411	418	399
Midwest [3]	9,301	7,401	1,133	767	8,588	7,171	840	577
Central [4]	4,780	3,683	740	357	5,745	4,750	671	324
West [5]	3,919	3,300	361	258	5,291	4,580	447	263
New order value, total .	**4,459**	**3,396**	**500**	**563**	**4,494**	**3,563**	**459**	**472**
Northeast [1]	722	593	63	66	748	598	75	74
South [2]	665	490	73	103	636	512	56	68
Midwest [3]	1,899	1,440	185	275	1,645	1,268	150	227
Central [4]	712	488	126	98	784	601	100	83
West [5]	460	386	54	20	682	584	78	20
Export order units [6]	1,721	1,329	214	178	2,317	1,837	206	274
Export order value [6]	483	352	49	82	569	416	60	94

[1] Covers Maine, New Hampshire, Vermont, New York, Massachusetts, Connecticut, Rhode Island, New Jersey, and Pennsylvania. [2] Covers Delaware, Maryland, Virginia, West Virginia, Kentucky, North Carolina, South Carolina, Tennessee, Mississippi, Alabama, Georgia, and Florida. [3] Covers Wisconsin, Michigan, Ohio, Illinois, and Indiana. [4] Covers Minnesota, North Dakota, South Dakota, Montana, Wyoming, Idaho, Iowa, Nebraska, Kansas, Missouri, Oklahoma, Arkansas, Louisiana, Texas, New Mexico, Colorado, and Utah. [5] Covers Washington, Oregon, California, Nevada, and Arizona. [6] Represents orders placed with U.S. builders.

Source: The Association for Manufacturing Technology, Mclean, VA, (copyright); and American Machine Tool Distributors Association, Rockville, MD, *U.S. Machine Tool Consumption Report*, monthly.

No. 981. Metalworking Machinery—Value of Shipments: 1990 to 2000

[In millions of dollars (3,426.1 represents $3,426,100,000)]

Product	NAICS product code	1990	1995	1996	1997	1998	1999	2000
Metalworking machinery	**(X)**	**3,426.1**	**4,547.1**	**4,607.8**	**5,010.3**	**4,817.1**	**3,783.3**	**3,632.4**
Metal cutting type [1]	(X)	2,371.3	3,036.6	3,141.1	3,583.3	3,481.8	2,512.6	2,552.4
Boring machines	333512A1	([2])	172.4	88.9	80.2	73.6	53.8	87.2
Drilling machines [2]	333512A1	184.1	78.9	99.5	89.2	102.9	50.6	23.7
Gear cutting machines	33351211	102.7	137.1	164.3	213.5	197.7	132.0	180.6
Grinding and polishing machines . . .	33351220	433.6	549.6	541.3	595.0	535.5	477.1	454.3
Lathes [3]	33351230	355.6	478.0	451.1	480.7	472.9	297.4	287.0
Milling machines [4]	33351240	214.3	194.8	199.7	280.2	281.1	200.5	150.5
Machining centers [5]	33351270	437.0	698.8	779.4	931.6	897.3	597.9	629.7
Station type machines	33351280	502.1	477.0	498.6	551.9	571.0	407.1	401.8
Other metal cutting machine tools [6] .	33351290	141.9	246.2	316.0	358.3	344.6	291.7	333.2
Metal forming type	(X)	1,080.2	1,510.5	1,466.6	1,427.0	1,335.3	1,270.7	1,080.0
Punching and shearing machines . . .	33351310 pt.	200.1	326.3	331.4	319.2	254.3	220.0	203.8
Bending and forming machines	33351310 pt.	222.9	256.9	283.0	258.5	262.7	265.8	262.4
Presses, except forging	33351330	308.3	379.2	402.0	422.4	399.5	433.7	303.1
Forging machines [7]	33351350 pt.	73.9	(D)	(D)	(D)	(D)	(D)	(D)
Other metal forming [7]	33351350 pt.	275.0	548.1	450.2	426.9	418.8	351.2	310.7

D Data withheld to avoid disclosure. X Not applicable. [1] Data for "All lathes (turning machines)" and "All milling machines," valued at under $3,025 each are included in total "Metal cutting type" for 1995 through 2000. [2] For 1990, data for "Boring machines" were combined with "Drilling machines" to avoid disclosing individual company data. [3] For 1995 through 2000 product code 33351230, "Lathes," excludes the value for product code 3335123031, All lathes valued under $3,025 each. [4] For 1995 through 2000 product code 33351240, "Milling machines," excludes the value for product code 3335124001, "All milling machines valued under $3,025 each." [5] Multi-function numerically controlled machines. [6] Excludes those designed primarily for home workshops, labs, etc. [7] For 1995 through 2000, data for "Forging machines" have been combined with "Other metal forming machines" to avoid disclosing individual company data.

Source: U.S. Census Bureau, 1990, *Current Industrial Reports*, Series MQ35W; and thereafter, MQ333W. See also <http://www.census.gov/ftp/pub/industry/1/mq35w005.pdf> (revised 06 June 2001).

Manufactures 625

No. 982. Selected Types of Construction Machinery—Value of Shipments: 1990 to 2000

[In millions of dollars (2,235.9 represents 2,235,900,000]

Product description	Product code	1990	1995	1997	1998	1999	2000
Tractor shovel loaders	33312014	2,235.9	3,041.8	3,912.5	4,235.9	4,049.2	4,188.6
Power cranes, draglines, and shovels	33312011	1,511.8	2,561.4	2,927.4	3,289.2	3,124.7	3,037.3
Mixers, pavers, and related equipment	33312012	609.6	1,168.8	1,283.8	1,480.3	1,608.2	1,494.2
Off-highway trucks, truck-type tractor, chassis trailers, coal haulers, or wagons	33312013	957.7	1,326.9	1,596.3	1,425.6	834.6	855.2
Motor graders and light maintainers	33312016	408.0	479.9	(D)	(D)	(D)	(D)
Rough terrain forklifts	33312016	209.3	355.4	499.5	668.1	616.8	549.2
Self-propelled continuous ditchers and trenchers	33312016	129.7	193.5	238.7	266.7	287.4	283.5
Construction machinery for mounting on trucks, tractors, and other prime movers . . .	33312017	(X)	(D)	258.6	278.3	274.8	311.2
Aerial work platforms	33392372	814.9	1,131.1	(D)	2,055.2	2,491.8	2,682.7

D Withheld to avoid disclosing figures for individual companies.   X Not applicable.

Source: U.S. Census Bureau, 1990-1998, *Current Industry Reports,* Series MA35D; thereafter, Series, MA333D. See also <http://www.census.gov/ftp/pub/industry/1/ma35d00.pdf> (released 27 July 2001).

No. 983. Mining and Mineral Processing Equipment—Shipments: 1999 and 2000

Product	Product code	Number of companies, 2000	Quantity (units)		Value (mil. dol.)	
			1999	2000	1999	2000
Mining and mineral processing equipment . .	(X)	(X)	(X)	(X)	1,338	1,261
Portable crushing, screening, washing, and combination plants	33312081	16	957	834	165	135
Underground mining machinery [1]	33313110	26	17,488	16,564	333	297
Crushing/pulverizing/screening machinery [2]	33313150	36	4,604	5,118	324	309
Drills and other mining machinery, n.e.c. [1][3]	33313171	25	24,206	16,274	156	133
Portable drilling rigs and parts	3331327	23	(X)	(X)	361	387

X Not applicable.   [1] Excludes parts.   [2] Excludes portables and parts.   [3] N.e.c. = Not elsewhere classified.

Source: U.S. Census Bureau, *Current Industrial Reports,* Series MA333F. See also <http://www.census.gov/ftp/pub/industry/1/ma35f00.pdf> (issued July 2001).

No. 984. Engines, Refrigeration and Heating Equipment, and Pumps and Compressors—Shipments: 1995 to 2000

[23,274 represents 23,274,000]

Product	Unit	1995	1997	1998	1999	2000
Internal combustion engines produced	1,000	23,274	25,077	27,523	27,069	24,431
Gasoline (except outboard, aircraft, and auto) . . .	1,000	22,287	23,989	26,352	25,781	23,263
Nonautomotive diesel (except aircraft)	1,000	246	300	296	344	299
Automotive diesel	1,000	732	771	851	927	849
Natural gas and LPG	1,000	9	18	24	16	19
Air-conditioning, heating equipment shipments:						
Heat transfer equipment	Mil. dol . . .	(NA)	4,246	4,472	5,065	4,656
Room air-conditioners and dehumidifiers	Mil. dol . . .	(NA)	1,020	1,098	1,144	1,208
Motor vehicle mechanical air-conditioning systems	Mil. dol . . .	(NA)	2,221	2,100	2,057	2,362
Compressors and compressor units	Mil. dol . . .	(NA)	2,796	2,814	2,972	2,977
Automotive air-conditioning compressors	Mil. dol . . .	(NA)	1,951	1,977	2,152	2,097
Nonelectric warm air furnaces and dehumidifiers .	Mil. dol . . .	(NA)	1,558	1,607	1,517	1,564
Unitary air conditioners	Mil. dol . . .	(NA)	4,615	5,229	5,614	5,348
Air source heat pumps	Mil. dol . . .	(NA)	917	1,054	1,025	997
Pumps and compressors [1] **. . . . .**	**Mil. dol . . .**	**7,373**	**8,879**	**8,759**	**8,515**	**8,660**
Industrial pumps	Mil. dol . . .	2,700	2,732	2,968	2,592	2,794
Domestic water systems	Mil. dol . . .	329	357	414	471	468
Air and gas compressors	Mil. dol . . .	2,466	2,635	2,520	2,561	2,462

NA Not available.   [1] Includes products not shown separately.

Source: U.S. Census Bureau, *Current Industrial Reports,* Series MA333L, MA333M, and MA333P. See also <http://www.census.gov/ftp/pub/industry/1/ma35l00.pdf> (released August 2001); <http://www.census.gov/ftp/pub/industry/1/ma35m00.pdf> (released September 2001); and <http://www.census.gov/ftp/pub/industry/1/ma35p00.pdf> (released November 2001).

No. 985. Computers and Office and Accounting Machines—Value of Shipments: 1990 to 2000

[In millions of dollars (25,630 represents 25,630,000,000)]

Selected products	1990	1995	1997	1998	1999	2000
Electronic computers [1]	25,630	49,038	50,250	56,892	64,696	62,072
Host computers (multi-users)	(NA)	(NA)	12,240	15,010	21,089	22,366
Single user computers	(NA)	(NA)	36,988	41,002	42,765	38,721
Other computers	(NA)	(NA)	(D)	48	(D)	(D)
Loaded computer processor boards and board subassemblies [2]	2,247	24,448	27,040	26,047	30,091	35,992
Computer storage devices & equipment	7,488	7,903	8,837	9,319	9,827	9,532
Parts for computer storage devices & subassemblies	955	2,236	2,382	2,310	2,254	1,424
Computer terminals	2,067	1,086	781	529	541	425
Computer peripheral equipment, n.e.c.	7,697	12,331	13,555	12,145	12,889	12,706
Parts for input/output equipment	3,706	2,391	2,628	2,630	2,388	2,637
Calculating and accounting machines	(D)	1,279	1,622	1,061	1,196	800
Magnetic and optical recording media	3,695	5,106	5,739	4,736	3,907	3,412

D Withheld to avoid disclosing data for individual companies.   NA Not available.   [1] Beginning 1997, computer industry data are not entirely comparable to previous years.   [2] These data are collected on two Current Industrial Report forms, MA35R, Computers and Office and Accounting Machines (Shipments) and MA36Q, Semiconductors, Printed Circuit Boards, And Other Electronic Components.
Source: U.S. Census Bureau, *Current Industrial Reports,* Series MA334R. See also <http://www.census.gov/ftp/pub/industry/1/ma35r00.pdf> (released September 2001).

No. 986. Computers and Office and Accounting Machines—Shipments: 1999 and 2000

[Quantity in thousands of units (30,335 represents 30,335,000, value in millions of dollars (64,696 represents $64,696,000,000)]

Product	Number of companies, 2000	Quantity (1,000)		Value (mil. dol.)	
		1999	2000	1999	2000
Electronic computers (automatic data processors)	132	30,335	27,704	64,696	62,072
Host computers (multi-users):					
Large scale systems and unix servers	16	1,393	1,526	6,885	7,168
Medium-scale systems and unix servers	24	1,074	(D)	10,760	(D)
PC servers	24	638	(D)	2,886	(D)
Other host computers	9	29	15	559	191
Single user computers:					
Personal computers	36	19,610	15,900	26,827	22,588
Workstations	36	1,586	2,702	7,191	5,606
Laptops (AC/DC)	10	(D)	7	(D)	13
Notebooks, subnotebooks (battery operated)	18	(D)	4,109	(D)	9,000
Personal digital assistants	5	(D)	(D)	(D)	(D)
Other portable computers	6	(D)	(D)	(D)	(D)
Other single user computers	5	207	217	110	107
Other computers	35	1,492	284	841	986
Computer storage devices and equipment	71	(X)	(X)	9,827	9,532
Parts for computer storage devices and subassemblies	18	(X)	(X)	2,253	1,424
Computer terminals	37	(X)	(X)	541	425
Computer peripheral equipment, n.e.c. [1]	220	(X)	(X)	12,889	12,706
Keyboards	25	10,702	(D)	735	(D)
Computer printers:					
Laser	27	1,879	3,369	3,319	2,989
Inkjet	12	11,435	7,691	1,036	741
Calculating and accounting machines	33	(X)	(X)	1,196	800
Printed circuit assemblies	748	(X)	(X)	30,091	35,992
Magnetic and optical recording media	53	(X)	(X)	3,907	3,412

D Withheld to avoid disclosure of individual companies.   X Not applicable.   [1] N.e.c. = Not elsewhere classsified.
Source: U.S. Census Bureau, *Current Industrial Reports,* Series MA334R; and <http://www.census.gov/ftp/pub/industry/1/ma35r00.pdf> (released September 2001).

No. 987. Computers and Industrial Electronics—Factory Shipments: 1990 to 1999

[In millions of dollars (50,793 represents $50,793,000,000)]

Item	1990	1995	1996	1997	1998	1999
Computer and peripheral equipment, total	50,793	73,555	78,278	76,287	78,356	85,216
Computers	25,973	49,038	50,682	50,250	56,892	62,712
Peripheral equipment	24,820	24,517	27,597	26,037	21,464	22,504
Industrial electronics, total	26,183	33,732	35,472	38,108	36,887	37,288
Controlling, processing equipment	12,728	16,450	17,051	18,212	18,082	18,310
Testing, measuring equipment	6,859	10,109	11,224	11,966	11,213	11,585
Nuclear electronic equipment	567	501	491	516	560	527
Robots, accessories, and components	275	(NA)	(NA)	(NA)	(NA)	(NA)
Other electronic equipment	5,754	6,672	6,706	7,414	7,033	6,867

NA Not available.
Source: Consumer Electronics Association, Washington, DC, *Electronic Market Data Book,* annual (copyright).

No. 988. Consumer Electronics and Electronic Components—Factory Sales by Product Category: 1990 to 2000

[In millions of dollars (43,033 representes $43,033,000,000). Factory sales include imports]

Product category	1990	1995	1996	1997	1998	1999	2000
Total [1]	43,033	64,530	74,690	78,818	84,684	95,117	93,082
Video products:							
Direct-view color TV	6,197	6,798	6,026	6,122	6,199	6,503	4,990
LCD color TV	50	44	38	39	36	36	42
Projection TV	626	1,417	1,361	1,577	1,632	1,481	1,057
TV/VCR combinations	178	723	684	831	1,014	968	986
Monochrome TV	99	34	27	23	20	15	15
LCD Monochrome TV	33	31	30	28	25	25	20
Other video:							
VCR decks	2,439	2,767	2,618	2,409	2,333	1,869	1,099
Camcorders	2,260	2,130	1,894	2,144	2,448	2,838	2,247
Laserdisc players	72	108	25	10	3	3	(NA)
Home satellite earth stations	421	1,265	726	733	957	535	921
Videocassette players	65	59	39	21	15	14	5
Digital versatile disc players (DVD)	(NA)	(NA)	171	421	1,099	1,717	2,145
Home and portable products:							
Compact audio systems	1,270	1,162	1,419	1,557	1,695	1,776	1,357
Separate audio components	1,935	1,911	1,609	1,565	1,530	1,545	1,425
Home radios	360	284	300	300	348	351	315
Portable audio equipment	1,645	2,506	2,033	2,146	1,987	2,155	1,959
Mobile electronics:							
Aftermarket autosound equipment	1,192	1,931	1,811	1,859	2,070	2,169	2,100
Factory installed autosound	3,100	3,100	2,710	2,540	2,610	2,700	2,850
Wireless (cellular) telephones	1,133	2,574	5,940	6,000	6,066	8,995	8,651
Pagers	118	300	460	550	660	750	790
Vehicle security	190	142	210	213	205	218	266
Home office products:							
Cordless telephones	842	1,141	1,679	1,745	1,808	1,562	1,960
Corded telephones	638	557	528	489	483	386	320
Telephone answering devices	827	1,077	1,020	1,104	1,044	994	1,074
Home computers	4,187	12,600	15,950	16,640	16,390	16,400	12,960
Computer printers	(NA)	2,430	3,900	4,188	4,500	5,116	5,245
Modems/fax modems	(NA)	770	1,170	1,305	1,460	1,564	1,564
Computer peripherals	1,980	816	1,212	1,440	1,950	2,150	2,365
Computer software (incl. CD-ROM)	971	2,500	3,450	3,930	4,480	5,062	5,771
Home fax machines	920	919	1,139	647	455	386	349
Digital cameras	(NA)	(NA)	483	519	1,207	1,825	2,033
Electronic gaming:							
Electronic gaming hardware	975	1,500	1,650	1,980	2,250	2,700	3,250
Electronic gaming software	2,400	3,000	3,900	4,480	5,100	5,850	6,725
Blank media:							
Blank audio cassettes	376	334	281	248	208	162	128
Blank videocassettes	948	708	695	639	590	351	438
Blank floppy diskettes	314	373	500	700	900	1,200	1,550
Accessories and batteries:							
Electronic accessories	793	944	982	1,178	1,398	1,356	1,450
Total primary batteries	1,383	2,600	2,869	2,963	3,620	4,943	4,590

NA Not available.   [1] Includes categories, not shown separately.

Source: Consumer Electronics Association, Washington, DC, *Electronic Market Data Book*, annual (copyright).

No. 989. Communication Equipment—Value of Shipments: 1990 to 2000

[In millions of dollars (36,990 represents $36,990,000,000)]

Product description	Product code	1990	1995	1997	1998	1999	2000
Total	(X)	36,990	56,362	73,588	82,198	89,557	104,389
Telephone switching and switchboard equipment	3342101	7,537	8,178	10,302	12,422	13,742	15,174
Carrier line equipment and modems	3342104	5,014	5,869	7,278	9,379	9,263	13,112
Other telephone and telegraph equipment and components	3342107	3,181	10,510	16,488	19,897	23,258	28,971
Communication systems and equipment (except broadcast)	3342201	14,768	23,032	29,416	31,128	33,281	36,357
Broadcast, studio, and related electronic equipment	3342203	1,856	2,845	3,360	3,625	4,000	4,029
Intercommunications systems, including inductive paging systems (selective calling)	3342903	346	296	256	249	401	447
Alarm systems	3342901	1,027	1,662	1,926	2,024	2,218	2,755
Vehicular and pedestrian traffic control equipment and electrical railway signals and attachments	3342902	471	711	964	912	952	838
Electronic teaching machines, teaching aids, trainers and simulators	3333197	1,209	913	872	713	701	782
Laser sources [1]	3359997	(NA)	788	992	(S)	(S)	(S)
Ultrasonic equipment	335999A	109	172	213	205	226	272
Other electronic systems and equipment, n.e.c [2]	335999C	1,473	1,387	1,520	1,645	1,515	1,652

NA Not available.   S Does not meet publication standards.   X Not applicable.   [1] Beginning in 1995, data for laser equipment, instrumentation, and components were eliminated from this survey. Only laser sources are being collected.   [2] Not elsewhere classified.

Source: U.S. Census Bureau, *Current Industrial Reports,* Series MA334P. See also <http://www.census.gov/ftp/pub/industry/1/ma36p00.pdf> (issued October 2001).

No. 990. Semiconductors, Printed Circuit Boards, and Other Electronic Components—Value of Shipments by Class of Product: 1990 to 2000

[In millions of dollars (56,301 represents $56,301,000,000). N.e.c.=not elsewhere classified]

Class of product	Product code	1990	1995	1997	1998	1999	2000
Total	(X)	56,301	118,906	131,512	130,386	141,662	168,269
Transmittal, industrial, and special-purpose electron tubes (except x-ray)	3344111	1,097	855	656	630	673	706
Electron tubes, receiving type	(X)	24	(1)	(1)	(1)	(1)	(1)
Receiving type electron tubes and cathode ray picture tubes	3344114	1,344	12,907	13,434	13,367	13,579	13,458
Electron tube parts	3344117	143	120	161	147	136	143
Printed circuit boards	3344120	7,175	8,367	8,702	8,473	9,150	11,129
Integrated microcircuits (semiconductor networks)	3344131	16,623	48,438	57,019	57,644	62,868	76,508
Transistors	3344134	682	943	1,500	887	994	1,375
Diodes and rectifiers	3344137	668	1,067	1,191	908	1,038	629
Other semiconductor devices	334413A	5,741	12,639	10,262	11,056	11,745	11,871
Capacitors for electronic applications	3344140	1,392	1,785	2,099	1,947	2,035	2,663
Resistors	3344150	800	953	993	945	971	1,026
Coils, transformers, reactors, and chokes for electronic applications	3344160	976	1,412	1,426	1,368	1,423	1,680
Coaxial connectors	3344171	420	732	581	590	631	782
Cylindrical connectors	3344174	514	553	555	580	550	659
Rack and panel connectors	3344177	500	541	658	746	391	676
Printed circuit connectors	334417A	805	1,026	1,277	1,125	1,376	2,389
Other connectors including parts	334417D	1,085	1,402	2,209	1,973	2,041	2,206
Filters (except microwave) and piezoelectric devices	3344191	457	729	815	798	858	1,076
Microwave components and devices	3342207	1,369	1,233	1,440	1,581	1,622	2,450
Transducers, electrical/electronic input or output	3344194	741	1,111	1,220	1,373	1,331	1,408
Switches, mechanical types for electronic circuitry	3344197	579	666	791	883	883	901
Printed circuit assemblies	334418A	8,269	24,448	27,040	26,047	30,091	35,992
All other electronic components n.e.c	334419D	4,898	6,978	7,485	7,322	7,276	8,542

X Not applicable. 1 Product codes combined to avoid disclosing figures for individual companies.

Source: U.S Census Bureau, *Current Industrial Reports,* Series MA334Q. See also <http://www.census.gov/ftp/pub/industry/1/ma36q00.pdf> (released September 2001).

No. 991. Selected Instruments and Related Products—Value of Shipments: 1990 to 2000

[In millions of dollars (1,418 represents $1,418,000,000]

Product description	Product code	1990	1995	1997	1998	1999	2000
Total	(X)	64,928	65,688	72,990	71,272	71,672	77,342
Automatic regulating and control valves	332911F	1,418	1,860	2,097	2,082	2,347	2,344
Solenoid-operated valves (except nuclear and fluid power transfer)	332911H	346	464	541	524	486	476
Aeronautical, nautical, and navigational instruments	3345111	2,518	2,125	2,531	2,504	2,800	2,773
Search & detection, navigation & guidance systems and equipment	3345113	32,420	24,697	26,584	26,031	24,598	25,558
Laboratory apparatus and laboratory furniture	3391110	1,675	1,837	1,888	1,843	1,782	1,964
Controls for monitoring residential and commercial environments and appliance	3345120	1,982	2,533	2,717	2,860	3,013	3,259
Process control instruments	3345130	5,224	6,439	7,073	6,637	6,825	7,185
Integrating and totalizing meters for gas and liquids	3345141	725	915	1,079	1,147	1,081	1,063
Counting devices	3345143	210	364	435	394	391	507
Motor vehicle instruments	3345145	1,457	2,193	2,245	2,436	2,851	3,104
Integrating instruments, electrical	3345151	396	445	457	460	473	490
Test equipment for testing electrical, radio and communication circuits, and motors	3345153	6,156	9,255	11,639	10,454	11,034	14,017
Instruments to measure electricity	3345155	586	555	456	377	365	425
Analytical, scientific instruments (except optical)	3345160	4,412	5,737	6,059	6,162	6,410	6,441
Sighting, tracking, and fire-control equipment, optical type	3333141	581	655	575	510	534	475
Optical instruments and lenses	3333143	1,252	1,579	2,005	2,068	2,354	2,790
Aircraft engine instruments (except flight)	3345191	579	430	521	657	658	694
Physical properties and kinematic testing equip.	3345193	1,012	1,374	1,523	1,728	1,736	1,743
Nuclear radiation detection and monitoring instruments	3345195	567	501	530	567	539	569
Commercial, geophysical, meteorological, and general purpose instruments	3345197	1,140	1,373	1,677	1,534	1,081	1,139
Surveying and drafting instruments	3345199	274	356	360	297	314	326

X Not applicable.

Source: U.S. Census Bureau, 1990, *Current Industrial Reports,* Series MA38B; thereafter Series MA334B. See also <http://www.census.gov/ftp/pub/industry/1/ma38b00.pdf> (issued October 2001).

Manufactures 629

No. 992. Motor Vehicle Manufactures—Summary by Selected Industry: 2000

[1,170,194 represents 1,170,194,000. Based on the Annual Survey of Manufactures; see Appendix III]

Industry	NAICS code [1]	All employees [2] Number	All employees [2] Payroll Total (mil. dol.)	All employees [2] Payroll Per employee (dol.)	Production workers [2]	Value of shipments [3] (mil. dol.)
Motor vehicle manufacturing, total	3361-3363	1,170,194	54,032	46,174	955,936	471,677
Motor vehicle, total	3361	230,525	14,559	63,155	200,916	239,396
Automobile & light duty motor vehicle	33611	195,492	12,947	66,229	172,526	220,068
Automobile	336111	94,883	6,018	63,426	82,336	98,921
Light truck & utility vehicle	336112	100,609	6,929	68,872	90,191	121,147
Heavy duty truck	33612	35,033	1,612	46,003	28,390	19,328
Motor vehicle body & trailer	3362	136,621	4,194	30,697	111,081	27,516
Motor vehicle body & trailer.	33621	136,621	4,194	30,697	111,081	27,516
Motor vehicle body.	336211	44,360	1,447	32,625	34,096	10,651
Truck trailer.	336212	34,259	1,010	29,496	28,859	6,380
Motor home	336213	18,160	542	29,825	15,035	4,212
Travel trailer & camper	336214	39,843	1,194	29,978	33,092	6,273
Motor vehicle parts	3363	803,048	35,280	43,932	643,939	204,765
Motor vehicle gasoline engine & engine parts. .	33631	97,306	4,742	48,730	79,966	31,465
Carburetor, piston, piston ring, & valve.	336311	18,581	784	42,220	15,203	3,273
Gasoline engine & engine parts	336312	78,725	3,957	50,266	64,763	28,192
Motor vehicle electrical & electronic equip.	33632	118,826	4,605	38,754	87,596	26,062
Vehicular lighting equipment.	336321	15,055	646	42,885	11,135	3,000
Other motor vehicle electrical & electronic equip	336322	103,771	3,959	38,155	76,461	23,062
Motor vehicle steering & suspension components, ex. spring.	33633	51,010	2,507	49,152	41,740	11,256
Motor vehicle brake system.	33634	44,156	1,599	36,222	34,803	12,229
Motor vehicle transmission & power train parts .	33635	112,244	6,147	54,764	91,851	35,103
Motor vehicle seating & interior trim	33636	56,473	1,980	35,069	44,660	15,359
Motor vehicle metal stamping	33637	116,062	5,988	51,594	97,592	24,069
Other motor vehicle parts	33639	206,972	7,711	37,255	165,731	49,222

[1] North American Industrial Classification System, 1997; see Text, Section 15, Business Enterprise. [2] Includes employment and payroll at administrative offices and auxiliary units. All employees represents the average of production workers plus all other employees for the payroll period ended nearest the 12th of March. Production workers represents the average of the employment for the payroll periods ended nearest the 12th of March, May, August, and November. [3] Includes extensive and unmeasurable duplication from shipments between establishments in the same industry classification.

Source: U.S. Census Bureau, *Annual Survey of Manufactures, Statistics for Industry Groups and Industries,* Series M00(AS)-1. See also <http://www.census.gov/prod/2001pubs/m00-as1.pdf> (issued February 2002).

No. 993. Motor Vehicle Manufactures—Employees, Payroll, and Shipments by Major State: 2000

[14,559 represents $14,559,000,000. Industry based on the North American Industrial Classification System (NAICS); see text, Section 15, Business Enterprise]

Major state based on employment	Motor vehicle manufacturing (NAICS 3361) Employees, total	Payroll (mil. dol.)	Shipments (mil. dol.)	Motor vehicle body and trailer manufacturing (NAICS 3362) Employees, total	Payroll (mil. dol.)	Shipments (mil. dol.)	Motor vehicle parts manufacturing (NAICS 3363) Employees, total	Payroll (mil. dol.)	Shipments (mil. dol.)
United States. .	230,525	14,559	239,396	136,621	4,194	27,516	803,048	35,280	204,765
Alabama.	(D)	(D)	(D)	3,779	107	798	12,549	618	3,444
Arkansas	(NA)	(NA)	(NA)	1,383	32	258	7,613	184	972
California	7,242	373	3,047	9,745	279	1,323	27,426	786	3,987
Florida	(NA)	(NA)	(NA)	4,403	148	765	4,444	123	618
Georgia	8,307	494	9,795	3,926	108	698	9,864	296	2,232
Illinois	8,901	588	10,255	4,651	140	878	29,687	1,046	5,762
Indiana.	9,476	527	10,466	27,805	988	6,260	103,672	4,890	25,055
Iowa	(NA)	(NA)	(NA)	8,694	259	1,539	9,597	326	1,868
Kentucky	19,276	1,351	24,525	(NA)	(NA)	(NA)	27,188	900	7,459
Michigan.	49,710	3,473	59,173	3,486	105	613	200,047	10,849	58,348
Mississippi	(NA)	(NA)	(NA)	1,117	29	159	11,291	318	1,828
Missouri	(D)	(D)	(D)	2,442	67	276	18,616	548	4,340
Nebraska	(NA)	(NA)	(NA)	1,476	37	246	4,410	140	706
New York	(NA)	(NA)	(NA)	1,041	31	239	32,521	1,895	9,810
North Carolina	(D)	(D)	(D)	4,019	162	877	20,314	679	5,314
Ohio	32,956	2,024	35,267	5,111	159	793	17,861	854	7,454
Oklahoma.	(D)	(D)	(D)	5,230	117	691	6,351	182	1,099
Oregon.	2,987	108	1,621	3,827	116	655	2,837	112	594
Pennsylvania.	(D)	(D)	(D)	8,025	213	1,345	15,778	626	3,509
South Carolina.	5,697	303	3,853	878	17	49	16,009	541	4,386
Tennessee	14,818	972	9,278	2,010	61	423	34,737	1,129	8,606
Texas.	(D)	(D)	(D)	6,134	176	949	16,857	473	3,317
Utah	(NA)	(NA)	(NA)	1,484	38	225	7,098	241	2,022
Virginia.	(D)	(D)	(D)	(D)	(D)	(D)	10,455	347	2,293
Wisconsin.	(D)	(D)	(D)	6,112	202	1,113	23,665	1,035	6,505

D Withheld to avoid disclosing data on individual companies.   NA Not available.

Source: U.S. Census Bureau, *Annual Survey of Manufactures, Geographic Area Statistics* Series M00(AS)-3. See also <http://www.census.gov/prod/2002pubs/m00as-3.pdf> (issued March 2002).

No. 994. Aerospace—Sales, New Orders, and Backlog: 1990 to 2000

[In billions of dollars (136.6 represents $136,600,000,000), except as indicated. Reported by establishments in which the principal business is the development and/or production of aerospace products]

Item	1990	1995	1996	1997	1998	1999	2000
Net sales	**136.6**	**102.8**	**103.1**	**114.9**	**119.2**	**124.2**	**110.7**
Percent U.S. Government	53.8	49.5	49.8	40.3	39.9	45.1	40.8
Complete aircraft and parts [1]	49.9	42.5	41.8	54.5	63.6	68.0	58.0
Aircraft engines and parts	16.4	12.5	15.7	12.1	12.8	14.4	12.5
Missiles and space vehicles, parts . . .	22.0	18.4	18.5	21.0	16.1	15.7	16.7
Other products, services	48.3	29.4	27.1	27.0	26.7	26.1	23.5
Net, new orders	146.0	109.1	126.3	119.0	109.9	115.2	138.9
Backlog, Dec. 31	250.1	202.6	229.9	219.0	200.2	188.4	215.7

[1] Except engines sold separately.

Source: U.S. Census Bureau, 1990-1997, *Current Industrial Reports,* Series M37G; thereafter M336G. See also <http://www.census.gov/ftp/pub/industry/1/m37g0013.pdf> (released October 2001).

No. 995. Net Orders for U.S. Civil Jet Transport Aircraft: 1990 to 2001

[1990 data are net new firm orders; beginning 1995, net announced orders. Minus sign (-) indicates net cancellations. In 1997 Boeing acquired McDonnell Douglas]

Type of aircraft and customer	1990	1995	1996	1997	1998	1999	2000	2001
Total number [1]	**670**	**421**	**595**	**501**	**601**	**346**	**585**	**271**
U.S. customers	259	138	408	258	392	192	412	49
Foreign customers	411	283	187	243	209	70	193	130
Boeing 737, total	189	189	349	280	350	258	378	184
U.S. customers	38	85	284	120	207	155	302	51
Foreign customers	151	104	65	160	143	45	86	73
Boeing 747, total	153	35	66	37	-4	22	24	16
U.S. customers	24	2	22	15	1	1	1	7
Foreign customers	129	33	44	22	-5	19	18	13
Boeing 757, total	66	-7	44	45	47	18	43	23
U.S. customers	33	-6	35	25	34	7	38	15
Foreign customers	33	-1	9	20	13	2	14	6
Boeing 767, total	60	26	10	96	40	32	6	32
U.S. customers	23	4	11	85	31	21	-2	-1
Foreign customers	37	22	-1	11	9	1	14	9
Boeing 777, total	34	83	88	46	65	21	113	30
U.S. customers	34	-	37	24	42	8	60	-
Foreign customers	-	83	51	22	23	8	53	20
McDonnell Douglas MD-11, total . . .	52	-6	9	11	12	-	-	-
U.S. customers	16	3	1	-	3	-	-	-
Foreign customers	36	-9	8	11	9	-	-	-
McDonnell Douglas MD-80/90, total .	116	51	29	-14	26	-20	-	-
U.S. customers	91	-	18	-11	24	-	-	-
Foreign customers	25	51	11	-3	2	-20	-	-
McDonnell Douglas MD-95, total . . .	-	50	-	-	65	15	21	-14
U.S. customers	-	50	-	-	50	-	13	-23
Foreign customers	-	-	-	-	15	15	8	9

- Represents zero.   [1] Includes types of aircraft not shown separately. Beginning 1999, includes unidentified customers.

Source: Aerospace Industries Association of America, Washington, DC, Research Center, Statistical Series 23, Internet site at <http://www.aia-aerospace.org/stats/aerostats/aerostats.cfm> (15 May 2002).

No. 996. U.S. Aircraft Shipments: 1980 to 2002

[Value in millions of dollars (18,929 represents $18,929,000,000)]

Year	Total		Civil						Military	
			Large transports		General aviation [1]		Helicopters			
	Units	Value	Units	Value	Units	Value	Units	Value	Units	Value
1980	14,677	18,929	387	9,895	11,877	2,486	1,366	656	1,047	5,892
1985	3,610	27,269	278	8,448	2,029	1,431	384	506	919	16,884
1990	3,321	38,585	521	22,215	1,144	2,007	603	254	1,053	14,109
1991	3,092	44,657	589	26,856	1,021	1,968	571	211	911	15,622
1992	2,585	47,397	567	28,750	941	1,840	324	142	753	16,665
1993	2,585	41,166	408	24,133	964	2,144	258	113	955	14,776
1994	2,309	36,568	309	18,124	928	2,357	308	185	764	15,902
1995	2,436	33,658	256	15,263	1,077	2,842	292	194	811	15,359
1996	2,235	36,247	269	17,564	1,130	3,127	278	193	558	15,363
1997	2,777	42,614	374	25,810	1,569	4,674	346	231	488	11,899
1998	3,560	55,286	559	36,880	2,220	5,874	363	252	418	12,280
1999	3,849	58,128	620	38,475	2,525	7,935	345	200	359	11,518
2000	4,027	51,664	485	31,171	2,816	8,558	493	270	233	11,665
2001	3,809	56,470	526	35,056	2,618	8,517	415	247	250	12,650
2002, prel.	2,956	47,532	388	27,500	1,940	7,110	373	222	255	12,700

[1] Excludes off-the-shelf military aircraft.
Source: U.S. Department of Commerce, International Trade Administration, Internet site <http://www.ita.doc.gov/td/aerospace/inform/information.htm>

Manufactures   631

No. 997. Aerospace Industry Sales by Product Group and Customer: 1990 to 2002

[In billions of dollars (134.4 represents $134,400,000,000). Due to reporting practices and tabulating methods, figures may differ from those in Table 994]

Product group and customer	Current dollars					Constant (1987) dollars [3]				
	1990	1995	2000	2001 [1]	2002 [2]	1990	1995	2000	2001 [1]	2002 [2]
Total sales.	134.4	107.8	146.2	151.0	144.4	123.7	86.6	109.8	110.5	104.6
PRODUCT GROUP										
Aircraft, total	71.4	55.0	82.1	84.1	76.1	65.7	44.2	61.7	61.6	55.1
Civil [4]	31.3	24.0	48.4	50.4	39.2	28.8	19.2	36.4	36.9	28.4
Military	40.1	31.1	33.7	33.7	36.9	36.9	25.0	25.3	24.7	26.7
Missiles	14.2	7.4	9.5	10.8	12.9	13.1	5.9	7.1	7.9	9.4
Space	26.4	27.4	30.3	31.0	31.3	24.4	22.0	22.8	22.6	22.7
Related products and services [5] . .	22.4	18.0	24.4	25.2	24.1	20.6	14.4	18.3	18.4	17.4
CUSTOMER GROUP										
Aerospace, total.	112.0	89.8	121.8	125.9	120.3	103.1	72.1	91.5	92.1	87.1
DOD [6]	60.5	42.4	47.0	48.7	53.8	55.7	34.1	35.3	35.6	38.9
NASA [7] and other agencies . . .	11.1	11.4	13.3	14.3	13.9	10.0	9.2	10.0	10.4	10.1
Other customers [8].	40.4	36.0	61.5	62.9	52.6	36.5	28.9	46.2	46.0	38.1
Related products and services [5] . .	22.4	18.0	24.4	25.2	24.1	20.6	14.4	18.3	18.4	17.4

[1] Preliminary. [2] Estimate. [3] Based on AIA's aerospace composite price deflator. [4] All civil sales of aircraft (domestic and export sales of jet transports, commuters, business, and personal aircraft and helicopters). [5] Electronics, software, and ground support equipment, plus sales of non-aerospace products which are produced by aerospace-manufacturing use technology, processes, and materials derived from aerospace products. [6] Department of Defense. [7] National Aeronautics and Space Administration. [8] Includes civil aircraft sales (see footnote 4), commercial space sales, all exports of military aircraft and missiles and related propulsion and parts.

Source: Aerospace Industries Association of America, Inc., Washington, DC, *2001 Year-end Review and Forecast*, Internet site <http://www.aia-aerospace.org>.

No. 998. Major Household Appliances—Value of Shipments: 1990 to 2001

[In millions of dollars (1,659.8 represents $1,659,800,000)]

Product	NAICS Product code	1990	1995	1997	1998	1999	2000	2001
Total	33522	11,670.0	13,966.2	15,225.0	15,551.4	16,622.3	17,041.0	17,381.3
Electric household ranges, ovens, and surface cooking units, equipment and parts.	3352211110	1,659.8	1,791.8	2,099.9	2,242.9	2,197.1	2,170.3	1,926.9
Gas household ranges, ovens, and surfacecooking units, equipment and parts.	3352213000	739.4	654.1	606.8	696.7	786.3	779.1	902.0
Other household ranges, cooking equipment outdoor cooking equipment incl. parts and accessories	3352215000	581.1	911.6	1,082.0	1,029.0	1,218.6	1,251.1	1,096.6
Household refrigerators [1] [2]	3352221000	3,208.1	4,739.4	5,272.4	5,035.6	4,968.8	5,395.8	5,227.1
Food freezers, complete units, for freezing and/or storing frozen food (household type) [2].	3352222000	226.6	(D)	(D)	(D)	(D)	(D)	(D)
Parts and attachments for household refrigerators and freezers	3352223000	134.0	111.8	155.8	89.7	92.4	99.4	114.0
Household laundry machines and parts.	3352240000	2,924.5	3,095.4	3,191.5	3,327.3	4,029.7	4,046.6	4,149.7
Water heaters, electric.	3352281000	433.8	513.0	552.3	541.3	580.0	572.7	555.7
Water heaters, except electric	3352283000	577.2	681.8	748.7	810.7	842.8	843.6	798.4
Household appliances, n.e.c. and parts.	3352285000	1,185.5	1,579.2	1,671.4	1,867.9	1,998.8	2,066.1	2,051.0

D Withheld to avoid disclosing data for individual companies. [1] Includes combination refrigerator-freezers. [2] Product code 33522210000 and 3352222000 are combined to avoid disclosing data for individual companies.

Source: U.S. Census Bureau, 1990, *Current Industrial Reports, Series MA36F;* thereafter Series MA335F. See also <http://www.census.gov/ftp/pub/industry/1/ma335f01.pdf> (issued August 2002).

Section 22
Domestic Trade

This section presents statistics relating to the distributive trades, specifically wholesale trade and retail trade. Data shown for the trades are classified by kind of business and cover sales or receipts, establishments, employees, payrolls, and other items. The principal sources of these data are from the Census Bureau and include the *1997 Economic Census* reports, annual survey reports, and the *County Business Patterns* program. These data are supplemented by several tables from trade associations such as the National Automobile Dealers Association (Table 1009). Several notable research groups are also represented such as Claritas (Table 1006), National Research Bureau and the International Council of Shopping Centers (Tables 1023 and 1024), Jupiter Media Matrix (Table 1018), and Forrester Research, Inc. (Table 1017).

Data on retail and wholesale trade appear in several other sections. For instance, labor force employment and earnings data (Table 603) appear in Section 12, Labor Force, Employment, and Earnings; gross domestic product of the industry (Table 632) appear in the Section 13, Income, Expenditures, and Wealth; financial data (several tables) from the quarterly *Statistics of Income Bulletin,* published by the Internal Revenue Service, appear in Section 15, Business Enterprise.

Censuses—Censuses of retail trade and wholesale trade have been taken at various intervals since 1929. Beginning with the 1967 census, legislation provides for a census of each area to be conducted every 5 years (for years ending in "2" and "7"). For more information on these censuses, see the *History of the 1997 Economic Census* found at <http://www.census.gov/prod/ec97/pol00-hec.pdf>. The industries covered in the censuses and surveys of business are those classified in 13 sectors defined in the *North American Industry Classification System,* called NAICS (see below). *Retail trade* refers to places of business primarily

engaged in retailing merchandise generally in small quantities to the general public; and *wholesale trade,* to establishments primarily engaged in selling goods to other businesses and normally operate from a warehouse or office that have little or no display of merchandise. All Census Bureau tables in this section are utilizing the new NAICS codes, which replaced the Standard Industrial Classification (SIC) system. NAICS makes substantial structural improvements and identifies over 350 new industries. At the same time, it causes breaks in time series far more profound than any prior revision of the previously used SIC system. For information on this system and how it affects the comparability of retail and wholesale statistics historically, see text, Section 15, Business Enterprise, and especially the Census Bureau Web site at <http://www.census.gov/epcd/www/naics.html>. In general, the 1997 Economic Census has two series of publications and documents for these two sectors subject series with reports on such as commodity line sales and establishment and firm sizes and geographic reports with individual reports for each state. For information on these series, see the Census Bureau Web site at <http://www.census.gov/epcd/www/97EC42.htm> and <http://www.census.gov/epcd/www/97EC44.htm>.

Current surveys—Current sample surveys conducted by the Census Bureau cover various aspects of the retail and wholesale trade. Its *Monthly Retail Trade and Food Services* contains monthly estimates of sales, inventories, and inventory/sales ratios, purchases, and accounts receivable for the United States, by kind of business. Annual figures on sales, year-end inventories, and inventory/sales ratios, by kind of business, appear in the *Annual Benchmark Report for Retail Trade and Food Services.* Statistics from the Bureau's monthly wholesale trade survey include national estimates of merchant wholesalers' sales, inventories, and inventory/ sales ratios by major summary groups "durable and non-durable," and selected kinds of business. Merchant wholesalers are those wholesalers who take title to the goods they sell (e.g., jobbers, exporters, importers, industrial distributors). These data, based on reports submitted by a sample of firms, appear in the *Monthly Wholesale Trade Report*. Annual figures on sales, inventory/sales ratios, year-end inventories, and purchases appear in the *Annual Benchmark Report for Wholesale Trade*. The reports just mentioned may appear in print in some cases, but principally are available as documents on the Census Bureau Web site at <http://www.census.gov/econ/www/retmenu.html>.

E-commerce—Electronic commerce (or e-commerce) are sales of goods and services over the Internet and extranet, electronic data interchange (EDI), or other online systems. Payment may or may not be made online. This edition has several tables on e-commerce sales such as Tables 1020 to 1022 in this section, 959 in Section 21, Manufactures, and 1247 in Section 27, Accommodation, Food Services, and Other Services. Also, there are several private sources for similar data such as Forrester Research Inc., Cambridge MA; BizRate.com, Los Angeles, CA; and Jupiter Media Matrix, New York, NY. These sources show estimated and projected online retail sales by key categories from business to consumers or to other businesses. Their methods of collecting the data vary widely between the sources and consequently these estimates of this activity vary also. Users of these estimates may want to contact the sources for descriptions of their methodology.

Statistical reliability—For a discussion of statistical collection and estimation, sampling procedures, and measures of statistical reliability applicable to Census Bureau data, see Appendix III.

No. 999. Wholesale and Retail Trade—Establishments, Employees, and Payroll by State: 1999 and 2000

[5,972 represents 5,972,000. Covers establishments with payroll. Employees are for the week including March 12. Excludes most government employees, railroad employees, and self-employed persons. Kind-of-business classification based on North American Industry Classification System (NAICS); see text, Section 15, Business Enterprise. For statement on methodology, see Appendix III]

State	Wholesale establishments (NAICS 42)						Retail establishments (NAICS 44,45)					
	Number of establishments		Number of employees (1,000)		Annual payroll (mil. dol.)		Number of establishments		Number of employees (1,000)		Annual payroll (mil. dol.)	
	1999	2000	1999	2000	1999	2000	1999	2000	1999	2000	1999	2000
U.S.	450,030	446,237	5,972	6,112	249,998	270,122	1,111,260	1,113,573	14,477	14,841	281,946	302,553
AL.	6,226	6,132	82	82	2,746	2,892	19,867	19,723	224	230	3,939	4,074
AK.	765	752	7	7	282	281	2,762	2,733	32	33	772	790
AZ.	6,724	6,731	86	86	3,341	3,627	16,616	16,911	249	255	5,126	5,694
AR.	3,545	3,505	42	45	1,293	1,402	12,236	12,211	131	135	2,182	2,268
CA.	58,194	58,326	773	808	35,452	40,011	106,864	107,987	1,421	1,491	32,621	36,073
CO	7,452	7,452	95	97	4,330	4,906	18,379	18,748	241	252	5,156	5,883
CT.	5,179	5,076	76	77	4,185	4,481	14,258	14,111	194	191	4,277	4,540
DE.	1,001	1,009	16	19	835	1,117	3,757	3,742	50	52	959	1,048
DC	377	372	5	5	294	282	1,935	1,945	19	19	396	431
FL.	30,816	30,671	302	315	11,224	12,536	66,928	67,396	889	903	16,959	18,044
GA	14,033	13,892	198	199	8,581	9,064	33,375	33,788	441	464	8,593	9,365
HI	1,812	1,809	18	19	600	627	4,903	4,924	60	63	1,263	1,313
ID	2,011	2,012	24	24	775	845	5,896	5,871	67	70	1,252	1,347
IL	21,764	21,509	338	344	16,077	16,683	44,017	43,800	636	637	12,214	12,992
IN	8,788	8,642	119	120	4,384	4,607	24,431	24,261	348	354	6,071	6,332
IA	5,256	5,155	65	65	2,111	2,173	14,494	14,382	180	184	3,032	3,169
KS.	4,964	4,876	65	62	2,560	2,333	12,286	12,261	150	153	2,646	2,747
KY.	4,986	4,939	73	74	2,408	2,536	17,105	16,988	216	221	3,620	3,804
LA.	6,331	6,192	79	79	2,635	2,723	17,655	17,755	231	232	3,895	4,032
ME	1,739	1,740	22	22	720	744	6,977	7,015	75	77	1,353	1,436
MD	6,197	6,098	94	95	4,274	4,526	19,573	19,539	279	285	5,642	6,062
MA	9,873	9,735	148	156	7,606	9,114	25,924	25,813	350	353	7,132	7,729
MI	13,689	13,576	190	191	8,556	8,887	39,262	38,862	542	545	10,268	10,667
MN	9,344	9,294	138	137	6,091	6,399	20,869	20,862	297	304	5,535	5,980
MS	3,137	3,116	39	40	1,187	1,222	12,744	12,794	138	141	2,355	2,384
MO	9,342	9,072	134	146	5,057	5,458	24,023	23,911	308	318	5,815	6,258
MT	1,555	1,537	15	15	420	433	5,038	5,101	51	52	873	920
NE.	3,090	3,061	41	41	1,330	1,346	8,155	8,248	105	110	1,743	1,895
NV.	2,600	2,556	30	31	1,168	1,238	6,793	6,940	102	108	2,279	2,533
NH	2,140	2,105	24	25	1,043	1,184	6,607	6,545	91	93	1,762	1,930
NJ.	17,436	17,157	276	279	13,827	14,724	34,582	34,841	422	439	9,238	9,897
NM	2,163	2,162	21	22	684	753	7,359	7,249	92	91	1,673	1,745
NY.	36,868	36,606	416	422	19,418	20,941	74,912	75,500	813	844	16,644	18,116
NC	12,409	12,364	169	173	6,640	7,153	35,684	35,785	436	450	8,111	8,739
ND	1,568	1,543	17	18	502	532	3,499	3,435	42	42	685	719
OH	16,944	16,646	256	261	9,929	10,437	43,270	42,708	629	644	11,402	11,903
OK	5,049	5,005	60	62	2,002	2,126	14,296	14,147	168	168	2,787	2,913
OR	5,870	5,836	80	79	3,108	3,266	14,200	14,256	186	193	3,894	4,126
PA.	16,909	16,796	237	243	9,626	10,287	48,978	48,518	653	668	11,897	12,556
RI	1,534	1,530	19	21	702	768	4,182	4,342	48	53	931	1,149
SC.	5,099	5,091	61	65	2,162	2,353	18,511	18,619	218	224	3,770	4,083
SD.	1,425	1,390	17	16	475	472	4,183	4,181	47	50	825	879
TN.	8,125	8,006	129	127	4,761	4,848	24,532	24,624	310	311	5,680	5,908
TX.	32,997	32,631	443	458	18,333	20,176	74,023	74,758	1,006	1,021	20,153	21,846
UT.	3,336	3,294	44	44	1,513	1,583	7,778	7,952	119	124	2,175	2,455
VT.	930	889	11	11	369	401	3,968	3,974	38	38	701	750
VA.	7,935	7,893	107	110	4,214	4,651	28,803	28,794	396	399	7,455	7,949
WA	9,988	9,869	122	125	4,951	5,412	22,582	22,700	303	313	6,681	7,181
WV	1,893	1,869	22	22	685	698	7,883	7,788	90	92	1,424	1,493
WI	7,941	7,928	117	119	4,339	4,636	21,409	21,354	316	322	5,570	5,891
WY	781	790	6	7	190	229	2,897	2,881	28	28	490	515

Source: U.S. Census Bureau, *County Business Patterns*, annual. See also <http://www.census.gov/prod/2002pubs/cbp00/cbp00-1.pdf> (issued May 2002).

U.S. Census Bureau, Statistical Abstract of the United States: 2002

No. 1000. Retail Trade—Establishments, Employees, and Payroll: 1999 and 2000

[1,111.3 represents 1,111,300 except as indicated. Covers establishments with payroll. Employees are for the week including March 12. Most government employees are excluded. For statement on methodology, see Appendix III]

Kind of business	NAICS code [1]	Establishments (1,000)		Employees (1,000)		Payroll (bil. dol.)	
		1999	2000	1999	2000	1999	2000
Retail trade, total	**44,45**	**1,111.3**	**1,113.6**	**14,477**	**14,841**	**281.9**	**302.6**
Motor vehicle & parts dealers	441	123.9	124.5	1,804	1,866	60.2	63.9
Automobile dealers	4411	50.1	50.9	1,175	1,222	45.2	47.8
New car dealers	44111	26.1	26.2	1,070	1,112	42.3	44.8
Used car dealers	44112	24.0	24.7	105	110	2.9	3.1
Other motor vehicle dealers	4412	14.1	14.5	115	127	3.4	3.8
Recreational vehicle dealers	44121	3.0	3.1	33	36	1.1	1.1
Motorcycle & boat & other MV dealers	44122	11.0	11.4	82	91	2.3	2.7
Motorcycle dealers	441221	3.8	4.0	33	38	1.0	1.2
Boat dealers	441222	5.3	5.3	38	40	1.0	1.1
All other motor vehicle dealers	441229	1.9	2.1	11	13	0.3	0.4
Automotive parts, accessories & tire stores	4413	59.7	59.1	514	517	11.6	12.2
Automotive parts, accessories & tire stores	44131	41.9	41.1	354	355	7.4	7.8
Tire dealers	44132	17.8	18.0	160	162	4.2	4.4
Furniture & home furnishing stores	442	64.3	64.8	525	549	12.4	13.4
Furniture stores	4421	29.6	29.7	270	284	7.0	7.5
Home furnishings stores	4422	34.7	35.1	255	265	5.4	5.9
Floor covering stores	44221	15.7	15.8	100	103	3.0	3.2
Other home furnishings stores	44229	19.0	19.3	155	162	2.5	2.7
Window treatment stores	442291	2.3	2.3	10	10	0.2	0.2
All other home furnishings stores	442299	16.7	17.0	145	152	2.3	2.5
Electronics & appliance stores	443	45.2	45.6	384	407	9.6	11.2
Appliance, TV & all other electronics stores	44311	29.0	29.6	258	279	5.9	6.6
Household appliance stores	443111	10.0	9.8	63	62	1.4	1.5
Radio, television & other electronics stores	443112	19.0	19.8	195	217	4.5	5.1
Computer & software stores	44312	13.0	12.9	105	106	3.2	4.2
Camera & photographic supplies stores	44313	3.1	3.1	21	22	0.4	0.4
Bldg material & garden equip & supp dealers	444	92.3	91.9	1,184	1,235	30.2	32.5
Building material & supplies dealers	4441	71.2	70.9	1,012	1,055	26.4	28.4
Home centers	44411	4.4	4.4	325	351	6.8	7.6
Paint & wallpaper stores	44412	8.4	8.4	43	46	1.1	1.2
Hardware stores	44413	15.3	15.0	145	146	2.3	2.5
Other building material dealers	44419	43.2	43.1	499	512	16.2	17.2
Lawn & garden equip & supplies stores	4442	21.1	21.0	172	180	3.8	4.0
Outdoor power equipment stores	44421	4.6	4.6	27	29	0.6	0.7
Nursery & garden centers	44422	16.4	16.5	144	152	3.2	3.4
Food & beverage stores	445	151.5	154.5	3,015	3,004	45.9	48.4
Grocery stores	4451	97.4	98.3	2,743	2,717	41.9	44.0
Grocery (except convenience) stores	44511	69.0	68.8	2,584	2,544	39.9	41.8
Convenience stores	44512	28.4	29.5	159	173	1.9	2.2
Specialty food stores	4452	25.9	27.8	141	154	2.1	2.4
Meat markets	44521	6.5	6.5	40	41	0.6	0.6
Fish & seafood markets	44522	1.8	1.9	8	8	0.1	0.1
Fruit & vegetable markets	44523	3.2	3.2	18	18	0.3	0.3
Other specialty food stores	44529	14.4	16.2	75	86	1.1	1.3
Baked goods stores	445291	4.9	5.5	29	33	0.5	0.6
Confectionery & nut stores	445292	3.9	4.0	21	21	0.2	0.2
All other specialty food stores	445299	5.6	6.8	25	32	0.3	0.4
Beer, wine & liquor stores [2]	4453	28.1	28.5	131	134	1.9	2.1
Health & personal care stores	446	82.4	81.2	938	914	17.8	19.3
Pharmacies & drug stores	44611	41.8	40.6	709	680	13.4	14.5
Cosmetics, beauty supplies & perfume stores	44612	9.6	9.6	62	61	0.8	0.8
Optical goods stores	44613	14.7	14.3	76	74	1.6	1.7
Other health & personal care stores	44619	16.3	16.7	91	98	2.0	2.2
Food (health) supplement stores	446191	8.4	8.7	45	49	0.6	0.7
All other health & personal care stores	446199	7.9	8.0	46	49	1.4	1.5
Gasoline stations	447	121.1	119.6	930	937	12.8	13.3
Gasoline stations with convenience stores	44711	81.5	80.5	646	653	8.4	8.9
Other gasoline stations	44719	39.6	39.1	284	284	4.4	4.4

See footnotes at end of table.

U.S. Census Bureau, Statistical Abstract of the United States: 2002

[See headnote, page 636]

Kind of business	NAICS code [1]	Establishments (1,000)		Employees (1,000)		Payroll (bil. dol.)	
		1999	2000	1999	2000	1999	2000
Clothing & clothing accessories stores	448	151.7	150.9	1,293	1,369	19.1	20.2
Clothing stores	4481	91.0	90.0	944	1,015	13.0	13.7
Men's clothing stores	44811	11.4	10.7	85	85	1.5	1.6
Women's clothing stores	44812	36.2	35.6	284	302	3.7	3.9
Children's & infants' clothing stores	44813	5.3	5.6	51	59	0.6	0.7
Family clothing stores	44814	20.9	20.6	420	453	5.7	5.9
Clothing accessories stores	44815	5.5	5.7	29	28	0.4	0.4
Other clothing stores	44819	11.7	11.8	76	88	1.1	1.2
Shoe stores	4482	30.0	29.7	189	185	2.6	2.6
Jewelry, luggage & leather goods stores	4483	30.6	31.3	161	168	3.6	3.9
Jewelry stores	44831	28.6	29.3	149	156	3.3	3.6
Luggage & leather goods stores	44832	2.0	2.0	12	12	0.2	0.2
Sporting goods, hobby, book & music stores	451	66.1	65.0	590	616	8.2	8.8
Sporting goods, hobby, musical instrument stores .	4511	44.2	43.6	383	389	5.7	6.0
Sporting goods stores	45111	23.1	22.6	182	185	2.8	2.9
Hobby, toy & game stores	45112	10.8	10.9	125	131	1.7	1.8
Sewing, needlework & piece goods stores	45113	5.9	5.7	45	39	0.5	0.5
Musical instrument & supplies stores	45114	4.4	4.4	32	33	0.7	0.8
Book, periodical & music stores	4512	21.8	21.4	207	228	2.6	2.8
Book stores & news dealers	45121	14.1	13.7	140	152	1.8	1.9
Book stores	451211	12.0	11.7	130	142	1.6	1.7
News dealers & newsstands	451212	2.1	2.0	9	10	0.1	0.2
Prerecorded tape, CD & record stores	45122	7.8	7.7	67	76	0.8	0.9
General merchandise stores	452	38.1	39.6	2,445	2,526	36.6	39.8
Department stores	4521	10.5	10.4	1,731	1,766	25.3	27.2
Other general merchandise stores	4529	27.6	29.2	714	760	11.2	12.6
Warehouse clubs & superstores	45291	1.8	2.0	462	478	7.9	8.7
All other general merchandise stores	45299	25.8	27.2	252	283	3.3	3.8
Miscellaneous store retailers	453	131.2	131.0	829	850	13.0	13.8
Florists	4531	24.8	24.2	122	122	1.5	1.6
Office supplies, stationery & gift stores	4532	43.6	43.0	339	350	4.8	5.2
Office supplies & stationery stores	45321	8.4	8.6	124	135	2.4	2.7
Gift, novelty & souvenir stores	45322	35.2	34.4	215	215	2.4	2.5
Used merchandise stores	4533	18.0	17.5	110	114	1.5	1.6
Other miscellaneous store retailers	4539	44.8	46.4	258	264	5.1	5.4
Pet & pet supplies stores	45391	8.2	8.1	66	68	0.9	0.9
Art dealers	45392	5.9	6.0	25	22	0.6	0.6
Manufactured (mobile) home dealers	45393	6.0	6.2	46	43	1.4	1.3
All other miscellaneous store retailers	45399	24.7	26.1	121	131	2.3	2.6
Tobacco stores	453991	4.8	5.5	19	22	0.3	0.4
All other misc. store retailers (exc. tobacco) .	453998	20.0	20.6	102	108	2.0	2.2
Nonstore retailers	454	43.6	44.8	540	567	16.1	18.1
Electronic shopping & mail-order houses	4541	10.6	11.8	255	277	8.9	10.4
Vending machine operators	4542	6.3	6.2	67	67	1.5	1.5
Direct selling establishments	4543	26.7	26.8	218	223	5.8	6.1
Fuel dealers	45431	12.2	11.8	107	106	3.0	3.1
Heating oil dealers	454311	5.4	5.2	55	54	1.7	1.7
Liquified petroleum gas (bottled gas) dealers .	454312	6.5	6.3	51	51	1.3	1.4
Other fuel dealers	454319	0.3	0.3	1	1	-	-
Other direct selling establishments	45439	14.5	15.0	111	117	2.8	3.0

- Represents or rounds to zero.   [1] Based on North American Industrial Classification System; see text, Section 15, Business Enterprise   [2] Includes government employees.

Source: U.S. Census Bureau, *County Business Patterns,* annual. See also <http://www.census.gov/prod/2002pubs/cbp00/cbp00-1.pdf> (issued May 2002).

[2,460,886 represents $2,460,886,000,000. Covers only establishments with payroll. See Appendix III]

Kind of business	NAICS code [1]	Estab-lish-ments (number)	Sales Total (mil. dol.)	Sales Per paid employee (dol.)	Annual payroll Total (mil. dol.)	Annual payroll Per paid employee (dol.)	Paid employee for pay period including March 12 (1,000)
Retail trade	44,45	1,118,447	2,460,886	175,889	237,196	16,953	13,991.1
Motor vehicle & parts dealers	441	122,633	645,368	375,440	50,239	29,226	1,719.0
Automobile dealers	4411	49,237	553,652	486,088	37,400	32,836	1,139.0
New car dealers.................	44111	25,897	518,972	496,034	35,203	33,647	1,046.2
Used car dealers	44112	23,340	34,680	373,905	2,197	23,691	92.8
Other motor vehicle dealers...........	4412	13,589	28,891	281,124	2,570	25,007	102.8
Recreational vehicle dealers...........	44121	3,014	10,070	341,776	814	27,627	29.5
Motorcycle, boat, & other motor vehicle dealers....................	44122	10,575	18,821	256,746	1,756	23,954	73.3
Motorcycle dealers	441221	3,635	7,369	253,885	712	24,532	29.0
Boat dealers	441222	5,262	8,934	254,290	839	23,888	35.1
All other motor vehicle dealers	441229	1,678	2,517	275,262	205	22,372	9.1
Automotive parts, accessories, & tire stores	4413	59,807	62,825	131,653	10,269	21,519	477.2
Automotive parts & accessories stores..	44131	42,519	43,166	129,024	6,718	20,081	334.6
Tire dealers..................	44132	17,288	19,659	137,821	3,551	24,892	142.6
Furniture & home furnishings stores	442	64,725	71,691	148,476	9,959	20,627	482.8
Furniture stores.................	4421	29,461	40,968	163,026	5,620	22,362	251.3
Home furnishings stores	4422	35,264	30,722	132,685	4,340	18,743	231.5
Floor covering stores	44221	16,603	16,472	171,250	2,458	25,557	96.2
Other home furnishings stores	44229	18,661	14,251	105,281	1,882	13,901	135.4
Window treatment stores	442291	2,126	915	107,078	149	17,380	8.5
All other home furnishings stores....	442299	16,535	13,335	105,159	1,733	13,667	126.8
Electronics & appliance stores...........	443	43,373	68,561	198,704	7,064	20,473	345.0
Appliance, television, & other electronics stores	44311	28,789	42,251	178,249	4,462	18,826	237.0
Household appliance stores	443111	10,484	10,083	167,434	1,218	20,218	60.2
Radio, television, & other electronics stores	443112	18,305	32,168	181,933	3,245	18,352	176.8
Computer & software stores	44312	11,741	24,059	265,839	2,278	25,168	90.5
Computer stores (custom assembly) ...	4431201	3,801	3,983	234,142	395	23,228	17.0
Other computer stores	4431202	5,670	17,230	294,075	1,466	25,014	58.6
Prepackaged software stores	4431203	2,270	2,845	190,975	417	27,990	14.9
Camera & photographic supplies stores...	44313	2,843	2,252	128,609	324	18,504	17.5
Building material & garden equipment & supplies dealers	444	93,117	227,566	203,564	25,609	22,908	1,117.9
Building material & supplies dealers	4441	71,916	195,888	205,701	22,313	23,431	952.3
Home centers	44411	3,997	51,628	181,883	4,996	17,602	283.9
Paint & wallpaper stores	44412	8,429	7,943	182,536	1,011	23,235	43.5
Hardware stores	44413	15,748	13,605	98,710	2,095	15,202	137.8
Other building material dealers	44419	43,742	122,712	251,925	14,210	29,173	487.1
Retail lumber yards	4441901	11,046	41,846	243,920	4,452	25,948	171.6
All other building material dealers ...	4441902	32,696	80,866	256,278	9,759	30,927	315.5
Lawn & garden equipment & supplies stores	4442	21,201	31,678	191,273	3,296	19,900	165.6
Outdoor power equipment stores	44421	4,769	4,069	153,676	535	20,222	26.5
Nursery & garden centers	44422	16,432	27,609	198,428	2,760	19,839	139.1
Food & beverage stores...............	445	148,528	401,764	138,871	40,581	14,027	2,893.1
Grocery stores	4451	96,542	368,250	139,298	37,426	14,157	2,643.6
Supermarkets & other grocery (except convenience) stores	44511	69,461	351,403	141,141	35,828	14,390	2,489.7
Convenience stores	44512	27,081	16,848	109,481	1,598	10,387	153.9
Specialty food stores	4452	22,373	10,830	91,137	1,456	12,250	118.8
Meat markets	44521	7,214	4,347	109,041	544	13,656	39.9
Fish & seafood markets............	44522	1,634	1,038	145,724	102	14,316	7.1
Fruit & vegetable markets	44523	3,179	2,107	122,128	237	13,736	17.3
Other specialty food stores [2]	44529	10,346	3,339	61,152	572	10,483	54.6
Baked goods stores	445291	2,790	890	60,115	191	12,899	14.8
Confectionery & nut stores	445292	3,684	1,228	56,907	191	8,842	21.6
Beer, wine, & liquor stores	4453	29,613	22,684	173,645	1,699	13,008	130.6
Health & personal care stores	446	82,941	117,701	130,244	15,191	16,809	903.7
Pharmacies & drug stores.............	44611	43,615	98,631	140,150	11,588	16,465	703.8
Cosmetics, beauty supplies, & perfume stores	44612	9,014	4,419	94,977	604	12,973	46.5
Optical goods stores	44613	15,192	6,432	88,052	1,401	19,182	73.0
Other health & personal care stores	44619	15,120	8,219	102,269	1,598	19,888	80.4
Gasoline stations	447	126,889	198,166	214,916	11,482	12,453	922.1
Gasoline stations with convenience stores.	44711	81,684	127,609	207,847	7,229	11,774	614.0
Other gasoline stations..............	44719	45,205	70,557	229,002	4,254	13,805	308.1
Clothing & clothing accessories stores	448	156,601	100,090	100,548	16,597	12,965	1,280.2
Clothing stores	4481	94,740	95,918	103,368	11,225	12,097	927.9
Men's clothing stores	44811	12,143	9,865	118,025	1,325	15,855	83.6
Women's clothing stores	44812	39,672	27,258	89,169	3,366	11,011	305.7
Children's & infant's clothing stores	44813	5,115	4,638	99,699	474	10,198	46.5
Family clothing stores	44814	20,450	44,796	114,197	4,797	12,229	392.3
Clothing accessories stores	44815	5,860	2,132	82,794	314	12,184	25.8
Other clothing stores..............	44819	11,500	7,229	97,535	949	12,799	74.1

See footnotes at end of table.

U.S. Census Bureau, Statistical Abstract of the United States: 2002

[See headnote, page 638]

Kind of business	NAICS code [1]	Estab- lish- ments (number)	Sales Total (mil. dol.)	Sales Per paid employee (dol.)	Annual payroll Total (mil. dol.)	Annual payroll Per paid employee (dol.)	Paid employee for pay period including March 12 (1,000)
Shoe stores	4482	31,399	20,543	110,565	2,349	12,640	185.8
Men's shoe stores	4482101	2,376	1,317	133,360	177	17,941	9.9
Women's shoe stores	4482102	4,466	2,343	87,356	325	12,122	26.8
Children's & juvenile's shoe stores	4482103	1,047	459	81,581	67	11,902	5.6
Family shoe stores	4482104	18,233	10,499	112,517	1,159	12,424	93.3
Athletic footwear stores	4482105	5,277	5,924	118,111	620	12,359	50.2
Jewelry, luggage, & leather goods stores	4483	30,462	19,936	119,795	3,024	18,169	166.4
Jewelry stores	44831	28,336	18,511	119,523	2,836	18,311	154.9
Luggage & leather goods stores	44832	2,126	1,425	123,448	188	16,259	11.5
Sporting goods, hobby, book, & music stores	451	69,149	62,011	110,568	7,113	12,683	560.8
Sporting goods, hobby, & musical instrument stores	4511	46,315	41,415	114,100	4,819	13,276	363.0
Sporting goods stores	45111	24,424	20,043	113,760	2,388	13,553	176.2
General-line sporting goods stores	4511101	7,458	9,312	115,429	1,005	12,462	80.7
Specialty-line sporting goods stores	4511102	16,966	10,732	112,349	1,383	14,475	95.5
Hobby, toy, & game stores	45112	10,824	14,388	128,746	1,369	12,247	111.8
Sewing, needlework, & piece goods stores	45113	6,590	3,183	70,184	495	10,910	45.4
Musical instrument & supplies stores	45114	4,477	3,801	128,078	567	19,119	29.7
Book, periodical, & music stores	4512	22,834	20,596	104,089	2,295	11,597	197.9
Book stores & news dealers	45121	14,676	13,229	100,797	1,567	11,936	131.2
Book stores	451211	12,363	12,375	101,875	1,447	11,915	121.5
Book stores, general	4512111	7,693	8,167	103,517	965	12,228	78.9
Specialty book stores	4512112	2,980	1,419	76,614	199	10,762	18.5
College book stores	4512113	1,690	2,789	115,933	283	11,774	24.1
News dealers & newsstands	451212	2,313	854	87,391	119	12,208	9.8
Prerecorded tape, compact disc, & record stores	45122	8,158	7,367	110,575	728	10,927	66.6
General merchandise stores	452	36,171	330,444	131,780	30,871	12,311	2,507.5
Department stores (incl. leased depts.) [3]	4521	10,366	223,232	(NA)	(NA)	(NA)	(NA)
Conventional department stores (incl. leased depts.) [3]	4521101	2,100	53,293	(NA)	(NA)	(NA)	(NA)
Discount or mass merch. dept. stores (incl. leased depts.) [3]	4521102	6,378	128,214	(NA)	(NA)	(NA)	(NA)
National chain department stores (incl. leased depts.) [3]	4521103	1,888	41,726	(NA)	(NA)	(NA)	(NA)
Department stores (excl. leased depts.)	4521	10,366	220,108	122,584	22,083	12,299	1,795.6
Conventional department stores (excl. leased depts.)	4521101	2,100	52,453	126,411	6,061	14,607	414.9
Discount or mass merchandising dept. stores (excl. leased depts.)	4521102	6,378	126,123	122,219	11,330	10,979	1,031.9
National chain department stores (excl. leased depts.)	4521103	1,888	41,532	119,107	4,693	13,458	348.7
Other general merchandise stores	4529	25,805	110,336	154,975	8,788	12,343	712.0
Warehouse clubs & superstores	45291	1,530	81,919	191,239	5,863	13,686	428.4
All other general merchandise stores	45299	24,275	28,418	100,201	2,925	10,314	283.6
Miscellaneous store retailers	453	129,838	78,109	103,733	10,165	13,500	753.0
Florists	4531	26,200	6,555	52,359	1,396	11,154	125.2
Office supplies, stationery, & gift stores	4532	44,615	31,573	103,014	3,637	11,868	306.5
Office supplies & stationery stores	45321	7,330	17,076	174,027	1,581	16,110	98.1
Stationery stores	4532101	1,202	513	83,321	75	12,191	6.2
Office supplies stores	4532102	6,128	16,563	180,099	1,506	16,372	92.0
Gift, novelty, & souvenir stores	45322	37,285	14,497	69,574	2,057	9,870	208.4
Used merchandise stores	4533	17,990	6,044	61,692	1,204	12,286	98.0
Other miscellaneous store retailers	4539	41,033	33,937	151,958	3,928	17,588	223.3
Pet & pet supplies stores	45391	8,318	5,493	89,763	709	11,588	61.2
Art dealers	45392	5,698	3,001	153,808	401	20,561	19.5
Manufactured (mobile) home dealers	45393	5,485	13,347	330,375	1,123	27,790	40.4
All other miscellaneous store retailers	45399	21,532	12,096	118,324	1,695	16,581	102.2
Nonstore retailers	454	44,482	123,107	243,297	12,323	24,355	506.0
Electronic shopping & mail-order houses	4541	10,013	79,018	361,795	5,743	26,297	218.4
Vending machine operators	4542	7,070	6,884	103,763	1,333	20,097	66.3
Direct selling establishments	4543	27,399	37,204	168,161	5,246	23,714	221.2
Fuel dealers [2]	45431	12,532	22,622	217,987	2,755	26,550	103.8
Heating oil dealers	454311	5,657	13,867	256,289	1,528	28,238	54.1
Liquefied petroleum gas (bottled gas) dealers	454312	6,623	8,657	177,082	1,216	24,873	48.9
Other direct selling establishments	45439	14,867	14,582	124,140	2,491	21,209	117.5
Direct selling, furniture, home furnishings, electronics, & appl.	4543901	4,284	3,617	122,608	551	18,678	29.5
Direct selling, books, periodicals, videos & compact discs	4543902	1,263	1,752	89,956	324	16,648	19.5
Direct selling, other merchandise	4543903	9,320	9,212	134,521	1,616	23,596	68.5

NA Not available.   [1] North American Industry Classification System, 1997; see text, Section 15, Business Enterprise.   [2] Includes other kinds of business not shown separately.   [3] Not included in broader kind-of-business totals.

Source: U.S. Census Bureau, *1997 Economic Census, Retail Trade, Geographic Area,* Series EC97R44A-US(RV), issued March 2000.

Domestic Trade   639

No. 1002. Retail Trade and Food Services—Estimated Per Capita Sales by Selected Kinds of Business: 1992 to 2001

[As of Dec. 31. In dollars. Based on estimated resident population estimates as of July 1. For statement on methodology, see Appendix III]

Kind of business	NAICS code [1]	1992	1993	1994	1995	1996	1997	1998	1999	2000	2001
Retail sales, total	**44-45**	7,259	7,673	8,248	8,595	9,057	9,371	9,747	10,518	10,843	11,123
Total (Excluding motor vehicle and parts dealers)	*44-45*	*5,582*	*5,804*	*6,135*	*6,358*	*6,662*	*6,904*	*7,159*	*7,658*	*7,949*	*8,112*
Motor vehicle and parts dealers	441	1,677	1,870	2,113	2,237	2,395	2,467	2,588	2,860	2,895	3,011
Furniture, home furnishings	442	216	225	241	249	262	277	291	312	324	321
Electronics and appliance stores	443	168	189	221	247	258	262	281	301	310	308
Building material and garden equipment and supply stores	444	628	666	733	757	802	857	901	968	986	1,045
Food and beverage stores	445	1,456	1,456	1,480	1,489	1,516	1,532	1,560	1,623	1,628	1,659
Health and personal care stores	446	356	363	374	390	415	445	482	533	558	598
Gasoline stations	447	614	631	658	690	734	746	710	768	866	834
Clothing and clothing accessories stores	448	472	485	497	501	516	525	553	586	594	594
Sporting goods, hobby, book, and music stores	451	193	203	221	232	242	245	257	272	277	298
General merchandise stores	452	972	1,032	1,096	1,144	1,189	1,238	1,302	1,399	1,439	1,511
Miscellaneous store retailers	453	219	243	271	294	317	342	369	388	386	393
Nonstore retailers	454	288	310	343	365	411	435	453	508	581	549
Food services and drinking places	**722**	**798**	**838**	**867**	**889**	**916**	**964**	**1,009**	**1,047**	**1,085**	**1,126**

[1] North American Industry Classification System, 1997; see text, Section 15, Business Enterprise.
Source: U.S. Census Bureau, *Current Business Reports, Annual Benchmark Report for Retail Trade and Food Services: January 1992 Through March 2002*, Series BR/01-A, and Population Division, Population Estimates Program.

No. 1003. Retail Trade—Estimated Purchases by Kind of Business: 1992 to 2000

[In billions of dollars (1,347.5 represents $1,347,500,000,000)]

Kind of business	NAICS code [1]	1992	1994	1995	1996	1997	1998	1999	2000
Total	**44,45**	1,347.5	1,572.2	1,646.0	1,749.9	1,830.5	1,917.6	2,096.6	2,234.0
Total (excl. motor vehicle and parts dealers)	*(X)*	1,004.8	1,128.3	1,174.6	1,239.4	1,295.8	1,348.8	1,460.0	1,565.9
Motor vehicle and parts dealers	441	342.6	443.9	471.4	510.5	534.8	568.9	636.6	668.1
Furniture and home furnishings stores	442	32.1	36.7	38.3	40.6	43.0	45.2	48.7	51.9
Electronics and appliance stores	443	30.8	42.5	49.0	51.5	52.1	56.6	61.1	64.4
Building material, garden equipment and supplies dealers	444	115.9	139.0	145.2	155.1	169.8	177.9	193.2	201.6
Food and beverage stores	445	279.2	289.0	290.3	298.2	303.6	310.0	323.5	332.8
Health and personal care stores	446	63.7	68.3	72.3	77.3	83.0	90.5	102.0	110.3
Gasoline stations	447	125.4	134.9	140.1	151.2	155.7	149.6	165.1	194.1
Clothing and clothing accessories stores	448	71.7	76.8	78.3	81.1	83.5	87.3	92.7	98.4
Sporting goods, hobby, book, and music stores	451	31.1	36.9	39.2	40.9	41.1	44.4	47.2	50.1
General merchandise stores	452	182.0	212.5	223.1	232.7	243.4	257.0	280.3	298.8
Miscellaneous store retailers	453	31.5	41.0	44.8	48.6	53.1	58.7	62.8	64.7
Nonstore retailers	454	41.6	50.7	54.0	62.3	67.5	71.6	83.5	98.8
Electronic shopping and mail order	4541	19.3	26.9	30.1	35.2	41.2	47.8	57.9	68.1

X Not applicable. [1] North American Industry Classification System, 1997; see text, Section 15, Business Enterprise.
Source: U.S. Census Bureau, *Current Business Reports, Annual Benchmark Report for Retail Trade and Food Services, January 1992 Through March 2002*, Series BR/01-A, and unpublished data.

No. 1004. Retail Trade—Merchandise Inventories and Inventory/Sales Ratio by Kind of Business: 1992 to 2001

[Inventories in billions of dollars (267.8 represents $267,800,000,000). As of Dec. 31. Estimates exclude food services. Includes warehouses. Adjusted for seasonal variations. Sales data also adjusted for holiday and trading-day differences]

Kind of business	NAICS code [1]	Inventories				Inventory/sales ratio			
		1992	1995	2000	2001	1992	1995	2000	2001
Total	**44,45**	267.8	329.5	416.5	395.8	1.69	1.70	1.62	1.48
Excluding motor vehicle and parts dealers	*44,45 ex 441*	*196.4*	*234.3*	*285.7*	*280.0*	*1.61*	*1.64*	*1.50*	*1.45*
Motor vehicle and parts dealers	441	71.4	95.2	130.8	115.8	1.93	1.87	1.96	1.57
Furniture, home furnishings, electronics, and appliance stores	442,443	16.5	22.1	25.8	25.0	1.99	1.95	1.80	1.59
Building material and garden equipment and supplies dealers	444	25.3	31.2	40.7	39.8	1.92	1.80	1.71	1.63
Food and beverage stores	445	27.4	28.6	32.8	33.0	0.00	0.00	0.84	0.84
Clothing and clothing accessories stores	448	27.5	29.4	35.9	33.0	2.64	2.62	2.53	2.29
General merchandise stores	452	49.6	59.6	65.4	65.1	2.27	2.33	1.88	1.74
Department stores	4521	38.0	43.3	42.6	41.3	2.48	2.49	2.16	2.14

[1] North American Industry Classification System, 1997; see text, Section 15, Business Enterprise.
Source: U.S. Census Bureau, *Current Business Reports, Annual Benchmark Report for Retail Trade and Food Services: January 1992 Through March 2002*, Series BR/01-A, and unpublished data.

U.S. Census Bureau, *Statistical Abstract of the United States: 2002*

No. 1005. Retail Trade and Food Services—Sales by Kind of Business: 1992 to 2001

[In billions of dollars (2,054.6 represents $2,054,600,000,000)]

Kind of business	NAICS code [1]	1992	1994	1995	1996	1998	1999	2000	2001
Retail and food services sales, total ..	**44, 45, 72**	**2,054.6**	**2,372.8**	**2,492.4**	**2,645.2**	**2,906.7**	**3,153.6**	**3,365.1**	**3,488.6**
Retail sales, total	**44, 45**	**1,851.2**	**2,147.2**	**2,258.8**	**2,402.3**	**2,634.1**	**2,868.2**	**3,059.1**	**3,167.8**
GAFO, total [2]		536.9	619.6	653.0	685.3	762.6	822.8	873.1	907.5
Motor vehicle and parts dealers	441	427.6	550.1	588.0	635.3	699.5	780.0	816.7	857.6
Automobile and other motor vehicle dealers	4411, 4412	377.2	492.8	528.7	572.9	631.9	708.2	743.0	784.9
Automobile dealers	4411	359.1	468.9	502.5	544.8	597.5	669.8	700.3	735.0
New car dealers.	44111	333.8	435.7	464.6	502.3	545.1	611.9	638.0	669.6
Used cars dealers	44112	25.3	33.2	37.8	42.4	52.3	57.9	62.4	65.4
Auto parts, access., and tire stores	4413	50.4	57.3	59.3	62.3	67.6	71.7	73.6	72.7
Furniture, home furnishings, electronics and appliance stores	442, 443	97.8	120.2	130.4	137.9	154.6	167.2	178.8	179.2
Furniture and home furnishings stores ..	442	55.0	62.8	65.5	69.4	78.6	85.1	91.4	91.5
Furniture stores.	4421	31.6	35.6	37.0	39.2	44.1	47.0	50.5	50.4
Home furnishings stores	4422	23.4	27.2	28.5	30.2	34.4	38.2	40.9	41.2
Electronics and appliance stores [3]	443	42.8	57.4	64.9	68.5	76.0	82.0	87.5	87.7
Appl. TV, and other elect. stores.	44311	29.0	37.9	42.1	43.3	46.3	51.5	57.3	59.1
Household appliance stores	443111	8.4	9.1	10.0	10.2	10.8	11.5	11.8	12.3
Radio, TV, and other elect. stores .	443112	20.6	28.9	32.2	33.1	35.5	40.0	45.5	46.7
Computer and software stores	44312	11.5	17.2	20.5	22.9	27.2	27.8	27.2	25.4
Building mat. garden equip. & supply stores..........................	444	160.2	190.8	199.1	212.8	243.5	264.0	278.1	297.7
Building mat. & supply dealers	4441	135.5	165.2	172.3	183.3	210.0	229.6	241.7	256.4
Hardware stores	44413	12.7	13.8	13.8	14.0	14.8	15.1	15.4	16.5
Food and beverage stores [3]	445	371.5	385.3	391.3	402.0	421.6	442.6	459.2	472.6
Grocery stores	4451	337.9	351.1	356.9	366.1	382.4	401.8	415.3	425.4
Beer, wine and liquor stores	4453	21.8	22.2	22.1	23.3	25.7	27.0	29.0	30.6
Health and personal care stores	446	90.8	97.3	102.5	110.2	130.2	145.4	157.5	170.3
Pharmacies and drug stores	44611	77.8	82.0	85.9	91.8	108.3	122.7	131.3	143.0
Gasoline stations	447	156.6	171.4	181.3	194.6	191.7	209.4	244.5	237.7
Clothing and clothing access. stores [3]	448	120.3	129.3	131.6	136.9	149.4	159.9	167.5	169.1
Clothing stores [3]	4481	85.9	90.8	91.4	94.5	104.9	112.4	118.6	121.0
Men's clothing stores	44811	10.2	10.0	9.3	9.6	10.6	10.5	10.8	10.6
Women's clothing stores	44812	31.8	30.6	28.7	28.3	28.7	30.2	32.5	32.8
Family clothing stores.	44814	33.2	38.1	40.0	42.3	49.5	53.8	56.5	57.3
Shoe stores.................	4482	18.1	19.4	19.8	20.6	21.5	21.8	21.9	21.7
Jewelry stores	44831	15.2	18.0	19.2	20.3	21.5	24.1	25.3	24.8
Sporting goods, hobby, book & music stores..........................	451	49.3	57.5	60.9	64.1	69.5	74.0	78.1	84.8
Sporting goods stores	45111	15.7	19.0	20.0	20.9	22.6	24.2	26.1	27.9
Book stores	451211	8.3	10.1	11.2	11.9	13.4	14.5	15.4	16.7
General merchandise stores. . . , ...	452	248.0	285.3	300.6	315.4	351.8	381.4	405.9	430.5
Department stores (excl. L.D. [4]).	4521	177.1	200.4	207.7	213.9	221.2	231.0	233.6	230.1
Discount dept. stores	4521102	91.9	111.0	118.4	121.7	126.5	133.7	136.3	137.8
Conventional and national chain dept.	4521101, 4521103	85.2	89.4	89.3	92.2	94.6	97.3	97.4	92.3
Department stores (incl. L.D. [4])	4521	181.3	205.3	212.8	218.7	226.0	236.1	238.7	234.7
Discount dept. stores	4521102	93.9	113.3	120.5	123.7	128.5	135.7	138.4	139.9
Conventional and national chain dept.	4521101, 4521103	87.4	92.0	92.3	95.1	97.5	100.4	100.4	94.8
Other general merchandise stores	4529	70.9	84.9	92.9	101.5	130.6	150.4	172.3	200.4
Warehouse clubs and superstores ...	45291	40.0	56.3	63.3	71.4	101.2	119.2	140.0	164.5
All other Gen. merchandise stores ...	45299	30.9	28.6	29.6	30.1	29.4	31.2	32.3	35.8
Miscellaneous stores retail	453	55.8	70.6	77.2	84.1	99.8	105.7	109.0	112.0
Nonstore retailers.................	454	73.4	89.4	95.9	109.1	122.5	138.4	163.8	156.4
Electronic shopping and mail order.	4541	35.3	47.1	52.7	61.2	79.5	92.9	109.9	106.5
Fuel dealers	45431	19.3	20.8	21.6	24.1	19.7	20.8	27.9	26.0
Food services and drinking places [3]....................	**722**	**203.4**	**225.6**	**233.6**	**242.9**	**272.6**	**285.5**	**306.0**	**320.7**
Full service restaurants	7221	86.5	97.1	99.4	104.5	119.7	124.6	132.9	137.6
Limited service eating places	7222	87.4	98.4	103.1	106.2	116.8	122.2	131.4	138.2
Drinking places	7224	12.4	11.8	12.5	13.0	14.1	14.7	15.7	16.8

[1] North American Industry Classification System, 1997; see text, Section 15, Business Enterprise. [2] GAFO represents stores classified in the following NAICS codes: 442,443,448,451,452, and 4532. [3] Includes other kinds of business not shown separately. [4] L.D. represents leased departments.

Source: U.S. Census Bureau, Current Business Reports, Annual Benchmark Report for Retail Trade and Food Services, January 1992 Through March 2002, Series BR/01-A.

No. 1006. Retail Trade and Food Services—Sales by Type of Store and State: 2001

[In millions of dollars, (3,324,957 represents $3,324,957,000,000) except as indicated. Kind-of-business classification based on North American Industry Classification System (NAICS); see text, Section 15, Business Enterprise. Data are estimates]

State	All retail stores [1] (NAICS 44, 45)	Total retail sales + food and drink	Motor vehicle and parts dealers (NAICS 441)	Furniture and home furnishings (NAICS 442)	Electronics and appliances (NAICS 443)	Bldg. material & garden equip. & supp dealers (NAICS 444)	Food and beverage stores (NAICS 445)	Health and personal care (NAICS 446)
U.S...	3,324,957	3,658,749	961,940	97,673	95,700	285,912	493,963	163,680
AL	45,174	49,494	13,638	1,129	736	4,124	6,215	2,012
AK	7,549	8,427	1,805	117	160	881	1,468	117
AZ	64,152	70,071	19,317	2,055	1,862	4,952	9,399	2,912
AR	27,368	29,653	8,568	568	476	2,507	3,156	944
CA	392,114	436,531	112,317	12,468	18,029	31,932	62,429	19,088
CO	58,342	64,382	16,769	2,206	2,008	5,752	9,160	1,701
CT	46,624	50,728	12,780	1,428	1,420	4,052	7,651	2,657
DE	11,180	12,271	3,171	478	424	1,111	1,562	658
DC	2,540	3,994	138	114	84	198	568	337
FL.....	195,869	213,757	63,565	6,002	5,428	13,999	31,793	10,390
GA	99,789	110,074	30,825	3,386	2,535	10,608	14,638	3,656
HI.....	12,308	14,505	2,289	199	201	580	2,337	884
ID.....	15,563	16,754	4,639	420	393	1,805	2,304	360
IL.....	138,373	154,272	39,602	4,044	3,960	11,768	20,524	8,153
IN.....	73,717	80,757	22,327	1,773	1,671	6,908	8,951	3,706
IA	34,875	37,645	10,763	883	830	4,170	4,840	1,381
KS	34,662	37,358	9,971	972	1,014	2,860	5,029	1,251
KY	41,201	46,131	11,374	844	667	4,090	5,967	2,083
LA	45,044	49,918	13,612	957	747	3,915	6,519	2,141
ME	17,793	19,096	4,536	322	222	1,606	3,624	609
MD	60,240	66,360	16,483	1,906	2,054	4,741	11,253	3,268
MA	81,369	91,407	21,653	2,182	1,757	5,849	13,666	5,182
MI.....	124,085	135,390	38,446	3,407	3,085	9,791	14,390	7,937
MN	73,837	79,832	19,802	2,531	2,615	7,708	8,934	3,181
MS	28,351	30,639	8,559	745	444	2,818	4,185	1,152
MO	67,548	73,955	21,229	1,607	1,490	5,486	8,601	2,684
MT	9,133	10,144	2,485	218	195	1,131	1,672	254
NE	20,214	22,084	5,351	902	422	2,246	2,833	775
NV	26,257	29,439	6,899	766	834	2,264	4,002	1,067
NH	22,720	24,308	7,137	613	754	1,656	3,338	812
NJ.....	104,969	113,988	28,746	3,494	3,444	6,719	17,105	7,655
NM	20,125	22,006	5,342	603	409	1,568	2,736	907
NY	185,761	206,352	43,783	5,689	5,470	13,945	30,224	13,986
NC	93,780	103,573	28,291	3,586	2,190	10,302	13,170	4,060
ND	7,844	8,487	2,100	188	169	1,374	823	358
OH	135,446	148,948	39,924	4,101	4,028	11,788	18,386	8,019
OK	35,455	38,976	11,558	944	961	2,599	4,405	1,459
OR	45,834	50,235	13,243	1,192	1,134	4,734	6,315	1,245
PA	134,331	147,088	39,501	3,127	2,695	10,892	21,354	8,215
RI.....	10,136	11,546	2,654	274	212	610	1,926	917
SC	45,266	49,994	12,825	1,267	787	5,609	6,813	1,889
SD	14,448	15,247	2,758	194	175	1,204	1,314	339
TN	70,106	76,919	20,694	1,910	1,242	5,892	12,115	3,039
TX	262,791	288,536	83,426	7,643	8,247	19,580	34,349	8,904
UT	26,877	28,959	7,551	1,043	856	2,808	4,979	401
VT	7,466	8,091	2,235	157	172	816	1,269	341
VA	81,954	89,613	22,511	2,900	2,895	7,365	11,929	3,466
WA	72,294	80,954	18,276	2,044	2,029	7,203	10,545	3,124
WV	17,415	18,960	4,908	318	224	1,499	2,633	1,218
WI.....	68,292	73,982	19,753	1,641	1,752	7,341	9,579	2,670
WY	6,376	6,917	1,809	116	94	557	988	116

See footnotes at end of table.

U.S. Census Bureau, Statistical Abstract of the United States: 2002

No. 1006. Retail Trade and Food Services—Sales by Type of Store and State: 2001—Con.

[See headnote, page 642]

State	Gasoline stations (NAICS 447)	Clothing and clothing accessories (NAICS 448)	Sporting goods, hobby, book & music stores (NAICS 451)	General merchandise (NAICS 452)	Miscellaneous stores (NAICS 453)	Nonstore retailers (NAICS 454)	Food services & drinking places (NAICS 722)
U.S...	**261,964**	**178,525**	**85,849**	**441,892**	**108,738**	**149,120**	**333,792**
AL	4,541	2,232	769	7,532	1,419	829	4,320
AK	545	335	197	1,441	217	268	878
AZ	5,685	2,221	1,757	8,240	2,727	3,026	5,919
AR	2,811	1,028	486	5,440	869	516	2,285
CA	28,144	23,766	11,890	49,221	12,523	10,307	44,417
CO	4,353	2,519	2,177	7,430	2,235	2,031	6,040
CT	2,959	3,125	1,378	3,624	1,495	4,056	4,104
DE	626	621	371	1,379	388	393	1,091
DC	212	392	181	108	160	47	1,454
FL.	13,476	10,788	4,416	23,134	6,120	6,758	17,888
GA	9,350	5,029	1,844	12,938	3,015	1,966	10,284
HI.....	915	1,509	399	2,336	563	95	2,198
ID.....	1,288	456	435	2,061	564	840	1,191
IL.....	9,734	8,832	3,384	16,551	3,990	7,830	15,899
IN.....	6,690	2,693	1,386	11,281	2,136	4,194	7,040
IA	3,854	1,150	641	4,603	800	962	2,770
KS	3,219	1,601	785	6,212	1,058	689	2,696
KY	4,414	1,532	746	7,231	1,513	739	4,930
LA	4,745	2,070	760	7,626	1,235	717	4,874
ME	1,475	899	384	1,826	513	1,776	1,303
MD	4,056	4,030	1,963	6,828	1,888	1,770	6,121
MA	5,394	6,151	2,724	8,716	2,797	5,298	10,038
MI.....	8,540	5,221	4,101	20,820	5,172	3,176	11,305
MN	6,108	2,823	2,569	9,076	2,490	6,001	5,994
MS	3,070	1,021	363	4,721	828	443	2,289
MO	7,244	2,457	1,361	9,916	2,058	3,415	6,407
MT	792	268	280	1,381	275	182	1,011
NE	1,793	820	424	2,751	464	1,432	1,870
NV	1,919	2,067	671	2,714	1,294	1,758	3,182
NH	1,461	1,026	657	2,856	646	1,763	1,588
NJ.....	5,856	7,136	3,578	10,563	3,687	6,984	9,019
NM	1,975	781	505	3,103	1,169	1,026	1,882
NY	10,704	18,848	6,520	19,884	7,894	8,814	20,591
NC	7,007	4,317	1,751	11,785	3,754	2,688	9,794
ND	703	220	216	1,196	215	281	642
OH	10,558	6,099	2,981	19,912	3,677	5,972	13,502
OK	3,869	1,031	713	6,110	1,097	708	3,522
OR	3,072	1,890	1,318	7,897	1,758	2,035	4,401
PA	9,654	7,557	3,093	15,008	3,492	9,740	12,757
RI.....	771	573	290	916	319	675	1,411
SC	4,354	2,290	737	6,110	1,869	716	4,728
SD	976	302	204	1,228	327	5,427	800
TN	6,240	3,584	1,309	10,678	2,173	1,230	6,813
TX	22,156	12,865	5,783	36,286	7,775	15,777	25,744
UT	2,094	1,081	812	3,738	547	967	2,082
VT	669	299	204	485	221	599	625
VA	7,394	4,615	1,927	11,424	2,179	3,349	7,659
WA	4,763	3,372	2,524	12,028	2,791	3,596	8,660
WV	1,935	688	279	2,926	504	283	1,544
WI.....	5,912	2,126	1,471	9,650	1,628	4,768	5,690
WY	1,009	168	132	967	208	210	542

[1] Includes other types of stores, not shown separately.

Source: Market Statistics, a division of Claritas Inc., Arlington, VA, *The Survey of Buying Power Data Service*, annual (copyright).

U.S. Census Bureau, Statistical Abstract of the United States: 2002

No. 1007. Retail Trade—Establishments and Sales by Merchandise Lines: 1997

[2,460,886 represents $2,460,886,000,000. Covers only establishments with payroll]

Merchandise lines	NAICS code [1] and ML code [2]	Establishments handling merchandise line		Merchandise line sales		
					As a percentage of total sales of—	
		Number	Total sales (mil. dol.)	Amount (mil. dol.)	Establishments handling line	All establishments
Retail trade [3]	**44,45**	**1,118,447**	**(X)**	**2,460,886**	**(X)**	**100.0**
Groceries & other foods for human consumption off the premises	100	322,867	934,996	367,224	39.3	14.9
Packaged liquor, wine, & beer	140	148,792	467,821	41,951	9.0	1.7
Cigars, cigarettes, tobacco, & smokers accessories	150	234,100	777,117	36,819	4.7	1.5
Drugs, health aids, & beauty aids (including cosmetics)	160	231,126	872,109	159,483	18.3	6.5
Men's wear	200	122,978	478,641	58,249	12.2	2.4
Women's, juniors, & misses wear	220	149,920	497,405	101,860	20.5	4.1
Children's wear	240	78,123	387,512	27,365	7.1	1.1
Footwear (including accessories)	260	119,579	406,513	39,182	9.6	1.6
Audio equipment & musical instruments & supplies	330	71,151	227,531	27,657	12.2	1.1
Furniture & sleep equipment	340	73,407	302,790	47,541	15.7	1.9
Computer hardware, software, & supplies	370	35,312	172,469	56,573	32.8	2.3
Kitchenware & home furnishings	380	154,091	586,734	32,382	5.5	1.3
Jewelry	400	126,364	440,843	31,358	7.1	1.3
Toys, hobby goods, & games	460	98,308	429,322	24,035	5.6	1.0
Sporting goods	500	74,961	351,311	35,612	10.1	1.4
Hardware, tools, & plumbing & electrical supplies	600	100,472	507,610	76,821	15.1	3.1
Lawn, garden, & farm equipment & supplies, cut flowers, etc.	620	118,805	541,974	52,123	9.6	2.1
Automobiles, vans, trucks, & other powered trans. vehicles	700	55,920	566,370	483,863	85.4	19.7
Automotive fuels	720	137,668	248,978	143,818	57.8	5.8
Automotive tires, tubes, batteries, parts, & accessories	740	152,701	773,034	82,182	10.6	3.3

X Not applicable.   [1] Based on North American Industry Classification System; see text, Section 15, Business Enterprise.
[2] ML is merchandise line code.   [3] Includes other merchandise lines not shown separately.
Source: U.S. Census Bureau, *1997 Economic Census, Merchandise Line Sales*, Series EC97R44S-LS(RV), January 2001.

No. 1008. Retail Trade—Nonemployer Establishments and Receipts by Kind of Business: 1997 to 1999

[1,831 represents 1,831,000. Includes only firms subject to federal income tax. Nonemployers are businesses with no paid employees. Based on the North American Industry Classification System (NAICS), see text, Section 15, Business Enterprise]

Kind of business	NAICS code	Establishments (1,000)			Receipts (mil. dol.)		
		1997	1998	1999	1997	1998	1999
Retail trade, total	**44-45**	**1,831**	**1,762**	**1,761**	**69,418**	**70,971**	**73,314**
Motor vehicle & parts dealers [1]	441	118	119	121	15,314	16,180	17,184
Used car dealers	44112	74	73	74	11,857	12,525	13,212
Motorcycle & boat & other MV dealers	44122	19	20	20	1,628	1,713	1,874
Automotive parts, accessories, & tire stores	4413	23	24	24	1,607	1,694	1,839
Furniture & home furnishings stores	442	40	38	37	2,402	2,534	2,542
Furniture stores	4421	15	14	14	977	1,025	1,026
Home furnishings stores	4422	25	24	23	1,424	1,510	1,516
Electronics & appliance stores	443	28	29	30	1,649	1,716	1,741
Bldg material & garden equip. & supp dealers [1]	444	29	28	28	1,923	2,032	2,165
Building material & supplies dealers	4441	20	20	20	1,487	1,578	1,685
Food & beverage stores	445	91	87	84	8,523	8,503	8,465
Grocery stores	4451	45	42	40	4,821	4,706	4,597
Specialty food stores	4452	36	35	34	2,163	2,151	2,141
Beer, wine, & liquor stores	4453	10	10	10	1,538	1,646	1,727
Health & personal care stores	446	60	80	89	1,355	1,607	1,813
Gasoline stations	447	11	11	10	1,690	1,739	1,713
Clothing & clothing accessories stores [1]	448	95	89	88	4,168	4,250	4,389
Clothing stores	4481	66	60	60	2,588	2,580	2,647
Jewelry stores	44831	23	23	23	1,267	1,348	1,406
Sporting goods, hobby, book, & music stores [1]	451	96	97	98	3,561	3,655	3,775
Sporting goods stores	45111	26	25	24	1,243	1,301	1,330
Book, periodical, & music stores	4512	31	32	33	1,054	1,024	1,025
General merchandise stores	452	21	24	26	1,009	1,170	1,250
Miscellaneous store retailers [1]	453	401	367	350	13,561	13,324	13,169
Gift, novelty, & souvenir stores	45322	70	71	72	1,924	2,072	2,130
Used merchandise stores	4533	87	84	80	2,260	2,200	2,243
Nonstore retailers [1]	454	844	793	799	14,263	14,261	15,109
Electronic shopping & mail-order houses	4541	56	42	45	1,103	1,100	1,260
Direct selling establishments	4543	750	713	717	12,246	12,203	12,860

[1] Includes other kinds of business not shown separately.
Source: U.S. Census Bureau, "Nonemployer Statistics"; published 28 March 2002; <http://www.census.gov/epcd/nonemployer/>.

No. 1009. Franchised New Car Dealerships—Summary: 1980 to 2001

[130.5 represents $130,500,000,000]

Item	Unit	1980	1985	1990	1995	1996	1997	1998	1999	2000	2001
Dealerships [1]	Number .	27,900	24,725	24,825	22,800	22,750	22,700	22,600	22,400	22,250	21,800
Sales	Bil. dol . .	130.5	251.6	316.0	456.2	490.0	507.5	546.3	606.5	650.3	690.4
New cars sold [2]	1,000. .	8,979	11,042	9,300	8,635	8,527	8,272	8,137	8,699	8,847	8,423
Used vehicles sold	Millions .	9.72	13.30	14.18	18.48	19.17	19.19	19.33	20.07	20.45	21.39
Employment	1,000. .	745	856	924	996	1,031	1,046	1,048	1,081	1,114	1,130
Annual payroll	Bil. dol . .	11.0	20.1	24.0	33.1	35.4	37.4	39.8	42.5	46.1	48.0
Advertising expenses	Bil. dol . .	1.2	2.8	3.7	4.6	5.0	5.1	5.3	5.6	6.4	6.6
Dealer pretax profits as a percentage of sales	Percent .	0.6	2.2	1.0	1.4	1.5	1.4	1.7	1.8	1.6	2.0
Inventory: [3] Domestic: [4]											
Total	1,000. . .	2,112	2,339	2,537	2,974	2,856	2,813	2,732	2,901	3,183	2,824
Days' supply	Days . . .	57	60	73	71	66	66	63	62	68	63
Imported: [4]											
Total	1,000. . .	269	345	707	445	317	338	350	378	468	508
Days' supply	Days . . .	31	30	72	72	58	54	54	47	50	51

[1] At beginning of year. [2] Data provided by "Ward's Automotive Reports." [3] Annual average. Includes light trucks. [4] Classification based on where automobiles are produced (i.e., automobiles manufactured by foreign companies but produced in the United States are classified as domestic).

Source: National Automobile Dealers Association, McLean, VA, *NADA Data*, annual.

No. 1010. New Motor Vehicle Sales and Expenditures by Model Year: 1990 to 2001

[In thousands of units (14,169 represents 14,169,000), except as indicated. A model year begins on Oct. 1 and ends on Sept. 30. It covers the fourth quarter of one calendar year and the first three quarters of the next calendar year]

Sales and expenditures	1990	1995	1996	1997	1998	1999	2000	2001
New motor vehicle sales	**14,169**	**15,204**	**15,459**	**15,498**	**15,963**	**17,414**	**17,817**	**17,472**
New-car sales	9,436	8,687	8,527	8,273	8,142	8,697	8,852	8,422
Domestic	6,790	7,178	7,254	6,906	6,764	6,982	6,833	6,323
Import	2,645	1,510	1,273	1,366	1,378	1,715	2,019	2,099
New-truck sales	4,733	6,517	6,932	7,226	7,821	8,717	8,965	9,050
Light	4,428	6,089	6,521	6,797	7,297	8,072	8,387	8,607
Domestic	3,996	5,694	6,089	6,226	6,651	7,310	7,546	7,629
Import	432	395	432	571	646	763	841	978
Other	306	429	411	429	524	645	578	443
Domestic-car production	6,231	6,351	6,081	5,927	5,547	5,637	5,540	4,882
Avg. expenditure per new car [1] (dollar) . .	14,371	17,959	18,777	19,531	20,370	20,672	20,427	21,605
Domestic (dollar)	13,936	16,864	17,468	17,907	18,485	18,639	18,897	19,654
Import (dollar)	15,510	23,202	26,205	27,722	29,615	28,974	27,767	27,477

[1] BEA estimate based on the manufacturer's suggested retail price.

Source: U.S. Bureau of Economic Analysis, *Survey of Current Business*, February 2001 and unpublished data. Data on unit sales and production are mainly from "Ward's Automotive Reports" published by Ward's Communications, Southfield, MI.

No. 1011. New and Used Car Sales and Leases: 1990 to 1999

[In thousands, except as indicated (46,830 represents 46,830,000]

Item	1990	1992	1993	1994	1995	1996	1997	1998	1999
Total car sales	**46,830**	**45,163**	**46,575**	**49,132**	**50,393**	**49,354**	**48,542**	**48,359**	**(NA)**
New passenger car sales [1]	9,300	8,213	8,518	8,991	8,635	8,526	8,272	8,139	(NA)
Used passenger car sales [2]	37,530	36,950	38,057	40,141	41,758	40,828	40,270	40,220	40,890
Value of transactions (bil. dol.)	219	247	279	312	338	337	338	335	361
Average price (dol.)	5,830	6,693	7,335	7,781	8,093	8,257	8,399	8,341	8,828
New passenger car leases [3]	**534**	**882**	**1,197**	**1,715**	**1,795**	**1,806**	**2,062**	**2,174**	**2,271**

NA Not available. [1] Includes leased cars. [2] Used car sales include sales from franchised dealers, independent dealers, and casual sales. [3] Consumer leases only.

Source: U.S. Bureau of Transportation Statistics, *National Transportation Statistics 2000*. Data supplied by following sources: New passenger car sales: 1994-98, American Automobile Manufacturers Association, *Motor Vehicle Facts & Figures, 1999*, Southfield, MI; Used passenger car sales: ADT Automotive, *2000 Used Car Market Report* Nashville, TN; Leased passenger cars: CNW Marketing/Research, Bandon, OR, personal communication, May 31, 2000.

U.S. Census Bureau, Statistical Abstract of the United States: 2002

No. 1012. Toy Industry—Retail Sales by Type of Product: 2000 and 2001

[In millions of dollars (31,149 represents $31,149,000,000), except as indicated. Minus sign (-) indicates decrease]

Product	Sales 2000	Sales 2001	Percent change, 2000-2001	Product	Sales 2000	Sales 2001	Percent change, 2000-2001
Total [1]	31,149	34,388	10	Games/puzzles	2,492	2,237	-10
Video games	6,581	9,409	43	Building/construction	722	882	22
Traditional toy industry	24,568	24,979	2	Arts & crafts	2,357	2,630	12
Infant/preschool	2,772	3,154	14	Models/accessories	266	281	6
Dolls	2,835	3,061	8	Learning/exploration	491	464	-6
Plush	2,336	2,031	-13	Pretend play	565	479	-15
Action figure toys	1,187	1,618	36	Trading cards/accessories	440	318	-28
Vehicles	2,624	2,821	8	Sports	2,135	1,528	-29
Ride-ons	664	773	17	All other toys	2,681	2,703	1

[1] Includes items not shown separately.

Source: NPD Group, Inc., Port Washington, NY and Toy Industry Association, Inc., New York, NY, *Toy Industry Fact Book*, annual (copyright).

No. 1013. Retail Food Stores—Number and Sales by Type: 1990 to 2000

[282.6 represents 282,600]

Type of food store	Number [1] (1,000)					Sales [2] (bil. dol.)					Percent distribution			
											Number		Sales	
	1990	1995	1998	1999	2000	1990	1995	1998	1999	2000	1990	2000	1990	2000
Total	282.6	264.4	251.9	247.8	243.8	368.3	402.5	435.4	458.3	483.7	100.0	100.0	100.0	100.0
Grocery stores	190.3	176.9	168.5	165.8	163.2	348.2	382.2	412.7	434.7	458.3	67.3	66.9	94.5	94.7
Supermarkets [3]	24.5	25.3	24.4	24.4	24.6	261.7	300.4	316.2	325.7	337.3	8.7	10.1	71.1	69.7
Conventional	13.2	12.3	10.9	10.3	9.9	92.3	76.4	65.3	63.6	63.4	4.7	4.1	25.1	13.1
Superstore [4]	5.8	6.8	7.4	7.6	7.9	87.6	116.7	133.8	138.9	142.4	2.1	3.2	23.8	29.4
Warehouse [5]	3.4	2.7	2.2	2.4	2.4	33.1	20.7	19.3	20.9	22.0	1.2	1.0	9.0	4.5
Combination food and drug [6]	1.6	2.7	3.2	3.4	3.7	29.3	59.3	72.0	75.5	81.8	0.6	1.5	8.0	16.9
Superwarehouse [7]	0.3	0.6	0.5	0.5	0.5	12.6	17.8	16.7	17.1	17.4	0.1	0.2	3.4	3.6
Hypermarket [8]	0.1	0.2	0.2	0.2	0.2	6.8	9.5	9.1	9.7	10.3	(Z)	0.1	1.8	2.1
Convenience stores [9]	93.0	86.9	83.9	82.9	81.9	37.0	42.4	45.3	47.6	48.5	32.9	33.6	10.0	10.0
Superette [10]	72.8	64.7	60.2	58.5	56.7	49.5	39.4	51.2	61.4	72.5	25.8	23.3	13.4	15.0
Specialized food stores [11]	92.3	87.5	83.3	82.0	80.6	20.1	20.3	22.7	23.6	25.4	32.7	33.1	5.5	5.3

Z Less than 0.05 percent. [1] Estimated. [2] Includes nonfood items. [3] A grocery store, primarily self-service in operation, providing a full range of departments, and having at least $2.5 million in annual sales in 1985 dollars. [4] Contains greater variety of products than conventional supermarkets, including specialty and service departments, and considerable nonfood (general merchandise) products. [5] Contains limited product variety and fewer services provided, incorporating case lot stocking and shelving practices. [6] Contains a pharmacy, a nonprescription drug department, and a greater variety of health and beauty aids than that carried by conventional supermarkets. [7] A larger warehouse store that offers expanded product variety and often service meat, deli, or seafood departments. [8] A very large store offering a greater variety of general merchandise—like clothes, hardware, and seasonal goods—and personal care products than other grocery stores. [9] A small grocery store selling a limited variety of food and nonfood products, typically open extended hours. [10] A grocery store, primarily self-service in operation, selling a wide variety of food and nonfood products with annual sales below $2.5 million (1985 dollars). [11] Primarily engaged in the retail sale of a single food category such as meat and seafood stores and retail bakeries.

Source: U.S. Dept. of Agriculture, Economic Research Service, *Food Marketing Review*, annual.

No. 1014. Food Sales by Nontraditional Retailers: 1997

[308,780 represents $308,780,000,000]

Sales outlet	Retail food sales (mil. dol.)	Share of total retail food sales (percent)	Sales outlet	Retail food sales (mil. dol.)	Share of total retail food sales (percent)
Traditional foodstores, total	**308,780**	**82.6**	Other stores:		
Supermarkets	222,003	59.4	Drugstores	5,007	1.3
Convenience stores	14,216	3.8	Eating and drinking places	923	0.2
Other grocery stores	50,331	13.5	Furniture stores	133	(Z)
Specialized food stores	22,230	5.9	Gasoline service stations	10,398	2.8
			Miscellaneous stores:		
Nontraditional foodstores, total [1]	**64,867**	**17.4**	Gift, novelty, and souvenir shops	199	0.1
General merchandise stores:			Hobby, toy, and game shops	266	0.1
Department stores	244	0.1	Liquor stores	1,234	0.3
Discount/mass merchandise stores	26,336	7.0	Nonstore retailers:		
Variety stores	896	0.2	Catalog and mail order	1,008	0.3
Warehouse club stores	7,964	2.1	Vending machine operators	4,134	1.1
Other general merchandise stores	795	0.2	Direct sales (mobile, door to door)	5,052	1.4

Z Less than 0.05 percent. [1] Includes other types of stores not shown separately.

Source: U.S. Dept. of Agriculture, Economic Research Service, *Food Marketing Review*, September-December 1998.

No. 1015. Percent of Supermarkets Offering Selected Services and Product Lines: 1990 to 2001

[In percent. Based on a sample survey of chain and independent supermarkets and subject to sampling variability; for details, see source]

Service or product line offered	1990	1992	1993	1996	1997	1998	1999	2000	2001
Service delicatessen	73	78	79	80	81	81	81	81	80
Service bakery	60	60	62	69	69	69	69	71	72
Service meat	42	48	47	74	60	59	60	62	66
Service seafood	33	41	37	46	43	43	45	45	51
Specialty cheese department	33	33	34	31	30	31	32	33	42
Salad bar	18	22	19	27	24	24	24	25	22
Automated teller machines (ATMs). . .	20	28	38	60	62	62	63	64	65
Banking in store	(NA)	(NA)	(NA)	14	22	21	22	21	20
Pharmacy	15	18	20	26	26	32	30	32	36
Warehouse aisle.	(NA)	(NA)	(NA)	10	16	17	17	16	14

NA Not available.

Source: Progressive Grocer, New York, NY, *Progressive Grocer 66th Annual Report* (copyright). Used by permission of Progressive Grocer magazine.

No. 1016. Food and Alcoholic Beverage Sales by Sales Outlet: 1990 to 2001

[In billions of dollars (578.3 represents $578,300,000,000)]

Sales outlet	1990	1993	1994	1995	1996	1997	1998	1999	2000	2001
Food sales, total [1]	**578.3**	**609.6**	**636.5**	**656.4**	**681.6**	**705.7**	**737.5**	**779.4**	**813.4**	**844.2**
Food at home.	316.0	329.4	343.6	352.4	367.6	376.9	391.0	415.7	430.9	443.9
Food stores [2]	267.1	266.7	274.0	276.1	285.4	289.4	295.7	308.9	319.4	328.1
Other stores [3]	29.5	42.1	47.3	52.8	57.1	61.8	69.6	79.9	83.1	87.8
Home-delivered, mail order	5.3	6.8	7.9	8.7	10.1	10.6	10.7	11.5	12.2	11.3
Farmers, manufacturers, wholesalers.	6.3	7.1	7.2	7.8	8.2	8.8	8.7	9.0	9.5	9.7
Home production and donations .	7.7	6.7	7.1	7.0	6.8	6.4	6.4	6.6	6.8	7.0
Food away from home [4]	262.3	280.1	292.9	304.1	314.0	328.8	346.5	363.7	382.4	400.3
Alcoholic beverage sales, total.	**72.9**	**75.9**	**78.3**	**80.4**	**83.6**	**86.4**	**92.0**	**97.1**	**102.0**	**106.4**
Packaged alcoholic beverages. . . .	38.1	38.9	40.4	41.5	43.5	44.8	48.4	51.7	53.6	55.6
Liquor stores.	18.6	18.5	19.0	18.9	20.0	20.9	22.1	23.2	25.0	26.3
Food stores	12.9	11.1	11.8	12.3	13.0	12.8	13.9	14.6	15.1	15.4
All other.	6.6	9.3	9.7	10.2	10.6	11.2	12.4	13.9	13.6	13.9
Alcoholic drinks.	34.8	36.9	37.9	38.9	40.1	41.5	43.6	45.5	48.4	50.8
Eating and drinking places [5]	26.8	28.5	29.4	30.3	31.5	33.5	35.0	36.5	38.9	40.9
Hotels and motels [5]	3.8	3.8	3.9	3.9	3.9	4.0	4.1	4.3	4.6	4.7
All other.	4.2	4.7	4.7	4.7	4.7	4.0	4.4	4.7	4.9	5.2

[1] Includes taxes and tips.   [2] Excludes sales to restaurants and institutions.   [3] Includes eating and drinking establishments, trailer parks, commissary stores, and military exchanges.   [4] Includes food furnished and donations.   [5] Includes tips.

Source: U.S. Department of Agriculture, Economic Research Service, food cpi, prices, and expenditures: food expenditure tables; published 18 June 2002; <http://www.ers.usda.gov/briefing/CPIFoodAndExpenditures/Data/>.

No. 1017. U.S. Online Retail E-Commerce Projections: 2000 to 2002

[In millions of dollars (44,784 represents $44,784,000,000), except as indicated]

Online product or service	Projected online sales			Percent change	
	2000	2001	2002	2000-2001	2001-2002
Retail trade, total [1]	**44,784**	**73,926**	**110,748**	**65.1**	**49.8**
Media.	6,670	9,807	13,019	47.0	32.8
Event tickets	350	933	1,986	166.6	112.9
Flowers	760	1,266	1,812	66.6	43.1
Recreation	2,626	4,148	5,916	58.0	42.6
Apparel	5,040	8,915	14,461	76.9	62.2
Electronics	6,096	11,856	18,306	94.5	54.4
Leisure travel.	12,200	16,700	21,000	36.9	25.7
Automobiles	2,845	5,315	9,360	86.8	76.1
Home products	2,232	4,659	8,256	108.7	77.2
Pet supplies	624	1,523	2,519	144.1	65.4
Health and beauty	1,352	2,656	4,460	96.4	67.9
Food and beverage	1,131	2,455	5,063	117.1	106.2

[1] Includes items sold to consumers in product categories not shown separately.

Source: Forrester Research, Inc., Cambridge, MA, *Online Retail Ripple Effect* (copyright).

U.S. Census Bureau, Statistical Abstract of the United States: 2002

No. 1018. Online Consumer Spending Forecast by Kind of Business: 2000 to 2002

[Forecast date: October 2001. (24.1 represents $24,100,000,000). Figures below reflect a partial revision of the Jupiter Internet Shopping Model]

Category	Online retail spending (bil. dol.)			Percentage of spending online			Number of online buyers (mil.)			Percentage of online buyers that purchase within category		
	2000	2001	2002	2000	2001	2002	2000	2001	2002	2000	2001	2002
Total	24.1	30.0	39.3	(X)	(X)	(X)	(X)	(X)	(X)	(X)	(X)	(X)
PCs	6.1	6.9	7.4	25.3	30.1	32.1	4.3	5.4	6.8	9	8	8
Peripherals	1.8	1.9	2.2	18.7	20.2	22.4	8.9	10.9	13.3	18	17	16
Software	1.4	1.9	2.6	17.4	24.4	32.2	15.9	20.4	24.4	32	31	30
Consumer electronics	1.1	1.4	1.9	2.4	3.2	4.2	3.8	5.3	7.4	8	8	9
Books	2.2	2.3	2.6	8.9	10.2	11.5	23.2	32.3	41.3	47	49	51
Music	0.7	0.9	1.2	4.6	6.4	8.7	20.7	30.3	40.4	43	46	50
Videos	0.5	0.6	0.8	3.9	4.8	6.0	10.1	14.4	18.9	21	22	23
Movie tickets	0.1	0.2	0.3	1.4	2.2	3.2	2.7	5.3	8.8	5	8	11
Event tickets	1.0	1.4	1.9	6.2	8.3	10.8	9.9	13.6	17.4	20	21	21
Over-the-counter drugs	0.1	0.1	0.1	0.3	0.3	0.6	3.2	5.6	8.6	6	9	11
Nutraceuticals	0.1	0.1	0.1	0.6	0.4	0.8	6.2	8.6	11.2	13	13	14
Medical supplies and contact lenses	0.1	0.1	0.3	0.9	1.0	1.8	2.7	4.4	6.4	6	7	8
Personal care	0.1	0.1	0.3	0.3	0.3	0.8	4.5	7.3	10.7	9	11	13
Apparel	2.3	3.2	4.6	1.2	1.7	2.2	17.5	26.3	35.4	36	40	43
Footwear	0.3	0.5	0.8	0.6	1.0	1.4	4.0	7.0	10.6	8	11	13
Jewelry	0.8	0.9	1.1	2.6	2.9	3.5	4.2	5.2	6.9	9	8	9
Grocery	0.6	0.6	1.0	0.1	0.1	0.2	1.1	1.1	1.5	2	2	2
Pets	0.1	0.1	0.2	0.3	0.6	1.0	1.6	2.4	3.5	3	4	4
Toys	0.8	1.0	1.1	2.9	3.2	3.7	14.1	18.4	22.3	29	28	27
Sporting goods	0.5	0.7	0.9	2.1	2.8	3.8	4.7	7.6	11.1	10	12	14
Flowers	0.4	0.6	0.8	2.9	3.7	4.7	7.6	11.8	16.2	16	18	20
Specialty gifts	0.4	0.6	0.8	1.2	1.6	2.2	7.8	10.9	14.1	16	17	17
Furniture	0.1	0.1	0.2	0.1	0.2	0.4	0.3	0.5	1.1	1	1	1
Large appliances	0.1	0.3	0.4	0.7	1.3	2.0	0.2	0.5	0.8	1	1	1
Housewares/small appliances	0.3	0.6	1.0	0.5	0.9	1.5	4.0	5.9	8.3	8	9	10
Art and collectibles	0.2	0.3	0.5	0.8	1.1	1.6	1.0	1.4	2.1	2	2	3
Home improvement	0.1	0.3	0.5	0.1	0.2	0.4	2.1	3.7	6.1	4	6	7
Garden supplies	0.1	0.1	0.2	0.2	0.3	0.5	1.7	2.3	3.3	3	4	4
Office products	0.3	0.6	1.1	1.1	2.0	3.3	5.4	8.8	12.9	11	13	16
Auto parts	-	-	0.1	-	-	-	0.1	0.3	0.9	-	-	1
Other	1.4	1.7	2.4	(NA)	(NA)	(NA)	(NA)	(NA)	(NA)	(NA)	(NA)	(NA)

- Represents or rounds to zero.   NA Not available.   X Not applicable.

Source: Jupiter Media Metrix, Inc., New York, NY, unpublished data (copyright).

No. 1019. Electronic Shopping and Mail-Order Houses—Total and E-Commerce Sales by Merchandise Line: 2000

[107,664 represents $107,664,000,000 in sales. Represents NAICS code 454110. Covers establishments with payroll. Based on 2000 Annual Retail Trade Survey, see Appendix III]

Merchandise line	Value of sales		E-commerce as percent of total sales	Percent distribution of total sales	Percent distribution of E-commerce sales
	Total (mil. dol.)	E-commerce (mil. dol.)			
Electronic shopping and mail-order houses, total [1]	107,664	21,368	19.8	100.0	100.0
Books and magazines	4,250	2,083	49.0	3.9	9.7
Clothing and clothing accessories (includes footwear)	14,419	1,960	13.6	13.4	9.2
Computer hardware	26,456	6,077	23.0	24.6	28.4
Computer software	3,566	1,115	31.3	3.3	5.2
Drugs, health aids, beauty aids	12,258	671	5.5	11.4	3.1
Electronics and appliances	3,446	1,071	31.1	3.2	5.0
Food, beer and wine	1,906	568	29.8	1.8	2.7
Furniture and home furnishings	6,437	849	13.2	6.0	4.0
Music and videos	4,463	1,282	28.7	4.1	6.0
Office equipment and supplies	6,929	1,432	20.7	6.4	6.7
Toys, hobby goods, and games	2,956	795	26.9	2.7	3.7
Other merchandise [2]	17,359	2,361	13.6	16.1	11.0
Nonmerchandise receipts [3]	3,219	1,104	34.3	3.0	5.2

[1] This industry comprises businesses primarily engaged in retailing all types of merchandise through catalogs, television, and the Internet. Data are preliminary and, therefore, subject to revision.   [2] Includes other merchandise such as jewelry, sporting goods, collectibles, souvenirs, auto parts and accessories, hardware, and lawn and garden equipment and supplies.   [3] Includes nonmerchandise receipts such as auction commissions, shipping and handling, customer training, customer support, and online advertising.

Source: U.S. Census Bureau, "2000 E-commerce Multi-Sector Report;" published 18 March 2002; <http://www.census.gov/eos/www/ebusiness614.htm>

No. 1020. Retail E-Commerce Sales, Number of Orders, and Average Purchase Amount in Key Categories: 2000 and 2001

[253.1 represents 253,100,000). **As of fourth quarter.** Based on a point-of-sale survey of online buyers covering approximately 1,000 merchants. Minus sign (-) indicates decrease]

Category	Orders (mil.)			Sales (mil. dol.) [1]			Average purchase amount (dol.) [1]		
	2000	2001	Percent change, 2000-2001	2000	2001	Percent change, 2000-2001	2000	2001	Percent change, 2000-2001
Total	253.1	285.8	12.9	28,910	35,873	24.1	114	125	9.9
Apparel	22.7	28.0	23.2	2,219	2,882	29.9	98	103	5.4
Computer goods . . .	43.6	41.9	-3.9	12,793	13,948	9.0	294	333	13.4
Consumer goods . . .	19.6	23.8	21.3	3,635	5,332	46.7	185	224	20.9
Entertainment	69.1	59.7	-13.6	4,194	4,332	3.3	61	73	19.6
Food/wine	16.1	18.0	11.6	831	853	2.7	51	47	-7.9
Gifts	67.5	100.0	48.1	4,097	7,017	71.2	61	70	15.6
Home & garden	3.8	4.6	21.5	309	519	68.0	82	113	38.3
Toys	10.7	9.9	-7.2	831	990	19.1	78	100	28.4

[1] Includes shipping and handling charges.

Source: BizRate.Com, Los Angeles, CA, *Consumer Online Report, Fourth Quarter, 2001* (copyright).

No. 1021. Retail Trade Sales—Total and E-Commerce by Kind of Business: 2000

[**3,060,748 represents $3,060,748,000,000.** Covers retailers with and without payroll. Based on 2000 Annual Retail Trade Survey; see Appendix III]

Kind of business	NAICS code [1]	Value of sales (mil. dol.)		E-commerce as percent of total sales	Percent distribution of E-commerce sales
		Total	E-commerce		
Retail trade, total	44,45	3,060,748	28,824	0.9	100.0
Motor vehicle and parts dealers	441	817,761	4,628	0.6	16.1
Furniture and home furnishings stores	442	91,629	(S)	(S)	(S)
Electronics and appliance stores	443	87,598	548	0.6	1.9
Building material and garden equipment supplies stores . .	444	278,326	449	0.2	1.6
Food and beverage stores	445	459,594	(S)	(S)	(S)
Health and personal care stores	446	157,143	(S)	(S)	(S)
Gasoline stations	447	247,222	(Z)	(Z)	(Z)
Clothing and clothing acces. stores	448	167,385	259	0.2	0.9
Sporting goods, hobby, book and music stores	451	77,942	419	0.5	1.5
General merchandise stores	452	404,590	(S)	(S)	(S)
Miscellaneous store retailers	453	109,827	392	0.4	1.4
Nonstore retailers	454	161,731	21,688	13.3	74.9
Electronic shopping and mail-order houses	454110	107,664	21,368	19.8	74.1

S Data do not meet publication standards because of high sampling variability or poor response quality. Unpublished estimates derived from this table by subtraction should be used with caution and not be attributed to the U.S. Census Bureau. For more information on methodology visit <www.census.gov/estats>. Z Less than $500,000 or 0.05 percent. [1] North American Industry Classification System; see text, Section 15, Business Enterprise.

No. 1022. Merchant Wholesale Trade Sales—Total and E-Commerce: 2000

[**2,751,761 represents $2,751,761,000,000.** Covers only businesses with paid employees. Based on 2000 Annual Trade Survey; see Appendix III]

Kind of business	NAICS code [1]	Value of sales (mil. dol.)		E-commerce as percent of total revenue	Percent distribution of E-commerce revenue
		Total	E-commerce		
Merchant wholesale trade, total	42	2,751,761	213,050	7.7	100.0
Durable goods [2]	421	1,435,014	107,672	7.5	50.5
Motor vehicles, parts and supplies	4211	199,560	39,960	20.0	18.8
Furniture and home furnishings	4212	46,468	2,669	5.7	1.3
Professional & commercial equipment & supplies	4214	282,669	27,968	9.9	13.0
Computer, peripheral equipment and software	42143	165,195	18,113	11.0	8.5
Electrical goods	4216	238,026	9,688	4.1	4.6
Hardware, and plumbing and heating equipment and supplies	4217	66,212	6,004	9.1	2.8
Machinery, equipment and supplies	4218	253,628	8,103	3.2	3.8
Miscellaneous durable goods	4219	174,636	10,367	5.9	4.9
Nondurable goods [2]	422	1,316,747	105,378	8.0	49.5
Drugs and druggists' sundries	4222	166,524	65,767	39.5	31.0
Apparel, piece goods and notions	4223	88,647	8,348	9.4	3.9
Groceries and related products	4224	383,306	6,010	1.6	2.7
Farm product raw materials	4225	106,389	3,263	3.1	1.5

[1] North American Industry Classification System; see text, Section 15, Business Enterprise. [2] Includes kinds of business not shown separately.

Source of Tables 1021 and 1022: U.S. Census Bureau, "2000 E-Commerce Multi-Sector Report"; published 18 March 2002; <http://www.census.gov/eos/www/ebusiness614.htm>.

No. 1023. Shopping Centers—Number, Gross Leasable Area, and Retail Sales by Gross Leasable Area: 1990 to 2001

[4,390 represents 4,390,000,000. As of December 31. A shopping center is a group of architecturally unified commercial establishments built on a site that is planned, developed, owned, and managed as an operating unit related in its location, size, and type of shops to the trade area that the unit serves. The unit provides on-site parking in definite relationship to the types and total size of the stores. The data base attempts to include all centers with three or more stores. Estimates are based on a sample of data available on shopping center properties; for details, contact source]

Year	Gross leasable area (sq. ft.)						
	Total	Less than 100,001	100,001- 200,000	200,001- 400,000	400,001- 800,000	800,001- 1,000,000	More than 1 million
NUMBER							
1990	36,515	23,231	8,756	2,781	1,102	288	357
1995	41,235	26,001	9,974	3,345	1,234	301	380
1999	44,426	27,696	10,770	3,834	1,398	324	404
2000	45,115	28,062	10,958	3,935	1,424	326	410
2001	45,827	28,474	11,100	4,038	1,466	329	420
Percent distribution	100.0	62.1	24.2	8.8	3.2	0.7	0.9
Percent change, 2000-2001	1.6	1.5	1.3	2.6	2.9	0.9	2.4
GROSS LEASABLE AREA							
1990 (mil. sq. ft.)	4,390	1,125	1,197	734	618	259	457
1995 (mil. sq. ft.)	4,967	1,267	1,368	886	689	271	486
1999 (mil. sq. ft.)	5,463	1,362	1,486	1,030	776	292	519
2000 (mil. sq. ft.)	5,566	1,383	1,514	1,059	790	294	526
2001 (mil. sq. ft.)	5,679	1,406	1,534	1,091	812	296	539
Percent distribution	100.0	24.8	27.0	19.2	14.3	5.2	9.5
Percent change, 2000-2001	2.0	1.6	1.4	2.9	2.9	0.9	2.5
RETAIL SALES							
1990 (bil. dol.)	706.4	205.1	179.5	108.0	91.7	45.1	77.0
1995 (bil. dol.)	893.8	259.6	227.1	136.4	115.8	57.0	97.8
1999 (bil. dol.)	1,105.3	320.8	280.7	168.9	143.0	70.4	121.4
2000 (bil. dol.)	1,181.1	342.8	300.0	180.5	152.8	75.2	129.8
2001 (bil. dol.)	1,221.7	354.5	310.3	186.8	158.0	77.8	134.4
Percent distribution	100.0	29.0	25.4	15.3	12.9	6.4	11.0
Percent change, 2000-01	3.4	3.4	3.4	3.5	3.4	3.4	3.5

No. 1024. Shopping Centers—Gross Leasable Area and Retail Sales by State: 2001

[5,679 represents 5,679,000,000. See headnote, Table 1023]

State	Gross leasable area, (mil. sq. ft.)	Retail sales, (bil. dol.)	Retail sales per sq. ft. (dol.)	Percent change, 2000-2001		State	Gross leasable area, (mil. sq. ft.)	Retail sales, (bil. dol.)	Retail sales per sq. ft. (dol.)	Percent change, 2000-2001	
				Gross leasable area	Retail sales					Gross leasable area	Retail sales
U.S.	**5,679**	**1,221.7**	**215**	**2.0**	**3.4**						
						MO	118	26.6	226	1.8	3.3
AL	79	17.9	227	2.4	2.9	MT	10	2.4	240	-	3.4
AK	8	2.5	326	-	4.3	NE	37	6.7	179	3.5	3.2
AZ	134	29.2	217	5.4	3.5	NV	53	8.0	150	7.9	3.7
AR	37	8.6	230	0.6	2.7	NH	25	5.5	217	1.3	5.0
CA	713	146.6	206	1.2	3.4						
						NJ	179	34.1	191	1.5	3.9
CO	107	27.5	256	3.4	3.8	NM	32	7.4	235	4.3	3.0
CT	98	22.7	233	1.4	4.2	NY	253	52.4	207	0.7	3.3
DE	23	5.3	232	-	4.1	NC	184	34.0	185	2.3	3.3
DC	10	2.0	211	2.7	3.4	ND	10	2.5	251	5.8	3.4
FL	452	112.5	249	2.8	3.8						
						OH	257	48.6	189	2.3	3.2
GA	190	36.9	194	3.4	3.2	OK	61	15.0	245	0.5	2.6
HI	20	5.3	264	-	5.1	OR	61	11.2	185	2.8	3.7
ID	20	3.8	191	-	2.9	PA	255	47.7	187	2.8	3.5
IL	267	50.0	187	1.2	3.6	RI	20	4.5	224	-	3.5
IN	124	25.0	201	1.9	3.1						
						SC	88	18.2	208	4.1	3.1
IA	45	8.8	196	0.8	3.2	SD	7	1.5	216	-	3.2
KS	60	13.6	227	2.7	3.2	TN	138	27.0	196	0.9	3.3
KY	69	16.1	235	1.4	3.1	TX	385	102.5	267	2.2	3.3
LA	86	21.8	253	1.4	3.2	UT	39	7.5	194	6.6	2.9
ME	18	5.1	285	2.3	4.3						
						VT	8	2.2	259	-	4.1
MD	132	29.4	223	1.2	3.4	VA	177	37.8	213	2.0	3.6
MA	116	28.0	240	0.4	3.7	WA	102	21.1	207	0.2	3.6
MI	148	29.7	201	3.7	3.3	WV	23	4.3	187	-	2.6
MN	71	10.5	231	2.3	3.4	WI	79	17.3	219	1.5	3.5
MS	45	9.3	208	0.9	2.5	WY	6	1.6	254	3.5	2.9

- Represents or rounds to zero.

Source of Tables 1023 and 1024: National Research Bureau, Chicago, IL. Data for 1995-2001 published by International Council of Shopping Centers in *Shopping Centers Today*, April issues (copyright—Trade Dimensions International, Inc.).

No. 1025. Merchant Wholesalers—Summary: 1992 to 2001

[In billions of dollars (1,731.6 represents $1,731,600,000,000) except ratios. Inventories and stock/sales ratios, as of December, seasonally adjusted. Data reflect latest revision. Based on Annual Trade Survey; see Appendix III]

Kind of business	NAICS code [1]	1992	1994	1996	1998	1999	2000	2001
SALES (bil. dol.)								
Merchant wholesalers	(X)	1,731.6	1,933.6	2,239.8	2,379.8	2,541.1	2,751.8	2,715.8
Durable goods	(X)	832.8	1,004.2	1,156.6	1,265.8	1,354.7	1,435.0	1,371.3
Motor vehicles, parts, and supplies	4211	149.6	163.4	165.7	173.2	196.0	199.6	204.4
Furniture and homefurnishings	4212	28.5	31.3	36.5	40.4	42.7	46.5	43.5
Lumber and construction materials	4213	45.8	56.0	59.1	63.7	71.5	71.2	73.5
Professional and commercial equipment	4214	133.5	165.4	220.2	254.1	275.1	282.7	266.2
Computer, peripheral equipment and software	42143	(NA)	(NA)	(NA)	150.8	162.3	165.2	146.2
Metals and minerals, except petroleum	4215	76.7	89.1	94.5	97.1	94.8	102.6	93.0
Electrical goods	4216	98.2	141.3	171.5	186.7	208.0	238.0	213.3
Hardware, plumbing and heating equipment	4217	41.3	49.2	54.3	60.4	63.4	66.2	63.1
Machinery, equipment and supplies	4218	147.5	174.4	206.6	242.5	244.5	253.6	256.4
Miscellaneous durable goods	4219	111.5	134.0	148.2	147.7	158.8	174.6	157.8
Nondurable goods	(X)	898.8	929.4	1,083.2	1,114.1	1,186.4	1,316.7	1,344.5
Paper and paper products	4221	48.1	55.4	64.8	69.9	74.9	80.1	76.6
Drugs, proprietaries, and sundries	4222	67.1	76.4	94.3	124.6	146.7	166.5	193.4
Apparel, piece goods, and notions	4223	62.7	68.5	73.1	84.2	85.7	88.6	80.6
Groceries and related products	4224	274.8	289.9	317.8	344.4	360.3	383.3	402.9
Farm-product raw materials	4225	106.2	99.1	137.5	108.0	101.6	106.4	106.1
Chemicals and allied products	4226	39.2	43.3	53.6	55.1	55.2	59.8	59.0
Petroleum and petroleum products	4227	137.5	125.4	143.5	116.4	136.2	186.6	178.0
Beer, wine, and distilled beverages	4228	50.4	52.0	55.9	61.8	67.4	71.2	72.6
Miscellaneous nondurable goods	4229	112.8	119.4	142.5	149.7	158.4	174.2	175.3
INVENTORIES (bil. dol.)								
Merchant wholesalers	(X)	194.5	219.8	238.8	269.4	285.7	304.7	288.0
Durable goods	(X)	119.8	138.4	153.2	174.6	184.7	194.2	174.0
Motor vehicles, parts, and supplies	4211	21.4	21.5	21.6	22.8	25.3	26.1	24.0
Furniture and homefurnishings	4212	4.2	4.4	4.8	5.1	5.4	5.9	5.4
Lumber and construction materials	4213	4.8	5.4	5.7	5.9	6.6	6.8	6.7
Professional and commercial equipment	4214	16.9	21.0	24.6	26.5	27.8	27.4	23.0
Computer, peripheral equipment, and software	42143	(NA)	(NA)	(NA)	12.4	12.5	11.3	8.0
Metals and minerals, except petroleum	4215	10.3	12.6	12.7	14.3	14.2	14.4	12.4
Electrical goods	4216	14.9	18.5	21.3	23.3	26.2	29.8	24.2
Hardware, plumbing and heating equipment	4217	6.4	7.8	8.6	9.6	9.8	10.7	10.3
Machinery, equipment and supplies	4218	28.0	31.6	37.7	48.2	49.3	50.0	47.8
Miscellaneous durable goods	4219	12.9	15.5	16.3	18.9	20.1	23.1	20.3
Nondurable goods	(X)	74.6	81.4	85.6	94.8	101.0	110.5	114.0
Paper and paper products	4221	4.6	4.9	5.3	0.0	6.2	7.1	6.3
Drugs, proprietaries, and sundries	4222	9.3	10.8	11.9	15.4	18.4	22.4	28.1
Apparel, piece goods, and notions	4223	10.5	12.0	12.0	13.6	12.7	12.9	12.8
Groceries and related products	4224	18.0	17.9	18.2	19.3	21.3	21.9	21.3
Farm-product raw materials	4225	8.1	9.9	9.5	10.1	9.9	11.0	9.9
Chemicals and allied products	4226	3.8	4.6	5.3	5.8	6.1	6.0	6.1
Petroleum and petroleum products	4227	3.9	4.2	4.5	3.4	3.8	4.5	4.4
Beer, wine, and distilled beverages	4228	4.3	4.6	5.1	5.8	6.2	6.6	6.4
Miscellaneous nondurable goods	4229	12.2	12.5	13.9	15.4	16.6	18.2	18.5
STOCK/SALES RATIO								
Merchant wholesalers	(X)	1.34	1.29	1.26	1.34	1.28	1.30	1.31
Durable goods	(X)	1.68	1.55	1.57	1.65	1.55	1.64	1.58
Motor vehicles, parts, and supplies	4211	1.72	1.57	1.56	1.54	1.49	1.57	1.42
Furniture and homefurnishings	4212	1.70	1.55	1.50	1.51	1.45	1.54	1.55
Lumber and construction materials	4213	1.28	1.10	1.13	1.06	1.07	1.15	1.05
Professional and commercial equipment	4214	1.44	1.37	1.33	1.24	1.15	1.23	1.07
Computer, peripheral equipment and software	42143	(NA)	(NA)	(NA)	1.02	0.87	0.90	0.69
Metals and minerals, except petroleum	4215	1.58	1.58	1.59	1.85	1.69	1.73	1.77
Electrical goods	4216	1.72	1.44	1.57	1.50	1.37	1.49	1.43
Hardware, plumbing and heating equipment	4217	1.84	1.76	1.84	1.85	1.85	1.97	1.92
Machinery, equipment and supplies	4218	2.23	2.04	2.09	2.39	2.39	2.34	2.38
Miscellaneous durable goods	4219	1.32	1.30	1.25	1.57	1.38	1.61	1.61
Nondurable goods	(X)	1.01	1.01	0.94	1.00	0.97	0.95	1.03
Paper and paper products	4221	1.11	0.94	0.98	1.00	0.97	1.05	1.01
Drugs, proprietaries, and sundries	4222	1.63	1.66	1.43	1.37	1.40	1.52	1.62
Apparel, piece goods, and notions	4223	1.94	2.16	1.79	2.02	1.74	1.73	1.92
Groceries and related products	4224	0.78	0.71	0.70	0.66	0.68	0.65	0.63
Farm-product raw materials	4225	0.94	1.12	0.86	1.10	1.20	1.16	1.21
Chemicals and allied products	4226	1.13	1.16	1.20	1.28	1.25	1.16	1.27
Petroleum and petroleum products	4227	0.36	0.40	0.35	0.37	0.29	0.26	0.36
Beer, wine, and distilled beverages	4228	1.04	1.03	1.09	1.08	1.07	1.08	1.01
Miscellaneous nondurable goods	4229	1.39	1.19	1.19	1.14	1.17	1.21	1.32

NA Not available.   X Not applicable.   [1] North American Industry Classification System, 1997; see text, Section 15, Business Enterprise.

Source: U.S. Census Bureau, *Current Business Reports, Annual Benchmark Report for Wholesale Trade, January 1992 through February 2002*, Series BW/01-A.

Domestic Trade   651

No. 1026. Wholesale Trade—Establishments, Sales, Payroll, and Employees by Kind of Business: 1997

[4,059,658 represents $4,059,658,000,000. Covers only establishments with payroll]

Kind of business	NAICS code [1]	Estab-lish-ments (number)	Sales		Annual payroll		Paid employ-ees for pay period including March 12 (1,000)
			Total (mil. dol.)	Per paid em-ployee (dol.)	Total (mil. dol.)	Per paid em-ployee (dol.)	
Wholesale trade	42	453,470	4,059,658	700,357	214,915	37,076	5,796.6
Wholesale trade, durable goods	421	290,629	2,179,717	641,421	133,237	39,207	3,398.3
Motor vehicle & motor vehicle parts & supplies wholesale.	4211	29,328	533,352	1,419,505	11,459	30,497	375.7
Furniture & home furnishings wholesale.	4212	15,246	75,006	476,337	5,317	33,766	157.5
Lumber & other construction materials wholesale.	4213	14,267	89,176	573,349	5,296	34,051	155.5
Professional & commercial equipment & supplies wholesale.	4214	45,351	367,384	513,025	33,292	46,490	716.1
Metal & mineral (except petroleum) wholesale.	4215	12,583	150,494	864,762	6,898	39,637	174.0
Electrical goods wholesalers.	4216	38,234	357,692	751,823	22,525	47,344	475.8
Hardware, & plumbing & heating equip. & supplies wholesale.	4217	21,194	92,190	420,510	7,978	36,390	219.2
Machinery, equipment, & supplies, wholesale. .	4218	76,643	328,968	425,821	29,402	38,058	772.6
Misc. durable goods wholesale..	4219	37,783	185,456	527,104	11,070	31,464	351.8
Wholesale trade, nondurable goods	422	162,841	1,879,940	783,865	81,678	34,057	2,398.3
Paper & paper product wholesalers.	4221	15,848	117,062	546,128	7,730	36,064	214.4
Drugs & druggists' sundries wholesalers.	4222	8,053	203,148	1,068,485	8,395	44,154	190.1
Apparel, piece goods & notions wholesalers. . .	4223	20,707	124,104	597,880	7,760	37,382	207.6
Grocery & related products wholesalers.	4224	41,760	588,970	688,919	26,778	31,322	854.9
Farm-product raw material wholesalers.	4225	10,343	166,786	1,710,260	2,306	23,646	97.5
Chemical & allied products wholesalers.	4226	15,920	128,923	777,735	7,241	43,683	165.8
Petroleum & petroleum products wholesalers. .	4227	11,297	267,624	1,941,710	4,480	32,503	137.8
Beer, wine & distilled alcoholic bev., wholesalers.	4228	4,850	69,703	459,550	5,667	37,363	151.7
Misc. nondurable goods wholesale	4229	34,063	213,619	564,336	11,321	29,909	378.5
Merchant wholesalers.	(X)	376,330	2,333,131	508,187	158,373	34,496	4,591.1
Manufacturers' sales branches & sales offices . .	(X)	29,305	1,258,875	1,365,066	45,912	49,785	922.2
Agents, brokers and commission merchants	(X)	47,835	467,652	1,650,981	10,630	37,529	283.3

X Not applicable.   [1] North American Industry Classification System, 1997; see text, Section 15, Business Enterprise.

Source: U.S. Census Bureau, *1997 Economic Census, Wholesale Trade,* Series EC97W42A-US(RV), issued March 2000.

No. 1027. Wholesale Trade—Establishments, Employees, and Payroll: 1999 and 2000

[450.0 represents 450,000. Covers establishments with payroll. Employees are for the week including March 12. Excludes most government employees, railroad employees, and self-employed persons. Kind-of-business classification based on North American Industry Classification System (NAICS); see text, Section 15, Business Enterprise. For statement on methodology, see Appendix III]

Kind of business	NAICS code	Establishments (1,000)		Employees (1,000)		Payroll (bil. dol.)	
		1999	2000	1999	2000	1999	2000
Wholesale trade	42	450.0	446.2	5,972	6,112	250.0	270.1
Wholesale trade, durable goods	421	290.1	288.6	3,528	3,625	158.8	171.8
Motor vehicle/motor vehicle pt & supply whsle . .	4211	28.3	28.4	392	402	13.6	14.1
Furniture & home furnishing whsle	4212	15.0	14.9	162	167	6.1	6.6
Lumber & other construction materials whsle . . .	4213	14.9	15.1	169	184	6.5	7.2
Professional & commercial equip & supp whsle. .	4214	45.2	44.4	751	763	41.8	44.9
Metal & mineral (except petroleum) whsle	4215	12.3	12.1	170	173	7.2	7.6
Electrical goods whsle	4216	38.5	38.3	507	535	29.2	33.9
Hardware, & plumb & heating equip & sup whsle	4217	21.5	21.4	238	249	9.6	10.4
Machinery, equipment, & supplies whsle	4218	75.4	73.7	803	796	33.2	34.2
Miscellaneous durable goods whsle	4219	38.9	40.2	336	355	11.7	12.9
Wholesale trade, nondurable goods	422	160.0	157.7	2,444	2,487	91.2	98.4
Paper & paper product whsle	4221	15.4	14.9	229	232	8.3	8.9
Drugs & druggists' sundries whsle	4222	7.5	7.4	200	210	10.1	12.0
Apparel, piece goods & notions whsle	4223	20.3	20.0	209	214	8.4	8.9
Grocery & related product whsle	4224	40.6	39.7	876	875	30.1	31.6
Farm product raw material whsle	4225	9.8	9.5	92	92	2.4	2.5
Chemical & allied products whsle	4226	15.4	15.3	160	166	7.7	8.3
Petroleum & petroleum products whsle	4227	11.2	10.7	134	132	4.9	5.2
Beer/wine/distilled alcoholic beverage whsle . . .	4228	4.7	4.6	153	157	6.3	6.8
Miscellaneous nondurable goods whsle	4229	35.2	35.4	392	409	13.1	14.3

Source: U.S. Census Bureau, *County Business Patterns,* annual. See also <http://www.census.gov/prod/2002pubs/cbp00/cbp00-1.pdf> (issued May 2002).

This section presents data on civil air transportation, both passenger and cargo, and on water transportation, including inland waterways, oceanborne commerce, the merchant marine, cargo, and vessel tonnages.

This section also presents statistics on revenues, passenger and freight traffic volume, and employment in various revenue-producing modes of the transportation industry, including motor vehicles, trains, and pipelines. Data are also presented on highway mileage and finances, motor vehicle travel, accidents, and registrations; and characteristics of public transit, railroads, and pipelines.

Principal sources of air and water transportation data are the annual *National Transportation Statistics,* issued by the U.S. Bureau of Transportation Statistics; the *Annual Report* issued by the Air Transport Association of America, Washington, DC; and the annual *Waterborne Commerce of the United States* issued by the Corps of Engineers of the Department of the Army. In addition, the U.S. Census Bureau in its commodity transportation survey (part of the census of transportation, taken every 5 years through 1997, for years ending in "2" and "7") provides data on the type, weight, and value of commodities shipped by manufacturing establishments in the United States, by means of transportation, origin, and destination. The latest complete reports for 1997 are part of the 1997 Economic Census. See text, Section 15, Business Enterprise, for a discussion of the 1997 Economic Census.

Additional sources of data on water transportation include *Merchant Fleets of the World,* issued periodically by the U.S. Maritime Administration; *The Bulletin,* issued monthly by the American Bureau of Shipping, New York, NY; and the annual *World Fleet Statistics.*

The principal compiler of data on public roads and on operation of motor vehicles is the U.S. Department of Transportation's (DOT) Federal Highway Administration (FHWA). These data appear in FHWA's annual *Highway Statistics* and other publications.

The U.S. National Highway Traffic Safety Administration issues data on traffic accident deaths and death rates in two annual reports: the *Fact Book* and the *Fatal Accident Reporting System Annual Report.* DOTs Federal Railroad Administration presents data on accidents involving railroads in its annual *Accident/Incident Bulletin,* and the *Rail-Highway Crossing Accident/Incident and Inventory Bulletin.*

The data for the truck transportation component of the 1997 Economic Census are presented in the *Truck Inventory and Use Survey.*

Data are also presented in many nongovernment publications. Among them are the weekly and annual *Cars of Revenue Freight Loaded* and the annual *Yearbook of Railroad Facts,* both published by the Association of American Railroads, Washington, DC; *Transit Fact Book,* containing electric railway and motorbus statistics, published annually by the American Public Transit Association, Washington, DC.; *Accident Facts,* issued by the National Safety Council, Chicago, IL; and *Transportation in America,* issued by the Eno Foundation for Transportation, Westport, Connecticut.

Civil aviation—Federal promotion and regulation of civil aviation have been carried out by the FAA and the Civil Aeronautics Board (CAB). The CAB promoted and regulated the civil air transportation industry within the United States and between the United States and foreign countries. The Board granted licenses to provide air transportation service, approved or disapproved proposed rates and fares, and approved or disapproved

U.S. Census Bureau, Statistical Abstract of the United States: 2002

proposed agreements and corporate relationships involving air carriers. In December 1984, the CAB ceased to exist as an agency. Some of its functions were transferred to the Department of Transportation (DOT), as outlined below. The responsibility for investigation of aviation accidents resides with the National Transportation Safety Board.

The Office of the Secretary, DOT aviation activities include: negotiation of international air transportation rights, selection of U.S. air carriers to serve capacity controlled international markets, oversight of international rates and fares, maintenance of essential air service to small communities, and consumer affairs. DOT's Bureau of Transportation Statistics (BTS) handles aviation information functions formerly assigned to CAB. Prior to BTS, the Research and Special Programs Administration handled these functions.

The principal activities of the FAA include: the promotion of air safety; controlling the use of navigable airspace; prescribing regulations dealing with the competency of airmen, airworthiness of aircraft and air traffic control; operation of air route traffic control centers, airport traffic control towers, and flight service stations; the design, construction, maintenance, and inspection of navigation, traffic control, and communications equipment; and the development of general aviation.

The CAB published monthly and quarterly financial and traffic statistical data for the certificated route air carriers. BTS continues these publications, including both certificated and noncertificated (commuter) air carriers. The FAA publishes annually data on the use of airway facilities; data related to the location of airmen, aircraft, and airports; the volume of activity in the field of nonair carrier (general aviation) flying; and aircraft production and registration.

General aviation comprises all civil flying (including such commercial operations as small demand air taxis, agriculture application, powerline patrol, etc.) but excludes certificated route air carriers, supplemental operators, large-aircraft commercial operators, and commuter airlines.

Air carriers and service—The CAB previously issued "certificates of public convenience and necessity" under Section 401 of the Federal Aviation Act of 1958 for scheduled and nonscheduled (charter) passenger services and cargo services. It also issued certificates under Section 418 of the Act to cargo air carriers for domestic all-cargo service only. The DOT Office of the Secretary now issues the certificates under a "fit, willing, and able" test of air carrier operations. Carriers operating only a 60-seat-or-less aircraft are given exemption authority to carry passengers, cargo, and mail in scheduled and nonscheduled service under Part 298 of the DOT (formerly CAB) regulations. Exemption authority carriers who offer scheduled passenger service to an essential air service point must meet the "fit, willing, and able" test.

Vessel shipments, entrances, and clearances—Shipments by dry cargo vessels comprise shipments on all types of watercraft, except tanker vessels; shipments by tanker vessels comprise all types of cargo, liquid and dry, carried by tanker vessels.

A vessel is reported as entered only at the first port which it enters in the United States, whether or not cargo is unloaded at that port. A vessel is reported as cleared only at the last port at which clearance is made to a foreign port, whether or not it takes on cargo. Army and Navy vessels entering or clearing without commercial cargo are not included in the figures.

Units of measurement—Cargo (or freight) tonnage and shipping weight both represent the gross weight of the cargo including the weight of containers, wrappings, crates, etc. However, shipping weight excludes lift and cargo vans and similar substantial outer containers. Other tonnage figures generally refer to stowing capacity of vessels, 100 cubic feet being called 1 ton. Gross tonnage comprises the space within the frames and the ceiling of the hull, together with those closed-in spaces above deck available for cargo, stores, passengers, or crew, with certain minor exceptions. Net or registered tonnage is the gross tonnage less the spaces occupied by the propelling machinery, fuel, crew quarters, master's cabin, and navigation spaces. Substantially, it represents space available for cargo and passengers. The net tonnage capacity of a ship may bear little relation to weight of cargo. Deadweight tonnage is the weight in long tons required to depress a vessel from light water line (that is, with only the machinery and equipment on board) to load line. It is, therefore, the weight of the cargo, fuel, etc., which a vessel is designed to carry with safety.

Federal-aid highway systems—The Intermodal Surface Transportation Efficiency Act (ISTEA) of 1991 eliminated the historical Federal-Aid Highway Systems and created the National Highway System (NHS) and other federal-aid highway categories. The final NHS was approved by Congress in December of 1995 under the National Highway System Designation Act.

Functional systems—Roads and streets are assigned to groups according to the character of service intended. The functional systems are (1) arterial highways that generally handle the long trips, (2) collector facilities that collect and disperse traffic between the arterials and the lower systems, and (3) local roads and streets that primarily serve direct access to residential areas, farms, and other local areas.

Regulatory bodies—The ICC, created by the U.S. Congress to regulate transportation in interstate commerce, has jurisdiction over railroads, trucking companies, bus lines, freight forwarders, water carriers, coal slurry pipelines, and transportation brokers. The Federal Energy Regulatory Commission is responsible for setting rates and charges for transportation and sale of natural gas and for establishing rates or charges for transportation.

Motor carriers—For 1960-73, Class I for-hire motor carriers of freight were classified by the ICC as those with $1 million or more of gross annual operating revenue; 1974-79, the class minimum was $3 million. Effective January 1, 1980, Class I carriers are those with $5 million or more in revenue. For 1960-68, Class I motor carriers of passengers were classified by the

ICC as those with $200,000 or more of gross annual operating revenue; for 1969-76, as those with revenues of $1 million or more; and since 1977, as those with $3 million or more. Effective January 1, 1988, Class I motor carriers of passengers are those with $5 million or more in operating revenues; Class II less than $5 million in operating revenues.

Railroads—Railroad companies reporting to the ICC are divided into specific groups as follows: (1) Regular line-haul (interstate) railroads (and their nonoperating subsidiaries), (2) switching and terminal railroads, (3) private railroads prior to 1964 (identified by ICC as "circular" because they reported on brief circulars), and (4) unofficial railroads, so designated when their reports are received too late for tabulation. For the most part, the last three groups are not included in the statistics shown here.

For years prior to 1978, Class I railroads were those with annual revenues of $1 million or more for 1950-55; $3 million or more for 1956-64; $5 million or more for 1965-75; and $10 million or more for 1976-77. In 1978, the classification became Class I, those having more than $50 million gross annual operating revenue; Class II, from $10 million to $50 million+; and Class III, less than $10 million. Effective January 1, 1982, the ICC adopted a procedure to adjust the threshold for inflation by restating current revenues in constant 1978 dollars. In 1988, the criteria for Class I and Class II railroads were $92.0 million and $18.4 million, respectively. Also effective January 1, 1982, the ICC adopted a Carrier Classification Index Survey Form for carriers not filing annual report Form R-1 with the commission. Class II and Class III railroads are currently exempted from filing any financial report with the Commission. The form is used for reclassifying carriers.

The Surface Transportation Board (STB) was established pursuant to the ICC Termination Act of 1995, Pub. L. No. 104-88, 109 Stat. 803 (1995) (ICCTA), to assume certain of the regulatory functions that had been administered by the Interstate Commerce Commission. The Board has broad economic regulatory oversight of railroads, addressing such matters as rate

Transportation 655

reasonableness, car service and interchange, mergers and line acquisitions,
line construction, and line abandonments.
49 U.S.C. 10101-11908. Other ICC regulatory functions were either eliminated or
transferred to the Federal Highway
Administration or the Bureau of Transportation Statistics within DOT.

Class I Railroads are regulated by the STB
and subject to the Uniform System of
Accounts and required to file annual and
periodic reports. Railroads are classified
based on their annual operating revenues.
The class to which a carrier belongs is
determined by comparing its adjusted
operating revenues for 3 consecutive
years to the following scale: Class I, $250
million or more, Class II $20 million to
$250 million, and Class III $0 to 20 million.

Postal Service—The Postal Service
provides mail processing and delivery
services within the United States. The
Postal Reorganization Act of 1970 created
the Postal Service, effective July 1971, as
an independent establishment of the Federal Executive Branch.

Revenue and cost analysis describes the
Postal Service's system of attributing revenues and costs to classes of mail and
service. This system draws primarily upon
probability sampling techniques to
develop estimates of revenues, volumes,
and weights, as well as costs by class of
mail and special service. The costs attributed to classes of mail and special services are primarily incremental costs which
vary in response to changes in volume;
they account for roughly 60 percent of
the total costs of the Postal Service. The
balance represents "institutional costs."
Statistics on revenues, volume of mail,
and distribution of expenditures are presented in the Postal Service's annual
report, *Cost and Revenue Analysis,* and its
Annual Report of the Postmaster General
and its annual *Comprehensive Statement
on Postal Operations.*

Statistical reliability—For a discussion
of statistical collection and estimation,
sampling procedures, and measures of
statistical reliability applicable to Census
Bureau data, see Appendix III.

U.S. Census Bureau, Statistical Abstract of the United States: 2002

No. 1028.Transportation-Related Components of U.S. Gross Domestic Product: 1980 to 2000

[In billions dollars (349.4 represents $349,400,000,000), except percent]

Item	1980	1985	1990	1995	2000
CURRENT DOLLARS					
Total transportation-related final demand	**349.4**	**495.9**	**616.7**	**782.0**	**1,053.6**
Total gross domestic product (GDP)	2,795.6	4,213.0	5,803.2	7,400.5	9,872.9
Transportation-related final demand as a percent of GDP	12.5	11.8	10.6	10.6	10.7
Personal consumption of transportation	238.4	372.9	455.5	560.3	784.9
Motor vehicles and parts	87.0	175.7	206.4	249.3	346.8
Gasoline and oil	86.7	97.2	107.3	113.3	165.3
Transportation services	64.7	100.0	141.8	197.7	272.8
Gross private domestic investment	52.1	74.0	78.7	130.5	201.1
Transportation structures	3.7	4.3	3.0	4.4	5.2
Transportation equipment	48.4	69.7	75.7	126.1	195.9
Net exports of transportation-related goods and service [1]	-1.1	-34.7	-28.5	-43.3	-108.4
Exports (+)	45.7	57.5	106.0	132.9	179.2
Civilian aircraft, engines, and parts	14.1	13.5	32.2	26.1	48.1
Automotive vehicles, engines, and parts	17.4	24.9	36.5	61.8	80.2
Passenger fares	2.6	4.4	15.3	18.9	20.7
Other transportation	11.6	14.7	22.0	26.1	30.2
Imports (-)	46.8	92.2	134.5	176.2	287.6
Civilian aircraft, engines, and parts	3.1	5.3	10.5	10.7	26.4
Automotive vehicles, engines, and parts	28.3	64.9	88.5	123.8	195.9
Passenger fares	3.6	6.4	10.5	14.7	24.2
Other transportation	11.8	15.6	25.0	27.0	41.1
Government transportation-related purchases	60.0	83.7	111.0	134.5	176.0
Federal purchases [2]	7.0	10.0	12.9	16.3	19.5
State and local purchases [2]	48.8	67.5	90.1	109.8	147.6
Defense-related purchases [3]	4.2	6.2	8.0	8.4	8.9
Total domestic transportation-related final demand [4]	350.5	530.6	645.2	825.3	1,162.0
Total gross domestic demand (GDD)	2,810.5	4,327.2	5,874.6	7,484.7	10,236.9
Transportation-related final demand as a percent of GDP	12.5	12.3	11.0	11.0	11.4
CHAINED (1996) DOLLARS					
Total transportation-related final demand	**537.4**	**643.3**	**719.8**	**802.8**	**992.0**
Total gross domestic product (GDP)	4,900.9	5,717.1	6,707.9	7,543.8	9,224.0
Transportation-related final demand as a percent of GDP	11.0	11.3	10.7	10.6	10.8
Personal consumption of transportation	362.2	494.3	532.6	574.6	736.2
Motor vehicles and parts	142.7	236.0	246.1	253.4	348.3
Gasoline and oil	94.8	104.8	113.1	120.2	136.6
Transportation services	124.7	152.6	173.4	201.0	251.3
Gross private domestic investment	84.0	99.7	91.1	132.8	197.8
Transportation structures	6.5	5.8	3.7	4.6	5.1
Transportation equipment	77.5	93.9	87.4	128.2	192.7
Net exports of transportation-related goods and service [1]	-5.1	-56.2	-31.3	-43.1	-102.8
Exports (+)	76.2	76.0	123.7	135.4	169.2
Civilian aircraft, engines, and parts	26.9	19.5	40.9	27.2	43.1
Automotive vehicles, engines, and parts	28.3	30.5	39.8	62.5	78.3
Passenger fares	4.5	7.1	19.1	18.9	19.7
Other transportation	16.5	18.9	23.9	26.8	28.1
Imports (-)	81.3	132.2	155.0	178.5	272.0
Civilian aircraft, engines, and parts	6.0	7.7	13.5	11.2	23.9
Automotive vehicles, engines, and parts	52.5	95.9	101.6	124.6	192.5
Passenger fares	5.5	9.3	12.7	14.9	20.7
Other transportation	17.3	19.3	27.2	27.8	34.9
Government transportation-related purchases	96.4	105.5	127.4	138.5	160.8
Federal purchases [2]	13.3	13.9	16.1	17.2	19.4
State and local purchases [2]	77.3	83.5	101.1	112.6	132.8
Defense-related purchases [4]	5.8	8.1	10.3	8.7	8.6
Total domestic transportation-related final demand [4]	542.6	699.5	751.2	845.9	1,094.8
Total gross domestic demand (GDD)	4,890.9	5,866.2	6,764.4	7,622.2	9,623.1
Transportation-related final demand as a percent of GDP	11.1	11.9	11.1	11.1	11.4

[1] Sum of exports and imports.   [2] Federal purchases and state and local purchases are the sum of consumption expenditures and gross investment.   [3] Defense-related purchases are the sum of transportation of material and travel.   [4] Sum of total personal consumption of transportation, total gross private domestic investment, net exports of transportation-related goods and services, and total government transportation-related purchases.

Source: U.S. Bureau or Transportation Statistics, *National Transportation Statistics, 2001.*

U.S. Census Bureau, Statistical Abstract of the United States: 2002

No. 1029. Passenger and Freight Transportation Outlays by Type of Transport: 1990 to 1999

[In billions of dollars (517.2 represents $517,200,000,000). Freight data include outlays for mail and express]

Type of transport	1990	1992	1993	1994	1995	1996	1997	1998	1999
Passenger:									
Private transportation	517.2	523.6	560.2	610.5	642.0	684.0	719.9	738.9	805.0
Automobiles [1][2]	507.3	515.0	551.6	601.2	631.7	672.4	706.1	722.5	787.4
New and used cars	148.1	141.2	153.2	172.2	169.6	174.6	178.0	183.7	200.2
Tires, tubes, accessories	32.9	33.6	35.6	38.7	40.6	42.6	43.6	45.9	49.3
Gasoline and oil	118.0	115.4	117.3	119.9	124.6	136.6	140.9	126.7	141.1
Insurance less claims	19.9	28.3	29.7	30.6	32.7	35.0	39.9	41.8	43.0
Interest on debt	28.2	25.7	28.0	29.3	38.0	39.1	40.3	37.8	40.6
Auto registration fees.	6.1	7.1	7.4	7.4	7.0	7.7	8.2	9.6	9.1
Operators' permit fees	0.6	0.8	0.7	0.8	0.8	0.9	0.9	0.9	1.0
Repair, greasing, washing, . . . parking, leasing, rentals [3] . . .	93.4	99.3	107.4	121.0	134.4	147.6	160.9	168.4	178.3
Air.	9.9	8.6	8.6	9.3	10.4	11.6	13.8	16.4	17.6
For-hire transportation	124.8	103.2	104.7	107.2	117.2	115.8	126.9	128.6	132.0
Local [2]	31.6	32.8	34.3	35.7	41.0	39.6	41.5	41.6	41.7
Bus and transit [4].	16.7	18.0	18.8	20.1	21.6	21.3	21.9	21.4	21.7
School bus	8.0	8.1	7.6	7.8	9.9	9.1	10.4	10.3	10.3
Taxi	4.0	4.0	4.3	4.7	5.0	5.4	5.7	6.4	6.2
Railroad commutation	2.8	2.7	3.5	3.1	4.5	3.8	3.5	3.5	3.5
Intercity	53.1	53.1	52.8	54.9	57.8	57.6	65.9	68.1	71.1
Air	49.5	49.2	49.3	50.5	54.0	53.9	61.8	64.0	67.0
Rail [5]	1.8	1.9	1.8	1.8	2.2	2.1	2.3	2.2	2.1
Bus	1.8	1.9	1.7	1.4	1.5	1.5	1.6	1.8	1.8
International	14.9	17.3	17.6	17.7	18.4	18.5	19.5	18.9	19.2
Freight, total [2]	350.9	375.1	396.6	420.3	442.4	467.2	494.9	528.8	561.8
Highway [2]	270.8	292.9	311.9	330.7	348.1	368.5	396.7	427.2	456.8
Truck, intercity	162.3	176.8	189.7	204.9	219.6	235.4	257.8	282.8	304.6
Truck, local	108.4	116.0	122.1	125.7	128.4	133.0	138.7	144.3	152.1
Rail	30.1	30.5	30.8	33.1	34.4	35.1	35.3	35.3	35.9
Water	20.1	19.9	20.8	21.2	22.7	24.6	21.0	22.5	24.5
Oil pipeline	8.5	8.5	8.5	8.7	9.1	8.6	8.6	8.6	9.1
Air carrier	13.7	15.0	15.8	17.2	18.8	20.4	22.8	24.2	25.3

[1] Includes business-owned vehicles. [2] Includes items not shown separately. [3] Includes storage. [4] Includes federal, state, and local government operating subsidies and capital grants. [5] Includes federal operating subsidies and capital grants for Amtrak.

Source: Eno Transportation Foundation, Inc., Washington, D.C. *Transportation in America,* annual (copyright).

No. 1030. Volume of Domestic Intercity Freight and Passenger Traffic by Type of Transport: 1980 to 1999

[Freight traffic in bil. ton-miles (2,487 represents 2,487,000,000,000); passenger traffic in bil. passenger-miles. A ton-mile is the movement of 1 ton (2,000 pounds) of freight for the distance of 1 mile. A passenger-mile is the movement of one passenger for the distance of 1 mile. Comprises public and private traffic, both revenue and nonrevenue. ICC = Interstate Commerce Commission]

Type of transport	1980	1985	1990	1992	1993	1994	1995	1996	1997	1998	1999
Freight traffic, total . . .	2,487	2,458	2,896	3,023	3,105	3,261	3,407	3,516	3,534	3,591	3,715
Railroads	932	895	1,091	1,138	1,183	1,275	1,375	1,426	1,421	1,442	1,499
Truck:											
ICC truck.	242	250	311	342	365	391	401	428	436	459	499
Non-ICC truck	313	360	424	473	496	517	520	544	560	568	594
Water:											
Rivers/canals	311	306	390	393	373	388	406	408	413	(NA)	(NA)
Great Lakes.	96	76	85	77	83	87	91	93	95	96	95
Oil pipelines	588	564	584	589	593	591	601	619	617	620	623
Domestic airways [1]	5	7	10	11	12	12	13	14	14	14	14
Passenger traffic, total .	1,468	1,636	1,847	1,946	1,985	2,065	2,098	2,182	2,247	2,328	2,400
Private automobiles	1,210	1,310	1,452	1,544	1,575	1,625	1,641	1,693	1,740	1,806	1,850
Domestic airways [2]	15	12	13	11	10	10	11	12	13	13	14
Air, public carrier	204	278	346	354	362	388	404	435	453	(NA)	(NA)
Bus [3]	27	24	23	23	25	28	28	29	31	32	35
Railroads [4]	11	11	13	14	14	14	14	13	13	14	14

NA Not available. [1] Revenue service only for scheduled and nonscheduled carriers, with small section 418 all-cargo carriers included from 1980. Includes express mail, and excess baggage. [2] Includes general aviation (mostly private business) flying. [3] Excludes school and urban transit buses. [4] Includes intercity (Amtrak) and rail commuter service.

Source: Eno Transportation Foundation, Inc., Washington, DC, *Transportation in America,* annual (copyright).

U.S. Census Bureau, Statistical Abstract of the United States: 2002

No. 1031. Transportation and Warehousing—Establishments, Employees, and Payroll by Kind of Business (NAICS Basis): 1999 and 2000

[3,627.1 represents 3,627,100. For establishments with payroll. See Appendix III. County Business Patterns excludes rail transportation (NAICS 482) and the National Postal Service (NAICS 491)]

Industry	NAICS code [1]	Establishments		Paid employees [2] (1,000)		Annual payroll (mil. dol.)	
		1999	2000	1999	2000	1999	2000
Transportation & warehousing.	**48-49**	**187,339**	**190,044**	**3,627.1**	**3,790.0**	**116,682.2**	**125,592.4**
Air transportation	481	5,285	5,429	582.8	615.6	24,414.4	26,569.3
Scheduled air transportation	4811	3,237	3,324	540.0	570.9	22,506.2	24,484.5
Scheduled passenger air transportation .	481111	2,698	2,740	506.1	536.2	21,434.4	23,470.7
Scheduled freight air transportation. . . .	481112	539	584	33.9	34.7	1,071.8	1,013.8
Nonscheduled air transportation.	4812	2,048	2,105	42.8	44.7	1,908.2	2,084.8
Water transportation	483	1,950	1,900	71.8	67.6	3,039.5	3,003.2
Deep sea, coastal, & Great Lakes water transportation	4831	1,307	1,254	52.5	47.8	2,312.4	2,214.2
Inland water transportation	4832	643	646	19.3	19.7	727.1	789.0
Inland water freight transportation.	483211	396	402	15.9	16.3	626.4	673.9
Inland water passenger transportation . .	483212	247	244	3.4	3.5	100.7	115.1
Truck transportation	484	108,749	110,416	1,384.2	1,415.8	43,626.2	46,451.5
General freight trucking	4841	52,724	55,874	897.6	922.7	29,343.4	31,614.0
General freight trucking, local.	48411	18,737	20,329	141.6	153.3	4,087.5	4,529.8
General freight trucking, long distance. .	48412	33987	35,545	756.0	769.5	25,256.0	27,084.2
Specialized freight trucking	4842	56,025	54,542	486.6	493.1	14,282.7	14,837.5
Used household & office goods moving .	48421	9,219	9,147	127.0	128.9	3,453.7	3,661.4
Specialized freight (except used goods) trucking, local	48422	33,459	32,493	197.5	200.4	5,457.2	5,692.4
Specialized freight (except used goods) trucking, long-distance	48423	13,347	12,902	162.1	163.7	5,371.9	5,483.7
Transit & ground passenger transportation . .	485	16,254	16,383	370.0	386.9	6,729.3	7,214.7
Urban transit systems	4851	723	705	40.1	43.1	1,226.1	1,295.8
Mixed mode systems	485111	163	152	6.1	6.2	144.7	146.9
Commuter rail	485112	13	15	(D)	(D)	(D)	(D)
Bus and other motor vehicle mode systems	485113	520	505	29.3	31.4	853.7	925.1
Other.	485119	27	33	(D)	(D)	(D)	(D)
Interurban & rural bus transportation.	4852	440	444	21.8	26.8	654.4	709.7
Taxi & limousine service.	4853	6,605	6,806	63.4	67.8	1,131.2	1,244.3
Taxi service	48531	3,102	3,116	28.6	30.4	459.3	485.2
Limousine service	48532	3,503	3,690	34.8	37.5	671.9	759.1
School & employee bus transportation . . .	4854	4,341	4,217	161.9	162.9	2,178.7	2,322.6
Charter bus industry	4855	1,480	1,451	33.6	34.1	651.4	668.7
Other transit & ground passenger transportation	4059	2,665	2,760	40.2	52.2	887.5	973.6
Special needs transpiration	485991	1,860	1,914	33.4	34.8	585.8	648.9
Pipeline transportation.	486	2,550	2,802	48.1	53.0	3,032.7	3,828.6
Pipeline transportation of crude oil	4861	327	307	7.1	6.7	453.4	425.6
Pipeline transportation of natural gas . . .	4862	1,683	1,938	34.5	39.2	2,205.4	2,961.1
Other pipeline transportation	4869	540	557	6.5	7.0	373.9	441.9
Scenic & sightseeing transportation	487	2,267	2,254	22.9	23.6	540.7	583.5
Scenic & sightseeing transportation, land. .	4871	458	454	8.7	8.7	188.3	192.8
Scenic & sightseeing transportation, water.	4872	1,649	1,642	12.3	13.0	295.5	331.2
Scenic & sightseeing transportation, other .	4879	160	158	1.9	2.0	56.9	59.5
Support activities for transportation	488	31,392	31,440	440.2	472.4	14,915.6	16,507.0
Support activities for air transportation . . .	4881	4,305	4,368	118.8	126.7	3,454.2	3,634.0
Airport operations	48811	1,834	1,834	62.9	67.9	1,431.1	1,569.5
Air traffic control.	488111	135	137	0.7	0.8	27.3	29.9
Other support activities for air transportation	48819	2,471	2,534	55.9	58.8	2,023.1	2,064.6
Support activities for rail transportation . . .	4882	837	821	21.0	21.4	672.5	714.4
Support activities for water transportation . .	4883	2,593	2,543	71.4	81.6	2,995.3	3,250.7
Port and harbor operations	48831	199	196	7.4	7.4	264.7	265.8
Marine cargo handling	48832	601	607	43.8	53.5	2,016.1	2,194.7
Navigational services to shipping	48833	891	863	11.4	11.8	430.1	478.7
Other.	48839	902	877	8.8	8.9	284.5	311.5
Support activities for road transportation . .	4884	6,943	7,010	50.5	56.2	1,148.7	1,308.8
Motor vehicle towing.	48841	6,145	6,078	39.9	41.8	878.7	961.7
Freight transportation arrangement.	4885	15,464	15,177	157.5	161.7	5,885.9	6,620.3
Other support activities for transportation. .	4889	1,250	1,521	20.8	24.7	759.1	978.6
Couriers & messengers	492	11,938	12,297	578.4	619.3	16,726.0	17,399.4
Couriers	4921	6,309	6,667	508.6	548.9	15,289.5	15,890.5
Local messengers & local delivery	4922	5,629	5,630	69.8	70.5	1,436.5	1,508.9
Warehousing & storage	493	6,954	7,123	128.6	135.9	3,657.9	4,035.3

D Figure withheld to avoid disclosure pertaining to individual companies. [1] North American Industry Classification System, 1997; see text, Section 15, Business Enterprise. [2] For employees on the payroll for the pay period including March 12.

Source: U.S. Census Bureau, "County Business Patterns"; 2000 data published 30 May 2002; <http://www.census.gov/epcd/cbp/view/cbpview.html>.

U.S. Census Bureau, Statistical Abstract of the United States: 2002

No. 1032. Transportation and Warehousing—Establishments, Revenue, Payroll, by Kind of Business (NAICS Basis): 1997

[318,245 represents $318,245,000,000. For establishments with payroll. Based on the 1997 Economic Census; see Appendix III]

Industry	NAICS code [1]	Estab-lish-ments (number)	Revenue Total (mil. dol.)	Revenue Per paid employee (dol.)	Annual payroll Total (mil. dol.)	Annual payroll Per paid employee (dol.)	Paid employee for pay period including March 12 (1,000)
Transportation & warehousing [2] [3] ...	48,49	178,025	318,245	108,959	82,346	28,193	2,920.8
Air transportation [2]	481	3,598	20,249	227,198	2,748	30,834	89.1
Scheduled air transportation [2]	4811	1,798	16,285	246,786	1,921	29,110	66.0
Nonscheduled air transportation	4812	1,800	3,964	171,332	827	35,750	23.1
Water transportation	483	1,921	24,019	329,676	2,834	38,900	72.9
Deep sea, coastal, & Great Lakes water transportation	4831	1,308	20,339	374,565	2,198	40,472	54.3
Inland water transportation	4832	613	3,680	198,323	637	34,300	18.6
Truck transportation.	484	103,798	141,225	109,156	38,471	29,735	1,293.8
General freight trucking	4841	44,781	88,426	107,901	25,722	31,387	819.5
Specialized freight trucking	4842	59,017	52,800	111,326	12,749	26,881	474.3
Transit & ground passenger transportation. . .	485	16,013	13,792	40,616	5,549	16,342	339.6
Urban transit systems.	4851	618	1,519	46,096	973	29,542	32.9
Interurban & rural bus transportation.	4852	407	1,147	57,660	550	27,624	19.9
Taxi & limousine service	4853	6,418	3,155	55,070	881	15,374	57.3
School & employee bus transportation. . . .	4854	4,484	4,393	28,964	1,878	12,382	151.7
Charter bus industry.	4855	1,531	1,768	56,164	548	17,407	31.5
Other transit & ground passenger transportation	4859	2,555	1,811	39,107	720	15,547	46.3
Pipeline transportation	486	2,311	26,837	544,582	2,661	53,989	49.3
Pipeline transportation of crude oil	4861	382	4,365	548,311	480	60,240	8.0
Pipeline transportation of natural gas	4862	1,450	19,627	548,404	1,871	52,277	35.8
Other pipeline transportation	4869	479	2,846	514,483	310	56,069	5.5
Scenic & sightseeing transportation	487	2,325	1,893	79,200	492	20,600	23.9
Scenic & sightseeing transportation, land. .	4871	454	558	67,777	170	20,619	8.2
Scenic & sightseeing transportation, water .	4872	1,692	1,129	79,565	283	19,940	14.2
Scenic & sightseeing transportation, other .	4879	179	207	138,604	40	26,757	1.5
Support activities for transportation	488	30,675	39,758	96,585	12,592	30,591	411.6
Support activities for air transportation. . . .	4881	4,231	9,153	79,279	2,820	24,425	115.5
Support activities for rail transportation . . .	4882	816	2,067	109,555	515	27,276	18.9
Support activities for water transportation. .	4883	2,525	7,515	103,681	2,763	38,125	72.5
Support activities for road transportation . .	4884	6,424	2,683	60,535	901	20,327	44.3
Freight transportation arrangement	4885	15,782	16,251	114,856	5,015	35,442	141.5
Other support activities for transportation . .	4889	897	2,090	109,826	579	30,427	19.0
Couriers & messengers	492	10,887	39,812	74,999	14,072	26,508	530.8
Couriers.	4921	5,503	36,293	78,315	12,830	27,685	463.4
Local messengers & local delivery	4922	5,384	3,519	52,202	1,242	18,420	67.4
Warehousing & storage	493	6,497	10,658	97,102	2,926	26,659	109.8

[1] North American Industry Classification System, 1997; see text, Section 15, Business Enterprise.   [2] Data do not include large certificated passenger carriers that report to the Office of Airline Statistics, U.S. Department of Transportation.   [3] Railroad transportation and U.S. Postal Service are out of scope for the 1997 Economic Census.

Source: U.S. Census Bureau, *1997 Economic Census, Transportation & Warehousing,* Series EC97T48A-US, issued January 2000.

No. 1033. Employment and Earnings in Transportation by Industry: 1980 to 2001

[2,960 represents 2,960,000. Annual average of monthly figures. Based on Current Employment Statistics program; see Appendix III]

Industry	SIC code [1]	1980	1990	1995	1997	1998	1999	2000	2001
NUMBER (1,000)									
Total transportation	(X)	2,960	3,511	3,904	4,123	4,273	4,411	4,529	4,530
Railroads.	40	532	279	238	227	231	235	236	227
Class I railroads, plus Amtrak	4011	482	241	212	202	205	204	194	188
Local and interurban passengers. . . .	41	265	338	419	452	469	478	476	482
Trucking and warehousing	42	(NA)	1,395	1,587	1,677	1,744	1,810	1,856	1,854
Water transportation	44	211	177	175	179	181	186	196	203
Air transportation	45	(NA)	968	1,068	1,134	1,181	1,227	1,281	1,287
Pipelines, exc. natural gas	46	21	19	15	14	14	14	14	14
Transportation services	47	(NA)	336	401	441	454	463	471	464
AVG. WEEKLY EARNINGS [2] (dol.)									
Class I railroads	4011	427	727	811	892	845	797	799	782
Local and interurban passengers. . . .	41	217	310	358	375	387	395	412	424
Trucking and warehousing	42	(NA)	450	504	532	545	561	579	583
Pipelines, exc. natural gas	46	441	711	888	902	918	944	956	957

NA Not available.   X Not applicable.   [1] 1987 Standard Industrial Classification, see text, Section 15, Business Enterprise.   [2] For nonsupervisory workers.

Source: U.S. Bureau of Labor Statistics, *Employment and Earnings,* March and June issues; and Internet site: <http://www.bls.gov/ces/>.

660 Transportation

No. 1034. Transportation Accidents, Deaths, and Injuries: 1980 to 2000

[6,216 represents 6,216,000]

Year and casualty	Motor ve-hicle [1] (1,000)	Rail-road [2]	Air-lines [3]	Air (Com-muter air car-riers [4])	On demand air car-riers [5]	General aviation	Recre-ational boat-ing [6]	Pipeline [7] (Gas)	Hazard-ous liquid	Water-borne [8]	Rail Rapid Trans-it [9]	Hazard-ous materi-als [10]
Accidents:												
1980....	6,216	8,205	19	38	171	3,590	5,513	1,524	246	4,624	6,789	15,719
1990....	6,471	2,879	24	15	106	2,215	6,411	198	180	3,613	12,178	8,880
1995....	6,699	2,459	36	12	75	2,053	8,019	161	188	4,298	14,327	14,743
1999....	6,279	2,768	52	13	73	1,913	7,931	175	168	4,036	(NA)	17,085
2000....	6,394	2,983	54	12	80	1,835	7,740	234	146	3,791	(NA)	17,224
Deaths:												
1980....	51.1	584	1	37	105	1,239	1,360	15	4	206	83	19
1990....	44.6	599	39	7	50	767	865	6	3	85	117	8
1995....	41.8	567	168	9	52	734	829	18	3	46	51	7
1999....	41.7	530	12	12	38	630	734	22	4	44	57	7
2000....	41.8	512	92	5	71	592	701	37	1	(NA)	32	12
Injuries:												
1980....	2,848	58,696	19	14	43	681	2,650	177	15	180	6,801	626
1990....	3,231	22,736	29	11	36	402	3,822	69	7	175	10,036	423
1995....	3,465	12,546	25	25	14	395	4,141	53	11	145	11,238	400
1999....	3,236	10,304	58	2	14	326	4,315	93	20	131	(NA)	252
2000....	3,189	10,424	26	7	10	329	4,355	77	4	125	(NA)	240

NA Not available. [1] Data on deaths are from U.S. National Highway Traffic Safety Administration and are based on 30 day definition. Includes only police reported crashes. For more detail, see Table 1077. [2] Accidents which result in damages to railroad property. Grade crossing accidents are also included when classified as a train accident. Deaths exclude fatalities in railroad-highway grade crossing accidents. [3] Includes scheduled and nonscheduled (charter) air carriers. Represents serious injuries. [4] All scheduled service. Represents serious injuries. [5] All nonscheduled service. Represents serious injuries. [6] Accidents resulting in death; injury or requiring medical treatment beyond first aid; damages exceeding $500; or a person's disappearance. [7] Beginning 1990, pipeline accidents/incidents are credited to year of occurrence; 1980 data are credited to the year filed. [8] Covers accidents involving commercial vessels which must be reported to U.S. Coast Guard if there is property damage exceeding $25,000; material damage affecting the seaworthiness or efficiency of a vessel; stranding or grounding; loss of life; or injury causing a person's incapacity for more than 3 days. [9] Reporting criteria and source of data changed between 1989 and 1990; these data from 1990 to present are not comparable to earlier years. [10] Accidents, deaths, and injuries involving hazardous materials cover all types of transport.
Source: U.S. Bureau of Transportation Statistics, *National Transportation Statistics, annual.*

No. 1035. U.S. Scheduled Airline Industry—Summary: 1990 to 2000

[For calendar years or Dec. 31 (465.6 represents 465,600,000). For domestic and international operations. Covers carriers certificated under Section 401 of the Federal Aviation Act. Minus sign (-) indicates loss]

Item	Unit	1990	1994	1995	1996	1997	1998	1999	2000
SCHEDULED SERVICE									
Revenue passengers enplaned .	Mil.	465.6	528.8	547.8	581.2	594.7	612.9	636.0	665.5
Revenue passenger miles.....	Bil......	457.9	519.4	540.7	578.7	603.4	618.1	652.0	692.5
Available seat miles.......	Bil......	733.4	784.3	807.1	835.1	857.2	874.1	918.4	956.5
Revenue passenger load factor .	Percent .	62.4	66.2	67.0	69.3	70.4	70.7	71.0	72.4
Mean passenger trip length [1].	Miles ...	984	982	987	996	1,015	1,008	1,025	1,041
Freight and express ton miles ..	Mil.	10,546	13,792	14,578	15,301	17,959	18,131	19,317	21,143
Aircraft departures........	1,000 ...	6,924	7,531	8,062	8,230	8,127	8,292	8,627	8,992
FINANCES									
Total operating revenue [2] ..	**Mil. dol. .**	**76,142**	**88,313**	**94,578**	**101,937**	**109,568**	**113,465**	**119,038**	**129,463**
Passenger revenue	Mil. dol. .	58,453	65,422	69,594	75,286	79,471	80,985	84,317	93,573
Freight and express revenue...	Mil. dol. .	5,432	7,284	8,616	9,679	10,477	10,697	11,415	11,993
Mail revenue	Mil. dol. .	970	1,183	1,266	1,279	1,362	1,708	1,739	1,975
Charter revenue	Mil. dol. .	2,877	3,548	3,485	3,447	3,575	3,821	4,030	4,365
Total operating expense	Mil. dol. .	78,054	85,600	88,718	95,728	100,981	104,137	110,635	122,389
Operating profit...........	Mil. dol. .	-1,912	2,713	5,860	6,209	8,587	9,328	8,403	7,074
Interest expense	Mil. dol. .	1,978	2,347	2,424	1,981	1,733	1,742	1,821	2,165
Net profit...............	Mil. dol. .	-3,921	-344	2,314	2,804	5,168	4,903	5,360	2,637
Revenue per passenger mile...	Cents...	12.8	12.6	12.9	13.0	13.2	13.1	12.9	13.5
Rate of return on investment...	Percent .	-6.0	5.2	11.9	11.5	14.7	12.0	11.1	6.6
Operating profit margin.......	Percent .	-2.5	3.1	6.2	6.1	7.8	8.2	7.1	5.5
Net profit margin...........	Percent .	-5.1	-0.4	2.4	2.8	4.7	4.3	4.5	2.0
EMPLOYEES [3]									
Total..............	**1,000 ...**	**545.8**	**539.8**	**547.0**	**564.4**	**586.5**	**621.1**	**646.4**	**680.0**
Pilots and copilots..........	1,000 ...	47.1	52.9	55.4	57.6	60.4	64.1	67.2	72.6
Other flight personnel........	1,000 ...	8.9	7.7	8.6	8.9	10.7	11.1	12.4	11.5
Flight attendants	1,000 ...	83.4	86.5	86.7	89.1	96.2	97.6	105.6	113.7
Mechanics	1,000 ...	61.0	55.8	50.5	50.8	65.5	69.9	70.3	72.8
Aircraft and traffic servicing personnel	1,000 ...	251.2	247.2	251.1	266.5	269.6	290.1	295.6	311.1
All other...............	1,000 ...	94.2	89.7	94.8	91.6	84.1	88.3	95.3	98.4

[1] For definition of mean, see Guide to Tabular Presentation. [2] Includes other types of revenues, not shown separately. [3] Average number of full time equivalents.
Source: Air Transport Association of America, Washington, DC, *Air Transport,* annual, and *Air Transport, Facts and Figures,* annual.

U.S. Census Bureau, Statistical Abstract of the United States: 2002

No. 1036. Airline Cost Indexes: 1980 to 2000

[Covers U.S. major and national service carriers. Major carriers have operating revenues of $1 billion or more; nationals have operating revenues from $75 million to $1 billion]

Index	Index (1982=100)								Percent distribution of total operating expenses [1]			
	1980	1985	1990	1995	1997	1998	1999	2000	1980	1990	1995	2000
Composite index	86.8	102.8	122.6	131.3	137.4	134.8	137.2	150.2	100.0	100.0	100.0	100.0
Labor costs:												
Passenger carriers.	85.8	110.5	121.7	155.7	163.0	164.5	166.6	176.3	35.2	31.6	35.5	35.2
Cargo carriers	78.3	116.0	148.8	151.7	156.0	159.1	164.8	170.1	27.3	30.0	40.0	27.9
Fuel	89.7	79.6	77.2	55.3	62.5	49.4	51.4	78.3	30.0	17.3	12.0	14.0
Aircraft fleet [2][3]	88.1	123.7	177.0	222.8	223.4	228.2	229.8	252.0	5.2	7.9	9.7	9.2
Interest [2][4]	88.1	98.0	96.0	93.5	72.1	67.4	68.9	59.9	3.2	2.6	3.1	1.8
Insurance	80.4	155.3	68.2	111.6	96.0	64.5	44.3	41.9	0.3	0.3	0.8	0.3
Maintenance material.	104.9	119.9	190.5	153.4	191.0	201.2	187.0	200.5	2.5	3.4	2.8	3.1
Landing fee	87.2	99.9	139.0	176.6	184.0	177.4	186.8	186.4	1.7	1.8	2.2	1.8
Traffic commissions [2].	75.4	112.9	169.2	139.4	126.9	113.0	97.9	80.4	4.9	9.4	8.6	4.6
Communication [2]	65.8	96.6	111.2	116.0	110.4	119.0	138.1	135.8	1.1	1.4	1.6	1.6
Advertising and promotion [2] . .	67.1	96.2	97.8	63.6	54.7	59.2	59.7	57.0	1.6	2.0	1.5	1.2
Passenger food [2]	90.6	98.9	128.4	110.9	102.8	105.2	106.8	104.9	2.9	3.5	3.4	3.0
All other	86.3	111.3	130.6	147.6	153.2	155.0	158.0	161.6	11.8	19.1	22.7	25.3

[1] Total operating expenses plus interest on long term debt, less depreciation and amortization. [2] Passenger airlines only. [3] Includes lease, aircraft and engine rentals, depreciation and amortization. [4] Interest on debt.

Source: Air Transport Association of America, Washington, DC, *Air Transport*, annual; and unpublished data.

No. 1037. Top 40 Airports in 2001—Passengers Enplaned: 1991 and 2001

[In thousands (432,473 represents 432,473,000), except rank. For calendar year. Airports ranked by total passengers enplaned by large certificated air carriers, 2001]

Airport	1991		2001		Airport	1991		2001	
	Total	Rank	Total	Rank		Total	Rank	Total	Rank
All Airports	432,473	(X)	595,946	(X)	Boston, (Logan Intl), MA	8,917	15	10,017	20
Top 40 Airports	327,718	(X)	462,085	(X)	New York, (JFK), NY.	8,354	17	9,647	21
Atlanta (Hartsfield Intl), GA. . .	17,737	4	36,384	1	Baltimore, MD	4,278	31	9,451	22
Chicago (O'Hare Intl), IL	26,053	1	28,626	2	Pittsburgh, PA	7,728	20	8,711	23
Dallas/Ft. Worth Intl, TX	22,834	2	25,198	3	Cincinnati, OH	4,337	29	8,352	24
Los Angeles Intl, CA	18,335	3	22,873	4	Salt Lake City, UT	5,476	25	7,840	25
Phoenix Sky Harbor Intl, AZ . .	10,981	7	16,540	5	Honolulu, HI	8,776	16	7,795	26
Denver Intl, CO	12,461	6	16,397	6	Tampa, FL	4,352	28	7,458	27
Las Vegas (McCarran Intl)					Miami/Ft. Lauderdale, FL. . . .	3,465	37	7,372	28
NV.	9,011	14	16,121	7	San Diego (Intl-				
Minneapolis-St. Paul Intl, MN .	9,207	12	15,648	8	Lindbergh), CA.	5,389	26	7,254	29
Houston International, TX	7,850	18	15,640	9	Chicago, IL (Midway)	2,937	43	7,063	30
Detroit (Wayne County), MI . .	9,800	8	15,467	10	Portland, OR	3,172	39	6,005	31
San Francisco Intl, CA	14,038	5	13,863	11	San Jose Muni, CA.	3,153	41	5,866	32
Newark, NJ.	9,742	9	13,823	12	Washington (Reagan				
St Louis (Lambert-St.					National), DC.	6,632	23	5,785	33
Louis Muni), MO.	9,453	10	12,864	13	Washington (Dulles Intl), DC .	4,715	27	5,754	34
Seattle-Tacoma Intl, WA	7,723	21	12,705	14	Cleveland (Hopkins Intl), OH .	3,558	35	5,529	35
Orlando Intl, FL	7,755	19	12,620	15	Kansas City, MO	3,319	38	5,496	36
Miami Intl, FL	9,350	11	11,505	16	Oakland Metro Intl, CA	2,965	42	5,487	37
Philadelphia, PA.	6,553	24	10,387	17	Memphis, TN.	3,502	36	4,785	38
New York (LaGuardia), NY. . .	9,195	13	10,311	18	New Orleans, LA	3,163	40	4,683	39
Charlotte (Douglas Muni),					San Juan, (Luis Munoz				
NC.	7,679	22	10,226	19	Marin Intl), PR	3,774	33	4,538	40

X Not applicable.

Source: U.S. Bureau of Transportation Statistics, Office of Airline Information, BTS Form 41, Schedule T-3, unpublished data.

No. 1038. Domestic Airline Markets: 2000

[In thousands (3,637 represents 3,637,000). For calendar year. Data are for the 30 top markets and include all commercial airports in each metro area. Data do not include connecting passengers]

Market	Passengers	Market	Passengers
New York to—from Los Angeles	3,637	Honolulu to—from Lihue, Kauai	1,733
New York to—from Chicago	3,067	New York to—from Las Vegas.	1,602
New York to—from Orlando	2,978	Los Angeles to—from Oakland	1,590
New York to—from Boston	2,966	New York to—from Dallas/Ft. Worth	1,583
New York to—from San Francisco	2,807	New York to—from West Palm Beach. . . .	1,563
New York to—from Atlanta	2,771	Chicago to—from Detroit	1,524
New York to—from Ft. Lauderdale	2,671	Chicago to—from Atlanta	1,513
Honolulu to—from Kahului, Maui	2,607	Chicago to—from Dallas/Ft. Worth	1,478
New York to—from Miami	2,542	Honolulu to—from Kona, Hawaii	1,466
New York to—from Washington	2,504	Chicago to—from Minneapolis/St. Paul . . .	1,447
Los Angeles to—from Las Vegas	2,405	Atlanta to—from Washington	1,428
Dallas/Ft. Worth to—from Houston.	2,289	Chicago to—from Lax Vegas	1,410
New York to—from San Juan	1,986	New York to—from Houston	1,382
Los Angeles to—from San Francisco	1,959	Boston to—from Washington.	1,381
Chicago to—from Los Angeles	1,817	Los Angeles to—from Phoenix	1,376

Source: Air Transport Association of America, Washington, DC, *Air Transport 2001*.

No. 1039. Worldwide Airline Fatalities: 1987 to 2001

[For scheduled air transport operations]

Year	Fatal accidents	Passenger deaths	Death rate [1]	Death rate [2]	Year	Fatal accidents	Passenger deaths	Death rate [1]	Death rate [2]
1987	25	900	0.09	0.06	1995	25	711	0.05	0.03
1988	29	742	0.07	0.04	1996	24	1,146	0.07	0.05
1989	29	879	0.08	0.05	1997	26	929	0.06	0.04
1990	27	544	0.05	0.03	1998	20	904	0.05	0.03
1991	29	638	0.06	0.03	1999	21	499	0.03	0.02
1992	28	1,076	0.09	0.06	2000	18	755	0.04	0.03
1993	33	864	0.07	0.04	2001	13	577	0.03	0.02
1994	27	1,171	0.09	0.06					

[1] Rate per 100 million passenger miles flown.   [2] Rate per 100 million passenger kilometers flown.

Source: International Civil Aviation Organization, Montreal, Canada, *Civil Aviation Statistics of the World,* annual.

No. 1040. Airline Passenger Screening Results: 1980 to 2000

[Calendar year data (585 represents 585,000,000)]

Item	1980	1985	1990	1995	1997	1998	1999	2000
Persons screened (mil.)	585	993	1,145	1,263	1,660	1,903	1,754	1,812
WEAPONS DETECTED								
Firearms, total	1,914	2,913	2,549	2,390	2,067	1,515	1,552	1,937
Handguns................	1,878	2,823	2,490	2,230	1,905	1,401	1,421	1,643
Long guns	36	90	59	160	162	114	131	294
Other/other dangerous articles........	108	74	304	(X)	(X)	(X)	(X)	(X)
Explosive/incendiary devices.........	8	12	15	(X)	(X)	(X)	(X)	(X)
Persons arrested:								
Carrying firearms/explosives	1,031	1,310	1,336	1,194	924	660	633	600
Giving false information.	32	42	18	68	72	86	58	61
Bomb threats received:								
Against airports	1,179	477	448	346	(NA)	(NA)	(NA)	(NA)
Against aircraft	268	153	338	327	(NA)	(NA)	(NA)	(NA)

NA Not available.   X Not applicable.

Source: U.S. Bureau of Transportation Statistics, *National Transportation Statistics, 2001,* Internet site <http://www.bts.gov/btsprod/nts/>.

No. 1041. Aircraft Accidents: 1982 to 2001

[For years ending December 31]

Item	Unit	1982	1985	1990	1995	1999	2000	2001, prel.
Air carrier accidents, all services [1].......	Number...	18	21	24	36	52	57	40
Fatal accidents..................	Number...	5	7	6	3	2	3	6
Fatalities	Number...	235	526	39	168	12	92	531
Aboard.....................	Number...	223	525	12	162	11	92	525
Rates per 100,000 flight hours:								
Accidents..................	Rate.....	0.241	0.241	0.198	0.267	0.299	0.312	0.215
Fatal accidents	Rate.....	0.057	0.080	0.049	0.022	0.012	0.016	0.012
Commuter air carrier accidents [2]........	Number...	26	18	15	12	13	12	7
Fatal accidents..................	Number...	5	7	3	2	5	1	2
Fatalities	Number...	14	37	6	9	12	5	13
Aboard.....................	Number...	14	36	4	9	12	5	13
Rates per 100,000 flight hours:								
Accidents..................	Rate.....	2.000	1.036	0.641	0.457	2.118	3.212	2.118
Fatal accidents	Rate.....	0.385	0.403	0.128	0.076	1.459	0.268	0.605
On-demand air taxi accidents [3].........	Number...	132	157	107	75	73	81	72
Fatal accidents..................	Number...	31	35	29	24	12	22	18
Fatalities	Number...	72	76	51	52	38	71	60
Aboard.....................	Number...	72	75	49	52	38	68	59
Rates per 100,000 flight hours:								
Accidents..................	Rate.....	4.39	6.11	4.76	3.02	2.21	2.28	2.12
Fatal accidents	Rate.....	1.03	1.36	1.29	0.97	0.36	0.62	0.53
General aviation accidents [4]..........	Number...	3,233	2,739	2,241	2,056	1,906	1,838	1,721
Fatal accidents..................	Number...	591	498	443	413	340	343	321
Fatalities	Number...	1,187	956	767	735	619	594	553
Aboard.....................	Number...	1,170	945	762	728	615	584	549
Rates per 100,000 flight hours:								
Accidents..................	Rate.....	10.90	9.66	7.86	8.24	6.41	6.33	6.56
Fatal accidents	Rate.....	1.99	1.75	1.55	1.65	1.14	1.18	1.22

[1] U.S. air carriers operating under 14 CFR 121. Beginning 1999, includes aircraft with 10 or more seats, previously operating under 14 CFR 135.   [2] All scheduled service of U.S. air carriers operating under 14 CFR 135. Beginning 1999, only aircraft with fewer than 10 seats.   [3] All nonscheduled service of U.S. air carriers operating under 14 CFR 135.   [4] U.S. civil registered aircraft not operated under 14 CFR 121 or 135.

Source: U.S. National Transportation Safety Board, Internet site <http://www.ntsb.gov/aviation/stats.htm> (accessed 28 May 2002).

No. 1042. On-Time Flight Arrivals and Departures at Major U.S. Airports: 2001

[In percent. Quarterly, based on gate arrival and departure times for domestic scheduled operations of U.S. major airlines. All U.S. airlines with 1 percent or more of total U.S. domestic scheduled airline passenger revenues are required to report on-time data. A flight is considered on time if it operated less than 15 minutes after the scheduled time shown in the carrier's computerized reservation system. Cancelled and diverted flights are considered late. See source for data on individual airlines]

Airport	On-time arrivals				On-time departures			
	1st qtr.	2d qtr.	3d qtr.	4th qtr.	1st. qtr.	2d qtr.	3d qtr.	4th qtr.
Total, all airports	74.5	78.7	74.2	83.2	78.1	81.9	76.7	84.7
Total major airports.	74.0	78.2	73.4	83.4	76.8	80.7	75.0	84.0
Atlanta, Hartsfield International	73.2	77.7	74.3	85.9	75.4	78.1	74.6	84.5
Baltimore/Washington International	79.0	80.9	75.3	82.6	79.3	82.3	77.3	78.6
Boston, Logan International	66.3	71.8	66.0	86.2	69.4	75.9	67.4	83.8
Charlotte Douglas.	81.8	83.6	76.4	86.6	81.6	82.5	78.7	85.6
Chicago Midway.	80.8	84.3	80.3	86.9	78.9	80.4	77.0	81.7
Chicago, O'Hare	71.5	72.5	86.3	80.3	73.5	73.7	68.7	82.1
Cincinnati International	80.5	86.0	78.1	87.7	84.4	87.0	78.9	89.5
Dallas/Ft. Worth Regional	76.5	82.2	77.0	84.3	77.7	81.5	74.1	82.0
Denver International	75.9	78.8	72.7	84.0	75.3	78.9	70.7	85.8
Detroit, Metro Wayne	82.1	83.6	77.8	85.2	79.8	82.3	77.1	80.9
Fort Lauderdale	71.3	78.2	73.5	83.2	75.8	82.6	78.9	87.2
Houston George Bush.	81.0	83.7	77.1	84.2	85.7	86.0	79.8	87.7
Las Vegas, McCarran International	73.4	80.1	73.1	82.8	72.4	80.0	76.6	83.0
Los Angeles International.	68.1	73.2	73.0	83.7	73.6	79.2	76.9	84.8
Miami International	73.0	77.9	72.4	79.3	77.6	80.9	72.5	83.6
Minneapolis/St. Paul International	80.7	81.2	78.1	85.7	80.2	82.2	78.2	85.4
Newark International	72.1	75.1	68.7	85.3	78.2	81.8	74.7	87.7
New York, Kennedy International.	66.6	69.0	63.3	81.0	69.6	74.2	66.8	75.2
New York, LaGuardia	64.6	70.6	64.0	87.7	72.2	78.9	70.7	87.5
Orlando International	73.9	80.5	75.5	85.4	79.4	85.5	79.5	90.4
Philadelphia International.	70.8	73.2	66.2	80.0	74.2	77.9	72.0	81.0
Phoenix, Sky Harbor International	71.0	80.7	78.5	86.0	72.5	80.3	76.7	83.8
Pittsburgh, Greater International	80.5	82.2	73.9	86.4	82.6	84.6	76.4	86.9
Portland International	75.4	78.6	75.5	77.4	81.9	85.8	79.5	81.4
Ronald Reagan National	77.8	79.8	65.4	84.7	84.1	85.2	70.3	87.7
St. Louis, Lambert	77.2	83.1	80.9	84.8	78.6	83.7	81.3	84.2
Salt Lake City International	74.9	83.0	80.9	83.5	79.2	88.0	81.4	86.6
San Diego International, Lindbergh	72.0	77.8	75.1	80.6	77.0	82.0	79.0	82.8
San Francisco International	68.7	75.8	88.1	73.2	74.9	83.1	74.5	80.8
Seattle-Tacoma International	65.3	71.3	68.1	72.9	73.5	80.0	73.6	80.4
Tampa International	73.4	78.8	75.0	83.9	79.4	84.7	79.9	88.0
Washington/Dulles	79.0	77.3	70.9	82.9	80.7	80.4	73.8	84.6

Source: U.S. Department of Transportation, Office of Consumer Affairs, *Air Travel Consumer Report*, monthly.

No. 1043. Consumer Complaints Against U.S. Airlines: 1990 to 2001

[Calendar year data. Represents complaints filed by consumers to the U.S. Department of Transportation, Aviation Consumer Protection Division, regarding service problems with air carrier personnel. See source for data on individual airlines]

Complaint category	1990	1994	1995	1996	1997	1998	1999	2000	2001
Total	7,703	5,179	4,629	5,782	6,394	7,980	17,345	20,564	14,076
Flight problems [1]	3,034	1,586	1,133	1,628	1,699	2,270	6,449	8,698	5,046
Customer service [2].	758	805	667	999	1,418	1,716	3,657	4,074	2,700
Baggage.	1,329	761	628	882	826	1,105	2,351	2,753	1,965
Ticketing/boarding [3]	624	598	666	857	904	805	1,329	1,405	1,310
Refunds	701	393	576	521	531	601	935	803	942
Fares [4].	312	267	185	180	195	276	584	708	568
Oversales [5].	399	301	263	353	414	387	673	759	539
Disability [6]	(NA)	(NA)	(NA)	(NA)	(NA)	331	520	612	454
Advertising	96	94	66	61	57	39	57	42	42
Tours	29	127	18	16	13	23	28	25	11
Animals	(NA)	(NA)	(NA)	(NA)	(NA)	(NA)	(NA)	1	6
Smoking.	74	20	15	13	5	(7)	(7)	(7)	(7)
Credit.	5	2	4	3	1	(7)	(7)	(7)	(7)
Other.	342	225	408	269	331	427	762	684	493

NA Not available. [1] Cancellations, delays, etc. from schedule. [2] Unhelpful employees, inadequate meals or cabin service, treatment of delayed passengers. [3] Errors in reservations and ticketing; problems in making reservations and obtaining tickets. [4] Incorrect or incomplete information about fares, discount fare conditions, and availability, etc. [5] All bumping problems, whether or not airline complied with DOT regulations. [6] Prior to 1998, included in ticketing/boarding. [7] Included in "Other" beginning 1998.

Source: U.S. Dept. of Transportation, Office of Consumer Affairs, *Air Travel Consumer Report*, monthly.

No. 1044. Commuter/Regional Airline Operations—Summary: 1980 to 2000

[Calendar year data (14.8 represents 14,800,000). Commuter/regional airlines operate primarily aircraft of predominately 75 passengers or less and 18,000 pounds of payload capacity serving short haul and small community markets. Represents operations within all North America by U.S. Regional Carriers. Averages are means. For definition of mean, see Guide to Tabular Presentation]

Item	Unit	1980	1985	1990	1995	1997	1998	1999	2000
Passenger carriers operating	Number.	214	179	150	124	104	97	97	94
Passengers enplaned	Millions .	14.8	[1]26.0	42.1	57.2	66.3	71.1	78.1	84.6
Average passengers enplaned per carrier. .	1,000 . .	69.2	152.4	277.5	461.4	637.5	733.0	804.7	830.4
Revenue passenger miles (RPM)	Billions .	1.92	[1]4.41	7.61	12.75	15.30	17.42	20.81	25.27
Average RPMs per carrier	Millions .	8.97	[1]24.64	50.75	102.80	147.09	179.64	214.49	268.83
Airports served	Number.	732	854	811	780	766	773	734	729
Average trip length	Miles. . .	129	173	183	223	231	245	267	299
Passenger aircraft operated	Number.	1,339	1,745	1,917	2,138	2,104	2,150	2,187	2,271
Average seating capacity (seats).	Number.	13.9	19.2	22.1	24.6	25.9	27.7	29.8	31.8
Fleet flying hours [2]	1,000 . .	1,740	2,854	3,447	4,659	4,695	4,631	5,058	5,363
Average annual utilization per aircraft.	Hours . .	1,299	1,635	1,798	2,179	2,231	2,154	2,313	2,368

[1] Adjusted to exclude a merger in 1986.   [2] Prior to 1995, utilization results reflected airborne rather than block hours. Data inclusive of carriers which may have operated during only part of calendar year 1996.

Source: Regional Airline Association and AvStat Associates, Washington, DC, *Annual Report of the Regional Airline Industry* (copyright).

No. 1045. Airports, Aircraft, and Airmen: 1980 to 1999

[As of Dec. 31 or for years ending Dec. 31]

Item	1980	1985	1990	1995	1996	1997	1998	1999
Airports, total [1]	**15,161**	**16,319**	**17,490**	**18,224**	**18,292**	**18,345**	**18,770**	**19,098**
Public	4,814	5,858	5,589	5,415	5,389	5,357	5,352	5,354
Percent—With lighted runways	66.2	68.1	71.4	74.3	74.5	74.6	74.8	76.2
With paved runways	72.3	66.7	70.7	73.3	73.7	74.0	74.2	74.2
Private	10,347	10,461	11,901	12,809	12,903	12,988	13,418	13,774
Percent—With lighted runways	15.2	9.1	7.0	6.4	6.4	6.4	6.3	6.7
With paved runways	13.3	17.4	31.5	33.0	32.9	33.0	33.2	31.8
Certificated [2].	730	700	680	667	671	660	660	655
Civil	(X)	(X)	(X)	572	577	566	566	565
Civil military.	(X)	(X)	(X)	95	94	94	94	90
General aviation	14,431	15,619	16,810	17,557	17,621	17,685	18,110	18,443
Active air carrier fleet [3].	**3,808**	**4,678**	**6,083**	**7,411**	**7,478**	**5,093**	**5,335**	**(NA)**
Fixed wing	3,803	4,673	6,072	7,293	7,357	5,093	5,335	(NA)
Helicopter.	2	5	11	118	121	(NA)	(NA)	(NA)
General aviation fleet [4].	211,043	196,500	198,000	188,089	191,129	192,414	204,710	(NA)
Fixed-wing	200,097	184,700	184,500	162,342	163,691	166,854	175,203	(NA)
Turbojet	2,992	4,100	4,100	4,559	4,424	5,178	6,066	(NA)
Turboprop	4,090	5,000	5,300	4,905	5,716	5,619	6,174	(NA)
Piston.	193,014	175,600	175,200	152,788	153,551	156,056	162,963	(NA)
Rotocraft	6,001	6,000	6,900	5,830	6,570	6,786	7,425	(NA)
Other.	4,945	5,800	6,600	4,741	4,244	4,092	5,580	(NA)
Gliders	(NA)	(NA)	(NA)	2,182	1,934	2,016	2,105	(NA)
Lighter than air.	(NA)	(NA)	(NA)	2,559	2,310	2,075	3,475	(NA)
Experimental.	(NA)	(NA)	(NA)	15,176	16,625	14,680	16,502	(NA)
Airman certificates held: [5]								
Pilot, total	827,071	709,540	702,659	639,184	622,261	616,342	618,298	635,472
Women	52,902	43,082	40,515	38,032	36,433	35,531	35,762	37,373
Student.	199,833	146,652	128,663	101,279	94,947	96,101	97,736	97,359
Recreational	(NA)	(NA)	87	232	265	284	305	343
Airplane:								
Private	357,479	311,086	299,111	261,399	254,002	247,604	247,226	258,749
Commercial	183,442	151,632	149,666	133,980	129,187	125,300	122,053	124,261
Air transport	69,569	82,740	107,732	123,877	127,486	130,858	134,612	137,642
Rotocraft only [6]	6,030	8,123	9,567	7,183	6,961	6,801	6,964	7,728
Glider only.	7,039	8,168	7,833	11,234	9,413	9,394	9,402	9,390
Flight instructor certificates	60,440	58,940	63,775	77,613	78,551	78,102	79,171	79,694
Instrument ratings	260,462	258,559	297,073	298,798	297,895	297,409	300,183	308,951
Nonpilot [7].	368,356	395,139	492,237	651,341	534,427	540,892	549,588	538,264
Mechanic	250,157	274,100	344,282	405,294	329,239	332,254	336,670	340,402
Repairmen	(NA)	(NA)	(NA)	61,233	50,768	51,643	52,909	35,989
Parachute rigger.	9,547	9,395	10,094	11,824	10,269	10,336	10,459	10,447
Ground instructor	61,550	58,214	66,882	96,165	68,573	69,366	70,334	71,238
Dispatcher.	6,799	8,511	11,002	15,642	13,272	13,967	14,804	15,655
Flight navigator	1,936	1,542	1,290	916	847	782	712	642
Flight engineer.	38,367	43,377	58,687	60,267	61,459	62,544	63,700	63,891

NA Not available.   X Not applicable.   [1] Existing airports, heliports, seaplane bases, etc. recorded with FAA. Includes military airports with joint civil and military use. Includes U.S. outlying areas. Airport-type definitions: Public—publicly owned and under control of a public agency; private—owned by a private individual or corporation. May or may not be open for public use.   [2] Certificated airports serve air-carriers with aircraft seating more that 30 passengers.   [3] Air-carrier aircraft are aircraft carrying passengers or cargo for hire under 14 CFR 121 (large aircraft—more than 30 seats) and 14 CFR 135 (small aircraft— 30 seats or fewer).   [4] Beginning 1995 excludes commuters.   [5] Source: U.S. Federal Aviation Administration. See Internet site <http://api.hq.faa.gov/civilair/index.htm> for data beginning 1990 (accessed 19 June 2002). Prior years in the *Statistical Handbook of Aviation*, annual.   [6] Data for 1980 and 1985 are for helicopters only.   [7] All certificates on record. No medical examination required. Data for 1996 and 1997 are limited to certificates held by those under 70 years of age.

Source: Except as noted, U.S. Bureau of Transportation Statistics, *National Transportation Statistics, 2000.*

Transportation   665

No. 1046. Federal Expenditures for Civil Functions of the Corps of Engineers, United States Army: 1970 to 1999

[In millions of dollars (1,128 represents $1,128,000,000). For fiscal years ending in year shown, see text, Section 8, State and Local Government Finances and Employment. These expenditures represent the work of the Corps of Engineers to plan, design, construct, operate, and maintain civil works projects and activities, particularly in the management and improvement of rivers, harbors, and waterways for navigation, flood control, and multiple purposes. The amounts listed below do not include the expenditure of funds contributed, advanced, or reimbursed by other government agencies or local interests. Includes Puerto Rico and outlying areas]

Fiscal year	Total program [1]	Navigation	Flood control	Multiple purpose	Fiscal year	Total program [1]	Navigation	Flood control	Multiple purpose
1970	1,128	398	379	331	1992	3,675	1,562	1,469	469
1980	3,061	1,225	1,228	551	1993	3,335	1,461	1,243	464
1985	2,956	1,234	1,187	419	1994	3,727	1,607	1,436	521
1987	2,937	1,135	1,272	411	1995	3,796	1,620	1,399	598
1988	3,086	1,271	1,271	423	1996	3,627	1,566	1,349	557
1989	3,252	1,395	1,253	462	1997	3,745	1,620	1,430	545
1990	3,297	1,391	1,397	375	1998	4,091	1,660	1,523	618
1991	3,511	1,473	1,447	443	1999	4,429	1,709	1,774	592

[1] Includes expenditures which are not associated with a specific purpose (e.g., headquarters staff supervision, management, and administration activities, and some research and development activities).

Source: U.S. Army Corps of Engineers, *Report of Civil Works Expenditures by State and Fiscal Year,* annual.

No. 1047. Freight Carried on Major U.S. Waterways: 1980 to 1999

[In millions of tons (4.0 represents 4,000,000)]

Item	1980	1985	1990	1994	1995	1996	1997	1998	1999
Atlantic intracoastal waterway	4.0	3.1	4.2	3.7	3.5	4.3	3.6	3.8	3.4
Great Lakes.	183.5	148.1	167.1	175.3	177.7	181.8	188.6	192.2	182.9
Gulf intracoastal waterway	94.5	102.5	115.5	117.6	117.9	118.0	118.1	113.8	109.6
Mississippi River system [1]	584.2	527.8	659.6	693.3	710.1	701.8	707.1	708.3	716.9
Mississippi River mainstem	441.5	384.0	475.6	496.8	520.2	505.6	504.7	504.4	512.3
Ohio River system [2].	179.3	203.9	260.0	270.5	267.6	270.9	274.9	278.8	277.9
Columbia River.	49.2	42.4	51.4	50.9	57.1	51.2	52.7	49.1	50.7
Snake River.	5.1	3.5	4.8	5.9	6.8	5.7	6.1	5.8	5.8

[1] Main channels and all tributaries of the Mississippi, Illinois, Missouri and Ohio Rivers. [2] Main channels and all navigable tributaries and embayments of the Ohio, Tennessee, and Cumberland Rivers.

Source: U.S. Army Corps of Engineers, *Waterborne Commerce of the United States,* annual.

No. 1048. Waterborne Commerce by Type of Commodity: 1990 to 2000

[In millions of short tons (2,163.9 represents 2,163,900,000). Domestic trade includes all commercial movements between United States ports and on inland rivers, Great Lakes, canals, and connecting channels of the United States, Puerto Rico, and Virgin Islands]

Commodity	1990	1995	1999	2000 Total	2000 Domestic	2000 Foreign imports	2000 Foreign exports
Total [1].	2,163.9	2,240.4	2,322.6	2,461.6	1,069.8	976.8	415.0
Coal.	339.9	324.5	289.2	297.0	220.7	15.5	60.9
Petroleum and petroleum products	923.2	907.1	979.1	1,081.0	370.6	651.7	58.7
Crude petroleum.	485.7	504.6	533.4	608.5	83.8	521.6	3.1
Petroleum products [1].	437.5	402.5	445.7	472.4	286.8	130.0	55.6
Gasoline	116.9	114.4	110.6	125.2	94.6	24.1	6.4
Distillate fuel oil	77.4	76.7	93.1	91.7	65.6	21.1	4.9
Residual fuel oil.	145.2	111.9	124.0	131.5	78.5	40.3	12.6
Chemicals and related products	123.8	153.7	155.7	172.4	76.0	38.5	57.9
Crude material, inedible [1].	374.7	381.7	386.6	380.3	234.2	97.3	48.7
Forest products, wood and chips	55.7	47.2	38.9	33.1	13.5	5.5	14.1
Pulp and waste paper	11.8	14.9	12.0	13.6	0.2	1.2	12.3
Soil, sand, gravel, rock, and stone	144.2	152.5	175.5	165.0	132.3	29.1	3.6
Primary manufactured goods [1]	76.0	106.3	147.4	153.0	45.8	92.0	15.3
Papers products	10.7	13.1	12.8	12.1	0.4	4.8	6.8
Lime, cement and glass	28.3	33.9	58.3	55.9	20.6	33.8	1.6
Primary iron and steel products	25.1	44.1	56.2	57.1	18.4	37.4	1.3
Food and farm products [1]	267.5	303.2	287.9	283.3	96.9	30.0	156.3
Fish	3.2	3.6	2.1	2.4	0.2	1.3	0.9
Grain [1]	157.3	167.9	152.7	145.2	54.6	1.6	89.0
Corn	96.1	105.0	95.9	88.2	38.0	0.2	50.0
Wheat	44.5	48.5	44.5	43.4	13.0	0.1	30.4
Oilseeds	36.0	46.1	48.9	57.6	24.6	0.7	32.3
Soybeans.	32.2	42.0	43.0	47.3	20.2	-	27.0
Vegetables products	6.7	9.0	9.1	8.0	1.0	0.0	4.0
Processed grain and animal feed.	28.2	33.0	29.7	23.1	8.2	0.8	14.2

- Represents or rounds to zero.   [1] Includes categories not shown separately.

Source: U.S. Army Corps of Engineers, *Waterborne Commerce of the United States,* annual.

666   Transportation

No. 1049. Cargo-Carrying U.S.-Flag Fleet by Area of Operation: 2001

[Tons in thousands of metric tons (31,877 represents 31,877,000. As of October 1, except all vessels engaged in domestic trade and all nonself-propelled vessels (except ITBs) as of January 1. One ton equals 100 cubic feet of space. Represents active vessels]

Area of operation	Total fleet		Liquid carriers		Dry bulk carriers		Containerships		Other freighters	
	Number	Tons	Number	Tons	Number	Tons	Number	Tons	Number	Tons
VESSELS OF 1,000 GROSS TONS AND OVER										
Grand total	**3,835**	**31,877**	**2,148**	**16,400**	**760**	**5,970**	**126**	**3,424**	**801**	**6,083**
Foreign waterborne trade [1]	336	6,292	66	1,353	164	1,468	64	2,558	42	913
Domestic trade	3,326	22,224	2,054	14,163	596	4,502	57	780	619	2,779
Coastal	1,346	14,098	580	9,369	327	2,044	57	780	382	1,905
Inland waterway	1,901	6,085	1,466	4,750	214	529	-	-	221	806
Great Lakes	79	2,041	8	44	55	1,929	-	-	16	68
Government	173	3,361	28	884	-	-	5	86	140	2,391
Total self-propelled	467	16,276	122	7,177	62	2,464	91	3,200	192	3,435
Foreign waterborne trade [1]	139	5,282	17	1,043	17	788	64	2,558	41	893
Domestic trade	155	7,633	77	5,250	45	1,676	22	556	11	151
Coastal	109	5,976	75	5,231	2	59	22	556	10	130
Inland waterway	-	-	-	-	-	-	-	-	-	-
Great Lakes	46	1,657	2	19	43	1,617	-	-	1	21
Government	173	3,361	28	884	-	-	5	86	140	2,391
Total nonself-propelled [2]	3,368	15,601	2,026	9,223	698	3,506	35	224	609	2,648
Foreign waterborne trade [1]	197	1,010	49	310	147	680	-	-	1	20
Domestic trade	3,171	14,591	1,977	8,913	551	2,826	35	224	608	2,628
Coastal	1,237	8,122	505	4,138	325	1,985	35	224	372	1,775
Inland waterway	1,901	6,085	1,466	4,750	214	529	-	-	221	806
Great Lakes	33	384	6	25	12	312	-	-	15	47
VESSELS LESS THAN 1,000 GROSS TONS										
Grand total	**27,552**	**40,939**	**1,767**	**2,689**	**21,705**	**34,449**	**4**	**2**	**4,076**	**3,799**
Foreign waterborne trade [1]	101	51	6	4	95	47	-	-	-	-
Domestic trade	27,451	40,888	1,761	2,685	21,610	34,402	4	2	4,076	3,799
Coastal	1,847	1,432	110	117	380	549	1	1	1,356	765
Inland waterway	25,493	39,301	1,647	2,565	21,211	33,828	3	1	2,632	2,907
Great Lakes	111	155	4	3	19	25	-	-	88	127
Total self-propelled	111	56	20	14	3	2	-	-	88	40
Domestic trade	111	56	20	14	3	2	-	-	88	40
Coastal	75	31	17	10	-	-	-	-	58	21
Inland waterway	27	21	1	3	-	-	-	-	26	18
Great Lakes	9	4	2	1	3	2	-	-	4	1
Total nonself-propelled [2]	27,441	40,883	1,747	2,675	21,702	34,447	4	2	3,988	3,759
Foreign waterborne trade [1]	101	51	6	4	95	47	-	-	-	-
Domestic trade	27,340	40,832	1,741	2,671	21,607	34,400	4	2	3,988	3,759
Coastal	1,772	1,401	93	107	380	549	1	1	1,298	744
Inland waterway	25,466	39,280	1,646	2,562	21,211	33,828	3	1	2,606	2,889
Great Lakes	102	151	2	2	16	23	-	-	84	126

- Represents zero.   [1] Includes U.S./Canada TransLakes.   [2] Includes integrated tug barge (ITB) units as of October 1, 2001.

Source: U.S. Maritime Administration, Office of Statistical & Economic Analysis; adapted from Corps of Engineers, Lloyds Maritime Information Service, U.S. Coast Guard and Customs Service data.

No. 1050. Jobs on U.S. Deep Sea Commercial Fleet and Typical Basic Monthly Wage for Able-Bodied Seamen: 1975 to 2000

[Employment in thousands (20.5 represents 20,500)]

Year	Employ-ment [1]	Year	Employ-ment [1]	Year	East coast wage rate [2]	West coast wage rate [2]	Year	East coast wage rate [2]	West coast wage rate [2]
1975......	20.5	1995	7.9	1975	612	900	1995	1,918	2,637
1980......	19.6	1996	7.5	1980	967	1,414	1996	2,014	2,769
1985......	13.1	1997	8.6	1985	1,419	2,029	1997	2,094	2,879
1990......	11.1	1998	7.9	1990	1,505	2,218	1998	2,178	2,994
1993......	9.3	1999	7.3	1993	1,721	2,438	1999	2,265	3,114
1994......	9.1	2000	6.6	1994	1,790	2,536	2000	2,453	3,114

[1] As of June 30, except beginning 1980, as of Sept. 30. Estimates of personnel employed on merchant ships, 1,000 gross tons and over. Excludes vessels on inland waterways, Great Lakes, and those owned by, or operated for, U.S. Army and Navy, and special types such as cable ships, tugs, etc.   [2] As of January. Basic monthly wage, over and above subsistence (board and room); excludes overtime and fringe pay benefits. West coast incorporates extra pay for Saturdays and Sundays at sea into base wages but east coast does not.

Source: U.S. Maritime Administration, Office of Maritime Labor, Training and Safety.

No. 1051. Merchant Fleets of the World: 2001

[Vessels of 1,000 gross tons and over. As of October 1. Specified countries have 100 or more ships]

Country of registry, 2001	Total	Tanker	Dry bulk [1]	Container-ship	Roll-on/roll-off	Cruise/passenger	Other [2]
World total, 2001	28,070	7,053	5,714	2,661	1,513	305	10,824
United States	444	131	17	91	60	13	132
Privately-owned	261	104	17	86	28	2	24
Government-owned.........	183	27	-	5	32	11	108
Foreign total	27,626	6,922	5,697	2,570	1,453	292	10,692
Panama	4,758	1,141	1,449	525	308	42	1,293
Liberia	1,505	583	353	277	58	28	206
Russia	1,477	271	97	21	8	6	1,074
China, People's Republic of ...	1,451	268	325	103	16	3	736
Malta	1,339	339	436	57	56	4	447
Cyprus	1,244	167	451	120	29	8	469
Bahamas.................	996	248	162	60	65	74	387
Singapore	862	410	130	165	32	-	125
Saint Vincent & the Grenadines.	750	91	138	28	32	5	456
Greece	717	287	277	46	24	16	67
Norway (NIS) [3]	650	311	85	5	69	9	171
Antigua & Barbuda	620	17	20	164	24	-	395
Japan..................	607	246	153	21	120	6	61
Indonesia	562	127	27	26	12	-	370
Turkey	536	94	149	23	26	3	241
Netherlands..............	518	66	2	48	17	9	376
Korea (South)	491	138	101	47	9	3	193
Italy	424	216	48	28	81	12	39
Hong Kong	414	48	249	62	3	-	52
Philippines	406	55	143	6	31	1	170
Cambodia	389	10	32	1	3	-	343
Germany.................	362	13	-	223	10	3	113
Malaysia	351	115	54	50	8	2	122
Belize..................	348	54	16	8	4	-	266
Denmark (DIS) [3]	302	73	7	73	13	-	136
India...................	301	100	113	7	-	-	81
Thailand	283	93	28	13	-	1	148
Marshall Islands	250	113	81	38	1	-	17
Honduras	213	44	13	2	3	2	149
United Kingdom	201	61	6	51	32	16	35
Ukraine	195	16	6	3	2	7	161
Isle of Man	188	84	23	17	21	-	43
Sweden	172	61	7	-	60	-	44
China,, Republic of (Taiwan) ...	166	17	49	67	1	-	32
Brazil..................	148	68	39	7	9	-	25
Iran	138	31	47	7	2	-	51
Vietnam	138	24	12	2	1	-	99
Syria...................	130	1	8	-	1	-	120
Netherlands Antilles.........	121	8	1	20	3	1	88
Cayman Islands...........	119	52	24	3	1	-	39
Portugal (MAR) [3]	108	32	9	3	10	1	53
Egypt..................	104	15	20	2	7	-	60
Korea (North).............	100	4	5	-	-	1	90
All other	2,472	710	302	141	241	29	1,049

- Represents zero.   [1] Includes bulk/oil, ore/oil, and ore/bulk/oil carriers.   [2] Breakbulk ships, partial containerships, refrigerated cargo ships, barge and specialized cargo ships.   [3] International Shipping Registry which is an open registry under which the ship files the flag of the specified nation but is exempt from certain taxation and other regulations.

Source: U.S. Maritime Administration, *Merchant Fleets of the World,* summary report, annual; and unpublished data.

No. 1052. Highway Mileage—Urban and Rural by Ownership: 1980 to 2000

[In thousands (3,955 represents 3,955,000). As of Dec. 31. Includes Puerto Rico beginning 1996]

Type and control	1980	1985	1990	1995	1996	1997	1998	1999	2000
Total mileage [1]	[2]3,955	3,862	3,880	3,912	3,934	3,959	3,920	3,932	3,951
Urban mileage [3]	624	691	757	819	834	843	849	853	859
Under state control	79	111	96	112	113	114	111	111	110
Under local control	543	578	661	706	719	728	736	740	746
Rural mileage	[2]3,331	3,171	3,123	3,093	3,100	3,116	3,072	3,079	3,092
Under state control	702	773	703	691	693	695	663	663	664
Under local control	2,270	2,173	2,242	2,231	2,238	2,254	2,291	2,299	2,311
Under federal control	262	225	178	170	169	167	118	117	117

[1] Beginning 1985, includes only public road mileage as defined 23 USC 402.   [2] Includes 98,000 miles of nonpublic road mileage previously contained in other rural categories.   [3] Includes a small amount of road owned by the federal government, such as roads in federal parks that are not part of a state or local highway system.

Source: U.S. Federal Highway Administration, *Highway Statistics,* annual.

No. 1053. Highway Mileage—Functional Systems and Urban/Rural: 2000

[As of Dec. 31. Excludes Puerto Rico. For definition of functional systems see text, this section]

State	Functional systems						Urban	Rural
	Total	Interstate	Other free-ways and express-ways	Arterial	Collector	Local		
U.S	3,936,229	46,427	9,140	379,586	793,136	2,707,940	852,241	3,083,988
AL	94,311	906	21	8,783	20,426	64,175	20,672	73,639
AK	12,823	1,083	-	1,504	2,736	7,500	1,809	11,014
AZ	55,195	1,168	126	4,756	8,527	40,618	18,206	36,989
AR	97,600	656	86	6,828	20,131	69,899	10,626	86,974
CA	168,076	2,453	1,343	27,044	31,920	105,316	84,648	83,428
CO	85,409	951	224	8,179	16,606	59,449	14,463	70,946
CT	20,845	346	197	2,842	3,007	14,453	11,804	9,041
DE	5,779	41	13	625	939	4,161	1,984	3,795
DC	1,425	13	19	264	153	976	1,425	-
FL	116,649	1,471	464	12,123	14,372	88,219	49,227	67,422
GA	114,727	1,244	165	13,133	23,285	76,900	27,606	87,121
HI	4,281	55	34	755	829	2,608	2,104	2,177
ID	46,456	611	-	3,787	9,843	32,215	4,082	42,374
IL	138,372	2,165	84	13,944	21,572	100,607	36,347	102,025
IN	93,608	1,169	137	7,944	22,639	61,719	19,944	73,664
IA	113,377	782	-	9,538	31,528	71,529	9,864	103,513
KS	134,502	872	13b	9,184	33,357	91,034	10,207	124,375
KY	79,267	762	90	5,492	17,636	55,287	11,826	67,441
LA	60,900	894	48	5,298	12,543	42,117	13,941	46,959
ME	22,670	367	18	2,291	5,974	14,020	2,634	20,036
MD	30,494	481	234	3,559	5,024	21,196	14,429	16,065
MA	35,311	566	199	5,633	5,486	23,427	23,101	12,210
MI	121,979	1,241	224	12,267	25,710	82,537	30,007	91,972
MN	132,250	912	150	12,658	29,458	89,072	16,018	116,232
MS	73,498	685	41	7,105	15,531	50,136	8,055	65,443
MO	123,039	1,178	320	9,386	24,978	87,177	16,370	106,669
MT	69,567	1,191	-	6,014	16,344	46,018	2,491	67,076
NE	92,791	482	17	7,884	20,796	63,612	5,186	87,605
NV	37,854	560	43	2,864	5,222	29,165	5,533	32,321
NH	15,211	224	40	1,545	2,706	10,696	2,938	12,273
NJ	36,022	420	311	5,348	4,573	25,370	24,184	11,838
NM	59,927	1,000	3	4,549	6,953	47,422	6,110	53,817
NY	112,783	1,667	792	13,467	20,560	76,297	40,993	71,790
NC	99,813	1,024	279	8,957	17,759	71,794	23,628	76,185
ND	86,609	572	-	5,872	11,541	68,624	1,834	84,775
OH	116,964	1,572	392	10,628	22,105	82,267	33,545	83,419
OK	112,634	930	138	7,853	25,381	78,332	13,361	99,273
OR	66,902	727	55	6,724	17,449	41,947	11,064	55,838
PA	119,642	1,757	486	13,162	19,784	84,453	34,250	85,392
RI	6,052	70	69	845	857	4,211	4,719	1,333
SC	64,921	829	71	6,818	13,388	43,815	10,621	54,300
SD	83,471	678	-	6,294	19,280	57,219	2,017	81,454
TN	87,419	1,073	121	8,710	18,062	59,453	17,740	69,679
TX	301,035	3,234	1,200	28,444	63,311	204,846	82,394	218,641
UT	41,852	938	8	3,334	7,820	29,752	7,521	34,331
VT	14,273	320	19	1,297	3,121	9,516	1,379	12,894
VA	70,393	1,118	218	8,156	14,118	46,783	18,938	51,455
WA	80,209	764	314	7,300	16,796	55,035	18,197	62,012
WV	37,277	549	9	3,237	8,777	24,705	3,251	34,026
WI	112,359	743	180	11,693	21,536	78,207	16,650	95,709
WY	27,326	913	3	3,669	10,687	12,054	2,298	25,028

- Represents zero.

Source: U.S. Federal Highway Administration, *Highway Statistics,* annual.

U.S. Census Bureau, Statistical Abstract of the United States: 2002

No. 1054. Commodity Shipments—Value, Tons, and Ton-Miles: 1993 and 1997

[Based on the 1997 Economic Census; see Appendix III]

Mode of transportation	Value 1993	Value 1997	Tons 1993	Tons 1997	Ton-miles 1993	Ton-miles 1997
All modes	5,846,334	6,943,988	9,688,493	11,089,733	2,420,915	2,661,363
Single modes	4,941,452	5,719,558	8,922,286	10,436,538	2,136,873	2,383,473
Truck [1]	4,403,494	4,981,531	6,385,915	7,700,675	869,536	1,023,506
For-hire truck	2,625,093	2,901,345	2,808,279	3,402,605	629,000	741,117
Private truck.	1,755,837	2,036,528	3,543,513	4,137,294	235,897	268,592
Rail	247,394	319,629	1,544,148	1,549,817	942,561	1,022,547
Water.	61,628	75,840	505,440	563,369	271,998	261,747
Shallow draft	40,707	53,897	362,454	414,758	164,371	189,284
Great Lakes.	(S)	1,504	33,041	38,421	12,395	13,415
Deep draft	19,749	20,439	109,945	110,191	95,232	59,047
Air (includes truck and air)	139,086	229,062	3,139	4,475	4,009	6,233
Pipeline [2]	89,849	113,497	483,645	618,202	(S)	(S)
Multiple modes	662,603	945,874	225,676	216,673	191,461	204,514
Parcel, U.S. Postal Service or courier .	563,277	855,897	18,892	23,689	13,151	17,994
Truck and rail	83,082	75,695	40,624	54,246	37,675	55,561
Truck and water.	9,392	8,241	67,995	33,215	40,610	34,767
Rail and water.	3,636	1,771	79,222	79,275	70,219	77,590
Other multiple modes	3,216	4,269	18,943	26,248	(S)	18,603
Other and unknown modes	242,279	278,555	540,530	436,521	92,581	73,376

S Data do not meet publication standards due to high sampling variability or other reasons.   [1] Truck as a single mode includes shipments that went by private truck only, for hire truck only, or a combination of private truck and for-hire truck.   [2] Commodity Flow Survey data exclude most shipments of crude oil.

Source: U.S. Bureau of Transportation Statistics and U.S. Census Bureau, *1997 Economic Census, Transportation, 1997 Commodity Flow Survey,* Series EC97TCF-US, issued December 1999. Internet site: <http://www.census.gov/econ/www/cfsnew. html>.

No. 1055. Hazardous Material Shipment Characteristics: 1997

[466,407 represents $466,407,000,000. Based on the 1997 Economic Census; see Appendix III]

Item	Value Amount (mil. dol.)	Value Percent	Tons Number (1,000)	Tons Percent	Ton-miles Number (mil.)	Ton-miles Percent	Average miles per shipment
MODE OF TRANSPORTATION							
All modes	466,407	100.0	1,565,196	100.0	263,809	100.0	113
Single modes	452,727	97.1	1,541,716	98.5	258,912	98.1	95
Truck [1]	298,173	63.9	869,796	55.6	74,939	28.4	73
For-hire truck	134,308	28.8	336,363	21.5	45,234	17.1	260
Private truck.	160,693	34.5	522,666	33.4	28,847	10.9	35
Rail	33,340	7.1	96,626	6.2	74,711	28.3	853
Water.	26,951	5.8	143,152	9.1	68,212	25.9	(S)
Air (includes truck and air)	8,558	1.8	66	-	95	-	1,462
Pipeline [2]	85,706	18.4	432,075	27.6	(S)	(S)	(S)
Multiple modes	5,735	1.2	6,022	0.4	3,061	1.2	645
Parcel, U.S. Postal Service or courier.	2,874	0.6	143	-	78	-	697
Other multiple modes	2,861	0.6	5,879	0.4	2,982	1.1	(S)
Other and unknown modes	7,945	1.7	17,459	1.1	1,837	0.7	38
HAZARDOUS CLASS AND DESCRIPTION							
Total	466,407	100.0	1,565,196	100.0	263,809	100.0	113
Class 1, explosives.	4,342	0.9	1,517	0.1	(S)	(S)	549
Class 2, gases.	40,884	8.8	115,021	7.3	21,842	8.3	66
Class 3, flammable liquids	335,619	72.0	1,264,281	80.8	159,979	60.6	73
Class 4, flammable solids	3,898	0.8	11,804	0.8	9,618	3.6	838
Class 5, oxidizers and organic peroxides . . .	4,485	1.0	9,239	0.6	4,471	1.7	193
Class 6, toxic (poison).	10,086	2.2	6,366	0.4	2,824	1.1	402
Class 7, radioactive materials	2,722	0.6	87	-	48	-	445
Class 8, corrosive materials	40,423	8.7	91,564	5.9	41,161	15.6	201
Class 9, misc. dangerous goods	23,946	5.1	65,317	4.2	22,727	8.6	323

- Represents or rounds to zero.   S Data do not meet publication standards because of high sampling variability or other reasons.   [1] "Truck" as a single mode includes shipments which went by private truck only, for-hire truck only or a combination of private truck and for-hire truck.   [2] Commodity Flow Survey data exclude most shipments of crude oil.

Source: U.S. Bureau of Transportation Statistics and U.S. Census Bureau, *1997 Economic Census, Transportation, 1997 Commodity Flow Survey, Hazardous Materials,* Series EC97TCF-US(HM)RV, issued April 2000. Internet site: <http://www. census.gov/econ/www/cfsnew.html>.

No. 1056. Bridge Inventory—Total and Deficient, 1996 to 2001, and by State, 2001

[As of December, except 2000 as of August. Based on the National Bridge Inventory program]

State and year	Number of bridges	Total number	Percent	Deficient and obsolete			
				Structurally deficient [1]		Functionally obsolete [2]	
				Number	Percent	Number	Percent
1996, total	581,862	182,726	31.4	101,518	17.4	81,208	14.0
1997, total	582,751	175,885	30.2	98,475	16.9	77,410	13.3
1998, total	582,984	172,582	29.6	93,076	16.0	79,506	13.6
1999, total	585,542	170,050	29.0	88,150	15.1	81,900	14.0
2000, total	587,755	167,993	28.6	87,106	14.8	80,887	13.8
U.S. total, 2001	**590,066**	**165,099**	**28.0**	**83,630**	**14.2**	**81,469**	**13.8**
Alabama.	15,641	4,922	31.5	2,677	17.1	2,245	14.4
Alaska	1,433	412	28.8	169	11.8	243	17.0
Arizona.	6,918	735	10.6	194	2.8	541	7.8
Arkansas	12,434	3,475	27.9	1,479	11.9	1,996	16.1
California	23,770	6,840	28.8	2,636	11.1	4,204	17.7
Colorado.	8,082	1,443	17.9	596	7.4	847	10.5
Connecticut.	4,171	1,305	31.3	362	8.7	943	22.6
Delaware	829	129	15.6	47	5.7	82	9.9
District of Columbia	243	161	66.3	25	10.3	136	56.0
Florida	11,303	2,114	18.7	300	2.7	1,814	16.0
Georgia	14,394	3,502	24.3	1,578	11.0	1,924	13.4
Hawaii	1,071	537	50.1	193	18.0	344	32.1
Idaho.	4,069	756	18.6	320	7.9	436	10.7
Illinois	25,529	4,824	18.9	2,725	10.7	2,099	8.2
Indiana.	18,067	4,418	24.5	2,257	12.5	2,161	12.0
Iowa	25,030	7,096	28.3	5,036	20.1	2,060	8.2
Kansas.	25,638	6,424	25.1	3,465	13.5	2,959	11.5
Kentucky	13,442	4,053	30.2	1,189	8.8	2,864	21.3
Louisiana	13,426	4,591	34.2	2,425	18.1	2,166	16.1
Maine.	2,367	866	36.6	354	15.0	512	21.6
Maryland	4,957	1,446	29.2	436	8.8	1,010	20.4
Massachusetts.	4,986	2,488	49.9	696	14.0	1,792	35.9
Michigan.	10,631	3,366	31.7	2,012	18.9	1,354	12.7
Minnesota.	12,830	1,784	13.9	1,221	9.5	563	4.4
Mississippi	16,825	5,002	29.7	3,694	22.0	1,308	7.8
Missouri	23,604	8,830	37.4	6,083	25.8	2,747	11.6
Montana	5,009	1,130	22.6	570	11.4	560	11.2
Nebraska	15,493	4,337	28.0	2,676	17.3	1,661	10.7
Nevada	1,510	221	14.6	67	4.4	154	10.2
Now Hampshire	2,354	802	34.1	387	16.4	415	17.6
New Jersey.	6,366	2,350	36.9	930	14.6	1,420	22.3
New Mexico	3,790	703	18.5	348	9.2	355	9.4
New York	17,378	6,588	37.9	2,406	13.8	4,182	24.1
North Carolina	16,991	5,307	31.2	2,513	14.8	2,794	16.4
North Dakota.	4,517	1,137	25.2	871	19.3	266	5.9
Ohio	27,952	7,166	25.6	3,304	11.8	3,862	13.8
Oklahoma.	22,708	9,123	40.2	7,605	33.5	1,518	6.7
Oregon.	7,309	1,653	22.6	362	5.0	1,291	17.7
Pennsylvania.	22,092	9,440	42.7	5,418	24.5	4,022	18.2
Rhode Island.	749	379	50.6	187	25.0	192	25.6
South Carolina.	9,064	2,056	22.7	1,187	13.1	869	9.6
South Dakota	6,001	1,744	29.1	1,398	23.3	346	5.8
Tennessee	19,362	4,701	24.3	1,761	9.1	2,940	15.2
Texas.	48,085	10,555	22.0	3,182	6.6	7,373	15.3
Utah	2,743	634	23.1	389	14.2	245	8.9
Vermont	2,714	955	35.2	452	16.7	503	18.5
Virginia.	12,789	3,465	27.1	1,222	9.6	2,243	17.5
Washington	7,939	2,142	27.0	551	6.9	1,591	20.0
West Virginia.	6,767	2,667	39.4	1,172	17.3	1,495	22.1
Wisconsin	13,516	2,657	19.7	1,862	13.8	795	5.9
Wyoming	3,076	642	20.9	389	12.6	253	8.2
Puerto Rico.	2,102	1,026	48.8	252	12.0	774	36.8

[1] Bridges are structurally deficient if they have been restricted to light vehicles, require immediate rehabilitation to remain open, or are closed.   [2] Bridges are functionally obsolete if they have deck geometry, load caring capacity, clearance or approach roadway alignment that no longer meet the criteria for the system of which the bridge is a part.

Source: U.S. Federal Highway Administration, Office of Bridge Technology, Internet site <http://www.fhwa.dot.gov/bridge/britab.htm>.

No. 1057. Funding for Highways and Disposition of Highway-User Revenue: 1990 to 2000

[In millions of dollars (75,444 represents $75,444,000,000). Data compiled from reports of state and local authorities]

Type	1990	1994	1995	1996	1997	1998	1999	2000
Total receipts	75,444	91,312	96,269	102,771	107,421	109,881	117,878	128,745
Current income.	69,880	84,017	87,620	94,972	98,667	100,975	106,602	117,501
Highway user revenues	44,346	55,387	59,331	64,052	66,266	69,227	73,897	81,006
Other taxes and fees	19,827	21,598	21,732	23,830	25,424	24,274	25,989	28,997
Investment income, other receipts . . .	5,707	7,032	6,557	7,090	6,977	7,474	6,715	7,498
Bond issue proceeds [1]	5,564	7,295	8,649	7,799	8,754	8,906	11,276	11,244
Funds from (+) or to (-) reserves.	-36	-1,120	-2,791	-4,689	-5,468	-2,689	-444	-1,286
Total funds available	75,408	90,192	93,478	98,082	101,953	107,192	117,434	127,459
Total disbursements	75,408	90,192	93,478	98,082	101,953	107,192	117,434	127,459
Current disbursements.	72,457	85,645	88,994	93,492	97,320	101,995	111,963	121,731
Capital outlay	35,151	42,379	44,228	46,810	48,360	51,614	59,499	64,647
Maintenance and traffic services.	20,365	23,553	24,319	25,564	26,777	27,235	29,212	30,984
Administration and research	6,501	8,376	8,419	8,445	8,256	8,519	8,722	10,328
Law enforcement and safety	7,235	7,673	8,218	8,897	9,761	10,155	9,946	10,721
Interest on debt.	3,205	3,664	3,810	3,776	4,166	4,472	4,584	5,051
Bond retirement [1]	2,951	4,547	4,484	4,590	4,633	5,197	5,471	5,728

[1] Excludes issue and redemption of short-term notes or refunding bonds.
Source: U.S. Federal Highway Administration, *Highway Statistics,* annual; and releases.

No. 1058. Federal Aid to State and Local Governments for Highway Trust Fund and Federal Transit Administration (FTA) by State: 2001

[Year ending Sept. 30. (26,452 represents $26,452,000,000)]

State	Highway trust fund		FTA		State	Highway trust fund		FTA		State	Highway trust fund		FTA	
	Total (mil. dol.)	Per capita (dol.) [1]	Total (mil. dol.)	Per capita (dol.) [1]		Total (mil. dol.)	Per capita (dol.) [1]	Total (mil. dol.)	Per capita (dol.) [1]		Total (mil. dol.)	Per capita (dol.) [1]	Total (mil. dol.)	Per capita (dol.) [1]
U.S. [2] .	26,452	(NA)	7,561	(NA)	KS. . . .	246	91.4	15	5.6	ND . . .	177	278.6	6	9.6
U.S. [3].	26,067	91.5	7,256	25.5	KY. . . .	510	125.5	25	6.3	OH . . .	880	77.3	167	14.7
AL. . . .	634	142.0	38	8.6	LA. . . .	1	0.2	43	9.7	OK . . .	298	86.2	25	7.1
AK. . . .	352	554.0	26	40.4	ME . . .	152	118.3	19	14.8	OR . . .	319	91.9	107	30.9
AZ. . . .	481	90.7	46	8.7	MD . . .	478	88.8	127	23.6	PA . . .	1,426	116.1	368	30.0
AR. . . .	267	99.3	15	5.7	MA . . .	476	74.6	218	34.2	RI	171	161.9	35	32.9
CA. . . .	2,051	59.4	1,421	41.2	MI	851	85.2	116	11.6	SC. . . .	375	92.2	22	5.3
CO . . .	372	84.3	109	24.6	MN . . .	409	82.3	147	29.5	SD. . . .	226	299.2	5	6.3
CT. . . .	399	116.5	98	28.7	MS . . .	289	101.0	11	3.7	TN. . . .	493	85.9	36	6.3
DE. . . .	119	149.6	11	13.5	MO . . .	633	112.4	148	26.4	TX. . . .	1,846	86.6	441	20.7
DC . . .	191	333.6	183	320.7	MT . . .	266	293.9	6	6.9	UT. . . .	220	97.0	63	27.9
FL. . . .	1,492	91.0	229	14.0	NE. . . .	162	94.4	11	6.7	VT. . . .	140	228.8	18	28.6
GA . . .	790	94.2	172	20.5	NV. . . .	186	88.4	20	9.6	VA. . . .	755	105.1	91	12.6
HI	157	128.0	48	39.1	NH . . .	133	105.7	9	6.8	WA . . .	522	87.3	212	35.3
ID	203	153.6	8	6.1	NJ	586	69.1	592	69.7	WV . . .	386	214.1	14	7.9
IL	883	70.7	382	30.6	NM . . .	298	163.2	17	9.2	WI	529	97.9	82	15.1
IN	621	101.6	75	12.3	NY	1,272	66.9	1,097	57.7	WY . . .	173	350.1	2	4.5
IA	309	105.7	25	8.7	NC . . .	861	105.1	53	6.5					

NA Not available. [1] Based on estimated resident population as of July 1. [2] Includes outlying areas and undistributed funds not shown separately. [3] For the 50 states and DC.
Source: U.S. Census Bureau, *Federal Aid to States for Fiscal Year, 2001.*

No. 1059. State Motor Fuel Tax Receipts, 1999 and 2000, and Gasoline Tax Rates, 2000

[571 represents $571,000,000]

State	Net receipts (mil. dol.)		Tax rate, [1] 2000	State	Net receipts (mil. dol.)		Tax rate, [1] 2000	State	Net receipts (mil. dol.)		Tax rate, [1] 2000
	1999	2000			1999	2000			1999	2000	
AL	571	580	18.00	KY	488	440	16.40	ND	95	102	21.00
AK	25	28	8.00	LA	537	544	20.00	OH	1,464	1,484	22.00
AZ	560	566	18.00	ME	155	174	19.00	OK	401	414	17.00
AR	366	399	19.50	MD	672	643	23.50	OR	390	385	24.00
CA	2,936	2,945	18.00	MA	628	644	21.00	PA	1,678	1,698	25.90
CO	512	522	22.00	MI	1,048	1,048	19.00	RI	133	135	29.00
CT	498	546	32.00	MN	580	596	20.00	SC	424	468	16.00
DE	103	104	23.00	MS	367	398	18.40	SD	112	116	22.00
DC	33	32	20.00	MO	642	674	17.00	TN	703	778	20.00
FL	1,525	1,612	13.10	MT	173	195	27.00	TX	2,593	2,700	20.00
GA	406	431	7.50	NE	275	307	22.80	UT	311	314	24.50
HI	66	69	16.00	NV	280	305	24.75	VT	80	87	20.00
ID	200	200	25.00	NH	130	136	19.50	VA	771	774	17.50
IL	1,212	1,232	19.00	NJ	501	525	10.50	WA	716	725	23.00
IN	739	746	15.00	NM	249	239	18.50	WV	298	295	25.40
IA	399	394	20.00	NY	1,472	1,406	29.30	WI	783	795	25.40
KS	338	359	20.00	NC	1,017	1,055	21.20	WY	90	100	14.00

[1] Cents per gallon. In effect Dec. 31.
Source: U.S. Federal Highway Administration, *Highway Statistics,* annual.

No. 1060. Public Highway Debt—State and Local Governments: 1980 to 2000

[In millions of dollars (2,381 represents $2,381,000,000). Long-term obligations. Data are for varying calendar and fiscal years. Excludes duplicated and interunit obligations]

Item	1980	1985	1990	1995	1996	1997	1998	1999	2000
Total debt issued..........	2,381	8,194	5,708	11,305	9,728	12,347	16,412	12,822	(NA)
State..................	1,160	5,397	3,147	4,718	6,653	8,174	9,789	9,554	9,067
Local [1]..............	1,221	2,797	2,561	6,587	3,075	4,173	6,623	3,268	(NA)
Total debt redeemed.......	1,987	5,294	3,120	5,634	6,380	7,043	11,735	5,808	(NA)
State..................	1,114	3,835	1,648	2,939	4,161	4,228	6,466	3,609	3,897
Local [1]..............	873	1,459	1,472	2,695	2,219	2,815	5,269	2,199	(NA)
Total debt outstanding [2].....	27,616	32,690	46,586	68,733	72,197	77,501	82,599	89,778	(NA)
State..................	20,210	21,277	28,362	39,228	41,720	45,666	49,182	55,646	61,434
Local [1]..............	7,406	11,413	18,224	29,505	30,477	31,835	33,417	34,132	(NA)

NA Not available.   [1] Local data estimated.   [2] End-of-year.
Source: U.S. Federal Highway Administration, *Highway Statistics*, annual.

No. 1061. State Disbursements for Highways by State: 1995 to 2000

[In millions of dollars (67,615 represents $67,615,000,000). Comprises disbursements from current revenues or loans for construction, maintenance, interest and principal payments on highway bonds, transfers to local units, and miscellaneous. Includes transactions by state toll authorities. Excludes amounts allocated for collection expenses and nonhighway purposes, and bonds redeemed by refunding]

State	1995	1996	1997	1998	1999	2000
United States....................	67,615	71,736	73,994	80,518	83,675	89,832
Alabama.......................	1,002	1,064	1,019	1,053	1,085	1,246
Alaska........................	438	453	435	404	416	501
Arizona.......................	1,199	1,532	1,359	1,430	1,860	2,040
Arkansas......................	666	755	832	815	736	817
California.....................	5,966	5,831	6,219	6,574	6,876	6,750
Colorado......................	922	922	887	1,166	1,260	1,392
Connecticut...................	1,153	1,202	1,173	1,427	1,094	1,304
Delaware......................	441	452	449	647	507	595
District of Columbia............	140	163	151	259	242	244
Florida........................	3,421	3,472	3,734	4,024	3,992	4,208
Georgia.......................	1,437	1,675	1,372	1,613	1,763	1,567
Hawaii........................	360	405	387	326	355	272
Idaho.........................	350	369	403	414	445	492
Illinois........................	3,006	3,097	2,992	3,306	2,957	3,447
Indiana.......................	1,433	1,444	1,636	1,652	1,522	1,932
Iowa..........................	1,078	1,128	1,173	1,177	1,253	1,494
Kansas.......................	1,019	1,162	1,087	1,306	1,155	1,206
Kentucky......................	1,397	1,072	1,331	1,181	1,578	1,651
Louisiana.....................	1,198	1,417	1,189	1,400	1,237	1,301
Maine.........................	379	509	474	485	458	488
Maryland......................	1,289	1,449	1,489	1,492	1,554	1,599
Massachusetts.................	2,501	2,545	3,287	3,351	4,407	3,524
Michigan......................	1,974	1,966	2,100	2,745	2,629	2,748
Minnesota.....................	1,210	1,374	1,450	1,377	1,534	1,692
Mississippi....................	662	826	809	843	968	1,039
Missouri......................	1,313	1,402	1,492	1,438	1,600	1,818
Montana......................	388	377	379	378	434	474
Nebraska.....................	578	595	611	589	681	745
Nevada.......................	484	468	431	446	557	651
New Hampshire................	328	346	360	371	416	387
New Jersey....................	2,102	2,928	2,247	2,513	2,905	4,503
New Mexico...................	535	532	546	570	753	1,162
New York	4,584	4,424	4,778	6,051	5,347	5,307
North Carolina................	1,871	1,939	2,099	2,352	2,441	2,621
North Dakota..................	270	266	326	306	413	385
Ohio..........................	2,637	2,709	2,940	3,327	3,158	3,351
Oklahoma.....................	828	918	867	944	1,322	1,417
Oregon.......................	888	995	992	1,051	1,009	1,010
Pennsylvania..................	3,153	3,118	3,764	3,902	4,143	4,517
Rhode Island..................	290	297	225	339	316	256
South Carolina................	668	678	741	766	885	970
South Dakota.................	286	289	349	305	371	466
Tennessee....................	1,230	1,283	1,351	1,420	1,398	1,440
Texas........................	3,593	4,312	4,253	4,295	4,840	5,665
Utah..........................	431	457	802	1,129	1,072	1,072
Vermont......................	194	192	213	222	252	287
Virginia.......................	2,107	2,321	2,358	2,619	2,771	2,678
Washington...................	1,909	1,766	1,851	1,805	1,780	1,871
West Virginia..................	781	935	940	893	930	1,170
Wisconsin....................	1,252	1,324	1,354	1,398	1,614	1,663
Wyoming.....................	272	283	284	321	386	396

Source: U.S. Federal Highway Administration, *Highway Statistics*, annual.

Transportation   673

No. 1062. State Motor Vehicle Registrations: 1980 to 2000

[In thousands (155,796 represents 155,796,000). Compiled principally from information obtained from state authorities, but it was necessary to draw on other sources and to make numerous estimates in order to complete series. Includes Alaska and Hawaii. See also Table 1065]

Item	1980	1990	1995	1997	1998	1999	2000
All motor vehicles	**155,796**	**188,798**	**201,530**	**207,754**	**211,617**	**216,309**	**221,475**
Private and commercial	153,265	185,541	197,941	204,079	207,841	212,474	217,567
Publicly owned	2,531	3,257	3,589	3,674	3,776	3,834	3,908
Automobiles [1]	121,601	133,700	128,387	129,749	131,839	132,432	133,621
Private and commercial	120,743	132,164	126,900	128,450	130,500	131,077	132,247
Publicly owned	857	1,536	1,487	1,299	1,339	1,355	1,374
Buses	529	627	686	698	716	729	746
Private and commercial	254	275	288	294	302	307	314
Publicly owned	275	351	398	403	413	422	432
Trucks [1]	33,667	54,470	72,458	77,307	79,062	83,148	87,108
Private and commercial	32,268	53,101	70,754	75,335	77,039	81,091	85,005
Publicly owned	1,399	1,369	1,704	1,972	2,024	2,057	2,103

[1] Trucks include pickups, panels and delivery vans. Beginning 1990, personal passenger vans, passenger minivans and utility-type vehicles are no longer included in automobiles but are included in trucks.

Source: U.S. Federal Highway Administration, *Highway Statistics,* annual.

No. 1063. Alternative Fueled Vehicles in Use by Fuel Type: 1999 to 2001

[339,340 represents 339,340,000]

Fuel type	Alternative fueled vehicles			Fuel consumption (1,000) gasoline-equivalent gallons)		
	1999	2000	2001	1999	2000	2001
Total	**406,841**	**432,344**	**456,306**	**339,340**	**353,760**	**366,331**
Liquified petroleum gases (LPG)	267,000	268,000	269,000	242,141	242,695	243,196
Compressed natural gas (CNG)	89,556	100,530	109,730	86,286	97,568	107,476
Liquified natural gas (LNG).	1,681	1,900	2,039	5,828	6,847	7,566
M85 (Mixture: 85% methanol + 15% gasoline) . . .	18,964	18,365	16,918	1,073	996	918
Neat methanol (M100)	198	195	184	447	437	406
E85 (Mixture: 85% ethanol+15% gasoline)	22,464	34,680	48,022	2,075	3,344	4,575
E95 (Mixture: 95% ethanol + 5% gasoline)	14	13	13	59	54	51
Electricity	6,964	8,661	10,400	1,431	1,819	2,143

Source: Energy Information Administration, *Alternatives to Traditional Transportation Fuels: 1992-2001.*

No. 1064. Number of Households Leasing Vehicles and Number of Vehicles Leased Per Household: 1989 to 1998

Item	Share of households leasing a vehicle for personal use (percent)				Average number of leased vehicles, among households having such vehicles			
	1989	1992	1995	1998	1989	1992	1995	1998
All households	**2.5**	**2.9**	**4.5**	**6.4**	**1.1**	**1.1**	**1.1**	**1.2**
Household income:								
Less than $10,000	(Z)	(Z)	(Z)	(Z)	(Z)	(Z)	(Z)	1.2
$10,000 to $24,999	(Z)	(Z)	1.5	4.0	(Z)	(Z)	1.0	1.1
$25,000 to $49,999	(Z)	3.3	3.4	5.0	(Z)	1.1	1.0	1.1
$50,000 to $99,999	6.1	4.1	9.4	9.5	1.1	1.1	1.2	1.2
$100,000 and over	5.0	9.6	14.2	14.8	1.2	1.1	1.3	1.3
Age of household head:								
Less than 35 years	4.2	3.2	4.8	8.2	1.1	1.0	1.0	1.1
35 to 44 years	3.0	4.2	5.4	8.3	1.0	1.1	1.1	1.1
45 to 54 years	3.3	3.2	7.8	7.6	1.1	1.2	1.2	1.3
55 to 64 years	(Z)	3.2	4.1	4.4	1.6	1.2	1.2	1.1
65 to 74 years	(Z)	1.0	1.3	2.9	(Z)	1.0	1.1	1.2
75 years and over	(Z)	(Z)	0.5	1.9	(Z)	(Z)	1.0	1.0
Race/ethnicity of respondent:								
White non-Hispanic	2.7	3.1	4.4	6.3	1.1	1.1	1.1	1.1
Non-White and Hispanic	(Z)	2.3	4.9	6.5	(7)	1.1	1.1	1.3
Work status of household head:								
Work for someone else	3.5	3.4	6.0	8.1	1.1	1.1	1.1	1.2
Self employed	3.4	7.2	5.2	9.0	1.0	1.1	1.3	1.1
Retired	(Z)	0.7	1.3	1.5	(Z)	1.3	1.0	1.2
Other not working	(Z)	(Z)	3.0	(Z)	(Z)	(Z)	1.0	(Z)
Homeownership status:								
Owner	2.2	3.5	5.8	7.2	1.1	1.1	1.2	1.2
Renter or other	3.0	1.8	2.3	4.8	1.1	1.1	1.1	1.1
Net worth percentile:								
Bottom 25 percent	(Z)	2.1	2.7	4.8	(7)	1.1	1.1	1.1
25 to 49.9 percent	2.8	(Z)	4.2	5.4	1.1	(Z)	1.0	1.1
50 to 74.9 percent	2.5	3.1	4.2	6.8	1.1	1.1	1.1	1.2
75 to 89.9 percent	2.9	3.5	6.2	7.8	1.0	1.0	1.2	1.2
Top 10 percent	2.5	6.4	8.3	9.5	1.3	1.2	1.3	1.2

Z Ten or fewer observations.
Source: Board of Governors of the Federal Reserve System, *Federal Reserve Bulletin,* January 2000, and unpublished revisions.

No. 1065. State Motor Vehicle Registrations, 1980 to 2000, and Licensed Drivers and Motorcycle Registrations by State: 2000

[**In thousands (155,796 represents 155,796,000).** Motor vehicle registrations cover publicly, privately, and commercially owned vehicles. For uniformity, data have been adjusted to a calendar-year basis as registration years in states differ; figures represent net numbers where possible, excluding re-registrations and nonresident registrations. See also Table 1062]

State	Motor vehicle registrations [1]								2000	
							2000		Motor-	
								Auto-mobiles (incl. taxis)	cycle registra-tion (incl. official) [2]	Licensed drivers
	1980	1985	1990	1995	1998	1999	Total			
U.S	155,796	171,689	188,798	201,530	211,617	216,309	221,475	133,621	4,304	190,625
AL......	2,938	3,383	3,744	3,553	3,859	3,957	3,960	1,962	54	3,521
AK......	262	353	477	542	546	571	594	244	16	465
AZ......	1,917	2,235	2,825	2,873	2,944	3,606	3,795	2,163	164	3,434
AR......	1,574	1,384	1,448	1,613	1,754	1,818	1,840	951	25	1,948
CA......	16,873	18,899	21,926	22,432	25,600	26,362	27,698	17,321	434	21,244
CO	2,342	2,759	3,155	2,812	3,466	3,858	3,626	1,921	98	3,107
CT......	2,147	2,465	2,623	2,622	2,701	2,766	2,853	2,009	54	2,653
DE......	397	465	526	592	616	616	630	400	11	557
DC	268	306	262	243	229	235	242	200	1	348
FL......	7,614	9,865	10,950	10,369	11,276	11,390	11,781	7,353	249	12,853
GA	3,818	4,580	5,489	6,120	6,893	6,973	7,155	4,067	87	5,550
HI	570	651	771	802	704	718	738	460	20	769
ID	834	854	1,054	1,043	1,119	1,130	1,178	515	42	884
IL	7,477	7,527	7,873	8,973	9,307	9,355	8,973	5,954	195	7,961
IN	3,826	3,824	4,366	5,072	5,372	5,495	5,571	3,245	117	3,976
IA	2,329	2,696	2,632	2,814	3,053	3,050	3,106	1,752	126	1,953
KS......	2,007	2,148	2,012	2,085	2,121	2,224	2,296	826	50	1,908
KY......	2,593	2,615	2,909	2,631	2,845	2,662	2,826	1,674	44	2,694
LA......	2,779	3,012	2,995	3,286	3,431	3,505	3,557	1,965	48	2,759
ME	724	840	977	967	930	915	1,024	618	29	920
MD	2,803	3,276	3,607	3,654	3,750	3,896	3,848	2,606	49	3,382
MA	3,749	3,738	3,726	4,502	5,159	5,333	5,265	3,674	107	4,490
MI......	6,488	6,727	7,209	7,674	8,128	8,290	8,436	5,023	182	6,925
MN	3,091	3,385	3,508	3,882	4,178	4,010	4,630	2,626	143	2,941
MS	1,577	1,746	1,875	2,144	2,256	2,317	2,289	1,319	32	2,008
MO	3,271	3,558	3,905	4,255	4,378	4,404	4,580	2,715	61	3,856
MT	680	652	783	968	988	998	1,026	467	26	679
NE......	1,254	1,258	1,384	1,467	1,526	1,570	1,619	852	21	1,195
NV......	655	709	853	1,047	1,220	1,162	1,220	656	24	1,371
NH	704	974	946	1,122	1,038	1,051	1,052	670	49	930
NJ......	4,761	5,164	5,652	5,906	5,780	6,103	6,390	4,451	111	5,655
NM	1,068	1,226	1,301	1,484	1,595	1,576	1,529	730	28	1,239
NY......	8,002	9,042	10,196	10,274	10,422	10,756	10,235	7,501	106	10,871
NC......	4,532	4,501	5,162	5,682	5,862	5,690	6,223	3,743	82	5,690
ND	627	655	630	695	672	704	694	339	17	459
OH	7,771	8,102	8,410	9,810	10,039	10,236	10,467	6,710	254	8,206
OK	2,583	2,911	2,649	2,856	2,919	2,931	3,014	1,587	57	2,295
OR	2,081	2,204	2,445	2,785	2,980	3,013	3,022	1,541	69	2,495
PA......	6,926	7,209	7,971	8,481	8,979	9,009	9,260	6,032	215	8,229
RI	623	610	672	699	715	747	760	539	19	654
SC......	1,996	2,222	2,521	2,833	2,893	3,026	3,095	1,924	51	2,843
SD......	601	657	704	709	769	782	793	380	29	544
TN......	3,271	3,754	4,444	5,400	4,469	4,427	4,820	2,855	71	4,251
TX......	10,475	12,444	12,800	13,682	13,324	14,069	14,070	7,616	182	13,462
UT......	992	1,099	1,206	1,447	1,532	1,577	1,628	867	28	1,463
VT......	347	398	462	492	496	518	515	296	22	506
VA......	3,626	4,253	4,938	5,613	5,818	5,871	6,046	3,874	60	4,837
WA	3,225	3,526	4,257	4,503	4,824	4,862	5,116	2,891	118	4,155
WV	1,320	1,143	1,225	1,425	1,378	1,379	1,442	795	26	1,347
WI	2,941	3,187	3,815	3,993	4,203	4,266	4,366	2,527	179	3,770
WY	467	500	528	601	559	528	586	215	19	371

[1] Automobiles, trucks, and buses. Excludes vehicles owned by military services. [2] Private and commercial.

Source: U.S. Federal Highway Administration, *Highway Statistics*, annual; and *Selected Highway Statistics and Charts*, annual.

No. 1066. Roadway Congestion: 2000

[**15,375 represents** 15,375,000 Various federal, state, and local information sources were used to develop the data base with the primary source being the Federal Highway Administration's Highway Performance Monitoring System. Areas shown are rated the top 70 in annual per person hours of delay]

Urbanized areas	Freeway daily vehicle miles of travel		Annual person hours of delay		Annual congestion cost		
	Total miles (1,000)	Per lane-mile of freeway	Total hours (1,000)	Per person	Per person (dol.)	Delay and fuel cost (mil. dol.)	Fuel wasted (gal. per person)
Total, average	**15,375**	**16,035**	**47,595**	**27**	**505**	**900**	**43**
Albany-Schenectady-Troy NY	5,500	10,000	2,980	6	115	60	10
Albuquerque NM	3,770	16,045	12,240	21	380	225	32
Atlanta GA	42,940	18,550	97,245	33	635	1,885	56
Austin TX	8,800	15,305	20,640	28	550	400	48
Bakersfield CA.	1,930	10,160	1,585	4	60	25	7
Baltimore MD	22,660	15,365	44,385	20	395	860	35
Beaumont TX	1,560	11,555	850	6	105	15	7
Birmingham AL	8,685	12,865	9,610	14	285	190	25
Boston MA	22,890	17,610	84,845	28	525	1,595	45
Boulder CO.	490	9,800	510	5	45	5	3
Buffalo-Niagara Falls NY	6,365	10,025	5,560	5	95	105	8
Charleston SC	2,815	11,980	5,625	12	220	100	20
Charlotte NC	7,640	15,915	13,950	22	410	265	37
Chicago IL-Northwestern IN	48,400	18,160	221,300	27	505	4,095	43
Cincinnati OH-KY	15,745	16,150	25,385	20	395	505	34
Cleveland OH	17,285	13,505	15,965	8	165	315	15
Colorado Springs CO	2,515	10,935	5,880	13	235	110	19
Columbus OH	11,850	13,940	17,790	17	330	345	30
Dallas-Fort Worth TX	48,700	15,460	141,125	37	695	2,640	60
Denver CO	16,905	16,335	66,165	35	640	1,225	55
Detroit MI	31,125	17,150	101,340	25	475	1,905	41
El Paso TX-NM	3,975	14,195	6,360	10	185	120	15
Eugene-Springfield OR	1,335	12,135	1,445	7	115	25	9
Fort Myers-Cape Coral FL	400	8,890	2,115	7	105	30	14
Fresno CA	2,550	12,750	6,145	11	215	120	18
Ft. Lauderdale-Hollywood-Pompano Beach FL	12,750	17,585	44,445	28	520	810	44
Hartford-Middletown CT	8,405	13,450	6,805	11	215	140	19
Honolulu HI	5,625	14,065	7,690	11	225	155	19
Houston TX	37,900	15,315	120,945	36	675	2,285	59
Indianapolis IN	11,260	15,530	20,630	20	385	395	34
Jacksonville FL	9,835	13,565	12,585	15	285	245	24
Kansas City MO-KS	19,310	11,160	12,395	9	175	245	16
Las Vegas NV	6,850	16,505	21,650	18	345	415	28
Los Angeles CA	126,495	23,425	791,970	62	1,155	14,635	94
Louisville KY-IN	10,040	14,985	17,855	21	400	335	37
Memphis TN-AR-MS	6,890	13,645	15,460	16	290	285	26
Miami-Hialeah FL	13,585	18,115	74,850	33	600	1,365	51
Milwaukee WI	9,700	15,770	20,360	15	285	390	25
Minneapolis-St. Paul MN	27,095	17,150	63,135	26	495	1,220	44
Nashville TN	10,000	13,160	14,170	20	395	275	34
New Orleans LA.	5,615	13,530	11,425	10	195	215	17
New York NY-Northeastern NJ . . .	101,295	15,350	400,115	23	450	7,660	39
Norfolk-Newport News-Virginia Beach VA	11,270	12,880	17,420	12	230	345	20
Oklahoma City OK	8,930	12,070	6,260	6	115	125	10
Omaha NE-IA	3,300	11,000	7,070	11	200	125	18
Orlando FL	9,430	12,920	37,385	31	575	690	48
Pensacola FL	1,130	10,275	3,430	11	165	50	16
Philadelphia PA-NJ	25,445	14,625	70,630	15	290	1,325	25
Phoenix AZ	19,425	18,860	72,590	28	525	1,360	44
Pittsburgh PA	11,130	9,355	12,510	7	130	235	11
Portland-Vancouver OR-WA	12,595	17,865	34,360	23	445	670	38
Providence-Pawtucket RI-MA	8,465	13,125	17,130	19	365	335	32
Richmond VA	7,000	11,025	6,495	10	195	125	17
Sacramento CA	12,170	17,765	27,140	19	385	540	33
Salem OR.	1,190	11,900	1,340	7	130	25	10
Salt Lake City UT	6,415	12,830	8,410	9	190	170	17
San Antonio TX	15,775	14,810	25,505	20	380	475	34
San Bernardino-Riverside CA	16,600	18,865	41,825	30	575	810	48
San Diego CA	33,745	18,800	65,305	24	480	1,295	41
San Francisco-Oakland CA	47,980	20,550	167,200	41	795	3,210	67
San Jose CA	16,530	18,680	55,920	33	635	1,065	53
Seattle-Everett WA	22,455	17,475	67,550	34	660	1,315	56
Spokane WA	1,500	11,110	1,760	5	90	30	9
St. Louis MO-IL	25,740	14,460	41,690	20	395	805	35
Tacoma WA	5,305	17,685	8,470	14	280	170	23
Tampa-St. Petersburg-Clearwater FL	8,460	13,115	41,285	21	380	745	32
Tucson AZ	2,150	11,620	7,680	11	220	150	18
Tulsa OK	6,270	11,720	6,965	9	170	135	14
Washington DC-MD-VA	34,535	18,320	123,190	35	655	2,325	56
West Palm Beach-Boca Raton-Delray Beach FL	8,365	16,400	21,010	20	385	395	33

Source: Texas Transportation Institute, College Station, Texas; *2002 Urban Mobility Study* (issued June 2002). (Copyright). See <http://mobility.tamu.edu/ums/>.

No. 1067. Travel in the United States by Selected Trip Characteristics: 1995

[656,462 represents 656,462,000. Trips of 100 miles or more, one way. U.S. destinations only. Data based on a sample and subject to sampling variability. For information and definitions of terms, see source]

Trip characteristic	Household trips		Person trips		Person miles		Personal use vehicle trips		Personal use vehicle miles	
	Number (1,000)	Per-cent	Number (1,000)	Per-cent	Number (1,000)	Per-cent	Number (1,000)	Per-cent	Number (1,000)	Per-cent
Total	**656,462**	**100.0**	**1,001,319**	**100.0**	**826,804**	**100.0**	**505,154**	**100.0**	**280,127**	**100.0**
Principal means of transportation:										
Personal use vehicles	505,154	77.0	813,858	81.3	451,590	54.6	505,154	100.0	280,127	100.0
Airplane.	129,164	19.7	161,165	16.1	355,286	43.0	(X)	(X)	(X)	(X)
Commercial airplane.	124,884	19.0	155,936	15.6	347,934	42.1	(X)	(X)	(X)	(X)
Bus [1]	17,340	2.6	20,445	2.0	13,309	1.6	(X)	(X)	(X)	(X)
Intercity bus	2,755	0.4	3,244	0.3	2,723	0.3	(X)	(X)	(X)	(X)
Charter, tour, or school bus	11,890	1.8	14,247	1.4	9,363	1.1	(X)	(X)	(X)	(X)
Train.	4,200	0.6	4,994	0.5	4,356	0.5	(X)	(X)	(X)	(X)
Ship, boat, or ferry	391	0.1	614	0.1	1,834	0.2	(X)	(X)	(X)	(X)
Other	213	-	243	-	429	0.1	(X)	(X)	(X)	(X)
Round trip distance:										
Less than 300 miles	194,098	29.6	306,433	30.6	74,658	9.0	185,418	36.7	45,159	16.1
300 to 499 miles	174,389	26.6	274,045	27.4	106,007	12.8	159,743	31.6	61,779	22.1
500 to 999 miles	140,046	21.3	214,006	21.4	146,631	17.7	106,846	21.2	72,114	25.7
1,000 to 1,999 miles	76,110	11.6	108,331	10.8	153,316	18.5	36,722	7.3	49,953	17.8
2,000 miles or more	71,819	10.9	98,503	9.8	346,192	41.9	16,425	3.3	51,123	18.3
Mean (miles)	872	(X)	827	(X)	(X)	(X)	555	(X)	(X)	(X)
Median [2] (miles)	438	(X)	425	(X)	(X)	(X)	368	(X)	(X)	(X)
Main purpose of trip: Business	192,537	29.3	224,835	22.5	212,189	25.7	125,036	24.8	61,929	22.1
Pleasure	372,586	56.8	630,110	62.9	506,971	61.3	305,571	60.5	177,698	63.4
Visit friends or relatives.	195,468	29.8	330,755	33.0	264,769	32.0	159,981	31.7	92,190	32.9
Leisure [3]	177,119	27.0	299,355	29.9	242,201	29.3	145,590	28.8	85,508	30.5
Rest or relaxation	65,017	9.9	115,154	11.5	100,838	12.2	53,780	10.6	33,598	12.0
Sightseeing	24,272	3.7	42,649	4.3	50,781	6.1	18,069	3.6	14,654	5.2
Outdoor recreation	39,899	6.1	65,418	6.5	41,620	5.0	35,987	7.1	19,407	6.9
Entertainment	37,456	5.7	58,757	5.9	42,929	5.2	27,920	5.5	14,531	5.2
Personal business	91,319	13.9	146,338	14.6	107,621	13.0	74,532	14.8	40,490	14.5
Other	19	-	36	-	23	-	16	-	9	-

- Represents or rounds to zero.   X Not applicable.   [1] Includes other types of buses.   [2] For definition of median, see Guide to Tabular Presentation.   [3] Includes other leisure activities not shown separately.

Source: U.S. Bureau of Transportation Statistics. *1995 American Travel Survey.*

No. 1068. National Personal Transportation Survey (NPTS)—Summary of Travel Trends: 1969 to 1995

[87,284 represents 87,284,000,000. Data obtained by collecting information on all trips taken by the respondent on a specific day (known as travel day), combined with longer trips taken over a 2-week period (known as travel period). For compatibility with previous survey data, all data are based only on trips taken during travel day. Be aware that terminology changes from survey to survey. See source for details. 1995 data not comparable with previous years]

Characteristics	Unit	1969 [1]	1977	1983	1990	1995
Vehicle trips	Millions . . .	87,284	108,826	126,874	158,927	229,745
Vehicle miles of travel (VMT)	Millions . . .	775,940	907,603	1,002,139	1,409,600	2,068,368
Person trips	Millions . . .	145,146	211,778	224,385	249,562	378,930
Person miles of travel	Millions . . .	1,404,137	1,879,215	1,946,662	2,315,300	3,411,122
Average annual VMT per household [2]	Miles.	12,423	12,036	11,739	15,100	20,895
To or from work.	Miles.	4,183	3,815	3,538	4,853	6,492
Shopping.	Miles.	929	1,336	1,567	1,743	2,807
Other family or personal business	Miles.	1,270	1,444	1,816	3,014	4,307
Social and recreational.	Miles.	4,094	3,286	3,534	4,060	4,764
Average annual vehicle trips per household [2] . . .	Number. . .	1,396	1,442	1,486	1,702	2,321
To or from work.	Number. . .	445	423	414	448	553
Shopping.	Number. . .	213	268	297	345	501
Other family or personal business	Number. . .	195	215	272	411	626
Social and recreational.	Number. . .	312	320	335	349	427
Average vehicle trip length [2].	Miles.	8.90	8.35	7.90	8.98	9.06
To or from work.	Miles.	9.40	9.02	8.55	10.97	11.80
Shopping.	Miles.	4.36	4.99	5.28	5.10	5.64
Other family or personal business	Miles.	6.51	6.72	6.68	7.43	6.93
Social and recreational.	Miles.	13.12	10.27	10.55	11.80	11.24
Average vehicle occupancy [2]	Persons. . .	(NA)	1.9	1.75	1.64	1.59
To or from work.	Persons. . .	(NA)	1.3	1.29	1.14	1.14
Shopping.	Persons. . .	(NA)	2.1	1.79	1.71	1.74
Other family or personal business	Persons. . .	(NA)	2.0	1.81	1.84	1.78
Social and recreational.	Persons. . .	(NA)	2.4	2.12	2.08	2.04
Workers by usual mode to work	Percent . . .	100.0	100.0	100.0	100.0	100.0
Auto.	Percent . . .	90.8	93.0	92.4	87.8	91.0
Public transit	Percent . . .	8.4	4.7	5.8	5.3	5.1
Other	Percent . . .	0.8	2.3	1.8	6.9	3.9

NA Not available.   [1] Excludes pickups and other light-trucks as household vehicles.   [2] Includes other purposes not shown separately.

Source: U.S. Federal Highway Administration, *Summary of Travel Trends, 1995 National Personal Transportation Survey,* December 1999.

No. 1069. Motor Vehicle Accidents—Number and Deaths: 1980 to 2000

[17.9 represents 17,900,000]

Item	Unit	1980	1985	1990	1995	1996	1997	1998	1999	2000
Motor vehicle accidents [1]	Million .	17.9	19.3	11.5	10.7	11.2	13.8	12.7	11.4	13.4
Vehicles involved:										
Cars	Million .	22.8	25.6	14.3	12.3	13.3	16.0	13.8	11.6	15.9
Trucks	Million .	5.5	6.1	4.4	4.5	4.8	7.7	7.3	6.2	8.8
Motorcycles	1,000 .	560	480	180	152	135	138	100	70	130
Motor vehicle deaths within 1 yr. [2]	1,000 .	53.2	45.9	46.8	43.4	43.6	43.5	41.8	41.3	43.0
Noncollision accidents	1,000 .	14.7	12.6	4.9	4.4	4.6	4.4	4.2	4.3	4.6
Collision accidents:										
With other motor vehicles	1,000 .	23.0	19.9	19.9	19	19.6	19.9	18.5	18.8	20.6
With pedestrians	1,000 .	9.7	8.5	7.3	6.4	6.1	5.9	5.9	5.8	5.3
With fixed objects	1,000 .	3.7	3.2	13.1	12.1	12.1	12.0	12.0	11.1	11.2
Deaths within 30 days [3]	1,000 .	51.1	43.8	44.6	41.8	42.1	42.0	41.5	41.7	41.8
Occupants	1,000 .	41.9	36.0	37.1	35.3	35.7	35.7	35.4	35.9	36.2
Passenger cars	1,000 .	27.4	23.2	24.1	22.4	22.5	22.2	21.2	20.9	20.5
Light trucks	1,000 .	7.5	6.7	8.6	9.6	9.9	10.2	10.7	11.3	11.4
Large trucks	1,000 .	1.3	1.0	0.7	0.6	0.6	0.7	0.7	0.8	0.7
Motorcycles	1,000 .	5.1	4.6	3.2	2.2	2.2	2.1	2.3	2.5	2.9
Buses	1,000 .	(Z)	0.1	(Z)	(Z)	(Z)	(Z)	(Z)	0.1	(Z)
Other/unknown	1,000 .	0.5	0.5	0.5	0.4	0.5	0.4	0.4	0.4	0.7
Nonoccupants	1,000 .	9.2	7.8	7.5	6.5	6.4	6.3	6.1	5.8	5.6
Pedestrians	1,000 .	8.1	6.8	6.5	5.6	5.4	5.3	5.2	4.9	4.7
Pedicyclist	1,000 .	1.0	0.9	0.9	0.8	0.8	0.8	0.8	0.8	0.7
Other/unknown	1,000 .	0.1	0.1	0.1	0.1	0.2	0.2	0.1	0.1	0.1
Traffic death rates: [3][4]										
Per 100 million vehicle miles	Rate . .	3.3	2.5	2.1	1.7	1.7	1.6	1.6	1.6	1.5
Per 100,000 licensed drivers	Rate . .	35.2	27.9	26.7	23.7	23.4	23.0	22.4	22.3	21.9
Per 100,000 registered vehicles	Rate . .	34.8	26.4	24.2	21.2	20.9	20.6	20.0	19.6	19.3
Per 100,000 resident population	Rate . .	22.5	18.4	17.9	15.9	15.9	15.7	15.4	15.3	15.2

Z Fewer than 50. [1] Covers only accidents occurring on the road. [2] Deaths that occur within 1 year of accident. Includes collision categories not shown separately. [3] Within 30 days of accident. Source: U.S. National Highway Traffic Safety Administration, *Traffic Safety Facts, 2000*; and unpublished data. [4] Based on 30-day definition of traffic deaths.

Source: Except as noted, National Safety Council, Itasca, IL, *Injury Facts,* annual (copyright).

No. 1070. Motor Vehicle Deaths by State: 1980 to 2000

[For deaths within 30 days of the accident]

State	1980	1990	1999	2000	Fatality rate [1] 1980	Fatality rate [1] 2000	State	1980	1990	1999	2000	Fatality rate [1] 1980	Fatality rate [1] 2000
U.S. [1]	51,091	44,599	41,717	41,821	3.3	1.5	MO	1,175	1,097	1,094	1,157	3.4	1.7
							MT	325	212	220	237	4.9	2.4
AL	940	1,121	1,138	995	3.2	1.8	NE	396	262	295	276	3.5	1.5
AK	88	98	79	103	3.3	2.2	NV	346	343	350	323	5.7	1.8
AZ	947	869	1,024	1,036	5.3	2.1	NH	194	158	140	126	3.0	1.0
AR	588	604	604	652	3.6	2.2	NJ	1,120	886	726	731	2.2	1.1
CA	5,496	5,192	3,559	3,753	3.5	1.2	NM	606	499	460	430	5.4	1.9
CO	709	544	626	681	3.2	1.6	NY	2,610	2,217	1,599	1,458	3.4	1.1
CT	575	385	301	342	3.0	1.1	NC	1,503	1,385	1,505	1,472	3.6	1.6
DE	153	138	100	123	3.6	1.5	ND	151	112	119	86	2.9	1.2
DC	41	48	41	49	1.2	1.4	OH	2,033	1,638	1,430	1,351	2.8	1.3
FL	2,825	2,891	2,920	2,999	3.6	2.0	OK	959	641	741	652	3.5	1.5
GA	1,508	1,562	1,508	1,541	3.5	1.5	OR	646	579	414	451	3.4	1.3
HI	186	177	98	131	3.3	1.5	PA	2,089	1,646	1,549	1,520	2.9	1.5
ID	331	244	278	276	4.8	2.0	RI	129	84	88	80	2.4	1.0
IL	1,975	1,589	1,456	1,418	3.0	1.4	SC	852	979	1,065	1,065	3.8	2.3
IN	1,166	1,049	1,020	875	3.0	1.2	SD	228	153	150	173	3.7	2.1
IA	626	465	490	445	3.3	1.5	TN	1,153	1,177	1,302	1,306	3.4	2.0
KS	595	444	540	461	3.4	1.6	TX	4,366	3,250	3,522	3,769	3.8	1.7
KY	820	849	814	820	3.2	1.8	UT	334	272	360	373	3.1	1.7
LA	1,219	959	938	937	5.0	2.3	VT	137	90	90	79	3.7	1.2
ME	265	213	181	169	3.5	1.2	VA	1,045	1,079	878	930	2.7	1.2
MD	756	707	590	588	2.6	1.2	WA	971	825	637	632	3.4	1.2
MA	881	605	414	433	2.5	0.8	WV	523	481	395	410	4.9	2.1
MI	1,750	1,571	1,382	1,382	2.8	1.4	WI	972	769	745	799	3.1	1.4
MN	848	566	626	625	3.0	1.2	WY	245	125	189	152	4.9	1.9
MS	695	750	927	949	4.2	2.7							

[1] Deaths per 100 million vehicle miles traveled.

Source: U.S. National Highway Safety Traffic Administration, *Traffic Safety Facts, 2000.*

U.S. Census Bureau, Statistical Abstract of the United States: 2002

No. 1071. Fatal Motor Vehicle Accidents—National Summary: 1990 to 2000

[Based on data from the Fatal Accident Reporting System (FARS). FARS gathers data on accidents that result in loss of human life. FARS is operated and maintained by National Highway Traffic Safety Administration's (NHTSA) National Center for Statistics and Analysis (NCSA). FARS data are gathered on motor vehicle accidents that occurred on a roadway customarily open to the public, resulting in the death of a person within 30 days of the accident. Collection of these data depend on the use of police, hospital, medical examiner/coroner, and Emergency Medical Services reports; State vehicle registration, driver licensing, and highway department files; and vital statistics documents and death certificates. See source for further detail]

Item	1990	1994	1995	1996	1997	1998	1999	2000
Fatal crashes, total	**39,836**	**36,254**	**37,241**	**37,494**	**37,324**	**37,107**	**37,140**	**37,409**
One vehicle involved	23,445	20,526	21,250	21,134	20,807	20,900	20,911	21,052
Two or more vehicles involved	16,391	15,728	15,991	16,360	16,517	16,207	16,229	16,357
Persons killed in fatal crashes	**44,599**	**40,716**	**41,817**	**42,065**	**42,013**	**41,501**	**41,717**	**41,821**
Occupants	37,134	34,318	35,291	35,695	35,725	35,382	35,875	36,249
Drivers	25,750	23,691	24,390	24,534	24,667	24,743	25,257	25,492
Passengers	11,276	10,518	10,782	11,058	10,944	10,530	10,521	10,669
Other	108	109	119	103	114	109	97	88
Nonmotorists	7,465	6,398	6,526	6,370	6,288	6,119	5,842	5,572
Pedestrians	6,482	5,489	5,584	5,449	5,321	5,228	4,939	4,739
Pedalcyclists	859	802	833	765	814	760	754	690
Other	124	107	109	156	153	131	149	143
Occupants killed by vehicle type:								
Passenger cars	24,092	21,997	22,423	22,505	22,199	21,194	20,862	20,492
Mini-compact (95 inches)	3,556	2,339	2,207	2,037	1,763	1,480	1,224	1,096
Subcompact (95 to 99 inches)	4,753	4,721	4,584	4,581	4,457	4,034	3,663	3,622
Compact (100 to 104 inches)	5,310	6,322	6,899	7,288	7,195	6,804	6,942	6,933
Intermediate (105 to 109) inches	4,849	4,407	4,666	4,670	4,794	4,617	4,721	5,131
Full size (110 to 114) inches	2,386	2,074	2,116	2,147	2,242	2,014	2,179	2,259
Largest (115 inches and over)	2,249	1,486	1,297	1,270	1,239	1,092	708	884
Unknown	989	648	654	512	509	1,153	1,425	567
Motorcycles	3,129	2,190	2,114	2,046	2,028	2,186	2,374	2,747
Other motorized cycles	115	130	113	115	88	108	109	115
Light Trucks	8,601	8,904	9,568	9,932	10,249	10,705	11,265	11,418
Pickup	5,979	5,574	5,938	5,904	5,887	5,921	6,127	5,953
Utility	1,214	1,757	1,935	2,147	2,380	2,713	3,026	3,324
Van	1,154	1,508	1,639	1,832	1,914	2,042	2,088	2,104
Other	254	65	56	49	68	29	24	37
Medium trucks	134	109	96	87	122	99	90	101
Heavy trucks	571	561	552	534	601	643	669	640
Buses	32	18	33	21	18	38	59	22
Other vehicles	296	317	307	340	343	336	355	398
Unknown	164	92	85	115	77	73	92	316
Persons involved in fatal crashes	**107,777**	**98,945**	**102,102**	**103,347**	**102,197**	**101,100**	**100,666**	**100,397**
Occupants	99,297	91,644	94,621	96,159	95,050	94,241	93,959	94,030
Drivers	58,893	54,549	56,164	57,001	56,688	56,604	56,502	57,090
Passengers	40,229	36,898	38,252	38,913	38,184	37,448	37,280	36,787
Other	175	197	205	245	178	189	177	153
Nonoccupants	8,480	7,301	7,481	7,188	7,147	6,859	6,707	6,367
Vehicle miles traveled (VMT) (100 mil)	21,444	23,576	24,227	24,858	25,617	26,315	26,911	27,498
Licensed drivers (1,000)	167,015	175,403	176,628	179,539	182,709	184,980	187,170	190,625
Registered vehicles (1,000)	184,275	192,497	197,065	201,631	203,568	208,076	212,685	217,028
Percent distribution of fatal accidents by the highest blood alcohol concentration (BAC) in accident:								
0.00 percent	50.6	59.1	58.7	59.1	61.5	61.3	61.6	60.3
0.01 to 0.09 percent	9.7	8.4	8.6	8.7	8.1	8.3	8.3	8.8
0.10 percent and over	39.7	32.5	32.6	32.1	30.3	30.4	30.1	30.9
Fatalities per 100,000 population:								
Under 5 years old	4.9	4.8	4.3	4.6	4.1	4.0	3.9	3.7
5 years to 15 years old	6.4	6.0	6.0	5.7	5.6	5.2	5.1	4.8
16 years to 24 years old	35.2	30.6	30.7	30.7	29.3	28.5	28.9	29.1
25 years to 44 years old	19.7	16.3	17.2	16.9	16.6	16.4	16.4	16.6
45 years to 64 years old	14.9	13.3	13.6	13.8	14.2	14.0	13.8	13.9
65 years to 79 years old	18.8	18.7	18.5	18.7	19.2	18.7	18.3	17.1
80 years old and over	26.8	28.0	28.0	27.8	29.2	28.4	27.3	24.9
Fatalities per 100 million VMT	2.1	1.7	1.7	1.7	1.6	1.6	1.6	1.5
Fatalities per 100,000 licensed drivers	26.7	23.2	23.7	23.4	23.0	22.4	22.3	21.9
Licensed driver per person	0.7	0.7	0.7	0.7	0.7	0.7	0.7	0.7
VMT per registered vehicle	11,637	12,247	12,294	12,329	12,584	12,647	12,653	12,670
Fatalities per 100,000 registered vehicles	24.2	21.2	21.2	20.9	20.6	19.9	19.6	19.3
Fatal crashes per 100 million VMT	1.9	1.5	1.5	1.5	1.5	1.4	1.4	1.4
Involved vehicles per fatal crash	1.5	1.5	1.5	1.5	1.5	1.5	1.5	1.5
Fatalities per fatal crash	1.1	1.1	1.1	1.1	1.1	1.1	1.1	1.1
Average occupants per fatal crash	2.5	2.5	2.5	2.6	2.5	2.5	2.5	2.5
Fatalities per 100,000 population	17.9	15.6	15.9	15.9	15.7	15.4	15.3	15.2

Source: U.S. National Highway Traffic Safety Administration, *Fatal Accident Reporting System,* annual.

U.S. Census Bureau, Statistical Abstract of the United States: 2002

No. 1072. Motor Vehicle Occupants and Nonoccupants Killed and Injured: 1985 to 2000

[For deaths within 30 days of the accident (3,416 represents 3,416,000)]

Year	Total	Occupants							Nonoccupants			
		Total	Passenger cars	Light trucks	Large trucks[1]	Motorcycles[2]	Buses	Other/unknown	Total	Pedestrian	Pedalcyclist	Other/unknown
KILLED												
1985	43,825	36,043	23,212	6,689	977	4,564	57	544	7,782	6,808	890	84
1986	46,087	38,234	24,944	7,317	926	4,566	39	442	7,853	6,779	941	133
1987	46,390	38,565	25,132	8,058	852	4,036	51	436	7,825	6,745	948	132
1988	47,087	39,170	25,808	8,306	911	3,662	54	429	7,917	6,870	911	136
1989	45,582	38,087	25,063	8,551	858	3,141	50	424	7,495	6,556	832	107
1990	44,599	37,134	24,092	8,601	705	3,244	32	460	7,465	6,482	859	124
1991	41,508	34,740	22,385	8,391	661	2,806	31	466	6,768	5,801	843	124
1992	39,250	32,880	21,387	8,098	585	2,395	28	387	6,370	5,549	723	98
1993	40,150	33,574	21,566	8,511	605	2,449	18	425	6,576	5,649	816	111
1994	40,716	34,318	21,997	8,904	670	2,320	18	409	6,398	5,489	802	107
1995	41,817	35,291	22,423	9,568	648	2,227	33	392	6,526	5,584	833	109
1996 [3] ..	42,065	35,695	22,505	9,932	621	2,161	21	455	6,368	5,449	765	154
1997	42,013	35,725	22,199	10,249	723	2,116	18	420	6,288	5,321	814	153
1998	41,501	35,382	21,194	10,705	742	2,294	38	409	6,119	5,228	760	131
1999	41,717	35,875	20,862	11,265	759	2,483	59	447	5,842	4,939	754	149
2000	41,821	36,249	20,492	11,418	741	2,862	22	714	5,572	4,739	690	143
INJURED (1,000)												
1988	3,416	3,224	2,585	478	37	105	15	4	192	110	75	8
1989	3,284	3,088	2,431	511	43	83	15	5	196	112	73	11
1990	3,231	3,044	2,376	505	42	84	33	4	187	105	75	7
1991	3,097	2,931	2,235	563	28	80	21	4	166	88	67	11
1992	3,070	2,908	2,232	545	34	65	20	12	162	89	63	10
1993	3,149	2,978	2,265	601	32	59	17	4	171	94	68	9
1994	3,266	3,102	2,364	631	30	57	16	4	164	92	62	9
1995	3,465	3,303	2,469	722	30	57	19	4	162	86	67	10
1996	3,483	3,332	2,458	761	33	55	20	4	151	82	58	11
1997	3,348	3,201	2,341	755	31	53	17	6	146	77	58	11
1998	3,192	3,061	2,201	763	29	49	16	4	131	69	53	8
1999	3,236	3,097	2,138	847	33	50	22	7	140	85	51	3
2000	3,189	3,055	2,052	887	31	58	18	10	134	78	51	5

[1] Medium and heavy trucks. [2] Includes motorized cycles. [3] Includes two fatalities of unknown type.

Source: U.S. National Highway Traffic Safety Administration, *Traffic Safety Facts, 2000;* and unpublished data.

No. 1073. Large Truck Involvement in Fatal Crashes by State: 2000

[Medium/heavy trucks represents trucks over 10,000 pounds gross vehicle weight, including single unit trucks]

State	Large trucks involved in fatal crashes				State	Large trucks involved in fatal crashes			
	Total vehicles involved in fatal crashes	Number	Percent of total vehicles	Percent of U.S. total for large trucks		Total vehicles involved in fatal crashes	Number	Percent of total vehicles	Percent of U.S. total for large trucks
United States .	57,403	4,930	8.6	100.0	Missouri	1,584	165	10.4	3.3
Alabama........	1,367	153	11.2	3.1	Montana	288	24	8.3	0.5
Alaska	121	4	3.3	0.1	Nebraska	372	52	14.0	1.1
Arizona.........	1,367	100	7.3	2.0	Nevada.........	402	36	9.0	0.7
Arkansas........	853	109	12.8	2.2	New Hampshire ...	170	10	5.9	0.2
California.......	5,123	364	7.1	7.4					
Colorado........	933	65	7.0	1.3	New Jersey	1,056	88	8.3	1.8
Connecticut......	470	36	7.7	0.7	New Mexico......	557	43	7.7	0.9
Delaware........	182	21	11.5	0.4	New York	2,020	153	7.6	3.1
District of Columbia.	67	3	4.5	0.1	North Carolina	2,043	170	8.3	3.4
Florida	4,276	302	7.1	6.1	North Dakota	106	11	10.4	0.2
					Ohio...........	1,912	182	9.5	3.7
Georgia	2,158	208	9.6	4.2	Oklahoma	895	107	12.0	2.2
Hawaii	172	1	0.6	(Z)	Oregon.........	633	60	9.5	1.2
Idaho..........	338	26	7.7	0.5	Pennsylvania.....	2,126	177	8.3	3.6
Illinois.........	1,977	163	8.2	3.3	Rhode Island.....	96	1	1.0	0.0
Indiana.........	1,274	166	13.0	3.4					
Iowa...........	635	84	13.2	1.7	South Carolina....	1,417	86	6.1	1.7
Kansas.........	642	79	12.3	1.6	South Dakota.....	219	22	10.0	0.4
Kentucky........	1,084	97	8.9	2.0	Tennessee.......	1,754	157	9.0	3.2
Louisiana	1,235	113	9.1	2.3	Texas	5,083	444	8.7	9.0
Maine..........	231	24	10.4	0.5	Utah...........	467	39	8.4	0.8
					Vermont	95	8	8.4	0.2
Maryland........	882	62	7.0	1.4	Virginia.........	1,288	96	7.5	1.9
Massachusetts....	608	46	7.6	0.9	Washington	868	64	7.4	1.3
Michigan........	2,016	147	7.3	3.0	West Virginia.....	523	48	9.2	1.0
Minnesota.......	884	75	8.5	1.5	Wisconsin	1,115	98	8.8	2.0
Mississippi.......	1,237	118	9.5	2.4	Wyoming........	182	18	9.9	0.4

Z Less than 0.05 percent.

Source: U.S. National Highway Traffic Safety Administration, *Traffic Safety Facts,* annual; and unpublished data.

No. 1074. Speeding-Related Traffic Fatalities by Road Type and Speed Limit: 2000

[Speeding consists of exceeding the posted speed limit or driving too fast for the road conditions]

State	Traffic fatalities, total	Speeding-related fatalities by road type and speed limit								
			Interstate		NonInterstate					
		Total [1]	Over 55 mph	At or under 55 mph	55 mph	50 mph	45 mph	40 mph	35 mph	Under 35 mph
United States	41,821	12,350	1,309	395	3,306	480	1,431	785	1,305	1,245
Alabama	995	369	38	3	88	7	133	28	35	20
Alaska	103	49	6	5	11	4	6	1	5	5
Arizona	1,036	354	43	10	63	34	66	35	18	33
Arkansas	652	144	19	2	75	4	10	4	11	11
California	3,753	1,331	219	29	327	55	92	105	186	106
Colorado	681	281	32	14	40	13	29	27	42	57
Connecticut	342	121	7	16	7	1	10	10	17	45
Delaware	123	27	1	2	3	14	1	1	4	1
District of Columbia	49	15	-	-	-	-	-	-	1	14
Florida	2,999	525	60	7	60	11	106	43	57	73
Georgia	1,541	342	33	16	123	6	52	23	45	27
Hawaii	131	54	-	-	4	1	3	-	15	10
Idaho	276	86	16	-	11	14	5	-	12	10
Illinois	1,418	492	27	46	180	6	54	27	77	73
Indiana	875	226	22	12	44	11	29	14	8	20
Iowa	445	51	5	-	26	3	4	-	2	5
Kansas	461	123	11	-	21	-	2	6	6	14
Kentucky	820	169	16	3	114	1	6	1	18	6
Louisiana	937	111	3	2	44	5	19	8	14	12
Maine	169	71	4	2	3	5	27	8	6	13
Maryland	588	195	9	13	18	27	14	28	24	29
Massachusetts	433	151	19	4	9	4	10	18	25	60
Michigan	1,382	276	25	4	126	9	31	5	20	36
Minnesota	625	171	14	8	86	7	5	5	2	31
Mississippi	949	221	21	-	77	16	40	9	23	17
Missouri	1,157	456	70	16	170	5	20	19	34	37
Montana	237	96	14	-	2	1	5	-	8	4
Nebraska	276	64	20	-	4	21	-	2	3	4
Nevada	323	122	10	4	12	4	22	2	23	11
New Hampshire	126	35	1	2	4	2	1	6	7	5
New Jersey	731	57	6	4	3	6	5	6	10	12
New Mexico	430	164	19	3	46	6	17	9	17	14
New York	1,458	434	7	29	104	17	25	25	19	00
North Carolina	1,472	519	27	7	296	11	106	5	54	4
North Dakota	86	34	1	-	19	-	-	3	-	5
Ohio	1,351	318	10	1	-	-	-	-	-	1
Oklahoma	652	245	55	2	44	8	42	16	7	5
Oregon	451	146	7	6	79	-	9	12	14	13
Pennsylvania	1,520	582	35	23	157	10	117	75	112	47
Rhode Island	80	39	-	5	3	2	3	5	8	13
South Carolina	1,065	312	40	2	103	7	62	12	42	14
South Dakota	173	59	10	2	16	-	5	4	2	3
Tennessee	1,306	320	23	15	92	14	66	35	25	34
Texas	3,769	1,446	168	59	230	44	100	87	134	116
Utah	373	109	22	2	17	8	4	11	9	8
Vermont	79	31	5	-	-	18	-	-	3	3
Virginia	930	166	17	11	79	-	22	1	18	16
Washington	632	242	37	-	30	32	9	24	50	28
West Virginia	410	117	16	2	51	4	10	13	14	5
Wisconsin	799	220	16	1	121	1	27	7	19	22
Wyoming	152	62	23	1	4	1	-	-	-	5

- Represents zero.   [1] Includes fatalities that occurred on roads for which the speed limit was unknown.

Source: U.S. National Highway Traffic Safety Administration, *Traffic Safety Facts 1995, Speeding. Traffic Safety Facts, Speeding,* annual; and unpublished data.

Transportation   681

No. 1075. Traffic Fatalities by State and Highest Blood Alcohol Concentration (BAC) in the Crash: 2000

[BAC means blood alcohol concentration; g/dl means grams per deciliter]

State	Traffic fatalities, total	No alcohol (BAC=0.00 g/dl)		Any alcohol (BAC=0.01 g/dl) or more					
				Total		Low alcohol (BAC=0.01-0.09 g/dl)		High alcohol (BAC=0.10 g/dl or more)	
		Number	Percent	number	Percent	Number	Percent	Number	Percent
United States	41,821	25,168	60	16,653	40	3,761	9	12,892	31
Alabama.	995	596	60	399	40	74	7	326	33
Alaska	103	50	48	53	52	9	9	44	43
Arizona.	1,036	580	56	456	44	102	10	354	34
Arkansas	652	452	69	200	31	61	9	139	21
California	3,753	2,352	63	1,401	37	340	9	1,061	28
Colorado.	681	425	62	256	38	58	8	198	29
Connecticut.	342	184	54	158	46	40	12	119	35
Delaware.	123	63	51	60	49	11	9	49	40
District of Columbia	49	30	61	19	39	5	10	14	29
Florida	2,999	1,808	60	1,191	40	261	9	930	31
Georgia	1,541	971	63	570	37	132	9	438	28
Hawaii	131	77	59	54	41	17	13	37	28
Idaho	276	162	59	114	41	33	12	81	29
Illinois	1,418	804	57	614	43	126	9	489	34
Indiana.	875	605	69	270	31	56	6	214	24
Iowa	445	321	72	124	28	24	6	100	22
Kansas.	461	307	67	154	33	36	8	118	26
Kentucky	820	564	69	256	31	53	6	203	25
Louisiana	937	490	52	447	48	95	10	352	38
Maine.	169	118	70	51	30	13	7	38	22
Maryland	588	363	62	225	38	64	11	161	27
Massachusetts.	433	215	50	218	50	65	15	153	35
Michigan.	1,382	876	63	506	37	109	8	397	29
Minnesota.	625	370	59	255	41	48	8	207	33
Mississippi	949	570	60	379	40	89	9	289	30
Missouri	1,157	646	56	511	44	124	11	387	33
Montana.	237	127	54	110	46	18	8	92	39
Nebraska	276	173	63	103	37	33	12	70	25
Nevada	323	178	55	145	45	32	10	112	35
New Hampshire	126	77	61	49	39	9	7	40	31
New Jersey.	731	412	56	319	44	88	12	231	32
New Mexico	430	225	52	205	48	46	11	159	37
New York	1,458	1,039	71	419	29	126	9	293	20
North Carolina	1,472	949	64	523	36	103	7	419	28
North Dakota.	86	45	52	41	48	5	6	36	42
Ohio	1,351	835	62	516	38	105	8	411	30
Oklahoma.	652	431	66	221	34	53	8	169	26
Oregon.	451	263	58	188	42	56	12	132	29
Pennsylvania.	1,520	902	59	618	41	107	7	511	34
Rhode Island.	80	39	49	41	51	10	12	31	38
South Carolina.	1,065	643	60	422	40	94	9	329	31
South Dakota	173	92	53	81	47	15	9	66	38
Tennessee	1,306	795	61	511	39	112	9	399	31
Texas.	3,769	1,871	50	1,898	50	448	12	1,450	38
Utah	373	284	76	89	24	21	6	68	18
Vermont	79	48	61	31	39	4	5	27	34
Virginia.	930	589	63	341	37	85	9	257	28
Washington.	632	357	56	275	44	59	9	217	34
West Virginia.	410	235	57	175	43	26	6	149	36
Wisconsin.	799	454	57	345	43	57	7	288	36
Wyoming	152	107	70	45	30	6	4	40	26

Source: U.S. National Highway Traffic Safety Administration, *Traffic Safety Facts*, annual; and unpublished data.

No. 1076. Fatalities by Highest Blood Alcohol Concentration in the Crash: 1985 to 2000

[BAC means blood alcohol concentration; g/dl means grams per deciliter]

Item	1985	1990	1993	1994	1995	1996	1997	1998	1999	2000
Total fatalities.	43,825	44,599	40,150	40,716	41,817	42,065	42,013	41,501	41,717	41,821
Fatalities in alcohol-related crashes	22,716	22,084	17,473	16,580	17,247	17,218	16,189	16,020	15,976	16,653
Percent.	51.8	49.5	43.5	40.7	41.2	40.9	38.5	38.6	38.3	39.8
BAC = 0.01-0.09 g/dl:										
Number	4,604	4,434	3,496	3,480	3,746	3,774	3,480	3,526	3,523	3,761
Percent.	10.5	9.9	8.7	8.5	9	9	8.3	8.5	8.4	9.0
BAC = 0.10 g/dl or more:										
Number	18,111	17,650	13,977	13,100	13,501	13,444	12,710	12,494	12,453	12,892
Percent.	41.3	39.6	34.8	32.2	32.3	32	30.3	30.1	29.9	30.8
Fatalities with BAC = 0.00 g/dl:										
Number	21,109	22,515	22,677	24,136	24,570	24,847	25,824	25,481	25,741	25,168
Percent	48.2	50.5	56.5	59.3	58.8	59.1	61.5	61.4	61.7	60.2

Source: U.S. National Highway Traffic Safety Administration, *Traffic Safety Facts*, annual; and unpublished data.

U.S. Census Bureau, Statistical Abstract of the United States: 2002

No. 1077. Crashes by Crash Severity: 1990 to 2000

[6,471 represents 6,471,000. A crash is a police-reported event that produces injury and/or property damage, involves a vehicle in transport and occurs on a trafficway or while the vehicle is in motion after running off the trafficway]

Item	1990	1993	1994	1995	1996	1997	1998	1999	2000
Crashes (1,000).	**6,471**	**6,106**	**6,496**	**6,699**	**6,770**	**6,624**	**6,335**	**6,279**	**6,394**
Fatal	39.8	35.8	36.3	37.2	37.5	37.3	37.1	37.1	37.4
Nonfatal injury.	2,122	2,022	2,123	2,217	2,238	2,149	2,029	2,054	2,070
Property damage only	4,309	4,048	4,336	4,446	4,494	4,438	4,269	4,188	4,286
Percent of total crashes:									
Fatal	0.6	0.6	0.6	0.6	0.6	0.6	0.6	0.6	0.6
Nonfatal injury.	32.8	33.1	32.7	33.1	33.1	32.4	32.0	32.7	32.4
Property damage only	66.6	66.3	66.8	66.4	66.4	67.0	67.4	66.7	67.0

Source: U.S. National Highway Safety Traffic Administration, *Traffic Safety Facts, 2000.*

No. 1078. Alcohol Involvement for Drivers in Fatal Crashes: 1990 and 2000

[BAC = blood alcohol concentration]

Drivers involved in fatal crashes	1990		2000	
	Number of drivers	Percentage with BAC of 0.10% or greater	Number of drivers	Percentage with BAC of 0.10% or greater
Total drivers [1]	**58,893**	**25**	**57,090**	**18**
Drivers by age group:				
16 to 20 years old.	8,821	21	7,956	15
21 to 24 years old.	7,195	35	5,895	27
25 to 34 years old.	15,764	33	11,630	24
35 to 44 years old.	10,177	26	11,039	22
45 to 64 years old.	9,935	16	12,857	14
65 years old and over	5,501	6	6,226	5
Drivers by sex:				
Male.	44,281	28	41,407	20
Female.	13,726	14	14,654	11
Drivers by vehicle type:				
Passenger cars	33,893	24	27,356	19
Light trucks.	15,501	29	20,192	20
Large trucks.	4,709	2	4,883	1
Motorcycles.	3,269	39	2,936	27

[1] Includes age, sex, and types of vehicles unknown.

Source: U.S. National Highway Safety Traffic Administration, *Traffic Safety Facts, 2000.*

No. 1079. Licensed Drivers and Number in Accidents by Age: 2000

[189,800 represents 189,800,000]

Age group	Licensed drivers		Drivers in accidents				Accidents per number of drivers	
			Fatal		All			
	Number (1,000)	Percent	Number	Percent	Number (1,000)	Percent	Fatal [1]	All [2]
Total	**189,800**	**100.0**	**61,400**	**100.0**	**25,100**	**100.0**	**32**	**13**
Under 16 years old.	31	(Z)	600	1.0	180	0.7	([3])	([3])
16 years old	1,448	0.8	1,600	2.6	840	3.3	110	58
17 years old	2,310	1.2	2,000	3.3	1,030	4.1	87	45
18 years old	2,849	1.5	2,300	3.7	1,020	4.1	81	36
19 years old	2,986	1.6	2,100	3.4	960	3.8	70	32
19 years old and under	9,624	5.1	8,600	14.0	4,030	16.1	89	42
20 years old	3,251	1.7	2,000	3.3	870	3.5	62	27
21 years old	3,191	1.7	1,600	2.6	480	1.9	50	15
22 years old	3,173	1.7	1,300	2.1	440	1.8	41	14
23 years old	3,284	1.7	1,300	2.1	400	1.6	40	12
24 years old	3,182	1.7	1,000	1.6	370	1.5	31	12
20 to 24 years old	16,081	8.5	7,200	11.7	2,560	10.2	45	16
25 to 34 years old	35,915	18.9	11,600	18.9	5,540	22.1	32	15
35 to 44 years old	41,815	22.0	12,200	19.9	5,240	20.9	29	13
45 to 54 years old	36,573	19.3	9,300	15.1	3,690	14.7	25	10
55 to 64 years old	22,778	12.0	5,000	8.1	1,960	7.8	22	9
65 to 74 years old	15,741	8.3	3,700	6.0	1,190	4.7	24	8
75 years old and over	11,273	5.9	3,800	6.2	890	3.5	34	8

Z Less than 0.05.   [1] Per 100,000 licensed drivers.   [2] Per 100 licensed drivers.   [3] Rates for drivers under age 16 are substantially overstated due to the high proportion of unlicensed drivers involved.

Source: National Safety Council, Itasca, IL, *Injury Facts, 2001,* (copyright).

U.S. Census Bureau, *Statistical Abstract of the United States: 2002*

No. 1080. Motor Vehicle Distance Traveled by Type of Vehicle: 1970 to 2000

[1,110 represents 1,110,000,000,000. Travel estimates based on automatic traffic recorder data. Speed trend data for 1970 were collected by several state highway agencies, normally during summer months; beginning 1980 all states have monitored speeds at locations on several highway systems Monitoring Program]

Year	Vehicle-miles of travel (bil.)					Avg. miles per vehicle (1,000)				
		Passenger cars					Passenger cars			
	Total	Cars [1]	Buses [2]	Vans, pickups, SUVs	Trucks [3]	Total	Cars [1]	Buses [2]	Vans, pickups, SUVs	Trucks [3]
1970	1,110	920	4.5	123	62	10.0	10.0	12.0	8.7	13.6
1980	1,527	1,122	6.1	291	108	9.5	8.8	11.5	10.4	18.7
1985	1,775	1,256	4.5	391	124	10.0	9.4	7.5	10.5	20.6
1990	2,144	1,418	5.7	575	146	11.1	10.3	9.1	11.9	23.6
1991	2,172	1,367	5.8	649	150	11.3	10.3	9.1	12.2	24.2
1992	2,247	1,381	5.8	707	153	11.6	10.6	9.0	12.4	25.4
1993	2,296	1,385	6.1	746	160	11.6	10.5	9.4	12.4	26.3
1994	2,358	1,416	6.4	765	170	11.7	10.8	9.6	12.2	25.8
1995	2,423	1,438	6.4	790	178	11.8	11.2	9.4	12.0	26.5
1996	2,486	1,470	6.6	817	183	11.8	11.3	9.4	11.8	26.1
1997	2,562	1,503	6.8	851	191	12.1	11.6	9.8	12.1	27.0
1998	2,632	1,550	7.0	868	196	12.2	11.8	9.8	12.2	25.4
1999	2,691	1,569	7.7	901	203	12.2	11.9	10.5	12.0	26.0
2000	2,750	1,602	7.7	924	206	12.2	11.9	10.2	11.7	25.7

[1] Includes motorcycles through 1994; thereafter in total, not shown separately. [2] Includes school buses. [3] Includes combinations.

Source: U.S. Federal Highway Administration, *Highway Statistics,* annual.

No. 1081. Passenger Transit Industry—Summary: 1980 to 2000

[6,510 represents $6,510,000,000. Includes Puerto Rico. Includes aggregate information for all transit systems in the United States. Excludes nontransit services such as taxicab, school bus, unregulated jitney, sightseeing bus, intercity bus, and special application mass transportation systems (e.g., amusement parks, airports, island, and urban park ferries). Includes active vehicles only]

Item	Unit	1980	1985	1990	1995	1998	1999	2000
Operating systems	Number. . .	1,044	4,972	5,078	5,973	6,000	6,000	6,000
Motor bus systems	Number. . .	1,040	2,631	2,688	2,250	2,262	2,262	2,262
Passenger vehicles, active [1]	Number. . .	75,388	94,368	92,961	115,874	123,855	128,516	131,493
Motor bus	Number. . .	59,411	64,258	58,714	67,107	72,142	74,228	75,013
Trolley bus	Number. . .	823	676	832	885	880	859	951
Heavy rail	Number. . .	9,641	9,326	10,419	10,157	10,301	10,306	10,591
Light rail	Number. . .	1,013	717	913	999	1,220	1,297	1,577
Commuter rail	Number. . .	4,500	4,035	4,415	4,565	4,963	4,883	5,073
Demand response	Number. . .	(NA)	14,490	16,471	29,352	29,646	31,884	33,080
Operating funding, total.	Mil. dol . . .	6,510	12,195	16,053	18,241	21,062	22,220	24,243
Passenger funding	Mil. dol . . .	2,557	4,575	5,891	6,801	7,969	8,282	8,746
Other operating funding [2]	Mil. dol . . .	248	702	895	2,812	3,685	3,648	4,217
Operating assistance.	Mil. dol . . .	3,705	6,918	9,267	8,628	9,407	10,290	11,280
Federal [3]	Mil. dol . . .	1,094	940	970	817	751	872	994
Local [3]	Mil. dol . . .	2,611	5,979	5,327	3,981	4,377	4,540	5,319
State [3]	Mil. dol . . .	(NA)	(NA)	2,970	3,830	4,279	4,878	4,967
Total expense	Mil. dol . . .	6,711	14,077	17,979	21,540	24,318	25,538	28,194
Operating expense	Mil. dol . . .	6,247	12,381	15,742	17,849	19,739	20,512	22,646
Reconciling expense	Mil. dol . . .	464	1,696	2,237	3,691	4,579	5,025	5,548
Capital and planning grants, federal [4] .	Mil. dol . . .	2,787	2,559	2,428	5,534	4,225	5,395	7,366
Capital expenditures	Million	(NA)	(NA)	(NA)	7,230	7,893	8,975	9,587
Vehicle-miles operated [1]	Million	2,287	2,791	3,242	3,550	3,794	3,972	4,081
Motor bus	Million	1,677	1,863	2,130	2,184	2,175	2,276	2,315
Trolley bus	Million	13	16	14	14	14	14	14
Heavy rail	Million	385	451	537	537	566	578	595
Light rail	Million	18	17	24	35	44	49	53
Commuter rail	Million	179	183	213	238	260	266	271
Demand response	Million	(NA)	247	306	507	671	718	759
Passengers carried [1]	Million	8,567	8,636	8,799	7,763	8,750	9,168	9,363
Motor bus	Million	5,837	5,675	5,677	4,848	5,399	5,648	5,678
Trolley bus	Million	142	142	126	119	117	120	122
Heavy rail	Million	2,108	2,290	2,346	2,033	2,393	2,521	2,632
Light rail	Million	133	132	175	251	276	292	320
Commuter rail	Million	280	275	328	344	381	396	413
Demand response	Million	(NA)	59	68	88	95	100	105
Avg. funding per passenger	Cents	29.8	53.0	66.9	87.6	87.1	90.3	93
Employees, number (avg.) [5]	1,000	187	270	273	311	339	350	358
Payroll, employee	Mil. dol . . .	3,281	5,843	7,226	8,213	9,211	9,495	10,400
Fringe benefits, employee	Mil. dol . . .	1,353	2,868	3,986	4,484	4,844	5,052	5,413

NA Not available. [1] Includes other categories not shown separately. [2] Beginning 1995, includes taxes levied directly by transit agency and other dedicated funds, formerly included in Local. [3] Includes other operating revenue, nonoperating revenue, and auxiliary income. Data for 1985 are state and local combined. [4] For 1980, capital grants only. [5] Through 1990, represents employee equivalents of 2,080 hours = one employee; beginning 1995, equals actual employees.

Source: American Public Transportation Association, Washington, DC, *Public Transportation Fact Book,* annual.

No. 1082. Domestic Motor Fuel Consumption by Type of Vehicle: 1970 to 2000

[92.3 represents 92,300,000,000. Comprises all fuel types used for propulsion of vehicles under state motor fuels laws. Excludes federal purchases for military use. Minus sign (-)indicates decrease]

Year	Annual fuel consumption (bil. gal)					Average miles per gallon				
	All vehicles	Avg. annual percent change [1]	Cars [2]	Vans, pickups, SUVs	Buses [3]	Trucks [4] (bil. gal.)	All vehicles	Cars [2]	Vans, pickups, SUVs	Buses [3]	Trucks [4] (bil. gal.)
1970 ..	92.3	4.8	67.8	12.3	0.8	11.3	12.0	13.5	10.0	5.5	5.5
1975 ..	109.0	2.5	74.3	19.1	1.1	14.6	12.2	14.0	10.5	5.8	5.6
1980 ..	115.0	-5.9	70.2	23.8	1.0	20.0	13.3	16.0	12.2	6.0	5.4
1981 ..	114.5	-0.4	69.3	23.7	1.1	20.4	13.6	16.5	12.5	5.9	5.3
1982 ..	113.4	-1.0	69.3	22.7	1.0	20.4	14.1	16.9	13.5	5.9	5.5
1983 ..	116.1	2.4	70.5	23.9	0.9	20.8	14.2	17.1	13.7	5.9	5.6
1984 ..	118.7	2.2	70.8	25.6	0.8	21.4	14.5	17.4	14.0	5.7	5.7
1985 ..	121.3	2.2	71.7	27.4	0.8	21.4	14.6	17.5	14.3	5.4	5.8
1986 ..	125.2	3.2	73.4	29.1	0.9	21.9	14.7	17.4	14.6	5.3	5.8
1987 ..	127.5	1.8	73.5	30.6	0.9	22.5	15.1	18.0	14.9	5.8	5.9
1988 ..	130.1	2.0	73.5	32.7	0.9	22.9	15.6	18.8	15.4	5.8	6.0
1989 ..	131.9	1.4	74.1	33.3	0.9	23.5	15.9	18.0	16.1	6.0	6.1
1990 ..	130.8	-0.8	69.8	35.6	0.9	24.5	16.4	20.3	16.1	6.4	6.0
1991 ..	128.6	-1.7	64.5	38.2	0.9	25.0	16.9	21.2	17.0	6.7	6.0
1992 ..	132.9	3.3	65.6	40.9	0.9	25.5	16.9	21.0	17.3	6.6	6.0
1993 ..	137.3	3.3	67.2	42.9	0.9	26.2	16.7	20.6	17.4	6.6	6.1
1994 ..	140.8	2.5	68.1	44.1	1.0	27.7	16.7	20.8	17.3	6.6	6.1
1995 ..	143.8	2.1	68.1	45.6	1.0	29.0	16.8	21.1	17.3	6.6	6.1
1996 ..	147.4	2.5	69.2	47.4	1.0	29.6	16.9	21.2	17.2	6.6	6.2
1997 ..	150.4	2.0	69.9	49.4	1.0	29.9	17.0	21.5	17.2	6.7	6.4
1998 ..	155.4	3.3	71.7	50.5	1.1	32.0	16.9	21.6	17.2	6.7	6.1
1999 ..	161.4	3.9	73.2	52.8	1.1	33.9	16.7	21.4	17.0	6.7	6.0
2000 ..	162.3	0.7	72.9	52.8	1.1	35.2	16.9	22.0	17.5	6.8	5.8

[1] Change from immediate prior year.   [2] Includes motorcycles through 1994; thereafter in total, not shown separately.
[3] Includes school buses.   [4] Includes combinations.

Source: U.S. Federal Highway Administration, *Highway Statistics*, annual.

No. 1083. Class I Intercity Motor Carriers of Passengers: 1990 to 2000

[943 represents $943,000,000. For carriers whose adjusted annual gross operating revenues are $5 million or more. Intercity carriers have intercity revenues which are 50 percent or more of their total operating revenues. Minus sign (-) indicated deficit]

Item	Unit	1990	1992	1993	1994	1995	1996	1997	1998	1999	2000
Number of intercity carriers [1]	Number.	21	21	21	20	20	17	17	15	14	12
Operating revenue	Mil. dol..	943	938	928	870	917	912	1,000	999	1,268	1,088
Intercity regular route	Mil. dol..	739	755	747	718	767	771	834	860	1,075	920
Other	Mil. dol..	204	182	182	152	150	141	165	139	192	168
Operating expenses	Mil. dol..	1,026	874	880	919	899	878	948	947	1,258	1,035
Operating income	Mil. dol..	-83	63	48	-48	18	33	52	52	9	53
Revenue passengers..........	Million..	44	41	40	41	43	37	52	47	54	33
Intercity regular route passengers.	Million..	37	36	35	36	38	34	41	37	42	31
Other passengers	Million..	7	5	5	4	5	4	12	10	12	2
Average fare, intercity regular route .	Dol.	20.22	21.15	21.32	19.77	20.10	22.85	20.57	23.14	25.56	29.46

[1] Excludes carriers preponderantly in local or suburban service and carriers engaged in transportation of both property and passengers.

Source: U.S. Bureau of Transportation Statistics, *Selected Earnings Data, Class I Motor Carriers of Passengers. Carriers of Passengers, 1988-1997, 1998, 1999*, and *2000*.

U.S. Census Bureau, Statistical Abstract of the United States: 2002

No. 1084. Bus Profile: 1990 to 2000

[7,605 represents $7,605,000,000]

Item	Unit	1990	1995	1998	1999	2000
FINANCIAL						
Expenditures, school bus	Mil. dol. .	7,605	9,889	10,326	10,340	(NA)
Operating revenues, intercity bus, Class I [1]	Mil. dol. .	943	1,189	1,075	1,327	1,134
Operating expenses, intercity bus, Class I [1]	Mil. dol. .	1,026	1,254	1,016	1,314	1,078
INVENTORY						
Operating companies, intercity bus, Class I	Number .	31	24	20	18	15
Vehicles:						
Commercial and Federal bus	Number .	118,726	125,057	133,070	136,748	140,097
School & other bus	Number .	508,261	560,447	582,470	592,029	606,028
Employees:						
Intercity & rural bus.	Number .	26,300	23,800	24,400	23,700	(NA)
School bus	Number .	111,200	131,100	141,000	146,700	(NA)
PERFORMANCE						
Vehicle-miles, all buses:						
Rural & urban highway	Millions .	5,726	6,383	7,007	7,662	7,601
Rural highway	Millions .	3,444	3,817	4,251	4,667	4,498
Urban highway	Millions .	2,283	2,566	2,756	2,995	3,103
Revenue:						
Passenger miles, intercity bus	Millions .	121,400	136,104	148,558	162,445	161,152
Passengers, intercity bus	1,000. . .	334,000	366,500	357,600	358,900	(NA)
Avg. miles traveled per vehicle, all buses	Miles . . .	9,133	9,312	9,793	10514	10,187
Avg. annual fuel consumption, all buses	Gallon . .	1,428	1,412	1,454	1,576	1,488
Avg. miles per gallon, all buses	Mpg . . .	6.4	6.6	6.7	6.7	6.8
Average revenue per passenger mile	Cents . .	11.6	12.2	12.8	12.8	(NA)
SAFETY						
Fatalities:						
School bus related	Number .	115	123	126	164	144
School bus occupants	Number .	11	13	6	10	12
Other vehicle occupants	Number .	64	72	90	126	98
Nonoccupants	Number .	40	38	30	28	34
Vehicles involved in fatal accidents, all buses	Number .	340	271	289	319	322
Occupant fatality rate:						
Per 100 million vehicle-miles, all buses.	Rate . . .	0.5	0.5	0.5	0.8	0.3
Per 10,000 registered vehicles, all buses	Rate . . .	0.5	0.5	0.5	0.8	0.3

NA Not available.   [1] Beginning 1995, data include intercity regular route carriers plus other carriers that are not predominantly in intercity regular route service.
Source: U.S. Bureau of Transportation Statistics, *National Transportation Statistics*, annual.

No. 1085. Truck Profile: 1990 to 2000

[6,196 represents 6,196,000]

Item	Unit	1990	1995	1998	1999	2000
INVENTORY						
Truck registrations, total	1,000 . . .	6,196	6,719	7,732	7,792	8,023
Single-unit 2-axle 6-tire vehicle	1,000 . . .	4,487	5,024	5,735	5,763	5,926
Combination trucks.	1,000 . . .	1,709	1,696	1,997	2,029	2,097
Employees:						
Trucking & courier services	1,000 . . .	1,274	1,440	1,569	1,611	(NA)
Truck drivers & deliverymen	1,000 . . .	2,148	2,861	2,685	2,643	(NA)
PERFORMANCE						
Vehicle miles, total.	Millions . .	146,242	178,156	196,380	202,688	205,791
Rural highway, total	Millions . .	89,692	106,031	115,142	117,941	120,631
Urban highway, total	Millions . .	56,550	72,125	81,238	84,747	85,160
Single unit 2-axle 6-tire vehicle	Millions . .	51,901	62,705	68,021	70,304	70,583
Combination trucks	Millions . .	94,341	115,451	128,359	132,384	135,208
Passenger miles:						
Single unit 2-axle 6-tire vehicle	Millions . .	51,901	62,705	68,021	70,304	70,583
Combination trucks.	Millions . .	94,341	115,451	128,359	132,384	135,208
Average miles traveled per vehicle:						
All trucks, total.	Avg. miles.	23,603	26,514	25,397	26,014	25,651
Single unit 2-axle 6-tire vehicle	Avg. miles.	11,567	12,482	11,861	12,199	11,911
Combination trucks	Avg. miles.	55,206	68,083	64,265	65,260	64,489
Ton-miles, intercity.	Millions . .	735,000	921,000	1,027,000	1,093,000	(NA)
Fuel consumed, all trucks	Mil. gal . .	24,490	28,993	31,975	33,909	35,193
Single unit 2-axle 6-tire vehicle	Mil. gal .	8,357	9,216	6,817	9,372	9,548
Combination trucks.	Mil. gal .	16,133	19,777	25,158	24,537	25,645
Average fuel consumption per vehicle	Gallons . .	3,953	4,315	4,135	4,352	4,387
Single unit 2-axle 6-tire vehicle	Gallons . .	1,862	1,835	1,189	1,626	1,611
Combination trucks.	Gallons . .	9,441	11,663	12,596	12,096	12,232
Highway-user taxes, total	Mil. dol .	19,356	25,116	28,697	(NA)	(NA)
SAFETY						
Occupant fatalities.	Number. .	9,306	10,216	11,447	12,024	12,159
Light trucks.	Number. .	8,601	9,568	10,705	11,265	11,418
Large trucks	Number. .	705	648	742	759	741
Vehicle involvement, total (per 100 million vehicle-miles)	Rate. . . .	2.9	2.4	2.3	2.2	2.2

NA Not available.
Source: U.S. Bureau of Transportation Statistics, *National Transportation Statistics*, annual.

No. 1086. Trucks by Use, Body Type, Miles, and Acquisition: 1992 and 1997

[In thousands (59,200.8 represents 59,200,800), **except percent change.** Based on the 1997 Economic Census; see Appendix III. Minus sign (-) indicates decrease]

Vehicular and operational characteristics	All trucks			Trucks, excluding pickups, panels, minivans, sport, utilities, and station wagons		
	1992	1997	Percent change, 1992-97	1992	1997	Percent change, 1992-97
MAJOR USE						
Total.	59,200.8	72,800.3	23.0	5,112.4	5,664.7	10.8
Agriculture.	3,554.6	3,377.8	-5.0	898.7	854.7	-4.9
Forestry and lumbering	264.5	276.7	4.6	100.6	112.1	11.4
Mining and quarrying.	220.4	250.7	13.7	79.2	82.1	3.7
Construction	4,986.3	6,033.9	21.0	1,015.4	1,161.8	14.4
Manufacturing	786.7	729.4	-7.3	257.6	258.6	0.4
Wholesale trade	1,136.1	1,264.6	11.3	438.3	440.4	0.5
Retail trade	1,950.9	2,243.8	15.0	434.9	469.3	7.9
For-hire transportation	889.2	1,059.4	19.1	769.6	938.2	21.9
Utilities	541.2	663.8	22.7	183.4	204.9	11.7
Services	3,123.3	4,233.5	35.5	421.2	591.4	40.4
Daily rental	307.6	508.0	65.1	90.6	171.2	89.0
One-way rental.	17.1	31.2	82.5	14.1	28.3	100.7
Personal transportation	40,441.9	50,934.5	25.9	231.0	183.0	-20.8
Not in use	981.0	1,193.1	21.6	177.8	168.6	-5.2
BODY TYPE						
Pickup	33,659.6	36,191.8	7.5	(X)	(X)	(X)
Minivan.	6,129.6	9,837.9	60.5	(X)	(X)	(X)
Panel or van	5,701.0	5,572.7	-2.3	(X)	(X)	(X)
Utility vehicle	8,598.1	15,533.1	80.7	(X)	(X)	(X)
Sport utility.	7,140.2	13,762.5	92.7	(X)	(X)	(X)
Station wagon.	1,457.9	1,770.7	21.5	(X)	(X)	(X)
Multistop or stepvan	408.4	560.4	37.2	408.4	560.4	37.2
Platform with added devices	295.7	308.2	4.2	295.7	308.2	4.2
Low boy or depressed center	89.8	111.1	23.7	89.8	111.1	23.7
Basic platform	1,183.3	1,176.1	-0.6	1,183.3	1,176.1	-0.6
Livestock truck	48.3	39.1	-19.0	48.3	39.1	-19.0
Insulated nonrefrigerated van	23.3	34.5	48.1	23.3	34.5	48.1
Insulated refrigerated van.	204.8	234.0	14.3	204.8	234.0	14.3
Drop-frame van	60.1	54.9	-8.7	60.1	54.9	-8.7
Open-top van.	20.1	20.8	3.5	20.1	20.8	3.5
Basic enclosed van.	785.4	1,009.0	28.5	785.4	1,009.0	28.5
Beverage	73.0	70.2	-3.8	73.0	70.2	-3.8
Public utility	157.0	152.0	-3.2	157.0	152.0	-3.2
Winch or crane.	58.8	55.0	-6.5	58.8	55.0	-6.5
Wrecker	104.1	111.9	7.5	104.1	111.9	7.5
Pole or logging.	53.9	55.7	3.3	53.9	55.7	3.3
Auto transport	22.3	20.1	-9.9	22.3	20.1	-9.9
Service truck	144.1	168.6	17.0	144.1	168.6	17.0
Yard tractor	8.1	10.8	33.3	8.1	10.8	33.3
Oilfield truck	26.5	26.1	-1.5	26.5	26.1	-1.5
Grain body	310.8	299.1	-3.8	310.8	299.1	-3.8
Garbage hauler	72.4	91.6	26.5	72.4	91.6	26.5
Dump truck	611.9	670.8	9.6	611.9	670.8	9.6
Tank truck (liquids or gases)	231.9	249.4	7.5	231.9	249.4	7.5
Tank truck (dry bulk)	33.8	39.7	17.5	33.8	39.7	17.5
Concrete mixer.	61.0	73.1	19.8	61.0	73.1	19.8
Other	23.7	22.6	-4.6	23.7	22.6	-4.6
ANNUAL MILES						
Less than 5,000	12,284.3	13,045.1	6.2	1,663.1	1,554.2	-6.5
5,000 to 9,999	12,273.1	13,465.5	9.7	751.9	753.4	0.2
10,000 to 19,999	22,656.5	29,974.6	32.3	978.6	1,128.8	15.3
20,000 to 29,999	7,499.5	10,198.5	36.0	512.6	585.4	14.2
30,000 to 49,999	3,215.3	4,349.9	35.3	458.8	571.1	24.5
50,000 to 74,999	717.0	951.3	32.7	284.9	374.5	31.4
75,000 or more	554.9	815.5	47.0	462.3	697.3	50.8
VEHICLE ACQUISITION						
Purchased new	26,967.2	30,052.9	11.4	2,091.2	2,323.6	11.1
Purchased used	30,417.3	37,834.5	24.4	2,601.1	2,762.6	6.2
Leased from someone else	1,397.1	4,039.3	189.1	373.6	522.2	39.8
Other and not reported	419.1	873.6	108.4	46.5	56.3	21.1

X Not applicable.

Source: U.S. Census Bureau, *1997 Economic Census, Vehicle Inventory and Use Survey, 1997,* Series EC97TV-US, issued October 1999.

Transportation 687

No. 1087. Truck Transportation, Couriers and Messengers, and Warehousing and Storage—Estimated Revenue: 1999 and 2000

[In millions of dollars (221,729 represents $221,729,000,000), except percent. For taxable and tax-exempt employer firms. Estimates have been adjusted to the results of the 1997 Economic Census. Based on the North American Industry Classification System; see text, Section 15, Business Enterprise. Minus sign (-) indicates decrease]

Kind of business	NAICS code [1]	1999	2000	Percent change, 1999-2000
Selected transportation industries.	**48, 49**	**221,729**	**237,296**	**7.0**
Truck transportation	484	162,083	171,691	5.9
General freight trucking	4841	101,817	109,347	7.4
General freight trucking, local	48411	14,273	15,152	6.2
General freight trucking, long-distance	48412	87,544	94,195	7.6
General freight trucking, long-distance, truckload	484121	57,851	61,932	7.1
General freight trucking, long-distance, less than truckload	484122	29,693	32,263	8.7
Specialized freight trucking	4842	60,266	62,344	3.4
Used household and office goods moving	48421	14,931	15,875	6.3
Specialized freight (except used goods) trucking, local. . .	48422	24,088	25,332	5.2
Specialized freight (except used goods) trucking, long-distance	48423	21,247	21,138	-0.5
Couriers and messengers	492	47,355	52,773	11.4
Couriers	4921	43,157	48,293	11.9
Local messengers and local delivery	4922	4,198	4,480	6.7
Warehousing and storage	493	12,291	12,832	4.4
General warehousing and storage	49311	6,592	7,004	6.2
Refrigerated warehousing and storage	49312	2,400	2,471	3.0
Farm product warehousing and storage	49313	642	647	0.7
Other warehousing and storage	49319	2,656	2,710	2.0

[1] Based on the North American Industry Classification System; 1997; see text Section 15, Business Enterprise.
Source: U.S. Census Bureau, 2000 Service Annual Survey, *Truck Transportation, Messenger Services and Warehousing.*
Internet site: <http://www.census.gov/econ/www/tasmenu.html>.

No. 1088. Truck Transportation—Summary: 1999 and 2000

[In millions of dollars (162,083 represents $162,083,000,000), except as indicated. For taxable and tax-exempt employer firms. Covers NAICS 484. Estimates have been adjusted to the results of the 1997 Economic Census. Based on the North American Industry Classification System; see text, Section 15, Business Enterprise. Minus sign (-) indicates decrease]

Item	1999	2000	Percent change, 1999-2000
Total operating revenue	**162,083**	**171,691**	**5.9**
Total motor carrier revenue	152,158	160,290	5.3
Local trucking [1]	49,164	51,860	5.5
Long-distance trucking [1]	102,994	108,430	5.3
Size of shipments:			
Less-than-truckload	44,526	48,157	8.2
Truckload.	107,632	112,132	4.2
Commodities handled:			
Agricultural and fish products.	12,232	12,064	-1.4
Grains, alcohol, and tobacco products.	5,441	5,717	5.1
Stone, nonmetallic minerals, and metallic ores	9,502	10,293	8.3
Coal and petroleum products.	5,530	5,915	7.0
Pharmaceutical and chemical products	8,794	9,330	6.1
Wood products, textiles, and leathers	14,804	16,126	8.9
Base metal and machinery	11,674	12,527	7.3
Electronic, motorized vehicles, and precision instruments	9,010	9,896	9.8
Used household and office goods.	9,878	10,297	4.2
New furniture and miscellaneous manufactured products	15,189	15,529	2.2
Other goods	50,104	52,596	5.0
Hazardous materials	9,535	9,969	4.6
Origin and destination of shipments:			
U.S. to U.S.	146,476	154,270	5.3
U.S. to Canada.	1,791	1,749	-2.4
U.S. to Mexico	1,218	1,284	5.5
Canada to U.S.	1,180	1,222	3.6
Mexico to U.S.	881	1,118	26.9
All other destinations	612	646	5.6
Inventory of revenue generating equipment (1,000):			
Trucks	204	211	3.4
Owned	168	178	6.0
Leased	37	33	-10.8
Truck-tractors.	900	938	4.2
Owned	763	793	3.9
Leased	137	145	5.8
Trailers	1,857	1,931	4.0
Owned	1,550	1,605	3.5
Leased	307	326	6.2
Highway miles traveled (mil.).			
Total.	83,055	86,576	4.2
By loaded or partially loaded vehicles	66,595	68,672	3.1
By empty vehicles	16,460	17,905	8.8

[1] Local trucking is the carrying of goods within a single metro area and its adjacent nonurban areas; long-distance trucking is the carrying of goods between metro areas.
Source: U.S. Census Bureau, 2000 Service Annual Survey, *Truck Transportation, Messenger Services and Warehousing.*
Internet site: <http://www.census.gov/econ/www/tasmenu.html>.

No. 1089. Railroads, Class I—Summary: 1990 to 2000

[As of Dec. 31, or calendar year data, except as noted (216 represents 216,000). Compiled from annual reports of class I railroads only except where noted. Minus sign (-) indicates deficit]

Item	Unit	1990	1993	1994	1995	1996	1997	1998	1999	2000
Class I line-hauling companies [1]	Number.	14	13	13	11	10	9	9	9	8
Employees [2]	1,000	216	193	190	188	182	178	178	178	168
Compensation	Mil. dol.	8,654	8,732	8,874	9,070	9,202	9,235	9,938	9,603	9,623
Average per hour	Dollars	15.83	17.90	18.50	19.0	20.1	20.3	21.3	21.0	21.5
Average per year	Dollars	39,987	45,354	46,714	48,188	50,611	51,882	55,764	54,082	57,157
Mileage:										
Railroad line owned [3]	1,000	146	140	138	137	136	133	132	122	121
Railroad track owned [4]	1,000	244	236	232	228	228	225	224	207	205
Equipment:										
Locomotives in service	Number.	18,835	18,161	18,505	18,812	19,269	19,684	20,261	20,256	20,028
Average horsepower	1,000 lb.	2,665	2,777	2,832	2,927	2,985	3,060	3,126	3,200	3,261
Cars in service:										
Freight train [5]	1,000	1,212	1,173	1,192	1,219	1,241	1,270	1316	1,369	1,381
Freight cars [6]	1,000	659	587	591	583	571	568	576	579	560
Income and expenses:										
Operating revenues	Mil. dol.	28,370	28,825	30,809	32,279	32,693	33,118	33,151	33,521	34,102
Operating expenses	Mil. dol.	24,652	24,517	25,511	27,897	26,331	27,291	27,916	28,011	29,040
Net revenue from operations	Mil. dol.	3,718	4,308	5,298	4,383	6,361	5,827	5,235	5,510	5,062
Income before fixed charges	Mil. dol.	4,627	4,990	6,184	5,016	7,055	6,168	5,803	6,001	5,361
Provision for taxes [7]	Mil. dol.	1,088	1,810	1,935	1,556	2,056	1,886	1,573	1,664	1,430
Ordinary income	Mil. dol.	1,961	2,258	3,315	2,439	3,885	3,156	2,807	2,976	2,501
Net income	Mil. dol.	1,977	2,240	3,298	2,324	3,885	3,156	2,807	2,971	2,500
Net railway operating income	Mil. dol.	2,648	2,517	3,392	2,858	4,338	3,984	3,698	4,047	3,924
Total taxes [8]	Mil. dol.	3,780	4,343	4,512	4,075	4,669	4,514	4,411	4,459	4,379
Indus. return on net investment	Percent.	8.1	7.1	9.4	7.0	9.4	7.6	7	6.9	6.5
Gross capital expenditures	Mil. dol.	3,591	4,504	5,035	5,720	6,550	6,737	7,357	6,193	5,290
Equipment	Mil. dol.	996	1,382	1,734	2,343	2,202	2,146	2,321	2,183	1,508
Roadway and structures	Mil. dol.	2,644	2,795	3,152	3,651	3,899	4,121	4,875	4,446	4,549
Other	Mil. dol.	-49	327	150	-275	449	471	161	-436	-767
Balance sheet:										
Total property investment	Mil. dol.	70,348	75,217	78,384	86,186	90,046	96,058	102,171	103,424	106,136
Accrued depreciation and amortization	Mil. dol.	22,222	23,892	24,200	23,439	23,932	21,862	23,338	23,177	23,989
Net investment	Mil. dol.	48,126	51,325	54,184	62,746	66,113	74,196	78,832	80,247	82,147
Shareholder's equity	Mil. dol.	23,662	24,658	27,389	31,419	32,255	34,996	32,976	30,478	32,401
Net working capital	Mil. dol.	-3,505	-3,295	-3,059	-2,634	-2,942	-3,434	-4,443	-4,834	-5,783
Cash dividends	Mil. dol.	2,074	1,054	1,398	1,518	3,937	995	1,521	2,084	819
AMTRAK passenger traffic:										
Passenger revenue	Mil. dol.	941.9	777.6	717.9	734.1	756.2	792.1	821.5	1067.8	1201.6
Revenue passengers carried	1,000	22,382	21,511	21,239	20,349	19,700	20,200	21,248	21,544	22,985
Revenue passenger miles	Million.	6,125	6,068	5,869	5,401	5,066	5,166	5,325	5,289	5,574
Averages:										
Revenue per passenger	Dollars	42.1	36.1	33.8	36.1	38.4	39.2	38.7	49.6	52.3
Revenue per passenger mile	Cents	15.4	12.8	12.2	13.6	14.9	15.3	15.4	20.2	21.6
Freight service										
Freight revenue	Mil. dol.	24,471	27,991	29,931	31,356	31,889	32,322	32,247	32,680	33,083
Per ton-mile	Cents	2.7	2.5	2.5	2.4	2.4	2.4	2.3	2.3	2.3
Per ton originated	Dollar	19.3	20.0	20.4	20.2	19.8	20.4	19.6	19.0	19.0
Revenue-tons originated	Million.	1,425	1,397	1,470	1,550	1,611	1,585	1,649	1,717	1,738
Revenue-tons carried	Million.	2,024	2,047	2,185	2,322	2,229	2,114	2,158	2,155	2,179
Tons carried one mile	Billion.	1,034	1,109	1,201	1,306	1,356	1,349	1,377	1,433	1,466
Average miles of road operated	1,000	133	124	123	125	127	122	120	121	121
Revenue ton-miles per mile of road	1,000	7,763	8,965	9,735	10,439	10,704	11,087	11,491	11,848	12,156
Revenue per ton-mile	Cents	3	3	2	2	2	2	2	2	2
Train miles	Million.	380	405	441	458	469	475	475	490	504
Net ton-miles per train-mile [9]	Number.	2,755	2,759	2,746	2,870	2,912	2,861	2,923	2,947	2,923
Net ton-miles per loaded car-mile [9]	Number.	69.1	71.6	72.2	73.6	75.0	74.0	73.2	73.8	73.1
Train-miles per train-hour	Miles	23.7	23.1	22.4	21.8	22.0	19.2	19	20	21
Haul per ton, U.S. as a system	Miles	726	794	817	843	842	851	835	835	843
Accidents/incidents: [10]										
Casualties—all railroads:										
Persons killed	Number.	1,297	1,279	1,226	1,146	1,039	1,063	1,008	932	937
Persons injured	Number.	25,143	19,121	16,812	14,440	12,558	11,767	11,459	11,700	11,643

[1] See text, this section, for definition of Class I. [2] Average midmonth count. [3] Represents the aggregate length of roadway of all line-haul railroads. Excludes yard tracks, sidings, and parallel lines. (Includes estimate for class II and III railroads.) [4] Includes multiple main tracks, yard tracks, and sidings owned by both line-haul and switching and terminal. (Includes estimate for class II and III railroads). [5] Includes cars owned by all railroads, private car companies, and shippers. [6] Class I railroads only. [7] Includes State income taxes. [8] Includes payroll, income, and other taxes. [9] Revenue and nonrevenue freight. [10] Source: Federal Railroad Admin., *Accident Bulletin*, annual. Includes highway grade crossing casualties.

Source: Except as noted, Association of American Railroads, Washington, DC, *Railroad Facts, Statistics of Railroads of Class I*, annual, and *Analysis of Class I Railroads*, annual.

Transportation 689

No. 1090. Railroads, Class I-Cars of Revenue Freight Loaded, 1970 to 2001, and by Commodity Group, 2000 and 2001

[In thousands (27,160 represents 27,160,000). Figures are 52-week totals]

Year	Carloads [1]	Commodity group	Carloads 2000 [3]	Carloads 2001, [3] prel.	Commodity group	Carloads 2000 [3]	Carloads 2001, [3] prel.
1970 ..	27,160	Coal	6,620	6,978	Metals and products	661	593
1980 ..	22,598	Metallic ores	301	228	Stone, clay, and glass products . .	500	483
1990 ..	16,177	Chemicals, allied products. . . .	1,485	1,405	Crushed stone, gravel, sand	841	879
1993 ..	15,911	Grain.	1,119	1,117	Nonmetallic minerals	419	360
1994 ..	16,763	Motor vehicles and equipment .	1,282	1,200	Waste and scrap materials	466	434
1995 ..	16,763	Pulp, paper, allied products . . .	469	427	Lumber, wood products	275	267
1996 [2]	16,521	Primary forest products.	246	213	Coke	200	193
1997 [2]	16,568	Food and kindred products . . .	428	444	Petroleum products	296	294
1998 [2]	16,914	Grain mill products.	451	468	All other carloads	298	296
1999 [2]	16,407						
2000 [3]	16,354						
2001 [3]	16,280						

[1] Beginning 1990 excludes intermodal.   [2] Excludes 2 Class I railroads.   [3] Excludes 3 Class I railroads.

Source: Association of American Railroads, Washington, DC, *Weekly Railroad Traffic*, annual.

No. 1091. Railroads, Class I Line-Haul-Revenue Freight Originated by Commodity Group: 1990 to 2000

[21,401 represents 21,401,000]

Commodity group	1990	1993	1994	1995	1996	1997	1998	1999	2000
Carloads (1,000) [1]	**21,401**	**21,683**	**23,179**	**23,726**	**24,159**	**25,016**	**25,705**	**27,096**	**27,763**
Farm products.	1,689	1,636	1,459	1,692	1,530	1,408	1,404	1,477	1,437
Metallic ores	508	443	440	463	443	327	311	295	322
Coal.	5,912	5,310	5,681	6,095	6,746	6,703	7,027	6,965	6,954
Nonmetallic minerals.	1,202	1,044	1,138	1,159	1,176	1,160	1,256	1,306	1,309
Food and kindred products	1,307	1,380	1,381	1,377	1,302	1,295	1,282	1,354	1,377
Lumber and wood products	780	710	771	719	682	669	645	673	648
Pulp, paper, allied products	611	620	651	628	589	582	547	612	633
Chemicals, allied products	1,531	1,606	1,695	1,642	1,639	1,674	1,653	1,814	1,820
Petroleum and coal products . . .	573	584	602	596	567	534	510	543	565
Stone, clay, and glass products. . .	539	487	512	516	491	485	475	538	541
Primary metal products	477	528	579	575	597	604	644	682	723
Fabricated metal products	31	37	37	32	29	29	27	27	30
Machinery, exc. electrical.	39	37	40	41	40	43	37	34	35
Transportation equipment	1,091	1,355	1,448	1,473	1,442	1,485	1,671	1,896	1,984
Waste and scrap materials.	439	558	604	623	605	608	581	624	619
Tons (mil.) [1]	**1,425**	**1,397**	**1,470**	**1,550**	**1,611**	**1,585**	**1,649**	**1,717**	**1,738**
Farm products.	147	147	131	154	142	126	129	139	136
Metallic ores	47	41	40	44	42	32	31	29	32
Coal.	579	534	574	627	705	705	749	751	758
Nonmetallic minerals.	109	96	106	110	113	109	120	125	126
Food and kindred products	81	88	88	91	87	86	87	92	94
Lumber and wood products	53	49	54	51	49	48	47	50	49
Pulp, paper, allied products	33	34	37	36	33	32	31	35	36
Chemicals, allied products	126	134	142	138	139	140	139	154	155
Petroleum and coal products . . .	40	41	43	43	42	39	38	40	42
Stone, clay, and glass products. . .	44	40	42	43	42	41	41	47	48
Primary metal products	38	43	47	47	49	50	53	56	60
Fabricated metal products	1	1	1	1	1	1	1	1	1
Machinery, exc. electrical.	1	1	1	1	1	1	1	1	1
Transportation equipment	23	29	30	30	29	31	36	40	42
Waste and scrap materials.	28	35	37	38	38	37	36	40	40
Gross revenue (mil. dol.) [1] .	**29,775**	**30,376**	**32,424**	**33,782**	**34,310**	**34,964**	**34,898**	**35,441**	**36,331**
Farm products.	2,422	2,528	2,407	3,020	2,807	2,645	2,529	2,720	2,673
Metallic ores	408	385	378	394	382	399	373	336	338
Coal.	6,954	6,481	7,021	7,356	7,706	7,698	7,997	7,739	7,794
Nonmetallic minerals.	885	818	862	875	895	899	920	955	969
Food and kindred products	2,188	2,336	2,427	2,464	2,378	2,385	2,378	2,400	2,424
Lumber and wood products	1,390	1,324	1,421	1,385	1,409	1,471	1,487	1,528	1,524
Pulp, paper, allied products	1,486	1,511	1,510	1,543	1,485	1,507	1,472	1,457	1,526
Chemicals, allied products	3,933	4,277	4,520	4,553	4,660	4,764	4,610	4,616	4,636
Petroleum and coal products . . .	918	929	967	997	1,013	1,028	991	980	1,010
Stone, clay, and glass products. . .	931	944	1,009	1,044	1,033	1,063	1,056	1,089	1,113
Primary metal products	979	1,021	1,114	1,199	1,254	1,294	1,304	1,289	1,371
Fabricated metal products	42	50	50	44	41	41	37	38	48
Machinery, exc. electrical.	67	59	65	69	70	73	64	55	61
Transportation equipment	3,100	3,021	3,257	3,269	3,390	3,462	3,339	3,582	3,843
Waste and scrap materials.	504	613	655	665	702	711	693	689	706

[1] Includes commodity groups and small packaged freight shipments, not shown separately.

Source: Association of American Railroads, Washington, DC, *Freight Commodity Statistics*, annual.

690   Transportation

No. 1092. Railroad Freight—Producer Price Indexes: 1990 to 2001

[Dec. 1984=100. Reflects prices for shipping a fixed set of commodities under specified and unchanging conditions]

Commodity	1990	1995	1996	1997	1998	1999	2000	2001, prel.
Railroad line-haul operating.	**107.5**	**111.7**	**111.5**	**112.1**	**113.4**	**113.0**	**114.5**	**116.9**
Coal.	104.2	107.3	106.7	107.0	108.7	107.3	108.7	110.8
Farm products	110.4	115.6	115.7	120.4	123.9	121.7	123.1	124.3
Food products	105.4	111.2	108.5	107.6	107.4	99.7	100.4	102.8
Metallic ores	106.5	101.9	103.5	103.4	104.4	103.8	105.9	107.1
Chemicals and allied products.	111.7	120.0	119.2	119.6	120.1	119.1	121.3	122.3
Nonmetallic minerals	111.7	119.5	119.2	120.6	121.5	121.7	122.1	122.8
Lumber and wood products	107.5	110.0	112.8	111.0	110.3	109.8	109.0	112.1
Transportation equipment.	107.5	112.8	114.0	113.2	113.4	113.3	112.6	121.6
Pulp, paper, and allied products	108.0	108.7	(NA)	111.2	113.7	115.5	119.0	122.5
Primary metal products	113.1	115.6	115.4	114.0	116.1	118.4	124.1	128.1
Stone, clay, glass, and concrete products	114.1	121.4	121.1	119.8	121.8	122.6	128.7	129.0
Petroleum and coal products	109.2	114.3	114.1	120.5	122.5	123.0	124.6	126.9

NA Not available.

Source: U.S. Bureau of Labor Statistics, *Producer Price Indexes,* monthly and annual.

No. 1093. Petroleum Pipeline Companies—Characteristics: 1980 to 2000

[173 represents 173,000. Covers pipeline companies operating in interstate commerce and subject to jurisdiction of Federal Energy Regulatory Commission]

Item	Unit	1980	1985	1990	1995	1996	1997	1998	1999	2000
Miles of pipeline, total	1,000.	173	171	168	177	169	160	157	154	152
Gathering lines	1,000.	36	35	32	35	32	31	21	20	18
Trunk lines	1,000.	136	136	136	142	137	130	136	134	134
Total deliveries	Mil. bbl.	10,600	10,745	11,378	12,862	12,635	12,481	12,914	13,317	14,450
Crude oil	Mil. bbl.	6,405	6,239	6,563	6,952	6,975	6,795	7,639	7,551	6,923
Products	Mil. bbl.	4,195	4,506	4,816	5,910	5,660	5,686	5,275	5,766	7,527
Total trunk line traffic	Bil. bbl-miles .	3,405	3,342	3,500	3,619	3,734	3,683	3,442	3,738	3,508
Crude oil	Bil. bbl-miles .	1,948	1,842	1,891	1,899	1,912	1,901	1,747	1,815	1,602
Products	Bil. bbl-miles .	1,458	1,500	1,609	1,720	1,822	1,782	1,696	1,923	1,906
Carrier property value	Mil. dol.	19,752	21,605	25,828	27,460	28,043	30,655	30,181	33,780	29,648
Operating revenues.	Mil. dol.	6,356	7,461	7,149	7,711	7,321	7,215	6,890	7,220	7,483
Net income	Mil. dol.	1,912	2,431	2,340	2,670	2,372	2,255	2,051	2,928	2,705

Source: PennWell Publishing Co., Houston, Texas, *Oil & Gas Journal,* annual (copyright).

No. 1094. U.S. Postal Service Rates for Letters and Post Cards: 1958 to 2002

[Domestic airmail letters discontinued in 1973 at 13 cents per ounce; superseded by express mail. Prior to February 3, 1991, international airmail rates were based on international zones which have been discontinued. Rates exclude Canada and Mexico]

Domestic mail date rate of change	Surface mail					International air mail date of rate change	Letters				
	Letters						First 1/2 ounce	Second 1/2 ounce	Each added 1/2 ounce	Post cards	Aero-gram-mes
	Each ounce	First ounce	Each added ounce	Post cards	Express mail [1]						
1958 (Aug. 1) . .	$0.04	(X)	(X)	$0.03	(X)	1961 (July 1) . .	(X)	(X)	(X)	$0.11	$0.11
1963 (Jan. 7). . .	$0.05	(X)	(X)	$0.04	(X)	1967 (May 1) . .	(X)	(X)	(X)	$0.13	$0.13
1968 (Jan. 7). . .	$0.06	(X)	(X)	$0.05	(X)	1971 (July 1) . .	(X)	(X)	(X)	$0.13	$0.13
1971 (May 16) . .	$0.08	(X)	(X)	$0.06	(X)	1974 (Mar. 2) . .	(X)	(X)	(X)	$0.18	$0.18
1974 (Mar. 2). . .	$0.10	(X)	(X)	$0.08	(X)	1976 (Jan. 3) . .	(X)	(X)	(X)	$0.21	$0.22
1975 (Sept. 14) .	(X)	$0.10	$0.09	$0.07	(X)	1981 (Jan. 1) . .	(X)	(X)	(X)	$0.28	$0.30
1975 (Dec. 31). .	[2](X)	[2]$0.13	[2]$0.11	[2]$0.09	(X)	1985 (Feb. 17) .	(X)	(X)	(X)	$0.33	$0.36
1978 (May 29). .	(X)	$0.15	$0.13	$0.10	(X)	1988 (Apr. 17) .	(X)	(X)	[3]$0.36	$0.36	$0.39
1981 (Mar. 22). .	(X)	$0.18	$0.17	$0.12	(X)	1991 (Feb. 3) . .	$0.50	$0.45	[3]$0.39	$0.40	$0.45
1981 (Nov. 1) . .	(X)	$0.20	$0.17	$0.13	$9.35	1995 (July 9) . .	$0.60	[3]$0.40	(X)	$0.40	$0.45
1985 (Feb.17) . .	(X)	$0.22	$0.17	$0.14	$10.75	1999 (Jan. 10) .	$0.60	[3]$0.40	(X)	$0.50	$0.50
1988 (Apr. 3). . .	(X)	$0.25	$0.20	$0.15	[4]$12.00	2001 (Jan. 7) . .	[3][5]$0.80	[3][5]$1.70	(X)	$0.70	$0.70
1991 (Feb. 3) . .	(X)	$0.29	$0.23	$0.19	[4]$13.95	2002 (June 30) .	[3]$0.80	[3]$1.70	(X)	$0.70	$0.70
1995 (Jan. 1). . .	(X)	$0.32	$0.23	$0.20	[4]$15.00						
1999 (Jan. 10). .	(X)	$0.33	$0.22	$0.20	[4]$15.75						
2001 (Jan. 7). . .	(X)	$0.34	$0.21	$0.20	[4]$16.00						
2002 (June 30) .	(X)	$0.37	$0.23	$0.23	[4]$17.85						

X Not applicable. [1] Post Office to addressee rates. Rates shown are for weights up to 2 pounds, all zones. Beginning Feb. 17, 1985, for weights between 2 and 5 lbs, $12.85 is charged. Prior to Nov. 1, 1981, rate varied by weight and distances. Over 5 pounds still varies by distance. [2] As of October 11, 1975, surface mail service upgraded to level of airmail. [3] Up to the limit of 64 ounces. [4] Over 8 ounces and up to 2 pounds. [5] The rate increments changed to 1 oz.

Source: U.S. Postal Service, "United States Domestic Postage Rate: Recent History," and unpublished data.

No. 1095. U.S. Postal Service—Summary: 1980 to 2001

[**106,311 represents 106,311,000,000.** For fiscal years; see text, Section 8, State and Local Government Finances and Employment. Includes Puerto Rico and all outlying areas. See text, this section]

Item	1980	1990	1995	1998	1999	2000	2001
Offices, stations, and branches	**39,486**	**40,067**	**39,149**	**38,159**	**38,169**	**38,060**	**38,123**
Number of post offices	30,326	28,959	28,392	27,952	27,893	27,876	27,876
Number of stations and branches	9,160	11,108	10,757	10,207	10,276	10,184	10,247
Pieces of mail handled (mil.)	**106,311**	**166,301**	**180,734**	**196,905**	**201,644**	**207,882**	**207,463**
Domestic [1]	105,348	165,503	179,933	195,961	200,613	206,782	206,381
First class [2]	60,276	89,270	96,296	100,434	101,937	103,526	103,656
Express Mail	17	59	57	66	69	71	70
Priority Mail	248	518	869	1,174	1,190	1,223	1,118
Periodicals (formerly 2d class)	10,220	10,680	10,194	10,317	10,274	10,365	10,077
Standard A (formerly 3d class)	30,381	63,725	71,112	82,508	85,662	90,057	89,938
Standard B (formerly 4th class)	633	663	936	1,023	1,043	1,128	1,093
Mailgram	39	14	5	4	4	4	3
U.S. Postal Service	(NA)	538	412	380	382	363	381
Free for the blind	28	35	52	53	53	47	45
International surface	450	166	106	96	103	79	60
International air	513	632	696	848	928	1,021	1,022
Employees, total (1,000)	**667**	**843**	**875**	**905**	**906**	**901**	**891**
Career	643	761	753	792	798	788	776
Headquarters	3	2	2	2	2	2	2
Headquarters support	(NA)	6	4	4	4	6	6
Inspection Service	5	4	4	4	4	4	4
Inspector General	(X)	(X)	(X)	(Z)	(Z)	1	1
Field Career	635	747	745	781	786	775	764
Postmasters	29	27	27	26	26	26	26
Supervisors/managers	36	43	35	37	39	39	39
Professional, administrative, and technical	5	10	11	12	11	10	10
Clerks	263	290	274	294	292	282	270
Mail handlers	37	51	57	62	62	61	60
City carriers	187	236	240	241	242	241	240
Motor vehicle operators	6	7	8	9	9	9	9
Rural carriers	33	42	46	52	55	57	60
Special delivery messengers	3	2	2	(X)	(X)	(X)	(X)
Building and equipment maintenance	27	33	38	41	42	42	43
Vehicle maintenance	5	5	5	6	6	6	6
Other [3]	4	1	2	2	2	2	1
Noncareer	25	83	122	113	108	114	115
Casuals	5	27	26	26	25	30	30
Transitional	(X)	(X)	32	17	12	13	14
Rural substitutes	20	43	50	56	57	58	58
Relief/Leave replacements	(X)	12	13	13	12	12	12
Nonbargaining temporary	(X)	(Z)	1	1	1	1	1
Compensation and employee benefits (mil. dol.)	16,541	34,214	41,931	45,596	47,333	49,532	51,351
Avg. salary per employee (dol.) [4]	24,799	37,570	45,001	50,117	48,111	50,103	54,481
Pieces of mail per employee, (1,000)	159	197	207	218	223	231	233
Total revenue (mil. dol.) [5]	**19,253**	**40,074**	**54,509**	**60,116**	**62,755**	**64,581**	**65,900**
Operating postal revenue	17,143	39,201	54,176	60,005	62,655	64,476	65,766
Mail revenue [6]	16,377	37,892	52,490	58,033	60,418	62,284	63,425
First class mail	10,146	24,023	31,955	33,861	34,933	35,516	35,876
Priority mail [7]	612	1,555	3,075	4,187	4,533	4,837	4,917
Express mail [8]	184	630	711	855	942	996	996
Mailgram	15	8	2	2	2	2	1
Periodicals (formerly 2d class)	863	1,509	1,972	2,072	2,115	2,171	2,205
Standard mail A (formerly 3d class)	2,412	8,082	11,792	13,702	14,436	15,193	15,705
Standard mail B (formerly 4th class)	805	919	1,525	1,754	1,829	1,912	1,994
International surface	154	222	205	184	194	180	178
International air	442	941	1,254	1,416	1,434	1,477	1,554
Service revenue [9]	765	1,310	1,687	1,972	2,237	2,191	2,341
Registry [9]	157	174	118	89	95	98	98
Certified [9]	120	310	560	386	377	385	495
Insurance [9]	55	47	52	73	92	109	123
Collection-on-delivery	21	26	21	18	20	22	15
Special delivery [10]	73	6	3	(X)	(X)	(X)	(X)
Money orders	95	155	196	210	228	235	225
Other [9]	244	592	737	1,197	1,425	1,342	1,385
Operating expenses (mil. dol.) [11]	19,413	40,490	50,730	57,786	60,642	62,992	65,640

NA Not available. X Not applicable. Z Fewer than 500. [1] Data for 1980 includes penalty and franked mail, not shown separately. [2] Items mailed at 1st class rates and weighing 11 ounces or less. [3] Includes discontinued operations, area offices, and nurses. [4] For career bargaining unit employees. Includes fringe benefits. [5] Net revenues after refunds of postage. Includes operating reimbursements, stamped envelope purchases, indemnity claims, and miscellaneous revenue and expenditure offsets. Shown in year which gave rise to the earnings. [6] For 1980, includes penalty and franked mail, not shown separately. Later years have that mail distributed into the appropriate class. [7] Provides 2 to 3 day delivery service. [8] Overnight delivery of packages weighing up to 70 pounds. [9] Beginning 1998, return receipt revenue broken out from registry, certified, and insurance and included in "other." [10] Special delivery discontinued June 8, 1997. [11] Shown in year in which obligation was incurred.

Source: U.S. Postal Service, *Annual Report of the Postmaster General* and *Comprehensive Statement on Postal Operations*, annual; and unpublished data.

This section presents statistics on the various information and communications media: publishing, including newspapers, periodicals, books, and software; motion pictures, sound recordings, broadcasting, and telecommunications; and information services, such as libraries. Statistics on computer use and Internet access are also included. Data on the usage, finances, and operations of the Postal Service previously shown in this section are now presented in Section 23, Transportation.

Information industry—The U.S. Census Bureau's *Service Annual Survey, Information Services Sector,* provides estimates of operating revenue of taxable firms and revenues and expenses of firms exempt from federal taxes for industries in the information sector of the economy. Similar estimates were previously issued in the *Annual Survey of Communications Services.* Data beginning 1998 are based on the North American Industry Classification System (NAICS) and the information sector is a newly created economic sector. It comprises establishments engaged in the following processes: (a) producing and distributing information and cultural products, (b) providing the means to transmit or distribute these products as well as data or communications, and (c) processing data. It includes establishments previously classified in the Standard Industrial Classification (SIC) in manufacturing (publishing); transportation, communications, and utilities (telecommunications and broadcasting); and services (software publishing, motion picture production, data processing, online information services, and libraries).

This new sector is comprised of industries which existed previously, were revised from previous industry definitions, or are completely new industries. Among those which existed previously are newspaper publishers, motion picture and video production, and online information services.

Revised industries include book publishers and libraries and archives. Newly created industries include database and directory publishers, record production, music publishers, sound recording studios, cable networks, wired telecommunications carriers, paging, and satellite telecommunications. The following URL contains detailed information about NAICS and provides a comparison of the SIC and NAICS <http://www.census.gov/epcd/www/naics.html>. See also the text in Section 15, Business Enterprise.

The 1997 Economic Census was the first economic census to cover the new information sector of the economy. The census, conducted every 5-years, for the years ending "2" and "7," provides information on the number of establishments, receipts, payroll, and paid employees for the United States and various geographic levels.

The Federal Communications Commission (FCC), established in 1934, regulates wire and radio communications. Only the largest carriers and holding companies file annual financial reports which are publically available. The FCC has jurisdiction over interstate and foreign communication services but not over intrastate or local services. The gross operating revenues of the telephone carriers reporting publically available data annually to the FCC, however, are estimated to cover about 90 percent of the revenues of all U.S. telephone companies. Data are not comparable with Census Bureau *Annual Survey* because of coverage and different accounting practices for those telephone companies which report to the FCC.

Reports filed by the broadcasting industry cover all radio and television stations operating in the United States. The private radio services represent the largest and most diverse group of licensees regulated by the FCC. These services provide voice, data communications, point-to-point, and point-to-multipoint radio communications for fixed and mobile communicators. Major users of these services are small businesses, the aviation industry, the maritime trades, the land transportation industry, the manufacturing industry, state and local public safety and governmental authorities, emergency medical service providers, amateur radio operators, and personal radio operations (CB and the General Mobile Radio Service). The FCC also licenses entities as private and common carriers. Private and common carriers provide fixed and land mobile communications service on a for-profit basis. Principal sources of wire, radio, and television data are the FCC's *Annual Report* and its annual *Statistics of Communications Common Carriers*.

Statistics on publishing are available from the Census Bureau, as well as from various private agencies. Editor & Publisher Co., New York, NY, presents annual data on the number and circulation of daily and Sunday newspapers in its *International Year Book*. Data on book production and prices are available from Information Today, Medford, NJ. The Book Industry Study Group, New York, NY, collects data on books sold and domestic consumer expenditures. Book purchasing data are from Ipsos, NPD, Inc., Rosemont, IL. Data on academic and public libraries are collected by the U.S. National Center for Education Statistics. Public library data are also gathered by Information Today, Medford, NJ, and the National Commission on Libraries and Information Science, Washington, DC.

Advertising—Data on advertising previously shown in this section are now presented in Section 27, Accommodation, Food Services, and Other Services.

Statistical reliability—For a discussion of statistical collection and estimation, sampling procedures, and measures of statistical reliability applicable to Census Bureau data, see Appendix III.

U.S. Census Bureau, Statistical Abstract of the United States: 2002

No. 1096. Information Industries—Establishments, Receipts, Payroll, and Employees by Kind of Business (NAICS Basis): 1997

[623,214 represents $623,214,000,000. For establishments with payroll. Based on the 1997 Economic Census; see Appendix III]

Industry	NAICS code [1]	Estab-lish-ments (number)	Receipts		Annual payroll		Paid employee for pay period including March 12 (1,000)
			Total (mil. dol.)	Per paid employee (dol.)	Total (mil. dol.)	Per paid employee (dol.)	
Information industries	51	114,475	623,214	203,255	129,482	42,229	3,066.2
Publishing industries	511	33,896	179,035	177,930	43,358	43,090	1,006.2
Newspaper, periodical, book, & database publishers [2]	5111	21,806	117,336	158,598	24,971	33,753	739.8
Newspaper publishers	51111	8,758	41,601	103,137	11,789	29,228	403.4
Periodical publishers.	51112	6,298	29,885	217,265	5,993	43,571	137.6
Book publishers	51113	2,684	22,648	251,933	3,643	40,522	89.9
Database & directory publishers	51114	1,458	12,258	284,312	1,655	38,384	43.1
Software publishers	5112	12,090	61,699	231,622	18,387	69,025	266.4
Motion picture & sound recording industries. .	512	22,204	55,926	202,643	9,392	34,032	276.0
Motion picture & video industries	5121	19,269	44,786	175,998	8,280	32,540	254.5
Sound recording industries	5122	2,935	11,140	517,797	1,112	51,671	21.5
Broadcasting & telecommunications	513	43,480	346,316	241,427	63,480	44,253	1,434.5
Radio & television broadcasting	5131	8,789	40,425	161,885	9,869	39,521	249.7
Radio broadcasting.	51311	6,894	10,648	84,060	3,604	28,455	126.7
Television broadcasting	51312	1,895	29,777	242,007	6,264	50,913	123.0
Cable networks & program distribution . . .	5132	4,679	45,390	260,334	6,151	35,280	174.4
Telecommunications [2].	5133	30,012	260,501	257,822	47,460	46,972	1,010.4
Wired telecommunications carriers	51331	20,815	208,791	256,051	39,565	48,520	815.4
Wireless telecommunications carriers (except satellite).	51332	6,386	37,889	258,977	5,839	39,913	146.3
Information services & data processing services. [2]	514	14,895	41,937	119,986	13,252	37,915	349.5
Information services [2].	5141	7,307	11,101	127,202	3,478	39,854	87.3
Libraries & archives	51412	2,298	861	39,055	373	16,928	22.0
Other information services	51419	4,482	8,837	158,544	2,639	47,351	55.7
Online information services.	514191	4,165	8,043	161,061	2,356	47,181	49.9
Data processing services	5142	7,588	30,837	117,585	9,774	37,269	262.3

[1] North American Industry Classification System, 1997; see text this section and, Section 15, Business Enterprise.
[2] Includes other industries, not shown separately.

Source: U.S. Census Bureau, *1997 Economic Census, Information,* Series EC97551A-US, issued October 1999.

No. 1097. Information Sector Services—Estimated Revenue: 1998 to 2000

[In millions of dollars (694,293 represents $694,293,000,000), except percent. For taxable and tax-exempt employer and nonemployer firms. Except as indicated, estimates adjusted to the results of the 1997 Economic Census]

Industry	NAICS Code [1]	1998	1999	2000	Percent change, 1999-00
Information industries	51	694,293	774,394	857,710	10.8
Publishing industries	511	202,876	220,631	235,215	6.6
Newspaper, periodical, book, database, and other publishers [2]	5111	130,332	139,145	146,590	5.4
Newspaper publishers	51111	45,691	48,603	51,710	6.4
Periodical publishers	51112	35,969	38,370	40,349	5.2
Book publishers.	51113	22,706	24,356	25,483	4.6
Database and directory publishers	51114	14,321	15,526	16,740	7.8
Software publishers.	5112	72,544	81,486	88,625	8.8
Motion picture and sound recording industries	512	60,592	65,051	68,198	4.8
Motion picture and video	5121	49,557	52,850	55,407	4.8
Sound recording [2].	5122	11,035	12,201	12,791	4.8
Broadcasting and telecommunications	513	382,429	426,755	475,369	11.4
Radio and television broadcasting	5131	44,089	47,593	53,017	11.4
Radio broadcasting	51311	11,763	13,208	15,019	13.7
Television broadcasting	51312	32,326	34,386	37,998	10.5
Cable networks and program distribution [2].	5132	52,469	60,059	68,143	13.5
Telecommunications [3]	5133	285,871	319,102	354,209	11.0
Wired telecommunications carriers	51331	228,148	247,828	269,903	8.9
Wireless telecommunications carriers (except satellite) [2]	51332	42,634	53,771	64,716	20.4
Information services and data processing services	514	48,396	61,958	78,929	27.4
Information services.	[3]5141	15,148	23,995	36,037	50.2
Libraries and archives.	51412	1,037	1,133	1,276	12.6
Other information services.	51419	12,474	20,967	32,691	55.9
Online information services	514191	11,444	18,795	27,697	47.4
Data processing services	5142	33,248	37,963	42,891	13.0

[1] Based in the North American Industry Classification System; see text this section and Section 15, Business Enterprise.
[2] Estimates not adjusted to the 1997 Economic Census. [3] Includes other industries, not shown separately.

Source: U.S. Bureau of the Census, *2000 Service Annual Survey, Information Sector Services.* See <http://www.census.gov/econ/www/servmenu.html> (released 29 November 2001).

Information and Communications 695

No. 1098. Information Industries—Establishments, Payroll, and Employees: 1999 and 2000

[For establishments with payroll (3,234.5 represents 3,234,500). Excludes most government employees, railroad employees and self-employed persons]

Industry	NAICS code [1]	Establishment		Paid employees [2] (1,000)		Annual payroll (mil. dol.)	
		1999	2000	1999	2000	1999	2000
Information industries	51	126,510	133,590	3,234.5	3,545.7	170,282	209,394
Publishing industries	511	32,377	32,545	1,004.7	1,080.7	54,516	75,348
Newspaper, periodical, book, & database publishers.	5111	21,245	21,946	700.0	749.2	26,821	31,258
Newspaper publishers.	51111	8,625	8,586	393.5	412.6	12,740	14,216
Periodical publishers.	51112	5,984	6,252	126.8	135.6	6,412	7,676
Book publishers	51113	2,646	2,661	81.4	87.2	3,767	4,310
Database & directory publishers	51114	970	1,370	31.7	46.2	1,455	2,418
Other publishers	51119	3,020	3,077	66.6	67.5	2,446	2,637
Greeting card publishers	511191	108	112	18.2	17.8	627	631
All other publishers	511199	2,912	2,965	48.5	49.7	1,820	2,006
Software publishers	5112	11,132	10,599	304.7	331.5	27,696	44,090
Motion picture & sound recording industries. .	512	23,102	22,899	293.4	304.2	10,531	11,736
Motion picture & video industries	5121	19,889	19,730	270.2	276.6	9,175	9,806
Motion picture & video production	51211	9,796	10,018	72.5	84.5	5,301	5,723
Motion picture & video distribution.	51212	706	678	27.7	13.9	1,058	1,119
Motion picture & video exhibition.	51213	6,197	5,884	137.1	144.0	1,134	1,130
Motion picture theaters (except drive-ins)	512131	5,885	5,593	135.2	142.3	1,111	1,107
Drive-in motion picture theaters	512132	312	291	1.9	1.7	22	23
Post production & other motion picture & video industries	51219	3,190	3,150	32.9	34.2	1,682	1,834
Teleproduction & other postproduction services.	512191	2,851	2,816	28.5	29.7	1,468	1,591
Other motion picture & video industries.	512199	339	334	4.4	4.5	214	243
Sound recording industries	5122	3,213	3,169	23.2	27.6	1,356	1,930
Record production	51221	274	276	1.0	1.1	53	55
Integrated record production/distribution .	51222	289	310	6.7	9.0	677	1,100
Music publishers	51223	701	670	5.2	5.1	252	283
Sound recording studios	51224	1,553	1,516	7.3	8.1	267	327
Other sound recording industries.	51229	396	397	3.0	4.3	108	166
Broadcasting & telecommunications	513	50,852	54,971	1,504.2	1,631.8	76,011	88,766
Radio & television broadcasting	5131	8,546	8,492	250.3	253.6	11,364	12,292
Radio broadcasting.	51311	6,537	6,442	123.5	121.5	4,541	4,841
Radio networks	513111	339	334	8.6	9.3	454	516
Radio stations	513112	6,198	6,108	114.8	112.1	4,087	4,325
Television broadcasting	51312	2,009	2,050	126.8	132.2	6,824	7,451
Cable networks & program distribution . . .	5132	5,364	5,270	182.1	212.7	8,060	10,084
Cable networks	51321	755	689	33.2	39.1	2,057	2,654
Cable & other program distribution	51322	4,609	4,581	148.9	173.6	6,002	7,430
Telecommunications.	5133	36,942	41,209	1,071.9	1,165.5	56,586	66,389
Wired telecommunications carriers	51331	23,461	26,223	815.7	870.2	44,614	49,010
Wireless telecommunications carriers (except satellite).	51332	9,263	10,424	186.0	202.5	8,102	11,027
Paging	513321	4,099	4,098	71.2	72.4	3,059	3,396
Cellular & other wireless telecommunications	513322	5,164	6,326	114.8	130.1	5,043	7,631
Telecommunications resellers	51333	2,208	2,458	43.6	54.6	2,167	3,342
Satellite telecommunications	51334	791	728	17.6	21.3	1,235	1,680
Other telecommunications	51339	1,219	1,379	8.9	16.9	469	1,330
Information services & data processing services.	514	20,179	23,175	432.2	529.0	29,224	33,544
Information services.	5141	11,265	14,139	149.2	232.5	16,473	19,023
News syndicates	51411	564	567	11.4	11.3	612	648
Libraries & archives	51412	2,590	2,754	31.0	33.8	566	679
Other information services	51419	8,111	10,818	106.8	187.4	15,295	17,696
Online information services.	514191	7,714	10,257	98.9	177.3	12,816	15,690
All other information services	514199	397	561	8.0	10.1	2,479	2,006
Data processing services	5142	8,914	9,036	283.0	296.6	12,751	14,521

[1] North American Industry Classification System code; see text this section and Section 15, Business Enterprise. [2] For employees on the payroll for the pay period including March 12.

Source: U.S. Census Bureau, "County Business Patterns"; 2000 data published 30 May 2002; <http://www.census.gov/epcd/cbp/view/cbpview.html>.

No. 1099. Gross Domestic Income in Information Technologies (IT) Industries: 1992 to 2000

[In millions of dollars (353,202 represents $353,202,000,000), except as noted]

Industry	NAICS [1] code	1992	1995	1998	1999	2000 est.
Total IT-producing industries.........	**(X)**	**353,202**	**470,912**	**646,930**	**718,151**	**796,56[?]**
Percent share of the economy........	(X)	5.6	6.4	7.3	7.7	8.0
Hardware............................	(X)	110,050	155,409	210,914	225,368	251,655
Computers and equipment, calc. machines..	([2])	24,102	31,036	39,211	38,583	46,223
Computers and equipment wholesale sales..	421430pt.,3pt.	39,743	51,114	75,084	81,016	87,676
Computer and equipment retail sales......	443120pt.	1,915	2,861	3,407	3,676	3,985
Electron tubes......................	334411	1,053	1,206	1,316	1,349	1,525
Printed circuit boards...................	334412	3,556	4,406	5,527	5,908	5,985
Semiconductors.....................	334413	18,308	40,836	57,055	64,072	72,293
Passive electronic components..........	334414,5,6,8pt.,9	13,494	15,310	12,072	12,881	14,503
Industrial instruments for measurement.....	334513	2,552	2,526	4,874	5,010	5,156
Instruments for measuring electricity.......	334514pt.,334515	3,493	3,981	8,383	8,659	9,212
Laboratory analytical instruments.........	334516	1,835	2,134	3,986	4,213	5,098
Software and services [3]................	(X)	75,490	111,350	185,609	213,986	245,656
Computer programming services.........	541511	18,624	26,119	47,796	55,013	62,715
Prepackaged software................	511210,334611	14,554	22,768	34,497	40,016	46,419
Computer integrated system design.......	541512	11,814	13,599	24,691	28,420	32,598
Computer processing, data preparation....	514210	12,554	21,844	28,062	32,300	37,048
Information retrieval services............	514191,8	2,879	3,910	8,977	10,333	11,852
Computer services management.........	541513	1,910	2,090	2,942	3,386	3,884
Computer rental and leasing............	532420	1,528	1,880	2,944	3,389	3,887
Computer maintenance and repair.......	811212	4,989	6,949	10,029	11,544	13,241
Computer related services, n.e.c. [4].......	541519	4,406	9,305	21,261	24,471	28,081
Communications hardware [3]............	(X)	23,970	30,775	46,709	51,431	61,464
Telephone equipment, exc. ext. modems...	334210,334418pt.	10,251	12,139	21,807	24,968	29,712
Radio & TV communications equipment....	334220, 334290	10,134	14,310	20,642	22,252	26,524
Communications services..............	(X)	143,692	173,378	203,698	227,366	237,792
Telephone and telegraph communications...	([5])	128,700	151,600	173,900	195,100	204,075
Cable and other pay TV services........	513210,20	14,992	21,778	29,798	32,266	33,718

X Not applicable.   [1] North American Industry Classification System; see text, Section 15, Business Enterprise.   [2] NAICS 334111,2,3,9, 334418pt., 333311pt.,3pt.   [3] Includes other industries, not shown separately.   [4]N.e.c. means not elsewhere classified.   [5] NAICS 513310,21,22,30,40,90.

No. 1100. Information Technologies (IT)—Employment and Wages: 1995 to 2000

[97,885 represents 97,885,000]

Industry	1987 SIC [1] code	Employment (1,000)			Annual wages per worker (dol.)		
		1995	1999	2000	1995	1999	2000
Total private................	**(X)**	**97,885**	**108,709**	**111,079**	**27,200**	**32,900**	**35,000**
Total IT-producing industries........	**(X)**	**4,004.2**	**5,256.0**	**5,596.6**	**46,900**	**65,600**	**73,800**
Hardware............................	(X)	1,475.3	1,707.2	1,748.7	46,300	65,900	77,200
Electronic computers.............	3571	190.0	195.7	198.0	59,600	98,000	124,300
Computers and equipment wholesalers..	5045pt	285.1	392.0	387.7	54,300	80,400	88,200
Computers and equipment retailers.....	5734pt	93.7	136.8	142.5	33,700	43,300	47,900
Computer storage devices & peripheral equipment.....................	3572,7	104.5	114.8	107.3	46,500	65,600	84,200
Computer terminals, office & accounting, machines.....................	3575,8,9	57.7	57.0	56.1	46,600	64,300	67,600
Electron tubes..................	3671	24.0	20.7	20.1	41,900	48,400	59,900
Semiconductors.................	3674	235.2	272.1	293.9	53,800	74,900	93,500
Printed circuit boards, electronic capacitors....................	3672,5-8	187.0	195.6	210.5	28,300	35,100	39,800
Electronic components, n.e.c. [2]........	3679	134.6	152.4	157.7	32,900	41,800	45,900
Industrial instruments for measurement..	3823	64.2	69.9	72.6	38,400	48,500	54,300
Instruments for measuring electricity....	3825	71.2	68.3	69.6	51,600	70,600	82,500
Analytical instruments............	3826	28.1	31.9	32.7	44,200	58,700	75,400
Software/services [3]................	(X)	1,109.6	1,903.2	2,122.8	50,700	72,200	80,900
Computer programming services.......	7371	245.3	454.7	518.7	52,700	69,000	81,600
Prepackaged software.............	7372	180.8	270.1	299.9	63,700	115,400	117,400
Computer integrated systems design....	7373	129.9	210.7	223.5	54,700	69,400	78,700
Computer processing & data preparation..	7374	223.1	276.1	284.8	39,700	49,200	52,300
Information retrieval services.........	7375	56.9	158.4	243.0	42,200	73,200	89,500
Computer maintenance & repair......	7378	48.6	58.2	53.7	37,800	42,700	44,800
Computer services management, rental & leasing......................	7376,7,9	205.3	447.2	471.3	51,800	68,400	74,900
Communications equipment [3].........	(X)	337.3	334.5	341.5	43,200	59,200	68,300
Telephone and telegraph equipment....	3661	111.7	120.9	126.7	49,900	70,700	80,500
Radio and TV communications equipment, n.e.c. [2]...............	3663,9	153.2	147.6	149.5	42,700	57,200	68,200
Communication services..............	(X)	1,081.9	1,311.1	1,383.6	45,100	57,300	60,100
Telephone communications.........	481	899.7	1,078.7	1,133.9	46,800	58,800	62,100
Telephone & telegraph communications..	482,489	26.7	33.2	33.9	48,500	71,200	76,500
Cable & other pay TV services........	4841	155.5	199.2	215.8	34,600	47,000	47,200

X Not applicable.   [1] 1987 Standard Industrial Classification code. See text, Section 12, Labor Force, Employment, and Earnings.   [2] N.e.c. means not elsewhere classified.   [3] Includes other industries, not shown separately.

Source of Tables 1099 and 1100: U.S. Department of Commerce, Economics and Statistics Administration, *The Digital Economy 2002,* March 2002. See Internet site <http://www.esa.doc.gov/508/esa/DIGITALECONOMY2002.htm>.

U.S. Census Bureau, Statistical Abstract of the United States: 2002

No. 1101. Communications Industry—Finances: 1997 to 2000

[In millions of dollars (180,814 represents $180,814,000,000). Covers publicly reporting media and communications companies with revenues of over $1 million in 13 media and communication industry segments. Minus sign (-) indicates loss]

Industry	Revenue				Operating income			
	1997	1998	1999	2000	1997	1998	1999	2000
Total	180,814	206,226	232,600	276,383	22,738	25,687	22,643	11,780
Broadcast television.	23,933	26,483	28,372	33,266	4,888	5,057	5,137	6,825
Television network companies	17,977	20,147	21,459	25,612	3,093	3,179	3,363	4,834
Television station broadcasters......	5,956	6,336	6,914	7,655	1,795	1,878	1,774	1,992
Cable and satellite television	36,276	38,332	44,146	57,053	3,388	3,561	1,931	1,617
Cable and satellite providers	27,027	27,508	32,315	43,047	2,049	1,638	200	-401
Radio broadcasting	3,101	3,518	4,681	7,001	672	804	1,107	1,516
Entertainment	27,362	36,243	39,510	42,443	1,769	3,561	4,095	3,455
Filmed entertainment	14,406	17,582	18,424	18,378	747	1,020	1,251	1,112
Recorded music.	8,788	9,544	10,672	11,433	534	604	627	1,078
Interactive entertainment and information	4,168	9,117	10,414	12,631	487	1,936	2,217	1,265
The Internet	4,596	5,717	9,067	14,756	-757	-1,485	-4,457	-13,080
Internet content providers	177	355	838	1,700	-353	-367	-1,165	-2,908
Internet search engines.	100	304	679	1,346	-64	-60	7	143
Internet service providers	4,318	5,059	7,551	11,710	-340	-1,059	-3,299	-10,315
Newspaper publishing	21,120	22,200	23,941	25,016	4,368	4,552	5,272	5,419
Consumer book publishing	3,584	3,375	3,359	3,408	273	129	230	365
Consumer magazine publishing	7,230	7,550	7,378	7,458	803	879	963	975
Business-to-business communications. ..	1,674	1,831	2,003	2,157	244	231	253	345
Professional, educational and training...	9,656	10,957	12,494	14,643	632	989	976	-1,316
Business information services	18,632	21,513	23,637	28,127	3,360	3,697	3,463	2,516
Financial information.	12,195	13,477	14,458	16,421	2,557	2,680	2,728	2,562
Marketing services.	20,715	25,341	30,631	37,405	2,243	2,838	2,708	2,036
Marketing services holding companies.	13,885	16,199	18,407	20,407	1,491	1,924	2,141	2,476
E-marketers	806	1,127	1,816	2,533	-114	-205	-573	-1,395
Miscellaneous publishing	2,934	3,166	3,380	3,649	856	875	966	1,108

Source: Veronis Suhler Stevenson, New York, NY, *Communications Industry Report,* annual (copyright).

No. 1102. Media Usage and Consumer Spending: 1996 to 2005

[Estimates of time spent were derived using rating data for television, cable and satellite and radio, survey research and consumer purchase data for books, home video, Internet, magazines, movies in theaters, newspapers, recorded music, and video games. Adults 18 and older except for radio, recorded music, movies in theaters, video games and Internet where estimates include persons 12 and older]

Item	1996	1997	1998	1999	2000	2001, proj.	2002, proj.	2003, proj.	2004, proj.	2005, proj.
HOURS PER PERSON PER YEAR										
Total	3,297	3,279	3,306	3,434	3,472	3,519	3,560	3,583	3,619	3,649
Television	1,559	1,544	1,551	1,588	1,633	1,643	1,655	1,649	1,673	1,679
Broadcast TV	985	923	884	867	862	867	865	847	852	847
Network stations [1]	809	750	710	706	801	806	804	787	791	786
Independent stations [1]......	176	173	174	162	60	61	61	61	61	62
Cable and satellite	573	620	667	720	771	776	789	802	821	832
Basic cable and satellite	485	519	566	617	635	639	653	666	669	678
Premium cable and satellite ..	88	101	101	103	136	137	137	136	152	154
Radio	973	964	936	967	961	981	985	990	995	998
Recorded music	292	270	283	289	263	250	247	246	244	243
Daily newspapers	162	159	156	154	151	149	148	146	145	144
Consumer magazines	112	112	111	110	107	106	104	103	101	100
Consumer books.	100	95	97	98	90	89	88	88	86	84
Home video [2]	54	53	55	55	59	62	67	70	74	81
Video games	25	36	43	61	70	79	90	97	103	115
Box office	12	13	13	13	12	12	12	12	12	12
Consumer Internet.	10	34	61	99	124	149	164	182	187	194
CONSUMER SPENDING PER PERSON PER YEAR (dol.)										
Total	496.87	523.49	564.43	613.05	640.86	678.06	714.28	748.97	771.55	795.50
Television	138.96	153.11	165.56	179.89	192.82	207.17	222.76	237.50	251.60	266.33
Broadcast TV	-	-	-	-	-	-	-	-	-	-
Cable and satellite	138.96	153.11	165.56	179.89	192.82	207.17	222.76	237.50	251.60	266.33
Radio	-	-	-	-	-	-	-	-	-	-
Recorded music	57.47	55.51	61.67	65.13	62.80	61.98	62.38	63.80	65.16	66.59
Daily newspapers	52.84	52.81	53.30	53.65	53.32	54.30	55.21	55.87	56.44	56.70
Consumer magazines	39.51	40.33	40.57	40.30	39.50	40.02	40.48	40.95	41.42	42.50
Consumer books.	72.68	72.26	75.62	80.43	77.64	78.90	81.24	83.97	83.66	83.37
Home video [2]	85.98	85.63	92.38	95.39	109.22	120.20	124.98	129.71	131.42	132.40
Video games	11.47	16.45	18.49	24.45	24.65	27.69	31.01	33.28	35.01	38.49
Box office	27.11	28.88	31.23	33.11	32.49	33.13	34.17	34.96	35.08	36.46
Consumer Internet.	13.24	20.87	27.63	41.77	50.63	57.37	64.90	71.90	75.15	76.38

- Represents zero.   [1] Independent stations included UPN, WB, and PAX affiliates through 1999. UPN, WB, and PAX affiliates moved to network stations in 2000.   [2] Playback of prerecorded tapes only.

Source: Veronis Suhler Stevenson, New York, NY, *Communications Industry Forecast,* annual (copyright).

U.S. Census Bureau, Statistical Abstract of the United States: 2002

No. 1103. Utilization of Selected Media: 1970 to 2000

[62.0 represents 62,000,000]

Item	Unit	1970	1980	1990	1994	1995	1996	1997	1998	1999	2000
Households with—											
Telephone service [1]	Percent	87.0	93.0	93.3	93.9	93.9	93.8	93.9	94.1	94.2	94.4
Radio [2]	Millions	62.0	78.6	94.4	98.0	98.0	98.0	98.0	(NA)	(NA)	(NA)
Percent of total households	Percent	98.6	99.0	99.0	99.0	99.0	99.0	99.0	99.0	99.0	99.0
Average number of sets	Number	5.1	5.5	5.6	5.6	5.6	5.6	5.6	5.6	5.6	5.6
Television [3]	Millions	59	76	92	94	95	96	97	98	99	101
Percent of total households	Percent	95.3	97.9	98.2	98.3	98.3	98.3	98.4	98.3	98.2	98.2
Television sets in homes	Millions	81	128	193	211	217	223	229	235	240	245
Average number of sets per home	Number	1.4	1.7	2.1	2.2	2.3	2.3	2.4	2.4	2.4	2.4
Color set households	Millions	21	63	90	93	94	95	97	98	99	101
Cable television [4]	Millions	4	15	52	59	60	63	64	66	67	69
Percent of TV households	Percent	6.7	19.9	56.4	62.4	63.4	65.3	66.5	67.2	67.5	68.0
VCRs [4]	Millions	(NA)	1	63	74	77	79	82	83	84	86
Percent of TV households	Percent	(NA)	1.1	68.6	79.0	81.0	82.2	84.2	84.6	84.6	85.1
Commercial radio stations: [2]											
AM	Number	4,323	4,589	4,987	4,913	4,909	4,857	4,762	4,793	4,783	4,685
FM	Number	2,196	3,282	4,392	5,109	5,296	5,419	5,542	5,662	5,766	5,892
Television stations: [5] Total	Number	862	1,011	1,442	1,512	1,532	1,533	1,564	1,589	1,615	1,663
Commercial	Number	677	734	1,092	1,145	1,161	1,174	1,195	1,221	1,243	1,288
VHF	Number	501	516	547	561	562	554	555	561	561	567
UHF	Number	176	218	545	584	599	620	640	660	682	721
Cable television:											
Systems [6]	Number	2,490	4,225	9,575	11,214	11,218	11,119	10,950	10,845	10,700	10,243
Households served [7]	Millions	4.5	17.7	54.9	60.5	63.0	64.6	65.9	67.0	68.5	69.3
Daily newspaper circulation [8]	Millions	62.1	62.2	62.3	59.3	58.2	57.0	56.7	56.2	56.0	55.8

NA Not available. [1] For occupied housing units. 1970 and 1980 as of April 1; all other years as of March. Source: U.S. Census Bureau, *1970* and *1980 Census of Housing*, Vol. 1; thereafter Federal Communications Commission, *Trends in Telephone Service*, annual. [2] 1980-1995 as of December 31, except as noted. Source: M Street Corp. as reported by Radio Advertising Bureau New York, NY, through 1990, *Radio Facts*, annual, (copyright); beginning 1994, *Radio Marketing Guide and Fact Book for Advertisers*, annual, (copyright). Number of stations on the air compiled from Federal Communications Commission reports. Beginning 1996, Federal Communications Commission, unpublished data as of Sept. 30. [3] 1970, as of September of prior year; all other years as of January of year shown. Excludes Alaska and Hawaii. Source: Television Bureau of Advertising, Inc., *Trends in Television*, annual (copyright). [4] As of February. Excludes Alaska and Hawaii. Source: See footnote 3. [5] Source: Beginning 1997, Federal Communications Commission, unpublished data. 1997 and 1998 as of December; beginning 1999, as of September. For prior years data, see footnote 3. [6] As of January 1. Source: Warren Communications News, Washington DC, *Television and Cable Factbook* (copyright). [7] Source: Nielsen Media Research, New York, NY, *Nielsen Station Index*, November estimates (copyright) [8] As of September 30. Source: Editor & Publisher, Co., New York, NY, *Editor & Publisher International Year Book*, annual (copyright).

Source: Compiled from sources mentioned in footnotes.

No. 1104. Multimedia Audiences—Summary: 2001

[In percent, except total (201,715 represents 201,715,000). As of spring. For persons 18 years old and over. Represents the percent of persons participating during the prior week, except as indicated. Based on sample and subject to sampling error; see source for details]

Item	Total population (1,000)	Television viewing	Television prime time viewing	Cable viewing [1]	Radio listening	Newspaper reading	Accessed Internet [2]
Total	201,715	93.6	82.5	73.1	84.4	79.3	52.1
18 to 24 years old	26,356	90.5	73.5	67.4	92.2	75.3	64.4
25 to 34 years old	38,298	92.3	80.3	72.0	90.0	75.6	63.3
35 to 44 years old	44,981	92.7	80.8	75.4	91.0	81.1	61.2
45 to 54 years old	36,085	94.3	85.4	76.1	88.7	82.5	60.2
55 to 64 years old	23,293	95.3	86.7	76.5	77.8	80.4	41.8
65 years old and over	32,702	96.9	88.6	70.1	62.4	80.3	14.7
Male	96,590	94.1	81.9	74.1	86.3	79.9	53.0
Female	105,125	93.1	83.1	72.1	82.6	78.9	51.2
White	168,905	93.5	82.6	74.4	84.3	79.5	53.8
Black	23,919	94.8	83.0	67.4	87.6	81.2	37.4
Asian	5,649	91.5	80.2	64.9	79.7	74.9	67.2
Other	3,241	93.5	76.9	59.0	71.9	64.6	45.0
Spanish speaking	23,046	94.0	82.4	61.0	86.8	66.5	41.5
Not high school graduate	34,691	92.0	80.1	60.0	74.3	61.3	16.3
High school graduate	66,416	95.1	84.9	74.1	82.5	78.8	36.8
Attended college	54,127	93.5	81.3	76.7	89.1	82.9	66.6
College graduate	46,481	93.5	82.8	77.6	89.2	86.5	76.5
Employed:							
Full time	112,508	92.8	81.2	75.6	91.7	81.9	64.3
Part time	19,483	92.9	79.9	72.2	87.9	79.7	64.0
Not employed	69,725	95.1	85.4	69.3	71.6	75.1	28.9
Household income:							
Less than $10,000	13,333	92.4	81.5	53.8	73.4	65.6	18.1
$10,000 to $19,999	23,325	93.9	83.5	58.4	72.4	69.1	18.5
$20,000 to $29,999	24,853	93.6	82.7	66.3	79.0	73.1	28.0
$30,000 to $34,999	11,984	93.6	81.5	68.0	82.8	77.4	34.8
$35,000 to $39,999	11,487	93.2	81.3	70.4	85.2	78.4	46.1
$40,000 to $49,999	21,354	94.2	82.8	75.6	87.0	78.4	53.5
$50,000 or more	95,378	93.6	82.6	81.6	89.8	86.0	73.9

[1] In the past 7 days. [2] In the last 30 days.
Source: Mediamark Research Inc., New York, NY, *Multimedia Audiences*, spring 2001 (copyright).

Information and Communications 699

No. 1105. Newspapers and Periodicals—Number by Type: 1980 to 2001

[Data refer to year of compilation of the directory cited as the source, i.e., generally to year preceding year shown. Data for 1995 and prior years include Canada and Mexico]

Type	1980	1985	1990	1995	1996	1997	1998	1999	2000	2001
Newspapers [1] .	9,620	9,134	11,471	12,246	10,466	10,042	10,504	10,530	10,696	10,739
Semiweekly.	537	517	579	705	612	558	557	560	558	573
Weekly.	7,159	6,811	8,420	9,011	7,655	7,191	7,267	7,471	7,594	7,622
Daily	1,744	1,701	1,788	1,710	1,537	1,582	1,461	1,647	1,661	1,656
Periodicals [1] . .	10,236	11,090	11,092	11,179	9,843	8,530	12,448	11,751	13,019	13,878
Weekly.	1,716	1,367	553	513	442	350	382	366	402	407
Semimonthly [2]	645	801	435	216	307	139	262	123	149	150
Monthly	3,985	4,088	4,239	4,067	3,554	3,067	3,378	3,204	3,572	3,636
Bimonthly	1,114	1,361	2,087	2,568	2,216	1,943	2,184	2,034	2,294	2,358
Quarterly	1,444	1,759	2,758	3,621	3,280	2,893	3,386	3,158	3,578	3,814

[1] Includes other items not shown separately.   [2] Includes fortnightly (every 2 weeks).

Source: Gale Group, Farmington Hills, MI, *Gale Directory of Publications and Broadcast Media,* annual (copyright).

No. 1106. Newspaper, Periodical, Database, and Directory Publishers—Estimated Revenue, Printing Expenses, and Inventories: 1999 and 2000

[In millions of dollars (48,414 represents $48,414,000,000), except percent. For taxable and tax-exempt employer firms. Estimates have not been adjusted to the results of the 1997 Economic Census. Based on the North American Industry Classification System; see text, this section, and Section 15, Business Enterprise. Minus sign (-) indicates decrease]

Item	Newspaper publishers (NAICS 51111)			Periodical publishers (NAICS 51112)			Database and directory publishers (NAICS 51114)		
	1999	2000	Percent change, 1999-00	1999	2000	Percent change, 1999-00	1999	2000	Percent change, 1999-00
Revenue	48,414	51,507	6.4	37,901	39,834	5.1	15,433	16,657	7.9
Single copy and subscription sales, total	8,818	9,149	3.8	14,912	14,397	-3.5	1,409	1,682	19.4
Print	8,760	9,085	3.7	13,943	13,458	-3.5	605	598	-1.2
Electronic.	(S)	(S)	(S)	969	939	-3.1	804	1,085	34.9
Advertising sales, total	35,513	38,222	7.6	17,820	19,415	9.0	10,679	11,158	4.5
Print	35,376	38,012	7.4	17,597	19,058	8.3	10,590	11,054	4.4
Electronic.	136	210	54.3	223	357	60.0	89	104	16.8
Contract printing	1,765	1,750	-0.9	1,140	1,062	-6.8	143	142	-0.7
Other revenue	2,318	2,386	2.9	4,028	4,960	23.1	3,202	3,674	14.7
Expenses: Purchased printing	3,427	3,352	-2.2	4,287	4,981	16.2	1,198	1,112	-7.2
Inventories at end of year.	737	786	6.7	1,258	1,340	6.6	408	398	-2.5
Finished goods and work-in-process	43	51	18.4	877	879	0.2	383	370	-3.5
Materials, supplies, fuel, etc	694	736	6.0	381	462	21.2	(S)	(S)	(S)

S Data do not meet publication standards.

Source: U.S. Census Bureau, *2000 Service Annual Survey, Information Sector Services.* See <http://www.census.gov/econ/www/servmenu.html> (released 29 November 2001).

No. 1107. Daily and Sunday Newspapers—Number and Circulation: 1970 to 2001

[Number of newspapers as of February 1 the following year. Circulation figures as of September 30 of year shown (62.1 represents 62,100,000). For English language newspapers only]

Type	1970	1975	1980	1985	1990	1995	1996	1997	1998	1999	2000	2001
NUMBER												
Daily: Total [1]	1,748	1,756	1,745	1,676	1,611	1,533	1,520	1,509	1,489	1,483	1,480	1,468
Morning	334	339	387	482	559	656	686	705	721	736	766	776
Evening	1,429	1,436	1,388	1,220	1,084	891	846	816	781	760	727	704
Sunday	586	639	736	798	863	888	890	903	898	905	917	913
CIRCULATION (mil.)												
Daily: Total [1]	62.1	60.7	62.2	62.8	62.3	58.2	57.0	56.7	56.2	56.0	55.8	55.6
Morning	25.9	25.5	29.4	36.4	41.3	44.3	44.8	45.4	45.6	46.0	46.8	46.8
Evening	36.2	35.2	32.8	26.4	21.0	13.9	12.2	11.3	10.5	10.0	9.0	8.8
Sunday	49.2	51.1	54.7	58.8	62.6	61.5	60.8	60.5	60.1	59.9	59.4	59.1
PER CAPITA CIRCULATION [2]												
Daily: Total [1]	0.30	0.28	0.27	0.26	0.25	0.22	0.21	0.21	0.20	0.20	0.20	0.20
Morning	0.13	0.12	0.13	0.15	0.17	0.17	0.17	0.17	0.17	0.16	0.17	0.16
Evening	0.18	0.16	0.14	0.11	0.08	0.05	0.05	0.04	0.04	0.04	0.03	0.03
Sunday	0.24	0.24	0.24	0.25	0.25	0.23	0.23	0.22	0.22	0.21	0.21	0.21

[1] All-day newspapers are counted in both morning and evening columns, but only once in total. Circulation is divided equally between morning and evening.   [2] Based on U.S. Census Bureau estimated resident population as of July 1, except 2000, enumerated resident population as of April 1.

Source: Editor & Publisher Co., New York, NY, *Editor & Publisher International Year Book,* annual (copyright).

No. 1108. Daily Newspapers—Number and Circulation by Size of City: 1980 to 2001

[Number of newspapers as of February 1 the following year. Circulation as of September 30 (29,413 represents 29,413,000). For English language newspapers only. See Table 31 for number of cities by population size. All-day newspapers are counted in both morning and evening columns; circulation is divided equally between morning and evening]

Type of daily and population-size class	Number					Net paid circulation (1,000)				
	1980	1990	1995	2000	2001	1980	1990	1995	2000	2001
Morning dailies, total ..	**387**	**559**	**656**	**766**	**776**	**29,413**	**41,311**	**44,310**	**46,772**	**46,821**
In cities of—										
1,000,001 or more	20	18	25	26	26	8,795	6,508	10,173	10,820	10,541
500,001 to 1,000,000.	27	22	22	25	31	5,705	4,804	5,587	5,412	6,568
100,001 to 500,000.	99	138	153	163	162	8,996	20,051	17,214	17,469	17,149
50,001 to 100,000.	75	100	138	162	159	2,973	4,373	5,602	5,887	5,718
25,001 to 50,000	64	102	115	141	148	1,701	3,209	3,150	3,899	3,740
Less than 25,000	102	179	203	249	250	1,243	2,365	2,584	3,285	3,104
Evening dailies, total ..	**1,388**	**1,084**	**891**	**727**	**704**	**32,788**	**21,017**	**13,883**	**9,000**	**8,757**
In cities of—										
1,000,001 or more	11	7	3	1	1	2,984	1,423	390	1	1
500,001 to 1,000,000. . . . ,	23	12	7	3	6	4,101	1,350	1,017	519	851
100,001 to 500,000.	123	71	45	32	28	8,178	4,687	2,529	1,603	1,322
50,001 to 100,000.	156	94	72	54	51	4,896	2,941	2,029	1,332	1,346
25,001 to 50,000	246	204	158	124	123	5,106	4,278	2,819	1,898	1,801
Less than 25,000	829	696	606	513	495	7,523	6,338	5,099	3,648	3,435

Source: Editor & Publisher Co., New York, NY, *Editor & Publisher International Year Book,* annual (copyright).

No. 1109. Daily and Sunday Newspapers—Number and Circulation, 1991 to 2000 and by State: 2001

[Number of newspapers as of February 1 the following year. Circulation as of September 30 (60,687 represents 60,687,000). For English language newspapers only. California, New York, Massachusetts, and Virginia Sunday newspapers include national circulation]

State	Daily			Sunday		State	Daily			Sunday	
	Circulation [1]				Net paid circu-lation (1,000)		Circulation [1]				Net paid circu-lation (1,000)
	Num-ber	Net paid (1,000)	Per capita [2]	Num-ber			Num-ber	Net paid (1,000)	Per capita [2]	Num-ber	
Total, 1991 ..	1,586	60,687	0.24	875	62,068	Maine.	7	230	0.18	4	191
Total, 1992 ..	1,570	60,164	0.23	891	62,160	Maryland	14	642	0.12	8	883
Total, 1993 ..	1,556	59,812	0.23	884	62,566	Massachusetts. .	32	1,626	0.25	16	1,564
Total, 1994 ..	1,548	59,305	0.23	886	62,294	Michigan.	49	1,691	0.17	26	1,938
Total, 1995 ..	1,533	58,193	0.22	888	61,529	Minnesota.	25	835	0.17	14	1,129
Total, 1996 ..	1,520	56,983	0.21	890	60,798	Mississippi	23	376	0.13	18	423
Total, 1997 ..	1,509	56,728	0.21	903	60,484	Missouri	43	945	0.17	23	1,196
Total, 1998 ..	1,489	56,182	0.20	898	60,066	Montana.	11	183	0.20	7	188
Total, 1999 ..	1,483	55,979	0.20	905	59,894	Nebraska	17	416	0.24	6	392
Total, 2000 ..	1,480	55,773	0.20	917	59,421	Nevada	8	301	0.14	4	323
						New Hampshire .	11	221	0.18	8	232
Total, 2001 ..	**1,468**	**55,578**	**0.20**	**913**	**59,090**	New Jersey. . . .	18	1,344	0.16	15	1,647
Alabama.	24	644	0.14	20	723	New Mexico . . .	18	282	0.15	13	282
Alaska	7	109	0.17	5	125	New York	58	6,432	0.34	37	5,475
Arizona.	16	782	0.15	11	888	North Carolina. .	47	1,321	0.16	39	1,555
Arkansas	28	474	0.18	16	536	North Dakota. . .	10	163	0.26	7	167
California	92	6,019	0.17	60	6,643	Ohio	84	2,369	0.21	42	2,650
Colorado.	29	1,045	0.24	15	1,204	Oklahoma.	43	619	0.18	36	769
Connecticut. . . .	17	715	0.21	13	794	Oregon.	19	683	0.20	11	731
Delaware	2	140	0.18	2	160	Pennsylvania. . .	83	2,706	0.22	41	3,065
District of						Rhode Island. . .	6	221	0.21	3	265
Columbia	2	863	1.51	2	1,108	South Carolina. .	15	618	0.15	14	723
Florida	42	3,028	0.18	38	3,820	South Dakota . .	11	156	0.21	4	135
Georgia	33	1,018	0.12	28	1,309	Tennessee	25	843	0.15	17	1,024
Hawaii	6	276	0.23	6	311	Texas.	87	2,964	0.14	83	3,819
Idaho	12	209	0.16	8	230	Utah	6	329	0.14	6	364
Illinois	66	2,345	0.19	30	2,476	Vermont	8	121	0.20	3	95
Indiana.	68	1,295	0.21	23	1,259	Virginia.	26	3,168	0.44	17	1,159
Iowa	37	611	0.21	12	624	Washington. . . .	24	1,103	0.18	18	1,252
Kansas.	44	428	0.16	14	374	West Virginia. . .	22	358	0.20	12	363
Kentucky	23	599	0.15	14	631	Wisconsin.	35	918	0.17	18	1,019
Louisiana	26	702	0.16	21	785	Wyoming	9	87	0.18	5	71

[1] Circulation figures based on the principal community served by a newspaper which is not necessarily the same location as the publisher's office.   [2] Per capita based on estimated resident population as of July 1, except 2000, enumerated resident population as of April 1.

Source: Editor & Publisher Co., New York, NY, *Editor & Publisher International Year Book,* annual (copyright).

Information and Communications 701

No. 1110. Periodicals—Average Retail Prices: 1998 to 2002

[In dollars]

Subject	1998	1999	2000	2001	2002
Agriculture	442.00	467.35	507.42	532.98	572.89
Anthropology	267.23	290.67	306.35	306.43	332.10
Art and architecture	103.29	104.57	107.72	111.03	113.66
Astronomy	1,033.38	1,074.54	1,061.96	1,120.34	1,249.42
Biology	831.23	909.11	973.96	1,030.06	1,097.01
Botany	660.69	701.17	752.46	781.78	819.61
Business and economics	367.82	409.72	461.32	503.02	552.67
Chemistry	1,543.67	1,651.51	1,790.18	1,920.53	2,143.22
Education	185.65	204.54	226.21	249.81	272.79
Engineering and technology	891.59	971.49	1,060.98	1,155.88	1,249.96
Food science	542.13	620.80	675.65	731.26	763.48
General science	638.23	702.96	776.77	855.06	929.85
General works	82.17	85.00	87.37	88.35	94.86
Geography	529.88	558.19	625.70	672.33	745.23
Geology	746.07	784.54	846.77	903.81	977.05
Health sciences	569.76	624.06	677.43	729.83	784.81
History	97.66	105.98	112.34	119.26	126.35
Language and literature	88.17	94.25	97.91	103.06	110.51
Law	129.33	137.74	145.67	156.65	172.10
Library and information science	217.90	235.80	248.55	266.13	283.66
Math and computer science	835.68	893.19	963.78	1,031.53	1,107.20
Military and naval science	258.67	282.33	308.11	360.56	354.20
Music	72.97	80.23	82.03	84.32	91.63
Philosophy and religion	114.85	123.53	130.53	136.37	146.60
Physics	1,653.07	1,755.92	1,900.36	2,038.03	2,218.82
Political science	181.76	206.16	226.37	254.73	284.93
Psychology	241.08	274.05	302.59	330.07	361.93
Recreation	97.12	108.14	116.07	128.90	148.35
Sociology	225.08	250.62	275.25	304.14	333.29
Technology	790.65	865.48	941.24	1,023.84	1,111.20
Zoology	670.22	739.25	807.88	861.88	933.80

Source: Library Journal, New York, NY, *Library Journal*, April 15, 2002. (Copyright 2002, used with permission of Library Journal, a publication of Reed Business Information, a division of Reed Elsevier).

No. 1111. Quantity of Books Sold and Value of U.S. Domestic Consumer Expenditures: 1995 to 2001

[**2,346 represents 2,346,000,000.** Includes all titles released by publishers in the United States and imports which appear under the imprints of American publishers. Multivolume sets, such as encyclopedias, are counted as one unit]

Type of publication and distribution area	Net publishers shipments [1] (mil.)					Domestic consumer expenditures (mil. dol.)				
	1995	1998	1999	2000	2001	1995	1998	1999	2000	2001
Total [1]	2,346	2,402	2,505	2,493	2,410	25,154	28,786	30,027	32,050	31,880
Hardback	879	895	929	926	(NA)	15,011	17,016	18,438	18,973	(NA)
Paperback	1,467	1,507	1,576	1,567	(NA)	10,143	11,770	11,589	13,077	(NA)
Trade	842	860	935	904	846	9,340	10,350	10,788	11,514	11,052
Adult	485	497	529	457	442	7,060	7,791	8,142	8,691	8,448
Juvenile	357	364	406	447	403	2,280	2,558	2,646	2,824	2,603
Mass market paperbacks-rack sized	530	484	485	471	455	2,322	2,348	2,457	2,622	2,602
Bookclubs	126	142	146	143	144	949	1,176	1,233	1,316	1,369
Mail order publications	96	78	66	65	52	578	487	553	590	551
Religious	157	171	174	171	174	1,792	2,037	2,150	2,295	2,413
Professional	165	170	178	187	168	4,153	4,751	4,959	5,293	4,870
University press	28	30	32	31	27	394	455	474	506	497
Elhi text	247	302	305	334	349	2,384	3,216	3,294	3,516	3,798
College text	155	176	184	186	194	2,708	3,365	3,483	3,718	4,020
Subscription reference	1	1	1	1	1	532	603	636	679	706
Domestic distribution	2,196	2,254	2,348	2,332	2,262	25,154	28,786	30,027	32,050	31,880
General retailers	1,145	1,143	1,199	1,181	1,141	11,888	13,102	13,813	14,557	14,389
College stores	284	291	299	301	294	4,311	5,122	5,279	5,699	5,718
Libraries and institutions [2]	97	102	105	106	102	2,111	2,394	2,496	2,664	2,640
Schools [2]	273	326	326	343	341	2,896	3,780	3,764	4,234	4,351
Direct to consumers	289	293	312	304	286	3,544	3,989	4,239	4,448	4,344
Other	108	99	108	104	99	404	399	435	449	438
Exports	149	149	157	155	149	(X)	(X)	(X)	(X)	(X)

NA Not available.   X Not applicable.   [1] Net, after returns.   [2] Elhi libraries included in schools.

Source: Book Industry Study Group, Inc., New York, NY, *Book Industry Trends, 2002*, annual (copyright).

No. 1112. American Book Title Production: 1999 and 2000

[Data compiled from R.R. Bowker's Books in Print database. Includes the output of small presses and self publishers]

Subject	Total		Hardcover		Mass market [1]		Trade [2]	
	1999	2000, prel.	1999	2000, prel.	1999	2000, prel.	1999	2000, prel.
Total.	119,357	96,080	53,109	44,695	8,281	6,114	57,967	45,271
Agriculture	1,037	881	504	457	10	8	523	416
Art.	4,795	3,896	2,293	2,010	22	15	2,480	1,871
Biography.	4,051	2,898	2,227	1,569	111	59	1,713	1,270
Business	3,789	2,761	1,408	1,305	14	20	2,367	1,436
Education	3,408	2,639	1,175	877	44	14	2,189	1,748
Fiction	12,372	11,808	3,992	3,532	4,217	3,468	4,163	4,808
General works.	1,456	878	732	396	42	14	682	468
History	7,486	6,948	3,841	3,906	35	32	3,610	3,010
Home economics	2,564	1,982	1,160	872	55	33	1,349	1,077
Juvenile	9,438	6,708	5,469	4,007	2,653	1,843	1,316	858
Language	2,565	2,132	1,035	1,029	48	25	1,482	1,078
Law.	3,078	2,299	1,406	1,129	6	2	1,666	1,168
Literature	3,646	2,803	2,068	1,501	137	43	1,441	1,259
Medicine.	6,153	4,817	2,758	2,190	114	88	3,281	2,539
Music.	1,593	987	550	446	25	11	1,018	530
Philosophy, psychology	5,861	4,317	2,415	1,885	216	83	3,230	2,349
Poetry and drama	2,455	1,860	936	550	50	35	1,469	1,275
Religion	6,044	5,086	2,446	2,191	136	85	3,462	2,810
Science	7,862	7,140	4,658	4,426	89	62	3,115	2,652
Sociology, economics	14,579	12,039	6,855	6,209	119	75	7,605	5,755
Sports, recreation.	3,252	2,695	1,143	1,041	95	66	2,014	1,588
Technology	8,896	6,449	3,436	2,698	24	13	5,436	3,738
Travel	2,977	2,057	602	469	19	20	2,356	1,568

[1] "Pocket-sized" books sold primarily through magazine and news outlets, supermarkets, variety stores, etc.   [2] All paperbound books, except mass market.

Source: Information Today, Inc., Medford, NJ, *The Bowker Annual Library and Book Trade Almanac, 2001.* (Copyright 2001 by Information Today, Inc.)

No. 1113. Average Per Volume Book Prices: 1999 and 2000

[In dollars. Data compiled from R.R. Bowker's Books in Print database. Includes the output of small presses and self publishers]

Subject	Hardcover		Mass market [1]		Trade [2]	
	1999	2000	1999	2000	1999	2000
Total.	62.32	60.80	5.64	5.76	32.93	29.48
Agriculture	55.40	67.24	6.42	7.86	39.26	45.68
Art.	59.31	48.35	6.95	7.84	26.54	25.83
Biography.	45.20	45.41	6.37	6.18	19.99	18.91
Business	131.50	134.26	7.61	8.16	48.85	50.82
Education	59.75	57.75	7.39	7.25	29.18	27.60
Fiction	27.95	25.33	5.58	5.81	16.09	15.75
General works.	153.98	137.29	7.01	6.95	40.76	41.44
History	52.25	51.46	6.65	6.79	26.05	26.49
Home economics	38.52	40.16	6.99	7.04	19.32	18.89
Juvenile	23.06	19.91	5.12	5.18	19.47	17.52
Language	55.92	56.01	7.13	6.94	30.17	26.58
Law.	100.13	100.35	6.66	6.99	49.52	49.21
Literature	73.92	56.84	6.49	7.26	20.52	20.47
Medicine.	90.03	82.25	6.32	5.62	44.41	34.36
Music.	55.55	50.63	6.64	8.65	21.71	23.94
Philosophy, psychology	54.01	50.53	7.20	7.53	23.49	20.97
Poetry and drama	46.11	36.98	6.26	5.61	16.04	16.19
Religion	44.68	41.89	7.48	8.20	20.40	18.38
Science	94.55	85.77	6.34	5.80	49.33	38.62
Sociology, economics	62.24	64.67	6.53	6.87	39.20	38.30
Sports, recreation.	38.45	37.75	6.73	6.31	22.62	20.99
Technology	100.53	93.86	6.89	6.60	59.82	51.40
Travel	40.31	40.17	8.35	8.29	21.56	19.24

[1] "Pocket-sized" books sold primarily through magazine and news outlets, supermarkets, variety stores, etc.   [2] All paperbound books, except mass market.

Source: Information Today, Inc., Medford, NJ, *The Bowker Annual Library and Book Trade Almanac, 2001.* (Copyright 2001 by Information Today, Inc.)

Information and Communications   703

No. 1114. Book Publishers—Estimated Revenue, Printing Expenses, and Inventories: 1998 to 2000

[In millions of dollars (22,480 represents $22,480,000,000), except percent. For taxable and tax-exempt employer firms. For NAICS 51113. Estimates have not been adjusted to the results of the 1997 Economic Census. Based on the North American Industry Classification System; see text, this section, and Section 15, Business Enterprise. Minus sign (-) indicates decrease]

Item	1998	1999	2000	Percent change, 1999-00
Revenue, total	**22,480**	**24,129**	**25,236**	**4.6**
Revenue from the sale of printed material.	18,622	19,840	20,975	5.7
Revenue from the sale of electronic or nonprinted material (except audio), total.	2,168	2,434	2,305	-5.3
Multimedia.	748	811	805	-0.7
Online.	1,420	1,623	1,500	-7.6
Revenue from the sale of audio books	191	198	176	-11.4
Revenue from the sale of publication rights	235	247	289	17.0
Contract printing.	428	361	264	-26.8
Other revenues	836	1,048	1,227	17.0
Expenses: Purchased printing	3,908	4,104	4,229	3.0
Inventories at end of year	2,737	2,984	3,463	16.1
Finished goods and work-in-process.	2,510	2,723	3,200	17.5
Materials, supplies, fuel, etc..	227	261	263	1.1

Source: U.S. Census Bureau, *2000 Service Annual Survey, Information Sector Services.* See <http://www.census.gov/econ/www/servmenu.html> (released 29 November 2001).

No. 1115. Book Purchasing for Adults: 1991 and 2001

[In percent. Excludes all children's books and books purchased for children under age 14. Based on an ongoing survey of 12,000 households conducted over 12 months ending in December of year shown. For details, see source]

Characteristic	Total		Mass market [1]		Trade [2]		Hardcover		Audio [3] 2001
	1991	2001	1991	2001	1991	2001	1991	2001	
Total	**100.0**	**100.0**	**100.0**	**100.0**	**100.0**	**100.0**	**100.0**	**100.0**	**100.0**
Age of purchaser:									
Under 25 years old	4.4	4.6	3.8	3.1	5.2	6.7	4.4	4.0	5.1
25 to 34 years old	18.7	12.5	14.0	10.3	25.5	14.9	19.6	12.7	7.4
35 to 44 years old	23.7	20.2	22.7	15.6	25.1	23.2	23.7	21.9	22.9
45 to 54 years old	22.4	24.4	26.0	22.6	18.5	24.9	20.6	25.1	32.3
55 to 64 years old	15.6	19.5	15.8	22.4	13.9	16.9	17.2	19.4	17.2
65 years old and over	15.2	18.8	17.7	26.0	11.8	13.4	14.5	16.9	15.1
Education of household head:									
Not a high school graduate.	8.2	6.5	11.6	8.3	5.0	5.2	5.9	5.6	13.4
High school graduate	53.5	54.4	61.2	57.8	44.4	51.0	49.9	54.4	56.0
College graduate.	19.0	21.7	15.1	20.1	23.9	22.6	20.3	22.5	17.9
Post college	19.3	17.4	12.1	13.8	26.7	21.2	23.9	17.5	12.7
Occupation of household head:									
Professional/managerial	39.2	38.0	32.0	30.0	47.9	45.0	42.1	39.8	25.1
Sales/service	7.7	9.3	6.6	6.8	8.2	10.7	9.2	10.6	9.7
Blue collar	23.2	18.7	27.0	19.8	19.6	17.0	20.6	18.7	27.6
Retired/unemployed	25.9	32.2	30.4	42.3	20.2	25.0	24.3	28.9	32.6
Other	4.0	1.8	4.0	1.1	4.1	2.3	3.8	2.0	5.0
Household income:									
Under $30,000	41.8	25.8	46.1	31.0	36.8	23.1	39.4	22.8	28.4
$30,000 to 49,999	30.6	21.1	30.2	21.9	31.3	20.1	30.6	21.2	24.5
$50,000 to 74,999	20.1	19.6	18.6	19.1	22.0	19.4	20.6	20.2	21.0
$75,000 and over	7.5	33.5	5.1	28.0	9.9	37.4	9.4	35.8	26.1
Household size:									
One member	20.8	16	17.7	17.7	24.1	15	22.8	15.4	12.1
Two members.	40.4	43.6	42.3	44.7	38.0	42.6	39.7	43.5	44.4
Three or more members	38.8	40.4	40.0	37.6	37.9	42.4	37.5	41.1	43.5
Age of intended reader:									
Under 25 years old	7.4	7.0	5.2	4.4	10.2	10.4	7.7	6.2	7.0
25 to 34 years old	18.6	13.1	14.1	10.4	24.6	15.9	19.8	13.5	7.2
35 to 44 years old	22.9	19.6	22.3	15.0	23.9	22.5	22.7	21.6	22.5
45 to 54 years old	20.8	23.1	24.9	22.2	16.5	22.9	18.5	23.8	29.8
55 to 64 years old	14.9	18.8	15.9	22.0	12.8	15.9	15.7	18.5	17.6
65 years old and over	15.4	18.4	17.6	26.0	12.0	12.4	15.6	16.4	15.9
Category of book:									
Popular fiction.	54.9	56.4	93.0	95.5	14.9	23.1	31.8	48.8	64.2
General nonfiction	10.3	7.8	3.6	1.8	15.6	10.2	16.5	11.8	9.3
Cooking/crafts.	10.8	9.1	0.4	0.1	20.6	16	18.2	12	1.1
Other	24.0	26.7	3.0	2.6	48.9	50.7	33.5	27.4	25.4
Where purchased (channel):									
Book stores [4]	57.3	41.3	48.4	35.2	73.7	49.9	54.7	39.6	22.9
Mass merchandisers	4.7	5.7	8.7	11.7	1.0	1.9	1.6	3.0	9.5
Book clubs	16.6	20	17.8	23.6	9.5	13.5	22.6	22.8	25.3
Online retailer/Internet	(NA)	7.5	(NA)	4.4	(NA)	9.1	(NA)	9.2	6.8
Other [5]	21.4	25.5	25.1	25.1	15.8	25.6	21.1	25.4	35.5

NA Not available. [1] "Pocket size" books sold primarily through magazine and news outlets, supermarkets, variety stores, etc. [2] All paperbound books, except mass market. [3] Audio and digital books were added to questionnaire in January 2001. Sample size for digital book purchasing (i.e. eBooks) was too small to show detailed breaks. [4] Includes independent, chain and used bookstores. [5] Includes mail order, price clubs, discount stores, food/drug stores, multimedia, and other outlets.

Source: Ipsos-NPD, Inc., Rosemont IL., *Ipsos BookTrends,* a service mark of Ipsos-NPD, Inc. (copyright).

No. 1116. Software Publishers—Estimated Revenue, Expenses, and Inventories: 1998 to 2000

[In millions of dollars (72,098 represents $72,098,000,000), except percent. For taxable and tax-exempt employer firms. Covers NAICS 5112. Estimates have been adjusted to the results of the 1997 Economic Census. Based on the North American Industry Classification System; see text, this section, and Section 15, Business Enterprise. Minus sign (-) indicates decrease]

Item	1998	1999	2000	Percent change, 1999-00
Revenue	72,098	80,959	88,042	8.7
Personal computer software revenue, total	11,818	12,940	13,819	6.8
Enterprise software revenue, total	20,580	22,849	24,755	8.3
Systems and systems management software revenue	10,130	12,261	13,809	12.6
Electronic commerce enabling technologies and software . . .	(S)	(S)	(S)	(S)
Mainframe computer software revenue, total	8,065	8,676	8,700	0.3
Other services revenue, total	13,625	16,076	17,443	8.5
Implementation and customization	4,597	5,428	5,727	5.5
Software upgrades and maintenance	7,224	8,575	9,431	10.0
Software user training	1,201	1,313	1,580	20.3
Internet access fees	(S)	(S)	(S)	(S)
Web hosting and design	(S)	(S)	(S)	(S)
Web site advertising	15	35	49	39.9
Other revenues	7,117	6,883	6,800	-1.2
Expenses: Selected purchases, total	4,751	5,460	6,060	11.0
Purchased printing	627	693	769	11.0
Purchased software reproduction	2,136	2,413	2,777	15.1
Purchased programming services	1,987	2,354	2,514	6.8
Inventories at end of year	784	863	1,020	18.2
Finished goods and work-in-process	665	697	864	24.0
Materials, supplies, fuel, etc.	119	167	157	-6.1

S Data do not meet publication standards.

Source: U.S. Census Bureau, *2000 Service Annual Survey, Information Sector Services.* See <http://www.census.gov/econ/www/servmenu.html> (released 29 November 2001).

No. 1117. Motion Picture and Sound Recording Industries—Estimated Revenue and Inventories: 1998 to 2000

[In millions of dollars (58,759 represents $58,759,000,000), except percent. For taxable and tax-exempt employer firms. For NAICS 512. Except where indicated, estimates have been adjusted to the results of the 1997 Economic Census. Based on the North American Industry Classification System; see text, this section, and Section 15, Business Enterprise. Minus sign (-) indicates decrease]

Item	1998	1999	2000	Percent change, 1999-00
Motion picture and recording industries (NAICS 512):				
Operating revenue	58,759	63,091	66,107	4.8
Total inventories	14,370	15,407	15,796	2.5
Finished goods and work-in-process	14,208	15,230	15,593	2.4
Materials, supplies, fuel, etc.	163	177	203	14.8
Motion picture and video (NAICS 5121):				
Operating revenue	48,002	51,227	53,660	4.8
Total inventories	14,053	15,101	15,437	2.2
Finished goods and work-in-process	13,942	14,983	15,308	2.2
Materials, supplies, fuel, etc.	112	118	130	9.8
Sound recording (NAICS 5122): [1]				
Operating revenue	10,758	11,864	12,447	4.9
Total inventories	317	306	359	17.1
Finished goods and work-in-process	266	248	286	15.3
Materials, supplies, fuel, etc.	51	58	73	25.0

[1] Estimates not adjusted to the results of the 1997 Economic Census.

Source: U.S. Census Bureau, *2000 Service Annual Survey, Information Sector Services.* See <http://www.census.gov/econ/www/servmenu.html> (released 29 November 2001).

U.S. Census Bureau, Statistical Abstract of the United States: 2002

No. 1118. Recording Media—Manufacturers' Shipments and Value: 1982 to 2001

[577.4 represents 577,400,000. Domestic shipments based on reports of manufacturers representing more than 90 percent of the market in 2001. Domestic value data based on list prices of records and other media. Minus sign (-) indicates returns greater than shipments]

Medium	1982	1985	1990	1995	1997	1998	1999	2000	2001
UNIT SHIPMENTS [1] (mil.)									
Total [2]	577.4	653.0	865.7	1,112.7	1,063.4	1,123.9	1,160.6	1,079.2	968.5
CDs	(X)	22.6	286.5	722.9	753.1	847.0	938.9	942.5	881.9
CD singles	(X)	(X)	1.1	21.5	66.7	56.0	55.9	34.2	17.3
Cassettes	182.3	339.1	442.2	272.6	172.6	158.5	123.6	76.0	45.0
Cassette singles	(X)	(X)	87.4	70.7	42.2	26.4	14.2	1.3	-1.5
Albums—LPs and EPs	243.9	167.0	11.7	2.2	2.7	3.4	2.9	2.2	2.3
Vinyl singles	137.2	120.7	27.6	10.2	7.5	5.4	5.3	4.8	5.5
Music video	(X)	(X)	9.2	12.6	18.6	27.2	19.8	18.2	17.7
DVD video	(X)	(X)	(X)	(X)	(X)	0.5	2.5	3.3	7.9
DVD audio	(X)	(X)	(X)	(X)	(X)	(X)	(X)	(X)	0.3
VALUE (mil. dol.)									
Total [2]	3,641.6	4,378.8	7,541.1	12,320.3	12,236.8	13,711.2	14,584.7	14,323.7	13,740.9
CDs	(X)	389.5	3,451.6	9,377.4	9,915.1	11,416.0	12,816.3	13,214.5	12,909.4
CD singles	(X)	(X)	6.0	110.9	272.7	213.2	222.4	142.7	79.4
Cassettes	1,384.5	2,411.5	3,472.4	2,303.6	1,522.7	1,419.9	1,061.6	626.0	363.4
Cassette singles	(X)	(X)	257.9	236.3	133.5	94.4	48.0	4.6	-5.3
Albums—LPs and EPs	1,925.1	1,280.5	86.5	25.1	33.3	34.0	31.8	27.7	27.4
Vinyl singles	283.0	281.0	94.4	46.7	35.6	25.7	27.9	26.3	31.4
Music video	(X)	(X)	172.3	220.3	323.9	508.0	376.7	281.9	329.2
DVD video	(X)	(X)	(X)	(X)	(X)	12.2	66.3	80.3	190.7
DVD audio	(X)	(X)	(X)	(X)	(X)	(X)	(X)	(X)	6.0

X Not applicable. [1] Net units, after returns. [2] Includes discontinued media.

Source: Recording Industry Association of America, Washington, DC, *2001 Yearend Statistics*. See Internet site <http://www.riaa.com> (accessed 8 August 2002).

No. 1119. Profile of Consumer Expenditures for Sound Recordings: 1990 to 2001

[In percent, except total value (7,541.1 represents $7,541,100,000). Based on monthly telephone surveys of the population 10 years old and over]

Item	1990	1995	1996	1997	1998	1999	2000	2001
Total value (mil. dol.)	7,541.1	12,320.3	12,533.8	12,236.8	13,723.5	14,584.5	14,323.0	13,740.9
PERCENT DISTRIBUTION [1]								
Age: 10 to 14 years	7.6	8.0	7.9	8.9	9.1	8.5	8.9	8.5
15 to 19 years	18.3	17.1	17.2	16.8	15.8	12.6	12.9	13.0
20 to 24 years	16.5	15.3	15.0	13.8	12.2	12.6	12.5	12.2
25 to 29 years	14.6	12.3	12.5	11.7	11.4	10.5	10.6	10.9
30 to 34 years	13.2	12.1	11.4	11.0	11.4	10.1	9.8	10.3
35 to 39 years	10.2	10.8	11.1	11.6	12.6	10.4	10.6	10.2
40 to 44 years	7.8	7.5	9.1	8.8	8.3	9.3	9.6	10.3
45 years and over	11.1	16.1	15.1	16.5	18.1	24.7	23.8	23.7
Sex: Male	54.4	53.0	50.9	48.6	48.7	50.3	50.6	48.8
Female	45.6	47.0	49.1	51.4	51.3	49.7	49.4	51.2
Sales outlet:								
Record store	69.8	52.0	49.9	51.8	50.8	44.5	42.4	42.5
Other store	18.5	28.2	31.5	31.9	34.4	38.3	40.8	42.4
Music club	8.9	14.3	14.3	11.6	9.0	7.9	7.6	6.1
Ad or 800 number	2.5	4.0	2.9	2.7	2.9	2.5	2.4	3.0
Internet [2]	(NA)	(NA)	(NA)	0.3	1.1	2.4	3.2	2.9
Music type: [3]								
Rock	36.1	33.5	32.6	32.5	25.7	25.2	24.8	24.4
Pop	13.7	10.1	9.3	9.4	10.0	10.3	11.0	12.1
Rap/Hip Hop	8.5	6.7	8.9	10.1	9.7	10.8	12.9	11.4
R&B/Urban	11.6	11.3	12.1	11.2	12.8	10.5	9.7	10.6
Country	9.6	16.7	14.7	14.4	14.1	10.8	10.7	10.5
Religious	2.5	3.1	4.3	4.5	6.3	5.1	4.8	6.7
Jazz	4.8	3.0	3.3	2.8	1.9	3.0	2.9	3.4
Classical	3.1	2.9	3.4	2.8	3.3	3.5	2.7	3.2
Soundtracks	0.8	0.9	0.8	1.2	1.7	0.8	0.7	1.4
New age	1.1	0.7	0.7	0.8	0.6	0.5	0.5	1.0
Oldies	0.8	1.0	0.8	0.8	0.7	0.7	0.9	0.8
Children's	0.5	0.5	0.7	0.9	0.4	0.4	0.6	0.5
Other	5.6	7.0	5.2	5.7	7.9	9.1	8.3	7.9
Media type:								
CDs	31.1	65.0	68.4	70.2	74.8	83.2	89.3	89.2
Cassettes	54.7	25.1	19.3	18.2	14.8	8.0	4.9	3.4
Singles (all types)	8.7	7.5	9.3	9.3	6.8	5.4	2.5	2.4
Music video [4]	(NA)	0.9	1.0	0.6	1.0	0.9	0.8	1.1
Vinyl LPs	4.7	0.5	0.6	0.7	0.7	0.5	0.5	0.6

NA Not available. [1] Percent distributions exclude nonresponses and responses of don't know. [2] Excludes record club purchases over the Internet. [3] As classified by respondent. [4] Beginning 2001 includes video DVDs.

Source: Recording Industry Association of America, Inc., Washington, DC, *2000 Consumer Profile*. See Internet site <http://www.riaa.com> (accessed 6 August 2002).

No. 1120. Radio and Television Broadcasting—Estimated Revenue and Expenses: 1999 and 2000

[In millions of dollars (47,292 represents $47,292,000,000), except percent. For taxable and tax-exempt employer firms. Covers NAICS 5131. Estimates have been adjusted to the results of the 1997 Economic Census. Based on the North American Industry Classification System; see text, this section, and Section 15, Business Enterprise. Minus sign (-) indicates decrease]

Item	Total (NAICS 5131)			Radio broadcasting (NAICS 51311)			TV broadcasting (NAICS 51312)		
	1999	2000	Percent change 1999-00	1999	2000	Percent change 1999-00	1999	2000	Percent change 1999-00
Operating revenue	**47,292**	**52,668**	**11.4**	**13,030**	**14,811**	**13.7**	**34,262**	**37,858**	**10.5**
Station time sales	29,771	33,126	11.3	11,258	12,726	13.0	18,513	20,400	10.2
Network compensation	657	606	-7.8	97	109	12.2	561	498	-11.2
National/regional advertising	10,277	11,762	14.5	2,658	3,013	13.3	7,618	8,749	14.8
Local advertising revenue	18,837	20,757	10.2	8,503	9,604	12.9	10,334	11,153	7.9
Network time sales	13,514	15,732	16.4	996	1,195	20.0	12,518	14,537	16.1
Other operating revenue	4,007	3,811	-4.9	776	890	14.7	3,231	2,921	-9.6
Expenses	**37,551**	**40,366**	**7.5**	**10,308**	**11,406**	**10.6**	**27,243**	**28,960**	**6.3**
Annual payroll	10,814	11,280	4.3	4,165	4,458	7.0	6,649	6,821	2.6
Employer contributions to Social Security and other supplemental benefits	1,427	1,535	7.6	503	590	17.3	924	945	2.3
Broadcast rights and music license fees	11,438	12,754	11.5	626	713	13.9	10,811	12,041	11.4
Depreciation	3,411	3,648	6.9	1,579	1,638	3.7	1,832	2,010	9.7
Lease and rental	616	655	6.4	268	294	9.7	349	362	3.7
Purchased repairs	266	276	3.6	86	91	5.3	180	185	2.7
Purchased communications and utilities	601	634	5.4	258	273	5.8	343	361	5.2
Purchased advertising	1,458	1,534	5.1	393	455	15.8	1,066	1,079	1.2
Other operating expenses (including network compensation fees)	7,521	8,052	7.1	2,431	2,896	19.1	5,090	5157	1.3

Source: U.S. Census Bureau, *2000 Service Annual Survey, Information Sector Services*. See <http://www.census.gov/econ/www/servmenu.html> (released 29 November 2001).

No. 1121. Cable and Pay TV—Summary: 1975 to 2001

[9,800 represents 9,800,000. Cable TV for calendar year. Pay TV as of Dec. 31 of year shown]

Year	Cable TV				Pay TV					
	Avg. basic subscribers (1,000)	Avg. monthly basic rate (dol.)	Revenue [1] (mil. dol.)		Units [2] (1,000)			Monthly rate (dol.)		
			Total	Basic	Total pay [3]	Pay cable	Noncable delivered premium	All pay weighted average [3]	Pay cable	Noncable delivered premium
1975	9,800	6.50	804	764	194	194	(NA)	(NA)	7.85	(NA)
1976	11,000	6.45	932	851	611	568	(NA)	7.96	7.87	(NA)
1977	12,200	6.86	1,207	1,004	1,138	1,047	(NA)	8.03	7.92	(NA)
1978	13,400	7.13	1,513	1,147	2,473	2,182	(NA)	8.16	8.01	(NA)
1979	15,000	7.40	1,942	1,332	5,157	4,480	(NA)	8.54	8.24	(NA)
1980	17,500	7.69	2,609	1,615	8,581	7,336	(NA)	8.91	8.62	(NA)
1981	21,100	7.99	3,675	2,023	14,310	12,239	(NA)	9.16	8.92	(NA)
1982	25,250	8.30	5,032	2,515	19,395	17,007	(NA)	9.49	9.30	(NA)
1983	29,430	8.61	6,485	3,041	24,515	22,818	(NA)	9.82	9.70	(NA)
1984	32,800	8.98	7,738	3,534	28,815	27,754	(NA)	10.03	9.96	(NA)
1985	35,440	9.73	8,831	4,138	29,885	29,418	(NA)	10.29	10.25	(NA)
1986	38,170	10.67	9,955	4,887	31,033	30,668	(NA)	10.35	10.31	(NA)
1987	41,160	12.18	11,563	6,016	33,528	33,232	(NA)	10.25	10.23	(NA)
1988	44,160	13.86	13,409	7,345	37,085	36,777	(NA)	10.24	10.17	(NA)
1989	47,500	15.21	15,378	8,670	39,055	38,916	(NA)	10.25	10.20	(NA)
1990	50,520	16.78	17,582	10,174	39,902	39,751	(NA)	10.35	10.30	(NA)
1991	52,570	18.10	19,426	11,418	39,983	36,569	(NA)	10.35	10.27	(NA)
1992	54,300	19.08	21,079	12,433	40,893	36,879	(NA)	10.29	10.17	(NA)
1993	56,200	[4]19.39	22,809	13,528	42,010	37,113	(NA)	9.27	9.11	(NA)
1994	58,450	21.62	23,160	15,164	47,478	42,528	4,950	8.64	8.83	6.99
1995	60,900	23.07	24,904	16,860	55,723	46,798	8,925	8.29	8.54	6.99
1996	62,800	24.41	27,295	18,395	63,705	49,728	13,977	8.05	8.35	6.99
1997	64,135	26.48	30,066	20,383	72,785	51,933	20,852	7.91	8.29	6.99
1998	65,418	27.81	32,446	21,830	80,605	55,280	25,325	7.82	8.20	6.99
1999	66,660	28.92	35,037	23,135	88,455	59,005	29,450	7.69	8.04	6.99
2000	67,860	30.37	38,179	24,729	102,590	65,918	36,672	7.64	8.00	6.99
2001, est. . .	68,523	32.87	43,769	27,031	115,330	75,193	40,137	7.65	7.96	7.06

NA Not available. [1] Includes installation revenue, subscriber revenue, and nonsubscriber revenue; excludes telephony and high-speed access. [2] Individual program services sold to subscribers. [3] Includes multipoint distribution service (MDS), satellite TV (STV), multipoint multichannel distribution service (MMDS), satellite master antenna TV (SMATV, C-band satellite, and DBS satellite. Includes average pay unit price based on data for major premium pay movie services. [4] Weighted average representing 8 months of unregulated basic rate and 4 months of FCC rolled-back rate.

Source: Kagan World Media, a Media Central/Primedia Company. From the *Broadband Cable Financial Databook 2001* (copyright); and *The Pay TV Newsletter,* May 31, 2001, and various other publications.

Information and Communications 707

No. 1122. Cable Networks and Program Distribution Services—Estimated Revenue and Expenses: 1998 to 2000

[In millions of dollars (52,310 represents $52,310,000,000), except percent. For taxable and tax-exempt employer firms. Covers NAICS 5132. Estimates have not been adjusted to the results of the 1997 Economic Census. Based on the North American Industry Classification System; see text, this section, and Section 15, Business Enterprise]

Item	1998	1999	2000	Percent change, 1999-00
Operating revenue.	52,310	59,895	67,930	13.4
Advertising revenue (net)	8,034	9,767	12,009	23.0
Program revenue.	9,454	10,301	10,970	6.5
Basic service tier.	23,541	26,890	29,509	9.7
Pay-per-view service	1,445	1,676	1,746	4.2
Other premium service	4,624	4,769	5,053	5.9
Installation, startup, and reconnect fees.	740	765	714	-6.7
Other cable and pay TV revenue	2,021	2,428	3,064	26.2
Internet access fees.	138	274	903	229.6
Local telephone service	144	220	451	104.7
Long-distance telephone service.	(S)	(S)	63	(S)
Other communication service revenue.	228	522	454	-13.0
Other operating revenue.	1,915	2,237	2,995	33.9
Operating expenses.	45,231	52,952	62,039	17.2
Annual payroll.	7,138	8,388	9,696	15.6
Employer contributions to social security and other supplemental benefits.	1,443	1,666	1,929	15.8
Program and production costs.	14,601	16,525	19,077	15.4
Depreciation.	9,425	11,498	13,965	21.4
Lease and rental.	760	878	1,005	14.5
Purchased repairs.	662	721	684	-5.0
Purchased communications and utilities.	736	840	921	9.7
Purchased advertising	1,590	1,836	2251	22.6
Other operating expenses.	8,876	10,600	12,510	18.0

S Data do not meet publication standards.

Source: U.S. Census Bureau, *2000 Service Annual Survey, Information Sector Services.* See <http://www.census.gov/econ/www/servmenu.html> (released 29 November 2001).

No. 1123. Telecommunications—Estimated Revenue and Expenses: 1999 and 2000

[In millions of dollars (318,097 represents $318,097,000,000), except percent. For taxable and tax-exempt employer firms. Except for NAICS 51332, wireless telecommunications carriers (except satellite), estimates have been adjusted to the results of the 1997 Economic Census. Based on the North American Industry Classification System; see text, this section, and Section 15, Business Enterprise. Minus sign (-) indicates decrease. See Table 1124 for wireless telecommunications carriers, NAICS 51332]

Item	Telecommunications (NAICS 5133)			Wired telecommunications carriers (NAICS 51331)		
	1999	2000	Percent change, 1999-00	1999	2000	Percent change, 1999-00
Operating revenue	318,097	352,950	11.0	247,532	269,545	8.9
Wired telecommunications services	228,321	243,575	6.7	221,439	235,879	6.5
Local service	76,414	87,284	14.2	74,807	85,526	14.3
Basic local service	60,463	70,463	16.5	58,892	68,754	16.7
Value-added services	15,952	16,821	5.5	15,915	16,772	5.4
Long-distance service	102,251	102,343	0.1	97,670	97,677	(Z)
Network access	49,656	53,948	8.6	48,962	52,675	7.6
Cellular telephone, PCS, and SMR	45,061	57,012	26.5	(S)	(S)	(S)
Basic monthly charges	19,633	25,734	31.1	120	162	35.6
Airtime	14,966	19,734	31.9	101	126	24.3
Long-distance service	2,156	2,400	11.3	(Z)	(Z)	-50.0
Roaming	5,293	5,580	5.4	6	8	43.9
Other	3,014	3,565	18.3	(S)	(S)	(S)
Directory advertising	1,788	1,750	-2.1	1,783	1,744	-2.2
Other communications services.	13,736	16,317	18.8	1,586	3,748	136.3
Other operating revenue	29,191	34,299	17.5	22,213	27,562	24.1
Operating expenses	266,792	306,706	15.0	200,833	230,098	14.6
Annual payroll.	54,447	65,306	19.9	43,193	52,517	21.6
Employer contributions to Social Security and other supplemental benefits	12,415	14,119	13.7	10,106	11,414	12.9
Access charges	37,581	40,530	7.8	31,657	32,891	3.9
Depreciation	49,929	59,725	19.6	38,120	44,075	15.6
Lease and rental	6,349	8,010	26.2	3,368	4,476	32.9
Purchased repairs.	3,581	4,477	25.0	2,830	3,504	23.8
Purchased communications and utilities	14,330	15,890	10.9	12,437	12,929	4.0
Purchased advertising	7,122	8,499	19.3	4,532	4,909	8.3
Universal service, contributions, and other similar charges	5,527	5,658	2.4	5,017	5,037	0.4
Other operating expenses	75,602	84,492	11.8	49,665	58,344	17.5

S Data do not meet publication standards. Z Less than 0.05 percent or $500,000.

Source: U.S. Census Bureau, *2000 Service Annual Survey, Information Sector Services.* See <http://www.census.gov/econ/www/servmenu.html> (released 29 November 2001).

No. 1124. Wireless Telecommunications Carriers (Except Satellite)— Estimated Revenue, and Expenses: 1998 to 2000

[In millions of dollars (42,363 represents $42,363,000,000), except percent. For taxable and tax-exempt employer firms. For NAICS 51332. Estimates have not been adjusted to the results of the 1997 Economic Census. Based on the North American Industry Classification System; see text, this section, and Section 15, Business Enterprise . Minus sign (-) indicates decrease. See Table 1123 for telecommunications total and wired carriers (NAICS 5133 and 51331)]

Item	1998	1999	2000	Percent change, 1999-00
Operating revenue	**42,363**	**53,485**	**64,309**	**20.2**
Cellular telephone, PCS, and SMR	32,844	42,654	54,578	28.0
Basic monthly charges	15,490	19,269	25,272	31.2
Airtime	11,557	14,723	19,473	32.3
Long-distance service	1,528	1,919	2,193	14.3
Roaming	3,162	5,115	5,326	4.1
Other	1,107	1,629	2,314	42.1
Other communications services [1]	6,423	6,920	6,164	-10.9
Other operating revenue	3,096	3,911	3,567	-8.8
Operating expenses	**39,720**	**50,381**	**59,214**	**17.5**
Annual payroll	6,722	8,259	9,224	11.7
Employer contributions to social security and other supplemental benefits	1,490	1,787	2,095	17.2
Access charges	2,233	3,371	5,038	49.4
Depreciation	8,743	10,376	13,275	17.9
Lease and rental	1,923	2,328	2,793	20.0
Purchased repairs	719	660	846	28.3
Purchased communications and utilities	1,051	1,311	1,757	34.0
Purchased advertising	2,467	2,343	3,330	42.1
Universal service, contributions, and other similar charges	325	441	526	19.2
Other operating expenses	14,047	19,505	20,329	4.2

[1] Includes wired telecommunications services revenue.

Source: U.S. Census Bureau, *2000 Service Annual Survey, Information Sector Services*. See <http://www.census.gov/econ/www/servmenu.html> (released 29 November 2001).

No. 1125. Telecommunications Industry—Carriers and Revenue: 1995 to 2000

[Revenue in millions of dollars (190,076 represents $190,076,000,000). Data based on carrier filings to the FCC. Because of reporting changes, data beginning 1997 are not strictly comparable with previous years; see source for details]

Category	Carriers					Telecommunications revenue				
	1995	1997	1998	1999	2000	1995	1997	1998	1999	2000
Total [1]	**3,058**	**3,604**	**4,121**	**4,822**	**4,850**	**190,076**	**231,168**	**246,392**	**268,505**	**292,762**
Local service providers	1,675	2,066	2,239	2,589	2,617	103,792	108,568	113,369	119,938	128,075
Incumbent local exchange carriers (ILECs) [2]	1,347	1,410	1,348	1,335	1,327	102,820	105,154	108,234	112,216	116,158
Pay telephone providers	271	509	615	758	683	349	933	1,101	1,213	972
Competitors of ILECs	57	147	276	496	607	623	2,481	4,034	6,508	10,945
CAPs and CLECs [3]	57	129	212	349	485	623	1,919	3,348	5,652	9,814
Local resellers	(4)	11	54	87	82	(4)	206	410	511	879
Other local exchange carriers	(4)	3	10	60	40	(4)	157	36	171	11
Private carriers	(4)	2	(4)	(4)	(4)	(4)	112	147	87	39
Shared tenant service providers	(4)	2	(4)	(4)	(4)	(4)	87	93	87	202
Wireless service providers [5]	930	969	1,235	1,495	1,451	18,627	33,030	37,032	50,152	63,280
Telephony [6]	792	732	808	806	810	17,208	29,944	33,139	46,513	59,823
Paging service providers	138	137	303	427	418	(4)	2,861	3,161	3,232	3,102
Toll service providers	453	569	647	738	782	76,447	89,570	95,992	98,414	101,407
Interexchange carriers	130	151	171	204	202	70,938	79,080	83,443	87,570	87,311
Operator service providers	25	32	24	21	21	500	603	590	337	635
Prepaid service providers	8	18	20	21	24	16	519	888	866	727
Satellite service carriers	(4)	13	13	21	24	(4)	1,011	475	280	336
Toll resellers	260	340	388	454	482	4,220	8,010	9,885	9,211	10,641
Other toll carriers	30	15	31	17	29	773	348	710	150	1,758

[1] Revenue data include adjustments, not shown separately. Through 1997, revenue data include some nontelecommunications revenue, formerly reported as local exchange wireless revenue. [2] Fewer ILECs filed in 1998 than in 1997 because of consolidation of study areas. [3] Competitive access providers and competitive local exchange carriers. [4] Data not available separately. [5] Includes specialized mobile radio services and other services, not shown separately. [6] Cellular service, personal communications service, and specialized mobile radio.

Source: U.S. Federal Communications Commission, *Trends in Telephone Service*, annual.

U.S. Census Bureau, Statistical Abstract of the United States: 2002

No. 1126. Telephone Systems—Summary: 1985 to 2000

[**112 represents 112,000,000.** Covers principal carriers filing annual reports with Federal Communications Commission]

Item	Unit	1985	1990	1994	1995	1996	1997	1998	1999	2000
LOCAL EXCHANGE CARRIERS [1]										
Carriers [2]	Number .	55	51	52	53	51	51	52	52	52
Access lines	Millions. .	112	130	157	166	178	194	205	228	245
Business access lines	Millions. .	31	36	42	46	49	53	57	57	58
Residential access lines	Millions. .	79	89	98	101	104	108	110	115	115
Other access lines (public, mobile, special)	Millions . .	2	6	17	19	25	33	38	55	72
Number of local calls (originating)	Billions . .	365	402	465	484	504	522	544	554	537
Number of toll calls (originating)	Billions . .	(NA)	63	83	94	95	101	97	102	106
Gross book cost of plant	Bil. dol. .	191	240	272	284	296	309	325	342	362
Depreciation and amortization reserves. .	Bil. dol. .	49	89	116	127	138	149	163	176	190
Net plant	Bil. dol. .	142	151	157	157	158	160	161	166	172
Total assets	Bil. dol. .	162	180	196	197	198	198	200	204	214
Total stockholders equity	Bil. dol. .	63	74	72	72	74	72	70	67	72
Operating revenues	Bil. dol. .	73	84	93	96	101	103	108	113	117
Local revenues . . [3]	Bil. dol. .	32	37	43	46	50	52	55	58	60
Operating expenses [3]	Bil. dol. .	48	62	70	72	74	75	78	79	81
Net operating income [4]	Bil. dol. .	13	14	13	14	16	16	18	20	20
Net income	Bil. dol. .	9	11	9	11	13	12	12	13	15
Employees	(1,000) .	(NA)	569	474	447	437	435	436	436	434
Compensation of employees	Bil. dol. .	(NA)	23	22	21	23	22	23	24	24
Average monthly residential local telephone rate [5]	Dollars . .	(NA)	19.24	19.81	20.01	19.95	19.88	19.76	19.93	20.78
Average monthly single-line business telephone rate [5]	Dollars . .	(NA)	41.21	41.64	41.80	41.81	41.67	41.29	41.21	41.80
LONG DISTANCE CARRIERS										
Number of carriers with presubscribed lines	Number .	(NA)	325	511	583	621	(NA)	(NA)	(NA)	(NA)
Number of presubscribed lines	Millions. .	(NA)	132	148	153	159	(NA)	(NA)	(NA)	(NA)
Total toll service revenues	Bil. dol. .	43	52	67	74	82	89	94	99	100
Interstate switched access minutes	Bil. min. .	167	307	401	432	468	497	519	553	567
INTERNATIONAL TELEPHONE SERVICE [6]										
Number of U.S. billed calls	Millions. .	425	984	2,347	2,830	3,520	4,259	4,477	5,305	6,627
Number of U.S. billed minutes	Millions. .	3,446	8,030	13,616	15,889	19,325	22,753	24,250	28,515	29,216
U.S. billed revenues	Mil. dol. .	3,487	8,059	12,543	14,335	14,598	15,662	14,726	14,980	14,901
U.S. carrier revenue net of settlements with foreign carriers	Mil. dol. .	2,332	5,188	7,966	9,054	8,434	9,691	9,681	9,869	10,237
Revenue from private-line service	Mil. dol. .	172	201	441	514	661	851	921	1,216	1,480
Revenue from resale service	Mil. dol. .	(NA)	167	1,121	1,756	3,637	4,112	4,798	4,528	7,366

NA Not available.   [1] Gross operating revenues, gross plant, and total assets of reporting carriers estimated at more than 90 percent of total industry. New accounting rules became effective in 1990; prior years may not be directly comparable on a one-to-one basis. Includes Virgin Islands, and prior to 1994, Puerto Rico.   [2] The reporting threshold for carriers is $100 million in annual operating revenue.   [3] Excludes taxes.   [4] After tax deductions.   [5] Based on surveys conducted by FCC. [6] Beginning 1994, data are for all U.S. points, and include calls to and from Alaska, Hawaii, Puerto Rico, Guam, the U.S. Virgin Islands, and offshore U.S. points. Beginning 1994, carriers first started reporting traffic to and from Canada and Mexico. Data for Canada and Mexico in prior years are staff estimates.

Source: U.S. Federal Communications Commission, *Statistics of Communications Common Carriers*, annual; *Trends in Telephone Service*, annual; and *Trends in the International Telecommunications Industry*, annual.

No. 1127. Cellular Telephone Industry: 1990 to 2001

[**Calendar year data, except as noted (5,283 represents 5,283,000).** Based on a survey mailed to all cellular, personal communications services, and enhanced special mobile radio (ESMR) systems. For 2001 data, the universe was 2,587 systems and the response rate was 87 percent. The number of operational systems beginning 2000 differs from that reported for previous periods as a result of the consolidated operation of ESMR systems in a broader service area instead of by a city-to-city basis]

Item	Unit	1990	1995	1996	1997	1998	1999	2000	2001
Systems	Number .	751	1,627	1,740	2,228	3,073	3,518	2,440	2,587
Subscribers	1,000 . .	5,283	33,786	44,043	55,312	69,209	86,047	109,478	128,375
Cell sites [1]	Number .	5,616	22,663	30,045	51,600	65,887	81,698	104,288	127,540
Employees	Number .	21,382	68,165	84,161	109,387	134,754	155,817	184,449	203,580
Service revenue . . [2]	Mil. dol. .	4,548	19,081	23,635	27,486	33,133	40,018	52,466	65,016
Roamer revenue [2]	Mil. dol. .	456	2,542	2,781	2,974	3,501	4,085	3,883	3,936
Capital investment	Mil. dol. .	6,282	24,080	32,574	46,058	60,543	71,265	89,624	105,030
Average monthly bill [3]	Dollars. .	80.90	51.00	47.70	42.78	39.43	41.24	45.27	47.37
Average length of call [3]	Minutes .	2.20	2.15	2.32	2.31	2.39	2.38	2.56	2.74

[1] The basic geographic unit of a wireless PCS or cellular system. A city or county is divided into smaller "cells," each of which is equipped with a low-powered radio transmitter/receiver. The cells can vary in size depending upon terrain, capacity demands, etc. By controlling the transmission power, the radio frequencies assigned to one cell can be limited to the boundaries of that cell. When a wireless PCS or cellular phone moves from one cell toward another, a computer at the Switching Office monitors the movement and at the proper time, transfers or hands off the phone call to the new cell and another radio frequency.   [2] Service revenue generated by subscribers' calls outside of their system areas.   [3] As of December 31.

Source: Cellular Telecommunications & Internet Association, Washington, DC, *Semiannual Wireless Survey* (copyright).

U.S. Census Bureau, *Statistical Abstract of the United States: 2002*

No. 1128. Information Services and Data Processing Services—Estimated Revenue: 1998 to 2000

[In millions of dollars (46,994 represents $46,994,000,000), except percent. For taxable and tax-exempt employer firms. Covers NAICS 514. Except as indicated, estimates adjusted to results of the 1997 Economic Census. Based on the North American Industry Classification System; see text, this section, and Section 15, Business Enterprise. Minus sign (-) indicates decrease]

Item	1998	1999	2000	Percent change, 1999-00
Total (NAICS 514)	**46,994**	**60,105**	**76,524**	**27.3**
News syndicates (NAICS 51411):				
Revenue................................	1,586	1,823	1,986	8.9
Libraries and archives (NAICS 51412):				
Revenue................................	954	1,018	1,151	13.1
Subsidies, contributions, gifts, and grants	631	698	794	13.8
Other revenue	323	320	357	11.6
On-line information services (NAICS 514191):				
Revenue................................	10,882	18,012	26,577	47.6
Internet access fees	5,499	8,966	12,345	37.7
Advertising.............................	725	1,355	3,507	158.9
Web hosting and design.......................	261	520	1,136	118.5
Online sales commissions.....................	(S)	(S)	(S)	(S)
Other revenue	4,322	7,038	9,421	33.9
All other information services [1] (NAICS 514199):				
Revenue................................	985	2,109	4,861	130.5
Internet access fees	(S)	(S)	(S)	(S)
Advertising.............................	658	1,477	3,002	103.3
Web hosting and design.......................	(S)	(S)	(S)	(S)
Online sales commissions.....................	(S)	(S)	(S)	(S)
Other revenue	(S)	(S)	(S)	(S)
Data processing services (NAICS 5142):				
Revenue................................	32,588	37,143	41,950	12.9
Transaction processing and data exchange	19,511	22,151	24,885	12.3
Data capture and imaging.....................	1,161	1,308	1,438	9.9
Computer timesharing services	748	764	749	-1.9
Web hosting and design.......................	(S)	(S)	1,292	(S)
Other data processing services	5,160	5,997	5,616	-6.3
All other revenue	6,008	6,645	7,969	19.9

S Data do not meet publication standards.   [1] Estimates not adjusted to the results of the 1997 Economic Census.

Source: U.S. Census Bureau, *2000 Service Annual Survey, Information Sector Services.* See <http://www.census.gov/econ/www/servmenu.html> (released 29 November 2001).

No. 1129. Academic Libraries—Summary: 1998

[For fiscal year. For 2- and 4-year degree granting institutions. Based on survey; see source for details]

Item	Number of libraries	Circulation (1,000) General	Circulation (1,000) Reserve	Paper volumes held (1,000)[1]	Staff [2] Total	Staff [2] Librarians (percent)	Expenditures Total (mil. dol.)	Expenditures Salary [3] (percent)	Percent with access from within library to— Electronic catalog	Percent with access from within library to— Internet
Total	**3,658**	**175,409**	**40,658**	**878,906**	**96,709**	**25.7**	**4,593**	**50.4**	**84.2**	**94.6**
Control:										
Public...............	1,583	116,158	25,267	521,817	58,314	25.0	2,780	52.4	95.7	97.5
Private	2,075	59,251	15,391	357,090	38,395	26.6	1,813	47.4	75.0	92.3
Level: [4]										
4-year degree and above [5].	2,220	150,575	34,453	821,965	82,533	25.4	4,072	48.5	86.7	95.4
Doctor's............	570	105,614	22,469	569,295	54,478	24.5	2,924	47.1	94.8	97.3
Master's............	944	33,869	8,747	186,922	20,547	27.2	868	52.4	87.9	95.7
Bachelor's	703	11,083	3,236	65,645	7,499	27.0	280	51.0	78.3	93.5
Less than 4-year........	1,438	24,834	6,205	56,941	14,176	27.4	520	65.4	80.1	93.3
Enrollment: [2]										
Less than 1,500	2,041	24,946	6,173	117,188	14,949	29.3	567	52.0	73.0	91.4
1,500 to 4,999	1,053	33,992	9,259	172,047	22,221	27.2	947	52.8	96.4	98.7
5,000 of more	564	116,472	25,226	589,671	59,539	24.2	3,078	49.3	99.1	98.0

[1] At end-of-year. [2] Full-time equivalent. [3] Salary and wages. [4] Level of highest degree offered. [5] Includes three institutions granting "other" degrees, not shown separately.

Source: U.S. National Center for Education Statistics, *Academic Libraries, 1998,* NCES 2001-341, July 2001.

U.S. Census Bureau, Statistical Abstract of the United States: 2002

No. 1130. Libraries—Number by Type: 1980 to 2000

Type	1980	1985	1990	2000	Type	1980	1985	1990	2000
Total [1]	31,564	32,323	34,613	37,024	Junior college . . .	1,191	1,188	1,233	1,283
					Colleges,				
United States . . .	28,638	29,843	30,761	32,914	universities	3,400	3,846	3,360	3,494
Public.	8,717	8,849	9,060	9,480	Departmental .	1,489	1,824	1,454	1,454
Public branches . . .	5,936	6,330	5,833	6,957	Law,				
Special [2]	7,649	7,530	9,051	9,948	medicine,				
Medicine	1,674	1,667	1,861	1,955	religious . . .	269	531	501	418
Religious	913	839	946	1,015	Government. . . .	1,260	1,574	1,735	1,411
Law [3]	417	435	647	1,172	Armed Forces	485	526	489	341
Academic	4,591	5,034	4,593	4,777	Outlying areas . .	113	114	110	(NA)

NA Not available. [1] Includes Canadian libraries, and libraries in regions administered by the United States, not shown separately. Data are exclusive of elementary and secondary school libraries. Law libraries with fewer than 10,000 volumes are included only if they specialize in a particular field. [2] Includes other types of special libraries, not shown separately. Increase between 1985 and 1990 is due mainly to revised criteria for identifying special libraries and improved methods of counting. [3] Increase in 2000 due to increased effort in identifying special libraries.

Source: Information Today, Inc., Medford, NJ, *The Bowker Annual Library and Book Trade Almanac* and *American Library Directory,* annual. (Copyright 2001 by Information Today, Inc.)

No. 1131. Public Libraries by Selected Characteristics: 2000

[**7,703 represents $7,703,000,000.** Based on survey of public libraries. Data are for public libraries in the 50 states and the District of Columbia. The response rates for these items are between 98 and 99 percent]

Population of service area	Number of—		Operating income—			Paid staff [3]		
				Source (percent)				
	Public libraries	Stationary outlets [1]	Total (mil. dol.) [2]	State government	Local government	Total	Librarians with ALA-MLS [4]	Libraries with Internet access
Total	9,074	16,298	7,703	12.8	77.1	130,102	29,519	8,638
1,000,000 or more	24	987	1,133	10.0	77.1	16,005	4,607	24
500,000 to 999,000	52	1,102	1,252	16.5	74.7	18,464	4,727	52
250,000 to 499,999	90	1,037	859	13.0	79.0	13,687	3,441	90
100,000 to 249,999	323	1,974	1,246	11.6	80.2	21,805	4,858	323
50,000 to 99,999	522	1,612	968	15.2	76.0	16,926	3,761	521
25,000 to 49,999	877	1,680	907	13.3	78.0	16,241	3,710	872
10,000 to 24,999	1,741	2,228	838	11.3	76.7	15,479	3,194	1,723
5,000 to 9,999	1,467	1,642	288	11.0	74.4	6,135	870	1,445
2,500 to 4,999	1,346	1,392	120	6.8	74.2	2,871	235	1,301
1,000 to 2,499	1,629	1,641	71	6.3	65.8	1,848	98	1,520
Fewer than 1,000	1,003	1,003	21	7.0	62.6	640	18	767

[1] The sum of central and branches libraries. The total number of central libraries was 8,915; the total of branch libraries was 7,383. [2] Includes income from the federal government (0.7%) and other sources (9.4%), not shown separately. [3] Full-time equivalents. [4] Librarians with master's degrees from a graduate library education program accredited by the American Library Association (ALA). Total librarians, including those without ALA-MLS, were 43,818.

Source: U.S. National Center for Education Statistics, *Public Libraries in the United States: 2000,* NCES 2002-344, July 2002.

No. 1132. Public Library Use of the Internet: 2000

[**In percent, except number of outlets. As of spring**. Based on sample survey; see source for details]

Item		Metropolitan status [1]			Poverty status [2]		
	Total	Urban	Suburban	Rural	Less than 20 percent	20 to 40 percent	More than 40 percent
All libraries outlets [3]	16,004	2,742	4,764	8,498	12,847	2,832	325
Connected to the Internet	95.7	98.3	98.5	93.3	95.6	96.3	92.8
Connected with public access.	94.5	97.7	97.3	91.9	94.3	95.8	93.5
Average number of workstations.	8.3	17.3	8.7	4.9	7.3	12.3	7.2
Speed of access:							
Less than 56kpbs.	5.8	1.0	2.5	9.4	6.7	2.6	0.0
56kpbs dial-up.	15.5	1.0	7.4	25.3	17.7	5.7	16.2
56kpbs direct connect	25.0	10.0	25.6	29.8	24.4	27.6	26.3
Greater than 56kpbs	53.6	88.2	64.6	35.4	51.3	64.1	57.4
Special software/hardware for persons with disabilities on—							
All workstations	8.5	8.7	7.0	9.3	5.8	20.4	7.5
Some workstations	20.3	26.6	23.9	6.1	18.5	29.6	10.5
No workstations	71.2	64.7	69.1	74.6	75.7	49.9	82.0
On public access workstations—							
No Internet filtering/blocking	75.5	70.8	69.8	80.4	75.9	73.3	77.9
Internet filtering/blocking on some stations	15.0	18.5	21.8	9.7	14.6	16.7	14.5
With acceptable use policies	95.5	96.8	97.1	94.0	94.7	99.4	91.7
With acceptable use policies which differentiate between users (e.g. adults and children)	43.6	31.4	41.1	49.2	43.2	43.9	53.8

[1] Urban = inside central city; Suburban = in metro area, outside of a central city; Rural = outside a metro area. [2] Determined by the 1990 poverty status of the service area of the outlet. [3] Central libraries and branches; excludes bookmobiles.

Source: National Commission on Libraries and Information Science, Washington, DC, *Public Libraries and the Internet 2000: Summary Findings and Data Tables,* September 2000, by John Carlo Bartot and Charles R. McClure, Florida State University, Tallahassee, FL.

No. 1133. Internet Access and Usage, and Online Service Usage: 2002

[For persons 18 years old and over (203,836 represents 203,836,000). As of spring. Based on sample and subject to sampling error; see source for details]

Item	Total adults	Any online/ Internet usage	Have Internet access			Used the Internet in the last 30 days			Used any online service in the past 30 days
			Home or work or other	Home only	Work only	Home or work or other	Home only	Work only	
Total adults (1,000)	203,836	117,802	150,852	112,714	65,220	114,230	94,483	54,040	117,802
PERCENT DISTRIBUTION									
Age:									
18 to 34 years old.	31.7	38.1	34.8	33.2	34.3	38.6	35.8	34.3	38.1
35 to 54 years old.	40.5	46.0	44.3	47.6	54.2	46.0	47.7	54.9	46.0
55 years old and over	27.8	15.8	20.9	19.2	11.5	15.4	16.5	10.8	15.8
Sex:									
Male.	47.9	49.1	48.7	50.2	50.5	49.0	49.7	51.0	49.1
Female	52.1	50.9	51.3	49.8	49.5	51.0	50.3	49.0	50.9
Household size:									
1 to 2 persons	46.6	40.2	42.0	38.8	41.1	40.3	39.5	41.5	40.2
3 to 4 persons	38.1	43.9	42.4	44.8	44.8	43.8	44.5	44.8	43.9
5 or more persons.	15.2	15.9	15.6	16.3	14.1	15.9	16.0	13.7	15.9
Any child in household. . . .	42.0	47.0	45.3	47.4	47.6	46.9	47.3	47.7	47.0
Marital status:									
Single.	24.0	27.0	25.3	22.9	23.9	27.2	24.5	23.2	27.0
Married.	57.2	60.8	59.9	65.3	63.6	60.5	64.3	64.3	60.8
Other	18.8	12.3	14.8	11.8	12.5	12.3	11.2	12.5	12.3
Educational attainment:									
Graduated college plus . . .	23.5	35.2	29.7	34.7	46.0	35.9	37.9	50.3	35.2
Attended college.	27.2	34.1	31.5	32.5	31.4	34.3	34.1	31.0	34.1
Did not attend college	49.3	30.7	38.8	32.8	22.6	29.8	28.0	18.7	30.7
Household income:									
Less than $50,000	50.5	32.9	39.8	31.6	21.9	32.5	29.7	18.9	32.9
$50,000 to $74,999	20.7	25.2	23.9	25.2	25.8	25.3	25.2	25.8	25.2
$75,000 to $149,999	22.9	33.0	28.6	33.6	40.4	33.2	35.0	42.4	33.0
$150,000 or more	5.9	8.9	7.7	9.5	11.9	9.0	10.1	12.9	8.9

Source: Mediamark Research Inc., New York, NY, *CyberStats,* spring 2002 (copyright). Internet site <http://www.mriplus.com/pocketpiece.html> (accessed 6 August 2002).

No. 1134. Computers and Internet Use by Individuals: 1997 and 2001

[255,689 represents 255,689, 000. As of October 1997 and September 2001. For persons 3 years old and over, except as indicated. Based on the Current Population Survey and subject to sampling error; see source for details. See also Section 1, Population, and Appendix III]

Characteristic	Population (1,000)		Computer use from any location				Internet use from any location			
			Number (1,000)		Percent of population		Number (1,000)		Percent of population	
	1997	2001	1997	2001	1997	2001	1997	2001	1997	2001
Total [1]	255,689	265,180	136,900	174,051	53.5	65.6	56,774	142,823	22.2	53.9
Sex:										
Male.	124,590	129,152	66,978	84,539	53.8	65.5	30,311	69,580	24.3	53.9
Female	131,099	136,028	69,921	89,512	53.3	65.8	26,464	73,243	20.2	53.8
Age:										
3 to 8 years old	24,445	23,763	14,412	16,877	59.0	71.0	1,748	6,637	7.2	27.9
9 to 17 years old	35,469	37,118	30,188	34,356	85.1	92.6	11,791	25,480	33.2	68.6
18 to 24 years old.	24,973	27,137	14,528	19,361	58.2	71.3	7,884	17,673	31.6	65.0
25 to 49 years old.	101,853	101,890	58,745	71,491	57.7	70.2	27,639	65,138	27.1	63.9
50 years old and over	68,949	75,272	19,026	31,965	27.6	42.5	7,712	27,895	11.2	37.1
Race/ethnicity:										
White, non-Hispanic	184,295	186,793	105,957	130,848	57.5	70.0	46,678	111,942	25.3	59.9
Black, non-Hispanic.	31,786	33,305	13,854	18,544	43.6	55.7	4,197	13,237	13.2	39.8
Asian American and Pacific Islander.	9,225	10,674	5,306	7,600	57.5	71.2	2,432	6,452	26.4	60.4
Hispanic	28,233	32,146	10,729	15,690	38.0	48.8	3,101	10,141	11.0	31.6
Family income:										
Less than $15,000	44,284	31,354	13,182	11,681	29.8	37.3	4,069	7,848	9.2	25.0
$15,000 to $24,999	32,423	26,649	12,115	12,464	37.4	46.8	3,760	8,893	11.6	33.4
$25,000 to $34,999	33,178	28,571	16,360	16,495	49.3	57.7	5,666	12,591	17.1	44.1
$35,000 to $49,999	38,776	36,044	23,440	25,233	60.4	70.0	8,824	20,587	22.8	57.1
$50,000 to $74,999	41,910	44,692	30,043	35,465	71.7	79.4	13,552	30,071	32.3	67.3
$75,000 and over	36,572	56,446	29,542	49,672	80.8	88.0	16,276	44,547	44.5	78.9
Educational attainment: [2]										
Less than high school	29,114	27,484	2,331	4,672	7.9	17.0	516	3,506	1.8	12.8
High school diploma/GED. .	57,487	57,386	19,256	27,118	33.5	47.3	5,589	22,847	9.7	39.8
Some college.	42,544	45,420	24,595	31,551	57.8	69.5	10,548	28,321	24.8	62.4
Bachelor's degree	27,795	30,588	20,640	25,965	74.3	84.9	11,503	24,726	41.4	80.8
More than BA degree	13,863	16,283	10,970	14,151	79.1	86.9	7,195	13,633	51.9	83.7
Employment status: [3]										
Employed	130,857	135,089	80,687	98,819	61.7	73.2	37,254	88,396	28.5	65.4
Not employed or not in labor force	72,911	77,268	18,074	31,487	24.8	40.8	9,012	28,531	12.4	36.9

[1] Includes other races and unreported income and education. [2] For persons 25 years old and over. [3] For persons 16 years old and over.

Source: U.S. Dept. of Commerce, National Telecommunications and Information Administration, *A Nation Online: How Americans Are Expanding Their Use of the Internet,* February 2002. Internet site <http://www.ntia.doc.gov/ntiahome/dn/index.html> (accessed 17 April 2002).

Information and Communications 713

No. 1135. Households With Computers and Internet Access by Selected Characteristic: 2001

[In percent. Based on the Current Population Survey and subject to sampling error; for details, see source. See also text, Section 1, Population and Appendix III]

Characteristic	Households with computers				Households with Internet access			
	Total	Rural [1]	Urban [1]	Central city [1]	Total	Rural [1]	Urban [1]	Central city [1]
All households	**56.5**	**55.6**	**56.7**	**51.5**	**50.5**	**48.7**	**51.1**	**45.7**
Age of householder:								
Under 25 years old	51.1	41.3	53.0	50.9	44.7	33.5	46.7	45.3
25 to 34 years old	62.5	61.5	62.8	57.5	57.3	55.4	58.8	53.9
35 to 44 years old	69.9	71.2	69.4	62.1	62.6	62.3	63.4	54.3
45 to 54 years old	66.9	68.0	66.4	59.9	60.9	61.1	61.3	53.4
55 years old or over	39.1	38.0	39.5	35.5	33.9	32.1	35.0	29.9
Householder race/ethnicity:								
White [2]	61.1	58.0	62.4	60.0	55.4	51.0	56.8	54.8
Black [2]	37.1	31.5	37.7	[3]33.9	30.8	24.4	30.9	27.4
American, Indian, Eskimo, Aleut [2]	44.7	37.6	49.5	[3]49.5	38.7	31.4	41.5	[3]44.1
Asian or Pacific Islander [2]	72.7	[3]69.4	72.8	67.4	68.1	68.2	64.1	63.1
Hispanic	40.0	36.6	40.3	38.1	32.0	29.9	32.6	29.8
Household type:								
Married couple with children under 18	78.9	78.6	79.0	72.4	71.6	69.7	73.6	64.6
Male householder with children under 18	55.1	53.6	55.6	51.8	44.9	39.9	47.2	44.3
Female householder with children under 18	49.2	51.0	48.9	41.6	40.0	40.9	42.3	33.5
Family households without children	58.8	55.0	60.4	55.2	53.2	48.9	55.3	49.7
Nonfamily households	39.2	31.6	40.9	41.4	35.0	26.9	36.2	37.0
Education of householder:								
Elementary	16.0	13.4	17.1	16.9	11.2	10.4	11.6	11.5
Some high school	28.2	27.6	28.4	25.5	22.7	22.4	22.6	19.8
High school graduate or GED	46.5	50.0	45.0	39.0	39.8	42.1	39.3	32.5
Some college	64.5	68.5	63.2	58.4	57.7	60.2	57.3	52.0
Bachelor's degree or more	79.8	81.1	79.5	76.7	75.2	75.1	75.0	72.0
Household income:								
Under $5,000	25.9	17.9	28.2	24.5	20.5	12.5	23.0	20.2
$5,000 to $9,999	19.2	16.4	20.1	20.6	14.4	11.0	15.5	14.5
$10,000 to $14,999	25.7	24.3	26.3	24.3	19.4	18.1	20.7	19.3
$15,000 to $19,999	31.8	29.4	32.6	33.9	23.6	21.0	25.3	24.6
$20,000 to $24,999	40.1	40.0	40.1	36.4	31.8	31.7	32.4	28.7
$25,000 to $34,999	49.7	49.4	49.9	49.9	42.2	40.5	43.7	41.3
$35,000 to $49,999	64.3	64.7	64.2	64.4	56.4	55.0	57.5	56.2
$50,000 to $74,999	77.7	78.1	77.6	75.8	71.4	70.6	71.7	70.5
$75,000 and over	89.0	89.0	88.9	86.4	85.4	84.8	85.5	83.8

[1] See text, Section 1, Population.   [2] Non-Hispanic.   [3] Figure does not meet standards of reliability or precision.

Source: U.S. Dept. of Commerce, National Telecommunications and Information Administration, *A Nation Online: How Americans Are Expanding Their Use of the Internet,* February 2002. Internet site <http://www.ntia.doc.gov/ntiahome/dn/index.html> (accessed 17 April 2002).

No. 1136. Households With Computers and Internet Access: 1998 and 2001

[In percent. Based on the Current Population Survey and subject to sampling error; for details, see source. See also text, Section 1, Population and Appendix III]

State	1998		2001		State	1998		2001	
	Computers	Internet access	Computers	Internet access		Computers	Internet access	Computers	Internet access
U.S.	**42.1**	**26.2**	**56.5**	**50.5**	MO	41.8	24.3	56.0	47.5
AL	34.3	21.6	43.7	37.6	MT	40.9	21.5	55.6	45.5
AK	62.4	44.1	68.7	64.1	NE	42.9	22.9	58.2	52.5
AZ	44.3	29.3	59.4	51.9	NV	41.6	26.5	55.0	50.2
AR	29.8	14.7	46.8	36.9	NH	54.2	37.1	61.2	57.2
CA	47.5	30.7	61.5	55.3	NJ	48.1	31.3	67.7	61.6
CO	55.3	34.5	64.7	58.5	NM	42.2	25.8	50.6	43.1
CT	43.8	31.8	58.7	55.0	NY	37.3	23.7	50.1	44.5
DE	40.5	25.1	58.4	52.5	NC	35.0	19.9	53.0	46.5
DC	41.4	24.2	55.9	52.8	ND	40.2	20.6	57.6	50.9
FL	39.5	27.8	52.4	46.7	OH	40.7	24.6	49.9	43.8
GA	35.8	23.9	63.1	55.2	OK	37.8	20.4	65.8	58.2
HI	42.3	27.9	62.8	52.7	OR	51.3	32.7	53.5	48.7
ID	50.0	27.4	53.0	46.9	PA	39.3	24.9	58.6	53.1
IL	42.7	26.5	53.2	47.3	RI	41.0	27.1	52.2	45.0
IN	43.5	26.1	59.4	51.0	SC	35.7	21.4	55.3	47.6
IA	41.4	21.8	57.5	50.9	SD	41.6	23.9	51.3	44.8
KS	43.7	25.7	49.8	44.2	TN	37.5	21.3	53.7	47.7
KY	35.9	21.1	45.7	40.2	TX	40.9	24.5	67.7	54.1
LA	31.1	17.8	62.8	53.3	UT	60.1	35.8	60.4	53.4
ME	43.4	26.0	64.1	57.8	VT	48.7	31.8	58.8	54.9
MD	46.3	31.0	59.1	54.7	VA	46.4	27.9	49.3	41.4
MA	43.4	28.1	58.3	51.2	WA	56.3	36.6	66.5	60.4
MI	44.0	25.4	64.6	55.6	WV	28.3	17.6	48.0	40.7
MN	47.6	29.0	41.9	36.1	WI	43.0	25.1	56.4	50.2
MS	25.7	13.6	55.3	49.9	WY	46.1	22.7	58.1	51.0

Source: U.S. Department of Commerce, National Telecommunications and Information Administration, *Falling through the Net: Defining the Digital Divide,* July 1999 and *A Nation Online: How Americans Are Expanding Their Use of the Internet,* February 2002. Internet site <http://www.ntia.doc.gov/ntiahome/dn/index.html> (accessed 17 April 2002).

Section 25
Banking, Finance, and Insurance

This section presents data on the nation's finances, various types of financial institutions, money and credit, securities, insurance, and real estate. The primary sources of these data are publications of several departments of the federal government, especially the Treasury Department, and independent agencies such as the Federal Deposit Insurance Corporation, the Federal Reserve System, and the Securities and Exchange Commission. National data on insurance are available primarily from private organizations, such as the American Council of Life Insurers.

Flow of funds—The flow of funds accounts of the Federal Reserve System bring together statistics on all of the major forms of financial instruments to present an economy-wide view of asset and liability relationships. In flow form, the accounts relate borrowing and lending to one another and to the nonfinancial activities that generate income and production. Each claim outstanding is included simultaneously as an asset of the lender and as a liability of the debtor. The accounts also indicate the balance between asset totals and liability totals over the economy as a whole. Several publications of the Board of Governors of the Federal Reserve System contain information on the flow of funds accounts: Summary data on flows and outstandings, in the *Federal Reserve Bulletin*, and *Flow of Funds Accounts of the United States* (quarterly); and concepts and organization of the accounts, in *Guide to the Flow of Funds Accounts* (2000). Data are also available at the Boards Web site <http://www. federalreserve.gov/releases/>.

Banking system—Banks in this country are organized under the laws of both the states and the federal government and are regulated by several bank supervisory agencies. National banks are supervised by the Comptroller of the Currency. *Reports of Condition* have been collected

from national banks since 1863. Summaries of these reports are published in the Comptroller's *Annual Report,* which also presents data on the structure of the national banking system.

The Federal Reserve System was established in 1913 to exercise central banking functions, some of which are shared with the U.S. Treasury. It includes national banks and such state banks that voluntarily join the system. Statements of state bank members are consolidated by the Board of Governors of the Federal Reserve System with data for national banks collected by the Comptroller of the Currency into totals for all member banks of the system. Balance sheet data for member banks and other commercial banks are published quarterly in the *Federal Reserve Bulletin.* The Federal Deposit Insurance Corporation (FDIC), established in 1933, insures each depositor up to $100,000. Major item balance sheet and income data for all commercial banks are published in the *FDIC Quarterly Banking Profile.* This publication is also available on the Internet at the following address: <http://www.fdic.gov>. Balance sheet and income data for individual institutions are also available at this site in the Institution Directory (ID) system.

The FDIC is the primary federal regulator of state-chartered banks that are not members of the Federal Reserve System and of most savings banks insured by the Bank Insurance Fund (BIF). The agency also has certain backup supervisory authority, for safety and soundness purposes, over state-chartered banks that are members of the Federal Reserve System, national banks, and savings associations.

Savings institutions—Savings institutions are primarily involved in credit extension in the form of mortgage loans. Statistics on savings institutions are collected by the U.S. Office of Thrift Supervision and the FDIC. The Financial Institutions Reform, Recovery, and Enforcement

U.S. Census Bureau, Statistical Abstract of the United States: 2002

Act of 1989 (FIRREA) authorized the establishment of the Resolution Trust Corporation (RTC) which was responsible for the disposal of assets from failed savings institutions. FIRREA gave the FDIC the job of managing the federal deposit insurance fund for savings institutions (SAIF= Savings Association Insurance Fund). Major balance sheet and income data for all insured savings institutions are published in the *FDIC Quarterly Banking Profile*.

Credit unions—Federally chartered credit unions are under the supervision of the National Credit Union Administration. State-chartered credit unions are supervised by the respective state supervisory authorities. The administration publishes comprehensive program and statistical information on all federal and federally insured state credit unions in the *Annual Report of the National Credit Union Administration*. Deposit insurance (up to $100,000 per account) is provided to members of all federal and those state credit unions that are federally-insured by the National Credit Union Share Insurance Fund which was established in 1970. Deposit insurance for state chartered credit unions is also available in some states under private or state-administered insurance programs.

Other credit agencies—Insurance companies, finance companies dealing primarily in installment sales financing, and personal loan companies represent important sources of funds for the credit market. Statistics on loans, investments, cash, etc., of life insurance companies are published principally by the American Council of Life Insurers in its *Life Insurers Fact Book*. Consumer credit data are published currently in the *Federal Reserve Bulletin*.

Government corporations and credit agencies make available credit of specified types or to specified groups of private borrowers, either by lending directly or by insuring or guaranteeing loans made by private lending institutions. Data on operations of government credit agencies, along with other government corporations, are available in reports of individual agencies; data on their debt outstanding are published in the *Federal Reserve Bulletin*.

Currency—Currency, including coin and paper money, represents about 46 percent of all media of exchange in the United States, with most payments made by check. All currency is now issued by the Federal Reserve Banks.

Securities—The Securities and Exchange Commission (SEC) was established in 1934 to protect the interests of the public and investors against malpractices in the securities and financial markets and to provide the fullest possible disclosure of information regarding securities to the investing public. Statistical data are published in the *SEC Annual Report*.

Insurance—Insuring companies, which are regulated by the various states or the District of Columbia, are classified as either life or property. Both life and property insurance companies may underwrite health insurance. Insuring companies, other than those classified as life, are permitted to underwrite one or more property lines provided they are so licensed and have the necessary capital or surplus.

There are a number of published sources for statistics on the various classes of insurance—life, health, fire, marine, and casualty. Organizations representing certain classes of insurers publish reports for these classes. The American Council of Life Insurers publishes statistics on life insurance purchases, ownership, benefit payments, and assets in its *Life Insurers Fact Book*.

No. 1137. Gross Domestic Product in Finance, Insurance, and Real Estate in Current and Real (1996) Dollars: 1990 to 2000

[In billions of dollars, except percent (1,010.3 represents $1,010,300,000,000). For definition of gross domestic product, see text, Section 13, Income, Expenditures, and Wealth. Based on 1987 Standard Industrial Classification; see text, Section 15, Business Enterprise]

Industry	Current dollars				Chained (1996) dollars [1]			
	1990	1995	1999	2000	1990	1995	1999	2000
Finance, insurance, real estate, total . . .	1,010.3	1,347.2	1,810.6	1,936.2	1,250.6	1,393.0	1,713.5	1,809.5
Percent of gross domestic product	17.4	18.2	19.5	19.6	18.6	18.5	19.3	19.6
Depository institutions	171.3	227.4	325.6	366.5	244.0	242.4	268.1	288.2
Nondepository institutions	23.3	34.1	53.7	59.0	26.3	33.4	60.6	66.8
Security and commodity brokers	42.3	77.7	138.8	144.2	42.0	76.5	210.0	290.7
Insurance carriers.	64.6	120.2	158.3	167.7	112.2	129.9	135.2	131.1
Insurance agents, brokers, and service	37.7	47.2	65.4	67.3	61.4	49.9	58.9	60.1
Real estate	665.7	832.6	1,051.2	1,116.3	763.4	852.8	986.2	1,018.3
Nonfarm housing services	488.3	628.9	764.4	810.5	580.1	648.0	701.3	721.1
Other real estate.	177.3	203.7	286.8	305.8	182.9	204.9	286.6	299.3
Holding and other investment offices	5.5	8.0	17.6	15.4	10.2	9.9	10.6	7.4

[1] See text, Section 13, Income, Expenditures, and Wealth.

Source: U.S. Bureau of Economic Analysis, *National Income and Product Accounts, 1929-97*; and *Survey of Current Business*, November 2001.

No. 1138. Finance and Insurance—Establishments, Revenue, Payroll, and Employees by Kind of Business: 1997

[2,234,737 represents $2,234,737,000,000. Covers taxable firms only. For statement on methodology, see Appendix III]

Kind of business	NAICS code [1]	All firms		Employer firms			
		Establishments (number)	Revenue (mil. dol.)	Establishments (number)	Revenue (mil. dol.)	Annual payroll (mil. dol.)	Paid employees [2] (1,000)
Finance & insurance	52	1,074,360	2,234,737	395,203	2,197,771	264,551	5,835.2
Monetary authorities—central bank	521	42	24,582	42	24,582	903	21.7
Credit intermediation & related activities	522	330,563	817,504	166,882	808,811	98,723	2,744.9
Depository credit intermediation	5221	109,389	533,349	102,916	533,134	70,230	2,017.7
Commercial banking	52211	(NA)	(NA)	70,860	421,759	57,247	1,575.4
Savings institutions	52212	(NA)	(NA)	16,264	78,947	8,409	264.8
Credit unions.	52213	(NA)	(NA)	15,640	29,694	4,308	172.1
Other depository credit intermediation . .	52219	(NA)	(NA)	152	2,734	266	5.4
Nondepository credit intermediation	5222	190,287	237,134	47,556	229,214	22,661	556.7
Credit card issuing	52221	(NA)	(NA)	588	24,503	1,783	58.8
Sales financing	52222	(NA)	(NA)	8,143	78,133	6,163	127.8
Other nondepository credit intermediation	52229	(NA)	(NA)	38,825	126,577	14,715	370.1
Activities related to credit intermediation . .	5223	30,887	47,021	16,410	46,463	5,833	170.5
Mortgage & nonmortgage loan brokers. .	52231	(NA)	(NA)	8,967	5,087	1,896	49.3
Financial clearinghouse & reserve activities	52232	(NA)	(NA)	1,239	34,780	2,257	63.7
Other credit intermediation activities . . .	52239	(NA)	(NA)	6,204	6,596	1,680	57.4
Security, commodity contracts & like activity .	523	242,901	291,425	54,491	274,987	71,281	706.1
Scrty & comdty contracts intermed & brokerage.	5231	55,307	202,576	26,049	196,417	49,983	449.2
Investment banking & securities dealing .	52311	7,661	119,338	4,136	118,386	22,330	140.8
Securities brokerage	52312	39,937	77,044	19,869	72,756	26,520	290.7
Commodity contracts dealing	52313	1,800	2,586	630	2,241	341	4.5
Commodity contracts brokerage	52314	5,909	3,608	1,414	3,034	792	13.2
Securities & commodity exchanges.	5232	1,193	2,215	30	1,900	442	6.7
Other financial investment activities	5239	186,401	86,634	28,412	76,669	20,857	250.1
Miscellaneous intermediation	52391	(NA)	(NA)	7,190	15,346	1,592	30.4
Portfolio management	52392	(NA)	(NA)	10,888	43,643	13,553	124.0
Investment advice	52393	(NA)	(NA)	7,807	9,398	3,197	42.9
All other financial investment activities . .	52399	(NA)	(NA)	2,527	8,282	2,534	52.9
Insurance carriers & related activities	524	499,365	1,084,618	172,299	1,072,784	92,230	2,327.3
Insurance carriers	5241	39,640	995,588	38,739	995,512	65,858	1,588.0
Direct life/health/medical insurance carriers.	52411	(NA)	(NA)	14,615	666,532	34,474	889.0
Other direct insurance carriers	52412	(NA)	(NA)	23,561	307,695	30,374	683.1
Reinsurance carriers.	52413	(NA)	(NA)	563	21,285	1,010	15.9
Agencies & other insurance related activities.	5242	459,725	89,030	133,560	77,272	26,372	739.3
Insurance agencies & brokerages	52421	378,410	68,893	120,392	59,174	19,533	557.7
Other insurance related activities	52429	81,315	20,138	13,168	18,098	6,839	181.6
Funds, trusts, & other financial vehicles (part)	525	1,489	16,608	1,489	16,608	1,413	35.3
Other investment pools & funds (part)	5259	1,489	16,608	1,489	16,608	1,413	35.3
Real Estate Investment Trusts (REITs). .	52593	1,489	16,608	1,489	16,608	1,413	35.3

NA Not available. [1] North American Industry Classification System, 1997; see text, Section 15, Business Enterprise. [2] For pay period including March 12.

Source: U.S. Census Bureau, *1997 Economic Census, Geographic Area Series* and *Nonemployer Statistics*.

No. 1139. Finance and Insurance—Establishments, Employees, and Payroll: 1999 and 2000

[**418.3 represents 418,300.** Covers establishments with payroll. Employees are for the week including March 12. Most government employees are excluded. For statement on methodology, see Appendix III]

Kind of business	NAICS code [1]	Establishments (1,000)		Employees (1,000)		Payroll (bil. dol.)	
		1999	2000	1999	2000	1999	2000
Finance & insurance, total	52	418.3	423.7	5,965	5,963	313.2	346.8
Monetary authorities—central bank	521	(Z)	0.1	22	22	1.0	1.1
Credit intermediation & related activities	522	173.8	176.3	2,781	2,753	112.6	116.1
Depository credit intermediation [2] . .	5221	104.0	105.6	1,937	1,935	75.9	78.5
Commercial banking.	52211	72.5	73.9	1,494	1,493	61.5	63.6
Savings institutions.	52212	15.9	15.9	254	244	9.1	9.2
Credit unions.	52213	15.5	15.6	184	192	4.9	5.4
Nondepository credit intermediation	5222	49.6	49.3	645	621	29.2	29.6
Credit card issuing	52221	0.8	0.8	59	68	1.9	2.5
Sales financing	52222	7.8	7.4	154	154	8.2	8.8
Other nondepository credit intermediation [2] . .	52229	41.0	41.1	432	399	19.1	18.2
Real estate credit	522292	20.5	19.8	275	238	12.5	10.8
Activities related to credit intermediation	5223	20.2	21.4	199	198	7.5	7.9
Security, commodity contracts & like activity	523	66.4	72.9	780	866	92.9	119.5
Scrty & comdty contracts intermed & brokerage [2]	5231	34.5	38.1	491	539	63.2	80.2
Investment banking & securities dealing. . . .	52311	5.9	6.3	130	138	23.7	31.2
Securities brokerage.	52312	26.3	29.5	340	378	37.9	47.0
Securities & commodity exchanges. [2]	5232	0.1	(Z)	7	7	0.5	0.5
Other financial investment activities [2]	5239	31.7	34.8	282	320	29.3	38.8
Portfolio management.	52392	11.4	11.6	140	156	18.5	24.9
Insurance carriers & related activities	524	176.1	172.2	2,346	2,290	104.8	108.1
Insurance carriers [2]	5241	42.3	37.4	1,549	1,489	72.6	74.7
Direct life/health/medical insurance carriers. .	52411	14.5	13.9	859	813	38.7	40.0
Direct life insurance carriers	524113	11.2	10.7	541	491	25.3	25.7
Direct health & medical insurance carriers.	524114	3.2	3.1	317	322	13.4	14.3
Other direct insurance carriers [2]	52412	27.2	23.0	672	660	32.5	33.5
Direct property & casualty insurance carriers	524126	24.0	19.8	621	609	30.2	31.1
Agencies & other insurance related activities [2] .	5242	133.9	134.8	797	801	32.2	33.3
Insurance agencies & brokerages	52421	120.3	121.5	593	596	23.8	24.7
Funds, trusts, & other financial vehicles (part) . . .	525	2.0	2.3	36	32	1.9	2.1

Z Less than 500. [1] North American Industry Classification System; see text, Section 15, Business Enterprise. [2] Includes industries not shown separately.

Source: U.S. Census Bureau, *County Business Patterns*, annual, <http://www.census.gov/prod/2002pubs/cbp00/cbp00-1.pdf> (issued May 2002).

No. 1140. Flow of Funds Accounts—Financial Assets of Financial and Nonfinancial Institutions by Holder Sector: 1990 to 2001

[In billions of dollars (36,359 represents $36,359,000,000,000). As of Dec. 31]

Sector	1990	1993	1994	1995	1996	1997	1998	1999	2000	2001
All sectors	36,359	45,321	47,610	53,812	59,848	67,830	76,840	87,353	89,323	90,580
Households [1]	14,854	18,400	19,036	21,619	24,004	27,429	30,503	35,064	33,680	32,098
Nonfinancial business	3,979	4,673	5,006	5,566	6,160	6,643	7,982	8,893	9,570	9,892
Farm business	47	57	59	61	61	62	64	65	65	67
Nonfarm noncorporate	356	408	470	546	641	772	1,102	1,264	1,394	1,500
Nonfinancial corporations	3,575	4,207	4,477	4,959	5,458	5,809	6,816	7,564	8,112	8,325
State and local government	963	1,083	1,026	994	1,008	1,033	1,180	1,268	1,321	1,406
U.S. Government	442	491	440	441	441	438	443	557	507	609
Monetary authorities	342	424	452	472	495	534	567	697	636	683
Commercial banking	3,337	3,892	4,160	4,494	4,710	5,175	5,642	5,980	6,462	6,876
U.S.-chartered commercial banks. . . .	2,644	2,932	3,123	3,322	3,445	3,742	4,094	4,433	4,773	5,010
Foreign banking offices in U.S.	367	542	590	666	715	811	806	747	784	851
Bank holding companies.	298	388	414	467	511	575	686	741	842	943
Banks in U.S.-affiliated areas.	28	29	33	39	40	46	56	59	63	72
Savings institutions	1,323	1,020	1,009	1,013	1,032	1,029	1,088	1,151	1,219	1,298
Credit unions	217	282	294	311	330	354	391	415	441	506
Bank personal trusts, estates	522	661	670	775	841	918	976	1,104	992	885
Life insurance	1,351	1,755	1,863	2,064	2,246	2,515	2,770	3,068	3,136	3,306
Other insurance	533	642	678	740	770	843	879	876	872	881
Private pension funds	1,634	2,304	2,460	2,923	3,251	3,747	4,178	4,645	4,538	4,161
State and local govt. retirement funds. . .	801	1,051	1,088	1,303	1,495	1,817	2,054	2,227	2,290	2,177
Money market funds	493	560	600	741	887	1,043	1,330	1,579	1,812	2,241
Mutual funds	608	1,375	1,477	1,853	2,342	2,989	3,613	4,538	4,435	4,136
Closed-end and exchange-traded investment funds.	53	117	118	135	147	156	167	185	204	209
U.S. Govt.-sponsored enterprises	478	631	782	897	989	1,099	1,404	1,721	1,969	2,301
Federally-related mortgage pools.	1,020	1,357	1,472	1,570	1,711	1,826	2,018	2,292	2,492	2,828
Asset-backed securities issuers.	270	492	568	709	855	1,066	1,385	1,612	1,823	2,105
Finance companies.	547	557	600	672	717	764	853	1,003	1,138	1,153
Mortgage companies.	49	60	36	33	41	32	35	36	36	37
Real estate investment trusts	28	30	31	33	38	64	71	68	62	77
Security brokers and dealers.	262	479	455	568	636	779	921	1,001	1,221	1,437
Funding corporations	251	337	380	394	499	613	717	973	1,100	1,086
Rest of the world	1,998	2,648	2,910	3,491	4,203	4,926	5,672	6,400	7,369	8,192

[1] Includes nonprofit organizations.

Source: Board of Governors of the Federal Reserve System, "Federal Reserve Statistical Release, Z.1, Flow of Funds Accounts of the United States"; published: 7 March 2002; <http://www.federalreserve.gov/releases/Z1/20020307/data.htm>.

No. 1141. Flow of Funds Accounts—Financial Assets and Liabilities of Foreign Sector: 1990 to 2001

[In billions of dollars (1,998 represents $1,998,000,000,000). As of Dec. 31]

Type of instrument	1990	1993	1994	1995	1996	1997	1998	1999	2000	2001
Total financial assets [1]	1,998	2,648	2,910	3,491	4,203	4,926	5,672	6,400	7,369	8,192
Net interbank assets	53	125	218	229	177	173	146	140	163	156
U.S. checkable deposits and currency . .	107	155	180	194	214	244	258	298	290	314
U.S. time deposits.	49	55	56	50	61	74	87	102	107	92
Security RPs [2]	20	59	47	68	71	91	72	80	91	121
Credit market instruments.	889	1,109	1,216	1,531	1,927	2,257	2,540	2,676	3,005	3,431
Open market paper	11	19	25	43	58	78	115	102	111	119
U.S. government securities	488	702	758	996	1,290	1,499	1,622	1,634	1,772	1,961
Official holdings	291	382	407	498	610	615	620	629	677	706
Treasury	286	373	397	483	591	590	589	578	582	594
Agency	5	9	10	15	20	25	31	51	95	112
Private holdings	197	321	351	498	679	884	1,002	1,005	1,095	1,255
Treasury	152	222	236	359	503	662	730	661	640	655
Agency	45	99	115	140	176	222	272	344	456	600
U.S. corporate bonds [3]	217	273	311	369	453	538	660	821	1,004	1,234
Loans to U.S. corporate business. . . .	172	114	122	122	126	143	142	120	117	116
U.S. corporate equities	244	374	398	528	657	920	1,175	1,538	1,748	1,693
Miscellaneous assets.	591	722	742	841	1,040	1,108	1,343	1,519	1,912	2,323
Foreign direct investment in U.S [4] . . .	505	593	618	680	746	823	912	1,094	1,370	1,551
Other	86	128	124	161	294	285	430	424	543	773
Total liabilities [1]	1,389	1,585	1,743	2,012	2,317	2,561	2,789	3,073	3,499	4,068
U.S. private deposits	298	272	374	419	522	618	642	704	825	887
Credit market instruments [1]	289	389	375	454	542	608	652	680	747	705
Commercial paper.	75	69	43	56	67	65	73	89	121	107
Bonds	115	230	242	299	366	428	463	479	505	487
Bank loans n.e.c. [5]	19	25	26	35	44	52	59	59	71	63
U.S. government loans	63	57	56	55	55	53	52	48	47	48
Trade payables	27	36	40	45	44	49	46	51	52	52
Miscellaneous liabilities [1]	713	836	901	1,030	1,156	1,237	1,389	1,589	1,830	2,378
U.S. direct investment abroad [3][4] . . .	629	724	787	886	987	1,067	1,197	1,328	1,445	1,613

[1] Includes other items not shown separately.   [2] Repurchase agreements.   [3] Through 1992, corporate bonds include net issues by Netherlands Antillean financial subsidiaries; U.S. direct investment abroad excludes net inflows from those bond issues.   [4] Direct investment is valued on a current-cost basis.   [5] Not elsewhere classified.

No. 1142. Flow of Funds Accounts—Credit Market Debt Outstanding: 1990 to 2001

[In billions of dollars (13,755 represents $13,755,000,000,000). As of Dec. 31. N.e.c.=Not elsewhere classified]

Item	1990	1993	1994	1995	1996	1997	1998	1999	2000	2001
Credit market debt.	13,755	16,169	17,199	18,440	19,812	21,310	23,488	25,736	27,521	29,496
U.S. Government.	2,498	3,336	3,492	3,637	3,782	3,805	3,752	3,681	3,385	3,380
Nonfederal domestic nonfinancial	8,352	9,098	9,509	10,071	10,659	11,439	12,539	13,745	14,932	16,041
Households [1]	3,625	4,260	4,575	4,914	5,224	5,557	6,023	6,540	7,114	7,724
Corporations	2,507	2,524	2,655	2,880	3,093	3,383	3,789	4,265	4,694	4,962
Nonfarm noncorporate business	1,093	1,008	1,016	1,062	1,129	1,224	1,364	1,519	1,665	1,781
Farm business.	135	138	142	145	150	156	164	169	180	188
State and local government	992	1,168	1,122	1,070	1,063	1,119	1,200	1,252	1,279	1,386
Rest of the world	289	389	375	454	542	608	652	680	747	705
Financial sectors	2,616	3,346	3,822	4,279	4,829	5,458	6,545	7,630	8,457	9,370
Commercial banking	198	208	228	251	264	309	382	449	509	564
Thrift institutions [2]	140	100	113	115	141	161	214	264	291	299
Life insurance companies . . . . . . [3]	-	-	1	1	2	2	2	3	2	3
Government-sponsored enterprises [3] .	399	528	701	807	897	995	1,274	1,592	1,826	2,115
Federally-related mortgage pools. . . .	1,020	1,357	1,472	1,570	1,711	1,826	2,018	2,292	2,492	2,828
Asset-backed securities issuers.	271	494	570	713	863	1,077	1,398	1,621	1,830	2,110
Finance companies.	374	385	434	484	534	568	625	696	777	770
Mortgage companies.	25	30	19	17	21	16	18	18	18	19
Real estate investment trusts	28	30	40	45	56	96	159	165	168	171
Security brokers and dealers	15	34	34	29	27	35	43	25	41	42
Funding corporations	147	180	211	249	312	373	413	504	504	451
CORPORATE CREDIT MARKET DEBT OUTSTANDING, BY TYPE OF INSTRUMENT										
Total	2,507	2,524	2,655	2,880	3,093	3,383	3,789	4,265	4,694	4,962
Commercial paper	117	118	139	157	156	169	193	230	278	190
Municipal securities [4]	115	125	132	135	138	142	148	153	154	157
Corporate bonds	1,008	1,230	1,253	1,344	1,460	1,611	1,830	2,059	2,231	2,559
Bank loans, n.e.c.	545	480	527	602	642	693	774	847	922	865
Other loans and advances.	473	388	421	454	468	508	562	596	670	671
Savings institutions.	17	5	5	6	8	9	12	15	20	21
Finance companies.	241	224	247	271	274	274	307	356	413	402
U.S. Government	9	8	8	10	9	8	8	8	8	7
Acceptance liabilities to banks	29	17	15	14	13	11	7	4	4	4
Rest of the world	172	114	122	122	126	143	142	120	117	116
Asset-backed securities issuers.	4	19	24	30	38	62	86	94	108	120
Mortgages	248	183	183	188	228	261	282	378	439	520

- Represents or rounds to zero.   [1] Includes nonprofit organizations.   [2] Covers savings institutions and credit unions.   [3] U.S. government.   [4] Industrial revenue bonds. Issued by state and local governments to finance private investment and secured in interest and principal by the industrial user of the funds.

Source of Tables 1141 and 1142: Board of Governors of the Federal Reserve System, "Federal Reserve Statistical Release, Z.1, Flow of Funds Accounts of the United States"; published: 7 March 2002; <http://www.federalreserve.gov/releases/Z1/20020307/data.htm>.

No. 1143. Flow of Funds Accounts—Assets and Liabilities of Households: 1990 to 2001

[As of December 31 (14,854 represents $14,854,000,000,000). Includes nonprofit organizations]

Type of instrument	Total (bil. dol.)								Percent distribution	
	1990	1995	1996	1997	1998	1999	2000	2001	1990	2001
Total financial assets	14,854	21,619	24,004	27,429	30,503	35,064	33,680	32,098	100.0	100.0
Deposits.	3,274	3,315	3,469	3,645	3,958	4,142	4,531	4,967	22.0	15.5
Foreign deposits.	13	23	35	37	38	44	51	47	0.1	0.1
Checkable deposits and currency . .	427	561	499	460	440	395	339	390	2.9	1.2
Time and savings deposits	2,465	2,281	2,434	2,566	2,733	2,831	3,138	3,391	16.6	10.6
Money market fund shares	369	450	501	582	747	872	1,003	1,139	2.5	3.5
Credit market instruments	1,556	1,928	2,087	2,030	2,044	2,281	2,070	1,894	10.5	5.9
Open-market paper.	63	48	55	56	64	68	73	53	0.4	0.2
U.S. Government securities	555	900	998	864	758	931	707	539	3.7	1.7
Treasury issues.	495	801	827	688	602	688	462	439	3.3	1.4
Savings bonds.	126	185	187	186	187	186	185	190	0.8	0.6
Other Treasury	369	616	640	501	415	501	277	249	2.5	0.8
Agency issues	60	99	171	177	157	243	245	100	0.4	0.3
Municipal securities.	575	455	433	469	488	527	542	582	3.9	1.8
Corporate and foreign bonds.	219	415	491	532	624	646	637	608	1.5	1.9
Mortgages	144	109	110	110	110	110	111	112	1.0	0.3
Corporate equities [1]	1,781	4,161	4,896	6,302	7,174	9,197	7,317	5,832	12.0	18.2
Mutual fund shares.	457	1,159	1,495	1,941	2,406	3,128	3,125	2,993	3.1	9.3
Security credit	62	128	163	215	277	324	412	443	0.4	1.4
Life insurance reserves.	392	566	611	665	718	784	819	868	2.6	2.7
Pension fund reserves [2]	3,376	5,671	6,325	7,323	8,209	9,080	9,091	8,723	22.7	27.2
Investment in bank personal trusts . . .	552	803	871	943	1,001	1,130	1,019	912	3.7	2.8
Equity in noncorporate business	3,179	3,596	3,786	4,051	4,394	4,663	4,956	5,106	21.4	15.9
Miscellaneous assets	224	292	301	312	321	334	339	359	1.5	1.1
Total liabilities	3,747	5,111	5,446	5,825	6,320	6,920	7,507	8,083	100.0	100.0
Credit market instruments	3,625	4,914	5,224	5,557	6,023	6,540	7,114	7,724	96.7	95.6
Home mortgages [3]	2,532	3,383	3,578	3,818	4,168	4,557	4,940	5,430	67.6	67.2
Consumer credit.	805	1,123	1,214	1,272	1,347	1,446	1,593	1,688	21.5	20.9
Municipal securities.	87	98	105	115	127	137	143	154	2.3	1.9
Bank loans, n.e.c. [4].	18	57	58	66	73	65	74	57	0.5	0.7
Other loans	101	160	173	191	204	219	246	264	2.7	3.3
Commercial mortgages	83	92	97	95	105	115	118	130	2.2	1.6
Security credit	39	79	94	131	153	228	235	195	1.0	2.4
Trade payables	67	101	109	118	127	133	139	145	1.8	1.8
Unpaid life insurance premiums [5]	16	18	18	19	17	19	20	20	0.4	0.2

[1] Only those directly held and those in closed-end and exchange-traded funds. Other equities are included in mutual funds, life insurance and pension reserves, and bank personal trusts. [2] See also Table 1194. [3] Includes loans made under home equity lines of credit and home equity loans secured by junior liens. [4] Not elsewhere classified. [5] Includes deferred premiums.

Source: Board of Governors of the Federal Reserve System, "Federal Reserve Statistical Release, Z.1, Flow of Funds Accounts of the United States"; published: 7 March 2002; <http://www.federalreserve.gov/releases/Z1/20020307/data.htm>.

No. 1144. Percent of Families Owning Financial Assets by Type of Asset: 1992 to 1998

[Families include one-person units; for definition of family, see text, Section 1, Population. Based on Survey of Consumer Finance; see Appendix III]

Age of family head and family income	Any financial asset [1]	Transac- tion accounts [2]	Certifi- cates of deposit	Savings bonds	Stocks [3]	Mutual funds [4]	Retirement accounts [5]	Life insur- ance [6]	Other man- aged [7]
1992, total	90.2	86.9	16.7	22.3	17.0	10.4	39.6	34.9	4.0
1995, total	91.0	87.0	14.3	22.8	15.2	12.3	45.2	32.0	3.9
1998, total	92.9	90.5	15.3	19.3	19.2	16.5	48.8	29.6	5.9
Under 35 years old	88.6	84.6	6.2	17.2	13.1	12.2	39.8	18.0	1.9
35 to 44 years old.	93.3	90.5	9.4	24.9	18.9	16.0	59.5	29.0	3.9
45 to 54 years old.	94.9	93.5	11.8	21.8	22.6	23.0	59.2	32.9	6.5
55 to 64 years old.	95.6	93.9	18.6	18.1	25.0	15.2	58.3	35.8	6.5
65 to 74 years old.	95.6	94.1	29.9	16.1	21.0	18.0	46.1	39.1	11.8
75 years old and over	92.1	89.7	35.9	12.0	18.0	15.1	16.7	32.6	11.6
Less than $10,000.	70.6	61.9	7.7	3.5	3.8	1.9	6.4	15.7	(B)
$10,000 to $24,999	89.9	86.5	16.8	10.2	7.2	7.6	25.4	20.9	4.9
$25,000 to $49,999	97.3	95.8	15.9	20.4	17.7	14.0	54.2	28.1	3.9
$50,000 to $99,999	99.8	99.3	16.4	30.6	27.7	25.8	73.5	39.8	8.0
$100,000 and more	100.0	100.0	16.8	32.3	56.6	44.8	88.6	50.1	15.8

B Base figure too small. [1] Includes other types of financial assets, not shown separately. [2] Checking, savings, and money market deposit accounts, money market mutual funds, and call accounts at brokerages. [3] Covers only those stocks that are directly held by families outside mutual funds, retirement accounts and other managed assets. [4] Excludes money market mutual funds and funds held through retirement accounts or other managed assets. [5] Covers IRAs, Keogh accounts, and certain employer-sponsored accounts. [6] Cash value. [7] Includes personal annuities and trusts with an equity interest and managed investment accounts.

Source: Board of Governors of the Federal Reserve System, *Federal Reserve Bulletin*, January 2000, and unpublished revisions.

No. 1145. Percent of Families Holding Financial Debt by Type of Debt: 1992 to 1998

[See headnote, Table 1144]

Age of family head and family income	Any debt	Home-secured debt [1]	Installment	Other lines of credit	Credit card balances [2]	Other residential property	Other debt [3]
1992, total	73.2	39.1	46.0	2.3	43.7	5.7	8.4
1995, total	74.5	41.0	45.9	1.9	47.3	4.7	8.5
1998, total	**74.1**	**43.1**	**43.7**	**2.3**	**44.1**	**5.1**	**8.8**
Under 35 years old	81.2	33.2	60.0	2.4	50.7	2.0	9.6
35 to 44 years old	87.6	58.7	53.3	3.6	51.3	6.7	11.4
45 to 54 years old	87.0	58.8	51.2	3.6	52.5	6.7	11.1
55 to 64 years old	76.4	49.4	37.9	1.6	45.7	7.8	8.3
65 to 74 years old	51.4	26.0	20.2	(B)	29.2	5.1	4.1
75 years old and over	24.6	11.5	4.2	(B)	11.2	1.8	2.0
Less than $10,000.	41.7	8.3	25.7	(B)	20.6	(B)	3.6
$10,000 to $24,999	63.7	21.3	34.4	1.2	37.9	1.8	7.0
$25,000 to $49,999	79.6	43.7	50.0	2.9	49.9	4.1	7.7
$50,000 to $99,999	89.4	71.0	55.0	3.3	56.7	7.7	12.2
$100,000 and more	87.8	73.4	43.2	2.6	40.4	16.4	14.8

B Base figure too small. [1] First and second mortgages and home equity loans and lines of credit secured by the primary residence. [2] Families that had an outstanding balance on any of their credit cards after paying their most recent bills. [3] Includes loans on insurance policies, loans against pension accounts, borrowing on margin accounts and unclassified loans.

Source: Board of Governors of the Federal Reserve System, *Federal Reserve Bulletin*, January 2000, and unpublished revisions.

No. 1146. Household Debt-Service Payments as a Percentage of Disposable Personal Income: 1980 to 2001

[In percent. As of end of year. Seasonally adjusted. The household debt-service burden is an estimate of the ratio of debt payments to disposable personal income. Debt payments consist of the estimated required payments on outstanding mortgage and consumer debt]

Year	Total	Consumer	Mortgage	Year	Total	Consumer	Mortgage
1980	12.53	7.96	4.57	1991	12.77	6.51	6.26
1981	12.49	7.60	4.89	1992	11.89	5.97	5.92
1982	12.49	7.45	5.04	1993	11.84	6.09	5.75
1983	12.51	7.46	5.05	1994	12.25	6.48	5.76
1984	12.99	7.81	5.19	1995	12.92	7.04	5.88
1985	13.93	8.29	5.64	1996	13.28	7.44	5.84
1986	14.38	8.48	5.89	1997	13.39	7.50	5.89
1987	13.79	7.91	5.87	1998	13.40	7.59	5.82
1988	13.47	7.58	5.89	1999	13.77	7.74	6.03
1989	13.71	7.58	6.13	2000	14.09	7.88	6.21
1990	13.41	7.10	6.31	2001	14.32	8.00	6.32

Source: Board of Governors of the Federal Reserve System, *"Household Debt Service Burden;"* published: 16 July 2002; <http://www.federalreserve.gov/releases/housedebt/default.htm>.

No. 1147. Banking Offices by Type of Bank: 1990 to 2001

[As of December 31. Includes Puerto Rico and outlying areas. Covers all FDIC-insured commercial banks and savings institutions. Commercial banks include insured branches of foreign banks]

Item	1990	1994	1995	1996	1997	1998	1999	2000	2001
All banking offices	**84,378**	**81,688**	**81,907**	**83,075**	**84,314**	**85,374**	**86,994**	**86,652**	**87,545**
Number of banks	15,162	12,604	11,972	11,456	10,923	10,464	10,223	9,904	9,613
Number of branches	69,216	69,084	69,935	71,619	73,391	74,910	76,771	76,748	77,932
Commercial banks	62,753	65,597	66,454	67,319	69,468	70,731	72,265	72,394	73,644
Number of banks.	12,347	10,452	9,942	9,530	9,143	8,774	8,581	8,315	8,080
Number of branches	50,406	55,145	56,512	57,789	60,325	61,957	63,684	64,079	65,564
Savings institutions	21,625	16,091	15,453	15,756	14,846	14,643	14,729	14,258	13,901
Number of banks.	2,815	2,152	2,030	1,926	1,780	1,690	1,642	1,589	1,533
Number of branches	18,810	13,939	13,423	13,830	13,066	12,953	13,087	12,669	12,368

Source: U.S. Federal Deposit Insurance Corporation, *Statistics on Banking*, annual; *Historical Statistics on Banking*; and *The FDIC Quarterly Banking Profile Graph Book*.

No. 1148. Selected Financial Institutions—Number and Assets by Asset Size: 2001

[As of December (6,569.2 represents $6,569,200,000,000). FDIC=Federal Deposit Insurance Corporation]

Asset size	Number of institutions			Assets (bil. dol.)		
	F.D.I.C.-insured			F.D.I.C.-insured		
	Commercial banks	Savings institutions	Credit unions [1]	Commercial banks [2]	Savings institutions	Credit unions [1]
Total................	8,080	1,533	9,984	6,569.2	1,299.0	501.6
Less than $5.0 million.........	30	12	3,798	0.1	(Z)	7.3
$5.0 million to $9.9 million......	98	26	1,552	0.8	0.2	11.2
$10.0 million to $24.9 million	746	75	1,827	13.6	1.4	29.4
$25.0 million to $49.9 million	1,548	171	1,129	58.2	6.3	40.3
$50.0 million to $99.9 million	2,062	291	720	148.8	21.4	51.1
$100.0 million to $499.9 million...	2,861	681	793	592.0	158.9	169.4
$500.0 million to $999.9 million...	335	132	109	227.6	92.6	74.9
$1.0 billion to $2.9 billion.......	219	89	48	362.8	147.0	72.2
$3.0 billion or more..........	181	56	8	5,165.4	871.1	45.7
	Percent distribution					
Total................	100.0	100.0	100.0	100.0	100.0	100.0
Less than $5.0 million.........	0.4	0.8	38.0	(Z)	(Z)	1.5
$5.0 million to $9.9 million.......	1.2	1.7	15.5	(Z)	(Z)	2.2
$10.0 million to $24.9 million	9.2	4.9	18.3	0.2	0.1	5.9
$25.0 million to $49.9 million	19.2	11.2	11.3	0.9	0.5	8.0
$50.0 million to $99.9 million	25.5	19.0	7.2	2.3	1.7	10.2
$100.0 million to $499.9 million...	35.4	44.4	7.9	9.0	12.2	33.8
$500.0 million to $999.9 million...	4.1	8.6	1.1	3.5	7.1	14.9
$1.0 billion to $2.9 billion.......	2.7	5.8	0.5	5.5	11.3	14.4
$3.0 billion or more..........	2.2	3.7	0.1	78.6	67.1	9.1

Z Less than $50 million or 0.05 percent.   [1] Source: National Credit Union Administration, *National Credit Union Administration Yearend Statistics 2001.* Excludes nonfederally insured state chartered credit unions and federally insured corporate credit unions.   [2] Includes foreign branches of U.S. banks.

Source: Except as noted, U.S. Federal Deposit Insurance Corporation, *Statistics on Banking, 2001.*

No. 1149. Insured Commercial Banks—Assets and Liabilities: 1990 to 2001

[In billions of dollars, except as indicated (3,389 represents $3,389,000,000,000). As of Dec. 31. 2001 data preliminary. Includes outlying areas. Except as noted, includes foreign branches of U.S. banks]

Item	1990	1994	1995	1996	1997	1998	1999	2000	2001
Number of banks reporting........	12,343	10,450	9,940	9,528	9,142	8,774	8,580	8,315	8,080
Assets, total.............	3,389	4,011	4,313	4,578	5,015	5,443	5,735	6,245	6,569
Net loans and leases............	2,055	2,306	2,550	2,758	2,916	3,181	3,433	3,755	3,823
Real estate loans............	830	998	1,080	1,139	1,245	1,346	1,510	1,673	1,804
Home equity loans [1]........	61	76	79	85	98	97	102	128	154
Commercial and industrial loans...	615	589	661	710	795	899	971	1,051	982
Loans to individuals...........	404	487	535	562	561	571	558	607	631
Credit cards and related plans ..	134	187	216	232	231	229	212	249	232
Farm loans................	33	39	40	41	45	46	45	48	48
Other loans and leases.........	242	251	292	364	329	381	410	443	433
Less: Reserve for losses........	56	52	53	53	55	57	59	64	72
Less: Unearned income	14	6	6	5	4	4	4	3	3
Investment securities............	605	823	811	801	872	980	1,046	1,079	1,180
Other	730	881	952	1,020	1,227	1,282	1,256	1,410	1,566
Domestic office assets...........	2,999	3,483	3,728	3,906	4,267	4,719	4,995	5,485	5,803
Foreign office assets...........	390	527	585	672	748	723	739	760	766
Liabilities and capital, total.....	3,389	4,011	4,313	4,578	5,015	5,443	5,735	6,245	6,569
Noninterest-bearing deposits.......	489	572	612	664	677	720	703	757	874
Interest-bearing deposits	2,162	2,302	2,416	2,533	2,745	2,961	3,127	3,423	3,518
Subordinated debt..............	24	41	44	51	62	73	76	87	95
Other liabilities	496	783	892	955	1,113	1,226	1,348	1,447	1,485
Equity capital	219	312	350	375	418	462	480	531	597
Domestic office deposits...........	2,357	2,443	2,573	2,724	2,896	3,109	3,175	3,473	3,762
Foreign office deposits...........	293	432	454	474	526	572	656	707	630

[1] For one- to four-family residential properties.

Source: U.S. Federal Deposit Insurance Corporation, *The FDIC Quarterly Banking Profile, Annual Report,* and *Statistics on Banking,* annual.

No. 1150. Insured Commercial Banks—Income and Selected Measures of Financial Condition: 1990 to 2001

[In billions of dollars, except as indicated (320.5 represents $320,500,000,000). 2001 data preliminary. Includes outlying areas. Includes foreign branches of U.S. banks]

Item	1990	1994	1995	1996	1997	1998	1999	2000	2001
Interest income	320.5	257.8	302.4	312.7	339.5	362.0	367.3	428.4	402.9
Interest expense	204.9	111.3	148.2	150.0	165.0	179.3	175.1	224.5	187.7
Net interest income	115.5	146.6	154.2	162.8	174.5	182.8	192.2	204.0	215.2
Provisions for loan losses	32.1	11.0	12.6	16.3	19.9	22.2	21.8	30.0	43.1
Noninterest income.	54.9	76.3	82.4	93.6	104.5	123.7	144.4	153.5	157.2
Percent of net operating revenue [1]	32.2	34.2	34.8	36.5	37.5	40.4	42.9	42.9	42.2
Noninterest expense.	115.7	144.2	149.7	160.7	170.0	194.1	204.2	216.1	222.3
Income taxes.	7.7	22.4	26.1	28.2	31.9	31.9	39.4	38.0	36.9
Net income	16.0	44.6	48.7	52.4	59.2	61.8	71.6	71.0	74.3
From domestic operations	14.2	39.3	43.1	46.0	53.1	56.6	64.8	63.8	67.4
From foreign operations.	1.8	5.3	5.7	6.3	6.1	5.2	6.7	7.2	6.9
PERFORMANCE RATIOS									
Return on assets [2] (percent)	0.48	1.15	1.17	1.19	1.23	1.19	1.31	1.19	1.16
Return on equity [3] (percent).	7.45	14.61	14.66	14.45	14.68	13.93	15.31	14.02	13.10
Net interest margin [4] (percent)	3.94	4.36	4.29	4.27	4.21	4.07	4.07	3.95	3.90
Net charge-offs [5]	29.7	11.2	12.2	15.5	18.3	20.7	20.4	24.8	36.5
Net charge-offs to loans and leases, total (percent).	1.43	0.50	0.49	0.58	0.64	0.67	0.61	0.65	0.94
Net charge-off rate, credit card loans (percent). .	3.86	3.00	3.98	4.66	5.34	5.26	4.48	4.70	6.26
CONDITION RATIOS									
Equity capital to assets (percent).	6.45	7.78	8.11	8.20	8.33	8.49	8.37	8.50	9.09
Noncurrent assets plus other real estate owned to assets [6] (percent)	2.94	1.01	0.85	0.75	0.66	0.65	0.63	0.74	0.92
Percentage of banks losing money	13.4	4.0	3.6	4.3	4.8	6.1	7.5	7.3	7.5

[1] Net operating revenue equals net interest income plus noninterest income. [2] Net income (including securities transactions and nonrecurring items) as a percentage of average total assets. [3] Net income as a percentage of average total equity capital. [4] Interest income less interest expense as a percentage of average earning assets (i.e. the profit margin a bank earns on its loans and investments). [5] Total loans and leases charged off (removed from balance sheet because of uncollectibility), less amounts recovered on loans and leases previously charged off. [6] The sum of loans, leases, debt securities and other assets that are 90 days or more past due, or in nonaccrual status plus foreclosed property.

No. 1151. Insured Commercial Banks—Selected Measures of Financial Condition by Asset Size and Region: 2001

[In percent, except as indicated. Preliminary. See headnote, Table 1150]

Asset size and region	Number of banks	Return on assets	Return on equity	Equity capital to assets	Net charge-offs to loans and leases	Percentage of banks losing money
Total	**8,080**	**1.16**	**13.10**	**9.09**	**0.94**	**7.5**
Less than $100 million	4,486	0.91	8.07	10.90	0.34	11.2
$100 million to $1 billion	3,194	1.20	12.24	9.68	0.41	3.0
$1 billion to $10 billion.	320	1.31	13.77	9.76	1.03	3.1
$10 billion or more	80	1.13	13.43	8.77	1.06	1.3
Northeast [1]	651	1.05	12.74	8.60	1.20	10.6
Southeast [2]	1,392	1.13	12.22	9.73	0.74	12.3
Central [3]	1,721	1.04	12.36	8.45	0.80	5.6
Midwest [4]	2,094	1.49	16.50	8.93	0.87	4.2
Southwest [5]	1,342	1.17	12.16	9.49	0.44	5.4
West [6]	880	1.63	15.96	10.34	1.24	12.7

[1] CT, DE, DC, ME, MD, MA, NH, NJ, NY, PA, PR, RI, and VT. [2] AL, FL, GA, MS, NC, SC, TN, VA, and WV. [3] IL, IN, KY, MI, OH, and WI. [4] IA, KS, MN, MO, NE, ND, and SD. [5] AR, LA, NM, OK, and TX. [6] AK, AZ, CA, CO, HI, ID, MT, NV, OR, Pacific Islands, UT, WA, and WY.

Source of Tables 1150 and 1151: U.S. Federal Deposit Insurance Corporation, *Annual Report; Statistics on Banking*, annual; and *FDIC Quarterly Banking Profile*.

No. 1152. Insured Commercial Banks—Delinquency Rates on Loans: 1990 to 2001

[In percent. Annual averages of quarterly figures, not seasonally adjusted. Delinquent loans are those past due 30 days or more and still accruing interest as well as those in nonaccrual status. They are measured as a percentage of end-of-period loans]

Type of loan	1990	1994	1995	1996	1997	1998	1999	2000	2001
Total loans.	**5.34**	**2.78**	**2.48**	**2.40**	**2.27**	**2.18**	**2.13**	**2.18**	**2.58**
Real estate	6.33	3.64	3.03	2.75	2.43	2.21	1.98	1.93	2.10
Residential [1]	(NA)	2.35	2.26	2.37	2.37	2.21	2.12	2.15	2.30
Commercial [2]	(NA)	5.40	4.07	3.23	2.45	2.10	1.73	1.53	1.80
Consumer	3.88	2.76	3.08	3.52	3.71	3.72	3.60	3.54	3.68
Credit cards	(NA)	3.35	3.73	4.33	4.69	4.70	4.53	4.50	4.33
Other	(NA)	2.42	2.67	2.98	3.07	3.12	3.08	2.97	3.27
Leases	1.97	0.93	0.79	1.06	1.08	1.04	1.28	1.59	2.09
Commercial and industrial	5.18	2.17	1.89	1.82	1.62	1.64	1.86	2.18	3.06
Agricultural	4.20	2.51	2.49	2.96	2.56	2.61	2.80	2.34	2.82

NA Not available. [1] Residential real estate loans include loans secured by one- to four-family properties, including home equity lines of credit. [2] Commercial real estate loans include construction and land development loans, loans secured by multifamily residences, and loans secured by nonfarm, nonresidential real estate.

Source: Federal Financial Institutions Examination Council (FFIEC), *Consolidated Reports of Condition and Income* (1990-2000: FFIEC 031 through 034; 2001: FFIEC 031 & 041).

No. 1153. U.S. Banking Offices of Foreign Banks—Summary: 1990 to 2001

[In billions of dollars, except as indicated (791 represents $791,000,000,000). As of December. Data cover foreign-bank branches and agencies in the 50 states and the District of Columbia, New York investment companies (through September 1996) and U.S. commercial banks of which more than 25 percent is owned by foreign banks, and International Banking Facilities. Foreign banks are those owned by institutions located outside of the United States and its affiliated insular areas]

Item	1990	1995	1996	1997	1998	1999	2000	2001	Share [1] 1990	1995	2000	2001
Assets	791	984	991	1,126	1,118	1,228	1,299	1,385	21.4	21.7	19.9	20.2
Loans, total	398	461	461	495	494	499	531	523	18.0	17.3	13.7	13.4
Business	193	249	265	282	280	279	296	271	30.8	35.1	27.1	26.4
Deposits	384	523	535	603	558	697	709	743	14.5	17.6	17.6	17.4

[1] Percent of "domestically owned" commercial banks plus U.S. offices of foreign banks.

Source: Board of Governors of the Federal Reserve System, "Share Data for U.S. Offices of Foreign Banks"; published 20 March 2002; <http://www.federalreserve.gov/releases/Iba/Share/SHRTBL1.html>.

No. 1154. Claims of U.S. Banking Organizations on Foreign Counterparties by Type of Claim: 2001

[In millions of dollars (881,938 represents $881,938,000,000). As of December. Adjusted cross-border claims are those booked outside the foreign counterparty's home country, usually at a U.S. bank's head office in the United States, and are adjusted for any guarantees. Cross-border claims are usually denominated in U.S. dollars. Local claims on foreign counterparties are those booked in the local offices of the reporting bank, that is, offices located in the country of the counterparty. These claims are usually, but not always, booked in local currency. Revaluation gains stem from the value of foreign exchange and derivatives contracts. U.S. banking organizations continually determine the market value of these contracts - "revaluing" them - to see if a positive or negative value results (based on movements in market factors or other variables)]

Country	Total claims	Adjusted cross-border claims	Local claims	Revalu-ation gains	Country	Total claims	Adjusted cross-border claims	Local claims	Revalu-ation gains
Total [1]	881,938	438,429	371,250	72,259	Italy	38,561	27,684	5,470	5,407
					Japan	57,311	16,462	34,429	6,420
Argentina	19,869	6,292	13,018	559	Korea, South	17,533	6,485	10,412	636
Australia	22,458	5,171	15,632	1,655	Mexico	78,000	19,056	57,598	1,346
Belgium	14,262	9,522	2,727	2,013	Netherlands	31,904	27,444	345	4,115
Brazil	39,012	17,848	19,818	1,346	Singapore	16,636	3,324	13,081	231
Canada	54,330	18,225	32,549	3,556	Spain	18,754	11,817	4,446	2,491
Cayman Islands	8,309	5,345	439	2,525	Sweden	8,429	6,614	413	1,402
France	40,823	31,054	4,838	4,931	Switzerland	16,961	11,775	2,212	2,974
Germany	123,145	98,793	15,324	9,028	Taiwan [2]	11,409	2,740	8,547	122
Hong Kong	18,478	3,821	14,296	361	United Kingdom	102,583	36,337	57,287	8,959

[1] Includes other countries not shown separately. [2] See footnote 2, Table 1308.

Source: Federal Financial Institutions Examination Council, "Statistical Release E.16, Country Exposure Lending Survey," quarterly, <http://www.ffiec.gov/E16.htm>.

No. 1155. Retail Fees and Services of Depository Institutions: 2000 and 2001

[In dollars, except as noted. As of June. For most services, fees are reported in terms of (1) the proportion of those institutions offering a service that charge for the service and (2) the average fee charged by the institutions that charge for the service. Based on a random sample of depository institutions belonging to the Bank Insurance Fund, whose members are predominantly commercial banks, or the Savings Association Insurance Fund, whose members are predominantly savings and loans associations]

Type of account or service	2000	2001	Type of account or service	2000	2001
NONINTEREST CHECKING ACCOUNT			AUTOMATED TELLER MACHINES (ATMs)		
Percent offering	95.4	96.7	Percent offering	88.8	90.9
Single-balance, single-fee account: [1]			Annual fee:		
Percent offering	37.4	29.6	Percent charging	13.1	10.7
Monthly fee (low balance)	7.19	7.12	Average	10.79	10.35
Minimum balance to avoid fee	485	527			
Fee-only account: [2]			Fees for customer withdrawals on us: [4]		
Percent offering	40.2	37.7	Percent charging	6.2	3.6
Monthly fee	5.16	4.74	Average	0.71	0.81
NOW ACCOUNTS [3]			Fees for customer withdrawals on others: [4]		
Percent offering	94.4	96.2	Percent charging	72.7	78.5
Single-fee account: [1]			Average	1.16	1.17
Percent offering	47.0	49.5	Surcharge: [5]		
Monthly fee (low balance)	8.49	8.15	Percent charging	75.4	88.5
Minimum balance to avoid fee	1,029	1,132	Average	1.26	1.32

[1] A monthly fee for balances below the minimum, no monthly fee for balances above the minimum, and no other charges. [2] A monthly fee, no minimum balance to eliminate the fee, and a charge per check in some cases. [3] NOW (negotiable order of withdrawal) accounts are checking accounts that pay interest and often have fee structures that differ from those of noninterest checking accounts. [4] An institution's "customer" is one who has an account at the institution. A customer's ATM transactions in which the machine used is that of the customer's institution are called "on us"; a customer's transactions in which the machine used is that of another institution are called "on others." [5] An ATM surcharge is a fee imposed by the ATM's institution, typically on every transaction by the machine's noncustomer users.

Source: Board of Governors of the Federal Reserve System, Annual Report to the Congress on Retail Fees and Services of Depository Institutions, June 2002.

No. 1156. Insured Savings Institutions—Financial Summary: 1990 to 2001

[In billions of dollars, except number of institutions (1,259 represents $1,259,000,000,000). As of December 31. Includes Puerto Rico, Guam, and Virgin Islands. Covers SAIF (Savings Association Insurance Fund)- and BIF (Bank Insurance Fund)-insured savings institutions. Excludes institutions in Resolution Trust Corporation conservatorship and, beginning 1993, excludes one self-liquidating institution. Minus sign (-) indicates loss]

Item	1990	1993	1994	1995	1996	1997	1998	1999	2000	2001
Number of institutions	2,815	2,262	2,152	2,030	1,925	1,780	1,689	1,641	1,589	1,533
Assets, total	1,259	1,001	1,009	1,026	1,028	1,026	1,088	1,149	1,217	1,299
Loans and leases, net	812	626	635	648	681	692	714	755	821	864
Liabilities, total.	1,192	922	929	940	942	937	994	1,054	1,114	1,189
Deposits	987	774	737	742	728	704	705	707	732	798
Equity capital.	68	78	80	86	86	89	95	95	103	110
Interest and fee income.	117	66	63	71	72	69	71	74	84	84
Interest expense	91	35	33	43	42	41	42	43	52	47
Net interest income.	26	32	30	28	30	29	29	31	32	37
Net income	-5	7	6	8	7	9	10	11	11	13

Source: U.S. Federal Deposit Insurance Corporation, *Statistics on Banking*, annual and *FDIC Quarterly Banking Profile*.

No. 1157. Federal and State-Chartered Credit Unions—Summary: 1990 to 2001

[Except as noted, as of December 31 (36,241 represents 36,241,000). Federal data include District of Columbia, Puerto Rico, Guam, and Virgin Islands. Excludes state-insured, privately-insured, and noninsured state-chartered credit unions and corporate central credit unions which have mainly other credit unions as members]

Year	Operating credit unions		Number of failed institutions [1]	Members (1,000)		Assets (mil. dol.)		Loans outstanding (mil. dol.)		Savings (mil. dol.)	
	Federal	State		Federal	State	Federal	State	Federal	State	Federal	State
1990 . . .	8,511	4,349	164	36,241	19,454	130,073	68,133	83,029	44,102	117,892	62,082
1995 . . .	7,329	4,358	26	42,163	24,927	193,781	112,860	120,514	71,606	170,300	99,838
1996 . . .	7,152	4,240	19	43,546	25,652	206,695	120,193	134,127	79,661	180,969	105,743
1997 . . .	6,981	4,257	16	43,491	27,921	215,104	136,074	140,104	92,117	187,822	119,359
1998 . . .	6,814	4,181	17	43,865	29,674	231,890	156,811	144,849	100,890	202,651	137,348
1999 . . .	6,566	4,062	23	44,076	31,308	239,316	172,086	155,578	116,366	207,614	149,305
2000 . . .	6,336	3,980	29	43,883	33,705	242,881	195,363	163,851	137,485	210,188	169,053
2001 . . .	6,118	3,866	22	43,817	35,560	270,123	231,432	170,326	152,112	235,201	201,923

[1] 1990 for year ending September 30; 1995 reflects 15-month period from October 1994 through December 1995, beginning 1996 reflects calendar year. A failed institution is defined as a credit union which has ceased operation because it was involuntarily liquidated or merged with assistance from the National Credit Union Share Insurance Fund.

Source: National Credit Union Administration, *Annual Report of the National Credit Union Administration*, and unpublished data.

No. 1158. Characteristics of Conventional First Mortgage Loans for Purchase of Single-Family Homes: 1990 to 2001

[In percent, except as indicated (154.1 represents $154,100). Annual averages. Covers fully amortized conventional mortgage loans used to purchase single-family nonfarm homes. Excludes refinancing loans, nonamortized and balloon loans, loans insured by the Federal Housing Administration, and loans guaranteed by the Veterans Administration. Based on a sample of mortgage lenders, including savings and loans associations, savings banks, commercial banks, and mortgage companies]

Loan characteristics	New homes						Previously occupied homes					
	1990	1995	1998	1999	2000	2001	1990	1995	1998	1999	2000	2001
Contract interest rate, [1]												
all loans	9.7	7.7	6.9	6.9	7.4	6.9	9.8	7.7	7.0	7.2	7.9	7.0
Fixed-rate loans	10.1	8.0	7.1	7.3	8.0	7.0	10.1	8.0	7.1	7.3	8.2	7.0
Adjustable-rate loans [2]	8.9	7.2	6.4	6.3	6.5	6.4	8.9	7.0	6.3	6.5	7.2	6.3
Initial fees, charges [3]	1.98	1.20	0.88	0.76	0.69	0.67	1.74	0.93	0.84	0.73	0.66	0.51
Effective interest rate, [4]												
all loans	10.1	7.9	7.1	7.0	7.5	7.0	10.1	7.8	7.1	7.3	8.1	7.0
Fixed-rate loans	10.4	8.2	7.2	7.4	8.2	7.1	10.4	8.2	7.2	7.4	8.3	7.1
Adjustable-rate loans [2]	9.2	7.4	6.5	6.3	6.5	6.4	9.2	7.1	6.5	6.6	7.2	6.4
Term to maturity (years)	27.3	27.7	28.4	28.8	29.2	28.8	27.0	27.4	27.7	28.1	28.6	27.5
Purchase price ($1,000)	154.1	175.4	195.0	210.7	234.9	244.8	140.3	137.3	169.5	179.3	191.8	211.5
Loan to price ratio	74.9	78.6	80.1	78.8	77.4	77.3	74.9	80.1	78.7	78.4	77.9	76.0
Percent of number of loans with adjustable rates.	31	37	17	35	40	18	27	31	12	18	21	11

[1] Initial interest rate paid by the borrower as specified in the loan contract. [2] Loans with a contractual provision for periodic adjustments in the contract interest rate. [3] Includes all fees, commissions, discounts and "points" paid by the borrower, or seller, in order to obtain the loan. Excludes those charges for mortgage, credit, life or property insurance; for property transfer; and for title search and insurance. [4] Contract interest rate plus fees and charges amortized over a 10-year period.

Source: U.S. Federal Housing Finance Board, *Rates & Terms on Conventional Home Mortgages, Annual Summary*.

U.S. Census Bureau, Statistical Abstract of the United States: 2002

No. 1159. Mortgage Debt Outstanding by Type of Property and Holder: 1990 to 2001

[In billions of dollars (3,808 represents $3,808,000,000,000). As of Dec. 31. Includes Puerto Rico and Guam]

Type of property and holder	1990	1992	1993	1994	1995	1996	1997	1998	1999	2000	2001
Mortgage debt, total	3,808	4,254	4,209	4,381	4,577	4,865	5,203	5,723	6,360	6,887	7,596
Residential nonfarm	2,932	3,434	3,411	3,593	3,778	4,009	4,281	4,703	5,181	5,612	6,194
One- to four-family homes	2,647	3,153	3,145	3,327	3,505	3,720	3,979	4,369	4,804	5,206	5,740
Savings institutions	600	490	470	478	482	514	521	534	549	595	621
Mortgage pools or trusts [1]	1,046	1,569	1,518	1,656	1,768	1,935	2,099	2,375	2,690	2,925	3,323
Government National Mortgage Association	392	580	405	441	461	494	523	522	565	593	570
Federal Home Loan Mortgage Corp	308	402	443	488	512	552	577	643	745	817	941
Federal National Mortgage Assoc	291	436	487	521	570	633	688	804	925	1,016	1,238
Private mortgage conduits [2]	55	151	184	206	224	256	311	405	455	500	575
Commercial banks	430	479	532	590	647	678	746	798	880	967	1,025
Individuals and others [3]	403	411	386	367	370	367	393	437	471	491	524
Federal and related agencies [4]	153	194	230	228	229	220	213	217	206	223	242
Federal National Mortgage Assoc	94	124	151	159	164	155	150	148	141	144	155
Life insurance companies	13	11	9	9	9	7	7	7	6	5	5
Five or more units	286	280	266	266	272	289	302	334	377	406	453
Nonfarm, nonresidential	797	740	717	705	714	769	831	923	1,076	1,167	1,286
Farm	79	80	81	83	85	87	90	97	103	109	116
TYPE OF HOLDER											
Savings institutions	802	628	598	596	597	628	632	644	669	724	758
Commercial banks	849	901	948	1,013	1,090	1,145	1,245	1,338	1,497	1,661	1,793
Life insurance companies	268	242	224	216	213	208	207	214	231	235	242
Individuals and others [3]	562	565	532	515	520	550	600	652	694	683	729
Mortgage pools or trusts [1]	1,088	1,633	1,580	1,725	1,848	2,038	2,232	2,581	2,948	3,231	3,698
Government National Mortgage Assoc.	404	600	414	451	472	506	537	537	582	612	591
Federal Home Loan Mortgage Corp	316	408	447	491	515	554	579	646	749	822	948
Federal National Mortgage Association	300	445	496	530	583	651	710	835	961	1,058	1,290
Farmers Home Administration	(Z)	(Z)	(Z)	(Z)	(Z)	(Z)	(Z)	(Z)	-	-	-
Private mortgage conduits	68	180	224	253	278	326	406	563	656	740	867
Federal and related agencies [4]	239	286	326	316	308	295	286	294	322	344	377
Federal National Mortgage Association	105	137	166	174	179	169	161	158	152	155	170
Farmers Home Administration	41	42	41	42	42	42	41	41	74	73	72
Federal Land Banks	29	29	28	29	28	30	31	33	34	36	41
Federal Home Loan Mortgage Corp	22	34	47	42	44	47	48	57	57	59	63
Federal Housing and Veterans Admin	9	13	12	11	10	6	4	4	4	4	3
Government National Mortgage Assoc.	(Z)	(Z)	(Z)	(Z)	(Z)	(Z)	(Z)	(Z)	(Z)	(Z)	(Z)
Federal Deposit Insurance Corp	(X)	(X)	14	8	4	2	1	(Z)	(Z)	(Z)	(Z)
Resolution Trust Corporation	33	32	17	10	2	(X)	(X)	(X)	(X)	(X)	(X)

- Represents zero.   X Not applicable.   Z Less than $500 million.   [1] Outstanding principal balances of mortgage pools backing securities insured or guaranteed by the agency indicated. Includes other pools not shown separately.   [2] Includes securitized home equity loans.   [3] Includes mortgage companies, real estate investment trusts, state and local retirement funds, noninsured pension funds, state and local credit agencies, credit unions, and finance companies.   [4] Includes other agencies not shown separately.

Source: Board of Governors of the Federal Reserve System, *Federal Reserve Bulletin*, monthly.

No. 1160. Mortgage Delinquency and Foreclosure Rates: 1990 to 2001

[In percent. Covers one- to four-family residential nonfarm mortgage loans]

Item	1990	1995	1996	1997	1998	1999	2000	2001
Delinquency rates: [1]								
Total	4.7	4.3	4.3	4.3	4.4	4.0	4.0	4.6
Conventional loans	3.0	2.8	2.8	2.8	2.9	2.5	2.5	3.0
VA loans	6.4	6.4	6.7	6.9	7.1	6.8	6.8	7.7
FHA loans	6.7	7.6	8.0	8.1	8.5	8.6	9.1	10.8
Foreclosure rates: [2]								
Total	0.9	0.9	1.0	1.1	1.1	1.0	0.9	1.0
Conventional loans	0.7	0.7	0.7	0.8	0.7	0.6	0.6	0.8
VA loans	1.2	1.3	1.6	1.8	1.9	1.7	1.2	1.3
FHA loans	1.3	1.3	1.8	2.1	2.4	2.0	1.7	2.2

[1] Number of loans delinquent 30 days or more as percentage of mortgage loans serviced in survey. Annual average of quarterly figures.   [2] Percentage of loans in the foreclosure process at yearend, not seasonally adjusted.

Source: Mortgage Bankers Association of America, Washington, DC, *National Delinquency Survey*, quarterly.

No. 1161. Percent of U.S. Households That Use Selected Payment Instruments: 1995 and 1998

[In percent. Based on Survey of Consumer Finance conducted by the Board of Governors of the Federal Reserve System; see Appendix III]

Age and education	Any of these instruments		ATM [1]		Debit card		Direct deposit		Automatic bill paying		Smart card	
	1995	1998	1995	1998	1995	1998	1995	1998	1995	1998	1995	1998
All households	**76.5**	**85.5**	**61.2**	**67.2**	**17.6**	**33.8**	**46.8**	**60.5**	**21.8**	**36.0**	**1.2**	**1.9**
Under 30 years old	75.2	80.2	71.1	75.6	24.5	45.0	31.1	45.2	17.9	30.5	1.8	2.6
30 to 60 years old.	77.4	87.4	67.2	75.9	19.7	38.6	42.9	58.0	24.5	38.6	1.5	2.3
61 years old and over	75.2	83.7	43.1	41.6	9.6	16.0	63.2	74.8	18.2	33.0	0.3	0.5
No college degree.	69.8	80.7	52.8	59.9	14.3	29.2	40.4	54.4	18.2	30.2	0.8	1.8
College degree.	91.5	95.1	80.1	81.9	25.2	43.1	61.0	72.6	30.1	47.7	2.1	2.0

[1] The question on automatic teller machines (ATMs) asked whether any member of the household had an ATM card, not whether the member used it.

Source: Mester, Loretta J., "Changes in the Use of Electronic Means of Payment," *Business Review*, Third Quarter 2001, published by Federal Reserve Bank of Philadelphia.

No. 1162. Consumer Payment Systems by Method of Payment, 1990 and 2001, and Projections, 2005

[73.7 represents 73,700,000,000]

Method of payment	Transactions						Volume					
	Number (bil.)			Percent distribution			Amount (bil. dol.)			Percent distribution		
	1990	2001	2005, proj.	1990		2005, proj.	1990	2001	2005, proj.	1990		2005, proj.
Total	**73.7**	**117.2**	**132.3**	**100.0**		**100.0**	**2,325**	**5,478**	**6,735**	**100.0**		**100.0**
Paper	62.8	81.4	82.0	85.2		69.5	1,864	3,431	3,455	80.2		62.6
Direct check payments [1]	28.0	29.2	24.9	38.0		24.9	1,188	2,250	2,056	51.1		41.1
Cash	33.4	51.0	55.7	45.3		43.5	582	1,058	1,246	25.0		19.3
Money orders	0.9	0.9	1.1	1.2		0.8	61	88	114	2.6		1.6
Travelers cheques	0.4	0.2	0.2	0.6		0.2	22	13	12	0.9		0.2
Official checks [2]	0.1	0.1	0.1	0.1		0.1	11	23	27	0.5		0.4
Cards	10.6	33.5	44.5	14.4		28.6	441	1,771	2,535	19.0		32.3
Credit cards [3]	10.4	21.1	24.7	14.1		18.0	432	1,341	1,727	18.6		24.5
Debit cards [4]	0.3	10.5	17.0	0.3		8.9	9	384	726	0.4		7.0
Stored value cards [5]	-	1.4	2.0	-		1.2	-	32	59	-		0.6
EBT cards and food stamps [6] . .	-	0.6	0.8	-		0.5	-	14	23	-		0.3
Electronic	0.3	2.3	5.8	0.4		2.0	20	275	745	0.9		5.0
Preauthorized payments [7]	0.3	1.5	2.7	0.4		1.3	18	200	390	0.8		3.6
Remote payments [8]	-	0.8	3.1	-		0.6	2	75	355	0.1		1.4

- Represents or rounds to zero. [1] Excludes consumer check repayments and prepayments involving other payment systems as well as all commercial and government checks. [2] Official checks include cashier's checks, teller checks, and certified checks purchased from financial institutions. Excludes those purchased by businesses. [3] Credit cards include general purpose cards usable at all kinds of merchants and proprietary cards usable only at selected outlets. Includes some purchases on personal cards for government, commercial, and business-related spending. Cash advances are excluded. [4] Debit cards include general purpose cards carrying the Visa or MasterCard brand, electronic funds transfer (EFT) brands of regional EFT systems, proprietary commercial cards issued by private firms to drivers in the long-haul trucking and business aviation industry, and proprietary consumer cards issued by supermarkets. Cash withdrawals at ATMs and cash back over the counter are excluded. [5] Stored value cards are used primarily for gift certificates and telephone calls. [6] Electronic benefits transfer cards are replacements for paper scrip food stamps. [7] Preauthorized payments are handled electronically "end-to-end" through an automated clearing house. [8] Remote payments are made using a telephone or a computer and include point-of-sale check conversions and utility-bill payments made at ATMs, self-service clerk-assisted electronic banking machines kiosks and clerk-assisted machines at supermarkets.

Source: HSN Consultants Inc., Oxnard, CA, *The Nilson Report*, twice-monthly. (Copyright used by permission.)

No. 1163. Debit Cards—Holders, Number, Transactions, and Volume, 1990 and 2000, and Projections, 2005

[160 represents 160,000,000]

Type of debit card	Cardholders (mil.)		Number of cards (mil.)			Number of transactions (mil.)			Volume (bil. dol.)		
	2000	2005, proj.	1990	2000	2005, proj.	1990	2000	2005, proj.	1990	2000	2005, proj.
Total [1]	**160**	**181**	**164**	**235**	**269**	**274**	**9,550**	**19,065**	**12**	**419**	**923**
Bank [2]	120	156	9	136	190	127	6,450	12,703	8	296	623
EFT systems [3]	159	180	160	223	258	129	3,039	6,295	3	119	295
Other [4]	11	11	4	12	12	17	61	68	1	3	5

[1] Cardholders may hold more than one type of card. Bank cards and EFT cards are the same pieces of plastic that carry multiple brands. The total card figure shown does not include any duplication. [2] Visa Check Card and MasterCard MasterMoney. [3] Cards issued by financial institution members of regional and national switches. EFT=Electronic funds transfer. [4] Commercial fuel cards issued by private-label firms plus retail cards such as those issued by supermarkets and oil companies.

Source: HSN Consultants Inc., Oxnard, CA, *The Nilson Report*, twice-monthly. (Copyright used by permission.)

Banking, Finance, and Insurance   727

No. 1164. Consumer Credit Outstanding and Finance Rates: 1990 to 2001

[In billions of dollars, except percent (789.1 represents $789,100,000,000). Covers most short- and intermediate-term credit extended to individuals, excluding loans secured by real estate. Estimated amounts of seasonally adjusted credit outstanding as of end of year; finance rates, annual averages]

Type of credit	1990	1993	1994	1995	1996	1997	1998	1999	2000	2001
Total	789.1	838.8	960.4	1,095.8	1,185.1	1,243.0	1,317.5	1,416.3	1,560.6	1,667.5
Revolving	238.6	309.9	365.6	443.1	498.9	531.0	562.5	597.7	666.5	699.4
Nonrevolving [1]	550.5	528.8	594.9	652.7	686.1	712.0	755.0	818.6	894.0	968.0
FINANCE RATES (percent)										
Commercial banks:										
New automobiles (48 months)	11.78	8.09	8.12	9.57	9.05	9.02	8.72	8.44	9.34	8.50
Other consumer goods (24 months)	15.46	13.47	13.19	13.94	13.54	13.90	13.74	13.39	13.90	13.22
Credit-card plans	18.17	16.83	16.04	15.90	15.63	15.77	15.71	15.21	15.71	14.89
Finance companies:										
New automobiles	12.54	9.48	9.79	11.19	9.83	7.12	6.30	6.66	6.61	5.65
Used automobiles	15.99	12.79	13.49	14.48	13.53	13.27	12.64	12.60	13.55	(NA)

NA Not available.   [1] Comprises automobile loans and all other loans not included in revolving credit, such as loans for mobile homes, education, boats, trailers, or vacations. These loans may be secured or unsecured.

Source: Board of Governors of the Federal Reserve System, *Federal Reserve Bulletin*, monthly.

No. 1165. Credit Cards—Holders, Number, Spending, and Debt, 1990 and 2000, and Projections, 2005

[122 represents 122,000,000]

Type of credit card	Cardholders (mil.)			Number of cards (mil.)			Credit card spending (bil. dol.)			Credit card debt outstanding (bil. dol.)		
	1990	2000	2005, proj.	1990	2000	2005, proj.	1990	2000	2005, proj.	1990	2000	2005, proj.
Total [1]	122	159	173	1,012	1,440	1,615	466	1,463	2,052	243	683	985
Bank [2]	79	107	120	213	453	569	243	937	1,337	154	479	715
Oil company	85	76	74	123	97	85	27	50	77	3	5	7
Phone	97	125	130	141	181	188	14	21	24	2	3	3
Store	96	114	120	459	615	661	75	124	157	51	96	113
Travel and entertainment [3]	16	25	32	28	35	41	85	235	320	20	52	77
Other [4]	10	7	7	49	59	71	23	97	138	13	49	69

[1] Cardholders may hold more than one type of card.   [2] Visa and MasterCard credit cards. Excludes debit cards.   [3] Includes American Express and Diners Club.   [4] Includes UATP, automobile rental, other airline including business aviation, hotel, restaurant, and club cards, Discover (except for cardholders), and miscellaneous cards.

Source: HSN Consultants Inc., Oxnard, CA, *The Nilson Report*, twice-monthly. (Copyright used by permission.)

No. 1166. Usage of General Purpose Credit Cards by Families: 1989 to 1998

[General purpose credit cards include Mastercard, Visa, Optima, and Discover cards. Excludes cards used only for business purposes. All dollar figures are given in constant 1998 dollars based on consumer price index data as published by U.S. Bureau of Labor Statistics. Families include one-person units; for definition of family, see text, Section 1, Population. Based on Survey of Consumer Finance; see Appendix III. For definition of median, see Guide to Tabular Presentation]

Age of family head and family income	Percent having a general purpose credit card	Median number of cards	Median new charges on last month's bills	Percent having a balance after last month's bills	Median balance [1]	Percent of cardholding families who—		
						Almost always pay off the balance	Sometimes pay off the balance	Hardly ever pay off the balance
1989, total	56.0	2	$100	52.1	$1,300	52.9	21.2	25.8
1992, total	62.4	2	100	52.6	1,100	53.0	19.6	27.4
1995, total	66.4	2	200	56.0	1,600	52.4	20.1	27.5
1998, total	67.5	2	200	54.7	1,900	53.8	19.3	26.9
Under 35 years old	58.3	2	200	71.6	1,500	39.0	22.5	38.5
35 to 44 years old	71.3	2	200	62.5	2,000	46.5	19.1	34.4
45 to 54 years old	75.3	2	200	59.2	2,000	48.2	22.7	29.1
55 to 64 years old	76.0	2	200	48.8	2,300	61.0	20.1	18.9
65 to 74 years old	71.2	2	200	33.9	1,000	74.0	14.9	11.1
75 years old and over	50.8	1	100	16.7	700	86.3	7.8	5.9
Less than $10,000	23.2	2	100	64.0	900	46.4	19.9	33.8
$10,000 to $24,999	50.8	2	100	56.9	1,200	52.3	19.3	28.4
$25,000 to $49,999	73.2	2	100	58.2	1,700	48.3	20.5	31.2
$50,000 to $99,999	89.6	2	200	55.9	2,400	53.9	20.2	25.9
$100,000 and more	97.9	2	800	36.4	3,100	72.0	13.8	14.1

[1] Among families having a balance.

Source: Board of Governors of the Federal Reserve System, unpublished data.

No. 1167. Money Stock: 1980 to 2001

[In billions of dollars (408 represents $408,000,000,000). As of December. Seasonally adjusted averages of daily figures]

Item	1980	1984	1985	1986	1987	1988	1989	1990	1991	1992	1993	1994	1995	1996	1997	1998	1999	2000	2001
M1, total[1]	**408**	**551**	**619**	**724**	**749**	**786**	**792**	**824**	**896**	**1,024**	**1,129**	**1,150**	**1,127**	**1,079**	**1,072**	**1,096**	**1,124**	**1,089**	**1,178**
Currency[1]	115	156	168	180	197	212	222	246	267	292	322	354	372	394	424	459	517	530	580
Travelers checks[2]	3	4	5	5	6	6	6	7	7	7	7	8	8	8	8	8	8	8	8
Demand deposits[3]	261	243	267	303	287	287	279	277	290	340	385	384	389	401	394	378	354	310	329
Other checkable deposits[4]	28	147	180	236	260	281	285	294	332	384	415	404	357	276	246	251	245	241	261
M2, total	**1,600**	**2,312**	**2,495**	**2,732**	**2,831**	**2,994**	**3,158**	**3,277**	**3,377**	**3,431**	**3,484**	**3,497**	**3,640**	**3,813**	**4,031**	**4,386**	**4,655**	**4,942**	**5,463**
M1	408	551	619	724	749	786	792	824	896	1,024	1,129	1,150	1,127	1,079	1,072	1,096	1,124	1,089	1,178
Non-M1 components in M2	1,192	1,760	1,876	2,008	2,082	2,208	2,366	2,453	2,480	2,407	2,355	2,347	2,514	2,734	2,959	3,290	3,531	3,853	4,285
Money market funds, retail	64	167	175	209	223	245	321	357	371	352	353	381	448	515	590	736	837	934	1,005
Savings deposits (including MMDAs[5])	400	705	815	941	937	926	894	923	1,044	1,187	1,219	1,150	1,134	1,273	1,400	1,602	1,739	1,876	2,307
Commercial banks	186	389	457	534	535	542	541	581	664	754	785	753	775	905	1,023	1,187	1,289	1,424	1,746
Thrift institutions	215	315	359	407	403	384	353	342	379	433	434	397	359	367	377	415	450	452	561
Small time deposits[6]	729	889	886	858	921	1,037	1,151	1,173	1,066	868	782	816	931	947	968	952	955	1,044	972
Commercial banks	286	388	386	369	392	451	534	611	602	508	468	503	575	593	625	626	635	699	639
Thrift institutions	442	501	499	489	529	586	618	563	463	360	314	314	357	354	343	326	320	345	334
M3, total	**1,996**	**2,993**	**3,208**	**3,499**	**3,686**	**3,928**	**4,076**	**4,152**	**4,205**	**4,216**	**4,278**	**4,360**	**4,626**	**4,972**	**5,452**	**6,042**	**6,542**	**7,116**	**8,030**
M2	1,600	2,312	2,495	2,732	2,831	2,994	3,158	3,277	3,377	3,431	3,484	3,497	3,640	3,813	4,031	4,386	4,655	4,942	5,463
Non-M2 components in M3	396	681	713	767	855	934	918	875	828	785	794	863	986	1,159	1,421	1,656	1,887	2,174	2,567
Large time deposits[8]	260	403	422	419	462	512	528	480	415	350	332	370	429	511	621	672	743	821	787
Commercial banks[8]	215	256	270	269	299	338	366	358	331	283	270	306	355	433	535	583	652	718	673
Thrift institutions	45	147	152	150	163	175	161	121	83	67	62	65	74	78	85	89	91	103	114
Repurchase agreements[9]	58	107	121	146	178	197	169	151	131	142	173	196	198	210	254	293	336	364	372
Eurodollars[9]	61	109	104	116	121	132	109	103	92	80	73	86	94	115	151	152	174	196	211
Money market funds, institution only	16	62	65	86	94	94	112	140	190	213	217	210	264	323	396	538	634	792	1,197

[1] Currency outside U.S. Treasury, Federal Reserve Banks and the vaults of depository institutions. [2] Outstanding amount of nonbank issuers. [3] At commercial banks and foreign-related institutions. [4] Consists of negotiable order of withdrawal (NOW) and automatic transfer service (ATS) accounts at all depository institutions, credit union share draft balances, and demand deposits at thrift institutions. [5] Money market deposit accounts (MMDA). [6] Issued in amounts of less than $100,000. Includes retail repurchase agreements. Excludes individual retirement accounts (IRAs) and Keogh accounts. [7] Issued in amounts of $100,000 or more. Excludes those booked at international banking facilities. [8] Excludes those held by money market mutual funds, depository institutions, U.S. Government, foreign banks and official institutions. [9] Excludes those held by depository institutions and money market mutual funds.

Source: Board of Governors of the Federal Reserve System, Federal Reserve Bulletin, monthly, and Money Stock Measures, Federal Reserve Statistical Release H.6, weekly.

No. 1168. Money Market Interest Rates and Mortgage Rates: 1980 to 2001

[Percent per year. Annual averages of monthly data, except as indicated]

Type	1980	1985	1990	1991	1992	1993	1994	1995	1996	1997	1998	1999	2000	2001
Federal funds, effective rate	13.35	8.10	8.10	5.69	3.52	3.02	4.21	5.83	5.30	5.46	5.35	4.97	6.24	3.88
Prime rate charged by banks	15.26	9.93	10.01	8.46	6.25	6.00	7.15	8.83	8.27	8.44	8.35	8.00	9.23	6.94
Discount rate [1]	11.77	7.69	6.98	5.45	3.25	3.00	3.60	5.21	5.02	5.00	4.92	4.62	5.73	3.40
Eurodollar deposits, 3-month	14.00	8.27	8.16	5.86	3.70	3.18	4.63	5.93	5.38	5.61	5.45	5.31	6.45	3.70
Large negotiable CDs:														
3-month, secondary market	13.07	8.05	8.15	5.83	3.68	3.17	4.63	5.92	5.39	5.62	5.47	5.19	6.35	3.71
6-month, secondary market [2]	12.94	8.24	8.17	5.91	3.76	3.28	4.96	5.98	5.47	5.73	5.44	5.33	6.46	3.66
Taxable money market funds [2]	12.68	7.71	7.82	5.71	3.36	2.70	3.75	5.48	4.95	5.10	5.04	4.64	5.89	3.67
Tax-exempt money market funds [2]	(NA)	4.90	5.45	4.13	2.58	1.97	2.38	3.39	2.99	3.14	2.94	2.72	3.54	2.24
Certificates of deposit (CDs): [3]														
6-month	(NA)	8.05	7.79	5.80	3.51	2.88	3.42	4.92	4.68	4.86	4.58	4.27	5.09	3.43
1-year	(NA)	8.53	7.92	6.03	3.78	3.16	4.01	5.39	4.95	5.15	4.81	4.56	5.46	3.60
2½-year	(NA)	9.32	7.96	6.46	4.56	3.80	4.58	5.69	5.14	5.40	4.93	4.74	5.64	3.97
5-year	(NA)	9.99	8.06	7.02	5.76	4.98	5.42	6.00	6.46	5.66	5.08	4.93	5.97	4.58
U.S. Government securities:														
Secondary market: [4]														
3-month Treasury bill	11.39	7.47	7.50	5.38	3.43	3.00	4.25	5.49	5.01	5.06	4.78	4.64	5.82	3.40
6-month Treasury bill	11.32	7.65	7.46	5.44	3.54	3.12	4.64	5.56	5.08	5.18	4.83	4.75	5.90	3.34
1-year Treasury bill	10.85	7.81	7.35	5.52	3.71	3.29	5.02	5.60	5.22	5.36	4.80	4.81	5.78	3.84
Auction average: [5]														
3-month Treasury bill	11.51	7.47	7.51	5.42	3.45	3.02	4.29	5.51	5.02	5.07	4.81	4.66	5.85	3.45
Home mortgages														
New-home mortgage yields [6]	12.70	11.60	10.05	9.32	8.24	7.20	7.49	7.87	7.80	7.71	7.07	7.04	7.52	7.00
Conventional, 5 yr. fixed [3]	(NA)	11.48	9.73	8.76	7.80	6.65	7.77	7.39	7.28	7.16	6.58	7.09	7.76	6.53
Conventional, 30 yr. fixed [3]	(NA)	11.85	9.97	9.09	8.27	7.17	8.28	7.86	7.76	7.57	6.92	7.46	8.08	7.01

NA Not available. [1] Rate for the Federal Reserve Bank of New York. [2] 12 month return for period ending December 31. Source: iMoneyNet, Inc., Westborough, MA, *Money Market Insight*, monthly, <http://www.imoneynet.com> (copyright). [3] Annual averages. Source: Bankrate, Inc., North Palm Beach, FL, *Bank Rate Monitor*, weekly (copyright). [4] Averages based on daily closing bid yields in secondary market; bank discount basis. [5] Averages computed on an issue-date basis; bank discount basis. Source: U.S. Council of Economic Advisors, *Economic Indicators*, monthly. [6] Effective rate (in the primary market) on conventional mortgages, reflecting fees and charges as well as contract rate and assumed, on the average, repayment at end of ten years. Source: U.S. Federal Housing Finance Board, *Rates & Terms on Conventional Home Mortgages Annual Summary*.

Source: Except as noted, Board of Governors of the Federal Reserve System, *Federal Reserve Bulletin*, monthly.

No. 1169. Bond Yields: 1980 to 2001

[**Percent per year**. Annual averages of daily figures, except as indicated]

Type	1980	1985	1990	1994	1995	1996	1997	1998	1999	2000	2001
U.S. Treasury, constant maturities: [1] [2]											
1-year	12.00	8.42	7.89	5.32	5.94	5.52	5.63	5.05	5.08	6.11	3.49
2-year	11.73	9.27	8.16	5.94	6.15	5.84	5.99	5.13	5.43	6.26	3.83
3-year	11.51	9.64	8.26	6.27	6.25	5.99	6.10	5.14	5.49	6.22	4.09
5-year	11.45	10.12	8.37	6.69	6.38	6.18	6.22	5.15	5.55	6.16	4.56
7-year	11.40	10.50	8.52	6.91	6.50	6.34	6.33	5.28	5.79	6.20	4.88
10-year	11.43	10.62	8.55	7.09	6.57	6.44	6.35	5.26	5.65	6.03	5.02
20-year	(NA)	(NA)	(NA)	7.47	6.95	6.83	6.69	5.72	6.20	6.23	5.63
30-year	11.27	10.79	8.61	7.37	6.88	6.71	6.61	5.58	5.87	5.94	5.49
U.S. Govt., long-term bonds [2] [3] . .	10.81	10.75	8.74	7.41	6.93	6.80	6.67	5.69	6.14	6.41	(NA)
State and local govt. bonds, Aaa	7.86	8.60	6.96	5.78	5.79	5.52	5.32	4.93	5.29	5.58	4.99
State and local govt. bonds, Baa	9.02	9.59	7.30	6.18	6.05	5.79	5.50	5.14	5.70	6.19	5.75
Municipal (Bond Buyer, 20 bonds) . . .	8.55	9.11	7.27	6.19	5.95	5.76	5.52	5.09	5.43	5.71	5.15
Corporate Aaa seasoned [4]	11.94	11.37	9.32	7.96	7.59	7.37	7.26	6.53	7.05	7.62	7.08
Corporate Baa seasoned [4]	13.67	12.71	10.36	8.62	8.20	8.05	7.86	7.22	7.88	8.37	7.95
Corporate seasoned, all industries [4] . .	12.75	12.05	9.77	8.25	7.84	7.67	7.53	6.87	7.45	7.98	7.49

NA Not available.   [1] Yields on the more actively traded issues adjusted to constant maturities by the U.S. Treasury.
[2] Through September 1996, yields are based on closing bid prices quoted by at least five dealers. Beginning October 1996, yields are based on closing indicative prices quoted by secondary market participants.   [3] Averages (to maturity or call) for all outstanding bonds neither due nor callable in less than 10 years, including several very low yielding "flower" bonds.   [4] Source: Moody's Investors Service, New York, NY.

Source: Except as noted, Board of Governors of the Federal Reserve System, *Federal Reserve Bulletin*, monthly.

No. 1170. Volume of Debt Markets by Type of Security: 1990 to 2001

[**In billions of dollars** (2,764 represents $2,764,000,000,000). Covers debt markets as represented by the source]

Type of security	1990	1995	1997	1998	1999	2000	2001
NEW ISSUE VOLUME							
Total	2,764	6,789	9,322	10,320	11,054	12,520	15,885
U.S. Treasury securities [1]	1,531	2,331	2,169	1,969	2,028	2,038	2,743
Federal agency debt	637	3,531	5,751	6,348	7,077	8,746	10,496
Municipal . . . . [2]	163	198	267	321	264	241	343
Mortgage-backed securities [2]	235	269	368	727	687	483	1,089
Asset-backed securities [3]	50	143	286	343	359	387	420
Corporate debt [4]	149	317	481	612	639	625	795
DAILY TRADING VOLUME							
Total	111.2	246.3	300.5	352.8	316.5	357.7	508.8
U.S. Treasury securities [1] [5]	111.2	193.2	212.1	226.6	186.5	206.6	297.9
Federal agency debt [5]	(NA)	23.7	40.2	47.6	54.6	72.8	90.2
Municipal [6] . . . . [2] [5]	(NA)	(NA)	1.1	7.7	8.3	8.8	8.8
Mortgage-backed securities [2] [5]	(NA)	29.4	47.1	70.9	67.1	69.5	112.0
VOLUME OF SECURITIES OUTSTANDING							
Total	7,745	11,229	13,102	14,447	16,026	17,056	18,566
U.S. Treasury securities [1]	2,196	3,307	3,457	3,356	3,281	2,967	2,968
Federal agency debt [7]	435	845	1,023	1,297	1,617	1,852	2,143
Municipal	1,184	1,294	1,368	1,464	1,533	1,568	1,688
Mortgage-backed securities [2]	1,333	2,352	2,680	2,955	3,334	3,565	4,126
Asset-backed securities [3] [7]	90	316	536	732	901	1,072	1,281
Money market instruments [8]	1,157	1,177	1,693	1,978	2,339	2,661	2,542
Corporate debt [4] [7]	1,350	1,938	2,346	2,666	3,023	3,372	3,818

NA Not available.   [1] Marketable public debt.   [2] Includes only Government National Mortgage Association (GNMA), Federal National Mortgage Association (FNMA), Federal Home Loan Mortgage Corporation (FHLMC) mortgage-backed securities and collateralized mortgage obligations (CMOs) and private-label MBS/CMOs.   [3] Excludes mortgage-backed assets.   [4] Includes non-convertible corporate debt, Yankee bonds, and MTNs (Medium-Term Notes), but excludes federal agency debt and all CDs.   [5] Primary dealer transactions.   [6] Beginning September 1998 includes customer-to-dealer and dealer-to-dealer transactions.   [7] The Bond Market Association estimates.   [8] Commercial paper, bankers acceptances, and large time deposits.
Source: The Bond Market Association, New York, NY. Copyright. Based on data supplied by Board of Governors of the Federal Reserve System, U.S. Dept. of Treasury, Thompson Financial Securities Data Company, Inside MBS & ABS, FHLMC, FNMA, GNMA, Federal Home Loan Banks, Student Loan Marketing Association, Federal Farm Credit Banks, Tennessee Valley Authority, and Municipal Securities Rulemaking Board.

No. 1171. Commercial Paper Outstanding by Type of Company: 1990 to 2001

[**In billions of dollars** (563 represents $563,000,000,000). As of December 31. Seasonally adjusted. Commercial paper is an unsecured promissory note having a fixed maturity of no more than 270 days]

Type of company	1990	1992	1993	1994	1995	1996	1997	1998	1999	2000	2001
All issuers	563	546	555	595	675	775	967	1,163	1,403	1,615	1,439
Financial companies [1]	415	398	399	431	487	591	766	936	1,124	1,272	1,214
Dealer-placed paper [2]	215	227	219	223	276	361	513	614	787	973	989
Directly-placed paper [3]	200	172	180	208	211	230	253	322	337	299	225
Nonfinancial companies [4]	148	148	156	165	188	185	201	227	279	343	225

[1] Institutions engaged primarily in commercial, savings, and mortgage banking; sales, personal, and mortgage financing; factoring, finance leasing, and other business lending; insurance underwriting; and other investment activities.   [2] Includes all financial company paper sold by dealers in the open market.   [3] As reported by financial companies that place their paper directly with investors.   [4] Includes public utilities and firms engaged primarily in such activities as communications, construction, manufacturing, mining, wholesale and retail trade, transportation, and services.
Source: Board of Governors of the Federal Reserve System, *Federal Reserve Bulletin*, monthly.

Banking, Finance, and Insurance   731

No. 1172. Total Returns of Stocks, Bonds, and Treasury Bills: 1950 to 2001

[In percent. Average annual percent change. Stock return data are based on the Standard & Poor's 500 index. Minus sign indicates loss]

Period	Stocks				Treasury bills, total return	Bonds (10-year), total return
	Total return	Capital gains	Dividends and reinvestment	Total return after inflation		
1950 to 1959	19.28	13.58	5.02	16.69	2.02	0.73
1960 to 1969	7.78	4.39	3.62	5.13	4.06	2.42
1970 to 1979	5.82	1.60	4.15	-0.14	6.42	5.84
1980 to 1989	17.54	12.59	4.42	11.87	9.21	13.06
1990 to 1999	18.17	15.31	2.48	15.09	5.01	7.96
2000 to 2001	-10.51	-11.60	0.99	-13.43	4.73	11.52

Source: Global Financial Data, Los Angeles, CA, "Stocks, Bills, Bonds And Inflation Sector Total Returns In The United States, 1871-1996"; <http://www.globalfindata.com/trial/trd.html>; and unpublished data. (copyright).

No. 1173. Equities, Corporate Bonds, and Municipal Securities—Holdings and Net Purchases by Type of Investor: 1990 to 2001

[In billions of dollars (3,543 represents $3,543,000,000,000). Holdings as of Dec. 31. Minus sign (-) indicates net sales]

Type of investor	Holdings					Net purchases				
	1990	1995	1999	2000	2001	1990	1995	1999	2000	2001
EQUITIES [1]										
Total [2]	3,543	8,475	19,581	17,566	15,186	-45.7	-0.2	-34.6	-45.3	67.7
Household sector [3]	1,781	4,161	9,197	7,317	5,832	-48.6	-91.6	-327.0	-498.6	-298.3
Rest of the world [4]	244	528	1,538	1,748	1,693	-16.0	16.6	112.3	193.8	124.7
Bank personal trusts and estates . . .	190	225	338	280	226	0.5	1.6	-40.4	-20.0	-20.0
Life insurance companies	82	315	965	941	935	-5.7	18.6	111.9	105.9	74.9
Other insurance companies.	80	134	208	194	185	-7.0	-0.6	-1.7	0.7	5.0
Private pension funds	606	1,289	2,326	2,195	1,902	0.9	-69.5	-29.1	-49.9	-17.1
State and local retirement funds. . . .	285	679	1,343	1,335	1,216	22.5	18.2	-6.2	-18.4	16.1
Mutual funds	233	1,025	3,377	3,227	2,837	14.4	87.4	136.4	189.1	109.7
CORPORATE & FOREIGN BONDS										
Total [2]	1,706	2,848	4,636	5,050	5,662	123.4	344.1	465.0	402.2	611.6
Household sector [3]	219	415	646	637	608	57.1	85.5	23.4	-21.1	-28.6
Rest of the world [4]	217	369	821	1,004	1,234	5.3	58.1	160.8	183.1	230.2
Commercial banking	89	111	220	277	372	4.6	8.4	38.8	57.6	95.0
Life insurance companies	567	870	1,173	1,222	1,337	56.5	90.7	41.5	49.0	114.3
Other insurance companies.	89	123	181	188	194	10.4	12.7	10.0	6.4	6.4
Private pension funds	158	242	311	326	346	19.9	13.4	9.7	15.0	20.0
State and local retirement funds.	142	189	310	340	343	-10.5	10.1	30.4	29.7	3.3
Money market mutual funds	2	22	124	162	163	-1.7	6.4	42.5	38.2	1.1
Mutual funds	59	196	368	362	420	4.7	23.3	29.2	-6.2	58.2
Government-sponsored enterprises .	-	31	91	117	146	-	10.3	23.7	25.8	28.2
Brokers and dealers.	29	76	93	113	161	-4.0	12.0	12.0	19.3	48.3
MUNICIPAL SECURITIES [5]										
Total [2]	1,184	1,293	1,532	1,568	1,688	49.3	-48.2	68.2	35.3	120.6
Household sector [3]	575	455	527	542	582	27.6	-44.8	40.2	15.0	40.7
Other insurance companies.	137	161	199	184	188	1.8	7.0	-9.1	-14.9	3.9
Money market mutual funds	84	128	210	245	281	13.9	14.3	17.5	34.3	36.2
Mutual funds	113	210	239	230	252	13.9	3.2	-3.2	-8.9	21.8

- Represents or rounds to zero. [1] Excludes mutual fund shares. [2] Includes other types not shown separately. [3] Includes nonprofit organizations. [4] Holdings of U.S. issues by foreign residents. [5] Includes loans.
Source: Board of Governors of the Federal Reserve System, "Federal Reserve Statistical Release, Z.1, Flow of Funds Accounts of the United States"; published: 7 March 2002; <http://www.federalreserve.gov/releases/Z1/20020307/data.htm>.

No. 1174. New Security Issues of Corporations by Type of Offering: 1990 to 2001

[In billions of dollars (339.1 represents $339,100,000,000). Represents gross proceeds of issues maturing in more than one year. Figures are the principal amount or the number of units multiplied by the offering price. Excludes secondary offerings, employee stock plans, investment companies other than closed-end, intracorporate transactions, equities sold abroad, and Yankee bonds. Stock data include equity investments made by limited partnerships]

Type of offering	1990	1993	1994	1995	1996	1997	1998	1999	2000	2001
Total	339.1	768.3	582.5	666.4	750.5	867.8	1,052.8	1,016.5	1,000.8	842.2
Bonds, total	298.9	645.8	498.0	573.0	592.7	695.0	846.8	778.7	686.4	621.2
Public, domestic	188.8	486.2	364.8	408.5	465.6	536.8	731.0	627.6	546.0	549.2
Private placement, domestic . . .	87.0	121.2	76.1	87.5	43.7	55.0	37.8	28.5	18.0	15.6
Sold abroad	23.1	38.4	56.8	76.8	83.4	103.2	78.0	122.6	122.4	56.4
Stocks, total	40.2	122.5	84.5	93.4	157.8	172.8	206.0	237.8	314.4	221.0
Preferred	4.0	18.9	12.1	11.3	32.2	29.5	38.4	19.3	9.0	39.5
Common	19.4	82.7	47.6	56.3	82.4	81.4	82.9	105.7	120.0	81.4
Private placement	16.7	20.9	24.8	25.8	43.2	61.9	84.7	112.7	185.4	100.0

Source: Board of Governors of the Federal Reserve System, *Federal Reserve Bulletin*, monthly.

No. 1175. Purchases and Sales by U.S. Investors of Foreign Bonds and Stocks, 1990 to 2001, and by Selected Country, 2001

[In billions of dollars (31.2 represents $31,200,000,000). Covers transactions in all types of long-term foreign securities as reported by banks, brokers, and other entities in the United States. Data cover new issues of securities, transactions in outstanding issues, and redemptions of securities. Includes transactions executed in the United States for the account of foreigners, and transactions executed abroad for the account of reporting institutions and their domestic customers. Data by country show the country of domicile of the foreign buyers and sellers of the securities; in the case of outstanding issues, this may differ from the country of the original issuer. The term "foreigner" covers all institutions and individuals domiciled outside the United States, including U.S. citizens domiciled abroad, and the foreign branches, subsidiaries and other affiliates abroad of U.S. banks and businesses; the central governments, central banks, and other official institutions of foreign countries; and international and regional organizations. "Foreigner" also includes persons in the United States to the extent that they are known by reporting institutions to be acting on behalf of foreigners. Minus sign (-) indicates net sales by U.S. investors or a net inflow of capital into the United States]

Year and country	Net purchases			Total transactions [1]			Bonds		Stocks	
	Total	Bonds	Stocks	Total	Bonds	Stocks	Purchases	Sales	Purchases	Sales
1990	31.2	21.9	9.2	907	652	255	337	315	132	123
1991	46.8	14.8	32.0	949	675	273	345	330	153	121
1992	47.9	15.6	32.3	1,375	1,043	332	529	514	182	150
1993	143.1	80.4	62.7	2,126	1,572	554	826	746	308	245
1994	57.3	9.2	48.1	2,526	1,706	820	858	848	434	386
1995	98.7	48.4	50.3	2,569	1,827	741	938	890	396	346
1996	110.6	51.4	59.3	3,239	2,279	960	1,165	1,114	510	450
1997	89.1	48.1	40.9	4,505	2,952	1,553	1,500	1,452	797	756
1998	11.1	17.3	-6.2	4,527	2,674	1,853	1,346	1,328	923	930
1999	-10.0	5.7	-15.6	3,941	1,602	2,339	804	798	1,162	1,177
2000	17.1	4.1	13.1	5,539	1,922	3,617	963	959	1,815	1,802
2001, total [2]	19.9	-30.6	50.5	5,129	2,285	2,844	1,127	1,158	1,447	1,397
United Kingdom	27.4	5.5	21.9	2,389	1,263	1,126	634	629	574	552
Japan	20.1	0.2	19.9	434	85	349	42	42	185	165
Cayman Islands	1.6	2.4	-0.8	383	166	216	84	82	108	109
Canada	-2.5	-0.8	-1.7	222	77	145	38	39	72	74
Bermuda	2.2	-2.7	4.9	204	127	77	62	65	41	36
Hong Kong	1.5	-3.3	4.8	147	18	129	7	11	67	62
Germany	-2.0	-2.4	0.4	141	54	86	26	28	43	43
France	-1.8	0.5	-2.3	101	26	76	13	13	37	39
Singapore	-2.8	-0.3	-2.5	83	38	45	19	19	21	24
Bahamas, The	1.2	-0.2	1.4	82	42	39	21	21	20	19
Netherlands	-3.6	-0.4	-3.2	70	16	53	8	8	25	28
Ireland	-2.1	-3.0	0.9	66	32	34	15	18	17	16
Switzerland	-2.7	-1.0	-1.7	65	15	50	7	8	24	26
Brazil	2.6	2.7	-0.1	60	39	22	21	18	11	11
Italy	1.2	-0.9	2.1	58	24	35	11	12	18	16
Argentina	-3.3	-3.2	-0.1	51	45	5	21	24	3	3

[1] Total purchases plus total sales.   [2] Includes other countries, not shown separately.

Source: U.S. Dept. of Treasury, *Treasury Bulletin*, quarterly.

No. 1176. U.S. Holdings of Foreign Stocks and Bonds by Country: 1999 to 2001

[In billions of dollars (2,026.6 represents $2,026,600,000,000)]

Country	Stocks			Country	Bonds		
	1999	2000	2001		1999	2000	2001
Total holdings	2,026.6	1,832.4	1,564.7	Total holdings	556.7	557.0	545.8
Western Europe [1]	1,167.8	1,119.7	932.7	Western Europe [1]	195.8	203.3	186.2
United Kingdom	374.8	365.7	335.0	United Kingdom	61.0	67.8	62.1
Finland	58.4	51.4	39.4	France	12.7	13.6	15.4
France	183.2	183.3	140.4	Germany	43.9	49.2	51.3
Germany	117.6	94.7	91.0	Italy	12.6	11.5	11.7
Ireland	18.2	16.8	14.4	Netherlands	12.4	16.8	17.8
Italy	53.5	50.1	38.2	Sweden	12.2	11.8	11.7
Netherlands	141.9	137.8	103.8	Canada	104.4	93.4	92.4
Spain	35.7	30.7	24.8	Japan	27.4	25.4	23.2
Sweden	74.8	65.9	53.0	Latin America [1]	104.6	115.6	121.1
Switzerland	64.3	75.5	57.2	Argentina	26.2	24.1	20.2
Canada	100.7	123.3	99.6	Brazil	19.6	20.2	22.9
Japan	273.7	182.2	143.5	Mexico	38.7	36.5	34.6
Latin America [1]	89.1	73.7	60.2	Other Western Hemisphere [1] ..	26.3	26.0	28.1
Argentina	11.3	9.7	8.1	Cayman Islands	14.0	9.3	11.8
Brazil	28.9	27.7	23.1	Other countries [1]	83.5	80.0	83.1
Mexico	30.2	25.1	20.0	Australia	28.7	27.3	26.5
Other Western Hemisphere [1] ..	129.0	144.2	141.7	Korea, South	12.5	10.7	8.8
Bermuda	45.9	36.3	34.8	International organizations	14.7	13.3	11.7
Netherlands Antilles	26.7	34.4	28.3				
Other countries [1]	266.3	189.3	187.0				
Australia	39.2	35.1	37.9				
Hong Kong	38.7	34.3	32.2				
Singapore	16.3	8.6	4.0				

[1] Includes other countries not shown separately.

Source: U.S. Bureau of Economic Analysis, *Survey of Current Business*, July 2002.

No. 1177. Foreign Purchases and Sales of U.S. Securities by Type of Security, 1990 to 2001, and by Selected Country, 2001

[In billions of dollars (18.7 represents $18,700,000,000). Covers transactions in all types of long-term domestic securities by foreigners as reported by banks, brokers, and other entities in the United States (except nonmarketable U.S. Treasury notes, foreign series; and nonmarketable U.S. Treasury bonds and notes, foreign currency series). See headnote, Table 1175. Minus sign (-) indicates net sales by foreigners or a net outflow of capital from the United States]

Year and country	Net purchases					Total transactions [4]				
	Total	Treasury bonds and notes [1]	U.S. Govt. corporations [2] bonds	Corporate bonds [3]	Corporate stocks	Total	Treasury bonds and notes [1]	U.S. Govt. corporations [2] bonds	Corporate bonds [3]	Corporate stocks
1990	18.7	17.9	6.3	9.7	-15.1	4,204	3,620	104	117	362
1991	58.1	19.9	10.2	16.9	11.1	4,706	4,016	124	155	411
1992	73.2	39.3	18.3	20.8	-5.1	5,282	4,444	204	187	448
1993	111.1	23.6	35.4	30.6	21.6	6,314	5,195	263	239	618
1994	140.4	78.8	21.7	38.0	1.9	6,562	5,343	297	222	699
1995	231.9	134.1	28.7	57.9	11.2	7,243	5,828	222	278	915
1996	370.2	232.2	41.7	83.7	12.5	8,965	7,134	241	422	1,169
1997	388.0	184.2	49.9	84.4	69.6	12,759	9,546	469	617	2,126
1998	277.8	49.0	56.8	121.9	50.0	14,989	10,259	992	641	3,097
1999	350.2	-10.0	92.2	160.4	107.5	14,617	8,586	880	577	4,574
2000	457.8	-54.0	152.8	184.1	174.9	16,910	7,795	1,305	775	7,036
2001, total [5]	529.7	18.5	165.4	229.4	116.4	19,994	10,517	2,239	1,252	5,986
United Kingdom	192.4	-7.2	44.8	116.3	38.5	5,875	3,700	365	576	1,233
Cayman Islands	50.7	13.0	6.2	27.7	3.7	3,317	1,046	856	228	1,188
Bermuda	16.6	3.6	6.9	17.7	-11.6	1,360	447	75	81	757
Japan	58.7	17.8	28.0	6.1	6.8	1,215	810	235	35	134
Canada	11.4	-4.1	1.3	3.3	11.0	883	591	43	29	219
France	6.7	-4.3	2.0	3.0	5.9	875	481	28	20	346
Germany	19.1	-1.7	6.5	5.9	8.4	547	331	44	19	153
Ireland	3.9	0.2	0.5	1.2	1.9	521	377	23	19	102
Netherlands Antilles	-6.6	-10.7	0.1	3.5	0.5	490	230	14	14	233
Hong Kong	29.9	7.2	17.8	4.2	0.7	411	262	104	10	36
Netherlands	5.7	-6.7	-1.0	2.5	10.9	350	230	30	11	80
Bahamas, The	-0.3	-4.5	0.5	1.8	1.9	333	195	8	35	95
Switzerland	10.6	1.4	3.0	2.7	3.5	260	76	19	14	151
Singapore	15.5	-7.9	2.9	5.4	15.1	254	113	32	19	89
Italy	-1.7	-2.0	-2.1	0.2	2.2	251	105	9	5	132

[1] Marketable bonds and notes.   [2] Includes federally-sponsored agencies.   [3] Includes transactions in directly placed issues abroad by U.S. corporations and issues of states and municipalities.   [4] Total purchases plus total sales.   [5] Includes other countries, not shown separately.

Source: U.S. Dept. of Treasury, *Treasury Bulletin*, quarterly.

No. 1178. Foreign Holdings of U.S. Securities by Country: 1999 to 2001

[In billions of dollars (1,080.4 represents $1,080,400,000,000)]

Country	U.S. Treasury securities			Country	Corporate and agency bonds			Corporate stocks		
	1999	2000	2001		1999	2000	2001	1999	2000	2001
Total holdings	1,080.4	1,026.1	1,039.5	Total holdings	825.2	1,076.0	1,392.6	1,526.1	1,547.6	1,464.0
Japan	301.0	325.6	331.3	Western Europe [1]	568.4	712.5	912.0	948.7	1,016.2	969.5
China [2]	63.1	62.3	81.8	United Kingdom	401.7	517.1	691.4	356.8	381.0	368.9
Germany	58.9	50.7	50.3	France	9.9	11.2	15.8	46.3	46.9	46.0
Hong Kong	40.9	39.8	49.5	Germany	39.2	42.7	51.8	91.1	111.0	104.9
Taiwan [2]	42.7	34.5	37.0	Italy	2.7	4.0	2.2	28.3	39.8	36.6
Korea, South	23.0	29.7	33.3	Netherlands	19.6	20.5	19.7	103.3	97.4	95.6
Middle East OPEC members	18.4	19.8	22.0	Canada	14.4	24.0	25.1	164.5	156.6	147.9
Singapore	34.6	28.9	21.5	Japan	66.0	99.7	120.6	143.3	134.4	123.4
France	35.4	25.4	21.1	Latin America	10.1	18.7	24.7	29.0	28.7	32.3
Switzerland	28.6	16.6	19.0	Other Western Hemisphere	130.9	172.7	231.5	159.0	125.1	102.4
				Other countries	35.4	48.4	78.7	81.6	86.6	88.5

[1] Includes other countries not shown separately.   [2] With the establishment of diplomatic relations with China on January 1, 1979, the U.S. government recognized the People's Republic of China as the sole legal government of China and acknowledged the Chinese position that there is only one China and that Taiwan is part of China.

Source: U.S. Bureau of Economic Analysis, *Survey of Current Business*, July 2002.

No. 1179. Stock Prices and Yields: 1990 to 2001

[Closing values as of end of December, except as noted]

Index	1990	1995	1997	1998	1999	2000	2001
STOCK PRICES							
Standard & Poor's indices: [1]							
S&P 500 composite (1941-43=10)	330.2	615.9	970.4	1,229.2	1,469.3	1,320.3	1,148.1
S&P 400 MidCap Index (1982=100)	100.0	217.8	333.4	392.3	444.7	516.7	508.3
S&P 600 Small Cap Index (Dec. 31, 1993=100) . .	(NA)	121.1	181.2	177.4	197.8	219.6	232.2
S&P 500/Barra Value Index (Dec. 31, 1974=35) . .	177.7	325.1	490.4	551.6	610.6	636.2	552.0
S&P 500/Barra Growth Index (Dec. 31, 1974=35) .	159.9	302.0	496.0	697.3	887.3	687.6	594.6
Russell indices: [2]							
Russell 1000 (Dec. 31, 1986=130)	171.2	328.9	513.8	642.9	768.0	700.1	604.9
Russell 2000 (Dec. 31, 1986=135)	132.2	316.0	437.0	422.0	504.8	483.5	488.5
Russell 3000 (Dec. 31, 1986=140)	180.9	351.9	543.1	664.3	793.3	725.8	634.2
N.Y. Stock Exchange common stock index							
Composite (Dec. 31, 1965=50)	180.5	329.5	511.2	596.1	650.3	656.9	589.8
Yearly high	201.6	331.7	515.2	601.8	663.5	681.2	667.7
Yearly low	161.8	249.9	386.4	462.7	572.4	575.0	494.6
Industrial (Dec. 31, 1965=50).	223.6	413.3	630.4	743.7	828.2	803.3	735.7
Transportation (Dec. 31, 1965=50)	141.5	302.0	466.3	482.4	466.7	462.8	438.8
Utility (Dec. 31, 1965=100)	182.6	252.9	335.2	445.9	511.2	440.5	329.8
Finance (Dec. 31, 1965=50)	122.1	274.3	496.0	521.4	516.6	647.0	593.7
American Stock Exchange Composite Index							
(Dec. 29, 1995=550)	(NA)	550.0	684.6	689.0	877.0	897.8	847.6
NASDAQ composite index (Feb. 5, 1971=100) . .	373.8	1,052.1	1,570.4	2,192.7	4,069.3	2,470.5	1,950.4
Nasdaq-100 (Jan. 31, 1985=125).	200.5	576.2	990.8	1,836.0	3,708.0	2,341.7	1,577.1
Industrial (Feb. 5, 1971=100)	406.1	964.7	1,221.0	1,304.3	2,239.0	1,483.0	1,389.2
Banks (Feb. 5, 1971=100)	254.9	1,009.4	2,083.2	1,838.0	1,691.3	1,939.5	2,134.9
Dow-Jones and Co., Inc.:							
Composite (65 stocks)	920.6	1,693.2	2,607.4	2,870.8	3,214.4	3,317.4	2,892.2
Industrial (30 stocks)	2,633.7	5,117.1	7,908.3	9,181.4	11,497.1	10,786.9	10,021.5
Transportation (20 stocks).	910.2	1,981.0	3,256.5	3,149.3	2,977.2	2,946.6	2,640.0
Utility (15 stocks).	209.7	225.4	273.1	312.3	283.4	412.2	293.9
Wilshire 5000 Total Market Index [3]							
(Dec. 31, 1980=1404.596)	3,101.4	6,057.2	9,298.2	11,317.6	13,812.7	12,175.9	10,818.6
COMMON STOCK YIELDS (percent)							
Standard & Poor's composite index (500 stocks): [4]							
Dividend-price ratio [5]	3.61	2.56	1.77	1.49	1.25	1.15	1.32
Earnings-price ratio [6]	6.47	6.09	4.57	3.46	3.17	3.63	2.95

NA Not available.   [1] Standard & Poor's Indices are market-value weighted and are chosen for market size, liquidity, and industry group representation. The S&P 500 index represents the 500 largest publicly traded companies. The S&P MidCap Index tracks mid-cap companies. The S&P SmallCap Index consists of 600 domestic small-cap stocks.   [2] The Russell 1000 and 3000 indices show respectively the 1000 and 3000 largest capitalization stocks in the United States. The Russell 2000 index shows the 2000 largest capitalization stocks in the United States after the first 1000.   [3] The Wilshire 5000 Total Market Index measures the performance of all U.S. headquartered equity securities with readily available prices.   [4] Source: U.S. Council of Economic Advisors, *Economic Report of the President*, annual.   [5] Aggregate cash dividends (based on latest known annual rate) divided by aggregate market value based on Wednesday closing prices. Averages of monthly figures.   [6] Averages of quarterly ratios which are ratio of earnings (after taxes) for four quarters ending with particular quarter to price index for last day of that quarter.

Source: Except as noted, Global Financial Data, Los Angeles, CA, <http://www.globalfindata.com/trial/trd.html>; (copyright).

No. 1180. Dow-Jones U.S. Equity Market Index by Industry: 1995 to 2001

[As of end of year]

Industry	1995	1996	1997	1998	1999	2000	2001
U.S. Equity Market Index, total	147.49	176.38	228.67	281.61	341.57	306.88	266.71
Basic materials	139.19	153.17	167.34	150.23	187.16	154.49	153.22
Consumer, cyclical	140.43	158.20	210.75	282.76	341.88	277.68	278.19
Consumer, noncyclical.	134.27	164.39	213.66	246.00	244.64	215.56	217.96
Energy	134.70	167.75	200.81	186.15	219.71	272.96	236.74
Financial	176.95	230.89	337.27	356.05	354.55	440.91	404.50
Healthcare	127.76	149.13	201.53	277.52	263.62	360.18	310.76
Industrial	156.26	187.88	224.43	245.89	308.19	276.11	245.14
Technology	229.07	311.29	381.45	648.08	1,188.60	749.01	535.89
Telecommunications	154.78	150.20	205.40	305.76	356.97	210.38	180.62
Utilities	109.20	107.18	130.82	141.84	118.12	177.80	127.04

Source: Dow Jones & Company, Inc., New York, NY, *Dow Jones Indexes*, (copyright).

No. 1181. NASDAQ—Securities Listed and Volume of Trading: 1990 to 2001

Item	Unit	1990	1993	1994	1995	1996	1997	1998	1999	2000	2001
Member firms	Number. . .	5,827	5,296	5,426	5,451	5,553	5,597	5,592	5,482	5,579	5,499
Branch offices.	Number. . .	24,457	44,181	57,105	58,119	60,151	62,966	70,752	80,035	82,126	88,168
Companies listed.	Number. . .	4,132	4,611	4,902	5,112	5,556	5,487	5,068	4,829	4,734	4,109
Issues	Number. . .	4,706	5,393	5,761	5,955	6,384	6,208	5,583	5,210	5,053	4,363
Shares traded	Billion	33.4	66.5	74.4	101.2	138.1	163.9	202.0	272.6	442.8	471.2
Average daily volume . .	Million	132	263	295	401	544	648	802	1,082	1,757	1,907
Value of shares traded . . .	Bil. dol. . . .	452	1,350	1,449	2,398	3,302	4,482	5,759	11,013	20,395	10,935

Source: National Association of Securities Dealers, Washington, DC, *NASD Annual Report* (copyright).

No. 1182. Sales of Stocks on Registered Exchanges: 1990 to 2001

[1,752 represents $1,752,000,000,000. Excludes over-the-counter trading]

Exchange	Unit	1990	1993	1994	1995	1996	1997	1998	1999	2000	2001
Market value of all sales, all exchanges [1][2]	Bil. dol. .	1,752	2,734	2,966	3,690	4,735	6,879	8,698	11,220	14,552	13,327
New York	Bil. dol . .	1,394	2,278	2,483	3,078	4,013	5,848	7,275	9,087	11,217	10,720
American.	Bil. dol . .	65	83	83	105	131	204	355	543	915	883
Chicago	Bil. dol . .	74	107	98	114	136	213	326	540	1,038	702
CBOE [3]	Bil. dol . .	81	65	87	107	130	179	214	271	330	197
Pacific	Bil. dol . .	53	70	70	94	108	151	182	255	248	96
Philadelphia.	Bil. dol . .	41	55	51	59	68	89	97	103	165	130
STOCKS [4]											
Shares sold, all exchanges [2]. . .	Billion. . .	53.3	82.8	90.5	106.4	125.7	159.7	206.4	244.1	317.7	371.0
New York	Billion. . .	43.8	68.7	76.7	90.1	108.2	138.8	178.9	207.7	265.7	312.7
American	Billion. . .	3.1	4.5	4.3	4.8	5.3	6.2	7.6	8.7	11.9	15.3
Chicago	Billion. . .	2.5	3.8	3.5	3.9	4.2	6.0	9.5	14.4	24.1	27.3
Pacific	Billion. . .	1.7	2.3	2.1	2.7	3.0	3.2	4.0	4.9	4.1	1.5
Market value, all exchanges [2] . .	Bil. dol . .	1,612	2,610	2,817	3,507	4,511	6,559	8,307	10,680	13,691	12,732
New York	Bil. dol . .	1,390	2,276	2,482	3,076	4,011	5,847	7,274	9,087	11,216	10,720
American	Bil. dol . .	36	54	56	73	86	139	280	446	758	806
Chicago	Bil. dol . .	74	107	98	114	136	213	326	540	1,038	702
Pacific	Bil. dol . .	45	62	59	79	92	123	148	206	163	46

[1] Includes market value of stocks, rights, warrants, and options trading. [2] Includes other registered exchanges, not shown separately. [3] Chicago Board Options Exchange, Inc. [4] Includes voting trust certificates, American Depository Receipts, and certificate of deposit for stocks.

Source: U.S. Securities and Exchange Commission, *Annual Report*.

No. 1183. Volume of Trading on New York Stock Exchange: 1990 to 2001

[39,946 represents 39,946,000,000. *Round lot*: A unit of trading or a multiple thereof. On the NYSE the unit of trading is generally 100 shares in stocks. For some inactive stocks, the unit of trading is 10 shares. *Odd lot*: An amount of stock less than the established 100-share unit or 10-share unit of trading]

Item	Unit	1990	1994	1995	1996	1997	1998	1999	2000	2001
Shares traded	Million .	39,946	74,003	87,873	105,477	134,404	171,188	206,299	265,499	311,290
Round lots	Million . .	39,665	73,420	87,218	104,636	133,312	169,745	203,914	262,478	307,509
Average daily shares	Million . .	157	291	346	412	527	674	809	1,042	1,240
High day	Million . .	292	483	653	681	1,201	1,216	1,350	1,560	2,368
Low day	Million . .	57	114	118	130	155	247	312	403	414
Odd lots	Million . .	282	583	656	841	1,091	1,443	2,384	3,021	3,781
Value of shares traded .	Bil. dol .	1,336	2,477	3,110	4,102	5,833	7,395	9,073	11,205	10,645
Round lots	Bil. dol. .	1,325	2,454	3,083	4,064	5,778	7,318	8,945	11,060	10,489
Odd lots	Bil. dol. .	11	22	27	38	56	77	128	145	155
Bond volume [1]	Mil. dol .	10,893	7,197	6,979	5,529	5,046	3,838	3,221	2,328	2,668
Daily average	Mil. dol .	43.1	28.6	27.7	21.8	19.9	15.2	12.8	9.2	10.8

[1] Par value.

Source: New York Stock Exchange, Inc., New York, NY, *Fact Book, 2001* (copyright).

No. 1184. Securities Listed on New York Stock Exchange: 1990 to 2001

[As of December 31, except cash dividends are for calendar year (1,689 represents $1,689,000,000,000)]

Item	Unit	1990	1992	1993	1994	1995	1996	1997	1998	1999	2000	2001
BONDS												
Number of issuers	Number .	743	636	574	583	564	563	533	474	416	392	369
Number of issues	Number .	2,912	2,354	2,103	2,141	2,097	2,064	1,965	1,858	1,736	1,627	1,447
Face value	Bil. dol . .	1,689	2,009	2,342	2,526	2,773	2,845	2,625	2,554	2,402	2,125	1,654
STOCKS												
Companies	Number .	1,774	2,088	2,361	2,570	2,675	2,907	3,047	3,114	3,025	2,862	2,798
Number of issues	Number .	2,284	2,658	2,904	3,060	3,126	3,285	3,358	3,382	3,286	3,072	2,984
Shares listed	Billion. . .	90.7	115.8	131.1	142.3	154.7	176.9	207.1	239.3	280.9	313.9	341.5
Market value	Bil. dol . .	2,820	4,035	4,541	4,448	6,013	7,300	9,413	10,864	12,296	12,372	11,714
Average price	Dollars .	31.08	34.83	34.65	31.26	38.86	41.26	45.45	45.40	43.77	42.14	34.11
Cash dividends on common stock [1]	Bil. dol . .	103.2	109.7	120.2	130.0	147.0	150.6	159.4	179.0	174.7	165.6	186.0

[1] Estimate based on average annual yield of the NYSE composite index.

Source: New York Stock Exchange, Inc., New York, NY, *Fact Book, 2001* (copyright).

No. 1185. Stock Ownership by Age of Head of Family and Family Income: 1992 to 1998

[**Median value in thousands of constant 1998 dollars (12.0 represents $12,000)**. Constant dollar figures are based on consumer price index data published by U.S. Bureau of Labor Statistics. Families include one-person units; for definition of family, see text, Section 1, Population. Based on Survey of Consumer Finance; see Appendix III. For definition of median, see Guide to Tabular Presentation]

Age of family head and family income (constant (1998) dollars)	Families having direct or indirect stock holdings [1] (percent)			Median value among families with holdings			Stock holdings' share of group's financial assets (percent)		
	1992	1995	1998	1992	1995	1998	1992	1995	1998
All families	**36.7**	**40.4**	**48.8**	**12.0**	**15.4**	**25.0**	**33.7**	**40.0**	**53.9**
Under 35 years old	28.3	36.6	40.7	4.0	5.4	7.0	24.8	27.2	44.8
35 to 44 years old	42.4	46.4	56.5	8.6	10.6	20.0	31.0	39.5	54.7
45 to 54 years old	46.4	48.9	58.6	17.1	27.6	38.0	40.6	42.9	55.7
55 to 64 years old	45.3	40.0	55.9	28.5	32.9	47.0	37.3	44.4	58.3
65 to 74 years old	30.2	34.4	42.6	18.3	36.1	56.0	31.6	35.8	51.3
75 years old and over	25.7	27.9	29.4	28.5	21.2	60.0	25.4	39.8	48.7
Less than $10,000	6.8	5.4	7.7	6.2	3.2	4.0	15.9	12.9	24.8
$10,000 to $24,999	17.8	22.2	24.7	4.6	6.4	9.0	15.3	26.7	27.5
$25,000 to $49,999	40.2	45.4	52.7	7.2	8.5	11.5	23.7	30.3	39.1
$50,000 to $99,999	62.5	65.4	74.3	15.4	23.6	35.7	33.5	39.9	48.8
$100,000 and more	78.3	81.6	91.0	71.9	85.5	150.0	40.2	46.4	63.0

[1] Indirect holdings are those in mutual funds, retirement accounts, and other managed assets.
Source: Board of Governors of the Federal Reserve System, *Federal Reserve Bulletin*, January 2000, and unpublished data.

No. 1186. Household Ownership of Equities: 1999

[**49.2 represents 49,200,000**. Based on a national probability sample of 4,842 household financial decisionmakers. Of these, 2,336 decisionmakers who indicated they owned equities were asked further questions about equity ownership]

Type of holding	Households owning equities		Number of individual investors (mil.)
	Number (mil.)	Percent of all households	
Any type of equity (net) [1]	49.2	48.2	78.7
Any equity inside employer-sponsored retirement plans	32.5	31.8	52.0
Any equity outside employer-sponsored retirement plans	36.3	35.5	61.6
Individual stock (net) [1]	26.7	26.1	40.0
Individual stock inside employer-sponsored retirement plans	10.7	10.5	14.0
Individual stock outside employer-sponsored retirement plans	21.9	21.4	32.8
Stock mutual funds (net) [1]	41.8	40.9	66.8
Stock mutual funds inside employer-sponsored retirement plans	28.5	27.9	39.9
Stock mutual funds outside employer-sponsored retirement plans . . .	27.8	27.2	44.4

[1] Multiple responses included.

No. 1187. Characteristics of Equity Owners: 1999

[**In percent, except as indicated**. See headnote, Table 1186. For definition of median, see Guide to Tabular Presentation]

Item	Total	Age				Household income		
		19 to 35 years old	36 to 54 years old	55 to 74 years old	75 years old and over	Less than $50,000	$50,000 to $99,999	$100,000 and over
Median age of owner (years)	47	29	44	61	78	45	44	48
Median household income (dol.)	60,000	47,000	62,500	53,000	30,000	34,000	65,000	125,000
Median household financial assets [1] (dol.)	85,000	25,000	88,000	200,000	200,000	42,500	89,000	300,000
Equity investments owned:								
Individual stock (net) [2]	54	45	52	58	63	44	52	67
Inside employer-sponsored retirement plans . .	20	21	23	17	6	15	20	29
Outside employer-sponsored retirement plans.	44	35	43	51	59	34	44	61
Stock mutual funds (net) [2]	85	83	88	84	80	81	89	88
Inside employer-sponsored retirement plans . .	58	64	67	47	12	49	66	69
Outside employer-sponsored retirement plans .	57	45	57	62	72	51	55	66
Non-equity investments owned: [2]								
Savings accounts, MMDAs, or CDs [3]	83	82	84	82	86	79	84	86
Bond investments (net) [2]	22	14	21	24	44	15	19	31
Individual bonds	9	4	8	11	25	4	7	15
Bond mutual funds.	16	11	16	19	30	12	15	23
Fixed or variable annuities	21	9	20	30	35	17	20	25
Hybrid mutual funds	39	33	42	41	35	33	42	46
Money market mutual funds	26	17	26	32	30	20	26	38
Investment real estate	26	17	26	34	24	18	26	40
Have employer-sponsored retirement plan coverage.	80	83	86	73	49	73	86	84
Have Individual Retirement Account (IRA).	53	37	53	67	39	41	55	67

[1] Includes assets in employer-sponsored retirement plans but excludes value of primary residence.   [2] Multiple responses included.   [3] MMDA=money market deposit account; CD=certificate of deposit.
Source of Tables 1186 and 1187: Investment Company Institute, Washington, DC, and Securities Industry Association, New York, NY, *Equity Ownership in America, Fall 1999* (copyright).

Banking, Finance, and Insurance 737

No. 1188. Households Owning Mutual Funds by Age and Income: 2000 and 2001

[In percent. Includes money market, stock, bond and hybrid, variable annuity, IRA, Keogh, and employer-sponsored retirement plan fund owners. An estimated 54,800,000 households own mutual funds in May 2001. Based on a sample survey of 3,019 households; for details, see source]

Age of household head and household income	Percent distribu- tion, 2000	As percent of all households		Age of household head and household income	Percent distribu- tion, 2000	As percent of all households	
		2000	2001			2000	2001
Total	100	49	52	Less than $25,000	9	17	21
Less than 25 years old .	2	23	32	$25,000 to $34,999. . . .	11	37	38
25 to 34 years old.	18	49	50	$35,000 to $49,999. . . .	19	49	49
35 to 44 years old.	28	58	60	$50,000 to $74,999. . . .	28	66	66
45 to 54 years old.	25	59	60	$75,000 to $99,999. . . .	14	77	78
55 to 64 years old.	13	54	54	$100,000 and over	19	79	85
65 years old and over . .	14	32	41				

Source: Investment Company Institute, Washington, DC, *Fundamentals, Investment Company Institute Research in Brief*, Vol. 9, No. 4, August 2000 and Vol. 10, No. 4, September 2001 (copyright).

No. 1189. Characteristics of Mutual Fund Owners: 2001

[In percent, except as indicated. Mutual fund ownership includes holdings of money market, stock, bond, and hybrid mutual funds; and funds owned through variable annuities, Individual Retirement Accounts (IRAs), Keoghs, and employer-sponsored retirement plans. Based on a national probability sample of 2,592 primary financial decisionmakers in households with mutual fund investments. For definition of median, see Guide to Tabular Presentation]

Characteristic	Total	Age			Household income		
		18 to 39 years old	40 to 54 years old	55 years old and over	Less than $50,000	$50,000 to $100,000	Over $100,000
Median age (years).	46	33	47	63	43	45	46
Median household income (dol.)	62,100	60,000	70,000	60,000	32,500	65,000	130,000
Median household financial assets [1] (dol.).	100,000	50,000	129,700	250,000	40,000	100,000	300,000
Own an IRA.	60	59	60	58	51	60	66
Household has a defined contribution retirement plan(s), net [2]	81	87	86	69	75	88	86
401(k) plan.	64	76	71	37	55	68	72
403(b) plan	11	12	11	11	9	12	13
State, local, or federal government plan.	35	31	35	40	34	38	38
Median mutual fund assets (dol.).	40,000	20,000	58,500	62,500	17,500	44,800	120,000
Median number of mutual funds owned	4	4	5	4	3	4	6
Own: [2] Equity funds	88	90	91	83	86	87	96
Bond funds	37	32	39	41	31	34	44
Hybrid funds.	34	34	36	35	33	32	43
Money market mutual funds	48	42	51	53	44	44	53
Own mutual funds bought: [2]							
Outside employer-sponsored retirement plan(s).	69	57	65	82	60	60	75
Inside employer-sponsored retirement plan(s). .	62	72	72	42	57	69	76

[1] Includes assets in employer-sponsored retirement plans but excludes value of primary residence. [2] Multiple responses included.

Source: Investment Company Institute, Washington, DC, *2001 Profile of Mutual Fund Shareholders*, 2001 (copyright).

No. 1190. Mutual Funds—Summary: 1990 to 2001

[Number of funds and assets as of December 31 (1,065 represents $1,065,000,000,000). A mutual fund is an open-end investment company that continuously issues and redeems shares that represent an interest in a pool of financial assets. Excludes data for funds that invest in other mutual funds. Minus sign (-) indicates net redemptions]

Type of fund	Unit	1990	1994	1995	1996	1997	1998	1999	2000	2001
Number of funds, total	Number. .	3,079	5,325	5,725	6,248	6,684	7,314	7,791	8,155	8,307
Equity funds	Number . .	1,099	1,886	2,139	2,570	2,951	3,513	3,952	4,385	4,717
Hybrid funds	Number . .	193	361	412	466	501	525	532	523	484
Bond funds	Number . .	1,046	2,115	2,177	2,224	2,219	2,250	2,262	2,208	2,091
Money market funds, taxable [1] . . .	Number . .	506	646	674	666	682	685	702	703	689
Money market funds, tax-exempt [2]. .	Number . .	235	317	323	322	331	341	343	336	326
Assets, total	Bil. dol . .	1,065	2,155	2,811	3,526	4,468	5,525	6,846	6,965	6,975
Equity funds	Bil. dol . .	240	853	1,249	1,726	2,368	2,978	4,042	3,962	3,418
Hybrid funds	Bil. dol . .	36	164	210	253	317	365	379	346	346
Bond funds	Bil. dol . .	291	527	599	645	724	831	813	811	925
Money market funds, taxable [1] . . .	Bil. dol . .	415	501	630	762	898	1,163	1,409	1,607	2,013
Money market funds, tax-exempt [2]. .	Bil. dol . .	84	110	123	140	161	189	204	238	272
Equity, hybrid and bond funds:										
Sales	Bil. dol . .	149	472	475	681	869	1,058	1,274	1,630	1,383
Redemptions	Bil. dol . .	98	329	313	397	541	748	1,021	1,330	1,177
Net sales	Bil. dol . .	51	143	163	284	328	310	252	300	206
Money market funds, taxable: [1]										
Sales	Bil. dol . .	1,219	2,234	2,729	3,524	4,395	5,534	7,083	8,691	10,701
Redemptions	Bil. dol . .	1,183	2,229	2,617	3,415	4,265	5,289	6,866	8,499	10,314
Net sales	Bil. dol . .	36	5	112	108	129	244	217	192	387
Money market funds, tax-exempt: [2]										
Sales	Bil. dol . .	197	369	396	467	536	639	687	788	783
Redemptions	Bil. dol . .	190	370	385	453	518	612	675	757	751
Net sales	Bil. dol . .	7	-1	11	13	18	27	12	31	31

[1] Funds invest in short-term, high-grade securities sold in the money market. [2] Funds invest in municipal securities with relatively short maturities.

Source: Investment Company Institute, Washington, DC, *Mutual Fund Fact Book*, annual (copyright).

No. 1191. Mutual Fund Shares—Holdings and Net Purchases by Type of Investor: 1990 to 2001

[In billions of dollars (608 represents $608,000,000,000). Holdings as of Dec. 31. Minus sign (-) indicates net sales]

Type of investor	Holdings					Net purchases				
	1990	1995	1999	2000	2001	1990	1995	1999	2000	2001
Total	608	1,853	4,538	4,435	4,136	53.7	147.4	191.2	235.0	201.6
Households, nonprofit organizations	457	1,159	3,128	3,125	2,993	22.5	66.0	173.7	252.1	211.5
Nonfinancial corporate business...	10	46	114	99	85	-1.0	4.6	-1.8	-1.8	-1.8
State and local governments.....	5	35	26	26	32	3.3	5.9	4.3	0.8	5.1
Commercial banking	2	2	11	14	20	-0.3	0.3	1.2	2.5	7.8
Credit unions	1	3	3	2	4	0.2	0.2	-1.1	-0.3	1.5
Bank personal trusts and estates..	63	254	461	387	320	9.7	11.9	-1.5	-30.5	-20.0
Life insurance companies	31	28	43	48	44	12.6	13.5	15.0	11.0	2.0
Private pension funds	40	327	754	734	639	6.6	45.0	1.6	1.2	-4.4

Source: Board of Governors of the Federal Reserve System, "Federal Reserve Statistical Release, Z.1, Flow of Funds Accounts of the United States"; published: 7 March 2002; <http://www.federalreserve.gov/releases/Z1/20020307/data.htm>.

No. 1192. Mutual Fund Retirement Assets: 1990 to 2001

[In billions of dollars, except percent (207 represents $207,000,000,000). Based on data from the Institute's Annual Questionnaire for Retirement Statistics. The 2001 survey gathered data from 11,783 mutual fund share classes representing approximately 81 percent of mutual fund industry assets. Assets were estimated for all nonreporting funds. Estimates of retirement assets in street name and omnibus accounts were derived from data reported on the Annual Questionnaire for Retirement Statistics and the Annual Institutional Survey]

Type of account	1990	1995	1996	1997	1998	1999	2000	2001
Mutual fund retirement assets ...	207	916	1,169	1,527	1,924	2,500	2,445	2,311
Percent of total retirement assets.	5	13	15	17	19	22	21	21
Individual retirement accounts (IRAs) ...	140	476	598	777	975	1,264	1,237	1,173
Employer-sponsored defined contribution retirement plans	67	439	571	750	950	1,236	1,208	1,138
401(k) plans [1]	35	266	349	473	605	793	798	765
Percent of total 401(k) assets	9	31	33	37	39	44	44	44
403(b) plans [2]	15	119	146	184	228	283	258	231
457 plans [3]	2	8	11	16	23	38	37	35
Other defined contribution plans [4]....	15	46	65	77	94	122	115	107
Percent of all mutual funds:								
Mutual fund retirement assets	19	33	33	34	35	37	35	33
Individual retirement accounts (IRAs) ...	13	17	17	17	18	18	18	17
Employer-sponsored retirement plans ...	6	16	16	17	17	18	17	16

[1] See headnote, Table 527. Predominantly 401(k) assets, but may also include some profit-sharing plan assets that do not have a 401(k) feature.   [2] Section 403(b) of the Internal Revenue Code permits employees of certain charitable organizations, nonprofit hospitals, universities, and public schools to establish tax-sheltered retirement programs. These plans may invest in either annuity contracts or mutual fund shares.   [3] These plans are deferred compensation arrangements for government employees and employees of certain tax-exempt organizations.   [4] Includes Keoghs; target benefit plans; thrift savings plans, stock bonus plans, and money purchase plans without a 401(k) feature; and all other defined contribution plans not specified elsewhere.

Source: Investment Company Institute, Washington, DC, *Fundamentals, Investment Company Institute Research in Brief, "Mutual Funds and the Retirement Market in 2001"*; Vol. 11, No. 2, June 2002 <http://www.ici.org> (copyright).

No. 1193. Individual Retirement Accounts (IRA) Plans—Value by Institution: 1990 to 2001

[As of December 31 (637 represents $637,000,000,000). Estimated]

Institution	Amount (bil. dol.)									Percent distribution		
	1990	1994	1995	1996	1997	1998	1999	2000	2001	1990	2000	2001
Total IRA assets..	637	1,056	1,288	1,467	1,728	2,150	2,542	2,507	2,399	100	100	100
Bank and thrift deposits [1] ...	266	255	261	258	254	249	244	252	255	42	10	11
Life insurance companies [2]...	40	69	81	92	135	156	201	202	200	6	8	8
Mutual funds	140	350	476	597	776	974	1,263	1,236	1,168	22	49	49
Securities held in brokerage accounts	190	382	471	519	563	771	834	817	777	30	33	32

[1] Includes Keogh deposits.   [2] Annuities held by IRAs, excluding variable annuity mutual fund IRA assets.

Source: Investment Company Institute, Washington, DC, *Mutual Fund Fact Book*, annual (copyright).

No. 1194. Assets of Private and Public Pension Funds by Type of Fund: 1990 to 2001

[In billions of dollars (3,005 represents $3,005,000,000,000). As of end of year. Except for corporate equities, represents book value. Excludes social security trust funds and U.S. Government pension funds; see Tables 518 and 522]

Type of pension fund	1990	1994	1995	1996	1997	1998	1999	2000	2001
Total, all types	3,005	4,345	5,107	5,700	6,650	7,481	8,303	8,284	7,846
Private funds	2,204	3,256	3,804	4,205	4,833	5,426	6,076	5,994	5,669
Insured [1]	570	797	881	954	1,086	1,248	1,431	1,456	1,508
Noninsured [2][3]	1,634	2,460	2,923	3,251	3,747	4,178	4,645	4,538	4,161
Credit market instruments [3] . .	472	611	631	627	675	652	677	717	735
U.S. Government securities [3] . .	263	351	356	343	355	307	318	344	342
Agency	133	212	214	204	211	195	206	232	239
Corporate and foreign bonds . .	158	229	242	245	279	301	311	326	346
Corporate equities	606	1,020	1,289	1,464	1,696	1,991	2,326	2,195	1,902
Mutual fund shares	40	206	327	412	570	668	754	734	639
Unallocated insurance contracts [4].	215	298	332	361	382	385	393	378	363
State and local pension funds [3] . . .	801	1,088	1,303	1,495	1,817	2,054	2,227	2,290	2,177
Credit market instruments [3]	402	491	530	565	632	705	751	806	791
U.S. Government securities	231	268	291	308	340	360	376	399	374
Corporate and foreign bonds	142	179	189	211	245	280	310	340	343
Corporate equities	285	508	679	828	1,085	1,234	1,343	1,335	1,216

[1] Annuity reserves held by life insurance companies, excluding unallocated contracts held by private pension funds.
[2] Private defined benefit plans and defined contribution plans (including 401(k) type plans). Also includes Federal Employees Retirement System (FERS) Thrift Savings Plan. [3] Includes other types of assets not shown separately. [4] Assets held at life insurance companies (e.g., guaranteed investment contracts (GICs), variable annuities).
Source: Board of Governors of the Federal Reserve System, "Federal Reserve Statistical Release, Z.1, Flow of Funds Accounts of the United States"; published: 7 March 2002; <http://www.federalreserve.gov/releases/Z1/20020307/data.htm>.

No. 1195. Annual Revenues for Selected Securities Industries: 1998 to 2000

[In millions of dollars (245,736 represents $245,736,000,000). Covers taxable employer firms only. Based on the North American Industry Classification System (NAICS); see text, Section 15, Business Enterprise. Based on Service Annual Survey; see Appendix III]

Kind of business	NAICS code	1998	1999	2000
Total	523x	245,736	295,302	348,923
Securities and commodity contracts				
intermediation and brokerage	5231	168,188	203,744	243,649
Investment banking & securities dealing	52311	92,500	113,907	130,581
Securities brokerage	52312	71,242	85,282	108,404
Commodity contracts dealing	52313	1,632	1,807	1,920
Commodity contracts brokerage	52314	2,814	2,748	2,744
Other financial investment activities [1]	5239x	77,548	91,558	105,273
Portfolio management	52392	66,143	76,275	88,012
Investment advice	52393	11,405	15,283	17,261

[1] Excludes NAICS 52391 (miscellaneous intermediation) and NAICS 52399 (all other financial investment activities).

No. 1196. Revenues of Selected Securities Industries by Source of Revenues: 1998 to 2000

[In billions of dollars (245.7 represents $245,700,000,000). See headnote, Table 1195]

Source of revenue	Total (NAICS 523x)			Security and commodity contracts intermediation and brokerage (NAICS 5231)			Portfolio management and investment advice [1]		
	1998	1999	2000	1998	1999	2000	1998	1999	2000
Total	245.7	295.3	348.9	168.2	203.7	243.6	77.5	91.6	105.3
Commissions from the sale of securities and commodities	52.0	63.4	71.2	47.5	58.2	64.7	4.5	5.2	6.5
Gains (losses) on trading accounts in securities and commodities (net)	34.1	45.0	53.7	31.1	42.8	49.5	(S)	(S)	(S)
Interest income from trading accounts in securities	14.2	15.5	16.3	13.2	14.5	13.9	1.0	1.0	2.4
Gains (losses) from trading accounts in securities	16.7	26.1	34.7	14.7	25.0	33.1	(S)	(S)	(S)
Gains (losses) from trading accounts in commodities	3.1	3.4	2.6	3.2	3.4	2.5	(S)	(S)	(S)
Gains from underwriting and selling groups of securities (net)	11.1	15.1	19.7	10.9	14.8	19.5	0.2	0.4	(S)
MBS, CMO, and REMIC transactions [2] . .	2.6	3.0	4.0	2.5	2.8	3.9	(S)	(S)	(S)
All other securities transactions	8.5	12.1	15.7	8.4	12.0	15.7	0.1	0.1	(S)
Gains on investment accounts (net)	2.8	4.1	5.6	2.2	3.7	3.5	(S)	(S)	(S)
Dividend income	1.9	2.5	2.5	1.0	1.4	1.3	(S)	(S)	(S)
Margin interest and other interest income . .	42.4	51.3	62.5	34.5	39.9	53.1	(S)	(S)	(S)
Other investment income	13.4	12.7	13.1	9.4	8.1	8.6	4.1	4.6	4.5
Asset/Portfolio management fees	65.7	76.1	91.5	21.1	23.1	30.7	44.5	53.0	60.8
Other revenue	22.5	25.1	29.2	10.5	11.7	12.8	(S)	(S)	(S)

S Data do not meet publication standards because of high sampling variability or poor response quality. [1] Excludes NAICS 52391 (miscellaneous intermediation) and NAICS 52399 (all other financial investment activities). [2] MBS=Mortgage-backed securities; CMO=Collateralized mortgage obligation; REMIC=Real estate mortgage investment conduit.
Source of Tables 1195 and 1196: U.S. Census Bureau, *Service Annual Survey: 2000.*

No. 1197. Securities Industry—Revenues and Expenses: 1990 to 2000

[In millions of dollars (71,356 represents $71,356,000,000)]

Type	1990	1992	1993	1994	1995	1996	1997	1998	1999	2000
Revenues, total	71,356	90,584	108,844	112,758	143,414	172,411	207,245	234,964	266,809	349,493
Commissions............	12,032	16,249	19,905	19,847	23,215	27,866	32,662	36,696	45,937	54,107
Trading/investment gains....	15,746	21,838	25,427	20,219	28,963	30,768	35,958	32,754	55,464	70,778
Underwriting profits........	3,728	8,300	11,249	6,844	8,865	12,613	14,611	16,237	17,782	18,718
Margin interest...........	3,179	2,690	3,235	4,668	6,470	7,386	10,630	12,732	15,247	24,547
Mutual fund sales.........	3,242	5,950	8,115	6,887	7,434	10,081	12,422	14,845	16,688	19,395
Other.................	33,428	35,557	40,913	54,293	68,468	83,697	100,961	121,700	115,692	161,949
Expenses, total	70,566	81,467	95,805	109,266	132,089	155,433	187,281	217,780	237,693	310,390
Interest expense	28,093	24,576	26,616	40,250	56,877	64,698	80,659	98,095	87,508	131,877
Compensation	22,931	32,071	39,125	37,595	41,541	51,033	58,558	65,027	81,737	95,206
Commissions/clearance paid .	2,959	3,722	5,338	5,360	5,700	7,364	8,864	10,326	13,488	15,523
Other.................	16,583	21,098	24,726	26,060	27,970	32,338	39,200	44,332	54,959	67,784
Net income, pretax....	790	9,117	13,039	3,492	11,325	16,978	19,964	17,184	29,116	39,103

Source: U.S. Securities and Exchange Commission, *Annual Report*.

No. 1198. Life Insurance in Force in the United States—Summary: 1990 to 2000

[As of December 31 or calendar year, as applicable (389 represents 389,000,000). Covers life insurance with life insurance companies only. Represents all life insurance in force on lives of U.S. residents whether issued by U.S. or foreign companies. For definition of household, see text, Section 1, Population]

Year	Number of policies, total (mil.)	Life insurance in force — Value (bil. dol.) Total	Ordinary [1]	Group	Industrial	Credit [2]	Average size policy in force (dollars) Ordinary [1]	Group	Industrial	Credit [2]	Average amount ($1,000) Per household	Per insured household	Disposable personal income per household ($1,000)
1990 .	389	9,393	5,367	3,754	24	248	37,910	26,630	670	3,500	98.4	124.5	44.6
1992 .	366	10,406	5,942	4,241	21	202	42,960	29,930	700	3,610	106.6	136.6	48.2
1993 .	363	11,105	6,428	4,456	20	200	45,770	31,430	700	3,850	111.6	143.1	49.7
1994 .	390	11,057	6,407	4,442	19	189	45,870	26,338	659	3,609	113.9	146.3	51.7
1995 .	393	11,638	6,816	4,603	18	201	49,090	27,051	664	3,554	119.1	148.9	54.3
1996 .	355	12,704	7,408	5,068	18	211	52,912	36,459	695	4,215	128.6	157.3	56.6
1997 .	351	13,364	7,855	5,279	18	212	57,333	37,176	720	4,516	134.1	167.6	58.1
1998 .	358	14,471	8,506	5,735	17	213	62,543	37,732	724	4,629	141.1	178.6	58.8
1999 .	367	15,496	9,172	6,110	(¹)	213	56,620	38,429	(¹)	4,640	149.2	189.8	63.9
2000 .	369	15,953	9,376	6,376	(¹)	201	57,682	40,800	(¹)	3,997	151.2	200.8	66.7

[1] Beginning 1999 industrial policies are included in ordinary.   [2] Insures borrower to cover consumer loan in case of death.

Source: American Council of Life Insurers, Washington, DC, *Life Insurers Fact Book*, annual (copyright).

No. 1199. Life Insurance Purchases in the United States—Number and Amount: 1990 to 2000

[28,791 represents 28,791,000. Excludes revivals, increases, dividend additions, and reinsurance acquired. Includes long-term credit insurance (life insurance on loans of more than 10 years' duration). See also headnote, Table 1198]

Year	Number of policies purchased (1,000) Total	Ordinary [1]	Group	Industrial	Amount purchased (bil. dol.) Total	Ordinary [1]	Group	Industrial
1990	28,791	14,066	14,592	133	1,529	1,070	459	(Z)
1992	28,382	13,350	14,930	102	1,489	1,048	441	(Z)
1993	31,238	13,574	17,574	90	1,678	1,101	577	(Z)
1994	32,225	13,675	18,390	160	1,611	1,051	560	(Z)
1995	31,999	12,466	19,404	129	1,543	1,005	538	(Z)
1996	30,783	11,926	18,761	96	1,704	1,089	615	(Z)
1997	31,708	11,667	19,973	68	1,893	1,204	689	(Z)
1998	31,891	11,522	20,332	37	2,065	1,325	740	(Z)
1999	38,584	11,673	26,912	(¹)	2,367	1,400	967	(¹)
2000	34,913	13,376	21,537	(¹)	2,515	1,594	921	(¹)

Z Less than $500 million.   [1] Beginning 1999 industrial policies are included in ordinary.

Source: American Council of Life Insurers, Washington, DC, *Life Insurers Fact Book*, annual (copyright).

U.S. Census Bureau, Statistical Abstract of the United States: 2002

No. 1200. U.S. Life Insurance Companies—Summary: 1990 to 2000

[As of December 31 or calendar year, as applicable (402.2 represents $402,200,000,000). Covers domestic and foreign business of U.S. companies. Beginning 1994 includes annual statement data for companies that primarily are health insurance companies]

Item	Unit	1990	1992	1993	1994	1995	1996	1997	1998	1999	2000
U.S. companies [1]	Number .	2,195	1,944	1,844	2,136	2,079	1,679	1,620	1,563	1,470	1,268
Income	**Bil. dol.**	**402.2**	**426.9**	**466.4**	**492.6**	**528.1**	**561.1**	**610.6**	**663.4**	**726.9**	**826.6**
Life insurance premiums	Bil. dol ..	76.7	83.9	94.4	98.9	102.8	107.6	115.0	119.9	120.3	130.6
Annuity considerations	Bil. dol ..	129.1	132.6	156.4	153.0	158.4	178.4	197.5	229.5	270.2	303.1
Health insurance premiums .	Bil. dol ..	58.3	65.5	68.7	86.2	90.0	92.2	92.7	94.9	100.0	105.6
Investment and other	Bil. dol ..	138.2	144.9	146.8	154.5	176.9	182.9	205.3	219.1	236.4	287.3
Payments to life insurance beneficiaries	Bil. dol ..	24.6	27.2	28.8	32.6	34.5	36.3	37.5	40.1	41.4	44.1
Payments under life insurance and annuity contracts	Bil. dol ..	63.8	67.8	71.2	168.2	193.1	210.7	239.1	261.8	313.9	331.1
Surrender values under life insurance [2]	Bil. dol ..	18.0	16.8	16.9	18.0	19.5	24.5	24.0	26.8	32.8	27.2
Surrender values under annuity policies [2]	Bil. dol ..	(NA)	(NA)	(NA)	92.8	105.4	115.7	140.8	154.5	198.3	214.0
Policy dividends	Bil. dol ..	12.0	12.2	12.7	15.9	17.8	18.1	18.0	18.9	19.1	20.0
Annuity payments	Bil. dol ..	32.6	37.6	40.3	40.4	48.5	51.1	55.1	60.4	62.5	68.7
Matured endowments	Bil. dol ..	0.7	0.6	0.6	0.6	1.0	0.7	0.6	0.6	0.5	0.6
Other payments	Bil. dol ..	0.6	0.6	0.6	0.5	0.9	0.6	0.6	0.6	0.6	0.6
Health insurance benefit payments	Bil. dol ..	40.0	45.0	46.0	60.1	64.7	66.7	67.4	70.0	74.5	78.8
BALANCE SHEET											
Assets	**Bil. dol ..**	**1,408**	**1,665**	**1,839**	**1,942**	**2,144**	**2,328**	**2,579**	**2,827**	**3,071**	**3,186**
Government securities	Bil. dol ..	211	320	384	396	409	411	391	379	362	363
Corporate securities	Bil. dol ..	711	863	982	1,072	1,241	1,416	1,658	1,896	2,180	2,232
Percent of total assets	Percent	50.5	51.8	53.4	55.2	57.9	60.8	64.3	67.1	71.0	70.1
Bonds	Bil. dol ..	583	670	730	791	869	962	1,060	1,140	1,190	1,240
Stocks	Bil. dol ..	128	192	252	282	372	454	598	758	990	992
Mortgages	Bil. dol ..	270	247	229	215	212	212	210	216	230	237
Real estate	Bil. dol ..	43	51	54	54	52	50	46	41	38	36
Policy loans	Bil. dol ..	63	72	78	85	96	102	105	105	99	102
Other	Bil. dol ..	110	112	112	120	133	137	169	187	163	216
Interest earned on assets [3]	Percent	8.89	8.08	7.52	7.14	7.34	7.25	7.35	6.95	6.71	7.10
Obligations and surplus funds [4]	Bil. dol ..	1,408	1,665	1,839	1,942	2,144	2,328	2,579	2,827	3,071	3,186
Policy reserves [5]	**Bil. dol ..**	**1,197**	**1,407**	**1,550**	**1,644**	**1,812**	**1,966**	**2,165**	**2,377**	**2,610**	**2,711**
Annuities [6]	Bil. dol ..	798	940	1,041	1,095	1,213	1,312	1,455	1,608	1,781	1,841
Group	Bil. dol ..	516	560	602	612	619	690	762	845	907	960
Individual	Bil. dol ..	282	381	439	482	594	622	693	763	874	881
Life insurance	Bil. dol ..	349	402	436	468	511	556	606	656	705	742
Health insurance	Bil. dol ..	33	45	51	58	63	70	75	82	92	95
Asset valuation reserve	Bil. dol ..	15	21	25	25	30	33	36	38	40	38
Capital and surplus	Bil. dol ..	91	115	128	137	151	147	160	173	181	192

NA Not available. [1] Beginning 1994 includes life insurance companies that sell accident and health insurance. [2] Beginning with 1994, "surrender values" include annuity withdrawals of funds, which were not included in prior years. [3] Net rate. [4] Includes other obligations not shown separately. [5] Includes the business of health insurance departments of life companies. Includes reserves for supplementary contracts with and without life contingencies, not shown separately. [6] Beginning 1996 data are not comparable with prior years' data due to a change in the treatment of separate account annuities.

Source: American Council of Life Insurers, Washington, DC, Life Insurers Fact Book, annual (copyright).

No. 1201. Property and Casualty Insurance—Summary: 1990 to 2000

[In billions of dollars (217.8 represents $217,800,000,000). Minus sign (-) indicates loss]

Item	1990	1994	1995	1996	1997	1998	1999	2000
Premiums, net written	**217.8**	**250.7**	**259.8**	**268.6**	**276.4**	**281.5**	**286.9**	**299.6**
Automobile, private [1]	78.4	96.8	102.0	107.7	113.6	117.3	118.6	119.6
Automobile, commercial [1]	17.0	16.7	17.2	17.6	18.0	18.1	18.1	19.5
Liability other than auto	22.1	23.6	23.4	24.5	25.0	24.2	23.9	25.5
Fire and allied lines	7.1	8.7	9.4	9.9	8.4	8.4	8.1	8.3
Homeowners' multiple peril	18.6	22.6	24.0	25.4	26.9	29.0	30.6	32.4
Commercial multiple peril	17.7	17.8	18.8	18.9	19.0	19.0	18.9	19.8
Workers' compensation	31.0	28.9	26.2	25.1	24.1	23.2	22.2	24.8
Marine, inland and ocean	5.7	6.7	7.1	7.5	7.6	7.6	7.7	8.1
Accident and health	5.0	7.2	7.8	7.8	8.3	9.8	11.1	13.3
Other lines	15.2	21.7	23.9	24.2	25.5	24.9	27.7	28.3
Losses and expenses	234.7	263.3	268.4	277.1	272.6	289.7	302.6	321.4
Underwriting gain/loss	-20.9	-22.2	-17.7	-16.7	-5.8	-16.8	-23.1	-31.2
Net investment income	32.9	33.7	36.8	38.0	41.5	39.9	38.9	40.7
Operating earnings after taxes	9.0	10.9	20.6	24.4	36.8	30.8	21.9	20.6
Assets	556.3	704.6	765.2	802.3	870.1	907.8	918.3	912.0
Policyholders' surplus	138.4	193.3	230.0	255.5	308.5	333.3	334.3	317.4

[1] Includes premiums for automobile liability and physical damage.

Source: Insurance Information Institute, New York, NY, The Fact Book; Property/Casualty Insurance Facts, annual (copyright).

No. 1202. Automobile Insurance—Average Expenditures Per Insured Vehicle by State: 1995 to 2000

[In dollars. The average expenditures for automobile insurance in a state are affected by a number of factors, including the underlying rate structure, the coverages purchased, the deductibles and limits selected, the types of vehicles insured, and the distribution of driver characteristics]

State	1995	1999	2000	State	1995	1999	2000	State	1995	1999	2000
U.S.	667	685	687	KS	474	542	558	ND	381	469	477
				KY	555	610	616	OH	531	578	579
AL	549	612	594	LA	788	813	806	OK	526	576	603
AK	730	751	770	ME	472	514	528	OR	565	621	625
AZ	727	789	792	MD	732	757	757	PA	667	691	699
AR	500	597	606	MA	898	889	946	RI	870	824	825
CA	794	668	658	MI	645	705	702	SC	582	593	612
CO	722	744	755	MN	628	688	696	SD	428	484	478
CT	881	861	871	MS	579	655	654	TN	519	582	592
DE	784	861	849	MO	573	605	612	TX	711	696	678
DC	959	986	996	MT	468	511	530	UT	547	615	620
FL	739	742	746	NE	452	523	533	VT	512	556	568
GA	597	672	674	NV	759	821	829	VA	553	566	576
HI	963	700	700	NH	609	650	665	WA	650	697	722
ID	447	493	505	NJ	1,013	1,015	977	WV	646	684	680
IL	612	646	652	NM	639	664	674	WI	506	547	551
IN	542	582	570	NY	906	930	936	WY	433	491	496
IA	429	466	479	NC	501	567	564				

Source: National Association of Insurance Commissioners (NAIC), Kansas City, MO, *State Average Expenditures and Premiums for Personal Automobile Insurance*, annual. Reprinted with permission. Further reprint or distribution strictly prohibited without written permission of the NAIC (copyright).

No. 1203. Average Premiums For Renters and Homeowners Insurance by State: 1999

[In dollars. Average premium equals premiums divided by exposure per house-years. A house-year is equal to 365 days of insured coverage for a single dwelling and is the standard measurement for homeowners insurance]

State	Renters [1]	Home-owners [2]	State	Renters [1]	Home-owners [2]	State	Renters [1]	Home-owners [2]
U.S.	171	487	KS	162	576	ND	100	403
			KY	137	394	OH	138	314
AL	159	457	LA	241	714	OK	203	594
AK	160	601	ME	116	336	OR	150	334
AZ	194	418	MD	133	372	PA	134	403
AR	189	501	MA	182	526	RI	169	520
CA	262	578	MI	153	417	SC	171	505
CO	168	559	MN	125	390	SD	106	378
CT	182	546	MS	224	594	TN	187	474
DE	136	317	MO	156	441	TX [3] ...	228	861
DC	160	617	MT	132	429	UT	142	369
FL	222	657	NE	124	467	VT	123	414
GA	203	448	NV	232	474	VA	133	345
HI	201	606	NH	136	410	WA	155	413
ID	137	319	NJ	167	497	WV	134	388
IL	157	387	NM	197	451	WI	105	266
IN	143	373	NY	197	533	WY	154	491
IA	124	347	NC	167	427			

[1] Based on the HO-4 renters insurance policy for tenants. Includes broad named-peril coverage for the personal property of tenants. [2] Based on the HO-3 homeowner package policy for owner-occupied dwellings, 1-4 family units. Provides "all risks" coverage (except those specifically excluded in the policy) on buildings, broad named-peril coverage on personal property, and is the most common package written. [3] The Texas Insurance Commissioner promulgates residential policy forms which are similar but not identical to the standard forms. Insurers can use State-promulgated or standard forms.
Source: National Association of Insurance Commissioners (NAIC), Kansas City, MO, *Dwelling Fire, Homeowners Owner-Occupied, and Homeowners Tenant and Condominium/Cooperative Unit Owners Insurance* (copyright). Reprinted with permission. Further reprint or distribution strictly prohibited without written permission of the NAIC.

No. 1204. Real Estate, Rental, and Leasing—Establishments, Revenue, Payroll, and Employees by Kind of Business: 1997

[342,621 represents $342,621,000,000. See Appendix III for comments on methodology]

Kind of business	NAICS code [1]	All firms		Employer firms			
		Establish-ments (number)	Revenue (mil. dol.)	Establish-ments (number)	Revenue (mil. dol.)	Annual payroll (mil. dol.)	Paid employ-ees [2] (1,000)
Real estate & rental & leasing	53	1,684,976	342,621	288,273	240,918	41,591	1,702.4
Real estate	531	1,557,556	252,120	221,650	153,275	27,947	1,117.2
Lessors of real estate	5311	681,796	154,509	110,226	85,791	9,484	469.4
Offices of real estate agents & brokers	5312	590,388	56,502	60,620	38,945	6,792	219.6
Activities related to real estate	5313	285,372	41,109	50,804	28,538	11,671	428.2
Rental & leasing services	532	124,792	79,184	64,472	76,379	12,569	559.4
Automotive equipment rental & leasing	5321	25,395	29,513	10,542	28,922	3,871	158.1
Consumer goods rental	5322	49,212	14,917	35,423	14,396	3,097	230.0
General rental centers	5323	7,328	3,963	6,509	3,911	941	40.3
Commercial/industrial equip rental & leasing .	5324	42,857	30,791	11,998	29,150	4,660	131.0
Lessors of other nonfinancial intangible assets .	533	2,628	11,317	2,151	11,264	1,074	25.8

[1] North American Industry Classification System, 1997; see text, Section 15, Business Enterprise. [2] For pay period including March 12.
Source: U.S. Census Bureau, *1997 Economic Census, Geographic Area Series* and *Nonemployer Statistics*.

No. 1205. Real Estate, Rental, and Leasing—Nonemployer Establishments and Receipts by Kind of Business: 1997 to 1999

[1,397 represents 1,397,000. Includes only firms subject to federal income tax. Nonemployers are businesses with no paid employees. Based on the North American Industry Classification System (NAICS), see text, Section 15, Business Enterprise]

Kind of business	NAICS code	Establishments (1,000)			Receipts (mil. dol.)		
		1997	1998	1999	1997	1998	1999
Real estate & rental & leasing, total....................	53	1,397	1,565	1,648	101,704	131,728	125,513
Real estate	531	1,336	1,492	1,569	98,845	126,566	120,409
Lessors of real estate	5311	572	710	683	68,718	88,023	81,152
Offices of real estate agents & brokers . . .	5312	530	496	524	17,556	20,265	22,066
Activities related to real estate........	5313	235	286	362	12,571	18,278	17,191
Rental & leasing services..............	532	60	72	78	2,806	5,071	5,013
Automotive equipment rental & leasing . . .	5321	15	17	18	591	1,002	962
Consumer goods rental [1]	5322	14	16	17	521	754	748
Video tape & disk rental	53223	8	7	6	282	299	278
General rental centers..............	5323	1	2	2	53	176	203
Commercial/industrial equipment rental & leasing.............	5324	31	37	40	1,641	3,139	3,100
Lessors of other nonfinancial intangible asset	533	(Z)	1	1	53	91	90

Z Less than 500.   [1] Includes other kinds of business not shown separately.

Source: U.S. Census Bureau, "Nonemployer Statistics"; published 28 March 2002; <http://www.census.gov/epcd/nonemployer/>.

No. 1206. Real Estate, Rental and Leasing—Establishments, Employees, and Payroll: 1999 and 2000

[298.1 represents 298,100. Covers establishments with payroll. Employees are for the week including March 12. Most government employees are excluded. For statement on methodology, see Appendix III]

Kind of business	NAICS code [1]	Establishments (1,000)		Employees (1,000)		Payroll (bil. dol.)	
		1999	2000	1999	2000	1999	2000
Real estate & rental & leasing, total . .	53	298.1	300.2	1,874	1,942	54.1	59.2
Real estate	531	231.3	234.9	1,226	1,280	36.6	40.4
Lessors of real estate	5311	107.5	108.2	484	501	11.4	12.5
Offices of real estate agents & brokers . . .	5312	64.3	65.1	260	271	9.6	10.6
Activities related to real estate	5313	59.5	61.6	482	507	15.6	17.3
Rental & leasing services	532	64.6	63.2	622	636	16.0	17.2
Automotive equipment rental & leasing . . .	5321	11.2	11.1	179	182	4.9	5.1
Passenger car rental & leasing	53211	5.5	5.2	127	129	3.2	3.4
Truck, utility trailer & RV rental & leasing	53212	5.8	5.8	52	53	1.6	1.7
Consumer goods rental [2]............	5322	34.5	33.1	255	255	4.0	4.2
Video tape & disc rental.............	53223	20.9	19.6	156	152	1.5	1.6
General rental centers	5323	6.4	6.4	42	42	1.1	1.2
Commercial/industrial equip rental & leasing........................	5324	12.5	12.6	145	157	6.1	6.7
Lessors of other nonfinancial intangible asset.	533	2.1	2.1	26	26	1.5	1.6

[1] North American Industry Classification System; see text, Section 15, Business Enterprise.   [2] Includes other kinds of businesses not shown separately.

Source: U.S. Census Bureau, *County Business Patterns*, annual, <http://www.census.gov/prod/2002pubs/cbp00/cbp00-1.pdf> (issued May 2002).

No. 1207. Rental and Leasing Services—Revenue by Kind of Business: 1998 to 2000

[In millions of dollars (90,073 represents $90,073,000,000). Based on the North American Industry Classification System (NAICS); see text, Section 15, Business Enterprise. Estimates have been adjusted using the results of the 1997 Economic Census. Based on Service Annual Survey; see Appendix III]

Kind of business	NAICS code	Employer and nonemployer firms			Employer firms		
		1998	1999	2000	1998	1999	2000
Rental & leasing services	532	90,073	98,171	106,453	85,002	93,156	100,899
Automotive equipment rental & leasing.......	5321	31,920	35,094	37,529	30,918	34,132	36,501
Passenger car rental & leasing	53211	20,663	22,705	24,366	20,072	22,137	23,769
Truck, utility trailer, & RV rental & leasing . . .	53212	11,257	12,389	13,163	10,846	11,994	12,732
Consumer goods rental [1]................	5322	16,530	17,648	18,821	15,776	16,900	17,999
Video tape & disc rental...............	53223	7,944	8,712	9,014	7,646	8,434	8,700
General rental centers.................	5323	4,493	5,117	5,593	4,317	4,914	5,268
Commercial/industrial equip rental & leasing . . .	5324	37,131	40,311	44,510	33,992	37,211	41,130

[1] Includes other kinds of businesses not shown separately.

Source: U.S. Census Bureau, *Service Annual Survey: 2000*.

744   Banking, Finance, and Insurance

Section 26
Arts, Entertainment, and Recreation

This section presents data on the arts, entertainment, and recreation economic sector of the economy, and personal recreational activities, the arts and humanities, and domestic and foreign travel.

Arts, Entertainment, and Recreation Industry—The U.S. Census Bureau's *Service Annual Survey, Arts, Entertainment, and Recreation Sector,* provides estimates of operation revenue of taxable firms and revenues and expenses of firms exempt from federal taxes for industries in this sector of the economy. Data beginning 1998 are based on the North American Industry Classification System (NAICS). Most establishments were previously classified in the Standard Industrial Classification (SIC) in services, some in retail trade.

This new sector is comprised of industries which existed previously, were revised from previous industry definitions, or are completely new industries. Among those which existed previously are amusement and theme parks. Revised industries include museums. New industries include theater companies and dinner theaters. The following URL contains detailed information about NAICS and provides a comparison of the SIC and NAICS <http://www.census.gov/epcd/www/naics.html>. See also the text in Section 15, Business Enterprise.

The 1997 Economic Census was the first economic census to cover the new Information Sector of the economy. The Census, conducted every 5-years, for the years ending "2" and "7," provides information on the number of establishments, receipts, payroll and paid employees for the U.S. and various geographic levels.

Recreation and leisure activities—Data on the participation in various recreation and leisure time activities are based on several sample surveys. Data on participation in fishing, hunting, and other forms of wildlife-associated recreation are published periodically by the U.S. Department of Interior, Fish and Wildlife Service. The most recent data are from the 2001 survey. Data on participation in various sports recreation activities are published by the National Sporting Goods Association. Mediamark, Inc. also conducts periodic surveys on sports and leisure activities, as well as other topics.

Parks and recreation—The Department of the Interior has responsibility for administering the national parks. The National Park Service publishes information on visits to national park areas in its annual report, *National Park Statistical Abstract. The National Parks: Index (year)* is a biannual report which contains brief descriptions, with acreages, of each area administered by the service, plus certain "related" areas. The annual *Federal Recreation Fee Report* summarizes the prior year's recreation fee receipts and recreation visitation statistics for seven federal land managing agencies. Statistics for state parks are compiled by the National Association of State Park Directors which issues its *Annual Information Exchange.*

Travel—Statistics on arrivals to the United States are reported by the International Trade Administration (ITA). Statistics on departures from the United States include the Department of Transportation's *International Air Travel Statistics* and other sources. Data on domestic travel, business receipts and employment of the travel industry, and travel expenditures are published by the U.S. Travel Data Center, which is the research department of the Travel Industry Association and the national nonprofit center for travel and tourism research located in Washington, DC. Other data on household transportation characteristics are in Section 23, Transportation.

Statistical reliability—For a discussion of statistical collection and estimation, sampling procedures, and measures of statistical reliability applicable to Census Bureau data, see Appendix III.

U.S. Census Bureau, Statistical Abstract of the United States: 2002

No. 1208. Arts, Entertainment, and Recreation—Establishments, Receipts, Payroll, and Employees by Kind of Business (NAICS Basis): 1997

[For establishments with payroll (85,088 represents $85,088,000,000). Based on the 1997 Economic Census; see Appendix III]

Industry	NAICS code [1]	Establishments (number)	Receipts [2] Total (mil. dol.)	Receipts [2] Per paid employee (dol.)	Annual payroll Total (mil. dol.)	Annual payroll Per paid employee (dol.)	Paid employee for pay period including March 12 (1,000)
Taxable establishments	**71**	**79,636**	**85,088**	**70,474**	**26,104**	**21,620**	**1,207.4**
Performing arts, spectator sports	711	25,942	32,744	138,788	12,834	54,400	235.9
Performing arts companies	7111	5,883	5,272	101,763	1,452	28,033	51.8
Spectator sports	7112	3,881	13,656	147,804	6,151	66,577	92.4
Sports teams & clubs	711211	483	7,809	234,284	4,922	147,686	33.3
Racetracks	711212	807	4,142	92,291	797	17,764	44.9
Other spectator sports.	711219	2,591	1,705	120,238	432	30,428	14.2
Promoters of performing arts, sports, & similar events	7113	2,633	5,045	98,133	1,053	20,475	51.4
Agents/managers for artists, athletes, & other public figures.	7114	2,532	2,410	182,032	911	68,800	13.2
Independent artists, writers, & performers .	7115	11,013	6,361	234,888	3,268	120,657	27.1
Museums, historical sites [3]	712	787	484	66,431	122	16,811	7.3
Amusement, gambling, & recreation industries	713	52,907	51,861	53,789	13,147	13,636	964.2
Amusement parks & arcades	7131	3,344	8,418	60,595	1,962	14,121	138.9
Amusement & theme parks	71311	607	7,172	64,733	1,690	15,258	110.8
Amusement arcades.	71312	2,737	1,247	44,305	271	9,647	28.1
Gambling industries	7132	2,099	15,542	92,217	3,222	19,117	168.5
Casinos (except casino hotels)	71321	447	10,186	88,413	2,305	20,004	115.2
Other gambling industries	71329	1,652	5,355	100,437	917	17,200	53.3
Other amusement & recreation services . .	7139	47,464	27,901	42,487	7,963	12,126	656.7
Golf courses & country clubs	71391	8,546	8,637	53,941	2,732	17,062	160.1
Skiing facilities.	71392	379	1,341	22,915	431	7,368	58.5
Marinas	71393	4,217	2,541	111,640	517	22,692	22.8
Fitness & recreational sports centers . . .	71394	16,604	7,945	30,987	2,405	9,380	256.4
Bowling centers	71395	5,590	2,821	32,037	821	9,325	88.0
All other amusement & recreation industries	71399	12,128	4,616	65,140	1,058	14,925	70.9
Tax-exempt establishments	**71**	**19,463**	**19,627**	**51,610**	**6,683**	**17,575**	**380.3**
Performing arts, spectator sports	711	4,624	4,876	53,681	1,622	17,852	90.8
Performing arts companies	7111	3,316	3,299	46,987	1,273	18,135	70.2
Theater companies & dinner theaters. . .	71111	1,647	1,776	54,135	631	19,223	32.8
Dance companies	71112	371	323	47,399	131	19,208	6.8
Musical groups & artists	71113	1,211	1,154	38,767	499	16,756	29.8
Other performing arts companies	71119	87	45	56,119	13	15,726	0.8
Promoters of performing arts, sports, & similar events	7113	1,308	1,577	76,461	348	16,890	20.6
Museums, historical sites [3]	712	4,793	6,280	74,328	1,715	20,294	84.5
Museums.	71211	3,434	4,529	75,334	1,212	20,167	60.1
Historical sites	71212	814	343	50,704	101	15,020	6.8
Zoos & botanical gardens	71213	269	1,279	81,326	364	23,162	15.7
Nature parks & other similar institutions . .	71219	276	129	68,539	36	19,319	1.9
Other amusement & recreation industries . .	713	10,046	8,470	41,327	3,347	16,331	205.0
Golf courses & country clubs	71391	3,212	5,583	48,145	2,291	19,761	116.0
Fitness & recreational sports centers.	71394	4,679	2,217	29,288	859	11,343	75.7
All other amusement & recreational industries	71399	2,155	670	50,410	197	14,809	13.3

[1] North American Industry Classification System, 1997; see text, this section and Section 15, Business Enterprise. [2] Revenue for tax-exempt establishments. [3] And in similar institutions.
Source: U.S. Census Bureau, *1997 Economic Census, Arts, Entertainment, and Recreation,* Series EC97571A-US(RV), issued April 2000.

No. 1209. Arts, Entertainment and Recreation Services—Estimated Revenue: 1999 and 2000

[In millions of dollars (115,366 represents $115,366,000,000), except percent. For taxable and tax-exempt employer firms. Except as indicated, estimates adjusted to the results of the 1997 Economic Census. Minus sign (-) represents decrease. See Appendix III]

Industry	NAICS code [1]	Total 1999	Total 2000	Total Percent change, 1999-00	Taxable 1999	Taxable 2000	Taxable Percent change, 1999-00
Arts, entertainment, and recreation	71	115,366	122,722	6.4	94,119	100,170	6.4
Performing arts, spectator sports	711	41,141	43,792	6.4	36,053	38,273	6.2
Performing arts companies [2]	7111	8,816	9,199	4.3	5,458	5,508	0.9
Spectator sports	7112	15,765	17,449	10.7	15,765	17,449	10.7
Sports teams and clubs	711211	8,973	10,404	16.0	8,973	10,404	16.0
Racetracks	711212	5,106	5,235	2.5	5,106	5,235	2.5
Other spectator sports.	711219	1,686	1,809	7.3	1,686	1,809	7.3
Promoters of performing arts, sports and similar events	7113	7,168	7,434	3.7	5,438	5,606	3.1
Agents and managers for artists, athletes, entertainers and other public figures	7114	3,054	3,249	6.4	3,054	3,249	6.4

See footnotes at end of table.

746 Arts, Entertainment, and Recreation

No. 1209. Arts, Entertainment and Recreation Services—Estimated Revenue: 1999 and 2000—Con.

[See headnote, page 746]

Industry	NAICS code [1]	Total			Taxable		
		1999	2000	Percent change, 1999-00	1999	2000	Percent change, 1999-00
Independent artists, writers, and performers . . .	7115	6,338	6,461	1.9	6,338	6,461	1.9
Museums, historical sites, and similar institutions .	712	7,625	8,239	8.1	703	836	19.0
Amusement, gambling, and recreation industries .	713	66,601	70,691	6.1	57,363	61,060	6.4
Amusement parks and arcades	7131	8,683	9,295	7.0	8,683	9,295	7.0
Amusement and theme parks.	71311	7,512	8,155	8.5	7,512	8,155	8.5
Amusement arcades	71312	1,171	1,141	-2.6	1,171	1,141	-2.6
Gambling industries.	7132	16,955	18,807	10.9	16,955	18,807	10.9
Casinos (except casino hotels).	71321	11,752	13,105	11.5	11,752	13,105	11.5
Other gambling industries	71329	5,204	5,702	9.6	5,204	5,702	9.6
Other amusement and recreation industries.	7139	40,963	42,589	4.0	31,725	32,958	3.9
Golf courses and country clubs	71391	16,116	16,540	2.6	10,099	10,374	2.7
Skiing facilities	71392	1,372	1,489	8.5	1,372	1,489	8.5
Marinas [3]	71393	3,037	3,254	7.2	3,037	3,254	7.2
Fitness and recreational sports centers	71394	11,836	12,603	6.5	9,292	9,864	6.2
Bowling centers.	71395	2,949	2,977	1.0	2,949	2,977	1.0
All other amusement and recreation	71399	5,654	5,726	1.3	4,977	5,000	0.5

[1] Based in the North American Industry Classification System; see text, this section and Section 15, Business Enterprise.
[2] Estimates for NAICS 71113 and 71119 not adjusted to the 1997 Economic Census. [3] Estimates not adjusted to the 1997 Economic Census.
Source: U.S. Census Bureau, *2000 Service Annual Survey, Information Sector Services.* See <http://www.census.gov/econ/www/servmenu.html> (released 29 November 2001).

No. 1210. Arts, Entertainment, and Recreation—Establishments, Payroll, and Employees by Kind of Business (NAICS Basis): 1999 and 2000

[For establishments with payroll (1,640.0 represents 1,640,000). See Appendix III]

Industry	NAICS code [1]	Establishments		Paid employees [2] (1,000)		Annual payroll (mil. dol.)	
		1999	2000	1999	2000	1999	2000
Arts, entertainment, & recreation, total . . .	**71**	**102,786**	**103,816**	**1,640.0**	**1,741.5**	**39,416**	**43,204**
Performing arts, spectator sports	711	32,906	33,859	330.4	351.9	17,381	19,090
Performing arts companies	7111	9,342	9,253	122.0	126.4	3,053	3,251
Theater companies & dinner theaters.	71111	3,322	3,367	61.7	63.4	1,350	1,469
Dance companies.	71112	591	584	10.2	10.7	195	216
Musical groups & artists.	71113	4,604	4,497	42.6	44.0	1,289	1,341
Other performing arts companies.	71119	825	805	7.4	8.3	219	226
Spectator sports	7112	4,372	4,461	91.0	100.2	8,159	9,215
Sports teams & clubs	711211	667	684	32.0	36.3	6,708	7,587
Racetracks	711212	888	899	42.5	45.8	880	994
Other spectator sports.	711219	2,817	2,878	16.5	18.1	571	633
Promoters of performing arts, sports, & similar events.	7113	4,224	4,394	65.4	71.8	1,673	1,917
Promoters of performing arts, sports, & similar events with facilities.	71131	1,030	1,107	41.2	44.3	782	787
Promoters of performing arts, sports, & similar events without facilities.	71132	3,194	3,287	24.2	27.6	891	1,130
Agents/managers for artists, athletes, & other public figures.	7114	2,837	3,048	15.1	16.0	1,037	1,117
Independent artists, writers, & performers.	7115	12,131	12,703	36.9	37.5	3,459	3,589
Museums, historical sites, & similar institutions . . .	712	5,714	5,777	104.6	110.4	2,321	2,549
Museums.	71211	3,940	3,988	71.4	75.4	1,603	1,765
Historical sites.	71212	891	892	8.0	8.3	131	143
Zoos & botanical gardens	71213	404	414	19.6	20.5	469	509
Nature parks & other similar institutions	71219	479	483	5.7	6.2	118	133
Amusement, gambling, & recreation industries . . .	713	64,166	64,180	1,205.0	1,279.2	19,714	21,564
Amusement parks & arcades	7131	3,135	2,879	127.4	124.0	2,266	2,277
Amusement & theme parks	71311	689	716	102.1	102.8	1,963	2,011
Amusement arcades	71312	2,446	2,163	25.3	21.3	304	266
Gambling industries	7132	2,238	2,191	178.7	202.6	4,099	4,757
Casinos (except casino hotels)	71321	546	537	128.4	150.2	3,077	3,592
Other gambling industries	71329	1,692	1,654	50.2	52.4	1,021	1,165
Other amusement & recreation services.	7139	58,793	59,110	898.9	952.6	13,349	14,531
Golf courses & country clubs	71391	11,809	11,885	280.1	297.9	5,817	6,243
Skiing facilities.	71392	395	389	60.1	56.9	426	452
Marinas	71393	4,170	4,126	24.0	24.8	599	640
Fitness & recreational sports centers	71394	22,401	23,003	357.5	382.8	4,035	4,499
Bowling centers	71395	5,291	5,234	84.2	87.9	847	888
All other amusement & recreation industries	71399	14,727	14,473	93.1	102.4	1,626	1,808

[1] North American Industry Classification System code; see text, this section and Section 15, Business Enterprise. [2] For employees on the payroll for the period including March 12.
Source: U.S. Census Bureau, "County Business Patterns"; 2000 data published 30 May 2002; <http://www.census.gov/epcd/cbp/view/cbpview.html>.

No. 1211. Arts, Entertainment, and Recreation—Nonemployer Establishments, and Receipts by Kind of Business (NAICS Basis): 1997 to 1999

[693.3 represents 693,300. Includes only firms subject to federal income tax. Nonemployers are businesses with no paid employees]

Kind of business	NAICS code[1]	Establishments (1,000)			Receipts (mil. dol.)		
		1997	1998	1999	1997	1998	1999
Arts, entertainment, and recreation . .	**71**	**693.3**	**713.1**	**748.7**	**14,366.1**	**15,324.6**	**16,656.4**
Performing arts, spectator sports, and related industries	711	536.0	571.1	611.2	10,251.8	11,002.1	12,178.3
Performing arts companies	7111	10.8	15.3	17.5	320.2	439.8	501.6
Spectator sports	7112	65.8	64.4	65.8	1,433.4	1,382.5	1,398.1
Promoters of performing arts, sports, and similar events	7113	12.8	18.5	21.1	513.1	714.7	830.6
Agents/managers for artists, athletes, and other public figures	7114	15.5	21.8	25.0	529.0	677.9	776.4
Independent artists, writers and performers	7115	431.1	451.1	481.8	7,456.1	7,787.2	8,671.6
Museums, historical sites, and similar institutions	712	1.8	2.7	3.3	37.5	42.1	47.0
Amusement, gambling, and recreation industries	713	155.6	139.3	134.2	4,076.8	4,280.4	4,431.2
Amusement parks and arcades	7131	7.2	6.6	5.6	463.1	413.3	324.7
Gambling industries	7132	2.7	4.1	5.6	196.6	318.3	475.2
Other amusement and recreation services .	7139	145.7	128.5	123.0	3,417.0	3,548.8	3,631.2

[1] Based on the North American Industry Classification System (NAICS), see text, Section 15, Business Enterprise.

Source: U.S. Census Bureau, "Nonemployer Statistics"; published 28 March 2002; <http://www.census.gov/epcd/nonemployer/>.

No. 1212. Expenditures Per Consumer Unit for Entertainment and Reading: 1985 to 2000

[Data are annual averages. In dollars, except as indicated. Based on Consumer Expenditure Survey; see text, Section 13, Income, Expenditure, and Wealth, for description of survey. See also headnote, Table 650. For composition of regions, see map, inside front cover]

Year and characteristic	Entertainment and reading		Entertainment				
	Total	Percent of total expenditures	Total	Fees and admissions	Television, radios, and sound equipment	Other equipment and services [1]	Reading
1985	1,311	5.6	1,170	320	371	479	141
1990	1,575	5.6	1,422	371	454	597	153
1991	1,635	5.5	1,472	378	468	627	163
1992	1,662	5.6	1,500	379	492	629	162
1993	1,792	5.8	1,626	414	590	621	166
1994	1,732	5.5	1,567	439	533	595	165
1995	1,775	5.5	1,612	433	542	637	163
1996	1,993	5.9	1,834	459	561	814	159
1997	1,977	5.7	1,813	471	577	766	164
1998	1,907	5.4	1,746	449	535	762	161
1999	2,050	5.5	1,891	459	608	824	159
2000, total	**2,009**	**5.3**	**1,863**	**515**	**622**	**727**	**146**
Age of reference person:							
Under 25 years old	1,148	5.1	1,091	271	473	348	57
25 to 34 years old	1,994	5.1	1,876	460	680	736	118
35 to 44 years old	2,615	5.8	2,464	715	789	960	151
45 to 54 years old	2,409	5.2	2,231	637	696	898	178
55 to 64 years old	2,134	5.4	1,955	509	581	865	179
65 to 74 years old	1,569	5.1	1,403	416	468	519	166
75 years old and over	835	3.8	707	214	325	167	128
Origin of reference person:							
Hispanic	1,245	3.8	1,186	262	545	380	59
Non-Hispanic	2,083	5.4	1,928	539	629	760	155
Race of reference person:							
White and other	2,137	5.4	1,980	561	629	791	157
Black	1,086	3.9	1,014	181	567	266	72
Region of residence:							
Northeast	2,087	5.4	1,915	577	627	711	172
Midwest	2,204	5.6	2,040	566	665	809	164
South	1,731	5.0	1,617	395	574	648	114
West	2,179	5.3	2,021	595	640	770	150

[1] Other equipment and services includes pets, toys, and playground equipment; sports, exercise, and photographic equipment; and recreational vehicles.

Source: U.S. Bureau of Labor Statistics, *Consumer Expenditure Survey*, annual.

No. 1213. Personal Consumption Expenditures for Recreation: 1990 to 2000

[In billions of dollars (284.9 represents $284,900,000,000), except percent. Represents market value of purchases of goods and services by individuals and nonprofit institutions]

Type of product or service	1990	1995	1996	1997	1998	1999	2000
Total recreation expenditures	**284.9**	**401.6**	**429.6**	**456.6**	**489.1**	**527.9**	**574.2**
Percent of total personal consumption [1]	7.4	8.1	8.2	8.3	8.4	8.4	8.5
Books and maps	16.2	23.1	24.9	26.3	28.2	30.7	33.9
Magazines, newspapers, and sheet music	21.6	26.2	27.6	29.1	31	32.9	36.8
Nondurable toys and sport supplies	32.8	47.2	50.6	53.2	56.5	60.4	64.6
Wheel goods, sports and photographic equipment [2]	29.7	38.5	40.5	42.8	46.2	50.3	58.3
Video and audio products, computer equipment, and musical instruments	52.9	77	80	83.7	90.3	98.0	106.9
Video and audio goods, including musical instruments	43.9	55.9	56.4	57.9	61.6	66.6	72.7
Computers, peripherals, and software	8.9	21	23.6	25.9	28.7	31.4	34.3
Radio and television repair	3.7	3.6	3.7	4	4.1	4.3	4.9
Flowers, seeds, and potted plants	10.9	13.8	14.9	15.3	15.9	16.6	17.5
Admissions to specified spectator amusements	14.8	19.2	20.7	22.1	23.4	25.8	27.3
Motion picture theaters	5.1	5.5	5.8	6.3	6.9	7.6	8.1
Legitimate theaters and opera, and entertainments of nonprofit institutions [3]	5.2	7.6	8	8.6	8.7	9.3	9.8
Spectator sports [4]	4.5	6.1	6.9	7.1	7.7	8.8	9.3
Clubs and fraternal organizations except insurance [5]	8.7	12.7	14	14.6	14.9	15.9	16.8
Commercial participant amusements [6]	24.6	43.9	48.3	52.8	57.3	63.2	69.2
Pari-mutuel net receipts	3.5	3.5	3.5	3.6	4.3	4.5	4.7
Other [7]	65.4	93.1	100.8	109.1	117	125.3	133.4

[1] See Table 639. [2] Includes boats and pleasure aircraft. [3] Except athletic. [4] Consists of admissions to professional and amateur athletic events and to racetracks, including horse, dog, and auto. [5] Consists of dues and fees excluding insurance premiums. [6] Consists of billiard parlors; bowling alleys; dancing, riding, shooting, skating, and swimming places; amusement devices and parks; golf courses; sightseeing buses and guides; private flying operations; casino gambling; and other commercial participant amusements. [7] Consists of net receipts of lotteries and expenditures for purchases of pets and pet care services, cable TV, film processing, photographic studios, sporting and recreation camps, video cassette rentals, and recreational services, not elsewhere classified.

Source: U.S. Bureau of Economic Analysis, *National Income and Product Accounts, Volume 1, 1929-97*, and *Survey of Current Business*, August 2001. See also <http://www.bea.gov/bea/dn/nipaweb/selecttable.asp>, (released as of 29 April 02).

No. 1214. Performing Arts—Selected Data: 1985 to 2000

[Sales, receipts, and expenditures in millions of dollars (209 represents $209,000,000). For season ending in year shown, except as indicated]

Item	1985	1990	1993	1994	1995	1996	1997	1998	1999	2000
Legitimate theater: [1]										
Broadway shows:										
New productions	33	40	34	39	33	38	37	33	39	37
Attendance (mil.) [2][3]	7.3	8.0	7.9	8.1	9.0	9.5	10.6	11.5	11.7	11.4
Playing weeks [2][3]	1,078	1,070	1,019	1,066	1,120	1,146	1,349	1,442	1,441	1,464
Gross ticket sales	209	282	328	356	406	436	499	558	588	603
Broadway road tours:										
Attendance (mil.)	8.2	11.1	14.9	16.0	15.6	18.1	17.6	15.2	14.6	11.7
Playing weeks	993	944	1,296	1,249	1,242	1,345	1,334	1,127	1,082	888
Gross ticket sales	226	367	626	705	701	796	782	721	707	572
Nonprofit professional theatres: [4]										
Companies reporting	217	185	177	231	215	228	197	189	313	262
Gross income	234.7	307.6	342.5	455.1	444.4	450.7	565.0	570.0	740.0	791.0
Earned income	146.1	188.4	209.7	277.4	281.2	274.0	349.9	342.0	442.0	466.0
Contributed income	88.6	119.2	132.8	177.7	163.1	176.7	215.1	228.0	298.0	325.0
Gross expenses	239.3	306.3	349.3	460.2	444.9	439.5	526.6	518.5	701.0	708.0
Productions	2,710	2,265	2,319	2,929	2,646	3,074	2,295	2,135	3,921	3,241
Performances	52,341	46,131	44,933	59,542	56,608	56,954	51,453	46,628	64,556	66,123
Total attendance (mil.)	14.2	15.2	16.5	20.7	18.6	17.1	17.2	14.6	18.0	22.0
OPERA America professional member companies: [5]										
Number of companies reporting [6]	97	98	85	86	88	83	91	89	95	98
Expenses [6]	216.4	321.2	389.5	404.9	435.0	466.7	534.1	556.3	591.1	636.7
Performances [7]	1,909	2,336	1,945	1,982	2,251	2,019	2,137	2,222	2,200	2,153
Total attendance (mil.) [7][8]	6.7	7.5	5.5	6.0	6.5	6.5	6.9	6.6	6.6	6.7
Main season attendance (mil.) [7][9]	3.3	4.1	3.6	3.7	3.9	3.9	4.0	3.7	4.0	4.3
Symphony orchestras: [10]										
Concerts	19,573	18,931	18,389	17,795	29,328	28,887	26,906	31,766	31,549	33,154
Attendance (mil.)	24.0	24.7	24.0	24.4	30.9	31.1	31.9	32.2	30.8	31.7
Gross revenue	252.4	377.5	430.5	442.5	536.2	558.9	575.5	627.6	671.8	734.0
Operating expenses	426.1	621.7	689.9	710.0	858.8	892.4	937.1	1,012.0	1,088.0	1,126.3
Support	188.1	257.8	293.0	293.1	351.0	382.8	401.1	459.7	486.0	521.0

[1] Source: The League of American Theaters and Producers, Inc., New York, NY. For season ending in year shown. [2] All shows (new productions and holdovers from previous seasons). [3] Eight performances constitute one playing week. [4] Source: Theatre Communications Group, New York, NY. For years ending on or prior to Aug. 31. [5] Source: OPERA America, Washington, DC. For years ending on or prior to Aug 31. [6] United States companies. [7] Prior to 1993 and for 1999, United States and Canadian companies; 1993 to 1998, U.S. companies only. [8] Includes educational performances, outreach, etc. [9] For paid performances. [10] Source: American Symphony Orchestra League, Inc., New York, NY. For years ending Aug. 31. Prior to 1995 represents 254 U.S. orchestras; beginning 1995, represents all U.S. orchestras, excluding college/university and youth orchestras. Also, beginning 1995, data based on 1,200 orchestras.

Source: Compiled from sources listed in footnotes.

No. 1215. Arts and Humanities—Selected Federal Aid Programs: 1980 to 2000

[In millions of dollars (188.1 represents $188,100,000), except as indicated. **For fiscal years ending in year shown,** see text, Section 8, State and Local Government Finances and Employment]

Type of fund and program	1980	1985	1990	1995	1996	1997	1998	1999	2000
National Endowment for the Arts:									
Funds available [1]	188.1	171.7	170.8	152.1	86.9	98.4	85.3	85.0	85.2
Program appropriation	97.0	118.7	124.3	109.0	63.5	65.8	64.3	66.0	66.0
Matching funds [2]	42.9	29.5	32.4	28.5	17.2	16.8	16.8	14.5	13.0
Grants awarded (number)	5,505	4,801	4,475	3,685	1,751	1,098	1,459	1,675	1,882
Funds obligated [3][4]	166.4	149.4	157.6	147.9	75.3	94.4	82.3	82.6	83.5
Partnership agreements	22.1	24.4	26.1	39.2	25.9	30.0	33.4	33.8	33.4
Music	13.6	15.3	16.5	10.9	5.4	(X)	(X)	(X)	(X)
Museums	11.2	11.9	12.1	9.0	3.8	(X)	(X)	(X)	(X)
Theater	8.4	10.6	10.6	7.3	5.2	(X)	(X)	(X)	(X)
Dance	8.0	9.0	9.6	7.1	4.2	(X)	(X)	(X)	(X)
Media arts	8.4	9.9	13.9	8.9	3.0	(X)	(X)	(X)	(X)
Challenge [5]	50.8	20.7	19.7	21.1	4.0	(X)	(X)	(X)	(X)
Visual arts	7.3	6.2	5.9	4.4	1.2	(X)	(X)	(X)	(X)
Other	36.6	41.3	43.1	40.0	22.6	(X)	(X)	(X)	(X)
National Endowment for the Humanities:									
Funds available [1]	186.2	125.6	140.6	152.3	93.9	94.8	94	95.5	102.6
Program appropriation	100.3	95.2	114.2	125.7	77.2	80.0	80.0	80.0	82.5
Matching funds [2]	38.4	30.4	26.3	25.7	15.9	13.9	13.9	13.9	15.3
Grants awarded (number)	2,917	2,241	2,195	1,871	815	900	852	874	1,230
Funds obligated [3]	185.5	125.7	141.0	151.8	93.4	94.8	92.7	92.1	100
Education programs	18.3	17.9	16.3	19.2	13.5	10.5	10.8	10.3	13
State programs	26.0	24.4	29.6	32.0	29.0	29.5	29.1	29.3	30.6
Research grants	32.0	24.4	22.5	22.2	5.1	8.5	7.7	6.6	6.9
Fellowship program	18.0	15.3	15.3	16.5	5.1	5.6	5.7	5.6	6.1
Challenge [5]	53.5	19.6	14.6	13.8	9.9	9.9	9.9	9.9	10.8
Public programs	25.1	24.1	25.4	25.8	12.5	12.6	11.1	12.2	11.8
Preservation and access	(X)	(X)	17.5	22.2	18.3	18.2	18.4	18.2	20.7
National Capital Arts and Cultural Affairs Program	(X)	(X)	(X)	(X)	(X)	(X)	(X)	(X)	(X)
Other	12.6	(X)	(X)	(X)	(X)	(X)	(X)	(X)	(X)

X Not applicable.   [1] Includes other funds, shown separately. Excludes administrative funds. Gifts are included in 1980; excluded thereafter.   [2] Represents federal funds obligated only upon receipt or certification by Endowment of matching nonfederal gifts.   [3] Includes obligations for new grants, supplemental awards on previous years' grants, and program contracts.   [4] Beginning with 1997 data, the grantmaking structure changed from discipline-based categories to thematic ones.   [5] Program designed to stimulate new sources and higher levels of giving to institutions for the purpose of guaranteeing long-term stability and financial independence. Program usually requires a match of at least 3 private dollars to each federal dollar. Funds for challenge grants are not allocated by program area because they are awarded on a grant-by-grant basis.

Source: U.S. National Endowment for the Arts, *Annual Report;* and U.S. National Endowment for the Humanities, *Annual Report.*

No. 1216. Attendance Rates for Various Arts Activities: 1997

[In percent. For persons 18 years old and over. Represents attendance at least once in the prior 12 months. Excludes elementary and high school performances. Based on the 1997 household survey Public Participation in the Arts. Data are subject to sampling error; see source. See also Tables 1218 and 1219]

Item	Jazz performance	Classical music performance	Opera	Musical play	Non-musical play	Ballet	Art museum	Historic park	Arts/craft fairs
Total	12	16	5	25	16	6	35	47	48
Sex:									
Male	13	14	4	22	15	4	34	48	42
Female	11	17	5	27	17	8	36	46	53
Race:									
Hispanic	7	8	3	16	10	5	29	33	34
White	12	18	5	27	17	7	36	51	52
African American	16	10	2	22	16	4	31	37	34
American Indian	11	9	5	15	5	1	22	42	47
Asian	10	16	7	20	18	4	42	44	39
Age:									
18 to 24 years old	15	16	5	26	20	7	38	46	44
25 to 34 years old	13	11	4	23	13	5	37	49	49
35 to 44 years old	14	14	4	26	15	7	37	52	54
45 to 54 years old	13	20	6	29	20	7	40	54	56
55 to 64 years old	9	16	5	23	14	5	30	45	44
65 to 74 years old	8	18	4	24	15	5	28	37	40
75 years old and over	4	14	3	15	13	4	20	25	24
Education:									
Grade school	2	2	-	6	3	2	6	13	13
Some high school	3	4	2	13	7	2	14	27	27
High school graduate	7	8	2	16	9	4	25	41	43
Some college	15	18	5	28	19	7	43	56	58
College graduate	21	28	10	44	28	11	58	67	65
Graduate school	28	45	14	50	37	14	70	73	69

- Represents or rounds to zero.

Source: U.S. National Endowment for the Arts, *1997 Survey of Public Participation in the Arts,* Research Division Report No. 39, December 1998.

No. 1217. Public School Supplemental Arts Education Programs by School Characteristic: 1998-99

[In percent. For activities during 1998-99 school year. Based on survey of school principals, during the 1999-2000 school year. For details, see source]

School characteristic	Public elementary schools				Public secondary schools			
	Field trips to arts performances	Field trips to art galleries or museums	Visiting artist(s)	Artist(s)-in-residence	Field trips to arts performances	Field trips to art galleries or museums	Visiting artist(s)	Artist(s)-in-residence
All schools	**77**	**65**	**38**	**22**	**69**	**68**	**34**	**18**
Enrollment size: [1]								
Less than 300	67	60	32	18	(NA)	(NA)	(NA)	(NA)
300 to 599	79	65	40	21	(NA)	(NA)	(NA)	(NA)
600 or more	86	70	41	28	(NA)	(NA)	(NA)	(NA)
Less than 400	(NA)	(NA)	(NA)	(NA)	65	64	33	15
400 to 999	(NA)	(NA)	(NA)	(NA)	69	64	32	21
1,000 or more	(NA)	(NA)	(NA)	(NA)	77	82	38	18
Region: [2]								
Northeast	79	73	47	31	78	80	37	33
Southeast	82	57	37	17	67	63	33	14
Central	74	61	35	23	71	67	34	16
West	77	67	34	19	64	68	33	15
Percent minority enrollment:								
5 percent or less	70	58	33	17	71	72	32	20
6 to 20 percent	79	69	39	25	71	67	38	18
21 to 50 percent	87	64	40	22	64	70	36	19
More than 50 percent	75	68	38	24	72	66	28	15
Percent of students eligible for free or reduced-price lunch:								
Less than 35 percent	79	71	41	26	74	74	34	19
35 to 49 percent	82	62	34	17	67	62	36	26
50 to 74 percent	79	56	40	20	61	60	34	15
75 percent or more	72	65	35	21	63	68	28	14

NA Not available.   [1] As of October 1, 1999.   [2] For composition of regions, see map, inside front cover.

Source: U.S. National Center for Education Statistics, *Arts Education in Public Elementary and Secondary Schools: 1999-2000*, NCES 2002-131.

No. 1218. Participation in Various Leisure Activities: 1997

[In percent, except as indicated (195.6 represents 195,600,000). Covers activities engaged in at least once in the prior 12 months. See headnote, Table 1216. See also Table 1219]

Item	Adult population (mil.)	Attendance at—			Participation in—				
		Movies	Sports events	Amusement park	Exercise program	Playing sports	Charity work	Home improvement/ repair	Computer hobbies
Total	**195.6**	**66**	**41**	**57**	**76**	**45**	**43**	**66**	**40**
Sex:									
Male	94.2	66	49	58	75	56	40	71	44
Female	101.4	65	34	57	77	35	46	61	37
Race:									
Hispanic	19.1	59	35	66	69	35	31	61	25
White	146.1	68	44	56	78	48	45	70	43
African American	22.1	60	35	55	74	34	44	51	37
American Indian	3.0	65	34	59	83	49	34	58	37
Asian	5.3	76	29	58	70	48	41	58	62
Age:									
18 to 24 years old	23.7	88	51	76	85	67	35	57	68
25 to 34 years old	40.1	79	51	70	82	63	41	63	51
35 to 44 years old	45.3	73	46	68	79	52	50	76	47
45 to 54 years old	33.7	65	42	53	77	40	46	75	40
55 to 64 years old	20.9	46	33	40	69	19	44	71	23
65 to 74 years old	19.6	38	21	29	65	23	40	55	11
75 years old and over	12.3	28	16	18	56	13	40	44	7
Education:									
Grade school	13.7	14	13	34	46	13	20	40	1
Some high school	26.9	52	25	54	66	30	31	59	19
High school graduate	62.0	62	38	58	74	41	36	65	35
Some college	50.3	78	48	64	81	54	50	71	52
College graduate	25.2	82	59	61	87	61	55	76	63
Graduate school	17.4	81	55	53	88	57	67	73	59
Income:									
$10,000 or less	15.0	37	15	39	55	19	32	42	19
$10,001 to $20,000	26.5	46	26	51	69	27	34	53	22
$20,001 to $30,000	29.4	56	28	55	72	40	37	61	30
$30,001 to $40,000	32.1	71	42	64	77	46	47	68	40
$40,001 to $50,000	25.9	73	51	67	80	51	42	75	47
$50,001 to $75,000	35.0	82	54	65	86	60	50	80	54
$75,001 to $100,000	16.2	81	66	64	86	61	51	79	64
Over $100,000	15.5	87	65	56	90	66	59	81	69

Source: U.S. National Endowment for the Arts, *1997 Survey of Public Participation in the Arts*, Research Division Report No. 39, December 1998.

Arts, Entertainment, and Recreation   751

No. 1219. Participation in Various Arts Activities: 1997

[In percent. Covers activities engaged in at least once in the prior 12 months. See Table 1218 and headnote, Table 1216]

Item	Playing classical music	Modern dancing [1]	Drawing	Pottery work [2]	Weaving	Photog- raphy [3]	Creative writing	Buying art work	Singing in groups
Total	1	13	16	15	28	17	12	35	10
Sex:									
Male	9	13	15	16	5	16	10	36	9
Female	13	12	17	14	49	18	14	34	12
Race:									
Hispanic	7	14	17	11	17	12	8	33	7
White	12	12	15	16	30	17	12	36	8
African American	8	11	16	11	25	18	14	43	26
American Indian	9	21	18	25	28	28	10	35	7
Asian	12	17	27	13	28	22	21	19	9
Age:									
18 to 24 years old	13	20	39	21	22	28	32	42	14
25 to 34 years old	10	13	18	17	25	18	13	43	9
35 to 44 years old	11	13	15	18	29	18	12	40	9
45 to 54 years old	15	11	13	18	29	18	10	37	13
55 to 64 years old	9	8	9	10	29	10	5	31	11
65 to 74 years old	6	14	7	10	32	10	5	23	10
75 years old and over . .	6	9	4	3	28	5	6	8	7
Education:									
Grade school	2	4	4	7	14	8	2	24	11
Some high school	4	11	13	15	22	12	8	35	9
High school graduate . . .	8	12	15	16	28	13	9	31	9
Some college	14	16	20	18	32	22	17	35	13
College graduate	18	10	18	13	32	23	14	41	9
Graduate school	20	15	18	13	26	22	19	41	12
Income:									
$10,000 or less	5	9	15	8	28	11	8	29	13
$10,001 to $20,000	7	10	13	12	27	14	8	27	9
$20,001 to $30,000	8	12	17	16	26	14	12	26	11
$30,001 to $40,000	10	14	15	20	29	18	11	44	13
$40,001 to $50,000	11	12	16	17	29	18	13	35	8
$50,001 to $75,000	15	13	17	18	28	18	17	32	10
$70,001 to $100,000 . . .	15	18	18	17	24	23	13	41	11
Over $100,000	18	12	12	14	23	23	11	46	9

[1] Dancing other than ballet (e.g. folk and tap). [2] Includes ceramics, jewelry, leatherwork, and metalwork. [3] Includes making movies or video as an artistic activity.

Source: U.S. National Endowment for the Arts, *1997 Survey of Public Participation in the Arts,* Research Division Report No. 39, December 1998.

No. 1220. Retail Sales and Household Participation in Lawn and Garden Activities: 1997 to 2001

[For calendar year. (26,639 represents $26,639,000,000). Based on national household sample survey conducted by the Gallup Organization. Subject to sampling variability; see source]

Activity	Retail sales (mil. dol.)					Percent households engaged in activity				
	1997	1998	1999	2000	2001	1997	1998	1999	2000	2001
Total	26,639	30,188	33,519	33,404	37,734	67	65	64	72	80
Lawn care	6,366	8,543	8,986	9,794	12,672	45	47	43	50	56
Indoor houseplants	1,107	1,159	1,270	1,332	1,784	29	29	32	39	46
Flower gardening	3,404	3,965	3,976	4,167	3,926	38	39	45	45	43
Insect control.	1,342	1,671	1,214	1,232	2,058	21	22	23	27	33
Shrub care	1,441	1,635	1,376	1,429	1,298	24	25	29	31	30
Vegetable gardening	1,914	2,006	2,595	2,169	1,535	23	24	29	27	25
Tree care	1,892	1,733	1,732	1,872	2,121	18	18	20	23	25
Landscaping	6,153	6,435	8,585	6,809	6,310	23	22	25	30	37
Flower bulbs	573	579	657	912	1,188	21	21	23	28	31
Fruit trees	455	301	264	284	748	11	10	13	13	15
Container gardening	558	783	1,020	1,257	1,202	11	11	15	18	22
Raising transplants [1]	383	160	302	334	291	7	7	12	11	12
Herb gardening	168	146	185	204	413	8	7	11	12	14
Growing berries	60	82	87	147	227	5	5	7	8	8
Ornamental gardening.	251	333	464	519	756	6	5	6	8	9
Water gardening	572	659	806	943	1,205	5	4	7	10	13

[1] Starting plants in advance of planting in ground.

Source: The National Gardening Association, Burlington, VT, *National Gardening Survey,* annual (copyright).

No. 1221. Household Pet Ownership: 2001

[Based on a sample survey of 80,000 households in 2001; for details, see source]

Item	Unit	Dog	Cat	Pet bird	Horse
Percent of households owning companion pets [1]	Percent . . .	36.1	31.6	4.6	1.7
Average number owned	Number . . .	1.6	2.1	2.1	3.0
Households obtaining veterinary care [2]	Percent . . .	85.0	66.8	12.9	56.7
Average visits per household per year	Number . . .	2.8	1.9	0.3	2.2
PERCENT OF HOUSEHOLDS OWNING PETS					
Annual household income:					
Under $20,000	Percent . . .	29.7	28.1	5.1	1.0
$20,000 to $34,999	Percent . . .	33.9	30.9	4.5	1.3
$35,000 to $54,999	Percent . . .	37.9	32.2	4.8	2.0
$55,000 to $84,999	Percent . . .	40.5	34.3	4.4	2.1
$85,000 and over	Percent . . .	39.7	33.7	4.2	2.1
Household size: [1]					
One person	Percent . . .	20.8	23.5	2.8	0.7
Two persons	Percent . . .	34.3	31.3	4.0	1.6
Three persons	Percent . . .	46.2	37.4	5.9	2.2
Four persons	Percent . . .	50.6	38.2	6.3	2.3
Five or more persons.	Percent . . .	53.0	39.7	8.3	3.2

[1] As of December 31, 2001.   [2] During 2001.
Source: American Veterinary Medical Association, Schaumburg, IL, *U.S. Pet Ownership and Demographics Sourcebook, 2002* (copyright).

No. 1222. Adult Attendance at Sports Events: 2001

[In thousands (9,234 represents 9,234,000), except percent. For fall 2001. Based on survey and subject to sampling error; see source]

Event	Attend one or more times a month		Attend less than once a month		Event	Attend one or more times a month		Attend less than once a month	
	Number	Percent	Number	Percent		Number	Percent	Number	Percent
Baseball	9,234	4.6	19,000	9.4	Golf	1,799	0.9	4,357	2.2
Basketball:					High school sports	11,516	5.7	7,622	3.8
College games	4,289	2.1	6,289	3.1	Horse racing:				
Professional games	3,266	1.6	8,349	4.1	Flats, runners	1,311	0.7	3,103	1.5
Bowling	1,749	0.9	2,564	1.3	Trotters/harness	755	0.4	2,079	1.0
Boxing	975	0.5	2,442	1.2	Ice hockey	2,460	1.2	6,679	3.3
Equestrian events	716	0.4	2,405	1.2	Motorcycle racing	802	0.4	2,462	1.2
Figure skating.	468	0.2	2,640	1.3	Pro beach volleyball.	127	0.1	1,790	0.9
Fishing tournaments.	617	0.3	2,231	1.1	Rodeo	1,120	0.6	3,690	1.8
Football:					Soccer.	3,245	1.6	3,497	1.7
College games	5,078	2.5	7,664	3.8	Tennis	792	0.4	2,722	1.3
Monday night professional					Truck and tractor pull/mud				
games	2,261	1.1	3,732	1.8	racing	881	0.4	3,114	1.5
Weekend professional					Wrestling—professional	1,148	0.6	3,651	1.8
games	3,831	1.9	8,646	4.3					

Source: Mediamark Research, Inc., New York, NY *Top-line Reports* (copyright). Internet site <http://www.mediamark.com/mri/docs/TopLineReports.html>

No. 1223. Adult Participation in Selected Leisure Activities by Frequency: 2001

[In thousands (30,391 represents 30,391,000), except percent. For fall 2001. Based on sample and subject to sampling error; see source]

Activity	Participated in the last 12 months		Frequency of participation							
			Two or more times a week		Once a week		Two to three times a month		Once a month	
	Number	Percent	Number	Percent	Number	Percent	Number	Percent	Number	Percent
Attend music performances [1] .	30,391	15.0	569	0.3	745	0.4	1,272	0.6	2,919	1.4
Baking	37,581	18.5	7,635	3.8	6,164	3.0	8,922	4.4	4,828	2.4
Barbecuing	66,588	32.8	10,171	5.0	10,867	5.4	15,394	7.6	9,157	4.5
Board games	35,789	17.7	2,812	1.4	3,425	1.7	6,186	3.1	6,372	3.1
Cooking for fun	34,374	17.0	10,510	5.2	6,539	3.2	5,481	2.7	3,493	1.7
Crossword puzzles	30,801	15.2	12,240	6.0	4,192	2.1	2,711	1.3	2,057	1.0
Dining out	104,989	51.8	21,503	10.6	26,281	13.0	25,053	12.4	11,800	5.8
Entertain friends or relatives at home	79,711	39.3	6,894	3.4	10,523	5.2	17,405	8.6	17,338	8.6
Go to bars/night clubs	41,806	20.6	3,506	1.7	5,766	2.8	8,165	4.0	6,192	3.1
Go to beach	52,187	25.7	3,265	1.6	2,578	1.3	4,974	2.5	5,377	2.7
Go to live theater	29,738	14.7	308	0.2	423	0.2	1,157	0.6	2,955	1.5
Play cards	42,504	21.0	5,353	2.6	4,228	2.1	6,312	3.1	7,280	3.6
Reading books	87,670	43.2	48,322	23.8	8,289	4.1	8,611	4.3	6,341	3.1
Surf the Net	54,851	27.1	32,820	16.2	7,574	3.7	4,432	2.2	2,182	1.1

[1] Excluding country and rock.
Source: Mediamark Research, Inc., New York, NY, *Top-line Reports* (copyright). Internet site <http://www.mediamark.com/mri/docs/TopLineReports.html>.

Arts, Entertainment, and Recreation   753

No. 1224. Selected Spectator Sports: 1985 to 2000

[47,742 represents 47,742,000]

Sport	Unit	1985	1987	1990	1995	1997	1998	1999	2000
Baseball, major leagues: [1]									
Attendance	1,000	47,742	53,182	55,512	51,288	64,921	71,930	71,558	74,316
Regular season	1,000	46,824	52,011	54,824	50,469	63,168	70,372	70,139	72,635
National League	1,000	22,292	24,734	24,492	25,110	31,885	38,424	38,323	39,738
American League	1,000	24,532	27,277	30,332	25,359	31,283	31,948	31,817	32,898
Playoffs [2]	1,000	591	784	479	533	1,349	1,314	1,202	1,314
World Series	1,000	327	387	209	286	404	243	216	366
Players' salaries: [3]									
Average	$1,000	371	412	598	1,111	1,337	1,399	1,607	(NA)
Basketball: [4] [5]									
NCAA—Men's college:									
Teams	Number	753	760	767	868	865	895	926	932
Attendance	1,000	26,584	26,798	28,741	28,548	27,738	28,032	28,505	29,025
NCAA—Women's college:									
Teams	Number	746	756	782	864	879	911	940	956
Attendance	1,000	2,072	2,156	2,777	4,962	6,734	7,387	8,010	8,698
Pro: [6]									
Teams	Number	23	23	27	27	29	29	29	29
Attendance, total [7]	1,000	11,534	13,191	18,586	19,883	21,677	21,801	13,450	21,503
Regular season	1,000	10,506	12,065	17,369	18,516	20,305	20,373	12,135	20,059
Average per game	Number	11,141	12,795	15,690	16,727	17,077	17,135	16,738	16,870
Playoffs	1,000	985	1,091	1,203	1,347	1,352	1,409	1,315	1,427
Average	Number	14,479	15,364	16,704	18,457	18,774	19,851	19,926	19,202
All-star game	1,000	43.1	34.3	14.8	18.8	20.6	18.3	(X)	18.3
Players' salaries:									
Average	$1,000	325	440	750	1,900	2,200	3,000	3,000	3,600
Football:									
NCAA College: [5]									
Teams	Number	509	507	533	565	581	595	601	606
Attendance	1,000	34,952	35,008	35,330	35,638	36,858	37,491	39,483	39,059
National Football League: [8]									
Teams	Number	28	28	28	30	31	31	32	31
Attendance, total [9]	1,000	14,058	[10]15,180	17,666	19,203	19,050	19,742	20,763	20,954
Regular season	1,000	13,345	[10]11,406	13,960	15,044	14,967	15,365	16,207	16,387
Average per game	Number	59,567	[10]54,315	62,321	62,682	62,364	64,020	65,349	66,078
Postseason games [11]	1,000	711	656	848	(NA)	(NA)	823	794	809
Players' salaries: [12]									
Average	$1,000	245	244	395	717	737	993	1,056	1,116
Median base salary	$1,000	137	135	191	295	290	385	400	420
National Hockey League: [13]									
Regular season attendance	1,000	11,634	11,856	12,580	9,234	17,641	17,265	17,152	18,831
Playoffs attendance	1,000	1,108	1,384	1,356	1,329	1,495	1,507	1,472	1,516
Horseracing: [14] [15]									
Racing days	Number	13,745	14,208	13,841	13,243	11,958	11,380	11,398	11,348
Attendance	1,000	73,346	70,105	63,803	38,934	41,846	37,728	(NA)	(NA)
Pari-mutuel turnover	Mil. dol	12,222	13,122	7,162	14,592	15,220	15,561	15,828	16,040
Revenue to government	Mil. dol	625	608	624	456	422	432	392	368
Greyhound: [14]									
Total performances	Number	9,590	11,156	14,915	16,110	14,557	14,943	14,455	14,403
Attendance	1,000	23,853	26,215	28,660	(NA)	14,306	(NA)	(NA)	(NA)
Pari-mutuel turnover	Mil. dol	2,702	3,193	3,422	2,730	2,291	2,237	2,130	2,054
Revenue to government	Mil. dol	201	221	235	157	114	109	101	98
Jai alai: [14]									
Total performances	Number	2,736	2,906	3,620	2,748	2,648	2,600	2,119	2,034
Games played	Number	32,260	38,476	(NA)	37,052	(NA)	37,175	28,706	27,461
Attendance	1,000	4,722	6,816	5,329	3,208	2,125	(NA)	(NA)	(NA)
Total handle	Mil. dol	664.0	707.5	545.5	296.4	251	153	119	1,959
Revenue to government	Mil. dol	50	51	39	13	10	9	5	4
Professional rodeo: [16]									
Rodeos	Number	617	637	754	739	729	703	700	688
Performances	Number	1,887	1,832	2,159	2,217	2,213	2,125	2,128	2,081
Members	Number	5,239	5,342	5,693	6,894	7,178	7,301	7,403	6,255
Permit-holders (rookies)	Number	2,534	2,746	3,290	3,835	4,197	4,117	3,511	3,249
Total prize money	Mil. dol	15.1	14.9	18.2	24.5	28.0	29.9	31.1	32.3

NA Not available.   X Not applicable.   [1] Source: Major League Baseball (previously, The National League of Professional Baseball Clubs), New York, NY, *National League Green Book;* and The American League of Professional Baseball Clubs, New York, NY, *American League Red Book.*   [2] Beginning 1997, two rounds of playoffs were played. Prior years had one round.   [3] Source: Major League Baseball Players Association, New York, NY.   [4] Season ending in year shown.   [5] Source: National Collegiate Athletic Assn., Indianapolis, IN. For women's attendance total, excludes double-headers with men's teams.   [6] Source: National Basketball Assn., New York, NY. For season ending in year shown.   [7] Includes All-Star game, not shown separately.   [8] Source: National Football League, New York, NY.   [9] Beginning 1987 includes preseason attendance, not shown separately.   [10] Season was interrupted by a strike.   [11] Includes Pro Bowl, a nonchampionship game and Super Bowl.   [12] Source: National Football League Players Association, Washington, DC.   [13] For season ending in year shown. Source: National Hockey League, Montreal, Quebec.   [14] Source: Association of Racing Commissioners International, Inc., Lexington, KY.   [15] Includes thoroughbred, harness, quarter horse, and fairs.   [16] Source: Professional Rodeo Cowboys Association, Colorado Springs, CO., *Official Professional Rodeo Media Guide,* annual (copyright).

Source: Compiled from sources listed in footnotes.

No. 1225. Selected Recreational Activities: 1975 to 2000

[26 represents 26,000,000]

Activity	Unit	1975	1980	1985	1990	1995	1998	1999	2000
Softball, amateur: [1]									
Total participants [2]	Million..	26	30	41	41	42	40	35	32
Youth participants	1,000 ..	450	650	712	1,100	1,350	1,400	1,411	1,375
Adult teams [3]	1,000 ..	66	110	152	188	187	166	163	157
Youth teams [3]	1,000 ..	9	18	31	46	74	81	83	81
Golfers (one round or more) [4][5]	1,000 ..	13,036	15,112	17,520	27,800	25,000	26,427	26,446	26,738
Golf rounds played [4][5]	1,000 ..	308,562	357,701	414,777	502,000	490,200	528,500	564,100	587,100
Golf facilities [4]	Number.	11,370	12,005	12,346	12,846	14,074	14,900	15,195	15,489
Classification:									
Private	Number.	4,770	4,839	4,861	4,810	4,324	4,251	4,285	4,290
Daily fee	Number.	5,014	5,372	5,573	6,024	7,491	8,247	8,470	8,761
Municipal	Number.	1,586	1,794	1,912	2,012	2,259	2,402	2,440	2,438
Tennis: [6]									
Players	1,000 ..	[7]34,000	(NA)	13,000	21,000	17,820	(NA)	20,000	20,000
Courts	1,000 ..	130	(NA)	220	220	240	(NA)	(NA)	(NA)
Indoor	1,000 ..	8	(NA)	14	14	15	(NA)	(NA)	(NA)
Tenpin bowling: [8]									
Participants, total	Million..	62.5	72.0	67.0	71.0	79.0	91.0	91.0	91.0
Male	Million..	29.9	34.0	32.0	35.4	36.3	41.8	41.8	41.8
Female	Million..	32.6	38.0	35.0	35.6	42.6	49.2	49.2	49.2
Establishments	Number.	8,577	8,591	8,275	7,611	7,049	6,398	6,398	6,247
Lanes	1,000 ..	141	154	155	148	139	128	128	125
Membership, total [9]	1,000 ..	8,751	9,664	8,064	6,588	4,925	4,156	4,156	3,756
American Bowling Congress	1,000 ..	4,300	4,688	3,657	3,036	2,370	2,027	2,027	1,866
Women's Bowling Congress	1,000 ..	3,692	4,187	3,714	2,859	2,036	1,678	1,678	1,481
Young American Bowling Alliance [10]	1,000 ..	759	789	693	693	519	451	451	409
Motion picture screens [11]	1,000 ..	15	18	21	24	28	34	37	37
Indoor	1,000 ..	11	14	18	23	27	33	36	37
Drive-in	1,000 ..	4	4	3	1	1	1	1	1
Receipts, box office	Mil. dol.	2,115	2,749	3,749	5,022	5,494	6,949	7,448	7,661
Admission, average price	Dollars .	2.05	2.69	3.55	4.23	4.35	4.69	5.08	5.39
Attendance	Million.	1,033	1,022	1,056	1,189	1,263	1,481	1,465	1,421
Boating: [12]									
Recreational boats owned	1,000 ..	(NA)	11,832	13,778	15,987	15,375	16,657	16,791	16,991
Retail expenditures on boating [13]	Mil. dol..	4,800	7,370	13,284	13,731	17,226	19,001	21,736	25,025
Retail units purchased:									
Total all boats [14]	1,000 ..	(NA)	643	675	525	664	576	585	574
Outboard boats	1,000 ..	(NA)	290	305	227	231	214	230	241
Inboard boats	1,000 ..	(NA)	8	17	15	12	18	19	22
Sterndrive boats	1,000 ..	(NA)	56	115	97	94	78	80	78
Jet boats	1,000 ..	(NA)	(NA)	(NA)	(NA)	15	10	8	7
Personal watercraft	1,000 ..	(NA)	(NA)	(NA)	(NA)	200	130	106	92
Sailboats	1,000 ..	(NA)	73	38	21	14	19	21	22
Canoes	1,000 ..	(NA)	105	79	75	98	108	121	112
Inflatable boats	1,000 ..	(NA)	16	34	27	(NA)	(NA)	(NA)	(NA)
Sailboard	1,000 ..	(NA)	21	50	42	(NA)	(NA)	(NA)	(NA)
Boat trailers	1,000 ..	(NA)	176	192	165	207	174	168	159
Outboard motors	1,000 ..	(NA)	315	392	352	317	314	332	349
Sterndrive and inboard engines	1,000 ..	(NA)	88	155	134	120	105	109	110

NA Not available. [1] Source: Amateur Softball Association, Oklahoma City, OK. [2] Amateur Softball Association teams and other amateur softball teams. [3] Amateur Softball Association teams only. [4] Source: National Golf Foundation, Jupiter, FL. [5] Prior to 1990, for persons 5 years of age and over; thereafter for persons 12 years of age and over. [6] Source: Tennis Industry Association, Hilton Head, SC. Players for persons 12 years old and over who played at least once. [7] 1974 data. [8] For season ending in year shown. Persons 5 years old and over. Source: Bowling Headquarters, Greendale, WI. [9] Membership totals are for U.S., Canada and for U.S. military personnel worldwide. [10] Prior to 1985, represents American Jr. Bowling Congress and ABC/WIBC Collegiate Division. [11] Source: Motion Picture Association of America, Inc., Encino, CA. 1975 figures represent theaters. [12] Source: National Marine Manufacturers Association, Chicago, IL. (copyright). [13] Represents estimated expenditures for new and used boats, motors and engines, accessories, safety equipment, fuel, insurance, docking, maintenance, launching, storage, repairs, and other expenses. [14] 1980 through 1990 includes other boats, not shown separately.

Source: Compiled from sources listed in footnotes.

U.S. Census Bureau, Statistical Abstract of the United States: 2002

No. 1226. Participation in Selected Sports Activities: 2000

[In thousands (248,518 represents 248,518,000), except rank. For persons 7 years of age or older. Except as indicated, a participant plays a sport more than once in the year]

Activity	All persons		Sex		Age								Household income (dol.)					
	Number	Rank	Male	Female	7-11 years	12-17 years	18-24 years	25-34 years	35-44 years	45-54 years	55-64 years	65 years and over	Under 15,000	15,000-24,999	25,000-34,999	35,000-49,000	50,000-74,999	75,000 and over
Total	248,518	(X)	120,931	127,587	20,232	23,537	26,594	37,440	44,894	37,107	24,001	34,714	35,897	29,022	37,037	45,396	52,009	49,159
SERIES I SPORTS [1]																		
Number participated in— [2]																		
Aerobic exercising [3]	28,633	9	6,575	22,057	924	2,082	4,636	6,994	5,491	3,773	2,051	2,682	3,313	2,968	4,118	5,133	5,957	7,144
Backpacking [3]	15,356	17	8,831	6,525	1,759	2,360	2,530	3,476	2,973	1,725	374	159	2,064	1,524	2,763	3,046	3,169	2,790
Badminton	4,897	28	2,247	2,651	865	1,000	532	907	996	347	190	62	435	553	746	1,496	954	712
Baseball	15,636	16	11,748	3,888	4,860	3,945	1,803	1,582	2,121	737	241	346	1,866	1,613	2,324	3,075	3,682	3,076
Basketball	27,084	10	18,486	8,598	6,187	7,659	3,850	4,470	3,325	1,089	261	244	2,761	2,173	4,497	5,318	6,515	5,820
Bicycle riding [2]	43,135	6	22,174	20,962	10,026	7,583	3,700	6,376	6,808	4,526	2,208	1,905	4,590	3,859	6,563	8,503	10,114	9,506
Billiards [2]	32,548	8	19,281	13,267	1,496	3,373	6,861	8,940	6,783	3,352	1,079	665	3,972	3,808	5,376	6,523	6,992	5,876
Bowling [2]	43,133	7	21,046	22,086	5,819	6,263	6,878	8,184	7,821	4,203	1,841	2,125	5,236	4,239	6,272	8,238	10,613	8,534
Calisthenics [2]	13,847	19	6,295	7,553	1,578	2,834	1,582	2,156	2,522	1,438	623	1,114	1,453	1,149	2,058	2,323	2,715	3,341
Camping [4]	49,881	3	25,610	24,271	6,182	6,279	6,318	9,417	10,412	6,646	2,611	2,014	6,042	5,292	8,279	10,568	11,086	8,614
Exercise walking [2]	86,296	1	28,668	57,627	3,350	4,177	7,631	14,085	15,966	15,210	10,039	15,838	13,028	9,741	12,426	15,425	16,978	18,697
Exercising with equipment [2]	44,820	4	20,439	24,380	1,208	4,248	5,708	9,067	9,184	7,588	3,978	3,839	3,993	3,798	5,881	7,617	9,828	13,704
Fishing—fresh water	44,389	5	29,227	15,161	5,420	4,818	5,343	7,947	9,020	5,838	3,249	2,753	5,817	5,432	7,628	9,570	8,440	7,503
Fishing——salt water	11,395	22	7,690	3,705	1,012	988	1,182	1,835	2,443	1,969	1,106	860	950	1,194	1,616	2,062	2,715	2,858
Football—tackle	7,477	26	6,738	739	1,437	2,769	1,459	925	542	177	97	72	688	868	1,429	1,499	1,631	1,361
Football—touch	9,794	24	7,843	1,951	2,521	2,887	1,333	1,539	1,020	276	146	72	1,131	1,116	1,405	2,222	2,419	1,501
Golf	26,401	11	20,080	6,322	1,043	2,451	2,532	5,108	5,610	4,040	2,495	3,122	1,552	1,520	3,002	4,709	6,707	8,911
Hiking	24,288	13	12,066	12,223	2,587	2,671	3,098	4,504	5,315	3,598	1,366	1,149	2,420	2,311	3,549	4,322	5,664	6,021
Hunting with firearms	19,144	15	16,467	2,677	891	2,089	2,981	3,845	4,428	2,690	1,231	991	2,237	2,233	3,162	4,421	4,245	2,846
Martial arts	5,438	27	3,257	2,181	1,400	980	804	877	653	559	91	74	608	553	818	1,338	1,144	978
Racquetball	3,222	29	2,295	926	104	310	646	961	631	436	83	50	209	196	432	592	899	893
Running/jogging [2]	22,812	14	11,509	11,303	1,727	3,743	4,269	5,390	3,539	2,475	1,053	615	2,003	1,972	2,956	4,277	5,321	6,281
Soccer	12,899	20	7,537	5,363	5,666	3,584	1,025	1,221	733	289	226	154	1,487	876	1,634	2,375	3,556	2,971
Softball	13,979	18	7,338	6,641	2,235	3,135	1,778	2,924	2,502	936	333	136	1,384	1,502	2,209	2,686	3,660	2,537
Swimming [2]	60,758	2	26,404	34,353	10,415	10,015	6,802	9,376	10,556	6,458	3,290	3,844	6,231	5,260	8,375	11,847	15,090	13,953
Table tennis	7,709	25	4,408	3,301	943	1,701	1,294	1,087	1,169	887	260	368	683	352	943	1,563	2,128	2,040
Tennis	10,032	23	4,954	5,078	848	1,620	1,843	1,849	1,784	836	771	486	749	680	1,091	1,718	2,593	3,202
Volleyball	12,261	21	5,388	6,874	1,437	3,586	1,807	2,723	1,690	766	216	37	1,224	1,085	1,870	2,829	2,971	2,283
Weightlifting	24,843	12	15,944	8,899	636	3,917	4,676	6,116	4,925	2,633	1,200	739	2,324	1,967	3,404	4,753	5,458	6,936

See footnotes at end of table.

U.S. Census Bureau, Statistical Abstract of the United States: 2002

Activity	All persons — Number	Rank	Sex — Male	Female	Age — 7-11 years	12-17 years	18-24 years	25-34 years	35-44 years	45-54 years	55-64 years	65 years and over	Household income (dol.) — Under 15,000	15,000-24,999	25,000-34,999	35,000-49,999	50,000-74,999	75,000 and over
Total	**248,755**	(X)	**120,932**	**127,821**	**20,285**	**23,537**	**26,594**	**37,440**	**44,894**	**37,166**	**24,001**	**34,928**	**31,714**	**30,019**	**36,452**	**44,248**	**54,798**	**51,522**

SERIES II SPORTS [5]

Number participating in—

Activity	Number	Rank	Male	Female	7-11 years	12-17 years	18-24 years	25-34 years	35-44 years	45-54 years	55-64 years	65 years and over	Under 15,000	15,000-24,999	25,000-34,999	35,000-49,999	50,000-74,999	75,000 and over
Archery (target)	4,524	19	3,730	794	958	897	435	754	880	388	154	59	307	481	656	1,162	1,053	866
Boating, motor/power	24,233	1	14,029	10,204	2,317	2,638	3,075	4,281	5,324	3,241	2,147	1,238	1,245	1,909	3,092	4,457	6,474	7,055
Canoeing	6,232	13	3,845	2,388	544	978	982	1,000	1,268	898	339	223	362	512	863	1,436	1,590	1,469
Dart throwing	17,436	4	10,518	6,918	1,511	1,984	2,676	4,995	3,942	1,585	524	219	1,978	1,793	2,801	3,395	4,525	2,945
Hunting with bow and arrow	4,691	18	4,407	285	234	369	606	1,108	1,340	488	303	245	339	625	770	1,107	1,169	681
Ice hockey	1,939	26	1,589	350	374	441	293	249	357	128	53	44	124	104	284	221	667	539
Ice/figure skating	6,724	12	2,566	4,157	1,936	1,386	872	892	1,018	391	160	70	446	354	892	1,104	1,794	2,135
Kayaking/rafting	3,137	21	1,864	1,273	367	396	473	643	525	451	193	88	149	279	499	525	650	1,036
Mountain biking-off road	7,056	11	4,846	2,210	775	1,069	916	2,081	1,330	570	225	91	566	699	1,014	1,329	1,667	1,781
Mountain biking-on road	14,297	6	8,244	6,053	1,977	1,750	1,879	3,845	2,763	1,353	590	155	1,069	1,266	1,725	2,470	3,274	4,492
Muzzleloading	2,867	22	2,693	174	54	125	236	677	812	569	246	147	176	337	605	617	647	486
Paintball games	5,349	17	4,463	886	501	1,949	1,219	836	527	221	49	47	493	328	757	1,158	1,256	1,357
Roller hockey	2,163	25	1,741	422	757	515	285	197	242	91	22	53	83	143	307	284	774	572
Roller skating/in-line wheels	21,817	3	10,570	11,247	8,060	5,964	2,282	2,769	1,871	532	200	139	1,362	1,879	3,001	3,785	6,444	5,348
Roller skating/traditional (2x2 wheel)	7,210	10	2,737	4,473	2,541	1,476	607	1,161	852	280	173	119	908	737	1,041	1,530	1,939	1,055
Sailing	2,454	23	1,252	1,202	96	184	76	423	565	494	336	280	201	90	328	372	516	948
Scooter riding	11,621	7	6,732	4,890	6,844	2,843	505	607	491	116	118	97	757	780	1,484	2,347	2,868	3,385
Scuba (open water)	1,647	27	1,018	629	24	112	131	371	506	299	171	32	64	41	127	198	441	776
Skateboarding	9,059	8	7,506	1,553	3,892	3,460	822	399	221	75	44	144	628	904	1,275	1,610	2,479	2,161
Skiing—alpine	7,392	9	4,352	3,040	711	1,278	906	1,313	1,676	985	379	143	105	341	625	926	1,595	3,799
Skiing—cross country	2,338	24	1,162	1,176	133	261	207	445	509	452	175	155	138	109	256	469	664	700
Snorkeling	5,451	16	2,954	2,497	380	598	700	994	1,271	988	410	110	148	420	369	632	1,281	2,600
Snowboarding	4,347	20	3,222	1,125	845	1,696	973	491	197	87	31	27	324	523	386	741	1,242	1,132
Step aerobics	6,089	14	523	5,566	59	204	1,003	1,742	1,453	793	425	426	656	524	857	1,075	1,410	1,566
Target shooting	14,829	5	11,465	3,364	763	1,654	2,143	3,332	3,632	1,903	822	581	1,052	1,519	2,378	3,141	3,811	2,929
Water skiing	5,921	15	3,542	2,379	323	1,002	1,336	1,353	1,211	386	232	79	256	557	595	1,127	1,579	1,808
Wind surfing	501	28	417	84	62	80	80	53	92	30	83	38	62	27	31	60	121	200
Work-out at club	24,071	2	11,134	12,936	420	1,400	4,488	5,743	5,013	3,537	1,759	1,737	1,553	1,681	2,809	3,561	5,521	8,945

X Not applicable. ¹ Based on a sampling of 15,000 households. ² Participant engaged in activity at least six times in the year. ³ Includes wilderness camping. ⁴ Vacation/overnight. ⁵ Based on a sampling of 20,000 households.

Source: National Sporting Goods Association, Mt. Prospect, IL, Sports Participation in 2000: Series I and Series II (copyright).

Arts, Entertainment, and Recreation 757

No. 1227. High School Students Engaged in Organized Physical Activity by Sex, Race, and Hispanic Origin: 2001

[In percent. For students in grades 9 to 12. Based on the Youth Risk Behavior Survey, a school-based survey and subject to sampling error; for details see source]

Characteristic	Enrolled in physical education class			Played on a sports team
	Total	Attended daily	Exercised 20 minutes or more per class [1]	
All students.	**51.7**	**32.2**	**83.4**	**55.2**
Male	55.6	36.3	87.7	60.9
Grade 9	74.0	48.2	85.0	63.5
Grade 10.	58.4	37.4	87.7	61.6
Grade 11.	46.7	30.0	90.6	61.5
Grade 12.	36.9	26.1	91.2	55.9
Female.	48.0	28.4	78.8	49.9
Grade 9	73.4	49.3	78.9	56.7
Grade 10.	49.9	26.1	80.3	50.8
Grade 11.	31.6	15.6	79.1	47.7
Grade 12.	26.0	14.7	75.0	41.4
White, non-Hispanic	48.3	29.5	85.2	57.4
Male.	52.0	33.8	90.3	61.7
Female	44.9	25.6	79.7	53.3
Black, non-Hispanic	60.5	40.8	76.4	52.7
Male.	67.4	46.3	81.0	64.4
Female	54.0	35.6	71.0	41.6
Hispanic.	58.4	38.7	81.9	48.8
Male.	61.6	41.9	84.6	57.8
Female	55.3	35.7	79.2	40.1

[1] For students enrolled in physical education classes.

Source: U.S. Centers for Disease Control and Prevention, Atlanta, GA, *Youth Risk Behavior Surveillance—United States, 2001, Morbidity and Mortality Weekly Report,* Vol. 51, No. SS-4, June 28, 2002.

No. 1228. Participation in High School Athletic Programs by Sex: 1971 to 2001

[Data based on number of state associations reporting and may underrepresent the number of schools with and participants in athletic programs]

Year	Participants [1]		Sex and sport	Most popular sports, 2000-2001 [2]	
	Males	Females		Schools	Participants
1971	3,666,917	294,105	MALES		
1972-73	3,770,621	817,073			
1973-74	4,070,125	1,300,169	Football (11-player)	13,454	1,012,420
1975-76	4,109,021	1,645,039	Basketball	17,135	539,749
1977-78	4,367,442	2,083,040	Track & field (outdoor)	15,016	491,822
1978-79	3,709,512	1,854,400	Baseball	14,791	450,513
1979-80	3,517,829	1,750,264	Soccer	9,746	332,750
1980-81	3,503,124	1,853,789	Wrestling	9,404	244,984
1981-82	3,409,081	1,810,671	Cross country.	12,245	188,420
1982-83	3,355,558	1,779,972	Golf	12,812	161,757
1983-84	3,303,599	1,747,346	Tennis.	9,767	143,650
1984-85	3,354,284	1,757,884	Swimming & diving	5,396	88,811
1985-86	3,344,275	1,807,121	FEMALE		
1986-87	3,364,082	1,836,356			
1987-88	3,425,777	1,849,684	Basketball	16,756	452,728
1988-89	3,416,844	1,839,352	Track & field (outdoor)	14,789	415,666
1989-90	3,398,192	1,858,659	Volleyball.	13,761	390,814
1990-91	3,406,355	1,892,316	Softball (fast pitch).	12,947	350,197
1991-92	3,429,853	1,940,801	Soccer	8,934	292,086
1992-93	3,416,389	1,997,489	Tennis.	9,606	164,282
1993-94	3,472,967	2,130,315	Cross country.	11,736	158,516
1994-95	3,536,359	2,240,461	Swimming & diving	5,733	139,601
1995-96	3,634,052	2,367,936	Competitive spirit squads	3,262	88,561
1996-97	3,706,225	2,474,043	Golf	1,613	60,918
1997-98	3,763,120	2,570,333			
1998-99	3,832,352	2,652,726			
1999-00	3,861,749	2,675,874			
2000-01	3,921,069	2,784,154			

[1] A participant is counted in the number of sports participated in.   [2] Ten most popular sports for each sex in terms of number of participants.

Source: National Federation of State High School Associations, Indianapolis, IN, *The 2000-2001 High School Athletics Participation Survey* (copyright).

No. 1229. Participation in NCAA Sports: 2000-01

Sport	Males			Females		
	Teams	Athletes	Average squad	Teams	Athletes	Average squad
Total [1]	7,832	208,866	(X)	8,414	150,916	(X)
Baseball	838	25,542	30.5	(X)	(X)	(X)
Basketball	967	15,706	16.2	995	14,439	14.5
Bowling [2]	1	16	16	23	197	8.6
Cross country	817	10,626	13	874	11,721	13.4
Equestrian [2]	8	110	13.8	40	1,048	26.2
Fencing [3]	37	642	17.4	45	670	14.9
Field hockey	(X)	(X)	(X)	239	5,152	21.6
Football	603	56,804	94.2	(X)	(X)	(X)
Golf	717	7,639	10.7	402	3,256	8.1
Gymnastics	24	367	15.3	89	1,397	15.7
Ice hockey [4]	129	3,758	29.1	60	1,319	22
Lacrosse	202	6,591	32.6	229	5,070	22.1
Rifle [3]	33	357	10.8	39	248	6.4
Rowing [5]	48	1,560	32.5	132	6,111	46.3
Sailing [2]	17	239	14.1	(X)	(X)	(X)
Skiing [3]	40	552	13.8	44	526	11.9
Soccer	710	18,093	25.2	824	18,548	22.5
Softball [2]	(X)	(X)	(X)	850	15,041	17.7
Squash [2]	20	350	17.5	25	361	14.4
Swimming/diving . . . . . . [4] .	370	7,265	19.6	454	10,108	22.3
Synchronized swimming [4] . .	(X)	(X)	(X)	8	116	14.5
Tennis	745	7,376	9.9	852	8,231	9.7
Track, indoor	525	17,086	32.5	564	15,962	28.3
Track, outdoor	638	20,271	31.8	673	18,339	27.3
Volleyball	73	1,055	14.4	947	12,978	13.7
Water polo	44	879	20	45	954	21.2
Wrestling	225	5,966	26.5	(X)	(X)	(X)

X Not applicable.   [1] Includes other sports, not shown separately.   [2] Sport recognized by the NCAA but does not have an NCAA championship.   [3] Co-ed championship sport.   [4] Sport recognized by the NCAA but does not have an NCAA championship for women.   [5] Sport recognized by the NCAA but does not have an NCAA championship for men.
Source: The National Collegiate Athletic Association (NCAA), Indianapolis, IN, 2000-01 Participation Study.

No. 1230. Participants in Wildlife Related Recreation Activities: 2001

[Preliminary. In thousands (37,805 represents 37,805,000). For persons 16 years old and over engaging in activity at least once in 2001. Based on survey and subject to sampling error; see source for details]

Participant	Number	Days of participation	Trips	Participant	Number	Days of participation
Total sportsmen [1]	37,805	785,762	636,787	Wildlife watchers [1]	66,105	(X)
Total anglers	34,067	557,394	436,662	Nonresidential [2]	21,823	372,006
Freshwater	28,439	466,984	365,076	Observe wildlife	20,080	295,345
Excluding Great Lakes .	27,913	443,247	349,188	Photograph wildlife . .	9,427	76,324
Great Lakes	1,847	23,138	15,888	Feed wildlife	7,077	103,307
Saltwater	9,051	90,838	71,586			
				Residential [3]	62,928	(X)
Total hunters	13,034	228,368	200,125	Observe wildlife	42,111	(X)
Big game	10,911	153,191	114,445	Photograph wildlife . .	13,937	(X)
Small game	5,434	60,142	46,450	Feed wild birds [4]	53,988	(X)
Migratory birds	2,956	29,310	24,155	Visit public parks	10,981	(X)
Other animals	1,047	19,207	15,074	Maintain plantings or .		
				natural areas	13,072	(X)

X Not applicable.   [1] Detail does not add to total due to multiple responses and nonresponse.   [2] Persons taking a trip of at least 1 mile for activity.   [3] Activity within 1 mile of home.   [4] Or other wildlife.

No. 1231. Expenditures for Wildlife Related Recreation Activities: 2001

[Preliminary. See headnote, Table 1230. (35,632 represents $35,632,000,000)]

Type of expenditure	Fishing			Hunting			Wildlife watching		
		Spenders			Spenders			Spenders	
	Expenditures (mil. dol.)	Number (1,000)	Percent of anglers	Expenditures (mil. dol.)	Number (1,000)	Percent of hunters	Expenditures (mil. dol.)	Number (1,000)	Percent of watchers
Total [1]	35,632	31,946	94	20,611	12,585	97	39,991	52,083	79
Food and lodging	5,881	25,603	75	2,450	10,073	77	4,818	15,365	70
Food	4,141	25,406	75	1,980	10,057	77	2,836	15,263	70
Lodging	1,740	6,473	19	469	1,701	13	1,983	5,648	26
Transportation	3,516	25,146	74	1,789	10,502	81	2,596	17,091	78
Public	400	1,254	4	186	452	3	702	1,986	9
Private	3,115	24,816	73	1,603	10,421	80	1,893	16,495	76
Other trip-related costs . . .	5,259	25,658	75	1,013	3,479	27	748	6,350	29
Sport specific equipment [2] .	4,617	21,224	62	4,562	9,516	73	7,354	45,802	69
Auxiliary equipment [3]	721	4,347	13	1,203	4,584	35	717	3,807	6
Special equipment [4]	11,625	2,319	7	4,597	573	4	17,046	1,410	2
Other expenditures [5]	4,013	(NA)	(NA)	4,998	(NA)	(NA)	6,712	(NA)	(NA)

NA Not available.   [1] Total not adjusted for multiple responses or nonresponse.   [2] Items owned primarily for each specific activity, such as rods and reels for fishing and guns and rifles for hunting.   [3] Equipment such as camping gear owned for wildlife-associated recreation.   [4] "Big ticket" equipment such as campers and boats owned for wildlife-associated recreation.   [5] Books, magazines, membership dues and contributions, land leasing and ownership, licenses and plantings.
Source of Tables 1230 and 1231: U.S. Fish and Wildlife Service, 2001 National Survey of Fishing, Hunting, and Wildlife Associated Recreation, May 2002.

Arts, Entertainment, and Recreation   759

No. 1232. Sporting Goods Sales by Product Category: 1990 to 2001

[In millions of dollars (50,725 represents $50,725,000,000), except percent. Based on a sample survey of consumer purchases of 80,000 households, (100,000 beginning 1995), except recreational transport, which was provided by industry associations. Excludes Alaska and Hawaii. Minus sign (-) indicates decrease]

Selected product category	1990	1994	1995	1996	1997	1998	1999	2000	2001, proj.
Sales, all products	50,725	56,162	59,794	62,818	67,333	69,848	71,161	74,507	74,403
Annual percent change [1]	(NA)	8.2	6.5	5.1	7.2	3.7	1.9	4.7	-0.1
Percent of retail sales	(NA)	2.6	2.6	2.6	2.7	2.7	2.5	2.4	2.3
Athletic and sport clothing [2]	10,130	9,521	10,311	11,127	12,035	12,844	10,307	11,072	11,570
Athletic and sport footwear [2]	11,654	11,120	11,415	12,815	13,319	13,068	12,546	13,026	13,593
Aerobic shoes	611	356	372	401	380	334	275	292	289
Basketball shoes	918	867	999	1,192	1,134	1,000	821	786	834
Cross training shoes	679	1,101	1,191	1,417	1,450	1,402	1,364	1,528	1,605
Golf shoes	226	238	225	231	239	220	208	226	235
Gym shoes, sneakers	2,536	1,869	1,741	1,996	1,980	2,010	1,936	1,871	1,927
Jogging and running shoes	1,110	1,069	1,043	1,132	1,482	1,469	1,502	1,638	1,720
Tennis shoes	740	556	480	541	545	515	505	533	549
Walking shoes	2,950	2,543	2,841	3,079	3,236	3,192	3,099	3,317	3,483
Athletic and sport equipment [2]	14,439	17,966	18,809	18,988	19,033	19,192	20,343	21,373	21,931
Archery	265	306	287	276	270	255	262	254	262
Baseball and softball	217	295	251	277	290	304	329	319	332
Billiards and pool	192	313	304	271	242	347	354	359	363
Camping	1,072	1,017	1,205	1,127	1,153	1,204	1,265	1,344	1,397
Exercise equipment	1,824	2,781	2,960	3,232	2,968	3,233	3,396	3,643	3,825
Fishing tackle	1,910	1,951	2,010	1,970	1,891	1,903	1,917	2,030	2,152
Golf	2,514	2,747	3,194	3,560	3,703	3,658	3,567	3,744	3,894
Hunting and firearms	2,202	3,523	3,003	2,521	2,562	2,200	2,437	2,256	2,211
In-line skating and wheel sports	150	545	646	590	562	509	473	1,074	860
Optics	438	503	655	673	690	710	718	729	736
Skin diving and scuba	294	322	328	340	332	345	363	355	362
Skiing, alpine	475	609	562	707	723	718	648	548	575
Tennis	333	313	297	296	319	318	338	378	393
Recreational transport	14,502	17,555	19,259	19,888	22,946	24,743	27,965	29,036	27,309
Bicycles and supplies	2,423	3,470	3,390	3,187	4,860	4,957	4,770	5,131	5,133
Pleasure boats	7,644	7,679	9,064	9,399	10,208	10,539	11,962	13,504	13,497
Recreational vehicles	4,113	5,690	5,895	6,327	6,904	8,364	10,413	9,529	7,781
Snowmobiles	322	715	910	974	975	883	820	872	898

NA Not available. [1] Represents change from immediate prior year. [2] Includes other products not shown separately.

Source: National Sporting Goods Association, Mt. Prospect, IL, *The Sporting Goods Market in 2001*; and prior issues (copyright).

No. 1233. Consumer Purchases of Sporting Goods by Consumer Characteristics: 2000

[In percent. Based on sample survey of consumer purchases of 100,000 households. Excludes Alaska and Hawaii]

Characteristic	Footwear					Equipment					
	Total households	Aerobic shoes	Gym shoes/ sneakers	Jogging/ running shoes	Skateboarding	Walking shoes	Fishing tackle	Camping equipment	Exercise equipment	Hunting equipment	Golf equipment
Total	100	100	100	100	100	100	100	100	100	100	100
Age of user:											
Under 14 years old	20	6	47	14	43	6	4	16	1	3	1
14 to 17 years old	6	5	12	13	33	4	2	9	4	2	6
18 to 24 years old	10	9	6	11	14	4	5	9	3	5	4
25 to 34 years old	13	23	9	20	6	9	22	17	21	26	14
35 to 44 years old	16	27	10	18	2	15	22	18	23	17	18
45 to 64 years old	22	26	12	22	2	41	36	20	38	37	45
65 years old and over	13	4	4	2	-	21	5	3	8	9	12
Multiple ages	-	-	-	-	-	-	4	8	2	1	-
Sex of user:											
Male	49	14	52	55	84	37	86	56	43	86	88
Female	51	86	48	45	16	63	10	31	52	12	12
Both sexes	-	-	-	-	-	-	4	13	5	2	-
Education of household head:											
Less than high school	8	3	6	3	3	6	11	6	3	6	1
High school	24	20	23	15	24	22	27	17	18	31	12
Some college	36	37	40	32	47	38	37	39	33	36	30
College graduate	32	40	31	50	26	34	25	38	46	27	57
Annual household income:											
Under $15,000	17	9	9	5	7	11	12	9	6	13	2
$15,000 to $24,999	13	8	10	8	9	10	12	10	7	8	6
$25,000 to $34,999	13	11	13	10	11	12	11	12	8	11	9
$35,000 to $49,999	16	16	19	16	19	17	10	18	18	16	13
$50,000 to $74,999	19	22	24	24	17	23	21	22	21	25	23
$75,000 to $99,999	12	19	15	18	24	14	18	16	20	12	18
$100,000 and over	10	15	10	19	13	13	16	13	20	15	29

- Represents or rounds to zero.

Source: National Sporting Goods Association, Mt. Prospect, IL, *The Sporting Goods Market in 2000* (copyright).

No. 1234. National Park System—Summary: 1990 to 2000

[For fiscal years ending in year shown, except as noted; see text, Section 9, Federal Government Finances and Employment (986.1 represents $986,100,000). Includes data for five areas in Puerto Rico and Virgin Islands, one area in American Samoa, and one area in Guam]

Item	1990	1994	1995	1996	1997	1998	1999	2000
Finances (mil. dol.): [1]								
Expenditures reported	986.1	1,404.0	1,445.0	1,391.0	1,473.0	1,604.0	1,530.0	1,833.0
Salaries and wages	459.1	627.2	633.0	650.0	683.0	721.0	733.0	799.0
Improvements, maintenance	160.0	222.9	234.0	234.0	246.0	255.0	289.0	299.0
Construction	108.5	205.6	192.0	168.0	188.0	191.0	62.0	215.0
Other	258.5	348.3	386.0	339.0	356.0	437.0	446.0	520.0
Funds available	1,505.5	2,307.7	2,225.0	2,116.0	2,301.0	2,658.0	2,972.0	3,316.0
Appropriations	1,052.5	1,388.8	1,325.0	1,346.0	1,625.0	1,765.0	1,867.0	1,881.0
Other [2]	453.0	918.9	900.0	770.0	676.0	893.0	1,105.0	1,435.0
Revenue from operations	78.6	97.0	106.3	133.2	174.8	202.8	215.3	233.8
Recreation visits (millions): [3]								
All areas	258.7	268.6	269.6	265.8	275.3	286.7	287.1	285.9
National parks [4]	57.7	63.0	64.8	63.1	65.3	64.5	64.3	66.1
National monuments	23.9	23.6	23.5	23.6	24.1	23.6	24.3	23.8
National historical, commemorative, archaeological [5]	57.5	59.5	56.9	59.0	63.0	74.2	72.6	72.2
National parkways	29.1	29.3	31.3	30.9	31.6	32.8	34.6	34.0
National recreation areas [4]	47.2	52.3	53.7	52.6	51.6	53.0	52.8	50.0
National seashores and lakeshores . . .	23.3	24.0	22.5	20.3	22.4	22.6	22.7	22.5
National Capital Parks	7.5	5.4	5.5	6.1	5.1	4.2	3.9	5.4
Recreation overnight stays (millions) [3] . .	17.6	18.3	16.8	16.6	15.8	15.6	15.9	15.4
In commercial lodgings	3.9	3.9	3.8	3.7	3.6	3.6	3.7	3.7
In Park Service campgrounds	7.9	7.6	7.1	6.5	6.3	6.1	6.2	5.9
In backcountry	1.7	2.4	2.2	2.1	2.2	2.1	2.0	1.9
Other	4.2	4.4	3.7	3.7	3.8	3.9	4.1	3.8
Land (1,000 acres): [6]								
Total	76,362	74,905	77,355	77,458	77,457	77,654	78,166	78,153
Parks	46,089	48,111	49,307	49,315	49,384	49,416	49,859	49,785
Recreation areas	3,344	3,351	3,353	3,353	3,329	3,361	3,404	3,388
Other	26,929	23,443	24,695	24,790	24,744	24,877	24,903	24,980
Acquisition, net	21	32	27	98	61	95	44	222

[1] Financial data are those associated with the National Park System. Certain other functions of the National Park Service (principally the activities absorbed from the former Heritage Conservation and Recreation Service in 1981) are excluded. [2] Includes funds carried over from prior years. [3] For calendar year. Includes other areas, not shown separately. [4] For 1990, combined data for North Cascades National Park and two adjacent National Recreation Areas are included in National Parks total. [5] Includes military areas. [6] Federal land only, as of Dec. 31. Federal land acreages, in addition to National Park Service administered lands, also include lands within national park system area boundaries but under the administration of other agencies. Year-to-year changes in the federal lands figures include changes in the acreages of these other lands and hence often differ from "net acquisition."

Source: U.S. National Park Service, Visits, *National Park Statistical Abstract*, annual; and unpublished data. Other data are unpublished.

No. 1235. State Parks and Recreation Areas by State: 2001

[For year ending June 30 (13,030 represents 13,030,000). Data are shown as reported by state park directors. In some states, park agency has under its control forests, fish and wildlife areas, and/or other areas. In other states, agency is responsible for state parks only]

State	Acreage (1,000)	Visitors (1,000) [1]	Revenue Total ($1,000)	Percent of operating expenditures	State	Acreage (1,000)	Visitors (1,000) [1]	Revenue Total ($1,000)	Percent of operating expenditures
United States .	13,030	766,021	690,119	38.9	Missouri	138	17,892	6,995	22.9
					Montana	65	1,340	1,457	27.1
Alabama	50	5,456	25,503	85.5	Nebraska	134	9,898	10,870	58.8
Alaska	3,291	3,662	2,344	42.9	Nevada	133	3,425	1,991	24.8
Arizona	58	2,516	7,153	44.4	New Hampshire . . .	79	6,689	7,480	96.5
Arkansas	50	7,746	13,984	47.0	New Jersey	358	15,064	7,288	20.1
California	1,416	80,306	49,381	17.2	New Mexico	91	4,003	4,394	27.5
Colorado	431	10,528	14,316	58.6	New York	1,158	55,529	63,422	41.9
Connecticut	185	7,453	3,145	25.7	North Carolina	168	11,995	3,624	15.4
Delaware	21	3,189	7,248	35.5	North Dakota	19	1,104	1,183	51.2
Florida	571	18,133	29,893	45.9	Ohio	204	59,369	26,540	41.0
Georgia	79	15,348	20,516	41.3	Oklahoma	72	15,125	23,897	47.2
Hawaii	28	18,665	1,793	27.7	Oregon	95	39,758	16,179	42.8
Idaho	43	2,430	4,061	44.6	Pennsylvania	289	36,436	16,574	21.5
Illinois	287	44,064	5,435	10.6	Rhode Island	9	6,351	3,126	57.7
Indiana	179	17,595	32,081	79.8	South Carolina	80	8,763	15,970	57.4
Iowa	63	15,203	3,130	29.5	South Dakota	102	7,568	7,694	68.3
Kansas	32	7,485	4,379	57.6	Tennessee	143	28,821	30,325	50.3
Kentucky	44	7,831	50,818	65.7	Texas	593	11,540	24,269	47.0
Louisiana	37	1,970	3,690	19.1	Utah	114	6,296	7,929	35.5
Maine	94	2,281	1,843	27.2	Vermont	69	820	5,665	97.7
Maryland	259	9,838	14,750	36.6	Virginia	62	6,011	7,912	43.8
Massachusetts	291	12,282	7,218	21.6	Washington	262	47,774	12,122	28.0
Michigan	351	25,499	29,432	54.6	West Virginia	196	8,026	18,852	60.1
Minnesota	258	8,343	11,351	37.5	Wisconsin	132	15,994	13,246	75.4
Mississippi	24	4,236	6,260	39.7	Wyoming	121	2,372	1,390	29.0

[1] Includes overnight visitors.

Source: National Association of State Park Directors, Tucson, AZ, *2001 Annual Information Exchange*.

No. 1236. Travel by U.S. Residents—Summary: 1994 to 2001

[In millions (564.8 represents 564,800,000), except party size. See headnote, Table 1237]

Type of trip	1994	1995	1996	1997	1998	1999	2000	2001
All travel:								
Total trips [1]	564.8	577.6	575.7	581.9	594.1	580.8	579.9	585.5
Person trips	968.0	994.8	994.2	1,026.6	1,035.6	1,019.6	1,032.7	1,051.6
Party size	1.7	1.7	1.7	1.8	1.7	2.0	2.0	2.0
Auto travel:								
Total trips	386.4	396.2	400.7	402.7	410.5	387.7	386.3	396.1
Person trips	729.9	751.0	758.6	781.2	784.0	752.5	760.5	781.1
Party size	1.9	1.9	1.9	1.9	1.9	2.2	2.2	2.2
Air travel:								
Total trips	136.7	138.6	134.1	136.2	140.8	141.2	141.8	137.1
Person trips	182.0	185.0	180.9	185.8	192.6	195.5	198.0	194.7
Party size	1.3	1.3	1.3	1.4	1.4	1.5	1.5	1.3
Business travel:								
Total trips	168.3	173.9	167.5	165.8	171.7	167.4	161.0	154.5
Person trips	213.0	219.8	212.8	213.5	219.5	214.1	209.4	201.6
Party size	1.3	1.3	1.3	1.3	1.3	1.4	1.4	1.4
Pleasure travel:								
Total trips	335.5	338.5	341.4	347.4	348.1	333.7	336.2	345.7
Person trips	644.7	653.6	656.2	682.7	681.4	658.3	669.3	689.5
Party size	1.9	1.9	1.9	2.0	2.0	2.2	2.2	2.3

[1] Includes other trips (e.g. medical, funerals, weddings), not shown separately.

Source: Travel Industry Association of America, Washington, DC, *TravelScope*, annual (copyright).

No. 1237. Characteristics of Pleasure Trips by U.S. Residents: 1995 to 2001

[338.5 represents 338,500,000. Represents trips to destinations 50 miles or more, one-way, away from home or one or more overnight trips. Based on a monthly mail panel survey of 20,000 U.S. households. For details, see source]

Characteristic	Unit	1995	1997	1998	1999	2000	2001
Total trips	**Millions**	**338.5**	**347.4**	**348.1**	**333.7**	**336.2**	**345.7**
Average household members on trip	Number	1.9	2.0	2.0	2.2	2.2	2.3
Average nights per trip [1]	Number	3.7	3.6	3.6	3.7	3.6	3.6
Traveled primarily by auto/truck/RV rental car	Percent	77	78	77	81	81	81
Traveled primarily by air	Percent	17	16	16	14	15	14
Used a rental car while on trip [2]	Percent	7	7	7	5	5	5
Stayed in a hotel while on trip	Percent	33	33	34	35	35	36
Household income:							
Less than $40,000	Percent	51	47	44	41	38	32
$40,000 or more	Percent	49	53	56	59	62	68

[1] Includes overnight and non overnight stays. [2] As a secondary mode of transportation.

Source: Travel Industry Association of America, Washington, DC, *TravelScope*, annual (copyright).

No. 1238. Domestic Travel Expenditures by State: 2000

[490,263 represents $490,263,000,000. Represents U.S. spending on domestic overnight trips and day trips of 50 miles or more, one way, away from home. Excludes spending by foreign visitors and by U.S. residents in U.S. territories and abroad. Includes travelers' expenditures in Indian casino gaming]

State	Total (mil. dol.)	Share of total (per-cent)	Rank	State	Total (mil. dol.)	Share of total (per-cent)	Rank	State	Total (mil. dol.)	Share of total (per-cent)	Rank
U.S., total	**490,263**	**100.0**	**(X)**	KS	3,582	0.7	38	ND	1,155	0.2	50
				KY	5,206	1.1	29	OH	12,952	2.6	11
AL	5,205	1.1	30	LA	8,503	1.7	19	OK	3,848	0.8	34
AK	1,381	0.3	49	ME	1,928	0.4	43	OR	5,544	1.1	28
AZ	8,869	1.8	18	MD	8,399	1.7	20	PA	14,726	3.0	8
AR	3,794	0.8	37	MA	11,133	2.3	14	RI	1,427	0.3	46
CA	63,700	13.0	1	MI	12,063	2.5	13	SC	6,982	1.4	24
CO	9,320	1.9	17	MN	7,793	1.6	23	SD	1,402	0.3	47
CT	6,780	1.4	26	MS	4,995	1.0	31	TN	9,867	2.0	15
DE	1,051	0.2	51	MO	9,619	2.0	16	TX	32,307	6.6	3
DC	4,439	0.9	32	MT	1,963	0.4	42	UT	3,831	0.8	35
FL	41,692	8.5	2	NE	2,654	0.5	39	VT	1,389	0.3	48
GA	14,269	2.9	9	NV	19,581	4.0	6	VA	13,294	2.7	10
HI	7,810	1.6	22	NH	2,502	0.5	40	WA	8,093	1.7	21
ID	2,198	0.4	41	NJ	14,756	3.0	7	WV	1,721	0.4	44
IL	21,931	4.5	5	NM	3,795	0.8	36	WI	6,793	1.4	25
IN	6,464	1.3	27	NY	29,296	6.0	4	WY	1,554	0.3	45
IA	4,367	0.9	33	NC	12,249	2.5	12				

X Not applicable.

Source: Travel Industry Association of America, Washington, DC, *Impact of Travel on State Economies, 2000* (copyright).

No. 1239. International Travelers and Expenditures: 1990 to 1999

[47,880 represents $47,880,000,000. For coverage, see Table 1240. Some traveler data revised since originally issued]

Year	Travel and passenger fare (mil. dol.)				U.S. net travel and passenger payments (mil. dol.)	U.S. travelers to foreign countries (1,000)	International visitors to the U.S. (1,000)
	Payments by U.S. travelers		Receipts from foreign visitors				
	Total [1]	Expenditures abroad	Total [1]	Travel receipts			
1990	47,880	37,349	58,305	43,007	10,425	44,623	39,363
1991	45,334	35,322	64,239	48,385	18,905	41,566	42,674
1992	49,155	38,552	71,360	54,742	22,205	43,898	47,261
1993	52,123	40,713	74,403	57,875	22,280	44,411	45,779
1994	56,844	43,782	75,414	58,417	18,570	46,450	44,753
1995	59,579	44,916	82,304	63,395	22,725	50,835	43,318
1996	63,887	48,078	90,231	69,809	26,344	52,311	46,489
1997	70,189	52,051	94,294	73,426	24,105	52,944	47,766
1998	76,480	56,509	91,384	71,286	14,904	56,300	46,395
1999	80,756	59,351	94,657	74,881	13,901	57,502	48,491

[1] Includes passenger fares not shown separately.
Source: U.S. Dept. of Commerce, International Trade Administration, Tourism Industries, Internet site <http://www.tinet.ita.doc.gov>.

No. 1240. Foreign Travel: 1990 to 2000

[In thousands (44,623 represents 44,623,000). U.S. travelers cover residents of the United States, its territories and possessions. Foreign travelers to the U.S. include travelers for business and pleasure, international travelers in transit through the United States, and students; excludes travel by international personnel and international businessmen employed in the United States]

Item and area	1990	1994	1995	1996	1997	1998	1999	2000
U.S. travelers to foreign countries. . . .	44,623	46,450	50,835	52,311	52,944	56,300	57,502	60,816
Canada	12,252	12,542	13,005	12,909	13,401	14,893	15,180	15,114
Mexico.	16,381	15,759	18,771	19,616	17,909	18,338	17,743	18,849
Total overseas.	15,990	18,149	19,059	19,786	21,634	23,069	24,579	26,853
Europe	8,043	8,167	8,596	8,706	9,800	11,143	11,577	13,373
Foreign travelers to the U.S.	39,363	44,753	43,317	46,489	47,766	46,396	48,491	50,891
Canada	17,263	14,974	14,662	15,301	15,127	13,422	14,110	14,594
Mexico.	7,041	11,321	8,016	8,530	8,445	9,276	9,915	10,322
Total overseas.	15,059	18,458	20,639	22,658	24,194	23,698	24,466	25,975
Europe	6,659	8,119	8,793	9,727	10,390	10,675	11,243	11,597
South America	1,328	2,112	2,449	2,461	2,831	2,957	2,733	2,941
Central America	412	513	509	524	564	697	731	822
Caribbean	1,137	1,031	1,044	1,133	1,189	1,161	1,258	1,331
Far East	4,360	5,551	6,616	7,500	7,756	6,724	6,935	7,554
Middle East	365	403	454	480	552	587	625	702
Oceania	662	556	588	629	680	639	667	731
Africa	137	173	186	205	234	258	274	295

Source: U.S. Dept. of Commerce, International Trade Administration, Tourism Industries, Internet site <http://www.tinet.ita.doc.gov> (accessed 22 August 2002).

No. 1241. Top States and Cities Visited by Overseas Travelers: 1999 and 2000

[24,466 represents 24,466,000. Includes travelers for business and pleasure, international travelers in transit through the United States, and students; excludes travel by international personnel and international businessmen employed in the United States]

State	Overseas visitors (1,000)		Market share (percent)		City	Overseas visitors (1,000)		Market share (percent)	
	1999	2000	1999	2000		1999	2000	1999	2000
Total overseas travelers [1].	24,466	25,975	100.0	100.0	New York City, NY	5,505	5,714	22.5	22.0
California	6,239	6,364	25.5	24.5	Los Angeles, CA	3,572	3,533	14.6	13.6
Florida	5,798	6,026	23.7	23.2	Orlando, FL	2,863	3,013	11.7	11.6
New York	5,798	5,922	23.7	22.8	Miami, FL.	2,863	2,935	11.7	11.3
Hawaiian Islands	2,740	2,727	11.2	10.5	San Francisco, CA.	2,789	2,831	11.4	10.9
Nevada	2,373	2,364	9.7	9.1	Las Vegas, NV	2,251	2,260	9.2	8.7
Massachusetts.	1,321	1,429	5.4	5.5	Oahu/Honolulu, HI	2,202	2,234	9.0	8.6
Illinois	1,321	1,377	5.4	5.3	Washington, DC	1,297	1,481	5.3	5.7
Guam	1,028	1,325	4.2	5.1	Chicago, IL.	1,272	1,351	5.2	5.2
Texas.	1,052	1,169	4.3	4.5	Boston, MA	1,199	1,325	4.9	5.1
New Jersey.	905	909	3.7	3.5	San Diego, CA	807	701	3.3	2.7
Arizona.	881	883	3.6	3.4	Atlanta, GA.	538	701	2.2	2.7
Georgia	612	805	2.5	3.1	Tampa/St. Petersburg, FL .	489	519	2.0	2.0
Pennsylvania.	538	649	2.2	2.5	San Jose, CA	514	494	2.1	1.9
Colorado.	465	519	1.9	2.0	Anaheim, CA	465	494	1.9	1.9
Michigan.	416	494	1.7	1.9	Dallas/Ft. Worth, TX	416	494	1.7	1.9
Washington.	514	468	2.1	1.8	Ft. Lauderdale, FL	465	468	1.9	1.8
Utah	391	416	1.6	1.6	Houston, TX	416	442	1.7	1.7
North Carolina	294	416	1.2	1.6	Maui, HI.	367	442	1.5	1.7
Louisiana	367	390	1.5	1.5	Seattle, WA	465	416	1.9	1.6
Ohio	367	390	1.5	1.5	Philadelphia, PA	343	390	1.4	1.5
Virginia.	343	364	1.4	1.4	New Orleans, LA	294	364	1.2	1.4
Minnesota.	220	364	0.9	1.4	Detroit, MI	294	338	1.2	1.3

[1] Includes other states and cities, not shown separately.

Source: U.S. Dept. of Commerce, International Trade Administration, Internet site <http://www.tinet.ita.doc.gov> (accessed 22 August 2002).

Arts, Entertainment, and Recreation 763

No. 1242. Impact of International Travel on States Economies: 2000

[Preliminary. (79,265.9 represents $79,265,900,000)]

State	Travel expenditures (mil. dol.)	Travel generated payroll (mil. dol.)	Travel generated employment (1,000)	Travel generated tax receipts (mil. dol.)	State	Travel expenditures (mil. dol.)	Travel generated payroll (mil. dol.)	Travel generated employment (1,000)	Travel generated tax receipts (mil. dol.)
U.S., total...	79,265.9	21,628.8	1,003.8	13,665.5	MO	177.7	49.0	2.6	32.9
AL	90.2	21.0	1.4	12.3	MT	101.4	24.3	2.0	13.8
AK	162.9	67.4	3.0	32.0	NE	63.7	17.7	1.2	11.2
AZ	1,746.9	494.9	25.4	288.2	NV	2,865.2	915.4	41.9	393.3
AR	50.3	13.2	0.9	7.6	NH	122.0	28.8	1.7	14.8
CA	15,079.7	3,999.0	179.1	2,417.1	NJ	933.0	252.6	10.8	188.3
CO	877.5	293.9	14.6	204.2	NM	114.9	27.4	1.9	16.0
CT	211.8	46.9	2.1	34.0	NY	10,271.5	2,793.5	108.1	2,164.9
DE	90.8	21.6	1.2	15.4	NC	584.3	185.3	9.2	107.6
DC	1,961.0	431.8	16.6	288.5	ND	46.4	12.2	1.0	10.7
FL	18,171.9	4,767.7	235.9	2,899.3	OH	620.9	176.5	9.6	121.6
GA	1,246.6	475.1	19.3	318.2	OK	90.1	34.5	1.7	16.0
HI	7,436.1	1,773.4	78.1	1,053.7	OR	371.5	104.5	6.2	61.6
ID	113.6	28.6	1.9	21.1	PA	1,246.2	364.8	17.7	227.4
IL	1,796.4	490.6	22.5	354.2	RI	119.4	26.1	1.5	15.8
IN	244.0	75.6	4.1	45.1	SC	491.8	124.2	7.7	76.3
IA	143.3	35.5	2.5	21.7	SD	40.1	10.7	0.9	5.6
KS	104.9	25.2	1.7	15.8	TN	442.2	197.3	7.7	105.2
KY	130.6	55.2	2.7	28.3	TX	3,751.3	1,162.0	54.3	705.2
LA	514.9	118.4	7.1	72.7	UT	381.1	130.2	8.0	76.5
ME	193.6	44.9	3.2	26.4	VT	144.5	35.5	2.2	20.5
MD	447.3	130.1	5.7	91.3	VA	500.8	151.7	8.1	82.1
MA	2,178.3	564.4	25.1	359.5	WA	909.3	249.4	12.3	172.7
MI	764.7	205.4	11.2	141.5	WV	32.2	8.0	0.5	5.0
MN	620.6	231.0	10.7	195.6	WI	334.4	90.2	6.0	57.9
MS	57.2	26.4	1.4	9.5	WY	75.1	19.7	1.6	9.3

Source: Travel Industry Association of America, Washington, DC, *Impact of Travel on State Economies, 2000* (copyright).

No. 1243. Foreign Visitors for Pleasure Admitted by Country of Last Residence: 1985 to 2000

[In thousands (6,609 represents 6,609,000). For years ending September 30. Represents non-U.S. citizens admitted to the country for a temporary period of time (also known as nonimmigrants)]

Country	1985	1990	1995	2000	Country	1985	1990	1995	2000
All countries [1]	6,609	13,418	17,612	30,511	United Arab Emirates ...	6	7	14	36
					Africa [1]	101	105	137	327
Europe [1]	2,048	5,383	7,012	11,806	South Africa	26	26	59	114
United Kingdom	598	1,899	2,342	4,671	Egypt	16	16	16	44
Germany [2]	373	969	1,550	1,925	Nigeria	25	11	10	27
France	226	566	738	1,113	Oceania [1]	282	562	478	748
Italy	155	308	427	626	Australia	195	380	327	535
Netherlands	82	214	308	559	New Zealand [4]	74	153	115	170
Switzerland	110	236	321	400	North America [1]	1,664	2,463	2,240	6,501
Spain	64	183	248	370	Canada	79	119	127	277
Ireland	55	81	126	325	Mexico	773	1,061	893	3,972
Sweden	71	230	142	321	Caribbean [1]	584	963	831	1,404
Belgium	39	95	153	254	Bahamas, The	211	332	234	377
Austria	34	87	146	182	Jamaica	74	132	130	240
Denmark	36	75	78	150	Dominican Republic	57	137	138	195
Norway	41	80	71	144	Trinidad and Tobago	71	81	64	133
Poland	40	55	36	116	Haiti	56	57	43	72
Finland	24	83	47	95	Barbados	17	34	36	57
Portugal	18	30	40	86	Cayman Islands	18	31	31	53
Russia	(X)	(X)	33	74	Netherlands Antilles	27	31	32	43
Greece	34	43	44	60	British Virgin Islands	4	8	9	31
Hungary	10	15	29	58	Aruba	(Z)	10	19	24
Czech Republic	(X)	(X)	12	44	Central America [1]	228	320	387	792
Iceland	5	10	14	27	Guatemala	53	91	99	177
Asia [1]	1,866	3,830	5,666	7,853	El Salvador	38	46	63	175
Japan	1,277	2,846	3,986	4,946	Costa Rica	41	62	91	172
China [3]	83	187	378	656	Panama	38	43	54	106
Korea	26	120	427	606	Honduras	37	52	37	87
Israel	80	128	160	319	Nicaragua	14	13	28	47
India	52	75	75	253	South America [1]	606	1,016	1,978	2,867
Hong Kong	64	111	162	195	Brazil	148	300	710	706
Philippines	59	76	85	163	Venezuela	122	199	400	570
Singapore	23	32	61	131	Argentina	66	136	320	515
Turkey	9	20	27	93	Colombia	123	122	174	411
Thailand	15	25	59	76	Chile	28	54	117	194
Saudi Arabia	31	33	45	67	Peru	44	97	98	190
Malaysia	19	27	40	64	Ecuador	42	57	77	122
Indonesia	19	28	44	62	Uruguay	7	16	37	66
Pakistan	17	27	27	47	Bolivia	10	14	16	48

X Not applicable. Z Fewer than 500. [1] Includes other countries and countries unknown, not shown separately. [2] Data for 1985 and 1990 are for former West Germany. [3] Includes People's Republic of China and Taiwan. [4] Prior to fiscal year 1995, data for Niue are included in New Zealand.

Source: U.S. Immigration and Naturalization Service, *Statistical Yearbook, 2000,* annual. Internet site <http://www.ins.usdoj.gov/graphics/aboutins/statistics/ybpage.htm> (accessed 23 August 2002).

This section presents statistics relating to services other than those covered in the previous few sections (22 to 26) on domestic trade, transportation, communications, financial services, and recreation services. Data shown for the services are classified by kind of business and cover sales or receipts, establishments, employees, payrolls, and other items. The principal sources of these data are from the Census Bureau and include the *1997 Economic Census* reports, annual surveys, and the *County Business Patterns* program. These data are supplemented by data from several sources such as the National Restaurant Association on food and drink sales (Table 1250), the American Hotel & Motel Association on lodging (Table 1248), and McCann-Erickson, Inc. and Publishers Information Bureau on advertising (Tables 1253 and 1254, respectively).

Data on these services also appear in several other sections. For instance, labor force employment and earnings data (Table 603) appear in Section 12, Labor Force; gross domestic product of the industry (Table 632) appear in Section 13, Income, Expenditures, and Wealth; and financial data (several tables) from the quarterly *Statistics of Income Bulletin,* published by the Internal Revenue Service, appear in Section 15, Business Enterprise.

Censuses—Limited coverage of the services industries started in 1933. Beginning with the 1967 census, legislation provides for a census of each area to be conducted every 5 years (for years ending in "2" and "7"). For more information on the most current census, see the *History of the 1997 Economic Census* found at <http://www.census.gov/prod/ec97/pol00-hec.pdf>. The industries covered in the censuses and surveys of business are those classified in 13 sectors defined in the *North American Industry Classification System,* called NAICS (see below). All Census Bureau tables in this section are utilizing the new NAICS codes, which replaced the Standard Industrial Classification (SIC) system. NAICS makes substantial structural improvements and identifies over 350 new industries. At the same time, it causes breaks in time series far more profound than any prior revision of the previously used SIC system. For information on this system and how it affects the comparability of statistics historically, see text, Section 15, Business Enterprise, and especially the Census Web site at <http://www.census.gov/epcd/www/naics.html>.

The *Accommodation and Food Services sector* (NAICS sector 72) comprises establishments providing customers with lodging and/or prepared meals, snacks, and beverages for immediate consumption. The *Other Services (Except Public Administration) sector* (NAICS sector 81) covers establishments with payroll engaged in providing services not specifically provided for elsewhere in the NAICS. Establishments in this sector are primarily engaged in activities such as repair and maintenance of equipment and machinery, personal and laundry services, and religious, grantmaking, civic, professional, and similar organizations. Establishments providing death care services, pet care services, photofinishing services, temporary parking services, and dating services are also included. Private households that employ workers on or about the premises in activities primarily concerned with the operation of the household are included in this sector but are not included in the scope of the census. In general, the 1997 Economic Census has two series of publications and documents for these two sectors: 1) subject series with reports on such as commodity line sales and establishment and firm sizes and 2) geographic reports with individual reports for each state. For information on these series, see the Census Web site at <http://www.census.gov/epcd/www/97EC72.htm> and <http://www.census.gov/epcd/www/97EC81.htm>.

Current surveys—The Service Annual Survey provides annual estimates of nationwide receipts for selected personal, business, leasing and repair, amusement and entertainment, social and health, and other professional service industries in the United States. For selected accommodation, social, health, and other professional service industries, separate estimates are developed for receipts of taxable firms and revenue and expenses for firms and organizations exempt from federal income taxes. Several service sectors from this survey are covered in other sections of this publication. The estimates for tax exempt firms in these industries are derived from a sample of employer firms only. Estimates obtained from annual and monthly surveys are based on sample data and are not expected to agree exactly with results that would be obtained from a complete census of all establishments. Data include estimates for sampling units not reporting.

Statistical reliability—For a discussion of statistical collection and estimation, sampling procedures, and measures of statistical reliability applicable to Census Bureau data, see Appendix III.

Figure 27.1
Advertising Expenditures: 1990 to 2001

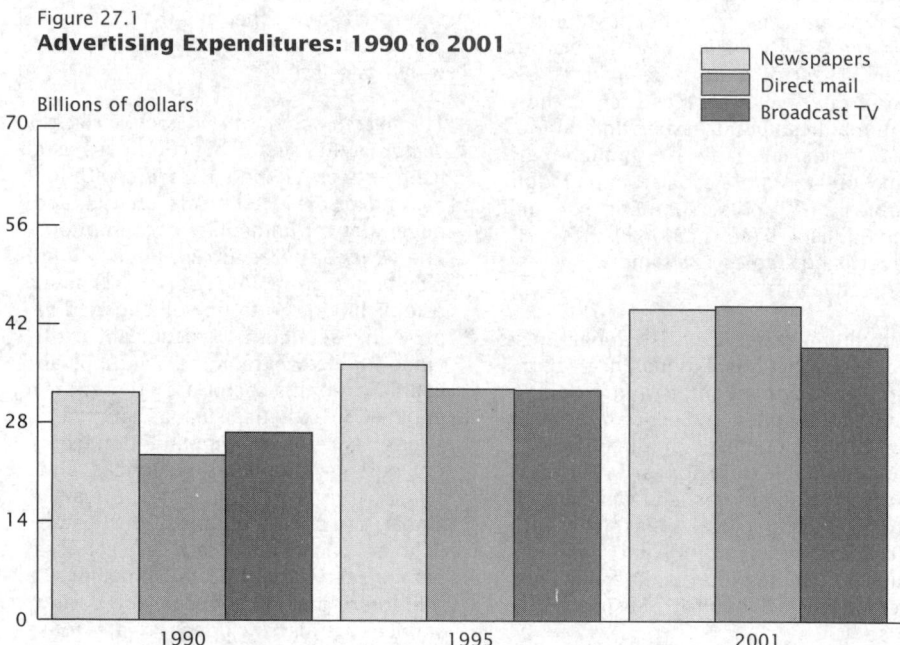

Source: Chart prepared by U.S. Census Bureau. For data, see Table 1253.

U.S. Census Bureau, Statistical Abstract of the United States: 2002

No. 1244. Service-Related Industries—Establishments, Employees, and Payroll by Industry: 1999 and 2000

[7,008 represents 7,008,000. Covers establishments with payroll. Employees are for the week including March 12. Excludes most government employees, railroad employees, and self-employed persons. Kind-of-business classification based on North American Industry Classification System (NAICS); see text, Section 15, Business Enterprise. For statement on methodology, see Appendix III]

Kind of business	NAICS code	Establishments (1,000)		Employees (1,000)		Payroll (bil. dol.)	
		1999	2000	1999	2000	1999	2000
All industries, total	(X)	7,008	7,070	110,706	114,065	3,555	3,879
Service-related industries, total	(X)	3,790	3,842	59,049	61,662	1,752	1,740
Transportation & warehousing	48-49	187	190	3,627	3,790	117	126
Air transportation	481	5	5	583	616	24	27
Water transportation	483	2	2	72	68	3	3
Truck transportation	484	109	110	1,384	1,416	44	46
Transit & ground passenger transportation	485	16	16	370	387	7	7
Pipeline transportation	486	3	3	48	53	3	4
Scenic & sightseeing transportation.	487	2	2	23	24	1	1
Transportation support activities	488	31	31	440	472	15	17
Couriers & messengers.	492	12	12	578	619	17	17
Warehousing & storage.	493	7	7	129	136	4	4
Information.	51	127	134	3,235	3,546	170	209
Publishing industries.	511	32	33	1,005	1,081	55	75
Motion picture & sound recording industries	512	23	23	293	304	11	12
Broadcasting & telecommunications	513	51	55	1,504	1,632	76	89
Information & data processing services	514	20	23	432	529	29	34
Real estate & rental & leasing.	53	298	300	1,874	1,942	54	59
Real estate	531	231	235	1,226	1,280	37	40
Rental & leasing services	532	65	63	622	636	16	17
Lessors of other nonfinancial intangible asset . . .	533	2	2	26	26	1	2
Professional, scientific, & technical services	54	705	723	6,432	6,816	311	362
Professional, scientific, & technical services	541	705	723	6,432	6,816	311	362
Legal services	5411	177	177	1,082	1,089	57	62
Accounting/tax prep/bookkeep/payroll services. .	5412	99	100	1,094	1,164	33	38
Architectural, engineering & related services . .	5413	103	102	1,213	1,213	60	65
Specialized design services	5414	28	28	131	140	5	6
Computer systems design & related services. . .	5415	94	100	1,013	1,171	66	85
Management, sci & tech consulting services . . .	5416	91	97	660	712	39	44
Scientific R&D services	5417	12	13	338	359	20	25
Advertising & related services.	5418	40	40	443	472	20	23
Oth professional/scientific/technical svc	5419	60	65	459	496	12	14
Management of companies & enterprises.	55	47	47	2,788	2,874	192	211
Admin/support waste mgt/remediation services . .	56	350	352	8,367	9,138	183	210
Administrative & support services [1]	561	334	336	8,079	8,847	173	200
Employment services	5613	41	42	3,993	4,573	81	98
Temporary help services.	66132	27	28	2,726	3,013	51	59
Business support services	5614	35	35	671	702	15	17
Travel arrangement & reservation services	5615	35	33	301	308	9	10
Waste management & remediation services	562	16	16	287	291	10	11
Educational services	61	66	68	2,432	2,532	57	62
Health care & social assistance	62	650	659	13,865	14,109	409	431
Ambulatory health care services	621	456	459	4,466	4,566	170	180
Hospitals	622	7	7	5,001	5,015	163	170
Nursing & residential care facilities	623	62	63	2,568	2,592	47	50
Social assistance.	624	126	129	1,830	1,936	28	31
Arts, entertainment, & recreation.	71	103	104	1,640	1,741	39	43
Perform arts, spectator sports, and related ind [1] . .	711	33	34	330	352	17	19
Performing arts companies.	7111	9	9	122	126	3	3
Spectator sports.	7112	4	4	91	100	8	9
Museums, historical sites, & like institutions . . .	712	6	6	105	110	2	3
Amusement, gambling, & recreation industries [1] . .	713	64	64	1,205	1,279	20	22
Gambling industries	7132	2	2	179	203	4	5
Accommodation & food services.	72	540	542	9,638	9,881	117	126
Accommodation [1].	721	59	60	1,738	1,768	32	35
Traveler accommodation	7211	49	50	1,685	1,714	31	34
RV parks & recreational camps.	7212	7	7	37	38	1	1
Food services & drinking places	722	480	483	7,900	8,113	85	91
Full-service restaurants	7221	191	192	3,788	3,897	43	47
Limited-service eating places	7222	211	211	3,319	3,385	31	33
Special food services	7223	27	29	469	502	7	7
Drinking places (alcoholic beverages).	7224	51	51	325	329	3	3
Other services (except public administration). . . .	81	718	723	5,151	5,293	102	110
Repair & maintenance [1]	811	235	233	1,318	1,334	34	37
Automotive R&M	8111	165	164	843	856	19	21
Electronic & precision equipment R&M.	8112	16	15	142	144	5	7
Personal and laundry services	812	195	199	1,261	1,293	22	23
Religious/grantmaking/prof/like organizations. . . .	813	288	291	2,572	2,666	46	50

X Not applicable. [1] Includes other kinds of business not shown separately.

Source: U.S. Census Bureau, *County Business Patterns*, annual. See also <http://www.census.gov/epcd/cbp/view/cbpview.html>.

Accommodation, Food Services, and Other Services 767

No. 1245. Service-Related Industries—Establishments, Employees, and Annual Payroll by State: 2000

[Covers establishments with payroll. Employees are for the week including March 12. Excludes most government employees, railroad employees, and self-employed persons. Kind-of-business classification based on North American Industry Classification System (NAICS); see text, Section 15, Business Enterprise. For statement on methodology, see Appendix III]

State	Professional, scientific, & technical services (NAICS 54)			Admin/support waste mgt/remediation services (NAICS 56)			Accommodation and food services (NAICS 72)		
	Estab-lish-ments	Employ-ees	Annual payroll (mil. dol.)	Estab-lish-ments	Employ-ees	Annual payroll (mil. dol.)	Estab-lish-ments	Employ-ees	Annual payroll (mil. dol.)
United States..	722,698	6,816,216	362,008	351,528	9,138,100	210,281	542,411	9,880,923	125,582
Alabama.........	8,221	72,572	3,056	3,958	124,939	2,188	6,885	129,601	1,258
Alaska..........	1,629	10,918	527	930	10,280	319	1,766	21,402	378
Arizona.........	12,259	113,687	4,566	6,859	200,421	4,295	9,283	202,756	2,477
Arkansas	4,816	32,262	1,028	2,236	59,870	1,009	4,421	75,968	712
California	94,060	1,061,160	64,840	41,154	1,161,377	28,402	63,206	1,111,310	15,688
Colorado........	17,570	138,730	8,048	7,282	176,492	4,496	10,195	201,654	2,586
Connecticut......	10,183	93,567	5,857	5,398	105,808	2,813	6,757	97,850	1,420
Delaware	2,169	18,090	968	1,183	29,887	635	1,560	26,522	386
District of Columbia .	4,211	77,111	5,964	1,124	31,153	920	1,644	42,710	917
Florida	50,697	380,240	17,071	27,194	911,443	18,478	28,317	599,197	7,867
Georgia	21,832	202,537	10,598	10,564	330,441	7,481	14,432	295,906	3,533
Hawaii	2,751	18,804	788	1,696	33,498	724	3,021	84,935	1,645
Idaho..........	2,968	25,582	1,002	1,664	26,955	453	2,872	44,657	432
Illinois	35,182	355,199	20,176	15,793	488,513	11,729	23,423	406,601	5,136
Indiana.........	11,333	90,126	3,265	6,737	153,442	3,262	11,698	221,882	2,308
Iowa	5,513	38,618	1,300	3,208	64,275	1,207	6,527	105,078	995
Kansas.........	6,424	53,304	2,057	3,307	69,926	1,389	5,536	97,071	927
Kentucky	7,173	54,483	1,827	3,609	81,575	1,411	6,592	136,151	1,456
Louisiana	10,067	76,375	2,791	4,195	100,273	1,960	7,263	161,533	1,886
Maine..........	3,098	20,695	794	1,716	26,937	604	3,651	43,356	578
Maryland	16,557	192,610	10,390	7,259	170,918	4,124	8,849	166,041	2,117
Massachusetts.....	21,103	232,109	16,877	9,467	209,131	6,023	14,580	238,108	3,485
Michigan........	21,311	208,560	9,887	11,713	315,030	7,932	18,610	325,162	3,495
Minnesota........	14,910	122,574	6,371	6,636	157,529	4,646	9,904	191,401	2,188
Mississippi	4,162	26,724	914	2,120	51,020	805	4,161	99,374	1,232
Missouri	12,278	119,221	5,381	6,632	148,457	2,881	10,899	211,839	2,385
Montana........	2,592	14,727	435	1,225	12,440	199	3,144	38,619	384
Nebraska	3,636	32,705	1,354	2,367	53,539	1,200	3,964	62,687	588
Nevada	5,563	40,793	1,824	3,193	65,058	1,642	3,907	278,651	6,461
New Hampshire....	3,856	24,267	1,244	1,879	41,323	1,021	3,027	48,566	627
New Jersey.......	30,103	262,672	15,885	13,147	299,523	7,432	16,443	255,132	4,326
New Mexico	4,179	37,349	1,689	1,796	35,510	794	3,677	67,997	732
New York	52,847	535,845	33,951	22,954	516,806	14,287	37,663	499,707	8,022
North Carolina....	17,653	149,863	6,591	10,092	230,790	4,793	15,065	275,353	3,046
North Dakota.....	1,247	9,081	260	761	10,626	198	1,730	25,740	228
Ohio	23,700	229,546	10,011	13,659	358,907	7,038	22,408	416,901	4,301
Oklahoma........	7,969	52,662	1,947	3,700	85,377	1,600	6,329	111,952	1,047
Oregon..........	9,600	66,901	3,030	4,664	85,973	1,903	8,424	127,030	1,540
Pennsylvania......	26,830	295,444	15,577	13,509	298,970	6,581	24,039	374,828	4,152
Rhode Island.....	2,742	18,152	776	1,608	30,281	671	2,597	36,732	463
South Carolina.....	7,865	60,460	2,448	4,672	146,915	2,896	7,988	153,905	1,695
South Dakota	1,509	8,298	246	853	9,658	147	2,189	31,188	295
Tennessee	9,919	95,083	4,060	6,253	187,636	3,799	9,630	197,957	2,249
Texas...........	48,854	445,044	23,499	22,507	793,625	19,913	34,990	707,597	8,457
Utah	5,390	50,856	2,096	2,715	101,852	1,967	3,884	79,987	817
Vermont.........	1,922	11,160	434	892	9,158	217	1,849	29,154	341
Virginia.........	21,210	287,437	16,811	9,195	237,626	5,358	12,531	246,896	2,976
Washington.......	16,044	136,540	7,116	7,887	131,871	3,426	13,051	201,736	2,630
West Virginia.....	2,869	20,135	574	1,423	26,019	509	3,238	52,550	542
Wisconsin........	10,652	89,025	3,616	6,205	123,292	2,410	12,855	197,751	1,909
Wyoming........	1,470	6,313	192	738	5,735	100	1,737	24,242	271

Source: U.S. Census Bureau, *County Business Patterns,* annual. See also <http://www.census.gov/epcd/cbp/view/cbpview.html>.

U.S. Census Bureau, Statistical Abstract of the United States: 2002

No. 1246. Service-Related Industries—Nonemployer Establishments and Receipts by Kind of Business: 1997 to 1999

[2,650 represents 2,650,000. Includes only firms subject to federal income tax. Nonemployers are businesses with no paid employees. Based on the North American Industry Classification System (NAICS), see text, Section 15, Business Enterprise]

Kind of business	NAICS code	Establishments (1,000)			Receipts (mil. dol.)		
		1997	1998	1999	1997	1998	1999
Professional, scientific & technical services....	54	2,650	2,415	2,388	81,165	83,081	85,443
Management, sci & tech consulting services .	5416	564	427	392	17,374	16,367	16,350
Admin/support waste mgt/remediation services .	56	892	925	990	16,975	19,237	21,777
Administrative & support services.........	561	872	908	974	16,230	18,407	20,919
Accommodation & food services...........	72	191	198	210	9,035	11,757	12,594
Accommodation	721	48	48	50	2,936	3,142	3,310
Food services & drinking places	722	143	151	160	6,098	8,615	9,284
Other services (except public administration) [1]..	81	1,936	2,209	2,293	43,299	48,438	51,876
Repair & maintenance [1]	811	565	599	619	17,732	19,044	20,245
Automotive R&M	8111	274	266	265	10,212	10,634	11,091
Personal & household goods R&M	8114	200	239	257	4,662	5,261	5,775
Personal & laundry services	812	1,350	1,451	1,512	25,161	27,037	29,226
Personal care services	8121	519	549	574	8,961	9,726	10,670

[1] Includes other kinds of business not shown separately.

Source: U.S. Census Bureau, "Nonemployer Statistics"; published 28 March 2002; <http://www.census.gov/epcd/nonemployer/>.

No. 1247. Selected Service Industries—E-Commerce Revenue: 1999 and 2000

[25,285 represents $25,285,000,000. Includes data only for businesses with paid employees, except for accommodation and food services, which also includes businesses with and without paid employees. Except as noted, based on the Service Annual Survey.

Kind of business	NAICS code [1]	E-commerce revenue (mil. dol.)		E-commerce as percent of total revenue, 2000	E-commerce revenue, percent distribution, 2000
		1999	2000		
Selected service industries, total	(X)	25,285	37,312	0.8	100
Selected transportation and warehousing [2]	48-49	3,019	3,691	1.6	9.9
Information	51	5,214	9,305	1.1	24.9
Publishing industries	511	3,069	4,748	2.0	12.7
Online information services..................	51419	1,020	1,997	6.4	5.4
Selected finance [3]	52	3,996	5,976	1.7	16.0
Securities and commodity contracts intermediation and brokerage	5231	3,831	5,664	2.3	15.2
Rental and leasing services	532	(S)	(S)	(S)	(S)
Selected professional, scientific, and technical services [4]	54	4,127	5,550	0.7	14.9
Computer systems design and related services	5415	2,869	3,541	2.0	9.5
Selected administrative and support and waste management and remediation services [5]	56	6,990	9,680	2.4	25.9
Health care and social assistance services	62	(S)	(S)	(S)	(S)
Arts, entertainment, and recreation services	71	(S)	(S)	(S)	(S)
Accommodation and food services [6]	72	(S)	(S)	(S)	(S)
Selected other services [7].....................	81	364	554	0.2	1.5

S Data do not meet publication standards because of high sampling variability or poor response quality. X Not applicable. [1] North American Industry Classification System; see text Section 15, Business Enterprise. [2] Excludes NAICS 481 (air transportation), 482 (rail transportation), 483 (water transportation), 485 (transit and ground passenger transportation), 487 (scenic and sightseeing transportation), 488 (support activities for transportation) and 491 (postal service). [3] Excludes NAICS 521 (monetary authorities-central bank), 522 (credit intermediation and related activities), 5232 (securities and commodity exchanges), NAICS 52391 (miscellaneous intermediation), 52399 (all other financial investment activities), 524 (insurance carriers and related activities) and 525 (funds and trusts). [4] Excludes NAICS 54112 (offices of notaries) and 54132 (landscape architectural services). [5] Excludes NAICS 56173 (landscaping services). [6] Based on Annual Retail Trade Survey. [7] Excludes NAICS 81311 (religious organizations), 81393 (labor and similar organizations), 81394 (political organizations) and 814 (private households).

Source: U.S. Census Bureau, "E-Stats"; published 18 March 2002; <http://www.census.gov/eos/www/ebusiness614.htm>.

No. 1248. Lodging Industry Summary: 1990 to 2000

Year	Average occupancy rate (percent)	Average room rate (dol.)	Room size of property	2000		Item	2000	
				Establishments	Rooms (mil.)		Business traveler	Leisure traveler
1990	63.3	57.96	Total	53,500	4.1	Typical night:		
1993	63.6	60.53				Made reservations .	91%	83%
1994	65.2	62.86	Percent:			Amount paid......	$91.00	$84.00
1995	65.5	66.65	Under 75 rooms...	51.5	22.5			
1996	65.2	70.93	75-149 rooms	33.5	35.1	Length of stay:		
1997	64.5	75.31	150-299 rooms ...	10.9	21.3	One night	36%	43%
1998	64.0	78.62	300-500 rooms ...	2.8	9.9	Two nights	25%	28%
1999	63.2	81.33	Over 500 rooms...	1.3	11.2	Three or more	39%	29%
2000	63.7	85.89						

Source: American Hotel & Motel Association, Washington, DC, Lodging Industry Profile (copyright).

No. 1249. Accommodation and Food Services—Establishments, Employees, and Payroll by Kind of Business: 1999 and 2000

[9,638.0 represents 9,638,000. Covers establishments with payroll. Employees are for the week including March 12. Excludes most government employees, railroad employees, and self-employed persons. Kind-of-business classification based on North American Industry Classification System (NAICS); see text, Section 15, Business Enterprise. For statement on methodology, see Appendix III]

Kind of business	NAICS code	Establishments (number)		Employees (1,000)		Payroll (mil. dol.)	
		1999	2000	1999	2000	1999	2000
Accommodation & food services, total	72	539,576	542,411	9,638.0	9,880.9	116,925	125,582
Accommodation	721	59,278	59,851	1,737.7	1,767.8	32,200	34,708
Traveler accommodation	7211	48,962	49,736	1,685.5	1,714.1	31,220	33,661
Hotels (exc casino hotels) & motels	72111	44,832	45,554	1,364.3	1,378.8	23,290	25,181
Casino hotels	72112	279	288	298.9	311.6	7,635	8,143
Other traveler accommodation	72119	3,851	3,894	22.3	23.7	295	337
Bed & breakfast inns	721191	3,000	2,999	18.2	19.0	229	254
All other traveler accommodation	721199	851	895	4.1	4.6	67	83
RV parks & recreational camps	7212	7,123	6,975	37.1	38.1	796	843
RV parks & campgrounds	721211	3,783	3,691	17.5	17.7	326	334
Recreational/vacation camps (exc campgrounds)	721214	3,340	3,284	19.7	20.4	471	509
Rooming & boarding houses	7213	3,193	3,140	15.1	15.6	184	204
Food services & drinking places	722	480,298	482,560	7,900.3	8,113.1	84,725	90,874
Full-service restaurants	7221	190,788	192,342	3,788.1	3,897.1	43,411	46,707
Limited-service eating places	7222	210,920	210,895	3,318.5	3,385.5	31,475	33,454
Limited-service restaurants	722211	170,421	170,565	2,924.6	2,967.9	27,468	28,852
Cafeterias	722212	4,250	4,199	74.3	69.9	871	875
Snack & nonalcoholic beverage bars	722213	36,249	36,131	319.7	347.7	3,137	3,728
Special food services	7223	27,413	28,745	468.8	501.9	6,701	7,367
Food service contractors	72231	16,455	16,894	356.7	377.5	5,187	5,632
Caterers	72232	8,171	8,714	99.3	108.6	1,293	1,470
Mobile food services	72233	2,787	3,137	12.8	15.8	221	265
Drinking places (alcoholic beverages)	7224	51,177	50,578	324.8	328.6	3,138	3,345

Source: U.S. Census Bureau, *County Business Patterns*, annual. See also <http://www.census.gov/epcd/cbp/view/cbpview.html>.

No. 1250. Commercial and Noncommercial Groups—Food and Drink Establishments and Sales: 1990 to 2002

[Sales in millions of dollars (238,149 represents $238,149,000,000). Excludes military. Data refer to sales to consumers of food and alcoholic beverages. Sales are estimated. For details, see source]

Type of group	Establishments, 1999	Sales (mil. dol.)						
		1990	1995	1998	1999	2000	2001	2002[1]
Total	856,597	238,149	294,631	339,827	358,017	377,811	391,083	406,277
Commercial restaurant services [2][3]	672,115	211,606	265,910	308,816	326,567	345,168	358,212	372,985
Eating places [2]	433,118	155,552	198,293	232,131	245,786	259,814	271,324	282,862
Full-service restaurants	200,534	77,811	96,396	117,774	125,430	134,461	140,393	146,711
Limited-service restaurants [4]	180,160	[5]69,798	[5]92,901	98,120	103,026	107,252	111,112	115,223
Snack and nonalcoholic beverage bars	41,830	(5)	(5)	10,570	11,548	12,204	13,877	14,920
Bars and taverns [6]	51,665	9,533	9,948	11,498	11,912	12,257	12,810	13,258
Managed services [2]	18,991	14,149	18,186	21,991	23,382	24,844	25,772	26,820
Manufacturing and industrial plants	(NA)	3,856	4,814	5,769	5,984	6,221	6,283	6,335
Colleges and universities	(NA)	2,788	3,989	5,068	5,443	5,933	6,308	6,649
Lodging places [2]	13,092	13,568	15,561	17,153	18,032	19,120	18,124	18,585
Retail hosts [2][7]	131,975	9,513	12,589	13,115	13,996	14,947	15,756	16,662
Department store restaurants	4,111	876	1,038	833	873	(NA)	(NA)	(NA)
Grocery store restaurants [7]	60,435	5,432	6,624	6,495	6,823	(NA)	(NA)	(NA)
Gasoline service stations	51,162	1,718	2,520	3,928	4,289	(NA)	(NA)	(NA)
Recreation and sports	15,902	2,871	3,866	4,456	4,623	4,868	4,921	5,088
Noncommercial restaurant services [2]	184,482	26,543	28,722	31,011	31,450	32,644	32,871	33,291
Employee restaurant services	5,133	1,864	1,364	1,120	1,036	990	921	877
Industrial, commercial organizations	1,928	1,603	1,129	864	775	(NA)	(NA)	(NA)
Educational restaurant services	101,195	7,671	9,059	9,737	9,831	10,060	10,121	10,138
Elementary and secondary schools	97,039	3,700	4,533	4,948	4,993	5,063	5,115	5,099
Hospitals	5,869	8,968	9,219	9,787	9,734	10,068	10,096	10,288
Miscellaneous [3]	35,591	2,892	3,673	4,285	4,630	4,933	5,068	5,123
Clubs	10,514	1,993	2,278	2,691	2,971	(NA)	(NA)	(NA)

NA Not available. [1] Projection. [2] Includes other types of groups, not shown separately. [3] Data for establishments with payroll. [4] Fast-food restaurants. [5] Snack and nonalcoholic beverage bars included in limited service restaurants. [6] For establishments serving food. [7] Includes a portion of delicatessen sales in grocery stores.

Source: National Restaurant Association, Washington, DC, *Restaurant Numbers: 25 Year History, 1970-1995*, 1998; *Restaurant Industry in Review*, annual; and *National Restaurant Association Restaurant Industry Forecast*, December 2001 (copyright).

No. 1251. Professional, Scientific, & Technical Services (Taxable)— Establishments, Receipts, Payroll, and Employees by Kind of Business: 1997

[579,542 represents $579,542,000,000. Covers only establishments with payroll]

Kind of business	NAICS code [1]	Estab- lish- ments (number)	Receipts		Annual payroll		Paid employ- ees for pay period including March 12 (1,000)
			Total (mil. dol.)	Per paid employee (dol.)	Total (mil. dol.)	Per paid employee (dol.)	
Professional, scientific, & technical services	**54**	**615,305**	**579,542**	**111,178**	**225,376**	**43,236**	**5,212.7**
Professional, scientific, & technical services	541	615,305	579,542	111,178	225,376	43,236	5,212.7
Legal services	5411	173,716	127,052	125,534	49,060	48,474	1,012.1
Offices of lawyers	54111	165,757	122,617	128,250	47,410	49,588	956.1
Other legal services	54119	7,959	4,436	79,180	1,650	29,462	56.0
Accounting, tax return prep, bookkeeping, & payroll services	5412	97,512	61,117	63,234	26,104	27,008	966.5
Architectural, engineering, & related services[2]	5413	92,710	116,986	112,669	46,943	45,210	1,038.3
Architectural services	54131	20,602	16,988	115,802	6,469	44,093	146.7
Engineering services	54133	52,526	88,181	120,788	35,338	48,405	730.0
Geophysical surveying & mapping services	54136	587	1,088	109,822	446	44,987	9.9
Surveying & mapping (except geophysical) services	54137	8,864	3,042	58,708	1,432	27,630	51.8
Testing laboratories	54138	5,488	6,443	78,550	2,709	33,024	82.0
Specialized design services[2]	5414	26,436	14,254	126,103	4,088	36,166	113.0
Interior design services	54141	9,612	4,945	145,816	1,022	30,120	33.9
Industrial design services	54142	1,322	1,363	100,170	583	42,816	13.6
Graphic design services	54143	14,631	7,555	122,601	2,355	38,212	61.6
Computer systems design & related services	5415	72,278	108,968	142,505	42,151	55,123	764.7
Management, scientific, & technical consulting services	5416	80,426	63,429	124,066	26,582	51,993	511.3
Management consulting services	54161	60,794	52,225	127,054	22,297	54,244	411.0
Environmental consulting services	54162	6,725	4,781	103,603	1,778	38,522	46.1
Other scientific & technical consulting services	54169	12,907	6,423	118,811	2,507	46,377	54.1
Scientific research & development services	5417	7,830	23,078	130,405	9,322	52,675	177.0
R&D in the physical, engineering, & life sciences	54171	6,855	21,822	135,283	8,821	54,683	161.3
Research & development in the social sciences & humanities	54172	975	1,257	80,188	502	32,008	15.7
Advertising & related services[2]	5418	38,832	49,290	118,141	16,012	38,379	417.2
Advertising agencies	54181	13,390	16,872	120,955	7,557	54,177	139.5
Public relations agencies	54182	6,513	4,772	123,195	1,952	50,384	38.7
Media representatives	54184	2,686	3,309	125,153	1,061	40,115	26.4
Display advertising	54185	2,261	4,639	112,169	823	19,901	41.4
Direct mail advertising	54186	3,454	8,672	101,229	2,427	28,325	85.7
Other services related to advertising	54189	9,086	9,140	135,706	1,596	23,702	67.4
Other professional, scientific, & technical services[2]	5419	25,565	15,368	72,261	5,115	24,049	212.7
Marketing research & public opinion polling	54191	4,030	7,880	73,266	2,963	27,553	107.6
Photographic services	54192	17,573	5,571	66,399	1,540	18,353	83.9
All other professional, scientific, & technical services	54199	3,058	1,502	91,866	469	28,690	16.3

[1] North American Industry Classification System, 1997; see text, Section 15, Business Enterprise. [2]Includes other kinds of business not shown separately.

No. 1252. Professional, Scientific, and Technical Services (Tax-Exempt)— Establishments, Revenue, Payroll, and Employees by Kind of Business: 1997

[15,709 represents $15,709,000,000. Covers only establishments with payroll]

Kind of business	NAICS code [1]	Estab- lish- ments (number)	Revenue		Annual payroll		Paid employees for pay period including March 12 (1,000)
			Total (mil. dol.)	Per paid employee (dol.)	Total (mil. dol.)	Per paid employee (dol.)	
Professional, scientific, & technical services	**54**	**5,824**	**15,709**	**105,806**	**6,023**	**40,567**	**148.5**
Professional, scientific, & technical services	541	5,824	15,709	105,806	6,023	40,567	148.5
Legal services	5411	2,532	1,497	64,197	797	34,168	23.3
Scientific R&D services	5417	3,292	14,212	113,558	5,226	41,759	125.1
R&D in physical, engineering, & life sciences	54171	2,318	12,324	114,312	4,593	42,606	107.8
R&D in social sciences & humanities	54172	974	1,888	108,873	633	36,488	17.3

[1] North American Industry Classification System, 1997; see text, Section 15, Business Enterprise.
Source of Tables 1251 and 1252: U.S. Census Bureau, *1997 Economic Census, Professional, Scientific, and Technical Services,* Series EC97554A-US, issued December 1999.

Accommodation, Food Services, and Other Services 771

No. 1253. Advertising—Estimated Expenditures by Medium: 1990 to 2001

[In millions of dollars (129,968 represents $129,968,000,000). See source for definitions of types of advertising]

Medium	1990	1994	1995	1996	1997	1998	1999	2000	2001
Total	129,968	153,024	165,147	178,113	191,307	206,697	222,308	247,472	231,287
National	73,638	69,124	96,933	105,054	112,809	122,271	132,170	151,664	141,797
Local	56,330	63,900	68,214	73,059	78,498	84,426	90,138	95,808	89,490
Newspapers	32,281	34,356	36,317	38,402	41,670	44,292	46,648	49,050	44,255
National	3,867	3,906	3,996	4,400	5,016	5,402	6,358	7,229	6,615
Local	28,414	30,450	32,321	34,002	36,654	38,890	40,290	41,821	37,640
Magazines	6,803	7,916	8,580	9,010	9,821	10,518	11,433	12,370	11,095
Broadcast TV	26,616	31,133	32,720	36,046	36,893	39,173	40,011	44,802	38,881
Four TV networks	9,863	10,942	11,600	13,081	13,020	13,736	13,961	15,888	14,300
Syndication	1,109	1,734	2,016	2,218	2,438	2,609	2,870	3,108	3,102
Spot (National)	7,788	8,993	9,119	9,803	9,999	10,659	10,500	12,264	9,223
Spot (Local)	7,856	9,464	9,985	10,944	11,436	12,169	12,680	13,542	12,256
Cable TV	2,631	5,209	6,166	7,778	8,750	10,340	12,570	15,455	15,536
Cable TV networks	2,000	3,885	4,500	5,695	6,450	7,640	9,405	11,765	11,883
Spot (Local)	631	1,324	1,666	2,083	2,300	2,700	3,165	3,690	3,653
Radio	8,726	10,529	11,338	12,269	13,491	15,073	17,215	19,295	17,861
Network	482	463	480	523	560	622	684	780	711
Spot (National)	1,635	1,902	1,959	2,135	2,455	2,823	3,275	3,668	2,956
Local (Local)	6,609	8,164	8,899	9,611	10,476	11,628	13,256	14,847	14,194
Yellow Pages	8,926	9,825	10,236	10,849	11,423	11,990	12,652	13,228	13,592
National	1,132	1,314	1,410	1,555	1,711	1,870	1,986	2,093	2,087
Local	7,794	8,511	8,826	9,294	9,712	10,120	10,666	11,135	11,505
Direct mail	23,370	29,638	32,866	34,509	36,890	39,620	41,403	44,591	44,725
Business papers	2,875	3,358	3,559	3,808	4,109	4,232	4,274	4,915	4,468
Out of home [1]	1,084	1,167	1,263	1,339	1,455	1,576	1,725	5,176	5,134
National	640	648	701	743	795	845	925	2,068	2,051
Local	444	519	562	596	660	731	800	3,108	3,083
Internet	(NA)	(NA)	(NA)	(NA)	800	1,383	2,832	6,507	5,752
Miscellaneous [2]	16,656	19,893	22,102	24,103	26,005	28,500	31,545	32,083	29,988
National	12,074	14,425	16,147	17,574	18,745	20,312	22,264	24,418	22,829
Local	4,582	5,468	5,955	6,529	7,260	8,188	9,281	7,665	7,159

NA Not available. [1] Prior to 2000, represents only "outdoor" billboards. Beginning 2000 includes other forms of outdoor advertising (i.e. transportation vehicles, bus shelters, telephone kiosks, etc.) previously covered under "Miscellaneous." [2] Beginning 2000, part of miscellaneous now included under "Out of home" advertising. See footnote 1.
Source: McCann-Erickson, Inc., New York, NY. Compiled for Crain Communications, Inc. in Advertising Age (copyright).

No. 1254. Magazine Advertising Revenue by Category: 1999 to 2001

[15,508 represents $15,508,000,000. Represents the volume of advertising in the consumer magazines belonging to the Publishers Information Bureau]

Category	Pages			Volume (mil. dol.)		
	1999	2000	2001	1999	2000	2001
Total [1]	255,146	269,016	237,613	15,508	17,052	16,214
Automotive	24,753	22,295	19,837	1,844	1,730	1,688
Automotive accessories and equipment	24,502	22,012	19,636	1,833	1,711	1,676
Technology [1]	22,009	26,536	17,426	1,385	1,736	1,236
Telecommunications	4,734	4,812	3,231	312	311	223
Computers and software	13,252	17,156	10,141	894	1,205	817
Home furnishings and supplies [1]	17,273	16,611	15,539	1,185	1,197	1,196
Household furnishings and accessories	4,709	4,597	4,056	283	272	264
Audio and video equipment and supplies	5,057	4,507	4,453	277	284	304
Toiletries and cosmetics [1]	15,857	15,741	16,696	1,143	1,218	1,401
Cosmetics and beauty aids [2]	8,484	8,781	9,304	578	640	759
Personal hygiene and health [2]	3,238	2,818	2,801	287	271	284
Hair products and accessories [2]	2,589	2,837	3,332	185	217	264
Direct response companies	22,163	19,554	19,353	1,121	1,034	1,096
Apparel and accessories [1]	24,774	26,576	25,043	1,120	1,295	1,316
Ready-to-wear	12,771	13,648	12,179	499	586	560
Footwear	3,349	4,058	4,281	158	218	221
Jewelry and watches	4,214	5,021	4,600	210	282	293
Financial, insurance and real estate	16,253	16,976	13,112	1,023	1,154	962
Financial	12,557	13,453	9,596	757	894	694
Insurance and real estate	3,697	3,524	3,516	266	260	268
Food and food products [1]	9,894	10,693	10,687	1,003	1,140	1,207
Prepared foods	1,919	1,961	1,883	194	212	223
Dairy, produce, meat and bakery goods	2,809	2,858	3,239	288	315	378
Beverages	1,854	1,981	2,086	166	197	213
Drugs and remedies	11,759	12,470	12,550	977	1,121	1,217
Medicines and proprietary remedies	10,272	10,506	10,255	850	965	1,011
Media and advertising	11,418	15,328	11,713	846	1,145	966
Retail stores	15,798	19,263	15,312	826	1,056	882
Retail stores [3]	12,786	15,869	12,227	671	863	692
Public transportation, hotels, and resorts	15,231	15,421	14,947	705	743	745
Cigarettes, tobacco and accessories	6,034	4,677	3,057	481	388	256
Beer, wine and liquor	4,565	5,016	4,924	299	360	391
Liquor	3,600	3,874	3,768	235	280	307
Miscellaneous services and amusements	5,424	5,803	5,100	277	310	287
Sporting goods	10,503	13,752	13,774	240	263	279

[1] Includes other categories, not shown separately. [2] Women's, men's, and unisex. [3] Includes apparel, business, drugs and toiletries, and food and beverage.
Source: Publishers Information Bureau, Inc., New York, NY, as compiled by Competitive Media Reporting.

No. 1255. Administrative and Support and Waste Management and Remediation Services—Establishments, Receipts, Payroll, and Employees by Kind of Business: 1997

[295,936 represents $295,936,000,000. Covers only establishments with payroll]

| Kind of business | NAICS code [1] | Estab- lish- ments (number) | Receipts | | Annual payroll | | Paid employ- ees for pay period including March 12 (1,000) |
			Total (mil. dol.)	Per paid employee (dol.)	Total (mil. dol.)	Per paid employee (dol.)	
Admin/support waste mgt/remediation services.........	56	276,393	295,936	40,278	137,337	18,692	7,347.4
Administrative & support services	561	260,025	256,591	36,310	128,438	18,175	7,066.7
Office administrative services	5611	24,537	28,054	82,906	11,971	35,377	338.4
Facilities support services...............	5612	2,490	7,576	67,558	3,280	29,251	112.1
Employment services [2]	5613	34,569	86,133	23,780	62,127	17,153	3,622.0
Temporary help services............	56132	23,522	57,221	21,901	40,256	15,408	2,612.7
Employee leasing services	56133	4,766	24,125	26,943	19,224	21,469	895.4
Business support services [2]	5614	32,920	36,026	59,590	11,900	19,683	604.6
Telephone call centers	56142	6,271	11,983	40,992	4,574	15,646	292.3
Business service centers	56143	10,130	8,504	79,699	2,076	19,459	106.7
Travel arrangement & reservation services [2] .	5615	36,578	21,484	71,493	7,699	25,622	300.5
Travel agencies...................	56151	29,332	9,977	54,467	4,464	24,369	183.2
Other travel arrangement & reservation services	56159	3,745	8,725	110,786	2,201	27,949	78.8
Investigation & security services	5616	21,494	20,444	29,938	10,698	15,665	682.9
Investigation, guard, & armored car services	56161	12,539	12,370	22,052	7,759	13,832	561.0
Security guards & patrol services	561612	6,644	9,133	19,146	6,256	13,116	477.0
Security systems services	56162	8,955	8,074	66,224	2,938	24,100	121.9
Services to buildings & dwellings	5617	80,807	29,915	28,599	13,317	12,731	1,046.0
Janitorial services	56172	55,157	21,128	23,678	10,106	11,326	892.3
Other support services..............	5619	26,630	26,958	74,859	7,446	20,677	360.1
Waste management & remediation services ...	562	16,368	39,346	140,166	8,899	31,702	280.7
Waste collection	5621	8,324	20,145	131,885	4,566	29,893	152.7
Waste treatment & disposal	5622	2,314	10,251	192,225	1,933	36,249	53.3
Remediation & other waste management services............................	5629	5,730	8,950	119,914	2,400	32,154	74.6

[1] North American Industry Classification System, 1997; see text, Section 15, Business Enterprise. [2] Includes other kinds of business not shown separately.

Source: U.S. Census Bureau, *1997 Economic Census, Administrative & Support and Waste Management & Remediation Services,* Series EC97556A-US, issued January 2000.

No. 1256. Administrative and Support and Waste Management and Remediation Services—Estimated Revenue: 1998 to 2000

[In millions of dollars (337,806 represents $337,806,000,000), except percent. For taxable and tax-exempt employer firms. Except as indicated, estimates adjusted to the results of the 1997 Economic Census. Based on the Service Annual Survey; see Appendix III]

Kind of business	NAICS code [1]	1998	1999	2000	Percent change, 1999-2000
Admin/support waste mgt/remediation services...............	56	337,806	374,339	410,638	9.7
Administrative & support services	561	295,279	327,287	361,859	10.6
Office administrative services	56111	34,896	41,322	48,732	17.9
Facilities support services..................	56121	7,542	8,055	9,109	13.1
Employment services [2]....................	5613	102,040	114,361	125,618	9.8
Temporary help services	56132	65,656	71,504	74,492	4.2
Employee leasing services	56133	30,680	35,964	42,855	19.2
Business support services [2]	5614	39,928	43,346	47,636	9.9
Telephone call centers	56142	13,713	14,817	16,115	8.8
Business service centers................	56143	8,923	9,667	10,397	7.5
Travel arrangement & reservation services [2]	5615	23,092	24,996	26,306	5.2
Travel agencies........................	56151	10,137	10,770	10,766	(-Z)
Other travel arrangement & reservation services ...	56159	10,092	11,152	12,485	12.0
Investigation and security services	5616	22,013	23,917	25,286	5.7
Investigation, guard, & armored car services......	56161	13,051	14,281	14,910	4.4
Security guards & patrol services	561612	9,252	10,316	10,735	4.1
Security systems services	56162	8,962	9,637	10,376	7.7
Services to buildings & dwellings	5617	33,712	36,949	41,065	11.1
Janitorial services	56172	24,181	26,712	30,097	12.7
Other support services	5619	32,056	34,341	38,107	11.0
Convention & trade show organizers	56192	7,303	7,779	9,383	20.6
Waste management & remediation services	562	42,527	47,052	48,779	3.7
Waste collection	5621	22,316	25,295	26,823	6.0
Waste treatment & disposal [3]	5622	10,020	11,101	11,689	5.3
Remediation & other waste management services....	5629	10,191	10,655	10,267	-3.6

Z Less than 0.05 percent. [1] North American Industry Classification System, 1997; see text, Section 15, Business Enterprise. [2] Includes other kinds of business not shown separately. [3] Estimates have not been adjusted to the results of the 1997 Economic Census.

Source: U.S. Census Bureau, "Service Annual Survey 2000"; published December 2001; <http://www.census.gov/svsd/www/sas00rpt.pdf>.

No. 1257. Other Services—Establishments, Receipts, Payroll, and Employees by Kind of Business: 1997

[163,033 represents $163,033,000,000. Covers only taxable establishments with payroll]

Kind of business	NAICS code [1]	Estab-lish-ments (number)	Receipts		Annual payroll		Paid employees for pay period including March 12 (1,000)
			Total (mil. dol.)	Per paid employee (dol.)	Total (mil. dol.)	Per paid employee (dol.)	
Other services (except public administration)	**81**	**420,950**	**163,033**	**65,381**	**48,453**	**19,431**	**2,493.6**
Repair & maintenance	811	235,466	105,154	82,384	29,875	23,406	1,276.4
Automotive R&M	8111	164,360	62,201	76,306	16,865	20,690	815.1
Automotive mechanical & electrical R&M	81111	99,444	33,510	86,966	8,634	22,406	385.3
General automotive repair	811111	77,751	25,598	88,078	6,439	22,154	290.6
Automotive body/paint/interior & glass repair	81112	41,168	20,905	89,202	5,926	25,285	234.4
Other automotive R&M	81119	23,748	7,785	39,829	2,306	11,796	195.5
Electronic & precision equipment R&M	8112	17,634	14,558	106,087	4,497	32,769	137.2
Computer & office machine R&M	811212	7,729	8,502	120,716	2,546	36,154	70.4
Commercial equipment (exc auto & electr) R&M	8113	20,290	17,506	104,851	5,172	30,978	167.0
Personal & household goods R&M	8114	33,182	10,889	69,335	3,341	21,274	157.1
Home/garden equipment & appliance R&M	81141	9,790	4,976	77,690	1,536	23,985	64.1
Reupholstery & furniture repair	81142	6,598	1,193	53,480	389	17,416	22.3
Footwear & leather goods repair	81143	2,153	261	47,790	73	13,320	5.5
Other personal & household goods R&M	81149	14,641	4,458	68,361	1,343	20,599	65.2
Personal & laundry services	812	185,484	57,879	47,552	18,577	15,263	1,217.2
Personal care services	8121	95,708	14,241	30,154	5,972	12,645	472.3
Hair, nail, & skin care services	81211	83,991	12,057	29,335	5,378	13,084	411.0
Barber shops	812111	4,242	428	32,085	194	14,561	13.3
Beauty shops	812112	74,493	11,209	29,273	5,032	13,142	382.9
Nail salons	812113	5,256	419	28,463	151	10,242	14.7
Other personal care services	81219	11,717	2,184	35,646	594	9,696	61.3
Death care services	8122	23,015	12,621	76,571	3,519	21,349	164.8
Funeral homes	81221	16,338	9,633	91,423	2,444	23,192	105.4
Cemeteries & crematories	81222	6,677	2,988	50,252	1,075	18,082	59.5
Drycleaning & laundry services	8123	44,782	17,913	45,303	5,939	15,021	395.4
Coin-operated laundries & drycleaners	81231	13,883	2,873	54,191	606	11,435	53.0
Drycleaning & laundry services (exc coin-op)	81232	27,939	7,092	34,803	2,575	12,637	203.8
Linen & uniform supply	81233	2,960	7,948	57,339	2,758	19,896	138.6
Other personal services	8129	21,979	13,105	70,959	3,148	17,044	184.7
Photofinishing	81292	7,055	5,520	76,671	1,583	21,986	72.0
Parking lots & garages	81293	10,358	5,175	67,940	968	12,705	76.2
All other personal services	81299	4,566	2,410	65,996	597	16,350	36.5

[1] North American Industry Classification System, 1997; see text, Section 15, Business Enterprise.

Source: U.S. Census Bureau, *1997 Economic Census, Other Services,* Series EC97S81A-US, issued December 1999.

No. 1258. Other Services—Estimated Revenue For Employer and Nonemployer Firms: 1998 to 2000

[In millions of dollars (333,934 represents $333,934,000,000), except percent. Except where indicated, results have been adjusted to the results of the 1997 Economic Census. Based on the Service Annual Survey. See text, this section and Appendix III]

Kind of business	NAICS code [1]	1998	1999	2000	Percent change, 1999-2000
Other services (except public administration, religious, labor, and political organizations, and private households)	81	333,934	353,370	375,786	6.3
Repair & maintenance.	811	133,797	139,734	146,399	4.8
Automotive R&M.	8111	77,969	81,588	85,995	5.4
Automotive mechanical & electrical R&M	81111	41,415	42,648	44,666	4.7
Automotive body/paint/interior & glass repair.	81112	25,436	26,988	28,655	6.2
Other automotive R&M. . . . .[2].	811119	11,118	11,953	12,674	6.0
Electronic and precision equipment R&M [2].	8112	17,598	18,745	18,758	0.1
Commercial equipment (exc auto elec) R&M	8113	21,179	21,305	22,909	7.5
Personal and household goods R&M	8114	17,051	18,096	18,737	3.5
Home/garden equipment & appliance R&M.	81141	6,075	6,476	6,449	-0.4
Reupholstery & furniture repair.	81142	2,141	2,320	2,458	6.0
Footwear & leather goods repair.	81143	382	396	376	-5.2
Other personal & household goods R&M	81149	8,453	8,904	9,454	6.2
Personal & laundry services	812	88,436	94,009	100,920	7.4
Personal care services.	8121	25,048	26,605	29,031	9.1
Hair, nail, & skin care services	81211	21,501	22,716	24,899	9.6
Barber shops.	812111	1,850	1,962	2,065	5.3
Beauty salons	812112	18,243	18,880	20,619	9.2
Nail salons	812113	1,409	1,874	2,214	18.2
Other personal care services	81219	3,547	3,889	4,132	6.2
Death care services.	8122	13,760	13,957	13,847	-0.8
Funeral homes	81221	10,857	10,998	10,949	-0.4
Cemeteries & crematories	81222	2,903	2,959	2,898	-2.1
Drycleaning & laundry services	8123	20,496	21,668	22,329	3.0
Coin-operated laundries & drycleaners.	81231	3,607	3,908	4,325	10.7
Drycleaning and laundry services, (exc coin-op) . . .	81232	8,353	8,756	9,045	3.3
Linen & uniform supply	81233	8,537	9,004	8,959	-0.5
Other personal services	8129	29,132	31,779	35,714	12.4
Photofinishing	81292	5,822	5,925	5,860	-1.1
Parking lots & garages	81293	6,432	6,998	7,725	10.4
All other personal services.	81299	16,879	18,856	22,128	17.4
Religious/grantmaking/prof/like organizations (except religious, labor, and political organizations) [3] . . .	813	111,702	119,627	128,467	7.4

[1] North American Industry Classification System, 1997; see text, Section 15, Business Enterprise.   [2] Estimates for NAICS 811219 (other electronics and precision equipment repair and maintenance) have not been adjusted to the results of the 1997 Economic Census.   [3] Estimates for NAICS 813211 (grantmaking foundations) have not been adjusted to the results of the 1997 Economic Census.

Source: U.S. Census Bureau, "Service Annual Survey 2000"; published December 2001; <http://www.census.gov/svsd/www/sas00rpt.pdf>.

U.S. Census Bureau, Statistical Abstract of the United States: 2002

No. 1259. Other Services (Tax-Exempt)—Establishments, Revenue, Payroll, and Employees by Kind of Business: 1997

[102,864 represents $102,864,000,000. Covers only establishments with payroll.]

Kind of business	NAICS code [1]	Estab-lish-ments (number)	Revenue		Annual payroll		Paid employees for pay period including March 12 (1,000)
			Total (mil. dol.)	Per paid employee (dol.)	Total (mil. dol.)	Per paid employee (dol.)	
Other services (except public administration)	81	98,765	102,864	134,886	17,068	22,381	762.6
Grantmaking & giving services	8132	11,906	48,957	467,113	3,080	29,391	104.8
Social advocacy organizations.	8133	10,120	7,525	88,481	2,003	23,554	85.0
Civic & social organizations	8134	28,364	9,916	37,956	2,683	10,269	261.3
Business/labor/political/like organizations. ...	8139	48,375	36,467	117,071	9,301	29,860	311.5
Business associations	81391	16,928	14,859	128,000	4,180	36,007	116.1
Professional organizations	81392	7,239	8,292	132,942	2,265	36,306	62.4
Other similar org. (exc. business, prof/labor/political)	81399	24,208	13,316	100,094	2,857	21,474	133.0

[1] North American Industry Classification System, 1997; see text, Section 15, Business Enterprise.

Source: U.S. Census Bureau, *1997 Economic Census, Other Services*, Series EC97581A-US.

No. 1260. Religious, Grantmaking, Civic, and Professional Service Firms—Revenue and Expenses for Tax-Exempt Employer Firms: 1998 to 2000

[In millions of dollars (111,702 represents $111,702,000,000), except as indicated. Based on the Service Annual Survey; subject to sampling variability. See text, this section, and Appendix III]

Kind of business	NAICS code [1]	Revenue				Expenses, 2000
		1998	1999	2000	Percent change, 1999-2000	
Religious/grantmaking/prof/ like organizations (except religious, labor, and political organizations)	813	111,702	119,627	128,467	7.4	98,864
Grantmaking and giving services [2]	8132	52,213	57,667	63,057	9.3	38,861
Social advocacy organizations	8133	8,877	9,882	10,438	5.6	9,382
Civic & social organizations	8134	10,908	11,408	12,175	6.7	11,264
Business, professional, and other organizations (except labor and political organizations)	8139	39,704	40,670	42,798	5.2	39,357

[1] North American Industry Classification System, 1997; see text, Section 15, Business Enterprise. [2] Estimates for NAICS 813211 (grantmaking foundations) have not been adjusted to the results of the 1997 Economic Census.

Source: U.S. Census Bureau, "Service Annual Survey 2000"; published December 2001; <http://www.census.gov/svsd/www/sas00rpt.pdf>.

No. 1261. National Nonprofit Associations—Number by Type: 1980 to 2001

[Data compiled during last few months of year previous to year shown and the beginning months of year shown]

Type	1980	1990	2000	2001	Type	1980	1990	2000	2001
Total	**14,726**	**22,289**	**21,840**	**22,449**	Public affairs	1,068	2,249	1,776	1,857
					Fraternal, nationality, ethnic .	435	573	525	537
Trade, business, commercial.	3,118	3,918	3,880	3,922	Religious.	797	1,172	1,123	1,160
Agriculture and environment .	677	940	1,103	1,120	Veteran, hereditary, patriotic .	208	462	835	834
Legal, governmental,					Hobby, avocational	910	1,475	1,330	1,408
public admin., military	529	792	790	807	Athletic sports	504	840	717	762
Scientific, engineering, tech .	1,039	1,417	1,302	1,317	Labor unions .... [2] .	235	253	232	233
Educational	[1]2,376	1,291	1,297	1,346	Chambers of Commerce [2] ..	105	168	143	142
Cultural.	([1])	1,886	1,786	1,812	Greek and non-Greek				
Social welfare	994	1,705	1,829	1,925	letter societies	318	340	296	312
Health, medical	1,413	2,227	2,495	2,574	Fan clubs	(NA)	581	381	381

NA Not available. [1] Data for cultural associations included with educational associations. [2] National and binational. Includes trade and tourism organizations.

Source: Gale Group, Farmington Hills, MI. Compiled from *Encyclopedia of Associations*, annual (copyright).

Section 28
Foreign Commerce and Aid

This section presents data on the flow of goods, services, and capital between the United States and other countries; changes in official reserve assets of the United States; international investments; and foreign assistance programs.

The Bureau of Economic Analysis publishes current figures on U.S. international transactions and the U.S. international investment position in its monthly *Survey of Current Business*. Statistics for the foreign aid programs are presented by the Agency for International Development (AID) in its annual *U.S. Overseas Loans and Grants and Assistance from International Organizations* and by the Department of Agriculture in its *Foreign Agricultural Trade of the United States*.

The principal source of merchandise import and export data is the U.S. Census Bureau. Current data are presented monthly in *U.S. International Trade in Goods and Services* report Series FT 900. The *Guide to Foreign Trade Statistics* found on the Census Bureau Web site at <http://www.census.gov/foreign-trade/guide/index.html> lists the Bureau's monthly and annual products and services in this field. In addition, the International Trade Administration and the Bureau of Economic Analysis present summary as well as selected commodity and country data for U.S. foreign trade in the *U.S. Foreign Trade Highlights* and the *Survey of Current Business*, respectively. The merchandise trade data in the latter source include balance of payments adjustments to the Census Bureau data. The Treasury Department's *Monthly Treasury Statement of Receipts and Outlays of the United States Government* contains information on import duties.

International accounts—The international transactions tables (Nos. 1262 to 1263) show, for given time periods, the transfer of goods, services, grants, and financial assets and liabilities between the United States and the rest of the world.

The international investment position table (No. 1265) presents, for specific dates, the value of U.S. investments abroad and of foreign investments in the United States. The movement of foreign and U.S. capital as presented in the balance of payments is not the only factor affecting the total value of foreign investments. Among the other factors are changes in the valuation of assets or liabilities, including changes in prices of securities, defaults, expropriations, and write-offs.

Direct investment abroad means the ownership or control, directly or indirectly, by one person of 10 percent or more of the voting securities of an incorporated business enterprise or an equivalent interest in an unincorporated business enterprise. Direct investment position is the value of U.S. parents claims on the equity of and receivables due from foreign affiliates, less foreign affiliates receivables due from their U.S. parent's. Income consists of parents shares in the earnings of their affiliates' plus net interest received by parents' on intercompany accounts, less withholding taxes on dividends and interest.

Foreign aid—Foreign assistance is divided into three major categories—grants (military supplies and services and other grants), credits, and other assistance (through net accumulation of foreign currency claims from the sale of agricultural commodities). *Grants* are transfers for which no payment is expected (other than a limited percentage of the foreign currency "counterpart" funds generated by the grant), or which at most involve an obligation on the part of the receiver to extend aid to the United States or other countries to achieve a common objective. *Credits* are loan disbursements or transfers under other agreements which give rise to specific obligations to repay, over a period of years, usually with interest. All known returns to the U.S. government stemming from grants and credits (reverse grants,

Foreign Commerce and Aid   777

returns of grants, and payments of principal) are taken into account in net grants and net credits, but no allowance is made for interest or commissions. *Other assistance* represents the transfer of U.S. farm products in exchange for foreign currencies (plus, since enactment of Public Law 87-128, currency claims from principal and interest collected on credits extended under the farm products program), less the government's disbursements of the currencies as grants, credits, or for purchases. The net acquisition of currencies represents net transfers of resources to foreign countries under the agricultural programs, in addition to those classified as grants or credits.

The basic instrument for extending military aid to friendly nations has been the Mutual Defense Assistance Program authorized by the Congress in 1949. Prior to 1952, economic and technical aid was authorized in the Foreign Assistance Act of 1948, the 1950 Act for International Development, and other legislation which set up programs for specific countries. In 1952, these economic, technical, and military aid programs were combine under the Mutual Security Act, which in turn was followed by the Foreign Assistance Act passed in 1961. Appropriations to provide military assistance were also made in the Department of Defense Appropriation Act (rather than the Foreign Assistance Appropriation Act) beginning in 1966 for certain countries in Southeast Asia and in other legislation concerning program for specific countries (such as Israel). Figures on activity under the Foreign Assistance Act as reported in the *Foreign Grants and Credits* series differ from data published by AID or its immediate predecessors, due largely to differences in reporting, timing, and treatment of particular items.

Exports—The Census Bureau compiles export data primarily from Shipper's Export Declarations required to be filed with customs officials for shipments leaving the United States. They include U.S. exports under mutual security programs and exclude shipments to U.S. Armed Forces for their own use.

The value reported in the export statistics is generally equivalent to a free alongside ship (f.a.s.) value at the U.S. port of export, based on the transaction price, including inland freight, insurance, and other charges incurred in placing the merchandise alongside the carrier at the U.S. port of exportation. This value, as defined, excludes the cost of loading merchandise aboard the exporting carrier and also excludes freight, insurance, and any other charges or transportation and other costs beyond the U.S. port of exportation. The country of destination is defined as the country of ultimate destination or country where the merchandise is to be consumed, further processed, or manufactured, as known to the shipper at the time of exportation. When ultimate destination is not known, the shipment is statistically credited to the last country to which the shipper knows the merchandise will be shipped in the same form as exported.

Effective January 1990, the United States began substituting Canadian import statistics for U.S. exports to Canada. As a result of the data exchange between the United States and Canada, the United States has adopted the Canadian import exemption level for its export statistics based on shipments to Canada.

Data are estimated for shipments valued under $2,501 to all countries, except Canada, using factors based on the ratios of low-valued shipments to individual country totals.

Prior to 1989, exports were based on Schedule B, Statistical Classification of Domestic and Foreign Commodities Exported from the United States. These statistics were retabulated and published using Schedule E, Standard International Trade Classification, Revision 2. Beginning in 1989, Schedule B classifications were based on the Harmonized System and made to coincide with the Standard International Trade Classification, Revision 3. This revision will affect the comparability of most export series beginning with the 1989 data for commodities.

Imports—The Census Bureau compiles import data from various customs forms required to be filed with customs officials. Data on import values are presented on two valuations bases in this section: The c.i.f. (cost, insurance, and freight) and the customs import value (as appraised by the U.S. Customs Service in accordance with legal requirements of the Tariff Act of 1930, as amended). This latter valuation, primarily used for collection of import duties, frequently does not reflect the actual transaction value. Country of origin is defined as country where the merchandise was grown, mined, or manufactured. If country of origin is unknown, country of shipment is reported.

Imports are classified either as "General imports" or "Imports for consumption." *General imports* are a combination of entries for immediate consumption, entries into customs bonded warehouses, and entries into U.S. Foreign Trade Zones, thus generally reflecting total arrivals of merchandise. *Imports for consumption* are a combination of entries for immediate consumption, withdrawals from warehouses for consumption, and entries of merchandise into U.S. customs territory from U.S. Foreign Trade Zones, thus generally reflecting the total of the commodities entered into U.S. consumption channels.

Prior to 1989, imports were based on the Tariff Schedule of the United States Annotated. The statistics were retabulated and published using Schedule A, Standard International Trade Classification, Revision 2. Beginning in 1989, the statistics are based on the Harmonized Tariff Schedule of the United States, which coincides with the Standard International Trade Classification, Revision 3. This revision will affect the comparability of most import series beginning with the 1989 data.

Area coverage—Except as noted, the geographic area covered by the export and import trade statistics is the United States Customs area (includes the 50 states, the District of Columbia, and Puerto Rico), the U.S. Virgin Islands (effective January 1981), and U.S. Foreign Trade Zones (effective July 1982). Data for selected tables and total values for 1980 have been revised to reflect the U.S. Virgin Islands' trade with foreign countries, where possible.

Statistical reliability—For a discussion of statistical collection and estimation, sampling procedures, and measures of statistical reliability applicable to Census Bureau data, see Appendix III.

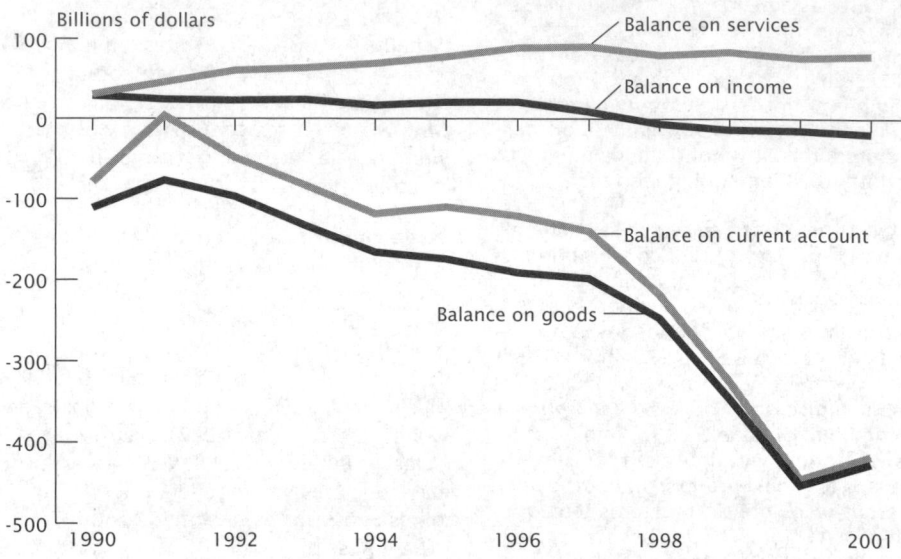

Figure 28.1
U.S. International Transaction Balances: 1990 to 2001

Billions of dollars

Balance on services

Balance on income

Balance on current account

Balance on goods

Source: Chart prepared by U.S. Census Bureau. For data, see Table 1262.

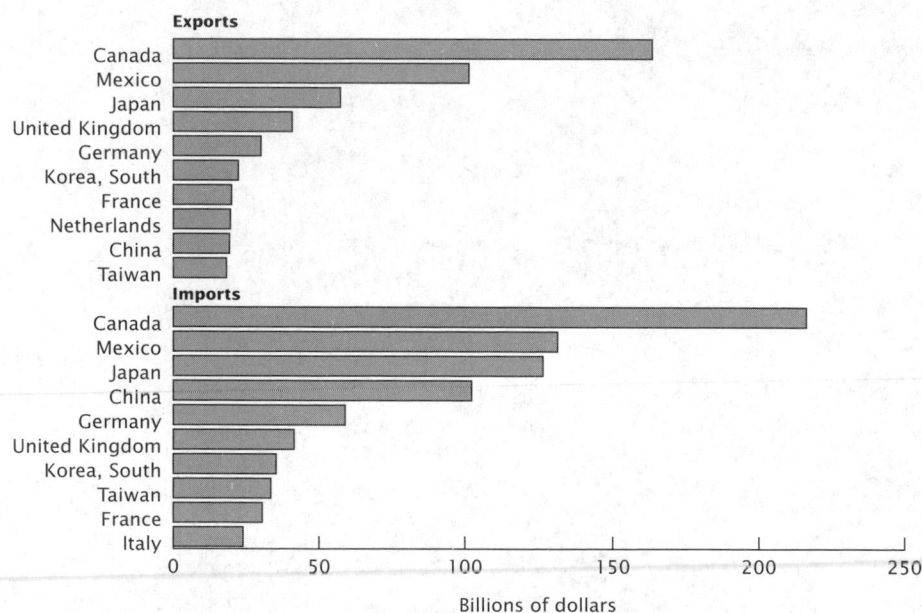

Figure 28.2
Top Purchasers of U.S. Exports and Suppliers of U.S General Imports: 2001

Exports

Canada
Mexico
Japan
United Kingdom
Germany
Korea, South
France
Netherlands
China
Taiwan

Imports

Canada
Mexico
Japan
China
Germany
United Kingdom
Korea, South
Taiwan
France
Italy

Billions of dollars

Source: Chart prepared by U.S. Census Bureau. For data, see Table 1283.

U.S. Census Bureau, Statistical Abstract of the United States: 2002

No. 1262. U.S. International Transactions by Type of Transaction: 1990 to 2001

[In millions of dollars (706,975 represents $706,975,000,000). Minus sign (-) indicates debits]

Type of transaction	1990	1992	1993	1994	1995	1996	1997	1998	1999	2000	2001
Exports of goods and services and income receipts	**706,975**	**749,324**	**777,044**	**869,328**	**1,005,935**	**1,077,966**	**1,195,538**	**1,191,932**	**1,242,655**	**1,418,568**	**1,298,397**
Exports of goods and services	535,233	617,268	642,884	703,890	794,433	852,120	934,980	932,694	957,353	1,065,702	1,004,589
Goods, balance of payments basis [1]	387,401	440,352	456,943	502,859	575,204	612,113	678,366	670,416	684,553	772,210	720,831
Services [2]	147,832	176,916	185,941	201,031	219,229	240,007	256,614	262,278	272,800	293,492	263,758
Transfers under U.S. military agency sales contracts [3]	9,932	12,387	13,471	12,787	14,643	16,446	16,675	17,450	15,920	14,060	12,813
Travel	43,007	54,742	57,875	58,417	63,395	69,809	73,426	71,286	74,731	82,042	72,295
Passenger fares	15,298	16,618	16,528	16,997	18,909	20,422	20,868	20,098	19,785	20,745	17,734
Other transportation	22,042	21,531	21,958	23,754	26,081	26,074	27,006	25,604	26,916	30,185	28,292
Royalties and license fees [5]	16,634	20,841	21,695	26,712	30,289	32,470	33,228	35,626	36,420	38,030	38,875
Other private services [5]	40,251	49,956	53,532	61,477	65,094	73,858	84,456	91,288	98,143	107,568	112,892
U.S. Government miscellaneous services	668	841	883	887	818	928	955	955	885	862	857
Income receipts	171,742	132,056	134,159	165,438	211,502	225,846	260,558	259,238	285,302	352,886	293,808
Income receipts on U.S.-owned assets abroad	170,570	130,631	132,725	163,895	209,741	224,090	258,756	257,304	283,092	350,525	291,342
Direct investment receipts	65,973	57,538	67,246	77,344	95,260	102,505	115,323	103,835	123,718	149,240	132,651
Other private receipts	94,072	65,977	60,353	82,423	109,768	116,994	139,874	149,868	156,177	197,440	155,175
U.S. Government receipts	10,525	7,115	5,126	4,128	4,713	4,591	3,559	3,601	3,197	3,845	3,516
Compensation of employees	1,172	1,425	1,434	1,543	1,761	1,756	1,802	1,934	2,210	2,341	2,466
Imports of goods and services and income payments	**-759,287**	**-762,105**	**-821,930**	**-949,312**	**-1,081,776**	**-1,158,822**	**-1,294,029**	**-1,364,962**	**-1,518,106**	**-1,809,099**	**-1,665,325**
Imports of goods and services	-616,094	-653,004	-711,675	-800,568	-890,821	-953,963	-1,042,869	-1,099,522	-1,219,191	-1,441,441	-1,352,399
Goods, balance of payments basis	-498,435	-536,528	-589,394	-668,690	-749,374	-803,113	-876,367	-917,112	-1,029,987	-1,224,417	-1,147,446
Services [2]	-117,659	-116,476	-122,281	-131,878	-141,447	-150,850	-166,502	-182,410	-189,204	-217,024	-204,953
Direct defense expenditures	-17,531	-13,835	-12,086	-10,217	-10,043	-11,061	-11,698	-12,185	-13,334	-13,560	-14,775
Travel	-37,349	-38,552	-40,713	-43,782	-44,916	-48,078	-52,051	-56,509	-58,865	-64,537	-58,921
Passenger fares	-10,531	-10,603	-11,410	-13,062	-14,663	-15,809	-18,138	-19,971	-21,315	-24,197	-23,407
Other transportation	-24,966	-23,767	-24,524	-26,019	-27,034	-27,403	-28,959	-30,363	-34,139	-41,058	-38,230
Royalties and license fees [5]	-3,135	-5,161	-5,032	-5,852	-6,919	-7,837	-9,614	-11,235	-12,613	-16,106	-16,399
Other private services [5]	-22,229	[4] -22,296	-26,261	-30,386	-35,249	-37,975	-43,280	-49,298	-46,117	-54,687	-50,289
U.S. Government miscellaneous services	-1,919	-2,263	-2,255	-2,560	-2,623	-2,687	-2,762	-2,849	-2,881	-2,879	-2,932
Income payments	-143,192	-109,101	-110,255	-148,744	-190,955	-204,859	-251,160	-265,440	-298,915	-367,658	-312,926
Income payments on foreign-owned assets in the U.S.	-139,728	-104,349	-105,123	-142,792	-184,692	-198,559	-244,494	-258,515	-291,603	-360,146	-305,096
Direct investment payments	-3,450	-2,189	-7,943	-22,150	-30,318	-33,093	-43,601	-37,582	-56,674	-68,009	-37,430
Other private payments	-95,508	-63,079	-57,804	-76,450	-97,004	-97,826	-112,843	-129,814	-139,798	-184,465	-163,353
U.S. Government payments	-40,770	-39,081	-39,376	-44,192	-57,370	-67,640	-88,050	-91,119	-95,131	-107,672	-104,313
Compensation of employees	-3,464	-4,752	-5,132	-5,952	-6,263	-6,300	-6,666	-6,925	-7,312	-7,512	-7,830
Unilateral current transfers, net [3]	**-26,654**	**-35,013**	**-37,637**	**-38,260**	**-34,057**	**-40,081**	**-40,794**	**-44,427**	**-48,913**	**-54,136**	**-50,501**
U.S. Government grants [3]	-10,359	-16,320	-17,036	-14,978	-11,190	-15,401	-12,472	-13,270	-13,774	-16,821	-11,334
U.S. Government pensions and other transfers	-3,224	-4,043	-4,104	-4,556	-3,451	-4,466	-4,191	-4,305	-4,406	-4,705	-5,804
Private remittances and other transfers [6]	-13,070	-14,650	-16,497	-18,726	-19,416	-20,214	-24,131	-26,852	-30,733	-32,610	-33,363

See footnotes at end of table.

U.S. Census Bureau, Statistical Abstract of the United States: 2002

No. 1262. U.S. International Transactions by Type of Transaction: 1990 to 2001—Con.

[See headnote, page 781]

Type of transaction	1990	1992	1993	1994	1995	1996	1997	1998	1999	2000	2001
Capital account transactions, net	-6,579	612	-88	-469	372	693	350	678	-3,491	705	726
U.S. assets abroad, net (increase/financial outflow (-))	-81,234	-74,410	-200,552	-176,056	-352,376	-413,923	-488,940	-359,632	-437,067	-580,952	-439,563
U.S. official reserve assets, net	-2,158	3,901	-1,379	5,346	-9,742	6,668	-1,010	-6,783	8,747	-290	-4,911
Gold [7]	-	-	-	-	-	-	-	-	-	-	-
Special drawing rights	-192	2,316	-537	-441	-808	370	-350	-147	10	-722	-630
Reserve position in the International Monetary Fund	731	-2,692	-44	494	-2,466	-1,280	-3,575	-5,119	5,484	2,308	-3,600
Foreign currencies	-2,697	4,277	-797	5,293	-6,466	7,578	2,915	-1,517	3,253	-1,876	-681
U.S. govt. assets, other than official reserve assets, net	2,317	-1,667	-351	-390	-984	-989	68	-422	2,751	-944	-573
U.S. credits and other long-term assets	-8,410	-7,408	-6,311	-5,383	-4,859	-5,025	-5,417	-4,678	-6,175	-5,177	-4,450
Repayments on U.S. credits and other long-term assets [8]	10,856	5,807	6,270	5,088	4,125	3,930	5,438	4,111	9,560	4,257	3,801
U.S. foreign currency holdings and U.S. short-term assets, net	-130	-66	-310	-95	-250	106	47	145	-634	-24	76
U.S. private assets, net	-81,393	-76,644	-198,822	-181,012	-341,650	-419,602	-487,998	-352,427	-448,565	-579,718	-434,079
Direct investments abroad	-37,183	-48,266	-83,950	-80,167	-98,750	-91,885	-105,016	-142,516	-155,385	-152,437	-156,019
Foreign securities	-28,765	-49,166	-146,253	-60,309	-122,506	-149,829	-118,976	-136,135	-131,217	-124,935	-97,661
U.S. claims on unaffiliated foreigners reported by U.S. nonbanking concerns	-27,824	-387	766	-36,336	-45,286	-86,333	-122,888	-38,204	-85,700	-163,846	-76,067
U.S. claims reported by U.S. banks, n.i.e.	12,379	21,175	30,615	-4,200	-75,108	-91,555	-141,118	-35,572	-76,263	-138,500	-104,332
Foreign assets in the U.S., net (increase/financial inflow (+))	141,571	170,663	282,040	305,989	465,684	586,038	759,290	504,464	813,744	1,024,218	895,459
Foreign official assets in the U.S., net	33,910	40,477	71,753	39,583	109,880	126,724	19,036	-19,948	43,551	37,619	6,092
Other foreign assets in the U.S., net	107,661	130,186	210,287	266,406	355,804	459,314	740,254	524,412	770,193	986,599	889,367
Direct investments in U.S.	48,494	19,823	51,362	46,121	57,776	86,502	105,603	178,209	301,006	287,655	157,936
U.S. Treasury securities	-2,534	37,131	24,381	34,274	99,548	154,996	146,433	48,581	-20,490	-52,792	15,779
U.S. securities other than U.S. Treasury securities	1,592	30,043	80,092	56,971	96,367	130,240	197,892	218,091	343,963	485,644	498,433
U.S. currency flows	18,800	13,400	18,900	23,400	12,300	17,362	24,782	16,622	22,407	1,129	23,783
U.S. liabilities to unaffiliated foreigners reported by U.S. nonbanking concerns	45,133	13,573	10,489	1,302	59,637	53,736	116,518	23,140	69,075	177,010	98,222
U.S. liabilities reported by U.S. banks, n.i.e.	-3,824	16,216	25,063	104,338	30,176	16,478	149,026	39,769	54,232	87,953	95,214
Statistical discrepancy	23,204	-49,141	1,281	-11,220	-3,782	-51,871	-132,232	71,947	-48,822	696	-39,193
Balance on goods	-111,034	-96,897	-132,451	-165,831	-174,170	-191,000	-198,119	-246,696	-345,434	-452,207	-426,615
Balance on services	30,173	60,440	63,660	69,153	77,782	89,157	90,354	79,868	83,596	76,468	78,805
Balance on income	28,550	22,954	23,904	16,694	20,547	20,987	8,750	-6,202	-13,613	-14,792	-19,118
Balance on current account [9]	-78,965	-48,515	-82,523	-118,244	-109,898	-120,937	-139,809	-217,457	-324,364	-444,667	-417,429

- Represents or rounds to zero. [1] Excludes exports of goods under U.S. military agency sales contracts identified in Census export documents, excludes imports of goods under direct defense expenditures identified in Census import documents, and reflects various other adjustments (for valuation, coverage, and timing) of Census statistics to balance of payments basis. [2] Includes some goods: Mainly military equipment included in "Transfers under U.S. military agency sales contracts"; major equipment, other materials, supplies, and petroleum products purchased abroad by U.S. military agencies included in "Direct defense expenditures" under "Imports," and fuels purchased by airline and steamship operators included in "Other transportation" under "Exports" and "Imports." [3] Includes transfers of goods and services under U.S. military grant programs. [4] Break in series. See Technical Notes in the June 1989, 1990, 1992, 1993, 1995, and July 1996-99 issues of the Survey. [5] These lines are presented on a gross basis. Exports exclude U.S. parents' payments to foreign affiliates and to include U.S. affiliates' receipts from foreign parents. Imports include U.S. parents' payments to foreign affiliates and to exclude U.S. affiliates' receipts from foreign parents. [6] The "other" transfers' component includes taxes paid by U.S. private residents to foreign governments and taxes paid by private nonresidents to the U.S. government. [7] At the present time, all U.S. Treasury-owned gold is held in the United States. [8] Includes sales of foreign obligations to foreigners. [9] Conceptually, "Balance on current account" is equal to "net foreign investment" in the national income and product accounts (NIPAs). However, the foreign transactions account in the NIPAs (a) includes adjustments to the international transactions accounts for the treatment of gold, (b) includes adjustments for the different geographical treatment of transactions with U.S. territories and Puerto Rico, and (c) includes services furnished without payment by financial pension plans except life insurance carriers and private noninsured pension plans.

Source: U.S. Bureau of Economic Analysis, Survey of Current Business, July 2001 and April 2002.

No. 1263. U.S. Balances on International Transactions by Area and Selected Country: 2000 and 2001

[In millions of dollars (-452,207 represents -$452,207,000,000). Minus sign (-) indicates debits]

Area or country	2000, balance on—				2001, balance on—			
	Goods [1]	Services	Income	Current account	Goods [1]	Services	Income	Current account
All areas	-452,207	76,468	-14,792	-444,667	-426,615	78,805	-19,118	-417,429
Western Europe.	-64,633	9,627	-29,257	-85,556	-69,364	15,087	-31,486	-87,305
European Economic [2]	-57,363	10,733	-29,633	-76,431	-63,564	13,746	-31,360	-81,242
Belgium-Luxembourg	4,008	1,128	-5,583	-528	(NA)	(NA)	(NA)	(NA)
France.	-9,573	-414	-353	-10,648	(NA)	(NA)	(NA)	(NA)
Germany	-29,578	453	1,944	-26,691	(NA)	(NA)	(NA)	(NA)
Italy	-14,080	-554	2,702	-12,278	(NA)	(NA)	(NA)	(NA)
Netherlands	12,093	1,868	4,580	18,462	(NA)	(NA)	(NA)	(NA)
United Kingdom	-2,661	2,890	-40,984	-39,477	-1,292	4,459	-48,982	-44,401
Eastern Europe	-10,176	1,687	1,760	-10,396	-7,627	1,838	1,193	-8,134
Canada	-54,691	6,832	17,881	-30,702	-55,649	7,261	21,656	-27,484
Latin America, other Western								
Hemisphere.	-39,917	16,928	4,178	-34,445	-40,234	15,291	1,147	-40,842
Mexico	-25,640	2,851	-1,113	-29,938	(NA)	(NA)	(NA)	(NA)
Venezuela	-13,115	2,896	-157	-10,509	(NA)	(NA)	(NA)	(NA)
Japan [3]	-82,921	16,189	-30,507	-97,491	-70,607	14,743	-27,612	-83,779
Other Asia and Africa	-205,637	19,556	-1,857	-210,188	-187,285	18,869	-5,988	-192,686
Australia	5,767	2,375	5,371	13,208	4,151	2,067	5,683	11,554
South Africa.	-1,128	510	841	-7	(NA)	(NA)	(NA)	(NA)
International and unallocated	1	3,274	17,639	10,903	(NA)	3,649	16,289	11,247

NA Not available. [1] Adjusted to balance of payments basis; excludes exports under U.S. military sales contracts and imports under direct defense expenditures. [2] Includes Denmark, Greece, Ireland, Spain, Portugal, European Atomic Energy Community, European Coal and Steel Community, and European Investment Bank, not shown separately. [3] Includes Ryukyu Islands.
Source: U.S. Bureau of Economic Analysis, *Survey of Current Business,* April 2002 issue.

No. 1264. Private International Service Transactions by Type of Service and Country: 1990 to 2001

[In millions of dollars (137,232 represents $137,232,000,000). For all transactions, see Table 1262]

Type of service and country	Exports				Imports			
	1990	1995	2000	2001	1990	1995	2000	2001
Total private services	137,232	203,768	278,570	270,088	98,210	128,781	200,585	187,246
Travel	43,007	63,395	82,042	72,295	37,349	44,916	64,537	58,921
Overseas	30,807	54,331	70,050	(NA)	28,929	35,281	51,524	(NA)
Canada	7,093	6,207	7,055	6,300	3,541	4,319	6,367	6,397
Mexico.	5,107	2,857	4,937	(NA)	4,879	5,316	6,646	(NA)
Passenger fares	15,298	18,909	20,745	17,734	10,531	14,663	24,197	23,407
Other transportation.	22,042	26,081	30,185	28,292	24,966	27,034	41,058	38,230
Freight.	8,379	11,273	13,236	12,094	15,046	16,455	26,979	24,981
Port services.	13,662	14,809	16,950	16,198	9,920	10,579	14,083	13,249
Royalties and license fees	16,634	30,289	38,030	38,875	3,135	5,919	16,106	16,399
Other private services	40,251	65,094	107,568	112,892	22,229	35,249	54,687	50,289
Affiliated services.	13,622	20,483	31,628	35,385	9,117	13,634	25,300	29,484
Unaffiliated services	26,629	44,611	75,940	77,507	13,111	21,615	29,387	20,805
Education	5,126	7,515	10,287	10,959	658	1,125	2,140	2,496
Financial services.	4,417	7,029	17,042	14,498	2,475	2,472	4,482	3,936
Insurance, net	230	1,296	2,412	3,209	1,910	5,360	9,189	1,341
Telecommunications	2,735	3,228	3,843	4,178	5,583	7,305	5,360	5,002
Business, professional, and technical services	7,752	16,078	28,026	29,224	2,093	4,822	7,776	7,574
Advertising.	130	425	518	(NA)	243	833	804	(NA)
Computer and data processing services.	1,031	1,340	2,464	(NA)	44	126	837	(NA)
Management, consulting, and public relations services	354	1,489	1,834	(NA)	135	465	708	(NA)
Legal services	451	1,667	3,214	(NA)	111	469	839	(NA)
Construction, engineering, architectural, & mining services .	867	2,550	5,252	(NA)	170	345	422	(NA)
Canada	15,684	17,927	23,206	24,130	9,130	11,160	16,313	16,734
Europe	48,192	73,092	103,501	99,453	39,815	52,708	86,662	76,779
France.	5,542	7,965	10,300	(NA)	4,169	5,951	10,472	(NA)
Germany	7,364	12,692	15,993	(NA)	6,819	7,586	11,402	(NA)
Italy.	3,279	4,533	5,392	(NA)	3,469	3,743	5,168	(NA)
Netherlands	3,269	6,119	6,855	(NA)	1,935	3,191	5,234	(NA)
Switzerland	(NA)	3,843	5,596	(NA)	(NA)	2,285	5,367	(NA)
United Kingdom.	12,989	18,625	30,093	28,607	11,564	16,063	26,913	23,795
Latin America and other Western Hemisphere	21,957	32,872	54,110	52,024	18,643	24,252	37,383	36,711
Brazil.	(NA)	4,997	5,960	(NA)	(NA)	1,165	1,906	(NA)
Mexico.	8,590	8,705	14,013	(NA)	6,731	7,930	10,986	(NA)
Venezuela	1,273	2,496	3,495	(NA)	659	701	590	(NA)
Other countries.	45,321	74,508	91,615	(NA)	27,976	38,542	57,361	(NA)
Australia	3,260	4,266	5,413	5,088	2,290	2,142	3,263	3,116
Japan	21,159	33,240	34,241	32,413	10,529	13,463	17,249	16,905
Korea, Republic of	(NA)	5,693	6,940	(NA)	(NA)	3,581	4,188	(NA)
Taiwan.	(NA)	4,429	4,712	(NA)	(NA)	2,856	3,676	(NA)
Int'l organizations and unallocated	6,077	5,365	6,140	6,180	2,646	2,119	2,866	2,531

NA Not available.
Source: U.S. Bureau of Economic Analysis, *Survey of Current Business,* October 2001 and April 2002.

Foreign Commerce and Aid   783

No. 1265. International Investment Position by Type of Investment: 1990 to 2000

[In millions of dollars (-245,347 represents -$245,347,000,000). Estimates for end of year; subject to considerable error due to nature of basic data]

Type of investment	1990	1995	1996	1997	1998	1999	2000
U.S. net international investment position:							
Current cost	-245,347	-514,637	-595,168	-972,605	-1,128,699	-1,099,786	-1,842,663
Market value	-164,495	-418,648	-542,234	-1,076,134	-1,423,988	-1,525,347	-2,187,444
U.S.-owned assets abroad:							
Current cost	2,178,978	3,451,983	4,012,746	4,567,279	5,091,616	5,921,099	6,167,212
Market value	2,294,085	3,873,632	4,549,179	5,278,032	6,063,175	7,206,320	7,189,792
U.S. official reserve assets	174,664	176,061	160,739	134,836	146,006	136,418	128,400
Gold	102,406	101,279	96,698	75,929	75,291	75,950	71,799
Special drawing rights	10,989	11,037	10,312	10,027	10,603	10,336	10,539
Reserve position in IMF	9,076	14,649	15,435	18,071	24,111	17,950	14,824
Foreign currencies	52,193	49,096	38,294	30,809	36,001	32,182	31,238
U.S. Government assets, other	84,344	85,064	86,123	86,198	86,768	84,227	85,171
U.S. loans and other long-term assets	83,716	82,802	83,999	84,130	84,850	81,657	82,577
Repayable in dollars	82,602	82,358	83,606	83,780	84,528	81,367	82,296
Other	1,114	444	393	350	322	290	281
U.S. foreign currency holdings and short-term assets	628	2,262	2,124	2,068	1,918	2,570	2,594
U.S. private assets:							
Current cost	1,919,970	3,190,858	3,765,884	4,346,245	4,858,842	5,700,454	5,953,641
Market value	2,035,077	3,612,507	4,302,317	5,056,998	5,830,401	6,985,675	6,976,221
Direct investments abroad:							
Current cost	616,655	885,506	989,810	1,067,436	1,196,765	1,327,954	1,445,177
Market value	731,762	1,307,155	1,526,243	1,778,189	2,168,324	2,613,175	2,467,757
Foreign securities	342,313	1,169,636	1,467,985	1,751,183	2,052,929	2,604,383	2,406,504
Bonds	144,717	392,827	465,057	543,396	576,745	577,745	577,694
Corporate stocks	197,596	776,809	1,002,928	1,207,787	1,476,184	2,026,638	1,828,810
U.S. claims on unaffiliated foreigners [1]	265,315	367,567	450,578	545,524	588,322	667,732	825,251
U.S. claims reported by U.S. banks [2]	695,687	768,149	857,511	982,102	1,020,826	1,100,385	1,276,709
Foreign-owned assets in the U.S.:							
Current cost	2,424,325	3,966,620	4,607,914	5,539,884	6,220,315	7,020,885	8,009,875
Market value	2,458,580	4,292,280	5,091,413	6,354,166	7,487,163	8,731,667	9,377,236
Foreign official assets in the U.S.	373,293	671,710	798,368	835,962	838,041	870,364	922,429
U.S. Government securities	291,228	497,776	610,469	614,530	620,285	628,907	676,897
U.S. Treasury securities	285,911	482,773	590,704	589,792	589,023	578,225	582,344
Other	5,317	15,003	19,765	24,738	31,262	50,682	94,553
Other U.S. Government liabilities	17,243	23,573	22,592	21,712	18,340	15,486	13,499
U.S. liabilities reported by U.S. banks [2]	39,880	107,394	113,098	135,384	125,883	138,847	144,650
Other foreign official assets	24,942	42,967	52,209	64,336	73,533	87,124	87,383
Other foreign assets in the U.S.:							
Current cost	2,051,032	3,294,910	3,809,546	4,703,922	5,382,274	6,150,521	7,087,446
Market value	2,085,287	3,620,570	4,293,045	5,518,204	6,649,122	7,861,303	8,454,807
Direct investments:							
Current cost	505,346	680,066	745,619	823,126	912,187	1,094,439	1,369,505
Market value	539,601	1,005,726	1,229,118	1,637,408	2,179,035	2,805,221	2,736,866
U.S. Treasury securities	152,452	358,537	502,562	662,228	729,738	660,693	639,684
U.S. currency	85,933	169,484	186,846	211,628	228,250	250,657	251,786
U.S. securities other than U.S. Treasury securities	460,644	971,356	1,199,461	1,578,694	2,012,429	2,522,009	2,963,973
Corporate and other bonds	238,903	481,214	588,044	715,196	902,153	1,061,924	1,374,259
Corporate stocks	221,741	490,142	611,417	863,498	1,110,276	1,460,085	1,589,714
U.S. liabilities to unaffiliated foreigners [1]	213,406	300,424	346,810	459,407	485,675	555,566	722,738
U.S. liabilities reported by U.S. banks [2]	633,251	815,043	828,248	968,839	1,013,995	1,067,157	1,139,760

[1] Reported by U.S. nonbanking concerns.   [2] Not included elsewhere.

Source: U.S. Bureau of Economic Analysis, *Survey of Current Business*, July 2001.

No. 1266. U.S. Reserve Assets: 1990 to 2001

[In billions of dollars (83.3 represents $83,300,000,000). As of end of year, except as indicated]

Type	1990	1994	1995	1996	1997	1998	1999	2000	2001
Total	83.3	74.3	85.8	75.1	70.0	81.8	71.5	67.6	68.7
Gold stock	11.1	11.1	11.1	11.0	11.0	11.0	11.0	11.0	11.0
Special drawing rights	11.0	10.0	11.0	10.3	10.0	10.6	10.3	10.5	10.8
Foreign currencies	52.2	41.2	49.1	38.3	30.8	36.0	32.2	31.2	29.0
Reserve position in IMF [1]	9.1	12.0	14.6	15.4	18.1	24.1	18.0	14.8	17.9

[1] International Monetary Fund.

Source: Board of Governors of the Federal Reserve System, *Federal Reserve Bulletin*, monthly; and Department of the Treasury, *Treasury Bulletin*, monthly.

No. 1267. Foreign Direct Investment Position in the United States on a Historical-Cost Basis by Industry and Selected Country: 1999 and 2000

[In millions of dollars (965,632 represents $965,632,000,000)]

Country	1999				2000			
	Total [1]	Petro-leum	Manufac-turing	Whole-sale	Total [1]	Petro-leum	Manufac-turing	Whole-sale
All countries.	965,632	51,890	399,525	94,657	1,238,627	92,856	496,578	109,611
Canada	76,526	2,926	34,116	5,117	100,822	4,508	50,117	3,565
Europe	670,030	46,792	310,205	40,351	890,611	82,563	384,368	50,028
Austria	3,203	(D)	866	334	3,172	-	943	385
Belgium	10,037	6	3,783	93	14,186	4	6,688	577
Denmark	5,226	-2	1,322	3,493	5,905	(Z)	3,675	1,656
Finland	4,967	(D)	2,122	(D)	5,473	(D)	2,191	2,485
France	82,276	(D)	54,781	2,220	119,069	(D)	66,056	2,947
Germany	111,706	160	56,354	10,987	122,846	232	59,824	10,039
Ireland	15,621	596	4,476	2,192	23,031	(D)	6,333	7,025
Italy	4,709	(D)	957	310	6,409	(D)	1,064	212
Luxembourg	57,047	(D)	44,751	1,457	83,304	(D)	63,685	1,514
Netherlands	125,775	10,733	42,988	7,958	152,432	13,195	50,840	7,673
Norway	3,089	255	1,805	-313	2,441	(D)	2,079	-437
Spain	2,746	-6	982	151	8,860	-1	1,172	143
Sweden	20,843	(D)	10,992	363	27,389	(D)	12,711	(D)
Switzerland	53,706	736	25,782	2,645	81,698	1,107	36,594	3,632
United Kingdom	166,900	32,418	57,333	5,823	229,762	66,086	67,881	6,993
Latin America and other								
Western Hemisphere	38,104	1,313	3,021	2,905	42,700	1,563	3,891	3,503
South and Central America	8,365	-394	165	495	8,671	504	-2392	569
Mexico	1,730	-8	328	528	2,471	-5	258	533
Panama	5,475	14	114	-6	4,004	24	(D)	-35
Other Western Hemisphere	29,739	1,707	2,855	2,410	34,029	1,059	6,283	2,933
Bahamas	1,581	(D)	135	243	1,385	(D)	294	262
Netherlands Antilles	3,153	160	1,089	(D)	3,515	(D)	793	484
United Kingdom Islands, Caribbean .	11,082	979	1,472	1,546	12,513	281	3,997	1,652
Africa	1,547	18	234	410	2,119	(D)	168	344
Middle East	4,432	847	808	126	8,373	(D)	1,253	154
Israel	2,485	-	811	135	3,183	-	1,258	155
Kuwait	916	(D)	1	(Z)	957	-5	2	(Z)
Saudi Arabia	946	(D)	-1	(D)	(D)	(D)	4	-
Asia and Pacific	174,993	-5	51,141	45,749	194,002	147	56,781	52,018
Australia	13,230	62	3,458	29	14,487	62	5,491	84
Hong Kong	883	(D)	251	252	1,494	(D)	491	406
Japan	153,119	145	45,617	43,061	163,215	602	43,724	48,428
Singapore	1,370	-12	109	175	7,661	10	(D)	178
Taiwan	2,990	-4	1,168	583	3,224	-4	1,179	722

- Represents or rounds to zero.   D Suppressed to avoid disclosure of data of individual companies.   Z Less than $500,000.   [1] Includes other industries not shown separately.
Source: U.S. Bureau of Economic Analysis, *Survey of Current Business,* September 2001.

No. 1268. U.S. Affiliates of Foreign Companies—Assets, Sales, Employment, Land, Exports, and Imports: 1999

[A U.S. affiliate is a U.S. business enterprise in which one foreign owner (individual, branch, partnership, association, trust, corporation, or government) has a direct or indirect voting interest of 10 percent or more. Estimates cover the universe of nonbank affiliates. These data are now on a North American Industry Classification System (NAICS) basis and not comparable to previous data, which were based on the Standard Industrial Classification system]

Industry	Total assets (mil. dol.)	Sales (mil. dol.) [1]	Employ-ment (1,000) [2]	Employee compen-sation (mil. dol.)	Gross book value (mil. dol.)		Merchan-dise exports [4] (mil. dol.)	Merchan-dise imports [4] (mil. dol.)
					P & E [3]	Land		
All industries	4,135,217	2,035,356	6,003.3	289,958	1,015,352	53,857	152,229	307,111
Manufacturing [5]	982,809	906,382	2,616.7	143,419	525,361	15,464	96,527	140,924
Petroleum and coal products	108,252	109,551	60.7	5,032	116,826	2,007	3,139	13,661
Chemicals	206,151	142,527	363.2	25,693	96,020	2,399	14,575	15,373
Computers and electronic products .	98,773	108,226	291.0	18,792	34,832	846	16,991	33,685
Transportation equipment	185,592	201,609	422.6	23,606	88,249	838	30,476	45,064
Wholesale trade [5]	303,806	500,839	518.4	30,096	96,136	3,151	48,629	157,366
Motor vehicles and motor vehicle parts and supplies	83,519	112,896	66.1	4,222	42,000	794	2,651	50,070
Petroleum and petroleum products . .	21,788	54,988	10.2	983	6,265	297	3,221	7,968
Retail trade	70,956	114,300	737.0	16,794	34,605	3,089	1,521	4,303
Information	212,450	91,453	332.2	19,534	76,748	1,055	1,053	160
Finance (except depository institutions) and insurance	2,162,809	206,641	263.6	27,760	50,599	1,273	-	1
Real estate and rental and leasing . . .	131,014	26,037	52.2	2,650	90,840	17,706	(D)	562
Professional, scientific, and technical services	27,319	21,865	119.3	8,021	5,875	239	(D)	357
Other industries	244,053	167,840	1,363.7	41,684	135,187	11,881	3,777	3,440

- Represents or rounds to zero.   D Withheld to avoid disclosure of data of individual companies.   [1] Excludes returns, discounts, allowances, and sales and excise taxes.   [2] Average number of full-time and part-time employees.   [3] Plant and equipment (P & E). Includes mineral rights and minor amounts of property other than land.   [4] F.a.s. value at port of exportation.   [5] Includes industries not shown separately.
Source: U.S. Bureau of Economic Analysis, *Survey of Current Business,* August 2001; and *Foreign Direct Investment in the United States, Operations of U.S. Affiliates of Foreign Companies, Preliminary 1999 Estimates.*

Foreign Commerce and Aid   785

No. 1269. Foreign Direct Investment in the United States—Gross Book Value and Employment of U.S. Affiliates of Foreign Companies by State: 1990 to 1999

[578,355 represents $578,355,000,000. A U.S. affiliate is a U.S. business enterprise in which one foreign owner (individual, branch, partnership, association, trust corporation, or government) has a direct or indirect voting interest of 10 percent or more. Estimates cover the universe of nonbank U.S. affiliates]

State and other area	Gross book value of property, plant, and equipment (mil. dol.)				Total employment				
								1999, prel.	
	1990	1995	1998	1999, prel.	1990 (1,000)	1995 (1,000)	1998 (1,000)	Total (1,000)	Percent of all businesses
Total	578,355	769,491	990,332	1,069,209	4,734.5	4,941.8	5,646.1	6,003.3	(X)
United States	552,902	733,089	925,476	990,916	4,704.4	4,898.9	5,622.0	5,978.3	5.3
Alabama.	7,300	10,598	16,284	16,775	55.7	60.6	73.9	78.3	4.8
Alaska	19,435	25,558	27,582	28,226	13.2	9.8	10.5	10.5	5.0
Arizona.	7,234	6,699	9,887	11,076	57.1	51.9	64.4	70.8	3.7
Arkansas	2,344	3,666	4,068	4,437	29.2	32.1	37.2	37.8	3.9
California	75,768	96,576	104,758	115,630	555.9	548.6	598.7	638.8	5.1
Colorado.	6,544	8,602	9,501	10,476	56.3	72.2	77.3	91.4	4.9
Connecticut.	5,357	8,466	9,705	11,381	75.9	73.3	98.9	103.4	6.9
Delaware	5,818	2,919	4,528	5,280	43.1	15.8	24.8	28.3	7.7
District of Columbia	3,869	4,983	3,635	3,807	11.4	13.4	13.8	15.3	3.5
Florida	18,659	24,865	34,669	36,632	205.7	210.0	263.2	285.0	4.7
Georgia	16,729	22,432	26,871	27,548	161.0	180.1	202.0	216.0	6.4
Hawaii	11,830	15,972	12,453	11,363	53.0	48.9	43.4	44.4	10.1
Idaho	776	1,026	1,853	2,247	11.7	11.3	14.3	18.4	4.0
Illinois	23,420	34,305	40,826	45,300	245.8	237.0	267.3	283.5	5.4
Indiana.	13,426	18,782	28,117	29,372	126.9	136.9	160.9	165.1	6.2
Iowa	2,712	4,527	6,412	7,447	32.8	35.8	36.1	40.1	3.2
Kansas	5,134	3,233	7,461	7,069	29.6	34.0	43.9	55.1	4.9
Kentucky	9,229	15,136	21,175	20,785	65.7	83.4	93.8	97.7	6.4
Louisiana	17,432	20,543	29,648	31,934	61.4	51.0	59.8	63.1	4.0
Maine.	2,080	3,885	4,321	4,386	26.6	29.1	32.9	32.6	6.5
Maryland	5,713	9,197	10,619	11,436	79.6	95.0	95.5	98.7	4.9
Massachusetts.	8,890	12,707	16,364	17,781	131.2	141.5	177.6	194.1	6.6
Michigan.	12,012	21,370	37,477	41,981	139.6	170.3	236.5	246.1	6.1
Minnesota.	11,972	8,688	10,413	11,396	89.8	79.8	84.8	91.8	4.0
Mississippi	2,989	3,055	3,717	5,172	23.6	22.6	23.8	25.6	2.7
Missouri	5,757	8,327	13,838	15,217	73.7	79.3	92.9	100.5	4.2
Montana.	2,181	1,938	2,474	2,484	5.1	4.4	7.0	13.7	4.4
Nebraska	776	1,320	2,263	2,660	14.9	15.7	21.5	25.3	3.3
Nevada	5,450	8,242	9,315	9,917	22.7	25.0	28.3	32.7	3.6
New Hampshire	1,446	2,212	2,825	2,976	25.9	30.0	35.6	36.1	6.7
New Jersey.	18,608	26,175	33,852	35,378	227.0	205.2	237.2	245.1	7.3
New Mexico	4,312	4,363	6,025	5,474	17.4	16.2	17.8	16.4	2.9
New York	36,424	52,992	57,742	63,105	347.5	343.8	389.2	410.2	5.7
North Carolina	15,234	21,475	25,850	28,658	181.0	225.3	239.9	258.8	7.7
North Dakota.	1,251	915	1,701	1,799	3.1	3.2	5.6	7.7	2.9
Ohio	20,549	29,932	37,911	38,759	219.1	222.1	258.7	260.1	5.3
Oklahoma.	6,049	5,448	8,891	6,825	43.6	34.2	40.2	43.9	3.6
Oregon.	3,427	5,807	9,119	9,612	39.1	49.7	55.2	58.3	4.3
Pennsylvania.	16,587	24,432	27,980	34,060	221.6	231.6	241.4	261.5	5.2
Rhode Island.	1,120	2,240	2,698	2,502	13.3	16.2	22.2	21.6	5.2
South Carolina.	10,067	13,438	19,792	21,494	104.7	111.6	126.3	136.0	8.7
South Dakota	553	665	1,060	932	4.5	4.6	10.4	6.5	2.1
Tennessee	10,280	14,227	18,186	19,638	116.9	136.3	148.7	151.8	6.4
Texas.	57,079	68,142	90,499	96,550	299.5	326.4	385.7	410.2	5.2
Utah	3,918	5,612	8,821	9,332	21.0	28.6	33.9	35.0	3.9
Vermont	631	1,037	1,373	1,253	7.7	10.4	11.2	11.9	4.7
Virginia.	10,702	15,129	20,421	21,601	113.3	141.4	155.0	170.5	6.0
Washington.	7,985	11,462	16,084	18,030	77.5	83.0	91.4	96.7	4.3
West Virginia.	7,975	7,809	7,474	7,317	34.9	31.9	29.1	27.8	4.8
Wisconsin.	5,088	7,415	9,660	11,013	81.4	71.5	88.9	100.4	4.1
Wyoming	2,782	4,544	7,277	5,392	5.8	6.9	7.8	6.7	3.7
Puerto Rico.	1,499	2,174	1,772	2,176	16.1	27.4	17.0	17.2	(NA)
Other territories and offshore	18,484	17,798	29,223	28,986	9.0	13.1	7.1	7.7	(NA)
Foreign.	5,470	16,430	1,519	1,724	5.0	2.4	(Z)	0.1	(NA)
Unspecified [1]	(NA)	(NA)	32,342	45,407	(NA)	(NA)	(NA)	(NA)	(NA)

NA Not available.   X Not applicable.   Z Less than 50.   [1] Covers property, plant, and equipment not located in a particular state, including aircraft, railroad rolling stock, satellites, undersea cable, and trucks engaged in interstate transportation.

Source: U.S. Bureau of Economic Analysis, *Survey of Current Business,* August 2001 issue, and *Foreign Direct Investment in the United States, Operations of U.S. Affiliates of Foreign Companies,* annual.

786   Foreign Commerce and Aid

No. 1270. U.S. Businesses Acquired or Established by Foreign Direct Investors— Investment Outlays by Industry of U.S. Business Enterprise and Country of Ultimate Beneficial Owner: 1990 to 2000

[In millions of dollars (65,932 represents $65,932,000,000). Foreign direct investment is the ownership or control directly or indirectly, by one foreign individual branch, partnership, association, trust, corporation, or government of 10 percent or more of the voting securities of a U.S. business enterprise or an equivalent interest in an unincorporated one. Data represent number and full cost of acquisitions of existing U.S. business enterprises, including business segments or operating units of existing U.S. business enterprises and establishments of new enterprises. Investments may be made by the foreign direct investor itself, or indirectly by an existing U.S. affiliate of the foreign direct investor. Covers investments in U.S. business enterprises with assets of over $1 million, or ownership of 200 acres of U.S. land. These industry data are now on a North American Industry Classification System (NAICS) basis and not comparable to previous data, which were based on the Standard Industrial Classification system]

Industry and country	1990	1994	1995	1996	1997	1998	1999	2000, prel.
Total	65,932	45,626	57,195	79,929	69,708	215,256	274,956	320,858
INDUSTRY								
Manufacturing................	(NA)	(NA)	(NA)	(NA)	(NA)	149,243	73,122	144,871
Wholesale trade	(NA)	(NA)	(NA)	(NA)	(NA)	3,321	(D)	7,486
Retail trade	(NA)	(NA)	(NA)	(NA)	(NA)	1,153	3,458	(D)
Information..................	(NA)	(NA)	(NA)	(NA)	(NA)	13,399	90,855	62,198
Depository institutions	(NA)	(NA)	(NA)	(NA)	(NA)	1,563	(D)	(D)
Finance, (except depository institutions) and insurance....	(NA)	(NA)	(NA)	(NA)	(NA)	21,057	46,380	44,117
Real estate and rental and leasing	(NA)	(NA)	(NA)	(NA)	(NA)	6,299	5,206	3,197
Professional, scientific, and technical services	(NA)	(NA)	(NA)	(NA)	(NA)	4,289	9,366	31,999
Other industries	(NA)	(NA)	(NA)	(NA)	(NA)	14,932	32,680	23,283
COUNTRY [1]								
Canada......................	3,430	4,128	8,029	9,700	11,755	22,635	9,271	27,536
Europe	36,011	31,920	38,195	49,427	44,014	170,173	196,288	244,705
France......................	10,217	1,404	1,129	6,021	2,578	14,493	23,750	26,508
Germany	2,363	3,328	13,117	12,858	6,464	39,873	21,514	16,887
Netherlands	2,247	1,537	1,061	6,476	10,244	19,009	22,265	47,909
Switzerland	3,905	5,044	7,533	4,910	6,745	4,525	7,512	22,485
United Kingdom..............	13,096	17,261	9,094	14,757	11,834	84,995	109,226	107,666
Other Europe	4,183	3,346	6,261	4,405	6,149	7,278	12,021	23,250
Latin America and other Western Hemisphere	796	1,352	1,550	1,790	924	11,354	33,046	13,072
South and Central America	399	(D)	1,283	(D)	166	920	1,622	(D)
Other Western Hemisphere	397	(D)	267	(D)	758	10,433	31,424	(D)
Africa	(D)	(D)	(D)	(D)	(D)	212	(D)	(D)
Middle East	472	(D)	447	(D)	847	2,810	848	(D)
Asia and Pacific	23,170	5,263	8,688	12,751	11,786	7,329	15,100	33,278
Australia....................	1,412	1,522	2,270	2,222	7,600	(D)	(D)	(D)
Japan	19,933	2,715	3,602	8,813	2,326	4,862	11,696	25,343
Other Asia and Pacific	1,825	1,026	2,816	1,716	1,860	(D)	(D)	(D)

D Suppressed to avoid disclosure of data of individual companies.   NA Not available.   [1] For investments in which more than one investor participated, each investor and each investor's outlays are classified by country of each ultimate beneficial owner.

Source: U.S. Bureau of Economic Analysis, *Survey of Current Business*, June 2001, and previous June issues.

No. 1271. U.S. Direct Investment Position Abroad, Capital Outflows, and Income by Industry of Foreign Affiliates: 1998 to 2000

[In millions of dollars (1,000,713 represents $1,000,713,000,000)]

Industry	Direct investment position on a historical-cost basis			Capital outflows (inflows (-))			Income		
	1998	1999	2000	1998	1999	2000	1998	1999	2000
All industries, total ..	1,000,703	1,130,789	1,244,654	131,004	142,551	139,257	90,676	109,179	134,787
Petroleum	91,248	97,864	105,486	7,491	11,676	10,403	7,227	10,094	18,524
Manufacturing..........	290,070	312,072	343,992	23,122	34,102	44,101	29,683	33,966	39,268
Food and kindred products...............	35,304	35,151	36,840	2,133	257	2,645	4,306	3,805	3,847
Chemicals and allied products	79,446	83,524	86,081	6,110	7,960	4,210	8,213	9,356	9,995
Primary and fabricated metals	18,379	18,930	18,713	2,897	1,213	477	1,234	1,432	1,709
Industrial machinery and equipment.........	30,928	34,944	42,523	1,789	4,877	8,521	5,699	4,379	6,839
Electronic and other electric equipment	32,077	37,474	43,441	2,820	5,716	9,113	2,053	4,153	5,177
Transportation equipment	33,888	36,133	41,099	-1,356	5,736	7,254	2,417	4,556	3,646
Other manufacturing....	60,048	65,916	75,294	8,728	8,344	11,882	5,762	6,284	8,055
Wholesale trade	68,742	80,254	88,090	5,524	11,849	10,288	8,992	10,477	13,079
Depository institutions ...	40,020	38,382	37,155	2,112	-1,338	-2,306	734	1,655	1,788
Finance, insurance, and real estate [1]	375,368	443,263	497,267	62,229	55,011	58,344	34,765	41,429	50,996
Services	59,148	70,398	79,857	11,934	11,632	11,455	6,089	8,486	8,738
Other industries	76,108	88,556	92,809	18,591	19,618	6,971	3,186	3,072	2,395

[1] Excludes depository institutions.

Source: U.S. Bureau of Economic Analysis, *Survey of Current Business*, September 2000.

No. 1272. U.S. Direct Investment Position Abroad on a Historical-Cost Basis by Country: 1990 to 2000

[In millions of dollars (430,521 represents 430,521,000,000). U.S. direct investment abroad is the ownership or control by one U.S. person of 10 percent or more of the voting securities of an incorporated foreign business enterprise or an equivalent interest in a unincorporated foreign business enterprise. Negative position can occur when a U.S. parent company's liabilities to the foreign affiliate are greater than its equity in, and loans to the foreign affiliate]

Country	1990	1994	1995	1996	1997	1998	1999	2000
All countries	430,521	612,893	699,015	795,195	871,316	1,000,703	1,130,789	1,244,654
Canada	69,508	74,221	83,498	89,592	96,626	98,200	111,051	126,421
Europe	214,739	297,133	344,596	389,378	425,139	518,433	588,341	648,731
Austria	1,113	2,197	2,829	2,854	2,646	3,856	3,711	3,676
Belgium	9,464	14,714	18,706	18,740	17,337	17,899	17,347	16,409
Denmark	1,726	2,030	2,161	2,554	2,385	2,764	4,123	5,618
Finland	544	761	965	1,070	1,311	1,628	1,290	1,279
France	19,164	27,322	33,358	35,200	36,630	42,328	40,009	39,087
Germany	27,609	38,878	44,242	41,281	40,726	47,685	50,892	53,610
Greece	282	482	533	566	634	648	604	672
Ireland	5,894	7,239	7,996	10,133	11,339	21,825	26,084	33,369
Italy	14,063	14,808	17,096	16,193	15,547	15,548	17,914	23,622
Luxembourg	1,697	6,310	5,929	7,753	10,258	14,571	16,484	19,470
Netherlands	19,120	29,889	42,113	54,118	68,619	89,978	105,571	115,506
Norway	4,209	5,026	4,741	5,483	6,633	6,897	6,181	6,303
Portugal	897	1,181	1,413	1,423	1,399	1,360	1,463	1,784
Spain	7,868	9,572	10,856	12,252	11,541	14,221	13,244	14,561
Sweden	1,787	1,905	6,816	5,248	3,542	5,237	10,200	11,371
Switzerland	25,099	27,908	31,125	30,744	30,634	38,225	48,849	54,873
Turkey	522	874	973	1,059	1,033	1,014	1,235	1,378
United Kingdom	72,707	100,817	106,332	134,559	154,462	183,035	212,007	233,384
Other	974	5,219	6,412	8,148	8,464	9,713	11,135	12,760
Latin America and other								
Western Hemisphere	71,413	116,478	131,377	155,925	180,818	196,755	220,705	239,388
South America	22,933	37,673	49,170	57,372	69,507	72,593	74,743	79,354
Argentina	2,531	5,692	7,660	7,893	10,980	12,327	14,175	14,489
Brazil	14,384	17,885	25,002	29,105	35,778	37,195	34,276	35,560
Chile	1,896	5,062	6,216	8,156	9,148	9,029	10,105	10,846
Colombia	1,677	3,463	3,506	3,531	4,097	3,749	3,854	4,423
Ecuador	280	784	889	922	838	904	1,035	838
Peru	599	971	1,335	2,281	2,147	2,148	2,705	3,317
Venezuela	1,087	3,087	3,634	4,474	5,339	5,912	7,342	8,423
Other	479	728	928	1,010	1,182	1,329	1,251	1,456
Central America	20,415	30,083	33,493	37,667	48,549	56,035	68,456	74,754
Costa Rica	251	607	921	1,223	1,529	2,074	1,539	1,983
Guatemala	130	200	233	331	358	498	578	904
Honduras	262	140	68	129	183	111	126	115
Mexico	10,313	16,968	16,873	19,351	24,050	26,657	32,262	35,414
Panama	9,289	11,905	15,123	16,335	22,016	25,924	33,027	35,407
Other	169	262	273	298	413	771	923	931
Other Western Hemisphere . .	28,065	48,722	48,714	60,886	62,761	68,127	77,506	85,280
Bahamas	4,004	2,808	1,768	1,876	1,569	-282	702	668
Barbados	252	391	698	848	787	929	1,065	1,227
Bermuda	20,169	28,355	28,374	37,091	38,071	41,908	47,119	54,114
Dominican Republic	529	266	330	400	488	645	956	1,126
Jamaica	625	1,167	1,287	1,583	1,952	1,960	2,311	2,596
Netherlands Antilles	-4,501	6,739	6,835	7,597	4,415	3,897	3,652	3,725
Trinidad and Tobago	485	529	673	786	639	1,004	1,329	1,331
U.K. Islands, Caribbean . . .	5,929	7,858	8,358	10,121	14,044	17,434	19,767	20,165
Other	574	608	392	583	797	632	605	329
Africa	3,650	5,760	6,017	8,162	11,330	14,061	14,884	15,813
Egypt	1,231	1,090	1,093	1,366	1,603	1,963	2,190	2,735
Nigeria	-401	605	629	1,020	1,396	1,686	1,462	1,283
South Africa	775	1,132	1,422	1,495	2,499	2,344	2,905	2,826
Other	2,045	2,933	2,873	4,281	5,833	8,068	8,326	8,969
Middle East	3,959	6,367	7,198	8,294	8,836	10,739	10,519	11,851
Israel	746	1,483	1,831	2,045	2,071	2,837	3,051	3,426
Saudi Arabia	1,899	2,100	2,741	3,476	3,821	4,672	4,426	4,784
United Arab Emirates	409	357	500	598	567	674	557	573
Other	905	2,427	2,126	2,174	2,377	2,556	2,486	3,069
Asia and Pacific	64,716	108,528	122,712	139,548	144,815	159,678	181,882	199,599
Australia	15,110	20,196	24,328	30,006	28,404	31,483	34,776	35,324
China	354	2,557	2,765	3,848	5,150	6,350	8,058	9,577
Hong Kong	6,055	11,092	11,768	14,391	17,315	17,548	20,092	23,308
India	372	1,030	1,105	1,344	1,563	1,592	1,402	1,258
Indonesia	3,207	6,355	6,777	8,322	6,729	8,104	10,495	11,605
Japan	22,599	34,117	37,309	34,578	33,854	41,423	49,438	55,606
Korea, South	2,695	4,334	5,557	6,508	6,467	7,365	8,559	9,432
Malaysia	1,466	3,148	4,237	5,663	6,530	5,629	5,820	5,995
New Zealand	3,156	3,893	4,601	5,940	7,160	6,021	5,433	5,340
Philippines	1,355	2,484	2,719	3,541	3,219	3,931	3,136	2,910
Singapore	3,975	10,940	12,140	14,912	18,026	17,550	20,117	23,245
Taiwan	2,226	3,775	4,293	4,476	5,007	6,295	6,513	7,737
Thailand	1,790	3,585	4,283	5,000	4,332	5,209	6,809	7,124
Other	356	1,022	830	1,019	1,058	1,177	1,235	1,138
International	2,535	4,406	3,618	4,295	3,752	2,837	3,406	2,851

Source: U.S. Bureau of Economic Analysis, *Survey of Current Business,* September 2001, and earlier issues.

No. 1273. U.S. Government Foreign Grants and Credits by Type and Country: 1990 to 2000

[In millions of dollars (14,396 represents $14,396,000,000). See text, this section. Negative figures (-) occur when the total of grant returns, principal repayments, and/or foreign currencies disbursed by the U.S. Government exceeds new grants and new credits utilized and/or acquisitions of foreign currencies through new sales of farm products]

Country	1990	1994	1995	1996	1997	1998	1999	2000
Total, net	**14,396**	**16,429**	**12,666**	**16,701**	**12,833**	**14,029**	**18,656**	**17,945**
Investment in financial institutions	1,304	1,430	1,517	1,833	1,588	1,580	1,451	1,500
Western Europe	**-103**	**176**	**177**	**197**	**390**	**317**	**428**	**178**
Austria	-10	-1	-1	-1	-1	(Z)	-	-
Belgium and Luxembourg	-9	-	-	-	-	-	-	-
Denmark	-	-	-	-	-	-	-	-
Finland	-8	-1	-1	-1	-1	(Z)	-	-
France	-15	-1	-	-	(Z)	-	-	-
Germany	-338	-	(Z)	(Z)	-	-	-	-
Iceland	(Z)	-	-	-	-	-	-	-
Ireland	2	36	-	11	39	8	-	-
Italy	-30	-	(Z)	-	-	-	-	-
Netherlands	-	-	-	-	-	-	-	-
Norway	-	-	-	-	-	-	-	-
Portugal	56	115	-16	-3	-	26	4	-80
Spain	-122	-55	-59	-48	-37	-37	-28	-19
Sweden	-	-	-	-	-	-	-	-
United Kingdom	-111	-118	-120	-125	-127	-130	-136	-135
Yugoslavia [1]	-39	-1	(X)	-1	(X)	-1	(X)	1
Former Yugoslavia: [1]								
Bosnia and Hercegovina	(X)	84	94	161	311	236	188	52
Croatia	(X)	52	9	-10	-7	-11	1	3
Macedonia	(X)	3	1	3	18	7	20	50
Slovenia	(X)	-17	-24	-27	-15	-15	2	1
Former Yugoslavia - Regional [3]	(X)	(Z)	(Z)	1	-8	8	21	74
Other [2] and unspecified [3]	520	81	293	236	220	229	355	234
Eastern Europe	**973**	**2,910**	**1,979**	**1,957**	**1,410**	**1,790**	**2,152**	**1,818**
Albania	-	16	15	58	11	16	4	25
Bulgaria	-	8	6	13	14	14	26	45
Czechoslovakia	(Z)	1	-2	3	-11	(X)	(X)	1
Czech Republic	(X)	2	3	10	5	5	8	9
Estonia	(X)	(Z)	2	7	4	6	4	5
Hungary	1	4	36	15	-16	13	13	11
Latvia	(X)	3	2	10	4	8	9	6
Lithuania	(X)	15	28	17	23	15	4	-14
Poland	912	8	6	50	29	38	24	38
Romania	79	18	9	30	5	28	10	37
Slovakia	-	1	2	12	11	6	8	6
Soviet Union	-30	(X)	(X)	(X)	(X)	(X)	(X)	-
Newly Independent States:								
Armenia	-	127	102	80	26	39	35	20
Azerbaijan	-	24	19	14	4	6	6	8
Belarus	-	37	50	31	19	3	6	1
Georgia	-	86	89	79	38	28	23	35
Kazakhstan	-	17	17	60	52	70	45	42
Kyrgyzstan	-	36	33	38	26	30	15	15
Moldova	-	22	19	15	8	5	32	31
Russia	-	1,184	465	423	361	444	968	796
Tajikistan	-	30	34	32	27	30	6	8
Turkmenistan	-	13	16	19	1	3	3	3
Ukraine	-	105	171	233	97	172	318	137
Uzbekistan	-	6	1	5	2	7	19	21
Former Soviet Union - Regional [3]	-	735	613	579	582	603	506	501
Other [2] and unspecified [3]	11	413	241	124	85	200	61	29
Near East and South Asia	**6,656**	**7,042**	**3,025**	**7,666**	**4,675**	**5,045**	**4,378**	**7,669**
Afghanistan	57	9	10	14	17	-	2	5
Bangladesh	181	202	87	48	42	24	65	42
Cyprus	16	16	6	11	10	14	-	-
Egypt	4,976	2,258	1,639	1,621	1,375	2,018	2,093	3,090
Greece	282	262	261	12	-210	-240	-145	-169
India	13	45	48	55	238	167	-79	-64
Iran	-	-	-	-21	-	-	-	-
Iraq [4]	-7	135	128	119	11	-	-	31
Israel	4,380	3,106	420	5,294	2,896	2,842	2,221	3,932
Jordan	155	98	129	168	279	217	186	301
Kuwait	-2,506	-	-	-	-	-	-	-
Lebanon	9	5	5	11	3	2	9	22
Nepal	20	21	20	21	24	20	19	15
Oman	4	1	4	12	26	20	-6	-6
Pakistan	531	-158	-187	-164	-62	-82	79	366
Saudi Arabia	-1,614	-	-	-	-	-	-	-
Sri Lanka	72	41	27	6	7	1	-6	-15
Syria	(Z)	-	-	-	-	-	-	-
Turkey	367	224	147	51	-129	-159	-259	-87
United Arab Emirates	-361	-	-	-	-	-	-	-
Yemen (Sanaa)	(X)	(X)	(X)	(X)	(X)	(X)	(X)	-
Yemen	43	1	3	5	12	5	10	15
UNRWA [5]	7	7	103	72	59	78	93	97
West Bank-Gaza	1	64	58	33	53	80	88	64
Other and unspecified [3]	29	705	118	298	25	39	10	30

See footnotes at end of table.

[In millions of dollars. See headnote, p. 789]

Country	1990	1994	1995	1996	1997	1998	1999	2000
Africa	**1,883**	**2,031**	**2,217**	**1,957**	**1,354**	**1,366**	**841**	**1,033**
Algeria	59	28	755	644	93	45	-46	-53
Angola	-15	58	37	42	41	38	21	31
Benin	5	17	14	13	23	14	23	22
Botswana	17	15	18	9	9	5	3	1
Burkina	15	14	23	11	15	17	9	7
Burundi	18	55	39	2	4	9	6	3
Cameroon	42	13	4	4	(Z)	6	2	1
Cape Verde	8	7	11	10	11	6	1	1
Chad	24	10	14	8	6	3	2	2
Congo, Democratic Republic of the (former Zaire)	242	1	1	(Z)	(Z)	1	2	9
Cote d'Ivoire	18	38	16	22	16	8	11	9
Eritrea	-	28	9	18	17	21	7	48
Ethiopia	57	168	127	104	77	162	44	142
Ghana	14	65	63	34	55	40	38	40
Guinea	16	38	28	29	28	18	22	19
Kenya	115	54	35	6	27	37	31	43
Lesotho	16	8	13	4	5	3	1	1
Liberia	32	66	67	58	28	19	26	19
Madagascar	34	23	33	42	35	44	30	21
Malawi	35	37	64	36	30	23	30	45
Mali	31	30	31	12	11	36	36	49
Mauritania	13	2	2	2	5	4	2	2
Morocco	96	27	-48	-4	-42	-48	-28	-10
Mozambique	83	82	115	53	79	81	74	119
Niger	34	16	31	15	11	13	7	5
Nigeria	156	52	1	-4	-10	-4	-38	-18
Rwanda	13	220	138	93	88	32	29	26
Senegal	61	33	24	38	36	18	26	26
Sierra Leone	2	10	11	28	18	14	5	10
Somalia	80	34	26	10	10	4	12	7
South Africa	20	71	112	101	113	90	91	67
Sudan	150	60	11	16	24	28	16	17
Swaziland	14	10	13	21	12	14	-	-
Tanzania	51	24	19	16	18	27	22	15
Togo	10	8	3	1	1	2	2	2
Tunisia	44	2	-4	-20	-6	-19	-22	-21
Uganda	43	57	56	41	56	19	51	92
Zambia	63	21	27	21	47	14	27	44
Zimbabwe	10	34	29	22	21	47	18	22
Other and unspecified [3]	157	492	246	397	343	475	248	168
Far East and Pacific	**39**	**751**	**753**	**783**	**137**	**759**	**1,145**	**545**
Australia	-34	-1	-	-	-	-	-	-
Burma	1	-2	-2	-2	-2	-2	-0	-0
Cambodia	5	16	39	36	28	35	16	23
China	71	6	136	113	227	248	293	167
Hong Kong	-8	1	73	133	44	17	-17	-15
Indonesia	46	24	25	44	-48	24	483	270
Japan and Ryukyu Islands	-635	-1	(Z)	(Z)	-	-	-	-
Korea, Republic of	-192	-55	-49	-62	-51	-52	330	-132
Laos	(Z)	2	3	4	4	5	4	5
Malaysia	-1	1	(Z)	1	1	2	-	133
Mongolia	-	18	11	7	13	23	14	8
New Zealand	-2	-	-	-	-	-	-	-
Pacific Islands, Trust Territory of the [6]	220	317	209	215	140	175	145	145
Philippines	557	-52	56	65	-46	297	-34	19
Singapore	(Z)	(Z)	1	(Z)	-	-	-	-
Taiwan	-7	-8	-5	-3	-1	-1	-1	-1
Thailand	-19	247	205	199	-285	-63	-120	-104
Vietnam	1	(Z)	(Z)	-	49	-9	-6	1
Other and unspecified [3]	38	238	51	34	63	58	36	26
Western Hemisphere	**2,025**	**1,005**	**485**	**511**	**663**	**1,033**	**5,120**	**1,167**
Argentina	64	33	-26	-43	-82	-84	-96	-74
Bolivia	114	156	101	100	122	97	104	135
Brazil	261	-59	-204	-191	-31	90	38	195
Canada	-41	-120	-	-	-	-	-	-
Chile	-32	-33	-24	-3	-2	5	-8	-22
Colombia	-30	20	5	27	27	43	173	32
Costa Rica	108	-5	-28	-43	-30	-27	-37	-34
Dominican Republic	28	(Z)	-15	-19	-29	-14	-13	-58
Ecuador	61	18	5	6	6	3	14	14
El Salvador	303	92	119	79	92	41	38	27

See footnotes at end of table.

U.S. Census Bureau, Statistical Abstract of the United States: 2002

No. 1273. U.S. Government Foreign Grants and Credits by Type and Country: 1990 to 2000—Con.

[In millions of dollars. See headnote, p. 789]

Country	1990	1994	1995	1996	1997	1998	1999	2000
Western Hemisphere—Continued:								
Guatemala	98	57	39	4	37	36	45	49
Guyana	42	11	10	11	12	12	5	5
Haiti	54	125	156	82	93	88	86	63
Honduras	226	54	77	31	29	31	82	100
Jamaica	108	99	30	-13	-30	-21	-24	-34
Mexico	140	-229	-198	-130	-75	-127	-118	-124
Nicaragua	105	46	41	37	44	50	53	53
Panama [7]	102	8	8	-4	-15	-20	4,100	-14
Paraguay	(Z)	3	1	2	3	2	6	4
Peru	93	157	151	76	134	113	101	86
Trinidad and Tobago	5	-9	-14	-15	5	205	-39	-19
Uruguay	-3	2	1	3	2	1	2	-2
Venezuela	-18	2	-2	2	3	5	4	133
Other [8] and unspecified [3]	236	579	251	512	351	505	605	652
Other international organizations and unspecified areas [3]	1,619	1,084	2,513	1,798	2,616	2,138	3,141	4,036

- Represents zero or rounds to zero.   X Not applicable.   Z Less than $500,000.   [1] In 1992, some successor countries assumed portions of outstanding credits of the former Yugoslavia (assignment of the remaining portions is pending). Subsequent negative totals reflect payments to the United States on these assumed credits which were greater than the extension of new credits and grants to these countries.   [2] Includes European Atomic Energy Community, European Coal and Steel Community, European Payments Union, European Productivity Agency, North Atlantic Treaty Organization, and Organization for European Economic Cooperation.   [3] In recent years, significant amounts of foreign assistance has been reported on a regional, inter-regional, and worldwide basis. Country totals in this table may understate actual assistance to many countries.   [4] Foreign assistance to Iraq in 1994-96 was direct humanitarian assistance to ethnic minorities of Northern Iraq after the conflict in the Persian Gulf.   [5] United Nations Relief and Works Agency for Palestine refugees.   [6] Excludes transactions with Commonwealth of the Northern Mariana Islands after October 1986; includes transactions with Federated States of Micronesia, Republic of the Marshall Islands, and Republic of Palau.   [7] Includes transfer of Panama Canal to the Republic of Panama on December 1999.   [8] Includes Andean Development Corporation, Caribbean Development Bank, Central American Bank for Economic Integration, Eastern Caribbean Central Bank, Inter-American Institute of Agricultural Science, Organizations of American States, and Pan American Health Organization.

Source: U.S. Bureau of Economic Analysis, press releases, and unpublished data.

No. 1274. U.S. Foreign Economic and Military Aid Programs: 1980 to 2000

[In millions of dollars (9,695 represents $9,695,000,000). For years ending September 30. Economic aid shown here represents U.S. economic aid—not just aid under the Foreign Assistance Act. Major components in recent years include AID, Food for Peace, Peace Corps, and paid-in subscriptions to international financial institutions, such as IBRD, and IDB. Annual figures are gross unadjusted program figures]

Year and region	Total economic and military aid	Economic aid			Military aid		
		Total	Loans	Grants	Total	Loans	Grants
1980	9,695	7,573	1,993	5,580	2,122	1,450	672
1981	10,550	7,305	1,460	5,845	3,245	2,546	699
1982	12,324	8,129	1,454	6,675	4,195	3,084	1,111
1983	14,202	8,603	1,619	6,984	5,599	3,932	1,667
1984	15,524	9,038	1,621	7,417	6,486	4,401	2,085
1985	18,128	12,327	1,579	10,748	5,801	2,365	3,436
1986	16,739	10,900	1,330	9,570	5,839	1,980	3,859
1987	14,488	9,386	1,138	8,248	5,102	953	4,149
1988	13,792	8,961	852	8,109	4,831	763	4,068
1989	14,688	9,860	694	9,166	4,828	410	4,418
1990	15,727	10,834	756	10,078	4,893	404	4,489
1991	16,663	11,904	354	11,550	4,760	428	4,332
1992	15,589	11,242	494	10,748	4,347	345	4,002
1993	28,196	24,054	462	23,593	4,143	855	3,288
1994	15,870	11,940	887	11,053	3,931	770	3,161
1995	15,108	11,295	190	11,105	3,813	558	3,255
1996	13,559	9,589	329	9,260	3,970	544	3,426
1997	13,037	9,171	218	8,953	3,866	298	3,568
1998	13,907	10,318	271	10,047	3,589	100	3,489
1999	15,987	12,308	408	11,899	3,679	152	3,527
2000, total	16,943	11,740	304	11,436	5,204	-	5,204
Near East	6,860	2,180	10	2,170	4,680	-	4,680
Sub Saharan Africa	1,553	1,499	9	1,490	54	-	54
Latin America	1,977	1,960	23	1,937	17	-	17
Asia	862	845	45	800	18	-	18
Eastern Europe	9	9	-	9	1	-	1
Western Europe	1,141	1,124	212	911	17	-	17
Eurasia	899	748	5	744	150	-	150
Oceania and other	3	-	-	-	3	-	3
Nonregional	3,639	3,375	-	3,375	263	-	263

- Represents zero.

Source: U.S. Agency for International Development, *U.S. Overseas Loans and Grants and Assistance from International Organizations,* annual.

U.S. Census Bureau, Statistical Abstract of the United States: 2002

No. 1275. U.S. Foreign Military Aid by Major Recipient Country: 1997 to 2000

[In millions of dollars (3,864.4 represents $3,864,400,000), except as indicated. For years ending Sept. 30. Military aid data include Military Assistance Program (MAP) grants, foreign military credit sales, International Military Education and Training, and excess defense articles]

Recipient country	1997	1998	1999	2000 Total (mil. dol.)	2000 Rank	2000 Percent of total assistance
Total [1]	3,864.4	3,589.0	3,678.9	5,204.0	(X)	30.7
Albania	0.7	2.3	4.7	2.2	27	3.5
Bosnia Hercegovina	0.5	0.6	4.6	51.9	4	34.7
Bulgaria	0.9	5.2	9.5	5.8	13	13.1
Croatia	0.4	0.5	0.4	4.5	19	8.3
Czech Republic	0.7	17.2	8.3	7.4	10	100.0
East Timor	-	-	-	8.5	9	24.0
Egypt	1,301.0	1,301.0	1,301.0	1,301.0	2	63.7
Estonia	0.6	9.0	5.4	4.8	16	87.8
Georgia	0.3	5.8	8.3	3.4	22	3.2
Haiti	0.3	0.3	0.5	4.3	20	5.0
Hungary	1.0	17.1	8.6	7.4	10	100.0
Iraq	-	-	-	25.0	6	100.0
Israel	1,800.0	1,800.0	1,860.0	3,120.0	1	76.7
Jordan	31.7	51.6	76.1	226.4	3	47.8
Kazakhstan	0.4	3.2	2.2	2.1	28	4.0
Latvia	0.5	7.0	5.4	4.7	17	77.1
Lithuania	0.5	7.7	5.4	5.2	14	75.0
Moldova	0.3	4.0	1.7	1.7	29	3.8
Morocco	0.8	0.9	4.9	2.4	25	5.8
Nigeria	-	-	0.1	10.5	7	11.8
Philippines	1.3	1.3	2.3	4.9	15	6.2
Poland	1.0	125.0	8.2	9.7	8	50.4
Romania	0.9	15.0	7.6	7.1	12	15.8
Slovakia	0.6	3.8	3.8	3.2	23	34.4
Slovenia	0.4	3.2	3.3	2.6	24	100.0
Thailand	1.6	2.0	1.7	1.7	29	29.3
Tunisia	0.8	0.9	2.9	3.9	21	100.0
Ukraine	1.0	5.1	5.4	4.6	18	2.6
Uzbekistan	0.3	2.1	2.2	2.3	26	6.8
Yugoslavia (Kosovo)	-	-	-	33.4	5	17.1

- Represents zero. X Not applicable. [1] Includes countries not shown separately.

Source: U.S. Agency for International Development, *U.S. Overseas Loans and Grants,* annual.

No. 1276. U.S. Foreign Economic Aid by Major Recipient Country: 1997 to 2000

[In millions of dollars (9,170.3 represents $9,170,300,000), except as indicated. For years ending Sept. 30]

Recipient country	1997	1998	1999	2000 Total (mil. dol.)	2000 Rank	2000 Percent of total assistance
Total [1]	9,170.3	10,318.0	12,307.6	11,740.0	(X)	69.3
Albania	7.7	32.0	49.1	62.8	28	96.5
Angola	49.2	62.8	48.5	92.3	17	100.0
Armenia	16.8	74.3	74.3	93.0	16	100.0
Bangladesh	77.8	97.4	190.2	71.5	25	99.4
Bolivia	131.2	108.9	133.3	231.9	7	99.8
Bosnia Hercegovina	183.6	282.9	185.0	97.5	15	65.3
Colombia	35.1	60.9	211.9	1,026.1	1	99.9
Egypt	810.7	828.4	860.3	741.4	3	36.3
Ethiopa	79.2	113.8	126.1	240.8	6	99.9
Georgia	1.7	75.4	93.0	101.6	14	96.8
Ghana	47.3	48.6	74.4	62.0	29	99.3
Guatemala	61.4	82.5	101.4	66.2	27	99.7
Haiti	101.5	102.7	94.1	81.9	19	95.0
India	125.6	126.7	172.6	168.1	11	99.7
Indonesia	34.8	98.7	197.1	201.2	8	100.0
Israel	1,200.0	1,200.0	1,080.0	949.1	2	23.3
Jordan	152.7	88.0	214.0	246.9	5	52.2
Kenya	28.9	66.6	78.3	79.4	20	99.5
Korea, North	0.0	70.4	156.6	79.4	21	100.0
Mozambique	55.0	72.2	78.4	82.0	18	99.8
Nigeria	1.3	9.6	23.6	78.5	22	88.2
Peru	126.2	168.0	196.3	190.5	9	99.8
Philippines	40.4	68.3	66.8	73.3	24	93.8
Russia	65.0	135.2	688.9	438.9	4	99.8
South Africa	79.5	75.2	57.8	51.7	34	98.3
Uganda	64.9	84.9	72.8	75.0	23	99.7
Ukraine	49.7	159.6	222.5	173.7	10	97.4
West Bank/Gaza	67.0	60.7	79.6	121.4	13	100.0
Yugoslavia (Montenegro)	-	-	1.7	162.3	12	82.9
Serbia	0.9	9.9	-	71.3	26	100.0

- Represents zero. X Not applicable. [1] Includes countries not shown separately.

Source: U.S. Agency for International Development, *U.S. Overseas Loans and Grants,* annual.

U.S. Census Bureau, Statistical Abstract of the United States: 2002

No. 1277. U.S. International Trade in Goods and Services: 1999 to 2001

[In millions of dollars (957,146 represents $957,146,000,000). Data presented on a balance of payments basis and will not agree with the following merchandise trade Tables 1278 to 1284]

Category	Exports			Imports			Trade balance		
	1999	2000	2001	1999	2000	2001	1999	2000	2001
Total	957,146	1,064,239	998,022	1,219,383	1,442,920	1,356,312	-262,237	-378,681	-358,290
Goods.	683,965	771,994	718,762	1,029,987	1,224,417	1,145,927	-346,022	-452,423	-427,165
Services	273,181	292,245	279,260	189,396	218,503	210,385	83,785	73,742	68,875
Travel	74,731	82,267	73,119	58,865	64,788	60,117	15,866	17,479	13,002
Passenger fares	19,785	20,760	18,007	21,315	24,306	22,418	-1,530	-3,546	-4,411
Other transportation	26,916	30,137	28,306	34,139	41,598	38,823	-7,223	-11,461	-10,517
Royalties and license fees	36,902	39,607	38,668	12,609	16,115	16,359	24,293	23,492	22,309
Other private services. . .	98,158	104,707	108,109	46,313	55,253	54,588	51,845	49,454	53,521
Other [1]	15,804	13,981	12,220	13,334	13,560	15,198	2,470	421	-2,978
U.S. government miscel. services	885	786	831	2,821	2,883	2,882	-1,936	-2,097	-2,051

[1] Represents transfers under U.S. military sales contracts for exports and direct defense expenditures for imports.

Source: U.S. Census Bureau, *U.S. International Trade in Goods and Services,* Series FT-900(01-12) and FT-900 (02-02). See also <http://www.census.gov/foreign-trade/Press-Release/2001pr/FinalRevisions2001/> (released 22 August 2002).

No. 1278. U.S. Exports, General Imports, and Trade Balance in Goods: 1970 to 2001

[In billions of dollars (43.8 represents $43,800,000,000). Domestic and foreign exports, are f.a.s. value basis; general imports are on customs value basis]

Year	Total goods [1]			Manufactured goods [2][3]			Agricultural products [4]			Mineral fuels [3][5]		
	Exports	Imports	Balance	Exports	Imports	Balance	Exports	Imports	Balance	Exports	Imports	Balance
1970 . .	43.8	40.4	3.4	31.7	27.3	4.4	7.3	5.8	1.6	1.6	3.1	-1.5
1971 . .	44.7	46.2	-1.5	32.9	32.1	0.8	7.8	5.8	2.0	1.5	3.7	-2.2
1972 . .	50.5	56.4	-5.9	36.5	39.7	-3.2	9.5	6.5	3.0	1.6	4.8	-3.2
1973 . .	72.5	70.5	2.0	48.5	47.1	1.3	17.9	8.5	9.4	1.7	8.2	-6.5
1974 . .	100.0	102.6	-2.6	68.5	57.8	10.7	22.3	10.4	11.9	3.4	25.5	-22.0
1975 . .	109.3	98.5	10.8	76.9	54.0	22.9	22.1	9.5	12.6	4.5	26.5	-22.0
1976 . .	117.0	123.5	-6.5	83.1	67.6	15.5	23.3	11.2	12.1	4.2	34.0	-29.8
1977 . .	123.2	151.0	-27.8	88.9	80.5	8.4	24.2	13.6	10.6	4.2	47.2	-43.0
1978 . .	145.9	174.8	-28.9	103.6	104.3	-0.7	29.8	15.0	14.8	3.9	42.0	-38.1
1979 . .	186.5	209.5	-23.0	132.7	117.1	15.6	35.2	16.9	18.3	5.7	59.9	-54.2
1980 . .	225.7	245.3	-19.6	160.7	133.0	27.7	41.8	17.4	24.3	8.2	78.9	-70.7
1981 . .	238.7	261.0	-22.3	171.7	149.8	22.0	43.8	17.2	26.6	10.3	81.2	-70.9
1982 . .	216.4	244.0	-27.6	155.3	151.7	3.6	37.0	15.7	21.3	12.8	65.3	-52.5
1983 . .	205.6	258.0	-52.4	148.5	171.2	-22.7	36.5	16.5	19.9	9.8	57.8	-48.0
1983 . .	205.6	258.0	-52.4	148.7	170.9	-22.2	36.1	16.0	20.2	9.8	57.8	-48.0
1984 . .	224.0	330.7	-106.7	164.1	230.9	-66.8	37.9	19.3	18.6	9.7	60.8	-51.1
1985 . .	218.8	336.5	-117.7	168.0	257.5	-89.5	29.3	19.5	9.8	10.3	53.7	-43.4
1986 . .	227.2	365.4	-138.2	179.8	296.7	-116.8	26.3	20.9	5.4	8.4	37.2	-28.8
1987 . .	254.1	406.2	-152.1	199.9	324.4	-124.6	28.7	20.3	8.4	8.0	44.1	-36.1
1988 . .	322.4	441.0	-118.6	255.6	361.4	-105.7	37.1	20.7	16.4	8.5	41.0	-32.5
1989 . .	363.8	473.2	-109.4	287.0	379.4	-92.4	41.6	21.1	20.5	9.9	52.6	-42.7
1990 . .	393.6	495.3	-101.7	315.4	388.8	-73.5	39.6	22.3	17.2	12.4	64.7	-52.3
1991 . .	421.7	488.5	-66.8	345.1	392.4	-47.3	39.4	22.1	17.2	12.3	54.1	-41.8
1992 . .	448.2	532.7	-84.5	368.5	434.3	-65.9	43.1	23.4	19.8	11.3	55.3	-43.9
1993 . .	465.1	580.7	-115.6	388.7	479.9	-91.2	42.8	23.6	19.2	9.9	55.9	-46.0
1994 . .	512.6	663.3	-150.7	431.1	557.3	-126.3	45.9	26.0	20.0	9.0	56.4	-47.4
1995 . .	584.7	743.4	-158.7	486.7	629.7	-143.0	56.0	29.3	26.8	10.5	59.1	-48.6
1996 . .	625.1	795.3	-170.2	524.7	658.8	-134.1	60.6	32.6	28.1	12.4	78.1	-65.7
1997 . .	689.2	870.7	-181.5	592.5	728.9	-136.4	57.1	35.2	21.9	13.0	78.3	-65.3
1998 . .	682.1	911.9	-229.8	596.6	790.8	-194.2	52.0	35.7	16.3	10.4	57.3	-47.0
1999 . .	695.8	1,024.6	-328.8	611.6	882.7	-271.1	48.2	36.7	11.5	9.9	75.2	-65.3
2000 . .	781.9	1,218.0	-436.1	691.5	1,012.7	-321.3	53.0	39.2	13.8	13.4	135.4	-122.0
2001 . .	730.9	1,141.0	-410.1	640.2	950.7	-310.4	55.2	39.5	15.7	12.7	121.9	-109.2

[1] Includes nonmonetary gold, military grant aid, special category shipments, trade between the U.S. Virgin Islands and foreign countries and undocumented exports to Canada. Adjustments were also made for carryover. Import values are based on transaction prices whenever possible (f.a.s. for 1974-1979 and Customs value thereafter). Import data before 1974 do not exist on a transaction price valuation basis. [2] Manufactured goods include commodity Sections 5-9 under Schedules A and E for 1970-1982 and SITC Rev. 3 for 1983-forward. Manufactures include undocumented exports to Canada, nonmonetary gold (excluding gold ore, scrap, and base bullion), and special category shipments. [3] Data for 1970-1980 exclude trade between the U.S. Virgin Islands and foreign countries. Census data concordances link the 1980-92 trade figures into time series that are as consistent as possible. Data for 1970-79 are not linked and are from published sources. Import values are f.a.s. for 1974-1979 and Customs value thereafter; these values are based on transaction prices while maintaining a data series as consistent as possible over time. Import data before 1974 do not exist on a transaction price valuation basis. 1991 Imports include revisions for passenger cars, trucks, petroleum and petroleum products not included elsewhere. [4] Agricultural products for 1983-forward utilize the latest census definition that excludes manufactured goods that were previously classified as manufactured agricultural products. [5] Mineral fuels include commodity Section 3 under SITC Rev. 1 for 1970-1976, SITC Rev. 2 for 1977-1982 and SITC Rev. 3 for 1983-forward.

Source: U.S. International Trade Administration, through 1996, *U.S. Foreign Trade Highlights,* annual; and thereafter, <http://www.ita.doc.gov/td/industry/otea/usfth/aggregate/H01T03.html> (released 20 June 2002).

Foreign Commerce and Aid   793

No. 1279. U.S. Exports and Imports for Consumption of Merchandise by Customs District: 1990 to 2001

[In billions of dollars (393.0 represents $393,000,000,000). Exports are f.a.s. (free alongside ship) value all years; imports are on customs value basis]

Customs district	Exports					Imports for consumption				
	1990	1995	1999	2000	2001	1990	1995	1999	2000	2001
Total [1]	393.0	584.7	695.8	780.0	731.0	490.6	738.6	1,016.9	1,205.6	1,132.6
Anchorage, AK	3.7	5.9	8.8	5.9	7.7	0.7	5.7	9.2	13.4	11.5
Baltimore, MD	6.7	9.0	5.9	6.2	5.7	11.2	14.4	17.7	18.6	18.4
Boston, ...	5.6	4.6	6.8	7.0	7.0	12.2	13.4	16.0	18.7	16.8
Buffalo, NY . . . [2]	15.8	30.5	37.5	38.2	31.1	19.2	29.1	39.7	38.4	34.7
Charleston, SC [2]	6.7	10.1	11.5	12.6	13.5	6.8	10.4	14.5	16.9	17.2
Chicago, IL	10.2	18.4	19.1	21.7	21.5	18.3	31.3	43.1	51.1	49.1
Cleveland, OH	4.0	7.8	17.5	22.7	18.0	11.3	21.7	29.7	36.5	35.2
Dallas/Fort Worth, TX	3.4	4.4	8.4	11.5	10.2	4.8	8.8	15.2	18.8	19.7
Detroit, MI	35.6	56.8	77.6	79.4	77.2	37.8	64.7	87.9	97.6	91.3
Duluth, MN	0.8	1.4	1.5	1.5	1.3	3.9	6.0	5.5	7.0	6.4
El Paso, TX	3.9	7.9	13.2	18.0	16.3	5.0	12.9	20.9	24.1	23.9
Great Falls, MT	2.4	3.0	4.3	5.0	6.1	4.7	6.9	11.0	14.3	17.6
Honolulu, HI	0.5	1.1	1.2	0.7	0.6	2.1	2.7	2.3	2.9	2.3
Houston/Galveston, TX . . .	17.6	27.4	25.7	29.7	29.5	21.6	23.4	27.8	40.9	39.3
Laredo, TX	15.2	24.3	45.2	57.7	52.1	10.0	24.7	51.1	62.7	62.3
Los Angeles, CA	42.1	67.0	66.4	77.6	69.1	64.1	96.3	128.8	150.1	141.7
Miami, FL	11.2	22.7	28.5	31.0	29.9	7.1	11.9	21.4	23.3	22.5
Milwaukee, WI	0.1	0.1	0.1	0.1	0.2	1.1	1.5	1.5	1.5	1.3
Minneapolis, MN	0.9	1.3	1.2	1.4	1.4	2.0	2.8	4.0	4.3	3.8
Mobile, AL [2]	1.9	3.4	3.3	4.0	4.8	3.4	3.9	5.5	7.9	7.3
New Orleans, LA	18.0	28.4	28.8	35.9	33.1	24.1	34.4	40.2	54.0	47.8
New York, NY	50.9	61.4	67.2	79.5	76.2	68.0	87.6	122.1	145.6	137.8
Nogales, AZ	2.1	4.0	5.6	7.3	6.2	4.2	7.7	11.6	14.1	12.9
Norfolk, VA [2]	11.7	14.4	12.9	12.4	12.4	7.4	8.6	12.1	13.6	12.8
Ogdensburg, NY	7.9	9.2	11.0	12.4	11.6	9.8	14.4	19.8	23.7	22.0
Pembina, ND	3.4	5.5	6.9	8.7	8.2	4.1	7.2	8.8	11.0	10.3
Philadelphia, PA	4.0	6.7	6.9	6.0	8.0	18.3	18.3	21.3	28.3	28.1
Port Arthur, TX	0.9	1.3	0.9	1.2	1.0	3.2	4.8	6.2	10.9	9.0
Portland, ME	1.7	2.1	2.4	2.6	2.3	4.3	4.4	6.9	8.7	9.2
Portland, OR	5.8	10.2	7.5	7.2	6.1	5.6	7.9	10.9	12.5	12.4
Providence, RI	(Z)	0.1	(Z)	(Z)	(Z)	1.3	0.9	1.2	1.3	1.4
San Diego, CA	3.4	6.1	10.7	12.7	12.3	4.3	8.9	19.0	22.2	21.2
San Francisco, CA	23.1	43.7	44.8	58.3	45.8	28.0	58.8	59.1	68.6	49.1
San Juan, PR	2.5	2.6	4.8	4.8	5.8	5.4	6.8	10.8	11.8	12.9
Savannah, GA	7.4	10.9	13.9	15.9	15.5	9.8	14.7	21.8	26.1	25.2
Seattle, WA	32.6	31.4	44.7	40.4	41.4	20.9	24.1	36.8	40.5	38.0
St. Albans, VT	4.0	4.4	4.3	4.5	3.1	5.2	7.4	8.6	9.4	9.2
St. Louis, MO.	0.3	0.3	1.9	1.3	0.8	3.0	4.4	6.6	7.9	7.1
Tampa, FL	4.3	6.7	5.6	4.8	4.7	7.0	9.2	13.6	14.7	13.4
Virgin Islands of the U.S. . . .	0.2	0.2	0.2	0.3	0.3	2.1	2.1	2.9	4.8	3.9
Washington, DC	1.1	2.3	2.7	2.8	3.0	0.8	1.2	2.0	2.6	2.3
Wilmington, NC	3.0	4.4	2.6	2.5	2.3	3.3	7.4	9.9	10.6	10.8

Z Less than $50 million. [1] Totals shown for exports reflect the value of estimated parcel post and Special Category shipments, and beginning 1990, adjustments for undocumented exports to Canada which are not distributed by customs district. The value of bituminous coal exported through Norfolk, VA; Charleston, SC; and Mobile, AL is reflected in the total but not distributed by district. [2] Excludes exports of bituminous coal, which are included in the "Total" line.

Source: U.S. Census Bureau, 1990, *U.S. Merchandise Trade: Selected Highlights,* Series FT 920, monthly; beginning 1995, *U.S. Export History* and *U.S. Import History* on compact disc.

No. 1280. Export and Import Unit Value Indexes—Selected Countries: 1997 to 2001

[Indexes in U.S. dollars, 1995=100. A unit value is an implicit price derived from value and quantity data]

Country	Export unit value					Import unit value				
	1997	1998	1999	2000	2001	1997	1998	1999	2000	2001
United States	99.2	95.9	94.7	96.2	95.4	98.5	92.6	93.4	99.4	95.9
Australia	97.7	86.7	82.7	81.1	73.8	94.6	86.8	87.2	85.3	72.0
Belgium.	89.1	87.9	83.6	79.6	78.8	90.5	87.4	84.5	82.6	82.1
Canada	99.3	92.3	93.0	100.6	96.5	99.4	96.0	95.7	98.0	93.9
Denmark	87.8	85.8	83.1	78.4	(NA)	88.1	86.6	82.8	77.0	(NA)
France	87.5	85.9	81.6	71.7	(NA)	88.3	86.4	82.4	75.5	(NA)
Germany	81.1	79.5	75.1	67.3	(NA)	83.2	80.1	75.4	72.4	(NA)
Greece	92.2	87.8	84.8	81.1	80.7	88.0	85.8	83.4	76.5	76.5
Ireland	95.1	91.7	91.8	83.5	82.0	94.0	90.3	88.3	82.9	82.9
Italy	100.3	99.3	94.6	86.3	87.4	97.0	92.6	87.6	86.4	85.7
Japan	86.5	80.5	85.2	89.2	83.6	95.1	83.0	83.8	92.6	86.3
Korea	73.2	61.0	61.5	61.8	(NA)	93.7	76.4	74.5	85.7	(NA)
Norway	98.7	81.9	88.4	111.2	106.9	88.3	84.0	79.5	73.9	73.7
Singapore	93.2	81.1	80.2	83.4	77.2	92.9	80.9	81.2	87.0	84.0
Spain	88.8	87.1	82.6	75.8	75.6	88.5	81.8	81.0	79.1	70.4
Switzerland	85.3	84.5	82.7	76.0	77.6	85.8	82.4	78.0	73.5	74.7
United Kingdom	99.2	95.1	92.1	89.2	85.0	96.9	92.1	88.9	86.5	82.0

NA Not available.

Source: International Monetary Fund, Washington, DC, *International Financial Statistics,* monthly, (copyright).

794 Foreign Commerce and Aid

No. 1281. U.S. Exports by State of Origin: 1990 to 2001

[In millions of dollars (394,045 represents $394,045,000,000). Exports are on a f.a.s. value basis. Exports are based on origin of movement]

State and other area	1990	2000	2001 Total	2001 Rank	State and other area	1990	2000	2001 Total	2001 Rank
Total	394,045	782,429	730,897	(X)	Montana	229	541	489	49
					Nebraska	693	2,511	2,702	35
United States	315,065	712,055	678,756	(X)	Nevada	394	1,482	1,423	43
Alabama	2,834	7,317	7,570	25	New Hampshire	973	2,373	2,401	38
Alaska	2,850	2,464	2,418	37	New Jersey	7,633	18,638	18,946	9
Arizona	3,729	14,334	12,513	16	New Mexico	249	2,391	1,405	44
Arkansas	920	2,599	2,911	33	New York	22,072	42,846	42,172	3
California	44,520	119,640	106,777	1	North Carolina	8,010	17,946	16,799	12
					North Dakota	360	626	806	46
Colorado	2,274	6,593	6,125	27					
Connecticut	4,356	8,047	8,610	24	Ohio	13,378	26,322	27,095	8
Delaware	1,344	2,197	1,985	41	Oklahoma	1,646	3,072	2,661	36
District of Columbia	320	1,003	1,034	(X)	Oregon	4,065	11,441	8,900	23
Florida	11,634	26,543	27,185	7	Pennsylvania	8,491	18,792	17,433	11
					Rhode Island	595	1,186	1,269	45
Georgia	5,763	14,925	14,644	14					
Hawaii	179	387	370	50	South Carolina	3,116	8,565	9,956	21
Idaho	898	3,559	2,122	40	South Dakota	205	679	595	47
Illinois	12,965	31,438	30,434	6	Tennessee	3,746	11,592	11,320	18
Indiana	5,273	15,386	14,365	15	Texas	32,931	103,866	94,995	2
					Utah	1,596	3,221	3,506	32
Iowa	2,189	4,466	4,660	30					
Kansas	2,113	5,145	5,005	28	Vermont	1,154	4,097	2,830	34
Kentucky	3,175	9,612	9,048	22	Virginia	9,333	11,698	11,631	17
Louisiana	14,199	16,814	16,589	13	Washington	24,432	32,215	34,929	4
Maine	870	1,779	1,813	42	West Virginia	1,550	2,219	2,241	39
					Wisconsin	5,158	10,508	10,489	20
Maryland	2,592	4,593	4,975	29	Wyoming	264	503	503	48
Massachusetts	9,501	20,514	17,490	10					
Michigan	18,474	33,845	32,366	5	Puerto Rico	3,600	9,735	10,573	(X)
Minnesota	5,091	10,303	10,524	19	Virgin Islands	51	174	187	(X)
Mississippi	1,605	2,726	3,557	31	Other [1]	75,328	60,464	41,377	(X)
Missouri	3,130	6,497	6,173	26					

X Not applicable.   [1] Includes unreported, not specified, special category, estimated shipments, foreign trade zone, re-exports, and any timing adjustments.

Source: U.S. Census Bureau, *U.S. International Trade in Goods and Services,* Series FT-900, December issues. For most recent release, see <http://www.census.gov/foreign-trade/Press-Release/2001pr/12/> (released 21 February 2002).

No. 1282. U.S. Agriculture Exports by State: 1997 to 2001

[In millions of dollars (57,269 represents $57,269,000,000). Fiscal years]

State	1997	1998	1999	2000	2001	State	1997	1998	1999	2000	2001
U.S.	57,269	53,653	49,043	50,744	52,735	MT	441	422	393	388	321
						NE	3,255	2,814	2,804	2,980	2,915
AL	544	466	374	390	408	NV	5	5	4	17	17
AK	(Z)	(Z)	(Z)	(Z)	1	NH	131	129	127	130	134
AZ	456	444	389	439	448	NJ	222	193	181	184	234
AR	1,832	1,733	1,301	1,371	1,385						
CA	8,265	8,007	7,366	7,982	8,698	NM	83	98	75	105	84
CO	848	785	807	919	869	NY	424	402	407	432	456
CT	82	97	95	110	78	NC	1,556	1,467	1,215	1,194	1,389
DE	152	131	106	107	139	ND	1,437	1,243	1,239	996	1,203
FL	1,309	1,131	1,097	1,222	1,242	OH	1,229	1,302	1,082	993	1,135
GA	1,340	1,166	909	1,005	1,107	OK	410	450	462	442	540
						OR	720	659	645	618	681
HI	132	128	132	147	163	PA	668	596	584	614	732
ID	832	803	773	808	820	RI	2	1	1	1	1
IL	3,627	3,151	2,812	2,876	3,057	SC	358	318	240	237	317
IN	1,725	1,606	1,415	1,410	1,546						
IA	4,058	3,569	3,231	3,327	3,259	SD	1,245	1,098	1,104	1,092	1,106
KS	2,892	2,954	3,024	3,243	3,099	TN	664	580	463	462	549
KY	1,084	926	860	790	1,010	TX	3,330	3,376	2,791	3,407	3,333
LA	863	750	565	686	765	UT	153	137	147	184	198
ME	35	38	37	57	60	VT	11	10	10	12	2
MD	285	230	180	188	246	VA	532	451	387	417	450
						WA	1,930	1,705	1,820	1,666	1,938
MA	88	90	72	83	28	WV	32	28	20	23	36
MI	836	884	744	816	776	WI	1,184	1,203	1,190	1,268	1,307
MN	2,607	2,289	2,207	2,204	2,299	WY	40	44	32	49	53
MS	870	826	549	620	620						
MO	1,448	1,328	1,024	990	1,151	Unallocated	1,000	1,392	1,547	1,045	328

Z Less than $500,000.

Source: U.S. Dept. of Agriculture, Economic Research Service, *Foreign Agricultural Trade of the United States* (FATUS), annual. See also <http://www.ers.usda.gov/publications/fau/july02/fau6602/fau6602.pdf> (revised August 2002).

No. 1283. U.S. Exports, Imports, and Merchandise Trade Balance by Country: 1997 to 2001

[In millions of dollars (689,182.4 represents $689,182,400,000). Includes silver ore and bullion. Country totals include exports of special category commodities, if any. Data include nonmonetary gold and includes trade of Virgin Islands with foreign countries. Minus sign (-) denotes an excess of imports over exports]

Country[1]	Exports, domestic and foreign					General imports					Merchandise trade balance				
	1997	1998	1999	2000	2001	1997	1998	1999	2000	2001	1997	1998	1999	2000	2001
Total [1]	689,182.4	682,137.7	695,797.2	781,917.7	729,100.3	870,670.7	911,896.1	1,024,618.2	1,218,022.0	1,140,999.4	-181,488.2	-229,758.4	-328,821.0	-436,104.3	-411,899.1
Afghanistan	11.5	7.0	18.0	8.2	5.8	10.0	16.7	9.3	0.8	0.8	1.5	-9.7	8.8	7.4	5.0
Albania	3.1	14.9	24.8	20.9	15.5	11.7	12.4	9.0	7.8	7.3	-8.6	2.5	15.8	13.1	8.2
Algeria	691.6	651.4	458.8	861.8	1,037.8	2,439.5	1,638.0	1,824.4	2,724.3	2,701.9	-1,747.9	-986.6	-1,365.5	-1,862.5	-1,664.1
Andorra	21.7	22.4	7.8	10.2	8.2	0.3	0.1	0.1	0.3	0.2	21.4	22.3	7.7	9.9	8.0
Angola	280.6	354.7	252.0	225.3	275.9	2,779.1	2,240.9	2,418.3	3,555.3	3,095.9	-2,498.6	-1,886.2	-2,166.3	-3,330.0	-2,820.0
Anguilla	18.1	16.7	22.2	29.9	20.1	0.7	2.1	2.3	1.7	1.8	17.4	14.6	19.9	28.2	18.3
Antigua	84.5	96.7	95.2	138.0	95.1	4.8	1.8	1.8	2.3	3.7	79.6	94.8	93.4	135.7	91.8
Argentina	5,810.0	5,885.8	4,949.9	4,695.6	3,920.2	2,228.2	2,230.9	2,598.3	3,099.5	3,013.4	3,581.8	3,654.9	2,351.5	1,596.1	906.8
Armenia	62.1	51.4	51.2	51.2	49.9	6.0	16.7	15.3	18.6	32.9	56.1	34.7	35.9	32.6	17.0
Aruba	238.4	351.2	307.2	291.4	276.5	610.2	469.5	674.8	1,535.5	1,034.0	-371.8	-118.3	-367.6	-1,244.1	-757.5
Australia	12,062.9	11,917.6	11,818.4	12,482.3	10,930.5	4,602.3	5,386.8	5,280.1	6,438.1	6,477.9	7,460.6	6,530.8	6,538.2	6,044.2	4,452.6
Austria	2,074.7	2,142.9	2,588.2	2,591.5	2,604.7	2,368.4	2,561.0	2,909.3	3,226.6	3,968.5	-293.7	-418.1	-321.1	-635.1	-1,363.8
Azerbaijan	62.3	123.1	54.8	209.6	64.3	5.7	4.9	26.3	20.9	20.6	56.6	118.2	28.6	188.7	43.7
Bahamas, The	809.5	815.6	842.0	1,069.3	1,026.3	154.9	142.4	195.3	275.0	313.9	654.6	673.2	646.7	794.3	712.4
Bahrain	406.1	294.6	347.8	449.0	432.7	116.4	155.5	225.4	337.6	424.1	289.8	139.1	122.3	111.4	8.6
Bangladesh	259.0	318.4	274.2	239.1	306.9	1,679.4	1,845.9	1,918.2	2,417.6	2,359.0	-1,420.4	-1,527.5	-1,644.0	-2,178.5	-2,052.1
Barbados	280.9	281.4	304.9	306.9	286.6	42.1	34.5	58.9	38.6	39.5	238.7	246.9	246.0	268.3	247.1
Byelarus	40.6	30.4	26.1	31.1	34.9	66.0	105.4	93.6	104.0	108.2	-25.4	-75.0	-67.6	-72.9	-73.3
Belgium	13,420.3	13,917.8	12,381.4	13,925.7	13,502.3	7,911.9	8,440.0	9,196.1	9,929.3	10,158.4	5,508.4	5,477.8	3,185.4	3,996.4	3,343.9
Belize	114.8	120.2	135.8	208.4	173.2	77.3	65.9	80.6	93.6	97.4	37.5	54.3	55.2	114.8	75.8
Benin	51.6	43.6	31.4	26.4	32.2	7.7	3.6	17.8	2.4	1.3	43.9	40.0	13.5	24.0	30.9
Bermuda	338.1	400.3	343.8	428.5	371.0	29.8	11.5	24.6	39.0	65.6	308.2	388.8	319.2	389.5	305.4
Bolivia	295.1	298.3	298.3	253.0	215.9	223.3	223.6	223.7	184.8	166.4	71.9	74.6	74.6	68.2	49.5
Bosnia and Herzegovina	102.5	40.0	43.7	44.1	43.1	8.3	7.4	14.9	17.8	11.9	94.2	32.6	28.8	26.3	31.2
Brazil	15,914.7	15,142.0	13,202.6	15,320.9	15,879.5	9,625.5	10,101.9	11,313.8	13,852.5	14,446.4	6,289.2	5,040.1	1,888.8	1,468.4	1,433.1
British Virgin Islands	64.6	62.6	60.1	63.4	74.7	13.1	7.5	22.3	30.9	11.9	51.5	55.1	37.8	32.5	62.8
Brunei	178.1	122.8	66.7	156.3	104.0	55.8	211.2	388.7	383.8	398.9	122.3	-88.4	-322.0	-227.5	-294.9
Bulgaria	109.6	112.4	102.8	114.0	108.4	171.4	219.1	198.8	235.6	337.0	-61.8	-106.7	-96.0	-121.6	-228.6
Burkina Faso	18.3	16.1	10.9	15.9	4.4	1.0	0.6	2.8	2.5	5.0	17.3	15.5	8.1	13.4	-0.6
Burma	19.9	31.9	8.6	17.1	11.4	114.9	163.7	232.1	470.7	469.9	-95.0	-131.8	-223.5	-453.6	-458.5
Cameroon	121.4	75.1	37.0	59.3	184.0	57.2	53.3	77.4	155.1	101.6	64.3	21.8	-40.4	-95.8	82.4
Canada	151,766.7	156,603.4	166,600.0	178,941.0	163,424.1	168,200.9	173,256.1	198,711.1	230,838.3	216,267.8	-16,434.2	-16,652.7	-32,111.1	-51,897.3	-52,843.7
Cayman Islands	270.3	421.9	368.8	354.5	261.8	19.6	18.1	9.4	6.6	6.8	250.7	403.8	359.4	347.9	255.0
Chad	3.1	3.5	2.7	10.8	137.0	2.9	7.5	6.9	4.6	5.7	0.2	-4.0	-4.3	6.2	131.3
Chile	4,368.4	3,979.3	3,078.3	3,460.3	3,118.4	2,293.1	2,452.5	2,953.1	3,269.0	3,495.3	2,075.3	1,526.8	125.2	191.3	-376.9
China	12,862.3	14,241.3	13,111.0	16,185.3	19,182.3	62,557.6	71,168.6	81,788.2	100,018.4	102,278.3	-49,695.3	-56,927.4	-68,677.2	-83,833.1	-83,096.0
Colombia	5,197.0	4,816.0	3,559.5	3,671.2	3,583.1	4,737.3	4,656.2	6,259.0	6,968.1	5,710.3	459.7	159.8	-2,699.4	-3,296.9	-2,127.2
Congo (Brazzaville)	74.7	92.0	47.0	81.7	90.0	471.5	315.4	414.6	531.7	473.8	-396.8	-223.4	-367.6	-450.0	-383.8
Congo (Kinshasa)	37.8	34.1	21.0	10.0	18.6	281.8	171.1	229.0	214.8	154.0	-244.0	-137.0	-207.9	-204.8	-135.4
Costa Rica	2,024.4	2,296.5	2,380.6	2,460.4	2,502.3	2,323.2	2,744.9	3,967.8	3,538.7	2,886.1	-298.8	-448.4	-1,587.2	-1,078.3	-383.8
Cote d'Ivoire	150.9	151.4	151.4	94.8	96.8	289.0	425.9	425.9	383.9	333.1	-138.1	-274.5	-274.5	-289.1	-236.3
Croatia	138.7	96.8	107.5	89.9	109.8	82.8	72.6	110.0	141.0	139.0	55.9	24.2	-2.5	-51.1	-29.2
Cyprus	244.5	161.9	191.7	190.1	267.9	16.4	31.8	31.4	23.4	35.1	228.1	130.1	160.2	166.7	232.8
Czech Republic	589.8	569.0	609.7	735.8	706.1	609.8	673.4	753.6	1,070.2	1,116.2	-20.0	-104.4	-143.9	-334.4	-410.1

See footnotes at end of table.

U.S. Census Bureau, Statistical Abstract of the United States: 2002

Country	Exports, domestic and foreign 1997	1998	1999	2000	2001	General imports 1997	1998	1999	2000	2001	Merchandise trade balance 1997	1998	1999	2000	2001
Denmark	1,756.9	1,874.3	1,725.6	1,506.8	1,609.2	2,137.7	2,395.0	2,818.7	2,965.0	3,406.1	-380.8	-520.7	-1,093.1	-1,458.2	-1,797.5
Djibouti	7.3	20.4	26.4	16.8	18.6	-	0.5	0.1	0.4	1.0	7.3	19.9	26.3	16.4	17.6
Dominica	37.4	52.1	38.6	37.5	30.7	9.1	6.4	19.1	6.9	5.3	28.3	45.7	19.5	30.6	25.4
Dominican Republic	3,924.0	3,943.8	4,100.4	4,472.8	4,397.6	4,326.8	4,441.2	4,286.7	4,383.3	4,183.4	-402.8	-497.4	-186.3	89.5	214.2
Ecuador	1,525.9	1,683.1	909.9	1,037.8	1,412.1	2,054.8	1,752.1	1,821.3	2,237.8	2,009.7	-528.9	-69.0	-911.4	-1,200.0	-597.6
Egypt	3,835.4	3,058.6	3,000.8	3,333.9	3,564.4	657.5	660.3	617.6	887.7	882.0	3,177.9	2,398.3	2,383.2	2,446.2	2,682.4
El Salvador	1,400.1	1,513.5	1,519.1	1,780.2	1,759.5	1,346.2	1,437.9	1,605.0	1,932.9	1,880.2	53.8	75.6	-85.9	-152.7	-120.7
Estonia	47.4	87.4	162.9	88.0	57.7	76.8	125.4	237.0	572.9	241.1	-29.3	-38.0	-74.0	-484.9	-183.4
Ethiopia	121.2	88.9	163.5	165.3	61.1	69.7	52.3	30.2	28.7	29.1	51.5	36.6	133.3	136.6	32.0
Fiji	32.8	74.2	126.4	23.0	19.4	84.6	101.1	99.8	146.8	182.3	-51.8	-26.9	26.6	-123.8	-162.9
Finland	1,741.1	1,914.8	1,668.8	1,570.9	1,554.0	2,391.5	2,595.6	2,907.7	3,250.8	3,393.8	-650.4	-680.8	-1,238.9	-1,679.9	-1,839.8
France	15,964.9	17,728.7	18,877.4	20,361.5	19,864.5	20,636.4	24,015.9	25,708.6	29,800.1	30,408.2	-4,671.5	-6,287.2	-6,831.2	-9,438.6	-10,543.7
French Guiana	493.7	246.5	194.2	17.0	129.9	2.4	3.2	4.2	2.3	0.4	491.4	243.3	190.0	14.7	129.5
French Polynesia	105.2	99.7	93.5	93.9	83.0	35.4	32.7	42.7	43.9	48.0	69.9	67.0	50.9	50.0	35.0
Gabon	84.5	61.6	45.4	9.1	73.0	2,202.3	1,258.8	1,543.2	2,196.5	1,659.7	-2,117.7	-1,197.2	-1,497.8	-2,133.0	-1,586.7
Gambia, The	9.7	9.9	9.6	9.1	8.4	2.9	2.0	0.2	0.4	0.5	6.8	7.9	9.4	8.7	7.9
Georgia	140.6	136.5	83.5	109.5	105.9	7.0	14.2	18.3	31.9	30.7	133.6	122.3	65.3	77.6	75.2
Germany	24,458.3	26,657.4	26,800.2	29,448.4	29,995.3	43,121.5	49,842.0	55,228.4	58,512.8	59,076.7	-18,663.2	-23,184.6	-28,428.2	-29,064.4	-29,081.4
Ghana	315.0	225.1	232.7	191.2	199.6	155.3	143.2	208.6	204.5	186.9	159.8	81.9	24.1	-13.3	12.7
Gibraltar	8.8	8.8	4.1	15.1	10.4	2.8	6.0	9.6	1.4	2.6	6.0	2.8	-5.5	13.7	7.8
Greece	949.3	1,355.2	995.5	1,221.8	1,293.6	453.2	466.7	563.1	591.4	505.2	496.2	888.5	432.3	630.4	788.4
Greenland	4.9	6.1	3.1	1.1	4.7	7.9	7.3	13.2	15.7	28.8	-3.0	-1.2	-10.1	-14.6	-24.1
Grenada	40.6	56.4	66.2	79.5	59.9	6.5	12.1	19.8	27.1	24.1	34.1	44.3	46.4	52.4	35.8
Guadeloupe	57.6	64.0	63.2	85.9	58.8	3.5	2.3	2.8	9.6	10.6	54.1	61.7	60.4	76.3	48.2
Guatemala	1,729.6	1,937.8	1,811.9	1,900.7	1,869.6	1,990.2	2,071.6	2,265.2	2,607.4	2,588.6	-260.6	-133.8	-453.2	-706.7	-719.0
Guinea	82.8	65.4	54.6	68.0	73.3	127.7	115.3	116.9	88.4	87.8	-44.9	-49.9	-62.4	-20.4	-14.5
Guyana	142.5	145.6	145.1	159.2	141.3	112.8	137.0	120.5	139.9	140.3	29.7	8.6	24.5	19.3	1.0
Haiti	499.1	548.6	613.8	576.6	550.4	188.2	271.8	301.1	296.9	263.1	310.9	276.8	312.7	279.7	287.3
Honduras	2,018.9	2,317.5	2,369.8	2,584.0	2,415.9	2,322.2	2,544.4	2,713.3	3,090.2	3,126.5	-303.4	-226.9	-343.5	-506.2	-710.6
Hong Kong	15,117.1	12,925.3	12,651.8	14,582.0	14,027.5	10,287.8	10,538.2	10,527.9	11,449.0	9,646.3	4,829.3	2,387.1	2,123.9	3,133.0	4,381.2
Hungary	485.5	482.6	504.1	569.1	685.5	1,078.9	1,566.5	1,892.6	2,715.2	2,964.6	-593.5	-1,083.9	-1,388.5	-2,146.1	-2,279.1
Iceland	179.2	236.5	297.6	255.6	255.4	230.8	267.9	303.7	259.8	262.5	-51.6	-31.4	-6.1	-4.2	-7.1
India	3,607.6	3,564.4	3,687.8	3,667.2	3,757.0	7,322.4	8,237.2	9,070.8	10,686.6	9,737.2	-3,714.8	-4,672.8	-5,383.0	-7,019.4	-5,980.2
Indonesia	4,522.3	2,298.9	2,038.3	2,401.9	2,520.6	9,188.4	9,340.6	9,525.4	10,367.0	10,103.6	-4,666.1	-7,041.7	-7,487.0	-7,965.1	-7,583.0
Iran	1.1	(NA)	48.1	16.8	8.1	0.1	16.4	2.4	168.8	143.4	1.0	-16.4	45.7	-152.0	-135.3
Iraq	82.0	106.4	9.5	10.4	46.2	311.9	1,183.2	4,226.4	6,065.9	5,820.3	-229.9	-1,076.8	-4,216.9	-6,055.5	-5,774.1
Ireland	4,642.2	5,646.8	6,383.6	7,713.5	7,144.0	5,866.6	8,400.9	10,994.3	16,463.6	18,499.3	-1,224.4	-2,754.1	-4,610.7	-8,750.1	-11,355.3
Israel	5,994.9	6,983.3	7,690.8	7,745.9	7,475.3	7,326.0	8,640.4	9,864.3	12,964.4	11,959.0	-1,331.0	-1,657.1	-2,173.5	-5,218.5	-4,483.7
Italy	8,994.7	8,990.8	10,090.5	11,000.3	9,915.6	19,407.5	20,959.1	22,355.5	24,982.7	23,789.9	-10,412.8	-11,968.3	-12,265.0	-13,982.4	-13,874.3
Jamaica	1,416.5	1,304.2	1,292.9	1,375.8	1,405.5	738.0	755.0	678.1	648.2	460.6	678.4	549.2	614.8	727.6	944.9
Japan	65,548.5	57,831.0	57,465.7	64,924.4	57,451.6	121,663.2	121,845.6	130,863.9	146,479.4	126,473.3	-56,114.8	-64,014.0	-73,398.2	-81,555.0	-69,021.7
Jordan	402.5	352.9	275.6	316.7	339.0	25.3	16.4	30.9	73.3	229.1	377.1	336.5	244.7	243.4	109.9
Kazakhstan	346.3	103.1	179.5	124.2	160.3	128.9	168.7	229.1	429.0	351.8	217.4	-65.6	-49.6	-304.8	-191.5
Kenya	225.3	198.9	189.2	237.6	577.7	114.0	98.5	106.3	110.1	128.3	111.4	100.4	82.8	127.5	449.4

See footnotes at end of table.

U.S. Census Bureau, Statistical Abstract of the United States: 2002

No. 1283. U.S. Exports, Imports, and Merchandise Trade Balance by Country: 1997 to 2001—Con.

[See headnote, page 796]

Country	Exports, domestic and foreign					General imports					Merchandise trade balance				
	1997	1998	1999	2000	2001	1997	1998	1999	2000	2001	1997	1998	1999	2000	2001
Korea, South	25,046.1	16,485.5	22,958.4	27,830.0	22,180.6	23,173.1	23,941.8	31,178.6	40,307.7	35,181.4	1,873.0	-7,456.3	-8,220.2	-12,477.7	-13,000.8
Kuwait	1,390.0	1,524.1	864.4	787.0	902.4	1,816.4	1,266.0	1,439.2	2,781.2	1,990.7	-426.4	258.1	-574.9	-1,994.2	-1,088.3
Kyrgyzstan	28.4	20.6	22.8	22.8	27.7	2.4	0.3	0.5	1.9	3.3	25.9	20.3	22.3	20.9	24.4
Latvia	217.8	186.8	218.2	133.6	110.5	145.1	114.7	228.8	287.7	144.5	72.7	72.1	-10.6	-154.1	-34.0
Lebanon	551.9	513.8	356.5	354.7	418.2	77.8	82.5	51.4	76.8	89.6	474.2	431.3	305.1	277.9	328.6
Lesotho	2.4	1.4	0.7	0.9	0.8	86.5	100.0	110.8	140.3	215.3	-84.2	-98.6	-110.1	-139.4	-214.5
Liberia	42.9	50.1	44.7	43.1	36.8	4.8	25.1	30.3	45.4	42.6	38.1	25.0	14.4	-2.3	-5.8
Liechtenstein	12.5	7.3	9.1	13.9	7.1	116.5	242.6	276.8	278.2	224.2	-104.0	-235.3	-267.8	-264.3	-217.1
Lithuania	87.4	62.2	66.0	59.4	99.8	79.8	80.9	96.8	135.0	164.2	7.6	-18.7	-30.8	-75.6	-64.4
Luxembourg	712.1	605.8	983.4	397.4	548.6	238.8	373.1	313.9	331.6	305.6	473.2	232.7	669.5	65.8	243.0
Macau	65.0	40.7	41.9	70.5	70.1	1,021.0	1,108.6	1,124.4	1,266.3	1,225.1	-956.0	-1,067.9	-1,082.5	-1,195.8	-1,155.0
Macedonia	33.8	14.8	56.2	68.5	32.9	147.1	175.4	136.5	151.8	111.6	-113.3	-160.6	-80.3	-83.3	-78.7
Madagascar	11.5	14.9	105.8	15.4	21.0	62.6	71.4	80.3	157.8	271.6	-51.0	-56.5	25.5	-142.4	-250.6
Malawi	17.6	14.5	7.4	13.7	12.8	82.8	60.4	72.5	55.4	77.9	-65.3	-45.9	-65.1	-41.7	-65.1
Malaysia	10,780.0	8,957.0	9,060.0	10,937.5	9,357.7	18,026.7	19,000.0	21,424.3	25,568.2	22,340.3	-7,246.7	-10,043.0	-12,364.3	-14,630.7	-12,982.6
Maldives	5.5	4.8	8.5	6.1	6.4	19.4	32.9	54.9	94.1	97.7	-13.9	-28.1	-46.4	-88.0	-91.3
Mali	26.2	25.3	29.8	32.0	32.7	3.8	3.4	9.8	6.1	5.5	22.3	21.9	20.8	22.2	26.6
Malta	120.9	267.0	190.4	334.7	258.9	223.6	340.3	325.0	482.4	368.9	-102.7	-73.3	-134.6	-147.7	-110.0
Marshall Islands	23.6	25.0	35.8	60.2	26.5	7.3	3.8	9.8	1.7	5.5	16.3	21.2	26.0	55.2	21.0
Martinique	33.9	26.4	34.9	21.6	23.2	2.4	1.0	0.8	1.7	0.6	31.4	25.4	34.1	19.9	22.6
Mauritania	20.9	19.5	25.2	16.2	25.4	0.2	0.4	0.4	0.4	0.3	20.6	19.1	24.4	15.8	25.1
Mauritius	31.4	23.2	39.0	23.9	29.0	238.4	271.6	259.3	285.9	277.9	-207.0	-248.4	-220.3	-262.0	-248.9
Mexico	71,388.4	78,772.5	86,908.9	111,349.0	101,296.5	85,937.5	94,629.0	109,720.6	135,926.4	131,337.9	-14,549.1	-15,856.5	-22,811.6	-24,577.4	-30,041.4
Micronesia, Federated States of	29.0	31.0	25.0	29.1	30.0	11.9	12.6	10.1	13.7	20.8	17.2	18.4	14.9	15.4	9.2
Moldova	19.7	20.6	10.6	27.3	35.5	53.7	109.3	87.1	105.4	68.3	-34.0	-88.7	-76.6	-78.1	-32.8
Monaco	6.9	6.4	12.6	28.2	15.0	19.6	25.7	14.3	22.9	15.0	-12.7	-19.3	-1.7	5.3	–
Mongolia	34.3	20.3	10.1	17.7	12.1	42.4	41.8	60.8	116.7	143.8	-8.1	-21.5	-50.7	-99.0	-131.7
Morocco	434.7	561.4	565.8	523.2	282.2	295.9	343.0	386.4	440.8	434.6	138.9	218.4	179.5	82.4	-152.4
Mozambique	45.6	45.7	34.8	57.0	28.4	30.5	25.8	10.3	24.4	7.1	15.1	19.9	24.5	32.6	21.3
Namibia	25.0	51.2	195.6	80.4	255.6	63.0	51.8	29.7	45.0	37.3	-38.1	-0.6	165.9	35.4	218.3
Netherlands	19,826.7	18,977.7	19,436.6	21,836.0	19,484.7	7,292.8	7,599.3	8,475.0	9,670.6	9,515.3	12,533.8	11,378.4	10,961.6	12,165.4	9,969.4
Netherlands Antilles	475.2	750.7	597.4	673.9	816.4	579.8	308.2	384.3	718.7	484.6	-104.6	442.5	213.1	-44.8	331.8
New Caledonia	34.4	19.2	41.7	19.3	25.1	51.9	21.7	8.6	31.4	14.6	-17.5	-2.5	33.0	-12.1	10.5
New Zealand	1,962.1	1,886.5	1,923.4	1,970.3	2,110.5	1,579.2	1,644.6	1,748.2	2,080.2	2,199.2	382.9	241.9	175.2	-109.9	-88.7
Nicaragua	289.8	336.5	373.7	380.1	443.1	439.3	452.7	495.2	588.5	603.6	-149.5	-116.2	-121.5	-208.4	-160.5
Niger	24.8	18.2	18.5	36.5	63.4	29.8	1.7	12.1	7.0	4.6	-5.0	16.5	6.4	29.5	58.8
Nigeria	813.1	816.8	627.8	721.8	955.1	6,349.4	4,194.0	4,385.1	10,537.6	8,774.8	-5,536.4	-3,377.2	-3,757.3	-9,815.8	-7,819.7
Norway	1,721.3	1,709.3	1,439.4	1,547.2	1,834.7	3,752.0	2,871.6	4,042.6	5,706.1	5,202.8	-2,030.7	-1,162.3	-2,603.2	-4,158.9	-3,368.1
Oman	340.8	302.7	188.2	199.8	306.2	242.4	216.8	219.5	257.5	420.1	98.4	85.9	-31.3	-57.7	-113.9
Pakistan	1,240.1	720.4	496.7	462.2	541.3	1,442.2	1,691.7	1,740.7	2,166.8	2,249.4	-202.2	-971.3	-1,244.0	-1,704.6	-1,708.1
Panama	1,536.1	1,753.0	1,742.3	1,612.4	1,330.5	367.2	312.3	364.8	307.0	290.7	1,168.9	1,440.7	1,377.5	1,305.4	1,039.8
Papua New Guinea	116.6	65.3	37.1	23.0	22.2	64.5	129.6	144.5	34.5	39.3	52.1	-64.3	-107.3	-11.5	-17.1
Paraguay	913.4	785.9	514.7	445.8	388.8	40.7	33.5	48.1	40.9	32.6	872.8	752.4	466.6	404.9	356.2
Peru	1,953.3	2,062.6	1,696.5	1,659.9	1,564.3	1,772.3	1,975.5	1,928.4	1,994.9	1,843.8	181.0	87.1	-231.9	-335.0	-279.5
Philippines	7,417.3	6,736.6	7,222.1	8,799.2	7,660.0	10,445.0	11,947.3	12,352.8	13,934.7	11,325.4	-3,027.6	-5,210.7	-5,130.6	-5,135.5	-3,665.4
Poland	1,169.9	882.0	826.2	757.2	787.7	695.6	783.7	816.2	1,041.3	952.6	474.4	98.3	10.0	-284.1	-164.9

See footnotes at end of table.

U.S. Census Bureau, Statistical Abstract of the United States: 2002

Country	Exports, domestic and foreign					General imports					Merchandise trade balance [1]				
	1997	1998	1999	2000	2001	1997	1998	1999	2000	2001	1997	1998	1999	2000	2001
Portugal	954.2	888.3	1,091.8	984.2	1,239.7	1,138.0	1,265.3	1,355.8	1,578.5	1,555.4	-183.8	-377.0	-264.0	-594.3	-315.7
Qatar	379.0	354.4	145.5	191.1	335.9	157.4	220.4	272.2	485.6	502.2	221.7	134.0	-126.7	-294.5	-166.3
Romania	258.0	336.6	176.0	232.7	374.5	399.8	393.3	442.4	472.8	519.9	-141.8	-56.7	-266.4	-240.1	-145.4
Russia	3,364.9	3,552.6	2,059.8	2,092.4	2,716.1	4,319.0	5,747.2	5,920.8	7,658.7	6,264.4	-954.0	-2,194.6	-3,861.0	-5,566.3	-3,548.3
Saudi Arabia	8,437.8	10,519.8	7,911.9	6,234.1	5,957.5	9,364.8	6,241.3	8,253.5	14,364.7	13,272.2	-927.0	4,278.5	-341.6	-8,130.6	-7,314.7
Senegal	51.8	59.1	63.4	81.7	79.5	6.8	5.2	9.2	4.2	103.8	44.9	53.9	54.3	77.5	-24.3
Singapore	17,696.2	15,693.6	16,247.3	17,806.3	17,651.7	20,074.6	18,355.7	18,191.4	19,178.3	15,000.0	-2,378.4	-2,662.1	-1,944.1	-1,372.0	2,651.7
Slovakia	82.0	110.6	127.2	110.1	69.8	165.6	165.7	169.3	240.8	237.6	-83.6	-55.1	-42.1	-130.7	-167.8
Somalia	2.8	2.7	2.8	4.9	6.6	0.3	0.6	0.2	0.5	0.3	2.4	2.1	2.6	4.4	6.3
South Africa	2,997.2	3,628.0	2,585.5	3,089.5	2,959.6	2,510.1	3,049.1	3,194.4	4,210.1	4,432.6	487.2	578.9	-609.0	-1,120.6	-1,473.0
Spain	5,538.7	5,453.6	6,133.4	6,322.3	5,756.0	4,605.5	4,780.2	5,059.2	5,713.3	5,197.3	933.3	673.4	1,074.2	609.0	558.7
Sri Lanka	154.7	190.4	167.1	204.7	183.0	1,620.0	1,766.5	1,742.2	2,001.9	1,984.2	-1,465.3	-1,576.1	-1,575.1	-1,797.2	-1,801.2
St. Lucia	89.3	92.4	98.1	107.4	86.7	34.2	22.4	28.0	22.3	28.9	55.1	70.0	70.1	85.1	57.8
St. Vincent	54.4	274.2	92.1	37.9	38.8	4.3	4.8	8.2	8.9	22.5	50.0	269.4	83.8	29.0	16.3
Sudan	36.4	44.2	21.0	17.4	17.0	12.1	106.1	0.1	1.8	3.4	24.3	-61.9	20.9	15.6	13.6
Suriname	183.0	187.2	143.8	134.2	155.3	91.5	81.1	122.9	135.2	142.9	91.5	106.1	20.9	-1.0	12.4
Sweden	3,314.1	3,822.1	4,250.5	4,553.7	3,541.0	7,298.9	7,848.0	8,102.7	9,597.1	8,908.5	-3,984.8	-4,025.9	-3,852.2	-5,043.4	-5,367.5
Switzerland	8,306.9	7,247.4	8,371.3	9,953.6	9,807.3	8,405.1	8,690.3	9,538.6	10,159.9	9,669.6	-98.2	-1,442.9	-1,167.4	-206.3	137.7
Syria	180.4	161.4	173.1	226.0	231.6	27.9	45.9	94.4	158.6	158.5	152.6	115.5	78.2	67.4	72.9
Taiwan	20,365.7	18,164.5	19,131.4	24,405.9	18,121.6	32,628.5	33,124.8	35,204.4	40,502.8	33,374.5	-12,262.8	-14,960.3	-16,073.1	-16,096.9	-15,252.9
Tajikistan	18.6	12.2	13.8	12.1	28.6	8.5	32.6	22.7	9.0	5.2	10.0	-20.4	-8.9	3.1	23.4
Tanzania	64.9	66.9	68.4	44.7	64.0	26.6	31.5	35.4	32.2	27.9	38.3	35.4	33.0	12.5	36.1
Thailand	7,349.4	5,238.6	4,984.6	6,617.5	5,989.4	12,601.5	13,436.4	14,329.9	16,385.3	14,727.2	-5,252.1	-8,197.8	-9,345.3	-9,767.8	-8,737.8
Togo	25.6	25.4	25.7	10.6	16.3	9.4	2.2	2.2	6.0	12.6	16.2	23.2	22.5	4.6	3.7
Trinidad and Tobago	1,105.9	983.1	785.3	1,099.6	1,087.1	1,134.3	976.9	1,286.7	2,228.8	2,380.0	-28.3	6.2	-501.4	-1,129.2	-1,292.9
Tunisia	252.3	195.6	280.2	288.9	276.0	63.1	61.5	74.6	93.9	121.7	189.2	134.1	205.6	195.0	154.3
Turkey	3,539.5	3,505.5	3,217.1	3,720.1	3,094.7	2,121.1	2,542.7	2,629.4	3,041.5	3,054.8	1,418.5	962.8	587.7	678.6	39.9
Turkmenistan	117.7	28.0	18.4	84.4	248.4	2.1	2.8	8.5	28.0	45.5	115.6	25.2	9.9	56.4	202.9
Turks and Caicos Islands	58.6	63.8	94.8	88.6	77.1	5.3	4.6	6.3	5.9	8.1	53.3	59.2	88.5	82.7	69.0
Uganda	35.2	29.8	25.0	28.2	31.7	37.8	15.1	20.3	29.1	17.7	-2.5	14.7	4.7	-0.9	14.0
Ukraine	402.9	367.5	204.6	191.0	200.1	410.0	531.4	528.9	872.2	673.6	-7.1	-163.9	-324.3	-681.2	-473.5
United Arab Emirates	2,607.1	2,365.9	2,707.8	2,284.7	2,637.9	920.1	659.9	714.3	971.8	1,194.2	1,687.0	1,706.0	1,993.5	1,312.9	1,443.7
United Kingdom	36,425.3	39,058.2	38,407.1	41,570.4	40,714.2	32,659.3	34,838.2	39,237.2	43,345.1	41,368.8	3,766.0	4,220.0	-830.1	-1,774.7	-654.6
Uruguay	547.6	591.3	494.5	406.9	406.3	228.9	255.7	198.6	313.0	227.7	318.7	335.6	295.9	93.9	178.6
Uzbekistan	234.1	147.3	339.0	157.7	144.9	39.1	34.1	25.6	41.2	53.5	195.1	113.2	313.4	116.5	91.4
Venezuela	6,601.6	6,515.8	5,353.5	5,549.9	5,642.1	13,477.2	9,181.4	11,334.5	18,623.2	15,250.5	-6,875.6	-2,665.6	-5,981.0	-13,073.3	-9,608.4
Vietnam	286.6	274.1	291.5	367.6	460.3	388.5	554.1	608.3	821.4	1,052.9	-101.9	-280.0	-316.8	-453.8	-592.6
Western Samoa	11.1	10.4	12.4	64.0	69.9	2.5	6.8	5.3	5.5	7.3	8.6	3.6	7.0	58.5	62.6
Yemen, Republic of	153.4	177.7	157.0	189.4	185.4	16.0	37.6	23.6	255.6	202.4	137.4	140.1	133.4	-66.2	-17.0
Yugoslavia, Fed. Rep. of	49.1	74.4	58.6	29.9	66.2	10.4	12.6	4.5	2.3	6.1	38.7	61.8	54.1	27.6	60.1
Zambia	29.3	21.7	19.8	19.1	31.2	55.9	47.3	37.7	17.7	15.6	-26.6	-25.6	-17.8	1.4	15.6
Zimbabwe	81.9	93.1	60.9	52.4	31.2	139.5	127.2	132.8	112.4	90.8	-57.5	-34.1	-71.9	-60.0	-59.6

- Represents zero or rounds to zero. [1] Includes timing adjustment and unidentified countries, not shown separately.

Source: U.S. Census Bureau, U.S. International Trade in Goods and Services, Series FT-900(01-12) and FT-900 (02-02). See also <http://www.census.gov/foreign-trade/Press-Release/2001pr/FinalRevisions2001/> (released 22 August 2002).

No. 1284. U.S. Exports and General Imports by Selected SITC Commodity Groups: 1998 to 2001

[In millions of dollars (682,138 represents $682,138,000,000). SITC=Standard International Trade Classification. N.e.s.=Not elsewhere specified]

Selected commodities	Exports [1]				General imports [2]			
	1998	1999	2000	2001	1998	1999	2000	2001
Total	682,138	695,797	781,918	729,100	911,896	1,024,618	1,218,022	1,140,999
Agricultural commodities	**50,654**	**47,091**	**51,296**	**53,705**	**35,748**	**36,681**	**39,186**	**39,544**
Animal feeds	4,054	3,372	3,780	4,221	607	564	597	574
Coffee.	10	9	9	16	3,069	2,534	2,350	1,357
Corn.	4,618	5,126	4,695	4,755	142	156	160	135
Cotton, raw and linters.	2,572	968	1,893	2,174	19	148	28	27
Hides and skins	1,130	1,020	1,426	1,813	110	100	109	100
Meat and preparations.	6,427	6,506	7,004	7,231	2,848	3,259	3,841	4,254
Soybeans	4,885	4,569	5,284	5,429	54	29	31	31
Sugar	3	4	4	3	715	557	461	480
Tobacco, unmanufactured.	1,459	1,312	1,204	1,269	780	753	569	710
Vegetables and fruits.	7,324	7,152	7,477	7,415	8,365	9,259	9,286	9,517
Wheat.	3,690	3,578	3,374	3,375	283	273	229	282
Manufactured goods	**552,778**	**565,490**	**625,894**	**577,714**	**790,754**	**882,013**	**1,012,855**	**950,679**
ADP equipment, office machinery . .	40,735	40,787	46,595	39,240	76,755	84,430	92,133	75,859
Airplane parts.	15,035	12,141	15,062	15,735	5,912	5,827	5,572	6,287
Airplanes.	35,242	32,665	24,777	26,961	7,052	9,222	12,412	14,884
Alcoholic bev, distilled	385	432	424	489	2,296	2,618	2,946	3,063
Aluminum	3,606	3,564	3,780	3,253	5,970	6,269	6,949	6,406
Artwork/antiques	1,140	1,148	1,387	1,637	3,976	4,890	5,864	5,458
Basketware, etc	2,583	2,872	3,309	3,579	3,834	4,378	4,840	5,591
Chemicals, cosmetics	4,763	4,853	5,292	5,825	2,895	3,148	3,539	3,750
Chemicals, dyeing.	3,471	3,620	4,089	3,782	2,472	2,633	2,667	2,478
Chemicals, fertilizers	3,231	2,921	2,249	2,077	1,570	1,501	1,684	1,890
Chemicals, inorganic	4,709	4,632	5,359	5,578	5,126	5,167	6,108	6,153
Chemicals, medicinal.	9,341	11,203	12,893	15,031	10,908	13,497	14,685	18,628
Chemicals, n.e.s.	10,838	11,068	12,264	12,382	4,833	5,084	5,725	5,927
Chemicals, organic	14,920	15,376	17,990	16,424	18,327	21,896	28,578	29,712
Chemicals, plastics	16,608	16,832	19,519	18,485	8,565	9,279	10,647	10,401
Cigarettes	4,165	3,226	3,304	2,118	102	151	258	238
Clothing	8,497	7,962	8,191	6,510	53,742	56,412	64,296	63,856
Cork, wood, lumber.	4,091	4,253	4,320	3,533	7,616	8,925	8,227	7,968
Crude fertilizers	1,600	1,536	1,724	1,654	1,300	1,268	1,401	1,318
Electrical machinery	65,575	75,249	89,917	72,055	79,365	88,620	108,747	84,670
Fish and preparations	2,172	2,742	2,806	3,069	8,104	8,910	9,907	9,742
Footwear.	720	694	663	639	13,881	14,064	14,842	15,234
Furniture and parts	4,411	4,343	4,744	4,255	13,339	16,181	18,923	18,610
Gem diamonds	124	312	1,289	1,714	8,497	9,885	12,068	10,616
General industrial machinery	30,121	29,882	33,094	32,153	28,811	31,467	34,667	33,264
Gold, nonmonetary	5,464	5,226	5,898	4,872	3,587	3,032	2,657	2,079
Iron and steel mill products.	5,481	4,989	5,715	5,482	17,159	13,369	15,807	12,449
Lighting, plumbing.	1,405	1,298	1,384	1,321	3,393	4,330	5,104	4,895
Metal manufactures, n.e.s.	10,699	11,185	13,453	11,365	13,506	14,414	16,204	15,510
Metal ores; scrap	3,581	3,484	4,234	4,420	4,099	3,647	3,817	3,237
Metalworking machinery.	5,270	5,268	6,191	4,703	7,926	6,782	7,726	6,587
Optical goods.	1,907	2,231	3,246	3,036	2,727	3,077	4,019	3,455
Paper and paperboard	9,930	9,863	10,640	10,042	12,793	13,400	15,185	14,815
Photographic equipment.	3,481	3,624	4,236	3,281	5,661	6,111	6,896	5,596
Plastic articles, n.e.s.	5,554	6,362	7,607	7,065	6,137	7,013	8,034	8,257
Platinum	388	503	888	962	3,051	3,613	5,566	5,240
Power generating machinery.	28,743	30,894	32,743	33,577	28,160	31,551	33,773	36,118
Printed materials.	4,671	4,581	4,776	4,746	3,075	3,323	3,680	3,721
Pulp and waste paper	3,443	3,528	4,576	3,690	2,442	2,597	3,381	2,630
Records/magnetic media	6,057	5,802	5,395	4,611	4,383	4,703	5,172	4,883
Rubber articles, n.e.s.	1,301	1,401	1,673	1,569	1,645	1,791	1,962	1,979
Rubber tires and tubes	2,554	2,400	2,379	2,287	4,095	4,638	4,785	4,209
Scientific instruments.	24,169	25,644	30,984	29,123	15,500	17,658	22,007	21,356
Ships, boats.	1,716	1,632	1,070	1,801	1,132	1,127	1,178	1,209
Silver and bullion	629	214	227	234	662	630	775	530
Spacecraft.	1,102	641	158	201	91	245	217	71
Specialized industrial machinery . . .	27,305	24,941	30,959	25,747	22,986	21,596	22,711	19,554
Television, VCR, etc.	23,417	24,404	27,921	24,230	42,449	50,936	70,468	62,836
Textile yarn, fabric.	8,976	9,245	10,534	10,074	12,896	13,578	15,171	14,616
Toys/games/sporting goods.	3,342	3,315	3,609	3,217	18,695	18,987	20,011	20,901
Travel goods	302	329	351	308	3,946	4,148	4,430	4,300
Vehicles	53,536	54,299	57,421	54,347	119,726	145,927	161,544	157,400
Watches/clocks/parts.	312	334	348	277	3,210	3,258	3,481	3,048
Wood manufactures	1,690	1,739	1,842	1,568	5,647	7,089	7,228	6,998
Mineral fuel	**10,251**	**9,880**	**13,179**	**12,494**	**57,323**	**75,803**	**135,367**	**121,923**
Coal	3,176	2,268	2,162	1,915	724	665	805	1,022
Crude oil	895	772	463	187	37,252	50,890	89,876	74,293
Petroleum preparations	2,857	3,414	5,746	5,034	10,947	14,183	25,673	24,620
Natural gas	243	218	411	536	5,273	6,669	12,594	15,417
Reexports	45,683	50,969	68,203	64,780	(X)	(X)	(X)	(X)

X Not applicable. [1] F.a.s. basis. Exports by commodity are only for domestic exports. [2] Customs value basis.

Source: U.S. Census Bureau, *U.S. International Trade in Goods and Services*, Series FT-900(01-12) and FT-900 (02-02). See also <http://www.census.gov/foreign-trade/Press-Release/2001pr/FinalRevisions2001/> (released 22 August 2002).

No. 1285. United States Total and Aerospace Foreign Trade: 1980 to 2001

[In millions of dollars (245,262 represents $245,262,000,000), except percent. Data are reported as exports of domestic merchandise, including Department of Defense shipments and undocumented exports to Canada, f.a.s. (free alongside ship) basis, and imports for consumption, customs value basis. Minus sign (-) indicates deficit]

Year	Merchandise trade			Aerospace trade						
				Trade balance	Imports	Exports				
						Total	Percent of U.S. exports	Civil		Military
	Trade balance	Imports	Exports					Total	Trans-ports	
1980	-19,696	245,262	225,566	11,952	3,554	15,506	6.9	13,248	6,727	2,258
1981	-22,267	260,982	238,715	13,134	4,500	17,634	7.4	13,312	7,180	4,322
1982	-27,510	243,952	216,442	11,035	4,568	15,603	7.2	9,608	3,834	5,995
1983	-52,409	258,048	205,639	12,619	3,446	16,065	7.8	10,595	4,683	5,470
1984	-106,703	330,678	223,976	10,082	4,926	15,008	6.7	9,659	3,195	5,350
1985	-117,712	336,526	218,815	12,593	6,132	18,725	8.6	12,942	5,518	5,783
1986	-138,279	365,438	227,159	11,826	7,902	19,728	8.7	14,851	6,276	4,875
1987	-152,119	406,241	254,122	14,575	7,905	22,480	8.8	15,768	6,377	6,714
1988	-118,526	440,952	322,426	17,860	9,087	26,947	8.4	20,298	8,766	6,651
1989	-109,399	473,211	363,812	22,083	10,028	32,111	8.8	25,619	12,313	6,492
1990	-101,718	495,311	393,592	27,282	11,801	39,083	9.9	31,517	16,691	7,566
1991	-66,723	488,453	421,730	30,785	13,003	43,788	10.4	35,548	20,881	8,239
1992	-84,501	532,665	448,164	31,356	13,662	45,018	10.0	36,906	22,379	8,111
1993	-115,568	580,659	465,091	27,235	12,183	39,418	8.5	31,823	18,146	7,596
1994	-150,630	663,256	512,626	25,010	12,363	37,373	7.3	30,050	15,931	7,322
1995	-158,801	743,543	584,742	21,561	11,509	33,071	5.7	25,079	10,606	7,991
1996	-170,214	795,289	625,075	26,602	13,668	40,270	6.4	29,477	13,624	10,792
1997	-180,522	869,704	689,182	32,239	18,134	50,374	7.3	40,075	21,028	10,299
1998	-229,758	911,896	682,138	40,960	23,110	64,071	9.4	51,999	29,168	12,072
1999	-328,821	1,024,618	695,797	37,381	25,063	62,444	9.0	50,624	25,694	11,820
2000	-436,104	1,218,022	781,918	26,734	27,944	54,679	7.0	45,566	19,615	9,113
2001	-411,042	1,141,954	730,912	26,035	32,473	58,508	8.0	49,371	22,151	9,137

Source: Aerospace Industries Association of America, Washington, DC, *Aerospace Facts and Figures*, annual.

No. 1286. U.S. Exporting Companies Profile by Company Type and Employment-Size Class: 1992 and 1999

Company type and employment-size class	Number of exporters		Known export value [1] (mil. dol.)		Percent of—			
					Number of exporters		Known export value	
	1992	1999	1992	1999	1992	1999	1992	1999
All companies, total	112,854	231,420	348,960	584,724	100.0	100.0	100.0	100.0
No employees	15,534	66,764	9,178	35,592	13.8	28.8	2.6	6.1
1 to 19 employees	51,186	92,474	29,397	38,479	45.4	40.0	8.4	6.6
20 to 49 employees	18,501	30,022	17,005	21,613	16.4	13.0	4.9	3.7
50 to 99 employees	10,505	16,317	13,840	21,109	9.3	7.1	4.0	3.6
100 to 249 employees	8,679	12,904	18,371	27,554	7.7	5.6	5.3	4.7
250 to 499 employees	3,621	5,200	15,055	24,195	3.2	2.2	4.3	4.1
500 or more employees	4,828	7,739	246,114	416,183	4.3	3.3	70.5	71.2
Manufacturers	(NA)	65,795	(NA)	407,214	(NA)	28.4	(NA)	69.6
No employees	(NA)	10,851	(NA)	11,323	(NA)	4.7	(NA)	1.9
1 to 19 employees	(NA)	18,953	(NA)	3,879	(NA)	8.2	(NA)	0.7
20 to 49 employees	(NA)	13,486	(NA)	6,146	(NA)	5.8	(NA)	1.1
50 to 99 employees	(NA)	8,799	(NA)	6,595	(NA)	3.8	(NA)	1.1
100 to 249 employees	(NA)	7,322	(NA)	14,039	(NA)	3.2	(NA)	2.4
250 to 499 employees	(NA)	2,875	(NA)	15,515	(NA)	1.2	(NA)	2.7
500 or more employees	(NA)	3,509	(NA)	349,718	(NA)	1.5	(NA)	59.8
Wholesalers	(NA)	68,100	(NA)	82,188	(NA)	29.4	(NA)	14.1
No employees	(NA)	14,988	(NA)	6,787	(NA)	6.5	(NA)	1.2
1 to 19 employees	(NA)	37,815	(NA)	19,457	(NA)	16.3	(NA)	3.3
20 to 49 employees	(NA)	8,289	(NA)	7,431	(NA)	3.6	(NA)	1.3
50 to 99 employees	(NA)	3,425	(NA)	6,173	(NA)	1.5	(NA)	1.1
100 to 249 employees	(NA)	2,163	(NA)	7,744	(NA)	0.9	(NA)	1.3
250 to 499 employees	(NA)	719	(NA)	3,165	(NA)	0.3	(NA)	0.5
500 or more employees	(NA)	701	(NA)	31,432	(NA)	0.3	(NA)	5.4
Other companies	(NA)	84,578	(NA)	84,966	(NA)	36.5	(NA)	14.5
No employees	(NA)	32,300	(NA)	12,963	(NA)	14.0	(NA)	2.2
1 to 19 employees	(NA)	34,157	(NA)	13,753	(NA)	14.8	(NA)	2.4
20 to 49 employees	(NA)	6,902	(NA)	7,132	(NA)	3.0	(NA)	1.2
50 to 99 employees	(NA)	3,400	(NA)	7,392	(NA)	1.5	(NA)	1.3
100 to 249 employees	(NA)	2,954	(NA)	4,984	(NA)	1.3	(NA)	0.9
250 to 499 employees	(NA)	1,501	(NA)	5,295	(NA)	0.6	(NA)	0.9
500 or more employees	(NA)	3,364	(NA)	33,446	(NA)	1.5	(NA)	5.7
Unclassified companies	(NA)	12,947	(NA)	10,356	(NA)	5.6	(NA)	1.8

NA Not available. [1] Known value is defined as the value of exports by known exporters, i.e., those export transactions that could be matched to specific companies. Export values are on f.a.s. or free alongside ship basis. Total export value was $251 billion in 1987 and $448 billion in 1992.

Source: U.S. Census Bureau, *A Profile of U.S. Exporting Companies, 1992* and *1998-1999*. See also <http://www.census.gov/foreign-trade/aip/edbrel-9899.pdf>.

No. 1287. Domestic Exports and Imports for Consumption of Merchandise by Selected Product Category: 1990 to 2001

[In millions of dollars (374,537 represents $374,537,000,000). Includes nonmonetary gold. 1990 to 1999, product categories based on SIC; beginning 2000, product categories based on NAICS and are not entirely comparable with SIC based data]

Product category	1990	1995	1997	1998	1999	2000	2001
Domestic exports, total [1]	**374,537**	**547,300**	**644,520**	**637,208**	**644,326**	**714,298**	**665,892**
Agricultural, forestry and fishery products	26,225	33,418	31,224	26,603	25,618	29,153	29,666
Agricultural products	22,597	29,391	27,460	23,336	21,960	23,596	24,068
Livestock and livestock products	829	920	1,132	1,110	1,029	1,255	1,309
Forestry products	281	272	279	257	233	1,644	1,436
Fish, fresh or chilled; and other marine products [2]	2,518	2,836	2,352	1,900	2,395	2,658	2,854
Mineral commodities	7,335	7,159	7,598	6,644	5,832	6,186	5,403
Minerals and ores	1,137	1,562	1,250	981	965	[3]4,481	[3]4,141
Oil and natural gas	638	729	1,566	1,251	1,445	1,706	1,261
Manufactured commodities	330,403	496,421	596,539	595,453	601,279	646,798	597,079
Food and kindred products	16,160	26,021	28,488	27,294	25,216	24,966	26,486
Beverages and tobacco	5,040	5,222	4,956	4,827	3,882	5,568	4,334
Textile mill products	3,635	5,696	7,081	7,180	7,541	2,236	1,991
Apparel and related products	2,848	7,190	9,279	9,474	8,541	8,104	6,469
Lumber and related products	6,523	7,424	7,312	5,960	6,236	4,854	3,944
Furniture and fixtures	1,589	2,953	3,643	3,958	2,304	2,882	2,418
Paper and allied products	8,631	14,943	14,512	13,713	13,839	15,539	14,045
Printing and publishing	3,150	4,471	4,791	4,865	4,719	4,869	4,867
Chemicals and allied products	37,806	57,897	65,080	63,896	66,296	77,649	76,837
Petroleum and coal products	6,794	6,014	7,331	5,668	2,892	8,862	8,214
Rubber and misc. plastics products	6,398	11,025	14,187	14,664	15,826	16,970	15,745
Leather and leather products	1,388	1,565	1,907	1,815	2,248	2,322	2,285
Primary metal products	13,116	20,191	22,694	21,737	19,893	20,126	18,150
Fabricated metal products	11,138	15,161	17,921	19,607	21,644	21,738	19,547
Machinery, except electrical	61,229	95,909	117,531	110,247	108,275	85,038	76,572
Computers and electronic products	39,807	76,235	93,767	92,230	97,990	114,700	134,263
Electrical equipment, appliances, and components	(NA)	(NA)	(NA)	(NA)	(NA)	25,401	22,764
Transportation equipment	68,113	82,699	108,465	119,981	119,175	121,701	122,877
Misc. manufactured commodities	4,296	7,383	7,279	6,653	7,047	[4]19,328	[4]20,815
Imports for consumption, total [1]	**490,554**	**739,661**	**862,426**	**907,647**	**1,017,435**	**1,205,339**	**1,132,635**
Agricultural, forestry and fishery products	12,750	19,799	22,817	22,859	22,968	24,378	23,599
Agricultural products	5,925	9,803	12,231	12,178	12,100	11,771	11,290
Livestock and livestock products	1,453	2,450	2,483	2,472	2,680	3,085	3,445
Forestry products	1,015	1,932	1,625	1,447	1,097	1,409	1,158
Fish, fresh or chilled; and other marine products [2]	4,357	5,614	6,478	6,761	7,090	8,113	7,706
Mineral commodities	51,391	51,050	53,313	38,619	46,043	79,841	76,243
Minerals and ores	1,500	1,413	1,406	1,509	1,185	[3]3,675	[3]3,553
Oil and natural gas	48,917	48,495	50,030	35,323	42,981	76,166	72,690
Manufactured commodities	407,043	639,729	750,206	803,384	906,665	1,040,329	972,669
Food and kindred products	16,564	18,326	22,600	23,811	25,487	18,944	19,646
Beverages and tobacco	94	169	463	437	413	502	8,723
Textile mill products	6,807	6,965	8,370	8,779	9,044	7,347	7,581
Apparel and accessories	24,644	41,208	50,191	55,838	59,156	62,928	62,429
Lumber and related products	5,446	10,406	13,531	14,042	17,480	15,388	14,968
Furniture and fixtures	5,235	8,303	11,008	13,127	11,799	15,607	15,266
Paper and allied products	11,669	16,757	14,839	15,857	16,460	19,080	18,170
Printing and publishing	1,849	2,902	3,210	3,461	3,786	4,197	4,143
Chemicals and allied products	21,611	38,079	48,382	52,355	62,149	76,606	80,681
Petroleum and coal products	14,472	8,971	22,149	18,689	21,972	40,156	35,222
Rubber and misc. plastics products	9,731	15,973	18,320	19,651	18,330	17,326	16,887
Leather and allied products	10,944	13,628	15,459	15,736	19,767	21,463	21,865
Primary metal products	23,232	33,519	37,727	42,771	39,036	43,833	36,350
Fabricated metal products	11,608	16,213	19,316	21,189	26,074	27,974	26,386
Machinery, except electrical	55,021	106,391	125,777	133,119	126,673	79,366	72,124
Computers and electronic products	55,736	114,912	120,879	125,321	163,981	250,694	204,950
Electrical equipment, appliances, and components	(NA)	(NA)	(NA)	(NA)	(NA)	39,567	38,949
Transportation equipment	89,599	122,344	140,684	155,753	182,428	213,110	212,013
Misc. manufactured commodities	20,090	28,694	35,579	38,715	42,492	[4]56,578	[4]56,427

NA Not available. [1] Includes scrap and waste, used or secondhand merchandise, manufactured commodities not identified by kind, and timing adjustments. [2] Includes frozen and packaged fish. [3] Beginning 2000, includes coal and nonmetallic minerals. Data are not comparable with prior years. [4] Beginning 2000, includes stone, clay, and glass products and instruments. Data are not comparable with prior years.

Source: U.S. Census Bureau, *U.S. International Trade in Goods and Services*, Series FT-900, December issues; and unpublished data.

Section 29
Outlying Areas

This section presents summary economic and social statistics for Puerto Rico, Virgin Islands, Guam, American Samoa, and the Northern Mariana Islands. Primary sources are the decennial censuses of population and housing and the censuses of agriculture, business, manufactures, and construction (taken every 5 years) conducted by the U.S. Census Bureau; the annual *Vital Statistics of the United States,* issued by the National Center for Health Statistics; and the annual *Income and Product* of the Puerto Rico Planning Board, San Juan.

Jurisdiction—The United States gained jurisdiction over these areas as follows: The islands of *Puerto Rico* and *Guam,* surrendered by Spain to the United States in October 1898, were ceded to the United States by the Treaty of Paris, ratified in 1899. Puerto Rico became a commonwealth on July 25, 1952, thereby achieving a high degree of local autonomy under its own constitution. The *Virgin Islands,* comprising 50 islands and cays, was purchased by the United States from Denmark in 1917. *American Samoa,* a group of seven islands, was acquired by the United States in accordance with a convention among the United States, Great Britain, and Germany, ratified in 1900 (Swains Island was annexed in 1925). By an agreement approved by the Security Council and the United States, the Northern Mariana Islands, previously under Japanese mandate, was administered by the United States between 1947 and 1986 under the United Nations trusteeship system. The Northern Mariana Islands became a commonwealth in 1986.

Censuses—Because characteristics of the outlying areas differ, the presentation of census data for them is not uniform. The 1960 Census of Population covered all of the places listed above except the Northern Mariana Islands (their census was conducted in April 1958 by the Office of the High Commissioner), while the 1960 Census of Housing also excluded American Samoa. The 1970, 1980, and 1990 Censuses of Population and Housing covered all five areas. The 1959, 1969, and 1978 Censuses of Agriculture covered Puerto Rico, American Samoa, Guam, and the Virgin Islands; the 1964, 1974, and 1982 censuses covered the same areas except American Samoa; and the 1969, 1978, 1987, 1992, and 1997 censuses included the Northern Mariana Islands. Beginning in 1967, Congress authorized the economic censuses, to be taken at 5-year intervals, for years ending in "2" and "7." Prior economic censuses were conducted in Puerto Rico for 1949, 1954, 1958, and 1963 and in Guam and the Virgin Islands for 1958 and 1963. In 1967, the census of construction industries was added for the first time in Puerto Rico; in 1972, Virgin Islands and Guam were covered. For 1982, 1987, 1992, and 1997 the economic censuses covered the Northern Mariana Islands.

Information in other sections—In addition to the statistics presented in this section, other data are included as integral parts of many tables showing distribution by states in various sections of the *Abstract.* See "Outlying areas of the United States" in the Index. For definition and explanation of terms used, see Section 1, Population; Section 4, Education; Section 17, Agriculture; Section 20, Construction and Housing; Section 21, Manufactures; and Section 22, Domestic Trade.

U.S. Census Bureau, Statistical Abstract of the United States: 2002

Figure 29.1
Selected Outlying Areas of the United States

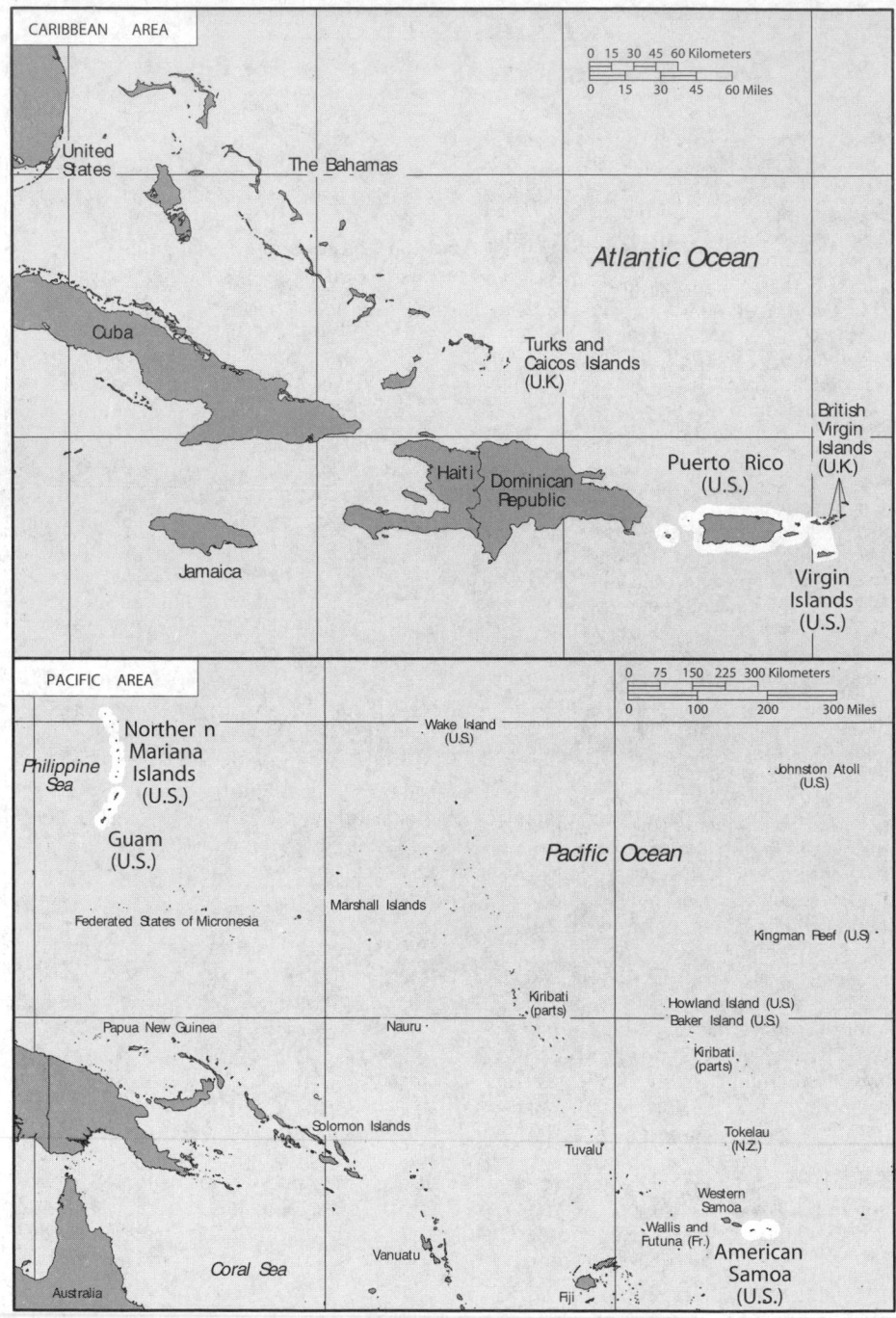

U.S. Census Bureau, Statistical Abstract of the United States: 2002

No. 1288. Estimated Resident Population With Projections: 1970 to 2010

[In thousands (2,722 represents 2,722,000). **Population as of July 1.** Population data generally are de facto figures for the present territory. Data for 1990 to 2000 are adjusted to the 2000 Census of Population for Puerto Rico only. See text, Section 30, for general comments regarding the data. For details of methodology, coverage, and reliability, see source]

Area	1970	1980	1990	1995	1996	1997	1998	1999	2000	2010, proj.
Puerto Rico.............	2,722	3,210	3,537	3,683	3,725	3,759	3,781	3,800	3,816	4,027
American Samoa...........	27	32	47	57	59	60	62	64	57	(NA)
Guam	86	107	134	144	145	146	149	152	155	(NA)
Virgin Islands.............	63	98	104	114	115	117	118	120	109	(NA)
Northern Mariana Islands.......	12	17	44	58	61	64	67	69	69	(NA)

NA Not available.
Source: U.S. Bureau of the Census, International Data Base. See Internet site: <http://census.gov/ipc/www/idbnew.html>.

No. 1289. Vital Statistics—Specified Areas: 1970 to 2000

[Data by place of residence. Rates for 1960, 1970, 1980, and 1990 based on population enumerated as of **April 1;** for other years, on population estimated as of **July 1**]

Area and year	Births		Deaths		Infant deaths	
	Number	Rate [1]	Number	Rate [1]	Number	Rate [2]
Puerto Rico: 1970	67,628	24.8	18,080	6.7	1,930	28.5
1980.............	72,986	22.8	20,413	6.4	1,351	18.5
1990.............	66,417	18.8	25,957	7.3	888	13.4
1995.............	63,425	17.0	30,032	8.1	804	12.7
2000 [3]	59,333	15.2	28,369	7.2	(NA)	(NA)
Guam: 1970	2,842	28.8	355	5.8	62	21.6
1980.............	2,945	27.8	393	3.7	43	14.6
1990.............	3,839	28.6	520	3.9	31	8.1
1995.............	4,180	29.0	592	4.1	38	9.4
2000 [3]	3,766	24.4	648	4.2	(NA)	(NA)
Virgin Islands: 1970	2,898	46.8	469	7.9	72	24.8
1980.............	2,504	25.9	504	5.2	61	24.4
1990.............	2,267	21.8	480	4.6	33	14.6
1995.............	2,063	18.1	664	5.8	34	16.6
2000 [3]	1,564	12.9	644	5.3	(NA)	(NA)
American Samoa: 1997..	1,634	27.1	257	4.3	17	(B)
2000.............	1,731	20.4	(NA)	(NA)	(NA)	(NA)
Northern Marianas: 1998 .	1,462	21.9	162	2.4	13	(B)
2000.............	1,431	19.9	(NA)	(NA)	(NA)	(NA)

B Base figure too small to meet statistical standards of reliability.   NA Not available.   [1] Per 1,000 population.   [2] Per 1,000 live births.   [3] Mortality data for 2000 are preliminary.
Source: U.S. National Center for Health Statistics, *Vital Statistics of the United States*, annual; *National Vital Statistics Reports* (NVSR); and unpublished data.

No. 1290. Population Characteristics by Area: 2000

[**As of April 1.** Based on the Census of Population; see Appendix III. See Table 335 for land area. For definition of median, see Guide to Tabular Presentation]

Item	United States	Puerto Rico	Virgin Islands	Guam	American Samoa	Northern Mariana Islands
Total resident population.............	281,421,906	3,808,610	108,612	154,805	57,291	69,221
Percent increase, 1990-2000........	13.2	8.1	6.7	16.3	22.5	59.7
Male........................	138,053,563	1,833,577	51,864	79,181	29,264	31,984
Female......................	143,368,343	1,975,033	56,748	75,624	28,027	37,237
Males per 100 females...........	96.3	92.8	91.4	104.7	104.4	85.9
Median age (years)..............	35.3	32.1	33.4	27.4	21.3	28.7
Marital status, persons 15 years and over..	221,148,671	2,903,329	80,207	107,649	35,079	53,632
Never married.................	59,913,370	813,784	32,764	37,711	12,741	22,462
Now married, excludes separated	120,231,273	1,509,403	31,223	57,505	19,519	28,224
Separated	4,769,220	104,897	2,639	1,453	437	916
Widowed.....................	14,674,500	197,123	4,078	4,253	1,570	1,121
Divorced	21,560,308	278,122	9,503	6,727	812	909
Households and families:						
Households	105,480,101	1,261,325	40,648	38,769	9,349	14,055
Family households (families) [1]	71,787,347	1,004,080	26,636	32,367	8,706	9,407
With own children under 18 years....	34,588,368	486,409	14,107	19,678	6,297	6,569
Married-couple family............	54,493,232	682,804	13,498	22,693	6,596	6,445
With own children under 18 years....	24,835,505	337,190	5,905	13,964	5,261	4,526
Female household, no husband present ..	12,900,103	268,476	10,132	6,284	1,398	1,663
With own children under 18 years....	7,561,874	131,584	6,450	3,753	640	1,106
Nonfamily households...............	33,692,754	257,245	14,012	6,402	643	4,648
Average household size	2.59	2.98	2.64	3.89	6.05	3.66
Average family size	3.14	3.41	3.34	4.27	6.24	4.16

[1] Includes other family types, not shown separately.
Source: U.S. Census Bureau, United States and Puerto Rico: DP-1, "Profile of General Demographic Characteristics: 2000 (area)" and DP-2, "Profile of Selected Social Characteristics: 2000 (area)"; Virgin Islands, Guan, and Northern Mariana Islands: "Population and Housing Profile: 2000 (area)." See Internet sites: <http://www.census.gov/population/www/cen2000/islandareas.html> and <http://www.census.gov/census2000/states/pr.html>.

Outlying Areas 805

No. 1291. Puerto Rico—General Demographic Characteristics: 1990 and 2000

[As of April 1. Based on the Censuses of Population and Housing, see Appendix III]

Characteristic	1990, number	2000 Number	2000 Per-cent	Characteristic	1990, number	2000 Number	2000 Per-cent
Total population	3,522,037	3,808,610	100.0	Mexican	(NA)	11,546	0.3
				Puerto Rican	(NA)	3,623,392	95.1
Male	1,705,642	1,833,577	48.1	Cuban	(NA)	19,973	0.5
Female	1,816,395	1,975,033	51.9	Other Hispanic or Latino	(NA)	107,835	2.8
				Not Hispanic or Latino	(NA)	45,864	1.2
Under 5 years	302,173	295,406	7.8	White alone	(NA)	33,966	0.9
5 to 9 years	316,473	305,162	8.0				
10 to 14 years	339,573	305,800	8.0	**RELATIONSHIP**			
15 to 19 years	326,717	313,436	8.2				
20 to 24 years	287,227	301,191	7.9	**Total population**	3,522,037	3,808,610	100.0
25 to 34 years	524,849	534,332	14.0	In households	3,487,667	3,761,836	98.8
35 to 44 years	462,479	515,663	13.5	Householder	1,054,924	1,261,325	33.1
45 to 54 years	355,858	463,036	12.2	Spouse	634,872	682,804	17.9
55 to 59 years	140,952	188,883	5.0	Child	1,475,741	1,431,769	37.6
60 to 64 years	124,852	160,564	4.2	Own child under 18 years	1,013,894	936,719	24.6
65 years and over	340,884	425,137	11.2	Other relatives	270,181	305,075	8.0
65 to 74 years	199,397	240,951	6.3	Under 18 years	128,384	139,420	3.7
75 to 84 years	108,822	136,480	3.6	Nonrelatives	51,949	80,863	2.1
85 years and over	32,665	47,706	1.3	Unmarried partner [3]	22,200	40,238	1.1
				In group quarters	34,370	46,774	1.2
Median age (years)	28.4	32.1	(X)	Institutionalized population	18,734	28,803	0.8
18 years and over	2,367,510	2,716,509	71.3	Noninstitutionalized			
Male	1,118,038	1,274,998	33.5	population	15,636	17,971	0.5
Female	1,249,472	1,441,511	37.8				
21 years and over	2,177,303	2,524,211	66.3	**HOUSEHOLD TYPE**			
62 years and over	416,445	518,249	13.6				
65 years and over	340,884	425,137	11.2	**Total households**	1,054,924	1,261,325	100.0
Male	156,226	186,203	4.9	Family households (families)	886,339	1,004,080	79.6
Female	184,658	238,934	6.3	With own children under			
				18 years	487,058	486,409	38.6
RACE [1]				Married-couple family	634,872	682,804	54.1
One race	(NA)	3,650,195	95.8	With own children under			
White	(NA)	3,064,862	80.5	18 years	363,989	337,190	26.7
Black or African American	(NA)	302,933	8.0	Female householder, no			
American Indian and				husband present	205,508	268,476	21.3
Alaska Native	(NA)	13,336	0.4	With own children under			
Asian	(NA)	7,960	0.2	18 years	105,085	131,584	10.4
Asian Indian	(NA)	4,789	0.1	Nonfamily households	168,585	257,245	20.4
Chinese	(NA)	1,873	-	Householder living alone	155,151	232,560	18.4
Filipino	(NA)	394	-	Householder 65 years			
Japanese	(NA)	251	-	and over	66,187	92,673	7.3
Korean	(NA)	244	-	Households with individuals			
Vietnamese	(NA)	195	-	under 18 years	552,367	565,692	44.8
Other Asian	(NA)	214	-	Households with individuals			
Native Hawaiian and				65 years and over	260,132	320,485	25.4
Other Pacific Islander	(NA)	1,093	-				
Native Hawaiian	(NA)	341	-	Average household size	3.31	2.98	(X)
Guamanian or Chamorro	(NA)	149	-	Average family size	3.69	3.41	(X)
Samoan	(NA)	347	-				
Other Pacific Islander	(NA)	256	-	**HOUSING OCCUPANCY**			
Some other race	(NA)	260,011	6.8				
Two or more races	(NA)	158,415	4.2	**Total housing units**	1,188,985	1,418,476	100.0
Race alone or in combination				Occupied housing units	1,054,924	1,261,325	88.9
with one or more other				Vacant housing units	134,061	157,151	11.1
races: [2]				For seasonal, recreational,			
White	(NA)	3,199,547	84.0	or occasional use	21,413	32,041	2.3
Black or African American	(NA)	416,296	10.9				
American Indian and Alaska				Homeowner vacancy rate			
Native	(NA)	26,871	0.7	(percent)	1.7	1.7	(X)
Asian	(NA)	17,279	0.5	Rental vacancy rate (percent)	7.3	7.4	(X)
Native Hawaiian and Other							
Pacific Islander	(NA)	2,894	0.1	**HOUSING TENURE**			
Some other race	(NA)	317,059	8.3				
				Housing units	1,054,924	1,261,325	100.0
HISPANIC OR LATINO AND RACE [1]				Owner-occupied housing units	760,233	919,769	72.9
				Renter-occupied housing units	294,691	341,556	27.1
Total population	3,522,037	3,808,610	100.0	Average household size of			
Hispanic or Latino (of any				owner-occupied units	3.36	3	(X)
race)	(NA)	3,762,746	98.8	Average household size of			
				renter-occupied units	3.17	2.94	(X)

- Less than .05 percent. NA Not available. X Not applicable. [1] Data on race and Hispanic origin were not collected in the 1990 census. [2] In combination with one or more of the races listed. Persons could report more than one race. [3] Sample data on unmarried partner households.

Source: U.S. Census Bureau, "Profile of General Demographic Characteristics for Puerto Rico," DP-1, 1990 and 2000. See Internet site <http://www.census.gov/Press-Release/www/2001/tables/redistpr.html#demoprofile> (released 03 July 2001).

No. 1292. Selected Social and Economic Characteristics by Area: 2000

[As of April 1. Based on the Decennial Census of Population and Housing; see Appendix III]

Characteristic	United States	Puerto Rico	Virgin Islands	Guam	American Samoa	Northern Mariana Islands
EDUCATIONAL ATTAINMENT						
Persons 25 years and over......	182,211,639	2,288,326	65,603	83,281	25,380	42,123
Less than 9th grade	13,755,477	581,225	12,133	7,843	3,120	5,794
9th to 12th grade, no diploma.......	21,960,148	335,179	13,743	11,862	5,476	7,181
High school graduate	52,168,981	509,856	17,044	26,544	9,983	14,986
Some college or associate degree....	49,864,428	443,813	11,694	20,398	4,928	7,634
Bachelor's degree or higher	44,462,605	418,253	10,989	16,634	1,873	6,528
EMPLOYMENT STATUS						
Persons, 16 years old and over....	217,168,077	2,842,876	78,265	105,014	33,945	52,898
In labor force..................	138,820,935	1,156,532	51,042	68,894	17,664	44,471
Percent of total	63.9	40.7	65.2	65.6	52.0	84.1
Armed forces.................	1,152,137	4,669	109	4,442	37	6
Civilian labor force	137,668,798	1,151,863	50,933	64,452	17,627	44,465
Employed..................	129,721,512	930,865	46,565	57,053	16,718	42,753
Unemployed...............	7,947,286	220,998	4,368	7,399	909	1,712
Percent of civilian labor force ..	5.8	19.2	8.6	11.5	5.2	3.9
Not in labor force..............	78,347,142	1,686,344	27,223	36,120	16,281	8,427
FAMILY INCOME IN 1999						
Families..................	72,261,780	1,008,555	26,636	32,367	8,706	9,407
Less than $10,000	4,155,386	316,675	5,584	3,955	2,107	1,553
$10,000 to $14,999	3,115,586	150,199	2,142	1,734	1,449	1,162
$15,000 to $24,999	7,757,397	202,824	4,203	3,923	1,995	1,864
$25,000 to $34,999	8,684,429	123,810	3,529	4,082	1,146	1,280
$35,000 to $49,999	12,377,108	101,047	4,011	5,400	969	1,301
$50,000 to $74,999	16,130,100	64,839	3,782	6,267	677	1,191
$75,000 or more	20,041,774	49,161	3,385	7,006	363	1,056
Median family income (dollars)	50,046	16,543	28,553	41,229	18,357	25,853
RESIDENCE IN 1995						
Persons 5 years and over	262,375,152	3,515,228	100,059	138,020	49,471	63,429
Same house	142,027,478	2,560,034	61,879	73,120	37,103	23,989
Different house in this area	112,851,828	820,514	27,688	40,945	5,763	15,576
Outside area	7,495,846	134,680	10,492	23,955	6,605	23,864
LANGUAGE SPOKEN AT HOME						
Persons 5 years and over	262,375,152	3,515,228	100,059	138,020	49,471	63,429
Speak only English at home........	215,423,557	506,661	74,740	52,831	1,440	6,819

Source: U.S. Census Bureau, United States and Puerto Rico: DP-1, "Profile of General Demographic Characteristics: 2000 (area)" and DP-2, "Profile of Selected Social Characteristics: 2000 (area)"; Virgin Islands, Guam, and Northern Mariana Islands: "Population and Housing Profile: 2000 (area)." See Internet sites: <http://www.census.gov/population/www/cen2000/islandareas.html> and <http://www.census.gov/census2000/states/pr.html>.

No. 1293. Federal Direct Payments: 2001

[In thousands of dollars (5,242,033 represents $5,242,033,000). For fiscal years ending September 30]

Selected program payments	Puerto Rico	Guam	Virgin Islands	American Samoa	Northern Mariana Islands	Marshall Islands	Micro-nisa	Palau
Direct payments to individuals for retirement and disability [1]........	5,242,033	190,545	131,874	39,761	20,545	867	419	352
Social Security:								
Retirement insurance.........	2,014,723	55,408	72,038	8,993	4,361	521	97	132
Survivors insurance..........	902,663	23,174	20,169	9,867	3,997	224	18	66
Disability insurance..........	1,642,711	13,335	17,979	12,257	1,390	15	2	25
Federal retirement and disability:								
Civilian [2]	192,573	60,542	14,369	1,532	4,527	78	240	97
Military....................	87,318	29,003	4,389	3,248	1,438	-	-	-
Veterans benefits:								
Service connected disability.....	215,692	6,442	1,647	3,005	385	9	56	5
Other	163,610	1,700	685	818	67	21	5	27
Other direct payments [1]...........	2,696,710	74,664	101,527	654	3,969	11	3,435	164
Medicare:								
Hospital insurance...........	519,805	741	13,031	-	-	-	-	-
Supplemental medical insurance .	796,591	487	8,751	-	-	-	-	-
Food stamp payments [3].........	-	37,172	17,631	-	-	-	-	-
Housing assistance...........	487,892	17,901	53,413	-	2,327	-	85	164
Agriculture assistance..........	26,265	-	781	-	108	-	-	-
Federal employees life and health insurance..................	62,555	13,006	-	-	-	-	-	-
Other	555,381	5,357	3,968	654	1,534	11	3,350	-

- Represents zero or rounds to zero. [1] Includes other payments, not shown separately. [2] Includes retirement and disability payments to former U.S. Postal Service employees. [3] Food stamp program in Puerto Rico was replaced by the Nutrition Assistance Grant Program in 1982.

Source: U.S. Census Bureau, *Consolidated Federal Funds Report for Fiscal Year, 2001* (issued April 2002). See also <http://www.census.gov/govs/www/cffr.html>.

Outlying Areas 807

No. 1294. Public Elementary and Secondary Schools by Area: 2000

[For school year ending in year shown, unless otherwise indicated (2,111,182 represents $2,111,182,000).]

Item	Puerto Rico	Guam	Virgin Islands	American Samoa	Item	Puerto Rico	Guam	Virgin Islands	American Samoa
Enrollment, fall	612,725	32,473	19,459	15,702	School staff	45,391	3,310	2,101	1,158
Elementary (kindergarten-					Teachers	37,620	1,975	1,511	820
grade 8)	445,463	23,698	13,906	11,895	Student support staff.	3,518	55	273	67
Secondary (grades 9-12 and post					Other support services staff.	17,866	145	294	296
graduates)	167,262	8,775	5,553	3,807					
Staff, fall	68,952	3,836	2,899	1,639	Current expenditures [1]				
School district staff .	2,177	326	231	118	($1,000)	2,111,182	194,156	146,474	36,895

[1] Public elementary and secondary day schools.

Source: U.S. National Center for Education Statistics, *Digest of Education Statistics*, annual; and unpublished data. See Internet site <http://nces.ed.gov/pubs2001/2001034.pdf>.

No. 1295. Puerto Rico—Summary: 1980 to 2001

[(3,184.0 represents 3,184,000).]

Item	Unit	1980	1990	1995	1997	1998	1999	2000	2001
POPULATION									
Total [1]	1,000	3,184.0	3,512.4	3,641.1	3,700.2	3,731.9	3,765.1	3,799.9	3,834.2
Persons per family	Number. . .	4.3	3.7	3.5	3.5	3.4	3.4	3.4	3.4
EDUCATION [2]									
Enrollment, total.	1,000	941.4	953.0	932.7	934.9	936.9	907.1	918.8	(NA)
Public (except public colleges or universities)	1,000	716.1	651.2	621.4	618.9	617.2	613.9	612.3	615.4
Private schools	1,000	95.2	145.8	145.9	143.1	144.1	118.7	131.9	(NA)
College and university	1,000	130.1	156.0	165.4	172.9	175.6	174.5	174.6	(NA)
Expenses	Mil. dol. . . .	825.0	1,686.4	2,555.8	3,629.1	3,748.7	3,902.0	4,158.0	4,341.9
As percent of GNP	Percent . . .	7.5	7.8	9.0	7.5	10.7	10.2	10.0	9.8
Public	Mil. dol. . . .	612.2	1,054.2	1,689.4	2,747.8	2,857.9	2,970.0	3,160.4	3,298.9
Private	Mil. dol. . . .	212.8	644.2	866.4	881.3	890.8	932.0	997.6	1,043.0
LABOR FORCE [3]									
Total [4]	1,000	907	1,124	1,219	1,298	1,317	1,310	1,303	1,293
Employed [5]	1,000	753	963	1,051	1,128	1,137	1,147	1,159	1,158
Agriculture [6]	1,000	38	36	34	31	31	27	24	22
Manufacturing.	1,000	143	168	172	162	161	159	159	159
Trade	1,000	138	185	211	228	236	229	239	242
Government	1,000	184	222	232	261	244	246	249	251
Unemployed	1,000	154	161	168	170	179	163	143	135
Unemployment rate [7]	Rate	17.0	14.0	14.0	13.1	13.6	12.5	11.0	10.5
Compensation of employees	Mil. dol. . . .	7,200.0	13,639.0	17,773.0	20,261.5	21,155.8	22,098.1	22,965.0	24,460.0
Avg. compensation	Dollar	9,563	14,854	16,911	17,962	18,607	19,266	19,814	21,123
Salary and wages	Mil. dol. . . .	7,200	13,639	17,773	20,262	21,156	22,098	22,965	24,460
INCOME [8]									
Personal income:									
Current dollars	Mil. dol. . . .	11,002.0	21,105.0	27,377.6	32,663.3	34,340.2	36,614.5	38,543.3	41,472.1
Constant (1954) dollars	Mil. dol. . . .	3,985.0	5,551.0	6,546.5	7,578.5	7,806.4	8,250.2	8,432.1	8,807.0
Disposable personal income:									
Current dollars	Mil. dol. . . .	10,403.0	19,914.0	25,590.9	30,607.2	32,065.8	34,041.7	35,775.2	38,883.5
Constant (1954) dollars	Mil. dol. . . .	3,768.0	5,238.0	6,119.3	7,101.4	7,289.3	7,670.5	7,826.6	8,257.3
Average family income:									
Current dollars	Dollar	14,858	22,232	26,316	30,896	31,286	33,064	34,487	36,776
Constant (1954) dollars	Dollar	5,381	5,847	6,293	7,168	7,112	7,450	7,545	7,810
BANKING [9]									
Assets	Mil. dol. . . .	10,223	27,902	39,859	42,380	46,088	53,338	58,813	55,701
TOURISM [8]									
Number of visitors	1,000	2,140.0	3,425.8	4,086.6	4,349.7	4,670.8	4,221.3	4,566.0	4,907.8
Visitor expenditures	Mil. dol. . . .	618.7	1,366.4	1,827.6	2,046.3	2,232.9	2,138.5	2,387.9	2,728.1
Average per visitor	Dollar	289	399	447	470	478	507	523	556
Net income from tourism	Mil. dol. . . .	202.2	383.3	498.7	553.5	597.9	577.1	615.4	663.1

NA Not available. [1] 1980, and 1990 enumerated as of April 1; all other years estimated as of July 1. [2] Enrollment for the first school month. Expenses for school year ending in year shown. "Public" includes: Public Preschool, Public Elementary, Public Intermediate, Public High School, Public Post-High School, Public Technological, Public Adult Education, Public Vocational Education, and Public Special Education. "College and university" includes both public and private colleges and universities. [3] Annual average of monthly figures. For fiscal years. [4] For population 16 years old and over. [5] Includes other employment not shown separately. [6] Includes forestry and fisheries. [7] Percent unemployed of the labor force. [8] For fiscal years. [9] As of June 30. Does not include federal savings banks and international banking entities.

Source: Puerto Rico Planning Board, San Juan, PR, *Income and Product* annual; and *Socioeconomics Statistics*, annual.

No. 1296. Puerto Rico—Gross Product and Net Income: 1990 to 2001

[In millions of dollars (21,619 represents $21,619,000,000). For fiscal years ending June 30. Data for 2001 are preliminary]

Item	1990	1995	1997	1998	1999	2000	2001
Gross product	21,619	28,452	32,343	35,111	38,281	41,442	44,211
Agriculture.	434	318	466	437	336	527	487
Manufacturing	12,126	17,867	19,302	22,994	23,312	23,375	27,099
Contract construction and mining [1]	720	1,006	1,257	1,482	1,668	1,833	1,977
Transportation & other public services [2]	2,468	3,276	3,751	3,978	4,032	4,312	4,704
Trade	4,728	5,989	6,724	7,287	8,112	8,421	8,717
Finance, insurance, real estate	3,896	5,730	6,917	7,672	8,183	9,903	11,181
Services	3,015	4,724	5,314	5,723	6,140	6,490	6,887
Government	3,337	4,440	5,220	5,251	5,530	5,478	6,011
Commonwealth.	2,884	3,793	4,457	4,462	4,693	4,601	5,103
Municipalities	453	647	763	789	836	877	908
Rest of the world	-8,985	-14,195	-15,844	-18,976	-19,560	-19,603	-23,686
Statistical discrepancy.	*-121*	*-703*	*-765*	*-739*	*529*	*706*	*835*
Net income	17,941	23,653	26,968	28,824	29,908	32,351	34,429
Agriculture.	486	442	638	594	619	667	648
Manufacturing	11,277	16,685	17,969	21,529	21,662	21,604	25,322
Mining	26	30	34	35	34	37	40
Contract construction	679	903	1,127	1,313	1,474	1,624	1,753
Transportation and other public services [2]. . .	1,778	2,360	2,691	2,784	2,632	2,980	3,140
Trade.	3,420	4,108	4,709	5,060	5,462	5,811	6,008
Finance, insurance, and real estate	3,280	4,735	5,773	6,251	6,743	8,139	9,224
Services	2,643	4,146	4,652	4,983	5,313	5,615	5,970
Commonwealth government [3].	3,337	4,440	5,220	5,251	5,530	5,478	6,011
Rest of the world	-8,985	-14,195	-15,844	-18,976	-19,560	-19,603	-23,686

[1] Mining includes only quarries.   [2] Includes other public utilities, and radio and television broadcasting.   [3] Includes public enterprises not elsewhere classified.

No. 1297. Puerto Rico—Transfer Payments: 1990 to 2001

[In millions of dollars (4,871 represents $4,871,000,000). Data represent transfer payments between federal and state governments and other nonresidents. See headnote, Table 1296]

Item	1990	1995	1997	1998	1999	2000	2001
Total receipts	4,871	6,236	7,399	7,758	8,627	8,662	9,504
Federal Government.	4,649	5,912	7,077	7,364	8,057	7,968	8,715
Transfers to individuals [1]	4,577	5,838	6,943	7,175	7,866	7,870	8,614
Veterans benefits.	349	440	484	495	479	491	491
Medicare	368	661	1,164	1,117	1,112	1,196	1,262
Old age, disability, survivors (social							
security).	2,055	2,912	3,282	3,472	3,556	3,863	4,336
Nutritional assistance	880	1,063	1,087	1,109	1,088	1,193	1,208
Industry subsidies	72	74	134	189	191	98	101
U.S. state governments	18	18	17	18	17	15	11
Other nonresidents	205	307	306	376	553	679	778
Total payments.	1,801	2,301	2,394	2,551	2,565	2,713	2,885
Federal Government.	1,756	2,132	2,355	2,496	2,499	2,643	2,830
Transfers from individuals.	817	1,052	1,158	1,231	1,237	1,301	1,402
Contribution to Medicare.	97	162	165	173	182	191	205
Employee contribution for social security . .	720	888	991	1,056	1,053	1,108	1,194
Transfers from industries	16	49	48	45	47	51	50
Unemployment insurance	247	184	202	217	216	234	233
Employer contribution for social security	675	847	946	1,003	999	1,056	1,145
Other nonresidents [2].	45	164	39	55	66	70	55
Net balance	3,070	3,935	5,005	5,207	6,062	5,949	6,619
Federal government	2,893	3,780	4,721	4,868	5,558	5,325	5,885
U.S. state governments	16	13	13	14	12	10	6
Other nonresidents	162	143	271	325	492	614	728

[1] Includes other receipts and payments not shown separately.   [2] Includes U.S. state governments.

Source of Tables 1296 and 1297: Puerto Rico Planning Board, San Juan, PR, *Economic Report of the Governor,* annual.

No. 1298. Puerto Rico—Merchandise Imports and Exports: 1980 to 2001

[In millions of dollars (9,018 represents $9,018,000,000). Imports are imports for consumption; see text, Section 28, Foreign Commerce and Aid]

Item	1980	1985	1990	1993	1994	1995	1996	1997	1998	1999	2000	2001
Imports.	9,018	10,162	16,200	16,124	17,152	18,969	19,422	21,928	21,706	26,697	27,199	27,642
From U.S	5,345	6,130	10,792	11,179	11,455	12,213	12,220	13,904	13,318	15,949	15,171	14,718
From other. . .	3,673	4,032	5,408	4,945	5,697	6,756	7,202	8,024	8,388	10,748	12,027	12,924
Exports	6,576	11,087	20,402	20,351	22,711	23,573	22,379	26,653	31,501	37,779	43,191	46,806
To U.S.	5,643	9,873	17,915	17,613	20,098	20,986	19,907	25,045	28,109	33,173	38,335	40,981
To other	933	1,214	2,487	2,738	2,613	2,587	2,472	1,608	3,392	4,606	4,856	5,825

Source: U.S. Census Bureau, *Foreign Commerce and Navigation of the United States,* annual; *U.S. Trade with Puerto Rico and U.S. Possessions, FT 895;* and, through 1985, *Highlights of U.S. Export and Import Trade, FT990;* thereafter, *FT920* supplement.

No. 1299. Puerto Rico—Agricultural Summary: 1993 and 1998

[1 cuerda = 0.97 acre]

All farms	Unit	1993	1998	All farms	Unit	1993	1998
Farms.	Number .	22,350	19,951	Average size of farm by operator:			
Farm land	Cuerdas .	826,893	865,478	Full owners	Cuerdas .	26.6	29.3
Average size of farm .	Cuerdas .	37.0	43.4	Part owners	Cuerdas .	92.3	111.7
				Tenants	Cuerdas .	63.4	75.9
Approximate land area. .	Cuerdas .	2,254,365	2,254,365	Farms by type of organization:			
Proportion in farms . .	Percent .	36.7	38.4				
				Individual or family. . .	Number .	19,911	17,887
Farms by size:				Partnership	Number .	288	211
Less than 10 cuerdas.	Number .	10,413	7,759	Corporation	Number .	382	437
10 to 19 cuerdas. . . .	Number .	4,475	4,473	Other	Number .	1,769	1,416
20 to 49 cuerdas. . . .	Number .	3,966	4,023	Farms by value of sales:			
50 to 99 cuerdas. . . .	Number .	1,723	1,792	Less than $1,200 . . .	Number .	4,456	3,307
100 to 174 cuerdas . .	Number .	820	809	$1,200 to $2,499. . . .	Number .	4,591	3,633
175 to 259 cuerdas . .	Number .	366	421	$2,500 to $4,499. . . .	Number .	4,593	3,900
260 cuerdas or more .	Number .	587	674	$5,000 to $7,499. . . .	Number .	2,566	2,408
				$7,500 to $9,999. . . .	Number .	1,248	1,233
Tenure of operator:				$10,000 to $19,999 . .	Number .	2,115	2,366
Operators	Number .	22,350	19,951	$20,000 to $39,999 . .	Number .	1,071	1,247
Full owners	Number .	17,759	15,620	$40,000 to $59,999 . .	Number .	348	405
Part owners	Number .	2,218	2,207	$60,000 or more	Number .	1,362	1,452
Tenants	Number .	2,373	2,124				

No. 1300. Puerto Rico—Farms and Market Value of Products Sold: 1998

[593,082 represents $593,082,000]

Type of product	Number of farms	Market value ($1,000)	Average value per farm (dol.)	Type of product	Number of farms	Market value ($1,000)	Average value per farm (dol.)
Total	**19,951**	**593,082**	**29,727**	Horticultural specialties . .	490	39,399	80,406
Crops, specialties	15,863	225,780	(NA)	Grasses and other crops .	288	5,464	18,971
Sugarcane	162	6,973	43,042	Livestock, poultry, and			
Coffee	10,441	55,486	5,314	their products	7,580	367,302	48,457
Pineapples	35	3,275	93,569	Cattle and calves.	5,602	53,442	9,540
Plantains	6,229	46,021	7,388	Poultry and poultry			
Bananas	3,836	11,854	3,090	products	1,153	99,208	86,043
Grains	1,256	4,170	3,320	Dairy products.	447	193,615	433,143
Root crops or tubers. . . .	2,517	7,624	3,029	Hogs and pigs.	1,368	11,365	8,308
Fruits and coconuts	4,201	17,343	4,128	Sheep and goats	377	380	1,009
Vegetables or melons. . .	1,639	28,172	17,189	Other.	858	9,292	10,830

NA Not available.
Source of Tables 1299 and 1300: U.S. Dept. of Agriculture, National Agricultural Statistics Service, *1998 Census of Agriculture-Area Data, Puerto Rico, Volume 1* (AC97-A-52).

No. 1301. Puerto Rico—Economic Census of Manufactures by Industry: 1997

[3,319 represents $3,319,000,000. Covers all establishments in operation at any time during the year. Employees are for the pay period including March 12. Based on the 1997 Economic Census; see Appendix III]

Manufacturing industries	1987 SIC code [1]	Total establish-ments (number)	Propri-etors and part-ners (number)	Unpaid family workers (number)	All employees Total (number)	All employees Payroll (mil. dol.)	Value added by manu-facture (mil. dol.)	Cost of materi-als (mil. dol.)	Value of ship-ments (mil. dol.)
Total	**(X)**	**2,092**	**601**	**108**	**163,605**	**3,319**	**36,427**	**10,343**	**46,876**
Food and kindred products	20	287	94	14	18,094	352	3,532	1,803	5,333
Tobacco products	21	4	(D)	-	(2)	(D)	(D)	(D)	(D)
Textile mill products	22	20	8	2	2,555	32	89	38	129
Apparel and other textile products	23	223	55	15	21,818	233	678	404	1,080
Lumber and wood products	24	117	(D)	(D)	(2)	(D)	(D)	(D)	(D)
Furniture and fixtures	25	146	65	7	2,472	30	97	69	165
Paper and allied products	26	41	2	1	2,152	43	162	121	283
Printing and publishing	27	208	93	27	6,469	126	430	284	713
Chemicals and allied products	28	186	11	2	37,860	1,149	21,393	3,919	25,418
Petroleum and coal products	29	28	-	3	1,555	49	849	379	1,220
Rubber and miscellaneous plastic products.	30	71	5	1	4,924	87	377	236	613
Leather and leather products	31	25	4	-	5,752	80	218	205	426
Stone, clay and glass products	32	159	37	5	5,298	106	565	161	726
Primary metal industries	33	24	7	1	727	13	77	37	111
Fabricated metal products	34	229	87	11	6,048	91	405	214	623
Industrial machinery and equipment.	35	78	29	5	4,301	107	2,665	262	2,940
Electronic and other electrical equipment . .	36	87	6	1	24,931	456	2,897	1,471	4,360
Transportation equipment	37	34	9	2	1,484	27	118	47	166
Instruments and related products	38	64	3	-	12,260	255	1,521	556	2,077
Miscellaneous manufacturing industries . . .	39	61	18	3	2,208	39	164	55	218

- Represents zero. D Withheld to avoid disclosure of information pertaining to a specific organization or individual. X Not applicable. [1] 1987 Standard Industrial Classification (SIC) code; see text, Section 12, Labor Force, Employment, and Earnings. [2] Represents 1,000 to 2,499 employees.
Source: U.S. Census Bureau, *1997 Economic Census of Puerto Rico and the Island Areas*, Series OA97E-4. See also <http://www.census.gov/prod/ec97/oa97e-4.pdf>.

No. 1302. Puerto Rico—Economic Summary by Industry: 1992 and 1997

[**2,551.0 represents $2,551,000,000** covers establishments with payroll. Employees are for the pay period including March 12. Based on the 1992 and 1997 Economic Censuses, see Appendix III]

Industry	1987 SIC code [1]	Establish-ments (number)		Sales/receipts/ shipments (mil. dol.)		Annual payroll (mil. dol.)		Paid employees (number)	
		1992	1997	1992	1997	1992	1997	1992	1997
Construction industries	C	1,529	1,957	2,551.0	3,965.3	506.6	697.2	47,666	57,123
General contractors and operative builders	15	574	798	1,226.8	1,998.8	234.4	324.1	22,676	27,460
Heavy construction other than buildings const.	16	196	195	554.1	916.5	96.4	156.0	8,462	11,208
Special trade contractors . . . . . . [2]	17	732	880	746.6	936.2	171.9	207.6	16,134	17,638
Subdividers and developers, n.e.c. [2]	6552	27	84	23.5	113.9	3.9	9.5	394	817
Manufacturing	D	2,258	2,092	31,325.8	46,876.0	2,706.5	3,318.9	158,181	163,605
Food and kindred products	20	331	287	5,240.0	5,333.0	310.3	351.8	20,193	18,094
Tobacco products	21	6	4	(D)	(D)	(D)	(D)	(D)	(D)
Textile mill products.	22	26	20	180.1	129.4	34.8	31.9	3,324	2,555
Apparel and other textile products . .	23	285	223	1,412.3	1,079.7	312.3	232.5	31,320	21,818
Lumber & wood products	24	106	117	(D)	(D)	(D)	(D)	(D)	(D)
Furniture and fixtures.	25	143	146	179.4	164.7	22.5	29.7	2,310	2,472
Paper and allied products.	26	55	41	321.6	283.3	43.8	42.8	2,732	2,152
Printing and publishing.	27	192	208	448.3	712.8	82.3	126.2	4,121	6,469
Chemicals and allied products.	28	190	186	13,253.4	25,418.3	861.3	1,149.5	31,161	37,860
Petroleum and coal products.	29	24	28	1,707.5	1,219.9	47.2	48.6	1,562	1,555
Rubber and misc. plastic products . .	30	92	71	415.7	612.7	65.8	86.9	4,252	4,924
Leather and leather products	31	31	25	387.5	426.1	65.0	80.3	5,785	5,752
Stone, clay, and glass products	32	174	159	518.6	726.5	81.3	106.0	4,517	5,298
Primary metal industries.	33	27	24	(D)	110.9	(D)	13.2	(D)	727
Fabricated metal products	34	211	229	492.0	622.9	67.4	90.9	4,924	6,048
Industrial machinery and equip	35	74	78	1,292.0	2,940.0	109.5	106.8	5,373	4,301
Electronic and other electronic equip	36	114	87	2,779.0	4,360.2	277.2	455.8	17,224	24,931
Transportation equipment.	37	34	34	151.5	165.8	20.5	26.9	1,315	1,484
Instruments and related products. . .	38	65	64	1,873.8	2,076.6	220.3	254.9	12,398	12,260
Miscellaneous manufacturing products	39	78	61	264.8	217.6	39.7	38.7	2,754	2,208
Wholesale trade.	F	2,651	2,809	10,187.7	12,594.6	673.2	850.9	34,996	39,582
Durable goods	50	1,343	1,468	3,472.9	4,462.3	275.0	375.2	14,688	17,719
Nondurable goods	51	1,308	1,341	6,711.7	8,102.0	398.2	475.7	20,308	21,863
Merchant wholesalers	(X)	2,408	2,453	8,494.0	9,386.3	487.4	582.2	28,682	31,211
Other operating types	(X)	243	356	1,693.7	3,208.4	185.8	268.7	6,314	8,371
Retail trade	G	13,534	14,582	11,707.0	17,088.0	1,114.0	1,593.2	119,615	153,746
Building materials, garden supplies .	52	991	987	615.8	972.9	60.0	93.4	5,577	7,499
General merchandise stores	53	485	389	1,503.0	2,229.9	162.7	194.6	15,690	19,282
Food stores	54	1,988	2,066	2,959.8	3,620.6	215.9	266.8	26,026	29,088
Automotive dealers and service stations	55, ex. 554	1,118	1,281	1,688.3	3,395.8	95.5	182.5	7,074	11,418
Gasoline service stations	554	1,060	1,115	710.5	1,141.3	32.8	54.7	4,115	5,550
Apparel and accessory stores	56	2,032	1,972	1,205.1	1,413.6	131.1	167.2	16,061	18,208
Furniture and home furnishings	57	1,048	1,096	772.2	1,119.4	77.0	105.6	6,188	8,089
Eating and drinking places	58	2,356	3,021	934.3	1,444.6	185.1	307.9	23,951	36,996
Drug stores & proprietary stores . . .	591	790	756	656.9	896.7	69.6	108.4	6,377	7,949
Miscellaneous retail.	59, ex. 591	1,666	1,899	660.9	853.0	84.3	112.0	8,556	9,667
Service industries [3]	I	6,356	8,048	3,110.3	5,823.0	893.6	1,546.1	71,378	111,125
Arrangement of passenger transportation	472	384	384	115.2	166.6	15.3	19.9	1,240	1,459
Hotels, paradores & motels.	701	166	206	412.3	791.5	130.9	238.9	8,774	14,932
Personal services	72	828	983	137.8	208.6	37.2	52.4	3,958	4,944
Business services	73	1,302	1,861	1,030.6	2,251.9	384.5	698.7	36,159	57,109
Auto repair, services, and parking . .	75	972	1,235	329.5	476.9	56.9	79.2	4,851	6,285
Miscellaneous repair services	76	480	564	172.6	239.1	37.1	50.1	2,853	3,919
Motion pictures.	78	135	179	107.0	136.4	15.1	22.2	1,414	2,335
Amusement and recreation services .	79	219	345	132.0	268.6	23.2	50.8	2,150	4,498
Dental laboratories	80	29	39	4.8	(D)	1.4	(D)	144	(D)
Legal services	81	1,153	1,280	288.7	463.0	90.5	122.3	4,169	5,057
Museum, art galleries, botanical, and zoological gardens	84	15	17	(D)	6.3	(D)	1.3	(D)	110
Engineering and management services.	87, ex. 872	671	950	375.8	805.4	100.8	208.6	5,580	10,277

D Data withheld to avoid disclosing individual company data.   X Not applicable.   [1] 1987 Standard Industrial Classification (SIC) code; see text, Section 12, Labor Force, Employment, and Earnings.   [2] Excludes cemeteries. N.e.c. means not elsewhere classified.
[3] Includes other establishments not shown separately.

Source: U.S. Census Bureau, *Economic Census of Puerto Rico and the Island Areas.* See Internet site <http://www.census.gov/csd/ia/index.html>.

No. 1303. Guam, Virgin Islands, and Northern Mariana Islands—Economic Summary: 1997

[Sales and payroll in millions of dollars (4,640 represents $4,640,000,000). Based on the 1997 Economic Census; see Appendix III]

Item	Guam	Virgin Islands	No. Mariana Islands	Item	Guam	Virgin Islands	No. Mariana Islands
Total: Establishments	2,707	2,032	1,232	Wholesale trade:			
Sales.	4,640	2,296	2,083	Establishments	270	115	87
Annual payroll	750	382	323	Sales.	941	252	223
Paid employees [1]	42,477	21,216	28,906	Annual payroll	77	27	9
				Paid employees [1]	3,393	1,144	745
Construction: Establishments. .	354	203	85	Retail trade:			
Sales.	506	185	88	Establishments	1,091	973	519
Annual payroll	139	52	21	Sales.	1,840	1,058	570
Paid employees [1]	7,094	2,623	2,302	Annual payroll	221	136	54
Manufacturing:				Paid employees [1]	15,334	8,966	4,811
Establishments	60	74	84	Services: Establishments	932	667	457
Sales.	165	146	762	Sales.	1,188	655	440
Annual payroll	33	28	147	Annual payroll	280	139	91
Paid employees [1]	1,320	1,194	13,715	Paid employees [1]	15,336	7,289	7,333

[1] For pay period including March 12.

Source: U.S. Census Bureau, *1997 Economic Census of Puerto Rico and the Island Areas,* OA97-E-5 to OA97-E-7. See Internet site <http://www.census.gov/csd/ia/index.html>.

No. 1304. Puerto Rico, Guam, Virgin Islands, American Samoa, and Northern Mariana Islands—Population, Selected Areas: 1990 and 2000

[As of April 1. Minus sign (-) indicates decrease]

Area	1990	2000	Population change, 1990 to 2000 Number	Percent
PUERTO RICO				
Municipio:				
San Juan	437,745	434,374	-3,371	-0.8
Bayamon.	220,262	224,044	3,782	1.7
Ponce.	187,749	186,475	-1,274	-0.7
Carolina	177,806	186,076	8,270	4.7
Caguas	133,447	140,502	7,055	5.3
Arecibo	93,385	100,131	6,746	7.2
Guaynabo	92,886	100,053	7,167	7.7
Mayaguez	100,371	98,434	-1,937	-1.9
Toa Baja	89,454	94,085	4,631	5.2
Trujillo Alto.	61,120	75,728	14,608	23.9
Aguadilla.	59,335	64,685	5,350	9.0
Toa Alta	44,101	63,929	19,828	45.0
Vega Baja	55,997	61,929	5,932	10.6
Humacao	55,203	59,035	3,832	6.9
Rio Grande	45,648	52,362	6,714	14.7
Place:				
San Juan zona urbana.	426,832	421,958	-4,874	-1.1
Bayamon zona urbana.	202,103	203,499	1,396	0.7
Carolina zona urbana	162,404	168,164	5,760	3.5
Ponce zona urbana	159,151	155,038	-4,113	-2.6
Caguas zona urbana	92,429	88,680	-3,749	-4.1
Guaynabo zona urbana	73,385	78,806	5,421	7.4
Mayaguez zona urbana	83,010	78,647	-4,363	-5.3
Trujillo Alto zona urbana.	44,336	50,841	6,505	14.7
Arecibo zona urbana	49,545	49,318	-227	-0.5
Fajardo zona urbana	31,659	33,286	1,627	5.1
Levittown comunidad zona urbana	30,807	30,140	-667	-2.2
Catano zona urbana	34,587	30,071	-4,516	-13.1
GUAM				
Dedido District	31,728	42,980	11,252	35.5
Yigo District.	14,213	19,474	5,261	37.0
Mangilao District	10,483	13,313	2,830	27.0
U.S. VIRGIN ISLANDS				
St Croix Island.	50,139	53,234	3,095	6.2
St Thomas Island	48,166	51,181	3,015	6.3
Charlotte Amalie subdistrict.	20,589	18,914	-1,675	-8.1
St John Island	3,504	4,197	693	19.8
AMERICAN SAMOA				
Eastern District	21,175	23,441	2,266	10.7
Ma'oputasi County	10,640	11,695	1,055	9.9
Western District	23,868	32,435	8,567	35.9
Tualauta County	14,724	22,025	7,301	49.6
NORTHERN MARIANA ISLANDS				
Saipan Municipality.	38,896	62,392	23,496	60.4

Source: U.S. Census Bureau, Internet releases (03 July 2001) <http://www.census.gov/Press-Release/www/2001/tables/redistpr.html#demoprofile>; <http://www.census.gov/Press-Release/www/2001/tables/redistgu.html>; <http://www.census.gov/Press-Release/www/2001/tables/redistvi.html>; <http://www.census.gov/Press-Release/www/2001/tables/redistas.html>; <http://www.census.gov/Press-Release/www/2001/tables/redistnmi.html>.

Section 30
Comparative International Statistics

This section presents statistics for the world as a whole and for many countries on a comparative basis with the United States. Data are shown for population, births and deaths, social and industrial indicators, finances, agriculture, communication, and military affairs.

Statistics of the individual nations may be found primarily in official national publications, generally in the form of yearbooks, issued by most of the nations at various intervals in their own national languages and expressed in their own or customary units of measure. (For a listing of selected publications, see Guide to Sources.) For handier reference, especially for international comparisons, the United Nations Statistics Division compiles data as submitted by member countries and issues a number of international summary publications, generally in English and French. Among these are the *Statistical Yearbook*; the *Demographic Yearbook*; *International Trade Statistics Yearbook*; *National Accounts Statistics: Main Aggregates and Detailed Tables*; *Population and Vital Statistics Reports* (quarterly); the *Monthly Bulletin of Statistics*; and the *Energy Statistics Yearbook*. Specialized agencies of the United Nations also issue international summary publications on agricultural, labor, health, and education statistics. Among these are the *Production Yearbook* and *Trade Yearbook* issued by the Food and Agriculture Organization, the *Yearbook of Labour Statistics* issued by the International Labour Office, *World Health Statistics* issued by the World Health Organization, and the *Statistical Yearbook* issued by the Educational, Scientific, and Cultural Organization.

The U.S. Census Bureau presents estimates and projections of basic demographic measures for countries and regions of the world in the *World Population Reports* (WP) series. The *International Population Reports* (Series IPC), and *International Briefs* (Series IB) also present population figures for many foreign

countries. Detailed population statistics are also available from the Census Bureau's International Data Base (http://www.census.gov/ipc/www/idb new.html>.

The International Monetary Fund (IMF) and the Organization for Economic Cooperation and Development (OECD) also compile data on international statistics. The IMF publishes a series of reports relating to financial data. These include *International Financial Statistics, Direction of Trade,* and *Balance of Payments Yearbook,* published in English, French, and Spanish. The OECD publishes a vast number of statistical publications in various fields such as economics, health, and education. Among these are *OECD in Figures, Main Economic Indicators, Economic Outlook, National Accounts, Labour Force Statistics, OECD Health Data,* and *Education at a Glance.*

Statistical coverage, country names, and classifications—Problems of space and availability of data limit the number of countries and the extent of statistical coverage shown. The list of countries included and the spelling of country names are based almost entirely on the list of sovereign nations, dependencies, and areas of special sovereignty provided by the U.S. Department of State.

In recent years, several important changes took place in the status of the world's nations. In 1990, a unified Germany was formed from the Federal Republic of Germany (West) and the German Democratic Republic (East). The Republic of Yemen was formed by union of the Yemen Arab Republic and the People's Democratic Republic of Yemen. Also in 1990, Namibia, once a United Nations mandate, realized its independence from South Africa.

In 1991, the Soviet Union broke up into 15 independent countries: Armenia, Azerbaijan, Belarus, Estonia, Georgia, Kazakhstan, Kyrgyzstan, Latvia, Lithuania,

Moldova, Russia, Tajikistan, Turkmenistan, Ukraine, and Uzbekistan.

Following the breakup of the Socialist Federal Republic of Yugoslavia in 1992, the United States recognized Bosnia and Herzegovina, Croatia, Slovenia, and The Former Yugoslav Republic of Macedonia as independent countries.

On January 1, 1993, Czechoslovakia was succeeded by two independent countries: the Czech Republic and Slovakia. Eritrea announced its independence from Ethiopia in April 1993 and was subsequently recognized as an independent nation by the United States.

The population estimates and projections used in Tables 1305, 1306, 1308, 1309, and 1312 were prepared by the Census Bureau. For each country, the data on population, by age and sex, fertility, mortality, and international migration were evaluated and, where necessary, adjusted for inconsistencies and errors in the data. In most instances, comprehensive projections were made by the component method, resulting in distributions of the population by age and sex and requiring an assessment of probable future trends of fertility, mortality, and international migration.

Economic associations—The Organization for European Economic Co-Operation (OEEC), a regional grouping of Western European countries established in 1948 for the purpose of harmonizing national economic policies and conditions, was succeeded on September 30, 1961, by the Organization for Economic Cooperation and Development (OECD). The member nations of the OECD are Australia, Austria, Belgium, Canada, Czech Republic, Denmark, Finland, France, Germany, Greece, Hungary, Iceland, Ireland, Italy, Japan, Luxembourg, Mexico, the Netherlands, New Zealand, Norway, Poland, Portugal, Slovakia, South Korea, Spain, Sweden, Switzerland, Turkey, the United Kingdom, and the United States.

Quality and comparability of the data—The quality and comparability of the data presented here are affected by a number of factors:

(1) The year for which data are presented may not be the same for all subjects for a particular country or for a given subject for different countries, though the data shown are the most recent available. All such variations have been noted. The data shown are for calendar years except as otherwise specified.

(2) The bases, methods of estimating, methods of data collection, extent of coverage, precision of definition, scope of territory, and margins of error may vary for different items within a particular country, and for like items for different countries. Footnotes and headnotes to the tables give a few of the major time-periods and coverage qualifications attached to the figures; considerably more detail is presented in the source publications. Many of the measures shown are, at best, merely rough indicators of magnitude.

(3) Figures shown in this section for the United States may not always agree with figures shown in the preceding sections. Disagreements may be attributable to the use of differing original sources, a difference in the definition of geographic limits (the 50 states, conterminous United States only, or the United States including certain outlying areas and possessions), or to possible adjustments made in the United States figures by other sources in order to make them more comparable with figures from other countries.

International comparisons of national accounts data—In order to compare national accounts data for different countries, it is necessary to convert each country's data into a common unit of currency, usually the U.S. dollar. The market exchange rates which are often used in converting national currencies do not necessarily reflect the relative purchasing power in the various countries. It is necessary that the goods and services produced in different countries be valued consistently if the differences observed are meant to reflect real differences in the volumes of goods and services produced. The use of purchasing power parities (see Table 1320) instead of exchange rates is intended to achieve this objective.

814   Comparative International Statistics

The method used to present the data shown in Table 1320 is to construct volume measures directly by revaluing the goods and services sold in different countries at a common set of international prices. By dividing the ratio of the gross domestic products of two countries expressed in their own national currencies by the corresponding ratio calculated at constant international prices, it is possible to derive the implied purchasing power parity (PPP) between the two currencies concerned. PPPs show how many units of currency are needed in one country to buy the same amount of goods and services which one unit of currency will buy in the other country. For further information, see *National Accounts, Main Aggregates, Volume I,* issued annually by the Organization for Economic Cooperation and Development, Paris, France.

International Standard Industrial Classification—The original version of the International Standard Industrial Classification of All Economic Activities (ISIC) was adopted in 1948. Wide use has been made both nationally and internationally in classifying data according to kind of economic activity in the fields of production, employment, national income, and other economic statistics. A number of countries have utilized the ISIC as the basis for devising their industrial classification scheme.

Substantial comparability has been attained between the industrial classifications of many other countries, including the United States and the ISIC by ensuring, as far as practicable, that the categories at detailed levels of classification in national schemes fitted into only one category of the ISIC. The United Nations, the International Labour Organization, the Food and Agriculture Organization, and other international bodies have utilized the ISIC in publishing and analyzing statistical data. Revisions of the ISIC were issued in 1958, 1968, and 1989.

International maps—A series of regional world maps is provided on pages 816-822. References are included in Table 1308 for easy location of individual countries on the maps. The Robinson map projection is used for this series of maps. A map projection is used to portray all or part of the round Earth on a flat surface, but this cannot be done without some distortion. For the Robinson projection, distortion is very low along the Equator and within 45 degrees of the center but is greatest near the poles. For additional information on map projections and maps, please contact the Earth Science Information Center, U.S. Geological Survey, 507 National Center, Reston, VA 22092.

U.S. Census Bureau, Statistical Abstract of the United States: 2002

World

S5 (Asia and Russia)

S6 (Australia, Southeast Asia, and Pacific Islands)

S3 (Europe)

S4 (Africa)

S2 (South America)

S1 (North and Central America)

S6 (Australia, Southeast Asia, and Pacific Islands)

U.S. Census Bureau, Statistical Abstract of the United States: 2002

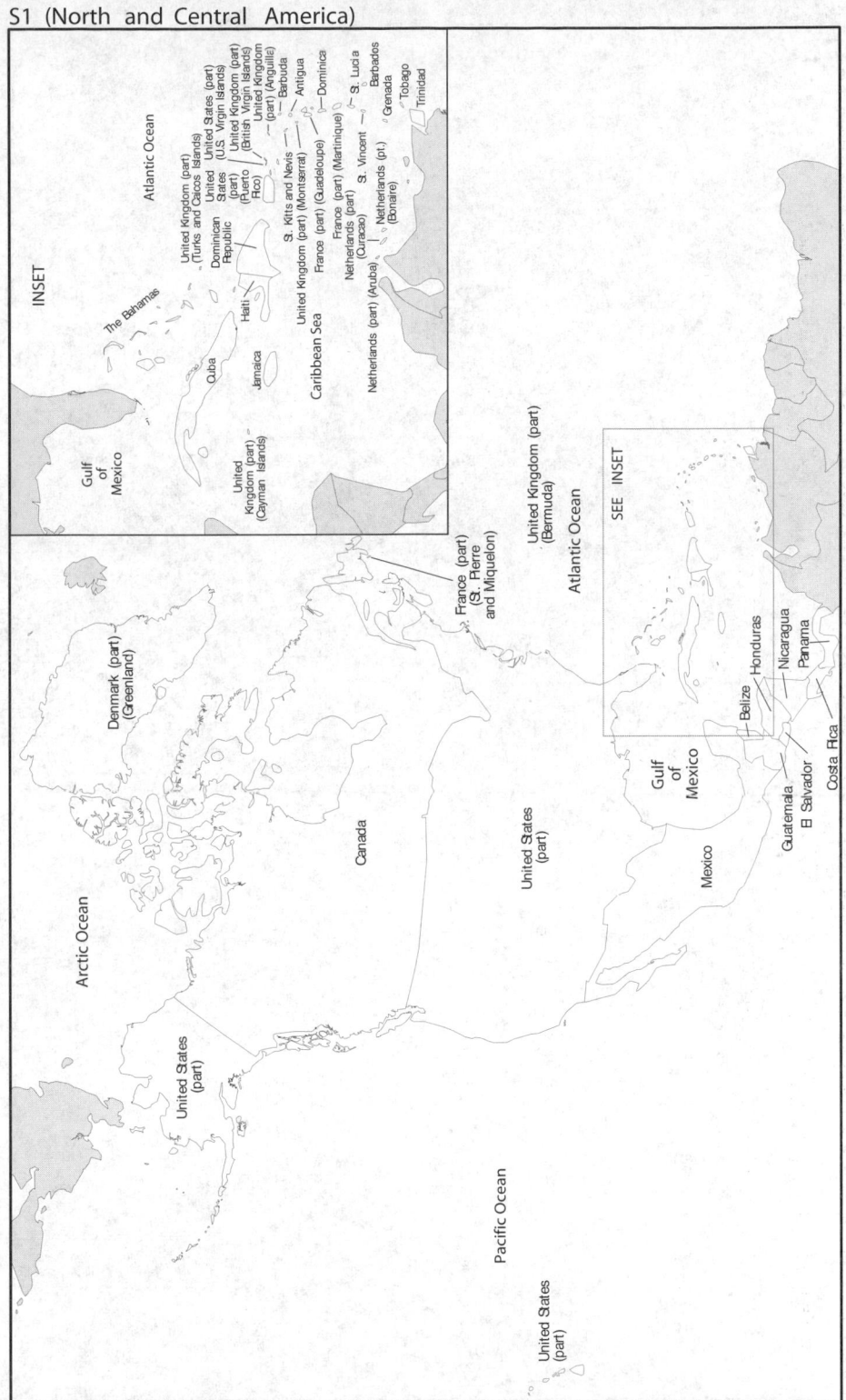

INSET

Atlantic Ocean

United Kingdom (part)
(Turks and Caicos Islands)
United States (part)
(U.S. Virgin Islands)
United Kingdom (part)
(British Virgin Islands)
United Kingdom (part) (Anguilla)
Barbuda
Antigua
Dominica
St. Lucia
Barbados
Tobago
Grenada
Trinidad

United States
(Puerto
Rico)

St. Kitts and Nevis
United Kingdom (part) (Montserrat)
France (part) (Guadeloupe)
France (part) (Martinique)
St. Vincent
Netherlands (pt)
(Bonaire)

Dominican
Republic

Haiti

Netherlands (part)
(Curaçao)
Netherlands (part) (Aruba)

The Bahamas

Cuba

Jamaica

Caribbean Sea

Gulf
of
Mexico

United
Kingdom (part)
(Cayman Islands)

France (part)
(St. Pierre
and Miquelon)

United Kingdom (part)
(Bermuda)

Atlantic Ocean

SEE INSET

Denmark (part)
(Greenland)

Arctic Ocean

Canada

United States
(part)

Gulf
of
Mexico

Belize
Honduras
Nicaragua
Panama

Mexico

Guatemala
El Salvador
Costa Rica

United States
(part)

Pacific Ocean

United States
(part)

U.S. Census Bureau, Statistical Abstract of the United States: 2002

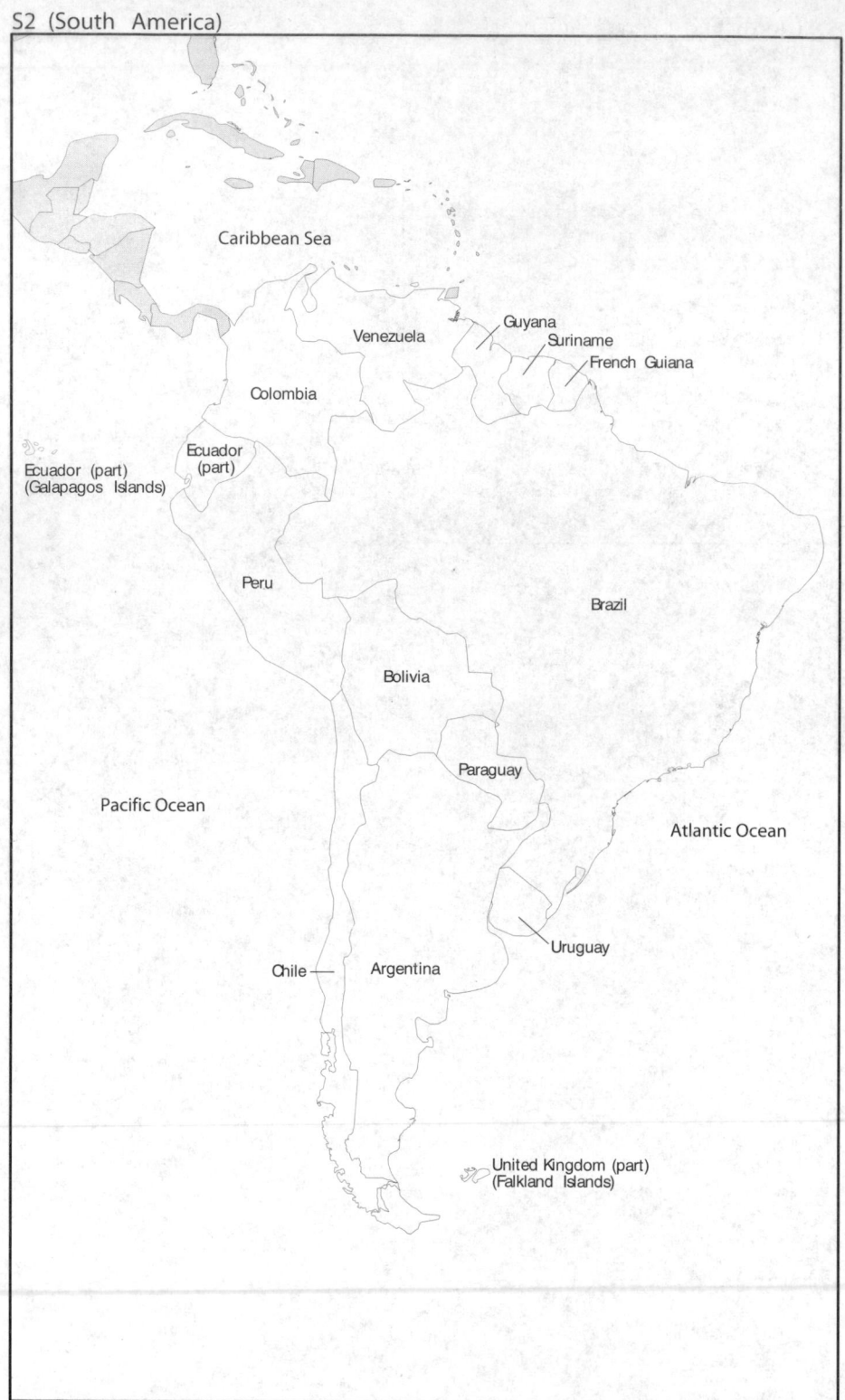

U.S. Census Bureau, Statistical Abstract of the United States: 2002

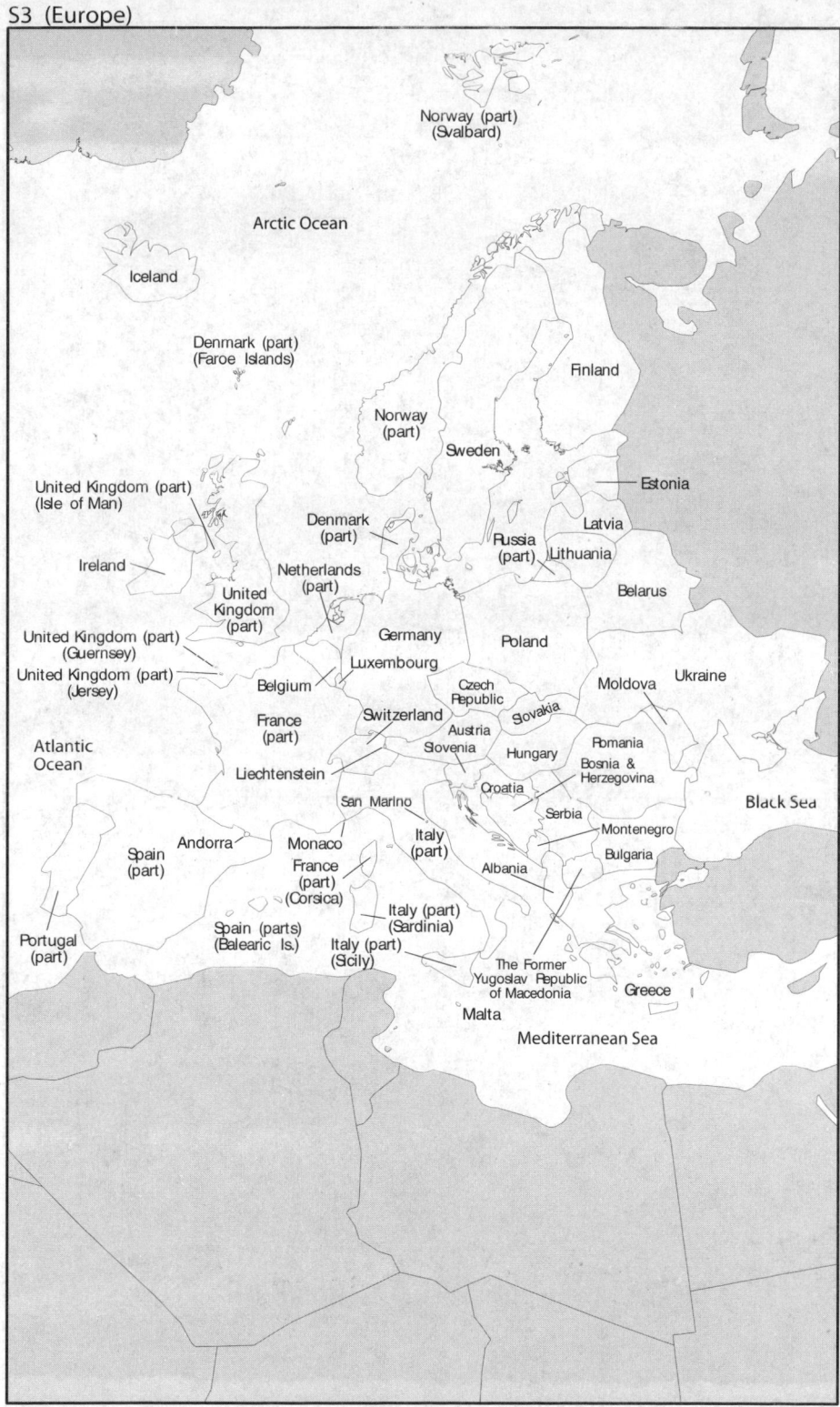

Norway (part)
(Svalbard)

Arctic Ocean

Iceland

Denmark (part)
(Faroe Islands)

Finland

Norway
(part)

Sweden

Estonia

United Kingdom (part)
(Isle of Man)

Denmark
(part)

Latvia

Russia
(part)

Lithuania

Ireland

Netherlands
(part)

Belarus

United
Kingdom
(part)

Germany

Poland

United Kingdom (part)
(Guernsey)

Luxembourg

Moldova

Ukraine

United Kingdom (part)
(Jersey)

Belgium

Czech
Republic

Slovakia

France
(part)

Switzerland

Austria

Hungary

Romania

Atlantic
Ocean

Liechtenstein

Slovenia

Croatia

Bosnia &
Herzegovina

Black Sea

San Marino

Andorra

Monaco

Italy
(part)

Serbia

Montenegro

Spain
(part)

France
(part)
(Corsica)

Albania

Bulgaria

Spain (parts)
(Balearic Is.)

Italy (part)
(Sardinia)

Portugal
(part)

Italy (part)
(Sicily)

The Former
Yugoslav Republic
of Macedonia

Greece

Malta

Mediterranean Sea

U.S. Census Bureau, Statistical Abstract of the United States: 2002

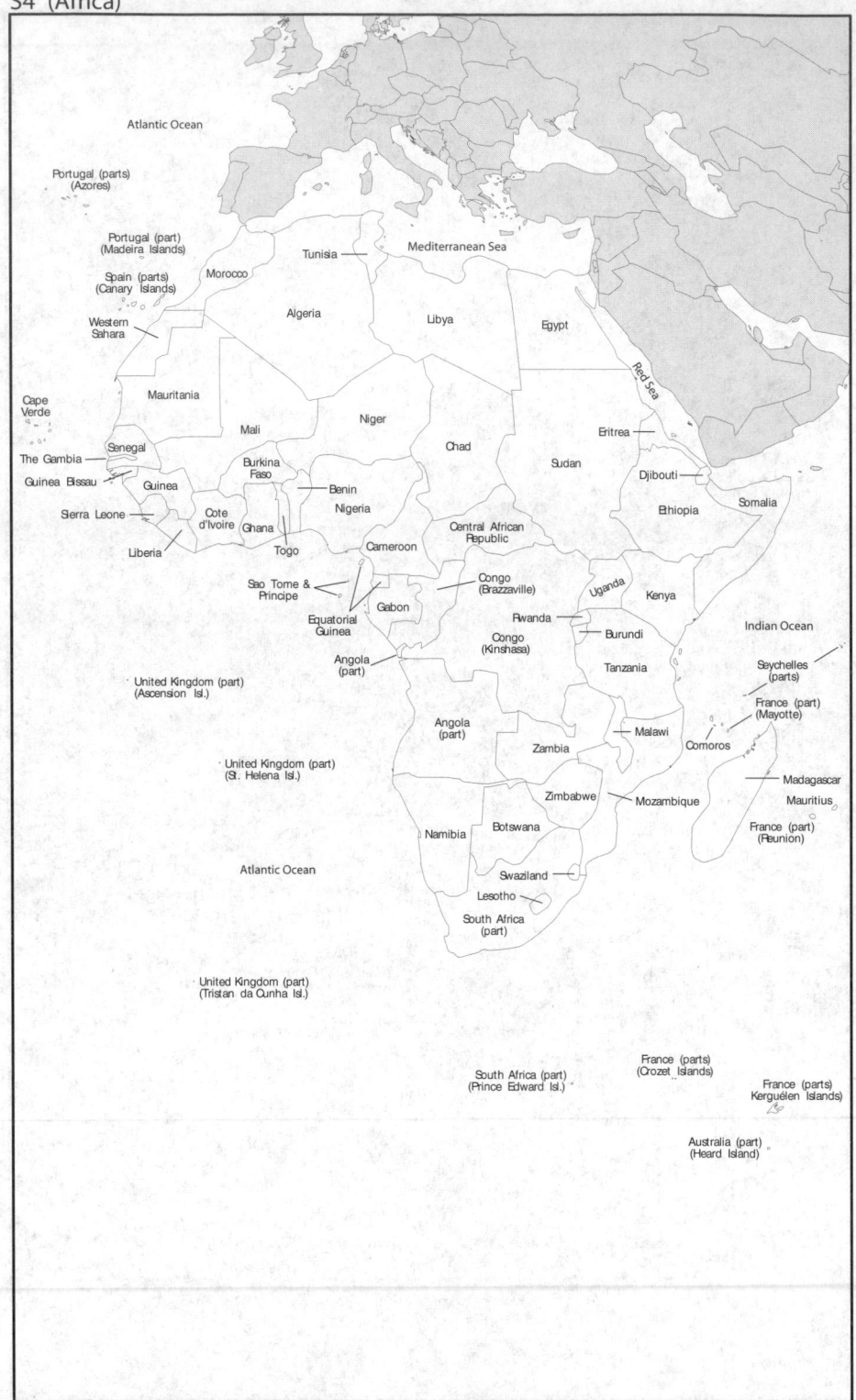

Atlantic Ocean

Portugal (parts)
(Azores)

Portugal (part)
(Madeira Islands)

Spain (parts)
(Canary Islands)

Western
Sahara

Cape
Verde

The Gambia

Guinea Bissau

Sierra Leone

Liberia

Tunisia

Morocco

Algeria

Mauritania

Mali

Senegal

Burkina
Faso

Guinea

Cote
d'Ivoire

Ghana

Togo

Benin

Nigeria

Cameroon

Sao Tome &
Principe

Equatorial
Guinea

Gabon

Angola
(part)

United Kingdom (part)
(Ascension Isl.)

United Kingdom (part)
(St. Helena Isl.)

Atlantic Ocean

United Kingdom (part)
(Tristan da Cunha Isl.)

Mediterranean Sea

Libya

Egypt

Red Sea

Niger

Chad

Sudan

Eritrea

Djibouti

Ethiopia

Somalia

Central African
Republic

Congo
(Brazzaville)

Uganda

Kenya

Rwanda

Congo
(Kinshasa)

Burundi

Tanzania

Angola
(part)

Zambia

Malawi

Indian Ocean

Seychelles
(parts)

France (part)
(Mayotte)

Comoros

Zimbabwe

Mozambique

Madagascar

Mauritius

France (part)
(Reunion)

Namibia

Botswana

Swaziland

Lesotho

South Africa
(part)

France (parts)
(Crozet Islands)

South Africa (part)
(Prince Edward Isl.)

France (parts)
Kerguélen Islands)

Australia (part)
(Heard Island)

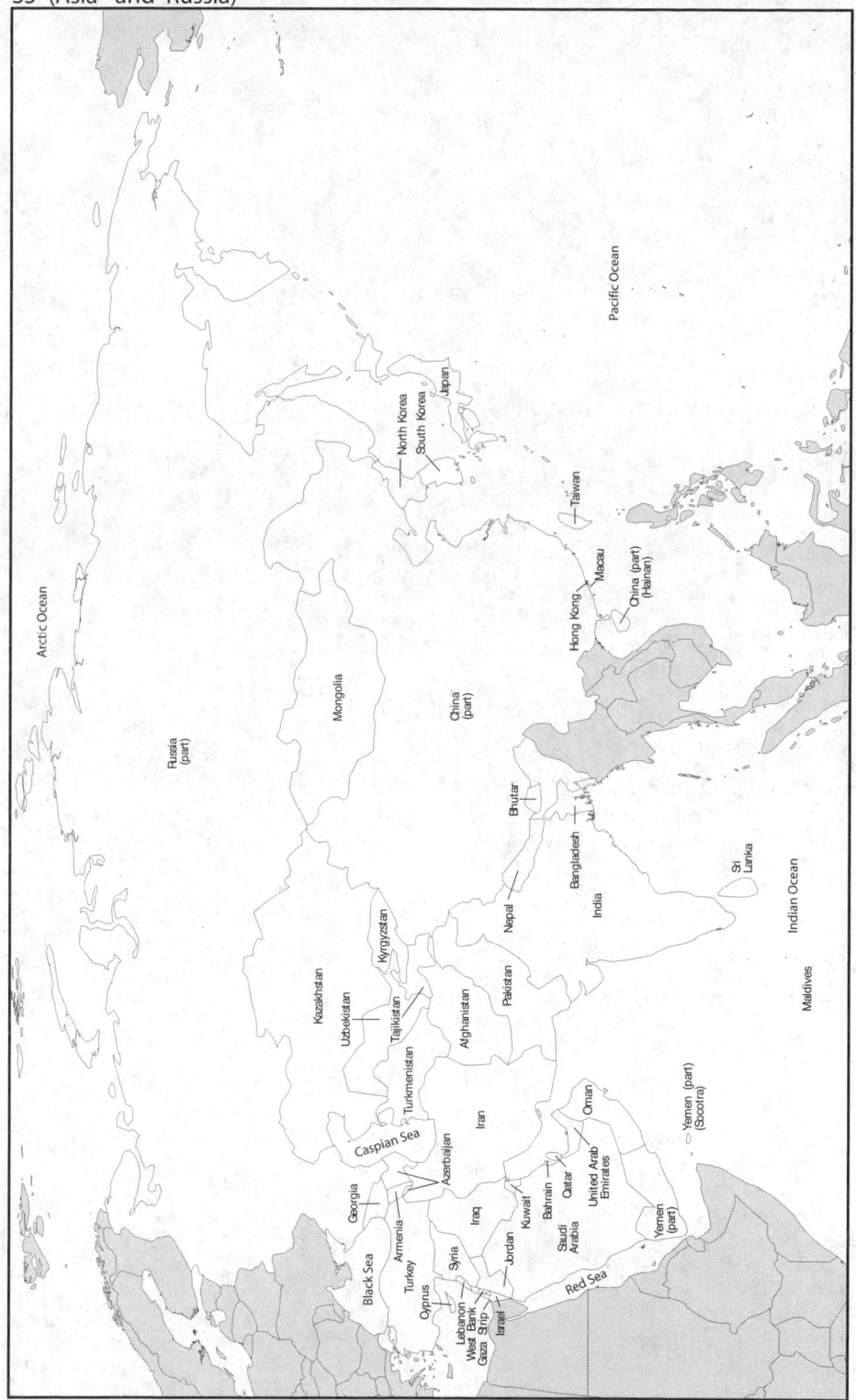

U.S. Census Bureau, Statistical Abstract of the United States: 2002

United Kingdom (part) (Pitcairn Islands)

France (parts) (French Polynesia)

France (parts) (French Polynesia)

France (parts) (French Polynesia)

New Zealand (part) (Cook Islands)

Kiribati (parts)

United States (part) (Jarvis Island)

Kiribati (parts)

United States (part) (Johnston Atoll)

United States (part) (Midway Islands)

United States (part) (Howland Island)

United States (part) (Baker Island)

Kiribati (part)

New Zealand (part) (Tokelau)

Western Samoa

United States (part) (American Samoa)

Niue

Tonga

Pacific Ocean

United States (part) (Wake Island)

Kiribati (parts)

Tuvalu

France (part) (Wallis and Futuna)

Fiji

Nauru

Vanuatu

France (part) (New Caledonia)

New Zealand (part)

Marshall Islands

Solomon Islands

United States (part) (Northern Mariana Islands)

United States (part) (Guam)

Federated States of Micronesia

Papua New Guinea

Australia (part)

Palau

Philippines

East Timor

Indonesia

Australia (part)

Vietnam

Brunei

Cambodia

Malaysia

Singapore

Laos

Thailand

Indian Ocean

Burma

No. 1305. Total World Population: 1980 to 2050

[As of midyear (4,457 represents 4,457,000,000)]

Year	Population (mil.)	Average annual [1] Growth rate (percent)	Average annual [1] Population change (mil.)	Year	Population (mil.)	Average annual [1] Growth rate (percent)	Average annual [1] Population change (mil.)
1980	4,457	1.70	76.3	2015	7,176	0.97	69.6
1985	4,855	1.70	83.0	2020	7,518	0.88	66.4
1990	5,284	1.56	83.2	2025	7,841	0.78	61.7
1995	5,691	1.36	77.7	2030	8,140	0.70	57.2
2000	6,080	1.26	77.3	2035	8,417	0.62	52.3
2001	6,157	1.24	76.8	2040	8,668	0.55	47.5
2005	6,461	1.14	73.8	2045	8,897	0.48	43.2
2010	6,824	1.03	70.8	2050	9,104	(NA)	(NA)

NA Not available.   [1] Represents change from year shown to immediate succeeding year.

Source: U.S. Census Bureau, "Total Midyear Population for the World: 1950-2050," published 10 May 2000; <http://www.census.gov/ipc/www/worldpop.html>.

No. 1306. Population by Continent: 1980 to 2050

[In millions, except percent (4,457 represents 4,457,000,000)]

Year	World	Africa	North America	South America	Asia	Europe	Oceania
1980	4,457	472	373	242	2,654	694	23
1990	5,284	629	424	296	3,186	721	27
2000	6,080	805	481	347	3,688	729	31
2010	6,824	985	534	387	4,155	728	35
2020	7,518	1,173	587	421	4,578	722	38
2030	8,140	1,378	636	449	4,931	705	41
2040	8,668	1,603	682	468	5,194	678	44
2050	9,104	1,846	722	480	5,369	642	45
PERCENT DISTRIBUTION							
1980	100.0	10.6	8.4	5.4	59.5	15.6	0.5
2000	100.0	13.2	7.9	5.7	60.7	12.0	0.5
2050	100.0	20.3	7.9	5.3	59.0	7.1	0.5

Source: U.S. Census Bureau, "International Data Base" (as of August 2002); <http://www.census.gov/ipc/www/idbnew.html>.

No. 1307. World Summary: 1980 to 2000

[4.8 represents 4,800,000. See text of this section for general comments concerning quality of the data]

Item	Unit	1980	1985	1990	1995	1996	1997	1998	1999	2000
Agriculture, forestry, fishing:										
Coffee	Mil. metric tons .	4.8	5.8	6.1	5.5	6.2	6.0	6.6	6.6	7.3
Cotton (lint)	Mil. metric tons .	13.9	17.3	18.4	20.3	19.2	19.0	18.1	18.1	18.4
Tobacco	Mil. metric tons .	5.3	7.1	7.1	6.3	7.4	9.0	7.0	7.0	6.8
Roundwood	Mil. cubic meters.	2,920	3,167	3,382	3,243	3,231	3,286	3,182	3,291	3,353
Fish catches	Mil. metric tons .	72.3	87.2	99.0	91.9	93.5	93.8	86.9	92.9	(NA)
Textile fiber production, total: [1]	Billion pounds . .	67.5	78.7	87.2	95.9	96.8	103.5	102.3	107.0	109.2
Rayon and acetate	Billion pounds . .	7.1	6.5	6.1	5.3	5.0	5.1	4.9	4.6	4.8
Noncellulosic fibers	Billion pounds . .	23.1	27.5	32.8	40.5	43.6	49.4	51.3	54.0	57.3
Cotton	Billion pounds . .	31.4	38.5	41.8	44.9	43.2	44.2	41.2	41.6	42.3
Wool, clean	Billion pounds . .	3.7	3.8	4.4	3.3	3.3	3.1	3.1	3.0	3.0
Silk	Billion pounds . .	0.1	0.2	0.1	0.2	0.2	0.2	0.2	0.2	0.2
Flax	Billion pounds . .	1.4	1.6	1.6	1.5	1.4	1.4	1.4	1.4	1.5
Hemp [2]	Billion pounds . .	0.6	0.5	0.4	0.2	0.1	0.1	0.2	0.2	0.2
Industrial production:										
Wine	Mil. hectoliters .	352.1	309.5	279.6	241.9	270	263.3	261.1	283.1	288.8
Sugar	Mil. metric tons .	79.0	90.8	111.2	118.5	125.8	125.9	128.8	134.0	131.8
Wheat flour	Mil. metric tons .	229.7	267.9	241.2	240.7	248.1	253	245.7	249.1	(NA)
Pig iron and ferroalloys [3]	Mil. metric tons .	542	507	517	518	511	534	528	532	(NA)
Crude steel . [4]	Mil. metric tons .	699	685	773	686	703	692	700	693	739
Sawnwood . [5]	Mil. cubic meters.	451	468	505	426	431	431	421	434	(NA)
Woodpulp . [6]	Mil. metric tons .	125.8	141.8	155.1	161.7	156.6	162.7	160.4	163.8	171.3
Newsprint	Mil. metric tons .	25.4	28.3	30.1	35.9	35.3	36.3	36.7	37.8	(NA)
Merchant vessels, launched .	Mil. gross tons .	13.9	17.3	14.8	23.0	15.5	22.2	23.0	(NA)	25.2
External trade:										
Imports, c.i.f	Bil. U.S. dollars .	2,045	1,998	3,557	5,084	5,328	5,492	5,420	5,656	6,189
Exports, f.o.b	Bil. U.S. dollars .	2,001	1,921	3,438	5,045	5,257	5,444	5,363	5,554	6,020
Civil aviation, kilometers flown [7]	Millions	(NA)	(NA)	(NA)	19,470	20,601	21,635	22,430	23,672	(NA)

NA Not available.   [1] Source: U.S. Dept. of Agriculture, Economic Research Service, *Cotton and Wool Situation and Outlook Yearbook*. Data from International Wool Textile Organization.   [2] Beginning 1996 not comparable with earlier years.   [3] Pig iron (foundry and steel making) plus other ferro alloys (spiegeleisen and ferro-manganese).   [4] Castings and ingots.   [5] Broadleaved and coniferous.   [6] Mechanical plus dissolving grades plus sulphate and soda plus sulphate and semi-chemical.   [7] Scheduled services of members of International Civil Aviation Organization.

Source: Except as noted, Statistical Division of the United Nations, New York, NY, *Monthly Bulletin of Statistics*, (copyright).

No. 1308. Population by Country: 1990 to 2010

[5,283,755 represents 5,283,755,000. Population data generally are de facto figures for the present territory. Population estimates were derived from information available as of spring 2000. East Timor became independent of Indonesia, but population data will not be available until the next update of the International Data Base. See text of this section for general comments concerning the data. For details of methodology, coverage, and reliability, see coverage, and reliability, see source. Minus sign (-) indicates decrease]

| Country or area | Map reference | Midyear population (1,000) | | | | Population rank, 2001 | Annual rate of growth,[1] 2000-2010 (percent) | Population per sq. mile, 2001 | Area (sq. mile) |
		1990	2000	2001	2010, proj.				
World	S0	5,283,755	6,080,142	6,157,401	6,823,635	(X)	1.2	122	50,580,319
Afghanistan	S5	14,750	25,889	26,813	33,864	39	2.7	107	250,000
Albania	S3	3,258	3,490	3,510	3,827	128	0.9	332	10,579
Algeria	S4	25,341	31,194	31,736	36,589	34	1.6	35	919,591
Andorra	S3	53	67	68	74	204	1.0	388	174
Angola	S4	8,056	10,145	10,366	12,646	71	2.2	22	481,351
Antigua and Barbuda	S1	63	66	67	71	206	0.6	394	170
Argentina	S2	32,634	36,955	37,385	41,082	31	1.1	35	1,056,637
Armenia	S5	3,366	3,344	3,336	3,365	130	0.1	290	11,506
Australia	S6	17,022	19,165	19,358	20,925	53	0.9	7	2,941,285
Austria	S3	7,718	8,131	8,151	8,278	86	0.2	255	31,942
Azerbaijan	S5	7,200	7,748	7,771	8,221	87	0.6	232	33,436
Bahamas, The	S1	257	295	298	315	176	0.7	77	3,888
Bahrain	S4	500	634	645	737	162	1.5	2,700	239
Bangladesh	S5	109,897	129,194	131,270	150,392	8	1.5	2,539	51,703
Barbados	S1	263	274	275	287	178	0.4	1,658	166
Belarus	S3	10,215	10,367	10,350	10,294	73	-0.1	129	80,154
Belgium	S3	9,969	10,242	10,259	10,340	76	0.1	879	11,672
Belize	S1	191	249	256	320	179	2.5	29	8,803
Benin	S4	4,656	6,396	6,591	8,411	95	2.7	154	42,710
Bhutan	S5	1,598	2,005	2,049	2,476	142	2.1	113	18,147
Bolivia	S2	6,574	8,153	8,300	9,499	85	1.5	20	418,683
Bosnia and Herzegovina	S3	4,424	3,836	3,922	4,103	121	0.7	199	19,741
Botswana	S4	1,304	1,576	1,586	1,502	147	-0.5	7	226,012
Brazil	S2	151,053	172,860	174,469	186,823	5	0.8	53	3,265,061
Brunei	S6	258	336	344	408	174	1.9	169	2,035
Bulgaria	S3	8,894	7,797	7,707	7,006	88	-1.1	181	42,683
Burkina Faso	S4	9,037	11,946	12,272	15,424	65	2.6	116	105,714
Burma	S5	38,519	41,735	41,995	43,674	27	0.5	165	253,954
Burundi	S4	5,285	6,055	6,224	7,669	99	2.4	628	9,903
Cambodia	S5	8,965	12,212	12,492	15,233	64	2.2	183	68,154
Cameroon	S4	11,761	15,422	15,803	19,202	60	2.2	87	181,251
Canada	S1	27,791	31,278	31,593	34,253	35	0.9	9	3,560,219
Cape Verde	S1	349	401	405	431	172	0.7	260	1,556
Central African Republic	S4	2,803	3,513	3,577	4,135	127	1.6	15	240,533
Chad	S4	6,018	8,425	8,707	11,616	83	3.2	18	486,178
Chile	S2	13,128	15,154	15,328	16,727	61	1.0	53	289,112
China [2]	S5	1,138,895	1,261,832	1,273,111	1,359,141	1	0.7	354	3,600,930
Colombia	S2	32,859	39,686	40,349	46,109	28	1.5	101	401,042
Comoros	S4	429	578	596	773	163	2.9	712	838
Congo (Brazzaville) [3]	S4	2,218	2,831	2,894	3,491	132	2.1	22	131,853
Congo (Kinshasa) [3]	S4	37,991	51,965	53,625	69,846	23	3.0	61	875,521
Costa Rica	S2	3,027	3,711	3,773	4,306	124	1.5	193	19,560
Cote d'Ivoire	S4	11,919	15,981	16,393	20,003	57	2.2	134	122,780
Croatia	S3	4,508	4,282	4,334	4,505	117	0.5	199	21,829
Cuba	S1	10,545	11,142	11,184	11,526	67	0.3	261	42,803
Cyprus	S5	681	758	763	801	158	0.5	214	3,568
Czech Republic	S3	10,310	10,272	10,264	10,157	75	-0.1	338	30,365
Denmark	S3	5,141	5,336	5,353	5,474	105	0.3	327	16,359
Djibouti	S4	370	451	461	579	166	2.5	54	8,486
Dominica	S1	73	72	71	70	202	-0.2	244	290
Dominican Republic	S1	7,098	8,443	8,581	9,884	84	1.6	459	18,680
Ecuador	S2	10,317	12,920	13,184	15,518	62	1.8	123	106,888
Egypt	S4	56,106	68,360	69,537	79,811	15	1.5	181	384,344
El Salvador	S1	5,100	6,123	6,238	7,293	98	1.7	780	8,000
Equatorial Guinea	S4	368	474	486	604	164	2.4	45	10,830
Eritrea	S4	2,945	4,136	4,298	5,709	119	3.2	92	46,842
Estonia	S3	1,573	1,431	1,423	1,372	148	-0.4	82	17,413
Ethiopia	S4	48,335	64,117	65,892	82,312	18	2.5	152	432,310
Fiji	S6	738	832	844	958	156	1.4	120	7,054
Finland	S3	4,986	5,167	5,176	5,228	107	0.1	44	117,942
France	S3	56,735	59,330	59,551	61,069	21	0.3	283	210,668
Gabon	S4	1,069	1,208	1,221	1,309	151	0.8	12	99,486
Gambia, The	S4	962	1,367	1,411	1,833	149	2.9	366	3,861
Georgia	S5	5,457	5,020	4,989	4,815	111	-0.4	185	26,911
Germany	S3	79,380	82,797	83,030	84,616	12	0.2	614	135,236
Ghana	S4	15,360	19,534	19,894	22,650	50	1.5	224	88,811
Greece	S3	10,158	10,602	10,624	10,758	69	0.1	210	50,502
Grenada	S2	92	89	89	91	197	0.2	682	131
Guatemala	S1	9,630	12,640	12,974	16,194	63	2.5	310	41,865
Guinea	S4	5,936	7,466	7,614	9,281	89	2.2	80	94,927
Guinea-Bissau	S4	996	1,286	1,316	1,614	150	2.3	122	10,811
Guyana	S2	742	697	697	729	160	0.4	9	76,004
Haiti	S1	6,028	6,868	6,965	7,950	94	1.5	655	10,641
Honduras	C1	4,772	6,250	6,406	7,683	97	2.1	148	43,201
Hungary	S3	10,372	10,139	10,106	9,831	77	-0.3	283	35,653
Iceland	S1	255	276	278	289	177	0.4	7	38,707
India	S5	850,558	1,014,004	1,029,991	1,168,205	2	1.4	897	1,147,950
Indonesia	S6	188,651	224,784	228,438	259,743	4	1.4	324	705,189
Iran	S5	55,717	65,620	66,129	73,772	17	1.2	105	631,660

See footnotes at end of table.

U.S. Census Bureau, Statistical Abstract of the United States: 2002

[See headnote, page 824]

Country or area	Map refer- ence	Midyear population (1,000)				Popu- lation rank, 2001	Annual rate of growth, [1] 2000- 2010 (percent)	Popula- tion per sq. mile, 2001	Area (sq. mile)
		1990	2000	2001	2010, proj.				
Iraq	S5	18,135	22,676	23,332	29,672	44	2.7	139	167,556
Ireland	S3	3,508	3,797	3,841	4,161	123	0.9	144	26,598
Israel	S4	4,512	5,842	5,938	6,645	100	1.3	757	7,849
Italy	S3	56,758	57,634	57,680	57,409	22	-	508	113,521
Jamaica	S1	2,463	2,653	2,666	2,851	135	0.7	638	4,181
Japan	S5	123,537	126,550	126,772	127,252	9	0.1	832	152,411
Jordan	S4	3,262	4,999	5,153	6,486	108	2.6	146	35,344
Kazakhstan	S5	16,708	16,733	16,731	17,276	55	0.3	16	1,049,150
Kenya	S4	23,767	30,340	30,766	33,068	36	0.9	140	219,788
Kiribati	S6	71	92	94	115	195	2.3	340	277
Korea, North	S5	20,019	21,688	21,968	23,753	49	0.9	473	46,490
Korea, South	S5	42,869	47,471	47,904	51,097	25	0.7	1,264	37,911
Kuwait	S5	2,142	1,974	2,042	2,788	144	3.5	297	6,880
Kyrgyzstan	S5	4,390	4,685	4,753	5,444	113	1.5	62	76,641
Laos	S5	4,210	5,497	5,636	6,993	102	2.4	63	89,112
Latvia	S3	2,672	2,405	2,385	2,252	139	-0.7	96	24,903
Lebanon	S4	3,147	3,578	3,628	4,056	125	1.3	918	3,950
Lesotho	S4	1,732	2,143	2,177	2,339	140	0.9	186	11,718
Liberia	S4	2,190	3,164	3,226	4,073	131	2.5	87	37,189
Libya	S4	4,140	5,115	5,241	6,447	106	2.3	8	679,359
Liechtenstein	S3	29	32	33	35	213	0.8	523	62
Lithuania	S5	3,702	3,621	3,611	3,560	126	-0.2	143	25,174
Luxembourg	S3	382	437	443	493	168	1.2	444	998
Macedonia, The Former Yugoslav Republic of	S3	1,893	2,041	2,046	2,115	143	0.4	206	9,928
Madagascar	S4	11,522	15,506	15,983	20,993	58	3.0	71	224,533
Malawi	S4	9,219	10,386	10,548	11,621	70	1.1	290	36,324
Malaysia	S6	17,504	21,793	22,229	26,144	48	1.8	175	126,853
Maldives	S5	216	301	311	400	175	2.8	2,683	116
Mali	S4	8,228	10,686	11,009	14,349	68	2.9	23	471,042
Malta	S4	359	392	395	420	173	0.7	3,184	124
Marshall Islands	S6	46	68	71	100	201	3.9	1,013	70
Mauritania	S4	1,984	2,668	2,747	3,561	134	2.9	7	397,838
Mauritius	S4	1,074	1,179	1,190	1,280	152	0.8	1,667	714
Mexico	S1	84,446	100,350	101,879	114,995	11	1.4	137	742,486
Micronesia, Federated States of	S6	109	133	135	141	191	0.6	497	271
Moldova	S5	4,398	4,431	4,432	4,535	116	0.2	341	13,012
Monaco	S3	30	32	32	33	214	0.4	41,235	1
Mongolia	S5	2,218	2,616	2,655	3,040	136	1.5	4	604,247
Morocco	S4	24,686	30,122	30,645	35,301	37	1.6	178	172,317
Mozambique	S4	14,276	19,105	19,371	20,504	52	0.7	64	302,737
Namibia	S4	1,409	1,771	1,798	1,908	146	0.7	6	317,873
Nauru	S6	9	12	12	14	223	1.9	1,491	8
Nepal	S5	19,325	24,702	25,284	30,758	40	2.2	479	52,819
Netherlands	S3	14,952	15,892	15,981	16,617	59	0.4	1,220	13,104
New Zealand	S6	3,360	3,820	3,864	4,228	122	1.0	37	103,734
Nicaragua	S2	3,643	4,813	4,918	5,839	112	1.9	106	46,430
Niger	S4	7,627	10,076	10,355	13,140	72	2.7	21	489,073
Nigeria	S4	92,483	123,338	126,636	155,588	10	2.3	360	351,649
Norway	S3	4,242	4,481	4,503	4,677	115	0.4	38	118,865
Oman	S5	1,773	2,533	2,622	3,523	137	3.3	32	82,031
Pakistan	S5	113,975	141,554	144,617	171,373	7	1.9	481	300,664
Palau	S6	15	19	19	22	219	1.4	108	177
Panama	S2	2,388	2,808	2,846	3,150	133	1.1	97	29,340
Papua New Guinea	S6	3,825	4,927	5,049	6,171	110	2.3	29	174,405
Paraguay	S2	4,236	5,586	5,734	7,162	101	2.5	37	153,398
Peru	S2	21,989	27,013	27,484	31,471	38	1.5	56	494,208
Philippines	S6	65,037	81,160	82,842	97,898	13	1.9	720	115,124
Poland	S3	38,119	38,646	38,634	38,691	30	-	329	117,571
Portugal	S3	9,923	10,048	10,066	10,183	78	0.1	285	35,382
Qatar	S5	481	744	769	970	157	2.6	181	4,247
Romania	S5	22,866	22,411	22,364	21,930	47	-0.2	251	88,934
Russia	S5	148,082	146,001	145,470	142,328	6	-0.3	22	6,592,817
Rwanda	S4	6,962	7,229	7,313	7,876	91	0.9	759	9,633
Saint Kitts and Nevis	S1	41	39	39	40	211	0.4	279	139
Saint Lucia	S1	140	156	158	177	189	1.3	671	236
Saint Vincent and the Grenadines	S1	107	115	116	119	193	0.3	886	131
Samoa	S0	170	179	179	176	185	-0.2	163	1,100
San Marino	S3	23	27	27	31	216	1.3	1,180	23
Sao Tome and Principe	S4	119	160	165	219	187	3.1	445	371
Saudi Arabia	S4	15,847	22,024	22,757	30,546	45	3.3	27	829,996
Senegal	S4	7,360	9,987	10,285	13,221	74	2.8	139	74,131
Seychelles	S4	73	79	80	83	198	0.4	453	176
Sierra Leone	S4	4,227	5,233	5,427	6,930	103	2.8	196	27,653
Singapore	S6	3,016	4,152	4,300	5,776	118	3.3	17,849	241
Slovakia	S3	5,263	5,408	5,415	5,475	104	0.1	287	18,842
Slovenia	S3	1,896	1,928	1,930	1,947	145	0.1	247	7,819
Solomon Islands	S6	335	466	480	610	165	2.7	45	10,633
Somalia	S4	6,675	7,253	7,489	9,922	90	3.1	31	242,216
South Africa	S4	38,176	43,421	43,586	41,108	26	-0.5	92	471,444
Spain	S3	39,351	39,997	40,038	40,157	29	-	208	192,819
Sri Lanka	S5	17,193	19,239	19,409	20,832	51	0.8	776	24,996

See footnotes at end of table.

U.S. Census Bureau, Statistical Abstract of the United States: 2002

No. 1308. Population by Country: 1990 to 2010—Con.

[See headnote, page 824]

Country or area	Map refer-ence	Midyear population (1,000) 1990	2000	2001	2010, proj.	Popu-lation rank, 2001	Annual rate of growth,[1] 2000-2010 (percent)	Popula-tion per sq. mile, 2001	Area (sq. mile)
Sudan	S4	26,627	35,080	36,080	45,485	33	2.6	39	917,375
Suriname	S2	395	431	434	450	169	0.4	7	62,344
Swaziland	S4	852	1,083	1,104	1,216	155	1.2	166	6,641
Sweden	S3	8,559	8,873	8,875	8,882	82	-	56	158,927
Switzerland	S3	6,838	7,262	7,283	7,385	92	0.2	474	15,355
Syria	S4	12,436	16,306	16,729	20,606	56	2.3	235	71,062
Tajikistan	S5	5,332	6,441	6,579	8,007	96	2.2	119	55,251
Tanzania	S4	26,224	35,306	36,232	44,957	32	2.4	106	342,100
Thailand	S5	55,052	61,231	61,798	66,291	19	0.8	313	197,595
Togo	S4	3,691	5,019	5,153	6,245	109	2.2	245	21,000
Tonga	S0	92	102	104	123	194	1.8	376	277
Trinidad and Tobago	S2	1,198	1,176	1,170	1,115	154	-0.5	590	1,981
Tunisia	S4	8,207	9,593	9,705	10,661	81	1.1	162	59,985
Turkey	S5	56,085	65,667	66,494	73,322	16	1.1	223	297,591
Turkmenistan	S5	3,668	4,518	4,603	5,431	114	1.8	24	188,456
Tuvalu	S6	9	11	11	13	224	1.5	1,095	10
Uganda	S4	17,186	23,318	23,986	31,395	42	3.0	311	77,108
Ukraine	S5	51,658	49,153	48,760	46,193	24	-0.6	209	233,089
United Arab Emirates	S5	1,951	2,369	2,407	2,763	138	1.5	75	32,278
United Kingdom	S3	57,621	59,508	59,648	60,602	20	0.2	639	93,278
United States	S1	249,948	275,563	278,059	300,118	3	0.9	79	3,539,227
Uruguay	S2	3,106	3,334	3,360	3,600	129	0.8	50	67,035
Uzbekistan	S5	20,624	24,756	25,155	29,280	41	1.7	146	172,741
Vanuatu	S6	154	190	193	221	184	1.5	34	5,699
Venezuela	S2	19,325	23,543	23,917	27,134	43	1.4	70	340,560
Vietnam	S5	66,338	78,774	79,939	90,192	14	1.4	636	125,622
Yemen	S5	12,023	17,479	18,078	24,637	54	3.4	89	203,849
Zambia	S4	7,851	9,582	9,770	11,482	80	1.8	34	285,992
Zimbabwe	S4	10,103	11,343	11,365	11,057	66	-0.3	76	149,293
OTHER									
Montenegro	S3	565	680	674	713	161	0.5	126	5,333
Serbia	S3	9,201	9,982	10,003	9,954	79	-	293	34,116
Taiwan [2]	S5	20,279	22,191	22,370	23,873	46	0.7	1,796	12,456
AREAS OF SPECIAL SOVEREIGNTY AND DEPENDENCIES									
American Samoa	S0	47	65	67	81	205	2.1	873	77
Anguilla	S1	8	12	12	14	222	1.8	345	35
Aruba	S1	67	70	70	73	203	0.5	939	75
Bermuda	S1	58	63	64	67	208	0.6	3,357	19
Cayman Islands	S1	26	35	36	42	212	1.8	354	100
Cook Islands	S0	18	20	21	22	218	0.9	222	93
Faroe Islands	S3	47	45	46	48	210	0.6	84	541
French Guiana	S2	116	173	178	214	186	2.1	5	34,421
French Polynesia	S0	202	249	254	291	180	1.5	179	1,413
Gaza Strip [4]	S4	643	1,132	1,178	1,651	153	3.8	8,009	147
Gibraltar	S3	29	28	28	28	215	0.2	11,935	2
Greenland	S1	56	56	56	56	209	-	(Z)	131,931
Guadeloupe	S1	378	426	431	468	170	0.9	634	680
Guam	S6	134	155	158	184	190	1.7	754	209
Guernsey	S3	63	64	64	66	207	0.3	859	75
Hong Kong	S5	5,688	7,116	7,211	7,981	93	1.1	18,883	382
Jersey	S3	84	89	89	92	196	0.3	1,978	45
Macau	S6	352	446	454	527	167	1.7	73,448	6
Man, Isle of	S3	69	73	73	77	200	0.5	324	227
Martinique	S1	374	415	418	448	171	0.8	1,023	409
Mayotte	S4	90	156	163	231	188	3.9	1,125	145
Montserrat	S1	11	6	8	10	225	4.3	196	39
Netherlands Antilles	S2	189	210	212	228	182	0.8	572	371
New Caledonia	S6	168	202	205	230	183	1.3	28	7,243
Northern Mariana Islands	S6	44	72	75	99	199	3.1	405	184
Puerto Rico	S1	3,537	3,916	3,937	4,088	120	0.4	1,138	3,459
Reunion	S4	597	721	733	829	159	1.4	759	965
Saint Helena	S4	7	7	7	8	226	0.6	46	158
Saint Pierre and Miquelon	S1	6	7	7	7	227	0.2	74	93
Turks and Caicos Islands	S1	12	18	18	24	220	3.0	109	166
Virgin Islands	S1	104	121	122	133	192	1.0	904	135
Virgin Islands, British	S1	16	20	21	25	217	2.0	359	58
Wallis and Futuna	S6	14	15	15	17	221	0.9	146	106
West Bank [4]	S4	1,255	2,020	2,091	2,765	141	3.1	960	2,178
Western Sahara	S4	191	245	251	301	181	2.1	2	102,703

- Represents or rounds to zero.   X Not applicable.   Z Less than one person per square mile.   [1] Computed by the exponential method. For explanation of average annual percent change, see Guide to Tabular Presentation   [2] With the establishment of diplomatic relations with China on January 1, 1979, the U.S. government recognized the People's Republic of China as the sole legal government of China and acknowledged the Chinese position that there is only one China and that Taiwan is part of China.   [3] "Congo" is the official short-form name for both the Republic of Congo and the Democratic Republic of the Congo. To distinguish one from the other the U.S. Dept. of State adds the capital in parentheses. This practice is unofficial and provisional.   [4] The Gaza Strip and West Bank are Israeli occupied with interim status subject to Israeli/Palestinian negotiations. The final status is to be determined.

Source: U.S. Census Bureau, "International Data Base" (as of August 2002); <http://www.census.gov/ipc/www/idbnew.html>.

U.S. Census Bureau, Statistical Abstract of the United States: 2002

No. 1309. Age Distribution by Country: 2001 and 2010

[In percent. Covers countries with 10 million or more population in 2001]

Country or area	2001 Under 15 years old	2001 65 years old and over	2010, proj. Under 15 years old	2010, proj. 65 years old and over	Country or area	2001 Under 15 years old	2001 65 years old and over	2010, proj. Under 15 years old	2010, proj. 65 years old and over
World	**29.6**	**7.0**	**30.0**	**8.6**	Japan	14.6	17.5	14.5	21.9
Afghanistan	42.2	2.8	53.0	3.9	Jordan	37.2	3.3	39.6	5.6
Albania	29.5	7.0	26.7	9.3	Kazakhstan	26.7	7.2	24.9	7.8
Algeria	34.2	4.1	33.5	5.2	Kenya	41.9	2.8	38.0	3.7
American Samoa	38.4	5.0	38.1	8.5	Korea, North	25.5	6.8	24.6	10.7
Andorra	15.3	12.6	15.3	17.1	Korea, South	21.6	7.3	21.6	10.6
Angola	43.3	2.7	53.4	3.4	Kuwait	28.8	2.4	37.0	4.2
Argentina	26.5	10.4	27.3	12.3	Kyrgyzstan	35.0	6.1	36.9	6.1
Armenia	23.2	9.7	18.2	10.3	Laos	42.7	3.3	51.5	3.9
Aruba	21.3	10.2	18.6	14.6	Latvia	16.6	15.3	12.4	16.2
Australia	20.6	12.5	20.4	15.2	Lebanon	27.6	6.7	29.0	8.1
Austria	16.6	15.4	14.8	18.1	Libya	35.4	3.9	41.5	5.5
Azerbaijan	28.9	7.1	26.0	7.3	Lithuania	18.7	13.6	15.8	14.5
Bahamas, The	29.4	6.1	27.0	8.7	Luxembourg	18.9	14.1	20.3	16.3
Bahrain	29.6	3.0	29.6	4.8	Macau	22.7	7.2	21.0	9.1
Bangladesh	35.0	3.4	34.5	4.5	Madagascar	45.0	3.2	60.2	3.9
Barbados	21.7	8.9	19.8	9.7	Malawi	44.4	2.8	45.0	3.4
Belarus	17.9	13.9	15.5	13.5	Malaysia	34.5	4.2	37.2	6.1
Belgium	17.5	16.9	16.1	18.1	Mali	47.2	3.1	62.1	3.8
Benin	47.3	2.3	59.4	3.1	Mauritania	46.1	2.3	59.9	2.9
Bermuda	19.4	11.2	18.2	14.6	Mexico	33.3	4.4	33.2	6.3
Bolivia	38.5	4.5	37.4	5.7	Monaco	15.3	22.5	15.1	24.1
Bosnia and					Mongolia	33.0	3.9	31.9	4.8
Herzegovina	20.1	9.1	19.1	12.6	Montenegro	21.7	12.1	21.7	13.8
Brazil	28.6	5.5	26.4	7.5	Morocco	34.4	4.7	34.7	6.1
Bulgaria	15.1	16.7	11.0	16.3	Mozambique	42.7	2.8	43.1	3.5
Burkina Faso	47.5	2.9	59.1	3.5	Nepal	40.3	3.5	46.5	4.8
Burma	29.1	4.8	26.5	5.5	Netherlands	18.4	13.7	17.6	16.0
Burundi	46.8	2.8	56.1	3.1	New Zealand	22.4	11.5	22.2	13.6
Cambodia	41.3	3.5	47.3	4.5	Nicaragua	39.0	2.9	40.2	4.2
Cameroon	42.4	3.4	49.5	4.7	Niger	48.0	2.3	60.0	3.0
Canada	18.9	12.8	18.2	15.5	Nigeria	43.7	2.8	53.5	3.8
Cape Verde	42.8	6.5	36.7	6.8	Norway	20.0	15.1	19.2	16.2
Central African					Oman	41.5	2.4	59.2	4.0
Republic	43.2	3.8	47.8	4.7	Pakistan	40.5	4.1	41.9	5.3
Chad	47.7	2.8	65.0	3.7	Panama	30.1	6.0	27.7	8.3
Chile	27.3	7.4	25.1	10.2	Paraguay	38.9	4.7	46.8	6.6
China [1]	25.0	7.1	22.5	8.9	Peru	34.4	4.8	34.3	6.7
Colombia	31.9	4.8	33.1	6.6	Philippines	36.9	3.7	40.1	5.2
Congo (Brazzaville) [2]	42.4	3.3	50.7	3.9	Poland	18.4	12.4	15.7	13.1
Congo (Kinshasa) [2]	48.2	2.5	63.2	3.2	Portugal	17.0	15.6	16.8	17.1
Costa Rica	31.4	5.3	30.5	7.3	Romania	17.9	13.5	15.5	14.1
Cote d'Ivoire	46.2	2.2	54.9	3.1	Russia	17.4	12.8	14.9	12.7
Croatia	18.2	15.2	19.6	16.7	Rwanda	42.4	2.9	41.2	3.0
Cuba	21.0	9.9	18.1	12.5	Samoa	31.9	5.7	23.2	6.9
Czech Republic	16.1	13.9	13.2	15.8	Saudi Arabia	42.5	2.7	58.0	5.1
Denmark	18.6	14.9	17.9	17.2	Senegal	44.1	3.1	53.6	4.0
Dominican Republic	34.1	4.9	36.0	6.9	Serbia	19.7	15.1	18.2	15.5
Ecuador	35.8	4.4	37.9	6.0	Sierra Leone	44.7	3.1	57.6	4.4
Egypt	34.6	3.8	34.9	5.2	Singapore	17.9	7.0	22.1	10.5
El Salvador	37.7	5.1	41.7	6.4	Slovakia	18.9	11.5	15.4	12.9
Estonia	17.1	14.8	13.7	15.6	Slovenia	16.1	14.3	14.1	16.0
Ethiopia	47.2	2.8	60.3	3.6	Somalia	44.5	2.8	61.5	3.4
Finland	18.0	15.0	16.3	17.3	South Africa	32.0	4.9	26.8	5.8
France	18.7	16.1	18.0	17.3	Spain	14.6	17.2	13.9	18.5
French Guiana	30.5	5.5	34.4	8.9	Sri Lanka	26.0	6.6	24.4	8.9
Gabon	33.3	5.9	35.8	8.5	Sudan	44.6	2.1	52.8	3.5
Gambia, The	45.2	2.7	58.1	3.8	Swaziland	45.5	2.6	49.8	3.5
Germany	15.6	16.6	14.3	20.1	Sweden	18.2	17.3	14.9	19.2
Ghana	41.2	3.5	39.4	4.4	Switzerland	17.0	15.3	15.0	18.2
Greece	15.0	17.7	14.7	19.8	Syria	39.9	3.2	44.8	4.3
Greenland	26.7	5.4	22.8	7.9	Taiwan [1]	21.2	8.8	21.4	11.1
Grenada	37.0	3.9	32.2	2.8	Tajikistan	41.2	4.6	45.9	5.2
Guam	35.1	6.2	37.2	8.7	Tanzania	44.8	2.9	54.6	3.9
Guatemala	42.1	3.6	50.4	4.9	Thailand	23.4	6.6	23.7	9.2
Guinea	43.1	2.7	50.5	3.5	Trinidad and Tobago	24.1	6.7	17.9	7.9
Guinea-Bissau	42.1	2.9	50.8	3.9	Tunisia	28.7	6.1	25.4	7.9
Guyana	28.2	4.9	25.7	6.1	Turkey	28.4	6.1	26.2	8.1
Haiti	40.3	4.2	41.6	5.1	Uganda	51.1	2.1	66.0	2.6
Honduras	42.2	3.6	46.0	5.1	Ukraine	17.3	14.1	14.4	13.9
Hungary	16.6	14.7	13.9	15.6	United Arab Emirates	28.9	2.4	28.7	6.7
Iceland	23.2	11.8	21.1	13.5	United Kingdom	18.9	15.7	17.1	17.0
India	33.1	4.7	33.6	6.1	**United States**	**21.1**	**12.6**	**21.6**	**14.4**
Indonesia	30.3	4.6	31.9	6.7	Uruguay	24.4	13.0	25.7	14.3
Iran	33.0	4.6	28.5	5.3	Uzbekistan	36.3	4.6	37.5	5.0
Iraq	41.6	3.1	50.3	3.9	Venezuela	32.1	4.7	30.7	6.6
Ireland	21.6	11.4	22.7	13.4	Vietnam	32.1	5.4	30.9	6.2
Israel	27.4	9.9	28.9	11.3	Yemen	47.2	3.0	65.0	3.5
Italy	14.2	18.3	13.1	20.5	Zambia	47.4	2.5	54.2	3.0
Jamaica	29.7	6.8	26.3	7.6	Zimbabwe	38.7	3.6	32.6	4.4

[1] See footnote 2, Table 1308.   [2] See footnote 3, Table 1308.

Source: U.S. Census Bureau, "International Data Base" (as of 10 May 2000); <http://www.census.gov/ipc/www/idbnew.html>.

No. 1310. Foreign or Foreign-Born Population and Labor Force in Selected OECD Countries: 1988 and 1999

[In Australia, Canada, and the United States the data refer to people present in the country who are foreign born. In the European countries and Japan they generally refer to foreigners and represent the nationalities of residents]

Country	Foreign population [1]				Foreign labor force [2]			
	Number (1,000)		Percent of total population		Number (1,000)		Percent of total labor force	
	1988	1999	1988	1999	1988	1999	1988	1999
United States [3]	[4]19,767	28,180	7.9	10.3	[4]11,565	16,114	9.4	11.7
Australia [3]	[5]3,965	4,419	22.9	23.3	[5]2,182	2,310	25.7	(NA)
Austria	344	748	4.5	9.2	161	334	5.4	10.0
Belgium [3]	869	897	8.8	8.8	[6]291	(NA)	7.2	(NA)
Canada [3]	[5]4,343	(NA)	16.1	(NA)	[5]2,681	(NA)	18.5	(NA)
Denmark	142	259.4	2.8	4.9	65	(NA)	2.2	(NA)
France	[7]3,714	3,263	6.8	(NA)	1,557	1,594	6.4	5.8
Germany	4,489	7,344	7.3	8.9	1,911	3,545	7.0	8.8
Italy	645	1,252	1.1	2.2	[5]285	748	1.3	3.6
Japan	941	1,556	0.8	1.2	[8]86	126	0.1	0.2
Luxembourg	106	159.4	27.4	36.0	[9]69	146	39.9	57.3
Netherlands	624	651.5	4.2	4.1	176	(NA)	3.0	(NA)
Spain	360	801	0.9	2.0	58	173	0.4	1.0
Sweden	421	487	5.0	5.5	220	222	4.9	5.1
Switzerland	1,007	1,369	15.2	19.2	[10]608	701	16.7	18.1
United Kingdom	1,821	2,208	3.2	3.8	871	1,005	3.4	3.7

NA Not available   [1] Data are from population registers except for France (census), the United Kingdom (labor force survey), Japan and Switzerland (register of foreigners) and Italy, and Spain (residence permits).   [2] Includes unemployed except for Italy, Luxembourg, Netherlands, and United Kingdom. Data for Austria, Germany, and Luxembourg are from social security registers, for Denmark from the register of population. Data for Italy, Spain, and Switzerland are from residence or work permits. Figures for Japan and Netherlands are estimates. Data for other countries are from labor force surveys.   [3] Census data except 1999 data for the United States from Current Population Survey.   [4] 1990 data.   [5] 1991 data.   [6] 1989 data.   [7] 1982 data.   [8] 1992 data.   [9] Includes cross-border workers.   [10] Foreigners with an annual residence permit or a settlement permit who engage in gainful activity. Seasonal and cross-border workers are excluded.

Source: Organization for Economic Cooperation and Development, Paris, France, *Trends in International Migration (2000 and 2001 Editions)* (copyright).

No. 1311. Medical Doctors and Inpatient Care—Selected Countries: 1990 to 2000

Country	Medical doctors per 1,000 population			Inpatient care					
				Beds per 1,000 population			Average length of stay (days)		
	1990	1999	2000	1990	1999	2000	1990	1999	2000
United States	2.4	(NA)	(NA)	4.9	3.6	(NA)	9.1	7.0	(NA)
Australia	(NA)	(NA)	(NA)	(NA)	(NA)	(NA)	(NA)	(NA)	(NA)
Austria	2.2	3.0	(NA)	10.2	8.7	(NA)	13.0	8.9	(NA)
Belgium	3.3	3.8	(NA)	8.0	(NA)	(NA)	13.8	(NA)	(NA)
Canada	2.1	2.1	(NA)	6.3	(NA)	(NA)	13.0	(NA)	(NA)
Czech Republic	2.8	3.0	3.1	11.3	8.7	8.8	15.4	11.3	11.4
Denmark	3.1	3.4	(NA)	5.6	(NA)	(NA)	8.2	(NA)	(NA)
Finland	2.4	3.1	(NA)	12.5	7.5	(NA)	18.2	10.6	(NA)
France	2.6	(NA)	(NA)	9.7	(NA)	(NA)	13.3	10.6	(NA)
Germany	3.1	3.5	(NA)	10.4	9.2	(NA)	17.2	12.0	(NA)
Greece	3.4	(NA)	(NA)	5.1	(NA)	(NA)	9.9	(NA)	(NA)
Hungary	2.9	3.2	(NA)	10.1	8.3	(NA)	12.6	10.0	9.7
Iceland	2.8	(NA)	(NA)	16.7	(NA)	(NA)	18.3	(NA)	(NA)
Ireland	1.6	2.3	(NA)	10.5	(NA)	(NA)	7.9	7.6	(NA)
Italy	4.7	5.9	(NA)	7.2	(NA)	(NA)	11.7	(NA)	(NA)
Japan	1.7	(NA)	(NA)	16.0	16.4	(NA)	50.5	39.8	(NA)
Korea, South	0.8	1.3	(NA)	3.1	5.5	(NA)	13.0	12.0	(NA)
Luxembourg	2.0	3.1	(NA)	11.7	(NA)	(NA)	17.6	(NA)	(NA)
Mexico	1.1	1.7	(NA)	0.8	1.1	(NA)	4.4	4.2	(NA)
Netherlands	2.5	3.1	(NA)	11.5	11.3	(NA)	34.1	(NA)	(NA)
New Zealand	1.9	2.3	2.2	8.5	(NA)	(NA)	9.6	8.5	(NA)
Norway	3.1	2.8	(NA)	(NA)	14.4	(NA)	(NA)	8.7	(NA)
Poland	2.1	2.3	(NA)	5.7	5.1	4.9	12.5	9.3	8.9
Portugal	2.8	3.2	(NA)	4.6	(NA)	(NA)	10.8	(NA)	(NA)
Spain	2.3	3.1	3.3	4.3	(NA)	(NA)	12.2	(NA)	(NA)
Sweden	2.9	3.1	3.1	12.4	3.7	(NA)	18.0	(NA)	(NA)
Switzerland	3.0	3.4	(NA)	(NA)	(NA)	(NA)	(NA)	(NA)	(NA)
Turkey	0.9	1.2	(NA)	2.1	2.6	(NA)	6.9	6.0	(NA)
United Kingdom	1.4	1.8	(NA)	5.9	4.1	(NA)	15.6	(NA)	(NA)

NA Not available.

Source: Organization for Economic Cooperation and Development, Paris, France, *OECD Health Data 2001* (copyright).

No. 1312. Vital Statistics, by Country: 2001 and 2010

[Covers countries with 10 million or more population in 2001]

Country or area	Crude birth rate [1] 2001	2010, proj.	Crude death rate [2] 2001	2010, proj.	Expectation of life at birth (years) 2001	2010, proj.	Infant mortality rate [3] 2001	2010, proj.	Total fertility rate per woman [4] 2001	2010, proj.
United States	14.2	14.3	8.7	8.6	77.3	78.5	6.8	6.2	2.06	2.12
Afghanistan	41.4	37.3	17.7	15.2	46.2	49.6	147.0	126.5	5.79	5.09
Algeria	22.8	19.9	5.2	4.9	70.0	72.5	40.6	28.9	2.72	2.17
Angola	46.5	42.9	24.7	21.6	38.6	41.3	193.7	174.7	6.48	5.94
Argentina	18.4	16.6	7.6	7.5	75.3	77.1	17.8	13.3	2.44	2.19
Australia	12.9	11.7	7.2	7.7	79.9	81.0	5.0	4.4	1.77	1.75
Bangladesh	25.3	22.1	8.6	7.6	60.5	63.9	69.9	54.3	2.78	2.30
Belarus	9.6	12.1	14.0	13.5	68.1	70.6	14.4	11.5	1.28	1.57
Belgium	10.7	9.9	10.1	10.7	78.0	79.4	4.7	4.2	1.61	1.63
Brazil	18.5	15.6	9.3	9.1	63.2	66.3	37.0	27.8	2.09	1.81
Burkina Faso	44.8	40.9	17.1	16.7	46.4	45.3	106.9	92.1	6.35	5.54
Burma	20.1	17.0	12.3	12.0	55.2	57.7	73.7	59.7	2.30	1.86
Cambodia	33.2	30.8	10.7	9.5	56.8	59.8	65.4	53.0	4.74	4.00
Cameroon	36.1	32.0	12.0	12.9	54.6	52.7	69.8	60.4	4.80	4.08
Canada	11.2	10.7	7.5	8.0	79.6	80.7	5.0	4.5	1.60	1.62
Chile	16.8	14.5	5.6	6.0	75.9	77.7	9.4	7.4	2.16	1.90
China [5]	16.0	13.1	6.7	7.1	71.6	73.9	28.1	20.5	1.82	1.82
Colombia	22.4	19.3	5.7	5.6	70.6	73.1	24.0	17.8	2.66	2.44
Congo (Kinshasa) [6] .	46.0	42.4	15.2	13.4	48.9	50.7	99.9	83.2	6.84	6.11
Cote d'Ivoire	40.4	36.4	16.7	17.5	44.9	43.4	93.7	80.0	5.70	4.79
Cuba	12.4	11.0	7.3	7.7	76.4	78.1	7.4	6.4	1.60	1.62
Czech Republic	9.1	8.4	10.8	11.2	74.7	76.7	5.6	4.8	1.18	1.23
Ecuador	26.0	21.8	5.4	5.0	71.3	73.8	34.1	25.3	3.12	2.62
Egypt	24.9	20.9	7.7	6.9	63.7	66.9	60.5	44.8	3.07	2.48
Ethiopia	44.7	41.6	17.8	18.7	44.7	42.1	100.0	87.8	7.00	6.36
France	12.1	11.0	9.1	9.8	78.9	80.2	4.5	4.1	1.75	1.74
Germany	9.2	8.7	10.4	11.0	77.6	79.1	4.7	4.2	1.38	1.44
Ghana	29.0	23.3	10.3	11.5	57.2	55.5	56.5	48.9	3.82	2.81
Greece	9.8	9.2	9.7	10.7	78.6	79.9	6.4	5.3	1.33	1.40
Guatemala	34.6	30.4	6.8	5.8	66.5	69.5	45.8	35.2	4.58	3.91
Hungary	9.3	8.9	13.2	12.9	71.6	74.0	9.0	7.4	1.25	1.29
India	24.3	20.7	8.7	7.9	62.9	66.1	63.2	48.5	3.04	2.55
Indonesia	22.3	18.7	6.3	6.3	68.3	71.1	40.9	30.0	2.58	2.28
Iran	17.1	19.7	5.4	5.3	70.0	72.6	29.0	21.0	2.02	1.96
Iraq	34.6	29.4	6.2	4.9	67.0	70.3	60.1	42.2	4.75	3.76
Italy	9.1	7.5	10.1	11.2	79.1	80.2	5.8	5.1	1.18	1.22
Japan	10.0	8.9	8.3	10.2	80.8	81.7	3.9	3.6	1.41	1.47
Kazakhstan	17.3	20.9	10.6	10.4	63.3	65.7	59.2	52.5	2.07	2.38
Kenya	28.5	21.9	14.4	17.9	47.5	44.3	68.0	60.4	3.50	2.40
Korea, North	19.1	13.9	6.9	7.5	71.0	73.5	23.6	17.6	2.26	1.90
Korea, South	14.9	12.2	5.9	6.8	74.7	76.6	7.7	6.6	1.72	1.72
Madagascar	42.7	40.5	12.4	10.1	55.4	58.9	83.6	68.7	5.80	5.47
Malawi	37.8	31.8	22.8	24.1	37.1	35.8	121.1	110.0	5.18	3.94
Malaysia	24.8	22.1	5.2	5.1	71.1	73.6	20.3	15.0	3.24	2.92
Mali	48.8	44.6	18.7	15.3	47.0	50.5	121.4	105.1	6.81	6.06
Mexico	22.8	19.3	5.0	5.0	71.8	74.1	25.4	18.5	2.62	2.27
Morocco	24.2	20.6	5.9	5.4	69.4	72.1	48.1	34.7	3.05	2.46
Mozambique	37.2	31.1	24.2	29.9	36.5	31.4	139.2	131.8	4.82	3.85
Nepal	33.4	28.8	10.2	8.7	58.2	61.7	74.1	58.7	4.58	3.73
Netherlands	11.9	10.1	8.7	8.9	78.4	79.8	4.4	3.9	1.65	1.66
Niger	50.7	45.5	22.7	19.1	41.6	44.6	123.6	111.3	7.08	6.28
Nigeria	39.7	35.3	13.9	15.9	51.1	47.0	73.3	66.1	5.57	4.79
Pakistan	31.2	24.8	9.3	7.5	61.5	64.8	80.5	63.3	4.41	3.16
Peru	23.9	19.8	5.8	5.6	70.3	72.9	39.4	29.3	2.96	2.41
Philippines	27.4	23.3	6.0	5.5	67.8	70.6	28.7	21.8	3.42	2.89
Poland	10.2	10.9	10.0	10.3	73.4	75.6	9.4	7.6	1.37	1.42
Portugal	11.5	10.4	10.2	10.6	75.9	77.7	5.9	5.1	1.48	1.52
Romania	10.8	10.6	12.3	12.4	70.2	72.5	19.4	14.9	1.35	1.42
Russia	9.4	12.1	13.9	14.5	67.3	68.8	20.1	17.7	1.27	1.56
Saudi Arabia	37.3	37.1	5.9	5.4	68.1	70.9	51.3	37.4	6.25	5.74
Senegal	37.5	33.0	8.4	6.7	62.6	65.8	56.8	45.1	5.12	4.29
Serbia	12.5	12.0	10.7	11.3	73.4	75.5	18.0	14.1	1.73	1.69
South Africa	21.1	17.8	16.8	30.3	48.1	35.5	60.3	67.4	2.43	2.09
Spain	9.3	8.5	9.1	10.1	78.9	80.2	4.9	4.4	1.15	1.22
Sri Lanka	16.6	14.8	6.4	6.6	72.1	74.4	16.1	12.5	1.95	1.78
Sudan	37.9	31.8	10.0	8.3	56.9	60.5	68.7	55.2	5.35	4.21
Syria	30.6	25.2	5.2	4.6	68.8	71.5	33.8	25.0	3.95	3.02
Taiwan [5]	14.3	13.0	6.0	6.8	76.5	78.2	6.9	5.9	1.76	1.75
Tanzania	39.7	34.9	13.0	13.4	52.0	50.5	79.4	65.8	5.42	4.62
Thailand	16.6	14.2	7.5	7.8	68.9	71.7	30.5	22.2	1.87	1.80
Turkey	18.3	15.6	6.0	6.1	71.2	73.7	47.3	34.3	2.12	1.82
Uganda	47.5	45.2	18.0	15.1	43.4	46.6	91.3	75.4	6.88	6.12
Ukraine	9.3	11.6	16.4	15.7	66.2	68.5	21.4	17.5	1.29	1.58
United Kingdom	11.5	10.6	10.4	10.2	77.8	79.3	5.5	4.8	1.73	1.72
Uzbekistan	26.1	26.1	8.0	7.4	63.8	66.2	71.9	65.6	3.06	2.80
Venezuela	20.7	17.8	4.9	5.0	73.3	75.5	25.4	18.9	2.46	2.13
Vietnam	21.2	18.3	6.2	5.8	69.6	72.2	30.2	22.7	2.49	2.10
Yemen	43.4	41.8	9.6	7.4	60.2	63.6	68.5	53.4	6.97	6.23
Zimbabwe	24.7	23.0	23.2	31.6	37.1	32.5	62.6	65.9	3.28	2.63

[1] Number of births during 1 year per 1,000 persons (based on midyear population). [2] Number of deaths during 1 year per 1,000 persons (based on midyear population). [3] Number of deaths of children under 1 year of age per 1,000 live births in a calendar year. [4] Average number of children that would be born if all women lived to the end of their childbearing years and, at each year of age, they experienced the birth rates occurring in the specified year. [5] See footnote 2, Table 1308. [6] See footnote 3, Table 1308.

Source: U.S. Census Bureau, "International Data Base" (as of 10 May 2000); <http://www.census.gov/ipc/www/idbnew.html>.

Comparative International Statistics 829

No. 1313. Health Expenditures as Percent of GDP by Country: 1980 to 2000

[In percent. G.D.P.=gross domestic product; for explanation, see text, Section 13, Income, Expenditures, and Wealth]

Country	Total health expenditures 1980	1990	1998	1999	2000	Public health expenditures 1980	1990	1998	1999	2000
United States	8.7	11.9	12.9	12.9	(NA)	3.6	4.7	5.8	5.7	(NA)
Australia	7.0	7.9	8.6	(NA)	(NA)	4.4	5.3	6.0	(NA)	(NA)
Austria	7.6	7.1	8.0	8.2	(NA)	5.2	5.2	5.8	5.9	(NA)
Belgium	6.4	7.4	8.6	8.8	(NA)	(NA)	(NA)	6.1	6.3	(NA)
Canada	7.1	9.0	9.3	9.3	9.2	5.4	6.7	6.5	6.6	6.5
Czech Republic	3.8	5.0	7.1	7.4	(NA)	3.7	4.8	6.5	6.7	(NA)
Denmark	9.1	8.5	8.3	8.4	(NA)	8.0	7.0	6.8	6.9	6.7
Finland	6.4	7.9	6.9	6.8	(NA)	5.0	6.4	5.3	5.2	(NA)
France	7.4	8.6	9.3	9.3	(NA)	5.8	6.6	7.1	7.1	(NA)
Germany [1]	8.8	8.7	10.3	(NA)	(NA)	6.9	6.7	7.8	(NA)	(NA)
Greece	6.5	7.5	8.4	(NA)	(NA)	3.6	4.7	4.7	(NA)	(NA)
Hungary	(NA)	(NA)	6.8	6.8	(NA)	(NA)	(NA)	5.6	5.5	5.2
Iceland	6.1	7.9	8.4	8.7	(NA)	5.4	6.8	7.0	7.4	(NA)
Ireland	8.4	6.7	6.8	(NA)	(NA)	6.8	4.8	5.2	(NA)	(NA)
Italy	7.0	8.0	7.7	7.9	(NA)	5.6	6.4	5.5	5.7	5.7
Japan	6.5	6.1	7.5	(NA)	(NA)	4.6	4.7	5.8	(NA)	(NA)
Korea, South	(NA)	4.8	5.1	5.4	(NA)	(NA)	1.7	2.4	2.4	(NA)
Luxembourg	5.9	6.1	6.0	6.1	(NA)	5.5	5.7	5.5	5.7	(NA)
Mexico	(NA)	4.4	5.3	(NA)	(NA)	(NA)	1.8	2.6	(NA)	(NA)
Netherlands	8.0	8.5	8.7	8.7	(NA)	5.6	5.7	6.0	6.0	(NA)
New Zealand	6.0	7.0	8.1	8.1	(NA)	5.3	5.8	6.3	6.3	(NA)
Norway	7.0	7.8	8.6	8.5	(NA)	5.9	6.4	7.1	7.0	(NA)
Poland	(NA)	5.3	6.4	6.2	(NA)	(NA)	4.8	4.2	4.6	(NA)
Portugal	5.6	6.2	7.7	(NA)	(NA)	3.6	4.1	5.1	(NA)	(NA)
Spain	5.4	6.6	7.0	(NA)	(NA)	4.3	5.2	5.4	(NA)	(NA)
Sweden	9.1	8.5	7.9	(NA)	(NA)	8.4	7.6	6.6	(NA)	(NA)
Switzerland	7.3	8.3	10.4	(NA)	(NA)	4.8	5.7	7.6	(NA)	(NA)
Turkey	3.3	3.6	4.8	(NA)	(NA)	0.9	2.2	3.5	(NA)	(NA)
United Kingdom	5.6	6.0	6.8	6.9	(NA)	5.0	5.1	5.7	5.8	(NA)

NA Not available.   [1] Data prior to 1991 are for former West Germany.

Source: Organization for Economic Cooperation and Development, Paris, France, *OECD Health Data 2001* (copyright).

No. 1314. Average Temperatures and Precipitation—Selected International Cities

[In degrees Fahrenheit, except as noted. Data are generally based on a standard 30-year period; for details, see source. For data on U.S. cities, see Tables 363-366]

City	January Average high	Average low	Warmest	Coldest	Average precipitation (inches)	July Average high	Average low	Warmest	Coldest	Average precipitation (inches)
Amsterdam, Netherlands .	41	34	57	3	3.1	69	55	90	39	2.9
Athens, Greece	55	44	70	28	1.9	89	73	108	61	0.2
Baghdad, Iraq	58	38	75	25	1.1	110	78	122	61	-
Bangkok, Thailand	89	71	95	54	0.4	90	78	99	72	6.2
Beijing, China	34	17	54	1	0.2	86	72	104	63	8.8
Berlin, Germany	35	26	58	-11	(NA)	73	56	95	41	(NA)
Bogota, Colombia	66	43	84	27	1.9	64	47	82	32	1.8
Brasilia, Brazil	81	64	95	54	(NA)	79	52	97	37	(NA)
Buenos Aires, Argentina .	85	64	104	44	4.2	58	41	88	23	2.3
Cairo, Egypt	65	49	86	32	0.2	93	72	108	63	-
Frankfurt, Germany	38	30	56	-4	1.8	75	57	97	38	2.4
Geneva, Switzerland	39	29	57	-2	2.2	77	56	96	41	2.8
Hong Kong, China	67	58	79	43	1.1	89	81	97	70	14.3
Istanbul, Turkey	46	37	64	16	3.7	82	66	100	50	0.7
Jakarta, Indonesia	83	75	92	72	(NA)	88	74	92	67	(NA)
Kabul, Afghanistan	36	23	64	-4	1.3	88	67	102	49	0.2
Karachi, Pakistan	76	55	93	39	0.3	89	83	109	68	3.5
Lagos, Nigeria	82	79	93	64	(NA)	79	76	88	70	(NA)
London, England	45	36	61	15	2.4	72	56	93	45	1.8
Madrid, Spain	51	32	68	14	1.8	90	61	104	46	0.4
Manila, Philippines	86	71	95	61	0.8	88	76	99	70	15.9
Mexico City, Mexico	70	45	86	26	0.3	74	56	86	37	5.1
Montreal, Canada	21	7	52	-31	2.8	79	61	93	43	3.4
Moscow, Russia	21	11	46	-33	1.4	71	55	95	41	3.2
Nairobi, Kenya	77	58	88	45	1.8	71	54	85	43	0.5
New Delhi, India	68	48	85	32	0.9	93	81	111	70	7.9
Paris, France	43	34	59	1	(NA)	75	58	95	41	(NA)
Rio De Janeiro, Brazil . . .	91	74	109	64	5.3	81	64	102	52	1.8
Rome, Italy	55	39	64	19	3.2	83	66	100	55	0.6
Seoul, Korea	33	21	55	-1	(NA)	82	71	97	55	(NA)
Singapore, Singapore . . .	85	73	100	66	9.4	86	76	99	70	5.9
Sydney, Australia	79	65	109	49	4.0	62	44	80	32	2.5
Tel Aviv, Israel	62	46	84	32	(NA)	87	69	100	50	(NA)
Tokyo, Japan	40	35	00	25	2.0	02	71	05	55	5.0
Toronto, Canada	28	15	59	-24	1.9	79	60	99	45	2.8

- Represents zero.   NA Not available.

Source: U.S. National Oceanic and Atmospheric Administration, *Climates of the World*.

No. 1315. Selected Environmental Data—OECD Countries

[Figures are for 1998 or the latest available year. Varying definitions and survey methods can limit the comparability across countries]

| Country | Air pollutant emissions per capita | | | Waste generated | | | |
| | | | | | Nuclear [3] | | |
	Sulfur oxides (kilograms)	Nitrogen oxides (kilograms)	Carbon dioxide [1] (tons)	Municipal [2] (kilograms per capita)	Amount (tons)	Per unit of energy (tons per Mtoe) [4]	Per 1,000 persons (kilograms)
United States	69	80	20	720	2,100	0.9	8.0
Australia............	101	118	17	690	-	-	-
Austria.............	7	21	8	510	-	-	-
Belgium	24	33	12	480	80	2.8	11.9
Canada	90	68	16	500	1,340	6.5	57.1
Czech Republic	68	41	12	310	45	1.0	4.5
Denmark............	21	47	11	560	-	-	-
Finland.............	20	51	12	410	71	2.2	13.3
France.............	16	29	6	590	1,130	4.6	20.6
Germany	16	22	10	[5]460	450	1.3	5.8
Greece.............	48	35	8	370	-	-	-
Hungary	65	19	6	490	55	3.2	5.1
Iceland.............	32	106	8	650	-	-	-
Ireland	49	34	10	560	-	-	-
Italy...............	23	31	7	460	-	-	-
Japan	7	11	9	400	964	1.8	7.3
Korea, South........	33	28	8	400	364	2.3	4.8
Luxembourg	8	40	17	590	-	-	-
Mexico.............	24	17	4	310	42	0.1	0.2
Netherlands	8	28	11	560	12	0.2	0.9
New Zealand........	12	46	8	[6]350	-	-	-
Norway.............	7	51	8	600	-	-	-
Poland	61	30	8	320	(NA)	(NA)	(NA)
Portugal	38	37	5	440	-	-	-
Spain..............	49	32	6	390	192	0.9	4.3
Sweden	10	38	6	360	238	4.5	24.1
Switzerland.........	5	18	6	600	64	2.4	10.9
Turkey	30	15	3	330	-	-	-
United Kingdom	34	35	9	480	820	3.7	29.2

- Represents zero.   NA Not available.   [1] Carbon dioxide from energy use only. Excludes international marine bunkers.
[2] Municipal waste is that which is collected and treated by or for municipalities: household waste and bulky waste as well as comparable waste from small communities or industrial enterprises; and market and garden residue.   [3] Wastes from spent fuel arising in nuclear power plants, measured in terms of heavy metal.   [4] Mtoe=million tons of oil equivalent (primary energy supply).   [5] Includes separate collection by private sector.   [6] Household waste only.

Source: Organization for Economic Cooperation and Development, Paris, France, *OECD Environmental Data Compendium*, 1999 (copyright).

No. 1316. Carbon Dioxide Emissions from Consumption of Fossil Fuels by Country 1990 to 2000, and Projections, 2005 and 2010

[In million metric tons of carbon (5,873 represents 5,873,000,000). Includes carbon dioxide emissions from the consumption of petroleum, natural gas, and coal, and the flaring of natural gas]

Country	1990	1995	1996	1997	1998	1999	2000, prel.	2005	2010
World, total..........	5,873	6,075	6,214	6,275	6,254	6,323	6,443	7,015	7,835
Australia..............	72	80	81	90	90	96	97	(NA)	(NA)
Brazil................	63	82	84	87	88	92	95	108	139
Canada	128	135	138	146	149	153	158	158	165
China [1]	617	788	803	824	805	792	775	889	1,131
France...............	102	101	106	104	110	109	109	116	120
Germany	(X)	239	240	239	235	223	220	246	252
India	156	226	228	231	235	240	253	300	351
Indonesia	41	58	64	67	64	67	69	(NA)	(NA)
Iran.................	56	71	71	79	78	80	81	(NA)	(NA)
Italy.................	112	118	118	113	115	113	117	131	137
Japan	269	298	308	309	300	307	314	324	330
Korea, South.........	61	109	112	118	101	105	115	128	144
Mexico...............	84	87	92	95	104	104	103	124	145
Netherlands	58	61	62	64	62	61	64	66	67
Poland	89	83	78	91	85	82	81	(NA)	(NA)
Russia...............	(X)	445	445	395	396	440	451	(NA)	(NA)
Saudi Arabia	59	69	73	72	70	71	75	(NA)	(NA)
South Africa	81	96	91	107	113	105	106	(NA)	(NA)
Spain................	62	67	64	73	74	79	81	(NA)	(NA)
Taiwan [1]............	32	52	56	58	61	67	69	(NA)	(NA)
Thailand.............	23	43	46	46	43	45	45	(NA)	(NA)
Turkey	35	41	46	49	50	49	55	57	66
Ukraine	(X)	122	109	102	100	105	104	(NA)	(NA)
United Kingdom	164	153	160	154	149	144	148	168	177
United States	1,355	1,430	1,481	1,503	1,504	1,526	1,571	1,690	1,809

NA Not available.   X Not applicable.   [1] See footnote 2, Table 1308.

Source: U.S. Energy Information Administration, *International Energy Annual, 2002*, and *International Energy Outlook, 2001.*

No. 1317. Educational Attainment by Country: 1999

[Percent distribution. Persons 25 to 64 years old]

Country	Total	Preprimary and primary education	Lower secondary education	Upper secondary education	Post-secondary nontertiary education [1]	Non-university tertiary education [2]	University education
United States ...	100	5	8	[3]51	(3)	8	27
Australia	100	(4)	[4]43	[3]31	(3)	9	18
Austria [5]	100	(4)	[4]26	57	6	5	6
Belgium	100	20	23	[3]31	(3)	14	12
Canada	100	7	[4]13	28	13	20	19
Czech Republic	100	(4)	14	[3]76	(3)	(6)	[6]11
Denmark	100	(Z)	20	[3]54	(3)	20	7
Finland [5]	100	(4)	[4]28	[3]40	(3)	17	14
France	100	20	18	41	(Z)	10	11
Germany	100	2	17	53	5	10	13
Greece [5]	100	41	9	27	5	6	12
Hungary	100	4	29	34	[7]20	(7)	[7]14
Iceland	100	2	35	30	10	5	18
Ireland [5]	100	23	26	[8]30	(8)	[8]10	11
Italy	100	25	32	30	4	(6)	[6]9
Japan	100	(4)	[4]19	49	(NA)	13	18
Korea, South	100	18	16	44	(X)	6	17
Mexico	100	59	21	7	(X)	1	12
Netherlands	100	12	23	42	(9)	[9]2	[9]20
New Zealand	100	(4)	[4]	39	7	14	13
Norway [5]	100	(Z)	15	56	1	2	25
Poland [5]	100	(4)	[4]22	64	3	(6)	[6]11
Portugal	100	67	12	[3]11	(3)	3	7
Spain	100	42	23	14	(10)	[10]6	15
Sweden	100	11	12	48	(10)	[10]16	13
Switzerland	100	(4)	[4]18	[3]58	(3)	9	15
Turkey	100	68	10	14	(X)	(6)	[6]8
United Kingdom	100	(4)	[4]18	57	(NA)	8	17

NA Not available. X Not applicable. Z Less than 0.5 percent. [1] This level straddles the boundary between upper secondary and postsecondary education from an international point of view, even though it might clearly be considered upper secondary or postsecondary in a national context. Although the content may not be significantly more advanced than upper secondary programs, it serves to broaden the knowledge of participants who have already gained an upper secondary qualification. [2] These programs focus on practical, technical, or occupational skills for direct entry into the labor market, although some theoretical foundations may be covered. They have a minimum duration of two years full-time equivalent at the tertiary level. [3] Postsecondary nontertiary included in upper secondary. [4] Preprimary and primary education included in lower secondary. [5] Data for 1998. [6] Nonuniversity tertiary included in university. [7] Nonuniversity tertiary included in postsecondary nontertiary and university. [8] Postsecondary nontertiary included in upper secondary and nonuniversity tertiary. [9] Postsecondary nontertiary included in nonuniversity tertiary and university. [10] Postsecondary nontertiary included in nonuniversity tertiary.

Source: Organization for Economic Cooperation and Development, Paris, France, Education at a Glance, annual, (copyright).

No. 1318. Participation in Job-Related Continuing Education and Training by Country

[Percentage of the employed population 25 to 64 years old. Data refer to all job-related education and training organized, financed, or sponsored by authorities, provided by employers, or self-financed. Job-related continuing education and training refers to all organized, systematic education and training activities in which people take part in order to obtain knowledge and/or learn new skills for a current or a future job, to increase earnings, improve job and/or career opportunities in current or other fields, and generally to improve their opportunities for advancement and promotion. Data are based on International Adult Literacy Survey 1994-1998 and national household surveys on adult education and training]

Country	Time period	Total	Male	Female
United States	1999	41	40	42
Australia	1996-97	47	46	50
Canada	1997	28	26	30
Czech Republic	1998-99	27	31	23
Denmark	1998-99	55	52	58
Finland	1995	51	46	56
Germany	1997	42	43	40
Hungary	1998-99	20	17	23
Ireland	1995-96	24	21	29
Italy	1998-99	25	25	25
Netherlands	1994-95	33	35	29
New Zealand	1995-96	47	46	47
Norway	1998-99	51	49	54
Poland	1994-95	17	16	17
Switzerland	1998-99	37	39	35
United Kingdom	1995-96	52	51	53

Source: Organization for Economic Cooperation and Development, Paris, France, Education at a Glance, annual (copyright).

U.S. Census Bureau, Statistical Abstract of the United States: 2002

No. 1319. Gross National Product by Country: 1990 and 2000

[61 represents $61,000,000,000]

Country	Gross national product [1]				GNP on purchasing power parity basis [2]			
	Total (bil. dol.)		Per capita (dol.)		Total (bil. dol.)		Per capita (dol.)	
	1990	2000	1990	2000	1990	2000	1990	2000
Algeria	61	48	2,440	1,580	109	153	4,350	5,040
Argentina	104	276	3,190	7,460	240	446	7,380	12,050
Australia	300	388	17,590	20,240	280	479	16,430	24,970
Bangladesh	31	48	280	370	110	209	1,000	1,590
Belarus	35	29	3,460	2,870	72	76	7,030	7,550
Belgium	183	252	18,340	24,540	192	282	19,270	27,470
Brazil	411	610	2,780	3,580	801	1,243	5,410	7,300
Bulgaria	20	12	2,260	1,520	47	45	5,340	5,560
Canada	550	650	19,790	21,130	539	836	19,400	27,170
Chile	29	70	2,190	4,590	61	138	4,690	9,100
China [3]	368	1,063	320	840	1,587	4,951	1,400	3,920
Colombia [4]	41	85	1,180	2,020	239	256	6,820	6,060
Congo (Kinshasa) [4]	8	(NA)	230	(NA)	44	(NA)	1,180	(NA)
Costa Rica	5	15	1,790	3,810	15	30	5,050	7,980
Cote d'Ivoire	9	10	780	600	16	24	1,320	1,500
Croatia	(NA)	20	(NA)	4,620	34	35	7,080	7,960
Czech Republic	(NA)	54	(NA)	5,250	119	142	11,500	13,780
Denmark	120	172	23,430	32,280	97	145	18,930	27,250
Ecuador	10	15	970	1,210	26	37	2,540	2,910
Egypt	42	95	810	1,490	128	235	2,450	3,670
El Salvador	5	13	940	2,000	15	28	2,920	4,410
Ethiopia	8	7	160	100	25	43	480	660
Finland	124	130	24,890	25,130	86	127	17,310	24,570
France	[5] 1,142	[5] 1,438	19,860	24,090	1,015	1,438	17,900	24,420
Germany	1,612	2,064	20,290	25,120	1,459	2,047	18,370	24,920
Greece	79	126	7,770	11,960	120	178	11,770	16,860
Guatemala	8	19	970	1,680	24	43	2,770	3,770
Hong Kong	72	176	12,680	25,920	95	174	16,730	25,590
Hungary	30	47	2,880	4,710	94	120	9,030	11,990
India	332	455	390	450	1,175	2,375	1,380	2,340
Indonesia	111	120	620	570	332	596	1,860	2,830
Iran	141	107	2,590	1,680	212	376	3,890	5,910
Ireland	42	86	11,960	22,660	41	97	11,680	25,520
Israel	51	104	10,860	16,710	61	121	13,130	19,330
Italy	988	1,163	17,420	20,160	974	1,354	17,170	23,470
Japan	3,348	4,519	27,100	35,620	2,509	3,436	20,310	27,080
Kazakhstan	(NA)	19	(NA)	1,260	99	82	6,100	5,490
Korea, South	246	421	5,740	8,910	381	818	8,880	17,300
Lebanon	(NA)	17	(NA)	4,010	8	20	2,280	4,550
Luxembourg	12	18	31,350	42,060	10	20	24,900	45,470
Malaysia	43	79	2,380	3,380	83	194	4,540	8,330
Mexico	236	497	2,830	5,070	514	861	6,170	8,790
Morocco	25	34	1,030	1,180	67	99	2,780	3,450
Netherlands	285	398	19,070	24,970	263	412	17,560	25,850
New Zealand	43	50	12,410	12,990	46	71	13,360	18,530
Nigeria	26	33	270	260	66	102	690	800
Norway	108	155	25,490	34,530	80	133	18,950	29,630
Pakistan	43	61	390	440	147	257	1,360	1,860
Peru	17	53	780	2,080	68	120	3,150	4,660
Philippines	45	79	740	1,040	202	319	3,310	4,220
Poland	(NA)	162	(NA)	4,190	204	348	5,360	9,000
Portugal	64	111	6,420	11,120	110	170	11,110	16,990
Romania	40	37	1,720	1,670	145	143	6,240	6,360
Russia	(NA)	241	(NA)	1,660	1,492	1,165	10,060	8,010
Saudi Arabia	105	150	6,620	7,230	160	236	10,120	11,390
Singapore	36	99	11,740	24,740	40	100	13,130	24,910
Slovakia	18	20	3,340	3,700	48	60	9,040	11,040
Slovenia	(NA)	20	(NA)	10,050	24	34	12,070	17,310
South Africa	102	129	2,890	3,020	280	392	7,950	9,160
Spain	458	595	11,790	15,080	498	760	12,810	19,260
Sri Lanka	8	16	470	850	34	67	1,990	3,460
Sweden	214	241	25,050	27,140	151	213	17,610	23,970
Switzerland	225	274	33,510	38,140	169	219	25,190	30,450
Syria	11	15	940	940	26	54	2,150	3,340
Thailand	84	122	1,520	2,000	211	384	3,790	6,320
Turkey	128	202	2,280	3,100	274	459	4,890	7,030
Ukraine	83	35	1,600	700	355	183	6,850	3,700
United Arab Emirates	37	(NA)	19,930	(NA)	40	(NA)	21,520	(NA)
United Kingdom	934	1,459	16,220	24,430	952	1,407	16,540	23,550
United States	**5,846**	**9,602**	**23,440**	**34,100**	**5,847**	**9,601**	**23,440**	**34,100**
Uruguay	9	20	2,870	6,000	18	30	5,950	8,880
Uzbekistan	(NA)	9	(NA)	360	51	58	2,510	2,360
Venezuela	52	104	2,650	4,310	96	139	4,900	5,740
Vietnam	(NA)	30	(NA)	390	64	157	970	2,000

NA Not available. [1] Gross national product calculated using the World Bank Atlas method; for details, see source. [2] See footnote 2, Table 1320. [3] See footnote 2, Table 1308. [4] See footnote 3, Table 1308. [5] GNP and GNP per capita estimates include the French overseas departments of French Guiana, Guadeloupe, Martinique, and Reunion.

Source: The World Bank, Washington, DC, *World Development Indicators CD-ROM*, annual (copyright).

No. 1320. Gross Domestic Product (GDP) by Country: 1995 to 2000

[23,666 represents $23,666,000,000,000. Except as noted, based on the System of National Accounts, 1993; for details, see source]

Country	Current price levels and exchange rates (bil. dol.)					Constant (1995) price levels and exchange rates [1] (bil. dol.)					GDP per capita, 2000 based on current	
	1995	1997	1998	1999	2000	1995	1997	1998	1999	2000	Exchange rates	PPPs [2]
OECD, total [3]	23,666	23,424	23,594	24,844	25,213	23,666	25,119	25,704	26,444	27,391	23,834	24,746
OECD Europe [4]	9,244	8,865	9,162	9,150	8,466	9,244	9,647	9,925	10,165	10,506	18,515	21,921
European Union [4]	8,614	8,257	8,544	8,544	7,857	8,614	8,970	9,231	9,472	9,786	20,759	24,395
Australia	373	417	372	406	389	373	404	425	443	452	20,278	26,495
Austria	235	206	211	210	189	235	244	252	259	267	23,270	27,001
Belgium	277	245	251	251	229	277	290	297	306	318	22,313	26,169
Canada	583	629	608	646	701	583	618	642	675	705	22,783	28,015
Czech Republic	52	53	57	55	51	52	54	53	53	55	4,942	14,285
Denmark	180	169	175	176	163	180	190	196	200	206	30,489	29,495
Finland [5]	129	122	129	128	121	129	143	151	157	166	23,437	25,260
France [5]	1,553	1,406	1,452	1,438	1,294	1,553	1,600	1,655	1,703	1,756	21,417	24,215
Germany	2,458	2,111	2,145	2,103	1,866	2,458	2,512	2,561	2,608	2,687	22,712	25,893
Greece	118	121	122	126	113	118	125	129	133	139	10,733	16,817
Hungary	45	46	47	48	46	45	47	50	52	54	4,623	12,435
Iceland	7	7	8	9	9	7	8	8	8	9	30,462	29,302
Ireland	67	80	87	95	95	67	80	86	96	107	25,173	29,174
Italy	1,097	1,167	1,197	1,180	1,074	1,097	1,132	1,152	1,171	1,205	18,604	25,161
Japan	5,292	4,313	3,941	4,494	4,765	5,292	5,574	5,513	5,550	5,681	37,546	25,968
Korea, South	489	477	317	406	457	489	549	512	568	618	9,671	15,055
Luxembourg	18	18	19	20	19	18	20	22	23	25	42,922	46,743
Mexico	286	401	421	480	574	286	321	338	350	374	5,903	9,152
Netherlands	415	377	394	398	370	415	444	463	480	497	23,212	27,836
New Zealand [6]	61	66	54	56	51	61	64	61	67	69	13,255	20,285
Norway	147	155	148	154	162	147	161	165	167	171	36,021	30,168
Poland	127	144	159	155	158	127	144	151	157	163	4,082	9,588
Portugal	107	107	113	115	106	107	116	121	125	129	10,613	18,021
Slovakia	18	20	21	20	19	18	21	22	22	23	3,568	11,643
Spain	584	562	588	603	561	584	623	650	676	704	14,048	20,124
Sweden [6]	240	239	240	243	229	240	248	257	268	278	25,818	24,843
Switzerland [6]	307	256	262	259	239	307	314	321	326	336	33,326	30,138
Turkey	169	190	200	185	200	169	195	201	191	205	2,991	6,439
United Kingdom	1,135	1,328	1,424	1,458	1,427	1,135	1,205	1,241	1,267	1,304	23,887	24,398
United States	**7,338**	**8,257**	**8,720**	**9,207**	**9,810**	**7,338**	**7,943**	**8,286**	**8,627**	**8,987**	**35,619**	**35,619**

[1] Based on constant (1995) price data converted to U.S. dollars using 1995 exchange rates. [2] The goods and services produced in different countries should be valued consistently if the differences observed are meant to reflect real differences in the volumes of goods and services produced. The use of purchasing power parities (PPP) instead of exchange rates is intended to achieve this objective. PPP's show how many units of currency are needed in one country to buy the same amount of goods and services which one unit of currency will buy in the other country. See text of this section. [3] Excluding Czech Republic, Hungary, Poland, and Slovakia. [4] European Union: Austria, Belgium, Denmark, Finland, France, Germany, Greece, Ireland, Italy, Luxembourg, Netherlands, Portugal, Spain, Sweden, and United Kingdom. [5] Includes overseas departments. [6] Based on System of National Accounts, 1968.

Source: Organization for Economic Cooperation and Development, Paris, France, "National Accounts of OECD Countries 1989-2000," Vol. 1; published July 2002.

834   Comparative International Statistics

No. 1321. Selected International Economic Indicators by Country: 1980 to 2000

[Data cover gross domestic product (GDP) at market prices. Gross fixed capital formation covers private and government sectors except military. Savings data are calculated by deducting outlays—such as personal consumption expenditures, interest paid, and transfer payments to foreigners—from disposable personal income]

Year	United States	France	Germany	Italy	Netherlands	United Kingdom	Japan	Canada
Ratio of gross fixed capital formation to GDP (current prices):								
1980	19.9	23.8	22.6	25.2	22.9	18.8	31.7	23.1
1985	19.2	20.3	19.5	21.8	21.0	18.1	27.7	19.8
1990	17.0	22.6	20.9	21.5	22.3	20.6	32.2	20.8
1995	17.5	18.8	22.4	18.3	20.3	16.3	27.8	17.0
1998	19.4	18.4	21.3	18.5	21.5	17.4	26.9	19.3
1999	20.0	19.1	21.3	19.0	22.2	17.7	26.2	19.5
2000	20.7	19.7	21.4	19.6	22.3	17.7	26.0	19.3
Ratio of savings to disposable personal income:								
1980	10.2	15.8	14.2	25.1	7.8	11.7	17.9	15.5
1985	9.2	13.8	12.8	21.0	5.6	9.1	19.0	15.7
1990	7.8	13.1	14.7	18.4	11.6	7.4	13.9	12.9
1995	5.6	16.0	11.2	16.6	14.9	10.3	12.3	9.2
1998	4.2	15.6	10.2	12.8	13.4	5.8	11.8	4.4
1999	2.2	15.4	9.9	11.5	10.6	5.2	11.1	4.2
2000	-0.1	15.9	9.8	10.3	9.4	4.5	11.1	3.9

Source: U.S. Dept. of Commerce, International Trade Administration, Office of Trade and Economic Analysis, based on official statistics of listed countries.

No. 1322. International Economic Composite Indexes by Country: 1980 to 2000

[**Average annual percent change from previous year; derived from indexes with base 1990=100.** The coincident index changes are for calendar years and the leading index changes are for years ending June 30 because they lead the coincident indexes by about 6 months, on average. The G-7 countries are United States, Canada, France, Germany, Italy, United Kingdom, and Japan. Minus sign (-) indicates decrease]

Country	1980	1985	1990	1992	1993	1994	1995	1996	1997	1998	1999	2000
LEADING INDEX												
Total, 13 countries	2.9	2.9	2.7	-1.1	-0.9	3.9	6.9	-0.6	3.0	2.2	-0.4	6.2
12 countries, excluding U.S.	7.7	5.5	4.4	-3.2	-3.3	3.7	6.1	-0.7	1.5	0.5	-1.6	5.3
G-7 countries	2.9	2.0	2.6	-1.6	-1.4	3.5	7.3	-0.6	3.2	2.4	-0.5	6.2
North America	-2.7	-0.4	-0.5	2.3	3.2	4.5	8.3	-0.4	5.1	4.5	1.1	7.4
United States	-3.1	-0.7	-0.4	2.6	3.1	4.2	8.2	-0.4	5.1	4.5	1.1	7.3
Canada	2.0	3.2	-2.6	-1.1	4.5	8.5	10.0	-0.9	5.3	4.6	0.7	9.4
Four European countries	3.1	2.8	1.5	0.3	-1.3	4.1	6.2	-2.3	0.1	5.4	-0.1	1.6
France	3.2	0.8	-1.0	2.7	-0.3	4.7	3.5	-3.4	1.3	3.1	-1.4	-2.0
Germany	2.0	2.1	4.4	-1.1	-4.5	2.0	8.8	-3.5	1.7	7.3	1.3	1.9
Italy	6.1	6.5	1.0	-0.9	-1.0	7.1	9.9	-0.9	-4.4	10.9	-0.6	5.6
United Kingdom	2.5	3.5	0.4	0.8	2.8	4.1	2.3	-	0.1	0.3	-0.5	1.6
Seven Pacific region countries	16.3	9.4	8.0	-6.6	-6.0	2.9	5.5	1.0	2.6	-5.3	-3.7	9.1
Australia	5.7	7.6	0.3	4.9	5.9	7.1	11.3	6.0	3.1	5.9	7.6	7.6
Taiwan [1]	2.6	5.6	6.1	8.4	4.0	8.1	3.1	-1.6	4.2	3.8	-	4.1
Thailand	4.0	7.1	14.4	7.5	9.2	12.0	5.7	2.0	-3.3	-6.0	-1.6	5.9
Japan	19.8	10.3	8.7	-9.7	-9.3	0.6	6.5	1.5	3.5	-6.9	-5.4	10.6
Korea, South	0.4	6.9	7.1	7.0	6.3	13.1	3.1	-0.7	-2.2	-5.3	1.8	8.5
Malaysia	4.9	-1.0	2.0	-1.2	0.7	7.6	1.5	0.2	0.9	-1.0	-1.1	3.8
New Zealand	2.3	6.0	1.8	3.5	4.5	2.7	0.9	-	2.3	1.2	0.1	7.0
COINCIDENT INDEX												
Total, 13 countries	-	3.5	4.0	0.3	-0.9	2.6	5.4	5.5	6.2	4.6	8.1	7.4
12 countries, excluding U.S.	1.9	3.4	6.5	-0.4	-2.6	1.5	4.6	5.3	4.8	2.2	8.8	7.5
G-7 countries	-0.2	3.4	3.9	-	-1.3	2.2	5.2	5.7	6.3	5.2	8.3	7.4
North America	-2.5	3.7	-	1.2	2.1	4.7	8.2	9.5	9.8	7.7	12.0	6.6
United States	-2.9	3.5	-	1.4	2.1	4.7	6.7	6.1	8.4	8.5	7.3	7.4
Canada	2.2	6.3	-0.1	-0.2	1.9	5.1	13.3	20.3	13.9	5.5	24.7	4.9
Four European countries	0.6	2.3	5.4	-1.6	-5.2	1.3	4.2	1.4	4.1	9.1	9.3	13.9
France	-2.3	-1.6	6.0	-2.6	-8.6	1.0	9.0	2.7	7.9	15.8	16.8	21.3
Germany	1.9	3.1	7.3	-0.7	-4.0	1.0	3.9	-1.2	0.5	8.0	7.8	12.3
Italy	6.9	4.1	6.4	-0.9	-8.4	-1.2	-1.5	3.5	5.4	7.1	9.3	16.8
United Kingdom	-2.1	4.1	0.9	-2.7	-	4.3	3.0	2.8	5.0	3.5	0.9	1.9
Seven Pacific region countries	3.5	4.3	8.4	0.7	-0.6	1.3	2.0	2.8	1.3	-5.3	-0.8	2.3
Australia	4.2	7.2	0.6	-2.0	1.3	9.2	8.8	3.8	4.3	6.7	8.0	6.4
Taiwan [1]	8.5	4.3	5.2	8.4	6.9	7.1	2.6	0.2	4.6	3.0	2.6	3.9
Thailand	4.2	3.3	13.0	7.1	11.8	10.2	4.5	1.6	-6.2	-12.3	6.7	3.8
Japan	4.0	4.4	9.1	-0.1	-2.2	-1.0	0.5	2.3	0.7	-5.4	-3.7	-0.1
Korea, South	-7.1	6.7	11.5	5.0	4.5	11.5	7.8	6.4	3.0	-16.9	12.4	14.9
Malaysia	-2.7	-8.2	-0.3	3.1	4.7	4.8	10.7	8.5	6.1	-5.1	5.7	10.8
New Zealand	1.4	1.3	0.6	0.8	3.3	5.4	10.6	10.3	5.5	0.6	8.4	4.6

- Represents or rounds to zero.   [1] See footnote 2, Table 1308.

Source: Foundation for International Business and Economic Research, New York, NY, *International Economic Indicators*, monthly.

Comparative International Statistics   835

No. 1323. Index of Industrial Production by Country: 1980 to 2001

[Annual averages of monthly data. Industrial production index measures output in the manufacturing, mining, and electric, gas and water utilities industries. Minus sign (-) indicates decrease]

Country	Index (1995=100)								Annual percent change				
	1980	1985	1990	1994	1998	1999	2000	2001	1996-97	1997-98	1998-99	1999-00	2000-01
OECD, total	(NA)	(NA)	(NA)	(NA)	110.6	114.4	120.8	117.7	5.0	2.2	3.4	5.6	-2.6
Canada	71.8	83.0	88.4	95.7	108.3	116.7	123.2	119.6	5.5	0.9	7.8	5.6	-2.9
Mexico [1]	80.3	85.0	95.7	108.5	127.9	133.3	141.5	136.5	9.3	6.3	4.2	6.2	-3.5
Australia	70.1	77.8	92.9	99.5	107.7	112.5	118.5	118.0	1.6	2.1	4.5	5.3	-0.4
Japan [2]	69.9	82.8	103.2	96.8	99.0	99.8	105.4	97.8	3.6	-6.6	0.8	5.6	-7.2
Korea, South [2]	22.0	36.2	66.4	89.3	106.2	131.9	154.0	156.7	5.3	-7.2	24.2	16.8	1.8
New Zealand.	74.0	85.0	87.0	96.0	105.0	101.0	105.0	104.0	1.9	-	-3.8	4.0	-1.0
Austria	70.2	76.6	92.3	95.3	116.2	123.2	134.1	134.3	5.9	8.6	6.0	8.8	0.1
Belgium [2]	83.4	86.8	99.3	93.9	108.8	109.7	115.6	114.8	4.7	3.4	0.8	5.4	-0.7
Czech Republic [2] . . .	(X)	(X)	144.9	100.7	108.3	104.8	110.5	118.0	4.4	1.7	-3.2	5.4	6.8
Denmark.	63.0	77.0	86.0	96.0	110.0	113.0	120.0	122.0	5.9	1.9	2.7	6.2	1.7
Finland.	66.4	76.7	86.9	94.1	122.5	129.0	143.9	142.2	9.3	8.1	5.3	11.6	-1.2
France	89.5	89.5	100.4	98.0	110.0	112.4	116.3	117.3	3.9	5.7	2.2	3.5	0.9
Germany	85.6	88.3	103.2	98.8	108.5	110.4	117.2	117.9	3.5	4.2	1.8	6.2	0.6
Greece [2].	92.6	99.2	101.9	98.2	109.8	114.1	114.7	(NA)	1.3	7.1	3.9	0.5	(NA)
Hungary [2]	116.7	128.1	113.8	95.5	129.1	142.4	168.3	175.2	11.1	12.5	10.3	18.2	4.1
Ireland	34.2	43.9	63.2	84.1	142.3	174.6	201.5	221.0	15.3	14.3	22.7	15.4	9.7
Italy	77.2	73.9	93.2	95.2	102.9	102.9	107.8	106.5	3.8	1.1	-	4.8	-1.2
Luxembourg	71.0	79.8	97.1	95.0	105.8	118.0	123.0	125.2	5.8	-0.1	11.5	4.2	1.8
Netherlands	78.7	83.1	90.6	95.4	105.1	106.8	110.9	109.9	2.6	-1.3	1.6	3.8	-0.9
Norway.	50.6	61.5	78.6	94.4	108.4	108.1	111.2	111.0	3.4	-0.6	-0.3	2.9	-0.2
Poland	(X)	107.3	87.7	90.4	127.4	133.5	143.5	144.1	11.2	4.7	4.8	7.5	0.4
Portugal	62.1	71.7	97.0	89.6	114.1	117.6	118.1	120.9	2.6	5.6	3.1	0.4	2.4
Spain.	80.1	82.7	96.6	95.4	111.4	114.2	119.2	117.5	7.0	5.5	2.5	4.4	-1.4
Sweden [3][4]	73.0	80.5	88.0	91.1	112.1	115.6	125.3	123.2	6.5	4.2	3.1	8.4	-1.7
Switzerland	77.0	80.0	96.0	98.0	108.0	112.0	122.0	125.0	5.0	2.9	3.7	8.9	2.5
Turkey	38.2	57.2	81.3	88.7	120.5	116.0	123.0	112.4	10.7	1.3	-3.7	6.0	-8.6
United Kingdom	76.8	83.0	94.1	98.2	102.8	104.1	105.8	103.5	1.1	0.7	1.3	1.6	-2.2
United States	69.6	76.9	86.4	95.3	117.2	121.9	127.4	122.5	6.0	5.8	4.0	4.5	-3.8

- Represents or rounds to zero. NA Not available. X Not applicable. [1] Including construction. [2] Not adjusted for unequal number of working days in the month. [3] Mining and manufacturing. [4] Annual figures correspond to official annual figures and differ from the average of the monthly figures.

Source: Organization for Economic Cooperation and Development, Paris, France, *Main Economic Indicators*, monthly (copyright).

No. 1324. Labor Productivity and Hours Worked by Country: 1990 to 2001

[**Annual percent change for period shown**. Data are derived from an annual database supported by the source. The Groningen Growth and Development Centre at the University of Groningen, Netherlands, maintains the database. For OECD countries and Eastern Europe, estimates are based on gross domestic product per hour worked, converted at purchasing power parities for 1996. Hence, estimates expressed in U.S. dollars at the price level of 1996 are corrected for differences in relative price levels. Minus sign (-) indicates decrease]

Country	Labor productivity		Total hours worked	
	1990-1995	1995-2001	1990-1995	1995-2001
OECD, total	1.8	1.8	0.2	1.0
OECD, excl. United States	1.9	1.6	-0.2	0.8
European Union [1]	2.5	1.3	-1.0	1.2
Australia.	2.4	2.3	1.0	1.7
Austria.	1.8	2.6	0.3	-0.3
Belgium	2.2	2.1	-0.7	0.4
Canada.	1.3	0.9	0.2	2.2
Czech Republic.	-0.6	1.6	-0.3	-0.5
Denmark.	2.4	1.2	-0.4	1.3
Finland	2.8	2.5	-3.4	1.8
France.	1.5	1.0	-0.4	1.4
Germany	3.2	1.5	-1.5	0.1
Greece	0.6	2.6	0.7	0.8
Hungary.	3.0	2.4	-5.2	1.5
Ireland	3.5	5.1	1.1	3.6
Italy.	3.1	0.7	-1.8	1.1
Japan	1.8	1.8	-0.4	-0.6
Mexico.	-1.1	1.9	2.7	2.6
Netherlands	1.1	0.9	1.0	2.3
New Zealand	0.9	0.7	2.1	1.7
Norway	3.4	1.7	0.3	1.2
Poland.	4.9	4.7	-2.6	-0.1
Portugal.	3.6	2.0	-1.8	1.3
South Korea	5.1	3.7	2.2	0.6
Spain	2.3	0.1	-1.0	3.5
Sweden	1.9	1.6	-1.3	1.0
Switzerland.	0.6	1.3	-0.6	0.5
Turkey	1.7	1.7	1.5	0.3
United Kingdom.	2.5	1.7	-0.9	1.0
United States.	1.1	2.0	1.2	1.6

[1] For countries, see text of this section.

Source: The Conference Board, New York, NY, *Performance 2001: Productivity, Employment, and Income in the World's Economies*, by Robert H. McGuckin and Bart van Ark, 2002 (copyright).

836 Comparative International Statistics

No. 1325. Patents by Country: 2000

[Includes only U.S. patents granted to residents of areas outside of the United States and its territories]

Country	Total [1]	Inventions	Designs	Country	Total [1]	Inventions	Designs
Total	**79,062**	**72,425**	**6,128**	Sweden	1,738	1,577	160
				Netherlands	1,410	1,241	66
Japan	32,921	31,296	1,497	Switzerland	1,458	1,322	132
Germany	10,822	10,234	505	Australia	859	704	139
Taiwan [2]	5,806	4,667	1,135	Israel	836	783	46
France	4,173	3,819	338	Belgium	756	694	48
United Kingdom	4,087	3,667	372	Finland	649	618	30
Korea, South	3,472	3,314	150	Denmark	509	436	47
Canada	3,923	3,419	484	Austria	537	505	30
Italy	1,967	1,714	247	Other countries	3,139	2,415	702

[1] Includes patents for botanical plants and reissues, not shown separately.   [2] See footnote 2, Table 1308.
Source: U.S. Patent and Trademark Office, Technology Assessment and Forecast Database.

No. 1326. Annual Percent Changes in Consumer Prices by Country: 1995 to 2001

[Change from previous year. See text of this section for general comments concerning the data. For additional qualifications of the data for individual countries, see source. Minus sign (-) indicates decrease]

Country	1995	1998	1999	2000	2001	Country	1995	1998	1999	2000	2001
United States	**2.8**	**1.6**	**2.2**	**3.4**	**2.8**	Japan	-0.1	0.7	-0.3	-0.7	-0.7
						Kenya	0.8	6.6	3.5	6.2	0.8
Argentina	3.4	0.9	-1.2	-0.9	-1.1	Korea, South	4.5	7.5	0.8	2.3	4.3
Australia	4.6	0.9	1.5	4.5	4.4	Malaysia	5.3	5.3	2.7	1.5	1.4
Austria	2.3	0.9	0.6	2.4	2.7	Mexico	35.0	15.9	16.6	9.5	6.4
Bangladesh	5.8	8.3	6.2	2.4	(NA)	Netherlands	1.9	2.0	2.2	2.5	4.5
Belgium	1.5	1.0	1.1	2.5	2.5	Nigeria	72.8	10.3	6.6	6.9	(NA)
Bolivia	10.2	7.7	2.2	4.6	1.6	Norway	2.5	2.3	2.3	3.1	3.0
Brazil	66.0	3.2	4.9	7.0	6.9	Pakistan	12.3	6.2	4.1	4.4	(NA)
Canada	2.2	1.0	1.7	2.7	2.5	Peru	11.1	7.2	3.5	3.8	2.0
Chile	8.2	5.1	3.3	3.8	3.6	Philippines	8.0	9.7	6.7	4.3	6.1
Colombia	21.0	20.4	11.2	9.5	8.7	Portugal	4.1	2.8	2.3	2.9	4.4
Egypt	15.7	4.2	3.1	2.7	2.3	Romania	32.2	59.1	45.8	45.7	34.5
France	1.8	0.7	0.5	1.7	1.6	Russia	197.4	27.7	85.7	20.8	21.5
Germany	1.8	0.9	0.6	1.9	2.5	South Africa	8.6	6.9	5.2	5.3	(NA)
Ghana	59.5	14.6	12.4	25.2	32.9	Spain	4.7	1.8	2.3	3.4	3.6
Greece	8.9	4.8	2.6	3.2	3.4	Sri Lanka	7.7	9.4	4.7	6.2	14.2
Guatemala	8.4	7.0	4.9	6.0	7.6	Sweden	2.5	-0.1	0.5	1.0	2.4
India	10.2	13.2	4.7	4.0	3.7	Switzerland	1.8	0.1	0.7	1.6	1.0
Indonesia	9.4	57.6	20.5	3.7	11.5	Thailand	5.8	8.1	0.3	1.5	1.7
Iran	49.6	17.9	20.1	14.5	11.3	Turkey	88.1	84.6	64.9	54.9	54.4
Israel	10.0	5.4	5.2	1.1	(NA)	United Kingdom	3.4	3.4	1.6	2.9	1.8
Italy	5.2	2.0	1.7	2.5	2.8	Venezuela	59.9	35.8	23.6	16.2	12.5

NA Not available.
Source: International Monetary Fund, Washington, DC, *International Financial Statistics*, monthly (copyright).

No. 1327. Comparative Price Levels—Selected OECD Countries: 2002

[**As of May.** Example of data: An item that costs $1.00 in the United States would cost $1.29 (U.S. dollars) in Japan]

Country	United States (U.S. dollar)	Canada (Canadian dollar)	Mexico (new peso)	Japan (yen)	France (franc)	Germany (Deutsche mark)	Italy (lire)	United Kingdom (pound)
United States	**100**	**126**	**130**	**77**	**118**	**118**	**141**	**99**
Australia [1]	75	94	97	58	88	88	105	74
Austria	83	104	107	64	98	98	116	81
Canada	79	100	103	61	94	94	111	78
Denmark	100	127	130	78	119	119	141	99
Finland	99	124	128	76	117	117	139	97
France	85	107	110	65	100	100	119	83
Germany	85	107	110	66	100	100	119	83
Hungary	46	58	59	35	54	54	64	45
Ireland	91	114	118	70	107	107	127	89
Italy	71	90	92	55	84	84	100	70
Japan	129	163	168	100	153	153	182	127
Korea, South	61	77	79	47	72	72	86	60
Mexico	77	97	100	60	91	91	108	76
Netherlands	82	104	106	64	97	97	115	81
New Zealand [1]	64	80	83	49	75	75	89	63
Norway	112	142	146	87	133	133	158	111
Poland	53	67	69	41	63	62	74	52
Portugal	61	77	79	47	72	72	86	60
Spain	69	87	90	54	82	82	97	68
Sweden	97	123	126	75	115	115	137	96
Switzerland	114	144	148	88	135	135	160	112
Turkey	49	62	63	38	58	58	69	48
United Kingdom	101	128	132	79	120	120	143	100

[1] Estimates based on quarterly consumer prices.
Source: Organization for Economic Cooperation and Development, Paris, France, *Main Economic Indicators*, June 2002 (copyright).

No. 1328. Gross Public Debt, Expenditures, and Receipts by Country: 1990 to 2001

[Percent of nominal gross domestic product. 2001 data estimated. Expenditures cover current outlays plus net capital outlays. Receipts cover current receipts but exclude capital receipts. Nontax current receipts include operating surpluses of public enterprises, property income, fees, charges, fines, etc]

Country	Gross debt			Expenditures			Receipts		
	1990	1995	2001	1990	1995	2001	1990	1995	2001
United States [1]	66.6	74.5	54.6	33.6	32.9	29.0	29.3	29.8	31.6
Australia	22.6	42.9	24.3	33.0	35.4	31.0	31.8	31.7	31.7
Austria	56.9	69.1	62.4	48.5	52.4	48.1	46.1	47.3	47.3
Belgium [2]	124.9	129.8	105.4	50.8	50.3	45.8	44.1	46.0	46.1
Canada [2]	93.3	120.6	100.5	46.0	45.3	37.4	40.1	40.0	39.5
Czech Republic	(X)	(NA)	(NA)	(X)	(NA)	47.1	(X)	(NA)	40.6
Denmark.	65.8	73.9	46.2	53.6	56.6	50.6	52.5	54.3	53.5
Finland.	14.3	57.2	39.7	44.4	54.3	43.1	49.6	50.6	48.0
France . . .́	39.5	59.3	63.6	49.6	53.6	49.4	47.4	48.0	49.3
Germany [3]	42.0	57.1	57.8	43.8	46.3	44.5	41.8	43.0	42.8
Greece	89.0	108.7	99.7	47.8	46.6	43.0	31.7	36.4	42.6
Hungary	(NA)	(NA)	(NA)	(NA)	51.2	43.0	(NA)	43.6	39.5
Iceland.	36.7	60.1	33.4	39.0	39.2	38.6	35.8	36.2	41.0
Ireland	92.4	80.0	26.7	39.5	37.6	26.7	36.7	35.4	33.2
Italy . .́	103.7	123.1	108.3	53.1	52.3	47.1	42.1	44.7	46.0
Japan [4]	61.5	76.2	118.6	31.3	35.6	38.3	34.2	32.0	32.3
Korea, South	8.2	6.3	9.7	18.3	19.3	23.4	21.8	23.5	28.1
Netherlands	75.6	75.5	53.1	49.4	47.7	40.1	43.7	43.6	41.1
New Zealand.	(NA)	(NA)	(NA)	48.8	38.8	40.2	44.0	41.9	41.2
Norway.	29.5	35.4	25.6	49.7	47.6	38.8	52.3	51.1	53.7
Portugal	(NA)	64.2	53.8	(NA)	41.2	42.4	(NA)	36.6	41.0
Spain	48.5	71.7	66.5	41.4	44.0	38.2	37.2	37.4	38.4
Sweden	42.7	76.9	48.6	55.8	62.1	53.1	59.8	54.2	56.4
United Kingdom	44.5	61.1	50.7	41.9	44.4	38.8	40.4	38.6	40.9

NA Not available.   X Not applicable.   [1] Includes funded part of central government employee pension liabilities amounting to 8.3 percent of GDP in 1999. Expenditures data includes outlays net of surpluses of public enterprises. Receipts exclude the operating surpluses of public enterprises.   [2] Includes funded government employee pension liabilities amounting to 19 percent of GDP in 1999. This overstates the Canadian debt position relative to countries that have large unfunded liabilities for such pensions which are not counted in those countries' debt figures.   [3] Debt data include accounts of the Inherited Debt Fund from 1995 on. The 1995 outlays are net of the debt taken on this year from the Inherited Debt funds.   [4] Debt data include debt of the Japan Railway Settlement Corporation and the National Forest Special Account from 1998 on. The 1998 expenditures would have risen by 5.4 percentage points of GDP if account were taken of the assumption by the central government of the debt of these two entities.

Source: Organization for Economic Cooperation and Development, Paris, France, *OECD Economic Outlook*, December 2001 (copyright).

No. 1329. Percent Distribution of Tax Receipts by Country: 1980 to 1999

Country	Income and profits taxes [2]				Social security contributions			Taxes on goods and services [5]		
	Total [1]	Total [3]	Individual	Corporate	Total [4]	Employees	Employers	Total [3]	General consumption taxes [6]	Taxes on specific goods, services [7]
United States: 1980	100.0	49.8	39.1	10.8	21.9	9.2	11.9	17.6	7.0	8.3
1990	100.0	45.4	37.7	7.7	25.9	11.0	13.4	17.3	8.0	7.1
1999	100.0	49.1	40.7	8.3	23.9	10.5	12.2	16.4	7.6	6.8
Canada: 1980	100.0	46.6	34.1	11.6	10.5	3.7	6.6	32.6	11.5	13.0
1990	100.0	48.5	40.8	7.0	12.1	4.3	7.5	26.0	14.1	10.3
1999	100.0	48.9	38.1	9.8	13.6	5.3	8.0	24.7	14.3	8.7
France: 1980.	100.0	16.8	11.6	5.1	42.7	11.1	28.4	30.4	21.1	8.4
1990.	100.0	16.1	10.7	5.3	44.1	13.2	27.2	28.4	18.8	8.7
1999.	100.0	24.0	17.6	6.4	36.1	8.8	25.0	26.8	17.3	8.6
Germany: 1980 [8]	100.0	35.1	29.6	5.5	34.3	15.3	18.4	27.1	16.6	9.3
1990	100.0	32.4	27.6	4.8	37.5	16.2	19.1	26.7	16.6	9.2
1999	100.0	29.8	25.1	4.8	39.3	17.3	19.3	28.0	18.4	8.7
Italy: 1980.	100.0	31.1	23.1	7.8	38.0	6.9	28.4	26.5	15.6	9.7
1990	100.0	36.5	26.3	10.0	32.9	6.3	23.6	28.0	14.7	10.6
1999	100.0	34.0	26.4	7.7	28.5	5.5	20.0	27.5	13.7	11.2
Japan: 1980	100.0	46.1	24.3	21.8	29.1	10.2	14.8	16.3	-	14.1
1990	100.0	48.5	26.8	21.6	29.0	11.0	15.0	13.2	4.3	7.3
1999	100.0	31.4	18.5	12.9	37.2	14.4	19.1	20.1	9.6	8.2
Netherlands: 1980	100.0	32.8	26.3	6.6	38.1	15.7	17.8	25.2	15.8	7.3
1990	100.0	32.2	24.7	7.5	37.4	23.1	7.5	26.4	16.5	7.5
1999	100.0	25.3	15.2	10.1	40.0	-	11.6	28.0	16.9	8.7
Sweden: 1980	100.0	43.5	41.0	2.5	28.8	0.1	27.6	24.0	13.4	9.2
1990	100.0	41.6	38.5	3.1	27.2	0.1	26.0	25.0	14.9	9.2
1999	100.0	41.6	35.6	6.0	25.3	5.8	19.1	21.4	13.8	7.0
United Kingdom: 1980. . .	100.0	37.8	29.4	8.4	16.7	6.4	10.1	29.1	14.7	13.3
1990 . . .	100.0	39.5	27.9	11.6	17.2	6.6	10.0	31.1	17.0	12.7
1999 . . .	100.0	39.2	28.8	10.4	17.1	7.3	9.7	32.3	18.8	11.9

- Represents zero.   [1] Includes property taxes, employer payroll taxes other than social security contributions, and miscellaneous taxes, not shown separately.   [2] Includes taxes on capital gains.   [3] Includes other taxes not shown separately.   [4] Includes contributions of self-employed not shown separately.   [5] Taxes on the production, sales, transfer, leasing, and delivery of goods and services and rendering of services.   [6] Primary value-added and sales taxes.   [7] For example, excise taxes on alcohol, tobacco, and gasoline.   [8] Data are for former West Germany.

Source: Organization for Economic Cooperation and Development, Paris, France, *Revenue Statistics of OECD Member Countries*, annual (copyright).

838 Comparative International Statistics

No. 1330. Income Tax and Social Security Contributions as Percent of Labor Costs: 2000

[Data are for single individual at the income level of the average production worker]

Country	Labor costs [1] (dol.)	Percent of labor costs			
		Total [2]	Income tax	Social security contributions	
				Employee	Employer [3]
Belgium	42,216	56	21	11	25
Germany	38,945	52	18	17	17
Switzerland.	36,194	29	9	10	10
Italy.	33,340	47	14	7	25
Netherlands	36,017	45	7	25	14
Denmark.	32,789	44	32	12	-
Canada	32,246	31	19	6	6
Norway.	28,231	37	19	7	11
United States	33,283	31	17	7	7
Luxembourg	32,429	35	11	12	12
Austria	31,025	45	7	14	24
Sweden	31,678	50	19	5	25
Australia	31,731	23	23	-	-
Finland.	31,215	47	21	6	21
United Kingdom.	30,924	30	14	7	9
France	29,421	48	9	9	29
Japan	31,141	24	6	9	9
Ireland	26,234	29	14	5	11
Spain	24,655	38	9	5	23
New Zealand.	25,039	19	19	-	-
Korea, South.	33,730	17	2	6	8
Iceland.	23,720	25	20	-	5
Greece.	18,852	36	2	12	22
Turkey	24,185	40	12	12	16
Czech Republic	17,832	43	8	9	26
Portugal	14,569	34	5	9	19
Poland	14,100	43	5	21	17
Hungary	12,400	52	14	9	29
Mexico	9,291	15	1	1	13

- Represents or rounds to zero.   [1] Adjusted for purchasing power parities, see text of this section. Labor costs include gross wages plus employers compulsory social security contributions.   [2] Due to rounding total may differ one percentage point from aggregate columns for income tax and social security contributions.   [3] Includes reported payroll taxes.

Source: Organization for Economic Cooperation and Development, Paris, France, *Taxing Wages, 2000-2001* (copyright).

No. 1331. Age of Withdrawal From Labor Force and Retirement Duration: 1999

[This table shows the median age at which people completely withdraw from the labor force. For example, half of Canadian men leave the labor force at age 62.4 or before and live another 18.2 years without working. A quarter of Canadian men leave the labor force before the age of 57.8 and another quarter after the age of 66.5.]

Country	First and third quartiles: a quarter of the population				Median age of withdrawal		Duration of complete retirement	
	Withdraws earlier than age		Never withdraws or later than age					
	Men	Women	Men	Women	Men	Women	Men	Women
Nine-country average	58.1	57.2	67.0	65.1	62.3	61.1	17.8	23.0
Canada	57.8	56.8	66.5	65.2	62.4	60.8	18.2	23.5
Finland.	56.0	56.8	63.0	62.5	59.6	59.8	18.9	23.7
Germany [1]	57.4	57.8	63.9	62.4	60.3	60.1	18.8	23.2
Italy	54.5	53.4	63.4	61.9	58.8	57.9	20.7	26.2
Japan	62.7	59.1	77.7	73.2	68.5	64.7	14.9	22.3
Netherlands [1]	57.8	56.9	64.1	62.4	60.4	59.8	18.2	23.2
Sweden	59.9	59.1	66.7	65.3	63.7	62.7	17.5	22.0
United Kingdom	57.8	57.2	66.5	64.5	62.6	60.4	16.8	22.3
United States	59.4	59.0	71.4	68.8	64.6	63.4	16.3	20.4

[1] 1998 data.

Source: Organization for Economic Cooperation and Development, Paris, France, *Ageing and Income, 2001* (copyright).

Comparative International Statistics   839

U.S. Census Bureau, Statistical Abstract of the United States: 2002

No. 1332. Civilian Labor Force, Employment, and Unemployment by Country: 1980 to 2001

[**106,940 represents 106,940,000**. Data based on U.S. labor force definitions (see source) except that minimum age for population base varies as follows: United States, Canada, France, Sweden, and United Kingdom, 16 years; Australia, Japan, Netherlands, Germany, and Italy (beginning 1995), 15 years; and Italy (1980 and 1990) 14 years]

Year	United States	Canada	Australia	Japan	France	Germany [1]	Italy	Netherlands	Sweden	United Kingdom
Civilian labor force (1,000):										
1980	106,940	11,707	6,693	55,740	22,930	27,260	21,120	5,870	4,312	26,520
1990	[2]125,840	14,044	8,440	63,050	24,280	29,410	[2]22,670	[2]6,640	[2]4,597	28,730
1995	[2]132,304	14,517	8,995	65,990	[2]24,830	[2]38,980	[2]22,460	7,260	4,460	28,560
1999	[2]139,368	15,536	9,466	67,090	25,830	39,800	23,130	7,900	4,430	29,300
2000	[2]140,863	15,789	9,678	66,990	25,980	39,750	23,340	8,050	4,489	29,450
2001	141,815	16,027	9,817	[3]66,870	(NA)	(NA)	23,540	(NA)	[3]4,537	(NA)
Labor force participation rate: [4]										
1980	63.8	64.9	62.1	62.6	57.5	54.7	48.2	55.4	66.9	62.5
1990	[2]66.5	67.3	64.7	62.6	55.9	55.3	[2]47.2	[2]56.1	[2]67.4	64.1
1995	[2]66.6	64.9	64.6	62.9	[2]55.6	[2]57.1	[2]47.1	59.2	64.1	62.7
1999	[2]67.1	65.8	64.2	62.4	56.4	57.6	47.8	62.8	62.8	63.2
2000	[2]67.2	65.9	64.7	62.0	56.4	57.5	48.1	63.5	63.8	63.3
2001	66.9	66.0	64.7	[3]61.6	(NA)	(NA)	(NA)	(NA)	[3]64.2	(NA)
Civilian employment (1,000):										
1980	99,303	10,857	6,284	54,600	21,440	26,490	20,200	5,520	4,226	24,670
1990	[2]118,793	12,961	7,877	61,710	22,080	27,950	[2]21,080	[2]6,230	[2]4,513	26,740
1995	[2]124,900	13,271	8,256	63,890	21,910	[3]35,780	[2]19,820	6,760	4,056	26,070
1999	[2]133,488	14,456	8,808	63,920	22,940	36,360	20,460	7,640	4,117	27,530
2000	[2]135,208	14,827	9,068	63,790	23,530	36,540	20,840	7,810	4,229	27,830
2001	135,073	14,997	9,154	[3]63,470	(NA)	(NA)	[3]21,280	(NA)	4,309	(NA)
Employment-population ratio: [5]										
1980	59.2	60.2	58.3	61.3	53.8	53.1	46.1	52.1	65.6	58.1
1990	[2]62.8	62.2	60.4	61.3	50.9	52.6	[2]43.9	[2]52.6	[2]66.1	59.6
1995	[2]62.9	59.4	59.2	60.9	49.0	[2]52.4	[2]41.5	55.1	58.3	57.2
1999	[2]64.3	61.3	59.8	59.4	50.1	52.6	42.3	60.8	58.4	59.4
2000	[2]64.5	62.1	60.6	59.0	51.1	52.8	42.9	61.6	60.1	59.8
2001	63.8	61.9	60.3	[3]58.4	(NA)	(NA)	(NA)	(NA)	[3]61.0	(NA)
Unemployment rate:										
1980	7.1	7.3	6.1	2.0	6.5	2.8	4.4	6.0	2.0	7.0
1990	[2]5.6	7.7	6.7	2.1	9.1	5.0	[2]7.0	[2]6.2	[2]1.8	6.9
1995	[2]5.6	8.6	8.2	3.2	[2]11.8	[2]8.2	[2]11.8	6.9	9.1	8.7
1999	[2]4.2	7.0	7.0	4.7	11.2	8.6	11.5	3.4	7.1	6.0
2000	[2]4.0	6.1	6.3	4.8	9.4	8.1	10.7	3.0	5.8	5.5
2001	4.8	6.4	6.7	[3]5.1	[3]8.7	[3]8.0	[3]9.6	(NA)	[3]5.0	(NA)
Under 25 years old	10.6	11.8	(NA)	(NA)	(NA)	(NA)	(NA)	(NA)	(NA)	10.5
Teenagers [6]	14.7	15.4	(NA)	(NA)	(NA)	(NA)	(NA)	(NA)	(NA)	(NA)
20 to 24 years old	8.3	9.6	(NA)	(NA)	(NA)	(NA)	(NA)	(NA)	(NA)	(NA)
25 years old and over	3.7	5.4	(NA)	(NA)	(NA)	(NA)	(NA)	(NA)	(NA)	3.8

NA Not available. [1] Unified Germany for 1991 onward. Prior to 1991, data relate to the former West Germany. [2] Break in series. Data not comparable with prior years. [3] Preliminary. [4] Civilian labor force as a percent of the civilian working age population. Germany and Japan include the institutionalized population as part of the working age population. [5] Civilian employment as a percent of the civilian working age population. Germany and Japan include the institutionalized population as part of the working age population. [6] 16-to 19-year-olds in the United States, Canada, France, Sweden, and the United Kingdom; 15-to 19-year-olds in Australia, Japan, Germany, and Italy.

Source: U.S. Bureau of Labor Statistics, *Comparative Civilian Labor Force Statistics, Ten Countries, 1959-2001*, March 2002, and *Monthly Labor Review*.

No. 1333. Percent of Persons 15 to 24 Years Old Not in Education or at Work by Age Group and Sex: 1999

[Represents those persons not in education and either unemployed or not in the labor force]

Country	15 to 19 years old			20 to 24 years old		
	Total	Male	Female	Total	Male	Female
Australia	7.4	7.3	7.5	14.5	10.9	18.3
Belgium	7.0	7.5	6.4	15.9	14.7	17.1
Canada	6.9	7.7	6.0	11.7	10.8	12.7
Czech Republic	20.9	21.8	20.0	20.6	12.5	29.0
Denmark	3.4	4.2	2.6	7.6	6.1	8.9
Finland	8.7	12.2	5.2	16.9	17.8	15.9
France	3.3	3.5	3.1	17.5	15.9	19.1
Germany	4.5	4.2	4.9	16.7	14.5	19.0
Greece	10.1	8.0	12.1	25.7	17.1	33.5
Hungary	10.2	9.7	10.8	21.4	16.8	26.1
Italy	14.8	14.1	15.6	29.9	27.4	32.4
Luxembourg	5.0	3.6	6.3	9.6	6.9	12.5
Mexico	17.9	6.2	29.3	26.2	5.1	45.5
Netherlands	3.8	3.6	4.0	8.0	5.7	10.4
Poland	4.6	5.2	3.9	27.2	23.4	30.8
Portugal	8.4	6.9	9.8	12.3	8.8	15.7
Spain	13.8	15.6	12.0	18.8	17.3	20.5
Sweden	4.8	6.3	3.3	11.4	11.7	11.1
Switzerland	[1]6.0	8.0	7.1	8.4	7.4	9.4
United States [2]	7.3	6.5	8.2	14.4	9.7	19.0

[1] Represents only those not in education and not in labor force. [2] Data for 1998.
Source: Organization for Economic Cooperation and Development, Paris, France, *Education at a Glance 2001* (copyright).

No. 1334. Unemployment Rates by Country: 1995 to 2001

[**Annual averages.** The standardized unemployment rates shown here are calculated as the number of unemployed persons as a percentage of the civilian labor force. The unemployed are persons of working age who, in the reference period, are without work, available for work and have taken specific steps to find work]

Country	1995	1999	2000	2001	Country	1995	1999	2000	2001
OECD, total	**7.5**	**6.8**	**6.3**	**6.5**	Ireland	12.3	5.6	4.2	3.8
European Union [1] . .	10.7	9.0	8.1	7.6	Italy	11.9	11.2	10.4	9.5
					Japan.	3.1	4.7	4.7	5.0
United States.	5.6	4.2	4.0	4.8	Korea, South	(NA)	(NA)	4.3	3.9
Australia	8.6	7.0	6.3	6.7	Luxembourg	2.9	2.4	2.4	2.4
Austria	3.9	4.0	3.7	3.6	Netherlands.	6.9	3.2	2.8	2.4
Belgium	9.9	8.6	6.9	6.6	New Zealand	6.3	6.8	6.0	5.3
Canada.	9.5	7.6	6.8	7.2	Norway.	5.0	3.2	3.5	3.6
Czech Republic . . .	(NA)	8.8	8.9	8.2	Poland	(NA)	(NA)	16.1	18.2
Denmark.	7.2	4.8	4.4	4.3	Portugal	7.3	4.5	4.1	4.1
Finland	16.2	10.2	9.7	9.1	Spain	22.9	15.8	14.0	13.0
France	11.7	10.7	9.3	8.6	Sweden	8.8	7.2	5.9	5.1
Germany.	8.2	8.6	7.9	7.9	Switzerland	3.5	3.0	2.6	(NA)
Hungary.	(NA)	7.1	6.5	5.8	United Kingdom . . .	8.7	5.9	5.4	5.0

NA Not available.   [1] See footnote 4, Table 1320.

Source: Organization for Economic Cooperation and Development, Paris, France, *Main Economic Indicators*, April 2002 and earlier releases.

No. 1335. Female Labor Force Participation Rates by Country: 1980 to 1999

[**In percent**. Female labor force of all ages divided by female population 15-64 years old]

Country	1980	1990	1995	1999	Country	1980	1990	1995	1999
Australia	52.7	62.9	64.8	64.4	Korea, South	(NA)	51.3	53.2	53.1
Austria.	48.7	55.4	62.3	62.2	Luxembourg	39.9	50.7	58.0	64.6
Belgium	47.0	52.4	56.1	57.8	Mexico	33.7	23.6	40.1	42.1
Canada	57.8	67.8	67.6	69.6	Netherlands	35.5	[1]53.1	[1]59.0	64.5
Czech Republic.	(X)	69.1	[1]65.4	64.9	New Zealand	44.6	[1]62.9	63.3	67.7
Denmark	(NA)	78.5	73.6	75.8	Norway	62.3	71.2	72.4	76.3
Finland	70.1	72.9	70.3	71.3	Poland.	(NA)	(NA)	61.1	59.0
France.	54.4	57.6	59.4	60.8	Portugal.	54.3	62.9	62.4	66.8
Germany [2]	52.8	57.4	61.7	62.8	Spain	32.2	41.2	45.1	48.9
Greece	33.0	43.6	45.9	49.0	Sweden	74.1	[1]80.5	76.1	74.6
Hungary.	(NA)	(NA)	50.5	52.1	Switzerland	54.1	59.6	[1]67.8	70.3
Iceland	(NA)	65.6	81.9	83.1	Turkey.	(NA)	36.7	34.2	34.0
Ireland.	36.3	38.9	47.8	54.9	United Kingdom	58.3	65.5	66.6	67.5
Italy	39.6	45.9	[1]43.3	46.0	**United States. . . . .**	**59.7**	**[1]68.8**	**70.7**	**71.7**
Japan	54.8	60.4	62.2	63.8					

NA Not available.   X Not applicable.   [1] Break in series. Data not comparable with prior years.   [2] Prior to 1991 data are for former West Germany.

Source: Organization for Economic Cooperation and Development, Paris, France, *OECD in Figures*, annual (copyright).

No. 1336. Civilian Employment-Population Ratio: 1980 to 2001

[Civilian employment as a percent of the civilian working age population. See headnote, Table 1332]

Country	Women					Men				
	1980	1990	1995	2000	2001	1980	1990	1995	2000	2001
United States . .	**51.5**	**[1]57.5**	**58.9**	**[1]60.2**	**60.1**	**77.4**	**[1]76.4**	**75.0**	**[1]74.7**	**74.4**
Canada	50.8	58.4	57.3	59.4	59.5	79.4	76.6	72.8	72.7	72.6
Australia	45.5	53.2	54.7	56.0	[2]56.4	79.1	76.4	74.7	73.4	[2]73.1
Japan	46.6	49.1	49.3	48.6	[2]48.5	79.6	77.0	77.5	76.2	[2]75.5
France	44.5	47.0	48.0	49.6	(NA)	72.0	66.0	63.9	64.0	(NA)
Germany [3]	40.3	[1]43.6	47.1	48.7	(NA)	71.3	68.4	68.1	66.9	(NA)
Italy	30.1	[1]32.7	33.4	35.7	(NA)	67.9	63.0	62.1	61.6	(NA)
Netherlands . . .	34.3	42.9	48.3	53.8	(NA)	77.4	69.8	70.4	73.5	(NA)
Sweden	59.3	63.0	59.5	59.3	(NA)	74.9	72.0	68.9	68.6	(NA)
United Kingdom .	47.8	53.2	53.5	55.3	(NA)	78.7	75.9	72.4	71.8	(NA)

NA Not available.   [1] Break in series. Data not comparable with previous years.   [2] Preliminary.   [3] Unified Germany for 1991 onward. Prior to 1991, data relate to the former West Germany.

Source: U.S. Bureau of Labor Statistics, *Comparative Civilian Labor Force Statistics, Ten Countries, 1959-2001*, March 2002, and *Monthly Labor Review*.

Comparative International Statistics   841

No. 1337. Civilian Employment by Industry and Country: 1990 and 2001

[118,793 represents 118,793,000. Data based on U.S. labor force definitions except that minimum age for population base varies as follows: United States, Canada, France, Sweden, and United Kingdom, 16 years; Australia, Germany, Italy, Japan, 15 years; and Italy (1990), 14 years. Industries based on International Standard Industrial Classification; see text of this section]

Industry	United States	Canada	Australia	Japan	France	Germany [1]	Italy	Sweden	United Kingdom
TOTAL EMPLOYMENT (1,000)									
1990, total	118,793	13,084	7,877	61,710	22,082	27,952	21,080	4,501	26,818
Agriculture, forestry, fishing [2] . . .	3,394	559	441	4,270	1,262	965	1,879	178	573
Industry [3]	29,834	3,063	1,879	20,890	6,403	10,875	6,842	1,268	8,128
Manufacturing	21,346	2,053	1,184	15,010	(NA)	8,839	4,755	943	[4]5,971
Services [5]	85,565	9,462	5,557	36,550	14,417	16,112	12,355	3,056	18,117
2001, total	135,073	15,077	9,157	[6]63,790	[6]23,531	[6][7]36,541	[6]20,843	[6]4,217	[6]27,677
Agriculture, forestry, fishing [2] . . .	3,277	435	435	[6]3,080	[6]931	[6][7]1,036	[6]1,113	[6]122	[6]426
Industry [3]	29,118	3,305	1,873	[6]19,710	[6]5,547	[6][7]12,270	[6]6,761	[6]999	[6]6,855
Manufacturing	18,970	2,274	1,113	[6]13,180	[6](NA)	[6][7]8,796	[6]5,144	[6]761	[6]4,753
Services [5]	102,678	11,337	6,849	[6]41,000	[6][7]17,053	[6][7]23,235	[6]12,970	[6]3,096	[6]20,396
PERCENT DISTRIBUTION									
1990, total	100.0	100.0	100.0	100.0	100.0	100.0	100.0	100.0	100.0
Agriculture, forestry, fishing [2] . . .	2.9	4.3	5.6	6.9	5.7	3.5	8.9	4.0	2.1
Industry [3]	25.1	23.4	23.9	33.9	29.0	38.9	32.5	28.2	30.3
Manufacturing	18.0	15.7	15.0	24.3	(NA)	31.6	22.6	20.9	[4]22.3
Services [5]	72.0	72.3	70.5	59.2	65.3	57.6	58.6	67.9	67.6
2001, total	100.0	100.0	100.0	100.0	100.0	100.0	100.0	100.0	100.0
Agriculture, forestry, fishing [2] . . .	2.4	2.9	4.8	[6]4.8	[6]4.0	[6][7]2.8	[6]5.3	[6]2.9	[6]1.5
Industry [3]	21.6	21.9	20.5	[6]30.9	[6][7]23.6	[6][7]33.6	[6]32.4	[6]23.7	[6]24.8
Manufacturing	14.0	15.1	12.2	[6]20.7	[6](NA)	[6][7]24.1	[6]24.7	[6]18.1	[6]17.2
Services [5]	76.0	75.2	74.8	[6]64.3	[6][7]72.5	[6][7]63.6	[6]62.2	[6]73.4	[6]73.7

NA Not available.   [1] Data for 1990 are for former West Germany (prior to unification); data for 2001 are for unified Germany.   [2] Includes hunting.   [3] Includes mining and construction.   [4] Includes mining.   [5] Transportation, communication, public utilities, trade, finance, public administration, private household services, and miscellaneous services.   [6] 2000 data.   [7] Preliminary.

Source: U.S. Bureau of Labor Statistics, *Comparative Civilian Labor Force Statistics, Ten Countries, 1959-2001*, March 2002 and unpublished data.

No. 1338. World Food Production by Commodity: 1990 to 2001

[In millions of metric tons (1,768.8 represents 1,768,800,000)]

Commodity	1990	1994	1995	1996	1997	1998	1999	2000	2001
Grains, total	1,768.8	1,712.8	1,759.8	1,717.8	1,870.7	1,880.0	1,871.8	1,871.1	1,836.6
Wheat.	588.0	524.0	538.4	581.9	609.2	588.7	585.9	582.3	577.0
Coarse grains.	828.7	871.3	802.9	908.5	883.9	889.0	876.5	856.9	873.2
Corn	482.3	560.3	517.4	592.2	575.2	605.6	606.8	585.0	589.5
Rice, milled	352.0	364.5	371.5	380.3	386.9	394.1	408.7	397.4	395.3
Oils	58.1	70.0	72.8	75.6	76.2	80.6	80.6	85.9	89.0
Soybeans	104.1	137.7	124.9	132.2	158.1	159.8	159.9	175.2	184.8
Rapeseed	25.1	30.3	34.4	31.5	33.2	35.9	42.5	37.5	35.9
Pulses [1]	58.3	56.0	55.6	54.0	55.0	56.2	57.1	54.6	52.4
Vegetables and melons [1]	461.6	531.8	559.8	593.6	608.1	631.0	667.6	691.9	698.1
Fruits [1]	352.6	393.8	407.0	425.5	442.5	433.8	457.8	466.4	466.3
Nuts [1]	4.6	5.6	5.4	5.8	6.2	6.3	6.6	6.8	7.0
Beef and pork	117.2	116.7	122.1	116.6	122.1	127.1	130.3	131.1	138.9
Poultry	37.4	43.2	47.5	50.4	53.7	54.6	57.7	59.7	61.9
Milk	441.3	(NA)	(NA)	364.4	365.6	368.4	372.0	375.9	376.3

NA Not available.   [1] Data from Food and Agriculture Organization of the United Nations, Rome, Italy.
Source: U.S. Dept. of Agriculture, Economic Research Service, *Agricultural Outlook*, monthly.

No. 1339. Fisheries—Commercial Catch by Country: 1990 to 1999

[In thousands of metric tons, live weight (97,854 represents 97,854,000). Catch of fish, crustaceans, mollusks (including weight of shells). Does not include marine mammals and aquatic plants]

Country	1990	1995	1998	1999	Country	1990	1995	1998	1999
World [1]	97,854	116,042	117,727	126,177	Thailand	2,786	3,573	3,507	3,607
					Norway	1,745	2,803	3,259	3,086
China [2]	12,095	28,418	38,025	40,030	Korea, South	1,745	2,688	2,354	2,423
Japan	10,354	6,787	6,030	5,936	Philippines	2,210	2,222	2,146	2,199
India.	3,794	4,906	5,245	5,352	Iceland	1,508	1,616	1,686	1,740
United States	5,868	5,638	5,154	5,228	Vietnam	960	1,394	1,653	1,795
Russia	7,808	4,374	4,518	4,210	Denmark	1,518	2,044	1,600	1,448
Indonesia	3,044	4,139	4,595	4,797	Bangladesh	848	1,170	1,354	1,544
Peru.	6,875	8,943	4,346	8,400	Spain	1,380	1,391	1,529	1,485
Chile	5,195	7,591	3,558	5,325	Mexico	1,401	1,355	1,216	1,251

[1] Includes other countries, not shown separately.   [2] See footnote 2, Table 1308.

Source: U.S. National Oceanic and Atmospheric Administration, National Marine Fisheries Service, *Fisheries of the United States*, annual. Data from Food and Agriculture Organization of the United Nations, Rome, Italy.

No. 1340. Meat Production by Type and Country: 1998 to 2000

[In thousand metric tons (48,604 represents 48,604,000). Carcass weight basis for beef, veal, and pork. Excludes offals and rabbit]

Country	Beef and veal 1998	Beef and veal 1999, prel.	Country	Pork [1] 1998	Pork [1] 1999, prel.	Country	Poultry meat 1999	Poultry meat 2000, prel.
World [2]	48,604	49,342	World [2]	78,940	81,240	World [2]	56,504	58,010
United States	11,804	12,124	China [3]	38,837	40,056	United States	15,990	16,422
Brazil [3]	6,140	6,270	United States	8,623	8,758	China [3]	11,150	11,350
China [3]	4,799	5,054	Germany	3,833	4,113	Brazil	5,641	5,987
Argentina	2,600	2,840	Spain	2,667	2,892	France	2,228	2,240
Australia	1,989	1,956	France	2,328	2,378	Mexico	1,922	2,036
Russia	2,090	1,900	Brazil	1,690	1,835	United Kingdom	1,516	1,535
Mexico	1,800	1,860	Poland	1,690	1,730	Japan	1,189	1,170
India	1,593	1,660	Netherlands	1,717	1,711	South Africa	1,121	1,150
France	1,593	1,568	Denmark	1,632	1,650	Thailand	1,025	1,117
Germany	1,367	1,374	Canada	1,338	1,562	Italy	1,135	1,098

[1] Includes edible pork fat, but excludes lard and inedible greases (except United States). [2] Includes other countries, not shown separately. [3] See footnote 2, Table 1308.

Source: U.S. Dept. of Agriculture, National Agricultural Statistics Service, *Agricultural Statistics*, annual.

No. 1341. Meat Consumption by Type and Country: 2000 and 2001

[In thousand metric tons (12,503 represents 12,503,000). Carcass weight basis for beef, veal, and pork. Broiler (chicken 16 week-old) weight based on ready to cook equivalent.]

Country	Beef and veal 2000	Beef and veal 2001 [1]	Country	Pork 2000	Pork 2001 [1]	Country	Poultry meat 2000	Poultry meat 2001 [1]
United States	12,503	12,349	China [2]	40,291	42,325	United States	11,259	11,229
European Union [3]	7,300	6,740	European Union [3]	16,168	16,346	European Union [3]	6,080	6,473
Brazil	6,090	6,190	United States	8,457	8,391	China [2]	5,539	5,611
China [2]	5,291	5,558	Japan	2,228	2,269	Brazil	5,044	5,288
Argentina	2,540	2,475	Russia	2,007	2,079	Mexico	2,155	2,224
Russia	2,308	2,437	Brazil	1,827	1,898	Japan	1,788	1,795
Mexico	2,309	2,341	Poland	1,544	1,476	Russia	1,324	1,705
India	1,400	1,395	Mexico	1,252	1,298	Canada	891	920
Japan	1,534	1,381	South Korea	1,057	1,144	Thailand	730	810
Canada	992	961	Canada	1,047	1,082	South Korea	458	486
South Africa	671	676	Philippines	1,026	1,075	Poland	375	400
Colombia	669	672	Taiwan	975	925	Hong Kong [2]	297	299

[1] Preliminary data. [2] Hong Kong & China data series has been revised to more accurately reflect actual demand and not just transshipments. [3] See footnote 3, Table 1320.

Source: U.S. Department of Agriculture, Foreign Agricultural Service, *Livestock and Poultry: World Markets and Trade*, annual. <http://www.fas.usda.gov/dlp/circular/2002/02-03l P/dlp102.pdf>.

No. 1342. Wheat, Rice, and Corn Production by Country: 1995 to 2001

[In thousands of metric tons (538,410 represents 538,410,000). Rice data cover paddy. Data for each country pertain to the calendar year in which all or most of the crop was harvested. See text of this section for general comments concerning quality of the data]

Country	Wheat 1995	Wheat 2000	Wheat 2001	Rice 1995	Rice 2000	Rice 2001	Corn 1995	Corn 2000	Corn 2001
World	538,410	583,727	580,323	551,363	591,865	588,900	517,406	585,049	589,452
Argentina	8,600	16,230	15,500	877	846	631	11,100	15,400	12,800
Australia	16,504	23,766	24,000	966	1,761	1,250	311	355	460
Bangladesh	1,245	1,673	1,750	26,533	37,633	38,254	-	-	-
Brazil	1,526	1,660	3,000	10,026	10,385	11,000	32,480	41,536	36,000
Burma	150	100	100	17,000	18,571	17,000	270	353	375
Canada	25,037	26,804	21,300	-	9	-	7,271	6,827	8,200
China [1]	102,215	99,640	94,000	185,214	187,909	180,000	112,000	106,000	110,000
Egypt	5,700	6,350	6,230	4,399	6,100	5,500	5,353	5,636	6,160
France	30,862	37,560	31,500	124	107	103	12,394	16,227	16,100
Germany	17,763	21,622	22,899	-	-	-	2,395	3,324	3,470
India	65,470	76,369	68,763	119,442	127,319	133,513	9,530	12,068	11,500
Indonesia	-	-	-	51,100	51,899	52,389	6,000	5,500	6,000
Italy	7,653	7,282	6,308	1,311	1,240	1,273	8,454	10,137	10,367
Mexico	3,468	3,300	3,250	349	322	277	17,780	17,700	19,000
Pakistan	17,002	21,079	19,023	5,951	7,051	5,611	1,283	1,250	1,250
Russia	30,100	34,450	46,900	462	585	497	1,700	1,550	800
Thailand	-	-	-	21,800	25,608	25,000	3,700	4,700	4,400
Turkey	15,500	18,000	15,500	346	354	320	1,800	2,100	2,000
United Kingdom	14,310	16,700	11,570	-	-	-	-	-	-
United States	59,404	60,758	53,278	7,887	8,658	9,663	187,970	251,854	241,485

- Represents or rounds to zero. [1] See footnote 2, Table 1308.

Source: U.S. Department of Agriculture, Economic Research Service, unpublished data from the PS&D (Production, supply and distribution) database.

U.S. Census Bureau, Statistical Abstract of the United States: 2002

No. 1343. Wheat, Rice, and Corn—Exports and Imports of Leading Countries: 1995 to 2001

[In thousands of metric tons (32,003 represents 32,003,000). Wheat data are for trade year beginning in July of year shown; rice data are for calendar year; corn data are for trade year beginning in October of year shown. Countries listed are the ten leading exporters or importers in 2001]

Leading exporters	Exports			Leading importers	Imports		
	1995	2000	2001		1995	2000	2001
WHEAT				WHEAT			
European Union [1]	32,003	38,808	31,800	European Union [1]	21,505	26,716	29,825
United States	33,778	28,866	26,535	Brazil	5,600	7,289	6,500
Australia	13,311	15,930	18,500	Iran	3,029	6,284	6,000
Canada	16,342	17,316	16,000	Egypt	5,932	6,050	5,800
Argentina	4,483	11,272	10,800	Japan	6,101	5,911	5,800
Ukraine	1,343	78	5,000	Algeria	3,782	5,600	4,500
Kazakhstan	4,279	3,668	3,500	Indonesia	3,632	4,068	4,000
India	1,500	1,569	3,000	Philippines	1,980	3,050	3,300
Russia	206	696	2,500	Iraq	515	3,300	3,300
Hungary	2,239	988	2,000	Mexico	1,581	3,066	3,200
RICE				RICE			
Thailand	5,281	7,521	7,250	Indonesia	1,081	1,500	2,500
Vietnam	3,040	3,528	3,500	European Union [1]	1,680	1,828	1,808
United States	2,694	2,690	2,714	Nigeria	300	1,250	1,800
Pakistan	1,632	2,429	1,250	Iran	1,574	1,000	1,250
China [2]	265	1,859	1,500	Iraq	234	1,000	1,000
India	3,700	1,600	3,250	Saudi Arabia	618	992	970
European Union [1]	902	1,390	1,368	Senegal	500	502	850
Egypt	338	705	700	Japan	451	730	700
Burma	265	668	800	Philippines	975	1,410	650
Australia	550	610	575	Brazil	770	730	625
CORN				CORN			
United States	56,589	49,156	48,897	Japan	15,976	16,340	15,300
European Union [1]	7,480	8,898	9,417	European Union [1]	10,420	11,338	11,825
Argentina	7,494	10,000	8,250	Korea, South	8,963	8,743	7,500
China [2]	168	7,276	4,000	Mexico	6,433	5,929	5,500
Hungary	120	730	2,500	Egypt	2,257	5,268	5,200
Brazil	218	6,400	1,600	Taiwan [2]	5,734	4,902	4,700
South Africa	2,650	1,500	1,300	Canada	855	2,538	3,300
Canada	642	107	300	Malaysia	2,309	2,481	2,200
Ukraine	58	395	300	Colombia	1,430	1,857	1,800
Paraguay	124	351	300	Algeria	488	1,600	1,650

[1] See footnote 3, Table 1320.   [2] See footnote 2, Table 1308.

Source: U.S. Department of Agriculture, Economic Research Service, unpublished data from the PS&D (Production, supply and distribution) database.

No. 1344. Unmanufactured Tobacco and Cigarettes—Selected Countries: 1995 to 2001

[5,546 represents 5,546,000. Tobacco is on dry weight basis]

Country	Unmanufactured tobacco (1,000 metric tons)			Country	Cigarettes (bil. pieces)		
	1995	2000	2001		1995	2000	2001
PRODUCTION				PRODUCTION			
World, total	5,546	5,896	5,690	World, total	5,599	5,576	5,542
China [1]	2,083	2,162	2,200	China [1]	1,735	1,699	1,685
India	528	599	530	United States	746	595	577
Brazil	324	493	455	Russia	141	310	315
United States	513	408	367	Japan	263	258	256
Zimbabwe	179	211	172	Indonesia	186	232	230
				United Kingdom	156	150	150
EXPORTS				Turkey	100	128	129
World, total	1,767	1,966	1,974				
Brazil	256	342	355	EXPORTS			
Zimbabwe	174	182	185	World, total	987	851	851
United States	209	183	185	United States	231	148	135
Malawi	99	101	101	United Kingdom	85	111	120
Greece	133	101	101	Netherlands	82	106	103
				Germany	85	91	91
IMPORTS				Singapore	50	59	59
World, total	1,781	1,973	1,983	Hong Kong	74	28	29
Russia	148	285	300	Indonesia	21	16	14
Germany	210	263	263	China [1]	63	13	13
United States	199	197	215				
United Kingdom	141	108	104	IMPORTS			
Japan	115	94	92	World, total	668	685	695
				Japan	72	83	84
CONSUMPTION				France	61	68	68
World, total	6,305	6,301	6,315	Singapore	38	49	49
China [1]	2,209	2,196	2,524	Italy	39	56	57
India	464	474	470	United Kingdom	20	45	54
United States	699	436	434	Hong Kong	59	24	45
Russia	142	301	302	Russia	78	20	15
Japan	197	169	174				

[1] See footnote 2, Table 1308.

Source: U.S. Dept. of Agriculture, Foreign Agricultural Service, *Tobacco: World Markets and Trade*, April 2002.

No. 1345. Wood Products—Production, Exports, and Consumption for Selected Countries: 1990 to 2001

[In thousand cubic meters (5,830 represents 5,830,000)]

Country	Production 1990	Production 2000	Production 2001	Exports 1990	Exports 2000	Exports 2001	Consumption 1990	Consumption 2000	Consumption 2001
SOFTWOOD LOGS									
Australia	5,830	12,475	11,400	-	988	900	5,830	11,488	10,501
Canada	122,000	163,000	157,000	800	2,595	2,800	125,289	164,926	158,800
China [1]	69,080	29,891	25,715	8	1	1	72,836	36,288	33,456
Finland	19,600	29,000	29,000	161	700	700	19,734	31,800	31,800
France [2]	14,189	17,000	18,000	477	900	800	13,969	16,210	17,320
Germany [2]	(NA)	31,653	17,000	1,947	4,083	3,200	(NA)	30,523	16,800
Japan	16,775	14,520	14,000	11	2	2	33,446	26,758	25,998
New Zealand	8,361	15,500	16,000	2,931	6,897	6,975	5,435	8,607	9,029
Russia	(NA)	64,000	64,000	(NA)	20,000	20,000	(NA)	44,000	44,000
Sweden	24,700	30,200	30,000	336	1,397	1,500	24,787	35,952	36,000
SOFTWOOD LUMBER									
Canada	53,777	68,557	66,500	37,008	48,607	46,600	17,767	20,719	20,500
China [1]	17,650	3,997	3,397	15	88	132	17,733	4,377	3,803
Finland	7,400	11,750	11,750	4,152	8,500	8,500	3,261	3,400	3,400
Germany [2]	12,145	15,010	14,600	839	3,202	3,300	15,551	17,108	15,600
Japan	26,551	16,403	16,000	7	2	2	33,854	25,208	24,698
Russia	(NA)	14,000	14,000	(NA)	4,500	4,350	(NA)	9,500	9,650
Sweden	11,785	14,839	15,000	6,500	11,188	11,200	5,431	3,832	4,000
TEMPERATE HARDWOOD LOGS									
China [1]	42,340	13,187	12,660	83	20	12	42,286	17,970	17,931
France	10,157	9,500	9,000	1,655	1,600	1,400	8,621	8,275	7,985
Russia	(NA)	22,300	23,000	(NA)	8,580	9,200	(NA)	13,720	13,800
TEMPERATE HARDWOOD LUMBER									
China [1]	10,819	2,217	1,995	65	332	335	10,755	4,400	4,376
France	3,303	3,000	3,000	646	820	800	2,767	2,530	2,550
Russia	(NA)	4,700	4,650	(NA)	320	360	(NA)	4,380	4,290
TROPICAL HARDWOOD LOGS									
Brazil	33,000	27,850	28,270	(NA)	236	130	33,146	27,986	28,320
Indonesia	27,000	25,500	26,500	-	-	-	27,068	25,500	26,500
Malaysia	39,655	23,074	21,000	20,378	6,804	6,000	19,286	16,852	16,000
TROPICAL HARDWOOD LUMBER									
Brazil	8,500	14,400	14,800	525	901	950	8,252	13,656	13,990
Indonesia	9,000	6,600	6,400	561	(NA)	(NA)	8,439	6,600	6,400
Malaysia	8,780	5,589	5,200	5,247	2,901	2,600	3,568	3,973	4,200

- Represents zero.   NA Not available.   [1] See footnote 2, Table 1308.   [2] Data for 1990 do not include East Germany.
Source: U.S. Dept. of Agriculture, Foreign Agricultural Service, *Wood Products: International Trade and Foreign Markets, Biennial Production, Consumption, and Trade Edition*, Circular Series WP-1-01, March 2002.

No. 1346. World Production of Major Mineral Commodities: 1990 to 2000

[5,386 represents 5,386,000,000]

Country	Unit	1990	1995	1999	2000, prel.	Leading producers, 1999
MINERAL FUELS						
Coal	Mil. short tons	5,386	5,218	5,053	5,059	China, United States, India
Dry natural gas	Tril. cu. ft.	73.6	78.0	84.9	88.0	Russia, United States, Canada
Natural gas plant liquids [1]	Mil. barrels [2]	1,691	2,005	2,187	2,279	United States, Saudi Arabia, Canada
Petroleum, crude	Mil. barrels [2]	22,107	22,752	24,035	24,858	Saudi Arabia, Russia, United States
NONMETALLIC MINERALS						
Cement, hydraulic	Mil. metric tons	1,160	1,444	1,600	1,700	China, India, United States
Diamond, gem and industrial	Mil. carats	111	113	117	(NA)	(NA)
Nitrogen in ammonia	Mil. metric tons	97.5	100.0	108.0	104.0	China, United States, India
Phosphate rock	Mil. metric tons	162	130	141	139	United States, China, Morocco
Potash, marketable	Mil. metric tons	27.5	24.6	25.7	26.5	Canada, Russia, Belarus
Salt	Mil. metric tons	183	192	209	210	United States, China, Germany
Sulfur, elemental basis	Mil. metric tons	57.8	53.2	57.1	57.4	United States, Canada, China
METALS						
Aluminum [3]	Mil. metric tons	19.3	19.7	23.1	23.9	United States, Russia, China
Bauxite, gross weight	Mil. metric tons	113.0	112.0	127.0	127.0	Australia, Guinea, Brazil
Chromite, gross weight [1]	1,000 metric tons	13,200	14,300	13,500	13,700	South Africa, Kazakhstan, Turkey
Copper, metal content [4]	1,000 metric tons	8,950	10,100	12,600	12,900	Chile, United States, Indonesia
Gold, metal content	Metric tons	2,180	2,210	2,540	2,445	South Africa, United States, Australia
Iron ore, gross weight [5]	Mil. metric tons	983	1,031	994	1,010	China, Brazil, Australia
Lead, metal content [4]	1,000 metric tons	3,370	2,820	3,020	2,980	Australia, United States, China
Nickel, metal content [4]	1,000 metric tons	974	1,030	1,120	1,230	Russia, Canada, Australia
Tin, metal content [4]	1,000 metric tons	221	193	198	200	China, Indonesia, Peru
Zinc, metal content [4]	1,000 metric tons	7,150	7,280	8,040	8,000	China, Australia, Canada

NA Not available.   [1] Excludes China.   [2] 42-gallon barrels.   [3] Unalloyed ingot metal.   [4] Mine output.   [5] Includes iron ore concentrates and iron ore agglomerates.
Source: Mineral fuels, U.S. Energy Information Administration, *International Energy Annual*; nonmetallic minerals and metals, 1990, U.S. Bureau of Mines, thereafter, U.S. Geological Survey, *Minerals Yearbook; Annual Reports;* and *Mineral Commodity Summaries, 2000.*

No. 1347. World Primary Energy Production by Region and Type: 1980 to 2000

[In quadrillion Btu (286.4 represents 286,400,000,000,000,000). Btu=British thermal units. For Btu conversion factors, see source]

Region and type	1980	1985	1990	1994	1995	1996	1997	1998	1999	2000 [1]
World total [2]	286.4	304.2	351.0	358.5	367.4	376.8	384.4	387.7	387.7	397.5
North America	80.9	84.6	92.0	95.4	96.2	98.6	99.2	99.9	99.0	99.1
United States	64.8	64.9	70.9	70.9	71.3	72.6	72.6	73.1	72.2	71.6
Central and South America	12.1	13.6	16.7	19.9	21.3	22.6	24.3	25.0	24.5	25.8
Western Europe	30.7	37.3	38.5	40.5	41.7	44.0	44.1	43.9	44.2	44.1
Eastern Europe and former U.S.S.R.	66.7	75.0	81.9	61.4	60.0	60.1	58.2	57.7	59.5	62.3
Middle East	42.2	25.8	41.0	46.9	48.0	49.0	51.3	54.5	53.3	57.1
Africa	18.1	19.3	21.6	24.1	25.4	26.2	27.9	28.0	28.3	29.3
Far East and Oceania . . .	35.8	48.7	59.3	70.2	74.9	76.3	79.4	78.9	79.0	79.7
Crude oil	128.1	115.4	129.5	130.5	133.3	136.6	140.5	143.2	140.8	146.0
Natural gas	52.7	61.4	75.9	79.2	80.3	84.0	84.0	85.7	87.6	90.8
Natural gas liquids	5.1	5.8	6.9	7.9	8.2	8.3	8.5	8.8	8.9	9.3
Coal	74.5	85.8	91.9	89.4	91.8	92.6	95.8	94.0	92.7	92.5
Hydroelectric power	18.1	20.6	22.6	24.5	25.7	26.1	26.7	26.7	27.1	27.5
Nuclear electric power . . .	7.6	15.4	20.4	22.5	23.3	24.1	23.9	24.4	25.2	25.7
Geothermal, solar, wind, wood, and waste	0.4	0.6	1.7	2.2	2.3	2.4	2.5	2.6	2.9	3.0

[1] Preliminary.   [2] Includes geothermal, solar, and wood and waste energy produced in the United States and not used for generating electricity, not shown separately by type.

No. 1348. World Primary Energy Consumption by Region and Type: 1980 to 2000

[In quadrillion Btu (282.6 represents 282,600,000,000,000,000). Btu=British thermal units. For Btu conversion factors, see source]

Region and type	1980	1985	1990	1994	1995	1996	1997	1998	1999	2000 [1]
World total [2]	282.6	307.5	346.2	358.4	368.0	377.4	381.8	383.1	389.9	397.4
North America	89.3	88.3	100.1	106.3	108.1	111.6	112.4	112.8	115.6	118.1
United States	76.0	74.0	84.2	89.3	91.0	94.0	94.4	94.7	96.8	98.8
Central and South America	11.4	12.3	14.1	16.9	17.7	18.5	19.5	20.3	20.4	21.1
Western Europe	58.6	59.9	63.9	64.7	66.7	68.5	69.0	70.4	70.3	71.3
Eastern Europe and former U.S.S.R.	61.4	70.7	74.2	54.7	53.2	52.5	49.8	48.8	50.1	51.1
Middle East	5.9	8.6	11.1	13.4	14.0	14.7	15.5	16.1	16.4	16.8
Africa	6.8	8.5	9.3	10.3	10.7	10.8	11.6	11.8	11.7	11.9
Far East and Oceania . . .	49.2	59.3	73.4	92.2	97.7	100.8	104.1	103.0	105.5	107.2
Petroleum	130.9	123.1	134.9	139.4	142.7	145.8	148.3	150.0	152.8	154.3
Natural gas	54.2	63.7	74.5	78.4	80.3	84.0	83.8	84.6	87.0	90.2
Coal	71.6	84.2	90.0	89.1	91.2	92.5	94.1	92.4	92.4	94.2
Hydroelectric power	18.3	21.0	22.7	24.8	26.0	26.4	27.0	26.9	27.3	27.8
Nuclear electric power . . .	7.6	15.4	20.4	22.5	23.3	24.1	23.9	24.4	25.2	25.7
Geothermal, solar, wind, wood, and waste	0.3	0.5	1.7	2.2	2.3	2.4	2.5	2.6	2.9	3.0

[1] Preliminary.   [2] See footnote 2, Table 1347.

Source of Tables 1347 and 1348: U.S. Energy Information Administration, *International Energy Annual*.

No. 1349. World Energy Consumption by Region and Energy Source, 1990 to 1999, and Projections, 2005 to 2020

[In quadrillion Btu (346.2 represents 346,200,000,000,000,000). Btu=British thermal units. For Btu conversion factors, see source]

Region and energy source	1990	1998	1999	Projections			
				2005	2010	2015	2020
World, total	346.2	379.7	381.9	438.6	492.6	551.7	611.5
North America	100.1	112.7	115.7	129.3	140.5	151.3	161.3
United States	84.2	94.6	97.0	107.6	115.6	123.6	130.9
Western Europe	59.8	65.8	66.0	71.5	74.7	77.7	81.5
Industrialized Asia	22.8	27.6	27.9	29.7	31.5	33.2	34.9
Eastern Europe and former Soviet Union . . .	76.3	50.6	50.4	56.8	61.8	68.2	73.4
Developing Asia	51.0	72.9	70.9	92.5	113.9	137.1	162.2
Middle East	13.1	19.1	19.3	22.0	26.3	30.5	34.8
Africa	9.3	11.6	11.8	14.0	15.7	18.1	20.3
Central and South America	13.7	19.4	19.8	22.7	28.3	35.6	43.1
Oil	134.9	149.8	152.2	173.4	195.4	219.0	241.8
Natural gas	74.5	84.5	86.9	105.2	123.4	145.8	168.6
Coal	90.0	80.3	84.8	95.6	104.7	112.8	122.3
Nuclear	20.4	24.4	25.3	26.9	27.5	27.7	28.0
Other	26.5	32.0	33.1	37.6	41.6	46.4	50.7

Source: 1990, 1998, 1999: U.S. Energy Information Administration (EIA), *International Energy Annual 1999*; Projections: *International Energy Outlook 2002*.

U.S. Census Bureau, Statistical Abstract of the United States: 2002

No. 1350. Energy Consumption and Production by Country: 1990 and 2000

[**346.2 represents 346,200,000,000,000,000**. See text of this section for general comments about the data. For data qualifications for countries, see source]

Country	Primary energy consumed				Dry natural gas production (tril. cu. ft)		Crude petroleum production (1,000 barrels per day)		Coal production (mil. short tons)	
	Total (quad. Btu)		Per capita (mil. Btu)							
	1990	2000, prel.	1990	2000, prel.	1990	2000, prel.	1990	2000, prel.	1990	2000, prel.
World	346.2	397.4	66	65	73.6	88.0	60,566	68,103	5,441	5,059
United States	84.2	98.8	337	351	17.8	19.0	7,355	5,822	1,029	1,074
Algeria	1.2	1.2	49	39	1.8	2.9	1,175	1,244	(Z)	(Z)
Argentina	1.9	2.7	58	73	0.6	1.3	483	761	(Z)	(Z)
Australia	3.7	4.9	215	255	0.7	1.1	575	722	226	337
Austria	1.2	1.4	151	174	0.1	0.1	22	19	3	1
Bahrain	0.3	0.4	520	536	0.2	0.3	42	(NA)	(NA)	(NA)
Bangladesh	0.3	0.5	2	4	0.2	0.3	1	3	(NA)	(NA)
Belarus	(X)	1.1	(X)	106	(X)	(Z)	(X)	37	(X)	(NA)
Belgium	2.2	2.8	217	268	(Z)	-	(NA)	(NA)	3	(Z)
Brazil	5.7	9.1	39	54	0.1	0.3	631	1,269	5	7
Bulgaria	1.3	0.9	145	115	(Z)	-	4	1	39	30
Burma	(NA)	(NA)	(NA)	(Z)	(Z)	0.1	13	8	(Z)	(Z)
Canada	10.9	13.1	394	425	3.9	6.5	1,553	1,977	75	76
Chile	0.6	1.0	43	68	0.1	(Z)	20	7	2	(Z)
China [1]	27.0	36.7	23	29	0.5	1.0	2,774	3,249	1,190	1,314
Colombia [2]	0.9	1.2	25	28	0.2	0.2	440	691	23	42
Congo (Kinshasa) [2]	(NA)	(NA)	(NA)	(NA)	(NA)	(NA)	29	25	(Z)	(Z)
Cuba	0.5	0.4	47	35	(Z)	(Z)	14	43	(NA)	(NA)
Czech Republic	(X)	1.5	(X)	141	(X)	(Z)	(X)	6	(X)	72
Denmark	0.8	0.9	160	165	0.1	0.3	121	363	(NA)	(NA)
Ecuador	(NA)	(NA)	(NA)	(NA)	(Z)	(Z)	285	395	(NA)	(NA)
Egypt	1.4	2.0	27	32	0.3	0.7	873	748	-	(Z)
Finland	1.1	1.3	226	251	(NA)	(NA)	(NA)	(NA)	(NA)	(NA)
France	8.8	10.4	155	177	0.1	0.1	61	29	15	5
Germany	(X)	14.0	(X)	170	(X)	0.8	(X)	64	(X)	225
Greece	1.1	1.3	103	126	(Z)	(Z)	15	5	57	69
Hong Kong	0.5	0.8	84	118	(NA)	(NA)	(NA)	(NA)	(NA)	(NA)
Hungary	1.3	1.1	122	105	0.2	0.1	40	27	20	15
India	7.8	12.7	9	13	0.4	0.8	660	646	233	345
Indonesia	2.3	3.9	13	18	1.5	2.4	1,462	1,423	12	74
Iran	3.1	4.7	57	74	0.8	2.1	3,088	3,696	1	1
Iraq	0.9	1.1	51	47	0.2	0.1	2,040	2,571	(NA)	(NA)
Ireland	0.4	0.6	105	156	0.1	(Z)	(NA)	(NA)	(Z)	(NA)
Israel	0.5	0.8	97	129	(Z)	(Z)	(Z)	(Z)	(NA)	(NA)
Italy	7.0	8.0	123	138	0.6	0.6	87	90	1	(Z)
Japan	17.9	21.8	145	172	0.1	0.1	11	7	11	3
Korea, North	1.6	2.8	80	128	(NA)	(NA)	(NA)	(NA)	99	101
Korea, South	3.7	7.9	85	167	(NA)	(NA)	(NA)	(NA)	19	5
Kuwait	0.5	1.0	210	452	0.2	0.3	1,175	2,126	(NA)	(NA)
Libya	0.5	0.6	123	110	0.2	0.2	1,375	1,410	(NA)	(NA)
Malaysia	1.0	1.9	55	80	0.7	1.5	619	690	(Z)	(Z)
Mexico	5.0	6.2	60	63	0.9	1.3	2,553	3,012	9	11
Morocco	0.3	0.4	13	15	(Z)	(Z)	(Z)	(Z)	1	(Z)
Netherlands	3.4	3.9	225	247	2.7	2.6	70	29	(NA)	(NA)
New Zealand	0.7	0.8	217	217	0.2	0.2	40	36	3	4
Nigeria	0.7	0.8	8	7	0.1	0.4	1,810	2,144	(Z)	(Z)
Norway	1.6	1.8	373	399	1.0	1.8	1,704	3,197	(Z)	1
Pakistan	1.2	1.9	10	13	0.5	0.9	62	54	3	4
Peru	(NA)	(NA)	(NA)	(NA)	(Z)	(Z)	129	97	(Z)	(Z)
Philippines	0.7	1.2	12	16	-	(Z)	5	1	1	1
Poland	4.0	3.7	104	95	0.2	0.2	2	13	237	179
Portugal	0.8	1.1	76	108	(NA)	(NA)	(NA)	(NA)	(Z)	-
Romania	2.9	1.6	124	71	1.0	0.5	163	120	42	32
Russia	(X)	28.1	(X)	193	(X)	20.6	(X)	6,479	(X)	281
Saudi Arabia	3.2	4.6	212	225	1.1	1.8	6,410	8,404	(NA)	(NA)
Serbia and Montenegro	(X)	(X)	(X)	(X)	(X)	(X)	(X)	(X)	(X)	(NA)
South Africa	3.4	4.6	91	106	-	0.1	-	26	248	326
Spain	3.9	5.4	101	137	0.1	(Z)	16	5	40	26
Sweden	2.2	2.3	254	254	(NA)	(NA)	(Z)	(NA)	(Z)	(NA)
Switzerland	1.2	1.2	174	173	(Z)	-	(NA)	(NA)	(NA)	(NA)
Syria	0.6	0.8	49	50	0.1	0.2	388	523	(NA)	(NA)
Taiwan [1]	2.0	3.8	100	170	0.1	(Z)	3	1	1	(Z)
Thailand	1.3	2.6	22	41	0.2	0.7	44	110	14	20
Trinidad and Tobago	(NA)	(NA)	(NA)	(NA)	0.2	0.5	150	122	(NA)	(NA)
Tunisia	(NA)	(NA)	(NA)	(NA)	(Z)	0.1	93	79	(NA)	(NA)
Turkey	2.0	3.2	35	47	(Z)	(Z)	73	53	52	74
Ukraine	(X)	6.5	(X)	130	(X)	0.6	(X)	74	(X)	90
United Arab Emirates	1.2	1.7	641	561	0.8	1.4	2,117	2,368	(NA)	(NA)
United Kingdom	9.3	9.9	161	166	1.8	3.8	1,820	2,275	104	35
Venezuela	2.1	2.7	107	113	0.8	1.0	2,137	2,949	2	9
Vietnam	0.3	0.7	4	9	(Z)	(Z)	50	316	5	10

- Represents zero.   NA Not available.   X Not applicable.   Z Less than 50 billion cubic feet, 500 barrels per day, or 500,000 short tons.   [1] See footnote 2, Table 1308.   [2] See footnote 3, Table 1308.

Source: U.S. Energy Information Administration, *International Energy Annual*.

No. 1351. Net Electricity Generation by Type and Country: 1999

[14,064.9 represents 14,064,900,000,000]

Country	Total [1] (bil. kWh)	Ther-mal [2]	Hydro	Nuclear	Country	Total [1] (bil. kWh)	Ther-mal [2]	Hydro	Nuclear
World, total	14,064.9	62.8	18.5	17.0	Korea, South	250.3	59.2	1.6	39.1
					Malaysia	61.5	88.0	12.0	-
Argentina	74.9	62.1	28.7	8.9	Mexico	183.0	73.9	17.8	5.2
Australia	195.2	89.7	8.5	-	Netherlands	85.3	90.3	0.1	4.2
Austria	59.3	29.5	67.6	-	New Zealand	37.6	30.1	62.0	-
Belgium	80.0	40.0	0.4	58.3	Norway	120.8	0.7	99.1	-
Brazil	327.0	6.2	88.7	1.2	Pakistan	62.4	64.3	35.6	0.2
Bulgaria	36.3	50.4	8.3	41.3	Paraguay	51.5	-	99.8	-
Canada	567.1	26.2	60.3	12.3	Poland	132.2	98.0	1.6	-
China [3]	1,175.2	79.7	19.0	1.2	Romania	48.5	52.8	37.3	9.9
Colombia	43.4	22.4	76.5	-	Russia	801.1	66.0	19.9	13.8
Czech Republic	61.3	75.4	2.8	20.7	Saudi Arabia	119.0	100.0	-	-
Denmark	38.2	88.2	-	-	Serbia and Montene-gro	(NA)	(NA)	(NA)	(NA)
Egypt	64.7	76.5	23.3	-	South Africa	186.9	92.7	0.4	6.8
Finland	74.4	42.5	17.1	29.3	Spain	198.5	57.7	11.4	28.2
France	499.5	9.9	14.4	75.1	Sweden	150.5	6.2	47.1	44.3
Germany	529.5	63.2	3.6	30.4	Switzerland	67.2	3.7	58.9	35.3
Greece	46.8	89.7	9.6	-	Taiwan [3]	139.7	67.2	6.3	26.4
Hungary	35.2	61.1	0.6	38.1	Thailand	86.0	94.8	4.1	-
India	454.2	79.5	17.8	2.5	Turkey	111.4	68.9	30.8	-
Indonesia	81.8	81.2	14.1	-	Ukraine	162.0	51.2	7.2	41.5
Iran	106.1	95.4	4.6	-	United Kingdom	350.6	70.1	1.5	26.1
Italy	247.7	79.1	18.1	-	United States	3,704.5	69.6	8.5	19.7
Japan	1,016.5	60.1	8.4	29.6	Uzbekistan	42.9	86.7	13.1	-
Kazakhstan	45.0	86.4	13.6	-	Venezuela	73.9	25.4	74.6	-
Korea, North	30.8	32.1	67.9	-					

- Represents zero. NA Not available. [1] Includes geothermal, solar, wind, and wood and waste generation, not shown separately. [2] Electricity generated from coal, oil, and gas. [3] See footnote 2, Table 1308.

Source: U.S. Energy Information Administration, *International Energy Annual 2000*.

No. 1352. Commercial Nuclear Power Generation by Country: 1990 to 2001

[Generation for calendar years; other data as of December (1,743.9 represents 1,743,900,000,000)]

Country	Reactors				Gross electricity generated (bil. kWh)				Gross capacity (1,000 kW)			
	1990	1995	2000	2001	1990	1995	2000	2001	1990	1995	2000	2001
Total	368	423	433	427	1,743.9	2,271.7	2,540.5	2,602.8	301,745	358,414	373,804	370,366
United States	112	109	104	104	606.4	705.7	789.1	794.5	105,998	105,810	103,129	103,759
Argentina	2	2	2	2	7.0	7.0	6.2	7.1	1,005	1,005	1,005	1,005
Armenia	(NA)	1	1	1	(NA)	0.3	(NA)	(NA)	(NA)	408	408	408
Belgium	7	7	7	7	42.7	41.3	48.2	46.3	5,740	5,911	5,995	5,995
Brazil	1	1	2	2	2.0	2.5	6.1	14.3	657	657	1,966	2,007
Bulgaria	(NA)	6	6	(NA)	(NA)	17.1	(NA)	(NA)	(NA)	3,760	3,760	(NA)
Canada	19	22	21	21	74.0	100.2	73.8	77.5	13,855	16,699	15,795	15,795
China [1]	(NA)	(NA)	2	2	(NA)	(NA)	14.7	14.9	(NA)	(NA)	1,968	1,968
Czech Republic	(NA)	(NA)	4	4	(NA)	(NA)	13.6	13.6	(NA)	(NA)	1,760	1,760
Finland	4	4	4	4	18.9	18.9	22.5	22.8	2,400	2,400	2,760	2,760
France	58	56	57	57	314.1	377.2	395.7	409.4	58,862	60,674	62,920	62,920
Germany	22	21	19	19	147.2	154.1	169.7	171.3	23,973	24,035	22,234	22,365
Great Britain	42	34	33	31	68.8	82.7	83.6	90.5	15,274	14,022	15,272	14,612
Hungary	4	4	4	4	13.6	14.0	14.1	14.1	1,760	1,840	1,851	1,866
India	6	10	13	14	6.0	7.6	15.5	19.2	1,330	2,270	2,960	2,720
Italy	2	(NA)	(NA)	(NA)	-	(NA)	(NA)	(NA)	1,132	(NA)	(NA)	(NA)
Japan	40	50	52	52	191.9	286.0	319.8	319.3	31,645	41,356	45,082	45,082
Korea, South	9	10	16	16	52.8	63.9	108.9	112.1	7,616	8,615	13,768	13,768
Lithuania	(NA)	2	2	2	(NA)	9.6	7.8	11.4	(NA)	3,000	3,000	3,000
Mexico	1	2	2	2	2.1	7.9	8.2	8.7	675	1,350	1,350	1,350
Netherlands	2	2	1	1	3.4	4.0	3.9	3.9	540	540	480	480
Pakistan	1	1	1	2	0.4	0.5	0.4	2.2	137	137	137	462
Romania	(NA)	(NA)	1	1	(NA)	(NA)	5.5	5.4	(NA)	(NA)	706	706
Russia	(NA)	29	29	30	(NA)	98.7	128.9	134.5	(NA)	21,266	21,266	22,266
Slovakia	(NA)	(NA)	6	6	(NA)	(NA)	16.5	17.1	(NA)	(NA)	2,640	2,640
Slovenia	1	1	1	1	4.6	4.7	4.8	5.3	664	664	664	707
South Africa	2	2	2	2	8.9	11.9	13.6	11.3	1,930	1,930	1,930	1,930
Spain	10	9	9	9	54.3	55.4	62.2	63.7	7,984	7,400	7,808	7,815
Sweden	12	12	11	11	68.2	69.9	57.3	72.2	10,344	10,442	9,844	9,844
Switzerland	5	5	5	5	23.6	24.8	26.3	26.7	3,079	3,200	3,322	3,352
Taiwan [1]	6	6	6	6	32.9	35.3	38.5	35.5	5,146	5,144	5,144	5,144
Ukraine	(NA)	15	14	13	(NA)	70.5	77.3	76.2	(NA)	13,880	12,880	11,880

- Represents zero. NA Not available. [1] See footnote 2, Table 1308.

Source: McGraw-Hill, Inc., New York, NY, *Nucleonics Week,* March issues (copyright).

U.S. Census Bureau, Statistical Abstract of the United States: 2002

No. 1353. Selected Indexes of Manufacturing Activity by Country: 1980 to 2000

[1992=100. Data relate to employees (wage and salary earners) in Belgium and Italy, and to all employed persons (employees, self-employed workers, and unpaid family workers) in the other countries. Minus sign (-) indicates decrease. For explanation of average annual percent change, see Guide to Tabular Presentation]

Index	United States	Can-ada	Japan	Bel-gium	France	Ger-many	Italy	Neth-erlands	Nor-way	Swe-den	United King-dom
Output per hour:											
1980.	70.5	74.4	63.2	65.4	66.6	(NA)	70.8	68.8	76.7	73.1	54.3
1985.	86.0	92.2	76.5	87.0	79.1	(NA)	83.3	88.5	90.2	86.2	71.1
1990.	96.9	94.7	94.4	96.8	93.6	(NA)	93.9	98.5	96.6	94.6	89.1
1995.	113.8	111.3	111.0	113.2	114.7	112.3	111.2	118.2	102.0	121.9	104.9
1999.	135.3	114.9	126.9	129.5	132.9	120.5	113.5	128.5	103.1	143.5	111.6
2000.	142.8	116.3	134.1	133.4	141.1	128.0	117.8	133.8	104.2	150.4	117.6
Average annual percent change:											
1979-85.	3.5	3.4	3.5	6.0	3.0	(NA)	3.5	4.4	2.4	3.1	4.4
1985-90.	2.4	0.5	4.3	2.2	3.4	(NA)	2.4	2.2	1.4	1.9	4.6
1990-2000.	4.1	2.1	3.5	3.2	4.1	(NA)	2.3	(NA)	0.8	4.7	2.7
Compensation per hour, national currency basis: [1]											
1980.	55.6	47.6	58.5	52.5	40.8	(NA)	29.0	64.4	39.0	37.3	32.1
1985.	75.1	71.9	72.4	75.3	72.8	(NA)	60.2	81.9	63.4	58.6	52.9
1990.	90.8	88.3	90.5	90.1	90.6	(NA)	85.8	90.9	92.3	87.8	82.9
1995.	107.9	106.0	108.3	109.2	108.5	117.6	114.6	110.7	109.2	106.5	107.9
1999.	122.1	113.1	115.2	118.3	118.7	129.3	129.4	124.0	133.4	127.5	129.6
2000.	130.7	117.0	114.5	121.1	125.7	133.5	133.6	131.0	140.1	130.7	134.7
Average annual percent change:											
1979-85.	7.2	9.1	4.7	8.1	12.8	(NA)	15.9	5.0	10.0	9.8	12.2
1985-90.	3.9	4.2	4.6	3.7	4.5	(NA)	7.4	2.1	7.8	8.4	9.4
1990-2000. [1] [2]	3.7	2.9	2.5	2.9	3.3	(NA)	4.5	(NA)	4.3	4.1	4.7
Real hourly compensation: [1] [2]											
1980.	91.6	91.6	75.2	86.5	79.6	(NA)	81.4	87.5	86.0	87.7	66.7
1985.	95.5	96.6	81.2	88.3	89.7	(NA)	88.7	90.8	90.8	87.4	77.5
1990.	96.6	94.7	95.0	95.2	96.0	(NA)	96.0	96.7	97.7	97.6	91.0
1995.	100.4	101.7	106.3	102.3	102.8	107.7	100.3	103.0	102.7	97.6	100.2
1999.	104.6	102.4	110.6	104.7	107.6	113.0	102.9	106.2	115.6	109.4	108.5
2000.	108.3	103.1	110.7	104.5	112.1	114.4	103.6	109.3	117.7	115.8	109.5
Average annual percent change:											
1979-85.	0.8	1.1	1.1	1.1	2.3	(NA)	0.8	0.4	0.6	-0.5	3.0
1985-90.	0.2	-0.4	3.2	1.5	1.4	(NA)	1.6	1.3	1.5	2.2	3.3
1990-2000.	1.1	0.9	1.5	0.9	1.6	(NA)	0.8	(NA)	1.9	1.7	1.9
Unit labor costs, national currency:											
1980.	78.8	63.9	92.5	80.3	61.3	(NA)	41.0	93.7	50.8	51.0	59.0
1985.	87.3	78.0	94.6	86.5	92.0	(NA)	72.2	92.5	70.2	68.0	74.4
1990.	93.7	93.3	95.9	93.0	96.8	(NA)	91.5	92.3	95.6	92.9	93.0
1995.	94.8	95.2	97.6	96.4	94.6	104.7	103.0	93.7	107.0	87.4	102.9
1999.	90.2	98.4	90.8	91.4	89.3	107.4	114.0	96.6	129.5	88.8	116.1
2000.	91.5	100.6	85.4	90.8	89.1	104.3	113.4	97.9	134.5	86.9	114.5
Average annual percent change:											
1979-85.	3.6	5.5	1.1	2.0	9.5	(NA)	12.0	0.5	7.4	6.5	7.5
1985-90.	1.4	3.7	0.3	1.5	1.0	(NA)	4.8	-0.1	6.4	6.4	4.5
1990-2000.	-0.4	0.8	-1.2	-0.3	-0.9	(NA)	2.2	(NA)	3.5	-0.7	1.9
Unit labor costs, U.S. dollar basis: [3]											
1980.	78.8	66.1	51.8	88.3	76.7	(NA)	59.0	82.9	63.9	70.2	77.7
1985.	87.3	69.0	50.3	46.9	54.2	(NA)	46.6	49.0	50.8	46.1	54.7
1990.	93.7	96.6	83.8	89.5	94.0	(NA)	94.1	89.1	95.0	91.3	93.9
1995.	94.8	83.8	131.7	105.2	100.5	114.2	77.9	102.7	105.0	71.3	92.0
1999.	90.2	80.0	101.2	77.6	76.8	91.3	77.3	82.1	103.1	62.5	06.3
2000.	91.5	81.8	100.4	66.8	66.4	76.9	66.6	72.1	94.8	55.2	98.3
Average annual percent change:											
1979-85.	3.6	2.8	-0.3	-9.3	-3.3	(NA)	-2.5	-7.6	-1.7	-5.2	-1.0
1985-90.	1.4	7.0	10.8	13.8	11.6	(NA)	15.1	12.7	13.3	14.7	11.4
1990-2000.	-0.4	-1.6	2.0	-2.9	-3.5	(NA)	-3.4	(NA)	-	-4.9	0.3
Employment:											
1980.	111.6	115.1	88.9	119.3	125.0	(NA)	122.6	107.8	134.5	130.9	151.8
1985.	106.0	106.8	93.5	104.0	110.3	(NA)	105.8	95.4	120.7	122.0	120.6
1990.	105.4	113.2	97.5	102.5	105.4	(NA)	104.6	101.1	105.4	117.2	115.4
1995.	102.5	104.8	90.1	91.9	92.1	86.2	95.6	91.3	107.2	97.9	98.9
1999.	102.4	118.5	83.2	88.8	89.7	82.1	97.3	92.4	111.6	98.7	96.9
2000.	101.7	123.7	81.7	89.1	90.4	82.7	97.1	93.0	108.7	100.0	93.4
Average annual percent change:											
1979-85.	-1.4	-1.3	1.2	-2.6	-2.3	(NA)	-2.3	-2.2	-1.8	-1.2	-4.6
1985-90.	-0.1	1.2	0.8	-0.3	-0.9	(NA)	-0.2	1.2	-2.7	-0.8	-0.9
1990-2000.	-0.4	0.9	-1.8	-1.3	-1.5	(NA)	-0.7	(NA)	0.3	-1.6	-2.1
Aggregate hours:											
1980.	107.5	114.6	95.6	119.7	133.2	(NA)	119.3	111.7	135.0	124.0	160.5
1985.	104.6	106.4	100.3	102.4	110.4	(NA)	101.8	96.6	120.2	119.4	125.2
1990.	104.8	113.5	102.9	104.3	105.9	(NA)	105.9	101.4	103.7	116.4	118.1
1995.	104.0	106.4	89.1	92.0	91.5	84.9	96.4	91.5	106.8	105.3	102.7
1999.	104.3	122.6	80.3	91.1	88.3	79.6	97.1	92.0	110.6	107.1	99.5
2000.	102.9	128.0	80.2	91.7	85.9	79.5	96.7	92.5	106.4	108.6	96.3
Average annual percent change:											
1979-85.	-1.2	-1.5	1.1	-3.2	-3.3	(NA)	-2.9	-2.5	-1.8	-0.8	-5.3
1985-90.	-	1.3	0.5	0.4	-0.8	(NA)	1.3	1.0	-2.9	-0.5	-1.2
1990-2000.	-0.1	1.2	-2.4	-1.3	-2.0	(NA)	-0.9	(NA)	0.3	-0.7	-2.0

- Represents or rounds to zero.   NA Not available.   [1] Compensation includes, but real hourly compensation excludes, adjustments for payroll and employment taxes that are not compensation to employees, but are labor costs to employers.   [2] Index of hourly compensation divided by the index of consumer prices to adjust for changes in purchasing power.   [3] Indexes in national currency adjusted for changes in prevailing exchange rates.

Source: U.S. Bureau of Labor Statistics, *International Comparisons of Manufacturing Productivity and Unit Labor Cost Trends*, September 26, 2002.

Comparative International Statistics   849

No. 1354. Indexes of Hourly Compensation Costs for Production Workers in Manufacturing by Country: 1980 to 2000

[United States=100. Compensation costs include pay for time worked, other direct pay (including holiday and vacation pay, bonuses, other direct payments, and the cost of pay in kind), employer expenditures for legally required insurance programs and contractual and private benefit plans, and for some countries, other labor taxes. Data adjusted for exchange rates. Area averages are trade-weighted to account for difference in countries' relative importance to U.S. trade in manufactured goods. The trade weights used are the sum of U.S. imports of manufactured products for consumption (customs value) and U.S. exports of domestic manufactured products (f.a.s. value) in 1992; see source for detail]

Area or country	1980	1985	1990	1995	1999	2000	Area or country	1980	1985	1990	1995	1999	2000
United States	100	100	100	100	100	100	Austria[7]	90	58	119	147	114	98
Total[1]	67	52	83	95	80	76	Belgium.	133	69	129	161	125	106
OECD[2]	74	57	90	103	86	82	Denmark	110	63	121	140	120	103
Europe	100	61	116	128	107	93	Finland[8]	84	63	141	140	112	98
Asian newly industrial-izing economies[3] . . .	12	13	25	37	33	34	France	91	58	104	116	94	83
Canada	88	84	107	94	82	81	Germany[7][9]	124	73	146	184	140	121
Mexico	22	12	11	9	11	12	Greece	38	28	45	53	(NA)	(NA)
Australia[4]	86	63	88	89	82	71	Ireland	61	46	79	80	71	63
Hong Kong[5]	15	13	22	28	29	28	Italy	83	59	117	94	87	74
Israel	38	31	57	61	62	65	Luxembourg.	122	60	112	132	98	84
Japan	56	49	86	139	109	111	Netherlands	122	67	121	140	112	96
Korea, South	10	10	25	42	37	41	Norway	117	80	144	142	125	111
New Zealand	53	34	55	58	48	41	Portugal	21	12	25	31	28	24
Singapore	15	19	25	43	37	37	Spain	60	36	76	75	63	55
Sri Lanka.	2	2	2	3	2	(NA)	Sweden.	127	74	140	125	113	101
Taiwan[6]	10	12	26	35	29	30	Switzerland	112	74	140	170	123	107
							United Kingdom	77	48	85	80	86	80

NA Not available. [1] The 28 foreign economies shown below. [2] Organization for Economic Cooperation and Development; see text of this section. [3] Hong Kong, South Korea, Singapore, and Taiwan. [4] Includes nonproduction workers, except in managerial, executive, professional, and higher supervisory positions. [5] Average of selected manufacturing industries. [6] See footnote 2, Table 1308. [7] Excludes workers in establishments considered handicraft manufactures (including all printing and publishing and miscellaneous manufacturing in Austria). [8] Includes workers in mining and electrical power plants. [9] Former West Germany.

Source: U.S. Bureau of Labor Statistics, *News Release* USDL 01-311, September 25, 2001.

No. 1355. Motor Vehicle Transportation Indicators for Selected Countries: 1999

[132,432 represents 132,432,000]

Item	United States	Canada	France	Germany	Japan	Mexico	Sweden	United Kingdom
NUMBER[1] (1,000)								
Automobiles[2][3]	132,432	13,887	27,480	42,324	49,896	9,842	3,867	22,115
Motorcycles[2][3]	4,152	334	(NA)	4,560	14,537	270	252	684
Buses.	729	68	80	85	238	110	15	80
Trucks.	83,148	3,626	5,740	4,382	20,814	4,640	353	3,089
Per 1,000 persons:								
Automobiles[2][3]	480.6	444.0	463.2	511.2	394.3	98.1	435.8	371.6
Motorcycles[2][3]	15.1	10.7	(NA)	55.1	114.9	2.7	28.4	11.5
Buses	2.6	2.2	1.3	1.0	1.9	1.1	1.7	1.3
Trucks	301.7	115.9	96.7	52.9	164.5	46.2	39.8	51.9
ROADS[4]								
Total kilometers (1,000)	6,328	902	894	656	1,156	319	211	372
Kilometers per 1,000 persons	22.96	28.83	15.06	7.93	9.14	3.18	23.77	6.25
Kilometers per square kilometer.	0.69	0.10	1.64	1.88	3.09	0.17	0.47	1.54
VEHICLE KILOMETERS OF TRAVEL[5]								
Automobiles (bil.)	2,529	(NA)	402	528	483	(NA)	57	380
Motorcycles (bil.).	17	(NA)	4	15	(NA)	(NA)	1	5
Buses (bil.).	12	(NA)	2	4	7	(NA)	1	5
Trucks (bil.)[6]	1,773	(NA)	112	58	257	(NA)	9	77
AVERAGE VEHICLE KILOMETERS PER VEHICLE[5]								
Automobiles	19,099	(NA)	14,629	12,475	9,671	(NA)	15,029	17,187
Motorcycles	4,109	(NA)	1,723	3,377	(NA)	(NA)	2,378	6,725
Buses	16,363	(NA)	28,750	43,690	27,429	(NA)	77,616	62,500
Trucks[6].	16,363	(NA)	19,512	13,192	12,347	(NA)	25,544	25,025

NA Not available. [1] Data for Japan, UK, and Canada are for 1998. [2] Includes mopeds. [3] Data for Germany and Sweden are from 1998; data for Mexico are from 1996. [4] Data for Japan, Sweden, and Mexico are from 1998; data for Canada are from 1995. [5] Data for Japan, Germany, and Sweden are from 1998. [6] U.S. data are light 2-axle 4-tire trucks such as vans, sport utility vehicles, pickup trucks, heavy single-unit trucks, and combination trucks. Non-U.S. data does not include travel by combination trucks.

Source: U.S. Federal Highway Administration, *Highway Statistics, 2000*

No. 1356. Information and Communication Technology (ICT) Sector—Employment by Country: 1997

[196 represents 196,000. The information and communication technology sector is defined as including the International Standard Industrial Classification (ISIC): Manufacturing— 3000-Office, accounting and computing machinery; 3130-Insulated wire and cable; 3210-Electronic valves and tubes and other electronic components; 3220-Television and radio transmitters and apparatus for line telephony and line telegraphy; 3230-Television and radio receivers, sound or video recording or reproducing apparatus, and associated goods; 3312-Instruments and appliances for measuring, checking, testing, navigating and other purposes, except industrial process equipment; 3313-Industrial process control equipment; Services— 5150-Wholesaling of machinery, equipment and supplies (where possible, member countries were asked to limit this class to include only the wholesaling of ICT goods as shown in the manufacturing component of the definition shown above); 7123-Renting of office machinery and equipment (including computers); 6420-Telecommunications; 72-Computer and related activities]

Country	Total ICT employment (1,000)	Percent of employment in total business sector	Country	Total ICT employment (1,000)	Percent of employment in total business sector
Australia [1]	196	2.6	Italy	671	3.5
Austria [2]	165	4.9	Japan [3]	2,060	3.4
Belgium	130	4.3	Korea, South [3]	462	2.5
Canada	430	4.6	Netherlands [3]	199	3.8
Czech Republic [2]	152	3.3	New Zealand	31	2.1
Denmark	96	5.1	Norway [4]	74	5.3
Finland	88	5.6	Portugal [2]	94	2.7
France	681	4.0	Sweden	174	6.3
Germany [3]	974	3.1	Switzerland [5]	172	6.0
Hungary [2]	157	5.7	Turkey [3]	100	0.5
Iceland [4]	4	4.2	United Kingdom	1,112	4.8
Ireland [3]	56	4.6	**United States**	**4,521**	**3.9**

[1] Data for 1998-99. [2] Includes all of Wholesale of machinery, equipment and supplies (ISIC 5150). [3] Excludes all of Wholesale of machinery, equipment and supplies (ISIC 5150). [4] Data for 1996. [5] Data for 1998.

No. 1357. Information and Communication Technology (ICT) Sector—Foreign Trade by Country: 1998

[In millions of dollars, except as indicated (645,996 represents $645,996,000,000). See headnote, Table 1356]

Country	ICT goods and services		Share of ICT in—		Country	ICT goods and services		Share of ICT in—	
	Imports	Exports	Total imports (percent)	Total exports (percent)		Imports	Exports	Total imports (percent)	Total exports (percent)
OECD, total	**645,996**	**620,358**	**13.2**	**12.5**	Ireland [3]	13,563	19,373	33.9	32.6
European Union [1]	297,578	270,366	11.8	10.1	Italy	23,377	13,742	8.5	4.4
G7 countries [2]	443,055	425,054	13.5	12.8	Japan	47,026	101,358	13.5	24.0
					Korea, South [4]	20,590	34,169	18.0	21.8
Australia	10,257	3,194	13.1	4.4	Mexico [4]	24,513	27,761	17.7	21.4
Austria	7,862	4,754	8.2	5.0	Netherlands	36,206	34,758	16.7	14.6
Belgium-Luxembourg	13,331	12,755	7.4	6.7	New Zealand	1,759	561	11.3	3.5
Canada	30,229	18,024	12.4	7.2	Norway	4,230	1,889	7.8	3.5
Czech Republic	3,629	1,876	10.5	5.5	Poland	5,100	1,954	9.6	4.4
Denmark [3]	5,442	3,910	12.7	8.3	Portugal	3,729	2,149	8.4	6.3
Finland	6,226	9,829	16.1	19.6	Spain	13,489	8,409	8.6	5.3
France	37,808	35,426	11.1	9.4	Sweden	12,700	15,515	14.2	14.9
Germany [3]	64,173	53,580	11.0	8.6	Switzerland [4]	9,005	5,640	9.4	5.3
Greece [3]	2,177	334	8.6	4.2	Turkey [3]	3,992	1,309	8.6	4.7
Hungary	4,880	5,127	19.7	21.5	United Kingdom	57,497	55,831	14.9	15.0
Iceland	264	39	8.1	1.3	**United States**	**182,945**	**147,092**	**16.4**	**15.2**

[1] For countries, see footnote 3, Table 1320. [2] For countries, see headnote, Table 1322. [3] Trade of ICT goods only. Total imports and total exports include goods only. [4] Excludes computer and information services.

Source of Tables 1356 and 1357: Organization for Economic Cooperation and Development, Paris, France, *Measuring the ICT Sector*, 2000.

No. 1358. Key Global Telecom Indicators for the World Telecommunication Service Sector: 1995 to 2002

[In billions U.S. dollars (778 represents $778,000,000,000), except where noted. All data were converted by annual average exchange rates. Country fiscal year data was aggregated to obtain calendar year estimates]

Indicators	1995	1996	1997	1998	1999	2000	2001	2002, prel.
Telecom market total revenue	778	885	946	1,015	1,112	1,210	1,320	1,445
Telecom telephone services revenue [1]	428	444	437	456	470	489	509	529
Other statistics:								
Main telephone lines [2]	691	741	795	849	907	986	1,040	1,115
Mobile cellular subscribers [2]	91	144	215	319	491	741	1,030	1,390
International telephone traffic minutes [3]	63	71	79	89	99	110	120	135
Personal computers [2]	230	260	320	370	430	500	550	605
Internet users [2]	34	58	96	155	241	361	505	655

[1] Revenue from installation, subscription and local, trunk and international call charges for fixed telephone service. [2] Data are in millions. [3] From 1994 including traffic between countries of former Soviet Union.

Source: International Telecommunication Union, Geneva Switzerland, 2002; <http://www.itu.int/ITU-D/ict/statistics/atglance/KeyTelecom99.html>.

No. 1359. Newspapers, Radio, Television, Telephones, and Computers by Country

[Rates per 1,000 persons. See text of this section for general comments about the data. For data qualifications for countries, see source]

Country	Daily newspaper circulation,[1] 1996	Radio receivers,[2] 1997	Television receivers,[3] 1997	Telephone main lines, 2000	Cellular phone subscribers, 2000	Personal computers,[4] 2000
Algeria	38	242	105	[5]52	[5]2	[5]6
Argentina	123	681	223	215	[5]121	51
Australia	296	1,391	554	524	446	465
Austria	296	751	525	474	786	276
Belgium	161	797	466	499	549	344
Brazil	40	434	223	[5]149	136	44
Bulgaria	254	537	394	[5]354	90	[5]27
Canada	158	1,067	710	[5]654	[5]225	390
Chile	98	354	215	221	224	85
China [6]	(NA)	335	321	[5]86	67	16
Colombia	46	524	115	[5]160	[5]75	[5]34
Cuba	118	352	239	44	1	[5]10
Czech Republic	254	803	531	[5]371	422	122
Denmark	311	1,145	594	705	665	432
Dominican Republic	52	178	95	[5]98	[5]50	(NA)
Ecuador	70	348	130	[5]91	[5]31	[5]20
Egypt	38	317	119	81	20	[5]12
Finland	455	1,498	622	[5]552	726	396
France	218	946	595	580	494	305
Germany	311	948	567	601	586	336
Ghana	14	236	93	12	6	[5]3
Greece	(NA)	475	240	[5]528	559	70
Guatemala	33	79	61	57	[5]30	[5]10
Honduras	55	410	95	46	24	[5]10
Hungary	186	690	435	[5]371	293	85
India	(NA)	120	65	32	4	5
Indonesia	23	155	68	31	17	10
Iran	26	263	71	149	15	[5]56
Iraq	20	229	83	[5]30	[5]_	(NA)
Ireland	149	697	402	[5]478	597	365
Israel	288	524	288	463	702	254
Italy	104	880	528	[5]462	737	209
Jamaica	63	483	183	199	142	[5]43
Japan	578	956	686	[5]558	526	315
Korea, South	(NA)	1,039	348	464	567	190
Kuwait	377	678	505	[5]240	[5]158	[5]121
Lebanon	141	907	375	[5]201	[5]194	[5]46
Malaysia	163	434	172	211	155	105
Mexico	97	329	272	125	142	51
Morocco	27	247	115	50	83	[5]11
Netherlands	306	980	519	[5]607	671	395
New Zealand	216	997	512	[5]496	[5]366	360
Norway	590	917	462	729	703	491
Pakistan	(NA)	94	22	[5]22	[5]2	[5]4
Panama	62	299	187	[5]164	[5]83	[5]32
Peru	84	273	126	64	[5]40	[5]36
Philippines	82	161	52	40	84	20
Poland	113	522	337	[5]263	181	69
Portugal	75	306	336	431	665	105
Puerto Rico	127	714	270	[5]333	[5]209	(NA)
Romania	(NA)	319	233	[5]167	112	[5]27
Russia	105	417	410	217	19	43
Saudi Arabia	59	321	262	[5]129	[5]40	[5]57
Singapore	324	744	388	485	684	483
South Africa	34	355	134	[5]125	[5]120	62
Spain	99	331	409	421	609	143
Sweden	445	932	519	[5]665	703	507
Switzerland	331	979	457	720	645	[5]502
Syria	20	278	70	104	2	[5]14
Taiwan [6]	[7]156	(NA)	(NA)	568	803	225
Thailand	64	234	254	[5]86	44	24
Turkey	110	178	330	280	246	38
United Kingdom	331	1,443	521	[5]567	670	338
United States	**212**	**2,116**	**806**	**[5]673**	**400**	**585**
Uruguay	293	603	239	[5]271	[5]95	[5]100
Venezuela	206	472	180	[5]109	[5]143	46

- Represents or rounds to zero.   NA Not available.   [1] Publications containing general news and appearing at least 4 times a week; may range in size from a single sheet to 50 or more pages. Circulation data refer to average circulation per issue or number of printed copies per issue and include copies sold outside the country.   [2] Data cover estimated number of receivers in use and apply to all types of receivers for radio broadcasts to the public, including receivers connected to a radio "redistribution system" but excluding television sets.   [3] Estimated number of sets in use.   [4] In many countries mainframe computers are used extensively, and thousands of users can be connected to a single mainframe computer; thus the number of PCs understates the total use of computers.   [5] 1999 data.   [6] See footnote 2, Table 1308.   [7] 1998 data. Source: U.S. Census Bureau. Data from Republic of China publications.

Source: Except as noted, Newspapers, radio, and television—United Nations Educational, Scientific, and Cultural Organization, Montreal, Canada, *Statistical Yearbook*, (copyright); telephones, cellular phones, and personal computers— International Telecommunications Union, Geneva, Switzerland, *World Telecommunication Indicators*, (copyright).

No. 1360. Dow-Jones World Stock Index by Country and Industry: 1995 to 2001

[Index figures shown are as of December 31. Based on share prices denominated in U.S. dollars. Stocks in countries that impose significant restrictions on foreign ownership are included in the world index in the same proportion that shares are available to foreign investors]

Country and industry	1995	1999	2000	2001	Country and industry	1995	1999	2000	2001
World, total	**132.4**	**245.3**	**210.9**	**175.7**	Asia/Pacific	118.5	133.3	93.0	73.2
Americas.	145.3	330.5	299.1	259.5	Australia	132.9	173.4	156.2	154.1
United States	147.5	341.6	306.9	266.7	Hong Kong.	201.9	288.8	245.6	195.2
Canada	112.9	223.4	225.4	180.1	Indonesia.	174.7	71.7	31.2	25.4
Mexico	79.0	170.1	132.2	157.4	Japan	111.1	128.3	88.3	62.3
Europe	131.0	269.2	241.1	189.2	Malaysia	224.3	111.8	88.5	91.6
Austria	103.5	101.9	86.1	86.2	New Zealand	178.8	141.4	96.7	102.7
Belgium	144.0	228.8	196.7	170.5	Singapore	187.8	177.3	135.3	108.4
Denmark	113.0	199.9	243.9	187.3	Thailand	196.6	55.4	27.2	28.4
Finland	267.1	1,814.0	1,536.0	955.0					
France	117.9	274.5	252.6	193.4	Basic materials.	128.1	134.6	117.7	109.8
Germany	133.9	260.7	218.8	165.8	Consumer, cyclical	131.7	240.0	188.0	171.4
Ireland.	155.6	290.8	312.0	301.0	Consumer, noncyclical. .	125.5	205.2	180.8	173.2
Italy	80.3	203.3	192.0	137.8	Energy	132.7	211.2	230.7	206.4
Netherlands	176.0	365.0	335.3	257.2	Financial	134.9	192.2	207.1	175.5
Norway	129.8	163.6	167.4	125.0	Healthcare	133.3	254.0	329.8	281.7
Spain	111.2	259.0	193.3	167.3	Industrial	124.0	199.3	167.1	138.5
Sweden	157.0	409.2	338.9	236.1	Technology	188.1	856.8	552.4	377.3
Switzerland	225.7	357.5	415.5	293.9	Telecommunications . . .	146.8	458.3	273.3	208.6
United Kingdom	122.5	234.0	199.8	166.7	Utilities	118.8	133.6	156.0	123.3

Source: Dow Jones & Company, Inc., New York, NY, *Dow Jones Indexes*, (copyright).

No. 1361. Foreign Stock Market Activity—Morgan Stanley Capital International Indexes: 1995 to 2001

[Index figures shown are as of December 31. January 1, 1970=100, except as noted. Based on share prices denominated in U.S. dollars. EM=Emerging Markets]

Index and country	Index			Percent change [1]		Index and country	Index			Percent change [1]	
	1995	2000	2001	2000	2001		1995	2000	2001	2000	2001
ALL COUNTRY (AC) INDEXES						Switzerland	1,569	2,695	2,104	4.9	-21.9
						United Kingdom	716.4	1,146	962.0	-13.6	-16.1
AC World index	182.0	289.8	(NA)	-15.1	(NA)	Hong Kong	4,818	5,475	4,314	-17.0	-21.2
AC World index except						Japan	3,348	2,552	1,789	-28.5	-29.9
USA.	153.8	195.4	(NA)	-16.3	(NA)	Singapore	2,735	2,081	1,560	-28.7	-25.0
AC Asia Pacific	124.5	92.7	(NA)	-28.9	(NA)						
AC Europe	201.9	376.5	297.2	-10.4	-21.1	**EMERGING MARKETS**					
European Union.	189.2	361.5	284.5	-11.5	-21.3						
						EM Far East index . .	263.7	123.8	140.0	-41.8	9.5
DEVELOPED MARKETS						India [5]	98.8	114.5	90.3	-22.8	-21.2
						Indonesia	508.2	78.2	69.4	-63.0	-10.9
World index [2]	734.0	1,221	1,004	-14.1	-17.8	Korea, South	173.8	78.7	114.8	-50.4	46.0
EAFE index [3]	1,136	1,492	1,155	-15.2	-22.6	Malaysia	347.0	160.9	164.3	-16.6	2.3
Europe index	733.4	1,378	1,086	-9.7	-21.2	Pakistan [5]	91.5	44.3	29.0	-13.8	-35.0
Pacific index	2,362	1,832	1,352	-26.4	-26.2	Philippines	442.5	142.2	117.8	-42.5	-19.7
Far East index	3,384	2,583	1,833	-27.6	-29.1	Sri Lanka [5]	105.6	36.3	49.4	-43.9	36.1
						Taiwan [6]	227.9	191.7	208.6	-45.4	8.8
United States	581.1	1,250	1,085	-13.6	-13.2	Thailand	523.3	56.9	60.6	-53.2	2.9
Canada	403.9	832.5	654.2	4.4	-21.4						
						EM Latin America . . .	781.8	1,002	876.2	-15.9	-4.3
Australia	304.2	317.7	315.8	-12.0	-0.6	Argentina	1,239	1,233	959.6	-26.1	-22.2
New Zealand [4]	114.2	56.4	59.6	-36.3	5.6	Brazil	578.1	869.9	597.1	-8.7	-21.8
Austria	890.4	708.3	655.6	-13.4	-7.4	Chile	902.8	604.7	568.7	-17.0	-6.0
Belgium	897.0	1,222	1,063	-18.6	-13.0	Colombia [5]	110.2	42.1	57.7	-41.2	37.1
Denmark.	1,124	2,201	1,850	2.7	-15.9	Mexico	744.5	1,197	1,698	-21.5	15.9
Finland [4]	128.8	921.8	561.7	-14.7	-39.1	Peru [5]	221.3	125.0	144.1	-26.7	15.3
France	672.1	1,509	1,160	-5.1	-23.2	Venezuela.	75.4	106.1	95.4	0.8	-10.0
Germany	818.1	1,436	1,099	-16.5	-23.5						
Ireland [4]	215.7	308.4	295.6	-14.3	-4.13	Czech Republic	(NA)	79.9	76.6	0.7	-4.2
Italy	208.6	447.2	322.4	-2.7	-27.9	Greece [4]	238.2	475.8	326.6	-42.5	31.4
Luxembourg	(NA)	491.9	265.4	2.2	-46.0	Hungary	(NA)	233.6	209.1	-27.7	-10.5
Netherlands	1,192	2,177	1,665	-5.4	-23.5	Jordan	96.1	55.1	71.1	-24.7	29.0
Norway.	1,023	1,181	1,018	-2.4	-13.8	Poland	(NA)	499.0	355.8	-4.6	-28.7
Portugal [4]	68.4	127.8	98.4	-12.2	-23.0	Russia	(NA)	155.2	237.8	-30.4	53.2
Spain	162.3	347.1	302.7	-16.8	-12.8	South Africa	(NA)	157.6	125.6	-19.6	-20.3
Sweden	1,796	4,240	3,047	-21.9	-28.2	Turkey	103.1	247.7	164.1	-46.2	-33.7

NA Not available.   [1] Percent change during calendar year (e.g. December 31, 2000, through December 31, 2001). Adjusted for foreign exchange fluctuations relative to U.S. dollar.   [2] Includes South African gold mines quoted in London.   [3] Europe, Australasia, Far East Index. Comprises all European and Far East countries listed under developed markets plus Australia, Malaysia, and New Zealand.   [4] January 1, 1988=100.   [5] December 1992=100.   [6] See footnote 2, Table 1308.

Source: Morgan Stanley Capital International, New York, NY, <http://www.msci.com/equity/index.html> (copyright). This information may not be reproduced or redisseminated in any form without prior written permission from Morgan Stanley Capital International. This information is provided on an "as is" basis. Neither Morgan Stanley or any other party makes any representation or warranty of any kind either express or implied, with respect to this information (or the results to be obtained by the use thereof) and Morgan Stanley expressly disclaims any and all warranties of originality, accuracy, completeness, merchantability, and fitness for any particular purpose. The user of this information assumes the entire risk of any use made of the information. In no event shall Morgan Stanley or any other part be liable to the user for any direct or indirect damages, including without limitation, any lost profits, lost savings, or other incidental or consequential damages arising out of use of this information.

U.S. Census Bureau, Statistical Abstract of the United States: 2002

No. 1362. Foreign Stock Market Indices: 1985 to 2001

[**As of year end**. The DAX index is a total return index which includes dividends, whereas the other foreign indices are price indices which exclude dividends]

Year	London FTSE 100	Tokyo Nikkei 225	Hong Kong Hang Seng	Germany DAX-30	Paris CAC-40
1985	1,413	13,113	1,752	1,366	(X)
1990	2,144	23,849	3,025	1,398	1,518
1991	2,493	22,984	4,297	1,578	1,766
1992	2,847	16,925	5,512	1,545	1,858
1993	3,418	17,417	11,888	2,267	2,268
1994	3,066	19,723	8,191	2,107	1,881
1995	3,689	19,868	10,073	2,254	1,872
1996	4,119	19,361	13,452	2,889	2,316
1997	5,136	15,259	10,723	4,250	2,999
1998	5,883	13,842	9,507	5,002	3,943
1999	6,930	18,934	16,962	6,958	5,958
2000	6,223	13,786	15,096	6,434	5,926
2001	5,217	10,543	11,397	5,160	4,625

X Not applicable.

Source: Global Financial Data, Los Angeles, CA, <http://www.globalfindata.com>, unpublished data (copyright).

No. 1363. United States and Foreign Stock Markets—Market Capitalization and Value of Shares Traded: 1990 to 2001

[**In billions of U.S. dollars (3,059.4 represents $3,059,400,000,000)**. Market capitalization is the market value of all domestic listed companies at the end of the year. The market value of a company is the share price times the number of shares outstanding. Value of shares traded is the annual total turnover of listed company shares]

Country	Market capitalization				Value of shares traded			
	1990	1995	2000	2001	1990	1995	2000	2001
United States	3,059.4	6,857.6	15,104.0	13,983.9	1,751.3	5,108.6	31,862.5	23,030.5
Argentina	3.3	37.8	166.1	192.5	0.9	4.6	6.0	6.6
Australia	107.6	245.2	372.8	374.3	40.1	98.7	226.3	240.0
Austria	11.5	32.5	29.9	25.2	18.6	25.8	9.4	7.7
Belgium	65.4	105.0	182.5	1,843.5	6.4	15.2	38.0	3,172.6
Brazil	16.4	147.6	226.2	186.2	5.6	79.2	101.3	57.9
Canada	241.9	366.3	841.4	615.3	71.3	183.7	634.7	446.3
Chile	13.6	73.9	60.4	56.7	0.8	11.1	6.1	4.1
China [1]	(NA)	42.1	581.0	524.0	(NA)	49.8	721.5	718.2
Denmark	39.1	56.2	107.7	85.2	11.1	25.9	91.6	91.8
Egypt	1.8	8.1	28.7	24.2	0.1	0.7	11.1	6.9
Finland	22.7	44.1	293.6	190.5	3.9	19.0	206.6	29.8
France	314.4	522.1	1,446.6	1,843.5	116.9	364.6	1,083.3	3,172.6
Germany	355.1	577.4	1,270.2	1,071.8	501.8	573.5	1,069.1	1,434.5
Greece	15.2	17.1	110.8	84.2	3.9	6.1	95.1	37.3
Hong Kong	83.4	303.7	623.4	506.1	34.6	106.9	377.9	196.4
India	38.6	127.2	148.1	110.4	21.9	13.7	509.8	249.3
Indonesia	8.1	66.6	26.8	23.0	4.0	14.4	14.3	23.3
Iran	(NA)	6.6	34.0	9.7	(NA)	0.7	5.0	1.1
Ireland	(NA)	25.8	81.9	78.7	(NA)	13.2	14.4	23.6
Israel	3.3	36.4	64.1	57.6	5.5	9.2	23.4	15.0
Italy	148.8	209.5	768.4	672.1	42.6	86.9	778.4	546.4
Japan	2,917.7	3,667.3	3,157.2	3,910.0	1,602.4	1,231.6	2,693.9	1,696.7
Korea, South	110.6	182.0	171.6	232.1	75.9	185.2	1,067.7	694.2
Luxembourg	10.5	30.4	34.0	22.7	0.1	0.2	1.2	0.7
Malaysia	48.6	222.7	116.9	119.0	10.9	76.8	58.5	23.6
Mexico	32.7	90.7	125.2	126.6	12.2	34.4	45.3	60.4
Morocco	1.0	6.0	10.9	9.1	0.1	2.4	1.1	1.2
Netherlands	119.8	356.5	640.5	1,843.5	40.2	248.6	677.2	3,172.6
New Zealand	8.8	32.0	18.6	17.8	1.9	8.4	10.8	8.4
Norway	26.1	44.6	65.0	69.1	14.0	24.4	60.1	52.4
Philippines	5.9	58.9	51.6	21.3	1.2	14.7	8.2	3.0
Poland	(NA)	4.6	31.3	25.9	(NA)	2.8	14.6	10.6
Portugal	9.2	18.4	60.7	60.7	1.7	4.2	54.4	34.8
Russia	(NA)	15.9	38.9	76.2	(NA)	0.5	20.3	22.9
Saudi Arabia	(NA)	40.9	67.2	73.2	(NA)	6.2	17.3	22.3
Singapore	34.3	148.0	152.8	117.1	20.3	60.5	91.5	63.0
Sweden	97.9	178.0	328.3	232.6	17.6	93.2	390.0	294.9
Switzerland	160.0	433.6	792.3	521.2	(NA)	310.9	609.1	576.9
Taiwan [1]	100.7	187.2	247.6	293.5	715.0	383.1	983.5	524.4
Thailand	23.9	141.5	29.5	36.3	22.9	57.0	23.3	31.1
Turkey	19.1	20.8	69.7	47.7	5.8	51.4	179.2	64.7
United Kingdom	848.9	1,407.7	2,580.0	2,149.5	278.7	510.1	1,835.3	4,594.1

NA Not available.   [1] See footnote 2, Table 1308.

Source: Standard and Poor's, New York, NY, *Standard & Poor's Emerging Stock Markets Factbook 2002* (copyright).

No. 1364. Foreign Exchange Rates: 2001

[**Foreign currency units per U.S. dollar**. Rates shown include market, official, principal, and secondary rates, as published by the International Monetary Fund in *International Financial Statistics*]

Country	Currency	2001	Country	Currency	2001
Afghanistan [1]	Afghanis	3,000.00	Laos	Kip	8,954.58
Albania	Leks	143.49	Latvia	Lats	0.63
Algeria	Algerian Dinar	77.22	Lebanon	Lebanese Pounds	1,507.50
Antigua and Barbuda	E. Caribbean Dollar	2.70	Lesotho	Maloti	8.61
Argentina	Pesos	1.00	Liberia	Liberian Dollar	48.58
Armenia	Dram	555.08	Libya [1]	Libyan Dinars	0.60
Aruba	Aruban Florins	1.79	Lithuania	Litai	4.00
Australia	Australian Dollar	1.93	Luxembourg [2]	Euro	1.12
Austria [2]	Euro	1.12	Macedonia, The Former		
Bahamas, The	Bahamian Dollar	1.00	Yugoslav Republic of	Denar	68.04
Bahrain	Dinars	0.38	Madagascar	Malagasy Francs	6,588.49
Bangladesh	Taka	55.81	Malaysia	Ringgit	3.80
Barbados	Barbados Dollar	2.00	Mali	Cfa Francs	733.04
Belarus	Rubel	1,390.00	Malta	Maltese Liri	0.45
Belgium [2]	Euro	1.12	Mauritania	Ouguiyas	255.25
Belize	Belize Dollar	2.00	Mauritius	Rupees	29.13
Benin	Cfa Francs	733.04	Mexico	New Pesos	9.34
Bolivia	Bolivianos	6.61	Moldova	Lei	12.87
Botswana	Pula	5.84	Mongolia	Tugriks	1,097.70
Brazil	Reals	2.36	Morocco	Dirhams	11.30
Bulgaria	Leva	2.18	Mozambique	Meticais	20,703.6
Burkina Faso	Cfa Francs	733.04	Namibia	Namibia Dollar	8.61
Burma [1]	Kyat	6.75	Nepal	Rupees	74.95
Cambodia	Riels	3,916.33	Netherlands [2]	Euro	1.12
Cameroon	Cfa Francs	733.04	Netherlands Antilles	Euro	(NA)
Canada	Canadian Dollar	1.55	New Zealand	New Zealand Dollar	2.38
Central African Republic	Cfa Francs	733.04	Nicaragua	Cordobas	13.37
Chad	Cfa Francs	733.04	Niger	Cfa Francs	733.04
Chile	Pesos	634.94	Nigeria	Naira	111.23
China [3]	Yuan	8.28	Norway	Kroner	8.99
Colombia	Pesos	2,299.63	Oman	Rials Omani	0.38
Comoros	Comorian Francs	549.78	Pakistan	Rupees	61.93
Congo (Brazzaville) [4]	Cfa Francs	733.04	Panama	Balboas	1.00
Costa Rica	Colones	328.87	Papua New Guinea	Kina	3.39
Cote d'Ivoire	Cfa Francs	(NA)	Paraguay	Guaranies	4,105.92
Croatia	Kuna	8.34	Peru	Nuevos Soles	3.51
Cyprus	Cyprus Pounds	0.64	Philippines	Pesos	50.99
Czech Republic	Koruny	38.04	Poland	Zlotys	4.09
Denmark	Kroner	8.32	Portugal [2]	Euro	1.12
Djibouti	Djibouti Francs	177.72	Qatar	Riyals	3.64
Dominica	E.Caribbean Dollar	2.70	Romania	Lei	29,060.8
Dominican Republic	Pesos	16.95	Russia	Rubles	29.17
Ecuador	U.S. Dollar	25,000.0	Rwanda	Rwanda Francs	442.99
Egypt	Egyptian Pounds	3.97	Saint Kitts and Nevis	E.Caribbean Dollar	2.70
El Salvador	Colones	8.75	Saint Lucia	E.Caribbean Dollar	2.70
Equatorial Guinea	Cfa Francs	733.04	Saint Vincent and the		
Estonia	Krooni	17.56	Grenadines	E.Caribbean Dollar	2.70
Ethiopia [1]	Birr	8.46	Saudi Arabia	Riyals	3.75
Euro area (EMU-11) [2]	Euro	1.12	Senegal	Cfa Francs	733.04
Fiji	Fiji Dollar	2.28	Sierra Leone	Leones	1,986.15
Finland [2]	Euro	1.12	Singapore	Singapore Dollar	1.79
France [2]	Euro	1.12	Slovakia	Koruny	48.35
Gabon	Cfa Francs	733.04	Slovenia	Tolars	242.75
Georgia	Lari	2.07	South Africa	Rand	8.61
Germany [2]	Euro	1.12	Spain [2]	Euro	1.12
Greece	Euro	1.12	Sri Lanka	Rupees	89.38
Guatemala	Quetzales	7.86	Sudan	Sudanese Dinars	258.70
Guyana	Guyana Dollar	187.32	Suriname [1]	Guilders	2,178.50
Haiti	Gourdes	24.43	Swaziland	Emalangeni	8.61
Honduras	Lempiras	15.47	Sweden	Kronor	10.33
Hong Kong	Hong Kong Dollar	7.80	Switzerland	Swiss Francs	1.69
Hungary	Forint	286.49	Syria	Syrian Pounds	11.23
Iceland	Kronur	97.42	Tanzania	Tanzania Shilling	876.41
India	Rupees	47.19	Thailand	Baht	44.43
Indonesia	Rupiah	10,260.8	Togo	Cfa Francs	733.04
Iran	Rials	1,753.56	Trinidad and Tobago	Tt Dollars	6.23
Iraq	Dinars	0.31	Tunisia	Dinars	1.44
Ireland [2]	Euro	1.12	Turkey	Liras	1,225,590
Israel	New Sheqalim	4.21	Uganda	Uganda Shilling	1,755.66
Italy [2]	Euro	1.12	Ukraine	Hryvnias	5.37
Jamaica	Jamaica Dollars	46.00	United Arab Emirates	Dirhams	3.67
Japan	Yen	121.53	United Kingdom	Pounds Sterling	0.69
Jordan	Dinars	0.71	Uruguay	Pesos	13.32
Kazakhstan	Tenge	146.74	Vanuatu	Vatu	145.31
Kenya	Kenya Shillings	78.56	Venezuela	Bolivares	723.67
Korea, South	Won	1,290.99	Yemen	Rials	168.67
Kuwait	Dinars	0.31	Zambia	Kwacha	3,610.93
Kyrgyzstan	Soms	(NA)	Zimbabwe	Zimbabwe Dollar	55.05

NA Not available.

[1] End-of-year values were used if annual averages were unavailable. Some values were estimated using partial year data.
[2] The euro became the official currency of the 11 Euro Area (EMU) nations.   [3] See footnote 2, Table 1308.   [4] See footnote 3, Table 1308.

Source: U.S. Dept. of Commerce, International Trade Administration, "Foreign Exchange Rates, 1994-01"; accessed August 2002; <http://www.ita.doc.gov/td/industry/otea/usfth/tabcon.html>.

No. 1365. Reserve Assets and International Transaction Balances by Country: 1995 to 2001

[In millions of U.S. dollars (74,780 represents $74,780,000,000). Assets include holdings of convertible foreign currencies, special drawing rights, and reserve position in International Monetary Fund and exclude gold holdings. Minus sign (-) indicates debits]

Country	Total reserve assets				Current account balance			Merchandise trade balance		
			2001							
	1995	2000	Total	Currency holdings[1]	1995	2000	2001	1995	2000	2001
United States	74,780	56,600	57,630	28,980	-109,890	-444,690	(NA)	-172,330	-449,570	(NA)
Algeria	2,005	12,024	18,081	17,963	(NA)	(NA)	(NA)	(NA)	(NA)	(NA)
Argentina	14,288	25,147	14,553	14,542	-5,210	-8,970	(NA)	2,358	2,558	(NA)
Australia	11,896	18,118	17,955	16,434	-19,323	-15,330	(NA)	-4,223	-4,711	(NA)
Austria	18,730	14,318	12,509	11,444	-5,448	-5,205	(NA)	-6,656	-2,732	(NA)
Bangladesh	2,340	1,486	1,275	1,274	-824	-306	(NA)	-2,324	1,654	(NA)
Belgium	16,177	9,994	11,266	8,743	14,232	11,360	13,037	9,555	2,225	3,315
Brazil	49,708	32,488	35,740	35,729	-18,136	-24,632	-23,208	-3,157	-696	2,645
Burma	561	223	(NA)	(NA)	-259	-243	(NA)	-823	-516	(NA)
Cameroon	4	212	332	331	90	(NA)	(NA)	627	(NA)	(NA)
Canada	15,049	31,924	33,962	30,484	-4,328	18,014	18,884	25,855	39,833	39,819
Chile	14,140	14,729	14,219	13,882	-1,350	-991	(NA)	1,381	1,438	(NA)
China [2]	75,377	168,278	215,605	212,165	1,618	20,518	(NA)	18,050	34,474	(NA)
Colombia . . . . . . [3]	8,349	8,916	10,154	9,659	-4,596	355	-1,693	-2,545	2,531	492
Congo (Kinshasa) [3] .	59	222	69	68	-650	(NA)	(NA)	516	(NA)	(NA)
Cote d'Ivoire	529	668	1,019	1,018	-492	-13	(NA)	1,376	1,797	(NA)
Denmark	11,016	15,108	17,110	16,117	1,855	2,507	(NA)	6,528	6,758	(NA)
Ecuador	1,628	947	840	816	-994	928	(NA)	-66	1,395	(NA)
Egypt	16,181	13,118	12,926	12,891	-254	-971	(NA)	-7,597	-8,321	(NA)
Finland	10,038	8,465	7,983	7,192	5,231	8,854	(NA)	12,437	13,684	(NA)
France	26,853	37,039	31,749	26,363	10,840	20,430	25,640	11,000	1,130	6,000
Germany	85,005	56,890	51,309	43,615	-18,930	-18,710	3,820	65,110	57,290	82,830
Ghana	698	232	(NA)	(NA)	-145	-413	(NA)	-257	-843	(NA)
Greece	14,780	13,424	5,154	4,787	-2,864	-9,820	(NA)	-14,425	-20,239	(NA)
Hungary	11,974	11,190	10,727	10,302	-2,530	-1,494	(NA)	-2,433	-2,106	(NA)
India	17,922	37,902	45,870	45,251	-5,563	-4,198	(NA)	-6,719	-12,193	(NA)
Indonesia	13,708	28,502	27,246	27,048	-6,431	7,986	(NA)	6,533	25,040	(NA)
Ireland	8,630	5,360	5,587	5,196	1,721	-593	(NA)	13,557	25,416	(NA)
Israel	8,119	23,281	23,379	23,179	-4,994	-1,416	-1,730	-7,261	-3,350	-3,549
Italy	34,905	25,566	24,419	20,905	25,076	-5,670	(NA)	38,729	10,717	(NA)
Japan	183,250	354,902	395,155	387,727	111,040	116,880	(NA)	131,790	116,720	(NA)
Kenya	353	898	1,065	1,048	-400	-238	(NA)	-750	-1,271	(NA)
Korea, South	32,678	96,131	102,753	102,488	-8,507	12,241	8,617	-4,444	16,872	13,392
Kuwait	3,561	7,082	9,897	9,191	5,016	14,865	(NA)	5,579	12,730	(NA)
Malaysia	23,774	29,523	30,474	29,585	-8,644	8,409	(NA)	-103	20,854	(NA)
Mexico	16,847	35,509	44,741	44,384	-1,576	-18,157	(NA)	7,089	-8,003	(NA)
Morocco	3,601	4,823	8,474	8,262	-1,296	-501	(NA)	-2,482	-3,235	(NA)
Nepal	586	947	1,038	1,030	-356	-277	(NA)	-961	-793	(NA)
Netherlands	33,714	9,643	9,034	5,930	25,759	11,156	12,405	23,812	21,278	23,588
Nigeria	1,443	(NA)	(NA)	(NA)	-2,578	(NA)	(NA)	3,513	(NA)	(NA)
Norway	22,518	20,164	15,488	14,408	4,854	22,986	24,078	8,571	25,500	24,973
Pakistan	1,733	1,513	3,640	3,636	-3,349	-96	(NA)	-2,891	-1,159	(NA)
Peru	8,222	8,374	8,618	8,670	-4,125	-1,628	(NA)	-2,168	-323	(NA)
Philippines	6,372	13,052	13,443	13,319	-1,980	9,081	(NA)	-8,944	6,917	(NA)
Poland	14,774	26,562	25,648	25,162	854	-9,997	(NA)	-1,646	-12,308	(NA)
Portugal	15,850	8,908	9,666	9,228	-132	-10,990	-10,080	-8,910	-13,936	-12,979
Romania	1,579	3,922	5,442	5,435	-1,780	-1,359	(NA)	-1,577	-1,684	(NA)
Saudi Arabia	8,622	19,585	17,596	14,796	-5,325	14,336	(NA)	24,390	49,843	(NA)
Singapore	68,695	80,132	75,375	74,851	14,900	21,797	(NA)	976	11,400	(NA)
South Africa	2,820	6,083	6,045	5,765	-2,205	-470	(NA)	2,667	4,231	(NA)
Spain	34,485	30,989	29,582	27,905	792	-19,237	-15,082	-18,415	-34,820	-31,500
Sri Lanka	2,088	1,039	1,287	1,226	-770	-1,042	(NA)	-985	-1,044	(NA)
Sudan	163	247	(NA)	(NA)	-500	-557	(NA)	-510	440	(NA)
Sweden	24,051	14,863	(NA)	(NA)	4,940	6,617	6,696	15,978	15,215	13,832
Switzerland	36,413	32,272	31,999	30,134	21,804	32,542	(NA)	3,258	389	(NA)
Syria	(NA)	(NA)	(NA)	(NA)	263	1,062	(NA)	-146	1,423	(NA)
Thailand	35,982	32,016	32,355	32,350	-13,554	9,313	6,195	-7,968	11,700	8,582
Trinidad and Tobago .	358	1,386	1,907	1,876	294	(NA)	(NA)	588	(NA)	(NA)
Turkey	12,442	22,488	18,879	18,733	-2,338	-9,819	(NA)	-13,212	-22,377	(NA)
United Kingdom	42,020	43,890	37,280	31,940	-14,290	-25,590	(NA)	19,010	-45,430	(NA)
Venezuela	6,283	13,088	9,239	8,825	2,014	13,111	(NA)	7,013	17,544	(NA)

NA Not available. [1] Holdings of convertible foreign currencies. [2] See footnote 2, Table 1308. [3] See footnote 3, Table 1308.

Source: International Monetary Fund, Washington, DC, *International Financial Statistics*, monthly, (copyright).

No. 1366. Foreign Trade—Destination of Exports and Source of Imports for Selected Countries: 2000

[In billions of dollars (1,217.9 represents $1,217,900,000,000), except as indicated]

Country	United States		Canada		Australia		Japan		France		Germany		Italy		United Kingdom	
	Imports	Exports	Imports	Exports	Imprts	Exports	Imports	Exports	Imports	Exports	Imports	Exports	Imports	Exports	Imports	Exports
World [1]	1,217.9	781.8	240.0	277.6	67.8	63.8	379.7	479.2	304.0	295.6	500.8	549.6	235.4	236.5	340.2	284.5
Canada	230.8	178.9	–	–	1.1	7.5	8.7	7.5	1.9	2.4	3.1	3.8	1.8	1.7	6.1	5.3
Mexico	135.9	111.3	4.5	1.4	0.3	0.2	2.4	5.2	0.5	1.2	1.3	4.5	0.3	1.7	1.0	1.0
United States	–	–	154.4	241.8	13.5	6.3	72.5	144.0	26.8	26.0	40.9	55.4	12.4	24.5	45.0	45.0
Australia	6.4	12.5	1.0	0.8	–	–	14.8	8.6	0.7	1.3	1.1	3.0	1.3	1.8	2.4	4.0
Japan	146.5	64.9	11.2	6.1	12.6	12.6	–	–	11.5	5.0	24.3	11.9	5.9	4.0	15.9	5.5
Korea	40.3	27.8	3.5	1.5	2.8	5.2	20.4	30.7	2.2	2.5	5.3	4.0	2.1	1.7	5.3	2.0
Czech Republic	1.1	0.7	0.1	(Z)	(Z)	(Z)	0.2	0.3	1.2	1.7	11.6	11.4	1.0	1.5	1.2	1.4
Hungary	2.7	0.6	0.1	(Z)	0.1	(Z)	0.4	0.8	1.9	1.1	9.6	9.4	1.6	2.2	1.1	0.9
Norway	5.7	1.5	2.9	0.5	(Z)	(Z)	1.2	1.0	7.1	1.1	6.9	3.9	0.8	0.9	8.8	3.2
Poland	1.0	0.8	0.2	0.1	0.1	0.1	0.1	0.4	2.8	2.8	10.8	13.2	1.9	3.5	1.4	2.0
Switzerland	10.4	10.0	0.9	0.4	0.7	0.2	3.3	2.1	6.9	9.9	16.9	23.1	7.0	7.9	8.7	4.8
Russia	7.7	2.1	0.4	0.1	(Z)	0.1	4.6	0.6	4.3	1.6	9.7	6.0	4.8	2.3	2.3	1.0
Algeria	2.7	0.9	0.8	0.3	(Z)	(Z)	(Z)	0.1	2.3	2.7	1.6	0.6	1.4	0.8	0.7	0.2
Egypt	0.9	3.3	(Z)	0.1	(Z)	0.1	0.2	0.7	0.3	1.1	0.2	1.4	1.0	1.4	0.6	0.8
Nigeria	10.5	0.7	0.3	(Z)	(Z)	(Z)	0.2	0.3	1.1	0.6	0.5	0.6	0.3	0.4	0.1	0.8
South Africa	4.3	3.2	0.4	0.2	0.5	0.3	3.0	1.9	0.8	1.1	2.8	3.4	2.3	0.9	4.1	2.2
Columbia	7.0	3.7	0.2	0.2	(Z)	(Z)	0.3	0.6	0.2	0.2	0.5	0.5	0.3	0.2	0.4	0.2
Brazil	13.9	15.3	1.0	0.7	0.4	0.1	3.0	2.5	2.2	2.1	3.5	4.5	2.4	2.2	1.8	1.2
Argentina	3.1	4.7	0.2	0.2	0.2	0.1	0.5	0.7	0.5	1.0	0.8	1.1	0.9	1.0	0.3	0.4
Israel	13.0	7.8	0.4	0.2	0.2	0.1	0.9	1.3	0.9	1.1	1.7	2.4	0.8	1.4	1.6	2.3
Saudi Arabia	14.4	6.2	0.6	0.2	0.8	0.3	14.2	3.1	3.2	1.3	1.0	2.4	2.0	0.8	1.6	2.4
Iran	0.2	(Z)	0.1	0.1	(Z)	0.1	5.4	0.6	1.1	0.7	0.5	1.4	2.2	0.2	0.1	0.4
Pakistan	2.2	0.5	0.2	0.4	0.1	0.2	0.3	0.6	0.4	0.9	0.5	1.9	0.8	0.2	0.6	0.3
India	10.7	3.7	0.8	0.4	0.4	0.3	2.6	2.5	1.3	0.7	2.2	1.7	1.5	0.9	2.6	3.1
Thailand	16.4	6.6	1.1	0.2	1.6	1.1	10.6	13.6	1.7	0.7	2.4	1.7	1.0	0.5	2.5	0.9
Malaysia	25.6	10.9	1.7	0.3	2.5	1.4	14.5	13.9	1.8	0.9	3.5	1.9	1.5	0.9	3.6	1.4
Indonesia	10.4	2.4	0.6	0.5	1.6	1.7	16.4	7.6	1.2	0.4	2.3	1.1	0.9	0.4	1.8	0.6
China [2]	100.0	16.2	7.6	2.4	5.3	3.5	55.1	30.4	9.6	3.0	16.8	8.5	6.4	2.2	7.6	2.2
European Union [3]	220.0	165.1	24.8	12.8	14.7	7.2	46.8	78.3	180.9	184.4	254.8	303.3	131.2	129.0	163.5	153.7
Denmark	3.0	1.5	0.4	0.5	0.3	0.1	2.1	0.7	2.1	2.3	7.5	8.4	1.6	1.8	3.6	3.4
Sweden	9.6	4.6	1.2	0.2	0.9	0.1	2.7	2.1	4.3	4.6	9.4	12.3	3.5	2.4	7.4	6.1
United Kingdom	43.3	41.6	8.7	3.9	4.0	2.2	6.6	14.8	24.2	29.1	34.5	44.8	12.8	16.2	–	–
Austria	3.2	2.6	0.5	0.2	0.3	(Z)	0.9	1.1	2.5	3.1	18.8	28.6	5.4	5.2		
Belgium-Luxembourg	10.3	14.3	0.7	1.5	0.5	0.6	1.9	5.4	21.6	22.1	25.2	29.4	10.1	6.7	2.1	1.7
France	29.8	20.4	2.8	1.3	1.4	0.8	6.4	7.5	–	–	47.6	61.5	26.3	29.5	15.1	14.7
Germany	58.5	29.4	5.2	2.1	3.4	0.3	12.7	20.0	49.3	44.5	–	–	41.1	35.5	26.1	25.9
Finland	3.3	1.6	0.4	0.2	0.4	0.1	0.9	1.2	2.7	1.5	5.0	6.3	2.0	1.0	4.1	2.1
Ireland	16.5	7.7	0.6	0.2	0.6	0.1	3.7	2.0	6.2	2.8	10.1	3.2	3.2	1.7	14.0	19.0
Italy	25.0	11.1	2.5	1.2	1.8	1.1	5.3	5.8	26.5	26.3	33.1	40.9	–	–	14.5	12.1
Netherlands	9.7	21.8	0.9	1.0	0.6	1.1	2.0	12.6	14.6	12.9	41.7	33.6	13.3	6.2	22.8	21.6
Spain	5.7	6.3	0.6	0.4	0.4	0.4	1.4	3.3	20.7	28.6	15.0	24.6	9.7	14.7	9.0	11.8

- Represents zero.   Z Less than 50,000,000.   [1] Includes other countries not shown separately.   [2] See footnote 2, Table 1308.   [3] Includes other countries not shown separately.

Source: Organization for Economic Cooperation and Development, Paris, France, OECD International Trade by Commodities Statistics, 2000.

U.S. Census Bureau, Statistical Abstract of the United States: 2002

No. 1367. International Tourism Arrivals, Expenditures, and Receipts—Leading Countries: 1990 to 2000

[Expenditures and receipts in millions of dollars; arrivals in thousands of visitors (457,298 represents 457,298,000). Excludes international transport receipts]

Country	Arrivals [1]					Expenditures					Receipts				
	1990	1995	1998	1999	2000	1990	1995	1998	1999	2000	1990	1995	1998	1999	2000
World, total [1]	457,298	568,750	641,326	656,598	697,454	244,026	363,175	NA	NA	NA	263,364	406,399	443,154	455,144	477,348
United States	39,363	43,317	46,395	48,491	50,891	37,349	44,916	56,509	59,351	65,044	43,007	63,395	71,286	74,881	85,153
Spain	34,085	34,920	43,396	46,776	47,898	4,254	4,461	5,001	5,523	5,572	18,593	25,388	29,839	32,497	31,454
France	52,497	60,033	70,040	73,042	75,595	10,304	16,328	17,791	18,631	17,166	20,184	27,527	29,931	31,507	29,900
Italy	26,679	31,052	34,933	36,516	41,181	13,826	14,827	17,653	16,913	15,693	16,458	28,729	29,866	28,359	27,500
Ireland	3,666	4,818	6,064	6,403	6,749	1,163	2,034	2,374	2,620	2,957	1,883	2,691	3,267	3,392	3,387
United Kingdom	18,013	23,537	25,745	25,394	25,209	17,560	24,268	32,267	35,631	36,267	13,762	18,554	20,978	20,223	19,544
Germany	17,045	14,847	16,511	17,116	18,983	33,771	54,007	48,911	48,495	47,785	14,288	18,135	16,766	16,730	17,879
Austria	19,011	17,173	17,352	17,467	17,982	7,748	10,267	10,324	9,803	9,291	13,417	14,586	9,396	10,171	10,031
Canada	15,209	16,968	18,870	19,411	19,650	10,931	11,663	10,765	11,345	12,140	6,339	7,882	12,628	12,533	10,704
Greece	8,873	10,130	10,916	12,164	12,500	1,090	1,323	1,756	3,989	4,558	2,587	4,136	6,188	8,783	9,219
Australia	2,215	3,726	4,167	4,459	4,946	4,535	4,587	5,388	5,792	5,740	4,088	7,857	7,335	7,525	8,006
Switzerland	13,200	11,500	10,900	10,700	11,000	5,873	7,346	6,798	6,718	6,238	7,411	9,365	7,973	7,769	7,500
Russia	(NA)	10,290	15,805	18,496	21,169	(NA)	11,599	8,279	7,434	(NA)	(NA)	4,312	6,508	7,510	(NA)
Poland	3,400	19,215	18,780	17,950	17,400	423	5,500	4,430	3,600	3,600	358	6,614	7,946	6,100	6,100
Hungary	20,510	39,240	33,624	28,803	31,141	477	1,056	1,115	1,191	1,061	824	2,640	3,514	3,394	3,429
Czech Republic	7,278	3,381	5,482	4,232	4,666	455	1,633	1,869	1,474	1,257	419	2,875	3,719	3,035	2,869
Ukraine	(NA)	3,716	6,208	3,805	4,406	729	3,041	2,021	1,774	568	(NA)	3,865	3,317	2,124	(NA)
Croatia	7,049	1,485	4,499	5,107	5,831	1,559	422	600	751		1,704	1,349	2,733	2,493	2,758
Brazil	1,091	1,991	4,818	5,107	5,313	5,519	3,412	5,731	3,085	3,893	1,444	2,097	3,678	3,994	4,228
Mexico	17,176	20,241	19,392	19,043	20,641	7,376	3,171	4,209	4,541	5,499	5,467	6,179	7,493	7,223	8,295
Netherlands	5,795	6,574	9,312	9,874	10,003	5,477	11,661	11,996	12,045	12,198	4,155	6,563	6,792	6,998	7,206
Belgium	5,147	5,560	6,179	6,369	6,457	470	9,003	8,794	10,426	10,151	3,721	5,859	5,443	7,331	7,422
China [2]	10,484	20,034	25,073	27,047	31,229	(NA)	3,688	9,205	10,864	13,114	2,218	8,733	12,602	14,099	16,224
Hong Kong	6,581	10,484	10,160	11,328	13,059	(NA)	(NA)	(NA)	(NA)	(NA)	5,032	9,604	7,496	7,210	7,886
Macau	2,513	4,202	4,517	5,050	6,688	(NA)	(NA)	(NA)	(NA)	(NA)	1,473	5,587	2,638	2,466	2,999
Korea, South	2,959	3,753	4,250	4,660	5,322	3,166	5,903	2,640	3,975	6,174	3,559	7,664	6,865	6,802	6,811
Thailand	5,299	6,952	7,843	8,651	9,579	854	3,373	1,448	1,843	2,065	4,326	5,934	5,934	6,695	7,112
Malaysia	7,446	7,469	5,551	7,931	10,222	1,450	2,314	1,785	1,973	(NA)	1,667	8,390	2,456	3,540	4,936
Singapore	4,842	6,422	5,631	6,258	6,917	1,893	4,631	4,707	4,666	4,970	4,937	2,684	5,402	5,859	6,018
Egypt	2,411	2,871	3,213	4,490	5,116	129	1,278	1,148	1,078	1,073	1,100	4,957	2,565	3,903	4,345
Turkey	4,799	7,083	8,960	6,893	9,586	520	912	1,754	1,471	1,711	3,225	4,339	7,809	5,203	7,636
Portugal	8,020	9,511	11,295	11,632	12,097	867	2,141	2,319	2,260	2,230	3,555	5,302	5,302	5,261	5,257
Indonesia	2,178	4,324	4,606	4,728	5,064	836	2,172	2,102	2,353	3,197	2,105	5,229	4,331	4,710	5,749
South Africa	1,029	4,684	5,898	6,026	6,000	1,117	1,849	1,908	2,028	2,004	992	2,126	2,717	2,637	2,707
Tunisia	3,204	4,120	4,718	4,832	5,057	179	251	235	239	263	948	1,393	1,557	1,560	1,496

NA Not available. [1] Includes other countries not shown separately. [2] See footnote 2, Table 1308.

Source: World Tourism Organization, Madrid, Spain, Yearbook of Tourism Statistics (copyright).

U.S. Census Bureau, Statistical Abstract of the United States: 2002

No. 1368. Net Flow of Financial Resources to Developing Countries and Multilateral Organizations: 1995 to 2000

[165,182 represents $165,182,000,000. Net flow covers loans, grants, and grant-like flows minus amortization on loans. Military flows are excluded. Developing countries cover countries designated by Development Assistance Committee as developing. GNP=gross national product]

Type of aid and country	Amount (mil. dol.)					Percent of GNP	
	1995	1997	1998	1999	2000	1999	2000
Total net flows..................	165,182	185,436	182,407	193,740	130,673	0.75	0.54
Official Development Assistance [1]	58,926	48,497	52,084	56,378	(NA)	(X)	(X)
Other Official Flows [2]	9,872	6,125	13,491	15,477	(NA)	(X)	(X)
Private flows at market terms [3]	90,411	125,623	111,223	110,404	(NA)	(X)	(X)
Net grants by nongovernment organizations	5,973	5,191	5,609	6,684	(NA)	(X)	(X)
United States......................	46,984	74,991	48,421	50,138	25,252	0.65	0.25
Australia	2,536	-3,043	1,745	1,279	1,491	0.76	0.40
Austria	906	1,661	889	1,963	1,067	0.39	0.57
Belgium	-234	-10,636	7,725	5,528	2,281	-0.09	1.00
Canada............................	5,724	10,536	9,227	6,992	6,483	1.04	0.95
Denmark...........................	1,799	1,928	1,806	1,992	2,176	1.07	1.39
Finland	604	449	1,633	858	1,050	0.50	0.88
France	12,477	13,979	8,402	9,160	5,557	0.81	0.43
Germany...........................	21,197	19,785	22,436	20,006	12,420	0.87	0.67
Greece	-	185	189	195	229	-	0.20
Ireland	247	323	333	251	741	0.46	0.93
Italy...............................	2,800	8,116	13,171	11,337	10,846	0.26	1.01
Japan.............................	42,295	29,509	17,902	20,794	11,264	0.82	0.23
Luxembourg	72	100	118	124	133	0.40	0.74
Netherlands........................	6,795	8,683	12,752	7,985	6,947	1.71	1.85
New Zealand	166	182	154	163	142	0.31	0.32
Norway............................	1,670	1,647	1,983	2,060	1,437	1.16	0.91
Portugal	395	1,337	2,015	2,457	4,622	0.38	4.45
Spain	2,025	7,411	11,841	29,029	23,471	0.37	4.25
Sweden	2,224	2,092	2,847	2,892	3,952	1.00	1.76
Switzerland	1,118	-3,457	4,683	3,241	2,054	0.35	0.80
United Kingdom	13,382	19,659	12,136	15,299	7,058	1.19	0.50

- Represents zero.   NA Not available.   X Not applicable.   [1] Grants or loans to countries and territories on Part I of the DAC List of Aid Recipients (developing countries which are: (a) undertaken by the official sector; (b) with promotion of economic development and welfare a the main objective; (c) at concessional financial terms (if a loan, having a grant element of at least 25 per cent). Technical cooperation is included in aid.   [2] Transactions by the official sector with countries on the List of Aid Recipients which do not meet the conditions for eligibility as Official Development Assistance or Official Aid, either because they are not primarily aimed at development, or because they have a grant element of less than 25 per cent.   [3] Consists of flows at market terms financed out of private sector resources (i.e. changes in holdings of long term assets held by residents of the reporting country) and private grants (i.e. grants by nongovernment organizations, net of subsidies received from the official sector).

Source: Organization for Economic Cooperation and Development, Paris, France, *Annual Reports of the Development Assistance Committee* (copyright).

No. 1369. External Debt by Country: 1990 to 2000

[In millions of dollars (27,877 represents $27,877,000,000). Total external debt is debt owed to nonresidents repayable in foreign currency, goods, or services. It is the sum of public, publicly guaranteed, and private nonguaranteed long-term debt, use of IMF credit, and short-term debt. Short-term debt includes all debt having an original maturity of one year or less and interest in arrears on long-term debt. Public debt comprises long-term external obligations of public debtors, including the national government and political subdivisions (or an agency of either) and autonomous public bodies, and external obligations of private debtors that are guaranteed for repayment by a public entity]

Country	1990	1995	1999	2000	Country	1990	1995	1999	2000
Algeria	27,877	32,772	28,004	25,002	Lebanon	1,779	2,966	8,235	10,311
Angola	8,594	11,380	11,029	10,146	Malaysia	15,328	34,343	41,902	41,797
Argentina	62,232	98,802	145,294	146,172	Mexico	104,442	166,874	167,626	150,288
Bangladesh......	12,439	15,924	16,533	15,609	Morocco........	24,458	22,665	19,190	17,944
Bolivia	4,275	5,275	5,548	5,762	Mozambique	4,650	7,458	6,982	7,135
Brazil...........	119,964	160,505	243,650	237,953	Nicaragua	10,745	10,402	7,094	7,019
Bulgaria	10,890	10,259	9,810	10,026	Nigeria	33,439	34,093	29,230	34,134
Burma	4,695	5,771	6,004	6,046	Pakistan........	20,663	30,229	33,899	32,091
Cameroon.......	6,676	9,385	9,444	9,241	Panama	6,506	6,098	6,837	7,056
Chile	19,226	22,038	34,269	36,978	Peru	20,064	30,852	28,896	28,560
China [1].	55,301	118,090	154,223	149,800	Philippines	30,580	37,829	53,019	50,063
Colombia	17,222	25,048	34,678	34,081	Poland.........	49,364	44,263	60,579	63,561
Congo (Kinshasa) [2].	10,274	13,239	11,999	11,645	Russia	59,340	121,735	174,360	160,300
Cote d'Ivoire	17,251	18,898	13,170	12,138	Slovakia	2,008	5,821	9,150	
Croatia.........	(NA)	3,829	11,027	12,120	South Africa	(NA)	25,358	23,907	24,861
Czech Republic	6,383	16,218	22,653	21,299	Sri Lanka	5,863	8,370	9,797	9,065
Ecuador	12,107	13,994	15,305	13,281	Sudan	14,762	17,603	16,132	15,741
Egypt...........	33,017	33,337	30,802	28,957	Syria	17,259	21,415	22,369	21,657
Hungary.........	21,202	31,649	29,833	29,415	Thailand........	28,095	100,039	96,769	79,675
India	83,628	94,469	98,158	100,367	Turkey	49,424	73,790	102,068	116,209
Indonesia	69,872	124,398	150,844	141,803	Ukraine	(NA)	8,429	13,941	12,166
Iran	9,020	21,879	10,357	7,953	Uruguay	4,415	5,318	7,500	8,196
Jordan	8,177	8,064	8,910	8,226	Venezuela........	33,170	35,538	38,192	38,196
Kenya	7,058	7,412	6,487	6,295	Vietnam........	23,270	25,427	23,260	12,787
Korea, South	34,968	85,810	130,316	134,417	Yugoslavia	17,792	11,137	11,253	11,960

NA Not available.   [1] See footnote 2, Table 1308.   [2] See footnote 3, Table 1308.

Source: The World Bank, Washington, DC, *2001 World Development Indicators CD-ROM* (copyright).

Comparative International Statistics   859

No. 1370. Military Budget by Country: 2001

[**Figures are for latest year available, usually 2001 except where noted.** Expenditures are used in a few cases where official budgets are significantly lower than actual spending]

Country	Amount (bil. dol.)	Country	Amount (bil. dol.)
Argentina [1]	3.1	Luxembourg	0.9
Australia	6.6	Netherlands	5.6
Belgium	2.2	North Korea	1.3
Brazil [1]	17.9	Norway	2.8
Canada	7.7	Pakistan	2.6
China [1]	42.0	Philippines	1.1
Colombia	2.1	Poland	3.7
Cuba	0.7	Portugal	1.3
Czech Republic	1.1	Russia [1]	60.0
Denmark	2.4	Saudi Arabia	27.2
Egypt	2.1	Singapore	4.3
France	25.3	South Korea	11.8
Germany	21.0	Spain	6.9
Greece	3.3	Sudan	0.6
Hungary	0.8	Sweden	4.2
India	15.6	Syria	0.8
Iran	9.1	Taiwan	8.2
Iraq	1.4	Turkey	5.1
Israel	9.0	United Arab Emirates [1]	3.9
Italy	15.5	United Kingdom	34.0
Japan	40.4	United States	396.1
Kuwait	2.6	Vietnam	1.8
Libya	1.2	Yugoslavia	0.5

[1] 2000 funding.

Source: Data from U.S. Dept. of Defense, and International Institute for Strategic Studies, Center for Defense Information, Washington, DC, "Last of the Big Time Spenders: U.S. Military Budget Still the World's Largest, and Growing"; published 4 February, 2002; <http://www.cdi.org/issues/wme/spendersFY03.html>.

No. 1371. Military Manpower Fit for Military Service by Country: 2001

[Covers males ages 15-49]

Country	Number	Country	Number
Afghanistan	3,561,957	Israel [3]	1,245,757
Albania	712,763	Italy	12,244,166
Algeria	5,383,770	Jamaica	517,077
Argentina	7,625,425	Japan	25,876,484
Australia	4,303,966	Kazakhstan	3,598,859
Austria	1,731,383	Korea, South	8,979,778
Bahrain	121,833	Kuwait	466,521
Bangladesh	21,362,279	Laos	710,627
Belarus	2,138,743	Lebanon	605,332
Belgium	2,079,624	Libya	866,012
Bolivia	1,306,452	Malaysia	3,514,023
Bosnia and Herzegovina	895,780	Mexico	19,394,184
Brazil	32,388,786	Morocco	5,160,374
Bulgaria	1,581,697	Mozambique	2,670,933
Burma [1]	6,425,514	Netherlands	3,555,501
Cambodia	1,610,761	New Zealand	841,915
Canada	7,114,851	Nicaragua	779,267
Chile	3,003,134	Nigeria	17,201,367
China	200,886,946	Norway	913,534
Colombia	7,205,211	Oman	429,811
Congo (Kinshasa)	5,915,251	Pakistan	21,897,366
Congo (Brazzaville)	347,946	Peru	4,847,250
Cote d'Ivoire	2,010,862	Philippines	14,942,363
Croatia	859,621	Poland	8,139,245
Cuba [2]	1,911,160	Russia	30,337,743
Czech Republic	2,024,070	Saudi Arabia	3,291,185
Denmark	1,106,094	Sierra Leone	563,631
Dominican Republic	1,430,776	Singapore	959,636
Ecuador	2,280,899	South Africa	6,977,328
Egypt	12,020,059	Spain	8,448,150
El Salvador	929,263	Sudan	5,194,862
Ethiopia	7,581,815	Sweden	1,803,995
Finland	1,033,188	Switzerland	1,570,918
France	12,127,793	Syria	2,448,630
Germany	17,760,412	Thailand	10,646,818
Greece	2,040,227	Turkey	11,432,438
Guatemala	2,018,636	Ukraine	9,630,184
Honduras	902,220	United Arab Emirates	420,484
Hungary	2,050,404	United Kingdom	12,139,930
Iceland	62,704	United States	(NA)
India	164,410,461	Venezuela	4,701,062
Indonesia	37,418,755	Vietnam	13,673,438
Iran	10,872,407	Yugoslavia	2,088,595
Iraq	3,301,880	Taiwan	5,025,856
Ireland	809,808		

NA Not available. [1] 6,419,677 females ages 15-49 fit for service. [2] 1,867,958 females ages 15-49 fit for service. [3] 1,208,973 females ages 15-49 fit for service.

Source: Central Intelligence Agency, *The World Factbook, 2001*. See also <http://www.cia.gov/cia/publications/factbook/index.html> (accessed June 2002).

2000 Census Data Sampler

This section presents a selection of data from the *2000 Census of Population and Housing* that became available too late to be incorporated into the topical sections of the *Abstract*. Data are presented for the states and, for some series, the 25 largest metro areas and cities. Most of these data are taken from the Census Bureau's *Demographic Profiles* presenting sample items from the decennial census. These data were asked of persons from a sample of housing units and persons in group quarters (e.g. college dormitories). The sample data include topics, such as school enrollment, educational attainment, marital status, grandparents as caregivers, veteran status, disability status of the civilian noninstitutionalized population, residence, nativity and place of birth, region of birth of the foreign born, language spoken at home, ancestry, employment status, commuting to work, occupation, industry, class of worker, income, and poverty status. The sample items also include sample housing topics, such as units in structure, year structure built, rooms, year householder moved into unit, vehicles available, house heating fuel, occupants per room, value, mortgage status and selected monthly owner costs, selected monthly owner costs as a percentage of household income, gross rent, and gross rent as a percentage of household income. The *Demographic Profiles* also contain data collected from the entire population, such as sex, age, race, and household type, for example. For complete access to the *Demographic Profiles* see: <http://www.census.gov/Press-Release/www/2002/demoprofiles.html>.

No. 1372. Urban and Rural Population by State: 2000

[In thousands, except percent (281,422 represents 281,422,000). As of April 1. Resident population]

State	Total	Urban Number	Urban Percent	Rural	State	Total	Urban Number	Urban Percent	Rural
U.S., total . . .	**281,422**	**222,361**	**79.0**	**59,061**					
					MO	5,595	3,883	69.4	1,712
AL.	4,447	2,466	55.4	1,981	MT	902	488	54.1	414
AK.	627	411	65.6	216	NE.	1,711	1,194	69.8	518
AZ.	5,131	4,524	88.2	607	NV.	1,998	1,829	91.5	170
AR.	2,673	1,404	52.5	1,269	NH	1,236	732	59.3	503
CA.	33,872	31,990	94.4	1,882					
					NJ.	8,414	7,939	94.4	475
CO	4,301	3,633	84.5	668	NM	1,819	1,364	75.0	456
CT.	3,406	2,988	87.7	418	NY.	18,976	16,603	87.5	2,374
DE.	784	628	80.1	156	NC	8,049	4,849	60.2	3,200
DC	572	572	100.0	-	ND	642	359	55.9	283
FL.	15,982	14,270	89.3	1,712					
					OH	11,353	8,782	77.4	2,571
GA	8,186	5,864	71.6	2,322	OK	3,451	2,255	65.3	1,196
HI	1,212	1,108	91.5	103	OR	3,421	2,694	78.7	727
ID	1,294	859	66.4	434	PA.	12,281	9,464	77.1	2,817
IL	12,419	10,910	87.8	1,510	RI	1,048	953	90.9	95
IN	6,080	4,304	70.8	1,776					
					SC.	4,012	2,427	60.5	1,585
IA	2,926	1,787	61.1	1,139	SD.	755	391	51.9	363
KS.	2,688	1,921	71.4	768	TN.	5,689	3,620	63.6	2,069
KY.	4,042	2,254	55.8	1,788	TX.	20,852	17,204	82.5	3,648
LA.	4,469	3,246	72.6	1,223	UT.	2,233	1,970	88.2	263
ME	1,275	513	40.2	762					
					VT.	609	232	38.2	376
MD	5,296	4,559	86.1	738	VA.	7,079	5,170	73.0	1,909
MA	6,349	5,801	91.4	548	WA	5,894	4,831	82.0	1,063
MI	9,938	7,419	74.7	2,519	WV	1,808	833	46.1	976
MN	4,919	3,490	70.9	1,429	WI	5,364	3,664	68.3	1,700
MS	2,845	1,387	48.8	1,457	WY	494	321	65.1	172

- Represents zero.

Source: U.S. Census Bureau, Census 2000 Summary File 1 Final National File, 2002.

No. 1373. Profile of Selected Social Characteristics—United States Summary: 2000

[As of April 1. Based on sample data from the 2000 Census of Population and Housing; see text Section 1, Population, and Appendix III]

Subject	Number	Percent	Subject	Number	Percent
SCHOOL ENROLLMENT			NATIVITY AND PLACE OF BIRTH		
Population 3 years and over enrolled in school	**76,632,927**	**100.0**	Total population	281,421,906	100.0
Nursery school, preschool	4,957,582	6.5	Native	250,314,017	88.9
Kindergarten	4,157,491	5.4	Born in United States	246,786,466	87.7
Elementary school (grades 1-8)	33,653,641	43.9	State of residence	168,729,388	60.0
High school (grades 9-12)	16,380,951	21.4	Different state	78,057,078	27.7
College or graduate school	17,483,262	22.8	Born outside United States	3,527,551	1.3
			Foreign born	31,107,889	11.1
EDUCATIONAL ATTAINMENT			Entered 1990 to March 2000	13,178,276	4.7
Population 25 years and over	**182,211,639**	**100.0**	Naturalized citizen	12,542,626	4.5
Less than 9th grade	13,755,477	7.5	Not a citizen	18,565,263	6.6
9th to 12th grade, no diploma	21,960,148	12.1			
High school graduate (includes equivalency)	52,168,981	28.6	REGION OF BIRTH OF FOREIGN BORN		
Some college, no degree	38,351,595	21.0	**Total (excluding born at sea)**	**31,107,573**	**100.0**
Associate degree	11,512,833	6.3	Europe	4,915,557	15.8
Bachelor's degree	28,317,792	15.5	Asia	8,226,254	26.4
Graduate or professional degree	16,144,813	8.9	Africa	881,300	2.8
			Oceania	168,046	0.5
Percent high school graduate or higher	80.4	(X)	Latin America	16,086,974	51.7
Percent bachelor's degree or higher	24.4	(X)	Northern America	829,442	2.7
MARITAL STATUS			LANGUAGE SPOKEN AT HOME		
Population 15 years and over	**221,148,671**	**100.0**	**Population 5 years and over**	**262,375,152**	**100.0**
Never married	59,913,370	27.1	English only	215,423,557	82.1
Now married, except separated	120,231,273	54.4	Language other than English [1]	46,951,595	17.9
Separated	4,769,220	2.2	Speak English less than "very well"	21,320,407	8.1
Widowed	14,674,500	6.6	Spanish	28,101,052	10.7
Female	11,975,325	5.4	Speak English less than "very well"	13,751,256	5.2
Divorced	21,560,308	9.7	Other Indo-European languages	10,017,989	3.8
Female	12,305,294	5.6	Speak English less than "very well"	3,390,301	1.3
GRANDPARENTS AS CAREGIVERS			Asian and Pacific Island languages	6,960,065	2.7
Grandparent living in household with one or more own grandchildren under 18 years	**5,771,671**	**100.0**	Speak English less than "very well"	3,590,024	1.4
Grandparent responsible for grandchildren	2,426,730	42.0	ANCESTRY (single or multiple)		
VETERAN STATUS			Total population	281,421,906	100.0
			Total ancestries reported	287,304,886	102.1
Civilian population 18 years and over	**208,130,352**	**100.0**	Arab [2]	1,202,871	0.4
Civilian veterans	26,403,703	12.7	Czech [2]	1,703,930	0.6
			Danish	1,430,897	0.5
DISABILITY STATUS OF THE CIVILIAN NONINSTITUTIONALIZED POPULATION			Dutch	4,542,494	1.6
			English	24,515,138	8.7
Population 5 to 20 years	**64,689,357**	**100.0**	French (except Basque) [2]	8,325,509	3.0
With a disability	5,214,334	8.1	French Canadian [2]	2,435,098	0.9
Population 21 to 64 years	**159,131,544**	**100.0**	German	42,885,162	15.2
With a disability	30,553,796	19.2	Greek	1,153,307	0.4
Percent employed	56.6	(X)	Hungarian	1,398,724	0.5
No disability	128,577,748	80.8	Irish [2]	30,594,130	10.9
Percent employed	77.2	(X)	Italian	15,723,555	5.6
Population 65 years and over	**33,346,626**	**100.0**	Lithuanian	659,992	0.2
With a disability	13,978,118	41.9	Norwegian	4,477,725	1.6
			Polish	8,977,444	3.2
RESIDENCE IN 1995			Portuguese	1,177,112	0.4
Population 5 years and over	**262,375,152**	**100.0**	Russian	2,652,214	0.9
Same house in 1995	142,027,478	54.1	Scotch-Irish	4,319,232	1.5
Different house in the U.S. in 1995	112,851,828	43.0	Scottish	4,890,581	1.7
Same county	65,435,013	24.9	Slovak	797,764	0.3
Different county	47,416,815	18.1	Subsaharan African	1,781,877	0.6
Same state	25,327,355	9.7	Swedish	3,998,310	1.4
Different state	22,089,460	8.4	Swiss	911,502	0.3
Elsewhere in 1995	7,495,846	2.9	Ukrainian	892,922	0.3
			United States or American	20,625,093	7.3
			Welsh	1,753,794	0.6
			West Indian (excluding Hispanic groups)	1,869,504	0.7
			Other ancestries	91,609,005	32.6

X Not applicable. [1] Includes other languages, not shown separately. [2] The data represent a combination of two ancestries shown separately in Summary File 3. Czech includes Czechoslovakian. French includes Alsatian. French Canadian includes Acadian/Cajun. Irish includes Celtic.

Source: U.S. Census Bureau, "2000 Census of Population and Housing, Profiles of General Demographic Characteristics"; <http://www.census.gov/Press-Release/www/2002/demoprofiles.html>.

No. 1374. Profile of Selected Economic Characteristics—United States Summary: 2000

[As of April 1. Based on sample data from the 2000 Census of Population and Housing; see text Section 1, Population, and Appendix III. For definition of median, see Guide to Tabular Presentation]

Subject	Number	Percent	Subject	Number	Percent
EMPLOYMENT STATUS			Government workers	18,923,353	14.6
			Self-employed workers in own not		
Population 16 years and over.	**217,168,077**	**100.0**	incorporated business.	8,603,761	6.6
In labor force	138,820,935	63.9	Unpaid family workers	400,037	0.3
Civilian labor force	137,668,798	63.4			
Employed	129,721,512	59.7	**INCOME IN 1999**		
Unemployed	7,947,286	3.7			
Percent of civilian labor force.	5.8	(X)	**Households . . . .**	**105,539,122**	**100.0**
Armed Forces	1,152,137	0.5	Less than $10,000.	10,067,027	9.5
Not in labor force.	78,347,142	36.1	$10,000 to $14,999	6,657,228	6.3
			$15,000 to $24,999	13,536,965	12.8
Females 16 years and over . . .	112,185,795	100.0	$25,000 to $34,999	13,519,242	12.8
In labor force	64,547,732	57.5	$35,000 to $49,999	17,446,272	16.5
Civilian labor force	64,383,493	57.4	$50,000 to $74,999	20,540,604	19.5
Employed	60,630,069	54.0	$75,000 to $99,999	10,799,245	10.2
			$100,000 to $149,999	8,147,826	7.7
Own children under 6 years.	21,833,613	100.0	$150,000 to $199,999	2,322,038	2.2
All parents in family in labor force. . .	12,787,501	58.6	$200,000 or more	2,502,675	2.4
			Median household income (dollars) . .	41,994	(X)
COMMUTING TO WORK			With earnings	84,962,743	80.5
Workers 16 years and over. . . .	**128,279,228**	**100.0**	Mean earnings (dollars)	56,604	(X)
Car, truck, or van—drove alone	97,102,050	75.7	With Social Security income	27,084,417	25.7
Car, truck, or van—carpooled	15,634,051	12.2	Mean Social Security income		
Public transportation (including taxi-			(dollars)	11,320	(X)
cab)	6,067,703	4.7	With Supplemental Security Income .	4,615,885	4.4
Walked	3,758,982	2.9	Mean Supplemental Security		
Other means	1,532,219	1.2	Income (dollars)	6,320	(X)
Worked at home	4,184,223	3.3	With public assistance income	3,629,732	3.4
Mean travel time to work (minutes) .	25.5	(X)	Mean public assistance income		
			(dollars)	3,032	(X)
OCCUPATION			With retirement income.	17,659,058	16.7
			Mean retirement income		
Employed civilian population			(dollars)	17,376	(X)
16 years and over	**129,721,512**	**100.0**			
Management, professional, and			**Families. . . . .**	**72,261,780**	**100.0**
related occupations	43,646,731	33.6	Less than $10,000.	4,155,386	5.8
Service occupations.	19,276,947	14.9	$10,000 to $14,999	3,115,586	4.3
Sales and office occupations	34,621,390	26.7	$15,000 to $24,999	7,757,397	10.7
Farming, fishing, and forestry occu-			$25,000 to $34,999	8,684,429	12.0
pations.	951,810	0.7	$35,000 to $49,999	12,377,108	17.1
Construction, extraction, and mainte-			$50,000 to $74,999	16,130,100	22.3
nance occupations	12,256,138	9.4	$75,000 to $99,999	9,009,327	12.5
Production, transportation, and			$100,000 to $149,999	6,936,210	9.6
material moving occupations	18,968,496	14.6	$150,000 to $199,999	1,983,673	2.7
			$200,000 or more	2,112,564	2.9
INDUSTRY			Median family income (dollars).	50,046	(X)
Employed civilian population			Per capita income (dollars) [1]	21,587	(X)
16 years and over	**129,721,512**	**100.0**			
Agriculture, forestry, fishing and			Median earnings (dollars):		
hunting, and mining	2,426,053	1.9	Male full-time, year-round workers .	37,057	(X)
Construction.	8,801,507	6.8	Female full-time, year-round		
Manufacturing.	18,286,005	14.1	workers	27,194	(X)
Wholesale trade	4,666,757	3.6			
Retail trade	15,221,716	11.7	**POVERTY STATUS IN 1999**		
Transportation and warehousing,					
and utilities.	6,740,102	5.2	**Families below poverty level .**	**6,620,945**	**9.2**
Information.	3,996,564	3.1	With related children under 18 years.	5,155,866	13.6
Finance, insurance, real estate,			With related children under 5		
and rental and leasing	8,934,972	6.9	years	2,562,263	17.0
Professional, scientific, management,					
administrative, and waste manage-			**Families with female house-**		
ment services	12,061,865	9.3	**holder, no husband present**		
Educational, health and social			**below poverty level . . . .**	**3,315,916**	**26.5**
services.	25,843,029	19.9	With related children under 18 years.	2,940,459	34.3
Arts, entertainment, recreation,			With related children under 5		
accommodation and food services .	10,210,295	7.9	years	1,401,493	46.4
Other services (except public					
administration).	6,320,632	4.9	**Individuals below poverty**		
Public administration	6,212,015	4.8	**level. . . . .**	**33,899,812**	**12.4**
			18 years and over	22,152,954	10.9
CLASS OF WORKER			65 years and over	3,287,774	9.9
			Related children under 18 years. . . .	11,386,031	16.1
Employed civilian population			Related children 5 to 17 years . . .	7,974,006	15.4
16 years and over	**129,721,512**	**100.0**	Unrelated individuals 15 years and		
Private wage and salary workers . . .	101,794,361	78.5	over	10,721,935	22.7

X Not applicable.

Source: U.S. Census Bureau, "2000 Census of Population and Housing, Profiles of General Demographic Characteristics"; <http://www.census.gov/Press-Release/www/2002/demoprofiles.html>.

No. 1375. Profile of Selected Housing Characteristics—United States Summary: 2000

[As of April 1. Based on sample data from the 2000 Census of Population and Housing; see text Section 1, Population, and Appendix III. For definition of median, see Guide to Tabular Presentation]

Subject	Number	Percent	Subject	Number	Percent
Total housing units	**115,904,641**	**100.0**	OCCUPANTS PER ROOM		
UNITS IN STRUCTURE			1.00 or less	99,406,609	94.2
			1.01 to 1.50	3,198,596	3.0
1-unit, detached	69,865,957	60.3	1.51 or more	2,874,896	2.7
1-unit, attached	6,447,453	5.6	**Specified owner-occupied**		
2 units	4,995,350	4.3	**units**	**55,212,108**	**100.0**
3 or 4 units	5,494,280	4.7			
5 to 9 units	5,414,988	4.7	VALUE		
10 to 19 units	4,636,717	4.0			
20 or more units	10,008,058	8.6	Less than $50,000	5,457,817	9.9
Mobile home	8,779,228	7.6	$50,000 to $99,999	16,778,971	30.4
Boat, RV, van, etc	262,610	0.2	$100,000 to $149,999	13,110,384	23.7
			$150,000 to $199,999	8,075,904	14.6
YEAR STRUCTURE BUILT			$200,000 to $299,999	6,583,049	11.9
			$300,000 to $499,999	3,584,108	6.5
1999 to March 2000	2,755,075	2.4	$500,000 to $999,999	1,308,116	2.4
1995 to 1998	8,478,975	7.3	$1,000,000 or more	313,759	0.6
1990 to 1994	8,467,008	7.3	Median (dollars)	119,600	(X)
1980 to 1989	18,326,847	15.8			
1970 to 1979	21,438,863	18.5	MORTGAGE STATUS AND		
1960 to 1969	15,911,903	13.7	SELECTED MONTHLY		
1940 to 1959	23,145,917	20.0	OWNER COSTS		
1939 or earlier	17,380,053	15.0			
			With a mortgage	38,663,887	70.0
ROOMS			Less than $300	255,243	0.5
1 room	2,551,061	2.2	$300 to $499	2,149,992	3.9
2 rooms	5,578,182	4.8	$500 to $699	4,943,283	9.0
3 rooms	11,405,588	9.8	$700 to $999	9,612,512	17.4
4 rooms	18,514,383	16.0	$1,000 to $1,499	11,679,988	21.2
5 rooms	24,214,071	20.9	$1,500 to $1,999	5,555,203	10.1
6 rooms	21,385,794	18.5	$2,000 or more	4,467,666	8.1
7 rooms	13,981,917	12.1	Median (dollars)	1,088	(X)
8 rooms	9,343,740	8.1	Not mortgaged	16,548,221	30.0
9 or more rooms	8,929,905	7.7	Median (dollars)	295	(X)
Median (rooms)	5.3	(X)			
Occupied housing units	**105,480,101**	**100.0**	SELECTED MONTHLY OWNER		
			COSTS AS A PERCENTAGE OF		
YEAR HOUSEHOLDER MOVED			HOUSEHOLD INCOME IN 1999		
INTO UNIT					
			Less than 15.0 percent	20,165,963	36.5
1999 to March 2000	21,041,090	19.9	15.0 to 19.9 percent	9,661,469	17.5
1995 to 1998	30,479,848	28.9	20.0 to 24.9 percent	7,688,019	13.9
1990 to 1994	16,948,257	16.1	25.0 to 29.9 percent	5,210,523	9.4
1980 to 1989	16,429,173	15.6	30.0 to 34.9 percent	3,325,083	6.0
1970 to 1979	10,399,015	9.9	35.0 percent or more	8,719,648	15.8
1969 or earlier	10,182,718	9.7	Not computed	441,403	0.8
			Specified renter-occupied		
VEHICLES AVAILABLE			**units**	**35,199,502**	**100.0**
None	10,861,067	10.3	GROSS RENT		
1	36,123,613	34.2			
2	40,461,920	38.4	Less than $200	1,844,181	5.2
3 or more	18,033,501	17.1	$200 to $299	1,818,764	5.2
			$300 to $499	7,739,515	22.0
HOUSE HEATING FUEL			$500 to $749	11,860,298	33.7
			$750 to $999	6,045,173	17.2
Utility gas	54,027,880	51.2	$1,000 to $1,499	3,054,099	8.7
Bottled, tank, or LP gas	6,880,185	6.5	$1,500 or more	1,024,296	2.9
Electricity	32,010,401	30.3	No cash rent	1,813,176	5.2
Fuel oil, kerosene, etc	9,457,850	9.0	Median (dollars)	602	(X)
Coal or coke	142,876	0.1			
Wood	1,769,781	1.7	GROSS RENT AS A PERCENTAGE		
Solar energy	47,069	(Z)	OF HOUSEHOLD INCOME IN 1999		
Other fuel	412,553	0.4			
No fuel used	731,506	0.7	Less than 15.0 percent	6,370,263	18.1
			15.0 to 19.9 percent	5,037,981	14.3
SELECTED CHARACTERISTICS			20.0 to 24.9 percent	4,498,604	12.8
			25.0 to 29.9 percent	3,666,233	10.4
Lacking complete plumbing facilities .	670,986	0.6	30.0 to 34.9 percent	2,585,327	7.3
Lacking complete kitchen facilities . .	715,535	0.7	35.0 percent or more	10,383,959	29.5
No telephone service	2,570,705	2.4	Not computed	2,657,135	7.5

X Not applicable.   Z Less than 0.05 percent.

Source: U.S. Census Bureau, "2000 Census of Population and Housing, Profiles of General Demographic Characteristics"; <http://www.census.gov/Press-Release/www/2002/demoprofiles.html>.

U.S. Census Bureau, Statistical Abstract of the United States: 2002

No. 1376. Educational Attainment by State: 2000

[In percent, except as indicated (182,212 represents 182,212,000). As of April 1. For persons 25 years old and over. Based on sample data from the 2000 Census of Population and Housing; see text, Section 1, Population, and Appendix III]

State	Population (1,000)	Less than 9th grade	9th to 12th grade, no diploma	High school graduate	With some college, but no degree	Associate degree	Bachelor's degree	Graduate or professional degree	High school graduate or more	College graduate or more
U.S. ...	182,212	7.5	12.1	28.6	21.0	6.3	15.5	8.9	80.4	24.4
AL......	2,887	8.3	16.4	30.4	20.5	5.4	12.2	6.9	75.3	19.0
AK......	380	4.1	7.5	27.9	28.6	7.2	16.1	8.6	88.3	24.7
AZ......	3,256	7.8	11.2	24.3	26.4	6.7	15.2	8.4	81.0	23.5
AR......	1,731	9.4	15.3	34.1	20.5	4.0	11.0	5.7	75.3	16.7
CA......	21,299	11.5	11.7	20.1	22.9	7.1	17.1	9.5	76.8	26.6
CO	2,777	4.8	8.2	23.2	24.0	7.0	21.6	11.1	86.9	32.7
CT......	2,296	5.8	10.2	28.5	17.5	6.6	18.2	13.3	84.0	31.4
DE......	515	5.0	12.4	31.4	19.5	6.6	15.6	9.4	82.6	25.0
DC	385	7.8	14.4	20.6	15.4	2.8	18.1	21.0	77.8	39.1
FL	11,025	6.7	13.4	28.7	21.8	7.0	14.3	8.1	79.9	22.3
GA	5,186	7.6	13.8	28.7	20.4	5.2	16.0	8.3	78.6	24.3
HI	802	7.2	8.2	28.5	21.8	8.1	17.8	8.4	84.6	26.2
ID	788	5.2	10.1	28.5	27.3	7.2	14.8	6.8	84.7	21.7
IL	7,974	7.5	11.1	27.7	21.6	6.1	16.5	9.5	81.4	26.1
IN	3,893	5.3	12.6	37.2	19.7	5.8	12.2	7.2	82.1	19.4
IA	1,896	5.6	8.3	36.1	21.4	7.4	14.7	6.5	86.1	21.2
KS......	1,701	5.2	8.8	29.8	24.6	5.8	17.1	8.7	86.0	25.8
KY......	2,646	11.7	14.2	33.6	18.5	4.9	10.3	6.9	74.1	17.1
LA......	2,775	9.3	15.9	32.4	20.2	3.5	12.2	6.5	74.8	18.7
ME	870	5.4	9.2	36.2	19.0	7.3	14.9	7.9	85.4	22.9
MD	3,496	5.1	11.1	26.7	20.3	5.3	18.0	13.4	83.8	31.4
MA	4,273	5.8	9.4	27.3	17.1	7.2	19.5	13.7	84.8	33.2
MI	6,416	4.7	11.9	31.3	23.3	7.0	13.7	8.1	83.4	21.8
MN	3,164	5.0	7.0	28.8	24.0	7.7	19.1	8.3	87.9	27.4
MS	1,758	9.6	17.5	29.4	20.9	5.7	11.1	5.8	72.9	16.9
MO	3,635	6.5	12.1	32.7	21.9	5.1	14.0	7.6	81.3	21.6
MT......	587	4.3	8.6	31.3	25.6	5.9	17.2	7.2	87.2	24.4
NE......	1,087	5.4	8.0	31.3	24.3	7.3	16.5	7.3	86.6	23.7
NV......	1,310	6.4	12.9	29.3	27.0	6.2	12.1	6.1	80.7	18.2
NH	824	3.9	8.7	30.1	20.0	8.7	18.7	10.0	87.4	28.7
NJ......	5,658	6.6	11.3	29.4	17.7	5.3	18.8	11.0	82.1	29.8
NM......	1,135	9.3	11.9	26.6	22.9	5.9	13.6	9.8	78.9	23.5
NY......	12,543	8.0	12.9	27.8	16.8	7.2	15.6	11.8	79.1	27.4
NC	5,283	7.0	14.0	28.4	20.5	6.8	15.3	7.2	78.1	22.5
ND	409	8.7	7.4	27.9	24.5	9.4	16.5	5.5	83.9	22.0
OH	7,412	4.5	12.6	36.1	19.9	5.9	13.7	7.4	83.0	21.1
OK	2,203	6.1	13.3	31.5	23.4	5.4	13.5	6.8	80.6	20.3
OR	2,251	5.0	9.9	26.3	27.1	6.6	16.4	8.7	85.1	25.1
PA......	8,266	5.5	12.6	38.1	15.5	5.9	14.0	8.4	81.9	22.4
RI	695	8.1	13.9	27.8	17.6	7.0	15.9	9.7	78.0	25.6
SC......	2,596	8.3	15.4	30.0	19.3	6.7	13.5	6.9	76.3	20.4
SD......	474	7.5	8.0	32.9	23.0	7.1	15.5	6.0	84.6	21.5
TN......	3,745	9.6	14.5	31.6	20.0	4.7	12.8	6.8	75.9	19.6
TX......	12,791	11.5	12.9	24.8	22.4	5.2	15.6	7.6	75.7	23.2
UT......	1,198	3.2	9.1	24.6	29.1	7.9	17.9	8.3	87.7	26.1
VT......	404	5.1	8.4	32.4	16.9	7.7	18.3	11.1	86.4	29.4
VA......	4,667	7.2	11.3	26.0	20.4	5.6	17.9	11.6	81.5	29.5
WA	3,828	4.3	8.6	24.9	26.4	8.0	18.4	9.3	87.1	27.7
WV	1,234	10.0	14.8	39.4	16.6	4.3	8.9	5.9	75.2	14.8
WI......	3,476	5.4	9.6	34.6	20.6	7.5	15.3	7.2	85.1	22.4
WY......	316	3.4	8.8	31.0	27.0	8.0	14.9	7.0	87.9	21.9

Source: U.S. Census Bureau, "2000 Census of Population and Housing, Profiles of General Demographic Characteristics"; <http://www.census.gov/Press-Release/www/2002/demoprofiles.html>.

2000 Census Data Sampler   865

No. 1377. Disability Status of Population by State: 2000

[In thousands except percent (64,689 represents 64,689,000). As of April. Covers civilian noninstitutionalized population. A disability is a long-lasting physical, mental, or emotional condition. This condition can make it difficult for a person to do activities such as walking, climbing stairs, dressing, bathing, learning, or remembering. This condition can also impede a person from being able to go outside the home alone or to work at a job or business. Based on sample data from the 2000 Census of Population and Housing; see text, Section 1, Population, and Appendix III]

State	Population 5 to 20 years			Population 21 to 64 years			Population 65 years and over		
		With a disability			With a disability			With a disability	
	Total	Number	Percent of total	Total	Number	Percent of total	Total	Number	Percent of total
U.S. . . .	64,689	5,214	8.1	159,132	30,554	19.2	33,347	13,978	41.9
AL	1,018	91	9.0	2,498	579	23.2	555	275	49.5
AK	166	11	6.9	358	56	15.6	34	16	46.2
AZ	1,200	96	8.0	2,813	547	19.4	654	260	39.7
AR	613	58	9.4	1,474	345	23.4	355	173	48.9
CA	8,172	609	7.5	19,211	3,848	20.0	3,470	1,466	42.2
CO	977	73	7.4	2,550	407	15.9	399	159	40.0
CT	736	56	7.6	1,945	328	16.8	440	163	37.0
DE	177	16	8.9	443	80	18.0	97	37	37.7
DC	113	11	10.0	350	76	21.9	66	28	42.5
FL	3,264	285	8.7	8,746	1,915	21.9	2,720	1,076	39.5
GA	1,915	158	8.2	4,733	940	19.9	755	359	47.5
HI	260	17	6.6	670	119	17.7	158	64	40.6
ID	332	24	7.2	702	117	16.7	141	60	42.5
IL	2,881	222	7.7	7,053	1,204	17.1	1,416	574	40.5
IN	1,422	118	8.3	3,434	636	18.5	707	302	42.6
IA	681	50	7.3	1,602	244	15.2	404	153	37.8
KS	645	47	7.2	1,465	246	16.8	331	137	41.5
KY	897	81	9.0	2,322	558	24.0	477	235	49.3
LA	1,111	104	9.3	2,446	541	22.1	490	235	48.1
ME	279	25	9.0	733	141	19.2	175	72	41.1
MD	1,194	97	8.1	3,076	530	17.2	573	228	39.8
MA	1,356	116	8.6	3,698	663	17.9	807	305	37.8
MI	2,336	198	8.5	5,631	1,018	18.1	1,171	496	42.3
MN	1,168	83	7.1	2,804	392	14.0	554	204	36.9
MS	707	61	8.6	1,542	378	24.5	326	168	51.7
MO	1,289	103	8.0	3,121	567	18.2	711	303	42.6
MT	213	15	7.1	505	85	16.9	114	45	39.6
NE	409	27	6.7	936	143	15.2	217	80	37.1
NV	436	33	7.7	1,173	256	21.8	214	87	40.6
NH	282	24	8.4	725	117	16.1	139	54	38.5
NJ	1,807	134	7.4	4,864	845	17.4	1,064	411	38.6
NM	457	37	8.1	997	209	21.0	206	92	44.8
NY	4,198	371	8.8	10,933	2,295	21.0	2,334	941	40.3
NC	1,750	148	8.5	4,643	970	20.9	924	423	45.7
ND	154	11	7.2	345	53	15.4	87	34	38.5
OH	2,601	206	7.9	6,395	1,121	17.5	1,422	583	41.0
OK	810	70	8.7	1,886	405	21.5	430	201	46.7
OR	762	63	8.2	1,973	355	18.0	423	176	41.5
PA	2,690	202	7.5	6,837	1,197	17.5	1,809	713	39.4
RI	234	22	9.3	590	116	19.7	144	58	40.3
SC	917	82	9.0	2,270	515	22.7	466	213	45.8
SD	186	13	6.8	400	62	15.6	101	40	39.5
TN	1,256	110	8.8	3,291	720	21.9	668	320	47.8
TX	5,183	410	7.9	11,612	2,315	19.9	1,966	880	44.8
UT	639	44	6.9	1,176	181	15.4	184	73	39.9
VT	141	12	8.3	354	57	16.2	73	28	38.6
VA	1,550	126	8.1	4,074	712	17.5	754	317	42.1
WA	1,356	104	7.7	3,400	607	17.8	640	270	42.3
WV	377	34	9.1	1,039	247	23.8	266	129	48.6
WI	1,258	99	7.9	3,019	450	14.9	663	242	36.5
WY	119	9	7.7	277	46	16.8	55	21	39.3

Source: U.S. Census Bureau, "2000 Census of Population and Housing, Profiles of General Demographic Characteristics"; <http://www.census.gov/Press-Release/www/2002/demoprofiles.html>.

U.S. Census Bureau, Statistical Abstract of the United States: 2002

No. 1378. Disability Status of Population—25 Largest Metropolitan Areas: 2000

[In thousands except percent (944 represents 944,000). As of April. Covers civilian noninstitutionalized population. See headnote, Table 1377. Covers metropolitan statistical areas (MSAs) and consolidated metropolitan statistical areas (CMSAs) as defined by the U.S. Office of Management and Budget as of June 30, 1999. For definitions and components of metropolitan areas, see Appendix II]

Metropolitan area	Population 5 to 20 years			Population 21 to 64 years			Population 65 years and over		
		With a disability			With a disability			With a disability	
	Total	Number	Percent of total	Total	Number	Percent of total	Total	Number	Percent of total
Atlanta, GA MSA	944	72	7.6	2,520	427	16.9	301	132	44.0
Boston-Worcester-Lawrence, MA-NH-ME-CT CMSA	1,245	103	8.3	3,435	590	17.2	688	261	38.0
Chicago-Gary-Kenosha, IL-IN-WI CMSA	2,139	164	7.7	5,293	916	17.3	949	387	40.7
Cincinnati-Hamilton, OH-KY-IN CMSA	467	38	8.1	1,129	194	17.1	218	88	40.4
Cleveland-Akron, OH CMSA	657	51	7.8	1,661	282	17.0	399	162	40.5
Dallas-Fort Worth, TX CMSA	1,257	101	8.0	3,095	570	18.4	397	169	42.6
Denver-Boulder-Greeley, CO CMSA	581	44	7.6	1,574	247	15.7	221	87	39.3
Detroit-Ann Arbor-Flint, MI CMSA	1,261	105	8.3	3,149	579	18.4	617	266	43.0
Houston-Galveston-Brazoria, TX CMSA	1,172	90	7.7	2,727	531	19.5	344	150	43.6
Kansas City, MO-KS MSA	406	30	7.5	1,026	173	16.8	190	78	41.0
Los Angeles-Riverside-Orange County, CA CMSA	4,092	305	7.5	9,277	1,933	20.8	1,569	676	43.1
Miami-Fort Lauderdale, FL CMSA	828	65	7.9	2,210	482	21.8	546	237	43.4
Minneapolis-St. Paul, MN-WI MSA	696	49	7.0	1,764	232	13.1	268	97	36.2
New York-Northern New Jersey-Long Island, NY-NJ-CT-PA CMSA	4,558	374	8.2	12,410	2,513	20.2	2,569	1,028	40.0
Philadelphia-Wilmington-Atlantic City, PA-NJ-DE-MD CMSA	1,406	111	7.9	3,486	642	18.4	790	311	39.4
Phoenix-Mesa, AZ MSA	754	60	7.9	1,822	335	18.4	380	146	38.4
Pittsburgh, PA MSA	480	33	6.8	1,317	216	16.4	398	156	39.3
Portland-Salem, OR-WA CMSA	511	41	8.0	1,336	227	17.0	234	97	41.4
Sacramento-Yolo, CA CMSA	437	34	7.7	1,021	199	19.5	196	81	41.5
St. Louis, MO-IL MSA	610	50	8.2	1,467	244	16.6	317	128	40.4
San Diego, CA MSA	640	45	7.1	1,562	279	17.9	304	124	40.8
San Francisco-Oakland-San Jose, CA CMSA	1,465	102	7.0	4,291	739	17.2	755	303	40.2
Seattle-Tacoma-Bremerton, WA CMSA	780	59	7.5	2,117	355	16.8	354	146	41.3
Tampa-St. Petersburg-Clearwater, FL MSA	463	42	9.0	1,318	302	22.9	446	181	40.7
Washington-Baltimore, DC-MD-VA-WV CMSA	1,671	132	7.9	4,540	737	16.2	737	288	39.1

Source: U.S. Census Bureau, "2000 Census of Population and Housing, Profiles of General Demographic Characteristics"; <http://www.census.gov/Press-Release/www/2002/demoprofiles.html>.

No. 1379. Disability Status of Population—25 Largest Cities: 2000

[In thousands except percent (143 represents 143,000). As of April. Covers civilian noninstitutionalized population. See headnote, Table 1377]

City	Population 5 to 20 years			Population 21 to 64 years			Population 65 years and over		
		With a disability			With a disability			With a disability	
	Total	Number	Percent of total	Total	Number	Percent of total	Total	Number	Percent of total
Austin, TX	143	12	8.3	418	64	15.3	42	18	42.7
Baltimore, MD	151	18	11.7	363	102	28.1	82	42	51.2
Boston, MA	123	13	10.7	369	81	21.9	57	26	45.7
Chicago, IL	665	66	10.0	1,697	401	23.6	289	137	47.6
Columbus, OH	158	14	9.2	436	79	18.0	59	26	43.5
Dallas, TX	268	27	9.9	710	165	23.2	97	42	43.8
Denver, CO	105	11	10.1	346	70	20.3	60	25	41.7
Detroit, MI	258	29	11.4	510	164	32.1	96	52	54.0
El Paso, TX	153	11	7.3	297	64	21.5	59	28	47.8
Houston, TX	460	40	8.6	1,157	255	22.0	158	70	44.3
Indianapolis, IN [1]	173	16	9.1	459	94	20.4	81	35	43.9
Jacksonville, FL	171	15	8.9	417	93	22.3	72	33	46.2
Los Angeles, CA	860	72	8.4	2,175	504	23.2	345	158	45.7
Memphis, TN	159	16	9.8	361	91	25.1	67	33	48.5
Milwaukee, WI	155	17	11.2	327	77	23.6	61	27	43.2
Nashville-Davidson, TN [1]	112	11	9.7	330	64	19.5	57	27	46.4
New York, NY	1,717	172	10.0	4,780	1,226	25.6	902	417	46.2
Philadelphia, PA	358	34	9.6	835	223	26.7	205	97	47.4
Phoenix, AZ	327	29	8.9	761	153	20.1	105	46	43.5
San Antonio, TX	285	26	9.0	628	142	22.6	114	54	46.9
San Diego, CA	266	19	7.1	708	124	17.5	124	51	41.3
San Francisco, CA	103	8	8.1	533	96	17.9	105	46	44.1
San Jose, CA	204	14	7.1	547	107	19.6	71	30	42.8
Seattle, WA	87	6	7.4	377	57	15.1	66	28	42.0
Washington, DC	113	11	10.0	350	76	21.9	66	28	42.5

[1] Represents the portion of a consolidated city that is not within one or more separately incorporated places.

Source: U.S. Census Bureau, "2000 Census of Population and Housing, Profiles of General Demographic Characteristics"; <http://www.census.gov/Press-Release/www/2002/demoprofiles.html>.

U.S. Census Bureau, Statistical Abstract of the United States: 2002

No. 1380. Mobility Status of Resident Population by State: 2000

[In thousands, except percent (262,375 represents 262,375,000). As of April 1. Based on comparison of place of residence in 1995 and 2000. Based on sample data from the 2000 Census of Population and Housing; see text, Section 1, Population, and Appendix III]

State	Population 5 years and over	Same house in 1995	Different house in United States in 1995 — Total — Number	Different house in United States in 1995 — Total — Percent of population 5 yrs. and over	Same county	Different county — Total	Different county — Same state	Different county — Different state	Elsewhere in 1995
U.S. . . .	262,375	142,027	112,852	43.0	65,435	47,417	25,327	22,089	7,496
AL.	4,152	2,385	1,719	41.4	1,027	692	366	326	49
AK.	580	268	299	51.6	160	139	43	96	13
AZ.	4,753	2,104	2,466	51.9	1,456	1,009	213	796	183
AR.	2,492	1,327	1,131	45.4	618	513	261	252	34
CA.	31,417	15,758	14,251	45.4	9,714	4,537	3,088	1,449	1,408
CO	4,006	1,769	2,103	52.5	920	1,183	539	644	135
CT.	3,185	1,853	1,228	38.6	799	429	168	261	104
DE.	732	410	305	41.7	187	118	17	101	17
DC	540	269	240	44.5	127	113	(X)	113	30
FL.	15,044	7,352	7,039	46.8	3,866	3,173	1,312	1,861	653
GA.	7,594	3,736	3,615	47.6	1,605	2,010	1,045	966	243
HI	1,134	644	444	39.1	295	149	24	125	47
ID	1,197	594	582	48.6	286	296	113	183	21
IL	11,548	6,558	4,635	40.1	3,011	1,624	959	665	354
IN	5,658	3,111	2,472	43.7	1,444	1,028	576	451	75
IA	2,738	1,558	1,142	41.7	637	504	290	215	38
KS.	2,500	1,310	1,139	45.5	606	533	256	277	51
KY.	3,776	2,112	1,618	42.8	933	686	367	319	46
LA.	4,153	2,452	1,659	39.9	1,017	642	388	254	42
ME	1,204	717	476	39.5	276	201	93	108	11
MD	4,945	2,752	2,046	41.4	1,085	960	465	495	147
MA	5,954	3,482	2,267	38.1	1,356	911	464	447	206
MI	9,269	5,307	3,802	41.0	2,324	1,478	1,010	468	160
MN	4,591	2,618	1,889	41.1	934	955	600	355	85
MS	2,641	1,545	1,071	40.6	595	476	249	227	25
MO	5,226	2,803	2,355	45.1	1,229	1,126	653	473	67
MT	847	454	386	45.6	191	195	84	112	7
NE.	1,595	872	694	43.5	373	321	167	154	28
NV.	1,854	693	1,086	58.6	567	519	53	466	75
NH	1,160	642	501	43.2	259	242	80	162	17
NJ.	7,856	4,697	2,847	36.2	1,628	1,219	684	535	312
NM	1,690	920	731	43.3	400	331	126	205	39
NY.	17,749	10,961	6,067	34.2	3,876	2,190	1,464	726	721
NC	7,513	3,980	3,337	44.4	1,679	1,658	739	919	196
ND	603	342	253	42.0	131	122	62	60	7
OH	10,600	6,096	4,384	41.4	2,793	1,591	1,002	589	121
OK	3,216	1,650	1,510	47.0	808	702	379	323	55
OR	3,199	1,497	1,619	50.6	863	756	357	399	83
PA	11,556	7,334	4,057	35.1	2,513	1,544	875	669	165
RI	985	572	387	39.3	240	147	50	97	26
SC.	3,749	2,097	1,592	42.5	837	755	313	442	59
SD.	704	392	305	43.3	149	156	83	73	7
TN.	5,316	2,866	2,372	44.6	1,341	1,032	464	568	78
TX.	19,242	9,545	8,970	46.6	5,204	3,766	2,403	1,363	726
UT.	2,024	998	961	47.5	538	422	180	242	65
VT.	575	340	228	39.6	122	106	36	70	7
VA.	6,619	3,453	2,960	44.7	1,197	1,763	942	822	205
WA	5,501	2,676	2,650	48.2	1,511	1,139	521	618	176
WV	1,707	1,081	618	36.2	359	259	120	138	8
WI	5,022	2,836	2,121	42.2	1,233	888	550	338	65
WY	463	238	220	47.6	111	109	36	73	5

X Not applicable.

Source: U.S. Census Bureau, "2000 Census of Population and Housing, Profiles of General Demographic Characteristics"; <http://www.census.gov/Press-Release/www/2002/demoprofiles.html>.

U.S. Census Bureau, Statistical Abstract of the United States: 2002

No. 1381. Nativity and Place of Birth of Resident Population by State: 2000

[In thousands, except percent (281,422 represents 281,422,000). As of April 1. Based on sample data from the 2000 Census of Population and Housing; see text, Section 1, Population, and Appendix III]

State	Native population						Foreign born population			
		Born in United States					Total		Entered 1990 to March 2000	
	Total popula-tion	Total	Total	State of residence	Different state	Born outside United States	Number	Percent of total popula-tion	Number	Percent of foreign-born population
U.S. . . .	**281,422**	**250,314**	**246,786**	**168,729**	**78,057**	**3,528**	**31,108**	**11.1**	**13,178**	**42.4**
AL	4,447	4,359	4,328	3,262	1,066	31	88	2.0	47	53.0
AK	627	590	580	239	341	10	37	5.9	15	39.7
AZ	5,131	4,474	4,419	1,779	2,639	56	656	12.8	317	48.4
AR	2,673	2,600	2,586	1,708	878	14	74	2.8	41	55.3
CA	33,872	25,007	24,634	17,019	7,615	374	8,864	26.2	3,271	36.9
CO	4,301	3,931	3,876	1,767	2,109	55	370	8.6	201	54.4
CT	3,406	3,036	2,922	1,941	982	114	370	10.9	144	39.0
DE	784	739	727	379	348	12	45	5.7	21	47.2
DC	572	498	491	224	267	7	74	12.9	38	51.0
FL	15,982	13,312	12,890	5,232	7,659	421	2,671	16.7	1,030	38.6
GA	8,186	7,609	7,520	4,736	2,784	90	577	7.1	345	59.7
HI	1,212	999	969	689	280	30	212	17.5	72	34.1
ID	1,294	1,230	1,219	611	608	11	64	5.0	31	47.7
IL	12,419	10,890	10,768	8,336	2,433	122	1,529	12.3	688	45.0
IN	6,080	5,894	5,862	4,216	1,646	32	187	3.1	97	52.2
IA	2,926	2,835	2,824	2,188	635	11	91	3.1	52	57.5
KS	2,688	2,554	2,533	1,600	932	21	135	5.0	74	55.1
KY	4,042	3,961	3,941	2,980	960	21	80	2.0	47	58.8
LA	4,469	4,353	4,328	3,547	781	25	116	2.6	43	37.0
ME	1,275	1,238	1,226	858	369	12	37	2.9	10	28.3
MD	5,296	4,778	4,718	2,611	2,107	60	518	9.8	228	44.1
MA	6,349	5,576	5,433	4,197	1,236	143	773	12.2	312	40.4
MI	9,938	9,415	9,358	7,490	1,868	57	524	5.3	235	44.9
MN	4,919	4,659	4,633	3,452	1,181	26	260	5.3	142	54.5
MS	2,845	2,805	2,791	2,114	677	14	40	1.4	20	49.6
MO	5,595	5,444	5,413	3,792	1,620	31	151	2.7	79	52.4
MT	902	886	879	506	373	7	16	1.8	5	29.0
NE	1,711	1,637	1,626	1,148	479	10	75	4.4	43	57.8
NV	1,998	1,682	1,655	426	1,230	26	317	15.8	139	44.0
NH	1,236	1,182	1,170	535	636	11	54	4.4	20	37.3
NJ	8,414	6,938	6,738	4,491	2,248	200	1,476	17.5	614	41.6
NM	1,819	1,669	1,651	937	714	19	150	8.2	58	39.1
NY	18,976	15,108	14,589	12,385	2,204	519	3,868	20.4	1,562	40.4
NC	8,049	7,619	7,548	5,073	2,475	71	430	5.3	268	62.4
ND	642	630	626	466	160	4	12	1.9	6	52.3
OH	11,353	11,014	10,940	8,486	2,455	73	339	3.0	143	42.2
OK	3,451	3,319	3,290	2,159	1,132	28	132	3.8	70	53.0
OR	3,421	3,132	3,102	1,549	1,553	30	290	8.5	145	50.0
PA	12,281	11,773	11,620	9,544	2,076	152	508	4.1	209	41.1
RI	1,048	929	910	644	266	19	119	11.4	41	34.8
SC	4,012	3,896	3,862	2,569	1,294	34	116	2.9	61	52.4
SD	755	741	738	514	224	4	13	1.8	7	55.0
TN	5,689	5,530	5,493	3,679	1,814	37	159	2.8	92	57.7
TX	20,852	17,952	17,727	12,970	4,757	225	2,900	13.9	1,336	46.1
UT	2,233	2,075	2,055	1,405	649	20	159	7.1	91	57.2
VT	609	586	581	331	250	5	23	3.8	8	35.3
VA	7,079	6,508	6,403	3,676	2,726	106	570	8.1	269	47.2
WA	5,894	5,280	5,196	2,781	2,414	84	614	10.4	286	46.6
WV	1,808	1,789	1,782	1,343	440	7	19	1.1	7	35.7
WI	5,364	5,170	5,137	3,939	1,198	33	194	3.6	91	46.8
WY	494	483	479	210	269	4	11	2.3	4	37.8

Source: U.S. Census Bureau, "2000 Census of Population and Housing, Profiles of General Demographic Characteristics"; <http://www.census.gov/Press-Release/www/2002/demoprofiles.html>.

U.S. Census Bureau, Statistical Abstract of the United States: 2002

No. 1382. Nativity and Place of Birth of Resident Population—25 Largest Metropolitan Areas: 2000

[In thousands except percent (4,112 represents 4,112,000). As of April. See headnote, Table 1381. Covers metropolitan statistical areas (MSAs) and consolidated metropolitan statistical areas (CMSAs) as defined by the U.S. Office of Management and Budget as of June 30, 1999. For definitions and components of metropolitan areas, see Appendix II]

| Metropolitan area | Native population | | | | Foreign-born population | | | |
| | Total popula-tion | Total | Born in United States | Born outside United States | Total | | Entered 1990 to March 2000 | |
					Number	Percent of total popula-tion	Number	Percent of foreign-born popula-tion
Atlanta, GA MSA	4,112	3,689	3,643	46	423	10.3	257	60.6
Boston-Worcester-Lawrence, MA-NH-ME-CT CMSA	5,819	5,098	4,987	111	721	12.4	301	41.8
Chicago-Gary-Kenosha, IL-IN-WI CMSA	9,158	7,691	7,581	110	1,467	16.0	653	44.5
Cincinnati-Hamilton, OH-KY-IN CMSA	1,979	1,928	1,919	9	51	2.6	25	49.5
Cleveland-Akron, OH CMSA	2,946	2,810	2,780	30	135	4.6	49	35.9
Dallas-Fort Worth, TX CMSA	5,222	4,437	4,388	49	785	15.0	431	54.9
Denver-Boulder-Greeley, CO CMSA	2,582	2,304	2,276	28	277	10.7	156	56.3
Detroit-Ann Arbor-Flint, MI CMSA	5,456	5,072	5,039	33	384	7.0	169	44.0
Houston-Galveston-Brazoria, TX CMSA	4,670	3,774	3,729	45	896	19.2	433	48.3
Kansas City, MO-KS MSA	1,776	1,696	1,683	13	81	4.5	44	54.7
Los Angeles-Riverside-Orange County, CA CMSA	16,374	11,306	11,154	152	5,068	30.9	1,775	35.0
Miami-Fort Lauderdale, FL CMSA	3,876	2,318	2,208	110	1,558	40.2	584	37.5
Minneapolis-St. Paul, MN-WI MSA	2,969	2,758	2,740	18	210	7.1	117	55.5
New York-Northern New Jersey-Long Island, NY-NJ-CT-PA CMSA	21,200	16,018	15,360	658	5,182	24.4	2,127	41.1
Philadelphia-Wilmington-Atlantic City, PA-NJ-DE-MD CMSA	6,188	5,755	5,633	122	434	7.0	183	42.1
Phoenix-Mesa, AZ MSA	3,252	2,794	2,761	33	457	14.1	245	53.6
Pittsburgh, PA MSA	2,359	2,296	2,286	11	62	2.6	25	40.0
Portland-Salem, OR-WA CMSA	2,265	2,017	1,996	21	248	11.0	132	53.1
Sacramento-Yolo, CA CMSA	1,797	1,537	1,515	21	260	14.5	113	43.6
St. Louis, MO-IL MSA	2,604	2,523	2,508	15	81	3.1	41	50.7
San Diego, CA MSA	2,814	2,208	2,162	45	606	21.5	216	35.5
San Francisco-Oakland-San Jose, CA CMSA	7,039	5,137	5,047	90	1,902	27.0	777	40.9
Seattle-Tacoma-Bremerton, WA CMSA	3,555	3,140	3,079	61	414	11.7	188	45.4
Tampa-St. Petersburg-Clearwater, FL MSA	2,396	2,162	2,102	60	234	9.8	90	38.5
Washington-Baltimore, DC-MD-VA-WV CMSA	7,608	6,627	6,516	111	981	12.9	457	46.6

Source: U.S. Census Bureau, "2000 Census of Population and Housing, Profiles of General Demographic Characteristics"; <http://www.census.gov/Press-Release/www/2002/demoprofiles.html>.

No. 1383. Nativity and Place of Birth of Resident Population—25 Largest Cities: 2000

[In thousands except percent (656 represents 656,000). As of April. See headnote, Table 1381]

| City | Native population | | | | Foreign-born population | | | |
| | Total population | Total | Born in United States | Born outside United States | Total | | Entered 1990 to March 2000 | |
					Number	Percent of total population	Number	Percent of foreign-born population
Austin, TX	656	547	537	10	109	16.6	66	60.6
Baltimore, MD	651	622	617	4	30	4.6	14	47.4
Boston, MA	589	437	418	19	152	25.8	74	48.5
Chicago, IL	2,896	2,267	2,206	61	629	21.7	292	46.4
Columbus, OH	712	664	659	5	48	6.7	30	63.7
Dallas, TX	1,188	898	888	9	290	24.4	174	60.0
Denver, CO	555	458	452	6	97	17.4	60	62.4
Detroit, MI	951	906	899	6	46	4.8	26	56.5
El Paso, TX	564	417	405	12	148	26.1	45	30.3
Houston, TX	1,955	1,439	1,420	19	516	26.4	269	52.2
Indianapolis, IN [1]	782	746	741	5	36	4.6	22	60.5
Jacksonville, FL	736	692	678	14	44	5.9	19	43.1
Los Angeles, CA	3,695	2,182	2,150	32	1,513	40.9	570	37.7
Memphis, TN	650	624	620	3	26	4.0	17	66.4
Milwaukee, WI	597	551	540	11	46	7.7	24	52.2
Nashville-Davidson, TN [1]	546	507	502	5	39	7.1	26	67.7
New York, NY	8,008	5,137	4,763	374	2,871	35.9	1,225	42.7
Philadelphia, PA	1,518	1,380	1,332	48	137	9.0	64	46.4
Phoenix, AZ	1,321	1,064	1,051	13	257	19.5	150	58.4
San Antonio, TX	1,145	1,011	989	22	134	11.7	47	35.4
San Diego, CA	1,223	909	889	20	314	25.7	118	37.4
San Francisco, CA	777	401	470	12	200	30.0	100	37.2
San Jose, CA	894	564	554	11	330	36.9	145	44.1
Seattle, WA	563	468	459	10	95	16.9	44	46.5
Washington, DC	572	498	491	7	74	12.9	38	51.0

[1] Represents the portion of a consolidated city that is not within one or more separately incorporated places.
Source: U.S. Census Bureau, "2000 Census of Population and Housing, Profiles of General Demographic Characteristics"; <http://www.census.gov/Press-Release/www/2002/demoprofiles.html>.

U.S. Census Bureau, Statistical Abstract of the United States: 2002

No. 1384. Language Spoken at Home by Resident Population by State: 2000

[In thousands, except percent (262,375 represents 262,375,000). As of April. Based on sample data from the 2000 Census of Population and Housing; see text, Section 1, Population, and Appendix III]

State	Population 5 years and over	English only	Language other than English, total [1] — Total — Number	Total — Percent of population 5 yrs. and over	Speak English less than "very well"	Spanish — Total	Spanish — Speak English less than "very well"	Other Indo-European languages — Total	Other Indo-European languages — Speak English less than "very well"	Asian and Pacific Island languages — Total	Asian and Pacific Island languages — Speak English less than "very well"
U.S.	262,375	215,424	46,952	17.9	21,320	28,101	13,751	10,018	3,390	6,960	3,590
AL	4,152	3,990	162	3.9	64	90	40	44	11	22	11
AK	580	497	83	14.3	31	17	6	13	4	22	12
AZ	4,753	3,523	1,229	25.9	540	927	435	102	27	62	28
AR	2,492	2,368	124	5.0	58	82	44	23	5	15	8
CA	31,417	19,015	12,402	39.5	6,278	8,106	4,304	1,335	454	2,709	1,439
CO	4,006	3,402	604	15.1	268	422	203	100	27	64	32
CT	3,185	2,601	584	18.3	235	268	117	251	90	48	23
DE	732	663	70	9.5	28	35	17	23	6	9	4
DC	540	449	90	16.8	38	49	25	24	6	9	5
FL	15,044	11,570	3,474	23.1	1,555	2,477	1,187	755	268	165	76
GA	7,594	6,843	751	9.9	374	426	246	169	53	116	63
HI.	1,134	832	302	26.6	144	19	5	14	3	267	135
ID.	1,197	1,085	112	9.3	47	80	36	19	5	8	4
IL.	11,548	9,327	2,221	19.2	1,055	1,254	666	640	253	249	111
IN.	5,658	5,296	362	6.4	143	186	84	127	38	37	18
IA.	2,738	2,578	160	5.8	68	79	37	49	16	25	14
KS	2,500	2,282	219	8.7	98	137	68	41	11	33	17
KY	3,776	3,628	148	3.9	59	70	31	51	15	21	11
LA	4,153	3,771	382	9.2	117	105	39	226	54	42	22
ME	1,204	1,110	94	7.8	24	10	3	76	18	6	2
MD	4,945	4,322	623	12.6	246	231	109	199	59	136	66
MA	5,954	4,839	1,116	18.7	459	370	163	530	194	171	90
MI	9,269	8,487	781	8.4	295	247	101	303	97	104	48
MN	4,591	4,202	390	8.5	168	132	62	111	30	104	58
MS	2,641	2,546	96	3.6	36	51	21	24	6	14	6
MO	5,226	4,962	264	5.1	103	111	46	98	31	42	21
MT	847	803	44	5.2	13	13	3	18	5	3	1
NE	1,595	1,469	126	7.9	58	78	40	28	8	15	8
NV	1,854	1,426	428	23.1	208	300	162	47	12	69	29
NH	1,160	1,064	96	8.3	28	19	7	64	16	10	5
NJ	7,856	5,855	2,002	25.5	873	968	483	659	242	276	120
NM	1,690	1,073	617	36.5	201	486	159	22	5	12	5
NY	17,749	12,786	4,963	28.0	2,310	2,416	1,182	1,655	664	671	395
NC	7,513	6,910	604	8.0	298	379	219	120	32	78	39
ND	603	565	38	6.3	11	8	3	24	7	2	1
OH	10,600	9,951	648	6.1	234	213	77	297	99	85	41
OK	3,216	2,977	239	7.4	99	141	65	37	9	35	18
OR	3,199	2,811	389	12.1	189	218	117	83	28	75	40
PA	11,556	10,583	972	8.4	368	357	141	428	139	144	76
RI.	985	789	197	20.0	84	79	40	91	32	20	10
SC	3,749	3,552	196	5.2	82	110	54	55	14	26	12
SD	704	658	46	6.5	16	10	4	20	8	3	2
TN	5,316	5,059	257	4.8	108	134	64	69	19	40	20
TX	19,242	13,231	6,011	31.2	2,670	5,195	2,369	358	92	374	187
UT	2,024	1,771	253	12.5	106	150	71	50	13	38	16
VT	575	541	34	5.9	9	6	1	24	6	3	2
VA	6,619	5,884	735	11.1	304	316	152	196	53	170	82
WA	5,501	4,731	771	14.0	351	321	155	177	62	243	123
WV	1,707	1,661	46	2.7	14	18	6	19	5	6	2
WI	5,022	4,653	369	7.3	149	169	77	125	37	61	32
WY	463	433	29	6.4	9	19	6	6	1	2	1

[1] Includes other language groups not shown separately.

Source: U.S. Census Bureau, "2000 Census of Population and Housing, Profiles of General Demographic Characteristics"; <http://www.census.gov/Press-Release/www/2002/demoprofiles.html>.

U.S. Census Bureau, Statistical Abstract of the United States: 2002

No. 1385. Language Spoken at Home by Resident Population—25 Largest Metropolitan Areas: 2000

[In thousands except percent (3,805 represents 3,805,000). As of April. See headnote, Table 1384. Covers metropolitan statistical areas (MSAs) and consolidated metropolitan statistical areas (CMSAs) as defined by the U.S. Office of Management and Budget as of June 30, 1999. For definitions and components of metropolitan areas, see Appendix II]

Metropolitan area	Population 5 years and over	English only	Language other than English, total [1]				Other Indo-European languages	Asian and Pacific Island languages
			Number	Percent of population 5 yrs. and over	Speak English less than "very well"	Spanish		
Atlanta, GA MSA	3,805	3,299	507	13.3	258	263	121	88
Boston-Worcester-Lawrence, MA-NH-ME-CT CMSA	5,447	4,450	997	18.3	409	313	476	166
Chicago-Gary-Kenosha, IL-IN-WI CMSA	8,482	6,366	2,116	24.9	1,015	1,210	607	226
Cincinnati-Hamilton, OH-KY-IN CMSA	1,840	1,755	86	4.6	29	30	35	15
Cleveland-Akron, OH CMSA	2,753	2,517	236	8.6	87	71	118	24
Dallas-Fort Worth, TX CMSA	4,806	3,643	1,164	24.2	593	894	106	130
Denver-Boulder-Greeley, CO CMSA	2,399	1,989	410	17.1	198	282	66	50
Detroit-Ann Arbor-Flint, MI CMSA	5,078	4,555	523	10.3	200	120	220	73
Houston-Galveston-Brazoria, TX CMSA	4,297	2,925	1,372	31.9	665	1,074	117	148
Kansas City, MO-KS MSA	1,648	1,523	125	7.6	55	70	30	20
Los Angeles-Riverside-Orange County, CA CMSA	15,116	8,035	7,080	46.8	3,708	5,007	646	1,292
Miami-Fort Lauderdale, FL CMSA	3,629	1,759	1,870	51.5	905	1,497	313	35
Minneapolis-St. Paul, MN-WI MSA	2,757	2,477	280	10.2	127	88	71	90
New York-Northern New Jersey-Long Island, NY-NJ-CT-PA CMSA	19,775	13,154	6,622	33.5	3,076	3,271	2,159	890
Philadelphia-Wilmington-Atlantic City, PA-NJ-DE-MD CMSA	5,791	5,070	721	12.4	294	302	256	131
Phoenix-Mesa, AZ MSA	3,000	2,274	726	24.2	344	577	73	46
Pittsburgh, PA MSA	2,228	2,112	116	5.2	35	26	69	16
Portland-Salem, OR-WA CMSA	2,105	1,791	314	14.9	160	154	78	71
Sacramento-Yolo, CA CMSA	1,674	1,307	367	21.9	173	168	84	108
St. Louis, MO-IL MSA	2,430	2,301	129	5.3	49	43	55	24
San Diego, CA MSA	2,618	1,753	865	33.0	392	574	80	186
San Francisco-Oakland-San Jose, CA CMSA	6,592	4,223	2,368	35.9	1,139	995	385	931
Seattle-Tacoma-Bremerton, WA CMSA	3,325	2,838	486	14.6	212	125	124	214
Tampa-St. Petersburg-Clearwater, FL MSA	2,260	1,915	345	15.3	136	209	94	31
Washington-Baltimore, DC-MD-VA-WV CMSA	7,093	5,934	1,159	16.3	483	469	327	256

[1] Includes other language groups not shown separately.
Source: U.S. Census Bureau, "2000 Census of Population and Housing, Profiles of General Demographic Characteristics"; <http://www.census.gov/Press-Release/www/2002/demoprofiles.html>.

No. 1386. Language Spoken at Home by Resident Population—25 Largest Cities: 2000

[In thousands except percent (610 represents 610,000). As of April. See headnote, Table 1384]

City	Population 5 years and over	English only	Language other than English, total [1]				Other Indo-European languages	Asian and Pacific Island languages
			Number	Percent of population 5 yrs. and over	Speak English less than "very well"	Spanish		
Austin, TX	610	420	190	31.1	85	149	17	21
Baltimore, MD	609	562	47	7.8	18	18	18	7
Boston, MA	557	371	186	33.4	91	76	68	35
Chicago, IL	2,679	1,727	952	35.5	494	625	213	83
Columbus, OH	659	593	66	10.0	28	19	19	17
Dallas, TX	1,090	686	404	37.1	237	348	23	22
Denver, CO	517	378	139	27.0	75	109	15	11
Detroit, MI	875	795	80	9.2	38	43	18	6
El Paso, TX	517	148	369	71.3	159	357	7	4
Houston, TX	1,795	1,053	742	41.3	395	597	54	71
Indianapolis, IN [2]	725	672	53	7.3	25	30	14	6
Jacksonville, FL	682	617	65	9.5	23	28	18	14
Los Angeles, CA	3,413	1,439	1,974	57.8	1,113	1,422	225	278
Memphis, TN	600	558	42	7.0	20	23	9	7
Milwaukee, WI	550	462	87	15.9	42	55	16	13
Nashville-Davidson, TN [2]	509	458	51	10.1	25	26	13	8
New York, NY	7,476	3,921	3,555	47.6	1,769	1,832	1,046	515
Philadelphia, PA	1,420	1,168	252	17.7	114	110	79	50
Phoenix, AZ	1,207	819	388	32.2	206	326	30	17
San Antonio, TX	1,053	561	492	46.7	171	463	14	12
San Diego, CA	1,142	714	427	37.4	199	244	44	126
San Francisco, CA	746	405	341	45.7	186	90	50	195
San Jose, CA	826	403	423	51.2	222	187	49	178
Seattle, WA	538	429	108	20.2	50	22	21	56
Washington, DC	540	449	90	16.8	38	49	24	9

[1] Includes other language groups not shown separately.
[2] Represents the portion of a consolidated city that is not within one or more separately incorporated places.
Source: U.S. Census Bureau, "2000 Census of Population and Housing, Profiles of General Demographic Characteristics"; <http://www.census.gov/Press-Release/www/2002/demoprofiles.html>.

U.S. Census Bureau, Statistical Abstract of the United States: 2002

No. 1387. Ancestry of Resident Population by State: 2000

[In thousands (281,422 represents 281,422,000). As of April. Covers single and multiple ancestries. Based on sample data from the 2000 Census of Population and Housing; see text, Section 1, Population, and Appendix III]

State	Total population [1]	English	French (except Basque) [2]	German	Irish [2]	Italian	Polish	Scottish	United States or American
U.S.	281,422	24,515	8,326	42,885	30,594	15,724	8,977	4,891	20,625
AL.	4,447	345	65	254	343	56	23	69	756
AK.	627	60	20	104	68	18	13	16	36
AZ.	5,131	532	147	800	526	225	127	103	240
AR.	2,673	211	51	250	255	35	19	36	425
CA.	33,872	2,521	784	3,332	2,622	1,451	491	542	1,141
CO	4,301	515	143	948	528	202	101	114	221
CT.	3,406	349	214	336	566	634	284	67	111
DE.	784	95	16	112	130	73	41	15	47
DC	572	25	7	27	28	13	8	7	10
FL.	15,982	1,469	445	1,888	1,648	1,004	430	294	1,279
GA	8,186	665	126	571	643	163	83	141	1,102
HI	1,212	52	18	70	53	22	11	13	17
ID	1,294	234	38	244	130	35	15	41	108
IL	12,419	832	268	2,441	1,513	744	933	150	569
IN	6,080	540	149	1,378	656	141	184	100	730
IA	2,926	277	76	1,046	396	49	33	43	197
KS.	2,688	290	83	695	310	51	35	50	237
KY.	4,042	392	66	515	424	62	28	60	846
LA	4,469	233	546	315	315	196	19	38	450
ME	1,275	274	182	86	193	59	25	61	120
MD	5,296	476	96	834	623	268	184	90	306
MA	6,349	722	509	377	1,428	860	323	162	245
MI	9,938	989	490	2,028	1,069	451	855	225	518
MN	4,919	310	203	1,807	553	111	240	62	143
MS	2,845	174	66	129	196	40	10	35	404
MO	5,595	529	196	1,314	712	176	90	83	587
MT	902	114	38	244	134	28	18	27	46
NE	1,711	164	45	661	230	43	62	23	77
NV	1,998	201	63	282	220	133	47	38	96
NH	1,236	223	181	106	241	106	51	54	74
NJ.	8,414	522	125	1,063	1,337	1,504	576	107	264
NM	1,819	138	37	179	134	43	21	29	93
NY.	18,976	1,140	479	2,123	2,454	2,737	986	212	717
NC	8,049	768	128	762	596	182	88	178	1,115
ND	642	32	25	282	49	5	18	8	15
OH	11,353	1,047	272	2,867	1,448	676	433	197	982
OK	3,451	292	79	435	355	50	27	52	392
OR	3,421	453	127	701	409	111	55	109	219
PA.	12,281	966	211	3,116	1,983	1,418	824	185	633
RI	1,048	125	114	56	193	199	43	20	31
SC.	4,012	328	71	338	318	81	37	74	558
SD.	755	53	22	307	78	8	12	8	29
TN.	5,689	517	94	475	528	94	46	103	998
TX.	20,852	1,463	467	2,069	1,508	363	228	290	1,554
UT.	2,233	648	51	258	132	58	17	99	151
VT.	609	112	88	55	100	39	20	28	50
VA.	7,079	789	143	829	696	257	125	153	808
WA	5,894	707	215	1,103	673	191	103	178	316
WV	1,808	176	25	253	198	70	29	28	341
WI	5,364	348	206	2,290	583	173	498	56	189
WY	494	79	17	128	66	15	10	16	32

[1] Includes persons of other ancestries not shown separately.   [2] Data represent a combination of two ancestries. French includes Alsatian. Irish includes Celtic.

Source: U.S. Census Bureau, "2000 Census of Population and Housing, Profiles of General Demographic Characteristics"; <http://www.census.gov/Press-Release/www/2002/demoprofiles.html>.

No. 1388. Commuting to Work by State: 2000

[In percent, except as indicated (128,279 represents 128,279,000). As of April 1. For workers 16 years old and over. Based on sample data from the 2000 Census of Population and Housing; see text Section 1, Population, and Appendix III]

State	Total workers (1,000)	Commuted by car, truck, or van		Used public transporta- tion [1]	Walked	Used other means	Worked at home	Mean travel time to work (min.)
		Drove alone	Carpooled					
U.S. . . .	**128,279**	**75.7**	**12.2**	**4.7**	**2.9**	**1.2**	**3.3**	**25.5**
AL.	1,900	83.0	12.3	0.5	1.3	0.8	2.1	24.8
AK.	291	66.5	15.5	1.8	7.3	4.8	4.1	19.6
AZ.	2,210	74.1	15.4	1.9	2.6	2.3	3.7	24.9
AR.	1,160	79.9	14.1	0.4	1.9	1.0	2.6	21.9
CA.	14,525	71.8	14.5	5.1	2.9	1.9	3.8	27.7
CO.	2,192	75.1	12.2	3.2	3.0	1.5	4.9	24.3
CT.	1,641	80.0	9.4	4.0	2.7	0.7	3.1	24.4
DE.	373	79.2	11.5	2.8	2.6	1.0	3.0	24.0
DC	261	38.4	11.0	33.2	11.8	1.9	3.8	29.7
FL.	6,910	78.8	12.9	1.9	1.7	1.7	3.0	26.2
GA	3,833	77.5	14.5	2.3	1.7	1.1	2.8	27.7
HI	563	63.9	19.0	6.3	4.8	2.4	3.6	26.1
ID	595	77.0	12.3	1.1	3.5	1.4	4.7	20.0
IL	5,746	73.2	10.9	8.7	3.1	1.0	3.1	28.0
IN	2,911	81.8	11.0	1.0	2.4	0.9	2.9	22.6
IA	1,470	78.6	10.8	1.0	4.0	0.9	4.7	18.5
KS.	1,311	81.5	10.6	0.5	2.5	0.9	4.0	19.0
KY.	1,782	80.2	12.6	1.2	2.4	0.9	2.7	23.5
LA.	1,831	78.1	13.6	2.4	2.2	1.6	2.1	25.7
ME	615	78.6	11.3	0.8	4.0	0.9	4.4	22.7
MD	2,592	73.7	12.4	7.2	2.5	0.8	3.3	31.2
MA	3,103	73.8	9.0	8.7	4.3	1.0	3.1	27.0
MI.	4,540	83.2	9.7	1.3	2.2	0.7	2.8	24.1
MN	2,542	77.6	10.4	3.2	3.3	0.9	4.6	21.9
MS	1,164	79.4	15.2	0.6	1.9	1.0	1.9	24.6
MO	2,629	80.5	11.6	1.5	2.1	0.8	3.5	23.8
MT	422	73.9	11.9	0.7	5.5	1.7	6.4	17.7
NE.	873	80.0	10.5	0.7	3.2	0.9	4.6	18.0
NV.	923	74.5	14.7	3.9	2.7	1.6	2.6	23.3
NH	639	81.8	9.8	0.7	2.9	0.8	4.0	25.3
NJ.	3,876	73.0	10.6	9.6	3.1	0.9	2.7	30.0
NM	759	75.8	14.8	0.8	2.8	1.6	4.2	21.9
NY.	8,212	56.3	9.2	24.4	6.2	0.8	3.0	31.7
NC	3,838	79.4	14.0	0.9	1.9	1.1	2.7	24.0
ND	319	77.7	10.0	0.4	5.0	0.8	6.0	15.8
OH	5,308	82.8	9.3	2.1	2.4	0.7	2.8	22.9
OK	1,540	80.0	13.2	0.5	2.1	1.1	3.1	21.7
OR	1,601	73.2	12.2	4.2	3.6	1.9	5.0	22.2
PA.	5,556	76.5	10.4	5.2	4.1	0.8	3.0	25.2
RI	491	80.1	10.4	2.5	3.8	1.0	2.2	22.5
SC.	1,823	79.4	14.0	0.8	2.3	1.3	2.1	24.3
SD.	373	77.3	10.4	0.5	4.5	0.8	6.5	16.6
TN.	2,618	81.7	12.5	0.8	1.5	0.8	2.6	24.5
TX.	9,158	77.7	14.5	1.9	1.9	1.3	2.8	25.4
UT.	1,033	75.5	14.1	2.2	2.8	1.2	4.2	21.3
VT.	312	75.2	11.9	0.7	5.6	0.9	5.7	21.6
VA.	3,482	77.1	12.7	3.6	2.3	1.2	3.2	27.0
WA	2,785	73.3	12.8	4.9	3.2	1.4	4.3	25.5
WV	718	80.3	12.7	0.8	2.9	0.9	2.4	26.2
WI	2,691	79.5	9.9	2.0	3.7	0.9	3.9	20.8
WY	240	75.4	13.2	1.4	4.4	1.3	4.3	17.8

[1] Including taxicabs.

Source: U.S. Census Bureau, "2000 Census of Population and Housing, Profiles of General Demographic Characteristics"; <http://www.census.gov/Press-Release/www/2002/demoprofiles.html>.

No. 1389. Commuting to Work—25 Largest Metropolitan Areas: 2000

[In percent, except as indicated (2,060.6 represents 2,060,600). As of April 1. For workers 16 years old and over. Based on sample data from the 2000 Census of Population and Housing; see text Section 1, Population, and Appendix III. Covers metropolitan statistical area (MSAs) and consolidated metropolitan statistical areas (CMSAs) as defined by the U.S. Office of Management and Budget as of June 30, 1999. For definitions and components of metropolitan areas see Appendix II]

		Percent of workers who—						
	Total	Commuted by car, truck, or van		Used public transpor-tation [1]	Walked	Used other means	Worked at home	Mean travel time to work (min.)
Metropolitan area	workers (1,000)	Drove alone	Car-pooled					
Atlanta, GA MSA.	2,060.6	77.0	13.6	3.7	1.3	1.0	3.5	31.2
Boston-Worcester-Lawrence, MA-NH-ME-CT CMSA	2,898.7	73.9	8.8	9.0	4.1	1.0	3.2	27.8
Chicago-Gary-Kenosha, IL-IN-WI CMSA .	4,218.1	70.5	11.0	11.5	3.1	1.0	2.9	31.0
Cincinnati-Hamilton, OH-KY-IN CMSA. . .	951.7	81.4	10.0	2.9	2.3	0.6	2.7	24.3
Cleveland-Akron, OH CMSA	1,375.8	82.3	8.7	3.4	2.1	0.7	2.7	24.0
Dallas-Fort Worth, TX CMSA.	2,527.6	78.8	14.0	1.8	1.5	1.0	3.0	27.5
Denver-Boulder-Greeley, CO CMSA	1,346.0	75.6	11.5	4.3	2.4	1.4	4.7	25.9
Detroit-Ann Arbor-Flint, MI CMSA.	2,482.5	84.2	9.3	1.8	1.8	0.7	2.3	26.1
Houston-Galveston-Brazoria, TX CMSA. .	2,081.6	77.0	14.2	3.3	1.6	1.3	2.5	28.8
Kansas City, MO-KS MSA.	881.3	82.8	10.4	1.3	1.4	0.7	3.4	22.9
Los Angeles-Riverside-Orange County, CA CMSA	6,767.6	72.4	15.2	4.7	2.6	1.6	3.6	29.1
Miami-Fort Lauderdale, FL CMSA	1,642.9	76.6	13.4	3.9	1.8	1.5	2.8	28.9
Minneapolis-St. Paul, MN-WI MSA.	1,595.6	78.3	10.0	4.5	2.4	0.9	3.8	23.7
New York-Northern New Jersey-Long Island, NY-NJ-CT-PA CMSA.	9,319.2	56.3	9.4	24.9	5.6	0.9	3.0	34.0
Philadelphia-Wilmington-Atlantic City, PA-NJ-DE-MD CMSA.	2,815.4	73.3	10.3	8.7	3.9	1.0	2.8	27.9
Phoenix-Mesa, AZ MSA	1,466.4	74.6	15.3	2.0	2.1	2.2	3.7	26.1
Pittsburgh, PA MSA	1,057.4	77.4	9.7	6.2	3.6	0.7	2.4	25.3
Portland-Salem, OR-WA CMSA	1,105.1	73.1	12.1	5.7	3.0	1.5	4.6	24.4
Sacramento-Yolo, CA CMSA	800.0	75.3	13.5	2.7	2.2	2.2	4.0	25.6
St. Louis, MO-IL MSA	1,239.0	82.6	9.9	2.4	1.6	0.6	2.8	25.5
San Diego, CA MSA	1,299.5	73.9	13.0	3.4	3.4	1.9	4.4	25.3
San Francisco-Oakland-San Jose, CA CMSA	3,432.2	68.1	12.9	9.5	3.3	2.2	4.1	29.3
Seattle-Tacoma-Bremerton, WA CMSA . .	1,776.2	71.6	12.8	6.8	3.2	1.4	4.2	27.7
Tampa-St. Petersburg-Clearwater, FL MSA	1,064.0	79.7	12.4	1.4	1.7	1.7	3.1	25.6
Washington-Baltimore, DC-MD-VA-WV CMSA	3,839.1	70.4	12.8	9.4	3.0	0.9	3.5	31.7

[1] Includes taxicabs.

Source: U.S. Census Bureau, "2000 Census of Population and Housing, Profiles of General Demographic Characteristics"; <http://www.census.gov/Press-Release/www/2002/demoprofiles.html>.

No. 1390. Commuting to Work—25 Largest Cities: 2000

[In percent, except as indicated (353.1 represents 353,100). As of April 1. For workers 16 years old and over. Based on sample data from the 2000 Census of Population and Housing; see text Section 1, Population, and Appendix III]

		Percent of workers who—						
	Total	Commuted by car, truck, or van		Used pub-lic trans-portation [1]	Walked	Used other means	Worked at home	Mean travel time to work (min.)
City	workers (1,000)	Drove alone	Carpooled					
Austin, TX.	353.1	73.6	13.9	4.5	2.5	2.1	3.4	22.4
Baltimore, MD	249.4	54.7	15.2	19.5	7.1	1.1	2.3	31.1
Boston, MA.	278.5	41.5	9.2	32.3	13.0	1.6	2.4	28.8
Chicago, IL	1,192.1	50.1	14.5	26.1	5.7	1.3	2.4	35.2
Columbus, OH.	367.4	79.0	10.8	3.9	3.2	0.8	2.3	21.9
Dallas, TX.	537.0	70.8	17.8	5.5	1.9	1.2	2.8	26.9
Denver, CO	278.7	68.3	13.5	8.4	4.3	1.8	3.7	24.5
Detroit, MI.	319.4	68.6	17.1	8.7	2.8	1.1	1.8	28.4
El Paso, TX.	208.1	76.5	15.8	2.3	2.0	1.2	2.2	22.4
Houston, TX	841.7	71.8	15.9	5.9	2.3	1.7	2.3	27.4
Indianapolis, IN [2]	385.2	80.0	12.3	2.4	2.0	0.8	2.5	22.7
Jacksonville, FL	350.5	79.2	13.4	2.1	1.8	1.6	1.9	25.2
Los Angeles, CA	1,494.9	65.7	14.7	10.2	3.6	1.6	4.1	29.6
Memphis, TN.	274.9	76.6	15.7	3.0	1.9	1.0	1.7	23.0
Milwaukee, WI.	249.9	68.8	13.6	10.3	4.7	0.9	1.7	22.5
Nashville-Davidson, TN [2] . . .	274.0	78.5	13.5	1.8	2.4	0.9	3.0	23.3
New York, NY	3,192.1	24.9	8.0	52.8	10.4	1.0	2.9	40.0
Philadelphia, PA.	569.8	49.2	12.8	25.4	9.1	1.6	1.9	32.0
Phoenix, AZ	599.6	71.7	17.4	3.3	2.2	2.2	3.3	26.1
San Antonio, TX.	491.4	75.6	15.2	3.8	2.2	1.1	2.2	23.8
San Diego, CA.	580.3	74.0	12.2	4.2	3.6	2.0	4.0	23.2
San Francisco, CA	418.6	40.5	10.8	31.1	9.4	3.6	4.6	30.7
San Jose, CA	428.0	76.4	14.1	4.1	1.4	1.5	2.5	27.8
Seattle, WA.	316.5	56.5	11.2	17.6	7.4	2.7	4.6	24.8
Washington, DC.	260.9	38.4	11.0	33.2	11.8	1.9	3.8	29.7

[1] Includes taxicabs. [2] Represents the portion of a consolidated city that is not within one or more separately incorporated places.

Source: U.S. Census Bureau, "2000 Census of Population and Housing, Profiles of General Demographic Characteristics"; <http://www.census.gov/Press-Release/www/2002/demoprofiles.html>.

2000 Census Data Sampler 875

No. 1391. Occupation of Employed Civilians by State: 2000

[**129,722 represents 129,722,000. As of April 1.** For employed civilians 16 years old and over. Based on sample data from the 2000 Census of Population and Housing; see text, Section 1, Population, and Appendix III]

State	Total (1,000)	Management, professional, and related	Service	Sales and office	Farming, fishing, and forestry	Construction, extraction, and maintenance	Production, transportation, and material moving
							Percent of employed
U.S. . . .	**129,722**	**33.6**	**14.9**	**26.7**	**0.7**	**9.4**	**14.6**
AL.	1,920	29.5	13.5	25.9	0.8	11.3	19.0
AK.	282	34.4	15.6	26.1	1.5	11.6	10.8
AZ.	2,233	32.7	16.2	28.5	0.6	11.0	10.9
AR.	1,173	27.7	14.1	25.1	1.5	10.6	21.0
CA.	14,719	36.0	14.8	26.8	1.3	8.4	12.7
CO	2,205	37.4	13.9	27.2	0.6	10.5	10.5
CT.	1,664	39.1	14.3	26.5	0.2	8.0	12.0
DE.	377	35.3	14.6	27.6	0.5	9.5	12.5
DC	263	51.1	16.1	22.8	0.1	4.8	5.2
FL.	6,995	31.5	16.9	29.5	0.9	10.3	10.8
GA	3,840	32.7	13.4	26.8	0.6	10.8	15.7
HI	538	32.2	20.9	28.1	1.3	8.6	8.9
ID	599	31.4	15.6	25.3	2.7	10.8	14.2
IL	5,833	34.2	13.9	27.6	0.3	8.2	15.7
IN	2,965	28.7	14.2	25.3	0.4	10.0	21.4
IA	1,490	31.3	14.8	25.9	1.1	8.9	18.1
KS.	1,316	33.9	14.4	25.8	1.0	9.9	15.0
KY.	1,798	28.7	14.3	25.4	0.9	11.0	19.7
LA	1,852	29.9	16.7	26.8	0.8	11.7	14.1
ME	624	31.5	15.3	25.9	1.7	10.3	15.3
MD	2,608	41.3	13.9	26.4	0.3	8.6	9.5
MA	3,161	41.1	14.1	25.9	0.2	7.5	11.3
MI	4,637	31.5	14.8	25.6	0.5	9.2	18.5
MN	2,580	35.8	13.7	26.5	0.7	8.4	14.9
MS	1,173	27.4	14.9	24.9	1.2	11.2	20.4
MO	2,658	31.5	15.0	26.9	0.6	9.8	16.3
MT	426	33.1	17.2	25.5	2.2	10.7	11.2
NE.	877	33.0	14.6	26.4	1.6	9.3	15.1
NV.	933	25.7	24.6	27.6	0.3	11.4	10.4
NH	651	35.8	13.0	26.6	0.4	9.4	14.8
NJ.	3,950	38.0	13.6	28.5	0.2	7.8	12.0
NM	763	34.0	17.0	25.9	1.0	11.4	10.7
NY.	8,383	36.7	16.6	27.1	0.3	7.6	11.7
NC	3,825	31.2	13.5	24.8	0.8	11.0	18.7
ND	317	33.3	16.7	26.1	1.7	9.8	12.4
OH	5,402	31.0	14.6	26.4	0.3	8.7	19.0
OK	1,545	30.3	15.5	26.6	0.9	11.3	15.4
OR	1,628	33.1	15.3	26.1	1.7	9.1	14.7
PA.	5,654	32.6	14.8	27.0	0.5	8.9	16.3
RI	501	33.9	15.7	27.1	0.3	7.7	15.2
SC.	1,825	29.1	14.7	25.2	0.6	11.5	19.0
SD.	374	32.6	15.6	26.5	1.9	9.1	14.2
TN.	2,652	29.5	13.7	26.1	0.6	10.3	19.9
TX.	9,234	33.3	14.6	27.2	0.7	10.9	13.2
UT.	1,044	32.5	14.0	28.9	0.5	10.6	13.5
VT.	317	36.3	14.6	24.5	1.3	9.3	14.0
VA.	3,413	38.2	13.7	25.5	0.5	9.6	12.5
WA	2,794	35.6	14.9	25.9	1.6	9.4	12.7
WV	733	27.9	16.6	26.1	0.7	12.3	16.4
WI	2,735	31.3	14.0	25.2	0.9	8.7	19.8
WY	241	30.0	16.7	24.2	1.5	14.8	12.8

Source: U.S. Census Bureau, "2000 Census of Population and Housing, Profiles of General Demographic Characteristics"; <http://www.census.gov/Press-Release/www/2002/demoprofiles.html>.

U.S. Census Bureau, Statistical Abstract of the United States: 2002

No. 1392. Household Income—Distribution by Income Level and State: 1999

[**Households as of April 2000.** Based on sample data from the 2000 Census of Population and Housing; see text, Section 1, Population, and Appendix III]

State	Number of households (1,000)	Number of households by income level (1,000)							Median income (dol.)
		Under $15,000	$15,000-$24,999	$25,000-$34,999	$35,000-$49,999	$50,000-$74,999	$75,000-$99,999	$100,000 and over	
U.S. . . .	**105,539**	**16,724**	**13,537**	**13,519**	**17,446**	**20,541**	**10,799**	**12,973**	**41,994**
AL	1,737	391	257	237	287	298	134	133	34,135
AK	222	23	23	25	36	49	30	36	51,571
AZ	1,902	284	264	266	333	365	184	206	40,558
AR	1,043	229	174	157	183	170	67	62	32,182
CA	11,512	1,616	1,318	1,315	1,746	2,203	1,327	1,987	47,493
CO	1,659	197	186	209	282	352	197	236	47,203
CT	1,302	157	126	131	188	265	173	262	53,935
DE	299	36	34	36	51	64	36	42	47,381
DC	249	52	28	31	35	40	22	41	40,127
FL	6,341	1,034	918	901	1,104	1,171	552	661	38,819
GA	3,008	481	369	379	503	593	312	371	42,433
HI	404	51	42	46	63	83	51	67	49,820
ID	470	74	72	70	90	90	39	34	37,572
IL	4,593	636	518	546	745	953	532	663	46,590
IN	2,337	334	315	320	418	500	237	214	41,567
IA	1,150	171	165	169	218	242	101	84	39,469
KS	1,039	155	143	145	188	211	100	96	40,624
KY	1,592	355	245	220	262	275	122	114	33,672
LA	1,657	400	248	223	261	275	127	123	32,566
ME	518	92	77	74	95	100	43	37	37,240
MD	1,982	221	188	212	306	427	269	359	52,868
MA	2,445	352	248	253	355	491	313	432	50,502
MI	3,789	533	469	470	624	779	433	480	44,667
MN	1,896	230	216	234	323	425	229	239	47,111
MS	1,048	261	165	148	171	168	71	63	31,330
MO	2,197	376	320	315	385	416	194	192	37,934
MT	359	72	62	55	65	62	23	20	33,024
NE	667	99	99	98	123	136	58	54	39,250
NV	752	93	93	98	136	163	83	85	44,581
NH	475	51	51	55	82	109	60	65	49,467
NJ	3,066	358	289	305	437	608	414	654	55,146
NM	678	141	107	97	115	112	53	52	34,133
NY	7,061	1,263	823	807	1,047	1,298	746	1,077	43,393
NC	3,133	530	432	436	553	609	279	295	39,184
ND	257	49	41	40	48	48	17	15	34,604
OH	4,447	692	594	603	771	905	445	436	40,956
OK	1,344	278	219	201	230	228	97	89	33,400
OR	1,335	202	179	186	236	269	129	133	40,916
PA	4,779	799	657	634	809	930	457	492	40,106
RI	408	72	51	48	64	82	44	47	42,090
SC	1,534	288	220	214	270	289	130	124	37,082
SD	290	53	47	44	55	54	20	17	35,282
TN	2,234	429	326	320	388	405	180	186	36,360
TX	7,397	1,259	1,004	996	1,219	1,359	706	854	39,927
UT	702	76	83	93	133	158	80	78	45,726
VT	241	35	34	33	45	50	23	21	40,856
VA	2,700	356	309	327	445	549	307	408	46,677
WA	2,272	297	265	285	389	486	264	285	45,776
WV	737	187	128	107	121	111	45	37	29,696
WI	2,086	270	265	276	378	474	226	197	43,791
WY	194	32	29	28	35	39	17	13	37,892

Source: U.S. Census Bureau, "2000 Census of Population and Housing, Profiles of General Demographic Characteristics"; <http://www.census.gov/Press-Release/www/2002/demoprofiles.html>.

U.S. Census Bureau, Statistical Abstract of the United States: 2002

No. 1393. Families and Persons Below Poverty Level by State: 1999

[In thousands (6,621 represents 6,621,000), except percent. Families and individuals as of April 2000. Based on sample data from the 2000 Census of Population and Housing; see text, Section 1, Population, and Appendix III. For information about poverty, see text, Section 13, Income, Expenditures, and Wealth]

State	Families				Persons					
	Total		Families with female householder [1]		Total		65 years old and over		Related children under 18 years old	
	Number	Percent	Number	Percent	Number	Percent	Number	Percent	Number	Percent
U.S.	**6,621**	**9.2**	**3,316**	**26.5**	**33,900**	**12.4**	**3,288**	**9.9**	**11,386**	**16.1**
AL.	153	12.5	86	35.6	698	16.1	86	15.5	234	21.2
AK.	10	6.7	5	20.0	58	9.4	2	6.8	21	11.2
AZ.	128	9.9	52	25.8	699	13.9	55	8.4	249	18.8
AR.	88	12.0	43	34.7	412	15.8	49	13.8	142	21.4
CA.	846	10.6	350	25.0	4,706	14.2	280	8.1	1,706	19.0
CO	68	6.2	31	20.6	389	9.3	30	7.4	116	10.8
CT.	50	5.6	30	19.6	260	7.9	31	7.0	83	10.0
DE.	13	6.5	8	20.4	70	9.2	8	7.9	23	11.9
DC	19	16.7	14	30.0	110	20.2	11	16.4	34	31.1
FL.	383	9.0	187	25.3	1,953	12.5	247	9.1	608	17.2
GA	210	9.9	120	28.5	1,034	13.0	102	13.5	355	16.7
HI	22	7.6	10	20.6	126	10.7	12	7.4	39	13.5
ID	28	8.3	11	27.7	149	11.8	12	8.3	50	13.8
IL	244	7.8	131	24.1	1,292	10.7	118	8.3	443	14.0
IN	108	6.7	58	23.4	559	9.5	54	7.7	180	11.7
IA	47	6.0	22	23.4	258	9.1	31	7.7	75	10.5
KS.	47	6.7	22	23.5	258	9.9	27	8.1	80	11.5
KY.	141	12.7	61	33.1	621	15.8	67	14.2	198	20.4
LA.	183	15.8	110	40.6	851	19.6	82	16.7	314	26.3
ME	27	7.8	13	28.1	136	10.9	18	10.2	38	13.0
MD	83	6.1	50	18.4	439	8.5	49	8.5	136	10.3
MA	106	6.7	62	22.1	573	9.3	71	8.9	171	11.6
MI	192	7.4	111	24.0	1,022	10.5	96	8.2	340	13.4
MN	64	5.1	31	19.3	380	7.9	45	8.2	115	9.2
MS	120	16.0	72	40.2	548	19.9	61	18.8	203	26.7
MO	127	8.6	65	26.1	638	11.7	70	9.9	212	15.3
MT	25	10.5	10	33.2	128	14.6	10	9.1	41	18.4
NE.	30	6.7	14	24.0	161	9.7	17	8.0	52	11.8
NV.	38	7.5	17	20.5	206	10.5	15	7.1	67	13.5
NH	14	4.3	7	17.6	79	6.5	10	7.2	22	7.3
NJ	136	6.3	72	19.4	700	8.5	83	7.8	221	10.8
NM	68	14.5	30	34.1	329	18.4	26	12.8	122	24.6
NY.	536	11.5	295	29.2	2,692	14.6	264	11.3	894	19.6
NC	196	9.0	104	27.4	959	12.3	122	13.2	302	15.7
ND	14	8.3	6	30.6	73	11.9	10	11.1	21	13.5
OH	235	7.8	137	26.3	1,171	10.6	116	8.1	397	14.0
OK	104	11.2	47	32.0	491	14.7	48	11.1	166	19.1
OR	70	7.9	32	25.9	389	11.6	32	7.6	115	14.0
PA.	250	7.8	135	24.9	1,304	11.0	164	9.1	408	14.3
RI	24	8.9	15	29.1	121	11.9	15	10.6	40	16.5
SC.	116	10.7	67	30.6	548	14.1	65	13.9	183	18.5
SD.	18	9.3	8	30.4	96	13.2	11	11.1	33	16.7
TN.	161	10.3	83	29.5	747	13.5	90	13.5	241	17.6
TX.	633	12.0	267	29.5	3,118	15.4	251	12.8	1,162	20.2
UT.	35	6.5	14	22.1	206	9.4	11	5.8	68	9.7
VT.	10	6.3	5	24.1	56	9.4	6	8.5	15	10.7
VA.	130	7.0	71	23.0	657	9.6	72	9.5	202	11.9
WA	111	7.3	52	24.1	612	10.6	48	7.5	194	13.2
WV	70	13.9	27	35.5	316	17.9	32	11.9	94	23.9
WI	78	5.6	42	21.7	452	8.7	49	7.4	144	10.8
WY	11	8.0	5	30.9	55	11.4	5	8.9	17	13.8

[1] No husband present.

Source: U.S. Census Bureau, "2000 Census of Population and Housing, Profiles of General Demographic Characteristics"; <http://www.census.gov/Press-Release/www/2002/demoprofiles.html>.

No. 1394. Household Income—Distribution by Income Level—25 Largest Metropolitan Areas: 1999

[In thousands except percent (1,506 represents 1,506,000), see headnote, Table 1392. Covers metropolitan statistical areas (MSAs) and consolidated metropolitan statistical areas as defined by the U.S. Office of Management and Budget as of June 30, 1999. For definitions and components of metropolitan areas see Appendix II]

Metropolitan area	Number of house-holds (1,000)	Percent distribution of households by income level							Median income (dol.)
		Under $15,000	$15,000-$24,999	$25,000-$34,999	$35,000-$49,999	$50,000-$74,999	$75,000-$99,999	$100,000 and over	
Atlanta, GA MSA	1,506	10.6	9.5	11.1	16.3	21.9	13.1	17.6	51,948
Boston-Worcester-Lawrence, MA-NH-ME-CT CMSA.	2,221	13.2	9.5	9.9	14.3	20.4	13.4	19.3	52,792
Chicago-Gary-Kenosha, IL-IN-WI CMSA	3,303	12.5	9.9	10.8	15.5	21.0	12.8	17.4	51,046
Cincinnati-Hamilton, OH-KY-IN CMSA . .	768	14.0	12.0	12.5	16.7	20.9	11.3	12.7	44,914
Cleveland-Akron, OH CMSA	1,167	15.3	12.8	12.9	16.7	20.3	10.7	11.2	42,215
Dallas-Fort Worth, TX CMSA	1,908	11.9	11.1	12.6	16.6	20.4	11.7	15.6	47,418
Denver-Boulder-Greeley, CO CMSA . . .	1,004	10.5	9.8	11.9	16.4	21.7	13.0	16.7	51,088
Detroit-Ann Arbor-Flint, MI CMSA	2,083	13.3	11.0	11.2	15.2	20.5	12.8	16.0	49,160
Houston-Galveston-Brazoria, TX CMSA .	1,641	14.3	12.0	12.6	15.9	18.9	11.1	15.1	44,761
Kansas City, MO-KS MSA	695	12.3	11.4	13.0	17.3	21.8	11.8	12.5	46,193
Los Angeles-Riverside-Orange County, CA CMSA.	5,352	14.8	11.9	11.7	15.2	18.9	11.2	16.2	45,903
Miami-Fort Lauderdale, FL CMSA	1,432	18.8	13.8	13.0	16.0	17.7	9.0	11.7	38,632
Minneapolis-St. Paul, MN-WI MSA	1,137	9.2	9.2	11.0	15.8	23.3	14.6	16.9	54,304
New York-Northern New Jersey-Long Island, NY-NJ-CT-PA CMSA.	7,739	15.6	9.8	10.0	13.7	18.4	12.1	20.3	50,795
Philadelphia-Wilmington-Atlantic City, PA-NJ-DE-MD CMSA	2,322	14.5	10.9	11.4	15.4	20.1	12.2	15.5	47,528
Phoenix-Mesa, AZ MSA	1,194	12.4	12.4	13.3	17.6	20.6	11.0	12.9	44,752
Pittsburgh, PA MSA	967	18.2	15.1	13.5	16.6	18.6	8.8	9.2	37,467
Portland-Salem, OR-WA CMSA	867	12.2	11.4	12.9	17.7	22.0	11.5	12.3	46,090
Sacramento-Yolo, CA CMSA	666	13.5	11.5	12.3	16.6	20.6	11.6	14.0	46,106
St. Louis, MO-IL MSA.	1,013	13.9	12.2	12.8	16.8	21.1	11.1	12.2	44,437
San Diego, CA MSA.	995	12.5	11.8	12.3	16.0	20.1	11.5	15.7	47,067
San Francisco-Oakland-San Jose, CA CMSA	2,559	10.0	7.8	8.7	13.2	19.5	14.0	26.7	62,024
Seattle-Tacoma-Bremerton, WA CMSA.	1,393	10.8	10.0	11.6	16.6	22.3	13.3	15.3	50,733
Tampa-St. Petersburg-Clearwater, FL MSA	1,010	16.2	15.4	15.0	17.8	18.1	8.2	9.4	37,406
Washington-Baltimore, DC-MD-VA-WV CMSA	2,874	10.1	8.4	9.9	14.6	21.2	14.2	21.6	57,291

No. 1395. Families and Persons Below Poverty Level—25 Largest Metropolitan Areas: 1999

[Number in thousands (72.0 represents 72,000), except percent. See headnote, Table 1393]

Metropolitan area	Families				Persons			
	Total		Families with female householder [1]		Total		Related children under 18 years old	
	Number	Percent	Number	Percent	Number	Percent	Number	Percent
Atlanta, GA MSA.	72.0	6.9	41.0	20.7	379.9	9.4	125.6	11.7
Boston-Worcester-Lawrence, MA-NH-ME-CT CMSA	87.3	6.0	49.7	20.5	482.7	8.6	138.9	10.2
Chicago-Gary-Kenosha, IL-IN-WI CMSA	178.7	7.9	98.1	23.0	943.0	10.5	337.6	14.0
Cincinnati-Hamilton, OH-KY-IN CMSA	36.1	6.9	22.7	25.0	184.3	9.5	62.2	12.1
Cleveland-Akron, OH CMSA	61.8	8.0	39.5	26.1	305.0	10.6	109.5	15.0
Dallas-Fort Worth, TX CMSA.	108.2	8.1	48.8	22.2	556.1	10.8	198.8	13.9
Denver-Boulder-Greeley, CO CMSA	36.5	5.6	17.1	18.1	217.2	8.6	64.6	10.0
Detroit-Ann Arbor-Flint, MI CMSA	109.3	7.7	67.6	23.5	571.1	10.6	202.0	14.4
Houston-Galveston-Brazoria, TX CMSA.	128.0	10.9	55.0	26.5	628.4	13.7	233.8	17.6
Kansas City, MO-KS MSA.	28.7	6.1	16.6	21.1	147.7	8.5	50.5	10.9
Los Angeles-Riverside-Orange County, CA CMSA	461.1	12.2	185.6	26.5	2,510.1	15.6	943.8	20.8
Miami-Fort Lauderdale, FL CMSA	116.1	12.0	54.8	26.1	581.6	15.3	181.7	19.8
Minneapolis-St. Paul, MN-WI MSA	31.7	4.2	17.4	16.5	195.3	6.7	63.7	8.2
New York-Northern New Jersey-Long Island, NY-NJ-CT-PA CMSA	536.7	10.2	291.1	26.3	2,678.8	12.9	880.5	17.2
Philadelphia-Wilmington-Atlantic City, PA-NJ-DE-MD CMSA.	124.8	7.9	75.2	23.3	653.8	10.9	215.4	14.0
Phoenix-Mesa, AZ MSA	67.0	8.2	26.0	21.2	383.5	12.0	134.9	15.9
Pittsburgh, PA MSA	49.2	7.8	27.2	25.5	248.6	10.8	74.2	14.4
Portland-Salem, OR-WA CMSA	38.8	6.8	18.4	22.1	222.6	10.0	68.4	12.1
Sacramento-Yolo, CA CMSA	39.2	8.7	18.1	22.1	224.9	12.7	79.6	16.8
St. Louis, MO-IL MSA	51.0	7.4	32.4	24.3	253.8	9.9	91.7	13.7
San Diego, CA MSA	59.2	8.9	25.8	22.8	338.4	12.4	115.9	16.5
San Francisco-Oakland-San Jose, CA CMSA. .	95.7	5.7	42.7	16.0	602.7	8.7	162.9	10.1
Seattle-Tacoma-Bremerton, WA CMSA	52.0	5.8	25.9	19.7	297.4	8.5	85.7	10.0
Tampa-St. Petersburg-Clearwater, FL MSA . .	50.2	7.8	24.8	22.5	262.4	11.2	80.2	15.7
Washington-Baltimore, DC-MD-VA-WV CMSA.	113.0	5.9	67.7	18.3	613.8	8.3	187.8	10.0

[1] No husband present.

Source of Tables 1394 and 1395: U.S. Census Bureau, "2000 Census of Population and Housing, Profiles of General Demographic Characteristics"; <http://www.census.gov/Press-Release/www/2002/demoprofiles.html>.

No. 1396. Selected Housing Characteristics by State: 2000

[In percent, except as indicated (115,905 represents 115,905,000). As of April 1. Based on sample data from the 2000 Census of Population and Housing; see text, Section 1, Population, and Appendix III]

State	Total housing units (1,000)	Percent of units by units in structure— 1-unit detached	1-unit attached	2 units	3 or 4 units	5 to 9 units	10 to 19 units	20 or more units	Mobile homes	Boat, RV, van, etc.
U.S.	115,905	60.3	5.6	4.3	4.7	4.7	4.0	8.6	7.6	0.2
AL.	1,964	66.2	2.0	2.2	3.3	3.8	2.4	3.6	16.3	0.3
AK.	261	58.5	7.0	5.5	7.4	5.7	3.0	5.4	6.8	0.7
AZ.	2,189	56.8	6.0	1.5	3.4	3.8	3.7	9.7	13.8	1.3
AR.	1,173	69.0	1.8	3.2	3.0	2.7	2.3	2.8	14.9	0.4
CA.	12,215	56.4	7.6	2.7	5.7	5.9	5.1	12.0	4.4	0.3
CO	1,808	62.1	6.3	2.1	3.8	4.6	5.6	9.7	5.7	0.2
CT.	1,386	58.9	5.1	8.6	9.2	5.5	3.8	7.9	0.8	(Z)
DE.	343	55.9	14.1	2.0	2.6	3.7	5.5	4.9	11.2	0.2
DC	275	13.2	26.4	3.0	8.0	7.9	10.3	30.9	0.1	0.1
FL.	7,303	52.3	5.9	2.7	4.3	5.0	5.0	12.9	11.6	0.4
GA	3,282	64.2	2.9	2.8	4.0	5.3	3.9	4.7	12.0	0.1
HI	461	52.0	8.3	2.3	4.6	6.7	5.0	20.8	0.2	0.1
ID	528	70.1	2.9	2.8	4.1	2.7	1.8	3.0	12.2	0.5
IL	4,886	57.9	4.8	6.9	6.5	6.2	4.3	10.1	3.2	(Z)
IN	2,532	71.2	2.9	3.4	4.0	4.6	3.2	4.1	6.6	0.1
IA	1,233	74.0	2.3	3.2	3.9	3.7	3.1	4.6	5.3	0.1
KS.	1,131	72.4	3.5	3.0	3.6	3.5	3.1	4.4	6.4	0.1
KY.	1,751	66.0	2.1	3.2	4.1	4.3	3.1	2.9	14.1	0.1
LA.	1,847	64.1	3.8	4.0	4.5	3.1	2.2	4.9	13.0	0.3
ME	652	67.4	2.2	5.6	5.8	4.3	1.7	2.9	9.8	0.3
MD	2,145	51.2	21.0	2.1	2.9	5.6	7.9	7.2	1.9	(Z)
MA	2,622	52.4	4.0	11.6	11.4	6.0	4.3	9.3	0.9	(Z)
MI	4,234	70.6	3.9	3.5	2.8	4.0	3.4	5.1	6.5	0.2
MN	2,066	67.8	5.2	3.0	2.3	2.4	3.8	10.7	4.5	0.3
MS	1,162	68.1	1.7	2.4	3.3	3.4	1.5	2.7	16.6	0.2
MO	2,442	68.8	2.7	3.9	5.1	3.8	3.2	4.1	8.2	0.3
MT	413	67.0	2.7	3.3	4.6	2.9	1.8	3.1	14.3	0.3
NE.	723	71.9	2.9	2.6	3.0	3.8	4.5	6.1	5.1	0.1
NV.	827	52.3	5.4	1.5	7.3	8.0	5.4	10.0	9.7	0.5
NH	547	62.4	4.4	6.5	6.0	5.0	3.2	5.8	6.5	0.1
NJ.	3,310	54.2	8.6	10.0	6.8	4.8	4.9	9.6	1.0	(Z)
NM	781	61.0	4.5	2.0	3.5	2.5	2.3	5.1	18.6	0.6
NY.	7,679	41.7	4.9	10.9	7.3	5.3	4.3	22.9	2.7	0.1
NC	3,524	64.4	3.0	2.5	3.2	4.3	3.2	2.9	16.4	0.2
ND	290	62.1	4.1	2.5	4.3	4.2	5.3	8.6	9.0	0.1
OH	4,783	67.4	3.8	5.2	4.8	4.8	3.9	5.5	4.6	0.1
OK	1,514	71.4	2.4	1.9	2.8	3.6	2.7	4.2	10.7	0.4
OR	1,453	62.8	3.3	3.0	4.2	4.3	3.8	7.8	10.3	0.6
PA.	5,250	55.9	17.9	5.2	4.6	3.4	2.5	5.4	4.9	0.1
RI	440	54.8	2.9	12.3	12.8	5.2	3.4	7.5	1.0	(Z)
SC.	1,754	61.5	2.3	2.5	3.3	4.4	2.4	3.2	20.3	0.1
SD.	323	67.4	2.3	2.7	3.7	3.5	3.4	5.6	11.4	0.1
TN.	2,439	67.3	2.8	3.4	3.4	4.4	3.1	4.3	11.0	0.2
TX.	8,158	63.4	3.1	2.1	3.3	4.4	4.3	10.0	9.0	0.4
UT.	769	67.7	4.9	3.8	4.8	3.6	3.9	5.8	5.1	0.3
VT.	294	65.6	3.4	7.2	6.4	5.1	1.5	2.8	7.7	0.2
VA.	2,904	62.3	9.6	2.1	3.3	5.0	5.3	5.9	6.4	0.1
WA	2,451	62.3	3.1	2.8	3.8	4.6	5.1	9.3	8.5	0.5
WV	845	69.1	1.6	2.6	2.9	2.6	1.5	2.4	16.9	0.4
WI	2,321	66.0	3.4	8.2	3.9	4.6	3.3	6.2	4.4	0.1
WY	224	64.9	3.6	2.5	4.6	3.0	1.9	3.2	15.9	0.4

Z Less than 0.05 percent.

Source: U.S. Census Bureau, "2000 Census of Population and Housing, Profiles of General Demographic Characteristics"; <http://www.census.gov/Press-Release/www/2002/demoprofiles.html>.

U.S. Census Bureau, Statistical Abstract of the United States: 2002

No. 1397. Specified Owner-Occupied Housing Units, Value, and Costs by State: 2000

[In percent, except as indicated (55,212 represents 55,212,000). As of April 1. Specified owner-occupied units are owner-occupied, one-family, attached and detached houses on less than 10 acres without a business or medical office on the property. Based on sample data from the 2000 Census of Population and Housing; see text, Section 1, Population, and Appendix III. For definition of median, see Guide to Tabular Presentation]

State	Total (1,000)	Percent of units with value of—			Median value (dol.)	Median selected monthly owner costs [1] (dol.)	Selected monthly owner costs as a percent of household income, 1999			
		$99,999 or less	$100,000 to $199,999	$200,000 or more			Less than 15 percent	15 to 24 percent	25 to 34 percent	35 percent or more
U.S. . . .	55,212	40.3	38.4	21.4	119,600	1,088	36.5	31.4	15.5	15.8
AL.	919	61.9	28.8	9.3	85,100	816	43.5	29.1	12.1	13.9
AK.	106	22.5	57.9	19.7	144,200	1,315	32.6	33.3	17.4	16.2
AZ.	1,032	35.6	45.9	18.5	121,300	1,039	34.8	31.8	16.3	16.2
AR.	513	72.3	22.0	5.7	72,800	737	45.3	29.0	11.8	12.7
CA.	5,528	11.6	35.5	52.9	211,500	1,478	28.0	28.7	19.3	23.2
CO	903	13.3	52.4	34.3	166,600	1,197	32.2	32.5	18.2	16.6
CT.	728	12.5	50.6	36.9	166,900	1,426	31.8	32.9	17.7	17.1
DE.	177	28.1	54.0	17.9	130,400	1,101	38.5	32.2	14.8	13.8
DC	76	18.6	43.5	37.8	157,200	1,291	38.2	27.0	14.6	18.6
FL.	3,242	46.9	38.5	14.7	105,500	1,004	34.2	30.5	15.8	18.5
GA	1,596	43.7	39.1	17.2	111,200	1,039	36.4	32.5	15.0	15.2
HI	174	6.7	21.7	71.5	272,700	1,571	35.7	23.7	17.9	22.1
ID	255	45.2	43.9	10.9	106,300	887	36.6	32.6	15.6	14.5
IL	2,470	35.7	41.0	23.3	130,800	1,198	36.1	32.4	15.9	14.9
IN	1,379	55.3	36.4	8.3	94,300	869	42.7	32.5	12.9	11.2
IA	665	65.7	28.2	6.1	82,500	829	45.2	32.4	12.2	9.6
KS.	582	61.6	29.9	8.4	83,500	888	43.5	32.8	12.5	10.5
KY.	806	61.8	30.2	8.1	86,700	816	44.3	30.1	12.3	12.3
LA.	865	62.3	29.2	8.5	85,000	816	45.7	27.0	11.4	14.2
ME	255	51.3	38.1	10.7	98,700	923	35.8	33.8	15.2	14.7
MD	1,179	23.1	50.3	26.6	146,000	1,296	32.1	33.7	17.6	16.1
MA	1,188	9.5	46.4	44.1	185,700	1,353	33.4	33.1	16.7	16.2
MI	2,269	41.3	41.6	17.2	115,600	972	41.8	31.5	13.2	12.7
MN	1,117	35.1	49.4	15.5	122,400	1,044	38.7	34.9	14.9	11.1
MS	532	72.5	21.8	5.7	71,400	752	42.4	27.5	12.3	16.0
MO	1,188	58.1	32.0	9.9	89,900	861	43.4	31.6	12.6	11.6
MT	165	50.5	40.2	9.3	99,500	863	38.0	30.9	15.1	15.3
NE.	370	61.4	31.7	6.9	88,000	895	42.1	33.1	13.6	10.6
NV.	363	15.7	63.7	20.6	142,000	1,190	28.0	32.1	19.2	19.8
NH	249	26.7	54.2	19.1	133,300	1,226	28.8	36.7	18.7	15.3
NJ	1,702	15.2	46.7	38.0	170,800	1,534	27.0	32.6	19.3	20.5
NM	340	45.2	40.3	14.6	108,100	929	40.3	27.9	14.6	16.0
NY.	2,690	32.2	35.7	32.1	148,700	1,357	31.5	31.4	16.8	19.6
NC	1,616	45.3	39.7	15.0	108,300	985	37.7	31.5	14.8	15.0
ND	122	73.3	23.5	3.3	74,400	818	44.9	32.5	12.1	9.7
OH	2,613	47.7	40.8	11.4	103,700	963	38.6	33.1	14.5	13.2
OK	699	73.8	21.4	4.9	70,700	764	45.3	29.6	11.9	12.1
OR	654	17.0	56.4	26.6	152,100	1,125	32.2	32.0	17.8	17.5
PA.	2,889	52.4	36.2	11.3	97,000	1,010	37.8	31.5	14.8	15.1
RI	202	20.5	61.1	18.3	133,000	1,205	30.2	33.6	18.5	17.1
SC	784	54.1	33.2	12.7	94,900	894	40.9	30.2	13.5	14.3
SD.	138	68.9	26.0	5.1	79,600	828	43.4	32.5	13.0	10.4
TN.	1,206	55.9	33.0	11.1	93,000	882	40.4	30.4	13.8	14.4
TX.	3,850	63.3	26.9	9.8	82,500	986	40.7	31.5	13.2	13.6
UT.	427	16.1	60.8	23.1	146,100	1,102	34.9	30.4	18.1	16.2
VT.	106	41.0	48.2	10.8	111,500	1,021	30.1	35.6	17.7	16.2
VA.	1,511	36.7	40.2	23.1	125,400	1,144	35.5	33.5	16.3	14.1
WA	1,157	15.1	48.5	36.4	168,300	1,268	30.3	31.9	19.1	18.1
WV	393	73.8	21.7	4.6	72,800	713	50.8	25.7	10.4	11.9
WI	1,122	41.9	46.1	12.0	112,200	1,024	36.8	35.1	15.6	12.0
WY	96	53.6	37.2	9.2	96,600	825	45.1	30.3	12.7	11.3

[1] Includes mortgages, deeds of trust, taxes, utilities, etc.

Source: U.S. Census Bureau, "2000 Census of Population and Housing, Profiles of General Demographic Characteristics"; <http://www.census.gov/Press-Release/www/2002/demoprofiles.html>.

2000 Census Data Sampler   881

No. 1398. Specified Owner-Occupied Housing Units, Value, and Costs— 25 Largest Metropolitan Areas: 2000

[In percent, except as indicated (884.3 represents 884,300). As of April 1. Specified owner-occupied units are owner-occupied, one-family, attached and detached houses on less than 10 acres without a business or medical office on the property. Based on sample data from the 2000 Census of Population and Housing; see text Section 1, Population, and Appendix III. See headnote Table 1401 for information regarding metropolitan areas]

Metropolitan area	Total (1,000)	Percent of units with value of— $99,999 or less	$200,000 or more	Median value (dol.)	Median selected monthly owner costs[1] (dol.)	Selected monthly owner costs as a percent of household income, 1999 Less than 15 percent	15 to 24 percent	25 to 34 percent	35 percent or more
Atlanta, GA MSA	884.3	27.9	24.3	135,300	1,165	32.8	34.9	16.3	15.4
Boston-Worcester-Lawrence, MA-NH-ME-CT CMSA	1,067.8	7.4	46.8	192,500	1,415	32.0	34.0	17.3	16.2
Chicago-Gary-Kenosha, IL-IN-WI CMSA	1,717.3	18.4	32.0	159,000	1,347	31.5	33.1	17.8	17.0
Cincinnati-Hamilton, OH-KY-IN CMSA	439.2	38.8	15.5	116,500	1,064	36.3	35.3	15.5	12.4
Cleveland-Akron, OH CMSA	711.1	37.7	15.3	117,900	1,049	35.5	33.2	15.6	15.1
Dallas-Fort Worth, TX CMSA	1,003.7	50.0	14.6	100,000	1,148	35.7	34.9	14.9	13.7
Denver-Boulder-Greeley, CO CMSA	565.3	6.1	39.7	179,500	1,271	30.7	33.4	18.8	16.6
Detroit-Ann Arbor-Flint, MI CMSA	1,305.3	32.4	22.7	132,600	1,076	40.1	31.6	13.7	13.8
Houston-Galveston-Brazoria, TX CMSA	863.4	57.4	12.2	89,700	1,072	39.4	32.6	13.1	13.8
Kansas City, MO-KS MSA	418.0	47.3	12.4	104,700	986	39.5	34.4	13.7	11.8
Los Angeles-Riverside-Orange County, CA CMSA	2,498.4	9.6	51.0	203,300	1,494	26.4	28.3	19.5	25.0
Miami-Fort Lauderdale, FL CMSA	634.5	33.1	18.3	126,100	1,225	24.2	30.0	18.8	25.9
Minneapolis-St. Paul, MN-WI MSA	704.0	18.3	21.2	141,200	1,157	34.2	37.1	16.7	11.8
New York-Northern New Jersey-Long Island, NY-NJ-CT-PA CMSA	3,088.9	7.0	51.0	203,100	1,679	27.8	30.7	18.5	22.3
Philadelphia-Wilmington-Atlantic City, PA-NJ-DE-MD CMSA	1,456.0	37.3	18.2	122,300	1,224	32.3	32.2	16.8	17.8
Phoenix-Mesa, AZ MSA	689.5	30.5	20.5	127,900	1,088	33.0	33.1	17.0	16.2
Pittsburgh, PA MSA	601.3	62.0	8.2	86,100	937	40.2	30.8	13.7	14.4
Portland-Salem, OR-WA CMSA	453.7	8.3	31.8	165,400	1,232	29.0	32.9	19.4	18.2
Sacramento-Yolo, CA CMSA	359.8	14.2	31.2	159,700	1,298	28.7	31.6	19.4	19.7
St. Louis, MO-IL MSA	624.4	50.4	13.5	99,400	953	42.0	32.8	12.9	11.6
San Diego, CA MSA	457.3	3.5	59.8	227,200	1,541	27.7	28.4	19.9	23.2
San Francisco-Oakland-San Jose, CA CMSA	1,258.0	2.7	82.5	353,500	1,822	29.4	28.2	19.5	22.2
Seattle-Tacoma-Bremerton, WA CMSA	719.2	6.2	47.8	195,400	1,399	27.8	32.3	20.3	19.0
Tampa-St. Petersburg-Clearwater, FL MSA	540.9	55.5	11.0	93,800	938	35.1	31.6	15.5	16.9
Washington-Baltimore, DC-MD-VA-WV CMSA	1,621.6	17.4	34.2	161,600	1,382	31.7	34.6	17.7	15.5

[1] For homes with a mortgage. Includes mortgages, deeds of trust, taxes, utilities, etc.

No. 1399. Specified Owner-Occupied Housing Units, Value, and Costs— 25 Largest Cities: 2000

[In percent, except as indicated (104.8 represents 104,800). As of April 1. See headnote, Table 1398 for coverage]

City	Total (1,000)	Percent of units with value of— $99,999 or less	$100,000 to $199,999	$200,000 or more	Median value (dol.)	Median selected monthly owner costs[1] (dol.)	Selected monthly owner costs as a percent of household income, 1999 Less than 15 percent	15 to 24 percent	25 to 34 percent	35 percent or more
Austin, TX	104.8	35.5	40.9	23.6	124,700	1,181	34.3	34.3	16.0	14.8
Baltimore, MD	116.6	83.3	12.5	4.3	69,100	853	35.0	28.0	14.8	20.5
Boston, MA	30.5	5.8	49.5	44.7	190,600	1,370	33.1	30.9	15.0	20.0
Chicago, IL	263.9	31.3	48.3	20.5	132,400	1,216	32.6	28.7	16.2	21.2
Columbus, OH	134.0	49.0	45.3	5.7	101,400	987	30.9	36.3	17.2	15.0
Dallas, TX	173.6	55.2	25.0	19.7	89,800	1,054	38.9	29.3	13.6	16.9
Denver, CO	104.3	10.7	55.6	33.7	165,800	1,134	33.2	29.7	17.2	19.2
Detroit, MI	164.2	84.8	12.9	2.3	63,600	769	41.1	23.9	12.0	20.4
El Paso, TX	102.0	79.9	16.4	3.7	71,300	810	38.4	30.3	14.4	15.7
Houston, TX	295.5	64.4	22.6	13.0	79,300	965	41.7	28.8	12.3	15.6
Indianapolis, IN [2]	172.7	51.7	39.6	8.7	98,200	928	37.6	33.6	14.5	13.5
Jacksonville, FL	157.7	61.3	30.4	8.4	87,800	902	37.2	32.4	14.2	15.2
Los Angeles, CA	412.8	4.6	39.7	55.7	221,600	1,556	27.2	24.8	17.4	29.4
Memphis, TN	130.7	73.2	19.3	7.5	72,800	838	34.0	29.4	15.1	19.8
Milwaukee, WI	82.3	73.0	24.8	2.2	80,400	863	36.7	32.5	15.0	15.0
Nashville-Davidson, TN [2]	109.1	41.2	43.3	15.5	113,300	1,006	35.6	32.1	16.2	15.3
New York, NY	391.4	4.2	40.8	55.0	211,900	1,535	30.4	25.3	15.8	26.8
Philadelphia, PA	315.4	84.9	12.6	2.5	59,700	800	39.2	26.3	12.8	19.4
Phoenix, AZ	250.1	41.9	41.0	17.1	112,600	1,021	30.7	33.6	17.0	17.8
San Antonio, TX	217.3	74.9	20.4	4.7	68,800	881	40.4	30.9	13.8	13.9
San Diego, CA	188.0	4.0	34.6	61.4	233,100	1,526	29.2	28.1	19.1	22.8
San Francisco, CA	79.5	5.6	3.6	90.8	396,400	1,693	36.9	23.7	15.6	22.9
San Jose, CA	146.9	2.1	3.4	94.5	394,000	1,717	27.5	30.1	20.0	21.8
Seattle, WA	102.7	2.5	25.9	71.6	259,600	1,497	32.0	29.0	18.7	19.7
Washington, DC	76.3	18.6	43.5	37.8	157,200	1,291	38.2	27.0	14.6	18.6

[1] For homes with a mortgage. Includes mortgages, deeds of trust, taxes, utilities, etc. [2] Represents the portion of a consolidated city that is not within one or more separately incorporated places.

Source of Tables 1398 and 1399: U.S. Census Bureau, "2000 Census of Population and Housing, Profiles of General Demographic Characteristics"; <http://www.census.gov/Press-Release/www/2002/demoprofiles.html>.

No. 1400. Specified Renter-Occupied Housing Units, Gross Rent by State: 2000

[In percent, except as indicated (35,200 represents 35,200,000). As of April 1. Specified renter-occupied units include all renter-occupied units except 1-unit attached or detached houses on 10 acres or more. Based on sample data from the 2000 Census of Population and Housing; see text, Section 1, Population, and Appendix III. For definition of median, see Guide to Tabular Presentation]

State	Total [1] (1,000)	Percent of units with gross rent of—					Median gross rent (dol.)	Gross rent as a percent of household income, 1999			
		$299 or less	$300 to $499	$500 to $749	$750 to $999	$1,000 or more		Less than 15 percent	15 to 24 percent	25 to 34 percent	35 percent or more
U.S. ...	35,200	10.4	22.0	33.7	17.2	11.6	602	18.1	27.1	17.8	29.5
AL.......	469	20.3	34.1	26.3	6.4	2.5	447	19.6	24.0	15.1	27.4
AK.......	82	4.0	11.7	31.7	22.4	16.9	720	17.3	26.1	17.2	25.4
AZ.......	605	6.8	20.6	38.8	18.3	10.1	619	15.8	26.9	18.8	30.9
AR.......	310	16.6	37.1	27.5	5.8	2.0	453	19.4	25.1	15.3	26.7
CA.......	4,922	4.9	12.6	31.3	23.6	24.5	747	14.6	26.7	19.2	34.1
CO	534	7.2	16.3	35.2	21.4	16.4	671	15.2	28.8	20.4	30.4
CT.......	429	9.6	12.8	35.6	22.7	15.0	681	18.4	27.5	18.5	29.0
DE.......	82	10.1	14.3	41.6	19.4	8.8	639	19.5	28.6	17.8	26.7
DC.......	147	12.8	17.6	34.5	16.8	15.4	618	20.0	26.9	17.8	28.2
FL.......	1,889	7.2	18.4	38.3	20.8	10.7	641	14.6	26.3	18.6	33.0
GA	964	11.9	20.9	31.2	20.8	9.2	613	18.4	27.4	17.5	28.1
HI.......	174	6.7	8.6	24.8	22.8	23.8	779	14.2	23.6	17.2	29.1
ID.......	126	12.7	30.4	34.0	10.9	3.7	515	17.5	27.1	17.6	28.1
IL.......	1,488	10.6	21.2	36.1	17.5	10.8	605	20.0	28.3	17.1	28.3
IN.......	654	11.9	31.2	38.4	9.7	3.4	521	21.0	28.3	17.0	26.4
IA.......	302	17.1	35.8	31.2	7.1	2.6	470	22.4	28.2	16.8	24.8
KS.......	310	13.9	33.4	31.4	10.3	4.8	498	21.1	29.3	16.7	25.0
KY.......	449	18.9	36.8	26.2	6.1	2.1	445	20.8	25.5	16.0	25.6
LA.......	526	17.3	34.4	28.7	7.0	2.9	466	18.6	23.3	14.8	29.8
ME	144	16.2	30.7	32.5	10.0	3.3	497	16.9	28.1	19.2	27.4
MD	632	8.7	14.2	33.6	24.3	14.9	689	18.2	29.3	19.1	27.0
MA	932	13.0	14.1	28.7	21.8	18.8	684	18.9	26.8	19.5	28.6
MI.......	976	10.8	28.3	38.3	12.5	5.7	546	20.9	27.2	16.8	28.4
MN	471	14.4	23.3	35.6	15.5	7.5	566	18.7	29.5	19.6	27.1
MS	283	21.1	33.3	25.9	6.0	1.9	439	18.9	23.4	14.8	27.6
MO	633	15.1	34.9	31.8	8.6	3.3	484	20.3	28.2	16.8	26.3
MT	105	18.6	36.9	26.4	6.1	2.4	447	18.2	25.6	16.9	28.2
NE.......	207	14.2	34.6	32.9	8.3	3.8	491	21.4	30.2	17.2	23.5
NV.......	293	4.1	12.2	40.7	26.7	13.0	699	15.2	28.5	20.2	30.5
NH	141	9.0	15.8	39.9	21.5	9.8	646	18.0	31.7	19.2	25.6
NJ.......	1,049	7.9	8.6	31.8	29.9	18.6	751	18.5	27.6	18.3	29.9
NM	201	13.4	31.3	28.9	10.8	5.8	503	16.6	24.5	16.8	30.5
NY.......	3,302	10.2	15.7	32.5	21.2	17.3	672	19.1	24.2	16.9	33.4
NC.......	944	11.2	26.8	34.7	13.7	5.3	548	19.3	27.2	16.3	26.7
ND	83	22.9	40.7	21.9	3.9	1.7	412	22.7	28.9	15.4	22.6
OH	1,353	12.7	32.0	36.1	10.3	4.0	515	20.5	28.1	17.0	27.4
OK	414	15.2	39.6	27.5	6.4	2.6	456	19.8	26.4	16.0	26.7
OR	468	7.4	18.9	42.4	18.0	9.4	620	14.7	28.0	19.6	32.2
PA.......	1,349	13.0	28.9	33.7	12.4	6.3	531	19.2	26.6	17.3	28.6
RI.......	163	15.6	22.6	38.5	12.9	6.5	553	18.7	26.5	19.4	28.9
SC.......	421	14.1	29.1	33.0	9.7	4.1	510	19.1	26.1	15.4	26.8
SD.......	88	22.9	35.7	25.3	4.7	2.0	426	20.9	29.2	16.3	22.7
TN.......	657	15.3	30.0	33.3	10.1	3.7	505	18.9	26.7	17.3	27.2
TX.......	2,649	9.1	25.1	37.1	15.4	7.9	574	18.8	28.8	17.4	27.1
UT.......	199	7.7	21.0	42.2	15.3	8.5	597	18.1	28.7	18.8	27.7
VT.......	67	11.6	25.2	38.1	14.0	5.4	553	15.9	27.7	20.1	29.5
VA.......	843	9.3	18.9	30.7	20.3	15.0	650	18.2	29.3	18.5	26.3
WA	796	7.3	16.4	36.4	21.6	14.0	663	15.1	28.4	19.8	30.8
WV	176	22.8	38.8	19.7	3.3	1.2	401	18.9	21.3	14.6	28.3
WI.......	642	10.5	29.5	39.7	12.3	4.3	540	21.1	30.8	17.5	25.4
WY	56	16.4	42.0	23.6	5.5	2.7	437	24.1	26.3	15.2	23.3

[1] Includes units with no cash rent.

Source: U.S. Census Bureau, "2000 Census of Population and Housing, Profiles of General Demographic Characteristics"; <http://www.census.gov/Press-Release/www/2002/demoprofiles.html>.

No. 1401. Specified Renter-Occupied Housing Units, Gross Rent—25 Largest Metropolitan Areas: 2000

[In percent, except as indicated (501.9 represents 501,900). As of April 1. Specified renter-occupied units include all renter-occupied units except 1-unit attached or detached houses on 10 acres or more. Based on sample data from the 2000 Census of Population and Housing; see text Section 1, Population, and Appendix III. Covers metropolitan statistical areas (MSAs) and consolidated metropolitan statistical areas (CMSAs) as defined by the U.S. Office of Management and Budget as of June 30, 1999. For definitions and components of metropolitan areas, see Appendix II. For definition of median, see Guide to Tabular Presentation]

Metropolitan area	Percent of units with gross rent of—			Median gross rent (dol.)	Gross rent as a percent of household income, 1999			
	Total [1] (1,000)	$499 or less	$500 to $749	$750 or more		Less than 15 percent	15 to 24 percent	25 to 34 percent	35 percent or more
Atlanta, GA MSA	501.9	16.3	33.0	48.0	746	17.1	29.9	19.4	28.5
Boston-Worcester-Lawrence, MA-NH-ME-CT CMSA	847.2	23.6	28.3	44.9	720	18.7	27.6	19.6	28.3
Chicago-Gary-Kenosha, IL-IN-WI CMSA	1,145.5	23.5	39.0	34.8	659	19.2	28.7	17.5	29.1
Cincinnati-Hamilton, OH-KY-IN CMSA	250.3	45.4	34.4	16.7	516	21.2	28.9	16.9	27.4
Cleveland-Akron, OH CMSA	360.8	38.9	39.5	17.6	545	18.9	27.6	17.6	29.3
Dallas-Fort Worth, TX CMSA	750.9	21.7	42.9	32.8	649	18.9	32.0	19.0	25.4
Denver-Boulder-Greeley, CO CMSA	334.3	19.2	35.8	42.7	706	15.1	29.3	21.0	30.5
Detroit-Ann Arbor-Flint, MI CMSA	574.0	33.0	39.9	23.4	584	21.2	26.9	16.5	29.0
Houston-Galveston-Brazoria, TX CMSA	643.0	30.6	41.5	24.7	589	20.3	30.0	17.4	26.2
Kansas City, MO-KS MSA	219.9	34.2	39.8	21.9	575	20.2	31.2	17.6	24.7
Los Angeles-Riverside-Orange County, CA CMSA	2,412.5	16.2	35.0	46.4	733	14.2	26.3	19.1	35.2
Miami-Fort Lauderdale, FL CMSA	526.4	20.8	36.9	39.3	689	12.3	24.1	18.9	37.7
Minneapolis-St. Paul, MN-WI MSA	310.9	24.7	41.7	31.5	641	17.3	30.9	20.3	28.0
New York-Northern New Jersey-Long Island, NY-NJ-CT-PA CMSA	3,627.1	19.8	30.4	47.2	740	19.5	24.9	17.2	32.5
Philadelphia-Wilmington-Atlantic City, PA-NJ-DE-MD CMSA	695.1	24.0	38.9	33.0	651	17.3	26.8	17.7	31.2
Phoenix-Mesa, AZ MSA	381.2	20.4	41.6	34.3	661	15.3	28.2	19.7	30.9
Pittsburgh, PA MSA	275.0	50.3	31.3	12.3	482	20.2	25.7	17.2	28.5
Portland-Salem, OR-WA CMSA	317.1	18.8	45.0	33.4	660	14.8	29.7	20.2	30.9
Sacramento-Yolo, CA CMSA	255.9	20.6	40.6	36.2	673	14.9	27.6	19.1	33.8
St. Louis, MO-IL MSA	287.5	42.7	37.1	15.5	525	20.6	28.4	16.5	27.6
San Diego, CA MSA	441.6	13.0	33.4	49.4	761	12.6	27.0	20.3	34.1
San Francisco-Oakland-San Jose, CA CMSA	1,072.2	11.0	17.2	69.2	968	16.4	28.5	19.7	31.0
Seattle-Tacoma-Bremerton, WA CMSA	514.8	16.9	35.7	44.1	723	14.9	29.8	20.6	29.8
Tampa-St. Petersburg-Clearwater, FL MSA	294.3	27.8	42.6	25.5	608	15.7	28.3	19.0	30.7
Washington-Baltimore, DC-MD-VA-WV CMSA	996.7	19.1	29.9	47.5	744	18.6	30.3	19.2	26.2

[1] Includes units with no cash rent.

No. 1402. Specified Renter-Occupied Housing Units, Gross Rent—25 Largest Cities: 2000

[In percent, except as indicated (146.1 represents 146,100). As of April 1. See Table 1401 for coverage]

City	Percent of units with gross rent of—					Median gross rent (dol.)	Gross rent as a percent of household income, 1999			
	Total [1] (1,000)	$299 or less	$300 to $499	$500 to $749	$750 to $999	$1,000 or more		Less than 15 percent	15 to 24 percent	25 to 34 percent	35 percent or more
Austin, TX	146.1	3.2	9.0	41.0	28.9	16.1	724	14.4	28.3	19.4	33.5
Baltimore, MD	127.6	19.3	29.8	34.3	9.7	4.3	498	18.8	23.7	17.9	33.0
Boston, MA	162.1	15.6	8.8	19.2	24.0	30.5	803	17.2	24.2	20.0	32.1
Chicago, IL	596.1	10.1	18.8	39.6	17.4	12.1	616	19.3	27.4	16.9	30.8
Columbus, OH	153.3	8.1	23.5	46.5	14.9	5.3	586	18.3	30.3	18.0	29.0
Dallas, TX	256.1	5.4	19.2	45.3	18.4	10.0	623	18.8	30.6	19.2	26.8
Denver, CO	113.4	9.5	18.1	37.6	19.8	13.0	631	16.5	28.4	20.3	30.6
Detroit, MI	150.8	13.5	37.4	33.8	8.5	2.8	486	21.1	21.2	14.8	33.9
El Paso, TX	70.3	17.3	35.3	30.7	8.3	3.3	474	15.9	25.1	18.9	32.0
Houston, TX [2]	388.6	5.1	27.9	42.0	14.9	7.8	575	19.9	29.5	17.7	27.0
Indianapolis, IN [2]	132.1	7.3	26.9	45.5	13.8	4.2	567	18.6	30.3	17.9	28.5
Jacksonville, FL	104.5	10.3	21.0	40.3	18.5	5.8	598	17.5	30.1	18.8	26.8
Los Angeles, CA	782.2	5.7	15.8	38.4	20.7	17.5	672	14.1	24.4	18.8	37.1
Memphis, TN	110.4	12.9	26.5	40.5	13.0	3.8	548	17.7	26.2	17.7	31.8
Milwaukee, WI	126.7	10.3	32.5	42.4	9.2	3.7	527	18.8	27.6	17.0	32.0
Nashville-Davidson, TN [2]	103.1	11.0	16.6	44.8	17.4	7.3	614	17.1	29.9	20.1	27.8
New York, NY	2,108.5	11.0	12.0	32.2	23.5	19.4	705	20.5	23.5	16.4	33.7
Philadelphia, PA	240.0	10.9	24.8	38.3	14.7	7.5	569	16.1	22.9	15.9	36.0
Phoenix, AZ	183.0	5.3	19.2	44.3	19.5	9.2	622	15.6	28.3	20.3	30.9
San Antonio, TX	169.7	10.7	28.1	37.9	13.3	6.0	549	17.5	29.7	18.3	28.0
San Diego, CA	227.2	4.1	11.0	31.4	23.6	25.9	763	12.8	26.6	20.0	34.4
San Francisco, CA	214.2	7.6	9.1	18.1	19.6	43.6	928	20.9	28.2	18.6	28.2
San Jose, CA	105.4	3.5	4.2	9.2	21.3	59.9	1,123	14.3	28.6	20.9	32.3
Seattle, WA	133.3	8.6	9.7	35.3	24.3	20.2	721	14.6	29.4	21.5	30.6
Washington, DC	146.0	12.8	17.6	31.6	16.8	16.4	618	20.0	26.0	17.0	20.2

[1] Includes units with no cash rent. [2] Represents the portion of a consolidated city that is not within one or more separately incorporated places.

Source of Tables 1401 and 1402: U.S. Census Bureau, "2000 Census of Population and Housing, Profiles of General Demographic Characteristics"; <http://www.census.gov/Press-Release/www/2002/demoprofiles.html>

Guide to—Sources of Statistics, State Statistical Abstracts, and Foreign Statistical Abstracts

Alphabetically arranged, this guide contains references to the important primary sources of statistical information for the United States published since 1990. Secondary sources have been included if the information contained in them is presented in a particularly convenient form or if primary sources are not readily available. Nonrecurrent publications presenting compilations or estimates for years later than 1990 or types of data not available in regular series are also included. Much data are also available in press releases.

Much valuable information may also be found in state reports, foreign statistical abstracts, which are included at the end of this appendix, and in reports for particular commodities, industries, or similar segments of our economic and social structures, many of which are not included here.

Publications listed under each subject are divided into two main groups: "U.S. Government" and "Nongovernment." The location of the publisher of each report is given except for federal agencies located in Washington, DC. Most federal publications may be purchased from the Superintendent of Documents, U.S. Government Printing Office, Washington, DC 20402, tel. 202-512-1800, (Web site <http.www.access.gpo.gov> or from Government Printing Office bookstores in certain major cities. In some cases, federal publications may be obtained from the issuing agency.

U.S. GOVERNMENT

Administrative Office of the United States Courts
http://www.uscourts.gov
Calendar Year Reports on Authorized Wiretaps. (State and Federal.)
Federal Court Management Statistics. Annual.
Federal Judicial Caseload Statistics. Annual.
Judicial Business of the United States Courts.
Statistical Tables for the Federal Judiciary. Semiannual.

Agency for International Development
http://www.usaid.gov
U.S. Overseas Loans and Grants and Assistance From International Organizations. Annual.

Army, Corps of Engineers
http://www.usace.army.mil
Waterborne Commerce of the United States (in five parts). Annual.

Board of Governors of the Federal Reserve System
http://www.federalreserve.gov
Annual Statistical Digest.

Board of Governors of the Federal Reserve System —Con.
Domestic Offices, Commercial Bank Assets and Liabilities Consolidated Report of Condition. Quarterly.
Federal Reserve Banks. Monthly review published by each Bank with special reference to its own Federal Reserve District.
Federal Reserve Bulletin. Monthly. (Also monthly releases on industrial production indexes.)
Flow of Funds Accounts of the United States: Flows and Outstandings. Z.1(780). Quarterly.
Industrial Production and Capacity Utilization G.17. Monthly.
Money Stock and Debt Measures. H.6. Weekly.

Bureau of Alcohol, Tobacco, and Firearms
http://www.atf.treas.gov
Alcohol and Tobacco Summary Statistics. Annual.

Bureau of Economic Analysis
http://www.bea.doc.gov
National Income and Product Accounts of the United States, 1929-1997: Statistical Tables, early 2001.

Bureau of Economic Analysis —Con.

Survey of Current Business. Monthly. (March, June, September, and December issues contain data on U.S. international transactions. Articles on foreign direct investment in the United States, U.S. direct investment abroad, and other topics appear periodically in other issues.)

U.S. Direct Investment Abroad: 1994 Benchmark Survey, 1998.

U.S. Direct Investment Abroad: Operations of U.S. Parent Companies and their Foreign Affiliates. Preliminary, 1997. Estimates, 1999

Bureau of Justice Statistics

http://www.ojp.usdoj.gov

Age Patterns of Victims of Serious Violent Crimes. September 1997.

Alcohol and Crime: An analysis of national data on the prevalence of alcohol involvement in crime. April 1998.

Background Checks for Firearm Transfers, 1999. June 2000.

Campus Law Enforcement Agencies, 1995. December 1996.

Capital Punishment. Annual.

Carjacking in U.S., 1992-96. March 1999.

Census of State and Local Law Enforcement Agencies, 1996. July 1998.

Characteristics of Adults on Probation, 1995, December 1997.

Child Victimizers: Violent offenders and their victims. March 1996.

Civil Rights Complaints in U.S. District Courts, 1990-98. January 2000.

Civil Trial Cases and Verdicts in Large Counties: Civil Justice Survey of State Courts, 1996. September 1999.

Correctional Populations in the United States. Annual.

Crimes Against Persons Age 65 or Older, 1992-97. January 2000.

Criminal Victimization 2000: Changes 1999-00: with trends 1993-00. June 2001.

Federal Criminal Case Processing, 1999: with trends 1982-99. February 2001.

Federal Law Enforcement Officers, 1998. March 2000.

Federal Tort Trials and Verdicts, 1996-97. March 1999.

Felony Defendants in Large Urban Counties. Biennial.

Felony Sentences in State Courts. Biennial.

Firearm Injury From Crime: Firearms, crime, and criminal justice. April 1996.

HIV in Prisons. Annual.

Incarcerated Parents and Their Children. August 2000.

Indicators of School Crime and Safety. Annual.

Indigent Defense Services in Large Counties, 1999. November 2000.

Intimate Partner Violence. May 2000.

Bureau of Justice Statistics —Con.

Jails in Indian Country, 1998 and 1999. July 2000.

Justice Expenditure and Employment in the United States, 1995. November 1999.

Lifetime Likelihood of Going to State or Federal Prison. March 1997.

Local Police Departments. Quadrennial.

Medical Problems of Inmates, 1997. January 2001.

National Corrections Reporting Program. Annual.

Prior Abuse Reported by Inmates and Probationers. April 1999.

Prison and Jail Inmates. Annual.

Prisoners. Annual.

Profile of State Prisoners Under Age 18, 1985-97. February 2000.

Prosecutors in State Courts. Biennial.

Sex Offenses and Offenders. February 1997.

Sheriffs' Department. Quadrennial.

Sourcebook of Criminal Justice Statistics. CD-ROM. Annual.

State Court Sentencing of Convicted Felons. Biennial.

Substance Abuse and Treatment, State and Federal Prisoners, 1997. December 1998.

Survey of State Criminal History Information Systems. Annual.

Time Served in Prison by Federal Offenders. 1986-97. June 1999.

Urban, Suburban, and Rural Victimization, 1993-98. October 2000.

Veterans in Prison or Jail. January 2000.

Violence-Related Injuries Treated in Hospital Emergency Departments. August 1997.

Bureau of Labor Statistics

http://www.bls.gov

Comparative Labor Force Statistics, Ten Countries. Annual.

Compensation and Working Conditions. Quarterly.

Consumer Expenditure Survey, Integrated Diary and Interview Survey data.

Consumer Prices: Energy and Food. Monthly.

CPI Detailed Report. Monthly.

Employee Benefits in Medium and Large Firms. Biennial.

Employee Benefits in Small Private Establishments. Biennial.

Employee Benefits in State and Local Governments. Biennial.

Employer Costs for Employee Compensation. Annual.

Employment and Earnings. Monthly.

Employment and Wages. Annual.

Employment Cost Index. Quarterly.

Employment Cost Indexes and Levels. Annual.

Bureau of Labor Statistics —Con.

Employment, Hours, and Earnings, United States, 1988-96. 1996. (Bulletin 2481.)

Employment Outlook: 1994-2005. (Bulletin 2472.)

The Employment Situation. Monthly.

Geographic Profile of Employment and Unemployment. Annual.

International Comparisons of Hourly Compensation Costs for Production Workers in Manufacturing. Annual.

International Comparisons of Manufacturing Productivity and Unit Labor Cost Trends. Annual.

Monthly Labor Review.

Occupational Injuries and Illnesses in the United States by Industry. Annual.

Occupational Projections and Training Data. Biennial.

Producer Price Indexes. Detailed report. Monthly, with annual supplement.

Productivity Measures for Selected Industries and Government Services. Annual.

Real Earnings. Monthly.

Regional and State Employment and Unemployment. Monthly.

Relative Importance of Components in the Consumer Price Indexes. Annual.

Metropolitan Area Employment and Unemployment. Monthly.

U.S. Import and Export Price Indexes. Monthly.

Usual Weekly Earnings of Wage and Salary Workers. Quarterly.

Work Experience of the Population. Annual.

Bureau of Land Management

http://www.blm.gov

Public Land Statistics. Annual.

Census Bureau

http://www.census.gov

Major reports, such as the Census of Population, which consist of many volumes, are listed by their general, all-inclusive titles. In most cases, separate reports of the most recent censuses are available for each state, subject, industry, etc.

1997 Economic Census.

Comparative Statistics.

Bridge Between NAICS and SIC.

Business Expenses.

Nonemployer Statistics.

Minority- and Women-Owned Business Enterprises.

Annual Benchmark Report for Retail Trade.

Annual Benchmark Report for Wholesale Trade and Food Services.

Annual Survey of Manufactures. (1996, most recent.)

Census of Governments. Quinquennial.

Compendium of Public Employment. Series GC, Vol. 3.

Census Bureau —Con.

Employee-Retirement Systems of State and Local Governments. Series GC, Vol. 4.

Employment of Major Local Governments. Series GC, Vol. 3.

Finances of County Governments. Series GC, Vol. 4.

Government Organization. Series GC, Vol. 1.

Public Education Finances. Series GC, Vol. 4.

Census of Housing. Decennial. (2000, most recent.)

Census of Population. Decennial. (2000, most recent.)

CFFR Consolidated Federal Funds Report. Annual.

 Volume I County Areas

 Volume II Subcounty Areas

County Business Patterns. Annual.

Current Construction Reports: New Residential Construction and New Residential Sales: Press Releases and Web Sites. Value of Construction Put in Place, C30 (monthly with occasional historical supplement); Residential Improvements and Repairs, C50 (quarterly and annual).

Current Housing Reports: Housing Vacancies, H111 (quarterly and annual); Who Can Afford to Buy a House, H121 (biennial) Market Absorption of Apartments, H130 (quarterly and annual); Characteristics of Apartments Completed, H131 (annual); American Housing Survey for the United States, H150 (biennial); American Housing Survey for Selected Metropolitan Areas, H170; Survey for Selected Metropolitan Areas, H171.

Current Population Reports. (Series P20.)

Consumer Income and Poverty, P60 and Household Economic Studies, P70.

Economic Census. Quinquennial.

Economic Census of Outlying Areas. Quinquennial.

FAS Federal Aid to States for Fiscal Year. Annual.

International Briefs. (Series IB.)

International Population Reports. (Series IPC.)

Manufacturing Profiles. (Series MP-1.) Annual.

Manufacturers' Shipments, Inventories, and Orders. Monthly.

Manufacturers' Shipments, Inventories, and Orders: 1992-2000.

Population Profile of the United States. (Biennial Series P23.)

Quarterly Financial Report for Manufacturing, Mining, and Trade Corporations.

Service Annual Survey Report.

Summary of U.S. International Trade in Goods and Services: includes cumulative data. (FT 900.)

Survey of Plant Capacity Utilization. (Current Industrial Reports MQ-C1.)

U.S. Census Bureau, Statistical Abstract of the United States: 2002

Census Bureau —Con.

U.S. Trade with Puerto Rico and U.S. Possessions. Monthly and Annual. (FT 895.)

Vehicle Inventory and Use Survey. Quinquennial.

World Population Profile: 1998 (Series WP.)

Centers for Disease Control and Prevention, Atlanta, GA

http://www.cdc.gov

Morbidity and Mortality Weekly Report. Annual.

Health Care Financing Administration

http://www.hcfa.gov

Centers for Medicare and Medicaid Services (CMS)

Health Care Financing Review. Medicare and Medicaid Statistical Supplement. Annual.

Health Care Financing Research Reports. Occasional.

Health Care Financing Review. Quarterly.

Coast Guard

http://www.uscg.mil

Annual Report of the Secretary of Transportation.

Marine Casualty Statistics. Annual.

Polluting Incidents in and Around U.S. Waters. Annual.

Comptroller of the Currency

http://www.occ.treas.gov

Quarterly Journal.

Congressional Clerk of the House

http://clerkweb.house.gov

Statistics of the Presidential and Congressional Election Years. Biennial.

Council of Economic Advisers

http://www.whitehouse.gov

Economic Indicators. Monthly.

Economic Report of the President. Annual.

Council on Environmental Quality

http://www.whitehouse.gov/ceq

Environmental Quality. Annual.

Department of Agriculture

http://www.usda.gov

Agricultural Chemical Usage. Field crops, vegetables (fruits and vegetables alternate years), restricted use pesticides. Chemical application rates and acres treated, selected states and U.S. Annual.

Agricultural Income and Finance. Situation and Outlook Report. Quarterly.

Agricultural Outlook. 11 issues per year.

Agricultural Price Reports. Reports on prices received for farm commodities, prices paid for farm supplies, indexes and parity ratios. Monthly and annual.

Agriculture and Trade Reports (five per year).

Western Europe

Department of Agriculture —Con.

China

Developing Economies

Pacific Rim

USSR

CATFISH. Catfish and Trout Production. Annual.

Census of Agriculture. Quinquennial. (1997, most recent.)

Cotton Ginnings and Winter Wheat Seedings.

Crop Production Reports. Acreage, yield, and production of various commodities. Monthly and annual.

Crop Values Report. Price and value of various commodities. Annual.

Dairy Product Prices. U.S. cheddar cheese, butter, nonfat dry milk, and dry whey prices and sales volumes. Regional cheddar cheese prices and sales volumes. Weekly.

Farm Labor. Quarterly.

Farmline. 11 issues per year.

Farm Numbers, Value. Farm numbers and land in farms, agricultural cash rents, agricultural land values, foreign ownership of U.S. Agricultural Land (ERS). Annual.

Financial Characteristics of U.S. (Agriculture Information Bulletin. No. 569.) Annual.

Food Consumption, Prices, and Expenditures, 1970-97. (Statistical Bulletin No. 928.) Revised annually.

Food Marketing Review, (Agricultural Economic Report No. 743). Revised annually.

Food Review. Quarterly.

Food Spending in American Households. (Statistical Bulletin No. 824.) Annual.

Foreign Agricultural Trade of the United States (FATUS). Bimonthly with annual supplements on calendar year and fiscal year trade statistics.

Fruit and Vegetable Reports. Acreage, yield, production, value, and utilization of various fruits and vegetables. Periodic.

Geographic Area Series (Internet, CD-ROM, Print), Volume 1

Journal of Agricultural Economics Research. Quarterly.

Livestock Reports. Cattle, Cattle on Feed, Hogs and Pigs. Sheep, Goats, Wool, and Mohair. Monthly, Quarterly, and Annual.

Milk and Dairy Products Reports. Milk cows, milk production, and dairy products. Monthly and Annual.

Winter Wheat Seedings.

National Resource and Conservation Service

http://www.nrcs.usda.gov

National Resources Inventory. Periodic.

Other Reports. Reports on varied items including cold storage, catfish, cherries, cranberries, trout, farm employment and wages, farm production expenditures, mink, mushrooms, and floriculture crops. Monthly and annual.

National Resource and Conservation Service —Con.

Poultry and Egg Reports. Reports covering eggs, chickens, turkeys, hatcheries, egg products, and poultry slaughter. Weekly, monthly, annual.

Rural Conditions and Trends. Quarterly.

Rural Development Perspectives. Three issues per year.

Situation and Outlook Reports. Issued for agricultural exports, cotton and wool, dairy, feed, fruit and tree nuts, agricultural resources, livestock and poultry, oil crops, rice, aquaculture, sugar and sweeteners, tobacco, vegetables, wheat, and world agriculture. Periodic.

Stock Reports. Stocks of grain, hops, peanuts, potatoes, rice, and soybeans. Quarterly, annual, periodic.

Usual planting and harvesting dates. Dates for major field crops. Periodic.

Weekly Weather and Crop Bulletin. Report summarizing weather and its effect on crops the previous week. Weekly.

Department of Agriculture, Food and Nutrition Service
http://www.fns.usda.gov
Annual Historical Review:
Food and Consumer Service Programs.

Department of Defense
http://www.defenselink.mil
Foreign Military Sales and Military Assistance Facts. Annual.

Department of Education
http://www.ed.gov
Rehabilitation Services Administration
http://www.ed.gov
Annual Report.

Department of Health and Human Services
http://www.os.dhhs.gov
Annual Report.

Department of Housing and Urban Development
http://www.hud.gov
Survey of Mortgage Lending Activity. Monthly and quarterly press releases.

Department of Labor
http://www.dol.gov
Annual Report of the Secretary.

Department of State
http://www.state.gov
United States Contribution to International Organizations. Issued in the House Documents series. Annual.

Department of State, Bureau of Consular Affairs
http://travel.state.gov
Report of the Visa Office. Annual. (Dept. of State Pub. 8810.)
Summary of Passport Statistics. Annual.

Department of Transportation
http://www.faa.gov
Airport Activity Statistics of Certified Route Air Carriers. Annual.

Condition and Performance Report. 1999. Biennial.

National Transportation Statistics, 1998.

Report of Passenger Travel Between the United States and Foreign Countries. Annual, semiannual, quarterly. Monthly.

Transportation Safety Information Report. Quarterly.

U.S. International Air Travel Statistics. Annual.

Department of the Treasury
http://www.irs.ustreas.gov
Active Foreign Credits of the United States Government. Quarterly.

Consolidated Financial Statements of the United States Government. (Prototype.)

Daily Treasury Statement.

Monthly Statement of the Public Debt of the United States.

Monthly Treasury Statement of Receipts and Outlays of the United States Government.

Statement of United States Currency and Coin. Monthly.

Treasury Bulletin. Quarterly.

United States Government Annual Report and Appendix.

Department of Veterans Affairs
http://www.va.gov
Annual Report of The Secretary of Veterans Affairs.

Disability Compensation, Pension, and Death Pension Data. Annual.

Government Life Insurance Programs for Veterans and Members of the Service. Annual.

Loan Guaranty Highlights. Quarterly.

Projections of The Veteran Population by State and County to the Year 2010.

Selected Compensation and Pension Data by State of Residence. Annual.

State and County Veteran Population Estimates. Annual.

Summary of Medical Programs. Annual.

Drug Enforcement Administration
http://www.whitehousedrugpolicy.gov
Drug Abuse and Law Enforcement Statistics. Irregular.

Employment and Training Administration
http://www.doleta.gov
Employment and Training Report of the President. Annual.

Unemployment Insurance Claims. Weekly.

Energy Information Administration
http://www.eia.doe.gov
Annual Energy Outlook. 2002.

Annual Energy Review. 2000.

Energy Information Administration —Con.

Coal Industry. 1999. Annual.

Cost and Quality of Fuels for Electric Utility Plants. Annual.

Electric Power. 2000 Volume 1. Annual.

Electric Power. Monthly.

Electric Sales and Revenue.

Emmissions of Greenhouse Gases in the U.S. 2000. Annual

Financial Statistics of Publicly-Owned Electric Utilities. 2000.

Financial Statistics of Selected Electric Utilities. Annual

Foreign Direct Investment in U.S. Energy. 1999. (Web only).

International Energy. Annual.

International Energy Outlook.

Inventory of Electric Utility Power Plants in the United States. 2000. Annual.

Inventory of Nonutility Power Plants in the United States. 2000.

Monthly Energy Review.

Natural Gas. 2000. Annual.

Natural Gas. 2000. Issues & Trends. (Web Only)

Natural Gas. Monthly.

Performance Profiles of Major Energy Producers. Annual.

Petroleum Marketing. 2000. Annual.

Petroleum Marketing. Monthly.

Petroleum Supply. 2000 Volume 1. Annual.

Petroleum Supply. 2000 Volume 2. Annual. (Web Only).

Petroleum Supply Monthly.

Quarterly Coal Report.

Renewable Energy Annual.

Residential Energy Consumption Survey: Housing Characteristics. Triennial.

Residential Transportation Energy Consumption Survey. Triennial.

Short-Term Energy Outlook. Quarterly. (Web Only)

State Energy Data Report. 1999. Annual.

State Energy Price and Expenditure Report. 1998. Annual.

Uranium Industry. 2000. Annual.

U.S. Crude Oil, Natural Gas, and Natural Gas Liquids Reserves. 2000. Annual.

Weekly Coal Production. (Electronic Only)

Environmental Protection Agency

http://www.epa.gov

Air Quality Data. Annual.

Cost of Clean Water. Annual.

Drinking Water Infrastructure Needs Survey. Second Report to Congress (EPA 816-R-01-004, February 2001).

Federal Certification Test Results for Motor Vehicles. Annual.

Municipal Water Facilities Inventory. Quinquennial.

Environmental Protection Agency —Con.

National Air Quality and Emissions Trends Report. 1999. Annual

Needs Survey, Conveyance and Treatment of Municipal Wastewater Summaries of Technical Data. Biennial.

Pesticides Monitoring Journal. Quarterly.

Radiation Data and Reports. Monthly.

Sewage Facility Construction. Annual.

Summary of Water Enforcement Actions Pursued by EPA since December 3, 1970. (Updated continuously)

Toxics Release Inventory (EPA 260-R-01-001). Annual (Most Recent 1999).

Water Quality Report to Congress, 1998. Biennial.

Export-Import Bank of the United States

http://www.exim.gov

Annual Report.

Report to the U.S. Congress on Export Credit Competition and the Export-Import Bank of the United States. Annual.

Farm Credit Administration.

http://www.fca.gov

Annual Report on the Work of the Cooperative Farm Credit System.

Loans and Discounts of Farm Credit Banks and Associations. Annual.

Production Credit Association: Summary of Operations. Annual.

Report to the Federal Land Bank Associations. Annual.

Federal Bureau of Investigation

http://www.fbi.gov

Bomb Summary. Annual.

Crime in the United States. Annual.

Hate Crime Statistics. Annual.

Law Enforcement Officers Killed and Assaulted. Annual.

Federal Communications Commission

http://www.fcc.gov

Annual Report.

Statistics of Communications Common Carriers. Annual.

Federal Deposit Insurance Corporation

http://www.fdic.gov

Annual Report.

Data Book-Operating Banks and Branches. Annual.

Quarterly Banking Profile.

Quarterly Banking Review.

Statistics on Banking. Annual, and Historical 1934-1996, Volume I.

Trust Assets of Insured Commercial Banks. Annual.

Federal Highway Administration

http://www.fhwa.dot.gov

Highway Statistics. Annual.

Federal Railroad Administration
http://www.fra.dot.gov
  Accident/Incident Bulletin. Summary,
    statistics, and analysis of accidents on
    railroads in the United States. Annual.
  Rail-Highway Crossing Accident/Incident
    and Inventory Bulletin. Annual.

Forest Service
http://www.fs.fed.us
  An Analysis of the Timber Situation in the
    United States. 1996-2050.
  Land Areas of the National Forest System.
    Annual.
  The 1993 RPA Timber Assessment Update.
    Forthcoming.
  U.S. Timber Production, Trade, Consump-
    tion, and Price Statistics. 2001.

Fish and Wildlife Service
http://endangered.fws.gov
  Federal Aid in Fish and Wildlife Restoration.
    Annual.
  1996 National Survey of Fishing, Hunting,
    and Wildlife Associated Recreation.

General Services Administration
http://www.gsa.gov
  Inventory Report on Real Property Leased to
    the United States Throughout the World.
    Annual.
  Inventory Report on Real Property Owned
    by the United States Throughout the
    World. Annual.

Geological Survey
http://ask.usgs.gov
  A Statistical Summary of Data from the U.S.
    Geological Survey's National Water Quality
    Networks. (Open-File Report 83-533.)
  Mineral Commodity Summaries. Annual.
  Mineral Industry Surveys. (Monthly,
    quarterly, or annual report.)
  Minerals Yearbook. (Monthly, quarterly, or
    annual report.)

Immigration and Naturalization Service
http://www.ins.gov
  I&N Reporter. Quarterly.
  Statistical Yearbook of the Immigration and
    Naturalization Service. Annual.
  Wage Statistics of Class I Railroads in the
    United States. Annual. (Statement No.
    300.)

International Trade Administration
http://www.ita.doc.gov
  International Construction Review.
    Quarterly.
  Electric Current Abroad. Irregular. (1998,
    most recent.)
  U.S. Foreign Trade Highlights. Annual.
  U.S. Global Trade Outlook. Irregular.
    Discontinued
  U.S. Industry and Trade Outlook. Annual.
    (2000, most recent.)

International Trade Commission
http://www.usitc.gov
  Synthetic Organic Chemicals, U.S.
    Production and Sales. Annual.

Internal Revenue Service
http://www.irs.ustreas.gov
  Corporation Income Tax Returns. Annual.
  Individual Income Tax Returns. Annual.
  IRS Data Book.
  Statistics of Income Bulletin. Quarterly.
  Statistics of Income Division. (Annual report
    on Corporation Income Tax Returns.
    Periodic compendiums on Studies of
    International Income and Taxes.)

Library of Congress
http://www.loc.gov
  Annual Report.

Maritime Administration
http://www.marad.dot.gov
  Annual Report.
  Cargo-Carrying U.S. Flag Fleet by Area of
    Operation. (Semiannual)
  Merchant Fleet Ocean-Going Vessels 1,000
    Gross Tons and Over. Quarterly.
  Seafaring Wage Rates. Biennial.

Mine Safety and Health Administration
http://www.msha.gov
  Informational Reports by Mining Industry:
    Coal; Metallic Minerals; Nonmetallic
    Minerals (except stone and coal); Stone,
    Sand, and Gravel. Annual.
  Mine Injuries and Worktime. (Some
    preliminary data.) Quarterly.

**National Aeronautics and Space
  Administration**
http://ifmp.nasa.gov
  Annual Procurement Report.
  The Civil Service Work Force.

National Center for Education Statistics
http://nces.ed.gov
  College and University Library Survey.
  The Condition of Education. Annual.
  Digest of Education Statistics. Annual.
  Earned Degrees Conferred. Annual.
  Faculty Salaries, Tenure, and Benefits.
    Annual.
  Fall Enrollment in Degree-Granting
    Institutions. Annual.
  Fall Staff in Postsecondary Institutions.
    Biennial.
  Financial Statistics of Higher Education.
  National Assessment of Educational
    Progress.
  Private School Survey. Biennial.
  Projections of Education Statistics. Annual.
  Revenues and Expenditures for Public
    Elementary and Secondary Education.
    Annual.
  School and Staffing Survey. Quadrennial.

National Center for Education Statistics —Con.

Statistics of Public Elementary and Secondary School Systems. Fall. Annual.

National Center for Health Statistics
http://www.cdc.gov/nchs/

Ambulatory Care Visits to Physician Offices, Hospital Outpatient Departments and Emergency Departments. Annual.

Health: United States. Annual. (DHHS Pub. No. PHS year-1232.)

National Hospital Discharge Survey: Annual Summary. Annual.

National Vital Statistics Reports (NVRS.) Monthly.

Vital and Health Statistics. (A series of statistical reports covering health-related topics.)

Series 10: Health Interview Survey Statistics. Irregular.

Current Estimates from the Health Interview Survey. Annual.

Series 11: Health and Nutrition Examination Survey Statistics. Irregular.

Series 13: Health Resources Utilization Statistics. Irregular.

Series 14: Health Resources: Manpower and Facilities Statistics. Irregular.

Series 20: Mortality Data. Irregular.

Series 21: Natality, Marriage, and Divorce Data. Irregular.

Series 23: National Survey of Family Growth Statistics. Irregular.

Vital Statistics of the United States. Annual.

Volume I, Natality

Volume II, Mortality

Volume III, Marriage and Divorce

National Credit Union Administration
http://www.ncua.gov

Annual Report.

Midyear Statistics.

Year-end Statistics.

National Guard Bureau
http://www.ngb.dtic.mil

Annual Review of the Chief.

The National Library of Medicine (for clinical medical reports)
http://www.nlm.nih.gov

Annual Report.

National Oceanic and Atmospheric Administration
http://www.lib.noaa.gov

Climates of the World, HCS 6-4. Monthly and annual.

Climatological Data. Issued in sections for states and outlying areas. Monthly with annual summary.

Climatography of the United States, No. 20, Supplement No. 1, Freeze/Frost Data.

Comparative Climatic Data. Annual.

National Oceanic and Atmospheric Administration —Con.

Daily Normals of Temp, Precip, HDD, & CDD/Clim 84. Periodic.

General Summary of Tornadoes. Annual.

Hourly Precipitation Data. Monthly with annual summary; for each state.

Local Climatological Data. Monthly with annual summary; for major cities.

Monthly Climatic Data for the World. Monthly.

Monthly Normals of Temp, Precip, HDD, & CDD/Clim 84. Periodic.

Our Living Oceans. Periodic.

Storm Data. Monthly.

Weekly Weather and Crop Bulletin. National summary.

National Park Service
http://www.nps.gov

Federal Recreation Fee Report. Annual.

National Park Statistical Abstract. Annual.

National Science Foundation
http://www.nsf.gov

Academic Research and Development Expenditures. Detailed Statistical Tables. Annual

Academic Science and Engineering: Graduate Enrollment and Support: Detailed Statistical Tables. Annual

Characteristics of Doctoral Scientists and Engineers in the United States. Detailed Statistical Tables. Biennial.

Characteristics of Recent Science/Engineering Graduates. Detailed Statistical Tables. Biennial.

Federal Funds for Research and Development. Detailed Statistical Tables. Annual.

Federal R&D Funding by Budget Function. Report. Annual.

Federal Science and Engineering Support to Universities, Colleges, and Nonprofit Institutions. Detailed Statistical Tables. Annual.

Federal Support to Universities, Colleges, and Nonprofit Institutions. Detailed Statistical Tables. Annual.

Graduate Students and Post-doctorates in Science and Engineering. Annual.

Immigrant Scientists, Engineers and Technicians. Detailed Statistical Tables. Annual.

International Science and Technology Data Update. Report. Annual.

National Patterns of R&D Resources. Report. Annual.

Planned R&D Expenditures of Major U.S. Firms. Special Report. (NSF 91-306.)

Research and Development in Industry. Detailed Statistical Tables. Annual.

Science and Engineering Degrees. Annual.

Science and Engineering Degrees, by Race/Ethnicity of Recipients. Detailed Statistical Tables. Annual.

National Science Foundation —Con.

Science and Engineering Doctorates Awards. Detailed Statistical Tables. Annual.

Science and Engineering Indicators. Report. Biennial.

Science and Engineering Personnel: A National Overview. Report. Biennial.

Science and Engineering Profiles. Annual.

Science and Technology Pocket Data Book. Report. Annual.

Science Resources Studies. Data Brief. Frequent.

Scientific and Engineering Research Facilities at Universities and Colleges. Report. Biennial.

Scientists, Engineers, and Technicians in Manufacturing Industries. Detailed Statistical Tables. Triennial.

Scientists, Engineers, and Technicians in Nonmanufacturing Industries. Detailed Statistical Tables. Triennial.

Scientists, Engineers, and Technicians in Trade and Regulated Industries. Detailed Statistical Tables. Triennial.

Survey of Direct U.S. Private Capital Investment in Research and Development Facilities in Japan. Report. (NSH 91-312.)

U.S. Scientists and Engineers. Detailed Statistical Tables. Biennial.

Women, Minorities, and Persons with Disabilities. Report. Biennial

Woman, Minorities in Science and Engineering. Report. Biennial.

National Transportation Safety Board
http://www.ntsb.gov
Accidents; Air Carriers. Annual.
Accidents; General Aviation. Annual.

Office of Management and Budget
http://www.whitehouse.gov/omb
The Budget of the United States Government. Annual.

Office of Personnel Management
http://www.opm.gov
Civil Service Retirement and Disability Fund. Report. Annual.

Demographic Profile of the Federal Workforce. Biennial. (Even years.)

Employment and Trends. Bimonthly. (Odd months.)

Employment by Geographic Area. Biennial. (Even years.)

The Fact Book. Annual.

Occupations of Federal White-Collar and Blue-Collar Workers. Biennial. (Odd years.)

Pay Structure of the Federal Civil Service. Annual.

Office of Personnel Management —Con.

Statistical Abstract for the Federal Employee Benefit Programs. Annual.

Work Years and Personnel Costs. Annual.

Office of Thrift Supervision
http://www.ots.treas.gov
Annual Report.

Patent and Trademark Office
http://www.uspto.gov
Commissioner of Patents and Trademarks Annual Report.

Technology Assessment and Forecast Reports

"All Technologies." Annual.

"Patenting Trends in the United States." Annual.

"State Country." Annual.

Railroad Retirement Board, Chicago, IL
http://www.rrb.gov
Annual Report.

Monthly Benefit Statistics.

Statistical Supplement to the Annual Report.

Rehabilitation Services Administration. Annual Report.

Caseload Statistics of State Vocational Rehabilitation Agencies in Fiscal Year. Annual.

Securities and Exchange Commission
http://www.sec.gov
Annual Report.

Small Business Administration
http://www.sbaonline.sba.gov
Annual Report.

Handbook of Small Business Data.

The State of Small Business.

Social Security Administration
http://www.ssa.gov
Income of the Population 55 and over, 1994, 1996, 1998, 2000.

Social Security Beneficiaries by State and County Data. Annual.

Social Security Bulletin. Quarterly with annual statistical supplement. (Data on Social Security Benefits, OASDI, Supplemental Security Income, Aid to Families with Dependent Children, Medicare, Medicaid, Low Income Home Energy Assistance, Food Stamps, Black Lung benefits, and other programs.)

Social Security Programs in the United States, 1997.

State Assistance Programs for SSI Recipients. Annual.

Supplemental Security Income, State and County Data. Annual.

U.S. Census Bureau, Statistical Abstract of the United States: 2002

NONGOVERNMENT

**AAFRC Trust For Philanthropy,
Indianapolis, IN**
http://www.aafrc.org
Giving USA. Annual.

**Advisory Commission on
Intergovernmental Relations,
Washington, DC**
*http://www.library.unt.edu/gpo/ACIR/
acir.html*
Characteristics of Federal Grant-in-Aid
Programs to State and Local Govern-
ments: Grants Funded FY 93. (Every
3 years.)
Changing Public Attitudes on Governments
and Taxes. Annual.
Significant Features of Fiscal Federalism.
Annual.

**Aerospace Industries Association,
Washington, DC**
http://www.aia-aerospace.org
Aerospace Facts and Figures. Annual.
Aerospace Industry Year-End Review and
Forecast. Annual.
Commercial Helicopter Shipments.
Quarterly.
Employment in the Aerospace Industry.
Monthly, Tabulated Quarterly.
Exports of Aerospace Products. Quarterly.
Imports of Aerospace Products. Quarterly.
Manufacturing Production, Capacity, and
Utilization in Aerospace and Aircraft and
parts. Monthly, Tabulated Quarterly.
Orders, Shipments, Backlog and inventories
for Aircraft, Missiles, & Parts. Monthly,
Tabulated Quarterly.

**Air Transport Association of America,
Inc., Washington, DC**
http://www.airlines.org
Air Transport Association, Annual Report.

**The Alan Guttmacher Institute, New York,
NY**
http://www.guttmacher.org
Perspectives on Sexual and Reproductive
Health. Bimonthly.

**American Bureau of Metal Statistics, Inc.,
Secaucus, NJ**
http://www.abms.com
Nonferrous Metal Data.

**American Council on Education,
Washington, DC**
http://www.acenet.edu
A Fact Book on Higher Education. Quarterly.
National Norms for Entering College
Freshmen. Annual.

**American Council of Life Insurance,
Washington, DC**
http://www.acli.com
Life Insurance Fact Book. Biennial.
(Odd years)

**American Dental Association,
Chicago, IL**
http://www.ada.org
Dental Statistics Handbook. Triennial.
Dental Students' Register. Annual.
Distribution of Dentists in the United States
by Region and State. Triennial.
Survey of Dental Practice. Annual.

**American Financial Services Association,
Washington, DC**
http://www.americanfinsvcs.com
AFSA Annual Research Report and Second
Mortgage Lending Report on Finance
Companies. Annual.
AFSA Annual Research Report and Second
Mortgage Lending Report Supplements.
Annual.

**American Forest & Paper Association,
Washington, DC**
http://www.afandpa.org
Statistical Roundup.
Statistics of Paper, Paperboard, and Wood
Pulp. Annual.
Wood Pulp and Fiber Statistics. Annual.

**American Frozen Food Institute,
Burlingame, CA**
http://www.affi.com
Frozen Food Pack Statistics. Annual.

**American Gas Association, Arlington,
VA**
http://www.aga.org
Gas Facts. Annual.

**American Iron and Steel Institute,
Washington, DC**
http://www.steel.org
Annual Statistical Report.

**American Jewish Committee, New York,
NY**
http://www.ajc.org
American Jewish Year Book.

**American Medical Association, Chicago,
IL**
http://www.ama-assn.org
Physician Characteristics and Distribution in
the U.S. Annual.
Physician Marketplace Statistics. Annual.
Physician Socioeconomic Statistics.
1991-2000.
Socioeconomic Characteristics of Medical
Practice. 1997/98.
U.S. Medical Licensure Statistics, and
License Requirements. Annual.

**American Metal Market, New York,
NY**
http://www.amm.com
Daily Newspapers.
Metal Statistics. Annual.

American Osteopathic Association, Chicago, IL
http://www.aoa-net.org
Yearbook and Directory of Osteopathic Physicians. Annual.

American Petroleum Institute, Washington, DC
http://www.api.org
American Petroleum Institute, Independent Petroleum Association of America, and Mid-Continent Oil and Gas Association
The Basic Petroleum Data Book. Annual.
Petroleum Industry Environmental Report. Annual.
Quarterly Well Completion Report.

American Public Transportation Association, Washington, DC
http://www.apta.com
Public Transportation Fact Book. Annual.

Association of American Railroads, Washington, DC
http://www.aar.org
Analysis of Class I Railroads. Annual.
Cars of Revenue Freight Loaded. Weekly with annual summary.
Freight Commodity Statistics, Class I Railroads in the United States. Annual.
Yearbook of Railroad Facts.

Association of Racing Commissioners International, Inc., Lexington, KY
http://www.arci.com
Statistical Reports on Greyhound Racing in the United States. Annual.
Statistical Reports on Horse Racing in the United States. Annual.
Statistical Reports on Jai Alai in the United States. Annual.

Book Industry Study Group, Inc., New York, NY
http://www.bisg.org
Consumer Research Study on Book Purchasing. Annual.

Boy Scouts of America, Irving, TX
http://www.bsa.scouting.org
Annual Report.

Bridge Commodity Research Bureau, a Bridge Information Systems Inc., Chicago, IL.
http://www.crbindex.com
The Blue Line. Daily
Bridge News Summaries. Daily
Commodity Year Book Update Disk. (Three editions annually.)
CRB Commodity Index Report. Weekly.
CRB Commodity Year Book. Annual.
CRB Futures Perspective. Weekly.
CRB Infotech. CD
Electronic Futures Trend Analyzer. Daily.
Final Markets. End of day.
Futures Market Service. Weekly.

Bridge Commodity Research Bureau, a Bridge Information Systems Inc., Chicago, IL. —Con.
Futures Market Service Fundamental & Technical Commentary. Daily and weekly.
Price Service. Daily

The Bureau of National Affairs, Inc., Washington, DC
http://www.bna.com
Basic Patterns in Union Contracts. Annual.
BNA's Employment Outlook. Quarterly.
BNA's Job Absence and Turnover. Quarterly.
Briefing Sessions on Employee Relations Workbook. Annual.
Calendar of Negotiations. Annual.
Directory of U.S. Labor Organizations. Annual.
National Labor Relations Board Election Statistics. Annual.
NLRB Representation and Decertification Elections Statistics. Quarterly.
PPF Survey (Personnel Policies Forum.) Three times a year.

Cahners Business Information Unit, New York, NY
http://www.cahners.com
Library Journal. Semimonthly.
Publishers Weekly.
School Library Journal. Monthly.

Carl H. Pforzheimer & Co., New York, NY
(No Web site)
Comparative Oil Company Statistics, 1999. Annual.

Chronicle of Higher Education, Inc., Washington, DC
http://chronicle.com
Almanac. Annual.

College Entrance Examination Board, Princeton, NJ
http://www.collegeboard.com
National Report on College-Bound Seniors. Annual.

The Conference Board, New York, NY
http://www.conference-board.com
The Conference Board Economic Times. Monthly.

Congressional Quarterly Inc., Washington, DC
http://www.cq.com
America Votes. A handbook of contemporary American election statistics, compiled and edited by Richard M. Scammon, Alice V. McGillivray and Rhodes Cook. Biennial.

Corporation for Public Broadcasting, Washington, DC
http://www.cpb.org
Average Revenue Profiles for Public Broadcasting Grantees. Annual.
Frequently asked Questions About Public Broadcasting Periodic.

Corporation for Public Broadcasting, Washington, DC —Con.

Public Broadcasting Stations' Income from State Governments and State Colleges & Universities Ranked State-By-State. Annual.

Public Radio and Television Programming Content by Category. Biennial.

The Council of State Governments, Lexington, KY

http://www.statesnews.org

The Book of the States. Annual.

State Administrative Officials Classified by Function. Annual.

State Elective Officials and the Legislatures. Annual.

State Legislative Leadership, Committees, and Staff. Annual.

Credit Union National Association, Inc., Madison, WI

http://www.cuna.org

The Credit Union Report. Annual.

Credit Union Services Profile. Annual.

Operating Ratios and Spreads. Semiannual.

Dodge, F.W., National Information Services Division, McGraw-Hill Information Systems Co., New York, NY

http://www.fwdodge.com

Dodge Construction Potentials. Monthly.

Dow Jones & Co., New York, NY.

http://www.dj.com

Wall Street Journal.

Daily except Saturdays, Sundays, and holidays.

The Dun & Bradstreet Corporation, Murray Hill, NJ.

http://www.dnb.com

The Business Failure Record. Annual.

The Business Starts Record. Annual.

Monthly Business Failure Report.

Monthly Business Starts Report.

Monthly New Business Incorporations Report.

Edison Electric Institute, Washington, DC

http://www.eei.org

Statistical Yearbook of the Electric Utility Industry. Annual.

Editor & Publisher Co., New York, NY

http://www.editorandpublisher.com

Editor & Publisher. Weekly.

International Year Book. Annual.

Market Guide. Annual.

Electronic Industries Alliance, Arlington, VA

http://www.eia.org

Electronic Market Data Book. Annual.

Electronic Market Trends. Monthly.

Electronics Foreign Trade. Monthly.

ENO Transportation Foundation, Leesburg, VA

http://www.enotrans.com

Transportation in America. Midyear, Annually with Periodic Supplements.

Euromonitor, London, England

http://www.euromonitor.com

Consumer Asia. Annual.

Consumer China. Annual.

Consumer Eastern Europe. Annual.

Consumer Europe. Annual.

Consumer International. Annual.

Consumer Latin America. Annual.

European Marketing Data and Statistics. Annual.

International Marketing Data and Statistics. Annual.

World Economic Factbook. Annual.

Federal National Mortgage Association, Washington, DC

http://www.fanniemae.com

Annual Report.

Food and Agriculture Organization of the United Nations, Rome, Italy

http://www.fao.org

Production Yearbook.

Trade Yearbook.

Yearbook of Fishery Statistics.

Yearbook of Forest Products.

Fortune (Time Warner), New York, NY

http://www.fortunedatastore.com

The Fortune Directory of the 500 Largest Industrial Corporations.

The Fortune Directory of the 500 Global Industrial Corporations.

The Foundation Center, New York, NY

http://www.fdncenter.org

Foundation Giving Trends. Annual.

Foundation Yearbook. Annual.

Gale Research Inc., Farmington Hills, MI

http://www.galegroup.com

Gale Directory of Publications and Broadcast Media. 1999.

General Aviation Manufacturers Association, Washington, DC

http://www.generalaviation.org

Shipment Report. Quarterly and Annual.

Statistical Databook. Annual.

Girl Scouts of the U.S.A., New York, NY

www.gsusa.org

Annual Report.

Health Forum, L.L.C., American Hospital Association, Company, Chicago, IL.

http://www.healthforum.com

Annual Report.

Health Insurance Association of America, Washington, DC

http://www.hiaa.org

U.S. Census Bureau, Statistical Abstract of the United States: 2002

Health Insurance Association of America, Washington, DC —Con.
   Source Book of Health Insurance Data. Annual.

Independent Petroleum Association of America, Washington, DC
   http://www.ipaa.org
   IPAA Weekly Oil Trends.
   IPAA Wholesale Oil Prices. Monthly.
   The Oil & Natural Gas Producing Industry in Your State. Annual.
   U.S. Petroleum Statistics. Semiannual.

Information Today, Inc., Medford, NJ
   http://www.infotoday.com
   American Library Directory. Annual.
   Bowker Annual Library and Book Trade Almanac.

Institute for Criminal Justice Ethics, New York, NY
   http://www.lib.jjay.cuny.edu/cje/html/institute.html
   Criminal Justice Ethics. Semiannual.

Insurance Information Institute, New York, NY
   http://www.iii.org
   Insurance Facts. Annual.

Inter-American Development Bank, Washington, DC
   http://www.iadb.org
   Annual Report.
   Economic and Social Progress in Latin America. Annual Survey.

International City Management Association, Washington, DC
   http://www.icma.org
   Baseline Data Reports. Bimonthly.
   Compensation: An Annual Report on Local Government Executive Salaries and Fringe Benefits.
   Municipal Year Book. Annual.
   Special Data Issues. Periodical.

International Labour Office, Geneva, Switzerland
   http://www.ilo.org
   Yearbook of Labour Statistics.

International Monetary Fund, Washington, DC
   http://www.imf.org
   Annual Report.
   Balance of Payments Statistics. Monthly with annual yearbook.
   Direction of Trade Statistics. Monthly with annual yearbook.
   Government Finance Statistics Yearbook.
   International Financial Statistics. Monthly with annual yearbook.

Investment Company Institute, Washington, DC
   http://www.ici.org
   Mutual Fund Fact Book. Annual.

Jane's Information Group, Coulsdon, UK and Alexandria, VA
   http://www.janes.com
   Jane's Air-Launched Weapons. (Binder-4 monthly update.)
   Jane's All the World's Aircraft. Annual.
   Jane's Armour and Artillery. Annual.
   Jane's Avionics. Annual.
   Jane's Fighting Ships. Annual.
   Jane's Infantry Weapons. Annual.
   Jane's Merchant Ships. Annual.
   Jane's Military Communications. Annual.
   Jane's Military Logistics. Annual.
   Jane's Military Training Systems. Annual.
   Jane's NATO Handbook. Annual.
   Jane's Spaceflight Directory. Annual.

Joint Center for Political and Economic Studies, Washington, DC
   http://www.jointcenter.org
   Black Elected Officials: A National Roster. Annual.

Laventhol & Horwath, Philadelphia, PA
   http://www.legalcasedocs.com
   The Executive Conference Center: A Statistical and Financial Profile. Annual.
   Gaming Industry Study. Annual.
   Lifecare Industry. Annual. (Analysis of facilities by size and section of the country for selected financial data, resident census information, and medical costs.)
   National Trends of Business in the Lodging Industry. Monthly. (Analysis of nationwide trends in sales, occupancy, and room rates of hotels, motor hotels, and economy lodging facilities.)
   Separate reports on the segments of lodging industries. Annuals. (Reports covering economy, all-suite, and resort.)
   U.S. Lodging Industry. Annual. (Report on hotel and motor hotel operations.)
   Worldwide Lodging Industry. Annual. (Report on international hotel operations.)

Lebhar-Friedman, Inc., New York, NY
   http://www.lf.com
   Accounting Today. Biweekly.
   Apparel Merchandising. Monthly.

McGraw-Hill Informations Service Co., Washington, DC
   http://www.fwdodge.com
   Electrical world Directory of Electric Utilities. Annual.
   Engineering and Mining Journal. Monthly.
   Keystone Coal Industry Manual. Annual.

Metropolitan Life Insurance Company, New York, NY
   http://www.metlife.com
   Health and Safety Education.

Moody's Investors Service, New York, NY
   http://www.moodys.com

**National Academy of Sciences,
Washington, DC**
  http://www.pnas.org
  Science, Engineering, and Humanities
    Doctorates in the United States. Biennial.
  Summary Report. Doctorate Recipients from
    United States Universities. Annual.

**National Association of Latino Elected and
Appointed Officials, Washington, DC**
  http://www.naleo.org
  National Roster of Hispanic Elected
    Officials. Annual.

**National Association of Realtors.
Washington, DC**
  http://nar.realtor.com
  Real Estate Outlook: Market Trends &
    Insights. Monthly.

**National Association of State Budget
Officers, Washington, DC**
  http://www.nasbo.org
  "State Expenditure Report". Annual.
  Fiscal Survey of the States. Semiannual.

**National Association of State Park
Directors, Tuscon, AZ**
  http://www.naspd.org
  Annual Information Exchange.

**National Catholic Educational Association,
Washington, DC**
  http://www.ncea.org
  Catholic Schools in America. Annual.
  United States Catholic Elementary and
    Secondary Schools. Staffing and
    Enrollment. Annual.
  U.S. Catholic Elementary Schools and their
    Finances. Biennial.
  U.S. Catholic Secondary Schools and their
    Finances. Biennial.

**National Center for State Courts,
Williamsburg, VA**
  http://www.ncsc.dni.us
  State Court Caseload Statistics. Annual.

**National Council of the Churches of Christ
in the U.S.A., New York, NY**
  http://www.ncccusa.org
  Yearbook of American and Canadian
    Churches. Annual.

**National Council of Savings Institutions,
Washington, DC**
  http://www.bankmag.com
  Fact Book of National Council of Savings
    Institutions. Annual.

**National Education Association,
Washington, DC**
  http://www.nea.org
  Estimates of School Statistics. Annual.
  Rankings of the States. Annual.
  Status of the American Public School
    Teacher, 1995-96. Quinquennial.

**National Fire Protection Association,
Quincy, MA**
  http://www.nfpa.org
  NFPA Journal. Bimonthly.

**National Food Processors Association,
Washington, DC**
  http://www.nfpa-food.org
  Canned Fruit and Vegetable Pack and Stock
    Situation Reports. Quarterly.

National Golf Foundation, Jupiter, FL
  http://www.ngf.org
  Americans' Attitudes on Golf (in their
    communities).
  Commercial Golf Range Participation and
    Supply in the U.S.
  Commercial Golf Ranges in the U.S.
  Directory of Executive and Par-3 Golf
    Courses in U.S.
  Directory of Golf: The People and
    Businesses in Golf. Annual.
  Directory of U.S. Golf Courses.
  Directory of U.S. Golf Practice Ranges and
    Learning Centers.
  Directory of Golf Retailers: Off-Course Golf
    Retail Stores in U.S.
  Golf Consumer Potential.
  Golf Consumer Spending in the U.S.
  Golf Facilities in Canada.
  Golf Facilities in the U.S. - 1998.
  Golf Facility Employee Compensation Study.
  Golf Participation in Canada.
  Golf Participation in U.S. - 1998.
  Golf Travel Market Report for the U.S.
  High-Interest Women Golfers—Target
    Marketing for Success.
  Hot Spots for Golf Course Construction
    Activity in the USA.
  NGF's *Infosearch: Accessing the World's
    Largest Golf Business Library.*
  Operating and Financial Performance
    Profiles of Golf Facilities in the U.S.
  Senior Golfer Profile.
  Trends in the Golf Industry. Annually.
  Women in Golf—1991-1996

**National Marine Manufacturers
Association, Chicago, IL.**
  http://www.nmma.org
  Boating. (A Statistical Report on America's
    Top Family Sport.) Annual.
  State Boat Registration. Annual.

**National Restaurant Association,
Washington, DC**
  http://www.restaurant.org
  Compensation for Salaried Personnel in
    Restaurants. 2001.
  Ethnic Cuisines II. 2000.
  Holiday Dining. 2001.

National Restaurant Association, Washington, DC —Con.

Meal Consumption Behavior. 2001.

Quick-Service Restaurant Trends. Annual.

Restaurant Economic Trends. Monthly.

Restaurant Industry Employee Profile. Annual.

Restaurant Industry Forecast. Annual.

Restaurant Industry in Review. Annual.

Restaurant Industry Operations Report. Annual.

Restaurant Industry Pocket Factbook. Annual.

Restaurant Industry 2010. 1999.

Restaurant Numbers: 25-Year History, 1970-95. 1998.

Restaurant Spending. Annual. Restaurants USA. Monthly.

Tableservice Restaurant Trends. Annual

Takeout Foods: A Consumer Study of Carry-out and Delivery. 1998

The Economic Impact of the Nation's Eating and Drinking Places. Annual.

National Sporting Goods Association, Mt. Prospect, IL

http://www.nsga.org

The Sporting Goods Market in 2001. Annual.

Sports Participation in 2000. Annual.

New York Stock Exchange, Inc., New York, NY

http://www.nyse.com

Fact Book. Annual.

Organization for Economic Cooperation and Development, Paris, France

http://www.oecd.org

Annual Oil Market Report.

Basic Science and Technology Statistics, 2000 Edition on CD-Rom. Annual

Bank Profitability: Financial Statements of Banks. 2000. Annual

Central Government Debt: Statistical Yearbook. 2000. Annual

Coal Information. Annual.

Education at a Glance: OECD Indicators 2001. Annual

Energy Balances of OECD Countries. 1998-1999. 2001 Edition. Annual.

Energy Prices and Taxes. Quarterly.

Energy Statistics of OECD Countries. 1998-1999. 2001 Edition. Annual.

External Debt Statistics: The Debt of Developing Countries and Countries in Transition. Annual.

Financial Market Trends. Triennial.

Food Consumption Statistics. Irregular.

Geographical Distribution of Financial Flows to Developing Countries.

Geographical Distribution of Financial Flows to Aid Recipients. 2001. Annual

Historical Statistics of Foreign Trade Series A. Annual.

Organization for Economic Cooperation and Development, Paris, France —Con.

Indicators of Industrial Activity. Quarterly.

International Development Statistics CD-ROM and Online Database. 2001. Annual

International Trade by Commodities. Series C. Annual.

Iron and Steel Industry in 1999. 2001 Edition. Annual.

Labour Force Statistics. Annual.

Latest Information on National Accounts of Developing Countries. Annual.

Main Economic Indicators. Monthly.

Main Science and Technology Indicators. Biennial.

Maritime Transport. Annual.

Meat Balances in OECD Countries. Annual.

Milk and Milk Products Balances in OECD Countries. Annual.

Monthly Statistics of International Trade. Series A. Monthly.

National Accounts of OECD Countries. Annual.

Vol. I: Main Aggregates.

Vol. II: Detailed Tables.

OECD Agricultural Outlook. 2001-2006. 2001 Edition. Annual

OECD Economic Outlook. Biannual. Historical Statistics. Annual.

OECD Economic Studies. Annual for member countries.

OECD Economic Surveys. Annual.

OECD Employment Outlook. Annual.

OECD Environmental Outlook 2000. Annual.

OECD Financial Statistics. Annual (three vols.) and monthly supplements.

OECD Health Data. 2001. Annual.

OECD Health Systems: Facts and Trends.

OECD Historical Statistics. (2000 Edition). Annual.

OECD Indicators of Industrial Activity. Quarterly.

OECD Main Economic Indicators. Monthly.

OECD Microtables on Foreign Trade by Commodities covering Series B (individual reporting countries) and Series C (total reporting countries). Annual from 1977.

OECD Observer. Bimonthly.

Oil and Gas Information. Annual.

Oil, Gas, Coal, and Electricity Quarterly Statistics. Quarterly.

The Pulp and Paper Industry. Annual.

Quarterly Labor Force Statistics.

Quarterly National Accounts.

Quarterly Oil Statistics and Energy Balances.

Revenue Statistics of OECD Member Countries. Annual.

Review of Fisheries in OECD Member Countries. Annual.

Statistical Report on Road Accidents. 1997-1998. Annual.

Organization for Economic Cooperation and Development, Paris, France —Con.

Statistical Trends in Transport (ECMT.)

Statistics of Area Production and Field of Crop Products in OECD Member Countries.

Structural Statistics for Industry and Services: Core Data. Annual.

Taxing Wages. 2000. Annual

Statistics of Foreign Trade:

Monthly Statistics of Foreign Trade. (Series A.)

Foreign Trade by Commodities. (Series C.) Annual.

Tourism Policy and International Tourism in OECD Member Countries. Annual.

Uranium Resources Production and Demand. Biennial.

World Energy Statistics and Balances.

Pan American Health Organization, Washington, DC

http://www.paho.org

Health Conditions in the Americas. Quadrennial.

PennWell Publishing Co., Tulsa, OK

http://www.pennwell.com

Offshore. Monthly.

Oil and Gas Journal. Weekly.

Population Association of America, Washington, DC

http://www.popassoc.org

Demography. Quarterly.

Population Index. (Princeton University, Princeton, NJ, Woodrow Wilson School of Public and International Affairs for the Population Association of America, Inc.) Quarterly.

Puerto Rico Planning Board, San Juan, PR

http://http://www.jp.gobierno.pr

Balance of Payments—Puerto Rico. Annual.

Economic Activity Index. Monthly.

Economic Indicators. Monthly.

Economic Projections. Annual.

Economic Report to the Governor. Annual.

External Trade Statistics-Puerto Rico. Annual.

Income and Product. Annual.

Input-Output—Puerto Rico. Every 5 years.

Statistical Appendix to the Economic Report to the Government. Annual.

Radio Advertising Bureau, New York, NY

http://www.rab.com

Radio Facts. Annual.

Reed Elsevier, Inc., Newton, MA

http://www.reed-elsevier.com

Broadcasting & Cable Yearbook.

Regional Airline Association, Washington, DC

http://www.raa.org

Annual Report.

Broadcasting Magazine. Weekly.

Research Associates of Washington, Arlington, VA

http://www.rschassoc.com

Inflation Measures for Schools, Colleges, and Libraries. Periodic.

Securities Industry Association, New York, NY

http://www.sia.com

Foreign Activity Report. Quarterly.

Securities Industry Trends. Periodic.

SIA Securities Industry Fact Book. Annual.

Shipbuilders Council of America, Arlington, VA

http://www.shipbuilders.org

Annual Report.

Simmons Market Research Bureau, Chicago, IL

http://www.smrb.com

Study of Media Markets. Annual.

Standard and Poor's Corporation, New York, NY

http://www.standardandpoors.com

Analyst's Handbook. Annual with monthly cumulative supplements.

Corporation Records. Six basic volumes; News Supplements, daily; Dividend Record, daily, and cumulative monthly and annual.

Daily Stock Price Records. Quarterly.

Security Owner's Stock Guide. Monthly.

Statistical Service. (Security Price Index Record; business and financial basic statistics with monthly supplement.)

United Nations Educational, Scientific and Cultural Organization, Paris, France

http://www.unesco.org

Statistical Yearbook.

United Nations Statistics Division, New York, NY

http://www.un.org

Compendium of Human Settlements Statistics. (Series N.)

Demographic Yearbook. (Series R.)

Energy Balances and Electricity Profiles. (Series W.)

Energy Statistics Yearbook. (Series J.)

Industrial Statistics Yearbook: (Series P.)

Commodity Production Statistics.

International Trade Statistics Yearbook. (Series G.)

Monthly Bulletin of Statistics. (Series Q.)

National Accounts Statistics: (Series X, Annually.)

United Nations Statistics Division, New York, NY —Con.

   Main Aggregates and Detailed Tables.
   Analysis of Main Aggregates.
Population and Vital Statistics Report. (Series A, Quarterly.)
Social Statistics and Indicators: (Series K, Occasional.)
   The World's Women: Trends and Statistics.
   Women's Indicators and Statistics Database (CD and diskette only.)
Statistical Yearbook. (Series; also available in CD-ROM, Series S/CD)
World Statistics Pocketbook. (Series V, Annually.)

United States League of Savings Institutions, Chicago, IL

http://www.westernleague.org
Savings Institutions Sourcebook. Annual.

United States Telephone Association, Washington, DC

http://www.usta.org
Statistics of the Local Exchange Carriers. Annual.

United Way of America, Alexandria, VA

http://www.unitedway.org
Annual Directory.

University of Michigan, Center for Political Studies, Institute for Social Research, Ann Arbor, MI

http://www.umich.edu
National Election Studies Cumulative Datafile. Biennial.

Warren Publishing, Inc., Washington, DC

http://www.law.emory.edu
Cable Action Update. Weekly.
Cable and Station Coverage Atlas. Annual.
Television Action Update. Weekly.
Television and Cable Factbook. Annual.
TV Station & Cable Ownership Directory. Semiannual.

World Almanac, New York, NY

http://www.worldalmanac.com
The World Almanac and Book of Facts. Annual.

World Health Organization, Geneva, Switzerland

http://www.who.int
Epidemiological and Vital Statistics Report. Monthly.
World Health Statistics. Quarterly and annual.

Guide to State Statistical Abstracts

This bibliography includes the most recent statistical abstracts for states published since 1995 plus those that will be issued in late 2002. For some states, a near equivalent has been listed in substitution for, or in addition to, a statistical abstract. All sources contain statistical tables on a variety of subjects for the state as a whole, its component parts, or both. The page counts given for publications are approximate. Internet sites also contain statistical data.

Alabama

University of Alabama, Center for Business and Economic Research, Box 870221, Tuscaloosa 35487-0221. 205-348-6191. Internet site <http://cber.cba.ua.edu/>

Economic Abstract of Alabama. 2000. 534 pp.

Alabama Economic Outlook, 2002. (Revised annually.)

Alaska

Department of Commerce, Department of Economic Development, Division of Community and Business Development, P.O. Box 110809, Juneau 99811-0809. 907-465-2017. Internet site <http://www.dced.state.ak.us/cbd/AEIS/AEIS_Home.htm/>

The Alaska Economy Performance Report. 1996. Online.

Arizona

University of Arizona, Economic and Business Research, Eller College of Business and Public Administration, McClelland Hall 103, Tucson 85721-0108. 520-621-2523. Fax: 520-621-2150. Internet site <http://www.ebr.eller.arizona.edu/>

Arizona Statistical Abstract, 2002, 600 pp.

*Arizona's Economy.*16-20 pp. Quarterly newsletter.

Arizona Economic Indicators 52 pp. Biennial.

Economic Outlook-Annual Forecast.

Arkansas

University of Arkansas at Little Rock, Institute for Economic Advancement, Economic Research, 2801 South University, Little Rock 72204. 501-569-8551.

Arkansas State and County Economic Data, 2002. 16 pp. (Revised annually.)

Arkansas Personal Income Handbook, 2002. 98 pp.

University of Arkansas at Little Rock, Institute for Economic Advancement, Census State Data Center, 2801 South University, Little Rock 72204. 501-569-8533. Internet site <http://www.aiea.ualr.edu/>

Arkansas Statistical Abstract, 2000. 740 pp. (Revised biennially.)

California

Department of Finance, 915 L Street, 8th Floor, Sacramento 95814. 916-322-2263. Internet site <http://www.dof.ca.gov/html/fsdata/stat-abs/sahome.htm>

California Statistical Abstract, 2001.

Colorado

University of Colorado, Boulder 80309-0420. 303-492-8227. Internet site <http://www.colorado.edu/libraries/govpubs/online.htm/>

Colorado by the Numbers-online only.

Connecticut

Connecticut Department of Economic & Community Development, 505 Hudson St., Hartford 06106. 1-860-270-8165. Internet site <http://www.state.ct.us/ecd/>

Connecticut Town Profiles, 2000. 340 pp.

Delaware

Delaware Economic Development Office, 99 Kings Highway, Dover 19901. 302-739-4271. Fax 302-739-2027. Internet site <http://www.state.de.us/dedo/newwebsite/>

Delaware Statistical Overview, 2002. 160 pp.

District of Columbia

Office of Planning, Data Management Division, 801 North Capitol St., N.E. Washington 20002. 202-442-7603

Office of Policy and Evaluation, Executive Office of the Mayor, 1 Judiciary Square, Suite 920 So., 441 4th St., NW, Washington 20001. 202-727-6979.

Indices—A Statistical Index to DC Services, Dec. 1997-98. 273 pp.

Florida

University of Florida, Bureau of Economic and Business Research, 221 Matherly Hall, Gainesville 32611-7145. 352-392-0171. Internet site <http://www.bebr.ufl.edu/>

Florida Statistical Abstract, 2001. 35th ed. 821 pp. Also available on diskette or CD-ROM.

Florida County Perspectives, 2001. One profile for each county. Annual. Available on CD-ROM.

Florida County Rankings, 2001, 8th edition. Annual. Available on CD-ROM.

Florida and the Nation, 2002. 6th edition. Annual. Available on CD-ROM.

Georgia

University of Georgia, Selig Center for Economic Growth, Terry College of Business, Athens 30602-6269. 706-542-4085. Internet site <http://www.selig.uga.edu/>

Georgia Statistical Abstract, 2000-01. 500 pp.

Georgia Statistical Abstract, 2002-03. 500 pp.

The University of Georgia, Center for Agri-business and Economic Development, Athens 30602-4356. 706-542-8938. Fax 706-542-8934. Internet site <http://www.georgiastats.uga.edu/>

The Georgia County Guide, 2002. 21st ed. Annual. 200 pp.

Hawaii

Hawaii State Department of Business, and Economic Development & Tourism, Research and Economic Analysis Division, Statistics Branch P.O. Box 2359, Honolulu 96804. Inquiries 808-586-2481; Copies 808-586-2423. Internet site <http://www.hawaii.gov/dbedt/stats.html/>

The State of Hawaii Data Book 2001: A Statistical Abstract. 700 pp.

Idaho

Department of Commerce, 700 West State St., P.O. Box 83720, Boise 83720-0093. 208-334-2470. Internet site <http://www.idoc.state.id.us/data/community/index.html/>

County Profiles of Idaho, 2001. 367 pp.

Idaho Community Profiles, 2001.

Profile of Rural Idaho, 2002.

University of Idaho, Center for Business Development and Entrepreneurship, Moscow 83844-3227. 208-885-6611. Internet site <http://www.uidaho.edu/cbde/>

Illinois

University of Illinois, Bureau of Economic and Business Research, 430 Wohlers Hall, 1206 South 6th Street, Champaign 61820. 217-333-2330. Internet site <http://www.cba.uiuc.edu/ research/>

Illinois Statistical Abstract, 2000. 15th edition. 759 pp.

Indiana

Indiana University, Indiana Business Research Center, Kelly School of Business, Ste 3110, 1275 E. 10th Street, Blooming-ton 47405. 812-855-5507. Internet site <http://www. ibrc.indiana.edu/>

Kansas

University of Kansas, Policy Research Institute, 607 Blake Hall, Lawrence 66044-3177. 785-864-3701. Internet site <http://www.ukans.edu/>

Kansas Statistical Abstract, 2000. 35th ed. 480 pp.

Kansas Statistical Abstract, 2001. 36th ed. 480 pp.

Kentucky

Kentucky Cabinet for Economic Development, Division of Research, 500 Mero Street, Capital Plaza Tower, Frankfort 40601. 502-564-4886. Internet site <http://www.edc.state.ky.us/kyedc/edevlinks.asp/>

Kentucky Deskbook of Economic Statistics. 34th ed. 1998.

Louisiana

University of New Orleans, Division of Business and Economic Research, New Orleans 70148. 504-280-6240. Internet site <http://leap.nlu.edu/STAAB.HTM/>

Statistical Abstract of Louisiana. 10th ed. 1997.

Maine

Maine State Planning Office, Station #38, Augusta 04333. 207-287-2989. Internet site <http://www.econdevmaine.com/>.

Maryland

RESI, 8000 York Road, Towson University, Towson 212520001. 410-704-3792. Fax 410-704-4115. Internet site <http://www.resiusa.org/>.

Maryland Statistical Abstract, 2000. 356 pp.

Massachusetts

Massachusetts Institute for Social and Economic Research, University of Massa-chusetts, 128 Thompson Hall, 200 Hicks Way, Amherst 01003-9277. 413-545-3460. Fax 413-545-3686. Internet site <http://www.umass.edu/miser/>.

Minnesota

Department of Trade and Economic Development, Analysis and Evaluation Office, 121 East 7th Place 500 Metro Square Building, St. Paul 55101-2146. 651-297-2335. Internet site <http://www.dted.state.mn.us/>.

Compare Minnesota: Profiles of Minnesota's Economy and Population, 2002-2003.

Office of State Demographer, Minnesota Planning, Rm. 300 Centennial Bldg., 658 Cedar Street, St. Paul 55155. 651-296-2557. Internet site <http://www.mnplan.state.mn.us/demography/>.

Mississippi

Mississippi State University, College of Business and Industry, Division of Research, P.O. Box 5288 Mississippi State 39762. 662-325-3817. Fax 662-325-8686.

Mississippi Statistical Abstract. 2001. 540 pp.

County Data Book, 2001. 540 pp.

Missouri

University of Missouri, Economic and Policy Analysis Research Center, 10 Professional Bldg., Columbia 65211. 573-882-4805. Internet site <http://econ.missouri.edu/eparc/>.

Statistical Abstract for Missouri, 2001. 423 pp. Biennial.

Montana

Census and Economic Information Center, Montana Department of Commerce, 301 S. Park, P.O. Box 200505, Helena 59620. 406-841-2740. Internet site <http://ceic.commerce.state.mt.us/otherlinks.html.

Nebraska

Nebraska Department of Economic Development, Box 94666, Lincoln 68509-4666. 402-471-3111. Fax 402-471-3788. Internet site <http://info.neded.org/>.

Nebraska Data Book, 2000. 300 pp. (Available only on Internet).

Nevada

Department of Administration, Budget and Planning Division, 209 East Musser Street, Suite 200, Carson City 89701. 775-684-0222. Internet site <http://www.budget.state.nv.us/>

Nevada Statistical Abstract. 2001. 50 pp.

A Biennial Report of Nevada State Agencies, 2001-2002.

New Hampshire

Office of State Planning, 2 1/2 Beacon St., Concord 03301-4497. 603-271-2155. Fax 603-271-1728. Internet site <http://www.state.nh.us/osp/>.

New Jersey

New Jersey State Data Center, NJ Department of Labor, P.O. Box 388, Trenton 08625-0388. 609-984-2595. Internet site <http://www.state.nj.us/labor/lra/njsdc.html/>.

Labor Market Information (Internet only).

New Mexico

University of New Mexico, Bureau of Business and Economic Research, 1920 Lomas N.E. Albuquerque 87131-6021. 505-277-6626. Fax 505-277-2773. Internet site <http://www.unm.edu/bber/>.

New Mexico Business, Current Economic Report (monthly).

FOR-UNM Bulletin (quarterly).

Population Projections by Age and Sex (periodic).

New York

Nelson A. Rockefeller Institute of Government, 411 State Street, Albany 12203-1003. 518-443-5522. Internet site <http:// www.rockinst.org/>

New York State Statistical Yearbook, 2000. 25th ed. 604 pp. 2001 26th ed. 618 pp.

North Carolina

Office of Governor, Office of State Budget and Management, Management Section, Data Services Unit, 20321 Mail Service Center, Raleigh 27699-0321. 919-733-7061. Fax 919-7153562. Internet site <http://www.osbpm.state.nc.us/>

Population Estimate Projection <http://demography.state.nc.us>; and, 2000 census <http://census.state.nc.us>

North Dakota

North Dakota Department of Commerce, P.O. Box 2057, 400 E. Broadway, Suite 50, Bismarck 58502-2057. 701-328-5300. Internet site <http://www.ndcommerce.com/>

North Dakota Economic Roadmap 2002. Job Service North Dakota. 135 pp.

Ohio

Department of Development, Office of Strategic Research, P.O. Box 1001, Columbus 43216-1001. 614-466-2116. Internet site <http://www.odod.state.oh.us/osr/census2000.htm>

Research products and services. (Updated continuously.)

Ohio County Profiles; Ohio County Indicators (updated periodically.)

Oklahoma

University of Oklahoma, Center for Economic and Management Research, 307 West Brooks Street, Room 4, Norman 73019. 405-325-2931. Fax 405-325-7688. Internet site <http://cemr.ou.edu/>

Statistical Abstract of Oklahoma, 2001. Annual. 401 pp.

Oregon

Secretary of State, Archives Division, Archives Bldg., 800 Summer Street, NE Salem 97310. 503-373-0701. Internet site <http://www.sos.state.or.us/>

Oregon Blue Book. 2001-2002. Biennial. 465 pp. (2002-2003 ed. will be out in March 2003)

Pennsylvania

Pennsylvania State Data Center, Institute of State and Regional Affairs, Penn State Harrisburg, 777 West Harrisburg Pike, Middletown Pennsylvania 17057-4898. 717-948-6310. Internet site <http://pasdc.hbg.psu.edu/pasdc/>

Pennsylvania Statistical Abstract, 2002. 295 pp.

Rhode Island

Rhode Island Economic Development Corporation, 1 West Exchange Street, Providence 02903. 401-222-2601. Fax 401-2222102. Internet site <http://www.riedc.com/>

Annual Trends and Time Series of Key Statistics, 2002. 12 pp. (Excel Spreadsheets).

South Carolina

Budget and Control Board, Office of Research and Statistics, Room 425, 1000 Assembly Street, Columbia 29201. 803-734-3780. Internet site <http://www.ors.state.sc.us/>

South Carolina Statistical Abstract: 2002. 400 pp.

South Dakota

University of South Dakota, State Data Center, Business Research Bureau, 404 E. Clark Street, Vermillion 57069-2390. 605-677-5287. Internet site <http://www.usd.edu/brbinfo/>

2001 South Dakota Community Abstracts. 400 pp.

Tennessee

University of Tennessee at Knoxville, Center for Business and Economic Research, College of Business Administration, 100 Glocker, Knoxville 37996-4170. 865-974-5441. Internet site <http://cber.bus.utk.edu/tnsdc/sdcmain.htm./>

Tennessee Statistical Abstract, 2000. 17th ed. 738 pp. Biennial.

Texas

Dallas Morning News, Communications Center, P.O. Box 655237, Dallas 75265-5237. 214-977-8261. Internet site <http://www.texasalmanac.com/texasrank2000.shtml>

Texas Almanac, 2002-2003. 672 pp.

Utah

University of Utah, Bureau of Economic and Business Research, David Eccles School of Business 1645 East Campus Center Drive, Salt Lake City 84112-9302. 801-581-6333. Internet site <http://www.business.utah.edu/bebr/>

Statistical Abstract of Utah. 1996. (Centennial.) (Last in paper format-Online only)

Utah Foundation, 5242 College Drive, Suite 390, Salt Lake City 84123-1544. 801-288-1838. Fax 801-263-6492. Internet site <http://www.utahfoundation.org/>

Statistical Review of Government in Utah. 1999. (Online only)

Vermont

Labor Market Information, Department of Employment and Training, 5 Green Mountain Drive, P.O. Box 488, Montpelier 05601-0488. 802-828-4202. Internet site <http://www.vtlmi.info/>

Economic and Demographic Profiles. Annual. 62 pp.

Virginia

Weldon Cooper Center, 918 Emmet Street, North, Charlottesville 22903-4832. 434-982-5522. Internet site <http://www.ccps.virginia.edu/demographics/>

Virginia Statistical Abstract, 2000. Biennial. 1,100 pp.

Washington

Washington State Office of Financial Management, Forecasting Division P.O. Box 43113 Olympia 98504-3113. 360-902-0599. Fax 360-664-8941. Internet site <http://www.ofm.wa.gov/data Book/index.htm/>

Washington State Data Book, 2001. 309 pp.

West Virginia

West Virginia University, College of Business and Economics, Bureau of Business and Economic Research, P.O. Box 6025, Morgantown 26506-6025. 304-293-7835. Internet site <http://www.bber.wvu.edu/>

Regional Economic Outlook. Semiannual. 8 pp.

West Virginia Research League, Inc., P.O. Box 11176, Charleston 25339. 304-766-9495.

The 1999 Statistical Handbook. 94 pp.

The 2000 Statistical Handbook. 94 pp.

The 2001 Statistical Handbook. 94 pp.

Wisconsin

Wisconsin Legislative Reference Bureau, P.O. Box 2037, Madison 53701-2037. 608-266-0342 Internet site <http://www.legis.state.wi.us/lrb/bb/>

2001-2002 State of Wisconsin Blue Book. 989 pp. Biennial.

Wyoming

Department of Administration and Information, Division of Economic Analysis, 1807 Capitol Avenue, Suite 206, Cheyenne 82002-0060. 307-777-7504. Internet site <http://eadiv.state.Wy.us/>

The Equality State Almanac 2000. 8th ed. 134 pp.

Guide to Foreign Statistical Abstracts

This bibliography presents recent statistical abstracts for member nations of the Organization for Economic Cooperation and Development, Slovakia, and Russia. All sources contain statistical tables on a variety of subjects for the individual countries. Many of the following publications provide text in English as well as in the national language(s). For further information on these publications, contact the named statistical agency which is responsible for editing the publication.

Australia
Australian Bureau of Statistics, Canberra
Year Book Australia. Annual. 2002. 893 pp. (In English.)

Austria
Statistik Austria, A-1033 Wien
Statistisches Jahrbuch Osterreichs. Annual. 2002. 608 pp. With CD-ROM. (In German.) With English translations of table headings.

Belgium
Institut National de Statistique, Rue de Louvain, 44-1000 Bruxelles
Annuaire statistique de la Belgique. Annual. 1995. 820 pp. (In French.)

Canada
Statistics Canada, Ottawa, Ontario, KIA OT6
Canada Yearbook: A review of economic, social and political developments in Canada. 2001. 564 pp. Irregular. (In English.)

Czech Republic
Czech Statistical Office, Sokolovska 142, 186 04 Praha 8
Statisticka Rocenka Ceske Rpubliky 2001. 773 pp. (In English and Czech.)

Denmark
Danmarks Statistik, Sejrograde 11, 2100 Kobenhava O
Statistisk ARBOG. 2001. Annual. 603 pp. (In Danish only.)

Finland
Statistics Finland, Helsinki
Statistical Yearbook of Finland. Annual. 2001. 699 pp. with CD-ROM (In English, Finnish, and Swedish.)

France
Institut National de la Statistique et des Etudes Economiques, Paris 18, Bld. Adolphe Pinard, 75675 Paris (Cedex 14)
Annuaire Statistique de la France. Annual. 2002. 968 pp. (In French.)

Germany
Statistische Bundesamt, D-65180 Wiesbaden
Statistisches Jahrbuch fur die Bundesrepublic Deutschland. Annual. 2001. 762 pp. (In German.)
Statistisches Jahrbuch fur das Ausland. 2001. 411 pp.

Greece
National Statistical Service of Greece, Athens
Concise Statistical Yearbook 2000. 276 pp. (plus13 pages of graphs) (In English and Greek)
Statistical Yearbook of Greece. Annual. 2000. 549 pp. (plus 8 pages of graphs). (In English and Greek.)

Hungary
Hungarian Central Statistical Office, 1024 Budapest
Statistical Yearbook of Hungary, 2000. 591 pp. (In English and Hungarian)

Iceland
Hagstofa Islands/Statistics Iceland
Statistical Yearbook of Iceland. 2001 with CD-ROM. Irregular. 325 pp. (In English and Icelandic.)

Ireland
Central Statistics Office, Skehard Road, Cort
Statistical Abstract. Annual. 1998-99. 419 pp. (In English)

Italy
ISTAT (Istituto Centrale di Statistica), Via Cesare Balbo 16 Roma
Annuario Statistico Italiano. Annual. 2001 with CD-ROM. 714 pp. (In Italian.)

Japan
Statistics Bureau, Ministry of Public Management, Home Affairs Posts and Telecommunications, Japan
Japan Statistical Yearbook. Annual. 2002. 921 pp. (In English and Japanese.)

Korea, South
National Statistical Office, Government
Complex, #920 Dunsan-dong Seo-gu
Daejeon 302-701

Korea Statistical Yearbook. Annual.
2001. 793 pp. (In Korean and English)

Luxembourg
STATEC (Service Central de la Statistique
et des Etudes), P.O. Box 304, L-2013,
Luxembourg

Annuaire Statistique. Annual. 2001.
(In French.) (Alphabetical numbering
system)

Mexico
Instituto Nacional de Estadistica Geografia e
Informatica, Avda. Insurgentes Sur No.
795-PH Col. Napoles, Del. Benito Juarez
03810 Mexico, D.F.

*Anuario estadistico de los Estados Unidos
Mexicanos*. Annual. 1998.
714 pp. Also on disc. (In Spanish.)
Agenda Estadistica 1999. 149 pp.

Netherlands
Statistics Netherlands, R L Vellekoop Prinses
Beatrixiaan 428, 2273 X Z Voorburg
Statistical Yearbook 2002 of the
Netherlands. 559 pp. (In English.)

Statistisch Jaarboek 2002. 569 pp. with
CD-ROM

New Zealand
Department of Statistics, Wellington

New Zealand Official Yearbook. Annual.
1998. 606 pp. (In English.)

Norway
Statistics Norway, Oslo/Kongsvinger

Statistical Yearbook. Annual. 2001.
539 pp. (In English.)

Poland
Central Statistical Office al. Niepodleglosci
208, 00-925 Warsaw

Concise Statistical Yearbook 2001.
653 pp. (In Polish and English)
Statistical Yearbook of the Republic of
Poland 2000. 800 pp. (In Polish and
English)

Portugal
INE (Instituto Nacional de Estatistica),
Avenida Antonio Jose de Almeida
P-1000-043 Lisboa

Anuario Estatistico: de Portugal. 2000.
358 pp. (In Portuguese and English.)

Russia
State Committee of Statistics of Russia,
Moscow

Statistical Yearbook. 2001. 679 pp.
(In Russian.)

Slovakia
Statistical Office of the Slovak Republic,
Bradacova 7, 852 86 Bratislava

Statisticka Rocenka Slovensak 2000.
719 pp. Plus 16 pages of graphs.
(In English and Slovak)

Spain
INE (Instituto Nacional de Estadistica),
Paseo de la Castellana, 183, Madrid 16

Espana Anuaria Estadistico Annual.
1996. 848 pp. + 16 pages of graphs
(In Spanish.)

Sweden
Statistics Sweden, S-11581 Stockholm

Statistisk Arsbok for Sverige. Annual.
2002. 697 pp. (In English and Swedish.)

Switzerland
Bundesamt fur Statistik, Hallwylstrasse 15,
CH-3003, Bern

Statistisches Jahrbuch der Schweiz.
Annual. 2002. 894 pp. with CD-ROM
(In French and German.)

Turkey
State Institute of Statistics, Prime Ministry,
114 Necatibey Caddesi, Bakanliklar,
Yenisehir, Ankara

Statistical Yearbook of Turkey. 1999.
721 pp. (In English and Turkish.)
Turkey in Statistics 1999 144 pp.
(In English and Turkish.)

United Kingdom
The Stationary Office, P.O. Box 29, Norwich,
NR3 1GN

Annual Abstract of Statistics. Annual.
2002. 429 pp. (In English.)

Appendix II
Metropolitan Areas: Concepts, Components, and Population

Statistics for metropolitan areas (MAs) shown in the *Statistical Abstract* represent areas designated by the U.S. Office of Management and Budget (OMB) according to published standards that are applied to Census Bureau data. The general concept of an MA is that of a core area containing a large population nucleus, together with adjacent communities having a high degree of economic and social integration with that core. Currently defined MAs are based on application of 1990 standards (which appeared in the Federal Register on March 30, 1990) to 1990 decennial census data and to subsequent Census Bureau population estimates, special census data, and 2000 census results. Current MA definitions were announced by OMB effective June 30, 1999. MAs include metropolitan statistical areas (MSAs), consolidated metropolitan statistical areas (CMSAs), and primary metropolitan statistical areas (PMSAs), as well as New England county metropolitan areas (NECMAs), the county-based alternative metropolitan areas for the city- and town-based MSAs and CMSAs of the six New England states.

Standards for designating metropolitan areas were first issued in 1949 by the then
Bureau of the Budget (predecessor of OMB), under the designation "standard metropolitan area" (SMA). The term was changed to "standard metropolitan statistical area" (SMSA) in 1959 and to "metropolitan statistical area" (MSA) in 1983. The collective term "metropolitan area" (MA) became effective in 1990.

OMB has been responsible for the official metropolitan areas since they were first defined, except for the period 1977 to 1981, when they were the responsibility of the Office of Federal Statistical Policy and Standards, Department of Commerce. The standards for designating metropolitan areas were modified in 1958, 1971,

1975, 1980, and 1990. They were modified again in 2000, but OMB will not redesignate areas until 2003.

Designating MSAs, CMSAs, and PMSAs— The current standards provide that each newly qualifying MSA must include at least: one city with 50,000 or more inhabitants, or a Census Bureau-defined urbanized area (of at least 50,000 inhabitants) and a total metropolitan population of at least 100,000 (75,000 in New England). Under the standards, the county (or counties) that contains the largest city becomes the "central county" (counties), along with any adjacent counties that have at least 50 percent of their population in the urbanized area surrounding the largest city. Additional "outlying counties" are included in the MSA if they meet specified requirements of commuting to the central counties and other selected requirements of metropolitan character (such as population density and percent urban). In New England, the MSAs are defined in terms of county subdivisions (primarily cities and towns) rather than counties. An area that meets these requirements for recognition as an MSA and also has a population of 1 million or more may be recognized as a CMSA if separate component areas can be identified within the entire area by meeting statistical criteria specified in the standards, and local opinion indicates support for recognizing the component areas. If recognized, the component areas are designated PMSAs, and the entire area becomes a CMSA. PMSAs, like the CMSAs that contain them, are composed of entire counties, except in New England where they are composed of county subdivisions. If no PMSAs are recognized, the entire area is designated as an MSA. As of the June 30, 1999, OMB announcement, there were 258 MSAs, and 18 CMSAs containing 73 PMSAs in the United States. In addition, there were three MSAs, one CMSA, and three PMSAs in Puerto Rico.

Central cities and MA titles—The largest city in each MSA/CMSA is designated a "central city." Additional cities qualify if specified requirements are met concerning population size and commuting patterns. The title of each MSA consists of the names of up to three of its central cities and the name of each state into which the MSA extends. However, a central city with less than 250,000 population and less than one-third the population of the area's largest city is not included in an MSA title unless local opinion supports its inclusion. Titles of PMSAs also typically are based on central city names, but in certain cases consist of county names. Generally, titles of CMSAs are based on the titles of their component PMSAs.

Defining New England County Metropolitan Areas (NECMAs)—The OMB defines NECMAs as a county-based alternative to the county subdivision based New England MSAs and CMSAs. The NECMA for an MSA or CMSA includes: the county containing the first-named city in that MSA/CMSA title (this county may include the first-named cities of other MSAs/CMSAs as well), and each additional county having at least half its population in the MSAs/CMSAs whose first-named cities are in the previously identified county. NECMAs are not identified for individual PMSAs. There are 12 NECMAs, including 1 for the Boston-Worcester-Lawrence, MA-NH-ME-CT CMSA and 1 for

the Connecticut portion of the New York-Northern New Jersey-Long Island, NY-NJ-CT-PA CMSA. Central cities of a NECMA are those cities in the NECMA that qualify as central cities of an MSA or a CMSA. NECMA titles derive from names of central cities.

Changes in MAs over time—Changes in MAs since the 1950 census have consisted chiefly of the recognition of new areas as they reached the minimum required city or area population, and the addition of counties (or county subdivisions in New England) to existing areas as new decennial census data showed them to qualify. In some instances, formerly separate MAs have been merged, a component of an MA has been transferred from one MA to another, or a component has been dropped from an MA. The large majority of changes have taken place on the basis of decennial census data. However, Census Bureau population estimates and special censuses serve as the basis for intercensal updates.

Because of these historical changes in geographic definitions, users must be cautious in comparing MA data from different dates. For some purposes, comparisons of data for MAs as designated at given dates may be appropriate; for other purposes, it may be preferable to maintain consistent MA definitions.

Table A. New England County Metropolitan Areas (NECMAs) as of June 30, 1999

[In thousands (145 represents 145,000). As of July]

NECMA	Population, 2001	NECMA	Population, 2001	NECMA	Population, 2001
Bangor, ME	145	**Burlington, VT**	201	**New London-Norwich, CT**	259
Penobscot County	145	Chittenden County	148	New London County	259
Barnstable-Yarmouth, MA	227	Franklin County	46	**Pittsfield, MA**	134
Barnstable County	227	Grand Isle County	7	Berkshire County	134
Boston-Worcester-Lawrence-		**Hartford, CT**	1,158	**Portland, ME**	267
Lowell-Brockton, MA-NH	6,099	Hartford County	861	Cumberland County	267
Bristol County, MA	540	Middlesex County	158	**Providence-Warwick-**	
Essex County, MA	730	Tolland County	139	**Pawtucket, RI**	974
Middlesex County, MA	1,463	**Lewiston-Auburn, ME**	104	Bristol County	51
Norfolk County, MA	653	Androscoggin County	104	Kent County	169
Plymouth County, MA	481			Providence County	627
Suffolk County, MA	682	**New Haven-Bridgeport-**		Washington County	126
Worcester County, MA	762	**Stamford-Waterbury-**			
Hillsborough County, NH	388	**Danbury, CT**	1,714	**Springfield, MA**	609
Rockingham County, NH	284	Fairfield County	885	Hampden County	456
Strafford County, NH	115	New Haven County	828	Hampshire County	153

Source: U.S. Census Bureau, "Time Series of Population Estimates by County: April 1, 2000 to July 1, 2001"; published 23 May 2002; <http://eire.census.gov/popest/data/counties/tables/CO-EST2001-07.php>.

U.S. Census Bureau, Statistical Abstract of the United States: 2002

Table B. Metropolitan Areas Outside of New England and Their Components as of June 30, 1999

[**Population as of July 2001. 124 represents 124,000.** All metropolitan areas are arranged alphabetically. PMSAs are included under their respective CMSAs, see CMSA entry]

Metropolitan area and component county	Popu-lation, 2001 (1,000)	Metropolitan area and component county	Popu-lation, 2001 (1,000)	Metropolitan area and component county	Popu-lation, 2001 (1,000)
Abilene, TX MSA	124	Gwinnett County	622	**Bloomington, IN MSA**	120
Taylor County	124	Henry County	133	Monroe County	120
		Newton County	68	**Bloomington-Normal, IL**	
Albany, GA MSA	121	Paulding County	90	**MSA**	152
Dougherty County	96	Pickens County	25	McLean County	152
Lee County	26	Rockdale County	72		
		Spalding County	59	**Boise City, ID MSA**	452
Albany-Schenectady-Troy,		Walton County	65	Ada County	312
NY MSA	878			Canyon County	140
Albany County	294	**Auburn-Opelika, AL**	117		
Montgomery County	49	Lee County	117	**Brownsville-Harlingen, TX**	
Rensselaer County	153			**MSA**	345
Saratoga County	204	**Augusta-Aiken, GA-SC**		Cameron County	345
Schenectady County	146	**MSA**	480		
Schoharie County	31	Columbia County, GA	92	**Bryan-College Station, TX**	
		McDuffie County, GA	21	**MSA**	152
Albuquerque, NM MSA	723	Richmond County, GA	198	Brazos County	152
Bernalillo County	562	Aiken County, SC	144		
Sandoval County	94	Edgefield County, SC	24	**Buffalo-Niagara Falls, NY**	
Valencia County	67			**MSA**	1,163
		Austin-San Marcos, TX		Erie County	944
Alexandria, LA MSA	127	**MSA**	1,313	Niagara County	219
Rapides Parish	127	Bastrop County	62		
		Caldwell County	34	**Canton-Massillon, OH**	
Allentown-Bethlehem-		Hays County	105	**MSA**	407
Easton, PA MSA	643	Travis County	834	Carroll County	29
Carbon County	60	Williamson County	278	Stark County	377
Lehigh County	314				
Northampton County	270	**Bakersfield, CA MSA**	676	**Casper, WY MSA**	67
		Kern County	676	Natrona County	67
Altoona, PA MSA	128				
Blair County	128	**Baton Rouge, LA MSA**	608	**Cedar Rapids, IA MSA**	193
		Ascension Parish	80	Linn County	193
Amarillo, TX MSA	219	East Baton Rouge Parish	410		
Potter County	114	Livingston Parish	96	**Champaign-Urbana,**	
Randall County	106	West Baton Rouge Parish	22	**IL MSA**	180
				Champaign County	180
Anchorage, AK MSA	265	**Beaumont-Port Arthur, TX**			
Anchorage Borough	265	**MSA**	383	**Charleston-North**	
		Hardin County	49	**Charleston, SC MSA**	555
Anniston, AL MSA	111	Jefferson County	250	Berkeley County	144
Calhoun County	111	Orange County	85	Charleston County	312
				Dorchester County	99
Appleton-Oshkosh-Neenah,		**Bellingham, WA MSA**	171		
WI MSA	363	Whatcom County	171	**Charleston, WV MSA**	249
Calumet County	42			Kanawha County	197
Outagamie County	164	**Benton Harbor, MI MSA**	162	Putnam County	52
Winnebago County	157	Berrien County	162		
				Charlotte-Gastonia-Rock	
Asheville, NC MSA	229	**Billings, MT MSA**	130	**Hill, NC-SC MSA**	1,545
Buncombe County	209	Yellowstone County	130	Cabarrus County, NC	136
Madison County	20			Gaston County, NC	192
		Biloxi-Gulfport-Pascagoula,		Lincoln County, NC	65
Athens, GA MSA	155	**MS MSA**	366	Mecklenburg County, NC	716
Clarke County	102	Hancock County	44	Rowan County, NC	132
Madison County	26	Harrison County	189	Union County, NC	133
Oconee County	27	Jackson County	133	York County, SC	170
Atlanta, GA MSA	4,263	**Binghamton, NY MSA**	251	**Charlottesville, VA MSA**	162
Barrow County	49	Broome County	199	Albemarle County	80
Bartow County	80	Tioga County	52	Fluvanna County	21
Carroll County	92			Greene County	16
Cherokee County	152	**Birmingham, AL MSA**	928	Charlottesville city	44
Clayton County	247	Blount County	52		
Cobb County	632	Jefferson County	660	**Chattanooga, TN-GA MSA**	468
Coweta County	95	St. Clair County	66	Hamilton County, TN	307
DeKalb County	665	Shelby County	150	Marion County, TN	28
Douglas County	96			Catoosa County, GA	55
Fayette County	96	**Bismarck, ND MSA**	95	Dade County, GA	16
Forsyth County	110	Burleigh County	70	Walker County, GA	62
Fulton County	017	Morton County	25		

U.S. Census Bureau, Statistical Abstract of the United States: 2002

Metropolitan area and component county	Population, 2001 (1,000)	Metropolitan area and component county	Population, 2001 (1,000)	Metropolitan area and component county	Population, 2001 (1,000)
Cheyenne, WY MSA	**82**	**Columbus, OH MSA**	**1,560**	**Detroit-Ann Arbor-Flint, MI**	
Laramie County	82	Delaware County	120	**CMSA**	**5,478**
		Fairfield County	127	**Ann Arbor, MI PMSA**	**591**
Chicago-Gary-Kenosha,		Franklin County	1,072	Lenawee County	100
IL-IN-WI CMSA	**9,233**	Licking County	148	Livingston County	165
Chicago, IL PMSA	**8,342**	Madison County	40	Washtenaw County	327
Cook County, IL	5,350	Pickaway County	53	**Detroit, MI PMSA**	**4,448**
DeKalb County, IL	90			Lapeer County	90
DuPage County, IL	912	**Corpus Christi, TX MSA**	**380**	Macomb County	800
Grundy County, IL	38	Nueces County	312	Monroe County	148
Kane County, IL	426	San Patricio County	67	Oakland County	1,199
Kendall County, IL	58			St. Clair County	167
Lake County, IL	661	**Corvallis, OR MSA**	**78**	Wayne County	2,045
McHenry County, IL	271	Benton County	78	**Flint, MI PMSA**	**439**
Will County, IL	536			Genesee County	439
Gary, IN PMSA	**634**	**Cumberland, MD-WV MSA**	**101**		
Lake County, IN	485	Allegany County, MD	74	**Dothan, AL MSA**	**138**
Porter County, IN	149	Mineral County, WV	27	Dale County	49
Kankakee, IL PMSA	**104**			Houston County	89
Kankakee County, IL	104	**Dallas-Fort Worth, TX**			
Kenosha, WI PMSA	**153**	**CMSA**	**5,401**	**Dover, DE MSA**	**129**
Kenosha County, WI	153	**Dallas, TX PMSA**	**3,646**	Kent County	129
		Collin County	541		
Chico-Paradise, CA MSA	**206**	Dallas County	2,245	**Dubuque, IA MSA**	**89**
Butte County	206	Denton County	466	Dubuque County	89
		Ellis County	117		
		Henderson County	75	**Duluth, MN-WI MSA**	**243**
Cincinnati-Hamilton, OH-		Hunt County	78	St. Louis County, MN	199
KY-IN CMSA	**1,995**	Kaufman County	76	Douglas County, WI	43
Cincinnati, OH-KY-IN		Rockwall County	48		
PMSA	**1,658**	**Fort Worth-Arlington, TX**		**Eau Claire, WI MSA**	**149**
Brown County, OH	43	**PMSA**	**1,755**	Chippewa County	56
Clermont County, OH	182	Hood County	43	Eau Claire County	93
Hamilton County, OH	835	Johnson County	132		
Warren County, OH	169	Parker County	93	**El Paso, TX MSA**	**688**
Boone County, KY	90	Tarrant County	1,486	El Paso County	688
Campbell County, KY	88				
Gallatin County, KY	8			**Elkhart-Goshen, IN MSA**	**184**
Grant County, KY	23	**Danville, VA MSA**	**110**	Elkhart County	184
Kenton County, KY	151	Pittsylvania County	62		
Pendleton County, KY	15	Danville city	48	**Elmira, NY MSA**	**91**
Dearborn County, IN	47			Chemung County	91
Ohio County, IN	6	**Davenport-Moline-**			
Hamilton-Middletown, OH		**Rock Island, IA-IL MSA**	**358**	**Enid, OK MSA**	**57**
PMSA	**337**	Scott County, IA	158	Garfield County	57
Butler County, OH	337	Henry County, IL	51		
		Rock Island County, IL	148	**Erie, PA MSA**	**280**
Clarksville-Hopkinsville,				Erie County	280
TN-KY MSA	**207**	**Dayton-Springfield, OH**			
Montgomery County, TN	135	**MSA**	**946**	**Eugene-Springfield, OR**	
Christian County, KY	72	Clark County	144	**MSA**	**324**
		Greene County	148	Lane County	324
Cleveland-Akron, OH		Miami County	99		
CMSA	**2,943**	Montgomery County	554	**Evansville-Henderson,**	
Akron, OH PMSA	**697**			**IN-KY MSA**	**296**
Portage County	153	**Daytona Beach, FL MSA**	**510**	Posey County, IN	27
Summit County	544	Flagler County	55	Vanderburgh County, IN	171
Cleveland-Lorain-Elyria,		Volusia County	455	Warrick County, IN	53
OH PMSA	**2,246**			Henderson County, KY	45
Ashtabula County	103	**Decatur, AL MSA**	**146**		
Cuyahoga County	1,380	Lawrence County	35	**Fargo-Moorhead, ND-MN**	
Geauga County	92	Morgan County	111	**MSA**	**176**
Lake County	228			Cass County, ND	124
Lorain County	287	**Decatur, IL MSA**	**113**	Clay County, MN	52
Medina County	156	Macon County	113		
				Fayetteville, NC MSA	**299**
Colorado Springs, CO		**Denver-Boulder-Greeley,**		Cumberland County	299
MSA	**533**	**CO CMSA**	**2,653**		
El Paso County	533	**Boulder-Longmont, CO**		**Fayetteville-Springdale-**	
		PMSA	**298**	**Rogers, AR MSA**	**322**
Columbia, MO MSA	**137**	Boulder County	298	Benton County	160
Boone County	137	**Denver, CO PMSA**	**2,161**	Washington County	162
		Adams County	375		
Columbia, SC MSA	**544**	Arapahoe County	501	**Flagstaff, AZ-UT MSA**	**124**
Lexington County	220	Denver County	554	Coconino County, AZ	118
Richland County	323	Douglas County	200	Kane County, UT	6
		Jefferson County	531		
Columbus, GA-AL MSA	**273**	**Greeley, CO PMSA**	**195**	**Florence, AL MSA**	**143**
Chattahoochee County,		Weld County	195	Colbert County	55
GA	15	**Des Moines, IA MSA**	**463**	Lauderdale County	87
Harris County, GA	25	Dallas County	43		
Muscogee County, GA	184	Polk County	379	**Florence, SC MSA**	**127**
Russell County, AL	50	Warren County	41	Florence County	127

U.S. Census Bureau, Statistical Abstract of the United States: 2002

Metropolitan area and component county	Popu- lation, 2001 (1,000)	Metropolitan area and component county	Popu- lation, 2001 (1,000)	Metropolitan area and component county	Popu- lation, 2001 (1,000)
Fort Collins-Loveland, CO MSA	259	**Greenville-Spartanburg-Anderson, SC MSA**	978	**Jackson, TN MSA**	108
Larimer County	259	Anderson County	169	Chester County	16
		Cherokee County	53	Madison County	92
Fort Myers-Cape Coral, FL MSA	462	Greenville County	387	**Jacksonville, FL MSA**	1,131
Lee County	462	Pickens County	112	Clay County	148
		Spartanburg County	257	Duval County	792
Fort Pierce-Port St. Lucie, FL MSA	330			Nassau County	60
Martin County	130	**Harrisburg-Lebanon-Carlisle, PA MSA**	632	St. Johns County	132
St. Lucie County	200	Cumberland County	216	**Jacksonville, NC MSA**	146
		Dauphin County	251	Onslow County	146
Fort Smith, AR-OK MSA	209	Lebanon County	121		
Crawford County, AR	54	Perry County	44	**Jamestown, NY MSA**	139
Sebastian County, AR	116			Chautauqua County	139
Sequoyah County, OK	39	**Hattiesburg, MS MSA**	113		
		Forrest County	73	**Janesville-Beloit, WI MSA**	153
Fort Walton Beach, FL MSA	173	Lamar County	40	Rock County	153
Okaloosa County	173				
		Hickory-Morganton-Lenoir, NC MSA	347	**Johnson City-Kingsport-Bristol, TN-VA MSA**	482
Fort Wayne, IN MSA	504	Alexander County	34	Carter County, TN	57
Adams County	33	Burke County	89	Hawkins County, TN	54
Allen County	334	Caldwell County	78	Sullivan County, TN	153
De Kalb County	40	Catawba County	145	Unicoi County, TN	18
Huntington County	38			Washington County, TN	108
Wells County	28	**Honolulu, HI MSA**	881	Scott County, VA	23
Whitley County	31	Honolulu County	881	Washington County, VA	51
				Bristol city, VA	17
Fresno, CA MSA	942	**Houma, LA MSA**	195		
Fresno County	816	Lafourche Parish	90	**Johnstown, PA MSA**	230
Madera County	126	Terrebonne Parish	105	Cambria County	151
				Somerset County	80
Gadsden, AL MSA	103	**Houston-Galveston-Brazoria, TX CMSA**	4,796		
Etowah County	103	**Brazoria, TX PMSA**	250	**Jonesboro, AR MSA**	83
		Brazoria County	250	Craighead County	83
Gainesville, FL MSA	219	**Galveston-Texas City, TX PMSA**	256		
Alachua County	219	Galveston County	256	**Joplin, MO MSA**	159
		Houston, TX PMSA	4,290	Jasper County	106
Glens Falls, NY MSA	125	Chambers County	27	Newton County	53
Warren County	64	Fort Bend County	381		
Washington County	61	Harris County	3,461	**Kalamazoo-Battle Creek, MI MSA**	453
		Liberty County	73	Calhoun County	138
Goldsboro, NC MSA	113	Montgomery County	315	Kalamazoo County	239
Wayne County	113	Waller County	34	Van Buren County	77
Grand Forks, ND-MN MSA	96	**Huntington-Ashland, WV-KY-OH MSA**	314	**Kansas City, MO-KS MSA**	1,803
Grand Forks County, ND	64	Cabell County, WV	96	Cass County, MO	86
Polk County, MN	31	Wayne County, WV	43	Clay County, MO	188
		Boyd County, KY	50	Clinton County, MO	20
Grand Junction, CO MSA	119	Carter County, KY	27	Jackson County, MO	656
Mesa County	119	Greenup County, KY	37	Lafayette County, MO	33
		Lawrence County, OH	62	Platte County, MO	76
Grand Rapids-Muskegon-Holland, MI MSA	1,103			Ray County, MO	23
Allegan County	108	**Huntsville, AL MSA**	349	Johnson County, KS	465
Kent County	580	Limestone County	67	Leavenworth County, KS	70
Muskegon County	171	Madison County	282	Miami County, KS	29
Ottawa County	244			Wyandotte County, KS	157
		Indianapolis, IN MSA	1,632		
Great Falls, MT MSA	79	Boone County	47	**Killeen-Temple, TX MSA**	314
Cascade County	79	Hamilton County	197	Bell County	240
		Hancock County	57	Coryell County	74
Green Bay, WI MSA	229	Hendricks County	111		
Brown County	229	Johnson County	119	**Knoxville, TN MSA**	698
		Madison County	132	Anderson County	71
Greensboro-Winston-Salem-High Point, NC MSA	1,269	Marion County	857	Blount County	108
Alamance County	133	Morgan County	68	Knox County	386
Davidson County	150	Shelby County	44	Loudon County	40
Davie County	36			Sevier County	74
Forsyth County	310	**Iowa City, IA MSA**	111	Union County	18
Guilford County	425	Johnson County	111		
Randolph County	132			**Kokomo, IN MSA**	101
Stokes County	45	**Jackson, MI MSA**	160	Howard County	85
Yadkin County	37	Jackson County	160	Tipton County	17
Greenville, NC MSA	135	**Jackson, MS MSA**	445	**La Crosse, WI-MN MSA**	120
Pitt County	135	Hinds County	210	La Crosse County, WI	108
		Madison County	77	Houston County, MN	20
		Rankin County	119		

U.S. Census Bureau, Statistical Abstract of the United States: 2002

Metropolitan area and component county	Popu-lation, 2001 (1,000)
Lafayette, LA MSA	387
Acadia Parish	59
Lafayette Parish	191
St. Landry Parish	88
St. Martin Parish	49
Lafayette, IN MSA	183
Clinton County	34
Tippecanoe County	149
Lake Charles, LA MSA	183
Calcasieu Parish	183
Lakeland-Winter Haven, FL MSA	493
Polk County	493
Lancaster, PA MSA	475
Lancaster County	475
Lansing-East Lansing, MI MSA	449
Clinton County	66
Eaton County	105
Ingham County	278
Laredo, TX MSA	201
Webb County	201
Las Cruces, NM MSA	177
Dona Ana County	177
Las Vegas, NV-AZ MSA	1,661
Clark County, NV	1,465
Nye County, NV	34
Mohave County, AZ	162
Lawrence, KS MSA	100
Douglas County	100
Lawton, OK MSA	112
Comanche County	112
Lexington, KY MSA	484
Bourbon County	19
Clark County	33
Fayette County	260
Jessamine County	40
Madison County	72
Scott County	35
Woodford County	23
Lima, OH MSA	155
Allen County	108
Auglaize County	47
Lincoln, NE MSA	252
Lancaster County	252
Little Rock-North Little Rock, AR MSA	590
Faulkner County	88
Lonoke County	54
Pulaski County	362
Saline County	86
Longview-Marshall, TX MSA	210
Gregg County	112
Harrison County	62
Upshur County	36
Los Angeles-Riverside-Orange County, CA CMSA	16,701
Los Angeles-Long Beach, CA PMSA	9,637
Los Angeles County	9,637
Orange County, CA PMSA	2,890
Orange County	2,890
Riverside-San Bernardino, CA PMSA	3,402
Riverside County	1,636
San Bernardino County	1,766
Ventura, CA PMSA	771
Ventura County	771

Metropolitan area and component county	Popu-lation, 2001 (1,000)
Louisville, KY-IN MSA	1,031
Bullitt County, KY	63
Jefferson County, KY	693
Oldham County, KY	48
Clark County, IN	97
Floyd County, IN	71
Harrison County, IN	35
Scott County, IN	23
Lubbock, TX MSA	244
Lubbock County	244
Lynchburg, VA MSA	215
Amherst County	32
Bedford County	61
Campbell County	51
Bedford city	6
Lynchburg city	64
Macon, GA MSA	326
Bibb County	154
Houston County	113
Jones County	24
Peach County	24
Twiggs County	11
Madison, WI MSA	433
Dane County	433
Mansfield, OH MSA	175
Crawford County	47
Richland County	128
McAllen-Edinburg-Mission, TX MSA	590
Hidalgo County	590
Medford-Ashland, OR MSA	185
Jackson County	185
Melbourne-Titusville-Palm Bay, FL MSA	490
Brevard County	490
Memphis, TN-AR-MS MSA	1,145
Fayette County, TN	31
Shelby County, TN	896
Tipton County, TN	53
Crittenden County, AR	51
DeSoto County, MS	114
Merced, CA MSA	219
Merced County	219
Miami-Fort Lauderdale, FL CMSA	3,958
Fort Lauderdale, FL PMSA	1,669
Broward County	1,669
Miami, FL PMSA	2,290
Miami-Dade County	2,290
Milwaukee-Racine, WI CMSA	1,692
Milwaukee-Waukesha, WI PMSA	1,502
Milwaukee County	932
Ozaukee County	84
Washington County	120
Waukesha County	367
Racine, WI PMSA	190
Racine County	190
Minneapolis-St. Paul, MN-WI MSA	3,016
Anoka County, MN	306
Carver County, MN	73
Chisago County, MN	43
Dakota County, MN	364
Hennepin County, MN	1,115
Isanti County, MN	33
Ramsey County, MN	509
Scott County, MN	98
Sherburne County, MN	69
Washington County, MN	208
Wright County, MN	95

Metropolitan area and component county	Popu-lation, 2001 (1,000)
Pierce County, WI	37
St. Croix County, WI	66
Missoula, MT MSA	96
Missoula County	96
Mobile, AL MSA	546
Baldwin County	146
Mobile County	400
Modesto, CA MSA	469
Stanislaus County	469
Monroe, LA MSA	147
Ouachita Parish	147
Montgomery, AL MSA	334
Autauga County	45
Elmore County	67
Montgomery County	222
Muncie, IN MSA	119
Delaware County	119
Myrtle Beach, SC MSA	202
Horry County	202
Naples, FL MSA	266
Collier County	266
Nashville, TN MSA	1,252
Cheatham County	37
Davidson County	565
Dickson County	44
Robertson County	56
Rutherford County	190
Sumner County	134
Williamson County	134
Wilson County	92
New Orleans, LA MSA	1,333
Jefferson Parish	451
Orleans Parish	476
Plaquemines Parish	27
St. Bernard Parish	66
St. Charles Parish	49
St. James Parish	21
St. John the Baptist Parish	44
St. Tammany Parish	198
New York-Northern New Jersey-Long Island, NY-NJ-CT-PA CMSA [1]	19,504
Bergen-Passaic, NJ PMSA	1,378
Bergen County, NJ	887
Passaic County, NJ	491
Dutchess County, NY PMSA	284
Dutchess County, NY	284
Jersey City, NJ PMSA	608
Hudson County, NJ	608
Middlesex-Somerset-Hunterdon, NJ PMSA	1,184
Hunterdon County, NJ	125
Middlesex County, NJ	757
Somerset County, NJ	302
Monmouth-Ocean, NJ PMSA	1,150
Monmouth County, NJ	623
Ocean County, NJ	527
Nassau-Suffolk, NY PMSA	2,774
Nassau County, NY	1,335
Suffolk County, NY	1,439
New York, NY PMSA	9,334
Bronx County, NY	1,338
Kings County, NY	2,465
New York County, NY	1,541
Putnam County, NY	97
Queens County, NY	2,225
Richmond County, NY	450
Rockland County, NY	289
Westchester County, NY	929

U.S. Census Bureau, Statistical Abstract of the United States: 2002

Metropolitan area and component county	Population, 2001 (1,000)	Metropolitan area and component county	Population, 2001 (1,000)	Metropolitan area and component county	Population, 2001 (1,000)
Newark, NJ PMSA	**2,042**	**Philadelphia, PA-NJ**		**Richmond-Petersburg, VA**	
Essex County, NJ	793	**PMSA**	**5,117**	**MSA**	**1,010**
Morris County, NJ	473	Bucks County, PA	605	Charles City County	7
Sussex County, NJ	147	Chester County, PA	443	Chesterfield County	267
Union County, NJ	523	Delaware County, PA	551	Dinwiddie County	25
Warren County, NJ	106	Montgomery County, PA	760	Goochland County	17
Newburgh, NY-PA		Philadelphia County, PA	1,492	Hanover County	90
PMSA	**397**	Burlington County, NJ	432	Henrico County	265
Orange County, NY	349	Camden County, NJ	509	New Kent County	14
Pike County, PA	49	Gloucester County, NJ	259	Powhatan County	23
Trenton, NJ PMSA	**354**	Salem County, NJ	64	Prince George County	34
Mercer County, NJ	354	**Vineland-Millville-**		Colonial Heights city	17
		Bridgeton, NJ PMSA	**146**	Hopewell city	22
Norfolk-Virginia Beach-		Cumberland County, NJ	146	Petersburg city	33
Newport News, VA-NC		**Wilmington-Newark,**		Richmond city	196
MSA	**1,583**	**DE-MD PMSA**	**595**		
Gloucester County, VA	35	New Castle County, DE	506	**Roanoke, VA MSA**	**236**
Isle of Wight County, VA	31	Cecil County, MD	89	Botetourt County	31
James City County, VA	50			Roanoke County	86
Mathews County, VA	9	**Phoenix-Mesa, AZ MSA**	**3,384**	Roanoke city	94
York County, VA	58	Maricopa County	3,195	Salem city	25
Chesapeake city, VA	204	Pinal County	189		
Hampton city, VA	146			**Rochester, MN MSA**	**126**
Newport News city, VA	180	**Pine Bluff, AR MSA**	**84**	Olmsted County	126
Norfolk city, VA	233	Jefferson County	84		
Poquoson city, VA	12			**Rochester, NY MSA**	**1,097**
Portsmouth city, VA	99	**Pittsburgh, PA MSA**	**2,347**	Genesee County	60
Suffolk city, VA	67	Allegheny County	1,271	Livingston County	64
Virginia Beach city, VA	427	Beaver County	180	Monroe County	734
Williamsburg city, VA	12	Butler County	177	Ontario County	101
Currituck County, NC	19	Fayette County	147	Orleans County	44
		Washington County	204	Wayne County	94
Ocala, FL MSA	**268**	Westmoreland County	369		
Marion County	268			**Rockford, IL MSA**	**375**
		Pocatello, ID MSA	**75**	Boone County	43
Odessa-Midland, TX MSA	**238**	Bannock County	75	Ogle County	52
Ector County	121			Winnebago County	280
Midland County	116	**Portland-Salem, OR-WA**			
		CMSA	**2,317**	**Rocky Mount, NC MSA**	**143**
Oklahoma City, OK MSA	**1,092**	**Portland-Vancouver,**		Edgecombe County	55
Canadian County	90	**OR-WA PMSA**	**1,965**	Nash County	88
Cleveland County	212	Clackamas County, OR	347		
Logan County	34	Columbia County, OR	45	**Sacramento-Yolo, CA**	
McClain County	28	Multnomah County, OR	666	**CMSA**	**1,875**
Oklahoma County	662	Washington County, OR	461	**Sacramento, CA**	
Pottawatomie County	66	Yamhill County, OR	87	**PMSA**	**1,700**
		Clark County, WA	361	El Dorado County	163
Omaha, NE-IA MSA	**723**	**Salem, OR PMSA**	**352**	Placer County	269
Cass County, NE	25	Marion County, OR	288	Sacramento County	1,269
Douglas County, NE	466	Polk County, OR	64	**Yolo, CA PMSA**	**175**
Sarpy County, NE	126			Yolo County	175
Washington County, NE	19	**Provo-Orem, UT MSA**	**377**		
Pottawattamie County, IA	88	Utah County	377	**Saginaw-Bay City-**	
				Midland, MI MSA	**403**
Orlando, FL MSA	**1,707**	**Pueblo, CO MSA**	**145**	Bay County	110
Lake County	228	Pueblo County	145	Midland County	84
Orange County	923			Saginaw County	209
Osceola County	182	**Punta Gorda, FL MSA**	**147**		
Seminole County	374	Charlotte County	147	**St. Cloud, MN MSA**	**170**
				Benton County	35
Owensboro, KY MSA	**92**	**Raleigh-Durham-Chapel**		Stearns County	135
Daviess County	92	**Hill, NC MSA**	**1,232**		
		Chatham County	52	**St. Joseph, MO MSA**	**102**
Panama City, FL MSA	**150**	Durham County	227	Andrew County	17
Bay County	150	Franklin County	49	Buchanan County	85
		Johnston County	128		
Parkersburg-Marietta,		Orange County	120	**St. Louis, MO-IL MSA**	**2,618**
WV-OH MSA	**151**	Wake County	656	Franklin County, MO	95
Wood County, WV	88			Jefferson County, MO	202
Washington County, OH	63	**Rapid City, SD MSA**	**90**	Lincoln County, MO	41
		Pennington County	90	St. Charles County, MO	297
Pensacola, FL MSA	**416**			St. Louis County, MO	1,015
Escambia County	293	**Reading, PA MSA**	**378**	Warren County, MO	25
Santa Rosa County	123	Berks County	378	St. Louis city, MO	339
				Clinton County, IL	36
Peoria-Pekin, IL MSA	**346**	**Redding, CA MSA**	**168**	Jersey County, IL	22
Peoria County	182	Shasta County	168	Madison County, IL	260
Tazewell County	128			Monroe County, IL	29
Woodford County	36	**Reno, NV MSA**	**353**	St. Clair County, IL	257
		Washoe County	353		
Philadelphia-Wilmington-				**Salinas, CA MSA**	**408**
Atlantic City, PA-NJ-DE-		**Richland-Kennewick-Pasco,**		Monterey County	408
MD CMSA	**6,216**	**WA MSA**	**198**		
Atlantic-Cape May, NJ		Benton County	147		
PMSA	**358**	Franklin County	51		
Atlantic County, NJ	255				
Cape May County, NJ	102				

914   Appendix II

Metropolitan area and component county	Popu-lation, 2001 (1,000)	Metropolitan area and component county	Popu-lation, 2001 (1,000)	Metropolitan area and component county	Popu-lation, 2001 (1,000)
Salt Lake City-Ogden, UT MSA	**1,349**	**Seattle-Bellevue-Everett, WA PMSA**	**2,439**	**Terre Haute, IN MSA**	**148**
Davis County	245	Island County	74	Clay County	27
Salt Lake County	904	King County	1,742	Vermillion County	17
Weber County	199	Snohomish County	623	Vigo County	105
		Tacoma, WA PMSA	**719**		
San Angelo, TX MSA	**103**	Pierce County	719	**Texarkana, TX-Texarkana, AR MSA**	**131**
Tom Green County	103			Bowie County, TX	90
		Sharon, PA MSA	**120**	Miller County, AR	41
San Antonio, TX MSA	**1,627**	Mercer County	120		
Bexar County	1,418			**Toledo, OH MSA**	**618**
Comal County	83	**Sheboygan, WI MSA**	**113**	Fulton County	42
Guadalupe County	93	Sheboygan County	113	Lucas County	453
Wilson County	34			Wood County	122
		Sherman-Denison, TX MSA	**113**		
San Diego, CA MSA	**2,863**	Grayson County	113	**Topeka, KS MSA**	**170**
San Diego County	2,863			Shawnee County	170
		Shreveport-Bossier City, LA MSA	**392**		
San Francisco-Oakland-San Jose, CA CMSA	**7,073**	Bossier Parish	99	**Tucson, AZ MSA**	**863**
Oakland, CA PMSA	**2,434**	Caddo Parish	251	Pima County	863
Alameda County	1,458	Webster Parish	41		
Contra Costa County	976			**Tulsa, OK MSA**	**811**
San Francisco, CA PMSA	**1,720**	**Sioux City, IA-NE MSA**	**123**	Creek County	68
Marin County	248	Woodbury County, IA.	103	Osage County	45
San Francisco County	771	Dakota County, NE	20	Rogers County	74
San Mateo County	702			Tulsa County	564
San Jose, CA PMSA	**1,668**	**Sioux Falls, SD MSA**	**177**	Wagoner County	59
Santa Clara County	1,668	Lincoln County	26		
Santa Cruz-Watsonville, CA PMSA	**255**	Minnehaha County	150	**Tuscaloosa, AL MSA**	**165**
Santa Cruz County	255			Tuscaloosa County	165
Santa Rosa, CA PMSA	**464**	**South Bend, IN MSA**	**265**		
Sonoma County	464	St. Joseph County	265	**Tyler, TX MSA**	**179**
Vallejo-Fairfield-Napa, CA PMSA	**532**			Smith County	179
Napa County	128	**Spokane, WA MSA**	**423**		
Solano County	404	Spokane County	423	**Utica-Rome, NY MSA**	**298**
				Herkimer County	64
San Luis Obispo-Atascadero-Paso Robles, CA MSA	**251**	**Springfield, IL MSA**	**202**	Oneida County	234
San Luis Obispo County	251	Menard County	13		
		Sangamon County	189	**Victoria, TX MSA**	**85**
Santa Barbara-Santa Maria-Lompoc, CA MSA	**400**	**Springfield, MO MSA**	**331**	Victoria County	85
Santa Barbara County	400	Christian County	57	**Visalia-Tulare-Porterville, CA MSA**	**374**
		Greene County	242	Tulare County	374
Santa Fe, NM MSA	**149**	Webster County	32		
Los Alamos County	18			**Waco, TX MSA**	**215**
Santa Fe County	131	**State College, PA MSA**	**136**	McLennan County	215
		Centre County	136		
Sarasota-Bradenton, FL MSA	**610**			**Washington-Baltimore, DC-MD-VA-WV CMSA**	**7,760**
Manatee County	275	**Steubenville-Weirton, OH-WV MSA**	**130**	**Baltimore, MD PMSA**	**2,573**
Sarasota County	335	Jefferson County, OH	73	Anne Arundel County, MD	498
		Brooke County, WV	25	Baltimore County, MD	762
Savannah, GA MSA	**296**	Hancock County, WV	32	Carroll County, MD	156
Bryan County	25			Harford County, MD	224
Chatham County	232	**Stockton-Lodi, CA MSA**	**595**	Howard County, MD	256
Effingham County	40	San Joaquin County	595	Queen Anne's County, MD	42
				Baltimore city, MD	635
Scranton—Wilkes-Barre—Hazleton, PA MSA	**620**	**Sumter, SC MSA**	**104**	**Hagerstown, MD PMSA**	**133**
Columbia County	64	Sumter County	104	Washington County, MD	133
Lackawanna County	212			**Washington, DC-MD-VA-WV PMSA**	**5,054**
Luzerne County	316	**Syracuse, NY MSA**	**731**	District of Columbia, DC.	572
Wyoming County	28	Cayuga County	81	Calvert County, MD	78
		Madison County	70	Charles County, MD	125
Seattle-Tacoma-Bremerton, WA CMSA	**3,605**	Onondaga County	458	Frederick County, MD	204
Bremerton, WA PMSA	**233**	Oswego County	122	Montgomery County, MD	891
Kitsap County	233			Prince George's County, MD	817
Olympia, WA PMSA	**214**	**Tallahassee, FL MSA**	**285**	Arlington County, VA	187
Thurston County	214	Gadsden County	45	Clarke County, VA	13
		Leon County	239	Culpeper County, VA	36
		Tampa-St. Petersburg-Clearwater, FL MSA	**2,450**	Fairfax County, VA	985
		Hernando County	136	Fauquier County, VA	58
		Hillsborough County	1,027	King George County, VA.	17
		Pasco County	363	Loudoun County, VA	191
		Pinellas County	925		

U.S. Census Bureau, Statistical Abstract of the United States: 2002

Metropolitan area and component county	Population, 2001 (1,000)	Metropolitan area and component county	Population, 2001 (1,000)	Metropolitan area and component county	Population, 2001 (1,000)
Prince William County, VA	299	**West Palm Beach-Boca Raton, FL MSA**	**1,165**	**Wilmington, NC MSA**	**241**
Spotsylvania County, VA	98	Palm Beach County	1,165	Brunswick County	77
Stafford County, VA	100			New Hanover County	163
Warren County, VA	32	**Wheeling, WV-OH MSA**	**151**	**Yakima, WA MSA**	**224**
Alexandria city, VA	129	Marshall County, WV	35	Yakima County	224
Fairfax city, VA	22	Ohio County, WV	47		
Falls Church city, VA	11	Belmont County, OH	69	**York, PA MSA**	**386**
Fredericksburg city, VA	20			York County	386
Manassas city, VA	36	**Wichita, KS MSA**	**549**	**Youngstown-Warren, OH MSA**	**591**
Manassas Park city, VA	11	Butler County	60	Columbiana County	112
Berkeley County, WV	79	Harvey County	33	Mahoning County	255
Jefferson County, WV	44	Sedgwick County	456	Trumbull County	224
Waterloo-Cedar Falls, IA MSA	**126**	**Wichita Falls, TX MSA**	**137**	**Yuba City, CA MSA**	**141**
Black Hawk County	126	Archer County	9	Sutter County	81
		Wichita County	128	Yuba County	61
Wausau, WI MSA	**126**	**Williamsport, PA MSA**	**119**	**Yuma, AZ MSA**	**165**
Marathon County	126	Lycoming County	119	Yuma County	165

[1] Five PMSAs of the New York-Northern New Jersey-Long Island, NY-NJ-CT-PA CMSA are in Connecticut and therefore do not appear in this table; also the CMSA's population shown here reflects the absence of those PMSAs.

Source: U.S. Census Bureau, "Time Series of Population Estimates by County: April 1, 2000 to July 1, 2001"; published 23 May 2002; <http://eire.census.gov/popest/data/counties/tables/CO-EST2001-07.php>.

Appendix III
Limitations of the Data

Introduction—The data presented in this *Statistical Abstract* came from many sources. The sources include not only Federal statistical bureaus and other organizations that collect and issue statistics as their principal activity, but also governmental administrative and regulatory agencies, private research bodies, trade associations, insurance companies, health associations, and private organizations such as the National Education Association and philanthropic foundations. Consequently, the data vary considerably as to reference periods, definitions of terms and, for ongoing series, the number and frequency of time periods for which data are available.

The statistics presented were obtained and tabulated by various means. Some statistics are based on complete enumerations or censuses while others are based on samples. Some information is extracted from records kept for administrative or regulatory purposes (school enrollment, hospital records, securities registration, financial accounts, social security records, income tax returns, etc.), while other information is obtained explicitly for statistical purposes through interviews or by mail. The estimation procedures used vary from highly sophisticated scientific techniques, to crude "informed guesses."

Each set of data relates to a group of individuals or units of interest referred to as the *target universe* or *target population*, or simply as the *universe* or *population*. Prior to data collection the target universe should be clearly defined. For example, if data are to be collected for the universe of households in the United States, it is necessary to define a "household." The target universe may not be completely tractable. Cost and other considerations may restrict data collection to a *survey universe* based on some available list, such list may be it of date. This list is called a *survey frame* or *sampling frame*.

The data in many tables are based on data obtained for all population units, *a census,* or on data obtained for only a portion, or *sample,* of the population units. When the data presented are based on a sample, the sample is usually a scientifically selected *probability sample.* This is a sample selected from a list or sampling frame in such a way that every possible sample has a known chance of selection and usually each unit selected can be assigned a number, greater than zero and less than or equal to one, representing its likelihood or probability of selection.

For large-scale sample surveys, the probability sample of units is often selected as a multistage sample. The first stage of a multistage sample is the selection of a probability sample of large groups of population members, referred to as primary sampling units (PSUs). For example, in a national multistage household sample, PSUs are often counties or groups of counties. The second stage of a multistage sample is the selection, within each PSU selected at the first stage, of smaller groups of population units, referred to as secondary sampling units. In subsequent stages of selection, smaller and smaller nested groups are chosen until the ultimate sample of population units is obtained. To qualify a multistage sample as a probability sample, all stages of sampling must be carried out using probability sampling methods.

Prior to selection at each stage of a multistage (or a single stage) sample, a list of the sampling units or sampling frame for that stage must be obtained. For example, for the first stage of selection of a national household sample, a list of the counties and county groups that form the PSUs must be obtained. For the final stage of selection, lists of households, and sometimes persons within the households, have to be compiled in the field. For surveys of economic entities and for the economic censuses the Bureau generally uses a frame constructed from the Bureau's Business Register. The Business Register contains all establishments with payroll in the United States including small single establishment firms as well as large multi-establishment firms.

Wherever the quantities in a table refer to an entire universe, but are constructed from data collected in a sample survey, the table quantities are referred to as *sample estimates*. In constructing a sample estimate, an attempt is made to come as close as is feasible to the corresponding universe quantity that would be obtained from a complete census of the universe. Estimates based on a sample will, however, generally differ from the hypothetical census figures. Two classifications of errors are associated with estimates based on sample surveys: (1) *sampling error*—the error arising from the use of a sample, rather than a census, to estimate population quantities and (2) *nonsampling error*—those errors arising from nonsampling sources. As discussed below, the magnitude of the sampling error for an estimate can usually be estimated from the sample data. However, the magnitude of the nonsampling error for an estimate can rarely be estimated. Consequently, actual error in an estimate exceeds the error that can be estimated.

The particular sample used in a survey is only one of a large number of possible samples of the same size which could have been selected using the same sampling procedure. Estimates derived from the different samples would, in general, differ from each other. The *standard error* (SE) is a measure of the variation among the estimates derived from all possible samples. The standard error is the most commonly used measure of the sampling error of an estimate. Valid estimates of the standard errors of survey estimates can usually be calculated from the data collected in a probability sample. For convenience, the standard error is sometimes expressed as a percent of the estimate and is called the relative standard error or *coefficient of variation* (CV). For example, an estimate of 200 units with an estimated standard error of 10 units has an estimated CV of 5 percent.

A sample estimate and an estimate of its standard error or CV can be used to construct interval estimates that have a prescribed confidence that the interval includes the average of the estimates derived from all possible samples with a known probability. To illustrate, if all possible samples were selected under essentially the same general conditions, and using the same sample design, and if an estimate and its estimated standard error were calculated from each sample, then: 1) Approximately 68 percent of the intervals from one standard error below the estimate to one standard error above the estimate would include the average estimate derived from all possible samples; 2) approximately 90 percent of the intervals from 1.6 standard errors below the estimate to 1.6 standard errors above the estimate would include the average estimate derived from all possible samples; and 3) approximately 95 percent of the intervals from two standard errors below the estimate to two standard errors above the estimate would include the average estimate derived from all possible samples.

Thus, for a particular sample, one can say with the appropriate level of confidence (e.g., 90 percent or 95 percent) that the average of all possible samples is included in the constructed interval. Example of a confidence interval: An estimate is 200 units with a standard error of 10 units. An approximately 90 percent confidence interval (plus or minus 1.6 standard errors) is from 184 to 216.

All surveys and censuses are subject to nonsampling errors. Nonsampling errors are of two kinds—*random* and *nonrandom*. Random nonsampling errors arise because of the varying interpretation of questions (by respondents or interviewers) and varying actions of coders, keyers, and other processors. Some randomness is also introduced when respondents must estimate. Nonrandom nonsampling errors result from total nonresponse (no usable data obtained for a sampled unit), partial or item nonresponse (only a portion of a response may be usable), inability or unwillingness on the part of respondents to provide correct information, difficulty interpreting questions, mistakes

U.S. Census Bureau, Statistical Abstract of the United States: 2002

in recording or keying data, errors of collection or processing, and coverage problems (overcoverage and undercoverage of the target universe). Random nonresponse errors usually, but not always, result in an understatement of sampling errors and thus an overstatement of the precision of survey estimates. Estimating the magnitude of nonsampling errors would require special experiments or access to independent data and, consequently, the magnitudes are seldom available.

Nearly all types of nonsampling errors that affect surveys also occur in complete censuses. Since surveys can be conducted on a smaller scale than censuses, nonsampling errors can presumably be controlled more tightly. Relatively more funds and effort can perhaps be expended toward eliciting responses, detecting and correcting response error, and reducing processing errors. As a result, survey results can sometimes be more accurate than census results.

To compensate for suspected nonrandom errors, adjustments of the sample estimates are often made. For example, adjustments are frequently made for nonresponse, both total and partial. Adjustments made for either type of nonresponse are often referred to as *imputations*. Imputation for total nonresponse is usually made by substituting for the questionnaire responses of the nonrespondents the "average" questionnaire responses of the respondents. These imputations usually are made separately within various groups of sample members, formed by attempting to place respondents and nonrespondents together that have "similar" design or ancillary characteristics. Imputation for item nonresponse is usually made by substituting for a missing item the response to that item of a respondent having characteristics that are "similar" to those of the nonrespondent.

For an estimate calculated from a sample survey, the *total error* in the estimate is composed of the sampling error, which can usually be estimated from the sample, and the nonsampling error, which usually cannot be estimated from the

sample. The total error present in a population quantity obtained from a complete census is composed of only nonsampling errors. Ideally, estimates of the total error associated with data given in the *Statistical Abstract* tables should be given. However, due to the unavailability of estimates of nonsampling errors, only estimates of the levels of sampling errors, in terms of estimated standard errors or coefficients of variation, are available. To obtain estimates of the estimated standard errors from the sample of interest, obtain a copy of the referenced report which appears at the end of each table.

Principal data bases—Beginning below are brief descriptions of 41 of the sample surveys and censuses that provide a substantial portion of the data contained in this *Abstract*.

U.S. DEPARTMENT OF AGRICULTURE, National Agriculture Statistics Service

Census of Agriculture

Universe, Frequency, and Types of Data: Complete count of U.S. farms and ranches conducted once every 5 years with data at the national, state, and county level. Data published on farm numbers and related items/ characteristics.

Type of Data Collection Operation: Complete census for— number of farms; land in farms; estimated market value of land and buildings, agriculture products sold; total cropland; irrigated land; farm operator characteristics; livestock and poultry inventory and sales; and selected crops harvested. Total farm production expenses, machinery and equipment, fertilizer and chemicals, and farm labor are estimated from a sample of farms.

Data Collection and Imputation Procedures: Data collection is by mailing questionnaires to all farmers and ranchers. Nonrespondents are contacted by telephone and correspondence followups. Imputations were made for all nonresponse item/characteristics.

Estimates of Sampling Error: Variability in the estimates is due to the sample selection and estimation for items collected

U.S. Census Bureau, Statistical Abstract of the United States: 2002

by sample and census nonresponse estimation procedures. The CVs for national and state estimates are generally very small. Approximately 85 percent response rate.

Other (nonsampling) Errors: Nonsampling errors are due to incompleteness of the census mailing list, duplications on the list, respondent reporting errors, errors in editing reported data, and in imputation for missing data. Evaluation studies are conducted to measure certain nonsampling errors such as list coverage and classification error. Results from the evaluation program for the 1997 census indicate the net under coverage amounted to about 13 percent of the nations total farms.

Sources of Additional Material: U.S. Department of Agriculture (NASS), *1997 Census of Agriculture,* Volume 2, Subject Series—Part 1, *Agriculture Atlas of the U.S.;* Part 2, *Coverage Evaluation;* Part 3, *Rankings of States and Counties;* Part 4, *History;* Part 5, *ZIP Code Tabulation of Selected Items;* and Volume 3 *Special Studies,* Part 1, *Farm and Ranch Irrigation Survey;* Part 2, *Census of Horticultural Specialities;* Part 3, *Census of Aquaculture.*

Basic Area Frame Sample

Universe, Frequency, and Types of Data: June agricultural survey collects data on planted acreage and livestock inventories. The survey also serves to measure list incompleteness and is subsampled for multiple frame surveys.

Type of Data Collection Operation: Stratified probability sample of about 11,000 land area units of about 1 sq. mile (range from 0.1 sq. mile in cities to several sq. miles in open grazing areas). Sample includes 42,000 parcels of agricultural land. About 20 percent of the sample replaced annually.

Data Collection and Imputation Procedures: Data collection is by personal enumeration. Imputation is based on enumerator observation or data reported by respondents having similar agricultural characteristics.

Estimates of Sampling Error: Estimated CVs range from 1 percent to 2 percent for regional estimates to 3 percent to 6 percent for state estimates of major crop acres and livestock inventories.

Other (nonsampling) Errors: Minimized through rigid quality controls on the collection process and careful review of all reported data.

Sources of Additional Material: U.S. Department of Agriculture, SRS, *Scope and Methods of the Statistical Reporting Service,* (name changed to National Agricultural Statistics Service), Miscellaneous Publication No. 1308, September 1983 (revised).

Multiple Frame Surveys

Universe, Frequency, and Types of Data: Surveys of U.S. farm operators to obtain data on major livestock inventories, selected crop acreage and production, grain stocks, and farm labor characteristics; farm economic data and chemical use data.

Type of Data Collection Operation: Primary frame is obtained from general or special purpose lists, supplemented by a probability sample of land areas used to estimate for list incompleteness.

Data Collection and Imputation Procedures: Mail, telephone, or personal interviews used for initial data collection. Mail nonrespondent followup by phone and personal interviews. Imputation based on average of respondents.

Estimates of Sampling Error: Estimated CV for number of hired farm workers is about 3 percent. Estimated CVs range from 1 percent to 2 percent for regional estimates to 3 percent to 6 percent for state estimates of livestock inventories and crop acreage.

Other (nonsampling) Errors: In addition to above, replicated sampling procedures used to monitor effects of changes in survey procedures.

Sources of Additional Material: U.S. Department of Agriculture, SRS, *Scope and Methods of the Statistical Reporting Service,* (name changed to National Agricultural Statistics Service), Miscellaneous Publication No. 1308, September 1983 (revised).

Objective Yield Surveys

Universe, Frequency, and Types of Data: Surveys for data on corn, cotton, potatoes, soybeans, and wheat, to forecast and estimate yields.

Type of Data Collection Operation: Random location of plots in probability sample. Corn, cotton, soybeans, spring wheat, and durum wheat selected in June from Basic Area Frame Sample (see above). Winter wheat and potatoes selected from March and June multiple frame surveys, respectively.

Data Collection and Imputation Procedures: Enumerators count and measure plant characteristics in sample fields. Production measured from plots at harvest. Harvest loss measured from post harvest gleanings.

Estimates of Sampling Error: CVs for national estimates of production are about 2-3 percent.

Other (nonsampling) Errors: In addition to above, replicated sampling procedures used to monitor effects of changes in survey procedures.

Sources of Additional Material: U.S. Department of Agriculture, SRS, *Scope and Methods of the Statistical Reporting Service,* (name changed to National Agricultural Statistics Service), Miscellaneous Publication No. 1308, September 1983 (revised).

U.S. CENSUS BUREAU

County Business Patterns

Universe, Frequency, and Types of Data: Annual tabulation of basic data items extracted from the Business Register, a file of all known single and multi establishment companies maintained and updated by the Census Bureau. Data include number of establishments, number of employees, first quarter and annual payrolls, and number of establishments by employment size class. Data are excluded for self-employed persons, domestic service workers, railroad employees, agricultural production workers, and most government employees.

Type of Data Collection Operation: The annual Company Organization Survey provides individual establishment data for multi establishment companies. Data for single establishment companies are obtained from various Census Bureau programs, such as the Annual Survey of

Manufactures and Current Business Surveys, as well as from administrative records of the Internal Revenue Service and the Social Security Administration.

Estimates of Sampling Error: Not Applicable. Other (nonsampling) Error: Response rates of greater than 85 percent for the 2000 Company Organization Survey.

Sources of Additional Materials: U.S. Census Bureau, General Explanation of County Business Patterns.

Census of Manufactures

Universe, Frequency, and Types of Data: Conducted every 5 years to obtain information on labor, materials, capital input and output characteristics, plant location, and legal form of organization for all plants in the United States with one or more paid employees. Universe was 365,000 manufacturing establishments in 1997.

Type of Data Collection Operation: Complete enumeration of data items obtained from 210,000 firms. Administrative records from Internal Revenue Service (IRS) and Social Security Administration (SSA) are used for 155,000 smaller single-location firms, which were determined by various cutoffs based on size and industry.

Data Collection and Imputation Procedures: Five mail and telephone follow-ups for larger nonrespondents. Data for small single-location firms (generally those with fewer than 10 employees) not mailed census questionnaires were estimated from administrative records of IRS and SSA. Data for nonrespondents were imputed from related responses or administrative records from IRS and SSA. Approximately 8 percent of total value of shipments was represented by fully imputed records in 1987.

Estimates of Sampling Error: Not applicable.

Other (nonsampling) Errors: Based on evaluation studies, estimates of nonsampling errors for 1972 were about 1.3 percent for estimated total payroll; 2 percent for total employment; and 1 percent for value of shipments. Estimates for later years are not available.

Foreign Trade—Export Statistics

Sources of Additional Material: U.S. Census Bureau, *1987 Census of Manufactures, Industry Series, Geographic Area Series,* and *Subject Series.*

Foreign Trade—Export Statistics

Universe, Frequency, and Types of Data: The export declarations collected by Customs are processed each month to obtain data on the movement of U.S. merchandise exports to foreign countries. Data obtained include value, quantity, and shipping weight of exports by commodity, country of destination, Customs district of exportation, and mode of transportation.

Type of Data Collection Operation: Shipper's Export Declarations (paper and electronic) are required to be filed for the exportation of merchandise valued over $1,500 - $2,500. Customs officials collect and transmit the documents to the Census Bureau on a flow basis for data compilation. Value data for shipments valued under $2,501 are estimated, based on established percentages of individual country totals.

Data Collection and Imputation Procedures: Statistical copies of Shipper's Export Declarations are received on a daily basis from Customs ports throughout the country and subjected to a monthly processing cycle. They are fully processed to the extent they reflect items valued over $2,500. Estimates for shipments valued at $2,500 or less are made, based on established percentages of individual country totals.

Estimates of Sampling Error: Not applicable.

Other (nonsampling) Errors: Clerical and complex computer checks intercept most processing errors and minimize otherwise significant reporting errors; other nonsampling errors are caused by undercounting of exports to Canada due to the nonreceipt of some Shipper's Export Declarations.

Sources of Additional Material: U.S. Census Bureau, U.S. *International Trade in Goods and Services: Exports, General Imports, and Imports for Consumption, SITC, Commodity by Country,* FT 925 (discontinued after 1996), *U.S. Imports of Merchandise,* and *U.S. Exports of Merchandise.*

Foreign Trade—Import Statistics

Universe, Frequency, and Types of Data: The import entry documents collected are processed each month to obtain data on the movement of merchandise imported into the United States. Data obtained include value, quantity, and shipping weight by commodity, country of origin, Customs district of entry, and mode of transportation.

Type of Data Collection Operation: Import entry documents, either paper or electronic, are required to be filed for the importation of goods into the United States valued over $2,000 or for articles which must be reported on formal entries. Customs officials collect and transmit statistical copies of the documents to the Census Bureau on a flow basis for data compilation. Estimates for shipments valued under $2,001 and not reported on formal entries are based on estimated established percentages of individual country totals.

Data Collection and Imputation Procedures: Statistical copies of import entry documents, received on a daily basis from Customs ports of entry throughout the country, are subjected to a monthly processing cycle. They are fully processed to the extent they reflect items valued at $2,501 and over or items which must be reported on formal entries.

Estimates of Sampling Error: Not applicable.

Other (nonsampling) Errors: Verification of statistical data reporting by Customs officials prior to transmittal and a subsequent program of clerical and computer checks are utilized to hold nonsampling errors arising from reporting and/or processing errors to a minimum.

Sources of Additional Material: U.S. Census Bureau, U.S. *International Trade in Goods and Services: Exports, General Imports, and Imports for Consumption, SITC, Commodity by Country,* FT 925 (discontinued after 1996), *U.S. Imports of Merchandise,* and *U.S. Exports of Merchandise.*

Census of Governments

Universe, Frequency, and Types of Data: Survey of all governmental units in the United States conducted every 5 years to obtain data on government revenue, expenditures, debt, assets, employment and employee retirement systems, property values, public school systems, and number, size, and structure of governments.

Type of Data Collection Operation: Complete census. List of units derived through classification of government units recently authorized in each state and identification, counting, and classification of existing local governments and public school systems.

Data Collection and Imputation Procedures: Data collected through field and office compilation of financial data from official records and reports for states and large local governments; mail canvass of selected data items, like state tax revenue and employee retirement systems; and collection of local government statistics through central collection arrangements with state governments.

Estimates of Sampling Error: Not applicable.

Other (nonsampling) Errors: Some nonsampling errors may arise due to possible inaccuracies in classification, response, and processing.

Sources of Additional Material: U.S. Census Bureau, *Census of Governments, 1997,* various reports, and *State Government Finances: 1992,* GF 92, No. 3.

Annual Surveys of State and Local Government

Universe, Frequency, and Types of Data: Sample survey conducted annually to obtain data on revenue, expenditure, debt, and employment of state and local governments. Universe is all governmental units in the United States (about 87,500).

Type of Data Collection Operation: Sample survey includes all state governments, county governments with 100,000+ population, municipalities with 75,000+ population, townships with 50,000+ population, all school districts with 10,000+ enrollment in March 1999, and other governments meeting certain criteria; probability sample for remaining units.

Data Collection and Imputation Procedures: Field and office compilation of data from official records and reports

for states and large local governments; central collection of local governmental financial data through cooperative agreements with a number of state governments; mail canvass of other units with mail and telephone follow-ups of nonrespondents. Data for nonresponses are imputed from previous year data or obtained from secondary sources, if available.

Estimates of Sampling Error: State and local government totals are generally subject to sampling variability of less than 3 percent.

Other (nonsampling) Errors: Nonresponse rate is less than 15 percent for local governments. Other possible errors may result from undetected inaccuracies in classification, response, and processing.

Sources of Additional Material: U.S. Census Bureau, *Public Employment in 1992,* GE 92, No. 1, *Governmental Finances in 1991-1992,* GF 92, No. 5, and *Census of Governments, 1997,* various reports. Web site references: Employment - state and local site: <http://www.census.gov/govs/www/ apes.html>. Finance - state and local site: <http://www.census.gov/govs/estimate.html>. Finance - state site: <http://www.census.gov/govs/ www/state.html>.

American Housing Survey

Universe, Frequency, and Types of Data: Conducted nationally in the fall in odd numbered years to obtain data on the approximately 116 million occupied or vacant housing units in the United States (group quarters are excluded). Data include characteristics of occupied housing units, vacant units, new housing and mobile home units, financial characteristics, recent mover households, housing and neighborhood quality indicators, and energy characteristics.

Type of Data Collection Operation: The national sample was a multistage probability sample with about 53,000 units eligible for interview in 2001. Sample units, selected within 394 PSUs, were surveyed over a 4-month period.

Data Collection and Imputation Procedures: For 2001, the survey was conducted by personal interviews. The interviewers obtained the information from the occupants or, if the unit was vacant, from informed persons such as landlords, rental agents, or knowledgeable neighbors.

Estimates of Sampling Error: For the national sample, illustrations of the S.E. of the estimates are provided in the Appendix D of the 2001 report. As an example, the estimated CV is about 0.2 percent for the estimated percentage of owner occupied units with two persons.

Other (nonsampling) Errors: Response rate was about 93 percent. Nonsampling errors may result from incorrect or incomplete responses, errors in coding and recording, and processing errors. For the 2001 national sample, approximately 1.9 percent of the total housing inventory was not adequately represented by the AHS sample.

Sources of Additional Material: U.S. Census Bureau, *Current Housing Reports,* Series H-150 and H-170, *American Housing Survey.*

Monthly Survey of Construction

Universe, Frequency, and Types of Data: Survey conducted monthly of newly constructed housing units (excluding mobile homes). Data are collected on the start, completion, and sale of housing. (Annual figures are aggregates of monthly estimates.)

Type of Data Collection Operation: Probability sample of housing units obtained from building permits selected from 17,000 places. For nonpermit places, multistage probability sample of new housing units selected in 169 PSUs. In those areas, all roads are canvassed in selected enumeration districts.

Data Collection and Imputation Procedures: Data are obtained by telephone inquiry and field visit.

Estimates of Sampling Error: Estimated CV of 3 percent to 4 percent for estimates of national totals, but may be higher than 20 percent for estimated totals of more detailed characteristics, such as housing units in multiunit structures.

Other (nonsampling) Errors: Response rate is over 90 percent for most items. Nonsampling errors are attributed to definitional problems, differences in interpretation of questions, incorrect reporting, inability to obtain information about all cases in the sample, and processing errors.

Sources of Additional Material: All data are available on the Internet at <http://www.census.gov/const/www/newsresconstindex.html>. Further documentation of the survey is also available at that site.

Value of Construction Put in Place

Universe, Frequency, and Types of Data: Survey conducted monthly on total value of all construction put in place in the current month, both public and private projects. Construction values include costs of materials and labor, contractors' profits, overhead costs, cost of architectural and engineering work, and miscellaneous project costs. (Annual figures are aggregates of monthly estimates.)

Type of Data Collection Operation: Varies by type of activity: Total cost of private one-family houses started each month is distributed into value put in place using fixed patterns of monthly construction progress; using a multistage probability sample, data for private multifamily housing are obtained by mail from owners of multiunit projects. Data for residential additions and alterations are obtained in a quarterly survey measuring expenditures; monthly estimates are interpolated from quarterly data. Estimates of value of private nonresidential construction, and state and local government construction are obtained by mail from owners (or agents) for a probability sample of projects. Estimates of farm nonresidential construction expenditures are based on U.S. Department of Agriculture annual estimates of construction; public utility estimates are obtained from reports submitted to Federal regulatory agencies and from private utility companies; estimates of Federal construction are based on monthly data supplied by Federal agencies.

Data Collection and Imputation Procedures: See "Type of Data Collection Operation." Imputation accounts for approximately 20 percent of estimated value of construction each month.

924 Appendix III

Estimates of Sampling Error: CV estimates for private nonresidential construction range from 3 percent for estimated value of industrial buildings to 9 percent for religious buildings. CV is approximately 2 percent for total new private nonresidential buildings.

Other (nonsampling) Errors: For directly measured data series based on samples, some nonsampling errors may arise from processing errors, imputations, and misunderstanding of questions. Indirect data series are dependent on the validity of the underlying assumptions and procedures.

Sources of Additional Material: U.S. Census Bureau, *Construction Reports,* Series C30, *Value of Construction Put in Place.*

Annual Survey of Manufactures

Universe, Frequency, and Types of Data: The Annual Survey of Manufactures (ASM) is conducted annually, except for years ending in 2 and 7 for all manufacturing establishments having one or more paid employees. The purpose of the ASM is to provide key intercensal measures of manufacturing activity, products, and location for the public and private sectors. The ASM provides statistics on employment, payroll, worker hours, payroll supplements, cost of materials, value added by manufacturing, capital expenditures, inventories, and energy consumption. It also provides estimates of value of shipments for 1,500 classes of manufactured products.

Type of Data Collection Operation: The ASM includes approximately 55,000 establishments selected from the census universe of 365,000 manufacturing establishments. Some 25,000 large establishments are selected with certainty, and some 30,000 other establishments are selected with probability proportional to a composite measure of establishment size. The survey is updated from two sources; Internal Revenue Service administrative records are used to include new single-unit manufacturers and the Company organization Survey identifies new establishments of multi-unit forms.

Data Collection and Imputation Procedures: Survey is conducted by mail with phone and mail follow-ups of nonrespondents. Imputation (for all nonresponse items) is based on previous year reports, or for new establishments in survey, on industry averages.

Estimates of Sampling Error: Estimated standard errors for number of employees, new expenditure, and for value added totals are given in annual publications. For U.S. level industry statistics, most estimated standard errors are 2 percent or less, but vary considerably for detailed characteristics.

Other (nonsampling) Errors: Response rate is about 85 percent. Nonsampling errors include those due to collection, reporting, and transcription errors, many of which are corrected through computer and clerical checks.

Sources of Additional Material: U.S. Census Bureau, *Annual Survey of Manufactures,* and Technical Paper 24.

Census of Population

Universe, Frequency, and Types of Data: Complete count of U.S. population conducted every 10 years since 1790. Data obtained on number and characteristics of people in the U.S.

Type of Data Collection Operation: In 1970, 1980, 1990 and 2000 complete census for some items—age, sex, race, and relationship to householder. In 1970, other items collected from a 5 percent and a 15 percent probability (systematic) sample of the population. In 1980, approximately 19 percent of the housing units were included in the sample; in 1990 and 2000, approximately 17 percent.

Data Collection and Imputation Procedures: In 1970, extensive use of mail questionnaires in urban areas; personal interviews in most rural areas. In 1980, 1990, and 2000, mail questionnaires were used in even more areas than in 1970, with personal interviews in the remainder. Extensive telephone and personal followup for nonrespondents was done in the censuses. Imputations were made for missing characteristics.

Estimates of Sampling Error: Sampling errors for data are estimated for all items collected by sample and vary by characteristic and geographic area. The CVs for national and state estimates are generally very small.

Other (nonsampling) Errors: Since 1950, evaluation programs have been conducted to provide information on the magnitude of some sources of nonsampling errors such as response bias and undercoverage in each census. Results from the evaluation program for the 1990 census indicate that the estimated net under coverage amounted to about 1.5 percent of the total resident population.

Sources of Additional Material: U.S. Census Bureau, The Coverage of Population in the 1980 Census, PHC80-E4; *Content Reinterview Study: Accuracy of Data for Selected Population and Housing Characteristics as Measured by Reinterview,* PHC80-E2; *1980 Census of Population,* Vol. 1, (PC80-1), Appendixes B, C, and D.

Current Population Survey (CPS)

Universe, Frequency, and Types of Data: Nationwide monthly sample survey of civilian noninstitutional population, 15 years old or over, to obtain data on employment, unemployment, and a number of other characteristics.

Type of Data Collection Operation: Multistage probability sample of about 50,000 households in 754 PSUs in 1996 expanded to about 60,000 households in July 2001. Over-sampling in some states and the largest MSAs to improve reliability for those areas of employment data on annual average basis. A continual sample rotation system is used. Households are in sample 4 months, out for 8 months, and in for 4 more. Month-to-month overlap is 75 percent; year-to-year overlap is 50 percent.

Data Collection and Imputation Procedures: For first and fifth months that a household is in sample, personal interviews; other months, approximately, 85 percent of the data collected by phone. Imputation is done for both item and total nonresponse. Adjustment for total nonresponse is done by a predefined cluster of units, by MSA size and residence; for item nonresponse imputation varies by subject matter.

Estimates of Sampling Error: Estimated CVs on national annual averages for labor force, total employment, and nonagricultural employment, 0.2 percent; for total unemployment and agricultural employment, 1.0 percent to 2.5 percent. The estimated CVs for family income and poverty rate for all persons in 1986 are 0.5 percent and 1.5 percent, respectively. CVs for subnational areas, such as states, would be larger and would vary by area.

Other (nonsampling) Errors: Estimates of response bias on unemployment are not available, but estimates of unemployment are usually 5 percent to 9 percent lower than estimates from reinterviews. Six to 7.0 percent of sample households unavailable for interviews.

Sources of Additional Material: U.S. Census Bureau and Bureau of Labor Statistics, *Current Population Survey; Design and Methodology,* (Tech. Paper 63), available on Internet <www.bls.census. gov/cps/tp/tp63.htm> and Bureau of Labor Statistics, *Employment and Earnings,* monthly, Explanatory Notes and Estimates of Error, Tables 1-A through 1-D and *BLS Handbook of Methods,* Chapter 1 (Bulletin 2490.)

Surveys of Minority- and Women-Owned Business Enterprises (SMOBE/SWOBE)

Universe, Frequency, and Types of Data: The surveys provide basic economic data on businesses owned by Blacks, Hispanics, Asians, Pacific Islanders, Alaska Natives, American Indians, and Women. All firms operating during 1997, except those classified as agricultural,are represented. The lists of all firms (or sample frames) are compiled from a combination of business tax returns and data collected on other economic census reports. The published data include the number of firms, gross receipts, number of paid employees, and annual payroll. The data are presented by geographic area, industry, size of firm, and legal form of organization of firm.

Type of Data Collection Operation: The surveys are based on a stratified probability sample of approximately 2.5 million firms from a universe of approximately 20.8 million firms. There were approximately 5.3 million firms with paid employees and 15.5 million firms with no paid employees. The data are based on the entire firm rather than on individual locations of a firm.

Data Collection and Imputation Procedures: Data were collected through a mailout/mailback operation. Compensation for missing data is addressed through reweighting, edit correction, and standard statistical imputation methods.

Estimates of Sampling Error: Variability in the estimates is due to the sample selection and estimation for items collected by SMOBE/SWOBE. CVs are applicable to only published cells in which sample cases are tabulated. The CVs for number of firms and receipts at the national level range from 1 to 4 percent. Other (nonsampling) Error: Nonsampling errors are attributed to many sources: inability to obtain information for all cases in the universe, adjustments to the weights of respondents to compensate for nonrespondents, imputation for missing data, data errors and biases, mistakes in recording or keying data, errors in collection or processing, and coverage problems.

Sources of Additional Materials: U.S. Census Bureau, Guide to the 1997 Economic Census and Related Statistics.

1997 Economic Census
(Geographic Area Series and Subject Series Reports) (for NAICS sectors 22, 42, 4445, 48-49, and 51-81)

Universe, Frequency, and Types of Data: Conducted every 5 years to obtain data on number of establishments, number of employees, total payroll size, total sales, and other industry specific statistics. In 1997, the universe was all employer and nonemployer establishments primarily engaged in wholesale, retail, utilities, finance & insurance, real estate, transportation & warehousing, and other service industries.

Type of Data Collection Operation: All large employer firms were surveyed (i.e. all employer firms above the payroll size cutoff established to separate large from small employers) plus a 5 percent to 25 percent sample of the small employer firms. Firms with no employees were not required to file a census return.

Data Collection and Imputation Procedures: Mail questionnaires were used with both mail and telephone followups for nonrespondents. Data for nonrespondents and for small employer firms not mailed a questionnaire were obtained from administrative records of the IRS and Social Security Administration or imputed. Nonemployer data were obtained exclusively from IRS 1997 income tax returns.

Estimates of Sampling Error: Not applicable for basic data such as sales, revenue, payroll, etc. Other (nonsampling)Errors: Trade area level unit response rates in 1997 ranged from 85 percent to 99 percent. Item response rates ranged from 60 percent to 90 percent with lower rates for the more detailed questions. Nonsampling errors may occur during the collection, reporting, and keying of data, and industry misclassification.

Sources of Additional Material: U.S. Census Bureau, *1997 Economic Census: Geographic Area Series* and *Subject Series Reports* (by NAICS sector), Appendix C and <www.census.gov/con97. html>

Current Business Surveys

Universe, Frequency, and Types of Data: Provides monthly estimates of retail sales by kind of business, and end-of-month inventories of retail stores; wholesale sales and end-of-month inventories; and annual receipts of selected service industries.

Type of Data Collection Operation: Probability sample of all firms from a list frame and, additionally, for retail and service an area frame. The list frame is the Bureau's Standard Statistical Establishment List (SSEL) updated quarterly for recent birth Employer Identification (EI) Numbers issued by the Internal Revenue Service and assigned a kind-of-business code by the Social Security Administration. The largest firms are included monthly.

Data Collection and Imputation Procedures: Data are collected by mail questionnaire with telephone followups for nonrespondents. Imputation made for each nonresponse item and each item failing edit checks.

U.S. Census Bureau, Statistical Abstract of the United States: 2002

Estimates of Sampling Error: For the 2001 monthly surveys, median CVs are about 0.6 percent for estimated total retail sales, 1.4 percent for wholesale sales, 1.7 percent for wholesale inventories. For dollar volume of receipts, CVs from the Service Annual Survey vary by kind of business and range between 1.5 percent to 15.0 percent. Sampling errors are shown in monthly publications.

Other (nonsampling) Errors: Imputation rates are about 18 percent to 23 percent for monthly retail sales, 30 percent for wholesale sales, about 32 percent for monthly wholesale inventories and 14 percent for the *Service Annual Survey.*

Sources of Additional Material: U.S. Census Bureau, *Current Business Reports, Monthly Retail Trade, Monthly Wholesale Trade,* and *Service Annual Survey.*

Service Annual Surveys

Universe, Frequency, and Types of Data: Provides national estimates for taxable and tax-exempt firms on selected service industries as defined by the North American Industrial Classification System (NAICS). Industries covered by the Service Annual Survey include all or part of the following NAICS sectors: Transportation and Warehouse (NAICS 48-49); Information (NAICS 51); Finance (NAICS 52); Real Estate and Leasing (NAICS 53); Professional, Scientific, and Technical Services (NAICS 54); Administrative and Support and Waste Management and Remediation Services (NAICS 56); Health Care and Social Assistance (NAICS 62); Arts, Entertainment, and Recreation (NAICS 71); and Other Services, except Public Administration (NAICS 81). Items collected include total revenue and revenue from e-commerce transactions; and for selected industries, revenue from detailed service products, total expenses and expenses by major type, revenue from exported services, and inventories. The Service Annual Survey is mailed in January and collects calendar year data for the prior year. Data collection continues for approximately 14 weeks. The data are published approximately 12 months after the initial survey mailing.

Type of Data Collection Operation: Data are obtained from a mail-out/mail-back probability sample of approximately 50,000 selected service firms with paid employees. The survey is supplemented with business births on a quarterly basis. The sampling frame for the Service Annual Survey (SAS) has two types of sampling units represented-Employer Identification Numbers (EINS) and large, multiple-establishment firms. Both sampling units represent clusters of one or more establishments owned or controlled by the same firm. The information used to create these sampling units was extracted the Census Bureau's Business Register and includes information in the most recent Economic Census.

Estimates of Sampling Error: The estimates are based on a sample. Exact agreement with results that would be obtained from a complete enumeration of firms represented on the sampling frame using the same enumeration procedures is not expected. However, because each firm on the sampling frame has a known probability of being selected into the sample, it is possible to estimate the sampling variability of the survey estimates. The particular sample used in this survey is one of a large number of samples of the same size that could have been selected using the same design. If all possible samples had been surveyed under the same conditions, an estimate of an unknown population value could have been obtained from each sample. These samples give rise to a distribution of estimates for the unknown population value. A statistical measure of the variability among these estimates is the standard error, which can be approximated from any one sample.

Other (nonsampling) Errors: Nonsampling error encompasses all other factors that contribute to the total error of a sample survey estimate and may occur in Census. In the Service Annual Survey, nonsampling error can be attributed to many sources: inability to obtain information about all units in the sample; response errors; differences in the interpretation of the questions; mistakes in coding or keying the data obtained; and other errors of collection, response, coverage, and processing.

U.S. Census Bureau, Statistical Abstract of the United States: 2002

Wholesale Trade Survey

Universe, Frequency, and Types of Data: Provides monthly estimates of retail sales by kind of business, and end of month inventories of retail stores; wholesale sales and end of month inventories; and annual receipts of selected service industries.

Type of Data Collection Operation: Probability sample of all firms from a list frame and, additionally, for retail and service an area frame. The list frame is the Bureau's Standard Statistical Establishment List (SSEL) updated quarterly for recent birth Employer Identification (EI) Numbers issued by the Internal Revenue Service and assigned a kind of business code by the Social Security Administration. The largest firms are included monthly.

Data Collection and Imputation Procedures: Data are collected by mail questionnaire with telephone followups for nonrespondents. Imputation made for each nonresponse item and each item failing edit checks.

Estimates of Sampling Error: For the 2001 monthly surveys median CV's are about 0.6 percent for estimated total retail sales, 1.4 for wholesale sales, 1.7 for wholesale inventories. For dollar volume of receipts, CV's from the Service Annual Survey vary by kind of business and range between 1.5 percent to 15.0 percent. Sampling errors are shown in monthly publications.

Other (nonsampling) Errors: Imputation rates are about 18 percent to 23 percent for monthly retail sales, 30 percent for wholesale sales, about 32 percent for monthly wholesale inventories and 14 percent for the Service Annual Survey.

Sources of Additional Material: U.S. Census Bureau, Current Business Reports, Monthly Retail Trade, Monthly Wholesale Trade, and Service Annual Survey.

Monthly Retail Trade Survey

Universe, Frequency, and Types of Data: Provides monthly estimates of retail sales by kind of business and end of month inventories of retail stores; wholesale sales and end of month inventories; and annual receipts of selected service industries.

Type of Data Collection Operation: Probability sample of all firms from a list frame. The list frame is the Bureau's Standard Statistical Establishment List (SSEL) updated quarterly for recent birth Employer Identification (EI) Numbers issued by the Internal Revenue Service and assigned a kind of business code by the Social Security Administration. The largest firms are included monthly; a sample of others is included every month also.

Data Collection and Imputation Procedures: Data are collected by mail questionnaire with telephone followups for nonrespondents. Imputation made for each nonresponse item and each item failing edit checks.

Estimates of Sampling Error: For the 1989 monthly surveys, CV's are about 0.5 percent for estimated total retail sales, 0.99 percent for estimated total retail inventories, 1.2 percent for wholesale sales, 1.7 percent for wholesale inventories. For dollar volume of receipts, CV's from the Service Annual Survey vary by kind of business and range between 1.5 percent to 15.0 percent. Sampling errors are shown in monthly publications.

Other (nonsampling) Errors: Imputation rates are about 20 percent for monthly retail sales, 28 percent for monthly retail inventories, 30 percent for wholesale sales, about 32 percent for monthly wholesale inventories and 14 percent for the Service Annual Survey.

Sources of Additional Material: U.S. Census Bureau, Current Business Reports, Monthly Retail Trade, Monthly Wholesale Trade, Service Annual Survey.

U.S. DEPARTMENT OF
EDUCATION, National Center
for Education Statistics

Higher Education General Information Survey (HEGIS), Fall Enrollment in Institutions of Higher Education; beginning 1986, Integrated Postsecondary Education Data Survey (IPEDS), Fall Enrollment

Universe, Frequency, and Types of Data:
Annual survey of all institutions and
branches listed in the *Directory* to
obtain data on total enrollment by sex,
level of enrollment, type of program,
racial/ethnic characteristics (every other
year prior to 1989, then annually) and
attendance status of student, and on
first-time students.

Type of Data Collection Operation: Complete census.

*Data Collection and Imputation Proce-
dures:* Survey package is usually mailed
in the spring with surveys due at varying dates in the summer and fall; mail
and phone followup procedures for nonrespondents. Missing data are imputed
by using data of similar institutions.

Estimates of Sampling Error: Not applicable.

Other (nonsampling) Errors: For degree-
granting institutions approximately
96.9 percent response rate in fall 1999.

Sources of Additional Material: U.S.
Department of Education, National Center for Education Statistics, *Fall Enrollment in Higher Education,* annual.

Higher Education General Information Survey (HEGIS), Financial Statistics of Institutions of Higher Education; beginning 1986, Integrated Post-secondary Education Data Survey (IPEDS), Finance

Universe, Frequency, and Types of Data:
Annual survey of all institutions and
branches listed in the *Education Directory, Colleges and Universities* to obtain
data on financial status and operations,
including current funds revenues, current funds expenditures, and physical
plant assets.

Type of Data Collection Operation: Complete census.

*Data Collection and Imputation Proce-
dures:* Survey package is usually mailed
in the spring with surveys due at varying dates in the summer and fall; mail
and phone followup procedures for
nonrespondents. Missing data are
imputed by using data of similar institutions.

Estimates of Sampling Error: Not applicable.

Other (nonsampling) Errors: For 1997,
95 percent for degree-granting institutions.

Sources of Additional Material: U.S.
Department of Education, National Cen-
ter for Education Statistics, *Financial
Statistics.*

Higher Education General Information Survey (HEGIS), Degrees and Other Formal Awards Conferred. Beginning 1986, Integrated Postsecondary Education Data Survey (IPEDS), Completions

Universe, Frequency, and Types of Data:
Annual survey of all institutions and
branches listed in the *Education Directory, Colleges and Universities* to obtain
data on earned degrees and other formal awards, conferred by field of study,
level of degree, sex, and by racial/ethnic
characteristics (every other year prior to
1989, then annually).

Type of Data Collection Operation: Complete census.

*Data Collection and Imputation Proce-
dures:* Survey package is usually mailed
in the spring with surveys due at varying dates in the summer and fall; mail
and phone followup procedures for
nonrespondents. Missing data are
imputed by using data of similar institutions.

Estimates of Sampling Error: Not applicable.

Other (nonsampling) Errors: For 1999-
2000, approximately 84.4 percent
response rate for degree-granting institutions.

Sources of Additional Material: U.S.
Department of Education, National Center for Education Statistics, *Completions,*
annual.

U.S. ENERGY INFORMATION ADMINISTRATION

Residential Energy Consumption Survey

Universe, Frequency, and Types of Data: Quadriennial survey of households and fuel suppliers. Data are obtained on energy-related household characteristics, housing unit characteristics, use of fuels, and energy consumption and expenditures by fuel type.

Type of Data Collection Operation: Probability sample of 5,900 eligible units in 116 PSUs. For responding units, fuel consumption and expenditure data obtained from fuel suppliers to those households.

Data Collection and Imputation Procedures: Personal interviews. Extensive followup of nonrespondents including mail questionnaires for some households. Adjustments for nonrespondents were made in weighting for respondents. Most item nonresponses were imputed.

Estimates of Sampling Error: Estimated CVs for household averages: For consumption, 1.3 percent; for expenditures, 1.0 percent; for various fuels, values ranged from 2.0 percent for electricity to 7.0 percent for LPG.

Other (nonsampling) Errors: Household response rate of 81.0 percent. Nonconsumption data were mostly imputed for mail respondents (2.5 percent of eligible units). Usable responses from fuel suppliers for various fuels ranged from 80.7 percent for electricity to 56.6 percent for fuel oil.

Sources of Additional Material: U.S. Energy Information Administration, *A look at Residential Energy Consumption in 1997.*

U.S. NATIONAL CENTER FOR HEALTH STATISTICS (NCHS)

National Vital Statistics System

Universe, Frequency, and Types of Data: Annual data on births and deaths in the United States.

Type of Data Collection Operation: Mortality data based on complete file of death records, except 1972, based on 50 percent sample. Natality statistics 1951-71, based on 50 percent sample of birth certificates, except a 20 percent to 50 percent in 1967, received by NCHS. Beginning 1972, data from some states received through Vital Statistics Cooperative Program (VSCP) and complete file used; data from other states based on 50 percent sample. Beginning 1986, all reporting areas participated in the VSCP.

Data Collection and Imputation Procedures: Reports based on records from registration offices of all states, District of Columbia, New York City, Puerto Rico, Virgin Islands, Guam, American Samoa, and Northern Marianas.

Estimates of Sampling Error: For recent years, CVs for births are small due to large portion of total file in sample (except for very small estimated totals).

Other (nonsampling) Errors: Data on births and deaths believed to be at least 99 percent complete.

Sources of Additional Material: U.S. National Center for Health Statistics, *Vital Statistics of the United States,* Vol. I and Vol. II, annual, and *National Vital Statistics Report.*

National Health Interview Survey (NHIS)

Universe, Frequency, and Types of Data: Continuous data collection covering the civilian noninstitutional population to obtain information on personal and demographic characteristics, illnesses, injuries, impairments, and other health topics.

Type of Data Collection Operation: Multistage probability sample of 49,000 households (in 198 PSUs) from 1985 to 1994; 43,000 households (358 design PSUs) from 1995 on, selected in groups of about four adjacent households.

Data Collection and Imputation Procedures: Some missing data items (e.g., race, ethnicity) are imputed using a hot deck imputation value. Unit nonresponse is compensated for by an adjustment to the survey weights.

Estimates of Sampling Error: Estimates of Standard Error (SE): For 1997 medically attended injury or poisoning episodes rates in the past 12 months by falling for: females 47.70 (2.37), and males 36.92 (2.06) per 1,000 population; for

1997 injury episodes rates during the past 12 months inside the home - 29.38 (1.28) per 1,000 population.

Other (nonsampling) Errors: The response rate was 93.8 percent in 1996; in 1999, the total household response rate was 87.6 percent, with the final family response rate of 86.1 percent, and the final sample adult response rate of 69.6 percent; in 2000, the total household response rate was 88.9 percent, with the final family response rate of 72.1 percent, and the final sample adult response rate was 72.1 percent for the NHIS. (Note: The NHIS sample redesign was conducted in 1995, and the NHIS questionnaire was redesigned in 1997.)

Sources of Additional Material: U.S. National Center for Health Statistics, Summary Health Statistics for U.S. Children: National Health Interview Survey, 1997, Vital and Health Statistics, Series 10 #203; U.S. National Center for Health Statistics, Summary Health Statistics for the U.S. Population: National Health Interview Survey, 1997, Vital and Health Statistics, Series 10 #204; U.S. National Center for Health Statistics, Summary Health Statistics for U.S. Adults: National Health Interview Survey, 1997, Vital and Health Statistics, Series 10 #205 (In preparation); U.S. National Center for Health Statistics, Design and Estimation for the National Health Interview Survey, 1995-2004, Vital and Health Statistics, Series 2 #130; U.S. National Center for Health Statistics, Summary Health Statistics Technical Report: National Health Interview Survey, 1997-2003, Vital and Statistics, Series 2 #134.

U.S. BUREAU OF JUSTICE STATISTICS (BJS)

National Crime Victimization Survey

Universe, Frequency, and Types of Data: Monthly survey of individuals and households in the United States to obtain data on criminal victimization of those units for compilation of annual estimates.

Type of Data Collection Operation: National probability sample survey of about 50,000 interviewed households in 376 PSUs selected from a list of

addresses from the 1980 census, supplemented by new construction permits and an area sample where permits are not required.

Data Collection and Imputation Procedures: Interviews are conducted every 6 months for 3 years for each household in the sample; 8,300 households are interviewed monthly. Personal interviews are used in the first interview; the intervening interviews are conducted by telephone whenever possible.

Estimates of Sampling Error: CVs averaged over the period 1998-2001 are:" 3.7 percent for personal crimes (includes all crimes of violence plus purse snatching crimes), 3.8 percent for crimes of violence; 12.1 percent for estimate of rape/sexual assault counts; 7.9 percent for robbery counts; 4.1 percent for assault counts; 11.2 percent for purse snatching (it refers to purse snatching and pocket picking); 2.5 percent for property crimes; 3.8 percent for burglary counts; 2.7 percent for theft (of property); and 5.2 percent for motor vehicle theft counts.

Other (nonsampling) Errors: Respondent recall errors which may include reporting incidents for other than the reference period; interviewer coding and processing errors; and possible mistaken reporting or classifying of events. Adjustment is made for a household noninterview rate of about 7 percent and for a within-household noninterview rate of 10 percent.

Sources of Additional Material: U.S. Bureau of Justice Statistics, *Criminal Victimization in the United States,* annual.

U.S. FEDERAL BUREAU OF INVESTIGATION

Uniform Crime Reporting (UCR) Program

Universe, Frequency, and Types of Data: Monthly reports on the number of criminal offenses that become known to law enforcement agencies. Data are collected on crimes cleared by arrest, by age, sex, and race of offender, and on assaults on law enforcement officers.

Type of Data Collection Operation: Crime statistics are based on reports of crime data submitted either directly to the FBI by contributing law enforcement agencies or through cooperating state UCR programs.

Data Collection and Imputation Procedures: States with UCR programs collect data directly from individual law enforcement agencies and forward reports, prepared in accordance with UCR standards, to FBI. Accuracy and consistency edits are performed by FBI.

Estimates of Sampling Error: Not applicable.

Other (nonsampling) Errors: Coverage of 94 percent of the population (96 percent in MSA's, 87 percent in "other cities," and 88 percent in rural areas) by UCR program, though varying number of agencies report. Some error may be present through incorrect reporting.

Sources of Additional Material: U.S. Federal Bureau of Investigation, *Crime in the United States, Hate Crime Statistics,* annual, *Law Enforcement Officers Killed & Assaulted,* annual.

U.S. BUREAU OF LABOR STATISTICS

U.S. Census Bureau, Current Population Survey (CPS)

Universe, Frequency, and Types of Data: Nationwide monthly sample survey of civilian noninstitutional population, 15 years old or over, to obtain data on employment, unemployment, and a number of other characteristics.

Type of Data Collection Operation: Multistage probability sample of about 50,000 households in 754 PSUs in 1996, expanded to about 60,000 households in July 2001. Over-sampling in some states and the largest MSA's to improve reliability for those areas of employment data on annual average basis. A continual sample rotation system is used. Households are in sample 4 months, out for 8 months, and in for 4 more. Month-to-month overlap is 75 percent; year-to-year overlap is 50 percent.

Data Collection and Imputation Procedures: For first and fifth months that a household is in sample, personal interviews; other months, approximately, 85 percent of the data collected by phone. Imputation is done for both item and total nonresponse. Adjustment for total nonresponse is done by a predefined cluster of units, by MSA size and residence; for item nonresponse imputation varies by subject matter.

Estimates of Sampling Error: Estimated CVs on national annual averages for labor force, total employment, and nonagricultural employment, 0.2 percent; for total unemployment and agricultural employment, 1.0 percent to 2.5 percent. The estimated CVs for family income and poverty rate for all persons in 1986 are 0.5 percent and 1.5 percent, respectively. CVs for subnational areas, such as states, would be larger and would vary by area.

Other (nonsampling) Errors: Estimates of response bias on unemployment are not available, but estimates of unemployment are usually 5 percent to 9 percent lower than estimates from reinterviews. About 7.5 percent of sample households unavailable for interviews.

Sources of Additional Material: U.S. Census Bureau and Bureau of Labor Statistics, *Current Population Survey; Design and Methodology,* (Tech. Paper 63 RV), available on Internet <www.bls.census. gov/cps/tp/tp63.htm> and Bureau of Labor Statistics, *Employment and Earnings,* monthly, Explanatory Notes and Estimates of Error, Tables 1-A through 1-D and *BLS Handbook of Methods,* Chapter 1 (Bulletin 2490).

Consumer Price Index (CPI)

Universe, Frequency, and Types of Data: Monthly survey of price changes of all types of consumer goods and services purchased by urban wage earners and clerical workers prior to 1978, and urban consumers thereafter. Both indexes continue to be published.

Type of Data Collection Operation: Prior to 1978, sample of various consumer items in 87 urban areas; thereafter, in 85 PSUs, except from January 1987 through March 1988, when 91 areas were sampled.

Data Collection and Imputation Procedures: Prices of consumer items are obtained from about 50,000 housing units, and 23,000 other reporters in 87 areas. Prices of food, fuel, and a few other items are obtained monthly; prices of most other commodities and services

U.S. Census Bureau, Statistical Abstract of the United States: 2002

are collected every month in the three largest geographic areas and every other month in others.

Estimates of Sampling Error: Estimates of standard errors are available.

Other (nonsampling) Errors: Errors result from inaccurate reporting, difficulties in defining concepts and their operational implementation, and introduction of product quality changes and new products.

Sources of Additional Material: U.S. Bureau of Labor Statistics, Internet site <http://www.stats.bls.gov/cpihome.htm> and *BLS Handbook of Methods,* Chapter 17, Bulletin 2490. U.S. Bureau of Labor Statistics Internet sites <http://www.bls.gov/ppi>.

Producer Price Index (PPI)

Universe, Frequency, and Types of Data: Monthly survey of producing companies to determine price changes of all commodities produced in the United States for sale in commercial transactions. Data on agriculture, forestry, fishing, manufacturing, mining, gas, electricity, public utilities, and a few services.

Type of Data Collection Operation: Probability sample of approximately 30,000 establishments that result in about 100,000 price quotations per month.

Data Collection and Imputation Procedures: Data are collected by mail and facsimile. If transaction prices are not supplied, list prices are used. Some prices are obtained from trade publications, organized exchanges, and government agencies. To calculate index, price changes are multiplied by their relative weights taken from 1997 shipment values from the Census of Manufactures.

Estimates of Sampling Error: Not applicable.

Other (nonsampling) Errors: Not available at present.

Sources of Additional Material: U.S. Bureau of Labor Statistics, *BLS Handbook of Methods,* Chapter 14, Bulletin 2490. U.S. Bureau of Labor Statistics Internet sites <http:///www.bls.gov/ppi>.

Current Employment Statistics (CES) Program

Universe, Frequency, and Types of Data: Monthly survey covering about 7 million establishments to obtain data on employment, hours, and earnings, by industry.

Type of Data Collection Operation: Sample survey of over 300,000 establishments in June 2002.

Data Collection and Imputation Procedures: Cooperating state agencies mail questionnaires to sample establishments to develop state and local estimates; information is forwarded to BLS where national estimates are prepared.

Estimates of Sampling Error: Not available until survey redesign is completed.

Other (nonsampling) Errors: Estimates of employment adjusted annually to reflect complete universe. Average adjustment is 0.3 percent over the last decade.

Sources of Additional Material: U.S. Bureau of Labor Statistics, *Employment and Earnings,* monthly, Explanatory Notes and Estimates of Error, Tables 2-A through 2-H.

National Compensation Survey

Universe, Frequency, and Types of Data: Nationwide sample survey of establishments of all employment size classes, stratified by geographic area, in private industry and state and local government. Data collected include wages and salaries, employer costs of employer compensation, and employee benefits. Data produced include percent changes in the cost of employment cited in the ECI and costs per hour worked for individual benefits cited in the ECEC. The survey provides data by ownership (Private industry and state and local government), industry sector, major industry divisions, major occupational groups, bargaining status, metropolitan area status, and census region. ECEC also provides data by establishment size class.

Type of Data Collection Operation: Probability proportionate to size sample of establishments. The sample is replaced on a continual basis. Establishments are in the survey for approximately 5 years, with some establishments replaced each quarter.

Data Collection and Imputation Procedures: For the initial visit, data are primarily collected in a personal visit to the establishment. Quarterly updates are obtained primarily by mail, fax, and telephone. Imputation is done for individual benefits.

Estimates of Sampling Error: Because standard errors vary from quarter to quarter, the ECI uses a 5-year moving average of standard errors to evaluate published series. These standard errors are available at <http://www.bls.gov/ncs/ect/home.htm>.

Other (nonsampling) Errors: Nonsampling errors have a number of potential sources. The primary sources are (1) survey nonresponse and (2) data collection and processing errors. Nonsampling errors are not measured. Procedures have been implemented for reducing nonsampling errors, however, primarily through quality assurance programs. These programs include the use of data collection reinterviews, observed interviews, computer edits of the data, and systematic professional review of the reports on which the data are recorded. The programs also serve as a training device to provide feedback to the field economists, or data collectors, on errors. And, they provide information on the sources of error which can be remedied by improved collection instructions or computer processing edits. Extensive training of field economists is also conducted to maintain high standards in data collection.

Sources of Additional Material: Bureau of Labor Statistics, *BLS Handbook of Methods,* Chapter 8 (Bulletin 2490) and <http://www.bls.gov/ncs>.

BOARD OF GOVERNORS OF THE FEDERAL RESERVE SYSTEM

Survey of Consumer Finances

Universe, Frequency, and Types of Data: Periodic sample survey of families. In this survey a given household is divided into a primary economic unit and other economic units. The primary economic unity, which may be a single individual, is generally chosen as the unit that contains the person who either holds the title to the home or is the first person listed on the lease. The primary unit is used as the reference family. The survey collects detailed data on the composition of family balance sheets, the terms of loans, and relationships with financial institutions. It also gathered information on the employment history and pension rights of the survey respondent and the spouse or partner of the respondent.

Type of Data Collection Operation: The survey employs a two-part strategy for sampling families. Some families were selected by standard multistage area-probability sampling methods from the 48 contiguous states. The remaining families in the survey were selected using tax data under the strict rules governing confidentiality and the rights of potential respondents to refuse participation.

Data Collection and Imputation Procedures: The Survey Research Center at the University of Michigan collected the 1989 survey data between August 1989 and March 1990. Adjustments for nonresponse errors are made through systematic imputation of unanswered questions and through weighting adjustments based on data used in the sample design for families that refused participation.

Estimates of Sampling Error: Because of the complex design of the survey, the estimation of potential sampling errors is not straightforward.

Other (nonsampling) Errors: The achieved sample of 3,143 families represents a response rate of about 69 percent in the area-probability sample and a rate of about 34 percent in the tax-data sample. Proper training of interviewers and careful design of questionnaires were used to control inaccurate survey responses.

Sources of Additional Material: Board of Governors of the Federal Reserve System, "Changes in Family Finances from 1983 to 1989: Evidence from the Survey of Consumer Finances," *Federal Reserve Bulletin,* January 1992.

U.S. INTERNAL REVENUE SERVICE

Statistics of Income, Individual Income Tax Returns

Universe, Frequency, and Types of Data: Annual study of unaudited individual income tax returns, forms 1040, 1040A, and 1040EZ, filed by U.S. citizens and residents. Data provided on various financial characteristics by size of adjusted gross income, marital status, and by taxable and nontaxable returns. Data by state, based on 100 percent file, also include returns from 1040NR, filed by nonresident aliens plus certain self-employment tax returns.

Type of Data Collection Operation: Annual 1999 stratified probability sample of approximately 177,000 returns broken into sample strata based on the larger of total income or total loss amounts as well as the size of business plus farm receipts. Sampling rates for sample strata varied from 0.05 percent to 100 percent.

Data Collection and Imputation Procedures: Computer selection of sample of tax return records. Data adjusted during editing for incorrect, missing, or inconsistent entries to ensure consistency with other entries on return.

Estimates of Sampling Error: Estimated CVs for tax year 1999: Adjusted gross income less deficit 0.11 percent; salaries and wages 0.21 percent; and tax-exempt interest received 1.78 percent. (State data not subject to sampling error.)

Other (nonsampling) Errors: Processing errors and errors arising from the use of tolerance checks for the data.

Sources of Additional Material: U.S. Internal Revenue Service, *Statistics of Income, Individual Income Tax Returns,* annual.

Statistics of Income, Sole Proprietorship Returns and Statistics of Income Bulletin

Universe, Frequency, and Types of Data: Annual study of unaudited income tax returns of nonfarm sole proprietorships, form 1040 with business schedules. Data provided on various financial characteristics by industry.

Type of Data Collection Operation: Stratified probability sample of approximately 51,000 sole proprietorships for tax year 1999. The sample is classified based on presence or absence of certain business schedules; the larger of total income or loss; and size of business plus farm receipts. Sampling rates vary from 0.05 percent to 100 percent.

Data Collection and Imputation Procedures: Computer selection of sample of tax return records. Data adjusted during editing for incorrect, missing, or inconsistent entries to ensure consistency with other entries on return.

Estimates of Sampling Error: Estimated CVs for tax year 1999 are available. For sole proprietorships, business receipts, 0.71 percent; net income, (less loss), 1.05 percent; depreciation 1.42 percent.

Other (nonsampling) Errors: Processing errors and errors arising from the use of tolerance checks for the data.

Sources of Additional Material: U.S. Internal Revenue Service, *Statistics of Income, Sole Proprietorship Returns* (for years through 1980) and *Statistics of Income Bulletin,* Vol. 21, No. 1 (summer 2001).

Statistics of Income, Partnership Returns and Statistics of Income Bulletin

Universe, Frequency, and Types of Data: Annual study of unaudited income tax returns of partnerships, Form 1065. Data provided on various financial characteristics by industry.

Type of Data Collection Operation: Stratified probability sample of approximately 43,000 partnership returns from a population of 2.0 million filed during calendar year 1999. The sample is classified based on combinations of gross receipts, net income or loss, and total assets, and on industry. Sampling rates vary from 0.08 percent to 100 percent.

Data Collection and Imputation Procedures: Computer selection of sample of tax return records. Data are adjusted during editing for incorrect, missing, or inconsistent entries to ensure consistency with other entries on return. Data not available due to regulations are not imputed.

Estimates of Sampling Error: Estimated CVs for tax year 1999 (latest available): For number of partnerships, 0.3 percent; business receipts, 0.2 percent; net income, 0.5 percent; net loss, 1.6 percent.

Other (nonsampling) Errors: Processing errors and errors arising from the use of tolerance checks for the data.

Sources of Additional Material: U.S. Internal Revenue Service, *Statistics of Income, Partnership Returns* and *Statistics of Income Bulletin,* Vol. 21, No. 2 (fall 2001).

Corporation Income Tax Returns

Universe, Frequency, and Types of Data: Annual study of unaudited corporation income tax returns, Forms 1120 and 1120 (A, F, L, PC, REIT, RIC, and S), filed by corporations or businesses legally defined as corporations. Data provided on various financial characteristics by industry and size of total assets, and business receipts.

Type of Data Collection Operation: Stratified probability sample of approximately 141,400 returns for 1999, distributed by sample classes generally based on type of return, size of total assets, size of net income or deficit, and selected business activity. Sampling rates for sample strata varied from .25 percent to 100 percent.

Data Collection and Imputation Procedures: Computer selection of sample of tax return records. Data adjusted during editing for incorrect, missing, or inconsistent entries to ensure consistency with other entries on return and to achieve statistical definitions.

Estimates of Sampling Error: Estimated CVs for 1999: Number of returns in subgroups ranged from 0.2 percent with assets under $100,000, to 0 percent with assets over $100 mil.; for amount of net income 0.22 percent.

Other (nonsampling) Errors: Processing errors and errors arising from the use of tolerance checks for the data.

Sources of Additional Material: U.S. Internal Revenue Service, *Statistics of Income, Corporation Income Tax Returns,* annual.

U.S. SOCIAL SECURITY ADMINISTRATION

Benefit Data

Universe, Frequency, and Types of Data: All persons receiving monthly benefits under Title II of Social Security Act. Data on number and amount of benefits paid by type and state.

Type of Data Collection Operation: Data based on administrative records. Data based on 100 percent files, as well as 10 percent and 1 percent sample files.

Data Collection and Imputation Procedures: Records used consist of actions pursuant to applications dated by subsequent post-entitlement actions.

Estimates of Sampling Error: Varies by size of estimate and sample file size.

Other (nonsampling) Errors: Processing errors, which are believed to be small.

Sources of Additional Material: U.S. Social Security Administration, *Annual Statistical Supplement to the Social Security Bulletin.*

Supplemental Security Income (SSI) Program

Universe, Frequency, and Types of Data: All eligible aged, blind, or disabled persons receiving SSI benefit payments under SSI program. Data include number of persons receiving federally administered SSI, amounts paid, and state administered supplementation.

Type of Data Collection Operation: Data based on administrative records.

Data Collection and Imputation Procedures: Data adjusted to reflect returned checks and overpayment refunds. For federally administered payments, actual adjusted amounts are used.

Estimates of Sampling Error: Not applicable.

Other (nonsampling) Errors: Processing errors, which are believed to be small.

Sources of Additional Material: U.S. Social Security Administration, *Annual Statistical Supplement to the Social Security Bulletin.*

Appendix IV

Weights and Measures

[For assistance on metric usage, call or write the National Institute of Standards and Technology, Metric Program, 100 Bureau Drive, Stop 2000, Gaithersburg, MD 20899-2000 (301-975-3690) Internet site <http://www.nist.gov/> E-mail: metric_prg@nist.gov]

Symbol	When you know conventional	Multiply by	To find metric	Symbol
in	inch	2.54	centimeter	cm
ft	foot	30.48	centimeter	cm
yd	yard	0.91	meter	m
mi	mile	1.61	kilometer	km
in^2	square inch	6.45	square centimeter	cm^2
ft^2	square foot	0.09	square meter	m^2
yd^2	square yard	0.84	square meter	m^2
mi^2	square mile	2.59	square kilometer	km^2
	acre	0.41	hectare	ha
oz	ounce [1]	28.35	gram	g
lb	pound [1]	.45	kilograms	kg
oz (troy)	ounce [2]	31.10	gram	g
	short ton (2,000 lb)	0.91	metric ton	t
	long ton (2,240 lb)	1.02	metric ton	t
fl oz	fluid ounce	29.57	milliliter	mL
c	cup	0.24	liter	L
pt	pint	0.47	liter	L
qt	quart	0.95	liter	L
gal	gallon	3.78	liter	L
ft^3	cubic foot	0.03	cubic meter	m^3
yd^3	cubic yard	0.76	cubic meter	m^3
F	degrees Fahrenheit (subtract 32)	0.55	degrees Celsius	C

Symbol	When you know metric	Multiply by	To find conventional	Symbol
cm	centimeter	0.39	inch	in
cm	centimeter	0.03	foot	ft
m	meter	1.09	yard	yd
km	kilometer	0.62	mile	mi
cm^2	square centimeter	0.15	square inch	in^2
m^2	square meter	10.76	square foot	ft^2
m^2	square meter	1.20	square yard	yd^2
km^2	square kilometer	0.39	square mile	mi^2
ha	hectare	2.47	acre	
g	gram	.035	ounce [1]	oz
kg	kilogram	2.21	pounds [1]	lb
g	gram	.032	ounce [2]	oz (troy)
t	metric ton	1.10	short ton (2,000 lb)	
t	metric ton	0.98	long ton (2,240 lb)	
mL	milliliter	0.03	fluid ounce	fl oz
L	liter	4.24	cup	c
L	liter	2.13	pint (liquid)	pt
L	liter	1.05	quart (liquid)	qt
L	liter	0.26	gallon	gal
m^3	cubic meter	35.32	cubic foot	ft^3
m^3	cubic meter	1.32	cubic yard	yd^3
C	degrees Celsius (after multiplying, add 32)	1.80	degrees Fahrenheit	F

[1] For weighing ordinary commodities.   [2] For weighing precious metals, jewels, etc.

U.S. Census Bureau, Statistical Abstract of the United States: 2002

Tables Deleted From the
2001 Edition of the Statistical Abstract

Appendix VI
New Tables

Index

NOTE: Index citations refer to **table** numbers, not page numbers.

U.S. Census Bureau, Statistical Abstract of the United States: 2002

NOTE: Index citations refer to **table** numbers, not page numbers.

U.S. Census Bureau, Statistical Abstract of the United States: 2002

NOTE: Index citations refer to **table** numbers, not page numbers.

U.S. Census Bureau, Statistical Abstract of the United States: 2002

NOTE: Index citations refer to **table** numbers, not page numbers.

NOTE: Index citations refer to **table** numbers, not page numbers.

U.S. Census Bureau, Statistical Abstract of the United States: 2002

NOTE: Index citations refer to **table** numbers, not page numbers.

U.S. Census Bureau, Statistical Abstract of the United States: 2002

NOTE: Index citations refer to **table** numbers, not page numbers.

U.S. Census Bureau, Statistical Abstract of the United States: 2002

NOTE: Index citations refer to **table** numbers, not page numbers.

NOTE: Index citations refer to **table** numbers, not page numbers.

U.S. Census Bureau, Statistical Abstract of the United States: 2002

NOTE: Index citations refer to **table** numbers, not page numbers.

NOTE: Index citations refer to **table** numbers, not page numbers.

U.S. Census Bureau, Statistical Abstract of the United States: 2002

NOTE: Index citations refer to **table** numbers, not page numbers.

NOTE: Index citations refer to **table** numbers, not page numbers.

U.S. Census Bureau, Statistical Abstract of the United States: 2002

NOTE: Index citations refer to **table** numbers, not page numbers.

U.S. Census Bureau, Statistical Abstract of the United States: 2002

NOTE: Index citations refer to **table** numbers, not page numbers.

U.S. Census Bureau, Statistical Abstract of the United States: 2002

NOTE: Index citations refer to **table** numbers, not page numbers.

U.S. Census Bureau, Statistical Abstract of the United States: 2002

NOTE: Index citations refer to **table** numbers, not page numbers.

U.S. Census Bureau, Statistical Abstract of the United States: 2002

NOTE: Index citations refer to **table** numbers, not page numbers.

NOTE: Index citations refer to **table** numbers, not page numbers.

U.S. Census Bureau, Statistical Abstract of the United States: 2002

NOTE: Index citations refer to **table** numbers, not page numbers.

NOTE: Index citations refer to **table** numbers, not page numbers.

NOTE: Index citations refer to **table** numbers, not page numbers.

U.S. Census Bureau, Statistical Abstract of the United States: 2002

NOTE: Index citations refer to **table** numbers, not page numbers.

NOTE: Index citations refer to **table** numbers, not page numbers.

NOTE: Index citations refer to **table** numbers, not page numbers.

NOTE: Index citations refer to **table** numbers, not page numbers.

U.S. Census Bureau, Statistical Abstract of the United States: 2002

NOTE: Index citations refer to **table** numbers, not page numbers.

U.S. Census Bureau, Statistical Abstract of the United States: 2002

NOTE: Index citations refer to **table** numbers, not page numbers.

972   Index

U.S. Census Bureau, Statistical Abstract of the United States: 2002

NOTE: Index citations refer to **table** numbers, not page numbers.

U.S. Census Bureau, Statistical Abstract of the United States: 2002

NOTE: Index citations refer to **table** numbers, not page numbers.

NOTE: Index citations refer to **table** numbers, not page numbers.

U.S. Census Bureau, Statistical Abstract of the United States: 2002

NOTE: Index citations refer to **table** numbers, not page numbers.

NOTE: Index citations refer to **table** numbers, not page numbers.

U.S. Census Bureau, Statistical Abstract of the United States: 2002

NOTE: Index citations refer to **table** numbers, not page numbers.

NOTE: Index citations refer to **table** numbers, not page numbers.

NOTE: Index citations refer to **table** numbers, not page numbers.

U.S. Census Bureau, Statistical Abstract of the United States: 2002

NOTE: Index citations refer to **table** numbers, not page numbers.

NOTE: Index citations refer to **table** numbers, not page numbers.

U.S. Census Bureau, Statistical Abstract of the United States: 2002

NOTE: Index citations refer to **table** numbers, not page numbers.

U.S. Census Bureau, Statistical Abstract of the United States: 2002

NOTE: Index citations refer to **table** numbers, not page numbers.

U.S. Census Bureau, Statistical Abstract of the United States: 2002

NOTE: Index citations refer to **table** numbers, not page numbers.

U.S. Census Bureau, Statistical Abstract of the United States: 2002

NOTE: Index citations refer to **table** numbers, not page numbers.

U.S. Census Bureau, Statistical Abstract of the United States: 2002

NOTE: Index citations refer to **table** numbers, not page numbers.

U.S. Census Bureau, Statistical Abstract of the United States: 2002

NOTE: Index citations refer to **table** numbers, not page numbers.

U.S. Census Bureau, Statistical Abstract of the United States: 2002

NOTE: Index citations refer to **table** numbers, not page numbers.

NOTE: Index citations refer to **table** numbers, not page numbers.

NOTE: Index citations refer to **table** numbers, not page numbers.

U.S. Census Bureau, Statistical Abstract of the United States: 2002

NOTE: Index citations refer to **table** numbers, not page numbers.

NOTE: Index citations refer to **table** numbers, not page numbers.

U.S. Census Bureau, Statistical Abstract of the United States: 2002

NOTE: Index citations refer to **table** numbers, not page numbers.

NOTE: Index citations refer to **table** numbers, not page numbers.

U.S. Census Bureau, Statistical Abstract of the United States: 2002

NOTE: Index citations refer to **table** numbers, not page numbers.

U.S. Census Bureau, Statistical Abstract of the United States: 2002

NOTE: Index citations refer to **table** numbers, not page numbers.

U.S. Census Bureau, Statistical Abstract of the United States: 2002

NOTE: Index citations refer to **table** numbers, not page numbers.

U.S. Census Bureau, Statistical Abstract of the United States: 2002

NOTE: Index citations refer to **table** numbers, not page numbers.

U.S. Census Bureau, Statistical Abstract of the United States: 2002